USA

written and researched by

Samantha Cook, Tim Perry and Greg Ward

with additional contributions from

Nicky Agate, Alf Alderson, Virginie Boone, Jeff Cranmer, Jeff Dickey, Nick Edwards, Mark Ellwood, Michael Kohn, Rich McHugh, Todd Obolsky, Lesley Rose, Nick Thomson, Karl Turpeinen, Diane Vadino, Paul Whitfield, Christian Williams and Cameron Wilson

ROUGH GUIDES

www.roughguides.com

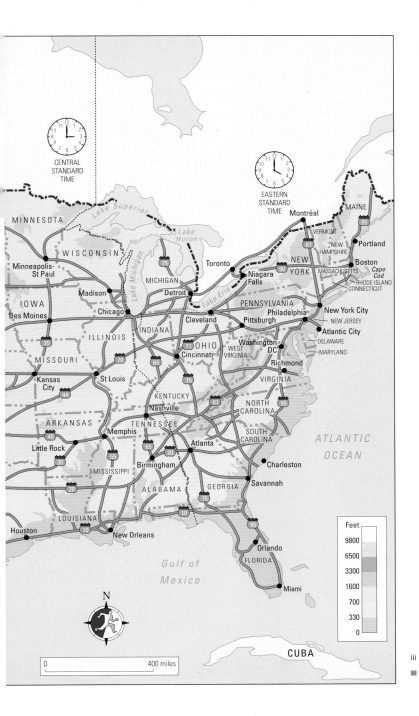

CENTRAL STANDARD TIME

EASTERN STANDARD TIME

MINNESOTA

WISCONSIN

Lake Superior

Lake Huron

Lake Michigan

Toronto

Niagara Falls

MICHIGAN

Detroit

Lake Erie

Montréal

MAINE

VERMONT

NEW HAMPSHIRE

Portland

NEW YORK

Boston

Cape Cod

MASSACHUSETTS

RHODE ISLAND

CONNECTICUT

Minneapolis-St Paul

Madison

IOWA

Des Moines

Chicago

ILLINOIS

INDIANA

OHIO

Cleveland

PENNSYLVANIA

Pittsburgh

Philadelphia

New York City

NEW JERSEY

Atlantic City

DELAWARE

MARYLAND

MISSOURI

Kansas City

St Louis

Cincinnati

WEST VIRGINIA

Washington DC

Richmond

KENTUCKY

Nashville

VIRGINIA

ARKANSAS

TENNESSEE

NORTH CAROLINA

Memphis

Little Rock

MISSISSIPPI

Birmingham

Atlanta

SOUTH CAROLINA

Charleston

Savannah

ATLANTIC OCEAN

ALABAMA

GEORGIA

LOUISIANA

Houston

New Orleans

Orlando

FLORIDA

Miami

Gulf of Mexico

N

CUBA

Feet	
9800	
6500	
3300	
1600	
700	
330	
0	

0   400 miles

iii

Times Square, New York City

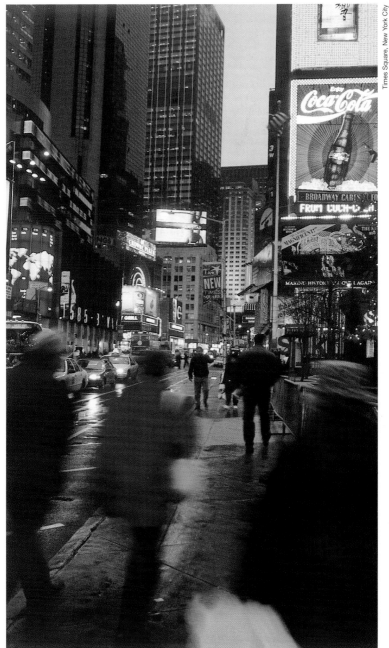

Introduction to the
USA

For five centuries, travelers have brought their hopes and dreams to America. For the earliest pioneers, it was a virgin wilderness ready to be shaped into a "New World," a potential paradise wasted on its native peoples. Millions of immigrants followed, to share in the building of the new nation and to better their lives, far from the hidebound societies of Europe and Asia. Eventually, slaves, who had been shipped over from Africa and the Caribbean, joined them as free citizens. As the United States expanded to fill the continent, something genuinely new was created: a vast country that took pride in defining itself in the eyes of the world.

Every traveler in the United States – be they foreigners on a coast-to-coast road trip or locals exploring their extraordinarily diverse land – has some idea of what to expect. American culture has become so thoroughly shared throughout the globe that one of the principal joys of getting to know the country is the repeated, delicious shock of the familiar. Yellow taxis on busy city streets; roadside mailboxes straight out of *Peanuts* cartoons; wooden porches overlooking the cottonfields; tumbleweed skittering across the desert; endless highways dotted with pick-up trucks and chrome-plated diners; the first sight of the Grand Canyon, or the Manhattan skyline – now more than ever an indelibly iconic image.

In this book, we've picked out the highlights across the entire USA, from Maine to Hawaii, and Alaska to Florida. We've divided the country region

Fact file

- The **US government** is divided into three branches: the executive, headed by the president; the legislative, which consists of the Senate and the House of Representatives; and the judicial, with the Supreme Court as its highest office.

- Despite New York's status as the cultural and economic center of the US, the **federal capital** is in Washington, DC, which doesn't even rank among the top twenty cities in terms of population (though officially, it is a "district," rather than a city).

- The **population** of the US (some 281 million) owns 200 million cars and trucks (roughly 1 vehicle for every 1.4 people), with more than 5.7 million miles of paved highway on which to drive them.

- With an area of 9.6 million square kilometers, the US is the **third largest country** in the world (ranking behind Russia and Canada).

- The US is the only country that contains all six major **climate zones**: tropical humid, dry, mild mid-latitude, severe mid-latitude, polar and highland.

- With its Aleutian Islands crossing the Greenwich Meridian, Alaska is technically home to both the **easternmost** and **westernmost** points in the US. Alaska also has the **highest point** in the US, Mount McKinley (20,320ft), and is the **largest state** by area (Rhode Island being the smallest).

by region and state by state, and covered every area of every state. As well as the big cities and national parks, we've explored the highways and byways, singling out detours worth making, and places to avoid. For every area covered, we've done more than simply provide up-to-date practicalities: we've delved into the history and provided background on the people who have made America what it is. Our hope is to inform and entertain travelers, and to point in unexpected directions as well as to the obvious landmarks, no matter whether you've lived here all your life or are seeing it all for the first time.

Where to go

Traveling in the United States is extremely easy; in a country where everyone seems to be forever on the move, there's rarely any problem finding a room for the night, and you can almost invariably depend on being able to eat well and inexpensively. The development of transportation has played a major role in the growth of the nation; the railroad opened the way for transcontinental migrations, while most of the great cities have been shaped by the automobile. Your experience of the country will be very much flavored by how you choose to get around.

By far the best way to explore the country is to **drive your own vehicle**: it takes a long time before the sheer pleasure of cruising down the highway, with the radio blaring blues or country music, the signs to Chicago, Memphis or Monument Valley flashing past, begins to pall. Car rental is a bargain, every main road is lined with budget motels charging around $40 per night

for a good room, and the price of gasoline remains relatively low.

We have also detailed **public transportation** options throughout; you can pretty much get to wherever you choose by a nationwide network of air, bus and rail. However, if you do travel this way, there's a real temptation to see America as a succession of big **cities**. True enough, **New York** and **Los Angeles** have an exhilarating dynamism and excitement,

The great outdoors

The horizon-spanning wildernesses of the North American heartland are magnificently uplifting. Any coast-to-coast drive is liable to leave you feeling dwarfed by the sheer scale of the continent, whether your route takes you across the sweeping deserts of the south or the forbidding mountains to the north. East of the Mississippi River, the vistas of Virginia's Blue Ridge Parkway and Tennessee's Great Smoky Mountains seem far removed from all civilization, while to the west stretch the snowy summits of Wyoming and Montana, the vast canyonlands of Utah and the mighty redwood forests of California. State and national parks (see p.48 for a rundown) provide the best opportunities to see wildlife, from the alligators of the Everglades to the wolves and bears of Yellowstone, and to escape your car by hiking out along the trails.

Jefferson Memorial, The Tidal Basin

and among their worthy rivals are **New Orleans**, the wonderfully decadent home of jazz, **Chicago**, a showcase of modern architecture, and **San Francisco**, on its beautiful Pacific bay. Few other cities – with the possible, and idiosyncratic, exception of **Las Vegas**, shimmering in the desert – can quite match this level of interest, however, and following a heavily urban itinerary will cut you off from the astonishing **landscapes** that make the USA truly distinctive. Especially in the vast open spaces of the West, the scenery is often breathtaking. The glacial splendor of **Yosemite**, the thermal wonderland of **Yellowstone**, the awesome redrock **canyons** of Arizona and Utah, and the spectacular **Rocky Mountains** are among many of the treasures preserved and protected in the splendid national park system. Once you reach such wilderness, the potential for **hiking** and **camping** is magnificent – but it's usually essential to have a car to get near these spots.

> There's rarely any problem finding a room for the night, and you can almost invariably depend on being able to eat well and inexpensively

Above all, travelers can enjoy the sheer thrill of experiencing American popular culture in the places where it began. Rock'n'roll place names spring to life; panoramas etched on our consciousness from a century of movies spread across the horizon; road trips taken by your favorite literary characters are still there to be traveled.

For **music** fans, the chance to hear country music in Nashville or rhythm and blues in New Orleans, to dance in a Mississippi jook-joint or to visit Elvis's shrine in Memphis, verges on a religious experience; readers brought up on the **books** of Mark Twain can ride a paddle wheeler on the Mississippi; **moviegoers** can live out their Wild West fantasies in the rugged Utah deserts.

The United States is all too often dismissed, even by its own inhabitants, as a land almost devoid of **history**. Though mainstream America tends to trace its roots back to the Pilgrims and Puritans of New England, the rest of the continent has a longer history, stretching back way beyond the French culture of Louisiana and the Spanish presence in California to the majestic cliff palaces built by the Ancestral Puebloans in the Southwest a thousand years ago. There are also any number of fascinating strands to America's post-revolutionary history: relics of the Gold Rush in California, of the Civil Rights years in the South, or of the Civil War anywhere east of the Mississippi.

Though we've had to structure this book regionally, the most invigorating expeditions are those that take in more than one area. You do not, however, have to cross the entire continent from shore to shore in order to appreciate its amazing diversity, or to be impressed by the way in which

Music

Music is the lifeblood of the USA, with every mile along the highways seeming to evoke a favorite song or performer. Devotees flock to the cities that gave birth to jazz, blues, country, soul and rap. Those worthy of special pilgrimages include the party town of New Orleans, which boasts an unrivaled jazz and R&B scene; Nashville, with its honky-tonks and rhinestone glitter; and of course Memphis, the home of Sun and Stax record labels as well as the ultimate rock'n'roll shrine, Graceland. Out in the country too, there's plenty of excitement. Explore rural Appalachia and you may find ensembles of backwoods fiddlers; Louisiana's sleepy bayous are enlivened by foot-stomping Cajun and zydeco sounds; and the jook-joints of Mississippi Delta hamlets enrapture blues purists. Hardcore rockers can head for Los Angeles, Boston and Seattle, while college towns like Austin, Texas, and Athens, Georgia, are the places to catch rising stars. And don't forget Las Vegas, where every act arrives in the end and Tom Jones seldom leaves.

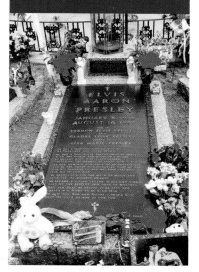

such an extraordinary range of topography and people has been melded into one nation. It would take a long time to see the whole place, and the more time you spend on the road simply getting from place to place – no matter how enjoyable in itself that can be – the less time you'll have to savor the small-town pleasures and back roads oddities that may well provide your strongest memories. It doesn't take long to realize that there is no such thing as a typical American person, any more than there is a typical American landscape, but there can be few places where strangers can feel so confident of a warm reception.

When to go

All US cities are pretty much year-round destinations (though Fairbanks, Alaska, in winter and Houston, Texas, in summer can be said to be less than ideal); national parks and mountain ranges sometimes less so.

The US **climate** is characterized by wide variations, not just from region to region and season to season, but also day to day and even hour to hour. Even setting aside far-flung Alaska and Hawaii, the main

It takes a long time before the sheer pleasure of cruising down the highway, with the radio blaring blues or country music, the signs to Chicago, Memphis or Monument Valley flashing past, begins to pall

body of the US is subject to dramatically shifting weather patterns, most notably produced by westerly winds sweeping across the continent from the Pacific.

In general, temperatures tend to rise the further south you go, and to fall the higher you climb, while the climate along either coast is, on the whole, milder and more uniform than inland.

The **Northeast**, from Maine down to Washington DC, experiences relatively low precipitation as a rule, but temperatures can range from bitterly cold in winter to uncomfortably hot (made worse by humidity) in the short summer. Farther south, summers get warmer and longer. **Florida**'s air temperatures are not necessarily dramatically high in summer, being kept down by the proximity of the sea both east and west. Florida, in winter, is warm and sunny enough to attract visitors from all over the country.

The **Great Plains**, which for climatic purposes can be said to extend from the Appalachians to the Rockies, are alternately exposed to icy Arctic winds streaming down from Canada and humid tropical airflows from the Caribbean and the Gulf of Mexico. Winters in the north, around the Great Lakes, can be abjectly cold, with driving winds and freezing rain. It can freeze or even snow in winter as far south as the Gulf of Mexico, though spring and fall get progressively longer and milder farther south through the Plains. Summer is much the wettest season in the **South** as a whole, the time when thunderstorms are most likely to strike. One or two hurricanes each year rage across Florida and/or the **Southeast**, from obscure origins in the Gulf of Mexico on the way to extinction out in the Atlantic. **Tornadoes** (or "twisters") are usually a much more local phenomenon, tending to cut a narrow swath of destruction in the wake of violent spring or summer thunderstorms. Average rainfall dwindles to lower and lower levels the further west you head across the plains.

Temperatures in the **Rockies** correlate closely with altitude; beyond the

The Wild West

Nowhere in the US is imbued with myth and history quite like the Wild West, much of which remains unchanged since the days of pioneers, prospectors and, of course, "cowboys and Indians." In Lincoln, New Mexico, you can trace the footsteps of Billy the Kid; in Tombstone, Arizona, you can re-live the gunfight at the OK Corral; and at Little Bighorn, Montana, you can climb the windswept hillside where General Custer made his "Last Stand." Colorado and California still abound with ghost towns abandoned when the gold and silver mines played out, while the great cattle drives are commemorated in Dodge City, Kansas, and Fort Worth, Texas. Above all, many Native Americans continue to inhabit their ancestral lands, especially in the Southwest, where the Hopi and the Acomans survive in remote mesa-top villages, the Navajo ride through Monument Valley, and the Havasupai still farm alongside magical waterfalls deep in the Grand Canyon.

Food

There's far more to American food than hotdogs and burgers (though to be sure, either can be had almost anywhere, done up in hundreds of different ways). In a place with a dozen types of sandwich (among them hoagies, subs, heroes and po-boys), the sheer variety of culinary experiences is overwhelming. One of the great pleasures of any road trip is discovering quirky diners dishing up delicious homecooked food – fiery chili, Cajun jambalaya, creamy clam chowder, hulking barbecue ribs and huge Southern feasts of fried chicken and catfish – while the major cities leave you spoiled for choice for world-class, affordable restaurants. Each region has its specialties, which we've detailed in relevant sections of the Guide. For more on food and drink, see p.53.

mountains in the south lie the extensive arid and inhospitable deserts of the **Southwest**. Much of this area is within the rain shadow of the California ranges. In cities such as Las Vegas and Phoenix, the mercury regularly soars above 100°F, though the atmosphere is not usually humid enough to be as enervating as that might sound.

West of the barrier of the Cascade Mountains, the fertile **Pacific Northwest** is the only region of the country where winter is the wettest season, and throughout the year the European-style climate is wet, mild and seldom hot. **California** weather more or less lives up to the popular idyllic image, though the climate is markedly hotter and drier in the south than in the north, and there's enough snow to make the mountains a major skiing destination. San Francisco is kept milder and colder than the surrounding district by the propensity of the Bay Area to attract sea fog, while the Los Angeles basin is prone to filling up with smog, as fog and pollution become trapped beneath a layer of warm air.

Average temperature (°F) and rainfall

To convert °F to °C, subtract 32 and multiply by 5/9

	Jan	Feb	Mar	Apr	May	June	July	Aug	Sept	Oct	Nov	Dec
Anchorage												
av. max temp	19	27	33	44	54	62	65	64	57	43	30	20
av. min temp	5	9	13	27	36	44	49	47	39	29	15	6
days of rain	7	6	5	4	5	6	10	15	14	12	7	6
Boston												
av. max temp	36	37	43	54	66	75	80	78	71	62	49	40
av. min temp	20	21	28	39	49	58	63	62	55	46	35	25
days of rain	12	10	12	11	11	10	10	10	9	9	10	11
Chicago												
av. max temp	32	34	43	55	65	75	81	79	73	61	47	36
av. min temp	18	20	29	40	50	60	66	65	58	47	34	23
days of rain	11	10	12	11	12	11	9	9	9	9	10	11
Honolulu												
av. max temp	76	76	77	78	80	81	82	83	83	82	80	78
av. min temp	69	67	67	68	70	72	73	74	74	72	70	69
days of rain	14	11	13	12	11	12	14	13	13	13	13	15
Las Vegas												
av. max temp	60	67	72	81	89	99	103	102	95	84	71	61
av. min temp	29	34	39	45	52	61	68	66	57	47	36	30
days of rain	2	2	2	1	1	1	2	2	1	1	1	2
Los Angeles												
av. max temp	65	66	67	70	72	76	81	82	81	76	73	67
av. min temp	46	47	48	50	53	56	60	60	58	54	50	47
days of rain	6	6	6	4	2	1	0	0	1	2	3	6
Miami												
av. max temp	74	75	78	80	84	86	88	88	87	83	78	76
av. min temp	61	61	64	67	71	74	76	76	75	72	66	62
days of rain	9	6	7	7	12	13	15	15	18	16	10	7
New Orleans												
av. max temp	62	65	71	77	83	88	90	90	86	79	70	64
av. min temp	47	50	55	61	68	74	76	76	73	64	55	48
days of rain	10	12	9	7	8	13	15	14	10	7	7	10
New York City												
av. max temp	37	38	45	57	68	77	82	80	79	69	51	41
av. min temp	24	24	30	42	53	60	66	66	60	49	37	29
days of rain	12	10	12	11	11	10	12	10	9	9	9	10
San Francisco												
av. max temp	55	59	61	62	63	66	65	65	69	68	63	57
av. min temp	45	47	48	49	51	52	53	53	55	54	51	47
days of rain	11	11	10	6	4	2	0	0	2	4	7	10
Seattle												
av. max temp	45	48	52	58	64	69	72	73	67	59	51	47
av. min temp	36	37	39	43	47	52	54	55	52	47	41	38
days of rain	18	16	16	13	12	9	4	5	8	13	17	19
Washington DC												
av. max temp	42	44	53	64	75	83	87	84	78	67	55	45
av. min temp	27	28	35	44	54	63	68	66	58	48	38	29
days of rain	11	10	12	11	12	11	11	11	8	8	9	10

things not to miss

It's not possible to see everything that the USA has to offer in one trip – and we don't suggest you try. What follows is a selective and subjective taste of the country's highlights: stimulating cities, memorable celebrations, dramatic drives, magnificent parks and natural phenomena. They're arranged in five color-coded categories to help you find the very best things to see, do and experience. All highlights have a page reference to take you straight into the guide, where you can find out more.

xiv

01 Yellowstone National Park, WY Page **890** • The national park that started it all has it all, from steaming fluorescent hot springs and spouting geysers to sheer canyons and meadows filled with wild flowers and assorted grazing beasts.

02 **Driving Highway 1** Page **1107** • The rugged Big Sur coastline, pounded by Pacific waves, makes an exhilarating route between San Francisco and LA.

03 **Monticello, VA** Page **450** • A squirrel's hop from the Blue Ridge Mountains, this elegant plantation was the home and final resting place of Thomas Jefferson, author of the Constitution and third US president.

04 **Baseball** Page **360** • America's summer pastime is a treat to watch wherever you are, but at Chicago's ivy-clad Wrigley Field, where the score and the pitchers' numbers are still changed by hand, it's simply irresistible.

05 **Skiing in the Rocky Mountains** Pages **841** & **1020** • The site for some of the best skiing anywhere, from glitzy resorts to atmospheric mining towns.

06 **Country Music Hall of Fame, Nashville, TN** Page **570** • Everything you ever wanted to know about country music, enshrined and explained in loving detail.

07 New England in the fall Page **195** • Fall in the northeast is a breathtaking spectacle, the copious foliage presenting an ever-changing palette of color and light.

08 Glacier National Park, MT Page **913** • Pressing hard against the Canadian border, Montana's loveliest park holds not only fifty glaciers, but also two thousand lakes, a thousand miles of rivers and the exhilarating Going-to-the-Sun road.

09 Swamps Page **668** • From the steamy Everglades of Florida to the ghostly bayous of Louisiana's Cajun country, America's swamplands harbor some pretty ornery critters.

10 Stern wheeler rides Page **561** • Just as they did in Mark Twain's day, steam-driven stern wheelers still ply the Mississippi from great old river towns like New Orleans, St Louis and Memphis.

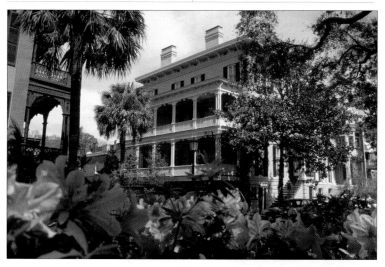

11 Savannah, GA Page **541** • Mint juleps on wide verandas, horsedrawn carriages on cobbled streets and lush foliage draped with Spanish moss; this historic cotton port remains the South's loveliest town.

12 South Philly cheese-steak, PA Page **164** • Born in Philadelphia's South Side, the cheesesteak is a sloppy feast that inspires passionate partisanship on behalf of its members.

13 Aurora borealis, AK Page **1277** • Winter visitors to Alaska see the skies ablaze with the shimmering veils of the Northern Lights.

14 **Miami's Art Deco, FL** Page **625** • This flamboyant city is justly famed for the colorful pastel architecture of its restored South Beach district.

15 **Mardi Gras, New Orleans, LA** Page **702** • Crazy, colorful, debauched and historic – this is the carnival to end them all.

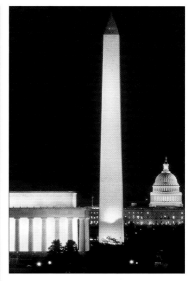

16 **The Mall, Washington DC** Page **412** • From the Lincoln Memorial to the US Capitol by way of the towering Washington Monument – the capital's Mall is an awesome showcase of American culture and history.

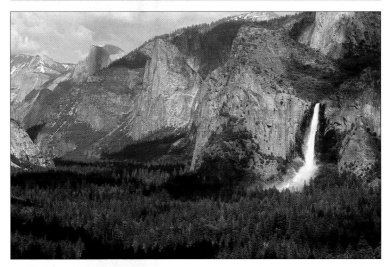

17 **Yosemite Valley, CA** Page **1121** • Enclosed by near-vertical, mile-high cliffs, and laced with hiking trails and climbing routes, the dramatic geology of Yosemite Valley is at the heart of California's best-loved park.

18 **Chicago's modern architecture, IL** Page **346** • The history of modern architecture is writ large on Chicago's dramatic skyline, where the world's first skyscrapers now stand in the shadow of sleek corporate monoliths.

19 **Niagara Falls, NY** Page **150** • The sheer power of Niagara Falls is even more overwhelming when seen from below, aboard the *Maid of the Mist*.

20 **Ancestral Puebloan sites** Page **994** • Scattered through desert landscapes like Arizona's magnificent Canyon de Chelly, the dwellings of the Ancestral Puebloans afford glimpses of an ancient and mysterious world.

21 **Mount St Helens, WA** Page 1027 • A breathtaking example of volcanic devastation, wrought by a powerful eruption in 1980.

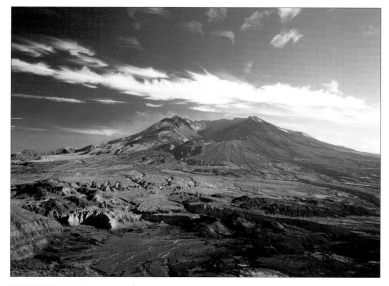

22 **Kentucky Derby, KY** Page 556 • Thousands gather in Louisville for a two-week binge of beer guzzling, wild partying – and even a spot of thoroughbred racing.

23 **San Francisco, CA** Page 1123 • Still bohemian and individualistic at heart.

24 **Mount Rushmore, SD** Page 829 • Preserved in the sternest granite, these four larger-than-life presidents now preside forever above the Black Hills of South Dakota.

25 Cheyenne Frontier Days, WY
Page **880** • Relive the Old West with some good ol' boys and girls at the world's most prestigious outdoor rodeo.

27 Austin nightlife, TX
Page **739** • Laid-back and progressive and home to an eclectic live-music scene – Austin is like nowhere else in the state.

26 Sweet Auburn, Atlanta, GA
Page **533** • This historic black district, just a stone's throw from downtown's ultra-modern skyscrapers, holds the birthplace of Dr Martin Luther King Jr, among other spots commemorating its native son.

28 Hawaii's volcanoes
Page **1299** • Hawaii's Big Island grows bigger by the minute, as the world's most active volcano pours molten lava into the ocean.

29 New York City
Page **67** • A city so special that we gave it its own chapter.

30 Big Bend National Park, TX Page **765** • Forcing the Rio Grande – and the Mexican frontier – to take a very big bend indeed, Texas' remote Chisos Mountains form a vast, barely charted enclave that bursts into color each spring.

31 Baltimore crabs, MD Page **473** • Delicious fresh steamed crabs are the pride of this characterful port city.

32 Saguaro cactus Page **966** • The astonishing Saguaro, which can reach fifty feet tall, grow as many as forty arms and live for two centuries, is emblematic of the desert Southwest.

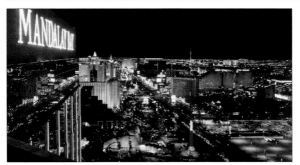

33 The Strip, Las Vegas, NV Page **1027** • With its erupting volcanoes, pirate battles, Eiffel Tower and Egyptian pyramid, the legendary Strip will blow your mind as well as your wallet.

ACTIVITIES | CONSUME | EVENTS | NATURE | SIGHTS |

34 Walt Disney World, Orlando, FL Page 652 •
Though each of Orlando's theme parks strives to outdo the rest, Walt Disney World remains the one to beat.

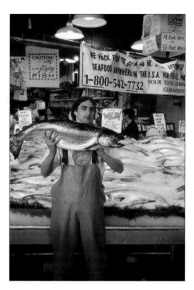

35 Pike Place Market, Seattle, WA Page 1183 •
Piled high with salmon, lobster, clams and crab, the oldest public market in the nation is also home to some great seafood restaurants.

xxiv

36 Hitting the open road •
There's no better way to experience the staggering diversity of places and peoples in this vast country.

contents

using the Rough Guide

We've tried to make this Rough Guide a good read and easy to use. The book is divided into five main sections, and you should be able to find whatever you want in one of them.

front section

The front color section offers a quick tour of the USA. The **introduction** aims to give you a feel for the place, with suggestions on where to go. We also tell you what the weather is like and include a basic country fact file. Next, our authors round up their favorite aspects of the USA in the **things not to miss** section – whether it's great food, amazing sights, or a special activity. Right after this comes the Rough Guide's full **contents** list.

basics

You've decided to go and the basics section covers all the **pre-departure** information to help you plan your trip. This is where to find out which airlines fly to your destination, what paperwork you'll need, what to do about money and insurance, about internet access, food, security, public transport, car rental – in fact just about every piece of **general practical information** you might need.

guide

This is the heart of the Rough Guide, divided into user-friendly chapters, each of which covers a specific city, state or region. Every chapter starts with a list of **highlights** and an **introduction** that helps you to decide where to go, depending on your time and budget. Likewise, introductions to the various towns and smaller regions within each chapter should help you plan your itinerary. We start most town accounts with information on arrival and accommodation, followed by a tour of the sights, and finally reviews of places to eat and drink, and details of nightlife.

contexts

Read Contexts to get a deeper understanding of how the USA ticks. We include a brief **history**, sections about **film** and **notable personalities** mentioned in the book, together with a detailed further-reading section that reviews dozens of **books** relating to the country.

index + small print

Apart from a **full index**, which includes maps as well as places, this section covers publishing information, credits and acknowledgments, and also has our contact details in case you want to send in updates and corrections to the book – or suggestions as to how we might improve it.

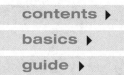

chapter map of the **USA**

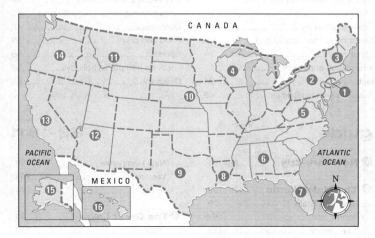

contents

contexts

index + small print

map symbols

maps are listed in the full index using colored text

-------	International border	✕	Battlefield
--- ---	State border	✦	Ski area
--- ---	Chapter division boundary	■	Restaurant
80	Interstate	●	Hotel
30	U.S. Highway	⚠	Campsite
1	Highway	✈	Airport
=====	Tunnel	✈	Airfield
-----	Path	P	Parking
■■■■	Railway	⊞	Hospital/medical center
— —	Ferry route	ⓘ	Information center
———	River	✉	Post office
⌂	Cave	▬▬▬	Wall
⋀⋀	Mountain range	↓	Church (regional maps)
▲	Mountain peak	■	Building
⫝	Waterfall	⊞	Church (town maps)
⸰	Marshland/swamp	✝✝	Cemetery
⚘	Viewpoint	▨	Park
☫	Lighthouse	⬚	Forest
●	Museum	⬚	Beach
🏛	Monument		

basics

basics

Getting there

Canadians and US citizens aside, you'll have to fly to get to the States – and the country is so vast that you'll have no end to the options of places to start and finish your travels. Clearly part of the battle is deciding which area to explore and then locating its hub, whether you're hitting the swamps of Florida, the frozen tundra of Alaska, the summer heat of Southern cities or the splendor of the Rockies and Southwest.

While flights to popular holiday destinations such as Florida tend to cost the same whenever you go, international airfares usually vary depending on the **season**. In general, **high season** is July to September, and then around Easter and Christmas. Fares drop during the **shoulder** seasons – April to June, and October. You'll get the best prices during the **low season**, November to March (excluding Easter, Christmas and New Year, when prices are hiked up and seats are at a premium). Certain destinations might actually be less costly and less crowded during high season: southern Florida and New Orleans, for example, are both extremely hot – almost swampy – between May and September, which counts as off-season. The extra you might spend on a summer flight can be more than compensated for by low prices once you're on the ground – as long as you can handle the heat. Watch for slack season bargains and check the exact dates of the seasons with your operator or airline. You might be able to save a lot by shifting your departure date by a week – or even a day. **Taxes** vary almost monthly, but creep relentlessly upward. Flying on weekends ordinarily adds a substantial amount to the round-trip fare; prices quoted below assume midweek travel.

You may cut costs by using a **specialist flight agent** – either a consolidator, who buys blocks of tickets from the airlines and sells them at a discount, or a **discount agent**, who deals with discounted flights and may also offer special student and youth fares and other services, including insurance, rail passes, car rentals and tours. Some agents specialize in **charter flights**, which may be cheaper than scheduled flights, but again departure dates are fixed and withdrawal penalties are high. For some of the more popular destinations, it may sometimes be cheaper to pick up a bargain **package deal** from one of the tour operators listed below and then find your own accommodation when you get there; however you won't find such deals often. Another possibility is to arrange a courier flight, although you'll need a flexible schedule, and it would also help if you are traveling alone with very little luggage. In return for shepherding a parcel through customs, you can expect to get a deeply discounted ticket. You'll probably also be restricted in the duration of your stay.

If the USA is only one stop on a longer journey, you might consider buying a Round-the-World ticket. Some travel agents can sell you an "off-the-shelf" RTW ticket that will have you touching down in about half a dozen cities (New York, Miami and Los Angeles are on many itineraries). Others will assemble one for you, tailored to your needs but apt to be more expensive. Figure on AU$2300/£800 for a RTW ticket including the US.

Booking flights online

Many airlines and discount travel websites offer you the opportunity to book your tickets online, cutting out the costs of agents and middlemen. Good deals can often be found through discount or auction sites, as well as through the airlines' own websites, but always check with a local or student travel agent too, as sometimes they will offer surprisingly attractive alternatives.

Online booking agents and general travel sites

ⓦ **www.cheapflights.com** Flight deals, travel agents, plus links to other travel sites. UK only.

ⓦ **www.cheaptickets.com** Discount flight specialists.

ⓦ **www.expedia.com/expedia.co.uk** Discount airfares, all-airline search engine and daily deals.

ⓦ **www.flyaow.com** Online air travel info and reservations site.

ⓦ **www.gaytravel.com** Gay online travel agent, concentrating mostly on accommodation.

ⓦ **www.hotwire.com** Bookings from the US only. Last-minute savings of up to forty percent on regular published fares. Travelers must be at least 18 and there are no refunds, transfers or changes allowed. Log-in required.

ⓦ **www.lastminute.com** Offers good last-minute holiday package and flight-only deals. UK only.

ⓦ **www.priceline.com** Name-your-own-price website that has deals at around forty percent off standard fares. You cannot specify flight times (although you do specify dates) and the tickets are nonrefundable, nontransferable and nonchangeable.

ⓦ **www.skyauction.com** Bookings from the US only. Auctions tickets and travel packages using a "second bid" scheme. The best strategy is to bid the maximum you're willing to pay, because if you win you'll pay just enough to beat the runner-up regardless of your maximum bid.

ⓦ **www.smilinjack.com/airlines.htm** Lists an up-to-date compilation of airline website addresses.

ⓦ **http://travel.yahoo.com** Incorporates a lot of Rough Guide material in its coverage of destination countries and cities across the world, with information about places to eat, sleep and so on.

ⓦ **wwww.travelocity.com** Destination guides, hot Web fares and best deals for car hire, accommodation and lodging as well as fares. Provides access to the travel agent system SABRE, the most comprehensive central reservations system in the US.

ⓦ **www.travelshop.com.au** Australian website offering discounted flights, packages, insurance, online bookings.

From the UK and Ireland

More than twenty US cities are accessible by nonstop flights from the UK. At these "gateway cities," airport hubs for US air carriers, you can connect with extensive networks of domestic flights on into the rest of the country. "Direct" services (which may land once or twice on the way, but are called direct if they keep the same flight number throughout their journey) fly from Britain to nearly every other major US city.

Nonstop flights to **Los Angeles** from London take eleven or twelve hours; the London–**Miami** flight takes eight hours; while flying time to **New York** is seven or so hours. Following winds ensure that return flights are always an hour or two shorter than outward journeys. One-stop direct flights to destinations beyond the east coast add time to the journey, but can work out cheaper than nonstop flights. They can even save you time, because customs and immigration are cleared on first touchdown into the US rather than the final destination, which may be a busy international gateway.

Only two airlines run nonstop scheduled services to the US **from Ireland**. From both Dublin and Shannon airports, Aer Lingus flies to New York, Chicago, Los Angeles and Boston, while Delta flies to New York and Atlanta. Both can arrange onward flights to any American destination, and may have good-value special deals. Otherwise the cheapest flights – if you're under 26 or a student – are available from USIT. Ordinary advance purchase – sometimes known as **Apex** – fares may be only marginally higher. These can come with a variety of restrictions, including having to travel at a certain time of day or on certain days of the week, or having to stay for a fixed length of time (usually including a Saturday night); tickets must be booked between 7 and 21 days in advance. Fares operate on a sliding scale, usually based on how far ahead you book.

Fares and airlines

Britain remains one of the best places in Europe to obtain flight bargains, though fares vary widely according to season, availability and the current level of inter-airline competition. The chart opposite) will give you a broad idea of typical rates offered by the operators listed opposite.

The comments that follow serve only as a general guide. The lowest-priced tickets usually must be booked in advance and may carry restrictions, with heavy penalties for

Sample air fares from Britain

The prices given below (in £ sterling) are a general indication of the (minimum) transatlantic air-fares obtainable from specialist companies for return (round-trip) flights; remember to add £45–60 airport tax to these figures. Each airline decides the exact dates of its own seasons.

LOW: Nov–March (not Christmas and Easter). HIGH: Easter, July–Sept, Christmas

London to	LOW return	HIGH return		LOW	HIGH
Boston	150	410	San Francisco	200	500
Chicago	200	540	Seattle	260	520
Denver	270	520	Washington	170	430
Houston	230	530			
Los Angeles	200	500	**Manchester to**		
Miami	200	540	Chicago	196	470
New York	150	420	Los Angeles	250	570
			New York	160	440

changes. The travel ads in the weekend papers and the holiday pages of ITV's *Teletext* give an idea of what's available; in London, scour *Time Out* and the *Evening Standard*. A good local travel agent will give you cost-saving advice as well as competitive quotes. Giveaway magazines aimed at young travelers, such as *TNT*, are also useful resources.

For an overview of the various offers, and unofficially discounted tickets, go straight to an agent specializing in low-cost flights. Especially if you're under 26 or a student, they may be able to knock up to thirty percent off the regular fares. In low or shoulder season, you should be able to find a return flight to east coast destinations such as New York for around £200, or to California for more like £300, while high-season rates tend to be from £100 to £200 more expensive. A Visit USA Airpass (VUSA) can be a good idea if you want to see a lot of the country. These are available only to non-US residents, and must be bought before reaching the US (see box on p.32).

With an open-jaw ticket you can fly into one city and out of another; fares are calculated by halving the return fares to each destination and adding the two figures together. Remember to check whether there is a high drop-off fee for returning a rental car in a different state from the one where you picked it up (see p.36).

If you're on a really tight budget you may want to consider flying as a courier, although these days the savings to be made are virtually negligible. Most of the major courier firms offer opportunities to travel cheaply in return for delivering a package, at rates of around £150 for a return to New York. As a rule, you're required to sacrifice your baggage allowance (only hand baggage is allowed) and fit in with some tight restrictions on when you travel – stays of much more than a fortnight are rare. For contacts see overleaf.

Nonstop flights

From London
(Heathrow, Gatwick or Stanstead)

Atlanta British Airways, Delta, United
Baltimore British Airways
Boston American Airlines, British Airways, Continental, United, Virgin Atlantic
Chicago Air India, American Airlines, British Airways, United, Thai Airways
Cincinnati Delta
Dallas/Fort Worth American Airlines, British Airways
Detroit Northwest, British Airways
Houston British Airways, Continental
Las Vegas Virgin Atlantic
Los Angeles Air New Zealand, American Airlines, British Airways, Continental, United, Virgin Atlantic
Miami American Airlines, British Airways, Continental, Virgin Atlantic
Minneapolis Northwest
New York Air India, American Airlines, British Airways, Continental, Kuwait Airways, United, Thai Airways, Virgin Atlantic
Orlando British Airways, Continental, Virgin Atlantic
Philadelphia British Airways, US Airways
Phoenix British Airways

Pittsburgh US Airways
Raleigh/Durham American Airlines
San Diego British Airways
St Louis TWA
San Francisco British Airways, Continental,
United, Virgin Atlantic
Seattle British Airways
Washington DC British Airways, Continental,
United, Virgin Atlantic

From Birmingham

New York Continental

From Manchester

Atlanta Delta
Chicago American Airlines, BMI (seasonal)
New York British Airways, Continental, Delta,
Pakistan International
Orlando Virgin Atlantic
Philadelphia US Airways, BMI (seasonal)

From Glasgow

Chicago American Airlines (seasonal)
New York British Airways, Continental

From Dublin/Shannon

Atlanta Aer Lingus
Boston Aer Lingus
Chicago Aer Lingus
Los Angeles Aer Lingus, Delta
New York Delta

Airlines

Aer Lingus (Ireland) ☏0645/737747,
ⓦwww.aerlingus.ie
Air India ☏020/8560 9996, ⓦwww.airindia.com
Air New Zealand ☏020/8741 2299,
ⓦwww.airnz.com
American Airlines ☏0345/789789,
ⓦwww.aa.com
British Airways ☏0345/222111, in Republic of
Ireland ☏01/222 2345, ⓦwww.british-airways.com
BMI ☏0870/607 0555, ⓦwww.flybmi.com
Continental ☏0800/776464, in Republic of
Ireland ☏01/814 5311, ⓦwww.continental.com
Delta (UK) ☏0800/414767, in Republic of Ireland
☏1-800/414 767, ⓦwww.delta.com
Delta (Ireland) ☏01/676 8080
Kuwait Airways ☏020/7412 0006,
ⓦwww.kuwait-airways.com
Northwest ☏0990/561000, ⓦwww.nwa.com
Pakistan International ☏0208/741 8066,
ⓦwww.fly-pia/com
Thai Airways ☏0870/606 0911,
ⓦwww.thaiairways.com

TWA ☏0345/333333, ⓦwww.twa.com
United ☏0845/844 4777, in Republic of Ireland
☏1-800/535-5300, ⓦwww.ual.com
US Airways ☏0845/600 3300,
ⓦwww.usairways.com
Virgin Atlantic ☏01293/747747, in Republic of
Ireland ☏01/873 3388, ⓦwww.virgin-
atlantic.com

Courier flights

International Association of Air Couriers
☏0800/074 6480 or 01305/216 930,
ⓦwww.aircourier.co.uk

Flight agents

Apex Travel Dublin ☏01/671 5933,
ⓦwww.apextravel.ie
Bridge The World London ☏020/7916 0990,
ⓦwww.bridgetheworld.com
CIE Tours International Dublin ☏01/703 1888,
ⓦwww.cietours.ie
Co-op Travel Care Belfast ☏028/9047 1717
Flightbookers London ☏020/7757 2444,
ⓦwww.ebookers.com
Joe Walsh Tours Dublin ☏01/676 0991,
ⓦwww.joewalshtours.ie
London Flight Centre London ☏020/7244
6411, ⓦwww.topdecktravel.co.uk
Premier Travel Derry ☏028/7126 3333,
ⓦwww.premiertravel.uk.com
STA Travel Nationwide ☏0870/160 0599,
ⓦwww.statravel.co.uk
Belfast   ☏028/9024 1469
Bristol   ☏0870/167 6777
Cambridge   ☏01223/366966
Edinburgh   ☏0131/226 7747
Glasgow   ☏0141/338 6000
Leeds   ☏0870/168 6878
Manchester   ☏0161/834 0668
Oxford   ☏0870/163 6873
Student & Group Travel (student groups, New York
and Boston) Dublin ☏01/677 7834
Trailfinders London ☏020/7628 7628,
ⓦwww.trailfinders.com
Birmingham   ☏0121/236 1234
Bristol   ☏0117/929 9000
Dublin   ☏01/677 7888
Glasgow   ☏0141/353 2224
Manchester   ☏0161/839 6969
The Travel Bag London ☏0870/900 1350,
ⓦwww.travelbag.co.uk
Twohigs Dublin ☏01/670 9750
USIT Campus National Call Centre ☏0870/
240 1010, ⓦwww.usitcampus.co.uk

USIT Now Belfast ☎028/9032 4073,
@ www.usitnow.ie

Cork ☎021/270900
Derry ☎028/7137 1888
Dublin ☎01/679 8833

Tour operators

Airtours ☎0870/241 2567, @www.airtours.co.uk
AmeriCan Adventures Tunbridge Wells ☎01892/
512700, @www.americanadventures.com
American Holidays Belfast ☎028/9023 8762,
Dublin ☎01/679 6011
Bon Voyage Southampton ☎0800/316 3012,
@www.bon-voyage.co.uk
British Airways Holidays Worldwide
☎0870/242 4245, @www.baholidays.co.uk
Florida & Fly Drives ☎0870/442 3800,
US cities ☎0870/242 4243
Explore Worldwide Aldershot ☎01252/760000,
@www.explore.co.uk
Greyhound International East Grinstead
☎01342/317317, @www.greyhound.com
North America Travel Service Leeds
☎0113/246 1466
Trans Atlantic Vacations Horley ☎01293/789400
Thomas Cook London ☎0870/566 6222,
@www.thomascook.co.uk
TrekAmerica Banbury ☎01295/256777,
@www.trekamerica.com
Unijet Haywards Heath ☎0870/600 8009,
@www.unijet.co.uk
United Vacations Heathrow Airport ☎0870/
606 2222, @www.unitedvacations.co.uk
Virgin Holidays Crawley ☎0870/220 2788,
@www.virginholidays.co.uk

Packages

Packages – fly-drive, flight-accommodation
deals and guided tours (or a combination of
all three) – can work out cheaper than
arranging the same trip yourself, especially
for a short-term stay. High street travel
agents have plenty of brochures and information.

Flight and accommodation deals

There are countless **flight and accommodation** packages to all the major American
cities. Although you can often do things
cheaper independently, these allow you to
leave the organizational hassles to someone
else. Drawbacks include the loss of flexibility
and the fact that you'll probably be made to
stay in hotels in the mid-range to expensive

bracket, even though less expensive
accommodation is almost always readily
available.

To take a typical example, a low-season
return flight plus middle-range midtown hotel
accommodation for three nights in New York
City starts at around £400–450 per person,
rising to more like £650 at peak periods.
Among the many tour operators, Virgin
Holidays is about the least expensive
(@www.virginholidays.co.uk): for example,
seven nights in San Francisco plus return
flight costs around £569–789 per person,
and the same deal for a Florida destination
can be as low as £439, both with car rental
included. Pre-booked accommodation
schemes, where you buy vouchers for use in
a specific group of hotels, are not normally
good value.

Fly-drive deals

Fly-drive deals, which give cut-rate (sometimes free) car rental when a traveler buys a
transatlantic ticket from an airline or tour
operator, are always cheaper than renting on
the spot and give great value if you intend to
do a lot of driving. On the other hand, you'll
probably have to pay more for the flight than
if you booked it through a discount agent.
Competition between airlines and tour operators means that it's well worth phoning to
check on current special promotions.

Getaway (☎020/797 3007) arranges fly-
drive deals with various carriers. Holiday
America (☎01424/224400, @www.holiday-
america.net) offers excellent deals for not
much more than an ordinary **Apex** fare (see
p.10). Several of the companies listed above
offer similar, and sometimes cheaper, packages. A good travel agent will put one
together for you. There will often be little to
choose between prices; the most important
determining factors are the current strength
of the dollar against the pound, and your
destination in the US. Florida and California
usually offer the lowest rates, ridiculously
cheap in off-peak times (and all year in
Florida), starting at around £16 per week for
a small family sedan or £116 for a seven-seat
passenger van (Northwest Flydrive). Watch
out for hidden extras, such as taxes, "drop-
off" charges and insurance; all are detailed
on p.36 onward.

Several of the operators listed overleaf go one stage further and book accommodation for self-drive tours. Bon Voyage, for example, arranges tailor-made packages in the Southwest, with two weeks in Arizona, including the flight to Phoenix and standard hotels, costing £1000–1200 per person.

Touring and adventure packages

A simple and exciting way to see a chunk of America's great outdoors, without being hassled by too many practical considerations, is to take a specialist **touring and adventure package**, which includes transportation, accommodation, food and a guide. Some of the more adventurous, such as AmeriCan Adventures and TrekAmerica, carry small groups around on minibuses and use a combination of budget hotels and camping (all equipment, except sleeping bags, is provided), or hostels on AmeriCan Adventures Roadrunner Hostelling Treks. Most concentrate on the West – ranging from Arizona to Alaska, and from seven days to five weeks; AmeriCan Adventures also covers the East, including the Florida Keys. Typical rates for a two-week trip – excluding transatlantic flights – range from £490 in low season up to £730 in midsummer, more for trips to Alaska.

From Australia and New Zealand

Other than seasonal bargains and all-in packages that may be on offer from time to time, the best deals from Australasia are available from the travel agents listed on pp.15–16. Various add-on fares and air passes valid in the continental US are available with your main ticket, allowing you to fly to destinations across the States. These must be bought before you go, though.

Fares

Whatever kind of ticket you're after, your first call should be to one of the **travel agents** listed on p.16, who can fill you in on all the latest fares and any special offers. The **most expensive** time to fly is during the northern summer (mid-May to end-Aug) and over the Christmas period (Dec to mid-

Jan); shoulder seasons cover March to mid-May and September, while the rest of the year is **low season**. The exact dates vary slightly between the airlines, so it's worth shopping around, especially if you have the flexibility to change your departure date by a day or two. Los Angeles is the main US gateway airport for flights **from Australia**; when they have surplus capacity, airlines frequently offer special fares to Los Angeles, which can be as low as A$1400 including tax from the eastern states, sometimes with a bonus A$99 return add-on fares to New York, Boston, Washington, Dallas, Chicago or Miami. Otherwise, the best you're likely to find are the regular Air New Zealand, Qantas and United flights to Los Angeles: low-season return fares cost around A$1575 including tax from the eastern states, rising to A$2000 from Western Australia; flying during peak season will add at least another A$500. Through-flights to New York start at A$1675 tax included, with Qantas or United from Sydney, Brisbane or Cairns. Expect to pay upwards of A$2100, including tax, from Perth to New York on Qantas.

From New Zealand, low-season fares from Auckland or Christchurch (add another NZ$150 for Wellington departures) start at around NZ$2150 to LA or San Francisco, NZ$2800 to New York.

Airlines

Air Canada 92 Pitt St, Sydney ☎1300/656 232 or 02/9232 5222, New Zealand ☎09/377 8833, ⓦwww.aircanada.ca
Air New Zealand 5 Elizabeth St, Sydney ☎13/2476; 139 Queen St, Auckland ☎09/357 3000 or 0800/737 000, ⓦwww.airnz.co.nz
America West Airlines 364 Kent St, Sydney ☎02/9290 2232, ⓦwww.americawest.com
American Airlines 8/80 Clarence St, Sydney ☎1300/650 747; Level 15, Jetset Centre, 48 Emily Place, Auckland ☎09/309 0735 or 0800/887 997, ⓦwww.aa.com
British Airways Qantas Centre, 70 Hunter St, Sydney ☎02/8904 8800; 154 Queen St, Auckland ☎09/356 8690, ⓦwww.british-airways.com
Continental Airlines 64 York St, Sydney ☎02/9244 2242, NZ ☎09/308 3350, ⓦwww.flycontinental.com
Delta Airlines Level 9, 189 Kent St, Sydney ☎02/9251 3211 or 800/500 992 or 18 Shortland

St, Auckland ☎09/379 3370 or ☎0800/440 876, ⊛www.delta-air.com

Japan Airlines 14/201 Sussex St, Sydney ☎02/9272 1111; 12/120 Albert St, Auckland ☎09/379 9906, ⊛www.japanair.com

KLM/Northwest 5 Elizabeth St, Sydney ☎1300/303 747; 16 Waverley St, Auckland ☎09/309 1782, ⊛www.klm.com

Korean Air 36 Carrington St, Sydney ☎02/9262 6000; 63 Albert St, Auckland ☎09/307 3687

Malaysia Airlines 16 Spring St, Sydney ☎13/2627; 12/12 Swanson St, Auckland ☎09/373 2741 or 0800/657 472, ⊛www.malaysiaair.com

Qantas 70 Hunter St, Sydney ☎13/1313; 154 Queen St, Auckland ☎09/357 8900 or 0800/808 767, ⊛www.qantas.com.au

Singapore Airlines 17 Bridge St, Sydney ☎13/1011; cnr Albert and Fanshawe sts, Auckland ☎09/303 2129 or 0800/808 909, ⊛www.singaporeair.com

South African Airways 5 Elizabeth St, Sydney ☎02/9223 4402; Walshes World, 87 Queen St, Auckland ☎09/379 3708, ⊛www.saa–usa.com

United Airlines 10 Barrack St, Sydney ☎13/17 77; 7 City Rd, Auckland ☎09/379 3800, ⊛www.ual.com

Virgin Atlantic Airways Level 8, 403 George St, Sydney ☎02/9244 2747, NZ ☎09/308 3377, ⊛www.virgin–atlantic.com

Air passes and RTW tickets

Unless you're combining your US trip with jaunts to Europe and/or Asia, US **air passes** (see p.32) and add-on fares generally offer greater savings and more flexibility than round-the-world (RTW) tickets. However, if the US is just one port of call on your big trip, there are endless possibilities for **RTW routings**; for example, prices for Sydney to Tahiti to Los Angeles, traveling overland to New York, then continuing to Frankfurt and Bangkok on the way back to Sydney, start at A$2699, flying with the "Star Alliance" (⊛www.star-alliance.com) which includes Air New Zealand, Lufthansa, United Airlines, Thai, Varig, SAS, Air Canada and Ansett Australia. The "Star Alliance" works on a mileage basis and is a flat rate year-round. If you're departing in low season, cheaper still is the "One World" (⊛www.oneworld.com) fare offered by Qantas and British Airways, in conjunction with American Airlines, Canadian Airlines and Cathay

Pacific, which covers four continents from A$2599. Kiwi travelers could start in Auckland and take in Sydney, Harare, Nairobi, London, New York, LA and Brisbane for around NZ$3239. Agents such as STA (see overleaf) specialize in putting together RTW airfares using various airlines, and can help you plan your trip.

Packages and tours

There are many variations on **package deals** available to Australasian travelers, from **fly-drive** deals to fully escorted bus tours, skiing packages and camping treks, which can work out cheaper than making the same arrangements yourself. Some of the no-frills fly-drive packages, for example, can cost less than a flight alone, and you'll often get extras, such as stopovers in Hawaii or Tahiti and passes to Disneyland, thrown in. Insight's eight-day "west coast" coach tour costs around A$2000, while Creative Holidays tours start at about A$1900 for seven days, including all accommodation, but excluding flights.

Small-group **hotel** and **camping tours** can get you further off the beaten track. TrekAmerica offers several itineraries ranging from one to nine weeks. Its seven-day "Western Wonder" tour starts and ends in LA, taking in Death Valley, Las Vegas and the Grand Canyon, and costs from A$1093/ NZ$1410, not including flights. The 24-day "Coast to Coast," which crosses the continent from Miami to San Francisco, or vice versa, starts at A$2275/NZ$2934 (again, airfares are extra).

Flight agents and tour operators

Anywhere Travel 345 Anzac Parade, Kingsford, Sydney ☎02/9663 0411, ⓔanywhere@ozemail.com.au

Budget Travel 16 Fort St, Auckland, plus branches around the city ☎09/366 0061 or 0800/808 040, ⊛www.budgettravel.co.nz

Destinations Unlimited 87 Albert St, Auckland ☎09/373 4033

Flight Centres 82 Elizabeth St, Sydney, plus branches throughout Australia ☎13/1600; 350 Queen St, Auckland ☎09/358 4310, plus branches throughout New Zealand; ⊛www.flightcentre.com.au

Northern Gateway 22 Cavenagh St, Darwin ☎08/8941 1394; ⓔoztravel@norgate.com.au

STA Travel 855 George St, Sydney; 256 Flinders St, Melbourne; other offices in state capitals and major universities (nearest branch ☎ 13/1776, fastfare telesales ☎ 1300/360 960); 10 High St, Auckland (☎ 09/309 0458, fastfare telesales ☎ 09/366 6673), plus branches in Wellington, Christchurch, Dunedin, Palmerston North, Hamilton and at major universities; ⊕ wwww.statravel.com.au, ⊛ www.statravel.co.nz

Student Uni Travel 92 Pitt St, Sydney ☎ 02/9232 8444, plus branches in Brisbane, Cairns, Darwin, Melbourne and Perth.

Thomas Cook 175 Pitt St, Sydney; 257 Collins St, Melbourne; plus branches in other state capitals (local branch ☎ 13/1771, Thomas Cook Direct telesales ☎ 1800/801 002); 191 Queen St, Auckland ☎ 09/379 3920, ⊛ www.thomascook.com.au

Trailfinders 8 Spring St, Sydney ☎ 02/9247 7666, ⊛ www.trailfinders.com

Usit Beyond cnr Shortland St and Jean Batten Place, Auckland ☎ 09/379 4224 or 0800/788 336, plus branches in Christchurch, Dunedin, Palmerston North, Hamilton and Wellington; ⊛ www.usitbeyond.co.nz

Specialist agents and operators

Adventure Specialists 1/69 Liverpool St, Sydney ☎ 02/9261 2927. Overland and adventure tour agent.

Adventure World 73 Walker St, North Sydney ☎ 02/9956 7766 or 1300/363 055, ⊛ www.adventureworld.com.au plus branches in Adelaide, Brisbane, Melbourne and Perth; 101

Great South Rd, Remuera, Auckland ☎ 09/524 5118, ⊛ www.adventureworld.co.nz. Agents for a vast array of international adventure travel companies that operate trips to every continent.

American Town and Country Holidays ☎ 03/9877 3322. Tailor-made trips, accommodation, car rental, and city ministays throughout the US.

American Travel Centre/Journeys Worldwide ☎ 07/3221 4788. Handles all aspects of travel to the US.

Canada and America Travel Specialists ☎ 02/9922 4600, ⊛ www.canada-americatravel.com.au. Wholesalers of Greyhound Ameripasses plus flights and accommodation in North America.

Creative Holidays 3/55 Grafton St, Woollahra, Sydney ☎ 02/9386 2111. Packages to New York, San Francisco, LA (eg Disneyland) and Hawaii.

Peregrine 258 Lonsdale St, Melbourne ☎ 03/9662 2700, ⊛ www.peregrine.net.au. Adventure tours in Asia, South America, Africa and the Pacific.

Snow Bookings Only 1141 Toorak Rd, Camberwell, Melbourne ☎ 03/9809 2699 or 1800/623 266. Skiing tours in the USA, France, Switzerland and Austria.

Sydney International Travel Centre ☎ 02/9299 8000, ⊛ www.sydneytravel.com.au. US flights, accommodation, city stays and car rental.

Wiltrans 10/189 Kent St, Sydney ☎ 02/9255 0899. Luxury cruise and tour specialist, concentrating on Egypt, southeastern Africa, the US, Patagonia and the Caribbean; Australian representative for Maupintour.

Entry requirements for foreign visitors

Under the Visa Waiver Scheme, designed to speed up immigration procedures, citizens of Britain, Ireland, Australia, New Zealand and most European countries in possession of full passports do not require visas for trips to the United States of less than ninety days. Visa waiver forms are handed out on incoming planes, and are processed during immigration control at your initial point of arrival on US soil. The form requires details of where you are staying on your first night, and the date you intend to leave the US. You should be able to prove that you have enough money to support yourself while in the US. You may experience difficulties if you admit to being HIV-positive or having AIDS or TB. Part of the form will be attached to your passport, where it must stay until you leave. The same form also covers entry across the land borders with Canada and Mexico.

Citizens of all other countries should contact their local US embassy or consulate for details of current entry requirements. Even those eligible for the visa waiver scheme *must* apply for a free tourist visa if they intend to stay in the US for more than ninety days; for advice on working or studying in the US, see p.19. Whatever your nationality, visas are not issued to convicted felons or to anybody who owns up to being a communist, fascist or drug dealer.

Customs

All passengers arriving in the US must present a completed **customs declaration form** (also handed out on incoming planes). Customs officers check whether you're carrying any fresh foods and ask if you've visited a farm in the last month: if you have, you could well lose your shoes. As well as foods and anything agricultural, it's prohibited to carry into the country any articles from such places as North Korea, Cambodia, Iraq, Libya or Cuba, obscene publications, lottery tickets, chocolate liqueurs or pre-Columbian artifacts. Anyone caught bringing drugs into the country will not only face prosecution but be entered in the records as an undesirable and probably denied entry for all time. The **duty-free allowance** if you're over 17 is 200 cigarettes and 100 cigars (*not* Cuban) and, if you're over 21, a liter of spirits.

US embassies and consulates elsewhere

Australia Embassy: 21 Moonah Place, Canberra, ACT 2600 ☏ 02/6214 5600, ⊛ www.usis–Australia .gov/embassy
Consulates: Melbourne: 553 St Kilda Rd, VIC 3004 ☏ 03/9526 5900, ⊛ www.usis-australia.gov/melbourne
Sydney: 19–29 Martin Place, NSW 2000 ☏ 02/9373 9200, ⊛ www.usconsydney.com
Perth: 16 St George's Terrace, 13th Floor, WA 6000 ☏ 08/9202 1224
Visa hotline ☏ 1902/941 641 (premium rated, $1.50 per minute)

Canadian visitors

Canadian citizens are in a particularly privileged position when it comes to crossing the border into the US. For a brief excursion, you do not necessarily need even a passport, just some form of ID; if you're obviously setting off on a longer trip, you should carry a passport, and if you plan to stay for more than ninety days you need a visa, too.

Bear in mind that if you cross into the States in your car, trunks and passenger compartments are subject to spot searches by US Customs personnel, and these are especially likely in the aftermath of the terrorist attacks on New York and Washington in September 2001. Remember, too, that Canadians are legally barred from seeking gainful employment in the US.

Canada

Embassy: 490 Sussex Drive, Ottawa, ON K1N 1G8
☎613/238-5335, ⦿www.usembassycanada.gov
Consulates: Calgary: 615 Macleod Trail SE, 10th
Floor, AB T2G 4T8 ☎403/266-8962
Halifax: Suite 904, Wharf Tower II, 1969 Upper
Water St, NS B3J 3R7 ☎902/429-2480
Montreal: 1155 St. Alexandre St, PQ H5B 1G1
☎514/398-9695
Québec City: 2 Place Terrasse Dufferin, PQ G1R
4T9 ☎418/692-2095
Toronto: 360 University Ave, ON M5G 1S4
☎416/595-1700
Vancouver: 1095 W Pender St, 21st Floor, BC V6E
2M6 ☎604/685-4311

Ireland

42 Elgin Rd, Ballsbridge, Dublin 4 ☎01/668 8777,
⦿www.usembassy.ie

New Zealand

Embassy: 29 Fitzherbert Terrace, Thorndon,
Wellington ☎04/462-2000,
⦿www.usembassy.state.gov/wellington
Consulate: 3rd Floor, Citibank Building, 23 Customs
St, Auckland ☎09/303 2724
Address for visa applications: Non-Immigrant
Visas, Private Bag 92022, Auckland 1

UK

London: 5 Upper Grosvenor St, W1A 1AE
☎020/7499 9000, visa hotline ☎0891/200290
Edinburgh: 3 Regent Terrace, EH7 5BW
☎0131/556 8315
Belfast: Queens House, 14 Queen St, BT1 6EQ
☎028/9032 8239

Foreign embassies and consulates in the US

Australia

1601 Massachusetts Ave NW, Washington DC
20036 ☎202/797-3000

Canada

Embassy: 501 Pennsylvania Ave NW, Washington
DC 20001 ☎202/682-1740,
⦿www.canadianembassy.org
Consulates: Boston: Three Copley Place, Suite 400,
MA 02216 ☎617/262-3760
Chicago: Two Prudential Plaza, 188 N Stetson Ave,
Suite 2400, IL 60601 ☎312/616-1860
Los Angeles: 558 S Hope St, 9th Floor, CA
90071–2627 ☎213/346-2700
New York: 1251 Avenue of the Americas, NY
10020–1175 ☎212/596-1793

San Francisco: 555 Montgomery St, Suite 1288,
CA 94111 ☎415/834-3180

Ireland

2234 Massachusetts Ave NW, Washington DC
20008 ☎202/462-3939, ⦿www.irelandemb.org

New Zealand

37 Observatory Circle NW, Washington DC 20008
☎202/328-4800, ⦿www.nzembassy.org

UK

Embassy: 3100 Massachusetts Ave NW,
Washington DC 20008 ☎202/588-6500,
⦿www.britain–usa.com/consular/embassy
Consulates: Boston: Federal Reserve Plaza, 25th
Floor, 600 Atlantic Ave, MA 022190 ☎617/
248-9555
Chicago: The Wrigley Building,
400 N Michigan Ave, Suite 1306, IL 60611
☎312/970-3800
Los Angeles: 11766 Wilshire Blvd, Suite 400, CA
90025 ☎310/477-3322
New York: 845 3rd Ave, NY 10022 ☎212/745-
0200
San Francisco: 1 Sansome St, Suite 850, CA
94104 ☎415/981-3030
Texas: Wells Fargo Plaza, 19th Floor,
1000 Louisiana, Suite 1900,
Houston, 77002 ☎713/659-6270

Extensions

The date stamped on your passport is the
latest you're legally allowed to stay. Leaving
a few days later may not matter, especially if
you're heading home, but more than a week
or so can result in a protracted, rather
unpleasant interrogation from officials, which
may cause you to miss your flight.
Overstaying may also cause you to be
turned away the next time you try to enter
the US.

To get an extension before your time is up,
apply at the nearest **US Immigration and
Naturalization Service** (INS) office (addresses
appear in the Federal Government Offices listings in local telephone directories; ⦿www.ins
.gov). They will assume that you're working
illegally and it's up to you to convince them
otherwise. Do this by providing evidence of
ample finances and, if you can, bring along an
upstanding American citizen to vouch for you.
You'll also have to explain why you didn't plan
for the extra time initially.

Work and study

Only the US Immigration and Naturalization Service can grant permission to **work** in the country. Contact your local embassy or consulate for advice on current regulations and INS addresses; however, unless you have relatives (parents or children over 21) or a prospective employer to sponsor you, your chances are at best slim.

Illegal work is not as easy to find as it once was, now that the government imposes fines up to $10,000 for companies caught employing anyone without the legal right to work in the US. Even in the traditionally more casual establishments, like restaurants and bars, things have really tightened up. If you do find work it's likely to be of the less visible, poorly paid kind – washer-up instead of waiter.

Students have the best chance to prolong their stay in the US. One way is to get onto an Exchange Visitor Program; participants get a J-1 visa that entitles them to accept paid summer employment and apply for a social security number. However, most of these visas are issued for jobs in American **summer camps**, which aren't everybody's idea of a good time; they fly you over, and after a summer's work you end up with around $500 and a month to six weeks in which to blow it. If you live in Britain and are interested, contact BUNAC, 16 Bowling Green Lane, London EC1 (☎020/7251 3472, ⓦwww.bunac.com/uk), or Camp America, 37a Queens Gate, London SW7 (☎020/7581 7373, ⓦwww.campamerica .co.uk). If you want to **study** at an American university, apply to that institution directly; once accepted, you're more or less entitled to unlimited visas so long as you remain enrolled in full-time education.

Applicants for **au pair visas** must prove that they have at least 200 hours' experience with infants, 24 hours' training in child development and eight hours' child safety training. Prospective employers must provide a written description of the job they expect their au pair to perform, so there is protection on both sides. The American Institute for Foreign Study runs a program called Au Pair in America (☎207/581-7322, ⓦwww.aifs.com/aupair/), open to men and women aged 18 to 26. There is a placement fee of $75, a $100 contribution toward insurance and a good-faith deposit of $400; the combined amount covers the interviewing and selection process, visa and flight to the US. On-the-job payment while in the US is about US$139 per week; if you last the whole year you get your good-faith deposit back in dollars.

Insurance, health and personal safety

Insurance

Though not compulsory, **travel insurance** is *essential* for **foreign travelers**. The US has no national health system. You can lose an arm and a leg (so to speak) having even minor medical treatment. Before spending on a new policy, however, it's worth checking whether you are already covered; this is recommended for US residents as well. Some all-risks home insurance policies, for example, may cover your possessions against loss or theft when overseas, and many private medical plans include cover when abroad, including baggage loss, cancellation or curtailment and cash replacement as well as sickness or accident. In Canada, provincial health plans usually provide partial coverage for medical mishaps in another country, while holders of official student/teacher/youth cards in Canada and the US are entitled to meager accident coverage and hospital inpatient benefits. Students will often find that their student health coverage extends during vacations and for one term beyond the date of last enrollment. Some bank and credit cards include certain levels of medical or other insurance, and you may automatically get travel insurance if you use a major credit card to pay for your trip.

After exhausting the possibilities above, you might want to contact a specialist travel insurance company, or consider the travel insurance deal we offer (see box). A typical travel insurance policy usually provides cover for the loss of baggage, tickets and – up to a certain limit – cash or checks, as well as cancellation or curtailment of your journey. Most of them exclude so-called dangerous sports unless an extra premium is paid: in the US this can mean scuba-diving, white-water rafting, windsurfing and trekking, though probably not kayaking or jeep safaris. Many policies can be chopped and changed to exclude coverage you don't need – for example, sickness and accident benefits can often be excluded or included at will. If you do take medical coverage, ascertain whether benefits will be paid as treatment proceeds or only after return home, and whether there is a 24-hour medical emergency number. When securing baggage cover, make sure that the per-article limit will cover your most valuable possession. If you need to make a claim, keep receipts for medicines and medical treatment, and in the event you have anything stolen, you must obtain an official statement from the police.

Rough Guide travel insurance

Rough Guides offers its own travel insurance, customized for our readers by a leading UK broker and backed by a Lloyds underwriter. It's available for anyone, of any nationality and any age, traveling anywhere in the world.

There are two main Rough Guide insurance plans: **Essential**, for basic, no-frills cover; and **Premier**, with more generous and extensive benefits. Alternatively, you can take out **annual multi-trip insurance**, which covers you for any number of trips throughout the year (with a maximum of 60 days for any one trip). Unlike many policies, the Rough Guides plans are calculated by the day, so if you're traveling for 27 days rather than a month, that's all you pay for. If you intend to be away for the whole year, the Adventurer policy will cover you for 365 days. Each plan can be supplemented with a "Hazardous Activities Premium" if you plan to indulge in sports considered dangerous, such as skiing, scuba-diving or trekking.

For a policy quote, call the Rough Guide Insurance Line on UK freefone ☎0800/015 0906; US toll-free ☎1-866/220 5588 or, if you're calling from elsewhere ☎+44 1243/621 046. Alternatively, get an online quote or buy online at ⊛ www.roughguides.com/insurance.

Health advice

If you have a serious **accident** while in the US, emergency medical services will get to you quickly and charge you later. For emergencies or ambulances, dial ☎911, the nationwide emergency number (or whatever variant may be on the information plate of the pay phone).

Should you need to see a doctor, consult the *Yellow Pages* of the telephone directory under "Clinics" or "Physicians and Surgeons." The basic consultation fee is $50–100, payable in advance. Medications aren't cheap either – keep all your receipts for later claims on your insurance policy.

Foreign visitors should bear in mind that many pills available over the counter at home – most codeine-based painkillers, for example – require a **prescription** in the US. Local brand names can be confusing; ask for advice at the **pharmacy** in any **drugstore**.

In general, **inoculations** aren't required for entry to the US.

Crime and personal safety

No one could pretend that America is trouble-free, although away from the urban centers **crime** is often remarkably low-key. Even the lawless reputations of Miami, Detroit or Los Angeles are far in excess of the truth, and most parts of these cities, by day at least, are safe; at night, though, some areas are completely off limits. All the major tourist areas and the main nightlife zones in cities are invariably brightly lit and well policed. By planning carefully and taking good care of your possessions, you should, generally speaking, have few real problems.

Mugging and theft

The biggest fear for most travelers is **mugging**, though it's nothing to get overly paranoid about. It's impossible to give hard and fast rules about what to do if confronted by a mugger. Whether to run, scream or fight depends on the situation – but most locals would just hand over their money.

Of course, the best thing is simply to avoid being mugged. Remember a few basic rules: *don't* flash money around; *don't* peer at your map (or this book) at every street corner, thereby announcing that you're a lost stranger; if drunk, take a taxi to your hotel; avoid dark streets; and in the wee hours stick to the street-side edge of the sidewalk, so you can run into the street to attract attention. If you must ask for directions, choose your target carefully. Consider carrying a wad of cash, perhaps $50, separate from the bulk of your holdings so that if you do get confronted you can hand over something of value without losing everything.

If the worst happens and your assailant is toting a gun or (more likely) a knife, try to stay calm: remember that he (for this is generally a male pursuit) is probably scared, too. Keep still, make no sudden movements – and hand over your money. When he's gone, find a phone and dial ☎**911**, or hail a cab and ask the driver to take you to the nearest police station. Here, report the theft and get a reference number on the report to claim insurance and travelers check refunds. If you're in a big city, call the local Travelers Aid (their numbers are listed in the telephone directory) for sympathy and practical advice. For specific advice for women in the case of mugging or attack, see p.43.

Hotel-room burglary is another potential problem. Always store valuables in the hotel safe when you go out; when inside, keep your door locked and don't open it to anyone who causes you to be suspicious. If they claim to be hotel staff and you don't believe them, call reception to check.

Obviously, losing your travel documents – and especially your passport – is a traveler's nightmare. If you are unlucky in this respect, go to the nearest consulate and get a **temporary passport** – little more than a sheet of paper saying you've reported the loss – which will suffice to get you out of America and back home.

Useful phone numbers to report stolen checks and cards

American Express checks ☎1-800/221-7282; cards ☎1-800/869–3016, ⊛www.travel.american express.com

Citibank ☎1-800/645-6556, ⊛www.citibank.com

Diners Club ☎1-800/234-6377, ⊛www.dinersclub.com

Mastercard ☎1-800/826-2181, ⊛www.mastercard.com

Thomas Cook/Mastercard ☎1-800/233-7373, ⊛www.us.thomascook.com

Visa checks ℡1-800/227-6811
Visa cards ℡1-800/847-2911,
ⓦwww.usa.visa.com

Car crime

Crimes committed against tourists driving **rented cars** aren't as common as they once were, but it still pays to be cautious. In major urban areas, any car you rent should have nothing on it – such as a particular license plate – that makes it easy to spot as a rental car. When driving, under no circumstances stop in any unlit or seemingly deserted urban area – and especially not if someone is waving you down and suggesting that there is something wrong with your car. Similarly, if you are "accidentally" rammed by the driver behind, do not stop immediately but drive on to the nearest well-lit, busy area and **call** ℡**911** for assistance. Keep your doors locked and windows never more than slightly open. Do not open your door or window if someone approaches your car on the pretext of asking directions. Hide any valuables out of sight, preferably locked in the trunk or in the glove compartment.

Costs and money

This book contains detailed price information for lodging and eating throughout the US. Accommodation rates are coded according to the system explained on p.45, which excludes any local taxes that may apply, while restaurant prices include food only and not drinks or tip. For museums and similar attractions, the entrance fees quoted are for adults, unless stated otherwise; if we do not list a discount for senior citizens or children, inquire if discounts are available. Costs may change during the life of this edition.

Costs

Traveling in the States can seem quite the deal or very expensive – depending in part on prices you're used to and where you're headed. New York prices, for example, are well above those in rural America. New England, Hawaii, Alaska and other areas can also be quite pricey.

Accommodation is likely to be your biggest single expense. Typical motel rooms in rural areas cost a few dollars either side of $40 per night, while hotel and motel rates in cities tend to start around $60. Hostels offering dorm beds – usually for $10 to $20 – are reasonably common, but don't save all that much money for two or more people traveling together. Camping, of course, is cheap, ranging from free to perhaps $20 per night, but is rarely practical in or around the big cities.

As for **food**, $20 a day is enough to get an adequate life-support diet, consisting of perhaps one full-scale meal in a local diner

Visa Travel Money

This is a **disposable debit card** pre-paid with dedicated travel funds that you can access from more than 457,000 Visa ATMs in 120 countries with a PIN that you select. When your funds are depleted, simply throw the card away. Because you can buy up to nine cards to access the same funds – useful for couples/families traveling together – it's recommended that you buy at least one extra as a backup in case your first is lost or stolen. You can call a 24-hour Visa global customer assistance services center from any of the 120 countries toll-free: ℡877/394-2247 or ℡800/847-2911 for lost cards; visit also ⓦwww.visa.com. In the UK and the US, many Thomas Cook outlets sell the card.

Money: a note for foreign travelers

US currency comes in $1 **bills** and coins, bills of $5, $10, $20, $50 and $100, plus various larger (and rarer) denominations. Confusingly, all are the same size and same green color, making it necessary to check each bill carefully. The dollar is made up of 100 cents in **coins** of 1 cent (usually called a **penny**), 5 cents (a **nickel**), 10 cents (a **dime**) and 25 cents (a **quarter**). Fifty-cent and $1 coins are less frequently seen. Change – especially quarters – is needed for buses, vending machines and telephones, so always carry plenty.

Generally speaking, one pound sterling will buy $1.40, one Canadian dollar is worth around 65¢, one Australian dollar equals about 50¢ and one New Zealand dollar is equivalent to about 42¢.

At the time of publication, the Euro equaled 89¢ but had not been phased in completely.

---

supplemented by a stash of groceries, while for a daily total of around $30 you can dine pretty well. Beyond this, everything hinges on how much sightseeing, taxi-taking, drinking and socializing you do. Much of any of these – especially in a major city – and you're likely to be getting through upwards of $50 a day. If you're visiting a significant number of national parks and monuments, buy a National Parks or Golden Eagle pass (see p.48); the $50 or $65 fee covers all passengers in your vehicle.

Renting a car, at around $150 per week, is a far more efficient way to explore the country than public transportation and, for a group of two or more, it's no more expensive either. Having your own vehicle also enables you to stay in budget motels along the interstates instead of expensive city-center hotels.

In almost every state, **sales tax**, at rates varying up to ten percent, is added to virtually everything you buy in shops, but it isn't part of the marked price (for more details, see p.61). The most economical possible vacation, therefore, with two people sharing a rental car, camping in state and federal parks most nights, and eating one restaurant meal per day, will work out at something over $200 per person per week.

Taking, changing and accessing money

Expect to pay most of your major expenses by **credit or debit card**; hotels and car rental agencies usually require a credit card imprint as security, even if you intend to settle the bill in cash, and you'll be at a serious disadvantage if you don't have one. Visa, MasterCard, Diners Club, American Express

and Discover are the most widely accepted.

You'll also need to carry a certain amount of **cash**. If you have a MasterCard or Visa, or a cash-dispensing card linked to an international network such as Cirrus, Plus, Maestro or Visa Debit – check with your home bank before you set off – you can not only withdraw cash from appropriate automatic teller machines (ATMs) but often use your debit card for purchases, as you would at home. For both American and foreign visitors, US dollar **travelers checks** are a better way to carry money than ordinary bills; they offer the great security of knowing that lost or stolen checks will be replaced. Checks such as American Express, Visa and Thomas Cook are universally accepted as cash in shops, restaurants and gas stations, and change from your transactions will be rendered in hard currency. Be sure to have plenty of $10 and $20 denominations, and don't be put off by "no checks" signs, which refer only to personal checks. Foreign travelers should not bring travelers checks issued in their own currencies; it can be hard to find a bank prepared to change them, and no other business is likely to accept them.

Emergencies

Having money wired from home using one of the companies listed in this section is never convenient or cheap, and should be considered a last resort. It's also possible to have money wired directly from a bank in your home country to a bank in the US, although this is somewhat less reliable because it involves two separate institutions. If you go this route, your home bank will need the address of the branch bank where you want to pick up the money and the address and telex number of the head office, which will act as the clearinghouse. Money wired this way normally takes two working days to arrive, and costs around the equivalent of $40 per transaction. Assuming you know someone prepared to send you money in a crisis, the quickest way is to have them take the cash to the nearest **Moneygram** (☎1-800/666-3947) office and have it instantaneously **wired** to the office nearest you. In the US this process should take no longer than ten minutes. They charge according to the amount sent (ranging from $12 to wire $100, to $70 for $1000). The fees differ slightly if the money is being sent from outside the US (from the UK, for example, it costs $20 to wire $100, and $50 to wire $1000). **Thomas Cook** (☎1-800/287-7362 or 1-888/823-4732 in Canada, ⓦwww.us .thomascook.com) and **Western Union** (US ☎1-800/325-6000, UK ☎0800/833833) offer a similar service, at slightly higher rates. If credit cards are involved, the latter charges an extra $10.

If you have a few days' leeway, it's cheaper to mail a **postal money order**, which is exchangeable at any post office. The equivalent for foreign travelers is the **international money order**, for which you need to allow up to seven days in the mail. An ordinary check sent from overseas takes two to three weeks to clear.

Telephones, mail, email and time zones

In general, keeping in touch is easy. The exception would be in rural areas where you may find it slightly frustrating getting to the nearest public phone – which may be many miles away.

US **telephones** are run by a large number of local companies, many of which were spun off from the previous Bell System monopoly – the successor to which is the nationwide AT&T network.

Public telephones usually work, and in cities at any rate can be found everywhere – on street corners, in train and bus stations, hotel lobbies, bars and restaurants. They take 25¢, 10¢ and 5¢ coins. The cost of a **local call** from a public phone is usually 25¢ – when necessary, a voice comes on the line telling you to pay more.

Some numbers covered by the same area code are considered so far apart that calls between them count as **non-local** (zone calls). These cost much more and sometimes require you to dial 1 before the seven-digit number. Pricier still are **long-distance calls** (to a different area code, again with the 1 in front), for which you'll need plenty of change. Non-local calls and long-distance calls are much less expensive if made between 6pm and 8am – the cheapest rates are 11pm–8am – and calls from **private phones** are always much cheaper than those from public phones. Detailed rates are listed at the front of the **telephone directory** (the *White Pages*, a copious source of information on many matters).

Making telephone calls from **hotel rooms** is usually more expensive than from a pay phone, though some budget hotels offer free local calls from rooms – ask when you check in. An increasing number of phones accept **credit cards**, while anyone who holds a credit card issued by an American bank can obtain an **AT&T calling card** (information at ☎1-800/225-5288).

International calls

International calls can be dialed direct from private or (more expensively) public phones. Most expensive of all is dialing direct from your hotel room, which often gets billed at the highest rate and then has a surcharge of

To make international calls from the US, dial
℡011 followed by the country code:

Australia 61
New Zealand 64
Republic of Ireland 353
UK and Northern Ireland 44

For codes not listed here, dial 0 for the
operator or check the front of the local
White Pages.

up to forty percent slapped on top – so
avoid doing this if at all possible. You can get
assistance from the **international operator**
(℡00), who may also interrupt every three
minutes asking for more money. The **lowest
rates** for international calls to Europe are
between 6pm and 7am, when the rate is
about $5 for the first three minutes.

One of the most convenient ways of phoning home from abroad is via a **telephone
charge card**. Using access codes for the
particular country you are in and a PIN number, you can make calls from most hotel, public and private phones that will be charged to
your own account. While rates are always
cheaper from a residential phone at off-peak
rates, that's normally not an option when
you're traveling. If you do use a calling card in
conjunction with a residential phone, when
you're staying as a guest, for instance, you
will be paying the calling card company's
rates, which will usually be more expensive
than the local operator's. You may be able to
use it to minimize hotel phone surcharges,
but don't depend on it. However, the benefit
of calling cards is mainly one of convenience,
as rates aren't necessarily cheaper than calling from a public phone while abroad and
can't compete with discounted off-peak times
many local phone companies offer. But
because most major charge cards are free to
obtain, it's certainly worth getting one at least
for emergencies; inquire first though whether
your destination is covered. If you like to chat
on the phone for a long time, consider the
city-specific cards on sale at delis and corner
stores in most major urban areas. They come
in denominations of $5, $10 and $20 and
allow bargain overseas rates – calls to the UK
work out around 3¢/minute.

In the **USA and Canada**, AT&T, MCI,
Sprint, Canada Direct and other North

American long-distance companies all
enable their customers to make credit-card
calls while overseas. Call your company's
customer service line to find out if they provide service from the US, and, if so, what the
toll-free access code is. Calls made from
overseas will automatically be billed to your
home number.

In **the UK and Ireland**, British Telecom
(℡0800/345144, 🌐www.chargecard.bt.com/)
will issue free to all BT customers the BT
Charge Card, which can be used in 116 countries; AT&T (Dial ℡0800/890 011, then 888
641 6123 when you hear the AT&T prompt to
be transferred to the Florida Call Center, free
24 hours) has the Global Calling Card. NTL
(℡0500/100 505) issues its own Global
Calling Card, which can be used in more than
sixty countries abroad, though the fees cannot
be charged to a normal phone bill.

To call **Australia and New Zealand** from
overseas, telephone charge cards such as
Telstra Telecard or Optus Calling Card in
Australia, and Telecom NZ's Calling Card can
be used. Fees are charged back to a domestic account or credit card. Apply to Telstra
(℡1800/038 000), Optus (℡1300/300 937)
or Telecom NZ (℡04/801 9000).

Toll-free numbers and area codes

Many government agencies, car rental
firms, hotels and so on have **toll-free numbers**, which usually have the prefix 1-800
(or increasingly, 1-888 or 1-877). From within the US, you can dial any number that
starts with those digits free of charge.
Phone numbers with the prefix 1-900 are
pay-per-call lines, generally quite expensive
and almost always involving either sports or
phone sex.

The US currently has about one hundred
area codes – three-digit numbers that must
precede the seven-figure number if you're
calling from abroad or from a region with a
different code. It can get confusing, especially as certain cities have several different area
codes within their boundaries; for clarity, in
this book, we've included the local area
codes in all telephone numbers.

Mail

Post offices are usually open Monday to
Friday from 9am until 5pm, and Saturday

Mobile phones

If you want to use your mobile in the USA, ask your phone provider if it will work abroad and what the call charges are. Unless you have a tri-band phone, it is unlikely that a mobile bought for use outside the US will work inside the US and vice versa. Many mobiles work only within the region designated by the area code in the phone number – 212 or 415, for example. They tend to be very expensive to own in the US, as users are billed for both incoming and outgoing calls. US residents should check with their phone provider about their calling options.

In the UK, for all but the very top-of-the-range packages, you'll have to inform your phone provider before going to the USA to get international access switched on. You may get charged extra for this depending on your existing package and your destination. You are also likely to be charged extra for incoming calls when abroad, as the people calling you will be paying the usual rate. If you want to retrieve messages while you're away, ask your provider for a new access code; your home one is unlikely to work in the USA. Tri-band phones will automatically switch to the US frequency, but these can be pricey, so you may want to rent a phone if you're travelling to the US. For further information about using your phone abroad, check out ⓦ www.telecomsadvice.org.uk/features/using_your_mobile_abroad.htm.

from 9am to noon, and there are blue **mail boxes** on many street corners. At time of publication, **mail within the US** cost 34¢ for a letter weighing up to an ounce. **Air mail** between the US and Europe may take a week. Postcards and aerograms are 70¢, while letters weighing up to an ounce (roughly four thin sheets) are 80¢. The last line of the address includes the city or town and an abbreviation denoting the state (California is "CA" and Texas is "TX," for example, though you can spell it in full if you're unsure; each abbreviation appears with the State Tourist Office addresses given on pp.28–29). The last line also includes a five-figure number – the **zip code** – denoting the local post office. (The additional four digits that you will sometimes see appended to zip codes are not essential.) Letters that don't carry the zip code may get lost or at least delayed; telephone directories carry a list for their service area. Alternatively, look on the USPS website: ⓦ www.usps.com.

Letters can be sent c/o **General Delivery** (what's known elsewhere as poste restante) to the one relevant post office in each city (which we've listed in the *Guide*). They *must* include the zip code and will be held for only thirty days before being returned to sender – so make sure there's a return address on the envelope. If you're receiving mail at someone else's address, it should include "c/o" and the regular occupant's name; otherwise it, too, is likely to be returned.

Rules on sending parcels are very rigid: packages must be in special containers bought from post offices and sealed according to their instructions, which are given at the start of the *Yellow Pages*. To send anything out of the country, you'll need a green customs declaration form, available from a post office.

Email

One way to keep in touch while traveling is to sign up for a free internet email address that can be accessed from anywhere. YahooMail or Hotmail, for example, are accessible through ⓦ www.yahoo.com and ⓦ www.hotmail.com. Once you've set up an account, use one of these sites to pick up and send mail from any internet café or hotel with internet access.

A useful website – ⓦ www.kropla.com – has information on how to plug in a laptop when abroad, phone country codes around the world and electrical systems in different countries. For a database of 8000 internet cafés and public access points worldwide, go to ⓦ www.cybercaptive.com.

Telegrams and faxes

To send a **telegram** (sometimes called a wire), go to a Western Union office (listed in the telephone directory). Credit card holders can dictate messages over the phone or send them via the internet at ⓦ www.westernunion.com. **International telegrams** cost slightly less than the cheapest international phone call ($9.95 for 250 words): one sent in the morning from the US should arrive at its overseas destination the following day. For domestic telegrams ask for a **mailgram**, which will be delivered to any address in the country the next morning.

Public **fax** machines, which may require your credit card to be "swiped" through an attached device, are found at photocopy centers and, occasionally, bookstores.

Time zones

The continental US spreads over four different time zones, plus one each for Alaska and Hawaii; these are shown on the map at the front of this book. The **Eastern** zone is five hours behind Greenwich Mean Time, so 10am London time is 5am in New York City. The **Central** zone, starting approximately on a line down from Chicago and spreading west to Texas and across the Great Plains, is an hour behind the East. The **Mountain** zone covers the Rocky Mountains and most of the Southwest and is two hours behind the east coast. The **Pacific** zone includes the three coastal states and Nevada and is three hours behind New York. **Alaska** is two hours behind the Pacific zone, as is Hawaii.

Information and maps

Each state has its own tourist office, as listed on pp.28–29. These offer prospective visitors a colossal range of free maps, leaflets and brochures. Contact them before you set off. Or, as you travel around the country, look for the state-run Welcome Centers, usually along main highways close to the state borders. In heavily visited states, these often have piles of discount coupons for cut-price accommodation and food. In addition, visitor centers in most towns and cities – often known as the "Convention and Visitors Bureau," or CVB, and listed throughout this book – provide details on the area.

The **USTTA** – United States Travel and Tourism Administration – has offices all over the world, usually in US embassies and consulates. They stock vast quantities of printed material, but are unable to answer queries on specific states or cities. In Britain, you can contact them only by telephone: ☎020/7495 4466 (Mon–Fri 10am–4pm).

Maps

The **free road maps** distributed by each state through its tourist offices and Welcome Centers are usually fine for general driving and route planning. For something more detailed, say for **hiking** purposes, camping shops generally have a good selection, and park ranger stations in national parks, state parks and wilderness areas all sell good-quality local hiking maps for $1–3.

Rand McNally produces maps for each state, bound together in the *Rand McNally Road Atlas*, and runs 24 US stores (☎1-800/333-0136, ext 2111, ⓦwww .randmcnally.com for their locations or maps by mail). Britain's best source for maps is Stanfords, at 12–14 Long Acre, London WC2E 9LP (☎020/7836 1321, ⓦwww.stan-fords.co.uk); it also has a mail-order service.

The American Automobile Association (AAA; ☎1-877/244-9790 or 303/753-8800, ⓦwww.aaa.com), based at 4100 E Arkansas Drive, Denver, CO 80222, provides free maps and assistance to its members, and to British members of the AA and RAC. Call the main number to get the location of a branch near you; bring your membership card, or at least know your membership number.

Alabama Alabama Bureau of Tourism & Travel, PO Box 4927, Montgomery AL 36103-4927, ☏ 334/242-4169 or 1-800/ALABAMA, ⓦ www.touralabama.org

Alaska Alaska Division of Tourism, PO Box 110801, Juneau, AK 99811 ☏ 907/465-2010, ⓦ www.dced.state.ak.is/tourism

Arizona Arizona Office of Tourism, 2702 N 3rd St, Suite 4015, Phoenix AZ 85009 ☏ 602/230-7733 or 1-888/520-3434, ⓦ www.arizonaguide.com

Arkansas Arkansas Dept of Parks & Tourism, One Capitol Mall, Little Rock AR 72201 ☏ 501/682-7777 or 1-800/NATURAL, ⓦ www.arkansas.com

California California Division of Tourism, PO Box 1499, Sacramento CA 95812 ☏ 916/856-5200 or 1-800/GO-CALIF, ⓦ www.gocalif.com

Colorado Colorado Tourism Office, 1625 Broadway, Suite 1700, Denver CO 80202 ☏ 303/832-6171 or 1-800/265-6723, ⓦ www.colorado.com

Connecticut Connecticut Tourism Division, 505 Hudson St, Hartford CT 06106 ☏ 860/270-8081 or 1-800/282-6863, ⓦ www.ctbound.org

Delaware Delaware State Tourism Office, 99 Kings Hwy, Dover DE 19901 ☏ 302/739-4271 or 1-866/284-7483, ⓦ www.visitdelaware.net

Florida Visit Florida, 661 E. Jefferson St, Tallahassee FL 32399 ☏ 850/488-5607 or 1-888/735-2872, ⓦ www.flausa.com

Georgia Georgia Dept of Industry, Trade & Tourism, 285 Peachtree Center Ave, Suite 1000, Atlanta GA 30303 ☏ 404/656-3590 or 1-800/847-4842, ⓦ www.georgia.org

Hawaii Hawaii Visitors Bureau, 2270 Kalakaua Ave, Suite 801, Honolulu HI 96815 ☏ 808/923-1811 or 1-800/464-2924, ⓦ www.gohawaii.com

Idaho Idaho Travel Council, 700 W State St, Boise ID 83720 ☏ 208/334-2470 or 1-800/842-5858, ⓦ www.visitid.org

Illinois Illinois Bureau of Tourism, 100 W Randolph St, Suite 3–400, Chicago IL 60601 ☏ 312/814-4732 or 1-800/226-6632, ⓦ www.enjoyillinois.com

Indiana Indiana Dept of Tourism, 1 N Capitol Ave, Suite 100, Indianapolis IN 46204-2288 ☏ 317/232-8860 or 1-888/365-6946, ⓦ www.indianatourism.com

Iowa Iowa Division of Tourism, 200 E Grand Ave, Des Moines IA 50309 ☏ 515/242-4705 or 1-888/472-6035, ⓦ www.traveliowa.com

Kansas Kansas Travel & Tourism Division, 700 SW Harrison St, Suite 1300, Topeka KS 66603 ☏ 785/296-2009 or 1-800/252-6727, ⓦ www.kansas-travel.com

Kentucky Kentucky Dept of Travel, 500 Mero St, Suite 2200 Frankfort KY 40601 ☏ 502/564-4930 or 1-800/225-8747, ⓦ www.kentuckytourism.com

Louisiana Louisiana Office of Tourism, Box 94291, Baton Rouge LA 70804-9291 ☏ 225/342-8100 or 1-800/344–8626, ⓦ www.louisianatravel.com

Maine Maine Office of Tourism, PO Box 2300, 235b Water St, Hallowell, ME 04347 ☏ 207/623-0363 or 1-888/624-6345, ⓦ www.mainetourism.com

Maryland Maryland Office of Tourism, 100 Light St, 12th Floor, Baltimore MD 21202 ☏ 410/659-7300 or 1-800/543-1036, ⓦ www.mdisfun.org

Massachusetts Massachusetts Division of Tourism, 10 Park Plaza, Suite 4150, Boston MA 02116 ☏ 617/973-8500 or 1-800/227-6277, ⓦ www.massvacation.com

Michigan Travel Michigan, PO Box 30226, Lansing MI 48909 ☏ 517/373-0670 or 1-888/784-7328, ⓦ www.michigan.org

Minnesota Minnesota Office of Tourism, 100 Metro Square, 121 7th Place E, St Paul MN 55101 ☏ 651/296-5029 or 1-800/657-3700, ⓦ www.exploreminnesota.com

Mississippi Mississippi Division of Tourism, PO Box 849, Jackson MS 39205-0849 ☏ 601/359-3297 or 1-800/927-6378, ⓦ www.visitmississippi.org

Missouri Missouri Division of Tourism, PO Box 1055, Jefferson City MO 65102 ☏ 573/751-4133 or 1-800/877-1234, ⓦ www.missouritourism.org

Montana Travel Montana, PO Box 200533, Helena MT 59620 ☏ 406/422-1962 or 1-800/541-1447, ⓦ www.visitmt.org

Nebraska Nebraska Travel & Tourism, PO Box 98907, Lincoln NE 68509 ☏ 402/471-3796 or 1-800/228-4307, ⓦ www.visitnebraska.org

Nevada Nevada Commission on Tourism, 401 N Carson St, Carson City NV 89701 ☏775/687-4322 or 1-800/638-2328, ⓦwww.travelnevada.com

New Hampshire New Hampshire Office of Travel, 172 Pembroke Rd, Concord NH 03302 ☏603/271-2655 or 1-800/386-4664, ⓦwww.visitnh.gov

New Jersey New Jersey Division of Travel & Tourism, PO Box 820, Trenton NJ 08625-820 ☏609/777-0855 or 1-800/847-4865, ⓦwww.visitnj.org

New Mexico New Mexico Dept of Tourism, 491 Old Santa Fe Trail, PO Box 20002, Santa Fe NM 87501 ☏505/827-7400 or 1-800/733-6396, ⓦwww.newmexico.org

New York City New York City CVB, 810 7th Ave, New York NY 10019 ☏212/484-1222 or 1-877/446-8313, ⓦwww.nycvisit.com

New York State Empire State Plaza, Main Concourse, Room 10, Albany NY 12220 ☏518/474-4116 or 1-800/225-5697, ⓦwww.iloveny.com

North Carolina North Carolina Travel & Tourism, 301 N Wilmington St, Raleigh NC 27601-2825 ☏919/733-8372 or 1-800/847-4862, ⓦwww.visitnc.com

North Dakota North Dakota Tourism Division, 604 E Boulevard Ave, Bismarck ND 58505 ☏701/328-2525 or 1-800/435-5663, ⓦwww.ndtourism.com

Ohio Ohio Office of Travel & Tourism, PO Box 1001, Columbus OH 43266 ☏614/466-8844 or 1-800/282-5393, ⓦwww.ohiotourism.com

Oklahoma Oklahoma Tourism & Recreation, 15 N Robinson St, Suite 801, Oklahoma City OK 73102 ☏405/521-2409 or 1-800/654-8240, ⓦwww.touroklahoma.com

Oregon Oregon Tourism Commission, 775 Summer St NE, Salem OR 97310 ☏503/986-0000 or 1-800/547-7842, ⓦwww.traveloregon.com

Pennsylvania Pennsylvania Bureau of Travel, Room 404, Forum Building, Harrisburg PA 17120 ☏717/787-5453 or 1-800/847-4872, ⓦwww.experiencepa.com

Rhode Island Rhode Island Tourism Division, One W Exchange St, Providence RI 02903 ☏401/222-2601 or 1-800/556-2484, ⓦwww.visitrhodeisland.com

South Carolina South Carolina Parks, Recreation and Tourism, Dept of International Marketing, 1205 Pendleton St, Columbia SC 29201 ☏803/734-0129 or 1-800/346-3634, ⓦwww.discoversouthcarolina.com

South Dakota South Dakota Dept of Tourism, c/o 500 E Capitol Ave, Pierre SD 57501 ☏605/773-3301 or 1-800/732-5682, ⓦwww.travelsd.com

Tennessee Tennessee Dept of Tourism, Rachel Jackson Building, 320 6th Ave, 5th Floor, Nashville TN 37243 ☏615/741-2158 or 1-800/462-8366, ⓦwww.tourism.state.tn.us

Texas Texas Dept of Commerce, Tourism Division, Box 141009, Austin TX 78714-1009 ☏512/462-9191 or 1-800/888-8839, ⓦwww.traveltex.com

Utah Utah Travel Council, Council Hall, Capitol Hill, Salt Lake City UT 84114 ☏801/538-1030 or 1-800/200-1160, ⓦwww.utah.com

Vermont Vermont Travel Division, 135 State St, Montpelier VT 05633 ☏802/828-3237 or 1-800/837-6668, ⓦwww.1-800-vermont.com

Virginia Virginia Tourism Corp, 901 E Bird St, Richmond VA 23219 ☏804/786-4484 or 1-800/321-3244, ⓦwww.virginia.org

Washington Washington State Tourism, PO Box 42500, Olympia WA 98504 ☏360/725-5052 or 1-800/544-1800, ⓦwww.tourism.wa.gov

Washington DC Washington DC Visitor Information, 1212 New York Ave NW, Suite 200, Washington DC 20005 ☏202/789-7000 or 1-800/422-8644, ⓦwww.washington.org

West Virginia West Virginia Division of Tourism, 2101 Washington St E, PO Box 50312, Charleston WV 25305 ☏304/558-2200 or 1-800/225-5982, ⓦwww.callwva.com

Wisconsin Wisconsin Dept of Tourism, 201 W Washington Ave, PO Box 7976, Madison WI 53707 ☏608/266-2161 or 1-800/432-8747, ⓦwww.travelwiscon.com

Wyoming Wyoming Division of Tourism, I-25 at College Drive, Cheyenne WY 82002 ☏307/777-7777 or 1-800/225-5996, ⓦwww.wyomingtourism.org

29

B

BASICS | Information and maps

Map outlets

USA and Canada

Adventurous Traveler Bookstore PO Box 64769, Burlington, VT 05406 ☎1-800/282-3963, Ⓦwww.AdventurousTraveler.com

Book Passage 51 Tamal Vista Blvd, Corte Madera, CA 94925 ☎415/927-0960, Ⓦwww.bookpassage.com

Distant Lands 56 S Raymond Ave, Pasadena, CA 91105 ☎1-800/310-3220, Ⓦwww.distantlands.com

Elliot Bay Book Company 101 S Main St, Seattle, WA 98104 ☎206/624-6600 or 1-800/962-5311, Ⓦwww.elliotbaybook.com

Forsyth Travel Library 226 Westchester Ave, White Plains, NY 10604 ☎1-800/367-7984, Ⓦwww.forsyth.com

Globe Corner Bookstore 28 Church St, Cambridge, MA 02138 ☎1-800/358-6013, Ⓦwww.globecorner.com

GORP Adventure Library ☎1-877/440-4677, Ⓦwww2.gorp.com

Map Link Inc 30 S La Patera Lane, Unit 5, Santa Barbara, CA 93117 ☎805/692-6777, Ⓦwww.maplink.com

Phileas Fogg's Travel Center #87 Stanford Shopping Center, Palo Alto, CA 94304 ☎1-800/533-3644, Ⓦwww.foggs.com

Rand McNally 444 N Michigan Ave, Chicago, IL 60611 ☎312/321-1751, Ⓦwww.randmcnally.com; 150 E 52nd St, New York, NY 10022 ☎212/758-7488; 595 Market St, San Francisco, CA 94105 ☎415/777-3131; other stores across the US – call ☎1-800/333-0136 ext 2111 or check the website for the nearest store.

Travel Books & Language Center 4437 Wisconsin Ave, Washington, DC 20016 ☎1-800/220-2665, Ⓦwww.bookweb.org/bookstore/travellers

The Travel Bug Bookstore 2667 W Broadway, Vancouver BC V6K 2G2 ☎604/737-1122, Ⓦwww.swifty.com/tbug

World of Maps 1235 Wellington St, Ottawa, ON K1Y 3A3 ☎613/724-6776, Ⓦwww.worldofmaps.com

UK and Ireland

Blackwell's Map and Travel Shop 53 Broad St, Oxford OX1 3BQ ☎01865/792 792, Ⓦwww.bookshop.blackwell.co.uk

Easons Bookshop 40 O'Connell St, Dublin 1 ☎01/873 3811, Ⓦwww.eason.ie

Heffers Map and Travel 20 Trinity St, Cambridge CB2 1TJ ☎01223/568 568, Ⓦwww.heffers.co.uk

Hodges Figgis Bookshop 56–58 Dawson St, Dublin 2 ☎01/677 4754, Ⓦwww.hodgesfiggis.com

John Smith and Sons 26 Colquhoun Ave, Glasgow G52 4PJ ☎0141/552 3377, Ⓦwww.johnsmith.co.uk

James Thin Melven's Bookshop 29 Union St, Inverness IV1 1QA ☎01463/233 500, Ⓦwww.jthin.co.uk

The Map Shop 30a Belvoir St, Leicester LE1 6QH ☎0116/247 1400

National Map Centre 22–24 Caxton St, SW1H 0QU ☎020/7222 2466, Ⓦwww.mapsnmc.co.uk

Newcastle Map Centre 55 Grey St, Newcastle upon Tyne NE1 6EF ☎0191/261 5622, Ⓦwww.traveller.ltd.uk

Ordnance Survey Service Phoenix Park, Dublin 8 ☎01/820 6100, Ⓦwww.irlgov.ie/osi/

Ordnance Survey of Northern Ireland Colby House, Stranmillis Ct, Belfast BT9 5BJ ☎028/9066 1244, Ⓦwww.osni.gov.uk

Stanfords 12–14 Long Acre, WC2E 9LP ☎020/7836 1321, Ⓦwww.stanfords.co.uk; maps by mail or phone order are available on this number and via Ⓔsales@stanfords.co.uk. Other branches within British Airways offices at 156 Regent St, W1R 5TA ☎020/7434 4744 and 29 Corn St, Bristol BS1 1HT ☎0117/929 9966

The Travel Bookshop 13–15 Blenheim Crescent, W11 2EE ☎020/7229 5260, Ⓦwww.thetravelbookshop.co.uk

Australia and New Zealand

The Map Shop 6 Peel St, Adelaide ☎08/8231 2033, Ⓦwww.mapshop.net.au

Mapland 372 Little Bourke St, Melbourne ☎03/9670 4383, Ⓦwww.mapland.com.au

Mapworld 173 Gloucester St, Christchurch ☎03/374 5399, Ⓕ03/374 5633, Ⓦwww.mapworld.co.nz

Perth Map Centre 1/884 Hay St, Perth ☎08/9322 5733, Ⓦwww.perthmap.com.au

Specialty Maps 46 Albert St, Auckland ☎09/307 2217, Ⓦwww.ubd-online.co.nz/maps

30

Getting around

Distances in the US are so great that it's essential to think carefully in advance about how you plan to get from place to place. Your choice of transportation will have a crucial impact on your trip. Amtrak provides a skeletal but often scenic rail service, and there are usually good bus links between the major cities – though Greyhound, the mainstay of the US bus network, has cut back on non-profitable routes of late. Things may get difficult only in isolated rural areas. Even here, by adroit advance planning, you can usually reach the main points of interest without too much trouble by using local buses and charter services, as detailed state-by-state throughout this book. In planning your public transportation timetable, keep enhanced concerns about security in mind.

Travel is almost always easier if you have a **car**. Many worthwhile and memorable US destinations are far removed from cities. Even if a bus or train can take you to the general vicinity of one of the great national parks, for example, it can be nearly impossible to explore the area without a vehicle. For that matter, the cities themselves can be so vast, and so heavily car-oriented, that the lack of a car can seriously impair your enjoyment.

By train

Traveling by **rail** is rarely the fastest way to get from A to B, though if you have the time it can be a pleasant and relaxing experience. As you will see from our map, on p.33, the Amtrak system isn't at all comprehensive – such popular destinations as Nashville and Santa Fe, and even some entire states, are left out altogether. What's more, the cross-country routes tend to be served by one or at most two trains per day, so in large areas of the nation the only train of the day passes through at three or four in the morning. That said, the train is by far the most comfortable way to travel, and especially on long-distance rides it can be a great way to meet people. A number of local train services connect stops on the Amtrak lines with towns and cities not on the main grid.

Amtrak also runs the coordinated Thruway bus service that connects some cities that their trains don't reach. However, this network is not in the least comprehensive.

For any one specific journey, the train can be more expensive than taking a Greyhound or even a plane – the standard fare from New York to Los Angeles, for example, is around $200 one-way – though special deals, especially in the off-peak seasons (Sept–May), bring the cost of a coast-to-coast round-trip down to well under $350 (closer to $250 at certain times). In addition to these, Amtrak's **All Aboard America** fares, allowing three stopovers en route, are available by region (Florida, for some reason, is excluded). Foreign travelers can benefit from the **passes** detailed overleaf.

Always **reserve** as far in advance as possible; all passengers must have seats, and some trains, especially between major east coast cities, are booked solid. **Sleeping compartments** (which are around $100 per night, including three full meals, for one or two people) and the plush Metroliner carriages cost extra. Even standard Amtrak carriages are surprisingly spacious, and there are additional dining cars and lounge cars (with full bars and sometimes glass-domed 360° viewing compartments).

Beautiful east coast Amtrak rides include the Hudson River Valley north of New York City (on several routes); along the Potomac

At the end of the introduction to each individual state in this book, a "**Getting Around**" section summarizes local transportation options.

Amtrak USA Rail Passes

Overseas travelers have a choice of the following **USA Rail Passes**, covering the areas shown on our map. The **Coastal Pass** permits unlimited train travel on the east and west coasts, but not between the two. The Northeast Pass is also available as a 5-day offer, for $149.

	15-day (June–Aug)	15-day (Sept–May)	30-day (June–Aug)	30-day (Sept–May)
East	$260	$210	$320	$265
Far West	$245	$190	$320	$250
Northeast	$205	$185	$240	$225
West	$325	$200	$405	$270
Coastal	–	–	$285	$235
National	$440	$295	$550	$385

On production of a passport issued outside the US or Canada, the passes can be bought at Amtrak stations in the US. The Amtrak website lists several places you can buy them internationally (see below).

Greyhound Discovery Passes

Foreign visitors, especially those inclined to venture beyond the major meccas, can – before leaving home – buy a Greyhound Discovery Pass. It offers unlimited travel within a set time limit. Most travel agents sell them. In the UK, they cost £92 (4-day), £113 (5-day), £146 (7-day), £174 (10–day), £205 (15-day), £235 (30-day), £256 (45–day) or £311 (60-day). No daily extensions are available. International agents are listed below.

On first use, the ticket clerk will date your pass (this is the commencement date of the ticket). Your destination is written on a page that the driver will tear out and keep as you board the bus. Repeat this procedure for every subsequent journey.

Where to buy Amtrak and Greyhound passes abroad

STA UK ☎ 0870/160 0599, ⊛ www.statravel .co.uk; Australia ☎ 1300/360 960, ⊛ www.statravel.com.au; New Zealand ☎ 0800/874 773, ⊛ www.statravel.co.nz
Trailfinders UK ☎ 020/7628 7628, ⊛ www.trailfinders.com; Ireland ☎ 01/ 677 7888, ⊛ www.trailfinders.ie; Australia ☎ 02/9247 6556, ⊛ www.trailfinders .com.au

USIT UK ☎ 0870/240 1010, ⊛ www .usitcampus.co.uk; Ireland ☎ 01/602 1600, ⊛ www.usitnow.ie; Australia ☎ 02/9232 8444, ⊛ www.usitbeyond.com.au; New Zealand ☎ 09/379 4224, ⊛ www .usitbeyond.co.nz
Walshes World Australia ☎ 02/9232 7499 or 1800/227 122; New Zealand ☎ 09/ 379 3708.

Air passes

The main American airlines (and British Airways in conjunction with various carriers) offer air passes for visitors who plan to fly a lot within the US. These must be bought in advance. In the UK they are usually sold with the proviso that you cross the Atlantic with the relevant airline. All the deals involve the purchase of between three and ten coupons; United, for instance, charges British travelers £292 for three **Visit USA** coupons and £479 to £499 for ten depending on the season. Each coupon is valid for a flight of any duration in the 48 contiguous US states – you purchase additional coupons for flights to Alaska, Hawaii, the Caribbean and Mexico at varying rates. American Airlines charge $429, Northwest $399 and Continental $269 for comparable itineraries. The situation is similar for Australasian visitors.

Other plans entitle foreign travelers to discounts on regular US domestic fares, again with the proviso that you buy the ticket before you leave home. However you do it, flying within the US is only a wise choice for travel in regions where fares are low anyway; flights within Florida, for example, are very expensive.

AMTRAK ROUTES

0 ————— 400 miles

N

CANADA

MEXICO

EAST REGION

WEST REGION

FAR WEST REGION

——— Amtrak Railroad

Seattle
Portland
San Francisco
Oakland
San Diego
Los Angeles
Bakersfield
Las Vegas
Reno
YOSEMITE
Phoenix
Tucson
Flagstaff
GRAND CANYON
Salt Lake City
Denver
Santa Fe
Albuquerque
El Paso
BIG BEND
YELLOWSTONE
MT. RUSHMORE
Duluth
Minneapolis St Paul
Omaha
Kansas City
Oklahoma City
Fort Worth
Dallas
San Antonio
Houston
Little Rock
St Louis
Madison
Milwaukee
Chicago
Lake Michigan
Lake Superior
Lake Huron
Lake Erie
Detroit
Toronto
Cleveland
Pittsburgh
Cincinnati
Louisville
Nashville
Memphis
Birmingham
Atlanta
New Orleans
Montréal
Boston
New York City
Atlantic City
Philadelphia
Niagara Falls
Washington DC
Charleston
Savannah
Jacksonville
Orlando
Tampa
Miami

River at Harpers Ferry, West Virginia (on the *Capitol Limited* out of Washington DC); and the New River Gorge (on the *Cardinal*). In the West, the *California Zephyr*, between Chicago and San Francisco, follows a stunning route west of Denver over the Rockies, rivaled a day later by the towering Sierra Nevada. The *Coast Starlight* gives unsurpassed views of the California coast on its journey between San Luis Obispo and Santa Barbara. Verify when you book your journey that the train passes through the scenic splendor during daylight hours.

Historic railroads

While Amtrak has a monopoly on long-distance rail travel, a number of **historic** or **scenic railways**, some steam-powered or running along narrow-gauge mining tracks, bring back the glory days of train travel. Many are purely tourist attractions, doing a full circuit through beautiful countryside in two or three hours, though some can drop you off in otherwise hard-to-reach wilderness areas. Popular lines include the **Cass Scenic Railroad** in West Virginia (☏304/456-4300 or 1-800/2255 982, ⌨www.neumedia.net/ ~cassar); the **Great Smoky Mountains Railroad** in North Carolina (☏1-800/872 4681, ⌨www.gsmr.com); the **Cumbres and Toltec** line in Chama, New Mexico (☏1–888/ 286-2737, ⌨www.cubrestoltec.com); **Durango & Silverton Narrow Gauge Railroad** in Colorado (☏1–800/872–4607, ⌨www.durangotrain.com); the **Big Trees and Roaring Camp Railroad** in Santa Cruz (☏831/335-4484, ⌨www.roaringcamprr .com) and the **Fort Bragg–Willits** line (☏707/964-6371 or 1–800/777 5865, ⌨www.skunktrain.com), both in California; and the **Mount Hood Railroad** (☏541/386-3556 or 1–800/872 4611, ⌨www.mthoodrr .com) outside Portland, Oregon.

For information on **Amtrak fares and schedules** in the US, and to make reservations, use the toll-free number: ☏**1-800/USA-RAIL**
Alternatively, check out the Amtrak **website**: ⌨www.amtrak.com
Do not phone individual stations.

By bus

If you're traveling on your own and making a lot of stops, **buses**, by far the cheapest way to get around, make a lot of sense. The main long-distance operator, **Greyhound**, links all major cities and many towns. Out in the country, buses are fairly scarce, sometimes appearing only once a day; here, you'll need to plot your route with care. But along the main highways, buses run around the clock to a fairly full timetable, stopping only for meal breaks (almost always fast-food dives) and driver changeovers. Greyhound buses are slightly less uncomfortable than you might expect. It's feasible to save on a night's accommodation by traveling overnight and sleeping on the bus – though you may not feel up to much the next day.

Greyhound's nationwide **toll-free information service** (☏1-800/229-9424) can give you routes and times, plus phone numbers and addresses of local terminals. You can also make reservations. Alternatively, check out the Greyhound **website**: ⌨www.grey-hound.com.

To avoid possible hassle, lone female travelers in particular should take care to sit as near to the driver as possible, and to arrive during daylight hours – many bus stations are in fairly dodgy areas. It used to be that any sizable community would have a Greyhound station; in some places the post office or a gas station doubles as the bus stop and ticket office, and in many others the bus service has been canceled altogether. **Reservations**, either in person at the station or on the toll-free number, are not essential, but recommended – if a bus is full you may be forced to wait until the next one, sometimes overnight or longer.

Fares on shorter journeys average about 11¢ a mile, but discounts are common on longer hauls (for example it will cost you $75 to get a round-trip ticket from Los Angeles to San Francisco, but for $218 you could get all the way to New York and back). For long-trip travel though, considering the time expended (around 65 hours coast-to-coast, if you eat and sleep on the bus), riding the bus is not necessarily a much better deal

Green Tortoise

One alternative to Long-Distance Bus Hell is the slightly countercultural **Green Tortoise**, whose buses, complete with foam cushions, bunks, fridges and rock music, ply the major cities of the west coast, running between Los Angeles, San Francisco and Seattle. In summer, they also cross the country to New York and Boston, trips that amount to mini-tours of the nation, taking about a dozen days (for between $469 and $499, not including food) and allowing plenty of stops for hiking, river-rafting and hot springs. Other Green Tortoise excursions go to the major national parks (in 16 days for $629), south to Mexico ($329–$549) and north to Alaska ($1500 for 28 days including airfare, or $699 for 14 days, excluding flight). The main office is at 494 Broadway, San Francisco, CA 94133 (☎415/956-7500 or 1-800/867–8647, ⊛www.greentortoise.com).

than flying. However, the bus is the best deal if you plan to visit a lot of places: Greyhound's **Ameripasses** for domestic travelers are good for unlimited travel nationwide for 7 days ($185), 10 days ($235), 15 days ($285), 21 days ($335), 30 days ($385), 45 days ($419) and 60 days ($509); the reduced rates for for-eign travelers (typically a saving of $20–40 per pass) are given in the box on p.32.

Greyhound produces a condensed **timetable** of major countrywide routes, but this is not distributed to travelers. To plan your route, pick up the free route-by-route timetables from larger stations.

By plane

Don't be misled by movie scenes in which characters stroll into large airports and casu-ally buy cross-country tickets. That kind of plane travel is outrageously expensive – $1000 for a one-way flight is not unheard of. However, with planning, **air travel** can work out reasonably cheap. Indeed, it can cost less than the train – especially if you take into account how much you save not paying for food and drink while on the move – and only a little more than the bus. Flying can also make sense for relatively short local hops, turning a full day's cross-desert $25 bus journey, for example, into a quick and scenic $50 flight of under an hour. We men-tion such options wherever appropriate.

Most airlines offer comparable **Apex** (see p.10) fares, but any good **travel agent**, especially student and youth-oriented ones like Council Travel and STA, can usually get you a much better deal. Phone the airlines to find out routes and schedules, then buy your ticket using the **Fare Assurance Program**, which processes all the ticket options to find

the cheapest fare, taking into account the requirements of individual travelers. One agent using the service is Travel Avenue (☎1-800/333-3335, ⊛www.travelavenue.com). Few standby fares are available, and the best discounts are usually offered on tickets booked and paid for at least two weeks in advance. These are almost always nonre-fundable and hard to change.

Toll-free airline numbers in the US

Aer Lingus ☎1-800/232-6537, ⊛www.aerlingus.ie
Air Canada ☎1-888/247-2262, ⊛www.aircanada.ca
Air France ☎1-800/237-2747, ⊛www.airfrance.com
Alaska Airlines ☎1-800/426-0333, ⊛www.alaskaair.com
Alitalia ☎1-800/223-5730, ⊛www.alitaliausa.com
America West ☎1-800/235-9292, ⊛www.americawest.com
American Airlines ☎1-800/433-7300, ⊛www.aa.com
American Trans Air ☎1-800/435-9282, ⊛www.ata.com
British Airways ☎1-800/247-9297, ⊛www.british-airways.com
Cathay Pacific ☎1-800/233-2742, ⊛www.cathay-usa.com
Continental Airlines ☎1-800/231-0856 (international), ☎1-800/523-3723 (domestic), ⊛www.continental.com
Delta Airlines ☎1-800/241-4141 (international), ☎1-800/221-1212 (domestic), ⊛www.delta.com
Hawaiian Airlines ☎1-800/367-5320, ⊛www.hawaiianair.com
Iberia ☎1-800/772-4642, ⊛www.iberia.com
Icelandair ☎1-800/223-5500, ⊛www.icelandair.com
Japan AirLines ☎1-800/525-3663, ⊛www.japanair.com

Jet Blue ☎1-800/538-2583, ⓦwww.jetblue.com
KLM ☎1-800/374-7747, ⓦwww.klm.com
Lufthansa ☎1-800/645-3880,
ⓦwww.lufthansa.com
Northwest Airlines ☎1-800/447-4747
(international) ☎1-800/225-2525 (domestic),
ⓦwww.qantas.com
SAS ☎1-800/221-2350, ⓦwww.scandinavian.net
Southwest ☎1-800/435-9792,
ⓦwww.southwest.com
Swissair ☎1-800/221-4750,
ⓦwww.swissair.com
TWA ☎1-800/892-4141 (international)
☎1-800/221-2000 (domestic), ⓦwww.twa.com
United Airlines ☎1-800/538-2929
(international), ☎1-800/241-6522 (domestic),
ⓦwww.ual.com
US Airways ☎1-800/622-1015 (international),
☎1-800/428-4322 (domestic)
ⓦwww.usairways.com
Virgin Atlantic ☎1-800/862-8621,
ⓦwww.virgin-atlantic.com

By car

For many people, the concept of cruising down a highway, preferably in an open-top convertible with the radio blaring, is one of the main reasons to set out on a tour of the US. The romantic images of countless road movies, from *Bonnie and Clyde* to *Thelma and Louise*, are not far from the truth, though you don't have to embark on a wild spree of drink, drugs, crime and murder to enjoy driving across America. Apart from anything else, a car makes it possible to choose your own itinerary and to explore the wide-open landscapes that may well provide your most enduring memories of the continent.

Driving in the **cities**, on the other hand, is not exactly fun, but places tend to be so large that a car is by far the most convenient way to negotiate your way around,

especially as public transportation may be spotty outside the major cities. Many cities, especially in the West, have grown up and assumed their present shapes since cars were invented. They sprawl for so many miles in all directions – Los Angeles and Houston are classic examples – that your hotel may be fifteen or twenty miles from the sights you came to see, or perhaps simply on the other side of a freeway that can't be crossed on foot. Only in a few cities, more often in the East, are the main attractions and facilities concentrated within walking distance of each other. Even in smaller towns the motels may be six miles or more out along the interstate, and the restaurants in a brand-new shopping mall on the far side of town.

Drivers wishing to **rent** cars are supposed to have held their licenses for at least one year (though this is rarely checked); people under 25 years old may encounter problems, and will probably get stuck with a higher than normal insurance premium. Car rental companies (listed on p.38) will also expect you to have a credit card; if you don't have one, they may let you leave a hefty deposit (at least $200), but don't count on it. The likeliest tactic for getting a good deal is to phone the major firms' toll-free numbers and ask for their best rates – most will try to beat the offers of their competitors, so it's worth haggling.

In general the lowest rates are available at the airport branches – $140 a week for a compact is a fairly good budget rate, but rates are always more expensive in the Northeast. Always be sure to get free unlimited mileage. Leaving the car in a different city from the one in which you rent it is likely to incur a **drop-off charge** – as much as

Driving for foreigners

Fly-drive deals are good value if you want to **rent** a car (see p.13), though you can save up to sixty percent simply by booking in advance with a major firm. If you choose not to pay until you arrive, be sure you take a written confirmation of the price with you. Remember that it's safer not to drive just after a long transatlantic flight – and that most standard rental cars have **automatic transmissions**.

UK nationals can drive in the US on a **full UK driving license** (International Driving Permits are not always regarded as sufficient). It's also easier and cheaper to book RVs in advance from Britain. Most travel agents who specialize in the US can arrange RV rental, and usually do it cheaper if you book a flight through them as well. A price of £400 for a five-berth van for two weeks is fairly typical.

Driving Distances In Miles

The distances shown on this chart represent the total mileages between selected cities and national parks in the US and Canada. They are calculated according to the shortest available route by road, and are thus higher than figures obtained by drawing a straight line on a map.

	Albuquerque	Atlanta	Boston	Chicago	Dallas	Denver	Grand Canyon NP	Great Smoky Mtns NP	Las Vegas	Los Angeles	Memphis	Miami	Nashville	New Orleans	New York	Orlando	St Louis	Salt Lake City	San Francisco	Seattle	Washington DC	Yellowstone NP	Yosemite NP	Montréal	Toronto
Atlanta GA	1404																								
Boston MA	2220	1108																							
Chicago IL	1312	708	994																						
Dallas TX	644	822	1753	921																					
Denver CO	437	1430	1998	1021	784																				
Grand Canyon NP AZ	407	1818	2627	1732	1051	708																			
Great Smoky Mtns NP	1457	177	917	585	905	1385	1831																		
Las Vegas NV	586	1979	2752	1780	1230	758	283	2036																	
Los Angeles CA	811	2191	3017	2048	1399	1031	555	2254	272																
Memphis TN	1010	382	1341	537	454	1043	1416	450	1603	1807															
Miami FL	1970	663	1520	1397	1343	2107	2499	614	2570	2716	997														
Nashville TN	1225	246	1092	466	659	1184	1610	221	2011	1811	209	910													
New Orleans LA	1157	480	1507	919	517	1277	1548	622	1858	1732	414	860	532												
New York NY	1997	854	208	809	1559	1794	2401	706	2794	2572	1102	1334	900	1335											
Orlando FL	1741	426	1301	1147	1098	1879	2271	614	2350	2429	688	229	648	1092	1004										
St Louis MO	1042	565	1207	289	655	863	1449	522	1620	1836	283	1226	321	696	976	1004									
Salt Lake City UT	604	1934	2376	1417	1257	534	365	1910	419	691	1551	2566	1703	1775	2189	2337	1362								
San Francisco CA	1109	2483	3128	2173	1752	1255	954	2592	570	387	2116	3093	2325	2278	2930	2871	2118	752							
Seattle WA	1453	2625	3016	2052	2131	1341	1213	2630	1180	1134	2317	3303	2242	2590	3088	3135	2135	848	810						
Washington DC	1849	618	448	709	1307	1616	2304	469	2420	2646	854	1057	659	1099	237	856	862	2048	2843	2721					
Yellowstone NP WY	973	1944	2382	1388	1343	563	755	1907	809	1081	1604	2568	1712	1840	2213	2432	1385	390	1027	827	2081				
Yosemite NP CA	971	2375	2961	2021	1634	1000	641	2384	358	348	1946	2928	2184	2096	2777	2708	1863	558	182	928	2616	1003			
Montréal Canada	2131	1199	310	847	1770	1824	2542	1035	2583	2855	1315	1649	1112	1651	382	1462	1101	2225	2959	2714	607	2009	2644		
Toronto Canada	1787	1011	609	515	1435	1492	2198	807	2251	2523	956	1494	776	1307	516	1346	749	1910	2823	2564	571	2303	2938	344	
Vancouver Canada	1590	2756	3155	2176	2234	1484	1357	2774	1322	1278	2461	3447	2566	2734	2943	3232	2191	990	954	144	2887	971	1072	3014	2820

Car rental companies

	US	UK	Ireland	Australia	New Zealand
Alamo ⓦwww.goalamo.com	☎1-800/354-2322	☎0870/400 4580			
Avis ⓦwww.avis.com	☎1-800/331-1084	☎0870/606 0100	☎09/153 0440	☎13 63 63	☎0800/651 5111
Budget www.budgetrentacar.com	☎1-800/527-0700	☎0800/181 181	☎01/878 7814	☎1300/362848	☎0800/652 227
Dollar ⓦwww.dollar.com	☎1-800/800-6000	☎01895/233300	☎1800/358008		
Enterprise ⓦwww.pickenterprise.com	☎1-800/325-8007				
Hertz ⓦwww.hertz.com	☎1-800/654-3001	☎0870/844 8844	☎01/813 3416	☎1800/550067	☎0800/655955
Holiday Autos ⓦwww.kemwel.com		☎1-800/422 7737	☎0990/300400	☎01/454 9090	
National ⓦwww.nationalcar.com	☎1-800/227-7368	☎0870/536 5365	☎028/9045 0904	☎13 19 08	☎09/537 2582
Rent-a-Wreck ⓦwww.rent-a-wreck.com	☎1-800/535 1391				
Thrifty ⓦwww.thrifty.com	☎1-800/367-2277	☎01494/751 4600	☎1300/367227	☎09/309 0111	

$200 or more, but these rules vary greatly depending on the rental company. Also, don't automatically go for the cheapest rate, as there's a big difference in the quality of cars from company to company; industry leaders like Alamo, Hertz and Avis tend to have newer, lower-mileage cars, often with air conditioning and stereo cassette decks as standard equipment – no small consideration on a 2000-mile desert drive.

Alternatively, various **local** companies rent out new and not so new vehicles. They are certainly cheaper than the big chains if you just want to spin around a city for a day, but free mileage is not included, so they work out far more costly for long-distance travel. Look for them in the *Yellow Pages* of the telephone directory.

When you rent a car, read the small print carefully for details on **Collision Damage Waiver (CDW)**, sometimes called Liability Damage Waiver (LDW), usually included in the price if you pre-pay outside the US, but well worth considering if it isn't. This form of insurance specifically covers the car that you are driving yourself – you are in any case insured for damage to other vehicles. At $9–13 a day, it can add substantially to the total cost, but without it you're liable for every scratch to the car – even those that aren't your fault. Some credit card companies offer automatic CDW coverage to Americans and Canadians using their card; read the fine print beforehand in any case.

Increasing numbers of states (New York for one) are requiring that this insurance be included in the weekly rental rate, and are regulating the amounts charged to cut down on rental-car company profiteering. Companies are also becoming more particular about checking up on the driving records of would-be renters and refusing to rent to high-risk drivers.

Another policy that rental companies try to get you to accept (and they've trained their staff to drive fear deep into your soul about this one) is **liability cover** if you cause injury to others while in a rental car. This usually costs around the same as CDW and when both these are taken together with taxes can double the cost of the rental. It's worth reading the small print of your holiday insurance to see if you are covered: the American Express annual Premier Plus policy, available only to UK residents, includes up to $50,000 CDW coverage and $1 million top-up liability

(☎0800/0287574 in the UK) and the policy pays for itself in two weeks.

In case you **break down** in a rented car, call the emergency number pinned to the dashboard. Otherwise, sit tight and wait for the highway patrol or state police, who cruise by regularly. Raising your car hood is a call for assistance, although women traveling alone should be wary of doing this. Another tip, for women especially, is to rent a **mobile telephone** from the car rental agency – you often have to pay only a nominal amount until you actually use it; in larger cities they increasingly come built into the car. Having a phone can be reassuring at least, and a potential lifesaver should something go wrong (see p.22).

> Specific information on public transportation and car rental for travelers with disabilities can be found on p.41.

Driveaways

One variation on renting is a **driveaway**: you drive a car from one place to another for the owner, paying only for the gas you use. The same rules as for renting apply, but look the car over before you take it; you'll be charged for any repair costs in addition to a large fuel bill if it's a big drinker. Some driveaway companies want a personal reference from someone either in the town you're leaving or in the car's eventual destination. Get in touch in advance, to spare yourself a week's wait for a car to turn up. The most common routes are between the coasts, but there's a fair chance of finding something that needs transporting to where you want to go. You needn't drive flat out, although four hundred miles a day is expected. Look under Automobile Transporters in the *Yellow Pages* and phone around for current offers, or try one of the sixty branches of Auto Driveaway, 310 S Michigan Ave, Chicago, IL 60604 (☎312/341-1900, ⓦwww.autodriveaway .com).

Renting an RV

Recreational vehicles (**RVs**) – those juggernauts that rumble down the highway, often complete with multiple bedrooms, bathrooms

and kitchens – can be rented from around $400 per week (plus mileage charges) for a basic camper on the back of a pickup truck. Though good for groups or families traveling together, these can be unwieldy on the road. Also, rental outlets are not as common as you might expect: people tend to own their RVs. On top of the rental fees, take into account the cost of gas (some RVs get twelve miles to the gallon or less) and any drop-off charges, in case you plan a one-way trip across the country. Also, it is rarely legal simply to pull off in an RV and spend the night at the roadside: you are expected to stay in designated RV parks that cost up to $20 per night. The Recreational Vehicle Dealers Association, 3930 University Drive, Fairfax, VA 22030 (☎703/591-7130, ⓦwww.rvda.org), publishes a newsletter and a directory of rental firms. Larger companies offering RV rentals include Cruise America (☎713/930–8133, ⓦwww .cruiseamerica.com) and Grand Travel Systems (☎602/939-6909 or 1-800/736-8678).

By bike

In general, **cycling** is a cheap and healthy way to get around all the big **cities**, some of which have cycle lanes and local buses equipped to carry bikes (strapped to the outside). For a $15 fee, Greyhound will take bikes (so long as they're in a box). Amtrak (for a $5 fee) asks you to reserve in advance and transport your bike in a container; space may be available for uncontained bikes. In **country areas**, roads are usually well maintained and have wide shoulders. A number of companies organize multiday cycle tours, with camping or stays in country inns; we've mentioned local firms where appropriate. The biggest nationwide organization is the not-for-profit Adventure Cycling Association (formerly Bikecentennial), 150 E Pine St, PO Box 8308–W, Missoula, MT 59807 (☎406/ 721-1776 or 1–800/755–2453, ⓦwww .adv-cycling.org), founded in 1974 to promote transcontinental cycle trips. It publishes **maps** ($11 each) of several 400-mile routes, detailing campgrounds, motels, restaurants, bike shops and sites of interest. Many individual states issue their own cycling guides; contact the tourist offices listed on pp.28–29. Backroads Bicycle

Tours, 801 Cedar St, Berkeley, CA 94710–1800 (☎510/527-1555 or 1-800/462-2848, ⓦwww.backroads.com), and the HI-AYH hosteling group (see p.47) also arrange group tours.

For more casual riding, bikes can be **rented** for $15 to $30 per day, or at discounted weekly rates, from outlets that are usually found close to beaches, university campuses and good cycling areas. Rates in heavily visited areas can be much higher. Local visitor centers should have details. Before setting out on a **long-distance cycling** trip, you'll need a good-quality, multispeed bike, panniers, tools and spares, maps, padded shorts and a **helmet** (some states and localities have laws requiring them) but a very good idea).

> The usual advice given to **hitchhikers** is that they should use their common sense; but common sense should tell anyone that hitchhiking in the United States is a **bad idea**. We do not recommend it under any circumstances.

Plan a route that avoids interstate highways (on which cycling is unpleasant and usually illegal). Of **problems** you'll encounter, the main one is traffic – RVs driven by buffoons who can't judge their width, and huge eighteen-wheelers (or in the western states, logging trucks) that scream past and create intense backdrafts capable of pulling you out into the middle of the road.

Travelers with disabilities

By international standards, the US is exceptionally accommodating for travelers with mobility problems or other physical disabilities. All public buildings, including hotels and restaurants, must be wheelchair accessible and provide suitable toilet facilities. Almost all street corners have dropped curbs. Most public transportation systems have such facilities as subways with elevators and buses that "kneel" to let people board.

Most states provide **information** for disabled travelers – contact the tourism departments listed on pp.28–29. SATH, the Society for Accessible Travel and Hospitality, 347 5th Ave, #610, New York, NY 10016 (☎212/447-7284 or 1-800/513-1126, ⓦwww.sath.org), is a not-for-profit travel-industry group of travel agents, tour operators, hotel and airline management and people with disabilities. They pass on any inquiry to the appropriate member; allow plenty of time for a response. Mobility International USA, PO Box 10767, Eugene, OR 97440 (☎541/343-1284, ⓦwww.miusa.org) offers travel tips to members ($35 a year) and operates an exchange program for disabled people.

The **Golden Access Passport**, issued without charge to permanently disabled US citizens, gives free lifetime admission to all national parks. *Easy Access to National Parks*, by Wendy Roth and Michael Tompane ($16), details every national park for people with disabilities, senior citizens and families with children. It's published by the Sierra Club, 85 Second St, 2nd Floor, San Francisco, CA 94105 (☎415/977-5500, ⓦwww.sierraclubbookstore.com). *Disabled Outdoors* is a quarterly magazine specializing in facilities for disabled travelers who wish to explore the great outdoors; its friendly office (see "Tour Operators," opposite) serves as a clearinghouse for all related information.

Other publications include *Travel for the Disabled* ($19.95), *Wheelchair Vagabond* ($14.95), *Directory of Accessible Van Rentals* ($9.95) and *Directory for Travel Agencies for the Disabled* ($19.95), all produced by Twin Peaks Press, PO Box 129, Vancouver, WA 98666 (℡360/694-2462, ⓦwww.pacifier.com/twinpeak).

Getting around

Most **airlines**, transatlantic and within the US, do what they can to ease your journey, and will usually let attendants of more seriously disabled people accompany them at no extra charge. The Americans with Disabilities Act (1990) obliges all air carriers to make the majority of their services accessible to travelers with disabilities.

Almost every Amtrak train includes one or more coaches with accommodation for handicapped passengers. Guide dogs travel free and may accompany blind, deaf or disabled passengers. Be sure to give 24 hours' notice. Hearing-impaired passengers can get information on ℡1-800/523-6590 (though it can take a while to get through; the service is poorly staffed).

Greyhound, however, is not recommended. Buses are not equipped with lifts for wheelchairs, though staff will assist with boarding (intercity carriers are required by law to do this), and the "Helping Hand" policy offers two-for-the-price-of-one tickets to passengers unable to travel alone (carry a doctor's certificate).

The American Public Transportation Association, 1666 K St, NW, Suite 1100, Washington, DC 20006 (℡202/496-4800, ⓦwww.apta.com), provides information about the accessibility of public transportation in cities.

The American Automobile Association (℡1-877/244-9790, ⓦwww.aaa.com) produces the *Handicapped Driver's Mobility Guide* for disabled drivers. The larger car rental companies provide cars with hand controls at no extra charge, though only on their full-size (most expensive) models; reserve well in advance.

Tour operators

A few **tour operators** cater to disabled travelers or arrange disabled group tours. Directions Unlimited, 123 Green Lane, Bedford Hills, NY 10507 (℡914/241-1700 or 1-800/533-5343, ℮cruisesusa@aol.com) and Wheels Up! (℡1-888/389-4335, ⓦwww.wheelsup.com) provide discounted airfares, tour and cruise prices for disabled travelers and a free monthly newsletter.

Senior Travelers

For many senior citizens, retirement brings the opportunity to explore the world in a style and at a pace that is the envy of younger travelers. As well as the obvious advantages of being free to travel during the quieter, more congenial and less expensive seasons, and for longer periods, anyone over age 62 with the appropriate ID can enjoy a vast range of discounts. Both Amtrak and Greyhound, for example, offer (smallish) percentage reductions on fares to older passengers.

Any US citizen or permanent resident 62 or over is entitled to free admission for life to all national parks, monuments and historic sites, using a **Golden Age Passport**, issued for a one-time fee of $10 at any such site. This free admission applies to all accompanying travelers in the same vehicle – a welcome encouragement to families to travel together – and also gives a fifty percent reduction on park user fees such as camping charges.

The **AARP** (formerly the American Association of Retired Persons), 601 E St NW, Washington, DC 20049 (℡202/434-2277 or 1-800/424-3410, ⓦwww.aarp.org), membership in which is open to US residents 50 or over for an annual $10 fee, organizes group travel for seniors and can provide discounts on accommodation and vehicle rental. **Elderhostel**, 75 Federal St, Boston, MA 02110 (☎1-877/426-8056, ⓦwww.elderhostel.com), runs an extensive network of educational and activity programs for people over sixty throughout the US, at prices broadly in line with those of commercial tours. Similar is **Saga Holidays**, 222 Berkeley St, Boston, MA 02116 (☎1-877/265-6862, ⓦwww.sagaholidays.com). Less educational group tours are available from **Vantage Travel** (☎1-800/322-6677, ⓦwww.vantagetravel.com).

Traveling with children

Traveling with kids in the United States is relatively problem-free. Children are readily accepted – indeed welcomed – in public places across the country.

Hotels and motels are quite accustomed to them, most state and national parks organize children's activities, every town or city has clean and safe playgrounds – and of course Disneyland in California and Disney World in Florida provide the ultimate in kids' entertainment.

Restaurants encourage parents to bring in their offspring. All the national chains provide highchairs and a special kids' menu, packed with huge, excellent-value (if not necessarily healthful) meals – cheeseburger and fries for 99¢, and so on.

Virtually all **museums** and tourist attractions offer reduced rates for kids. Most large cities have natural history museums or aquariums, and quite a few also have hands-on children's museums.

State tourist offices can provide specific information. **Guidebooks** for parents traveling with children include the *Unofficial Guide to California With Kids* ($17) and *New York City With Kids* ($16), both in the Frommer's Family Guides list, and the very helpful *Trouble Free Travel with Children* ($8.95), available through Publishers Group West.

Each of the John Muir Publications' *Kidding Around* series covers the history and sights of a major US city.

Getting around

Children under two years old **fly** free on domestic routes and for ten percent of the adult fare on international flights – though that doesn't mean they get a seat, let alone frequent-flier miles. When from two to twelve years old they are usually entitled to half-price tickets.

Traveling by **bus** may be the cheapest way to go, but it's also the most uncomfortable for kids. Under-twos travel (on your lap) for free. Children under twelve are charged half the standard fare.

Even if you discount the romance of the railroad, taking the **train** is by far the best option for long journeys – not only does everyone get to enjoy the scenery, but you can get up and walk around. Most cross-country trains have sleeping compartments, which may be quite expensive but are likely to be seen as a great adventure. Children's discounts are much the same as for bus or plane travel.

Most families choose to travel by **car**. If you hope to enjoy a driving vacation with your kids, make plans. Don't set unrealistic targets, pack sensible snacks and drinks, stop every couple of hours, arrive at your destination before sunset and avoid traveling through big cities during rush hour. Car rental companies usually provide **kids' car seats** for about $4 a day. You would, however, be advised to check, or bring your own; they are not always available.

Recreational Vehicles (RVs) are a good option for families, combining the convenience of kitchens and bedrooms with the freedom of the road (see "Getting Around," p.39).

Resources

Rascals in Paradise, 2107 Van Ness Ave, Suite 403, San Francisco CA 94109 (☏415/921-7000 or 1-800/872-7225, ⓦwww.rascalsinparadise.com) can arrange scheduled and customized itineraries built around activities for kids in the US and abroad, ranging from hiking and horseriding to mountain biking and watersports. **Travel With Your Children**, 40 Fifth Ave, New York, NY 10011 (☏212/477 5524 or 1-888/822-4388) publishes a newsletter, *Family Travel Times* (ⓦwww.familytraveltimes.com), and books on travel with children, including *Great Adventure Vacations With Your Kids*..

Women travelers

A woman traveling alone in America is not usually made to feel conspicuous, or liable to attract unwelcome attention. Cities can feel a lot safer than you might expect from recurrent media images of demented urban jungles, simply because there are so many people around. Like anywhere, though, particular care must be taken at night: walking through unlit, empty streets is never a good idea, and, if there's no bus service, take cabs. Women who look confident are less likely to encounter trouble – those who stand around looking lost and a bit scared are prime targets.

In the major urban centers, if you stick to the better parts of town, going into bars and clubs alone should pose few problems: there's generally a pretty healthy attitude toward women who do so, and your privacy will be respected. Lesbian bars are usually a trouble-free and welcoming alternative.

However, **small towns** may lack the same liberal or indifferent attitude toward lone women travelers. People seem to jump immediately to the conclusion that your car has broken down, or that you've suffered some strange misfortune; you may get fed up with well-meant offers of help. If your **vehicle** does **break down** on heavily traveled roads, wait in the car for a police or highway patrol car to arrive. Rent a portable telephone with your car, for a small charge – a potential lifesaver.

Rape statistics in the US are high. *Never* hitch alone – this is an invitation for trouble, and there's no shortage of weirdos to give it. If you have a car, be careful who you pick up: being in the driver's seat doesn't mean you're safe. Avoid traveling at night by public transportation – deserted bus stations, if not

actually threatening, will do little to make you feel secure. Where possible, team up with a fellow traveler (there really is safety in numbers). On Greyhound buses, sit near the driver. Should disaster strike, major towns have some kind of rape counseling service; if not, the local sheriff's office will arrange for you to get help and counseling, and, if necessary, get you home.

The **National Organization for Women** (ⓦwww.now.org) is a leader in seeking to advance issues of importance to women. NOW branches, listed in local phone directories, can provide information on rape crisis centers and counseling services, feminist bookstores and lesbian bars.

Also consult *Ferrari Guides: Women's Travel in Your Pocket* ($9.95), Ferrari Publications, PO Box 37887, Phoenix, AZ 85069 (☏602/863-2408 or 1-800/962-2912, ⓦwww.ferrariguides.com), an annual guide for women traveling in the US, Canada, the Caribbean and Mexico. The same company has a lesbian–specific travel website, ⓦwww.leznet.com.

Women's travel specialists in the US

Call of the Wild 2519 Cedar St, Berkeley, CA 94708 ☎510/849-9292 or 1-888/378-1978, ⓦwww.callwild.com. This established outfitter offers hiking adventures for women of all ages and abilities. Trips include visits to Native American ruins, backpacking in California national parks, cross-country skiing, yoga and jaunts to Hawaii.
Outdoor Vacations for Women over 40 PO Box 200, Groton, MA 01450 ☎508/448-3331, ⓔov40fun@aol.com. Activities include cross-country skiing, rafting, canoeing, biking, hiking and snorkeling. No previous experience is required.
Outward Bound 100 Mystery Point Rd, Garrison, NY 10524 ☎1-888/882-6863 or 914/424-4000,

ⓦwww.outwardbound.com. Year-round programs include canoeing, sledding, and desert and canyon hiking. No previous experience is required.
Prairie Women Adventures and Retreats RR1, Box 32, Matfield Green, KS 66862 ☎620/753-3416, ⓦwww.vacationranches.com/homestead/women.htm. The 5000-acre cattle ranch is owned by women. Guests can work alongside ranch hands, with free time to hike, bike, and ride horses.
Womanship 137 Conduit St, Annapolis, MD 21401 ☎ 410/267-6661 or 1-800/342-9295, ⓦwww.womanship.com. Live-aboard, learn-to-sail cruises for women of all ages. Destinations include Chesapeake Bay, Florida, the Pacific Northwest and Mystic, Connecticut. Choose trips of from three to seven days.

Gay and lesbian travelers

The gay scene in America is huge, albeit heavily concentrated in the major cities. San Francisco, where between a quarter and a third of the voting population is reckoned to be gay or lesbian, is arguably the world's premier gay city. New York runs a close second, and up and down both coasts gay men and women enjoy the kind of visibility and influence those in other places can only dream about. Gay officeholders and police officers are no longer a novelty. Resources, facilities and organizations are endless.

In the heartland, however, life looks more like the Fifties – away from large cities homosexuals are still oppressed and commonly reviled. Gay travelers need to watch their step to avoid hassles and possible aggression.

Virtually every major city has a predominantly gay area – **Chelsea**, **Avenue A** and **Christopher Street** in New York City, Los Angeles' **West Hollywood**, San Francisco's **Castro** district, Houston's **Montrose**, Seattle's **Capitol Hill** and so on.

Gay life exploded into the public eye in the 1970s, but since the 1980s the energies of gay men and women have been primarily directed toward protecting existing rights and increasing support and help for victims of the AIDS pandemic. Activist groups like ACT-UP (the AIDS Coalition To Unleash Power) and Queer Nation hold sit-ins (and kiss-ins) as part of continuing efforts to

maintain a high profile in the face of continued intolerance and isolation.

Things change quickly in the gay and lesbian (and emerging bisexual) scene, but we've tried to give an overview of local **resources**, **bars** and **clubs** in each major city.

National **publications** are available from any good bookstore. Bob Damron, PO Box 4222458, San Francisco, CA 94142 (☎415/255-0404 or 1-800/462-6654, ⓦwww.damron.com) produces the best. These include the *Men's Travel Guide*, a pocket-sized yearbook listing hotels, bars, clubs and resources for gay men ($18.95); the *Women's Traveler*, which provides similar listings for lesbians ($15.95); the *Road Atlas*, which shows lodging and entertainment in major cities ($18.95); and *Damron Accommodations*, which lists 1000 accommodations for gays and lesbians worldwide

($19.95). Buy these for twenty percent off on the website.

Gayellow Pages, PO Box 533, Village Station, New York, NY 10014 (☎212/674-0120, ⓦwww.gayellowpages.com) publishes a useful directory of businesses in the US and Canada ($16), plus regional directories for New England, New York and the South. *The Advocate*, Liberation Publications, PO Box 4371, Los Angeles, CA 90078 (ⓦwww.advocate.com; $2.95) is a bimonthly national gay news magazine, with features, general info and classified ads (not to be confused with *Advocate Men*, which is a soft-porn magazine).

Another useful lesbian publication is *Gaia's Guide*, 132 W 24th St, New York, NY 10014 ($6.95), a yearly international directory. Finally, the International Gay & Lesbian Travel Association (☎1-800/448-8550, ⓦwww.iglta .org) is a comprehensive, invaluable source for gay and lesbian travelers.

Accommodation

Accommodation costs form a significant proportion of the expenses for any traveler exploring the US – in part, because the standards of comfort and service can be high.

If you're on your own, it's possible to pare down what you pay by sleeping in dormitory-style hostels, where a bed usually costs between $10 and $20. However, with basic room prices away from the major cities starting at around $40 per night, groups of two or more will find it little more expensive to stay in the far more abundant motels and hotels. Many hotels will set up a third single bed for around $15 on top of the regular price, reducing costs for three people sharing. On the other hand, the lone traveler has a hard time of it: "singles" are usually double rooms at an only slightly reduced rate.

Wherever you stay, you'll be expected to **pay in advance**, at least for the first night and perhaps for further nights too. Most places ask for a credit card imprint when you arrive, but they'll also accept cash or US dollar travelers checks. **Reservations** – essential in busy areas in summer – are held only until 5 or 6pm unless you've warned the hotel you'll be arriving late.

Accommodation price codes

Throughout this book, accommodation prices have been graded with the symbols below, according to the cost of the least expensive double room throughout most of the year.

However, except at interstate budget motels, there's rarely such a thing as a set rate for a room. A basic motel in a seaside or mountain resort may double its prices according to the season, while a big-city hotel that charges $200 per room during the week will often slash its rate on the weekend. Because the high and low seasons for tourists vary widely across the country, astute planning can save a lot of money. Watch out also for local events, ranging from big spectacles such as Mardi Gras in New Orleans through Spring Break in Myrtle Beach down to college football games – which can raise rates far above normal.

Only where we explicitly say so do these room rates include local taxes.

❶ up to $35	❹ $75–100	❼ $160–200
❷ $35–50	❺ $100–130	❽ $200–250
❸ $50–75	❻ $130–160	❾ $250+

Hotels and motels

Drivers approaching any significant town encounter endless lines of motels along the highway, and the choice along major cross-country routes is phenomenal. **Hotels** and **motels** are essentially the same thing, although motels tend to be found beside the main roads away from city centers – and thus are much more accessible to drivers. The budget ones are pretty basic affairs, but in general there's a uniform standard of comfort everywhere – each room comes with a double bed (often two), a TV and phone, and an attached bathroom – and you don't get a much better deal by paying, say, $60 instead of $40. Over $60, the room and its fittings simply get bigger and more luxurious, and there'll probably be a swimming pool, free for guests.

The cheapest properties tend to be family-run, independent motels, but there's a lot to be said for paying a few dollars more to stay in motels belonging to the **national chains**. After a few days on the road, if you find that a particular chain consistently suits your requirements, you can use its central reservation number, listed above, to book ahead, and possibly obtain discounts as a regular guest.

During **off-peak periods** many motels and hotels struggle to fill their rooms, and it's worth **haggling** to get a few dollars off the asking price. Staying in the same place for more than one night will bring further reductions. Also, look for **discount coupons**, especially in the free magazines distributed by local visitor centers and interstate Welcome Centers. These can offer amazing value – $20 for a double room in a comfortable mid-range chain – but read the small print, as rates sometimes turn out to be a per-person charge for two people sharing and are often limited to midweek.

Few budget hotels or motels bother to compete with the ubiquitous diners by offering **breakfast**, although many provide free self-service coffee and sticky buns.

B&B has become an ever more popular option, often as a luxurious alternative to conventional hotels. Some B&Bs consist of no more than a couple of furnished rooms in someone's home, and even the larger establishments tend to have fewer than ten rooms, without TV or phone, but often laden with flowers, stuffed cushions and an almost over-contrived homey atmosphere.

The price you pay for a B&B – which varies from around $50 to $200 for a double room – always includes a huge and wholesome breakfast (sometimes a buffet on a sideboard, but more often a full-blown cooked meal). The crucial determining factor is whether each room has an en-suite bathroom; most B&Bs feel obliged to provide private bath facilities, although that can damage the authenticity of a fine old house. Prices in those that do tend to start at more like $60 or $70. At the top end of the spectrum, the distinction between a "hotel" and a "bed and breakfast inn" may amount to no more than that the B&B is owned by a private individual rather than a chain.

In many areas, B&Bs have united to form central **booking agencies**, making it much easier to find a room at short notice; we've given addresses and numbers for these where appropriate.

National chains

Best Western (③–⑥) ☎1-800/780-7234, ⓦwww.bestwestern.com
Baymont Inns & Suites (③) ☎1-877/229-6668, ⓦwww.baymontinns.com
Comfort Inns (③–⑤) ☎1-800/228-5150, ⓦwww.comfortinns.com
Courtyard by Marriott (⑤/⑥) ☎1-800/321-2211, ⓦwww.courtyard.com
Days Inn (④/⑤) ☎1-800/329-7466, ⓦwww.daysinn.com
Econolodge (②–④) ☎1-800/533-2666, ⓦwww.econolodge.com
Embassy Suites Hotels (⑥) ☎1-800/362-2779, ⓦwww.embassysuites.com
Fairfield Inns (④/⑤) ☎1-877/444-2800, ⓦwww.fairfieldinn.com
Hallmark Inns (②/③) ☎1-800/251-3294
Hampton Inns (④/⑤) ☎1-800/426-7866, ⓦwww.hamptoninn.com
Hilton Hotels (⑤ and up) ☎1-800/774-1500, ⓦwww.hilton.com
Holiday Inns (⑤ and up) ☎1-800/465-4329, ⓦwww.holiday-inn.com
Hosteling International – American Youth Hostels (①) ☎1-800/909-4776, ⓦwww.hiayh.org
Howard Johnson (②–④) ☎1-800/446-4656, ⓦwww.hojo.com
ITT Sheraton (⑤ and up) ☎1-800/625-5144
La Quinta Inns (④) ☎1-800/531-5900, ⓦwww.laquinta.com

Marriott Hotels(**⑤** and up) ☎1-888/236-2427, 🌐www.marriott.com
Motel 6(**②** ☎1-800/466-8356, 🌐www.motel6.com
Ramada Inns(**④** and up) ☎1-800/272-6232, 🌐www.ramada.com
Red Carpet Inns(**②** ☎1-800/251-1962, 🌐www.reservahost.com
Red Roof Inns(**③** ☎1-800/843-7663, 🌐www.redroof.com
Renaissance Hotels ☎1-800/468-3571 (**⑤** and up), 🌐www.renaissancehotels.com
Rodeway Inns(**③** ☎1-800/228-2000, 🌐www.rodeway.com
Scottish Inns(**②** ☎1-800/251-1962, 🌐www.reservahost.com
Select Inns(**②** ☎1-800/641-1000, 🌐www.selectinn.com
Sleep Inns(**③** ☎1-800/753-3746, 🌐www.sleepinn.com
YMCA(**②**/**③** ☎212/308-2899, 🌐www.ymcanyc.org

Ys and Youth Hostels

Although hostel-type accommodation is not as plentiful in the US as it is in Europe and elsewhere, provision for backpackers and low-budget travelers is on the increase. Unless you're traveling alone, most hostels work out little cheaper than motels; stay in them only if you prefer their youthful ambience and sociability. Many are not accessible on public transportation, or convenient for sightseeing in the towns and cities, let alone in rural areas.

The official **HI-AYH (Hostelling International–American Youth Hostels)** network has more than 150 hostels in major cities and rural locations throughout the US. Urban hostels tend to have 24-hour access, while rural ones may have a curfew and limited daytime hours. Annual membership is currently $25 and rates range from $12 to $29 for HI members; nonmembers generally pay an additional $3 per night. Check the HI-AYH website (🌐www.hiayh.org) for comprehensive listings.

A growing number of **independent** hostels, some of which fail to meet HI's fairly rigid criteria, choose not to be tied down by HI regulations. Many are no more than converted motels, where the "dorms" consist of a couple of bunk beds in a musty room, which is also let out as a private room on request. Others may be purpose-built rural properties, or at least converted and modernized to

For advice on **camping**, see the "Outdoors" section beginning overleaf.

B

Accommodation

a high standard. The American Association of Independent Hostels (AAIH) is a loose affiliation of independent hostels.

In addition, **YMCA/YWCA** hostels (known as "Ys"), provide mixed-sex or, in a few cases, women-only accommodation, at prices ranging from around $12 for a dormitory bed to $70 for a single or double room. Ys offering accommodation (and not all do, many being basically health clubs) are often in older buildings in less than ideal neighborhoods, but facilities can include a gym, a swimming pool and an inexpensive cafeteria. Especially in high season, **reserve ahead**; write to the relevant hostel and enclose a deposit. Some hostels will allow you to use a **sleeping bag**, though officially HI affiliates should insist on a **sheet sleeping bag**. The **maximum stay** is often restricted to three days, though this rule is often ignored if there's space. Few hostels provide meals but most have **cooking** facilities.

All the information in this book was accurate at press time; however, youth hostels are often shoestring organizations, prone to changing address or closing down altogether. Similarly, new ones appear each year; check the notice boards of other hostels for news. The *Hostel Handbook for the USA and Canada*, produced each May, lists four hundred hostels and is available for $5 from Jim Williams, *Sugar Hill House International House Hostel*, 722 St Nicholas Ave, New York, NY 10031 (☎212/926-7030, 🌐www .hostelhandbook.com). *Hostelling North America*, the HI guide to hostels in the USA and Canada, is available free of charge to any overnight guest at HI-AYH hostels or direct from the HI National Office, PO Box 37613, 733 15th St NW, Suite 840, Washington, DC 20005 (☎202/783-6161, 🌐www.hiayh.org).

Overseas travelers will find a comprehensive list of hostels in the *International Youth Hostel Handbook*. In the UK, it's available from the **Youth Hostel Association (YHA)**, Trevelyan House, 8 St Stephen's Hill, St Albans, Herts AL1 2DY (☎08708/708808, 🌐www.iyhf.org), from whom annual HI membership costs £12.50 (under-18s £6.25).

Outdoors

The United States is blessed with fabulous backcountry and wilderness areas, coated by dense forests, cut by deep canyons and capped by great mountains. Even the heavily populated east coast has its share of open space, notably along the Appalachian Trail, which winds from Mount Katahdin in Maine to the southern Appalachians in Georgia – some two thousand miles of untrammeled forest. In order to experience the full breathtaking sweep of America's wide-open stretches, however, head west to the Rockies, to the red-rock deserts of the Southwest, or right across the continent to the amazing wild spaces of the west coast states. In some areas, however, the shoreline is often disappointingly hard to access, with a high proportion firmly under private ownership.

National parks and monuments

The **National Park Service** administers both national parks and national monuments. The park service is sadly underfunded, and in style and design most of its visitor centers and other facilities still date conspicuously from the 1950s. Nonetheless, its rangers do a superb job of providing information and advice to visitors, maintaining trails, and organizing such activities as free guided hikes and campfire talks.

In principle, a **national park** preserves an area of outstanding natural beauty, encompassing a wide range of terrain and the very best examples of particular landforms and wildlife. **Yellowstone** has boiling geysers and herds of elk and bison. **Yosemite** offers towering granite walls and cascading waterfalls. The awesome and colorful **Grand Canyon** is so deep that you can barely see the river that carved it. A **national monument** is usually much smaller, focusing perhaps on just one archeological site or geological phenomenon, such as **Devil's Tower** in Wyoming. Altogether, there are more than 375 units of the national park system, including national seashores, lakeshores, battlefields and other historic sites.

National parks tend to be perfect places to **hike** – almost all have extensive trail networks – but they're all far too large for most people to tour on foot. (Yellowstone, for example, is bigger than the states of Delaware and Rhode Island combined.) Even in those rare cases where you can use public transportation to reach a park, you'll almost certainly need some sort of vehicle to explore it once you're there. The Alaskan parks are mostly howling wilderness, with virtually no roads or facilities for tourists – you're on your own.

Most parks and monuments charge **admission fees** ranging from $4 to $20, which cover a vehicle and all its occupants. For $50, they also sell the **National Parks pass**, which gives a named driver, and all passengers in the same vehicle, a year's unlimited access to (almost) every national park and monument. The more deluxe **Golden Eagle pass** ($65) allows access to absolutely all parks. Separate passes are available for disabled travelers and senior citizens – see p.40 and p.41, respectively.

While hotel-style **lodges** are found only in some major parks, every park or monument tends to have at least one well-organized **campground** for visitors. Often, a cluster of motels can be found not far outside the park boundaries. With appropriate free permits – subject to some restrictions in popular parks – backpackers can also usually camp in the **backcountry** (a general term for areas inaccessible by road).

For up-to-the-minute **information** on the national park system, access the official Park Service website at ⓦ www.nps.gov.

It features full details of the main attractions of the national parks, plus opening hours, the best times to visit, admission fees, hiking trails and visitor facilities.

Other public lands

National parks and monuments are often surrounded by tracts of **national forest**, also federally administered, but much less protected. These too tend to hold appealing rural campgrounds, but in the words of the slogan each is a "Land Of Many Uses," and usually allows logging and other land-based industry – ski resorts more often than strip mines.

Other government departments administer a whole range of wildlife refuges, national scenic rivers, recreation areas and the like. The **Bureau of Land Management** (BLM) has the largest holdings of all, most of it open rangeland, such as in Nevada and Utah, but also including some enticingly out-of-the-way reaches. **Environmentalists** engage in endless running battles with developers, ranchers and the extracting industries over uses – or alleged misuses – of the federal lands.

State parks and **state monuments**, administered by individual states, preserve sites of more limited, local significance. Many are explicitly designed for recreational use, and thus hold better campgrounds than their federal equivalents.

Camping and backpacking

The ideal way to see the great outdoors – especially if you're on a low budget – is to tour by car, and **camp** at night in state and federal campgrounds, which tend to be far more peaceful and scenic than their commercially run equivalents. Typical public campgrounds range in price from free (usually when there's no water available, which may be seasonal) to around $8 per night. Fees at the commercial campgrounds abundant near major towns – many of which resemble open-air hotels, complete with shops and restaurants – are more like $15–20. There may be plenty of campgrounds, but there are also plenty of people who want to use them: if you're camping in high season, either reserve in advance or avoid the most popular areas.

Backcountry camping in the national parks is usually free, by permit only. Before you set off on anything more than a half-day hike, and whenever you're headed for any-

where at all isolated, be sure to inform a ranger of your plans, and ask about weather conditions and specific local tips. Carry sufficient food and drink to cover emergencies, as well as all the necessary equipment and maps. Check that fires are permitted before you start one; even if they are, try to use a camp stove in preference to local materials – in some places firewood is scarce, although you may be allowed to use deadwood. In wilderness areas, try to camp on previously used sites. Where there are no toilets, bury human waste at least six inches into the ground and a hundred feet from the nearest water supply and campground. Burn what trash you can, and take the rest away.

Backpackers should **never drink** from rivers and streams, however clear and inviting they may look; you never know what acts people – or animals – have performed further upstream. **Giardia** – a water-borne bacteria that causes an intestinal disease, characterized by chronic diarrhea, abdominal cramps, fatigue and weight loss – is a serious problem. Water that doesn't come from a tap should be boiled for at least five minutes, or cleansed with an iodine-based purifier (such as Portable Aqua) or a Giardia-rated filter, available from any camping or sports store.

Hiking at lower elevations should present few problems, though the swarms of **mosquitoes** that you may encounter near water can drive you crazy; Avon Skin-so-soft hand cream or anything containing DEET are fairly reliable repellents. **Ticks** – tiny beetles that plunge their heads into your skin and swell up – are another hazard. They sometimes leave their heads inside, causing blood clots or infections, so get advice from a park ranger if you've been bitten. One species of tick causes **Lyme Disease**, a serious condition that can even affect the brain. Nightly inspections of your skin are strongly recommended.

Beware, too, of **poison oak**, an allergenic shrub that grows all over the western states, usually among oak trees. Its leaves come in groups of three (the middle one on a short stem) and are distinguished by prominent veins and shiny surfaces. If you come into contact with it, wash your skin (with soap and cold water) and clothes as soon as possible – and don't scratch. In

CANADA

Seattle

Salt Lake City

Denver

San Francisco

Las Vegas

Los Angeles

Santa Fe

Phoenix

PACIFIC
OCEAN

El Paso

MEXICO

CANADA

Anchorage

Juneau

ALASKA

HAWAII

Honolulu

1. Olympic, WA → p.1202
2. North Cascades, WA → p.1204
3. Mount Rainier, WA → p.1206
4. Crater Lake, OR → p.1232
5. Glacier, MT → p.913
6. Yellowstone, WY → p.890
7. Grand Teton, WY → p.897
8. T. Roosevelt (north), ND → p.837

9. T. Roosevelt (south), ND → p.838
10. Wind Cave, SD → p.832
11. Badlands, SD → p.823
12. Redwood, CA → p.1171
13. Lassen Volcanic, CA → p.1173
14. Yosemite, CA → p.1119
15. Kings Canyon, CA → p.1116
16. Sequoia, CA → p.1116

17. Death Valley, CA → p.1098
18. Joshua Tree, CA → p.1096
19. Great Basin, NV → p.1038
20. Zion, UT → p.1002
21. Bryce Canyon, UT → p.1006
22. Capitol Reef, UT → p.1009
23. Canyonlands, UT → p.1010
24. Arches, UT → p.1013

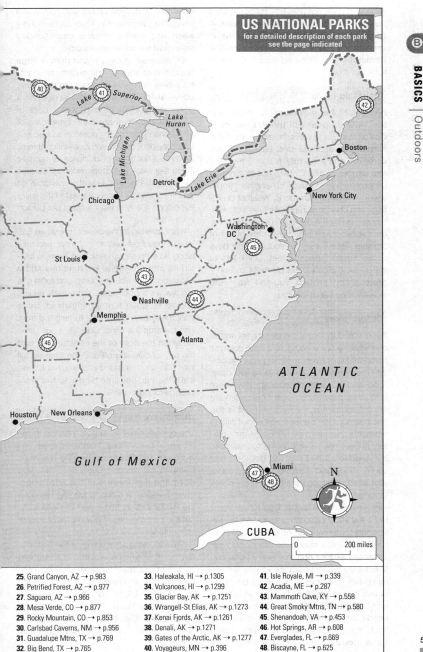

US NATIONAL PARKS
for a detailed description of each park
see the page indicated

Ⓑ

BASICS | Outdoors

Lake Superior

Lake Huron

Lake Michigan

Detroit

Lake Erie

Boston

Chicago

New York City

Washington DC

St Louis

Nashville

Memphis

Atlanta

Houston

New Orleans

Miami

ATLANTIC OCEAN

Gulf of Mexico

N

CUBA

0   200 miles

25. Grand Canyon, AZ → p.983
26. Petrified Forest, AZ → p.977
27. Saguaro, AZ → p.966
28. Mesa Verde, CO → p.877
29. Rocky Mountain, CO → p.853
30. Carlsbad Caverns, NM → p.956
31. Guadalupe Mtns, TX → p.769
32. Big Bend, TX → p.765

33. Haleakala, HI → p.1305
34. Volcanoes, HI → p.1299
35. Glacier Bay, AK → p.1251
36. Wrangell-St Elias, AK → p.1273
37. Kenai Fjords, AK → p.1261
38. Denali, AK → p.1271
39. Gates of the Arctic, AK → p.1277
40. Voyageurs, MN → p.396

41. Isle Royale, MI → p.339
42. Acadia, ME → p.287
43. Mammoth Cave, KY → p.558
44. Great Smoky Mtns, TN → p.580
45. Shenandoah, VA → p.453
46. Hot Springs, AR → p.608
47. Everglades, FL → p.669
48. Biscayne, FL → p.625

serious cases, hospital emergency rooms can give antihistamine or adrenaline jabs. A comparable curse is **poison ivy**, similar in appearance, found throughout the country. Remember the sage advice, "Leaves of three, let it be."

Mountain hikes

Hiking at **higher elevations**, for instance in the 14,000ft peaks of the Rockies or in California's Sierra Nevada, and certainly in Alaska, take especial care. Late snows are common, and especially in spring there's a real danger of avalanches, not to mention meltwaters that make otherwise simple stream crossings hazardous. Weather conditions can change abruptly. Altitude sickness, brought on by the depletion of oxygen in the atmosphere, can affect even the fittest of athletes. Take it easy for your first few days above seven thousand feet. Drink lots of water, avoid alcohol, eat plenty of carbohydrates, and protect yourself from the increased power of the sun.

Desert hikes

If you intend to hike in the **desert**, tell someone where you are going, and write down all pertinent information, including your expected time of return. Carry an extra two days' food and water and never go anywhere without a map. Cover most of your ground in early morning: the midday heat is too debilitating. Don't even think about hiking when the mercury tops 90°F (the temperature in California's Death Valley, for example, has reached 136°F). If you get lost, find some shade and wait. As long as you've registered, the rangers will eventually come looking for you.

However hot the day, at high elevations at night you should also be prepared for below-freezing temperatures. At any time of year, you'll stay cooler during the day if you wear full-length sleeves and trousers. Shorts and short sleeves will expose you to far too much sun – something you won't be aware of until it's too late. A wide-brimmed hat and good sunglasses will spare you the blinding headaches that can result from the desert light. You may also have to contend with **flash floods**, which can appear from nowhere: a distant cloud can turn a dry wash into a raging river. Never camp in a dry wash, and don't attempt to cross flooded areas until the water has receded.

It's essential to carry – and **drink** – large quantities of liquid in the desert. An eight-hour hike in typical summer temperatures above 100°F would require you to drink a phenomenal thirty pints of water. Loss of appetite and thirst are early symptoms of heat exhaustion, so it's possible to become seriously dehydrated without feeling thirsty. Watch out for signs of dizziness or nausea; if you feel weak and stop sweating, it's time to get to the doctor. Is water available on your trail? Rangers keep abreast of the latest conditions. Carry at least a quart per person even if it is.

When **driving** in the desert, carry two gallons of water per person in the car, and take along an emergency pack with flares, a first-aid kit and snakebite kit, matches and a compass. A shovel, tire pump and extra gas are always a good idea. If the car's engine overheats, don't turn it off; instead, try to cool the engine quickly by turning the front end towards the wind. Carefully pour some water on the front of the radiator, and turn the air conditioning off and the heat up full blast. In an emergency, never panic and leave the car: you'll be harder to find wandering around alone.

Adventure travel

The opportunities for active traveling in the US are all but endless, from whitewater rafting down the Colorado River, to mountain biking in the volcanic Cascades, canoeing down the headwaters of the Mississippi River, horseback riding in the Big Bend on the Rio Grande in Texas, and Big Wall rock-climbing on the sheer granite monoliths of Yosemite Valley.

While an exhaustive listing of the possibilities could fill another volume of this book, certain places have an especially high concentration of adventure opportunities, such as Moab, Utah (p.1015), or New Hampshire's White Mountains (p.258). Throughout the book we recommend guides, outfitters and local adventure tour operators.

Wildlife

Watch out for bears, deer, moose, mountain lions and rattlesnakes in the backcountry, and consider the effect your presence can have on their environment.

Other than in a national park, you're highly unlikely to encounter a **bear**. Even there, it's rare to stumble across one in the wilderness. If you do, don't run, just back away slowly. As friendly as they may appear, they are *wild* animals. Most fundamentally, they will be after your food, which should be stored in airtight containers when camping. Ideally, hang both food and garbage from a high branch (too weak to support the weight of a bear) some distance from your camp. Never attempt to feed bears (frequently they'll beg, but once fed will become aggressive in their demands for more), and never get between a mother and her young. Young animals are cute; irate mothers are not.

Snakes and creepy-crawlies

Though the deserts in particular are home to a wide assortment of **poisonous creatures**, these are rarely aggressive towards humans. To avoid trouble, observe obvious precautions. Don't attempt to handle wildlife. Keep your eyes open as you walk, and watch where you put your hands when scrambling over obstacles. Shake out shoes, clothing and bedding before use. Back off if you do spot a creature, to give it room to escape.

If you are bitten or stung, current medical thinking rejects the concept of cutting yourself open and attempting to suck out the venom. Whether snake, scorpion or spider is responsible, apply a cold compress to the wound, constrict the area with a tourniquet to prevent the spread of venom, drink lots of water, and bring your temperature down by resting in a shady area. Stay as calm as possible and seek medical help immediately.

Food and drink

"Fast food" may be America's most enduring contribution to the modern culinary world, but most travelers find the sheer variety – and, for the most part, quality – of the foods available around the US quite astonishing.

Whether it's for basic sustenance or for a special social occasion, most Americans love to **dine out** and, in the cities at least, you can pretty much eat whatever you want, whenever you want. Along all the highways and on every main street, restaurants, fast-food places and coffee shops try to outdo one another with flashing neon signs as well as bargains and special offers.

Whatever you eat and wherever you eat, service is usually enthusiastic – thanks in large part to the institution of **tipping**. Waiters depend on tips for the bulk of their earnings; fifteen to twenty percent is the standard rate, and a bare minimum in major cities.

Regional specialties

While the predictable enormous steaks, burgers and piles of ribs or half a chicken, served up with salads, cooked vegetables and bread, are found everywhere, many visitors find it more rewarding to explore the diverse regional and **ethnic cuisines** around the country. **Beef** is especially prominent in the Midwest and Texas, while **fish** and **seafood** dominate the menus in Florida, Louisiana, around Chesapeake Bay and in the Pacific Northwest. **Shellfish**, such as the highly rated Dungeness crab – smoother and creamier than the average crab – and the Chesapeake's unique soft-shell crab, highly spiced and eaten whole, is popular too. Maine lobsters and steamers (clams),

Coping as a vegetarian

In the big cities at least, being a **vegetarian** in the United States presents few problems. Most towns of any size boast at least one wholefood or vegetarian café. However, don't be too surprised in rural areas if you find yourself restricted to a diet of eggs, cheese sandwiches (you might have to ask them to leave the ham out), salads and pizza. In the southeast, most soul-food cafés offer great-value vegetable plates (four different vegetables, including potatoes) for around $5, but these are often cooked with pork fat. Similarly, baked beans, and the nutritious-sounding red beans and rice, usually contain bits of diced pork. Of the major fast-food chains, the Mexicanesque *Taco Bell*, selling good meatless tostadas and burritos, is your best bet.

eaten alone or mixed up in a chowder, are a great reason to visit New England.

Cajun food, which originated in the bayous of Louisiana as a way to use up leftovers, is centered on red beans and rice, enlivened with unusual seafood like crawfish and catfish, and always highly spiced. The oft-misunderstood distinction between Cajun and **Creole** cooking is explained in our "Louisiana" chapter, on p.696.

Southern American cooking – also known as "**soul food**" – is not always easy to find outside the South, but is worth seeking out. You may not fancy eating **grits** (ground white corn served hot, mixed with butter) for breakfast, but full meals can be delicious, and incredibly filling. Vegetables such as **collard greens**, **black-eyed peas**, fried **eggplant** and **okra** (a principal ingredient of the Cajun gumbo) are added to staples such as fried chicken, roast beef and **hogjaw** – meat from the mouth of a pig. **Chitterlings** (or chitlins) are a delicacy prepared from the innards of a pig. Meat dishes are usually accompanied by **cornbread** to soak up the thick gravy poured over everything; with fried fish, you'll often get **hush puppies** – fried corn balls with tiny bits of chopped onion.

By contrast, **California cuisine** is geared toward health and aesthetics. It's basically a development of French *nouvelle cuisine*, utilizing the wide mix of fresh, locally available ingredients. The theory is to eat only what you need, and what your body can process. Vegetables are harvested before maturity and steamed to preserve both vitamins and flavor. Seafood comes from oyster farms and the catches of small-time anglers, and what little meat there is tends to be from animals reared on organic farms. The result is small but beautifully presented portions and high, high

prices: not unusually $50 a head (or much more) for a full dinner with wine.

A spin-off from California cuisine is the so-called New New Mexican or **Santa Fe-style** food, again emphasizing ultrafresh and unusual ingredients, and spiced with chilis to reflect the Spanish and Mexican heritage of the Southwest desert region.

Although technically ethnic, **Mexican** food is so common it often seems like an indigenous cuisine, especially in southern California. In Texas, **Tex-Mex** food is a somewhat less spicy local version, whose distinguishing dish is beef and bean chili con carne. Day or night, this is the cheapest type of food to eat: even a full dinner with a few drinks will rarely be more than $10 anywhere except in the most upmarket establishment.

Mexican food in the States is different from that found in Mexico, making more use of fresh meats and vegetables. The essentials, however, are the same: lots of rice and pinto beans, often served refried (boiled, mashed and fried), with variations on the **tortilla**, a thin corndough or flour pancake that can be wrapped around food and eaten by hand (a **burrito**); folded, fried and filled (a **taco**); rolled, filled and baked in sauce (an **enchilada**); or fried flat and topped with a stack of filling (a **tostada**). Meals are usually served with complimentary **nachos** (chips) and a hot **salsa** dip. The **chile relleno** is a good vegetarian option – a green pepper stuffed with cheese, dipped in egg batter and fried.

Local variations in cuisine are endless. Many farming and ranching regions – Nevada in particular – have a surprising number of **Basque** restaurants; the **Amish** communities of Pennsylvania have their own traditions; and **Portuguese** restaurants, dating from whaling days, can be found in New England. **Chinese** food is everywhere and can often be as cheap as Mexican; **Japanese**, found especially on the coasts but increasingly in all big cities, is rather more expensive and fashionable. **Italian** food is popular, and specialist Italian regional cooking is catching on fast in the major cities. **French** food, too, is available, though usually pricey, and rarely found outside the larger cities. **Thai**, **Korean**, **Indian** and **Indonesian** food is similarly city-based, though usually cheaper.

Drinking

Across the country, **bars** and **cocktail lounges** are pretty true to their *Cheers*-celebrated popular image: long, dimly lit counters with a few customers perched on stools before a bartender-cum-guru, and tables and booths for those who don't want to join in the drunken bar-side debates. New York, Baltimore, Chicago, New Orleans and San Francisco are the consummate boozing towns, but, almost anywhere, men, at any rate, shouldn't have to search very hard for a comfortable place to drink.

To **buy and consume alcohol** in the US, you need to be 21, and could well be asked for ID even if you look much older. Utah, predominantly Mormon, has the most byzantine restrictions. Many other states prohibit selling alcohol on Sunday, during elections, or – in the case of many counties– at all, ever. The famous **distilleries** of Tennessee and Kentucky, including Jack Daniels (see p.577), can be visited – though maddeningly,

several are in "dry" counties so they don't offer samples. A few states – Vermont, Oklahoma, and, once more, Utah – restrict the alcohol content in beer to just 3.2 percent, half the usual strength. In more liberal areas, alcohol can be bought and drunk any time between 6am and 4am, seven days a week. (New Orleans is a law unto itself, with certain bars open 24 hours and a far from rigid policy on ID.)

Though for the most part American **beer** is limited to fizzy, light national brands like Budweiser, Miller and Coors, there are alternatives. On the east coast look for Boston-based Samuel Adams or New Amsterdam. The Texan brand Lone Star has its dedicated followers, as do Pete's Wicked Ales in Minnesota. In California, the full-bodied, San Francisco-brewed Anchor Steam beer is available all over, while the rarer Red Sail Ale is among the finest brews in the country.

Of special interest to travelers are **microbreweries** and **brewpubs**, originating in the West but now found in virtually every sizable US city and college town, in which you can drink excellent beers, brewed on the premises and often not available anywhere else. These are usually friendly and welcoming places, and almost all serve a wide range of good-value, hearty **food** to help soak up the drink.

As for **wine** and wineries, you'll find details of tours and tastings for visitors scattered throughout this book, for example in California on p.1167, Texas on p.761, Ohio on p.310, and even Hawaii on p.1307.

Sports

Besides being good fun, catching a baseball game at Chicago's Wrigley Field on a summer afternoon, or joining in with the screaming throngs at a Ravens football game in Baltimore, can give visitors an unforgettable insight into a town and its people. Professional teams almost always put on the most spectacular shows, but big games between college rivals, minor league baseball games and even Friday night high school football games provide an easy and enjoyable way to get on intimate terms with a place.

Sports are central to American life. Star athletes have been idolized by successive generations of children (and adults), and millions play the most popular games, if only on a dusty sandlot. However, American sports are experiencing a bit of a backlash. Some consider pro salaries obscene – one baseball player signed a quarter-billion-dollar (ten-year) contract. A number of college coaches make a million bucks a year in salaries and TV contracts, and many "student athletes" barely make it to class. More voters are objecting to building stadiums with tax dollars. Some pumped-up jocks are spending their weekends in jail rather than on the field. Critics regard an increase in empty seats and declines in TV ratings as healthy correctives. On the plus side, more opportunities to compete – both pro and collegiate – are now available for American women.

Baseball, because the major league teams play so many games – 162 in total, usually five or so a week throughout the summer – is probably the easiest sport to catch when traveling. The ballparks – such as Wrigley Field, Boston's Fenway Park, LA's glamorous Dodger Stadium, or Baltimore's evocative Camden Yards – are great places to spend time. It's also among the cheapest sports to watch (from around $7/8 a seat), and tickets are usually easy to come by.

Pro football is quite the opposite. Tickets are exorbitantly expensive and almost impossible to obtain (if the team is any good), and most games are played in anonymous municipal bunkers; you'll do better stopping in a bar to watch it on TV. (American football is not the game called football in other countries.)

College football is a whole lot better and more exciting, with chanting crowds, cheerleaders and cheaper tickets. Although New Year's Day games such as the Rose Bowl or the Orange Bowl are all but impossible to see in the flesh, big games like Nebraska vs Oklahoma, Michigan vs Ohio State, or Notre Dame vs anybody are not to be missed if you're anywhere nearby.

Basketball also brings out intense emotions. The interminable pro playoffs run well into June. The men's college tournament – "March Madness" – is acclaimed by many as the nation's most exciting sports extravaganza.

Hockey, long the preserve of Canada and cities in the far north of the US, is now penetrating the rest of the country. Tickets, particularly for successful teams, are hard to get.

The **Kentucky Derby**, held in Louisville on the first Saturday in May (see p.555), is the biggest event on the **horse-racing** calendar. Also in May, the **Indianapolis 500**, the largest **motor-racing** event in the world, fills that city with visitors throughout the month, with practice sessions and carnival events building up to the big race.

We've listed the major league teams for three sports on pp.57–58; local tourist offices can also help with schedules and ticket information.

Skiing

Skiing is the biggest mass-market participant sport, and downhill resorts can be found all over the US. The eastern resorts of Vermont and New York State, however, pale by comparison with those of the Rockies, such as Vail and Aspen in Colorado, and the

Skiing: How to save money

Especially in the Rocky Mountains, the US features some of the best **ski terrain** in the world, but without careful planning a ski vacation can be horribly expensive. In addition to the tips listed below, phone (toll-free) or write in advance to resorts for brochures and, when you get there, scan local newspapers for money-saving offers.

• Visit during early or late season to take advantage of lower accommodation rates.

• The more people in your party, the more money you save on lodgings. For groups of four to six, a condo unit costs much less than a standard motel.

• Before setting a date, ask the resort about package deals including flights, rooms and ski passes. This is the no-fuss and often highly economical way to book a ski vacation.

• Shop around for the best boot and ski rentals – prices often vary enormously.

• Purchase advance-sale lift tickets; for example, gas stations and supermarkets in Colorado offer savings of around thirty percent on ski-slope rates.

• If you must buy tickets at the resort, save money by purchasing multiday tickets.

• If you're an absolute beginner, look for resorts that offer free "never-ever" lessons with the purchase of a lift ticket.

• Finish your day's skiing in time to take advantage of happy hours and dining specials, which usually last from 4pm until 7pm.

Sierra Nevadas in California. You can usually rent equipment for about $20 per day, and expect to pay another $20 to $50 a day for lift tickets.

A cheaper option is **cross-country skiing**, or ski touring. Backcountry ski lodges dot mountainous areas along both coasts and in the Rockies. They offer a range of rustic accommodation, equipment rental and lessons, from as little as $10 a day for skis, boots and poles up to about $150 for an all-inclusive weekend tour.

Baseball

Major League Baseball ☏ 212/931-7800, ⊛ www.majorleaguebaseball.com
American League ☏ 212/931-7600
National League ☏ 212/931-7700
Anaheim Angels ☏ 1-888/796-4256
Arizona Diamondbacks ☏ 602/462-6500
Atlanta Braves ☏ 404/522-7630
Baltimore Orioles ☏ 410/685-9800
Boston Red Sox ☏ 617/267-9400
Chicago Cubs ☏ 773/404-2827
Chicago White Sox ☏ 312/674-1000
Cincinnati Reds ☏ 513/421-4510
Cleveland Indians ☏ 216/420-4636
Colorado Rockies ☏ 303/762-5437
Detroit Tigers ☏ 313/962-4000
Florida Marlins ☏ 305/626-7400
Houston Astros ☏ 713/259-8000
Kansas City Royals ☏ 816/921-8000
Los Angeles Dodgers ☏ 323/224-1500
Milwaukee Brewers ☏ 414/902-4400

Minnesota Twins ☏ 612/375-1366
New York Mets ☏ 718/507-6387
New York Yankees ☏ 718/293-4300
Oakland Athletics ☏ 510/638-4900
Philadelphia Phillies ☏ 215/463-6000
Pittsburgh Pirates ☏ 412/323-5000
St Louis Cardinals ☏ 314/421-3060
San Diego Padres ☏ 619/881-6500
San Francisco Giants ☏ 415/972-2000
Seattle Mariners ☏ 206/346-4000
Tampa Bay Devil Rays ☏ 727/825-3137
Texas Rangers ☏ 888/283-2254

Basketball

National Basketball Association (NBA) ☏ 212/407-8000, ⊛ www.nba.com
Atlanta Hawks ☏ 404/827-3865
Boston Celtics ☏ 617/523-6050
Charlotte Hornets ☏ 704/357-0252
Chicago Bulls ☏ 312/455-4000
Cleveland Cavaliers ☏ 216/420-2000
Dallas Mavericks ☏ 214/748-1808
Denver Nuggets ☏ 303/405-8555
Detroit Pistons ☏ 248/377-0100
Golden State Warriors ☏ 510/986-2200
Houston Rockets ☏ 713/627-3865
Indiana Pacers ☏ 317/263-2500
Los Angeles Clippers ☏ 310/426-6001
Los Angeles Lakers ☏ 310/419-3100
Memphis Grizzlies ☏ 901/888-4667
Miami Heat ☏ 305/577-4328
Milwaukee Bucks ☏ 414/227-0500
Minnesota Timberwolves ☏ 612/673-1600
New Jersey Nets ☏ 201/935-8888

New York Knicks ☎212/465-6000
Orlando Magic ☎407/649-3200
Philadelphia 76ers ☎215/339-7600
Phoenix Suns ☎602/379-7900
Portland Trailblazers ☎503/224-9291
Sacramento Kings ☎916/928-0000
San Antonio Spurs ☎210/554-7787
Seattle Supersonics ☎206/281-5800
Utah Jazz ☎801/325-2500
Washington Wizards ☎301/773-2255

Football

National Football League (NFL) ☎212/450-2000,
ⓦ www.nfl.com
Arizona Cardinals ☎602/379-0101
Atlanta Falcons ☎770/945-1111
Baltimore Ravens ☎410/654-6200
Buffalo Bills ☎716/649-0015
Carolina Panthers ☎704/358-7000
Chicago Bears ☎847/295-6600
Cincinnati Bengals ☎513/621-3550
Cleveland Browns ☎440/891-5000

Dallas Cowboys ☎972/556-9900
Denver Broncos ☎303/649-9000
Detroit Lions ☎248/335-4131
Green Bay Packers ☎920/496-5719
Indianapolis Colts ☎317/297-2658
Jacksonville Jaguars ☎904/633-6000
Kansas City Chiefs ☎816/920-9300
Miami Dolphins ☎954/452-7000
Minnesota Vikings ☎612/828-6500
New England Patriots ☎508/543-8200
New Orleans Saints ☎504/733-0255
New York Giants ☎201/935-8111
New York Jets ☎516/560-8100
Oakland Raiders ☎510/864-5000
Philadelphia Eagles ☎215/463-5500
Pittsburgh Steelers ☎412/323-1200
St Louis Rams ☎314/982-7267
San Diego Chargers ☎619/280-2121
San Francisco 49ers ☎408/562-4949
Seattle Seahawks ☎206/827-9777
Tampa Bay Buccaneers ☎813/879-2827
Tennessee Titans ☎888/313-8326
Washington Redskins ☎703/478-8900

Festivals and public holidays

Someone, somewhere is always celebrating something in the US, although, apart from national holidays, few festivities are shared throughout the country. Instead, there is a disparate multitude of local events: art and craft shows, county fairs, ethnic celebrations, music festivals, rodeos, sandcastle-building competitions, and many others of every hue and shade.

The box opposite contains a selection of the best local festivals covered in this book. In addition, tourist offices for each state (see pp.28–29) can provide full lists, or just phone the visitor center in a particular region ahead of your arrival and ask what's coming up. Certain festivities, such as **Mardi Gras** in New Orleans, are well worth planning your vacation around; obviously other people will have the same idea, and visiting during these times requires an extra amount of advance effort.

Public holidays

The biggest and most all-American of the **national festivals and holidays** is

Independence Day. On the Fourth of July, the entire country takes a time out as people picnic, drink, salute the flag and watch or participate in firework displays, marches, beauty pageants and more, all in commemoration of the signing of the Declaration of Independence in 1776. **Halloween** (October 31) lacks any such patriotic overtones, and is not a public holiday despite being one of the most popular yearly flings. Traditionally, masked kids run around the streets banging on doors and demanding "trick or treat," and are given candy. These days that sort of activity is mostly confined to rural and suburban areas, while in some bigger cities Halloween has grown into a massive gay-

For further details of the selected festivals and events listed below, including more precise dates, see the relevant page of the *Guide*, or contact the local authorities direct. The state tourist boards listed on pp.28–29 can provide fuller calendars for each area.

January

Elko NV: Cowboy Poetry Gathering p.1038
St Paul MN: Winter Carnival p.389

February

Cordova AK: Iceworm Festival p.1269
Daytona Beach FL: Daytona 500 Race p.643
Fort Worden WA: Hot Jazz Festival p.1199

March

Austin TX: South by Southwest p.744
Butte MT: St Patrick's Day p.908
Fairbanks AK: Ice Festival p.1274
Los Angeles CA: Academy Awards p.1089
New Orleans LA: Mardi Gras pp.702–703
also elsewhere in Louisiana p.708

April

Boston MA: Patriot's Day – Marathon p.215
Lafayette LA: Festival International de
Louisiane p.708
New Orleans LA: French Quarter Festival and
Jazz & Heritage Festival (into May) p.703
Santuario de Chimayó NM: Easter
Pilgrimage p.944

May

Black Mountain NC: Folk Festival p.515
Breaux Bridge LA: Crawfish Festival p.708
Charleston WV: Vandalia Festival of
Appalachian Culture p.464
Flagstaff AZ: Zuni Crafts Show p.978
Indianapolis IN: Indianapolis 500-Mile Race
p.343
Los Angeles CA: Cinco de Mayo (May 5)
p.1089
Louisville KY: Kentucky Derby p.555
Memphis TN: Memphis in May, including
Barbecue Cook-out p.569
San Antonio TX: International Conjunto
Festival p.738

June

Fort Worth TX: Chisholm Trail Round-up p.757
Hardin MT: Little Bighorn Days p.904
Nashville TN: Fan Fair p.576
Telluride CO: Bluegrass Festival p.874

July

Blowing Rock NC: Highland Games p.514
Cheyenne WY: Cheyenne Frontier Days p.880
Elko NV: National Basque Festival p.1039

Fairbanks AK: Eskimo/Indian Olympics p.1274
Flagstaff AZ: Hopi Crafts Show p.978
Navajo Crafts Show (into Aug) p.979
Fort Totten ND: Powwow and Rodeo p.836
Milwaukee WI: Great Circus Parade p.374
Minneapolis MN: Aquatennial p.388
Philadelphia PA: Freedom Fest p.166
Riverblues p.166
St Paul MN: Taste of Minnesota p.389
Talkeetna AK: Moose Dropping Festival p.1270
Traverse City MI: Cherry Festival p.333

August

Asheville NC: Mountain Dance & Folk Festival
p.515
Elkins WV: Augusta Festival of Appalachian
Culture p.461
Gallup NM: Inter-tribal Indian Ceremonial p.956
Memphis TN: Anniversary of Elvis's Death
p.567
Newport RI: Folk & Jazz festivals p.243
San Antonio TX: Texas Folklife Festival p.738
Santa Fe NM: Indian Market p.937
Sturgis SD: Motorcycle Rally & Races p.827

September

Fort Worth TX: Pioneer Days p.757
Greenville MS: Delta Blues Festival p.595
Lafayette LA: Festivals Acadiens p.708
Los Angeles CA: LA's Birthday (Sept 4) p.1089
LA County Fair p.1089
Lubbock TX: Panhandle South Plains Fair p.761
Monterey CA: Monterey Jazz Festival p.1112
New York, NY: Festa di San Gennaro p.84
Opelousas LA: Zydeco Festival p.708
Pendleton OR: Pendelton Round-up p.1235
Santa Fe NM: Fiestas de Santa Fe p.937
Savannah GA: Jazz Festival p.546
Tulsa OK: Chile Cookoff & Bluegrass Festival
p.777

October

Albuquerque NM: Hot-air Balloon Rally p.950
Charleston SC: Moja Arts Festival p.525
Custer State Park SD: Round-up of Bison
p.831
Helena AR: Blues Festival p.605
Opelousas LA: Louisiana Yambilee p.708
Tombstone AZ: Helldorado Days p.969

oriented celebration. In West Hollywood in LA, in New York's Greenwich Village and San Francisco's Castro district, the night is marked by mass cross-dressing, huge block parties and wee-hours partying. More sedate is **Thanksgiving Day**, on the fourth Thursday in November. Relatives return to the familial nest to stuff themselves with roast turkey and (supposedly) fondly recall the first harvest of the Pilgrims in Massachusetts. In fact, Thanksgiving was a national holiday before anyone thought to make that connection.

On the national **public holidays** listed below, shops, banks and offices are likely to be closed. Many states also have their own holidays, and in some places Good Friday is a half-day holiday. The traditional **summer season** for tourism runs from **Memorial Day** to **Labor Day**; some tourist attractions are open only during that period.

Jan 1 **New Year's Day**
Third Mon in Jan **Martin Luther King Jr's Birthday**
Third Mon in Feb **Presidents' Day**
Last Mon in May **Memorial Day**
July 4 **Independence Day**
First Mon in Sept **Labor Day**
Second Mon in Oct **Columbus Day**
Nov 11 **Veterans' Day**
Fourth Thurs in Nov **Thanksgiving Day**
December 25 **Christmas Day**

Directory

ADDRESSES Generally speaking, roads in built-up areas in the US are laid out on a grid system, creating "blocks" of buildings. The first one or two digits of a specific address refer to the block, which will be numbered in sequence from a central point, usually downtown; for example, 620 S Cedar Avenue will be six blocks south of downtown. It is crucial, therefore, to take note of components such as "NW" or "SE" in addresses; 3620 SW Washington Boulevard will be a very long way indeed from 3620 NE Washington Boulevard.

AIRPORT TAX This is invariably included in the price of your ticket.

CIGARETTES AND SMOKING The country that first gave tobacco to the world is now probably the most concerned about its detrimental effects on health. Smoking is generally frowned upon – though many Americans still smoke. Most cinemas are nonsmoking, restaurants are usually divided into nonsmoking and smoking sections (California and New York City have banned smoking altogether in most restaurants) and smoking is forbidden on public transportation and flights.

DATES In the American style, the date 1.8.02 means not 1 August but January 8.

ELECTRICITY 110V AC. All plugs are two-pronged and rather insubstantial. Some travel plug adapters don't fit American sockets.

FLOORS The first floor in the US is what would be the ground floor in Britain; the second floor would be the first floor, and so on.

ID: Should be carried at all times. Two pieces should suffice, one of which should have a photo: a passport and credit card(s) are your best bets. Not having your license with you while driving is an arrestable offense.

MEASUREMENTS AND SIZES US measurements are in inches, feet, yards and miles, and weights in ounces, pounds and tons. American pints and gallons are about four-fifths of Imperial ones. Clothing sizes are four figures less what they would be in the UK – a British women's size 12 is a US size 8 – while British shoe sizes are 1/2 below American ones for women, and one size below for men.

TAX A sales tax is added to virtually every-thing you buy in a shop, but isn't included in the marked price. The actual rate varies from place to place: in New York and parts of California it's above eight percent, while some states – Alaska, Delaware, Montana and Oregon – have no sales tax at all. A hotel tax will add five to fifteen percent to most bills. You also often must pay a tax on top of the cost of a car rental if you pick up the vehicle at an airport.

TEMPERATURES Always given in Fahrenheit.

TIME ZONES See p.27.

TIPPING Expected for all bar and restaurant service, at a rate of fifteen to twenty percent or so on the bill (unless the service is utterly abominable). About the same amount should be added to taxi fares. A hotel porter who has lugged your suitcases up several flights of stairs should get $3 to $5.

VIDEOS The standard format used for video cassettes in the US is different from that used in the United Kingdom, Ireland, Australia, New Zealand, and elsewhere. This means that you cannot buy prerecorded videotapes in the US compatible with a video player bought in another country. However, blank tapes in the US can be used with cameras bought elsewhere as the camera will format the tape to record and play in the correct standard.

BASICS | Directory

guide

guide

CHAPTER 1 # Highlights

* **Ellis Island** Once the first stop for millions of prospective immigrants from all over the world. See p.77

* **Grand Central Station tours** Admire the magnificent Beaux Arts building and savor the seafood in its subterranean Oyster Bar. See p.92

* **The Metropolitan Museum** The museum's mammoth collection could keep you busy for days. See p.98

* **Brooklyn Bridge** Take a stroll across this much-loved bridge for spec-

tacular views of the skyline. See p.80

* **Coney Island** The world's tallest Ferris wheel is among the landmark attractions at this beachside amusement spot. See p.107

* **Baseball game at Yankee Stadium** Between April and October, it would be a shame not to take in a ballgame. See p.124

* **Sylvia's Restaurant in Harlem** A Harlem institution celebrated for its soul food and gospel Sunday brunches. See p.113

New York City

T he most beguiling city in the world, **New York City** is an adrenaline-
charged, history-laden place that holds immense romantic appeal for
visitors. Wandering the streets here, you'll cut between buildings that
are icons to the modern age. Whether gazing at the flickering lights of
the midtown skyscrapers as you speed across the Queensboro Bridge, experiencing the 4am half-life downtown, or just wasting the morning on the Staten
Island ferry, you really would have to be made of stone not to be moved by it
all. There's no place quite like it.

While the events of September 11, 2001, which demolished the World Trade
Center, shook New York to its core, the populace responded resiliently under
the composed aegis of then-Mayor Rudy Giuliani. Until the attacks, New
Yorkers had mixed feelings about their mayor. Some were annoyed by his abra-
sive style. But most acknowledged that under his leadership, during the late
Nineties, New York had become cleaner, safer and more liveable, as the city took
on a truly international allure and shook off the more notorious aspects to its
reputation. Even in the aftermath of the destruction of the World Trade Center,
New York remains a unique and fascinating city – and one you'll likely want to
return to again and again.

New York City comprises the central island of **Manhattan** and four outer
boroughs – **Brooklyn**, **Queens**, the **Bronx** and **Staten Island**. Manhattan, to
many, *is* New York. You could spend weeks just in Manhattan and still barely
scratch the surface, but there are some key attractions – and some pleasures –
that you won't want to miss. These include the different **ethnic neighborhoods**, like Chinatown, and the more artsy concentrations of SoHo, TriBeCa,
and the East and West villages. Of course, there is the celebrated **architecture**
of corporate Manhattan, and there are the **museums**, not just the
Metropolitan and MoMA, but countless other smaller collections that afford
weeks of happy wandering. In between sights, you can **eat** just about anything,
at any time, cooked in any style; you can **drink** in any kind of company; and
sit through any number of obscure **movies**. The more established arts – **dance**,
theater, **music** – are superbly presented. For the avid consumer, the choice of
shops is vast, almost numbingly exhaustive in this heartland of the great capitalist dream.

Some history

The first European to see Manhattan Island, then inhabited by the Algonquin
Indians, was the Italian navigator Verrazano, in 1524. Dutch colonists established
the settlement of **New Amsterdam** exactly one hundred years later. The first

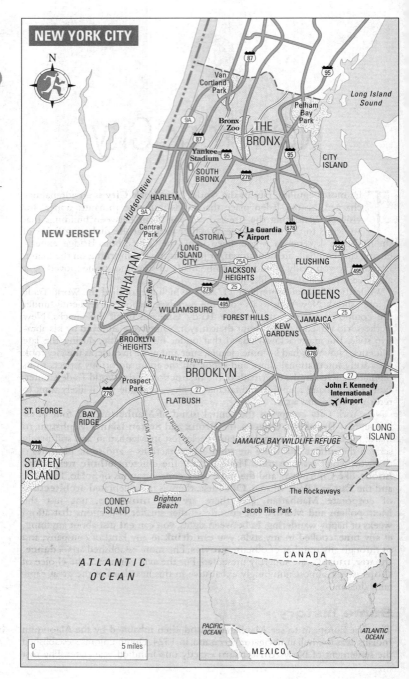

governor, Peter Minuit, was the man who "bought" the whole island for a handful of trinkets. Considering that the Indians he actually paid were not locals but only passing through, it might be said that they received a fine deal, too. A strong defensive wall – today's Wall Street follows its course – surrounded the colony. By the time the British laid claim to the area in 1664, the heavy-handed rule of governor **Peter Stuyvesant** had so alienated its inhabitants that control was handed over without a fight.

Renamed New York, the city prospered and grew, its population reaching 33,000 by the time of the American Revolution. The opening of the Erie Canal in 1825 facilitated trade farther inland, spurring the city to become the economic powerhouse of the nation, the base later in the century of **financiers** such as Cornelius Vanderbilt and Pierpont Morgan. The **Statue of Liberty** arrived in 1886, a symbol of the city's role as the gateway for generations of immigrants, and the early twentieth century saw the sudden proliferation of Manhattan's extraordinary **skyscrapers**, which cast New York as the city of the future in the eyes of an astonished world.

Almost a century later, the skyline remains *the* defining feature of New York, reproduced in countless forms; the events of September 11, 2001, while devastating, have only made it more iconic.

Arrival, information and getting around

New York City is served by two **international airports**: most flights use **John F. Kennedy (JFK)** (☎718/244-4444) in Queens, but some Virgin, British Airways and Continental flights touch down at **Newark** (☎973/961-6000) in New Jersey. In addition, most domestic arrivals land at **La Guardia** (☎718/533-3400), also in Queens. From all the airports, the cheapest and most straightforward way into Manhattan is by bus.

From JFK, New York Airport Service buses run to the Port Authority Bus Terminal, Grand Central Station, Penn Station and major Midtown hotels in Manhattan ($13 one-way; students $6; every 15–20min 6am–midnight; journey time 45min–1hr; ☎718/706-9658). The alternative bus/subway link (☎718/330-1234) costs just the $1.50 subway fare: take the free shuttle bus (labeled "Long-term parking") to the Howard Beach station on the #A subway line, then the ninety-minute train ride to central Manhattan (every 20min 6am–1am).

Olympia Airport Express buses take up to forty minutes to get **from Newark** to Manhattan, where they stop at Grand Central and Penn stations ($11; every 20–30min 6.15am–midnight; ☎212/964-6233 or in NJ ☎908/354-3330). New Jersey Transit buses also run to the Port Authority Terminal in Manhattan ($3.95; once per hour; ☎973/762-5100).

New York Airport Service buses **from La Guardia** take 45 minutes to Grand Central and the Port Authority. The fare is $10 (students $6); buses run every 15–30min 6am–midnight (to Grand Central and the Port Authority) with a somewhat more limited schedule in the other direction (☎718/706-9658). New York Airport Service buses also **link JFK and La Guardia**, taking 45 minutes or so ($11; every 30min 5.40am–11pm).

Taxis are pricey from the airports; expect to pay $16–22 from La Guardia, a flat rate of $35 from JFK and $35–55 from Newark (airport taxis at Newark will tell you their flat fares to different parts of Manhattan before you leave). **Car services** may cost a few dollars more. **Minibus shuttle services** are a decent mid-priced option if you are staying in Midtown and don't mind multiple stops along the way. Gray Line Air Shuttles run from all three airports between 7am–11.30pm; prices are roughly $15–20 per person depending on the airport. (☎212/315-3006 or 1-800/451-0455). Super Shuttle minivans are a similar 24-hour option (☎1-800/258-3826 or 212/258-3826). For **general information** on getting to and from the airports, call ☎1-800/AIR-RIDE.

Greyhound buses pull in at the Port Authority Bus Terminal, 42nd Street and Eighth Avenue (☎212/564-8484). **Amtrak** trains come in to Penn Station, at Seventh Avenue and 33rd Street (☎1-800/872-7245).

Information

The best place for information is the **New York Convention and Visitors' Bureau** at 810 Seventh Avenue at 53rd Street (Mon–Fri 8.30am–6pm, Sat & Sun 9am–5pm; ☎212/484-1222, ⓦwww.nycvisit.com). It has leaflets on what's going on in the arts and elsewhere, bus and subway maps and information on accommodation – though they can't actually book anything for you. You can also find lots of listings at ⓦnewyork.citysearch.com.

The main Manhattan **post office** is at 421 Eighth Avenue, between West 31st and 33rd streets (Mon–Sat 24hr for important services; zip code 10001).

City transportation

Few cities equal New York for sheer street-level stimulation, and **walking** is the most exciting way to explore. However, it's also exhausting, so you'll need to use some form of **public transportation**. The fastest way to get from A to B in Manhattan and the boroughs is the **subway**. Intimidating at first glance, the subway system is actually quite user-friendly. A number or letter identifies each subway train and route; most routes run uptown or downtown, following the great avenues, rather than crosstown. The subway is open 24 hours a day. Every journey, whether on the **express** lines, which stop only at major stations, or the **locals**, which stop at them all, costs $1.50, utilizing a token or the newer, more convenient **MetroCard** available at station booths or vending machines (or sometimes from newsstands). Both are also valid on buses (the MetroCard also allows free transfers within a two-hour period from bus to subway or vice-versa), and MetroCards can be purchased in any

La Guardia to JFK

Manhattan Airport Service links JFK and La Guardia airports between 5.40am and 11pm. Buses leave, on average, every 30 minutes (though it varies depending on your direction and the time of day) and take 45 minutes to 60 minutes; at select times they stop once along the way. The fare is $11 one way. Call ☎212/875-8200.

amount from $3 to $80; a $15 purchase allows 11 rides for the cost of 10. A 7–day pass ($17) and a 30–day pass ($63) allow unlimited rides. The "Fun Pass" is valid for 24 hours of unlimited rides but is unaccountably not sold at subway booths; you can usually find them in hotels and certain businesses such as Gristedes supermarkets. Call ☎212/638-7622 to find the nearest location that sells them.

Once you get past the turnstile, forget everything you've seen in the movies. New York City subways are generally quite safe in part because they are almost always crowded, even at night. The key to being safe is to use common sense. Always use the more crowded center subway cars late at night and, while you're waiting, keep to the area marked in yellow, where you can be seen by the booth attendants.

New York's **bus system** is clean, efficient and fairly frequent. Its one disadvantage is that it can be extremely slow – in peak hours almost down to walking pace – but it can be your best bet for traveling crosstown. Buses leave their route terminal points at five- to ten-minute intervals, and stop every two or three blocks. As noted above, anywhere in Manhattan the fare is payable on entry with a subway token, a MetroCard or $1.50 correct change – no pennies or dollar bills. If you're using a token, ask for a transfer if you need to change buses anywhere along your journey; transfers can only be used to continue in your direction, not for return trips on the same bus line.

Route maps for both the **subway** and **bus** networks are available at all token booths or from the New York Convention and Visitor's Bureau (see opposite) or the concourse office at Grand Central.

Taxis are reasonably priced and they're everywhere. Although the rudimentary English of many drivers is notorious, they can normally get you where you want to go. Knowing the exact address and its cross street is helpful.

Guided tours

Countless businesses and individuals compete to help you make sense of the city, offering all manner of **guided tours**. One of the more original – and least expensive – ways to get oriented is with Big Apple Greeter (1 Centre St, New York, NY 10007; ☎212/380-8159, ⓕ380-3685, ⓦwww.bigapplegreeter.org).

Walking tours

Big Onion Walking Tours ☎212/439-1090, ⓦwww.bigonion.com. The Onion guides peel off the many layers of the city's history (all guides hold advanced degrees in American history). From $10; call for schedules and meeting places.

Harlem Heritage Tours 230 W 116th St, Suite 5C ☎212/280-7888, ⓦwww .harlemheritage.com. Cultural walking tours of Harlem, general and specific (such as Harlem Jazz Clubs) are led mid-days and evenings for $15–20; reservations are recommended.

Municipal Arts Society 457 Madison Ave ☎212/935-3960 or 439-1049, ⓦwww.mas.org. Architectural and cultural tours. Weekday walking tours from $10–15; free Wednesday lunchtime tours of Grand Central Station begin at 12.30pm from the main information booth; Saturday walking and bus tours may need reservations.

The 92nd Street Y 1395 Lexington Ave ☎212/996-1100, ⓦwww.92ndsty.org. None better, with a mixed bag of walking tours, from art tours to political New York and pre-dawn visits to the wholesale meat and fish markets. $20 and up.

This not-for-profit group matches you with a local volunteer and points you to places that interest you. It's free (so get in touch well ahead of time).

Grayline, the biggest operator of guided bus tours, is based in Midtown Manhattan at Eighth Avenue and 42nd Street, in the Port Authority Bus Terminal (☎1-800/669-0051). Half-day tours, taking in the main sights of Manhattan, go for around $25, and a full day costs $30–60, bookable through any travel agent. City Sightseeing (Coach), at 1040 Sixth Avenue, also offers double-decker bus tours for about the same prices; call ☎1-800/876-9868.

The **Circle Line Ferry** sails around Manhattan in three hours from Pier 83 at the west end of 42nd Street (at 12th Avenue), taking in everything from the bustling Downtown to the more subdued stretches of Harlem, with a commentary and on-board bar ($22; March–Dec with varying regularity; ☎212/563-3200, ⓦwww.circleline.com). The **Staten Island Ferry** (see p.109) provides a panorama of the Downtown skyline for free.

Liberty Helicopter Tours, at the west end of 30th Street, near the Jacob Javits Convention Center (☎212/967-4550), offers **helicopter flights** from around $59 for 4 and a half minutes to $187 for 15 minutes.

Accommodation

Prices for **accommodation** in New York are well above the norm for the US as a whole. Most hotels charge more than $100 a night (although exceptions and decent double rooms from $75 a night do exist). You may be away from your lodgings for all your waking hours, so spending $150 on a bed doesn't make much sense. On the other hand, if you pay a bit more you can stay in a more central location.

Most of New York's **hotels** are in Midtown Manhattan – a good enough location, though you may well want to travel downtown for less expensive (and usually better) food and nightlife. **Booking ahead** is strongly advised; at certain times of the year – Christmas and early summer particularly – everything is likely to be full. Phone the hotels directly, or at no extra charge contact a booking service, such as Meegan's (☎718/995-9292 or 1-800/441-1115), CRS (☎407/740-6442 or 1-800/950-0232), The Room Exchange (Mon–Fri only ☎212/760-1000) or Express Reservations (Mon–Fri only ☎1-800/356-1123). Rates are often reduced at weekends – so it's always worth asking.

Bed and breakfast is an attractive alternative. Staying in a New Yorker's spare room or subletting an apartment is an increasingly popular (and somewhat less inexpensive) option. Reservations are normally arranged through an agency such as those listed below. Rates run about $80–100 for a double, or $100 and up a night for a studio apartment. Book well in advance.

Hostels

Chelsea Center Hostel 313 W 29th St at 8th Ave ⊤212/643-0214, ⑤473-3945. This small, clean and safe private hostel, with beds for $30, includes sheets, blankets and breakfast. Reservations are essential in high season. Cash only. ❶

Chelsea International Hostel 251 W 20th St, between 7th and 8th aves ⊤212/647-0010, ⑤727-7289. In the heart of Chelsea, this is the closest hostel to Downtown. Beds are $27 a night, with four or six sharing the clean, rudimentary rooms. Private double rooms are $65 a night. Guests must leave a $10 key deposit. No curfew; passport required. ❶

Gershwin 7 E 27th St, off 5th Ave ⊤212/545-8000, ⑤684-5546. This new hostel/hotel geared toward young travelers offers Pop Art decor, a small bar and well-priced restaurant, beds from $35 a night and private rooms from $59. Reservations are accepted for private rooms only. ❷

Hostelling International-New York 891 Amsterdam Ave at W 103rd St ⊤212/932-2300, ⑤932-2574. Dorms cost $32–38; facilities include a restaurant, library, travel shop and theater. Reserve well in advance – they're very busy. ❶

International House – Sugar Hill 722 St Nicholas Ave at 145th St ⊤212/926-7030, ⑤283-0108, ⓔsugarhill@hostelhandbook.com and its jointly run neighbor, **The Blue Rabbit**, at no. 730 ⊤/⑤ 212/491-3892. These noisy but adequate dorms in friendly, well-run hostels are way up on the Harlem-Washington Heights border, opposite the 145th St subway station (A or D train). $25 a night, limited number of doubles $30 per person; no curfew, no chores and no lockout. Both ❶

Jazz on the Park 36 W 106th St at Central Park W ⊤212/932-1600, ⓦwww.jazzhostel.com. This groovy bunkhouse boasts a TV/games room, rooftop barbecues, the *Java Joint Café* and lots of activities. The rooms sleep between 2 and 14, and are clean, bright and air-conditioned. Reservations are essential June–Oct and over Christmas and New Year. ❷

Vanderbilt YMCA 224 E 47th St between 2nd and 3rd aves ⊤212/756-9600. The Y is smaller and quieter than its handy Midtown location (a 5min walk from Grand Central Station) might suggest. It houses an inexpensive restaurant, swimming pool, gym and laundry. All rooms are air-conditioned. Singles $70, doubles $85. ❹

Bed and breakfast

Affordable New York City 21 E 10th St, NY 10003 ⊤212/533-4001, ⑤387-8732,

ⓦwww.affordablenewyorkcity.com. Detailed descriptions are provided for this established network of 120 properties (B&Bs and apartments) around the city. B&B accommodations from $85 (shared bath) and $100 (private), unhosted studios $140–175 and one-bedrooms $175–225. Cash or travelers' checks only; three-night minimum. Very customer-oriented and personable.

Bed and Breakfast Network of New York 130 Barrow St, NY 10014 ⊤212/345-8134. Write at least a month in advance. Hosted doubles ❺; unhosted accommodation ❻/❼

CitySonnet.com Village Station, PO Box 347, NY 10014-0347 ⊤212/614-3034, ⑤425/920-2384, ⓦwww.CitySonnet.com. This small, personalized B&B/short-term apartment agency (formerly West Village Reservations) offers accommodations all over the city, but specializes in Downtown and Greenwich Village. Singles start at $80, doubles are $100–155, and unhosted flats start at $140.

Colby International 139 Round Hey, Liverpool L28 1RG, England (in the UK ⊤0151/220 5848). Guaranteed B&B accommodations can be arranged from the UK. Book at least a fortnight ahead in high season for these excellent-value doubles ❹ and studios ❺

Urban Ventures PO Box 426, NY 10024. Personal callers welcome at Suite 1412, 38 W 32nd St ⊤212/594-5650, ⓦwww.nyurbanventures.com. The minimum stay is three nights for hosted and four nights for unhosted, and you can book until the last minute. Budget doubles ❹, "comfort range" rooms ❺, unhosted apartments ❻

Hotels

Algonquin 59 W 44th St ⊤212/840-6800. At New York's classic literary hangout, the decor remains little changed, though the bedrooms have been refurbished to good effect. Ask about summer and weekend specials. ❽/❾

Amsterdam Inn 340 Amsterdam Ave at 76th St ⊤212/579-7500. From the owners of the *Murray Hill Inn* (see below), this new hotel is within easy walks to Central Park, Lincoln Center and the American Museum of Natural History. Rooms are basic (no closets) but clean, with TVs, phones and maid service. The staff is friendly and there's a 24-hour concierge. ❺

Chelsea 222 W 23rd St ⊤212/243-3700. One of New York's most noted landmarks, this aging neo-Gothic building boasts a fabulous past (see p.93). Avoid the older rooms; ask for a renovated one, with wood floors, log-burning fireplaces and plenty of space for a few extra friends. Studio room ❼, suite ❾

Chelsea Lodge 318 W 20th St ☎212/243-4499, ☎243-7852. When you step through the (unmarked) door this gem of a place in a converted boarding house greets you with cheery Early American/Sportsman decor. The "lodge" rooms (shared toilet, most rooms don't have phones) are a little small for two, but the few deluxe rooms are a great value and have new full bathrooms. A three-day cancellation policy applies. ❼

Dylan 52 E 41st St ☎212/338-0500 or 1-866/55-DYLAN, ☎338-0569. The hardwood floors, warm light and vaguely lemony-tasting air floating through the lobby are indicative of the whole experience – classy and clever. If you can afford it, book the Alchemy Suite, a one-of-a-kind Gothic bedchamber with a vaulted ceiling and unusual stained glass windows. ❾

Edison 228 W 47th St ☎212/840-5000. The most striking thing about the funky 1000-room *Edison*, a good value for Midtown, is its beautifully restored Art Deco lobby. The rooms, though not fancy, have been recently renovated. ❼

Gramercy Park 2 Lexington Ave at E 21st St ☎212/475-4320. In a lovely location, this hotel is pleasant enough, with a mixture of newly renovated and tatty rooms. Guests get a key to the adjacent private park. ❼

Larchmont 27 W 11th St, between 5th and 6th aves ☎212/989-9333. A budget hotel in tree-lined Greenwich Village has small but nice, clean rooms. Good find. Singles ❹, doubles ❺

Lucerne 201 W 79th St at Amsterdam Ave ☎875-1000 or 1-800/492-8122, ☎721-1179. This beautifully restored 1904 brownstone, with its extravagantly baroque red terracotta entrance, charming rooms and friendly, helpful staff, is just a block from the Natural History Museum and close to the liveliest stretch of the Columbus Ave scene. ❽, with summer rates at ❼

Mansfield 12 W 44th St at 5th Ave ☎212/944-6050. A value alternative to the nearby *Algonquin* and *Royalton*, it offers above-average rooms (some triples and quads) and luxuries like thermo-vapor whirlpools and steam baths. Check out the steakhouse and the good deli off the lobby. ❼/❽

Milburn 242 W 76th St ☎212/362-1006. This welcoming and well-situated hotel, great for families, has recently been renovated in gracious style. Doubles ❼/❽; large two-room suites, with kitchenettes ❽

Murray Hill Inn 143 E 30th St between Lexington and 3rd aves ☎212/683-6900. The small and basic rooms do have air-conditioning, telephones, cable TV and a sink; some also have a private

bath. Packed with young travelers and backpackers, the inn offers great weekly rates. ❹/❺

Paramount 235 W 46th St between Broadway and 8th Ave ☎212/764-5500. A former budget hotel renovated by Ian Schrager (co-founder of Studio 54), it's now one of the hippest places in town to stay. The pop and media crowd comes to enjoy the Philippe Starck interior and to be waited on by sleek young things. It also boasts a trendy *Dean and DeLuca* coffee shop and a quality bar and restaurant. ❾; with summer specials at ❽

Pickwick Arms 230 E 51st St ☎212/355-0300. The thoroughly pleasant budget hotel is one of the best deals in Midtown. All 400 rooms are air-conditioned, with cable TV, direct dial phones and room service. The open-air roof deck has stunning views, and there are two restaurants (one French, one Mediterranean) downstairs. A single room with shared bath is $75. ❹

Roger Smith 501 Lexington Ave at E 47th St ☎212/755-1400. One of the best Midtown hotels, popular with bands, offers both style and helpful service. Plusses include individually decorated rooms, a great restaurant that doubles as a jazz club and art works on display in public spaces. Breakfast is included. ❾, summer at ❼

Royalton 44 W 44th St ☎212/869-4400. Attempting to capture the market for the arbiters of style, the Philippe Starck-designed *Royalton* aimed to be the *Algonquin* of the 1990s and beyond. It is as much a power-lunch venue for NYC's media and publishing set as a place to stay. ❾

Salisbury 123 W 57th St ☎212/246-1300. Good service, large rooms with kitchenettes and proximity to Central Park are the attractions here. The price includes a continental breakfast. ❽

Seventeen 225 E 17th St between 2nd and 3rd aves ☎212/475-2845. As you might expect in a budget accommodation, *Seventeen* has rudimentary bedrooms and bathrooms in the hall that have seen better days. But it's clean and friendly and nicely situated on a pleasant tree-lined street minutes from Union Square and the East Village. Check out the excellent weekly rates. Nightly rates ❹/❺

SoHo Grand 310 W Broadway at Grand St ☎212/965-3000. In a great location at the edge of SoHo, this hotel draws guests of the model/media-star/actor variety. Its appeal includes small but stylish rooms, a good bar, restaurant and fitness center. ❾

Stanford 43 W 32nd St, between Broadway and 5th Ave ☎1-800/365-1114 or 563-1500, ☎629-0043. In a clean, moderately expensive hotel on the block known as Little Korea, rooms are a tad small, but attractive and very quiet, and the hall-ways are narrow but well-lit. Free continental breakfast and valet laundry and the efficient and friendly staff would be welcome in hotels twice the price. **⑦**

W 541 Lexington Ave between 49th and 50th sts ☎212/755-1200. If the folks hanging out in the *Whisky Blue Bar*, dining at *Heartbeat* or just posing on the sidewalk are any indication, the *W*, which opened in 1998, might well be the hippest hotel in town. Stylish rooms. **⑨**

Washington Square 103 Waverly Place ☎212/777-9515. The ideal location in the heart of Greenwich Village is a stone's throw from the NYU campus. Don't be deceived by the posh-looking lobby – the rooms are what you'd expect for the price, and the staff can be surly. Continental breakfast is included. **⑥/⑦**

Wolcott 4 W 31st St at 5th Ave ☎212/268-2900. This relaxing, moderately priced hotel has a gilded, ornamented lobby and decent rooms, all with bathrooms – a very good deal. **⑥**

The City

New York City comprises the central island of Manhattan and four outer bor-oughs – Brooklyn, Queens, the Bronx and Staten Island. **Manhattan**, to many, *is* New York; certainly, this is where you're likely to spend most time, and to stay. The island is broadly divided into three areas: **downtown** (below 14th St), **midtown** (from 14th St to Central Park/57th St), and **uptown Manhattan** (north of 57th St). The southern (downtown) part of Manhattan was the first to be settled, which means that its streets have names and are somewhat ran-domly arranged. Above Houston Street (pronounced *How-stun*, not *Hew-stun*) on the East Side and 14th on the West Side, the streets follow a sensible grid pattern, numbers increasing as you move north.

Fifth Avenue, the greatest of the main avenues, begins downtown at the arch in Washington Square Park and cuts along the east side of Central Park, serv-ing as a dividing line between east streets ("the East Side") and west streets ("the West Side"). House numbers increase as you walk away from Fifth Avenue to either side; numbers on avenues increase as you move north. In most cases, **traffic** runs from east to west on odd-numbered streets, from west to east on even-numbered streets, and in both directions on major crosstown streets. Apart from Broadway and Park and Eleventh avenues, which run both ways in most stretches, avenues run in alternate directions.

Manhattan is a hard act to follow, and the four **outer boroughs**, essentially residential in character, inevitably pale in comparison. However, **Brooklyn Heights** is one of the city's most beautiful neighborhoods, and both the faded resort of **Coney Island** and nearby **Brighton Beach**, both in Brooklyn, deserve trips out on the subway, while a ride on the **Staten Island Ferry** is an attraction in itself.

Downtown Manhattan

DOWNTOWN MANHATTAN harbors its extremes in close proximity. Before the terrorist attack on the World Trade Center in September 2001, for some this area contained perhaps the most spectacular and glamorous skyline in the world; for others, parts of Downtown remain a somewhat run-down and seedy home. But whatever your perspective, it is undeniably archetypal New York.

The **Statue of Liberty** is the obvious focus – not so much for the vaunted symbol (though this is hard to ignore) as for the views of Manhattan. From here you can see up the straight, broad avenues as far as the East Village and sometimes beyond. This lower part of the island begins with the **Financial District** – Wall Street at its center – and then drifts, within half a mile, into the first of the city's ethnic districts: bustling, insular **Chinatown**, fast expanding into adjacent **Little Italy**. East of Chinatown and Little Italy, and also extending up to 14th Street east of First Avenue, is the **Lower East Side**, formerly Jewish, now more Dominican; working class and creative types mix here in a hotbed of artistic innovation and interesting nightlife options, but with areas of poverty also apparent. To the west of Chinatown and Little Italy, the one-time industrial areas of **SoHo** and **TriBeCa** are now expensive residential neighborhoods, home to Manhattan's art and film scenes. North of Houston Street, which cuts across the island, are **Greenwich Village** (on the west side) and the **East Village**, former bohemian enclaves now more traditional than their residents would like to believe.

The Statue of Liberty and Ellis Island

The tip of Manhattan Island and the shores of New Jersey, Staten Island and Brooklyn form the broad expanse of **New York Harbor**. One of the finest natural harbors in the world stretches as far as the Verrazano Narrows – the thin neck of land between Staten Island and Long Island. One can appreciate its expansive beauty by gazing out from the promenades in Battery Park and Brooklyn, but to get the best views of Manhattan's tip you should really take to the water.

You can do this on the **Staten Island Ferry** or by taking a **Circle Line ferry**. They go to both the Statue of Liberty and Ellis Island from the pier in Battery Park (sailings every 20min in summer, 8.30am–4.30pm; $8, children $3 round-trip; tickets from Castle Clinton in the park; ticket and schedule information ☎212/269-5755 or ⓦ www.statueoflibertyferry.com). If you take the last ferry, you can't visit both islands, so leave as early as possible, which will also help you to avoid the long queues. Liberty Island needs a good couple of hours, especially if the weather's nice and there aren't too many people; Ellis Island, too, demands at least two hours if you want to see the Museum of Immigration. There are no admission fees for either island. (Governor's Island, the third island in the bay, is currently inaccessible except through monthly tours led by Big Onion Walking Tours – see p.71).

The **Statue of Liberty**, torch in hand and clutching a stone tablet, has for more than a century served as a figurehead for the American Dream, with probably the most instantly recognizable profile in existence. Depicting Liberty throwing off her shackles and holding a beacon to light the world, it was the creation of the French sculptor Frédéric Auguste Bartholdi, crafted a hundred years after the American Revolution in recognition of fraternity between the French and American people (though he originally intended it for Alexandria in Egypt). Liberty, which consists of thin copper sheets bolted together and supported by an iron framework designed by Gustave Eiffel, was built in Paris between 1874 and 1884. Bartholdi enlarged his original terracotta model through four successive versions – one of which stands beside the Seine in Paris – to its present size. It was formally dedicated by President Grover Cleveland on October 28, 1886. You can climb up the 354 steps to the crown, though the cramped stairway to the torch remains closed to the public. Don't be surprised if you have to wait more than an hour to ascend.

Just across the water, a few minutes by ferry, **Ellis Island** was the first stop for more than twelve million prospective immigrants. Originally called Gibbet Island by the English (who used it for punishing unfortunate pirates), it became

The World Trade Center, 1973–2001

During its 28-year lifespan, the glorious twin towers of the **World Trade Center** became an integral part of New York's legendary skyline and a symbol of the city's social and economic success. However, on September 11, 2001, as many thousands of people began their working day in the towers, two hijacked planes crashed into each tower just 20 minutes apart. The subsequent collapse of both towers and other buildings in the World Trade Center complex served as a terrible wake-up call to an America, and a city, that had believed itself to be invincible. Hundreds of firefighters, police officers and rescue workers were among the 3000 or more who lost their lives amid the smoke and the falling debris.

While the WTC's claim to the world's two tallest buildings was quickly usurped by the Sears Tower in Chicago, and later by others, and despite the damage wrought by a terrorist bomb explosion on February 26, 1993, in which six people were killed, the Center was fully occupied and successful, and had become both a coveted workspace and a much-loved tourist destination.

Visitors to the Financial District should expect to be shocked and saddened by what remains of this integral part of the skyline. There is much talk of what should be installed in the towers' place, but any realization of that talk is likely a long way away. In the meantime, subways have been reconfigured and some streets may remain in a no-go zone: inquire locally for details.

an immigration station in 1892, mainly to handle the massive influx from southern and eastern Europe. It remained open until 1954, when it was left to fall into atmospheric ruin.

The immigrants who arrived at Ellis Island were all steerage class passengers; richer voyagers were processed at their leisure on board ship. Most families arrived hungry and penniless; con men preyed on them from all sides, stealing their baggage as it was checked and offering rip-off exchange rates for whatever money they had managed to bring. Each family was split up – men sent to one area, women and children to another – while a series of checks weeded out the undesirables and the infirm. Steamship carriers were obliged to return any immigrants not accepted to their original port, but according to official records only two percent were rejected. Many of those jumped into the sea and tried to swim to Manhattan rather than face going home.

By the time of its closure, Ellis Island was a formidable complex, the island having been expanded by landfill. In the turreted central building, **The Museum of Immigration** (daily 9.30am–5pm; free; ☎212/363-3200, ⓦwww .ellisisland.org) tries hard to recapture the spirit of the place with features such as "Ellis Island Stories," a stirring half-hour dramatic re-enactment of the immigrant experience based on oral histories (April–Sept, $3, children $2.50); the "Wall of Honor" (ⓦwww.wallofhonor.com), with the names of many who came through Ellis Island; and "Treasures From Home," a collection of family heirlooms, photos and other artifacts.

The Financial District

The **Financial District** has been synonymous with the Manhattan of the popular imagination for some time – its tall buildings and skyline, its symbols of economic strength and financial wheeling and dealing. So when the September 11, 2001 attacks on the World Trade Center resulted in the collapse of the Twin Towers and the death of thousands of New Yorkers (see box above), the widespread impact this had was no surprise. There is still plenty to see in the area, however, as this is the city's most historic district, with winding streets, old churches and great twentieth century architecture; in any case many visitors might find a pilgrimage to the site of the former Twin Towers – or as near as you can get – hard to resist.

When the Dutch arrived in New York and settled at the site of the future Financial District, they built a wooden wall at the edge of their small settlement to protect themselves from pro-British settlers to the north. Hence, the narrow canyon of Wall Street gained its name. Today, behind the Neoclassical mask of the **New York Stock Exchange** at Broad and Wall streets, the purse strings of the world are pulled – a process you can observe from the 3rd floor of the NYSE Interactive Education Center at 20 Wall St (Mon–Fri 8.45am–4.30pm; free; ℡212/656-3000, ⓦwww.nyse.com). The Exchange floor resembles a melee of brokers and buyers, scrambling for the elusive fractional cent on which to make a megabuck. The **Federal Hall National Memorial**, at 26 Wall St, looks a little foolish surrounded by skyscrapers. The building was once the Customs House, but the exhibition inside (Mon–Fri 9am–5pm; free; ℡212/825-6888, ⓦwww.nps.gov/feha) relates to the headier days of 1789, when George Washington was sworn in as president from a balcony on this site. Washington's statue stands, very properly, on the steps outside the daintily rotunded hall. At Wall Street's Western end, **Trinity Church** (Broadway between Rector and Church sts; guided tours daily at 2pm; free) is an ironic onlooker to the street's dealings, a knobbly neo-Gothic structure erected in 1846 and the city's tallest building for fifty years. It has much of the air of an English church, especially in its sheltered graveyard, the resting place of early luminaries, including the first secretary of the Treasury, Alexander Hamilton.

Broadway comes to a gentle end at **Bowling Green Park**, an oval of turf used for the game by eighteenth-century colonial Brits on a lease of "one peppercorn per year." Earlier still, the green was the site of one of Manhattan's more memorable business deals. Peter Minuit, first director general of the Dutch colony of New Amsterdam, bought the whole island from the Indians for a handful of baubles worth sixty guilders (about $25). At the green today, office workers picnic in the shadow of Cass Gilbert's 1907 **US Customs House**, a monument to New York's booming maritime economy. Four statues at the front (sculpted by Daniel Chester French, who also created the Lincoln Memorial in Washington, DC) represent the four continents, while the twelve near the top personify the world's commercial centers. The Customs House contains the superb **Smithsonian National Museum of the American Indian** (daily 10am–5pm; free; ℡212/514-3700, ⓦwww.si.edu/nmai), a fascinating assembly of artifacts from almost every tribe native to the Americas. The curators have been creative with the presentation of their material, which includes large wood and stone carvings from the Pacific Northwest; elegant featherwork from Amazonia; a large array of masks; Aztec mosaics; Mayan textiles; seven-foot house posts shaped like animals; some scalps; and a tribe's worth of elaborately beaded moccasins.

Downtown Manhattan lets out its breath in **Battery Park**, where the nineteenth-century Castle Clinton (daily 8.30am–5pm) once protected the southern tip of Manhattan and now sells ferry tickets to the Statue of Liberty and Ellis Island. At the **Museum of Jewish Heritage** (Sun–Wed 9am–5pm, Thurs until 8pm, Fri 9am–5pm, closed Jewish holidays; $7, children $5; ℡212/509-6130, ⓦwww.mjhnyc.org), three floors of exhibits range from the practical accoutrements of everyday Eastern European Jewish life to the prison garb survivors wore in Nazi concentration camps, along with photographs, personal belongings, multimedia presentations and narratives. The collection includes Nazi leader Heinrich Himmler's personal annotated copy of Hitler's *Mein Kampf*.

North up Water Street, at Pearl and Broad streets, stands the partly reconstructed **Fraunces Tavern** (Mon–Fri 9am–5pm; $3, children, seniors, students $2; ☎212/425-1778, ⓦwww.fraucestavernmuseum.org). Here, on December 4, 1783, with the British conclusively beaten, a weeping George Washington took leave of his assembled officers, intent on returning to rural life in Virginia. The second floor recreates the site's history with a series of illustrated panels; the restaurant is no longer in business.

Farther up Water Street, at the eastern end of Fulton Street, is the renovated **South Street Historic District**, formerly New York's sailship port, from where Robert Fulton started a ferry service to Brooklyn. Trade eventually moved elsewhere, and the blocks of warehouses and ship's chandlers were left to rot until they were renovated in the 1970s. Regular guided tours of the Seaport run from the **South Street Seaport Museum** at 207 Water St (April 1–Sept 30 daily 10am–6pm, Oct 1–March 31 daily 10am–5pm; $5, admission includes all tours, films, galleries and museum-owned ships, as well as **New York Unearthed**; ☎212/748-8600, ⓦwww.southstseaport.org). The tour features refitted ships and chubby tugboats (the largest US collection of sailing vessels by tonnage), plus a handful of maritime art and trade exhibits.

You might also look in on the **Fulton Fish Market**, a tatty building that wears its eighty years as the city's wholesale outlet with no pretensions. Visit while you still can (the market is scheduled to move to a somewhat unsavory location in the Bronx in 2003), preferably around 6am, when buyers' lorries park up beneath the highway to collect the catches – invigorating stuff. Tours can be arranged through the museum the first and third Wednesday of the month, April–Oct (☎212/748-8786). The adjacent **Pier 17 Pavilion**, an overdeveloped complex of restaurants and shops, sticks out like a sore thumb.

From just about anywhere in the seaport you can see the much-loved **Brooklyn Bridge**. Now just one of several spans across the East River, it was in its day a technological quantum leap. The first bridge to use steel cables, it towered over the low brick structures around it, and for twenty years after it opened in 1883 it was the world's largest suspension bridge. It didn't go up easily, though. John Augustus Roebling, its architect and engineer, crushed his foot taking measurements for the piers and died of gangrene three weeks later. His son Washington took over, only to be crippled by the bends from working in an insecure underwater caisson. He then directed the work from his sick bed. Twenty workers died during the construction and, a week after the opening day in 1883, twelve people were crushed to death in a panicked rush on the bridge's footpath. Despite this gory history, the beauty of the bridge itself and the spectacular views of Manhattan it offers make a walk across its wooden planks (from the Brooklyn side into the city) an essential part of any New York trip.

Further west, at the corner of Vesey Street and Broadway, the defiantly antique **St Paul's Chapel** seems decidedly out of place in this downtown temple to modernity. The oldest church in Manhattan dates from 1766 – eighty years earlier than Trinity Church and almost prehistoric by New York standards.

City Hall Park and the Civic Center

Immediately north of St Paul's Chapel, Broadway and Park Row form the apex of **City Hall Park**, a recently restored green and brightly flowered triangle now worthy of its handsome setting. Cass Gilbert's 1913 **Woolworth Building** (233

Broadway between Barclay St and Park Place) is a venerable onlooker. For many, this is New York's definitive skyscraper, its soaring lines fringed with Gothic decoration. Frank Woolworth made his fortune from "five and dime" stores and, true to his philosophy, he paid cash for his skyscraper. The whimsical reliefs at each corner of the lobby show him doing just that, counting out the money in nickels and dimes. Facing him in caricature are the architect (medievally clutching a model of his building), the renting agent and the builder. Within, vaulted ceilings ooze honey-gold mosaics, and even the mailboxes are magnificent.

At the top of the park, marking the beginning of the **Civic Center** and its incoherent jumble of municipal offices and courts, stands **City Hall** (Mon–Fri free tours at 10am, 11am and 2pm; ☎212/788-6865) completed in 1812. After the city saluted the hero aviator Charles A. Lindbergh in 1927, it became the traditional finishing point for Broadway ticker-tape parades given for astronauts, returned hostages and, more recently, the World Champion Yankees. Inside, it's an elegant meeting of arrogance and authority, with the sweeping spiral staircase delivering you to the precise geometry of the **Governor's Room** and the self-important rooms that formerly contained the **Board of Estimates Chamber**.

If City Hall is the acceptable face of municipal bureaucracy, **Tweed Courthouse** – where the **Museum of the City of New York** (see p.101) will move in 2003 – behind it at 52 Chambers St, is a reminder of a seamier underbelly. It was the brainchild of William Marcy "Boss" Tweed, who worked his way from nowhere to become chairman of the Democratic Central Committee at Tammany Hall in 1856, and manipulated the city's revenues into his own and his supporters' pockets. Deservedly, he died nearby in a jail he had built while holding public office.

Chinatown and Little Italy

A short stroll northeast from the Civic Center is **Chinatown**, Manhattan's most thriving ethnic neighborhood, which over recent years has extended north across Canal Street into Little Italy and east into the Lower East Side. With more than 150,000 residents (125,000 of them Chinese), seven Chinese newspapers, about 150 restaurants and more than 300 garment factories, it is a model for poor neighborhoods; it has the lowest crime rate, highest employment and least juvenile delinquency of any city district.

The Chinese began to arrive in New York in the mid-nineteenth century. Most had previously worked out West, building railroads and digging gold mines, and few intended to stay: their idea was simply to make a nest egg and retire to a life of leisure with their families (99 percent of the workers were men) back in China. Some did go back, but on the whole the big money took rather longer to accumulate than expected, and so Chinatown took shape as a permanent settlement. Budget restaurants boomed, thanks in part to the increase in working women who had no time to cook and bought food to take home. **Mott Street** is the main tourist thoroughfare and the streets around – Canal, Pell, Bayard, Doyers and the Bowery – host a positive glut of restaurants, tea and rice shops, and grocers.

On the north side of Canal Street, **Little Italy** is light years away from the solid ethnic enclave of old. Originally settled by the huge nineteenth-century influx of Italian immigrants, the neighborhood has far fewer Italians living here now. Families were driven away by the high rents or the encroaching expanse of Chinatown. The restaurants (of which there are plenty) tend to have high

Hoboken New Jersey

Hudson River

DOWNTOWN MANHATTAN

ACCOMMODATION

Chelsea Hotel	1
Chelsea International Hostel	3
Chelsea Lodge	4
Gramercy Park	2
Larchmont	6
Seventeen	5
SoHo Grand	8
Washington Square	7

TRIBECA

NORTH MOORE ST
FRANKLIN ST
LEONARD ST
WORTH ST
W BROADWAY

Former Site of
World Trade Center

Woolworth Building

GREENWICH ST
WEST STREET
WARREN ST
DUANE ST
READE ST
CHAMBERS ST
BARCLAY ST
PARK PL

BATTERY
PARK
CITY

Trinity Church

VESEY ST
LIBERTY ST
CEDAR ST

St Paul's
Chapel

New York
Stock Exchange

City Hall

Tweed
Courthouse

CHINATOWN

Columbus
Park

BAYARD ST
CENTRE ST

Museum of
Jewish Heritage

Castle Clinton
National Monument

Smithsonian
National Museum
of the American Indian

Battery
Park

Vietnam
Veterans'
Plaza

Frances
Tavern

South Street
Seaport
Museum

Fulton
Fish Market

South Street
Seaport
Pier 17

East River

FDR DRIVE

MANHATTAN BRIDGE

BROOKLYN BRIDGE

SOUTH ST

WATER ST

CHERRY ST

MONROE ST
MADISON ST
HENRY ST
MARKET ST
CATHERINE ST
DIVISION ST
EAST BROADWAY

RUTGERS ST

BROOKLYN

Staten Island

Statue of Liberty

Ellis Island

BROOKLYN BATTERY TUNNEL

N

Ⓜ Subway stations

0   1000 yds

prices and a touristy feel. However, some original bakeries and salumerias (Italian specialty food stores) do survive, and you can still indulge yourself with a cappuccino and pastry. September's ten-day **Festa di San Gennaro** is a wild and raucous splurge to celebrate the patron saint of Naples. Italians from all over the city converge on **Mulberry Street**, transforming Little Italy's main strip with food outlets and street stalls.

SoHo and TriBeCa

Since the mid-1960s, **SoHo**, the grid of streets that runs *South* of *Ho*uston Street, has meant fashion chic, urbane shopping, cosmopolitan galleries and **art**. Languishing outside the Financial District and Greenwich Village, it had long been a wasteland of manufacturers and wholesalers. However, as the Village declined in hipness, SoHo was suddenly "in." Its loft spaces were ideal for low-rent studios, and galleries quickly followed, attracting crowds, boutiques and restaurants. Gentrification came next, and what remains is a mix of chichi antique, art and clothes shops, and numerous **museums**. These include the **Guggenheim SoHo** at 575 Broadway (Thurs–Mon 11am–6pm; free; ☏212/423-3500, ⓦwww.guggenheim.org) and the **New Museum of Contemporary Art** at 583 Broadway (Wed & Sun noon–6pm, Thurs–Sat noon–8pm; $6, students and seniors $3, under 18s free, Thurs 6–8pm free; ☏212/219/1222, ⓦwww.newmuseum.org). SoHo now carries the veneer of the chic establishment – a loft in the area means money (and lots of it) – but it is still home to some good art galleries and some of the best cast-iron facades in America.

The technique of **cast-iron architecture** originated as a way of assembling buildings quickly and inexpensively, with iron beams rather than heavy walls carrying the weight of the floors. The result was the removal of supporting walls, greater space for windows and, most noticeably, decorative facades. Almost any style or whim could be cast in iron and pinned to a building, and architects indulged themselves in Baroque balustrades, forests of Renaissance columns and all the effusion of the French Second Empire to glorify SoHo's sweatshops. Have a look at 72–76 Greene St, a neat extravagance whose Corinthian portico stretches the whole five stories, all in painted metal, and at the strongly composed elaborations of its sister building at nos. 28–30. At the northeast corner of Broome Street and Broadway the magnificent **Haughwout Building** is perhaps the ultimate in the genre, with rhythmically repeated motifs of colonnaded arches framed behind taller columns in a thin sliver of a Venetian palace.

TriBeCa, the *Tri*angle *Be*low *Ca*nal Street, has caught some of the fallout of SoHo's artists (the rest went to Williamsburg in Brooklyn and to Chelsea), and has rapidly changed from a wholesale garment district to an upscale community. Less a triangle than a crumpled rectangle – the area bounded by Canal and Chambers streets, Broadway and the Hudson River – TriBeCa contains spacious industrial buildings that house the apartments of a new gentry, including Robert De Niro (whose film production company, TriBeCa Film Center, and restaurant, *TriBeCa Grill*, are at 375 Greenwich St).

Greenwich Village

For many visitors, **Greenwich Village** (or simply "the Village") is the most loved neighborhood in New York, despite having lost any radical edge long ago. Its bohemian image, however, endures well enough if you don't live in the city. It still sports many attractions that brought people here in the first place:

a busy street life that stays up later than many other parts of the city; more restaurants per head than anywhere else; and bars, seldom cheap, cluttering every corner.

Greenwich Village grew up as a rural retreat from the early and frenetic nucleus of New York City. During the yellow fever epidemic of 1822 it became a refuge from the infected streets downtown. Refined Federal and Greek Revival townhouses lured some of the city's highest society names and later proved fertile ground for struggling artists and intellectuals. By the turn of the last century Greenwich Village was on its way toward becoming New York's Left Bank.

The natural center of the Village, **Washington Square**, is not exactly elegant but it does retain its northern edging of redbrick rowhouses – the "solid, honorable dwellings" of Henry James's eponymous novel – and Stanford White's imposing **Triumphal Arch**, built in 1892 to commemorate the centenary of George Washington's inauguration. The artist Marcel Duchamp climbed the arch in 1913 to proclaim the Free Republic of Greenwich Village. These days, it's also the heart of the truly urban campus of NYU. As soon as the weather gets warm, the park becomes a sports field, performance space, chess tournament and social club, feverish with life as street entertainers strum, skateboards flip and the pulsing bass of hip-hop resounds through the whispered offers of the few surviving dope peddlers.

Follow **MacDougal Street** south and you hit **Bleecker Street** – the Village's main drag, packed with shops, bars, people and restaurants. This junction is also the area's best-known meeting place, a vibrant corner whose European-style sidewalk cafés have been turned from the literary hangouts of Modernist times to (in some cases) overpriced tourist draws (though they're still fun for a spot of luxury people-watching). Turning right takes you through the hubbub of Village life, stretching up **Sixth Avenue** to the unmistakable nineteenth-century bulk of the **Jefferson Market Courthouse**, voted, in 1885, fifth most beautiful building in America. It now serves as the local public library. Cut through from here to **Seventh Avenue** and you'll pass by **Bedford Street**, one of the Village's quietest and most desirable living areas. Nearby, **Christopher Street** joins Seventh at **Sheridan Square**, home of the *Stonewall Inn*'s gay bar where, in 1969, a police raid precipitated a siege that lasted the best part of an hour. If not a victory for gay rights, it was the first time that gay men had stood up to the police en masse, and as such represents a turning point in the struggle for equal rights, remembered by the annual **Gay Pride March**, held on the last Sunday in June.

The East Village

The **East Village** differs quite a bit from its western counterpart. Once, like the adjacent Lower East Side, the East Village was a refuge for immigrants and solidly working-class people. Home to New York's nonconformist intelligentsia in the early twentieth century, it later became the haunt of the **Beats** – Kerouac, Burroughs, Ginsberg, et al – who would get together at Ginsberg's house on East Seventh Street for declamatory poetry readings. Later, Andy Warhol debuted the Velvet Underground here; the Fillmore East hosted almost every band under the sun; and Richard Hell, Patti Smith and the Ramones invented punk rock in a hole-in-the-wall called **CBGB** (see p.118). Further east, **Alphabet City** (avenues A, B, C, D), a former Slavic enclave – and erstwhile turf of drug dealers and gangs – has recently gentrified at an alarming rate. Along Avenue A, you'll pass a number of worthwhile fashion and design shops as well as sushi bars, cafés and record stores. **Tompkins Square Park**, between avenues A and B and Seventh and Tenth streets, is considered the center of Alphabet City. The park – and the streets framing it – are welcoming, with plenty of offbeat restaurants and bars. However, while avenues A, B and C become more hip as you move east, Avenue D is a sombre and edgy affair, and no-one, bar the residents of the housing projects that line the East River, should have any need to go there, especially at night.

Much of the East Village has changed since the economic boom of the mid-1980s and the 1990s, not the least of which has been escalating rents and "yuppification," stripping the East Village of its former status as a hotbed of dissidence and creativity. Nevertheless, the area's main drag, the vaudevillian **St Mark's Place**, is still one of downtown's more vibrant strips, even if the thrift shops, panhandlers and political hustlers have given way to more sanitized forms of rebellion and a cluster of *Starbucks*.

Astor Place, at the western end of St Mark's Place, was one of the city's most desirable neighborhoods in the 1830s. The now-undistinguished Lafayette Street was home to such wealthy names as John Jacob Astor, one of New York's most hideously greedy tycoons. The antique Astor Place **subway station**, bang in the middle of the junction, discreetly remembers the man on its platforms, where colored reliefs of beavers recall Astor's first big killings – in the fur trade. More recently, though, Astor Place has begun looking like a mall, with chain superstore outlets hawking household goods, books and records.

A stone's throw from the subway, **Cooper Square** is dominated by the seven-story brownstone mass of **Cooper Union**, erected in 1859 by the industrialist Peter Cooper as a college for the poor. Early in 1860, Abraham Lincoln wowed top New Yorkers here with his "might makes right" speech, in which he boldly criticized the pro-slavery South and helped propel himself to the Republican nomination for president. Today, Cooper Union remains a prestigious art and architecture school.

The Lower East Side

South of Tompkins Square, the **Lower East Side** began life toward the end of the nineteenth century as an insular slum for more than half a million Jewish immigrants. Since then it has changed considerably, with many Puerto Rican and Chinese inhabitants. An even more recent influx of well-off students, artists, designers and the like has begun to send the neighborhood up the social ladder. South of East Houston Street, this area is so trendy its almost not again; it boasts a plethora of bars and cool clothing stores while retaining a slightly seedy edge.

You can still **buy** just about anything cut-price in the Lower East Side, especially on Sunday mornings, when **Orchard Street** is filled with stalls and stores selling off hats, clothes and designer labels at hefty discounts. Next to this melee is the **Lower East Side Tenement Museum**, 90 Orchard St between Broome and Delancey (Tues–Fri 1–5pm, Thurs until 8pm, Sat & Sun 11am–4.30pm; $9; ☎212/431-0233, ⓦwww.tenement.org) which offers the lowdown on the neighborhood's immigrant past. The museum gives tours through an 1863 tenement building, whose restored rooms re-create the poverty that many area residents withstood while trying to build a new life in America.

The **Bowery** runs up as far as Cooper Square on the edge of the East Village. This wide thoroughfare has gone through many changes: it took its name from *Bouwerie*, the Dutch word for farm, when it was the city's main agricultural supplier; later, in the closing decades of the nineteenth century, it was lined with music halls, theaters, hotels and restaurants, drawing people from all parts of Manhattan. The only city thoroughfare never to have been graced by a church, it is still – in some sections – a skid row, yet such days are limited as the demand for apartments continues and the tide of gentrification sweeps through the Lower East Side. The one – bizarre – focus is the **Bowery Savings Bank** at Grand Street. Designed by Stanford White in 1894, its splendid architecture makes the surrounding debris even more depressing much as does its sister bank on 42nd Street.

Midtown Manhattan

MIDTOWN MANHATTAN is the center of the city. Most of the hotels are here, and it's where you're most likely to arrive – at Penn or Grand Central stations, or the Port Authority Bus Terminal. New York's most glamorous (and most expensive) street, **Fifth Avenue**, cuts through its heart, with the neon theater strip of **Broadway** just to the west for much of the way. The character of Midtown undergoes a radical transformation depending on which side of Fifth you find yourself. On the avenue and to the east are the corporate businesses and prestigious skyscrapers – including Chrysler, Empire State, the Seagram buildings – as well as the residential neighborhoods of **Gramercy Park** and **Murray Hill**. West of Fifth, and in particular west of Broadway, the area progressively declines from the recently revitalized **Chelsea** – a new magnet for art galleries and commercial development – to the **Garment District**, whose wholesale apparel shop employees still roll racks of clothing through the streets. The **Theater District** is no longer sleazy, having benefited from the multimillion-dollar cleanup of **Times Square**. Even the folks at Disney have been impressed by the transformation, judging the area sanitized enough to be the home for their flagship store on 42nd Street and for a new Disney Hotel now under construction. **Clinton**, the former Hell's Kitchen neighborhood west of Broadway in the 40s and low 50s, has seen a crackdown on porn shops and other sleazy businesses, gentrifying slowly though still rough near the West Side Highway.

The East Side: Union Square to 42nd Street

Downtown Manhattan ends at 14th Street, which slices across from the housing projects of the East Side through rows of cut-price shops to the meat-packing warehouses on the Hudson. In the middle is **Union Square**, until the mid-1980s a scene of dope-pushing and street violence but since remodeled and therefore much more inviting, its shallow steps enticing passers-by to stroll the paths, feed the squirrels and admire the statuary. On any Monday, Wednesday, Friday or Saturday you'll find a terrific farmers' market. The stretch of **Broadway** north of here, once known as Ladies' Mile for its fancy stores and boutiques, has recently been reinvented as an urban mall, with large chain stores on every block in the 20s. The interesting architecture includes sculptured facades, massive windows and curvy lintels.

Turn right on East 20th Street for the faithful reproduction of **Theodore Roosevelt's Birthplace**, housed in the original building at no. 28 (Wed–Sun 9am–5pm; $2). The somber brownstone mansion boasts many of the original

▲ **1 2 3** The Cloisters, Columbia University & Harlem   ▲ Museum of the City of New York & El Barrio

ACCOMMODATION

Algonquin Hotel	14
Amsterdam Inn	6
Chelsea Center Hostel	21
Dylan	17
Edison	11
Gershwin	22
Hostelling International-New York	2
International House-Sugar Hill	3
Jazz on the Park	1
Lucerne	4
Mansfield	16
Milburn	5
Murray Hill Inn	20
Paramount	13
Pickwick Arms	8
Roger Smith	10
Royalton Hotel	15
Salisbury	7
Stanford	18
Vanderbilt YMCA	12
W	9
Wolcott	19

MIDTOWN/UPTOWN MANHATTAN

East River

QUEENS MIDTOWN TUNNEL

Humphriss Tunnel

FDR DRIVE

0   800 yds

N

Circle Line Ferry

LINCOLN TUNNEL TO N.J.

Jacob Javits Convention Center

Dewitt Clinton Park

THEATER DISTRICT

GARMENT DISTRICT

TIMES SQUARE

BROADWAY

Port Authority Bus Terminal

General Post Office

Madison Square Garden

Pennsylvania Station

Macy's

Carnegie Hall

Museum of Modern Art

Radio City Music Hall

Museum of TV & Radio

Rockefeller Center

Bryant Park

MURRAY HILL

New York Public Library

Pierpont Morgan Library

Empire State Building

Trump Tower

Citicorp Center

Seagram Building

St. Patrick's Cathedral

Waldorf-Astoria Hotel

Met-Life (Pan Am) Building

Grand Central Terminal

Chrysler Building

United Nations Headquarters

Metropolitan-Life Building

Madison Square Park

Chelsea Park

Flatiron Building

M Subway stations

TWELFTH AVENUE
ELEVENTH AVENUE
TENTH AVENUE
NINTH AVENUE
EIGHTH AVENUE
SEVENTH AVENUE
SIXTH AVENUE
FIFTH AVENUE
MADISON AVENUE
PARK AVENUE
LEXINGTON AVENUE
THIRD AVENUE
SECOND AVENUE
FIRST AVENUE

W. 57TH ST.
W. 56TH ST.
W. 55TH ST.
W. 54TH ST.
W. 53RD ST.
W. 52ND ST.
W. 51ST ST.
W. 50TH ST.
W. 49TH ST.
W. 48TH ST.
W. 47TH ST.
W. 46TH ST.
W. 45TH ST.
W. 44TH ST.
W. 43RD ST.
W. 42ND ST.
W. 41ST ST.
W. 40TH ST.
W. 39TH ST.
W. 38TH ST.
W. 37TH ST.
W. 36TH ST.
W. 35TH ST.
W. 34TH ST.
W. 33RD ST.
W. 32ND ST.
W. 31ST ST.
W. 30TH ST.
W. 29TH ST.
W. 28TH ST.

E. 57TH ST.
E. 56TH ST.
E. 54TH ST.
E. 53RD ST.
E. 52ND ST.
E. 50TH ST.
E. 49TH ST.
E. 48TH ST.
E. 47TH ST.
E. 46TH ST.
E. 45TH ST.
E. 44TH ST.
E. 43RD ST.
E. 42ND ST.
E. 40TH ST.
E. 39TH ST.
E. 38TH ST.
E. 37TH ST.
E. 35TH ST.
E. 34TH ST.
E. 33RD ST.
E. 32ND ST.
E. 31ST ST.
E. 30TH ST.
E. 29TH ST.
E. 27TH ST.
E. 26TH ST.
E. 25TH ST.
E. 24TH ST.

furnishings, some of Teddy's hunting trophies and a small gallery documenting the president's life.

Manhattan's clutter suddenly breaks into the ordered open space of **Gramercy Park** (between 20th and 21st sts where Lexington Ave becomes Irving Place). A former swamp reclaimed in 1831, it is one of the city's best squares, its center tidily planted and, most noticeably, completely empty for much of the day – principally because the only people who can gain access are those rich enough to live here and possess keys to the gate.

Broadway and Fifth Avenue meet at 23rd Street at **Madison Square**, by day a maelstrom of cars and cabs, but with a serenity that Union Square has lost. Most notable among the elegant structures that surround it, the **Flatiron Building** (175 Fifth Ave, between 22nd and 23rd sts), rises cheekily on a triangular plot of land on the square's southern side; its twenty stories dwarfed nearby structures when it was built in 1902. Its uncommonly thin, tapered shape creates unusual wind currents at ground level; years ago police officers prevented men from gathering to watch the wind raise the skirts of women passing on 23rd Street.

Farther up Fifth Avenue is New York's prime **shopping territory**, home to some heavyweight department stores, including Lord & Taylor between 38th and 39th streets. Overshadowing them all, however, is the **Empire State Building** (Ⓦwww.esbnyc.com) at 34th Street and Fifth Avenue, a muscular 102-story symbol of New York since being completed in 1931. After September 2001 it became, as once before, the city's tallest building. Inside, its basement is an underground marbled shopping precinct, finished everywhere with delicate Deco touches. The first elevator toward the top takes you to the 86th floor, summit of the building before the radio and TV mast was added. The views from the outside walkways here are as stunning as you'd expect; Manhattan spreads on all sides. If you have time, line up for the small single elevator and go to the Empire State's last reachable zenith, a small cylinder at the foot of the TV mast (part of a harebrained scheme to erect a mooring post for airships – a plan abandoned after some VIPs almost got swept away by the wind). You can't go outside, and the extra sixteen stories don't add a great deal to the view, but you can say you went all the way. Visit during the week if you are intent on rising to that apex: due to crowding, the 102nd Floor Observatory is closed on weekends during the summer (otherwise daily 9.30am–midnight; last trip 11.30pm; $9).

East of the Empire State Building, the residential district **Murray Hill** was once dominated by the crusty old financier J.P. Morgan and his son, J.P. Jr.; the latter's brownstone, at 37th Street and Madison Avenue, is now headquarters of the American Lutheran Church. The home of the elder Morgan, once adjacent to his son's, was razed to make way for the **Pierpont Morgan Library** (Tues–Thurs 10.30am–5pm, Fri 10.30am–8pm; Sat 10.30am–6pm, Sun noon– 6pm; July & Aug closed Sun; suggested donation $8, students $6). A gracious Italian-style nest built in 1917, the library, at 29 E 36th St (Ⓣ212/685-0610, Ⓦwww.morganlibrary.org), is filled with the fruits of the Morgans' magpie-like trips to Europe. Its two main rooms are off a corridor often lined with Rembrandt prints. The first, the **West Room**, remains much as it looked when it was Morgan's study, with a carved sixteenth-century Italian ceiling, paintings by Memling and Perugino, and a custom-carved desk. The domed and pillared hallway leads to the **East Room** or library, a sumptuous three-tiered cocoon of rare books, autographed musical manuscripts, and trinkets culled from European households and churches. A rotating permanent collection includes

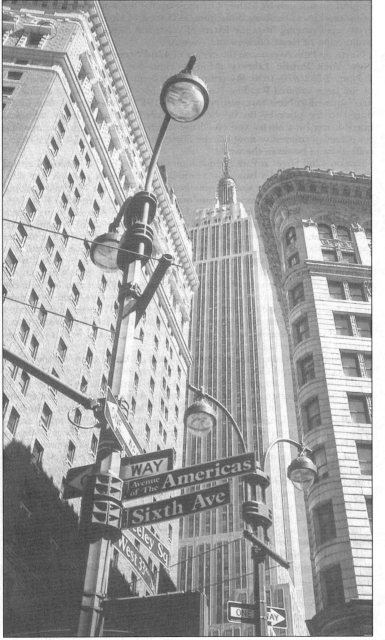

ONE WAY

WAY
Avenue of The **Americas**

Sixth Ave

eley Sq

West 33rd

ONE WAY

△ Empire State Building

original manuscripts by Mahler (the museum has the world's largest collection of his work); a Gutenberg Bible from 1455 (one of eleven surviving); and literary relics ranging from the letters of Vasari and George Washington to the manuscripts of Keats, Dickens and Thoreau.

North up Fifth Avenue, on the corner of **42nd Street**, stands the Beaux Arts **New York Public Library** (Mon & Thurs–Sat 10am–6pm, Wed 11am–7.30pm ☎212/870–1630, ⓦwww.nypl.org). Leon Trotsky worked on and off in the large coffered Reading Room at the back of the building during his brief sojourn in New York, just prior to the 1917 Russian Revolution, introduced to the place by his Bolshevik comrade Nikolai Bukharin, who was bowled over by a library you could use so late in the evening. The opening times are less impressive now, but the library still boasts one of the five largest collections of books in the world.

East on 42nd Street at Park Avenue looms the huge bulk of **Grand Central Station**, built around a basic iron frame but clothed with a Beaux Arts skin. The structure's immense size has now been dwarfed by the Met Life building behind it. Yet the main station's **concourse** is a sight to behold – 470ft long and 150ft high, it boasts a barrel-vaulted ceiling speckled like a Baroque church with a painted representation of the winter night sky. The 2500 stars are shown back to front, "as God would have seen them," the painter is reputed to have explained. Explore Grand Central on your own or take the Municipal Arts Society's excellent free tour. For the best view of the concourse – as well as the flow of commuters and commerce – climb up to the catwalks that span the sixty-foot-high windows on the Vanderbilt Avenue side. After that, seek out the station's more esoteric reaches, including the *Oyster Bar* – one of the city's most highly regarded seafood restaurants, deep in the terminal's bowels and crammed every lunchtime. Near the restaurant, testing an acoustical fluke, two visitors can stand on opposite sides of any of the vaulted spaces and hold a conversation just by whispering.

Across the street, the former **Bowery Savings Bank** (now *Cipriani 42nd Street*) echoes Grand Central's grandeur, extravagantly lauding the virtues of sound investment and savings. A Roman-style basilica, it has a floor paved with mosaics, columns (each fashioned from a different kind of marble), and bronze bas-reliefs on the elevator doors. The more famous **Chrysler Building**, at 405 Lexington Ave, also dates from a time (1930) when architects carried off prestige with grace and style. This was for a short while the world's tallest building and is one of Manhattan's best-loved structures. The car-motif friezes, jutting gargoyles and arched stainless-steel pinnacle give the solemn Midtown skyline a welcome touch of whimsy. Chrysler moved out some time ago, and for a while the building was left to degenerate by a company that didn't fully appreciate its spirited silliness, but the new owner has pledged to keep it lovingly intact. The lobby, once a car showroom, is for the moment all you can see, with its opulently inlaid elevators, walls covered in African marble and murals showing airplanes, machines and brawny builders who worked on the tower.

The **United Nations** complex, at the eastern end of 42nd Street, comprises the glass-curtained **Secretariat**, the curving sweep of the **General Assembly** and, connecting them, the low-rising **Conference Wing**. Guided tours leave from the monumental General Assembly lobby (daily every 20min, 9.30am–4.45pm; $7.50, students $5; ☎212/963-8687, ⓦwww.un.org/MoreInfo/pubsvs.html) and take in the UN conference chambers and its constituent parts.

The West Side: Chelsea, the Garment District and Times Square

Chelsea took shape in 1830 when its owner, Charles Clarke Moore, laid out his land for sale in broad lots. It failed to achieve the desirability it sought, taking until recent decades for real estate to get hot here, led by a thriving gay community. Walk up and down Eighth Avenue between 14th and 23rd streets and you'll see all manner of fashionable bars and restaurants mingled in with bodegas, frequented by the neighborhood's mixed clientele.

During the nineteenth century the area was a focus of New York's theater district. Nothing remains of that now, but the hotel that put up all the actors, writers and attendant entourages – the **Chelsea Hotel** – remains a New York landmark, with a down-at-the-heel Edwardian grandeur all its own. Mark Twain and Tennessee Williams lived here, Brendan Behan and Dylan Thomas staggered in and out during their New York visits, and in 1951 Jack Kerouac, armed with a customized typewriter (and a lot of Benzedrine), typed the first draft of *On the Road* nonstop onto a 120ft roll of paper. In the 1960s Andy Warhol and his doomed protégé Edie Sedgwick holed up here and made the film *Chelsea Girls* in (sort of) homage. In October 1978 Sid Vicious stabbed Nancy Spungen to death in their suite, a few months before his own life ended with an overdose of heroin. The hotel also inspired Joni Mitchell to write *Chelsea Morning* – which in turn inspired Bill and Hillary Clinton in naming their daughter.

To the west, **Chelsea Piers**, a 1.7 million-square-foot sports complex that opened in 1995, was built along the Hudson River around West 23rd Street; extending over four piers, it offers a host of indoor and outdoor facilities as well as some good spots to eat and drink. A block over, at West 22nd Street between Tenth and Eleventh avenues, is a patch of established **galleries**, many of which have relocated here from SoHo, driven away by rising rents and a lack of space.

A few blocks north at 32nd Street, Sixth Avenue collides with Broadway at **Greeley Square**, an overblown name for a trashy triangle celebrating Horace Greeley, founder of the *Tribune* newspaper, and known for his rallying call to "Go West, young man!"

The **Garment District**, a loosely defined patch between 34th and 42nd streets and Sixth and Eighth avenues, produces three-fourths of all the women's and children's clothes in America. You'd never guess it, though; the outlets are strictly wholesale with no need to woo customers. Retail stores, abound, however. **Macy's**, the famed old department store with two million square feet of floor space and $5 million in sales a day, is on **Herald Square** at 34th Street and Seventh Avenue.

The district's dominant landmark is the **Pennsylvania Station** and **Madison Square Garden** complex, a combined box and drum structure that swallows up millions of commuters in its train station below and accommodates the Knicks and Liberty basketball – and Rangers hockey – teams up top. The original Penn Station, demolished to make way for this, is now hailed as a lost masterpiece, which reworked the ideas of the Roman Baths of Caracalla to awesome effect: "Through it one entered the city like a god . . . One scuttles in now like a rat," mourned one observer. Immediately behind Penn Station, the same architects – McKim, Mead and White – were responsible for the **General Post Office**. The old joke is that it had to be this big to fit in the sonorous inscription above the columns – "Neither snow nor rain nor heat nor gloom of night stays these couriers from the swift completion of their appointed rounds." Another transportation hub, the **Port Authority Bus Terminal** at 40th–42nd streets and Eighth Avenue, serves as a gateway to the wonders of Times Square.

Forty-second Street meets Broadway at the southern margin of **Times Square**, the center of the theater district, where the pulsating neon suggests a heart for the city itself. Because of the major cleanup launched by the city and by business interests like Disney, the ambience along 42nd Street and north has changed dramatically. Traditionally a melting pot of debauchery, depravity and fun, the Square is now a largely sanitized universe of popular consumption, with refurbished theaters and blinking signage an homage to days gone by.

Not an actual square at all, Times Square was created by the intersection between straight-arrow Seventh Avenue and left-leaning Broadway; the latter more or less follows true north through much of the island, which tilts to the northeast. So narrow is the angle between these two thoroughfares that Broadway, which meets Seventh Avenue at 43rd Street, does not begin to strike off on its own until 48th Street. Here, in the intervening blocks and in the immediate side streets at midnight every December 31, hundreds of thousands of people watch a giant sparkling ball drop from the top of Times Tower.

At the southernmost end of the square was the headquarters of the *New York Times*, **Times Tower**, modeled on Giotto's *Campanile* in Florence. In 1928, the zipper sign displaying the news of the world was added; in 1965 the building was covered with lifeless marble slabs. The paper itself has long since moved around the corner to a handsome building with globe lamps on 43rd Street.

Further north, the **Equitable Center**, 757 7th Ave, houses Roy Lichtenstein's 68ft *Mural with Blue Brush Stroke*, which pokes you in the eye as you enter. Otherwise **Carnegie Hall**, an overblown, warehouse-like venue for opera and concerts at 154 W 57th St, is the thing to see. Tchaikovsky conducted the program on opening night and Mahler, Rachmaninov, Toscanini, Frank Sinatra and Judy Garland have played here; it has dropped in status since Lincoln Center opened (see pp.102 & 118), but the superb acoustics still ensure full houses most of the year (mid-Sept to June; tours available Mon, Tues, Thurs & Fri at 11.30am, 2pm & 3pm; $6; ☎212/247-7800).

Sixth Avenue is properly named "Avenue of the Americas," though no New Yorker ever calls it this and the only manifestation is the flags of Central and South American countries still flying on some blocks. If nothing else, Sixth's distinction is its width, a result of the Elevated Railway that once ran along here, now replaced by the Sixth Avenue subway underground. In its day the Sixth Avenue "El" marked the borderline between respectability to the east and vice to the west, and the avenue still separates the glamorous strips of Fifth, Madison and Park avenues from the less salubrious western districts. Worth a stop is the **Royalton** (44 W 44th St), one of the three New York hotels designed by Philippe Starck (the *Hudson* and the *Paramount* are the others). Its decor – which includes fountains and hidden doors in the toilets – seems straight out of *Alice in Wonderland*.

Farther up, Sixth Avenue is solidly corporate, especially between 47th and 50th streets. At 49th Street, the **Radio City Music Hall** is the last word in 1930s luxury. The staircase is regally resplendent with the world's largest chandeliers, the original murals from the men's toilets are now in the Museum of Modern Art and the huge auditorium looks like an extravagant scalloped shell. At the **AXA Financial Building** (1290 6th Ave), look for Thomas Hart Benton's *America Today* murals, a magnificent portrayal of ordinary American life in the days before the Depression.

Fifth Avenue and east: 42nd Street to Central Park

Fifth Avenue has been a great strip for as long as New York has been a great city, and its very name evokes wealth and opulence. All who consider themselves suave and cosmopolitan end up here, and the stores showcase New York's most conspicuous consumerism. That the shopping is beyond the means of most people needn't put you off, for Fifth Avenue has some of the city's best architecture; the boutiques and stores are just the icing on the cake.

At the heart of Fifth Avenue's glamour is **Rockefeller Center**, built between 1932 and 1940 by John D. Rockefeller Jr., son of the oil magnate. One of the finest pieces of urban planning anywhere balances office space with cafés, a theater, underground concourses and rooftop gardens that work together with a rare intelligence and grace. The **GE Building** here rises 850ft, its monumental lines matching the scale of Manhattan itself, though softened by symmetrical setbacks to prevent an overpowering expanse of wall. At its foot, the **Lower Plaza** holds a sunken restaurant in summer, linked visually to the downward flow of the building by Paul Manship's sparkling *Prometheus*; in winter, the plaza becomes an **ice rink**, allowing skaters to show off their skills to passers-by. Inside, the Center is no less impressive. In the GE lobby, José Maria Sert's murals, *American Progress* and *Time*, are a little faded but eagerly in tune with the Thirties Deco ambience – presumably more so than the original paintings by Diego Rivera, removed by John D.'s son Nelson when the artist refused to scrap a panel glorifying Lenin. A leaflet available from the lobby desk details a **self-guided tour** of the Center. Among the GE Building's many offices are the **NBC Studios** (daily 1hr tours leave regularly, 9.15am–5pm; reservations at the NBC Experience Store Tour Desk; $10). If you're a TV fan, pick up a free ticket for a **show recording** from the mezzanine lobby or out on the street. The most popular tickets evaporate before 9am. The newer glass-enclosed **Today Show** studio is at the southwest corner of the plaza at 49th Street, often surrounded by avid fans waiting to get on TV by way of the cameras that obligingly pan the crowds from time to time.

Almost opposite Rockefeller Center on 51st Street and Fifth Avenue, **St Patrick's Cathedral**, designed by James Renwick and completed in 1888, seems the result of a painstaking academic tour of the Gothic cathedrals of Europe – perfect in detail, but lifeless in spirit, with a sterility made all the more striking by the glass-black **Olympic Tower** next door, an exclusive apartment block where Jackie Onassis once lived. Between Fifth and Sixth avenues at 25 W 52nd St, the **Museum of Television and Radio** (Tues–Wed & Fri–Sun noon–6pm, Thurs noon–8pm; $6) holds an excellent archive of American TV and radio broadcasts. The museum's computerized reference system allows you to search for programs, then watch them on one of 96 video consoles.

Continuing north, the **Trump Tower** at 57th Street is the last word in Fifth Avenue opulence, with an outrageously over-the-top atrium, filled with designer stores, that is just short of repellent. Perfumed air, polished marble paneling and a five-story waterfall are calculated to knock you senseless with expensive yet somewhat garish taste. But the building is clever: a neat little outdoor garden is squeezed high in a corner, and each of the 230 apartments above the atrium gets views in three directions.

To the east, **Madison Avenue** makes for pleasant strolling, especially north of here, where it is filled with expensive galleries, haute couture shops and elegantly dressed East Siders. The next avenue east, **Park Avenue**, was said in

1929 to be the place "where wealth is so swollen that it almost bursts." Things haven't changed much: corporate headquarters and four-star hotels jostle in triumphal procession, led by the massive New York Central Building (now the **Helmsley Building**) that literally sits above Park Avenue at 46th Street and boasts a lewdly excessive Rococo lobby. In its day this formed a skillful punctuation mark to the avenue, but its thunder was stolen in 1963 by the **Met Life Building** (200 Park Ave at 45th St) that looms behind it.

Wherever you placed it, the solid mass of the **Waldorf Astoria Hotel** (Park Ave between 49th and 50th sts) would hold its own, a resplendent statement of Art Deco elegance. Crouched behind it is **St Bartholomew's Church**, a low-slung Byzantine hybrid that adds immeasurably to the street and gives the lumbering skyscrapers a much-needed sense of scale. The spiky-topped **General Electric Building** behind seems like a wild extension of the church, its slender shaft rising to a meshed crown of abstract sparks and lightning strokes that symbolizes the radio waves used by its original owner, RCA. The lobby (entrance at 570 Lexington) is yet another Deco delight.

Among all this it's difficult at first to see the originality of the **Seagram Building** between 52nd and 53rd. Designed by Mies van der Rohe with Philip Johnson and built in 1958, this was the seminal curtain-wall skyscraper, the floors supported internally, allowing a skin of smoky glass and whisky-bronze metal (Seagram's is known for distilled liquors), now weathered to a dull black. Every interior detail – from the fixtures to the lettering on the mailboxes – was specially designed. It was the supreme example of Modernist reason, and its opening was met by a wave of approval. The plaza, an open forecourt designed to set the building apart from its neighbors, was such a success as a public space that the city revised the zoning laws to encourage other highrise builders to supply plazas. Alas, you see the result in the windswept, sterile places all over the city.

A block east, the chisel-topped **Citicorp Center** on Lexington Avenue (between 53rd and 54th sts), finished in 1979, is one of Manhattan's most conspicuous landmarks. The slanted roof was designed to house solar panels to provide power for the building, but the idea was ahead of the technology and Citicorp had to content itself with adopting the distinctive top as a corporate logo.

MoMA on the Move

Founded in 1929, moved to its present home ten years later, and extensively updated in the mid-1980s so that its gallery space was doubled, the **Museum of Modern Art** (MoMA) at 11 W 53rd St offers probably the finest and most complete account of late nineteenth- and twentieth-century art you're likely to find. MoMA covers every medium – illustration and design, architecture and photography – but focuses primarily on painting and sculpture, and it's justly famous for its 14,000-plus film archive, often showing retrospectives and rare films you have little chance of seeing elsewhere.

However, MoMA at this site will be closed through early 2005, as it embarks on its most comprehensive reconfiguration ever, and most of the permanent collection has been moved to a facility in Queens (MoMAQueens, 45-20 33rd St at Queens Blvd, Ⓦwww.moma.org). Special Picasso and Matisse exhibits in the temporary space should soften the blow of losing (albeit temporarily) a vital ingredient of Manhattan's art culture.

Uptown Manhattan

UPTOWN MANHATTAN begins above 57th Street, where the businesslike bustle of Midtown gives way to the comfortable domesticity of the Upper East and West sides. In between, people come to **Central Park**, the city's back garden, to play, jog and escape Midtown's crowds in a particularly intelligent piece of urban landscaping.

The **Upper East Side** is at its most opulent in the several blocks just east of Central Park, and at its most prestigious in the Metropolitan and other great museums of "Museum Mile." The **Upper West Side** is less refined, though its Lincoln Center hosts New York's most prestigious arts performances. It is also predominantly residential, well-heeled on its southern fringe, especially along Columbus Avenue, but less so as you move north. The northern reaches embrace the monolithic Cathedral of St John the Divine and Columbia University. Still farther north is one of the city's most intriguing museums, the medieval arts collection of **The Cloisters**.

Central Park

"All radiant in the magic atmosphere of art and taste." So enthused *Harper's* magazine on the opening of **Central Park** in 1876, and, to this day, few New Yorkers could imagine life without it. Set just about smack in the middle of Manhattan, extending from 59th to 110th streets, it provides residents (and street-weary tourists) with a much-needed refuge from the harshness of big-city life. Whether you're into jogging, baseball, boating, botany or just plain walking, or even if you rarely go near the place, there's no question that Central Park makes New York a bearable (even enjoyable) place to live.

The poet and newspaper editor William Cullen Bryant had the idea for an open public space in 1844, and spent seven years trying to persuade City Hall to carry it out. Eventually 840 desolate and swampy acres north of the city limits, then occupied by a shantytown of squatters, were set aside. The two architects commissioned to design the landscape, **Frederick Olmsted** and **Calvert Vaux**, planned to create a rural paradise, a complete illusion of the countryside in the heart of Manhattan – even then growing at a fantastic rate. At its opening in 1876, Central Park was declared a "people's park" – though most of the impoverished masses it was allegedly built to serve had neither the time nor the carfare to come up from their downtown slums and enjoy it. But as New York grew and workers' leisure time increased, people began flooding in, and the park began to live up to its mission, sometimes in ways that might have scandalized its original builders. Today, in spite of the advent of motorized traffic, the sense of captured nature that they intended largely survives (thanks in large part to the not-for-profit Central Park Conservancy), although the skyline has changed greatly and some of the open space has been turned into asphalted playgrounds. For general park information call ☎212/360-3444 or call ☎1-888/NYPARKS for special events information.

One of the best ways to explore is to rent a **bicycle** from either the Loeb Boathouse (roughly $9 an hour) or Metro Bicycles (Lexington at 88th St; ☎212/427-4450; $7 per hour). The other is **on foot**, along the many footpaths that crisscross the park. There's little chance of getting lost, but to know exactly where you are, find the nearest lamppost: the first two figures signify the number of the nearest street. After dark, however, you'd be well advised not to enter on foot. If you want to see the buildings illuminated from the park, one option is to fork out for a **carriage ride**. You can pick up a hack along Central Park South, between Fifth and Sixth avenues. If you worry that the carriage business is cruel to the horses, bear in mind that city law requires that they cannot work more than nine hours per day, and must get fifteen-minute breaks every two hours. You might better worry about the damage to your wallet – a twenty-minute trot costs $34, excluding tip.

Most places of interest lie in the southern reaches of the park. Near **Grand Army Plaza**, the main entrance to the park at Fifth Avenue and 59th Street, is the **Central Park Wildlife Center**, which tries to keep caging to a minimum and the animals as close to the viewer as possible (Mon–Fri 10am–5pm, Sat, Sun & holidays 10am–5.30pm; ⊤212/439-6500; $3.50, ages 3–12 50¢, under 3 free). Beyond here, the **Dairy**, once a ranch building intended to provide milk for nursing mothers, now houses a visitor's center (Tues–Sun 10am–5pm; ⊤212/794-6564), distributing free leaflets and maps, selling books and putting on exhibitions. Weekend walking tours often leave from here; call for times.

Nearby, the **Wollman Rink** (63rd St at mid-park) is a lovely place to skate in winter, or to practice your in-line skating skills in the warmer months. From the rink you may wish to swing west past the restored **Sheep Meadow**, a dust bowl in the 1970s, now emerald green. Then head north up the formal Mall to the **Bandshell** and the terrace and sculptured birds and animals of **Bethesda Fountain**, on the shore of the **Central Park Lake**. To your left (west) is **Strawberry Fields**, a tranquil, shady spot dedicated to John Lennon by his widow, Yoko Ono, and the **Imagine mosaic** – both near his home at the Dakota, where he was shot dead in 1980. Rent a **boat** from the Loeb Boathouse on the eastern bank of the lake (March–Nov daily 10am–6pm, weather permitting; ⊤212/517-2233; rowboats are $10 for the first hour, $2.50 per 15mins after, with a $30 refundable deposit; **gondola rides**, given 5–10pm, cost $30 per 30min per group and require reservations) or cross the water by the elegant cast-iron **Bow Bridge**. Beyond this bridge, delve into the wild woods of **The Ramble** along a maze of paths and bridges. At 81st Street near the West Side stands the mock citadel of **Belvedere Castle**, another visitor center that has nature exhibits and boasts great views of the park from its terraces. Next to the castle is the **Delacorte Theater**, home to free **Shakespeare in the Park** performances in summer, and the immense **Great Lawn**, the preferred sprawling ground for many sun-loving New Yorkers. Near the north end of the park is the beautifully terraced and landscaped **Conservatory Garden** at 103rd Street, off Fifth Avenue, encompassing three distinct garden styles (English, Italian, and French).

The Metropolitan Museum of Art

The **Metropolitan Museum of Art** (usually simply the "Met"), one of the world's great art museums, juts into the park at Fifth Avenue and 82nd Street (Tues–Thurs & Sun 9.30am–5.15pm, Fri & Sat 9.30am–8.45pm, closed Mon; suggested donation $10, students $5, includes same-day admission to The Cloisters, see p.105). Its all-embracing collection amounts to more than two million works of art, spanning America and Europe as well as China, Africa, the Far East and the classical and Islamic worlds. You could spend weeks here and not see everything. The choice of works that follows – among the Met's greatest hits – is inevitably selective in the extreme.

If you can make just one visit, head for the **European Painting** galleries. Of the early (fifteenth and sixteenth century) **Flemish and Netherlandish paintings**, the best are by Jan van Eyck, who is generally credited with having started the tradition of North European realism, and Rogier van der Weyden, whose *Christ Appearing to His Mother* is one of his most beautiful works. Later canvases include Bruegel's *Harvesters*, part of the series of six paintings that included his familiar Christmas-card *Hunters in the Snow*. To the left from here are the **Spanish paintings**, including the very different landscape of El Greco's extraordinary *View of Toledo* and Velázquez's *Portrait of Juan de Pareja*. "All the rest are art, this alone is truth," remarked a critic of this somber portrait when it was first exhibited in 1650. The **Italian Renaissance** is less spectacularly represented here but a worthy selection includes an early *Madonna and Child Enthroned with Saints* by Raphael, a late Botticelli and Filippo Lippi's *Madonna and Child Enthroned with Two Angels*. The culmination of the European Galleries is the **Dutch paintings** section, dominated by the major works of Rembrandt, Vermeer and Hals. Vermeer, genius of the domestic interior, is represented by five works, most haunting of which is the *Portrait of a Young Woman*, and there are some fine portraits by Rembrandt – a beautiful painting of his common-law wife, Hendrike Stoffjels, painted three years before her early death, and a superb *Self-portrait* from 1660, the year he was declared bankrupt.

The **nineteenth-century galleries** house a startling array of **Impressionist** and **Post-Impressionist art**, beginning with Manet, the movement's most influential precursor, and his striking *Young Lady in 1866*. The prolific Monet is widely represented, including three superb works – *Rouen Cathedral*, *The Houses of Parliament (Effect of Fog)* and *The Doge's Palace Seen from San Giorgio Maggiore* – in which you can detect the beginnings of his final phase of near-Abstract Impressionism. Nearby is Courbet's erotic *Woman with a Parrot* (which inspired Manet's similar work), along with a casting of Degas' *Little Dancer*, complete with real tutu, bodice and shoes. The Post-Impressionists Paul Gauguin and Toulouse-Lautrec follow, and there are also major works by Van Gogh (including *Irises* and *Self Portrait with Straw Hat*), Pissarro and Seurat (*Circus Sideshow*).

Housed over two floors in the Lila Acheson Wallace Wing, the Met's compact **twentieth-century collection** features paintings such as Picasso's *Portrait of Gertrude Stein* and *The Blind Man's Meal*, alongside works by Klee, Hopper, Matisse, Braque and Klimt. Postwar pieces include Pollock's masterly *Autumn Rhythm (Number 30)*, Thomas Hart Benton's rural idyll *July Hay*, Charles DeMuth's *The Figure 5 in Gold*, and Warhol's *Last Self Portrait*, as well as works by Max Beckmann, Lichtenstein, Rothko, Johns and de Kooning.

The **American Wing**, in the northwest corner of the Met, is virtually a museum in its own right, with 25 furnished historical rooms, starting with the Early Colonial period and the Hart room of around 1674, and ending with Frank Lloyd Wright's Room from the Little House, Minneapolis, originally windowed on all four sides, demonstrating Wright's emphasis on minimal interior–exterior division. The **American paintings** include the nineteenth-century canvases of William Sidney Mount, who depicted genre scenes on his native Long Island, and the landscape artists of the Hudson Valley School, Thomas Cole and his pupil Frederick Church. Winslow Homer gets a gallery to himself, while later rooms bring the Met's American art into the twentieth century with works by Thomas Eakin (including the melancholic *Max Schmitt in a Single Scull*) and John Singer Sargent, whose *Portrait of Madam X* was one of the most famous pictures of its day, exhibited at the 1884 Paris Salon and considered so improper that Sargent had to leave the city.

The Met's **Medieval Galleries** are no less exhaustive, with displays of sumptuous Byzantine metalwork and jewelry donated by J.P. Morgan. The main sculpture hall is piled high with religious statuary and carvings, and surrounded by later period rooms – paneled Tudor bedrooms, florid Rococo boudoirs and salons from France, and an entire Renaissance patio from Vélez Blanco in Spain. The **Egyptian rooms** also have as much to see – huge statuary, smaller sculptural pieces and jewelry – although the most prominent exhibit is the **Temple of Dendur**, housed in its own huge gallery, designed to symbolize its original site on the banks of the Nile. Built by the Emperor Augustus in 15 BC for the Goddess Isis of Philae, the temple was moved here as a gift from the Egyptian people during the construction of the Aswan High Dam in 1965 – it would otherwise have been drowned.

The **Asian Art galleries** showcase plenty of murals, sculptures and textile art from Japan, China, Southeast and Central Asia and Korea, all around the galleries' highlight – the exquisite **Chinese Garden Court**, lovingly assembled by experts from the People's Republic. The **Greek and Roman galleries**, always rich in classical artifacts (including a near-fully restored Roman Cubiculum, replete with an uncomfortable-looking chaise), now also boast a formidable array of earlier Cypriot, Mycenaean, Etruscan and Italic painting, ornaments, vases and other objects.

Finally, if you have plenty of time on your hands, consider the Met's minor glories: stately rows of human and equine dummies clad for battle in the **Arms and Armor** exhibit; and the second-floor **Musical Instruments** collection, featuring eighteenth-century spinets and clavichords in surprisingly good condition. The **Costume Institute** on the ground floor puts on wonderfully imaginative special exhibits.

The Upper East Side

A two-square-mile grid, the **Upper East Side** has wealth as its defining characteristic, as you'll appreciate if you've seen any of the many Woody Allen movies set here. **Fifth Avenue** up here has been the patrician face of Manhattan since the opening of Central Park attracted the Carnegies, Astors and Whitneys to migrate north and build fashionable residences. **Grand Army Plaza**, at Central Park South and Fifth Avenue, flanked by the extended chateau of the swanky **Plaza Hotel**, and glowing with the gold statue of the Civil War's Gen. William Tecumseh Sherman, serves as the introduction.

On the corner of Fifth Avenue and 65th Street, America's largest reform synagogue, the **Temple Emanu-El**, strikes a sober tone. The brooding Romanesque–Byzantine cavern manages to be bigger inside than it seems from outside. The interior melts away into darkness, making you feel very small indeed (Mon–Fri & Sun 9am–5pm).

A block east, dominating a square block, is the **Seventh Regiment Armory** (Park Ave between 66th and 67th streets), built in the 1870s with pseudo-medieval crenellations and, inside, a grand double stairway and spidery wrought iron chandeliers – the only surviving building from the era before the New York Central's railroad tracks were roofed over and Park Avenue became an upscale residential neighborhood.

Back on Fifth Avenue, at 70th Street, you'll find Henry Clay Frick's house, a handsome spread and now the tranquil home of the **Frick Collection** (Tues–Sat 10am–6pm, Sun 1–6pm, closed Mon; $10, students $5). One of many prestigious museums in the area, the Frick is perhaps the most enjoyable of the big New York galleries; it is made up of the art treasures hoarded by Frick during his years as probably the most ruthless of New York's robber barons. The legacy of his self-aggrandizement is a revealing glimpse into the sumptuous life enjoyed by New York's big industrialists. The collection includes paintings by Reynolds, Hogarth, Gainsborough (*St James's Park*) and Bellini, whose *St Francis* suggests his vision of Christ by means of pervading light, a bent tree and an enraptured stare. El Greco's *St Jerome*, above the fireplace, reproachfully surveys the riches all around, and looks out to the South Hall, where one of Boucher's intimate depictions of his wife hangs near an early Vermeer, *Officer and Laughing Girl*. In the opposite direction are the library's British works, most notably one of Constable's *Salisbury Cathedral* series, and the North Hall, which holds an engaging and sensitive portrait of the Comtesse de Haussonville by Ingres. But the West Gallery holds Frick's greatest prizes: two Turners, views of Cologne and Dieppe; van Dyck's informal portraits of Frans Snyders and his wife – paintings reunited when Frick purchased them; and a set of piercing self-portraits by Rembrandt, along with the enigmatic *Polish Rider*. A tiny room on the other side of the West Gallery houses an exquisite set of Limoges enamels and a collection of small-scale paintings that includes a *Virgin and Child* by Jan van Eyck.

The **Guggenheim Museum**, farther up Fifth Avenue at 89th Street (Sun–Wed 9am–6pm, Fri & Sat 9am–8pm, closed Thurs; $12, seniors, students $8, children under 12 free, Fri 6–8pm pay what you wish), is better known for the building than its collection. This structure, designed by Frank Lloyd Wright, caused a storm of controversy when it was unveiled in 1959. Its centripetal spiral ramp, which wends you continuously all the way to its top floor (affording a vertiginous view of the lobby at the center), is still thought by some to favor Wright's talents over those of the exhibited artists. More outrage accompanied recent construction of a tower extension, but visitors will have difficulty understanding the fuss; it melds seamlessly with the ramp, and its galleries allow a much greater part of the museum's collection to be on rotational display. One of the newer additions is the Mapplethorpe Gallery, fittingly housing some of the museum's odder pieces, including Louise Bourgeois' wood-chip sculpture *Femme Volage* – and several Calder mobiles. Much of the building is still given over to temporary exhibitions, but the permanent collection includes work by Chagall, Léger, the major Cubists and, most completely, Kandinsky. Additionally, there are some late nineteenth-century paintings, not least the exquisite Degas' *Dancers*, Modigliani's *Jeanne Héburene with Yellow Sweater*, and some sensitive early Picassos.

South of here, the **Whitney Museum of American Art**, 945 Madison Ave at 75th Street (Tues–Thurs, Sat & Sun 11am–6pm, Fri 1–9pm, closed Mon; $10, students $8, Fri 6–9pm pay what you wish), brings things up to date: a pre-eminent collection of twentieth-century American art and a superb exhibition locale. Every other year the museum mounts the Whitney biennial show of contemporary American art – an event that has become a lightning rod for critical abuse since the 1995 show, when a giant mound of cooking fat presented as sculpture set right-wing aesthetes into a frenzy. When that's not on, check out the somewhat arbitrary Highlights of the Permanent Collection, arranged by both chronology and theme. Enjoy the prominent Abstract Expressionists collection, with great works by high priests Pollock and de Kooning, leading on to Rothko and the Color Field painters and the later Pop Art works of Warhol, Johns and Oldenburg. The museum is especially strong on Hopper, O'Keeffe and Calder, with galleries concentrating on each.

The Museum of the City of New York, on the corner of 103rd Street and Fifth Avenue (Wed–Sat 10am–5pm, Sun noon–5pm, closed Mon; suggested donation $7; ☎212/534-1672), might also grab your interest, with an informative rundown on the history of the city from Dutch times to the present day. It also runs Sunday walking tours of various New York neighborhoods.

(The museum is scheduled to relocate downtown to the Tweed Courthouse in the spring of 2003.)

At the northernmost part of the Upper East Side is well-tended **Carnegie Hill**, a Historic District bounded by 86th and 98th streets and Fifth and Lexington avenues. One of the highlights here is the **Russian Orthodox Cathedral of St Nicholas** at 15 E 97th St, most notable for its polychromatic Victorian body and five onion domes on top. Get too much past here, and the upscale living quickly fades.

Gracie Mansion at 88th Street overlooking the East River was built in 1799 on the site of a Revolutionary fort as a country manor house; it is one of the best-preserved colonial buildings in the city. Roughly contemporary with the Morris–Jumel Mansion (see p.105), Gracie Mansion has been the official residence of the mayor of New York City since 1942, when Fiorello LaGuardia, "man of the people" that he was, reluctantly set up house. "Mansion" is a bit overblown for what's a rather cramped clapboard cottage.

The Upper West Side

North of 59th Street, Manhattan's West Side becomes less commercial, fading north of Lincoln Center into a residential area of mixed charms. This is the **Upper West Side**, now one of the city's more desirable addresses, though in truth an area long favored by artists and intellectuals. Streets have been rechristened in honor of erstwhile residents like Isaac Bashevis Singer and Edgar Allan Poe. However, gentrification during the 1990s saw it become a bit yuppified and noticeably less funky than it once was.

Broadway sheers north from Columbus Circle to the **Lincoln Center for the Performing Arts**, a marble assembly of buildings put up in the early 1960s on the site of some of the city's worst slums. Home to the Metropolitan Opera and the New York Philharmonic and to a host of other smaller companies (see p.118), this is worth seeing even if you don't catch a performance (tours leave daily at 10.30am, 12.30pm, 2.30pm and 4.30pm from the ticket booth at the Met; phone to reserve; ℡212/875-5350; $9.50, students $8). At the center of the complex, the **Metropolitan Opera House** is an impressive marble and glass building, with murals by Marc Chagall behind each of its high front windows. On the left, *Le Triomphe de la Musique* is cast with a variety of well-known performers, landmarks snipped from the New York skyline and a portrait of Sir Rudolph Bing, the man who ran the Met for more than three decades, garbed as a gypsy. The other mural, *Les Sources de la Musique*, is reminiscent of Chagall's renowned set for the Met production of *The Magic Flute*: the god of music strums a lyre while a Tree of Life, Verdi and Wagner all float down the Hudson River.

The most famous of the monumental apartment buildings of **Central Park West** is the **Dakota**, a grandiose Renaissance-style mansion on 72nd Street, built in the late nineteenth century to persuade wealthy New Yorkers that life in an apartment could be just as luxurious as in a private house. Over the years, big-time tenants have included Lauren Bacall and Leonard Bernstein, and in the late 1960s the building was used as the setting for Polanski's film *Rosemary's Baby*. Most people now know it as the former home of **John Lennon** – and (still) of his wife Yoko Ono, who owns a number of the apartments. Outside the Dakota, on the night of December 8, 1980, Lennon was murdered – shot by a man who professed to be one of his greatest admirers (see p.98 to read about the nearby Lennon memorial in Central Park).

North up Central Park West, the often-overlooked **New-York Historical Society** at 77th Street (Tues–Sun 11am–5pm; suggested donation $5;

☎212/873-3400) is more a museum of American than of New York history. Its collection includes paintings by James Audubon, the Harlem naturalist who specialized in lovingly detailed watercolors of birds; a broad sweep of nineteenth-century American portraiture (including the picture of Alexander Hamilton that found its way onto the $10 bill) and Hudson River School landscapes (among them Thomas Cole's fantastically pompous *Course of Empire* series); and a glittering display of Tiffany glass, providing an excellent all-round view of Louis Tiffany's attempts "to provide good art for American homes."

Up the street looms the **American Museum of Natural History**, Central Park West at 79th Street (Sun–Thurs 10am–5.45pm, Fri & Sat 10am–8.45pm; suggested donation $10, students $7.50, children $6; IMAX films, the Hayden Planetarium and certain special exhibits cost extra, call for details; ☎212/769-5100, ⓦ www.amnh.org). The largest such museum in the world is a strange architectural melange of heavy Neoclassical and rustic Romanesque styles covering four city blocks. Restored in the mid-1990s, the museum boasts superb nature dioramas and anthropological collections, interactive and multimedia displays, lively signage and an awesome assemblage of bones, fossils and models.

Top attractions range from the **Dinosaur Halls** to the new **Hall of Biodiversity**, which focuses on both the ecological and evolutionary aspects of nature. Other delights include the massive totems in the **Hall of African Peoples**, the taxidermical marvels in **North American Mammals** (including a vividly staged bull moose fight), and the two thousand gems in the **Hall of Meteorites**, among them a dazzling two-ton hunk of raw copper. The **Rose Center for Earth and Space**, comprising the new **Hall of the Universe** and the **Hayden Planetarium** (contained in a huge central sphere), opened in 2000. Bearing no resemblance to the rather fusty old planetarium that was torn down, the center boasts all the latest technology and a truly innovative design, with open construction, spiral ramps and dramatic glass walls on three sides of the facility. One exhibit, "The Scales of the Universe," depicts the relative size of things, from galaxies, stars and planets down through cells and atoms, each in comparison to the central sphere. It's simply presented, and effective, yet the concepts still manage to boggle the mind. The Planetarium screens a 40-minute 3-D film "Passport to the Universe" which, though visually impressive, will roughly double the price of museum entry.

The Upper West Side's second best address after Central Park West is **Riverside Drive**, which weaves its way from 72nd Street up the western edge of Manhattan, flanked by palatial townhouses put up in the early twentieth century by those not quite rich enough to compete with the folks down on Fifth Avenue, and by **Riverside Park**, landscaped in 1873 by Frederick Olmsted of Central Park fame. Riverside Drive makes the most pleasant route up to the prestigious **Columbia University**, whose campus fills seven blocks between 114th and 121st streets and Amsterdam Avenue and Morningside Drive. The campus plazas were designed by McKim, Mead and White in grand Beaux Arts style. Regular guided tours start from the information office at 116th Street and Broadway.

The **Cathedral Church of St John the Divine** rises up at Amsterdam Avenue and 112th Street with a solid kind of majesty – far from finished but still one of New York's tourist gems. A curious mixture of Romanesque and Gothic styles, the church was begun in 1892, but building stopped with the outbreak of war in 1939 and only sporadically resumed in the early 1990s, albeit fraught with funding difficulties and controversy. It's still barely two-thirds finished; on completion, unlikely before 2050, it will be the largest cathedral structure in the world, its floor space – at 600ft long, and 320ft wide at the transepts – big enough to swallow both the cathedrals of Notre Dame and Chartres whole.

Harlem and the North

Home to a culturally and historically – if not economically – rich **black** community, **Harlem** is still a focus of black activism and culture, and well worth seeing. Up until recently, because of a near-total lack of support from federal and municipal funds, Harlem formed a self-reliant and inward-looking community. For many downtown Manhattanites, white and black, 125th Street was a physical and mental border not willingly crossed. Today, the fruits of a cooperative effort involving businesses, residents and City Hall funding are manifest in new housing, retail and community projects, and much has been made of former President Bill Clinton's new offices here as well. But while brownstones triple in value and Harlem's physical proximity to the Upper West Side is touted, poverty and unemployment are still evident in large patches. Though it's unlikely you'll be hassled in daytime, 125th Street, 145th Street, Convent Avenue and Malcolm X Boulevard (formerly Lenox Avenue) are the safest areas; at night, stick to the clubs.

Harlem's sights are very spread out; it's not a bad idea to get acquainted with the area via a **guided tour** (see p.71), and follow that up with further trips. Harlem's working center is 125th Street between Broadway and Fifth Avenue, a flattened expanse spiked with the occasional skyscraper. Number 253 is the famous **Apollo Theatre** – not much from the outside, but for many years the center of black entertainment in Northeast America. Almost all the great figures of jazz and blues played here – James Brown recorded his seminal *Live At The Apollo* album in 1962 – though a larger attraction today is the Wednesday Amateur Night, open to all. At no. 144 is the **Studio Museum in Harlem** (Wed & Thurs noon–6pm, Fri noon–8pm, Sat & Sun 10am–6pm, closed Mon & Tues; $5, students $3, free on the first Sat of every month), a small but vibrant collection of African and African-American art from all eras.

Close by, **Adam Clayton Powell Jr. Boulevard** pushes north, a broad and busy thoroughfare named after the 1930s minister who helped force the white-owned stores of Harlem to employ the blacks on whom their economic survival depended. Powell became the first black on the city council, then New York's first black representative in the US House. In 1967, amid rumors of the misuse of public funds, his House colleagues excluded him from Congress by majority vote. This failed to diminish his standing in Harlem, where voters twice re-elected him before his death in 1972. One street east, the **Schomburg Center for Research in Black Culture**, 515 Malcolm X Blvd at 135th Street (Mon–Wed noon–8pm, Thurs–Sat 10am–6pm; free), has displays on black history, and literally millions of artifacts, manuscripts, artwork and photographs in its archives. Just north at 132 W 138th St, Powell preached at the **Abyssinian Baptist Church**. The church is also famed for its revival-style Sunday morning services and a gospel choir of gut-busting vivacity. Cross over to 138th Street between Powell and Eighth, and you're in what many consider the finest, most articulate block of rowhouses in Manhattan – **Strivers' Row** – commissioned during the 1890s housing boom and taking in designs by three sets of architects. Within the burgeoning black community at the turn of the last century this came to be the desirable place for ambitious professionals to reside, hence its nickname.

From Park Avenue to the East River, Spanish Harlem, or **El Barrio**, dips down as far as East 96th Street to collide head on with the affluence of the

Upper East Side. The center of a large Puerto Rican community, it is quite different from Harlem in look and feel. El Barrio was originally a working-class Italian neighborhood (a small pocket of Italian families survives around 116th St and First Ave) and the quality of the architecture here is nowhere as good as that immediately to the west. The result is a shabbier and more intimidating atmosphere. Cultural roots are in evidence, however, at **La Marqueta** on Park Avenue between 111th and 116th, a five-block street market of tropical produce, sinister-looking meats and much shouting, and the **Museo del Barrio** at Fifth Avenue and 104th Street (Wed–Sun 11am–5pm; suggested donation $4), which showcases Latin American and Caribbean art and culture.

North of Harlem, starting from West 145th Street or so, is the neighborhood of **Washington Heights**, and **Audubon Terrace** at W 155th Street and Broadway (easily reached by subway #1 to 157th and Broadway or the #A to 155th) is a complex of nineteenth-century Beaux Arts buildings housing an odd array of museums. The **Hispanic Museum** (Tues–Sat 10am–4.30pm, Sun 1–4pm, closed Mon, Library closed Aug; free; ☎212/926-2234) houses one of the largest collections of Hispanic art outside Spain. The three thousand paintings include works by Goya, El Greco and Velázquez, and more than 6000 decorative works of art.

The **Morris–Jumel Mansion**, within easy walking distance on 160th Street between Amsterdam and Edgecombe (Wed–Sun 10am–4pm, closed Mon & Tues; $3; ☎212/923-8008), is another uptown surprise, its proud Georgian outlines faced with a later Federal portico. Built as a rural retreat in 1765 by Colonel Roger Morris, it was briefly Washington's headquarters before it fell to the British. Later, wine merchant Stephen Jumel bought the mansion and refurbished it for his wife Eliza, formerly a prostitute and his mistress. When Jumel died in 1832, Eliza married ex-Vice President Aaron Burr, twenty years her senior. The marriage lasted six months before old Burr upped and left, to die on the day of their divorce. Eliza battled on to the age of 91, and on the top floor of the house you'll find her obituary, a magnificently fictionalized account of a "scandalous" life.

From most western stretches of Washington Heights you get a glimpse of the **George Washington Bridge**, a dazzling concoction of metalwork and grace-ful lines that links Manhattan to New Jersey. Get even better views from **The Cloisters** in Fort Tryon Park. This reconstructed monastic complex houses the pick of the Metropolitan Museum's medieval collection (Subway A to 190th St–Ft Washington Ave; Tues–Sun 9.30am–5.15pm, closes 4.45pm Nov–Feb, closed Mon; suggested donation $10, students $5, includes admission to Metropolitan Museum on same day; hourly direct shuttle bus from the Met Fri & Sat June–Aug for $5; ☎212/923-3700). The collection is the handiwork of collectors George Barnard and John D. Rockefeller, who spent the early twentieth century shipping over all they could buy of medieval Europe. Among its larger artifacts are a monumental Romanesque Hall made up of French remnants and a frescoed Spanish Fuentiduena Chapel, both thirteenth-century. At the center of the museum is the Cuxa cloister from a twelfth-century Benedictine monastery in the French Pyrenees; its capitals are brilliant works of art, carved with weird, self-devouring grotesque creatures. The Early Gothic Hall houses smaller sculptures, among them a memorably tender *Virgin and Child*, carved in England in the fourteenth century. Tapestries include the spec-tacular *Unicorn Tapestries*. Campin's *Merode Altarpiece*, housed in its own antechamber, depicts the Annunciation in a typical Flemish interior of the day, while through the windows, life goes on in a fifteenth-century market square.

The amazing downstairs Treasury houses the *Belles Heures de Jean, Duc de Berry* – perhaps the greatest of all medieval Books of Hours, executed by the Limburg Brothers with dazzling genre miniatures of seasonal life – and the twelfth-century altar cross from Bury St Edmunds in England, a mass of tiny expressive characters from biblical stories.

The outer boroughs

Many visitors to New York don't stray off Manhattan. But if you're staying a while, choose to investigate the **outer boroughs** and you'll be well rewarded. **Brooklyn** is certainly worth a trip, primarily for the salubrious neighborhood of Brooklyn Heights just across the East River, bucolic Prospect Park and the Brooklyn Botanical Garden and the Brooklyn Museum. For inveterate nostalgics, Coney Island and its Russian neighbor, Brighton Beach, lie at the far end of the subway line. Few indeed make it to **Queens**, though it holds the bustling Greek community of Astoria and the Museum of the Moving Image. **Staten Island** has a couple of unusual museums, and the ferry ride out is fun in itself. The **Bronx**, renowned for the desolate and bleak environs of its southern reaches, which are in fact slowly improving, has the city's largest zoo and another glorious botanical garden.

Brooklyn

If it were still a separate city, **Brooklyn** would be the fourth largest in the US, but until as recently as the early 1800s it was no more than a group of autonomous towns and villages distinct from the already thriving Manhattan. Robert Fulton's steamship service across the water first changed the shape of Brooklyn, starting with the establishment of a leafy retreat at Brooklyn Heights. What really transformed things, though, was the opening of the Brooklyn Bridge. Thereafter development spread deeper inland, as housing was needed to service a more commercialized Manhattan. By 1900, Brooklyn was fully established as part of the newly incorporated New York City, and its fate as Manhattan's perennial kid brother was sealed.

Brooklyn Heights, one of New York City's most beautiful neighborhoods, has little in common with the rest of the borough. The peaceful, tree-lined enclave was settled by financiers from Wall Street and remains exclusive. Such noted literary figures as Truman Capote, Tennessee Williams and Norman Mailer lived here. Although there isn't much to see as you wander its perfectly preserved terraces and breathe in the air of civilized calm, students of urban architecture can have a field day. Begin your tour at the **Esplanade** – more commonly known as the **Promenade** – with its fine views of downtown Manhattan across the water. **Pierrepoint** and **Montague** streets, the Heights' main arteries, are studded with delightful brownstones, restaurants, bars and shops.

Farther into Brooklyn, Flatbush Avenue leads to **Grand Army Plaza**, a grandiose junction laid out by Calvert and Vaux late in the nineteenth century as a dramatic approach to their new Prospect Park just beyond. The triumphal **Soldiers and Sailors' Memorial Arch** was added thirty years later, topped with a fiery sculpture of Victory – Frederick William MacMonnies' rider, chariot, four horses and two heralds – in tribute to the Northern triumph in the Civil War. **Prospect Park** was landscaped in the early 1890s, and remains for the most part remarkably bucolic – far more so than Central Park. The same is true for the adjacent **Brooklyn Botanic Garden** (April–Sept Tues–Fri 8am–6pm, Sat & Sun 10am–6pm; Oct–March Tues–Fri 8am–4.30pm, Sat & Sun 10am–4.30pm; $3, free Tues & Sat before noon ☎718/623-7200, ⓦwww .bbg.org), one of the city's most enticing park and garden spaces, smaller and more immediately likeable than its more celebrated cousin in the Bronx.

The **Brooklyn Museum of Art**, 220 Eastern Parkway (Wed–Fri 10am–5pm, Sat & Sun 11am–6pm, first Sat of every month 11am–11pm, closed Mon & Tues; $6, students $3; ☎718/638-5000, ⓦwww.brooklynart.org), though doomed to stand perpetually in the shadow of the Met, is a major museum and a good reason to forsake Manhattan for an afternoon. The Beaux Arts entrance is currently being restored, with renovations due to be completed in early 2003. Highlights include the ethnographic department on the ground floor, the arts and applied arts from Oceania and the Americas and the classical and Egyptian antiquities on the second floor and the evocative American period rooms on the fourth floor. Look in on the top-story American and European Painting and Sculpture Galleries, where the eighteenth-century portraits include one of George Washington by Gilbert Stuart. Pastoral canvases by William Sidney Mount, alongside the heavily romantic Hudson River School and paintings by Eastman Johnson (such as the curious *Not at Home*) and John Singer Sargent, lead up to twentieth-century work by Charles Sheeler and Georgia O'Keeffe. European artists on display include Degas, Cézanne, Toulouse-Lautrec, Monet, Dufy and Rodin.

Generations of working-class New Yorkers came to relax at one of Brooklyn's farthest points, **Coney Island**, reachable from Manhattan on the #Q, #W, #F or #N subway lines. At its height, 100,000 people came here daily; now, however, it's one of the city's poorest districts and the amusement park is peeling and run-down. The boardwalk, though, has undergone extensive and successful renovation of late and, if you like down-at-the-heel seaside resorts, there's no better place on earth on a summer weekend. The beach, a broad swath of golden sand, is beautiful, although it is often crowded on hot days and the water might be less than clean. In late June, catch the **Mermaid Parade**, one of the country's oddest and glitziest small-town fancy dress parades. The **New York Aquarium** on the boardwalk opened in 1896 and is still going strong, displaying fish and invertebrates from the world over in its darkened halls, along with frequent open-air shows of marine mammals (Mon–Fri 10am–5pm, Sat, Sun & holidays 10am–5.30pm; $9.75; ☎718/265-3474).

Farther along the Boardwalk, **Brighton Beach**, or "Little Odessa," is home to the country's largest community of Russian émigrés – around 20,000, who arrived in the 1970s – and a long-established and now largely elderly Jewish population. Livelier than Coney Island, it's also more prosperous, especially along its main drag, **Brighton Beach Avenue**, which runs underneath the Q subway line in a hotchpotch of food shops and appetizing restaurants. In the evening, the restaurants really heat up, becoming a near-parody of a rowdy Russian night out with loud live music, much glass-clinking and the frenzied knocking back of vodka. Definitely worth a visit.

The Bronx

The city's northernmost borough, **The Bronx** was for a long time believed to be its toughest and most crime-ridden district, and presented as such in films like *Fort Apache, The Bronx* and books like *Bonfire of the Vanities*, even after urban renewal was underway. In fact, it's not much different from the other outer boroughs, though geographically it has more in common with Westchester County to the north than it does with the island regions of New York City:

steep hills, deep valleys and rocky outcroppings to the west, and marshy flatlands along Long Island Sound to the east. Settled in the seventeenth century by the Swede Jonas Bronk, it became, like Brooklyn, part of the city proper around the end of the nineteenth century, and soon became one of the most sought-after residential areas of the city. Its main thoroughfare, Grand Concourse, became lined with luxurious Art Deco apartment houses; many, though greatly run-down, still stand.

The **Bronx Zoo** (Mon–Fri 10am–5pm, Sat & Sun 10am–5.30pm; $9, kids $5, free every Wed; ☎718/367-1010, ⓦwww.wcs.org) is accessible either by its main gate on Fordham Road or by a second entrance on Bronx Park South. The latter is the entrance to use if you come directly here by subway (to E Tremont Ave on the #2 or #5). Even if you don't like zoos, the largest urban zoo in the US is better than most, and one of the first to realize that animals both looked and felt better out in the open. The "Wild Asia" exhibit is an almost forty-acre wilderness through which tigers, elephants and deer roam relatively free, visable from a monorail (May–Oct; $2). Look in also on the "World of Darkness," which holds nocturnal species, and the simulation of a Himalayan mountain area, holding endangered species such as the red panda and snow leopard.

Across the road from the zoo's main entrance is the back turnstile of the **New York Botanical Gardens** (Tues–Sun 10am–6pm; $3, students $2, kids $1, free Wed), which in parts is as wild as anything you're likely to see upstate. West of its main entrance, the **Poe Cottage** (Grand Concourse and E Kingsbridge Rd; Sat 10am–4pm, Sun 1–5pm; $2) is a tiny white clapboard shack that was Edgar Allan Poe's home for the last three, unhappy years of his life, which saw his wife's death and very little writing beyond the short, touching poem *Annabel Lee*. Poe left the cottage for the last time in 1849 to travel to Baltimore to secure backing for his own literary magazine; he disappeared and was eventually found delirious, dying in a hospital a few days later. The house, with its few meager furnishings spread thinly through half a dozen rooms, does little to uncover any mysteries.

Queens

Queens, named after the wife of Charles II of England, was one of the rare places where postwar immigrants could buy their own homes and establish their own communities. **Astoria**, for example, holds the world's largest concentration of Greeks outside Greece. It also has a long **filmmaking** tradition: Paramount had its studios here until the company was lured away by Hollywood's reliable weather. The area was then left empty and disused by all except the US Army, until Hollywood's stranglehold on the industry finally weakened. The new studios here – not open to the public – now rank as the country's fourth largest and are set for a major expansion. The **American Museum of the Moving Image** in the old Paramount complex at 35th Avenue at 36th Street (Tues–Fri noon–5pm, Sat & Sun 11am–6pm, closed Mon; $8.50, students/seniors $5.50; ☎718/784-0077, ⓦwww.ammi.org) is devoted to the history of film, video and TV. In addition to viewing posters and kitsch movie souvenirs from the 1930s and 1940s you can listen in on directors explaining sequences from famous movies; watch fun short films made up of well-known clips; add your own sound effects to movies; and see some original sets and costumes. A wonderful, mock-Egyptian pastiche of a 1920s movie theater shows kids' movies and TV classics.

From the summer of 2002 through early 2005, Queens is also the temporary home of the **Museum of Modern Art**, while it's being reconstructed on 53rd

Street in Manhattan. Along with the permanent collection, most of which will be moved to **MoMaQNS**, 45-20 33rd St at Queens Blvd (#7 to 33rd Street stop; ☎212/708-9400, ⓦwww.moma.org), there will be special Picasso and Matisse exhibits. Call ahead for the schedule.

If you're really keen on exploring Queens, the **Queens Museum of Art**, at Flushing Meadows-Corona Park (Tues–Fri 10am–5pm, Sat & Sun noon–5pm; suggested donation $5; ☎718/592-9700, ⓦwww.queensmuse.org) is another possible destination. Its one permanent item is an 18,000-square-foot model of the five boroughs of New York City, spectacularly lit, recently updated and originally conceived for the 1964 World's Fair by Robert Moses. Great fun if you know the city well, and useful orientation if you don't. Take the subway #7 to Willets Point–Shea Stadium.

Staten Island

Until 1964, **Staten Island** was isolated from the rest of the city – getting to it meant a ferry trip or a long ride through New Jersey, and commuting into Manhattan was a bit of a haul. The opening of the Verrazano Narrows Bridge changed things: upwardly mobile Brooklynites found inexpensive property on the island and swarmed over the bridge to buy their parcel of suburbia. Today Staten Island has swollen to accommodate dense residential neighborhoods amid the rambling greenery and endless backwaters of neat homes. Residents pining for a lost sense of isolation have voted to begin the long process of divorcing their borough from New York City altogether (though that seems unlikely to happen any time soon).

The Staten Island Ferry sails from Battery Park around the clock, with departures every 15–20 minutes during rush hours (between 7–9am and 5–7pm), every 30 minutes mid-day and evenings, and every 60 minutes late at night – weekends less frequently. Truly New York's best bargain, since 1997 the ferry has been giving great wide-angled views of the city – absolutely free. The ferry terminal quickly dispels any romance, but it's easy to escape to the adjoining bus station and catch the S74 bus to the Jacques Marchais Center of Tibetan Art at 338 Lighthouse Ave (April–Nov Wed–Sun 1–5pm; Dec–March Wed–Fri 1–5pm; ☎718/987-3500; $5, students/seniors $3; ⓦwww.tibetanmuseum.com). Jacques Marchais was the alias of Jacqueline Kleber, a New York art dealer who reckoned she'd get on better with a French name. In the 1920s and 30s, she assembled the largest collection of Tibetan art in the Western world and housed it in a hillside "Buddhist temple." The exhibition is small enough to be accessible, with magnificent bronze Bodhisattvas, fearsome deities in union with each other, musical instruments, costumes and decorations from Tibet. During the first or second week of October the museum hosts a harvest festival: Tibetan monks in maroon robes with saffron trim perform the traditional ceremonies, and Tibetan food and crafts are sold.

Back on the main Richmond Road, a short walk brings you to **Historic Richmond Town** (July & Aug Wed–Fri 10am–5pm, Sat & Sun 1–5pm; Sept–June Wed–Sun 1–5pm; ☎718/351-1611; $4, students $2.50), where a dozen or so old buildings have been transplanted from their original sites and grafted on to the eighteenth-century village of Richmond. Half-hourly tours negotiate the best of these – including the oldest elementary school in the country, a picture-book general store, and the atmospheric Guyon-Lake-Tysen House of 1740; craftspeople use old techniques to weave cloth and fire kilns. It's all carried off to picturesque and ungimmicky effect in rustic surroundings, a mere twelve miles from downtown Manhattan.

Eating

There isn't anything you can't eat in New York. The city has more restaurants per head than anywhere else in the States, and many New Yorkers not only eat out often but take their food incredibly seriously, obsessed with new cuisines, new dishes and new restaurants. Certain areas are pockets of ethnic restaurants: **Chinatown** (including Vietnamese) below Canal Street; **Little Italy** just to the north; and **Little India**, Sixth Street east of Second Avenue. On the **Upper West Side**, quite a few places offer the surprising combination of Cuban and Chinese. The **outer boroughs** of Brooklyn and Queens both have excellent dining opportunities.

New York does, however, have strict **public smoking laws**, so if smoking is important to you, call ahead to check if it's allowed.

Downtown Manhattan (to 14th Street)

Aquagrill 210 Spring St at 6th Ave ☏ 212/274-0505. The freshest seafood imaginable is inventively prepared (like the warm octopus salad), with a variety of mussels featured daily. With drinks, appetizer and dessert, it's about $50 a head.

Balthazar 80 Spring St between Crosby St and Broadway ☏ 212/965-1414. Ultra-popular when it first opened in April 1997, this is still one of the hottest reservations in town. The tastefully ornate Parisian decor and nonstop beautiful people keep your eyes busy until the food arrives; then all you can do is savor the fresh oysters and mussels, the exquisite pastries and everything in between.

Café Le Figaro 184 Bleecker St at MacDougal St ☏ 212/677-1100. Discover the ersatz Left Bank at its finest at a 1950s beat hangout. On the menu: good people-watching and first-rate snacks and meals.

Corner Bistro 331 W 4th St at Jane St ☏ 212/242-9502. The down-home pub with cavernous booths serves some of the best burgers and fries in town. An excellent place to unwind and refuel in a friendly neighborhood atmosphere, it's also a longstanding literary haunt; can get quite crowded.

Cowgirl Hall of Fame 519 Hudson St at W 10th St ☏ 212/633-1133. Don't let the theme-bar ambience put you off this great-value Tex Mex treat. A rowdy atmosphere, great margaritas and fried chicken, and a different cowgirl celebrated every week.

Cupping Room Café 359 W Broadway, between Broome and Grand sts ☏ 212/925-2898. An American/Continental restaurant that hosts live jazz on Friday and Saturday nights. It serves up an eclectic, creative mix, from steaks to Cajun to

French, mostly well pulled off. Though good for brunch, prepare to wait.

Day-O 103 Greenwich Ave at W 12th St ☏ 212/924-3161. A lively atmosphere and good food draw a young crowd to this downtown Caribbean/Southern joint. Highlights include fried catfish, jerk chicken and coconut shrimp. Deadly tropical drinks too.

Florent 69 Gansevoort St, between Washington and Greenwich sts ☏ 212/989-5779. In the heart of the meat-packing district, see and be seen at this almost-always-open ultrafashionable diner/bistro serving good moderate-to-pricey French food.

Gandhi 345 E 6th St, between 1st and 2nd aves ☏ 212/614-9718. Manhattan's curry capital is E 6th St, and this inexpensive place is one of its better entries – though superior Indian food can be found in Queens.

Jerry's 101 Prince St, between Greene and Mercer sts ☏ 212/966-9464. This American–French restaurant, with an upscale atmosphere and moderate prices – is casual and good for people-watching. It's closed Sun evening.

Joe's Shanghai 9 Pell St between Bowery and Mott sts ☏ 212/233-8888. Probably Chinatown's most famous restaurant, this place is always packed, with good reason. Try the soup dumplings and the seafood main courses; communal tables.

Jules 65 St Mark's Place at 1st Ave ☏ 212/477-5560. Step down into this relaxed, yet unmistakably hip, French bistro where live jazz on Thursdays accompanies the steak frites and salad frisee aux lardons. The weekend brunch is unbeatable.

Katz's 205 E Houston St at Ludlow St ☏ 212/254-2246. Wisecracking Lower East Side Jewish deli serving archetypal overstuffed pastrami and corned beef sandwiches. Best known as the site of the orgasm scene in *When Harry Met Sally*.

Lombardi's 32 Spring St, between Mott and Mulberry sts ☎212/941-7994. Arguably some of the best pizza in town, including an amazing clam pie; no slices though. Ask for roasted garlic on the side.

Lupe's East LA Diner 110 6th Ave at Watts St ☎212/966-1326. Good fun and inexpensive, this very laid-back hole-in-the-wall restaurant serves great beer and burritos.

Moustache 90 Bedford St, between Grove and Barrow sts ☎212/229-2220; 265 E 10th St between 1st Ave and Ave A ☎212/228-2022. A small, cheap Middle Eastern spot with a "pitza" specialty (pizzas of pita bread and eclectic toppings); also offers great hummus and falafel.

Nobu 105 Hudson St at Franklin St ☎212/219-0500. The very well-known restaurant's lavish woodland decor complements really superlative Japanese cuisine, especially sushi, at the ultra-high prices you would expect. If you can't get a reservation, try *Next Door Nobu*, located . . . just next door.

Petite Abeille 466 Hudson St ☎212/791-6479. Another popular remnant of the Belgian food craze that swept the city a few years back. The omelets, mussels and such at this very small place are well worth sampling.

Sevilla 62 Charles St at 4th St ☎212/929-3189. This wonderful Village old-timer is still a favorite neighborhood haunt. The dark, fragrant (from garlic) restaurant offers good, moderately priced food. Think terrific paella and large pitchers of strong sangria.

Second Avenue Deli 156 2nd Ave at E 10th St ☎212/677-0606. The East Village deli serves marvelous burgers, pastrami and other goodies in an ebullient, snap-happy style.

Thailand Restaurant 106 Bayard St at Baxter St ☎212/349-3132. The deep sea bass, crispy and spicy, is delicious at this Chinatown location.

Time Café 380 Lafayette St at Great Jones St ☎212/533-7000. The consistently great food has an organic edge. Salads, pasta and fish specials come moderate to expensive in a comfortable, airy setting. Also on the premises are the *Fez Lounge*, a faux Moroccan back-room bar, and a downstairs club with nightly live music. It all gets quite crowded at weekends.

Tortilla Flats 767 Washington St at W 12th St ☎212/243-1053. This over-decorated Mexican spot is a must-see. Check out the Elvis room and sample the potent margaritas and heaped portions of food. Theme nights include Ernest Borgnine Night, Hula Hoop Night and Bingo for Shots.

Two Boots 37 Ave A, between E 2nd and 3rd sts ☎212/505-2276; also 75 Greenwich Ave, between 7th Ave and 11th St ☎633-9096 (pizza only). Raucous, inexpensive pizza joint with a Cajun bent where anything goes on great, thin-crust pizza. Other dishes, like jambalaya and seafood creole, served as well.

Xunta 174 1st Ave, between 10th and 11th sts ☎212/614-0620. This electric East Village gem buzzes with hordes of young faces perched on rum barrels downing pitchers of sangria and choosing from the dizzying tapas menu – try the mussels in fresh tomato sauce, or shrimp with garlic. You can eat (and drink) very well for around $20.

Yama 40 Carmine St ☎212/989-9330. This intimate yet bustling Japanese restaurant features great sushi, great everything. Try the wasabi shu-mai dumplings.

Midtown Manhattan (14th St to 59th St)

Carmine's 200 W 44th St, between Broadway and 8th Ave ☎212/221-3800; also 2450 Broadway, between W 90th and W 91st sts ☎212/362-2200. Mountainous portions of tasty home-style southern Italian food are made to share at this large, loud favorite. Be prepared to wait; only parties of six or more can make reservations after 6pm.

Carnegie Deli 854 7th Ave, between W 54th and 55th sts ☎212/757-2245. At the famous Jewish deli, the most generously stuffed sandwiches in the city are served by the rudest waiters.

Eighteenth and Eighth 159 8th Ave at 18th St ☎212/242-5000. At this hip, gay little upscale diner in Chelsea, the prices are moderate, the crowd is beautiful, and even breakfast is trendy.

Emporio Brasil 15 W 46th St, between 5th and 6th aves ☎212/764-4646. Check out the great Brazilian food and atmosphere at reasonable prices for Midtown. Try the tasty feijoada (a stew of meaty pork and black beans, with rice), Brazil's national dish (Sat afternoon only).

Hallo Berlin 402 W 51st St, between 9th and 10th aves ☎212/541-6248. The best for wursts on the West Side, served by an owner who once sold them from a pushcart and made enough to open a restaurant with a pleasant bench-and-table beer-garden setting.

Jezebel 630 9th Ave at W 45th St ☎212/582-1045. Good, old-fashioned Southern cooking and a bordello atmosphere make this place stand out amid the Theater District clones. Serves dinner only, Tue through Sat.

Joe Allen's 326 W 46th St, between 8th and 9th aves ☎212/581-6464. The tried and true formula of checkered tablecloths, old-fashioned barroom feel and reliable American food at moderate prices works at this popular pre-theater spot. Reserve, unless you can arrive after 8pm.

Julian's 802 9th Ave, between W 53rd and 54th sts ☎212/262-4800. A bright, pleasing room and clever dining garden, offering light and inventive Mediterranean fare, is tucked into a Hell's Kitchen alley.

Les Halles 411 Park Ave S, between E 28th and 29th sts ☎212/679-4111. In this noisy, bustling bistro (not recommended for veggies), carcasses dangle in a butcher's shop in the front. Very pseudo Rive Gauche, it serves rabbit, steak frites and other staples. The entrees are $15-25.

Negril 362 W 23rd St off 9th Ave ☎212/807-6411. The lively Jamaican restaurant serves spicy jerk chicken or goat stews and other dishes (especially the lunch specials) at reasonable prices. Dinner entrees are $12 and up.

Oyster Bar Lower Level, Grand Central Terminal ☎212/490-6650. The wonderfully atmospheric old place, down in the vaulted dungeons of Grand Central, draws Midtown office workers for lunch (see p.92). Prices are moderate to expensive; you can eat more cheaply at the bar.

Pad Thai 114 8th Ave at 16th St ☎212/691-6226. Good noodle dishes, curries and other Thai classics are menued at reasonable prices – along with a wide array of vegetarian choices.

Shoebox Café Grand Central Station, Lower Food Concourse ☎212/986-5959. Instead of taking the train to the Deep South, just stop here, with authentic fried chicken and bourbon pecan country ham available. The muffins (sweet and savory options) are also worthy, if heavy. Open Monday through Friday until 7pm.

Sushi Zen 57 W 46th St, between 5th and 6th aves ☎212/302-0707. The food's on the expensive side, but enjoy the swimmingly fresh sushi, tranquility-inducing decor and the attentive service.

Union Square Café 21 E 16th St, between 5th Ave and Union Square W ☎212/243-4020. The California-style dining comes with a classy but comfortable downtown atmosphere. No one does salmon like Chef Danny Meyer. Prices average $150 for two – but the creative menu (and great people-watching) is a real treat.

Vong 200 E 54th St, between 2nd and 3rd aves ☎212/486-9592. The eccentrically decorated and expensive, yet still popular, restaurant brings a French colonial approach to Thai cooking. The chefs put mango in foie gras, and sesame and tamarind on Muscovy duck. Somehow, it works.

Uptown Manhattan (60th St and above)

Barking Dog Luncheonette 1678 3rd Ave at E 94th St ☎212/831-1800. This diner-like place offers outstanding, cheap American food (like mashed potatoes and gravy). Kids will feel at home, especially with the puppy motif.

Brother Jimmy's BBQ 1461 1st Ave at E 76th St ☎212/545-RIBS. This casual, fun barbecue restaurant's motto is "Pig Out!" There's quite a bar scene for those into its frat-party atmosphere.

Comfort Diner 142 E 86th St at Lexington Ave ☎212/369-8628 and 214 E 45th St, between 2nd and 3rd aves ☎212/867-4555. At one of the friendliest spots in town, this retro diner serves up hearty staples like meatloaf, fried chicken and macaroni & cheese. It's a great place to fill up and relax.

Dock's Oyster Bar 2427 Broadway, between W 89th and W 90th sts ☎212/724-5588 and 633 3rd Ave at E 40th St ☎212/986-8080. Both offer ultrafresh, moderate to expensive seafood. The Upper West Side branch is a bit cozier, but you may find slow service at both.

Ecco-la 1660 3rd Ave, between E 92nd and E 93rd sts ☎212/860-5609. Unique pasta combinations at very moderate prices make this one of the Upper East Side's most popular Italians. It's a real find if you don't mind waiting.

El Pollo 1746 1st Ave, between E 90th and E 91st sts ☎212/996-7810. Come here for fast food, like rotisserie chicken, Peruvian style – tasty and cheap. Bring your own wine.

Fujiyama Mama 467 Columbus Ave, between W 82nd and 83rd sts ☎212/769-1144. The West Side's best – and most boisterous – sushi bar comes with high-tech decor and loud music.

Gabriela's 685 Amsterdam Ave at 93rd St ☎212/961-0574. Count on good, inexpensive, authentic Mexican – not just your usual enchiladas and burritos, but also a wide array of regional chicken and seafood dishes in a large crowded room, noisy, lively and thoroughly enjoyable. Expect to wait.

Heidelburg 1648 2nd Ave between E 85th and 86th sts ☎212/628-2332. At one of the last Yorkville German joints, the food is the real deal, with excellent liver dumpling soup, Bauernfruestuck omelets and pancakes (both sweet and potato). Have a huge, boot-shaped glass of Weissbeer with anything.

La Caridad 2199 Broadway at W 78th St ☎212/874-2780. This neighborhood institution doles out plentiful and inexpensive Cuban–Chinese food (the Cuban is better, though). Bring your own beer and expect to wait.

Malaga 406 E 73rd St, between 1st and York aves ☎212/737-7659. An intimate local Spanish restaurant, it has good, wholesome food at moderate prices.

Mughlai 320 Columbus Ave at 75th St ☎212/724-6363. This uptown, upscale Indian spot lists entrees at $11–16.

Sarabeth's Kitchen 423 Amsterdam Ave between 80th and 81st sts ☎212/496-6280; 1295 Madison Ave between 92nd and 93rd sts ☎212/410-7335. Best for brunch, this country-style restaurant serves delectable baked goods and impressive omelets, and the long lines outside reflect this. Dinner is expensive.

Serendipity 3 225 E 60th St, between 2nd and 3rd aves ☎212/838-3531. The long-established eatery/ice-cream parlor, made more famous by the 2001 movie *Serendipity*, is adorned with Tiffany lamps. The frozen hot chocolate, a trademarked and copyrighted recipe, is out of this world, and the wealth of ice cream offerings are a real treat, too.

Sylvia's Restaurant 328 Lenox Ave, between W 126th and 127th sts ☎212/996-0660. The down-home Southern cooking at this Harlem institution makes it worth the trek uptown. Listen to live gospel music with Sunday brunch.

Vinnie's Pizza 285 Amsterdam Ave at W 73rd St ☎212/874-4382. For those who prefer their pizza thick, doughy, loaded with cheese and cheap, this Upper West Side place is for you.

Zula 1260 Amsterdam Ave at 122nd St ☎212/663-1670. High-quality and inexpensive ($8 up) Ethiopian food that's popular with the folk from Columbia University. Spicy chicken, beef and lamb dishes mainly.

The outer boroughs

Elias Corner 24-02 31st St (at 24th Ave), Astoria ☎718/932-1510. Pay close attention to the seafood on display as you enter, for this Astoria institution doesn't have menus and the staff is not always forthcoming. Serves some of the best and freshest fish: try the swordfish kebabs.

Jackson Diner 37-47 74th St between 37th Ave and Roosevelt Ave, Jackson Heights ☎718/672-1232. Come here hungry and stuff yourself silly with amazingly light and reasonably priced Indian fare. Samosas and mango lassis are not to be missed.

Peter Luger's Steak House 178 Broadway at Driggs Ave ☎718/387-7400. Catering to carnivores since 1873, *Peter Luger's* may just be the city's finest steakhouse. The service is surly and the decor plain, but the porterhouse steak – the only cut served – is divine. Cash only; expect to pay at least $60 a head.

Primorski 282 Brighton Beach Ave between 2nd and 3rd sts ☎718/891-3111. Perhaps the best of Brighton Beach's Russian hangouts, with a huge menu of authentic Russian dishes, including blintzes and stuffed cabbage, at absurdly cheap prices. Live music in the evening.

Drinking

New York's best **bars** are in **Downtown Manhattan** – Greenwich Village, the East Village, SoHo and the Lower East Side. The **Midtown** places tend to be geared to an after-hours office crowd and (with a few exceptions) are pricey and rather dull; **Uptown**, the Upper West Side at least, between 60th and 85th streets along Amsterdam and Columbus avenues, has several good places to drink. Most of the bars listed below serve food of some kind and have happy hours sometime between 4pm and 8pm during the week. See also the bars listed in "Gay and Lesbian New York" (p.122).

Downtown Manhattan (to 14th Street)

Barramundi 147 Ludlow St, between Stanton and Rivington ☎212/529-6900. The magical, fairy-lit garden, open until 10pm, makes this bar a blessed sanctuary from the painfully hip Lower East Side.

Blind Tiger Ale House 518 Hudson St at W 10th St ☎212/675-3848. The name is fitting. You could

easily leave here with things looking a bit foggy, after taking on 24 beers on tap, an eclectic bottled selection and assorted liquors.

Chumley's 86 Bedford St at Barrow St ☎212/675-4449. As much fun to find (there's no sign) as it is to drink in, this atmospheric former speakeasy has a great selection of beers and good bar food.

Decibel 240 E 9th St (between 2nd and 3rd aves) ☎212/979-2733. A rocking atmosphere (with good tunes) envelops the great, beautifully decorated underground sake bar. The inevitable wait for a wooden table will be worth it, guaranteed.

Double Happiness 174 Mott St at Broome ☎212/941-1282. Low ceilings, dark lighting, nooks, crannies and the superlative green tea martinis make this Asian-themed bar a decadently seductive place to be.

Drinkland 339 E 10th St, between aves A and B ☎212/228-2435. Dizzying psychedelic decor fused with DJs spinning big-beat and trip-hop – plus strong mixed drinks – make this place a favorite among downtown dwellers.

Ear Inn 326 Spring St, between Washington and Greenwich sts ☎212/226-9060. The 'Ear' is as in 'Bar' with half the neon 'B' chipped off. This cozy pub, a stone's throw from the Hudson River, has a good mix of beers on tap, serves basic, reasonably priced, American food and claims to be the second oldest bar in the city. It may also be one of the best.

Fanelli 94 Prince St at Mercer St ☎212/226-9412. The cozy bar, SoHo's oldest, serves up cheap and hearty food.

Grassroots Tavern 20 St Mark's Place, between 2nd and 3rd aves ☎212/475-9443. This roomy, wooden and wonderful underground den has Brooklyn beers for $3, an extended happy hour and at least three animals roaming around at any hour of the day or night.

Liquor Store Bar 225 W Broadway at White St ☎212/226-7121. Cozy little pub with sidewalk seating that feels like it's been around since colonial times. A welcome respite from the trendy local scene.

Max Fish 178 Ludlow St, (between Houston and Stanton ☎212/529-3959. This stalwart of the LES scene attracts visiting indie rock bands, lured by an unpretentious vibe and a juke box that rocks all others out of town.

OpenAir 121 St Mark's Place, between 1st Ave and Ave A ☎212/979-1459. This little newcomer is the antithesis of St Marks: beautifully designed, it somehow divides itself into a chill-out lounge, an eerie middle space lit by flickering flat screens and a front bar, all imbued with the same well-spun tunes from the DJ.

St Dymphna's 118 St Marks Place, between 1st Ave and Ave A ☎212/254-6636. A tempting menu and some of the city's best Guinness make this snug Irish watering hole a favorite among young East Villagers.

Sweet and Vicious 5 Spring St, between The Bowery and Elizabeth St ☎212/334-7915. Although this gem of a bar is said to be named

after the owner's cats, it could just as easily refer to the peachy-pink lighting and the two decrepit pistols (found while excavating the site) that hang next to the door.

White Horse Tavern 567 Hudson St at W 11th St ☎212/243-9260. At this convivial, inexpensive old-time Village institution, Dylan Thomas drank up before his last trip to the hospital.

Winnie's 104 Bayard St, between Mulberry and Baxter sts ☎212/732-2384. At this tiny Chinatown bar, New Yorkers belt out a few, karaoke-style. It's slightly seedy, but good fun all round.

Midtown Manhattan (14th Street to 59th Street)

Belmont Lounge 117 E 15th St, between Park Ave S and Irving Place ☎212/533-0009. Oversized couches, dark cavernous rooms and a tree-canopied backyard reel in a continuous stream of twenty-somethings. The drinks are strong.

Chelsea Commons 242 10th Ave at 24th St ☎212/929-9424. This personable bar is also a great place to eat, with reasonably priced and excellent burgers and other such pub grub. The popular local hangout has a summer garden, winter fireplace and the occasional impromptu puppet show.

The Coffee Shop 29 Union Square W at 16th St ☎212/243-7969. The former coffee shop has turned trendy bar and restaurant, and there's Brazilian-style food in the noisy adjacent restaurant.

McHale's 750 8th Ave at 46th St (no phone). A good, old-fashioned bar offers a respite from edgy Times Square. A regular menu of bar food (burgers, fries, nachos, wings) comes at affordable prices.

Old Town Bar and Restaurant 45 E 18th St, between Broadway and Park Ave S ☎212/473-8874. The atmospheric bar is popular with publishing types, models and photogs in the Flatiron district. Unpretentious and old-world, it has a good pub menu.

Park 118 10th Ave, between 17th and 18th sts ☎212/352-3313. It's easy to get lost in this vast warren of rooms filled with fireplaces, geodes and even a Canadian redwood in the middle of the floor. The garden is a treat though, and the servers are the best dressed in New York.

Passerby 436 W 15th St, between 9th and 10th aves ☎212/206-7321. This funky space is a welcome after a visit to owner–artist Gavin Brown's gallery next door. As you might suspect, it's full of black-clad lovelies, weird mirrors and art-world gossip.

P J Clarke's 915 3rd Ave at E 55th St
☎212/759-1650. Legendary spit-and-sawdust
alehouse with a not-so-cheap restaurant out back.
You may recognize it as a location for the movie
The Lost Weekend.

Pete's Tavern 129 E 18th St at Irving Place
☎212/473-7676. The former speakeasy claims to
be the oldest bar in New York – opened in 1864 –
though these days it inevitably trades on its history, which includes such illustrious patrons as John
F. Kennedy Jr. and O. Henry, who allegedly wrote
Gift of the Magi in his regular booth here.

Uptown Manhattan (60th Street and above)

Abbey Pub 237 W 105th St, between Broadway
and Amsterdam ☎212/222-8713. Half-a-century
old, the *Abbey* is still charming locals and students
alike with its stained glass windows and overheard
learned conversations whispered in wooden
booths. Not to mention the cheap beer.

Bear Bar East 1770 2nd Ave, between 92nd and
93rd sts ☎212/987-7580. The raucous, spit 'n'
sawdust sports bar offers hip-hop on Friday, free
drinks on Monday for the "ladies" and too many
cheap beer 'n' wings deals to list here.

Border Café 244 E 79th St ☎212/535-4347. This
friendly neighborhood hangout, down to earth
despite its upscale location, serves good frozen
margaritas.

The Cocktail Room 334 E 73rd St, between 1st
and 2nd aves ☎212/988-6100. This fancy-
schmanzy bar comes with couches, dim lighting
and a modish 60s theme. Popular with singles and
groups who lounge on couches in the back, this
neighborhood anomaly throbs on weekends.

Dead Poet 450 Amsterdam Ave, between 81st
and 82nd sts ☎212/595-5670. You'll be waxing
poetical and then dropping down dead if you stay
for the duration of this sweet little bar's happy
hour: it lasts from 8am to 8pm and offers draft
beer at $3 a pint. The backroom has armchairs,
books and a pool table.

Dublin House Tap Room 225 W 79th St, between
Broadway and Amsterdam ☎212/874-9528.
The lively Upper West Side Irish pub, pouring a
very nice Black & Tan, is dominated at night by the
young, inebriated and rowdy.

Lenox Lounge 288 Lenox Ave and 125th St
☎212/722-9566. The infamous Harlem jazz hangout with a great Art Deco interior always gives a
cool vibe throughout.

Metropolitan Museum of Art 1000 5th Ave at
82nd St ☎212/535-7710. It's hard to imagine a

more romantic spot to sip a glass of wine,
whether on the Cantor Roof Garden (open only in
warm weather), enjoying one of the best views in
the city, or on the Great Hall Balcony listening to
live chamber music (Fri and Sat 5–8pm).

Prohibition 530 Columbus Ave, between 84th and
85th sts ☎212/579-3100. A pool table, live jazz
and pavement tables combine to make this one of
the liveliest singles scenes on the Upper West
Side.

Ruby's Tap House 1754 2nd Ave at 92nd St
☎212/987-8179. Pool, darts and 26 tap beers,
plus the option for ladies to dance on the bar for
free drinks, make this a raucous and popular joint.

Smoke 2751 Broadway at 105th St ☎212/864-
9834. The unpretentious, mellow lounge is favored
by local jazz fans for its live music from 10pm. An
$8 cover is charged on weekends.

Subway Inn 143 E 60th St at Lexington Ave
☎212/223-8929. This downscale neighborhood
dive bar, across from Bloomingdale's, is great for a
late afternoon beer.

Time Out 349 Amsterdam Ave between 76th and
77th sts ☎212/362-5400. How strange . . . a
sports bar with a pleasant atmosphere. Count on a
good selection of cheap beers and pub grub,
friendly bonhomie and 24 screens of sporting
entertainment ($10 cover for special events).

The outer boroughs

Bohemian Hall and Park 29-19 24th Ave, Astoria
☎718/728-9776. Old world Czech Bohemians and
twenty-something bohemians mingle at New
York's largest beer garden, which features a variety of pilsners. Summer bands range in style from
polka to rock to hip hop.

Café-Bar 32-90 34th Ave, Astoria ☎718/204-
5273. With its plush couches and outdoor seating,
the ultra-relaxed *Café-Bar* is the perfect place to
kill time before a matinee at the nearby American
Museum of the Moving Image.

Galapagos 70 N 6th St, between Wythe and Kent
aves, Williamsburg ☎718/782-5188. Gorgeous
design – this converted factory features watery
pools and candelabras – and avant-garde movies
on Sunday and Monday nights.

Iona 180 Grand St, between Bedford Ave and
Driggs St, Williamsburg ☎718/384-5008. An Irish
bar for the young and the hip, *Iona* provides a
calm, tasteful respite from the moody lighting and
incestuous hip of the other bars all around. A
sweet outdoor garden and a great selection of
beer only add to this gem's appeal.

Nightlife and entertainment

New York's **music scene** reflects the city's diversity. Excellent traditional and contemporary **jazz** is still concentrated in Greenwich Village and Harlem, and you'll find a scattering of blues, hip-hop, Brazilian and West Indian music in Manhattan as well. Straight **rock music** is led these days by an enhanced indie scene, and there's also a widely unreliable range of **electronic** and **experimental dance** music clubs. Admission **prices** to venues vary, but most jazz clubs have a hefty cover and a minimum charge for food and drinks. Rock venues and dance clubs ask from nothing (rare) to around $30.

New York magazine carries good **what's on listings**, though the *Village Voice* (Ⓦ www.villagevoice.com) is better for things Downtown and anything vaguely "alternative." The Sunday *New York Times* "Weekly Guide" is also good for mainstream events. On Friday, the paper's "Weekend" section lists ticket availability for the major shows. The monthly *Paper* magazine (Ⓦ www.papermag.com) features club, bar and restaurant guides, offering a hip, "downtown" perspective, as does the free club life monthly, *Flyer*. Your best bet is probably *Time Out New York* (Ⓦ www.timeoutny.com), which simplifies the city with comprehensive listings and consumer information.

New York's **club life** is an amorphous creature. Parties change at a rapid pace, so be sure to check the listings in the *Village Voice*, *Paper*, *Time Out New York* or *Homo Xtra*, or pick up flyers in East Village record and second-hand clothing stores before you make any plans. Musically, **drum'n'bass**, **electronica**, **'80's nostalgia** and **house** hold sway at the moment – with the emphasis on the deep, vocal style that's always been popular in the city – but Latin freestyle, dancehall reggae, funk and hip-hop all retain interest. Nothing gets going much before midnight, so there's no point turning up earlier. During the week is the best time to club – prices are cheaper, crowds are smaller and service is better. All venues tend to be strict about **ID**.

In the world of film, revival cinemas are increasingly giving way to multiscreen "plexes," but some alternatives still exist.

Theater

New York is one of the world's great **theater** centers. You can find just about any kind of production here, from lavish, over-the-top musicals to experimental productions in converted garages. Venues are referred to as **Broadway, Off-Broadway or Off-Off Broadway**, representing a descending order of ticket price, production polish, elegance and comfort – but it doesn't necessarily have much to do with the address.

Broadway offerings consist primarily of large-scale musicals, comedies and dramas with big-name actors, with the occasional classic and one-person show. **Off-Broadway** theaters tend to combine high production qualities with a greater willingness to experiment. Off-Broadway is social and political drama, satire, ethnic plays and repertory: in short, anything that Broadway wouldn't consider a sure-fire money-spinner. **Off-Off Broadway** is the fringe – drama on a shoestring, perhaps with sensitive or uncommercial subjects. Most Broadway theaters are just east or west of Broadway between 40th and 52nd streets; Off- and Off-Off Broadway theaters are sprinkled throughout Manhattan, with a concentration in the East and West villages, Union Square, Chelsea and several in the 40s and 50s west of the Broadway Theater District. Specific Broadway listings appear in the free, widely available *Official Broadway Theater Guide*.

Nowhere are regular **tickets** inexpensive on Broadway: they range from $50–100; Off-Broadway prices have risen recently too, to as much as $55 in some cases: in general, expect to pay upwards of $25 Off-Broadway and $15 Off-Off. These prices can, however, be cut considerably if you can wait in line on the day of the performance at the Manhattan **TKTS** booth at Duffy Square, where Broadway and Seventh Avenue meet between 45th and 47th sts (open Mon–Sat 3–8pm, 10am–2pm for Wed & Sat matinees, 10–11am for Sun performances). The booth has at least one pair of tickets for every performance of every Broadway and Off-Broadway show available, at 50 to 75 percent off (plus a $2.50 ticket service charge), payable in cash or travelers' checks.

Twofer discount coupons are available at the New York Convention and Visitors' Bureau, as well as at many shops, banks, restaurants and hotel lobbies. The days are long gone when they really did offer two-for-the-price-of-one, but they still entitle two people to a hefty discount. Unlike TKTS, twofers make it possible to book ahead, though don't expect to find coupons for the latest shows. The **Hit Show Club**, 630 9th Ave at 44th St (☎212/581-4211) also provides discount vouchers up to 50 percent off that you present at the box office. In addition, same-day standing-room tickets are also available for some sold-out shows for $10–20. Check listings magazines for availability.

If you're prepared to pay **full price** you can, of course, either go directly to the theater or call one of the following ticket sales agencies. **Tele-Charge** (☎212/239-6200 or 1-800/432-7250 outside NY) and **Ticketmaster** (☎212/307-4100 or 1-800/755-4000 outside NY) sell tickets over the phone to Broadway shows, but note that no show is represented by both these agencies. You will need a credit card and should expect to pay a $5-7 surcharge per ticket. Make sure to ask the operator to explain where your seats will be – if you are unhappy with the seating arrangements, you must say so now. **Tickets Central** (☎212/279-4200) sells tickets to many Off-Broadway theaters 1–8pm daily. All these services charge a service fee of a couple of dollars or more. You can also buy theater tickets over the Internet at individual theater websites or at ⓦwww.ticketmaster.com and ⓦwww.telecharge.com.

Classical music, opera and dance

New Yorkers take **serious music** seriously. Long queues form for anything popular, many concerts sell out, and on summer evenings a quarter of a million people may turn up in Central Park for free performances by the **New York Philharmonic**.

Besides **Lincoln Center** (see box, overleaf), the most important venue is **Carnegie Hall**, 154 W 57th St (☎212/247-7800, ⓦwww.carnegiehall.org), where the greatest names from all schools of music have performed. The acoustics remain superb, and a recent renovation has amended years of structural neglect, restoring the place to its former glory.

When it comes to **dance** Lincoln Center once again serves as a showcase, but a number of other venues regularly host events. The **Brooklyn Academy of Music** (or BAM), 30 Lafayette St, Brooklyn (☎718/636-4100, ⓦwww.bam.org), is America's oldest performing arts academy and one of the most daring producers in New York – definitely worth crossing the river for. Six dance troupes are in residence at the **City Center**, 131 W 55th St (☎212/581-1212, ⓦwww.citycenter.org), including America's two undisputed choreographic giants, the Merce Cunningham Dance Company and the Paul Taylor Dance

Lincoln Center

Lincoln Center, on Broadway at 64th St (Ⓦ www.lincolncenter.org), is New York's powerhouse of performing art. Each major venue is in active use through the year.

New York State Theater ☏212/870-5570. Six months of the year home to the **New York City Ballet** (Ⓦ www.nycballet.com) – considered by many to be the greatest dance company in existence – this accessible venue is also where the New York City Opera plays David to the Met's Goliath. Seats go for less than half the Met's prices, and standing-room tickets are available if a performance sells out.

Avery Fisher Hall ☏212/875-5030. The permanent base of the New York Philharmonic, directed by Kurt Masur, is also a temporary one for visiting orchestras and soloists. Tickets $15–50.

Metropolitan Opera House ☏212/362-6000, Ⓦ www.metopera.org. It hosts the Metropolitan Opera Company from September until late April and the American Ballet Theater, early May to July. Tickets are outrageously expensive and difficult to get, though 175 standing-room tickets for $12–16 go on sale every Saturday morning at 10am (the line has been known to form at dawn).

Alice Tully Hall (Centercharge ☏212/721-6500). This smaller venue is used by chamber orchestras, string quartets and instrumentalists. Prices are similar to those in Avery Fisher Hall.

Company, as well as the Joffrey and Dance Theatre of Harlem and, in spring, American Ballet Theater. The most important space in Manhattan for small and mid-sized dance companies is the **Joyce Theater**, 175 8th Ave (☏212/242-0800, Ⓦ www.joyce.org). The Joyce hosts companies from around the world, and also has a small downtown satellite – Joyce SoHo – at 155 Mercer St (☏212/431-9233).

Larger performance venues

Beacon Theater 2124 Broadway at W 74th St ☏212/496-7070. A restored theater caters to a more mature rock crowd with everything from Spinal Tap to Cher. $25-$100.

Madison Square Garden W 31st–33rd sts, between 7th and 8th aves ☏212/465-6741. New York's principal large stage plays host to big rock acts. However, it's not the most atmospheric place to see a band, with seating for yourself and 20,000 of your closest friends.

Radio City Music Hall 6th Ave and 50th St ☏212/247-4777. Although not as prestigious a venue as it once was, the building is a luminous performance in itself.

Roseland 239 W 52nd St, between Broadway and 8th Ave ☏212/777-6800. This club has retained the grand ballroom feel of its heyday (take a gander at the shoes in the entryway and the elaborate powder rooms) but the $2.5 million renovations make it a great place to catch big names before they hit the arena/stadium circuit.

Rock and pop venues

Arlene Grocery 95 Stanton St, between Ludlow and Orchard sts ☏212/473-9831. This intimate, erstwhile bodega hosts free gigs by local indie talent during the week. Monday is "Punk and Heavy Metal Karaoke" night, and you can sing along with a live band. A $3-5 cover is collected on the weekend.

Baby Jupiter 170 Orchard St at Stanton St ☏212/982-2229. Past the mediocre diner, the excellent performance space in back hosts a spectrum of rock (indie to avant-garde) bands and experimental performances. $2–5.

The Bottom Line 15 W 4th St at Mercer St ☏212/228-7880. Established singer-songwriters appear in a cabaret setup, with tables crowding out any suggestion of a dance floor. Shows at 7.30pm and 10.30pm; $15–20, cash only.

Bowery Ballroom 6 Delancey St, corner of The Bowery ☏212/533-2111. A minimum of attitude, great sound and even better sightlines make this a local favorite to see well-known Britpop and indie rock bands. Shows $10–20.

Brownies 169 Ave A, between E 10th and 11th sts ℡ 212/420-8392. See major-label one-shots and bands on the cusp of making it big. $7–$10.

CBGB and OMFUG 315 Bowery at Bleecker St ℡ 212/982-4052. This legendary punk/art noise bastion has seen far better days. Run-of-the-mill rock bands crowd today's bills, often five or six acts playing a night starting at around 7pm. $5–10.

CB's 313 Gallery 313 Bowery at Bleecker St ℡ 212/677-0445. Seven nights a week, CBGB's clean, spacious counterpart features folk, acoustic, and experimental music. $5.

Fez (*Under Time Café*), 380 Lafayette St at Great Jones St ℡ 212/533-2680. The mirrored bar and sparkling gold stage curtain suggest a disco fantasy; the poetry readings and acoustic performances are high caliber. Around $10.

Irving Plaza 17 Irving Place, between E 15th and E 16th sts ℡ 212/777-6800. Once home to Off-Broadway musicals, this venue now hosts an impressive array of rock, electronic music and techno acts – a good place to see popular bands in a manageable setting. $10–25.

Mercury Lounge 217 E Houston St at Essex St ℡ 212/260-7400). The dark, medium-sized, innocuous space showcases a mix of local, national and international pop and rock acts. It's owned by the same crew as Bowery Ballroom – which has been getting the better bands. Around $7–12.

SOB's ("Sounds of Brazil") 204 Varick St at W Houston St ℡ 212/243-4940. The lively club/restaurant, with regular Caribbean, salsa and world music acts, puts on two performances a night. Admission $10–20 with $10–15 minimum cover at tables.

Jazz venues

The Blue Note 131 W 3rd St at 6th Ave ℡ 212/475-8592, ⓦ www.bluenote.net. Famous names here aren't really worth the high prices, cattle-herd atmosphere and minimal leg room. Cover charges vary wildly, from $7 to $65, plus a $5 minimum per person; all of this leads to a controlled ambience – the antithesis of the freeflow of jazz. Sets are at 9pm & 11.30pm.

Café Carlyle The Carlyle Hotel, 35 E 76th St at Madison Ave ℡ 212/744-1600. This intimate, special place is home to both Bobby Short and Woody Allen, who does the jazz thing here on Monday nights. $30–60 cover, no minimum.

Detour 349 E 13th St at 1st Ave ℡ 212/533-6212. This coffee and cocktail bar, presenting

modern jazz and experimental music, fancies itself as a bit of the Left Bank in the East Village. No cover.

Iridium Jazz Club 1650 Broadway at 51st St ℡ 212/582-2121. Contemporary jazz is performed 7 nights a week in a surrealist decor described as "Dolly meets Disney." The godfather of electric guitar, Les Paul, plays every Monday. Shows at 8.45pm and 10.45pm, extra Fri & Sat show at 12.15am. Cover $20–35, $10 food and drink minimum, Sunday jazz brunch.

Knitting Factory 74 Leonard St, between Church St and Broadway ℡ 212/219-3055, ⓦ www.knittingfactory.com. While this intimate downtown space is known for its avant-garde jazz, you can hear all other kinds of aural experimentation – from art rock to electronica – here, too. Recommended.

Smalls 183 W 10th St at 7th Ave S ℡ 212/929-7565, ⓦ www.smallsjazz.com. Hosting well-knowns and unknowns, this cozy West Village club offers four to ten hours of music for $10. Free juice and nonalcoholic beverages, or BYOB.

Smoke 2751 Broadway at 106th St ℡ 212/864-6662, ⓦ www.smokejazz.com. Voted the city's best club by *New York* magazine, this Upper West Side joint is a real neighborhood treat. Sets start at 9pm, 11pm and 12.30am; the first two weekend sets are smoke-free, and there's a retro happy hour with $3 cocktails Mon–Sun 5–8pm.

Tonic 107 Norfolk St, between Rivington and Delancey sts ℡ 212/358-7503, ⓦ www.tonicnyc.com. This hip Lower East Side avant-jazzerie flourishes on two levels, with no cover charge to the lower, Subtonic lounge. Occasional movies and Klezmer-accompanied brunch on a Sunday. Cover varies.

Village Vanguard 178 7th Ave at Greenwich St ℡ 212/255-4037. The jazz landmark still lays on a regular diet of big names. Admission $15; $10 drink minimum weekdays, $20 cover and $10 minimum at weekends.

Zinc Bar 90 W Houston at La Guardia St ℡ 212/477-8337. This great jazz venue with strong drinks and loyal regulars hosts new talent and established greats such as Max Roach and Grant Green, and schedules poetry readings at 6.30pm Sundays and comedy at 8pm Tuesdays. The blackboard at the entrance announces the evening's featured band. Cover is $5 with a one-drink minimum.

Spoken word and slam venues

13 35 E 13th St ℡ 212/979-6677. On Monday

nights this cozy bar is home to *A Little Bit Louder*, a superior evening of open mike and poetry slams. You can dance here, too – outside in summer – a rare treat.

Gathering of the tribes 285 E 3rd St, between aves C & D ☎212/674-3778. This super-cool venue, hidden away in the lowest of the Lower East Side, hosts one of the city's finest open mikes from 5pm to 7pm on Sunday nights. $3.

NuYorican Poet's Café 236 E 3rd St, between aves B & C ☎212/505–8183, ⓦwww.nuyorican .com. The godfather of all slam venues often features stars of the poetry world who pop in unannounced. SlamOpen on Wednesdays and the Friday Night Slam both cost $5 and come highly recommended.

Poetry Project at St Mark's Church, 131 E 10th St at 2nd Ave ☎212/674-0910, ⓦwww.poetryproject .com. The late Allen Ginsberg, a *Poetry Project* protégé, said, "The poetry project burns like red hot coal in New York's snow." Make of that what you will, the thrice-weekly reading series features some truly, ahem, hot stuff. Closed July and August.

Clubs and discos

Baktun 418 W 14th St ☎212/206-1590. If you're in the mood to trek this far west, the rewards are vast in one of the city's most unpretentious night clubs. They finally got their cabaret license, making "Direct Drive" Saturdays one of the best nights out a Manhattanite can have.

Centro-Fly 45 W 21st St ☎212/627-7770. If you can stand the attitude, the wait, the rough bouncers and the rope, Centro-Fly hosts some of the biggest names in commercial house at the weekends, especially at their Friday night GBH (Great British House) parties. $20 ($10 on guest list, ☎212/539-3916). Downstairs in the Pinky things are a little more low-key and sedate. Open till 6am.

Don Hill's 511 Greenwich St at Spring St ☎212/219-2850. Drag queens, creative types and slumming stars congregate at this dive on the outskirts of SoHo – your rubber gear won't get a second glance. Saturday night is *Tiswas*, featuring live bands and the best of Britpop. $10–15.

Filter 14 432 W 14th St ☎212/366-5680. This not-quite-finished (ever) space was once home to Mother, and almost to Armani (hence the perpetual unfinishedness). The Friday night deep house parties here are superb, with the talented guests such David Morales spinning top quality tunes.

Frying Pan Pier 63, Chelsea Piers at 23rd St

☎212/439-1147. This old lightship is one of the coolest club venues in the city. Great views, consistently good parties and a relaxed door policy all lend themselves to a damn fine time. $10.

Fun 130 Madison St ☎212/964-0303. This eclectic space under the Manhattan Bridge is fun, funky and as unpretentious as they come. Urban bible *Flyer* hosts parties here on the last Thursday of the month, to which a hugely varied selection of hipsters and international DJs come and play; $5–15.

Limelight 37 W 20th St at 6th Ave ☎212/807-7059. This is one of the most splendid party spaces in New York: a church designed by Trinity Church-builder Richard Upjohn. A scandalous past involving jailbird Michael Alig has led the club to clean up its ways and it now plays host to more measured monthly events such as Gatecrasher. $30.

Meow Mix 269 E Houston St at Suffolk St ☎212/254-0688. Lipstick lesbians, leather ladies and all types in between dance at this temple to *les femmes*; well-behaved men are welcome too. Free–$5.

Shine 285 W Broadway at Canal St ☎212/941-0900. Looking every bit like a nightclub should look, it features velvet ropes and angry bouncers outside and high ceilings, plush red curtains and dim lights inside. Once important for up-and-coming rock bands, it's still the place for music industry parties and the like. $10–20.

Spa 76 E 13th St ☎212/388-1062. This funky space has a stage, chill-out room and loads of pretty boys and girls. It hosts hip DJs like Paul Sevigny (brother of Chloe) at their popular Wednesday night party. $20 (free on guest list, ☎212/714-5075).

Vinyl 6 Hubert St, between Hudson and Greenwich sts ☎212/343-1379. This big warehouse is a techno sweatshop – full of rave kids and other slaves to the beat. Come Sunday afternoons 3–10pm for the super popular, heavy house Body and Soul parties with DJ François K. Expect a lengthy queue. $12–20.

Comedy clubs

Caroline's on Broadway 1626 Broadway at W 49th St ☎212/757-4100. This glitzy room books some of the best acts in town. Two-drink minimum. $12–22 cover; more expensive at weekends.

Chicago City Limits Theater 1105 1st Ave at 61st St ☎212/888-5233. New York's oldest improvization theater plays one show nightly, two on weekends. Closed Tues. Admission is $20, $10 on Mon.

Comedy Cellar 117 MacDougal St, between W 3rd and Bleecker sts, ☎212/254-3480. The popular Greenwich Village comedy club – now in its 19th year – is a good late-night hangout. $5 cover Sun–Thurs, $12 Fri–Sat. Two-drink minimum.

Comic Strip Live 1568 2nd Ave, between E 81st and E 82nd sts ☎212/861-9386. The famed showcase draws stand-up comics going for the big time. Three shows Fri & Sat. Cover $10–15, two-drink minimum.

Dangerfield's 1118 1st Ave at E 61st St ☎212/593-1650. The new-talent showcase is run by Rodney Dangerfield. Cover $12.50–15, no minimum.

Don't Tell Mama 343 W 46th St, between 8th and 9th aves ☎212/757-0788. The lively, convivial piano bar and cabaret features rising stars. Shows at 8 and 10pm. Two-drink minimum, cover varies.

Duplex 61 Christopher St at 7th Ave ☎212/841-5410. The Village cabaret is popular with a gay crowd. Two-drink minimum. Cover max $12. The rowdy piano bar downstairs is also worth a look.

Gotham Comedy Club 34 W 22nd St, between 5th and 6th aves ☎212/367-9000, ⒲www.gothamcomedyclub.com. A swanky and spacious comedy venue in the Flatiron district, highly respected by NY media types. Cover $10 Sun–Thurs, $15 Fri and Sat. Two-drink minimum.

Stand Up New York 236 W 78th St at Broadway ☎212/595-0850. The Upper West Side club is a

forum for established acts. Two nightly shows, sometimes three, at weekends. Two-drink minimum; cover $8 weeknights, $12 weekends.

Upright Citizens Brigade Theater 161 W 22nd St at 7th Ave ☎212/366-9716, ⒲www.ucbtheater.com. Consistently hilarious sketch-based comedy goes on seven nights a week. Thurs night is improv night, with a mere $5 cover.

Film

American Museum of the Moving Image 35th Ave and 36th St, Queens ☎718/784-0077, ⒲ammi.org Foreign and avant-garde films.

Angelika Film Center W Houston St at Mercer St ☎212/995-2000, ⒲www.angelikafilmcenter.com Latest non-Hollywood offerings and European art-house movies.

Anthology Film Archives 32–34 2nd Ave at Bond St ☎212/505-5181, ⒲www.anthologyfilmarchives.org. Shows many films you thought you'd never have the chance to see again.

Film Forum 209 W Houston St, between Varick St and 6th Ave ☎212/727-8110, ⒲www.filmforum.com. Shows the best in independent film and documentary, as well as themed revivals.

The Museum of Modern Art 11 W 53rd St ☎212/708-9480, ⒲www.moma.org (see p.96). A vast collection of well-chosen films, from Hollywood screwball comedies to hand-painted Super 8, entry to which is free with museum admission.

Gay and lesbian New York

There are few places in America – indeed in the world – where **gay culture** thrives as it does in New York. **Chelsea** (centered on Eighth Avenue between 14th and 23rd streets) and the **East Village** are the largest gay neighborhoods, and have largely replaced the **West Village** as the hub of gay New York, although a strong presence still lingers around Christopher Street. The other haven is Brooklyn's **Park Slope**, though perhaps more for women than for men and it's primarily a residential area and so a little harder to get to know. Gay and lesbian bars are listed overleaf, clubs opposite. For more information, get the **Gayellow Pages** (⒲www.gayellowpages.com - New York is in the East & South edition; $12), available from the bookstores below. Up-to-the-minute news can be found in *HomoXtra* (*HX*) or *Blade*, provocative weekly free-listings magazines.

Resources

ACT UP (AIDS Coalition to Unleash Power) 332 Bleecker Street, Suite G5, NY 10014 ☎212/966-4873, ⓦwww.actupny.org. Meets Mondays at the Center, 7.30pm.

Bluestockings 172 Allen St, between Stanton & Rivington sts ☎212/777-6028, ⓦwww.bluestock-ings.com. Collectively run feminist bookstore on the Lower East Side.

Center for Mental Health and Social Services at the Center, 208 W 13th St ☎212/620-7310. Free confidential counseling and referrals.

Creative Visions 548 Hudson St, between Perry and Charles sts ☎212/645-7573 or 1-800/997-9899, ⓦwww.creativevisions.citysearch.com. A well-stocked gay bookstore that also has a huge range of S&M videos and some vintage maga-zines.

Gay and Lesbian National Hotline ☎1-888/THE GLNH or 212/989-0999, ⓦwww.glnh.org (Mon–Fri 6–10pm, Sat noon–5pm). Information, help and referrals.

Gay Men's Health Crisis (GMHC) 119 W 24th St, between 6th and 7th aves ☎212/807-6664, ⓦwww.gmhc.org. Despite the name, this organi-zation – the oldest and largest not-for-profit AIDS organization in the world – provides information and referrals to everyone.

Lesbian Herstory Archives PO Box 1258, NY 10116 ☎718/768-DYKE (768-3953), ⓦwww .datalounge.com/lha. Celebrated and unmissable. Call or write for an appointment or for schedule of events in Park Slope.

Out of the Closet Thrift Shop 220 E 81st St, ☎212/472-3573. An excellent fundraising thrift store for AIDS groups open Tues–Sat 10am–5pm.

The Lesbian, Gay, Bisexual & Transgender Community Services Center 208 W 13th St, NY 10014 (w of 7th Ave) ☎212/620-7310, ⓦwww.gaycenter.org. The just-renovated, glis-tening new Center, which houses countless organizations (from ACT UP to the Metro Gay Wrestling Alliance), also sponsors workshops, dances, movie nights, guest speakers, youth services, programs for parents and kids, an archive and library, the annual Center Garden Party and lots more.

The Oscar Wilde Memorial Bookshop 15 Christopher St, between 6th & 7th aves ☎212/255-8097, ⓦwww.oscarwildebooks.com. The first gay bookstore in the US. Unbeatable.

Bars

The Bar 68 2nd Ave at E 4th St ☎212/674-9714;
The Boiler Room 86 E 4th St at 2nd Ave

☎212/254-7536. Two connected bars, very popu-lar in the East Village scene, attract a good mix of gay and lesbian patrons.

Barracuda 275 W 22nd St, between 7th and 8th aves ☎212/645-8613. A favorite spot in New York's gay scene, and as un-scene as you'll find in Chelsea. Check out the two-for-one happy hour from 4–9pm during the week, crazy drag shows and pick-up lines and a sweet hideaway lounge out back.

The Cock 188 Ave A at 12th St ☎212/777-6724. Unashamed of its theme, but without the overblown muscles and the tiny white tee. With amateur "talent" contests and strip karaoke to kill for, it's dirty, sleazy and a social hodgepodge – and a whole lot of fun.

g 223 W 19th St, between 7th and 8th aves ☎212/929-1085. Nearly as stylish as its "guppie" clientele, this large and deservedly very popular lounge also features a regular DJ and juice bar.

Ginger's 363 5th Ave, Park Slope, Brooklyn ☎718-788-0924. This new addition to Park Slope's sapphic scene is dark, moody and has a great happy hour.

Hell 59 Gansevoort St, between Greenwich and Washington sts ☎212/727-1666. Upscale lounge, male-dominated, on the upper fringes of the West Village.

Henrietta Hudson 438 Hudson St at Morton St ☎212/924-3347. This lesbian hangout serves food and gets fairly brimming at night. The loung-ing, pool and dancing areas are all separated, and guys are welcome too.

Julius 159 W 10th St at Waverly Place ☎212/929-9672. As the oldest gay bar in the city, dating from harder times, this quaint, wooden affair deserves at least one drink.

Marie's Crisis 59 Grove St ☎212/243-9323. A well-known cabaret/piano bar, popular with tourists and locals alike, features old-time singing sessions on Fri and Sat nights. Often packed, always fun.

Meow Mix 269 E Houston St at Suffolk St ☎212/254-0688. This place remains one of the girl-clubs of the moment, way east downtown. Bands or performances most nights; men are wel-come if they behave themselves. See also p.120.

The Monster 80 Grove St ☎212/924-3558. A venerable West Village institution, it has a dance floor, campy piano bar and cabaret.

Rubyfruit Bar & Grill 531 Hudson St at 10th St ☎212/929-3343. A cozy, friendly place for grown-up dykes, *Rubyfruit* is all about couches, cheap drinks and good company.

Stonewall 53 Christopher St between Waverly

Place and 7th Ave S ☎ 212/463-0950. The site of the seminal 1969 riot is mostly refurbished and flies the pride flag like they own it – which, one supposes, they do.

Wonder Bar 505 E 6th St, between aves A and B ☎ 212/777-9105. Cramped, festive and lesbian-friendly, this is a truly wonderful and unpretentious

find for the thinking boy. Still mainly for the men, though.

The Works 428 Columbus Ave at W 81st St ☎ 212/799-7365. The tropical theme bar brings in a fairly mixed crowd with its friendly, laid-back atmosphere – one of the few options for this part of town, but kinda kitschy nonetheless.

Shopping

When it comes to consumerism, New York is the capital of the world. You can **shop** for every possible taste, preference, creed and perversity, in any combination and often at any time of day or night. It can be extraordinarily cheap, too, like in the markets of the **East and West villages**, but move further uptown and it can also be phenomenally expensive. **Midtown Manhattan** is mainstream territory, with its department stores, big-name clothes designers and branches of the larger chains; Downtown plays host to a wide variety of more offbeat stores – **SoHo** is perhaps the most popular shopping neighborhood in these parts, and generally the most expensive, although with some affordable alternatives for the young and trendy. **Uptown**, the Upper East Side is uncompromisingly upmarket, while the funkier **Upper West Side** has an array of off-the-wall stores to compare with anything SoHo or the Village can offer.

Department stores

Bloomingdale's 1000 3rd Ave ☎ 212/705-2000; ⓦ www.bloomingdales.com. Perhaps Manhattan's most famous department store, it's packed with designer clothiers, perfume concessions and the like.

Macy's Broadway at 34th St ☎ 212/695-4400 or 1-800/289-6229, ⓦ www.macys.com. The world's largest department store embraces two buildings, two million square feet of floor space and ten floors (housing, unfortunately, fairly mediocre wares except for the excellent Cellar housewares department downstairs).

Saks Fifth Avenue 611 5th Ave at W 49th St ☎ 212/753-4000, ⓦ www.saks5thavenue.com. Although Saks remains virtually synonymous with style and quality, it has also updated itself to carry the merchandise of all the big designers.

Books

Barnes & Noble (ⓦ www.bn.com) Twelve super-store locations at 4 Astor Place at Broadway and Lafayette ☎ 212/420-1322; 385 5th Ave at 36th St ☎ 212/779-7677; 675 6th Ave at W 22nd St ☎ 212/727-1227; 600 5th Ave at W 48th St

☎ 212/765-0592; Citicorp Building at E 54th St and 3rd Ave ☎ 212/750-8033; 750 3rd Ave at 47th St ☎ 212/697-2251; 2289 Broadway at W 82nd St ☎ 212/362-8835; 240 E 86th St at 2nd Ave ☎ 212/794-1962; 1280 Lexington at E 86th St ☎ 212/423-9900; 1972 Broadway across from Lincoln Center ☎ 212/595-6859; 396 6th Ave Greenwich Village ☎ 212/674-8780 and 33 E 17th St at Union Square ☎ 212/253-0810. These mega-sized bookstores are way too bland and commercial for many a bibliophile, but offer generous selection, late hours, comfortable chairs and coffee bars.

Coliseum Books 1771 Broadway at 57th St ☎ 212/757-8381. Huge, if not flashy, general bookstore; knowledgeable staff and late hours.

Complete Traveler 199 Madison Ave at W 35th St ☎ 212/685-9007. Manhattan's premier travel bookshop, well stocked with both secondhand and new titles.

Drama Book Shop 723 7th Ave between W 48th and 49th sts ☎ 1-800/322-0595, ⓦ www .dramabookshop.com. The best theater and film bookstore around, with more than 50,000 titles and a very knowledgeable staff.

Gotham Book Mart 41 W 47th St ☎212/719-4448. Literary bookstore once frequented by e e cummings and Anaïs Nin. Has a good selection of drama and theater books. At the time of publication, plans were afoot to move to a new location.

Housing Works Used Books Café 126 Crosby St between Houston and Prince sts ☎212/334-3324. Very cheap books, comfy and spacious. Proceeds benefit AIDS charity.

Murder Ink 2486 Broadway between 92nd and 93rd sts ☎212/362-8905, ⊛www.murderink.com. The first store to specialize in mystery and detective fiction in the city is still the best.

Rizzoli 31 W 57th St ☎212/759-2424. The Manhattan branch of the Italian store has a good selection of foreign newspapers and magazines and high-quality art and photography books.

St Mark's Bookshop 31 3rd Ave between 8th and 9th sts ☎212/260-7853. Wonderfully eclectic selection of new titles from mainstream to alternative. Open late.

Strand Bookstore 828 Broadway at 12th St ☎212/473-1452. With about eight miles of books and a stock of 2.5 million+, this is the largest book operation in the city. Recent review copies and new books show up at half price; older books are from 50¢ up.

Records

Breakbeat Science 181 Orchard St ☎212/995-2592, ⊛www.breakbeatscience.com. The first drum'n'bass-only store to open in the US is still going strong.

Etherea 66 Ave A between 4th and 5th sts ☎212/358-1126. Their specialties are indie rock and electronica. Marketing domestic and imports, CDs and vinyl, this is one of the best shops in the city. Good used selection.

Footlight Records 113 E 12th St ☎212/533-1572, ⊛www.footlight.com. *The* place for show tunes, soundtracks and jazz.

Generation Records 210 Thompson St between Bleecker and W 3rd sts ☎212/254-1100. The focus here is on hardcore, metal and punk with some indie. New CDs and vinyl are upstairs, the used goodies downstairs.

House of Oldies 35 Carmine St between Bleecker St and 6th Ave ☎212/243-0500, ⊛www.houseofoldies.com. Just what the name says – oldies but goldies of all kinds. Vinyl only.

Kim's 6 St Mark's Place between 2nd and 3rd aves ☎212/598-9985; 144 Bleecker at La Guardia St ☎212/260-1010; and 350 Bleecker at 10th St. Extensive selection of new and used indie obscurities on CD and vinyl, some real cheap. Esoteric videos upstairs. Be warned: a serious

Sports in New York

Seeing either of New York's two **baseball** teams involves a trip across the East River to the outer boroughs. The Yankees play in the Bronx, at **Yankee Stadium**, 161st Street and River Avenue (☎718/293-6000). Get there on subway #C, #D or #4 direct to the 161st Street station. The Mets are based in Queens, at **Shea Stadium**, 126th Street at Roosevelt Avenue (☎718/507-8499). Take subway #7 to the Willets Point/Shea Stadium station. Tickets are priced between $8 and $50, depending on the team (Yankee tickets are generally more expensive) and where you sit. For an unbelievably raucous New York experience, show up on game day for bleacher seats at Yankee Stadium: the hooligan regulars and the bouncers who keep an eye on them are often more fun to watch than the game.

New York's football teams – the **Jets** and the **Giants** – play at the **Meadowlands Sports Complex**, East Rutherford, New Jersey (☎201/935-3900). Buses from the Port Authority Bus Terminal at 42nd Street and 8th Avenue (☎212/564-8484) serve the stadium. Call ahead first; tickets are hard to come by. If all else fails, catch the action on the big screen in any sports bar.

Basketball's two New York pro teams are the **Knicks** and the **Liberty**, the latter members of the WNBA. Both play at **Madison Square Garden** (☎212/465-6741), West 33rd and 7th Avenue, served by the #1, #2, #3, #A, #C and #E trains. Tickets for the Knicks are very expensive and, due to impossibly high demand, available in only limited numbers, if at all; however, the women's games are fairly exciting and cheaper at $8–58. Another area team, the New Jersey Nets, play in an arena at the Meadowlands Complex (see above); tickets range from $25–75.

attitude problem comes with the job description here.

Other Music 15 E 4th St ☏212/477-8150, ⓦwww.othermusic.com. Great selection of electronica, indie and "alternative."

Temple Records 29 Ave B between 2nd and 3rd sts ☏212/475-7552. Owned by New York's DJ Khan, this absolute temple to techno spans Detroit to Berlin – an obsessive wannabe turntablist's heaven.

Vinyl Mania 41 Carmine St ☏212/924-7223. First port of call for DJs seeking the newest, rarest releases and imports.

CHAPTER 2   # Highlights

✳ **Fire Island, Long Island, NY** A great weekend get-away from NYC, with fewer tourists and better beaches than the swanky Hamptons. See p.131

✳ **The Adirondacks, NY** A vast and rugged wilderness offering superb hiking, skiing and mountain-climbing opportunities. See p.141

✳ **Ithaca, NY** New York State's answer to San Francisco, built on a steep hill and complete with New Age stores, scores of vegetarian cafés (including Moosewood of cookbook fame) and a laid-back collegiate vibe. See p.144

✳ **Niagara Falls, NY** Take the memorable *Maid of the Mist* boat trip and stand close enough to feel the spray from these majestic falls. See p.150

✳ **Pennsylvania Dutch Country, PA** Rural back roads, bucolic fields and quaint roadside stalls selling shoo-fly pie and homemade root beer make for a perfect bike ride. See p.166

✳ **The Boardwalk, Atlantic City, NJ** Tacky and trashy it may be, but unmissable nonetheless – the Boardwalk is the heart and soul of this blue-collar seaside town. See p.187

The Mid-Atlantic

he three Mid-Atlantic states – **NEW YORK**, **PENNSYLVANIA** and **NEW JERSEY** – stand at the heart of the most populated and industrialized corner of the US. Although dominated in the popular imagination by the gray smokestacks of New Jersey and the coalfields and steel factories of Pennsylvania, these states also encompass lakes, forests, farmland, rolling green countryside and, in places, expanses of virtual wilderness.

European settlement was characterized by considerable shifts and turns: the **Dutch**, who arrived in the 1620s, were methodically squeezed out by the **English**, who in turn fought off the **French** challenge to secure control of the region by the mid-eighteenth century. The Native American population, including the **Iroquois Confederacy** and Lenni Lenape Indian, had sided with the French against the English, and were soon confined to reservations or pushed north into Canada. At first the economy depended on the fur trade, though by the 1730s English **Quakers**, along with **Amish** and **Mennonites** from Germany and a few Presbyterian **Irish**, had made farming a significant force, their holdings extending to the western limits of Pennsylvania and New York.

All three states were important during the **Revolution**: over half the battles were fought here, including major American victories at **Trenton** and **Princeton** in New Jersey. Upstate New York was geographically crucial, as the British forces knew that control of the Hudson River would effectively divide New England from the other colonies, and the long winter spent by the ragtag Continental Army at **Valley Forge** outside Philadelphia turned it into a well-organized force. After the Revolution, industry became the region's prime economic force, with **mill towns** springing up along the numerous rivers. By the mid-1850s the large **coalfields** of northeast Pennsylvania were powering the smoky steel mills of Pittsburgh, and the discovery of high-grade **crude oil** in 1859 marked the beginning of the automobile age. Though still significant, especially in the regions near New York City, heavy industry has now by and large been replaced by tourism as the economic engine.

Although many travelers to the east coast may not consider venturing much further than New York City itself (covered in Chapter One of this book) the region is much more than just an overspill of the Big Apple. Each region has a distinct identity. Just thirty minutes outside of Manhattan, **Long Island** offers both the crashing surf of the Atlantic Ocean and the cool calm of the Long Island Sound. **Upstate New York** is for outdoors enthusiasts: the wooded **Catskill Mountains** line the Hudson River (which Henry James claimed was "in the geography of the ideal"), the imposing **Adirondack Mountains** spread over a quarter of the state, and the **Finger Lakes** region offers a pastoral alternative to the industrial Erie Canal cities along I-90. In the northwest corner of the state, on the Canadian border, are the awesome **Niagara Falls**. **Pennsylvania** is best known for the fertile **Pennsylvania Dutch** country and the two great cities of **Philadelphia** and **Pittsburgh**. **New Jersey**, often pictured as one big industrial carbuncle, offers shameless tourist pleasures along the shore: day-trippers in their millions flock each year to the Boardwalk and casinos of **Atlantic City**.

The entire region is well covered by **public transportation**, with New York's JFK and New Jersey's Newark airports acting as major international gateways, and New York's La Guardia Airport serving domestic flights. In Pennsylvania, both Philadelphia and Pittsburgh have reasonably busy airports with a growing number of international flights. Amtrak **trains** run routes up and down the Northeast Corridor through New York, New Jersey and Pennsylvania, while the New Jersey Transit rail and bus network serves all of New Jersey, extending from Atlantic City west to Philadelphia and north to Manhattan. Greyhound **buses** follow the major interstates, with a few subsidiary lines running to more out-of-the-way places.

New York State

However much the tourist authorities try to encourage visitors, the large and rambling state of **NEW YORK** stands inevitably in the shadow of America's most celebrated city. The words "New York" bring to mind soaring skyscrapers and congested streets, not the 50,000 square miles of rolling dairy farmland, colonial villages, workaday towns, lakes, waterfalls and towering mountains that spread north and west from New York City and constitute **upstate New York**. Just an hour's drive north of Manhattan, the valley of the **Hudson River**, with the moody **Catskill Mountains** rising stealthily from the west bank, offers a respite from the intensity of the city. Much wilder and more rugged are the peaks of the vast **Adirondack Mountains** further north – far beyond the scope of a casual excursion, but holding some of eastern America's most enticing scenery. To the west, the slender *Finger Lake*s and endless miles of dairy farms and vineyards occupy the central portion of the state. Few of the cities hold much of interest, but the smaller towns, like Ivy League **Ithaca**, can be quite charming for a day or two, while the venerable spa town of **Saratoga Springs** attracts thousands of punters during the August horse racing season.

In the seventeenth and eighteenth centuries, as nation-molding political and military battles were taking place, semi-feudal **Dutch landowning dynasties** such as the Van Rensselaers held sway upstate. Their control over tens of thousands of tenant farmers was barely affected by the transfer of colonial power from Holland to Britain, or even by American independence. Only with the completion of the **Erie Canal** in 1825, linking New York City with the Great Lakes, did the interior start to open up; improved opportunities for trade enabled canal-side cities like **Rochester**, **Syracuse** and especially **Buffalo** to undergo massive expansion. On the other hand, this industrial and agricultural growth in the hinterland served, inevitably, to increase the financial standing of the Wall Street capitalists. The story of the past century and a half has been one of New York City's political and economic domination of New York State, though Governor George Pataki's popularity has buoyed upstate politicians, if not fully redressed the imbalance.

Getting around New York State

From New York City, the Long Island Railroad (leaving from Penn Station) and Metro North (leaving from Grand Central Station) shuttle commuters to and from the suburbs of Long Island and Westchester County respectively. For journeys further north, Greyhound and Adirondack Trailways **buses** run to all the major towns, while Amtrak operates a **train** service along a beautiful route through the Hudson Valley to the state capital, **Albany**; from there trains continue north to Montréal via the Adirondacks, and west along the Erie Canal to Buffalo and Niagara Falls. Many bus and train **stations** are several miles out from the town centers; the necessary walking can be unpleasant in the muggy heat of summer (not to mention the freezing winter).

Car rental in and around New York City is expensive, and restricted to drivers over 25 years of age; lower rates can be found by taking public transportation away from the metropolitan area. Be aware as well that the New York State Thruway (I-95 and I-87) is a **toll road**, which adds up to around $15 end-to-end. **Flying**, with occasional special deals of $150 for a New York to Buffalo round-trip, is another option, though you'll miss a lot of nice scenery; if you do decide to fly, the discount carrier serving the largest number of destinations in New York state is JetBlue (☎1–800/JETBLUE or 801/365-225, ⓦwww.jet-blue.com). **Cycling** is best enjoyed as a means of exploring areas such as the Finger Lakes or Catskills, and if you have a lot of time you may want to consider renting a **canal boat** and cruising the Erie or Champlain canals; contact the state tourist office (see p.29) for details on either of these options, and for general information on visiting New York state.

Long Island

Just east of New York City, **Long Island** unfurls for 125 miles of lush farmland and broad sandy beaches, and is perhaps best explored as an excursion of a few days from the metropolis. Its western end abuts the urban boroughs of Brooklyn and Queens, and for a while continues as a suburban sprawl of shopping malls and fast-food outlets; but further east, the settlements begin to thin out and the countryside can get surprisingly remote. The **north** and **south shores** differ greatly – the former more immediately beautiful, its cliffs topped with luxurious mansions and estates, while the South Shore is fringed by almost continuous sand, interspersed with holiday resorts such as **Jones Beach** and **Fire Island**. At its far end Long Island splits in two, the **North Fork** retaining a marked rural aspect while the **South Fork**, much of which is known as **The Hamptons**, sets itself apart as an enclave of New York's richest and most famous.

The quickest way to reach Long Island is via the reliable if rather worn **Long Island Railroad** from Penn Station (☎718/217-LIRR, ⓦwww.mta.nyc.ny.us/lirr/) though numerous **bus services** (operated by major companies and the Hampton Jitney ☎1–800/936-0440) cover most destinations. **Parking permits** for most of Long Island's beaches are issued only to local residents, so on the whole it works out to be less expensive to head to the beach on public transport. There's plenty of **accommodation**, listed in the text; A Reasonable Alternative (117 Spring St, Port Jefferson, NY 11777; ☎631/928-4034) offers a good range of B&B lodging throughout Long Island.

The South Shore and Fire Island

Long Island's **South Shore** merges gently with the wild Atlantic, with shallow, creamy sand beaches and rolling dunes like those at Long Beach and **Jones Beach,** which together run along fifty miles of seashore. These get less crowded the further east you go; once you get as far as **Gilgo** or **Oak Beach**, or cross the water to **Robert Moses State Park** on the western tip of Fire Island, you can find solitude. **Long Beach** has a die-hard surfer contingent that gathers at the **Long Beach Surf Shop**, 651 E Park Ave (☎631/897-7873); you can purchase a used board here for about $250. **Ocean Parkway** leads along the narrow offshore strand from Jones Beach to **Captree**, a good base for fishing and whale-watching trips organized by the Captree Boatman's Association (☎631/669-6484, ⓦwww.captreefleet.com) before crossing back to **Bay Shore**, a dull town that serves as a **ferry** terminal for Fire Island. This way you bypass the sprawling mess of **Amityville**, famous for its "horror" of twenty years ago. The house on the hill, from which a mysterious supernatural force is said to have driven the occupants, still stands.

Fire Island

Fire Island, a slim spit of land parallel to the South Shore, is in many ways a microcosm of New York City. On summer weekends half of Manhattan seems to be holed up in its tiny settlements. Though the population is definitely mixed, certain parts of the island are primarily known as **gay** resorts: gay women and a few older men make for **Cherry Grove**; the wealthier gay males for **The Pines**, where the social scene revolves around private house parties as opposed to bars. **Ocean Beach** has also a lively (straight) nightlife; and **Point O Woods** is the most exclusive of the lot. A mixed crowd hangs out in the **Sunken Forest** (aka Sailor's Haven), so called because it's the only part of the island that lies below sea level – and the pressure, barometric and otherwise, is less intense.

The **season** is as rigidly defined as the people. From Memorial Day onwards Fire Island hums with activity and is swamped with crowds, though it's always possible to escape for gorgeous wild walks along the sand (there is a national seashore here, with a beautiful restored lighthouse); after Labor Day, the weather may still be very warm, but the throngs diminish dramatically.

Most **ferries** dock at Ocean Beach, where trippers pile up groceries on trolleys (cars are forbidden) and set off for their vacation pads. Ferry schedules are subject to change; Fire Island Ferries (☎631/665-3600, ⓦ www.fireislandferries.com) and the Sayville Ferry Service (☎631/589-0810, ⓦ www.sayvilleferry.com) leave from Bay Shore, while the Davis Park Ferries (☎631/475-1665) leave from Patchogue; one-way rates are around $6 and the journey takes half an hour. All **accommodation** should be booked well in advance; options include *Jerry's*, 168 Cottage Walk, Ocean Beach (☎631583-8870; ❹), which doubles its rates at weekends; *Cleggs Hotel*, 478 Bayberry Walk, Ocean Beach (May–Oct; ☎631/583-5399; ❹), which offers garden apartments with full kitchens and baths as well as rooms; *Fire Island Hotel* at 25 Cayuga Walk in nearby Ocean Bay Park (☎631/583-8000; ❺), which used to be a Coast Guard station; and the *Boatel,* the only hotel in Fire Island Pines (☎631/597-6500; ❸–❺). *Giovanni's*, opposite the ferry terminal, is the best place to **eat** for under $10, or if you'd like to splash out, try *Matthew's* nearby for its terrific fish specials for around $25. At weekends, the *Ice Palace*, at the *Cherry Grove Beach Motel* on Main Walk, and *Flynn's* (same location as *Fire Island Hotel*) on Bay Walk, are good for riotous boozing and dancing. Pick up the *Fire Island News* ($1) at a newsstand to find out what's happening while you're there.

The North Shore and North Fork

Along the rugged **North Shore**, Long Island drops to the sea in a series of bluffs, coves and wooded headlands. The expressway beyond Queens leads straight onto the **Gold Coast**, where **Great Neck** was F. Scott Fitzgerald's West Egg in *The Great Gatsby*, home of Gatsby himself. Some of this real estate is so expensive that only the richest of the rich can afford to live here. The motley French Norman–style buildings at Falaise in **Sands Point**, on the sharp tip of the next peninsula, were once owned by the Guggenheims; they now house a self-celebratory **museum** (May–Oct Wed–Sun tours hourly noon–3pm; $6; ☎516/571-7900). The 209 acres of unkempt parkland offer great views over what Fitzgerald called "the most domesticated body of salt water in the Western hemisphere, the great barnyard of Long Island Sound." In Old Westbury, at 71 Old Westbury Rd, **Westbury Gardens** is a classier attraction: a Georgian mansion with beautiful, well-tended gardens and some pleasant works of art, including a few Gainsboroughs (April–Oct daily except Tues 10am–5pm, rest of year Wed–Sun 9am–4.30pm; $10; ☎516/333-0048).

Sagamore Hill, on the coast road six miles beyond Glen Cove, is the heavily touristed former country retreat where **Teddy Roosevelt** lived for thirty-odd years (April–Oct daily 9am–5pm, rest of year Wed–Sun; tours only; $5; ℡516/922-4788). Its 23 rooms are adorned everywhere with the great man's trophies, sprouting horns from walls or grinning toothily up from the firesides. The **Old Orchard Museum** near the parking lot recounts Teddy's political and personal life, but the real reason to come is to stroll the gorgeous grounds, where green lawns drop to Oyster Bay and the sea. It's a very pleasant trip altogether – with helpful and knowledgeable tour guides (often Roosevelt descendants) taking you around on 45-minute tours.

Nearby **COLD SPRING HARBOR** grew up as a whaling port, and retains some of its looks. A fully equipped whaleboat and a 400-piece assembly of scrimshaw work help its **Whaling Museum** (Tues–Sun 11am–5pm; $3; ℡631/367-3418) to recapture that era. The **Vanderbilt Mansion** just outside Centerport (Tues–Sun noon–5pm; $8; ℡631/854-5555) displays the dubious taste typical of Vanderbilt residences. In the style of a Baroque Spanish palace, it's heavily ornate both outside and in, with marble-encased galleries, swirling staircases and gaudy fireplaces. Oddly enough, they also have planetarium shows here.

On the less touristed **North Fork** – once an independent colony – the scenery is typical of the wild Atlantic coast. In **GREENPORT**, its most picturesque town, a clutter of narrow streets and alleys lead down to a harbor pierced by the masts of visiting yachts, where there's a small **maritime museum** nearby (May–Dec Wed–Sun 10am–5pm; free; ℡631/477-2100). Plentiful **accommodation** includes the *Bartlett House*, 503 Front St (℡631/477-0371; ❺), and *Watson's by the Bay*, 104 Bay Ave (May–Sept; ℡631/477-0426; ❹). Regular **ferries** connect with Shelter Island and the South Fork every fifteen minutes (foot passengers $1 each way; cars $8 round-trip); others cross to New London, Connecticut, described on p.248.

The South Fork

The US holds few wealthier quarters than the small towns of Long Island's **South Fork**, where huge mansions lurk among the trees or stand boldly on the flats behind the dunes. Nowhere is consumption as deliberately conspicuous as in **the Hamptons** – among the oldest communities in the state, settled by restless New Englanders in the mid-1650s, but relatively isolated until the rich began to turn up in their motor cars. The current generation of high rollers clog the roads in Range Rovers and Mercedes, and the sidewalks in slow, sauntering processions; pretty as the Hamptons are, avoid them if you are at all antisocial. Nightlife venues are expensive and notoriously changeable; pick up *Dan's Papers* or the *East Hampton Star* to find out what's happening.

Southampton

Long association with the smart set has left **SOUTHAMPTON** unashamedly upper class. Its streets are lined with galleries and clothing and jewelry stores, but the nearby beaches are superb. The **visitor center** at 76 Main St (Mon–Fri 10am–4pm, Sat & Sun 11am–4pm; ℡631/283-0402, ⓦ www.southamptonchamber.com) has lists of **B&Bs**, such as the *Mainstay*, 579 Hill St (℡631/283-4375; ❺). You can get marvelous fresh seafood in a number of **restaurants**, notably *Barrister's* at 36 Main St (℡631/283-6206) and the venerable *Southampton Publick House* at 40 Bowden Square (℡631/283-2800), which operated during Prohibition as "Mrs Cavanaugh's

Speakeasy." Relatively casual **nightspots** like *Southampton Tavern* on Tuckahoe Lane nestle next to impossibly upscale clubs, like *Jet East* on North Sea Road where super-rich regulars shell out hundreds of dollars to reserve Saturday night tables. The latest addition to the velvet-roped ranks of chic bars is *Conscience Point*, nearby on North Sea Road. It's owned by the same team as *Jet East* and features much the same crowd.

Sag Harbor

Historic **SAG HARBOR**, in its heyday a harbor second only to that of New York, was designated first Port of Entry to the New Country by George Washington; the **Old Custom House** (May–June, Sept–Oct Sat & Sun 10am–5pm; July–Aug Tues–Sun 10am–5pm; $3; ☎631/692-4664) dates from this era. The **Whaling Museum** on Main Street (mid-May to Sept Mon–Sat 10am–5pm, Sun 1–5pm; $3; ☎631/725-0770) commemorates the town's brief whaling days with guns and scrimshaw. Nearby the **Whaler's Presbyterian Church** is crenellated with jutting rows of whale blubber spades, and beautiful memorials in **Oakland Cemetery** commemorate young whalers.

   In summer, the windmill where John Steinbeck once lived serves as a **visitor center** (June–Sept daily 10am–5pm, Fri–Sat late night until 8pm; rest of year Sat & Sun only 10am–5pm; ☎631/725-0011, ⊛www.sagharborchamber.com). You can get a nice room at the *Baron's Cove Inn* at 31 W Water St (☎631/725-2100; ❺), but at the well-heeled *American Hotel* at 25 Main St (☎631/725-3535; ❼) you can also get a splendid French meal and a good cigar from the hotel's humidor. There are several good, less expensive **restaurants** along Main Street, such as the superb sushi bar *Sen* at no. 23 (☎631/725-1774). For **nightlife**, the *Boom Bistro,* right across from *Baron's Cove*, is the club of the moment and wildly popular.

East Hampton and Amagansett

East Hampton is the trendiest of the Hamptons, filled with the mansions of celebrities like Steven Spielberg, Jerry Seinfeld and Martha Stewart, as well as obnoxiously chic shops and restaurants. However if you're there, it's worth driving or biking around **Further Lane**, **Lily Pond** and some of the other exclusive neighborhoods just to catch sight of some of the spectacular (and just plain beautiful) homes. **Amagansett** is a village within East Hampton and, though crowded in the summer, tends to be more down to earth than the rest of town. Note the old shingle homes along quiet leafy side streets and enjoy the lively weekend scene (and fresh muffins) at *Farmer's Market* on Main Street and the partying at *Stephen Talkhouse* at no. 161, a terrific bar and music joint that gets well-known folk, jazz and rock performers year-round (☎631/267-3117).

Montauk

Blustery, wind-battered **MONTAUK**, beyond Amagansett on the farthest tip of Long Island, never quite made it as a resort; plans to develop it were shattered by the Wall Street Crash of 1929. This town isn't chic or quaint, but real people actually live here and it provides access to the rocky wilds of **Montauk Point**, whose rare beauty figures in all the tourist brochures. A **lighthouse** – New York state's oldest, dating from 1796 – forms an almost symbolic finale to this stretch of the American coast.

   Motels in the town center offer fairly priced rooms (a rarity in the eastern end of Long Island); rates at the *Oceanside Beach Resort* (☎631/668-9825; ❹–❻) at 626 Montauk Street Highway, vary seasonally but reasonably; if you want something fancier, try *Gurney's Inn* on Old Montauk Highway (☎631/668-2345; ❾). The ultimate Montauk **dining** experience is *The Lobster Roll* (☎631/267-3740) on the highway, which serves excellent fresh fish, including the eponymous sandwich. Other good options include the moderately priced *Shagwong* on Main Street (☎631/668-3050), as well as the delicious sushi at super-basic *Westlake Clam & Chowder House:* from the tables here, you can watch the fishermen bring home their catch and have it delivered to you via the kitchen in minutes.

The Hudson Valley and the Catskills

To the average commuter, the **Hudson River** is just an inconvenient barrier en route to New Jersey. However, you only need to travel a few miles north of Manhattan before the valley takes on a Rhine-like charm, with prodigious historic homes, such as those of the Roosevelt, Vanderbilt and van Cortland families, rising from its steep and thickly wooded banks. A little further on come the forests of the **Catskill Mountains**, whose brilliant fall colors rival anything to be seen in New England. Few of the cities along the Hudson, including the large but lackluster state capital of **Albany**, hold much to attract the visitor, but some of the small towns are worth checking out, most notably the New Agey village of **Woodstock**, nestled among the Catskills.

The lower Hudson Valley

A mere 25 miles north of central New York City, leafy **TARRYTOWN** was the original setting for Washington Irving's tales of *Rip Van Winkle* and *The Legend of Sleepy Hollow*. In 1835 the author rebuilt a farm cottage just south of town on West Sunnyside Lane (off US-9), which he named **Sunnyside**: "a little old-fashioned stone mansion, all made up of gable ends, and as full of angles and corners as an old cocked hat." Tours squeeze through its cozy rooms, enjoyable even if you've never read a word of Irving (March–Dec, daily except Tues 10am–4pm; $8; ☎914/591-8763). It's also worth looking around the neighboring village of **LYNDHURST**, where the spikily crenellated **Lyndhurst Castle** is as dapper a piece of nineteenth-century Gothic revivalism as you're likely to find (April–Oct Tues–Sun 10am–5pm; Nov–March Sat & Sun 10am–4pm; $10; ☎914/631-4481). Also of interest here is **Kykuit** (pronounced "Kigh-cut"), the old Rockefeller Estate; the mansion is filled with modern artwork (particularly sculpture) and the collection in the gardens and grounds is just as impressive, with works by Picasso, Calder, Henry Moore and many others (May–Nov; tours only; ☎914/631-9491).

About ten miles north of Tarrytown along US-9, the town of **OSSINING** holds two impressive mid-Victorian creations: one is a huge bridge carrying the **Old Croton Aqueduct**, New York City's first water supply; the other, just south of town, is **Sing Sing Prison**, which for over 150 years has been the place where New York City criminals get sent "up the river."

The west bank and Catskill Mountains

Rising above the west bank of the Hudson River, the magnificent crests of the **Catskills**, cloaked with maple and beech that turn orange, ochre and gold each fall, have a rich and absorbing beauty. This dislocated branch of the Appalachians is inspiring country, filled with amenities – campgrounds, hiking, fishing and, especially, skiing. To enjoy it to the full, venture onto the trails; the mountains are so tightly packed that good roadside overlooks are rare.

West Point

The first real place of interest on the west bank of the Hudson, sixty miles out of New York City, is the United States Military Academy at **WEST POINT**, which Congress established in 1802 after realizing that the ragged troops who had won the Revolutionary War had been knocked into shape almost exclusively by European officers. Homegrown skills had to be cultivated in case foreign help wasn't so readily forthcoming again. Since then, West Point has provided the military training for US Army generals Grant, Lee, MacArthur, Eisenhower, Patton and Schwarzkopf, to name but a famous few. Today, four-thousand-odd candidates on a tough four-year course fill the smart showpiece campus, which protectively overlooks the Hudson from a wide, strategic bluff. What draws most people are the stirringly patriotic parade ground drills, at their most frequent during spring and late summer/early fall; West Point's **visitor center** (daily 9am–4.45pm; ☎845/938-2638, ⓦwww.usma.edu) can provide a full schedule. The free **West Point Museum** (daily 10.30am–4.15pm) shows trophies of war including pistols that belonged to George Washington, Napoleon Bonaparte and Adolf Hitler and, disturbingly, the pin from the Nagasaki atomic bomb.

Kingston

Of the various towns on the fringes of the mountains, **KINGSTON** is one of the most pleasant and convenient places to stop. An agreeable mix of well-preserved old houses and neat little businesses lines **Green and Crown streets** at the center of town, much of which dates from the late eighteenth century, when Kingston played a vital political and military role in the fight for American independence.

Kingston is very easy to reach – it's just off I-87 (exit 19), and Adirondack Trailways buses heading north from New York City stop ten minutes' walk from the center. The town's two **visitor centers**, on Clinton Avenue (☎845/331-9506, ⓦwww.ci.kingston.ny.us) and Broadway (☎845/331-7517), have leaflets for suggested walking tours around the historic sights. If you want to **stay**, the large *Holiday Inn*, 503 Washington Ave (☎845/338-0400; ⑤), is probably the best value, complete with sauna, pool and games area, though its rates rise on summer weekends. The *Market Basket Deli*, 308 Wall St (☎845/338-2755), serves fresh breads and bagels, while the town's brewpub, the *Woodstock Brewing Co*, 20 St James St (☎845/331-2810), does good big platters of food as well as a range of home-brewed ale. Further **food and drink** options can be found across the river in Rhinebeck (see p.138).

Woodstock

West from Kingston, Hwy-28 meanders into the Catskills, looping past the lovely Ashokan Reservoir where Hwy-375 branches off to **WOODSTOCK**. The village, carved out of the lush deciduous woodlands and cut by fast-rushing creeks, was not actually the venue of the famed **psychedelic picnic** of August 1969. That was some sixty miles southwest in Bethel, where a monument at Herd and West Shore roads marks the site on the farm owned by Max Yasgur where the first festival was held. However, Woodstock has enjoyed a bohemian reputation since the foundation in 1902 of the **Byrdcliffe Arts Colony** (which runs summer residency courses; ☎845/679-2079, ⓦwww.woodstockguild.org), and during the 1960s it was a favorite stomping ground for the likes of Dylan, Hendrix and Van Morrison. It still bears signs of its **hippie** past: shops sell crystals and tie-dyed T-shirts and crystals, and there's even the odd commune out in the woods, but in the cafés you're just as likely to bump into a successful Manhattanite who owns a second home here as you would a long-haired beatnik-type. Woodstock's galleries and craft shops command a regional reputation and the village is also a hub for the performing arts: the **Maverick Concert** series (late June–Aug; around $15 per concert; ☎845/679-8217) has played host to some of the world's finest chamber musicians since 1916. Just west of Woodstock in the small town of Mount Tremper, the **Kaatskill Kaleidoscope** claims to be the world's largest, created by a local hippie artist and now knee-deep in psychedelic souvenirs and T-shirts. The kaleidoscope, in reality a 60ft-high converted grain silo, plays ten-minute sound and light shows throughout the day, and makes a tacky but entertaining roadside stop. (Wed–Mon 10am–7pm; $5; ☎1-888/303-3936).

Woodstock is a great base for exploring the Catskills, and the best option for **accommodation** is the cozy *Twin Gables Guest House* (☎845/679-9479; ❺), in the center of the village at 73 Tinker St. If this is full, as is often the case, the higher rates at *Woodstock Lodge* on Country Club Lane (☎845/679-2814; ❹–❻) will get you a cabin and breakfast. Alternatively, there are chain motels like *Howard Johnson*, 2764 Hwy-32 (☎845/246-9511; ❸), ten miles northeast in Saugerties. Between Saugerties and Woodstock are the *Rip Van Winkle* (May–Oct; $23.50 per tentsite; ☎845/246-8334) and *KOA* (May–Oct; $25 per tentsite; ☎845/246-4089) **campgrounds**, both of which have full facilities for both tents and RVs. The best **places to eat** are a little way out of the village: the menu at the *New World Home Cooking Company*, 882 Rte-12 (April–Oct; ☎845/246-0900), has Caribbean and Creole-influenced dishes for under $10, while two miles west of Woodstock on Hwy-212 in tiny **Bearsville**, the *Bear Café* (☎845/679-5555) serves French bistro food unparalleled in these parts with prices to match. Several **buses** each day take two and a half hours to reach Woodstock from New York City's Port Authority Bus Terminal (Adirondack Trailways; ☎1-800/858-8555). Sturdy **bikes** can be rented from Overlook Mountain Bikes, 93 Tinker St (Wed–Sat 10am–6pm, Sun 11am–6pm, closed Tues; ☎845/679-2122).

For more **information** visit the Chamber of Commerce booth on Rock City Road just off the village green (hours vary; ☎845/679-6234), tune into the local radio station, WDST (100.1 FM), or pick up the weekly *Woodstock Times*.

On through Catskill Park

As you continue along Hwy-28, the picturesque hamlet of **PHOENICIA**, in a hollow to the right of the road, is an ideal resting place and a great base for hiking trails in the area. You can catch the circular **Catskill Mountain Railroad** (Sat, Sun and holidays 11am–5pm; $6; ☎845/688-7400) through scenic Esopus Creek. The *Phoenicia Hotel*, on Main Street (☎845/688-7500; ❸), is a basic and inexpensive place to stay with an inviting (and cheap) bar attached. Next door is the *American Café* (☎845/688-2900), which serves great burgers plus a tasty selection of Mexican fare; the *Phoenicia Diner* is another good option on Hwy-28 (☎845/688-9957). A few miles further west, Hwy-49A affords a good vista of the rambling Catskills from the parking lot of the Belleayre ski resort. The *HI-AYH Hostel*, Main Street, Pine Hill (☎845/254-4200), has beds for $15 as well as private rooms and cabins (❷/❸); other accommodation in the village includes two large budget Victorian inns on Main Street – the *Colonial Inn* (☎845/254-5577; ❹) and the *Pine Hill Arms*

Century Old Inn (☎845/254-9811; ❸) – plus the six-room *Birchcreek Inn* (☎845/254-5222; ❺), in a wooded setting out on Hwy-28.

The return route to I-90 along Hwy-23A includes a breathtaking view of the dramatic **gorge** between the villages of Hunter and Catskill, along with the area's premier **ski runs** on Hunter Mountain. The resort's chair lifts also operate after the snow has melted (late June–Aug Fri–Sun 10am–5pm; $6; ☎518/263-4223). Accommodation rates rise significantly during the ski season: *Scribner Hollow Lodge*, half a mile from the mountain on Hwy-23A (☎518/263-4211; ❽/❾), boasts fireplaces in most of its 38 deluxe rooms and a fine-dining restaurant with great views, though places in the hamlet of Catskill, such as the *Red Ranch Motel* on Hwy-32 (☎518/678-3380 or 1-800/962-4560; ❷), are much more basic but affordable.

The east bank

HYDE PARK, set on a peaceful plateau on the east bank of the Hudson twenty miles south of Kingston, is not an especially attractive town, but is worth a stop for the homes of **Franklin D.** and **Eleanor Roosevelt**. Well-signposted off US-9 at 519 Albany Post Rd, the house where the "New Deal" president was born and spent much of his adult life is preserved here along with a library and a good **museum** (May–Oct daily 9am–5pm; Nov–April daily 9am–5pm; no charge for the grounds, guided house tour only $10, combination pass Val-Kill, Hyde Park and the Vanderbilt estate $18; ☎845/229-9115). The museum contains extensive photos and artifacts, including the specially adapted car he drove after being struck down by polio in 1921, and the letter from Einstein that led to the development of the atomic bomb.

FDR lies buried in the Rose Garden, beside his wife (and distant cousin) Eleanor, a gifted and influential Democratic politician without whose help his career might well not have survived his long bouts of illness. Unlike other president's wives, who had mainly served as hostesses at society functions, Eleanor Roosevelt played a prominent role in the New Deal programs, and toured the country and reported to FDR on the living conditions of the poor. After FDR's death in 1945 she moved to the nearby cottage, **Val-Kill**, from where she carried on her work as chair of the United Nations Human Rights Commission, receiving dignitaries such as Tito, Nehru, Khrushchev and John F. Kennedy until her death in 1962. Shuttle buses leave the FDR house every half-hour (May–Oct daily 9am–5pm; Nov–April Sat & Sun 9am–5pm; tours only $5; ☎845/229-9115).

A three-mile-long clifftop **path** along the Hudson from the Roosevelt complex winds up at the Beaux Arts **Vanderbilt Mansion**. This virtual palace is, believe it or not, the smallest of the family's residences, built for Frederick, a grandson of railroad baron Cornelius. The furnishings are quite garish, but the formal gardens are very pretty and offer a fine view of the Hudson River (daily 9am–5pm; $8). The grounds are open year-round, from dawn to dusk, at no charge.

Apart from these historic homes, Hyde Park has one other huge tourist draw, the excellent public dining rooms of the **Culinary Institute of America** (lunch and dinner daily; reservations ☎845/471-6608), the largest and most prestigious cooking school in the country. Housed in a huge Gothic-style red-brick castle along US-9, south of Hyde Park at 433 Albany Post Rd, the various restaurants here – ranging from the casual atmosphere and the pizza and vegetarian dishes at *St Andrew's Café* to the $25 fixed-price Italian dinners at *Caterina de Medici* and the four-star *American Bounty* and *Escoffier* rooms, where jackets are required – have trained some of America's best chefs.

Beyond Hyde Park, US-9 cuts slightly inland from the Hudson, passing through a number of sleepy towns on its way north toward Albany. **RHINEBECK**, six miles north of Hyde Park, is the first and most worthwhile of these, holding a number of good restaurants as well as **America's oldest hotel**. The lovely, white colonial *Beekman Arms*, at 6387 Mill St has been hosting and feeding travelers in its warm, wood-paneled rooms since 1766 (☎845/876-7077; ❺). Two other good places to eat on the same block of Mill Street are the *Calico Restaurant & Patisserie* (Wed–Sun; ☎845/876-2749), which offers tasty breakfast pastries and a lunch and dinner menu with strong Northern Italian and regional French influences at around $10 for a main course, and the all-American *Foster's Coachhouse Tavern* at 22 Montgomery St (☎845/876-8052). Nearby is the pricier but very authentic French *Le Petit Bistro* at 8 E Market St (Thurs–Mon; ☎845/876-7400). Rhinebeck is also home to the New Agey **Omega Institute for Holistic Studies**, which runs a wide range of self-improvement workshops at a large campus east of town on Lake Drive; call for details of current programs (☎845/266-4444 or 1-800/944-1001).

The other good stop on the east bank of the Hudson is **Olana**, the hilltop home of **Frederick Church** (1826–1900), one of the foremost artists of the Hudson River School. High above a bend in the river, across the bridge from the town of Catskill, the quirky but very attractive house rises in an odd blend of Persian and Moorish motifs; obligatory (and very popular) guided **tours** (April–May & Oct Wed–Sun 10am–5pm; June–Sept Wed–Sun 10am–6pm; $3; last tour one hour before closing; for reservations call ☎518/828-0135) take in the bric-a-brac clogged rooms, as well as a number of his picturesque paintings. The grounds are also open daily from 8am until sunset.

Albany

Founded by Dutch fur trappers in the early seventeenth century, **ALBANY** made its money by controlling trade along the Erie Canal, and its reputation by being capital of the state. It's not an unpleasant town, just rather boring, with its contemporary character almost exclusively shaped by political and bureaucratic affairs, though there are a few livelier areas on the fringes.

A good place to start a tour is the **Quackenbush House**, the city's oldest building, built along the river in 1736 and now serving as part of the **Albany Urban Culture Park**. The modern **visitor center** next door at Broadway and Clinton (Mon–Fri 9am–4pm, Sat & Sun 10am–4pm; ☎518/434-6311, Ⓦ www.albany.org) has free maps and occasionally leads guided **tours** of the downtown area, where there are a number of Revolutionary-era homes. It also has engaging displays tracing Albany's history, with a special emphasis on the impact of the Erie Canal, and maps detailing driving tours of the surrounding area, taking in a still-functioning set of **locks** from the original canal along with the impressive industrial legacy of **Troy**, across the Hudson via I-787 N.

Uphill from the waterfront, carved out from the heart of the city in the Sixties and Seventies as part of a controversial urban renewal project, Nelson A. Rockefeller's **Empire State Plaza** replaced 98 acres of nineteenth-century buildings (and displacing hundreds of Albanian families) with a complex that includes a subterranean retail arcade lined with impressive modern art. The view from the **Corning Tower**'s 42nd floor observation deck (daily 10am–2.30pm; free) looks out far across the state, beyond the twisting Hudson River to the Adirondack foothills, the Catskills and the Berkshires in Massachusetts. It also peers down on the neighboring Performing Arts Center, known locally as **"The Egg"** (☎518/473-1845) – which adds the only curves to the Plaza's harsh angularity.

The **New York State Museum** (daily 9.30am–5pm; free; ☎518/474-5877), one level down at the south end of the plaza, reveals everything you could want to know about New York State in imaginative if static tableaux. The excellent section on New York City history is better than anything like it in Manhattan itself, with exhibits on immigration and skyscraper construction, storefronts and trolley cars, and the original set of *Sesame Street*.

The most engaging part of Albany is the few blocks west of the plaza, stretching between Washington and Madison avenues to the open green spaces of **Washington Park**, laid out by Frederick Law Olmsted, the father of American landscape architecture. The recently renovated **Albany Institute of History and Art**, 125 Washington Ave (Tues–Sat 10am–5pm, Sun noon–5pm; $5, free Wed; ☎518/463-4478), has a good range of Hudson River School paintings, and the neighborhood is full of the same sort of nineteenth-century brick-built homes Rockefeller had pulled down to build his Empire State Plaza.

Practicalities

Arrive by Greyhound (☎518/434-0121) or Adirondack Trailways (☎518/436-9651) and it's a short, hilly walk to the heart of downtown; come in by Amtrak and you face a two-mile bus ride (☎518/462-5763) across the river in Rensselaer. If you intend to **stay** the night, bear in mind that downtown lodging is not particularly cheap. Suburban chain motels start at $50 a night while downtown options amount to the *Ramada Inn*, 300 Broadway (☎518/434-4111; ❹), the more comfortable *Albany Crowne Plaza* at State and Lodge streets ☎518/462-6611; ❻), and the exceptionally nice *Mansion Hill Inn*, 115 Philip St (☎518/465-2038; ❻), a B&B in a restored home just down the hill from the state governor's mansion; it also has a fine restaurant. Other good **places to eat** include *Jack's Oyster House*, 42 State St (☎518/465-8854), and the Indonesian *Yono's*, 64 Colvin Ave (☎518/436-7747). **Lark Street**, a few blocks west of the plaza, lit up by fairy lights between Washington and Madison, is the center of Albany's reasonably active gay scene, and the place where the city hangs out at night. *Justin's* at no. 301 (☎518/436-7008) and *Café Hollywood* at no. 275 (☎518/472-9043) serve good progressive American food at moderate prices, while the welcoming *MaMoun's*, 206 Washington Ave (☎518/434-3901), has great inexpensive lamb, chicken and vegetarian dishes. The *Lionheart Blues Café*, 256 Lark St (☎518/436-9530), puts on live music most nights. The college town of **TROY**, across the river, also has a number of lively spots.

North through the Adirondacks

Mountaineers, skiers and dedicated hikers form the majority of visitors to the vast northern region between Albany and the Canadian border. Outdoor pursuits are certainly the main attractions in the rugged wilderness of the **Adirondack Mountains**, though a few small resorts, especially the former Winter Olympic venue of **Lake Placid**, have a bit of life to offer, and the elegant spa town of **Saratoga Springs** nestles invitingly in the delicate countryside of the southern foothills.

Saratoga Springs

For well over a century, **SARATOGA SPRINGS**, just 42 miles north of Albany on I-87, was very much the place to be seen for the northeast's richest and most glittering names. At first, the town's curative waters were the main attraction; then John Morrisey, an Irish boxer, transformed things by opening a **racecourse** and **casino** during the 1860s. At one time, the Morgans, Vanderbilts and Whitneys all had houses in the town, and Diamond Jim Brady, the flashiest among the 1920s nouveau riche, was one of its most ostentatious visitors. Saratoga Springs retains the feel of an exclusive vintage resort during the August horse racing season, but for the rest of the summer it is accessible, affordable and fun. **Broadway**, the main axis, takes in just about every aspect of the modern town from lurid motel signs to the Gothic and Renaissance residential palaces on the northern tip of downtown; most of the town's many good bars are here or in the few blocks just east. The carefully cultivated **Congress Park**, off South Broadway, laid out for the *curistes*, remains a shady retreat from town center traffic. Three of the original mineral springs still flow up to the surface here, funneled out into drinking fountains (the water is tepid and salty, but some people swear by it). Also here is the original **casino**, which when built formed part of a whole city block; it now houses a small historical **museum** (May–Sept Mon–Sat 10am–4pm, Sun 1–4pm; Oct–April Wed–Sat 10am–4pm, Sun 1–4pm, closed Dec–Jan; $3; ☎518/584-6920). The **racetrack** (season runs late July through August, post time 1pm; grandstand $2; ☎518/584-6200) still functions in a rather grand, old-fashioned manner, though there is no longer a strict dress code (beyond shirt and shoes) for the grandstand or the clubhouse (no shorts or tank tops). There's no such pretension at the **harness track** on nearby Crescent Avenue (evening meetings several times a week May–Nov; $2). If you can't get to either, visit the array of paintings, trophies and audiovisual displays at the **National Museum of Racing and Thoroughbred Hall of Fame** on Union Avenue at Ludlow Street (Mon–Sat 10am–4.30pm, Sun noon–4.30pm; $7; ☎518/584-0400). On the southern edge of town, green **Saratoga State Park** (daily 8am–dusk; $4 per car) presents opportunities to swim in great old Victorian pools, picnic, hike or even bathe in one of two bathhouses (Wed–Mon 9am–4pm; ☎518/583-2880). The **Saratoga Performing Arts Center** (☎518/587-3330) – or SPAC – was built during the 1960s in a successful attempt to revive the town's fortunes. As well as being home to the New York City Opera in June, the New York City Ballet in July and the Philadelphia Orchestra in August, it hosts the Newport Jazz Festival in late June and promotes rock concerts by big-name stars.

Practicalities

Central Saratoga Springs is easily explored on foot. **Accommodation** is only a problem during August's race season, or if there's a big gig on at SPAC, when prices can more than double. Central motels include the *Spa Motel*, 73 Ballston Ave (☎518/587-5280 in season or 518/584-6032 during off season; ❸), and the *Turf and Spa*, 140 Broadway (☎518/584-2550 or 1-800/972-1779; ❸). The lavishly restored landmark *Adelphi Hotel*, 365 Broadway (☎518/587-4688; ❻), the *Sheraton*, a little further north at no. 534 Broadway (☎518/584-3000; ❺), and the grand *Gideon Putnam Hotel*, located right in Saratoga Springs State Park, have more character (☎518/584-1354; ❻/❾). The **Chamber of Commerce**, 494 Broadway (☎518/584-3255 or 1-800/526-8970, ⓦwww.saratoga.org), has full lists of accommodation, with prices. **Eating** is also easy.

One longtime favorite is the soul food at *Hattie's*, 45 Phila St (☎518/584-4790), where huge dinners cost under $15; another good bet is *Wheat Fields*, 440 Broadway (☎518/587-0534), with good salads and pasta served on an outdoor patio. *Beverly's*, 47 Phila St (☎518/583-2755), serves great but pricey breakfasts. There's usually good Irish **music** at the *Parting Glass Pub*, 40 Lake Ave (☎518/583-1916). *Nine Maple Avenue*, logically enough at 9 Maple Ave (☎518/583-2582), offers live jazz and blues until the early hours, and the folksy *Caffe Lena*, 47 Phila St (Thurs–Sun; ☎518/583-0022) – where Don McLean first inflicted *American Pie* on the world – still pulls in the crowds.

The Adirondacks

The **Adirondacks** are said by locals to be named after an Iroquois insult for enemies they'd driven into the forests and left to become "bark eaters," and cover an area larger than Connecticut and Rhode Island combined. Until recent decades the area has been almost the exclusive preserve of loggers, fur trappers and a few select New York millionaires who really knew how to get away from it all (E.L. Doctorow's novels *Loon Lake* and *Billy Bathgate* both describe the bucolic retreats of Manhattan mobsters). For sheer grandeur, the region is hard to beat. Forty-six peaks reach to over 4000ft; in summer the purple-green mountains span far into the distance in shaggy tiers, in fall the trees form a russet-red kaleidoscope.

Though Adirondack Trailways buses serve the area, you'll find it hard-going without a **car**. General **information** can be had from the Adirondack Region tourist office (☎1-800/487-6867) or the Welcome Center along I-87 south of Lake George (☎518/761-6366 or 1-800/365-1050). The Adirondack Mountain Club (ADK), PO Box 3055, Lake George, NY 12845 (☎518/668-4447), or the Adirondack Park **Visitor Interpretive Centers** (daily 9am–5pm) in Paul Smiths, north of Saranac Lake (☎518/327-3000) and in Newcomb on Hwy-28 N right in the heart of the park (☎518/582-2000), can provide details on hiking and camping.

Lake George

Though the undulating scenery around **LAKE GEORGE**, 25 miles up I-87 from Saratoga Springs, is undeniably some of the most gorgeous in the region, the village itself is overrun with cheap souvenir shops catering to the thousands of tourists who come here in search of a quick taste of the Adirondacks. The numerous sightseeing cruises, fun parks, factory outlet stores and other diversions now on offer, here and in neighboring Glens Falls, obscure the natural splendor, as well as the region's considerable history. James Fenimore Cooper's *Last of the Mohicans* was based on the Battle of **Fort William Henry**, which was fought here between the British and the French in 1757, but the replica fort (July & Aug daily 10am–9pm; May, June, Sept & Oct daily 10am–5pm; $9.95), along the lakeshore on Canada Street in the center of town, does little to evoke the era when this was the distant frontier.

Blue Mountain Lake

While Lake George and the eastern fringes of the Adirondacks in general hold little to compete with the interior, an hour's drive northwest along Hwy-28 takes you past the headwaters of the Hudson River to the tiny resort of **BLUE MOUNTAIN LAKE**. A handful of **motels** and lakeside **cabins** provide accommodation, and you can swim at the pretty little **beach** that fronts the village center. **Sagamore Great Camp**, about fifteen miles west, in the woods above Raquette Lake, is the only one of the many "Great Camps" that wealthy Easterners constructed in the Adirondacks around the end of the nineteenth century that is open to the public. Not to be confused with the four-star *Sagamore Resort* on an island in Lake George, Sagamore Great Camp was a summer home of the **Vanderbilts**, basically a huge and luxurious log cabin in which they entertained illustrious guests – including Hoagy Carmichael, who supposedly wrote the song *Stardust* while driving the four-mile dirt road that leads up to the house. The still-intact house and grounds are now used as a conference and educational center, and for cross-country skiing in winter; call for details of summer art and photography **classes**, or to reserve a place on a guided two-hour **tour** (July & Aug 10am & 1.30pm daily; Sept & Oct 10am & 1.30pm; rest of year call for details; $9; ℡315/354-5311). Alternatively, if you'd like to get closer to the other, still private Great Camps, you can take a short tour of the area by plane, which gives good views of several; it also gives a clear idea of how uninhabited the region really is. In Inlet, near Raquette Lake, try Bird's Seaplane Service (8.30am–dusk; $20 per person, $50 minimum; ℡315/357-3631) or Payne's ($20 per person, $50 minimum; ℡315/357-3971).

Just north of Blue Mountain Lake on Hwy-30, the twenty-building **Adirondack Museum** (late May to mid-Oct daily 9.30am–5.30pm; $10) has 22 rather bland exhibit areas spread over thirty acres on aspects of regional life, including art, sports, iron mining and wildlife. It's perhaps most memorable for its grand views out over the lake and surrounding mountains.

Lake Placid

The winter sports center of **LAKE PLACID**, twice the proud host of the Winter Olympics, lies thirty miles west of I-87 on Hwy-73. In winter there's thrilling alpine skiing at imposing Whiteface Mountain and all manner of Nordic disciplines at Mount Van Hoevenberg, and in summer you can watch luge athletes practice on refrigerated runs, freestyle skiers somersaulting off dry slopes into swimming pools, and top amateur ice hockey games; ask at the **information center** in the Olympic Center at 216 Main St (℡518/523-2445 or 1-800/44-PLACID, ⓦwww.lakeplacid.com). The mountain slopes also provide challenging terrain for hikers and cyclists; good **mountain bikes**, maps of local trails and **guided tours** are available from High Peaks Cyclery, 331 Main St (℡518/523-3764). In summer, the self-guided **Olympic Site Tour** package (℡518/523-1655; $17) takes you by chair lift to the top of the 393ft ski jump and eight miles up the sheer Whiteface Mountain toll road and back again. At **Mount Van Hoevenberg**, you can do a bobsled run ($30) or bike the extensive trail network ($18 bike rental; $5 trail fee; for information on both, call Olympic Sports Center on ℡518/523-4436).

The town itself is set on two lakes: **Mirror Lake**, which you can sail on in summer and skate on in winter, and larger **Lake Placid**, just to the west, on which you can take a narrated **cruise** in summer ($7.25; ℡518/523-9704). Other attractions include the **Olympic Center** on Main St (℡518/523-3330), which houses four ice rinks and the informative **1932 and 1980 Lake Placid Winter Olympic Museum** ($4). **John Brown's Farm and Grave**, on Hwy-73 outside the village, was where the famous abolitionist brought his family in 1849 to aid a small colony of black farmers and where he conceived his ill-fated raid on Harper's Ferry in an attempt to end slavery. The house is less interesting than his story (see p.458), but at least it's free (late May to late Oct Wed–Sat 10am–5pm, Sun 1–5pm; ℡518/523-3900).

Lake Placid's **accommodation** options range from the somewhat economical to the opulent. The casually elegant *Mirror Lake Inn*, 5 Mirror Lake Drive

(☎518/523-2544; ❺–❾), has over 120 rooms, the best of them palatial, but is as cozy as a small B&B. Facilities include pool, sauna, health club, private beach/skating rink and a top-notch restaurant. *Edelweiss Motel*, 14 Hwy-86 on the east side of town, has rooms which are clean, if a little retro (☎518/523-3821; ❸).The *Keene Valley Hostel* in nearby Keene Valley (☎518/576-2030; ❶) is a great base if you want to be within walking distance of all the best hiking trails.

Lake Placid is virtually a fast-food-free zone and it's possible to **eat well** for comparatively little. *Leslie's* is a much-loved local bakery at 99 Main St (☎518/523-4279), while *Nicola's Over Main*, 2 Marcy Road (☎518/523-4430), does Greek and Italian dinners, including good wood-fired pizza. *Goldberries* at 187 Main St (☎518/523-1799) offers standard fare but has good views of the lake. The waterfront *Cottage Café*, 5 Mirror Lake Drive (☎518/523-9845), is a café/pub serving snacks and unusual specials such as chilled strawberry soup. It's also the town's top après-ski spot, while the central *Hilton* is the main place for **live music**.

Saranac Lake

SARANAC LAKE, ten miles northwest of Lake Placid, is a smaller, more laid-back community. The tranquil lakeshore is lined with lovely gingerbread cottages, most of them built during the late 1800s when this was a popular middle-class retreat and spa. Robert Louis Stevenson spent the winter of 1888 in a small cottage here, now preserved as a **museum** (for details and directions contact the **Saranac Area Chamber of Commerce**, 30 Main St ☎518/891-1990, ⓦwww.saranaclake.com). Saranac Lake is still a rather quiet year-round resort, but makes a great alternative base to Lake Placid as it's close to all facilities and offers better-value accommodation. Among the many motels on Lake Flower Drive, *Sara-Placid Motor Inn*, 120 Lake Flower Drive (☎518/891-2729; ❸), has rooms and suites to suit most budgets, as well as friendly management.

The Thousand Islands

Beyond the Adirondacks, on the broad St Lawrence River that forms the border with Canada, are 1800 barely populated hunks of earth known as the **Thousand Islands**. They share their name with a salad dressing because one c.1900 visitor, George Boldt, president of New York's *Waldorf-Astoria Hotel*, is said to have asked the steward on his yacht to concoct something different for a special luncheon. The resultant orange goo is now famous the world over.

From both **Alexandria Bay** and the smaller fishing port of **Clayton**, boat excursions set out to explore the waterway; the tiny craft are all but swamped by the huge passing cargo ships, larger than many of the islands. For departure times, contact Uncle Sam's Tours (April–Oct daily; in Clayton ☎315/686-3511, in Alexandria Bay ☎315/482-2611 or 1-800/ALEXBAY).

The Finger Lakes

At the heart of the state, southwest of Syracuse on the far side of the Catskills from New York City, are the eleven **Finger Lakes**, narrow channels gouged out by glaciers that have left tell-tale signs in the form of drumlins, steep gorges and any number of waterfalls. With the exception of well-to-do **Ithaca** and tiny **Skaneatles**, few towns compete with the lakeshore scenery, but the area as a whole is a relaxing place to spend some time, particularly if you enjoy sampling **wine**: it comes as a surprise to many people, but the Finger Lakes region – and much of upstate New York – produces a number of good vintages.

Skaneatles and Seneca Falls

SKANEATLES (pronounced "Skinny-Atlas"), crouching at the neck of Skaneatles Lake, is perhaps the prettiest Finger Lakes town. It's also the best place to go swimming in the region: just a block from the town center, and lined by huge resort homes, the appealing bay sports a **beach** and a marina where you can take boat trips and rent watersports equipment. **Accommodation** is sparse, but the handful of motels includes the *Hi-Way Host*, 834 W Genessee St (☎315/685-7633; ❸), and the *Colonial Motel*, one mile west on Hwy-20 (☎315/685-5751; ❷), while the *Sherwood Inn* (☎315/685-3405; ❹), overlooking the lake, is not as expensive as it looks. It also has two good restaurants; cheaper but still scrumptious meals can be had at the ever-popular *Doug's Fish Fry*, 8 Jordan St (☎315/685-3288).

At **SENECA FALLS**, just west of the northern tip of Cayuga Lake, Elizabeth Cady Stanton and a few colleagues planned and held the first Women's Rights Convention in 1848 – 72 years before the Nineteenth Amendment gave all women in the US the right to vote. On the site of the **Wesleyan Chapel**, 136 Fall St, where the first campaign meeting was held, is the **Women's Rights National Historical Park** (daily 9am–5pm; $2; ☎315/568-2991), setting the early women's movement in its historical context. The center also offers a **walking tour** that takes in the small museum at the Cady Stanton house and passes the (privately owned) former home of **Amelia Bloomer**, whose crusade to urge women out of their cumbersome undergarments won her a place in the dictionary. A block east of the visitor center, the **National Women's Hall of Fame** (May–Oct Mon–Sat 9.30am–5pm, Sun noon–4pm; Nov–April Wed–Sat 10am–4pm, Sun noon–4pm; closed Jan; $3; ☎315/568-8060) at 76 Fall St, where over a hundred women, including Emily Dickinson and Sojourner Truth, have been honored for their efforts in fields such as humanitarianism, sports and the arts, makes an interesting stop.

The town itself is a blend of old mills and homes of various architectural styles, tucked away among the mature trees. If you want to stop over, the best **place to stay** is the *Guion House* B&B, at 32 Cayuga St (☎315/568-8129; ❹). There are several reasonable **cafés** along Fall Street. Hwy-89, between Seneca Falls and Ithaca, has been dubbed the **Cayuga Wine Trail**, with dozens of small wineries operating along the west shore of the largest of the Finger Lakes.

Ithaca

Cayuga Lake comes to a halt at its southern end at picturesque **ITHACA**, piled like a diminutive San Francisco high above the lakeshore and culminating in the towers, sweeping lawns and shaded parks of the Ivy League **Cornell University**. On campus, which is cut by striking gorges, creeks and lakes, the sleek, I.M. Pei-designed **Herbert F. Johnson Museum of Art** (Tues–Sun 10am–5pm; free; ☎607/255-6464) merits a visit more for its fifth-floor view of the town and lake than for the unspectacular collection of Asian and contemporary art. The pick of the countless **waterfalls** within a few miles of town is the slender 210ft **Taughannock Falls**, ten miles north, just off Hwy-89, which has a swimming beach close at hand and offers a pleasant trek through the countryside on your way to the falls. **Buttermilk Falls State Park**, two miles south of town on Rte-13, is another delightful spot. Cayuga Lake provides excellent boating and windsurfing opportunities; boards and boats can be rented from the nearby **visitor center** at 904 East Shore Drive, off Hwy-34 N (Mon–Fri 8am-5pm, summer Sat 10am–5pm, Sun 10am-4pm; ☎607/272-1313 or 1-800/28-ITHACA, ⊛www.visitithaca.com).

Greyhound and other **buses** operate out of the terminal at W State and N Fulton. Budget **places to stay** are scarce, though accommodation is on the whole reasonably priced; try the cramped *Hillside Inn*, 518 Stewart Ave (☎607/273-6864; ❸), the *Elmshade Guest House*, 402 S Albany St (☎607/273-1707; ❸), or *Paragon House*, 140 College Ave (☎607/272-0919; ❸), in **Collegetown**, further up the hill near Cornell. The rooms at the *Best Western University Inn*, 1020 Ellis Hollow Rd, on the east edge of campus (☎607/272-6100; ❸), are larger and probably worth the extra expense. Out of term, the *Statler Hotel* on East Avenue within the campus proper, is a pleasant option (☎607/257-2500 or 1-800/541-2501; ❺)

Ithaca boasts two dining and entertainment zones. Downtown, centered around the vehicle-free **Commons**, is the larger and better, and features the top-rated vegetarian **restaurant** of cookbook fame, *Moosewood* (☎607/273-9610), in DeWitt Mall as well as *Café DeWitt*, which offers healthy and filling salads at lunchtime. A block away, *Just a Taste*, 116 N Aurora St (☎607/277-9463), is a lively wine-and-tapas bar, while *Simeon's on the Commons*, 224 E State St (☎607/272-2212), does gourmet sandwiches. Numerous cheap student-oriented places to eat line the streets of Collegetown: check out the Italian *Little Joe's*, 410 Eddy St (☎607/273-2771), or *The Nines*, that serves up the best deep-dish pizza around and has live music, on 311 College Ave (☎607/272-1888). For news of the lively **music** scene – and gigs at the *Haunt*, 114 W Green St (☎607/273-3355) – get the free *Ithaca Times*.

Corning

Forty miles southwest of Ithaca, world-famous **Steuben Glass** has been manufactured in the otherwise undistinguished town of **CORNING** since Frederick Carder started making his characteristic Art Nouveau pieces in 1903. The excellent **Museum of Glass** in the Corning Glass Center traces its history from ancient heads and amulets to modern sculptures and paperweights. Also in the complex, where glass is omnipresent in mirrors and motifs, are the Hall of Science and Technology, full of push-button exhibits, and the Steuben Glass factory itself, where every stage of the production process can be viewed from behind (glass) screens (daily: July & Aug 9am–8pm; Sept–June 9am–5pm; ☎607/937-5371; $11).

The **Rockwell Museum**, ten minutes' stroll away at 111 Cedar St and Denison Parkway (Mon–Sat 9am–5pm, Sun noon–5pm; $5; ☎607/937-5386), has more than two thousand pieces of Steuben glass, plus antique toys and a strong collection of Western art – and is not to be confused with the Norman Rockwell Museum in Stockbridge, Massachusetts. For further information on these attractions, and for help in finding accommodation, contact the **visitors bureau** at 5 W Market St (☎607/936-6544 or 1-866/946-3386, ⊛http://corningsteuben.com).

Toward Niagara Falls: the Erie Canal towns

The fertile farming country stretching from Albany at the head of the Hudson to Buffalo on Lake Erie, along the route of the **Erie Canal**, comprises the agricultural heartland of New York State. The eastern parts – also known as **Central Leatherstocking**, after the protective leggings worn by the area's first settlers – are well off the conventional tourist trails. Unless you want to check out one of the specialist sports museums, like the Baseball Hall of Fame at **Cooperstown**, this is not a high-priority destination.

With the captivating exception of **Niagara Falls**, one of the continent's biggest crowd pullers, there's little to see in the northwest reaches of New York State. Standing out from the mostly flat farmland, the industrial giants of **Rochester**, **Syracuse** and **Buffalo** each possess a couple of worthy museums, but are best approached as bases for seeing the surrounding area (Buffalo, for example, is a good base for Niagara Falls).

Cooperstown

Seventy miles west of Albany, sitting gracefully on the wooded banks of tranquil Otsego Lake, is the almost aggressively pretty **COOPERSTOWN**, christened "Glimmerglass" by novelist James Fenimore Cooper, son of the town's founder. The fact that baseball is said to have originated here on Doubleday Field is commemorated by the inspired and spacious **National Baseball Hall of Fame**, on Main Street. Everything is displayed in such an attention-grabbing manner that even if you know nothing about the game it's difficult to remain uninterested. Babe Ruth gets a whole display to himself, while more of the greats are shown in action in photographs and videos (daily: May–Sept 9am–9pm; Oct–April 9am–5pm, Fri until 8pm; $9.50; ☎607/547-7200). In summer, Cooperstown hosts classical concerts and the Glimmerglass Opera, north on Hwy-80 by the lake.

The local chamber of commerce runs a really helpful little **visitor center** at 31 Chestnut St (Mon–Fri 9am–5pm; ☎607/547-9983, ⊛www.cooperstown-chamber.org). If you're here June through August, leave the car at one of the free parking lots on the edge of town and take the trolley around the various sights (trolley runs 8am–9pm; $2 all-day pass). **Accommodation** in the town itself is expensive, but there's a cluster of clean motels right on gorgeous Otsego Lake, a few miles north on Hwy-80; the *Lake'N Pines* (☎607/547-2790 or 1-800/615-5253; ❸) offers superb value. For **eating**, *Clete Boyer's*, three miles south on Hwy-28 (☎607/544-1112), serves gimmicky but tasty American food.

Canastota

Just before Syracuse, at exit 34 from I-90, nondescript **CANASTOTA** is the home of the **International Boxing Hall of Fame** (May–Sept daily 9am–5pm; Oct–April Mon–Sat 9am–5pm, Sun 9am–4pm; $4; ☎315/697-7095), a mecca for boxing enthusiasts but easily skipped by anyone else. Canastota's links with boxing go back to early in the nineteenth century, and this ten-thousand-strong village has produced two postwar world champions: Carmen Basilio, who took away the middleweight crown of Sugar Ray Robinson in an epic 1958 encounter, and Billy Backus, a welterweight title-holder during the early 1970s. All the greats are represented in the two-room museum, whether by picture, dressing-gown, mouthpiece, handwraps, gloves or bronze fist impressions, and there's a selection of big-fight videos.

Syracuse

A lively but largely unattractive modern city, busy **SYRACUSE** made its name first for the production of salt and, more importantly, for its central position on the Erie Canal. Despite a population nudging half a million, there's little to see, though the presence of Syracuse University gives downtown an active and youthful feel. The redevelopment of **Armory Square**, around Franklin and Fayette streets, as an area of specialty shops, galleries and cafés has gone some way toward adding character to the city center, but the city still feels dominated by the highways and railroads that slice through it.

The **Erie Canal Museum** (daily 10am–5pm; donation; ☎315/471-0593), housed in one of the few surviving canal-era buildings, an 1850s weighing station at 318 E Erie Blvd, tells the story of the long battle between politicians and taxpayers before work on the canal began in 1810. The waterway was designed to link the Great Lakes with New York City via the Hudson, thereby cutting hefty transportation costs – which it did by an average of ninety percent. At first, however, not everyone was in favor, critics speaking of a "big ditch" in which "would be buried the treasure of the state." The project eventually took fifteen years and one thousand lives, and went three million dollars over budget, but it spawned America's first generation of engineers, and after it opened in 1825, prosperous towns quickly sprung up alongside the canal. Erie Boulevard itself was created by filling in the old canal bed, and the industrial surroundings do little to evoke the era, though the reconstructed **canal boat** inside the museum is definitely worth a look.

Good-value **rooms** can be found in downtown's *Econolodge*, 454 James St (☎315/425-0015; ❷), and the fairly central *HI-Downing International Hostel*, 535 Oak St (☎315/472-5788), has $10 dorm beds. For **food**, *Clark's Ale House*, 122 W Jefferson St (☎315/479-9859), is locally famous for its roast beef sandwiches and cheese plates. The *Empire Brewing Co*, 120 Walton St (☎315/475-2337), has an eclectic menu and good beer brewed on the premises, while *Pastabilities*, 311 S Franklin St (☎315/474-1153), is health-conscious and popular. Student numbers ensure a lively **music** scene; consult the resourceful and free *Syracuse New Times*. Good hangouts include the loud, bluesy *Dinosaur BBQ*, 246 W Willow St (☎315/476-1662), and the small, punky *Lost Horizon*, 5863 Thompson Rd (☎315/446-1934). The city's **visitor center** is at 572 S Salina St (Mon–Fri 8.30am–5pm; ☎315/470-1800 or 1-800/234-4SYR, ⓦhttp://chamber.cny.com).

Rochester

In contrast to its sprawling suburbs, downtown **ROCHESTER** is a salubrious place, with its central office-block area bordered by well-heeled mansions on spacious boulevards. High-tech companies such as Bausch & Lomb and Xerox have brought capital to the city, but by far the most conspicuous names on view are those of **Kodak** and its founder, George Eastman. Legacies throughout the metropolitan area include Kodak Park, the Eastman Theater, and above all the **International Museum of Photography** at George Eastman House, two miles from downtown at 900 East Ave (Tues, Wed, Fri & Sat 10am–5pm, Thurs 10am–8pm, Sun 1–5pm; $6.50; ☎716/271-3361). In the modern annex at the rear, a first-rate exhibition of photographic history ranges from high-quality Civil War prints to modern experimental works, plus a space which houses temporary exhibitions, as well as an arthouse cinema. The house itself, fussily restored to its early twentieth-century glory, is mildly interesting; upstairs there's the fun, hands-on Discovery Room plus an informative exhibition on Eastman's. Fittingly, given Eastman's passion for horticulture, the gardens have been superbly maintained and are worth a visit in themselves.

An obsessive collector of anything and everything, local bigwig Margaret Woodbury Strong (1897–1969) bequeathed her estate to the city as the **Strong Museum** on Manhattan Square (Mon–Sat 10am–5pm, Sun 12–5pm; $6). Half devoted to a history of the American family, half obsessed with a history of American consumer culture, it's recently been radically updated to feature interactive exhibits such as a history of Barbie and *Sesame Street*. Pop culture addicts will enjoy its kitsch sensibility, which includes a fully working 1920s carousel and a 1950s diner shipped here wholesale from its original site in Pennsylvania. The theme of celebrating former Rochester denizens continues at the **Susan B. Anthony House** at 17 Madison St, where this groundbreaking suffragist lived from 1866–1906 (June–Aug Wed–Sun 11am–4pm; $6; ☎716/235-6124).

Practicalities

Greyhound drops off at Broad and Chestnut streets downtown. The Amtrak station, 320 Central Ave, is on the north side beyond the I-490 inner loop road; it's served by RTS **buses** (☎716/654-0200). Rochester's **visitor center** is at 45 East Ave between Chestnut and Main (Mon–Fri 8.30am–5pm, Sat 9am–5pm, Sun 10am–3pm; ☎716/546-3070, ⓦwww.visitrochester.com). **Accommodation** is somewhat expensive. Downtown choices include the excellent *428 Mt Vernon* B&B (☎716/271-0792; ❺), at the entrance to lush Highland Park, with private baths in all rooms. Among budget options in the south of the city, near the I-90 Thruway, is the *Red Roof Inn*, 4820 W Henrietta Rd, off I-90 exit 46 (☎716/359-1100; ❸).

Popular **places to eat** in the fairly lively downtown include *Aladdin's Natural Eatery*, 646 Monroe Ave (☎716/442-5000), serving inexpensive Middle Eastern food, the pub-style *Old Toad*, 277 Alexander St (☎716/232-2626), where British staff serve beer and cheap meals, and the restored Art Deco *Highland Park Diner*, 960 S Clinton Ave (☎716/461-5040). *Jine's Café*, 658 Park Ave, is good value for breakfast (☎716/461-1280) and if you want to sample a Garbage Plate, the local delicacy comprising a platter of just about anything that can be successfully deep fried, head over to *Nick Tahou Hots* at 320 Main St (☎716/436-0184). Keep an eye out, too, for the local soft drink, Jolt, which tastes like a normal cola but packs a big wallop of caffeine.

Out from Rochester

The **Lake Ontario State Parkway** is a quiet, scenic way of driving to Niagara Falls from Rochester, taking about an hour longer than the standard route along I-90 via Buffalo. The parkway starts eight miles from downtown at the end of Lake Avenue, near the popular **Ontario Beach Park**. This short golden strand of shore, rimmed by exclusive holiday homes, is a real poseur's paradise; you may well feel self-conscious if your shades don't match up to the ubiquitous (locally manufactured) Ray-Bans.

If big crowds and the churning noise of speedboats are not your thing, head twenty miles along the parkway to the more secluded **Hamlin Beach State Park** ($3 per car). The parkway passes through few towns, and the best place to stop for refreshments is the small and attractive Point Breeze harbor, ten miles on from Hamlin.

Buffalo

As I-90 sweeps down into the state's second largest city, **BUFFALO**, downtown looms up in a cluster of Art Deco spires and glass-box skyscrapers – Manhattan in miniature on Lake Erie. The city's early twentieth-century prosperity is reflected in such architecturally significant structures as the towering 1928 **City Hall** (the tallest in the country, and with a free observation deck on the top floor), the deep red terra-cotta relief of Louis Sullivan's **Guaranty Building** on Church Street, as well as major buildings by H.H. Richardson, Eliel Saarinen and Frank Lloyd Wright. However, the dereliction of the immediate environs suggests that the Rust Belt of rotting industrial towns may now have reached Buffalo. The city has only distant memories of the boom years, when the massive **grain elevators** along the Erie waterfront were busy 24 hours a day.

That Buffalo's wealthy merchants were a cultured lot is also apparent in the excellent **Albright–Knox Art Gallery**, 1285 Elmwood Ave (Tues–Sat 11am–5pm, Sun noon–5pm; $4; ☎716/882-8700), two miles north of downtown amid the green spaces of the F.L. Olmsted-designed **Delaware Park**. One of the top modern collections in the world, it's especially strong on recent American and European art: the Color Field painters, Abstract Expressionism, Pop, Op and Kinetic Art, with Pollock, Rothko, Warhol and Rauschenberg among the names. Other highlights include thirty large paintings by Clyfford Still, and a fine selection of pieces by earlier artists such as Matisse, Picasso and Monet. There's also a tasty, chic restaurant open daily for lunch from noon–3pm.

The area around Delaware Park is Buffalo's choicest neighborhood, featuring several homes designed by Frank Lloyd Wright (call ☎716/884-0095 for guided architectural tour information). Between here and downtown is **Allentown**, Buffalo's most bohemian quarter, its leafy streets lined by lovely Victorian homes as well as numerous good cafés, bars and restaurants. Allen Street between Main Street and Elmwood Avenue holds some of the best examples of nineteenth-century architecture; some of the area around Theatre Place downtown is also good (see overleaf).

Being a staunchly blue-collar city, Buffalo loves its professional **sports** teams: football's Bills (☎716/649-0015), ice hockey's Sabres (☎716/855-4100) and baseball's Bisons (☎716/846-2003 or 1-888/223-6000) who, as the top farm team for the Cleveland Indians, attract over a million fans per season to downtown's modern and very pleasant ballpark.

The **Lake Erie shoreline** west of Buffalo is lined by numerous beaches where **windsurfers** skim across the water and do flips in the waves, while the Miss Buffalo boat tours (☎716/856-6696; $12 and up), which leave from 79 Marine Drive next to the Naval and Servicemen's Park, provide a good view of the city skyline. To the south, in the town of Orchard Park, the **Burgwardt Bicycle Museum** (Mon–Sat 11am–5pm, Sun 1.30–5pm; $4.50; ☎716/662-3853) holds over two hundred antique bikes and engaging displays of cycling memorabilia.

Arrival, information and accommodation

Greyhound, Empire Trailways (☎716/852-1750), Metro Bus and Metro Rail, the city's new tramway (both ☎716/855-7211), all operate from the downtown depot at Ellicott and Church streets. To get to **Niagara Falls**, take bus #40 (1hr; hourly 7am–10pm; $1.85) or in high season you can also take the Tourist Express ($5). Amtrak **trains** to and from Niagara Falls and Toronto stop some six blocks away at Exchange and Washington streets; Chicago-bound trains only stop in the eastern suburb of Depew, eight miles from town but close to the **airport** (☎716/632-3115). There's a helpful **visitor center** at 617 Main St (☎716/852-0511 or 1-800/BUFFALO, ⓦwww.buffalocvb.org).

The Adam's Mark 120 Church St ☎716/845-5100, ⓦwww.adamsmark.com/buffalo/. Recently renovated, this hotel has comfortable, upscale rooms, plus an indoor pool and free use of the health club. **❻**

Hampton Inn & Suites 220 Delaware Ave ☎716/855-2223. A safe bet in the heart of the nightlife district downtown, with free breakfast. **❹**

HI-Buffalo Hostel 667 Main St ☎716/852-5222. Very central hostel with beds for $15. Nothing special, but the cheapest option by far.

Hotel Lenox 140 North St ☎716/884-1700 or 1-800/82-LENOX. The one moderately priced place to stay (besides the hostel) near downtown, with a $10 discount for students. **❸**

Roycroft Inn 40 S Grove St, East Aurora ☎716/652-5552 or 1-877/652-5552. Immaculately refurbished inn located a half-hour drive east of Buffalo, formerly the centerpiece of the Roycroft Arts and Crafts Community. The on-site restaurant serves tasty meals. **❺**

Eating, drinking and nightlife

The heart of blue-collar Buffalo's downtown centers on Chippewa and Main streets: plenty of restaurants are within easy reach and there's ample parking. For a quick **snack**, the cheap food stalls and tiny Polish cafés of ancient **Broadway Market**, 999 Broadway, are well worth perusing, too. The main nightlife drag, along Chippewa from Delaware Avenue to Main Street, has plenty of sports bars and nightclubs. The majority of theaters and venues that house the city's burgeoning **arts scene** are handily grouped nearby along Main Street between Chippewa and Tupper streets. For further information, pick up the free weeklies *Blue Dog Press* or *Art Voice*.

Anchor Bar 1047 Main St ☎716/886-8920. The city's specialty of buffalo (spicy chicken) wings with blue cheese and celery dressing is said to have been invented here. Lunch costs around $7, and there's occasionally live jazz at night.

Calumet Arts Café 56 W Chippewa St ☎716/855-2220. A good late-night bar and restaurant, with jazz, blues, folk and world music.

Colter Bay 561-565 Delaware Ave, Allentown ☎716/882-1330. Lively sports bar, with a good selection of dark beers and scotch.

Hemmingway's 492 Pearl St ☎716/852-1937.

Serves big portions of hearty if standard American food.

Nietzsche's 248 Allen St ☎716/886-8539. A neighborhood institution, with friendly staff, hosting a wide variety of live acts seven days a week; there's room for dancing in the back.

Osake 235 Delaware Ave ☎716/842-6261. This casual café serves cheap sushi and noodles; not a place to linger, but good value.

Spot Coffee 227 Delaware Ave ☎716/856-2739. A local joint serving basic food and good drinks; it's open 24hrs on weekends and hosts regular live music performances.

Niagara Falls

Every second, almost three quarters of a million gallons of water explode over the knife-edge **NIAGARA FALLS**, right on the border with Canada some twenty miles north of Buffalo on I-190. This awesome spectacle is made even more so by the variety of methods laid on to help you get closer to it: boats, catwalks, observation towers and helicopters all push as near to the curtain of gushing water as they dare. At night the falls are lit up, and the colored waters tumble dramatically into blackness, while in winter the whole scene changes as the falls freeze to form gigantic razor-tipped icicles.

Many visitors will, however, find the whole experience a bit too gimmicky; no commercial opening has been left unexploited (Oscar Wilde quipped that

NIAGARA FALLS

Whirlpool Rapids & Niagara Power Project

All Tucked Inn
WALNUT AVENUE

VICTORIA AVE

CANADA

Budget Inn
FERRY AVENUE 62

Helicopter Rides

MAIN STREET

1ST ST

2ND STREET

3RD STREET

4TH STREET

5TH STREET

6TH STREET

7TH STREET

8TH STREET

NIAGARA STREET

RAINBOW BRIDGE

Niagara River

NIAGARA PARKWAY RIVER ROAD

Maid of the Mist Boat Dock

PROSPECT ST

SO BOUND

NO BOUND

(i) Bus Station

Prospect Point Observation Tower

FALLS MALL

3RD STREET

Convention Center

American Falls

Luna Island

4TH STREET

Travelodge Falls View

Bridal Veil Falls

Green Island

Cave of the Winds

RAINBOW BOULEVARD

Terrapin Point

USA

BUFFALO AVENUE

Goat Island

ROBERT MOSES PARKWAY

Horseshoe Falls

Niagara River

Three Sisters Islands

0   400 yds

Buffalo

he would have been more impressed if the falls ran upwards; at least no one's tried that yet) and now corporate big-hitters like the *Hard Rock Café* have joined in the action, pushing the place closer to an aquatic Vegas (there's already a **casino** on the Canadian side). Don't expect too much; neither the small city of **Niagara Falls**, a smelly, shabby industrial eyesore despite recent efforts to spruce it up, nor the more developed tinsel town of **Niagara, Canada**, is a place to savor in any way. Once you've seen the falls, from as many different angles as you can manage, there's no point in sticking around, and you'll have a better time heading on to Buffalo (or Rochester, or anywhere) rather than trying to rustle up some fun here. However, one of the biggest **factory outlet malls** in the country is just north of the city, and seems to be almost as big a draw as the falls these days.

Arrival and information

Amtrak **trains**, en route between New York and Toronto, stop a long two miles from downtown at 27th Street and Lockwood Road. If you arrive at the **bus station** (☎716/285-9319), on 4h Street and Niagara Street, you're next door to the official **Welcome Center**, 310 4th St (daily: July & Aug 9am–8pm; Sept–June 9am–5pm; ☎716/285-2400 or 1-800/338-7890, ⊛www.nfcvb.com). There's also a kiosk in Prospect Park by the falls, as well as countless other places in town that claim to be visitor centers but are in fact just fronts for tour companies.

Arriving **by car**, follow the signs to the main parking lot, which is right next to the falls and costs $5 – watch out for the helpful but unofficial rangers who'll steer you into privately owned, high-priced lots just outside the park. Local Metro Transit System **buses** (☎716/285-9319) run to all areas of the city

($1.25) and to Buffalo (bus #40 or #60 express; $1.85 each way). To send the obligatory postcards, you'll need the **post office** at 615 Main St (Mon–Fri 8.30am–5pm, Sat 9am–noon; zip code 14302; ☎716/285-7561).

Accommodation

Places to stay in central Niagara can be quite expensive if you don't plan ahead or shop around, but US-62, east of Hwy-190, is lined with dozens of motels with rates beginning at $30. Many of these are pretty tacky, targeting the thousands of honeymoon couples who come here every year (despite Wilde's assertion that the falls "must be one of the earliest if not keenest disappointments of American married life"). With the falls under an hour's drive away, both **Rochester** and **Buffalo** make better bases.

The closest place to **camp** is seven miles from downtown at the **Niagara Falls Campground & Lodging**, 2405 Niagara Falls Blvd in Wheatfield (☎716/731-3434), for $18 a night.

All Tucked Inn B&B 574 3rd St ☎716/282-0919. Cozy B&B with nice if basic rooms. **❷**
Budget Inn 492 Main St ☎716/285-8366. No-frills downtown motel. **❸**
HI-Niagara Falls 1101 Ferry Ave ☎716/282-3700. Friendly, well-run hostel with beds for $13 ($15 nonmembers). Facilities include showers, kitchen and TV lounge. Preference is given to HI members and reservations are necessary in summer.

Park Place B&B 740 Park Place ☎716/282-4626. Comfortable home near downtown with full breakfast and afternoon pastries. **❸**
Travelodge Falls View 201 Rainbow Blvd ☎716/285-9321 or 1-800/876-3297. Landmark hotel with grand lobby but rather plain rooms. The rates fluctuate, dropping dramatically off-season. **❷**–**❺**

The Falls

Niagara Falls comprises three distinct cataracts. The tallest are the **American** and **Bridal Veil** falls on the American side, separated by tiny Luna Island and plunging over jagged rocks in a 180ft drop; the broad **Horseshoe Falls** which curve their way over to Canada are probably the most impressive. They date back a mere twelve thousand years, when the retreat of melting glaciers allowed water trapped in Lake Erie to gush north to Lake Ontario. Back then the falls were seven miles down river, but constant erosion has cut them back to their present site. The falls are colorfully lit up at night, and many say they're most beautiful in winter, when the grounds are covered in snow and the waters turn to ice.

Getting around Niagara Falls State Park is easy, thanks to the convenient but tacky **viewmobile** trolley ($4.50) which connects all car parks and the major sightseeing points. The best views on the American side are from the **Prospect Point Observation Tower** (daily 10am–5pm; 50¢), and from the area at its base where the water rushes past; Terrapin Point on **Goat Island** in the middle of the river has similar views of Horseshoe Falls. The nineteenth-century tightrope-walker Blondin crossed the Niagara repeatedly near here, and even carried passengers across on his back; other suicidal fools over the years have taken the plunge in barrels (see box opposite) The reasons such craziness has long been banned become self-evident when you approach the towering cascade on the not-to-be-missed **Maid of the Mist** boat trip from the foot of the observation tower (April–Oct Mon–Fri 10am–6pm every 30 mins, Sat & Sun 10am–6pm every 15 mins; $8.50; ☎716/284-4233). From Goat Island, the **Cave of the Winds** tour leads down to the base of the falls by elevator to within almost touching distance of the water and offers a magical nighttime view as it runs well into the evening (mid-May to late Oct; $6; ☎716/278-1730). A combination pass for these and other attractions costs $24. Rainbow

Maniacs and Miracles

Fifteen people have taken the plunge over Niagara's 170-foot **Horseshoe Falls** – and, remarkably, ten of them survived the fall. The first daredevil was 63-year-old Annie Taylor in 1901, who rode in a wooden barrel and suffered only minor bruises from her journey. Since then, thrillseekers have followed her lead, using everything from giant rubber balls to water tanks as craft: the last successful navigation of the falls was in 1995, by a man who'd already survived one attempt and had brought his girlfriend along for a second try. Those less lucky include Red Hill, killed in 1945 while using a vessel he called "The Thing" built of little more than inner tubes and netting. Other deaths have been equally pointless: from a would-be stuntman in a kayak, who refused a helmet for fear it would obscure his face on film, to a jet skier whose parachute, improperly packed, failed to open when he overshot the falls.

The most miraculous survival story, though, is that of Roger Woodward, a seven-year-old on a boat trip with his teenage sister in the upper Niagara River in the summer of 1960. When the boat developed motor trouble and capsized, they were thrown into the river, from where his sister was rescued. Roger and the captain, James Honeycutt, went over the falls wearing nothing but swimsuits and life preservers. Honeycutt was killed but the boy surfaced near a tour boat at the base of the falls, bruised and concussed but alive, making him the only person ever to survive an unprotected trip over the falls.

helicopter tours (☎716/284–2800) are a more expensive proposition at $50 per person for a ten-minute ride. To check the view out from Niagara, Ontario, it's a twenty-minute walk across the **Rainbow Bridge** to the Canadian side (25¢ each way; bring ID and check with the US Immigration officials before heading across), where you get an arguably better view, bigger crowds and even more tawdry commercialism. Driving across is inadvisable: the toll for a car is just 75¢, but parking on the other side can cost more than $15.

As you look on in awe, reflect that you're seeing only about half the volume of water – the rest is diverted to hydroelectric power stations. The full story of this engineering feat is related at the free **Niagara Power Project Visitors Center** in nearby Lewiston (daily 9am–5pm; free; ☎716/285-3211). With your own transportation it's also possible to trace the inhospitable Niagara Gorge two miles along the dramatic Robert Moses Parkway to the **Whirlpool Rapids**, a violent maelstrom swollen by broken trees and other flotsam. Ten miles east of Niagara Falls, the town of **LOCKPORT** takes its name from the series of locks that raise and lower boats some 65ft at the western end of the Erie Canal. You can see the impressive flight of locks from the Pine Street Bridge, or up close on canal boat **tours** (May–Oct daily at 12.30pm & 3pm, also 10am on Sat, June–Aug additional daily tours at 10am & 7pm; $11.50; ☎716/693-3260).

Eating and drinking

Though most of the **eating options** in Niagara Falls are fast-food joints of indifferent quality, there are a few decent local bars and restaurants – with some better places over in Canada.

Atrium 219 4th St ☎716/282-1734. Affordable American standards and pasta in the *Ramada Inn*.
The Bakery and Ports of Call Restaurant 3004 Niagara St ☎716/282-9498. A bit out of the way but offers a wide variety of European dishes for $10–20. The bar makes a good spot for a quiet drink.

Como's Restaurant 2200 Pine Ave ☎716/285-9341. A good, standard option with huge portions and a reasonably priced deli.
Riverside Inn 115 S Water St, Lewiston ☎716/754-8206. Waterfront property built in 1871, ten minutes' drive north of the falls, with a menu that approaches fine dining.

Pennsylvania

PENNSYLVANIA, which, but for a small stretch on Lake Erie is the only landlocked state in the northeast, was explored by the Dutch in the early 1600s, settled by the Swedes forty years later, and claimed by the British in 1664. Charles II of England, who owed a debt to the Penn family, rid himself of the potentially troublesome young **William Penn**, an enthusiastic advocate of religious freedom, by granting him land in the colony in 1682. Penn Jr. immediately established a "holy experiment" of "brotherly" love and tolerance, naming the state for his father and setting a good example by signing a peaceful cohabitation treaty with the Native Americans. Most of the early agricultural settlers were religious refugees: Quakers like Penn himself, Mennonites from Germany and Switzerland, to be joined later by Irish Catholics during the potato famines of the nineteenth century..

"The keystone state" was crucial in the development of the US. Politicians and thinkers like **Benjamin Franklin** congregated in Philadelphia – home of both the Declaration of Independence and the Constitution – and were prominent in articulating the ideas behind the Revolution. Later, the battle in Gettysburg, south Pennsylvania – best remembered for Abraham Lincoln's immortal **Gettysburg Address** – marked a turning point in the Civil War. Pennsylvania was also vital industrially: Pittsburgh, in the west, was the world's leading steel producer in the nineteenth century, and nearly all the nation's anthracite coal is still mined here.

The two great urban centers of **Philadelphia** and **Pittsburgh**, both lively and vibrant tourist destinations, are at opposite ends of the state. The three hundred miles between them, though predominantly agricultural, are topographically diverse. There are over one hundred state parks, with green rolling countryside in the east, brooding forests in the west, and in the northeast, the rivers, lakes and valleys of the Poconos. **Lancaster County**, home to traditional Amish farmers, and the **Gettysburg** battlefield both heave with busloads of day-trippers, while the Hershey chocolate factory, minutes away from **Harrisburg**, the capital, draws thousands of cocoa-loving visitors each year.

Getting around Pennsylvania

Although to appreciate the less-populated stretches of Pennsylvania you really need a **car**, public transportation is adequate if you organize your trip carefully. Both I-76 (the Pennsylvania Turnpike) and I-80 sweep all the way across to Ohio, nearly five hundred miles east to west. US-30 (the Lincoln Highway) also runs east–west between Philadelphia and Pittsburgh, past Lancaster City, York and Gettysburg, while the prettiest north–south route is US-15, from Maryland to New York State, which follows the Susquehanna River for about fifty miles.

Amtrak crosses daily from Philadelphia to Pittsburgh, stopping at Lancaster City, Harrisburg and other smaller towns. **Greyhound** covers all the major cities and some small towns not served by rail, but its routes can be circuitous; check arrival times when buying your ticket, especially if you need to make a connection.

Philadelphia

The original capital of the nation, **PHILADELPHIA** was laid out by William Penn Jr. in 1682, on a grid system that was to provide the pattern for most American cities. It was envisaged as a "greene countrie towne" and today, for all its historical and cultural significance, it still manages to retain a certain quaintness. Just a few blocks away from the noise, crowds, heat and dust of downtown, shady cobbled alleys stand lined with red-brick colonial houses, while the peace and quiet of huge Fairmount Park make it easy to forget you're in a major metropolis.

Settled by **Quakers**, Philadelphia prospered swiftly on the back of trade and commerce, and by the 1750s had become the second largest city in the British Empire. Economic power fueled strong revolutionary feeling, and the city was the capital during the **War of Independence** (except for nine months under British occupation in 1777–78). It also served as the US capital until 1800, while Washington, DC was being built. The **Declaration of Independence** was written, signed and first publicly read here in 1776, as was the **US Constitution** ten years later. Philadelphia was also a hotbed of new ideas in the arts and sciences, as epitomized by the scientist, philosopher, statesman, inventor and printer **Benjamin Franklin**.

Philadelphia, which translated from Greek means "City of Brotherly Love," is in fact one of the most **ethnically mixed** US cities, with substantial communities of Italians, Irish, Eastern Europeans and Asians living side by side among the majority black population. Many of the city's **black** residents are descendants of the migrants who flocked here after the Civil War when, like Chicago, Philadelphia was seen as a place of tolerance and liberalism. More recently, it voted in the nation's first black mayor, and has the country's best museum dedicated to African-American history and culture. On the downside, Philadelphia is also the place where, as part of a huge police effort to dislodge the black separatist group MOVE, a bomb dropped from a helicopter set fire to entire city blocks, killing women and children and leaving many hundreds homeless.

Once known as "Filthydelphia," and the butt of endless derision from W.C. Fields in the 1930s (as in his famous epitaph: "On the whole, I'd rather be in Philadelphia"), the city underwent a remarkable resurgence preparing for the nation's bicentennial celebrations in 1976. Philadelphia's strength today is its great energy – fueled by history, strong cultural institutions, and a new influx of income due to its new downtown convention center – grounded in its many staunchly traditional neighborhoods, especially Italian **South Philadelphia**. An impressive amount of new construction and revitalization is currently being undertaken in the downtown area, further testimony of the city's economic boom.

Arrival and information

Philadelphia's **International Airport** (☎215/937-6800) is eight miles southwest of the city off I-95. Taxis into town cost around $20 (try Yellow Cab; ☎215/829-4222), and the South East Pennsylvania Transit Authority (SEPTA) runs **trains** every thirty minutes (6am–midnight; $5.50; see transportation below) to three downtown destinations: 30th Street near the university, Suburban Station near City Hall and Market East, adjacent to the Greyhound terminal at 1001 Filbert St (☎215/931-4000). The very grand 30th Street Amtrak station, the second busiest in the US, is just across the Schuylkill River in the university area (Amtrak passengers can transfer downtown on SEPTA

PHILADELPHIA

Delaware River

Benjamin Franklin Bridge

Independence Seaport

0   400 yds

Eastern State Penitentiary

Philadelphia Museum of Art

Fairmount Park

PENNSYLVANIA AVENUE

Rodin Museum

Free Library

Franklin Institute Science Museum

BENJAMIN FRANKLIN PARKWAY

Schuylkill River

30th Street Station

Drexel University

University of Pennsylvania

Museum of Archeology & Anthropology

ARCH ST

WALNUT STREET

FAIRMONT AVENUE

WALLACE STREET

MT. VERNON STREET

GREEN STREET

SPRING GARDEN STREET

CALLOWHILL STREET

RACE STREET

VINE STREET EXPRESSWAY

JOHN F. KENNEDY BOULEVARD

MARKET STREET

CHESTNUT STREET

SANSOM STREET

WALNUT STREET

LOCUST STREET

SPRUCE STREET

PINE STREET

LOMBARD STREET

SOUTH STREET

RITTENHOUSE SQUARE

Pennsylvania Academy of the Fine Arts

CENTER CITY

Mutter Museum

Rosenbach Museum

BROAD STREET

JUNIPER STREET

City Hall

Convention Center

Reading Terminal Market

CHINATOWN

Edgar Allan Poe National Historic Site

Franklin Square

FRONT STREET

2ND STREET

3RD STREET

4TH STREET

5TH STREET

6TH STREET

7TH STREET

8TH STREET

9TH STREET

10TH STREET

11TH STREET

12TH STREET

13TH STREET

BROAD STREET

15TH STREET

16TH STREET

17TH STREET

18TH STREET

19TH STREET

20TH STREET

21ST STREET

22ND STREET

23RD STREET

24TH STREET

25TH STREET

26TH ST.

Betsy Ross House

ELFRETH'S ALLEY

Christ Church

American-Jewish History Museum

Free Quaker Meeting House

African American Museum in Philadelphia

Independence Mall

Liberty Bell

Independence National Historic Park

Independence Hall & Congress Hall

Philosophical Hall

Washington Square

First Bank of the US

INHP Visitor Center

DOCK STREET

Penn's Landing

OLD CITY

SOCIETY HILL

Physick House

Head House Square

Italian Market

Subway station

for free; ask when you purchase your ticket), opposite the city's main (24–hour) **post office** at 30th and Market (zip code 19104).

The excellent **visitor center**, 1525 JFK Blvd (daily 9am–5pm; ☎215/636-1666 or 1-800/537-7676, ⓦwww.gophila.com) at the Penn Center subway station in the heart of downtown, supplies a wealth of information and can help with accommodation.

City transportation

SEPTA (☎215/580-780 0) runs an extensive **bus** system and a **subway** (both 6.30am–1am). The most useful subway lines cross the city east–west (Market–Frankford line) and north–south (Broad Street line); the handiest bus route is **#76**, which runs from Penn's Landing and the Independence Hall area out along Market Street past City Hall to the museums and Fairmount Park. Bus and subway services require exact fares of $2; **day passes**, which are also good for a ride to or from the airport, go for $6. Bright purple **PHLASH** buses run a handy downtown loop (☎215/580-7500; $2 one way, $4 day pass, exact change required).

City tours

Philadelphia Trolley Works (☎215/925-TOUR) cruises the historic area and Fairmount Park in fake streetcars on ninety-minute narrated jaunts ($18 for a day pass – board at any of the trolley's 20 stops); you'd do much better to get a map and wander around on your own. The best, guided **walking tours** are offered by the Foundation for Architecture (☎215/569-3187; $8), while Poor Richard's Walking Tours (☎215/206-1682; call for prices) are run by University of Pennsylvania graduate students and are for serious history buffs. Alternatively, Centipede Tours offers candlelight walks through the hidden gardens and courtyards of Society Hill, complete with a costumed guide; the tours leave from the Welcome Park at 2nd and Walnut (June–Oct Fri–Sat 6.30pm; ☎215/735-3123; $5). Philadelphia Trolley Works (☎215/925-TOUR; from $16) offer tours around downtown and Fairmount Park with stops throughout the city, while companies such as the 76 Carriage Co (☎215/923-8516) run narrated thirty-minute horse-drawn tours around the historic district for $30 (1–4 people; daily 10am-6pm).

Accommodation

Philadelphia's luxury downtown **hotels** are prohibitively expensive, though at weekends there's a chance of getting a reduced rate. The visitor center is a great resource for accommodation discounts. **B&Bs** are a good option, but often need to be arranged in advance. B&B Center City, 1804 Pine St (☎215/735-1137), can arrange rooms throughout the metropolitan area for between $50 and $100 per night.

Comfort Inn 100 N Christopher Columbus Blvd ☎215/627-7900. High-rise hotel in a good location near Penn's Landing; rates include continental breakfast. ❹

HI-Bank Street Hostel 32 S Bank St ☎215/922-0222 or 1-800/392-HOST. Friendly hostel wedged between INHP (see overleaf) and Old City, with bunk beds for $18 (members), $21 (nonmembers), plus free tea and coffee. Closed 10am–4.30pm; curfew 12.30am, 1am Fri & Sat.

HI-Chamounix Mansion Philadelphia West Fairmount Park ☎215/878-3676 or 1-800/379-0017. Quaker country estate in a gorgeous park setting, but a bit of a trek from downtown (take bus #38 from Market St to Ford and Cranston and then walk for a mile). Midnight curfew, closed 11am–4.30pm and mid-Dec to mid-Jan; beds $13 HI members, $16 others.

Holiday Inn Cityline 4100 Presidential Blvd at City Ave ☎215/477-0200 or 1-800/642-8982.

Comfortable hotel with bar, restaurant and indoor pool in exclusive Main Line district, 10 miles from downtown. Handy for restaurants and stores in Manayunk and a 15min drive from downtown. ❹
International House 3701 Chestnut St ☎215/387-5125. Mostly single rooms with shared baths adjacent to the University of Pennsylvania. ❸
Penn's View Inn 14 N Front St ☎215/922-7600. Exceptional service and clean, comfortable rooms

in Old City, with a very fine wine bar next to the lobby. Continental breakfast included. ❼
Shippen Way Inn 418 Bainbridge St ☎215/627-7266. Newly renovated, family-run B&B a block from South St with nine cozy rooms. ❹
Thomas Bond House 129 S 2nd St ☎215/923-8523 or 1-800/845-BOND. Twelve-room 1769 B&B near INHP, slightly marred by an ugly parking lot at the rear. ❹/❺

The City

Philadelphia stretches for about two miles from the Schuylkill (pronounced *Schoolkill*) River on the west to the Delaware on the east; the urban area extends for many miles to the north and south, but everything you're likely to want to see is right in the central swath. The city's central districts are compact, walkable and readily accessible from each other; Penn's sensibly planned grid system makes for easy sightseeing.

Independence Hall National Park

Any tour of Philadelphia should start with **Independence National Historic Park**, or **INHP**, "America's most historic square mile," which covers a mere four blocks just west of the Delaware River between Walnut and Arch streets, but can take more than a day to explore in full. The solid redbrick buildings here, not all of which are open to the public, epitomize the Georgian (and after the Revolution, Federalist) obsession with balance and symmetry.

All INHP sites (unless otherwise specified) are open 365 days a year and admission is free; hours are usually 9am to 5pm, sometimes longer in summer. The **visitor center** at 6th and Market streets (daily 8:30am–5pm, closed Christmas, Thanksgiving & Easter; ☎215/965-7676 or 1-800/537-7676, ⓦ www.independencevisitorcenter.com) has maps and shows a short, somewhat ghostly film, *Independence*, directed by John Huston. Free **tours** set off from the rear of the east wing of Independence Hall, the single most important site, as well as from the visitor center itself – call to check schedules. Throughout the day, costumed actors perform patchy but informative skits in various locations across the site – pick up a copy of the *Historic Philadelphia Gazette* pamphlet for listings.

It's best to reach **Independence Hall** early, to avoid the hordes of tourists and school parties. Built in 1732 as the Pennsylvania State House, this was where the Declaration of Independence was prepared and signed and, after the pealing of the Liberty Bell, given its first public reading on July 8, 1776. Today, in the room in which Jefferson et al drafted and signed the United States Constitution, you can see George Washington's high-backed chair with the half-sun on the back – Franklin, in optimistic spirit, called it "the rising sun."

The **Liberty Bell** itself hung in Independence Hall from 1753, ringing to herald vital announcements such as victories and defeats in the Revolutionary War. Stories as to how it received its famous crack vary; one tells that it occurred while tolling the funeral of Chief Justice Marshall in 1835. Whatever the truth, it rang publicly for the very last time on George Washington's birthday in 1846.

Later in the century, the bell's inscription from Leviticus, advocating liberty "throughout all the land unto all the inhabitants," made it an anti-slavery symbol for the New England abolitionists – the first to call it the Liberty Bell. After the Civil War the silent bell was adopted as a symbol of reconciliation and embarked on a national rail tour. The well-traveled and somewhat lumpen icon now rests at eye level in a purpose-built concrete-and-glass **pavilion** on Market Street between 5th and 6th streets. After endless complaints about the pavilion's architecture, it's due to move in late 2002 to a neocolonial style home not far away that's been designed to better blend in with the rest of INHP.

Next door to Independence Hall on 6th and Chestnut streets, **Congress Hall**, built in 1787 as Philadelphia County Courthouse, is where members of the new United States Congress first took their places, and where all the patterns for today's government were established. The **First Bank of the United States** at 3rd and Chestnut streets was established in 1797 to formalize the new union's currency – a vital task given that even Rhode Island, the smallest state, had three different types of currency in use.

In 1774, delegates of the first Continental Congress – predecessor of the US Congress – chose defiantly to meet at **Carpenter's Hall**, 320 Chestnut St, rather than the more commodious State House, to air their grievances against the English king. Today the building exhibits early tools and furniture (Tues–Sun 10am–4pm). Directly north, **Franklin Court**, 313 Market St, is a tribute, on the site of his home, to Benjamin Franklin. The house no longer stands, but steel frames outline the original structure. An underground museum has dial-a-quote recordings of his pithy sayings and the musings of his contemporaries, and there's a working printshop. The **B Free Franklin Post Office**, 316 Market St, sells stamps and includes a small postal museum. Other buildings in the park include the original **Free Quaker Meeting House**, two blocks north of Market at 5th and Arch, built in 1783 by the small group of Quakers who actually fought in the Revolutionary War. There's also the **Philosophical Hall**, 104 S 5th St, still used today by the nation's first philosophical debating society (founded by Franklin). The building is closed to the public, but features a statue of Ben in intellectual mode, garbed in a fetching toga.

Old City

INHP runs north into **Old City**, Philadelphia's earliest commercial area, above Market Street near the riverfront. Washington, Franklin and Betsy Ross all worshiped at **Christ Church**, on 2nd Street just north of Market Street. Dating from 1727, it is surrounded by the gravestones of signatories to the Declaration of Independence (Mon–Sat 9am–5pm; donation). The church's official burial ground, two blocks west at 5th and Arch, includes **Benjamin Franklin's grave**. At 239 Arch St, the **Betsy Ross House** (daily 10am–5pm; donation; ☎215/686-1252), by means of unimpressive wax dummies, salutes the woman credited with making the first American flag. The story is probably apocryphal, as it wasn't until the centennial celebrations in 1876 that a man claiming to be Ross's grandson came forward to stake her claim. Even if she did live at 239 Arch St, the building that currently holds that address was not her home; the streets have been extensively renamed and renumbered since the Revolution. Inside the house, there's a gift shop and shady **garden**, an oasis away from the busy streets outside.

The claim of **Elfreth's Alley** – a pretty little cobbled way off 2nd Street between Arch and Race streets – to be the "oldest street in the United States" is somewhat dubious but it has been in continuous residential use since 1727, and its thirty houses, notable for their wrought-iron gates, water pumps, wooden shutters and attic rooms, date from the eighteenth century. No. 126 is the **Mantua Maker's Museum** where furniture was made for Philadelphia's elite in the eighteenth century (Tues–Sat 10am–4pm, Sun 12pm–4pm; $2; ☎215/574-0560).

The area north of Market Street also holds two excellent museums: the **National Museum of American Jewish History**, 55 N 5th St (Mon–Thurs 10am–5pm, Fri 10am–3pm, Sun noon–5pm; $3; ☎215/923-3811), which is dedicated to the experiences of Jews in the States and includes a synagogue; and the emotive and politically informed **African American Museum in Philadelphia**, 7th and Arch streets (Tues–Sat 10am–5pm, Sun noon–5pm; $6; ☎215/574-0380). The latter tells the stories of the thousands of blacks who migrated north to Philadelphia after Reconstruction and in the early twentieth century. As well as lectures, films and concerts, there are photos, personal memorabilia, poems by black poet Langston Hughes and a piped-in Billie Holiday soundtrack. The **Edgar Allan Poe National Historic Site**, 532 N 7th St, just north of Spring Garden Street (daily 9am–5pm; free; ☎215/597-8780), is the only one of Poe's five Philadelphia residences that survives; it's also where he wrote *The Black Cat* in 1843. The stripped-down walls and bare wood floors do little to evoke Poe's presence – and despite local efforts, restoration plans have still yet to get under way. However, if you're a true Poe fanatic, the staff in the small **museum** adjacent to the house can answer almost any Poe-related question. If you're keen on literary pilgrimages, you might also want to visit the grave of another key figure of American letters, **Walt Whitman**; he's buried in the Harleigh Cemetery, on Haddon Avenue across the river in Camden, New Jersey.

Penn's Landing

Just to the east of Old City along the Delaware River, where William Penn stepped off in 1682, spreads the huge and heavily industrialized port of Philadelphia. Along the port's southern reaches, on the river side of the I-95 freeway, the old docklands have been renovated as part of the **Penn's Landing** development, which includes the **Independence Seaport Museum** (daily 10am–5pm; $8; ☎215/925-5439) and a variety of historical **ships**, including the flagship *USS Olympia* and World War II submarine *Becuna* (both daily 10am–5pm; $5), and the three-masted Portuguese Tall Ship *Gazela*, built in 1883 (while in port, Sat & Sun 12.30–5.30pm; check on ☎215/923-9030; donation). All along the riverfront promenade are food stalls, landscaped pools and fountains, and there are regular outdoor concerts and festivals. A ferry crosses the Delaware (Riverlink Ferry; $5 round-trip; ☎215/925-LINK) to the down-at-heel town of Camden, where the main attraction is the **New Jersey State Aquarium** (daily: mid-March to mid-Sept 9.30am–5.30pm; mid-Sept to mid-March 10am–5pm; $10.95; ☎609/365-3300) – good for kids but otherwise eminently missable. A $21.50 River Pass covers the museum, ships, aquarium and a round-trip on the ferry.

Society Hill

Society Hill, an elegant residential area west of the Delaware and directly south of INHP, spreads between Walnut and Lombard streets. Though it is indeed Philadelphia's high society who live here now, the area was named for its first inhabitants, the Free Society of Traders – a rather more fun-loving bunch than the strict Quakers who lived to the north. After falling into disrepair, the Hill itself was flattened in the early 1970s to provide a building site for I.M. Pei's twin skyscrapers, Society Hill Towers. Luckily, the rest of the neighborhood has been restored to form one of the city's most picturesque districts: cobbled gas-lit streets are lined with immaculately kept colonial, Federal and Georgian homes, often featuring the state's namesake keystones on their window frames, and markers everywhere point out the area's rich history. One of the few buildings open to

△ Historic Philadelphia

the public is the **Physick House**, 321 S 4th St, home to Dr Philip Syng Physick, "the Father of American Surgery," and filled with eighteenth- and nineteenth-century decorative arts (Thurs–Sun 11am–2pm; $4).

Center City

Center City, Philadelphia's main business and commercial area, stretches from 8th Street west to the Schuylkill River, dominated by the endearing Baroque wedding cake of **City Hall** and its 37ft bronze statue of Penn. Before ascending thirty stories to the observation deck at Penn's feet, check out the quirky sculptures and carvings around the building, including the cats and mice at the south entrance. A couple of blocks north at Broad and Cherry streets, the **Museum of American Art** at the Pennsylvania Academy of Fine Arts (Tues–Sat 10am–5pm, Sun 11am–5pm; $5, free on Sun 3–5pm; ☎215/972-7600), housed in an elaborate, multicolored Victorian pile, exhibits three hundred years of American art, including works by Mary Cassatt, Thomas Eakins and Winslow Homer.

Beginning at 8th Street, Chinatown, marked by a 40ft oriental gate, has some of the best budget food in the city. A block over on 12th Street is the century-old **Reading Terminal Market** – where many Amish farmers come to the city to sell their produce. It's always good for a lively time and makes a great lunch spot. The $500-million Convention Center, which opened next door in 1993, signaled major changes for this once dodgy area, as flashy hotels, coffeehouses and restaurants have replaced the previously derelict shops and offices.

Rittenhouse Square

Grassy **Rittenhouse Square**, one of Penn's original city squares, is in a very fashionable part of town. On one side it borders chic Walnut Street, on the other a residential area of solid brownstones with beautifully carved doors and windows. The redbrick 1860 **Rosenbach Museum**, 2010 Delancey Place, holds over thirty thousand rare books and James Joyce's original hand-scrawled manuscripts of *Ulysses* (Tues–Sun 11am–4pm, last tours at 2.45pm; $3.50). On summer evenings there are free outdoor jazz and R&B concerts in the square.

Three blocks northwest from the square, the **Mutter Museum** (Mon–Sat 10am–4pm, Sun noon–4pm; $8; ☎215/563-3737), 19 S 22nd St in the College of Physicians (between Chestnut and Market), is not for the squeamish. Filled with weird pathological and medical oddities, including sickeningly lifelike wax models of tumors and skin infections, alongside closets full of skeletons, syphilitic skulls, pickled internal organs and the death cast of a pair of Siamese twins, it's unique to say the least.

The museums

The mile-long Benjamin Franklin Parkway, known as Museum Row – or, less convincingly, as "America's Champs-Elysees" – sweeps northwest from City Hall to the colossal Museum of Art in **Fairmount Park**, an area of countryside annexed by the city in the nineteenth century. Spanning nine hundred scenic acres on both sides of the Schuylkill River, this is one of the world's largest landscaped city parks, with jogging, biking and hiking trails, early American homes, an all-wars memorial to the state's black soldiers, and a zoo – the country's first – at 3400 Girard Ave (daily 9.30am–5pm, hours vary in summer; $10.50; ☎215/243-1100). In the late 1960s, local residents **Muhammad Ali** and Joe Frazier all but brought the city to a standstill with the announcement one afternoon that they were heading for Fairmount for an informal slug-out.

Sylvester Stallone later immortalized the steps of the **Philadelphia Museum of Art** (Tues & Thurs–Sun 10am–5pm, Wed 10am–8.45pm; $10, pay what you wish all day Sun), 26th Street and Franklin Parkway, by running up them in the film *Rocky*, but he missed out on a real treat inside: one of the finest collections in the US, with a twelfth-century French cloister, Renaissance art, a complete **Robert Adam** interior from a 1765 house in London's Berkeley Square, Rubens tapestries, Pennsylvania Dutch crafts and **Shaker furniture**, a strong **Impressionist** collection, and the world's most extensive collection of the works of **Marcel Duchamp**. Exhibits are displayed in an easy-to-follow chronological order. On Wednesday nights, there are excellent programs of live jazz and classical music along with film showings and artistic debate – all included in the admission price.

A few blocks away at Franklin Parkway and 22nd Street (Tues–Sun 10am–5pm; donation; ☎215/763-8100), the exquisite **Rodin Museum**, marble-walled and set in a shady garden with a green pool, holds the largest collection of Rodin's Impressionistic sculptures and casts outside Paris, including *The Thinker*, *The Burghers of Calais* and *The Gates of Hell*. Among the rare books at the **Free Library of Philadelphia**, 19th and Vine streets (Mon–Thurs 9am–9pm, Fri 9am–6pm, Sat 9am–5pm, tours at 11am; free; ☎215/686-5322), are cuneiform tablets from 3000 BC, medieval manuscripts, first editions of Dickens and Poe, and such intriguing titles as the 1807 *Inquiry into the Conduct of the Princess of Wales*.

Over the road in the vast **Franklin Institute Science Museum** (N 20th St and Benjamin Franklin Parkway; Sun–Thurs 9.30am–5pm, Fri–Sat 9am–9pm; ☎215/448-1200) are a **Planetarium** ($6), the four-story **OMNIVERSE movie theater** ($7.50) and the **Mandell Futures Center** ($9.75) – a state-of-the-art facility filled with entertaining gadgets such as a hugely popular machine on which you can see (disappointingly hazy) images of your face aged by 25 years. A **combination ticket** ($14.50) covers admission to all three. Continuing the educational theme, the nearby **Academy of Natural Sciences** exhibits dinosaurs, mummies and gems (Mon–Fri 10am–4.30pm, Sat & Sun 10am–5pm; $9; ☎215-299-1000), while the **Please Touch Museum**, 210 N 21st St (daily 9am–4.30pm; $6.50), is a hands-on adventureland aimed at youngsters.

Eastern State Penitentiary

One of Philadelphia's most significant historic sites stands, all but forgotten, just a short walk from the Fairmount Park museums. The **Eastern State Penitentiary**, whose gloomy Gothic fortifications fill an entire block of the residential neighborhood along Fairmount Avenue at 22nd Street, embodies an almost complete history of attitudes toward crime and punishment in the US. Since it opened in 1829, the Quaker-inspired prison's radical efforts to rehabilitate inmates via isolation, rather than punish them, attracted visitors from around the world; when Charles Dickens came to America in 1842, he wanted to see two things, this prison and Niagara Falls. Though it underwent substantial changes in its 140-year history, and has slowly decayed since its final closure in 1970, the bulk of the Panopticon-style radial prison survives, and preservationists have recently completed a major restoration program. **Guided tours** leave on the hour (June–Sept Wed–Sun 10am–6pm; May–June & Oct–Nov Sat & Sun 10am–5pm, last tour 4pm; $7; ☎215/236-7326) and point out its many novel architectural features, as well as the cell where Al Capone cooled his heels and the block where Tina Turner filmed a music video.

West Philadelphia

Across the Schuylkill River, **West Philadelphia** is home to the Ivy League **University of Pennsylvania**, where Franklin established the country's first medical school. The compact campus blends into fairly gritty urban areas, but has some great museums: the small **Institute of Contemporary Art**, 118 S 36th St, which displays cutting-edge traveling exhibitions in an airy white space (Wed–Fri noon–8pm, Sat & Sun 11am–5pm; $3; ☎215/898-7108), and the intriguing **Arthur Ross Gallery** (call ☎215/898-2083 for hours; free), 220 S 34th St, which has changing student displays. The superlative **Museum of Archeology and Anthropology**, 33rd and Spruce streets (Tues–Sat 10am–4.30pm, Sun 1–5pm; $5), is the university's top draw. Regarded by experts as one of the world's finest science museums, its exhibits span all the continents and their major epochs – from Nigerian Benin bronzes to Chinese crystal balls. Most astonishing is the priceless twelve-ton granite Sphinx of Rameses II, c.1293–1185 BC, in the **Lower Egyptian Gallery**, while the **Meso-American** and **Greco-Roman Galleries** also hold plenty of highlights.

South Philadelphia

Staunchly blue-collar **South Philadelphia**, center of Philadelphia's black community since the Civil War, is also home to many of the city's Italians; opera singer **Mario Lanza** (who has his own museum at 416 Queen St) and pop stars Fabian and Chubby Checker grew up here. It's also where to come for an authentic – and very messy – **cheesesteak**, and to rummage through the wonderful **Italian Market** (another *Rocky* location) which runs along 9th Street south from Christian Street. One of the last surviving urban markets in the US, the wooden market stalls that have stood here for generations are packed to overflowing with bric-a-brac, produce, secondhand Levis and live seafood.

South Street, the original boundary of the city, is now Philadelphia's main **nightlife** district, with dozens of cafés, bars, restaurants and nightclubs lined up along the few blocks west from Front Street, with a tie-dye ambience not unlike New York's St Mark's Place or San Francisco's Haight-Ashbury. During the day you can wander amongst the many good book, record and clothing **shops** (the Book Trader, 501 South St, is open daily until midnight). At night, it makes a lively, if highly commercial, evening out – and is perhaps best avoided on summer weekends when the throngs of visitors can be especially overwhelming.

Eating

Eating out in Philadelphia is a real treat: the ubiquitous street stands sell **soft pretzels** with mustard for around $1, while Chinatown and the Italian Market are good for ethnic food, and Reading Terminal Market makes a bargain lunch stop in Center City. South Street has plenty of fun, if well-touristed, eateries while hipper restaurants cluster along 2nd Street in the Old City. The South Philly **cheesesteak**, a sandwich of melted American cheese atop layers of wafer-thin roast beef, varies from joint to joint around town; some of the best are to be found in the Italian cafés around 9th and Passyunk in South Philadelphia. And bear in mind that a cheesesteak is hot, a **hoagie** (complete with lettuce and tomato) is not.

Alyan's 603 S 4th St ☎215/922-3553. Small Middle Eastern restaurant off South St. Dinner from $7. Bring your own bottle.

Brasil's 112 Chestnut St ☎215/413-1700. Good Brazilian food, live Latin and salsa music, and friendly service in a great atmosphere.

Circa 1518 Walnut St ☎215/545-6800. A stylish Center City restaurant decked out in marble, mirrors and chandeliers. Offers meat and seafood dinners with innovative twists for around $10. Great happy hours on Thurs & Fri; techno music later at night.

City Tavern 138 S 2nd St ☎215/413-1443. Reconstructed 1773 tavern in INHP, familiar to the city's founders, and called by John Adams "the most genteel tavern in America." Costumed staff serve "olde style" food (pasties, turkey rarebit) to a harpsichord accompaniment, but the prices, unfortunately, are as modern as they get, from about $16 for dinner. Lunch is less expensive.

The Continental 138 Market St ☎215-923-6069. Trendy retro diner, popular with a gay crowd, serving huge portions in a funky, all-white setting.

Delilah's Reading Terminal Market, 12th and Spruce sts ☎215/574-0929. Superb soul food but with scatty service. Nigerian stew with cornbread for under $5; beans and rice even less.

Jim's Steaks 400 South St ☎215/928-1911. Black-and-white-tiled Art Deco diner serving some of the biggest and best cheesesteaks in the city, as the constant line outside proves. Try and beat the record – 11 cheesesteaks in 90 minutes.

Montserrat 623 South St ☎215/627-4224. Wide variety of fresh, healthy food, with a vegetarian emphasis, served inside or on a large deck overlooking the South St parade.

Novelty 15 S 3rd St ☎215/627-7885. Upscale eatery, with a pricey but good selection of mainly fish dishes. Try the Novelty Box for a sampler of the restaurant's different specials.

Serrano 20 S 2nd St ☎215/928-0770. Intimate Old City café. Creative international cooking, with good fresh seafood. Try the appetizer tasting menu. Diners get preferential seating at the *Tin Angel* folk club upstairs (see overleaf).

Sonoma 4411 Main St, Manayunk ☎215/483-9400. Pleasant, reasonably priced California-style Italian restaurant.

South Street Diner 140 South St ☎215/627-5258. Huge menu with Greek and Italian specialties from $6. Open 24hrs seven days a week.

Tony Luke Jr's 118 S 18th St ☎215/568-4630. Excellent steak sandwiches and hoagies.

Tre Scalini 1533 S 11th St ☎215/551-3870. A taste of traditional South Philly Italian, with reasonably priced dishes and a low-key atmosphere.

White Dog Café 3420 Sansom St ☎215/386-9224. Trendy, creative food in an antique-filled room near the universities. Arty, student crowd; dinners cost $12–25.

Drinking

A trail of theme **bars** has sprung up along Penn's Landing and the Delaware River, but the most popular place for bar-hopping is **South Street**; although **2nd Street** in the Old City is rapidly becoming the area for the coolest bars. Philly's growing number of **cafés** are spread around the city; South Street and 2nd Street again have the densest concentrations, though several have opened in Center City over the past couple of years.

Cuba Libre 10 S 2nd St ☎215/627-0666. Newcomer serving decidedly average Cuban fare, redeemed by a small bar offering good cocktails and excellent *mojitos*.

Dickens Inn 421 S 2nd St ☎215/928-9307. English-style pub in Head House Square, with four large bars and over 130 different single-malt whiskeys. The exceptionally welcoming staff make it a great night out, and a decent lunch stop, too.

Irish Pub 2007 Walnut St ☎215/568-5603. Good music and atmosphere near Rittenhouse Square.

The Khyber 56 S 2nd St ☎215/238-5888. Philly's oldest and most congenial bar, with a huge range of beers; it's also a reliable place to hear local

bands (see listings, overleaf).

Last Drop Coffeehouse 1300 Pine St ☎215/893-9262. Trendy café, serving Philly's best espresso.

Society Hill 301 Chestnut St ☎215/925-1919. Tasty sandwiches in a bar with plenty of atmosphere, a stone's throw from the *Bank Street Hostel*. Live jazz piano music nightly.

Sugar Mom's Church Street Lounge 225 Church St ☎215/925-8219. Popular basement bar where the jukebox ranges from Tony Bennett to Sonic Youth, with a dozen international beers on tap.

Woody's Bar and Restaurant 202 S 13th St ☎215/545-1893. Large, friendly downtown beer bar popular with Philly's gay community.

Nightlife and entertainment

Few reminders are left of the 1970s "Philly Sound"; stars like Patti LaBelle, the O'Jays and Harold *If You Don't Love Me By Now* Melvin and the Blue Notes have waned, though their legacy is readily apparent in the smooth vocals of contemporary artists like Boyz II Men and the soulful rhymes of rapper Eve. It's also a decent place to see rock bands: most of the names that play New York come down here and tickets are half the price or even less. The world-famous **Philadelphia Orchestra** performs at the grand Academy of Music on Broad Street (☎215/893-1999), modeled after Milan's La Scala; nosebleed seats cost just $5 on the day, and they give free summer concerts at the Mann Music Center in Fairmount Park (☎215/567-0707). Philadelphia's other great strength is its **theater** scene: small venues abound. Check the **listings** in the free *City Paper* or *Philadelphia Weekly* newspapers, or call the 24-hour **event hotline** (☎215/573-2787). TIXSTOP, in the visitor center, sells half-price standby tickets (Tues–Thurs 11.30am–3.30pm, Fri & Sat 11.30am–5pm).

Annual events in Philadelphia include the fortnight-long Freedom Fest that leads up to the Fourth of July, and the superb Riverblues weekend festival on the Delaware River, at the end of July, which features top-name blues artists.

Katmandu Pier 25, N Delaware Ave ☎215/629-7400. Slightly tacky but fun tropical-themed bar, just north of the decidedly unexotic Franklin Bridge. Features a nightly outdoor barbecue.

The Khyber 56 S 2nd St ☎215/238-5888. Small, mainly alternative, rock venue with a gargoyle-lined bar, bluesy jukebox and casual young clientele. Cover $3–6 when bands are on.

Painted Bride Art Center 230 Vine St ☎215/925-9914. Art gallery with live folk, jazz and poetry performances after dark.

Silk City Lounge 5th and Spring Garden sts ☎215/592-8838. Very mixed musical bag – Sinatra, hip-hop, acid jazz, indie dance – in an ultratrendy but unflashy club. Live local bands play at the weekend.

Theater of Living Arts 334 South St ☎215/922-1011. Converted movie palace that's the best place to catch alternative-rock bands.

Tin Angel 20 S 2nd St ☎215/928-0978. Intimate upstairs bar and coffeehouse, featuring top local and nationally known folk and acoustic acts.

Trocadero 10th and Arch sts ☎215/922-LIVE. Trendy downtown dance club with occasional live alternative bands. Cover varies, and ID is essential.

Warmdaddy's 4 S Front St ☎215/627-2500. Live blues every night and a buzzing atmosphere; something of a Penn's Landing institution.

Zanzibar Blue 200 S Broad St in the *Bellevue Hotel* ☎215/732-5200. Classy club with contemporary New York-style jazz nightly, often by famous names, so expect a hefty cover charge and two-drink minimum.

Central Pennsylvania

Central Pennsylvania, cut north to south by the broad **Susquehanna River**, has no major cities, though the state capital, **Harrisburg**, is an excellent base from which to explore sights that include the **Hershey** chocolate empire and the rolling Amish farmlands of **Lancaster County** to the east, and the Civil War site of **Gettysburg** on the state's southern border. To the north, the mighty forests of the "Grand Canyon of Pennsylvania," around **Williamsport**, reveal the legacy of its great nineteenth-century lumber wealth in mansion-lined streets. Cities like **Johnstown**, beyond the dramatic Allegheny Mountains in the west, and **Scranton** are industrial towns with little of interest for the casual visitor.

Lancaster County – Pennsylvania Dutch Country

Lancaster County, fifty miles west of Philadelphia, stretches for about 45 miles from Churchtown in the east to the Susquehanna River in the west. Although Lancaster City, ten miles east of the river, was US capital for a day in September 1777, the region is famed more for its preponderance of agricultural religious communities, known collectively as the **Pennsylvania Dutch** (a mistaken derivation of *Deutsch*, or German).

The Pennsylvania Dutch

The people now known as the Pennsylvania Dutch originated as **Anabaptists** in sixteenth-century Switzerland, under the leadership of Menno Simons. His unorthodox advocacy of adult baptism and literal interpretation of the Bible led to the order's persecution; they were invited by William Penn to settle in Lancaster County in the 1720s. Today the twenty or so Pennsylvania Dutch include the "plain" Old Order **Amish** (a strict order that originally broke away from Simons in 1693) and freer-living **Mennonites**, as well as the "fancy" **Lutheran** groups (distinguished by the colorful circular "hex" signs on their barns). Living by an unwritten set of rules called Amish Ordnung, the Amish are the strictest and best known: the men with their wide-brimmed straw hats and beards (but no "military" moustaches), the women in bonnets, plain dresses (with no fripperies like buttons) and aprons. Shunning electricity and any exposure to the corrupting influence of the outside world, the Amish power their farms with generators, and travel (at roughly ten miles per hour) in hand-made horse-drawn buggies. For all their insularity, the Amish are very friendly and helpful; resist the temptation to photograph them, however, as the making of "graven images" offends their beliefs.

An extremely touristy place, even before it was brought to international fame by the movie *Witness*, Lancaster County has maintained its natural beauty in the face of encroaching commercialization. It is a region of gentle countryside and fertile farmlands, mule-drawn ploughs, tiny roadside bakeries crammed with jams and pies, Amish children wending on old-fashioned scooters to and from their one-room schoolhouses, and flower-filled, immaculate farmhouses. However, attempting to live a simple life away from the pressures of the outside world has proved too much for many Pennsylvania Dutch. A few (mainly Mennonites) have succumbed to commercial need by offering rides in their buggies and meals in their homes. Members of the stricter orders in particular have moved away from the ceaseless intrusions of privacy – as well as soaring land prices – to less touristed Ohio and Iowa. Remember, too, that as Sunday is a day of rest for the Amish, many attractions, restaurants and other amenities will be closed.

Arrival and information

The Pennsylvania Turnpike sweeps across the north of the region, but most activity is concentrated further south near the east–west US-30. Amtrak arrives at the train station at 53 McGovern Ave, as do buses from Capital Trailways and Greyhound (℡717/397-4861). The bustling **Pennsylvania Dutch Visitors Bureau**, just off US-30 at 501 Greenfield Rd (daily 8.30am–5pm, later closing in summer; ℡717/299-8901, ⓦwww.padutchcountry.com), does an excellent job of providing orientation and advice on accommodation. In Lancaster City itself, the smaller and less resourceful **visitor center** at 100 S Queen St in the Southern Farmers' Market (April–Oct Mon–Fri 8.30am–5pm, Sat 9am–4pm, Sun 10am–3pm; ℡717/397-3531) has maps for self-guided walking tours. It also organizes **guided tours** (April–Oct Mon–Sat 10am & 1.30pm, Sun 1.30pm; $7).

Visitors keen to learn about Pennsylvania Dutch culture should head to the excellent **People's Place**, Main Street, Intercourse, eleven miles east of Lancaster City, which has a well-stocked bookstore, an informative if sentimental slide show, an Amish museum and the film *Hazel's People*, plus displays of quilts and artwork (June–Aug Mon–Sat 9.30am–8pm, hours vary in winter; $5; ℡717/768-7171). The **Mennonite Information Center**, 2209 Millstream Rd off US-30, organizes lodging with Mennonite families. Call at least two hours ahead for a guide to take you on a two-hour, $28 tour in your car (Mon–Sat 8am–5pm; ☏717/299-0954, ⊛www.mennoniteinfoctr.com).

Getting around

Winding country lanes weave through Pennsylvania Dutch Country, passing small villages with eccentric-sounding names such as **Intercourse** (source of many droll postcards, but supposedly named for its location on the junction of two main roads). Although a car will get you to the quieter back roads that the tour buses miss, it's more fun to **ride a bike**. Only then can you feel the benefits of all that pure fresh air – and it shows more consideration for the horse-drawn buggies with which you share the road. Try Lancaster County Bicycle Tours in Bird-in-Hand (☏717/393-7600 or 1-866/BIKEFUN) for guided tours or Dreamride in Lancaster City (☏717/397-2503) for bike rental by the day or hour.

For those without transportation, Red Rose Excursions, 47 N Queen St in Lancaster City (☏717/397-3175), runs an extensive **bus** system. Amish Country Tours, on US-30 (☏717/768-3600), does four-and-a-half-hour farm-lands **tours** (Mon–Sat; $19.95, though some accommodation places offer a similar service for free). Ed's Buggy Rides on US-896, north of Strasburg, runs lolloping three-mile countryside excursions for $8 (☏717/687-0360).

Accommodation

Accommodation options in Pennsylvania Dutch Country range from reasonably priced **hotels** in and around Lancaster City, through **farm vacations** (ask at the Pennsylvania Dutch Visitors Bureau) to **campgrounds**. *White Oak Campgrounds*, 372 White Oak Rd, Quarryville, four miles north of Strasburg, overlooks the heart of the Dutch farmlands and hosts a county auction on Saturdays (reservations recommended; $18; ☏717/687-6207).

Brunswick Ramada Inn Chestnut and Queen sts ☏717/397-4801 or 1-800/233-0182. Seventies-style luxury hotel in the center of downtown Lancaster City, with spacious, comfortable rooms. **❺**

Countryside Motel 134 Hartman Bridge Rd ☏717/687-8431. Clean and simple place six miles east of Lancaster City on Hwy-896. **❸**

Historic Strasburg Inn Rte-896, Strasburg ☏717/687-7691 or 1-800/872-0201. One hundred luxury rooms tucked away in sixty rolling acres of land. **❻**

O'Flaherty's Dingledein House 1105 E King St ☏717/293-1723 or 1-800/779-7765. Friendly B&B near Lancaster City. Only seven rooms are available, so call ahead. Rates include a huge country breakfast. **❹**

Patchwork Inn 2319 Old Philadelphia Pike ☏717/293-9078. Homestyle rooms in a nineteenth-century farm between Lancaster City and Smoketown. **❹**

Red Caboose Motel Paradise Lane, Strasburg ☏717/687-5000. Quirky accommodation in converted train cabooses. **❷**

Village Inn 2695 Old Philadelphia Pike, Bird-in-Hand ☏717/293-8369 or 1-800/914-2473. Excellent old inn with modern amenities, large breakfast, deck, lawn and back pasture. Price includes 2hr tour of Amish Country and use of adjacent motel's pool. Offers off-season discounts. Book ahead. **❺**

Touring Pennsylvania Dutch Country

Though useful for a general overview and historical insight, the attractions that interpret Amish culture tend toward overkill. It's far more satisfying just to explore the countryside for yourself. Here, among the streams with their covered bridges and fields striped with corn, alfalfa and tobacco, the reality hits you – these aren't actors re-creating an ancient lifestyle, but a living, working community. There's no guarantee as to what you'll see: on Sunday, for example, there are no quilt sales or bake shops, and the farmers don't work the fields, but there may well be a large gathering of buggies outside one of the farms, indicating an Amish church service (in High German) or a "visiting day."

Among the widely spread formal "attractions," the **Ephrata Cloister**, 632 W Main St, Ephrata (on US-272 and 322), re-creates the eighteenth-century settlement of German Protestant celibates that acted, amongst other things, as an early publishing and printing center (April–Oct Mon–Sat 9am–5pm, Sun noon–5pm; $6; ☎717/733-6600). Further south, about three miles northeast of Lancaster City, the **Landis Valley Museum**, 2451 Kissell Hill Rd, is a living history museum of rural life, with demonstrations of local crafts and the like (Tues–Sat 9am–5pm, Sun noon–5pm; $7; ☎717/569-0401).

In Lancaster City itself, a stolid redbrick town with tree-lined avenues, the **Heritage Center Museum**, in Penn Square (Tues–Sat 10am–4pm; free; ☎717/299-6440), exhibits Lancaster master crafts, including wagons and rifles, ancient Amish calligraphy known as fraktur, clocks, wooden toys, weathervanes and quilts. At **Strasburg**, a mixture of tourist kitsch and historical authenticity southeast of Lancaster City on US-896, the **Strasburg Railroad** gives 45-minute round-trip rides in original steam trains through patchwork farmland to Paradise (daily, hours vary, call for updated schedule; $8.50; ☎717/687-7522, ⓦwww.strasburgrailroad.com). Disappointingly, **Paradise** holds no heavenly delights, but there are some good views on the way (if little that couldn't be seen by bike or car), and the train makes regular picnic stops. The oldest building in the county, the **Hans Herr House**, 1849 Hans Herr Drive, five miles south of downtown Lancaster City off US-222, is a 1719 Mennonite church with a pretty garden and orchard, a medieval German facade and exhibits on early farm life (April–Dec Mon–Sat 9am–4pm; $4; ☎717/464-4438).

Eating and nightlife

Lancaster County **food** is delicious: Germanic and served in vast quantities. There are no Amish-owned restaurants, but Amish roadside stalls sell fresh homemade root beer, jams, pickles, breads and pies. The huge "all-you-can-eat" **tourist restaurants** on US-30 and US-340 may look off-putting, all pseudo-rusticism with costumed waitresses, but most serve good meals (for around $13.50), "family-style" – you share long tables and mountains of fried chicken, sauerkraut, noodles, pickles, cottage cheese and apple butter, corn, hickory-smoked ham, *schnitz und knepp* (apple, ham and dumpling stew) and shoo-fly pie with crowds of other tourists. None stays open later than 8pm.

Rural Lancaster County, where people get up at the crack of dawn, is not known for its wild **nightlife** – or any nightlife for that matter; even the streets of Lancaster City are strangely quiet after dark. Options are not totally limited to early nights or cable TV, however: a couple of good – and very friendly – bars are worth exploring downtown. The Fulton Opera House, 12 N Prince St (☎717/394-7133), is a plush red-and-gold restored Victorian theater, hosting dance, plays and special events.

Central Market Penn Square, Lancaster City ☎717/291-4739. Covered market selling fresh farm produce and sandwiches. Tues & Fri 6am–4.30pm, Sat 6am–2pm.

Good 'n' Plenty East Brook Rd, US-896, Smoketown ☎717/394-7111. Not Amish-owned, but Amish women cook and serve food in the best of the family-style restaurants. Open Mon–Sat 11.30am–8pm. Closed mid-Dec to end of Jan.

Lancaster Dispensing Co 33–35 N Market St, Lancaster City ☎717/299-4602. Downtown

Lancaster's trendiest, friendliest bar, with live weekend jazz and blues, plus food.

Lancaster Malt Brewing Co Plum and Walnut sts, Lancaster City ☎717/391-MALT. Brewpub serving good bar food and three different microbrews. Tours given by appointment. Open daily.

Lapp's 2270 Lincoln Highway East ☎717/394-1606. A solid Lancaster County style diner, open seven days a week.

Molly's Pub 253 E Chestnut St, Lancaster City ☎717/396-0225. Neighborhood bar with lively

atmosphere and good burgers. Closed Sun.
Plain and Fancy 3121 Old Philadelphia Pike (Rte-340), Bird-in-Hand ☎717/768-4400. Standard family-style restaurant, the only one in the area that's open on Sundays.

Zinn's Diner Rte-272, Denver ☎717/336-2500. Well-established premises serving authentic Dutch and American favorites. Adjacent recreation park is ideal for an after-dinner stroll.

Harrisburg and Hershey

HARRISBURG, Pennsylvania's capital, lies on the Susquehanna River thirty or so miles northwest of Lancaster City. It's a surprisingly attractive small city, lined with shuttered colonial buildings and well complemented by its kitsch Chocolatetown neighbor **Hershey**. Harrisburg is also known as the site of the **Three Mile Island** nuclear facility, which stands along the river on the east side of town, and suffered a famous meltdown in the 1970s.

The ornate **capitol** at Third and State is undeniably beautiful; at its dedication in 1906, Theodore Roosevelt called it "the handsomest building I ever saw." Italian Renaissance in style, it has a dome modeled after St Peter's in Rome (Mon–Sat 9am–4pm; free). The complex includes the archeological and military artifacts, decorative arts, tools and machinery exhibited in the free four-floor **State Museum of Pennsylvania**, a cylindrical building that holds a planetarium, at Third and North (Tues–Sat 9am–5pm, Sun noon–5pm; free). But undoubtedly the real attraction here is the excellent new **National Civil War Museum**, at Lincoln Circle off Market Street (Mon–Fri 9am–5pm, Sat & Sun 10am–5pm; $7; ☎717/260-1861). Almost 730,000 Americans were killed in the Civil War – more than in all other conflicts since the Revolution combined - and the museum offers an intelligent analysis of the reasons for, and results of, the war. Especially evocative are the fictionalized monologues, playing on video screens in every gallery, that focus on the human cost of the conflict. There's also a good terrace café with great views across the city.

One of the best ways to spend a Harrisburg afternoon is to cross the Susquehanna along the Walnut Street footbridge and stroll through **City Island**, a waterfront development with vast sports facilities (including a family-filled concrete beach, a baseball stadium and a football ground), shady picnic areas, regular festivals and concerts and **paddlewheeler rides** (May–Oct; call ☎717/234-6500 for schedule; $5).

HERSHEY, ten miles east, was built in 1903 by candy magnate Milton S Hershey for his chocolate factory – so it has streets named Chocolate and Cocoa avenues, streetlamps in the shape of Hershey's Chocolate Kisses and air rich with the smell of cocoa. **Hershey Chocolate World** (daily 9am–4.45pm; longer hours in summer; ☎717/534-4900) offers a free mini-train ride through a simulated chocolate factory (accompanied by sugary, piped warblings of *It's a Chocolate, Chocolate World*). Those not content with the free sample given out at the end can gorge themselves in the vast gift and souvenir shops and cafés.

Hersheypark, which began in 1907 as a picnic ground for Hershey factory workers, is now a huge, if poorly organized **amusement park** with roller coasters and sundry other rides (mid-May to Sept daily hours vary; $27.95; ☎717/534-3090 or 1-800/HERSHEY). The adjacent **Hershey Museum of American Life** has exhibits on the Pennsylvania Dutch and tells the Milton S. Hershey story (daily 10am–5pm; $6).

Twenty-five miles south of Harrisburg, the blue-collar town of **YORK** is home to the final assembly plant of **Harley–Davidson**. The company runs free tours of its factory and is set to open a full-scale museum in late 2002 (Mon–Fri; call ☎1-877/746-7937).

Practicalities

Amtrak **trains** share the central station at Fourth and Chestnut with Greyhound, whose **buses** also stop in Hershey at 337 W Chocolate St (☎717/397-4861 or 1-800/231-2222). Harrisburg's **visitor center** at 114 Walnut St (☎717/232-1377, ⓦwww.visithhc.com) provides maps and a suggested downtown **walking tour**. **Hotels** on the outskirts of town, aimed toward business travelers and politicians, are a snip compared to prices in DC or Philly. *Quality Inn Riverfront*, 525 S Front St (☎717/233-1611; ❸), is in downtown Harrisburg, while just across the river in leafy Camp Hill is the *Radisson Penn Harris* (☎717/763-7117; ❹), with good-value rooms in relaxing surroundings. Alternatives in Hershey include the *Spinners Inn*, 845 E Chocolate Ave (☎717/533-9157 or 1-800/800-5845; ❹), with a decent restaurant, and (yes, really) the *Chocolatetown Motel* (March–Dec; ☎717/533-2330; ❸), a mile further on at no. 1806. More upscale lodging is available at the *Hotel Hershey* (☎717/533-2171; ❽/❾) complete with an onsite spa, offering kitschy, chocolate-based beauty treatments and strangely lacking any sense of fun. Call the Hershey Visitor's Information line ☎717/534-4900 for more listings.

Budget **restaurants** line Second Street in downtown Harrisburg, the best being *Fisaga*, Locust & N Second St (☎717/257-1328), which serves good basic sandwiches and pastas at reasonable prices. *Deweys Dry Dock & Deli*, 33 N Second St (☎717/233-3700), does good sandwiches and fries, while *Nick's 1014*, 1014 N Third St (☎717/238-8844), and *Scott's*, 212 Locust St (☎717/234-7599), are popular bar/grills with music some nights.

Gettysburg

The small town of **GETTYSBURG**, thirty miles south of Harrisburg near the Maryland border, gained tragic notoriety in July 1863 for the cataclysmic **Civil War** battle in which fifty thousand men died. There were more casualties during these three days than in any American battle before or since – a full third of those who fought were killed or wounded – and entire regiments were wiped out when the tide finally turned against the South.

Four months later, on November 19, Abraham Lincoln delivered his **Gettysburg Address** at the dedication of the National Cemetery. His two-minute speech, in memory of all the soldiers who died, is acknowledged as one of the most powerful orations in American history. Lincoln himself was convinced that it was a "flat failure," and prefaced his remarks with the words "the world will little note nor long remember what we say here . . ."; you'll be muttering it in your sleep by the time you leave.

Gettysburg, by far the most baldly commercialized of all the Civil War sites, is overwhelmingly geared toward **tourism**, relentlessly replaying the most minute details of the battle. Fortunately, it is perfectly feasible to avoid the crowds and commercial overkill and explore for yourself the rolling hills of the battlefield (now a national park) and the tidy town streets with their shuttered historic houses.

Information and getting around

Gettysburg Travel Council, 35 Carlisle St (daily 8.30am–5pm; ☎717/334-6274), is housed in the tiny historic train depot where Lincoln disembarked in November 1863 and should be the first stop on any visit. Though the town is compact and easy to walk around, there is no public transportation, and a car helps when touring the huge battlefield. **Bikes** can be rented in the battleground at the campground at 610 Taneytown Rd (April–Oct; $15 half day, $25 full day; ☎717/334–1288). Two-hour Battlefield Bus Tours, running through the town and making numerous stops in the battlefield, depart from 778 Baltimore St (daily every 30min; $18.95; ☎717/334–6296).

Accommodation

There are plenty of lodgings in and around Gettysburg, including many **B&Bs**. The most central place to **camp** is at Artillery Ridge Resort, 610 Taneytown Rd (April–Oct; $16.50; ☎717/334–1288).

Baltimore St B&B 449 Baltimore St ☎717/334-2454. Gothic facade and interior, with standard rooms. ❹

Blue Sky Motel 2585 Biglerville Rd ☎717/677-7736. Good-value motel four miles north of town. ❸

Doubleday Inn 104 Doubleday Ave ☎717/334-9119. A memorabilia-packed luxury B&B, the only one within the battlefield. ❺

Gettysburg Travelodge 64 Steinwehr Ave ☎717/334-9281. Standard motel between downtown and the battlefield. ❹

Historic Farnsworth House Inn 401 Baltimore St ☎717/334-8838. An 1810 townhouse, used as Union HQ in the war and still riddled with bullet holes. Includes four rooms, with breakfast, afternoon tea and ghost stories in the cellar. ❹

The Town

Pick just a couple of the numerous museums in town and follow the Travel Council's fourteen-block downtown walking tour for a sense of the history of the place. The **National Civil War Wax Museum**, 297 Steinwehr Ave (summer daily 9am–8.15pm; rest of year daily 9am–4.15pm; closed weekdays Jan–Feb; $5; ☎717/334–6245), uses dreadful dummies in its displays on the lead-up to the Civil War, the Underground Railroad for escapee slaves, abolitionist John Brown, and the famous Southern belle spies Rose Greenhow and Belle Boyd. Across the National Cemetery in the battlefield, there are yet more dummies in the **Hall of Presidents and Their First Ladies**, 504 Baltimore St (daily: June–Aug 9am–9pm; Sept 9am–7pm; Oct, Nov & March–May 9am–5pm; closed Dec–Feb; $5.95; ☎717/334–5717), complete with pearls of presidential wisdom and stirring patriotic music. The only civilian to die in the battle, twenty-year-old Jennie Wade, was killed by a stray bullet as she made bread for the Union troops in her sister's kitchen. The **Jennie Wade House**, next to the Gettysburg Tour Center on Baltimore Street (daily: June–Sept 9am–9pm; Oct–Nov & Mar–May 9am–7pm; closed Dec–Feb; $5.95; ☎717/334–4100), looks exactly as it did on July 3, 1863, with bullet holes in the front door and on the bedpost, an artillery shell hole ripped through the wall adjoining the neighboring house, and a macabre model of Jennie's corpse lying under a sheet in the cellar.

President Eisenhower, who retired to Gettysburg, is commemorated to the west of the park at the **Eisenhower National Historic Site**, where his Georgian-style mansion holds an array of memorabilia. The site is accessible only on shuttle bus tours from the National Park Visitor Center in Taneytown (daily 9am–4pm; $5.25; ☎717/334–1124).

The battleground

It takes most of a day to see the 3500-acre **Gettysburg National Military Park**, which surrounds the town (daily 6am–10pm; free). The **visitor center** on Taneytown Road (daily: summer 8am–6pm, rest of year 8am–5pm; ☎717/334–1124) doubles as the best **museum**, with guns, uniforms, surgical and musical instruments, tents and flags, as well as touching photos of the 1938 Joint Soldiers Reunion. A thirty-minute, painstakingly thorough **electric map show** ($3) plots the intricacies of the battle; at the visitor center, you can pick up details of a self-guided **driving route**, or a **guide** will join you in your car for a personalized two-hour tour ($35). The guides are available on a first come, first served basis, and the visitor center does not accept reservations, so it's best to arrive just before it opens at 8am to secure a guide for the same day.

Directly opposite the visitor center, the **Gettysburg National Cemetery** contains thousands of graves arranged in a semicircle around the Soldiers' National Monument on the site where Lincoln gave the Gettysburg Address. Most stirring of all are the hundreds of small marble gravestones marked only with numbers. A short walk away, the **Cyclorama Center** holds a 356ft circular painting of **Pickett's Charge**, the suicidal Confederate thrust across open wheatfields in broad daylight, and is accompanied by a recitation of the Gettysburg Address (daily 8am–5pm; $3). The earliest existing draft of the Address (not, as commonly believed, scrawled on the back of an envelope) sits in a hallowed cabinet in a dark room on the lower story. The battlegrounds themselves, golden fields reminiscent of an English country landscape, are peaceful now except for their names: **Valley of Death**, **Bloody Run**, **Cemetery Hill**. Uncanny statues of key figures stand at appropriate points and heavy stone monuments honor different regiments.

Eating and nightlife

Evenings in Gettysburg tend to be quiet; the tour buses have gone home and many people choose to drink in their hotel bars. However, there are some good **restaurants** and many in historically important buildings. If you're still hungry for battle trivia, you can contact James Getty, an Abe Lincoln lookalike, to find out about his next performance, where he answers questions and recounts his "memories" (call for details; ☎717/334-6049).

Blue Parrot Bistro 35 Chambersburg St ☎717/337-3739. Pasta and steaks with a good choice of sauces. Like most restaurants in town, things wind down soon after 8.30pm.
Dobbin House Tavern 89 Steinwehr Ave ☎717/334-2100. The oldest house in the city, dating from 1776 and once a hideout for slaves on the "underground railroad" to freedom. Lunch from $8, candlelit dinners are more expensive. Food veers between Pennsylvania Dutch and early American.

Western Pennsylvania

Western Pennsylvania, a key point for frontier trade and an important thoroughfare to the West, was the focus of the fighting between the English and the French in the seven-year French and Indian War for colonial and maritime power (1756–63). It grew to industrial prominence in the nineteenth century, with the exploitation of its coal resources gathering pace after the Civil War, and the opening of the world's first oil well at Titusville (now Drake Well Memorial Park) in northwestern Pennsylvania in 1859.

Today, tourism in western Pennsylvania, like the now-quiet coal and steel industries, is concentrated around the surprisingly appealing city of **Pittsburgh**. To the south of the city, the **Laurel Highlands** features Frank Lloyd Wright's not-to-be-missed architectural masterpiece, **Fallingwater**, as well as nearby **Ohiopyle State Park** and the **Youghiogheny River**, which offer plenty of outdoor activities. Another great wilderness area to explore is the lush **Allegheny National Forest** in the north, which begins twenty miles from I-80. Erie's **Presque Isle State Park,** in the very northwest corner of the state, is also worth a visit for its sandy beaches and wooded hiking trails.

Pittsburgh

The vibrant ten-block district known as the Golden Triangle, at the heart of downtown **PITTSBURGH**, stands at the confluence of the Monongahela, Allegheny and Ohio rivers, once bitterly fought over as the gateway to the West. The French built Fort Duquesne on the site in 1754, only for it to be destroyed four years later by the British, who replaced it with **Fort Pitt**. Industry began with the development of iron foundries in the early 1800s, and by the time of the Civil War, Pittsburgh was producing half of the iron and one third of the glass in the US. Soon after, the city became the world's leading producer of steel, thanks to the vigorous expansion programs of **Andrew Carnegie**, who, by 1870, was the richest man in the world. Present-day Pittsburgh is dotted with his cultural bequests, along with those of other wealthy forefathers including the Mellon bankers, the Frick coal merchants and the Heinz food producers.

Though saddled with a Victorian reputation for dirt and pollution, the city experienced a transformation after the 1950s. A face-lift involved large-scale demolition of abandoned steel mills, which freed up much of the downtown waterfront, but all-out yuppification has been kept in check by the student population and the small-town feel of the older ethnic neighborhoods to the north and south. Pittsburgh today is one of America's most attractive and most liveable cities; resilience and enthusiasm rather than coal fumes fill the air, and

ACCOMODATION				RESTAURANTS	
Appletree B&B	5	HI-Pittsburgh	8	Grand Concourse	D
Best Western University Center	6	The Priory	1	Grandview Saloon	C
Hampton Inn University Center	7	Ramada Plaza Suites	4	Seventh Street Grille	B
Hilton Pittsburgh	3	The Westin	2	Valhalla	A

sleek architecture and green parks supplant smokestacks and slums. The popular **Andy Warhol Museum**, opened in 1994, has bolstered Pittsburgh's image as a destination city, while an enormous new **Convention Center** will bring in major conferences, which is sure to add to the influx of visitors.

Each of Pittsburgh's close-knit neighborhoods – the **South Side** and **Mount Washington**, across the Monongahela River from the **Golden Triangle**, the **North Side** across the Allegheny River, and **Oakland**, the university area in the east – attests in its own way to the city's history and its resurgence. Easily accessible from each other, they retain individual identities while remaining part of a proud whole.

Arrival, information and getting around

Greyhound pulls in at Eleventh Street and Liberty Avenue downtown, across from Amtrak. From the modern, efficient **Pittsburgh International Airport** (☎412/472-3500), fifteen miles west, Airlines Transportation (☎412/321-4990) runs hourly **shuttles** downtown (daily 7am–10pm; $14 one-way, $24 round-trip) and to Oakland ($15 one-way, $26 round-trip). Almost as quick and significantly cheaper, the excellent **local bus** #28X runs roughly every 20min between the airport and Oakland via Robinson town center and downtown (daily 5am–midnight; $2). Pittsburgh's main **visitor center** is downtown on Liberty Avenue, adjacent to the Gateway Center (Mon–Fri 9am–4.45pm, Sat & Sun 9am–2.45pm; ☎412/281-7711 or 1-800/366-0093, �🖥www.visitpittsburgh.com), with subsidiary branches at the airport (Mon–Sat 8am–8pm, Sun noon–8pm), Station Square (daily 10am–5pm) and in the Senator John Heinz Pittsburgh Regional History Center (daily 10am–5pm). The main **post office** is at Seventh and Grant (Mon–Fri 7am–6pm, Sat 7am–2.30pm; ☎412/642-4472; zip code 15230).

Though Pittsburgh is a city of distinct districts, **transportation** between them is simple. **Buses** through town ($1.60), the Monongahela trolley incline to Mount Washington (daily until around midnight; $1.60) and a small "T" **subway** system (free downtown, $1 to cross the river to Station Square, $1.60 or $2 farther into South Hills) are all run by PAT (☎412/442-2000), which has a downtown service center at 534 Smithfield St (Mon & Thurs 9am–6pm, Tues, Wed & Fri 9am–5pm) where you can pick up timetables. Twenty-five cent transfers, which must be bought simultaneously with your fare if needed, allow you to connect with any of the system's vehicles within three hours. For **taxis**, call Yellow Cab (☎412/665-8100).

Accommodation

Pittsburgh's **hotels** and few **B&Bs** are generally pricey, although weekend packages at luxury downtown hotels can bring rates down to under $100. **Oakland** has a couple of reasonably priced business hotels, while the only real budget place is the affiliated **Youth Hostel** on the South Side. You can check out all of the Pittsburgh area's B&Bs at �🖥www.pittsburghbnb.com.

Appletree Bed & Breakfast 703 S Negley Ave ☎412/661-0631, �🖥www.appletreeb-b.com. Friendly upmarket establishment with eight cozy rooms in Shadyside. **❻**

Best Western University Center 3401 Blvd of the Allies ☎412/683-6100 or 1-800/245-4444, �🖥www.bestwestern-pittsburgh.com. Standard motel rooms, but one of the best deals in Oakland. **❹**

Hampton Inn University Center 3315 Hamlet St ☎412/681-1000 or 1-800/426-7866, ⍟www.hamptoninn.com. Welcoming branch of

chain in Oakland offering a generous self-service continental breakfast bar and free van shuttle to downtown and surrounding areas. **❺**

Hilton Pittsburgh, Gateway Center ☎412/391-4600 or 1-800/445-8667, ⍟www.hilton.com. This downtown branch offers all the usual amenities at surprisingly reasonable rates, as well as views across the Point. **❹**

HI-Pittsburgh 830 E Warrington Ave ☎412/431-1267, ⍟trfn.clpgh.org/ayh. New hostel housed in a former bank (vault still intact) with 48 beds

($19–22); located on the South Side in Allentown, 15–20min walk from Station Sq/E Carson St. Check-in 8–10am and 5pm–midnight. ❶
The Priory–A City Inn 614 Pressley St ☎412/231-3338, ⓦwww.thepriory.com. Recently restored 1880s inn, originally built to house travel-ing Benedictine monks and now constituting North Side's nicest B&B. ❺

Ramada Plaza Suites One Bigelow Square ☎412/281-5800, 1-800/225-5858, ⓦwww.plaza-suites.com. Convenient downtown suites with kitchens. ❺
The Westin 1000 Penn Ave ☎412/281-3700 or 1-800/937-8461, ⓦwww.westin.com. Flashy downtown tower with pool and gym. ❼

Downtown: the Golden Triangle

The *New York Times* once described Pittsburgh as "the only city with an entrance," and the view of the **Golden Triangle** skyline on emerging from the tunnel on the Fort Pitt Bridge is undeniably breathtaking. Surrounded by water and fronted with a huge fountain, Pittsburgh's downtown pays tribute to both its coal-grimed past and sunny future. In the core of the original city, the Triangle's imaginative contemporary architecture stands next to Gothic churches and red-brick warehouses. Philip Johnson's magnificent Postmodern concoction, the black-glass Gothic **PPG Place** complex, looms incongruously over the old **Market Square**, lined with historic restaurants and shops and a venue for free live lunchtime entertainment most weekdays. More recent history is apparent on the faded buildings along Liberty Avenue, with 1940s and 1950s fronts left in peace during successive face-lifts. At the flat end of the triangle, the spaceship-like dome of **Mellon Arena** looms above the transport stations – it hosts large concerts and exhibitions, and is home to the **Pittsburgh Penguins** ice hockey team (☎412/642-7367 for Penguins tickets).

Point State Park, at the peak of the Triangle, is where it all began, the site of five different forts during the French and Indian War. This popular gathering area has a 150ft fountain with a pool, as well as great views of port activity and across to the colorful old buildings on verdant Mount Washington. The park, a great place to view sunsets and an excellent venue for the city's outdoor festi-vals, contains the 1764 **Fort Pitt Blockhouse**, the city's oldest structure, a lookout of sandstone and rough brick.

Northeast of downtown along Penn Avenue, the characterful **Strip District** has a bustling early-morning market with wholesale outlets and fresh produce stalls, popular with bargain hunters and good for cheap breakfasts; it's also a place to head to at night. Down by the river is a growing entertainment com-plex, with restaurants, bars, a marina and a floating boardwalk. The seven-floor **Senator John Heinz Pittsburgh Regional History Center**, at 1212 Smallman St (daily 10am–5pm; $6; ☎412/454-6000, ⓦwww.pghhistory.org), does a good job of telling the city's story, paying particular attention to immi-grants of various eras. Nearby, right on the Allegheny River, the huge brand new **Convention Center** is due to open early in 2002.

South Side

In the nineteenth century, 400ft **Mount Washington**, across the Monongahela River, was the site of most of the city's coal mines. No longer dominated by belching steel mills and industry, the **South Side**, banked by the green "moun-tain," is an area of many churches, colorful houses nestled on steep hills, and old neighborhoods. These days only two survive of the twelve cable cars which, at the height of steel production, used to carry coal up the trolley inclines. The 1877 **Duquesne Incline**, from 1197 W Carson St to 1220 Grandview Ave, is the most interesting for its small **museum** of Pittsburgh history in the waiting room at the top: old photos of the city show workers struggling blindly through the streets in pitch-black midday smog (Mon–Sat 5.30am–12.45am, Sun 7.30am–12.45am; $1.60). The outdoor observation platform is a prime spot for **views** over the Golden Triangle to the hills on the horizon, which are especially awesome after dark. Not surprisingly, many (expensive) bars and restaurants here take advantage of the vista.

The best way to get to the South Side is across the 1883 blue-and-cream **Smithfield Street Bridge**, the oldest of fifteen downtown bridges and the most unusual-looking, thanks to its elliptical "fisheye" truss. Just to the west of the bridge stands redbrick **Station Square**, a complex of renovated railroad warehouses filled with restaurants and shops. Its showpiece is the beautiful stained glass and marble of the *Grand Concourse* seafood restaurant (see "Eating" p.180), filling the huge waiting room of the old Pittsburgh and Lake Erie train station. This is also the jetty for the enjoyable hour-long narrated Just Ducky Tours **river cruises**, which run every ninety minutes in summer, less frequently in the shoulder seasons (daily April–Oct, Sat & Sun only Nov 10am–6pm; $15, children $9; ℡412/402-3825).

Along the banks of the Monongahela, **East Carson Street** is the main drag of the lively mixed residential and commercial South Side, where a longstanding community of Polish and Ukrainian steelworkers has gradually absorbed an offbeat mix of cafés, bars and bookstores. Onion-domed churches stand alongside thrift stores and galleries, and the narrow backstreets are lined by brick rowhouses. This is also Pittsburgh's most extensive and varied **nightlife** center.

North Side

The star attraction on the **North Side**, annexed by Pittsburgh only in 1907, is undoubtedly the **Andy Warhol Museum**, 117 Sandusky St, just over the Seventh Street Bridge from downtown, which documents the life and work of Pittsburgh's most celebrated son over eight floors of a spacious Victorian warehouse (Tues–Thurs 10am–5pm, Fri 10am–10pm, Sat & Sun 10am–5pm, closed Mon; $8, students and children $4; Fri 5–10pm free; ℡412/237-8300, ⓦwww.warhol.org).

Born in Pittsburgh in 1928, Andy Warhol (born Andrew Warhola, the youngest son of working-class Carpatho-Rusyn immigrants) moved to New York at the age of 21, after graduating from Carnegie-Mellon University. By the end of the 1950s, he was one of the most successful commercial artists in the nation, before turning his attention to fine and Pop arts. During the early 1960s he started shooting 16mm films – *Empire*, *Chelsea Girls* and *Lonesome Cowboys* – and developed the "Exploding Plastic Inevitable" multimedia show, featuring erotic dancers and music by the Velvet Underground, whom he managed. After founding *Interview* magazine in 1969, Warhol became transfixed with the rich and famous and, up until his death in 1987, was perhaps best known for his celebrity portraits and his appearances at society events.

Although the majority of Warhol's most famous pieces are in the hands of private collectors, the museum boasts an impressive selection of work, with over five hundred items on display at any one time, including Pop Art (*Campbell's Soup Cans*) and portraiture (Elvis, Marilyn, Jackie Kennedy). It pays equal attention to archival material, and chronological self-guided tours give a good idea of Warhol's artistic development and his eventful lifestyle. A cinema shows two films or videos daily, one of which is usually a Warhol production. There's an excellent, informative Archives Study Department and a popular free **Weekend Factory** (call for details), where Warhol's techniques are explained and visitors can have a go themselves. During "**Good Fridays**" (Fri 5–10pm; free), there is a cash bar, and the lobby buzzes with live bands or other performance arts. The museum also has a well-stocked gift shop and a café.

Elsewhere on the North Side, revitalization centers around the intriguingly named **Mexican War Streets** on the northern edge of Allegheny Commons. In this unevenly restored, tree-lined area of nineteenth-century gray-brick and limestone terraces, old families, descendants of German and Scandinavian immigrants, live in an uneasy truce alongside young professionals. The excellent and highly unusual **Mattress Factory**, 500 Sampsonia Way (Tues–Sat 10am–5pm, Sun 1–5pm, closed Aug; $6, free on Thurs; ☎412/231-3169), has contemporary installations by top mixed-media artists, and is a must on any visit to the city. The **National Aviary**, Allegheny Commons West (daily 9am–4.30pm; $5; ☎412/323-7235), is a huge indoor bird sanctuary with over three hundred species, including foul-mouthed parrots, in free flight under a showpiece 30ft glass dome. Nearby, **The Pittsburgh Children's Museum**, 10 Children's Way, Allegheny Square (Tues–Thurs & Sat 10am–5pm, Fri 10am–8pm, Sun noon–5pm; $5, children 2–18 yrs $4.50, Thurs $3.50 all; ☎412/322-5058, ⓦwww.pittsburghkids.org), offers a plethora of games, events and special exhibitions.

The **USS Requin**, a 1945 submarine, bobs on the shores of the Allegheny River (daily 10am–5pm; $5) outside the huge state-of-the-art **Carnegie Science Center**, 1 Allegheny Ave, most of whose exhibits are aimed at children (daily 10am–5pm, Sat until 9pm; $14, children $10; ☎412/237-3400, ⓦwww .carnegiesciencecenter.com). One exhibit, "The Works," explores Pittsburgh's past by means of a working foundry, and it holds such wonders as the world's largest cockroach (from Florida). The Center also contains an impressive OMN-IMAX theater and a planetarium ($8 for one show, $12 for two); combination tickets are available ($18 for exhibits and one attraction, $21 for all). Next door, **Heinz Field** (call ☎412/432-7800 for tickets or tours), home to the **Pittsburgh Steelers** football team, is one of the two brand new sports venues that opened in 2001 to replace the shared Three Rivers Stadium. The other, further along the river toward 6th St Bridge, is **PNC Park** (☎1-800/289-2827), the new home of the **Pittsburgh Pirates** baseball team. Beautifully constructed so that from most seats you get a sweeping view of the Allegheny and downtown, it's a real treat to watch a game here on a balmy summer night.

Oakland and the East Side

Oakland, Pittsburgh's university area, which is dotted with the mansions of wealthy industrialists, houses the predictable mixture of students and more-established families. Sights concentrate around the campuses of **Carnegie-Mellon University**, the **University of Pittsburgh** (always known as "Pitt") and several other colleges. The 42-story Gothic-revival **Cathedral of Learning**, Fifth Avenue at Bigelow Boulevard, called by Frank Lloyd Wright "the world's largest Keep Off the Grass sign," is a university building with a difference: over twenty classrooms are furnished with antiques and specially crafted items donated by the city's different ethnic groups, from Lithuanian to Chinese to Irish. These beautiful rooms, far more interesting than they may sound, have been used by students since the 1930s; all are open to the public except the exotic Syria-Lebanon room and the Early American room, complete with trap door and secret passage, which are shown on ninety-minute **guided tours** only (Mon–Fri 9am–2.30pm, Sat 9.30am–2.30pm, Sun 11am–2.30pm; $3). Alternatively, you can do your own tape-recorded tour (also $3) or follow the useful booklet ($1.25). On the grounds behind the Cathedral of Learning is the French Gothic **Heinz Memorial Chapel**

(Mon–Fri 9am–5pm, Sun 1–5pm; free), notable for its long, narrow, stained-glass windows depicting political, literary and religious figures.

Across from the cathedral at 4400 Forbes Ave, the **Carnegie cultural complex** holds two great museums – the **Museum of Natural History**, famed for its extensive dinosaur relics and sparkling gems, and the **Museum of Art**, with Impressionist, Post-Impressionist and American regional art, as well as an excellent modern collection (Mon–Sat 10am–5pm, Thurs until 9pm, Sun 1–5pm, closed Mon Sept–June; $8, students $5). Schenley Park nearby includes the colorful flower gardens of **Phipps Conservatory** (Tues–Sun 9am–5pm, extended hours during shows; $6, students $4) and wild wooded areas beyond.

If you're coming to the East Side from downtown, be sure to avoid the area along Center Avenue known as **The Hill District**; this is one of Pittsburgh's toughest districts, especially after dark. Many cab drivers avoid it, but as it neighbors the college precincts, tourists can easily stumble into it. An alternative route from downtown is along Liberty Avenue via the predominantly Italian neighborhood of **Bloomfield**, a busy area of shops, restaurants and quaint rowhouses.

The stretch of Fifth Avenue from around the Cathedral of Learning up to Shadyside is lined with important and architecturally beautiful academic buildings, places of worship and early private mansions. The imposing **Soldiers and Sailors Memorial**, 4141 Fifth Ave (Tues–Sun 9am–4pm; $4), also serves as a museum and is filled with military paraphernalia and historic exhibits. Further on, opposite the exquisite external mural of the Byzantine Catholic **Church of the Holy Spirit**, is the humble broadcasting complex of **WQED**, notable for being the first publicly-funded TV station when it opened in April 1954 and home to the long-running kids' show *Mr Rogers' Neighborhood*.

Shadyside, on the eastern fringes of Oakland, is an upmarket, trendy neighborhood with the commercial section of Walnut Street being particularly chic. There are several art galleries, and the **Pittsburgh Center for the Arts**, at 6300 Fifth Ave in Mellon Park, showcases innovative Pittsburgh art in various media (Mon–Sat 10am–5.30pm, Sun noon–5pm; free). A short way to the south, **Squirrel Hill** is another lively area, housing a mixture of students and the city's largest Jewish community, with a fine selection of shops and restaurants lining Murray and Forbes avenues, plus two multiscreen cinemas.

Further east, the small **Frick Art Museum**, 7227 Reynolds St (Tues–Sat 10am–5pm, Sun noon–6pm; free), shows Italian, Flemish and French art from the fifteenth to the nineteenth centuries; its collection of decorative art includes two of Marie Antoinette's chairs. On the same grounds, **Clayton** is a mansion furnished exactly as it was when industrialist Henry Clay Frick lived there. Obligatory **guided tours** ($5) walk you around the house, pointing out the various late-Victorian decorative touches, as well as the bed where Frick recovered after being stabbed by an anarchist during the bitter Homestead Steel Strike. Frick and most of his family are buried, under tons of protective concrete and steel, just south of the family home, on the highest hill in **Homewood Cemetery**, which also holds the tombs of H.J. Heinz (of the ketchup and baked beans fortune) and sundry Mellons. Three miles north, bordering the Allegheny River, the green expanse of **Highland Park** contains the nicely landscaped and enjoyable **Pittsburgh Zoo** (daily in summer 10am–6pm, rest of year 9am–5pm; April–Nov $8, Dec–March $6), which has the distinction of having bred two baby elephants in recent years.

Eating

Eating downtown can prove expensive and the area is rather deserted at night, but there's a growing range of places in the adjacent **Strip District** and good neighborhood Mediterranean and Eastern European restaurants along and around **East Carson Street** on the South Side. **Station Square** and **Mount Washington** cater to a more upmarket crowd, while **Oakland** is, as you might expect, home to an array of cheap student hangouts – look out for the ultra-cheap mobile ethnic food vans at lunchtime. A little further east, **Shadyside** and **Squirrel Hill** have a number of good mid-priced places.

Grand Concourse 1 Station Square ☎412/261-1717. Pricey, plush seafood restaurant in a gorgeous setting inside the Station Square complex.

Grandview Saloon 1212 Grandview Ave ☎412/431-1400. Relaxed Mount Washington restaurant, usually packed with a young crowd enjoying huge plates of pasta. Arrive early for a deck table with a view.

Gullifty's 1922 Murray Ave ☎412/521-8222. Squirrel Hill establishment serving fine pastas, meat dishes and sumptuous sweets. Look out for the twice-yearly Garlic Festival (usually April and Oct).

Kaya 2000 Smallman St ☎412/261-6565. Stylish Caribbean restaurant in the Strip District with a varied vegetarian selection. Huge range of beers, rums and other spirits.

Kim's Coffee Shop 5447 Penn Ave ☎412/362-7019. Friendly, cozy and very cheap Vietnamese joint also serving some Chinese and Thai – the spicy cold Beef Siamese is a treat. Licensed but you can BYOB too. Closed Mon.

La Feria 5527 Walnut St ☎412/682-4501. Colorful upstairs Peruvian shop-cum-restaurant offering a limited but tasty selection of inexpensive specials from the Andes. BYOB.

Mallorca 2228 E Carson St ☎412/488-1818. In a smart setting on the South Side, this restaurant serves excellent paella and Mediterranean dishes, as well as fine sangria. Try the delicious goat in red wine sauce.

Penn Brewery Troy Hill Rd and Vinial St ☎412/237-9402. On the North Side, this is Pittsburgh's longest-established brewpub, serving decent German food.

Seventh Street Grille 130 7th St, Century Building ☎412/338-0303. Excellent Californian- and Italian-influenced menus strong on pasta and seafood. Very popular despite being a little pricey.

Star of India 412 S Craig St ☎412/682-3000. Indian restaurant in Oakland offering tasty North Indian cooking. Wash down the great lunch buffet with a smooth, creamy lassi.

Valhalla 1150 Smallman St ☎412/434-1440. At the start of the Strip, close to Greyhound, this trendy microbrewery with cool decor serves a range of specialties like mango salmon and veal veronese, as well as its own beer.

Yumwok/Lulu's Noodles 400 S Craig St ☎412/687-7777. Combined establishment serving filling noodles and good standard pan-Asian cuisine at bargain prices, justifiably popular with students. BYOB.

Nightlife and entertainment

With its recent cultural resurgence, Pittsburgh's **nightlife** offers rich pickings in everything from the classics to jazz and alternative rock. The nationally regarded City Theater, 57 S 13th St (☎412/431-4900), puts on groundbreaking productions in a converted South Side church. The widely traveled Pittsburgh Symphony Orchestra plays at the Heinz Hall, 600 Penn Ave (☎412/392-4900), and the city's ballet, dance and opera companies perform at the downtown Benedum Center for the Performing Arts, 7th Street and Penn Avenue (☎412/456-6666). *City Paper*, a free weekly newspaper published on Wednesdays, has extensive **listings**.

Bloomfield Bridge Tavern 4412 Liberty Ave ☎412/682-8611. Super-friendly Polish local pub just over the bridge from Oakland. Live music Thurs–Sat, from punk to polka, and there's also food – mostly greasy stuff, though the potato pancakes are great when washed down with vodka.

Club Café 56 S 12th St ☎412/431-4950. Laid-back South Side club with regular live (often acoustic) music.

Club Laga 3609 Forbes Ave ☎412/687-4636. Large, loud student disco that also hosts live rock bands of some standing.

Dee's 1314 Carson St ☎412/431-5400. South Side institution; great jukebox, pool, darts and a lively crowd.

M 1600 Smallman St ☎412/261-2232. Huge,

popular Strip District dance club (mainly techno and industrial) that also promotes some live rock. Next door to *Rosebud* (see below).

Nick's Fat City 1601 E Carson St ☎412/481-6880. Popular South Side pool bar with (usually) good live bands. Happy hour 10pm–midnight.

Rosebud 1650 Smallman St ☎412/261-2221. Generally considered Pittsburgh's best music venue, this atmospheric bar/restaurant features acoustic, rockabilly and indie acts.

The Sharp Edge 302 S St Clair ☎412/661-3537. Friendly beer emporium on the edge of Shadyside with good food and hundreds of imported and American beers, including cask ales. The jukebox plays rock tunes and there's sports on TV.

Smokin' Joe's 2001 E Carson St ☎412/431-6757. One of the South Side's most congenial bars, with a vast range of beers on tap and over 200 bottled brands.

31st St Pub 3101 Penn Ave ☎412/391-8334. It won't win any prizes for decor, but this place draws a crowd to hear up-and-coming local indie and hardcore bands and the odd underground celebrity act from out of town.

Around Pittsburgh: Fallingwater and Ohiopyle

Just over an hour southeast of Pittsburgh, the **Laurel Highlands** takes in seventy miles of rolling hills and valleys. The main reasons to come this way down Hwy-381 are to see one of Frank Lloyd Wright's most unique creations and to take advantage of some prime outdoor opportunities around the small town of Ohiopyle.

You do not need to be an architecture buff to appreciate Wright's **FALLING-WATER** (mid–March to late Nov Tues–Sun 10am–4pm; $10, weekends $15; ☎724/329-8501, ⊛www.paconserve.org), which was built in the late 1930s for the Kaufmann family, owners of Pittsburgh's premier department store. Signposted off Hwy-381 some twenty miles south of I-70, it is set on Bear Run Creek in the midst of gorgeous deciduous forest that constitutes the 5000-acre **Bear Run Nature Reserve**. It is the only one of Wright's buildings to be on display exactly as it was designed, and for good reason – it's built right into a set of cliffside waterfalls. Wright used a **cantilever** system to make the multi-tiered structure "cascade down the hill like the water down the falls"; the house's almost precarious position is truly stunning, and it is remarkable how well its predominantly rectangular shapes blend in with nature's less uniform lines. The well-presented hour-long tour (more extensive and expensive tours are available for experts) takes visitors up through the different levels of the building, allowing plenty of time to admire the setting from the various terraces as well as the beauty of the interior design. Among the house's pioneering features is a lack of load-bearing walls, which gives an extra sense of space, and **natural skylights**. When Edgar Kaufmann Jr. entrusted the house to the Western Pennsylvania Conservancy in 1963, he donated all the furnishings and artwork with it. Objects on display include some fine East Asian **sculpture** of Buddhas and Indian deities. Tours begin and end a few hundred yards from the house in the wooden reception pavilion, where there is a café and shop.

Ohiopyle and around

Five miles south of Fallingwater, tiny **OHIOPYLE** is the most convenient base from which to enjoy the wilds of **Ohiopyle State Park** or activities like whitewater rafting on the **Youghiogheny River**. The park fans out around the town and river, offering a maze of trails for hiking or biking, and natural delights such as **Cucumber Falls** and the unique habitat of the **Ferncliff Peninsula**, known for its wildflowers. At the built-up end of a massive steel and wooden footbridge high above the river, a small **visitor center** dispenses local information (daily 9am–5pm; ☎724/329-8591). Just beyond it the *Ohiopyle House Café*, 144 Grant St (☎724/329-1122), serves up tasty dishes like lobster ravioli and caramel pudding, while a couple of seasonal canteens and a general store sell basic snacks and provisions. The *Yough Plaza Motel* on Sherman St (T1-800/992-7238; ❸) has reasonable standard units; even better for budget travelers is the affiliated **Ohiopyle Youth Hostel** just north of the railway tracks at 113 Ferncliff Rd (T724/329-4476), with dorm beds from $15. If you want to camp or rent a cabin in the park itself, call the reservation service at T1-888/727-2757. For **rafting**, White Water Adventurers at 6 Negley St (T1-800/992-7238, Wwww.wwaraft.com) is one of several outfits that rent equipment and give instruction.

Three miles southwest of Ohiopyle, there is another Frank Lloyd Wright house, **Kentuck Knob** (Tues–Sun 10am–4pm; $10, weekends $15), also known as the I.N. Hagan House. A hexagonal structure of fieldstone and cypress, it sits on a hilltop giving wonderful views of the surrounding countryside. Further down the Youghiogheny, in the village of **Confluence,** the cozy *River's Edge Café* (T814/395-5059) serves good food at moderate prices right on the banks of the river.

Northwest Pennsylvania

The overwhelmingly rural northwestern corner of Pennsylvania offers nature lovers a treat in the shape of **Allegheny National Forest**, which spreads out between I-80 and the far western reaches of New York State. The only major conurbation is **Erie**, further northwest on the eponymous Great Lake.

Allegheny National Forest

Occupying over half a million acres and a sizeable portion of four counties, the pristine **ALLEGHENY NATIONAL FOREST** affords a bounty of opportunities for engaging in outdoor pursuits like hiking, fishing, snowmobiling and, best of all, admiring the fall foliage which rivals any in New England. In the north there are several points of interest within easy access of Hwy-6, the major route through the forest. Entering the region from the east, on the highway, it is worth a stop to admire the **Kinzua Viaduct** railroad bridge, the highest and longest in the world when constructed in 1882, which is accessible by foot and allows tremendous views of the creek below. It is possible to ride over the bridge on the **Knox Kane Kinzua Railroad**, whose office in Marienville (T814/927-6621) to the southwest can provide fare and schedule information. The dominant feature of the forest's northern section is the huge **Kinzua Reservoir**, created by a dam at the southern end. Swimming is possible at **Kinzua** and **Kiasatha beaches** or you can enjoy a picnic at **Rimrock Overlook** or at **Willow Bay** in the very north. The summer-only Kinzua Point Information Center on Hwy-59 (T814/726-1291) has details on trails and private campgrounds, or you can make **camping** reservations directly for any of the forest's 715 state-run sites on T1-877/444-6777.

Erie

The focal point of Pennsylvania's forty-mile slice of Lake Erie waterfront is the pleasant city of **ERIE** itself. It bears no resemblance to the major urban centers of Pittsburgh or Philadelphia, being entirely low-rise and extremely leafy; indeed you hardly realize you are downtown until you find yourself in the shady park-like town square, on 6th Street between the main thoroughfares of Peach and State streets. There are several places of cultural interest in the city, all within walking distance of here, including the Neoclassical **Court House** and several **museums** devoted to history, art and science; better than these, the **Erie Maritime Museum** at 150 E Front St in the Bayfront Historical District (Mon–Sat 9am–5pm, Sun noon–5pm; $4) has a fascinating display on the geological and ecological development of the Great Lakes and also focuses on warships of different periods; the elegant **US Brig Niagara** is usually moored outside and is part of the museum.

Undoubtedly, Erie's main attraction is the elongated comma-shaped peninsula of **Presque Isle State Park**, which bends east from its narrow neck three miles west of downtown until it almost touches the city's northernmost tip. The park is maintained as a nature preserve and has wide sandy **beaches** good for swimming, backed by thick woods offering a series of trails. The Park Office (daily 8am–4pm; ☎814/833-7424) provides general information and a map. Those without a vehicle can hop on the **Presque Isle Aquabus** (Mon noon–6pm, Tues–Sun 10am–6pm; $3 one-way, $5 round-trip), which leaves on the hour from Dobbins Landing on the Erie Bayfront.

Practicalities

Erie has frequent Greyhound **bus** connections to Pittsburgh, Cleveland and Buffalo; the station is at 5759 Peach St, some three miles out of downtown, and is served by local bus #9 to Mill Creek Mall. The **CVB**, downtown at 109 Boston Store Place (Mon–Fri 8.30am–5pm; ☎814/454-7191 or 1-800/524-3743, ⊛www.TourErie.com), is the place to go for information.

Accommodation is often twice as expensive in the summer as in the off-season. The centrally located *Holiday Inn* downtown, 18 W 18th St (☎814/456-2961 or 1-800/832-9101; ❹), provides the usual amenities but the elegant *Boothby Inn* B&B at 311 W 6th St (☎814/456-1888 or 1-866/266-8429; ❺) makes for a far more pleasant stay. Out by Presque Isle, *El Patio*, 2950 W 8th St (☎814/838-9772; ❹), is one of numerous motels lining Peninsula Drive and offers very good long-stay rates off-season. The *Sara Coyne Campground*, 50 Peninsula Drive (☎814/833-4560), is just before the entrance to Presque Isle, the best location of the various **campsites** in the Erie area. Nearby at 35 Peninsula Drive the friendly *Joe Root's Grill* (☎814/836-7668) serves up hearty portions; downtown try the *Marketplace Grill*, 319 State St (☎814/455-7272), for steaks and a filling pizza and pasta lunchtime buffet, or the cheap Chinese *Happy Garden*, 418 State St (☎814/452-4488).

New Jersey

The long, skinny state of **NEW JERSEY** has been at the heart of US history since the **Revolution**, when a battle was fought at **Princeton**, and George Washington spent two bleak winters at **Morristown**. As the **Civil War** came, the state's commitment to an industrial future ensured that, despite its border location along the Mason–Dixon line, it fought with the Union.

That commitment to industry has doomed New Jersey in modern times. Most travelers only see "the Garden State" (so called for the rich market garden territory at the state's heart) from the stupendously ugly New Jersey Turnpike toll road which, heavy with truck traffic, cuts through a landscape of gray smokestacks and industrial estates. Even the songs of **Bruce Springsteen**, Asbury Park's golden boy, paint his home state as a gritty **urban wasteland** of empty lots, gray highways, lost dreams and blue-collar tragedy. The majority of the refineries and factories hug only a mere fifteen-mile-wide swath along the turnpike, but bleak cities like **Newark**, home to the major airport, and **Trenton**, the capital, do little to improve the look of the place and the state suffers from a poor image problem.

But there is more to New Jersey than factories and pollution. Alongside its revolutionary history, Thomas Paine and Walt Whitman both wrote nostalgically of the happy years they spent there; while the **northwest corner** near the **Delaware Water Gap** is traced with picturesque lakes, streams and woodlands. Best of all, the **Atlantic shore** offers many bustling resorts, from the tattered glitz of Atlantic City to the glorious kitsch of Wildwoods and the old-world charm of Cape May.

Getting around New Jersey

With a **car**, New Jersey is easily accessible from New York City, via I-95, while the **New Jersey Turnpike** (a $6 toll road) sweeps from the northeast down to Philadelphia. The **Garden State Parkway** runs parallel to the Atlantic from New York to Cape May (with a 35¢ toll every twenty miles), and gives easy access to the shoreline resorts. One nice route in the north of the state is US-29, from Trenton along the Delaware River. In general, driving in the Garden State is not pleasurable, though, as New Jersey must have the worst and most confusing set of roadsigns in the States.

Newark International Airport (☎973/961-6000) is the fastest-growing gateway to the US, served by all the major international carriers and popular for its convenient access to Manhattan (a 30min bus ride away; $11) rather than for being in New Jersey.

Numerous Amtrak **trains** pass through Newark, Princeton and Trenton, en route between Philadelphia, New York and Washington, DC. There's also a service that links Philadelphia and Atlantic City. Greyhound covers most of the state, while New Jersey Transit (☎973/762-5100 or 1-800/772-2222) also provides a good train and bus service, extending to Philadelphia and New York as well as out to the coast. New Jersey's south coast is connected to Delaware by the Cape May–Lewes **ferry** (in Cape May ☎609/886-1725; in Lewes ☎302/645-6313).

Inland New Jersey

Traveling west on the interstates from the shore or from New York City, visitors see the New Jersey of popular imagination: heavily industrialized, a cultural desert, peppered with run-down cities like Trenton and Paterson. **Newark**, the state's largest city, is perhaps the nation's drabbest, redeemed only by its efficient airport, new performing arts center, and views over the Hudson to the Statue of Liberty (which is, incidentally, in New Jersey waters). The one place that holds interest in inland New Jersey is **Princeton**, an Ivy League town that makes a pretty if limited stopoff.

Princeton

Self-satisfied **PRINCETON**, on US-206 eleven miles north of Trenton, is home to **Princeton University** – the nation's fourth oldest, which broke away from the overly religious Yale in 1756. It began its days inauspiciously as Stony Brook in the late 1600s and then in 1724 became known as Princes Town, a coach stop between New York and Philadelphia. In January 1777, a week after Washington's triumph against the British at Trenton, the **Battle of Princeton** occurred southwest of town. This victory, a turning point in the Revolutionary effort, bolstered the morale of Washington's troops before their long winter encampment at Morristown to the north. After the war, in 1783, the **Continental Congress**, fearful of potential attack from incensed unpaid veterans in Philadelphia, met here for four months; the leafy, well-kept town was then left in peace to follow its academic pursuits. Graduates of the university include actor James Stewart, jazz-age writer F. Scott Fitzgerald, and presidents Wilson and Madison. Today, there is little to do in this sleepy place other than tour the university and see the historic sites.

Arrival, information and getting around

A shuttle bus, the Princeton Airporter, makes the run from Newark (1hr 30min) and JFK (2hr 40min) airports to town (daily every hour 7am–10pm; $23 and $38 respectively; ☎609/587-6600). The in-town train terminal, on campus at University Place, a block north of Alexander Road, is connected by SEPTA shuttles (☎215/580-7800) to Princeton Junction, three miles south, where both Amtrak and New Jersey Transit stop on their New York–Philadelphia runs. Suburban Transit **buses** from New York's Port Authority bus station (☎1-800/222-0492) stop every thirty minutes at Nassau Street.

Information is available from Stanhope Hall at the university (Mon–Fri 8.45am–5pm; ☎609/258-3600) or from the **Chamber of Commerce** at 216 Rockingham Row (Mon–Fri 8.30am-4.30pm; ☎609/683-1760, ⓦwww .princetonchamber.org). The **Historical Society museum**, 158 Nassau St (Tues–Sun noon–4pm), organizes **walking tours** through town (Sun 2pm; $6) and also provides **maps** so you can do it yourself.

The town and the university

Mercer Street, the long road that sweeps southwest past the university campus to Nassau Street, is lined with elegant colonial houses, graced with shutters, columns and wrought-iron fences. The **Princeton Battlefield State Park**, a mile out, includes the **Thomas Clarke House**, 500 Mercer St, a Quaker farmhouse that served as a hospital during the battle (park open daily dawn to dusk, house open Wed–Sat 10am–noon & 1–4pm, Sun 1–4pm; free; ☎609/921-0074). The simple house at 112 Mercer St, back toward town, is where **Albert Einstein** lived while teaching at the Institute of Advanced Study (however, it is not open to the public).

Princeton University's tranquil and shaded campus is a beautiful place for a stroll. Just inside the main gates on Nassau Street, **Nassau Hall** (tours Mon–Sat 10am, 11am, 1.30pm & 3.30pm, Sun 1.30pm & 3.30pm; free; ☎609/258-3606) was, when constructed in 1756, the largest stone building in the nation; its 26-inch-thick walls (now patterned with plaques and patches of ivy placed by graduating classes) withstood American and British fire during the Revolution. It was also the seat of government during Princeton's brief spell as national capital. The 1925 **chapel**, based on one at Kings College, Cambridge University, in England, has stained-glass windows showing scenes from works by Dante, Shakespeare and Milton, as well as the Bible, and the Prospect Gardens, a flowerbed in the shape of the university emblem, are a blaze of orange in summer. In the middle of the campus, fronted by the

Picasso sculpture *Head of a Woman*, the **University Art Museum**, not included on the standard tours, is well worth a look for its collection from the Renaissance to the present, including Modigliani, Van Gogh and Warhol, and Chinese and pre-Columbian art (Tues–Sat 10am–5pm, Sun 1–5pm; ☎609/452-3787; free).

While Princeton has found itself acting as a sanctuary and gathering place for exiled members of China's democracy movement since the **Tiananmen Square** massacre of 1989, a substantial number of those who visit are disarmingly conservative prospective students and their proud parents, soaking up the tales of old-boy pranks and superstitions that prop up the Ivy League tradition. The student-led **tours** may be complacent, but they are free; they leave from the Frist Campus Center, facing Washington Road (Mon–Sat 10am, 11am, 1.30pm & 3.30pm, Sun 1.30pm & 3.30pm; ☎609/258-3603).

Accommodation, eating and drinking

The only **hotel** in the center of Princeton is the pompous, ersatz-colonial *Nassau Inn* on Palmer Square (☎609/921-7500; **❼**). Budget **motels** can be found along US-1 and in the suburb of **Lawrenceville** a few miles south of town; there's the functional *Red Roof Inn*, 3203 US-1 (☎609/896-3388; **❷**), and the *McIntosh Inn* (☎609/896-3700; **❸**), by the Quaker Bridge Mall on US-1, along with the more relaxing *Best Western Palmer Inn*, 3499 US-1 at Alexander Road (☎609/452-2500; **❺**).

There's cheap diner-type **food** along Witherspoon Street. *Panera's*, 136 Nassau St (☎609/688-1692), serves tasty, reasonably priced sandwiches, or for a more upmarket feast, the popular *Annex*, 128 Nassau St (☎609/921-7555), serves quality Italian dinners by candlelight. *Mediterra* at 29 Hulfish St (☎609/252-9680) is an upscale Mediterranean restaurant with a welcoming atmosphere and well-prepared food. **Nightlife** is limited, especially out of term time, but the *Tap Room* bar downstairs at the *Nassau Inn* is usually full of ancient revelers drinking, reminiscing and enjoying live jazz.

New Jersey shore

New Jersey's Atlantic coast, a 130-mile stretch of almost uninterrupted **resorts** – some rowdy, many pitifully run-down and faded, a few undeveloped and peaceful – has long been reliant on farming and tourism. No profitable ports were established, nor did short-lived attempts at whaling come to anything. In the late 1980s the whole coastline suffered severe and well-publicized pollution from ocean dumping, but today the beaches, if occasionally somewhat crowded, are safe and clean: sandy, broad and lined by characteristic wooden **boardwalks**, some of which, in an attempt to maintain their condition, charge admission during the summer. The rundown glitz of **Atlantic City** is perhaps the shore's best known attraction, but there are also quieter resorts like **Spring Lake** and historic Victorian **Cape May**, plus local gems like **Wildwood** that are worth the journey further down the coast.

Spring Lake and Asbury Park

SPRING LAKE, about twenty miles down the Jersey coast, is one of the smallest, most uncommercial communities on the shore, a gentle respite on the road south to Atlantic City. Tourism in this elegant Victorian resort evolved slowly, without the booms, crises, resurgences and depressions of other seaside towns – partly due to the strict zoning laws prohibiting new building. You can walk the totally undeveloped two-mile **boardwalk** and watch the crashing ocean from battered gazebos, swim and bask on the white beaches (in summer, compulsory beach tags cost $6 per day, but most guesthouses provide them free) or sit in the shade by the town's namesake, **Spring Lake** itself. Wooden footbridges, swans and geese, and the grand St Catherine's Catholic Church on the banks of the lake give it the feel of a country village. For the moment, what little activity there is centers on the upmarket shops of Third Avenue.

Bruce Springsteen fans can use the town as a base for visiting nearby **ASBURY PARK**, a decaying old seaside town where The Boss lived for many years and played his first gigs. Almost nothing remains of the carousels and sea-side arcades that Springsteen wrote about on early albums such as his debut *Greetings from Asbury Park*; the sole survivor is Madame Marie's fortune-telling salon, which still stands amid the rubble and half-completed condominium developments that line the boardwalk. Also of interest is the *Stone Pony*, 913 Ocean Ave, where Springsteen played dozens of times in the mid-1970s and to which he returned even after becoming famous, for impromptu jam sessions and, in 1999, for his most recent reunion tour with the E Street Band.

Practicalities

Spring Lake is accessible by US-34 from the New Jersey Turnpike, and served by New Jersey Transit from New York. The Chamber of Commerce (☎732/449-0577) keeps erratic hours but the Spring Lake Hotel and Guest House Association (☎732/449-0577) can help find lodging, especially on sum-mer weekends. There are no cheap **motels**, and **B&Bs** can be expensive. The easygoing *Sea Crest by the Sea*, 19 Tuttle Ave (☎732/449-9031; ❼), is an 1885 inn with rooms furnished individually on quirky themes, and an excellent all-you-can-eat home-cooked breakfast. *Ashling Cottage*, 106 Sussex Ave (☎732/449-3553; closed Feb; ❻), overlooks the lake, while the *Chateau Inn*, 500 Warren Ave (☎732/974-2000 or 1-877/974-LAKE; ❹), is slightly less expensive. Adjacent to Asbury Park, in the much more attractive Victorian resort of **OCEAN GROVE**, friendly *Lillagaard B&B*, 5 Abbot Ave (☎732/988-1216; ❹), is right on the beach. Most of Spring Lake's **restaurants** are in the elegant Victorian hotels along the seafront, and can be pricey. The **North Pavilion** on the boardwalk sells cheap breakfasts and snacks, but there are no fast-food stands along the walk itself. *Who's On Third*, 1300 Third Ave (☎732/449-4233), is a no-nonsense café serving breakfast and lunch. For a blowout, the *Sandpiper*, 7 Atlantic Ave (☎732/449-6060), serves superb fresh fish and seafood in elegant, candlelit surroundings. Dinner costs around $20; bring your own bottle.

Atlantic City

What they wanted was Monte Carlo. They didn't want Las Vegas.
What they got was Las Vegas. We always knew that they would get Las Vegas.

Stuart Mendelson, Philadelphia Journal, 1978.

ATLANTIC CITY, on Absecon Island just off the midpoint of the Jersey shoreline, has been a tourist magnet since 1854, when Philadelphia speculators created it as a rail terminal resort. In 1909, at the peak of the seaside town's popularity, Baedeker wrote "there is something colossal about its vulgarity" – a quality which it sustains today, even while beset by bankruptcy and decay. The real-life model for the board game **Monopoly**, it has an impressive history of popular culture, boasting the nation's first **Boardwalk** (1870), the world's first **Big Wheel** (1892), the first color **postcards** (1893) and the first **Miss America Beauty Pageant** (cunningly devised to extend the tourist season in 1921, and still held here yearly). During Prohibition and the Depression, Atlantic City was a center for rum-running, packed with speakeasies and illegal gambling dens. Thereafter, in the face of increasing competition from Florida, it slipped into a steep decline, until desperate city officials decided in 1976 to open up the decrepit resort to legal **gambling**.

Arrival, information and getting around

Traveling to Atlantic City by bus can be a real money-spinner; casino-sponsored **buses** from New York, Philadelphia and other points along the coast give away vouchers exchangeable for cash and free meals to a value well above the fare. It's hoped that you will spend all this money and more in the casinos, but you can easily cash it and leave. The brand new bus terminal at Atlantic and Ohio is served by Greyhound (☎609/345-6617 or 1-800/231-2222) and New Jersey Transit (☎973/762-5100 or 1-800/772-3606) as well as several other bus companies connecting the city with New York, Washington, DC and Philadelphia.

New Jersey Transit trains ($6 one-way, $12 round-trip) run between Atlantic City and Philadelphia, from the new train station next to the Convention Center at 1 Miss America Way (☎1-800/AC-TRAIN). **Atlantic City International Airport** in Pomona (☎609/645-7895) has direct flights to Philadelphia, as well as further afield to cities in Florida and the Midwest; a shuttle bus service connects the airport with the city proper ($20; ☎1-888/640-2222). For maps and information, head for the **Atlantic City Convention and Visitors Association,** 2314 Pacific Ave (Mon–Fri 9am–5pm; ☎609/348-7100 or 1-888/228-4748, ⊛www.atlanticcitynj.com). Two satellite offices are open longer hours – try the helpful **visitor information desk** in Ocean One Mall on the Boardwalk (daily 11am–7pm) or the new **visitors center** on the AC Expressway one mile east of the Atlantic City toll plaza (summer Mon–Thurs 9am–5pm, Fri–Sun 9am–8pm, winter daily 9am–5pm; ☎609/449-7130 or 1-888/AC-VISIT).

Atlantic City is easy to **walk** around, although it is unwise to stray further from the five-mile Boardwalk along the ocean than the parallel Pacific, Atlantic and Arctic avenues, as other parts of the city can be dangerous at night. Ventnor and Margate, to the south on Absecon Island, are served by **buses** along Atlantic Avenue. Pale blue Jitneys (☎609/344-8642) offers a 24-hour minibus service the length of Pacific Avenue, the #1 route traveling as far as Ventnor ($1.50 exact change required).

Various **bike rental** stands along the Boardwalk charge about $3 per hour, although cycling is only permitted from 6am until 10am in the summer.

Accommodation

Atlantic City is not Vegas – there's no chance of getting a $40 room at one of the casinos. The already high **accommodation** rates rise at weekends and in summer, though rates plunge off-season; if you book ahead and business is slow many places will offer discounted **package deals**, with $200 suites going for under half-price. Otherwise room prices at the casinos are astronomical, but reasonably priced **motels** line Pacific and Atlantic avenues behind the Boardwalk, and things are cheaper in quiet Ocean City, a family resort to the south. The **Convention Center** above the train terminal offers over 12,000 hotel rooms: bland but convenient.

Casino on the Boardwalk at Delaware Ave ☎ 609/343-4000 or 1-800/621-0200. The most pleasant of the huge casino hotels, with luxury ocean-view rooms. ❺

The Irish Pub 164 St James Place ☎ 609/344-9063. Basic rooms above one of the town's best bars. ❷

Quality Inn Beach Block S Carolina & Pacific aves ☎ 609/345-7070 or 1-800/356-6044. Chain motel housed in a converted school. The lobby and shared areas are rather shabby, but the clean, newly refurbished rooms make up for it. ❹

Rodeway Inn 124 S Carolina Ave ☎ 609/345-0155. Clean and basic rooms close to the Boardwalk. ❷

Showboat Econolodge Boardwalk 117 S Kentucky Ave ☎ 09/344-9093 or 1-800/323-6410. Standard chain motel next to the Boardwalk and Sands Casino. ❸

Surfside Resort Hotel 18 S Mount Vernon Ave ☎ 609/347-SURF. A gay-friendly hotel with standard rooms and a lively club attached. ❸

Trump Taj Mahal Casino Resort 1000 Boardwalk ☎ 609/449-1000 or 1-800/825-8786. Nothing terribly exciting, but the closest Atlantic City gets to the way-out theme casinos of Vegas (see box, overleaf). ❼

The Town

Arriving by train, you'll be confronted by the monstrous **Convention Center**, which opened above the station in 1997, and houses a massive food court and standard mall shops, along with its meeting spaces and countless hotel rooms. Most of the hopeful new arrivals, however, head straight for the casinos, with an ample overspill flooding the Boardwalk and beach. Beyond the Boardwalk there is little to see in Atlantic City, although a quick walk around the eerily quiet slums of the South Inlet district makes a chilling contrast to the manic jollity a mere block away. This is not an area in which to linger for any length of time, or indeed at all at night – the **danger** is very real, though police have made considerable inroads over the past few years.

Atlantic City's wooden **Boardwalk** was originally built as a temporary walkway, raised above the beach so that vacationers could take a seaside stroll without treading sand into the grand hotels. Alongside the brash 99¢ shops and exotically named palm-readers, a few beautiful Victorian buildings that survived the wrecker's ball invoke past elegance, despite being dwarfed by the casinos and housing fast-food joints. Early in the morning, when the breezes from the ocean are at their most pleasant, the Boardwalk is peaceful, peopled only by keen cyclists and a few lost souls down on their luck.

The **Central Pier** offers all the fun of a fair, with rides, games and old-fashioned "guess your weight" challenges. A few blocks south, another pier has been remodeled into an ocean-liner-shaped shopping center. The small and faded **Arts Center and Historic Museum** (☎ 609/347-5837), on the Garden Pier at the quiet northern end of the Boardwalk, has a free collection of seaside memorabilia, postcards, photos and a special exhibit on Miss America, as well as traveling art shows. A block off the Boardwalk, where Pacific Avenue meets Rhode Island Avenue, and at the heart of some of the city's worst deprivation, stands the **Absecon Lighthouse.** Active until 1933, it's recently been fully restored and offers a terrific view from its 167ft tower (July–Aug daily 11am–4pm, Sat also 7pm–9pm; Sept–Dec and March–June Thurs–Mon 11am–4pm; call for Jan–Feb hours; $4; ☎ 609/449-1360).

Atlantic City's **beach** is free, family filled and surprisingly clean, considering its proximity to the Boardwalk. Beaches at well-to-do **Ventnor**, a jitney ride away, are quieter, but charge users $3 per week. For the same fee, New Jersey's beautiful people pose on the beaches of **Margate**, three miles south of Atlantic City; all watched over by Lucy, the Margate Elephant at 9200 Atlantic Ave. A 65ft wood and tin Victorian oddity, Lucy was built as a seaside attraction in 1881 and used variously as a tavern and a hotel. Today her huge belly is filled with a **museum** of Atlantic City memorabilia, and photos and artifacts from

The casinos of Atlantic City

Each of Atlantic City's dozen casinos, which also act as luxury hotels, conference centers and concert halls, has a slightly different image, despite the apparent uniformity of vast, richly ornamented halls, slot machines, relentless flashing lights and incessant noise, chandeliers, mirrors, and a disorienting absence of clocks or windows.

By far the most ostentatious (and "The Don" wouldn't have it any other way) is Donald Trump's Disneyesque **Taj Mahal**. Occupying nearly twenty acres and over forty stories high, this gigantic but oddly anticlimactic piece of Far Eastern kitsch stands opposite the arcade-packed Steel Pier at the north end of the Boardwalk, dotted with glittering minarets and onion domes. It is one of the largest gambling casinos on earth, precariously tottering on the edge of bankruptcy. At the other end of the scale, the **Claridge**, Indiana Avenue and the Boardwalk, dubs itself "the friendly casino" and is smaller, darker and more downmarket than the others. **Sands**, next door at South Indiana Avenue, is a noisy and popular venue with a vague circus theme. Both these properties are slightly off the Boardwalk, accessible by a glass-covered slow-moving sidewalk with accompanying taped music from the various stars who have played Atlantic City. **Caesars**, Arkansas Avenue and the Boardwalk, has an uninspired Roman theme, with statues of Greek gods, marble columns and laurel wreaths at every turn.

All casinos are **open 24 hours** a day, and have a strict minimum **age requirement**, so be prepared to show ID to prove you're 21 or older if you plan to gamble.

her own history (Apr–May and Sept–Oct Sat & Sun 10am–5pm; June–Aug Mon–Sat 10am–8pm, Sun 10am–5pm; closed Nov–Mar; $4; ☎609/823-6473).

Eating

One side-effect of Atlantic City's rabid commercialization is an abundance of **fast food**. The Boardwalk is lined with pizza, burger and sandwich joints, and the diners on Atlantic and Pacific avenues serve soul food and cheap breakfasts. All the large casinos boast several restaurants, ranging in price and menu, as well as all-you-can-eat **buffets** – most cost around $14 for lunch, and a little more for dinner. Some of the casinos offer half-price buffets to "members" or "VIPs" – all you have to do to join is fill in a form and give some proof of address. If money's running low after too many days in the casino, there are bargain buffets on the Boardwalk for less than $5 – but inevitably, you get what you pay for.

Hunan Chinese Restaurant 2323 Atlantic Ave ☎609/348-5946. Reasonably priced Chinese food two blocks from the Boardwalk. Combination plates from $7.

Los Amigos 1926 Atlantic Ave ☎609/344-2293. Great for cheap, late-night food, this Mexican restaurant is open until 5am Friday and Saturday, while its bar serves until 6am.

Pappa T's Pizza 1245 Boardwalk ☎609/348-5030. One of the better cheap and cheerful Boardwalk joints, with pizza and breakfast from $3.50.

Planet Hollywood at *Caesars*, 2100 Pacific Ave on the Boardwalk ☎ 609/347-STAR. Decent burgers and salads at hyped-up prices in a hyped-up atmosphere.

White House Sub Shop Mississippi and Arctic aves ☎ 609/345-8599. This bright and superefficient sandwich bar is where Bill Cosby gets his subs when in town. Prices range from $6 for half a French loaf crammed with omelette, to $12 for a full steak sandwich.

Entertainment and nightlife

Atlantic City sells itself as the fun nighttime city; but the **nightlife** centers on the casinos and Boardwalk amusements. Once you get bored with slot machines there is little else to do. Big-name entertainers perform regularly at the casinos, with tickets in the $30 range – the free weekly *Whoot* has listings. The Comedy Stop **comedy club** at the *Tropicana* (☎609/340-4000) has twice nightly shows, each costing $18. For cheaper informal fun, good neighborhood **bars** include the friendly, dark-paneled *Irish Pub*, 164 St James Place (☎609/345-9613), which serves cheap food and often has live Irish music, and *McGuire's Pittsburgh Café*, 142 S Tennessee Ave (☎609/345-9607).

Cape May

CAPE MAY was founded in 1620 by the Dutch Captain Mey, on the small hook at the very southern tip of the Jersey coast, jutting out into the Atlantic and washed by the Delaware Bay on the west. After being briefly settled by New England whalers in the late 1600s, it turned in the eighteenth century to more profitable farming and, soon after, to tourism. In 1745 the first advertisement for Cape May's restorative air and fine accommodation appeared in the Philadelphia press, heralding a period of great prosperity, when Southern plantation owners, desiring cool sea breezes without having to venture into Yankee land, flocked to the fashionable boarding houses of this genteel "resort of Presidents."

The Victorian era was Cape May's finest; nearly all its gingerbread architecture dates from a mass rebuilding after a severe fire in 1878. However, the increase in car travel after World War I meant that vacationers could go further, more quickly and more cheaply, and the little town found itself something of an anachronism, while the gaudier charms of Atlantic City became the brightest stars on the Jersey coast. During the 1950s, Cape May began to dust off its most valuable commodity: its history. Today the whole town is a National Historic Landmark, with over six hundred **Victorian buildings**, tree-lined streets and beautifully kept **gardens**, and a lucrative B&B industry. It teeters dangerously on self-parody at times, thanks to its glut of cutesy olde shoppes, but if you avoid the main drags and wander through the back streets, you'll find an appealing combination of historical authenticity and good **beaches**.

Arrival, information and getting around

New Jersey Transit (☎973/762-5100 or 1-800/772-3606) runs an express **bus** to Cape May from Philadelphia and the south Jersey coast, and services from New York and Atlantic City, while **ferries** connect the town to Lewes, Delaware (12 a day in the summer, 6 off-season; $4.50 per person, $18 per car; schedules on ☎609/886-1725 or book at 1-800/64-FERRY).

Maps and **information** are available from the **Welcome Center** at 405 Lafayette St (daily approx 9am-4.15pm; ☎609/884-9562, ⓦwww.cape-maynj.com) which can also help with finding accommodation. Other sources of information include a small booth in the paved mall at the southern end of Washington Street, and the tiny Chamber of Commerce, in the bus depot, 609 Lafayette St (Mon–Fri 9am–5pm; ☎609/884-5508).

Though Cape May itself is best enjoyed on foot, to venture out a bit further rent a **bike** from the Village Bike Shop near the bus terminal at 605 Lafayette (7am–7pm; $5 per hour, $12 per day; ☎609/884-8500). The Cape May Whale Watcher (☎609/884-5445 or 1-800/786-5445), at Second Avenue and Wilson Drive, offers three trips around Cape May Point daily: two **dolphin-watches** (2hr; 10am & 6.30pm; $17 and $18 respectively) and a **whale-watching voyage** (3hr; 1pm; $26). Boats leave from an inlet of the Cape May Canal, behind Wilson Drive.

Accommodation

Most of Cape May's pastel Victorian homes seem to be (pricey) **B&Bs** or **guesthouses**, and the resort is so popular that choice plummets on summer weekends. During July and August even old motor inns can command over $100 a night; June and September rates are often around half that. Standard **hotels** front the ocean on Beach Drive, and you can **camp** at *Seashore Campsites*, 720 Seashore Rd (reservations recommended July & Aug; ☎609/884-4010 or 1-800/313-2267). Another alternative is to stay at one of the numerous beachfront hotels in **Wildwood**, a short drive away (see opposite) – stop by or call the **visitor information center** at 3601 Boardwalk (summer Sun–Thurs 9am–10pm, Fri–Sat 9am–11pm, call for winter hours; ☎609/522-1407).

Abigail Adams Bed and Breakfast 12 Jackson St ☎609/884-1371. High-quality lodging 100ft from the beach. Rates include afternoon tea. ❹

Inn of Cape May Beach Drive and Ocean Ave ☎1-800/582-5933. Once a fashionable Victorian shorefront hotel, now with small adjoining modern motel wing. The cheapest rooms are those with shared baths in the main building. Open April–Oct, and weekends in Nov–Dec. ❹–❼

Manor House 612 Hughes St ☎609/884-4710. Great breakfasts and a relaxing porch in the heart of the historic district. ❺

The Montreal Inn Beach Drive and Madison Ave ☎609/884-7011 or 1/800-525-7011. Modern motel with standard rooms. ❺/❻

Queen Victoria 102 Ocean St ☎609/884-8702. Twenty-plus rooms in four buildings, including a cottage and a carriage house. Rates include bicycle loans, as well as breakfast (in bed if desired) and afternoon tea. ❺–❾

Sea Breeze Motel Pittsburgh and New York aves ☎609/884-3352. No-nonsense budget motel in a residential street a couple of blocks from the beach, a mile from downtown. ❸

Summer Cottage Inn 613 Columbia Ave ☎609/884-4948. 1867 inn with verandas and cupola. ❺–❼

The Town

Cape May's brightly colored houses were built by nouveau riche Victorians with a healthy disrespect for subtlety. Cluttered with cupolas, gazebos, balconies and "widow's walks," the houses follow no architectural rules except excess. They were known as "patternbook homes," with designs and features chosen from catalogs and thrown together in accordance with the owner's taste. The Victorian obsession with the Orient is everywhere: Moorish arches and onion domes sit comfortably next to gingerbread- and Queen Anne-style turrets.

The only old home open as a museum, the eighteen-room **Emlen Physick House**, 1048 Washington St (daily 10am–4pm; $8; ☎609/884-5404), was built by the popular Philadelphia architect Frank Furness. It has been restored to its 1879 glory, with whimsical "upside down" chimneys, a mock Tudor half-timbered facade, and much original furniture. Various B&Bs and hotels, given enough notice, also conduct informal tours of their premises: the *Mainstay Inn*, 635 Columbia Ave, was once an elaborate Italianate 1872 gambling club (main floor open for self-guided tours daily 11am–2pm; ☎609/884-8690), and the *Abbey*, Columbia Avenue and Gurney Street, is a Gothic mansion with a 60ft tower and blood-red etched windows (tours Tues, Thurs & Sat 4pm; $8; ☎609/884-4506).

West of town, where the Delaware Bay and the ocean meet, the 1859 **Cape May Lighthouse**, visible from 25 miles at sea, offers great views from a gallery below the lantern (199 steps up) and a small exhibit on its history at ground level (summer 9am–8pm, call for winter hours; $4; ☎609/884-8656). Three miles north of town on US-9, **Historic Cold Spring Village**, 735 Seashore Rd (June–Sept Tues–Sun 10am–4.30pm; $7; ☎609/898-2300), depicts a typical nineteenth-century south Jersey farming community. Restored buildings from the region house a jail, school, inn and shops, and there are various craft shows and special events.

Cape May's excellent **beaches** literally sparkle with quartz pebbles. Beach tags ($4 per day, $8 per week) must be worn from 10am until 6pm in the summer, and are available at the beach and from B&Bs, official vendors or from **City Hall**, 643 Washington St (℡609/884-9525).

Eating

Cape May lacks the usual boardwalk snack bars, but it has plenty of cheap **lunch** places. **Dinner**, however, is far more expensive. If you're staying at a B&B, you can always fill up there with homemade goodies, and make do with bar snacks at night. Cape May's liquor laws are stringent, which means that many restaurants are BYO – call to check, and pick up some drinks at a liquor store before you eat.

Bellevue Tavern 7–9 S Main St ℡609/463-1738. Functional c.1900 bar with inexpensive hot sandwiches at lunchtime; dinners average $14.
Gecko's Carpenter's Square Mall ℡609/898-7750. A good lunch stop with a tasty Southwestern menu and great desserts. Patio seating available.
The Lemon Tree 507 Washington St mall ℡609/884-2704. Good antidote to the twee coffee shops along the street, a cheap, cheerful deli

where nothing's over $6; the cheesesteaks are Philadelphia-quality.
Louie's Pizza 7 Gurney St ℡609/884-0305. Fresh pizza opposite the beach from $10, or $2 per slice.
Mad Batter 19 Jackson St ℡609/884-5970. Splash out on international meals (baked clams in a tomato pesto sauce) served by candlelight in the garden, from $16. Lunch from $8.

Nightlife and entertainment

Cape May is a friendly and laid-back place to be after dark; the day-trippers have gone home and the **bars** and **music venues** are enjoyed by locals and tourists alike. If you're after something a bit more lively, head a few miles north to the raucous nightclubs of **Wildwood**. Again, remember that you may have to travel a little farther than you expect to find a bar that serves alcohol.

Cabana's 429 Beach Ave ℡609/884-4800. Two-level bar which often hosts live music downstairs; upstairs is a low-key cocktail lounge.
Carney's 401 Beach Ave ℡609/884-4424. Spacious and relaxed Irish bar, with raucous live

music.
Ugly Mug Washington St mall and Decatur St ℡609/884-3459. Local favorite, with a friendly bar, plus chowder, sandwiches and seafood from $4.

Around Cape May: Wildwood

Little more than a hundred years old, the staunchly blue-collar resort of nearby **Wildwood** offers a counterpoint to the old-world fakery of Cape May. The increase in leisure time following WWII and the subsequent boom in the vacation industry created towns like Wildwood, which sprung up to house the newly idle sun-seekers. The 1950s architecture, left lovingly intact, includes dozens of gaudy but fun-looking hotels with names like *Pink Orchid Waikiki* and *The Shalimar,* all still featuring plastic palm trees, kidney-shaped swimming pools and plenty of aqua, orange and pink paint. To best appreciate the town's brash charm, take a stroll along the Boardwalk, and stop along the wide, if throbbing, beaches.

CHAPTER 3 # Highlights

* **Fenway Park, MA** With its odd dimensions and cozy feel, the Boston Red Sox's home is arguably the most atmospheric ballpark in the country. See p.215

* **Provincetown, MA** Wild beaches, lovely flower-filled streets and an alternative vibe on the outer reaches of Cape Cod. See p.222

* **Historic "summer cottages," Newport, RI** Conspicuous consumption gone crazy in yachtie WASP resort. See p.241

* **Mount Washington Hotel, Bretton Woods, NH** Splendid century-old hotel beneath the windswept mountain itself. See p.260

* **Kancamagus Highway, NH** Lovely drive through the White Mountains, dotted with hiking trails and wooded camp-grounds. See p.262

* **Acadia National Park, ME** Remote mountains and lakes, stunning beaches and the chance to catch the sun-rise before anyone else in the US. See p.287

New England

The six New England states of **MASSACHUSETTS, RHODE ISLAND, CONNECTICUT, NEW HAMPSHIRE, VERMONT** and **MAINE** like to view themselves as the repository of all that is intrinsically American. In this version of history, the tangled streets of old Boston, the farms of Connecticut and the village greens of Vermont are the cradle of the nation. Certainly, nostalgia is at the root of the region's tourist trade; while the real business of making a living happens in cities for the most part well off the tourist trail, innumerable small towns have been dolled up to recapture a past that is at best wishful, and at times purely fictional. Picturesque they may be, with white-spired churches beside immaculate rolling greens, but they're not always authentic: there's little to distinguish a clapboard house built last year from another, two hundred years old, which has just had its annual coat of white paint.

The genteel seaside towns of modern Cape Cod and Rhode Island are a far cry from the first European settlements in New England. While the Pilgrims congregated in neat and pristine communities, later arrivals, with so much land to choose from, felt no need to reconstruct the compact little villages they had left behind in Europe. Instead, they fanned out across the Native American fields, or straggled their farmhouses in endless strips along the newly built roadways (thus establishing a more genuinely American style of development). As the European foothold on the continent became more certain, the coastline came increasingly to be viewed as prime real estate, to be lined with grand patrician homes – from the Vanderbilt mansions of Newport to the presidential compounds of the Bush and Kennedy families.

The Ivy League colleges – Harvard, Yale, Brown, Dartmouth, et al – still embody New England's strong sense of its own superiority, though in fact the region's traditional role as home to the WASP elite is due more to the vagaries of history and ideology than to economic or cultural realities. Its thin soil and harsh climate made it difficult for the first pioneers to sustain an agricultural way of life, while the industrial prosperity of the nineteenth and early twentieth centuries is now for the most part a distant memory. Despite recent diversification, and the development of some high-tech industries, New England has pokets, mostly in rural Vermont and New Hampshire, that are as poor as any in the US economic base.

New England can be a rather pricey place to visit, especially in late September and October, when visitors flock to see the magnificent **fall foliage**. Its tourist facilities are aimed at weekenders from the big cities as much as outsiders; places like **Cape Cod** make convenient short breaks for locals, but they're not the bucolic retreats you might expect. **Connecticut** and

Rhode Island in particular clearly form part of the great east coast mega-lopolis, which stretches from Washington to Boston – you rarely escape the feeling that you're traveling through some vast suburb of New York. **Boston** itself, however, is a vibrant and stimulating city, while further up the coast the towns finally thin out and the scenery gets appealing (as does the **seafood**). Inland, too, the lakes and mountains of **New Hampshire**, and particularly

Maine, offer rural wildernesses to rival any in the nation. **Vermont** is slightly less diverse, but its country roads offer pleasant wandering through tiny villages and serene forests.

Some history

The **Native Americans** who first inhabited the northeast shoreline lived by farming and fishing along the coast in summer, retreating with their animals to the relative warmth of the inland valleys in winter. Though the Algonquin did not always live in harmony with each other, they did manage to repel the first European invaders, earning themselves five hundred years' grace, some time around 1000 AD, by forcing the Viking Leif Eriksson to abandon the settlement of **Vinland the Good** – which may have been anywhere between Newfoundland and Massachusetts.

Within five years of Columbus's first voyage, John Cabot nosed by in 1497, in search of the Northwest Passage. Over the next century, European fishermen began to return each year, but it was not until the early 1600s that the French and English attempted to found permanent colonies, in what is now Maine. The name – New England – was given in 1614 by explorer John Smith, who particularly appreciated the plentiful lobsters.

This was not promising land: as a character in Robert Lowell's *Endecott and the Cross* put it, "I'm not a birdwatcher or an Indian ... I don't see the point of this outpost of England." Without precious metals to be mined, or the potential to grow lucrative crops, the first major impetus for emigration was **religion**. Refugees from intolerance – notably the Puritans, beginning with the **Pilgrims** in 1620 – made the arduous voyage to search for the freedom to build their own communities. The Pilgrims only survived at first thanks to the Indians: they were aided by a certain Squanto, who had been kidnapped, sold as a slave in Spain and returned home via England. In return, the Pilgrims forced the natives from the terraces they had farmed for generations, dismissing as inappropriate their solution to the problems of survival in such terrain: "Their land is spacious and void, and there are few and do but run over the grass ... They are not industrious, neither have art, science, skill or faculty to use either the land or the commodities of it."

The possibility of a serious Native American threat was removed in **King Philip's War** of 1675–76, in which a leader of the Narragansett persuaded feuding groups to bury their differences in one last, and ultimately hopeless throw. By then, white colonization was beyond the stage where it could be controlled by a few high-minded zealots. The **Salem witch trials** of 1692 provided a salutary lesson on the potential dangers of fanaticism, and as immigration became less English-based, with influxes of Huguenots after 1680 and Irish in 1708, Puritan domination decreased and a definite class structure began to emerge.

While the strand of history that began with the Pilgrims is just one among many in the colonization of America – the Spanish were in Santa Fe before the Pilgrims ever left England – the metropolis of **Boston** deserves to be celebrated as the place where the great project of American **independence** first captured the popular imagination. The leading port of colonial America was always the likeliest focus of resentment against the latest impositions of the British government, and was ready to take up the challenge thrown down by British Prime Minister Townshend in 1766: "I dare tax America." So many of the seminal moments of the **Revolutionary War** took place here: the Boston Massacre of 1770, the Boston Tea Party of 1773, Paul Revere's ride and the first shots at Lexington and Concord in 1775.

Once nationhood was secured, however, New England's prosperity was ironically hit hard by the loss of trade with England, and Boston was slowly eclipsed by Philadelphia, New York and the new capital, Washington. The **Triangular Trade** in slaves, sugar and rum provided one substitute source of income, the brief heyday of **whaling** another. New England was also momentarily at the forefront of the **Industrial Revolution**, when water-powered mills created a booming textile industry, most of which quickly moved south where wages were scandalously cheaper. The attempt to farm the north, however, foundered: careless techniques served to exhaust the land, and as the vast spaces of the west opened to settlement many of the inland towns fell silent.

Massachusetts

To the first colonists of the **Massachusetts Bay Company**, their arrival near the site of modern Salem in 1630 marked a crucial moment in history. **Puritans** who had decided to leave England before it was engulfed by civil war, saw their purpose, in the words of Governor John Winthrop, as the establishment of a Utopian "**City upon a hill**." Their new colony of **MASSACHUSETTS** was to be a beacon to the rest of humanity, an exemplar of sober government along sound spiritual principles. Not all those who followed, however, shared the same motivation; the story is often told of the preacher who told his congregation that they had come to New England to build a new kingdom of God, only to be challenged by a vociferous parishioner who said he had come to fish.

In their own terms, the Puritans were not successful: as waves of immigration brought all kinds of dissenters and free-thinkers from Europe, society in New England inevitably became secular. However, their **influence** remained. A clarity of thought and forcefulness of purpose can be traced from the foundation of Harvard College in 1636, through the intellectual impetus behind the Revolution and the crusade against slavery, to the nineteenth-century achievements of **writers** such as Melville, Emerson, Hawthorne and Thoreau.

Other traditions, too, have helped shape the state – poor migrants from **Ireland** and **Italy**, freed and escaped **slaves** from the Southern states, **Portuguese** seamen – even if they have not always been welcome. The anti-immigrant "Know-Nothing" party of the 1850s acquired considerable public support; in 1927, the Italian anarchists **Sacco and Vanzetti** came up against conservative old Massachusetts, and were framed and executed on murder charges. As recently as the 1970s, Boston experienced racial conflicts that matched the bitterness of those erupting throughout the nation. This has been somewhat healed of late, as have any economic doldrums that plagued the city for the latter half of the century, and a new sense of confidence – so emblematic of Boston's storied past – has taken hold.

Boston is East Coast America at its best, and spending a few days there is strongly recommended. It's a place that isn't content to rest on its laurels – the history is visible, but there's a great deal of modern life and energy besides, thanks in part to the presence of **Cambridge**, the home of Harvard University, just across the river. Several further historic towns are within easy reach – **Salem** to the north, **Concord** and **Lexington** just inland, and **Plymouth** to the south. **Provincetown**, a three-hour ferry ride across the bay at the tip of Cape Cod, is great fun to visit, and the rest of the Cape offers historic towns, lovely beaches – and huge crowds. Except for a handful of college towns such as **Amherst**, **inland Massachusetts** is much quieter; its settlements are naturally concentrated where the land is fertile, such as along the Connecticut River valley and in the **Berkshires** to the west.

Getting around Massachusetts

With the single proviso that all roads in Massachusetts seem to lead to Boston, this is an easy state to tour on **public transportation**. Planes, trains and buses all radiate out from the one great city; the connections to **Cape Cod** in particular (see p.220) are legion. The Amtrak line that connects Boston with New York, Philadelphia and Washington is the best regional **train** service in the nation, and the east–west line via Worcester and Springfield gives access to Montréal, Toronto and Chicago. With the exception of local commuter lines, trains do not, however, continue north of Boston. The only service along the coast is the summer-only service south to Hyannis on Cape Cod. **Buses** from Boston are also plentiful, but the only major north–south route inland is Route 91 along the Connecticut River valley.

Boston

Although the metropolitan area of **BOSTON** has long since expanded to fill the shoreline of **Massachusetts Bay**, and stretches for miles inland as well, the seventeenth-century port at its heart is still discernible. Forget the neat grids of modern urban America; the twisting streets clustered around **Boston Common** are a reminder of how the nation started out, and the city is enjoyably human in scale.

Boston was, until 1755, the biggest city in America; as the one most directly affected by the latest whims of the British Crown, it was the natural birthplace for the opposition that culminated in the **Revolutionary War**. Numerous evocative sites from that era are preserved along the **Freedom Trail** through downtown. Since then, however, Boston has in effect turned its back on the sea. As the third busiest port in the British Empire (after London and Bristol), it stood on a narrow peninsula. What is now Washington Street provided the only access by land, and when the British set off to Lexington in 1775 they embarked in ships from the Common itself. During the nineteenth century, the Charles River marshlands were filled in to create the posh Back Bay residential area. Central Boston is now slightly set back from the water, separated by the hideous John Fitzgerald Expressway that carries I-93 across downtown. The city has been working on routing the traffic underground and disposing of this eyesore (a project a decade in the making known as "the Big Dig"), though the monumental task won't likely be completed before 2002, much to the frustration of locals.

There is a certain truth in the charge leveled by other Americans that Boston likes to live in the past; echoes of the "Brahmins" of a century ago can be heard in the upper-class drawl of the posher districts. But this is by no means just a city of WASPs: the Irish who began to arrive in large numbers after the Great

Famine had produced their first mayor as early as 1885, and the president of the whole country within a hundred years. The liberal tradition that spawned the Kennedys remains alive, fed in part by the presence in the city of more than one hundred universities and colleges, the most famous of which – **Harvard University** – actually stands in the city of Cambridge, just across the Charles River, and is fully integrated into the tourist experience thanks to the area's excellent subway system.

The slump of the Depression seemed to linger in Boston for years – even in the 1950s, the population was actually dwindling – but these days the place definitely has a rejuvenated feel to it. **Quincy Market** has served as a blueprint for urban development worldwide, and with its busy street life, imaginative museums and galleries, fine architecture and palpable history, Boston is the one destination in New England there's no excuse for missing.

Arrival and information

Boston may not be the "hub of the universe," as Oliver Wendell Holmes once said, but it is the center of New England's transportation networks. An increasing number of direct flights from Europe means that it provides many visitors with their first taste of America, while efficient rail and bus services from New York, Montréal and further afield make this an obvious starting point, wherever you're heading in New England.

Air

Logan Airport (☎617/561-1800 or 1-800/23-LOGAN), constantly busy with both international and domestic services, is a mere three miles from downtown Boston. It stands on an artificial peninsula jutting into Boston Harbor, created by leveling three islands and destroying Revolution Wharf. As driving within the city is not to be recommended (see opposite), it makes little sense to rent a car at the airport. A **taxi** into town costs $10–20, plus an extra $4.50 in fees and tolls; the trip should take twenty minutes, but most traffic passes through the Sumner or Callahan tunnels, which can get very congested. The construction of the Ted Williams Tunnel has alleviated the problem somewhat. Between 5.30am and 1am, free shuttle **buses** run every few minutes from all terminals to the airport **subway** station on the MBTA Blue line (see opposite), from where it's an easy ten-minute ride to the city center. Just as quick, and a lot more fun, is the **water shuttle**, which connects the terminal buses with Rowe's Wharf across the harbor, an easy gateway into the heart of north Boston (Mon–Fri every 15min 6am–8pm, Sat & Sun every 30min 10am–8pm; $10 one-way, $17 round-trip; ☎617/330-8680 or 1-800/23-LOGAN).

Trains

Amtrak (☎1-800/USA-RAIL, ⊛www.amtrak.com) trains along the Northeast Corridor from Providence, Washington, DC and New York, and from Chicago and Canada via Springfield, as well as the summer-only Cape Cod specials, arrive a short walk from downtown Boston near the waterfront at **South Station**, Summer Street and Atlantic Avenue. The renovated station houses information booths, newsstands, restaurants and a fantastic old clock, though no currency exchange. The Red subway line inside the station can whisk you to the center of town or out to Cambridge. Some Amtrak services also make an extra stop at **Back Bay Station**, 145 Dartmouth St, on the Orange subway line near Copley Square. **North Station** is used only by MBTA commuter trains.

Buses

Several **bus** companies provide direct links between Boston and the rest of New England. Vermont Transit (☎1-800/451-3292, ⓦwww.vermonttransit .com) covers western Massachusetts, New Hampshire's White Mountains, Vermont and Montréal; while Concord Trailways (☎1-800/639-3317, ⓦwww.concordtrailways.com) runs to southern New Hampshire and up the Maine coast. Heading south, Bonanza Bus Lines (☎1-800/556-3815, ⓦwww.bonanzabus.com) connects Providence and Newport, Cape Cod and New York City; and Peter Pan Bus Lines (☎617/343-9999, ⓦwww.peterpan-bus.com) services New York and western Massachusetts. Greyhound (☎1-800/231-2222, ⓦwww.greyhound.com), with its many connections, offers nationwide service. Plymouth and Brockton Bus Co (☎508/746-0378, ⓦwww.p-b.com), serving Hyannis, has buses that leave from Logan Airport; all other buses leave from South Station (see opposite).

Information

The most convenient place to get advice and maps is the **Visitor Information Center** (Mon–Sat 8.30am–5pm, Sun 9am–5pm; ☎617/536-4100 or 1-800/888-5515, ⓦwww.bostonusa.com) above the Park Street subway stop on the Tremont Street side of Boston Common. There are also information kiosks in **Quincy Market**, the **John Hancock Tower** at Copley Square in Back Bay, and in the **Prudential Center**, also in the Back Bay. For advance information, the **Boston By Phone** service (☎1-888/SEE-BOSTON) allows visitors anywhere in North America to connect directly with a wide range of hotels and services.

The city's main **post office** is at McCormack Station, Post Office Square (Mon–Fri 8am–5pm; ☎617/720-4754; zip code 02109).

Getting around

Much of the pleasure of visiting Boston comes from being in a city that was built long before cars were invented. Walking around it can be a joy; conversely, driving is an absolute nightmare. The freeways won't take you where you want to go, the one-way traffic systems can have you circling for hours, and if you ever do arrive, parking lots are thin on the ground and very expensive. There's no point renting a car in Boston until the day you leave, especially since the city's public transportation is so good and the local drivers so bad.

The Massachusetts Bay Transportation Authority (MBTA, known as the "**T**") is responsible for Boston's **subway** system and **trolleybuses**. The subway, which opened in 1897, is the oldest in the US; its first station, **Park Street**, remains its center (any train marked "inbound" is headed here), and is the place to pick up all schedules and information. Four lines – Red, Green, Blue and Orange – operate daily from 5am until 1am, although certain routes begin to shut down earlier. Away from downtown, the trains emerge from tunnels to run along the city's major arteries. Though maps are posted at each station, it's a good idea to pick up the widely available Rapid Transit maps for reference. Trains are fast and safe; only some parts of the Orange line might be said to be unsafe after dark.

Within the city, the standard fare is $1, paid with tokens inserted into turnstiles, but on some incoming aboveground routes you have to pay extra, up to $2.75 (conversely, some outbound aboveground routes are free). You can buy eleven tokens for the price of ten, and a **Boston Visitor Pass** covers all subway and local bus journeys at a cost of $6 for a day, $11 for three days, or $22 for a week. (For MBTA **information** call ☎617/222-3200 or 1-800/392-6100 or visit ⓦwww.mbta.com).

The normal fare on MBTA's **local buses** is 75¢, but longer distances, such as out to Salem or Marblehead, cost up to $2.75. MBTA also runs **commuter rail lines**, extending as far as Salem, Ipswich and Concord; these are based at the unlovely **North Station** (☏617/222-3200) on Causeway Street, under the Fleet Center.

In and around Boston are some eighty miles of **bike trails**, making it an excellent city to explore on two wheels. Bicycles can be rented from the Community Bike Shop at 490 Tremont St (☏617/542-8623) and Back Bay Bikes & Boards, 333 Newbury St (☏617/247-2336), from mid–March through mid–October. Rentals are around $10 for two hours; $20–25 per day.

City tours

It's easy enough to get to know Boston by following the **Freedom Trail** on foot (see p.206). If you prefer to be guided, narrated trips run throughout the day aboard the hundred-minute Old Town Trolley Tours (☏617/269-7010; $20, $7 kids aged 4–12) or the similarly priced Discover Boston Trolley Tours (☏617/742-1440, ⓦwww.discoverbostontours.com), which specializes in narrated audio tours in multiple languages. But nothing is as popular (or as novel) as a Boston Duck Tour (adults $22, kids 4–12 $12; ☏617/723-DUCK, ⓦwww.bostonducktours.com), a very entertaining romp by land and by sea aboard a real WWII amphibious landing vehicle. Same-day tickets are sold inside the Prudential Center daily April through November. Boston By Foot, 77 N Washington St (☏617/367-2345), conducts ninety-minute walking tours for $8. Also useful are the bus excursions further afield to Lexington, Concord, Salem and Plymouth with Brush Hill Tours/Gray Line (☏617/720-6342, ⓦwww.brushhilltours.com or www.grayline.com). Boston Bike Tours (☏617/308-5902, ⓦwww.bostonbiketours.com), on Boston Common, can take you around for a couple of gentle hours by bike. A two-hour tour costs $18, or only $8 if you have your own bike; either way, a helmet, map and water are included.

Accommodation

Good-quality budget **accommodation** is hard to find in Boston – any hotel room within walking distance of downtown for under $120 has to be considered a bargain. Citywide Reservation Services (☏617/267-7424 or 1-800/ 468-3593, ⓦwww.cityres.com) can often get discounts of ten percent or more at hotels, inns or guesthouses, though a more enjoyable and affordable way of staying in the Boston area is to use a **B&B agency**. The excellent B&B Agency of Boston (47 Commercial Wharf, Boston, MA 02110; ☏617/720-3540 or 1-800/248-9262; in the UK ☏0800/895128, ⓦwww.bbonline.com/ma /bnbagency/bnb.html) offers hundreds of properties across the city for $80–120. Host Homes of Boston (☏617/244-1308 or 1-800/600-1308, ⓦwww.hosthomesofboston.com) and Boston Reservations (☏617/332-4199, ⓦwww.bostonreservations.com) provide a similar service.

Hostels

Back Bay Summer Hostel 512 Beacon St ☏617/353-3294, ☏617/531-0459 off-season, ⓦwww.usahostels.org/about_bosback.shtml). A well-located Boston University dorm runs as a hostel in the summer months. HI members $24, others $29. **Beantown Hostel** 222 Friend St ☏617/742-3759. Dorm beds for $22 next door to and above

the *Irish Embassy* pub (232 Friend St), about 5 minutes' walk north of Faneuil Hall. Free admission to pub gigs on most nights, and free barbecues Tues and Sun.
Charlestown YMCA 150 2nd Ave, Charleston Navy Yard ☏617/241-8400. Rooms near the *USS Constitution*, popular with military personnel, with private bath and TV for $99 a night. Guests have

free use of the excellent gym.

HI-Boston 12 Hemenway St ☎617/536-9455,
ⓦwww.bostonhostel.org. In the Fenway area
(Hynes Convention Center "T" station), close to the
hip end of Newbury St and the Lansdowne St
clubs, this is the best hostel in town, with internet
access and a Council Travel office on the ground
floor (as well as no curfew). Dorms $27 for mem-
bers, $30 others. In summer book ahead, or check
in at 8am, to be sure of a place.

YMCA Central Branch 316 Huntington Ave
☎617/536-7800. Best budget rooms in the Back
Bay, next to Northeastern "T" station. Rates –
around $45 for one person, $65 for two – include
breakfast. Co-ed June–Sept, otherwise men-only.

YWCA 40 Berkeley St ☎617/375-2524,
ⓦwww.ywcaboston.org. Women-only singles
($65), doubles ($100) and triples ($120) in a con-
venient South End location, near Arlington and
Back Bay "T" stations. There's another YWCA
building nearby at 140 Clarendon St and rooms
can be arranged there, as well. Non-YWCA members pay $2 for temporary membership. Nightly
and weekly rates.

Hotels, motels and B&Bs

82 Chandler Street 82 Chandler St ☎617/482-
0408. One of Boston's best in-town B&Bs, this
refreshingly restored 1863 brownstone is on one
of the most up-and-coming streets of the South
End. Breakfasts are good, served communally on
the sun-splashed top floor – where you'll find the
best room in the house. ⑤/⑥

Best Western – Inn at Longwood Medical 342
Longwood Ave ☎617/731-4700 or 1-800/528-
1234. Above-average motel rooms near Longwood
"T" station and within walking distance of Fenway
Park. ⑥

Boston Park Plaza 64 Arlington St ☎617/426-
2000 or 1-800/225-2008. Spacious, high-ceilinged
rooms in Bill Clinton's favorite grand old Boston
hotel, in the Back Bay. The presence of the swank
Whiskey Park bar and several airline offices in the
hotel ensure that it's always a hub of activity.
⑥–⑧

A Cambridge House 2218 Massachusetts Ave,
Cambridge ☎617/491-6300 or 1-800/232-9989,
ⓦwww.acambridgehouse.com. Classy, restored
B&B near Porter Square, a 30min walk from
Harvard Square. Tasty breakfasts, served on the

patio in summer, and early-evening nibbles and
wine. ⑥

Charles Street Inn 94 Charles St ☎617/314-
8900, ⓦwww.charlesstreetinn.com. Pampered
luxury in the heart of Beacon Hill, with nine rooms,
each named after a famous local figure (Ralph
Waldo Emerson, Henry James and the like). ⑨

Copley Square Hotel 47 Huntington Ave
☎617/536-9000 or 1-800/225-7062. Situated on
the eastern fringe of Copley Square, this quiet
hotel is also home to the *Café Budapest*, widely
considered the most romantic restaurant in
Boston. ⑧/⑨

Eliot Hotel 370 Commonwealth Ave at
Massachusetts Ave ☎617/267-1607 or 1-
800/443-5468, ⓦwww.eliothotel.com). West Back
Bay's answer to the *Ritz*, at the busy crossroads of
Boston's upscale student enclave. Rooms have
luxurious Italian marble bathrooms and private
pantries. Nice breakfasts, too, and possibly the
best (if not the most expensive) restaurant in
Boston, *Clio*. ⑨

Harborside Inn 185 State St ☎617/723-7500,
ⓦwww.hagopianhotels.com. Luxurious hotel with
a Victorian accent in a renovated mercantile warehouse across from Quincy Market and the Custom
House. Rates drop some $30 a night Dec–March.
⑥/⑦

Howard Johnson Lodge 1271 Boylston St
☎617/267-8300 or 1-800/654-2000. Reasonably
priced motel rooms next to Fenway Park. The free
parking's a plus. ⑤

Lenox Hotel 710 Boylston St ☎617/536-5300 or
1-800/225-7676, ⓦwww.lenoxhotel.com. Lovingly
maintained, medium-sized hotel in Back Bay,
where the 200-plus rooms are graced with brass
chandeliers, dark wood furniture and marble bathrooms. ⑨

Newbury Guest House 261 Newbury St
☎617/437-7666 or 1-800/383-1550,
ⓦwww.hagopianhotels.com. Well-located, big, 32-
room Victorian brownstone house, with rates at the
lower end of Boston's price range. $10 parking
and free continental breakfast are also available.
Rates go down substantially Dec–Feb. ⑤/⑥

The Tremont Boston 275 Tremont St ☎617/426-
1400 or 1-800/331-9998, ⓦwww.wyndham.com.
Well-restored, 322-room Art Deco hotel, in the
Theater District two blocks from the Common.
⑤–⑨

ACCOMMODATION
82 Chandler Street	8
Back Bay Summer Hostel	13
Beantown Hostel	2
Best Western	17
Boston Park Plaza	4
Charles Street Inn	3
Copley Square Hotel	9
Eliot Hotel	12
Harborside Inn	1
HI-Boston	14
Howard Johnson Lodge	16
Lenox Hotel	10
Newbury Guest House	11
The Tremont Boston	5
YMCA Central Branch	15
YWCA The Berkeley	7
Residence	
YWCA Boston	6

0   400 yds

BOSTON

Charles River

CHINATOWN

THEATER DISTRICT

BACK BAY

SOUTH END

Public Garden

John Hancock Tower

Trinity Church

Prudential Center

Christian Science Center

Symphony Hall

▶ Kenmore Square

▶ Fenway Park, ⑯ & ⑰

▲ Cambridge

RESTAURANTS, BARS & CLUBS

The Black Rose	I
The Blue Diner	M
Bull and Finch Pub	Q
Buzzy's	L
Chaps	R
Commonwealth Brewery Company	J
Daily Catch	D
Division Sixteen	V
Durgin Park	G
Gabriele's	A
Giacomo's	B
Golden Palace	N
J J Foley's	K
Kingfish Hall	H
Legal Sea Foods	S
Mamma Maria	C
Other Side Cosmic Café	W
Pad Thai Café	X
Panificio Bakery	O
Rabia's	F
Sevens Ale House	P
Steve's Greek–American Cuisine	U
Trattoria Il Panino	E
Tremont 647	T

The City

Boston has grown up around **Boston Common**, which was set aside as public land in 1634. The obvious first stop on any tour of the city, it is also one of the gems in the string of nine parks (six of which were designed by Frederick Law Olmsted, America's foremost landscape architect) known as Boston's **Emerald Necklace**. Another gem is the lovely **Public Garden**, across Charles Street, where the two-ton **swan boats** ($1.50), which paddle across the main pond, are a less-than-natural, though whimsical, focal point.

The **visitor center** – the start of the **Freedom Trail** – is near the tapering north end of the Common. As you stand here, facing up Tremont Street with the **State House** away to your left, the main **shopping** district, **Quincy Market**, and the **waterfront** are slightly ahead and down to the right. The modern concrete wasteland of **Government Center** is straight up Tremont Street, with the **North End** beyond – first Irish, then Jewish, and now very definitely Italian. A short way behind you on the left rises **Beacon Hill**, every bit as elegant as when Henry James called Mount Vernon Street "the most prestigious address in America" (and far removed from its eighteenth-century nickname of "Mount Whoredom"). Heading away from the center down Tremont Street brings you to **Chinatown** and the **Theater District**, while grand boulevards such as Commonwealth Avenue lead west from the Public Garden into the **Back Bay**, where Harvard Bridge runs across the Charles River into **Cambridge**.

The Freedom Trail

Probably the best way to orient yourself in downtown Boston – and to appreciate the city's role in American history – is to walk some or all of the **Freedom Trail**. You can pick up or leave this easy self-guided route anywhere – a line of red bricks marking the trail is embedded in the pavement – but technically it begins on Boston Common at the **Visitor Information Center**.

From here, head for the golden dome of the **Massachusetts State House** (free tours Mon–Sat 10am–3.30pm), which was completed in 1798 to a design by Charles Bulfinch. It remains the seat of Massachusetts' government; its most famous feature, the wooden Sacred Cod symbolizing the wealth Boston accrued from its fisheries, hangs in front of the Speaker, and faces in different directions according to which party is in office.

Though **Park Street Church** (July & Aug Tues–Sat 9am–3pm; rest of year by appointment; free) is by no means "the most interesting mass of bricks and mortar in America" that Henry James claimed, its ornate white steeple is undeniably impressive. This was where the orator William Lloyd Garrison launched his campaign to free the slaves on July 4, 1829. The 1600 graves of the **Old Granary Burying Ground** just around the corner (daily 9am–5pm; free) include those of Paul Revere, Samuel Adams and John Hancock, as well as the reputed Mother Goose, a Bostonian named Elizabeth Vergoose (or Vertigoose), said to have collected nursery rhymes for her grandchildren; while **King's Chapel Burying Ground** (daily 9.30am–5pm; free) contains Boston's earliest colonists and the first governor, John Winthrop. A statue of Benjamin Franklin marks the site of **Boston Latin**, America's first public school, attended by Franklin and Samuel Adams. Guests at the nearby **Omni Parker House Hotel** (not officially on the Trail) have included Charles Dickens and John Kennedy, Malcolm X and Ho Chi Minh. The **Old Corner Bookstore** at School and Washington streets (Mon–Sat 9am–6pm, Sun noon–5pm) was a literary salon frequented by Longfellow, Thoreau and Hawthorne.

Next come the Trail's two most striking and significant buildings. At the **Old South Meeting House** (daily: April–Oct 9.30am–5pm; Nov–March 10am–4pm; $3), the largest building in colonial Boston and an old Puritan house of worship, Samuel Adams addressed the patriots about to carry out the Boston Tea Party on December 16, 1773. This was no raucous and unruly mob: they were solemn men, well aware of the likely impact of their actions. The elegant **Old State House**, built in 1712 and still proud, although dwarfed by surrounding skyscrapers, was the seat of colonial government. From its balcony the Declaration of Independence was read on July 18, 1776; exactly two hundred years later Queen Elizabeth II appeared on that same balcony. Inside is a **museum** of Boston history (daily 9am–5pm; $3). Outside, a plain ring of cobblestones set on a traffic island at the intersection of Devonshire and State streets marks the site of the **Boston Massacre** on March 5, 1770, when British soldiers fired on a crowd that was pelting them with stone-filled snowballs, and killed five, including the black Crispus Attucks.

Modern visitors gravitate to **Quincy Market** and **Faneuil Hall** (it rhymes with Daniel; daily 9am–5pm; free) for the lively shops, restaurants and takeaways that made this a pioneer example of successful urban renewal (by the developer who went on to transform London's Covent Garden). Faneuil Hall was, however, once known as the "Cradle of Liberty," a meeting place for Revolutionaries and, later, abolitionists. Nearby on Union Street, step off the Freedom Trail to visit **The New England Holocaust Memorial**, six tall hollow glass pillars built to resemble smokestacks and etched with quotes and facts about the Holocaust, with an unusual degree of attention to its non-Jewish victims.

Passing under the six-lane John Fitzgerald Expressway and into the North End, you reach **Paul Revere House**, Boston's last surviving seventeenth-century house (daily: mid-April to Oct 31 9.30am–5.15pm; Nov 1 to mid-April

The Black Heritage Trail

Massachusetts was the first state to declare slavery illegal, in 1783 – partly as a result of black participation in the Revolutionary War – and a large community of free blacks and escaped slaves swiftly grew in the North End and on Beacon Hill. Ironically, very few blacks now live on Beacon Hill, but the **Black Heritage Trail** through the area celebrates important sites in local black history (the various visitor centers provide maps).

Pick up the Trail either at 46 Joy St, where the **Abiel Smith School** contains a **Museum of Afro-American History** (summer daily 10am–4pm, rest of year Mon–Sat 10am–4pm; free), illustrating the national civil rights campaign as well as local history, or at the **African Meeting House** at 8 Smith Court (off Joy St), for displays and talks from well-informed rangers. Built in 1806 as the first African-American church in the United States, this became known as "Black Faneuil Hall" during the abolitionist campaign; Frederick Douglass issued his call here for all blacks to take up arms in the Civil War. Among those who responded were the volunteers of the **Massachusetts 54th Regiment**, commemorated by a monument at the edge of Boston Common, opposite the State House, which depicts their farewell march down Beacon Street. Robert Lowell won a Pulitzer Prize for his poem, *For the Union Dead*, about this monument, and the regiment's tragic end at Fort Wagner was depicted in the movie *Glory*. The Trail then winds around Beacon Hill, passing schools, other institutions, and residences ranging from the small, cream clapboard houses of Smith Court to the imposing **Lewis and Harriet Hayden House** at 66 Phillips St, once a stop on the famous "Underground Railroad," sheltering runaway slaves from pursuing bounty-hunters.

9.30am–4.15pm; closed Mon Jan–March; $2.50), built after the Great Fire of 1676, and home to Paul Revere – patriot, silversmith, Freemason and father of sixteen children – from 1770 until 1800. When Revere embarked upon his famous **ride** of April 18, 1775, to warn Lexington of imminent British attack, two lanterns were hung from the belfry of **Old North Church**, 193 Salem St (daily: June–Oct 9am–6pm; Nov–May 9am–5pm), to alert Charlestown in case he got caught. A little further up, from **Copp's Hill Burial Ground** (daily 9am–5pm; free), you can see across the harbor to Charlestown; as indeed could the British, who planted their artillery here for the Battle of Bunker Hill.

In theory, the Freedom Trail now crosses the Charlestown Bridge, but that's a long walk over. Its final two sites are better reached by the frequent **ferries** from Long Wharf to Charlestown Navy Yard (Mon–Fri every 15–30min 6.30am–8pm, Sat & Sun every 30min 10am–6pm; $1 each way). First is the **USS Constitution**, also known as "Old Ironsides," the oldest commissioned warship afloat in the world. Launched in Boston in 1797, it was prominent in the War of 1812. Every July 4 it is ceremonially turned around – sailed out into the bay and its cannon fired – mainly to equalize the weathering on its two sides. Unless it's closed due to ongoing rehabilitation work, free tours of the ship are led by costumed guides (daily 9.30am–3.50pm, ⓦ www.ussconstitution.navy.mil), or visit the **USS Constitution Museum** (daily: summer 9am–6pm; rest of year 10am–5pm; free). Above the museum, the **Bunker Hill Monument** sits on Breed's Hill, the actual site of the battle fought on June 17, 1775, which, although won by the British, did much to convince them that they could not hope to triumph in the end. A spiral staircase of almost three hundred steps leads to the top; a small **museum** (daily 9am–5pm; free) at the base has dated but informative exhibits on the battle.

The waterfront

It comes as a disappointment to realize that you can't walk along Boston's **waterfront** for any distance, broken up as it is by over a dozen heavily developed wharfs jutting into the harbor. However, if you head straight for the sea from Quincy Market, **Columbus Park**, next to the ugly *Marriott Long Wharf Hotel*, makes a nice place to sit. Faneuil Hall originally stood at the head of **Long Wharf**, which stuck out nearly two thousand feet into the harbor, and was the site of the final British evacuation on March 17, 1776. Later, a thousand-foot expanse of the waterfront was filled in, and the **Custom House Tower** erected to mark the end of the wharf, though it too now finds itself inland, as a further thousand feet of new land has been added.

Out on the water, **Boston Harbor Cruises** (ⓣ617/227-4321 or 1-877/733-9425, ⓦ www.bostonharborcruises.com; inner and outer harbor $17, inner harbor $8) from Long Wharf are not all that exciting. The port is nowhere near as busy as when fishing boats lined the quays three or four deep on all sides. Instead you pass vast rows of freshly imported Japanese cars on the quayside, and get a close-up view of the airport. You can get off one cruise in Charlestown, to see the *USS Constitution*, and catch the next one back for no extra charge.

Close by on Central Wharf, the **New England Aquarium** (July & Aug Mon, Tues & Fri 9am–6pm, Wed & Thurs 9am–8pm, Sat & Sun 9am–7pm; Aug–June Mon–Fri 9am–5pm, Sat & Sun 9am–6pm; $13) has an outdoor pool of basking sea otters. Inside, the colossal Giant Ocean Tank, a four-story glass cylinder, holds sharks, giant turtles and tropical marine life (with an unsettling emphasis on how "delicious" certain species are). Scuba divers hand-feed the fish five times a day, and sea lion shows are held in a floating amphitheater alongside.

If you follow the shoreline past **Rowe's Wharf** (the base for the water shuttles to the airport), a short distance before South Station the **Congress Street Bridge** leads off to the left across the Fort Point Channel. Moored to the bridge is the **Boston Tea Party Ship and Museum**, damaged by fire in 2001 and scheduled to reopen by spring 2002; for hours and admission fee call ☎617/338-1773 or visit ⓦ www.bostonteapartyship.com. This is not the original *Beaver*, one of the three ships stormed by patriots in 1773, but a replica, *Beaver II*, sailed here from Denmark in 1973. Neither is it the original mooring, which was on the now-demolished Griffin's Wharf; instead it's the site of the house where the conspirators prepared their assault.

On the far side of the bridge, a forty-foot **milk bottle**, which serves as an ice-cream parlor and sandwich bar, marks the **Children's Museum**, 300 Congress St (Mon–Thurs, Sat & Sun 10am–5pm, Fri 10am–9pm; $7, children $6, Fri 5–9pm $1 for all). The five floors of educational exhibits are designed to entice kids into learning by doing, with plenty of buttons to push, strings to pull and tunnels to crawl through, as well as costumes, water toys and climbing structures.

The **Museum of Science**, in the Science Park on the Charles River Dam at the northern end of the waterfront, not far from North Station (summer daily 9am–7pm; rest of year Mon–Thurs, Sat & Sun 9am–5pm, Fri 9am–9pm; $11, children $8), has several floors of hands-on exhibits illustrating basic principles of natural and physical science. An impressive OMNIMAX cinema takes up the full height of one end of the building, and the Hayden Planetarium pays its way with Pink Floyd laser shows and the like ($7.50, children $5.50; call ☎617/723-2500 for show times).

Back Bay and beyond

From 1857 onwards, the spacious boulevards and grand houses of **Back Bay** were built as each portion of the tidal flats of the Charles River was filled in. Thus a walk through the area from east to west provides an object lesson in Victorian architecture. One of the most architecturally significant – if not the prettiest – of its buildings is the Romanesque **Trinity Church** ($3) on Clarendon Street, supported on four thousand wooden pilings that have to be kept permanently moist. Towering over the church is Boston's signature skyscraper, the **John Hancock Tower**, an elegant wedge designed by I.M. Pei, and whose rooftop observatory affords a glorious panorama of Boston. (At the time of publication the observatory was closed indefinitely due to security concerns; call ☎617/572-6429 for the latest details.) Construction defects caused the Hancock Tower to shed three thousand panes of glass during its first year; the cost of insuring a neighboring hotel against damage was so prohibitive that it was cheaper for the developers to buy it outright. **Copley Square** nearby is an upmarket shopping mall with several good snack bars and restaurants.

The **Christian Science Center** at Huntington and Massachusetts avenues is the "Mother Church" of the First Church of Christ, Scientist, and the home of the *Christian Science Monitor* newspaper; Nelson Mandela made a point of paying a personal visit in 1990 to thank the paper for its support of his release from prison. The complex houses the **Mapparium** (Mon–Sat 10am–4pm; free), an impressive glass globe of the world, through which you can walk on a footbridge. Part of its interest is that it was built in 1932, and thus shows national boundaries as they were then.

Further south, beyond the boundaries of Back Bay and a long enough walk to warrant taking the Green subway line instead (take the train marked "E"), is the **Museum of Fine Arts** at 465 Huntington Ave (Mon & Tues

10am–4.45pm, Wed–Fri 10am–9.45pm, Sat & Sun 10am–5.45pm; $14, which includes a free repeat visit within 30 days, under-17s free, Ⓦwww.mfa.org). From its magnificent collections of Asian and ancient Egyptian art onwards, this holds sufficient marvels to detain you all day. High points include Edward Hopper's tranquil, hopeful *Room in Brooklyn* (American Modern room); Andrew Wyeth's *Corner of the Woods* (William Coolidge room); Degas' *The Little Dancer*; Gauguin's *Where do we come from, What are we, Where are we going?* (Impressionists room); and Millet's *The Sower* (English and French room). Don't miss the **American Decorative Arts**, either: a gloriously nostalgic jamboree of coffee urns, speak-your-weight machines and reconstructed living rooms. The I.M. Pei-designed West Wing holds special exhibits and the contemporary art collection.

A smaller-scale and rather more idiosyncratic collection of fine arts can be found at the **Isabella Stewart Gardner Museum**, down the road at 280 The Fenway (Tues–Sun 11am–5pm; $10, weekends $11). Styled after a fifteenth-century Venetian villa, the Gardner has a stunning central courtyard, and is crammed with a hodgepodge of works collected by the eccentric Boston socialite. Some of the most interesting pieces are unlabeled, such as the tapestry of a lion, a sea lion and an elephant above the door of the Italian room, or the sculpted pigeon on the nearby windowsill. Relaxing weekend music concerts are held Saturday and Sunday at 1.30pm and cost an additional $5.

Cambridge

The excursion across the Charles River to **Cambridge** merits at least half a day, starting with a fifteen-minute ride on the Red "T" line from Park Street to **Harvard Square**. This is not so much a square as a number of interlocking streets, filled with small shopping malls and bookstores, at the point where Massachusetts Avenue runs into JFK and Brattle streets. It's an exceptionally lively area, filled with students from nearby Harvard University and MIT; the café terrace at *Au Bon Pain* makes for enjoyable people-watching, and in summer street musicians are a common sight. The **Cambridge Visitor Information Booth** here (Mon–Sat 9am–5pm; ☎617/497-1630) sporadically organizes walking tours in summer, and sells local maps and guides. More thorough information is available from the **Harvard Events & Information Center**, Holyoke Center, 1350 Massachusetts Ave (Mon–Fri 9am–5pm; ☎617/495-1573, Ⓦwww.hno.harvard.edu), which also arranges student-led tours.

Feel free to wander into **Harvard Yard** and around the core of the university, founded in 1636; its enormous Widener Library (named for a victim of the *Titanic*) boasts a Gutenberg Bible and a first folio of Shakespeare. Five minutes' walk west along Brattle Street is the imposing yellow-fronted mansion at no. 105, known as **Longfellow House**, after the author of *Hiawatha*, who lived here until 1882. A century earlier it was briefly the headquarters of General George Washington. The site has been undergoing extensive renovation. Call ☎617/876-4491 or visit Ⓦwww.nps.gov/long to check hours and admission fee. Dexter Pratt, immortalized in Longfellow's *Under the spreading chestnut tree, the village smithy stands*, lived at 56 Brattle St, now a popular bakery and café.

Cambridge has several first-class art museums on offer, along with more specialized science museums with a few engaging exhibits of note. The **Harvard University Art Museums** (Mon–Sat 10am–5pm, Sun 1–5pm; $5, free on Wed; ☎617/495-9400) encompasses over 150,000 works of art across three museums. Highlights of Harvard's substantial collection of Western art are showcased in the **Fogg Art Museum**, at 32 Quincy St, while the **Busch-Reisinger**

NEW ENGLAND | Boston

Museum on the second floor has a small but excellent selection focusing on German Expressionists and the work of the Bauhaus. Just steps away at 485 Broadway, the **Arthur M. Sackler Museum** is devoted to classical, Asian and Islamic art. The **Harvard Museum of Natural History**, at 26 Oxford St (daily 9am–5pm; $6.50), operates three museums devoted to botany, zoology, and minerals and geology respectively.

A couple of miles southeast of Harvard Square is the **Massuchusetts Institute of Technology** (MIT), whose **List Visual Arts Center**, 20 Ames St (Tues–Thurs, Sat & Sun noon–6pm, Fri noon–8pm; ℡617/253-4680), exhibits contemporary art in all media, including photography and video, and often has accompanying lectures.

Lexington and Concord

On the night of April 18, 1775, **Paul Revere** rode down what is now Massachusetts Avenue from Boston, racing through Cambridge and Arlington on his way to warn the American patriots gathered at **Lexington** of an impending British attack. Close behind him was a force of more than four hundred British soldiers, intent on seizing the supplies that they knew the "rebels" had hoarded at **Concord** further north.

Although much of Revere's route has been turned into major freeways, the various settings of the first military confrontation of the Revolutionary War – "the shot heard round the world" – remain much as they were then. The triangular **Town Common** at Lexington was where the British encountered the opposition. Captain John Parker ordered his 77 American "**Minutemen**" to "stand your ground. Don't fire unless fired upon, but if they mean to have a war let it begin here." No one knows who fired the first shot, but the Minuteman Statue commemorates the eight Americans who died. Guides in period costume lead tours of the **Buckman Tavern**, where the Minutemen waited for the British to arrive; the **Hancock–Clarke House** a quarter of a mile north, where Samuel Adams and John Hancock were awakened by Paul Revere, is now a **museum**. All three sites are open Monday to Saturday from 10am to 5pm, on Sunday from noon to 5pm, and admission to each is $5 or $12 to visit all three.

By the time the soldiers marched on Concord the next morning the surrounding countryside was up in arms. In running battles in the town itself, and along the still-evocative **Battle Road** leading back toward Boston, 73 British soldiers and 49 colonials were killed over the next two days. The relevant sites now form the **Minuteman National Historic Park**, with visitor centers at the scenic North Bridge (174 Liberty St) in Concord and at Battle Road in Lexington. Paul Revere's ride and the Battle of Lexington are re-enacted annually on Patriot's Day, a city holiday on the third Monday in April that is also the day of the Boston Marathon.

South of Concord, **Walden Pond** was where Henry David Thoreau conducted the experiment in solitude and self-sufficiency described in his 1854 book *Walden*. "I did not feel crowded or confined in the least," he wrote of life in his simple log cabin. The site where it stood is now marked with stones, and at dawn you can still watch the pond "throwing off its nightly clothing of mist." Thoreau is interred, along with Ralph Waldo Emerson, Nathaniel Hawthorne and Louisa May Alcott, atop a hill in **Sleepy Hollow Cemetery**, just east of the center of Concord.

As well as guided **bus tours** from Boston (see p.202), **buses** run to Lexington from Alewife Station, at the northern end of the Red "T" line, and **trains** to Concord from North Station ($4 one-way).

Eating

There is far more to eating in Boston than its image as "Beantown" might suggest. Above all, there's the **seafood**, especially lobsters, scrod (a generic term for young, white-fleshed fish), clams (served steamed and dipped in butter, or as creamy chowder) and oysters (some of the world's best come fresh daily from Wellfleet and other Cape Cod spots). You could base a day's tour of the different neighborhoods around the foods on offer: breakfast in the cafés of **Beacon Hill**; lunch in the food plazas of **Quincy Market** or **The Garage** on JFK Street in Cambridge, or dim sum in **Chinatown**; for dinner, a budget **Indian** restaurant in Cambridge, an **Italian** place around Hanover Street in the North End, or expensive seafood overlooking the Harbor.

The central aisle of **Quincy Market**, lined with restaurants and brasseries, is superb for all kinds of takeaways, including fresh clams and lobster, ethnic dishes, fruit cocktails and cookies (all over the city, you'll find marvelous chocolate and ice cream), which you can buy from different vendors and eat in the central seating area.

Chinatown, where restaurants stay open until 2 or 3am, is the best place for **late-night eating**.

Boston

The Blue Diner 150 Kneeland St ☎617/695-0087. Classic restored Fifties diner with lively jukebox, slowly inching its way upmarket but with excellent traditional and unpretentious American food. Open till 4am on weekends.

Buzzy's 327 Cambridge St ☎617/242-7722 and 647 Massachusetts Ave, Cambridge ☎617/864-2333. Locally famous for fabulous roast beef sandwiches, hand-cut french fries, and the fact that they never close.

Daily Catch 323 Hanover St ☎617/523-8567 and 261 Northern Ave ☎617/338-3093. Sicilian-style seafood restaurant, noted for its many styles of calamari. Expect to pay from $10 to $40 for an entree.

Division Sixteen 955 Boylston St ☎617/353-0870. While the food is good and the wine list inspired, the real draw is the atmosphere, a converted police stable with a decidedly 1920s feel, in which locals sip martinis and any number of frozen concoctions.

Durgin Park 340 N Market St, Faneuil Hall ☎617/227-2038. Crowded, hurried and proud of its surly service, but a Boston institution for its chunky prime ribs and seafood specialties – not to mention the baked beans. Tables are shared, and no reservations are taken. Entrees start from $7.

Gabriele's 1 1st Ave, Charlestown Navy Yard ☎617/242-4040. Excellent upscale Italian restaurant, with a terrace for outdoor dining.

Giacomo's 355 Hanover St ☎617/523-9026. Fresh, flavorful food, with an emphasis on seafood and pasta specialties – the pumpkin tortellini in a sage butter sauce is a North End classic. Note the restaurant doesn't take reservations or credit cards.

Golden Palace 14–20 Tyler St ☎617/423-4565. Chinese restaurant open until 11.30pm, with excellent and reasonably priced dim sum daily until 3pm. Entrees $7 and upwards.

Kingfish Hall 188 S Market Bldg ☎617/523-8862. Well-regarded, stylish seafood house worth the splurge ($20 to $30 an entree).

Legal Sea Foods at the *Park Plaza Hotel*, 50 Park Plaza ☎617/426-4444. Citywide chain deservedly renowned for its top-quality seafood, especially their excellent oysters.

Mamma Maria 3 North Square ☎617/523-0077. Widely acknowledged as the best of the North End's traditional Italian restaurants, noted for seafood dishes and fresh breads. Expensive and also popular for special occasions.

Pad Thai Café 1116 Boylston St ☎617/247-3399. Fresh Thai soups, salads and curries, with highly recommended house specials, all in the $5–10 range. Popular with students, the place gets crowded fast. Open daily for lunch and dinner, *pad thai* also delivers after 5:30pm.

Panificio Bakery 144 Charles St ☎617/227-4340. Consistently rated the best bakery in Boston; try to make time for their brunch, served weekends from 10am–4:30pm.

Rabia's 73 Salem St ☎617/227-6637. The best thing about this small restaurant is its Express Lunch special from noon to 2pm, when you can pay under $7 for a heaping plate of Italian leftovers.

Steve's Greek–American Cuisine 316 Newbury St ☎617/267-1817. One of Boston's classic cheap eats, with heavenly Greek food and divine grilled chicken sandwiches.

Trattoria Il Panino 11 Parmenter St ☎617/720-1336. An old North End standby popular with

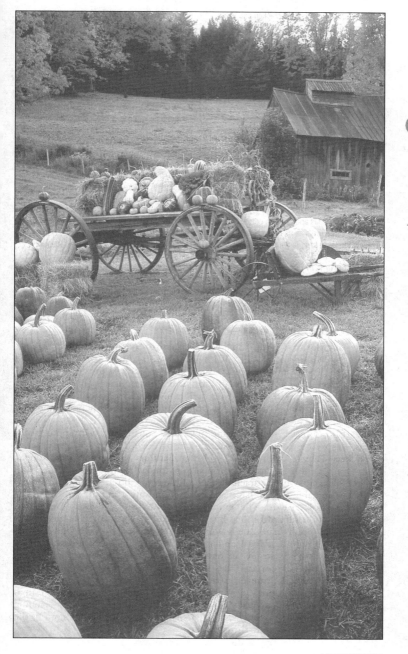

△ Vermont Pumpkins

locals. The great Amalfi-coast chicken and pasta dishes are complemented by a good wine list and friendly service.

Tremont 647 647 Tremont St ☎617/266-4600. Part of the burgeoning South End dining scene, with big portions of New American food, much of it grilled, as well as superb desserts and a good selection of wines.

Cambridge

Bombay Club 57 JFK St, second floor, Harvard Square ☎617/661-8100. One of the very best of Cambridge's many Indian restaurants, with a good-value lunch buffet.

Cambridge Sail Loft 1 Memorial Drive, Kendall Square ☎617/225-2222. Fine array of inexpensive seafood near MIT.

Dalí 415 Washington St, Somerville ☎617/661-3254. Excellent tapas and Spanish entrees amid decor nearly as surreal as its namesake. Often crowded, the lively sangria bar makes the long waits tolerable.

East Coast Grill 1271 Cambridge St, Inman Square ☎617/491-6568. Fairly pricey, but tasty Southern-style food – BBQ and the like – in a good restaurant area.

Elephant Walk 2067 Massachusetts Ave, Porter Square ☎617/492-6900 and 900 Beacon St, Boston ☎617/247-1500. Their French fare is very good, but the adventurous Cambodian side of the menu steals the show: try the excellent *poulet dhomei* – chicken with basil, bamboo shoots and pineapple.

John Harvard's Brew House 33 Dunster St, Harvard Square ☎617/868-3585. Cozy brewpub, serving a good menu with exciting little twists on American grill standards. $30 should suffice for a big meal with a couple of drinks.

Mr Bartley's Gourmet Burgers 1246 Massachusetts Ave, Harvard Square ☎617/354-6559. Delicious, shamelessly unhealthy burgers and other diner fare served in an Americana-festooned atmosphere.

Redbone's 55 Chester St, Somerville ☎617/628-2200. Excellent, inexpensive ribs, chicken and cat-fish with a big range of vegetable side dishes. Just off Davis Square, two "T" stops from Harvard Square.

Rhythm & Spice 315 Massachusetts Ave, Central Square ☎617/497-0977. Lively restaurant with a young clientele not far from MIT, serving good-value Caribbean food.

Nightlife and entertainment

Mainstream Boston's pride and joy, the **Boston Symphony Orchestra** is based at Symphony Hall, 301 Huntington Ave (☎617/266-1200, ⓦwww.bso.org), which Stravinsky called the best auditorium in the world – with a winter season followed by the **Boston Pops** concerts in May, June and on July 4. The city's **theater** scene divides into the safe productions of the Theater District (often Broadway cast-offs) and more experimental companies in Cambridge. The **Bostix** ticket kiosks (☎617/482-BTIX, ⓦwww.boston .com/artsboston) at Faneuil Hall and in Copley Square sell tickets for all major events – as well as tours, "T" passes, and so on – with some half-price same-day tickets. They're open Tuesday through Saturday 10am–6pm and Sunday 11am–4pm; Copley Square is also open on Monday 10am–6pm.

Seattle bands may have attracted much of the music business hype during the 1990s, but arguably Boston has made a more innovative and substantial contri-bution to **rock music**. The emergence in the late 1980s of the Pixies, Dinosaur Jr and Buffalo Tom has been followed by a fresh batch of guitar rock acts like Tracy Bonham and Letters to Cleo, and the live music circuit is dom-inated by the very best local and touring indie bands. Key nightlife zones include **Lansdowne Street**, an entire block of nightclubs next to Fenway Park; **Boylston Place**, on the south side of Boston Common; and Cambridge's **Central Square** district.

Note that the city's **bars** are unusually officious in demanding ID. Though not permitted to offer cut-price happy hours, some provide free early-evening snacks instead. The free weekly *Boston Phoenix* (ⓦwww.thephoenix.com) is the best source of up-to-date **listings**.

Boston bars, cafés and clubs

Avalon 15 Lansdowne St Ⓣ617/262-2424. An anchor on the Lansdowne St club scene, *Avalon* is a local favorite for late-night dancing with different themes on different nights (Saturday is techno night) and a live concert venue. Dress tends to be casual.

The Black Rose 160 State St Ⓣ617/742-2286. Large Irish pub beside Faneuil Hall, with traditional music every night and Guinness galore.

Bull and Finch Pub 84 Beacon St, Beacon Hill Ⓣ617/227-9605. Its status as the original setting of TV's *Cheers* makes this place totally touristy, but at least it's central and lively.

Chaps 100 Warrenton St, off Stuart St Ⓣ617/266-7778. Glitzy gay club filled with lots of decked-out young men.

Commonwealth Brewery Company 138 Portland St Ⓣ617/523-8383. Brewpub right by the Fleet Center near North Station, serving good pub food and its own ales.

J J Foley's 21 Kingston St Ⓣ617/338-7713. A blue-collar Irish bar in the heart of downtown, with decent food, sports on TV and a great jukebox. Around since 1909.

Other Side Cosmic Café 407 Newbury St Ⓣ617/536-9477. Popular and trendy café with great salads, sandwiches, beer, wine, coffee and tea. Across from Tower Records and the Mass Turnpike, and open late.

Sevens Ale House 77 Charles St, Beacon Hill Ⓣ617/523-9074. It may not look like much, but that's the point at this centrally located neighborhood watering hole.

Cambridge

The Cellar 991 Massachusetts Ave Ⓣ617/876-2580. An eclectic mix of students and locals gather in this laid-back niche between Harvard and Central squares. Two stories, two bars and some live entertainment on weekends.

Club Passim 47 Palmer St, Harvard Square Ⓣ617/492-5300. A four-decades-old, intimate "coffee house" that has been a noted folk/blues venue since Joan Baez performed here as an unknown 17-year-old.

House of Blues 96 Winthrop St, Harvard Square Ⓣ617/497-2229. The original, surprisingly small branch of this popular chain of live music venues features high-quality blues nightly. There's also a decent Cajun-themed restaurant and a heaving bar.

Man Ray 21 Brookline Ave, Central Square Ⓣ617/864-0400. Nightly themes draw very different crowds to Cambridge's most popular dance club. Wed is gothic/industrial, Thurs and Sat (when the club is known as *Campus*) draw a lively gay crowd, and Fri is reserved for the fetish/bondage scene.

Middle East 472/480 Massachusetts Ave, Central Square Ⓣ617/864-EAST. Cambridge's best alternative music venue with three stages and a good, inexpensive Arabic restaurant. Cover usually $3–10 in the main rooms with free music in the restaurant – acts to have played here gratis include Morphine, Buffalo Tom and Tracy Bonham.

Phoenix Landing 512 Massachusetts Ave, Central Square Ⓣ617/576-6260. Affable neighborhood bar and restaurant with soccer beamed in from Europe and a down-to-earth mix of music at weekends.

Ryles Jazz Club 212 Hampshire St Ⓣ617/876-9330. Eclectic jazz and world music club charging $10–20 covers.

Plough & Stars 912 Massachusetts Ave, between Harvard and Central squares Ⓣ617/441-3455. Time-worn Irish pub with music most nights. Cover free or up to $8.

Western Front 343 Western Ave, Central Square Ⓣ617/492-7772. This former jazz and blues club is now dedicated to reggae, with live music Fri and Sat nights, and Jamaican food Thurs–Sat.

Sports

The legendary Red Sox play **baseball** at Fenway Park (Kenmore subway on the Green "T" line). The whole stadium, squeezed in 1912 into the odd-shaped plot that was all its builders could buy, is painted green, including the 37ft, six-inch wall in the left field known as the "**Green Monster**" ($18–55; information Ⓣ617/267-8661, tickets Ⓣ617/267-1700, Ⓦwww.redsox.mlb.com). **Basketball**'s Celtics and **hockey**'s Bruins both play at the Fleet Center, 150 Causeway St near North Station (box office open daily 11am–7pm; call Ticketmaster for tickets by phone Ⓣ617/931-2000, Ⓦwww.fleetcenter.com).

The 26.2-mile **Boston Marathon**, first run in 1897, is now held on Patriot's Day, the third week in April, and finishes on Boylston Street at Copley Square (Ⓣ617/236-1652, Ⓦwww.bostonmarathon.org).

The North Shore

As you head northward out of Boston, you pass through a succession of rich little ports that have been all but swallowed up by the suburbs. The most obvious day-trip from Boston is the half-hour ride out to **Salem**. Nearby **Marblehead**, on the other hand, gave us the **US Navy**: George Washington's first five vessels were built there. If you have the time, the atmospheric old fishing ports of **Gloucester** and **Rockport**, further out on **Cape Ann**, have strong literary and artistic links: T.S. Eliot used to come here for his family vacations, and the *Dry Salvages* of the third of his *Four Quartets* are a group of offshore rocks. They're also the best places on the east coast for **whale-watch-**

BOSTON AND CAPE COD

ing trips: Cape Ann Whale Watch (☎978/283-5110 or 1-800/877-5110, ⓦwww.seethewhales.com) offers three- to four-hour trips for $28 between April and October.

Salem and Marblehead

Ironically, **SALEM** is remembered less as the site where the colony of Massachusetts was first established, with the most elevated of intentions, than as the place where just sixty years later Puritan self-righteousness reached its apogee in the horrific **witch trials** of 1692. While the town itself was to prosper as a port – as evidenced by its fine old buildings – the witch scare did much to discredit the idea that the New World conducted its affairs on a different moral plane than the Old. Nineteen Salem women were hanged as witches (and one man, Giles Corry, pressed to death with a boulder), thanks to a group of impressionable teenage girls who reported as truth a garbled mixture of fireside tales told by a West Indian slave, Tituba, and half-digested scare stories published by Cotton Mather, a pillar of the Puritan community.

That this unpleasant history is now the basis of a child-oriented tourist industry – all black hats and broomsticks – makes Salem an unsettling place. The **Salem Witch Museum** in Washington Square (daily: July & Aug 10am–7pm; rest of year 10am–5pm; $6) draws parallels with modern racism and political persecution, but is at heart a rather tacky show of illuminated dioramas and prerecorded commentary. Innumerable other witch-related attractions in town are best ignored. Salem's later seafaring years are remembered in the **Peabody Essex Museum** in East India Square (April–Oct Mon–Sat 10am–5pm, Sun noon–5pm; Nov–March closed Mon; $10), which since 1799 has assembled a remarkable collection of objects brought home by voyaging New Englanders. As well as extensive Japanese and Asian displays, it has one of only three existing breadfruit-wood idols of the Hawaiian god Ku, and details about the town's ships themselves.

Little of Salem's original waterfront remains, though the long **Derby Wharf** is still standing, together with the imposing **Custom House** at its head, where Nathaniel Hawthorne once worked. The **House of Seven Gables** at 54 Turner St, the star of his eponymous novel, is a rambling old mansion beside the sea (summer daily 10am–7pm; rest of year Mon–Sat 10am–5pm, Sun noon–5pm; $8). Hour-long guided tours of the complex also take in the author's birthplace, moved here from its original site on Union Street.

Regular MBTA **buses** run to Salem from Haymarket Station in Boston ($2.75 each way), and hourly **trains** (every 2hr at weekends) leave from North Station. If you want to **stay**, the best-value motel rooms are at the *Clipper Ship Inn*, 40 Bridge St (☎978/745-8022; ❸), while the *Salem Inn*, 7 Summer St (☎978/741-0680 or 1-800/446-2995, ⓦwww.saleminnma.com; ❺), a 39-room trio of Federal-style homes, is classier. *Nick's Firehouse Coffee Shoppe*, 30 Church St (☎978/745-9432), is the best deal in town for breakfast or lunch, where a burger can still be had for under $3. *Lyceum Bar & Grill*, 43 Church St (☎978/745-7665, ⓦwww.lyceumsalem.com), is more elegant and expensive.

When Salem's witch-related attractions grow tiresome, head five miles south and east along the bay to **MARBLEHEAD**, a lovely waterfront village whose historic homes date back as far as the mid-1700s. Free walking tour **maps** are available from the information booth in the center (☎781/639-8469, ⓦwww.marbleheadchamber.org) from June through October, while 250-year-old **Fort Sewall**, jutting into the harbor, gives pretty views. The *Seagull Inn*, 106 Harbor Ave (☎781/631-1893, ⓦwww.seagullinn.com; ❻), has comfortable B&B **rooms** overlooking the water, and the *Marblehead Inn*, 264 Pleasant

St (☎781/639-9999 or 1-800/399-5843, ⓦwww.marbleheadinn.com; ❺)
offers renovated two-room suites, some with fireplace; *Flynnie's*, 28 Atlantic Ave
(☎781/639-2100), serves fresh, inexpensive **seafood** and offers the same from
an outpost at Devereux Beach, *Flynnie's at the Beach*, from May through
October.

The South Shore

It can take a while to get clear of Boston heading south – especially on summer weekends, when the traffic down to Cape Cod can be horrendous. Two
historic towns, one north and one west of the Cape, are worth exploring –
Plymouth and **New Bedford**.

Plymouth

"America's Hometown," little **PLYMOUTH**, on the south shore of
Massachusetts Bay forty miles south of Boston, is given over to commemorat-
ing, in various degrees of taste, the landing here of the 102 **Pilgrims** in
December 1620.

A solemn pseudo-Greek temple by the sea encloses the nondescript
Plymouth Rock, where the Pilgrims are said to have touched land; as they
had already spent two months on Cape Cod, and there are no contemporary
references to the rock, it is of symbolic importance only. Two worthier memorials make no claim to authenticity, but meticulously reproduce the experience
of the Pilgrims. Both the replica of the **Mayflower** (the *Mayflower II*) in town,
and **Plimoth Plantation** three miles south, are staffed by costumed "inter-
preters," each of whom acts out the part of a specific Pilgrim, Indian or sailor.
The charade visitors are obliged to perform – pretending to have stepped back
into the seventeenth century – can be a little tiresome, but ultimately the sheer
depth of detail in both endeavors makes them fascinating. At the Plantation,
everything you see in the Pilgrim Village of 1627, and the Wampanoag Indian
Settlement, has been created using traditional techniques (both April–Nov
daily 9am–5pm; *Mayflower II* until 7pm in July & Aug; ☎508/746-1622;
Mayflower II alone $8 and Plantation alone $20, Plantation and *Mayflower II*
$22). A reasonably interesting way to pass time is at **Cranberry World**
(May–Nov daily 9.30am–5pm; $2), a slick little museum sponsored by Ocean
Spray, which details how the tart crimson berries are harvested from local bogs
and then processed into various products. The frequent tours end with free
samples of juice; if you've always wondered what "Cran-Raspberry" or
"Cranicot" taste like, here's your chance to find out.

Plymouth's **visitor center**, located on the Waterfront at no. 130 (☎508/747-
7525 or 1-800/USA-1620, ⓦwww.visit-plymouth.com). Plymouth & Brockton
(☎508/746-0378, ⓦwww.p-b.com), provides a regular **bus** service to and from
Boston or the Cape. There are also express ferries from Plymouth to
Provincetown (June–Sept daily 10am; $27; ☎508/747-2400 or 1-800/242-2469,
ⓦwww.provincetownferry.com). Standard **motels** include the *Blue Spruce Motel*,
710 State Rd (☎508/224-3990 or 1-800/370-7080, ⓦwww.bluespruce-motel
.com; ❸); the *Cold Spring*, 188 Court St (April–Dec; ☎508/746-2222 or 1-
800/678-8667; ❹); and *Clear Pond Motel*, 233 Carver Rd (☎508/746-4520; ❸);
while the *Governor Bradford Motor Inn*, 98 Water St (☎508/746-6200 or 1-
800/332-1620, ⓦwww.governorbradford.com; ❹), overlooking the harbor, has
slightly better facilities, including a heated outdoor pool. The *Lobster Hut*

(☎508/746-2270) and *McGrath's* (☎508/746-9751) are good, reasonably priced **seafood** places on the waterfront; *Al's Restaurant* (☎508/746-3383), also on the waterfront, specializes in pizza.

New Bedford

The famous old whaling port of **NEW BEDFORD**, 45 miles due south of Boston, is still home to one of the nation's most prosperous fishing fleets which, each year, haul in the largest catch on the east coast. Ongoing development and a waterfront highway have obscured some of its past, but on County Street the fine old houses still stand of which Melville commented:

New Bedford is a queer place. Had it not been for us whalemen, that tract of land would this day perhaps have been in as howling condition as the coast of Labrador . . . all these brave houses and flowery gardens came up from the Atlantic, Pacific and Indian oceans. One and all, they were harpooned and dragged hither from the bottom of the sea.

The roster of the whaling ship *Acushnet*, in the **New Bedford Whaling Museum** at 18 Johnny Cake Hill (daily 9am–5pm, second Thurs every month until 9pm; $6), shows Melville as one of the crew. Other evocative displays include a half-size replica of a whaling vessel. Immediately opposite stands the **Seamen's Bethel**; it really does have the ship-shaped pulpit described in *Moby Dick*, but this one was rebuilt after a fire in 1866.

The town's **visitor centers** at 47 N Second St (☎508/991-6200) and at Pier 3 (☎508/979-1745) can book **accommodation**; *The 1875 House* is an atmospheric little B&B at 36 Seventh St (☎508/997-6433; ❹). **Ferries** to Martha's Vineyard are detailed on p.227.

Cape Cod and the islands

Here a man may stand, and put all America behind him.

Henry David Thoreau

The trouble with standing on **Cape Cod** these days is that "all America" tends to be a lot closer behind you than you might prefer. Its main tourist haunts are packed in summer, its roads circled by a grim procession of crawling vehicles, searching in vain for some "unspoiled" bit of beach or "undiscovered" old town. Unless you have your own, preferably very secluded, place to stay, it's barely worth turning up at weekends, especially between June and August, and putting yourself through the hassle of trying to find what little available accommodation there is, invariably at premium prices. However, the place is undeniably beautiful and if you find yourself in the region midweek in May or September – when hotel prices are much lower, the crowds have thinned, and the weather usually very pleasant – it's certainly worth a visit.

Cape Cod was named by Bartholomew Gosnold in 1602, on account of the prodigious quantities of cod caught by his crew off Provincetown. Less than twenty years later the Pilgrims landed nearby; in the few months before moving on to Plymouth, they began the process, continued by generations of Europeans, of stripping the interior of the Cape bare of its original covering of thick woods. Today, much of the land on the Cape – from its salt marshes to its ever-eroding dunes – is considered a fragile and endangered ecosystem, a designation, however, that hasn't especially dampened the persistence of developers.

If you imagine the Cape as an arm, its **upper** section, the thirty-mile east-ward stretch closest to mainland Massachusetts, would be represented by the biceps. Much of the worst beachfront development lies along the southern shore, and **Hwy-28**, running from Falmouth via Hyannis to Chatham, gets especially clogged. Only once you get beyond the "elbow" and head north to the **Outer Cape** or, anatomically speaking, the forearm, past the spectacular dunes of **Cape Cod National Seashore**, do you get a feeling for why the Cape still has a reputation as a seaside wilderness. **Provincetown**, right at the end, is the one town on the Cape that can be unreservedly recommended.

Sadly, the islands of **Martha's Vineyard** and **Nantucket**, off the Cape to the south, are dependent on summer tourism for their livelihood. However, a trip out to Nantucket in particular does still evoke haunting memories of its proud seafaring days. Again, the off-season has a charm all its own, a time when you can sink into the rhythms of life on the island without the distraction of hordes of day-trippers.

Getting to the Cape

It was the Pilgrims who first suggested the construction of a canal between Cape Cod Bay and Buzzards Bay, so that coastal shipping could avoid the dangers of the open ocean; when finally completed at the start of the twentieth century, it left the peninsula as an island. Now all traffic to the Cape bottlenecks at one or other of the two enormous bridges – Bourne on Hwy-28 and Sagamore on Hwy-6 – across the canal, and you may regret trying to **drive** there on a summer Friday (or back on a Sunday). Each has an **information office** for the Cape (daily 9am–7pm) on its mainland side.

One way to dodge the traffic is to **fly**. US Airways affiliate Colgan Air (T1-800/428-4322, Wwww.colganair.com) serves Hyannis, Martha's Vineyard and Nantucket from Washington, DC, New York, Boston and points further north such as Augusta, Maine; and Cape Air (T1-800/352-0714, Wwww.flycapeair.com) flies several times daily from Boston, Providence and New Bedford to Hyannis, Provincetown and the islands. Bonanza **buses** run regularly from New York and Boston (T617/345-0539 or 1-800/556-3815, Wwww.bonanzabus.com), and the Plymouth & Brockton Bus Co (T508/746-0378, Wwww.p-b.com) runs daily to Hyannis and Provincetown from Rhode Island, Boston, Plymouth and New York (for other Boston services, see p.201). **Ferries** take 90 minutes to cross from Boston to Provincetown (see p.222); for boats to the various islands, see p.227.

You can also **cycle** from Boston on the 135-mile Boston–Cape Cod Bikeway, which extends all the way to Provincetown.

The Upper Cape

The **Upper Cape**, just across the bridges, was the first part of the peninsula to attract tourists in any numbers – and it shows. To see the various communities of the south coast as "pretty little villages" – the image they hope to project – you'd have to be wearing exceptionally rose-tinted spectacles, or blinders. Each is arranged around a prim central green; but you have to fight your way through thickets of malls, motels and fast-food joints to reach their artificial hearts.

It only makes sense to **stay** in one of these places if you're catching a **ferry** to the islands (see p.227). Thus one obvious base is **FALMOUTH**, where central motels include the comfortable *Shoreway Acres Inn*, 59 Shore St (T508/540-3000 or 1-800/352-7100, Wwww.shorewayacresinn.com; ❺), with indoor and outdoor pools, and the harborfront *Best Western Marina*

Tradewinds on Robbins Road (☎508/548-4300 or 1-800/341-5700, ⓦwww.vacationinnproperties.com; ❺). The luxurious clapboard *Village Green Inn*, 40 W Main St (☎508/548-5621 or 1-800/237-1119, ⓦwww.village-greeninn.com; ❹–❻), is a bargain in Cape terms; the oceanfront *Grafton Inn*, 261 Grand Ave (☎508/540-8688 or 1-800/642-4069, ⓦwww.graftoninn .com; ❻), in the Falmouth Heights district, is also good. The *Sippewissett Campground & Cabins*, a couple of miles out at 836 Palmer Ave (☎508/548-2542, ⓦwww.sippewissett.com; ❶), offers a free shuttle service to the ferries and beaches. Restaurants abound, though with the possible exception of *Betsy's Diner*, 457 Main St (☎508/540-0060), built in the Fifties and serving no-nonsense food from that era, the best food is to be found in the assorted moderately priced seafood places along the waterfront at **WOODS HOLE**, four miles southwest; the *Fishmonger's Café* at 56 Water St (☎508/548-9148) is a natural foods restaurant with seafood specials at lunch and dinner; eggs, granola and the like at breakfast. The Woods Hole Oceanographic Institution's **exhibition center** at 15 School St, near Little Harbor (May–Oct Tues–Sat 10am–4.30pm, Sun noon–4.30pm; Nov, Dec, March & April Fri & Sat 10am–4.30pm, Sun noon–4.30; free), focuses on the Institution's sensational discovery of the *Titanic* in 1986. Ocean Quest, a private nonprofit, runs ninety-minute research-based ocean cruises in summer (reservations recommended; $20; ☎1-800/37-OCEAN, ⓦwww.capecodnet/oceanquest).

The largest port on the Cape, and its main commercial hub, **HYANNIS** clings a little desperately to the glamour it earned when the **Kennedy compound** at Hyannisport placed it at the center of world affairs. Hence the existence of the **John F. Kennedy Museum**, 397 Main St (Mon–Sat 10am–5pm, Sun 1–5pm; $2), which shows photographs, newsclippings and film footage of the days JFK spent on the Cape. The Kennedys are still here, though their property can only be glimpsed, at a considerable distance, from the sea – Hy-Line Cruises, Ocean Street Dock ($10; ☎508/778-2600, ⓦwww.hy-linecruises.com), runs one-hour harbor cruises that peek in at the compound.

Sightseeing trips on the **Cape Cod Central Railroad** (May–Oct Tues–Sun; $13; ☎508/771-3800 or 1-888/797-7245, ⓦwww.capetrain.com) run from the corner of Main and Center streets in Hyannis along a meandering route west through cranberry bogs to Sandwich and to Buzzards Bay, and along the Cape Cod Canal.

There are many hotels in Hyannis, but you would have to find a pretty compelling reason to stay in one. A good **B&B** in Hyannis Port – and the only one – is the *Simmons Homestead Inn*, 288 Scudder Ave (☎508/778-4999 or 1-800/637-1649, ⓦwww.simmonshomesteadinn.com; ❻). *The Egg & I*, 521 Main St (☎508/771-1596), does a decent breakfast, while *Alberto's* at no. 360 (☎508/778-1770) offers good but pricey Italian meals. *Perry's*, 546 Main St (☎508/775-9711), is a great deli with three-decker clubs and other "stacked" sandwiches, and also serves breakfast.

The Mid-Cape

The middle stretch of Cape Cod holds some of its prettiest, most unspoiled places. Time-worn old fishing communities like Wellfleet and Chatham, along with dozens of carefully maintained, mildly touristy hamlets along the many winding roads, are what most people hope to find when they come to the Cape. Cutting across the middle, the **Cape Cod Rail Trail** follows a paved-over railroad track from Dennis to Eastham, through cranberry bogs and forests. It makes a good **cycling** trip; bikes can be rented in all the main towns.

One desirable destination is the whitewashed old fishing community of

Cape Cod National Seashore

After the bustle of Cape Cod's towns, the **Cape Cod National Seashore** really does come as the proverbial "breath of fresh air." These protected lands, spared by President Kennedy from the rampant development further south, take up virtually the entire Atlantic side of the Cape, from Chatham north to Provincetown. Most of the way you can park by the road, sometimes for a fee, and strike off across the dunes to windswept beaches – though in places parking is limited to local residents. A program of grass-planting helps to hold the whole place together; three feet of the lower Cape is washed away each year, and much of it is carried here by the sea to extend the seemingly endless beaches.

It was on these shifting sands, not then as denuded as today, that the **Pilgrims** made their first home. They obtained their water from Pilgrim Spring near Truro; at Corn Hill Beach they uncovered the freshly buried cache of Indian corn that kept them alive. After a couple of months, which they survived with the help of the Wampanoag Indians, they moved on to Plymouth (where the reconstructed Indian village at Plimoth Plantation, is based on one found at Eastham).

Displays and movies at the main **Salt Pond Visitor Center**, on US-6 just north of Eastham (daily 9am–5pm ☎508/255-3421, ⓦwww.nps.gov/caco/places/saltpond-vc.html), trace the geology and history of the Cape. A road and a hiking/cycling trail head east to the sands of **Coast Guard Beach** and **Nauset Light Beach**, both of which offer excellent swimming. Another fine beach is the **Head of the Meadow**, halfway between Truro and Provincetown on the northeast shore.

CHATHAM, tucked away in a protected harbor between Nantucket Sound and the open Atlantic Ocean. Hang out at the **Fish Pier** on Shore Road and wait for the fleet to come in mid-afternoon, or head a mile south on Hwy-28 to **Chatham Light**, one of many lighthouses built to protect mariners from the treacherous shoals. Tour **maps** are available from the booth at 533 Main St (☎508/945-5199 or 1-800/715-5567, ⓦwww.chathamcapecod.org). The *Impudent Oyster* (☎508/945-3545) serves excellent seafood just off Main Street at 15 Chatham Bars Ave; reservations are recommended. One of the nicest **places to stay** on the whole east coast is the romantic *Whalewalk Inn*, at 220 Bridge Rd in the town of **Eastham** (☎508/255-0617 or 1-800/440-1281, ⓦwww.whalewalkinn.com; ❼), where rates for the secluded B&B rooms and a converted barn and carriage house include free use of bicycles to ride the many nearby trails. Out on Queen Anne Road, a five-minute walk from downtown, the *Queen Anne Inn* at no. 70 (☎508/945-0394 or 1-800/545-INNS, ⓦwww.queenanneinn.com; ❻) and the *Bow Roof House* at no. 59 (☎508/945-1346; ❹) are two B&Bs where all rooms have private baths. The nearest **hostel**, with beds from $15, is the *HI-Mid Cape*, between Chatham and Provincetown at 75 Goody Halet Drive, Eastham (☎508/255-2785; ❶), open May through September.

Provincetown

The compact fishing village of **PROVINCETOWN** ("P-Town") is right on the knuckle of what would be Cape Cod's clenched fist. Silvery clapboard houses, with gloriously unruly gardens, line its tiny winding streets. Provincetown is far from secluded: its population of five thousand rises tenfold in summer. Self-professed **bohemians** and **artists** have always flocked here for the dazzling light and vast beaches, and in 1914 Eugene O'Neill established the Provincetown Playhouse in a small hut. It has also become renowned, since the

PROVINCETOWN

ACCOMMODATION

Dunes Edge Campground	1
Elephant Walk Inn	4
Land's End Inn	8
Outermost Hostel	2
Revere Guest House	6
Secret Garden Inn	7
Sunset Inn	3
Watership Inn	5

▲ HI-Truro

ATLANTIC OCEAN

Race Point Beach

CAPE COD NATIONAL SEASHORE

Province Lands Visitor Center

PROVINCE LANDS

RACE POINT ROAD

PROVINCE LANDS ROAD

CAPE COD NATIONAL SEASHORE

CEMETERY ROAD

OLD COLONY WAY

AUNT SUKEY WAY

HARRY KEMP WAY

MILLER HILL

ALDEN ST

PEARL ST

BREWSTER ST

DYER ST

WILLOW ST

HOWLAND STREET

CONWELL STREET

STANDISH ST

CENTER STREET

FREEMAN ST

ARCH ST

WINSLOW ST

JEROME ST

ALDEN ST

Pilgrim Monument

TOWN HILL

PRINCE ST

RYDER ST

GOSNOLD ST

MASONIC PL

CARVER STREET

COURT STREET

WINTHROP STREET

CENTRAL ST

ATLANTIC AVE

CONANT

MONTELLO

BRADFORD STREET

SHANK

PAINTER

BROWN ST

RACE ROAD

PLEASANT STREET

FRANKLIN ST

SCHOOL ST

MECHANIC ST

COTTAGE ST

NICKERSON ST

TREMONT STREET

CREEK ROAD

BLUEBERRY

WEST VINE ST

PILGRIM HEIGHTS

CREEK ROUND HILL

POINT ST

ATWOOD AVE

COMMERCIAL STREET

WEST END

EAST END

Provincetown Art Association & Museum

BRADFORD STREET

COMMERCIAL STREET

THISTLEMORE

ALLERTON ST

SNOWS ST

CONWAY ST

DUNCAN LANE

ATKINS MAYO ROAD

KENDALL LANE

HANCOCK ST

ATKINS LANE

ANTHONY ST

KILEY CT

LOVETTS CT

YOUNGS CT

WASHINGTON AVENUE

LAW ST

Whydah Museum

MacMillan Wharf

Fishermen's Wharf

Provincetown Heritage Museum

Coast Guard Station

Seth Nickerson House

Pilgrims Landing Place

Herring Cove Beach

Cape Cod Bay

▼ Long Point Beach

0 — 1 mile

N

beatnik 1950s, as a **gay** and **lesbian** center. Commercialism, though rampant, is countercultural: gay, environmentalist and feminist giftshops join arty (not craftsy) galleries, restaurants and bars on the aptly named **Commercial Street**.

Provincetown retains a firm grip on its past. Strict zoning ensures that there are few new buildings in town, and there is barely a sign of ugly development. Albeit crowded and raucous from July through September, P-Town remains a place where history, natural beauty and, above all, difference, are respected and celebrated.

Arrival, information and getting around

Provincetown lies 120 miles from Boston by land, but less than fifty by sea, nestled in the second largest natural harbor in the world (after Le Havre in France). By far the nicest way to arrive is on the **ferry**. Boston Harbor Cruises leave Long Wharf Ferry Terminal in Boston at 9am, arriving at MacMillan Wharf 90 minutes later, and return at 4pm (daily May to mid-June, additional departures on weekends in early June through early Oct; $25 one-way, $45 round-trip; ⊤617/227-4321 or 1-877/733-9425, Ⓦwww.bostonharborcruises .com). The tiny **visitor center** in the Chamber of Commerce, at the end of the wharf at 307 Commercial St, sells ferry tickets (summer daily 9am–5pm; rest of year Mon–Sat 9.30am–4.30pm; ⊤508/487-3424, Ⓦwww.ptownchamber.com).

It couldn't be easier to **walk** around tiny P-Town, but many visitors prefer to **cycle** the narrow streets, hills and the undulating Province Lands Bike Trail, a difficult six-mile route with great vistas. Bike rental outlets in town include Arnold's, 329 Commercial St (⊤508/487-0844), which charges about $15 a day. For those without transportation, **tours** to the more isolated dunes and moors include ones led by the Provincetown Trolley Inc from the town hall on Commercial Street (daily every half-hour from 10am–4pm or until 7pm in season; $8; ⊤508/487-9483, Ⓦwww.provincetowntrolley.com); Art's Sand Dune Tours are based at Commercial and Standish streets (April–Oct 10am–dusk; $12 daytime tour and $15 sunset tour; ⊤508/487-1950, Ⓦwww.artsdunetours.com). **Whale-watching** cruises leave from MacMillan Wharf between April and October 31; one of the main cruise operators is the Dolphin Fleet Whale Watch (⊤508/349-1900 or 1-800/826-9300, Ⓦwww.whalewatch.com); they have a ticket office within the Chamber of Commerce and sell tickets for about $20.

Accommodation

Besides the few motels on the outskirts, every second picturesque cottage in town seems to be a guesthouse. Prices are reasonable until mid-June, and during the off-season you can find some real bargains. The Provincetown Reservation System (⊤508/487-2400 or 1-800/648-0364) and the gay-oriented In Town Reservations (⊤508/487-1883 or 1-800/67P-TOWN, Ⓦwww.intownreservations.com) can usually rustle up lodging at busy times. The welcoming *Dunes' Edge Campground*, on Hwy-6 just east of the central stoplights (⊤508/487-9815, Ⓦwww.dunes-edge.com), charges $25 for its wooded sites and is only in operation May to September.

Elephant Walk Inn 156 Bradford St ⊤508/487-2543 or 1-800/889-WALK, Ⓦwww.elephant-walkinn.com. Central, spacious rooms with private baths and a video library. Free parking. ❸–❺
HI-Truro North Pamet Rd, Truro ⊤508/349-3889, Ⓦwww.hiayh.org/hostels/massach/truro.htm. Ten

miles south of Provincetown in a former coast-guard station. Dorm beds $15–19 a night. Mid-June to early Sept. Office hours 7.30–10am & 5–10pm.
Land's End Inn 22 Commercial St ⊤508/487-0706 or 1-800/276-7088,

@www.sunsol.com/landsend. Meticulously decorated rooms and suites, many with sweeping ocean views. **4**/**5**

Outermost Hostel 28 Winslow St ☎508/487-4378. Very basic five-dorm cabins with $15 beds. May–Oct.

Revere Guest House 14 Court St ☎508/487-2292 or 1-800/487-2292. B&B with relaxing garden patio and continental breakfast, and rooms with shared baths for around $65 in summer. **3**/**4**

Secret Garden Inn 300a Commercial St ☎508/487-9027 or 1-866/786-9646, @www.provincetown.com/secretgardeninn.

Homey five-room guesthouse in a quiet lane off the town center, with sundeck, sea views and fresh-baked goods. **3**

Sunset Inn 142 Bradford St ☎508/487-9810 or 1-800/965-1801, @www.sunsetinnptown.com. Clean, quiet rooms in a house full of art and close to the town center. Rooms with shared bath are $20–30 cheaper than those with private bath. **4**/**5**

Watership Inn 7 Winthrop St ☎508/487-0094 or 1-800/330-9413, @www.watershipinn.com. Fifteen rooms with private bath in an 1820s home; rates include a good continental breakfast. **4**

The town and the beaches

Visitors who head straight for the beaches miss out on Provincetown's tiny core, centered on the three narrow miles of **Commercial Street**. **MacMillan Wharf**, always busy with charters, yachts and fishing boats (which unload their catch each afternoon), splits the town in half. Not far away in the quieter **East End**, the **Heritage Museum**, at the intersection of Commercial and Center streets (daily 10am–6pm; $3), stands in an 1860 Methodist church. This well-tended collection of Provincetown memorabilia includes a 68-inch stuffed striped bass, a Portuguese altar, a model fishing schooner and a reconstruction of the beach hut of Harry Kemp, beach-bum poet and crony of Eugene O'Neill. It also has leaflets on walking tours. Further out, the delightful **Provincetown Art Association and Museum**, 460 Commercial St (May–Oct daily noon–5pm & 8–10pm; Nov–April Sat & Sun noon–4pm; $3), displays paintings by local artists.

The 252ft granite tower of the **Pilgrim Monument and Provincetown Museum** on High Pole Hill, in the pretty **West End** of P-Town, has an observation deck (only accessible by stairs and narrow ramps) which looks out over the whole of the Cape (daily: July & Aug 9am–7pm; April–June & Sept–Nov 9am–5pm; $6). At the bottom of the hill on Bradford Street, there's a bas-relief monument to the Pilgrims' 1620 **Mayflower Compact**, in which they agreed to unite as one body to build the first colony. Further from the wharf, the weathered clapboard houses have colored blinds, white picket fences, and wild-flowers spilling out of every crevice. The 1746 **Seth Nickerson House**, 72 Commercial St (June–Oct daily 10am–5pm; $2.50), is the oldest house in town, built by a ship's carpenter. Tours lead through the cabin-like rooms with slanting doors and crazy floorboards. A modest bronze plaque on a boulder at the western end of Commercial Street commemorates the Pilgrims' actual landing place.

A little way beyond the town's narrow strip of sand, undeveloped **beaches** are marked only by dunes and a few shabby beach huts. You can swim in the clear water from the uneven rocks of the two-mile breakwater, where the sea bed crunches with soft-shell clams, or head through scented wild roses and beach plums to find blissful isolation on undeveloped beaches nearby. West of town, **Herring Cove Beach**, easily reached by bike or through the dunes, is more crowded but never unbearably so. In the wild **Province Lands**, at the Cape's northern tip, vast sweeping moors and bushy dunes are buffeted by a deadly sea, site of three thousand known shipwrecks. The **visitor center** (April–Nov daily 9am–5pm; ☎508/487-1256), in the middle of the dunes on Race Point Road, has an observation deck from which you might spot a whale.

Eating

Food in Provincetown can be expensive: the snack bars around MacMillan Wharf are generally extortionate, and the – undeniably good – *nouvelle cuisine* in the trendy gay restaurants can be $10 for a salad and a coffee. Portuguese bakeries, relics of early settlement, and bland family restaurants abound on Commercial Street.

Bubala's by the Bay 183 Commercial St ☏ 508/487-0773. Breakfast, lunch or dinner on the water in a local and fun hangout serving all kinds of sandwiches, seafood and breakfast items.

Café Heaven 199 Commercial St ☏ 508/487-9639. Light and airy café serving all-day breakfasts, espresso coffee and creative salads from $5. Open 8am–3pm and 6–9.30pm.

Ciro & Sal's 4 Kiley Court ☏ 508/487-6444. Tasty, traditional Italian cooking, though quite expensive. Reservations are recommended.

Post Office Café 303 Commercial St ☏ 508/487-3892. Small, gay-run restaurant serving healthy lunches and dinners for $10–20. Gay/feminist cabaret performed nightly.

Spiritus Pizza 190 Commercial St ☏ 508/487-2808. Combination pizza place and coffee bar with a scene that intensifies as the night marches on.

The Squealing Pig 335 Commercial St ☏ 508/487-4822. Excellent pub with a classic name right in the middle of town, featuring live music some nights.

Nightlife and entertainment

Each weekend, boatloads of revelers from the mainland seek out P-Town's notoriously wild **nightlife**. From house music raves to drag cabarets, from torch singing to R&B, the variety is huge.

The Atlantic House 6 Masonic Place, behind Commercial St ☏ 508/487-3821. The "A-House" – a dark drinking hole favored by Tennessee Williams and Eugene O'Neill – is now a trendy gay music club and bar.

Governor Bradford 312 Commercial St ☏ 508/487-2781. Popular bar with live jazz, reggae and R&B.

The New Crown and Anchor 247 Commercial St ☏ 508/487-1430. Noisy pub with nightly drag cabaret and a mostly gay crowd.

Student Union 9–11 Carver St ☏ 508/487-3490. Lively dance club and video bar within the *Gifford House Inn* that has little to do with students.

Vixen 336 Commercial St ☏ 508/487-6424. High-energy lesbian club.

Martha's Vineyard

The island of **MARTHA'S VINEYARD**, just seven miles south of Cape Cod and twenty-four miles long by ten wide, may or may not have been named for Bartholomew Gosnold's daughter Martha (some ancient maps call it *Martin's* Vineyard). The "Vineyard" part, however, was for its "incredible store of vines"; considerably more fertile than bleak little Nantucket, it has never been quite so dependent on the sea to make a living. Now more than ever, tourism is at the root of the island's economy, boosted by the gaggle of celebrities, not least the Clintons, who show up year after year. The popularity of the island with the rich, famous, and/or well-connected has driven up housing prices and lowered availability to extremes. The many second-homeowners who spend the summer here get a better deal than mere day-trippers, though – some of the best beaches are off-limits to nonresidents.

Ferries to the island arrive either at **Oak Bluffs**, where genteel Victorian terraced cottages look down on the harbor and a colorful century-old fairground carousel sits near the jetty, or at the more upmarket **Vineyard Haven**. **Edgartown**, over to the east, is the oldest settlement on the island, and has been extravagantly dolled up for visitors (you may recognize it as the location for the *Jaws* films). A little ferry shuttles back and forth from Edgartown to adjacent **Chappaquiddick Island** (the bridge that Senator Edward Kennedy made infamous is on the far side).

Ferries to Martha's Vineyard and Nantucket

Unless otherwise specified, all the ferries below run several times daily in midsummer (mid-June to mid-Sept). Most have fewer services from May to mid-June, and between mid-September and October. There is at least a skeleton service to each island, though not on all routes, all year round. Round-trip passenger **fares** from Woods Hole and Falmouth to Martha's Vineyard are around $10; from Hyannis $27; to Nantucket $25; or high-speed ferry to Nantucket $58. Round-trip costs for cars (mid-May to mid-Sept) are $104 in the high season, not including passengers.

To Martha's Vineyard

From **Falmouth** to Oak Bluffs. Passengers only. The *Island Queen* (☏508/548-4800, ⓦ www.islandqueen.com).

From **Falmouth** to Edgartown. Passengers only. $18 round-trip. Falmouth Ferry Service (☏508/548-9400).

From **Woods Hole** to both Vineyard Haven and Oak Bluffs. Car ferry. Steamship Authority (☏508/477-8600, ⓦ www.islandferry.com).

From **Hyannis** to Oak Bluffs. Passengers only. Hy-Line (☏508/778-2600 in Hyannis; ☏508/693-0112 on Martha's Vineyard or 1-888/778-1132 from within North America, ⓦ www.hy-linecruises.com).

From **New Bedford** to Vineyard Haven. Passengers only. $20 round-trip. Cape-Island Express Lines (☏508/997-1688, ⓦ www.mvferry.com). Also Steamship Authority (☏508/477-8600, ⓦ www.islandferry.com).

From **New Bedford** to Oak Bluffs. Passengers only. $20 round-trip. Steamship Authority (☏508/477-8600, ⓦ www.islandferry.com).

From **New London** to Oak Bluffs. Passengers only. Seasonal service. Fox Navigation (☏1-888/SAILFOX, ⓦ www.foxnavigation.com).

From **Montauk**, Long Island, to Oak Bluffs. Passengers only; summer Thursdays only; $40. Viking Ferry (☏516/668-5700).

To Nantucket

From **Hyannis**. Cars on Steamship Authority (☏508/477-8600 for auto reservations; ☏508/548-5011 on the mainland; ☏508/228-0262 on Nantucket). Also Hy-Line (☏508/778-2600 in Hyannis; ☏508/228-3949 on Nantucket or 1-888/778-1132 within North America, ⓦ www.hy-linecruises.com).

From **Harwich Port**. Passengers only. Freedom Cruise Line (☏508/430-7772, ⓦ www.nantucketislandferry.com).

The Hy-Line ferry company in summer also runs a **connecting service** with three departures daily, for passengers only, between Oak Bluffs, Martha's Vineyard and Nantucket (☏508/693-0112). The journey takes about two hours, $27 round-trip.

The three principal island communities are connected by a regular bus service and offer full facilities and shops of every kind. They're quite mellow places to pass a summer's day, but a little exploring can yield some pleasant surprises, such as quiet beaches and bird-filled lagoons. Bringing a car over is expensive and pointless, as the island is jam-packed with cars throughout the summer and you can easily get around by **bike**; rent one at the rental places lined up by the ferry landing. The best bike ride is along the State Beach Park between Oak Bluffs and Edgartown, with the dunes to one side and marshy Sengekontacket Pond to the other; purpose-built cycle routes continue to the youth hostel at West Tisbury (see overleaf).

Trips around the west side of the island ("p-island") can be disappointing, with not a peep of the ocean beyond the private estates; however, you do eventually come to the **lighthouse** at **Gay Head Cliffs**, where the multicolored clay was once the main source of paint for the island's houses — anyone caught removing any clay faces a sizeable fine. The cliffs are not vast, and they're crumbling away so fast that it's not safe to get too close to them. From Gay Head public beach below, however, you can get some great views of this spectacular mass. Gay Head was once famous for its Wampanoag harpooneers, such as Tashtego in *Moby Dick*.

Accommodation

If accommodation is booked up, as is very likely, the main **Chamber of Commerce** office at Beach Road in Vineyard Haven (T 508/693-0085, W www.mvy.com) may be able to help. There is a **campground** in Vineyard Haven, at 569 Edgartown Rd (T 508/693-3772, W www.campmvfc.com); tentsites cost $36 per day for two people and include water and electricity hookups.

Attleboro House 42 Lake Ave, Oak Bluffs T 508/693-4346. Charming, old-fashioned guest-house on a distinguished harbor-view terrace. No private bathrooms, however. ❹

Colonial Inn 38 N Water St, Edgartown T 508/627-4711 or 1-800/627-4701, W www.colonialinnmvy.com. Extremely central white clapboard inn, part of a largish mall, with clean, airy rooms in view of the water. Some off-season bargains (❺) can be found, but midsummer rates are high. ❼

HI-Martha's Vineyard Edgartown–West Tisbury Rd T 508/693-2665, W www.hiayh.org/hostels/massach/martha.htms. In an appealing setting at the forest's edge and away from town, near the island's main bike path. Shuttle buses run to here from the ferry terminal. April to mid-Nov. $15 members, $19 others.

Nashua House B&B 30 Kennebec Ave across from the Post Office, Oak Bluffs T 508/693-0043, W www.nashuahouse.com. Small, sunny, Victorian-style rooms with shared baths and ocean views in the heart of Oak Bluffs. ❸/❹

Shiretown Inn 44 N Water St, Edgartown T 508/627-3353 or 1-800/541-0090, W www.shiretowninn.com. A variety of B&B rooms done up in different styles, including some very costly, but fancy ones, right in the center of town. ❻

Tuscany Inn 22 N Water St, Edgartown T 508/627-5999, W www.mvweb.com/tuscany. Savor an unexpected slice of Italy in the center of (somewhat stuffy) Edgartown. The owner has given her inn Tuscan touches, from the garden to the cooking classes that are taught on-site in the off-season. ❻

Wesley Hotel 70 Lake Ave, Oak Bluffs T 508/693-6611, W www.wesleyhotel.com. Large but characterful hotel near the ferries, with a great wraparound deck and pretty views. Most rooms are $110-plus, with prices rising dramatically in summer, all with private bath. ❺

Eating and drinking

It's not at all hard to find something to **eat** on Martha's Vineyard. The ports in particular have rows of places to tempt tourists just off the ferries. Only in Edgartown and Oak Bluffs can you order alcohol with meals, but you can bring your own elsewhere. Many pubs, too, serve inexpensive food, though the people partaking of it often look like they're on a break from a Ralph Lauren photo shoot. Wear Nautica if you want to blend in with the locals.

The Black Dog Bakery 480 State Rd, Vineyard Haven T 508/693-4786. Skip the overrated *Black Dog Tavern* next door and stock up on delicious muffins and breads for the ferry ride back.

Giordano's 107 Circuit Ave, Oak Bluffs T 508/693-0184. Crowded and reasonably priced Italian place, often closed out of season.

Lambert's Cove West Tisbury T 508/693-2298. The restaurant at this country inn is a gem, set in over seven acres of lawn and serving vegetables grown on the property; try the delectable soups. Reservations suggested.

Louis' 350 State Rd, Vineyard Haven T 508/693-3255. Lively, well-priced Italian place that also serves clams, located right near the ferry dock.

The Newes from America attached to the *Kelley House Inn*, 23 Kelley St, Edgartown T 508/627-4397. Swill 500 beers in this atmospheric pub (not necessarily all in the same night) and they'll name a stool after you.

The Wharf Lower Main St, Edgartown T 508/627-9966. One of the better-priced seafood joints on the island, on the east side of town, with home-brewed ales on the premises.

Zapotec 10 Kennebec Ave, Oak Bluffs T 508/693-6800. Exciting seafood variations based on Mexican cuisine.

Nantucket

The thirty-mile, two-hour sea crossing to **NANTUCKET** may not be an oceangoing odyssey, but it does set the "Little Grey Lady" apart from her larger, shore-hugging sister, Martha. Halfway here from Hyannis, neither mainland nor island is in sight, and once you've landed you can avert your eyes from the smart-money double-deck cruisers with names like *Pier Pressure* and *Loan Star* and let the place remind you that it hasn't always been a rich folk's playground. Indeed, despite the formidable prowess of its seamen (see box overleaf), survival for early settlers on the island's scrubby soil was always a struggle.

The tiny cobbled carriageways of **Nantucket Town** itself, once one of the largest cities in Massachusetts, were frozen in time by economic decline 150 years ago. Today, this area of delightful old restored houses – the town has more buildings on the National Register of Historic Places than Boston – is very much the center of activity. From the moment you get off the ferry you're besieged by bike rental places and tour companies. **Straight Wharf** leads directly onto **Main Street** with its shops and restaurants; the **information office** – which has a daily list of accommodation vacancies, but doesn't make reservations – is nearby at 25 Federal St (T 508/228-0925). The **Chamber of Commerce**, 48 Main St (T 508/228-1700, W www.nantucketchamber.org), carries the best range of island information. The main sights in town are the excellent **Whaling Museum** (daily 11am–4pm; $12) on Broad Street at the head of Steamboat Wharf, where you should look out especially for such scrimshaw artifacts as a set of twenty-one whale types carved from whale teeth, and the astonishing harpoon corkscrewed in the "lurry" or last struggle of a dying whale, and the **Peter Foulger Museum** ($5), which covers island history next door.

After a stroll around Nantucket Town, it's customary to cycle the seven flat miles east to the village of **Siasconset** (always abbreviated to 'Sconset), where the venerable cottages stand literally encrusted with salt, and then to meander back across the heaths and moorland. Buses also link Nantucket Town and 'Sconset. NRTA (T 508/228-7025) runs shuttles from late May through early October and charges $1 each way.

Accommodation

But for the **youth hostel**, accommodation on Nantucket is invariably expensive; the going rate in B&Bs and guesthouses starts at $85. There are no campgrounds.

Cliff Lodge 9 Cliff Rd T 508/228-9480, W www.nantucket.net/lodging/clifflodge. An 18th-century hilltop B&B with a rooftop deck and homemade muffins in the morning. The twelve rooms are sunlit; lower-priced singles are available in the off-season. ❻

Hawthorn House 2 Chestnut St T 508/228-1468, W www.hawthorn-house.com. Central, stunning and well-appointed guesthouse. Rates include vouchers for breakfast in town. ❻

HI-Nantucket Star of the Sea, Surfside T 508/228-0433, W www.hiayh.org. Dorm beds at Surfside Beach, just over 3 miles south of town. $15 members, $19 nonmembers. Lockout 10am–5pm, curfew 10pm. April–Oct only.

Hungry Whale 8 Derrymore Rd T 508/228-0793. Good-value, friendly B&B a short walk from the center. Five rooms, one with private bath. ❹

Jared Coffin House 29 Broad St T 508/228-2400 or 1-800/248-2405, W www.jaredcoffinhouse.com. Sixty rooms, all with period furniture in four adjacent buildings in the town center. There's also a superb restaurant and likeable bar on-site. ❻

The Nesbitt Inn 21 Broad St T 508/228-0156. The central location and affordable rooms, most with original furniture, compensate for the shared baths in this Victorian inn, built in 1872. ❹

The whalers of Nantucket

Scores of anonymous Captains have sailed out of Nantucket, that were as great, and greater than your Cook . . . For in their succorless empty-handedness, they, in the heathenish sharked waters, and by the beaches of unrecorded, javelin islands, battled with virgin wonders and terrors that Cook with all his marines and muskets would not have willingly dared.

Herman Melville, Moby Dick

In 1659, a sober group of 27 Quaker and Presbyterian families arrived on Nantucket and set about imposing order on the haphazard business of **whaling**. Whales had always beached themselves on the treacherous sandy shoals all around – up to a dozen might be washed ashore in a major storm – and the local **Indians** had become skilled in hunting them in nearby waters. At first, the white settlers treated the island itself as their vessel, erecting tall masts from which a permanent watch was kept for passing whales. As the years went by, they stopped waiting at home, and sent large ships out into the ocean to pursue their prey. The Wampanoag played an integral part in the process: the actual kill was effected by two rowboats working in tandem, and at least five of each thirteen-man crew, usually including the crucial **harpooneer**, would be Indian. (The common occurrence when an injured whale would speed away, dragging a boat helter-skelter behind it for endless terri-fying hours, was known as a "**Nantucket Sleighride**.")

The early chronicler Crèvecoeur provides an extensive account of Nantucket as it was in 1782 in his *Letters from an American Farmer*. Although perturbed by the islanders' universal habit of taking a dose of opium every morning, he held them up as a model of diligence and good self-government. Whaling was a disciplined pro-fession, unmarred by the stereotyped debauchery of sailors elsewhere, and to feed themselves and equip their ships the islanders kept up a shrewd and extensive trade with the mainland. At that time there were already more than a hundred ships. The whalers were not paid; instead each had a share (a *lay*) of the final proceeds of the voyage. Crèvecoeur was impressed by the Nantucketers' ambition: "Would you believe that they have already gone to the Falkland Islands and I have heard several of them talk of going to the South Sea."

They did indeed reach the Pacific – see Chapter Sixteen, Hawaii, for an account of their experiences there. The great days of Nantucket were immortalized by Herman Melville:

And thus have these naked Nantucketers, these sea hermits, issuing from their ant-hill in the sea, overrun and conquered the watery world like so many Alexanders . . . Two thirds of this terra-queous globe are the Nantucketer's. For the sea is his; he owns it, as Emperors own empires.

In fact *Moby Dick* is a valediction; by the time it was published in 1851, Nantucket's fortunes had gone into an abrupt decline. Soon after a devastating fire in 1846, reports of the Californian Gold Rush lured young men westwards; the discovery of underground oil in Pennsylvania came as the final blow. A magazine article of 1873 reported, "Let no traveler visit Nantucket with the expectation of witnessing the marks of a flourishing trade . . . of the great fleet of ships which dotted every sea, scarcely a vestige remains."

Eating

Crèvecoeur (see box above) reported that on Nantucket "Music, singing and dancing are holden in equal detestation." **Seafood** fortunately is not; the only trouble is that Nantucket's restaurants, good as they may be, tend to be excep-tionally expensive – easily costing $30–40 for an entree.

Arno's Main Street Grill 41 Main St ☎508/228-7001. Good-value snacks and lunches served in generous portions. The grill is usually saddled with pancakes, bacon and burgers, but *Arno's* excels at inventive seafood dishes and quesadillas. Breakfast served until 2pm, lunch until 4pm.

The Brotherhood of Thieves 23 Broad St (no phone). A lively old whaling bar serving up thick burgers and chowder. Cash only.

Espresso Café 40 Main St ☎508/228-6930. Inexpensive, healthy lunches, including some vegetarian dishes.

Rose and Crown 23 S Water St ☎508/228-2595. Seafood saloon with live music, DJs, karaoke nights and comedy. Cover charges vary, but are generally inexpensive.

Seagrille 45 Sparks Ave ☎508/325-5700. One of the best places in Nantucket for seafood, with a good wine list, and not too badly priced.

Topper's 120 Wauwinet Rd ☎508/228-8768. Pricey but outstanding New American cuisine in this quiet, upscale flagship restaurant at the *Wauwinet* hotel and resort a few miles outside Nantucket town.

Central and western Massachusetts

The 150 miles of Massachusetts that stretch inland to the west of Boston have always been obliged to play second fiddle to the state capital. Just ten years after the Revolution, the farmers who struggled to make a living from this indifferent soil so resented the imposition of taxes by the prosperous merchants of the east that they rose in **Shay's Rebellion**; their pitchforks were no match for the guns of the new nation.

These days the citizens of the west are eager to promote themselves as cultural rivals of the big city, with the **Berkshires** hosting the celebrated **Tanglewood** music festival in summer. **Amherst**, the home of such diverse talents as Emily Dickinson and Dinosaur Jr, is a stimulating little college community, as is its larger neighbor, **Northampton**; both have all the cafés, restaurants and bookstores you could want. Another delightful college town is **Williamstown** in the far northwest corner, set at the end of the incredibly scenic Mohawk Trail.

Worcester

Forty miles west of Boston on I-90, **WORCESTER** is Massachusetts' second largest city and the only industrial city in the US not beside a sea, lake or river. Abbie Hoffman's hometown is definitely not a place to spend a great deal of time, but if you're nearby you could visit the remarkable **Higgins Armory Museum**, at 100 Barber Ave (Tues–Sat 10am–4pm, Sun noon–4pm; $6.75), which houses weapons and armor from all over the world in a bizarre steel and glass office-cum-museum (note the conspicuous riveting). The enthusiasm for metalworking of the founder of the Worcester Pressed Steel Company led him to tour Europe after World War I, buying vast quantities of ancient armor. You might also drop by the **American Antiquarian Society**, 185 Salisbury St (Mon–Fri 9am–5pm, tours Wed 2pm), which holds copies of two-thirds of all the material published in America before 1821, more even than the Library of Congress. The **Worcester Art Museum**, 55 Salisbury St (Tues, Wed & Fri 11am–5pm, Thurs 11am–8pm, Sat 10am–5pm, Sun 11am–5pm; $8), is worth a stop for its collection of early American paintings and special exhibitions. A more consumerist attraction is the new **Worcester Common Fashion Outlet Mall**, just off I-290 exit 14 or 16, with over a hundred designer stores under one roof; one reason for its popularity is that there is no state sales tax on clothing purchases under $175.

Among local **accommodation**, the *Hampton Inn*, 110 Summer St (☎508/757-0400 or 1-800/426-7866, ⓦwww.hamptoninnworcester.com; ❺), has good clean rooms. The *Sole Proprietor*, 118 Highland St (☎508/798-3474,

ⓦ www.thesole.com), is a reliable fish **restaurant**. Outside Worcester but worth a detour is the *Salem Cross Inn* (off Route 9 in West Brookfield; ⓣ 508/867-2345, ⓦ www.salemcrossinn.com), a rambling restaurant in a restored 1705 farmhouse that serves consistently high-quality Yankee cooking.

Springfield

SPRINGFIELD, at the point where I-90 crosses I-91 – in an extremely confusing way – ninety miles from Boston at the southern end of the Pioneer Valley, has an odd assortment of claims to fame, including being the home of the Springfield rifle and the late children's author Dr Seuss. However, visitors are drawn to this unwieldy and unattractive city, split by the wide Connecticut River, by the 1890s invention of Dr James Naismith – the sport of **basketball**. Naismith designed the game as a way of providing exercise for athletes at the YMCA, and its popularity spread with amazing rapidity. After a trip to the Berlin Olympics in 1936, Naismith came up with another bright idea and established the **Basketball Hall of Fame** at 1150 W Columbus Ave, next to the river just south of Memorial Bridge (Jan–June & Sept–Dec daily 9.30am–5.30pm, July & Aug Mon–Sat 9am–7pm, Sun 9.30am–5.30pm; $10). This museum enjoyably traces the history of the game with movies, videos and plenty of memorabilia, and also lets you test your own skills.

Springfield's Amtrak station is very central, at 66 Lyman St (ⓣ 413/785-4230 or 1-800/USA-RAIL). Several **bus lines**, including Peter Pan (ⓣ 413/781-2900 or 1-800/237-8747, ⓦ www.peterpanbus.com), which provides daily services to and from Boston and New York, operate out of the nearby bus station at 1776 Main St. The **CVB** is downtown at 1441 Main St (ⓣ 413/787-1548 or 1-800/723-1548, ⓦ www.valleyvisitor.com). **Lodging** includes the *Comfort Inn & Suites*, 106 Capital Drive (ⓣ 413/736-5000 or 1-800/288-5150, ⓦ www.comfortinn.com; ④), and there are a number of budget motels over the river in West Springfield. If you're hungry, tiny Fort Street has been home to *The Student Prince/Fort Restaurant* (ⓣ 413/734-7475) for over 65 years – a local favorite serving German wiener schnitzel, goulash and sauerbraten.

Better still, head over to nearby **Amherst**, a typical New England college town, where *The Lord Jeffery Inn*, 30 Boltwood Ave (ⓣ 413/253-2576 or 1-800/742-0358, ⓦ www.lordjefferyinn.com; ④/⑤), offers comfortable rooms and the lively *Elijah Boltwood's Tavern* serves perfect Yankee pot roast. Tours of the Amherst campus can be arranged; call ⓣ 413/545-4237.

Old Sturbridge Village

Halfway between Worcester and Springfield on US-20, near the junction of I-90 and I-84, the restored and reconstructed **Old Sturbridge Village** (Jan Sat & Sun 10am–4pm; mid-Feb to March, Nov & Dec daily 10am–4pm; April–Oct daily 9am–5pm; $20), made up of preserved buildings brought from all over the region, gives a somewhat idealized but engaging portrait of a small New England town of the 1830s. As in other places like it, costumed interpreters act out roles – working in blacksmiths' shops, planting and harvesting vegetables, tending cows and the like – but they pull it off in an unusually convincing manner. The 200-acre site itself, with mature trees, ponds and dirt footpaths, is very pretty, and with all its crafts and diversions you could easily spend half a day here. The nearby *Old Sturbridge Village Lodges* (ⓣ 508/347-3327 or 1-800/SEE-1830, ⓦ www.osv.org/pages/lodges.htm; ④), owned by the museum, is a reasonable place to stay; the *American Motor Lodge*, on Hwy-20 W at I-84 exit 3B, Sturbridge (ⓣ 508/347-9121 or 1-877/738-4801, ⓦ www.americanmotorlodge.com; ③), costs a bit less.

The Berkshires

The **Berkshire Hills**, where Massachusetts borders New York, are a cross between the English Lake District and the grand seafront resort of Newport, Rhode Island. Especially in the area nearest the Massachusetts Turnpike (I-90), the green hillsides are dotted with ostentatious Victorian mansions, while the towns are chic, arty – if not snooty – summer tourist magnets. Further north, it's easier to escape civilization and get deep into the woods. The **Mohawk Trail** in the northwest corner passes through North Adams and **WILLIAMSTOWN**, following the very scenic route the Native Americans used to travel between the valleys of the Connecticut and Hudson rivers. Williamstown has two worthy art museums: the highlight of the **Sterling and Francine Clark Art Institute**, 225 South St (Tues–Sun 10am–5pm; June–Oct $10, rest of year, free), is the thirty-strong collection of Renoir paintings, while the **Williams College Museum of Art** on Main Street (Tues–Sat 10am–5pm, Sun 1–5pm; free) has good exhibits of ancient Middle Eastern and modern American art.

STOCKBRIDGE, just south of I-90 fifty miles west of Springfield, started out as "Indian Town," because the Nipmuck Indians had several villages in the area. The Reverend John Sergeant built the simple wooden **Mission House**, now located on Main Street, in 1739 in an attempt to live in close proximity with the local Native Americans and convert them to Christianity by sheer force of example. His success barely lasted beyond his own death; later settlers were far less keen on having the natives around.

That Stockbridge today looks the archetypal New England small town – most of all when there's snow on the ground – is due largely to the artist **Norman Rockwell**, who lived here for 25 years until his death in 1978. Many of his *Saturday Evening Post* covers, whose sentimentality was made palatable by his sharp wit, featured the town; a collection of covers can be seen at the $10 million **museum** on Hwy-183 (May–Oct daily 10am–5pm; Nov–April weekdays 10am–4pm, weekends 10am–5pm; $12). Some of the tour guides modeled for Rockwell as children and recall that for every few minutes they managed to hold still he'd slip them a coin from his large pile of nickels.

Magnificent houses in the hills around Stockbridge include **Chesterwood**, the luxurious home and studio of Daniel Chester French, sculptor of the Lincoln Memorial (late May to Oct daily 10am–5pm; $6.50), half a mile south of the new Rockwell Museum, and **Naumkeag**, which belonged to Joseph Choate, US ambassador to Queen Victoria (May–Oct daily 10am–5pm). Stockbridge was also the setting for Arlo Guthrie's song, and movie, *Alice's Restaurant*.

Well-heeled tourists flock to nearby **LENOX** each year for the summer season of the Boston Symphony Orchestra at **Tanglewood**. Open-air symphonic concerts are held every Friday, Saturday and Sunday in July and August, with chamber music and recitals given on other days; covered seats are pricey and often hard to get, but you can sit and picnic on the lush lawns for an admission fee of around $15. Some midweek rehearsals are also open to the public (℡413/637-1666 for details), and there's a **jazz** festival on Labor Day weekend (the first weekend of September). Further north on US-7, **Arrowhead** (June–Nov daily 9.30am–5pm; $5), near Pittsfield, was Herman Melville's home while he wrote *Moby Dick*; declining sales of his books eventually forced him to sell up and move to New York. The **Hancock Shaker Village**, five miles west of Pittsfield, survived from 1783 to 1960 (daily: June–Oct 9.30am–5pm; Nov–May 10am–3pm; $9). Its legacy includes the large dwelling place, in which almost one hundred people slept and ate; a round stone barn for their cattle; and the garage where the last Shakers kept their cars. A more important, and much less commercialized Shaker village, **Mount Lebanon**, is another five miles west on US-20, just over the New York state border; much has been dismantled and moved to museums, but self-guided **tours** give a sense of the Shaker way of life ($5).

Practicalities

Much of the **accommodation** in the Berkshires is concentrated in Lenox and neighboring Lee; when the Tanglewood concerts are on, prices naturally go through the roof and a last-minute vacancy is almost impossible to find. The only rooms in Lee for under $80 are in the *Super 8 Motel* at 170 Housatonic St (☎413/243-0143 or 1-800/800-8000; ❹). For slightly more, you can stay at the historic *Merrell Inn* in South Lee, an atmospheric 200-year-old roadside inn (1565 Pleasant St, Rte-102; ☎413/243-1794 or 1-800/243-1794, ⓦwww .merrell-inn.com; ❹–❻). In Lenox, the *Brook Farm Inn* at 15 Hawthorne St (☎413/637-3013, ⓦwww.brookfarm.com; ❺–❻) is a welcoming B&B; the *Best Western Black Swan Inn* (☎413/243-2700 or 1-800/876-7926; ❺) at 435 Laurel St on Rte-20 in Lee has lakefront doubles. Williamstown has several mid-priced motels, as well as some stately accommodation – like the 100-room *Williams Inn* on Main Street (☎413/458-9371 or 1-800/828-0133, ⓦwww.williamsinn.com; ❻). The *Red Lion Inn* is one of the grander edifices on Main Street, Stockbridge (☎413/298-5545; ❼); rooms are expensive, and the *Lion's Den* bar and restaurant downstairs is fun. If you're hungry, the *Church Street Cafe*, 65 Church St, Lenox (☎413/637-2745), is good value and the friendly *Sullivan Station*, a converted railroad station in Lee (☎413/243-2082), serves standard American food such as prime rib, pork chops and clam chowder, plus a selection of beers on tap.

Rhode Island

RHODE ISLAND is the smallest state of the Union, at a mere 48 miles long by 37 miles wide, and tends to be overlooked as a destination, even if it is home to more than twenty percent of the nation's historical landmarks. It was established by Roger Williams in 1635 as a "lively experiment" in religious freedom. He had been expelled from Puritan Salem for his radical ideas (including the notion that Indians should be paid for their land and that there should be a complete separation of church from state), and the Massachusetts Puritans liked to call the state "**Rogues Island**."

Despite its size, Rhode Island has over four hundred miles of coastline, hacked out of the Narragansett Bay; it is, in fact, made up of over thirty tiny islands, including Hope and Despair. The "**Ocean State**" therefore developed through sea trade, whaling and smuggling. Partly due to this commercial interest, Rhode Islanders, resenting the stringent economic pressures placed on them from England, were in the front rank of the Revolutionary groundswell. However, no Revolutionary battles were fought on Rhode Island soil, and unwilling at first to abandon its new-found freedom, it turned out to be the last state to ratify the Constitution. Between the Revolution and the Civil War, Rhode Island shifted from a maritime economy to lead the **Industrial Revolution** with Samuel Slater's creation of the nation's first water-powered **textile mill** in Pawtucket, just outside Providence. Today, although still heavily industrialized, the state's principal destinations are its two original ports: well-heeled **Newport**, yachting capital of the world, with good beaches and outrageously extravagant mansions, and the colonial college town of **Providence**. **Block Island**, about thirty miles south of Newport, has a popular state beach, while the rest of Rhode Island is largely made up of sleepy small towns and fishing ports.

Getting around Rhode Island

Rhode Island is tiny enough to make getting around ridiculously easy. I-95, the major interstate, runs through **Providence** on its way from Massachusetts to Connecticut. The more scenic US-1 follows the coast of Narragansett Bay into Connecticut. **Newport** is accessible from Hwy-138, which connects the small islands in Narragansett Bay to the mainland. **Public transportation** is good: local buses connect Providence and Newport, and Amtrak stops regularly in Providence. **Ferries** link Block Island and Newport.

Providence

Splayed across seven hills on the Providence and Seekonk rivers, **PROVIDENCE** was Rhode Island's first settlement, founded "in commemoration of God's providence" on land given to Roger Williams by the Narragansett Indians (his insistence that Indians should be paid for their land being waived in his own case). Now New England's fourth largest city, it has been the **state capital** since 1901, and flourished as one of the most important ports of call in the notorious "triangle trade," where New England rum was exchanged for African slaves, who were then sold for West Indian molasses. Since Slater's invention of the water-powered textile mill, port trade and industry have been the mainstays of the economy. Today Ivy League **Brown University** and the **Rhode Island School of Design** (RISD or "Rizdee") give the place a certain cultural verve (although this admittedly doesn't stray far beyond the immediate environs of College Hill on the east bank of the river), and the many original colonial homes on **Benefit Street** emphasize a historical importance almost absent from the somewhat drab downtown across the river. Ethnic diversity is provided by **Little Italy** on Federal Hill, west of the river, and by fairly voluble Greek and Portuguese – and especially Cape Verdean – communities.

Arrival, information and getting around

T.F. Green Airport (☎401/737-4000 or 1-888/268-7222) is in Warwick, nine miles south of Providence. In town, the Amtrak station (daily 5am-10.30pm; ☎401/351-8983 or 1-800/250-4989) is at 100 Gaspee St, in a domed building a short walk southwest of the capitol. Greyhound and Bonanza (☎401/751-8800 or 1-888/751-8800) **buses** stop downtown at Kennedy Plaza, while Plymouth & Brockton (☎508/746-0378, ⊛www.p-b.com) buses stop considerably further out at 1 Bonanza Way, exit 25 off I-95. Bus transportation within the city, and to the rest of the state, is provided by RIPTA (Mon–Fri 6.30am–10pm, Sat

9am–11pm, Sun 11am–6.30pm; ☎401/781-9400 or 1-800/244-0444, ⊕www
.ripta.com), with most local and all long-distance buses leaving from Kennedy
Plaza, where schedules are available from a rarely staffed information booth
(Mon–Fri 7am–6pm). However, sightseeing is best done on foot. RIPTA also runs
a daily ferry service between Providence and Newport from mid-April through
October ($8 round-trip). To get to **Block Island**, contact Island Hi-Speed Ferry
($14 each way; ☎1-877/733-9425, ⊕www.islandhighspeedferry.com) at the
State Pier, Port of Galilee. There are dozens of hotels, inns and cottages on the
resort island; the Block Island Tourism Council (☎1-800/383-BIRI, ⊕www
.blockislandinfo.com) can help.

The **CVB**, 1 W Exchange St (Mon–Fri 10am–5pm; ☎401/274-1636 or 1-
800/233-1636, ⊕www.providencecvb.com), provides maps and brochures, as
does the useful **Providence Preservation Society**, in the 1772 Shakespeare's
Head building at 21 Meeting St, which has self-guided walking tours of the
city's historic areas (Mon–Fri 9am–5pm; ☎401/831-7440, ⊕www.ppsri.org)
or 90-minute guided tours ($12) every Friday from April to October. There's
another **information center** in the Roger Williams National Memorial Park
Zoo, 282 N Main St (daily: summer 9am–5pm; rest of year 9am–4.30pm;
☎401/785-3510).

Accommodation

Downtown Providence has few budget **rooms**, but **B&B**s are a viable option.
Anna's Victorian Connection (☎1-800/884-4288) books rooms in Providence
and Newport. Motorists can take advantage of the mid-priced **motels** along
I-95, or north in Pawtucket, and south near the airport at Warwick.

Comfort Inn 2 George St, Pawtucket ☎401/723-6700 and 1940 Post Rd, Warwick ☎401/732-0470. Decent rooms near exit 27 off I-95 and Slater Mill, or by the airport. ❺
Days Hotel on the Harbor 220 India Point ☎401/272-5577 or 1-800/528-9931. Standard chain hotel with all the usual modern conveniences, plus a good Indian restaurant on-site. ❸
Holiday Inn Downtown 21 Atwells Ave ☎401/831-3900. Next to the Civic Center near Little Italy. ❻

The Old Court 144 Benefit St ☎401/751-2002, ⊕www.oldcourt.com. Luxury ten-room B&B in an old rectory. ❻
Providence 9 Kennedy Plaza ☎401/421-0700 or 1-800/294-7709, ⊕www.providencebiltmore.com. The Grand Dame of the city, around since the 1920s; centrally located, with all the amenities as well as good views. ❺/❻
State House Inn 43 Jewett St ☎401/351-6111, ⊕www.providence-inn.com. Pleasant, central B&B rooms in a restored old home. ❺/❻

The City

Providence's main attractions focus around three of its seven hills. Downtown,
which centers on **Kennedy Plaza**, is situated just below **Constitution Hill**.
City Hall, at the western end of the plaza, is mainly notable for the star-
spangled midnight-blue ceiling in the Alderman's Chamber. Though no longer
used as a train terminal, the nearby 1898 Beaux Arts **Union Station** is a fine
example of the historic restoration at which the city excels. Southeast of the
plaza, the 1828 **Westminster Arcade**, the oldest enclosed shopping mall in the
nation, features expensive clothes shops and a food court in a small, bright, skylit hall. The **Roger Williams National Memorial**, at N Main and Smith
streets, at the foot of Constitution Hill, includes part of city-founder Williams'
original settlement (daily 9am–4.30pm; free), while at the top of the hill, the
white marble **Rhode Island Statehouse** boasts a huge unsupported dome,
the fourth largest in the world, topped with a statue called *Independent Man*, an

Roger Williams Park and Zoo & T F Green Airport

11-foot-tall bronze figure created by George Brewster as a symbol of freedom and independence. A handsome full-length portrait of Washington adorns the Reception Room (Mon–Fri 8.30am–4.30pm; free guided tours between 9am & noon; ☎401/222-2357).

Laid-back **College Hill**, across the river, is an attractive district of colonial buildings and museums. Part of Williams' holy experiment was the establishment of the Baptist Church in 1638. The white clapboard **First Baptist Meeting House**, at the foot of the hill at 75 N Main St, dates from 1775, and is remarkable for its very tall steeple. This street leads into **South Main Street**, once bustling with waterfront activity, now a small stretch of potpourri and pottery shops. **Benefit Street**, a block up the hill, is Providence's "**mile of history**," lined with the ice-cream-colored former clapboard homes of merchants and sea captains. Now beautifully restored, the street was once just a dirt path leading to graveyards until it was improved in the nineteenth century for the "benefit of the people of Providence" – hence its name. The elegant **John Brown House**, 52 Power St at Benefit Street (March–Dec Tues–Sat 10am–5pm, Sun noon–4pm; Jan & Feb Fri & Sat 10am–5pm & Sun noon–4pm; $6), was home to the patriot and entrepreneur who made his fortune trading in slaves and with China. The first house built on the hill (nicely conspicuous from the river), it retains its original furnishings and holds displays on the formidable Brown family and the city itself.

237

Ivy League **Brown University** sets the tone for this three-centuries-old district with its relaxed, intellectual feel; for free tours, contact the admissions office, 45 Prospect St (Mon–Fri 8am–4pm; tours 10am, 11am, 1pm, 3pm & 4pm; 11am & 3pm only during Christmas & spring break; mid-Sept to mid-Nov Sat tours 10am, 11am & noon). At the eastern edge of College Hill, **Wickenden Street** buzzes with a creative assortment of bookstores, cafés, and antiques and thrift stores.

The small but excellent collection of the **RISD Museum of Art**, 224 Benefit St, is worthy of its status as one of the best art school museums in the country, and includes ancient and Oriental works, Impressionist and Post-Impressionist American art and one of Rodin's statues of Balzac (Tues–Sun 10am–5pm; $5). Also on the RISD campus, the **Woods–Gerry Gallery**, 62 Prospect St (Mon–Sat 10am–4pm, Sun 2–5pm; free), is a solid redbrick mansion set in a tree-shaded garden with heavy stone benches and exhibiting innovative student art.

Across the road, the Greek Revival **Providence Athenaeum**, 251 Benefit St (Mon–Thurs 10am–6pm, Fri–Sat 10am–5pm, Sun 1–5pm; free), is where Edgar Allan Poe unsuccessfully wooed fellow poet Sarah Whitman. Today the library holds original Audubon prints and rare books, and the place feels more like a living room, with its piano and hand-painted chairs in the cozy reading rooms.

Federal Hill, west of downtown, is Providence's **Little Italy**, entered through a large arch topped by a bronze pinecone at Atwells Avenue. Long a powerful Mafia stronghold, this area is one of the friendliest and safest in the city – alive with cafés, delis, bakeries and bars, and with a large Italianate fountain in the Piazza de Pasquale.

Pawtucket

In 1793, Samuel Slater used technology surreptitiously imported from England to shove Rhode Island into the industrial age. His landmark **Old Slater Mill** is still in operation, in suburban Pawtucket. A ten-minute drive north to exit 28 on I-95, the **Slater Mill Historic Site**, on Roosevelt Avenue, also includes in its museum of the Industrial Revolution the 1810 Wilkinson Mill and the 1758 **Sylvanus Brown House** (June–Nov Mon–Sat 10am–5pm, Sun noon–5pm; Dec to late April Sat & Sun 1–3pm; $7).

Eating

Studenty **Thayer Street** is lined with inexpensive lunch places, almost all of which remain open until late. **Wickenden Street** is more alternative, and more expensive. The family-run Italian restaurants on Federal Hill serve good food at reasonable prices, and the Westminster Arcade downtown is your best bet for a quick breakfast or lunch.

Angelo's 141 Atwells Ave ☏ 401/621-8171. Family-style restaurant offering inexpensive Italian standards.

CAV Restaurant, Antiques and Gifts 14 Imperial Place ☏ 401/751-9164. A hip restaurant with live entertainment after 9.30pm Thurs–Mon.

Coffee Exchange 207 Wickenden St ☏ 401/273-1198. Trendy coffee bar. A popular meeting place for arty intellectuals. Deckchairs and barrels act as sidewalk seating and tables.

Davio's 11 Dorrance St ☏ 401/274-4810. An upscale place to dine on Mediterranean specialties and an Italian-inspired menu of steak and seafood. The wine list is impressive.

Kabob 'n' Curry 261 Thayer St ☏ 401/273-8844. Above-average Indian meals in trendy Thayer St.

New Japan 145 Washington St ☏ 401/351-0300. Reasonably priced Japanese place, with sashimi six days a week and sushi on Sunday.

Nightlife and entertainment

As Providence's **nightlife** is largely student-oriented, things get quiet during the vacations, though Thayer Street is always lively. On summer evenings, a **party trolley** with balloons and noisy music rumbles through downtown. The $6 fee includes entry to six nightclubs on its route, and a half-price drink (Fri & Sat 8.30pm–2am; ℡401/861-1385). The Cable Car Cinema at 204 S Main St (℡401/272-3970), and the Avon Rep Cinema at 250 Thayer St (℡401/421-3315), show good independent and art **films**. The Providence Performing Arts Center, downtown at 220 Weybosset St, hosts various shows in a grand old Art Deco movie house (℡401/421-2787, ⓦ www.ppacri.org). The free weekly *Providence Phoenix* has complete entertainment listings.

AS220 115 Empire St ℡401/831-9327. Unabashedly artsy café/bar hangout for locals and students. Also a music venue featuring everything from mellow jazz to performance art. Gallery on second floor. Cover $2–5.

Finnegan's Wake 397 Westminster St ℡401/751-0290. Authentic Irish pub, right down to the corned beef and cabbage.

Snookers 145 Clifford St ℡401/351-7665. Lively pool hall with a variety of table games. Its green room features alternative DJs and is one of the city's most sociable spots. No cover.

Trinity Brewhouse 186 Fountain St ℡401/453-2337. Hang out here after a Providence Bruins (minor league hockey) or Friars (college basketball) game to imbibe microbrews either in celebration or despair.

Newport

Thirty miles south of Providence, **NEWPORT** stands at the southern tip of the largest island in Narragansett Bay, **Aquidneck Island**. It was established as a colony by William Coddington of Providence in 1639. Due to its excellent harbor, it grew rapidly as a port for the triangle trade and as a privateering center. **Religious tolerance** led to an influx of Jews, Quakers and Baptists who formed lucrative international trade links, but this great prosperity was severely knocked back by the **British occupation** of 1776–79, when half the population fled and much of the town was burned down. Fortunately, enough of its original eighteenth-century homes have survived for Newport to rival Boston in this respect.

In the 1850s the town became fashionable again as a resort for wealthy Southern merchants, and very soon nouveau riche industrialists such as the Astors, Belmonts and Vanderbilts were building "**summer cottages**" – better described as mansions – along the rocky coastline. The obscene ostentation of this era, now known by Mark Twain's disparaging phrase as the **Gilded Age**, shocked Massachusetts' old wealth to the core.

Depression killed off the decadence, but Newport kept going as a naval town until the 1970s. Today the town feeds off tourism; much of it caters to the tennis and yachting set, but there are as many people looking at – and envying – the wealth as enjoying it. Though sanitized by the ugly new **America's Cup Avenue**, which replaced the sea-salt rawness of the waterfront with bars and boutiques, the rough old port still rears its boozy head, with beer and R&B clubs as evident as cocktails and cruises, making it an essential stop, especially during the summer **festival season**.

Arrival, information and getting around

There are actually three towns on Aquidneck Island: **Portsmouth** is at the northern edge, and then comes the appropriately named **Middletown**, with **Newport**, the southernmost, just below it. The mainland is connected to the island from I-95 on US-138 by the **Jamestown Bridge** to Conanincut Island, and from there by the **Newport Bridge** ($2 toll each way).

Newport itself, spanning only ten miles, is easy to walk around. **Thames** (pronounced *Thaymz*) Street is the main road, with Bellevue Avenue, or Mansion Row, parallel to the east. Maps and advice are available from the large **visitor center** at 23 America's Cup Ave (daily: summer 8am–8pm; rest of year 9am–5pm; ☎401/849-8048 or 1-800/976-5122, ⓦwww.gonewport.com).

The adjacent **Gateway Center**, the least expensive place to park a car, is also the terminal for Bonanza (☎401/846-1820, ⓦwww.bonanzabus.com) and RIPTA **buses**; the latter run regularly through town, to the beaches and on to Providence ($1.25–3.50; ☎401/781-9400 or 1-800/244-0444, ⓦwww.ripta .com). Also based at the Center are free summer **shuttle buses** connecting the main sights and shopping areas (daily 10am–7pm) and Viking Tours, whose bus and harbor excursions take in admission to one or more mansions ($10–38; ☎401/847-6921). Rented **bikes**, good for getting to the quieter beaches, cost $5 per hour ($25 a day) at Ten Speed Spokes, 18 Elm St, next to the visitor center (Mon–Sat 9.30am–5.30pm, summer also Sun noon–5pm; ☎401/847-5609, ⓦwww.tenspeedspokes.com). The Newport Historical Society organizes **walking tours** through colonial Newport on Thursday, Friday and Saturday in summer at 10am (tours depart from the Museum of Natural History; usually $7; ☎401/841-8770). Easily the best and most relaxing way of getting a good look at the mansions and the town is on the beautiful *Madeleine* **schooner** (☎401/847-0298, ⓦwww.cruisenewport.com), which leaves several times daily from Bannister's Wharf; the $25 price for a ninety-minute tour is ultimately better value than the cheaper motorboat tours.

Accommodation

There are plenty of reasonably priced **guesthouses** in Newport, but it's a good idea to book ahead, especially on summer weekends (when prices jump). The visitor center (see above) has free phone links to inns and motels in all price ranges. **B&Bs** are by far the most prevalent form of lodging, and it's usually possible to get a decent room for around $60. Two established agencies are Bed and Breakfast of Rhode Island (free; ☎401/849-1298 or 1-800/828-0000, ⓦwww .visitnewport.com/bedandbreakfast), which can find rooms from around $65, and Anna's Victorian Connection, 5 Fowler Ave ($5 fee; ☎401/849-2489 or 1-800/884-4288), whose rooms start from $40.

Admiral Fitzroy Inn 398 Thames St ☎401/848-8000 or 1-866/848-8780, ⓦwww.admiralfitzroy .com. Cheerfully decorated B&B in the heart of the action, with a roof deck overlooking the harbor and excellent breakfasts. ➍/➎

Cliffside Inn 2 Seaview Ave ☎401/847-1811 or 1-800/845-1811, ⓦwww.cliffsideinn. Gorgeous and romantic Victorian manor house, one minute from the Cliff Walk and First Beach. ➐

Howard Johnson Inn 351 W Main Rd, Middletown ☎401/849-2000 or 1-800/654-2000, ⓦwww.hojo.com. Just two miles from downtown Newport, this chain offers the best hotel value in the area. Rates heavily reduced outside of July and August. ➍

The Melville House 39 Clarke St ☎401/847-0640, ⓦwww.melvillehouse.com. A quiet, colonial-style B&B serving delicious breakfasts two blocks from the harbor in Newport's Hill District, within walking distance of all the sights.

Villa Liberté 22 Liberty St ☎401/846-7444 or 1-800/392-3717. Fifteen comfortably appointed rooms, with black-and-white tiled baths, in a cheerfully restored one-time "house of the evening." ➍—➐

The Willows Romantic Inn 8–10 Willow St
⊤401/846-5486, ⓦ www.thewillowsofnewport
.com. A dreamy inn popular with newlyweds and
couples celebrating anniversaries, complete with
canopy beds and frilly bedspreads, and an outdoor
garden that frequently receives awards. Breakfast
is served in bed by staff in black-tie. ❼–❾

The Town

Newport's main attractions are obviously its **mansions**, but there is nothing to
be gained by attempting to tour them all, and while it's pleasant enough to
stroll around the predominantly colonial **downtown**, the ever-growing profusion of souvenir shops is somewhat off-putting. Otherwise, you'll do better following the crowds to one of the **beaches**.

The mansions

The phrase "**conspicuous consumption**" was coined by sociologist
Thorstein Veblen, who visited Newport c.1900 and witnessed the desperate
need of new, entrepreneurial **millionaires** to flaunt their wealth. More than
just a summer resort, Newport became an arena in which families competed
to outdo each other – though the "season" of wild and decadent parties lasted
only a few weeks, and many of the ten-million-dollar mansions lay empty for
years at a time.

It's difficult to grasp the sheer wealth involved by merely gawking at the mansions' facades, but after being herded in and rushed through more than a couple, the opulence rapidly begins to pall. Choose one to see, or two at the most.
The most important stand on **Bellevue Avenue**, **Ocean Drive** and **Harrison
Avenue**. The Astors' **Beechwood**, 580 Bellevue Ave (mid-May to Oct daily
10am–5pm; Nov & Dec daily 10am–4pm; Feb to mid-May Fri, Sat & Sun
10am–4pm; $10), is an entertaining antidote to the drier historical drills given
on other tours. Costumed actors welcome visitors as house guests who have
arrived for a party held by Mrs Astor, the self-proclaimed queen of American
society (she devised the notion of the **Four Hundred**, an elite of individuals
whose lineage had to go back at least three generations). Anecdotes, bitchy
asides and a constant stream of activity – as well as strawberry tea in the servants' kitchen – make it all great fun.

Also on Bellevue Avenue, the **Marble House** is the most over-the-top
example of Gilded Age excess, with a golden ballroom and a Chinese teahouse
in the grounds; both this and **Rosecliff**, with its colorful rose garden and
heart-shaped staircase, were used as sets during the filming of *The Great Gatsby*.
Kingscote, on Bellevue Avenue, is a quirky Arts and Crafts cottage with a
lovely interior, while the biggest and best of the lot, Cornelius Vanderbilt's **The
Breakers**, on Ochre Point Avenue, is a sumptuous Italian Renaissance palace,
overlooking the ocean. All except Beechwood are run by the **Preservation
Society of Newport County**, 424 Bellevue Ave (⊤401/847-1000,
ⓦ www.newportmansions.org), whose combination tickets slightly help to beat
the hefty individual admission prices of at least $10 (April–Sept daily
9am–5pm; rest of year schedules vary; *Breakers* costs $15, all others $10; all eight
Society properties $50).

One way to see the Bellevue Avenue mansions on the cheap is to peer in the
back gardens from the **Cliff Walk**, which begins on Memorial Avenue where
it meets First Beach. This three-and-a-half-mile oceanside path alternates from
jasmine and wild roses to unappealing concrete underpasses through perilous
rocks. For those with a car, Ocean Drive continues from Bellevue Avenue
where the Cliff Walk ends, following the coast eastwards and passing

Hammersmith Farm, John and Jackie Kennedy's 28-room shingled summer home, originally owned by Jackie's mother. Once open to visitors, the farm is now a private residence and closed to the public. The First Couple's wedding reception was held on the beautiful grounds.

Downtown

Newport's colonial, political and business center, **Washington Square**, lies just south of the Gateway Center, beginning where Thames Street meets the Brick Market. The 1762 market, off **Long Wharf** (the most important of Newport's colonial wharves), has been reconstructed to house galleries and pricey gift-shops. The **Old Colony House**, one of Rhode Island's few pre-Revolutionary brick buildings and seat of government from 1739 to 1900, stands across the square (July–Sept Mon–Fri 9.30am–noon & 1–4pm, Sat & Sun 9.30am–noon; free). To the north, the **Easton's Point** district, between Washington Street by the water and Spring Street to the east, is lined with the eighteenth-century homes of ships' captains; only the 1748 **Hunter House**, 54 Washington St, is open to the public (May–Oct daily 10am–5pm; $10).

The oldest religious building in town is the shabby 1699 **Great Friends Meeting House**, at Marlborough and Farewell streets, restored to its nineteenth-century appearance and completely free of adornment (tours by appointment; donation; ☎401/846-0813). In 1790, Newport's Jewish community wrote to George Washington expressing their hopes for his new government. His enthusiastic reply advocating religious liberty is exhibited at the Georgian **Touro Synagogue**, 85 Touro St, built in 1763 and the oldest in the nation (July to first Mon in Sept daily except Sat 10am–5pm; first Mon in Sept to Nov and May–July Mon–Fri 1–3pm, Sun 11am–3pm; rest of year Mon–Fri one tour at 1pm, Sun 11am–3pm; free; ☎401/847-4794, Ⓦwww.tourosynagogue.org). Down the hill, the newly opened **Museum of Newport History**, 127 Thames St (Mon & Wed–Sat 10am–4pm, Sun 1–4pm; $5), may be small, but it has a superb understanding of the evolution of not just Newport but the whole of maritime New England, displayed through photographs, artifacts and a huge computer database. A $7 combination ticket covers admission and **walking tours** organized by the **Newport Historical Society** (see p.240). The Society's offices at 82 Touro St also has changing exhibits on Newport's past (Tues–Fri 9.30am–4.30pm, Sat 9.30am–noon; free).

Washington himself worshiped at the 1726 **Trinity Church** on Queen Anne Square, a colonial structure based on the Old North Church in Boston and the designs of Sir Christopher Wren (daily: mid-June to early Sept 10am–4pm; May & mid-Sept to mid-Oct 1–4pm; rest of year 10am–1pm; free). A few blocks south, **St Mary's Church**, Spring Street and Memorial Boulevard, is the oldest Catholic Church in Rhode Island and the place where Jackie Bouvier married John Kennedy (Mon–Fri 7–11.30am; free).

Bellevue Avenue, the street lined with most of Newport's famous mansions, also has two museums of note. The **Newport Art Museum**, at no. 76, is housed in the 1864 mock-medieval Griswold House and exhibits New England art from the last two centuries (Mon, Wed–Sat 10am–5pm, Sun 1–5pm, closed Tues; $6). At no. 194, the grand **Newport Casino** was an early country club, which held the first national tennis championship in 1881. It is now the **International Tennis Hall of Fame**, and still keeps its grass courts open to the public. The museum includes exhibits on tennis fashion – or what has passed for it – and trophies (daily 9.30am–5pm; $8).

The beaches

The indubitable attraction of Newport's shoreline, with its many coves and gently sloping beaches, is slightly marred by the fact that many are strictly private. **Gooseberry Beach**, on the southern edge of the island, is surrounded by grand houses and charges $1 admission. The town beach, **First** (or Newport, or Easton's) **Beach**, is at the east end of Memorial Boulevard. **Second** and **Third** beaches are further along the same route toward Middletown. The visitor center (see p.240) provides a guide to them all.

Eating

Many of Newport's **restaurants** are smug and overpriced, and visitors on a budget will have to make do with snacks. However, there are some gems, even along touristy Thames Street, and the seafood here is well worth the blowout if you have the extra cash.

(see p.240)

Asterix & Obelisk 599 Thames St ☎ 401/841-8833. Happening, moderately priced eatery in a former garage, with abstract paintings on the walls and Oriental rugs on an orange cement floor. The eclectic menu is mainly American with a touch of Asian.

The Black Pearl Bannisters Wharf ☎ 401/846-5264. A Newport institution famous for its chunky clam chowder; repair to the Commodore Room for more formal dining.

Brick Alley Pub & Restaurant 140 Thames St ☎ 401/849-6334. Attracts a good mix of locals and tourists for lunch, dinner and cocktails.

Ocean Coffee Roasters 22 Washington Square ☎ 401/846-6060. Hip, upbeat café serving aspiring artists and poets rather than the yacht set. Crepes from $4, lunch specials with an international edge

from $5.50, flavored coffees and teas. Features occasional poetry readings and exhibitions.

Via Via I 112 William St ☎ 401/846-4074. Specialty oven-fired pizza – shrimp pesto or chicken and goat's cheese, for example – that can also be delivered until 2am. The slightly better situated *Via Via II* is nearby at 372 Thames St (☎ 401/848-0880).

West Deck Waites Wharf ☎ 401/847-3610. Inexpensive, family-style clam chowder, lobster and grilled sandwiches, with outdoor seating.

White Horse Tavern Marlborough and Farewell sts ☎ 401/849-3600. Intensely atmospheric restaurant (the building dates from 1687) serving solid American fare, such as New York sirloin, sauteed lobster and rack of lamb. More affordably priced at lunchtime.

Live music

Newport is historically famed for its duo of music festivals: the **Ben & Jerry's Folk Festival** in late July or August, followed by the **August Jazz Festival**. Both are held in Fort Adams State Park (☎ 401/847-3700), as is the **Rhythm & Blues Festival**. The lesser-known but arguably more memorable **Newport Music Festival**, with a focus on classical music, unfolds in the mansions during July (☎ 401/846-1133, ⓦ www.newportmusic.org).

Otherwise, there is plenty of shamelessly unrefined **nightlife**. Noisy bars abound near the waterfront, and among the **live music venues** in town, two of the best are the *Red Parrot*, 348 Thames St (☎ 401/847-3800), for live jazz and world music nightly, and the *Wharf Deli & Pub*, 37 Bowen's Wharf (☎ 401/846-9233), which puts on R&B and jazz.

Connecticut

CONNECTICUT was named Quinnehtukqut by the Native Americans for the "great tidal river" that splits it in two before spilling out into the Long Island Sound and washing the old whaling ports of the coast. This small and densely populated state is a sort of conservative, high-rent suburb of New York City, enabling commuters to earn Big Apple salaries while avoiding New York state and city taxes. Its first white settlers arrived in the 1630s: refugees from Massachusetts seeking liberty, good farmland and trading opportunities. Connecticut soon became a center for "**Yankee ingenuity**," prospering through the invention and marketing (often by the notorious and not always honorable Yankee peddlers) of many a useful little household object. Although hit very badly by English raids in the Revolutionary War, its role in providing the war effort with crucial supplies made it known as "the **provisions state**." After the war, the original charter of Connecticut's first colonists was used as a model for the American Constitution and gave rise to another nickname: "the **Constitution state**." It continued to prosper during the eighteenth and nineteenth centuries, with steady industrialization and lucrative whaling along the southeastern coast. Today, much of the old industry, especially in the north, has withered away, leaving areas of green countryside, untroubled by noisy interstates, many verdant forests and the idyllic rural villages that typify New England's PR image – but also unemployment and poverty. **New Haven** in particular, home to Yale University, faces distinctly urban problems like drug wars, homelessness and violent crime, which belie New England's myth of rural tranquility.

The linchpins of Connecticut's economy – insurance companies, medical research and military bases – hardly make for pleasing aesthetics, as demonstrated by the rather dull capital city, **Hartford**; and even the historic and otherwise attractive coastline is marred by some unfortunate stretches of sprawling gray concrete.

Getting around Connecticut

Except for a few isolated areas in the north, Connecticut is well connected with major **roads**: I-95 is the main interstate, running from New York to Rhode Island along the shore of the Long Island Sound. I-91 travels north from I-95 at New Haven, weaving its way along the Connecticut River to Vermont. However, in Connecticut, as with the other New England states, it's a shame to miss out on the quiet countryside scenery along the side roads, so it's worth getting off the interstates if you have the time. While the back roads can be poorly labeled, the distances involved are so small that you're not likely to run into major problems if you get lost.

All of the major east coast airlines **fly** to Bradley International Airport near Hartford, and Greyhound, Bonanza (☎1-800/556-3815, ⓦwww.bonanzabus.com) and Peter Pan Trailways (☎1-800/237-8747, ⓦwww.peterpanbus.com) **buses** run to most of the main towns. Connecticut Transit buses (☎860/525-9181 or 1-888/BUS-RIDE) serve the inland area around Hartford. Metro North (☎1-800/638-7646) **trains** carry passengers between New Haven and New York City, with connecting services to numerous other towns; Amtrak's line runs between New York City and Boston with various stops along the shore and a connection to Hartford.

Southeastern Connecticut

The much-visited **southeastern coast** of Connecticut spans fifteen miles from Stonington in the east to Niantic in the west, bisected by the Thames (pronounced *Thaymz*) River. Each of the handful of tiny, picturesque colonial communities and old whaling villages along the Long Island Sound is a mere stone's throw from the next. No longer are they the iniquitous and rumbustious ports that so inspired Melville, but they're still keen to preserve a sense of their history. The restored nineteenth-century **Mystic Seaport** justifies at least a day's visit; nearby are the less lovely US Naval submarine base at **Groton** and the pretty fishing harbor of **Stonington Borough**.

Mystic

The old whaling port and shipbuilding center of **MYSTIC**, the purists will tell you, does not in fact exist; it is an area governed partly by Groton and partly by Stonington. Nonetheless, it does have a small, well-kept, and somewhat touristy **downtown**, lined with typical New England-quaint clapboard galleries and antique shops. The old bridge across the bustling **Mystic River** that divides it down the middle still opens hourly, and self-guided walking tours take in the many old houses built by well-off sea captains. The **Olde Mistick Village**, at the intersection of I-95 and US-27, is a pleasant enough outdoor mall with over sixty upmarket shops in colonial-style buildings. For a scenic walk or bike ride away from the tourists, take the four-mile river road, which is protected from cars and development and passes by Downes Marsh, a sanctuary for osprey.

What brings the tourists to Mystic is the impeccably reconstructed seventeen-acre waterfront village of **Mystic Seaport**, at the mouth of the river, where more than sixty weathered buildings house old-style workshops, stores and a printing press. Its **Stillman Building** exhibits exquisitely carved scrimshaw and a vast amount of products made from whales' wax-like spermaceti, as well as showing film of a bloody whale capture. There are demonstrations of shanty-singing, fish-splitting and sail-setting, among other salty pastimes, as well as storytelling and theater, while in the **shipyard** you can watch the building, restoration and maintenance of wooden ships. The *pièce de résistance* is the restored *Charles W Morgan*, a three-masted wooden Yankee **whaling ship** built in 1841 (daily: summer 9am–6pm; rest of year 9am–5pm; $17, late-afternoon arrivals are granted free entrance on the next day; ℡1-888/9SEAPORT). The last of its kind, the *Morgan* is a remnant of an age of exploration and arrogant expansion remembered now with a mixture of nostalgia and shame. Done up ready to embark on a hypothetical two-year voyage, the ship is filled with whaling memorabilia; below deck, accessible by perilously narrow stairs, the blubber room is crowded with huge iron try-pots for melting down the stinking blubber.

Over six thousand weird and wonderful sea creatures glug about the **Mystic Aquarium**, at exit 90 off I-95. Hourly shows at the Marine Theater (daily: summer 9am–6pm; rest of year 9am–5pm; $16) showcase porpoises and a beluga whale, and the explanations of the creatures' behavior make this a step up from standard aquarium fare. For those interested in the history of underwater exploration, there's the high-tech "Challenge of the Deep" exhibit, hosted by Dr Robert D. Ballard of the team that found the *Titanic*.

Practicalities

Mystic has an **information office** in the Olde Mistick Village shopping mall (Mon–Sat 9.30am–6.30pm, Sun 10am–6pm; ℡860/536-1641 or 1-800/863-6569, ⓦwww.mysticmore.com). The office lists current rates and books **accommodation**: places to stay in town are at a premium in July and August. Options include the *Comfort Inn* (℡860/572-8531 or 1-800/228-5150, ⓦwww.whghotels.com/cimystic; ❸–❺), *Days Inn* (℡860/572-0574 or 1-800/572-3993, ⓦwww.whghotels.com/dimystic; ❸–❺) and the *Best Western Sovereign Hotel* (℡860/536-4281 or 1-800/363-1622; ❸–❺), which are all handy for the Seaport, on Whitehall Avenue just off I-95 exit 90. Slightly more memorable would be a stay at the *Inn at Mystic* (℡860/536-9604 or 1-800/237-2415, ⓦwww.innatmystic.com; ❻), a colonial revival mansion hidden away at the junction of routes 1 and 27. The rural colonial farmhouse *Applewood Farms Inn* is five minutes north of town at 528 Colonel Ledyard Highway, Ledyard (℡860/536-2022 or 1-800/717-4262, ⓦwww.visitmystic.com/applewoodfarmsinn; ❻); its owners will collect you from the train station if given notice. The *Seaport* **campground** is on US-184 in Old Mystic, three miles from the Seaport, but is only open April to mid-November (℡860/536-4044, ⓦwww.seaportcampground.com; $28 per night for up to two adults and two children, $21 per night April to mid-May & mid-Sept to mid-Nov).

Without a doubt the best-known **restaurant** is *Mystic Pizza*, at 56 W Main St (℡860/536-3700), a small, family-run pizza place that continues to serve huge, inexpensive and fresh "pies," unruffled by its movie-star status. The *Sea View Snack Bar*, on Hwy-27 between the visitor center and downtown (℡860/572-0096), serves seafood and sandwiches in a covered picnic area overlooking the Mystic River, while *The Green Marble*, 8 Steamboat Wharf (℡860/572-0012), roasts its own coffee, and *Kitchen Little*, 81 1/2 Greenmanville Ave (℡860/536-2122), serves a mean breakfast along the riverfront. Ten minutes' drive south in the small fishing port of **Noank**, the casual *Abbott's Lobster in the Rough*, 117 Pearl St (May through the second Monday in Oct daily noon–9pm; rest of year Fri–Sun, noon–7pm; ℡860/536-7719), serves superb fresh steamed lobster and seafood at outdoor picnic tables. A giant New England dinner for four costs $22 per person, a lobster plate around $14; bring your own alcohol.

Stonington Borough

STONINGTON BOROUGH, five miles east of Mystic, is an overwhelmingly pretty old fishing village, originally Portuguese but now very New England, characterized by appealing whitewashed cottages (which were once factory houses), white picket fences and colorful flower gardens. Its main street, **Water Street**, is chock-a-block with antique shops and upmarket thrift stores, crowded with well-heeled bargain hunters at the weekend. The **Lighthouse Museum** at no. 7 dates from 1823 and is full of local memorabilia, maps and drawings; fresh flowers everywhere add a nice touch. You can climb the stone steps and iron staircase to the top for views over the water and Connecticut's neighboring states (July & Aug daily 10am–5pm; May, June, Sept & Oct Tues–Sun 10am–5pm; $4). The waterfront itself is a great place to pass a few sunny hours, peaceful and quiet with a few bobbing fishing boats and clean water for swimming.

The most central **place to stay**, though not cheap, is *The Inn at Stonington* at 60 Water St (℡860/535-2000, ⓦwww.innatstonington.com; ❼), where summer weekend rates start at $175; weekday and winter rates go down considerably. Authentic New England clam chowder, and full meals, can be had at *Noah's*, 113 Water St (☎860/535-3925), an old Portuguese **restaurant** with a friendly, pine-table-trendy atmosphere and delicious home-baked cakes. Two seafood restaurants – *Water Street Café*, 142 Water St (☎860/535-2122), and *Skipper's Dock*, 66 Water St (☎860/535-0111) – are worth a visit; the former is elegant, the latter less expensive and rowdier, with an open deck sporting fabulous views of the ocean.

Groton

Seven miles west of Mystic Seaport, **GROTON** is a suitably unpleasant name for the hometown of the hideous **US Naval Submarine Base**, headquarters for the North Atlantic fleet. The **USS Nautilus**, the country's first nuclear-powered submarine, was built in Groton. In 1958, four years after it was launched, it became the first vessel to sail under the polar icecap. It's now moored on the Thames, and self-guided tours allow access to its terrifyingly claustrophobic corridors, one-person-wide in many places. The sub looks pretty much as it did in the 1950s, complete with pin-ups of Marilyn Monroe. The **Submarine Force Museum** next door has exhibits on the history of submersibles from the minuscule *American Turtle*, built in 1775, to the frighteningly powerful *Trident* (mid-May through Oct Mon & Wed–Sun 9am–5pm, Tues 1–5pm; Nov to mid-May Mon & Wed–Sun 9am–4pm; closed first full week of May and last full week of October; free; ☎860/694-3174 or 1-800/343-0079, ⒲www.ussnautilus.org).

New London

NEW LONDON, opposite Groton on the west side of the Thames, is the closest thing the region has to a city, although it spreads over only six square miles. Originally settled in 1646, it was a wealthy whaling port in the nineteenth century and today is home to the **US Coast Guard Academy**, 15 Mohegan Ave off I-95, where visitors can wander around a museum of Coast Guard history (Mon–Fri 9am–4.30pm, Sat 10am–5pm, Sun noon–5pm; free) and visit the training tall ship *USS Eagle* (Fri–Sun 1–5pm; call ☎860/444-8595 to find out when the ship is in port). Overlooking the academy is the **Lyman Allyn Art Museum** (Tues–Sat 10am–5pm, Sun 1–5pm; $4; ☎860/443-2545), part of Connecticut College at 625 Williams St and specializing in American Impressionist works and local decorative arts. A self-guided walking tour of downtown passes along prosperous Huntington Street, where four adjacent Greek Revival mansions are known as **Whale Oil Row**. For swimming and sunbathing, the **Ocean Beach Park**, on Ocean Avenue, has a sand beach and huge saltwater pool, as well as a wooden boardwalk (summer daily 9am–midnight; $2).

New London was the birthplace of boozy playwright **Eugene O'Neill**. His childhood home, the **Monte Cristo Cottage**, 325 Pequot Ave, is open for tours, complete with juicy details of his trauma-ridden early life – though they may already be familiar to you from his *Long Day's Journey into Night* (June–Aug Tues–Sat 10am–5pm, Sun 1-5pm; tours Tues–Sat 10am, noon, 2pm & 4pm, Sun 1:30pm and 3:30pm; $5). The writer's influence is further felt at the O'Neill Memorial Theater Center, 305 Great Neck Rd (I-95 exit 82) in nearby **Waterford**, an acclaimed testing ground for playwrights and actors, where audiences can take pot luck and watch new, often experimental, shows in rehearsal (performances held sporadically May–Aug; ☎860/443-5378).

Groton and New London practicalities

Groton–New London Airport (☎860/445-8549) has a limited service to the rest of New England, along with several car rental outlets on-site; you can also arrive year-round in New London by **car ferry** from Orient Point on Long Island (Cross Sound Ferry, 2 Ferry St, ☎860/443-5281, ⓦ www.longis-landferry.com). Reservations are strongly recommended. Greyhound and Bonanza both serve the town, which is also the center of SEAT's far from comprehensive local **bus** system (☎860/886-2631).

The **New London Trolley Info Station** has brochures and helpful staff at the corner of Golden Street and Eugene O'Neill Drive (☎860/444-7264). It's open daily in the summer, 10am–4pm; in winter, Fri–Sun 10am–4pm. The **Southeastern Connecticut Chamber of Commerce** has offices at 105 Huntington St (☎860/443-8332, ⓦ www.chambersect.org) but is only open weekdays. New London is generally a less expensive place to stay than Mystic, with reasonably priced **motels** along I-95, including the *Holiday Inn*, I-95 and Frontage Road (☎860/442-0631 or 1-800/HOLIDAY, ⓦ www.whghotels .com/hinewlon; ❺), and the *Red Roof Inn*, 707 Colman St (☎860/444-0001 or 1-800/RED-ROOF, ⓦ www.redroof.com; ❸). Additionally, in Groton there are plenty of budget motels off I-95 exit 86, including a *Super 8* (☎860/448-2818 or 1-800/800-8000; ❸).

Central Connecticut

Though **central Connecticut** is dominated by **Hartford**, the state's largest city is possibly one of the nation's dullest destinations. There's not a great deal of point in straying away from the coast, where **New Haven** is a whole lot more interesting.

Hartford

The unattractive modern capital of Connecticut, **HARTFORD**, on the Connecticut River, is also the insurance center of the United States. Its central gold-domed **state capitol**, sitting on a hill in Bushnell Park, houses a small museum of Connecticut history; free tours of the capitol are available during the week from 9.15am until 1.15pm (July and Aug until 2.15pm; April–Oct Sat 10.15am–2.15pm). Marginally more thrilling is the antique merry-go-round in the park, which gives jangling rides for 50¢. The **Museum of Connecticut History**, across the road at 231 Capitol Ave, holds Colt rifles and revolvers and the desk at which Abraham Lincoln signed the paper that emancipated all slaves during the Civil War (Mon–Fri 9am–4pm, Sat 10am–4pm, Sun noon–4pm; free).

Hartford's pride and joy is the Greek Revival **Wadsworth Atheneum**, 600 Main St, the nation's oldest continuously operating public art museum, holding some 45,000 pieces, among which are many fine and decorative arts, as well as Old Masters including Rubens' *The Return of the Holy Family from Egypt* and, in the French Impressionists collection, Renoir's *Monet Painting in His Garden at Argenteuil*. Lectures and films are put on at the Atheneum Theater, and there's an excellent café, too (Tues–Sun 11am–5pm; $7, free all day Thurs & before noon Sat).

About a mile west of downtown Hartford on Hwy-4, a hilltop community known as Nook Farm was home in the 1880s to next-door neighbors **Mark Twain** and **Harriet Beecher Stowe**. Today their Victorian homes, furnished much as they were then, are open for tours (Twain house summer Mon–Sat 9.30am–4pm, Sun noon–4pm; rest of year Mon & Wed–Sat 9.30am–4pm, Sun noon–4pm; $9; Stowe house year-round Tues–Sat 9.30am–4pm, Sun noon–4pm; open Mon June to mid-Oct and in Dec; $6.50). Twain lived at 351 Farmington Ave from 1874 until 1891, writing many of his classic works including *Huckleberry Finn*, and he spent a fair portion of his publishing royalties building and redecorating this outrageously ornate home, with its unusual black-and-orange brickwork and luxurious Tiffany stained-glass interior.

Practicalities

Hartford, which lies at the junction of I-91 (north–south) and I-84 (east–west), is easily accessible by car. Greyhound, Peter Pan and Bonanza **buses** and Amtrak **trains** all pull into the terminal at Union Place. If you have to stay the night, there are budget **motels** along I-91, including the *Super 8* at exit 33 (☏860/246-8888 or 1-800/800-8000, ⓦwww.super8motel.com; ❸); the *Red Roof Inn* (☏860/724-0222 or 1-800/843-7663; ❹) is off the same exit. Hotels in Hartford itself cater mainly to business visitors and are correspondingly pricey, though it's possible to get a room for under $130 at the central *Crowne Plaza Downtown*, 50 Morgan St (☏860/549-2400; ❻). The *YMCA*, 160 Jewell St (☏860/246-9622, ⓦwww.ghymca.org; ❶), often has rooms with shared bath for $19 and with private bath for $24, and the HI–affiliated *Mark Twain Hostel*, 131 Tremont St (☏860/523-7255), charges $18 and is open year-round. The *1895 House B&B*, 97 Girard Ave, off I-84 exit 46 (☏860/232-0014; ❸), has inexpensive rooms with shared bathrooms near the Twain House. A popular **restaurant** is *Black Eyed Sally's*, 350 Asylum St (☏860/278-7427), which serves hearty Cajun cooking with great selections of Cajun beer, plus live blues music Wednesday through Saturday. For tasty, inexpensive home-cooking check out *Timothy's*, 243 Zion St (☏860/728-9822), a popular hangout with local artists and musicians, feasting on classic American dishes; bring your own booze. For further information, visit Hartford's **CVB**, downtown at Civic Center Plaza (Mon–Fri 9am–4.30pm; ☏860/728-6789 or 1-800/466-7811, ⓦwww.enjoyhartford.com); or pick up a copy of the free local weekly, *The Hartford Advocate*.

New Haven

NEW HAVEN, founded in 1638 by a group of wealthy Puritans from London on a large natural harbor at the mouth of the Quinnipiac River, developed a solid economy based on shipping and, later, industry. In 1716 it became the seat of **Yale University**, the third oldest college in the States, but it was hardware, firearms, gas and other types of manufacturing in the nineteenth century that really brought the city into its own. New Haven churned out Winchester rifles, musical instruments, tools, carriages and corsets, and **Eli Whitney**, inventor of the revolutionary cotton gin, discovered in his workshop here a method of mass production that eliminated expensive skilled labor. Today, however, little manufacturing remains in New Haven, and the city has struggled for decades to revitalize and redevelop.

It's an uneasy place, half tension-ridden urban wasteland and half Ivy League idyll. Town–versus–gown conflicts are so marked as to give the city a crackling energy, and New Haven is certainly less WASPish and smug than many other Ivy League towns. Drug pushing, gang wars and homelessness notwithstanding, blacks and whites – and Italians, Irish and Asians – co-exist, uneasily. The city's ethnic diversity, and the undeniable vitality provided by the much-maligned Yalies, make it a stimulating place to spend some time.

Arrival, information and getting around

New Haven lies where the interstates I-91 and I-95 fork, and is on the main **train** line between Washington and Boston; services also run to Canada and New York. The Amtrak terminal is in the colossal and nicely renovated **Union Station**, on Union Avenue six blocks southeast of the Yale campus downtown. To or from New York, the Metro-North Commuter Railroad (℡203/497-2089 or 1-800/638-7646) is a better deal than Amtrak. Greyhound, Bonanza and Peter Pan **buses** from Boston arrive at 45 George St (℡203/772-2470). On arrival, it's advisable to catch a cab to your hotel, as the bus and train terminals are in potentially dodgy areas. One reputable firm is Metro Taxi (℡203/777-7777).

Public transportation to areas outside downtown is provided by Connecticut Transit (℡203/624-0151, ⓦwww.cttransit.com), 470 James St, but service is poor after 6pm. An **information booth** at 200 Orange St, two blocks east of the Green (the town's park), has schedules (Mon–Fri 9am–5pm). The **Greater New Haven CVB** is at 59 Elm St (Mon–Fri 8.30am–5pm; ℡203/777-8550 or 1-800/332-STAY, ⓦwww.newhavencvb.org).

Accommodation

New Haven has surprisingly few **hotels** for a city of its size; not even expensive ones for visiting Yalie parents. **B&Bs** from around $70 can be arranged in advance through Nutmeg Bed and Breakfast, PO Box 271117, West Hartford, CT 06127-1117 (℡860/236-6698 or 1-800/727-7592). The downtown hotels, although slightly overpriced, are worth it for their convenient location and safety. Because of the shortage of rooms, be sure to book ahead if you're going to be visiting during graduation in late May.

Best Western Executive–West Haven 490 Saw Mill Rd, West Haven ℡203/933-0344, ⓦwww.bestwestern.com/executivehotelwesthaven. Standard rooms not far from downtown New Haven at I-95 exit 42. Features indoor pool and fitness center. ❹

Colony Inn 1157 Chapel St ℡203/776-1234 or 1-800/458-8810, ⓦwww.colonyatyale.com. Downtown luxury hotel with wood furniture and modern amenities. ❹/❺

Hotel Duncan 1151 Chapel St ℡203/787-1273. Comfortable rooms in an old-fashioned hotel, a few steps away from Yale, with singles in the $45 range, doubles starting at $60. ❸

Holiday Inn 30 Whalley Ave ℡203/777-6221 or 1-800/HOLIDAY, ⓦwww.holiday-inn.com. Generic rooms in a good central Yale location. ❹

New Haven Hotel 229 George St ℡203/498-3100, ⓦwww.newhavenhotel.com. Central hotel with nice standard rooms and a health club. ❺

The City

A succession of remarkably ugly buildings built during the 1950s rather blighted New Haven, but its **downtown**, centering on the **Green**, remains both attractive and walkable, thanks in part to some sensitive restoration. This area, laid out in 1638, was the site of the city's original settlement; around the Green are three churches, a grand library and a number of stately government buildings. The park itself is now home to a handful of homeless residents, and borders the student-filled district centered around College and Chapel streets. The surrounding five blocks are a genuinely lively place in which to hang out, filled with bookstores, cafés, clubs and hip clothing stores; the **Neon Garage**, an art exhibit in a real parking lot on Crown Street, is especially notable for its glass and neon sculptures. There are some very rough pockets, but in general New Haven is reasonably safe to wander around, even at night, especially during term time.

New Haven's prime attraction, **Yale University**, stands proudly right in the center of things. You can wander at will, though free hour-long student-led tours set off daily from the Yale Visitor Information Center at 149 Elm St (T203/432-2300), across from the north side of the Green (Mon–Fri 9am–4.45pm, Sat & Sun 10am–4pm; tours Mon–Fri 10.30am & 2pm, Sat & Sun 1.30pm); it also supplies maps for self-guided tours. Tours will have you trooping to and fro quite a bit, starting with the beautiful old spires and ivy-strewn cobbled courtyards of the old campus (mostly built in the 1930s, but painstakingly distressed to look suitably ancient) and ending up at the remarkable **Beinecke Rare Books Library**, 121 Wall St, where venerable manuscripts and delicate hand-printed books are viewed with the aid of natural light seeping through the translucent marble walls (Mon–Fri 8.30am–5pm, Sat 10am–5pm, closed Sat in Aug; free). Other buildings of interest include the modernist, Louis Kahn-designed **Center for British Art**, 1080 Chapel St, where British paintings range from Elizabethan portraits to modern works by Peter Blake and Francis Bacon (Tues–Sat 10am–5pm, Sun noon–5pm; free). The impressive **Yale University Art Gallery**, just across the road at 1111 Chapel St (Tues–Sat 10am–5pm, Sun noon–5pm; closed mid-July to Aug; free), and the nation's oldest university art collection, holds American decorative arts, regional design and furniture, and African and pre-Columbian works. Among major European paintings is Van Gogh's famous *Night Café*, said by the artist to be "one of the ugliest pictures I have done." A quirky **Collection of Musical Instruments** is at 15 Hillhouse Ave (limited hours, phone ahead T203/432-0822), and the **Peabody Museum of Natural History**, 170 Whitney Ave, is a solid nineteenth-century collection of fossils, skeletons and gems (Mon–Sat 10am–5pm, Sun noon–5pm; $5).

Since 1900, New Haven's close-knit **Italian District** has been based among the well-kept brownstones and colorful window boxes of **Wooster Street**, just beyond Crown Street southeast of the Green. This was where the city's original Italian immigrants settled when they came to work on the railroad. There's little to see here, but there are some incredibly popular restaurants, and it's well worth stopping by when there's a festival on.

Eating

You can't leave New Haven without trying the local **pizza** (known locally as tomato pies). The *New York Times* discovered New Haven's pizzas several years ago, and since then queues have been forming down the street at all the family pizza restaurants in Wooster Square. There are also plenty of reasonably priced and innovative restaurants around the Green, on College and Chapel streets.

Atticus Bookstore Café 1082 Chapel St, next to the Yale Center for British Art T203/776-4040. Salads, soups, sandwiches, brioches and good coffee, in a relaxed bookstore open until midnight.
Café Pika Tapas 39 High St T203/865-1933. A bright, mural-filled place with diverse tapas and wines from Spain.
Claire's Corner Copia 1000 Chapel St T203/562-3888. Eclectic Mexican and Middle Eastern food, including vegetarian dishes, at moderate prices.
Frank Pepe's Pizzeria 157 Wooster St T203/865-5762. Most popular of the Wooster restaurants; plain, functional and friendly, with huge "combination pies" starting at $5, baked in coal-fired ovens.

Louis' Lunch 263 Crown St T203/562-5507. Small, dark and ancient burger house that claims to have served the first hamburger in the US, and presents the meat between two slices of toast. Highly popular, but worth the inevitable wait.
Willoughby's Coffee & Tea 1006 Chapel St T203/789-8400. Self-consciously trendy gourmet coffee bar frequented by hip intellectual types and fashionable locals. Superb coffee from $1, sticky cakes for slightly more. Three other locations around New Haven.
Yankee Doodle 260 Elm St T203/865-1074. Yalies' favorite coffee shop, with original Fifties fittings and shop sign, serving greasy spoon favorites such as burgers and cherry Cokes.

Nightlife and entertainment

New Haven has an undeniably rich **cultural scene**, and is especially strong on **theater**. The Yale Rep Company, 1120 Chapel St (☎203/432-1234), which boasts among its eminent past members Jodie Foster and Meryl Streep, turns out consistently good shows during the school year. The Long Wharf Theater (☎203/787-4282), 222 Sargent Drive, just off I-95, has a nationwide reputation for quality performances, as does the refurbished Schubert Performing Arts Center, 247 College St (☎203/562-5666).

Additionally, there are several good **bars** and **clubs**, concentrated on College and Chapel streets. The free biweekly paper *Hip*, available from the clothes shops along Chapel Street, has information on happenings in and around New Haven, while the *New Haven Advocate*, a free news and arts weekly, has more comprehensive listings.

Bar 254 Crown St ☎203/495-8924. Plain name, outrageous place – this is where the New Haven gay community lets its collective hair down.
Café Nine 250 State St ☎203/789-8281. Decades-old intimate, yet divey club with live jazz Wed through Sun nights and open blues jams on a regular basis.

Taboo 806 State St ☎203/777-6670. An expansive lounge in an old Polish American Club offering live music and a huge patio that's packed in nice weather.
Toad's Place 300 York St ☎203/624-8623. Mid-sized nationally renowned live music venue, where the likes of Dylan and the Stones "pop in" occasionally to play impromptu gigs. Tickets $10–25.

New Hampshire

Long after sailors, fishermen and agricultural colonists had domesticated the entire coastline of New England, the harsh, glacier-scarred interior of **NEW HAMPSHIRE**, with its dense forests and forbidding mountains, remained the exclusive preserve of the Algonquin Indians. Only the few miles of seashore held sizeable seventeenth-century communities of European settlers, such as Strawbery Banke at **Portsmouth**.

Even when the Indians were finally driven back, following the defeat of their French allies in Canada, the settlers could make little agricultural impact on the rocky terrain of this "granite state." Towns such as Nashua, Manchester and Concord grew up in the fertile Merrimack Valley, but not until the Industrial Revolution made possible the development of water-powered **textile** mills did the economy take off. For a while, ruthless **timber** companies looked set to strip all northern New Hampshire bare – very few of the trees you see now are original growth – but they were brought under control when the state recognized that the pristine landscape of the **White Mountains** might turn out to be its greatest asset. Large-scale **tourism** began towards the end of last century; at one stage fifty trains daily brought travelers up to Mount Washington.

Ever since becoming the first American state to declare independence, in January 1776, New Hampshire has been proud to go its own idiosyncratic way. The absence of a sales tax, or even a personal income tax, is seen as a fulfillment of the state motto, "Live Free or Die." Alternative sources of revenue include state-owned **liquor stores** in which, unlike in neighboring states, you are able to purchase alcohol on Sundays. The stores were set up after the failure of Prohibition, and have been enthusiastically promoted ever since: they even have them in freeway rest areas. The state has long gained inordinate political clout as the venue of the first **primary election** of each presidential campaign, with its villages well used to playing host to would-be world leaders.

One less ideological aspect of New Hampshire's individualism is the emphasis on a healthy outdoor lifestyle. Hiking, climbing, cycling and **skiing** are enjoyed both by energetic locals and by the many visitors who drive up from Boston and New York. The major destinations are **Lake Winnipesaukee**, and **Conway**, **Lincoln** and **Franconia** in the mountains further north. Some have grown rather too large and commercial for their own good, but if you steer clear of the paying "attractions," the lakes, islands and snowcapped peaks themselves remain spectacular. To see the bucolic rural scenery more usually associated with New England, take a detour off the main roads up the Merrimack Valley – to **Canterbury Shaker Village** near Concord, for example.

Getting around New Hampshire

Manchester has a small **airport**, but travelers coming to New Hampshire from far afield usually do so via Boston's Logan Airport, approximately 45 minutes to the south. Concord Trailways (⊕603/228-3300 or 1-800/639-3317, ⓦwww.concordtrailways.com) runs **buses** from there to Manchester, Concord, Conway and Franconia. Vermont Transit (⊕1-800/451-3292, ⓦvermonttransit.com) runs from Boston to Conway and Franconia, and at weekends (Fri, Sat & Sun) also connects Conway with Burlington and Montréal. The closest Amtrak service is to Claremont or on to White River Junction in Vermont, across the state line from Hanover. A surprising number of **cyclists** set out to tour the mountains.

The coast

Of all the US states with ocean access, New Hampshire has the shortest coastline – just eighteen miles. Driving north from Boston along either I-95 or the quieter US-1, you enter New Hampshire after roughly forty miles, to be confronted almost immediately by the nuclear power plant at **Seabrook Station**, which opened in 1990 after years of determined opposition, not least from the irate state of Massachusetts over the border.

HAMPTON BEACH, a little further on, is a traditional family-oriented, if somewhat tacky, seaside resort (its free information line has the optimistic number ⊕1-800/GET-A-TAN). The usual assortment of motels and fast-food places lines the approaches to the boardwalk and crowded beaches, but in a place this close to Boston summer **accommodation** rates are high. The *Breakers by the Sea Motel* at 409 Ocean Blvd (⊕603/926-7702, ⓦwww.breakersbythesea.com; ❸/❹), is one of the least expensive options, offering roomy one- or two-bedroom apartments; for a bit more comfort try the *Oceanside Inn* at 365 Ocean Blvd (⊕603/926-3542; ❹). Large local **campgrounds** include *Tuxbury Pond* in South Hampton (⊕603/394-7660 or 1-800/585-7660, ⓦwww.tuxburypond.com).

Portsmouth

New Hampshire's oldest community, **PORTSMOUTH**, might look like a major city on the map, but once you're there it has much more of the feel of a country town, and a pleasant lived-in atmosphere that places it well above some of the smaller, more tourist-focused communities along the coast. Its position at the mouth of the Piscataqua River has always made it an important port – it was the state capital until 1808 – but it has barely grown, and the spire of **North Church** in the central **Market Square** remains the highest building you'll see in town.

Of a striking selection of grand timber mansions, the 1758 gambrel-roofed, cream-and-white clapboard **John Paul Jones House** at 43 Middle St, on the corner of State Street, is the most distinctive (June to mid-Oct Mon–Sat 10am–4pm, Sun noon–4pm; $4). However, with so many old houses to see you can contentedly walk at random (or, better, get a *Harbour Trail* leaflet from the visitor center), and a visit to **Strawbery Banke** (see below) provides a better overview of local history. In **Prescott Park** along the waterfront, the **Sheafe Warehouse Museum** (free) has a fascinating collection of mostly nautical ephemera.

Indeed Portsmouth's fortunes have long rested with its **naval shipyard**, visible across the bay (in Kittery, Maine; see p.276). Founded in 1800 by John Paul Jones as the US government's first shipyard, it has remained active ever since – it launched 31 submarines in 1944 alone, and built the first Polaris in 1962. During World War I, **Humphrey Bogart**, as a junior naval rating, suffered injuries, while attempting to prevent the escape of a prisoner, that left him with his trademark sneer and a slight lisp.

Strawbery Banke

The lack of any great pressure on space has made it possible to preserve ten acres of Portsmouth's original site as **Strawbery Banke**, Hancock and Marcy streets at I-95 exit 7 (mid-April to Oct daily 10am–5pm, Nov to mid-April Wed–Sun guided tours hourly between 10am–2pm; $12 adults, $8 children, $28 family; tickets good for two consecutive days). This area began life as the home of wealthy shipbuilders, and was successively the lair of privateers and a red-light district before turning into respectable – and, in the 1950s, ultimately decaying – suburbia. It was then decided to re-create its former appearance, mainly by clearing away the newer buildings (only two of the houses on display had to be moved here). One or two people still live here, tucked away on the upper floors, but the whole complex serves as a living museum, which you can explore either on a guided tour or on your own, in which case several of the houses have well-informed attendants.

Each building is shown in its most interesting former incarnation, whether that be 1695 or 1955; in the **Drisco House**, the first you come to, each individual room dates from a different era. The 1766 **Pitt Tavern** holds most historic significance, having served as a meeting place during the Revolution for patriots and loyalists (it still functions as a Masonic lodge, one of the four oldest in the US – which explains why you can't go upstairs). Tiny glasses remind you that its clientele drank gin rather than beer (Masonics were usually known for their beer steins). Although you may have to struggle to keep ahead of school groups, Strawbery Banke continues to undertake serious academic research. Traditional **crafts** are studied and practiced here; in the **Dinsmore Shop**, an infinitely patient cooper manufactures barrels with the tools and methods of 1800. The Mills Zoldak **pottery** shop, open year-round, produces attractive low-priced ceramics; you can visit without paying admission.

Practicalities

C&J Trailways **buses** (☎1-800/258-7111) halt at 5 Congress St, on Market Square, en route between Boston and Portland. You can pick up information from the **visitor center** at 500 Market St (Mon–Fri 9.30am–5pm;

☎603/436-1118, ⓦwww.portsmouthchamber.org), and the outside tables of the *Café Brioche* in Market Square (☎603/430-9225) make an obvious point from which to get your bearings. Portsmouth Harbor Cruises (☎603/436-8084 or 1-800/776-0915, ⓦwww.portsmouthharbor.com) is among operators offering boat trips from $10.

Accommodation in the town center is restricted to expensive places such as the grand *Sise Inn* at 40 Court St (☎603/433-1200 or 1-800/746-3466, ⓦwww.someplacesdifferent.com; ⑥), a nicely preserved Queen Anne-style house with large rooms, and **B&Bs** like the peaceful, rambling seven-room *Inn at Strawbery Banke*, 314 Court St (☎603/436-7242 or 1-800/428-3933; ⑤), and the more formal *Martin Hill Inn*, 404 Islington St (☎603/436-2287; ⑤). Hotels and motels along US-1 include the *Comfort Inn at Yoken's* (☎603/433-3338 or 1-800/552-8484; ❹), which has a pool. The adjacent *Yoken's* (☎603/436-8224) is a popular and inexpensive ribs restaurant, housed in New England's largest **giftshop**, a veritable gold mine of trivia.

Of the in-town **restaurants**, the *Stockpot*, overlooking the river at 53 Bow St (☎603/431-1851), specializes in paella and stir-fries; *Porto Bello*, at no. 67 (☎603/431-2989), does superb Italian dishes at reasonable prices – reservations are recommended; and funky *Friendly Toast*, 121 Congress St (☎603/430-2154), makes for an inexpensive breakfast and lunch spot for the generous portions and homemade bread. At night, the *Portsmouth Brewery*, 56 Market St (☎603/431-1115), is raucous with live music and *The Press Room*, 77 Daniel St (☎603/431-5186), has live jazz and good bar food.

Odiorne Point State Park

The one brief patch of semi-wilderness along the New Hampshire coast is, ironically, where the first white settlers landed in 1623. Some of the scattered ruins in the marshy duneland of **Odiorne Point State Park** date from those early days; others, far more modern, were World War II defenses. The two park entrances are on Hwy-1A near **Rye**, four miles southeast of Portsmouth, where a summer-only visitor center is open daily from 10am until 4pm. The offshore **Isles of Shoals**, a supposed haunt of Blackbeard the pirate, can be visited by taking a boat trip from Portsmouth Harbor (☎603/431-5500 or 1-800/441-4620, ⓦwww.islesofshoals.com).

The Merrimack Valley

The financial and political heartland of New Hampshire is the **Merrimack Valley**, which – first by water and now by road – has always been the main thoroughfare north to the White Mountains and Québec. None of its towns is of any great interest to tourists, though all are pleasant enough, and equipped with relatively inexpensive motels.

The southernmost (and New Hampshire's second-biggest) town on the river, **Nashua**, was rated by *Money* magazine in 1997 as the number one place to live in America. Plenty of its citizens still choose to work in Boston, though Massachusetts no longer allows employees to escape state taxes by living across the border in New Hampshire. **MANCHESTER**, like its namesake in England, was a major nineteenth-century cotton producer. Although its massive Amoskeag Mills closed in the 1930s, it remains the largest city in the state, and is now notable mainly for the glassware, furniture and paintings in the **Currier Gallery of Art** at 201 Myrtle Way (Mon, Wed, Thurs, Sat & Sun

11am–5pm, Fri 9am–11pm; free). The focal point of **CONCORD** is the gold dome of the State House, the seat of New Hampshire's state legislature; despite its small size it has 424 members, making it the fourth largest such body in the world (after the parliaments of the United States, Britain and India). Local schoolteacher Christa McAuliffe, a victim of the *Challenger* shuttle tragedy, is commemorated by a planetarium, at 3 Institute Drive, off the I-93, exit 15E (Tues–Sat 10am–5pm, Sun noon–5pm, open until 10pm on Friday Skywatch nights; ☎603/271-7831).

Fifteen miles north of Concord on Hwy-106, **Canterbury Shaker Village** (May–Oct daily 10am–5pm; April, Nov & Dec, Sat & Sun 10am–5pm; $10) was the sixth Shaker community (see pp.236, 552 and 559) to be founded by Ann Lee in the 1780s, numbering 300-strong by 1860. Ninety-minute tours show Shaker crafts and techniques – such as box-making – and the attached *Creamery* restaurant serves Shaker food from April through December. South of Concord, outside Derry on Hwy-28, the **Robert Frost Farm** (summer daily 10am–5pm; rest of year Sat & Sun 10am–5pm; $3) has been evocatively restored to its condition when New England's poet laureate lived here from 1900 to 1911. Displays in the barn discuss his work, and a half-mile "poetry nature trail" leads past the sites that inspired many of his best-known poems.

The Lakes Region

Of the literally hundreds of lakes created by the snowmelt flowing south from the White Mountains, much the biggest is **Lake Winnipesaukee**, which forms the center of the vacation-oriented Lakes Region. Long segments of its 300-mile shoreline, especially in the east, consist of thick forests sweeping down to waters dotted with little islands, which are disturbed only by pleasure craft. The most sophisticated of the towns is **Wolfeboro**; the most fun to visit has to be **Weirs Beach**.

Ideally, you would bring your own small boat and get thoroughly lost in the maze of small channels and islets. Failing that, the **cruise ship** *Mount Washington* does daily two-and-a-half-hour tours of the more open stretches in summer, leaving Weirs Beach daily at 10am, 12.30pm and 3pm, Wolfeboro (except Mon & Thurs) at 11.15am and Meredith Mondays at noon and 2.30pm. The tours cost $18, and also call at either Center Harbor (Mon 11am) or Alton Bay (Thurs 11.15am). It's certainly a pretty ride, though it can seem a little long in the heat of the day, and you might prefer to take an evening dinner cruise instead for $35–39 (July & Aug Mon–Sat; ☎603/366-5531 or 1-888/843-6686, ⊛www.cruiseNH.com). A smaller mail-boat does more local round-trips from Weirs Beach for $14 (Mon–Sat 11am & 2pm; ☎603/569-1114) or from Wolfeboro daily at 10am, also $14.

Wolfeboro

Because Governor Wentworth of New Hampshire built his summer home nearby in 1768, tiny **WOLFEBORO** claims to be "the oldest summer resort in America." Sandwiched between lakes Winnipesaukee and Wentworth, it has little to show for that history, but it's a relaxing place to spend a few hours, along the short but bustling main street, next to the quay where the *Mount Washington* comes in.

The 1812 *Wolfeboro Inn* (☎603/569-3016 or 1-800/451-2389, ⊛www .wolfeboroinn.com; ❹–❻) stands in a dignified waterfront position at 90 N

Main St, just a few yards from the town proper; its *Wolfe's Tavern* serves good-value meals, and a complimentary cruise on the Inn's own *Winnipesaukee Belle* is included in season. *123 North Main B&B*, 123 N Main St (℡603/569-9191 or 1-800/577-9506; ❺/❻), is a relaxing place with friendly owners, close to both the town and lake. *Wolfeboro Campground* is on Haines Hill Road (℡603/569-9881; $16–17 per site), open mid-May to mid-October. *Garwoods* (℡603/569-7788), 6 N Main St, serves good-value **food** outdoors along the waterfront; *Lydia's Café* (℡603/569-3991), at 33 N Main St, is an excellent, veggie-oriented place for breakfast, lunch or smoothies.

The eastern shore of Lake Winnipesaukee is considerably less developed than the area around Weirs Beach, and makes for much better walking. One fascinating stopoff, a few miles north of Wolfeboro on Hwy-109, is the **Libby Museum** (summer Tues–Sat 10am–4pm, Sun noon–4pm; $2), where the obsession of c.1900 dentist Henry Forest Libby with evolution is illustrated by various ineptly stuffed animals (one can only hope that he was a better dentist than he was a taxidermist) and the skeletons of bears, orangutans and humans. There's also a mastodon's tooth, a "Niddy Noddy" spinning device, and a fingernail supposedly pulled out by its Chinese owner to demonstrate his new Christian faith. The front steps command a superb view over the lake itself.

Weirs Beach and Laconia

The short boardwalk at **WEIRS BEACH**, the very essence of seaside tackiness even if it is fifty miles inland, is in summer the social center of the Lakes Region. Its little wooden jetty throngs with vacationers, the amusement arcades jingle with cash, and there's even a neat little crescent of sandy beach, suitable for family swimming. The better of its two competing **water parks** is Surf Coaster (summer daily 10am–8pm, weather permitting; $20, less if you're under 4ft tall) on Hwy-11B just south of town, which offers dramatic rides and a powerful wave machine.

Nearby **LACONIA** controls the purse-strings for Weirs Beach but isn't really worth a visit of its own except for a stop at the White Mountain National Forest Headquarters at 719 Main St (Mon–Fri 8am–4.30pm; ℡603/528-8721, ⓦwww .fs.fed.us/r9/white), which has helpful maps and camping info. **Belknap Mill** here claims to be "the oldest unaltered brick textile mill building in the United States." Though now an arts center, the mill's machinery is still in working order amongst the gallery space, which is the venue for evening concerts and lecture programs.

On Father's Day weekend (the third in June), at least twenty thousand **bikers** cruise up for a gigantic motorcycle race and rally in **Loudon**, where the New Hampshire International Raceway hosts NASCAR on a regular basis. Even at quieter times, room rates in Laconia are high; the best choice is the *Landmark Inn of the Lakes Region*, 480 Main St (℡603/524-8000; ❸–❺), but motel options are abundant along Rte-3 between Weirs Beach and Meredith. Laconia's heartiest place to eat is *Water Street Café* (℡603/524-4144), at 141 Water St, which serves healthy helpings of old-fashioned food for breakfast, lunch and dinner. The nearest **campground** is the *Gunstock* (℡603/293-4341 or 1-800/486-7862, ⓦwww.gunstock.com; $24 per night for up to two adults and three children), near Gilford six miles south.

Meredith

MEREDITH, four miles north of Weirs Beach, is the last of Lake Winnipesaukee's resorts. The *Inn at Mill Falls,* Rte-3 (℡603/279-7006 or 1-800/622-MILL, ⓦwww.millfalls.com; ❹–❻), is an exceptionally comfortable place to stay overnight; rooms at the *Chieftain Motor Lodge*, 95 Pleasant St (☎603/279-8584, ⓦwww.chieftaininn.com; ❹), are much more basic, though the lakeside setting is nice enough. Inside the *Chase House Inn* at Mill Falls (along Rte-3), *Camp* (☎603/279-3003) is a good place for seafood or chicken pot pie, while *Mame's* (☎603/279-4631), at 8 Plymouth St, serves tavern fare in an old village home.

The **Winnipesaukee Railroad** (☎603/745-2135, ⓦwww.hoborr.com) operates two-hour scenic trips ($9.50; $6.95 for picnic lunch) along the lakeshore between Meredith and Weirs Beach, at weekends from the last Monday in May and then several times daily from mid-June to early September, including special fall foliage excursions.

Northwards to the mountains

Hwy-25 northeast from Meredith leads to Conway in the White Mountains; US-3 northwest, on the other hand, keeps you in the Lakes Region a little longer, leading past **Squam Lake**, where portions of the movie *On Golden Pond* were filmed. Educational tours of the **Squam Lakes Natural Science Center** at **Holderness** (May–Nov daily 9.30am–4.30pm; $8) lead through a largely natural landscape, in which animals such as deer, bobcat, otters, bears and foxes are kept (mostly short-term) in enclosures and loon-sighting cruises are offered on the lake. Squam Lake Tours also offers three tours daily, May through October (☎603/968-7577, ⓦwww.squamlaketours.org), as well as a sunset tour from June to August.

Five miles on from Holderness at **Plymouth**, you can either rejoin I-93 as it heads into the mountains, or continue another five miles west to the misleadingly named **Polar Caves**, actually little more than a cascade of clammy granite boulders tumbled against a hillside and entirely missable.

The White Mountains

Thanks to their accessibility from both Montréal to the north and Boston to the south, the **White Mountains** have become a year-round tourist destination, popular with summer hikers and winter skiers alike. Commercialized they may be, in built-up strips along the main highways, but the great granite massifs retain much of their majesty and power. **Mount Washington** can claim the severest weather in the world, and conditions are harsh enough for the timberline to be at four thousand feet, as compared to the norm in the Rockies of ten thousand.

Just a few high passes – here called "**notches**," discovered only after infinite pains by the early pioneers – pierce the range, and the roads through these gaps, such as the **Kancamagus Highway** between Lincoln and Conway, make for an enjoyable driving tour. However, you won't really have made the most of the White Mountains unless you also set off, on foot or on skis, across the long expanses of thick evergreen forest that separate them, with snowcapped peaks poking out in all directions. The best sources of **information** in the region are the White Mountains Attractions visitor center at I-93 exit 32 in North Woodstock (☎603/745-8720 or 1-800/FIND-MTS, ⓦwww.visitwhite-mountains.com) and the info center at Pinkham Notch (☎1-800/262-4455, ⓦwww.outdoors.org) on Rte-16, open daily year-round 6.30am–10pm.

White Mountains accommodation

Thanks to the influx of youthful hikers and skiers to the White Mountains, there's an abundance of **budget** accommodation in the area; hostels cost under $25, and while inns and B&Bs tend to start from around $80, haggling sometimes pays off at quiet times and rates vary dramatically between seasons, and from weekday to weekend. **Campers** can pitch their tents anywhere in the White Mountains National Forest below the treeline and away from the roads, provided they show consideration for the environment; there are also more than twenty official campgrounds ($14–16 per night; National Forest information ☎1-888/CAMPS-NH, reservations ☎877/444-6777 or ⓦwww.reserveUSA.com).

Hostels and mountain huts

Apart from the hostels at Crawford Notch and Pinkham Notch, accessible to motorists, the eight **Appalachian Mountain Club** huts along the Appalachian Trail can be reached only on foot. In summer, they provide meals and bedding for up to one hundred people per night. Prices in all of them range from $18 to $66, according to the amount of privacy (and food) you're after. Reservations are strongly recommended (☎603/466-2727, ⓕ466-3871, ⓦwww.outdoors.org), and you'll be expected to pay in full when you book the accommodation. The AMC runs a shuttle van service for hikers between major trailheads and the lodges from June to October ($8).

Hostels

Crawford Notch Hostel US-302, Carroll ☎603/466-2727, ⓦwww.outdoors.org. AMC hostel with two dorms and three cabins in the heart of the mountains just outside of Bretton Woods. Meals are optional. $18 per night for members; $20 for others. Open daily 7–10am and 4–9.30pm throughout the year. ❶/❷

Joe Dodge Lodge at Pinkham Notch Hwy-16, Pinkham Notch ☎603/466-2727, ⓦwww.outdoors.org. One of the more expensive AMC lodges, at $47–51 per bunk or $63–70 for a double room, but worth it. Near the base of the Mount Washington Auto Rd and filled with hikers. The visitor information center is open daily 6.30am–10pm; the lodge is also open year-round. ❷

Hiking, cycling, & skiing in the White Mountains

Hiking in the mountains is coordinated by the **Appalachian Mountain Club** (AMC), whose chain of information centers, hostels and huts along the Appalachian Trail, traversing the region from northeast to southwest, is detailed opposite; ring ☎603/466-2727 or 1-800/262-4455 for further information, and pick up a copy of the *AMC White Mountain Guide* ($21.95) before you attempt any serious expedition. Downhill and cross-country skiers can choose from several resorts that double up as summertime activity centers. Both Loon Mountain (☎603/745-8111 or 1-800/229-LOON, ⓦwww.loonmtn.com) and Bretton Woods Mountain Resort (☎603/278-3300, ⓦwww.brettonwoods.com) keep the chair lifts open through summer, and offer decent mountain-bike trails as well as rollerblading and horseback riding. General information on the skiing centers along I-93 is available from Ski NH (PO Box 10, North Woodstock, NH 03262; ☎603/745-9396, ⓦwww.skinh.com); those further east are covered by the very helpful Mount Washington Valley Chamber of Commerce on Hwy 16, North Conway (PO Box 2300, North Conway, NH 03860; ☎603/356-3171 or 1-800/367-3364, ⓦwww.mtwashingtonvalley.org). North Conway is the best place to rent equipment and other supplies.

Bikes can be rented from North Country Adventures on the Kancamagus Highway in Lincoln (☎603/745-8600, ⓦwww.e-northcountryadventures.com), from the Bretton Woods ski resort on Hwy-302, or from Joe Jones on Main Street in North Conway (☎603/356-9411, ⓦwww.joejonessports.com).

Motels, hotels and B&Bs

Boulder Motor Court junction of routes 3 and 302, Twin Mountain ☏1-866/846-5437, ⓦwww.bouldermotorcourt.com. One- and two-bedroom cottages with kitchens, fireplaces and other amenities. Snowmobile tours and rentals also available. ❸

Bungay Jar Easton Valley Rd/Hwy-116, Franconia ☏603/823-7775 or 1-800/421-0701, ⓦwww.bungayjar.com. B&B rooms (❺) in a superb woodland setting, with a separate cottage in town (❼).

Eagle Mountain House 2 Carter Notch Rd, Jackson ☏603/383-9111 or 1-800/966-5779, ⓦwww.eaglemt.com. Highly atmospheric inn with a roaring fireplace in the lobby and a wraparound porch filled with rocking chairs, far above the bustle of North Conway. Has its own golf course. ❸–❻

The Forest – A Country Inn Hwy-16A, Intervale ☏603/356-9772 or 1-800/448-3534, ⓦwww.for-est-inn.com. Welcoming B&B between North Conway and Jackson where many of the rooms include a fireplace. Organizes inn-to-inn cross-country skiing and biking holidays in conjunction with other B&Bs in the region. ❹/❺

Franconia Inn Easton Valley Rd/Hwy-116, Franconia ☏603/823-5542 or 1-800/473-5299, ⓦwww.franconiainn.com. Comfortable thirty-bed inn two miles south of town, with great views. Makes for a good cross-country ski base. ❺

Gale River Motel 1 Main St, Franconia ☏603/823-5655 or 1-800/255-7989, ⓦwww.galerivermotel.com. Sweet little ten-room motel. Two cottages, sleeping 4 to 6 people, are also available. ❸

Hillwinds Lodge Hwy-18, Franconia ☏603/823-5551 or 1-800/906-5292, ⓦwww.franconiainn.com/hillwinds.html. Standard rooms at a good price. ❸

The Inn at Jackson Thorn Hill Rd, Jackson ☏603/383-4321 or 1-800/289-8600,

ⓦwww.innatjackson.com. A nonsmoking inn in a 1902 Stanford White-designed building near Jackson Village. Rates include home-cooked breakfast. ❹/❺

Mount Washington Hotel Rte-302, Bretton Woods ☏603/278-1000 or 1-800/258-0330, ⓦwww.mtwashington.com. Beautiful hotel dating from 1902 (see opposite); also runs the less-fancy *Bretton Arms* (ⓦwww.brettonarms.com), on the same property, which is much cheaper, though rooms are still spacious (❺). ❾

New England Inn Hwy-16A, Intervale ☏603/356-5541 or 1-800/826-3466, ⓦwww.newenglandinn.com. Comfortable traditional white-clapboard inn owned by three brothers, near North Conway; rooms vary in quality; cottages are good value. ❸–❺

Snowvillage Inn Snowville ☏603/447-2818 or 1-800/447-4345, ⓦwww.snowvillageinn.com. Peaceful setting, on Stuart Rd six miles south of Conway. Big, country-style breakfasts are included in rates. ❺

Stonybrook Motel & Lodge Hwy-18, one mile south of Franconia ☏603/823-8192 or 1-800/722-3552, ⓦwww.stonybrookmotel.com. Comfortable, well-priced motel near the interstate. ❸

Swiss Chalets Village Inn Hwy-16A, Intervale ☏603/356-2232, ⓦwww.swisschaletsvillage.com. One of the nicest motels in the North Conway area, away from the bustle of the main drag. Many of the rooms come with a hot tub and fireplace. ❹–❻

Village House Hwy-16A, Jackson ☏603/383-8966 or 1-800/972-834. B&B just beyond the covered bridge, with private baths and a great big porch. ❸/❹

Woodstock Inn Hwy-3, North Woodstock ☏603/745-3951 or 1-800/321-3985, ⓦwww.woodstockinnnh.com. Sumptuous Victorian inn, with its own brewpub and good, popular restaurant. ❹

Franconia Notch and the Old Man of the Mountains

I-93, speeding up towards Canada, and the more leisurely US-3 merge briefly about ten miles beyond **Lincoln**, to pass through **Franconia Notch State Park**. From a roadside pullout you can look back and upwards to the **Old Man of the Mountain**. This natural rock formation, resembling an old man's profile, will no doubt already be familiar from powerfully magnified photographs – and New Hampshire's license plates. Seen from a thousand feet below, it's absolutely tiny but can be fun to try and find. It all has to be held together with wires, and one particular family has the annual responsibility of climbing up to plug the cracks made by the winter's ice.

Franconia Notch itself is a slender valley crammed between two great walls of stone. From the park **visitor center** (May–Oct daily 9am–4.30pm; ☎603/745-8391, ⓦwww.flumegorge.com), you can for $8 walk along a two-mile boardwalk–cum–nature trail to the **Flume** and look down on the Pemigewasset River as it rages through a narrow, rock-filled gorge; take a $10 **cable–car** ride up the sheer granite face of **Cannon Mountain** (May–Oct daily 9am–4.30pm; ☎603/823-8800, ⓦwww.cannonmt.com); or hike the various, well-marked trails up to panoramic views for free.

Further on, one mile south of **FRANCONIA**, the **Frost Place** on Ridge Road (July to second Mon in Oct daily except Tues 1–5pm, June weekends 1–5pm; $3) is a former home of poet Robert Frost, memorable largely for an inspiring panorama of unspoiled mountains. Each summer the place houses a poet, who will often give poetry readings during visiting hours; however, Frost's farm outside Concord (see p.256) makes a better destination.

Bretton Woods

The ease with which US-302 now crosses the middle of the mountains belies the effort that went into cutting a road through **Crawford Notch**, halfway between Franconia and Conway. Just north, the magnificent **Mount Washington Hotel** (see opposite) stands in splendid isolation in the wide mountain valley of **BRETTON WOODS**. Its glistening white facade, capped by red cupolas and framed by the western slopes of Mount Washington rising behind, has barely changed since the hotel opened in 1902. In its heyday, a stream of horse-drawn carriages brought families (and their servants) up from the train station, deliberately located at a distance to enhance the sense of grandeur. Displays in the grand lobby commemorate the Bretton Woods Conference of 1944, which laid the groundwork for the postwar financial structure of the capitalist world, by setting the gold standard at $35 an ounce (it's now $350) and creating the International Monetary Fund and the World Bank.

Restoration has ensured that the hotel remains marvelously evocative, with its quarter-mile terrace and white wicker furniture, and the place is worth checking out even if you're not staying. Weekend golfing and tennis packages are available, and there's skiing in winter.

Mount Washington

The 6288ft **Mount Washington** was named for George Washington before he became president, but over the years other mountains in this "Presidential Range" have taken the names of Madison, Jefferson, and even Eisenhower. (Mount Nancy was called that long before the Reagans were in the White House; and Mount Deception just happens to be close by.)

From the top of Mount Washington you can see on a clear day all the way to the Atlantic – and right into Canada – but the real interest in making the ascent lies in the extraordinary severity of the weather up there. The wind exceeds hurricane strength on more than a hundred days of the year, and in 1934 it reached the highest speed ever recorded anywhere in the world – 231mph. On the summit, you'll see the remarkable spectacle of buildings actually held down with great chains; many have been blown away over the years, including the old observatory, said to be the strongest wooden building ever constructed. There's now a viewing platform, with a weatherproof museum and café just below. Among the roll call of the 103 victims to have died on the mountain are two who attempted to slide down the Cog Railway on "improvised boards."

On the way to the top, you pass through four distinct climatic zones, starting with century-old fir and ash trees so stunted as to be below waist-height and ending with Arctic tundra. The drive up the **Mount Washington Auto Road** (mid–May to late Oct only – weather permitting, 7.30am–6pm in peak season, 7.30am–5.30pm after the first Monday in September; call ☎603/466-3988 to check weather conditions) isn't as hair-raising as you might expect, though the hairpin bends and lack of guardrails certainly keep you alert. There is a $16 **toll** for private cars and driver (plus $6 for each additional adult and $4 for kids), which comes with an audio tape or CD detailing the road's history. Specially adapted minibuses, named "stages" after the horse-drawn carriages that first used the road, give **narrated tours** ($22). Driving takes thirty or forty minutes under sane conditions, though rally-drivers have done it in less than ten. The record for the annual **running** race each June – heading up the mountain – now stands at an incredible 58 minutes 20 seconds.

Last but far from least, you can also ride to the top on the coal-fired steam train of the **Mount Washington Cog Railway**, which noisily climbs the exposed western flank of the mountain, ascending gradients of up to 38 percent on a track completed in 1869. It's truly a unique experience, inching up the steep wooden trestles while avoiding descending showers of coal smut. The three-hour round-trip costs $44 and trains leave hourly (mid-July to Sept 8am–5pm, less often during the rest of the year, weather permitting; ☎603/278-5404 or 1-800/922-8825, ⊛www.thecog.com) from a station off Rte-302 six miles northeast of Bretton Woods. Reservations are recommended.

North Conway

A few miles south of Mount Washington, heading past **Glen**, US-302 and Hwy-16 as they approach **NORTH CONWAY** become a hodgepodge of shopping malls, fast-food places and theme parks such as Heritage USA and Storyland. The strip between North Conway and **Conway** proper offers all sorts of "factory outlets" (including a branch of Maine's L.L. Bean – see p.280) for discount shopping. The towns are not terribly interesting, but there are plenty of secluded lodging options in the foothills to either side, and bars and restaurants in the malls (detailed below), as well as the very important **White Mountain National Forest Saco Ranger Station**, 33 Kancamagus Highway in Conway (☎603/447-5448), which sells maps and books and provides a ton of resources for travel planning. It also handles backcountry cabin rentals and sells parking permits ($3 for one day; $5 for five days), which are mandatory within the White Mountains region. If you're traveling through here in high season, be warned that it can take over half an hour to drive five miles due to congested roads.

The Kancamagus Highway

The **Kancamagus Highway** (Hwy-112) connecting Conway and Lincoln is the least busy road through the mountains, and makes for a very pleasant drive. Several campgrounds are situated in the woods to either side, and various walking trails are signposted. The half-mile hike to **Sabbaday Falls**, off to the south roughly halfway along, leads up a narrow rocky cleft in the forest to a succession of idyllic waterfalls.

White Mountains eating and drinking

Family restaurants and fast-food places line the main drags of major centers such as North Woodstock and North Conway. The best places are in less conspicuous areas and worth rooting out. Some of the hotels and B&Bs recommended on p.260 also serve food.

1785 Inn & Restaurant 3582 Hwy-16, just north of North Conway ☎603/356-9025 or 1-800/421-1785. The area's premier European fine-dining experience, with prices to match – around $40 a head with wine.

Polly's Pancake Parlor I-93 exit 38, Hwy-117, Sugar Hill ☎603/823-5575. Yes, it's in the middle of nowhere, but it's a scenic nowhere and well worth the schlep if you love pancakes.

Red Parka Pub US-302, Glen ☎603/383-4344.

Evening-only steakhouse with bar until 1am and live rock music at weekends.

Thompson House Eatery Hwy-16A, Jackson ☎603/383-9341. Huge portions of very reasonably priced American comfort food.

Truant's Taverne Main St, North Woodstock ☎603/745-2239. Cozy, affordable restaurant, serving well-cooked American grill fare for under $15 a plate.

West to Vermont

Much of the western side of New Hampshire, as you approach the Connecticut River that forms the entire border with Vermont, amounts to a less developed – and therefore less touristy – version of the Lakes Region. For a tranquil day or two the area around **Lake Sunapee** can be very appealing. Good bets for local inns include *The Back Side Inn*, 1171 Brook Rd, Goshen (☎603/863-5161, ⓦwww.bsideinn.com; ❹), behind Mount Sunapee, a former hostel and now family-run Victorian with ten simple but comfortable rooms and a sumptuous breakfast buffet; and the upmarket *Goddard Mansion* on Hillstead Road in Claremont (☎603/543-0603 or 1-800/736-0603, ⓦwww.goddardmansion.com; ❹), with fancy mountain-view rooms and an elegant dining room and parlor.

Hanover

HANOVER, near Lebanon and just across from Vermont, is home to the venerable and elegant **Dartmouth College**, founded in this remote spot in the eighteenth century "for the instruction of the Youth of Indian tribes . . . and others." The main attraction here is the small **Hood Museum of Art** on the college green (Tues & Thurs–Sat 10am–5pm, Wed 10am–9pm, Sun noon–5pm; free), which has works by Picasso and Monet alongside Assyrian bas-reliefs. In the adjacent cultural complex, the Dartmouth Film Society screens international art and classic movies year-round ($5).

Hanover itself is enjoyable to wander around, with lively places to **eat and drink** such as *Molly's Restaurant & Bar*, 43 S Main St (☎603/643-2570), and the always busy *Lou's Restaurant & Bakery*, 30 S Main St (☎603/643-3321). Its best **accommodation** is in the *Hanover Inn* (☎603/643-4300 or 1-800/443-7024, ⓦwww.hanoverinn.com; ❾), overlooking Dartmouth Green from the corner of Main and Wheelock streets; the *Chieftain Motor Inn*, 84 Lyme Rd (Rte-10 N) (☎603/643-2550, ⓦwww.chieftaininn.com; ❹/❺), represents the best budget option.

One secluded and memorable place to stay nearby is *Moose Mountain Lodge* (mid-June to mid-Oct and Dec 26 to early March; ☎603/643-3529, ⓦwww .moosemountainlodge.com; ❼, two-night stay required), a steep climb up in the hills above **Etna**, overlooking Vermont. All year it feels blissfully remote from the world below, but it really comes into its own for **cross-country skiing** in winter. The friendly owners, who love the country life, charge $100 per day per person, which includes a hearty breakfast, lunch and dinner.

Vermont

VERMONT comes closer than any New England state to realising the quintessential image of small-town Yankee America, with its white churches and red barns, covered bridges and clapboard houses, snowy woods and maple syrup. No city manages a population of more than forty thousand (only **Burlington** comes close) and the chief tourist attraction is Ben and Jerry's ice-cream factory in Waterbury. Though rural, the landscape is not all that agricultural, as much is covered by mountainous forests (the state's name comes from the French *vert mont*, or green mountain). The people who choose to live here are a mix of hippies and diehard conservatives working together to preserve their environment and lamenting the arrival of yet more ski resorts. One striking feature of Vermont is the absence of billboards, but the cutesy "country stores" which seem to grace every other crossroads can become tedious.

This was the last area of New England to be settled, early in the eighteenth century, with French explorers working their way down from Canada, and American colonists beginning to spread north. Even as that rivalry died down, another developed between settlers from New Hampshire and those from New York. The wealthy New York merchants who built fine homes along the Connecticut River valley thought of themselves as the "River Gods," but the hardy settlers of the lakes and mountains to the west had little time for their patrician ways. Their leader, the now-legendary **Ethan Allen**, formed his **Green Mountain Boys** in 1770, proclaiming that "the gods of the hills are not the gods of the valley." During the Revolutionary War, this all-but-autonomous force captured Fort Ticonderoga from the British and helped to win the decisive Battle of Bennington. By 1777, Vermont was an independent republic, with the first constitution in the world explicitly forbidding slavery and granting universal (male) suffrage, but once its boundaries with New York were agreed on, it joined the Union in 1791. Curiously, the two seminal figures of the **Mormon** religion were both born in Vermont shortly thereafter – Joseph Smith in 1805, and his lieutenant and successor Brigham Young in 1801.

With the occasional exception, such as the extraordinary assortment of Americana at the **Shelburne Museum** near Burlington, there are few specific goals for tourists. Visitors come in great numbers during two well-defined seasons: to see the **fall foliage** in the first two weeks of October, and to **ski** in the depths of winter, when the resorts of **Killington**, and **Stowe** further north (home of *The Sound of Music*'s Trapp family), spring into life. For the rest of the year, you might just as well explore any of the state's minor roads that take your fancy, confident that some picturesque village will be around the next corner. There are far too many to list; we've had to leave out such prime examples as **Peru**, **Grafton** and **Middlebury**. Further information can be picked up from the official Welcome Center on each interstate as it enters Vermont.

Getting around Vermont

Vermont Transit Lines (☎802/864-6811 or 1-800/642-3133 in Vermont; ☎1-800/451-3292 elsewhere in New England, ⓦwww.vermonttransit.com) **buses** connect Montréal with Boston and New York, passing through Burlington, Montpelier, Rutland, White River Junction, Killington and Brattleboro. Other services link Stowe with Burlington, cross the north from

Newport to Portland, Maine, and traverse the Green Mountains. Amtrak-affiliated Vermonter **trains** (☎1-800/872-7245, ⓦwww.northeast.amtrak.com/vermont) between Washington, DC and St Albans (the Ethan Allen Express) stop at Brattleboro, White River Junction, Montpelier, Waterbury and Burlington – in the early morning southbound and mid-evening going north. The main **airport** is in Burlington.

Lake Champlain Ferries (☎802/864-9804, ⓦwww.ferries.com) carries cars from Grand Isle, VT to Plattsburgh, NY; Burlington, VT to Port Kent, NY; and Charlotte, VT to Essex, NY; and a six-minute ferry journey links Larrabee's Point with Ticonderoga further south. Vermont Mountain Bike Tours (PO Box 541, Pittsfield, VT 05762; ☎802/746-8580) and Adventure Guides of Vermont (PO Box 3, North Ferrisburgh, VT 05473; ☎802/425-6211 or 1-800/425-8747) organize **cycling tours**.

Southern Vermont

Of the two low-key towns at either end of Vermont's southern corridor – a mere forty miles from east to west and linked by Hwy-9 – **Brattleboro** has the atmosphere of a college town, but no college, while **Bennington** has the college but not the atmosphere. The birthplace of Mormon prophet Brigham Young is marked by a monument at **Whitingham**, halfway between the two.

Brattleboro

If **BRATTLEBORO**, in the south-central section of the state, is your first taste of Vermont, it may come as a surprise. Not the quaint, 1950s-throwback village you might expect, its style owes more to the central and northern Massachusetts college towns, with numerous little stores catering to the youthful and vaguely "alternative" population that has moved into the surrounding hills over the last two decades. The town's one unlikely claim to fame is that this was where **Rudyard Kipling** wrote his two *Jungle Books*.

Trains follow the river into town and stop behind the Old Union Railroad Station, which, as the **Brattleboro Museum & Art Center** (mid-May through Oct Tues–Sun noon–6pm; $3), now displays locally made Estey organs and works of art. **Buses**, on the other hand, pick up and drop off next to exit 3 off the interstate, a couple of miles north. Much the best place to **stay** is in one of the lovely river-view rooms at the Art Deco *Latchis Hotel*, 50 Main St (☎802/254-6300, ⓦwww.brattleboro.com/latchis; ❺). There's also a good restaurant, the *Riverview Café*, serving dishes made with local ingredients in a waterfront setting (☎802/254-9841). The nearby *Common Ground Community Restaurant* at 25 Elliot St (☎802/257-0855) is a long-established worker-owned **vegetarian restaurant**, serving dinner, lunch and Sunday brunch in a very pleasant glassed-in conservatory. Homemade baked goods and specialty coffee make *Mocha Joe's* at 82 Main St (☎802/257-7794) a good place for a morning snack or evening dessert.

Bennington

Little has happened in **BENNINGTON** in the past two hundred years to match the excitement of the days when Ethan Allen's Green Mountain Boys – known as the "Bennington Mob" – were based here. A 306ft hilltop obelisk (mid-April to Oct daily 9am–5pm; $2) commemorates the **Battle of Bennington** of 1777, in which they were a crucial factor in defeating the

British under General Burgoyne (though the battle itself was fought just across the border in New York).

About a mile north of the sleepy intersection at the town center, three **covered bridges** span the Walloomsac River. Hikers set out from the southern end of the Long Trail (see below) roughly five miles east. Students from the small and exclusive arts-oriented Bennington College crowd into the *Blue Benn* **diner** at 102 Hunt St (☎802/442-5140). The *Fife 'n' Drum* **motel** (☎802/442-4074, ⓦwww.sover.net/~toberua/; ➌) is one of many south of town on US-7. Eight miles east of town on Hwy-9, by the Prospect Ski Mountain, is the *HI-Greenwood Lodge* **hostel** (open mid-May to mid-Oct; ☎802/442-2547, ⓦwww.campvermont.com/greenwood), with beds for $18.

The Green Mountains

The **Green Mountains** that form the backbone of Vermont are not as harsh as New Hampshire's White Mountains, though the forests for which they are named are invariably buried in snow for most of the winter, and the higher roads are liable to be blocked for long periods. Here and there, denuded patches mark where trees have been shaved away to create ski-runs, but for the most part the usually peaceful **Hwy-100** running up from the south offers unspoiled mountain views to either side.

In summer, hikers take up the challenge of the **Long Trail** along the central ridge, 264 miles from north to south. This trail predates the Appalachian Trail, which now joins its southern portion, and was constructed by the **Green Mountain Club** (4711 Waterbury-Stowe Rd, Waterbury Center, VT 05677; ☎802/244-7037), whose *Guidebook to the Long Trail* ($14.95) is invaluable.

Hwy-100 Scenic Drive: Weston

One of the prettiest villages along Hwy-100 is **WESTON**, spreading beside a little river and centering on a perfect green, where a somber stone slab commemorates the seventeen local soldiers who were killed on the same day during the Civil War, at Alexandria in Virginia. Nearby, the **Farrar-Mansur House** (July & Aug Wed–Sun 1–4pm; May, June, Sept & Oct Sat & Sun 1–4pm; $2 donation) is a 1795 house and tavern, which recreates early settler life with collections of clocks, dolls, guns and weaving equipment, while the **Weston Playhouse** is a typical little Vermont theater, putting on light summer and classic fall performances (Tues–Sun; $25–31; ☎802/824-5288).

Stores selling antiques, toys and fudge are scattered up and down the main street. The **Vermont Country Store**, south of the green, is larger than it looks from its modest facade. For all its seeming quaintness, the Vermont institution, known as the "Purveyors of the Practical and Hard-to-Find," is part of a chain of superstores that has a successful mail-order business. The **Weston Village Store** opposite leans more on the side of kitsch but is a fun place to browse all kinds of books, chairs, garden tools and kitchen implements.

Weston's nicest **accommodation** is the lovely *Inn at Weston* (☎802/824-6789, ⓦwww.innweston.com; ➎), whose homey rooms are complemented by an excellent restaurant and a cozy pub. Among decent alternatives are the family-run *Colonial House Inn & Motel* (☎802/824-6286 or 1-800/639-5033, ⓦwww.cohoinn.com; ➋/➌), less than two miles south on Hwy-100, and the *Friendly Acres Motel & Inn* (☎802/824-5851; ➍), a little closer to town on the same road. A small, but magnificent soda fountain dominates the 1885 mahogany bar of the lunch-only *Bryant House* **restaurant** (closed Sun; ☎802/824–6287), next door to the Vermont Country Store and run by the same management; the menu includes such country goodies as "johnny cakes" of cornbread with molasses.

Killington

The ski resort of **KILLINGTON**, in the center of the Green Mountains halfway between Woodstock to the east and Rutland to the west, has grown out of nothing since 1957. Despite a permanent population of about 700, it's estimated that in season there are enough beds within twenty miles to accommodate over ten thousand people each night. The resort sprawls over six peaks and is especially good for beginners and intermediates (for skiing information, call ☎802/422-3333 Mon–Fri 9am–5pm).

In winter, the Killington Access Road up from US-4 is humming with crowded bars and restaurants; most of which close in summer, though you can still take the **gondola** (☎802/422-3333; $13) up to the observation deck and cafeteria on the bleak summit. Hiking routes that meet here include the Long and Appalachian trails. The *Cortina Inn & Resort* (☎802/773-3333 or 1-800/451-6108, ⓦwww.cortinainn.com; ❺) is one of several **inns** on Hwy-4 offering reduced summer rates; the quiet *Val Roc Motel*, out on Hwy-4 just after the junction with Hwy-100 S (☎802/422-3881 or 1-800/238-8762, ⓦwww .valroc.com; ❸), is reasonably priced except during the busiest ski weekends.

Woodstock

Since the 1790s, **WOODSTOCK**, a few miles west of the Connecticut River up US-4, has been one of Vermont's more refined centers and a beautiful place to spend time. Its distinguished houses center around an oval green, now largely taken over by antiques stores and tearooms. It should most certainly not be confused with Woodstock, New York, of festival fame.

Woodstock has two main paying attractions. The first is the **Billings Farm and Museum** (May–Oct daily 10am–5pm; Nov Sat & Sun 10am–4pm; $7), part of which has been kept as it was on the death of its former owner in 1890 and is a nationally renowned museum of farm life, while the rest is run as a modern dairy farm with afternoon milkings daily at 3pm. The other is the **Vermont Raptor Center** on Church Hill Road (Mon–Sat 10am–4pm, $7), an educational center and nature preserve that treats injured birds of prey.

An information booth on the green in summer (☎802/457-3555) conducts free **walking tours** of the village (Mon, Wed & Sat 10.30am), and can help with **accommodation**. Options include the *Shire Motel*, 46 Pleasant St (☎802/457-2211, ⓦwww.shiremotel.com; ❸/❹), the upscale *Village Inn of Woodstock*, 41 Pleasant St (☎802/457-1255 or 1-800/722-4571, ⓦwww .villageinnofwoodstock.com; ❻), and the cozy *Applebutter Inn* (☎802/457-4158; ❹), just east on Hwy-4 in Taftsville. You don't have to be a guest at the riverside, nonsmoking *Lincoln Inn* (☎802/457-3312, ⓦwww.lincolninn.com; ❺), three miles west on Hwy-4, to **eat** in its reasonably priced dining room (Wed–Sun only), but if you are, a delicious breakfast is included in the rates; in Woodstock itself, *Bentley's*, 3 Elm St (☎802/457-3232), has a range of microbrews and upscale bar fare, as well as live music on weekends, while *The Prince and the Pauper*, 24 Elm St (☎802/457-1818), serves more expensive continental cuisine in a casual setting. *Pane e Salute*, 61 Central St (☎802/457-4882), has the area's best cappuccino and pastries. The nearest **hostel** is over twenty miles south in Ludlow: beds at the *Trojan Horse Hostel*, 44 Andover St (☎802/228-5244 or 1-800/547-7475), cost $15 in summer and $20 in winter.

Quechee

In recent years, the grand houses on the hills around **QUECHEE**, six miles east of Woodstock, have been joined by a proliferation of new condos and second homes. It's all reasonably well landscaped, but a shame nonetheless, and adds nothing to the environs of **Quechee State Park**, which was created in time to spare the splendors of the **Quechee Gorge**. A delicate bridge spans the 165ft chasm of the Ottauquechee River, and hiking trails lead down to the park through the fir trees, where you'll find Quechee Gorge State Park, one of Vermont's many state-run **campgrounds** (☎802/295-2990 or 1-800/299-3071, ⓦwww.vtstateparks.com/quechee; $12–19 per night). The *Quality Inn*, on Hwy-4 between Quechee Gorge and the Timber Village antiques mart (☎802/295-7600 or 1-800/732-4376, ⓦwww.choicehotels.com; ④), offers the best value **accommodation**.

A waterfall on the river turns the turbines of the **Simon Pearce Glass Mill** (daily 9am–9pm), housed in a former woolen mill along Rte-4 in Quechee itself. Here, you can watch bowls and pots being made and then eat off them at the onsite **restaurant**, which serves shepherd's pie and beef-and-Guinness stew for around $12, among other dishes; reservations recommended (☎802/295-1470).

White River Junction

Probably the most exciting thing ever to happen in **WHITE RIVER JUNCTION** was the first use of laughing gas as an anesthetic, in 1844. The town has little to offer on its own, but it's an invaluable transportation hub: Amtrak trains stop right by North Main Street, and buses run east into New Hampshire – **Hanover** (see p.263) is just across the river – and throughout Vermont.

A good old-fashioned railroad **hotel** – the *Hotel Coolidge* at 39 S Main St (☎802/295-3118 or 1-800/622-1124, ⓦwww.hotelcoolidge.com; ③) – still survives in the town center, and has recently added an HI-affiliated hostel wing with kitchen space and dorm beds ($19 HI-members, $29 others). In the same building, the *River City Café* serves good soups and sandwiches at bargain rates. Except for the *Super 8 Motel*, at I-91 exit 11 (☎802/295-7577 or 1-800/800-8000; ③), accommodation in the area is pricey.

Montpelier and Barre

Another fifty miles north up I-89, **MONTPELIER** is the smallest state capital in the nation, with about eight thousand inhabitants. Surrounded by leafy gardens, the golden domed **capitol** is well worth a free tour for its marble-floored and mural-lined hallways. Copious information on accommodation, here and throughout the state, is available from the **Vermont Travel Division** at 134 State St (Mon–Fri 7.45am–4.30pm; ☎1-800/VERMONT). **Budget rooms** can be had at the central *Montpelier Guest Home*, 22 North St (☎802/229-0878; ②), which has a relaxing deck and gardens, or the *Vermonter Hotel* (☎802/479-9014; ③), southeast on US-302. There's also the HI/AYH-affiliated *Capitol Home Hostel*, out on RD1 (phone for directions: ☎802/223-2104 before 9pm), with beds for $14.

For **food**, students from the local New England Culinary Institute run both the *Main St Grill & Bar* at 118 Main St (☎802/223-3188) and the more upmarket *Chef's Table* at the same address (☎802/229-9202), serving excellent and inexpensive – if experimental – dishes from all over the world. *Julio's*, 54 State St (☎802/229-9348), cooks up delicious Mexican specialties, and the *Mountain Café*, 7 Langdon St (☎802/223-0888), dishes up good organic breakfasts, lunches and Sunday brunches.

The immigrant stoneworkers of the adjacent town of **BARRE** (pronounced *BA-rie*) were famed for their union militancy at the start of the twentieth-century. Their most enduring legacy is the gravestones they carved themselves, in **Mount Hope Cemetery** on Hwy-14, though the Scots among them did also erect a rather incongruous statue of Robert Burns downtown. Southeast of town, you can watch workers cut huge blocks out of the earth at the world's biggest granite quarry, the **Rock of Ages** (May–Oct Mon–Sat 8.30am–5pm, Sun noon–5pm; free; guided tours June to mid-Oct Mon–Fri 9.15am–3pm; $4). The *Hollow Inn & Motel* at 278 S Main St (T802/479-9313 or 1-800/998-9444, W www.hollowinn.com; ❹) has rooms with TV, VCR and mini-kitchens. It also has a fitness center and provides complimentary continental breakfast. For other **meals**, the *Country House*, at 276 N Main St (T802/476-4282), serves affordable pasta and fish dishes.

Waterbury

Few people paid much attention to **WATERBURY** before 1978; even then, the opening of a homemade ice-cream stand run by a pair of hippies in the forecourt of a gas station excited little interest. However, **Ben & Jerry's Ice Cream Factory**, one mile north of I-89 on Rte-100 in the center of Waterbury, on the way up to Stowe, has grown so huge, so fast, that it is now the number-one tourist destination in Vermont. Half-hour tours (daily: July & Aug 9am–8pm; Sept & Oct 9am–6pm; Nov–May 10am–5pm; June 9am–5pm; $2; T802/882-1260) include a short film, a view of the workforce from an observation platform, and a free mini-scoop of the stuff that made it all possible – you can buy more at the overpriced giftshop and ice-cream stall outside. The omnipresent black-and-white cow logo, and the sanctimonious reminders to recycle, eat organic and buy milk from farming co-ops can get to be a bit much; if the summer crowds seem intolerable, bear in mind there are better things to do in Burlington and Stowe.

Waterbury is the closest Amtrak stop to Stowe – the station is just south of the interstate on Park Row – and Vermont Transit buses also pass through.

Stowe

There is still a beautiful nineteenth-century village at the heart of **STOWE**, with a white-spired meeting house and a green to stroll around, although a century's experience of catering to large crowds of skiers, summertime hikers, bikers and golfers, and autumn leaf-peepers has rather swamped the approach road to the main ski area with resort spas, equipment stores and sprawling condominium complexes. Nonetheless, the setting remains spectacular, at the foot of Vermont's highest mountain, the 4393ft **Mount Mansfield**.

Hwy-108 – **Mountain Road** – leads close to the mountain through the dramatic **Smugglers' Notch**, which is closed by snow through the winter. Weather permitting, you can get to the very top either by driving four and a half miles up the **Toll Road**, which itself starts seven miles up Mountain Road (mid-May to mid-Oct daily 9am–5pm; $14 per car plus $2 for each passenger), or by taking the **gondola** (mid-June to mid-Oct daily 10am–5pm; $11; T802/253-3500 or 1-888/253-4754, W www.stowe.com) up to the *Cliff House Restaurant*, and hiking for another half-hour from there. There's also a skate park ($10 a day) that offers rollerblading lessons and rentals, plus a 2300-foot long luge-type ride known as the Alpine Slide ($9 a ride). What really made Stowe's name as a **cross-country ski resort** was its connection to the **Trapp family**, of *The Sound of Music* fame. After fleeing Austria during World War II, they established the *Trapp Family Lodge* on Luce Hill Road (T802/253-8511 or

1-800/826-7000, Ⓦwww.trappfamily.com; ❼–❾).The original lodge, where Maria von Trapp held her singing camps, has burned down, and she herself died in 1987, but an equally luxurious building has taken its place; its *Austrian Tea Room* serves incredibly heavy Germanic cakes and pastries. Good hiking and cross–country ski trails lead out from the lodge.

The best of the plentiful **accommodation** includes the streamside *Inn at Turner Mill,* 56 Turner Mill Lane (Ⓣ802/253–2062; ❹); *Stoweflake Mountain Resort & Spa* at 1746 Mountain Rd (Ⓣ1-800/253–7355, Ⓦwww.stoweflake .com/home.php; ❺); the *Riverside Inn* at 1965 MountainView Rd (Ⓣ802/253–4217 or 1-800/966-4217, Ⓦwww.rivinn.com), where rates rise $15 or more in winter and during fall foliage; the small *1860 House* (Ⓣ1-800/248-1860, Ⓦwww.1860house.com; ❹), a nationally registered landmark on School Street; and the central 1833 *Green Mountain Inn* at 18 Main St (Ⓣ802/253-7301 or 1-800/253-7302, Ⓦwww.greenmountaininn.com; ❺). The *Gold Brook* **campground** is two miles south on Hwy-100 (Ⓣ802/253-7683; $18 per site).There are plenty of places to **eat** in and around Stowe. Best for breakfast is *McCarthy's* up on Mountain Road (Ⓣ802/253-8626); *Gracie's Restaurant* in the Carlson Building on Main Street (Ⓣ802/253-8741) does a good job with sandwiches, burgers and salads. In the evening, the *Shed Restaurant & Brew Pub* on Mountain Road (Ⓣ802/253-4364) has moderately priced dinners, while the *Blue Moon Café,* 35 School St (Ⓣ802/253-7006), offers an innovative menu with prices in the $15–20 range. The always crowded *Pie in the Sky,* 492 Mountain Rd (Ⓣ802/253-5100), serves relatively inexpensive pizza and pasta dishes.

The **visitor center** is on Main Street (Mon–Fri 9am–5pm, Sat & Sun 10am–5pm; Ⓣ802/253-7321 or 1-800/24-STOWE); for **skiing information**, contact Stowe Mountain Resort at 5781 Mountain Rd (Ⓣ802/253-3500 or 1-888/253-4849, Ⓦwww.stowe.com), Mount Mansfield (Ⓣ802/253-7311) or Smuggler's Notch (Ⓣ802/644-8851 or 1-800/451-8752, Ⓦwww.smuggs.com/sg). **Bikes** can be rented from the Mountain Sports & Bike Shop on Mountain Road (Ⓣ802/253-7919 or 1-800/MTBIKE4, Ⓦwww.mountainsportsvt.com); an excellent biking trail climbs the mountain. A ski museum is scheduled to open at the corner of Mountain and Main streets in 2002.

Lake Champlain

The 150-mile-long **Lake Champlain**, which forms the boundary between Vermont and NewYork state, and just nudges its way into Canada in the north, never exceeds twelve miles in width. Across the water from the flatlands of the Champlain Valley, the imposing Adirondacks are always visible, looming in the west.The first non–native to see the lake, Samuel de Champlain in 1609, who named it after himself, was also the first to claim that it held a sinuous Loch Ness-type monster, which is referred to affectionately in the region as "Champ".

The life and soul of the valley is the French-influenced city of **Burlington**, whose longstanding trade connections with Montréal has filled it with elegant nineteenth-century architecture. Within just a few miles of the center, US-2 leads north onto the supremely rural **Champlain Isles**, covered in meadows and orchards.

Vermont is one of the few states with designated **Underwater Historic Preserves** (details at Ⓣ802/475-2022, Ⓦwww.lcmm.org), where divers can

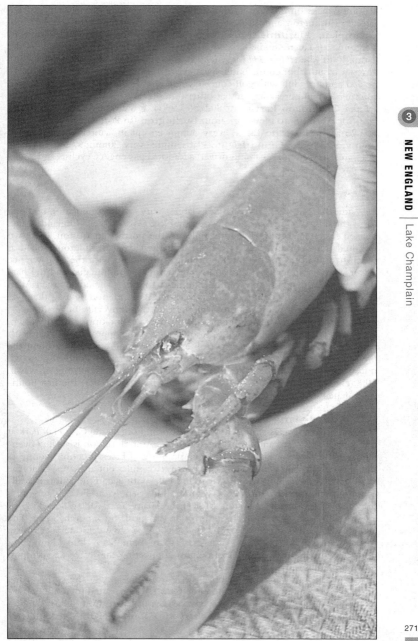

△ Lobster

see shipwrecks on the lake floor. Several of these underwater "state parks" are close to Burlington, and the best place to learn more about them is at the **Lake Champlain Maritime Museum** in Basin Harbor, seven miles west of Vergennes (May to mid-Oct daily 10am–5pm; $8). The museum is in the grounds of the *Basin Harbor Club* (☎802/475-2311 or 1-800/622-4000, ⓦwww.basinharbor.com), oddly part down-home family resort, part well-heeled country club with golf course, where rates include three meals a day in summer (⑥) and breakfast only at other times (⑤).

Lake Champlain Ferries (☎802/864-9804, ⓦwww.ferries.com) cross the lake from Vermont to New York from **Burlington** (to Port Kent; every 90min; $13.25); **Charlotte** (to Essex; every 30min except in winter when it leaves hourly; $7.50); and **Grand Isle** (to Plattsburgh; every 20min; $7.50). All these rates are one-way for a car and driver; additional passengers, cyclists and walk-ons pay $2.50–4.50.

Burlington

Lakeside **BURLINGTON**, Vermont's largest "city" with a population nudging forty thousand, is one of the most enjoyable towns in New England, a hip, relaxed fusion of Montréal, eighty miles to the north, and Boston, over two hundred miles southeast. In fact, from its earliest days, Burlington looked as much to Canada as to the south. Shipping connections with the St Lawrence River were far easier than the land routes across the mountains, and the harbor became a major supply center. The city's founders included Ethan Allen and family – far from being some impoverished Robin Hood figure, Ethan was a wealthy landowner, and his brother Ira set up the University of Vermont.

Burlington today is the definitive youthful, outward-looking university town. It's one of the few American cities to offer something approaching a café culture, with a downtown you can stroll around on foot, especially around the Church Street Marketplace, and plenty of open-air terraces. Politically, too, it's unusual: Bernard Saunders, the former "socialist" mayor of Burlington, was in 1990 elected to the House of Representatives from Vermont – the first political independent to go to Congress in forty years.

Arrival, information and getting around

Vermont Transit **buses** stop in downtown Burlington, beside City Hall Park at the corner of St Paul and Main streets, but the Amtrak station is an inconvenient five miles northeast, in the small community of Essex Junction (connecting buses every half-hour; $1). The airport is two miles out along US-2, in the same general direction. **Information** and help with accommodation is available from the **tourist center** at 60 Main St (July–Sept Mon–Fri 8.30am–5pm, Sat & Sun 11am–3pm; Oct–June Mon–Fri 8.30am–5pm; ☎802/863-3489 or 1-877/686-5253, ⓦwww.vermont.org), or the kiosk on Church Street. The local CCTA **bus** company (☎802/864-CCTA, ⓦwww.cctaride.org) runs a free shuttle (June to mid-Oct Mon–Fri 7.15am–9pm, Sat & Sun 11am–9pm; mid-Oct to May Mon–Fri 7.15am–6pm) connecting the university campus, downtown and the waterfront.

Lake Champlain Ferries (see above) leave from the jetty at the end of King Street; Lake Champlain Scenic Shoreline Cruises ($9 narrated tour; $36 lobster dinner cruise; ☎802/862-8300, ⓦwww.soea.com) departs from the Burlington Boathouse. Skirack, 85 Main St (☎802/658-3313 or 1-800/882-4530), rents **bikes**.

Accommodation

Burlington has no shortage of moderately priced accommodation, especially along Shelburne Road between Burlington and Shelburne, while for **camping** the lakeside *Northbeach Campsites* (T 802/862-0942) is less than two miles north on Institute Road.

Burlington Redstone B&B 497 S Willard St T 802/862-0508, W www.burlingtonredstone.com. A gorgeous home a few blocks south of town center with lake and mountain views. ❹

Colonial Motor Inn 462 Shelburne Rd T 802/862-5754. Sixties-era decor lends a campy touch to this clean motel with pool and cable TV. ❸

Econo Lodge 1961 Shelburne Rd T 802/985-3377 or 1-800/825-1882. On Rte-7 just west of I-89, with clean basic rooms and continental breakfast. ❹

Ho-Hum Motel 1660 Williston Rd T 802/863-4551 or 1-800/228-7031. Simple, reasonably priced motel, three miles east of downtown on US-2, near the airport. ❸

Holiday Inn 1068 Williston Rd T 802/863-6363 or 1-800/HOLIDAY, W www.holiday-inn.com/ burlingtonvt. Straightforward standard accommodation not far from town and right off I-89. ❺

Mid-Town Motel 230 Main St T 802/862-9686 or E mid-town@juno.com. Spartan, inexpensive quarters in the heart of downtown; the closest accommodation to the center. No phones. ❸

Mrs Farrell's Home Hostel (HI/AYH) 27 Arlington Court T 802/865-3730, W www.hiayh.org/hostels/vermont/burlin.htm). A few dorm beds three miles out from the center. $15 members, $18 others. 10pm curfew; reservations essential.

The City

Your natural inclination on setting out to explore Burlington might be to head for the **waterfront**. In fact, this is a surprisingly undeveloped area, though Battery Park at its northern end makes a good place to watch the sun go down over the Adirondacks – especially when there's a band playing, as there often is at weekends.

A better target is the pedestrianized **Church Street Marketplace**, a few blocks back, which holds Burlington's finest old buildings and its modern cafés and boutiques. The free **Robert Hull Fleming Museum** on Colchester Avenue (Tues–Fri 9am–4pm, Sun 1–5pm) has an interesting collection of art and artifacts from all over the world, including pre-Columbian pieces, while north on Hwy-127, the **Ethan Allen Homestead** (mid-May to mid-June daily 1–5pm; mid-June to mid-Oct Mon–Sat 10am–5pm, Sun 1–5pm; $4) offers a multifaceted look at the life and times of Vermont's controversial founding father.

The Shelburne Museum

It takes a whole day, if not more, to appreciate fully the remarkable fifty-acre collection of unalloyed **Americana** gathered at the **Shelburne Museum**, on Rte-7 in Shelburne, seven miles south of Burlington (June to mid-Oct daily 10am–5pm, guided tours at 11am, 1pm and 2:30pm; late Oct to late-May daily 1-4pm, only select buildings open; $17.50, valid for two successive days; $10 late Oct to late May). Created in 1947 by heiress Electra Webb, the museum is built around her parents' French Impressionist paintings, including works by Degas and Monet, displayed in a meticulous reconstruction of their New York City apartment. However, Electra's own interests ranged far wider, and she put together what is probably the nation's finest celebration of its own inventions outside of the Smithsonian.

More than thirty buildings, some original and some constructed especially for the museum, focus on aspects of everyday life over the past two centuries; most are staffed by well-informed attendants. The village includes a general store, complete with painted "**cigar store Indians**," an apothecary, a **Shaker barn**, a railroad station, and even an enormous **steam paddlewheeler** from Lake Champlain, the *SS Ticonderoga*, with its own rock–surrounded lighthouse.

Eating, drinking and entertainment

The presence of ten thousand students during term time ensures that Burlington has ample choice of inexpensive and good restaurants, as well as some pretty raucous night spots. Note that this is one of the most vehement **anti-smoking** towns in the East, and smoking is banned in most restaurants and some bars.

3

Bourbon Street Grill 213 College St ☎802/865-2800. Crowded and dimly lit place, with Cajun specials from $8.

Daily Planet 15 Center St behind Church Street Marketplace ☎802/862-9647. Innovative menu combining Asian and Mediterranean cooking with old-fashioned American comfort food.

Five Spice Café 175 Church St ☎802/864-4045. Excellent Southeast Asian food, including dim sum and vegetarian dishes.

Muddy Waters 184 Main St ☎802/658-0466. Dark-lit, wood-panelled, eclectic interior and colorful clientele distinguish this popular coffee house. The caffeine beverages pack quite a punch.

NECI Commons 25 Church St ☎802/862-6324. The Burlington outpost of the New England Culinary Institute offers wonderful food and attentive service. Brunch is a bargain, as are items to take away.

Pauline's Café & Restaurant 1834 Shelburne Rd, South Burlington ☎802/862-1081. Innovative American cuisine with a continental flavor. Light meals in a casual setting downstairs, more formality and higher prices upstairs.

Red Onion Café 140 1/2 Church St ☎802/865-2563. Inviting bakery with outdoor seating and the best sandwich shop around. Just try to resist the cookies.

Shanty Restaurant & Fish Company 181 Battery St ☎802/864-0238. Truly fresh seafood in a family-run, laid-back setting with views of Lake Champlain.

Smokejack's 156 Church St ☎802/658-1119. Creative meat and seafood dishes smoked over an oakwood grill, served with a great wine list and custom martinis.

Wine Works/Wine Bar 133 St Paul St ☎802/951-9463. A combined bar and store with wine-tasting events.

Maine

As big as the other five New England states combined, **MAINE** barely has the population of tiny Rhode Island. In theory, therefore, there's plenty of room for its massive summer influx of visitors; in reality, the majority of these make for the southern stretches of the extravagantly corrugated **coast**. You only really begin to appreciate the size and space of the state further north, or **inland**, where vast tracts of mountainous forest are dotted with lakes, and barely pierced by roads – more like the Alaskan interior than the RV-cluttered roads of the Vermont and New Hampshire mountains, and ideal territory for hiking and canoeing (and moose spotting).

Although Maine is in many ways inhospitable – the **Algonquin** called it "Land of the Frozen Ground" – it has been in contact with Europe ever since the arrival of the **Vikings**, around 1000 AD. For the navigator Verrazano, in 1524, the "crudity and evil manners" of the Indians made this the "Land of Bad People," but before long European fishermen were setting up camps each summer to dry their catch. Francis Bacon in turn said that the English were "worse than the very Savages, impudently lying with their Women, teaching their men to drink drunke, and . . . to fall together by the eares."

North America's first agricultural **colonies** were in Maine: de Champlain's **French** Protestants near Mount Desert Island in 1604, and an **English** group that survived one winter at the mouth of the Kennebec three years later. In the face of the unwillingness of subsequent English settlers to let them farm in peace, the local Indians formed a long-term alliance with the French, and until as late as 1700 regularly drove out streams of impoverished English refugees. By 1764, however, the official census could claim that even Maine's black population was more numerous than its Native Americans.

Originally part of Massachusetts, Maine became a separate entity only in 1820, when the Missouri Compromise made Maine a free, and Missouri a slave, state. In the nineteenth century, its people had a reputation for conservatism and resistance to immigration, manifested in anti-Irish riots. The state's **economy** has always been heavily based on the sea, although many of those who fish also farm, and long expeditions are now rare. Recently they have been selling their catch direct to Russian factory ships anchored just offshore. Lobster fishing in particular has defied gloomy predictions and has boomed again as evidenced by the many thriving lobster pounds.

Maine's climate is famously harsh. In winter, most of Maine is under ice; summer is short and usually heralded in early June by an infestation of tiny black flies. **Fall colors** begin to spread from the north in late September – when, unlike elsewhere in New England, off-season prices apply – but temperatures drop sharply, becoming quite frosty by mid-October.

Getting around Maine

The vast majority of visitors to Maine **drive**. The most enjoyable route to follow is US-1, which runs within a few miles of the coast all the way to Canada, with innumerable turnoffs to hidden seaside villages. If you're in a hurry, I-95, initially the (tolled) Maine Turnpike, offers speedy access to Portland and beyond. In the **interior**, the roads are quiet and the views spectacular; many belong to the lumber companies, who keep careful track of who you are and where you're going (and charge you for the privilege). At any time of year bad weather can render these roads suddenly impassable; be sure to check before setting off (Nov–April call ☎207/287-3427 or visit ⓦwww.state.me.us/mdot).

Public transportation, on the other hand, falls a long way short of meeting travelers' needs. The six-times-daily Greyhound service from Boston to Portland, three of which continue to Bangor, links the main towns of the southern coast, as does Concord Trailways (☎1-800/639-3317, ⓦwww.concordtrailways.com), but that's about all. Except in high summer, you can't get a bus any nearer to Acadia National Park or Bar Harbor than Bangor or Belfast, and nothing at all runs north. Sadly, in a state whose industry and tourism were once built on its railroads, there is no longer any Amtrak service. A Canadian train runs across the middle of the state to reach New Brunswick, traveling from McAdam to Brownville Junction.

The Maine coast

Considering that the state has a **coastline** of three thousand miles, finding access to the sea in Maine can be a frustrating business. The oceanfront is monopolized by an endless succession of private homes and vacation residences – most famously that of former president Bush at Kennebunkport. In fact, only two percent of the shore is publicly owned – and not all of that is beach. Rather than long walks on coastal footpaths, travelers can expect attractive if rather commercial harbor villages, linked mostly by roads set well back from the water and packed with diners, motels and factory outlets.

The liveliest destinations are **Portland** and **Bar Harbor** (at the edge of **Acadia National Park**); there's a wide choice of smaller seaside towns, such as **Belfast** and **Wiscasset**, if you're looking for a more peaceful base. **Beaches** are more common (and the sea warmer) further south, for example at **Ogunquit**.

The best way to see the coast itself must be by **boat**: ferries and excursions operate from even the smallest harbors, with major routes including the ferries to **Canada** from Portland and Bar Harbor, and the shorter trips to **Monhegan** and **Vinalhaven** islands from Boothbay Harbor and Rockland respectively.

South of Portland

I-95 crosses from Portsmouth, New Hampshire (see p.253), into an area of Maine so dense with little communities that Mark Twain alleged one couldn't "throw a brick without danger of disabling a postmaster." Three miles over the border, an **information center** at **Kittery** provides copious details on the whole state (daily: July–Aug 7am–9pm; Sept 9am–6pm; rest of year 9am–5pm; ☎207/439-1319 or 1-800/639-9645).

If you want to avoid the tolls on the interstate and follow more scenic US-1 instead, you'll soon find yourself in **YORK**, which was in 1639 the first English city to be chartered in North America. Its seventeenth-century **Old Gaol** now serves as a museum, commemorating its own past and that of the local Native Americans.

Ogunquit

The three-mile spit of sand that shields **OGUNQUIT** from the open ocean is Maine's finest **beach**, a long stretch of sand and calm surf that is ideal for long walks, but the town remains small enough to be a pleasant resort. The summer season at the **Ogunquit Playhouse** (☎207/646-5511) usually attracts a few big-name performers. Worth stopping into, if even just for a look, is the **Harbor Candy Shop** (☎207/646-8078), an old-style artisan candy shop piled with incredible confectionaries at 26 Main St; Bread & Roses Bakery (☎207/646-4227), next door, is just as tempting. Among dozens of **inns**, many of which close for the winter, are the *Betty Doon Motor Hotel* (☎207/646-2469, ⓦwww.bettydoon.com; ❷–❹), 5 Beach St (be sure to ask for the penthouse, a three-room suite with full kitchen, roof deck and room to sleep six; ❺), and *The Aspinquid* (☎207/646-7072, ⓦwww.aspinquid.com; ❸/❹), which has ocean-view rooms. *Pinederosa* (May–Sept; ☎207/646-2492, ⓦwww.pinederosa.com; $19.50 for two adults), the closest **campground** to town, is north of town off Captain Thomas Road and operates a free shuttle to Ogunquit Beach in July and August. The misnamed Marginal Way, a clifftop path, leads from central Ogunquit to **Perkins Cove** a mile south, where well-priced **seafront restaurants** include *Barnacle Billy's* (☎207/646-5575). For nightly entertainment, don't pass up the chance to sing show tunes at the packed **piano bar** on the corner of Main and Beach streets.

Kennebunkport

KENNEBUNKPORT was perfectly happy as a self-contained and exclusive residential district, before its worldwide exposure as the home of **George Bush**'s "summer White House." If anything, locals seem to feel that George lowered the tone of the place by becoming president. However, Kennebunkport is not actually all that different from anywhere else along the coast – which is presumably what's really bothering the locals. The best place to hang out (and eat seafood) is *Alisson's* at 8 Dock Square (☎207/967-4841), where dinner is served until 10pm and a pub menu available until 11pm; the bar stays open until 1am. There's no great point paying in-town hotel rates when there are so many motels along the highways.

Forty miles north of Kennebunkport is the **Cape Elizabeth lighthouse**, commissioned by George Washington in 1791 and familiar from postcards and posters. The *Lobster Shack* (☎207/799-1677) just below the light (and above the horn) is great for fresh seafood.

Portland

The largest city in Maine, **PORTLAND** was founded in 1632 in a superb position on the Casco Bay Peninsula, and quickly prospered, building ships and exporting the great inland pines for use as masts. A long line of wooden **wharves** stretched along the seafront, with the merchants' houses on the hill-side above. From the earliest days it was a cosmopolitan city, with a large free black population who traditionally worked as longshoremen; great bitterness arose when Irish immigrants began to muscle in on the scene in the 1830s. When the **railroads** came, the Canada Trunk Line had its terminus right on Portland's quayside, bringing the produce of Canada and the Great Plains one hundred miles closer to Europe than it would have been at any other major US port. Some of the wharves are now taken up by new condo developments, though **Custom House Wharf** remains much as it must have looked when Anthony Trollope passed through in 1861 and said, "I doubt whether I ever saw a town with more evident signs of prosperity." Most of what he saw of the town was destroyed by an accidental **fire** in 1866 (Indians in 1675, and the British in 1775, had previously burned Portland deliberately).

Grand Trunk Station was torn down in 1966, and downtown Portland appeared to be in terminal decline until a group of committed residents undertook the energetic redevelopment of the area now known as **Old Port Exchange**. Their success has revitalized the city, keeping it at the heart of Maine life – but you shouldn't expect a hive of energy. Portland is simply a pleasant, sophisticated, and in places very attractive town, not a major urban center.

Arrival, information and getting around

Both I-95 and US-1 skirt the promontory of Portland, within a few miles of the city center; **Portland International Jetport** (☎207/774-7301) is next to I-95, and connected with downtown by regular city buses. Congress Street is the main central thoroughfare, while Fore Street runs along the harbor just to the south. Concord Trailways (☎1-800/639-3317, ⓦwww.concordtrailways.com) and Greyhound are the principal **bus** operators along the coast, with frequent services to Boston, as well as north to Bangor (and, in summer, Bar Harbor). Vermont Transit Lines (☎207/772-6587 or 1-800/552-8737, ⓦwww.vermonttransit.com) runs to Montréal, New Hampshire and Vermont as well as destinations within Maine; the station is at 950 Congress St, on the eastern edge of downtown. The **visitor center** is at 305 Commercial St (mid-May to mid-Oct Mon–Fri 8am–6pm, Sat & Sun 10am–6pm; rest of year Mon–Fri 8am–5pm, Sat & Sun 10am–3pm; ☎207/772-5800, ⓦwww.visitportland.com).

Downtown Portland, though served by buses ($1) and trolleys, is compact enough to stroll around; Cyclemania, at 59 Federal St (☎207/774-2933), rents **bicycles** for $15 a day.

Between mid-May and late October, the Prince of Fundy Company's *Scotia Prince* **ferry** leaves Portland for **Yarmouth** in Nova Scotia at 8pm each evening, returning the next day. The sail takes eleven hours each way. High-season one-way fare is $105 per car, $86 per person, plus $32–175 extra for a cabin or suite, though there are various discount and excursion fares (details on ☎207/775-5616 or 1-800/☎845-4073, ⓦwww.scotiaprince.com).

Accommodation

Finding a room in Portland is no great problem, though you can expect to pay more to stay in town than in the **budget motels** around exit 8 off I-95. The closest **campground** is *Wassamki Springs*, off Hwy-114 toward Westbrook (May to mid-Oct only; ☎207/839-4276).

Best Western Merry Manor Inn 700 Main St ☎207/774-6151 or 1-800/528-1234, ⓦwww.bestwestern/merrymanorinn.com. Clean, comfortable and convenient, with a pool and on-site restaurant. ❹

The Danforth 163 Danforth St ☎207/879-8755 or 1-800/991-6557, ⓦwww.danforthmaine.com. Twelve rooms, ten with private baths and working fireplaces, in an 1820s Federal-style home near the Old Port. Full breakfast served. ❺/❻

The Eastland Park 157 High St ☎207/775-5411 or 1-888/671-8008, ⓦwww.eastlandparkhotel.com. A central luxury hotel that recently spent $4 million on a massive refurbishment; the fine dining restaurant and ornate lobby are jewels in the crown, but the well-appointed rooms are worth every penny as well. ❺

Embassy Suites 1050 Westbrook St ☎207/775-2200 or 1-800/EMBASSY, ⓦwww.embassysuites.com. Spacious suites for the price of a hotel room, overlooking Portland's tiny Jetport. Rates include full breakfast and afternoon cocktails and a free shuttle to and from the Jetport. ❼

Fairfield Inn 340 Park Ave ☎207/871-0611 or 1-800/228-2800, ⓦwww.marriott.com. Good-value doubles on the western edge of the peninsula near the Maine Medical Center. ❹–❻

Inn at St John 939 Congress St ☎207/773-6481 or 1-800/636-9127, ⓦwww.innatstjohn.com. Century-old hotel with small, central rooms near the museums. Free airport pick-up and breakfast. ❸

Oak Leaf Inn 51A Oak St ☎207/773-7882, ⓦwww.oakleafinn.com. Cozy rooms, near the Wadsworth-Longfellow House, available mostly by the week: $175/week for shared bath or $195 with private bath. Also serves as the *Portland Youth Hostel*, which used to be housed in Portland Hall. $22 members, $25 others.

Pomegranate Inn 49 Neal St ☎207/772-1006 or 1-800/356-0408, ⓦwww.pomegranateinn.com. Romantic B&B with eight rooms – some with fire-places – and a quiet garden. ❹–❻

YMCA 70 Forest Ave ☎207/874-1105. Men-only hostel accommodation north of Congress St near Deering Oaks Park. $27 per night for dorms; often full.

The City

Thanks to the various fires, not all that much of old Portland survives, though various grand mansions can be seen along Congress and Danforth streets. The **Wadsworth-Longfellow House/Maine Historical Society** at 485–489 Congress St was Portland's first brick house when built in 1785 by Peleg Wadsworth, but owes its fame primarily to Wadsworth's grandson, the poet Henry Wadsworth Longfellow, who spent his boyhood here. The gallery has changing displays of state history and art (June–Oct Mon–Sat 10am–4pm, Sun noon–4pm; $6, gallery only $4; tours on the hour and half-hour, 45min).

The **Portland Museum of Art** at 7 Congress Square is a much more modern affair, built in 1988 by the I.M. Pei partnership (Tues, Wed, Sat & Sun 10am–5pm, Thurs–Fri 10am–9pm; Mon 10am–5pm Memorial Day–Columbus Day; tours at 2pm daily & 6pm Thurs–Fri; ⓦwww.portlandmuseum.org; $6, free Friday 5–9pm). All parts of the museum give superb views over the bay; at times the collection seems subordinate to the design, which does not allow much room for extensive displays. The lower stories usually hold temporary exhibitions – though there's a lovely open-air garden café as well – while the works upstairs include a lively and flirtatious set of 1880s Winslow Homer engravings, some Andrew Wyeths, and an array of early nineteenth-century European ceramics commemorating heroes of the American Revolution.

For relaxed wandering, the restored **Old Port Exchange** near the quayside, between Exchange and Pearl streets, can be quite entertaining, with all sorts of redbrick antiquarian shops, specialist book and music stores (particularly on Exchange St), and other esoterica. Several companies operate **boat trips** from the nearby wharves: the *Palawan*, a vintage 58ft ocean racer, sails around the harbor and Casco Bay islands and lighthouses from DiMillo's Long Wharf off Commercial Street (daily in summer; 2hr trip; $20; T207/773-2163), and Bay View Cruises, 184 Commercial St, offers **seal-watching** tours (daily May–Oct; $10; T207/761-0496). Casco Bay Lines runs a twice-daily mail boat all year, and additional cruises in summer, to six of the innumerable **Calendar Islands** in Casco Bay, from its terminal at 56 Commercial and Franklin streets ($10.75; T207/774-7871, W www.cascobaylines.com). **Long**, **Peaks** and **Cliff islands** all have accommodation or camping facilities. If you follow Portland's waterfront to the end of the peninsula, you'll come to the **Eastern Promenade**, a remarkably peaceful two-mile harbor trail that connects to East End Beach, below the headland. Above the promenade, at the top of Munjoy Hill, at 138 Congress St, is the eight-sided shingled 1807 **Portland Observatory** (June–Sept daily 10am–5pm; $3), which affords an exhilarating view of the bay.

Eating

Not only is Portland rich in affordable **restaurants**, but most of its entertainment venues and bars, listed separately below, serve food as well. The bountiful Farmer's Market, in Monument Square (Wed, May–Nov) offers the perfect opportunity to sample local produce and culture.

Benkay 2 India St T 207/773-5555. Great sushi and other Japanese dishes keep this place packed for lunch and dinner.
Boone's 6 Custom House Wharf T 207/774-5725. Traditional waterfront restaurant in old wharf buildings, overlooking the fishing docks. Serves good lobster and grilled seafood in general.
Federal Spice 225 Federal St T 207/774-6404. Eclectic fare influenced by South American, Southeast Asian and Caribbean cuisine, all very hot and spicy.
Flatbread Company 72 Commercial St T 207/772-8777. Right next to the ferry terminal, a popular spot specializing in thin wood-fired pizzas.
Fresh Market 43 Exchange St T 207/773-7146.

Fresh pasta and noodles of all kinds, including ginger and squid's ink, at reasonable prices.
Great Lost Bear 540 Forest Ave T 207/772-0300. Serves good-value burgers and beer, as well as spicy chicken wings and the like.
Old Port Tavern 11 Moulton St T 207/774-0444. Old-style tavern with good food and Old-World atmosphere.
Silly's 40 Washington St T 207/772-0360. Burgers, pies and particularly fine milkshakes in a space adorned with wacky Americana.
Village Café 112 Newbury St T 207/772-5320. No-nonsense, well-priced family dining, with well-cooked steak and seafood plus several Italian dishes on the menu.

Nightlife and entertainment

Portland's formal entertainment possibilities range from the tiny and adventurous Mad Horse Theater Company at 92 Oak St (T207/828-1270, W www.madhorse.com) up to the large productions at the Portland Performing Arts Center, 25A Forest Ave (T207/774-0465, W www.portlandstage.com). Maine's biggest gigs take place each summer roughly ten miles south of Portland at **Old Orchard Beach**. The free *Portland Phoenix* has weekly listings of local events.

Fore Play Sports Pub 436 Fore St ☎207/780-1111. Popular sports bar with acres of pool tables, darts and enough TVs to satiate the most ardent sports fan.
Gritty McDuff's 396 Fore St ☎207/772-2739. Portland's first brewpub, serving food and their own Portland Head Pale Ale and Black Fly Stout at long wooden benches. There's sometimes folk music, and the friendly (if a little self-consciously British) atmosphere gets rowdy on Saturday night.
Three Dollar Dewey's 241 Commercial St ☎207/772-3310. Raucous beer hall, with a wide selection of draft beers and good food.

North along the coast from Portland

The coastal towns immediately north of Portland are no less commercialized than those to the south; **Freeport**, for example, is one long shopping mall, albeit a good one. However, soon after **Brunswick** I-95 veers inland toward Augusta (see p.290), and US-1 is left to run on alone parallel to the ocean. Things become much less frenetic, and prices a whole lot lower; even on the main road you'll find pleasant communities such as **Bath** and **Belfast**, while the many headlands can be even more peaceful.

Freeport

Much of the current prosperity of **FREEPORT**, fifteen miles north of Portland, rests on the invention by Leon L. Bean, in 1912, of a particularly ugly rubber-soled fishing boot. That original boot is still selling, and **L.L. Bean** has grown into a successful mail-order business with an enormous clothing store on Main Street that never closes. Originally, this was so predawn hunting expeditions could stock up; all the relevant equipment is available for rent or sale, and the store runs regular workshops to teach backcountry lore. However, with the outdoor look in vogue, L.L. Bean is now more of a fashion emporium. Freeport has expanded to welcome its 2.5 million annual customers a year with a mile-long strip of top-name **factory outlets** along US-1, most of which do give genuine reductions on usual shop prices.

Freeport is not an ideal place to stay – everything falls quiet once the shoppers have gone home – but if you need accommodation, the *Harraseeket Inn* at 162 Main St (☎207/865-9377 or 1-800/342-6423, Ⓦwww.harraseeketinn .com; ❼) is a wonderful clapboard B&B inn with some eighty rooms. The *Freeport Inn & Cafe*, 31 Hwy-1 S (☎207/865-3106 or 1-800/998-2583, Ⓦwww.freeportinn.com; ❺), provides good-value rooms and no-frills food, including all-day breakfasts.

For a complete change of pace, head a mile south of Freeport to the sea, where the *Harraseeket Lunch & Lobster Co* (☎207/865-3535), extending on its wooden jetty into the peaceful bay, makes a great outdoor lunch spot. The very green promontory visible just across the water is **Wolfe's Neck Woods State Park**. In summer, for $2, you can follow hiking and nature trails along the unspoiled fringes of the headland (☎207/865-4465).

Brunswick

Only a few miles further north from Freeport is **BRUNSWICK**, home since 1794 to the private Bowdoin College, which lists President Franklin Pierce and author Nathaniel Hawthorne among its alumni. Free tours of the college (Mon–Fri at 9am, 11am, 2pm & 4pm, Sat at 11am & noon; ☎207/725-3000) take in the intriguing **Peary-MacMillan Arctic Museum** (Tues–Sat 10am–5pm, Sun 2–5pm). After decades of controversy, experts now generally agree that former student Admiral Robert Peary really was the first man to reach the North Pole in 1909; whatever the truth, his assembled equipment and notebooks are a powerful testament to arctic exploration.

It was while her husband Calvin was teaching here in the early 1850s that Harriet Beecher Stowe wrote *Uncle Tom's Cabin*, a book whose portrait of slavery had such an impact that Lincoln is said to have greeted her with the words "so this is the little lady that made this big war." The rambling old **Harriet Beecher Stowe House** at 63 Federal St (☎207/729-7869 or 1-800/698-5548; ❹) is now a motel; guests stay in modern rooms around the back, but can use the lounge of the original house. There's also the friendly *Traveler's Inn*, 130 Pleasant St/US-1 (☎207/729-3364 or 1-800/457-3364; ❸). The *Great Impasta* at 42 Maine St (☎207/729-5858) serves excellent, well-priced Italian **food**; the *Broadway Deli*, 142 Maine St (☎207/729-7781), does all-day breakfasts (closed Tues in winter); and *Bohemian*, 111 Maine St (☎207/725-9095), is a pleasant sidewalk **café** with good coffee.

The ideal time to visit Brunswick would be Labor Day Weekend (first weekend in Sept), when the town hosts its **Bluegrass Festival** (☎207/725-6009) a little further on at Thomas Point Beach, reached by following Hwy-24 from Cook's Corner. The festival, among the best of its kind, attracts some of the biggest bluegrass names from the US and abroad. On the same road, **Orrs Island** has a well-equipped oceanfront **campground** (☎207/833-5595; $21 per day for two adults).

Bath

The small town of **BATH** has an exceptionally long history of **shipbuilding**: the first vessel to be constructed and launched here was the *Virginia* in 1607, by Sir George Popham's short-lived colony. **Bath Iron Works**, founded in 1833, attracted job-seeking Irishmen in such numbers as to provoke a mob of anti-immigrant "Know-Nothings" to burn down the local Catholic church in July 1854. The works continue to produce ships – during World War II, more destroyers were built here than in all Japan – and only admit visitors for special occasions such as ceremonial launchings. However, at the **Maine Maritime Museum**, 243 Washington St, next to the Iron Works two miles south of the town center (daily 9.30am–5pm; $9), you can tour a functioning shipyard where apprentices learn to build wooden schooners using traditional techniques.

As you head up the coast, **accommodation** starts to be better value. The *Inn at Bath* (☎207/443-4294 or 1-800/423-0964, ⓦwww.innatbath.com; ❹/❺), 969 Washington St, is a wonderful B&B with beautiful gardens and all the amenities. For a more rural experience, try the *Fairhaven Inn* on North Bath Road (☎207/443-4391 or 1-888/443-4391; ❹), which has shared and private bathrooms, serves a fine full breakfast, and offers hiking and cross-country skiing in season.

Places to eat include *Kristina's*, 160 Centre St (☎207/442-8577), specializing in inventive American dishes and serving up great breads and desserts; and *Beale Street Barbecue & Grill* (☎207/442-9514) on 215 Water St, offering slow-smoked chicken, pulled pork and ribs, to stay or to go. Be warned, however, that everything in Bath closes very early in the evenings.

Wiscasset and Boothbay Harbor

Achingly quaint, tiny **WISCASSET**, ten miles on from Bath, is dominated by the Wiscasset Bridge, which carries US-1 over the Sheepscot River. Tourism is catching on here; in fact, the town lumberyard, grocery and newsstand have all been replaced by antiques shops and art galleries to welcome visitors, changes that haven't been welcomed by locals. **Accommodation** possibilities in the area include the comfortable and modern *Wiscasset Motor Lodge* (April–Oct

207/882-7137 or 1-800/732-8168, Ⓦwww.wiscassetmotorlodge.com; ❷/❸), approximately three miles south on US-1. The lakeside **campground** *Down East Family Camping* (Ⓣ207/882-5431), at Gardiner Pond, four miles north on Hwy-27, features an impressive cathedral stand of Norway pines.

BOOTHBAY HARBOR, at the southern tip of Hwy-27, is one of Maine's most crowded resorts and it lays on boat trips of all kinds, including daily whale-watching trips (Ⓣ207/633-3500 or 1-888-WHALE-ME) that leave from Pier 6. There's no reason to stay overnight, but if you do pass by, the *Lobstermen's Co-op* at 99 Atlantic Ave (Ⓣ207/633-4900), a working lobster pound, dishes up ultrafresh lobsters at low prices, as well as a range of sandwiches. *Fisherman's Wharf Inn* at Pier 6, 22 Commercial St, serves good seafood in a more formal setting and also has waterfront rooms (Ⓣ207/633-5090 or 1-800/628-6872, Ⓦwww.fishermanswharfinn.com; ❺). *Moody's Diner* (Ⓣ207/832-7785) in **Waldoboro**, back on Hwy-1 east, is a longstanding haunt of police and truckers, open 24 hours and oozing nostalgia.

Rockland and Vinalhaven

ROCKLAND, where US-1 reaches Penobscot Bay roughly halfway between Portland and Bar Harbor, is the world's largest distributor of **lobsters**, and holds the Maine Lobster Festival over the first weekend of August (for more info call Ⓣ 1-800/LOB-CLAW, Ⓦwww.mainelobsterfestival.com). One of the best of its traditional lobster pounds is *Miller's* (Ⓣ207/594-7406), on the shore of Wheeler's Bay in an isolated cove at Spruce Head on Hwy-73, open from 10am until 7pm in season, for succulent lobsters and steamers. The *Brown Bag* bakery, 606 Main St (Ⓣ207/596-6372), has low-fat breads and lunches. The *White Gates*, four miles north on US-1 (Ⓣ207/594-4625; ❸), is the cleanest budget **motel** in the area. South of Rockland, the pretty **St George Peninsula**, in particular the village of Tenants Harbor, inspired writer Sarah Orne Jewett's classic Maine novel *Country of the Pointed Firs*. Boats leave from the hamlet of Port Clyde at the tip of the peninsula, fourteen miles south of Rockland, to tiny **Monhegan Island**, eleven miles off the coast and with a year-round population of less than a hundred. Lobsters are the main business on this rocky outcrop, though the stunning cliffs and isolated coves have long attracted artists – including Edward Hopper. Fifteen miles of hiking trails twist through the wilderness and past a magnificent 1824 lighthouse. **Accommodation** such as the *Island Inn* (May to mid-Oct; Ⓣ207/596-0371, Ⓦwww.islandinnmonhegan.com; ❹–❼) is pricey, though there are self-catering units available: try *The Monhegan House* (Ⓣ207/594-7983 or 1-800/599-7983, Ⓦwww.monheganhouse.com; ❸). However, it makes a great day-trip away from the tourist bustle of the mainland, aboard the *Laura B* (May–Oct daily; Nov–April Mon, Wed & Fri; three sailings a day in summer, fewer at other times; $27 round-trip; Ⓣ207/372-8848, Ⓦwww.monheganboat.com). Nature cruises and lighthouse tours are also available for $24 July through August.

Four to six **ferries** run daily throughout the year from Rockland to the island of **Vinalhaven**, which has one or two inns (but no campgrounds), a few shops, a museum and an impressive lighthouse; slightly fewer serve neighboring **North Haven**. Fares are $9 round-trip to either destination. The boats do carry cars and bikes, though what attracts many visitors are the hiking opportunities. The Maine State Ferry Service at 517A Main St (Ⓣ207/Ⓣ596-2202 or 1-800/491-4883, Ⓦwww.state.me.us/mdot/opt/ferry/ferry.htm) has full schedules; they also operate several daily services from **Lincolnville**, six miles north of Camden – where there's also a small but pleasant beach – across to **Islesboro**.

Camden and Rockport

The adjacent communities of **CAMDEN** and **ROCKPORT** split into two separate towns in 1891, in a dispute over who should pay for a new bridge over the Goose River between them. Rockport was at that time a major lime producer, but a fire at the kilns in 1907 not only put an end to that business but also destroyed the ice-houses that were the town's other main source of income. Now it's a quiet working port, among the prettiest on the Maine coast, home to numerous lobster boats, pleasure cruisers and little else; clearly, Camden has won the competition for tourists. The one essential stop in the area is **Camden Hills State Park**, two miles north of Camden ($2), where you can hike or drive up to a tower that affords one of the best views of the Maine coastline; on a clear day it's possible to see as far as Acadia National Park.

Camden and Rockport specialize in organizing sailing expeditions of up to six days in the large schooners known as **windjammers**. Expeditions sail late May into mid-October. Vessels include the *Timberwind* (☏207/236-0801 or 1-800/759-9250) for three- and six-day trips ($295–649) out of Rockport and the *Appledore* (☏207/236-8353), which does two-hour cruises for $20 from Camden. Maine Sport Outfitters in Rockport (☏1-800/722-0826, ⓦwww.mainesport.com) rents **kayaks** and **bikes**. Among busy **eating and drinking** spots in Camden are *Rathbone's* at 21 Bayview St (☏207/236-3272), for grilled pizzas and seafood, and the nearby *Waterfront* (☏207/236-3747), for gourmet sandwiches and a great harbor location. *Gilbert's Publick House* on Sharp's Wharf (☏207/236-4320) has pool tables and microbrews on tap, while the *Sea Dog*, 43 Mechanic St (☏207/236-6863), is the town's popular brew-pub.

Camden's information office is at the Public Landing (☏207/236-4404 or 1-800/223-5459, ⓦwww.visitcamden.com). The classy **place to stay** is the *Whitehall Inn*, 400 yards north of the center at 52 High St (☏207/236-3391 or 1-800/789-6565, ⓦwww.whitehall-inn.com), which in summer provides great evening meals with rates (❼) and during the rest of the year operates on a B&B basis (❺). The Castleview, 59 High St (☏1-800/272-8439, ⓦwww.castleviewinn.com; ❻/❻), is the only B&B in town oceanside, with the attendant views as well as great breakfasts. The nearby *Maine Stay*, 22 High St (☏207/236-9636; ❼), is a cozy 1813 white-clapboard inn, and the *Snow Hill Lodge*, north on Hwy-1 near Lincolnville Beach (☏207/236-3452 or 1-800/476-4775; ❷), ranks as a good budget option.

Belfast

Homely **BELFAST** feels like the most lived-in and liveable of the towns along the Maine coast. Here the shipbuilding boom is long since over (and the chicken-processing plant that regularly turned the bay blood red has also gone), and the town has declared the waterfront a historic district, sparing it from over-commercialization and condo development. As you stroll around, look out for the old-fashioned Greyhound and Western Union office (complete with jukebox) and any number of whitewashed Greek Revival houses. Belfast was a lively center in the 1960s, a fact still reflected in its stores, community theater groups, festivals and the WBYA (101.7 FM) radio station. However, except for its several eating establishments and one cinema, most businesses close early in the evening.

The convivial **information office** (☏207/338-5900, ⓦwww.belfast-maine.org), at the foot of Main Street by the bay, is next to the old **railroad station** used by the Belfast and Moosehead Lake Railroad (☏207/948-5500 or 1-800/392-5500, ⓦwww.belfastrailroad.com). Hour-long excursions ($18) in reconditioned Pullman cars run from here up the lush banks of the Passagassawakeag River, along tracks laid in 1870 to connect logging operations with the sea – though whatever impression you might get from their advertisements, the trains are pulled by diesel not steam. En route to the villages of Brooks and Burnham Junction, you pass through thick forests, at their most colorful in the fall. The same company offers **cruises** on an old-style paddleboat in Penobscot Bay ($15, combination rail–cruise ticket saves $3). Also right beside the rail terminal, *Weathervane Seafood* **restaurant** (T207/338-1774) has tables on the wooden jetty outside; across the bay, *Young's Lobster Pound* (T207/338-1160) serves $10 fresh-boiled lobster dinners, among the best in the state, with sunset views. Up the street, *Krazy Kones* scoops locally made Cranberry Tiger **ice cream** in its family-friendly parlor. Historic *Darby's Restaurant* on High Street serves tasty, inventive breakfasts, lunches and dinners to a congenial mix of locals and visitors. *Bay Wrap*, 20 Beaver St, has all kinds of gourmet wraps on offer. *Belfast Co-op Store and Deli*, 123 High St (T207/338-2532), offers a huge range of vegetarian food and picnic fixin's. For **accommodation**, try the *Alden House*, 63 Church St (T207/338-2151 or 1-877/337-8151, Wwww.thealdenhouse.com; ❹), a beautiful 1840 Greek Revival house run as a B&B; the comfortable *Thomas Pitcher House*, 19 Franklin St (T207/338-6454 or 1-888/338-6454, Wwww.thomaspitcherhouse.com; ❹); or the *Londonderry Inn*, 133 Belmont Ave (T207/338-2763 or 1-877/529-9566, Wwww.londonderry-inn.com; ❹), an old farmhouse that serves huge breakfasts. Along Hwy-1 across the Passagassawakeag River in East Belfast are several inexpensive motels, including the *Gull* (T207/338-4030; ❶–❹), and an oceanfront campground, *The Moorings* (T207/338-6860; $21 per tentsite), on Hwy-1 toward Searsport, open May through October.

Mount Desert Island

Considering that five million visitors come to **Mount Desert Island** each year, that it contains most of New England's only national park, and that it boasts not only a genuine fjord but also the highest headland on the entire Atlantic coast north of Rio de Janeiro, it is an astonishingly small place, measuring just sixteen miles by thirteen. It is, of course, simply one among innumerable rugged granite islands along the Maine coast; the reason to come here is that it is the most accessible, linked to the mainland by bridge since 1836, and has the best facilities.

The island was named *Monts Deserts* (bare mountains) by Samuel de Champlain in 1604 and fought over by the French and English for the rest of the century. Although all existing settlements date from long after the final defeat of the French, the name remains, still pronounced in French (more like *dessert*, actually).

The social center, **Bar Harbor**, has accommodation and restaurants to suit all pockets, while you'll find lower-key communities all over the island. **Acadia National Park**, which covers much of the island, offers active travelers with plenty of outdoor opportunities, including camping, cycling, canoeing, kayaking and bird-watching.

Getting there

If you're **driving**, Mount Desert is easy enough to get to, along Hwy-3 off US-1, though in high summer roads on the island get congested (and the horse-drawn tours don't help). **Public transportation**, however, is minimal. Greyhound buses run to Bar Harbor from Bangor for perhaps a couple of

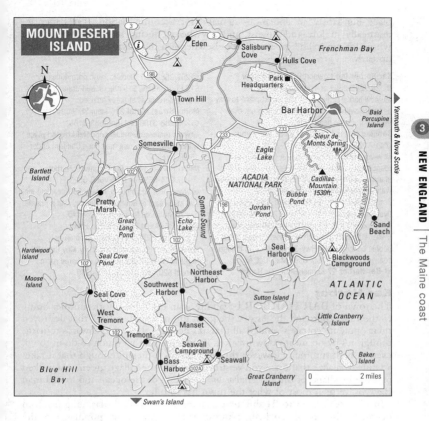

months in summer, starting in mid-June. Concord Trailways has a seasonal shuttle between Bar Harbor and the Bangor airport, with connecting service to Boston's Logan airport – reservations are required (☎207/942-8686 or 1-888/741-8686, ⓦwww.concordtrailways.com/bar_harbor.htm). West Coastal Connections (☎207/546-2823 or 1-800/596-2823) goes as far as Ellsworth and Bar Harbor, as does Downeast Transportation (Mon, Wed & Fri; ☎207/667-5796), which also runs buses across the island from Bar Harbor to Southwest Harbor (Mon & Thurs) and Northeast Harbor (Tues & Wed).

Nearby Hancock City/Bar Harbor Airport (☎207/667-7432) has a limited service run by Colgan Air (☎1-800/272-5488); Bangor International Airport, 45 miles away, is served by Northwest, Delta and Continental. The *Cat* **high-speed catamaran** takes under three hours to link Bar Harbor with Yarmouth, Nova Scotia (June–Sept $55; Oct to mid-June $45; ferries leave Bar Harbor daily 8am, return from Yarmouth 3.45pm, July–Aug 1pm, 3.45pm and 8.45pm). For reservations, contact Bay Ferries (☎207/288-3395 or 1-888/249-7245, ⓦwww.catferry.com) or visit their office at 65 Main St.

Accommodation on Mount Desert Island

Hwy-3 into and out of Bar Harbor (which becomes Main Street on the way south) is lined with budget **motels**, which do little to improve the look of the place but satisfy an enormous demand for accommodation. Rates increase drastically in July and August, and anywhere offering sea views will cost a whole lot more. The quieter places elsewhere on the island tend to be booked up early.

Bar Harbor Inn Newport Drive, Bar Harbor (☏ 207/288-3351 or 1-800/248-3351, ⓦ www.barharborinn.com. The nicest place to stay bar none, with spacious rooms looking out over the bay from the heart of town. ❼

Cadillac Motor Inn 336 Main St, Bar Harbor ☏ 207/288-3831 or 1-888/207-2593, ⓦ www.cadillacmotorinn.com. A quiet inn surrounded by woods near the center of town. Offers standard motel-type rooms and larger apartments with fireplaces and big kitchens. ❸–❺

Emery's Cottages on the Shore Sand Point Rd, five miles north of Bar Harbor ☏ 207/288-3432 or 1-888/240-3432, ⓦ www.emeryscottages.com. Sweet little cottages with kitchenettes on a private pebble beach just off Hwy-3. Weekly stays in high season cost $480–760. Open May–Oct. ❹

HI-Bar Harbor 27 Kennebec St, Bar Harbor ☏ 207/288-5587. Beds in large dormitories for $12 HI members, $15 others. Mid-June to Aug only; reservations strongly advised.

Maine Street Motel 315 Main St, Bar Harbor ☏ 207/288-3188 or 1-800/333-3188, ⓦ www.mainestreetmotel.com. Refurbished place, with its own restaurant next door. Children under 15 stay free. ❺

Moorings Inn Shore Rd, Southwest Harbor ☏ 207/244-5523 or 1-800/596-5523, ⓦ www.mooringsinn.com. Lovely 200-year-old inn, two miles east of Southwest Harbor, with a private beach and boats for rent next door. ❺

YWCA 36 Mount Desert St, Bar Harbor ☏ 207/288-5008. Very central, women-only accommodation, open sporadically May through September – call ahead. Beds in shared rooms start at $20, and go as high as $50.

Bar Harbor

The town of **BAR HARBOR** began life as an exclusive resort, summer home to the Vanderbilts and the Astors; the great fire of October 1947 that destroyed their opulent "cottages" ended all that. It's now firmly geared towards tourists, though it's by no means downmarket. There's not all that much to do in town, even in high summer. However, the ambience is sufficient enough that it takes a while to realize that once you've strolled around the village green, and walked past the headland of the *Bar Harbor Inn* for views of the ocean and Frenchman Bay, you've seen most of what the town has to offer.

In high season up to 21 different **sea trips** set off each day, ranging from deep-sea fishing to cocktail cruises. Among the most popular are the *Friendship V* and *Acadian* **whale-watching** expeditions, departing from Harbor Place, next to the Town Pier (June–Oct at least twice daily; ☏ 207/288-2386, ⓦ www.whalesrus.com), and the two-hour cruises on the impressive **two-masted schooners** *Young America* and *Margaret Todd* from the *Bar Harbor Inn* (daily June–Oct; *America* 10.30am, 2pm & 6.15pm; $22; *Margaret Todd* noon & 3.30pm; $27.50; ☏ 207/288-4585 or 207/288-2373, ⓦ www.downeastwindjammer.com).

One of the town sights in its heyday was the "Indian village," a summer encampment where Native Americans came to sell goods to tourists; it was cleared away in the 1930s to make room for a new ballpark. Now the only signs of the island's first inhabitants are the artifacts at the **Robert Abbe Museum**, which were found at Fernald Point near Southwest Harbor and attributed to a nomadic people who made birch-bark canoes. What became of them is summed up by a classic understatement on a map contrasting the tribal areas of 1600 with the modern reservations: "The native population did not view territorial boundaries as we do today." The museum is a couple of miles south of Bar Harbor – not a particularly pleasant walk – at Sieur de Monts Spring, just off the Park Loop Road (daily: July & Aug 9am–5pm; mid-May to June, Sept & Oct 10am–4pm; $2). A new branch of the Abbe is located downtown at 26

Mount Desert St (June to mid-Oct Sun–Wed 10am–5pm, Thurs–Sat 10am–9pm; mid-Oct to May Thurs–Sun 10am–5pm; $4.50) A free shuttle service travels to both locations in July and August.

Bar Harbor's main **tourist information** office is at the ferry terminal (℡207/288-5103); in summer there's another in the basement of the Municipal Building on Cottage Street that offers many free and comprehensive maps of the area.

Acadia National Park

Not all of **ACADIA NATIONAL PARK** is on Mount Desert Island – there are sections on the Isle au Haut to the west, reached by ferry from Stonington, and on the Schoodic peninsula to the east – but there's all you could want here in terms of mountains and lakes for secluded rambling, and **wildlife** such as seals, beavers, puffins and bald eagles. The two main geographical features are the narrow fjord of **Somes Sound**, which almost splits the island in two, and **Cadillac Mountain**, only 1530ft high but offering tremendous ocean views. The summit, the first place in the United States to see the sun rise each morning, can be reached either by a moderately strenuous climb – more than you'd want to do before breakfast – or by a very leisurely drive, winding up a low-gradient road.

The most enjoyable way to explore is to ride a rented **bicycle** around the fifty miles of gravel-surfaced "**carriage roads**," built by John D. Rockefeller to protest the 1917 vote allowing "infernal combustion engines" onto the island. Two Bar Harbor companies rent mountain bikes between 8am and 6pm, at around $10 for half a day, $16 all day: Bar Harbor Bicycle Shop, at 141 Cottage St on the edge of town (℡207/288-3886, ⓦwww.barharborbike .com), and Acadia Bike & Canoe, across from the post office at 48 Cottage St (℡207/288-9605 or 1-800/526-8615, ⓦwww.acadiabike.com). Southwest Cycle does the same on Main Street, Southwest Harbor (℡207/244-5856). All outlets provide excellent maps. Be sure to carry water, as there are very few refreshment stops inside the park. **Kayaks** can be rented (solo kayaks $32 all day), from mid-May to mid-October from National Park Outdoor Recreation Center, 137 Cottage St in Bar Harbor (℡207/288-0007 or 1-877/386-4124, ⓦwww.acadiakayak.com), which also offers guided sea kayaking trips and downhill bike rides from the top of Mount Cadillac. Another popular tour operator, Coastal Kayaking Tours (ⓦwww.acadiafun.com), has the same location and phone numbers as Acadia Bike.

Open all year, the park has a **visitor center** near the entrance to the Loop Road north of Bar Harbor (daily 8am–5.30pm; ℡207/288-3338), and its headquarters at Eagle Lake (mid-April to Oct Mon–Fri 8am–4.30pm; Nov to mid-April daily 8am–4.30pm; see visitor center for phone number). The entrance fee is $10 per vehicle or $7 per cycle, and is good for a four-day stay. There are two official **campgrounds**: *Blackwoods*, five miles south of Bar Harbor off Route 3 (reserve through Destinet, 9450 Canal Park Drive, San Diego, CA 92121-1256 or on ℡207/288-3338; $14–18 per tentsite), and *Seawall* on Hwy-102A, four miles south of Southwest Harbor (first-come, first-served; $12–18). Both are in woods, near the ocean, and have full facilities in summer; only *Blackwoods* is open in winter, with minimal facilities.

The one and only sizeable beach, five miles south of Bar Harbor, is a stunner: called simply **Sand Beach**, it's a gorgeous strand bounded by twin headlands, with restrooms, a parking lot and a few short hiking trails. The water, sadly, is usually arctic.

Eating, drinking and nightlife on Mount Desert Island

Mount Desert's most memorable **eating** experiences are to be found in the many **lobster pounds** all over the island, but for nightlife as such, Bar Harbor is where the people are. Cottage Street is a much more promising area to look for food and evening atmosphere than the surprisingly subdued waterfront. The Art Deco Criterion cinema at 35 Cottage St (☎207/288-3441) puts on 2pm matinees on rainy days, in addition to its usual showings.

The Alternative Market 16 Mount Desert St ☎207/288-8225. Bag lunches, big sandwiches, soups, smoothies and fresh-squeezed juices.

Beal's Lobster Pier Clark Point Rd, Southwest Harbor ☎207/244-3202. Fresh seafood for under $10, on a rickety wooden pier crammed full of lobsters.

Eat a Pita 326 Main St, Southwest Harbor ☎207/244-4344. A great casual, cozy and affordable spot for delicious, healthy gourmet food (pastas, salads, pita sandwiches, seafood), candlelit tables and friendly service. Lunch and dinner served. Credit cards not accepted.

Galyn's 17 Main St, Bar Harbor ☎207/288-9706. Delicious fish and prime ribs in an unpretentious setting.

Gringo's 30 Rodick St, Bar Harbor ☎207/288-BEAN. A fun, cheap place to get burritos and smoothies.

Jordan Pond House Park Loop Rd ☎207/276-3316. Worthy concession restaurant in the heart of Acadia National Park between Bar Harbor and Northeast Harbor. Serves light meals, ice cream and popovers (light, puffy egg muffins). Afternoon tea served in the beautiful lakeside garden 11.30am–5.30pm.

Lompoc Café & Brewpub 36 Rodick St, Bar Harbor ☎207/288-9392. A healthy Middle Eastern menu for $10–15, with local Thunder Hole Ale and other Atlantic Brewing Company beers on draft and live music every night. Open 11.30am–1am.

Preble Grille 14 Clark Point Rd, Southwest Harbor ☎207/244-3034. Classy and deservedly popular spot with flavorful grilled meats for $15–19 or pastas for about $12.

Rupununi 119 Main St ☎207/288-2886. Late-night pub grub – the burgers are best; the bar stays open until 1am.

Seafood Ketch McMullin Ave, Bass Harbor ☎207/244-7463. Great super-fresh fish and seafood, with views over Bass Harbor. Reservations recommended.

Thirsty Whale 40 Cottage St, Bar Harbor ☎207/288-9335. As rowdy as Bar Harbor gets. Live music every night of the week in season.

Village Green Bakery Café 195 Main St, Bar Harbor ☎207/288-9450. Great pastries, plus a full range of lunches and dinners, including the requisite boiled lobsters. Low prices and good for families.

XYZ Restaurant & Gallery across from Manset Town Dock, Shore Rd, Manset ☎207/244-5221. Ocean views from every table, seafood from $7 and Mexican specialties. Open mid-May to mid-Oct.

Downeast Maine: the coast to Canada

Looking at a map of the United States, you'd never dream that Canada stretches for five hundred miles beyond Maine to the east. In fact, few travelers venture far beyond Acadia National Park, which is one reason why what's known as **Downeast** Maine remains so little touched by change. Another reason is that this is bleak and windswept country, where high cliffs are battered by harsh seas. In summer, though, the weather is no worse than in the rest of Maine, and the coastal drive can be exhilarating. At those points where the road runs next to the sea, the overwhelming power of the ocean is undeniable, sweeping in as it does to create the highest tides in the nation.

A short way northeast of Acadia, a loop road leads from US-1 to the rocky outcrop of **Schoodic Point**, which offers good bird-watching, great views, and a splendid sense of solitude. Tourism is not big business in these parts, but each village has one or two B&Bs and low-priced restaurants. The fishing harbor at **JONESPORT** on Hwy-187, which deserves a detour, holds *Tootsies Bed and Breakfast* (☎207/497-5414; ❸). A glorious high-arched iron bridge leads to the nature reserve of **Beal's Island**. **MACHIAS**, back on US-1, is even more picturesque, with a little waterfall right in the middle, and was the unlikely scene of the first naval battle of the Revolutionary War, in 1775. The townsfolk commandeered the British schooner *Margaretta* and proceeded to terrorize all passing British shipping, an attack they planned in the still-standing gambrel-roofed **Burnham Tavern**. For good-value meals, there's *Helen's Restaurant*, 28 E Main St/Rte-1 (℡207/255-8423), part of the *Machias Motor Inn* (℡207/255-4861; ❸), which has sun decks and superb views.

Continuing east, and abandoning US-1 for Hwy-189, you come to the prominently striped **lighthouse** at **West Quoddy Head**, the easternmost point of the US, where an international bridge crosses to Campobello Island in Canada. The nearby settlement of **Bailey's Mistake** is named for a sea captain who beached his lumber vessel in thick fog in 1830, and chose to settle here with his crew, building homes with their erstwhile cargo, rather than face the wrath of the ship's owners back in Boston.

The border between the United States and Canada weaves through the center of **Passamaquoddy Bay**; the towns to either side get on so well that they refused to fight against each other in the War of 1812, and promote themselves jointly to tourists as the **Quoddy Loop** (information on ℡207/454-2597, ⓦ www.quoddyloop.com). It's perfectly feasible to take a "two-nation vacation," but each passage through customs and immigration between **CALAIS** (pronounced *callous*) in the States and **St Stephen** in Canada does take a little while – and be aware, though, that the towns are in different time zones. In town, the *Wickachee*, on Main Street (℡207/454-3400), serves big plates of seafood and steak. West Coastal Connections (℡207/546-2823 or 1-800/596-2823) runs a once-daily van from Calais to Ellsworth and Bar Harbor.

Inland Maine

The vast expanses of the **Maine interior**, stretching up into the cold far north, consist mostly of evergreen forests of pine, spruce and fir, interspersed with the white birches and maples responsible for the spectacular fall colors. Only in the remote north is much of it genuine wilderness, however; elsewhere, what you see is more likely to be woodlands cultivated by the timber companies.

Distances here are large. Once you get away from the two largest cities nearer the sea – **Augusta**, the state capital, and **Bangor** – it's roughly two hundred miles by road to the northern border at **Fort Kent**, while to drive between the two most likely inland bases, **Greenville** and **Rangeley** (where exiled psychologist Wilhelm Reich lived and is buried), takes three hours or more. Driving (there's no public transportation) through this mountainous scenery can be a great pleasure, but you do need to know where you're going. There are few places to stay, and beyond Bangor many roads are tolled access routes belonging to the lumber companies: gravel-surfaced, vulnerable to bad weather, and in any case often not heading anywhere in particular.

This landscape has evolved in a very unusual way. Many waterfront communities grew up without roads to serve them, in the days when the timber harvest was floated downriver to the sea; other more recent settlements have only ever been accessible by seaplane. Now that mighty trucks carry the tree-trunks instead, roads are finally being pushed through, amid complaints that they are ruining the feel of the place.

If you have the time, this is great territory in which to **hike** – the **Appalachian Trail** starts its 2000-mile course down to Georgia at the top of Mount Katahdin – or **raft** on the **Allagash Wilderness Waterway**. Especially around **Baxter State Park**, the forests are home to deer, beaver, a few bears, some recently introduced caribou – and plenty of **moose**. These endearingly gawky creatures (they look like badly drawn horses, and are virtually blind), tend to be seen at early morning or dusk; in spring they come to lick the winter's salt off the roads, while in summer you may spot them feeding in shallow water. They do, however, cause major havoc on the roads, particularly at night, and each year significant numbers of drivers (and moose) are killed in collisions.

Augusta

The capital of Maine since 1832, **AUGUSTA** is much quieter and less visited now than it was a hundred years ago. The lumber industry here really took off after the technique of making paper from wood was rediscovered in 1844, and Augusta also had a lucrative sideline – each winter hundreds of thousands of tons of **ice**, cut from the Kennebec River, were shipped out, as far south as the Caribbean, in a trade now all but forgotten by history. There are informative displays on Maine's landscape and industrial past at the lively **Maine State Museum**, a short way south of the capitol on State Street (Mon–Fri 9am–5pm, Sat 10am–4pm, Sun 1–4pm; free).

If you plan to stay in Augusta, the best-value **accommodation** is the *Best Inn* (T207/622-3776 or 1-800/237-8466, W www.bestinn.com; ❸), at 65 Whitten Road at the Maine Turnpike's Augusta-Winthrop exit. For **food**, the lobster rolls at *Burnsie's Homestyle Sandwiches* (T207/622-6425), on Hichborn Street next to the capitol, are favorites with the politicians, while *Curly's*, 750 Main St (T207/933-2745), does good, moderately priced seafood.

Bangor

In its prime, **BANGOR**, 120 miles northeast of Portland, was the undisputed "Lumber Capital of the World." Every winter its raucous population of "River Tigers" went upstream to brand the felled logs, which they then maneuvered down the Penobscot as the thaw came in April, reaching Bangor in time to carouse the summer away in the grog shops of Peppermint Row. Bangor exported ice to the West Indies – and got rum in return. Those days were coming to an end when, in October 1882, Oscar Wilde addressed a large crowd at the new Opera House and spoke diplomatically of "such advancement . . . in so small a city."

Bangor today is not a place to spend much time, although its plentiful motels and the big Bangor Mall on Hogan Road north of town make it a good last stop before the interior. Its twin claims to fame are that it's the unlikely home of Stephen King, the horror fiction writer (BookMarc's at 78 Harlow St stocks King paraphernalia), and that it possesses what, at 31ft, may well be the largest statue of **Paul Bunyan** in the world, excepting perhaps one or two in Minnesota – though it is easy to miss on the way into town.

From mid-May until the end of July there's **harness racing** at Bass Park on Main Street (T207/947-6744), just behind the statue; admission is $1 but the potential to lose money is unlimited. The same venue hosts the **Bangor State Fair**, in the last week of July and the first in August. A few miles north of Bangor, the Maine Center for the Arts (T207/581-1755), at the University of Maine in **Orono**, runs a series of big-name concerts each summer. Orono is named after the eighteenth-century Chief Joseph Orono; a small island nearby is now a rather sad reservation running summer bingo sessions.

Practicalities

Bangor is the last sizeable town along I-95, before it finally veers from the coast and heads up the Penobscot towards Canada. It's also the end of the line for Greyhound, the three daily services from Boston and Portland terminating at 158 Main St.

Accommodation possibilities include the *Main Street Inn*, opposite Paul Bunyan at 480 Main St (℡207/942-5282; ❸), and the *Phenix Inn*, right downtown at 20 Broad St on West Market Square (℡207/947-0411, ⓦwww.maineguide.com/bangor/phenixinn.com; ❹). The *Holiday Inn* at 500 Main St (℡207/947-8651 or 1-800/799-8651; ❺) houses Bangor's liveliest dance venue, the *Bounty Tavern*. For the best breakfasts in Bangor, try *Bagel Central*, 33 Central St (℡207/947-1654), the state's only kosher deli, or load up on subs and salads at Sweet's Market (℡207/947-5217), 26 Main St; other options include a handful of Indian and Pakistani places, and the massive Mexican *Pepino's* at 570 Stillwater Ave (℡207/947-1233). *Margarita's*, 15 Mill St in Orono (℡207/866-4863), is another lively, if unimaginatively named, Mexican restaurant.

Baxter State Park and the far north

Driving through northern Maine can feel as though you're trespassing on the private fiefdoms of the logging companies; only **Baxter State Park** is public land. However, you're pretty much free to hike, camp and explore anywhere you like, so long as you let people know what you're doing. The scenery is pretty much the same everywhere, although to experience what Thoreau described in his *Maine Woods*, you'll need to leave your car at some point and set off into the backwoods.

Five miles north of Brownsville Junction on Hwy-11, an inconspicuous left turn leads to the **Katahdin Iron Works** at Silver Lake (summer daily 9am–5pm), built in 1843. It's remarkable how little remains of what one hundred years ago was a thriving industrial community: one solitary brick oven and the tower of the blast furnace, stark and forlorn at the end of a few miles of gravel track. In good summer weather it's possible to continue along the track across the hills to Greenville.

Further north, **MILLINOCKET** is a genuine company town, built on a wilderness site by the Great Northern Paper Company in 1899–1900 as the "magic city of the North." Public curiosity was so great that three hundred people came on a special train from Bangor to see what was happening. Since then it has produced massive quantities of newsprint, but in 1990 the company was taken over by the Georgia Pacific Corporation, and although the townspeople made a killing from cashing in their stocks, their homes are almost unsaleable, and their jobs may well not last.

Next to **Millinocket Lake**, ten miles northwest, the splendidly ramshackle old *Big Moose Inn* (Box 98, Millinocket, ME 04462; ℡207/723-8391, ⓦwww.bigmoosecabins.com) with adjacent campground ($10 per person) makes a great place to stay; it also has some four-person cabins ($34–38). Unicorn Expeditions (℡207/725-2255 or 1-800/864-2676) uses the inn as a base for day **rafting** and **kayaking** expeditions, and there are **dogsled races** in February and March, as well as seaplane tours. A more standard place to stay is the clean *Katahdin Inn*, 740 Central St/Hwy-11 (℡207/723-4555 or 1-877/902-4555, ⓦwww.katahdininn.com; ❸), which provides a free continental breakfast.

Approaching the southern end of **Baxter State Park** itself, on a clear day the 5268ft peak of **Mount Katahdin** is visible from afar. The park was the single-handed creation of former Maine Governor Percival P. Baxter, who, having failed to persuade the state to buy Katahdin and the land around it, bought it himself between the 1930s and 1960s and deeded it bit by bit to the state on condition that it remain "forever wild."

The area's **chamber of commerce** resides in Millinocket at 1029 Central St (℡207/723-4443, Ⓦwww.katahdinmaine.com); the **Baxter State Park Authority** is at 64 Balsam Drive (℡207/723-5140).

North to Canada

The northernmost tip of Maine is taken up by Aroostook County, which covers an area larger than several individual states. Although its main activity is the large-scale cultivation of potatoes, it is also the location of the **Allagash Wilderness Waterway**; this is where most of the **whitewater rafting** companies mentioned in this section actually carry out their expeditions.

Britain and the United States all but went to war over Aroostook in 1839; at **Fort Kent**, the northern terminus of US-1 (which runs all the way from Key West, Florida), the main sight is the solid cedar **Fort Kent Blockhouse**, built to defend American integrity and looking like a throwback to early pioneer days. *Doris' Café* (℡207/834-6262), at Fort Kent Mills on Hwy-161, just off Hwy-11 toward Eagle Lake, serves big breakfasts.

Greenville

GREENVILLE, at the southern end of Moosehead Lake, is another nineteenth-century lumber town that now makes its living primarily from tourism. It's not exceptionally pretty or very large, but it is well positioned for exploring the Maine woods. In town, the main attraction is the restored **steamboat** *Katahdin*, which tours the lake and also serves as the (nonprofit) Moosehead Marine Museum (cruises at 12.15pm Tues, Thurs, Sat & Sun July–Aug; Sat & Sun only in June & Sept; $20–36).

The **Chamber of Commerce** on Main Street near the T-junction at the lake (summer daily 10am–5pm; rest of year Thurs–Tues 10am–4pm; ℡207/695-2702, Ⓦwww.mooseheadarea.com) has details on **accommodation**, including the *Kineo View Motor Lodge* (℡207/695-4470 or 1-800/659-VIEW, Ⓦwww.kineoview.com; ❸), overlooking the lake from deep in the woods on the hill three miles above town; the *Chalet Moosehead*, Birch Street (℡207/695-2950 or 1-800/290-3645, Ⓦwww.mooseheadlodging.com; ❸/❹), the only motel right on the lake; and the antiques-filled *Greenville Inn* on Norris Street (℡207/695-2206 or 1-888/695-6000, Ⓦwww.greenvilleinn.com; ❺). Among local **rafting** companies charging $90–110 for a day in the water is Wilderness Expeditions, The Birches, PO Box 41GC, North Rockwood, ME 04478 (℡207/534-2242 or 1-800/825-WILD). Greenville is also the largest **seaplane** base in New England; contact Currier's Flying Service (℡207/695-2778) or Folsom's (℡207/695-2821).

Rangeley

RANGELEY is only just in Maine, a little way east of New Hampshire and an even shorter distance south of the border with Québec. Furthermore, as the café-bar *Doc Grant's* (℡207/864-3449) on Main Street makes a great show of telling you, it's equidistant (at 3107.5 miles) from the North Pole and the Equator. That doesn't mean it's on the main road to anywhere, although if you're avoiding the coast altogether you can get here direct from the northern

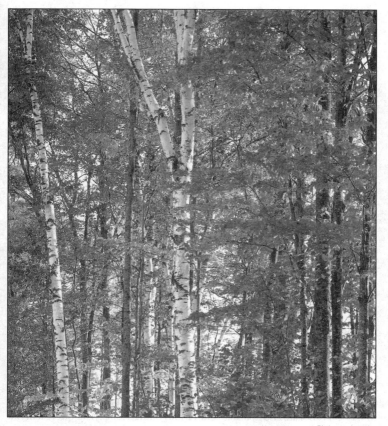

△ Birches and maples

side of the White Mountains (see p.258). It has always been a resort, served in 1900 by two train lines and several steamships (though now you have to get here on your own), with the main attraction then being the fishing in the spectacularly named Mooselookmeguntic Lake.

This small and very cozy one-street town, nestling amid a complex system of lakes and waterways, serves as base for summer explorations, and in winter as the nearest town to the **ski** area at **Saddleback Mountain**. Rangeley also has one unlikely tourist attraction, about halfway along the north side of Rangeley Lake, a mile up a side track off Route 16. The remote **Wilhelm Reich Museum** at **Orgonon** (PO Box 687, Rangeley, ME 04970; July & Aug Wed–Sun 1–5pm; Sept Sun 1–5pm; $4) is where Wilhelm Reich eventually made his American home after fleeing Germany in 1933. An associate of Freud in Vienna, who wrote the acclaimed *Mass Psychology of Fascism*, Reich is best remembered for developing the orgone energy accumulator, which he claimed could create rain and dissipate nuclear radiation. Skeptical authorities focused on the rather unspecific way in which it was said to collect and harness human sexual energy. In a tragic end to his career, Reich was imprisoned after a wayward student broke an injunction forbidding the transportation of his accumulators across state lines, and he died in the federal penitentiary in Lewisberg, Pennsylvania, in November 1957. He is buried here, amid the neat lawns and darting hummingbirds, and his house remains a center for the study of his work.

Practicalities

The *Rangeley Inn* on Main Street (℡207/864-3341 or 1-800/MOMENTS, Ⓦwww.rangeleyinn.com; ❺) stands between Rangeley Lake and the smaller bird sanctuary of Haley Pond, so you can stay right in town and have a room that backs onto a scene of utter tranquility; there's also a gorgeous old wooden dining room. *Northwoods B&B* on Main Street (℡207/864-2440 or 1-800/295-4968; ❺) is a good second choice. Otherwise, the Chamber of Commerce (see below), can provide lists of private home/condo rentals and remote campsites around the lake – which really are remote, several of them inaccessible by road. For **food**, try the *People's Choice* on Rte-4 (℡207/864-5220), where the portions are huge and the desserts divine.

Twenty miles north of Rangeley, the peaceful *Grant's Kennebago Camps* beside Kennebago Lake (PO Box 786, Rangeley, ME 04970; ℡207/864-3608) arranges fishing, canoeing and windsurfing, with accommodation in comfortable cabins, including all meals, costing around $90 per person per day; there are lower weekly rates. A more accessible campground is *Cathedral Pines* (℡207/246-3491), just north of **Stratton** on Eustis Road. At its entrance stands a memorial to Benedict Arnold's expedition to Québec in 1775, which passed this way, and to Colonel Timothy Bigelow, who climbed what is now Mount Bigelow in a –"vain endeavor to see the city of Québec."

Rangeley Lakes' **Chamber of Commerce**, down by Lakeside Park (℡207/864-5364 or 1-800/MT-LAKES, Ⓦwww.rangeleymaine.com), has details of various activities, including snowmobiling and dawn moose-watching **canoeing** expeditions (℡207/864-5136; $38). One really fun thing to do is to take a **seaplane** trip with the Mountain Air Service (℡207/864-5307) – a fifteen-minute tour, flying low over vast forests and tiny lakes, costing $25 per person. Boat cruises are also available, and various outfits along Main Street rent out canoes and mountain bikes.

Sugarloaf USA and Kingfield

The road east of Rangeley cuts through prime moose-watching territory – locals call Hwy-16 E "Moose Alley." After about fifty miles, in the Carrabassett Valley, looms the huge mountain of the **SUGARLOAF USA** ski resort (℡1-800/THE-LOAF, Ⓦwww.sugarloaf.com). A brilliant place for skiers of all abilities, this condo-studded center would be a more popular destination if it wasn't for the fact that the nearest airport is a two-hour drive away in Portland. In summer, one of the most likely places to spot a gangling **moose** is behind the check-in building on the resort's approach road. Other summer activities include guided **mountain bike tours** with the Sugarloaf Outdoor Center (℡207/237-6830).

The best base for Sugarloaf is fifteen miles south in the tiny town of **KINGFIELD**. The gorgeous *Inn on Winter's Hill*, 33 Winter Hill St (℡207/265-5421 or 1-800/233-WNTR, Ⓦwww.wintershill.com; ❹), is a lovingly restored Georgian Revival house with big rooms, an outdoor pool, hot tub, tennis court and the excellent *Julia's* dining room (winter only).

Down on the main street, the big white *Kingfield Herbert Hotel* (☎207/265-2000, Ⓦwww.mainemountaininn.com; ❹) has less attractive but functional rooms. *Anni's Café*, next to the gas station, is an inexpensive place to **eat**. Kingfield was the birthplace of twins Francis and Freelan Stanley, who invented, among other things, a steam-powered car and the dry plate photographic process (which they sold to Kodak). The **Stanley Museum** on School Street (May–Oct Tues–Sun 1–4pm; $2) celebrates their story. Part of the main room is given over to their sister, Chansonetta, a remarkable photographer whose studies of c.1900 rural and urban workers have been widely published.

CHAPTER 4 # Highlights

* **Wrigley Field, Chicago, IL** Soak in the old-world ambience of this ivy-covered ballpark with cold beer and a hot dog. See p.360

* **Chicago architecture, IL** Superb examples of modern architecture make up the city's distinctive skyline. See p.353

* **Rock and Roll Hall of Fame, Cleveland, OH** From rockabilly to Motown, punk to hip hop – it's all here inside this striking museum. See p.304

* **Cedar Point Amusement Park, Sandusky, OH** More stomach-churning rides than you're likely to find anywhere else in the US. See p.308

* **The Henry Ford Museum, Detroit, MI** Home to such oddities as the car JFK was riding in when he was shot. See p.327

* **Ann Arbor, MI** A plethora of bookshops, sidewalk cafés and cultural activities make this the quintessential college town. See p.329

* **Mall of America, Bloomington, MN** The mall you'll never have to leave: hundreds of stores, an amusement park, plus bars and nightclubs. See p.390

The Great Lakes

S wept by tumultuous storms and traversed by fleets of oceangoing tankers, the interconnected **Great Lakes** form the largest body of fresh water in the world; Lake Superior alone is more than three hundred miles from east to west. Left untouched, the shores of these inland seas can rival any coastline: Superior and the northern reaches of Lake Michigan offer stunning rocky peninsulas, craggy cliffs, tree-covered islands, mammoth dunes and deserted beaches. For lengthy stretches along Lake Erie, and the bottom lips of lakes Michigan and Huron, however, sluggish waters lap against large cities and the unused wharves of decaying ports.

To varying degrees, all the states that line the American side of the lakes – **OHIO**, **MICHIGAN**, **INDIANA**, **ILLINOIS**, **WISCONSIN** and **MINNESOTA** – share this mixture of natural beauty and aging industry. Cities such as Chicago and Detroit, with all their good and bad points – and **Chicago** in particular, with its magnificent architecture, museums, music and restaurants, is an unmissable destination – should not be seen as characterizing the entire region. Within the first hundred miles or so of the lakeshores, especially in Wisconsin and Minnesota, tens of thousands of smaller lakes and tumbling streams are scattered through a luxuriant rural wilderness; beyond that, you are soon in the heart of the Corn Belt, where you can drive for hours and encounter nothing more than a succession of crossroads communities, grain silos and giant barns. Garrison Keillor's wry stories about the fictional backwater town of Lake Wobegon (where "all the women are strong and all the men are beautiful"), set in Minnesota, carry more than a ring of truth.

The first foreigner to reach the Great Lakes, the French explorer Champlain in 1603, found the region inhabited mostly by tribes of Huron, Iroquois and Algonquin. France soon established a network of military forts, Jesuit missions and fur-trading posts – which entailed treating the native people as allies rather than subjects. Territorial disputes with their colonial rivals, however, culminated in the **French and Indian War** with Britain from 1754 to 1761. The victorious British felt under no constraints to deal equitably with the Native Americans, and things grew worse with large-scale American settlement after independence. The **Black Hawk War** of 1832 put a bloody end to traditional life.

Settlers from the east were followed to Wisconsin and Minnesota by waves of **Scandinavians** and **Germans**, while the lower halves of Illinois and Indiana attracted **Southerners**, who attempted to maintain slavery and resisted Union conscription during the Civil War. These areas often still have more in common with neighboring Kentucky and Tennessee than with the industrial cities of their own states.

The impetus given to **industry** by the Civil War was encouraged by abundant supplies of ores and fuel and efficient transportation by water and rail. As lakeshore cities like Chicago, Detroit and Cleveland grew, their populations swelled with hundreds of thousands of poor **blacks** who migrated from the Deep South in search of jobs. Many worked in munitions during the two world wars. But a lack of planning, inadequate housing and mass layoffs at times of low demand bred conditions that led to the riots of the late 1960s and current inner-city deprivation. Depression in the 1970s ravaged the economy – especially the **automobile** industry, on which so much else depended – and brought the unwanted title of "**Rust Belt**." Since then, urban centers have battled back, with **Cleveland**, Ohio, perhaps the most dramatic example of a turnaround in fortunes.

During the summer, breezes coming off the Great Lakes keep the **temperature** down to a comfortable average of 70°F, though heat waves can push temperatures over 100°F. Even in spring and fall, freezing occurs in the northern reaches of the region, where winter readings of -50°F are not uncommon and parts of the lakes are frozen solid.

Public transportation serves all the major towns. **Amtrak**'s national hub is in Chicago and its routes spread across the entire region; **Greyhound** operates reasonably frequent services to nearly all urban centers. The best way to appreciate the sculptured shorelines of the lakes themselves, however, is to travel the lonely minor roads by **car**. In the northwest, **cycling** alongside Superior and the northern parts of Lake Michigan can be quite enjoyable.

Ohio

OHIO, the farthest east of the Great Lakes states, lies to the south of shallow Lake Erie. This is one of the nation's most industrialized regions, but the industry is largely concentrated in the east, near the Ohio River. To the south the landscape becomes less populated and more forested. Ohio also has the world's largest **Amish** population. They farm in the northeast and west into mid-Indiana, and are much less of a tourist attraction than the highly publicized Pennsylvania Dutch (see p.167).

Enigmatic traces of Ohio's earliest inhabitants can be seen at the **Great Serpent Mound**, a grassy state park sixty miles east of Cincinnati, where a cleared hilltop high above a river was reshaped to represent a giant snake swallowing an egg, possibly by the Adena Indians around 800 BC. When the French claimed the area in 1699, it was inhabited by the **Iroquois**, in whose language Ohio means "something great." In the eighteenth century, its prime position between Lake Erie and the Ohio River made it the subject of fierce contention between the French and British. Once the British had acquired control of most of the French land east of the Mississippi, settlers from New England began to establish communities along both the Ohio River and the Iroquois War Trail paths on the shores of the lake.

During the Civil War, Ohio was at the forefront of the struggle, producing two great Union generals, Ulysses Grant and William Sherman, and sending more than twice its quota of volunteers to fight for the North. Its progress thereafter has followed the classic "Rust Belt" pattern: rapid industrialization, aided by its natural resources and crucial location, which during the 1970s foundered alarmingly and has only recently shown any signs of resurgence.

Although the state is dominated by its triumvirate of "C"s (**Cleveland**, **Columbus** and **Cincinnati**), its most visited destinations are the **Lake Erie Islands**, which have benefited from the recent cleanup of the polluted lake and now attract thousands of partying mainlanders. Cincinnati and Cleveland, the latter hit especially hard by the recession, have both undergone major face-lifts and are surprisingly attractive, as is the comparatively unassuming state capital of Columbus.

Getting around Ohio

Amtrak **trains** between New York or Washington and Chicago stop at either Cincinnati or Cleveland and Toledo. Ohio is well served by Greyhound **buses**, and there are major **airports** at Cleveland and Cincinnati.

Cleveland and around

Today, the great industrial port of **CLEVELAND** – for so long the butt of jokes after the heavily polluted Cuyahoga River caught fire in the early 1970s – is no longer the "Mistake on the Lake." Although the path back from acute recession (another 1970s legacy) is by no means complete on a citywide basis, the downtown area is now a hub of energy. Cleveland boasts a sensitive and fond restoration of the Lake Erie/Cuyahoga River waterfront, a superb constellation of museums, glittering city center malls and new downtown superstadiums. Add to that the recent arrival of several major corporate headquarters and classy hotels – and, of course, the **Rock and Roll Hall of Fame** – and there's an unmistakeable buzz about the place.

Founded in 1796, Cleveland profited greatly, thirty years later, from the opening of the **Ohio Canal** between the Ohio River and Lake Erie. During the city's heyday, which began with the Civil War and lasted until the 1920s, its vast iron and coal supplies made it one of the most important **steel** and **shipbuilding centers** in the world. **John D. Rockefeller** made his billions here, as did the many others whose now-decrepit old mansions line "Millionaires' Row." This has become a no-go area, along with several other bleak and faceless danger spots. Despite the investment of billions of dollars, the scars of deprivation are still visible if you wander too far off the tourist path.

South and west of the city are several spots of interest, including the quaint lakeshore community of **Vermilion**, the tiny liberal college sanctuary of **Oberlin**, and the charming hamlet of **Peninsula**.

Arrival, information and getting around

Cleveland Hopkins International Airport (℡216/265-6030) is ten miles southwest of downtown. The twenty-minute **taxi** ride into town costs around $20, but the Regional Transit Authority (RTA; ℡216/621-9500, Ⓦwww .gcrta.org) **train** is only $1.50 and takes just ten minutes longer. Greyhound arrives at 1465 Chester Ave, at the back of Playhouse Square, and the Amtrak station is on the lakefront at 200 Cleveland Memorial Shoreway NE.

Cleveland is concentrated in different pockets and, as the potentially dangerous areas are scattered pretty wide (it is not safe, for example, to stray into the
streets around the three-block-deep Cleveland Clinic, very close to the much-
frequented University Circle), you're safest in a **car**. The RTA runs an efficient
bus service ($1.25 or $1.50 for express services; 50¢ within downtown) and a
small Rapid train line ($1.50) until about 12.30am. A **light rail** system – the
Waterfront Line – connects Terminal Tower, the Flats, the Rock and Roll Hall
of Fame and other downtown sights; it costs $1.50 and runs every fifteen min-
utes between 7am and midnight. **City tours**, run by Trolley Tours of
Cleveland, leave from the Powerhouse on the west bank of the Flats (May–Oct
daily; Nov–April Fri & Sat; $9 for 1hr, $14 for 2hr, reservations required;
☏216/771-4484 or 1-800/848-0173, � www.lollytrolley.com).

Maps and **information** can be had in advance from the Cleveland **CVB**
(Mon–Fri 9am–9pm; ☏1-800/321-1004, � www.travelcleveland.com). The
handiest **visitor centers** are in the lobby of the Terminal Tower in Public
Square (summer daily 10am–5pm; rest of year Mon–Fri 9.30am–4.30pm, Sat
& Sun 11am–4pm; ☏216/621-7981) and on the east bank of the Flats next to
Hooter's (summer daily 11am–7pm; winter daily 11am–4pm; ☏216/621-2218).

Accommodation

Travelers without cars in Cleveland are largely limited to the somewhat
expensive downtown **hotels**. Most now offer packages that include admission
to the Rock and Roll Hall of Fame or other attractions. **B&Bs** can be
arranged through Private Lodgings, Box 18590, Cleveland, OH 44118
(☏216/321-3213).

Baymont Inn 4222 W 150th St ☏216/251-8500,
� www.baymontinns.com. Standard motel rooms;
easy downtown access via train and only two
miles to the airport. ❹

Comfort Inn Downtown 1800 Euclid Ave
☏216/861-0001, � www.comfortinn.com. The
standard *Comfort Inn* rooms are on the edge of
downtown, a little far to walk to bars and restaurants. ❺

Days Inn – Lakewood 12019 Lake Ave
☏216/226-4800, � www.daysinn.com. The plain
but adequate rooms are in the western suburb of
Lakewood five miles from downtown, though
accessible by bus #55CX. ❹

Embassy Suites Hotel 1701 E 12th St
☏216/523-8000, � www.es-cleveland.com.
These quality downtown rooms are near Playhouse
Square. ❼

Glidden House 1901 Ford Drive ☏216/231-
8900, � www.gliddenhouse.com. Your bed and
large continental breakfast are in a huge Gothic
mansion – it has 60 rooms – very handy for
University Circle. ❼

Holiday Inn – Lakeside 1111 Lakeside Ave
☏216/241-5100, � www.holiday-inn.com. This
functional, unexciting downtown hotel is near the
Rock and Roll Hall of Fame. ❻

Marriott Key Center 127 Public Square
☏216/696-9200, � www.marriotthotels.com.
Probably the best value of the downtown upscale
hotels, this venue is clean, bright and close to the
action. ❻

Omni International Hotel 2065 E 96th St
☏216/707-4300, 1-800/THE OMNI, � www
.omnihotels.com. This clean, luxury hotel in
University Circle is handy for Little Italy and
Coventry Village. Rooms are over $200 during the
week – ask about weekend discounts. ❼

Red Roof Inn 6020 Quarry Lane, Independence
☏216/447-0030, � www.redroof.com. Though
eleven miles south from downtown, it is served by
public transportation. ❸–❹

Wyndham Hotel 1260 Euclid Ave ☏216/615-7500,
� www.wyndham.com/playhousesquare/. The best
luxury option in the downtown theater district,
Playhouse Square. ❻

The City

The main streets in Cleveland lead to the stately nineteenth-century Beaux Arts
Public Square, at the very center of downtown, dominated by the landmark

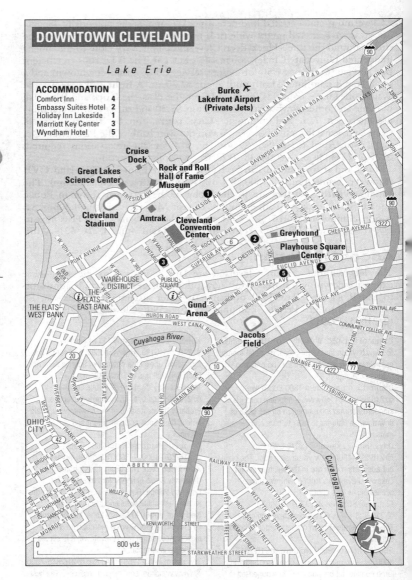

DOWNTOWN CLEVELAND

Lake Erie

ACCOMMODATION

Comfort Inn	4
Embassy Suites Hotel	2
Holiday Inn Lakeside	1
Marriott Key Center	3
Wyndham Hotel	5

Burke Lakefront Airport (Private Jets)

Cruise Dock

Great Lakes Science Center

Rock and Roll Hall of Fame Museum

Cleveland Stadium

Amtrak

Cleveland Convention Center

Greyhound

Playhouse Square Center

WAREHOUSE DISTRICT

PUBLIC SQUARE

THE FLATS EAST BANK

THE FLATS WEST BANK

Gund Arena

Jacobs Field

Cuyahoga River

OHIO CITY

Cuyahoga River

0   800 yds

N

Terminal Tower in its southwestern corner. **Ontario Street**, which runs north–south through the Square, divides the city into east and west. Cleveland's most interesting areas are at two opposite ends of the spectrum: the industrial romance of the **Flats** in the northwest, and the cultural institutions of **University Circle**, east of the river.

Downtown and around

Downtown Cleveland is once again a bustling place, and its recent redevelopment has seen the emergence of several distinct subsections. In its traditional heart, among the banks and corporate headquarters, stand glamorous shopping malls. One, the **Avenue at Tower City** in the Terminal Tower, has an **observation deck** on the 42nd floor (summer Sat & Sun 11am–4.30pm; rest of year Sat & Sun 11am–3.30pm; $2, tickets from the visitor center in the lobby). Another, the **Arcade**, is a skylit hall built in 1890. The **Playhouse Square Center** (☏216/241-6000, ⓦ www.playhousesquare.com), twelve blocks away at 1501 Euclid Ave, is an impressive complex of four renovated old theaters. Take a look at the gorgeous lobby of the small Ohio Theatre, with its starlit-sky ceiling.

Just to the southwest, in what were once mostly vacant lots, is the **Gateway District**. New restaurants and bars surround **Jacobs Field** stadium (☏216/420-4200, ⓦ www.indians.com) – home of the Indians baseball team – and the equally modern multipurpose **Gund Arena** (☏216/420-2000, ⓦ www.gundarena.com), which hosts the Cavaliers basketball team and major sporting and entertainment events.

West of the Gund is the **riverfront**, where one of the nation's busiest waterways shares space with excellent bars, clubs and restaurants strung out along a boardwalk. On both banks of the Cuyahoga River, the **Flats**, long known for its nightlife, relishes its industrial setting. Magnificent grimy old buildings, warehouses and slag heaps, set in among fourteen **bridges**, appear powerful and romantic rather than depressing, a proud testimony to Cleveland's manufacturing history.

A short but steep walk uphill leads to the **Warehouse District**, a nicely developing stretch of nineteenth-century commercial buildings between West Third and West Tenth streets, given over to shops, galleries, cafés and trendy new restaurants. North, on the other side of the busy Cleveland Memorial Shoreway (Hwy-2), the waters of Lake Erie lap gently into **North Coast Harbor**, the new showpiece of Midwest regeneration. To see the city from the water, try a two-hour cruise on the *Goodtime III* ($12.50; ☏216/861-5110) from the dock at East Ninth Street Pier, just beyond the I.M. Pei-designed **Rock and Roll Hall of Fame** (see box, overleaf). Next door to the Rock Hall – as Clevelanders refer to it – is the giant **Great Lakes Science Center** (daily 9.30am–5.30pm; OMNIMAX open until 9pm with shows on the hour; $7.75 for museum, $7.75 OMNIMAX theater, $10.95 combo ticket; ☏216/694-2000, ⓦ www.greatscience.com). Its white paneling and glass frontage perfectly complement its neighbor. There are no standout displays, though the cumulative effect of the 350 interactive exhibits (many on meteorological and aquatic themes) makes this a very enjoyable place to spend a few hours. Across the road, the futuristic, 72,000-seat **Cleveland Stadium** is the new home of the reincarnated Browns pro football team (☏440/891-5000, ⓦ www.clevelandbrowns .com). After living in NFL limbo for three years, Cleveland football fans joyously welcomed a new franchise for the 1999 season.

To the west of the river, **Ohio City** is one of Cleveland's hipper neighborhoods, with junk stores, Victorian clapboard houses and the busy **West Side Market** at Lorain Avenue and West 25th Street, selling all manner of ethnic foods (Mon & Wed 7am–4pm, Fri & Sat 7am–6pm). It's easily spotted by its redbrick Victorian clock tower.

Out from downtown

Five miles east of downtown, **University Circle** is a cluster of more than seventy cultural and medical institutions, and is also home to several major performing arts companies (see p.306). The eclectic **Museum of Art**, fronted

The Rock and Roll Hall of Fame

Cleveland, not the most obvious candidate, convincingly won a hotly contested bid to host the **Rock and Roll Hall of Fame** largely because **Alan Freed**, a local disc jockey, popularized the phrase "rock and roll" here back in 1951. Since then, Cleveland has hardly produced a roll call of rock icons – Joe Walsh, Pere Ubu, Nine Inch Nails and Bone Thugs 'N' Harmony are about the biggest names – but the city embraced the idea of the museum with enthusiasm. Few can now argue that it was not the correct choice. However, cynics are quick to snipe that Cleveland won out over Memphis, New York and other cities with a richer musical heritage because, quite simply, it bagged up the most cash – a financial package that some put as high as $65 million.

The idea for a definitive rock museum was first floated in 1983, with the establishment of the **Rock Hall of Fame Foundation** to honor all those who have made "an exceptional contribution to modern music." The inductees are selected annually by an international panel of rock "experts," but only those performers who have released a record 25 years prior to their nomination are eligible.

The museum's septuagenarian architect – **I.M. Pei** – wanted the building "to echo the energy of rock and roll." One of Pei's trademark tinted-glass pyramids (a smaller version of the one he did at the Louvre), a white concrete, steel and glass structure, strikes a bold pose on the shore of Lake Erie. A tall main tower supports sweeping geometric extensions and dramatic cantilevered offshoots in cylindrical, triangular and rectangular shapes, all fronted by the pyramid (or tent, as Pei likes to call it), which looks spectacular when lit up at night. The base of the pyramid extends into an impressive entrance plaza shaped like a turntable, complete with a stylus arm attachment. It might all look good, but Pei's lavish design means that most exhibits must be placed in the basement.

The museum is much more than an array of mementos and artifacts. Right from the start – the excellent twelve-minute films *Mystery Train* and *Kick Out the Jams* – the emphasis is on the contextualization of rock. The exhibits chart the art form's evolution and progress, acknowledging influences ranging from the blues singers of

by a lagoon at 11150 East Blvd (Tues, Thurs, Sat & Sun 10am–5pm, Wed and Fri 10am–9pm; free; ☎1-888/269-7829, ⓦwwwclemusart.com), ranges from Renaissance armor to African art, and has a good café. Also notable is the **Museum of Natural History**, Wade Oval, with exhibits on dinosaurs and Native American culture (Mon–Sat 10am–5pm, Sun noon–5pm; Wed until 10pm Sept–May; $6.50; ⓦwww.cmnh.org). The modest **Cleveland Botanical Garden**, 11030 East Blvd (daily dawn to dusk; free; ⓦwww.cbgarden.org/), is trying to increase its profile, with a $37 million face-lift scheduled for completion in 2002. Meanwhile, dotted along East and Martin Luther King Jr boulevards in Rockefeller Park, 24 small landscaped cultural **gardens** are dedicated to and tended by Cleveland's diverse ethnic groups, including Croatians, Estonians and Finns. **Murray Hill**, Cleveland's Little Italy, is adjacent to University Circle. Beyond this attractive area of brick streets, small delis and galleries is the trendy **Coventry Village** neighborhood.

Five miles southwest of downtown via I-71 (exit at W 25th or Fulton Rd), the **Cleveland Metroparks Zoo**, 3900 Brookside Drive (summer Mon–Fri 9am–5pm, Sat & Sun 9am–7pm; rest of year daily 9am–5pm; rainforest also open Wed until 8pm; $7, or $5 zoo only; ⓦwww.clemetzoo.com/), features a "Wolf Wilderness." Seven thousand plants and 118 species of animal, including orangutans, American crocodiles and Madagascan hissing cockroaches, populate a spectacular 164-acre **rainforest** building. The RTA runs special buses from downtown during summer.

the Delta to the hillbilly wailers of the Appalachians. Look for "The Beat Goes On" display – a bank of interactive computers that reveals the inspirational earlier artists who shaped the sound of a series of contemporary bands.

Elsewhere in the subterranean main exhibition hall, there's an in-depth look at seven crucial rock genres through the cities that spawned them: rockabilly (Memphis), R&B (New Orleans), Motown (Detroit), psychedelia (San Francisco), punk (London and New York), hip-hop (New York) and grunge (Seattle). Much space is taken up by exhibits on what the museum sees as key artists of all time, including Elvis Presley, the Beatles (featuring a collection of John Lennon's possessions donated by Yoko Ono), U2, George Clinton and the Rolling Stones. In 1999, the new exhibit "Beats and Rhymes" opened, tracing the development of hip-hop and rap with costumes, artifacts and special programs.

Above ground, Pei's airy structure feels like a modern art gallery. Several U2 Trabants are suspended from the ceiling, a giant inflatable teacher from Pink Floyd's *Wall* tour bursts forth every five minutes and photographic portraits by Annie Leibovitz and others adorn the area by the stairwells.

On the top floor is the **Hall of Fame** itself. Compared with the racket elsewhere, this is a self-consciously reverential darkened space. The images of the hundred-plus inductees are flicked up on tiny screens, beside which are their autographs etched on glass.

The museum is at North Coast Harbor (daily 10am–5.30pm, Wed until 9pm; $15; reservations ☏1-800/493-ROLL). It gets particularly crowded at weekends: if that's the only time you can make it, you'll need to book in advance and be given a time to turn up. However, because it takes a good half-day to see just a decent proportion of the exhibits, it's much better to go on a weekday morning, when you can take full advantage of the interactive displays. Plan a visit to coincide with the extensive series of seminars and workshops that feature Hall of Fame inductees and leading rock writers. Call up details of these events on the Rock Hall's website (ⓦwww.rockhall.com).

Eating

At first sight, corporate chains seem to dominate Cleveland – especially in the Flats – but the city has many culinary delights, many of them ethnic. The **West Side Market** in Ohio City is one of the best places for cheap and unusual picnic food, but there are also some excellent (if pricey) fine-dining restaurants downtown. Little Italy and the Coventry Village area, both just east of University Circle, are worth exploring for authentic food and coffee bars, respectively. The *Arabica* chain also serves up good quality espresso at locations around the city, and can be found downtown at 856 Euclid Ave (☏216/771-6869).

Cleveland Chophouse and Brewery 824 W St Clair ☏216/623-0909. Try the mashed potatos at Cleveland's choice for a spacious and casual brew-steakhouse.

Flat Iron Café 1114 Center St ☏216/696-6968. The landmark tavern on the east (downtown) bank of the Flats, with an Irish-American edge, serves up good sandwiches, salads and desserts, plus a smooth pint of Guinness.

Hornblower's Barge & Grille 1151 N Marginal Rd ☏216/363-1151. Reasonable-value pastas, sandwiches and seafood are offered in a good location overlooking Lake Erie and a short stroll from the Rock Hall.

Mama Santa 12301-05 Mayfield Rd ☏216/231-9567. Unpretentious and inexpensive southern Italian home cooking in Little Italy.

Nate's Deli & Restaurant 1923 W 25th St ☏216/696-7529. This daytime Middle Eastern café serves great gyros and plenty of vegetarian dishes. The hummus, in particular, has quite a reputation.

Ruthie & Moe's Diner 4002 Prospect Ave ☏216/431-8063. This clean, friendly, traditional diner is well worth the 5min drive from downtown for its breakfasts, lunches and huge desserts.

Tommy's 1824 Coventry Rd ☎216/321-7757. Great-value food, much of it Middle Eastern vegetarian, is dished up in a trendy, bright setting in lively Coventry Village. Try the famous shakes and check out the adjoining used bookstore.
Watermark Restaurant 1250 Old River Rd

☎216/241-1600. An excellent and extensive seafood menu is offered in a classy Flats location overlooking the river.
Que Tal? 1803 Coventry Rd ☎216/932-9800. The place to grab some quick Mexican food in Coventry Village.

Nightlife and entertainment

For after-dark entertainment, the **Flats** area boasts the greatest conglomeration of drinking, live music and dancing venues, although they tend to be cheesier than their counterparts in the **Warehouse District** and the more bohemian **Ohio City** across the river. Five miles east, both the **University Circle** and the youthful **Coventry Village** neighborhoods have good venues and bars, though the Circle contains no-go zones you shouldn't wander into. Cleveland's **rave** scene remains strong and mostly underground; if you're interested, look for flyers at Record Revolution (☎216/321-7661), 1828 Coventry Rd.

As for more refined entertainment, the **Cleveland Opera** (☎216/575–0900, ⓦ www.clevelandopera.org) and **Ballet** (☎216/861-5545) perform in **Playhouse Square Center** (☎216/241-6000), which also hosts drama. The well-respected **Cleveland Orchestra** (☎216/231-1111) is based in University Circle at Severance Hall, 11001 Euclid Ave, close to the leading regional theater of the **Cleveland Play House** (☎216/795-7000). For **what's on** information, try one of Cleveland's two free weeklies: the well-written *Free Times* covers all of the arts, while *Scene* concentrates mostly on music.

The Basement 1078 Old River Rd ☎216/344-0001. Dance club on the Flats east bank, voted the city's best four years running, offers Eighties music and occasional concerts.
Club Isabella 2025 University Hospitals Drive, University Circle ☎216/229-1177. The popular, reasonably priced Italian restaurant features live jazz.
Great Lakes Brewing Co 2516 Market St, Ohio City ☎216/771-4404. At this famous old joint, Cleveland's best brewpub, the huge mahogany bar still bears the bullet holes made during a 1920s shootout involving lawman Elliot Ness.

Grog Shop 1765 Coventry Rd, Cleveland Heights ☎216/321-5588. The dark, dank and sweaty collegiate punk and alternative venue is near Coventry Village.
Harbor Inn 1219 Main Ave ☎216/241-3232. Go to a great old-fashioned bar amid the hyped chain outfits of the Flats for 180 beers, video games and lots of character.
Mercury Lounge 1392 W 6th St ☎216/566-8840. This hip new martini lounge in the warehouse district tends to attract Cleveland's fashionable.

Around Cleveland

Less than an hour outside the city are several small towns and sights well worth exploring. **VERMILION**, beyond the western suburbs of Cleveland, is also known as Harbor Town because of its attractive lakeside area, which has thrived since 1837. Today it's a quaint old hamlet lined with clapboard houses, cedar trees and tidy gardens. Old-style galleries and shops hug the small downtown, a stone's throw from the boat rides, seafood restaurants and fishing boats on the dockside. Through models, pictures and artifacts, the **Inland Seas Maritime Museum**, 480 Main St (daily 10am–5pm; $5), does a worthy job of exploring shipping on the Great Lakes from the late seventeenth century to the wreckage of the *Edmund Fitzgerald* freighter almost 300 years later. Vermilion's **visitor center** is at 5741 Liberty Ave (Tues–Thurs 10am–4:30pm; ☎440/967-4262). The best place to **stay in town** is the comfortable *Motel Plaza*, 4645 Liberty Ave (☎440/967-3191; ❸). Just east in the industrial port town of **LORAIN**, the *Spitzer Plaza Hotel*, 301 Broadway Ave (☎440/246-5767 or 1-800/446-

7452, @www.plazahotel.spitzer.com; ❺), offers big rooms and good value.

Some twenty miles southeast of Vermilion, the famously liberal college town of **OBERLIN** clusters around the green acres of Tappan Square. Founded in 1834, **Oberlin College**, on the square's north and east sides, was America's first co-ed university and one of the first to enroll black students. From the start, it played a pivotal role in facilitating the movement of black slaves from the Deep South to Canada on the Underground Railroad. A **sculpture** of railroad tracks emerging from the earth, opposite the Conservatory of Music at South Professor Street, is one of several such commemorative sights detailed in a fascinating **walking tour** leaflet available from the **Chamber of Commerce**, 20 E College St (Mon–Fri 8.30am–5pm; ☎440/774-6262, @www.oberlin .org). Also of interest is the **Allen Memorial Art Museum**, 87 Main St (Tues–Sat 10am–5pm, Sun 1-5pm; free; @www.oberlin.edu/allenart/). Recognized as one of the best college museums in the US, it holds more than 14,000 objects, from ancient Egyptian icons to Japanese woodblock prints and a fine array of contemporary art.

There are plenty of good places to **stay** in town. The pleasant *Oberlin Inn* motel is at 7 N Main St (☎440/775-1111, @www.oberlininn.com; ❻). The *Ivy Tree Inn & Garden*, 195 S Professor St (☎440/774-4510; ❹), offers a well-tended garden in a comfortable B&B atmosphere. Oberlin also boasts half a dozen hip coffee houses and bars, with good organic **food** dished up at the *Two Trees Café* in the Co-op Bookstore, 37 W College St (☎440/774-3741).

Twenty miles south of Cleveland off US-77, the village of **PENINSULA** is nestled in the heart of the **Cuyahoga Valley National Recreation Area**, where the Ohio & Erie Canal Towpath's hiking and biking trail follows the meandering Cuyahoga River for twenty miles. A few miles south of town off Riverview Road, the sprawling **Hale Farm and Village** (Tues–Sat 10am–5pm, Sun noon–5pm; $9) brings to life the fictional 1848 Ohio township of Wheatfield, complete with good-natured role-playing townsfolk and artisans who demonstrate skills like brick-making and glass-blowing.

The best place to stay in the area is at *HI-Stanford House* (☎330/467-8711; ❶), 6093 Stanford Rd, a hostel in a lovely old farmhouse. Bike rental is easy to come by at Century Cycles, 1621 Main St ($5 first hour, $4 second hour, $3 each additional hour); the **Chamber of Commerce,** 1663 Main St, is just down the block.

A few miles farther south in **AKRON** (home of Goodyear Tire and Rubber Co), visitors can tour Goodyear co-founder F.A. Seiberling's palatial **Stan Hywet Hall and Gardens**, 714 N Portage Path (Jan–March Tues–Sat 10am–4pm, Sun 1–4pm; April–Dec daily 10am–4.30pm; $8, gardens only $4), a magnificent 65-room Tudor Revival country house finished in 1915, with secret passageways, hand-carved wood paneling and an indoor swimming pool.

The Lake Erie Islands

The **LAKE ERIE ISLANDS** – Kelleys Island and the three **Bass Islands** further north – were early stepping stones for the **Iroquois** on the route to what is now Ontario. French attempts to claim the islands in the 1640s met with considerable hostility, and they were left more or less in peace until 1813, when in the **Battle of Lake Erie**, fought off South Bass Island, the Americans established their control over the Great Lakes by destroying the entire English fleet (for the first time in history).

The islands first tasted prosperity in the 1860s, when a boom in **wine production** meant that nearly every available acre was planted with grapes. Tourism arrived almost simultaneously, as steamboats brought wealthy visitors to spend their summers in the grand hotels. However, the economy was hit hard by Prohibition and the emergence of the California wineries, as well as by the advent of car travel. In the 1970s, Lake Erie's appalling pollution was the final straw for many inhabitants, who undertook a huge cleanup, both literally, of the lake, and figuratively, of the islands' image. Their plan has worked; today the islands are heavily visited, especially in summer, with fishing, swimming and partying the main attractions. Those mainland towns, like **Sandusky**, that act as jump-off points for the islands are destinations in themselves.

The mainland

The large coal-shipping port of **SANDUSKY**, fifty miles west of Cleveland on US-2, is probably the most visited of the lakeshore towns, thanks to **Cedar Point Amusement Park**, five miles southeast of town (May–Oct daily 9am–10pm; $34, after 5pm $23). The largest ride park in the nation – and widely considered the best in the world – Cedar Point boasts no less than thirteen roller coasters. The neighboring **Soak City** water park provides a good way to cool off, with eighteen acres of water slides and a wave pool (May–Sept daily 10am–9pm; $21, both parks $46). Otherwise, Sandusky is a nice enough town in a pleasant farmland setting, but there's not much to it apart from its pretty downtown square and the fast-food spots lining US-2.

The smaller resort town of **PORT CLINTON**, twelve miles west across the Sandusky Bay Bridge, is another departure point for the islands. Its pleasant lakefront is dotted with decent cafés and jet ski-rental outlets. Try not to leave the area without exploring the rest of the peninsula, with glorious views particularly around tiny **MARBLEHEAD**, fourteen miles east of Port Clinton.

Eight miles south of Sandusky, tiny **MILAN** (pronounced *MY-lan*) boasts a pleasant, leafy village square and many well-preserved Greek Revival-style homes. Its most famous building is the two-story brick **Thomas Edison Birthplace**, 9 Edison Drive (summer Tues–Sat 10am–5pm, Sun 1–pm; rest of year Tues–Sun 1–5pm; $5), with guided tours and an adjacent museum dedicated to the inventor of the light bulb.

Practicalities

Amtrak **trains** pass through Sandusky once daily en route between Chicago and Boston or New York, via Cleveland. The station, at North Depot and Hayes avenues, is in a dodgy area, and unstaffed. Greyhound **buses** stop way out at 6513 Milan Rd. Sandusky's **visitor center** is at 4424 Milan Rd, Suite A (summer daily 8am–9pm; rest of year daily 8.30am–5pm; ℗419/625-2984 or 1-800/255-ERIE; ⓦwww.sanduskycounty.org).

Accommodation in Sandusky can be quite expensive in high season – it's not unheard-of for a standard motel room to cost $200-plus on peak weekends. The *Coronado Motel*, 4319 Venice Rd (℗419/625-2954, ⓦwww.sanduskymotel.com; ❷), two miles west of downtown, is affordable, its clean rooms equipped with microwaves and fridges. Along the main drag of Cleveland Road (US-6), the *Best Western Cedar Point* at no. 1530 (℗419/625-9234; ❺) has a pool. **Camping** is available at the *Bayshore Estates* at 2311 Cleveland Rd (℗419/625-7906) and at the *Milan Travel Park* just off US-80 at 11404 US 250 N (℗419/433-4277), which has laundry facilities, free showers and a pool. Also in **Milan**, the *Colonial Inn South*, 12111 Rte-250 (℗419/499-3403 or

Ferries to **Kelleys Island** are operated by Neuman Boats from the foot of Frances Street in **Marblehead** every hour from dawn until dusk, more frequently at weekends and during peak times (March–Dec; $9.50 round-trip, bikes $3.50; ℡419/798-5800 or ℡1-800/876-1907, ⓦwww.neumanferry.com). Kelleys Island Ferry Boat Lines (℡419/798-9763) offers a year-round service from Main Street, Marblehead, for the same prices. The *Island Rocket* (℡419/627-1500 or 1-800/854-8121, ⓦwww.islandrocket.com), a powerful "cigarette" boat, whisks through the water from Jackson Street Pier in **Sandusky** for $9 one-way.

You can also take the *Island Rocket* from **Sandusky** to **South Bass Island** for a one-way fare of $11. A better value is the *Island Rocket* same-day "island hopper" ticket, which allows you to visit both islands for $28. The *Jet Express* (April–Nov; $10 one-way; ℡1-800/2451-JET) takes a mere 22 minutes to reach **South Bass Island** from Port Clinton, and runs until 11.30pm in the summer. Watch for their discount days or take the boat after 4pm any day but Saturday and return before the end of the evening and the fare is $15 round-trip. Ferry boats are hourly by Miller Boats (March–Nov daily 7am–7.30pm; $5 one-way; ℡419/285-2421) from **Catawba Point**, at the end of US-53 N, to Lime Kiln Dock on the island's southern tip. **Cruises**, run by Goodtime (℡419/625-9692) from Sandusky's Jackson Street Pier, depart daily at 9.30am and stop at both Kelleys Island and South Bass Island, for a round-trip fare of $21.95.

All crossings generally operate from late March to early November, though weather can interfere with these plans.

Flights to both Kelleys Island and South Bass Island leave daily from Sandusky and Port Clinton and cost about $65.50 round-trip. Contact Griffing Airlines (℡419/626-5161).

1-800/886-9010; ❹), is a recently refurbished family–owned motel. In **Lakeside**, a quiet Methodist retreat across Sandusky Bay, the *Hotel Lakeside,* 236 Walnut Ave (℡419/798-4461; ❹), offers decent, simple rooms at great prices.

For a good **meal** and live music in fun surroundings (there's an on-site waterfall), head for *Margaritaville* in Sandusky, at the junction of highways 6 and 2 (℡419/627-8903).

Kelleys Island

KELLEYS ISLAND is about nine miles north of Sandusky, in the western basin of Lake Erie. Seven miles across at its widest, it's the largest American island on the lake, but it's also one of the most peaceful and picturesque, home to just 175 permanent residents. The whole island, green, sleepy and with few buildings less than a century old, is a National Historic District. Its seventy-plus archeological sites include **Inscription Rock**, a limestone slab carved with four-hundred-year-old pictographs, east of the dock on the southern shore. The **Glacial Grooves State Memorial**, on the west shore, is a four-hundred-foot trough of solid limestone, scoured with deep ridges by the glacier that carved the Great Lakes.

Settled in the 1830s, Kelleys was initially a working island, its economy based on lumber, then wine, and later limestone quarrying. All but the last have collapsed, though a steady tourist industry also developed. Today, hundreds of Clevelanders come here on weekends to swim from the sandy public beach on the north shore, bird–watch with the island's active Audubon Society and hike through some dramatic abandoned quarries, which now sprout cedars.

Practicalities

The Kelleys Island **Chamber of Commerce** (summer daily 10am–5pm; ☎419/746-2360) is on Division Street straight up from the *Island Rocket* dock. Getting around is easy; cars are heavily discouraged, and most people, when not strolling, use **bikes** ($2 per hour/$8 per day) or **golf carts** ($12 per hour/$65 per day), available from First Place Rentals, at the top of the Neuman ferry dock (☎419/746-2314). A few **B&Bs** and inns can be reserved through the chamber. One comfortable option is *The Inn on Kelleys Island,* 317 W Lakeshore Drive (☎866/878-2135, ⓦwww.aves.net/the-inn/; ❹), a restored nineteenth-century Victorian home with a great lake view and a private beach. You can **camp** for $15 at the first-come, first-served state park on the north bay near the beach. The jovial *Village Pump* (☎419/746-2281) serves good home-style **food and drink** until 2am. The menu at the *Island Café & Brew Pub* (☎419/746-2314) includes several options for vegetarians.

South Bass Island

SOUTH BASS ISLAND is the largest and southernmost of the Bass Island chain, three miles from the mainland northwest of Kelleys Island, and named for the excellent bass fishing in the surrounding waters. Also referred to as **Put-in-Bay** (the name of its one and only village), this is the most visited of the American Lake Erie Islands, with its permanent population of 450 swelling to ten times that in summer.

Just a year after its first white settlers arrived, British troops invaded the island during the War of 1812. The Battle of Lake Erie (1813), which took place on the island's southeastern edge, is commemorated by **Perry's Victory and International Peace Memorial** in a 25-acre park where the island dramatically nips in at the waist. You can see the ten miles to the battle site from an observation deck near the top of the 352ft stone Doric column (May–Oct daily 10am–7pm; $3).

After the war, with the lake safe from Canadian invasion, South Bass Island grew both as a port (transporting cedar to the mainland for the construction of steamboats) and as a tourist destination. In the 1890s its *Victory Hotel* was one of the largest hotels in the world. Wine was also big business, though only one of its 26 vineyards survived Prohibition (by producing grape juice) – the **Heineman Winery** (☎419/285-2811), 900 Catawba Ave. The winery tours include a glass of wine or grape juice (May–Sept daily 11am–5pm; $5).

All this history is well documented at the **Lake Erie Islands Historical Society**, 441 Catawba Ave, which features dozens of model ships, exhibits on the shipping and fishing industries, and memorabilia of life on the islands.

Despite the colorful past, and the island's undeniable beauty, visitors today may well be struck most by the hordes of boozers staggering between bars whose repertoire extends little beyond Jimmy Buffet songs.

Practicalities

Put-in-Bay's **visitor center** (summer daily 9am–6pm, call for hours out of season; ☎419/285-2832, ⓦwww.put-in-bay.com) is in Harbor Square, downtown, just next to the northern dock. To get around, as on Kelleys Island, most people rent either **golf carts** from Baycarts Rental on Harbor Square ($10–20 per hour; ☎419/285-5785) or bikes from Island Bike Rental at both docks ($9 per day; ☎419/285-2016). A **shuttle bus** runs between the northern dock, the winery and the state park ($1). A narrated jump-on/jump-off **tram tour** ($6) sets off from the dock every thirty minutes. The local **taxi** will take you anywhere on the island for $3 per person (8am–3am; ☎419/285-2311).

Hotel rooms are heavily booked on weekends and during the summer, and B&Bs often require a two-night minimum stay on weekends. The *Stagger Inn B&B*, 182 Concord Ave (℡419/285-2521; ❹), and the *Commodore Motel*, 272 Delaware Ave (℡419/285-3101; ❹), which has a pool, offer some of the most competitive rates. **Camp** for $12 in the state park (get there by 9am) or at the *Fox's Den Campground* ($25 for one or two; ℡419/285-5001) on the southern shore.

Food on the island is expensive everywhere. The grill meals and seafood sandwiches at *The Boardwalk* (℡419/285-3695) are no exception, but this is the only downtown restaurant directly on the water. Just over the street, *Frosty's* (℡419/285-3278) does good pizza. Put-in-Bay's wild **nightlife** – it really does get raucous here – pulls in revelers from the other islands and the mainland. Numerous **live music** venues include the *Beer Barrel Saloon* – said to have the longest uninterrupted bar in the world complete with 160 bar stools – and the appropriately named *Round House*. *The Brewer*, just around the corner from the main drag on Catawba Avenue, is a reasonable brewpub.

Columbus

Ohio's largest city, state capital and home to the massive Ohio State University, **COLUMBUS** is a likeable place to visit. Its position in the rural heart of the state also makes it the only center of culture for a good three-hour drive in any direction.

Ohio became a state in 1803, and after trying Zanesville and Chillicothe, legislators designated this former patch of rolling farmland on the high east bank of the Scioto River its capital in 1812. The fledgling city was built from scratch, and its considered town planning is evident today in broad thoroughfares and green spaces. Statuary forms another part of the cityscape, with monuments seemingly erected on any spare scrap of land, many of them of its namesake, **Christopher Columbus**; there's even a replica of his ship, the *Santa Maria*, docked downtown on the Scioto River. For the 1992 quincentennial of the explorer's discovery of North America, some city officials erroneously felt that a full-scale celebration would put their city (which has lagged behind Cincinnati and Cleveland in terms of public recognition) on the map. It bombed, with Native American and other ethnic groups branding the festivities as exploitation.

After that failure to capture national recognition, city boosters have pinned their hopes on **sport**. The Columbus Crew of professional soccer (who play in the nation's first stadium built specifically for pro soccer) have a huge following. So do the Ohio State Buckeyes college football team, and the year 2000 brought in Ohio's first NHL hockey team, the Columbus Blue Jackets.

However, until Columbus does manage to make it big, it's best enjoyed for what it is – a lively college city with a smattering of good **museums**, some gorgeous Germanic **architecture**, and a particularly vibrant **nightlife**, including Ohio's most active **gay scene**. The spacious, orderly and easygoing **downtown** area holds several attractions and the giant Columbus City Center mall. The main entertainment districts – the bohemian **Short North** and the more mainstream **Brewery District** – are on the north and south fringes, respectively.

Arrival, information and getting around

Port Columbus International Airport (☎614/239-4083) is seven miles northeast of downtown. **Taxis** into the center cost around $16–18, while a cheaper alternative is a bus named the Capital City Flyer run by COTA ($5; ☎614/228-1776, ⓦwww.cota.com). Greyhound stops at East Town and Third streets. COTA also runs a good central bus service connecting downtown with German Village, the Short North and North Campus; a day pass costs $2.50. The main **visitor center** is at 90 N High St (Mon–Fri 9am–5.30pm; ☎614/221-CITY or 1-800/345-4FUN, ⓦwww.surpriseitscolumbus.com, ⓦwww.columbuscvb.org), with another branch on the second level of the Columbus City Center mall, just south of the Ohio Statehouse at High and Rich streets (Mon–Sat 10am–9pm, Sun noon–6pm).

Accommodation

Compared with other cities in the region, Columbus offers a good choice of mid-range places to **stay** that are well placed to let you discover the city by day and night. Downtown rates are good while even more savings can be made by staying in the German Village/Brewery District locales.

Best Western Clarmont 650 S High St ☎614/228-6511. A 2min walk from the Brewery District and German Village, this chain motel is a little run-down but good value nonetheless. ❹

German Village Inn 920 S High St ☎614/443-6506. The family-run motel on the south edge of the German Village/Brewery District is similar to the *Clarmont*. ❸

Harrison House B&B 313 W 5th Ave ☎614/421-2202 or 1-800/827-4203, ⓦwww.columbus-bed-breakfast.com. This welcoming big home is in Victorian Village, an upcoming district close to the Short North. ❺

Holiday Inn City Center 175 E Town St ☎614/221-3281, ⓦwww.holidayinn.com. This reliable motel with a pool and bar is within easy walking distance of the main museums, German Village and the Statehouse. ❻

Hostelling International – Columbus 95 E 12th Ave ☎614/294-7157, ⓦwww.hiayh.org. For this excellent location on campus, reservations are advisable. $14 per night, $17 for non-HI members. ❶

The Westin Columbus 310 S High St ☎614/228-3800. Columbus's grand downtown Victorian hotel. ❼

Downtown

As good a place as any to start a walking tour of downtown is the **Ohio Statehouse** (Mon–Fri 7am–7pm, Sat & Sun 10am–5pm; tours Mon–Fri 9.30am–3pm, Sat & Sun 11.15am–3pm; free), pleasantly set in ten acres of park at the intersection of Broad and High streets, the two main downtown arteries. Highlights of the free guided tours in this recently renovated 1839 Greek Revival structure – one of the very few state capitols without a dome – are the ornate Senate and House chambers.

From here, most places of interest lie a few blocks east and west along Broad Street. The new incarnation of Columbus's **COSI** (Center of Science and Industry) is housed in a streamlined structure across the river at 333 W Broad St (Mon–Sun 10am–5pm; adults $12, kids $7; ⓦwww.cosi.org), and boasts more than 300,000 square feet of exhibit space, most of it geared toward children. Across from COSI's former location, the **Wendy's Original Restaurant** at 257 E Broad St (Mon–Fri 10am–8pm, Sat 10am–7pm, Sun 11am–6pm), pays homage to Dave Thomas's enduringly down-home national burger chain, started here in 1969. There's the usual menu, plus pictures of famous patrons, glass cases full of *Wendy* dolls, the original homemade dress Thomas's daughter Wendy wore when she posed for the logo that's still used today, and other memorabilia. Incidentally, the city also introduced the **White Castle** burger chain to the world in 1921, but some enthusiast of the greasy patties bought up the first castellated diner and moved it elsewhere as a private residence.

Three blocks east, a giant Henry Moore sculpture stands at the entrance to the inviting **Columbus Museum of Art**, 480 E Broad St (Tues–Wed & Fri–Sun 10am–5.30pm, Thurs 10am–8.30pm, closed Mon; $4, free Thurs 5.30–8.30pm), which also has a pleasant sculpture garden. Indoors, this airy space holds particularly good collections of Western and modernist art, including a dramatic mixed-media piece by Anselm Kiefer just by the entrance, a renowned photography gallery and touring exhibits.

The **Topiary Garden**, 480 E Town St, in Old Deaf School Park (daylight hours; free), at the corner of Washington Avenue and East Town Street south of the museum, provides a quirky photo opportunity. In the center of this verdant little park, a group of locals have re-created in topiary Georges Seurat's famous post-Impressionist work, *Sunday Afternoon on the Island of La Grande Jatte*. Believed to be the only painting reinterpreted in evergreen shrubbery, it features fifty pruned humans, three dogs, a monkey, a cat and eight leafy boats floating in a pond.

German Village and Brewery District

Just six blocks south of the Statehouse, I-70 separates downtown from the delightful **German Village** neighborhood. During the mid-nineteenth century, thousands of German immigrants settled in this part of Columbus, building neat redbrick homes, the most lavish of which surround the 23-acre **Schiller Park**. Their descendants, however, started leaving the area during World War I, and with Prohibition and World War II further depleting their numbers, few were left by the 1950s. The area, then known as the Old South End, soon became run-down, and by the 1960s the big corporations were eyeing it for office developments until a group of local preservationists, determined to save these gorgeous homes from the wrecker's ball, decided to designate the area as the German Village. They formed a preservation society, drew up a list of renovation guidelines for residents, and won a place on the National Register of Historic Places.

Today the eighteen-block village is the biggest privately funded body on that register, a professional residential district with a sizable gay community. The best way to explore its brick-paved streets, corner bars, old-style restaurants, Lutheran churches and grand homes is to call at the **German Village Meeting Haus**, 588 S 3rd St (April–Sept Mon–Fri 9am–4pm, Sat 10am–2pm; rest of year closed Sun), where popular walking tours run by the German Village Society start with a twelve-minute video presentation. The Society also oversees the immensely popular **Haus und Garten Tour** on the last Sunday in June, and the **Oktoberfest** celebrations in early September. The Village caters to book lovers; the **Book Loft**, 631 S 3rd St (daily 10am–11pm), crams its books, many of them discounted, into 32 rooms of a former residence.

Just across High Street (US-23) are the warehouses of the **Brewery District**, where, until Prohibition, the German immigrants brewed beer by traditional methods. Many of the original buildings still stand, but today the beer is produced by a handful of microbreweries such as **Columbus Brewing Co**, 525 Short St, which sometimes sets up free tours of the operation (by appointment, ☏614/224-3626). The area is also the focus of Columbus's more mainstream nightlife, with several restaurants, theme pubs, music venues and, inevitably, brewpubs.

North of downtown

Across Nationwide Boulevard at the top end of downtown is the **Short North**, a former red-light area that's now Columbus's most vibrant enclave. Standing on either side of High Street – the main north–south thoroughfare – two landmark buildings mark the transition into the area. To the left is the restored Victorian warehouse of **North Market** (see "Eating," below), while to the right is the strikingly deconstructivist **Greater Columbus Convention Center**, a massive pile of angled blocks designed by Peter Eisenman and completed in 1993. A few blocks further north across I-670 is the start of the trail of galleries, bars and restaurants that makes the area so popular with locals. The first Saturday of each month sees the **Gallery Hop**, when all the local art dealers throw open their doors – complementing the art works with wine, snacks and occasional performance pieces – and the socializing goes on well into the evening.

Businesses become a little more low-rent for a mile before High Street cuts through the **university campus** and suddenly sprouts cheap eating places and funky shopping emporia. For bargain vinyl, head to the basement Used Kids Records, 1992 N High St. On the other side of the street, the **Wexner Center for the Arts**, North High Street at 15th Avenue (Tues–Wed & Fri–Sun 10am–6pm, Thurs 10am–9pm; ☎614/292-3535, Ⓦ www.wexarts.org), is another recent Eisenman construction – even more extreme than the Convention Center – and it's home to cutting-edge contemporary art exhibitions, movies, mixed-media performances, a café and a bookstore.

Eating

The Short North and German Village neighborhoods are crammed with places to **eat**, be they bottom-dollar snack bars or stylish and adventurous bistros. For a wide range of ethnic and organic snacks during the day, try the **North Market** downtown at 59 Spruce St (Tues–Fri 9am–7pm, Sat 8am–5pm, Sun noon–5pm; ☎614/463-9664), which also sells fresh produce.

Barcelona 263 E Whittier St, German Village ☎614/444-1130. Noted for its tapas and desserts, this stylishly decorated local favorite also does tasty Mediterranean entrees.

Cap City Fine Diner 1299 Olentangy River Rd ☎614/291-3663. A self-proclaimed "upscale diner," this big, lively joint just off downtown serves up traditional food (meatloaf) with new twists (chili-onion rings and buttermilk mash). Huge portions, especially the desserts; lunch entrees around $8, dinner $14.

Cup O' Joe Coffee & Dessert House 627 S 3rd St, German Village ☎614/221-1JOE. Voted Columbus's best coffee house, it offers great desserts and coffees and comfy sofas.

Katzinger's 475 S 3rd St, German Village ☎614/228-3354. A mesmerizing range of sandwiches, Jewish munchies and cheesecakes, though prices are high for a deli.

Out on Main 122 E Main St ☎614/224-9520. Newish gay-themed restaurant with fabulous atmosphere and a great menu to match. *Planet Hollywood*esque exhibits include Melissa Etheridge's guitar, Greg Louganis's Speedo and a Liberace display.

Schmidt's Restaurant und Sausage Haus 240 E Kossuth St, German Village ☎614/444-6808. The Columbus landmark (since 1886) serves schnitzel and strudel in a former slaughterhouse.

Tapatio 491 N Park St, Short North ☎614/221-1085. Inventive Caribbean and South American food and a great patio.

Nightlife

Not long ago, Columbus was being tipped as "the next Seattle"; while that didn't happen, this youthful university town has a rich source of local **bands**, from country revivalists to experimental alternative acts. In addition to the German Village, the **gay scene** is concentrated in the Short North on and around North High Street, with a few additional bars and clubs downtown –

the biweekly *OUTlook* has complete listings. On most summer Friday evenings there are free concerts in downtown Bicentennial Park on the Scioto River. The *Other Paper* and *Columbus Alive* provide free details of what's happening.

Dick's Den 2417 N High St ☎614/268-9573. The campus dive bar has good jazz at the weekends.
Little Brother's 1100 N High St, Short North ☎614/421-2025. Underground sounds from alternative rock to swing and spoken word.
Ludlow's 485 S Front St, Brewery District ☎614/341-7284. Pick of the more mainstream Brewery District venues with live bands Thurs–Sat.
Oldfield's On High 2590 N High St ☎614/784-

0477. Predominantly collegiate campus bar with eclectic live music tastes.
Short North Tavern 674 N High St, Short North ☎614/221-2432. Oldest bar in the neighborhood; live bands at the weekend.
Union Station Video Café 630 N High St, Short North ☎614/228-3740. Popular gay video bar with a decent selection of appetizers and sandwiches, plus a pool table and internet access.

Cincinnati

CINCINNATI, just across the Ohio River from Kentucky and roughly three hundred miles from both Detroit and Chicago, is a dynamic commercial metropolis with a definite European flavor and a sense of the South. Its tidy center, rich in architecture and culture, lies within a few minutes' easy walk of the arty **Mount Adams** district, the attractive **riverfront** and the lively **Over-the-Rhine** area in the north end of downtown.

The city was founded in 1788 at the point where a Native American trading route crossed the river. Its name comes from a group of Revolutionary War admirers of the Roman general Cincinnatus, who saved Rome in 458 BC and then returned to his small farm and refused to accept any reward or glory. Cincinnati quickly became an important supply point for pioneers heading west on flatboats and rafts, and its population skyrocketed with the establishment of a major steamboat **riverport** in 1811. Tens of thousands of **German** immigrants poured in during the 1830s.

Loyalties were split by the **Civil War**. At first, merchants were perturbed by the loss of important markets; then they began to pick up lucrative government contracts, and the city decided that its future lay with the Union. In the prosperous postwar decade, Cincinnati acquired Fountain Square, the prodigious Music and Exhibition Hall, a zoo, art museum, public library and the country's first professional baseball team. **Sport** remains a great source of pride: downtown gift shops are decked out in the orange and black of the **Bengals** football team and the red and white of the baseball-playing **Reds**.

A Cincinnati success story is the **Rookwood Pottery**, started by Maria Storer in Mount Adams in 1880. Its distinctive tiles adorn countless downtown Art Deco landmarks, as well as the Union and Dixie train terminals.

Charles Dickens, Winston Churchill and Longfellow all admired Cincinnati; Mark Twain, on the other hand, said that he hoped to be in Cincinnati when the world ended, as it's always twenty years behind everywhere else.

Arrival, information and getting around

Cincinnati–Northern Kentucky International Airport (☎859/767-3151) is twelve miles south of downtown, in Covington, Kentucky. **Taxis** to the city center (☎859/586-5236) cost $24. The Greyhound station is on the eastern fringe of the center, just off Broadway, at 1005 Gilbert Ave. Amtrak **trains** arrive a mile northwest of downtown at the Union Terminal museum complex, which is on the daytime citywide Metro **bus** network (50¢;

CINCINNATI

0   400 yds

N

Vernon Manor Hotel

Eden Park

Cincinnati Art Museum

EDEN PARK DRIVE

MOUNT ADAMS DR

PARKSIDE PL.

PARADROME ST.

HATCH ST.

BELVEDERE ST

ST GREGORY ST

TALBI ST.

PAVILION ST.

Zoo

Holiday Inn Downtown

DORCHESTER AVENUE

CARMATT ST.

DORSEY STREET

MULBERRY STREET

PEETE STREET

MCMICKEN AVENUE

SYCAMORE TERRACE

JOSEPHINE STREET

CALVIN ST.

BURNETT AVENUE

RYAN AVENUE

CHANNING STREET

HIGHLAND AVENUE

RINGGOLD STREET

SLACK STREET

PEUBLO

BOAL STREET

MILTON STREET

LIBERTY HILL

READING ROAD

LIBERTY STREET

LIBERTY STREET

15TH STREET

14TH STREET

REPUBLIC STREET

CLAY STREET

13TH STREET

12TH STREET

READING ROAD

GILBERT AVENUE

VAN METER STREET

ELSINORE AVENUE

IDA STREET

MONASTERY STREET

WAREHAM DRIVE

CELESTIAL ST.

MOUNT ADAMS

OREGON STREET

BAUM STREET

KILGORE ST.

COLUMBIA PARKWAY

Music Hall

VINE STREET

12TH STREET

CENTRAL PARKWAY

Bus Station

EGGLESTON AVENUE

COURT STREET

COURT STREET

RACE ST.

ELM STREET

BOWEN STREET

MAIN STREET

WALNUT STREET

SYCAMORE STREET

8TH STREET

BROADWAY

9TH STREET

GARFIELD PLACE

7TH STREET

471

Taft Museum

Bicentennial Commons

PLUM STREET

DOWNTOWN

6TH STREET

5TH STREET

FOUNTAIN SQUARE

Contemporary Arts Center

PIKE ST.

Lytle Park

PETE ROSE WAY

L & N BRIDGE

CENTRAL AVENUE

Carew Tower

Westin Hotel

4TH STREET

Yeatman's Cove Park

75

3RD STREET

71

Riverfront Stadium

CENTRAL BRIDGE

71

PETE ROSE WAY

STADIUM DRIVE

PRODUCE DRIVE

MEHRING WAY

ROEBLING SUSPENSION BRIDGE

Ohio River

NEWPORT, KENTUCKY

Licking River

71
75

CLAY WADE BAILEY BRIDGE

Covington Landing

RIVERSIDE DRIVE

2ND STREET

COURT AVENUE

GREENUP STREET

SCOTT BLVD

RIVERCENTER

Marriott at River Center

COVINGTON, KENTUCKY

4TH STREET

$\textcircled{T}$ 513/621-4455). The best way to move between downtown Cincy and the sights across the river in Covington and Newport, KY, is via the South Bank Shuttle Tank **shuttle bus**, which picks up at Fountain Square in front of the *Westin* – and costs only 25¢. The city's taxis enforce a $3 minimum fare, though that will usually get you from downtown to most places of interest.

Cincinnati's main **visitor center** is at 300 W 6th St (Mon–Fri 9am–5pm; $\textcircled{T}$ 513/621-2142 or 1-800/CINCY-USA; $\textcircled{w}$ www.cincyusa.com); there's another – and perhaps more accessible – visitor center in Fountain Square, as well as information booths around Fountain Square and at 605 Philadelphia St in Covington (daily 10am–6pm; $\textcircled{T}$ 859/655-4159).

Accommodation

Although Cincinnati's quality **hotels** are reasonable by big-city standards, budget travelers may have problems finding affordable downtown rooms. Uptown **motels** – about two miles north – are much cheaper, but you'll need a car to get around safely at night.

Budget Host Inn 3356 Central Parkway $\textcircled{T}$ 513/559-1600, $\textcircled{w}$ www.budgethost.com. Just about the cheapest place in uptown Cincinnati, though doubles vary greatly in price. Three miles from downtown. ❸

Gateway B&B 326 E 6th St, Newport, KY $\textcircled{T}$ 859/581-6447. This comfortable, affordable Victorian place is five minutes from downtown Cincy and Covington, KY. ❺

Holiday Inn Downtown 800 W 8th St $\textcircled{T}$ 513/241-8660. Fairly priced downtown rooms. ❺

Marriott at River Center 10 W River Center Blvd, Covington, KY $\textcircled{T}$ 859/261-2900 or 1-800/228-9290, $\textcircled{w}$ www.marriotthotels.com. The new luxury hotel on the river has spacious rooms and great service, and an on-site pool and spa. ❻–❽

Vernon Manor Hotel 400 Oak St $\textcircled{T}$ 513/281-3300, $\textcircled{w}$ www.vernonmanor.com. The 1924 landmark, renovated in 1999, features huge suite rooms in an old-style hotel. Though a good location for the university and zoo, don't walk around at night. ❼

Westin Hotel 21 E 5th St $\textcircled{T}$ 513/621-770. Another top luxury option right downtown. ❼–❽

Downtown

Downtown Cincinnati rolls back from the Ohio River to fill the flat Basin area, ringed by a disarray of steep hills. During the city's emergent industrial years, the filth, disease, crime and general commotion of the so-called Sausage and Rat rows led the middle classes to abandon downtown en masse. Nowadays, however, attractive stores, street vendors, restaurants, cafés, open spaces and gardens occupy the area. The city's rich blend of architecture is best appreciated on the **walking tour** detailed in an excellent free booklet from the visitor centers. Over, among and even right through the hotel plazas, office lobbies and retail areas, the **Skywalk** network of air-conditioned passages and flyovers spans sixteen city blocks.

At the geographic center of downtown, the **Genius of the Waters** in **Fountain Square** sprays a cascade of hundreds of jets to symbolize the city's trading links. Surrounded by a tree-dotted plaza and all but enclosed by soaring facades of glass and steel, the area is a popular lunch spot and venue for daytime concerts. Looming above at Fifth and Vine streets, the 48-story Art Deco **Carew Tower** has a viewing gallery on its top floor that gives a wonderful panorama of the tight bends of the Ohio River and the surrounding hillsides (Mon–Thurs 9.30am–5.30pm, Fri & Sat 9.30am–9pm, Sun 11am–5pm; $2).

Just east of Fountain Square are the Art Deco headquarters of the detergents giant **Procter and Gamble**. The company was formed in 1837 by candlemaker William Procter and soapmaker James Gamble, to exploit the copious supply of animal fat from the slaughterhouses of "**Porkopolis**," as Cincinnati was then known. A shady style of management has spawned tales of dubious religious and political links; the corporate logo even had to be changed to counter accusations that it was a satanic symbol. By sponsoring radio's "Puddle Family" in 1932, the company created the world's first **soap opera**.

Nearby, the left-field multimedia modern art exhibitions at the superb **Contemporary Arts Center**, in the Mercantile Center at 115 E 5th St (Mon–Sat 10am–6pm, Sun noon–5pm; $3.50, free Mon; ☎513/721-0390, ⓦwww.spiral.org), lead to continual run-ins with Cincy's more conservative citizens. By contrast, the **Taft Museum**, just east of downtown in an immaculate 1820 Federal-style mansion at 316 Pike St (Mon–Sat 10am–5pm, Sun 1–5pm; $4), contains a priceless collection of works by Rembrandt, Goya, Turner and Gainsborough, plus some staggering Ming porcelain and French enamels. The statue of a weary Abraham Lincoln in **Lytle Park**, in front of the museum, was criticized as unpatriotic when unveiled in 1917; it's now seen as a great example of sculptural realism.

Mount Adams and Eden Park

Just over a mile northeast from downtown, the land rises suddenly and the streets – narrow courses with tight corners and abrupt dead ends – start to conform to the contours of **Mount Adams**. Century-old townhouses coexist with avant-garde galleries, stylish boutiques, trendy gift shops and international restaurants. During the late nineteenth century, the elegant dining rooms of Mount Adams entertained the rich and famous eager to escape the squalor and noise of the Basin. Today its lively bars attract yuppies, students, hedonists and iconoclasts from all over the city. From downtown, take a taxi or #49 bus.

Adjacent to this tightly packed neighborhood are the rolling lawns, verdant copses and scenic overlooks of **Eden Park**, its features reflected in the new **Mirror Lake**, a man-made pool installed as part of the city's Millenium Project. A loop road at the northern end of the park leads to the **Cincinnati Art Museum** on Art Museum Drive (Tues–Sat 10am–5pm, Sun noon–6pm; $5, free Sat; ☎513/721-5204, ⓦwww.cincinnatiartmuseum.org). Its one hundred labyrinthine galleries span five thousand years, taking in an excellent Islamic collection as well as a solid selection of European and American paintings by the likes of Matisse, Monet, Picasso, Edward Hopper and Grant Wood.

Riverside

The Cincinnati side of the Ohio River has been a mess recently, due to the massive redevelopment project underway to build two new stadia for the Bengals and the Reds. But just to the east, the riverside takes on a greater serenity – the mile-long **riverside walk** begins near the stadium at **Public Landing**, at the bottom of Broadway. The cobbled wharf here, on the original site of the city, is a great place to take a look at immaculately painted showboats and other river craft. Nearby, **Bicentennial Commons** was a two-hundredth-birthday present from the city to itself in 1988.

The Museum Center at Union Terminal

Cincinnati's latest attraction is its **Museum Center** (☎513/287-7000, ⓦwww.cincymuseum.org), housed in the magnificent Art Deco **Union Terminal** northwest of downtown, approached via a stately driveway off Ezzard Charles Drive. The restored lobby is absolutely stunning, complete with extraordinary mosaic murals and a Rookwood-tiled ice-cream parlor. Highlights of the **Museum of Natural History** are dioramas of Ice Age Cincinnati and "The Cavern," which houses a living bat colony. The

Historical Society holds a succession of well-presented, short-term exhibitions, and the **Cinergy Children's Museum** has a two-story treehouse and eight other interactive exhibit areas (Mon–Sat 10am–5pm, Sun 11am–6pm; museums $5.50 each, any two $9, all three $12, with OMNIMAX $15). The museums are time-consuming, so it's best to get a combination ticket (valid for six months) and use it over two days.

Covington and Newport, Kentucky

Covington, directly across the Ohio River on the Kentucky side, is very much a part of the Cincinnati hinterland. It can be reached from downtown Cincinnati by walking over the bright-blue 355-yard 1867 **John A. Roebling Suspension Bridge**, at the bottom of Walnut Street, which served as a prototype for the Brooklyn Bridge. Once across, you're confronted by the much-hyped **Covington Landing** – "the largest waterfront complex on inland waters" – a collection of cafés, shops and clubs on permanently moored boats that's little more than an upmarket mall on water. The BB riverboat company (☎859/261-8500) runs sightseeing cruises ($12.50) from the Landing – reservations are recommended.

Ten minutes' walk southwest of the bridge brings you to the attractive, narrow, tree-lined streets and nineteenth-century houses of **MainStrasse Village**. It's a Germanic neighborhood of antique shops, bars and restaurants that plays host to the lively **Maifest** on the third weekend of each May, and is the centerpiece of the citywide **Oktoberfest** on the weekend after Labor Day. At 6th and Philadelphia streets, 21 mechanical figures accompanied by glockenspiel music toll the hour on the German Gothic **Carroll Chimes Bell Tower**. Just beyond Covington at I-75 exit 186 is the **Oldenberg Brewery**, crammed with boozing memorabilia; tours of the microbrewery and its museum cost $3 (daily 10am–5pm).

Across the Licking River from Covington, the subdued town of **Newport** has gotten a lot livelier since the recent opening of the impressive **Newport Aquarium**, One Aquarium Way (daily 10am–6pm; ☎859/491-FINS or 1-800/406-FISH, ⓦ www.newportaquarium.com). Clear underwater tunnels and see-through floors allow visitors to literally be surrounded by sharks and snapping gators.

Eating

Cincinnati boasts enough excellent home-grown gourmet and continental restaurants to ensure that national chains have a low profile in the city. It's also famous for fast-food **Cincinnati chili** with chains such as *Skyline Chili*, open from breakfast to midnight at more than forty sites, including Vine and 7th streets downtown.

Aralia 815 Elm St ☎513/723-1217. Excellent Sri Lankan curries in a handy downtown location.
Courtyard Café 1211 Main St, Over-the-Rhine ☎513/723-1119. Good grill food, burgers and desserts at value-for-money prices.
Dee Felice 529 Main St, Covington, KY ☎859/261-2365. This small and atmospheric restaurant/jazz venue specializes in Cajun cuisine, with lots of fresh seafood dishes.
Longworth's 1108 St Gregory St, Mount Adams ☎513/651-2253. Good meals are menued at attractive prices in a delightful garden setting.

Food is served all day until midnight, with music until 2.30am.
Mullane's Parkside Café 723 Race St ☎513/381-1331. This friendly joint, bedecked with local art, has an excellent choice of vegetarian options.
Rookwood Pottery 1077 Celestial St, Mount Adams ☎513/721-5456. Steaks and sandwiches are served inside the former kilns of Cincinnati's celebrated pottery.
Scalea's Ristorante 320 Greenup St, Covington, KY ☎859/491-3334. An atmospheric and inventive

Italian eatery lists entrees at $12–25; the restaurant's attached deli/market offers cheaper options. Tucker's 1637 Vine St ☎513/721-7123 and 18 E 13th St, Over-the-Rhine ☎513/241-3354. Get a perfect start on your day with traditional and gourmet breakfasts in a 1950s setting.

Nightlife

After dark, the hottest area with the widest appeal is the **Over-the-Rhine** district, which fans out from Main Street, around 12th and 14th, and buzzes every night – though be careful where you park or walk as it backs onto some dodgy areas. The bars, restaurants and cafés of scenic **Mount Adams** offer a good choice of music, food and atmosphere, especially on warm summer nights, when the narrow streets are full of revelers. The studenty **Corryville** neighborhood, a five-minute drive northwest from downtown, has a lively undergraduate edge, while **Covington Landing**, Kentucky, is busy but bland. A proliferation of **brewpubs** has sprung up all over town in the past few years, always dependable for a good drink in friendly surroundings. What's-on **listings** for the whole city can be found in the free *Cincinnati CityBeat*.

Arnold's 210 E 8th St ☎513/421-6234. A fun and funky downtown spot, it's a favorite with jazz fans, though it also puts on roots and acoustic acts. Good restaurant upstairs.

Blind Lemon 936 Hatch St, Mount Adams ☎513/241-3885. Beyond the intimate, low-ceilinged bar, you'll find a relaxed patio crowd. Music (mostly acoustic) nightly at 9.30.

Bogart's 2621 Vine St, Corryville ☎513/281-8400. Established indie acts play this mid-sized venue directly opposite *Sudsy Malone's*.

BrewWorks 1115 Main St, Covington, KY ☎859/581-2739. This big, boisterous brewpub pours the best microbrewed ales in town.

The Pavilion 949 Pavilion St, Mount Adams ☎513/744-9200. The bar has great views of the city and the Ohio River from its terraced outdoor deck.

Rhythm & Blues Café 1142 Main St, Over-the-Rhine ☎513/684-0080. Good food and great atmosphere. Live rock, blues and various genres every Wed, Fri and Sat nights.

Sudsy Malone's Rock & Roll Laundry & Bar 2626 Vine St, Corryville ☎513/751-2300. You can drink beer, catch a live indie act and wash your clothes all at the same time in this fun Corryville landmark. Daily 7am–2am.

Warehouse 1313 Vine St, Over-the-Rhine ☎513/684-9313. A popular dance club, it plays alternative and industrial sounds midweek and the latest house at weekends.

Classical music, opera and theater

Music Hall, at 1243 Elm St (☎513/621-1919), an 1870s conglomeration of spires, arched windows and cornices, is said to have near-perfect acoustics. Home to Cincinnati's Opera and Symphony Orchestra, it also hosts the May Festival of choral music. The **Cincinnati Playhouse in the Park** (☎513/421-3888, ⓦ www.cincyplay.com), in Eden Park, puts on drama, musicals and comedies, with performances throughout the year (except Mon).

Michigan

Mention **MICHIGAN** and most people think of cars, heavy industry and inner-city Detroit. Midwesterners prefer to focus on its magnificent scenery. The beaches, dunes and cliffs along the 3200-mile shoreline of its two vividly contrasting **peninsulas** – bordering four of the five Great Lakes – rival many an oceanfront state.

The mitten-shaped **Lower Peninsula** is dominated from its southeastern corner by the industrial giant of **Detroit**, surrounded by satellite cities heavily devoted to the automotive industry. In the west, the scenic 350-mile Lake Michigan shore drive passes through likeable little ports before reaching the stunning **Sleeping Bear Dunes** and resort towns such as **Traverse City** in the peninsula's balmy northwest corner. The desolate, dramatic and thinly populated **Upper Peninsula**, reaching out from Wisconsin like a claw to separate lakes Superior and Michigan, is a far cry indeed from the cosmopolitan south.

In the mid-seventeenth century, **French explorers** forged a successful trading relationship with the Chippewa, Ontario and other tribes. The **British**, who acquired control after 1763, were far more brutal. Governor Henry Hamilton, the "Hair Buyer of Detroit," advocated taking scalps rather than prisoners. Ever since, Michigan's economy has developed in waves, the eighteenth-century fur, timber and copper booms culminating in the state establishing itself at the forefront of the nation's manufacturing capacity, thanks to its abundant raw materials, good transportation links, and the genius of innovators such as **Henry Ford**. Despite the slumps of the Seventies and Eighties, car production remains the major source of Michigan income – and tourism is now a four-season money-spinner.

Getting around Michigan

It's easy to be daunted by Michigan's sheer **size**: Detroit is more than seven hundred miles from Ironwood on the Wisconsin border (a **ferry** between Ludington and Manitowoc, Wisconsin, helps to cut driving time – see p.331). Greyhound **buses** run regularly throughout the south, but services elsewhere are less frequent, and those few buses that serve the remote Upper Peninsula travel through at night. Amtrak **trains** between New York and Chicago stop at Detroit, Dearborn and Ann Arbor; trains into Canada leave from Windsor, just over the river from Detroit. Michigan's principal **airport**, a hub for Northwest Airlines, is just outside Detroit. **Cycling** is both feasible and rewarding, particularly with the abundance of bike paths in and around Traverse City; Michigan Bicycle Touring (☎616/463-5885, ⓦ www.bikembt.com) in Kingsley organizes tours and can help with routes.

Detroit and around

DETROIT, the birthplace of the mass-production **car industry** and the **Motown** sound, has long had an image problem. It boasts a billion-dollar downtown development, ultramodern motor-manufacturing plants, some excellent museums and one of the nation's biggest art galleries. But since the 1960s, media attention has dwelt instead on its huge tracts of urban wasteland, where for block after block there's nothing but the occasional heavily fortified loan shop or food store. Although cities like Atlanta, Newark and Washington, DC post much worse crime statistics, the press has seemed intent on painting Detroit as some kind of war zone.

Such views incur the wrath of many Detroiters, who claim that the press has magnified the city's problems because blacks run Detroit and account for 75 percent of its population. That assertion certainly carries weight, but Detroit – which has lost nearly half its citizens, almost a million people, in forty years – has unarguably suffered. However, following the resurgence of Cleveland,

Pittsburgh and other Rust Belt cities, Detroit, under the leadership of Mayor Dennis Archer, showed signs of turning the corner. The Detroit Tigers opened Comerica Park, and Ford Field is scheduled for completion in 2002 for the pro football Lions. Three big-time casinos opened and plans are afoot to enhance the waterfront. While these developments won't wipe out the city's problems in one fell swoop, they're an exciting start.

Founded in 1701 by Antoine de Mothe **Cadillac**, as a trading post for the French to do business with the Chippewa, Detroit was no more than a medium-sized port two hundred years later. Then **Ford**, **Olds**, the **Chevrolets** and the **Dodge** brothers began to build their automobile empires. Thanks to the introduction of the mass assembly line, Detroit sped into high gear in the 1920s, expanding into the countryside and booming like a mining town – fast, compulsive and indifferent to the needs of its population. The auto barons sponsored the construction of segregated neighborhoods and unceremoniously dispensed with workers during times of low demand. Such policies created huge ghettos, and the city came to a boil in July 1967 in the bloodiest **riot** in the USA for fifty years. More than forty people died and 1300 buildings were destroyed. Nothing was solved, and little even improved. The inner city was left to fend for itself, and the all-important motor industry was rocked by the oil crises and Japanese competition.

No visitor to Detroit could fail to be disturbed by the divisions between rich and poor, and the fact that other industrial towns have been hit equally hard by the recession is little consolation. However, while heavily scarred and bruised, Detroit is not the apocalyptic mess some would have it. New businesses and theaters have already opened downtown, and suburban residents have started to return to its festivals, theaters, clubs and restaurants. However, it makes more sense to think of Detroit as a region rather than a European-style city and, so long as you plan your time and don't mind driving, it holds plenty to see and do. For the moment, **downtown** is not so much the heart of the giant as just another segment. Other segments include the huge **Cultural Center**, freewheeling **Royal Oak**, posh **Birmingham**, the Ford-town of **Dearborn** and even nearby **Windsor**, **Ontario**, and **Ann Arbor**, a short drive west.

Arrival, information and getting around

Flights come into **Detroit Wayne County Metropolitan Airport** in Romulus (℡734/942-3550), eighteen miles southwest of downtown and a hefty $30-plus taxi ride, though Metropolitan (℡734/727-1740) runs a shuttle for $22.

The main Greyhound (1001 Howard Ave) and Amtrak (2601 Rose St) terminals are in areas where it's inadvisable to walk around at night. Amtrak also stops ten miles out at 16121 Michigan Ave, Dearborn, near the Henry Ford Museum and several mid-range motels, and at unstaffed suburban stations at Birmingham, Pontiac and Royal Oak. The People Mover elevated **railway** loops around thirteen art-adorned stations downtown (Mon–Thurs 7am–11pm, Fri 7am–midnight, Sat 9am–midnight, Sun noon–8pm; 50¢). Otherwise, public transportation is inadequate. DOT **buses** (℡313/933-1300) run a patchy inner-city service for $1.25 per ride, while the slightly better SMART buses ($1.50; ℡313/962-5515) serve suburbia. Transportation in the Motor City is geared firmly towards the **car**; driving is not too much of a challenge, but you do need to know where you're heading. During the day, April–August, the Attractions Shuttle **minibuses** (℡313/259-8726) run between the major sights with unlimited stops for $4.

The Motown sound

Mo.town (mo'toun') adj [< a trademark for phonograph records, etc. <Mo(tor) Town, nickname for Detroit, Mich] designating or of style of rhythm and blues characterized by a strong, even beat.

Webster's New World Dictionary of the American Language

The legend that is Tamla Motown started in 1959 when Ford worker and part-time songwriter **Berry Gordy Jr** borrowed $800 to set up a studio. From his first hit onward – the prophetic *Money (That's What I Want)* – he set out to create a crossover style, targeting his records at white and black consumers alike.

Early Motown hits were pure **formula**. Gordy softened the blue notes of most contemporary black music in favor of a more danceable, poppy beat, with **gospel**-influenced singing and clapping. Prime examples of the early approach featured all-female groups like the **Marvelettes** (*Needle in a Haystack*), the **Supremes** (*Baby Love*) and **Martha Reeves and the Vandellas** (*Nowhere to Run*), as well as the all-male **Miracles** (*Tracks of My Tears*), featuring the sophisticated love lyrics of lead singer **Smokey Robinson**. Gordy's "Quality Control Department" scrutinized every beat, playing all recordings through speakers modeled on cheap transistor radios before the final mix.

The Motown organization was an intense, close-knit community: **Marvin Gaye** married Gordy's sister. "Little" **Stevie Wonder** was the baby of the family. It did, however, move with the times, utilizing such innovations as the wah-wah pedal and synthesizer. By the late 1960s its output had acquired a harder sound, crowned by the acid soul productions of Norman Whitfield with the versatile **Temptations**. In 1968 the organization outgrew its premises on Grand Avenue; four years later it abandoned Detroit altogether for LA, to be closer to Hollywood. Befitting the MOR tastes of the 1970s, the top sellers now were the high-society soul of **Diana Ross** and the ballads of the **Commodores**. White artists began to appear on the label: Tom Jones is said to have turned down a contract, though R. Dean Taylor (*Indiana Wants Me*) and the less successful Kiki Dee accepted.

The 1970s saw many top artists, dissatisfied with Gordy's constant intervention, leave the label. The crack songwriting team of Holland-Dozier-Holland, responsible for most of the **Four Tops**' hits, stayed in Detroit to produce the seminal **Chairmen of the Board** (*Gimme Just A Little More Time*), along with **Aretha Franklin** and **Jackie Wilson**.

Today Motown is owned by the giant **PolyGram** corporation. Artists on the label include Boyz II Men, Queen Latifah and, to this day, Stevie Wonder.

Detroit's main **visitor center** is downtown at 211 W Fort St on the tenth floor (Mon–Fri 9am–5pm; ☎1-800/DETROIT, ⓦ www.visitdetroit.com). An information booth is at the entrance to the Henry Ford Greenfield Village (May–Sept daily 9am–5pm; ☎313/271-1620). The main **post office** is at 1401 W Fort St, at Eighth Street (Mon–Fri 8.30am–5pm, Sat 8am–noon; zip code 48200).

Accommodation

Downtown Detroit caters well for expense-account travelers – its top-range hotels are as secure as any city's – but if your budget is restricted it's harder to find lodging that is both cheap and safe at night. A fifteen percent tax comes slapped onto room bills. If exchange rates are favorable it may be worth staying in Windsor, Ontario.

The Atheneum 1000 Brush St ☎313/962-2323 or 1-800/772-2323, ⓦ www.atheneumsuites.com. At this swish, newish, all-suite hotel in Greektown, some units fetch more than $300 a night; others are a third of that price. ❼

Best Western 1020 Washington Blvd ☎313/887-7000. This newly remodeled mid-range hotel offers a pool, athletic room and complimentary continental breakfast. ❹

Dobson House 1439 Bagley Ave ☎313/965-1887. A functional Victorian B&B near the former Tiger Stadium, it includes a continental breakfast in its rates. ❺

Fairfield Inn – Auburn Hills 1294 Opdyke Rd ☎248/373-2228. This clean new motel on the north edge of the metro area is close to Pontiac Silverdome. ❹

Fairfield Inn – Metro Airport 31119 Flynn Drive, Romulus ☎734/728-2322. It's the pick of the budget motels near the airport. ❹

HI-Country Grandma's Home Hostel 22330 Bell Rd, New Boston ☎734/753-4901. This friendly home hostel on the outskirts of Dearborn is halfway between Detroit and Ann Arbor. Beds are $11 for HI-AYH members, $14 for others. ❶

Holiday Inn Express 34952 Woodward Ave, Birmingham ☎248/646-7300. Recently renovated, it is reasonably placed for Birmingham and Royal Oak restaurants and bars. ❼

Hotel St Regis 3071 W Grand Blvd ☎313/873-3000. This nice old hotel is about four miles from downtown. Other than the Motown Museum, there's little to see in the immediate area, though it is well placed for those with a car. Weekend rates see a price drop of around $35. ❻

Hyatt Regency Dearborn Fairlane Town Center, Dearborn ☎313/593-1234 or 1-800/233-1234. A candy-brown colossus, it has every imaginable amenity. Though not cheap, it has special deals. ❼

Ramada Plaza Hotel & Suites 430 Ouellette Ave, Windsor, ON ☎519/256-4656 or 1-800/769-0949. This renovated hotel next to the Windsor Tunnel has a bar, restaurant and indoor pool. ❹

Red Roof Inn 24130 Michigan Ave, Dearborn ☎313/278-9732 or 1-800/843-7663. Clean, budget lodgings near the Henry Ford Museum. ❹

Renaissance Center/Marriott Hotel downtown at Beaubien St and E Jefferson Ave ☎313/568-8000 or 1-800/228-9290, ⓦwww.mariotthotels.com. A fun place to stay, it towers over the city by the river – ask for a room on the upper floors. ❻

Sagamore Motor Lodge 30776 N Woodward Ave ☎248/549-1600. Have a look at the room first; if it's all right you've got a bargain, close to a trendy suburb, Royal Oak. Follow Woodward Ave away from the river (north) for 8 miles. ❸

Shorecrest Motor Inn 1316 E Jefferson Ave ☎313/568-3000 or 1-800/992-9616. A friendly, family-run place in lively Rivertown, just off downtown, it has been newly re-done with clean, good-value rooms. ❹

Downtown

Futuristic glass-box office buildings and a tastefully revamped park overlook the deodorant-green **Detroit River**, but for the most part downtown seems rather empty – even in the middle of the day, its streets are quiet and uncrowded. One reason is that most offices and stores are squeezed into the six gleaming towers of the **Renaissance Center**, a virtual city within a city. Zooming up 73 stories from the riverbank, the towers offer a great view of the metropolis from an observation deck ($3). This giant business, convention and retail center, known locally as the RenCen, was one of many complexes developed by **Detroit Renaissance** (a joint public/private sector project) to rejuvenate downtown in the aftermath of the 1967 riot. Seen by some as the savior of the city, the consortium is viewed less favorably by those who were compelled to sell their small businesses and homes to make way for its mammoth projects. In 1996, General Motors bought the RenCen, promising to take down the concrete ramparts that make it so fort-like and alienated from the rest of the city center. (The ramparts still stood in 2001.) Landscaping plans include a glass-enclosed "Winter Garden" on the river and a riverfront boardwalk to Belle Isle (see p.326).

Rare green space comes among the fountains and sculptures of **Hart Plaza**, which rolls down to the river in the shade of the RenCen. It hosts free lunchtime concerts and lively weekend ethnic festivals all summer long. The US leg of the annual **Montreux–Detroit Jazz Festival** takes place here in early September. The plaza nestles between the towering RenCen and another

DOWNTOWN DETROIT

ACCOMMODATION

The Atheneum	3
Best Western	2
Dobson House	4
Marriott Hotel	6
Sagamore Motor Lodge	1
Shorecrest Motor Inn	5

massive chunk of steel and concrete, the **Cobo Convention Center**. This in turn is next to **Joe Louis Arena** (℡313/983-6859), home of Detroit's beloved Red Wings hockey team, 1997 and 1998 Stanley Cup champions.

Ten blocks north up Woodward Avenue is the **Theater District**, downtown's prime nightlife spot. Highlights are the magnificently restored Siamese–Byzantine **Fox Theatre**, 2211 Woodward Ave (℡313/983-6611), a huge old movie palace that is the city's top concert and drama venue, and the grand Italian Renaissance **State Theatre** nearby (℡313/961-5450). This area is at the center of the city's massive **Columbia Street** redevelopment project, with the new baseball and football stadia (see "Sports," p.329), alongside microbreweries, coffee houses and the inevitable themed restaurants, including a *Hard Rock Café*.

Three miles east of the RenCen, **Belle Isle Park** is a quiet inner-city island retreat with twenty miles of walkways, sports facilities, a marina and free attractions including an aquarium, a Great Lakes Museum and elaborate gardens. It's also home to the annual **Detroit Grand Prix** for Indy cars. Diamond Jack's River Tours (June–Sept; $12; ☎313/843-7676, Ⓦwww.diamondjack.com) depart from Hart Plaza downtown, last two hours and loop round Belle Isle; alternatively, take DOT bus #25 and transfer to #12 at MacArthur Bridge.

The Detroit Cultural Center

Three miles northwest of downtown, next to Wayne State University, the top-class museums of the **Detroit Cultural Center** cluster within easy walking distance of each other, and you can easily spend a whole day here.

One hundred galleries in the colossal **Detroit Institute of Arts**, 5200 Woodward Ave (Wed–Fri 11am–4pm, Sat & Sun 11am–5pm; $4; ☎313/833-7900, Ⓦwww.dia.org), trace a history of civilization, most notably Chinese, Persian, Egyptian, Greek, Roman, Italian, Dutch and American. No fewer than 93 Rembrandts, 77 Matisses and 67 Picassos are in its collection, as are masterpieces such as a Van Gogh self-portrait and Joos Van Cleeve's *Adoration of the Magi*. However, Diego Rivera's enormous 1932 mural *Detroit Industry* steals the show. Guided tours of what ranks as one of America's most prestigious art museums take place at 1pm with an extra tour at 2.30pm on Sunday, for no additional charge.

The impressive new Charles H. Wright **Museum of African American History**, 315 E Warren St (daily except Mon 9.30am–5pm; $5; Ⓦwww.maah-detroit.org), is the largest African-American museum in the world. Its massive core exhibit covers 600 years of history in eight distinct segments, starting with a chilling sculpture of a slave boat, before moving through the Civil War, the Depression, and the respective work of Dr Martin Luther King and Malcolm X before settling on contemporary African-American society. Also in the Cultural Center, the **Detroit Historical Museum**, 5401 Woodward Ave (Wed–Fri 9.30am–5pm, Sat & Sun 10am–5pm; $3; Ⓦwww.detroithistorical.org), interprets the city's past through its "**Streets of Old Detroit**" display. Its most interesting exhibit, not surprisingly, examines the automobile, with an automated display of the "body drop" process on an assembly line.

The Motown Museum

Unlike cities such as Memphis, Nashville and New Orleans, Detroit is devoid of the bars, clubs and homes of its musical heroes. The golden age of Motown was very much confined to a time and a place, and, disappointingly, only at the **Motown Museum**, 2648 W Grand Blvd (Tues–Sat 10am–5pm, Sun & Mon noon–5pm; $6), can Tamla fans now pay homage to the world's most celebrated record label. The museum, run independently as a not-for-profit organization, is housed in the small white-and-blue-clapboard house that served as Motown's recording studio from 1959 to 1972. On the ground floor, Studio A remains just as it was left: battered instruments stand piled up against the nicotine-stained acoustic wall-tiles, and a well-scuffed Steinway piano all but fills the room. Upstairs are the former living quarters of label founder Berry Gordy, while in the adjoining house (once Motown's publishing office), record sleeves, gold and platinum discs and other memorabilia are displayed. The enthusiastic and knowledgeable staff will quite happily give one person the full tour. The museum was restored and expanded in 1995. Each October, Motown legends contribute to its upkeep by performing at the annual 2648 Grand fundraiser.

The Henry Ford Museum, Greenfield Village and the Automotive Hall of Fame

The enormous **Henry Ford Museum** (Ⓦ www.hfmgv.org), ten miles from downtown at 20900 Oakwood Blvd, Dearborn, pays fulsome tribute to its founder (an inveterate collector of Americana) as a brilliant industrialist and do-gooder. The former is certainly true. The hero of the "second industrial revolution" and inventor of the assembly line didn't succeed by being a philanthropist. His Service Department of 3500 private policemen prompted the *New York Times* in 1928 to call him "an industrialist fascist – the Mussolini of Detroit." To Ford, unions were 'the worst things that ever struck the earth,' though he was forced to let the UAW into his factories in 1943, after only 34 out of 78,000 workers voted against joining a union. Ford also bowed to the economic necessity of employing blacks, though he banned them from the model communities he built for his white workers. Instead, the company constructed a separate town, which he sardonically named Inkster.

In addition to the massive "**The Automobile in American Life**" exhibit, the twelve-acre museum amounts to a giant curiosity shop, holding several planes and trains, rows and rows of domestic inventions, and cabinets full of schoolchild collectibles like dime novels, comics and baseball cards. Real oddities include the chair Lincoln was sitting in and the car Kennedy was riding in when each was shot, and even a test tube holding Edison's last breath. One pertinent item not on view, however, is the Iron Cross that Hitler presented to Ford (a notorious anti-Semite) in 1938.

Ford uprooted the houses of famous Americans from all over the country to relocate them in **Greenfield Village**. Among the 240 buildings, you'll find Ford's own birthplace, the Wright Brothers' cycle shop, Edison's laboratory and Firestone's farm. Costumed hosts demonstrate everything from weaving to puncture repairing.

Reached on SMART bus routes #200 and #250, the museum and village are open daily from 9am to 5pm, although the interiors of the village buildings are closed Jan 4 to March. Tickets are $12.50 for the museum or village, $24 for a two-day combination ticket. For further information, call ☎313/271-1620 or 1-800/835-5237.

Directly next door to the Ford sprawl, the **Automotive Hall of Fame**, 21400 Oakwood Blvd (summer daily 10am–5pm; rest of year closed Mon; $6; Ⓦ www.automotivehalloffame.org), is more interesting than it might at first sound. In paying homage to the innovators and inventors of the global (not just the Detroit) auto industry, the interactive exhibits let visitors see how they would have handled problems encountered by Buick, Honda and the like. It's not just for mechanical types, either – there's a chance to pit your wits against the dealmakers who set up General Motors.

New additions include the **Spirit of Ford** at 1151 Village Rd (daily 9am–5pm; $9), which takes a fun, highly interactive look behind the scenes at Ford Motor Company.

Windsor, Ontario

The riverside cafés of the easygoing Canadian city of **WINDSOR**, due south of Detroit across the river, offer surprisingly pleasant views of their larger neighbor's skyline. Like Detroit's, Windsor's main industry is auto manufacturing, but it's much smaller and more relaxed, and makes a good place simply to hang out. However, two downtown **casinos** have added significant traffic to the streets. For those not hooked on slots and blackjack, the most interesting attraction is booze-oriented: the **Hiram Walker plant**, where Canadian Club whiskey is distilled, stands just a short stroll from downtown at Riverside and Walker (free tours and samplings Mon–Fri; ☎519/254-5171).

Transit Windsor **buses** (☎519/944-4111) connect downtown Detroit and downtown Windsor for $2.35 each way. Bring proper identification for customs and immigration officials. To drive, take the tunnel ($2 toll). The **visitor center** has two locations, across the Ambassador Bridge at 1235 Huron Church Rd, and at 110 Park St E in the city center (both open Sun–Thurs 8.30am–5pm, Fri–Sat 8am–8pm; ☎519/973-1338 or 1-800/265-3633).

Eating

Detroit's **ethnic** restaurants dish up the best (and least expensive) food in the city. **Greektown**, basically one block of Monroe Avenue between Beaubien and St Antoine streets, is crammed with authentic Greek places, and also contains Trappers Alley, a small mall brimming with good stalls and shops. Less commercial, but offering just as high a standard, are the bakeries, bars and cantinas of **Mexican Town**, five minutes from downtown. **Royal Oak**, ten miles north, has a wide range of vaguely alternative wholefood places, along with bars, record stores and bookstores, making it the liveliest suburban hangout in this massive sprawling metropolis.

Atwater Block Brewery 237 Joseph Campau St ☎313/393-2073. The new, spacious Rivertown brewpub serves up excellent beer-battered fish, mushrooms, mussels, wings and whatever else the chefs can think of.

Fishbone's Rhythm Kitchen Café 400 Monroe Ave, Greektown ☎313/965-4600. Noisy, fun and often packed Cajun joint.

Intermezzo 1435 Randolph St ☎313/961-0707. The cigar-and-martini set hangs out at this modern downtown Italian place. Good food.

La-Shish 12918 Michigan Ave, Dearborn ☎313/584-4477. Juice bar with good, inexpensive Lebanese dishes.

New Hellas Café 583 Monroe St, Greektown ☎313/961-5544. The very authentic, reasonably priced Greektown institution also includes the *Top of the Hellas* café, serving coffees and desserts in grand, relaxing surroundings.

Original Pancake House 33703 Woodward Ave, Birmingham ☎248/642-5775. Amid uninspired decor, it offers a huge variety of superb crepes, waffles, omelets and pancakes. Top breakfast spot.

Pronto! 608 S Washington, Royal Oak ☎248/544-0123. Big salads and a huge selection of sandwiches are the specialties in a soothing pastel space.

Rattlesnake Club 300 River Place, Rivertown ☎313/567-4400. Owned by creative Detroit master chef Jimmy Schmidt, it contains a setting to match the exquisite food. Dinner will set you back $15–25 per main course; lunch costs a lot less.

Woodbridge Tavern 289 St Aubin St, Rivertown ☎313/259-0578. Excellent burgers and sandwiches come with the 1920s decor and a great outdoor terrace and live rock music Thurs–Sun.

Xochimilco 3409 Bagley Ave ☎313/843-0179. The cornerstone restaurant of Detroit's authentic Mexican Town area delivers on huge portions, great service and superb value. Open to 2am, but if it's full try *El Zocala* across the street.

Nightlife

There's lots to do late at night in Detroit – the city where the techno beat originated and is still going strong – though if you're unfamiliar with the layout it's best to travel by taxi. In the past few years young whites from the suburbs have started to come back downtown for nights out, particularly to the bars and clubs of the **Theater District**, while the **Rivertown** area is renowned for its chic bistros and funky jazz and blues bars, tucked in among rambling warehouses. The suburbs of upmarket **Birmingham** and youthful **Royal Oak** are good places to hang out, while there are a couple of fun establishments in the blue-collar neighborhood of **Hamtramck**. Way up on the northern fringe, once-deserted **Pontiac** now has a range of well-attended rock venues, dance clubs and lounges. Canadian **Windsor** also has some good nightlife, with an age limit of 19 as opposed to Michigan's 21.

For details of events in Detroit, Ann Arbor and Windsor, pick up the free weekly *Metro Times*.

Gusoline Alley 309 S Center St, Royal Oak ☏ 248/545-2235. Cramped and dark with a loaded jukebox, this is a legend among Detroit bars. Go early for a seat; the wildly mixed crowd is a people-watcher's dream.

Lili's 21 2390 Jacob St, Hamtramck ☏ 313/875-6555. Cool and quirky rock venue, five miles from downtown.

Magic Bag 22920 Woodward Ave, Ferndale ☏ 248/544-3030. About two miles south of Royal Oak, this popular club boasts a huge range of beers, blues artists and regular roots acts.

Magic Stick 4120 Woodward Ave ☏ 313/833-9700. This great venue incorporates a bowling alley and billiards lounge. It is next to the Majestic Theater, a venue for big rock shows and huge techno nights.

Moto 3515 Caniff St, Hamtramck ☏ 313/369-0090. The place to see and be seen, and to dance to techno and funk, also books occasional live acts.

Rhinocero 265 Riopelle St, Rivertown ☏ 313/292-9230. Poppy jazz hangout – a tight squeeze but fun.

Saint Andrew's Hall/Shelter 431 E Congress St ☏ 313/961-MELT. The cramped downtown club promotes top bands on the alternative circuit. It only holds 800, so get a ticket in advance. Downstairs is the *Shelter* club, with lesser-known touring bands followed by dance music.

Tonic 29 S Saginaw St, Pontiac ☏ 248/334-7411. It bills itself as the premiere concert after-party: three levels of dancing and all the DJ vibe you can handle.

Classical music, theater and opera

Most of Detroit's major arts venues are handily grouped together in the northwest sector of downtown. A sweeping staircase and giant chandeliers are part of the splendor of the new **Detroit Opera House**, 1526 Broadway (☏313/237-7464, Ⓦwww.detroitoperahouse.com). Close by, the **Music Hall Center for Performing Arts**, 350 Madison Ave (☏313/963-7622, Ⓦwww.musichall.org), is the primary venue for **dance** in the city and also promotes rock concerts, youth theater and Broadway shows. In the Theater District, the gorgeous **Fox Theatre**, 2211 Woodward Ave (☏313/983-6611), is the biggest draw, hosting the big Broadway shows, while the cozy 450-seater **Gem Theatre**, 333 Madison Ave (☏313/963-9800, Ⓦwww.gemtheatre.com), and the **Masonic Temple Theatre**, nearby at 500 Temple St (☏313/832-2232, Ⓦwww.themasonic.com), a hall with near-perfect acoustics, are also worth a visit. A little further on toward the Cultural Center, the Detroit Symphony Orchestra performs at the **Orchestra Hall**, 3711 Woodward Ave (☏313/576-5100).

Sport

Detroit is one of the few cities with franchises competing at the highest level in all four major team sports. The toast of the local fans are the 1997 and 1998 **hockey** champions Red Wings, who entertain at the downtown Joe Louis Arena (☏313/983-6859 Ⓦwww.detroitredwings.com). Tickets are virtually impossible to get, but plenty of bars put on promotions for games. **Baseball**'s Tigers (☏313/962-4000, Ⓦwww.detroittigers.com) said their goodbyes to venerable Tiger Stadium at Michigan and Trumbull, and moved east to snazzy **Comerica Park** in 2000. Soon they'll be joined by the **football**-playing Lions (☏248/335-4131, Ⓦwww.detroitlions.com), who will move into a $225-million domed venue next door. In the meantime, the Lions and **basketball**'s Pistons (☏248/377-0100, Ⓦwww.nba.com/pistons) are based 25 miles north in the Pontiac Silverdome and Palace of Auburn Hills.

Around Detroit: Ann Arbor

Although its population just tops 100,000, **ANN ARBOR**, 45 minutes' drive west of Detroit along I-94, offers a greater choice of restaurants, live music venues and cultural activities than most towns ten times its size. The **University of Michigan** has shaped the economy and character of the town ever since it was moved here from Detroit in 1837, providing the city with a very conspicuous radical edge.

Much the best thing to do in Ann Arbor is to stroll round downtown and the campus, which meet at South State and Liberty streets. Downtown's twelve blocks of brightly painted shops and sidewalk cafés offer all you would expect from a college town, with forty bookshops and more than a dozen record stores. Don't miss the huge flagship store of Border's Books at 612 E Liberty St or Encore Recordings, 417 E Liberty St (℡313/994-8031).

Though the huge university campus doesn't look particularly appealing, it does emanate a sense of excitement, especially around the central meeting place of the **Diag**. Worth a look are the **Museum of Natural History**, 1109 Geddes Ave (Mon–Sat 9am–5pm, Sun noon–5pm; free), packed with huge dinosaur skeletons, rare Native American artifacts and a planetarium, and the small but eclectic **Museum of Art**, 525 S State St (Tues–Sat 10am–4pm, Thurs until 9pm, Sun noon–5pm; free).

Practicalities

Frequent Greyhound services to both Detroit and Chicago stop at 116 W Huron St; Amtrak is on the north edge of downtown at 325 Depot St. The **visitor center** is at 120 W Huron St (Mon–Fri 9am–5pm; ℡734/995-7281, ⓦwww.annarbor.org).

Although most Ann Arbor **motels** target their rates at conventioneers and academics, the *Lamp Post Inn*, 2424 E Stadium Blvd (℡734/971-8000, ⓦwww.lamppostinn.com; ❸), is a good-value motel about a mile from campus. The choice place to stay is the *Campus Inn*, right downtown at 615 E Huron St (℡734/769-2200 or 1-800/666-8693, ⓦwww.campusinn.com; ❼). Good **B&Bs** include the unusual *Artful Lodger* on the edge of the university campus at 1547 Washtenaw Ave (℡734/769-0653, ⓦwww.artlodger.com; ❹), decorated with art, theater and music memorabilia. The modern downtown *YMCA*, 350 S Fifth Ave (℡734/663-0536; ❷), is open to both sexes. The nearest **campground** is ten miles east, at the *KOA*, 6680 Bunton Rd, in blue-collar Ypsilanti.

Restaurants worth trying include the good-value Indian *Raja Rani*, 400 S Division St (℡734/995-1545), and the wholefood *Seva*, 314 E Liberty Ave (℡734/662-1111). *Jerusalem Garden*, 307 S Fifth Ave (℡734/995-5060), serves the best falafel in town, while *Zingerman's*, 422 Detroit St (℡734/663-DELI), is an excellent if expensive deli. A pair of popular **brewpubs** – the *Arbor Brewing Co*, 114 E Washington St (℡734/213-1393), and the *Grizzly Peak Brewing Co*, 120 W Washington St (℡734/741-7325) – are within a couple of blocks of each other.

Ann Arbor's **live music** scene has enjoyed a nationwide reputation ever since the Stooges, MC5 and Bob Seger made their names here. Unlike many college towns, the place doesn't go to sleep during the summer. For news of gigs, grab a copy of *Current*, a free monthly. Likely venues include the jazzy *Bird of Paradise*, 312 S Main St (℡734/662-8310), and the often-crowded *Del Rio*, 122 W Washington Ave (℡734/761-2530), which serves good Mexican food and hosts free Sunday jazz sessions. The *Blind Pig*, 208 S First St (℡734/996-8555), is the best place to watch live rock, alternative and blues while *The Ark*, 316 S Main St (℡734/761-1451), is a nationally significant venue for folk, acoustic and roots music. From time to time there are also live bands at the beautiful Art Deco *Michigan Theater*, 603 E Liberty St (℡734/668-8480), otherwise a great place to watch movies on the cheap.

Festivals are a key part of Ann Arbor life. The orchestral May Festival kicks off activities, followed by the Frog Island Festival in Ypsilanti, which focuses on jazz and world music in mid-June. July sees the hectic Street Art Fair with hundreds of stalls, while early September brings the recently revived Ann Arbor Blues and Jazz Festival.

The rest of the Lower Peninsula

Between Ann Arbor and the Lake Michigan coast there's not a whole lot worth stopping for, though Kellogg's new **Cereal City USA**, 171 W Michigan Ave (℡616/962-6230, ⓦwww.kelloggscerealcity.org), in Battle Creek is a fun diversion that traces the history of cereal – and of course, magnate Kellogg's impact on it (summer Mon–Fri 9.30am–5pm, Sat 9.30am–6pm, Sun 11am–5pm; call for winter hours; $7.95). Further west, **St Joseph** is just the first of many small ports on the 350-mile trip north along Lake Michigan's eastern shore, the northwest reaches of the peninsula attracting sportspeople and tourists from all over the Midwest. Within striking distance of **Traverse City** are the beautiful **Sleeping Bear Dunes** and the charming towns of **Charlevoix** and **Petoskey**. At the northern tip, a revitalized **Mackinaw City** is the departure point for the state's major tour-bus attraction, old-world **Mackinac Island**.

Along Lake Michigan

Less than thirty miles north of Indiana, **ST JOSEPH** lies just north of "Harbor Country" – a string of small towns offering good swimming, boating and fishing opportunities. St Joseph's neat downtown perches on a high bluff, from which steep steps lead down to sandy Silver Beach, where each of the two parallel piers has its own lighthouse. When not swimming, watch the yachts go by while eating great **food** at *Clementine's Too* (℡616/983-0990), 1235 Broad St, or at a sidewalk table at *Schu's*, 501 Pleasant St (℡616/983-7248). **Places to stay** include the classy lakeside *Boulevard Suite Hotel*, 521 Lake Blvd (℡616/983-6600; ❺), where all the rooms are suites, and the good-value *Econolodge*, two miles from downtown at 2723 Niles Ave (℡616/983-6321; ❷). For general information on the area, call into the **visitor center** just off I-94 exit 29 (℡616/925-6301).

Fifty miles north, **HOLLAND** was settled in 1847 by Dutch religious dissidents. Today's residents lose no opportunity to let visitors know of their roots: tens of thousands of tulips brighten the town in early summer, while the Netherlands museum, a Dutch village, a clog factory and the inevitable windmill all attract tourist dollars. Twenty miles farther up the shoreline, **GRAND HAVEN** boasts one of the largest and best sandy beaches on the Great Lakes, seen on a leisurely stroll along the one-and-a-half-mile boardwalk (for the most part a concrete path). At the top of Dewey Hill stands a huge, electronically controlled musical fountain.

Just under one hundred miles farther north, a string of pleasant small villages starts with **LUDINGTON**, where **Ludington State Park**, eight miles north on Hwy-116, offers great hiking and sightseeing amid sweeping sand dunes and virgin pine forests; admission is $4 per car. **Camping** in some beautiful sites costs $15 a night. From downtown, the **Lake Michigan Car Ferry** departs for Manitowoc, Wisconsin ($40 per adult, $47 per car, not including driver; ☎231/845-5555 or 1-800/841-4243, ⊛www.ssbadger.com) – a comparative bargain when you weigh up the cost of braving the cross-Chicago traffic. The best place to **stay overnight** is *Snyder's Shoreline Inn*, 903 W Ludington Ave (☎231/845-1261 or 1-800/843-2177, ⊛www.snydersshoreinn.com; ❹), the only downtown property with uninterrupted views of the lakeshore. *House of Flavors*, 402 W Ludington Ave (☎231/845-5785), is a chrome-heavy diner serving breakfasts, burgers and a huge range of ice cream. *Scotty's*, 5910 E Ludington Ave (☎231/843-4033), is reliable for lunch and does steaks and seafood in the evenings. The **visitor center** is on the east side of town at 5827 US-10 (☎231/845-0324 or 1-800/542-4600).

Surrounded by forest, **MANISTEE**, 32 miles north, boasts an attractive Victorian downtown and a mile-long **boardwalk** that runs alongside the Manistee River onto Lake Michigan. One of several pretty lakeside areas is **Douglas Park** – with a good sandy beach, small marina and picnic area – next to the *Lake Shore Motel*, 101 S Lakeshore Drive (☎231/723-2667; ❺). To stay downtown, try the *Maples B&B*, 435 Fifth St (☎231/723-2904; ❸). The **Chamber of Commerce** is at 11 Cypress St (Mon–Fri 8am–5.30pm; ☎231/723-2575).

Thirty miles north, tiny **FRANKFORT** nestles under bluffs overlooking Lake Michigan. With a grassy park and a small beach at either end of its main street, it not only makes a charming stop for lunch or a picnic, but also provides cheaper **accommodation** than the Leelanau Peninsula towns just to the north. The *Harbor Lights Motel and Condos*, 15 Second St (☎231/352-9614; ❹), stands right on the beach. The *Still Grinning Inn*, 670 Crystal Ave (☎231/352-7669; ❷), provides great value B&B. Along the main drag, the *Frankfort Deli*, 327 Main St (☎231/352-3354), has good sandwiches. Directly across the street, the *Coho Café* (☎231/352-6053) serves up well-priced modern food. The **visitor center** (Mon–Fri 9am–noon & 1–5pm; ☎231/352-7251) is also on Main Street, opposite the park.

The Leelanau Peninsula

The southwestern edge of the heavily wooded **Leelanau Peninsula** is occupied by the **Sleeping Bear Dunes National Lakeshore**, a constantly re-sculptured area of towering dunes and precipitous 400ft drops. The area was named by the Chippewa, who saw the mist-shrouded North and South Manitou islands as the graves of two drowned bear cubs, and the massive mainland dune, covered with dark trees, as their grieving mother. Fierce winds off Lake Michigan cause the dunes to edge inland, burying trees that reappear years later stripped of foliage, while the continual attack of high water undercuts the massive sand banks, occasionally sending massive chunks into the lake. Stunning overlooks can be had along the hilly, nine-mile loop of the **Pierce Stocking Scenic Drive**, off Hwy-109. You can also clamber up the strenuous but enjoyable **Dune Climb**, four miles farther north on Hwy-109 (best done barefoot, as shoes soon fill with sand).

The **visitor center** (☎231/326-5134, ⊛www.leelanau.com), at the junction of highways 22 and 109, provides details on trails, campgrounds and beaches. Nearby, the village of **GLEN ARBOR**, dotted with some interesting galleries, is the closest community to the dunes. Decent places to **eat** here include *Le Bear*, 5707 Lake St (☎231/334-4640), where affordable lunches and costly seafood dinners are served on a waterfront deck, and *Art's Bar*, 6487 Western Ave (☎231/334-3754), a pleasant tavern delivering great hamburgers and inexpensive fried fish.

LELAND, fifteen miles north, makes an even better base. Its harbor, crammed with expensive launches, holds a quaint collection of well-weathered sheds, known as **Fishtown**, where the day's catch was once hauled in for gutting and smoking; most are now touristy knickknack shops. *The Cove*, at 111 River St (☎231/256-9834), serves up tasty Great Lakes fish dishes and a superb key lime pie. **Ferries** from Leland ($22 round-trip; ☎231/256-9061) go to the uninhabited North and South Manitou islands. **NORTHPORT**, on the tip of the peninsula, is another relaxing fishing village, where the *Beech Tree*, 202 Waukazoo St (☎231/386-5200), is an art gallery that's worth a look. Eleven miles south on the peninsula's east coast, **SUTTONS BAY** may not be as pretty but its main artery, St Joseph Avenue, has some of the area's best places to eat. *Hatties*, at no. 111 (☎231/271-6222), serves fine meals along the lines of chicken with cherry sauce and Thai scallops. *Café Bliss*, at no. 420 (☎231/271-5000), specializes in vegetarian and Native American cuisine with entrees around $12. The *Hose House Deli*, in a restored 1913 fire station at no. 303 (☎231/271-6303), serves large good-value sandwiches and coffee.

Nowhere on the peninsula is **accommodation** inexpensive. The best option is the *Leelanau Country Inn*, midway between Glen Arbor and Leland at 149 East Harbor Hwy, Maple City (☎231/228-5060, ⓦwww.leelanaucountryinn.com; ❸), a good-value Victorian B&B serving large breakfasts.

Traverse City

Smooth beaches and striking bay views help make lively **TRAVERSE CITY**, 242 miles northwest of Detroit, the favorite in-state resort for Michigan natives. A town of 15,000 year-round residents, it was saved from the stagnation that overtook many communities when their lumber mills closed down, because the stripped fields proved to be ideal for fruit-growing. Today, the area's claim to be "**Cherry Capital of the World**" is no idle boast. Thousands of acres of cherry orchards envelop the town, their wispy, pink blossoms bringing a delicate beauty each May. At the **National Cherry Festival** during the first full week in July, visitors can watch parades, fireworks and concerts and sample every imaginable cherry product. Coca-Cola chose the event to launch its cherry flavor in the 1980s.

Traverse City's neat **downtown** rests along the bottom of the west arm of **Grand Traverse Bay**, below the Old Mission Peninsula. This slender seventeen-mile strip of land, which divides the bay into two inlets, makes for a pleasant short driving tour. Narrow roads slice through miles of cherry orchards and vineyards, with tremendous simultaneous views of the bay on either side. Five sandy public beaches and a small harbor can be found around the town itself. Various companies offer boat, windsurfer, jet ski and mountain bike rental (the surrounding countryside is excellent for cycling). There are 36 **golf courses** – some of them among the most beautiful in the country – in the immediate area.

Practicalities

Greyhound stops near downtown at 3233 Cass Rd. The **visitor center**, downtown at 101 Grandview Parkway (summer Mon–Fri 9am–7pm, Sat 9am–6pm, Sun noon–4pm; rest of year Mon–Fri 9am–5pm, weekends vary; ☎231/947-1120 or 1-800/TRAVERS, ⓦwww.tcvisitors.com), can help with finding **accommodation**, though there's a dearth of central budget lodgings in summer. The attractive little *Bay Shore Motel*, near downtown at 833 E Front St (☎231/935-4400; ❻), has a private beach and nice rooms. The remodeled and very central *Park Place Hotel*, 300 E State St (☎231/946-5000 or 1-800/748-0133, ⊕www.park-place-hotel.com; ❻), is reliable, as are the well-maintained *Days Inn & Suites*, 420 Munson Ave (☎231/941-0208; ❺), and the basic but clean *Sierra Motel*, 230 Munson Ave (☎231/946-7720; ❹), both a couple of miles southeast. There's **camping** at Traverse City State Park, just outside town at 1132 US-31 N ($15/night; ☎231/922-5270).

Traverse City brochures may tout its exclusive country clubs, but more affordable **places to eat** are easy to find. Big breakfasts with home-baked bread are served at *Mabel's*, 472 Munson Ave (☎231/947-0252), while *Mode's Bum Steer*, 125 E State St (☎231/947-9832), is Traverse's premier rib joint. The best bet for a meal, particularly in the evening, is to drive north onto the Old Mission Peninsula where the *Boathouse*, 14039 Peninsula Drive (☎231/223-4030), dishes up fresh seafood, pasta and vegetarian food right by the lake. Farther up, on the peninsula's central spine road, the popular *Old Mission Tavern*, 17015 Center Rd (☎231/223-7280), has classic European dishes and lots of local art.

The *U & I Lounge*, 214 E Front St, is the best **bar** in town; it also serves up great gyros, burgers and salads. *Union Street Station*, 117 S Union St (☎231/941-1930), has pool tables and **live music** of all sorts most nights.

North of Traverse City

Scenic Hwy-31 skims along Lake Michigan and through **Charlevoix** and other pretty lakeside towns on its way north from Traverse City. The northern tip of the peninsula is occupied by the much improved **Mackinaw City**, where ferries take excursionists to much-hyped **Mackinac Island** – billboards advertise its attractions for fifty miles before you arrive.

Charlevoix, Petoskey and Harbor Springs

CHARLEVOIX boasts a positively idyllic setting, fronting onto three separate lakes: Michigan, Charlevoix and the beautiful, bowl-shaped Round Lake. Petunia-lined **Bridge Street**, the two-block downtown, looks over a picturesque, almost landlocked **harbor** on Round Lake, hemmed in on other sides by terraced ridges. An undeniably beautiful place, in recent years it has become a bit too fancy. Stop by the helpful **visitor center**, 408 E Bridge St (☎231/547-2101 or 1-800/367-8557). Two sandy beaches on the Michigan shoreline are great places to watch the sunset.

Lakeside **hotels**, such as the turreted *Weathervane Terrace*, 111 Pine River Lane (☎231/547-9955, ⊕www.weathervane-chx.com; ❼), may charge more than $300 on peak weekends. The *Charleboyne Motel*, at US-31 and Boyne City Road a mile north of town (☎231/547-9340; ❸), is small, basic and clean. One of the best value **B&Bs**, the *MacDougall House*, 109 Petoskey Ave (☎231/547-5788, ⊕www.michiganbandb.com; ❹), has private bathrooms and huge breakfasts. *Whitney's Oyster Bar*, 305 Bridge St (☎231/547-0818), serves fresh seafood and snacks until 2am with lots of beers and upstairs seating.

Bigger and busier **PETOSKEY**, sixteen miles north along US-31, high above Lake Michigan, feels more like a real town, with its grand Victorian houses encircling the nicely restored **Gaslight District** downtown. Ernest Hemingway spent many of his teenage summers here – his novel *The Torrents of Spring* alludes to several local landmarks. The most central and welcoming hotel is the venerable *Perry's Hotel*, at Bay and Lewis streets (☎231/347-4000 or 1-800/737-1899; ❺); its *Noggin Room Pub* has good snacks and pizza. The award-winning *Serenity B&B*, at 618 E Lake St (☎231/347-1338, www.serenitybb.com; ❻), is a big Victorian house serving superb full breakfasts. Budget lodging is sometimes available in the clean dorms at North Central Michigan College, 1515 Howard St (☏231/348-6611; ❶). One of Hemingway's favorite hangouts was *Jesperson's*, 312 Howard St (☏231/347-3601), which still does great pies and sandwiches. The locally popular *Mitchell Street Pub*, 426 E Mitchell St (☏231/347-1801), also offers decent snacks. The town's helpful **visitor center** is at 401 E Mitchell St (Mon–Fri 8am–4pm; ☏1-800/845-2828, www.petoskey.com).

Twelve miles up Hwy-119, **HARBOR SPRINGS** is a favorite with the Midwestern elite. Its charming main street and small shaded beach with park are certainly captivating, but the sheer ostentation puts many off this "Cornbelt Riviera" resort. The comfy *Harbor Springs Cottage Inn*, at Bay and Zoll streets (☏231/526-5431; ❺), has the only reasonably affordable rooms in town.

Mackinaw City

Forty miles northeast of Petoskey, **MACKINAW CITY** has long enjoyed a steady tourist trade as the major embarkation point for Mackinac Island (the other is the sleepier town of **St Ignace** just across the bridge).

Mackinaw City was once little more than a bland colony of cheap motels and fudge shops looking for business from those who couldn't get a place to stay on the island. The city was once a terminus for freight trains; the oil and other detritus they dumped put the city's sewer system under strain and for a decade or so there was a moratorium on new development. Now, the streets have been landscaped with trees that are lit up at night, and visitors flock to the new **Mackinaw Crossings** on South Huron Street. This mall-cum-entertainment zone has given the town a lift, offering vacationers several dozen niche retail stores, a food court, a multiscreen cinema and an amphitheater that hosts nightly live acts and a laser show at 10pm during the summer.

Several mid-priced **motels** have been built alongside the shore, among them the *Ramada Limited Waterfront*, 723 S Huron St (☏231/436-5055; ❺), and the *Best Western Dockside Waterfront* (☏231/436-5001; ❻–❽). A couple blocks north at 111 Langlade St, the *Welcome Inn* (☏231/436-5525; ❸) offers simple, clean rooms for a much better rate. A good **meal** can be had outdoors at the *Depo*, 250 S Huron St (☏231/436-7060), a refurbished train station in the Courtyards of Mackinaw City; enjoy the tasty grill food and seafood dips with a good view of the entertainment in the adjacent amphitheater.

Mackinac Island

Viewed from an approaching boat, the tree-blanketed rocky limestone outcrop of **MACKINAC ISLAND** (pronounced "Mackinaw"), suddenly thrusting out from the swirling waters, is an unforgettable sight. As you near the harbor, large Victorian houses come into view, dappling the hillsides with white and pastel. The most conspicuous is the imposing $250-plus-a-night *Grand Hotel* (☏906/847-3331, www.grandhotel.com; ❾), where just to enter the foyer costs $5. On disembarking, you'll see rows of horses and buggies (all motorized transportation is banned from the island, except for emergency vehicles) and inhale the omnipresent smell of fresh manure. Also ubiquitous on the island is **fudge**, relentlessly marketed as a Mackinac "delicacy."

Mackinac's crowded Main Street and the contrived nostalgia can get irritating, but the island is still worth visiting, not least for the ferry ride over and the chance to cycle along the hilly back roads. Underneath the tourist trimmings is a rich history. French priests established a mission to the Huron Indians here during the winter of 1670–71. The French built a fort in 1715 but within fifty years had lost control of the island to the British. Since independence Mackinac has been a base for John Jacob Astor's American Fur Company, a fishing port, and a jail for Confederate officers during the Civil War. The government acknowledged its beauty by designating it as the country's second national park, two years after Yellowstone in 1875, though management was handed over to the state of Michigan twenty years later. To get a feel for the history, hike or cycle up to the whitewashed stone **Fort Mackinac**, a US Army outpost until 1890. Its ramparts afford a great view of the village and lake below, though admission is a steep $8 (May to mid-Oct 9.30am–6.30pm).

Practicalities

Arnold Transit ($15.50; $6.50 for bikes; ☎906/847-3351 or 1-800/542-8528, ⓦwww.arnoldonline.com) is the only one of the three ferry companies to offer a high-speed catamaran **crossing from Mackinaw City** to the island.

The average **room** on Mackinac costs more than $130 per night. The least costly hotel is *Murray's* (☎906/847-3360 or 1-800/462-2546; ❺), which serves a large continental breakfast buffet. Unpretentious B&Bs such as the *Bogan Lane Inn* (☎906/847-3439, ⓦwww.mackinac.com/noganlane/; ❸) and the secluded *Small Point* (☎906/847-3758; ❹) are more affordable. *Haan's 1830 Inn* (☎906/847-6244; ❺) is a big Greek Revival home close by the harbor. The **information kiosk** on Main Street (☎906/847-3783) provides full details of accommodation, horseback rides and bike rental.

The Upper Peninsula

From the map, it would seem logical for Michigan's **Upper Peninsula**, separated from the rest of the state by the **Mackinac Straits**, to be part of Wisconsin. However, when Michigan entered the Union in 1837 (eleven years before Wisconsin), its legislators, keen to tap the peninsula's huge mineral wealth, incorporated it into their new state.

Before then the UP, as it's commonly known, figured prominently in French plans to create an empire in North America. Father Jacques Marquette and other missionaries made peace with the native people and established settlements, including the port of Sault Ste Marie in 1688. The French hoped to press further south, but before they could get much past Detroit, the British inflicted a severe military defeat in 1763.

Vast, lonesome and wild, the Upper Peninsula is full of stunning landmarks, exemplified by the **Pictured Rocks National Lakeshore**. Most of the eastern section is marked by low-lying, sometimes swampy land in between softly undulating limestone hills. The northwest corner is the most desolate, especially the rough and broken **Keewanaw Peninsula**, and **Isle Royale National Park** fifty miles offshore. The UP's only real city is **Marquette**, a college town with a quiet buzz – a good base from which to explore the UP's rugged terrain. Until 1957 you could get to the UP from lower Michigan only by ferry. Today, the five-mile **Mackinac Bridge** ($1.50 toll), lit up beautifully at night, stretches elegantly across the bottleneck Straits of Mackinac.

Sault Ste Marie

Perched at the northeast corner of the UP, 340 miles from Detroit, **SAULT STE MARIE** (known locally as *The Soo*) stands across St Mary's Rapids from the Canadian town bearing the same name. It's one of the oldest settlements in the US, not that you'd guess that from its bedraggled, 1950s-looking downtown and the industrial sprawl of the waterfront. The Soo owes most of its trade and industry to the St Mary's Locks, the only water connection between Superior and the other Great Lakes, built in 1855 and later expanded to take oceangoing vessels. Four giant reservoirs raise upbound boats 21 feet to the level of Lake Superior. To see this impressive operation, which accounts for more tonnage than the Suez and Panama canals combined, take one of the **Soo Locks boat tours** ($15; ☎906/632-6301, ⓦwww.soolocks.com) from Dock #1 or Dock #2 on East Portage Avenue, or watch for free from the visitor center (daily 7am–11pm).

Despite efforts to increase its tourist trade, the Soo is not a place where you'd want to spend much time. The *Crestview Thrifty Inn*, 1200 Ashmun St (☎906/635-5213; ❹), has clean, comfortable rooms. The *Bambi Motel*, further along at no. 1801 (☎906/632-7881; ❸), has one of the most garish signs you'll ever lock eyes on. *Antler's*, 804 E Portage Ave (☎906/632-3571), looks like a dive bar but is in fact an historic **pub**, where you can also get reasonable steaks and fish.

Paradise

Native Americans who lived in this area sixty miles west and north of the Soo called it *Tahquamenon* (Marsh of the Blueberries). Now it's called **PARADISE**, and in summer this elongated lakeside village can live up to its name, cut as it is out of thick, dark green forests and surrounded by small, reed-cluttered ultramarine lakes. Life is slow and easy here, but the choppy waters of Superior deny absolute calm to the beach. In winter, temperatures drop to -40°F and snowmobiles are the usual mode of transportation. Ten miles west on Hwy-123, one of the most popular spots on the UP for hiking, boating and camping, is the gorgeous **Tahquamenon Falls State Park** ($3 per car; ☎906/492-3415), where waters, dyed a translucent brown by tannic acid, spill over two sets of cataracts.

Whitefish Road winds eleven miles north of town to where shingly **Whitefish Point** nudges into the harsh waters of Lake Superior. Raging northwesterly winds building up over almost four hundred miles of open lake have contributed to more than five hundred shipwrecks along the eighty-mile stretch of lakeshore westward to Munising. That story is told there at the **Great Lakes Shipwreck Historical Museum** (mid-May to mid-Oct daily 10am–6pm; $7.50) with the help of subtle lighting and atmospheric background music. It's not all ancient history; the cargo ship *Edmund Fitzgerald* foundered in 96mph gusts on November 10, 1975, with the loss of its 29-strong crew.

Curley's Motel & Cabins (☎906/492-3445; ❸) is your best bet for **accommodation**: six-person cabins cost under $100, and there's a nice beach on site. Or check out the *Yukon Inn* (☎906/492-3264), full of stuffed trophies, across the road. A clean budget option is the *Vagabond Motel* (☎906/492-3477; ❷), while you can pitch a tent at the *Superior Campground* (☎906/492-3249), a mile south of town near *The Penguin*, a restaurant popular for its whitefish.

Pictured Rocks National Lakeshore

The 42 miles between the attractive fishing villages of **Grand Marais** and **Munising** form the **Pictured Rocks National Lakeshore**, a splendid array of multicolored cliffs, rolling dunes and secluded sandy beaches. Rain, wind, ice and sun have carved and gouged arches, columns and caves into the face of the lakeshore, all stained different hues. Hiking trails run along the clifftops and the partially unpaved Hwy-58 takes you close to the water, but the best way to see the cliffs is by **boat**. Pictured Rocks Cruises offers a three-hour narrated tour that leaves from the left of the City Pier in Munising (July & Aug 5-7 trips daily; June, Sept & early Oct 2 trips daily; $22; ℡906/387-2379). Less than a mile farther along the lake at 1204 Commercial St, Shipwreck Tours gives two-hour narrated cruises in a glass-bottom boat with surprisingly clear views of three shipwrecks – one intact (June to early Oct 2-3 trips daily; $20; ℡906/387-4477). Those in a hurry can get a glimpse by visiting the **Miners Castle Overlook**, just east of Munising, or **Munising Falls**, one of half a dozen nearby waterfalls, near the village's well-posted **visitor center** (℡906/387-2138). In Munising, *Scotty's Motel*, 415 Cedar St (℡906/387-2449; ❸), and the *Munising Motel*, 332 E Onota St (℡906/387-3187; ❹), are comfortable enough places to stay.

Marquette

Forty miles west of Munising is the unofficial capital of the UP, the bustling college town of **MARQUETTE**, also the center of the area's massive ore industry.

The helpful **state welcome center** (summer daily 9am–6pm, rest of year daily 9am–5pm; ℡906/249-9066), 2201 US-41 S just south of town, has vouchers for local hotel discounts and lots of information about Marquette's sights. Premier among them is rugged **Presque Isle Park**, north of town on Lakeshore Boulevard, almost completely surrounded by Lake Superior and with stunning views of the lake. Back at East Ridge Street and Lakeshore, the **Marquette Maritime Museum** (late May–Sept daily 10am–5pm; $3) has exhibits on the fishing and freighting industries, as well as a video about the fabled Superior wrecking of the *Edmund Fitzgerald*. The area's most curious sight, however, is the **Superior Dome**, on Northern Michigan University's campus at 1401 Presque Isle Ave, the largest wooden dome in the world.

Accommodations in Marquette are abundant and inexpensive. Cheap motels cluster west of town on US-41, but there are better, equally affordable options downtown. The *Village Inn* at 1301 N Third St (℡906/226-9400, 1-800/800-8909; ⓦwww.villageinnofmarquette.com; ❸/❹) offers high-quality, good-value rooms (some with kitchen), but by far the nicest place to stay is the grand **Landmark Inn** at 230 N Front St (℡906/228-2580, ⓦwww.thelandmarkinn .com; ❺/❻), with rooms overlooking the lake. You can camp at the *Tourist Park Campground* (℡906/228-0465) on Sugarloaf Avenue.

Downtown, *JJ's Shamrock,* 113 S Front St (℡906/226-6734), serves basic bar food along with occasional live music. For a more formal dining experience, locals favor the *Northwoods Supper Club* (℡906/228-4343), just west of town off US-41, with a meat-and-potatoes menu in a rustic setting. Popular drinkspots include *Remie's Bar*, 111 Third St (℡906/226-9133), with a rowdy local crowd and live music on Wednesdays.

The Keewanaw Peninsula

Beyond Marquette, the land becomes progressively more rough-hewn, culminating in the **Keewanaw Peninsula**, which juts like a dorsal fin eighty miles out into Lake Superior. Encircled by a dramatic shoreline and enriched by crags and precipices, it's a great place for a short driving tour, with roads winding through forests, past old copper workings and up and down steep hills.

Halfway up the peninsula in the small college town of **HOUGHTON** on Portage Lake, the *College Motel* at 1308 College Ave next to the Michigan Tech campus (☎906/482-2202; ❷) is good value. The luxury option is the 100-year-old *Charleston House Inn B&B*, 918 College Ave (☎906/482-7790, Ⓦwww.charlestonhouseinn.com; ❼), downtown by the water. The *Suomi Home Bakery and Restaurant* (☎906/482-3220), under the covered street downtown, serves cheap pasties and Finnish food. At the northern tip of Keewanaw, best reached along Hwy-26 (the Brockway Mountain Drive) from Eagle River, handsome little **COPPER HARBOR** was once so rich in minerals that early miners could pick up chunks of pure copper from the lakeshore. Today you can tour the **Delaware Mine** (☎906/289-4688, Ⓦwww.copper-harbor.org), ten miles west on US-41. Budget **accommodation** is available at the *Norland Motel* (☎906/289-4815; ❷), two miles east on US-41, next to Fort Wilkins State Park.

Isle Royale National Park

Much closer to Canada than the US, the 45-mile sliver of **ISLE ROYALE NATIONAL PARK**, fifty miles out in Lake Superior, is in a double sense as far as you can get in Michigan from Detroit. All cars are banned and, instead of freeways, 166 miles of hiking trails lead past windswept trees, swampy lakes and grazing moose. The park is open from mid-May until the end of September. Aside from other outdoors types the only traces of human life you're likely to see are ancient mineworks (thought to be two millennia old), shacks left behind by commercial fishermen in the 1940s and a few lighthouses and park buildings. Trekking, canoeing, fishing and scuba-diving among shipwrecks are the principal leisure activities. Camping is free, but visit the **park headquarters** at 800 E Lakeshore Drive (☎906/482-0984) in Houghton before you leave the mainland, for advice on water purity, mosquitoes and temperatures that can drop well below freezing even in summer. You can also stay in a self-catering cottage or a more expensive lodge room (including all meals) at the *Rock Harbor Lodge* (PO Box 605, Houghton, MI 49931; ☎906/337-4993, Oct–April ☎270/773-2191; see Ⓦwww.grand-isle-royale.com; ❻). The lodge rents canoes and motorboats for $22 and $48 per day, respectively, and offers cruises for $11.

Ferries leave from Copper Harbor ($40 one-way; ☎906/289-4437), Houghton ($47 one-way; ☎906/482-0984) and Grand Portage, Minnesota ($32–52 one-way; ☎715/392-5551). If there are enough in your party, it may be just as economical to charter a **plane** from Isle Royale Seaplane Service in Houghton (☎906/482-8850).

Indiana

Thanks to an early nineteenth-century influx of northward migrants, much of **INDIANA** still displays vestiges of the easygoing South. Among these early settlers was the family of Abraham Lincoln, who set up home near the present village of Santa Claus in 1816 and stayed for fourteen years before moving to Illinois. Unlike the abolitionist Lincolns, many brought slaves to this new territory; Indiana allowed a system of "voluntary servitude" to operate until 1843. At the outbreak of the Civil War, thousands of ex-Southerners rioted against the draft, in part expressing a concern that Indiana was every bit as subservient to the northeast as Deep South slaves were to their masters. However, since the 1870s, industrialization has integrated Indiana into the regional economy. The sports-happy state is at the forefront of the nation in automobile racing and high school basketball.

Despite some beautiful dunes and beaches, the most lasting memories provided by Indiana's fifty-mile **lakeshore** (by far the shortest of the Great Lake states) are of the grimy steel mills and poverty-stricken neighborhoods of towns like **Gary** and **East Chicago**. In northern Indiana, the area in and around **Elkhart** and **Goshen** contains one of the nation's largest **Amish settlements**. The central plains are characterized by small market towns, except for the sprawling capital, **Indianapolis**, which has brightened up its downtown in recent years to the point that it's not a bad stopover. Hilly southern Indiana, at its most appealing in the fall, is a welcome contrast to the central cornbelt, boasting several quaint towns such as **Nashville**, **Vincennes**, **Madison** and **Corydon**. Thriving **Columbus** exhibits a great array of contemporary architecture for such a small city, and former resort town **West Baden Springs** is restoring the elegant hotel that made it famous.

Dozens of explanations have been offered as to why residents of the state are called "**Hoosiers**"; the most believable is that its use spread from the days of the Ohio Falls Canal construction in the 1820s, when a contractor, Samuel Hoosier, gave employment preference to those living on the Indiana side of the Ohio River.

Getting around Indiana

Nine interstates – five of them slicing through Indianapolis – provide boring but fast ways of traversing Indiana. Greyhound runs frequent services, particularly on I-65 between Chicago and Louisville and I-70 between the East and St Louis. **Indianapolis**, **Michigan City** and **South Bend** are the major stops on the three different Amtrak routes that cut through the state. Flights from most Midwestern and Eastern cities land at **Indianapolis International Airport**.

Northern Indiana

Lying just off I-80/90, halfway along the northern fringe of Indiana, **SOUTH BEND** briefly rivaled Detroit as the country's leading car manufacturer during the early 1920s, when now-defunct Studebaker was going strong. These days it's better known for the **University of Notre Dame**, the most famous Roman Catholic college in the US and home of the Fighting Irish team that once dominated college football. Free tours of the campus (☎219/237-4872, ⓦ www.nd.edu) take in the gold-domed Administration Building and sights such as a replica of the grotto at Lourdes. If you are in for something more daring, head to the East Race Waterway, where you can kayak or raft the first man-made whitewater course in North America. For $2, navigate the one-third mile course that runs, believe it or not, through downtown South Bend. Once downtown, head to Niles Avenue near the Jefferson Street bridge and the Emporium Restaurant (☎219/299-4765; June–Aug only).

Budget **motels** are grouped along US-31 N. The *Book Inn B&B*, 508 W Washington St (☎219/288-1990 or 1-877/288-1990, ⓦwww.book-inn.com; ➎), offers gourmet breakfasts and has a used bookstore in the basement.

Forty miles west, smaller **MICHIGAN CITY** marks the start of the twenty-mile **Indiana Dunes National Lakeshore**, intended to prevent further encroachment on the state's shoreline. There's not much to the "city" itself but it is the handiest place to stay near the lake. The *Knights Inn*, 201 W Kieffer Rd (☎219/874-9500, ⓦwww.knightsinn.com; ➌), offers the best value. Just west of town, the impressive **Mount Baldy** is, in fact, a giant sand dune. Good swimming beaches and hiking trails through woods and marshes can be found at **Indiana Dunes State Park**, twelve miles farther along.

From here it's another fifteen miles west to the industrial mess of **GARY**, the largest US city founded in the twentieth century and mildly famous as the birthplace of Michael Jackson. Until the US Steel Corporation built a giant foundry here in 1906, this was uninhabited bogland. These days it's basically a depressed suburb of Chicago.

Indianapolis

INDIANAPOLIS began life in 1821, when a tract of barely inhabited marshes was designated the state capital. Its location in the middle of Indiana's rich farmland bore terrific commercial advantages, but the absence of a navigable river prohibited the transportation of bulky materials such as coal and iron to sustain heavy industry. Though home to more than sixty car manufacturers by 1910, the city never seriously threatened Detroit's supremacy. Nevertheless, it has become one of the biggest cities in the world not accessible by water, attracting food, paper and pharmaceutical industries, including the giant Eli Lilly Corporation.

Today the city has shaken off such nicknames as Naptown, India-no-place and Brickhouse in the Cornfield in favor of its chosen designation as the country's unofficial amateur sports capital – "amateur" events like the Pan-American Games and national Olympic trials being worth big money these days. (Major league pro teams include the basketball Pacers and the football Colts.) In recent years, it has constructed several world-class sports stadia (including the retro-styled **Conseco Fieldhouse** downtown) along with new hotels, a gaggle of top-class museums and a zoo – and its old downtown landmarks have become cultural, shopping and dining complexes. No longer is it (quite) true that nothing happens here except for the glamorous **Indianapolis 500 car race** each May – "the most televised annual event in the world" (see box, p.343).

Arrival and information
Indianapolis International Airport (☎317/487-9594) is twelve miles west of downtown, on the #8 bus route (☎317/635-3344; $1). A **taxi** (Yellow Cabs; ☎317/487-7777) into the center costs around $27. Greyhound arrives at 127 N Capitol Ave (☎1-800/231-2222), just off Monument Circle, while Amtrak, 350 S Illinois St (☎317/267-3071), is next to the fairly central Union Station complex. The **visitor center** is at 201 S Capitol St (Mon–Fri 10am–5.30pm, Sat 10am–5pm, Sun noon–5pm; ☎317/237-5200 or 1-800/824-INDY, ⓦwww.indy.org), beside the RCA Dome.

Accommodation

Indianapolis has plenty of quality **places to stay**, but few real budget downtown options, and prices can double during the race months of May, August and September.

Canterbury Hotel 123 S Illinois St ☎317/634-3000 or 1-800/538-8186. The gracious landmark hotel in the heart of downtown was built in 1928. Includes continental breakfast. **7**

Crowne Plaza Union Station 123 W Louisiana St ☎317/631-2221. Regular hotel rooms plus suites in converted railway carriages. **6**

Days Inn Downtown 401 E Washington St ☎317/637-6464 or 1-800/329-7466. Centrally located lodgings. **4**

Fall Creek YMCA 860 W 10th St ☎317/634-2478. Single rooms for men and women; $25. **1**

Hampton Inn Downtown 105 S Meridian St ☎317/261-1200 or 1-800/HAMPTON. Clean new rooms, next to Circle Centre. **5**

Ramada Plaza Waterbury Hotel 108 N Pennsylvania St ☎317/614-1400 or 1-800/272-6232. New rooms downtown in a recently converted, grand old bank building. Free parking. **5**

Renaissance Tower Historic Inn 230 E 9th St ☎317/261-1652. Just off central downtown. Rooms are occasionally very inexpensive, but at all times come complete with four-poster bed, toaster, coffeemaker and popcorn popper. **5**

Downtown

Though spacious and unhurried, downtown Indianapolis lacked a nerve center until the opening of the relatively tasteful **Circle Centre** shopping and entertainment complex in 1995. That year also saw the completion of the spectacular **Indianapolis Artsgarden**, an eight-story glass rotunda illuminated with fairy lights and suspended over the busy Washington and Illinois intersection. A performance and exhibition space, it also acts as a walkway to Circle Centre and several downtown hotels. One block north, streets radiate from **Monument Circle**, the starting point for a lengthy series of memorials and plazas dedicated to veterans. After climbing 32 flights of steep stairs to the top of the renovated 284ft **Soldiers and Sailors Monument** (there are often queues for the tiny elevator) you are rewarded with an unspectacular view of the city (daily 10am–7pm; free).

Five blocks east, the serene tree-shaded **Lockerbie Square Historic District**, starting at New York and East streets, is a small enclave of picturesque charm. Small wood-frame cottages, once home to nineteenth-century artisans, line the cobblestone streets. Many of them are painted in bright pinks, blues and yellows, with ornately carved porches. The nearby **Indiana State Museum**, 202 N Alabama St (Mon–Sat 9am–4.45pm, Sun noon–4.45pm; free; Ⓦ www.state.in.us/ism/museum/), gives a useful insight into the state's history through exhibits on everything from geology to sport.

The spectacular **Eiteljorg Museum of American Indians and Western Art** (June–Aug Mon–Sat 10am–5pm, Sun noon–5pm; rest of year closed Mon; tours at 2pm; $6) is housed in a stone, wood and adobe building on the western edge of downtown at 500 W Washington St. Harrison Eiteljorg, an industrialist who went West in the 1940s to speculate in minerals, fell so deeply in love with the art of the region that he brought as much of it back with him as possible. The work on display ranges from Georgia O'Keeffe to Frederic Remington and Andy Warhol. Tribal artifacts from all over North America are displayed on the upper level, while a 38ft Haida totem pole stands in the grounds. There are also frequent displays of beading and basket weaving, superb touring exhibits and a gorgeous gift shop. The Eiteljorg stands amid the rolling greenery of **White River State Park**, which is also home to the sizable **Indianapolis Zoo** and the lush new **White River Gardens** (Mon–Fri 9am–4pm, Sat & Sun 9am–5pm; $13; Ⓦ www.indyzoo.com). In the park's southeast corner stands the superb new **Victory Field**, home of the Indianapolis Indians (☎317/269-3545), the farm team for the Cincinnati Reds.

Out from downtown

Although the bodies of former president Benjamin Harrison and Hoosier poet James Whitcomb Riley lie in the enormous **Crown Hill Cemetery**, at 38th Street and Michigan Road, the most visited grave belongs to 1930s bank robber **John Dillinger**, supposedly buried at Section 44 Lot 94 (though some researchers allege another man was killed in his place). Designated Public Enemy Number One, he completed thirteen bank raids – killing four policemen, three FBI agents, one sheriff and an undetermined number of innocent bystanders – in a single-year career. Something of a folk hero, he escaped from jail twice, but was eventually ambushed by the FBI outside a Chicago theater in 1934 (see p.359).

Opposite the cemetery at 1200 W 38th St, more than 150 lush wooded acres accommodate the capacious **Indianapolis Museum of Art** (Tues, Wed, Fri & Sat 10am–5pm, Thurs 10am–8.30pm, Sun noon–5pm; free; ⓦ www.ima-art.org). The main building, surrounded by a lake, botanical garden, sculpture courtyard and concert terrace, is fronted by the original of Robert Indiana's Pop Art sculpture *LOVE*. Inside, the exceptional displays include neo-Impressionist works, the Eiteljorg Collection of African Art, the largest collection of Turner paintings outside Britain and an array of paintings and prints from Gauguin's Pont Aven school.

The Indianapolis 500

Seven miles northwest of downtown, the **Indianapolis Motor Speedway** stages only two events per year; but one does happen to be the legendary **Indianapolis 500** (the other is the prestigious NASCAR Brickyard 400 in August).

Held on the last Sunday in May, the Indy 500 is preceded by two weeks of qualification runs that whittle the hopeful entrants down to a final field of 33 drivers, one of whom will scoop the million-dollar first prize. The two-and-a-half-mile circuit was built as a test track for the city's motor manufacturers. The first 500-mile race held in 1911 – won in a time of 6hr 42min, at an average speed of 74.6mph – was a huge success, vindicating the organizers' belief that the distance was the optimum length for spectators' enjoyment. Cars now hit 225mph, though the official times of the winners are reduced by delays caused by accidents. The automotive technology is marvelous, but the living legends in the eyes of their fans are such championship drivers as A.J. Foyt, Mario Andretti and members of the Unser dynasty.

The big race crowns one of the nation's largest festivals, watched by up to 450,000. At first, the city's conservative hierarchy saw it as an infringement on the traditional observance of Memorial Day weekend. However, it brings so much money into the city, with thousands of "Indy" racing fanatics staying for up to two weeks, that it is now exploited to the full, with civic events such as the crowning of the Speedway Queen, a Mayor's Ball and a street parade. Seats for the race usually sell out well in advance, but you may gain admittance to the infield, where the giddy and boozy atmosphere makes up for the poor view.

Adjoining the track, the impressive display of race-car history at the **Indianapolis Motor Speedway Hall of Fame Museum**, 4790 W 16th St, provides a good background to the hysteria (daily 9am–5pm; $3; ⓦ www.indy500.com). For an extra two dollars, a rickety old bus saunters around the super-smooth asphalt track (only a small patch of bricks remains), ringed by huge banked grandstands. The circuit also holds four of the eighteen holes of the unique **Brickyard Crossing golf course** (☎317/484-6572; ⓦ www.brickyardcrossing.com), home to the annual Senior PGA Tournament; green fees are $90.

The city's most offbeat museum, the **Indiana Medical History Museum**, 3045 W Vermont St (Wed–Sat 10am–4pm, or by appointment; $5; ☎ 317/635-7329, ⓦ www.imhm.org), is housed in the old Pathology Building of what was once a huge psychiatric hospital. Pointing out the cabinets of preserved brains and similarly gruesome exhibits, the guides give a fascinating account of medical practice in the late nineteenth century.

The **Children's Museum of Indianapolis**, 3000 N Meridian St (summer daily 10am–5pm; rest of year closed Mon; $8, children $3.50; ☎ 317/921-4000, ⓦ www.childrensmuseum.org), is arguably the best of its kind in the country. There's a carousel, an excellent exhibit on African American storytelling, a big-screen IWERKS theater, interactive gadgets, and a planetarium that mounts laser shows to a Lollapalooza soundtrack.

Eating

Circle Centre, the swish mall at Illinois and Washington, houses dozens of places to eat, but most of these are chains. You'd do better to stick to the more established restaurants downtown or head up to **Broad Ripple Village** (bus #17) at College Avenue and 62nd Street, packed with bars, cafés, galleries and shops. At lunchtime, **City Market**, 222 E Market St, is a maze of lunch counters and tables where you can feast cheaply on all sorts of international food amid a cacophonous din.

Bazbeaux 334 Massachusetts Ave, downtown ☎ 317/636-7662 and 832 E Westfield Blvd, Broad Ripple Village ☎ 317/255-5711. The best pizzas in town are offered with a great range of toppings.
Elbow Room 605 N Pennsylvania St ☎ 317/635-3354. This pub serves specialty sandwiches and lots of import beers.
India Garden 830 Broad Ripple Ave ☎ 317/253-6060. Good Indian curries with a noted lunchtime buffet.
Rathskeller Restaurant 401 E Michigan St ☎ 317/636-0396. Continental dishes include lots of German specialties, set in the historic Atheneum, built in 1892 as a cultural center for the city's German-speaking population.

Ruthellen's 825 N Pennsylvania St ☎ 317/631-RUTH. The wildly baroque yet cozy atmosphere for upscale dining attracts a mixed clientele. Fri–Sat night piano bar. Closed Mon.
St Elmo Steak House 127 S Illinois St ☎ 317/635-0636. One of the most famous steak restaurants in the meat-mad Midwest, it is rather pompous and expensive. Expect to pay $25–30 for a meal.
Shapiro's 808 S Meridian St ☎ 317/631-4041. The landmark deli is just a few blocks off downtown. Fill up at the counter with lox, tongue or other specialties and eat in an old-style cafeteria atmosphere. Leave room for the huge desserts.

Nightlife and entertainment

The emerging area in downtown is Massachusetts Avenue, where along with some good bars and restaurants, the 3000-seater **Murat Centre** (502 N New Jersey St; ☎ 317/231-0000) provides a special venue for gigs and Broadway musicals; decorated in outlandish Byzantine style, the center is part of a huge Shriner temple. In summer, head north to chic **Broad Ripple Village**. See the free paper *NUVO* for full details of gigs and events.

The 1927 Spanish Baroque Indiana Repertory Theatre, 140 W Washington St (☎ 317/635-5252), puts on dramatic productions between October and May; the Indianapolis Symphony Orchestra has weekly concerts at the equally elaborate 1916 Hilbert Circle Theatre, 45 Monument Circle (☎ 317/639-4300).

Broad Ripple Brew Pub 840 E 65th St ☎ 317/253-2739. Atmospheric brewpub, six miles north.
Chatterbox 435 Massachusetts Ave ☎ 317/636-0584. Lively local bar, with jazz nightly except Sun.

Madame Walker Theatre Center 617 Indiana Ave ☎ 317/236-2099. Black cultural and heritage center. *Jazz on the Avenue* every Fri plus regular dance events, plays and concerts.
Slippery Noodle 372 S Meridian St ☎ 317/631-

6968. Indiana's oldest bar, established in 1850, is next to Union Station. Cheap beer Mon and Tues, live blues Wed–Sat.

Vogue 6259 N College Ave ☎317/259-7029. Popular Broad Ripple rock and indie venue with retro club nights.

Out from Indianapolis: Bloomington

BLOOMINGTON, by far the liveliest small city in Indiana, is 45 miles south-west of Indianapolis on Hwy-37. It owes its vibrancy to the main campus of Indiana University, east of downtown. The I.M. Pei-designed **Indiana University Art Museum** on East Seventh Street (Wed–Sat 10am–5pm, Sun noon–5pm; free) holds a fine international collection of painting and sculpture. Across the street from the pastoral campus, law student Hoagy Carmichael composed *Stardust* on the piano of a popular hangout. The architecturally rich downtown also features a host of good shops.

Practicalities

Greyhound, 409 S Walnut St (☎812/332-1522), runs a reliable **bus** service to Indianapolis. Bloomington's friendly **visitor center** can be found at 2855 N Walnut St (☎812/334-8900 or 1-800/678-9828, ⓦwww.visitbloomington.com).

The best budget **place to stay** in central Bloomington is the *Motel 6 – Bloomington University*, 1800 N Walnut St (☎812/332-0820; ❷), or there's the central Victorian *Grant Street Inn*, 310 N Grant St (☎812/334-2353, ⓦwww.grantstinn.com; ❻). The *Indiana Memorial Union* on Seventh and Park (☎812/856-6381), a good source of campus information, also offers a range of cheap places to **eat**. Student bars and cafés are strung out along Kirkwood Avenue, including the vegetarian *Laughing Planet*, at no. 322 E Fifth St (☎812/323-2233). Among the wide range of ethnic restaurants in town are the Tibetan *Snow Lion*, 113 S Grant Ave (☎812/336-0835), and the wonderful *Siam House*, 430 E Fourth St (☎812/331-1233). The *Runcible Spoon*, 412 E Sixth St (☎812/334-3997), is a favorite place for breakfast, coffee and dessert, while the *Brewpub at Lennie's*, 1795 E Tenth St (☎812/323-2112), is the best place in town for microbrewed ales.

Illinois

Nearly everything in **ILLINOIS** revolves around **Chicago**, the largest and most exciting of the Great Lakes cities. At the state's northeastern corner, on the shores of **Lake Michigan**, Chicago has a skyline to rival any city's, plus a gamut of top-rated museums, restaurants and cafés, and innumerable bars and nightclubs paying homage to the city's strong jazz and blues heritage. Seventy-five percent of the state's twelve million population live within commuting distance of Chicago's energetic center, which controls the bulk of the state economy – Illinois is the third largest agricultural producer in the US. The sole exception to the endless flat prairies elsewhere is far to the south, where the forested **Shawnee Hills** rise between the Mississippi and Ohio rivers.

The contrast between the quiet rural hinterlands and the buzzing urban center could hardly be greater. That said, Illinois does hold a few places to head for, though, apart from a couple of mildly exciting college towns, most are of historic rather than current interest. First explored and settled by the French, in 1763 the area that's now Illinois was sold to the English. Granted statehood in 1818, Illinois remained a distant frontier until the mid-1830s when, after a series of uprisings, the native **Sauk** were subjugated and settlers began to arrive in sizable numbers. Among these were the first followers of Joseph Smith, founder of the Mormon Church, who established a large colony along the Mississippi at Nauvoo. The **Mormons** met with suspicion and persecution and, after Smith was murdered by a lynch mob in 1844, fled west to Utah.

Other early immigrants included the young **Abraham Lincoln**, who practiced law from 1837 onward in **Springfield**, the state capital and home of a wide range of Lincolniana, including his restored home, his law offices and various other period buildings and artifacts, as well as his monumental tomb. Indeed, Illinois' self-proclaimed nickname – emblazoned on its car license plates – is "Land of Lincoln," and many other central Illinois towns claim important roles in the making of the sixteenth US president.

Getting around Illinois

Because Chicago is the site of **O'Hare Airport** (the world's busiest), as well as the hub of the national Amtrak **train** network, you're likely at least to pass through it. If you plan to spend time in the rest of Illinois, Amtrak, numerous commuter railroads and, to a lesser extent, Greyhound, make getting around on public transportation feasible, and **cycling** is generally easy on these endless flat plains.

Half a dozen **interstates** fan out across the country from Chicago. The famous Chicago-to-LA Route 66 has been defunct since the 1960s, though I-55 southwest to St Louis, followed by I-44 and I-40, follow its general route.

Chicago

CHICAGO is in many ways the nation's last great city. Sarah Bernhardt called it "the pulse of America" and, though long eclipsed by Los Angeles as the nation's second most populous city after New York, Chicago really does have it all, with less of the hassle and infrastructural problems of its coastal rivals.

Founded in the early 1800s, Chicago grew up with the country, serving as the main connection between the established east coast cities and the wide open Wild West frontier. This position on the sharp edge between civilization and wilderness made the city into a crucible of innovation. Many aspects of modern life, from skyscrapers to suburbia, had their start, and perhaps their finest expression, here on the shores of Lake Michigan.

Despite burning to the ground in the legendary fire of 1871, Chicago boomed thereafter, doubling in population every decade and reaching two million around 1900, swollen by **Irish** and **eastern European** immigrants (Chicago still has the largest Polish population in the world outside Warsaw). In the early years of the twentieth century, it cemented a reputation as a place of apparently limitless opportunity, with jobs aplenty for those willing to work. The attraction was strongest among Deep South **blacks**: from 1900 to

1920 African Americans poured in, with more than 75,000 arriving during the war years of 1916–18 alone. Long hours, poor pay and squalid working conditions were the catalysts that made Chicago the cradle of American **trade unions**. By around 1900 most workers were organized under the American Federation of Labor, and the 1894 Pullman strike saw black and white workers unite for almost the first time in the US. As hostilities intensified, the city's workers became the driving force behind the left-wing "Wobblies." Chicago has also long been an important center for black organization – both the Reverend Jesse Jackson's **Operation PUSH** (People United to Save Humanity) and the more militant **Nation of Islam**, founded by Elijah Mohammed in the 1940s, have their national headquarters on the city's South Side.

During the Roaring Twenties, Chicago's self-image as a no-holds-barred free market was pushed to the limit by a new breed of entrepreneur. Criminal syndicates, ruthlessly and brazenly run by the likes of **gangsters** like Al Capone and Bugsy Moran, took advantage of Prohibition to sell bootleg alcohol. Shootouts in the street between sharp-suited, Tommy-gun-wielding mobsters were not as common as legend would have it, but the backroom dealing and iron-handed control they pioneered was later perfected by politicians such as former mayor **Richard Daley** – father of the present mayor – who ran Chicago single-handedly from the 1950s until his death in 1976. His brutal handling of antiwar demonstrators at the **1968 Democratic convention** remains notorious. These days, the tourist authorities play down the mobster era; few traces of the hoodlum years exist, and those that do owe more to Hollywood than contemporary Chicago.

Today, Chicago's towering **skyline** – the city has one of the world's best collections of **modern architecture**, from Frank Lloyd Wright houses to the 110-story **Sears Tower** – dominates the pancake-flat prairies for hundreds of miles around. Chicago's status as the cultural and financial heart of middle America is beyond question. **The Loop** downtown holds the head offices of many major US companies and some of the nation's most important **commodity markets**, which together handle the buying and selling of one-third of the world's agricultural and industrial products.

For visitors, Chicago offers the **Art Institute of Chicago** and a wide range of excellent **museums** (many of which have one day of free admission per week), restaurants, sports and highbrow cultural activities. However, its strongest suit is **live music**, with a phenomenal array of **jazz** and **blues** clubs packed into the back rooms of its amiable bars and cafés. The **rock** scene is also one of the healthiest in the country with a prolific number of bands having come out of the city in the 1990s, including Smashing Pumpkins, Material Issue, Veruca Salt and Wilco. And almost everything is noticeably less expensive than in other US cities – **eating out**, for example, costs much less than in New York or LA, but is every bit as good. Though locals might deny it, the city has a surprisingly low-key and generally welcoming population – Chicagoans on the whole are proud of their city and usually keen to point out its best features. Two great ways to get a real feel for the city are to head out to ivy-covered **Wrigley Field** on a sunny summer afternoon to catch baseball's Cubs in action, or take a cruise boat under the bridges of the Chicago River at sunset.

Arrival, information and getting around

Chicago's **O'Hare International Airport** (☏773/686-2200, ⦿www.ohare .com), the national HQ for United, American and several other airlines, is seventeen miles northwest of downtown Chicago. It is connected to the center by

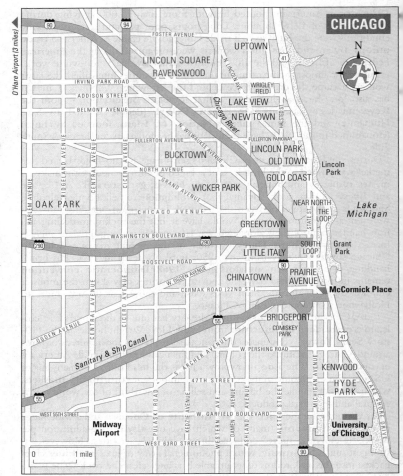

24-hour CTA (Blue Line) **trains** from the station under Terminal 4, which take around forty minutes and cost $1.50 (see opposite). **Midway Airport**, smaller than O'Hare but used by an increasing number of domestic airlines, is eleven miles southwest of downtown; take one of CTA's Midway (Orange Line) trains, which take thirty minutes, or the #99M Midway Express bus (weekday rush hours only). **Taxis** into town from O'Hare cost around $25–30 (there's also a shared ride program with a flat rate of $15), and take thirty minutes to an hour. From Midway the fare is about $25 (shared rides are $10) and the journey time twenty to forty minutes. Another option is Continental Air Transport's **express bus and van** service between the airports and downtown hotels ($20 from O'Hare, $15 from Midway; ☎312/454-7799, ⊛www.airportexpress.com). The highways are often clogged, so allow at least an hour for the trip from either airport.

Chicago is the hub of the nationwide Amtrak rail system, and almost every cross-country route passes through **Union Station** (☎312/558-1075) at Canal and Adam streets, west of the Loop. Greyhound and a number of regional bus companies pull into the large 24-hour **bus station** at 630 W Harrison St, three blocks southwest.

Arriving in Chicago **by road**, racing towards the gleaming glass towers of the Loop, can be memorable. Bear in mind, though, that traffic on the expressways to and from downtown can be bumper-to-bumper during rush hours. **Parking** can also be a problem. Meters are expensive (25¢ for 15min) and usually have a two-hour limit. Check street signs for additional restrictions, which are rigidly enforced – violations may result in your car being towed and impounded. Perhaps the best place to leave a car in the downtown area is in the garage under Grant Park at Columbus Drive and Monroe Drive ($13 for 24hr; ☎312/742-7644), close to the east side of the Art Institute.

Information

Pick up information and maps from the **Chicago Tourism Council**, in the lobby of the Chicago Cultural Center at the entrance on 77 E Randolph St (Mon–Wed 10am–7pm, Thurs 10am–9pm, Fri 10am–6pm, Sat 10am–5pm, Sun 11am–5pm; ☎312/744-6630 or 312/346-3278, ⓦwww.ci.chi.il.uc/). There are also **information centers** in the Historic Water Tower, 800 N Michigan Ave on the Magnificent Mile (Mon–Sat 9.30am–7pm, Sun 10am–6pm) and in the Illinois Market Place Visitor Information Center at Navy Pier, 700 E Grand Ave (Mon–Thurs 10am–9pm, Sun 10am–7pm).

Chicago's new main **post office**, the largest in the world, is at 433 W Harrison St (Mon–Sat 8am–5pm; ☎1-800/275-8777; zip code 85907). The Loop Station is at 211 S Clark St (Mon–Fri 7am–7pm).

City transportation

Getting around Chicago is simple and quick, thanks to buses and the "El," a system of elevated trains operated 24 hours a day by the Chicago Transit Authority (CTA; ☎312/836-7000, ⓦwww.transitchicago.com). Pick up a CTA System Map, available at most subway stations and visitor centers or from the CTA office on the seventh floor of the Merchandise Mart. **Buses** run every five to fifteen minutes during rush hours and every eight to twenty minutes at most other times. **Rapid transit trains** run every five to fifteen minutes during the day and every fifteen to sixty minutes all night. Lines are color-coded and denoted by route rather than destination. The Howard–Dan Ryan is the Red Line; Lake Englewood–Jackson Park is the Green Line; the O'Hare–Congress–Douglas is the Blue Line; the Ravenswood is the Brown Line (whose trains circle the Loop, giving the area its name); the Evanston Express is the Purple Line; and the Skokie Swift is the Yellow Line.

The CTA no longer accepts tokens; instead, riders purchase a **transit card** (available in all El stations) and add value to it. One ride costs $1.50; another ride within two hours costs just 30¢. If you plan to be on the move, passes good for one ($5), two ($9), three ($12) or five ($18) days of unlimited rides might be a good idea. They're available at O'Hare, Midway and Amtrak subway stations.

Chicago's **taxis**, despite a recent increase in fares, are more reasonable than those of many other major US cities. Charges are $1.50 at the drop of the flag, $1.20 per mile and 50¢ for each additional passenger. Cabs can be hailed anytime in the Loop and other central neighborhoods; otherwise call Yellow (☎312/829-4222) or Checker taxis (☎312/243-2537).

Guided tours

Various sightseeing companies run **guided bus tours** of the city center. Chicago Trolley (daily 9.30am–5pm; $20; $25 for two days, hop-on; ☏773/648 5000, ⓦwww.chicagotrolley.com) hour-long tours begin at the Sears Tower. Chicago Motor Coach ($10; ☏312/666-1000) runs double-decker buses that pick up at the Sears Tower, the Art Institute and Navy Pier. The former, though, is often ranked "best tour in Chicago" by Chicagoans.

The **Chicago Architecture Foundation**, in the Santa Fe Building at 224 S Michigan Ave (☏312/922-3432, ⓦwww.architecture.org), runs a number of highly recommended tours throughout the city. Among these are two information-packed walking tours of the Loop, giving a friendly in-depth introduction to Chicago's buildings and history ($10 for 2hr, $15 for both tours). It also offers walking tours of Frank Lloyd Wright's buildings in Oak Park, Historic Pullman and other neighborhoods; bus tours of the Loop and Near North ($15; 2hr), Hyde Park and Frank Lloyd Wright's Robie House ($25; 3hr 30min). Perhaps the most popular of all are the excellent ninety-minute Chicago Architecture by Boat tours, which leave from Michigan Avenue and Lower Wacker Drive (May–Oct Mon–Sat 3 departures, Sun 2 trips; $21). **Other sightseeing boat tours** include those offered along the river by Mercury (☏312/332-1368, ⓦwww.cruisechicago.com; $14) and Wendella (☏312/337-1446) during the summer season; and Spirit of Chicago Harbor Cruises ($17; ☏312/836-7888), who continue year-round, sailing from Navy Pier. Shoreline Sightseeing Tours ($17 for architectural cruises, $10 for lake cruises; ☏312/222-9328, ⓦwww.shorelinesightseeing.com) is another good option, with architectural river cruises as well as lake tours, a slightly different look at the architecture of Chicago.

A **River Bus** (April–Oct; $2; ☏312/337-1446) operates on the river during rush hour in summer, running from the Michigan Avenue Bridge to Union Station in eight minutes.

Accommodation

Most central **accommodation** is oriented towards business and convention trade rather than tourism, but there are still plenty of moderately priced rooms. A number of clean (if unexciting) prewar hotels in and around the Loop offer reasonable rates, especially at weekends, and motorists can pick from scores of motels along the interstates. Even top-class downtown hotels are, comparatively, not that expensive. Under the Chicago's Got It program, hotels in all price ranges offer discounts of fifteen to forty percent on Thursday to Sunday nights, when the business types have gone home, so you can often get a room in a really plush place for around $100. If you're stuck, Hot Rooms is a reservation service offering hotel rooms at discount rates (☏773/468-7666 or 1-800/468-3500). While they're not as prominent as elsewhere, **bed and breakfast** rooms are available from $75 per night through Chicago B&B, PO Box 14088, IL 85914 (☏312/951-0085). Just under fifteen percent room tax is added to all bills.

Allegro 179 W Randolph St ☏312/236-0123, ⓦwww.allegrochicago.com. The old *Bismarck Hotel* has been given a total face-lift and new name, and turned into a comfortable, business-class hotel. ❽

Arlington House International Hostel 616 W Arlington Place ☏773/929-5380 or 1-800/467-8355, ⓦwww.arlingtonhouse.com. The easygoing hostel, open 24hr, is close to Wrigley Field and loads of good bars. Segregated and mixed dorms. Members pay $19.50, others $3 extra. ❶

Best Western Grant Park 1100 S Michigan Ave ☏312/922-2900 or 1-800/528-1234, ⓦwww.bestwestern.com. A large hotel with outdoor pool, it's handy for Grant Park and lakeside attractions. Good value if a little far south. ❻

Blackstone 636 S Michigan Ave ☏312/427-4300. Recently designated a Chicago landmark, this resurgent, once-elegant c.1900 hotel (featured in *The Untouchables*), overlooks the lake near Grant Park. ❺

Cass 640 N Wabash Ave ☎312/787-4030, ⓦwww.casshotel.com. A clean and basic hotel, it's the best value in the Near North area. ❹

Chicago International Hostel 6318 N Winthrop Ave ☎773/262-1011, ⓦwww.hostels.com .chicagohostel/. A big hostel, open 24hr, 365 days a year, it's a short walk from the Loyola El station. Dorm beds cost $15. ❶

Comfort Inn Lincoln Park 601 W Diversey Parkway ☎773/348-2810 or 1-800/228-5150. Medium-sized motel, with free continental breakfast. ❻

Days Inn Lincoln Park North 644 W Diversey Parkway at Clark ☎773/525-7010; ⓦwww.lpdaysinn.com. This good, friendly motel is popular with visiting musicians and a convenient base for North Side nightlife. Free continental breakfast. ❺

The Drake 140 E Walton Place ☎312/787-2200 or 1-800/553-7256, ⓦwww.thedrakehotel.com. Chicago's society hotel, just off the Magnificent Mile, has been modernized without sacrificing its sedate charms. You can always just pop in for a drink. ❽/❾

Executive Plaza Hotel 71 E Wacker Drive ☎312/346-7100, ⓦwww.executive-plaza.com. In a magnificent setting by the Michigan Avenue Bridge, an extra $10 gets a river view. Big weekend discounts. ❼

Hampton Suites Hotel 33 W Illinois Ave ☎312/832-0330, ⓦwww.hamptoninn.com. New,

clean motel in a good River North location. ❼

HoJo Inn 720 N LaSalle St ☎312/664-8100 or 1-800/446-4656, ⓦwww.hojo.com. Standard *HoJo* rooms in a good Near North location. ❺

International House of Chicago 1414 E 59th St ☎773/753-2270. Plain, pleasant rooms are available in summer on the University of Chicago campus – not a nice part of town, for $37. Reservations are essential. ❷

J. Ira & Nicki Harris Hostel at HI-Chicago 24 E Congress ☎312/360-0300, ⓦwww.hichicago.org. New and huge and centrally located for easy downtown access. ❶

Lenox Suites Hotel 231 N Rush St ☎312/337-1000, ⓦwww.lenoxsuites.com. A great all-suite hotel, it's just a few blocks north of the river. ❼

Monaco 225 N Wabash ☎312/960-8500 or 1-800/397-7661, ⓦwww.monaco-chicago.com. A stylish and luxurious French Deco hotel. ❽

Red Roof Inn 162 E Ontario St ☎312/787-3580 or 1-800/733-7663. A few yards off the Magnificent Mile, this is a clean, no-frills accommodation in the center of the shopping action. ❺

Three Arts Club of Chicago 1300 N Dearborn St ☎312/944-6250, ⓦwww.threearts.org. This women's residence doubles as a co-ed hostel in summer. Breakfast and dinner, linens and towels are included. ❷

Wright's Cheney House B&B 520 N East Ave, Oak Park ☎708/524-2067. Frank Lloyd Wright designed this Prairie-style house in 1904, and most of the furnishings and fabrics in the lovely two-bedroom suites are Wright designs too. ❼

The City

Chicago is an easy city to negotiate: streets form a grid and numbering is consistent, beginning at State and Madison streets. State Street – "that great street" in Sinatra's song – is at zero east and west and Madison at zero north and south. **Lake Michigan**, which provides Chicago with some of its most attractive open space (twenty miles of lakeshore lie within the city limits), serves as a clear point of reference for getting your bearings – the lake is always to the east of the urban grid. **Michigan Avenue** is the city's main thoroughfare, running between the lakeside museums and parklands, the densely packed skyscrapers of downtown and the diverse low-rise neighborhoods that spread to the north, south and west. It's here that you might experience the full force of "The Hawk," the nickname given to the strong wind that blows off the lake. The nickname "**Windy City**" was coined by a New York newspaper editor describing the boastful claims of the city's promoters when pitching for the World's Columbian exhibition of 1893. The **Chicago River**, which cuts through the heart of downtown Chicago to Lake Michigan, separates the business district from the shopping and entertainment areas of the North Side. The latter include the upscale **Near North** and **Gold Coast** neighborhoods and the artists' lofts and galleries of **River North**, plus the modestly charming area

DOWNTOWN CHICAGO

N. CLYBOURN AVE.
GOETHE STREE
DIVISION STREET
E. SCOTT ST.
DIVISION STREET
GOLD
COAST
E. ELM ST.
E. CEDAR ST.
E. BELLEVUE PL.
E. OAK STREET
E. WALTON ST.
Oak Street Beach

② John Hancock Center

Lake Michigan

N. LARRABEE STREET
N. ORLEANS STREET
N. FRANKLIN STREET
N. WELLS STREET
N. LASALLE STREET
N. CLARK STREET
N. DEARBORN STREET
N. STATE STREET

W. CHICAGO AVENUE

Historic Water Tower

E. CHESTNUT ST.
E. PEARSON ST.

Museum of Contemporary Art

W. SUPERIOR STREET
E. SUPERIOR STREET

③ HoJo Inn
W. HURON ST.

④ Terra Museum of Art
W. ERIE STREET
⑤
W. ONTARIO STREET
⑥
W. OHIO STREET
W. GRAND AVENUE

Ohio Street Beach

41

Tribune Tower

N. MCCLURG CT.
N. FAIRBANKS CT.
N. ST. CLAIR ST.
RUSH ST.
N. WABASH AVE.
NORTH MICHIGAN AVENUE
MAGNIFICENT MILE

W. ILLINOIS STREET
Wrigley Building
⑦
W. HUBBARD STREET
W. KINZIE STREET

Merchandise Mart

Chicago River

MILWAUKEE AVENUE

IBM Building

E. NORTH WATER ST.

Chicago River

EAST WACKER DRIVE
⑧ Illinois Center

WEST WACKER DRIVE

GEORGE HALES DRIVE
FIELD BOULEVARD

⑨
Chicago Cultural Center

LAKE STREET

SOUTH JEFFERSON STREET
N. CLINTON STREET
S. FRANKLIN STREET
SOUTH WACKER DRIVE

E. RANDOLPH STREET
⑩ Marshall Field
E. WASHINGTON STREET
_i_

Chicago Mercantile Exchange

E. MADISON STREET
Carson Pirie Scott
E. MONROE STREET

THE LOOP

Sears Tower

E. ADAMS STREET

Art Institute

NORTH MICHIGAN AVENUE

Grant Park

Union Station (Amtrak)

E. JACKSON BOULEVARD
Board of Trade

VAN BUREN STREET

Symphony Center

290

Auditorium Theater
⑪

Buckingham Fountain

41

Lake Michigan

Greyhound Terminal

W. HARRISON STREET

CONGRESS PARKWAY

S. WELLS STREET
S. CLARK STREET
S. FEDERAL STREET
S. DEARBORN STREET
S. PLYMOUTH COURT
S. WABASH AVENUE

⑫
E. BALBO DRIVE

S. COLUMBUS DRIVE
SOUTH LAKE SHORE DRIVE

W. POLK STREET

SOUTH CANAL STREET

Chicago River

E. 8TH ST.
E. 9TH ST.

W. TAYLOR ST.
W. TAYLOR ST.

E. 11TH ST.
⑬

John G. Shedd Aquarium

SOUTH MICHIGAN AVENUE

W. ROOSEVELT ROAD

E. ROOSEVELT ROAD

Field Museum of Natural History

MCFETRIDGE

0   800 yds

– – – Elevated rail
• Stations

Soldier Field

Adler Planetarium

Navy Pier

② John Hancock Center

ACCOMMODATION

Allegro	10	The Drake	2	HoJo Inn	3	Monaco	9
Best Western Grant Park	13	Executive Plaza Hotel	8	HI-Chicago	11	Red Roof Inn	5
Blackstone	12	Hampton Suites Hotel	7	Lenox Suites Hotel	6	Three Arts Club	1
Cass	4						

of **Old Town**, the young professional enclaves of **Lincoln Park**, **Wrigleyville** and **Lakeview** and hip **Wicker Park**.

In contrast to the wealth and prosperity of the North Side, the deprived **South Side** is more like New York's South Bronx: a huge and, in places, desperately poor expanse with a justifiably dangerous reputation. But while large areas are definitely unsafe after dark and dodgy even at midday, a few corners of the South Side are well worth visiting – particularly the Gothic campus of the **University of Chicago**, and neighboring **Hyde Park**, site of the **Museum of Science and Industry** – one of the largest and most popular museums in the US. Apart from **Oak Park** to the west, which holds the childhood home of **Ernest Hemingway** and more than a dozen well-maintained examples of the influential architecture of **Frank Lloyd Wright**, suburban Chicago has little to offer.

Downtown Chicago: The Loop

Downtown Chicago puts on what is perhaps the finest display of **modern architecture** in the world, from the prototype skyscrapers of the 1890s to Mies van der Rohe's modernist masterpieces, and the second tallest building in the world, the quarter-mile-high **Sears Tower**. Just about all these edifices are workplaces of one kind or another; the whole place is bustling in the day and virtually empty later on.

The compact heart of Chicago is known as **the Loop**, because it's circled by the elevated tracks of the CTA "El" trains, For a first impression of downtown, start your explorations by seeing the energy, drive and unmasked greed exposed in the trading pits of the various **commodity marketplaces**. Half the world's wheat and corn (and pork belly futures) are bought and sold amid the cacophonic roar of the **Chicago Board of Trade**, housed in a gorgeous Art Deco tower, appropriately topped by a 30ft stainless steel statue of Ceres, Roman goddess of grain. From the entrance at 141 W Jackson St, where it intersects with LaSalle Street, take the elevator to the fifth-floor visitor gallery (Mon–Fri 8am–1.15pm; free), where displays trace the evolution of the various frantic shouts and signals by which trade is actually carried out. A similarly energetic ballet goes on from the early hours on Chicago's stock options exchange, the largest in the US. At the **Chicago Mercantile Exchange**, three blocks away at 30 S Wacker Drive (Mon–Fri 7.30am–3.15pm; free), precious metals, currencies and commodities are bought and sold to the tune of some $50 billion a day. The **best time to visit** the exchanges is just before the close of trade, when the pressure is at its peak and tempers are most frayed.

A couple of other buildings in the immediate vicinity are worth nosing around. Half a block from the Board of Trade, **The Rookery**, 209 S LaSalle St, built in 1886 by Burnham and Root, is one of the city's most celebrated and photographed edifices. Its forbidding Moorish Gothic exterior gives way to a wonderfully airy lobby, decked out in cool Italian marble and gold leaf in 1905 during a major remodeling by Frank Lloyd Wright and restored in 1992. The spiral cantilever staircase rising from the second floor must be seen to be appreciated. A couple of doors toward the Board of Trade, look in at the **Continental Illinois Bank** lobby, with its 28 Ionic marble columns and intricate murals.

Looking up at the proud facade of the **Reliance Building**, 32 N State St, you'd be forgiven for thinking it dated from the Art Deco 1930s, but it was in fact completed way back in 1895 by Daniel Burnham, who did much to shape the face of Chicago. His **Fisher Building**, with its tongue-in-cheek, aquatic-inspired ornamental terracotta, stands at 343 S Dearborn St. A block farther south, the 1890 **Manhattan Building** was the world's first tall all-steel-frame building, and is generally acknowledged as the progenitor of the modern curtain-walled skyscraper, Now converted into luxury apartments, it preserves some noteworthy exterior ornament.

The Loop holds some of Chicago's grandest c.1900 **department stores**. The best-looking of these, the 1899 **Carson Pirie Scott** store at 1 S State St, boasts a magnificent ironwork facade that blends botanic and geometric forms in an intuitive version of Art Moderne. Its architect, Louis Sullivan, was also responsible for the gorgeous spherical bronze clocks suspended from the corners of the **Marshall Field's** department store, two blocks north, at State and Washington streets. The comparatively bland exterior of Marshall Field's oldest and grandest branch masks one of the world's great stores, with seven floors of merchandise.

A newly resurrected stretch of the riverfront walk follows the west bank of the river, with open-air cafés and gardens. Farther south, and back on the Loop side at South Wacker Drive and Adams Street, is the 1468ft **Sears Tower**, the tallest building in the world until 1997, when Malaysia's Petronas Towers nudged it from the top by the length of an antenna. Various companies occupy the tower (Sears has moved to the suburbs), and it's so huge that it has more than one hundred elevators. Two ascend, in little more than a minute, from the ground-level shopping mall to the 103rd-floor **Skydeck Observatory** (March–Sept daily 9am–11pm; Oct–Feb daily 9am–10pm; $10), for breathtaking views that on a clear day take in four states – Illinois, Michigan, Wisconsin and Indiana. Look for the distinctive triangular **Metropolitan Detention Center**, where prisoners exercise on the grassy roof, beneath wire netting to ensure they don't get whisked away by helicopter.

The Chicago River

The Loop is usually said to end at the "El" tracks, but the blocks beyond this core, to either side of the Chicago River, hold plenty of interest. Broad, double-decked **Wacker Drive**, parallel to the water, was designed as a sophisticated promenade, lined by benches and obelisk-shaped lanterns, by Daniel Burnham in 1909. It was never completed but, despite the almost constant intrusion of construction works, it makes for a nice extended walk. The river itself had its direction reversed c.1900, in an engineering project more extensive than the digging of the Panama Canal. As a result, rather than letting its sewage and industrial waste flow east into Lake Michigan, Chicago now sends it all south into the Corn Belt.

A **boat tour** from beneath the Michigan Avenue Bridge gives magnificent views of downtown and a good insight into the city's history (see "Guided Tours" box, p.350). However, half an hour's walk, especially at lunchtime when the office workers are out in force, will do the trick. Burnham's promenade runs along both sides of the river, crossing back and forth over the twenty-odd drawbridges that open and close to let barges and an occasional sailboat pass. The **State Street Bridge** is a superb vantage point. On the south bank, at 35 E Wacker Drive, the elegant Beaux Arts **Jewelers Building** was built in 1926 and is capped on the seventeenth floor by a domed rotunda that once housed Al Capone's favorite speakeasy. Across the river stands what's commonly considered the masterpiece of Ludwig Mies van der Rohe – the 1971 **IBM Building** at 330 N Wabash Ave. The gentle play of light and shadow across the detailed bronze and smoked-glass facade has been the model for countless other less considered copies worldwide. The building is so huge that it acts as a funnel for winter winds off Lake Michigan, and heavy ropes sometimes must be tied across the broad plaza at its base to protect people from getting blown away.

Perhaps Chicago's most successful and acclaimed building of recent years stands four blocks west at **333 W Wacker Drive**. Towering over a broad bend in the river, and bowed to follow its curve, the green glass facade reflects the almost fluorescent green of the river (recently upgraded from "toxic" to merely "polluted"). On the lower floors, a more classically detailed stone base actively addresses its stalwart elder neighbors.

Farther west, the huge **Merchandise Mart**, a hulking retail building hugging the river, was the world's largest building when it opened in 1931. Shrewd business tycoon Joseph P. Kennedy snapped up the structure after the war just by paying its back taxes.

South Michigan Avenue and the Art Institute of Chicago

Many of Chicago's major cultural attractions are gathered on the eastern edge of the Loop, along Michigan Avenue between the city's commercial core and the shores of Lake Michigan. On the lake side of South Michigan Avenue, at the east end of Adams Street, the **Art Institute of Chicago** (Mon–Fri 10.30am–4.30pm, Tues until 8pm, Sat 10am–5pm, Sun noon–5pm; $10 suggested donation, free Tues; Ⓦ www.artic.edu) has an excellent collection of Impressionist and Post-Impressionist paintings, Asian art (particularly Japanese prints), photography and architectural drawings. The Neoclassical facade of the main entrance does its best to look dignified, but the numerous added-on wings can make it hard to find your way around inside.

Most visitors head straight upstairs to the Impressionist works, which include a wall full of Monet's *Haystacks* captured in various lights, next to Seurat's immediately familiar pointillist *Sunday Afternoon on La Grande Jatte*. A handful of Post-Impressionist masterpieces by Van Gogh, Gauguin and Matisse are arrayed nearby. Beyond here, a tortured, tuxedoed self-portrait by **Max Beckmann** – his last Berlin painting before fleeing the Nazis – welcomes you into a crowded gallery of early twentieth-century American and European works, in which moody portraits by Balthus and Picasso, and Surrealist landscapes by Max Ernst and Yves Tanguy hang side by side with Edward Hopper's lonely *Nighthawks* and Georgia O'Keeffe's *Black Cross, New Mexico*.

Also look for the pitchfork-holding farmer of Grant Woods' oft-reproduced *American Gothic* – a picture he painted as a student at the Art Institute school, and sold to the museum for $300 in 1930 – and for the delightful seventh-century Indonesian-sculptured stone monkeys in the Southeast Asia collections displayed around the McKinlock Court Garden – in summer an **open-air café**. Also here, in the east end of the complex, is the immaculately reconstructed Art Moderne trading room of the Chicago Stock Exchange, designed by Louis Sullivan in 1893 and moved here in the 1970s.

A few blocks north, the **Chicago Cultural Center** takes up most of the splendid old Public Library building at 78 E Washington St, and offers a range of free activities. As well as the city's main **visitor center**, it features various galleries (including some great photos of Chicago's most famous landmarks), major touring exhibits, and free lunchtime and evening recitals, readings and concerts (Ⓣ 312/346-3278 for details). The highlight is the **Museum of Broadcast Communications**, where you can watch old advertisements, newsreels and sporting moments (Mon–Sat 10am–4.30pm, Sun noon–5pm; Ⓦ www.mbcnet.org; free).

In 1900 this lakefront strip around the Art Institute on South Michigan

Avenue was the city's prime entertainment district. Many of that era's grand structures preserve a sense of its unabashed artistic aspirations. The world-renowned **Chicago Symphony Orchestra**, now run by Daniel Barenboim after many successful years under the baton of Sir Georg Solti, performs to sell-out crowds at the new **Symphony Center** at 220 S Michigan Ave (ⓦwww.cso.org/). Down the street, the **Fine Arts Building** (ⓦwww .fabgallery.com) at no. 410 once held the offices of *Wizard of Oz* author L. Frank Baum and the drafting studio of the young Frank Lloyd Wright. At no. 430, the stately 1889 **Auditorium Theater** (ⓦwww.auditoriumtheater .org) was originally funded by a group of Chicago's civic leaders who were embarrassed by the derision of the more established Eastern cities. They hoped this performance center, incorporating lavish use of gold, mosaics and murals, in addition to the acoustically perfect theater, would overcome the stigma.

Yet farther south on Michigan stand two of Chicago's most famous old **hotels**, including the recently renovated *Hilton,* the world's largest hotel when it opened in 1927 – and the more affordable and atmospheric *Blackstone*. South of here, the neighborhood income levels drop off sharply. Apart from the Prairie Avenue Historic District described on p.362, there's little of interest before the Hyde Park district three miles south. However, R&B fans may like to know that the southwest corner of Michigan Avenue and 21st Street held the studios and offices of **Chess Records**, immortalized in the early Rolling Stones song *2120 S Michigan Avenue*. Plans to turn this hallowed building into a museum and resource center for local musicians have so far failed to get beyond the argument stage.

Grant Park

East of the Art Institute toward Lake Michigan, **Grant Park** provides a welcome but not entirely complete break from the downtown urban grid – wide strips of high-speed road and railroad slice through it, so casual rambling can be frustrating. The northern half of the park centers on the immense **Buckingham Fountain**, which features daily light and water shows from dusk to 11pm. The whole two-hundred-acre swath is sprinkled with sculptures and monuments, from a moping Columbus to a proud Plains Indian on horseback. Nearly every weekend in summer sees a musical festival (be it gospel, blues, country, jazz or classical) held in the area around the Petrillo Music Shell, just behind the Art Institute. The **Taste of Chicago** in early July attracts more than two million people to a week-long feeding frenzy, garnished with concerts and other live entertainment (ⓦwww.tasteofchicago.com).

The major attractions are gathered in the newly landscaped southern half of Grant Park, known as **Museum Campus**. The extensive and engaging **Field Museum of Natural History**, 1200 S Lake Shore Drive at Roosevelt Road (daily 9am–5pm; $8, free Wed; ⓦwww.fmnh.org), is ten minutes' walk south of the Art Institute, in a huge marble-clad, Daniel Burnham–designed Greek temple. "Natural history" here includes anything non-white and non-European: the collection ranges from Egyptian tombs – the entire burial chamber of the son of a Fifth Dynasty Pharaoh was brought here in 1908 – to the man-eating lions of Tsavo. Folklorists in an earthen lodge in the Native American section tell myths and legends – intended for young kids but not overly sentimental or simple-minded. Also kid-oriented is "Underground Adventure," a simulated environment that "shrinks" you to 1/100th your size, giving you an entirely new perspective on the soil.

Just across busy Lake Shore Drive, on the shores of Lake Michigan, the **Shedd Aquarium** (summer daily 9am–6pm, rest of year Mon–Fri 9am–5pm,

Sat & Sun 9am–6pm; $15, $7 on Mon, when Aquarium section only is free; ⓦ www.sheddnet.org) proclaims itself the largest indoor aquarium in the world. The 1930s structure is rather old-fashioned, but the lighthearted and often tongue-in-cheek displays – some use *Far Side* cartoons – are informative and entertaining. The central exhibit, a 90,000-gallon re-creation of a coral reef complete with sharks (who get fed at 11am and 2pm daily), turtles and thousands of tropical fish, is surrounded by more than a hundred lesser tanks. Highlights include the sluggish and comical South American freckled sideneck turtles, housed across from a 4ft, 250lb alligator snapping turtle, who trundles to the surface to breathe every half-hour. The **Oceanarium** provides an enormous contrast, with its modern lake-view home for marine mammals such as Pacific dolphins and beluga whales. Designed to replicate a rocky Alaskan coastline, it's a carefully disguised amphitheater for such demonstrations of the animals' "natural behavior" as jumping out of the water and fetching plastic rings. Performances are four times daily and you need a ticket. At other times watch from underwater galleries as the animals cruise around the tank, and listen to the clicks, beeps and whistles they use to communicate with each other. Get to the Shedd early to beat the long lines and school groups.

In summer, Shoreline Marine Sightseeing ($9; ⓣ 312/222-9328, ⓦ www .shorelinesightseeing.com) runs hour-long **cruises** along the lakeshore from a jetty just north of the Aquarium. Nearby, the expanded and renovated **Adler Planetarium** (daily 9am–4:30pm, 1st Fri of month 9:30am–10pm; $10–15 determined by exhibits entered, free Tues; ⓦ www.adlerplanetarium.org) has added an interactive 360-degree movie theater; and offers one of the best views of the city skyline. The small Meigs Field Airport is just to the south, so don't be surprised if low-flying planes seem about to crash into the lake.

Chinatown

Close by the gentrified blocks of the South Loop neighborhoods, **Chinatown** – estimated population nine thousand within a narrow ten-block radius – looks much as it did in the mid-1900s. A colorful tile-covered gate at Wentworth and Cermak marks the edge of the district. Once through here you could just as well be in downtown Hong Kong – indeed, some older residents speak no English and rarely pass through the gate to the outer world. More than forty **restaurants** (the best of them listed on p.364) serve Mandarin, Szechuan, Shanghai and Cantonese cuisine; it's a good place to eat and to poke around the little groceries filled with spices, teas, herbs and vegetables.

The Near North Side

Chicago's **Near North Side**, where you're likely to spend much of your time, has few big-name attractions, but it's great for simply wandering around, chancing upon odd **shops**, neighborhood bars and historic sites in a generally low-rise tangle containing some of the city's most characteristic corners.

When the Michigan Avenue Bridge was built over the Chicago River in 1920, the warehouse district along its north bank quickly changed into one of the city's most upmarket quarters, now known as the **Magnificent Mile** and famed for its fashionable shops and department stores. Throughout the Roaring Twenties one glitzy tower after another was thrown up along Michigan Avenue. To the north, the opulent **Drake Hotel** rose off Lincoln Park. To the south, the white terracotta, wedding-cake colossus of the **Wrigley Building** was put up just over the river at 400 N Michigan Ave; it's spectacularly lit up at night. Built by the Chicago-based chewing-gum magnate, it was eclipsed almost immediately by the "Mag Mile's" most famous structure, the **Tribune Tower**. Still housing the editorial offices of Chicago's morning news-paper, as well as, on the ground floor, the studios of its main AM radio station, WGN (you can peer in from the street and watch the DJs in action), the tower was completed in 1925. Its flying buttresses and Gothic detailing turn their back on the then-prevalent Moderne style. Look closely at its lower floors and you'll see pieces of historic buildings – like the Parthenon and the Great Pyramid – pilfered from around the world by *Tribune* staffers and embedded here.

While the Tribune Tower anchors its southern end, the Mag Mile's northern reaches are dominated by the cross-braced steel **John Hancock Center** at 875 N Michigan Ave. Though it's about 325 feet shorter than the Sears Tower, the 360° panorama on a clear day from its 94th-floor **Skydeck Observatory** (daily 9am–midnight; $9) is unforgettable.

Back at ground level, you're right at the heart of Chicago's prime **shopping district**, where Neiman-Marcus and Tiffany & Co rub shoulders with Benetton and Nike Town. Some front onto Michigan Avenue, but most of the shops are enclosed within multistory complexes, or "vertical shopping malls." The oldest of these – and still the best – is **Water Tower Place**, 835 N Michigan Ave, with more than a hundred stores on seven floors plus a bustling food-court. The **900 N Michigan Avenue** mall offers a less-cramped space and more upscale shops, anchored by Bloomingdale's and including Gucci and Aquascutum.

Across from Water Tower Place, at the very center of this consumer paradise, stands the **Historic Water Tower** – a building you'll feel is either beautiful or grotesque. An exuberant but naive example of frontier Gothic, the stone castle, topped by a 100ft tower, was built in 1869 and is one of the very few struc-tures to have survived the 1871 fire. Two other museums are close at hand. The **Terra Museum of American Art**, 664 N Michigan Ave (Tues 10am–8pm, Wed–Sat 10am–6pm, Sun noon–5pm; $7, free on Tues; ⓦwww.terramuseum .org), holds good landscape paintings by Church and Cole, but it's the exten-sive collection of American Impressionist works that make it stand out. The **Museum of Contemporary Art**, at 200 E Chicago Ave (Wed–Sun 10am–5pm, Tues 10am–8pm; $10; ⓦwww.mcachicago.org), has lots of space for its wacky interactive displays, video presentations, and a permanent collec-tion featuring pieces by Calder, Nauman, Warhol and others. At the rear is a sculpture garden and patio where a café serves good bistro food.

Away from the Magnificent Mile, the area along the river between Michigan Avenue and the lake is at the center of a massive redevelopment project, at least partially attributed to the success of the renovated **Navy Pier** (ⓦwww.navypier .com), at East Illinois Street. Since undergoing a facelift in 1995, the pier has become the city's premier tourist destination, attracting more than eight million visitors annually to its shops, chain restaurants, 3D-IMAX theater and fifteen-story Ferris wheel. The pier, home to the **Chicago Children's Museum** (daily 10am–5pm; $6.50, free family night Thurs 5-8pm; ⓦwww.chichildrensmuseum .org), is also a venue for concerts and weekend festivals in summer and an embarkation point for several boat tours, including Shoreline Sightseeing Co ($9; ⓣ312/222-9328, ⓦwww.shorelinesightseeing.com). Shoreline runs thirty-minute **cruises** along the lakeshore from Navy Pier (weather permitting) year-round.

The more heavily industrial area west of Michigan Avenue is also experienc-ing a revival, though on a smaller scale and with a different character. In the rechristened **River North**, many old brick warehouses and factory premises have been converted to house avant-garde art galleries, restaurants and night-clubs. Huron and Superior streets, around their intersections with Wells Street, hold the most concentrated collection. Before you begin gallery-hopping, pick up a copy of the free *Chicago Gallery News*.

The Gold Coast and Old Town

As its name suggests, the **Gold Coast**, stretching north from the Magnificent Mile along the lakeshore, is one of Chicago's wealthiest and most desirable neighborhoods. This residential district is primarily notable for Chicago's most central (and style-conscious) beach. The broad strand of **Oak Street Beach** is accessible via a walkway under Lake Shore Drive, across from the *Drake Hotel*. After dark, the summertime crowds are apt to be found in the myriad bars of Rush and Division streets. The more northerly reaches of the Gold Coast, approaching Lincoln Park, are also its most exclusive, nowhere more so than the stretch of Astor Street running south from the park. **Old Town**, west of LaSalle Street to either side of North Avenue, has a much more lived-in look than does the dandified Gold Coast. Originally a German immigrant commu-nity based around the 1873 **St Michael's Church**, the neighborhood today boasts a broad ethnic and cultural mix. While its many century-old rowhouses and workers' cottages are now prime real estate, its then-shabby housing stock and derelict factories once attracted a variety of creative types. **Wells Street**, the main drag, emerged in the late 1960s as a mini-Haight–Ashbury. Although almost all signs of that era have vanished (or, as in the case of the folk club *Earl of Old Town*, moved uptown), at least one survivor, the Second City comedy club (see p.369), is still going strong. The rest of the neighborhood is packed with some of the city's best bars, galleries and barbecue joints, and makes for a diverting afternoon's wander. Especially noteworthy are the House of Glunz, at 1206 N Wells St, a wine shop dating to 1888, and neighborhood landmark Barbara's Bookstore (Mon–Sat 10am–10pm, Sun 11am–8pm; ☎312/642-5044) at 1350 N Wells St. This independent bookstore has an impressive fic-tion and children's section and frequent author readings.

Lincoln Park and Wrigleyville

In summer, Chicago's largest green space, **Lincoln Park**, gives a much-needed respite from the gridded pavements of the rest of the city. Unlike Grant Park to the south, Lincoln Park is packed with leafy nooks and crannies, monuments and sculptures, and has a couple of friendly, family-oriented **beaches**, at the eastern ends of North Avenue and Fullerton Avenue. Near the small **zoo** (daily 9am–5pm; free) at the heart of the park, you can rent paddleboats or bikes. If the weather's bad, head for the **conservatory**, 2400 N Stockton Drive (free), or visit the **Chicago Historical Society museum** (Mon–Sat 9.30am–4.30pm, Sun noon–5pm; $5), at the south end of the park at 1601 N Clark St, and bone up on Chicago's captivating past. It also has a nice, skylit café.

The Lincoln Park neighborhood, inland from the lake between North Avenue and Diversey Parkway, centers on **Lincoln Avenue** and **Clark Street**, which run diagonally from near the Historical Society; **Halsted Street**, with its blues bars and nightclubs, runs north–south through its heart. Any of these main roads merits an extended stroll, popping in to the many book and record stores, while smaller side streets show off why Lincoln Park is such a popular place to live. Look for the **Biograph Theatre** movie house, 2433 N Lincoln Ave, where **John Dillinger** was ambushed and killed by the FBI in 1934, thanks to a tip from his companion, the legendary Lady in Red. **Oz Park**, at Lincoln and Webster avenues, was the namesake, if not the inspiration, for

Chicago author L. Frank Baum's stories, set somewhere over the rainbow.

Chicago spreads north from Lincoln Park for block after low-rise block of houses and shops, many of which date from the late 1800s, when thousands of German immigrants settled in what was then the separate enclave of Lake View. This area is now dubbed **Wrigleyville** in honor of **Wrigley Field**, 1060 W Addison St at N Clark Street, the ivy-covered 1920s stadium of baseball's much-loved Cubs. This remains one of the best places to get a real feel for the game – the club is so traditional that it fought the installation of floodlights until 1988. Even if you know nothing about the rules, there are few more pleasant and relaxing ways to spend an afternoon than drinking beer, eating hot dogs and watching the Cubs struggle to win a ball game (they haven't won a World Series since 1908).

The West Side and Oak Park

Chicago's **West Side**, west of the Chicago River, was where the **Great Fire of 1871** started – supposedly when Mrs O'Leary's cow kicked over a lantern. The flames spread quickly east to engulf the entire central city, which was built of wood and fed the fire for three full days. Appropriately enough, the O'Leary cottage is now the site of the Chicago Fire Department training academy. The West Side also saw 1886's **Haymarket Riots**, when striking workers assembled at the old city market at Desplaines and Randolph streets; after a peaceful demonstration, as police began to break up the crowd, a bomb exploded, killing an officer. Six more policemen and four workers died in the resulting panic; four labor leaders were later found guilty of murder and hanged, despite the fact that none of them had been present at the event.

Though the West Side has little to see compared with the rest of the city, it does provide a good look at its day-to-day realities, having served as the port of entry for Chicago's myriad ethnic groups, now congregated in its distinct neighborhoods. **Milwaukee Avenue**, which stretches under the "El" tracks diagonally from the Loop out towards O'Hare Airport, has long been home to a sizable eastern European community, mainly Poles – over a million altogether, including some 60,000 who came to Chicago during the martial-law era of the 1980s. For an introduction, stop by the **Polish Museum of America** (daily noon–5pm; free; Ⓦ www.prcua.org/pma) at 984 N Milwaukee Ave, or the **Ukrainian National Museum**, 721 N Oakley (Thurs–Sun 11am–4pm and by appointment; free; Ⓦ www.ukrntlmuseum.org). **Greektown**, the few blocks of Halsted Street north of the I-290 freeway, and **Little Italy**, along Taylor Street west of Halsted, are both just a short walk from the University of Illinois subway station, on the CTA Congress line. Four blocks southeast of Little Italy is Maxwell Street and the site of the famed **Maxwell Street Market**. Although the city banned the market for various reasons in 1994, a new Maxwell Street Market was born on Canal Street and Roosevelt Road. It's still a lively place to visit on Sundays, when blues bands entertain on street corners and *kielbasa* replaces bagels among the stallholders.

Ten miles west of the Loop, the affluent and attractive c.1900 suburb of **Oak Park** has been preserved as a national historic district, thanks in part to its early influence on two very different but very American figures, **Ernest Hemingway** and **Frank Lloyd Wright**. Oak Park is easily accessible by public transportation: take the Green Line west to the Harlem Avenue stop. The **visitor center**, just over two blocks east of the station at 158 N Forest Ave (summer daily 10am–5pm; rest of year daily 10am–4pm; ☏ 708/524-7800, Ⓦ www.visitoakpark.com), has an excellent architectural walking tour map as well as guidebooks and free brochures.

Hemingway was born and bred in Oak Park, editing his high school newspaper and living a normal middle-class life. Both his birthplace (at 339 N Oak Park Ave) and his boyhood home (600 N Kenilworth Ave) bear commemorative plaques, and there's an engaging collection of memorabilia at the **Oak Park and River Forest Historical Society** (Thurs–Sun 1–4pm; Thurs is free; $4) at 217 Home Ave, a block south of the station.

In 1889, a decade before Hemingway's birth, an ambitious young architect named Frank Lloyd Wright arrived in Oak Park, which he used for the next twenty years as a testing ground for his innovative design theories. Most of the 25 buildings he put up here are in keeping with conventional Victorian design, and few are open to the public; fortunately, however, his most interesting and groundbreaking edifices are maintained as monuments. His ideal of an "organic architecture," in which all aspects of the design derive from a single unifying concept – quite at odds with the fussy "gingerbread" popular at the time – is exemplified by **Unity Temple** at 875 Lake St. Though the simplicity of this angular, reinforced-concrete structure was largely dictated by economics, its unembellished surfaces contribute to a masterful manipulation of space, especially in the skylit interior, where the subtle interplay of overlapping planes creates a dynamic spatial flow. Though little noticed in the US, Unity Temple was very influential in Europe as a precursor of modern architecture.

Wright built his small, brown-shingled **home and studio**, nearby at 951 Chicago Ave on the corner of Forest Avenue, at age 22 in 1889, and remodeled it repeatedly thereafter. It shows all his hallmarks: large fireplaces to symbolize the heart of the home and family; free-flowing, open-plan rooms; and the visual linking of interior and exterior spaces. The furniture of the kitchen and dining rooms is Wright's own design; he added a two-story studio in 1898, with a mezzanine drafting area suspended by chains from the roof beams. In 1909 Wright abandoned Oak Park and his family for new pastures; he was eventually to design such landmarks as New York's Guggenheim Museum. You can see the house itself on a 45-minute guided tour (Mon–Fri 11am, 1pm & 3pm, Sat & Sun every 20min, 11am–3.30pm; $9). Lengthier walking tours ($9 including use of Walkman) take in the dozen other Wright-designed houses within a two-block radius. Booking the walking and house tours at the same time will save you $2.

The South Side

The **South Side** of Chicago has always had a raw deal, cursed with the presence of bad-neighbor heavy industries like the sprawling **Chicago Stockyards**, the slaughterhouses and meatpackers that Upton Sinclair exposed in his 1906 novel *The Jungle*, and whose stink covered most of the South Side until the 1950s. The overriding impression is one of misery and downtrodden poverty, with block after block of deprived and dangerous neighborhoods. That said, there are exceptions: not just the **Prairie Avenue** and **Hyde Park** districts described overleaf, but also the buzzing **Chinatown** around Wentworth Avenue and 22nd Street; the artsy, predominantly Mexican **Pilsen** district, a few blocks north and west; and the largely Irish, blue-collar **Bridgeport**, around Halsted and 37th – Mayor Daley's old fiefdom, the home of Comiskey Park and baseball's White Sox (see p.369). To reach the South Side, double-decker Illinois Central commuter trains run beside the lake to Prairie Avenue (a block from the 18th St station) and Hyde Park (near the 59th St station). CTA bus #1 follows Michigan Avenue to the same places. Bus #8 runs every fifteen minutes, 24 hours a day, south through Pilsen to Bridgeport.

Two blocks east of Michigan Avenue, a mile from the Loop and only a quarter of a mile from the lake, **Prairie Avenue** started life as an exclusive suburb. Though just ten minutes' walk south from Grant Park and the Field Museum, it's best reached by cab, bus or train; the route is confusing and the streets are just not safe. As the one part of Chicago to remain unscathed in the Great Fire of 1871, this area had a brief moment of glory as the city's finest address. However, by 1900 the railroads had cut it off from Lake Michigan, and the expansion of the stockyards had encouraged the wealthy to flee back to their traditional North Side haunts.

One of the few structures to have survived the intervening years is the Romanesque 1886 **Glessner House**, Chicago's only surviving H.H. Richardson-designed house, standing sentry on the southwest corner of Prairie Avenue and 18th Street. Behind the forbidding stone facade, the house opens onto a garden court, its interior filled with Arts and Crafts furniture and swathed in William Morris fabrics and wall coverings. The place is maintained by the Chicago Architecture Foundation, which gives guided tours (Wed–Sun noon–3pm; $11 joint admission with Clarke House). A block away stands Chicago's oldest building, the **Clarke House** at 1855 S Indiana Ave (details as for Glessner House), a plain white 1836 Greek Revival pioneer home that spent many years as a community center before being gussied up as a minor museum of interior decor. Much more interesting, and proof of the wealth once concentrated here, is the lavish Gothic **Presbyterian Church**, a block away at 1936 S Michigan Ave, with its Burne-Jones and Tiffany stained-glass windows.

An island of middle-class prosperity surrounded by urban poverty, **Hyde Park** is the most attractive and sophisticated South Side Chicago neighborhood. It's also one of the more racially integrated areas of the city, and among its more erudite: the **University of Chicago**, endowed by Rockefeller in 1892 and now among the top institutions in the US, has encouraged a college-town atmosphere, with bookshops and numerous cafés around its compact campus, especially along East 57th Street. On the campus itself, two buildings are well worth searching out: the massive Gothic pile of the **Rockefeller Memorial Chapel**, at 59th Street and Woodlawn Avenue, and the Prairie-style **Robie House**, designed by Frank Lloyd Wright, two blocks north at 5757 S Woodlawn Ave. Campus tours start from the Ida Noyes Hall, 1212 E 59th St (Mon–Sat 10am).

Woodlawn Avenue runs north from the University of Chicago campus, passing one of the South Side's most popular taverns, *Jimmy's Woodlawn Tap* at 1172 E 55th St, before turning a whole lot grander. Besides its enormous mansions, Woodlawn Avenue illustrates the social and racial mix for which Hyde Park is renowned. Within two blocks of each other are the Midwest's largest Jewish temple, the ornate **Isaiah Israel** at 1100 E Hyde Park Blvd, and the home of **Minister Louis Farrakhan**, leader of the Nation of Islam, which was started here on the South Side in the 1940s by the late Elijah Muhammad. In between, at 4944 S Woodlawn Ave, stands the huge brick manor where boxer Muhammad Ali lived for many years.

Just west of the university, on the eastern edge of lush Washington Park, the **Du Sable Museum of African American History**, 740 E 56th Place, takes a look at the experience of Americans of African descent, from slavery to the present day (Mon–Sat 10am–5pm, Sun noon–5pm; $3; ⓦ www.dusablemuseum.org). Named for Jean Du Sable, the Haitian-born Francophone who was Chicago's first permanent settler, it focuses on the works of WPA-sponsored artists of the 1930s and on the civil rights movement of the 1960s.

Washington Park wraps around the south side of the University of Chicago campus, to join the long green strip of the **Midway** – one of the few reminders that in the late nineteenth century Chicago was the site of the **World's Columbian Exposition**. Attracting some thirty million spectators in the summer of 1893 (45 percent of the US population at the time), the Midway was then filled with full-sized model villages from around the globe, including an Irish market town and a mock-up of Cairo complete with belly dancers. These days it's used mainly by joggers and students tossing Frisbees. A short stroll east, in Jackson Park, the cavernous **Museum of Science and Industry**, 57th Street at Lake Shore Drive (summer Mon–Fri 9.30am– 5.30pm; rest of year Mon–Fri 9.30am–4pm, Sat & Sun 9.30am–5.30pm; $9; free on Thurs; ⓦ www.msichicago.org), was Chicago's single most popular tourist destination (and ranked second in the US) until it started charging admission in 1991. Besides interactive computer displays, the best of which explores the inner workings of the brain, exhibits include a captured German U-boat, a trip down a replica coal mine, and a simulated space-shuttle journey. It's fun for kids, but adults may not feel like staying very long. The complex also hosts a giant OMNIMAX movie dome; admission is $6 extra.

    Promontory Point juts into Lake Michigan east of the museum, giving great views of the Chicago skyline, including a close-up look at Mies van der Rohe's first high-rise, the Promontory Apartments at 5530 S Lake Shore Drive.

Eating

Chicago's cosmopolitan makeup is reflected in its plethora of ethnic restaurants. **Italian** food, ranging from hearty **deep-dish pizza** (developed in 1953 at *Pizzeria Uno*, see p.365) to delicately crafted creations presented at stylish trattorias, continues to dominate a very dynamic scene. In recent years there's been a surge of popularity for **New American** cuisine. **Thai** restaurants still thrive, as do ones with a broad **Mediterranean** slant, many of which serve tapas; and there are still plenty of opportunities to sample more longstanding Chicago cuisines – Eastern European, German, Mexican, Chinese, Indian, even Burmese and Ethiopian. Of course, a number of establishments serve good old-fashioned barbecue **ribs**, a legacy of Chicago's days as the nation's meatpacker. And no visit is complete without sampling a messy Italian beef sandwich, or a Chicago-style hot dog, laden with tomatoes, onions, hot peppers and a pickle.

    The largest concentration of restaurants is found north and west of the **Loop**. To the west, **Greektown**, around Halsted Street at Jackson Boulevard, and **Little Italy**, on and around Taylor Street, are worth a look. The **Near North** and **River North** areas harbor a good number of upscale places. **Chinatown**, though not pretty, is a predictably good neighborhood for Cantonese and Szechuan food. Many bars and cafés listed in the "Nightlife and Entertainment" section also serve snacks and light meals, and dozens of places in the Loop offer great breakfast and lunch specials.

Downtown

The Berghoff 17 W Adams St ☎ 312/427-3170. The beautifully preserved Chicago landmark, dating from 1893, offers plentiful Germanic specialties plus fish dishes and corned beef and cabbage. Try the draft or root beer. A bargain.

Billy Goat Tavern 430 N Michigan Ave, lower level ☎ 312/222-1525. This legendary journalists' haunt opens early and closes late, serving the 'cheezborgers' made famous by John Belushi's comedy skit. Very reasonable.

Everest One Financial Place, 440 S LaSalle St ☎ 312/663-8920. Take in the stunning vista from the 40th floor and tuck into chef Jean Joho's wild mushroom consommé and roasted Maine lobster. Very expensive; closed Sun, Mon.

Italian Village 71 W Monroe St ☎ 312/332-7005. Three Italian establishments flourish under one roof. The *Village* has traditional Italian-American food and a world-class wine cellar. The basement *La Cantina* serves chicken Vesuvio, a Chicago creation, among its reasonably priced dishes. The expensive *Vivere* (☎ 312/332-4040) has an adventurous menu, a mesmerizing wine list and a large pre-theater crowd (so arrive after 8pm).

Lou Mitchell's 565 W Jackson Ave ☎ 312/939-3111. Near Union Station, *Lou's* has been around since 1923, serving terrific omelets, waffles and hash browns all day long. Try the pecan-laden cookies.

Marché 833 W Randolph St ☎ 312/226-8399. Creative French cuisine – try the porcini-crusted Chilean sea bass – is served in an eclectic atmosphere in the Market District. Entrees $16–28.

Prairie 500 S Dearborn St, in the *Hyatt* ☎ 312/663-1143. Modeled on a Frank Lloyd Wright interior, this place uses only fresh Midwestern ingredients in dishes such as sirloin of buffalo and brandied loaf of duck.

Printers Row 550 S Dearborn St ☎ 312/461-0780. Seafood and game are highlights among the captivating New American concoctions devised by owner/chef Michael Foley. Quite pricey.

Russian Tea Time 77 E Adams St ☎ 312/360-0000. This Midwestern nod to New York's *Russian Tea Room* offers a sampling of authentic fare from the former Soviet empire. Pricey, but lunch can be a bargain.

Sorriso 321 N Clark St ☎ 312/644-0283. The alfresco dining comes with a spectacular view of the Loop riverfront and skyline. The menu features Italian and American dishes including *scungilli* (conch) salad. The piano bar occasionally serves free pizza during the cocktail hour.

Trattoria No 10 10 N Dearborn St ☎ 312/984-1718. This charming surprise, in a series of underground rooms, serves up delicious warm bread (stuffed with sun-dried tomatoes), grilled sea scallops and risotto.

Greektown and Little Italy

Costa's 340 S Halsted St ☎ 312/263-9700. At this casual Greek place, which is reasonably priced, try the Mussels Salonika, or the cheese-stuffed roasted peppers.

Gennaro's 1352 W Taylor St ☎ 312/243-1035. The speakeasy atmosphere is enhanced by the locked front door, opened after you're checked out through the peephole. Fine *gnocchi*.

Greek Islands 200 S Halsted St ☎ 312/782-9855. A large place, it has several rustic "taverna" nooks. The grilled sea bass and red snapper are fresh and flavorful.

Mia Francesca 1400 W Taylor St ☎ 312/829-2828. Here's the most subdued of the Francesca restaurant family. That said, it offers some of the best Italian in the city, period. Don't be surprised to find a crowd here all day.

Parthenon 314 S Halsted St ☎ 312/726-2407. One of the oldest places in Greektown: *saganaki* (fried cheese doused with Metaxa brandy and ignited) was invented here.

Pegasus 130 S Halsted St ☎ 312/226-3377. True hospitality and evocative wall murals add to the appeal of this popular establishment. Stuffed squid and pastitsio (macaroni, meat and cheese casserole) are recommended. The rooftop garden has a superb view of the Loop skyline.

Santorini 800 W Adams St ☎ 312/829-8820. The decor re-creates a Greek island village, and the food is beguiling, too; grilled octopus and lamb *exohiko* (wrapped in filo pastry and fried) are highlights.

Tufano's Vernon Park Tap 1073 W Vernon Park Place, near the United Center ☎ 312/733-3393. A neighborhood landmark for more than 60 years. Its recent face-lift has eroded some of the original charm, but the chalkboard specials, good service and moderate prices remain. The antipasto and homemade ravioli are standouts.

Tuscany 1014 W Taylor St ☎ 312/829-1990. The creative menu here includes wood-roasted chicken and terrific risottos. Service is very attentive, and there's a huge, bustling bar.

Chinatown

Emperor's Choice 2238 S Wentworth Ave ☎ 312/225-8800. The attractive storefront serves delicious egg rolls and seafood dishes. Try steamed clams, poached shrimp or the lobster.

Hong Min 221 W Cermak Rd ☎ 312/842-5026. Superb dim sum, with more than 36 lunch items. Cantonese and Mandarin specialties include West Lake duck with barbecued pork.

Seven Treasures 2312 S Wentworth Ave ☎ 312/225-2668. Cantonese and some spicier Szechuan dishes concentrate on soups, dumplings and noodles. Reasonable prices.

Sixty-Five 2414 S Wentworth Ave ☎ 312/225-7060. The two-story Cantonese restaurant emphasizes exceptional seafood. Try the family-style meals.

Near North Side and River North

Big Bowl Café 159 E Erie St ☎ 312/787-8297. Diner with an Asian accent. Filling soups and pot stickers make it a budget choice for weary shoppers.

Café Iberico 739 N LaSalle Blvd ☎/573-1510. At this authentic and reasonably priced tapas bar, you can share plates of eggplant stuffed with goat's cheese or grilled octopus on potatoes.

Eli's The Place For Steak 215 E Chicago Ave ☎312/642-1393. This glitzy room is perfect for celebrity-spotting and for great steaks, seafood and other nicely rendered dishes – and a famous cheesecake.

Frontera Grill & Topolobampo 445 N Clark St ☎312/661-1434. Wildly imaginative Mexican food: *La Frontera* is crowded and boisterous; *Topolobampo* is more refined and pricier.

Gino's East 633 N Wells St ☎312/943-1124. A Chicago tradition: huge deep-dish pizzas (no need for appetizers here) and graffiti-covered walls. Expect to wait.

Nacional 27 325 W Huron St ☎312/664-2727. A popular new Latin place serves food from a variety of Central American cuisines. Salsa dancing on weekends.

Pizzeria Uno 29 E Ohio St ☎312/321-1000. The place that put Chicago deep-dish pizza on the map.

Portillo's 100 W Ontario St ☎312/587-8930. This Chicago-area chain serves good Chicago hot dogs and the best Italian beef sandwich in the city.

Scoozi! 410 W Huron St ☎312/943-5900. At this ebullient mixture of nostalgic (there's an accordion player) and trendy (it's a place to be seen), the emphasis is on northern Italian, with splendid pizza and risotto.

Shaw's Crab House 21 E Hubbard St ☎312/527-2722. This large 1930s Key West-style dining room is crowded at lunch and after work; its consistently high-quality fare includes baked crab cakes, Dungeness crab in garlic butter, seafood gumbo and popcorn shrimp. Not cheap.

Star of Siam 11 E Illinois St ☎312/670-0100. Terrific Thai food served in a spacious, inviting setting. The *Tom yom* soup, Pad Thai noodle dish and curries are top-notch.

Old Town

Café Ba-Ba-Reeba! 2024 N Halsted St ☎773/935-5000. One of the city's Spanish hot spots, it delivers a good variety of hot and cold tapas, filling paella and, of course, sangria.

Flat Top Grill 319 W North Ave ☎312/787-7676. Create-your-own stir-fry with a wide variety of meats, vegetables and mild-to-spicy sauces.

Old Jerusalem 1411 N Wells St ☎312/944-0459. This old-time favorite serves reasonable Middle Eastern dishes; the falafel is great. Bring your own beer or wine.

Topo Gigio 1516 N Wells St ☎312/266-9355. The well-prepared Italian cuisine is served by the very friendly staff in a peaceful garden amid the Old Town bustle. The homemade tiramisu is fabulous.

Twin Anchors 1655 N Sedgwick St ☎312/266-1231. You'll wait for a seat in a neighborhood spot that's famed for its BBQ ribs, but the interesting clientele and 1950s-style bar make it worth it.

Lincoln Park and around

Ann Sather 929 W Belmont Ave ☎773/348-2378 and four other locations. This Chicago institution serves breakfast, brunch and some of the city's finest Scandinavian food. Only this location is open for dinner.

Brother Jimmy's BBQ 2909 N Sheffield Ave ☎773/528-0888. The BBQ chicken and three kinds of ribs (aficionados say Northern are the best) come with side orders such as candied yams or collard greens and corn bread. Moderate prices, and loud live music Thurs–Sun.

Charlie Trotter's 816 W Armitage Ave ☎773/248-6228. Prepare for a superb, and appropriately pricey, experience. Chef Trotter is a true artist and his daring creations, such as caviar-stuffed quail eggs or Maine salmon with blood sausage, are constantly evolving.

Chicago Diner 3411 N Halsted St ☎773/935-6696. This vegetarian restaurant incorporates international influences in its expansive menu. Soup, salads, tempe burgers and the macrobiotic plate are popular. Vegan dishes are served as well.

Little Bucharest 3001 N Ashland Ave ☎773/929-8640. A Romanian inn serves huge stews, roasts and sweetbreads. Rich desserts come with a complimentary *slivovitz* (plum brandy). A bargain.

Mia Francesca 3311 N Clark St ☎773/281-3310. Huge servings of pasta and tasty pizzas (try the *quattro formaggi*) ensure that this cozy Italian place with a no-reservations policy is always packed.

R J Grunts 2056 Lincoln Park W ☎773/929-5363. Check out the great burgers and a top-notch salad bar – purported to be the nation's first – in a casual neighborhood atmosphere.

Wishbone 1001 W Washington Blvd ☎312/850-2663 and 1800 W Grand Ave ☎312/829-3597. The rich, down-home Southern cooking come in large portions at reasonable prices. The yardbird chicken (served with a red-pepper sauce), baked ham and sweet potato pie are wonderful.

Yoshi's Café 3257 N Halsted St ☎773/248-6160. An East-West fusion with a French accent, it works especially well with tuna or fluke (sea urchin). More Asian is the three-course *kaiseki* menu of tiny dishes. Very expensive.

Wicker Park

Café Absinthe 1954 W North Ave ☎773/278-4488. Fine French dining in a romantic, casual setting. One of the city's best.

Irazu 1865 N Milwaukee Ave ☎773/252-5687. Wonderful Costa Rican diner; great burritos plus a small selection of authentic main courses.

Smoke Daddy 1804 W Division St ☎773/772-6656. Arguably Chicago's best BBQ, with jazz and blues nightly, also offers vegetarian options.

Soul Kitchen 1576 N Milwaukee Ave ☎773/342-9742. At this loud joint, a youthful crowd munches on the likes of pecan-breaded catfish and fire-and-spice lamb.

The South Side: Hyde Park

Dixie Kitchen 5225 S Harper, Harper Court

☎773/363-4943. The great soul food includes pulled pork sandwiches, breaded oysters with chili sauce and desserts like peach cobbler and pecan pie.

Medici on 57th 1327 E 57th St ☎773/667-7394. At this quintessential collegiate hangout next to the University of Chicago, the chummy crowd chows down on burgers, pizza, salads and ice cream.

Mellow Yellow 1508 E 53rd St ☎773/667-2000. A soul food emphasis is evident in the catfish, steaks, seafood and rotisserie chicken served at this casual, popular place – it does crepes and quiche, too.

Valois Cafeteria 1518 E 53rd St ☎773/667-0647. A budget-priced menu features baked chicken, barbecue ribs and pork sandwiches. Don't skip the freshly baked biscuits.

Drinking

If not quite as wild as in the bootlegging days of speakeasies and Prohibition, Chicago remains a consummate boozer's town and is one of the best US cities for **bars**, catering to just about every group and interest and many open to 3 or 4am, some until 5am. At **"sports bars"** – Chicago has more of them than anywhere else – banks of TV screens broadcast Cubs, Sox, Bears, Bulls and Blackhawks games. These are great places for beer drinking and male bonding, but not for thoughtful conversation. **Division Street**, in the two blocks west of State Street, is unreconstructed breeder-bar territory, with a handful of more subtle joints tucked away on side streets off the main drag. **Wicker Park**, a couple of miles north of Lincoln Park, is the trendiest hangout zone, while Halsted Street between Belmont and Addison is known as **Boystown** for its gay bars and clubs.

The hundred-plus **cafés and coffee houses** across the city may not have taken the place of the traditional taverns, but they're a growing alternative.

Saloons, pubs and bars

Bar Louie 226 W Chicago Ave ☎12/337-3313. The friendly, casual place in River North has tables out front and cheap bar food.

Berghoff's 17 W Adams St ☎312/427-3170. This former men-only stand-up bar in a showcase c.1900 tavern next to *The Berghoff* restaurant is crowded and congenial at lunchtime and after work.

Cavanaugh's 53 W Jackson St ☎312/939-325. Visit this Loop favorite in the historic Monadnock Building for an after-work drink. Experience the warm interior with antique woodwork, Harp on draft and the full menu.

Delilah's 2771 N Lincoln Ave ☎773/472-2771. At a dimly lit bar (playing underground records – from alternative country to ambient techno – at night), choose from a great selection of beers (150) and bourbons.

Goose Island Brewing Co 1800 N Clybourn Ave ☎312/915-0071. Forty ales and lagers, including the popular Honker's Ale, are brewed on the premises at this convivial Lincoln Park haunt.

Green Door Tavern 678 N Orleans St ☎312/664-5496. In an unlikely spot near the galleries of River North, this historic place is chock-full of Chicago memorabilia: some pure kitsch, others genuine antiques. Drink at the long bar or settle into a cozy back room to sample "home-style cooking."

O'Neil's 152 E Ontario St ☎312/787-5269. This dark little Near North space – formerly known as Howard's – is popular with media types and serves good burgers. Its ace card is the patio out back.

John Barleycorn 658 W Belden Ave ☎773/348-8899. The dimly lit Lincoln Park pub has retained its character. A lovely garden is open in summer. Daily all-you-can-eat specials.

Old Town Ale House 219 W North Ave
ⓣ 312/944-7020. An eclectic crowd of scruffy
regulars and yuppies mingle in this convivial
haunt, complete with a pinball machine and a
library of paperbacks.
Rainbo Club 1150 N Damen Ave ⓣ 773/489-
5999. Busy Wicker Park bar and hangout for indie-
rock types.
The Red Lion Pub 2446 N Lincoln Ave
ⓣ 773/348-2695. British ales and ciders, fish and
chips and shepherd's pie enhance an authentic
pub atmosphere, complete with sing-along piano.
Resis' Beerstube 2034 W Irving Park Rd
ⓣ 773/472-1749. The old-time German tavern features good imported draft and bottled beers, platters of wurst and a delightful shaded beer garden.

Sports bars

ESPNZone 43 E Ohio St ⓣ 312/644-3776. Part
futuristic game parlor, part megalithic sports
bar/restaurant, the *Zone* offers so-so food and
service is sluggish, but sports fans will probably
still pack it up.
Harry Caray's 33 W Kinzie St ⓣ 312/828-0966.
This great sports bar/Italian restaurant in an old
River North brick warehouse was founded by former Cubs radio and TV announcer Caray. The huge
bar, packed with beer drinkers until the early
hours, has floor-to-ceiling Cubs memorabilia.
Murphy's Bleachers 3655 N Sheffield Ave
ⓣ 773/281-5356. The bar to be at before, during,
and after Cubs games. It doesn't get much more
Chicago than this.

Slugger's 3540 N Clark St ⓣ 773/248-0055. At
probably the only bar in the world with its own
indoor batting cage, this raucous beer joint fairly
rattles and hums during Cubs, Bears and Bulls
games. Beer is ridiculously inexpensive during
happy hour.

Gay & lesbian bars

Big Chicks 5024 N Sheridan Rd, Andersonville
ⓣ 773/728-5511. This friendly place for a mixed
crowd has a free jukebox and free barbecues out
back on summer Sundays.
The Closet 3325 N Broadway ⓣ 773/477-8533. A
tiny, cramped but congenial lesbian bar, it attracts
gay men as well.
Gentry 440 N State St ⓣ 773/836-0933. The
cabaret and piano bar is popular with corporate
types after work.
Sidetrack 3349 N Halsted St ⓣ 773/477-9189.
One of the most popular bars along Halsted's gay
strip in Lakeview.

Cafés

The Bourgeois Pig 738 W Fullerton Ave
ⓣ 773/883-5282. Inventive sandwiches in a laid-
back student atmosphere.
Kopi, A Traveler's Café 5317 N Clark St,
Andersonville ⓣ 773/989-5674. A bit of a trek
from downtown will bring you to a really splendid
combo coffee-and-tea house, Indonesian art
gallery, boutique and bookstore stocked with travel
guides and literature. Live music and prose/poetry
readings.

Nightlife and entertainment

From its earliest frontier days, Chicago has had some of the best **nightlife** in
the US. "Sweet Home Chicago", birthplace of Muddy Waters' **urban blues**,
as well as R&B's Chess Records, is still going strong, inspiring the energetic
dance beat of 1980s **house music** as well as the groundbreaking **jazz** of the
Art Ensemble of Chicago. **Nightclubs** aplenty are all over town, especially
along Halsted Street, Lincoln Avenue and Clark Street on the North Side.
Uptown, at the intersection of North Broadway and Lawrence, is a bit down-
at-heel, but has half a dozen good venues. The best **gay clubs** congregate in
the Lincoln Park area. Highbrow pursuits are also well provided for: Chicago's
classical music, **dance** and **theater** are world-class.

For what's-on information, Chicagoans pick up the excellent **free newspaper**
The Reader (copies comes out Thursday afternoon and are usually all gone by
Saturday). The weekly *New City* and the gay and lesbian *Windy City Times* are
good sources as well. Full listings also appear in the Friday issues of the *Chicago
Sun–Times* and the *Chicago Tribune*, and *Chicago* magazine has useful arts and
restaurant listings. The Gramaphone Ltd record store at 2663 N Clark St
(ⓣ 773/472-3683) is the best place for details of one-shot **dance** nights.

Blues

B.L.U.E.S. 2519 N Halsted St ☎773/528-1012. Opened in the 1970s, it's still going strong, though a little over-touristed. The tiny stage has been graced by all the greats.

Blue Chicago 536 N Clark St ☎312/661-0100. The touristy blues joint features mostly female performers.

Buddy Guy's Legends 754 S Wabash Ave ☎312/427-0333. This South Loop club owned by veteran guitarist and vocalist Buddy Guy and offering great acoustics and atmosphere, aims to present the very best local and national acts. Not as touristy as other downtown blues clubs.

Checkerboard Lounge 423 E 43rd St ☎773/624-3240. Way down on the South Side, the *Checkerboard* has a fabulous history and retains the support of the best local acts.

Kingston Mines 2548 N Halsted St ☎773/477-4646. Top-notch local and national acts on two stages play to an up-for-it partying crowd.

Rosa's Lounge 3420 W Armitage Ave ☎773/342-0452. Run by Mama Rosa and her son and dedicated to the blues greats, this is undoubtedly the friendliest blues joint around. For real aficionados, it caters less to the tourist crowd.

Jazz

Andy's 11 E Hubbard St ☎312/642-6805. Very popular with the after-work crowd; informal with moderate prices.

The Cotton Club 1710 S Michigan Ave ☎312/341-9787. A sophisticated, live-music venue and disco, it attracts a well-dressed, mellow crowd.

Green Dolphin Street 2200 N Ashland Ave ☎773/395-0066. This swanky, pricey restaurant and jazz club offers a solid line-up of regular performers.

The Green Mill 4802 N Broadway ☎773/878-5552. This place had a checkered past during Prohibition and is in the tough Uptown neighborhood, but it is one of the best – and most beautiful – rooms for local and national talent.

Joe Segal's Jazz Showcase 59 W Grand Ave ☎312/670-2473. A classy, dressy room hosts premier jazz by top names.

Rock clubs

Cubby Bear 1059 W Addison St ☎773/327-1662. A sports bar during the day – right next to Wrigley Field – this place transforms itself after dark into one of the city's most boisterous and eclectic live venues, popular with aging dinosaurs more than new bands, but still fun.

Double Door 1572 N Milwaukee Ave ☎773/489-3160. This former biker bar, now a hip and eclectic

venue, anchors the music scene in the Wicker Park/Bucktown neighborhood. There's live music almost every night, and Sundays usually feature Liquid Soul, the acid jazz legends of Chicago.

Elbo 2871 N Lincoln Ave ☎773/549-5549. Mostly indie/alternative bands on the way up.

Empty Bottle 1035 N Western Ave ☎773/276-3600. More up-and-coming indie, along with avant-garde jazz, and progressive country.

House of Blues 329 N Dearborn St ☎312/527-2583. Despite its name, this Near North venue puts on all kinds of music.

Metro 3730 N Clark St ☎773/549-0203. Arguably the top spot in the city, this club, in an old cinema building, regularly hosts young English bands trying to break in Stateside, and DJ mixes.

Folk, country and world music clubs

Baby Doll Polka Club 6102 S Central Ave ☎773/582-9706. For 40 years, this Southwest Side club has been full of locals doing the polka, two-step and the occasional tango.

Fitzgerald's 6615 W Roosevelt, Berwyn ☎708/788-2118. Excellent venue for alternative country, Americana, Cajun and zydeco in the western suburb of Berwyn.

Old Town School of Folk Music 909 W Armitage Ave – and now a second location for concerts at 4544 N Lincoln Ave at W Montrose Ave ☎773/728-6000. Established in 1959, this place presents about 80 concerts a year, including just about every type of folk.

Schuba's 3159 N Southport Ave at Belmont Ave ☎773/525-2508. Some of the best alternative country and roots revival bands play this likeable bar at weekends.

Dance

Circus 901 W Weed St ☎312/266-1200. This celebrity hangout features cartoonish, technicolor decor and a live trapeze act.

Crobar 1543 N Kingsbury St ☎312/413-7000. The exclusive, hyper-trendy warehouse club near the river spins the newest techno and house. Sun is gay night.

Excalibur 632 N Dearborn St ☎312/266-1944. A city institution blasts out rock, R&B and Motown on several floors.

Iggy's 700 N Milwaukee Ave ☎312/829-4449. This place gets lively at about 3am on the weekend. The red-velvet interior looks like a bordello, and there's a cute patio.

Red Dog 1958 W North Ave ☎773/278-1009. This small Wicker Park club, or "funk parlor" as they like to call it, plays house, soul and funk. The entrance is in the alley.

Smart Bar 3730 N Clark St, underneath the Metro ☎773/549-0203. Great techno and house on the weekend in post-industrial Wrigleyville surroundings. Weekdays see a mix of punk, goth and Eighties. The whole complex is open late – until 5am Fri and Sat.

Voyeur 151 W Ohio St ☎312/832-1717. For clubgoers who take their people-watching seriously, this popular space offers two-way mirrors, fish-eye lenses, and closed-circuit TV cameras trained on the stainless-steel dance floor.

Theater and comedy

While it was once every Chicago actor's and playwright's ambition to end up in New York, many are now quite content to remain here. The city now supports numerous **theater** companies, many of them – notably Steppenwolf, John Malkovich's former company, at 1650 N Halsted St (☎312/335-1888, Ⓦ www.steppenwolf.org) – with reputations as good as any in the US. Notable Chicago theaters include the Court Theater, 5535 S Ellis St (☎773/753-4472), and Goodman Theater, 200 S Columbus Ave (☎312/443-3800). **Comedy**, too, is particularly vibrant; Chicago's improvisational scene is considered the best in the nation, with the troupe at Second City, 1231 N Wells St (☎312/337-3992, Ⓦ www.secondcity.com), especially renowned.

Classical music, opera and dance

Under Daniel Barenboim, who is committed to including more contemporary music in its repertoire, the profile of the world-renowned **Chicago Symphony Orchestra** – based at the Orchestra Hall, 220 S Michigan Ave (☎312/435-8122 or 312/435-8172, Ⓦ www.chicagosymphony.org) – looks like it's being raised yet higher. The 186-member **Symphony Chorus** performs both classical and contemporary choral works with the CSO, specifically in summer at the open-air **Ravinia Festival**, 25 miles north of downtown Chicago (Ⓦ www.ravinia.org). The **Lyric Opera of Chicago**, 20 N Wacker Drive (☎312/332-2244, Ⓦ www.lyricopera.org), now under the directorship of William Mason, performs in the beautiful Civic Opera House; its season is from mid-September to early February, and most performances are sold out.

The **Joffrey Ballet** is the city's prime classically oriented dance company, based at 70 E Lake St (☎312/739-0120, Ⓦ www.joffrey.com). **Hubbard Street Dance Chicago**, now in its new home at 1147 W Jackson Blvd (☎312/850-9744, Ⓦ www.hubbardstreetdance.com), is more contemporary but equally talented.

Sports

Staunchly blue-collar Chicago must be among the best US cities for watching **sports**, as Chicagoans are, for better or worse, loyally supportive of their teams. The city's most successful outfit in recent memory was the Michael Jordan-led **Chicago Bulls** basketball team, winner of six NBA championships in the 1990s. Now that Jordan has left, however, Bulls fans have little to cheer about. The Bulls play in the ultramodern United Center, 1901 W Madison St, as do hockey's **Blackhawks** (both ☎312/559-1212). The **Chicago Bears** football team (☎847/615-2327) can be seen at the 66,000-capacity Soldier's Field at 425 E McFetridge Drive, at the south end of Grant Park.

As for baseball, neither Chicago team – the Cubs or the White Sox – has won a World Series since 1917. The **Chicago White Sox** (☎312/831-1SOX) play at the modern Comiskey Park at 333 W 35th St on the South Side. To fans, the real tragedy of 1994's baseball strike was that the American League Central Division-leading Sox had a chance to bring the World Series title to Chicago for the first time in almost eighty years. The **Chicago Cubs** (☎312/831-

CUBS), meanwhile, are more consistent – they break North-Siders' hearts every year – but their games remain well-attended thanks to marquis players like Sammy Sosa and to the atmosphere conjured up at grand old Wrigley Field (see p.360), near Lincoln Park.

Central Illinois

Interstates 55 and 57 slice south through the Corn Belt of **central Illinois** from Chicago. Parallel to I-55, the legendary **Route 66** began its run here, cutting through the state and onto the Pacific Coast – you might try to catch a glimpse of it, as some old-time diners and other Americana still stand. One worthwhile stop, reachable by either interstate, is the state capital, **Springfield**, which interestingly commemorates President and former resident **Abraham Lincoln**. Otherwise, if you're on your way south, the college towns of **Bloomington-Normal** and **Champaign-Urbana** are the only rational urban stops, while if you're heading west from Chicago it's well worth pausing at the delightful old river town of **Galena**.

Springfield

The Illinois state capital, **SPRINGFIELD**, spreads out from a neat, leafy downtown grid, 199 miles south of Chicago. Abraham Lincoln honed his legal and political skills here, and tourists flock to his old homes, haunts and final resting place. What they find is neither tacky nor pompous. The sites portray the life of the sixteenth president of the USA and, as well, the uncertainty and turmoil of a nation on the brink of civil war.

Twenty miles northwest of Springfield on Hwy-97, **Lincoln's New Salem State Historic Site** marks where the future president first came to live in this area in 1831. In this backwoods clearing he clerked in a store, volunteered for the Black Hawk War, served as postmaster and failed in business before taking up legal studies and moving to Springfield to pursue his political career. Today the authentically re-created village features simple homes, workshops, a store and a tavern. The **visitor center** hosts a worthwhile exhibit on pioneer lifestyles (March–Oct daily 9am–5pm; Nov–Feb daily 8am–4pm). On summer weekends the park presents *Abraham!*, a musical that dramatizes Lincoln's New Salem years.

Pick up tickets at the **Lincoln Home Visitor Center**, at Eighth and Jackson in Springfield itself, for a narrated tour of the only house Lincoln ever owned, which he shared with his wife Mary from 1844 to 1861. Though tours are free (daily 8.30am–5pm, though often later; ℡217/523-0222), you can expect to wait. Various displays and a brief film at the visitor center are good ways to pass time.

In the restored Greek Revival **Old State Capitol**, three blocks away at Sixth and Adams (March–Oct daily 9am–5pm; Nov–Feb daily 9am–4pm; free; ℡217/785-7960), Lincoln attended at least 240 Supreme Court hearings, and proclaimed in 1858, "A house divided against itself cannot stand. I believe this government cannot endure permanently, half slave and half free." Objects, busts and papers relating to Lincoln and the Democrat Stephen A. Douglas, whom he debated in the 1858 US Senate election (Douglas won that election) and whom he defeated in the 1860 presidential election, can be found throughout the building. At the tastefully renovated **Lincoln Depot** on Tenth and Monroe (April–Aug daily 10am–4pm; free), the newly elected president said goodbye

to Springfield in February 1861 and boarded a train for his
Washington, DC (a slide show illustrates the twelve-day jo
time he returned was in his funeral train. **Lincoln's Tor**
Ridge Cemetery on the north side of town. The vault, ador
statuettes, is open to the public (March–Oct daily 9am–5
9am–4pm; free).

At the current **Illinois State Capitol**, in majestic lime
Capitol, tour highlights include the chambers of the state Senate and
Representatives, in striking red and blue, respectively (Mon–Fri 8am–4pm,
free; ☎217/782-2099). The **Illinois State Museum**, on Spring and Edwards,
is crammed with natural history and Native American and contemporary art
exhibits, along with the interactive "**At Home in the Heartland**" display
tracing Illinois family life from 1700 to 1970 (Mon–Sat 8.30am–5pm, Sun
noon–5pm; free). The **Dana–Thomas House**, 301 E Lawrence Ave, completed in 1904, survives as the best-preserved and most completely furnished
example of **Frank Lloyd Wright**'s early Prairie house, with more than four
hundred pieces of glasswork, original art and light fixtures (tours Wed–Sun
9am–4pm; $3). Just north of town, Bill Shea proudly displays 50 years' worth
of road signs, gas pumps, and Route 66 memorabilia at **Shea's Gas Station
Museum** (Tues–Fri 9am–4pm, Sat 9am–noon; free).

Practicalities

Amtrak **trains** from Chicago and St Louis roll in at Third and Washington
downtown, at manageable times. Greyhound drops off two miles east of downtown at 2351 S Dirksen Parkway. The **Convention and Visitors Bureau**, 109
N Seventh St (Mon–Fri 8am–5pm; ☎217/789-2360 or 1-800/545-7300), has
brochures and maps. The best selection of budget **accommodation**, including a *Days Inn* (☎217/529-0171; ❸), lies off I-55 at the Dirksen Parkway exit.
Downtown accommodation is reasonably priced – even the swanky politicians'
hotels offer affordable deals on the weekend. Central options include the *Best
Western Lincoln Plaza*, 101 E Adams St (☎217/523-5661 or 1-800/528-1234,
ⓦwww.bestwestern.com; ❹), next to the capitol and Amtrak, and the *Mansion
View Inn & Suites*, 529 S Fourth St (☎217/544-7411 or 1-800/252-1083,
ⓦwww.mansionview.com; ❹). *The Inn at 835*, 835 S Second Ave (☎217/523-
4466, ⓦwww.innat835.com; ❺), is a charming eleven-room **B&B** converted
from a 1900 downtown apartment block.

Springfield's cafés seem to have exclusive rights to a phenomenon known as
the **Horseshoe** – ostensibly a sandwich, but fried, covered in melted cheese
and very tasty. *Norb Andy's*, 518 E Capitol Ave (☎217/523-7777), musters up
the best Horseshoes around. The *Cozy Dog Drive-In* at 2935 S Sixth St
(☎217/525-1992) claims to be the birthplace of the **Cozy Dog** (also known
as the corn dog), a deep-fried, batter-drenched hot dog on a stick. At the other
end of the health spectrum, *Augie's Front Burner*, 2 W Old State Capitol Plaza
(☎217/544-6979), serves up good California-style and vegetarian meals, while
Sebastian's Hideout, 221 S Fifth St (☎217/789-8988), has a wide-ranging
Mediterranean menu with good couscous dishes and occasional jazz or blues.

Galena

The neat little town of **GALENA**, a few miles short of both Iowa and
Wisconsin in the far northwest corner of Illinois, can have changed little since
its nineteenth-century heyday. Thanks to its sheltered location just a few miles
up the Galena River, it was a major port of call for Mississippi River steamboats. These days the only traffic it gets are the day-trippers who come to

the gentle crescent of Main Street, tucked in behind an immaculate
levee. Its impeccable redbrick facades and graceful skyline of spires and
...ses place it among the most attractive river towns in the US. With the aid
: the free *Galenian* guide from the visitor center (see below), you can spend
an enjoyable few hours on a walking tour of the various historic sites along
both Main Street and Bench Street. The latter is squeezed onto a steep bluff
above Main street.

Galena boasts of having contributed nine generals to the Union army during
the Civil War, much the most significant of whom was **Ulysses Simpson
Grant**. Grant moved to the town in 1860, working as a clerk in a leather store
owned by his father and operated by his two brothers. Some contemporary
accounts speak of him as the town lush, the kind of person decent folk crossed
the street to avoid. However, his West Point education encouraged the townspeople to appoint him as colonel when they raised the 21st Illinois regiment
on the outbreak of war. When he came home, in August 1865, it was as overall commander of the victorious army.

The grateful citizens of Galena presented Grant with a **house**, a couple of
blocks up Bouthillier Street on the far side of the river (daily 9am–5pm; $2
suggested donation). It's not a grand place by any means, but it was in the
plainly furnished downstairs drawing room that Grant received the news of
his election as president in 1868. Although he went on to serve two terms, he
is commonly agreed to have been a better general than president. His administrations were plagued by scandal, and he lost all his own money through
unwise investments. The family fortunes were restored just before his death in
1885, when Mark Twain first persuaded him to write, and then published,
Grant's best-selling *Memoirs*.

Practicalities

The 1857 Railroad Museum, across the river from the town proper at 101
Bouthillier St, serves as the local **visitor center** (Mon–Thurs 9am–5pm, Fri &
Sat 9am–7pm, Sun 10am–5pm; ☎815/777-4390), and provides the most con-
venient short-term parking lot.

The plush *DeSoto House Hotel*, 230 S Main St (☎815/777-0090 or 1-
800/343-6562, ⓦwww.desotohouse.com; ❼), was Grant's campaign headquarters in 1868. Its grand *Generals' Restaurant* serves steak and seafood dinners. If
your budget won't stretch that far, the *Triangle Motel*, at highways 20 and 84
(☎877/425-3629; ❸), makes a good-value alternative. As for inexpensive spots
to **eat**, *Boone's Place*, 305 S Main St (☎815/777-4488), is a reliable espresso and
sandwich bar.

Wisconsin

As many cows as humans call **WISCONSIN** home. About four million of each
eat to their hearts' content in this rich, rolling farmland, which has a higher
proportion of overweight people than any other state. However, America's self-
proclaimed "Dairyland" is more than just one giant pasture. Beyond the massive

red barns and silvery silos lie endless pine forests, some 15,000 sky-blue lakes, postcard-pretty valleys and dramatic bluffs. The state, whose Ojibway name means "gathering of the waters," is bordered by Lake Michigan to the east, Lake Superior in the north and, to the west, the Mississippi and St Croix rivers. Only the southern boundary, with Illinois, is dry.

The **history** of Wisconsin exemplifies the standard formula for westward expansion. Seventeenth-century French and British explorers began by trading with the Native Americans and soon ousted them from their land. The European settlers who followed – predominantly Germans, Scandinavians and Poles – tended to be liberal and progressive; such major national social programs as labor laws for women and children, assistance for the elderly and the disabled, and unemployment compensation were rooted here. On the downside, Sen. Joseph McCarthy, the infamous 1950s witch-hunter, was born in Grand Chute, former headquarters of the right-wing John Birch Society.

Wisconsin today is best known for its liquids. The **milk** from all those cattle yields cheeses of all kinds, while the **beer**, as the song says, is what made **Milwaukee** famous. Sparkling Madison apart, Wisconsin's other cities – **LaCrosse**, **Green Bay**, **Oshkosh** – can veer toward the dull side, but they're also clean, safe and amiable. The smaller towns can be distinctive and charming.

Getting around Wisconsin

You'll be hard put to explore Wisconsin's remote north, or key locales like the Door County peninsula, without a vehicle. Public transportation is better in the south. Milwaukee and, to a lesser extent, Madison are hubs for Greyhound and Amtrak. Five **trains** daily connect Milwaukee and Chicago, a ninety-minute journey, while one crosses the state in the south en route for Seattle, via Columbus (near Madison), Portage, Wisconsin Dells, Tomah and LaCrosse.

Milwaukee

Bustling **MILWAUKEE**, the "Deutsch Athens" of southeastern Wisconsin, is a combination of the down-home and the sophisticated, known for its lakeside and ethnic **festivals** and huge **breweries**. Visually it's a mix of elegant Teutonic architecture, rambling Victorian warehouses and tasteful waterfront developments. Its prime position on the shores of Lake Michigan, at the confluence of three rivers, made it a meeting place for Native groups long before white settlers moved in, while the opulent mansions lining the lake commemorate the industrialists who helped make this Wisconsin's economic and manufacturing capital. By 1850, less than two decades old and with a population of twenty thousand, Milwaukee already had a dozen breweries and 225 saloons. The contemporary estimate of six thousand bars – one per hundred residents – is not necessarily apocryphal.

Arrival, information and getting around

Milwaukee is well served by air, rail and bus. Its **airport**, eight miles south of downtown at 5300 S Howell Ave, is connected with the city center by bus #80 ($1.35), and by limousine service ($9). A taxi will set you back about $17. Amtrak is at 433 W St Paul Ave, while Greyhound and Wisconsin Coach (☎414/272-2156), serving southeastern Wisconsin, operate out of the same terminal at 606 N James Lovell Drive. Badger Bus (☎414/276-7490, ⓦwww.badgerbus.com), across the street at no. 635, runs an express service to

Madison (six daily; $22 round-trip). Take care in and around the stations at night. **Getting around** Milwaukee is easy and inexpensive via the county's extensive **transportation system** (24-hour info ☎414/344-6711; flat fare $1.35). The Milwaukee Loop is a special trolley service connecting 18 stops in the city's center (Wed–Sat 10am–10pm, Sun till 6pm; $1 to hop on and off all day).

Milwaukee's **Convention and Visitors Bureau**, 510 W Kilbourn Ave (Mon–Fri 8am–5pm, Sat 9am–2pm; ☎414/273-3950 or 1-800/554-1448, Ⓦwww.milwaukee.org), has details on such **festivals** as the eleven-day Summerfest (late June to early July), Great Circus Parade (usually mid-July) and the Wisconsin State Fair (early Aug). The main **post office** is at 345 W St Paul Ave (Mon–Fri 7.30am–8pm; ☎1-800/275-8777; zip code 53203).

Accommodation

Lodgings in Milwaukee run the gamut from low-budget to upmarket chains to luxury hotels. Alternatively, Cedarburg is a tranquil and attractive Currier & Ives-type village twenty miles north; the *Washington House* (☎414/375-3550, Ⓦwww.washingtonhouseinn.com; ➍) and *Stagecoach* (☎414/375-0208 or 1-888/375-0208, Ⓦwww.stagecoach-inn-wi.com; ➍) inns here are charming.

The Astor 924 E Juneau Ave ☎414/271-4220 or 1-800/558-0200, in Wisconsin 1-800/242-0355, Ⓦwww.theastorhotel.com. The classy, historic 1920s hotel offers free continental breakfast and health club passes. Extended stays are available. ➎
HI–Red Barn 6750 W Loomis Rd ☎414/529-3299. Hostel 13 miles southwest, via Hwy-894 or buses #10 and #35 (best avoided at night). Hiking and biking trails. May–Oct only; $11 members, $14 others. Check-in 5–10pm. ➊
HI–Milwaukee Summer Hostel 1530 W

Wisconsin ☎414/288-3232, Ⓦwww.hostelling-wisconsin.org. New hostel in Marquette University dorm; operational June–Aug. ➊
Crane House B&B 346 E Wilson St ☎414/483-1512, Ⓦwww.cranhouse.com. The handsome B&B is in a self-contained suburb-that's-not-a-suburb, Bay View. Excellent breakfasts. ➍
Park East Hotel 916 E State St ☎414/276-8800 or 1-800/328-PARK, Ⓦwww.parkeasthotel.com. Clean, very comfortable rooms in a nice part of downtown. Good value compared with the bigger hotels. ➎

The City

Downtown Milwaukee, split north to south by the **Milwaukee River**, is only a mile long and a few blocks wide. Handsome old buildings and gleaming, modern steel-and-glass structures are comfortably corralled together on three sides by spaghetti-like strands of freeway. **Lake Michigan** forms the fourth boundary. To bolster the allure of downtown, the city has successfully poured millions into its **Riverwalk** development, now something of a nightlife center and the site of many public entertainment events. The **Milwaukee Art Museum**, 750 N Lincoln Memorial Drive (Tues, Wed, Fri & Sat 10am–5pm, Thurs noon–9pm, Sun noon–5pm; $6; Ⓦwww.mam.org), contains works by European masters and twentieth-century Americans. One wing – with stunning views of the lake – is devoted to a comprehensive collection of Post-Impressionist paintings. Architect Santiago Calatrava's spectacular $100 million expansion first opened on May 4, 2001. The **Museum Center** complex, downtown at 800 W Wells St, is a three-attraction entity (combination ticket $12). At the **Milwaukee Public Museum** (daily 9am–5pm; $6.50; Ⓦwww.mpm.edu), the intertwined histories and mysteries of the earth, nature and humankind are imaginatively presented through dioramas such as "The Streets of Old Milwaukee" and a battle of the dinosaurs. Next, **Discovery World – The James Lovell Museum of Science, Economics and Technology** (daily 9am–5pm; $5.50; Ⓦwww.discoveryworld.org), features popular hands-on exhibits and laser light shows. Lastly, the **Humphrey IMAX Dome Theater** has a giant, wraparound screen (Mon–Wed 11.30am–4.30pm, Thurs & Fri 11.30am–8.30pm, Sat 10.30am–8.30pm, Sun 10.30am–5.30pm; shows on the half-hour; weekday matinees $4, evenings $6.75; @www.mpm.edu/imax).

The blue-domed, neo-Byzantine **Annunciation Greek Orthodox Church** stands like a mushroom crossed with a spaceship at 9400 W Congress St. Completed in 1961, it was one of the last major works by native Wisconsin architect Frank Lloyd Wright. The interior is a jaw-dropping blend of the streamlined and the ornate. Unfortunately, tours have been phased out and visits discouraged. About the only way to see inside is to attend the Sunday service (9am summer, 9.30am rest of year; bus #57). The 37-room **Pabst Mansion**, 2000 W Wisconsin Ave (Mon–Sat 10am–3.30pm, Sun noon–3.30pm; $7), was completed in 1893 as the castle of a local beer baron and is a knockout example of ornate Flemish Renaissance architecture, featuring exquisite wood, glass and ironwork. Pabst Brewery has shut down, but the **Miller Brewing Company** at 4251 W State St still offers free behind-the-scenes tours (Mon–Sat, usually 10am–4pm but times updated daily; phone ☎414/931-2467 or 1-800/944-LITE; bus #71), culminating in generous samples for over-21s. The more primitive microbrewery **Sprecher**, 701 W Glendale Ave (Sat 1pm, 2pm & 3pm; also Mon–Fri 4pm in June, July, Aug & holiday weeks; reservations necessary; $2; ☎414/964-2739), serves samples straight out of the barrel. Schlitz, the "beer that made Milwaukee famous," was bought out by Stroh's in the late 1980s and is now produced in Detroit.

You can also take one-hour tours of the engine plant responsible for Milwaukee's other legendary brand name, **Harley-Davidson**, out in a rough area of town on 11700 W Capitol Drive at Hwy-45. It's really for Harley devotees; bikes aren't assembled here and if you don't know your shovelheads from your knuckleheads you might feel out of place (free tours Mon–Fri 9.30am, 11am & 1pm June–Aug; Mon, Wed and Fri in Sept–Dec; ☎414/535-3666). For those more interested in Harley chic, there's ample opportunity to purchase all kinds of merchandise throughout Milwaukee. Milwaukee Iron Motorcycle Tours (☎262/482-1525) provides safe, friendly chauffeured tours aboard Harleys at reasonable rates and tailored to clients' needs.

Eating

The Germans who first settled in Milwaukee determined its **eating** style – heavy on bratwurst, rye bread and beer. Subsequent immigrants threw the collective kitchen wide open, making for a culinary cornucopia. With Lake Michigan lapping the city's feet, freshwater fish can hardly be overlooked, especially on a Friday night when fish boils (see p.378) break out all over the place. Wherever you go, portions tend to be big.

J Pandl's Whitefish Bay Inn 1319 E Henry Clay St ☎414/964-3800. The suburban landmark is famous for reasonably priced grilled whitefish, colossal oven-baked pancakes and its stein collection.
The King & I 823 N 2nd St ☎414/276-4181. Good medium-priced Thai food, downtown.
Milwaukee Ale House 233 N Water St ☎414/226-BEER. Milwaukee's sole all-grain, old-style brewpub serves filling food and fresh Wisconsin-only beer.

Mimma's Café 1307 E Brady St ☎414/271-7737. This unmissable Italian restaurant is classy yet casual with imaginative, mouthwatering cuisine and an extensive wine list.
Old Town Serbian Gourmet House 522 W Lincoln Ave ☎414/672-0206. Tasty Serbian food on the Pole-dominated south side. Try a burek, a meat- or spinach-filled pie the size of a Frisbee. Live music Fri–Sun.

Nightlife and entertainment

The concept of neighborhoods is vital to Milwaukee's nightlife. **Brady Street** in the near northeast, a counterculture haven in the 1960s, is now filled with Italian restaurants and bars. **Walker's Point**, on the edge of downtown, has all sorts of gay and straight watering holes, while the Polish locals can be found farther south. Downtown gets busy on the weekend, especially either side of the river on **Water** and **Old World Third** streets between Juneau and State.

High culture in downtown Milwaukee revolves around the **Marcus Center for the Performing Arts**, 929 N Water St (☎414/273-7206 or 1-888/612-3500, ⓦwww.marcuscenter.org), and the plush, historic **Pabst Theater**, 144 E Wells St (☎414/286-3663). Nearby, the **Milwaukee Repertory Theater**, 108 E Wells St (☎414/224-9490, ⓦwww.milwaukeerep.com), has a reputation for risk-taking productions, as does the arty, eclectic **Theatre X** (☎414/278-0555), in the Broadway Theater Center in the Third Ward, a restored warehouse district on the edge of downtown. The Center, 158 N Broadway, is also home to the adventurous Skylight Opera (☎414/291-7800, ⓦwww.skylight-opera.com) and **Milwaukee Chamber Theatre** (☎414/276-8842, ⓦwww.chamber-theatre.com), where the focus is split between classical and contemporary plays.

Café Vecchio 1137 N Old World 3rd St ☎414/273-5700. Upscale European-style coffee/wine bar features 100-plus-bottle wine list, espresso drinks and twenty different martinis.
John Hawk's Pub 100 E Wisconsin Ave ☎414/272-3199. Riverside Brit-style establishment downtown. Food all day, jazz on Sat.
Safe House 779 N Front St ☎414/271-2007, ⓦwww.safe-house.com. This unique, tongue-in-cheek nightclub seems to come straight out of a spy film. Open from 11am, with light meals served.

Up and Under Pub 1216 Brady St ☎414/276-2677, ⓦwww.upandunderpub.com. Milwaukee's top blues bar.
Velvet Room 730 N Old World 3rd St ☎414/319-1190. Premier cocktail lounge with a fun, plush decor, billiards and "New American" menu.
Von Trier 2235 N Farwell Ave ☎414/272-1775. Black Forest decor and lots of imported beers – the Weise is a house specialty.
Zur Krone 839 S 2nd St ☎414/647-1910. This blue-collar bar has good atmosphere and beer selection.

Wisconsin's eastern shores

North of Milwaukee, **eastern Wisconsin** is a melange of the industrial and the maritime, with a nod to agriculture, shaped by its proximity to **Lake Michigan** and the smaller **Lake Winnebago**. Of its towns, Appleton was the birthplace of escapologist Harry Houdini, **Green Bay** is home to the legendary Packers, and **Oshkosh** is a household name for its overalls and baby clothes, but it's all best seen as a prelude to the most romanticized part of the state, **Door County**.

Green Bay

Few cities are as closely associated with a sports team as **GREEN BAY** is with the football Packers: 108 miles north of Milwaukee, it's the smallest city in the US to have a major-league professional sports franchise and the only one to own a team. **The Green Bay Packer Hall of Fame**, 855 Lombardi Ave (June–Aug daily 9am–6pm; rest of year daily 10am–5pm; $8; ⓦwww.packer-halloffame.com), celebrates the dynastic years of the 1960s when the Pack won Superbowls I and II, as well as more recent stars such as Antonio Freeman and

Brett Favre. Stuffed with hands-on displays, movie theaters and memorabilia, the museum offers more than enough to satisfy any football fan. Packer fans can also tour adjacent **Lambeau Field** (summer daily 9.30am–3.30pm; $7.50, or $10 combination ticket with Hall of Fame).

Also in this busy but not particularly attractive port, pride of place at the **National Railroad Museum**, 2285 S Broadway (May to Oct daily 9am–5pm; rest of year Mon–Fri 9am–5pm; $7 in summer including train ride, $6 in winter; ⓦwww.nationalrrmuseum.org), goes to the 1.1 million-ton 1941 *Union Pacific Big Boy* locomotive, one of many such trains that served Green Bay's still-enormous freight depot. West on Hwy-172, opposite the airport, stands Wisconsin's biggest casino – **Oneida Bingo & Casino**. Tribal history, and the way in which profits from blackjack, video poker and bingo have improved education and social and health facilities, are examined at the **Oneida Nation Museum**, seven miles west of Hwy-41 as it runs south from downtown (Tues–Fri 10am–6pm, Sat 10am–5pm; $2; ☎920/869-2768, ⓦwww.oneidanation.org).

The city's visitor center (☎920/494-9507 or 1-888/867-3342, ⓦwww .greenbay.com) sits in the shadow of the football stadium, off Lombardi Avenue, near the *Best Western Midway Hotel*, 780 Packer Drive (☎920/499-3161 or 1-800/528-1234, ⓦwww.bestwestern.com; ❹). *Titletown Brewing Company*, 200 Dousman St (☎920/437-2337), has a great setting for drinks in a former railroad depot downtown, while *Brett Favre's Steakhouse*, 1020 Advance St (☎920/490-9663) is an up-scale family restaurant/sportsbar serving Southern cuisine.

Door County

From **Sturgeon Bay**, 140 miles north of Milwaukee, **Door County** sticks into Lake Michigan like a gradually tapering candle for 42 miles. With thirteen light-houses and a dozen fishing villages, its coastline smacks more of New England than the midwest. The name derives from "Porte des Morts" or "**Door of the Dead**," French for the treacherous eight-mile strait that severs Washington Island at its tip. Despite drawing a million-plus warm-weather tourists, the peninsula (actually an island split off from Wisconsin by a canal) is not an extended theme park. Prices can get a little steep, but you get what you pay for – a small sliver of America devoid, for the most part, of crude billboards, sloppy diners, bland chain motels and tacky amusements. Activities include browsing around galleries and attending arts festivals, as well as hiking, fishing and boating. Renting a **bicycle** (Fish Creek's Nor-Door Cyclery has the best models; ☎920/868-2275, ⓦwww.nordoorsports.com) gives you the chance to follow an excellent **cycle trail**. Winter is considerably quieter with ice fishing, cross-country skiing and snowmobiling being the predominant outdoor activities.

Pick up road and trail maps at the visitor center at 1015 Green Bay Rd in Sturgeon Bay (☎920/743-4456 or 1-800/52-RELAX, ⓦwww.doorcounty vacations.com), where you can also phone local lodgings for free.

Exploring Door County

Door County's only sizable town, **Sturgeon Bay**, is a pleasant enough ship-building community, if not exactly abundant in small-town splendor. Ten miles north on Hwy-57 is the rolling **Whitefish Dunes State Park**, with its wispy sand dunes and popular mile-long beach (daily; $7 per car). A short trail leads to the spectacular rocky **Cave Point County Park** (free), studded with wind- and wave-sculptured caves that are particularly dramatic in winter. In general beaches are better this side of the peninsula; Jacksonport's (free) **Lakeside Park** ranks as the best of the lot. You can also swim in several placid inland lakes.

Over on the western side, biking and hiking trails traverse the thickly forested hills of **Peninsula State Park** (situated between tiny Fish Creek and elegant Mennonite **Ephraim**, with its resplendent white-clapboard architecture). An observation tower and lighthouse stand on the park's extensive shoreline. Just outside it on Hwy-42 is the anachronistic Skyway Drive-In movie theater (☎920/854-9938).

Washington Island, off the peninsula's northern tip, offers a different cultural perspective. During Prohibition, the Icelandic community here convinced authorities that (40 percent alcohol) bitters were an ancient cure for rheumatism and dyspepsia. Cases of the stuff were shipped in, and the habit stuck; go into the historic *Nelsen's Hall Bitters Pub and Restaurant* (☎920/847-2496), about two miles from the Detroit Harbor dock, and you're likely to find old-timers drinking bitters by the pint. Motel rooms are available on Washington, but there's no such luxury on the primitive neighboring 950-acre Rock Island. Once the private estate of a millionaire, it's dotted with stark, stone buildings; no cars are allowed, so see them by foot or bike.

The islands are served by the Washington Island Ferry from Northport at the tip of the peninsula (daily; $8 round-trip, cars $18, bikes $3; ☎920/847-2546 or 1-800/223-2094) and the Rock Island Ferry out of Jackson Harbor (June to mid-Oct daily; $7.50 round-trip; ☎920/847-2252).

Accommodation

Door County has a full range of **accommodation**, including some overpriced resorts. Prices given are for shoulder seasons (the best time to come); expect to pay up to 25 percent extra at the grander hotels in July and August, and a small weekend premium. Camping is idyllic. State park sites cost $10–15 (plus $9.50 reservation fee and $7 daily admission, annual $25). Recommended private campgrounds include *Path of Pines*, County Road F off Hwy-42, near Fish Creek (mid-May to mid-Oct; $17–28; ☎920/868-3332 or 1-800/868-7802).

Century Farm Motel 10068 Hwy-57 ☎920/854-4069. Basic cottages (sleeping up to six people) are set in farmland halfway between Sister Bay and Ephraim. Among the lowest prices on the peninsula. ❸

Chal-A-Motel 3910 Hwy-42, 57 Sturgeon Bay ☎920/743-6788. This offbeat, clean, year-round budget motel has a huge collection of dolls, toys and old autos you can see for $1 ($2 for nonguests). ❸

Liberty Park Lodge and Shore Cottages Hwy-42 N, Sister Bay ☎920/854-2025. Spotless complex with a lakeside porch and sandy beach. Good value. ❸

Twin Oaks Lodge City Rd/Hwy-42 ☎920/854-2633, ⓦ www.twinoaksdc.com. This cordial motor hotel is conveniently situated on the edge of Fish Creek at the quiet end of Peninsula State Park. Free use of bikes. ❸

Waterbury Inn Hwy-42, Ephraim ☎920/854-2821 or 1-800/720-1624, ⓦ www.waterburyinn.com. This luxury property has one-and two-bedroom suites with fully equipped kitchens. ❺

White Gull Inn 4225 Main St, Fish Creek ☎920/868-3517, ⓦ www.whitegullinn.com. An elegant old inn, next to delightful Sunset Park, is the county's crown jewel. Good restaurant (breakfast not included), and a fish boil (see below) every night in summer. ❻

Eating

One reward of a midsummer visit to Door County is the chance to sample the cherry in all its guises. Another traditional treat is the **fish boil**, a delicious outdoor ritual involving whitefish steaks, potatoes and onions cooked in a cauldron over a wood fire. Rounded off with coleslaw and cherry pie, it's widely available for between $10 and $16.

Al Johnson's Swedish Restaurant Hwy-42, Sister Bay ☎920/854-2626. Pancakes, meatballs and other fine Scandinavian dishes are featured. Goats are tethered atop the sod roof.
Bayside Tavern Main St, Fish Creek ☎920/868-3441. A convivial pub serves a celebrated chili, burgers and a mean Friday night perch-fry.
Dal Santo's 341 N 3rd Ave, Sturgeon Bay ☎920/743-6100. Pizza, pasta and bar snacks are served in an old railroad depot with a good micro-

brewery. The cherry ale is surprisingly palatable and refreshing.
Square Rigger Lodge and Galley 6332 Hwy-57, Jacksonport ☎920/823-2408. This cocktail lounge and restaurant, on a private sandy beach, presents one of the county's best fish boils.
Wilson's Hwy-42, Ephraim ☎920/854-2041. Burgers, sandwiches and (along with the Door County Ice Cream Factory in Sister Bay) the top ice cream on the peninsula.

Upstate Wisconsin

Sparsely settled **northern Wisconsin** has no large cities (and few small ones), and no interstates. It's a lake-studded wilderness, covered by enormous tracts of forest. Canoe its rivers, fish for record-breakers or ski or snowmobile cross-country trails without having to fight for space. **Bayfield** and the **Apostle Islands** in the northwest are the obvious destinations, but Hayward, southeast of Superior, is home to the amazing **National Freshwater Fishing Hall of Fame** (mid-April to Nov daily 10am–5pm; closed on weekends after Nov 1; $5). You're invited to "Walk through the biggest fish in the world!" – a four-story, 500-ton, fiberglass monster.

The Apostle Islands

All but one of the 22 islands scattered off **Bayfield Peninsula** in Lake Superior are part of the **Apostle Islands National Lakeshore** – a prized preserve for outdoors enthusiasts seeking to recharge depleted spiritual batteries.
    The jumping-off point for the islands, **BAYFIELD**, once a lumbering and fishing village, is now a pleasant soft-sell tourist trap. Its sumptuous *Old Rittenhouse Inn*, 301 Rittenhouse Ave (☎715/779-5111 or 1-800/779-2129, ⓦwww.rittenhouseinn.com; ❻), offers gourmet meals and swank **rooms**. *Tree Top House*, 225 N Fourth St (☎715/779-3293; ❷), has clean, simple doubles. *Island View Place*, Route 1, Box 46 (☎715/779-5307 or 1-800/484-8189, ⓦwww.island-view.com; ❹), a half-mile outside of town, is one of many waterside condominiums with nightly and weekly accommodations. Lodges and cottages are the centerpiece for the thirty gorgeous lakeside acres of Rocky Run (☎715/373-2551; ❺), a resort outside **Washburn** eleven miles south. Bayfield's visitor center is at 42 S Broad St (☎715/779-3335 or 1-800/447-4094). Campers heading for the islands require permits ($15; $30 for eight people or more) from the visitor center at 410 Washington Ave (summer daily; weekdays in winter; ☎715/779-3397). Apostle Island Cruise Service boats ($24.95; ☎715/779-3925, ⓦwww.apostleisland.com) twist their way past all of the islands, and will set down and pick up campers.

Madeline Island

By the fifteenth century **Madeline Island** was known to the Ojibway as Mon–a waun-a-kauning – home of the golden-shafted woodpecker. Frenchman Michel Cadotte founded a fur trading post there for the British in 1793, and subsequently married Equaysayway, daughter of a tribal leader, who took the name the island bears today. Madeline is now the only commercially developed Apostle island, but it all remains pretty low-key. Cadotte is buried in an overgrown cemetery in its sole town, **LA POINTE**.

La Pointe is accessible in summer via the twenty-minute ride on the Madeline Island Ferry Line from Bayfield (every 30min in peak season; passengers $4, bikes $1.75, cars $9.25; ☎715/747-2051, ⓦwww.madferry.com). Its 180 year-round residents maintain an interesting little **historical museum** (May–Oct daily 10am–6pm; $5). Assorted sandy beaches, wide bays, scenic points and forests can be explored along 45 miles of sometimes rough road. Rent **bikes** near the dock for $22 per day. The Ferry Line conducts two-hour bus tours (mid-June–Sep 10.30am and 1.30pm; $9).

A **visitor center** on Main Street (☎715/747-2801 or 1-888/ISLE-FUN, ⓦwww.madelineisland.com) can offer advice on places to stay; the *Madeline Island Motel* (☎715/747-3000; ❸) and *The Island Inn* (☎715/747-2000; ❹), both near the ferry dock, are probably the best value. Camping sites, on top of a bluff and close to caves at Big Bay State Park (☎1-888/947-2757, ⓦwww.wiparks.net), cost $10–14 plus a $9.50 reservation fee, and include park admission. A wooden footbridge across the lagoon leads to **Big Bay State Park** ($11–14; no reservations); the campgrounds share a splendid mile-long beach. Eating options include the new pub in *The Inn on Madeline Island* (☎715/747-6315 or 1-800/822-6315, ⓦwww.madisland.com; ❺), home-style meals in a casual harborside setting at *The Beach Club* (☎1-800/822-6315) or the low-cost *Grampa Tony's* (☎715/747-3911).

Southern Wisconsin

Assorted highways and back roads lace up **southern Wisconsin**, passing over rolling hills and deep dales. The immensely likeable lakeside college town of **Madison** doubles as the state capital. Cozy Madison area communities like **New Glarus** or **Mount Horeb**, and historic settlements like **Little Norway**, attest to a mixed European heritage. **Wisconsin Dells** has a picturesque setting, but may appeal only to those who revel in tacky attractions and Americana. Stretches of the **Mississippi River**, undulating down the western border, are designated as **The Great River Road**, a scenic highway that runs from near Canada to the Gulf of Mexico.

Madison

The history books record that **MADISON**, just over an hour west of Milwaukee, was little more than a wooded, mosquito-infested swamp when it was selected to be the political nucleus of the Wisconsin Territory in 1836. Today this stimulating, youthful metropolis is one of the most beautifully set cities in the US, with a handful of diverting museums.

Downtown is neatly laid out on an isthmus between lakes Mendota and Monona, with the sumptuous white granite **State Capitol** sitting benignly on a hill at its center, surrounded by shady trees, lawns and park benches. Capitol Square itself is the site of a fun **farmers' market** (May–Oct Sat 6am–2pm); browse late for bargains. **Madison Civic Center**, close by at 211 State St, houses a professional repertory theater (box office ☎608/266-9055) and **art museum** (☎608/257-0158) and also presents concerts and touring shows. Frank Lloyd Wright designed the **Unitarian Meeting House**, 900 University Bay Drive, in the late 1940s. With its sweeping, dramatically curved ceiling and triangle motif, it's definitely worth a look (May–Oct Tues–Fri 10am–4pm, Sat 9am–noon; $3). The lakeside **Monona Terrace Community and Convention Center**, 1 John Nolen Drive, is a more recently realized example of Wright's grand vision (daily tours 11am & 1pm; $2, free Mon & Tues). Surprisingly intimate and full of architectural detail, the Center, with its curves, arches and domes, echoes the State Capitol building just a few blocks away.

If the capitol is the city's governmental heart, the **University of Wisconsin** (average enrollment 46,000) is its spirited, liberal-thinking head, now mellowed since its protest heyday in the late 1960s. The **Memorial Union**, 800 Langdon St (☎608/262-1583), holds a budget cafeteria and pub, the *Rathskeller*, with tables strewn beneath huge, vaulted ceilings and live music most nights. Out back, the spacious **UW Terrace** offers beautiful sunset views over Lake Mendota. Capitol and campus are arterially connected by State Street, eight tree-lined, pedestrianized blocks of restaurants, cafés, bars and funky stores. Williamson Street, on the city's near-east side a few blocks from Monona Terrace, happily evinces its countercultural community roots.

Practicalities

Greyhound does regular **bus** runs to Milwaukee, Green Bay and beyond, while Badger Coaches make six trips daily to Milwaukee ($22 round-trip; ☎608/255-6771, ⊛www.badgerbus.com). Both operate out of the terminal at 2 S Bedford St. Van Galder buses depart from the Memorial Union to Chicago's O'Hare Airport (10 daily; $21; ☎608/752-5407 or 1-800/747-0994, ⊛www.vangalderbus.com). The **visitor center** is at 615 E Washington Ave (Mon–Fri 8am–4.30pm; ☎608/258-4959 or 1-800/373-MDSN, ⊛www.visitmadison.com).

Accommodation can be had all over the city, though the budget chains lie to the east, off I-90/94. *Collins House*, 704 E Gorham St (☎608/255-4230, ⊛www.collinshouse.com; ❺), is a beautiful B&B a few blocks from the capitol. The upscale *Madison Concourse Hotel*, 1 W Dayton St (☎608/257-6000 or 1-800/356-8293, ⊛www.concoursehotel.com; ❺), is even closer. *Canterbury Inn*, 315 W Gorham St (☎608/258-8899 or 1-800/838-3850, ⊛www.madisoncanterbury.com; ❼), has six splendid Chaucer-inspired rooms above a welcoming bookstore-cum-coffeehouse. There's also a new *Hostelling International* hostel at 141 S Butler St (☎608/441-0144, ⊛www.hiayh.org; ❶) with 28 beds and 4 private rooms, and all the usual amenities: kitchen, laundry, internet, storage and lockers.

State Street is a veritable smorgasbord of **food** and **drink**, from the tiny *Nepalese Himal Chuli* at no. 318 (☎608/251-9225) and its sister restaurant, *Chautara*, at no. 334 (☎608/251-3626), to the veteran *Ella's Deli* at 2902 E Washington (☎608/241-5291), with its kosher-style food and rich ice creams. *Deb & Lola's* at no. 227 (☎608/255-0820) serves fresh, eclectic Southwestern-influenced cuisine. The *Essen Haus*, 514 E Wilson St (☎608/255-4674), is a raucous *biergarten* with a phenomenal selection of beers. *Dotty Dumpling's Dowry*, 116 N Fairchild St (☎608/255-3175), is a local landmark thanks to its great burgers and kooky nostalgic decor.

There's plenty of **entertainment**, often free, on campus (call the events line on ☎608/265-3000). The soulful neighborhood *Crystal Corner*, 1302 Williamson St (☎608/256-2953), puts on blues acts, while *O'Cayz Corral*, 504 E Wilson St (☎608/256-1348), ranges through heavy metal, folk and acoustic. *The Cardinal*, 418 E Wilson St (☎608/251-0080), with its handsome 1908 decor, is one of the best dance club-cum-bars. The free weekly *Isthmus* carries full listings.

Baraboo

Between 1884 and 1912, the **Ringling Brothers' Circus** kept winter quarters in **BARABOO**, thirty miles northwest of Madison. The **Circus World Museum**, 426 Water St, successfully recaptures the pre–TV glory days of big-top history, via an enormous collection of memorabilia and daily performances including an old-time circus show that is both tawdry (elephants with bows on their tails do leg kicks to *New York, New York*) and irresistible (mid-July and Aug daily 9am–9pm, $11.95, with shows at 11am, 3pm and 7.30pm; May– early July daily 9am–6pm, same schedule, without 7.30pm show; Sept–April Mon–Sat 9am–5pm, Sun 11am–5pm museum only, no shows; $5–15, varies with season; ⓦ www.cicusworldmuseum.com). Every summer, usually in the first half of July, 75 meticulously restored circus wagons set out on a four-day rail journey through small-town Wisconsin and Illinois, culminating in a horse-drawn parade through downtown Milwaukee – an unbeatable extravaganza of Americana. Built in 1915 and modeled after the grand opera house at Versailles, the **Al Ringling Theatre** (summer tours, noon Thurs–Sun; $3; ⓦ www.alringling.com) in the town center is one of America's prettiest small playhouses.

Baraboo itself is calmer, quieter and more affordable than nearby Wisconsin Dells. The elegant *Victorian Gollmar Guest House B&B*, 422 Third St (☎608/356-9432, ⓦ www.gollmar.com; ❹), plays up the fact that it was once home to a circus family. More basic **rooms** are at the *Spinning Wheel*, 809 Eighth St (☎608/356-3933; ❷). *Kristina's Family Restaurant* at 506 W Pine (Hwy-12) (☎608/355-9213), serves low-cost **meals**. Baraboo's **visitor center** is at the intersection of highways 12, 33 and 136 (Mon–Fri 9am–4.30pm; ☎608/356-8333 or 1-800/227-2266, ⓦ www.baraboo.com).

Spring Green

During his seventy-year career, Wisconsin-born architect and social philosopher **Frank Lloyd Wright** designed such structures as New York's spiraling Guggenheim Museum and Tokyo's earthquake-proof *Imperial Hotel*. Three miles south of **SPRING GREEN**, itself forty miles west of Madison on Hwy-14, stand Wright's magnificent former residence, **Taliesin**, and his **Hillside Home School**. The streamlined geometry and functional grandeur of the latter, opened in 1932, exemplify Wright's break from the boxy, fustian Victorian style (May–Oct daily, tours on the hour 10am–4pm; $10). His studio is imposing; there's also a jewel-like theater space. Extensive and varied tours are also available of the house (daily except Wed at 9.30am & 1.30pm; reservation only; $40) and grounds (May–Oct daily at 10.45am & 1.45pm; $15). These and other, pricier, tours leave from the **Frank Lloyd Wright Visitor Center** (☎608/588-7900, ⓦ www.taliesinpreservation.org), designed by Wright in 1953 as a restaurant; it now features displays, a café and a bookstore. Among numerous other Wright-influenced buildings are the bank, pharmacy and the lounge of the *Post House*, 127 E Jefferson St (☎608/588-2595), a mid-priced restaurant downtown.

From 1944 onward, Alex Jordan built the **House on the Rock**, six miles south of Taliesin on Hwy-23, on and out of a natural, 60ft, chimney-like rock – for no discernible reason. He certainly never lived in it, nor did he intend it to become Wisconsin's number one tourist attraction (mid-March–Oct daily 9am–dusk; Nov–Dec holiday tour daily 10am–6pm; $19.50, or $12.50 Nov–Dec). Only the first section of this multilevel series of furnished nooks and chambers bears any resemblance to a house of any kind. With its low ceilings, indirect lighting, indoor pools, waterfalls, trees and pervasive shag carpeting, the style is a sort of Frank Lloyd Wright meets *The Flintstones*. The rest of the house is a logic-free labyrinth, containing Jordan's astounding collection of collections (antiques, nickelodeons and pneumatic music machines, miniature circuses, dolls and dolls' houses, maritime memorabilia, armor and firearms, ad infinitum), with little to indicate what is genuine or imitation, and no clue as to what it all means. The net effect is overwhelming and disorienting, alternately great fun and ghastly. Highlights include the **Infinity Room**, comprising three thousand small glass panels tapering to a point and cantilevered several hundred feet above the Wyoming Valley. A complex of other attractions has been added to the fifty-acre grounds, including the utterly dazzling **World's Largest Carousel** (with 269 fabulous figures and some 20,000 lights), a circus building, a giant doll's house and an old-style shopping street.

Practicalities

Spring Green is a pretty **place to stay**, but prices can be high in summer. *Round Barn Lodge*, Hwy-14 (☏608/588-2568, 🌐www.roundbarn.com; ❹), has a pool, sauna and family dining on a former dairy farm. *The Usonian Inn*, Hwy-14/Hwy-23 (☏608/588-2323, 🌐www.usonianinn.com; ❸), offers alternative, Taliesin-style lodgings. Locals and thespians hang out at *The Shed* (☏608/588-9049), an easygoing diner and bar on Lexington Street downtown. The **American Players Theatre** (☏608/588-2361, 🌐www.americanplayers.org) performs Shakespeare and other classics in a wooded amphitheater every evening from mid-June to October. For information, stop by the Winsted Shop on Hwy-23 or call ☏608/588-7544.

Minnesota

Though **MINNESOTA** is more than a thousand miles from either coast, it's virtually a seaboard state, thanks to **Lake Superior**, connected to the Atlantic via the St Lawrence Seaway. The glaciers that, millions of years ago, flattened all but its southeast corner gouged out more than 15,000 **lakes**, and major **rivers** run along the eastern and western borders. Ninety-five percent of the population lives within ten minutes of a body of water, and the very name Minnesota is a Sioux word meaning "land of sky-tinted water."

French explorers in the sixteenth century encountered prairies to the south and, in the north, dense forests whose abundant waterways were an ideal breeding ground for beavers and muskrats. **Fur trading**, **fishing** and **lumbering** flourished, and the Ojibway and Sioux were eased out by waves of French, British and American immigrants. Admitted to the Union in 1858, the new state of Minnesota was at first settled by Germans and Scandinavians, who farmed in the west and south. Other ethnic groups followed, many drawn by the massive **iron ore** deposits of north central Minnesota, which are expected to hold out for two more centuries.

Minnesota still thrives on its natural resources and on a progressive social outlook typified by such Democratic heavyweights as Hubert Humphrey, Walter

Mondale and Eugene McCarthy. Current governor **Jesse Ventura**, a former professional wrestler, has garnered attention nationally and beyond for his unconventional and outspoken approach to politics.

More than half of Minnesota's hardy inhabitants, who endure some of the fiercest winters in the nation, live in the southeast, around the so-called Twin Cities of **Minneapolis** and **St Paul**. These attractive and basically friendly rivals together rank as the Midwest's great civic double act for their combined cultural, recreational and business opportunities. Smaller cities include the northern shipping port of **Duluth**, the gateway to the **Scenic Hwy-61** lakeshore drive, and **Rochester**, near pretty river towns like Red Wing and Winona. The tranquil waters of **Voyageurs National Park** lie halfway along the state's boundary with Canada.

In recent years, the state has earned a reputation as the "Hollywood of the North," thanks to its increased use as an affordable, talent-rich filmmaking locale. Internationally acclaimed fraternal filmmakers Joel and Ethan Coen, responsible for the Oscar-winning, Minnesota-set *Fargo*, were raised in the Twin Cities' suburb of St Louis Park.

Getting around Minnesota

Minneapolis/St Paul **airport**, home base for Northwest Airlines, handles routes to Europe as well as domestic flights. Amtrak **trains** cross the state once a day east and west from Chicago and Seattle, with stops in Winona, Red Wing, St Paul, St Cloud, Staples and Detroit Lakes. Greyhound, founded upstate in Hibbing although no longer based there, is the largest of the several **bus** companies plying Minnesota's roads. Seven buses per day make the nine-hour journey to Chicago from the Twin Cities. Duluth, St Louis and Kansas City are also served several times daily from the state's major metropolises.

Minneapolis and St Paul

Commonly known as the **Twin Cities**, **MINNEAPOLIS** (a hybrid Sioux/Greek word meaning "water city") and **ST PAUL** are competitive yet complementary. Fraternally rather than identically twinned, they may be even better places to live than they are to visit, thanks to their good looks, cleanliness, cultural activity, social awareness and relatively low crime rates. About thirty of *Fortune Magazine's* 500 top corporations are based here; many extend substantial financial support to local arts, community projects and sports. Life for a majority of Twin Citians seems so vibrantly wholesome that the most significant threat would appear to be their own creeping complacency.

St Paul has been called "the last city of the east," making Minneapolis across the curving Mississippi "the first city of the west." Only a twenty-minute expressway ride separates their respective downtowns, but each has its own character, style and strengths. **St Paul**, the state capital – originally called Pig's Eye, after a scurrilous French-Canadian fur trader who sold whisky at a Mississippi River landing in the 1840s – is the staid, slightly older sibling, careful to preserve its buildings and traditions. Its residents are mainly German, Irish and Catholic. The compact but stately downtown is built, like Rome, on seven hills: the **Capitol** and the **Cathedral** occupy one each, august monuments that keep the city mindful of its responsibilities.

Minneapolis, founded on money generated by the Mississippi's hundreds of flour and saw mills, is livelier, artier and more modern, with skyscraping, up-to-date architecture and an upbeat and even brash attitude that never quite jeopardizes its essential affability. The mostly Slavonic, Nordic and Lutheran residents are spread over wider ground than in St Paul, with dozens of lakes and parks to underscore the city's appeal. The home-grown superstar **Prince** and the recording company Flyte Tyme cast a global spotlight on the local music scene.

Arrival, information and getting around

Twin Cities International Airport lies about ten miles south of either city in suburban Bloomington. Airport Express (☎612/827-7777 or 1-800/333-1532) shuttles travelers between the airport and major hotels for around $10, and some lodgings lay on their own transportation. **Taxis** to Minneapolis will set you back close to $25, to St Paul $15. Bus #7 goes to Minneapolis; #54 to St Paul (6am–midnight: $1–1.50). Amtrak is midway between the cities at 730 Transfer Rd, off University Avenue. The Greyhound terminals, both in convenient downtown locations, are at 950 Hawthorne St (☎612/371-3325) in Minneapolis and, less used, 166 W University Ave (☎651/222-0507) in St Paul. Metropolitan Council Transit Operations **buses** (☎612/349-7000 or 612/373-3333) make both cities relatively easy to explore without a car. Money-saving multiple-ride tickets can be bought at 719 Marquette Ave in Minneapolis or numerous locations in either city. Old-style **trolleys** run through both downtowns; St Paul's is a bargain 50¢ per ride, but in Minneapolis it costs $5 for a two-hour pass or $6 all day.

In Minneapolis, the **visitor center** is at 4000 Multifoods Tower, 33 S Sixth St (☎612/661-4700 or 1-800/445-7412), with an additional location on the second level of the City Center shopping complex (☎612/335-5827). In St Paul it's at 102 Norwest Center, 55 E Fifth St (☎612/297-6985 or 1-800/627-6101). The main Minneapolis **post office** is on First and Marquette (zip code 55401); St Paul's at 180 E Kellogg Blvd (zip code 55101). The state-run website (Ⓦwww.minneapolis.org) has loads of practical travel information. The same is true for the Minnesota Historical Society site (Ⓦwww.mnhs.org).

Accommodation

You're likely to pay more for lodgings downtown than in the suburbs, where dozens of cheap **motels** line I-494 near the airport, though some of the pricier central hotels offer reduced rates and special package deals on weekends. The pretty riverside community of **Stillwater**, 25 miles from St Paul via I-35 N and Hwy-36 E, has many grand old B&Bs and motels – (☎612/439-7700 for information). For **bed and breakfast** options in the Twin Cities, consult Ⓦwww.bedandbreakfast.com, as many B&Bs do not have their own site.

Minneapolis

Christopher Inn 201 Mill St, Excelsior ☎952/474-6816. The year-round suburban B&B on Lake Minnetonka offers good discounts off-season and midweek. ➎
City of Lakes International House 2400 Stevens Ave ☎612/871-3210. This conveniently situated independent hostel has $38 private rooms and $18 dorm beds. Bicycles $3. Reservations required. ➊/➋
Evelo's B&B 2301 Bryant Ave S ☎612/374-9656. Three comfortable rooms in a well-preserved

Victorian home near bus lines, lakes and downtown. Nonsmokers preferred. Also known as *The Bell House*. ➌
Hotel Amsterdam 830 Hennepin Ave ☎612/288-0459 or 1-800/649-9500. The friendly, low-cost gay/lesbian-owned hotel is above a noise-controlled saloon bar/disco downtown. ➋
Le Blanc House 302 University Ave NE ☎612/379-2570, Ⓦwww.leblanchouse.com. Gourmet breakfasts and fine rooms await you in a fancy Victorian home minutes from downtown. ➎
Minneapolis Hilton and Towers 1001 Marquette

Ave ☎612/376-1000, 🌐www.theunionstation
.com/minhilton/. The newest and classiest downtown lodgings feature a great gym and pool.
Weekend rates are around $100 a night. **❻**
Nicollet Island Inn 95 Merriam St ☎612/331-
1800, 🌐www.nicolletislandinn.com. This pricey,
mid-river establishment has the edge on other
downtown hotels because of its delightful location
and Minnesota-grown menu. **❻**

St Paul

Chatsworth B&B 984 Ashland Ave ☎612/227-
4288, 🌐www.chatsworth-bb.com. A beautiful
c.1900 home is now run as a welcoming B&B. **❹**
The Covington Inn Pier 1, Harriet Island
☎612/292-1411. A compact, one-of-a-kind B&B
occupies a converted towboat facing downtown,
with a café on the premises. **❻**
The Garden Gate B&B 925 Goodrich Avenue
☎651/227-8430, 🌐www.gardengatebandb
.com. Large Victorian home with four simple rooms
in St Paul's Crocus Hill neighborhood. **❹**

Embassy Suites 175 E 10th St ☎612/224-5400
or 1-800/EMBASSY, 🌐www.embassy-suites.com.
The tropical atrium is the outstanding feature of
this comfortable chain hotel on the edge of downtown. **❻**
Holiday Inn Express 1010 Bandana Blvd W
☎612/647-1637 or 1-800/HOLIDAY. This is a
unique lodging in a former railroad car repair shop
attached to a mall complex. Indoor pool and
sauna. **❺**
The Saint Paul Hotel 350 Market St ☎651/292-
9292 or 1-800-292-9292, 🌐www.stpaulhotel
.com. This grand 1910 establishment is rated
Minnesota's top hotel. Rooms tend to be smaller
than other luxury hotels, but the staff and atmosphere make up for it. The *St Paul Grill*, in the
hotel, provides some of the city's finest dining. The
classy bar has tons of great scotches and
cognacs. If nothing else, have a look at the
Courvoisier from Napolean's coronation in 1804.

Exploring Minneapolis

Downtown Minneapolis is laid out on a simple grid. The riverfront, dubbed
the **Mississippi Mile**, continues to be developed as a place for strolling, dining and entertainment. Each city has its own landing site for narrated summertime **paddleboat** cruises ($14; ☎1-800/543-3908). The vast Third Avenue
bridge makes an ideal vantage point for viewing **St Anthony Falls**, a controlled torrent in a wide stretch of the river. The missionary Father Hennepin
discovered the Falls in 1680. The first permanent settlement of present-day
Minneapolis was begun nearby in the early nineteenth century.

Downtown's major stores line up along the pedestrianized **Nicollet Mall**.
Hennepin Avenue, the other main drag, is a block west. It has been revitalized as an entertainment district in recent years thanks, in part, to the beautifully restored **Orpheum** and **State theaters**, twin hosts to top-quality
Broadway shows and concerts. The **IDS Center**, on the Mall, is the tallest
building in either city; its indoor glass atrium, the Crystal Court, is essentially modern Minneapolis's town square. Citizens escape weather extremes via a
skyway system of elevated, climate-controlled glass walkways, connecting
more than forty buildings. Culturally, Minneapolis would be poorer without
the **Walker Art Center**, Vineland Place (Tues, Wed, Fri & Sat 10am–5pm,
Thurs 10am–9pm, Sun 11am–5pm; $6, free Thurs and 1st Sat of month;
☎612/375-7622, 🌐www.walkerart.org), on the edge of downtown. This
multipurpose contemporary art and performance space balances its permanent collection of sculpture and paintings (such as German Expressionist
Franz Marc's *Blue Horses*) with exciting temporary exhibitions. The seven-acre
outdoor **Sculpture Garden** is a work of genius. Its most popular piece is the
gigantic whimsical *Spoonbridge and Cherry* (not exactly a bridge, more like a
fountain) by Claes Oldenburg and Coosje van Bruggen. One mile from
downtown, at 2400 Third Ave S (bus #9), the huge **Minneapolis Institute
of Arts** hosts a thoroughly comprehensive collection of art from 2000 BC to
the present (Tues, Wed, Fri & Sat 10am–5pm, Thurs 10am–9pm, Sun

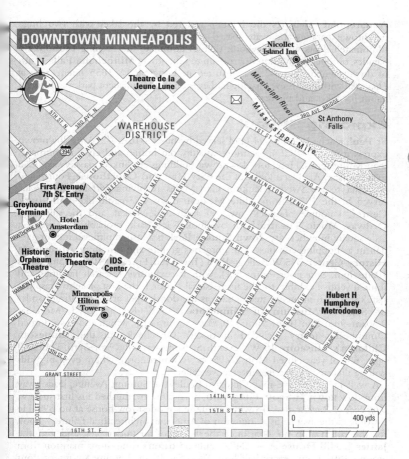

DOWNTOWN MINNEAPOLIS

N

Nicollet
Island Inn

MERRIAM ST.

Theatre de la
Jeune Lune

Mississippi River

3RD AVE. BRIDGE

St Anthony
Falls

5TH ST. N.

3RD AVE. N.

WAREHOUSE
DISTRICT

Mississippi Mile

1ST ST. S.

7TH ST. N.

394

2ND AVE. N.

1ST AVE. N.

WASHINGTON AVENUE

2ND ST. S.

HENNEPIN AVENUE

First Avenue/
7th St. Entry

NICOLLET MALL

1ST AVE. S.

3RD ST. S.

Greyhound
Terminal

MARQUETTE AVENUE

4TH ST. S.

HAWTHORNE AVE.

Hotel
Amsterdam

2ND AVE. S.

5TH ST. S.

Historic
Orpheum
Theatre

Historic State
Theatre

IDS
Center

3RD AVE. S.

6TH ST. S.

LASALLE AVENUE

7TH ST. S.

HARMON PLACE

8TH ST. S.

5TH AVE. S.

PORTLAND AVE. S.

PARK AVE.

CHICAGO AVENUE

Hubert H
Humphrey
Metrodome

Minneapolis
Hilton &
Towers

9TH ST. S.

9TH AVE. S.

YALE PL.

10TH ST. S.

10TH AVE. S.

12TH ST. S.

11TH ST. S.

11TH AVE. S.

13TH ST. S.

12TH AVE. S.

GRANT STREET

NICOLLET AVENUE

14TH ST. E.

15TH ST. E.

0   400 yds

16TH ST. E.

4

noon–5pm; free; Ⓦ www.artsmia.org). Antiques, crafts and artifacts fill the
exquisite c.1900 mansion setting of the nearby **American Swedish
Institute**, 2600 Park Ave S (Tues, Thurs, Fri & Sat noon–4pm, Wed
noon–8pm, Sun 1-5pm; $5). In stark contrast, changing exhibitions and the
University of Minnesota's permanent art collection share space in the controversial **Frederick R. Weisman Museum**, on campus at 333 E River Rd
(Tues, Wed & Fri 10am–5pm, Thurs 10am–8pm, Sat & Sun 11am–5pm; free;
Ⓦ www.weismanfoundation.org). Architect Frank O. Gehry's airy structure,
with its boldly irregular stainless steel west facade overlooking the Mississippi,
is the most startling love-it-or-hate-it design in the cities.

Arctic winters apart, hordes of Minneapolitans flock to the shores of lakes
Calhoun and **Harriet** and **Lake of the Isles**, all in residential areas within
two miles south of downtown. The **Hubert H. Humphrey Metrodome**,
900 S Fifth St (☎612/332-0386), squats on the eastern edge of downtown like
a giant white pincushion; the dome is home to the state's pro baseball and football teams, the Twins and the Vikings. Each July the **Minneapolis**

Aquatennial celebrates the lifestyle fostered by the lakes with two huge downtown parades and water-based events such as milk-carton boat races. Illuminated floats with storybook themes dominate the evening **Holidazzle** parades, on Nicollet Mall in the run-up to Christmas. **Minnehaha Falls**, south of downtown on bus #7, was featured in Longfellow's 1855 poem *Song of Hiawatha* without his ever having laid eyes on it. The adjacent park is a favorite haunt for hikes and picnics.

Exploring St Paul

St Paul, reached along I-94 (and served by buses #16A, #21A or downtown express route #94BCD), has more wealthy old homes and civic monuments than Minneapolis. Here, too, downtown buildings are linked via skyways. Call in at the jazzy Art Deco lobby of the **City Hall and Courthouse**, Fourth and Wabasha, to see Swedish sculptor Carl Milles' revolving 36ft *Vision of Peace*, carved in the 1930s from white Mexican onyx. The castle-like **Landmark Center**, a couple of blocks away at Fifth and Market, and the glittering **Ordway Music Theatre** both overlook Rice Park, probably the prettiest little square in either city. **Town Square Park** is a lush, multilevel indoor garden in a shopping complex. The gorgeous granite and limestone **Minnesota History Center**, 345 W Kellogg Blvd (Tues, Wed, Fri & Sat 10am–5pm, Thurs 10am–9pm, Sun noon–5pm; free), with its extensive research facilities and some inventive exhibits for the more casual visitor, is the best place to grasp the state's story. An immense steel iguana is the doorkeeper at the exciting hands-on **Science Museum of Minnesota**, 120 W Kellogg Blvd (Mon–Sat 9.30am–9pm, Sun 10am–9pm; $10; ⓦ www.smm.org), which also has a domed Omnitheater (entry included in ticket). Or check out the **Minnesota Children's Museum**, 10 W Seventh St (summer daily 9am–5pm, Thurs till 8pm; rest of year closed Mon; $5.95; ⓦ www.mcm.org), where even big kids will be diverted by the five interactive galleries.

A well-preserved five-mile Victorian boulevard, Summit Avenue, leads away from downtown. **F. Scott Fitzgerald**, born close by, finished his first success, *This Side of Paradise*, in 1918 while living in a modest row house at no. 599. He disparaged the avenue as a "museum of American architectural failures." Look for the coffin atop no. 465, once the home of an undertaker, and visit the **James J. Hill House** at no. 240, a railroad baron's sumptuous mansion from around 1891 (tours every half-hour Wed–Sat 10am–3.30pm; $6; reservations recommended; ⓣ651/297-2555). Territorial governor **Alexander Ramsey**'s house (tours on the hour May–Dec Tues–Sat 10am–3pm, Sun 1pm, 2pm & 3pm; $6; ⓣ651/296-8760s), nearby at 265 S Exchange St in the fashionable Irvine Park district, remains a showcase of Victorian high style.

The costumed staff does a fine job of interpreting Minnesota's frontier past at **Fort Snelling** (May–Oct Mon–Sat 10am–5pm, Sun noon–5pm; $6; ⓣ612/726-1171), near the airport off highways 5 and 55. Built between 1819 and 1825 on a strategic bluff at the confluence of the Mississippi and Minnesota rivers, this was Minnesota's first permanent structure – a successful attempt by the US government to establish an official presence in the wilderness that had recently been won from Great Britain. Another good bet is the venerable and picturesque **Como Park Zoo and Conservatory**, reached by taking I-94 to the Lexington Ave exit, then continuing north on Lexington for about three miles (summer daily 10am–6pm; rest of year daily 10am–4pm; free). Farther afield, in suburban Apple Valley, off Hwy-775 (take bus #77Z from the Mall of America), is the spacious, highly regarded **Minnesota Zoo**

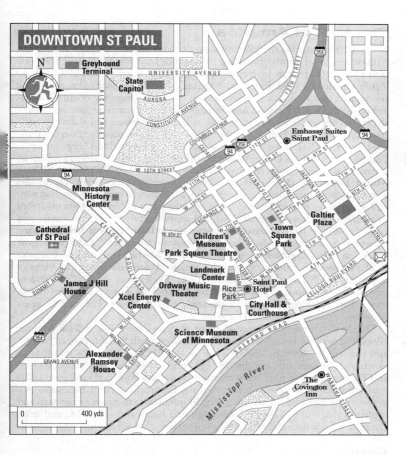

DOWNTOWN ST PAUL

N

Greyhound
Terminal
State
Capitol

UNIVERSITY AVENUE

AURORA

CONSTITUTION AVENUE

COLUMBUS AVENUE

CEDAR

RICE STREET

Embassy Suites
Saint Paul

E 12TH STREET

E. 11TH ST

E. 10TH ST

9TH ST

E 7TH ST

E. 8TH ST

W. 12TH STREET

Minnesota
History
Center

Cathedral
of St Paul

W 11TH ST

W. 10TH STREET

EXCHANGE ST

W 9TH ST

KELLOGG

MINNESOTA STREET

ROBERT STREET

JACKSON STREET

SIBLEY STREET

Galtier
Plaza

7TH

Children's
Museum

W 7TH ST
WABASHA ST

Town
Square
Park

Park Square Theatre

W. 9TH ST

5TH ST

Landmark
Center

ST PETER ST

4TH STREET

James J Hill
House

SUMMIT AVENUE

BOULEVARD

Ordway Music
Theater

Xcel Energy
Center

MARKET ST

Rice
Park

Saint Paul
Hotel

City Hall &
Courthouse

KELLOGG BOULEVARD

W 7TH ST

WALNUT ST

Science Museum
of Minnesota

Alexander
Ramsey
House

GRAND AVENUE

S EXCHANGE ST

CHESTNUT ST

SHEPARD ROAD

Mississippi River

The
Covington
Inn

WABASHA STREET

0   400 yds

(May–Sept Mon–Sat 9am–6pm, Sun 9am–8pm; Oct–April daily 9am–4pm; $8, or $14 combination ticket; ☎951/431-9500, @www.mnzoo.com). The animals reside in reconstructions of their natural habitats; the Komodo dragon exhibit, Imation IMAX Theater and new Discovery Bay aquatic center are outstanding.

Annual celebrations in St Paul include a beanfeast called **Taste of Minnesota** (tons of food, live entertainment, rides and fireworks) running from late June to July 4 and the nation's largest **State Fair** (end of Aug to early Sept). The **Winter Carnival** (late Jan to early Feb) is a frosty gala designed to make the most of the seasonal freeze with ice and snow sculpturing, hot-air ballooning, team sports, parades and more. Perhaps, though, the longest-running celebration here is **Hockey Season** – the non-summer months. The twin cities finally got a pro hockey squad again – the Minnesota Wild – and the new Xcel Energy Center (317 Washington St; ☎651/222-9543, @www.wild.com) is testament to the sport's importance round these parts.

The Mall of America

Shopping addicts make the pilgrimage to the Mall of America from all over the Midwest – and far beyond, including parties from Japan and the regular Shop 'Til You Drop packages run by British operator Major Travel (£300; ℡020/7485-7017). Opened in 1992, this mind-boggling 4.2-million-square-foot, four-story monument to squeaky-clean consumerism has fast become the country's most-visited destination, tallying 42 million visits in a recent year. The futuristic super-structure contains twice as much steel as the Eiffel Tower, and there's enough room to play a week's NFL games side by side. It incorporates more than five hundred stores, with a seven-acre theme park (the pay-per-ride Camp Snoopy). Featured rides include **UnderWater World** ($13.95), with 1.2 million gallons of water and amazing Gulf of Mexico and Caribbean tanks; and **NASCAR Silicon Motor Speedway** ($9.50), which offers simulated stock-car racing. There's also a comedy club, several dance and music bars, a multiscreen cinema, a bowling alley and a vast array of eateries. *Hotel Discovery*, the latest in 'diner-tainment,' serves international foods in simulated global and mythological settings. The science and educational store **Brainstorms**, the custom-made **Basic Brown Bear Factory** (where you can custom-design a cuddly ursine companion), **Lake Wobegon USA** (an eclectic giftstore inspired by folksy Minnesota humorist Garrison Keillor's fictional community) and the hands-on demonstrations at Oshman's Super Sports USA are the highlights of a tour. Evidence of the Mall's all-under-one-roof convenience is provided by the **Chapel of Love** retail store, where more than 1500 couples have legitimately tied the knot. The mall is open Mon–Sat 10am–9:30pm, Sun 11am–7pm.

The Mall is twenty minutes south of the cities on I-494 at 24th Avenue, Bloomington. Take bus #54M from St Paul's West Sixth Street (between Jackson and Kellogg) or #80AB, #5E, #7DEF or #19EFG from various locations in downtown Minneapolis. For the #80 bus, head to Nicollet Mall between Third and Twelfth streets; it runs every twenty minutes. All buses and taxis drop off at the Transit station on the lower level of the East parking ramp. Buses also run between the mall and the airport every 30 minutes. Taxis between the mall and the cities range from $20–25. Some high-end hotels run shuttles to and from the mall. Check with them directly; their service changes often.

Eating

Preconceptions of Midwestern blandness are swiftly put to rest by an almost bewildering array of **restaurants** in the Twin Cities. In Minneapolis, head for the downtown warehouse district, the southerly **Nicollet** neighborhood, the funky **Uptown** and **Lyn–Lake** areas, or the university's Dinkytown. In St Paul, try Galtier Plaza downtown, the **Asian** restaurants on University Avenue, or the horde of ethnic options all along **Grand Avenue**. Of local chains, *Lotus* serves budget Vietnamese meals, *LeeAnn Chin* has adequate Chinese cuisine, while *Keys* offers great breakfasts and fresh lunches. Be sure to sample **wild rice**, a Minnesota specialty.

Minneapolis

Broder's Cucina Italiana 2308 W 50th St, ℡612/925-3113. Terrific deli for eat-in or takeout. There's a full-service restaurant across the street. **Buc** 1204 Harmon Place ℡612/638-2225. This irresistibly festive Italian restaurant dishes out massive portions. There's another branch in St Paul. **Café Brenda** 300 1st Ave N ℡612/342-9230,

ⓦwww.cafebrenda.com. Excellent, moderately priced *nouvelle* vegetarian cuisine in arty downtown warehouse district. **Chez Bananas** 129 N 4th St ℡612/340-0032. Spicy, Caribbean-influenced food, and toys on the tables. **Café Havana** 1119 N Washington Ave ℡612/338-8484. A Cuban newcomer in the trendy warehouse

△ Mall of America

district offers classy decor, music, and excellent – though pricey - food.

Emily's Lebanese Deli 641 University Ave NE ⓣ612/379-4069. Warm, low-cost local place.

Goodfellows 40 S 7th St ⓣ612/332-4800. Award-winning and expensive American cuisine comes in a posh setting.

Modern Café 337 13th Ave NE ⓣ612/378-9882. Check out the eclectic, cheap, flavorsome food in a former neighborhood diner gone hip.

Monte Carlo 219 N 3rd Ave ⓣ612/333-5900. Locals swear by this century-old steakhouse. Pricey.

Odaa 408 Cedar Ave S ⓣ612/338-4459. Tasty all-you-can-eat Ethiopian finger food for $10 or less.

Palomino 825 Hennepin Ave ⓣ612/339-3800. The stylish, popular downtown Euro-bistro specializes in Mediterranean fare.

Pizza Luce 119 N 4th Street ⓣ612/333-7359. No frills decor, hip urban staff, and excellent pizza.

Peter's Grill 114 S 8th St ⓣ612/333-1981. This downtown lunch/early dinner institution is old-style, uncomplicated and quintessentially American. Past diners include President Clinton.

Sawatdee 607 Washington Ave S ⓣ612/338-6451. The toothsome Thai food is always well prepared; main courses are $8–15. There are several branches in the Twin Cities, and a new *Sawatdee* sushi restaurant next door. They have excellent late-night discounts on all sushi.

St Paul

Café DaVinci 400 Sibley St ⓣ612/222-4050. Exceptional northern Italian cuisine is served in a Leonardoesque setting.

Caravan Serai 2175 Ford Parkway ⓣ612/690-1935. Afghani food, tent-like space, pillow seats.

Mickey's Diner 36 W 7th St ⓣ612/222-5633. Landmark 24hr diner in 1930s dining car.

Moscow on the Hill 371 Selby Ave ⓣ612/291-1236. Exquisite Russo-European food, modest ambience.

St Paul Grill 350 Market St ⓣ612/292-9292. Traditional but inventive food in classic downtown hotel.

Taste of Scandinavia 75 W 5th St ⓣ612/222-1100. Delicious, authentic lunches and daytime snacks are served cafeteria-style in Landmark Center, – the most central of three locations.

W A Frost Selby and Western aves ⓣ612/224-5715. A former pharmacy and F. Scott Fitzgerald hangout has been converted into a plush restaurant with garden patio.

Nightlife and entertainment

The Greater Twin Cities have been dubbed a "cultural Eden on the prairie," where 2.5 million people support upwards of one hundred **theater** companies, more than forty **dance** troupes, twenty **classical music** ensembles, and more than a hundred art galleries. Sir Tyrone Guthrie began the theatrical boom back in 1963, enrolling large-scale local assistance to establish the classical repertory company (ⓣ612/377-2224 or 1-800/848-4912) named after him. The Guthrie Theater is at 725 Vineland Place, Minneapolis (ⓣ612/377-2224 or 1–877/44STAGE, Ⓦwww.guthrietheater.org). The cities now have more theaters per capita than anywhere in the US apart from New York City.

Unusually, **nightlife** in Minneapolis (and, to a lesser extent, St Paul) hasn't been siphoned off by suburbia – one hundred thousand students ensure a vibrant club scene. Before the Seattle music explosion, Minneapolis natives Bob Mould and Paul Westerberg pioneered the grunge sound with their seminal bands **Husker Du** and **The Replacements**. The city still churns out great guitar bands like Soul Asylum, while erstwhile **Prince Rogers Nelson** continues to meddle around in his multimedia **Paisley Park** studio in suburban Chanhassen. For complete entertainment information and listings, check out the ubiquitous free weekly *City Pages*. *Lavender* and *focus*POINT provide a similar service from a lesbian and gay perspective.

Minneapolis and St Paul theaters

Bryant-Lake Bowl Theatre 810 W Lake St, Minneapolis ⓣ612/825-3737, Ⓦwww.bryantlake-bowl.com. Performances, bowling, café and bar all under one funky roof.

Chanhassen Dinner Theater 521 W 78th St, Minneapolis ⓣ612/934-1525 or 1-800/362-3515, Ⓦwww.chanhassentheaters.com. Mainstream musicals, popular comedies and drama on four stages, plus meals. Thirty minutes from downtown.

Dudley Riggs' Brave New Workshop 2605 Hennepin Ave S, Minneapolis ☎612/332-6620. The grandparent of local satirical comedy troupes.
Fitzgerald Theater 10 E Exchange St, St Paul ☎651/290-1221, ❈www.fitzgeraldtheater.org. Best known as the venue for Garrison Keillor's weekly *A Prairie Home Companion* performance, it also hosts other concerts and lectures.
Great American History Theater 30 E 10th St, St Paul ☎612/292-4323. Original plays deal with events and personalities from the region's past.
Jungle Theater 709 W Lake St, Minneapolis ☎612/822-7063, ❈www.jungletheater.com. Hole-in-the-wall theater/cabaret.
Park Square 408 St Peter St, St Paul ☎651/291-7005, ❈www.parksquaretheater.org. Well-executed classic and contemporary plays.
Penumbra 270 N Kent St, St Paul ☎651/224-3180. Professional African-American company.
Red Eye Collaboration 15 W 14th St, Minneapolis ☎612/870-0309. Challenging experimental theater.
Theatre de la Jeune Lune 1st St and 1st Ave, Minneapolis ☎612/332-3986, ❈www.jeunelune.org. A unique ensemble of Parisians and Minneapolitans offer dynamic, highly physical productions from a commedia base.

Minneapolis bars and clubs

Backstage at BRAVO! 900 Hennepin Ave ☎612/338-0062, ❈www.backstageatbravo.com. Newish three-story restaurant/piano bar with theatrical leanings.
Figlio Calhoun Square, 3001 Hennepin Ave ☎612/822-1688. Top late-night dining and people-watching.
Fine Line 318 1st Ave ☎612/338-8100. Sleek, small and musically eclectic downtown club.
First Avenue and 7th St Entry 701 1st Ave ☎612/338-8388 or 612/332-1775, ❈www.first-avenue.com. The landmark rock venue where TAFKAP's *Purple Rain* was shot still packs 'em in with top bands and dance music.
Gay 90s 408 Hennepin Ave S ☎612/333-7755. This sprawling, predominantly gay club has two dance floors, a piano lounge, dining, and polished

weekend drag shows.
Ground Zero 15 NE 4th St ☎612/378-5115. The mixed clientele savors the great space, varied themes, gothic influences and occasional fetish nights.
Kieran's Irish Pub 330 2nd Ave S ☎612/339-4499. Friendly atmosphere built round good food, grog, music and poetry. Downtown location.
Loon Café 500 1st Ave N ☎612/332-8342. Try the chilis at this noisy, likeable sports bar offering great grub.
Loring Bohemian Bar and Café 1624 Harmon Place ☎612/338-6258 or 612/332-1617. Beautiful people with attitude drink, dine or drift upstairs to the dance/theater Playhouse.
New French Café & Bar 128 N 4th St ☎612/338-3790. Cozy warehouse district mainstay.
Nye's Polonaise Room 112 E Hennepin Ave ☎612/379-2021. Experience old-time atmosphere at the piano and polka bars and the Polish-American restaurant.
Quest 110 N 5th St ☎612/338-3383, ❈www.thequestclub.com. State-of-the-art dance club, with live acts. Dress flash.

St Paul bars and clubs

The Dakota Bar and Grill 1021 Bandana Blvd ☎651/642-1442, ❈www.dakotacooks.com. Gourmet Midwestern food and great local and national jazz in converted shopping mall locale.
Gallivan's 354 Wabasha St ☎651/227-6688. This downtown white-collar pub, one of St Paul's oldest bars, has a neighborhood feel.
McGovern's 225 W 7th St ☎651/224-5821. At a quintessential Irish pub, you're likely to strike up some decent conversation.
O'Gara's Bar and Grill 164 N Snelling Ave ☎651/644-3333. The mixed clientele is drawn by grub, grog and live bands in the adjoining *Garage*.
Tom Reid's Hockey City Pub 258 W 7th St ☎651/292-9916. At a pre- and post-game hangout, Minnesotans gather to honor their favorite sport.
Town House 1415 University Ave ☎651/646-7087. Gay/lesbian bar with dance, drag and C&W evenings, plus piano lounge.

Northern Minnesota

Minnesota's substantial **northern** half, covered with forested lakes, remains much as it was when the Europeans first traded with the Indians. The northeast – **the Arrowhead**, poking into Lake Superior – holds the greatest charm: most visitors choose secluded outdoor vacations centered on fishing, canoeing and snowmobiling, but there's infinite potential for driving tours in a wilderness comparable to the Alaskan interior.

The Arrowhead is anchored by busy **Duluth**. From here, **Scenic Hwy-61** skirts the clifftops around Lake Superior, passing waterfalls, state parks and neat little towns on the way northeast to the Canadian border. Sleepy little **Grand Marais** is poised at the edge of the wild **Boundary Waters Canoe Area Wilderness** and the **Gunflint Trail**. Inland, the **Iron Range** makes a scenic route north to the idyllic **Voyageurs National Park**. To the southwest, in **Itasca State Park**, the Mississippi River begins its great roll down to the Gulf of Mexico; you can cross the headwaters on stepping-stones. Everywhere you'll find campgrounds and Ma and Pa lakeside **resorts**, havens of homely simplicity dedicated to soothing urban-ravaged souls.

Duluth

DULUTH, at the western extremity of Lake Superior 150 miles north of Minneapolis and St Paul, forms a long crescent at the base of the Arrowhead. Named for a seventeenth-century French officer, Daniel Greysolon, Sieur du Lhut, it cascades down from the granite bluffs surrounding **Skyline Drive** (an exhilarating thirty-mile route) to a busy **harbor**, shared with Superior, Wisconsin. Together these 'twin ports' constitute the largest inland port in the US. Originally the main cargo was fur; now it ships grain, lumber and ore to the Atlantic via the St Lawrence Seaway.

In the 1980s, Duluth had a face-lift and began to encourage tourism. The main drawback is that it's **cold**. The seaway is frozen through the winter, and even spring and fall evenings can be chilly. Temperatures are always significantly cooler near the lake – as fate would have it, the location of nearly all the attractions and activities.

A short walk down Lake Avenue from the **Convention and Visitors Bureau office**, 100 Lake Place Drive (☏218/722-4011 or 1-800/4-DULUTH), leads to the free **Marine Museum** in Canal Park, a vantage point for watching big boats from around the world pass under the delightfully archaic Aerial Lift Bridge (June to early Sept daily 10am–9pm; rest of year times vary). Originating at Canal Park, Duluth's **Lakewalk** is the free way to take in the view, though in summer you can also take two-hour **harbor cruises** ($9.75; ☏218/722-6218, ⓦwww.visitduluth.com/vista). Also worthwhile is a visit to the stately lakeside Jacobean Revival mansion **Glensheen**, 3300 London Rd (May–Oct daily 9.30am–4pm; Nov–April 11am–2pm Fri–Sun only; two separate tours $10, reservations required on ☏218/726-8910 or 1-888/454-GLEN). Both the grounds and interior are impressive. On a grislier note, aged heiress Elisabeth Congdon was murdered on the premises in 1977, but the crisply efficient guide deflects any queries.

Rail excursions along the Superior shoreline to pretty **Two Harbors** (mid-May to mid-Oct; $18 for 6hr, $9.50 for 90min; ☏218/722-1273 or 1-800/423-1273, ⓦwww.lsrm.org) run from **The Depot** complex at 506 W Michigan St. The Depot also houses the Lake Superior Railroad Museum, a children's museum, cultural heritage center and art museum (summer 9.30am–6pm, winter 10am–5pm; $8.50), and is home to performing companies at night. The historic Lake Superior and Mississippi Railroad takes a ninety-minute journey along the scenic St Louis River 11am and 2pm on weekends, mid-June to early September ($7; departs from the parking lot on Grand Ave and 71st Ave W, across from the zoo; ⓦwww.lsmrr.org). Duluth's Spirit Mountain **ski area** (☏-800/642-6377, ⓦwww.spiritmt.com) boasts the best downhill runs in the Midwest.

Practicalities

From 4426 Grand Ave, Greyhound **buses** connect with the upper Midwest. **Accommodation** rates and availability fluctuate in summer. Victorian-styled B&Bs include the *Charles Weiss Inn*, 1615 E Superior St (☎218/724-7016 or 1-800/525-5243; ❺). Better **motels** include the *Best Western Edgewater East*, 2400 London Rd (☎218/728-3601 or 1-800/777-7925, ⓦwww.bestwestern.com; ❹), which has a good pool, and the central *Canal Park Inn*, 250 Canal Park Drive (☎218/727-8821 or 1-800/777-8560; ❹). *Indian Point* **campground**, at 75th and Grand, west off Hwy-23 (☎218/624-5637), has summer bayside sites: tents $15, full hook-up possible.

The Italian-American **food** at *Grandma's Saloon And Deli*, in view of the bridge at 522 Lake Ave S (☎218/727-4192), is not for dieters. *Grandma's Sports Garden* (☎218/722-4724), across a parking lot at no. 425, is similarly convivial, dishing up tasty food when not functioning as either dance floor or basketball court. Classiest of all is the revolving *Top of the Harbor* (☎218/727-8981, ⓦwww.radisson.com/duluthmn), atop the *Radisson Hotel*, 505 W Superior St, and there's also the lovely *Bennett's on the Lake*, 600 E Superior St (☎218/722-2829, ⓦwww.bennettsonthelake.com), featuring a superb lake view.

North from Duluth: Highway 61

Memorialized on vinyl by Minnesota native Bob Dylan, stunning Scenic Hwy-61 follows Lake Superior for 150 miles from Duluth to the border, its precipitous cliffs interspersed with pretty little ports and picture-postcard picnic sites.

At **Gooseberry River State Park**, forty miles northeast from Duluth, the river splashes over volcanic rock through waterfalls and cascades to its outlet in Lake Superior. Like all but one of the seven other state parks along Hwy-61, it provides access to the rugged two-hundred-mile **Superior Hiking Trail**, divided into easily manageable segments for day-trekkers. To camp at any of the state parks, reserve at ☎218/834-2700 or ☎1-800/246-CAMP.

Just beyond **Cascade River State Park**, the road dips into the somnolent little port of **GRAND MARAIS**, where a walk around the photogenic Circular Harbor will soon cure car-stiff legs. The **visitor center** at 13 N Broadway (☎218/387-2524 or 1-888/922-5000, ⓦwww.grandmarais.com) has lists of **outfitters** for those going into the Boundary Waters Canoe Area Wilderness. Inexpensive **room** options include the ultraclean *Sandgren Motel*, by the lights on Hwy-61 (☎218/387-2975 or 1-800/796-2975; ❸), and the appealing *Harbor Inn Motel* (☎218/387-1191 or 1-800/595-4566, ⓦwww.bytheharbor.com; ❸). *Naniboujou Lodge*, fifteen miles east on Hwy-61 (☎218/387-2688, ⓦwww.naniboujou.com; ❺), is a bit pricier, but it's worth dropping by this former 1920s private club just to see the restaurant's eye-popping Cree Indian designs. A backpacker haunt with a difference is *Spirit of the Land Island Hostel* (☎218/388-2241 or 1-800/454-2922; ❶), 58 miles inland from Grand Marais on an island in Seagull Lake; bunks cost $17–19, plus $2 extra for non-members. For herrings and imported beer, or just a well-priced snack, head for *Sven & Ole's Pizza*, 9 W Wisconsin St (☎218/387-1713).

The town of **GRAND PORTAGE**, just below the Canadian border, is at the lake end of the historic 8.5-mile portage route – so vital to the nineteenth century fur trade – now preserved in Grand Portage National Monument. A stockade has been superbly reconstructed. Residents of the Grand Portage Indian Reservation operate a casino in the town. In summer, ferries run daily to remote **Isle Royale National Park** (see p.339).

The canoeing wilderness and the Gunflint Trail

The huge **Boundary Waters Canoe Area Wilderness**, west of Grand Marais, is also accessible from Tofte and especially from easygoing **Ely**, home of the intriguing **International Wolf Center** (May–Oct daily 9am–5pm; Nov–April Fri–Sun 10am–5pm; $5.50). The wilderness is a paradise for canoeing, backpacking and fishing. Overland trails or "portages" link more than a thousand lakes; in winter you can ski and dogsled cross-country. The unpaved sixty-mile **Gunflint Trail** from Grand Marais cuts the wilderness in two; otherwise there are no roads in this outback, let alone electricity or telephones. Most lakes remain motor-free. Stringent rules limit entry to the wilderness. In summer you need a date-specific permit ($10 reservation fee and a $20 deposit; ☎1-800/745-3399, 1-877/550-6777 or 218/365-7561 or 7562), which local outfitters can issue. For those who don't want to rough it, several rustic lodges lie strung out along the trail. The **Gunflint Trail Association** can offer good advice at ☎1-800/338-6932 or 218/387-2870, ⓦwww.gunflint-trail.com.

The Iron Range

In the **Iron Range**, a few miles west of Ely, a number of fabulously rich mines continue to function more than a century after their inception. If you're interested in surveying old workings, it's possible to descend 2300ft at the **Soudan Underground Mine State Park** on Hwy-169 (summer daily 10am–4pm; $6, plus $4 vehicle fee).

Seventy miles southwest on Hwy-169 in **Chisholm**, the **Ironworld USA** cultural theme park (June 11 to Sept 12 9.30am–5pm; $7) turns ecological disaster into tourist spectacle, inviting you on a trolley ride to see "the scenic wonder of an open pit mine." Further opportunities to view such wonders (this time for free) occur during the ten-minute drive to **HIBBING** – a plain little community, of interest mainly as the birthplace of Robert Zimmerman in 1941. He's known today as Bob Dylan; oddly, the museum in City Hall has no exhibits on him.

Hibbing was also the home of America's biggest bus company. With the help of model buses and old advertisements the **Greyhound Origin Center**, 1201 Greyhound Blvd, looks back to its roots transporting local miners to and from the pits (mid-May to Sept 30 Mon–Sat 9am–5pm; $3). The Hull–Rust Mahoning Mine, once the world's largest open pit iron ore mine, can be toured or viewed from an overlook (mid-April to Sept 30 daily 9am–7pm; free).

Voyageurs National Park

Set along the border lakes between Minnesota and Canada, **VOYAGEURS NATIONAL PARK** is like no other in the US national park system. To see it properly, or indeed to grasp its immense beauty at all, you need to leave your car behind and venture into the wild by boat. Once out on the lakes, you're in a great, silent world. Kingfishers, osprey and eagles swoop down for their share of the abundant walleye. Moose and bear stalk the banks. Sunrises and sunsets inspire poets and photographers.

The park's name comes from the intrepid eighteenth-century French-Canadian trappers, who needed almost a year to get their pelts back to Montréal in primitive birchbark canoes. They paddled for sixteen hours a day, fighting off attacks from Native Americans – and each other. Their "customary waterway" became so established that the treaty of 1783 ending the American Revolution specified it as the international border.

You can't do Voyageurs justice on a day trip, though daily cruises from **Rainy Lake visitor center**, ten miles east of International Falls, do at least allow a peek at the lake country (late May to early Sept; $35 or more for a range of special tours; ⓦwww.nps.gov/voya/vvcenter/rlvc.htm). If you're here for a few days, rent a **boat** (reckon on $40 a day) and camp out. It's easy to get lost in this maze of islands and rocky outcrops, and unseen sandbanks lurk beneath the surface. If you're at all unsure, hire a guide from one of the resorts for the first day (around $200 per 8hr day). During **freeze-up** – usually from December until March – the park takes on a whole new aura, as a prime destination for skiers and snowmobilers (rentals from $120 per day).

INTERNATIONAL FALLS, the only sizable nearby community, might sound attractive, but it's a messy array of motels, duty-free shops, fast-food joints and lumber yards; the falls, never more than glorified rapids anyway, were dammed in 1906.

Practicalities

Most travelers access Voyageurs from Hwy-53, which runs northwest from Duluth. After just over one hundred miles, at Orr, comes Rte-23, which runs northeast toward **Crane Lake** at the eastern end of the park. About 28 and 31 miles further along Hwy-53, highways 129 and 122 lead, respectively, to the **visitor centers** at **Ash River** (May–Sept daily 9am–5pm; ☏218/374-3221) and **Kabetogama Lake** (May–Sept daily 9am–5pm; ☏218/875-2111). Another prime visitor center is at **Rainy Lake** (May–Sept daily 9am–5pm; rest of year times vary), at the westernmost entrance 36 miles farther on via International Falls (see above).

Once inside the park, you need to take a few **precautions**. Check (natural) mercury levels in fish before eating them, don't pick wild rice (only Native Americans may do this), be wary of Lyme Disease (a tick-induced gastric illness), boil drinking water, and watch out for bears. Discuss such matters and procedures, along with customs procedures in case you plan to paddle into Canadian waters, with a ranger before venturing out.

The definitive way to experience the park is to **camp** on one of its many scattered islands, most plentiful around Crane Lake (if you don't have your own boat, cruise operators can drop you off and pick you up at a later date). There are also first-come, first-served state-owned campgrounds on the mainland at Ash River and Woodenfrog, near Kabetogama. However, most visitors stay in one of more than sixty **resorts**. Basically family-run cottages, these usually cater for weekly stays, with all meals, though you can rent rooms nightly. Most popular are those around Kabetogama, such as *Watson's Harmony Beach* (☏218/ 875-2811, ⓦwww.fishandgame.com/harmonybeach/; ❸), a great place for picking up tips on the park; *Arrowhead Lodge* (☏218/875-2141, ⓦwww .arrowheadlodgeresort.com; ❸), well known for its restaurant; and the basic, cheap and cheerful *Driftwood Lodge* (☏218/875-3841, ⓦwww.driftwood-lodgeresort.com; ❶). You can book through the Kabetogama Lake Association (☏1-800/524-9085, ⓦwww.kabetogama.com). Resort associations for Crane Lake (☏218/993-2346), Ash River (☏1-800/950-2061) and Rainy Lake/ International Falls (☏218/283-9400) can also fix you up with lodgings, including houseboats (usually $1000 and up per week).

Southern Minnesota

Southern Minnesota is split between high plains, timbered ravines and slow-flowing Mississippi tributaries in the east, and the drier, flatter prairie and checkerboard farmland of the west. In the scenic **southeast**, spared a filing down by the last glacial advance, attractive small towns sit along the Mississippi, or on bluffs above it, in the ninety-mile **Hiawatha Valley**. Mississippi shipping helped sustain easygoing communities like **Winona**, **Red Wing**, **Lake City** (where water skiing was invented about 1922) and **Wabasha**, all of which share well-preserved old homes and hotels.

The agricultural and college center of **Northfield**, off I-35 thirty miles south of the Twin Cities, annually commemorates the Jesse James gang's foiled attempt to rob the town bank in September 1876. **Harmony**, almost in Iowa and near Minnesota's largest **Amish** colony; **Lanesboro**, with a storybook setting on the hillsides of the Root River; and **Mantorville** have all kept at least one foot in the nineteenth century. Further west, **New Prague** and **New Ulm** were prime targets for the beleaguered Sioux during a six-week war with the US government in 1862.

Rochester

The metropolis of **ROCHESTER**, a white-collar community in a rural setting about eighty miles southeast of Minneapolis and St Paul, was settled in the 1850s by migrants from Rochester, New York, as a humble crossroads campground for wagon trains. After a tornado devastated the town in 1883, Dr William Worral Mayo established the huge **Mayo Clinic**, 200 First St SW (☎507/284-2511, ⓦwww.mayohealth.org). Free tours serve as ninety-minute promotions for "the first and largest private group medical practice in the world" (Mon–Fri 10am; art tour Tues–Thurs 1.30pm). You can also tour the sprawling family home, **Mayowood**, 3720 Mayowood Rd southwest of Hwy-52 (☎507/282-9447; Sat and Sun, May to mid-June at 1pm, 2pm and 3pm, plus Sat at 11am; mid-June to Oct on Tues, Thurs, Sat and Sun, same hours; $10).

Rochester is rife with chain and budget **accommodation**, especially within the five-block radius of downtown, including the *Kahler Hotel*, 20 SW Second Ave (☎507/282-2581 or 1-800/533-1655, ⓦwww.kahler.com/kahlergrand/; ❹). *The Broadstreet Café and Bar*, 300 NW First Ave (☎507/281-2451), a bistro in a renovated warehouse, serves excellent meals; there's live music in the cozy *Redwood Room* downstairs.

Jefferson Union Bus Depot, 405 SW First Ave (☎507/289-4037), is the hub for **bus services**. Rochester Express (☎507/282-8673 or 1-800/479-7824) and Rochester Direct (☎507/280-9270 or 1-800/280-9270) make between eight and eleven van runs daily to the Minneapolis–St Paul International Airport or the Mall of America for $19 one-way, $36 round-trip. Rochester's **visitor center** is at 150 S Broadway (☎507/288-4331 or 1-800/634-8277, ⓦwww.rochestermn.com).

Pipestone National Monument

The town of **PIPESTONE**, eight miles east of the South Dakota border, is named for a soft red clay, within the local quartzite, that was used for centuries by Great Plains Indians to make ceremonial calumets, or peace pipes. The quarry site, a kind of neutral, inter-tribal United Nations, is now the **Pipestone National Monument** (daily 8am–5pm, longer on summer weekends; $2). A self-guided **trail** winds from the **visitor center** through stands of trees, past rock formations and exposed quarry pits and over a creek, complete with picturesque falls.

Pipestone's small **historic district** includes a sleepy county museum and a building with several amusing sandstone gargoyles. Pick up a walking-tour brochure from the **visitor center** (☎507/825-3316 or 1-800/336-6125), near the junction of highways 75 and 23. You can sleep and eat at the grand old *Calumet Inn*, 104 W Main St (☎507/825-5871 or 1-800/535-7610, ⓦwww.calumetinn.com; ④), though the *Arrow Motel*, Hwy-75 N, is less expensive (☎507/825-3331 or 1-888/825-9599; ②). Each late July to early August the town puts on the nine-day "Song of Hiawatha" **Indian pageant** in an outdoor amphitheater.

From a distance the red rocks at **Blue Mounds State Park**, sloping into a long cliff a few miles north of the junction of I-90 and US-75 at Luverne, create a great hump that appeared blue at sunset to approaching pioneers. Twice a year, at the equinoxes, the sun lines up with a curious 1250ft row of rocks, aligned on an east–west axis. There are seasonal **campgrounds** (☎1-800/246-CAMP) and a permanent small herd of buffalo. Ring the same number for picturesque **Split Rock Creek State Park**, only seven miles south of Pipestone and the site of a dam dating from 1935.

CHAPTER 5 # Highlights

* **Adams-Morgan and Georgetown, Washington, DC**. The best neighborhoods in which to discover that DC isn't all monuments, memorials and museums. See p.408

* **National Air and Space Museum, Washington DC** Soaring planes and real-life spacecraft make this the most popular of DC's Smithsonian Institution museums. See p.416

* **Colonial Williamsburg, VA** As good an insight as you could hope for into pre-Independence British America, apothecaries and all. See p.442

* **Charlottesville, VA** See Thomas Jefferson's architectural imprint and then head off into the Blue Ridge Mountains on gorgeous Skyline Drive. See p.450

* **Seneca Rocks, WV** These 1000ft limestone cliffs are just one of the highlights of the pristine Monongahela National Forest. See p.461

* **Cape Henlopen State Park, DE** With rolling sand dunes backed by pine forest, the park makes a fine base to enjoy the coast away from the more frenetic resorts. See p.488

5

The Capital Region

The city of **WASHINGTON DC** and the four states of **VIRGINIA**, **WEST VIRGINIA**, **MARYLAND** and **DELAWARE** constitute a cross-section of the nation. Since the days of the first American colonies, US history has been shaped here, from agitation towards independence to the battles of the Revolutionary and Civil wars. Now, the contrasts and incongruities of contemporary America are shown in high relief: the corridors of power in Washington are literally a stone's throw away from dire inner-city poverty while, nearby, dozens of time-worn farming and fishing towns seem straight out of some Norman Rockwell idyll.

Early in the seventeenth century, the first British settlements began to take root along the rich estuary of the **Chesapeake Bay**; the colonists hoped for gold, but found their fortunes growing tobacco. **Virginia**, the first settlement, was the largest and most populous; it originally included most of what are now Kentucky, Tennessee and Ohio, and as late as the 1790s had double the population of any other state. Fully half of these people were **slaves**, brought from Africa to do the backbreaking work of harvesting the tobacco. Despite its central position on the east coast, the whole region lies below the Mason–Dixon Line – the symbolic border between North and South, drawn up in 1763 as the boundary between slave and free states – and until the Civil War one of the country's busiest slave markets was just two blocks from the White House.

Besides generating the bulk of colonial wealth, the region also produced many of early America's great leaders, from firebrand politicians like **Patrick Henry** ("Give me Liberty or Give me Death") to patrician intellectuals such as **Thomas Jefferson**. Another Virginian, **George Washington**, led the Continental Army against the British in the Revolutionary War and served as the first president, while **James Madison** was the primary author of the Constitution.

For all its colonial importance, by the mid-nineteenth century the region had lost power and status to the industrial and mercantile centers of Philadelphia and New York. Tensions between North and South finally erupted into the **Civil War**, of which traces are still visible everywhere. The hundred miles between the capital of the Union – Washington DC – and that of the Confederacy – Richmond, Virginia – were a constant and bloody battleground for four long years. This sense of a nation divided against itself is especially acute at the grand manor of **Robert E. Lee**, the Confederacy's military leader: high on a hill overlooking the heart of Washington DC, its grounds are now filled with the war dead of the Arlington National Cemetery.

Washington DC itself, with its magnificent monumental architecture, is an essential stop on any tour of the region. **Virginia**, to the south, holds literally

New York City

Philadelphia, PA

Pittsburgh

76

81

78

79

79

70

77

79

PENNSYLVANIA

WEST VIRGINIA

Wheeling

Ohio River

77

64

Charleston

Beckley

Hinton

19

Lewisburg

Roanoke

New River Gorge

Monongahela National Forest

Elkins

Davis

Cumberland

Berkeley Springs

40

Cass

Hillsboro

92

Allegheny Mountains

New Market Battlefield

33

Staunton

Lexington

Lynchburg

Bedford

29

460

81

64

BLUE RIDGE PARKWAY

219

MOUNT ROGERS NATIONAL RECREATION AREA

81

77

Nashville, TN

CUMBERLAND GAP NATIONAL PARK

KENTUCKY

Ohio River

OHIO

MARYLAND

Thurmont

Frederick

Gettysburg Battlefield

Antietam Battlefield

Harpers Ferry

Berkeley Springs

Middleburg

66

Manassas Battlefield

SHENANDOAH NATIONAL PARK

15

270

Baltimore

Annapolis

WASHINGTON, D.C.

Alexandria

Mt. Vernon

Fredericksburg

Charlottesville

Appomattox

VIRGINIA

Richmond

Petersburg

95

460

85

NORTH CAROLINA

Wilmington

New Castle

NEW JERSEY

Delaware Bay

Cape May

Lewes

Rehoboth Beach

Ocean City

DELAWARE

Dover

13

Chestertown

St. Michaels

Oxford

Easton

Cambridge

Salisbury

Chincoteague

ASSATEAGUE ISLAND NATIONAL SEASHORE

ATLANTIC OCEAN

301

50

Solomon's Island

Pt. Lookout

Reedville

Chesapeake Bay

Potomac River

Rappahannock River

York R.

James River

Williamsburg

Jamestown

Yorktown

Norfolk

Portsmouth

Virginia Beach

360

58

64

95

95

N

CANADA

PACIFIC OCEAN

ATLANTIC OCEAN

MEXICO

0   50 miles

402

hundreds of historic sites, from the homes of early politicians to the colonial capital of **Williamsburg**, as well as the narrow forested heights of **Shenandoah National Park**, along the crest of the Blue Ridge Mountains. Much greater expanses of wilderness, crashing white-water rivers and innumerable backwoods villages await you in less-visited **West Virginia**.

Most tourists come to **Maryland** for the maritime traditions of **Chesapeake Bay** – though many of its quaint old villages have been gentrified by weekend pleasure-boaters. **Baltimore** is full of character and enjoyably unpretentious (and has a phenomenal concentration of bars), while **Annapolis**, the pleasant state capital, is linked by bridge and ferry to the **eastern shore**, where **Assateague Island** remains an Atlantic paradise. **New Castle**, across the border in **Delaware**, is a perfectly preserved colonial-era town; nearby are some of the east coast's best and least crowded beaches.

Washington DC

That the marshy swamp where **WASHINGTON DC** now stands was chosen as the site of the **capital** of the newly independent United States of America says a lot about then-prevalent attitudes toward government. Washington, District of Columbia (the boundaries of the two are identical) – also known as "DC" and "The District" – can be unbearably hot and humid in summer, and bitterly cold in winter. Such an unpleasant climate, it was hoped, would discourage elected leaders from making government a full-time job. This disdain for politics is still apparent: DC is run as a virtual colony of Congress, where residents have just one, nonvoting representative and couldn't vote in presidential elections until the 23rd Amendment was passed in 1961.

Other than the federal government, **tourism** is DC's biggest industry. The city attracts almost twenty million visitors each year. Conveniently, most arrive in midsummer, when the lawmakers have gone home, so overcrowding is rarely a problem. The nation's showcase puts on quite a display for its guests, and admission to virtually all major attractions is free. The most famous sites are concentrated along the central **Mall**, including the White House, individual memorials to four of the greatest presidents, and the superb museums of the Smithsonian Institution. Downtown, however (broadly speaking the area immediately north of the Mall, between the White House and the Capitol), can seem very empty, even intimidating, at night, and you're more likely to spend your evenings in the hotels and restaurants of the city's more motherly neighborhoods, such as historic **Georgetown**, arty **Dupont Circle** and the funkier **Adams–Morgan** district.

Some history

The decision to establish the national capital at this spot had much to do with the fact that it lies midway between the rural South and the northern cities of Boston, New York and Philadelphia (the last, the previous capital, was thought too exciting for a seat of government). It was also accessible from the sea, via the Potomac River – a bit too easily so, as demonstrated by the burning and ransacking of the city by the British during the War of 1812. Best of all, the land was cheap – the state of Maryland ceded sovereignty to the federal government, which had to pay only for the individual sites it chose for its buildings. Though the baroque plan of the city was laid out in 1791 – by a Frenchman, **Pierre L'Enfant**, assisted by the black American scientist **Benjamin Banneker** – few buildings were put up, apart from the actual houses of government, until near the end of the century. Charles Dickens, visiting in 1842, found "spacious avenues that begin in nothing and lead nowhere."

After the Civil War, thousands of Southern **blacks** arrived in search of a sanctuary from racial oppression; to some extent, they found one. Segregation was banned in public places, and **Howard University**, the only US institution of higher learning that enrolled black people, was set up in 1867. By the 1870s African-Americans made up more than a third of the 150,000 population, but economic resources were soon stretched to the breaking point. As poverty and squalor worsened, official **segregation** was reintroduced in 1920. Blacks were banned from government buildings – including, in an ironic twist, the Lincoln Memorial – and the jobs they had come to find.

After World War II, the city's economy and population boomed. Although segregation of public facilities was declared illegal in the 1950s, civil rights protests divided the city during the 1960s – culminating in the destructive downtown riots of 1968. The city's problems have changed little since: DC has one of the country's highest murder rates, as well as appalling levels of unemployment, illiteracy and drug abuse. After years of mismanagement by city leaders, a control board appointed by Congress took charge of the city's finances in 1995, in an attempt to turn around the massive budget deficit (which was due in part to a middle-class flight to the suburbs). The city rebounded under the board, which by virtue of its success put itself out of a job in 2001. Power was restored to the mayor, **Anthony Williams**, and the city council. The city's rising fortunes can be seen in lower crime rates, newly paved roads and a revitalized downtown, where restaurants, cultural happenings and sports events have begun to attract visitors to areas once overrun by drug dealers.

However, just as things seemed to be getting back on track, terror struck the capital. On September 11, 2001, terrorists hijacked a United Airlines jet and crashed it into the Pentagon, killing nearly 200 people, including those on the plane. Security throughout the capital was tightened in the aftermath of the attack. Government leaders and city officials then began to grapple with their next challenge: balancing the openness demanded of a democratic capital with the vital needs of public and national security, an issue likely to be at the forefront of the city's concerns for some time.

Arrival, information and getting around

Washington DC is served by three major **airports**, two on the outskirts and one right in the city center. **Dulles International Airport**, 26 miles west in northern Virginia, and **Baltimore–Washington International Airport** (BWI), halfway between DC and Baltimore, get the majority of the international traffic. **Ronald Reagan Washington National Airport** and its major state-of-the-art terminal, along the Potomac River just west of the Mall, is mostly used by domestic flights. Taking a **taxi** downtown from BWI or Dulles costs around $50, but **express buses** run from both airports to a downtown terminal at 1517 K St NW, just three blocks north of the White House.

Washington Flyer Express (☎1-800/927-4359) serves Dulles (every 30min; 40min journey; $16 one-way, $26 round-trip) and the SuperShuttle (☎1-800/BLUE-VAN) runs from BWI (every 30min; 1hr journey; $30 one-way). From Dulles, the cheapest method, though more time-consuming, is to take the Washington Flyer Express as far as West Falls Church Metro station ($8) and the Metro subway system (see below) from there. A SuperShuttle runs from National (every 30–60min; $13 one-way), though this airport is on the Metro system, just a short ride from downtown. Taxis downtown from National cost around $15.

By **train** – from Philadelphia, New York and Boston, as well as direct from BWI Airport – you arrive amid the gleaming malls of bustling **Union Station**, 50 Massachusetts Ave NE, two blocks north of the US Capitol and with its own Metro station. Greyhound and other **buses** stop at a modern station at 1005 First St NE, in a fairly dodgy part of the city, ten blocks from downtown; take a cab, especially at night, at least as far as Union Station Metro (around $6). **Driving** into DC is a sure way to experience some of the worst traffic on the east coast – the main I-95 and I-495 freeways circuit Washington on the **Beltway**, jammed eighteen hours a day.

Once in the city, stop at the **DC Chamber of Commerce Visitor Center**, Ronald Reagan Building, 1300 Pennsylvania Ave NW (Mon–Sat 8am–6pm, Sun noon–5pm; ☎202/328-4748), which can help with maps, tours, bookings and citywide information. Look for visitor information desks at the airports and Union Station. The **White House Visitor Information Center**, 1450 Pennsylvania Ave NW (daily 7.30am–4pm; ☎202/208-1631), supplies free maps and handy guides to museums and attractions; the most useful is the free *Washington DC Visitors Guide*.

The main **post office** is across from Union Station on Massachusetts Avenue and Capitol Street NE (Mon–Fri 7am–midnight, Sat & Sun 7am–8pm; ☎202/523-2628; zip code 20002).

City transportation

Getting around DC is a cinch. Most places downtown, including the Mall museums, the major monuments and the White House, are within walking distance of each other, and an excellent **public transportation** system reaches outlying sights and neighborhoods. The clean, efficient and still-growing **Metro subway** is the envy of other cities; one-way fares start at $1.10 (base rate, off-peak), with a slight rush-hour surcharge from 5.30–9.30am and 3–7pm. A One Day Pass, valid after 9.30am on weekdays, costs $5 (trains run Mon–Thurs 5.30am–midnight, Fri 5.30am–2am, Sat 8am–2am & Sun 8am–midnight; get route information at the Metro Center Sales Office, Metro Center station, 12th and F sts NW; ☎202/637-7000). The standard fare on the more extensive **bus** network is also $1.10. **Taxis** are a good-value alternative with most cross-town fares ranging $5–12.50. (Surcharges kick in during peak hours and for each additional passenger.) There are taxi stands at major hotels and transportation terminals (like Union Station), or call Yellow Cab (☎202/544-1212).

Tours

During the day, open-sided **Tourmobiles** (☎202/554-5100, ⊕www.tourmobile .com) connect the major museums and sites – allowing you to stop for as long as you choose at any of a dozen different locations. An $18 one-day ticket covers downtown DC and Arlington Cemetery, while an extra $25 gets you to Mount Vernon (see p.433) and back; tickets for the three-hour "twilight tour," which departs from Union Station (daily 6.30pm), also run $18. All can be bought from the main office on the Ellipse, just south of the White House, at kiosks on the Mall and in Union Station or on the tram itself.

If you want to **cycle** or **cruise** along the Potomac River or the historic C&O Canal, both Thompson's Boat Center, 2900 Virginia Ave NW at Rock Creek Parkway (℡202/333-4861), near the Watergate complex, and Fletcher's Boat House, 4940 Canal Rd NW, two miles farther up the canal towpath (℡202/244-0461), rent touring bikes, rowboats and canoes. You could also get to know the city on a three-hour cycling trip with Bike the Sites Inc ($40 per person including bike and helmet; ℡202/966-8662); or call Better Bikes (℡202/293-2080), which will deliver rental bikes anywhere in DC ($28-38 a day). In addition, mule-drawn **canal boats**, with costumed National Park Service guides, follow the old C&O Canal from behind 30th and M streets in Georgetown on a hour-long narrated cruise (April–Oct; $8; ℡202/653-5190). The city's best **walking tours** are led by Anthony S. Pitch ($10; ℡301/294-9514), who ambles around Adams-Morgan and Georgetown most Sunday mornings beginning at 11am.

In general, it's worth calling ahead to major sites for any changes to tour procedures due to heightened **security concerns**.

Accommodation

Most DC **hotels** cater to business travelers and political lobbyists, and during the week are quite expensive. At weekends, however, and throughout July and August, when Congress is in recess, many cut their rates by up to fifty percent – it's always worth asking about special rates. For a list of properties contact one of the city information offices or call Washington DC Accommodations (℡202/289-2220 or 1-800/554-2220, ⓦwww.washingtondcaccommodations.com), which provides a general hotel reservation and travel planning service.

Similarly, a number of **B&B** agencies offer comfortable doubles from around $55–65: try the B&B League (℡202/363-7767) or Bed & Breakfast Ltd (℡202/328-3510, ⓦwww.bedandbreakfastdc.com). There's no good **camping** anywhere near DC but, besides the **youth hostel**, both the Catholic University (℡202/319-5277) and Georgetown University (℡202/687-4560) offer **budget rooms** in summer; these must be arranged well in advance.

DC in summer is hot and humid, and **air conditioning** is essential for a good night's rest.

Adams Inn 1744 Lanier Place NW ℡202/745-3600 or 1-800/578-6807, ⓦwww.adamsinn.com. Clean, simply furnished B&B rooms, with and without bath, spread across three adjoining Victorian townhouses on a quiet Woodley Park street, near the zoo. ❸/❹

Allen Lee Hotel 2224 F St NW ℡202/331-1224 or 1-800/462-0186, ⓦwww.allenleehotel.com. Slightly faded, musty rooms come with clunky air conditioning, but the hotel is handy and cheap, two blocks from Foggy Bottom–GWU Metro. Pay the extra ten bucks or so for a private bath. ❹

The Brenton 1708 16th St NW ℡202/332-5550, ⓦwww.thebrenton.com/. Well-situated near Dupont's 17th Street scene, this Victorian B&B caters to a gay clientele with eight rooms plus a suite (with kitchen). ❺/❻

Brickskeller Inn 1523 22nd St NW ℡202/293-1885, ⓦwww.brickskeller.net/. Simple rooms, some with private baths, above a raucous late-opening bar near Dupont Circle. ❹

Doubletree Hotel Park Terrace 1515 Rhode Island Ave NW ℡202/232-7000 or 1-800/222-TREE. European elegance six blocks north of the

White House featuring comfortable rooms, marble bathrooms and free coffee-making facilities; the closest Metro is Dupont Circle. ⑥–⑧

Embassy Inn 1627 16th St NW ℡202/234-7800 or 1-800/423-9111. Welcoming inn on a residential side street in Dupont Circle East offering good-value rooms (with attractive weekend rates), free continental breakfast and an early evening sherry to speed you on your way. ⑤–⑥

Four Seasons 2800 Pennsylvania Ave NW ℡202/342-0444 or 1-800/332-3442, ⓦwww.fourseasons.com. DC's most luxurious hotel, a sympathetic modern redbrick at the eastern end of Georgetown, is stuffed with leisure facilities. ⑨

Harrington Hotel 1100 E St NW ℡202/628-8140 or 1-800/424-8532, ⓦhotel-harrington.com. Popular with groups, this large, old-fashioned hotel has a great location, between the Capitol and the White House, off Pennsylvania Ave. ⑤

Hay-Adams Hotel 1 Lafayette Square NW ℡202/638-6600 or 1-800/424-5054, ⓦwww.hayadams.com. Historic (and very expensive) townhouse hotel overlooking the White House. ⑨

Hereford House 604 South Carolina Ave SE ℡202/543-0102. Attractive townhouse B&B, with bright, reasonably sized rooms run in the "true British tradition," one block from Eastern Market Metro. ⑤

HI-Washington DC 1009 11th St NW ℡202/737-2333, ⓦwww.hiwashingtondc.org. Huge (270 beds), clean and very central hostel three blocks north of Metro Center. It may accept members only in busy spring and summer months. ①

India House Too 300 Carroll St NW ℡202/291-1195, ⓦwww.dchostel.com. A little way out in Upper Northwest (though near Takoma Park Metro), this few-frills townhouse-hostel has the cheapest dorm beds in DC ($14) and two equally affordable (though sought-after) doubles. Take passport or ID. ①/②

Kalorama Guest House 1854 Mintwood Place NW ℡202/667-6369 and 2700 Cathedral Ave NW ℡202/328-0860. Cozy, nicely furnished rooms (no TVs though) in several restored Victorian townhouses; rates include breakfast, coffee and an evening sherry. The first group is in the grander part of the lively Adams–Morgan neighborhood, the second is across Rock Creek near the zoo. ③/④

Monticello 1075 Thomas Jefferson St NW ℡202/337-0900, ⓦwww.hotelmonticello.com. All-suite hotel nicely situated off M Street near the canal towpath in Georgetown. Rates include complimentary breakfast and access to the business center. Ask for discounts on weekends. ⑧–⑨

Omni Shoreham 2500 Calvert St NW ℡202/234-0700, ⓦomnihotels.com. Plush Washington institution, near Woodley Park Metro, bursting with history. Every president since FDR has held an inaugural ball here. ⑧

Simpkins' B&B 1601 19th St NW ℡202/387-1328. A welcoming Victorian townhouse at Dupont Circle, provides a range of shared and private rooms, morning toast and tea included. High-speed internet access is free. Produce a passport, whether US or foreign. ②

State Plaza 2117 E St NW ℡202/861-8200 or 1-800/424-2859. Check out the excellent weekend rates for these spacious suites with fully equipped kitchens, close to Foggy Bottom Metro. ⑥

Swiss Inn 1204 Massachusetts Ave NW ℡202/371-1816 or 1-800/955-7947, ⓦtheswissinn.com. Friendly townhouse accommodation offering eight "efficiencies" (air-con rooms with kitchenettes, TV and bath), multilingual hosts and parking (free at weekends) outside. Book well in advance; prices don't get much better downtown. ③–⑤

Tabard Inn 1739 N St NW ℡202/785-1277, ⓦtabardinn. Very pleasant small hotel with individually decorated, antique-stocked rooms and a good restaurant, just two blocks from Dupont Circle Metro. Rates, for doubles with shared bath, include breakfast and a pass to the fully equipped YMCA gym nearby. ⑤–⑦

Topaz 1733 N St NW ℡202/393-3000, ⓦwww.topazhotel.com. A contemporary boutique hotel, a short hop from the Dupont scene, with 99 funky rooms, several of which are outfitted for exercise or yoga. ⑦–⑨

The William Lewis House 1309 R St NW ℡202/462-7574 or 1-800/465-7574, ⓦwww.wlewishous.com. A pair of elegantly decorated turn-of the century townhouses are home to this gay B&B near Logan Circle, where ten antique-filled rooms, all with shared bath and, out back, a porch and jacuzzi, make for a very relaxing stay. Reserve in advance. ④–⑤

Windsor Inn 1842 16th St NW ℡202/667-0300 or 1-800/423-9111. Under the same management as the *Embassy Inn*, the *Windsor* is a few blocks farther north, its rooms a shade larger. ⑤–⑥

Woodley Park Guest House 2647 Woodley Rd NW ℡202/667-0218 or 1-866/667-0218, ⓦwoodleyparkguesthouse.com. Sixteen cozy rooms (the cheapest share facilities) that come with free continental breakfast and cheap parking, too. Close to the zoo, the Metro and plenty of restaurants. ③/⑥

The City

Because the city was built from scratch, Washington's regular **town plan** is easy to grasp. Centered on Capitol Hill and its governmental monoliths, the District is divided into four **quadrants** – northeast, northwest, southeast and southwest. Dozens of broad **avenues**, all named after states, run diagonally across a standard grid of **streets**, meeting up at monumental traffic circles like Dupont Circle. North–south streets are numbered, east–west ones are lettered. There's no J Street, an intentional slight to early Supreme Court Justice John Jay, or X, Y or Z Street. I Street is often written Eye Street. Be sure to note the relevant two-letter code in any **address** (NW, NE, SW, SE), which shows its quadrant; 1600 Pennsylvania Ave NW is a *long* way from 1600 Pennsylvania Ave SE.

Until you get your bearings, stick to the established tourist trail; almost all the most famous sights are on **Capitol Hill** or in the comparatively affluent northwest quarter. To the west of the Capitol, the broad, green **Mall** holds monuments to presidents **Washington, Jefferson, Lincoln** and **Franklin D. Roosevelt**, as well as the **White House**, official home of the current president. Also here are the bulk of the city's many marvelous museums, including the national collections of the **Smithsonian Institution**.

However, there is more to Washington than an endless succession of museums and monuments, and it's well worth your time to search out the many attractive **neighborhoods**. Despite its reputation, most of the city is in surprisingly good shape, with row after row of nineteenth-century brick-fronted houses set along leafy boulevards. Between the Mall and the main spine of **Pennsylvania Avenue** – the parade route connecting Capitol Hill to the White House – the Neoclassical buildings of the **Federal Triangle** offer a sobering contrast to the rest of the city's neighborhoods. North and east of here, what's known as **Old Downtown** has been revitalized after years of neglect, and now features new plazas, galleries and restaurants alongside its traditional attractions, like the FBI Building, Old Post Office and the theater associated with President Lincoln's assassination. The area around the **MCI Center**, particularly along Seventh St NW, is fast developing as an entertainment and nightlife scene, with a good selection of bars and restaurants. The oldest area, **Georgetown**, where popular bars and restaurants now line M Street and Wisconsin Avenue above the **Potomac River**, actually precedes the establishment of the District. Georgetown is a fifteen-minute walk from the Foggy Bottom–GWU Metro but its Federal-era and Victorian townhouses and the towpath along the **C&O Canal** make it a fine target for a day's poking about. Other neighborhoods to check out – especially for eating and drinking – are **Dupont Circle** at Massachusetts, Connecticut and New Hampshire avenues, which pulls a dynamic mix of urban professionals of all stripes, and the gentrifying Latin immigrant community of **Adams–Morgan**, a favored destination of the weekend party crowd that's a short walk from Dupont Circle up 18th Street at Columbia Road.

Most DC visitors also take the short Metro ride to **Arlington** in Virginia to see the National Cemetery, President John F. Kennedy's burial place and the Pentagon.

Capitol Hill

Though there's more than one hill in Washington DC, when people talk about what's happening on "**The Hill**" they mean **Capitol Hill** – a shallow knoll topped by the giant white dome of the US Capitol building and rising at the very center of the city. When Washington DC was first laid out, Capitol Hill was intended to be both the symbolic and real seat of the federal government. Home of both the legislature – **Congress** – and the judiciary – the **Supreme Court** – this is still the place where the law of the land is made and refined; it also holds the newly refurbished **Library of Congress**.

US Capitol

Between Constitution and Independence aves at the east end of the Mall; closest Metro stop is Capitol South or Union Station. Summer daily 9am–6pm; rest of year daily 9am–4.30pm. Admission free. Tour information ☎ 202/225-6827, general information ☎ 202/224-3121, ⓦ www.aoc.gov

Visible from all over the city, and housing the nation's lawmakers and tax-takers, the **Senate** and the **House of Representatives**, the **US Capitol** provides an opportunity to appreciate the immense power wielded by the nation's elected officials – and watch them at work. The grand halls and public spaces are packed with monuments and statues of deceased political leaders, while the current crop of legislators can be seen arguing over the finer points of law and policy in committee rooms and the ornate main chambers. When the lantern above the dome is lit, Congress is in session.

Begun in 1793 – George Washington, in Masonic garb, laid the cornerstone – the Capitol was repeatedly expanded over the ensuing years, and is now a confusing hybrid, hard to find your way around, though the omnipresent Capitol police officers keep you on the right track. There's free, walk-in access to the building all year (from the East Front), though between April and September you can expect to wait in line first, for up to two hours. Once inside, the **free tours** (every 15min, 9am–3.45pm) are basically just a walk around the building. US citizens who want to see inside the legislative chambers must arrange "VIP tours" through their representatives. Visitors from other countries can simply show their passports at the House or Senate appointments desks, both on the first floor. Nine presidents, most recently JFK (Nixon declined in advance), have lain in state before burial in the impressive **Rotunda**, which, capped by a 180ft dome, links the two halves of the Capitol – the Senate is in the north wing, the House in the south.

Armed Forces' **bands** perform for free four nights a week (June–Aug) on the East Terrace of the Capitol. The National Symphony Orchestra follows suit on the West Terrace on Memorial Day, July 4 and Labor Day.

Library of Congress

Jefferson Building, 10 First St SE; Madison Building, 101 Independence Ave SE; closest Metro stop is Capitol South. Mon–Sat 10am–5.30pm. Admission free. ☎ 202/707-8000, ⓦ www.loc.gov

In the **Library of Congress**, the largest library in the world, more than 95 million books and manuscripts, and countless thousands of microfilm rolls and computer disks, are arrayed on six hundred miles of shelves. Set up in 1800, the entire library was burned by the British in 1814; to replace the loss, Thomas Jefferson sold the country his six-thousand-volume personal collection. In 1870, when the Library of Congress was declared the national copyright library, the need was felt to build a suitable home. The result was the exuberantly eclectic **Thomas Jefferson Building**, opened in 1897 across from the Capitol, complete with a domed octagonal **Reading Room**, and hundreds of mosaics, murals and sculptures in its stunning Great Hall. The **American Treasures** exhibit, on the second floor, includes a vast array of original documents and manuscripts, including Dr Martin Luther King Jr's "I Have a Dream" typescript

❶, ❷, ❸ & Cleveland Park ▲   ▲ ❹

KALORAMA RD.

ADAMS-MORGAN

Dumbarton Oaks Park

KALORAMA ROAD

CALIFORNIA STREET

Montrose Park

FLORIDA AVENUE

COLUMBIA ROAD

NEW HAMPSHIRE AVENUE

R STREET

S STREET ❻
❼

SHERIDAN CIRCLE

R STREET

29

Q STREET

DUPONT CIRCLE

6TH STREET ❾

Georgetown University

GEORGETOWN

Q STREET

P STREET

CONNECTICUT AVENUE

❿

⓫ DUPONT CIRCLE Ⓜ

P STREET

35TH STREET

33RD STREET

31ST STREET

30TH STREET

29TH STREET

28TH STREET

PROSPECT ST.

N STREET

POTOMAC PKWY

NEW HAMPSHIRE AVENUE

18TH STREET

SCOTT CIRCLE ⓬

⓭ ⓮

NEW DOWNTOWN

M STREET

16TH STREET

M STREET

⓯

THOMAS JEFFERSON ST.

⓰

23RD STREET

21ST STREET

FARRAGUT NORTH Ⓜ

MCPHERSON SQUARE

WHITEHURST FREEWAY

29

ROCK CREEK AND POTOMAC

WASHINGTON CIRCLE

K STREET

FARRAGUT WEST Ⓜ

PENNSYLVANIA AVENUE

I STREET ⓳

Francis Scott Key Memorial Bridge

FOGGY BOTTOM-GWU Ⓜ I STREET

George Washington University

H STREET

The White House

Potomac River

Little River

Theodore Roosevelt Island

⓴

21ST STREET

FOGGY BOTTOM

F STREET

19TH STREET

18TH STREET

17TH STREET

The Ellipse

66

Ⓜ ROSSLYN

GEORGE WASHINGTON MEMORIAL PKWY

Kennedy Center

㉑

VIRGINIA AVENUE

E STREET

E STREET

50

66

Department of State

C STREET

CONSTITUTION AVENUE

Theodore Roosevelt Bridge

Vietnam Veterans Memorial 🏛

Constitution Gardens

Washington Monument 🏛

Arlington Memorial Bridge

Lincoln Memorial 🏛

Korean War Veterans Memorial 🏛

INDEPENDENCE AVENUE

Holocaust Museum

Arlington National Cemetery

ARLINGTON CEMETERY Ⓜ

FDR Memorial 🏛

West Potomac Park

Tidal Basin

Bureau of Engraving & Printing

14th St Bridge

Jefferson Memorial 🏛

OHIO DRIVE

GEORGE WASHINGTON MEMORIAL PKWY

George Mason (14th St) Meml Bridge

US 1

Rochambeau Meml Bridge

JEFFERSON DAVIS HWY

BOUNDARY DRIVE

Pentagon

Ⓜ PENTAGON

SHIRLEY HIGHWAY

395

National Airport & Alexandria ▼

ACCOMMODATION

Adams Inn	4
Allen Lee Hotel	20
The Brenton	7
Brickskeller Inn	11
Doubletree Hotel Park Terrace	12
Embassy Inn	9
Four Seasons	15
Harrington Hotel	22
Hay-Adams Hotel	19
Hereford House	23
HI-Washington DC	18
India House Too	5
Kalorama Guest House	2
Monticello	16
Omni Shoreham	1
Simpkins' B&B	10
State Plaza	21
Swiss Inn	17
Tabard Inn	13
Topaz	14
The William Lewis House	8
Windsor Inn	6
Woodley Park Guest House	3

WASHINGTON DC

N

0   500 yds

Ⓜ Metro station

U STREET
CARDOZO Ⓜ

LEDROIT PARK

STREET

STREET

14TH STREET

SHAW-
HOWARD
UNIVERSITY Ⓜ

RHODE ISLAND AVENUE

R STREET

8

Q STREET

VERMONT AVENUE

9TH STREET

7TH STREET

P STREET

FLORIDA

LOGAN
CIRCLE

N STREET

MARYLAND AVENUE

NORTH CAPITOL ST

1ST STREET

AVENUE

MT VERNON
SQ-UDC Ⓜ

NEW JERSEY AVENUE

THOMAS
CIRCLE

M STREET

13TH STREET

12TH STREET

7TH STREET

50

MT. VERNON
SQUARE

1ST STREET

Greyhound
Bus Terminal

17

18

K STREET

K STREET

NORTH CAPITOL ST

1ST STREET

NEW YORK AVENUE

14TH STREET

13TH STREET

11TH STREET

Convention
Center

MASSACHUSETTS

AVENUE

3RD ST

395

H STREET

METRO CENTER Ⓜ

GALLERY
PLACE Ⓜ

9TH STREET

7TH STREET

6TH STREET

JUDICIARY
SQUARE Ⓜ

G STREET

UNION
STATION Ⓜ

Union
Station

F ST

2ND STREET

4TH STREET

6TH STREET

7TH STREET

22

PENNSYLVANIA AVENUE

OLD
DOWNTOWN

C STREET

1ST STREET

LOUISIANA AVENUE

DELAWARE AVE

Senate
Offices

D ST

STANTON
SQUARE

Ⓜ

1

FEDERAL TRIANGLE

Ⓜ

ARCHIVES-NAVY MEML

CONSTITUTION AVENUE

CAPITOL
HILL

MADISON DRIVE

The Mall

4TH ST

US Capitol

Library of
Congress

EAST CAPITOL STREET

JEFFERSON DRIVE

Ⓜ SMITHSONIAN

MARYLAND AVE

INDEPENDENCE AVENUE

N CAROLINA AVE

National Airport & Alexandria

12TH STREET

10TH STREET

9TH STREET

C STREET

FEDERAL
CENTER SW Ⓜ

2ND ST

WASHINGTON AVE

House
Offices

C STREET

SEWARD
SQUARE

D STREET

EASTERN
MARKET Ⓜ

L'ENFANT
PLAZA Ⓜ

E STREET

CAPITAL
SOUTH Ⓜ

NEW JERSEY

23

S CAROLINA AVE

E STREET

395

SOUTHWEST/
WATERFRONT

7TH STREET

I STREET

1ST STREET

SOUTH CAPITOL STREET

2ND STREET

SOUTHEAST FREEWAY

VIRGINIA AVENUE

G STREET

MAINE AVENUE

WATER STREET

K STREET

L STREET

M STREET

4TH STREET

NAVY YARD Ⓜ

Washington
Channel

Ⓜ WATERFRONT

4TH STREET

1ST STREET

N STREET

Washington
Navy Yard

Navy
Museum ■

Ohio Drive

East
Potomac
Park

OHIO DRIVE

6TH STREET

2ND STREET

P STREET

Anacostia River

Fort
McNair

Frederick
Douglass
Meml Bridge

ANACOSTIA Ⓜ

411

▼ Anacostia Museum

and architect Maya Lin's drawing of the Vietnam Veterans Memorial. Documents of special significance – those associated with Washington, Lincoln and Jefferson, among others – are shown in an environmentally controlled cabinet for short periods at a time. Free library **tours** – the only way to see the Jefferson Building – depart Monday to Saturday at 10.30am, 11.30am, 1.30pm and 2.30pm (with an additional tour at 3.30pm on weekdays), but are subject to change; check the information desk in the lobby of the Madison Building.

Supreme Court

First St NE and Maryland Ave NE; closest Metro stop is Union Station. Mon–Fri 9am–4.30pm. Admission free. ☎ *202/479-3211,* Ⓦ *www.supremecourtus.gov*
The **Supreme Court**, across from the US Capitol, is the nation's final arbiter of what is and isn't legal. Established in 1787, the court didn't receive its own building until 1935, when Cass Gilbert – architect of New York's Woolworth Building – designed this Corinthian masterpiece. The grand interior spaces, especially the marble and damask drapes of the courtroom itself – where guides give lectures (hourly, Mon–Fri 9.30am–3.30pm; free) when the court is not in session – make it worth climbing the gleaming white steps and going inside. Sessions run from October to June (Mon–Wed) and the cases to be heard are listed in the day's *Washington Post*. Sessions begin at 10am and last one hour per case. Arrive early to get one of the 150 seats, or join the separate line if you're happy to settle for a three-minute stroll through the standing gallery.

The Mall

One of the main features of L'Enfant's grand plan for Washington was a large central parkland. Today the two-mile-long **Mall** stretches west from the Capitol to the Potomac River. It wasn't always such a carefully manicured park, however: when the Capitol was built, it looked out across a muddy, bug-infested swamp and, by the 1870s, the south side was lined by meat-markets and warehouses and crisscrossed by railroad tracks. For a time a stark reminder of L'Enfant's unfulfilled dream, the Washington Monument was left unfinished for more than twenty years, an ugly stone stump cut off halfway.

The Mall has become DC's most popular green space, used for summer softball games and Fourth of July concerts. Yet its central role in a planned capital city also places it at the very heart of the country's political and social life. When there's a protest gesture to be made, the Mall is the place to make it, whether it's a demonstration by the Million Men marchers of black America, a mass prayer meeting of the Promise Keepers, or the unveiling of the commemorative AIDS Memorial Quilt. In addition to numerous museums, it boasts a quartet of presidential monuments, along with the White House and the powerful Vietnam and Korean war veterans memorials.

Washington Monument

15th St NW at Constitution Ave; closest Metro stop is Smithsonian. April–Aug daily 8am–midnight; Sept–March daily 9am–5pm. Admission free. Ⓦ *www.nps.gov/wamo*
The Mall's most prominent feature, the **Washington Monument** is an unadorned marble obelisk built in memory of George Washington. At 555ft it's the tallest all-masonry structure in the world. Volunteers started work on it in 1848, but various internal arguments, and later the Civil War, so disrupted construction that it wasn't completed until 1884. When the US Government took over the project in 1876, marble from a slightly different source was used; the transition line where work resumed at the 150ft level is readily apparent.

To visit the monument pick up a free ticket from the 15th Street kiosk (on the Mall, south of Constitution Ave), which allows you to turn up at a fixed time later in the day, or you can reserve with TicketMaster (☎1–800/505–5040; $1.50). The elevator up takes seventy seconds and deposits you at the 500ft level to enjoy the monument's panoramic 360° views of the city.

The White House

1600 Pennsylvania Ave NW; closest Metro stop is McPherson Square or Farragut West. Continuous free tours Tues–Sat 10am–noon; additional tours in summer. Tours (☎202/456-7041, ⓦ www.whitehouse.gov) start from the bleachers on the Ellipse, south of the White House. In winter simply join the queues. However, in spring and summer you must pick up tickets as early as possible (they've usually all gone by 8.30am – and on some days they've all been spoken for as early as 6.30am) from the Visitor Center at 1450 Pennsylvania Ave (daily 7.30am–4pm; ☎202/208-1631).

For nearly two hundred years, the **White House** has been the residence and office of the President of the United States. Standing at the edge of the Mall, due north from the Washington Monument, this grand, Neoclassical edifice was completed in 1800 by Irish immigrant James Hoban, who modeled it on the Georgian manors of Dublin. Each of its presidential occupants has made his mark: Thomas Jefferson added the first toilets, just before the British burned the place down in the War of 1812. It was quickly rebuilt and then expanded, often in such a hurry that the whole building was on the verge of collapse. Harry Truman had to move out for four years from 1948 while the structure was stabilized: all the rooms were dismantled and a modern steel frame was inserted. Truman also added the balcony to the familiar south side portico.

Though many visitors are surprised by how small and homey it is, security at the White House is every bit as tight as you'd imagine. Protesters are still allowed to set up camp opposite the main entrance, but the stretch of Pennsylvania Avenue immediately outside was closed to traffic in 1995, shortly after the bombing of a federal building in Oklahoma City.

White House **tours** consist of a lot of waiting around followed by a quick shuffle through the basement and up to the ground-floor reception rooms, then peeping in at a succession of plush, railed-off rooms filled with portraits of ex-presidents. In summer, the gardens are sometimes opened for afternoon tours, and at Christmas there are special evening tours of the festively decorated interior. US citizens may reserve tickets for a guided tour by contacting their Member of Congress – although this must be done well in advance.

If you're interested in the history of the place and its occupants, you may find the **Visitor Center**, a couple of blocks southeast on Pennsylvania Avenue, more rewarding than the White House itself. It's filled with photos and film footage of First Families and their distinguished guests, including a portly President Hoover playing "Hooverball" with a group of lumbering judges, and the Wright Brothers showing off their latest airplane. In one inaugural portrait after another, a drawn and exhausted president hands over power to his beaming successor.

Lincoln Memorial

West Potomac Park, at 23rd St between Constitution and Independence aves; closest Metro stop is Foggy Bottom–GWU. Daily 24hr, staffed 8am–midnight. Admission free. ⓦ www.nps.gov/linc/home.htm

At the far west end of the Mall, the **Lincoln Memorial** is modeled on a Doric temple, enclosed by a colonnade and fronted by a long reflecting pool. During the Civil Rights march on Washington in 1963, Dr King delivered his epic "I Have a Dream" speech here. Ironically, when this monument to the Great Emancipator was dedicated in 1922, the crowds were segregated by color – even black leader Dr Robert Moton, who gave an address, was forced to watch from a roped-off area to the side.

The Lincoln Memorial is a fitting tribute to the man who put down the southern rebellion during the Civil War and thereby preserved the Union and ended slavery in the US. A craggy likeness of Abraham Lincoln sits firmly grasping the arms of his throne-like chair, apparently deep in thought, while inscriptions of Lincoln's two most celebrated speeches – the Gettysburg Address and the Second Inaugural Address – are carved on the north and south walls.

Vietnam Veterans Memorial

Constitution Ave at 21st St NW; closest Metro stop is Foggy Bottom–GWU. Daily 24hr, staffed 8am–midnight. Admission free. Ⓦ *www.nps.gov/vive/home.htm*

Cutting sharply into the green lawn of the Mall, the small and simple **Vietnam Veterans Memorial** serves as a somber and powerful reminder of the nearly 60,000 US soldiers who died in Vietnam. The pathway that slopes down from the grass forms a gash in the earth, its increasing depth symbolizing the increasing involvement of US forces in the war. Alongside, a black marble wall is carved with the names of every soldier who died, in chronological order from 1959 to 1975.

The memorial was designed by Maya Lin, a 21-year-old architecture student. When it was first erected in 1982, there was some outcry from veterans' groups about its anti-war connotations. In 1984, to achieve a balance, a more traditional statue of three heroic soldiers was placed nearby, under a floodlit American flag. More lobbying led to the establishment in 1993 of the **Vietnam Women's Memorial**, which stands in a grove of trees at the east end of the main site; it honors the 11,000 American women who served in the conflict.

Korean War Veterans Memorial

West Potomac Park, south of Lincoln Memorial Reflecting Pool; closest Metro stop is Smithsonian. Daily 24hr, staffed 8am–midnight. Admission free. Ⓦ *www.nps.gov/kwvm/*

The **Korean War Veterans Memorial**, dedicated in 1995, incorporates a dramatic Field of Remembrance in which nineteen life-sized stainless steel combat troops advance across an open field toward the Stars and Stripes. Between 1950 and 1953, almost 55,000 Americans were killed in Korea (with 8000 more missing in action and more than 103,000 wounded). It's an affecting memorial to an often-forgotten conflict. The memorial lists 15 other countries that sent military forces to help prevent South Korea from falling to communism. A plaque at the flagstand proclaims: "Our nation honors her sons and daughters who answered the call to defend a country they never knew and a people they never met."

Jefferson Memorial

West Potomac Park, Tidal Basin near 15th St SW and Ohio Drive; closest Metro stop is Smithsonian. Daily 8am–midnight. Admission free. Ⓦ *www.nps.gov/thje/home.htm*

Completed in 1943 and modeled on his country home, Monticello (see p.450), the **Jefferson Memorial** consists of a shallow dome hovering over a bronze statue of Thomas Jefferson, the author of the Declaration of Independence and the third US president. The interior walls, encircled by an Ionic colonnade, are carved with Jefferson's words, and an inscription around the frieze reads: "I have sworn upon the altar of God eternal hostility against every form of tyranny over the mind of man."

The **Tidal Basin**, which fills most of the space between the Lincoln and Jefferson memorials, was created in order to prevent the western end of the Mall, including the spots where the two memorials sit, from being inundated by Potomac floods. The reflections off it are especially pretty in spring (usually early April), when the rows of Japanese cherry trees come out in full bloom.

FDR Memorial
West Potomac Park, south of the Korean Memorial, near the Tidal Basin. Daily 24hr, staffed 8am–midnight. Admission free. Ⓦ www.nps.gov/fdrm/home.htm

The **FDR Memorial** was opened in 1997, its four outdoor "gallery" rooms designed to highlight the achievements of Franklin Delano Roosevelt's twelve years as President. Bronze sculptures of FDR and his wife, Eleanor, along with waterfalls and remembrance pools, offset inscriptions from the president's best-known speeches. In a belated nod to the fact that FDR was crippled by polio (a fact kept from the American people throughout his presidency), it's the first memorial in DC purposely designed to be wheelchair-accessible.

The Smithsonian Institution

The cream of Washington DC's remarkable panoply of historical artifacts and fine art works comes under the general auspices of the **Smithsonian Institution**, which holds the US national collections of everything under the sun. Endowed by an Englishman – James Smithson, illegitimate son of the first Duke of Northumberland, who never even visited the US – the Smithsonian was established in 1846 "for the increase and diffusion of Knowledge." This broad brief is reflected in its impressive range of research centers and museums. Nine line up along the Mall, four more are just north, and the zoo is a few miles north beyond Rock Creek.

The original home of the Smithsonian, the 1849 Norman-style Smithsonian Institution Building, known as **The Castle**, stands on the Mall halfway between the Capitol and the Washington Monument. It was at first devoted to scientific research but, as the Smithsonian became more of a museum, the sheer accumulation of items necessitated the construction of the various other buildings along the Mall. The old Castle is now the Smithsonian headquarters and main **visitor center**, 1000 Jefferson Drive SW (daily 9am–5.30pm; ⊺202/357-2700), with the latest details on all the galleries available from the high-tech information desk. The ornate tomb of James Smithson (after death, he finally made it to the US) is in an alcove just off the Mall entrance, and the lovely flower-filled Enid A. Haupt Garden (daily: summer 7am–8pm; winter 7am–5.45pm) fronts the Castle on the south side. You can still get a feel for the days when the Smithsonian was known as "the nation's attic" by visiting the adjacent **Arts and Industries Building**, DC's first "National Museum," which once displayed the hundreds of objects sent here for safekeeping after the 1876 Centennial Exhibition in Philadelphia. Although some of the Victoriana artifacts remain on display, the building's main focus now is temporary exhibitions by the African-American History Center and the American Indian and Anacostia museums.

National Air and Space Museum

South side of the Mall between Fourth and Seventh sts SW; closest Metro stop is L'Enfant Plaza. ⓦ *www.nasm.si.edu*

The **National Air and Space Museum** is by far DC's most popular attraction, drawing nearly ten million people every year. Most of them may seem to be here on the day you come, but the hangar-like building can accommodate everyone without feeling crowded, and you can always see the hundreds of historic aircraft close up. Hanging from the rafters in the main entrance gallery, the "**Milestones in Flight**" include the handmade plane in which the **Wright Brothers** made the first powered flight in 1903; **Charles Lindbergh**'s *Spirit of St Louis*, which he flew solo across the Atlantic in 1927; the claustrophobic *Mercury* capsule in which **John Glenn** orbited the earth in 1962; and the ultralight *Voyager*, which flew around the world nonstop in 1986.

Most of the museum is taken up with exploring the space race from both American and Soviet perspectives, using models and actual spacecraft to show the development from Werner von Braun's V1 rockets up to a gawky-looking lunar module. "**Apollo to the Moon**" is one of the most fascinating galleries, centering on the Apollo 11 (1969) and 17 (1972) missions, the first and last, respectively. Check out Neil Armstrong's and Buzz Aldrin's spacesuits, navigation aids, space food, clothes and charts, and the astronaut's survival kit (complete with shark repellent). Further galleries include "**Rocketry and Space Flight**," a history of rocket propulsion dating to the twelfth century; "**Looking at Earth**," where the aerial photographs include Boston snapped from a balloon in 1860 and German castles recorded by camera-toting pigeons; and "**The Great War in the Air**," bursting with dogfighting biplanes.

The museum also shows a rotating program of super-large-screen **IMAX** movies ($6.50; ☎202/357-1686 for times), all of which have some connection with flying. The *Flight Line* **cafeteria** and the *Wright Place* **restaurant** enable star-struck families to stay in the building all day.

National Museum of Natural History

North side of the Mall, Tenth St NW and Constitution Ave; closest Metro stop is Smithsonian. ⓦ *www.mnh.si.edu*

The imposing three-story entrance rotunda of the **National Museum of Natural History** feels like the busiest and most boisterous crossroads in all of DC, with troops of screeching schoolkids endlessly chasing each other around a colossal African elephant. Hundreds of other stuffed animals, tracing evolution from fossilized four-billion-year-old plankton to dinosaurs' eggs and beyond, are on display all over the place – pick up floor plans and guides at the information desk at the elephant's feet.

Naturally enough, the "**Dinosaurs**" section is the most popular part of the museum, with hulking skeletons reassembled in imaginative poses and accompanied by informative text, written with a light touch, accessible to children. "**Exploring Marine Ecosystems**" uses videos, aquariums and the odd furry seal to illustrate life on the "Rocky Shore of Maine" and a "Coral Reef from the Caribbean." Nearby you can admire a rare specimen of the giant squid; scientists don't know quite where it lives, but reckon it grows to fifty feet in length.

Elsewhere, the museum seems firmly locked into a 1950s-style approach to natural history, with a lot of very dated anthropology. Displays on "**Native Cultures of the Americas**" include the Lucayans (originally from the Bahamas), said to have "vanished" shortly after encountering Columbus. Dioramas of the "primitive" pueblos of the Southwest stand alongside bison, bighorn sheep and other once-wild creatures. Similarly static exhibits cover peoples of the Pacific and Asia, as well as ancient Greece and Egypt.

Upstairs are hundreds of creepy-crawly critters – lizards, snakes, tarantulas and the like – as well as an **Insect Zoo**, filled with hundreds of bugs, which you can play with should you so desire. The museum also boasts a truly exceptional array of gemstones, including the legendary 45-carat **Hope Diamond** that once belonged to Marie Antoinette, on display in a new **Gem and Mineral Hall**, which features natural and reconstructed environments, interactive exhibits and hands-on specimens.

As at the Air and Space Museum, you'll also find a rotating selection of **IMAX** movies ($6.50; ☎202/663-7400 for times). As you'd expect, the films shown here portray more earth-bound themes, the massive screens plunging you far beneath the oceans or whisking you away to the Galapagos.

National Museum of American History

North side of the Mall, 14th St NW and Constitution Ave; closest Metro stop is Smithsonian. ⓦ *americanhistory.si.edu*
If you like kitsch, you won't want to miss the bizarre melange of cultural artifacts at the **National Museum of American History**. George Washington's wooden teeth, Muhammad Ali's boxing gloves, and the ruby slippers Judy Garland wore in *The Wizard of Oz* are set among didactic displays tracing the country's development. It's not so much a center for scholarly study as a sanctuary for vanishing Americana, incorporating Model T Fords, old post offices and even a restored, c.1900 ice-cream parlor, which still serves up banana splits.

As you enter from the Mall, directly onto the second floor, a display showcases the battered red, white and blue flag that inspired the US national anthem – the **Star-Spangled Banner** itself, which survived the British bombing of Baltimore harbor during the War of 1812. It's been under restoration for six years, a project slated for completion in 2002. Once restored, the relic will form the focus of a new display titled "For Which It Stands" and will presumably be shown in a manner conducive to its long-term preservation. The worthier exhibits are also on this floor: an account of the rural farm-based society of the early US stands across from an examination of the mass movement of African-Americans from Southern farms to the wartime industries of northern cities. A Woolworth lunch counter from Greensboro, North Carolina, evokes the sit-in of 1960. "American Encounters" focuses on New Mexico, looking at how tourism has affected communities such as the pueblo of Santa Clara and Hispanic Chimayo. On the first floor, the "**Information Age**" gallery traces communications from Morse's first telegraph to virtual reality tours of the Smithsonian. Separate galleries display in glorious profusion the artifacts and machines that have shaped modern America – from light bulbs and motorbikes to trains and atomic clocks. The top floor holds political memorabilia (much of it more than a century old), stamp and coin collections and old TV sets and typewriters. Two final outstanding exhibits inject a serious tone. "**Personal Legacy: the Healing of a Nation**" brings together some of the 25,000 items left by relatives at the Vietnam Memorial in DC. "**A More Perfect Union**" deals candidly with the shameful internment of Japanese-American citizens during World War II.

Hirshhorn Museum

South side of the Mall, Independence Ave at Seventh St SW; closest Metro stop is L'Enfant Plaza. Ⓦ *hirshhorn.si.edu/*

Housed in the most clearly modern building on the Mall – a windowless cylinder balanced on fifteen-foot stilts above a concrete plaza, looking like a spaceship poised for takeoff – the **Hirshhorn Museum and Sculpture Garden** holds an extensive collection of late nineteenth- and twentieth-century art. From the main entrance on Independence Avenue, escalators climb to the upper-floor galleries, where major works by Picasso, de Kooning, Mondrian, Pollock, Matisse and many more are on display. The gallery downstairs hosts touring exhibitions, and critically acclaimed films are shown in the evenings (Ⓣ202/357-1300 for details).

A stimulating collection of modern **sculpture** is displayed in an open-air garden across Jefferson Drive, on the Mall side of the museum. Alongside assorted Moores, Rodins, Smiths and Malliols are two expressive abstract figures by Marino Marini, and a stalwart *Yucatán Woman* by Mexican sculptor Francisco Zuniga. The landscaped garden, sunk below ground level, perhaps to spare members of Congress from having to look at modern art, is also a nice place for a picnic lunch.

National Museum of African Art

South side of the Mall at 950 Independence Ave SW; closest Metro stop is Smithsonian. Ⓦ *www.si.edu/nmafa*

Built in 1987, the curved and domed **National Museum of African Art** holds more than six thousand sculptures and artifacts, both spiritual and functional, from the numerous tribal cultures of sub-Saharan Africa. The permanent collection ranges from Nigerian carved-ivory cult figures to Zairean mother-and-child fertility fetishes and puppet heads from eastern Mali. Look out for an extraordinary seventeenth-century bronze from the Lower Niger, consisting of a vase swarmed over by eight bizarre chameleons, all cast in one piece. While the museum celebrates the "**Art of the Personal Object**," highlighting the grace of everyday objects such as combs and pipes, much of its sculpture is highly abstract, and its influence on the Cubists is obvious.

About half the space is devoted to changing exhibitions on specific regions, and the gift shop sells woven and dyed fabrics and clothes, as well as books and postcards.

Arthur M. Sackler Gallery

South side of the Mall at 1050 Independence Ave SW; closest Metro stop is Smithsonian. Ⓦ *www.asia.si.edu/*

The angular and pyramidal counterpart of the African Art museum, the **Arthur M. Sackler Gallery** contains art works and devotional objects from Asia and the Middle East. Most of the exhibitions are temporary, and occasionally draw from other museums' collections, so it's not possible to predict what will be on display at any one time. However, exhibitions might take in

Two important cogs in the Smithsonian system are closed for renovation until 2004. Separated from the main Mall galleries, the **Smithsonian American Art Museum**, Eighth and G streets NW (closest Metro stop is Gallery Place-Chinatown; Ⓦ www.nmaa.si.edu) may not get the traffic of the other museums, but it's perhaps the most worthwhile of all, and in the past has mounted thought-provoking shows. Opened in 1829, the museum was known as the National Gallery of Art before Andrew Mellon later usurped that name. Since 1968, it has shared the Greek Revival-style **Old Patent Office** with the National Portrait Gallery. The collection ranges from splendid nineteenth-century examples of "Art of the American West" – including almost 400 paintings by George Catlin, who spent six years on the Great Plains – to Revolutionary portraits and dramatic American landscapes. More recent pieces have been displayed on the top floor in the vaulted and colonnaded **Lincoln Gallery**, which in 1865 hosted President Lincoln's Inaugural Ball and remains one of DC's most celebrated interior spaces.

The **National Portrait Gallery** at Eighth and F streets NW (Ⓦ wwwnpg.si.edu) holds pretty much what you'd expect: paintings, sculptures and photographs of famous and not-so-famous people, from Pocahontas to Mark Twain, includes Gilbert Stuart's famous "Lansdowne" portrait of George Washington, as well as por-traits and sculptures of every president. There's also the odd masterpiece on show – like Edgar Degas' severe portrait of his friend, Impressionist Mary Cassatt.

Sackler's noted collection of translucent jade dragons and intricate, three-thousand-year-old bronzes from China; stone deities from India and Tibet; and lushly illustrated early Islamic texts from Iran, gorgeously colored in gilt, silver and crushed stone pigments. Inexpensive posters and prints are sold in the gift shop. Underground galleries – featuring temporary exhibitions – con-nect the Sackler to the Freer Gallery and the African Art museum.

Freer Gallery of Art

South side of the Mall, Jefferson Drive at 12th St SW; closest Metro stop is Smithsonian. Ⓦ *www.asia.si.edu/*
From the day it opened in 1923, the **Freer Gallery** has been one of the more unusual Smithsonian museums. Put together and paid for by railroad million-aire Charles Freer, it revolves around more than one thousand prints, drawings and paintings by London-based American artist **James McNeil Whistler** – the largest collection of his works anywhere. The collection also includes Chinese jades and bronzes, Byzantine illuminated manuscripts, Buddhist wall sculptures and pieces of Persian metalwork, all collected by Freer under Whistler's tutelage. Among other works are pieces by Whistler's contemporaries Winslow Homer, Albert Pinkham Ryder and John Singer Sargent.

In addition to his portraits and landscapes, Whistler is represented by an entire room – the **Peacock Room**. Its original owner commissioned Whistler to execute a painting for the mantelpiece; the artist later covered the walls and furnishings with blue and gold painted peacock feathers. His patron hated it, so Freer bought it and shipped it over from London (he also kept live peacocks in the museum's central courtyard).

The National Zoo

3001 Connecticut Ave NW; closest Metro stop is Woodley Park-Zoo. Buildings open daily May to mid-Sept 10am–6pm; rest of year 10am–4.30pm. Grounds daily May to mid-Sept 6am–8pm; rest of year 6am–6pm. Admission free. Ⓦ *www.si.edu/natzooo/*

Few people realize that the **National Zoo**, up in the north of town but a short walk from the Metro, forms part of the Smithsonian ensemble – which at least means that admission is free. It sprawls down the steep slopes of the gorge cut by Rock Creek, with trails through lush vegetation and comparatively humane simulations of the home environments of more than three thousand creatures. Among the zoo's star attractions are the **pandas** Mei Xiang and Tian Tian, who arrived from the People's Republic of China in December 2000. The pair fills the absence left by the passing of Ling Ling and Hsing Hsing, the famous pair presented by Beijing during Richard Nixon's 1972 visit. The best time to catch the duo is first thing in the morning. In addition to the expected menagerie of giraffes and elephants, birds and bees, and lions and tigers, the zoo (or BioPark as it likes to call itself) boasts an unusual feature in its **Think Tank**, where orangutans assemble, commuting to and from their cages as they please by means of overhead cables across public areas of the zoo.

Other museums and attractions

While you could easily spend a week wandering around the Smithsonian, the national collections are by no means the only worthwhile museums in DC – or, for that matter, along the Mall. The large **National Gallery of Art**, at the foot of the US Capitol, is the best art museum in the city, and one of the top ten in the world. In addition to more quality art galleries, you can tour various **federal buildings** – to watch the FBI track down criminals, or count brand-new dollar bills as they roll off the presses – or honor the nation's dead, including the Kennedy brothers, at **Arlington National Cemetery**.

National Gallery of Art

North side of the Mall, Constitution Ave between Third and Seventh sts NW; closest Metro stop is Archives-Navy Memorial. Mon–Sat 10am–5pm, Sun 11am–6pm. Admission free. ☎ 202/737-4215, ⓦ www.nga.gov

Though the visually stunning **National Gallery of Art**, the nearest of the Mall museums to the Capitol, is not in fact a government institution, it fully deserves its name. It owes its prominence to the efforts of the industrialist **Andrew Mellon**, who bought the building and donated most of the paintings. Many were purchased from the cash-poor post-revolutionary government of the USSR, where they had previously hung in the Hermitage in St Petersburg. Mellon's family has continued as benefactors, raising countless millions to build I.M. Pei's modernistic East Building in 1978.

The original Neoclassical gallery, designed by John Russell Pope in 1941, is now called the **West Building** and holds the bulk of the permanent collection. Parts of the collection are rotated or sent out on tour, and some rooms may be closed for renovation. To find a particular work, visit the interactive **Micro Gallery** in the West Building (main floor, Mall entrance).

From the domed central rotunda, where you can pick up a floor plan and gallery guide, a vaulted corridor runs the length of the building. If you only have limited time, latch onto one of the informative daily **free tours** – ask for a schedule at the information desk. Galleries to the west on the main floor display major works by Renaissance masters, arranged by nationality: half a dozen Rembrandts fill the **Dutch** gallery, Van Eyck and Rubens dominate the **Flemish**, and El Greco and Velázquez face off in the **Spanish**, near eight progressively darker Goyas. There's also the only Leonardo in the US, the 1474 *Ginevra de' Benci*, painted in oil on wood, plus works by Botticelli, Crivelli and Raphael – including the latter's celebrated *Alba Madonna* (1520), one of Mellon's purchases from the Hermitage. The other half of the West Building holds an exceptional collection of nineteenth-century **French** paintings – Gauguin from Pont-Aven to Tahiti, a couple of Van Goghs, some Monet studies of Rouen Cathedral and water lilies, Cézanne still lifes and the like. At either end of the building, the skylit, fountain-filled **Garden Courts** make an ideal place to rest weary feet, while Salvador Dalí's *The Last Supper* overlooks the escalators down to the café.

The triangular **East Building** houses **twentieth-century** paintings and sculpture. As in the Guggenheim in New York, the attention-grabbing spatial choreography of the architecture all but overpowers the works of art. You emerge from under the oppressively low entrance into a central atrium, from where an escalator, literally carved out of a 40ft granite wall, climbs to the main galleries – which, squeezed into the corners, can seem like an afterthought. Exhibitions change and go on tour throughout the year, so the bulk of the permanent collection is rarely on display. Nonetheless, you may catch Picasso's haunting *Family of Saltimbanques* and the very blue *The Tragedy*, as well as Giacometti bronzes and paintings, plenty of Alexander Calder (whose huge red-and-black mobile is usually in place), early Mirós, some Warhol soup cans and Chuck Close's *Fanny* – a finger painting *par excellence*. The underground concourse that links the two buildings contains a good bookstore, an espresso bar and a large cafeteria – topped by pyramidal skylights and bordered by a glassed-in waterfall.

National Archives

North side of the Mall at Seventh St and Constitution Ave NW; closest Metro stop is Archives-Navy Memorial. April to Labor Day daily 10am–9pm; rest of year daily 10am–5.30pm. Admission free. ☎ 202/501-5000, ⓦ www.archives.gov. The Archives' exhibit halls are closed for renovation until 2003.

On display at the **National Archives** are the three short texts upon which the United States is founded: the **Declaration of Independence**, the **Constitution** and the **Bill of Rights**. These three original sheets of parchment (three additional pages of the Constitution are not on display), drafted respectively in 1776, 1787 and 1789, are now contained in helium-filled glass cases, which drop underground in case of fire or other threat. You can usually look at them as long as you like, but if there's a crowd you have to shuffle on past. The impressive Neoclassical Greek temple – designed by John Russell Pope – also displays a 1297 revised copy of the **Magna Carta**, which established in Britain such basic concepts as trial by jury and equality before the law. The National Archives presents exhibitions and serves as the official repository of all US national records – census data, treaties (including the surrender of Japan in World War II), passport applications and genealogical records – most of which are kept in storage.

Federal Bureau of Investigation

On Pennsylvania Ave between Ninth and Tenth sts NW, just north of the Mall; closest Metro stop is Federal Triangle. Hour-long tours every 20–30min, Mon–Fri 8.45am–4.15pm, no reservations. Admission free. ☎ 202/324-3447, ⓦ www.fbi.gov

A fortress-like modern building on Pennsylvania Avenue holds the headquarters of the FBI – the **Federal Bureau of Investigation**, the nation's elite law-enforcement organization. Set up in 1908, the FBI came into its own chasing bootleggers and bank robbers like Al Capone and Machine Gun Kelly during the 1920s and 1930s. Hordes of visitors queue outside, sometimes for more than an hour, to join tours past displays on the infamous gangsters and dangerous subversives from whom the FBI shields the American people (they kept extensive files on Dr Martin Luther King Jr). Ideology aside (the FBI has only just begun to emerge from the shadow of its longtime iron-fisted director, J. Edgar Hoover), the tours rush you through an overview of fingerprinting, ballistics testing and other crime-fighting techniques. What really brings the crowds in, however, is the climactic display of sharpshooting and firepower: agents blast away at cut-out targets with a battery of small arms and automatic weapons.

Old Post Office

1100 Pennsylvania Ave NW, at 12th St. Closest Metro stop is Federal Triangle. Mid-April to mid-Sept Mon–Sat 10am–9pm, Sun noon–8pm; rest of year Mon–Sat 10am–7pm, Sun noon–8pm. Admission free. ☏ 202/289-4224, ⓦ www.oldpostofficedc.com

Built in 1899, the fanciful Romanesque **Old Post Office**, just across from the FBI, is one of the most recognizable of downtown's monuments. Its glorious galleried interior is now known as the Pavilion, in which guise it supports hundreds of shops, stalls and a food court. The more clued-up visitors make a bee-line here, rather than to the Washington Monument, for their first aerial view of the city. The **clock tower** (mid-April to mid-Sept daily 8am–11pm; closed Thurs 6.30–9.30pm; rest of year daily 10am–5.45pm; free; ☏202/606-8691) stands 270ft above Pennsylvania Avenue, and the glass elevator ride allows you to see the iron, glass and wood interior in all its fine glory.

Ford's Theater National Historic Site

511 Tenth St NW; closest Metro stop is Metro Center. Daily 9am–5pm; theater is closed during rehearsals or matinees, but Lincoln Museum and House Where Lincoln Died remain open. Admission free. ☏ 202/426-6924, ⓦ www.fordstheatre.org

Ford's Theater National Historic Site is a beautiful restoration of the nineteenth-century playhouse, which continues to stage regular productions of contemporary and period drama (see p.430). However, because of its role in one of the greatest national tragedies, it lives a double life as a tourist attraction in its own right. It was here, on April 14, 1865, a mere five days after the end of the Civil War, that **Abraham Lincoln** was shot by the actor and Southern sympathizer John Wilkes Booth during a performance of *Our American Cousin*.

Entertaining talks (hourly 9.15am–4.15pm; free) set the scene in the theater itself, after which you can file up to the circle for a view of the presidential box where it all happened, and finally go down to the basement **Lincoln Museum**. Macabre relics here include the clothes that Lincoln was wearing, Booth's .44 single-shot Derringer pistol and the assassin's diary, in which he wrote: "I hoped for no gain. I knew no private wrong. I struck for my country and that alone." The mortally wounded president was carried across the street to **The House Where Lincoln Died**, the Petersen House, where he died the next morning. That, too, is open to the public, who troop through its gloomy parlor rooms to see a replica of the bed on which Lincoln breathed his last.

Corcoran Gallery of Art

500 17th St NW; closest Metro stop is Farragut North or Farragut West. Mon, Wed & Fri–Sun 10am–5pm, Thurs 10am–9pm. Admission $5, free on Mon and on Thurs after 5pm. ☏ 202/639-1700, ⓦ www.corcoran.org/

Just down the street from the White House, the **Corcoran Gallery** is one of the oldest and most respected art museums in the US. It's also one of the nicest to visit in DC, with good guided tours (daily except Tues), an excellent gallery shop and a café that features rousing gospel Sunday brunches. Especially strong on American art – from frontier artists like Remington and Bierstadt, to portraiture by Mary Cassatt and Thomas Eakins, and modern works by Calder, Warhol and Rothko – it also includes a sampling of Dutch masters, medieval tapestries and French Impressionists. In the Salon Doré (Gilded Room), an eighteenth-century Parisian interior has been re-created to stunning effect, with floor-to-ceiling hand-carved paneling, gold-leaf decor and ceiling murals.

US Holocaust Memorial Museum

100 Raoul Wallenburg Place SW, off 14th St at Independence Ave. Closest Metro stop is Smithsonian. Daily 10am–5.30pm. Admission free. ☎ 202/488-0400, ⓦ www .ushmm.org

Nothing in DC is more disturbing than the large and generously laid-out **US Holocaust Memorial Museum**. Commemorating the persecution and murder of six million Jews by the Nazis, it places Hitler in historical perspective while personalizing the suffering of the individual victims.

In addition to case after case of newspapers and newsreels documenting Nazi activities from the early 1930s through the "Final Solution," reconstructions and in many cases actual relics of Warsaw Ghetto streets, railroad cattle-cars and concentration camp barracks fill the top floors. The sheer numbers of people killed is chillingly evoked throughout, first by a whole room filled with shoes stolen from deportees, later by a crisp glass wall etched with the names of the hundreds of Eastern European Jewish communities wiped off the map.

Tickets for specific entry times are available free of charge from 10am each day – with a limit of four per person – at the 14th Street entrance. You can also reserve in advance through Tickets.com (☎1-800/400-9373; fee charged). If you arrive without a ticket any later than mid-morning, you're unlikely to get into the permanent exhibition, but a certain number of temporary displays are usually open to all visitors.

The Bureau of Engraving and Printing

One block south of the Mall at 14th and C sts SW; closest Metro stop is Smithsonian. Mon–Fri 9am–2pm (with extended evening hours from 5–7pm in summer); May–Aug arrive early to pick up a timed ticket; Sept–April no ticket necessary. Closed Christmas to New Year. Admission free. ☎ 202/622-2000, ⓦ www.moneyfactory.com/

In most ways, a tour of the **Bureau of Engraving and Printing** is like visiting any other printing plant. The difference is that the presses here crank out millions of dollars in currency every day, $120 billion a year. It's a surprisingly low-tech operation: the bills come off in huge sheets, which are sliced up into single bills by ordinary paper cutters, checked for defects and loaded into large wheelbarrows. The Bureau also produces all US postage stamps. A short film explains the basics of intaglio printing, and you can watch it all happen from a glassed-in upstairs gallery.

Phillips Collection

1600 21st St at Q St NW; closest Metro stop is Dupont Circle. Tues–Wed 10am–5pm, Thurs 10am–8.30pm, Fri–Sat 10am–5pm, Sun noon–5pm. Admission $7.50. ☎ 202/387-2151, ⓦ www.phillipscollection.org

The **Phillips Collection**, one of the country's most extensive assemblies of modern paintings, starts off with a variety of proto-modern artists such as El Greco and Turner, before hurrying via French Impressionism to the real heart of the show – hundreds of works by Picasso, Matisse, Kandinsky, Van Gogh,

Rothko, O'Keeffe, Klee and many others. The building adds to the experience: part is displayed in the Phillips family's ornate 1890s mansion, the rest in a 1960s purpose-built gallery space, all of it recently renovated. Popular free concerts take place in the oak-paneled Music Room on Sundays (Sept–May 5pm); reserve in advance for free gallery tours on Wednesdays and Saturdays at 2pm and free gallery talks on the first and third Thursdays of the month at 12.30pm.

National Museum of Women in the Arts

1250 New York Ave NW; closest Metro stop is Metro Center. Mon–Sat 10am–5pm, Sun noon–5pm. Suggested donation $5. ☎ 202/783-5000, ⓦ www.nmwa.org

Housed in a converted Masonic Temple, the **National Museum of Women in the Arts**, which opened in 1987, is the country's only museum dedicated to women artists. It includes hundreds of works by "unknown" painters – a policy inspired by the fact that, as recently as the 1960s, not one female artist was mentioned in the leading American art history textbook. It also features sculptures by Barbara Hepworth and Camille Claudel (Rodin's mistress and assistant) and paintings by Helen Frankenthaler, Georgia O'Keeffe, Mary Cassatt and Elaine de Kooning – and has one of DC's better museum cafés, the *Mezzanine Café*.

Washington National Cathedral

Massachusetts and Wisconsin aves NW. Bus #30, #32, #34 or #36 from Pennsylvania Ave (downtown) or Wisconsin Ave (Georgetown), or #N2, #N4 or #N6 from Farragut Square. Mon–Fri 10am–5pm, Sat 10am–4.30pm, Sun 8am–4.30pm (open until 9pm on weekdays May–Sept). Suggested donation $3. ☎ 212/537-6200, ⓦ www.cathedral.org/cathedral.

The twin towers of **Washington National Cathedral** – the world's sixth largest cathedral – are visible long before you reach the church's perch on the heights of Mount St Alban in the northwest of town. Built from Indiana limestone and modeled entirely in the medieval English Gothic style, the Protestant church took 83 years to build and measures more than a tenth of a mile from the west end of the nave to the high altar at the opposite end. Among other things, you'll find the sarcophagus of **Woodrow Wilson**, the only president to be buried in the District, and the **Space Window**, whose stained glass incorporating a sliver of moon rock commemorates the flight of Apollo 11. From the south porch (near the Washington statue), an elevator ascends to the **Pilgrim Observation Gallery**, which affords stupendous city views.

For a floor plan and information, descend to the crypt floor, where there's an **information desk** and gift shop. **Guided tours** are available on request at the west entrance (Mon–Sat 10am–3.15pm, Sun 12.30–2.30pm; suggested donation $3); ask one of the purple-hatted docents.

Arlington National Cemetery

Across the Potomac River in Arlington, Virginia; closest Metro stop is Arlington Cemetery. April–Sept daily 8am–7pm; rest of year daily 8am–5pm. Admission free. ☎ 703/695-3250, ⓦ www.arlingtoncemetery.org

The vast sea of identical white headstones on the hillsides of **Arlington National Cemetery** is a poignant contrast to the grand monuments of the capital. The country's most honored final resting place was first used during the Civil War, when the grand mansion at the top of the hill, and all the surrounding land, belonged to Confederate leader **Robert E. Lee**. Nearly 200,000 US war dead lie here. Soldiers who died in world wars I and II, Korea and Vietnam are buried in the **Tomb of the Unknowns.** An eternal flame marks the grave of **President John F. Kennedy**, near his brother Robert and next to his widow, Jacqueline Kennedy Onassis. The gravesite of Pierre L'Enfant offers a superb view over the Mall and the District that he designed. The new **Women in Military Service Memorial**, by the main gate, is one of several **memorials** to celebrated personnel.

Unless you have strong legs and lots of time, the best way to see the vast cemetery is by Tourmobile (see p.405), which leaves from the visitor center at the entrance. You can also walk here from the Lincoln Memorial across the Arlington Bridge.

The Pentagon

Across the Potomac along I-395. Closest Metro stop is Pentagon. Mon–Fri 9.30am–5pm, last tour 3.30pm. Admission free. ☎ *703/695-1776,* ⓦ *www.defenselink .mil/pubs/pentagon/*

The headquarters of the US military establishment is one of the world's largest chunks of architecture: though it's only five stories tall, the total floor area – 6.5 million square feet – is three times that of the Empire State Building. Each of the five sides is more than 900ft long, and the combined length of all the internal corridors exceeds seventeen miles. These and other useless factoids are about all you get from visiting the behemoth building, apart from the opportunity to see at firsthand the people responsible for thwarting the country's adversaries. In the one novel departure from the norm, the service-personnel guides who accompany you walk backward the entire time to ensure that foreign agents posing as gawking tourists don't slip off into the restrooms.

Ninety-minute **guided tours** used to leave every thirty minutes from the small waiting area inside the entrance. Nowadays, you should call ahead to check on the status of tourist visits. Tours were suspended indefinitely after September 11, 2001, when terrorists crashed a hijacked airplane into the Pentagon, killing nearly two hundred people and destroying a sizable section of the building.

The Newseum

1101 Wilson Blvd, Arlington, VA. Closest Metro stop is Rosslyn. Wed–Sun 10am–5pm. Admission free. ☎ *703/284-3544,* ⓦ *www.newseum.org*

Under the auspices of the Freedom Forum, in whose headquarters it stands, the **Newseum** provides an interactive look at the history, theory and practice of news. A 126-foot-long video wall displays live satellite newsfeeds and daily front pages from around the world, and the News History Gallery features a storyboard timeline with historic front pages (*Jesse James Assassinated! Nixon Resigns!*). If you can beat the crowds, try your hand at editing, reporting or TV announcing. Outside, the **Freedom Park** (daily dawn to dusk; free) features various "icons" of freedom – parts of the Berlin Wall, a South African ballot box, and a toppled statue of Lenin among them. The world's first **Journalists Memorial**, a 24-foot-high spiraling glass prism, is etched with the names of nearly a thousand journalists killed while reporting. The Newseum is scheduled to move to downtown DC in 2005.

Eating

Just as the faces in government change with every election, so too do **restaurants** come and go more quickly in Washington DC than just about anywhere else in the US. Within this constant flux a few longstanding favorites endure.

Certain neighborhoods – Connecticut Avenue around **Dupont Circle**, 18th Street and **Columbia Road** in **Adams–Morgan**, M Street in **Georgetown** and downtown's **Seventh Street** and **Chinatown** – always seem to hold a good range of dining options. There are handy **food courts** in Union Station and at the Old Post Office and National Place, the last two both on Pennsylvania Avenue. A few citywide chains, like *Teaism*, *Firehook* and the *Chesapeake Bagel Bakery*, offer good coffee and quick snacks; otherwise, the cafés in the main museums are good for downtown lunch breaks.

Downtown

America Union Station, 50 Massachusetts Ave NE ☎202/682-9555; Union Station Metro. The huge, reasonably priced menu has been culled from all over the US. Choose between the double-decker restaurant inside and the concourse seating outside.

The Breadline 1751 Pennsylvania Ave NW ☎202/822-8900; Farragut West Metro. DC's best sandwiches are made with DC's best bread. Mon–Fri 7am–6pm.

Café Asia 1134 19th St NW ☎202/659-2696; Farragut North Metro. Situated in an old townhouse, the café serves excellent value dishes such as sashimi, Thai noodles and lemongrass-grilled chicken. Sushi happy hour Mon–Sat 5.30–7.30pm.

Coco Loco 810 7th St NW ☎202/289-2626; Gallery Place-Chinatown Metro. An in-crowd restaurant with a choice of superb Mexican tapas (snacks and appetizers) and all-you-can-eat Brazilian grills.

District Chophouse & Brewery 509 7th St NW ☎202/347-3434; Gallery Place-Chinatown Metro. This classy swing-era joint delivers great music, a grillhouse menu and good house beers on tap.

Grillfish 1200 New Hampshire Ave NW ☎202/331-7310; Dupont Circle or Foggy Bottom-GWU Metro. One of the best finds in DC offers casual dining, perfectly cooked fish and seafood and excellent desserts.

Jaleo 480 7th St NW ☎202/628-7949; Gallery Place-Chinatown Metro. Call in early for a glass of wine and nibbles, because the notoriously long waits at this fashionable, upscale tapas bar can spoil an otherwise perfect evening.

Malaysia Kopitiam 1827 M St NW ☎202/833-6232; Dupont Circle or Farragut North Metro. A no-frills basement eatery, where the extensive selection of Malay, Chinese and Indian fare is a first-class ticket to Southeast Asia.

The Mark 401 7th St NW ☎202/783-3133; Gallery Place-Chinatown Metro. This chic and expensive spot features seasonal menus of New American cuisine and a select choice of wines by the glass.

Old Ebbitt Grill 675 15th St NW ☎202/347-4801; Metro Center Metro. At this very plush, old-style downtown tavern, check out the immaculate mahogany bar, gilt mirrors and stylish clientele. Serves everything from burgers to oysters.

Oodles Noodles 1120 19th St NW ☎202/293-3138; Farragut North Metro. A lunch-crowd favorite serving flavorful, hearty bowls of noodles on the cheap. Closed Sun.

Red Sage 605 14th St NW ☎202/638-4444; Metro Center Metro. This renowned and expensive Southwestern restaurant (reservations essential) drips with Santa Fe chic, but you can also eat for less at the funky *Chili Bar*.

Reeve's Restaurant and Bakery 1306 G St NW ☎202/628-6350; Metro Center Metro. A classic daytime diner turns out big fried breakfasts, crisp-coated chicken at lunchtime and strawberry pies. Mon–Sat 7am–6pm.

Sholl's Colonial Cafeteria 1990 K St NW ☎202/296-3065; Farragut West Metro. The last of a disappearing breed – a remarkably cheap self-service café – dishes up home-cooked food, cakes and pies to long lines. Mon–Sat 7am–10.30am, 11am–2.30pm & 4–8pm.

Sky Terrace *Washington Hotel*, 515 15th St NW ☎202/638-5900; Metro Center Metro. From its hilltop perch above the White House, the restaurant has magnificent views that more than make up for the unremarkable food. May–Oct only.

Zuki Moon 824 New Hampshire Ave NW ☎202/333-3312; Foggy Bottom-GWU Metro. A spiffy Japanese-style noodle bar offering great-value noodle soups, tempura appetizers and green-tea ice cream. Closed Sat & Sun lunch.

Dupont Circle

Dupont Circle Metro is the nearest stop for all the places listed below.

Afterwords Café 1517 Connecticut Ave NW ☎202/387-1462. In the back of Kramerbooks (hence the punny name), the café serves imaginative meals and a fine Sunday brunch. It's open late every night and all night Fri & Sat, with live music Wed–Sat.

Annie's Paramount Steakhouse 1609 17th St NW ☎202/232-0395. This easy-going steakhouse, an institution in the Dupont gay scene, is open all-night Fri & Sat, when midnight brunch is served.

Bistro du Coin 1738 Connecticut Ave NW ☏202/234-6969. Visit a rare treat in DC – a classic bistro with a superb bar, boisterous atmosphere and genuine French food. Closed Mon.

Café Citron 1343 Connecticut Ave NW ☏202/530-8844. Bright restaurant serving tasty Caribbean-influenced Latin food – try the ceviche or fill up on one of their popular fajitas. Stick around for a smooth late-night scene at the bar.

Cyberstop Café 1513 17th St NW ☏202/234-2470. One of DC's few cybercafés, this laid-back neighborhood coffee shop serves good coffee, cakes and bagels with seating inside the arty townhouse or out on the sidewalk.

Johnny's Half Shelf 2002 P St NW ☏202/296-2021. Retro 1920s decor and a swank marble bar sit well with this bistro's down-to-earth menu, which features local seafood specialties. Closed Sun.

Lauriol Plaza 1801 18th St NW ☏202/387-0035. Lines form early in this packed, family-run Mexican–Spanish restaurant, renowned for its excellent food.

Luna Grill & Diner 1301 Connecticut Ave NW ☏202/835-2280. A quirky, comfy diner with wholesome blue-plate specials, "green plate" (vegetarian) dishes and organic coffees and teas; also makes an excellent weekend brunch spot.

The Newsroom 1803 Connecticut Ave NW ☏202/332-1489. The newsstand offers a wide selection of hipster magazines, British and French imports and hard-to-find newspapers plus internet access, coffee and snacks.

Pizzeria Paradiso 2029 P St NW ☏202/223-1245. Arguably DC's best pizzeria, with thunderingly good food, affordable house wine and a charming atmosphere – though you can expect to wait in line.

Sushi Taro 1507 17th St NW ☏202/462-8999. The steady stream of Japanese suits seeking a taste of home testifies that this is indeed one of DC's best Japanese restaurants. Closed Sat & Sun lunch.

Zorba's Café 1612 20th St NW ☏202/387-8555. A self-serve café where you'll find filling Greek combo platters, kebabs and pita-bread sandwiches. The sidewalk seating is hard to get in summer.

Adams-Morgan

Nearest Metros for Adams-Morgan are Woodley Park-Zoo or Dupont Circle.

Bukom Café 2442 18th St NW ☏202/265-4600. Wash down delicious West African dishes – such as *obe ila*, a soup with okra and smoked fish, and *nkatikwan*, chicken with peanuts (figure $10) – with African beer and music.

Cashion's Eat Place 1819 Columbia Rd NW ☏202/797-1819. A chef's restaurant, *Cashion's* serves fabulous – and expensive – New American cuisine. Book ahead or sip a proper cocktail at the very chic bar while you wait. Closed Mon. Dinner only.

The Diner 2453 18th St NW ☏202/232-8800. It's more stylish café than down-at-the-heels diner, but with greasy classics adorning the eggs-and-sandwich-rich menu, classic coffee counter and 24hr service, it's a winner.

Meskerem 2434 18th St NW ☏202/462-4100. At the District's favorite Ethiopian hangout, the *messob* platter gives you a taste of everything.

Meze 2437 18th St NW ☏202/797-0017. A wide array of delicious Turkish mezze (the Middle East's answer to tapas) is served up hot or cold in a fashionable setting.

Mixtec 1792 Columbia Rd NW ☏202/332-1011. The great-tasting, low-priced Mexican food includes superb tacos and tortillas, plus spit-roasted chicken, mussels steamed with chilis and a soothing *menudo*.

Pasta Mia 1790 Columbia Rd NW ☏202/328-9114. Expect long lines at this no-frills, family-run pasteria, which piles on the pasta at prices so low it's worth the wait. Mon–Sat 6.30pm–11pm.

Pizza Mart 2445 18th St NW ☏202/234-9700; Woodley Park-Zoo Metro. The elephantine slices at this hole-in-the-wall pizzeria are a club hopper's late night salvation. Open until 3am.

Rocky's Café 1817 Columbia Rd NW ☏202/387-2580. This easy-going bistro serving Creole–Cajun and Caribbean food is a solid choice in the Adams–Morgan scene – especially if you're in the mood for a laid-back Saturday brunch. Closed on Sun and for lunch Mon–Fri.

Saigonnais 2307 18th St NW ☏202/232-5300. The gourmet-quality Vietnamese food includes such specialties as whole steamed fish and an amazing fish soup. The food is worth the slightly higher prices.

Georgetown

Buses #30, #32, #34, #35 or #36 from Pennsylvania Ave NW; or Foggy Bottom-GWU Metro and a 20min walk.

Amma Vegetarian Kitchen 3291 M St NW ☏202/625-6625. A scrumptious haven for strict vegetarians, this South Indian joint specializes in *dosa* – lentil and rice flour wraps – but also has very good curries and yummy breads.

Au Pied de Cochon 1335 Wisconsin Ave NW ☏202/333-5440. This casual, enjoyable 24hr bistro offers conservatory dining, breakfasts and great-value early-bird dinners (around $10).

Café la Ruche 1039 31st St NW ☎ 202/965-2684. Seek out this relaxing, inexpensive bistro away from M Street's maddening crowds, with patio seating ideal for dining alone or in twos. Count on the onion soup, quiches and croques or drop by for a pastry and an espresso. Open until 10pm (weekends until midnight).

Dean & Deluca 3276 M St NW ☎ 202/342-2500. The conservatory-style café and attached deli-market are in one of Georgetown's handsomest redbrick buildings. Open until 8pm (weekends 10pm).

Enriqueta's 2811 M St NW ☎ 202/338-7772. A creative menu (by DC standards) showcases authentic Mexican food – try the generous mussels appetizer – and excellent margaritas. Closed Sat lunch and Sun.

J Paul's 3218 M St NW ☎ 202/333-3450. The best of Georgetown's saloons is not cheap, but worth it for the famous crab cakes and house-brewed Amber Ale.

Old Glory 3139 M St NW ☎ 202/337-3406. At this rollicking barbecue restaurant – a good-time place with live R&B bands three nights a week – hickory smoke rises in earnest from the kitchen.

Paolo's 1303 Wisconsin Ave NW ☎ 202/333-7353. Designer Italian dining – gourmet pizzas and even better pasta – is your reward. Compete for the few sidewalk tables.

Saigon Inn 2928 M St NW ☎ 202/337-5588. Bargain lunch deals bring in the crowds – though the Vietnamese food is a bit too Westernized to be authentic.

Red Ginger 1564 Wisconsin Ave NW ☎ 202/965-7009. The colorful Caribbean bistro brings a splash of the islands to Georgetown, with plenty of rum for everyone. Dinner only.

Upper Northwest

Spices 3333 Connecticut Ave NW ☎ 202/686-3833; Cleveland Park Metro. Stylish Pan-Asian restaurant serving everything from stir-fried basil chicken to sushi.

Lebanese Taverna 2641 Connecticut Ave NW ☎ 202/265-8681; Woodley Park-Zoo Metro. The delicious Middle Eastern joint lures with soothingly dark, authentic decor inside and ample sidewalk tables under shady umbrellas outside.

Nam Viet 3419 Connecticut Ave NW ☎ 202/237-1015; Cleveland Park Metro. You really can't go wrong at this no-frills Vietnamese spot: excellent food, heaping portions, extensive menu and exceptionally low prices.

Woodley Café 2619 Connecticut Ave NW ☎ 202/332-5773; Woodley Park-Zoo Metro. This roomy neighborhood café/bar attracts a mellow crowd. Breakfast and Sunday brunch are good, there's a full menu for lunch and dinner.

Entertainment and nightlife

DC's **bar** and **nightlife** scene is less developed than in more settled cities. Peak times for drinking tend to be the rush hours, and comparatively few people who work in the District during the week venture back into town at the weekend. However, things are slowly improving, and in the well-worn haunts of collegiate **Georgetown**, yuppified **Dupont Circle** and boisterous **Adams-Morgan** you should be able to pass a pleasant evening or two. For clubs, expect to pay a cover of $5 to $15 (highest at weekends); ticket prices for most gigs run $5 to $20. See the free weekly *CityPaper* for up-to-date **listings** of music, theater and other events in the area – as well as good alternative features and reporting. The *Washington Blade* and *Metro Weekly* focus on **gay** and **lesbian** life, which is at its most outgoing in Dupont Circle.

Badlands 1415 22nd St NW ☎ 202/296-0505; Dupont Circle Metro. The popular gay dance club, at its best on Friday and Saturday nights, draws a party crowd.

Bedrock Billiards 1841 Columbia Rd NW ☎ 202/667-7665. A comfortable, lively subterranean setting, top bartenders and loyal clientele set this funky pool hall apart from Adams–Morgan's more frenzied club scene.

The Big Hunt 1345 Connecticut Ave NW ☎ 202/785-2333; Dupont Circle Metro. More than 25 brews on tap and a good jukebox draw a groovy crowd.

The Black Cat 1811 14th St NW ☎ 202/667-7960; U St-Cardozo Metro. Showcases new bands and veteran alternative acts. The separate bar has no cover charge.

Blue Room 2321 18th St NW ☎ 202/332-0800. Classier than the typical Adams-Morgan fare, this swank venue boasts a bar worthy of Bogart's elbows.

Blues Alley 1073 Wisconsin Ave NW (rear) ☎202/337-4141. The small, celebrated Georgetown jazz bar, in business for more than thirty years, attracts top names. Book in advance.
The Brickskeller 1523 22nd St NW ☎202/293-1885; Dupont Circle Metro. Brick-lined basement saloon serves "the world's largest selection of beer" – more than 800 different types.
Capitol City Brewing Company 1100 New York Ave NW ☎202/628-2222; Metro Center Metro. DC's oldest microbrewery serves a changing menu of beers to an excitable crowd; there's a branch at 2 Massachusetts Ave NE, near Union Station.
Chi-Cha Lounge 1624 U St NW ☎202/234-8400; U St-Cardozo Metro. This upscale candlelit lounge oozes atmosphere, with live Latin music and regulars toking on fruit-cured tobacco from Middle Eastern-style hookahs.
The Common Share 2003 18th St NW ☎202/588-7180. The young set loads up on the District's cheapest pints and drinks at this welcoming if gritty dive before pushing on to the Adams–Morgan scene.
The Dubliner 520 N Capitol St NW, at the *Phoenix Park* ☎202/737-3773; Union Station Metro. At this bare-bones Irish bar, go for the Guinness on draft, live music and boisterous conversation.
Eighteenth Street Lounge 1212 18th St ☎202/466-3922; Dupont Circle Metro. An ultrahip club is housed discreetly in Teddy Roosevelt's former mansion, where the beats – mostly acid jazz, dub and trip-hop – are always smooth. Dress the part.
ESPN Zone 555 12th St NW ☎202/783-3776; Metro Center Metro. The sports empire's DC branch has hundreds of TVs – even above the urinals – all tuned into the games of the moment.
Fox and Hounds 1537 17th St NW ☎202/232-6307; Dupont Circle Metro. Smack in the middle of the 17th Street scene, this easygoing bar draws a diverse crowd, all there to enjoy the very stiff and very cheap rail drinks. Hit the patio in the summer.
Hawk and Dove 329 Pennsylvania Ave SE ☎202/543-3300; Capitol South Metro. The famous old pub rolls on with a battered bar and a young, loud crowd.
Habana Village 1834 Columbia Rd NW ☎202/462-6310. The intoxicating Latin dance

joint is infused with the eclectic spirit of the Adams–Morgan of old.
Irish Times 14 F St NW ☎202/543-5433; Union Station Metro. A crowded but comfortable pub, popular with Hill staffers and college students, offering a good range of beers and above-average bar food.
Lucky Bar 1221 Connecticut Ave NW ☎202/331-3733; Farragut North or Dupont Circle Metro. This everybody-knows-your-name kind of place has plenty of room and booths at the back to hang out in and shoot pool, plus $1 beer nights and English soccer on TV.
Nation 1015 Half St SE ☎202/554-1500; Navy Yard Metro. This mid-sized warehouse concert venue that doubles as a dance club boasts guest DJs from around the globe. The 18-and-over crowd raves at Buzz on Fridays, while Saturday's Velvet Nation is a favorite on the gay scene. Take a cab home as the neighborhood is not the place to linger.
Mr Smith's 3104 M St NW ☎202/333-3104. The brick-walled saloon bar on the Georgetown drag serves up decent burgers and beer and live bands Fri & Sat.
9:30 Club 815 V St NW ☎202/393-0930; U St-Cardozo Metro. An excellent indie, rock and pop venue, which also has a good bar.
Polly Esther's 605 12th St NW ☎202/737-1970; Metro Center Metro. Enthusiastic retro club, with multiple dance floors celebrating the hits of the 70s, 80s and 90s.
Red 1802 Jefferson Place NW ☎202/466-3475; Dupont Circle Metro. Hipsters show up well past midnight at this underground hideout to dance to deep house beats, often until dawn.
Rumba 2443 18th St NW ☎202/588-5501. Great Latin bands tuck into a tight space to set the atmosphere at this funky bar-restaurant.
Republic Gardens 1355 U St NW ☎202/232-2710; U St-Cardozo Metro. Hip-hop, soul and jazz vie for attention in one of U St's hottest clubs.
Sequoia 3000 K St NW ☎202/944-4200. The popular restaurant-bar at the eastern end of Washington Harbor provides outdoor terrace seating overlooking the river.
The Tombs 1226 36th St NW ☎202/337-6668. Basement Georgetown haunt for burgers and beers.

Culture and sports

With five different theater spaces, the **Kennedy Center**, 2700 F St NW (☎202/467-4600, ⓦwww.kennedy-center.org; Foggy Bottom Metro), next to the Watergate complex, hosts most of the capital's highbrow cultural events (including Washington Opera and Washington Ballet Company performances). It also presents nightly **film** screenings organized by the American Film

Institute (☎202/785-4600). The highly regarded, often pioneering **Arena Stage**, Sixth Street and Maine Avenue SW (☎202/488-3300, ⓦwww.arenastage.org; Waterfront Metro), puts on contemporary **theater** and performance pieces at its three-stage complex, while the historic **Ford's Theatre**, 511 Tenth St NW (☎202/426-6924; Metro Center Metro), has a family-friendly program of mainstream musicals and dramas, frequently historical in nature. The celebrated **Shakespeare Theatre**, 450 Seventh St NW (☎202/547-1122, ⓦwww.shakespearedc.org; Archives-Navy Memorial Metro), stages four productions a year, plus a free summer performance in Rock Creek Park. The experimental **Woolly Mammoth Theatre**, 1401 Church St NW (☎202/393-3939, ⓦwww.woollymammoth.net; Dupont Circle Metro), and the **Source Theatre Company**, 1835 14th St NW (☎202/462-1073; U St-Cardozo Metro), the anchor of DC's alternative theater scene, are also worth seeking out.

Out of the city, **Wolf Trap Farm Park**, 1551 Trap Rd, Vienna, VA (ⓦwww.wolftrap.org), is the country's first national park for the performing arts, presenting concerts, opera, ballet and dance at the outdoor **Filene Center** (☎703/255-1860) or the indoor **Barns** (☎703/938-2404). There's a Metro-shuttle bus service for most performances. For half-price, same-day theater **tickets**, call ☎202/TICKETS or visit the TicketPlace booth on the ground floor of the Old Post Office Pavilion on Pennsylvania Avenue NW; otherwise TicketMaster (☎202/432-7328 or 1-800/551-7328, ⓦwww.ticketmaster.com) has full-price tickets for all arts, music and sports events.

Tickets to the Washington Redskins **football** games at FedEx Field, just inside the Capital Beltway in Landover, Maryland (☎301/276-6050, ⓦwww.redskins.com/), are sold on a season ticket basis only. You'll have better luck catching the DC United **soccer** team at RFK Stadium, 2400 E Capitol St SE (☎703/478-6600; Stadium-Armory Metro). The huge downtown **MCI Center** (☎202/661-5500, ⓦwww.mcicenter.com; next to Gallery Place-Chinatown Metro) hosts home games of the pro **basketball** Washington Wizards (ⓦwww.nba.com/wizards) and Mystics (ⓦwww.wnba.com/mystics), as well as the pro **hockey** Washington Capitals (ⓦwww.washingtoncaps.com). The prospects for the woebegone Wizards rose when Michael Jordan left retirement to take the floor for them in 2001. The Caps added further star power to their line-up that same year by signing Czech superstar Jaromir Jagr, a prolific goal scorer and perennial all-star, to a seven-year $77 million contract.

Virginia

Traveling through **VIRGINIA**, the oldest, largest and wealthiest of the American colonies and the single most powerful influence on the early United States, is a nonstop history lesson. Pretty and rural it may be, but it's the past that predominates: wherever you go you're pointed towards this or that painstakingly restored two-hundred-year-old building, where something or other happened a long time ago. The more you know about it all, the more rewarding Virginia is to visit, but the historical plaques get a bit ridiculous after a while, marking every spot where George Washington slept, Thomas Jefferson thought, or Robert E. Lee tied his horse to a tree. You can see why Disney chose northern Virginia as the site of its proposed theme park of American history a few years back; and you'll also soon realize that Virginia takes itself a bit too seriously to allow such a project to get off the ground.

Virginia's recorded history began at **Jamestown**, just off the Chesapeake Bay, with the establishment in 1607 of the first successful British colony in North America. Though the first colonists hoped to find gold, it was **tobacco** that made their fortunes. The native strain – used for hundreds of years by Virginia's indigenous population, of whom almost no trace remains – was too strongly flavored for European tastes. When a smoother, more palatable variety was introduced in 1615 by John Rolfe – the same man whose shipwreck on Bermuda inspired Shakespeare's *The Tempest* – tobacco quickly became the colony's major cash crop. Before long, vast plantations, owned by a very few aristocratic families, sprang up along the many broad rivers that flow into Chesapeake Bay. To grow and harvest tobacco required both an immense amount of land – so the Native Americans had to go – and intensive labor which led to the plantation owners bringing in **slaves** from Africa. By the end of the seventeenth century, enslaved African Americans accounted for nearly half of the colony's 75,000 people; a hundred years later, they numbered over 300,000. Virginians had an enormous impact on the foundation of the nascent United States: George Mason, Thomas Jefferson and James Madison wrote the Declaration of Independence and the Constitution, and four of the first five US presidents were from Virginia. However, by the mid-1800s the state was in decline, its once fertile fields depleted by overuse and its agrarian economy increasingly eclipsed by the urban and industrialized North.

As the confrontation between North and South over slavery and related economic and political issues grew more divisive, Virginia was caught in the middle. Though this slaveholding state initially voted against secession from the Union, it joined the Confederacy when the **Civil War** broke out, providing its capital, Richmond, and its military leader, Robert E. Lee, who had previously turned down an offer to lead the Union army. Four long years later, Virginia was ravaged, its towns and cities wrecked, its farmlands ruined and most of its youth dead. It has never regained its early prosperity, or its prominence in national affairs.

Richmond itself was largely destroyed in the war; today it's a small city, with some good museums, and is the best starting point for seeing Virginia. The bulk of the **colonial** sites are concentrated just to the east, in what is known as the **Historic Triangle**. Here the remains of **Jamestown**, the original colony, **Williamsburg**, the restored colonial capital, and **Yorktown**, site of the final battle of the Revolutionary War, lie within half an hour's drive of each other. Another historic center, Thomas Jefferson's **Charlottesville**, sits at the foot of the gorgeous **Blue Ridge Mountains**, an hour west of Richmond. An attractive small college town in its own right, it's also within easy reach of the natural splendors of **Shenandoah National Park** and the little towns of the western valleys. **Northern Virginia**, often visited as a day-trip from Washington DC, features several posh suburbs and a number of restored historic homes, the closest colonial architecture to the capital in **Alexandria**, and **Manassas**, the scene of two important Civil War battles.

Getting around Virginia

Virginia is an easy place to explore. Two north–south Amtrak routes from Washington DC cross the state, one through Charlottesville towards Atlanta and the other through Fredericksburg and Richmond on the way to Florida; in addition, daily connections run east from Richmond to the Historic Triangle, and west from Charlottesville towards Chicago. Greyhound buses reaches dozens of smaller towns. **Drivers** heading south can take the stunning Blue Ridge Parkway along the Appalachians. If you've got the time, there's ample opportunity for **cycling**, whether on quiet country roads or up in the mountains, and **hiking** or **walking** are also worth thinking about.

Northern Virginia

Northern Virginia, almost all of which lies within commuting distance of Washington DC, holds some extremely exclusive suburbs, including McLean and the rest of Fairfax County, which are home to a high proportion of US senators. In contrast, **Alexandria**, nestled on the Potomac just beyond the limits of the nation's capital, seems at least two centuries removed from the modern political whirl. Further afield, this Anglophile heartland of Virginia's landed gentry – often called "Hunt Country" for their love of horses and fancy-dress blood sports – holds well-preserved eighteenth- and nineteenth-century stately homes, cottages, churches, barns and taverns tucked away along the quiet back roads. It's all very popular with tourists, nowhere more so than **Mount Vernon**, the longtime home of George Washington, while Manassas to the west was the site of the bloody battles of Bull Run.

Alexandria

The sheer amount of well-preserved eighteenth- and nineteenth-century architecture lining King Street, which extends a good half-mile up from the Potomac, and its cross streets, makes **ALEXANDRIA** a must, especially for those who are staying in Washington DC but do not have time to venture further afield in Virginia. Originally an important colonial trading post and a busy port named after the pioneer John Alexander, the town was actually ceded to the newly created nation's capital in 1801 until it was returned to Virginia in 1847. When the Civil War broke out, it was occupied by Union forces and was the only place in the South to remain so for the duration of the war, which must have been a sore point for Robert E. Lee, whose boyhood home was here. In earlier days, George Washington had also maintained close ties with Alexandria, owning property here and attending gatherings at the famous **Gadsby's Tavern**, 134 N Royal St, now a museum (April–Sept Tues–Sat 10am–5pm, Sun 1–5pm; Oct–March Tues–Sat 11am–4pm, Sun 1–4pm; $4). Among other meticulously restored buildings open to the public are **Carlyle House**, 121 N Fairfax St, a 1752 manor house that was home to five royal governors (Tues–Sat 10am–5pm, Sun noon–5pm; $4) and **Lee–Fendall House**, 614 Oronoco St (Tues–Sat 10am–4pm, Sun 1–4pm; $4), which belonged to the Lee family and contains many of their possessions. Down on the waterfront the **Alexandria Archaeology Museum** at 105 N Union St (Tues–Fri 10am–3pm, Sat 10am–5pm, Sun 1–5pm; free) displays various aspects of the town's history. The small, rectangular Georgian **Christ Church** at 118 N Washington St was built in 1773 and often counted Washington himself among its worshippers. Further along King Street towards the newer part of town stands the huge obelisk of the **George Washington National Masonic Memorial**, which is visible for miles around.

Practicalities

Alexandria has the distinct advantage of being on the Washington DC **metro** line, making it easy to reach from the city. For that reason few tourists choose to stay here; should you decide to, however, there is the usual range of major hotel chains, located mostly on the outskirts, such as the *Days Inn Landmark*, 110 S Bragg St (℡703/354-4950 or 1-800/329-7466, ⓦdaysinnalexandria .com; ❹). The friendly **visitor center** is located in the town's oldest house at 221 King St (℡703/838-4200, ⓦwww.FunSide.com) and can provide a useful walking itinerary map, as well all the usual tourist information. There is no shortage of **places to eat** - try the tasty seafood at *Fish Market*, 105 King St (℡703/836-5376), or the New Orleans-style Creole fare at *Two-Nineteen*, 219 King St (℡703/549-1141).

Mount Vernon – George Washington's home

Set on a shallow bluff overlooking the broad Potomac River, five miles south of Alexandria, **Mount Vernon** (daily: March & Sept–Oct 9am–5pm; April–Aug 8am–5pm; Nov–Feb 9am–4pm; $9) is among the most attractive historic houses in the US. The country estate of **George Washington**, with its eight thousand acres of landscaped and planted grounds, has been maintained virtually intact since Washington's death in 1799. Just fifteen miles from downtown DC, it's close enough to be reached as a day-trip on the city's Tourmobiles ($22; see p.405), or by bus from Huntington Metro station. Besides illuminating the life and times of the leader of the revolutionary armies and the first US president, Mount Vernon also provides an eye-opening look into the lifestyle of the colonial gentlemen who founded the United States of America.

A small museum gives an overview of Mount Vernon's history; in the house itself, the furnishings and decoration reflect Washington's preference for plain living, but few items – a reading chair with built-in fan, and a key to the destroyed Bastille, presented by Thomas Paine on behalf of Lafayette – give much of a sense of his character. The four-poster bed upon which he died stands in an upstairs bedroom; he and his wife Martha are buried in a simple tomb on the south side of the house.

Gunston Hall – George Mason's home

Gunston Hall, the 1755 Georgian brick home of Washington's contemporary **George Mason**, stands just around a bend in the river, ten minutes' drive south along Hwy-1 at the east end of Hwy-242 in Lorton (daily 9.30am–5pm; $5). It was Mason's revolutionary idea "that all men are by nature equally free and independent and have certain inherent rights" which Jefferson incorporated into the Declaration of Independence. Mason was later one of the main framers of the US Constitution, which he subsequently refused to support because it neither included a Bill of Rights nor abolished slavery. Unlike Washington and Jefferson, Mason eschewed public power, preferring to stay here with his family – which is understandable once you've seen the place. One of the most impressive works of architecture in Virginia, much of it was designed and constructed by William Buckland; the masterful interiors, particularly in the stately drawing room, feature exquisite carved ornamentation. The house fronts onto a large formal garden, and the extensive grounds are in turn surrounded by two riverfront state parks and wildlife refuges.

Manassas Battlefield National Park

MANASSAS BATTLEFIELD NATIONAL PARK extends over grassy hills at the western fringes of the Washington DC suburban belt, just off I-66.

Such is the power of these brooding hillsides you don't have to know the details of what happened here to get a sense of the site's historical importance. Soon after the first shots were fired at Fort Sumter, the first major land battle of the Civil War – known as the **Battle of Bull Run** – was fought here on the morning of July 21, 1861. Expecting an easy victory, some 25,000 Union troops attacked a Confederate detachment that controlled a vital railroad link to the Shenandoah Valley. The rebels proved powerful opponents, their strength in battle earning their commander, General Thomas Jackson, the famous nickname "Stonewall." He and General Lee also masterminded a second Confederate victory here in late August 1862.

Displays in the small **visitor center** at the entrance (daily 8.30am–5pm; June–Aug Sat & Sun until 6pm; park admission $2) describe how the first battle took shape, and detail other aspects of the war.

Richmond and the tidewater

At the very heart of Virginia, **Richmond** and the **Chesapeake Bay tidewater** are, in many ways, where the US was born. Not only does this fairly compact area hold some of the most important surviving colonial-era sites, it is also where the strength of the nation was tested by the Civil War. The greatest interest is to be found in the compact **Historic Triangle**, east of Richmond, and in **Fredericksburg**, to the north, around which several crucial battles were waged.

Richmond and around

Founded in 1737 at the furthest navigable point on the James River, **RICHMOND** remained a small outpost until just before the end of the colonial era, when independence-minded Virginians, realizing that their capital at Williamsburg was open to British attack, shifted it fifty miles further inland. The move to Richmond failed to offer much protection – the city was raided many times and twice put to the torch, once by troops under the command of Benedict Arnold.

Richmond subsequently flourished, its population reaching 100,000 by the time of the Civil War. When war broke out it was named the **capital of the Confederacy**, despite the fact that Virginia had voted two-to-one against secession from the Union just a month before. The massive **Tredegar Iron Works**, now a dedicated visitor center-cum-museum, became the main engine of the Confederate war machine. For four years the city was the focus of Southern defenses and Union attacks, but despite an almost constant state of siege – General McClellan came within six miles as early as 1862, and General Grant steamrolled remorselessly towards it through the last months of the war – it held on until the very end. It was less than a week after the fall of Richmond, on April 3, 1865, that General Lee surrendered to General Grant at Appomattox, a hundred miles west.

After the war, Richmond was devastated. Much of its downtown was burned, allegedly by fleeing Confederates who wanted to keep its stores of weapons, and its warehouses full of tobacco, out of the victors' hands. Rebuilding, however, was quick, and the city's economy has remained among the strongest in the South. Today's Richmond is a remarkably elegant city, with an extensive inventory of architecturally significant older buildings alongside its modern office towers. **Tobacco** is still a major industry – machine-rolled cigarettes were invented here in the 1870s, and Marlboro-maker **Phillip Morris** runs a huge manufacturing plant just south of downtown. Richmond is also a leading **banking** center.

Arrival, information and getting around

Two hours by car from Washington DC via I-95, which cuts through the east side of downtown, Richmond is also served by Amtrak which pulls into 7519 Staples Mill Rd, five miles northwest of downtown, and Greyhound, which stops just off I-64 at 2910 N Blvd, also a good way from the center. The large **airport**, ten miles east of downtown, is served by major carriers and has a small visitor center (Mon–Fri 9am–5pm; ☎804/236-2360) in the arrivals terminal.

Another small visitor center is located in the bell tower on the state capitol grounds (Mon–Fri 10am–4pm; ☎804/786-4484); the main **visitor center** (daily: June–Aug 9am–7pm; Sept–May 9am–5pm; ☎804/358-5511), which provides discounts for some of the area's hotels and advises on tours, joined the **CVB** head office in 2002 at 403 N 3rd St (☎804/782-2777 or 1-888/RICH-MOND, ⓦwww.richmondva.org).

Most of Richmond is compact enough to walk around, but to get to outlying places (like the stations or the Museum of Fine Arts) you might want to take a GRTC **bus** (zone system, most fares $1.25; ☎804/358-GRTC). More convenient for museum-hopping is the weekend-only **Cultural Connection bus** (June–Nov Sat 10am–5.30pm, Sun noon–5.30pm; $1; ☎804/266–8100), whose three separate routes link all major sites. **Bikes** are available for rent at Two Wheel Travel, a couple of miles from downtown at 2934 W Cary St (☎804/359-2453).

Accommodation

Finding well-priced **accommodation** in Richmond isn't difficult, with plenty of anonymous downtown hotels catering to the business and government trade. If you prefer to get a feel for the old city, stay the night in a **B&B** in one of the historic quarters.

The Berkeley 1200 E Cary St ☎804/780-1300 or 1-888/780-4422, ⓦwww.berkeleyhotel.com. Elegant small hotel on historic Shockoe Slip. ❻
The Jefferson 101 W Franklin St ☎804/788-8000 or 1-800/424-8014, ⓦwww. jefferson-hotel.com. Beautifully maintained, spacious grand hotel, with fabulous marble-columned lobby. ❼
Linden Row Inn 100 E Franklin St ☎804/783-7000 or 1-800/348-7424, ⓦwww.lindenrowinn.com. A magnificent row of redbrick Georgian terrace

houses, now a comfortable modern hotel with antique furnishings. ❹
Midtown Inn and Conference Center 3200 W Broad St ☎804/359-4061 or 1-800/866-0553, ⓦwww.briggshospitality/midtown.html. Good location, near the Fan District and Fine Arts Museum; has the usual hotel chain amenities. ❸
William Catlin House 2304 E Broad St ☎804/780-3746. Small, comfortable, upmarket B&B on Church Hill, across from St John's Church. ❹

Downtown Richmond

Richmond's **downtown** centers on a few blocks rising up from the James River to either side of Broad Street. Modern office towers front onto a riverside park, while up the hill in the **Court End District**, dozens of well-preserved antebellum homes provide a suitable backdrop for some important museums and historic sites. A **Richmond Citypass**, valid for one month and giving access to any five of nineteen attractions around town, is available for $15 from any visitor center or ticket desk at each attraction – well worth considering if you're in town for a few days.

The **Virginia State Capitol** (daily 9am–5pm; Jan–March closed Sun; last tour 4.15pm; free), which has been in use since 1788 as the seat of the state (and, during the Civil War, Confederate) government, is the focal point of the city, visible from all over Richmond and offering a sweeping view from its columned portico. Thomas Jefferson had a hand in the design, based on his favorite building, the Roman Maison Carré in Nîmes, France. The domed central rotunda, not visible from outside, holds the only marble statue of George Washington modeled from life, and busts of Jefferson and the seven other Virginia-born US presidents line the walls. Likenesses of famous Virginians, including a solemn bronze Robert E. Lee, fill the adjacent **Old House Chamber**, where Aaron Burr was tried and acquitted of treason in 1807.

Just two blocks north of the capitol, the **Museum of the Confederacy**, 1201 E Clay St (Mon–Sat 10am–5pm, Sun noon–5pm; $6), gives an even-handed history of the Civil War. Personal effects of Confederate leaders include J. E. B. Stuart's plumed hat, the tools used to amputate Stonewall Jackson's arms at Chancellorsville (he died), and Robert E. Lee's revolver and the pen he used to sign the surrender. An exhibition entitled "From Sunup to Sunup" highlights the reality of slavery. Next door, the so-called **White House of the Confederacy** (same hours; $7), a Neoclassical mansion where Jefferson Davis lived as Confederate president, has recently been restored to its 1860s appearance. Tours of the house itself are reverential and rather dull, though it's interesting to reflect that Abraham Lincoln came for a look just days before his death; far more engaging is the exhibition on Davis's staff, telling how some of his slaves were supposedly "bribed" into escaping north, and a small collection of domestic memorabilia with captions hurriedly written by Davis's wife. A $10 **combination ticket** allows access to both the house and museum.

Two blocks to the west, the 1812 **Wickham House** now forms part of the excellent **Valentine Museum** at 1015 E Clay St (Mon–Sat 10am–5pm, Sun noon–5pm; $5). This Neoclassical monolith houses a small local history museum, focusing on the experience of working-class and black Americans, as well as an extensive array of furniture and pre-Civil War clothing such as whalebone corsets and other *Gone with the Wind*-era apparel.

West of the Convention Center on Sixth Street is a neighborhood of early nineteenth-century houses, many fronted by ornate wrought-iron balconies similar to those in New Orleans' French Quarter. Known as **Jackson Ward**, and filling a dozen blocks around First and Clay streets, this has been the center of Richmond's African-American community since well before the Civil War, when Richmond had the largest free black population in the US. As well as covering local history, the **Maggie L. Walker House**, 110 E Leigh St (Wed–Sun 9am–5pm; free), traces the working life of the physically disabled black Richmond woman who, during the 1920s, founded and ran the first non-white-male-owned bank in the US, now the Consolidated Bank and Trust. Nearby, the **Black History Museum** at 00 Clay St (Tues–Sat 10am–5pm, Sun 1–5pm; $4) houses displays on Richmond's role as a center of Southern black society, and includes a well-presented gallery of the civil rights movement.

A refreshing example of recent urban revitalization is the landscaping of a 1.25-mile stretch of waterfront into **Canal Walk**, running between Downtown and Shockoe Bottom. For an interesting (and free) insight into the Confederate period, you can start or end your stroll at the **Richmond Civil War Visitor Center**, newly opened at the refurbished Tredegar Iron Works, down by the river below Fourth St. More of a museum in reality, it has a regular slide show about Civil War history and three floors of exhibits, including moving personal accounts of the war from ordinary soldiers.

Shockoe Bottom, the Poe Museum and Church Hill

A short walk southeast from the Court End District, a very different neighborhood allows a glimpse of another side of the Richmond story. Split down the middle by the raised I-95 freeway, the increasingly gentrified (and regularly flooded) riverfront warehouse district of **Shockoe Bottom** still holds a few palpable reminders of Richmond's industrial past among the restaurants and nightclubs on its cobblestone streets. From **Shockoe Slip**, a prettified old wharf area rebuilt in the 1890s after being destroyed in the Civil War, Cary Street runs east along the waterfront, lined by a wall of brick warehouses known as **Tobacco Row**.

Nearby, Richmond's oldest building, an appropriately gloomy two hundred-and-fifty-year-old stone house at 1914 E Main St, serves as the **Edgar Allan Poe Museum** (Tues–Sat 10am–4pm, Mon & Sun noon–5pm; $6). Poe spent much of his life in Richmond and considered it his hometown; he wrote the *Narrative of Arthur Gordon Pym* while working on the Richmond-based magazine *Southern Literary Messenger*. The museum displays Poe memorabilia plus a model of Richmond as it was in his day.

Church Hill, a few blocks northeast, is one of Richmond's oldest surviving residential districts, its decorative eighteenth-century houses, adorned with cast-iron porches and rambling magnolia-filled front gardens, looking out over the James River. Capping the hill at the heart of the neighborhood, **St John's Church** at 2401 E Broad St (Mon–Sat 10am–4pm, Sun 1–4pm, last tour 3.30pm; $3), which dates back to 1741, is best known as the place where, during a 1775 debate on whether the Virginia colony should raise a militia against the British, **Patrick Henry** made the impassioned plea: "Is life so dear, or peace so sweet, to be purchased at the price of chains of slavery? I know not what course others may take, but as for me, give me liberty or give me death." His speech is re-enacted by an actor every Sunday between Memorial and Labor days at 2pm, after the religious services.

The Fan District and Carytown

The newest and most opulent of Richmond's neighborhoods, called the **Fan District** because its tree-lined avenues fan out at oblique angles, spreads west from the downtown area, beyond Belvidere Street (US-1). Its centerpiece is **Monument Avenue**, lined with garish c.1900 mansions. Richmond's most imposing boulevard was laid out by unabashed city planners from 1889 onwards to commemorate key figures of the Confederacy. Four successive grand intersections hold statues of J.E.B. Stuart, Robert E. Lee, Stonewall Jackson and Jefferson Davis. In recent times, many of the city's black population expressed dissatisfaction with this choice of heroes, and in 1996 a statue of the late tennis champion **Arthur Ashe** was duly erected. A native of Richmond, Ashe felt obliged to leave the city in 1961 because its tennis courts were segregated. The statue shows Ashe's dedication to education as well as the game of tennis – he's encircled with children and holds books and tennis racquet aloft.

South of Monument Avenue, at 2800 Grove Ave, stands the **Virginia Museum of Fine Arts** (Tues–Sun 11am–5pm, Thurs until 8pm; $4 donation). An extensive collection of Impressionist and Post-Impressionist paintings is displayed alongside American paintings ranging from George Catlin's romantic images of Plains Indians to the Pop Art creations of Roy Lichtenstein and Claes Oldenburg in the vast West Wing. Other galleries contain such diverse items as Frank Lloyd Wright furniture, Lalique jewelry, and Hindu and Buddhist sculpture from the Himalayas; but perhaps the most popular part of the museum is a world-class array of over three hundred Carl Fabergé works, including four of his trademark jewel-encrusted Easter eggs crafted in the 1890s for the Russian tsars.

Just beyond the Fan District, **Carytown** is another up-and-coming area. Its abundance of trendy shops offering Asian art, tarot readings, and holistic medicines, alongside restaurants on Cary St, adding a definite flavor of eastern and New Age sensibilities to the capital of the Old South.

Eating

Richmond has a good choice of **eating** options at both ends of the price spectrum, with barbecue being a specialty.

Acacia 3325 W Cary St ℡804/354-6060. Quality regional cuisine with alfresco dining at this highly-rated Carytown establishment; good range of meats in barbecue and other flavorful sauces. Closed Sun & Mon.

Awful Arthur's Oyster Bar 101 N 18th St ℡804/643-1700. Shockoe Bottom hangout, with raw oysters and clams, shrimp and crabs, and steak for those not wanting seafood. All budgets catered for.

Millie's Diner 2603 E Main St ℡804/643-5512. Refurbished diner, complete with mini-jukeboxes on each table, somewhat adrift of downtown beyond Shockoe Bottom. A changing menu of fairly expensive but very tasty meals.

Peking Pavilion 1302 E Cary St ℡804/649-8888. Very good, inexpensive (especially at lunchtime) Chinese restaurant in Shockoe Slip serving Szechuan and Mandarin specialties. There's also a

branch at 5710 Grove Ave in the West End.

Penny Lane 207 N 7th St ℡804/780-1682. British-style establishment with a full menu of grills and other pub grub, plus a full range of English and other beers, and soccer on TV.

Strawberry Street Café 421 N Strawberry St ℡804/353-6860. Casual and comfortable Fan District neighborhood café offering mainly quiches, pastas and salads.

Third Street Diner 218 E Main St ℡804/788-4750. Relaxed 24hr diner with particularly good breakfasts and Greek dishes. Stylish student crowd, especially at night when it's also a bar.

The Tobacco Company 1201 E Cary St ℡804/782-9431. Inventive New American food in a stunningly restored three-story tobacco warehouse, with antique elevator. Cocktail bar with nightly live entertainment in the leafy ground-floor atrium.

Drinking and nightlife

Richmond's main **drinking and nightlife** spots are concentrated around the riverside **Shockoe Slip** and **Shockoe Bottom** areas, just east of downtown, where you'll find the likes of the *Richbrau Brewery*, 1214 E Cary St (℡804/644-3018), a watering hole that's especially lively at weekends; *Goodfellas*, 1722 E Main St (℡804/643-5022), a trendy club with a roaring sound system pumping out decent rock music; and the *Have a Nice Day Café*, 18th and Main (℡804/771-1700), a cheesy but fun retro-1970s café and nightclub. In the **Fan District**, try *Buddy's Place,* 325 N Robinson St (℡804/355-3701), or the *Border Chophouse and Bar,* 1501 W Main St (℡804/355-2907).

Between October and June, Theater Virginia (℡804/367-0831), in the Museum of Fine Arts, is Richmond's best bet for live **theater**. For news on music and events, check the listings in the free *Style Weekly* newspaper.

Fredericksburg

Only a mile off the I-95 freeway, about halfway to Richmond from Washington DC and easy to reach on Amtrak or Greyhound, **FREDER-ICKSBURG** is one of Virginia's prettiest historic towns, its elegant downtown streets backed by residential avenues lined with white picket fences. In colonial days, this was an important inland port, where tobacco and other plantation products were loaded onto boats that sailed down the Rappahannock River. Dozens of eighteenth- and nineteenth-century buildings along the waterfront now hold antique stores and secondhand bookshops.

Two blocks away, in the 1816 town hall, the **Fredericksburg Area Museum**, 907 Princess Anne St (March–Nov Mon–Sat 10am–5pm, Sun 1–5pm; Dec–Feb Mon–Sat 10am–4pm, Sun 1–4pm; $4), has a broad range of displays tracing local history from Native American settlements to the present day. The **Rising Sun Tavern**, by the river at 1304 Caroline St, was built as a home in the mid-1700s by George Washington's brother Charles. As an inn, it became a key meeting place for patriots and a hotbed of sedition. It is now a small "living history" **museum** (March–Nov Mon–Sat 9am–5pm, Sun 11am–5pm; Dec–Feb Mon–Sat 10am–4pm, Sun noon–4pm; $4), where costumed "wenches" guide visitors around a collection of pub games and ancient pewterware. They don't, however, serve food or drink any more, except for the glass of spiced herbal punch you get on the tour.

Fredericksburg's strategic location made it vital during the **Civil War**, and the land around the town was heavily fought over. More than 100,000 men lost their lives in the major battles of Fredericksburg, Chancellorsville, Spotsylvania and countless other bloody skirmishes. Indeed Stonewall Jackson himself was mistakenly killed by his own troops at Chancellorsville in May 1863. The **Fredericksburg and Spotsylvania National Battlefield Park**, south of town at 1013 Lafayette Blvd (visitor center open daily: summer 8.30am–6.30pm; rest of year 9am–5pm; $4 for a weekly pass), has informative exhibits and rents three-hour audio tours ($5 for tape and player) of the various battlefield sites.

Practicalities

Fredericksburg's **visitor center** at 706 Caroline St (daily: summer 9am–7pm; rest of year 9am–5pm; ℡540/373-1776 or 1-800/678-4748, Ⓦwww.fredericksburgva.com) can provide maps of walking tours and details about discounted tickets to the area's attractions. Thanks to a lot of weekend activity, the town has several good places to **eat** and **drink**. The closest contemporary equivalent to the bawdy *Rising Sun* is probably *Sammy T's,* 801 Caroline St (℡540/371-2008), a popular bar and diner with substantial sandwiches and a huge range of bottled beers. *Smythe's Cottage* at 303 Fauquier St (℡540/373-1645) serves up tasty southern cooking in an early nineteenth-century cottage. For a cappuccino, head diagonally across from the visitor center to *Java Connection* at 615 Caroline St. Heading north out of town at 2200 Princess Anne St, *Carl's* is one of the region's few surviving original ice cream parlours. The cozy pub in the basement of the eighteenth-century *Kenmore Inn*, 1200 Princess Anne St (restaurant closed Sun, also Mon lunchtime; ℡540/371-7622, Ⓦwww.kenmoreinn.com; ❹), serves old-fashioned steaks and fish, occasionally accompanied by live jazz, and has B&B rooms furnished with antiques. Another of Fredericksburg's many old-fashioned **B&Bs** is the *Richard Johnston Inn*, 711 Caroline St (℡540/899-7606; ❹); for a nice **motel** try the *Fredericksburg Colonial Inn*, 1707 Princess Anne St (℡540/371-5666, Ⓦwww.fci1.com; ❸).

The Historic Triangle: Jamestown, Williamsburg and Yorktown

The **Historic Triangle**, on the thin peninsula that stretches east of Richmond between the James and York rivers, holds by far the richest concentration of colonial-era sites in the US. **Jamestown**, founded in 1607, was Virginia's first settlement; **Williamsburg** is an animated, if overly theatrical, resurrection of the colonial capital; and it was at **Yorktown** that American independence from the English crown was finally secured. All three sites are within an hour by car, bus or train from the capital.

Although I-64 is the quickest way to cover the fifty miles from Richmond to Williamsburg, a far more pleasing drive along US-5 rolls through **plantation** country, where many eighteenth-century mansions, with invariably lovely grounds, are open to the public. Once you're in the Historic Triangle area, the best way to get around is along the lushly landscaped **Colonial Parkway**, which winds west to Jamestown and east to Yorktown, twenty miles end-to-end. Most of the area's numerous tourist facilities – this is the most visited destination in the state – are to be found around Williamsburg. We've listed a few suggestions under "Historic Triangle practicalities" on p.444.

Jamestown National Historic Site

The first successful English colony in the New World, **JAMESTOWN** was established as a commercial venture, sponsored by King James I but paid for and owned by the **Virginia Company**. On May 13, 1607, the colonists, thirty adventure-minded aristocrats and seventy-five indentured servants, arrived at the mouth of the Chesapeake Bay after four months at sea, and within two weeks had established a fortified settlement on a low-lying island forty miles up the James River.

Despite the fact that Jamestown was intended to be self-supporting, not one member of the party had any experience with farming or fishing – their leader, **John Smith**, wrote in 1608 that "though there be Fish in the Sea, and Foules in the ayre, and Beasts in the woods, their bounds are so large, they are so wilde, and we so weake and ignorant, we cannot much trouble them." The Virginia Company continued to send new recruits, but the loss of life was extreme: of more than seven thousand settlers who came to Jamestown in its first decade, six thousand perished within a year of arriving.

What saved Jamestown, besides the provisions brought by new settlers, was **tobacco**: by 1619 the colony was shipping some twenty tons a year back to England. As it expanded, the colony began to encroach upon the **Powhatan**, an Algonquin-speaking people who controlled most of tidewater Virginia and who until then had been fairly peaceable. In 1622 and again in 1644 provocations caused the Powhatan to attack the Jamestown colonists, killing around five hundred settlers each time. The most serious damage to Jamestown, however, was caused by the colonists themselves, when they burned the fort to the ground in 1675 in protest at the lack of protection offered them by the crown. Rather than rebuild the tiny island outpost, by the end of the 1600s they had shifted the capital and most of the commercial activity inland to Williamsburg, and Jamestown slowly disappeared.

The one bit of seventeenth-century Jamestown to survive, protected within the **Jamestown National Historic Site**, is the 50ft tower of the first brick church, built in 1639 – the rest was destroyed by fire in 1698. Around it are sundry unearthed foundations, as well as numerous memorial shrines and monuments.

From the **visitor center** (daily: June–Sept 8.30am–5.30pm; Oct–May 9am–5pm; $6 per car, or $9 if combined with the Yorktown battlefield, see p.444; ☎757/229-1733), where artists' drawings and audiovisual exhibits endeavor to conjure up the past; a footpath leads down to the river, where the remains of the original fortress, now underwater, are vaguely visible.

Jamestown Settlement

Next to the authentic site of Jamestown, the state of Virginia has created the **Jamestown Settlement** (daily 9am–5pm; $10.75, or $15.75 with Yorktown Victory Center, see p.444), a complex of museums and full-size replicas that elucidate the details of what went on here. A short film dramatizes Jamestown's early days, and displays explore Europe's need for colonies, documenting the economic and social conditions, in England especially, which led to the founding of Jamestown. There's also an informative section on the Powhatan.

Behind the museum, two groups of reconstructed buildings are inhabited by interpretive guides, dressed in period costume. In the **Powhatan Village**, women wearing buckskins practice weaving and pottery, while in the larger and more convincing replica of **James Fort**, some fifteen thatched, wattle-and-daub buildings – all built with period tools – act as a blacksmith's, a store-house and a church. Full-sized replicas of the three **ships** that carried the first settlers here – the *Godspeed* (which retraced the route from England in 1985), the *Susan Constant* and the *Discovery* – are moored below on the James River.

Williamsburg

A year after mosquito-plagued Jamestown burned down, the colonial capital was moved inland to a small village known as the Middle Plantation, soon rechristened **WILLIAMSBURG** in honor of King William III. To reflect the increasing wealth of the colony, a grand city was laid out, centering upon a mile-long, hundred-foot-wide avenue. Suitable buildings were constructed, beginning with the **capitol** in 1704 and culminating in the opulent **Governor's Palace** in 1720. By the mid-1700s, tobacco-rich Virginia was the most prosperous of the American colonies, and Williamsburg was its largest city – though with some two thousand residents, not on the scale of Philadelphia, New York or Boston. Williamsburg remained the seat of colonial government, and emerged as one of the leading centers of **revolutionary thought**: at the College of William and Mary, George Wythe, Thomas Jefferson, James Monroe and George Mason argued the finer points of law and democracy, while in the capitol, and in the many raucous taverns that surrounded it, firebrand politicians like Patrick Henry held forth on the iniquities of colonialism and organized the first resistance to British rule. When the Revolutionary War broke out, the government moved to the more secure Richmond, and Williamsburg slowly faded from view, all but unrecognized for its place in American history.

Fortunately, many of the colonial structures survived intact until the 1920s, when oil baron **John D. Rockefeller** answered the pleas of a local priest, W.

A. R. Goodwin, to support Williamsburg's restoration. Over the ensuing years, Rockefeller, with Goodwin acting as his agent, spent some $90 million buying and restoring the surviving structures to their original condition, in many cases building replicas from scratch. In 1934, **Colonial Williamsburg** opened as the first theme park in the US to use American history for amusement, with costumed guides as interpreters. While you have to buy a ticket to look inside most of the buildings (see box opposite), the entire historic area, which includes many fine gardens, is open all the time, and you can wander freely down the cobblestone streets and across the lush green commons. Cars are banned, and Williamsburg as a whole is a remarkably pleasant – if rather crowded – place.

Most of the **modern town** of Williamsburg lies to the west of the historical area and includes some fairly attractive architecture that is over a century old itself. It is dominated by the William and Mary College campus, whose students and staff comprise the majority of customers for the modest selection of shops and restaurants and inhabit the leafy residential streets further west. There is not much to the east of Colonial Williamsburg other than functional motels and drab commercial outlets.

Colonial Williamsburg

Crowds flock to **COLONIAL WILLIAMSBURG** in high summer, and tickets are very expensive, but a visit really is worth including in your itinerary. The meticulously restored buildings and the various interpretive activities and crafts workshops – encompassing over thirty colonial trades, from apothecary to wigmaker – are both entertaining and true to life. As Rockefeller's tidy influence has waned (his idea of restoration was that everything should be made to look new), Williamsburg has tried to come to grips with the less savory realities of colonial life. Thus people previously referred to as servants are now acknowledged to have been slaves – fully half of Williamsburg's population was African-American – and their lives and conditions are well covered. On another level, houses and outbuildings formerly repainted every year, are now left to age naturally, and once-manicured lawns are now allowed to become (at least slightly) overgrown.

From the **Wren Building** on the William and Mary campus, built in 1716 at the west end of Williamsburg and now separated from the historic area by a mock-colonial shopping center, **Duke of Gloucester Street** runs east through the historic area to the rebuilt capitol. The first of its eighteenth-century buildings, a hundred yards along, is the Episcopalian **Bruton Parish Church** where Goodwin preached (Mon–Sat 9am–5pm, Sun noon–5pm; donation). It was built in 1715, at a time when all white Virginians were required by law to attend services at least once a month. Behind it, the broad **Palace Green** spreads north to the rebuilt Governor's Palace (see opposite). West of the church, the **court house** – built in 1770 and still in use when Rockefeller bought it – and the octagonal **Powder Magazine** face each other in the midst of the Market Square. Further along, **Chowning's Tavern**, a reconstruction of an alehouse that stood here in 1766, is one of four functioning pubs in the district. As a law student, Thomas Jefferson rented a room in the (no longer used) **Market Square Tavern** across the street.

Various other buildings along Duke of Gloucester Street house blacksmiths' shops, printers and milliners, open only to Colonial Williamsburg ticket-holders. At the east end of the street, fife-and-drum corps and members of the militia assemble in front of the reconstructed capitol (see opposite) before the nightly march through town.

Tickets for Colonial Williamsburg

To set foot inside any of the more than two hundred assorted buildings that have been restored or rebuilt as part of Colonial Williamsburg, you need to buy a ticket, either from the main **visitor center** (daily 8.30am–8pm; ☎1-800/HISTORY), north of center off the Colonial Parkway, or from a smaller office at the west end of Duke of Gloucester Street. There are three types of **tickets**, all of which include an introductory guided tour and unlimited free parking at the visitor center. The basic **Day Pass** ($32, 6–17 yrs $16), valid for one day only, gets you into everything including Carter's Grove Plantation, six miles east on Route 60; the better-value **Freedom Pass** ($38, 6–17 yrs $19) gives you unlimited access to everything in Colonial Williamsburg for an entire year – you can upgrade it by paying the $6 difference if you're so impressed the first day that you decide to stick around. There are additional charges, however, for the various special entertainment and educational events offered by Colonial Williamsburg, such as staged trials in the courthouse, evening dances and candlelit walking tours. The **Liberty Pass** ($55, 6–17 yrs $23) gets you everything the Freedom Pass offers, but special events are free or discounted by 25 percent, and you also receive deals on dining and shopping. For those that prefer to have a quick wander around without buying a ticket for entry to the buildings, parking at the visitor center is free for two hours, but a flat $24 thereafter, so keep an eye on the time.

The real architectural highlight is the **capitol**, at the east end of Duke of Gloucester Street. The current building, a 1945 reconstruction of the 1705 original, has an open-air ground-floor **arcade** linking two keyhole-shaped wings. The east wing housed the elected, legislative body of the colonial government, the **House of Burgesses**, while the east wing held the chambers of the **General Court** – where alleged felons, including thirteen of Blackbeard's pirates, were tried. The eleven justices of the General Court, all of whom were appointed by the king, served as a second legislative body, much as the US House and Senate work today; if the two became deadlocked, they'd meet jointly in a conference chamber bridging the two wings.

A number of fully stocked giftshops along **Duke of Gloucester Street** have been done up as olde worlde apothecaries and silversmiths. The **Raleigh Tavern** was where the independence-minded colonial government reconvened after being dissolved by the loyalist governors in 1769 and again in 1774; the original tavern burned down in 1859. Considering that most Virginians of the time, even well-to-do landowners, lived in one- or two-room log cabins, the imposing two-story **Governor's Palace** at the north end of the Palace Green, with its grand ballroom and opulent furnishings, must have served as a telling declaration of the power vested within.

The smaller of the two conventional museums in Williamsburg, the recently expanded **Abby Aldrich Rockefeller Folk Art Center** on the south side of town, has an intriguing collection of household implements, children's toys, and general bric-a-brac, as well as fascinating paintings and sculptures by so-called primitive or natural artists. The other, the **DeWitt Wallace Decorative Arts Museum**, features fine furniture, porcelain and portraits. Its modern galleries are underground; the entrance is through the reconstructed facade of the **Public Hospital**, two blocks south of Bruton Parish Church. The first asylum in North America, the hospital now has reconstructions of the wire cages in which many early patients were kept, and exhibits tracing the evolution of the treatment of mental illness in the US.

Yorktown battlefield

YORKTOWN, along the York River on the north side of the peninsula, is not much of a town, but gave its name to the decisive final battle of the **Revolutionary War**. The smallest and least visited of the Historic Triangle sites, Yorktown was little more than farmland when, on October 18, 1781, overwhelmed and besieged British (and German) troops under the command of Cornwallis surrendered to the joint American and French forces commanded by George Washington. At the heart of the battlefield, a **visitor center** (daily 9am–5pm; $5 per car, or $9 combined with the Jamestown National Historic Site, see p.440) has informative interpretive displays, racks of military artifacts and a short audiovisual presentation on the war. The **Siege Line Overlook** on the roof gives good views of strategic points; maps and an audio tour ($3) are available if you want to explore in greater detail.

The **Moore House**, where the British surrender was agreed, survived later Civil War battles (and eventual use as a barn) before John D. Rockefeller had it restored; it stands along the York River, a mile east of the visitor center.

Yorktown Victory Center

Though Yorktown survived the battle more or less unscathed – the fighting took place on open fields to the east, and in the waters of Chesapeake Bay – much of the town was destroyed by fire in 1814, and very little of substance survives from the colonial days. Many of the surviving homes are privately owned, and not open to visitors. To make up for this, as at Jamestown, the state of Virginia and the National Park Service have constructed a mini-theme park – this time a re-created Continental Army encampment – as part of the **Yorktown Victory Center** (daily 9am–5pm; $7.75, or $15.75 with Jamestown Settlement, see p.441), west of the battlefield on US-17. It's not as extensive or convincing as the one at Jamestown, but the museum is better, focusing on the tobacco wealth of now-vanished York River towns and covering both sides, British and American, of events leading up to the Revolution. A final gallery deals with the course and impact of the war itself.

Historic Triangle practicalities

Of the three main sites, only Williamsburg is easily reached without a car. Amtrak **trains** and Greyhound **buses** stop at the **Transportation Center** at 408 N Boundary St, two blocks from the Governor's Palace. An airport shuttle from Norfolk Airport runs to Williamsburg for $34 (☎757/857-1231). Once there, the Colonial Parkway makes an excellent cycling route to Jamestown or Yorktown, but there's no other transportation available; rent a **bike** for $15 a day from Bikes Unlimited at 759 Scotland St in Williamsburg (☎757/229-4620). In Colonial Williamsburg, ticket-holders can use the hop-on, hop-off **shuttle buses** with an execrable recorded commentary that leave from the visitor center every ten minutes or so and stop at convenient points in the historic area.

Considering the wealth of historic structures, it's surprising how few hotels or B&Bs there are with any character. All central **accommodation** is handled by Colonial Williamsburg (☎1-800/HISTORY), which includes the range from motel to four-star luxury, and they even offer rooms in some of the restored eighteenth-century homes and inns within the historic area – for which you must reserve well in advance. Good-value packages are available, with meals, two nights' lodging and admission, from around $150 per person. Otherwise **places to stay** around the Historic Triangle are generally characterless and rarely cheap; to make your search easier, the Williamsburg

Hotel/Motel Association (☎757/220-3330 or 1-800/899-9462) can find you a bed at no extra charge. West of center US-60 is lined with endless motels, and there are several lower-end places just a few blocks east of the capitol, including the *Bassett Motel*, 800 York St (☎757/229-5175; ❷), and the recommended *Quarterpath Inn*, 620 York St ☎1-800/446-9222, ⓦwww.quarterpathinn.com; ❹). For a change of pace, the *Duke of York Motel*, 508 E Water St in Yorktown (☎757/898-3232; ❸), has reasonable beachfront doubles along the York River. Finally, there are several **campgrounds** along US-5 and US-60 west of Williamsburg that charge around $20 per tent.

The various old-style **restaurants** and taverns along Duke of Gloucester Street in Colonial Williamsburg feature good (though ludicrously overpriced) pub food as well as strolling entertainment, and can be fun; all except *Chowning's Tavern* must be reserved well in advance (☎1-800/HISTORY). West of the historic area, in the **Merchants Square** shopping mall, the excellent *Trellis Café* (☎757/229-8610) serves international food in an upmarket setting. There is also a clutch of restaurants near the William and Mary campus, including the *Green Leafe Café*, 765 Scotland St (☎757/220-3405), offering a solid dose of hearty fare and good beers.

The Atlantic coast

One of the busiest of the east coast ports, **Norfolk** sits midway along the coast at the point where the Chesapeake Bay empties into the Atlantic Ocean. Virginia's only heavily industrial center, it is not a particularly pretty place, but it does have a rich maritime and naval heritage, as well as the Chrysler Museum, one of the nation's best art galleries. Fifteen miles east of Norfolk, along the open Atlantic, low-key **Virginia Beach** draws summer sun-seekers to the state's only real resort, surrounded by broad beaches and tidal marshlands.

The rest of Virginia's Atlantic coast is on its isolated and sparsely populated **Eastern Shore**, where the attractive little island town of **Chincoteague** serves as the headquarters of a wildlife refuge that straddles the Maryland border and forms part of the Assateague Island National Seashore.

Norfolk

A strategic location at the broad mouth of the Chesapeake Bay, and an extensive deep-water harbor made colonial **NORFOLK** the main American trading port, and in the mid-eighteenth century it was the largest city in Virginia. After being burned by the British in 1775, and suffering naval bombardments during the Civil War, Norfolk never regained much character, and despite recent efforts to redevelop its waterfront, the modern city is little more than a supply depot for the vast naval shipyards. Along with Hampton and Newport News on the north side of the James River, Norfolk is home to the largest naval base outside Russia, and carriers, cruisers and all manner of gray-steel behemoths steam past incessantly

The Town

On the downtown waterfront is Norfolk's premier attraction, **Nauticus: The National Maritime Center** (June–Aug daily 10am–6pm; rest of year Tues–Sat 10am–5pm, Sun 12–5pm; $9.50; ⓦwww.nauticus.org), housed in a formidable replica battleship. The Nauticus's steep admission price is justified by the interactive oceanography exhibits, the giant-screen films and the country's first group virtual reality experience, where goggled visitors sink into Loch Ness and protect Nessie's eggs from unwelcome scientists. The more serious-minded will enjoy the on-site **Hampton Roads Naval Museum** (same hours; free), which documents the growth of naval operations in the area. The adjacent **International Pier** is frequented by colossal US (usually the *USS Wisconsin*) and foreign ships, which can be toured if they're docked for any length of time (call ☎757/664-1000 or 1-800/664-1080 for information). The small Elizabeth River **ferry** (Mon–Fri 7.15am–11.45pm, Sat & Sun 10.15am–11.45pm; 75¢; ☎757/640-6300) shuttles from nearby Waterside Park across the harbor to the historic **Portsmouth** neighborhood, where brick-lined streets are lined by eighteenth- and nineteenth-century houses.

Two blocks from the harbor, the **Douglas MacArthur Memorial** on Bank Street (Mon–Sat 10am–5pm, Sun 11am–5pm; free) houses the mortal remains and personal effects of the flamboyant US general. The leader of the Allied armies in the Pacific during World War II, who as head of the occupying armies wrote the constitution of Japan, MacArthur was relieved of his command during the Korean War, apparently because of his alarming desire to bomb China.

An extraordinary array of oriental antiquities is displayed in the intimate Tudor-style former home now known as the **Hermitage Foundation Museum**, on the Lafayette River at 7637 N Shore Rd (Mon–Sat 10am–5pm, Sun 1–5pm; $4, guided tours only). Its exhibits include Persian rugs, medieval tapestries, rare ancient Chinese ceremonial vessels, Roman glass and Art Nouveau.

The **Chrysler Museum**, half a mile north of the downtown waterfront on Olney Road and Mowlbray Arch (Wed 10am–9pm, Thurs–Sat 10am–5pm, Sun 1–5pm; $7, free on Wed), holds the eclectic collection of car magnate Walter Chrysler Jr. It includes a little bit of everything, from ancient Greek statuary to French Impressionist paintings, Franz Klein abstractions and Mayan funerary objects, as well as a world-class collection of Tiffany and Lalique glassware.

Practicalities

Airport Shuttle (☎757/857-1231) services connect downtown Norfolk with both **Norfolk International Airport** ($15), five miles northeast, and **Patrick Henry International Airport** ($43), twelve miles north. Amtrak bus connections from Newport News stop at the *Howard Johnson Waterside*, 700 Monticello Ave, and Greyhound stops opposite at no. 701. Norfolk's downtown **visitor center** is in the Nauticus Center on the waterfront (daily 10am–5pm; ☎757/664-1000 or 1-800/368-3097, ⓦwww.norfolkcvb.com); drivers can go to a larger visitor center at exit 273 off I-64, at Fourth View Street (daily 9am–7pm; ☎757/441-1852).

With far more accommodation options available nearby in the more pleasant surroundings of Virginia Beach, there should be no need to resort to the standard hotel and motel chains available in Norfolk, the only real affordable options in the city. You can **eat** Cajun-style seafood at the *Bienville Grille*, 723 W 21st St (☎757/625-5427), or try the eclectic Cajun–Asian blend at *The 219*, 219 Granby St (☎757/627-2896). **Waterside Park**, downtown at the mouth of the Elizabeth River, has something of a party atmosphere during summer weekends with live music, cheap beer and heaps of atmosphere. Also downtown, the ornate Art Nouveau Wells Theater (☎757/627-1234) puts on **plays** and small concerts.

Virginia Beach

In both character and geography **VIRGINIA BEACH** is about halfway between Maryland's huge, frenzied Ocean City and North Carolina's untamed open Outer Bank. Virginia's only real summer resort has grown to become the largest city in the state, but takes care to pitch itself as a family destination; among steps to deter the Spring Break crowd, Virginia Beach – home to evangelist/politician Pat Robertson's Regent College – has enacted anti-cruising laws that make it illegal to drive past the same spot twice within three hours. That said, the oceanfront vicinity can be a monument to tackiness, and there are several testosterone-filled surfer bars. Fortunately a multimillion dollar program to widen the beach keeps it from getting too sardine-like and the overall lazy atmosphere actually leads some to stay longer than planned.

The City

The city's focus is its long straight sandy beach, lined with all the usual hotels and motels, and backed by a boardwalk strip of bars, restaurants and nightclubs. The forty-block downtown area is too spread out to walk the length of, but you should find all you need within a smaller radius, as it's fairly homogenous. During the day, the main activities are sunbathing and playing in the waves; Virginia Beach is one of the main east coast surfing centers, hosting the summer-long Billabong competitions. You can rent surf, skim and boogie boards from Wave Riding Vehicles, at 19th and Cypress (☎757/422-8823). Away from the sands, most of the action is along Atlantic Avenue, the main beachfront drag.

High-tech interactive exhibits and an IMAX theater combine at the **Virginia Marine Museum**, 717 General Booth Blvd (daily: mid-June to early-Sept 9am–9pm; rest of year 9am–5pm; $9.95, or $14.95 with IMAX show; ⓦwww.vmsm.com), which features all things aquatic, from submarines to seabirds, and has a pleasant nature trail linking its two main buildings. The museum organizes regular **dolphin-watching** expeditions in summer ($17; reserve a day in advance at ☎757/437-BOAT).

The eccentric **A.R.E. Visitors Center** at the headquarters of the Association for Research and Enlightenment, at 67th Street and Atlantic Avenue (Mon–Sat 9am–8pm, Sun 11am–8pm; free), focuses on Edgar Cayce (1877–1945), a pioneer in hypnotism and ESP, known as "the sleeping prophet" because of his alleged ability, while in a trance, to diagnose and heal the ailments of individuals anywhere in the world. Visitors can use an enormous metaphysical library, or join "testings" of group ESP (daily June–Aug at 1pm; free).

Once the people-watching on the town beach starts to pall, head a few miles up or down the coast to find some beautiful and much more peaceful stretches of golden sand. To the south lie the four-mile-long **Back Bay National Wildlife Refuge**, where you can walk or fish but not officially swim or sunbathe, and False Cape State Park. Closer at hand to the north, the thick woodlands of **First Landing State Park** was the site at which the first English settlers touched land in 1607 before moving on to Jamestown; it is now popular with weekend boaters and cyclists, and has a beach on Chesapeake Bay. Several adventure organizations such as Sandbridge Eco Sports, 577 Sandbridge Rd (☎757/721-6210 or 1-800/695-4212), run **kayaking** and dolphin-watching expeditions in the area.

Practicalities

Greyhound stops at 1017 Laskin Rd, off 31st Street, while the Amtrak bus connection from Newport News arrives at 19th Street and Pacific Avenue. The **visitor center** is at the east end of I-264, half a mile west of the beach on 21st Street (daily: summer 9am–8pm, winter 9am–5pm; ☎757/437-4888 or 1-800/446-8038). Beach **trolleys** are the best mode of transportation in the area; there are four different routes covering the city, the most useful being up and down Atlantic Avenue (daily noon–midnight; 50¢; ☎757/222-6100).

Virginia Beach has one great boon for **budget travelers** – just a block from the beach, there are dorm beds from $18 (YHA members $14.50) and bargain B&B singles and doubles at *HI-Angie's Guest Cottage Hostel*, 302 24th St (☎757/428-4690, ⓦwww.angiescottage.com; ❶–❸). Typical rates at the seafront hotels tend to approach $100 in summer, with cheaper options at the appealingly old-styled *Thunderbird Motor Lodge* at 35th and Oceanfront (☎757/428-3024 or 1-800/633-6669, ⓦwww.ThunderbirdVirginiaBeach.com; ❸), which also has a nice café; the adjacent *Budget Lodge*, 34th and Oceanfront (☎757/428-4413 or 1-800/446-8388; ❷); and the smallish *Sea Side* at 27th and Atlantic Avenue (☎757/428-9341 or 1-800/348-7263; ❷); – a nice break from the surrounding high-rises. For details of the lovely oceanside **campground** at First Landing/Seashore State Park, call ☎757/412-2300 or 1-800/933-7275.

The town also offers some great **restaurants** and a frenetic **nightlife**. *Capt. John's Crabhouse*, 33rd and Atlantic (☎757/425-6263), has a fine seafood and meat evening buffet for $16.95, while *Mahi Mah's*, by the ocean at Seventh and Atlantic (☎757/437-8030), has a creative menu of sushi, sashimi and other seafood, plus a wide selection of beers. *Baja Cantina*, 206 23rd St (☎757/437-2920), is a friendly bar serving tasty Mexican food to a decent rock soundtrack. Check *Port Folio*, the listings newspaper, for details of live **music** events; the *Abbey Road Pub* at 203 22nd St (☎757/425-6330), is a lively bar with over a hundred different beers and nightly live rock'n'roll; hostelers congregate most nights at the *Jewish Mother*, 3108 Pacific Ave (☎757/422-5430), a daytime deli and late-night beer bar with free live music.

The eastern shore

Virginia's longest and least visited stretch of Atlantic coastline, the **eastern shore**, lies separated from the rest of the state on the far side of Chesapeake Bay. Only the southernmost segment of what's known as the Delmarva peninsula (see p.480) belongs to Virginia, by which point it has narrowed to become a flat spit of sand protected by a fringe of low-lying islands.

US-13, which runs straight down the center of the peninsula and provides a handy short cut from Philadelphia or points north, crosses seventeen miles of open sea at the mouth of Chesapeake Bay, via the **Chesapeake Bay Bridge-Tunnel** ($10 per car). For most of its length, the roadway runs just a few yards above the water, bringing you almost eye-to-eye with passing ships; it twice burrows beneath the surface between artificial islands, before reaching its southern extremity halfway between Norfolk and Virginia Beach. To either side of US-13, little villages and fishing harbors such as Nassawadox, Assawoman and Accomac are tucked away on rambling back roads.

Chincoteague

Much the most appealing destination on the eastern shore, **CHINCOTEAGUE** occupies a beautiful barrier island just south of the Maryland border. Although it's little more than a village, its two principal streets hold a fair assortment of motels and restaurants, and it makes an appropriately relaxed base for exploring **Assateague Island National Seashore**. The northern half of Assateague, which holds several popular hiking trails, can only be reached from Maryland (see p.483); the southern half, just a mile onwards from Chincoteague, is taken up by the **Chincoteague National Wildlife Refuge**, notable for its seabirds and wild ponies. Call in at the **visitor center** (daily 9am–5pm; ☎757/336-6122; $5 per car) for a schedule of ranger-guided wildlife safaris ($10); or if you just want a day at the beach, drive straight past to **Tom's Cove**. Families fill the area nearest the parking lot, but set off walking north and you may end up with several miles of sand to yourself. If you're in Chincoteague on the last Wednesday and Thursday of July, don't miss the annual **Pony Penning Carnival**, when the wild ponies that roam Assateague Island to the north are herded together and directed on a swim through the channel to Chincoteague Memorial Park to be sold by auction to help the local community. It can be a crowded event, but the sight of dozens of ponies swimming in convoy in such pristine surroundings is unforgettable.

Central **accommodation** options in Chincoteague include the grand *Island Manor House*, 4160 Main St (☎757/336-5436; ❺), an antique-furnished B&B, and the large but peaceful *Mariner Motel*, 6273 Maddox Rd (☎757/336-6565, ⓦwww.esva.net/~motel; ❸), on the main road to Assateague. Next door, at no. 6251, is *Steamers* (☎757/336-5478), a brightly lit **restaurant** serving all-you-can-eat spiced crab and/or shrimp meals for around $20. Located in the small waterfront plaza, *Landmark Crab House*, 6172 N Main St (☎757/336-5552), also serves tasty seafood.

Charlottesville and the Shenandoah Valley

The densely forested 4000ft peaks of the **Blue Ridge Mountains** form a definite barrier between the history-rich worlds of tidewater Virginia to the east and the rougher river-and-valley country to the west. In between the two, at the geographical center of the state, sits the friendly, manageably small college town of **Charlottesville,** which holds two great monuments to the mind of **Thomas Jefferson**. South of Charlottesville, the village of **Appommattox** is the place at which papers were signed to officially end the **Civil War**, and is now preserved as an engaging national historic site. To the west, the northern Blue Ridge Mountains, crowned by the dense forests of **Shenandoah National Park**, run south to Tennessee, culminating in 5729ft Mount Rogers. Little seems to have changed in the lush Shenandoah Valley, on the far side of the mountains, since it was a vital battleground during the Civil War.

I-81, the main highway through the Shenandoah Valley, is joined in the north by I-66 from Washington DC and in the middle by I-64 from Richmond through Charlottesville. Numerous scenic routes are slower but more worthwhile, such as **Skyline Drive** and the **Blue Ridge Parkway**, which weave along the four-hundred-mile-long mountain crest. You'll need a car to get the most out of the region, though cycling is a good option along the many back roads and, for hikers, the **Appalachian Trail** runs right down the middle. There are plenty of roadside motels, so you needn't be too concerned about advance planning – it's a great place for aimless exploration.

Charlottesville

If you only have a couple of days to see Virginia, **CHARLOTTESVILLE**, seventy miles west of Richmond, should be near the top of your itinerary. Abounding in history, and holding some of the finest examples of early American architecture, it is at once small enough to feel comfortable in and large enough to have good restaurants and nightspots. Its compact, low-rise center is crisscrossed by magnolia-shaded streets, and makes a fine area to amble around, particularly in the six pedestrianized blocks of **Main Street**, site of the nightly town promenade. However pleasant the town, the compelling attraction is the legacy of Thomas Jefferson, whose home and final resting place, **Monticello**, stands atop a hill just east of town, overlooking the beautifully landscaped Neoclassical campus of the University of Virginia.

The University of Virginia

Though he wrote the Declaration of Independence and served as the third US president, Thomas Jefferson took more pride in having established the **University of Virginia** than in any of his other achievements, and after a visit you may well understand why. In 1976 the university was officially designated the greatest piece of architecture in the US; it also reveals the ideology of its patron, who, besides designing every building down to the most minute detail, also planned the curriculum and selected the faculty. Uniquely for universities of the time, which functioned primarily as seminaries, the University of Virginia was not rooted in religious training, but emphasized instead a broadly based liberal arts education, not surprising as Jefferson had been one of the prime proponents of the separation of church and state.

The highlight and architectural focus of the campus is the redbrick, white-domed **Rotunda**, modeled on the Pantheon and completed in 1821 to house the library and classrooms. A basement gallery tells the story of the university, while upstairs three elliptical classrooms are linked by a richly decorated central hall. A staircase winds up to the **Dome Room**, where Corinthian columns rise to an ocular skylight. From the Rotunda, where 45-minute guided tours of the campus begin (daily 10am–4pm; free), twin colonnades stretch along either side of a lushly landscaped quadrangle, linking together a string of single-story student apartments and taller pavilions in which professors live and hold tutorials. While the overall feel is harmonious, each individual block is unique, the differing facades and rooflines designed to show off the various orders and styles of Neoclassical architecture.

Parallel to the quadrangle buildings, two further rows of dormitory buildings, the East and West ranges, front on to serpentine walled gardens. **Edgar Allan Poe** stayed in one of these dorms while studying at the University of Virginia in 1826, but was forced to drop out after his stepfather cut off his allowance, apparently because Edgar had lost all of his money gambling. His room – Number 13, of course – in the West Range is now restored to how it would have looked during his occupancy, and is virtually the only campus interior, apart from the Rotunda, that you can visit.

Monticello – Thomas Jefferson's home

One of America's most familiar buildings – it graces the back of the nickel coin – **Monticello**, three miles southeast of Charlottesville on Hwy-53, was the home of Thomas Jefferson for most of his life. A visit provides a distinctive insight into the most intriguing of America's founding fathers. Surrounded by acres of beautifully landscaped hilltop grounds, which once comprised an

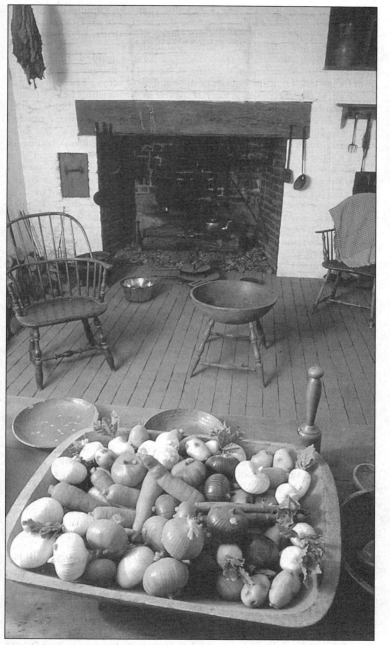

451

△ Inside Monticello

enormous plantation, with fine views out over the Virginia countryside, Monticello is a handsome house, whose symmetrical brick facade, centered upon a white Doric portico, belies the quirky irregularities of the interior – furnished as it was when Jefferson lived, and died, here.

To see Monticello you have to join one of the **guided tours** (daily: March–Oct 8am–5pm; rest of year 9am–4.30pm; $11) that leave continuously from the parking lot at the bottom of the hill. There's often a line, especially at weekends, so try to get there as early as possible in the morning. From the outside, Monticello looks like an elegant, Palladian-style country home, but as soon as you enter the domed entrance hall, with its funhouse mirror and displays of fossilized bones and elk antlers (from Lewis and Clark's epic 1804 journey across North America, which Jefferson sponsored as president), you begin to get a sense that Jefferson was a somewhat more interesting character than the sober statesman portrayed by most histories. His love of gadgets and odd little contraptions, which fill the house, marked him as something of an eccentric: examples of these include the elaborate dual-pen device he used to make automatic copies of all his letters, and the weather vane over the front porch which is connected to a dial so he could see which way the wind was blowing without having to step outside. Even Jefferson's **private chambers**, which can also be seen on the tour, are rather interesting: he slept in a tiny alcove linking his dressing room and his study, and would get up on the right side of the bed if he wanted to make some late-night notes, on the left if he wanted to get dressed. The upstairs rooms, where Jefferson's daughter lived, are not open to the public.

On the grounds around the house you get a feeling for how Monticello, a five thousand-acre plantation, really functioned. Extensive flower and vegetable gardens spread to the south and west, and a dank passage runs under the house from the kitchen and beer cellar (Jefferson was a keen home-brewer) to the remains of Mulberry Row, Monticello's **slave quarters**. Despite calling slavery an "abominable crime," Jefferson owned almost two hundred slaves and recent research indicates that he may have also sired a child with one of them. At the south end of Mulberry Row, a grove of ancient hardwood trees surrounds Jefferson's grave, marked by a simple stone obelisk; a footpath beyond winds back down to the bottom of the hill.

Charlottesville practicalities

Amtrak trains from DC stop in Charlottesville at 810 W Main St, and Greyhound pulls in a few blocks away at 310 W Main St. Once you arrive, you can get to everything on foot, including the new downtown **visitor center** at 108 2nd St SE (Mon-Sat 10am-5pm, Sun 11am-3pm; ☎434/977-6100 or 1-877/386-1102, ⊛www.charlottesvilletourism.org). The more established visitor center (daily 9am–5pm; ☎434/977-1783), well-signposted on Hwy-53 just south of I-64, houses a superb free exhibit called "Thomas Jefferson at Monticello," and is an excellent starting point for a trip to Monticello. Bus #8 from Market Street downtown goes there.

For its size, Charlottesville has quite a good range of **accommodation**. The usual motels line Emmet Street (US-29) at the west end of town, the least expensive being the *Budget Inn*, 140 Emmet St (☎434/293-5141 or 1-800/293-5144, ⊛www.budgetinn-charlottesville.com; ❸). *Hampton Inn & Suites* (☎434/923-8600 or 1-800/426-7866, ⊛www.hampton-inn.com; ❹) offers standard rooms right near the university at 900 W Main St, or good-value **B&B** is available at the two beautifully restored houses of the *200 South Street Inn*, 200 South St (☎434/979-0200, ⊛www.southstreetinn.com; ❺), and at the *1817 Historic Bed and Breakfast*, 1211 W Main St (☎434/979-7353; ❺). To arrange a stay in a B&B, call Guesthouses (☎434/979-7264).

The best **eating** and **drinking** is to be had near the university and on the downtown mall. In between the two, *Southern Culture*, 633 W Main St, (☎434/979-1990) is an inexpensive local favorite, with a slightly retro-1950s feel and fabulous tuna steak. *Metropolitan*, 214 W Water St ☎434/977-1043), is a suitably pricey downtown restaurant, but the fresh fish is worth every dollar. Just north of the downtown mall at Fifth and Market streets, *Tastings* (☎434/293-3663) offers grilled meats and a grand selection of wines, including many from the vineyards surrounding Charlottesville, while Virginia's best selection of beers, plus a range of light meals, can be sampled a block further north at the *Court Square Tavern*, 500 E Jefferson St (☎434/296-6111). The *C&O Restaurant*, 515 E Water St (☎434/971-7044), housed in an old railroad engineers' diner, offers bistro-style food in its humming bar and more upscale French *nouvelle cuisine* in the upstairs dining room.

Being a college town, Charlottesville isn't short of **nightlife**, whether at bars like the *Outback Lounge*, 110 N Fourth St (☎434/979-7211), or in its two main nightclubs, *Max's*, 120 S 11th St (☎434/295-6299), and *Starr Hill*, 709 W Main St (☎434/977-0017), which hosts live bands.

Appommattox

Settled amid the mild, roaming hills of central Virginia, some sixty miles south of Charlottesville on US-24, **APPOMMATTOX** marks the spot at which Robert E. Lee and Ulysses S. Grant met on April 9, 1865 to signify the end of the Civil War. After four years of enormous bloodshed on both sides, the Confederacy bowed out with a mere whimper. Grant's Union troops had cut off a nearby railroad line upon which Lee's final battalion depended for vital supplies, and the half-starved Confederate army had no choice but to submit. Final papers were signed in a private home near the Appommattox Court House. This event, a defining moment in American history, is remembered in the **Appommattox Court House National Historical Park** (daily 9am–5.30pm; $2), a place refreshingly free of the usual tourist baggage that accompanies most similarly important sites in the state. The tiny village has been handsomely restored, though the home and courthouse, now containing a museum, are reconstructions of the original.

Getting to Appommattox requires a car, and the nearest accommodation is available in the newer city of the same name, a few miles west. You're better off driving 20 miles further west, however, to **LYNCHBURG**, whose dramatic hills and tidy historic center make a fine place to spend an evening. Try the *Lynchburg Mansion Inn*, 405 Madison St (☎804/528-5400; ❺), a cozy Victorian B&B.

Shenandoah National Park

SHENANDOAH NATIONAL PARK, which contains seemingly endless acres of dark forests, deep rocky ravines and precipitous, surging waterfalls, has one of the most unusual histories of any US national park. Far from being untouched for the past three hundred years, this "natural" landscape was created when hundreds of small family farms and homesteads were bought up by the state and federal governments during the Depression, and the land was left to revert to its natural state.

Shenandoah, meaning "river of high mountains," has one of the most scenic byways in the US, the **Skyline Drive**, a thin ribbon of pavement curving along the crest of the Blue Ridge Mountains. It starts just off I-66 near the town of **Front Royal**, 75 miles west of DC, and winds south through the park, giving great views over the Piedmont to the east and lovely Shenandoah Valley to the west.

Admission to the park is $10 for cars and $5 for pedestrians, cyclists and motorcyclists; permits are good for six days. The views are especially fine, and the crowds especially large, in the fall, but at any time of year you can get the best of what the park has to offer by following one of the many **hiking trails** that split off from the ridge. One favorite leaves from the parking area of Big Meadows Lodge in the southern half of the park and winds along to tumbling **Dark Hollow Falls**; another, leaving Skyline Drive at mile marker 45, climbs up a fairly treacherous incline to the top of **Old Rag Mountain** for 360° views out over the whole of Virginia and the Allegheny Mountains in the west. More ambitious hikers, or those who want to spend the night out in the backcountry, head for the **Appalachian Trail**; details on any of these hikes, and free overnight camping permits, can be picked up at either of the **visitor centers** (mid–April–late Nov 8.30am–5pm; ☎540/999-3500, ⓦ www.nps.gov/shen), located along Skyline Drive four miles beyond the north entrance and at mile marker 51, in the middle of the park.

Three rustic **lodges**, near the center of the park, offer beds and food; reservations are handled by ARAMARK Services (☎540/743-5108 or 1–800/999-4714, ⓦ www.visitshenandoah.com). The northernmost and oldest, the 1894 *Skyland Lodge*, has cabins (❸) and modern hotel rooms (❺), as well as a large restaurant with panoramic views; *Big Meadows Lodge*, next to the larger visitor center ten miles south, has similar facilities and a campground; and *Lewis Mountain* has cabins (❸) and a first-come, first-served campground ($17). For more information on camping in the park call ☎1–800/365-2267.

The Shenandoah Valley

The small, character-filled towns of the **Shenandoah Valley**, down below Skyline Drive, are as rich in human history as any in Virginia. Many were left in ruins after the war, but have since been restored to their original antebellum condition, and numerous memorials, monuments and cemeteries line the back roads, surrounded by spacious horse farms and apple orchards.

Given its strategic importance and fertile soil, the Shenandoah Valley was inevitably one of the most fought-over battlegrounds in the Civil War, changing hands over seventy times at a cost of some 100,000 dead and maimed. The whole bloody story is told in evocative detail in the small but outstanding **museum** (daily 9am–5pm; $6) at the **New Market Battlefield**, just off I-81, thirty miles south of the I-66 junction. This was the scene of the legendary 1864 confrontation that involved a company of fourteen-year-old cadets from the Virginia Military Institute.

Besides its Civil War history, the northern Shenandoah Valley also holds half a dozen of Virginia's many underground **limestone caverns**. All are privately owned and cost $6–13.50 to enter. You'll no doubt see billboards advertising each one as the best; that title really belongs to the largest, **Luray Caverns**, twelve miles east of New Market off Hwy-211 (guided 1hr tours daily, every 20min from 9am to 6pm, 4pm in winter; $14), a subterranean wonderland featuring a bizarre underground "organ" with stalagmites as "pipes." Your ticket also gives access to the adjacent **Historic Car and Carriage** exhibit (daily 9am–7.30pm), a collection of vintage automobiles starring an 1892 Benz.

Further south, off Hwy-250 northwest of the town of **STAUNTON**, the **Museum of Frontier American Culture** (daily 9am–5pm; $8) brings to light how the various immigrants who settled here melded their traditions to develop a joint American culture. Most of the exhibits are about farming techniques and other somewhat mundane activities, but it's all engagingly presented and well worth a look. Close by, just off US-660 near Stuarts Draft, the lovely *Shenandoah Acres Resort* (☎540/337-1911 or 1-800/654-1714, Ⓦwww.shenacres.com; ❹) offers large cabins and motel units, as well as camping facilities ($22 per tent) and a man-made lake for swimming.

Lexington

Though it's one of the region's smaller towns, **LEXINGTON**, in the heart of the Shenandoah Valley, easily has the most to offer visitors. From horse-drawn carriages parading along its quiet, brick-lined streets, to the fine rolling countryside all around – displayed to great effect in the movie *Sommersby* – Lexington makes a great place to sit back and relax or, if you prefer, delve deep into Civil War and assorted other military memorabilia at its small museums and memorials.

The most engaging of these, the **Lee Chapel** (April–Oct Mon–Sat 9am–5pm, Sun 2–5pm; Nov–March Mon–Sat 9am-4pm, Sun 1-4pm; free), is on the attractive colonnaded campus of **Washington and Lee University**, a short walk north of the town center. A commodious and somber building, the chapel is named in honor of Confederate general Robert E. Lee, who taught here after the Civil War. Behind the pulpit is a marble statue of Lee in repose, surrounded by an array of authentic battle flags; along with many members of his family, Lee is interred downstairs in the chapel crypt, and his horse Traveler is buried just outside.

On the comparatively bland but formidable campus of the **Virginia Military Institute**, just east of the Lee Chapel, the **Military Museum** (daily 9am–5pm; free) tells the story of the state-supported, male-only military academy, which was founded in 1836 and has the dubious claim to fame of being the only university in US history to have sent its entire student body into battle. If possible, time your visit to coincide with the 4pm Friday full-dress parade held on the field in front of the museum.

At the opposite end of the parade ground, the **George C. Marshall Museum** (daily: March–Oct 9am–5pm; Nov–Feb 9am–4pm; $3) documents the life of World War II US general and later secretary of state George C. Marshall, whose plan for the reconstruction of postwar Europe earned him the Nobel Peace Prize in 1953.

The **Stonewall Jackson House**, 8 E Washington St (June–Aug Mon–Sat 9am–6pm, Sun 1–6pm; Sept–May Mon–Sat 9am–5pm, Sun 1–5pm; $5), is where the noted Confederate general and Virginia Military Institute philosophy professor lived for fifteen years before his death at the battle of Chancellorsville. His spartan brick townhouse is furnished as it was in the years before the war. Stonewall is buried, along with hundreds of his fellow soldiers, in the **Stonewall Jackson Memorial Cemetery** off South Main Street. This is now the prime destination for twilight **ghost tours**, leaving from the visitor center every evening at 8.30pm (May–Oct only; $8), which are great if you're traveling with kids.

Twenty miles south of Lexington on US-11 is the spectacular **Natural Bridge** (daily: June–Sept 9am–10pm; Oct–May 9am–5pm; $10), where meandering Cedar Creek has gradually carved away at the softer limestone, forming a 215ft archway that has dazzled several distinguished visitors over the years: George Washington allegedly carved his initials into the rock (though it takes a keen eye to see them), and Thomas Jefferson was so impressed that he bought the site and owned it for fifty years. It's worth the hefty admission price, but don't expect it to be "one of the Seven Natural Wonders of the World" as its publicists suggest. The Natural Bridge **Caverns** are also on site ($7), but it's best to save your money for the more spectacular Luray Caverns, further north (see p.454). Another option is the $17 combination ticket which gets you into the caverns, the Bridge and the cheesy **Wax Museum** that's also here.

Even if you're not thrilled by war stories and natural bridges, Lexington still makes a good stop, with dozens of fine old homes to see; pick up a walking tour map from the friendly **visitor center**, 102 E Washington St (daily: June–Aug 8.30am–6pm; Sept–May 9am–5pm; ☎540/463-3777, Ⓦwww.lexingtonvirginia.com). For **food**, the *Southern Inn Restaurant*, right in the center at 37 S Main St (☎540/463-3612) offers good ol' Southern cooking such as a scrumptious meatloaf; it's attached to a bar that churns out live **music** Friday and Saturday nights. If your taste tends towards tofu, you may prefer the *Blue Heron Café*, 4 E Washington St (☎540/463-2800), one block from the visitor center. A few blocks west stands Lexington's one remarkably cheap **place to stay**, the nicely maintained $10-a-night self-serve *Overnight Guests*, 216 W Washington St (☎540/463-3075; ❶); in addition to the usual motels along the highways, the comfy German- and French-speaking *Asherowe B&B*, 314 S Jefferson St (☎540/463-4219; ❸), is located six blocks southwest of the visitor center. There is also a **campground** along Rte-11 south of town, near Natural Bridge (☎540/291-2727).

The Blue Ridge Parkway

Once out of Shenandoah National Park, Skyline Drive becomes the **Blue Ridge Parkway**, which winds southwest along the crest of the Appalachians at an average elevation of three thousand feet. It's a beautiful drive, though **I-81**, sweeping along the flank of the mountains, is a more efficient way of getting from Virginia to North Carolina and on to the Great Smokies, a route covered in detail on p.512. In summer the *Rocky Knob Cabins* (☎540/593-3503; ❸), at milepost 174 on the Parkway itself, offers a memorable night's stay in the idyllic Meadows of Dan. Not far beyond milepost 214, the rambling old *HI-Blue Ridge Country* **hostel** (☎540/236-4962; ❶) has dorm beds for $15.65 ($18.65 for nonmembers). Of the nearby towns, **ROANOKE**, sandwiched between I-81 and the Parkway, is the largest community in western Virginia. Beyond its drab modern approaches, the leisurely, old-fashioned streets make for a pleasant stopoff, particularly to visit the still-functioning farmers' market (Mon–Sat) and the modern Center In The Square mall. The mall contains several museums, including the engaging **Roanoke Valley History Museum** (Tues–Fri 10am–4pm, Sat 10am–5pm, Sun 1–5pm; $2), which documents settlement of the region by the Scottish, Welsh and Germans, and the **Virginia Museum of Transportation**, 303 Norfolk Ave (Mon–Sat 10am–5pm, Sun noon–5pm; $6), which is home to the largest collection of steam locomotives in America, and hints at Roanoke's railroad foundations.

An excellent, helpful **visitor center** at 114 Market St (daily 9am–5pm; ☎540/345-8622 or 1-800/635-5535, Ⓦwww.visitroanokeva.com) can provide information and walking tour maps. The *Jefferson Lodge* at 616 S Jefferson St (☎540/342-2951; ❷) is basic but very centrally located, while the least expensive of the interstate motels is the *Rodeway Inn*, 526 Orange Ave NE, at exit 4E off I-581 (☎540/981-9341 or 1-800/228-2000; ❸). Campbell Avenue downtown sports a number of appealing **restaurants**, including *Awful Arthur's Seafood Co*, 108 Campbell Ave (☎540/344-2997), a good lunch or dinner spot with interesting specials. *Carlos*, at 312 Market St (☎540/345-7661), serves superb "international cuisine," predominantly Brazilian, while the *Tavern on the Market* at 32 Market Square (☎540/343-2957) serves up typical pub fare and a range of beers.

History buffs surfeited on the Civil War might want to call into the town of **BEDFORD**, about 20 miles east of Roanoke and not far from the Parkway. An unprepossessing place in itself, this small community of 3200 lost twenty-one men (out of thirty-five) at Omaha Beach during the Allied invasion of Normandy on June 6, 1944, the highest per capita loss of anywhere in the USA. For that reason, Bedford was chosen as the site for the massive **National D-Day Memorial** ($10 per car annual fee), which opened on the anniversary of the event in 2001. Situated on a beautifully landscaped hilltop, the various monuments, statues and structures culminate in the 44ft arch of Victory Plaza. It is signposted just off US-460, on the south side of town.

West Virginia

The people of **WEST VIRGINIA** are only half joking when they call their state the Ireland of the US. Generally poor and almost entirely rural, it shares a similar history of exploitation by outside powers, with **timber** and **coal-mining** companies taking advantage of the rich natural resources while giving little in return. But, quite apart from the almost Third World deprivation which endures in some areas, West Virginia is also, in places at least, incredibly beautiful, and can boast the longest white-water rivers and most extensive wilderness areas in the eastern US. The extreme topography, which has historically isolated its inhabitants, now makes the state a popular destination for hikers and outdoors enthusiasts, and the moonshiners of old have been replaced by ski instructors and mountain-bike guides. Pioneer settlers started to cross the mountains of western Virginia in significant numbers during the middle of the seventeenth century. Farming small plots of land with their own labor, they came to have ever less in common with the slave-holding plantation owners of old Virginia, and when the Civil War broke out, the area declined to secede from the Union. The Supreme Court never ruled whether West Virginia was legally entitled to declare itself a state, and Virginia itself has still not officially recognized the split. West Virginia has, however, developed a political and economic identity of its own. Around 1900, when railroads from the east coast first reached into the mountainous interior, timber companies clear-cut stand after stand of forest, setting up a succession of mill towns, each dismantled in its turn when they moved on somewhere new. **Cass**, now preserved within the Allegheny National Forest, is one of the few that was left intact. Later on, coal-mining conglomerates, especially in the south, perfected the "company town" approach, wherein workers were paid a little bit less each month than the amount they owed for their company-provided food and lodging. Coal companies still exert immense power in West Virginia, but the real key to the state's future prosperity is tourism, which in places now accounts for over half its income.

The state's most popular destination, the restored 1850s town of **Harpers**

Ferry, is barely in West Virginia at all, standing just across the broad rivers which form its Maryland and Virginia borders. To the west, the **Allegheny Mountains** stretch for over 150 miles; more than a million acres of hardwood forest rival New England for brilliant autumnal color. West Virginia's oldest and most attractive town, **Lewisburg**, sits just off I-64 at the mountains' southern foot, while the capital, **Charleston**, lies in the comparatively flat Ohio River valley of the west.

Getting around West Virginia

With its many mountains and rivers making straight, flat roads virtually non-existent, getting around West Virginia is as much a part of its attraction as is any specific destination – a bike and a stout pair of legs, or a motorcycle, would be ideal, but a car is pretty necessary if you really want to see the state. Greyhound is basically useless here, and Amtrak, apart from serving Harpers Ferry from Washington DC, has only one, albeit spectacular route, running through the New River Gorge to the capital, Charleston.

Harpers Ferry

HARPERS FERRY, a ruggedly sited eighteenth-century town now restored as a national historic park, gives many visitors their first and only look at West Virginia. Clinging to steep hillsides above the rocky confluence of the Potomac and Shenandoah rivers, many of the town's forty-odd brick and stone buildings date from the days when George Washington set up the country's first **national munitions factory** here to arm the young Republic. During the mid-1800s Harpers Ferry was a thriving industrial complex, home to some five thousand workers and linked to the capital by the B&O Railroad and the Chesapeake & Ohio Canal. After suffering the ravages of the Civil War and a series of torrential floods, however, it was all but abandoned, the empty shells of its homes and factories slowly becoming overgrown by the dense forest that covers the surrounding hills. Almost all of Harpers Ferry has since been reconstructed as an outdoor museum, combining historical importance and natural beauty.

However pretty Harpers Ferry may be – and in the fall, when the leaves blaze with color, it's hard to imagine a more picture-perfect setting – it's best known for its place in US history. The 1859 raid on its huge US arsenal by anti-slavery revolutionary **John Brown**, which rocked the already fragmenting nation, was the clearest foreshadowing of the Civil War, which broke out just sixteen months later. In the hope of fomenting a widespread slave revolt, Brown and twenty-one other abolitionist radicals, including two of his sons and five black men, seized the munitions factory and its large store of weapons on the night of October 16. They held out for two days before US troops, under the command of Robert E. Lee, stormed the buildings, killing many of the raiders and capturing Brown. He was taken to nearby Charles Town, put on trial just nine days later, and convicted of treason; by the time he was hanged on December 2, he was far from alone in regarding himself as a martyr to the abolitionist cause.

As one of only two places in the US with the capacity to manufacture munitions, Harpers Ferry was a major prize in the Civil War, and it never got back on its feet after the resultant devastation. The arsenal buildings were burned in 1861 to keep the weapons out of Confederate hands, while in 1862 Stonewall Jackson captured the town along with 12,500 Union soldiers. Enough of the original buildings and cobbled streets survive, however, to give a good sense of how things used to be, and the restoration project has so far managed to re-create the townscape without making it feel too much like a theme park.

The Town

Almost everyone who comes to Harpers Ferry drives. Parking is virtually banned in the old town area; shuttle buses run from the large **visitor center** on US-340 (visitor center and attractions open daily 8am–5pm; buses run 8am–5.45pm, 6.45pm in summer; ☎304/535-6299, ⓦ www.nps.gov/hafe) – where you pay the $3 per person, $5 per car entry fee – to the old town, dropping off outside the old balconied **Stagecoach Inn**, at the end of gas-lit Shenandoah Street in the heart of the restored area; inside there's an information desk with maps and a small bookshop. Across the street, displays in the **Master Armorer's House** will tell you everything you want to know about gun-making; adjacent buildings include a restored blacksmith's shop, a general store and a tavern, often peopled with costumed guides who describe and act out events from the town's history.

John Brown's **fort** – actually the armory's engine room, where he and his raiders were captured – originally stood directly across from the tavern, but was rebuilt a block away, near the point where the rivers meet. It's no more than an empty shell, however, and if you want to get the full story of the raid you'd do better to spend half an hour in the **John Brown Museum** opposite. Here, as throughout Harpers Ferry, debate continues to rage over Brown's sanity or sanctity; many regard him as a borderline psychotic. One monument on the wall of the building, erected by the Daughters of the Confederacy, salutes the attack's first victim, a free black railroad baggage master named Hayward Shepherd, as epitomizing the "character and faithfulness of thousands of negroes" in the old South; across from it stands another monument honoring Brown's "heroism."

Other museums, housing exhibits on the Civil War and local black history, line both sides of **High Street** as it climbs away from the river. At one point, a set of stone steps ascends between them through the residential area, to the 1782 **Harper House**, preserved as a typical worker's rooming house of the period.

A footpath continues uphill, past overgrown churchyards hemmed in by dry-stone walls, to **Jefferson Rock**, a huge gray boulder affording a great view over the two rivers; Thomas Jefferson said the vista was worth a voyage across the Atlantic. For a longer hike, two trails lead onwards into the surrounding forest: the **Appalachian Trail** continues from Jefferson Rock across the Shenandoah River into the Blue Ridge Mountains of Virginia, while the **Maryland Heights Trail** makes a four-mile round-trip around the headlands across the Potomac River. You can also float down the river in a **raft** or innertube provided by one of the many outfitters along the rivers east and south of town.

Practicalities

Harpers Ferry makes a popular excursion from Washington DC, served by several trains daily on the Maryland Rail Commuter network (☎1-800/325-7245), and by one daily Amtrak service, which arrives at 5.15pm, en route to Chicago. Greyhound, however, comes no closer than Frederick, Maryland (see p.475).

If you want to **spend the night**, the century-old *Hilltop House Hotel and Restaurant* on Ridge Street (☎304/535-2132 or 1-800/338-8319, ⓦ www.hilltophousehotel.com; ❸) may be showing its age, but still has reasonable prices and good views, while amiable **B&Bs** are sprinkled throughout the surrounding region, including *Harpers Ferry Guest House*, 800 Washington St (☎304/535-6955, ⓦ www.harpersferry-wv.com; ❹); nearby budget motels include the *Comfort Inn* on US-340 (☎304/535-6391 or 1-800/228-5150; ❸). The *HI-Harpers Ferry Lodge*, a couple of miles east at 19123 Sandy Hook Rd in Knoxville, MD (☎301/834-7652, ⓦwww.harpersferryhostel.org; closed Nov–March; ❶), has dorm beds from $14, and its own campground; there's plenty more **camping** along the Potomac River in the C&O Canal Historic Park. The park's **visitor center** has further details, as does the **Jefferson County tourist bureau** (☎304/535-2627 or 1-800/848-TOUR), across US-340. As for **eating**, old-style cafés line High Street up from the historic area – both the *Mountain House Café* (☎304/535-2339) and the *Garden of Food* (☎304/535-2202) are good and relatively inexpensive.

Around Harpers Ferry

Among small towns worth seeing nearby is **CHARLES TOWN**, four miles south of Harpers Ferry on US-340, where John Brown was tried and hanged; the **Jefferson County Museum** at Washington and Samuel (Mon–Sat 10am–4pm; free) tells the story of his trial, conviction and execution, and remembers his last words: "I, John Brown, am now quite certain that the crimes of this guilty land will never be purged away but with blood." **SHEPHERDS-TOWN**, a cozy village along the Potomac ten miles to the north, is prettier and better for wandering, with quaint ancient shops and cafés looking across the river to Maryland's infamous **Antietam Battlefield** (see p.475).

Further afield, and of more salubrious interest, is the old spa town of **BERKELEY SPRINGS**, now preserved as a state historic park, thirty miles west of Harpers Ferry on Hwy-9, seven miles south of I-70. The nearest early America ever came to having resorts like Bath in England, Berkeley Springs was a favorite summer retreat of the colonial elite – George Washington and Lord Fairfax were among the regulars who came here to take the waters – and assorted massage and steam bath treatments are still available at its many health spas. You can take a soak in the old **Roman Bath House** (call ☎304/258-2711 for details), in active use since 1815 and now run by the state. The town's **central square** is leafy and green, with footpaths fanning out in all directions, one climbing the hill up to the fortress-like mid-Victorian **Berkeley Castle**. Among the **B&Bs** in Berkeley Springs are the *Highlawn Inn*, 304 Market St (☎304/258-5700 or 1-888/290-4163, ⓦwww.highlawninn.com; ❹), and the *Manor Inn*, 415 Fairfax St (☎304/258-1552, ⓦwww.bathmanorinn.com; ❹).

The Allegheny Mountains

Considering that it's the most extensive wilderness area near the east coast, within just a few hours' drive of a dozen big cities, surprisingly few people have heard about, much less bothered to visit, the backcountry reaches of the **Allegheny Mountains**, West Virginia's segment of the Appalachian chain. The entire 140-mile crest is protected as part of the **Monongahela National Forest**, within which numerous state parks highlight the most spectacular sights. There are no cities and few towns, public transportation is nonexistent, and not much goes on after dark – to give an idea of how rural it is, whole counties do without a single traffic light – but if you like to backpack, ski, cycle, climb, canoe or just wander around the great outdoors, the Alleghenies are well worth a visit. For maps and more detailed information, contact the state tourist office (see p.28) or the Monongahela National Forest Supervisor, 200 Sycamore St, Elkins, WV 26241 (Mon–Fri 8am–4.45pm; ☎304/636-1800).

Blackwater Falls, the Canaan Valley and Seneca Rocks

Some of the most beautiful stretches of the Monongahela National Forest are in the central northern part of the state, where the thundering torrents of the **Blackwater Falls** pour over a 60ft limestone cliff before crashing down through a steeply walled canyon. South from here spreads the dense maple, oak, walnut and birch forest of broad **Canaan Valley**, while to the east rise the barren subarctic highlands of the **Dolly Sods Wilderness**, the whole area crisscrossed by hiking, cycling and skiing trails.

Rising up at the far end of the Canaan Valley, the state's highest point, 4861ft **Spruce Knob,** stands out over the headwaters of the Potomac River – you can actually drive all the way to the summit. Even more impressive views can be had from the top of **Seneca Rocks**, some twenty miles to the northeast, whose 1000ft limestone cliffs are commonly considered to present the most challenging rock-climb on the east coast. If you want to take the easy way up, a good trail leads in around the back of the North Peak, and takes well under an hour to the top. The helpful **Discovery Center** at the junction of US-33 and Hwy-28 (summer daily 8am–4.30pm; rest of year Sat & Sun only; ☏304/567-2827) has details of outdoor recreation opportunities in the entire region. *Yokum's* (☏304/567-2351 or 1-800/772-8342, ⊛www.yokum.com), near the base of Seneca Rocks, takes care of all your vital needs, with a cheap **motel** (❷), self-service **cabins** (❹), and a pretty riverside **campground** (from $5), plus a country store and down-home **restaurant** serving tasty, good value meals.

The old logging town of **DAVIS** (population 1000), just east of US-219 at the north end of the Canaan Valley, makes another convenient base, with a couple of **places to stay**: the *Best Western Alpine Lodge* (☏304/259-5245; ❸) has standard motel rooms, and the *Bright Morning Inn* (☏304/259-5119, ⊛www.brightmorninginn.com; ❸) on Williams Avenue doubles as the town **café**. *Muttley's* next door (☏304/259-4858) serves great-value steaks. Among local **outdoor guides and outfitters**, Blackwater Outdoor Adventures, nearly twenty miles away on Rte-72 at St. George (☏304/478-3775, ⊛www.raftboc.com), runs rafting, caving and canoeing trips, and also rents out bikes. Timberline Resort (☏304/866-4801 or 1-800/SNOWING, ⊛www.timberlineresort.com) operates the state's largest downhill ski area several miles southeast of town. For more information on the region, contact the **visitor center** on Main Street (daily 9am–5pm; ☏304/259-5315 or 1-800/782-2775, ⊛www.canaanvalley.org).

Elkins and the Augusta Festival

Despite its rather drab and functional appearance, one of the best places for visitors to experience the vibrant folk traditions of the West Virginia mountains is **ELKINS**, the biggest town in northern West Virginia, which lies just west of the Canaan Valley. The **Augusta Heritage Center**, which is part of Davis and Elkins College at 100 Sycamore St (☏304/637-1209), works to keep Appalachian cultural traditions alive in music, arts and crafts. Concerts and events are held throughout the summer, and there are celebrations of dulcimer-playing in April and fiddle music in October, but its major annual showcase is mid-August's **Augusta Festival**. This offers public workshops in such diverse down-home pursuits as banjo-playing, blacksmithing, quilt-making and folk dancing, and after dark, performers get together for a nightly hoedown, featuring storytellers, bluegrass bands and all-round good times.

Elkins' main **visitor center** (Mon–Fri 8.30am–5.30pm, Sat & Sun 9am–6pm; ☎304/636-2717 or 1-800/422-3304, ⓦwww.randolphcounty.com), half a mile east of the town center at the intersection where US-33 starts to climb into the mountains, can provide full details on local **accommodation**, including several B&Bs, while the *Super 8*, at the intersection of US-219 and US-250 (☎304/636-6500 or 1-800/800-8000, ⓦwww.super8.com; ❸), has inexpensive, clean motel rooms. The *Starr Café and Augusta Bookshop*, 224 Davis Ave (☎304/636-7273), is a friendly place to stop off for a coffee or snack in the center of town.

Pocahontas County

The southern half of the Monongahela National Forest is contained within hilly **Pocahontas County**, known as "the birthplace of rivers" because it holds the headwaters of the Greenbrier, Cheat, Gauley and other great West Virginia rivers. Like most of the Alleghenies, it's a mountainous, fairly inaccessible region – two roads, US-219 and Hwy-92, wind north-to-south, with a handful of minor roads twisting between them – offering outstanding outdoor recreation as well as endless scenic vistas.

Besides gorgeous scenery, Pocahontas County is also home to the state-run **Cass Scenic Railroad**, a restored, steam-powered logging railroad built in 1902. Running on narrow-gauge tracks, the chugging Shay locomotive carries visitors up to the top of 4842ft Bald Knob on a converted logging train (summer daily 10.50am, 1pm & 3pm, some evening dinner trains; $17, $19 weekends; ☎304/456-4300 or 1-800/CALL-WVA), starting at the old lumber-mill village of **CASS**, five miles west of Hwy-28 near the town of **Greenbank**. Cass was built by the local logging company to provide subsidized housing for its workers, thereby ensuring their faithful economic dependence; it has been preserved in its entirety as a historic park. You can wander around the eerily monotonous, white loggers' cabins, or even **stay the night** in one of several converted into self-service accommodation (☎1-800/CALL-WVA; ❸–❹) which have room for up to ten people. A short way west of Cass, *Whittaker Campground* (☎304/456-3218) offers basic camping facilities in a fine hillside setting.

Just outside of Greenbank, it's impossible to miss the gigantic white dish of the **Green Bank Telescope** and its smaller cousins, standing out against the mountain ridges. At sixteen million tons, the national radio astronomical telescope is the largest steerable object on the planet. The site, chosen because of the state's minimal radio interference, is open to the public, who can join free hourly tours on a shuttle bus, following an introductory lecture (June–Aug daily; May & Sept–Oct Sat & Sun 9am–4pm). Four miles north on Hwy-28 in Boyer, *Ryder's* restaurant (☎304/456-4308) dishes up good home-style cooking at bargain prices.

A rigorous five-mile walk downhill from Cass leads along the tracks to the start of the bicycle-friendly **Greenbrier River Trail**, which follows the river and the railroad for 75 miles, coming out near Lewisburg (see opposite). You can also rent a **mountain bike** from Elk River Touring Center (☎304/572-3771 or 1-888/572-3771, ⓦwww.ertc.com), fifteen miles north of **Marlinton**, the county seat, off US-219 in the hamlet of **Slatyfork**, and set off into the mountains. The company runs a shuttle service to the trailheads and organizes backcountry cycling trips and ski tours in winter, and its lovely year-round **hotel** (❸) has a hot tub and good-value restaurant. Larger cabins for groups are also available. The Pocahontas County **visitor center** in Marlinton (☎304/799-4636 or 1-800/336-7009) provides maps of the local area.

Another spot well worth visiting is **Cranberry Glades Botanical Area**, off

Hwy-39/55, five miles west of the junction with the exquisite Highland Scenic Highway (Rte-150). A half-mile boardwalk is set out around a rare patch of peat bogland; it's fun trying to identify the minute carnivorous plants that hide among the mosses and other flora. Leaflets and further information can be obtained from the Cranberry Mountain Nature Center (daily 9am–5pm; ☎304/653-4826) at the junction itself.

The other main attraction in this part of the Alleghenies is the birthplace of **Pearl S. Buck**, author of *The Good Earth* and one of only two American women – the other being Toni Morrison – to win the Nobel Prize for Literature. Her **home** at **HILLSBORO**, on US-219 halfway between Marlinton and Lewisburg, is packed with memorabilia.

Lewisburg and the Greenbrier Resort

Located just off I-64 on the southern edge of the Monongahela National Forest, **LEWISBURG** is the archetypal West Virginia town, its few square blocks of old buildings surrounded by rich pastureland, with good roads allowing quick access to the wilder mountain reaches. Originally a frontier outpost during the Indian Wars of the 1770s, Lewisburg was greatly prized during the Civil War for its location at the head of the Greenbrier Valley, but nowadays its attractions are those of a classic American small town, where everyone seems to know everyone else and where the houses and shops have remained in the same family for generations. In mid-August each year, Lewisburg plays host to the **West Virginia State Fair** (call ☎304/645-1090 for exact dates).

Washington Street, the four-block business district, is lined on both sides by brick-faced early nineteenth-century houses, and makes for pleasant wandering; no. 106 has been a two-chair barbershop for over a hundred years. A block away, in a small park at 200 N Jefferson St, stands the oldest surviving structure in Lewisburg, a rough-hewn limestone shed built in 1770 to protect a freshwater spring that is still flowing today.

The **visitor center**, 111 N Jefferson St (Mon–Fri 9am–5pm, Sat 10am–4pm; ☎304/645-1000 or 1-800/833-2068, ⓦwww.greenbrierwv.com), hands out walking tour maps of the town and can suggest driving tours around Greenbrier Valley. It can also put you in touch with various cozy **hotels**, such as the *General Lewis Inn*, 301 E Washington St (☎304/645-2600 or 1-800/628-4454, ⓦwww.generallewisinn.com; ❹), which also has a fine, moderately priced **restaurant**.

Just east of Lewisburg, outside the faded spa of **WHITE SULPHUR SPRINGS**, two dozen US presidents have escaped the pressures of politics in *The Greenbrier*, 300 W Main St (☎304/536-1110 or 1-800/624-6070, ⓦwww.greenbrier.com; ❾). The grandest and plushest hotel in West Virginia, it is five-star all the way, from the pillared entrance hall to the 6500 acres of lush grounds and golf courses. The hotel's four restaurants are all open to the public and require reservations.

The New River Gorge

One of West Virginia's most spectacular river canyons, the **New River Gorge** lies just thirty miles west of Lewisburg along I-64. Stretching for over fifty miles, and now protected as a national park, the thousand-foot cleft was carved through the limestone mountains by the New River – despite its name, one of the oldest rivers in North America. Apart from one daily train (see overleaf), there's no easy access to most of the gorge – to see it, you have to get out on the water, with the help of any of over fifty professional rafting companies;

visitor centers located near the most impressive spots give details of recreation opportunities. Just off US-19 northeast of **Fayetteville**, the **Canyon Rim visitor center** sits alongside the New River Gorge Bridge (daily: June–Aug 9am–8pm; Sept–Oct 9am–6pm; Nov–May 9am–5pm; ☎304/574-2115), the largest single-span steel arch in the country, which rises nine hundred feet above the river; the smaller **Grandview visitor center** is located at an elbow bend in the river, five miles north of I-64 near **Beckley** (same hours; ☎304/763-3715). Those traveling between Beckley and Charleston can find very cheap **accommodation** at the cozy *Avision Inn* (☎304/442-8446, 1-800/CALL-WVA) on Hwy-61 in Handley, where singles only cost $25 and the whole three-bedroomed self-catering cottage costs $65.

Fortunately for car-less travelers, Amtrak **trains** from Washington DC pass right through the gorge on one of the most stunning railway journeys in the East. Though the ride itself is memorable enough, for a close-up look you can get off at the southern end of the gorge at the c.1900 railroad town of **HINTON**. The train's only stop, it's a fascinating, if somewhat dilapidated remnant of the glory days of the railroads. An almost perfectly preserved purpose-built company town – the National Park Service intends someday to restore it as a living museum – it is beautifully sited, with brick-lined streets angling up from the water, lined by dozens of grand civic buildings as well as row after row of slowly decaying workers' houses. A walking tour map of Hinton is available from the Chamber of Commerce, 206 Temple St (Mon–Fri 9am-5pm; ☎304/466-5420).

Although the town has definitely seen better days, Hinton still makes a workable base for visitors to the gorge: there is another visitor center (same hours as the Canyon Rim visitor center; ☎304/466-0617), as well as a pair of decent budget **motels**, the *Coast-to-Coast* (☎304/466-2040; ❷) and the *Sandman* (☎304/466-1700; ❷), and a couple of riverfront taverns. Local **river-rafting** outfits include New River Tours (☎304/466-2288 or 1-800/292-0880) and Cantrell Canoes (☎304/466-0595 or 1-800/470-RAFT), both charging from $69 per person (with occasional specials) for trips through the gorge. All of these facilities are to be found on Hwy-20 just south of town.

Charleston

After leaving the gorge, the New River flows west into the Ohio and eventually the Mississippi, but not before passing through **CHARLESTON**, West Virginia's state capital and largest city. Charleston isn't a place many people set out to visit, mainly because there's not very much to see or do; the riverfront **state capitol**, designed by Lincoln Memorial architect Cass Gilbert and completed in 1932, is pleasant enough, with a small monument to black activist Booker T. Washington on its grounds, but nothing really grabs you. The **West Virginia Cultural Center** (Mon–Thurs 9am–8pm, Fri-Sat 9am–6pm, Sun 12–6pm, ⊛www.wvculture.org; free), in the same compound as the capitol, acts as the state museum with extensive displays in the basement on coalmining, forestry, wars and general social history. The main live showcase of traditional West Virginian culture takes place here during the annual **Vandalia Festival**, Appalachia's largest celebration of folk arts and crafts, held on Memorial Day weekend and featuring lively bluegrass music and tall-tale-telling contests. The annual **Regatta** on Labor Day weekend is one of the city's other big events.

There are three hundred **rooms** at the very central *Travelodge*, 2 Kanawha Blvd E (☎304/343-4521 or 1-800/578-7878; ❸), which also has a sauna and swimming pool; other motels abound along the interstates. *General Seafood*, 213 Broad St (Tues–Sat; ☎304/343-5671), is a restaurant attached to a fish market, and Capitol Street downtown boasts a string of eateries such as the *Mykonos Café* at no. 218 (☎304/347-9220), which does good Greek lunch specials. On the western edge of downtown, almost alongside I-64 between Lee and Quarrier streets, the gleaming new **Charleston Civic Center** mall is the liveliest area to while away a couple of hours.

Maryland

Founded as the sole Catholic colony in strongly Protestant America, and isolated as the northernmost slave state, **MARYLAND** has always been unusual. Within its small, irregularly-shaped area, its attractions range from the frantic, boardwalk beaches of **Ocean City** to the sleepy fishing villages of the **Chesapeake Bay**, and the bustling urban center of **Baltimore** to peaceful Appalachian hill country. Once one of the world's most productive fishing areas, Maryland's Chesapeake has recently been brought back from the brink of complete annihilation due to pollution and overfishing. Its abundant oyster stocks are a thing of the past, but legendary **soft-shell blue crabs** and sweet rockfish are more plentiful than ever, and now support a diverse, decentralized economy, buoyed by the hundreds of weekend boaters who cruise from one to another of its colonial-era towns.

Maryland's heritage isn't quite as obvious as Virginia's, with nowhere near as many historical sites, but it boasts plenty of firsts for the United States, including the first Catholic Cathedral, gas-lit street and telegraph line between Baltimore and Washington DC. Kent Island on Maryland's **Eastern Shore** was the third permanent English settlement (behind Jamestown and Plymouth Rock) in 1631. And during the War of 1812, the British forces attempted a last-ditch effort to wrest back the colonies, in which they burned down much of Washington DC and moved onto the shipyards of Baltimore. In a valiant battle, they were staved off at **Fort McHenry**; the fort's resistance inspired an onlooker, Francis Scott Key, to write the words to the United States' national anthem, **The Star-Spangled Banner**.

Maryland's largest city is the busy port of **Baltimore**, a quirky and engaging metropolis with a revitalized urban waterfront, thriving cultural scene and eclectic neighborhoods that characterize its diverse residents. **Western Maryland** stretches over a hundred miles to the Appalachian foothills, its rolling farmlands noteworthy chiefly for the Civil War battlefield at **Antietam**. Just twenty miles south of Baltimore, along the Chesapeake Bay, picturesque **Annapolis** has served as Maryland's capital since 1694. Some of the state's most worthwhile destinations, from the pretty fishing and yachting town of **St Michaels** to the untouched wilderness of **Assateague Island**, are across the Chesapeake Bay on the eastern shore, connected to the rest of the state by the US-50 bridge but otherwise still a world apart – except for the sprawling resort of Ocean City.

Getting around Maryland

The best way to get around Maryland is by **boat**, sailing around the gorgeous Chesapeake Bay. If you lack either the money or the good fortune needed to do this, you can hop aboard the *Chesapeake Flyer* **catamaran** (☎304/639-7241), which cruises the bay from Baltimore to Annapolis and the eastern shore towns of St Michaels and Rock Hall. **Cycling** is also a good option, especially on the eastern shore, where the roads are wide-shouldered and little-traveled, winding through cornfields from one colonial-era hamlet to another – the state tourist office (see p.28) puts out an excellent free map of the safest and most scenic routes. Baltimore is on the main Amtrak line between New York, Philadelphia and Washington DC, and is linked by regular buses with Annapolis.

5

Baltimore

I would never want to live anywhere but Baltimore. You can look far and wide, but you'll never discover a stranger city with such extreme style. It's as if every eccentric in the South decided to move north, ran out of gas in Baltimore, and decided to stay.

John Waters, Shock Value

BALTIMORE is among the more enjoyable stops on the east coast, and its closely knit neighborhoods and historic quarters provide an engaging backdrop to many diverse attractions, especially those along its celebrated **waterfront**, like the Inner Harbor's **National Aquarium** and the Pier 6 Concert Pavilion and Power Plant entertainment complex. The city also boasts top-rated **museums**, like the Walters Art Museum and the child-oriented, interactive Port Discovery, which cover everything from fine arts through black history to urban archeology. That Baltimore has been home to such diverse figures as writers Edgar Allan Poe and Anne Tyler and civil rights activists Frederick Douglass and Thurgood Marshall goes some way towards explaining its sometimes bizarrely varied character, but it's still hard to pin down exactly what makes it such an engaging city to visit, and to live in.

Arrival, information and getting around

The spacious, modern **Baltimore-Washington International Airport** (BWI), ten miles south of the city center and twenty-five miles northeast of DC, is one of the busier east coast hubs. The cheapest and best way to get into the city is on the MTA **light-rail** system (see p.468 for more details), which leaves every seventeen minutes and takes around twenty-five. Airport Shuttle **vans** ($11; ☎410/821-5387 or 1-800/BLUE-VAN) into Baltimore leave the terminal every twenty minutes, taking half an hour to reach downtown. **Taxis** cost around $20. **MARC** commuter trains (☎410/539-5000 or 1-800/325-RAIL; hourly; $3.25 one-way, $6 round-trip), operating weekdays from DC, stop at BWI airport before continuing on to the restored **Pennsylvania Station** (commonly known as Penn Station), half a mile north of downtown at 1525 N Charles St, which is also the arrival point of Amtrak **trains** (☎1-800/USA-RAIL) from all destinations. All Greyhound **buses** stop on the west side of downtown at 210 W Fayette St, but be careful in this area at night since it borders on the rougher part of the city.

Pick up free maps and the seasonal *Quick Guide* at the **Baltimore Area**

Pennsylvania Station & Baltimore Museum of Art

BALTIMORE

STATE CENTER

CHASE STREET

Great Blacks in Wax Museum (3/4 mile)

Mount Vernon

Maryland Historical Society

Mother Seton House

Washington Monument

Peabody Conservatory of Music

Walters Art Museum

Lexington Market

Greyhound Bus Station

Westminster Church & Edgar Allan Poe Grave

City Hall

Shot Tower

Flag House

Little Italy & Fell's Point, Canton

Port Discovery

World Trade Center

Harborplace

Baltimore Maritime Museum

USS Constellation

National Aquarium

Oriole Park at Camden Yards

Pier 6 Concert Pavilion

Inner Harbor

Maryland Science Center

American Visionary Museum

PSINet Stadium

FEDERAL HILL DISTRICT

Federal Hill Park

Cross St. Market

Water Taxi to Fell's Point

N

ACCOMMODATION

Admiral Fell Inn	5
Celie's Waterfront B&B	6
Days Inn Inner Harbor	4
The Inn at Government House	1
Mount Vernon Hotel	2
Radisson Plaza	3

RESTAURANTS

Donna's Coffee Bar	C
Five Seasons	E
Helmand	A
Thairish	B
Women's Industrial Exchange	D

M Metro station

0 — 400 yds

Fort McHenry

Convention and Visitors Association, on the West Wall of the Inner Harbor (☎ 410/837-4636 or 1-888/BALTIMORE, ⓦ www.baltimore.org), or from its booths at the airport and train station.

City transportation

Because the city is so compact – everything of interest is within a mile of the center – you could get around quite happily on foot. A **water taxi** nips between the Inner Harbor and more than forty area attractions, including the National Aquarium, Fell's Point, the Civil War Museum and Canton (April–Oct Mon–Fri 10am–11pm, Sat & Sun 10am–midnight; Nov–March Mon–Fri 11am–6pm, Sat & Sun 10am–11pm; all-day pass $5 – includes a trolley ride to Fort McHenry; ☎ 410/563-3901 or 1-800/658-8947). Several other operators run **harbor cruises**, including the one-hour George's Island (daily April–Oct; 11.30am, 1pm, 2:30pm, 4pm; $9, children $5), which docks near the visitor center. The city-operated **MTA** bus, subway and light-rail system ($1.35, day passes $3; ☎ 410/539-5000) covers many locations, including the airport, and runs from 6am (8am at weekends) until midnight. On buses, have exact change ready. **Taxi** companies include Yellow Cab (☎ 410/685-1212) and Royal Cab (☎ 410/327-0330).

Accommodation

Unfortunately, Baltimore has few budget options since the city's only youth hostel shut down, but the usual chain **hotels** provide moderately priced accommodation downtown. A more pleasant alternative – and certainly worth the price if barhopping is on your agenda – are the quaint **B&Bs** clustered around the historic waterfront area of Fell's Point. The Maryland Reservation Center (☎ 410/269-7550 or 1-800/654-9303) lists area inns and rooms in private homes from $50 per night. Any available hotel discounts may be found by phoning the Baltimore Hotel Hotline (☎ 1-800/964-6835).

Admiral Fell Inn 888 S Broadway ☎ 410/522-7377 or 1-800/292-4667, ⓦ www.AdmiralFell .com. Nicely restored historic hotel in the heart of Fell's Point, including breakfast and free parking. ❻–❽

Celie's Waterfront B&B 1714 Thames St ☎ 410/522-2323 or 1-800/432-0184, ⓦ www .Baltimore-Bed-Breakfast.com. Seven exquisite rooms, some with private balcony, and a rooftop deck with superb views of Fell's Point harbor. Celie is a welcoming and knowledgeable host. ❺

Days Inn Inner Harbor 100 Hopkins Place ☎ 410/576-1000 or 1-800/DAYSINN, ⓦ www.daysinnerharbor.com. Standard hotel chain with cheaper rates than the rest, centrally located within walking distance to most sights, including

Harborplace. ❺

The Inn at Government House 1125 N Calvert St ☎ 410/539-0566, ⓦ www.baltimorecity.gov. Elaborate Victorian mansion with antique-filled rooms, and breakfast included. The mayor of Baltimore is a regular in the splendid dining room. Substantially cheaper Oct–May. ❹–❺

Mount Vernon Hotel 24 W Franklin St ☎ 410/727-2000 or 1-800/245-5256, ⓦ www.bichotels.com. Formerly a youth hostel, this large hotel with comfortable rooms and a great location offers HI members a flat rate of $66; others pay regular rates. Book ahead in summer. ❹

Radisson Plaza 20–30 W Baltimore St ☎ 410/539-8400, ⓦ www.radisson.com. Plush downtown hotel, two blocks from the Inner Harbor. ❻

Downtown Baltimore

When the whole of **downtown Baltimore** burned to the ground in 1904, everything from the waterfront to the Mount Vernon area was destroyed, except for the domed 1867 **City Hall** at 100 N Holliday St. Though it wasn't a place to spend much time a few years ago, Baltimore has undergone a dramatic facelift, especially in the **Inner Harbor** area. The old power plant station is now outfitted with the country's first *ESPNZone* sports bar/restaurant and gaming center, as well as a Barnes & Noble bookstore and *Hard Rock Café*. Injected with new restaurants and bars, **Harborplace** – originally a tourist magnet for shopping – now makes for a pleasant stroll along the brick-lined waterfront, with attractions like the National Aquarium, Science Center and Baltimore-built Navy frigate *USS Constellation*. It is also in walking distance to the two **sports stadiums**, making it a good place for baseball and football fans to meet for a pre-game meal or post-game drink.

West of the central **Charles Street** – where you'll find the main cluster of businesses, restaurants and cafés – is Baltimore's original **shopping** district, now in decline as consumers head for the huge Harborplace Mall (see overleaf). Though many of the premises have been abandoned and boarded up, there are a few remaining, including the oldest and loudest of the city's covered markets, **Lexington Market**, at the center of which is *Faidley's*, the best (and cheapest) of many outlets serving oysters, clams, crabs and other Chesapeake Bay produce. Safely busy during the day, the surrounding streets can be threatening after dark, when the area is best avoided.

Three blocks up, at 600 N Paca St, the **Mother Seton House** (Sat & Sun 1–4pm; free) is a small, late eighteenth-century brick house, now a museum, where **Elizabeth Seton**, the first American woman to achieve sainthood, founded the Daughters of Charity Catholic order.

Just south of the market, **Westminster Church** was built in 1852 on top of the main Baltimore cemetery, and many ornate tombs now stand in dark catacombs underneath. Among the prominent citizens buried here is **Edgar Allan Poe**, who lived in Baltimore for three years in the 1830s, marrying his thirteen-year-old cousin and beginning a career in journalism before moving on to Richmond, Virginia. In 1849, while passing through Baltimore, Poe was found incoherent near a polling place and died soon afterwards. In 1875 his remains were moved from a pauper's grave and entombed within the stone memorial that stands along Green Street on the north side of the church.

A particularly fun place to visit is the narrow brick rowhouse where baseball great **Babe Ruth** was born in 1895, at 216 Emory St (April–Oct daily 10am–5pm; Nov–March daily 10am–4pm; 10am–7pm on days when the Orioles have a home game; $6; ☎410/727-1539). Chock-full of photographs, film clips and baseball memorabilia, it not only traces the life and achievements of the much-loved home-run hitter, but also serves as an enjoyable introduction to the game and its personalities.

Appropriately enough, **Oriole Park at Camden Yards,** the beautiful baseball stadium of the Baltimore Orioles, is just two blocks west, on the site of the old railroad terminal at Camden Yards (for tickets to a game, phone Ticketmaster ☎410/481-7328). Guided tours of the ballpark cost $5 (daily April–Sept; last tour 2pm; information on ☎410/547-6234), leaving from the ticket office at Eutaw and Camden streets; tickets can only be purchased in person. The centenary of the Babe's birth was marked by the unveiling of a bronze statue in the summer of 1995; see if you can spot the mistake, which was immediately picked up on by hardcore baseball buffs.

Just next door, looking very much like the mother ship just landed, is the **PSINet Stadium** – home to the **Baltimore Ravens** football team – which opened its 68,400 seats to a professional football team-hungry crowd in September 1998. Fans were amply rewarded by the team's unexpected Super Bowl victory in 2001. Tickets can be purchased through Ticketmaster (☎410/481-7328), and tours are offered daily (☎410/261-RAVE).

The Inner Harbor and the National Aquarium

Sooner or later, if you're in Baltimore you're bound to be drawn down to the **Inner Harbor**, a success story of urban revitalization. The rotting wharves and derelict warehouses that stood here through the 1970s have been replaced by the sparkling steel-and-glass **Harborplace** shopping mall, crammed with thriving restaurants like the *Cheesecake Factory*, *Wayne's BBQ*, and seafood specialist *Phillips*, as well as sports memorabilia and bric-a-brac shops that swarm day and night with tourists and locals. It is quite an enjoyable place, with the waterfront promenade enlivened by busking guitar players and the occasional fire-eating juggler. Sweeping views of the entire city and beyond can be admired from the observation deck of Baltimore's own **World Trade Center** on the north pier (Mon–Wed 10am–5pm, Thurs–Sat 10am–6.30pm, Sun 11am–5.30pm; $4).

Nothing in the Inner Harbor dates from before its rebuilding, but to lend an air of authenticity, remnants from the city's proud maritime past have been assembled here, including the graceful **USS Constellation** (daily Oct 15–April 30 10am–5pm; $6.50), an eighteenth-century, Baltimore-built frigate that was the first ship in the US Navy, and which has just undergone a $9 million renovation. Another collection of ships – a Coast Guard cutter that survived Pearl Harbor, a Chesapeake Bay lightship and a World War II submarine – and a charming lighthouse make up the **Baltimore Maritime Museum** (Mon–Thurs 10am–5.30pm, Fri-Sun 10am–6pm; $6.50) on the next pier.

In the southwest corner of the harbor at 601 Light St, the spanking new glass, steel and concrete **Maryland Science Center** (Mon–Fri 10am–5pm, Sat & Sun 10am–6pm; $14, IMAX show $7, combination ticket $18; Ⓦ www.mdsci.org) is especially fun for kids; it features imaginative and interactive displays on themes ranging from dinosaurs to space travel. Keep in mind that frequent special exhibits can extend visiting hours, as well as raise prices.

The National Aquarium

Far and away the biggest tourist attraction in Baltimore – on national holidays it rivals Walt Disney World as the most popular destination in the US – the **National Aquarium** is certainly well worth visiting, so long as you avoid the weekend throngs (July & Aug daily 9am–8pm; Sept–Oct & March–June Sat–Thurs 9am–5pm, Fri 9am–8pm; Nov–Feb Sat–Thurs 10am–5pm, Fri 10am–8pm; always open for two hours after last admission; $16, $5 after 5pm on Fridays; Ⓦ www.aqua.org). The main exhibition building, a rather gray, 1970s concrete space with a confusing jumble of escalators and ramps, rises in levels from a tankful of bat rays past a simulated South Pacific reef up to the rooftop rainforest garden. From here, another ramp winds down past the **Open Ocean Exhibit**, which features a number of slow-moving sharks.

While the displays in the main building are generally educational, if not all that innovative or thought-provoking, the separate **Marine Mammal Pavilion**, at the end of an adjacent pier, is a lot more entertaining: this is where the aquarium's trained **dolphins** and beluga **whales** are put through their paces. Half-hour shows are every ninety minutes, with the best views to be had from either end of the pavilion where transparent acrylic panels allow you to watch the animals above and below the water as they run the gamut of tail-walking, breaching, and spitting water into the audience. A slithery **snake** exhibit was added in recent years and, judging from the squeals of onlookers, it's a hit as well.

Mount Vernon

Baltimore's most elegant quarter is just north of downtown on the shallow rise known as **Mount Vernon**, where a couple of good museums sit amid rows of eighteenth-century brick townhouses. The neighborhood, good for strolling, takes its name from the country home of George Washington, whose likeness tops the 165ft marble column of the central **Washington Monument**, in a small leafy park next to the aspirational spire of the sham-Gothic Mount Vernon Methodist Church at Charles Street and Monument Place. You can climb the monument for a great view over the city, but it opens only on random days.

At the foot of the monument, the solemn stone facade of the **Peabody Conservatory of Music** hides one of the city's best interior spaces: the beautiful, skylit atrium of the **Peabody Library** (Mon–Fri 9am–3pm; free). Five tiers of intricate wrought-iron balconies rise above ground-floor displays of sixteenth-century books, including a wonderful illustrated 1555 edition of Boccaccio's *Decameron* and a 1493 printing of the *Nuremburg Chronicles*. Two blocks west, the **Maryland Historical Society** museum (Tues–Fri 10am–5pm, Sat 9am–5pm; $4, free on Sat 9–11am) has a fairly tame collection of portraits of Maryland society and documents tracing local history, though its antique-filled chambers give a strong sense of the maritime wealth created here through nineteenth-century trade. A small room off the lobby holds some nifty models of Chesapeake Bay boats, and upstairs the "War of 1812 Gallery" displays the original manuscript of the lyrics to *The Star-Spangled Banner*.

Walters Art Museum

Baltimore's best museum, the **Walters Art Museum** at 600 N Charles St, a block south of the Washington Monument, provides a comprehensive survey of art from ancient statuary to French Impressionist painting (Tues–Sun 10am–5pm; open the first Thurs of every month until 8pm; $8, kids free, free Sat 10am–1pm and first Thurs of month; ⓦ www.thewalters.org). Entry includes a free **audio tour**, except when museum entry is free, when it costs $3. The main building's core is a large sculpture court, modeled upon an Italian Renaissance palazzo, beyond which modern galleries show off Greek and Roman antiquities, medieval illuminated manuscripts, Islamic ceramics and some very fine Byzantine silver. The top floor is rather oddly-organized, with pre-Columbian stone carvings displayed in a narrow corridor at the end of a grand hall filled with late nineteenth-century paintings, including Manet's beer-drinking *At the Café*.

Almost everything on display was bought by William Walters, one of the first US collectors of **Chinese** and **Southeast Asian** art. The adjacent restored **Hackerman House** holds some especially fine pieces, including a roomful of Chinese jade figurines, a Ming dynasty handscroll, some lovely Japanese prints and a pair of polychrome and gilt temple doors carved to look like peacock feathers. A seventh-century lacquered wood statue of a svelte Buddha is perhaps the oldest such image in the world.

The Flag House and 1812 Museum and Little Italy

A quarter of a mile east of downtown and the Inner Harbor, across the busy Falls Expressway, the intriguing **Flag House and 1812 Museum** (Tues–Sat

10am–4pm; last tour at 3.30pm; $5) was where, in 1813, Mary Pickersgill sewed the 30ft-by-45ft US flag whose presence at the harbor fort attack inspired Francis Scott Key to write *The Star-Spangled Banner*. The actual banner is now in the Museum of American History in Washington DC (see p.417), but the house is full of other such patriotic tributes.

The densely tangled streets of **Little Italy**, still a strongly Italian neighborhood, spread to the south and east of downtown. Besides dozens of restaurants and cafés (many of them very good), the area holds plenty of Baltimore's trademark stone-fronted rowhouses, almost all with highly polished marble steps. As a sort of traditional local substitute for air conditioning, in the heat of summer residents move their furniture outdoors, thereby turning each street into an extended living room.

Fell's Point and Canton

Beyond Little Italy, separated from the renovated Inner Harbor by acres of derelict wharves and warehouses, stands Baltimore's oldest and liveliest quarter, **Fell's Point**. Projecting into the main harbor, its deepwater frontage made it the heart of the city's extensive shipbuilding industry; the shipyards are long gone, but many old bars and pubs have hung on to form one of the best nightlife districts in the country. While there is little in the way of sightseeing, the **Pink Flamingos** junk shop owned and run by Edith Massey – inspiration for many of John Waters' offbeat films – was at 728 S Broadway, a block from the water; it's now a novelty store specializing in Divine memorabilia. The NBC cop drama *Homicide* also called this area home for a while, using the abandoned police station and local coffee shops as a backdrop.

Canton is also an area awakening to new businesses and restaurants, quickly rivaling Fell's Point and Federal Hill for top billing in nightly entertainment. Heading east from Fell's Point, you'll see the first wave of trendy restaurants and bookstore cafés along Boston Street, but the main concentration of bars and eateries surround the square between the two branches of O'Donnell Street.

Other Baltimore attractions

The city's newest museum, designated by Congress as "America's official National Museum, Repository, and Education Center for the Best in original, self-taught artistry," is the **American Visionary Art Museum**, 800 Key Hwy (Tues–Sun 10am–6pm; $6; ⓦ www.avam.org), which holds an array of creatively displayed art handcrafted from everyday objects such as sand and stone; there's also a good organic café on site.

The **B&O Railroad Museum**, housed in an 1830 passenger station at 901 W Pratt St, just under a mile west of the Inner Harbor (daily 10am–5pm; $6.50), commemorates the first large-scale railroad in the US, founded in 1827. It holds dozens of ornate carriages, including some wacky parasol-covered early models, and row upon row of locomotives, from steam engines to sleek 1940s diesels.

Perhaps Baltimore's most unusual museum is about a mile northeast of the center, in an old fire station off Broadway at 1601 E North Ave. The **Great Blacks in Wax Museum** (mid-Jan to mid-Oct Tues–Sat 9am–6pm, Sun noon–6pm; mid-Oct to mid-Jan Tues–Sat 9am–5pm, Sun noon–5pm; $6) uses wax models to illustrate black history, from Egyptian pharaohs and early Muslims through to Dr Martin Luther King Jr, Marcus Garvey and Malcolm X. The models are posed in prop-filled dioramas – Rosa Parks being dragged off a Montgomery bus, for example, stands across from a pair of Jim Crow-era drinking fountains, a spotless enamel one labeled "Whites Only" and a rusty spigot for "Colored People." Upstairs, figures in the Maryland Room include Baltimore-born ragtime piano player and composer Eubie Blake, and blues diva Billie Holiday, who was born and raised on Dallas Street just around the corner.

Further out on the north side, at the top of Charles Street, two miles from downtown are the pseudoclassical modern galleries of the **Baltimore Museum of Art** (Wed–Fri 11am–5pm, Sat & Sun 11am–6pm; $6, free on first Thurs of the month; ⓦwww.artbma.org). As well as great Italian and Dutch works by Botticelli, Raphael, Rembrandt and Van Dyck, an overview of contemporary art spotlights Gilbert and George's *Hellish* self-portrait. One gallery in the West Wing is devoted to Warhol, while the American Wing holds furniture and decorative arts, as well as paintings. The highlight is the Cone Collection of works by Delacroix, Degas, Cézanne and Picasso, with over a hundred drawings and paintings by Henri Matisse.

A short walk south of the Inner Harbor, the predominantly residential **Federal Hill District** is a great place to escape from the crowds. Lined with interesting shops, its main thoroughfare, Light Street, leads to the indoor **Cross Street Market**, which, though smaller than its downtown counterpart, is considerably more welcoming, and boasts some excellent delis, seafood bars and fruit stalls. **Federal Hill Park** in the northeast is a quiet public space with fine views over the harbor and the downtown cityscape – in the summer months, it's a popular spot for sunset canoodling.

As part of the city's regeneration, the decrepit fish market across from the Harbor at 35 Market Place was relaunched as the gleaming **Port Discovery** (summer daily 10am–6pm, Sept–May Tues–Sat 10am–5pm, Sun noon–5pm; $11; ⓦwww.portdiscovery.org), an interactive children's museum packed to the ceiling with hands-on exhibits and – surprisingly – fun for visitors of all ages. You can even treat yourself to a bird's-eye view from the **HiFlyer**, a tethered helium balloon (summer Sun–Wed 10am–10pm, Thurs–Sat 10am–midnight; Sept–Oct & April–May Sun–Wed noon–8pm, Thurs–Sat noon–midnight; Nov–Mar Sat & Sun noon–8pm; $12, $15 after 8pm).

Eating

Baltimore is affectionately known as **Crab City**, and locals will argue to their graves that Maryland produces the best steamed **crabs** this side of heaven. The city has dozens of reasonably priced fresh **seafood** places, as well as the usual range of diners and more than a dozen good family-run restaurants side by side in Little Italy, just east of the Inner Harbor. Canton holds a wider selection, ranging from Irish to Mexican, while Fell's Point boasts numerous vegetarian and waterfront restaurants, and even high tea at Bertha's pub. The Colonnade Market in the Light Street Pavilion of **Harborplace Mall** holds a wide selection of fast-food outlets, including several Phillips counters offering steamed clams, soft-shell crab sandwiches and so on. In general the city's restaurants tend to be unpretentious, family oriented and reasonably priced.

Bertha's 734 S Broadway (☎410/327-5795). Casual and inexpensive yet stylish seafood restaurant, tucked away behind a tiny Fell's Point bar. **Crabby Dick's** 606 S Broadway (☎410/327-7900). Lively seafood restaurant-cum-sports bar offering lots of crab and shellfish specials plus pasta, sandwiches and BBQ dishes. **Da Mimmo** 217 S High St (☎410/727-6876).

Intimate, romantic Little Italy café, with live piano music, a wide-ranging menu, and even a complimentary limo service from any downtown location. Main dishes $10–15. **Donna's Coffee Bar** 2 W Madison at Charles ☎410/385-0180. Espressos, pastries and light, savory dishes in elegant Mount Vernon, with sidewalk seating.

Five Seasons 322 N Charles St ☎410/625-9787. Ethiopian restaurant serving meats like goat in rich Berbere sauces as well as dishes from Morocco, India and Japan. Also a dance venue with live DJs.

Helmand 806 N Charles St ☎410/752-0311. Inexpensive but chic dinner-only Afghan restaurant in Mount Vernon. Plenty of lamb dishes, plus *aushak* (leek-filled vegetarian ravioli) and the delicious *kaddo borawni*, a fried-pumpkin appetizer.

Obrycki's 1727 E Pratt St ☎410/732-6399. Baltimore's best and longest established seafood restaurant, with delicious fresh crabs at premium prices. Closed in winter.

Rick's Café Americain 2903 O'Donnell St ☎410/675-1880. Snazzy eatery with *Casablanca* theme in Canton. Good range of burgers, sandwiches and main courses; the wine list is quite pricey.

Thairish 804 N Charles St ☎410/752.5857. Tiny, basic and very cheap Mount Vernon spot with a limited but tasty range of authentic Thai favorites.

Women's Industrial Exchange Restaurant 333 N Charles St ☎410/685-4388. Excellent-value 1940s café with full breakfasts for under $3, huge plates of chicken gumbo for $5, and great crabcakes.

Drinking and nightlife

Baltimore's waterfront **Fell's Point** neighborhood may well have the densest assembly of drinking places in the US. One bar after another lines up along Broadway and the many smaller side streets; almost all feature some sort of entertainment, usually live bands, and on summer nights the sidewalks are packed solid with revelers. Those tired of long wait lines are now heading to the up-and-coming area around **Canton**, which offers plenty of venues – and more space – for the thirsty. The city's highbrow culture is concentrated northwest of the center, in the Mount Royal Avenue area, home to both the **Meyerhoff Symphony Hall** (☎410/783-8000) and the **Lyric Opera House** (☎410/727-6000).

For a full rundown of what's on and where, pick up a copy of the excellent free *City Paper*, at newsstands and book and record stores all over town, or check out Ⓦwww.marylandnightlife.com.

Bohagers 701 S Eden St ☎410/563-7220. Raucous dance club, with live bands several times a week and crabcakes every night.

Buddies Jazz Pub 313 N Charles St ☎410/332-4200. Evening jazz in this downtown location, for the price of a drink or two.

Cat's Eye Pub 1730 Thames St ☎410/276-9085. Cozy, crowded bar, with a good range of beers and live music nightly.

Eight by Ten 10 E Cross St ☎410/625-2000. Just west of Inner Harbor, this Federal Hill joint puts on live bands every night, with the emphasis on indie rock and reggae.

Looney's Pub 2900 O'Donnell St ☎410/675-9235. This animated hangout, serving up a variety of snacks and beers, is one of Canton's most

popular watering holes.

Max's on Broadway 735 S Broadway ☎410/675-6297. Huge corner venue with a very long bar, pool tables, and a rainbow of beer taps. Upstairs is a more refined atmosphere in the leather upholstered cigar lounge. Live bands play occasionally.

Mount Royal Tavern 1204 W Mount Royal Ave ☎410/669-6686. Welcoming bar, popular with art students as well as nightcapping musicians.

Sisson's 36 E Cross St ☎410/539-2093. A Federal Hill watering hole featuring six handcrafted beers, homemade root beer and cajun/creole munchies.

Wharf Rat Bar 801 S Ann St ☎410/276-9034. A convivial bar, well stocked with English ales, that packs in a trendy and discerning crowd.

Western Maryland

Stretched between West Virginia and the razor-straight Pennsylvania border, **western Maryland** ranges for some two hundred miles east to west, but is in places well under five miles across. In general, the further west you go, the more mountainous and backwoodsy the feel, quite similar to Maryland's Appalachian neighbors.

Though the countryside is very pretty and great for hiking and camping, spe-
cific points of interest are few. Apart from the Civil War battlefield at
Antietam, west of the only sizeable town, **Frederick**, the best reason to come
to this part of the state is to cycle or hike the footpath of the restored old
Chesapeake and Ohio Canal, which winds along the Maryland side of the
Potomac River from Washington DC for over 180 miles to **Cumberland** in
the western mountains. Even further west is the state's largest freshwater lake,
Deep Creek Lake, popular with watersports enthusiasts, which has more than
70,000 acres of public parks and forests surrounding it – some of which makes
smooth cross-country skiing during the winter.

Frederick and around

One of the first towns settled in northwestern Maryland, **FREDERICK**, at the
junction of I-70 and I-270 an hour west of Baltimore, was laid out in 1745 by
German farmers lured from Pennsylvania by the promise of cheap fertile land.
It grew to become a main stopover on the route west to the Ohio Valley, and
the bulk of today's tidy town survives from the early 1800s. A **visitor center**
(daily 9am–5pm; ☎301/228-2888 or 1-800/999-3613) at 19 E Church St has
walking tour maps of the town, pointing out such places as the **Schifferstadt
House** (Thurs–Sat 10am–4pm, Sun noon–4pm; donation), just off US-15, a
stonewalled farmhouse built in 1753 and largely unaltered since.

According to a romantic poem popular with around 1900 schoolchildren,
ninety-five-year-old Barbara Fritchie defiantly waved the US flag while
Confederate soldiers marched past her home, the tiny **Barbara Fritchie
House** (April–Sept Mon & Thurs–Sat 10am–4pm, Sun 1–4pm; $2) along
Carroll Creek on the west side of town. When Winston Churchill passed
through, he stopped at the house and recited the poem from memory.

Camp David, the mountain retreat used by US presidents since FDR,
where Jimmy Carter brought Menachem Begin and Anwar Sadat together in
1978 to sign the historic Camp David accords between Israel and Egypt, is hidden away in the mountains north of Frederick. Nearby **Cunningham Falls
State Park** and the **Catoctin Mountain Park** both hold seemingly endless
hardwood forests – great for fall color – in the midst of which are numerous
preserved remnants of early homesteaders. Pick up details on hiking and camping at the main **visitor center** (daily 10am–4pm; ☎301/663-9388), off Hwy-
77 two miles west of US-15.

Besides being a nice detour off the highway, Frederick is a good base for
exploring places such as **Antietam** (see below) and **Harpers Ferry** in West
Virginia (see p.458). There are **motels** along both I-70 and US-15, and in
town the *Tyler Spite House*, 112 W Church St (☎301/831-4455; ❻), is a pleasant **B&B** in an elegant 1814 mansion. For a bite to **eat**, try the soups and steaks
at the *Brown Pelican*, 5 E Church St, or the burgers and steamed crabs at *Cactus
Flats*, three miles north off US-15.

Antietam National Battlefield

The site of the single bloodiest battle in the Civil War, **Antietam National
Battlefield** spreads over unaltered farmlands outside the whitewashed and balconied village of **Sharpsburg**. Here, fifteen miles west of Frederick, on the
morning of September 17, 1862, in an effort to consolidate rebel gains after
their victory at 2nd Manassas, 40,000 troops faced a Union army twice that
number. Hours later, some 25,000 from both sides lay dead or dying. The
fiercest fighting, and the worst bloodshed, occurred in cornfields to the north;

Union general Joseph Hooker recorded: "In the time that I am writing, every stalk of corn in the northern and greater part of the field was cut as closely as could have been done with a knife, and the slain lay in rows precisely as they had stood in their ranks a few moments before."

The battle continued throughout the day without a clear result. It may not have been decisive, but the Confederates' lack of success lost them the support of their erstwhile ally Great Britain, while the Union performance encouraged Lincoln to issue the Emancipation Proclamation. Pick up a brochure and driving tour map of the park at the **visitor center**, a mile north of Sharpsburg off Hwy-65 (daily 8.30am–5pm; ☎301/432-5124), where you also pay the $2 park entry fee. Numerous plaques and memorials have been constructed around the fields, but otherwise the site, with its various farm buildings and country churches, is unchanged, and the entire park serves as a mute but evocative memorial to the conflict. Special events are always held around the battle's anniversary.

Cumberland and the C&O Canal

The only large town in the far west of Maryland, **CUMBERLAND** started life as a coal-mining center in the late 1700s. Often confused with Daniel Boone's Cumberland Gap in southwest Virginia, this Cumberland was also an important trans-Appalachian crossing, but its main place in history is as the terminus of the ill-fated **C&O (Chesapeake and Ohio) Canal**, an impressive engineering feat begun in 1813 but not completed until 1850, by which time the railroads had already made it obsolete.

The **visitor center** in the **Western Maryland Station Center** (Mon–Fri 9am–5pm, Sat & Sun 10am–4pm; ☎301/777-5905, ⓦwww.mdmountainside.com), at 13 Canal St, can provide information on hiking, cycling, canoeing and camping; in summer, the historic trains of the **Western Maryland Scenic Railroad** set off on ninety-minute rides through the surrounding mountains (May–Sept Wed–Sun; Oct daily; Nov–Dec 14 Sat & Sun, 11.30am; ☎301/759-4400 or 1-800/872-4650, ⓦwww.wmsr.com; $18, kids $10). The tiny black and white log cabin where George Washington served his first commission in the 1750s stands directly opposite the station on the other side of the canal.

About twenty miles before Cumberland, I-68 slices straight through a wedge of sedimentary rock, exposing a dramatic syncline that can be viewed from a platform at the excellent **Sideling Hill Exhibit Center** (daily 9am–5pm; ☎301/842-2155); there's a special **geologic exhibit** staffed by an on-site geologist, and the views east of the hill from the parking lot are quite stunning.

Annapolis and southern Maryland

While Baltimore has grown into the state's largest and busiest city, **Annapolis**, Maryland's colonial and current capital, has changed little in size and outward appearance. Before the US broke free from English rule, this was considered to be one of the most genteel and attractive colonial centers, and though its time-worn streets are now usually crowded, Annapolis is still among the more engaging small US cities. Its once-vital Chesapeake Bay **waterfront** now has little of the feel of colonial maritime life, but the real attractions of Annapolis, among its narrow streets, include fine homes, the Beaux Arts campus of the US Naval Academy, and the beautiful state capitol. If you like the look of

Annapolis, and want to get a better feel for the Chesapeake Bay region away from the crowds, head south to places like **St Mary's City** – the first capital of Maryland, completely reconstructed in the 1960s – or **Solomons Island**, one of many small Chesapeake Bay towns that seem not to have changed for decades.

Annapolis

At the center of **ANNAPOLIS**, overlooking the town's baroque web of streets, the **Maryland State House** (daily 9am–5pm, tours at 11am & 3pm; free) was completed in 1779 and soon after served as an early capitol of the US. It remains the oldest state house still in use. The **Old Senate Chamber**, to the right of the grand entrance hall, is where the Treaty of Paris was ratified in 1784, officially ending the Revolutionary War; a statue of George Washington stands on the spot where he resigned his commission as head of the Continental Army, and displays document the role Annapolis played in the life of the young Republic. Free guided tours are given twice a day, or you can wander around on your own, perhaps stopping by to listen to the proceedings of Maryland's current crop of legislators, who hold court from January to April in the more modern wing to the north of the old building. Also on the grounds of the State House is the cottage-sized **Old Treasury Building**, built in 1735 to hold colonial Maryland's currency reserves.

Many grand late eighteenth-century brick homes line the streets of Annapolis, but for substance and grace none surpasses the **Hammond–Harwood House**, two blocks west of the State House at 19 Maryland Ave, off King George Street (Mon–Sat 10am–4pm, Sun noon–4pm; $5 including tour). The warm redbrick Palladian villa, which consists of two symmetrical wings connected by a central hall, was built in 1774 to the designs of William Buckland, and is most notable for its beautifully carved decorative woodwork, especially evident in the intricate front doorway. Despite its architectural harmony, the house has had an unfortunate history, the architect himself becoming so obsessed with its construction that his fiancée left him, breaking his heart and causing his untimely death at the age of 38; the original owner also died in mysterious circumstances before the house was completed.

Another historic Annapolis mansion, the 1765 **William Paca House**, 186 Prince George St (March–Dec Mon–Sat 10am–4pm, Sun noon–4pm; Jan–Feb Fri & Sat 10am–4pm, Sun noon–4pm; $8 including tour), was a downmarket rooming house until the 1960s; it was restored to its period appearance in time for the 1976 Bicentennial; the interior is decorated in warm rich colors and fancy furniture, while the splendid formal garden, which you can peer into from King George Street, is being constantly landscaped and boasts an impressive viewing pavilion.

Besides such elite manors, dozens of pastel eighteenth-century clapboard cottages and commercial structures fill the narrow streets that run down to the waterfront. Of those that have escaped the gentrifiers, the **Tobacco Prise House**, 4 Pinkney St (by appointment, ☎410/267-7619; $2), is a colonial tobacco warehouse that now sets out to explain the handling and storage of the valuable leaves. Further along, the **Shiplap House**, 18 Pinkney St (Mon–Fri 2–4pm; free), was built in 1715 as a tavern; now it's a small museum of Annapolis history, with a herb garden to the rear containing assorted medicinal plants grown in colonial times.

The waterfront and US Naval Academy

Although few colonial sites survive along the modern **Chesapeake Bay waterfront** to give a sense of the port's former maritime strength, the rebuilt 1850s dockside city **Market House** is an early nineteenth-century replacement of a colonial warehouse used by the revolutionary army. Today, with its sidewalk cafés and stalls, it's a good spot for people-watching.

The rest of the waterfront, locally known as "city dock", is pleasant enough for an afternoon's wandering, especially on summer weekends when the harbor and bay are full of clanging halyards and billowing sails. In amongst the boat supply shops and harborside bars, the gray stone walls of the **US Naval Academy** (daily: March–Nov 9am–5pm; Dec–Feb 9am–4pm; free) seem designed to exacerbate the sensory deprivation endured by the over four thousand crew-cut young men and handful of women (all of whom line up in formation outside **King Hall**, the dining commons, every day at noon) who spend four strictly disciplined years here before embarking on careers as naval officers. The moment of transition, at the end of each summer's graduation ceremony, is marked by the traditional "Hat Toss." A small museum holds models of various British and US warships and other naval memorabilia. Superb guided tours of the Academy ($5.50) leave every half-hour from the **Armel–Leftwich Visitor Center** (same hours as the Academy) in Halsey Field House, through Gate 1 at the end of King George Street.

Practicalities

Compared to the rest of Maryland, Annapolis is easy to reach, on Greyhound and MTA (#210) buses from Baltimore. By road it's only about half an hour from Washington (via US-50) or Baltimore (via I-97), though parking can be difficult. A trolleybus (75¢) loops around the small and very walkable central area. Annapolis's **visitor center**, 26 West St (Mon–Fri 9am–5pm; ☎410/280-0445, ⓦwww.visit-annapolis.org), can provide free maps and practical information, including lists of **walking tour** operators and $12 **horseback riding** tours; if you'd rather see the city on your own, consider picking up one of the *Historic Annapolis* audio-cassette tours, narrated by newsman Walter Cronkite, from the Historic Annapolis Foundation Museum Store at 77 Main St.

Finding a **place to stay** is not usually a problem, though prices are fairly steep. There's a free accommodation bureau (☎1-800/715-1000), or you can choose from **B&Bs** like the central and characterful *Scot-Laur Inn*, 165 Main St (☎410/268-5665; ❹), the pricier *Prince George Inn*, 232 Prince George St (☎410/263-6418; ❺), or the attractive *Flag House Inn*, 26 Randall St (☎410/280-2721 or 1-800/437-4825, ⓦwww.flaghouseinn.com; ❹). Dozens of motels are to be found along US-50 on the west side of town.

Restaurants and **bars** are both plentiful and good: the no-frills *Chick and Ruth's Delly*, 165 Main St (☎410/269-6737), does big breakfasts and has a booth on permanent reserve for Maryland's governor; the ritzier *Harry Browne's*, 66 State Circle (☎410/263-4332), is popular with politicos and expense-account lobbyists. You can tuck into fish and chips while people-watching from the sunny porch of the waterfront *Middleton Tavern*, 2 Market Space (☎410/263-3323), one of the city's oldest buildings. The *King of France Tavern* in the historic *Maryland Inn*, 16 Church Circle (☎410/263-2641), puts on live jazz, while the *Market House* on the waterfront contains a good range of cheap snackbars with shared outside seating.

Southern Maryland

The little-visited back roads of **southern Maryland** resemble in many ways the agricultural Deep South. All along both main routes, US-301 from Baltimore and Hwy-2 from Annapolis, lush fields of corn and tobacco, dotted with aging wooden barns, fill the arable lands in scattered parcels, and narrow, tree-lined country lanes branch off suddenly onto rivers or the broad Chesapeake Bay.

Solomons Island

Towns in southern Maryland are few and far between, but a couple are worth seeking out. The old shipbuilding community of **SOLOMONS ISLAND**, sixty miles south of Annapolis via Hwy-2, is not actually an island but a narrow two-mile peninsula between the Patuxent River and Back Creek Bay. The entire waterfront is dotted with cozy **B&Bs**, like the *Locust Inn* (☎410/326-9817; ➌), and fresh seafood **restaurants**, including the *Lighthouse Inn* (☎410/326-2444) on the bay side, and *Solomon's Pier* (☎410/326-2424) across the road, both of which have tasty food and sunny outdoor decks. The best reason to stop here is the **Calvert Marine Museum** (daily 10am–5pm; $5), on Hwy-2 at the north end of town. This focuses specifically on the Patuxent River, and on the unique estuarine ecosystem of the Chesapeake Bay tidal areas. Its two protected marshland wildlife areas, one saltwater and one freshwater, can be explored on raised walkways. Inside the main building, exhibits follow the development of local boat-building and commercial fishing, and dozens of historic boats are on show. In summer, an old oyster bay-boat, the *William B. Tennison*, leaves from the museum dock on hour-long **cruises** (May–Oct Wed–Sun at 2pm; $5) around the bay.

St Mary's City and Point Lookout State Park

The reconstructed village of **ST MARY'S CITY** is well worth a look, both for its lovely location and the exemplary attention to detail in all the buildings and archeological sites. Set on a broad Potomac cove near the southern tip of the Maryland peninsula, twenty miles south of Solomons Island, St Mary's City is a small-scale but accurate reconstruction of Maryland's first colonial capital, established here in 1634 before being moved to Annapolis sixty years later. The entire complex, including a working tobacco plantation and a replica of the tiny *Maryland Dove* ship on which the first colonists arrived from England, is run as a sort of theme park, complete with costumed tour guides who are both approachable and very knowledgeable, even if their English accents need a bit of work (Wed–Sun 10am–5pm; $6.50; @ www.smcm.edu/hsmc). Its main feature is a reconstruction of the long-vanished **State House**, where in 1689 Protestant rebels seized control of what had been a Catholic-run colony; unfortunately it's all a bit too manicured to provide much of a sense of history. Nearby, and much more fun, living history **performances** are staged at the *Maryland Dove* dock, which are well acted and sensitive to the fact that this was British America, and long before Independence was even a thought; to a modern American, truly prehistoric.

South from St Mary's City, the very tip of the southern Maryland peninsula was used during the Civil War as a **prisoner-of-war camp** for rebel forces captured at the battle of Gettysburg. In just over a year, from March 1864 to June 1865, more than four thousand died due to the appalling conditions, including some seven hundred Union guards. Most of the Confederate soldiers were buried in a mass grave, now marked by a granite obelisk; the actual camp (the ramparts have been rebuilt and there's a small and somewhat gruesome museum) was a mile south. The point where the Potomac flows into the Chesapeake is a good place to watch the sun rise or set.

The eastern shore

Maryland's compelling **eastern shore** occupies over half of the broad Delmarva (*Dela*ware, *Mary*land, *Vir*ginia) peninsula that protects the Chesapeake from the open Atlantic. Its miles of back roads are perfectly suited to aimless exploration and sudden discovery of such sights as the odd wooden farmhouse or tobacco barn marooned in the middle of a field, or an old sailboat tied up at an apparently decrepit dock that springs to life when the fishing craft return. The US-50 bridge/tunnel, built across the Chesapeake Bay in the early 1960s, may have made the eastern shore more accessible, but it hasn't affected its air of somnolence. Branching off from US-50 as it races down to the beach resort of **Ocean City**, quiet country lanes lead to two-hundred-year-old waterfront towns like **Chestertown**, **St Michaels** and **Oxford**.

Chestertown and Rock Hall

A stopping place for travelers since colonial days, when it was a prime Chesapeake port, **CHESTERTOWN** is the northernmost town on the eastern shore. Stretching west along High Street from the Chester River, it is surprisingly intact, with its fine old riverfront homes, a courthouse square lined with ornate wooden cottages, and a generally languorous feel that makes it a popular weekend escape from Baltimore or DC. Many of the old houses, like the *Widow's Walk Inn*, 402 High St (T410/778-6455 or 1-888/778-6455, W www.chestertown.com/widow; ❹), have been converted into **B&Bs**, while others now house top-rated **restaurants** like the *Feast of Reason*, 203 High St (T410/778-3828; closed Sun), and the *Imperial Hotel* (T410/778-5000) across the street, with its swanky dining room. The **visitor center**, 400 S Cross St (Mon–Fri 9am–4pm, Sat 10am–2pm; T410/778-0416), has information about walking and cycling tours.

To the west of town, fifteen miles of country lanes lead down to the wharves and dockside restaurants of **ROCK HALL**, an old fishing port where you can watch the day's catch being unloaded while chewing on crab legs at the barebones *Waterman's Crabhouse* (T410/778-1803) on the main pier. The *Chesapeake Flyer* catamaran service lands here (see p.466), and bikes can be rented from the marina office.

St Michaels

A contender for prettiest harbor on the Chesapeake Bay, tiny **ST MICHAELS**, twelve miles west of US-50 on Hwy-33, is also one of its oldest ports. Founded during the mid-1600s, it grew into one of colonial America's prime shipbuilding centers, and its fast sloops and shallow-draft "bugeyes" evaded British blockades during the Revolutionary War. St Michaels languished while Baltimore blossomed, but since the early 1960s it has been rediscovered, its old buildings now gentrified into art galleries, boutiques and cozy B&Bs.

Some corners of the town survive intact, however; among them the old town green, **St Mary's Square**, a block off the main Talbot Street on Mulberry Street. To get a clear sense of the history of Chesapeake Bay, head north along the docks to the extensive and modern **Chesapeake Bay Maritime Museum** (daily March–May & Oct–Nov 9am–5pm; June–Sept 9am–6pm; Dec–Feb 9am–4pm; $7.50). This focuses on the restored **Hooper Strait Lighthouse**, at the foot of which float several Chesapeake Bay sailboats – designed to make the most of the bay's shallow waters. Nearby, some two hundred other boats include a Native American dugout canoe, while in the museum workshop skilled artisans and legions of volunteers restore and maintain historic boats using painstaking traditional techniques. If you left your boat at home and want to get out on the bay, Patriot Cruises (☎410/745-3100) run one-hour **excursions** for $10 while other companies operate shorter (and cheaper) trips. Among St Michaels' revered seafood **restaurants**, the *Crab Claw* (☎410/745-2900; March to mid-Dec) occupies a prime chunk of the waterfront alongside the Maritime Museum and boasts an extensive menu. Though many of its customers turn up for the beer and the views rather than anything else, the prime reason to come is to enjoy their all-you-can-eat **steamed crabs**. At weekends especially, the rest of the town's wharves and docks are filled with boaters who flock to restaurant-cum-bars such as the *Town Dock* (☎410/745-5577) and *St Michaels Crab House* (☎410/745-3737), both at the end of Mulberry Street. As a result, **B&Bs** such as the period-furnished *Hambleton Inn*, 202 Cherry St (☎410/745-3350 or 1-866/745-3350, ⓦwww.hambletoninn.com; ❺), and the *Kemp House Inn*, 412 S Talbot St (☎410/745-2243, ⓦwww.kemphouseinn.com; ❹), charge much higher rates at weekends and tend to be fully booked; for slightly cheaper rooms your choice is restricted to the *St Michaels Motor Inn* (☎410/745-3333 or 1-800/528-1234, ⓦwww.bestwestern.com; ❹), a branch of *Best Western* at 1228 S Talbot St on the rather featureless main road into town.

Tilghman Island

If you want to see the real, workaday Chesapeake, **TILGHMAN ISLAND**, west of St Michaels across the Knapps Narrows drawbridge (which rules over vehicle traffic and opens for every single boat coming through), was once home to most of the Chesapeake's skipjack fleet. Partly in response to the continued depletion of oyster stocks, the government has made it illegal to harvest oysters except from small, graceful and hopelessly outmoded sailing boats called **skipjacks**, of which just a handful are still in use. Most are moored at **Dogwood Harbor**, on the east side of the island; during the fall and winter harvest, they unload at the Harrison Oyster Packing Company, at the foot of the bridge. You can buy oysters fresh off the boat, or sample them and other local delicacies at two very good restaurants on either side of the bridge: the *Bay Hundred* (☎410/886-2622) and the more upscale *Bridge Restaurant* (☎410/886-2500). However, many locals and visiting weekend fisherman head straight for *Harrison's*, directly across from the bridge (☎410/886-2121), for a traditional Eastern Shore dinner stacked with corn on the cob and fresh fried chicken.

Oxford

Just west of US-50, or seven miles south of St Michaels via country lanes and a ferry, the leafy waterfront hamlet of **OXFORD** seems to have slumbered peacefully since colonial days. Along with Annapolis, this was one of the two ports of entry for all of colonial Maryland, a role remembered by the reconstructed one-room **Customs House** next to the ferry landing on the north side of town. After Independence, Oxford was all but forgotten; its full-time population is under a thousand and there's hardly any tourist trade. Wandering the quiet streets, however, or lolling on the lawns of the long riverfront promenade can be quite relaxing and enjoyable. A trip on the small **ferry** across the Tred Avon River, which made its maiden voyage in 1683 and has been in continuous service since 1836, makes for a nice excursion en route to or from St Michaels (every 20min; June–Aug Mon–Fri 7am–9pm, Sat & Sun 9am–9pm; Sept to mid-Dec & March–June Mon–Fri 7am–sunset, Sat & Sun 9am–sunset; $5.50 per car, $1.25 per passenger; ☎410/745-9023).

Schooner's Llanding (☎410/226-0160) is a friendly, inexpensive seafood **restaurant** with a large deck right on the main harbor, at the end of Tilghman Street; at the *Pier Street Marina & Restaurant* (☎410/226-5411), further south, you can sample fresh crabs in a spectacular waterfront setting. The ancient *Robert Morris Inn*, on Morris Street at The Strand (☎410/226-5111, ⓦ www.robertmorrisinn.com; ❺), named for the Oxford man who personally financed the Continental Army during the Revolutionary War, serves James Michener's favorite crabcakes. In the larger but less interesting town of **EASTON** on US-50, the ancient *Bishop's House B&B*, 214 Goldsborough St (☎410/820-7290 or 1-800/223-7290, ⓦ www.bishopshouse.com; ❺), offers a comfortable alternative to the highway motels.

Ocean City

With more than ten miles of broad Atlantic beach, a boisterous boardwalk amusement park and hundreds of thousands of visitors every weekend, **OCEAN CITY** is Maryland's number one summer resort. No matter how you get here – up or down the coastal highway or across the rural eastern shore along US-50 – its tower-block hotels and massive overcrowding will come as a shock; it is so overgrown, in fact, that its northern reaches now encroach into Delaware. If you're after a quiet weekend by the sea, avoid it like the plague, and take extra care to avoid college vacations.

Ocean City might be good for a day out, or even a long weekend, but it's hard to imagine anyone wanting to stay very long. It is, at least, easy to reach: Carolina Trailways **buses** from DC end up in the southern end of town at Second Street and Hwy-1 (☎410/289-9307). The **visitor center**, at 4001 Coastal Highway (daily 9am–5pm; ☎410/289-2800 or 1-800/626-2326, ⓦ www.ococean.com), has the usual brochures and can help with accommodation. Places to **stay** are plentiful except on summer weekends, and off-season rates are at least half prime-time ones, but pleasant accommodation is rare indeed. For bargains, check out ⓦ www.ocmdhotels.com. The *Summer Place*, a privately-run **hostel** near the bus station and boardwalk at 104 Dorchester St (April–Oct; ☎410/289-4542; ❷), rents rooms at a flat rate of $20 per person and does not accept reservations; if you're unlucky there, and want a **motel** in the same area, try the *Oceanic* on the tip of the peninsula at the south end of Baltimore Street (☎410/289-6498; ❸). The bright and breezy *Nassau Motel* further up at 60th and Oceanfront (☎410/524-6451, ⓦ www.ocnassaumotel.com; ❹) has reasonable rates. Other alternatives range from the faded seaside grandeur of the *Commander Hotel*, on the boardwalk at 14th Street (☎410/289-6166 or 1-888/289-6166, ⓦ www.commanderhotel.com; ❺), to the gleaming marble and glass of the *Coconut Malorie*, at 60th Street and The Bay (☎410/723-6100 or 1-800/767-6060, ⓦ www.coconutmalorie.com; ❼). The only campsite is at *Ocean City Campground*, 105 70th St (☎410/524-7601, ⓦ www.occamping.com).

Dominated by the boardwalk fast-food joints and the national franchises along Hwy-1 (there are no less than three all-night *McDonald's*), Ocean City has few good **eating** options. The *Angler Restaurant*, on the bay at Talbot Street

(☎410/289-7424), has fresh seafood and an all-you-can-eat salad bar; it also offers nice beers, wild tropical cocktails and nightly live bands. **Nightspots** include the frenetic *Big Kahuna Surf Club*, 18th and Hwy-1 (☎410/289-6331), and *Shenanigan's*, 4th and Boardwalk (☎410/289-7181), which has a full menu and live music until 2am. Pick up the free *Ocean City Today* to find out what's on.

Assateague Island National Seashore

If you find yourself in the Ocean City area in the peak of summer and want to escape the crowds, head just down the coast to **Assateague Island National Seashore** – a 37-mile stretch of entirely undeveloped beach and marshland stretching into Virginia. Until 1933 Assateague Island was attached to Ocean City; then a hurricane drove a wedge between them, and it became a separate barrier island, which is progressively being pushed by the elements back towards the mainland. Another storm in 1962 led to the abandonment of construction plans, under which nine thousand residential lots had been set aside, and instead the island was designated a national seashore.

Assateague's main **visitor center** (daily 9am–5pm; ☎410/641-1441, Ⓦwww.nps.gov/asis) is eight miles from Ocean City, just before the humpback bridge across to the island ($5 park entry per car, valid one week). If you plan to do any walking, pick up the $2.25 booklet detailing the park's three main trails. Of these, the *Life of the Marsh Trail* guides you along half a mile of boardwalks through low-lying leeward wetlands, while *Life of the Dunes*, on the thick white sands just back from the beach, is a little longer, and harder going. Most visitors, however, come strictly for the beaches themselves, which feel a world away from Ocean City. Seashore **camping facilities** on Assateague Island are available year-round (☎410/641-3030 or 1-888/432-2267; $10-14 per site), but if you want a bit more comfort, the best **lodging** is to be found near the southern half of the island, across the Virginia border in **Chincoteague** (see p.448).

Delaware

Though **DELAWARE** has its beautiful spots – including some of the mid-Atlantic's best beaches – its tourist boards have their work cut out. Most of the images potential visitors have of the state are negative: Delaware is known for the massive chemical plants of the **DuPont** Corporation and **Dover Air Force Base**, as well as for tolerating shady business practices – half of America's largest companies have their official bases in this tiny state, thanks to its permissive tax, banking and incorporation laws. The upside of this is that there's no sales tax, which certainly makes shoppers happy.

To downplay the state's dubious contemporary image, Delaware's promoters emphasize its past – for example, as the first ex-colony to ratify the Constitution, it claims the title of **America's First State**. Dutch whalers established a settlement at the mouth of the Delaware Bay in 1631, and soon afterwards the Swedes built a larger colony at present-day **Wilmington**. The two groups fought amongst themselves until the British took over in 1664. Delaware was part of neighboring Pennsylvania – Philadelphia is only ten miles north of the present, arching state border – until hiving itself off in 1776.

Much of Delaware's fortunes (and misfortunes) since then can be traced directly to the **du Pont family**, who, fleeing the wrath of revolutionary France, set up a gunpowder mill that became the main supplier of conventional explosives to the US Government. After World War I, the du Ponts went public and made millions in the stock market frenzies of the Roaring Twenties, since which time the company has diversified, its labs inventing such modern essentials as nylon and cellophane.

The du Ponts built huge mansions for themselves in the **Brandywine Valley** north of Wilmington, near the perfectly preserved old colonial capital, **New Castle**, on the Delaware Bay just five miles south of I-95. Further south, **Dover**, the capital, may not detain you long, but beyond it the small and amiable resorts of **Lewes** and **Rehoboth Beach** mark the northern extent of over twenty miles of unspoiled Atlantic beaches.

Getting around Delaware

Apart from Wilmington, which is on the main east coast **train** and **bus** lines, Delaware is hard to get around without a car. Greyhound services are limited to a summer-only route from DC to **Rehoboth**, and local public transportation is nonexistent.

I-95 and the New Jersey Turnpike converge at Wilmington, from where US-13 runs south through the state. More often called the **Du Pont Highway**, it was paid for and constructed by the industrialists so that they could ride in comfort between their Wilmington mansions and Dover. A direct car **ferry** connects Cape May, the southern tip of New Jersey and Lewes, at the mouth of the Delaware Bay (see p.488).

Wilmington and around

WILMINGTON may not be the most compelling place in America, but this medium-sized city can make for a refreshing break from the tourist trail: not only does it boast the excellent Delaware Art Museum and some pretty waterside parks, but the surrounding Brandywine Valley holds the manor homes and gardens (and factories) of the du Ponts, all open to the public and providing an inside look at the First State's First Family and America's de facto aristocracy.

If you arrive in Wilmington by train, on the Amtrak line between New York and Washington, you'll pull in to the quirky 1907 terracotta station on the somewhat dangerous and run-down south side of the city. From here, the two main streets, Market and King, run north for about a mile to the Brandywine River. Their partly pedestrianized lengths hold a standard array of stores and other small businesses, as well as a handful of restored eighteenth-century rowhouses clustered around the Georgian **Old Town Hall**, 512 Market St (March–Dec Tues–Fri noon–4pm, Sat 10am–4pm; free), now a small museum of local history. The faceless gray monoliths that tower over the cityscape house the headquarters of hundreds of national companies.

A short walk north of the downtown commercial district, at the top end of Market Street, **Brandywine Park** comes as a welcome relief from the concrete pavement, with its grassy knolls lining both banks of the Brandywine River. In the residential districts to the north are some of the city's oldest and most elegant houses, many dating from the Revolutionary War, when Wilmington's flour mills fed the American forces. The nearby **Delaware Art**

Museum, 2301 Kentmere Parkway (Tues & Thurs-Sat 9am–4pm, Wed 9am–9pm, Sun 10am–4pm; free; ⓦwww.delart.org), has a good range of works by American painters like Thomas Eakins, Winslow Homer and Edward Hopper, as well as a comprehensive collection of English Pre-Raphaelite painting and drawing.

Most of Wilmington's surprising number of important colonial sites are hidden away amid the decrepit and heavily industrialized waterfront to the east of downtown. A poorly signposted "Historic Wilmington" loop stops first at the foot of Seventh Street, where a small monument marks the site of Delaware's first European colony, **Fort Christina**, set up by Swedish settlers in 1638. Nearby, at 606 Church St, the **Hendrickson House Museum and Old Swedes Church** (Mon–Sat 10am–4pm; free) is one of the oldest houses of worship in the US, built in 1690 and still retaining its impressive black walnut pulpit.

The downtown **CVB** at 100 W 10th St (Mon–Sat 9am–5pm; ☎302/652-4088 or 1-800/489-6664, ⓦwww.VisitWilmingtonDe) has walking and driving tour maps and practical information. Few people choose to spend a night in Wilmington, but if you do, the standard **hotel** and motel chains exist, or you can shell out $309 on a night at the splendidly ornate *Hotel du Pont,* 100 W 11th St (☎302/594-3100 or 1-800/441-9019, ⓦwww.hoteldupont.com; ⑨). For **eating**, the excellent *Waterworks Café*, 16th and French streets in Brandywine Park (☎302/652-6022), is classy (and pricey), or you can scout around the happening Trolley Square area northwest of downtown, where *Kelly's Logan House*, 1701 Delaware Ave (☎302/652-9493), serves tasty burgers and other pub fare in a pleasant garden setting.

The du Pont mansions

Various generations of the du Pont family built opulent homes in the rural Brandywine Valley northwest of Wilmington. To learn how their fortune was made, stop first at the **Hagley Museum**, off Hwy-141 just north of Wilmington (mid–March to Dec daily 9.30am–4.30pm; Jan to mid–March Sat & Sun 9.30am–4.30pm; $9.75). Pierre du Pont, the patriarch, was minister of finance to Louis XVI, but the museum begins later with the founding in 1802 of a small water-powered gunpowder mill along the banks of the Brandywine River. Mirroring the development of nineteenth-century American industry, the complex grew over the next hundred years to include ever-larger steam-powered and eventually electrically-powered factories – almost all of which are still in working order.

The enormous pink **Nemours Mansion**, just a mile up the road, gives an idea of the wealth and power the family garnered (May–Nov Tues–Sat 9am–3pm, Sun 11am–3pm; tours every two hours; $10). It was built by Alfred du Pont in 1910, modeled upon the family's ancestral home in France and surrounded by a three-hundred-acre, Versailles-style formal garden. Two miles northwest, off Hwy-52, the one-time du Pont family estate of **Winterthur** (Mon–Sat 9am–5pm, Sun noon–5pm; $10, gardens only $5) has evolved into the country's finest museum of early American decorative arts. Since 1927, when Henry du Pont took over the twelve-room cottage to house himself and his antique furniture, Winterthur has grown into a vast private museum, each of its two hundred rooms showcasing a particular decorative style. Ranging from the simplicity of a Shaker cottage to a beautiful three-story elliptical staircase taken from a North Carolina plantation home, the various pieces of furniture, textiles, silverwork and paintings – all made in America between 1640 and 1860 – form a rich catalog of the diversity of American applied arts.

New Castle

Delaware's magnificently preserved first capital, **NEW CASTLE**, fronts the broad Delaware River, just six miles south of Wilmington via Hwy-141. Founded in the 1650s by the Dutch – who were intent on expanding from their colony at New Amsterdam, and taken over by the British in 1664, New Castle was the main stopping point between Baltimore and Philadelphia. William Penn first set foot in the New World here in October 1682. Largely bypassed when railroads and highways replaced the riverboats, it has managed to survive intact, its quiet cobbled streets and immaculate eighteenth-century brick houses shaded by ancient hardwood trees.

The heart of New Castle is the tree-filled **town green** that spreads east from the shops of Delaware Street. Laid out in 1655 by Peter Stuyvesant, and ringed by a cracked red-brick sidewalk, it is dominated by the stalwart tower of the Immanuel Episcopal Church, built in 1703 and bordered by tidy rows of two-hundred-year-old gravestones. The church's modern, pristine white interior was reconstructed after a disastrous fire in the 1980s. On the west edge of the green, the **Old Court House** (Tues–Sat 10am–3.30pm, Sun 1.30–4.30pm; free) was built in 1732 and served as the first state capitol. Its dainty cupola was the centerpoint from which surveyors determined the state's curved northern border, drawn up when Delaware seceded from Pennsylvania in 1776.

Fine colonial houses fill the few blocks around the town green. The largest, and only one regularly open to the public, is the **George Read II House** (Tues–Sat 10am–4pm, Sun noon–4pm; $4), two blocks south along the river at 42 The Strand. Built between 1797 and 1804 for a signatory of the Declaration of Independence, the original house burned down in 1824. The sumptuously detailed rebuilt version holds marble fireplaces, brightly painted walls, elaborately carved woodwork and some of the finest plasterwork ornamentation of the Federal period. The spacious gardens behind the building were laid out in 1847 to the picturesque designs of Andrew Jackson Downing. The large houses across the street, backing onto the Delaware River, also date from the early nineteenth century, and many are now run as B&Bs. A large riverfront park spreads south from the foot of Delaware Street, with rolling lawns and sheltered benches. Its pride and joy is a tiny white-clapboard ticket office, which dates from the opening of the town's first railroad in 1832 and stands next to a small piece of track.

Practicalities

Many visitors are content to see New Castle, just off the interstate, as a day-trip from Washington DC or Philadelphia, but there's enough here to merit a longer visit. For further information, or to pick up the self-guided **walking tour** map, drop in to the **visitor center** at the court house, which is open to the public at 211 Delaware St (Tues–Sat 10am–3.30pm, Sun 1.30–4.30pm; ☎302/323-4453), or call the Historic New Castle Visitor's Bureau at ☎1-800/758-1550. Comfortable **B&Bs** line the Delaware riverfront, ranging from the good-value *William Penn Guest House*, 206 Delaware St (☎302/328-7736; ❸), to the more luxurious and hospitable *Armitage Inn*, 2 The Strand (☎302/328-6618, ⓦwww.armitageinn.com; ❺). There's good beer and pub grub, including crabs and clams, at the popular *Jessop's Tavern*, 114 Delaware St (☎302/322-6111), while more refined taste buds will enjoy the French-influenced seafood dishes at the grand *Arsenal at Old New Castle*, next to the Church on Market Street (☎302/328-1290).

Dover

DOVER, the capital of Delaware, struggles to attract visitors as they bypass the city en route to the beach resorts of Rehoboth and Maryland's Ocean City. Located in the mostly agricultural center of the state, just west of US-13, Dover is basically a very small town, with a low-rise business district hemmed in by blocks of suburban houses. South of **Lockerman Street**, the main route through town, a few strangely somnolent governmental buildings center upon the 1792 **Old State House**, its old legislative chambers now restored as a museum (Tues–Sat 10am–4.30pm, Sun 1.30–4.30pm; free) and furnished with early American antiques. To the west, around the oval **town green**, lawyers and insurance brokers have taken over historic buildings such as the *Golden Fleece Tavern*, where Delaware's early legislators agreed to ratify the Constitution.

In the same building as the friendly **visitor center** (Mon–Sat 8.30am–4.30pm, Sun 1.30–4.30pm; ☎302/739-4266), at the corner of Duke of York and Federal streets next to the Old State House, the impressive **Biggs Museum of American Art** (Wed–Sat 10am–4pm, Sun 1.30–4.30pm; free) has historical and art displays downstairs, while the upper floor is given over to paintings, furniture, silver and other period housewares. The **Delaware State Museums** (Tues–Sat 10am–3.30pm; free; ⊛www.destatemuseums.org) includes the trio located a short walk west of the green; the **Archaeology Museum** and **Museum of Small Town Life** contain fairly tedious displays of anthropological detritus – Native American shell necklaces, wooden water pipes from early Wilmington and the like – but not to be missed is the **Johnson Victrola Museum**. The outwardly unassuming building houses a large collection of phonographs, dedicated to the memory of Dover-born engineer Eldridge Reeves Johnson, who helped to invent the **Victrola**. The layout is like a 1920s music store: dozens of "talking machines," from early wind-ups to prototype jukeboxes, play period recordings, and comical photographs document early, pre-electric recording techniques – entire orchestras crowd together around huge megaphones. Pride of place goes to a painting of a dog, Nipper, listening to a Victrola, an image made familiar as "His Master's Voice." In 1929 Johnson sold the rights to his machine, and to his trademark dog, to RCA for $29 million.

Every Tuesday and Friday for over fifty years, **Spence's Bazaar**, two blocks south on Queen Street at New Burton Road, has hosted a free-for-all **flea market**. All of Dover turns out for this, including dozens of local **Amish**, who ride here in their ancient horse-drawn buggies to sell homegrown fruits and vegetables. Though it's not as well known as the Amish community of Pennsylvania's Lancaster County (see p.167), the area around Dover has nearly as large an Amish population, concentrated in the farmlands to the west of town; happily for them, their presence has yet to become a tourist attraction. If you're not around on flea market days, Lockerman Street hosts a variety of street stalls every day during fine weather. Most of Dover's **restaurants** and **hotels** are concentrated on Lockerman Street and State Street in the town center, just north of the green. The *Tudor House B&B* at 228 N State St (☎302/736-1763 or 1-877/736-1763; ❸) is an amiable if somewhat dishevelled place to stay and *C'Moore's* at 24 Lockerman St (☎302/674-8875) is a fine spot to fill up on a homestyle cooked dinner or sandwiches. The US-13 highway also has some budget accommodation, such as the *Comfort Inn* (☎302/674-3300; ❸), two blocks south of Lockerman Street.

The Delaware coast

The thirty-mile-long Delaware coast is one of the little-known jewels of the east coast. Its only built-up resort, which is packed solid in summer, is the traditional seaside town of **Rehoboth Beach**. The historic fishing community of **Lewes** is also attractive, but what really sets the area apart is the ease with which you can find long stretches of sand to yourself. For every developed stretch, about ten times more has been preserved as open space, most extensively at **Delaware Seashore State Park**, which stretches south from Rehoboth to the Maryland border.

Lewes

Whether you come down Hwy-1, or cruise across on the ferry from Cape May, New Jersey, **LEWES** makes a good introduction to the Delaware coast. Its natural harbor at the mouth of Delaware Bay has attracted seafarers ever since a Dutch whaling company set up a small colony here in 1631. Lewes' current role as a summer resort hasn't obscured its substantial history, outlined in the mock-Dutch **Zwaanendael Museum**, in the heart of town on Savannah Road at Kings Highway (Tues–Sat 10am–4.30pm, Sun 1.30–4.30pm; free). The **CVB** next door (Mon–Fri 10am–4pm, Sat 10am–2pm; ☎302/645-8073 or 1-877-465-3937, ⊛www.leweschamber.com), housed inside a gambrel-roofed 1730s farmhouse, has walking tour maps of the town, which point out the handful of eighteenth-century houses and outbuildings collected from around the area to form the **Lewes Historical Complex** (mid June–early Sept Tues–Sat; $4) on Front Street three blocks north. Along the canal, keep an eye out for the **Overfalls Lightship**, which lit the entrance to Delaware Bay until 1961, and, lined up along the top of **Memorial Park,** the array of cannons, one said to be from an old pirate ship. You can walk almost everywhere in town, or **rent a bike** from Lewes Cycle Sports, 514 Savannah Rd (☎302/645-4544).

Though Lewes can justly boast of being "the First Town in the First State," most people come here for its beach rather than its history. There's an extensive strand along the usually calm Delaware Bay at the foot of the town, while three-thousand-acre **Cape Henlopen State Park** (☎302/645-8983), where the bay meets the open ocean just a mile east of the town center, offers the chance to camp beside the biggest sand dunes north of Cape Hatteras. For a nice day out, or a possible next leg of your journey, take the seventy-minute **ferry trip** across the Delaware Bay from beside the state park to the pleasant Victorian beach resort of **CAPE MAY**, New Jersey (6–15 services daily all year, first at 8am, last at 8pm, or 9.20pm mid–May to mid–Oct; $6.50 per person, $20 per car May–Oct; $4.50/$18 Nov–April; ☎302/645-6030 or 1-800/64-FERRY; see also p.191).

Except on peak summer weekends, Lewes is quiet enough that you should have no trouble finding a motel room along Savannah Road, such as *Vesuvio's* (☎302/645-2224; ❹), just before the drawbridge, or *The Captain's Quarters* (☎302/645-7924, ⊛www.captainsquartersmotel.com; ❹) on the far side. Most of the **restaurants**, not surprisingly, feature seafood, such as the *Lighthouse* (☎302/645-6271) by the bridge, where you get a free cruise if you dine between 4 and 6pm, or there is the more formal Italian dining at *La Rosa Negra* at 128 Second St (☎302/645-1980), back in the town center.

Rehoboth Beach

A nonstop parade of motels and shopping malls along the six miles of Hwy-1 links Lewes with **REHOBOTH BEACH**, Delaware's largest and liveliest beach resort, which merges into **Dewey Beach** at its southern end. Crowded all summer, but nearly empty the rest of the year, Rehoboth – which started life as a Methodist revival camp, and attracts so many escapees from DC that it's known as the Nation's Summer Capital – is more family oriented than other beach towns, lacking the nightlife of Ocean City but making up for it with miles of clean and uncrowded sands.

Rehoboth has less of a history than Lewes, though its wooden **boardwalk** is one of the last on the east coast. It stretches along the Atlantic to either side of Rehoboth Avenue – always "**The Avenue**" – which acts as the main drag, its four short blocks clogged with souvenir shoppers browsing though the usual array of T-shirts and seaside kitsch. Most of the **restaurants** and **nightspots** are concentrated here, with *Thrashers French Fries* stands and burger bars mixed in with the mock-Caribbean beach shack decor of the *Back Porch Café*, 59 Rehoboth Ave (☎302/227-3674), and the gaudy Mexican touch of the *Iguana Grill*, a block north at 52 Baltimore Ave (☎302/227-5957). After dark, the action shifts to the Anglophile environs of the *Country Squire*, 19 Rehoboth Ave (☎302/227-3985), which has the largest beer selection for miles.

If shopping is your passion, Rehoboth has the largest concentration of **outlet stores** in the Delmarva area, with more than 140 famous name shops like Nike, Donna Karan, Gap and Coach, where, as in all of Delaware, you can shop tax-free. You can't miss the blatant consumerism along Route 1 – just follow the tide of cars inching toward the latest bargains.

Apart from the peak times of July and August, it shouldn't be too difficult to find a bed in one of Rehoboth's many **motels**: just off the boardwalk are the *Sandcastle*, 123 Second St (☎302/227-0400 or 1-800/372-2112, ⓦwww .thesandcastlemotel.com; ❹), and the *Admiral*, a block south at 2 Baltimore Ave (☎302/227-2130 or 1-888/882-4188; ❸). **B&Bs** are a nice alternative by the beach; try the upmarket *Corner Cupboard Inn*, 50 Park Ave (☎302/227-8553, ⓦwww.cornercupboardinn.com; ❼), with a nice restaurant and just four blocks from the beach, or the *Rehoboth Guest House*, 40 Maryland Ave (☎302/227-4117 or 1-800/564-0493, ⓦwww.rehobothguesthouse.com; ❺). Room rates at all of the above can soar well above $100 on summer weekends. For more information, contact the **Chamber of Commerce**, 501 Rehoboth Ave (☎302/227-2233 or 1-800/441-1329, ⓦwww.beach-fun.com).

South of Rehoboth, **Delaware Seashore State Park** (☎302/227-2800, ⓦwww.destateparks.com) stretches for miles along a thin, sandy peninsula, split by Hwy-1 and bounded on the east by the Atlantic and on the west by various freshwater marshlands. There's little here apart from beachfront parking areas ($5) and the park's campground (☎302/539.7202 or 1-877/98PARKS) until you approach the Maryland border, where the concrete tower blocks of **Bethany Beach** do little to prepare you for the Costa del Sol-like concentrations of hotels and condos in Ocean City, ten miles further along (see p.482).

CHAPTER 6

Highlights

* **Blue Ridge Parkway, NC**
This tortuous but exhilarating wilderness highway makes a destination in itself. See p.512

* **Walking tours, Charleston, SC**
Whether you're into architecture or black heritage it's a delight to stroll the cobbled streets of this gorgeous historic port. See p.521

* **Martin Luther King birthplace, Atlanta, GA**
Engaging tours take you around King's childhood home, in the South's most dynamic city.
See p.534

* **Memphis, TN**
Especially exciting for music fans, who could spend days checking out Beale Street, Sun Studio, Al Green's church and, of course, Graceland. See p.560

* **Country Music Hall of Fame, Nashville, TN**
Bursting with memorabilia of the stars, including Elvis's gold Cadillac.
See p.576

* **The Mississippi Delta, MS** The birthplace of the blues holds an irresistible appeal, with Clarksdale as the obvious first port of call. See p.594

6

The South

As Mark Twain put it in 1882, "In the South, the [Civil] war is what AD is elsewhere; they date everything from it." Five generations later, the legacies of slavery and "The War Between the States" are still evident throughout the southern heartland states of **NORTH CAROLINA**, **SOUTH CAROLINA**, **GEORGIA**, **KENTUCKY**, **TENNESSEE**, **ALABAMA**, **MISSISSIPPI** and **ARKANSAS**. The war is the focal point for countless museums and shrines, and the Confederate "Stars and Bars" flag remains conspicuous in many places.

The area, however, is not entirely stuck in its ways. How far the "New South" differs from the old is still a matter for debate. Nonetheless, the last few decades have unquestionably seen the influx of high-tech industries, the emergence of liberal white political leaders such as Jimmy Carter and Bill Clinton, and the growth of such dynamic urban centers as **Atlanta**, the birthplace of Dr Martin Luther King Jr and venue for the 1996 Olympics. It took suffering and blood-shed to effect the changes of the 1950s and 1960s. Relations between black and white have improved, in the cities at least, though the countryside reveals levels of shocking iniquity and poverty where racial tension lies uneasily close to the surface.

The South has never been one uniform, homogenous unit. Even during the Civil War there were substantial pockets of pro-Union support, particularly in the mountains. Today the culture and makeup of the overwhelmingly black stretches in the cotton belt are markedly different from the white hill farms in Kentucky and Tennessee. Likewise, the Sun Belt industries of North Carolina and northern Alabama are far removed from the rural backwaters of southern Georgia.

The most exciting aspect of the Southern heritage is undoubtedly its **music**. Hundreds of thousands of fans make pilgrimages each year to the country and blues meccas of **Nashville** and **Memphis**, the homelands of Elvis Presley, Hank Williams, Robert Johnson, Dolly Parton and Otis Redding. As well, a substantial number of visitors seek out the backwoods barn dances in Appalachia or the blues jook-joints of the Mississippi Delta and South Carolina. The Southern experience is also reflected in a rich regional **literature**, its communities and people well documented by the likes of William Faulkner, Carson McCullers, Flannery O'Connor, Alice Walker, Eudora Welty, and the one-book-wonders Margaret Mitchell and Harper Lee.

Other major destinations for travelers include the elegant coastal cities of **Charleston** and **Savannah**, frenzied beach resorts such as **Myrtle Beach**, college towns like **Athens** and **Chapel Hill**, and the historic Mississippi River ports of **Natchez** and **Vicksburg**. Away from the urban areas, much Southern scenery consists of undulating, sun-scorched hillsides dotted with wooden shacks and rust-red barns, broken by occasional forests. Highlights include the misty Appalachian **mountains** of Kentucky, Tennessee and North Carolina, the subtropical **beaches** and tranquil **barrier islands** along the Atlantic and Gulf coasts and the river road through the tiny settlements of the flat Mississippi Delta.

During July and August, the daily high **temperature** is mostly a very humid 90°F. Virtually every motel, bar, restaurant and museum is air-conditioned, but you might want to schedule your visit a little to either side of these months. On the coasts, where the beaches offer a less expensive alternative to neighboring Florida, the main season is from June to August, and outside these dates many attractions are closed. The fall colors in the mountains (just as beautiful and a lot less expensive and congested than New England) are at their headiest during October.

Public transportation in rural areas is poor. In any case, it's best to take things at your own pace – you'll find things to see and do in the most unlikely places – so renting a car is a good idea. **Accommodation** in the South is generally good value. The region's varied **cuisine**, much of it dished out at simple roadside shacks, ranges from the ubiquitous grits (maize porridge) to highly calorific, irresistible **soul food** – fried chicken, wood-smoked barbecue and the like, along with turnip greens, spinach, macaroni and all manner of tasty vegetables. Fish is also good, from catfish (which has a sort of mild trout flavor), to the wonderful **Low Country Boils**, seafood stews served with rice, traditionally prepared on the sea islands. Look, too, for the distinctively Southern *Krispy Kreme* doughnut outlets, especially in the Carolinas and Georgia. The doughnuts are great, but it's the decor that steals the show – turquoise Formica, shiny chrome counter stools and fabulous 1950s signs.

Some history

The **Spanish** and **French** had begun to build settlements throughout the South as early as the 1520s. However, by the early seventeenth century the **British** had pushed them back to what are now Florida and Louisiana, and steered the region toward a role as supplier of **raw materials** to its **cotton** mills and **tobacco** factories. Both climate and soil favored staple agriculture, and massive labor-intensive **plantations** started to spring up. No self-respecting European would cross the Atlantic to pick cotton on a plantation, so the big landowners turned to **slavery** as the most profitable source of labor. Millions of blacks were brought into the country, primarily through the port of Charleston.

As the South became increasingly set in its ways, with little incentive to diversify, the Northern states surged ahead in both agriculture and industry. By the early nineteenth century the Southern economy was clearly subservient to that of the North: the South grew the crops, but Northern factories monopolized the more lucrative manufacturing of finished goods. Southern politicians and plantation-owners accused the North of political and economic aggression, and felt that unless slavery continued to spread into the territories and even the free states, they would progressively lose all say in the future of the nation. The election as president in late 1860 of **Abraham Lincoln**, a longtime critic of slavery, brought the crisis to a head, and in February 1861 six Southern states broke away to form the Confederate States of America. Jefferson Davis was sworn in as president of the Confederacy on February 18, 1861 – an occasion on which his vice president proudly proclaimed that this government was "the first in the history of the world, based upon this great physical and moral truth . . . that the Negro is not equal to the white man." **Secession** radically upped the stakes in the controversy. Most Northerners had been indifferent to the issue of slavery – even Lincoln, as late as mid-1861, said "I have no purpose . . . to interfere with slavery in the States where it exists" – but the potential destruction of the Union was seen as a far more serious, and treacherous, threat.

During the resultant **Civil War**, the South was outgunned and ultimately overwhelmed by the vast resources of the North. The Confederates fired the first shots and scored the first victory in April 1861, when the Union garrison at Fort Sumter (outside Charleston, South Carolina) surrendered. The Union was on the military defensive until mid-1862, when its navy blockaded the coast of Georgia and the Carolinas and occupied several key ports. Then Union forces in the west, under generals Grant and Sherman, swept through

Tennessee, and by the end of 1863 the North had taken Vicksburg, the final Confederate-held port on the Mississippi, as well as the strategic mountain-locked town of Chattanooga on the Tennessee–Georgia border. Grant proceeded north to Virginia, while Sherman captured the transportation nexus of Atlanta and began a bloody and ruthless march to the coast, burning everything in his way. With 228,000 men dead (a quarter of the South's adult white male population), the Confederacy's defeat was total, and General Robert E. Lee surrendered on April 9, 1865, at Appomattox in Virginia.

The war was followed by a period of **Reconstruction**, when the South was occupied by Union troops. The political administrations imposed and run by Northern Republicans ("carpetbaggers" or "scalawags") were characterized by corruption, but what galled Southerners most was that blacks were also involved in government. When this probationary era came to an end in the mid-1870s, the Southern states returned to Democratic Party control. Black politicians were intimidated out of office, in particular by the **Ku Klux Klan**, which was started in 1865 by ex-Confederate officers. "**Jim Crow**" segregation laws were imposed, and poll taxes, literacy tests and property qualifications disenfranchised virtually all blacks (and many poor whites).

The war left the South in chaos. Along with the devastating death toll, two-thirds of Southern wealth had been destroyed. From controlling thirty percent of the nation's assets in 1860, the South was down to twelve percent in 1870, while the spur the war gave to industrialization meant that the North was booming. With the abolition of slavery, the plantations were no longer viable. Instead, the Southern economy turned to **sharecropping**, a crude barter system under which landowners provided their tenants with land, housing and even food and implements, the cost of which was later deducted (along with a high rate of interest) from the sale of crops. Most farms, however, were too small to be economical. As a result, the freed slaves benefited little from the abolition of what southern states called their "peculiar institution": thousands were forced into debt, and there were mass migrations to cities like Memphis and Atlanta, as well as to the North.

After the uncertainties of Reconstruction, industrial growth accelerated (the impetus coming, ironically enough, from Northern investors, who took advantage of the cheap land and labor), but even by the 1929 stock market crash the South still lagged well behind the North. During the **Great Depression**, the region was especially hard hit because so many of its people were poor to begin with. President Franklin D. Roosevelt's New Deal program, particularly the establishment of the Tennessee Valley Authority (see p.560) and road-building projects, helped to alleviate immediate hardships and lay down an infrastructure to aid economic recovery. The war effort during the early Forties stimulated industrial growth. Since the Sixties, foreign companies, particularly from Japan, have opened thousands of new factories in the South, attracted by the anti-union "Right to Work" statutes upheld by most states. Also, the warm climate – the South is a large component of the US "**Sun Belt**" – has attracted many companies from the East and Midwest. Nonetheless, the overall lack of agricultural and industrial diversification still means that huge parts of the South remain disturbingly poor.

The political revolution wrought by Roosevelt's New Deal in the 1930s included a more liberal trend in federal law-making. A groundbreaking 1954 Supreme Court ruling outlawed segregation in schools, but individual Southern states were at best very slow to effect the required changes. The **civil rights movement**, which began when blacks campaigned for desegregation in education, soon expanded to encompass demonstrations and protests – such as the Montgomery bus boycott and the Greensboro lunch-counter sit-in – against racial barriers in other areas of life. Before civil rights legislation was finally imposed in the late Sixties, some southern whites, encouraged by firebrand politicians, put up a bloody resistance to change, and left behind a catalog of murder, attacks and harassment – particularly in Mississippi and Alabama. Modern travelers can follow in the footsteps of **Dr Martin Luther King Jr** throughout the South, from his birthplace in Atlanta, through his church in Montgomery, to the site of his assassination in Memphis, commemorated (some think rather inappropriately) by the National Civil Rights Museum.

The civil rights years had a marked effect on **party politics** in the South. Since the Civil War the region had voted almost *en bloc* for the **Democrats**, but as that party became more identified with liberal reforms, greater government intervention and, especially, racial integration, there was a marked shift toward the **Republican** Party, especially in presidential elections. Right-wing politicians have been forced to search for a party political home. Dinosaur Strom Thurmond of South Carolina and the equally vitriolic George Wallace campaigned for the US presidency under the banners of small segregationist parties. More recently, Senate Republican Leader Trent Lott has added to the traditional Southern demagoguery typified by fellow GOP Senator Jesse Helms of North Carolina. Meanwhile, many unreconstructed backwoodsmen still fight for white supremacy under the umbrella of the Democratic Party.

The dispossession of the **Native Americans** is often the forgotten chapter of Southern history. Colonial powers at best tolerated the Indians, for the most part peaceful agrarian tribes, and used them as allies in their imperialist wars with each other. However, after the Revolution, pressure from plantation owners and small farmers led to the forced removal in the 1830s of the "five civilized tribes" – the Cherokee, Creek, Choctaw, Chickasaw and Seminole – to malarial Oklahoma. Today only a few thousand Native Americans live in the South.

North Carolina

NORTH CAROLINA, though the most industrialized of the Southern states, remains relatively rural and poor, with just six million people spread over an area larger than England. It suffered heavily during the **Civil War**, and **Reconstruction** brought mixed fortunes: although poverty and hostility were still endemic the Democrats, once they regained control in 1870, were effective in stamping out the Ku Klux Klan. Since then there have been parallel traditions of radical black, and white racist, activity. **Greensboro**, for example, where **Jesse Jackson** served his political apprenticeship, was the site of the 1960 lunch-counter sit-in by black students, and also of the Greensboro Massacre of 1979, when Klansmen killed five people at a Communist Workers Party demonstration.

Geographically, North Carolina breaks down into three distinct areas – running from east to west, the coast, the Piedmont and the mountains – that help make it one of the more interesting states to tour around. For visitors, the coast is the most promising area, with good beaches, beautiful landscapes and a fascinating history. The inner coast consists largely of the less developed **Albemarle Peninsula**, with colonial **Edenton** nearby. The central **Piedmont** is dominated by manufacturing cities, and by the academic institutions of the prestigious Research Triangle: **Raleigh**, the state capital, is home to North Carolina State University. Duke University is at **Durham**, and the University of North Carolina at trendy **Chapel Hill**. **Winston–Salem** combines tobacco culture and Moravian heritage, while **Charlotte** bills itself as the next boom city of the South, though for the moment it's distinguished by little but its downtown skyscrapers. In the **mountains**, one of the most stunning stretches of Appalachia, the only towns of any size, **Boone** and **Asheville**, are linked by the spectacular **Blue Ridge Parkway**, while **Great Smoky Mountains National Park** overlaps the border with Tennessee.

Getting around North Carolina

North Carolina's major **airports** are at Charlotte, an arrival point for transatlantic flights, Raleigh-Durham and Wilmington, all of which will connect you with several major US cities. A tiny airport at Manteo in the Outer Banks (☏252/473-2227) runs charter flights to the barrier islands, but driving would be easier. Charlotte, Raleigh, Durham and Greensboro (with an express bus link to Winston–Salem) are served by **Amtrak**, but unfortunately there is no coastal route. Plenty of **buses** run within the Piedmont; schedules are much less frequent in the mountains and along the coast, both of which are best explored by car. North Carolina's **interstates** are some of the most attractive in the country, the medians carpeted with poppies and wildflowers. The state also has a good network of **cycling** routes along quiet country roads; for information, contact the Department of Transportation (☏919/733-2804).

The North Carolina coast

The **North Carolina coast**, which ranges through salt marshes, beaches, barrier islands and estuaries, holds most of the state's more interesting **historic sites**. The continent's earliest English colonists vanished inexplicably from **Roanoke Island** in 1590; just over three centuries later, the Wright brothers achieved the first powered flight a few miles up the road. The **Outer Banks**, the long reef of barrier islands that stretches down from Virginia, are in parts tacky and elsewhere beautifully unspoiled.

Edenton and the Albemarle

The huge and generally relaxed **Albemarle Peninsula** remains largely unexploited. Local towns try to make much of their **colonial history** – this was the first part of North Carolina to have permanent European settlements, around the end of the seventeenth century – but often there's not a lot left to see, except for restored eighteenth-century buildings that start to look similar after a while.

Edenton

EDENTON, set along a beautiful, placid Albemarle Sound **waterfront** roughly forty miles south of the Virginia border, was established as North Carolina's first state capital in 1722. A major center of unrest in the American Revolution, it remained a prosperous port until the early nineteenth century, when it began to fade. Today Edenton feels frozen, not unpleasantly, some time around 1960.

As you stroll around the town – possibly aided by the self-guided walking tour issued by the **Historic Edenton Visitor Center** (April–Oct Mon–Sat 9am–5pm, Sun 1–5pm; Nov–March Tues–Sat 10am–4pm, Sun 1–4pm; $3–5; ☏ 252/482-2637, ⓦ www.edenton.com; guided tours available, call ahead for times) – you'll come across an exceptional number of colonial and pre-Civil War **houses**, and the magnificent wooden **Cupola House**; **St Paul's Parish Church** and the Georgian **Chowan County Courthouse** overlooking the waterfront are fine mid-eighteenth-century structures. The main road, **Broad Street**, is also interesting in an offbeat way, with its Victorian facades, old-fashioned drugstores selling home-mixed sodas, and Fifties chrome signs.

A narrated slide show at the visitor center covers colonial history well, but is less explicit about slavery. There's no mention of the remarkable **Harriet Jacobs**, a runaway slave who hid for seven years in her grandmother's attic. She finally escaped to the North through such ruses as disguising herself as a male sailor, and was eventually reunited in Boston with the two children she had had by a white man in Edenton. She wrote this amazing story as *Incidents in the Life of a Slave Girl*, one of the most famous published slave narratives of the nineteenth century. None of the buildings mentioned in the book is still standing, but the visitor center provides walking and trolley tours to give you an idea of where places were. A map published by the Harvard University Press (1987) provides information on some historic sites.

If you like peace and quiet, Edenton is not a bad base for explorations of the coast. Luxurious **B&Bs** include the *Trestle House Inn*, 632 Soundside Rd (☏ 252/482-2282, ⓦ www.edenton.com/trestlehouse; ❺), and the bizarre *Granville Queen Themed Inn*, 108 S Granville St (☏ 252/482-5296 ⓦ www.edenton.com/granvillequeen; ❹/❻), in which every room is done out on a "queen" theme – ask for the Egyptian Queen, with its resident sphinxes. You won't need to eat for the rest of the day after their five-course breakfast. A reliable budget **motel** is the *Coach House*, 919 N Broad St (☏ 252/482-2107; ❷). For **eating,** the *Creekside Restaurant & Bar*, 406 W Queen St (☏ 252/482-0118), has a good, varied menu. For Carolina pit-cooked barbecue try *Lane's Family BBQ and Seafood*, 421 E Church St (☏ 252/482-4008). Closer to the water, there is the fishy *Waterman's Grill*, 427 S Broad St (☏ 252/482-7733).

Exploring the Albemarle

ALBEMARLE plantation life can be sampled at **Hope**, the home of David Stone, a state governor and US senator of the Revolutionary and Federal period. It's off Hwy-308, a few miles west of **Windsor**, about 25 miles southwest of Edenton (Jan to late Dec Mon–Sat 10am–4pm, Sun 2–5pm; $6.50). The house, built in 1803, is classic Southern myth: white, with a double balcony at the front, and filled with hand-carved wooden furniture. Admission includes entrance to the 1763 **King-Bazemore House**, a simple planter's home, which holds demonstrations of colonial cooking in its working kitchen.

A clearer picture of slave life is given by **Somerset Place State Historic Site**, a plantation 25 miles southeast of Edenton at **Cresswell** on US-64 (summer Mon–Sat 9am–5pm, Sun 1–5pm; rest of year Tues–Sat 10am–4pm, Sun 1–4pm; free; ☏ 252/797-4560). This is how the lowland plantations must have looked, with fields dissolving into marshland beyond huge oaks. The wooden shacks of the slaves' quarters have gone, but you can see the foundations of the tiny shed-sized slave "hospital." The director of the site is descended from slaves who worked here. Guided tours are available.

There's a **campground** at the neighboring **Pettigrew State Park** at 252 Phelps Lake ($12, first come first served; ☏919/797-4475), an area of mighty trees ranged around a shallow rainwater-fed lake, ideal for fishing. Even if you don't stay, go down to the tiny museum at the water's edge, where the interesting display on local Native Americans includes two 4000-year-old dugout canoes raised from the lake. Close by both, the Tyrrell County **Visitor's Center**, 203 S Ludington Drive (☏252/796-0723), has information on further exploring.

The southern shore of the Albemarle Peninsula holds less to see, though the marshy countryside and tree-lined roads make for a pleasant drive, and **Lake Mattamuskeet Wildlife Refuge** (☏252/926-4021), off Hwy-94 on the causeway across the lake, or off US-264 near New Holland, is an amazing sight in winter, when thousands of swans migrate here from Canada. It's also a sanctuary for endangered osprey.

The Outer Banks

The **OUTER BANKS** are a series of long sand bars, sprinkled with wispy sea oats, that stretch about 180 miles from the Virginia border to Cape Lookout, near Beaufort. They are a great place to wander at your own speed, although unfortunately there's no public transportation apart from the ferries between islands and to the mainland.

The main road from the north, US-158, crosses from the mainland on a low bridge, where you're greeted by a roadside **visitor center** (☏252/261-4644, ⓦwww.outerbanks.org). South along US-158 and the parallel shoreline Beach Road, the coastal towns of **Kitty Hawk**, **Kill Devil Hills** and **Nags Head** are strung out without a break, and the fine warm-water **beaches** are lined with motels and fast-food places mixed in with huge vacation "cottages." Note that when Outer Banks hotels describe themselves as "waterfront," it simply means they are on the coastal side of the road, not that they necessarily have ocean views.

Kill Devil Hills, Nags Head and Roanoke Island

The **Wright Brothers National Memorial** (summer daily 9am–6pm; rest of year daily 9am–5pm; $4 per car, $2 pedestrians; ☏252/441-7430), a large granite fin atop a hill just off the main road at **KILL DEVIL HILLS**, commemorates the plucky Orville Wright's **first powered flight**, on December 17, 1903. Most histories say the flight took place at **Kitty Hawk**, a town eight miles north, but that was just the name of the nearest post office. The flight in fact took place off Kill Devil Hill, in what is now the city of Kill Devil Hills. A boulder next to the **visitor center** marks where his first aircraft hit the ground, and successive numbered markers show the distance of each of his subsequent flights. A museum in the visitor center records the brothers' various experiments. After several years of trials with kites and gliders, visiting the Outer Banks for a few weeks at a time and living in makeshift shacks on the beach, Orville and Wilbur finally launched their powered plane on a cold December morning, shaking hands before the takeoff. As one of the locals acting as ground crew remarked, "We couldn't help notice how they held on to each other's hand, sort o' like folks parting who weren't sure they'd ever see one another again." The phlegmatic Orville recorded the historic moment of takeoff in his diary: "The machine lifted from the truck . . . I found control of the front rudder quite difficult . . . the machine would rise suddenly to about 10 feet and then as suddenly, on turning the rudder, dart for the ground . . . time about twelve seconds."

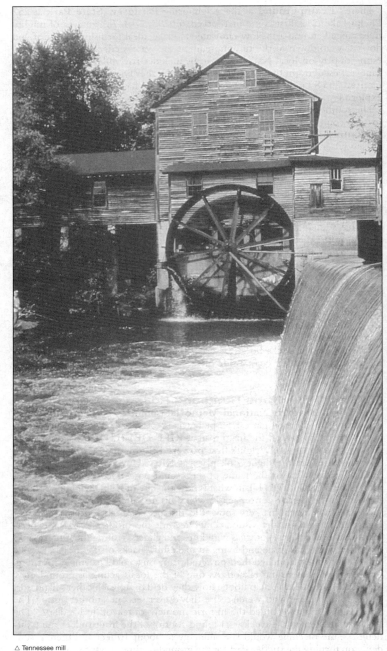

△ Tennessee mill

A few miles south in **NAGS HEAD**, at Hwy-158 milepost 12, **Jockey's Ridge State Park** (☎252/441-7132) boasts the largest sand dunes on the east coast. It's a particularly great place to be at sunset, while during the day instructors from Kitty Hawk Kites (☎252/441-4124) will teach you the basics of hang-gliding for $65.

ROANOKE ISLAND lies between the mainland and Bodie Island, a part of the Outer Banks. It is accessible from both by bridges. Roanoke Island was the **first English settlement** in North America, founded by **Sir Walter Raleigh** in 1585. The colonists survived initial difficulties with weather, disease and Indians, and were joined by one hundred more settlers brought over by John White in 1587. When White returned three years later, however, all trace of the colony had disappeared, except for the one mysterious word "Croatoan" carved on a tree. Theories as to the fate of the "Lost Colony" have varied, although it is generally assumed that the settlers were massacred by hostile natives – a key piece of early anti-Indian mythology. A rather fanciful version has it that settlers and Native Americans banded together and marched inland, forming what is now the small and very racially mixed Lumbee tribe in southwest North Carolina.

Nothing authentic survives of the Roanoke settlement, but **Fort Raleigh National Historic Site**, three miles north of **Manteo** off US-64, contains a conjectural and tiny reconstruction of the colonists' earthwork fort, set in a wooded glade with a canopy of Spanish moss (summer Sun–Fri 9am–8pm, Sat 9am–6pm; rest of the year daily 9am–5pm; free; ☎252/473-5772). A museum covers local Indian interaction with colonists, and an outdoor amphitheater on the ocean hosts performances of *The Lost Colony*, an undeniably impressive drama (June–Aug daily except Sat, 8.30pm; $16-20; ☎1-800/488-5012). Adjacent to the fort, the **Elizabethan Gardens** are elegantly landscaped with walkways, statues and subtropical blooms. The shade provided by the trees makes it a great place to go in high summer (open daily year-round, closing times vary with season; $5).

In Manteo itself, the recently renovated **Roanoke Island Festival Park** has a slew of well-done historical attractions that, if seen in full, take several hours (call for hours; $8 tickets valid for 2 days; ☎252/475-1500). Of particular note is the **Exhibit Hall**, where costumed employees walk you through the history of Virginia; also here is the *Elizabeth II*, a reconstruction of a sixteenth-century English **ship**, and a re-enactment of the ship's trip to Roanoke. Call ☎252/475-1506 for a current schedule of films, dance, music and dramatic presentations.

Motels line the beaches north of Oregon Inlet, which separates Bodie Island and Cape Hatteras National Seashore. The *Blue Heron Motel*, on Hwy-12 at Nags Head (☎252/441-7447; summer ❺, winter ❸), is one of the cleanest, with an oceanfront pool. The *First Colony Inn* is a great B&B at 6720 S Virginia Dare Trail, Nags Head (☎252/441-2343, ℱ252/441-9234, ⓦwww.first-colonyinn.com; ❼/❽), with friendly and knowledgeable staff. There's also nice **hostel** accommodation at *HI-Outerbanks* in Kitty Hawk at 1004 W Kitty Hawk Rd (☎252/261-2294, ℱ252/261-2294, ⓦwww.hiayh.org; ❶–❸), with dorm beds for $15–18 a night, camping and some private rooms available. The standard of **food** varies considerably, but the *Flying Fish Café*, on Hwy-158 in Kill Devil Hills (☎252/441-6894) prides itself on its Mediterranean/American cuisine, while the *Lone Cedar Café*, on the Manteo-Nags Causeway, Nag's Head, (☎252/441-5405) serves fresh seafood, pasta and steaks.

6

THE SOUTH | The North Carolina coast

Cape Hatteras National Seashore

CAPE HATTERAS NATIONAL SEASHORE stretches south onto **Hatteras** and **Ocracoke** islands, with wonderful unspoiled beaches on its seawardside. Most tourists just drive straight through on Hwy-12, and even in high season you can pull off the road and walk across the dunes to deserted beaches. The salt marshes on the western side are also beautiful, and at the northern end of Hatteras Island the **Pea Island National Wildlife Refuge** has trails and observation platforms from which you can see a wide variety of birdlife.

More than six hundred ships have been wrecked along this treacherous stretch of coast since the sixteenth century. At the south end of Hatteras Island, not far from the early nineteenth-century black-and-white-striped **Cape Hatteras Lighthouse**, a **visitor center** (summer daily 9am–6pm; rest of year daily 9am–5pm) has exhibits on the island's maritime history. The lighthouse itself was moved 2,900ft inland from its original location to protect it from encroaching Atlantic waters. At the village of **Frisco**, the **Native American Museum** is a loving collection of arts and crafts, including a drum from a Hopi *kiva* (Tues–Sun 11am–5pm, Mon by appointment; free; ☎252/995-4440).

Various **motels**, food shops and adequate **restaurants** are scattered through the fly-blown settlements along Hwy-12. The *Cape Hatteras Motel* in Buxton (mid-June to mid-Aug; ☎252/995-5611, ⓦwww.capehatterasmotel.com; ❽) is a big hit with windsurfers and has a relaxed, friendly atmosphere plus a fish-cleaning station. *Diamond Shoals* on Hwy-12 (☎252/995-5217) is a good central place for breakfast. **Camping** is best at one of the summer-only, first-come, first-served National Park Service campgrounds near Salvo, Buxton and Frisco. Ocracoke and Bodie Island ranger stations at the entrances to the seashore keep daily lists of what's available (call ☎252/473-2111).

Ocracoke Island

OCRACOKE ISLAND (pronounced *oke-ruhcoke*) is forty minutes by ferry from Hatteras – and is even more beautiful. This 14-mile ribbon of land is bisected by Hwy-12, and it's perfectly possible to drive along and pull over to find yourself a deserted patch of beach. Despite the crowds of tourists in the village of **OCRACOKE** itself, at its southern tip, the island somehow seems to have hung on to its atmosphere. There's nothing in particular to see on the island, except perhaps the harbor and squat brown lighthouse (you can't go in), and a tiny British World War II naval cemetery. It's nicer instead just to catch some rays, take a stroll or enjoy a cycle ride; **bike rental** places include Island Rentals on Silver Lake Road ($12–20; ☎252/928-5480).

Ocracoke ferries

In summer, **ferries between Ocracoke and Hatteras** leave both islands on the hour and half-hour all day, except between 5 and 7am and between 6.30pm and midnight when they are hourly. Winter sailings from Ocracoke and Hatteras are hourly between 5am and midnight. The crossing takes forty minutes, although you may have to wait if you have a car as there's room for only 30 cars, and it's loaded on a first-come, first-served basis.

Ferries from Ocracoke also head south down the coast to **Cedar Island** (2hr 15min; 8 daily each way between 7am and 8.30pm in summer, 4–6 daily in winter; $1 foot passenger, $2 bike, $10 car) and to **Swan Quarter**, on the Albemarle (2hr 30min; 3 daily all year; same fares as above). Both require motorists to reserve in summer (☎1-800/293-3779); at short notice you should get the day you want, if not the time.

Hotels and **B&Bs** in Ocracoke village get full in summer, and are fairly expensive; as elsewhere on the Outer Banks, rates drop in September. There is also a small, scenic **hostel** at **The Ocracoke Island Wayfarer Hostel**, 125 Lighthouse Rd (℡252/928-3411, @www.wayfarerhostel.com). Dorms are $19 and two private rooms are available for $39 each. The *Anchorage Inn*, on Route 12 (℡252/928-1101, @www.theanchorageinn.com; ❺), is comfortable, with a pool and complimentary continental breakfast and also offers apartments with kitchenettes; or you could sleep in one of the unusual "crow's-nest" rooms in the 1901 *Island Inn and Dining Room*, on Hwy-12 (℡1-877/456-3466, ℗252/928-4352; ❺), whose **restaurant** is renowned for its crabcakes (℡252/928-7821). Other, less expensive restaurants include the *Back Porch*, on Back Road (℡252/928-6401), which serves great fish, and the lively *Howard's Pub & Raw Bar*, a mile north of the village on Hwy-12 (℡252/928-4441), which has over two hundred beers and serves a full menu until 2am. The fairly isolated Park Service **campground**, a few miles north, tends to be the first of the Outer Banks sites to fill up. Tentsites start from $12.

Cape Lookout National Seashore

The mainland between Cedar Island and Beaufort is a rural backwater, sparsely settled and hardly touched by tourists. It's reasonably attractive to wander around, but towns such as **Davis** and **Smyrna** don't have any accommodation, and the most likely reason to pass through is to get to the all-but-deserted **CAPE LOOKOUT NATIONAL SEASHORE**, a narrow ribbon of sand stretching south of Ocracoke Island along three undeveloped Outer Banks, with no roads or habitation (the visitors center is at the eastern end of Harker's Island ℡252/728-2250). Its few visitors share a total of around 56 miles of beach along all three islands, with the marshes on the landward side supporting rich and unusual plant and birdlife adapted to the harsh, salty conditions.

At the northern tip of the **North Core Banks**, across from Ocracoke, stand the pretty, but eerie, ruins of the abandoned village of **Portsmouth Village**, whose last two residents left in 1971. The main ferry for the island, from **Atlantic** (Morris Marina, call for times and fares ℡252/225-4261), lands seventeen miles south of Portsmouth Village, which you can only reach on foot. Groups of travelers are taken by ferries to or from Ocracoke (around $15 per person; call Rudy Austin on ℡252/928-4361). **Cabins** on the island, operated by the marina, cost around $10 per person; otherwise there's only primitive **camping**, with neither drinking water nor food available.

The **South Core Banks** is served in summer by one private ferry each way per day from Davis ($13 round-trip; call Alger Willis on ℡252/729-2791). Here, too, the ferry company manages some wood **cabins** (the smallest sleeps four people; all work out at $12 per head if full). Camping is as primitive as on the north island, but the ferry can buy food for you on the mainland and bring it across. At the cabin area, showers and water are available. Three passenger ferries run to the southern tip of the south island from low-key **Harker's Island**, to within two or three miles of **Cape Lookout** itself and its lighthouse. Ferries also go to the peaceful **Shackleford Banks**, inhabited by feral horses since the early 1500s. Check with park headquarters for schedule (℡252/728-2250).

Beaufort

BEAUFORT, about 150 miles southeast of Raleigh, is probably the nicest of North Carolina's coastal towns: a relaxing place to hang out and drink cold beer, or just sit around on the waterfront, which heats up at night. The

Maritime Museum has good displays on local ecology and shipping history (Mon–Fri 9am–5pm, Sat 10am–5pm, Sun 2–5pm; free; ☎252/728-7317). In the restored area on Turner Street, off the waterfront, you'll find handsome **old houses**, an apothecary and the city jail. Across from the museum, you can take a more active excursion with The Watercraft Center (☎252/728-6330), who have guided kayak eco-tours of the surrounding waterways including the **Shackleford Banks** (tours start at $40, kayak rentals $10 per hour, $30 per half-day, $55 per day). The main house serves as the town **welcome center** (Mon–Sat 9am–5pm; ☎252/728-5225 or 1-800/575-SITE, ⓦ www.historicbeaufort.com).

Among the many historic **B&Bs** in the shady residential streets off Turner Street, *Langdon House*, 135 Craven St (☎252/728-5499, ℱ252/728-1717, ⓦ www.langdonhouse.com; ⑥), is friendly and relaxed, as is the *Cedars Inn*, 305 Front St (☎252/728-7036, ⓦ www.cedarsinn.com; ⑤ summer). The *Inlet Inn*, on the waterfront at 601 Front St (☎252/728-3600, ℱ252/728-5833, ⓦ www.inletinn.com; ⑤ summer), has huge hotel rooms, and also offers a continental breakfast served in your room. **Rates** everywhere increase considerably in summer. **Morehead City**, a couple of miles down the coast, and the Bogue Bank resorts boast plenty of **motels**.

As for **eating and nightlife**, Beaufort's waterfront is vibrant at night, milling with yachties and vacationers drinking, listening to live music and simply strolling. There are a number of decent bar-restaurants on the wooden **boardwalk** right on the water, but for exquisite – if pricey – New American cuisine, head for the stylish *Front Street Grill*, set back from the waterfront at 300 Front St (☎252/728-3118). The notable *Beaufort Grocery Co*, 117 Queen St (☎252/728-3899), prides itself on inventive dishes made from superbly fresh ingredients.

The beaches

South of Beaufort, the **beaches** along the twenty-mile offshore **Bogue Bank** are always pretty crowded, especially **Atlantic Beach** at the east end, with **Emerald Isle**, to the west, marginally less so. On **Bear Island** to the south, though – reached by ferry (April–Oct, hours vary; $2; ☎910/326-4881) with a strict limit on the number of daily passengers – the stunning **Hammocks Beach State Park** has high sand dunes, a wooded shore and perfect beaches. The entrance is four miles west of **Swansboro**; register at the small park center if you want to **camp** (☎910/326-4881; $8). No camping is permitted in turtle season (March and April), however, when **loggerhead sea turtles** come ashore to lay their eggs.

On the far side of the Camp Lejeune US Marine base, **Topsail Island**, yet another sand bar of resorts, is considerably less built up than Bogue Bank, presumably because its beaches aren't quite as good. **Surf City** and **Topsail** were once both slightly run-down family resorts, but seem to have improved nicely, possibly due in part to a beating from a couple of hurricanes. Public beach access points are signposted from the main road, but you can get down from lots of other places.

Wilmington

Though it's the largest town on North Carolina's coast, **WILMINGTON**, set back along the **Cape Fear River** fifty miles short of the southern border, has a welcoming down-home feel. During the Civil War, it was briefly the Confederacy's most important harbor, exporting cotton all over the world.

"**Blockade-runners**" would attempt to outrun the Union navy, racing into the safety of Fort Fisher's guns some twenty miles to the south of town; "Rebel Rose" Greenhow, glamorous Confederate spy, drowned here during a run in 1864. Dozens of blacks were murdered in Wilmington by white mobs in the **Race Riot** of 1898 – a backlash to the election of a "Fusionist" (Republican-Populist-black) governor two years earlier.

Wilmington today is attractive and friendly, with a historic district, starting on the south side of Market Street and stretching east along Third Street, that feels genuinely lived in. At 814 Market St, the **Cape Fear Museum** (summer Mon–Sat 9am–5pm, Sun 2–5pm; rest of year closed Mon; call for admission fee; ☎910/341-4350) gives a lively account of local history, while **Louise Wells Cameron Art Museum** (formerly St John's Museum of Art), 114 Orange St (Tues–Sat 10am–5pm, Sun noon–4pm; $3; ☎910/763-0281), features works by the nineteenth-century Impressionist Mary Cassatt. Architecture fans should head for the **Bellamy Mansion Museum of History and Design Arts**, an ornate antebellum mansion at Fifth and Market (Tues–Sat 9am–5pm, Sun 1–5pm; $6; ☎910/251-3700) which concentrates on restoration, preservation and local design. The extravagant houses, ornate **City Hall** and lovely old **Thalian Hall** demonstrate Wilmington's former wealth, but it's the cobbled streets of the weathered, boardwalked **waterfront**, dotted with laid-back cafés and restaurants, that really appeal. **Chandler's Wharf**, an upmarket shopping mall in a restored warehouse, is typical of the area's revitalization, while the **Cotton Exchange**, 321 N Front St, sells crafts and food in a group of buildings that housed a grain mill, warehouse and cotton business. The blocks back from the waterfront are lined with quirky thrift shops and memorabilia troves. Wilmington's notoriety as a popular film location has earned it the nickname "Hollywood East." *Blue Velvet* and *Teenage Mutant Ninja Turtles* were shot in the area, and EUE/Screen Gems Studios, at North 23rd Street, boasts the set of the hit teen-drama *Dawson's Creek* (tours Wed–Sun; $10; call Silver Screen Tours for reservations ☎910/675-8479).

Twenty miles south on Hwy-421, near Kure Beach, **Fort Fisher State Historic Site** commands a spectacular rocky position overlooking both the sea and the mouth of the Cape Fear River. A small **museum** focuses on the fort's days as a Confederate stronghold, with relics from sunken blockade runners and various weaponry (call for hours; free; ☎910/458-5798).

Practicalities

The **bus** station is at 201 Harnett St, a mile north of downtown off Third Street. Wilmington's **visitor center**, 24 N Third St (Mon–Fri 8.30am–5pm, Sat 9am–4pm, Sun 1–4pm; ☎910/341-4030 or 1-800/222-4757, ⓦwww.cape -fear.nc.us), has maps and walking tours; the funniest, most informative overviews of the city are given by Adventure Walking Tours, which leave from the flagpole at Market and Water streets (April–Oct 10am & 2pm; $10; ☎910/763-1785). There's also an **information** kiosk (April–Oct daily 9.30am–4.30pm) at the foot of Market Street, from where riverboat tours ($8) and a river taxi ($13) to and from the *USS North Carolina* depart. For local events, pick up a copy of the free listings magazine *Encore*.

Much of the accommodation is **B&Bs**: when the movie stars come to town, they stay at the *Graystone Inn* on Third and Dock, renowned for its elegance and romantic grandeur. (☎910/763-2000, ⓕ910/763-5555, ⓦwww.graystoneinn .com; ❼); another nice alternative is the *Inn on Orange*, 410 Orange St (☎910/815-0035 ⓕ910/762-2279, ⓦwww.innontheorange.com; ❺), which has spacious rooms, a pool and garden. Right on the riverfront, there's the excellent *Best Western Coastline Inn*, 503 Nutt St (☎910/763-2800, ⓕ910/763-2785, ⓦwww.coastlineinn.com; ➍), which delivers a free continental breakfast and newspaper to your room. You could also head a dozen miles east to **Wrightsville Beach**, where among the string of weatherworn condos and pricey resort hotels, the *Silver Gull*, 20 E Salisbury St, offers comfortable motel rooms next to the fishing pier (☎910/256-3728, ⓕ910/256-2909, ⓦwww.beachonline.com; ➎), though nowhere is particularly cheap, apart from the usual budget **motels** on Hwy-17.

For a quick **meal** try the *Underground Sandwich Shoppe*, 103 Market St (☎910/763-9686). For dinner *Paleo Sun Café*, 35 N Front St (☎910/762-7700), has something for almost everyone as well as live jazz, etc. The same can be said for the *Café Phoenix*, 9 S Front St (☎910/343-1395), with pasta, seafood, steaks and vegetarian selections and, possibly, the occasional film star. *Elijah's*, 2 Ann St at Chandler's Wharf (☎910/343-1448), is a popular seafood grill with riverfront dining. Wilmington has a fairly thriving **nightlife** – as well as a small gay scene. A fun-loving crowd heads to the *Reel Café*, 100 S Front St (☎910/251-1832), to hear live music or a DJ and eat on the patio, while the nearby *Barbary Coast*, 116 Front St (☎910/762-8996), is a rough hole-in-the-wall that has gained some cachet from being Mickey Rourke's favorite spot in town. *Thalian Hall*, 310 Chestnut St (☎1-800/523-2820, ⓦwww.thalianhall.com), built in 1858, is a vibrant performing arts center hosting dance, music, theatre and film.

The North Carolina Piedmont

North Carolina's **PIEDMONT** is a fairly industrialized area of textile and tobacco towns, mostly in decline. However, even close to the towns it can still be very rural, little changed since the 1950s. The main area of interest is the **Research Triangle** trio of neighboring college towns: **Raleigh**, the state capital; relaxed **Durham**, with its strong black community; and countercultural **Chapel Hill**. **Winston-Salem**, famous for its tobacco industry, boasts the excellent Old Salem village, while **Charlotte**'s international airport is the point of arrival for many European visitors.

Raleigh

RALEIGH, North Carolina's capital, stands on I-40 at the very heart of the state, focusing around the central, pedestrianized **Capitol Square**. The **Capitol** itself is worth a look if only to see the copy of Canova's bizarre statue of George Washington in Roman garb (Mon–Fri 8am–5pm, Sat 9am–5pm, Sun 1–5pm; free). Just steps away the **North Carolina Museum of History**, 5 E Edenton St (Tues–Sat 9am–5pm, Sun noon–5pm; free; ☎919/715-0200), is impressively far-reaching, a chronological trot through the state's history from the viewpoint of its people, with particularly strong sections on women. Opposite is the **North Carolina Museum of Natural Sciences**, 11 W Jones St (Mon–Sat 9am–5pm, Sun 1–5pm; free; ☎919/733-7450), which looks at local geology, as well as animal and plant life, going all the way back to the dinosaur age.

The four-block **City Market**, south of the capitol, arranged around Martin Street and Moore Square, holds a number of good shops and restaurants; check out the local artists and sculptors at work in **Artspace**, 201 E Davie St (Mon–Sat 9am–5pm). US President **Andrew Johnson** was born in a tiny hut just north of where the capitol now stands; his birthplace has since been moved to **Mordecai Historic Park**, north of town at 1 Mimosa St (Mon & Wed–Sat 10am–4pm, Sun 1–4pm; $3–6). Here you can also see the **Mordecai House**, built by a wealthy plantation–owner and continuously inhabited by the same family for two centuries. A little way out to the northwest via I-40, the impressive **North Carolina Museum of Art**, 2110 Blue Ridge Blvd (Tues–Thurs & Sat 9am–5pm, Fri 9am–9pm, Sun 11am–6pm; tours daily 1.30pm; free; ☎919/839-6262), has an eclectic display of works from Africa, Europe and the US. It also boasts the particularly good *Blue Ridge Restaurant* which is open for lunch Tuesday to Friday, for brunch at the weekend and dinner on Friday (☎919/833-3548).

Practicalities

Raleigh-Durham **airport** (☎919/840-2123) is off I-40, fifteen minutes northwest of town. The **taxi** ride into town costs around $30, while a circuitous shuttle service will charge a whole lot less ($18). Amtrak drops you off at 320 W Cabarrus St. The Greyhound station is in a seedy part of downtown at 321 W Jones St. A patchy local **bus** service (CAT or Capital Area Transit ☎919/828-7228) operates out of the transit mall at Blount and Martin streets. The **visitor center** at 301 N Blount St (Mon–Fri 8am–5pm, Sat 10am–5pm, Sun 1–5pm; ☎919/733-3456, ⊛www.raleighcvb.org) coordinates local walking and driving tours.

If you want to **stay**, avoid the more anonymous downtown hotels and try instead the *William Thomas House B&B*, at 530 N Blount St, just a few blocks from Capitol Square (☎919/755-9400, ⊛www.williamthomashouse.com; ❻), or head out to Hillsborough Street near North Carolina State University, where the *Velvet Cloak Inn* at no. 1505 offers comfortable rooms, free coffee, tea and cookies, and an indoor pool, at good weekend rates (☎919/828-0333, ⊛www.velvetcloakinn.com; ❸–❺).

Big Ed's, in the City Market at 220 Wolfe St (☎919/836-9909), serves Southern **home-style** breakfasts and is closed on Sundays. Across the street, *Greenshields Brewery*, 214 E Martin St (☎919/829-0214), offers very good English-style beer and pub food. More upmarket, but just as popular, the huge *42nd St Oyster Bar*, downtown at West and Jones streets (☎919/831-2811), is always buzzing with journalists, politicians and students enjoying fresh fish and seafood. **Hillsborough Street**, lined with bars, clubs and cafés, has some great places to eat and is the epicenter of Raleigh's excellent **nightlife**. *Rathskeller* at no. 2412 (☎919/821-5342) serves healthy, creative food in intimate wooden booths, and there's also a lively bar. Or try *Cup a Joe* at no. 3100 (☎919/828-9665), a bohemian coffee bar with live folk music on Friday and Saturday. For techno and house, make for the *Five O Café*, above the Studio arts cinema at no. 2526 (☎919/821-4419), while *The Brewery* at no. 3009 (☎919/834-7018) is a good venue in which to see the best regional rock and alternative bands. Away from Hillsborough Street, the *Berkeley Café*, at 217 W Martin (☎919/821-0777), specializes in roots and alternative country as well as rock. The *Tir Na Nog Irish Pub* on 218 S Blount (☎919/833-7795), is a lively bar with live music Tuesday to Saturday that also serves Irish food and a Sunday brunch. Pick up the free *Spectator* for nightlife listings.

Durham

Twenty miles northwest of Raleigh, **DURHAM** found itself at the center of the nation's tobacco industry after farmer Washington Duke came home from the Civil War with the idea of producing cigarettes – by 1890 he and his three sons had formed the **America Tobacco Company**, one of the nation's most powerful businesses. The **Duke Homestead Historical Site**, 2828 Duke Homestead Rd, about a half-mile north of I-85 (April–Oct Mon–Sat 9am–5pm, Sun 1–5pm; Nov–March Tues–Sat 10am–4pm, Sun 1–4pm; free), incorporates an even-handed and lively museum covering the social history of tobacco farming.

In 1924 the Duke family's $40 million endowment to the previously small-scale Trinity College enabled it to expand into a world-respected medical research facility, swiftly changing its name to **Duke University**. It's well worth visiting the campus: the **Museum of Art** on Campus Drive (Tues, Thurs & Fri 10am–5pm, Wed 10am–9pm, Sat 11am–2pm, Sun 2–5pm; free; ☎919/684-5135) has good African, pre-Columbian, medieval and Asian collections. The Gothic west campus centers on the soaring cathedral-style **chapel** (☎919/681-1704 for hours and services), which boasts one of the most powerful Flentrop organs in the world. Also on campus, the terraces and bowers of the beautifully landscaped **Sarah P. Duke Gardens** are a blaze of fragrance and color surrounded by pine forest, especially in May.

Elsewhere, the city has more of a blue-collar feel and takes pride in its vibrant **black heritage**. Based in a number of surprisingly small old plantation homes, set in 71 acres seven miles north of town in rural Treyburn Park, the **Stagville Preservation Center** (Mon–Fri 9am–4pm; free; ☎919/620-0120) is not a museum as such, but hosts various workshops and living history demonstrations, illustrating plantation life from the early 1800s to Reconstruction through the works of local black craftspeople.

At 5109 Farrington Rd, between Hwy-54 and Old Chapel Hill Road, and worth a detour, **Patterson's Mill Country Store** (closed Monday), at the end of a rutted country lane, looks like something straight out of *The Waltons*, selling everything from old signs and used books to crafts, candy, soap and spices. A back room is stuffed with vials and potions, and upstairs there's a bewildering panoply of tobacco memorabilia.

Practicalities

Greyhound **buses** stop in Durham at 820 W Morgan St. Pick up maps and local information from the Durham **visitor center**, at 101 E Morgan St (Mon–Fri 8.30am–5pm, Sat 10am–2pm; ☎919/687-0288, ⊛www.durham-nc.com).

Durham's **Brightleaf Square**, an upbeat, upmarket shopping area of restored tobacco warehouses off Main Street downtown, is a good bet for **restaurants**: try *Anotherthyme*, 109 N Gregson St (☎919/682-5225), which specializes in creative pasta and seafood dishes with a Southwestern flavor. Durham has historically been at the center of the North Carolina Piedmont **blues** scene, with musicians such as Reverend Gary Davis playing for tips in the 1920s at Raleigh's tobacco markets. The town hosts the **Bull Durham Blues Festival** for a weekend in September (☎919/983-1709).

Chapel Hill

The hip, villagey atmosphere of **CHAPEL HILL**, on the southwest outskirts of Durham, has benefited from the rise to national prominence of such local bands as Superchunk, Archers of Loaf and Ben Folds Five. It's also the hometown of James "Carolina on My Mind" Taylor. About fifty percent of the 45,000 population are students, and its position as a bastion of white liberalism in a poor rural state brings the town its detractors; that said, it's a pleasant enough place to hang out for a while, joining the hordes of students in the laid-back bars and coffeehouses along **Franklin Street**, which fringes the north side of campus. Franklin continues west into the adjacent city of **Carrboro**, though there's very little to distinguish the transition.

The **University of North Carolina**, dating from 1789, was the nation's first state university and holds some fine eighteenth-century buildings. The earliest is **Old East**, its original brick painted a fashionable tan in the 1840s. Evidence of the university's wealth can be seen at the splendid **Morehead Planetarium**, East Franklin Street (star shows $4.50, surrounding exhibits free; ☎919/549-1236), which serves as a NASA training center, and at the **Ackland Art Museum**, South Columbia and Franklin streets (Wed–Sat 10am–5pm, Sun 1–5pm; free; ☎919/966-5736), which is strong on Greek and Roman antiquities. The UNC **visitor center** (☎919/962-1630) is in the west lobby of the Planetarium, and they lend out Walkmans that allow you to do a self-guided tour of the campus.

Practicalities

Greyhound **buses** stop downtown at 138 E Franklin St in front of the Carolina Coffee Shop. There's a downtown **welcome center** at 179 E Franklin St (Tues–Sat 10am–4pm, ☎919/929-9700, ⓦwww.downtownchapelhill.com) or, if that's closed, you can try the Chapel Hill/Orange County **visitors bureau** at 501 W Franklin, (Mon–Fri 8.30am–5pm; ☎1-888/968-2060, ⓦwww .chocvb.org). Chapel Hill has few places to **stay**, and is often booked up; one of the most popular spots is the 1920s *The Carolina Inn* at 211 Pittsboro St, on campus (☎919/933-2001, ⓕ919/962-3400, ⓦwww.carolinainn.com; ❼). The *Hampton Inn*, 1740 Hwy-15/501 (☎919/968-3000, ⓕ919/929-0322; ❹), is a comfortable motel just out of town.

For **food**, *Crooks Corner*, 610 W Franklin St (☎919/929-7643), serves cordon bleu Southern cooking such as shrimp and grits or fried chicken and greens in smart surroundings. *Four Eleven West*, 411 W Franklin St (☎919/967-2782), is an excellent modern Italian restaurant. One of the best breakfast spots is *Elmo's Diner*, in the Carr Mill Mall in Carrboro at 200 N Greensboro St (☎919/929-2909). Adjacent to the mall is the community-owned *Weaver Street Market*, 101 E Weaver St (☎919/929-0010), featuring an inexpensive, tasty vegetarian buffet where you pay by the weight. For Chapel Hill **nightlife**, stay on Franklin Street: *The Cave*, 452 W Franklin St (☎919/968-9308), has live music from bluegrass to indie, with *Local 506*, 506 W Franklin St (☎919/942-5506), the next step up. Over in Carrboro, the *Cat's Cradle*, 300 E Main St (☎919/967-9053), has a reputation for booking the best bands on the national touring circuit, while the cozy 300-seater ArtsCenter, 300-G E Main St (☎919/929-2787), stages plays, dance shows and concerts.

Winston-Salem

Though synonymous with the brand names of its cigarettes, **WINSTON-SALEM**, 105 miles west of Raleigh, instead owes its spot on the tourist itinerary to the delightful **Old Salem**, a well-preserved twenty-block area that honors the heritage of the city's first Moravian settlers. Escaping religious persecution in what are now the Czech and Slovak republics, the first Moravians settled in this rolling area of the Piedmont in the mid-seventeenth century. They soon established trading links with the frontier settlers and founded the town of Salem on a communal basis – they permitted only those of the same religious faith to live here. The demand for their crafts helped establish the adjacent community of Winston, which, accruing tremendous wealth from tobacco, soon outgrew the older community. The two merged in 1913 to form Winston-Salem.

Today visitors can tour ten of Old Salem's buildings and, with the help of costumed guides, learn about the skills, trades and customs of the Moravians. Start at the **visitor center** at Academy and Old Salem Rd (Mon–Sat 9am–5pm, Sun 12.30–5pm; ☎336/721-7300), and if time is tight, prioritize the **Single Brothers House**, built in 1771, where unmarried men would sleep, worship and make items such as silverware, hats and paper. There's also a **tavern** at 736 S Main (☎336/748-8585) where beers and large lunches and dinners are served, and a **bakery** at 525 S Main that produces great cookies.

There isn't too much to see in Winston-Salem's downtown, although the city is trying to liven things up by introducing live music outdoors from April to October, Thursday through Sunday nights. On Thursdays, Live after Five is at Corpenington Plaza; Fridays, 4th Street is blocked off for jazz and blues performances; on Saturdays, Trade Street hosts a variety of music programs; and on Sundays there's VIP In The Park. Three miles northwest of downtown, the **Reynolda House Museum of American Art**, 2250 Reynolda Rd (Tues–Sat 9.30am–4.30pm, Sun 1.30–4.30pm; $6, free to college students; ☎336/725-5325), uniquely throws together pieces by all the top American artists from the eighteenth century to the present day in what was the home of tobacco baron Richard Joshua Reynolds. The mansion, designed by Charles Barton Keen, is set in lush, landscaped gardens, with a number of its surrounding buildings converted into fancy stores collectively known as **Historic Reynolda Village**. Close by, and integrating the former home of underwear manufacturer Charles Hanes, is the occasionally controversial **Southeastern Center for Contemporary Art (SECCA)**, 750 Marguerite Drive (Tues–Sat 10am–5pm, Sun 2pm–5pm; ☎336/725-1904), which gets all the area's major shows. About a mile east, **Whitaker Park**, off Reynolds Boulevard (☎336/741-2458; free), is the impressive, fully automated factory that churns out up to 275 million Winston, Salem and Camel cigarettes per day; unfortunately a video has replaced the previous tours and there's not much of a reason to stop by anymore. At Winston-Salem State University the renowned **Diggs Gallery**, 601 Martin Luther King Blvd (Tues–Sat 11am–5pm; ☎336/750-2458; free), has ten to fifteen different exhibits yearly, primarily on African-American art and various educational programs. Be sure to check out the colorful and somewhat perplexing murals *Origins* and *Ascension*, by John Biggers, in the nearby O'Kelly library.

Practicalities

Greyhound **buses** stop at 250 Greyhound Court on the east side of town by Hwy-52. Amtrak lays on buses to the *Salem Inn* for the short ride from the nearest station in Greensboro. Winston-Salem's resourceful **visitor center** is on the north edge of downtown at 601 N Cherry St (☎910/777-3796 or 1-800/331-7018, ⓦwww.visitwinstonsalem.com).

Brookstown Inn, 200 Brookstown Ave (☎336/725-1120 or 1-800/845-4262, ⓕ336/773-0147, ⓦwww.brookstoneinn.com; ⓞ), is a highly recommended small **hotel** in a former cotton warehouse, dishing up complimentary cheese and wine, cookies and milk, and continental breakfast. A less expensive option across the street, the *Salem Inn*, 127 S Cherry St (☎336/725-8561 or 1-800/533-8760, ⓕ336/725-2318, ⓦwww.saleminn.com; ⓞ), offers clean and central motel rooms.

Eating options aren't that exciting, though the *Twin City Diner*, 1425 W First

St (☎336/724-4462), is a popular place for sandwiches and grill food. The more upmarket *Bistro 420*, 420 W 4th St (☎336/721-1336), serves good Southern cuisine. The *Village Tavern*, in Reynolda Village (☎336/748-0221), is a great spot for a beer and some pub food. Touring roots, rock and reggae bands play the atmospheric *Ziggy's*, 433 Baity St (☎336/748-0810), out by Wake Forest University campus.

Charlotte

More than anywhere else in the region, **CHARLOTTE**, at the junction of I–77 and I-85 near the South Carolina border, can genuinely claim to have made it: a banking and transportation center that has become the largest city in the state, "boosted," in much the same way as Atlanta, by ambitious business and city leaders. They like to project the image of a sophisticated, fast-lane cultural metropolis – in fact its center is somewhat soulless, though many nearby neighborhoods are delightful and stuffed with good places to eat. Served by direct British Airways flights from London, however, it does make one of the best and most manageable arrival points in the region.

The chief attraction in **downtown** Charlotte, an unlovely mass of skyscrapers and concrete known as "uptown," is **Discovery Place**, 301 N Tryon St, a kids-oriented science museum with an indoor rainforest and an OMNIMAX theater hosting a planetarium (call ☎704/372-6261 for hours and prices). There's also the **Nature Museum** at 1658 Sterling Rd (Mon–Fri 9am–5pm, Sat 10am–5pm, Sun 1pm–5pm; ☎704/337-2671), geared toward children seven years and under, and replete with rabbits, hamsters and ponies, as well as puppet shows and a butterfly room. Another major landmark, on the east side of downtown, is the massive **Ericsson Stadium,** home of the NFL team, the Carolina Panthers.

Although most restaurants and stores are tucked away inside the city's skyscrapers, Tryon Street is downtown's busiest thoroughfare. At the intersection of Tryon and Trade streets is **Independence Square**, where at each corner giant modern statues stand – depicting transportation, commerce, industry and the future. Just a few blocks away, the newly renovated **Levine Museum of the New South**, 200 E 7th St (Tues–Sat 10am–5pm, Sun 1am–5pm; $6), looks at the growth of the region from Reconstruction onwards. Interesting vignettes examine musical history, with the spotlight falling on local names such as gospel legends the Golden Gate Quartet. The **Mint Museum of Art**, three miles further southeast at 2730 Randolph Rd on bus #15 (Tues 10am–10pm, Wed–Sat 10am–5pm, Sun noon–5pm; $6; ☎704/337-4820), has a good array of Indian, pre-Columbian and African art, plus a noted collection of pottery and porcelain. The **Mint Museum of Craft and Design** at 220 N Tryon St, is also worth a stop for its eclectic collection of metal, glass, wood, fiber and ceramic works (Tues–Thurs 10am–7pm, Fri 10am–9pm, Sat 10am–7pm, Sun noon–5pm; $6; ☎704/337-4920).

For those interested in **NASCAR** racing, fifteen minutes from downtown in the suburb of Concord is the **Lowe's Motor Speedway**, where guided tours are available, and in late May the Coca-Cola 600 comes to town.

Practicalities

Charlotte/Douglas International Airport (☎704/359-4000), seven miles west of town on Old Dowd Road or I-85, is served by the #5 **bus** ($1.45) running every 45min from downtown to the airport; **taxis** cost about $15 and **shuttle buses**, which leave from the lower level, $8. Greyhound stops centrally at 601

W Trade St, while Amtrak trains pull in at 1914 N Tryon St. The expansive **visitor center** is at 330 S Tryon St (Mon–Fri 8.30am–5pm, Sat 10am–4pm, Sun 1–4pm; ℡704/331-2753 or 1-800/231-4636, ⓦwww.cvb.org).

Most of Charlotte's **hotels** are aimed at the conference trade, though the *Dunhill Inn*, 237 N Tryon St (℡704/332-4141, ℻704/376-4117, ⓦwww.dun-hillhotel.com; ❺/❼), possesses old-world charm. The *Holiday Inn,* 230 N College St (℡704/335-5400, ℻704/376-4921, ⓦwww.holiday-inn.com; ❹/❻), has good facilities, and the *Days Inn*, 601 N Tryon St (℡704/333-4733, ℻704/372-9925; ❸), is a cheap central option. The *Morehead Inn B&B,* 1122 E Morehead St (℡704/376-3357, ℻704/335-1110, ⓦwww.morehead.com; ❺), offers a great location in the **Dilworth/South End** neighborhood, a pleasing mix of renovated commercial buildings and broad, tree-lined avenues. Just a mile southeast of uptown, is where you'll find the broadest range of **restaurants**, from the trendy *Providence Café*, 110 Perrin Place (℡704/376-2008), which offers vegetarian fare and New American cuisine, to the French bistro *Bijoux*, 201 N Tryon St (℡704/377-0900), and the *Southend Brewery & Smokehouse*, 2100 South Blvd (℡704/358-HOPS). *Lupie's Café*, 2718 Monroe Rd (℡704/374-1232), is an inexpensive option where you will find lip-smacking chili and other homestyle dishes. **Nightlife** is concentrated between the easily walked grid of Tryon, College, Seventh and Fifth streets, particularly around the Mint Museum of Art.

The North Carolina mountains

The best way to see the **mountains** of North Carolina is from the pristine **Blue Ridge Parkway**, which runs across the northwest from Virginia (see p.456) to the **Great Smoky Mountains National Park**. It's a delight to drive; the vast panoramic expanses of forested hillside, with barely a settlement in sight, may astonish travelers fresh from the crowded centers of the east coast. This predominantly poor region has been a breeding ground for **blue-grass** music, as played by Doc Watson and Earl Scruggs. The North Carolina High Country Host, 1700 Blowing Rock Rd, in Boone (℡1-800-438-7500) is a helpful **visitor center** that services most of the mountain area.

The Blue Ridge Parkway

The peak tourist season for the **BLUE RIDGE PARKWAY** is October, when the leaves of the deciduous trees which cover the landscape turn from bright yellow and gold through browns to vivid red. All year round, however, this magnificent, twisting mountain road – largely built in the 1930s by Roosevelt's Civilian Conservation Corps volunteers – is a worthwhile vacation destination in itself, peppered with state-run campgrounds, short hiking trails and dramatic overlooks. When planning your itinerary, take note that though the Parkway is closed to commercial vehicles, and only particularly crowded near one or two hyped beauty spots, the constant curves make it difficult to average anything approaching the 45mph speed limit.

Boone

BOONE is the most obvious northern base for exploring the mountains; the town itself holds little of interest, though as home to the Appalachian State University it does have a life of its own. On campus, just off Hwy-321, the small **Appalachian Cultural Museum** (Tues–Sat 10am–5pm, Sun 1–5pm;

Mountain activities

Organized **outdoor pursuits** available along the Blue Ridge Parkway include excellent **whitewater rafting** and **canoeing**, most of it on the Nolichucky River near the Tennessee border south of Johnson City, Tennessee, but also on the Watauga River and Wilson Creek. Companies running trips include Wahoo's Adventures (☎1-800/444-7238), based near Boone, and High Mountain Expeditions (☎1-800/262-9036), in Blowing Rock. Expect to pay $65 for a full day (safety equipment included).

Winter sees **skiing** at a number of slopes and resorts, particularly around **Banner Elk**, twelve miles southwest of Boone. Resort accommodation is expensive, ski passes less so ($20–30 for each weekday). Appalachian Ski Mountain (☎1-800/322-2373) is near Blowing Rock, and Ski Beech (☎1-800/222-2293) is at Beech Mountain; you can pick up full listings at visitor centers.

$2, free Tues) gives a good overview of the area, concentrating on such mountain pastimes as music, storytelling, stock-car racing and making moonshine whiskey. Corny family entertainments dot US-321 – the three-mile steam-driven Tweetsie Railroad, which also has other attractions, is all that remains of a line across the mountains to Johnson City, Tennessee (summer–fall daily 9am–6pm; $22) – while pretty back roads hold offbeat settlements such as **Valle Crucis** on US-194, where the 1883 Mast General Store (summer Mon–Sat 7am–6.30pm, Sun 1–6pm; winter hours vary) is well worth a look around.

Local public transportation is dire, so you'll need a **car** to get here and around. The **visitor center** is downtown at 208 Howard St (☎828/264-2225 or 1-800/852-9506, ⓦwww.visitboonenc.com). Bargain central **accommodation** can be had at the *Boone Trail Motel*, 275 E King St (☎828/264-8839; ❸). The *High Country Inn*, 1785 Hwy-105 (☎828/262-0073 or 1-800/334-5605, ⓦwww.highcountryinn.com; ❹), is a clean motel with a decent café and a sports bar, while the *Cat Pause Inn*, 2044 Broadstone Rd, Valle Crucis (☎828/963-7297, ⓦwww.catpauseinn.com; ❹), is great value. Back in Boone, the *Lovill House Inn* at 404 Old Bristol Rd (☎704/264-4204 or 1-800/849-9466, ⓦwww.lovillhouseinn.com; ❺) is a pleasant **B&B**. Most of the best places to **eat** or to have a beer are along King Street; the *Caribbean Café*, 489 W King St (☎828/265-2233), serves good, spicy food including vegetarian dishes; and the gourmet pizzas, pasta and Mexican food at the *Red Onion Café*, 227 Harden St (☎828/264-5470), are favorites among locals. For great vegetarian food and energizing smoothies try *Angelica's*, 506 W King St (☎828/265-0809).

South along the Parkway

Eight miles south of Boone, **BLOWING ROCK** is a pleasant if touristy resort just south of the Parkway, though the "Blowing Rock" itself (summer daily 8am–8pm; rest of year daily 10am–5pm; $4) is nothing as impressive as photos suggest. At the nearby **Parkway Craft Center** (☎828/295-7938), you can see traditional folk crafts being made. The **visitor center** (Mon–Sat 9am–5pm; ☎828/295-7851) is on Park Avenue. On Main Street you'll find **hotels** such as the *Boxwood Lodge* (☎828/295-9984, ⓦwww.boxwood.com; ❹). The least expensive local **campground** is at Julian Price Park, milepost 297 on the Parkway (no reservations, electricity or showers; $12; ☎828/963-5911). At *Woodland's* (☎828/295-3651), on Hwy-321 bypass, the pork barbecue is excellent; it's also a good spot to drink beer, as is the back porch of *The Canyons*, a comfy restaurant on Hwy-321 (☎828/295-7661).

The Canyons also has a fine view of the privately owned **Grandfather Mountain** (5964ft), fifteen miles further south with access near milepost 304 (summer daily 8am–7pm; rest of year daily 8am–5pm; $10). The price may be high, but the owners make a genuine attempt to protect this unique environment, and the prospect from the top – especially on the "mile-high swinging bridge" between the peaks – is superb, as are some of the trails. Bears, otters and other animals, including golden and bald eagles that were wounded by gunshot in their western homelands, are held in habitat-like settings. During the **Highland Games** and "Gathering of the Clans" in the second full week in July, distantly Scottish Americans (take a look at the local phone book and see just how many names begin with "Mc") dress up in kilts, toss cabers and tootle away on bagpipes.

Of various short and easy **trails** off the Parkway hereabouts, the one leading half a mile or so up to **Rough Ridge**, near milepost 301, is especially picturesque at dusk. Rough Ridge is one of several access points to the 13.5-mile **Tanawha Trail**, which runs along the ridge above the Parkway from Beacon Heights to Julian Price Park, looking out over the lush, dense forests to the east. If you plan a longer backpacking trip, equip yourself with a large-scale visitor center map; though the actual walking is not that difficult, it's easy to get lost in the woods.

Another good hike heads through the **Linville Gorge Wilderness**, near milepost 316 a couple of miles outside Linville Falls village. The high and spectacular **Linville Falls** themselves are at one end of the wilderness where the gorge begins. Breathtaking views from either side of the gorge look down 2000ft to the **Linville River** below, which has perfect, long, deep swimming pools. Be warned that ascents are steep, and some of the fainter paths are near-jungle. You can also climb **Hawksbill** or **Table Rock** mountains from the nearest unsurfaced forest road, which leaves Hwy-181 south of the village of Jonas Ridge (signposted "Gingercake Acres," with a small, low sign to Table Rock). The unremarkable but amiable villages of **Linville** and **Linville Falls** have the usual **motels** and restaurants; Linville Falls also has a **campground** (☏828/765-2681, ⒲www.linvillefalls.com), and *Spears Restaurant* (☏828/765-0026) is worth a detour for its hickory-smoked pork barbecue. Alternatively, travel south along the Parkway to milepost 328.3 and stock up on apple cider, homemade honey and fudge at the **Orchard at Altapass** (June–Oct; call ☏828/765-9531 for hayride details), where there's also live mountain music in the store at weekends.

The views from the Parkway in the **Mount Mitchell State Park** (☏828/675-4611) area, south toward Asheville, are tremendous. Sadly, however, this is largely because the trees around the summit of Mount Mitchell – the highest point in the eastern US, at 6684ft – have been ravaged by acid rain from coal-burning industries in the Chattanooga Basin to the west, and the large barren patches leave the horizon clear.

Asheville and Black Mountain

Encircled by a ring of interstates, and skirted to the east and south by the Parkway, modest **ASHEVILLE**, roughly 100 miles southwest of Boone, retains an appealing downtown core. It's also something of a New Age center, with ephemera stores, holistic healing sessions and a tradition among the region's farmers of growing medicinal herbs. Two miles south on Biltmore Avenue, the **Biltmore Estate** is the largest private mansion in the US (daily 8.30am–5pm; $33; ☏828/255-1776). Built in the late nineteenth century by George Vanderbilt and loosely modeled on a Loire chateau, it's a wild piece of nouveau riche folly, from the Victorian chic of the indoor palm court to the landscaped gardens.

Asheville's Greyhound/Trailways terminal is inconveniently located at 2 Tunnel Rd, two miles out of downtown on bus #13 or #4 stopping at the Innsbruck Mall. Central **motels** include the *American Court*, 85 Merrimon Ave (☎1-800/233-3582, ℱ828/253-2507, ⓦwww.americancourt.com; ❹); for a bit of pampering, head for the luxurious *Cedar Crest* **B&B**, 674 Biltmore Ave (☎828/252-1389, ℱ828/253-7667, ⓦwww.cedarcrestvictorianinn.com; ❻). The nearest **campground** is *Bear Creek RV Park*, 81 S Bear Creek Rd, off I-40 to the west (☎828/253-0798, ⓦwww.ashvillebearcreek.com; from $26 per night).

There are several upmarket **places to eat**, among them tiny *Salsas*, 6 Patton Ave (☎828/252-9805), serving up an aromatic blend of Mexican and Caribbean dishes, though tables can be hard to come by. The *Laughing Seed Café*, 40 Wall St (☎828/252-3445), has wonderful vegetarian food (check out the "meatloaf"), while *Beanstreets Coffee*, 3 Broadway (☎828/255-8180), is a fun place to hang out. Although Asheville is small, there are enough students to keep a reasonable **nightlife** scene going; *Barley's*, 42 Biltmore Ave (☎828/255-0504), is the best brewpub in town and offers good food and live music. *Ashville Music Zone*, 81 Broadway (☎828/255-8811), is a very popular venue which caters to all sorts of music tastes, and *Jack of the Wood*, 95 Patton Ave (☎828/252-5445), is an enjoyable pub.

Pick up information on the numerous local summer music and craft festivals from the downtown **visitor center**, 151 Haywood St (☎828/258-6101 or 1-800/257-1300, ⓦwww.ashvillechamber.org). August's **Mountain Dance and Folk Festival** features bluegrass and traditional dancing, while the hugely enjoyable **Leaf Festival**, a folk music and arts and crafts gathering held in mid-May and October in **BLACK MOUNTAIN**, fourteen miles east on I-40 (one bus a day), showcases Appalachian and world folk music, usually attracting major European and African musicians. There's little to do in Black Mountain otherwise, though the clear fresh air, pretty views and relaxed pace make a stroll worthwhile. The *Monte Vista* there, at 308 W State St (☎828/669-2119, ℱ828/669-0596, ⓦwww.montevistahotel.com; ❹), is a small, very comfortable **hotel** with regional decor, while the *Town Pump*, 143 Cherry St (☎828/669-4808), is a tavern/music venue.

Twenty miles southeast of the Parkway on US-64/74, the natural granite tower of **Chimney Rock** sticks out from the almost-sheer side of Hickory Nut Gorge (summer daily 8.30am–5.30pm; rest of year daily 8.30am–4.30pm; park stays open about an hour and a half past last ticket sale; $10; ☎828/625-9611 or 1-800/277-9611). After taking the elevator to the top, you can clamber up and down steps and walk along protected walkways atop the impressive cliffs. Many of the climactic moments of *The Last of the Mohicans* were filmed here; you may recognize the mighty waterfall that drops 400ft from the western end of the gorge. From the top you can see **Lake Lure**, where the movie *Dirty Dancing* was filmed.

Great Smoky Mountains National Park

West of Asheville, **GREAT SMOKY MOUNTAINS NATIONAL PARK** is the most visited national park in the US. It straddles the border with Tennessee, and is covered in more detail – with a map – in our Tennessee section on p.580. In summer and fall, the North Carolina approaches to the park are every bit as clogged with traffic as those in Tennessee, and all accommodation can be booked up weeks in advance.

The largest of the possible bases for touring the park is **CHEROKEE**, where a few Cherokee managed to hang on when the tribe was "removed" along the Trail of Tears to Oklahoma in 1838 (see p.583). Now known as the "Eastern Band of the Cherokee Nation," they have a small reservation on the edge of the park, which derives its main income from tourism. As a result, Cherokee itself is a mass of fast-food restaurants, cornily named motels, moccasin retailers and tacky giftshops – and the requisite casino. It's an odd place, where the presentation of Native Americans as noble savages all but equates them with the "cuddly" bears of the park as just another novelty for tourists.

Away from the kitsch and cliché, however, the **Museum of the Cherokee Indian** at the north end of town (mid-June to Aug Mon–Sat 9am–8pm, Sun 9am–5pm; Sept to mid-June daily 9am–5pm; $8; ☎828/497-3481) has good archeological displays and sections on Cherokee arts and history – including Sequoyah's invention of a syllabary in 1821, to preserve the oral Cherokee culture in writing. Qualla Arts and Crafts, across the street, is a Cherokee-run cooperative selling traditional crafts, principally basketwork. Nearby, the **Oconaluftee Indian Village** (mid-May to late Oct daily 9am–5.30pm; $12) is a reconstruction of a mid-eighteenth-century Cherokee village. Amid the log cabins, you can see demonstrations of weaving and basketmaking, as well as crafts and skills that have long since died out, such as dugout canoe construction and blowpipe hunting. During summer months an outdoor drama, *Unto these Hills*, re-enacts the Cherokee plight from Hernando De Soto's arrival to the Trail of Tears ($14; ☎336/725-5325). All three attractions can be seen by purchasing a value-ticket for $22 at any of the locations and can be spread over a series of days.

Cherokee is not much of a **place to stay**; though the motels are fine, there's not a single passable place to eat, and it's unbelievably dead between about October and March – and as a reservation town, it's also entirely dry. If you need to stay nearby, you're better driving on to Maggie Valley (see below), but if you're stuck, the **visitor center** (daily: June to Oct 8am–9pm; Aug–Oct 8am–6pm; Nov to mid-June 8am–5pm; ☎828/497-9195 or 1-800/438-1601), in the center of town, lists more than fifty motels; the central *Cherokee Plaza* (☎828/497-2301 or 1-800/535-4798, ℗828/497-7834; ❷/❹) overlooks the river. Incidentally, nearby, look out for the great sign at the *Pink Motel,* 34 Highway at 441 North Ave (☎828/497-3530; ❹), a 1950s Tinkerbell, swathed, of course, in fairytale pink.

The **Oconaluftee visitor center**, the headquarters of the North Carolina side of the park, is a short way out of Cherokee along US-441 (daily: summer 9am–7pm; fall & spring 9am–6pm; winter 9am–5pm; ☎828/926-1686, ⓦwww.maggievalley.com). It has good displays on Appalachian farming life, and a re-created pioneer village. Fifteen miles east, the small community of **MAGGIE VALLEY** boasts a string of motels with peaceful views over the valleys – one of the cheapest, the *Riverlet* (☎828/926-1900; ❸), on US-19, overlooks two streams and has a pool. It's all rather tranquil here, with trout farms, wooden shacks and clear, fresh air. Tourism focuses on hillbilly culture, with lots of hoedowns and the like, but if you're really desperate for kicks you could head for the nearby **Ghost Town in the Sky**, where a chairlift sweeps you up to a hokey Wild West re-creation complete with a saloon. During the last weekend in July, Maggie Valley hosts an **International Folk Festival**.

Southwestern North Carolina

The area west of Asheville, and south of the national park, holds a number of dramatic **waterfalls**. **Looking Glass Falls**, about twelve miles south of the

Parkway on US-276, is in a particularly beautiful section of the **Pisgah National Forest**. The falls drop 85 feet, with a great (albeit very cold) swimming hole at the bottom. **Connestee Falls**, a few miles south on US-276 toward Brevard, is a double waterfall and even higher. Unbridled optimists can pay to pan for **gemstones**, such as rubies, at outwashes of the numerous gem mines near the 250ft **Cullasaja Falls**, further west on US-64.

The far west corner of the state is famous for its superb **whitewater**, with plenty of companies offering canoeing and rafting on the **Nantahala River**. Guided raft expeditions cost around $33 for a three-hour trip; one company, Nantahala Outdoor Center (☎828/488-2175 or 1-800/232-7238), also runs a **hostel** (❶). Wildwater Ltd offers a five-hour train and rafting trip along the Nantahala with the Great Smoky Mountain Railway for around $60 (☎1-800/872-4681). Both companies offer excursions on neighboring rivers (Whitewater Ltd ☎1-800/451-9972).

West of the Nantahala, off US-129 almost in Tennessee, **Joyce Kilmer National Forest** is worth a detour, being one of the last remaining stands of unlogged virgin forest in the southeastern US, including some enormous hardwood trees.

South Carolina

The relatively small state of **SOUTH CAROLINA** remains, with Mississippi, one of the poorest and most rural pockets of the US, although the prime real estate along its coast has lately been developed into exclusive golf courses and tennis clubs. Politics in the first state to secede from the Union in 1860 have traditionally been conservative. Reconstruction was mired in terrible Klan violence, while demagogues openly espoused lynching and enforced "Jim Crow" laws with frightening zeal. The state contains two of the country's most right-wing minor universities – football-fixated Clemson, and Christian Bob Jones University in Greenville, a training ground for the fundamentalist right.

South Carolina's fascinating subtropical coastline of **sea islands**, great beaches, marshes and lush palmetto groves preserves traces of a virtually independent black culture (featuring the unique patois *gullah*), from the days when slaves escaped the mainland plantations. Beyond the grand old peninsular port of **Charleston**, arguably the most elegant city in the US with its rainbow-colored old buildings and magnificent, tree-lined avenues, restored plantations stretch as far north as **Georgetown**, en route toward the poseur's paradise of **Myrtle Beach**. Inland, the rolling Piedmont and flat coastal plain hold little to see.

Getting around South Carolina
Charleston has South Carolina's biggest **airport**, with flights to and from major towns on the east coast. Three Amtrak routes cut through the state, stopping at Greenville and Clemson in the west, Columbia and other towns in the center and Charleston on the coast. **Buses** run along I-85 between Charlotte, North Carolina, and Atlanta, and a less regular service operates along the coast, stopping at Myrtle Beach and Charleston.

Myrtle Beach and the north coast

Birthplace of *Wheel of Fortune* star Vanna White, **MYRTLE BEACH** is a brazen splurge of seaside fun, an unmitigated stretch of commercial development twenty miles down the coast from the North Carolina border at the center of the sixty-mile "Grand Strand." Predominantly a family resort, it's packed fit to burst during mid-term vacations with leering, jeering students in fluorescent beachwear – if you've seen the movie *Shag*, you'll know what to expect. Fans of crazy golf, water parks, factory outlet malls, funfairs and parasailing will be in heaven, and the **beach** itself isn't bad. The widest stretch is at North Myrtle Beach, a chain of small communities among which Ocean Drive is the center and Atlantic Beach is exclusively used by African Americans.

South of Myrtle Beach lie **Murells Inlet**, a fishing port with lots of good fish restaurants, and **Pawleys Island**, a secluded resort once favored by plantation-owners and today retaining a far slower pace than its neighbors. Between the two on Hwy-17 is the beautifully landscaped **Brookgreen Gardens** (summer daily 9.30am–9.30pm; rest of the year 9.30am–5pm; $8.50; ☎1-800/849-1931), a former rice and indigo plantation with an outdoor display of American figurative sculpture, and the setting for many of Julia Peterkin's novels of *gullah* life. There's also a wildlife sanctuary, where you're likely to spot alligator and deer, and an hour-and-a-half boat tour around the area.

Practicalities

US- or Hwy-17 (also called Kings Highway) is Myrtle Beach's main traffic thoroughfare, while the parallel Ocean Boulevard is lined with hotels and motels. Greyhound **buses** from Charleston and Wilmington come in at 511 7th Ave N (closed 1–3pm daily). Minimal transportation in the beach areas is provided by Coastal Rapid Public Transit buses (75¢–$2.10 one-way; ☎843/626-9138). Great American Trolley runs a route around the center beach area and out to the Myrtle Square Mall and Broadway at the Beach (July–Sept 8.30am–midnight; closes 10pm Oct 1–15; $2 each way; ☎1-800/395-6629).

The main **visitor center** at 1200 Oak St (☎1-800/356-3016) provides events listings and details of accommodation; there's also a branch at 2090 Hwy-501 E in Conway. Of the countless **motels**, the *Compass Cove*, 2311 S Ocean Blvd (☎1-800/228-9894, ⓕ843/448-5444, ⓦwww.compasscove.com; ❺), with turquoise pools and ocean views from the more expensive tower rooms, and the similar *Sands Beach Club* further north, at 9400 Shore Drive (☎843/449-1531 or 1-800/845-2202, ⓕ843/444-9344, ⓦwww.sandsresorts.com; ❼), are two solid choices. During the summer, rates increase dramatically; if traveling by yourself or with one other person it may be cheaper to stay in Conway about 11 miles to the west of US-501.

With ten campgrounds and two state parks, Myrtle Beach calls itself the "Seaside Camping Capital of the World"; this might be an apt description if you have a fairly broad definition of camping. You'll find most of the commercial **campgrounds** concentrated along Kings Highway – on this road in North Myrtle Beach you'll find the *Barefoot Camping Resort*, 4825 Hwy-17 (☎1-800/272-1790). Hours tend to fluctuate so call ahead.

If you want burgers, standard diner meals, "surf 'n' turf" in a themed bar or any one of a zillion varieties of ethnic fast food, you'll have no problem finding places to eat. Well-prepared **seafood** can be had at the classier *Sea Captain's House* at 3200 N Ocean Blvd (☎843/448-8082), or at a number of similar establishments in Murrells Inlet; for a Mediterranean meal and a view of art, stop by the *Collector's Café*, 7726 N Kings Hwy (℡843/449-9370).

As for **nightlife**, Celebrity Square at Broadway at the Beach, between 21st and 29th avenues off the Hwy-17 bypass (℡843/444-3200), is a compact area of bars and clubs, while the *House of Blues*, Barefoot Landing, 4640 Hwy-17 (℡843/272-3000), attracts top national rock, reggae and roots talent. More kitschy are the glut of **country music variety shows**; the longest-running is the *Carolina Opry*, Hwy-17 N (℡843/238-8888), where powerful singers belt out corny, family-oriented rock'n'roll, country and bluegrass with a couple of hymns thrown in for good measure. Next door at the Dolly Parton-owned *Dixie Stampede* (℡1-800/433-4401) you can see a lighthearted, surreal take on the Civil War with some impressive horsemanship, all while chowing down on a huge dinner without utensils.

South to Charleston: the plantations

The peaceful waterfront of **GEORGETOWN**, the first town beyond Myrtle Beach to be anything more than a beach town, makes a refreshing and quite extraordinary contrast, while the main street has a late-Fifties feel. Ask at the **visitor center**, 1001 Front St (℡1-800/777-7705), for a self-guided walking tour sheet to the fine antebellum and eighteenth-century houses in the 32-block historic district in the center. A quick stroll down the boardwalk, however, gives all-too-clear views of the monstrous steel works on the opposite bank. The **Rice Museum** (Mon–Sat 10am–4.30pm; $5), in the clock tower on Front Street, tells how the cultivation of rice flourished on the coast during the slavery period. On the north side of town, turning east after the bridge, is the **Belle W. Baruch Plantation** ($15; by appointment only; ℡843/546-4623). Though fairly overgrown, the plantation's original "**slave street**" is still standing, complete with wooden shacks and a church. It serves as a powerful reminder of the brutal basis of antebellum southern prosperity, and an interesting look at the home of Bernard M. Baruch, who gave economic advice to presidents Woodrow Wilson on up to JFK.

If you want to **stay** in Georgetown, the *Carolinian Clarion*, 706 Church St (℡843/546-5191; ❸), is a good bet, and has a pool. To **eat**, you needn't stray from the motel's restaurant, *Hook, Line and Sinker*, which serves superlative crabcakes, fish stews and Low Country Boils until 9pm daily except Sunday.

Hopsewee Plantation, the grand mansion home of Thomas Lynch, a signatory of the Declaration of Independence, is set in Spanish moss-draped grounds, twelve miles south of Georgetown on US-17 (March–Oct Mon–Fri;

Kudzu

The western Carolinas are badly afflicted by **kudzu**, a leafy climbing vine introduced from Japan in 1876 for decoration and shade. Its use was encouraged by the federal government from the 1930s to stop soil erosion. Unbelievably, it can grow as much as a foot a day in hot weather, and eventually kills trees by cutting off the sunlight. So far, it has covered about two million acres of forest. In places it's amazing, totally carpeting whole stands of trees and telegraph poles and wires. South Carolina folk poet James Dickey's poem *Kudzu* portrays it as a mysterious, evil invader from the east:

In Georgia, the legend says
that you must close your windows
at night to keep it out of the house
the glass is tinged with green, even so . . .

Nov–Feb by appointment only; $8; ☎843/546-7891). Clouds of large and ferocious mosquitoes drift up from the adjacent river, so think twice before visiting in summer. The less manicured, and slightly less mosquito-plagued **Hampton Plantation State Park**, further south, two miles off US-17 on Hwy-857, is probably closer to the look of a typical plantation. The grounds (9am–6pm; free) are pretty, but the house (summer Thurs–Mon 11am–4pm; rest of year 1pm–4pm; $2) is most impressive, a huge eighteenth-century Neoclassical monolith built by Huguenots, yet, while its exterior has been restored, the inside is pretty bare. The plantation itself is isolated in the heart of the dense **Francis Marion National Forest**. This heavily black area is particularly known for its sweetgrass basket-weaving, a craft that originated with the slaves in West Africa, using tight bundles of grasses to make intricate baskets and pots. Despite the enormously time-consuming work and the cost of materials, the baskets you see being made at roadside stalls here cost at most $20.

Further south, beyond the forest and a few miles north of Charleston, is the much-publicized **Boone Hall Plantation** (April–Aug Mon–Sat 8.30am–6.30pm, Sun 1–5pm; Sept–March Mon–Fri 9am–5pm, Sun 1–4pm; $12.50). A visit is a sanitized and annoying experience: the plantation may date from the late seventeenth century but the house is a twentieth-century reconstruction used for much television and movie filming. Tours are conducted by hapless young women in southern belle costumes, who rather overplay the connections with *Gone with the Wind*. The grounds are more interesting, with a long, tree-lined drive and another rare slave street, this time of small mid-eighteenth-century brick cabins that housed privileged slaves – domestic servants and skilled artisans.

Charleston

CHARLESTON, one of the finest-looking cities in the US, today spreads way beyond its original confines on the tip of a peninsula at the confluence of the Ashley and Cooper rivers, roughly one hundred miles south of Myrtle Beach and north of Savannah, Georgia. It's a compelling place to visit, its historic district lined with tall, narrow houses of peeling, multicolored stucco, adorned with wooden shutters and ironwork balconies wrought by slaves from Barbados. The Caribbean feel is augmented by palm trees, a tropical climate and easygoing atmosphere, while the town's pretty hidden gardens and leafy patios evoke New Orleans.

Founded in 1670 by a group of English aristocrats as a specifically money-making venture, Charles Towne swiftly boomed as a **port** serving the rice and cotton plantations. It became the region's dominant town, a commercial and cultural center which right from the start had a mixed population, with immigrants including French, Germans, Jews, Italians and Irish, as well as the English majority. One-third of all the nation's **slaves** came through Charleston, sold at the market on the riverfront and bringing with them their ironworking and building skills. The town had a sizeable **free black** community too, and its then unusually urban density allowed an anonymity and racial openness that, although still dominated by slavery, went a lot further than in the rest of the South. Nevertheless there was still slave unrest, culminating in the abortive Veysey slave revolt of 1823, after which the city built the Citadel armory and later the military university to control future uprisings.

The **Civil War** started on Charleston's very doorstep, at Fort Sumter in the harbor. Fire swept through the city, destroying large chunks, in 1861; more damage was inflicted when it was taken by Union troops in February 1865. The decline of the plantation economy and slump in cotton prices led to an economic crash after the war, made worse by a catastrophic earthquake in 1886. As the upcountry industrialized, capital steadily deserted the city, and it only really recovered when World War II restored its importance as a port and naval base. Since then, a steady program of preservation and restoration – not helped by the devastation of Hurricane Hugo in 1989 – has made **tourism** Charleston's main focus. Despite the crowds, however, it has kept its atmosphere, while maintaining all the energy and life of a real, working town. The *gullah* traditions of the sea islands are a tangible presence here, too: "basket ladies" weave their sweetgrass baskets all around the market and near the post office, and many people – black and white – speak the distinctive *gullah* dialect.

Arrival, information and getting around

Charleston International Airport is about twelve miles north of downtown, off I-526; the airport **shuttle** (☎843/767-7113) costs $10, while a **taxi** ride with Yellow Cabs (☎843/577-6565) costs around $21. Both Amtrak – 4565 Gaynor Ave, eight miles north of downtown – and Greyhound – at 3610 Dorchester Rd, out near I-26 – are in inconvenient and potentially dangerous locations. From downtown, a taxi ride to either location will cost $14. Local **public transportation** isn't bad, however: CARTA buses (75¢ in exact change; day pass $2, 3-day pass $5; ☎843/747-0922) cover most areas, including near Amtrak (due to an unavoidable walk down an embankment to the

Guided tours

Charleston is ideal for **walking tours**; the visitor center has details on scores of them. Charleston Strolls (Mon–Sat 9.30am; $16; ☎843/766-2080) leave from the *Palmetto Café* at the *Charleston Place Hotel*, 130 Market St, and from *Mills House Hotel*, 115 Meeting St, thirty minutes later; the Civil War Walking Tour sets out from *Mills House Hotel* (March–Dec daily 9am; $15; private tours also available throughout year; ☎843/722-7033), Architectural Walking Tours of Charleston run two two-hour tours – the morning tour covering the eighteenth century, the afternoon tour the nineteenth (Mon & Wed–Sat 10am & 2pm; $15; ☎1-800/931-7761); both leave from 173 Meeting St. In the fall, the Preservation Society, 147 King St (☎1-800/968-8175), organizes candlelit tours, visiting private old homes, with free tea and wafers (Sept & Oct Thurs–Sat 7pm; $35).

Much of Charleston's beauty is owed to the black slaves who built it, and there are two good **black history tours**: Al Miller's one- and two-hour van tours leave from the visitor center, and include material on slave uprisings, the Civil War and the lives of the freed slaves ($10/15; ☎843/762-0051), while Gullah Tours spice their tours with Charleston folktales told in *gullah* (by appointment only; call for times and prices ☎843/763-7551).

Horse and carriage tours, led by Carolina Polo and Carriage Company ($17, discount given on advance reservations; ☎843/577-6767), leave from the market, providing a lively but leisurely sixty-minute overview of the town. *Schooner Pride* (mid-March to Oct; $18; ☎843/559-9686) offers two-hour **cruises** around the harbor in the afternoon and at sunset. Among several **trolley** tours available, *Gray Line of Charleston* (☎843/722-4444 or 1-800/423-0444) offers entertaining and informative 75- and 90-minute Historic Charleston Tours ($15/$17) that depart daily from the visitor center.

train station, CARTA recommends a cab at night) and in front of Greyhound, for 75¢; Downtown Area Shuttles (DASH; ⓣ843/724-7420) runs a variety of routes through the historic district south of Calhoun Street, which all stop at the visitor center (Mon–Fri every 15min from 8am; last bus times vary; same prices). You can rent **bikes** from The Bicycle Shoppe, 280 Meeting St (ⓣ843/722-8168).

Charleston's huge and well-equipped **visitor center**, 375 Meeting St (summer daily 8.30am–5.30pm; rest of year daily 8.30am–5pm; ⓣ1-800/868-8118, ⓦwww.charlestoncvb.com), has discount coupons, leaflets and maps, and shows a film about the town ($2.50). The **post office** is at 557 E Bay St (Mon–Fri 8.30am–5.30pm, Sat 9.30am–2pm; zip code 29401).

Accommodation

Though Charleston is an expensive city, and **accommodation** options are limited if your budget's tight, it's really worth trying to stay within walking distance of downtown. As well as hotels, a lot of grand Historic-District houses serve as **B&Bs**, with prices starting at around $70. Agencies include Historic Charleston B&B, 57 Broad St (ⓣ843/722-6606). Further out, the usual **budget motels** cluster around US-17 in West Ashley and Mount Pleasant, and along I-26 in North Charleston.

Andrew Pinckney Inn 40 Pinckney St ⓣ843/937-8800 or 1-800/505-8983, ⓦwww.andrewpinckneyinn.com. Very comfortable inn located beside Charleston's historic markets. Continental breakfast served on the balcony overlooking the city. ④/⑤

Best Western King Charles Inn 237 Meeting St ⓣ843/723-7451, ⓦwww.charlestownmanagement.com. Clean, cozy premises in the Historic District with pool and complimentary afternoon tea. Ask for a room at the front – the rooms in the back are a bit scuzzy. ⑤–⑦

Cannonboro Inn B&B 184 Ashley Ave ⓣ843/723-8572, ⓕ843/723-8007, ⓦwww.charleston/sc/inns.com. Fine, columned house, all nonsmoking, with attractive patios and gardens. Very comfortable rooms, and with free use of bicycles. ⑤/⑥

Charleston Place Hotel 130 Market St ⓣ843/722-4900, ⓕ843/937-9024, ⓦwww.charlestonplacehotel.com. Charleston's premier hotel boasting unparalleled accommodations in the heart of the historic district. ⑦–⑨

Days Inn Historic District 155 Meeting St ⓣ843/722-8411 or 1-800/329-7466, ⓕ843/723-5361, ⓦwww.daysinn.com. Standard rooms with attractive wrought-iron balconies; one of the least expensive downtown options, near the market. ⑤–⑦

Eliot House Inn 78 Queen St ⓣ843/723-1855 or 1-800/729-1855, ⓕ8433/722-1567, ⓦwww.eliothouseinn.com. Luxurious B&B in an old Charleston building. Free wine and afternoon tea served in a pretty courtyard, which also has jacuzzi. Free bicycle use and a good continental breakfast. ⑤–⑦

Holiday Inn Historic District 125 Calhoun St ⓣ877/805-7900, ⓕ843/805-7700, ⓦwww.charlestonhotel.com. New downtown hotel with clean, comfortable rooms and friendly staff. ⑤–⑦

Maison Dupre 317 E Bay St ⓣ843/723-8691, ⓕ843/723-3722, ⓦwww.maisondupre.com. Beautiful inn in a crumbling 1804 European-style building. An idyllic garden holds fountains and a wishing well. Offers complimentary high teas and good continental breakfast. ⑦/⑧

Mills House Hotel 115 Meeting St ⓣ843-577-2400 or 1-800/874-9600. Actually a *Holiday Inn* and one of central Charleston's better large hotels. Elegantly furnished rooms with a nice bar featuring occasional live music. ⑤–⑦

The City

Charleston's **Historic District** is fairly self-contained, a predominantly residential area of leaning lines, weathered colors and exquisite hidden courtyards, bounded by Calhoun Street to the north and East Bay Street by the river. It's best taken in by strolling at your own pace – though that pace can get pretty slow at midday in high summer, when the heat is intense. Attractive spots to

Aiken-Rhett House

CHARLESTON

Charleston Museum

Joseph Manigault House

N

Ashley River

Avery Research Centre for African American History & Culture

Colonial Lake

Heyward-Washington House

Nathaniel-Russell House

Edmonston-Alston House

Calhoun Mansion

White Point Gardens

Cooper River

Charleston Market

Waterfront Park

0   400 yds

One way street

6

THE SOUTH | South Carolina

pause in the shade include the swinging benches at **Waterfront Park**, a beautifully landscaped piazza with boardwalks leading out over the river, and **White Point Gardens**, by the Battery on the tip of the peninsula, where the flower-filled lawns have good views across the water and a breeze even in the sweltering summer.

Opposite the visitor center, the **Charleston Museum**, 360 Meeting St (Mon–Sat 9am–5pm, Sun 1–5pm; $7, or $18 with the Joseph Manigault House and Heyward-Washington House; ☏843/722-2996), is the nation's oldest, dating from 1773 (although the original building no longer stands). It's something of a ragbag of city memorabilia, with video presentations on subjects from rice growing to the Huguenots. One intriguing room holds exhibits from its early collections, where pickled snakes once shared space with Egyptian mummies and casts from the British Museum in London. The "head of a New Zealand chief" and a "fine electrical machine," however, were destroyed in a fire of

1778. The tiny (and free) **Museum of Postal History** located in the Post Office, at 557 E Bay St, is packed with fascinating stuff, such as a postage stamp bearing the face of Confederate President Jefferson Davis that had to be withdrawn because it made him look too much like Lincoln.

Charleston's **market area** runs from Meeting Street to East Bay Street, focusing on a long, narrow line of enclosed, low-roofed, nineteenth-century sheds, but also spilling out onto the surrounding streets. Undeniably touristy, packed with hard-headed "basket ladies," this is one of the liveliest spots in town, selling junk, spices, tacky T-shirts, jewelry and rugs.

Most of the city's fine **houses** are private, and can only be admired from the outside. The late nineteenth-century **Calhoun Mansion**, 16 Meeting St, is among the more extreme, with its ornate plaster and woodwork, hand-painted porcelain ballroom chandeliers and other similar extravagances (Wed–Sun 10am–4pm, closed Jan; $15; ☎843/722-8205). The Charleston Museum's $18 combination ticket gets you into the 1803 **Joseph Manigault House**, opposite the museum, and the **Heyward–Washington House**, 87 Church St, built by a rice baron. In the heart of Catfish Row, this was the setting for Dubose Heyward's novel of black waterfront life, *Porgy*. Admission to each separately is $7 (Mon–Sat 10am–5pm, Sun 1–5pm). The stately antebellum **Edmonston-Alston House** overlooks the harbor at 21 E Battery St (Tues–Sat 10am–4.30pm, Mon & Sun 1.30–4.30pm; $8; ☎843/722-7171). The Neoclassical **Nathaniel–Russell House**, 51 Meeting St (☎ 843/724-8481), is noted for its daring flying staircase, which soars unsupported for three floors. Tremendously elegant both inside and out, its piazza-free design also sets it apart from the other mansions. A short walk north of the downtown area at the much scruffier and more faded **Aiken–Rhett House**, 48 Elizabeth St (☎843/723-1159), the work-yard and slave quarters are intact, but the mansion itself has been left almost entirely unfurnished, in fact almost empty – and all the better for it. (Mon–Sat 10am–5pm, Sun 2–5pm; $7 each or $12 for combination ticket). An additional source for black history is the **Avery Research Center for African–American History and Culture**, 125 Bull St (Mon–Sat noon–5pm; donation; ☎843/953-7609), where there is a retired nineteenth-century classroom and an archive of personal papers, photographs, oral histories and art, among other items; the center hosts periodic films, lectures and exhibits.

Fort Sumter

The first shots of the Civil War were fired on April 12, 1861, at **Fort Sumter**, on a small island some way out from Charleston, where the rivers meet the Atlantic. When South Carolina announced its secession, the federal government had to decide whether to reprovision its forts in the south. The commander of Fort Sumter, Major Robert Anderson, requested supplies in early 1861; when a relief expedition was sent, Confederate General Pierre Beauregard demanded the fort's surrender. In one of the ironies that so characterized the war, Beauregard, who personally coordinated the bombardment, had been the star pupil of Major Anderson's artillery classes at West Point. After a relentless barrage, the garrison gave in the next day, becoming the first prisoners of the war. The fort was retaken by Union troops on Good Friday 1865, the very day of Lincoln's assassination, and today holds a **museum** (summer daily 10am–6pm; rest of year daily 10am–5pm). Fort Sumter Tours operates **tour boats** to Fort Sumter from the City Marina, off Lockwood Boulevard and Patriot's Point in nearby Mount Pleasant ($11 boat & fort; call for schedule ☎843/722-2628).

Eating

Though the historic district crawls with mostly undistinguished seafood places, the town's elegant ambience lends itself very well to the classy "New" Southern **cooking** served up in a variety of innovative, upbeat restaurants. Cappuccino bars and cafés line Market and King streets.

Charleston Grill 224 King St ☎843/577-4522. Classy restaurant at the *Charleston Place* hotel with renowned chef Bob Waggoner and nightly live jazz. If you want to splurge, this is a good choice.

Gaulart and Maliclet (aka *French and French*) 98 Broad St ☎843/577-9797. Wonderful French bistro, seating only nine people. Fondue dinners and croissant breakfasts. Lunch only on Mon, closed Sun.

Hyman's Seafood 213-215 Meeting St ☎843/723-6000. Excellent seafood served in a very casual setting; the fried green tomatoes are great, too. Still a family-owned business and has been consistently expanding down the block since 1980.

Magnolias 185 E Bay St ☎843/577-7771. Splendid *nouvelle* Southern cuisine – shrimp with grits and such – in a stylish monochrome setting with a circular bar.

Mickey's 137 Market St ☎843/723-7121. Stylish Sixties diner with good-value all-day breakfast deals.

Mimi's Café 1241 Harborview Rd, James Island ☎843/795-4090. Family-owned restaurant not associated with the popular franchise. Good value with a broad menu and hearty Sunday brunch.

Old Towne Restaurant 229 King St ☎843/723-8170. Great-value Greek restaurant with excellent grilled seafood, chicken and steaks. Very centrally located.

Poogan's Porch 72 Queen St ☎843/577-2337. Delicious local food in big old Charleston house, including Low Country Boils, crabcakes and catfish. Very popular for Sunday brunch.

Slightly North of Broad 192 E Bay St ☎843/723-3424. One of the best, most fashionable restaurants in town, for truly great *nouvelle* Southern cooking – scallops with smoked sausage, Low Country sampler with Hopping John and butterbeans and the like – along with adventurous world cuisine.

Sticky Fingers 235 Meeting St ☎843/853-RIBS. Established Southern barbecue eatery that attracts tourists by the coachload.

Nightlife and entertainment

Charleston has a dynamic **nightlife**, albeit one that's geared toward tourist revelers, with a wide choice of **music venues**, **clubs** and **bars**, especially around the market. Ask at the visitor center about its many festivals, or pick up the free weekly *Citypaper*. There are also lively bars out at the Isle of Palms and Sullivan's Island (see overleaf). **Spoleto Festival USA** (☎843/722-2764), an international arts festival inspired by its Italian namesake, runs for seventeen days each year from May to June. Its funkier sibling, **Piccolo Spoleto** (☎843/724-7305, ⓦwww.piccolospoleto.com), runs concurrently, featuring many regional artists and free performances, as well as infusing the city with a carnival-like atmosphere. October's **Moja Arts Festival** (☎843/724-7305, ⓦwwwmojafestival.com) celebrates African/Caribbean theatre, dance and film, with all events free or low-priced.

Blind Tiger Pub 38 Broad St ☎843/577-0088. Local bar away from the market area with hidden entrance and busy beer garden.

Club Tango 39 John St, entrance in alley adjacent to *Embassy Suites* ☎843/577-2822. Hugely popular multilevel dance club, open Thurs through Sat.

Cumberland Grill 26 Cumberland St ☎843/577-9469. A nice bar and sandwich shop that puts on blues, bluegrass, rock, reggae and folk.

Henry's 54 N Market St ☎843/723-4363. Flash bar, with live music, serving appetizers, seafood and sandwiches.

Horse & Cart 347 King St ☎843/722-0797. Grungy bar/café, with over 100 beers and live music (of all genres) every night.

Mandalay King and Wentworth streets ☎843/577-7600. Trendy and very popular brewpub serving creative Thai dishes in a metal and glass decor.

Music Farm 32 Ann St ☎843/853-FARM. Best place in Charleston to see regional and national touring bands.

Vendue Inn 23 Vendue Range ☎843/723-0485. Busy rooftop bar and restaurant with great views over the city.

Around Charleston

The **river road**, Hwy-61, leads **west** from Charleston along the Ashley River, past a series of magnificent plantations. Many can be visited, although in best Southern tradition, house tours tend to dwell on the furniture and dining habits of the slave masters rather than provide a sense of social history. **Drayton Hall**, closest to Charleston at 3380 Ashley River Rd (daily: March–Oct 9.30am–4pm; Nov–Feb 9.30am–3pm; $10; ☎843/769-2600), is a particularly fine Georgian mansion, looking much as it did in the mid-eighteenth century with its handcarved wood and plasterwork. The nearby **Magnolia Plantation and Gardens**, ten miles from downtown Charleston, is most notable for its stunning ornamental gardens, particularly in spring when the azaleas are blooming. Tram tours cover the entire grounds (grounds open daily 8am–dusk; last tickets at 5.30pm; $12; house tours daily 9.30am–4.30pm; $6; tram tours $5; ☎843/571-1266 or 1-800/367-3517) but require purchase of general admission ticket. The **Audubon Swamp Garden** (☎1-800/367-3517), a pre-served swamp, complete with alligators and lush flowers, has a self-guided walking tour ($5), which does not require the general admission charge. You can also rent bicycles and canoes to roam the area for $3 per three hours. Across the Ashley River, on Hwy-171, west of the Ashley River Bridge, **Charles Towne Landing** is a 663-acre state park (daily: summer 8am–6pm; rest of year 9am–5pm; $5, tram tour $1; ☎843/852-4200) with a natural habitat zoo, a living history settler's village and a replica of a seventeenth-century merchant ship, as well as hiking and biking trails and bike and kayak rentals.

East of Charleston, **beaches** such as **Isle of Palms** and **Sullivan's Island** are heavily used by locals at weekends. The further you get from town, the more likely you are to find a stretch to yourself. The Isle of Palms **bus** (#8) from Charleston's Market Street, runs to both Isle of Palms and Sullivan's Island. If you want to stay, there are plenty of motels and eating places, and the odd decent bar, such as the *Windjammer*, 1000 Ocean Blvd, Isle of Palms (☎843/886-8596), open until 2am with live rock at weekends; *Bert's Island*, 2209 Middle St, Sullivan's Island (☎843/883-3924), is similar.

The sea islands

South of Charleston toward Savannah, the coastline dissolves into small, marshy islands. **Edisto Island**, south of US-17 on Hwy-174, is typical: huge live oaks festooned with great drapes of Spanish moss line the roads, beside bright green marshes with rich birdlife, and great beaches on the seaward side. If you want to stay, there are no budget motels, but the **campground** at **Edisto Beach State Park** (☎843/869-2156, ☎843/869-3022) is near a great beach lined with palmetto trees and other semitropical plants. Electrical and water hook-up costs $23, walk-ins $12.

BEAUFORT (pronounced *Byoofert*), the biggest town, is rather twee but the old district is lovely – offset somewhat by racial tensions and the baleful prox-imity of Parris Island US Marine Base, notorious for the brutality of its train-ing regime, as mythologized in Kubrick's Vietnam film *Full Metal Jacket*. The Greyhound **bus** station is two miles north of town on US-21. The **visitor cen-ter** at 1106 Carteret St (☎843/986-5406) has details of tours around the small historic district and discount coupons for the **motels** out on US-21. In town, the *Best Western Sea Island Inn*, 1015 Bay St (☎843/522-2090, ☎843/521-4858,

W www.sea-island-inn; **⑤/⑥**), has nice rooms with an old-fashioned feel. *Ultimate Eating,* 859 Sea Island Parkway (☎843/838-1314), serves nourishing Low Country and *gullah*-style dishes. For magnificent views of Beaufort River visit *Ollie's Seafood Restaurant* where the oysters are a specialty.

St Helena Island

Across the bridge to the southeast of Beaufort, **ST HELENA ISLAND** is among the least spoiled of the eastern sea islands. The **landscape** is gorgeous: amazing Spanish moss and enormous, wide views out across bright marshes, and small shrimp and oyster fishing communities. Occasionally you see what looks like a fleet of ships in the middle of a field, only to realize that in fact the boats are anchored in a small salt creek, hidden by bright green marsh reeds.

This is an area of strong **black communities**, descended from slaves, who were given parcels of land when they were freed by the Union army in February 1865 and who speak a dialect known as *gullah,* an Afro-English patois with many West African words. The **Gullah Institute** in the **Penn Center National Historic District** (☎843/838-2432), off US-21, houses the **school** started for freed slaves by Charlotte Forten, a black Massachusetts teacher, who remarked, "I have never seen children so eager to learn . . . the majority learn with wonderful rapidity. Many of the grown people are desirous of learning to read. It is wonderful how a people who have been so long crushed to the earth . . . can have so great a desire for knowledge, and such a capability for attaining it." The school was an important retreat for civil rights leaders in the 1960s, used by Dr Martin Luther King Jr's SCLC and others. Set back from the road is a **museum** containing fascinating old pictures of black fishermen and farmers, plus old tools and shrimp nets, and rattlesnake skins (donation; Tues–Fri 11am–4pm). Nearby, off US-21, the ruined black **Chapel of Ease**, nestled among the thick Spanish moss, with seashell-adorned interior walls, makes for an interesting visit if you have a half-hour to spare. Before the bridge across to Hunting Island is the *Shrimp Shack* (March–Dec Mon–Sat 11am–8.30pm; ☎843/838-2962), an excellent fresh **seafood** joint, where the "shrimp burger" has to be seen to be believed, and should ideally be eaten at one of the trestle tables overlooking the shrimp boats bobbing in the marshy shallows.

St Helena's main **beach**, nine miles beyond the museum at **Hunting Island State Park** on the east shore (daily dawn–dusk; $2), can get crowded, but it's simply idyllic: soft white sand, wide and gently shelving, scattered with shards of pearly shells and lined with palmettos, palm trees and sea oats. The water is incredibly warm. Pelicans come in to feed, particularly in the early morning, and the shrimp fleet sails past soon after. You can **stay** near the beach in weather-beaten cabins backing onto a glassy lagoon full of jumping fat fish, although you need to reserve from a year and a half to two years in advance; for reservations call ☎843/838-2011. There's also the larger Hunting Island campground: head first to the **park office**, next to a sluggish pool (Mon–Fri 9am–5pm, Sat & Sun 11am–5pm).

THE SOUTH | The sea islands

Georgia

Compared to the rest of **GEORGIA**, the largest of the Southern states, the bright lights of its capital **Atlanta** are a wild aberration. Apart from some beaches and towns on the highly indented coastline, this overwhelmingly rural state is composed of slow, easygoing settlements where the best, and sometimes the only, way to enjoy your time is to sip iced tea and have a chat on the porch.

Settlement in Georgia, the thirteenth British colony (named after King George II), started in 1733 at Savannah, intended as a haven of Christian principles for poor Britons, with both alcohol and slavery banned. However, under pressure from planters, **slavery** was introduced in 1752, and by the time of the **Civil War** almost half the population were black slaves. Little fighting took place on Georgian soil until Sherman's troops marched in from Tennessee, burned Atlanta to the ground and laid waste to all property on the way to the coast. The economy successfully re-established itself after the war, attracting substantial investment in the latter years of the nineteenth century.

Today, bustling **Atlanta** stands as the unofficial capital of the South. The city where **Dr Martin Luther King Jr** was born, preached and is buried bears little relation to *Gone with the Wind* stereotypes, and its forward-looking energy is upheld as a role model for other cities with large black populations – though it does still suffer high levels of urban poverty and violent crime.

Atlanta's main rival as a tourist destination is the **Georgia coast**, stretching south from beautiful old **Savannah** via the **sea islands** to the semitropical **Okefenokee Swamp**, inland near Florida. In the **northeast**, the **Appalachian foothills** are particularly fetching in fall, while **Athens** has a reputation for producing offbeat rock groups such as REM and the B-52's. Further **south**, the agricultural heartlands are rich in musical history, but only **Macon** and ancient **Ocmulgee** provide reasons to stop.

Getting around Georgia

Georgia's main points of interest are easily accessible, but local transportation is poor. Amtrak **trains** from Washington, DC to New Orleans and Florida call at Atlanta and Savannah respectively. **Bus** services in most areas are patchy and infrequent, though Atlanta has regular connections to the major cities, and several daily buses along the coast call at Savannah. Atlanta has the world's largest passenger **airport**, and Savannah has a reasonable service – but airfares between the two are high.

Atlanta

ATLANTA is a relatively young city: only incorporated in 1847, it was little more than a minor transportation center until the Civil War, when its accessibility made it a good site for the huge Confederacy munitions industry – and consequently a major target for the Union army. In 1864 Sherman's army **burned** the city, an act immortalized in *Gone with the Wind*. Recovery after the war took just a few years: Atlanta was the archetype of the aggressive, urban, industrial "New South," furiously championed by "**boosters**" – newspaper owners, bankers, politicians and city leaders. Industrial giants who based themselves here included **Coca–Cola**, source of a string of philanthropic gifts to the city. Heavy **black** immigration to Atlanta increased its already considerable black population and led to the establishment of a thriving community centered around **Auburn Avenue**.

Very few of Atlanta's buildings predate 1915, and nothing at all survives from before 1868. Its characters, on the other hand – politicians and newspaper people – have changed little, and the "booster" tradition has continued to the present, peaking spectacularly when Atlanta won the right to host the 1996 **Olympics**. The bid to convince the world of the city's prosperity and sophistication was led by city leaders such as ex-mayor **Andrew Young** (the first Southern black congressman since Reconstruction, who became Carter's ambassador to the UN) and flamboyant former CNN magnate **Ted Turner**.

Today's Atlanta is at first glance a typical large American city. Its population has reached 3.5 million, and urban sprawl is such a problem that each citizen is obliged to travel an average of 34 miles per day by car – the highest figure in the country. Cut off from each other by roaring freeways, bright lights and an enclave mentality, its neighborhoods tend to have distinct racial identities – broadly speaking, "white flight" was to the northern suburbs, while the southern districts are predominantly black. That said, the city is undeniably progressive, with little interest in lamenting a lost Southern past. Since voting in the nation's first black mayor, Maynard Jackson, in 1974, it has remained the most conspicuously black-run city in the US, and an estimated 200,000 black families streamed in from states further north in the 1980s alone. The Olympics may not have been the triumph Atlanta so eagerly anticipated – even before the Centennial Park bombing tarnished the event itself, years of disruption and grandiose construction projects had left many Atlantans wondering whether the city had lost more than it gained – but with its ever-increasing international profile, cosmopolitan blend of cultures and hip local neighborhoods, the spirit and dynamism of modern Atlanta is a far cry indeed from its much-mythologized Deep South roots.

Arrival, information and getting around

The colossal **Hartsfield International Airport** (☎404/530-6600), the busiest passenger airport in the US, is ten miles south of downtown Atlanta, just inside I-285 ("the perimeter"). Road **shuttle** services such as the Atlanta Airport Shuttle (daily every 15–20min 7am–11pm; ☎404/524-3400) run into the city for around $14, $22 round-trip good for thirty days, or a little more to get to Buckhead. The airport is also the southern terminus of the south line of the **subway**, fifteen minutes' ride from downtown ($1.75; see below). If you need a **taxi** to get downtown, call Checker Cab ($18 for one passenger, $19 between two, $24 for three or more; ☎404/351-1111). The Amtrak station, at 1688 Peachtree St, is too far north of downtown to walk to: take a taxi or bus #23 to the Arts Center subway stop, N5 on the northern line. Greyhound **buses** arrive south of downtown at 232 Forsyth St, near the Garnett Street subway station.

Atlanta's **subway** and wide network of **buses** are run by the Metropolitan Area Rapid Transit Authority (MARTA; ☎404/848-4711), and are clean, reliable and pretty safe, operating between 5am and 1am weekdays and Saturdays, and from 6am until 12.30am on Sundays. Fares are $1.75 per journey (daily pass $3.50, Fri–Sun pass $9, weekly pass $13).

A good way to explore the neighborhoods of Atlanta is on a ninety-minute **walking tour** with the Atlanta Preservation Center, 156 Seventh St ($5;

@404/876-2041). Destinations include the West End, Fox Theater, Sweet Auburn (with emphasis on the churches), an architectural tour of downtown and many more.

Information

Atlanta's principal **visitor center**, in the **Peachtree Center**, 233 Peachtree St (Mon–Fri 8.30am–5.30pm; @404/222-6600 or 1-800 ATLANTA, @www .atlanta.com), caters mostly to business travelers. A more useful branches for tourists, at Pryor and Atlanta streets in **Underground Atlanta** (Mon–Sat 10am–6pm, Sun noon–6pm; @404/222-6688), also handles bus tour reservations and sells half-price tickets for local events. Other branches can be found near the car rental offices in the **airport** (Mon–Fri 9am–9pm, Sat 9am–6pm, Sun 12.30–6pm; @404/305-8426) and in **Buckhead**'s Lenox Square mall (Tues–Sat 11am–5pm, Sun noon–6pm; @404/266-1398).

Accommodation

Your best bets for a place to stay in **downtown** Atlanta are the chain hotels, though with so many conventions around even these aren't particularly inexpensive. **Midtown** is cheaper, and puts you nearer the nightlife, while **Buckhead** boasts some of the swankiest hotels in the country. If you're driving to Georgia, you can save a good deal of money – not just at the interstate motels around the perimeter – by picking up **discount coupons** from state visitor centers (see above). The B&B Atlanta agency, 1608 Briarcliff Rd, #5 (@404/875-0525 or 1-800/967-3224), will reserve **B&B** rooms.

Ansley Inn 253 15th St @404/872-9000 or 1-800/446-5416, @404/892-2318, @www.ans-leyinn.com. Lovely, friendly midtown B&B, near Ansley Park, whose 33 rooms have stripped-wood floors, antique furnishings, wet bars and whirlpool tubs. **⑤**

Atlanta International Hostel 223 Ponce de Leon Ave @404/875-9449, @404/870-0042, @www.hostel-atlanta.com. Part of *Woodruff B&B* (see below) and close to the North Ave MARTA station. Dorms $19.

Days Inn Downtown 300 Spring St NW at Baker St @404/523-1144, @404/577-8495, @www.daysinn.com. Reliable chain hotel in the heart of downtown, with bar and outdoor pool. **❸/⑤**

Quality Hotel 89 Luckie St @404/524-7991 or 1800/228-5151, @404/524-0672. Very hospitable, central downtown hotel with views of the Atlanta skyline. Rates include continental breakfast. **❸/⑤**

Ritz-Carlton Buckhead 3434 Peachtree Rd NE at Phipps Drive @404/237-2700, @404/233-5168, @www.ritzcarlton.com. Exquisite, elegant hotel,

one of the finest in the Ritz-Carlton group, with Atlanta's best haute cuisine restaurant. **❼**

Sheraton Atlanta Hotel 165 Courtland St NE @404/659-6500 or 1800/833-8624, @404/524-1259, @www.sheratonatlantahotel.com. Luxury downtown hotel with wonderful indoor pool surrounded by foliage, and its own mini-shopping mall. **❹**

Super 8 111 Cone St @404/524-7000, @404/650-7521, @www.super8atlanta.com. Very atypical *Super 8*, housed in a converted downtown hotel and offering bargain rates for a great spot near Peachtree Plaza, CNN and Underground Atlanta. **❹**

Travelodge Downtown 311 Courtland St NE @404/659-4545, @404/659-5934, @www.trav-elodge.com. Small, central motel, offering standard rooms on the east side of downtown. **⑤**

Woodruff B&B 223 Ponce de Leon Ave @404/875-9449. Beautifully converted two-room former bordello; rates include full breakfast. Close to the North Ave MARTA station. **⑤**

The City

Atlanta's layout is confusing, following old Native American trails rather than a logical grid system, with no fewer than 32 streets named "Peachtree"; take care to note whether you're looking for Avenue, Road, Boulevard and so forth. The most important is **Peachtree Street**, which cuts a long north–south swath

ATLANTA

Ⓜ MARTA Station

Buckhead ▲   ▲ *Amtrak*

High Museum of Art
Woodruff Arts Center

Piedmont Park

Fox Theater

NORTH AVENUE

CIVIC CENTER

Centennial Olympic Park

Georgia Dome

CNN Center

WORLD CONGRESS CENTER

High Museum of Art

PEACHTREE CENTER

The APEX

DOWNTOWN

Underground Atlanta

World of Coca-Cola

Georgia State Capitol

GEORGIA STATE

MLK Jr Center

Ebenezer Baptist Church

MLK Jr. Birthhome

THE MARTIN LUTHER KING JR. HISTORIC DISTRICT

KING MEMORIAL

Oakland Cemetery

Turner Field

Cyclorama
Zoo Atlanta

Grant Park

0   800 yds

6

THE SOUTH | Atlanta

Virginia Highlands, Decatur

Little Five Points

ACCOMMODATION

Ansley Inn	1
Days Inn Downtown	4
Quality Hotel	7
Sheraton Atlanta Hotel	5

Super 8	6
Travelodge Downtown	3
Woodruff B&B	2

RESTAURANTS AND BARS

Beautiful Restaurant	H
Front Page News	B
Kaya Club and Bistro	C
Mary Mac's Tearoom	D
Mumbo Jumbo	G

Sylvia's	I
Tamarind Thai Restaurant	A
Thelma's Kitchen	F
The Varsity	E

531

through the city. Sights are scattered, but relatively easy to reach on public transportation. Once you're there, the **downtown** area, the Martin Luther King Jr Historic District ranged along **Auburn Avenue**, and the trendy neighborhoods of **Little Five Points** and **Virginia-Highland** are all easy to explore on foot.

Downtown Atlanta

Downtown Atlanta is for the most part the usual big-city concentration of glimmering skyscrapers, transformed and overhauled for the 1996 Olympics. Its highlight, however, and the only place open after dark, is **Underground Atlanta** (or "the Underground"), a four-block subterranean maze of shops, stalls, restaurants and bars on the original site of the city (effectively buried in the late nineteenth century by the construction of railroad viaducts). In the 1970s the district, ranged around Five Points MARTA station, was a crime-ridden wasteland, but, thanks to Andrew Young's dream of a revitalized downtown, it's now one of the liveliest – albeit very touristy – pockets of the city. The underground labyrinth of cobbled gas-lit streets, restored to their original appearance and dotted with historical markers, is reached by steps from a piazza buzzing with street performers.

The eastern side of the piazza is dominated by the super-glossy **World of Coca-Cola** pavilion (June–Aug Mon–Sat 9am–6pm, Sun 11am–6pm; Sept–May Mon–Sat 9am–5pm, Sun noon–6pm; $6, children $3; ☎404/676-5151). This three-story spin through Coca-Cola's history, from its origins in the non-air-conditioned nineteenth-century Hotlanta, through the evolution of the famed contour bottle "embraced by generations" to "the Real Thing," is surprisingly fun. On the third floor you can quench your thirst with a whole host of coke products from all over the world, such as Stoney Ginger Beer from South Africa or Japan's Vegita Beta.

Northwest of the Underground, the **CNN Center** – a structure that was originally an upmarket shopping mall, and still holds a few small stores – daily achieves a global reach undreamed of by Coca-Cola's founders. The Cable News Network is just one of eleven television networks in the empire developed by Ted Turner, and sold to Time-Warner in 1995. Aptly, among the thousands of MGM classics now stamped with the Turner logo is *Gone with the Wind* – witness the plethora of Tara, Scarlett and Rhett knickknacks in the giftshop. Unlike the Coke pavilion, this is a working facility – adrenalin-fueled, forty-minute **guided tours** (daily 9am–6pm, every 15min; $8) rush past frazzled producers and toothy anchorpersons – but you can videotape yourself reading the (real) news of the day ($15 in the giftshop). If you're desperate to be on TV, time your visit to coincide with the 3.30pm filming of *TalkBack Live*, when visitors are invited to be part of the audience.

Several downtown blocks just northeast of the CNN Center were razed prior to the 1996 Olympics to make way for the open space of **Centennial Park**, intended as a focus for public festivities during the Games; forced to close almost immediately by the pipe-bombing that killed two revelers, the park has failed to find a post-Olympic identity, and rumors abound that it too will soon be redeveloped.

The **Atlanta Public Library**, in Margaret Mitchell Square at Carnegie Way and Forsyth Street (Mon–Thurs 9am–9pm, Fri & Sat 9am–6pm, Sun 2–6pm), has a room devoted to *Gone with the Wind* author and Atlanta native **Margaret Mitchell**. The novel (1936) and film (1939) helped perpetuate popular images of the genteel plantation South – as well, of course, as the burning of Atlanta. Fantastically popular, the novel took just six weeks to sell enough copies to

The burning of Atlanta and the march to the sea

In summer 1864, following the comprehensive Confederate defeats of Spotsylvania and the Wilderness in May, Union General **William Tecumseh Sherman** invaded north Georgia. Outflanking the much smaller Confederate forces, he laid siege to Atlanta; the city eventually surrendered at the start of September.

Sherman announced that the entire population of the city must leave forthwith, and that he would burn their property as he deemed necessary. The Confederate commander, General Hood, powerless to resist, expostulated: "Sir, permit me to say that the unprecedented measure you propose transcends, in studied and ingenious cruelty, all acts ever before brought to my attention in the dark history of war. In the name of God and humanity, I protest." Sherman responded: "In the name of common sense, I ask you not to appeal to a just God in such a sacrilegious manner . . . Talk thus to the marines, but not to me." On November 16, Sherman put a torch to the city, and set out on his notorious "**March to the Sea.**" As he later exulted, "Behind us lay Atlanta, smoldering in ruins, the black smoke rising high in the air, and hanging like a pall over the ruined city."

Sherman's March is seen as an early example of total war; some accuse him of inventing the methods later followed in the Nazi *Blitzkrieg*. His explicit intention was to "make Georgia howl," via the systematic destruction of agricultural and industrial resources and terrorizing of civilians. One Georgia woman recorded in her diary that "there was hardly a fence left standing all the way from Sparta to Gordon. The fields were trampled down and the road was lined with carcasses of horses, hogs and cattles that the invaders, unable either to consume or carry away with them, had wantonly shot down, to starve out the people . . . the dwellings that were standing all showed signs of pillage, and on every plantation we saw . . . charred remains."

It was the final blow to the Southern war effort; though the Confederate armies struggled on for a few months after Sherman took Savannah, their fate was sealed.

form a tower fifty times higher than the Empire State Building. The tiny downtown branch of the **Atlanta History Center** is also here, with videos on city history and information on historical tours. Midtown's **High Museum of Art** (see p.535) has a downtown satellite gallery at 30 John Wesley Dobbs Ave at Peachtree Street, featuring smaller photography and folk art collections (Mon–Fri 11am–5pm; free).

Sweet Auburn

A mere half-mile east of downtown, **Auburn Avenue** provides a glimpse into Atlanta's black history. In its 1920s heyday, "**Sweet Auburn**" was a prosperous, progressive area of black-owned businesses and jazz clubs, but since the Depression it has declined, becoming yet another faceless strip of boarded-up barbers and beauty stores. Despite admirable efforts and promises of revitalization, it has yet to succeed in reincarnating itself as a living monument to black culture and heritage.

However, several blocks have been designated as the **Martin Luther King Jr National Historic Site** (☎404/331-6922), in honor of Auburn's most cherished native son, the reverend who won the Nobel Peace Prize at a time when he was being actively persecuted by agents of the US government. Despite the lack of attention given to it by the city, this short stretch of road is the most visited attraction in the entire state of Georgia, and it's a moving experience to watch the crowds of schoolkids listening patiently to the guided tours and waiting in turn to take photographs. Head first for the Park

Service's purpose-built **visitor center**, 450 Auburn Ave (daily 9am–5pm), which holds a powerful exhibition entitled " Courage To Lead" that covers King's life and campaigns. Across the street at no. 449, the **Martin Luther King Jr Center for Non-violent Change** is privately run by King's family (daily 9am–5pm; free). Chiefly an educational and research facility, it also features displays of treasured artifacts such as King's bibles and traveling case, as well as separate rooms devoted to Mahatma Gandhi and Rosa Parks. King's mortal remains were brought here from Memphis in the early 1970s, and his **memorial**, a simple slab inscribed with the words "Free at last, free at last, thank God Almighty I'm free at last," stands in the shallow, five-tiered Reflecting Pool outside, guarded by an eternal flame.

The **Ebenezer Baptist Church** next door, where King followed both his father and grandfather as pastor – and where his mother was assassinated while playing the organ in 1974 – has been converted into another museum (Mon–Sat 9am–5pm, Sun 1–5pm), while its congregation has decamped to a much larger new church over the road. Auburn remained the base for King's breathtakingly courageous campaigning during the Sixties, and his Southern Christian Leadership Conference (**SCLC**) still has its headquarters in the old Masonic building on the corner of Auburn Avenue and Hilliard Street.

King's **birthplace**, a block east at no. 501, is a small, neat Queen Anne-style shotgun house restored to its 1920s appearance, and now looking smarter than its neighbors. Home to Martin until he was 12, it remained in his family until 1971, since when it has been open for lively, anecdotal guided **tours** (daily 10am–5pm, 30min; free). These start from Fire Station no. 6, nearby at 501 Auburn Ave (daily 9am–5pm); you may have to be put on a waiting list, as schoolgroups often visit en masse.

Further west, at 184 Auburn, the recently reopened **Royal Peacock Club** was famed from the 1930s to the 1950s for performances by Cab Calloway, Louis Armstrong and Aretha Franklin, while the **Atlanta Life Insurance Co. Building** at no. 148, from 1920 to 1980 the headquarters of the nation's largest black-owned business, now holds a small selection of African-American art in the lobby.

The privately run **African-American Panoramic Experience** or **APEX** at 135 Auburn (Tues–Sat 10am–5pm; $3; ☎404/523-2739) has an eclectic collection on black history, including a reconstruction of a 1920s black-owned drugstore and an African art gallery.

Little Five Points to Emory University

Northeast of Auburn Avenue, around Euclid and Moreland avenues, the youthful **Little Five Points** district is the center of Atlanta's alternative community, a tangle of thrift stores, secondhand record stores, funky restaurants, body-piercing and branding parlors, bars and clubs. By way of contrast, just a few blocks north at 1 Copenhill Ave, on the hill where Sherman is said to have watched Atlanta burn, the **Carter Presidential Center** is devoted to the peanut farmer who rose to become Georgia state governor and the 39th president of the USA. In addition to viewing film footage and a reconstruction of his Oval Office (where he spent "tedious hours" in budget meetings, and in his final hours of office negotiated the release of the hostages in Iran), you can read twelve-year-old Jimmy's school essay on health, in which he earnestly urges his readers to keep their teeth clean (Mon–Sat 9am–4.45pm, Sun noon–4.45pm; $5, under 17 free).

Northeast of here, beyond the yuppie **Virginia-Highland** restaurant district, the trek to **Emory University**'s campus is rewarded by the stylish

Michael C. Carlos Museum, 571 S Kilgo St (Mon–Sat 10am–5pm, Sun noon–5pm; $3 donation; ☎404/727-4282), which has a huge collection of fine art and antiquities from all continents, in an airy building designed by Michael Graves. Sub-Saharan African art is unusually well represented, including Nigerian headcrests woven with snake-like tendrils; among the extraordinary pre-Columbian collection, note the Andean *Human as a Peanut*.

Midtown

Midtown stretches from Ponce de Leon Avenue, lined with funky restaurants, to 26th Street. In recent years, it has become dominated by massive skyscrapers – look out for **One Atlantic Center**, a spiky, futuristic monstrosity at 15th and Peachtree streets that was designed by Philip Johnson and John Burgee. The wildly flamboyant Art Deco **Fox Theater**, 660 Peachtree St at Ponce de Leon (☎404/881-2100, ⊛www.foxtheatre.com), with its strong Moorish theme, should also not be missed. Unless you buy a ticket for one of its fairly mainstream theatrical shows, the only way to see the theater is on an organized tour (Mon, Wed & Thurs 10am, Sat 10am & 11am; $5).

A few blocks north, the huge **Woodruff Arts Center** includes the main branch of the **High Museum of Art**, 1280 Peachtree St NE (Tues–Sat 10am–5pm, Sun noon–5pm; $8, free Thurs after 1pm; ☎404/773-HIGH, ⊛www.high.org). You'll find excellent contemporary and non-Western exhibitions – particularly strong on African art – on display in the ultra-white glass-and-steel building, designed by Richard Meier. There's also a good giftshop, and a peaceful little espresso bar in the airy atrium.

Buckhead

Further north, the affluent white suburb of **Buckhead** is a trendy area of glitzy, youthful malls and swanky hotels. Within the space of two and a half blocks of Peachtree at Paces Ferry Road, celebrity residents such as Elton John can enjoy over a hundred top-quality restaurants. Tucked away nearby, permanent exhibits at the superb **Atlanta History Center**, 130 W Paces Ferry Rd (Mon–Sat 10am–5.30pm, Sun noon–5.30pm; $10; ☎404/814-4000, ⊛www .atlantahistorycentre.com), cover everything from Civil War black politics to women's history, while temporary installations detail city-specific events and personalities. There are also tours of two houses in the extensive grounds: the **Swan House**, a ponderous 1920s mock-classical mansion, and the **Tullie Smith Farm**, an antebellum farmhouse and garden. For a further taste of the Tara-style Old South, tour the **Governors Mansion**, 391 W Paces Ferry Rd (Tues–Thurs 10–11.30am; free).

The West End

The **West End**, Atlanta's oldest quarter, dating from 1835, is a slightly shabby but slowly reviving district southwest of downtown. Historically a black residential area, it remains so today: a buzzy, more upbeat counterpoint to Sweet Auburn. Georgia's only museum dedicated to African-American and Haitian art is displayed at the **Hammonds House**, 503 Peeples St (Tues–Fri 10am–6pm, Sat & Sun 1–5pm; $2), and you can tour the 1910 Beaux Arts **Herndon Home**, 587 University Place (Tues–Sat 10am–4.30pm; $5), designed and lived in by Alonzo Herndon, the freed slave who became a barber, founded the Atlanta Life Insurance Company and went on to be the city's first black millionaire. Together with his wife (the director of Atlanta University's drama department), and such black luminaries as W.E.B. DuBois and Booker T. Washington, he participated in setting up progressive black institutions. The mansion's grand interior, built and crafted by black artisans, contains the family's original furnishings, including some fine Venetian glass.

The fascinating **Wren's Nest**, home of *Br'er Rabbit* author Joel Chandler Harris, at 1050 R.D. Abernathy Blvd (Tues–Sat 10am–4pm, Sun 1–4pm; $3), skewers preconceptions about the Uncle Remus stories propagated by the racist images of Disney's *Song of the South*. Harris, a friend of Mark Twain, was a respected journalist whose column for the *Atlanta Constitution* retold the slave stories he had heard while training as a printer on a plantation newspaper; recently the dialect has been reappraised as authentically African and the stories as valuable affirmation of a black folk tradition. Regular storytelling sessions take place in the peaceful, untamed garden.

Grant Park

Directly south of downtown, **Grant Park** is home to the **Cyclorama**, a huge circular painting (50ft by 900ft) depicting the Battle of Atlanta, executed by a group of German and Polish artists in 1885–86. Cycloramas used to travel around the country as entertainment in the days before movies; you sit inside the circle of the painting and the whole auditorium slowly rotates twice. During the second rotation, a guide provides interesting details about the painting; look out in particular for the hole in the wagon, originally used as a fire escape. In the accompanying museum, treating the war from the point of view of the average soldier, banks of distressing statistics are interspersed with photos and memorabilia (daily: summer 9.20am–5.30pm; rest of year 9.20am–4.30pm; $5). Adjacent, **Zoo Atlanta** (ⓦwww.zooatlanta.org) features giant pandas from Chengdu and re-creations of African rainforests and other habitats (daily: summer 9am–6.30pm; rest of year 9.30am–5.30pm; $15). In summer, a special zoo shuttle runs from Five Points MARTA station to the park.

Eating

Atlanta has scores of good **restaurants** to suit all budgets. Most of the downtown options close down fairly early and are quite upmarket – though with the Peachtree Center alone holding a dozen restaurants, a *Hard Rock Café*, a *Planet Hollywood*, and a food court, it's not hard to find something to suit any budget – while Buckhead is even glitzier. Southern **soul food** is best around Auburn Avenue, and **vegetarians** can get plenty of choice in Little Five Points and Virginia-Highland. For a good takeout lunch, try the **Dekalb Farmers' Market**, twenty minutes' drive toward Stone Mountain at 3000 E Ponce de Leon Ave, where stalls sell goat stew, tofu stir-fry and glazed duck; other goodies include fresh farm-fattened catfish and pretty blue crabs, and aromatic coffees from around the world.

Atlanta Fish Market 265 Pharr Rd NE ☎404/262-3165. Buckhead's top seafood specialist, with ultra-fresh oysters and crabs.

Beautiful Restaurant 397 Auburn Ave NE ☎404/223-0080. Famous down-home soul-food cafeteria serving up stewed chicken, corn bread, ribs and vegetable plates. Near the Ebenezer Baptist Church.

Buckhead Diner 3073 Piedmont Rd at E Paces Ferry ☎404/262-3336. Glitzy postmodern diner, always lively with locals enjoying Southern food with a twist, like crab egg rolls, stuffed grits, veal

and wild mushroom meatloaf. No reservations taken, so expect a wait.

Café Tu Tu Tango 220 Pharr Rd ☎404/841-6222. Hip Buckhead café, where local artists make and sell their work. Serves substantial portions of eclectic, delicious snacks and tapas from around the world. Open daily from 11.30am until late.

Dante's Down the Hatch 3380 Peachtree Rd ☎404/266-1600. Lively, subterranean fondue restaurant in the Underground, kitted out like an eighteenth-century sailing frigate, with wooden beams, dark nooks and crannies and a moat with live pointy-nosed crocs. Entrees cost around $25, and there's nightly live jazz for an extra $6.

Flying Biscuit 1655 McLendon Ave NE ☎404/687-8888. Tiny café near Little Five Points, renowned for breakfasts in particular and healthy New American food with a Southern twist.

Front Page News 1104 Crescent Ave ☎404/897-3500, ⓦwww.newsyoucanswallow.com. Late-closing midtown bar/grill popular for its Cajun dishes and outdoor seating.

Mary Mac's Tearoom 224 Ponce de Leon Ave ☎404/876-1800. A cute, small restaurant renowned for cheap traditional Southern cuisine. Mon–Sat 11am–8.30pm, Sun 11am–3pm.

Mumbo Jumbo 89 Park Place ☎404/523-0330. Very chic downtown restaurant, offering Tuscan/American cuisine, with an open kitchen and a bar full of posers.

Nava 3060 Peachtree Rd NW ☎404/240-1984. Spicy, modern Southwestern food plus mighty margaritas in glitzy Buckhead surroundings.

Sylvia's 241 Central SW ☎404/529-9692. This downtown affiliate of the legendary Harlem restaurant is a must if you're in the mood for soul food.

Tamarind 80 14th St NW ☎404/873-4888. Stylish midtown joint with a great selection of flavorful Thai dishes.

Thelma's Kitchen 768 Marietta St NW ☎404/688-5855. Inexpensive downtown soul-food institution forced to relocate when its much-loved former home was destroyed to build Centennial Park; try the salmon and grits for breakfast. Mon–Sat 8am–3pm.

The Varsity 61 North Ave NW ☎404/881-1706. Vast, packed midtown fast-food drive-in diner: a true Fifties throwback. Open till 11.30pm.

THE SOUTH | Atlanta

6

Nightlife

Atlanta is a place where you can have a very good time; budget for blowing some money hopping between its bars and clubs. The main concentrations are in the overlapping yuppie **Virginia–Highland** and punky **Little Five Points**, and the more upmarket **midtown**, the center of Atlanta's thriving **gay and lesbian** scene. **Buckhead** can be a lot of fun if you've got bags of cash. Up-to-the-minute listings for all venues can be found in the free weekly *Creative Loafing*.

Blind Willie's 828 N Highland Ave NE ☎404/873-2583. The best blues venue in town, with appearances by major artists, this Virginia-Highland hangout is also a lively bar. Daily 8pm–late.

Burkhart's Pub 1492 Piedmont Ave ☎404/872-4403. Midtown gay bar, with drag & karaoke nights that sometimes feature resident act "The Gospel Girls."

Club Rarity 1924 Piedmont Rd NE ☎404/875-5238. Predominantly but not exclusively lesbian midtown joint that's a glorious melange of cozy lounges and wild dance floors, with themed nights that range from rodeo to 1970s schlock on Sun.

Eddie's Attic 515B N McDonough St, Decatur ☎404/377-4976. Offers nightly acoustic music, from traditional fiddlers to contemporary singer-songwriters and occasional stand-up comedy.

Euclid Avenue Yacht Club 1136 Euclid Ave NE ☎404/688-2582. Classic neighborhood bar in Little Five Points, dishing up fine pork barbecue

and Brunswick stew.

Kaya Club & Bistro 1068 Peachtree St NE ☎404/874-4460. Midtown's hottest dance club covers the full spectrum, with Latin, reggae, jazz and hip-hop nights. Closed Sun & Mon.

Manuel's Tavern 602 N Highland Ave NE ☎404/525-3447. Relaxed, studenty neighborhood bar-cum-restaurant near the Carter Center. Wooden benches, ceiling fans and portraits of Jack Kennedy – plus the occasional presence of Jimmy himself.

Masquerade 695 North Ave NE ☎404/577-8178. Groovy grunge/punk hangout in midtown, split into rooms done up as Heaven, Hell and Purgatory, with a big outdoor auditorium. Live bands Wed–Sun.

Star Community Bar 437 Moreland Ave NE ☎404/681-9018. Enjoyable Little Five Points hangout, bursting with Elvis memorabilia, and offering drink and live music/disco. Cover charge. Closed Sun.

Stone Mountain

Just half an hour's drive east of Atlanta, **Stone Mountain State Park** (park daily 6am–midnight; attractions daily spring & summer 10am–9pm, rest of year 10am–5pm; $6 per vehicle) centers around a huge dome of granite with a five-mile circumference. You can climb it in around 45 minutes, or take a cable car to the top, and there are various train rides and so on, but most visitors come to see the massive 90ft by 190ft relief of Confederates Jefferson Davis, Robert E. Lee and Stonewall Jackson. Work on the colossal sculpture was started in 1924 by Gutzon Borglum, who went on to carve Mount Rushmore in South Dakota (see p.829), but was not completed until 1970. Concessions and gift-shops down below supply endless souvenir kitsch, and the nightly lasershow in summer culminates with Elvis's gut-wrenching rendition of *Dixie* (9.30pm; free with entrance to park).

North from Atlanta: the mountains

Atlanta is a short drive from some spectacular **Appalachian mountain scenery**, at its best in October when the leaves turn gold and red. A drive through the mountains on the secondary roads takes you through endless hairpins and narrow passes; Hwy-348 ascends a particularly impressive pass at the White County line, crossed at the top by the **Appalachian Trail**. Of the various towns and villages, **Dahlonega** makes the best base; most of the rest – like **Helen**, 35 miles northeast, now a pseudo-Bavarian village – are either kitsch or downright dull. The region does, however, abound in delightful **state parks**, several of which offer both camping and hotel-style lodges.

Dahlonega

The attractive small town of **DAHLONEGA**, in the Appalachian foothills fifty miles northeast of Atlanta on US-19, owes its origins to the first-ever **Gold Rush** in the US. Benjamin Parks discovered gold at Auraria, six miles south, in 1828; Dahlonega was established five years later, to serve as the seat of Lumpkin County. Within a further five years, enough gold had been unearthed for Dahlonega to acquire its own outpost of the US Mint, which, by the time production was terminated by the Civil War, had produced over $6 million of gold coin. The whole fascinating saga is recounted by videos and displays in the **Gold Museum**, housed in the handsome former courthouse on the main square (Mon–Sat 9am–5pm, Sun 10am–5pm; $3; ☎706/864-2257). You can also pan for gold at various small mines in the area, although you're unlikely to make your fortune. The town hosts one of Appalachia's biggest annual **bluegrass** festivals in the third week of June, and in October the **Gold Rush Days**, a real down-home hoedown, with food, crafts, clogging and music.

Dahlonega's **visitor center** is across from the courthouse (daily 9am–5.30pm; ☎706/864-3711). The *Smith House*, just down from the square at 84 S Chestatee St (☎706/867-7000 or 1-800/852-7564; ❹), is a classic round-table Southern **restaurant**, serving superb all-you-can-eat meals at low prices, and also offering comfortable double **rooms**.

Amicalola Falls State Park

Twenty miles west of Dahlonega on Hwy-52, **Amicalola Falls State Park** (daily 7am–10pm; $2 per vehicle; ☎706/265-4703) focuses on a dramatic multi-tiered waterfall that cascades down a steep wooded hillside. Having driven to the overlook at the top, continue for another half-mile to reach the park's modern **lodge** (☎706/265-8888 or 1-800/864-7275; ❹), which holds comfortable double rooms and a restaurant with panoramic views. For even more seclusion, hike for five miles toward the start of the **Appalachian Trail** from here to reach the *Len Foote Hike Inn* (☎770/389-7275; ❷), accessible only on foot, which offers basic rooms and food; you can also **camp** ($15) or stay in individual guest cabins (❹) closer to the park entrance.

Athens

The small and very likeable city of **ATHENS**, almost seventy miles northeast of Atlanta, is home to the 30,000-plus students of the University of Georgia, and has a liberal feel – and city government – unusual for the South. The compact downtown area north of the campus is alive with book and record stores, clubs, bars, restaurants and cafés; Broad Street in particular is lined with sidewalk tables. It has achieved world fame in recent years as the home of rock groups REM and the B-52s.

Pilgrims drawn by the REM connection will want to head straight for the original home of the **Automatic for the People** slogan – *Weaver D's* soul-food café, well within walking distance east of downtown at 1016 E Broad St (☎706/353-7797). Unaffected by its new sideline in memorabilia, it continues to serve its delicious Southern fried chicken and vegetables on molded styrofoam plates. The band started out playing at the *40 Watt Club*, originally housed at 171 College Ave but now resurrected in its third, and by far its largest, premises at 285 W Washington St (☎706/549-7871), and half-owned by Barrie Buck, wife of guitarist Peter. *Athens Music Factory*, 420 E Clayton (☎706/353-8869), holds a weekly open mic and puts on a "Battle of the Bands" contest each summer, while *Caledonia Lounge*, 256 W Clayton St (☎706/549-5577), is where you can hear new sounds from up-and-coming bands. On the other hand, the big-name bands tend to appear at the *Georgia Theatre*, 215 N Lumpkin St (☎706/353-3405), a converted movie theater that still shows films on quiet nights. You'll find information on all music events in the free weekly *Flagpole*.

Practicalities

Greyhound, based at 220 W Broad St, has a regular service to Atlanta, while the Athens Transit System operates buses around town (every 30min; 75¢ flat fare). The **visitor center** is situated in the city's oldest surviving residence, the Church-Waddel-Brumby House (c.1820), a couple of blocks north of campus at 280 E Dougherty St (Mon–Sat 10am–6pm, Sun 12–6pm; ☎706/353-1820, ⓦ www.visitathensga.com). Ask about their self-guided walking tour leaflet on Athens music history. An excellent ninety-minute bus tour of historic Athens (Classic City Tours; $10; ☎706/208-TOUR, reservations recommended), which includes the Church-Waddel-Brumby House, leaves from the visitor center daily at 2pm.

Lodging can be a problem during graduation or if there's a big football game on. Otherwise, choices include the good-value, business-oriented *Courtyard by Marriott*, 166 Finley St (☎706/369-7000, ⓕ706/548-4224, ⓦ www.courtyard .com/ahncy; ❹); the trusty *Holiday Inn Downtown*, 197 E Broad St (☎706/549-4433, ⓕ706/548-3031, ⓦ www.hi-athens.com; ❹); or *Magnolia Terrace B&B*, 277 Hill St (☎706/548-3860, ⓕ706/369-3439; ❹). For top-quality **food**, your best bet is *Harry Bissett's New Orleans Café & Oyster Bar*, a simulated French Quarter restaurant at 279 E Broad St (☎706/353-7065), or the vegetarian specials at the inexpensive *Grit*, 199 Prince Ave (☎706/543-6592). *Five Star Day Grill* serves good, cheap food in a funky setting; the daily pesto specials are a favorite. Athens has a thriving **bar** scene, although Georgia's blue laws require drinks-only bars to close on Sundays.

Among Athens' most hospitable bars is *The Globe*, 199 N Lumpkin St (closed Sun; ☎706/353-4721), where you can settle into an old rocking chair or leather sofa and select from a huge array of beers. *The Burnstone Brewhouse*, 140 E Washington St (☎706/549-5999), is a first-rate microbrewery with a grill, open seven days a week.

Central Georgia

The broad expanse of **central Georgia**, south of Atlanta, is famous more for its people than for places to see. **Otis Redding**, **James Brown**, **Little Richard** and the **Allman Brothers** were all born here or grew up in the area, while former president **Jimmy Carter** came from little Plains, roughly 120 miles due south of the capital.

Few of its small towns hold much of interest, though vegetable fanatics may enjoy tiny **Juliette**, twenty miles north of Macon, where the *Whistle Stop Café* dishes up the fried green tomatoes of book and movie fame (Mon–Sat 8am–2pm, Sun noon–7pm), and **Vidalia** further east, the self-proclaimed "Sweet Onion Capital of the World." The largest communities are the dull army center of **Columbus** and the likeable town of **Macon**.

Macon

MACON, eighty miles southeast of Atlanta on I-75, where I-16 branches off to the coast, makes an attractive stop en route to Savannah, especially when its 200,000 **cherry trees** erupt with frothy blossoms (celebrated by a festival in the third week of March). As the highest navigable point on the **Ocmulgee River**, Macon was laid out in 1823 and became a major cotton port. Downtown is no longer the commercial center it once was, particularly following the arrival of the huge **Macon Mall** near the intersection of the two freeways, but there are signs, everywhere, of an imminent urban renaissance. Chief among these is the excellent **Georgia Sports Hall of Fame** at 301 Cherry St (Mon–Sat 9am–5pm, Sun 1–5pm; $6; ☎478/752-1585), a handsome, state-of-the-art facility where you'll find an interactive Paralympics exhibit alongside a celebration of the long-standing football rivalry between the University of Georgia and Georgia Tech. Close by, at 355 Martin Luther King Blvd, is the restored **Douglass Theatre** (open for tours Mon–Sat 9am–6pm; donations; ☎478/742-2000), Macon's premier movie theatre and vaudeville hall for African Americans during the Thirties and Forties, hosting such blues greats as Ma Rainey, Ida Cox and Bessie Smith.

Macon was home to **Little Richard**, **Otis Redding** (the frankly unremarkable Otis Redding Memorial Bridge is just east of downtown) and the **Allman Brothers**. Duane Allman and Berry Oakley, killed here in motorcycle smashes in 1971 and 1972 respectively, are buried in **Rose Hill Cemetery** on Riverside Drive, the inspiration for various of the band's songs. That heritage is celebrated in the exuberant **Georgia Music Hall of Fame**, next door to the visitor center at Martin Luther King Jr Boulevard and Walnut Street (Mon–Sat 9am–5pm, Sun 1–5pm; $8; ☎478/750-8555). A huge roster of Georgian musicians are recalled by themed interactive displays that include a Gospel chapel, a rock'n'roll soda shop and a country café. As well as admiring Redding's trademark black sweater and the B-52s' wigs, you can watch footage of Ray Charles singing *Georgia on My Mind* to the state legislature, inspect a photo of James Brown confiding to the pope, and listen to seventy years' worth of jukebox recordings.

One of the best of its kind anywhere, the celebratory **Tubman African-American Museum**, 340 Walnut St (Mon–Sat 9am–5pm, Sun 2–5pm; $3), has a wonderful, eclectic collection, from African drums and textiles – which schoolchildren are encouraged to handle and play with – through intricate quilts, to angry, dazzling avant-garde work. There's a reading area, filled with black studies books, autobiographies and photograph collections, in a room quietly dominated by a heavy iron ankle brace and chain, which visitors are free to touch and lift. Note that the museum expects to move to larger premises sometime in 2003. A few minutes north of town at 4182 Forsyth Rd, the **Museum of Arts and Sciences** (Mon–Thurs & Sat 9am–5pm, Fri 9am–9pm, Sun 1–5pm; $7) is a creative ensemble of interactive exhibits geared toward kids and an indoor "natural habitat" complete with a treehouse from where you can observe animals such as antelope, leopards and deer.

Ocmulgee National Monument

Between 900 and 1100 AD, people of the Mississippian culture migrated from the Mississippi Valley to a spot a couple of miles east of modern downtown Macon, and leveled the site overlooking the Ocmulgee River that is now **OCMULGEE NATIONAL MONUMENT** (daily 9am–5pm; free). Their settlement of thatched huts has vanished, but two grassy mounds, each thought to have been topped by a temple, still rise prominently from the plateau. Near the visitor center, which holds artifacts from excavations in the area, you can enter the underground chamber of a ceremonial **earthlodge**. Modern wooden supports now hold up the roof, replacing the original timbers whose fiery destruction baked the clay floor, thereby preserving a ring of individually molded seats, and a striking bird-shaped altar or dais.

Practicalities

The imposing Terminal Station at the foot of Cherry Street houses Macon's **visitor center** (Mon–Sat 9am–5.30pm; ☎478/743-3401 or 1-800/768-3401, ⓦwww.maconga.com); it's the base for entertaining, customized two-hour **city tours** (Mon–Sat 10am & 2pm; $10).

Although a new Amtrak service is in the works, there are at present no trains to Macon. However, Greyhound provides good connections from 65 Spring St (where Little Richard is said to have written *Tutti Frutti* while washing dishes). Though motels surround the I-475/US-80 interchange, for **accommodation** you'd be better off heading **downtown.** If you want to bask in southern hospitality, you can do no better than the grand *1842 Inn*, 353 College St (☎478/741-1842; ❼), which throws in complimentary hors d'ouevres, as well as a full Southern breakfast in its lovely courtyard. Otherwise, there's the renovated *Crowne Plaza*, 108 First St (☎478/746-1461; ❹), which also has a very fine **restaurant**. The atmospheric, wood-paneled *Len Berg's*, at 240 Old Post Office Alley off Walnut Street (☎478/742-9255), serves down-home Southern lunches at bargain prices. For a true Southern **barbecue** experience drive 45 minutes north of town to the original *Fresh Air Barbecue*, on US-23 (☎478/775-3182): a roadside shack serving pork that's been hickory-smoked for 24 hours, along with succulent Brunswick stew and crisp coleslaw. You can hear live music at the bar/restaurant *The Rookery*, 543 Cherry St (☎478/746-8658), and at *Riverfront Blues*, 550 Riverside Drive (☎478/741-9970), but the most popular nightspot is the *Tic-Toc Room*, 408 Martin Luther King Blvd (☎478/744-0123), the former stomping ground of Redding and Little Richard.

Savannah

American towns don't come much nicer than **SAVANNAH**, seventeen miles up the Savannah River from the ocean, on the border with South Carolina. The appealing **Historic District**, ranged around Spanish-moss-swathed squares, formed the core of the original city, and today boasts examples of just about every architectural style of the eighteenth and nineteenth centuries, while the atmospheric cobbled waterfront on the **Savannah River**, key to the postwar economy, is edged by towering old cotton warehouses.

Savannah was founded in 1733 by James Oglethorpe as the first settlement of the new British colony of Georgia. His intention was to establish a haven for debtors, with no Catholics, lawyers or hard liquor, and above all, no slaves. However, with the arrival of North Carolinan settlers in the 1750s, plantation agriculture, based on slave labor, thrived. The town became a major export center, at the end of important railroad lines by which **cotton** was funneled from far away in the South. Sherman arrived here in December 1864 at the end of his March to the Sea; he offered the town to Abraham Lincoln as a Christmas gift, but at Lincoln's urging left it intact and set to work apportioning land to freed slaves. This was the first recognition of the need for "reconstruction," though such concrete economic provision for slaves was rarely to occur again.

The plantations floundered after the Civil War; cotton prices slumped, and Savannah went into decline. There was little industry beyond the port, and as that fell into disuse and decay, so too did Savannah's graceful townhouses and tree-lined boulevards. Not until the 1960s did local citizens start to organize what has been, on the whole, the successful restoration of their town – recently, and tentatively, extended to the predominantly black **Victorian District**.

Savannah has acquired a new notoriety of late thanks to its starring role in John Berendt's best-selling *Midnight in the Garden of Good and Evil*; both book and movie detailed a delicious brew of cross-dressing, voodoo and murder. For a sense of what goes on behind closed doors in the city, it's an unbeatable read, and locals delight in making dark hints as to how much they knew, or even did, themselves. If you want to look behind the closed doors for yourself, however, few locations in "The Book" – as it's universally known – are open to the public, and none is likely to satisfy your curiosity.

Arrival, information and getting around

Savannah's **airport**, served by several major airlines, is eight miles west of the city. A taxi to downtown costs around $20. The **bus station** is on the western edge of downtown at 610 W Oglethorpe Ave, while the **train station** is about three miles southwest, at 2611 Seaboard Coastline Drive. The latter isn't served by buses; a taxi from the station to downtown usually costs about $8.

The Historic District is best explored on foot, but if you want to get further out, Chatham Area Transit (CAT; ☎912/233-5767) operates a reasonable **bus** network (75¢) and a free **trolley** service that runs between downtown, the visitor center and the city market. Route maps are available from the **visitor center**, 301 Martin Luther King Jr Blvd (Mon–Fri 8.30am–5pm, Sat & Sun 9am–5pm; ☎912/944-0455 or 1-877/SAVANNAH, ⊛www.savannahvisit.com), which also has accommodation discount coupons and sells $8 DayPasses that entitle visitors to unlimited **parking** at all city meters and garages for two days. In addition, the visitor center can provide details of countless **walking tours**, and serves as the starting point for several different **trolley tours**, costing around $17–23 per hour. For $17, you can also join leisurely, breezier **horse-and-carriage tours**, most romantic by moonlight (☎912/236-6756). The best **black heritage tours** are run by the King-Tisdell Cottage (see p.545), while **river cruises** start from behind City Hall, for $14.95 and up (☎912/232-6404). **Bicycles** can be rented from Bicycle Link, 22 W Broughton St (☎912/233-9401).

Accommodation

By far the most appealing places to stay in Savannah are the central **B&Bs** in elegant private houses, but for those on a tight budget the usual insalubrious **hotels** congregate on and around Boundary Street near the Greyhound station, and there are chain **motels** further out on Ogeechee Road (US-17). The Last Minute Rooms service can arrange fifty percent discounts on one-night stays if you call on the day (☎912/238–1389).

The nearest **campground** is six miles southeast, at Skidaway Island State Park ($16 tents, $18 RVs; ☎912/598–2300), a barrier or "sea" island, with an interesting combination of salt- and freshwater habitats.

Bed and Breakfast Inn 117 W Gordon St at Chatham Square ☎912/238-0518, ☎912/233-2537. Great-value B&B in 1853 townhouse overlooking a shady square – reservations are essential. ⑥

Days Inn 201 W Bay St ☎912/236-4440, ☎912/232-2725, ⓦwww.daysinn.com. The most affordable hotel in the Historic District, if lacking the character of the B&Bs. ⑥

The Granite Steps 126 E Gaston St ☎912/233-5380, ☎912/236-3116, ⓦwww.granitesteps.com. Very friendly B&B with grand communal rooms, an enchanting courtyard with antiques in every suite. ⑨

Hamilton-Turner Inn 350 Abercorn St ☎912/233-1833 or 888/448-8849, ⓦwww.hamilton-turnerinn.com. Charming 1873 French Second Empire-style B&B once owned by "Mandy" from the book *Midnight in the Garden of Good and Evil*. ⑦

HI-Savannah 304 E Hall St ☎912/236-7744, ☎912/236-7744. Modernized youth hostel in a historic building, four blocks back from the river, with $16 dorms and a few basic private rooms (②); daytime lockout, but no curfew. Closed Dec, Jan & Feb.

Magnolia Place 503 Whitaker St ☎912/236-7674 or 1-800/238-7674, ⓦwww.magnoliaplaceinn.com. Well-appointed B&B with a gorgeous veranda overlooking Forsyth Park; however, the rooms have seen better days. ⑦

The Mulberry 601 E Bay St ☎912/238-1200, ☎912/236-2184, ⓦwww.savannahghotels.com. Friendly Holiday Inn-owned hotel with a B&B feel (free iced tea and cookies in the lounge). Rooftop jacuzzi, courtyard and luxurious riverview rooms. ⑤

The Town

Savannah's **Historic District** is flanked by the river, Martin Luther King Jr Boulevard in the west and, to the east, Broad Street, the old commercial main street, now a series of boarded-up stores and offices. Broughton Street has since become the main thoroughfare of downtown Savannah. You can get an overview at the **Savannah History Museum**, behind the visitor center, in the restored Railroad Station at 303 Martin Luther King Jr Blvd (daily 9am–5pm; $3), where an informative jaunt through Native American culture, colonial development, the river and the Civil War is let down slightly by a slide show that is less a history lesson than a hard-sell promotion of Savannah's considerable charms. A block south, the **Historic Railroad Shops** (daily 9am–4pm) is a worthwhile slice of industrial architecture.

The best way to get a feel for the place is simply to wander the "tabby" streets – made from a kind of primitive concrete mashed up with oyster shells – lined with shuttered Federal, Regency and antebellum houses adorned with intricate iron balconies, and intriguing details such as false "earthquake decorations." These sturdy iron rods embedded in the walls served no purpose, but were placed there simply to keep up with elegant South Carolina neighbor Charleston in architectural cachet. Note, too, the preponderance of light blue houses, washed in buttermilk and indigo to keep the ghosts away. The shady residential **squares**, ablaze with dogwood trees, azaleas and magnolias, offer peaceful respite from the blistering summer heat. Forrest Gump told his life story from a bench in **Chippewa Square**, but eager movie-buffs will find an imposing statue of James Oglethorpe, and no such bench.

Most visitors take in one or two of Savannah's old **mansions**, such as the

SAVANNAH

Savannah River

RIVERFRONT PLAZA Ⓐ

RIVER STREET Ⓑ

WILLIAMSON ST.

FACTORS WALK

W. BAY ST. Ⓐ Ⓒ E. BAY ST. Ⓓ

First African Baptist Church

W. BRYAN ST. E. BRYAN ST.

FRANKLIN SQUARE Ⓔ CITY MARKET

JOHNSON SQUARE REYNOLDS SQUARE Ⓒ WARREN SQUARE WASHINGTON SQUARE

Ⓕ Ⓖ Ⓗ W. CONGRESS ST. Ⓘ E. CONGRESS ST.

W. BROUGHTON ST. E. BROUGHTON ST.

Owens-Thomas House

Davenport House

W. STATE ST. E. STATE ST.

Telfair Museum of Art

TELFAIR SQUARE WRIGHT SQUARE OGLETHORPE SQUARE COLUMBIA SQUARE GREENE SQUARE

W. YORK ST. E. YORK ST.

W. OGLETHORPE AVE. E. OGLETHORPE AVE.

Second African Baptist Church

Civic Center

W. HULL ST. E. HULL ST. CRAWFORD SQUARE

ORLEANS SQUARE CHIPPEWA SQUARE E. HULL ST.

W. PERRY ST. E. PERRY ST.

Colonial Park Cemetery

Ⓙ

W. LIBERTY ST. E. LIBERTY ST.

Savannah History Museum

W. HARRIS ST. E. HARRIS ST.

PULASKI SQUARE MADISON SQUARE LAFAYETTE SQUARE TROUP SQUARE

Green-Meldrim House

W. CHARLTON ST. E. CHARLTON ST.

Ⓚ W. JONES ST. E. JONES ST.

CHATHAM SQUARE MONTEREY SQUARE CALHOUN SQUARE WHITEFIELD SQUARE

W. TAYLOR ST. E. TAYLOR ST.

Ⓛ

W. GORDON ST. E. GORDON ST.

Ⓞ Ⓢ Massie Heritage Interpretation Center Ⓞ

King-Tisdell Cottage

W. GASTON ST. E. GASTON ST.

Forsyth Park

W. HUNTINGDON ST. E. HUNTINGDON ST. Ⓞ

N

0 250 yds

Macon 16

ACCOMMODATION			
Bed and Breakfast Inn	4	HI-Savannah	8
Days Inn	1	Magnolia Place	5
The Gastonian	7	The Mulberry	2
The Granite Steps	6	Planters Inn	3

RESTAURANTS AND BARS			
606 East Café	G	Mrs Wilkes' Boarding House	K
Bistro Savannah	E	Nita's Place	L
Gallery Espresso	J	The Pirate's House	D
Garibaldi's	H	Savannah Blues	F
Huey's	A	The Shrimp Factory	B
Moon River Brewing Co	C	Velvet Elvis	I

English architect William Jay's neoclassical Regency style **Owen-Thomas House**, 124 Abercorn St (tours Mon noon–5pm, Tues–Sat 10am–5pm, Sun 2–5pm; $8; ☏912/233-9743), or the redbrick Georgian **Davenport House**, 324 E State St (Mon–Fri 10am–4.30pm, Sat 1pm-4.30pm; $4; ☏912/236-8097). The latter, the first restoration project of the Historic Savannah Foundation, is sparsely furnished but boasts a wonderful elliptical staircase and delicate plasterwork. The **Green-Meldrim House**, on Madison Square (Tues & Thurs–Sat 10am–4pm; $5; ☏912/232-1251), is a splendid Gothic Revival mansion with dramatic ironwork, which General Sherman used as his headquarters. At the southern edge of the Historic District, the **Massie Heritage Interpretation Center**, 207 E Gordon St (Mon–Fri 9am–4pm;

$3), is a simple, effective museum illuminating Savannah's architecture with displays on its neighborhoods and growth, and tracing influences from as far away as London and Beijing. While you can't go inside, the **Mercer House** on picturesque Monterey Square nearby is one of the grandest of the city's mansions and featured prominently in "The Book." Also worth a visit is another of Jay's Regency mansions, the **Telfair Museum of Art**, 124 Abercorn St (Mon noon–5pm, Tues–Sat 10am–5pm, Sun 1–5pm; $8, Sundays free; ☎912/232-1177), which also has the distinction of being the oldest art museum in the South.

Though the Spanish moss of the city proper may be redolent of the Old South, Savannah's **waterfront** area, at the foot of a steep little bluff below Bay Street and reached by assorted stone staircases and atmospheric alleyways, retains the look and feel of an eighteenth-century European port. The main thoroughfare, **River Street**, is cobbled with the ballast carried by long-vanished sailing ships, while its tall brick cotton warehouses are said to be haunted by the ghosts of the slave stevedores. It's now a lively commercial district, lined with seafood restaurants and salty bars that heave with partying crowds on Saturday nights; as certain businesses target themselves ever more directly toward the "Spring Break" student crowd, however, some of its former charm is being lost. Looking out over the water from the paved **Riverfront Plaza** across the way you can appreciate just how busy the port still is.

As the one-time point of entry for many of Georgia's slaves, Savannah has a strong **black history**. The predominantly black **Victorian District**, southeast of downtown, is being slowly restored, and has a couple of good, if underfunded, museums. The nerve center of the restoration process is the **King-Tisdell Cottage**, 514 E Huntingdon St, owned by a middle-class black family c.1900 (Tues–Fri noon–4.30pm, Sat 1–4pm; $3; ☎912/234-8000). In addition to a fine collection of *gullah* baskets and African woodcarving, it illustrates the history of slaves and free blacks before the Civil War, and of the freed slaves after, commemorating Savannah's role as the site of Sherman's famous "**Field Order #15**," which granted each freed slave forty acres and a mule. The museum also operates excellent **black heritage tours** (leaving from the visitor center, Mon–Sat 1pm & 3pm; $15; call a day in advance on ☎912/234-8000). The two-hour tours take in the **Second African Baptist Church**, 123 Houston St, where Field Order #15 was signed; the poor black **Yamacraw** neighborhood, now sadly run-down and depressed; and the 1777 **First African Baptist Church**, the oldest black church in North America, built by slaves. This last, at 23 Montgomery St in the Historic District, can also be visited independently (daily 10am–2pm). Note the decorative carvings by the pews and diamond-shaped holes in the floor, ventilation for slaves escaping on the Underground Railroad. Back in the Victorian District, the airy **Beach Institute**, 502 E Harris St (Tues–Sat noon–5pm; $3.50), Georgia's first school for freed slaves, today houses an African-American art gallery with a permanent display of extraordinary woodcarvings by folk artist Ulysses Davis.

A ten-minute drive east from Savannah will take you to the lovely **Bonaventure Cemetery** (dusk to dawn), swathed in trees and sloping down to the Wilmington River. The final resting place of luminaries such as Johnny Mercer and Conrad Aiken, it's also a major sight in "The Book" and written about there to great effect. Sylvia Shaw Judson's *Bird Girl* statue, which graces the cover and used to be situated here, has since been moved to the Telfair Museum of Art (see above).

Eating

Savannah has a large number of **restaurants**, with some great seafood places on the **riverfront**. The **City Market**, a couple of blocks south of W Factors Walk, is also a prime restaurant district, with a clutch of stylish New American places.

Bistro Savannah 309 W Congress St ☏912/233-6266. Near the City Market, the mainly seafood menu here is worthy of more expensive restaurants.

City Market Café 224 W St Julian St ☏912/ 236-7133. A good lunch stop; try the excellent sandwiches.

Gallery Espresso 6 E Liberty St ☏912/233-5348. Dim, arty, super-hip coffee bar with exquisite cakes, crumpets and muffins, vegetarian food and soup, along with the best coffee in town (try the Iced Thai) and wine. Open until 11pm.

Garibaldi's 315 W Congress St ☏912/232-7118. Lovely decor – cherry-red walls, pressed tin ceiling, fairy lights and gold mirrors – with a chatty crowd and great Northern Italian dishes, *nouvelle cuisine* and seafood. The specialty is grilled flounder, deliciously succulent with a crispy coating. Serves dinner only.

Huey's 115 E River St ☏912/234-7385. Riverfront restaurant serving excellent, authentic Cajun/Creole food; go straight for the Oysters Rockefeller. Live music wafts in from the adjoining bar, and there's a jazz brunch at weekends.

Moon River Brewing Co 21 W Bay St ☏912/447-0943. Brewpub near the riverfront, with solid American food and a good beer selection.

Mrs Wilkes' Boarding House 107 W Jones St ☏912/232-5997. Savannah's most famous eating place, a real Southern experience run by the redoubtable Mrs Wilkes, and serving all-you-can-eat breakfasts (8–9am; $6) and lunches (11am–3pm; $12) only. Everyone sits around large tables, helping themselves to delicious mounds of fried chicken, sweet potatoes, spinach, beans and spaghetti. There's no sign outside; just get there early and join the line.

Nita's Place 129 E Broughton St ☏912/238-8233. Friendly soul-food restaurant at the eastern edge of downtown, open for lunch only with an $8 fried chicken special.

The Shrimp Factor 313 E River St ☏912/236-4229. Good and unusual shrimp dishes on the waterfront, with typical entrees like Shrimp Stuffed Savannah for $21.95.

Voo-Doo Café 321 Habersham ☏912/447-1999. Arty café serving a full range of Spanish/ American fare.

Entertainment and nightlife

Savannah's **nightlife** is laid-back, if unusually strict about requiring ID. Everything is fairly close together, ranged between the City Market and the river. There's an annual **jazz festival** in late September. For information on this or other jazz events and venues, contact the Coastal Jazz Association at ☏912/232-2222; for **listings**, read the free *Creative Loafing* newspaper.

Club One 1 Jefferson St ☏912/232-0200. Gay club, where drag acts occasionally include Lady Chablis, from "The Book."

The Pirate's House, *Hannah's East/45 South* 20 E Broad St ☏912/233-5757. Cool jazz in an informal atmosphere. Jazz veteran Ben Tucker plays with a variety of big names after 9pm upstairs in *Hannah's East*. For American fine dining head for the *45 South* room.

Rail Pub 405 W Congress St ☏912/238-1311. Lively, endearingly shabby multilevel bar frequented by a young crowd near the market.

Savannah Blues 411 W Congress St ☏912/447-5044. City Market club that features live blues nightly from 10pm.

606 East Café 319 W Congress St ☏912/233-2887. Funky student hangout with dance floor, pool tables and drag acts, as well as inexpensive entrees ($6–16).

Velvet Elvis 127 W Congress St ☏912/236-0665. Vintage beerhall, decorated to match the name, near City Market. Live jazz, indie rock, ska or R&B Wed–Sat, plus a "Steamy Seafood Patio" serving salads and shellfish.

Out from Savannah

Tybee Island, eighteen miles east of the city on US-80, is served by three daily C&H buses (☏912/232-7099) from the Civic Center in Savannah. Here you'll find Savannah's best – and not too overdeveloped – **beach**, as well as a 154ft lighthouse, at 30 Meddin Drive, dating from 1736, and a small museum housed in a nearby gun battery (summer daily except Tues 9am–5.30pm; rest of year Mon & Wed–Fri noon–4pm, Sat & Sun 10am–4pm; $4). To get there take a left turn just before the beach. Abundant **accommodation** options include the *DeSoto Beach Hotel*, 212 Butler Ave (℡912/786-4542, ℗912/786-4543, ⓦwww.desotobeachhotel.com; ❺), yet another sight from "The Book." For great **Low Country food**, head for *The Crab Shack*, at 40 Estill Hammock Rd, Chimney Creek (℡912/786-9857), where you can dine on delicious crabs and shrimp in an old shack by the creek – worth a visit if you can find it. Take a right turn off the main road to the beach, about two miles before you reach the lighthouse turnoff. *Spanky's Beachside* at 1605 Strand Ave (℡912/786-5520) has live music at weekends.

FORT PULASKI NATIONAL MONUMENT, off US-80 E en route to Tybee Island, is the most interesting of several local forts (daily 8.30am–6.45pm; $2). An impressive Confederate stronghold, set on its own idyllic if rather buggy little island and ringed by a moat inhabited by the occasional alligator, it was nevertheless taken by Union troops, the first masonry fortress to be pierced by rifled cannon fire.

Ten miles south of Savannah at 7601 Skidaway Rd, **Wormsloe State Historic Site** (Tues–Sat 9am–5pm, Sun 2–5.30pm; $3; ℡912/353-3023) is the site of an eighteenth-century defensive plantation. The atmospheric tabby ruins of the fortified house of British settler Noble Jones are now overgrown with palms and lush forest. Inside the house, a museum covers the early settlement of Savannah, with archeological finds and demonstrations of the skills and crafts of the first settlers. Much of the Georgia coast is taken up by a string of **National Wildlife Refuges**, on the small marshy islands that make up the **barrier island chain**. It's well worth detouring or backtracking along the quiet side roads to cross to **Blackbeard Island**, **Wolf Island**, **Pinckney** or **Wassaw**, where tranquil swamps are filled with nesting birds and offer great fishing.

Brunswick and the southern coast

BRUNSWICK, the one sizeable settlement south of Savannah, is a hop-off point for the offshore **sea islands**. It's not in itself very exciting, although the shrimp docks can be quite interesting when the catch is brought in. The wonderful *Hostel in the Forest*, reached via an inconspicuous muddy driveway on the south side of US-82, is a couple of miles west of I-95 exit 6 (℡912/264-9738, no reservations); it charges $15 per night for dorm beds in a geodesic dome and for lodging in a few treehouses. In the unlikely event you'll need to stay in town, the **visitor center**, 4 Glynn Ave (daily 8.30am–5pm; ℡912/265-0620), has lists of budget **motels** and central **B&Bs**, such as the comfortable *Rose Manor Guest House*, 1108 Richmond St (℡912/267-6369; ❹). The best **food** nearby, in an unlikely setting next to a gas station at exit 6 on I-95, not far from the hostel, is at the superlative *Georgia Pig* (℡912/264-6664), where luscious smoky barbecue comes with the local Brunswick stew, coleslaw, honey-flavored baked beans and fragrant sauce.

The **Hofwyl–Broadfield Plantation**, ten miles north of Brunswick on US-17, gives a vivid idea of life under slavery (Tues–Sat 9am–5pm, Sun 2–5.30pm; $3.50). A good exhibit covers the rice cultivation that made the planters so wealthy, and you can see the surprisingly modest plantation house where their descendants lived until the 1970s. Occasional **gospel** concerts are held here on summer Saturdays, with soul food on sale.

The sea islands

Several of Georgia's **SEA ISLANDS**, like those of South Carolina, were divided among freed slaves after the Civil War. They remained poor, agricultural communities, however, and little now remains from those years for an outsider to see. Today they make handy alternatives to Florida as seashore breaks for tired inlanders.

Jekyll Island

The **southern islands** are the most developed, largely due to **JEKYLL ISLAND**, originally bought in 1887 for use as an exclusive "club" by a group of millionaires, among them the Rockefellers, Pulitzers, Macys and Vanderbilts, whose opulent residences are still standing, though in a perpetual state of refurbishment. There's a small **Welcome Center** on the causeway, but the **museum orientation center** (daily 9am–5pm; ☎912/635-4036) gives a more useful overview of the island's history and runs guided tours on the hour of the mansions for $10; to get there, turn left after paying the toll, then head along Riverview Drive onto Stable Road. It's in the middle of the "historic district" that centers on the **Radisson**, the original club building, which is now the **Jekyll Island Club** (☎912/635-2600, ℉912/635-2818, ⓦwww.jekyllclub.com; ❻). There are plenty of **accommodation** options strung along Beachview Drive next to the ocean: the *Ramada*, at no. 150 S Beachview Drive (☎912/635-2111 or 1-800/835-2110, ℉912/635-2758; ❹), has ocean views and a big Georgia-shaped pool. There's a **campground** a little further north (☎912/635-3021; $13), near the nesting sites of loggerhead turtles.

St Simon's Island and Cumberland Island

Most of **ST SIMON'S ISLAND**, reached across a green marsh inhabited by wading birds (35¢ toll), is still an evocative landscape of marshes, palms and live oaks covered with Spanish moss. The tiny village is pleasantly quiet, little more than a handful of T-shirt shops and cafés, with a small coastal museum, **St Simon's Island Museum** (Mon–Sat 10am–5pm, Sun 1.30–5pm; $4; ☎912/638-4666), concentrating on local events. You can rent **kayaks** at Southeast Adventures (☎912/638-6732), which also runs bird- and dolphin-watching tours. The beach by the village is not safe for swimming due to fierce currents, but the sand is nice and firm for strolling. The best swimming is on the east side of the island, where the flat, fine sand stretches out for miles. **FORT FREDERICA NATIONAL MONUMENT**, seven miles north of the causeway (summer daily 8am–5pm; $5; ☎912/638-3639), was built in 1736 by General Oglethorpe as the largest British fort in North America; it's now an atmospheric ruin.

As well as a number of **resorts**, the nicest of which is *Sea Palms*, 5445 Frederica Rd (☎912/638-3351 or 1-800/841-6268, ℉912/634-8029, ⓦwww.seapalms.com; ❹), with atmospheric rooms overlooking the marshes, **accommodation** options include *Saint Simon's Inn*, 609 Beachview Drive (☎912/638-1101, ℉912/638-0943, ⓦwww.stsimonsinn.com; ❸), just a block from the beach near the village. By far the best place to **eat** on the island is *Frannie's Place Restaurant*, 318 Mallery St, famed for its exceptional Brunswick stew; try also the specialty sandwiches, crabcakes and to-die-for desserts. At the **Sea Island Festival** in late August, you can hear traditional music and see folk crafts being made (☎912/638-9014).

To the south, **CUMBERLAND ISLAND** is a stunning wildlife refuge of marshes, beaches and semitropical forest roamed by wild horses, with the odd deserted planter's mansion. You can get there by ferry from the village of St Mary's, to the south near the Florida border (summer daily trips out at 9am & 11.45am, back at 10.15am, 2.45pm & 4.45pm; rest of year Thurs–Mon, trips out at 9am & 11.45am, back at 10.15am & 4.45pm; 45min; $16).

Okefenokee Swamp

The dense semitropical **OKEFENOKEE SWAMP** stretches over thirty miles down to Florida from a point roughly thirty miles southwest of Brunswick. Tucked away among its astonishing profusion of luxuriant plants and trees are something like 20,000 alligators, over thirty species of snake, as well as bears and pumas. You can only get in at the **Okefenokee Swamp Park**, a private charity-owned concession at the northeast end, on Hwy-177, off US-23/1, not served by public transportation (June–Aug daily 9am–6.30pm; Sept–May daily 9am–5.30pm; $14–18; ☎912/283-0583). Admission includes an hour and a half boat tour through the swamp (slick yourself with bug repellent), a serpentarium, a good interpretive center on wildlife, an observation tower, reconstructed pioneer buildings – and a lot of placid alligators sunning themselves in oblivious bliss.

Unlovely **WAYCROSS**, ten miles north, holds bargain **motels** such as the *Pinecrest*, 1761 Memorial Drive (☎912/283-3580; ❶). The town's **Okefenokee Heritage Center**, 1460 N Augusta Ave (Tues–Sun 9am–5pm; $4), has occasional displays on the history of the swamp.

Kentucky

Two hundred years after it was wrested from the Native Americans, **KENTUCKY** still hasn't quite made up its mind as to whether it belongs in the North or the South. Both the rival presidents in the Civil War, Abraham Lincoln and Jefferson Davis, were born here, and divisions were acute between slave-owning farmers and the merchants who depended on trade with the nearby cities of the industrial North. Officially neutral, seventy thousand Kentuckians joined the Union army and forty thousand the Confederates. After the war Kentucky sided with the South in its hostility to Reconstruction, and since then it has remained solidly Democrat.

Kentucky's rugged beauty is at its most appealing in the mountainous **east** and the small historic towns of the **Bluegrass Downs**, with visits enlivened by the varied attractions of bourbon whiskey, thoroughbred horses and bluegrass music. **Louisville**, home of the **Kentucky Derby**, is a busy manufacturing and arts center; the more reserved **Lexington**, eighty miles east, is a major horse-breeding market.

Getting around Kentucky

Kentucky's limited **public transportation** can be a real headache. There's full Greyhound service along the interstates south of Louisville and Lexington (and both have surprisingly good city transportation), but a lot of ground is left uncovered. Amtrak doesn't operate here at all. **Cycling** is a pleasant and manageable option; if you're **driving**, be sure to keep small change for the tolls on the state highways. Lexington has its own small airport, but it's also within easy reach of the airport for Cincinnati, Ohio, which is in Covington, Kentucky (see p.315). Louisville is served by Louisville International Airport.

Lexington, Bluegrass and eastern Kentucky

The fertile **Bluegrass Downs**, just eighty miles across, form the base of America's thoroughbred racing industry, with **Lexington** quietly prospering at its heart. The name comes from the unique steel-blue sheen of the buds in the meadows, only visible in early morning during April and May. Kentucky's first white pioneers, who trekked in the 1770s through the 150 miles of wilderness now called the **Daniel Boone National Forest**, were amazed to find this "Eden" deserted while the Indians lived in much less attractive terrain. Anthropologists have now discovered that the area's twelfth-century inhabitants were plagued by fatal bone diseases, due to mineral deficiencies in the soil.

Around modern Lexington are some of the oldest towns west of the Alleghenies. However, amid the fine scenery of the **Natural Bridge** and **Cumberland Gap** districts, eastern Kentucky suffers from acute rural poverty.

Lexington

The productivity of the bluegrass fields has kept **LEXINGTON**'s economy ticking over since 1775, though its lack of a navigable river always made its traders vulnerable to competition from Louisville. Eighty miles east of Louisville and ninety south of Cincinnati, Ohio, it still retains large numbers of fine antebellum houses. However, its current affluence dates from after World War I, when smoking caught on internationally and Lexington emerged as the world's largest burley **tobacco** market. Despite a population now exceeding 200,000, the city maintains an almost rustic atmosphere, with its most conspicuous activity the **horse** trade.

Arrival and information

Lexington's **airport** is six miles west of town on US-60 W, near Keeneland racetrack (handy for the jets of the horse-breeders). Greyhound drops off about a mile from downtown at 477 New Circle Rd – take bus #3 across the street from the bus station, in front of Wal-Mart, to get downtown. Lex-Tran (℡859/253-4636) operates a good service from downtown to the university and suburbs, but you need a car to reach the horse-related attractions. The **visitor center** is in the Civic Center at 301 E Vine St (Mon–Fri 8.30am–5pm, Sat 10am–5pm, Sundays June–Aug noon–5pm; ℡859/233-7299 or 1-800/845-3959, ⓦwww.visitlex.com). Check the free *ACE Weekly* for local events.

Accommodation

Lexington has very little accommodation to offer downtown, but budget **motels** can be found around the exits from I-75. If you're stuck, the visitor center (see above) helps find rooms. The best **campground** (℡859/233-4303, Ⅎ859/255-2690) is at the Horse Park ($18 per site).

Brand House B&B 461 N Limestone St ☎859/226-9464 or 1-800/366-4942, ℗859/367-0470, ⓦwww.brandhouselex.com. Immaculately restored antebellum house with modern amenities (including a pool table) and warm hospitality. Five blocks from the center of Lexington. ❼

Holiday Inn 1950 Newtown Pike ☎859/233-0512, ℗859/231-9285, ⓦwww.hilexingtonnorth .com. Vast, ranch-style affiliate of the *Holiday Inn* chain. Includes a swimming pool, badminton court and gym. ❺

Homewood B&B 5301 Bethel Rd ☎859/255-2814, ℗859/231-8681. Set on a 21-acre horse farm, this is an appealing rural retreat. ❺

La Quinta 1919 Stanton Way, junction of I-64 & I-75, exit 115 ☎859/231-7551, ℗859/281-6002. Handily placed motel with comfortable rooms and free cold-buffet breakfast. ❸

University of Kentucky 700 Woodland Ave ☎859/257-3721, ℗859/323-1900. A few fully equipped rooms available for short stays through the academic year, and plenty more during summer. ❶

Downtown Lexington

The plush hotels, glass office blocks, skywalks and shopping malls of Lexington's city center, set in a dip on the Bluegrass Downs, crowd in on fountain-filled **Triangle Park**. Despite its age, the city has few buildings of architectural interest; the early merchants threw up mostly functional structures, preferring to get on with making money. The redbrick, ivy-covered buildings of small 1780 **Transylvania University** are behind the Courthouse at N Broadway and Third Street (the name means "across the woods," an appropriate description of Kentucky at the time). On the other side of downtown, the **University of Kentucky Art Museum**, in the Singletary Center for the Arts at Rose Street and Euclid Avenue (Tues–Sun noon–5pm, Fri noon–8pm; free; ☎859/257-5716) displays contemporary American art and Native American artifacts.

The best photo opportunity comes in the form of **Thoroughbred Park**, at Main Street and Midland Avenue, an impressive life-size bronze sculpture of a horse race in progress.

Lexington's horses

Along **Paris** and **Ironworks pikes**, northeast of Lexington, in an idyllic Kentuckian landscape, sleek thoroughbred horses cavort in bluegrass meadows. Some farms are still staked out by miles of immaculate white-plank fences, though most now use the cheaper but much less attractive black creosote to protect the wood. You can watch the horses' early-morning workouts at **Keeneland racetrack** to the west (April–Oct daily dawn–10am; free; ☎859/254-3412 or 1-800/456-3412), and then eat a super-cheap breakfast at the adjacent *Keeneland Kitchen*. Tasteful dark-green grandstands emphasize the crisp white rails around the one-mile oval track. Until recently there was no public address system, which made for a unique atmosphere, with thousands of puzzled voices trying to work out which horse was which, breaking into cheers as they hurtled into the final furlong; even today, coverage is muted, in keeping with Keeneland tradition (racing for 3 weeks in April Tues–Sun 7.30pm; and 3 weeks in Oct Wed–Sun 1pm; call for reserved tickets; $3.50–25; ☎859/288-4299).

Tours of horse farms used to be very popular, but some owners have become reluctant to let the public get too close to the shy creatures. There are a handful of farms that allow visits; most are free, but you should tip the groom. One choice is **Calumet Farm** off Versailles Road (Mon & Wed 1.30pm, Fri 10.30am; free; ☎859/231-8272). **Three Chimneys** on Old Frankfort Pike is about fifteen minutes west of downtown and offers tours by appointment only (☎859/873-7053). Alternatively, try the comprehensive **Blue Grass Tours** (March–Oct 9am & 1.30pm, Nov–Feb by appointment only; $25; ☎859/252-5744 or 1-800/755-6956, ⓦwww.bluegrasstours.com), whose three-hour itinerary includes a stop at a private farm, a drive through another, and a visit to Keeneland racetrack and other horse-related areas. The **Thoroughbred Center**, 3380 Paris Pike (Mon–Fri tours 9am, 10.30am & 1pm; Sat 9am & 10.30am; ☎859/293-1853), allows you to watch trainers at work.

The enjoyable **Kentucky Horse Park** is a little further along at 4089 Ironworks Parkway (April–Oct daily 9am–5pm; rest of year Wed–Sun 9am–5pm; $10). Its museum traces the use of horses throughout history, from Roman chariot races through cavalry regiments, commercial haulage and modern sports. The 1032-acre park also features live specimens of over thirty different breeds and a working farm, and offers guided horseback rides ($14). Experienced equestrians can ride unsupervised or inexperienced with a guide at Whispering Woods, in Georgetown ($20 per hour; call ☎502/570-9663 for reservations).

Eating, drinking and nightlife

Lexington's large student population means it has several lively, youth-oriented **eating places**, besides the steakhouses catering for the horse crowd and conventioneers. Fast-food cafés, open until early evening, fill the third floor of central **Festival Market**, at Main Street and Broadway; the streets around the back hold a few lively bars, which flourish despite the Baptist-inspired 1am curfew on drinking places.

Alfalfa Restaurant 557 S Limestone St ☎859/253-0014. Hippy-ish café near the University of Kentucky. A wide range of inexpensive international food, with vegetarian dishes. Live music some nights and rotating art exhibits. Open until 9pm on weeknights, 10pm weekends.
Atomic Café, 265 N Limestone St ☎859/254-1969. Fun ambience with good spicy food and potent cocktails. Live reggae Thurs–Sat.
Cheapside Bar & Grill 131 Cheapside St ☎859/254-0046. Tasty food, a nice patio and good local bands make this a very popular downtown meeting spot.
Ed and Fred's Desert Moon 148 Grand Blvd

☎859/231-1161. Wacky decor, good Southwestern food and pizza. If driving, though, be careful where you park, to avoid getting towed.
Furlong's 735 E Main St ☎859/266-9000. Great tasting, reasonably priced Cajun cuisine.
Kentucky Theatre 214 E Main St ☎859/231-6997. Evocatively restored 1920s movie palace showing offbeat and art-house films, as well as being a great venue for rock, blues and jazz concerts. Also serves alcohol and decent snacks.
Ramsey's Diner 496 E High St ☎859/259-2708. Very popular and atmospheric with tasty sandwiches, burgers and meals for $4–8. Cheap snacks available from the bar after 10.30pm. Open until 1am.

Bluegrass country

Apart from the horse farms directly to the north of Lexington, most places of interest lie to the south, like the fine old towns of **Danville** and **Harrodsburg**, and the restored **Shaker Village** at Pleasant Hill. After about forty miles, the meadows give way to the striking **Knobs** – random lumpy outcrops, shrouded in trees and wispy low-hanging clouds, that are the eroded remnants of the Pennyrile Plateau.

The Shaker Village at Pleasant Hill

The utopian settlement of **PLEASANT HILL**, hidden among the bluegrass hillocks near Harrodsburg, was established by **Shaker missionaries** from New England around 1805. Within twenty years, five hundred villagers were producing seeds, tools and cloth, for sale as far away as New Orleans. During the Civil War, Union and Confederate troops alike were billeted upon the pacifist Shakers. Numbers thereafter declined until the last member died in 1923, but a nonprofit organization has since returned the village to its nineteenth-century appearance.

The Shaker values of absolute celibacy, hygiene, simplicity and communal ownership have left their mark on the 27 gray and pastel-colored dwellings, which women and men entered via different doors. There are demonstrations of broom-making, weaving, quilting and other traditional crafts, and also excursions on the sternwheeler *Dixie Belle* (April–Oct daily 9.30am–5.30pm; Nov–March daily 9am–5pm; $10, $14 with *Dixie Belle*). The inn (☎859/734-5411) houses a superb **restaurant** specializing in boiled ham, lemon pie and other Kentucky favorites, and an inn (❹). Both the restaurant and the inn, as well as the other rooms in the village should be reserved well in advance.

Berea

Thirty miles south of Lexington, just off I-75 in the foothills where Bluegrass Country meets Appalachia, the unique **Berea College** gives its 1500 mainly local students free tuition in return for work in any of 120 crafts, ranging from needlework to wrought ironwork. Founded in 1855 by abolitionists as a vocational college for the young people of East Kentucky – both white and black – it was forcefully shut down four years later by mobs opposed to the board's support for John Brown's raid at Harpers Ferry (see p.458).

The college's reputation has attracted many private art and craft galleries to little **BEREA**. Free tours leave from *Boone Tavern Hotel,* a student-run hotel and restaurant at Main and Prospect streets (☎859/986-9358, ℗859/985-3700, ⊛www.4berea.com/tavern/; ❹), and explore the campus and student craft workshops. The hotel includes a smoke-free **dining room** open to non-residents and free admission to the college fitness center. If you're on a tight **budget**, *Mario's Pizza*, 636 Chestnut St (☎606/986-2331), is a good option.

Daniel Boone National Forest

Almost the entire eastern length of Kentucky is taken up by the steep slopes, narrow valleys and sandstone cliffs of the unspoiled **DANIEL BOONE NATIONAL FOREST**. Few Americans can have been mythologized as much as **Daniel Boone**, said to have been one of Kentucky's earliest fur-trapping pioneers, in 1767. Perhaps the most famous legend tells of the time he was captured by Shawnee Indians and initiated as *Sheltowee*, or Big Turtle. Learning of their plans to attack pioneer communities, Big Turtle escaped just in time to warn the citizens of his own settlement at **Boonesborough**, southeast of Lexington. But all did not end happily ever after. Boone failed to legalize his land claims, and lost practically all of the land in Kentucky he had claimed for himself and his sponsors. The resultant animosity forced the ageing frontiersman to press further west to Missouri in 1798, where he died in 1820 aged 86.

Natural Bridge and around

The geological extravaganza of the **Red River Gorge**, sixty miles east of Lexington via the Mountain Parkway, is best seen by taking a thirty-mile loop drive from the **Natural Bridge State Resort Park** on Hwy-77, near the village of Slade. Natural Bridge itself is a large sandstone arch surrounded by steep hollows and exposed clifflines; for the best panoramic view, continue to the solid span of **Sky Bridge**, which stretches along the top of a thin ridge. As well as hiking trails, canoeing, fishing, rock-climbing and camping, there's cottage **accommodation** in secluded *Hemlock Lodge* (☎606/663-2214; ❸/❹), where weekends usually fill up a year in advance.

Toward the southeast

In 1940, "Colonel" Harlan Sanders opened a small diner at the back of a gas station in tiny **CORBIN**, ninety miles south of Lexington on I-75. His **Kentucky Fried Chicken** empire has since spread to over sixty countries. The original 100-seat restaurant, near the junction of US-25 E and US-25 W, has been restored with 1940s decor and memorabilia (daily 10am–10pm; ☎606/528-2163). The bespectacled Sanders (1890–1980) was not a soldier, but a member of the Honorable Order of Kentucky Colonels.

STEARNS, fifty miles southwest of Corbin on Hwy-92, is a classic former mining company town, one of many in the Appalachians, in which the company owned every building – from the shops and church to the sheriff's office. As one Thirties writer put it, "with their unpaved streets and unpainted buildings (they) come into view like blighted spots on the land, with all the inconveniences and few if any of the comforts of modern towns of equal size." The **McCreary County Museum** at 1 Henderson St (Tues–Sat 9am–4pm, Sun noon–4pm; $3) takes a sanitized look at this history. The highlight for visitors is the eleven-mile trip on the **Big South Fork Scenic Railway** (April to early Nov; $15; ☎606/376-5330 or 1-800/462-5664 for schedules), which traverses deep woodlands and descends a rugged 600ft gorge to **Blue Heron**, another former mining community or to **Barthell**, where a guided tour takes you through the town ($17).

On the tristate border of Kentucky, Tennessee and Virginia, the **CUMBER-LAND GAP NATIONAL HISTORIC PARK** is one of the most visited parts of the area. A natural passageway used by migrating deer and bison, it served as a gateway to the west for Boone and other pioneers. **Pinnacle Overlook**, a 1000ft lookout over the three states, is near the **visitor center** (daily: summer 8am–6pm; rest of year 9am–5pm; ☎606/248-2817) on US-25 E in **Middlesboro**.

Just outside the forest boundaries on the Virginia border, there are plenty of coalfields and lumber forests, but few people. The high death toll in underground mines and the ecological disasters of strip-mining have drawn national attention here, particularly during the violent struggles of the Thirties in places such as **Harlan County**, where striking miners were evicted from their homes and killed by armed company men.

Louisville, central and western Kentucky

In heavily rural Kentucky, the manufacturing giant of **Louisville** stands out, with its lively cultural and racial mix. Only occasionally does it bother with the laid-back Southern image other parts of the state are so keen to promote. In the **southern** hinterland, numerous small towns retain their tree-shaded squares and nineteenth-century townhouses – and their strict Baptist beliefs – while the endless caverns of **Mammoth Cave National Park** attract spelunkers and hikers in their thousands. The west, where the Ohio River meets the Mississippi, is flat, heavily forested and generally less attractive.

Louisville

LOUISVILLE, just south of Indiana across the Ohio River, is firmly embedded in the American national consciousness for its multimillion-dollar

Kentucky Derby. Each year, the horse race attracts over 500,000 fans to this cosmopolitan and well-diversified industrial city, which still bears the traces of the early French settlers who came upriver from New Orleans. Today a third of the country's bourbon is made here.

Louisville's history revolves around a perennial rivalry with Cincinnati, a mere one hundred miles upstream. For example, despite being pro-Union during the Civil War, it promoted itself thereafter – erecting Confederate statues and so on – as the place for Southern business to invest, as opposed to Midwestern Yankee cities like Cincinnati.

Besides a lively arts scene and lots of citywide festivals, Louisville boasts an unrivaled network of public parks, many designed by Frederick Law Olmsted. One native son who took advantage of the recreation facilities was three-time world heavyweight boxing champion **Muhammad Ali**, who used to do his early-morning training in the scenic environs of Chickasaw Park.

Arrival, information and getting around

Most major US airlines fly into **Louisville International Airport** (T502/367-4636), five miles south of downtown on I-65; take bus #2 or pay a $15 cab fare. Greyhound terminates at fairly central 720 W Muhammad Ali Blvd (T502/585-3331). An excellent **bus** service (75¢) makes getting around easy. Some routes operate as late as 2am, and downtown **trolleys** run from 7.30am to 6pm. The **visitor center** is at 3rd and Market streets (Mon–Fri 8.30am–5pm, Sat 9am–4pm, Sun 11am–4pm; T502/584-2121 or 1-800/626-5646, ext 321, Wwww.gotolouisville.com). For news of upcoming events, pick up a copy of the free listings magazine *LEO* (*Louisville Eccentric Observer*).

Accommodation

Most of the year, Louisville's **accommodation** is plentiful and reasonably priced, though of course it's solidly booked up for the Derby. You can **camp** just over the river in Indiana at the central *KOA*, 900 Marriott Drive, Clarksville, IN (T812/282-4474).

Doubletree Club Louisville Downtown 101 E Jefferson St T502/585-2200, F502/585-5486, Wwww.doubletree.com. Comfortable rooms come with complimentary breakfast and access to an indoor pool and fitness center. ⑤

The Columbine B&B 1707 S 3rd St T502/635-5000, Wwww.thecolumbine.com. Five rooms with private baths in this popular B&B close to the university. Great garden and gourmet breakfasts. ⑤

Galt House 140 4th St T502/589-5200, F502/589-3444, Wwww.galthouse.com. Located on the Ohio riverfront, this huge hotel has an unmistakable Kentucky feel, with grand ballrooms, sweeping staircases and avenue-like corridors. Also has great views over river. ⑤/⑥

Old Louisville Inn 1359 S 3rd St T502/635-1574. Luxurious Victorian B&B with a relaxed touch; whirlpool rooms available. ⑤

Super 8 Motel 927 S 2nd St T502/584-8888 or 1-800/800-8000, F502/584-8897, Wwww.super8.com. Downtown chain motel offering a fitness room and continental breakfast. Provides complimentary shuttle rides to public transportation. ③

Central Louisville

Downtown Louisville rolls gently down toward Main Street, then abruptly lunges down to the river. **Riverfront Plaza**, between Fifth and Sixth streets, is a prime observation point for the natural **Falls of the Ohio**. The *Belle of Louisville*, a 1914 steam sternwheeler, leaves from the wharf at 4th Street & River Road for daily cruises in the summer (Tues–Sun at noon, Tues & Thurs also at 6pm; $10; T502/574-2355).

No matter what you think of baseball, it's hard not to be impressed by the **Louisville Slugger Museum**, at 800 W Main St (Mon–Sat 9am–5pm; Sundays

April–Nov noon–5pm; $6; ☎502/588-7228). Frequent tours start with a short, emotive movie featuring prominent shots of Louisville Slugger bats being used to good effect, before visiting displays honoring key players, a batting cage that gives you an idea of just how rapid a 95mph fastball really is, and a working bat factory, explaining all the processes involved in the manufacturing of wooden bats. The trip ends with everyone getting a souvenir miniature bat.

The **Speed Art Museum**, at 2035 S 3rd St on the University of Louisville campus (Tues, Wed & Fri 10.30am–4pm, Thurs 10.30am–8pm, Sat 10.30am–5pm, Sun noon–5pm; free; ☎502/634-2700) hosts traveling exhibits and has a small, but interesting, permanent collection of art and sculpture from medieval to modern times, featuring works by Rembrandt, Monet, Rodin and Henry Moore.

Louisville's horses: the Kentucky Derby

The Kentucky Derby is one of the world's premier horse races; it's also, as Hunter S. Thompson put it, "decadent and depraved." Derby Day itself is the first Saturday in May, at the end of the two-week **Kentucky Derby Festival**. Since 1875, the leading lights of Southern society have gathered for an annual orgy of betting, haute cuisine and mint juleps in the plush grandstand, while tens of thousands of the beer-guzzling proletariat cram into the infield. Apart from the $40 infield tickets available on the day – offering virtually no chance of a decent view – all seats are sold out months in advance. The actual race, traditionally preceded by a mass drunken rendition of *My Old Kentucky Home*, is run over a distance of one and a quarter miles, lasts barely two minutes, and offers close to a million dollars in prize money. Only during the Superbowl do television commercials cost more. Thoroughbreds also race at **Churchill Downs**, three miles south of downtown at 700 Central Ave, from May to July, and October to November ($2; ☎502/636-4400).

The excellent hands-on **Kentucky Derby Museum** (daily 9am–5pm; $7), next to Churchill Downs at 704 Central Ave (bus #4), will appeal to horse-racing enthusiasts and ignoramuses alike. Admission includes a tour of Churchill Downs, a magnificent audiovisual display that captures the Derby Day atmosphere on a 360° screen.

Eating

Louisville's **restaurants** cater for all tastes, though downtown prices are fairly high.

Brasserie Dietrich's 2862 Frankfort Ave ☎502/897-6076. Atmospheric converted movie house in the Crescent Hill district, serving inventive seafood and meat dishes from a wood-burning grill.

Bristol Bar & Grille 1321 Bardstown Rd ☎502/456-1702. Very good bistro-style salads and entrees with great desserts; a perennial Louisville favorite. Branch at 300 N Hurstbourne Parkway ☎502/426-0627.

Heine Brothers Coffee 1295 Bardstown Rd ☎502/456-5108. Friendly espresso bar, attached to *Carmichael's*, a good independent bookstore.

Jicama 1538 Bardstown Rd ☎502/454-4383. Stylish Latin American grill in the busy Deer Park district. Prices range from $10 to $20 a head.

Lynn's Paradise Café 984 Barret Ave ☎502/583-

EGGS. Quite simply a place that has to be visited for its stone-age theme decor. Friendly staff serve big portions of standard American fare, a choice selection of beers, and the best breakfasts in the city. In the lively Highlands neighborhood close to downtown.

Ramsi's Café on the World 1293 Bardstown Rd ☎502/451-0700. Atmospheric café open late with eclectic and very tasty selections.

Rudyard Kipling 422 W Oak St ☎502/636-1311. The decor has a hint of *The Jungle Book*, but the food is local with a few Indian dishes thrown in. Live music, usually acoustic, most nights. Closed Sun.

Vietnam Kitchen 5339 S 3rd St ☎502/363-5154. A small basic eatery, fifteen minutes' drive out of downtown in the South End, where the city's Asian chefs eat on their days off. The menu is huge.

Nightlife and entertainment

The **Kentucky Center for the Arts**, 501 W Main between Fifth and Sixth avenues (℡502/584-7777 or 1-800/775-7777), and fronted by several outlandish sculptures, is Louisville's main venue for high culture. The **Actors' Theatre of Louisville** at 316 W Main St (℡502/584-1205), meanwhile, has a national reputation for its new productions. As for **drinking** and **live music**, the two-mile strip around Bardstown Road and Baxter Avenue (bus #17) is punctuated by fun bars and restaurants; the best **gay** clubs are on the eastern edge of downtown.

Brewery 426 Baxter Ave ℡502/583-3420. Sports-themed bar with live music. Open late.

Connections 130 S Floyd St ℡502/585-5752. The pick of Louisville's gay scene. At weekends this giant club, complete with terrace garden, holds over 2000.

Molly Malone's 933 Baxter Ave ℡502/473-1222. Fun Irish pub and restaurant with live music on the weekends.

Phoenix Hill Tavern 644 Baxter Ave ℡502/589-4957. Big bar with four different areas that gets in occasional national touring acts.

Stevie Ray's 230 E Main St ℡502/582-9945. As the name suggests, a rocking loud blues bar.

Twice Told Coffeehouse 1604 Bardstown Rd ℡502/456-0507. Cozy singer-songwriter venue that often gets noted names and surprise appearances.

Out from Louisville

South from Louisville to Tennessee, **central Kentucky** offers great scope for a one- or two-day driving tour. There's small-town charm in **Bardstown** and Abraham Lincoln's birthplace of **Hodgenville**, while the top natural attraction is the amazing **Mammoth Cave National Park**, the largest underground cave system in the world.

Kentucky's **western** stretches don't compare with the rugged east for scenic beauty; all the significant lakes were created by damming its rivers, and much of the land is scarred by strip mines, oilfields and commercial forests. There's little of real interest here except for the **Land Between the Lakes** recreation area, squeezed between Kentucky and Barkley lakes, overlapping the Tennessee border.

Fort Knox

Legendary **FORT KNOX** straddles 100,000 acres either side of US-31 W, thirty miles southwest of Louisville. The bomb-proof **Bullion Depository**, on Gold Vault Road, surrounded by security fences, machine-gun turrets, patrol guards and huge floodlights, stores nine million pounds of the federal gold reserve behind doors weighing twenty tons apiece. No visits are allowed at the depository; you can stop by the road for a maximum of five minutes.

Bardstown and the bourbon distilleries

Forty miles south of Louisville on US-31 E, attractive **BARDSTOWN** is the place to get acquainted with Kentucky **bourbon whiskey**, created in earliest pioneer days, so the story goes, when Elijah Craig, a Baptist minister, added corn to the usual rye and barley. Named for Bourbon County near Lexington, Kentucky's whiskey soon gained a national reputation, thanks to crisp limestone water and the skills of small-scale distillers. Under federal law, corn must make up at least 51 percent of all solid ingredients, and the drink must mature for two years in new oak barrels with charred interiors.

Get into the spirit at Bardstown's free **Oscar Getz Museum of Whiskey History**, 114 N Fifth St (May–Sept Mon–Sat 9am–5pm, Sun 1–5pm; rest of year Mon–Sat 10am–4pm, Sun 1–4pm). Fourteen miles west at **CLERMONT**, you can stop at **Jim Beam American Outpost** (Mon–Sat 9am–4.30pm, Sun 1–4pm; free), which has an informative museum, a film on the whiskey-making process, an outdoor moonshine still and barrel-making museum, and a Beam family home. **Maker's Mark Distillery**, twenty miles south of Bardstown near **Loretto**, is an out-of-the-way collection of beautifully restored black, red and gray plankhouses, in which whiskey is still made manually (Mon–Sat 10.30am–3.30pm, Sun 1.30–3.30pm; free; ☎502/865-2099). However, don't expect a sample at either distillery; like most of rural Kentucky, the area is **dry**.

Abraham Lincoln's birthplace

On February 12, 1809, **Abraham Lincoln**, the sixteenth president of the US, was born in a one-room log cabin in the frontier wilds, son of a wandering farmer and, if some accounts are to be believed, an illiterate and illegitimate mother. The **National Historic Site** (summer daily 8am–6.45pm; rest of year daily 8am–4.45pm; free), has a symbolic cabin of his birth, three miles south of **HODGENVILLE** on US-31 E, and is enclosed in a granite and marble Memorial Building with 56 steps, one for each year of Lincoln's life. The family moved in 1811 to the **Knob Creek** area, where Lincoln's earliest memory was of slaves being forcefully driven along the road. Here you can visit another re-creation of his boyhood home (daily April–Oct varying hours; $1). Knob Creek, which the Lincolns left in 1816 for Indiana, doesn't overplay the presidential connection, and its down-home cafés make it a good place to stop.

Mammoth Cave National Park

The three hundred and fifty miles of labyrinthine passages (with an average of five new miles discovered each year) and domed caverns of **MAMMOTH CAVE NATIONAL PARK** lie halfway between Louisville and Bowling Green, ten miles off I-65. Its amazing geological formations, carved by acidic water trickling through limestone, include a bewildering display of stalagmites and stalactites, a huge cascade of flowstone known as **Frozen Niagara**, and **Echo River**, 365ft below ground, populated by a unique species of colorless and sightless fish. Among traces of human occupation are Native American artifacts, a former saltpeter mine, and the remains of an experimental tuberculosis hospital, built in 1843 in the belief that the cool atmosphere of the cave would help clear patients' lungs. Access is by guided tours, available for most tastes and abilities, including the physically challenged ($7–35); tickets are available from the **visitor center** (summer daily 7.30am–7.30pm; fall daily 8am–6pm; rest of year Mon–Fri 9am–5pm, Sat & Sun 8am–5pm; ☎270/758-2328 for info and ☎1-800/967-2283 for tour reservations; ⒲www.mammoth-cave.com). Book ahead, especially in summer. Also keep in mind the temperature in the caves is a constant 54°F, so take a sweater or jacket.

The park's attractions are by no means all subterranean. The scenic **Green River** cuts through densely forested hillsides and jagged limestone cliffs; you can follow hiking trails, rent canoes or, for a more leisurely trip, take the *Miss Green River II* **cruise boat** ($6; ☎270/758-2243). **Camping** is free in the backcountry; however, a permit must be picked up first at the visitor center; the *Mammoth Cave Hotel* (☎270/758-2225) has cottages (❸) and motel **rooms** (❹).

The privately owned caves all around, many of which ruin the sights with garish light shows, and the "attractions" in nearby Cave City and Park City, are best ignored.

Bowling Green and around

BOWLING GREEN's main claim to fame is as the only place where you can buy a drink between Louisville and Nashville, just sixty miles further southwest. It's a lively enough place and offers a treat for **sports car** enthusiasts. One-hour tours of the **General Motors Corvette Assembly Plant**, on Louisville Road, off I-65, take a step-by-step look at the manufacture of one of the great symbols of the American Dream (Mon–Fri at 9am & 1pm; ☏502/745-8419; free; reservations advisable). For real Corvette junkies, there's also the **National Corvette Museum**, south of the plant at 350 Corvette Drive (daily: April–Sept 8am–5pm; Oct–March 8am–5pm; $8).

There's a former **Shaker settlement**, with furniture displays and crafts for sale, 11 miles west of Bowling Green off US-68/80, in **SOUTH UNION** (March–Dec Mon–Sat 9am–5pm, Sun 1–5pm; $5). A mile or two away on Hwy-73, the 1869 *Shaker Tavern* (☏270/542-6801 or 1-800/929-8701; ❹), a B&B, serves traditional Kentucky recipes such as chess pie. However, only guests and groups of six or more can eat at the tavern.

Tennessee

A shallow rectangle, only one hundred miles from north to south, **TENNESSEE** stretches 450 miles from the Mississippi to the Appalachians, and divides into three distinct regions. The marshy **western** third of the state occupies a low plateau edging down toward the Mississippi. Only in the far southwest corner do the bluffs rise high enough to permit a sizeable riverside settlement – the exhilarating port of **Memphis**. Tennessee's largest city is a magnet for music fans, as the birthplace of urban blues and long-time home of **Elvis**. The fine plantation homes and tidy old towns of **middle Tennessee**'s rolling farmland reflect the comfortable lifestyle of its pioneers; smack at the heart of this is **Nashville**, still **country music's** capital, despite upstart competition from Branson (see p.799) and Myrtle Beach (see p.518). The mountainous **east** shares its top attraction with North Carolina – the peaks, streams and meadows of **Great Smoky Mountains National Park**.

Tennessee's first white settlers, most of them British Protestants, arrived from across the mountains in the 1770s to settle in the hills and hollows of the Appalachians. Initially relations with the **Cherokee** were good. However, demand for land increased, and confrontations throughout the state culminated in 1838 with the forced removal of the Indians on the "Trail of Tears." One of the main congressional opponents of this process was **Davy Crockett**, familiar from legend as the heavy-drinking hunter in a coonskin cap. When **Civil War** came, the plantation owners of the west maneuvered Tennessee into the Confederacy, against the wishes of the nonslaveholding smallhold farmers in the east. The last state to secede became the primary battlefield in the west, the site of 424 battles and skirmishes.

Despite economic development to rival any in the country, soil erosion and farm mechanization led to a mass migration to the cities in the years before World War I. The fundamentalist beliefs of these transplanted hill-dwellers (whose folk and fiddle music served to spark Nashville's country scene) influenced a **prohibition** movement that kept all of Tennessee bone-dry until 1939, and still sees a majority of counties forbidding the sale of alcohol. The New Deal of the 1930s brought significant changes. In particular, the **Tennessee Valley Authority**, created in 1933, harnessed the flood-prone **Tennessee River**, providing much-needed jobs and cheap power, and ignited the transition from an agricultural to an industrial economy.

Getting around Tennessee

For such a popular tourist destination, Tennessee has disappointing **transportation** connections. Amtrak only calls at Memphis, and while Greyhound provides a reasonable service to major towns and cities, traveling by bus through the small towns in the east is very difficult. The **airports** at Memphis and Nashville have extensive connections throughout the US, though fares between the two are high. If you harbor fantasies of traveling by **boat** along the Mississippi, note that only luxury craft make the trip these days, at prohibitive prices (see p.563).

Memphis

The cotton-trading capital of the Delta, **MEMPHIS**, perched above the Mississippi two hundred miles west of Nashville and three hundred south of St Louis, is one of the great destinations of the South. Visitors come from all over the world to celebrate the city that virtually invented blues, soul and rock 'n' roll, as well as to chow down in the unrivaled barbecue capital of the nation. A visit to Memphis, the home of the Sun and Stax record labels, with its frequent festivals and vigorous nightlife, feels like an invitation to share in a genuine and enduring local culture.

Culturally and geographically, Memphis has more in common with the deltalands of Mississippi and Arkansas than with the rest of Tennessee. Founded in 1819 and named for Egypt's ancient Nile capital, its fortunes rose and fell with **cotton**. The Confederate defeat that ended the slave trade briefly plunged it into economic chaos, and severe yellow fever epidemics didn't help, but thanks to its potential for river and rail transportation Memphis soon bounced back. The nation's second largest inland port became a major stopping-off point for **black migrants** escaping the poverty of the Delta, and many stayed, significantly shaping the city's identity.

For a couple of decades after the 1968 **assassination** of Dr Martin Luther King Jr, Memphis tottered on the brink of terminal decline, with downtown hit by a massive case of "white flight." In the past decade, however, the city has regenerated itself yet again, its new self-confidence typified by the extraordinary 321ft stainless steel **Pyramid** that now dominates the riverfront skyline. The famous **blues** corridor of **Beale Street** is booming once more, perhaps a little ersatz but always entertaining, while Elvis Presley's **Graceland** – a refreshing change from the usual "gracious southern home" – provides an intimate and exuberant glimpse of Memphis's most famous son.

Arrival, information and getting around

Memphis International Airport is ten miles south of downtown – a long and complicated bus trip, but just fifteen minutes by the Yellow Cabs **limo/van** service ($10; ☎901/577-7777) or **taxi** ($20–25). Greyhound **buses**

stop at 203 Union Ave in downtown, while the Amtrak station at 545 S Main St is in a particularly seedy and unsafe area on the southern edge of downtown.

Slow and infrequent Memphis Area Transit Authority buses cover nearly all the city (☎901/274-6282); more useful is the downtown **trolley** service (☎901/274-6282) that runs along the Main Street Mall from the Pyramid to Beale Street and the Civil Rights Museum, until 6pm on Sundays and after midnight on all other days (60¢ flat fare; day pass $2.50).

Carriage tours at $30 per half-hour or $50 per hour (for 2 people) start from the *Peabody* and *Crowne Plaza* hotels, among others (Mon–Fri 5pm–1am, Sat & Sun 1pm–1am; ☎901/834-9945). **American Dream Safari** (☎901/527-8870) offers **driving tours** in a 1955 Cadillac that range from a gospel service at Al Green's church ($60 including lunch) up to week-long blues pilgrimages into the Delta. **Sternwheelers** offer ninety-minute sightseeing trips of the mighty Mississippi for $12.50, leaving Riverside Drive at Monroe Avenue (March–Nov daily 2.30pm & 5.30pm as well as dinner cruises in season; ☎901/527-5694).

Information

The spacious and modern **Tennessee Welcome Center** by the Pyramid, complete with nine-foot bronze Elvis, facing Mud Island at river level at 119 N Riverside Drive and Adams Avenue is open 24 hours a day every day. For advance information on the city call ☎901/543-5333 or visit ⓦwww .memphistravel.com. The **post office** is at 555 S Third St at Calhoun Avenue (Mon–Fri 8.30am–5.30pm, Sat 10am–2pm; ☎901/521-2245; zip code 38101).

Accommodation

Downtown Memphis has a reasonable mixture of grand hotels and inexpensive **places to stay**, though most budget motels are concentrated along Elvis Presley Boulevard to the south. The visitor center (see above) gives good advice, and is particularly helpful at busy times such as the anniversary of Elvis's death in mid-August. B&B in Memphis (PO Box 41621, TN 38174; ☎901/725-3958) runs a reservation service, with rooms costing $60 and upwards. The closest **campground** is the *Elvis Presley Blvd RV Park*, 3971 Elvis Presley Blvd (☎901/332-3633), three blocks south of Graceland.

Best Western Benchmark 164 Union Ave ☎901/527-4100, ☎901/525-1747, ⓦwww .bestwestern.com. Prime downtown location near the *Peabody* hotel (see below); good value and clean. ❹

Elvis Presley's Heartbreak Hotel 3677 Elvis Presley Blvd ☎901/332-1000, ☎901/332-2107, ⓦwww.elvis.com. Right across from Graceland, every room has a fridge and microwave plus 24hr Elvis videos. The hotel also boasts a heart-shaped pool, memorabilia of the King and package deals that include the other corporate Elvis attractions. ❺

French Quarter Suites 2144 Madison Ave ☎901/728-4000 or 1-800/843-0353, ☎901/278-1262, ⓦwww.memphisfrenchquarter.com. Upmarket suites in the only hotel in Overton Square.

Memphis Marriott Downtown 250 N Main St ☎901/527-7300, ☎901/526-1561, ⓦwww .marriotthotels.com. Good-quality large hotel with

pool and health club, opposite the Convention Center with views of the river and Pyramid. ❻

The Peabody 149 Union Ave ☎901/529-4000 or 1-800/PEABODY, ☎901/529-3646, ⓦwww.peabodymemphis.com. Opulent landmark hotel near Beale St. Don't miss the legendary ducks, who waddle from the elevator at 11am promptly to the strains of the *King Cotton March*, spend the day in the lobby fountain, and return to their penthouse at 5pm. ❼

Sleep Inn at Court Square 40 N Front St ☎901/522-9700, ☎901/522-9710, ⓦwww.sleepinn.com. Good-value motel in the heart of downtown, facing the river near Mud Island and backing right onto Main Street; rates include free breakfast. ❹

Talbot-Heirs Guesthouse 99 S 2nd St ☎901/527-9772, ⓦwww.talbothouse.com. Nine individually decorated rooms equipped with kitchens and internet access. ❻

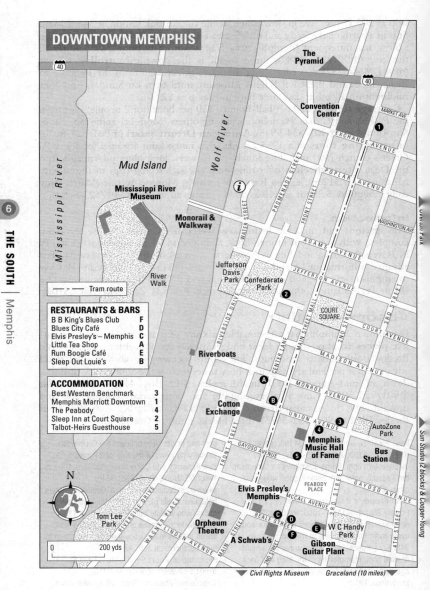

DOWNTOWN MEMPHIS

The Pyramid

Convention Center **1**

MARKET AVE

EXCHANGE AVENUE

POPLAR AVENUE

WASHINGTON AVE

Wolf River

PROMENADE STREET

FRONT STREET

Mud Island

Mississippi River Museum

ADAMS AVENUE

Monorail & Walkway

WATER STREET

i

JEFFERSON AVENUE

Mississippi River

Jefferson Davis Park

Confederate Park **2**

COURT SQUARE

2ND STREET

3RD STREET

River Walk

COURT AVENUE

RIVERSIDE DRIVE

MAIN STREET MALL

CENTER LANE

MADISON AVENUE

- - - Tram route

RESTAURANTS & BARS
B B King's Blues Club	**F**
Blues City Café	**D**
Elvis Presley's – Memphis	**C**
Little Tea Shop	**A**
Rum Boogie Café	**E**
Sleep Out Louie's	**B**

Riverboats

A

MONROE AVENUE

B

ACCOMMODATION
Best Western Benchmark	**3**
Memphis Marriott Downtown	**1**
The Peabody	**4**
Sleep Inn at Court Square	**2**
Talbot-Heirs Guesthouse	**5**

Cotton Exchange

UNION AVENUE

3

AutoZone Park

FRONT STREET

GAYOSO AVENUE

4

Memphis Music Hall of Fame

5

Bus Station

GAYOSO AVENUE

Elvis Presley's Memphis

PEABODY PLACE

MCCALL AVENUE

3RD STREET

4TH STREET

N

Tom Lee Park

RIVERSIDE DRIVE

WAGNER PLACE

BEALE STREET

C **D**

W C Handy Park

E

Orpheum Theatre

MAIN STREET

2ND STREET

A Schwab's

C

F

Gibson Guitar Plant

LINDEN AVENUE

0 200 yds

Civil Rights Museum   Graceland (10 miles)

THE SOUTH | Memphis

6

Overton Park

Sun Studio (2 blocks) & Cooper-Young

The City

Downtown Memphis has in the last few years started to come back to life, at the cost of losing some of its old cotton-era buildings. The central streets parallel to the river are steadily acquiring new hotels, restaurants and stores. **Beale Street** on downtown's southern fringes is the liveliest area to stroll around,

with Sun Studio nearby and the **Civil Rights Museum** just south. The huge
Mud Island on the river itself merits half a day, while **Graceland**, ten miles
out, should on no account be missed.

The riverfront

The northern boundary of downtown is marked by the surreal 32-story, 321ft
Pyramid, two-thirds the size of the Great Pyramid, and taller than the Statue
of Liberty. Completed in 1991, it was intended as a symbolic link with the Nile
Delta with permanent displays; today its 22,500-seat theater puts on Memphis's
biggest concerts and ball games (tours were suspended at press time; call
☏901/521-9675 for updates). Around here nearby **Main Street** is generally an
attractive pedestrianized mall (served by trolleys; see p.561), with wide paved
sidewalks and modern fountains, that is gradually rebuilding its retail activity.

From Riverside Drive, **monorail trains** and a walkway reach **Mud Island**
(April & May Tues–Sun 10am–5pm; June–Aug daily 10am–8pm; Sept & Oct
Tues–Sun 10am–5pm; grounds are free; museum $8, both free on Thurs after

The Big Muddy

I do not know much about gods; but I think that the river
Is a strong brown god – sullen, untamed and intractable.

St Louis-born T.S. Eliot, *The Four Quartets*

North America's principal waterway, the **Mississippi** – the name comes from the
Algonquin words for "big" and "river" – starts just ninety miles south of the Canadian
border at Lake Itasca, Minnesota, and winds its way 2348 miles to the Gulf of
Mexico, taking in over one hundred tributaries on the way and draining all or part of
thirty-one US states and two Canadian provinces.

The **"Big Muddy"** – it carries 2lb of dirt for every 1000lb of water – is one of the
busiest commercial rivers in the world, and one of the least conventional. Instead of
widening toward its mouth, like most rivers, the Mississippi grows narrower and
deeper. Its **"Delta,"** near Memphis, more than three hundred miles upstream from
the river's mouth, is not a delta at all, but an alluvial flood plain. Furthermore, its
estuary deposits, which extend the land six miles out to sea every century, are paltry compared to other rivers; gulf currents disperse the sediment before it has time
to settle.

The Mississippi is also, in the words of Mark Twain, who spent four years as a
riverboat pilot, "the **crookedest** river in the world." As it weaves and curls its way
extravagantly along its channel, it continually cuts through narrow necks of land to
shape and reshape oxbow lakes, meander scars, cutoffs and marshy backwaters. A
bar could operate one day in Arkansas and then find itself in dry Tennessee the next,
thanks to an overnight cutoff.

A more serious manifestation of the Mississippi's power is its propensity to **flood**.
Although the river builds its own levees, artificial embankments have since as early
as 1717 helped to safeguard crops and homes. Since the disastrous floods of 1927,
the federal government has installed a wide range of flood-protection measures; virtually the entire riverfront from Cape Girardeau, Missouri, to the sea is now walled
in, and it's even possible to drive along the top of the larger levees.

While it's no longer feasible to sail Twain's route for yourself, **riverboat excursions**
operate in most sizeable river towns. Longer cruises, on the luxurious *Delta Queen*
and *Mississippi Queen* **paddlewheelers**, are expensive; contact the Delta Queen
Steamboat Company, 30 Robin Street Wharf, New Orleans, LA 70130 (☏1-800/543-
1949).

4pm June–Aug) across Wolf Channel, which Tom Cruise had a hard time crossing in the movie version of John Grisham's *The Firm*. On the island, which
formed in 1910 when the river began depositing silt alongside a stationary
boat, the **Mississippi River Museum** is an enjoyable and ingenious romp
through the history of the river. Highlights include a full-size reconstructed
steam packet squeezed into the core of the building, a morbidly fascinating
"Theater of Disasters," and little-known characters such as keelboatman Mike
Fink, who in 1830 styled himself "half-horse, half-alligator"; there's also an
overview of Memphis music, featuring the original sign from Stax Records and
one of Elvis's Vegas-era white jumpsuits. Outside, the half-mile **River Walk** is
a scale model of the river itself, complete with town grids, which ends in the
"Gulf of Mexico" at a swimming pool and artificial beach. You can also visit
the original **Memphis Belle**, a World War II B17 bomber, nearby.

The small, tree-shaded **Jefferson Davis** and **Confederate parks** by the
Mississippi River are popular lunchtime meeting places. When the Union took
Memphis during the Civil War, thousands of dismayed residents watched from
these sites as seven out of eight Confederate gunboats were sunk. The imposing buildings of **Cotton Row**, halfway along Front Street, might have seen
busier days, but this is still the largest spot cotton market in the country. The
Cotton Exchange Building at 84 S Front St contains a small historical exhibit
on the cotton trade, but visitors are not allowed into the trading area. At the
south end of downtown, **Tom Lee Park**, the venue for major outdoor events
such as "Memphis in May," commemorates a black boatman who rescued 32
people from a sinking boat in 1925 – despite the fact that he couldn't swim.

Beale Street

Beale Street began life as one of Memphis's most exclusive enclaves; its elite
residents were driven out by the yellow fever epidemics, to be replaced by a
diverse mix of blacks, whites, Greeks, Jews, Chinese and Italians. But it was
Beale's **black culture** that gave the street its fame. This was where black
roustabouts, deckhands and travelers passing through Memphis immediately
headed for; rural blacks came for the bustling Saturday market; and, in times of
strict segregation, Beale acted as the center for black businesses, financiers and
professionals.

As the black main street of the mid-South, Beale in its Twenties' heyday was
jammed with vaudeville theaters, concert halls, bars and jook-joints (mostly
white-owned). Along with the frivolity came a reputation for heavy gambling,
voodoo, murder and prostitution. One appalled evangelist proclaimed that "if
whiskey ran ankle deep in Memphis…you could not get drunker quicker than
you can on Beale Street now."

Although Beale still drew huge crowds in the Forties, the drift to the suburbs
and, ironically, the success of the **civil rights** years in opening the rest of
Memphis to black businesses, almost killed it off. The **bulldozers** of the late
Sixties spared only the Orpheum Theatre and a few commercial buildings
between Second and Fourth streets.

Beale Street has now been restored as an **Historic District**, its shops, clubs
and cafés bedecked with Twenties-style facades and signs, while a Walk of
Fame with brass musical notes embedded into the sidewalk honors musical
greats such as B.B. King and Howlin' Wolf. Tourist money has led to extensive development, but with the exception of a few out-and-out souvenir
shops, most of the new businesses remain in tune with the past, and for blues
fans in particular its music venues showcase top regional talents. At its western end, 1997 saw the conversion of 126 Beale St – formerly home to

Lansky's, tailors to the Memphis stars – into *Elvis Presley's* – *Memphis Restaurant* (see p.569), which now rivals *B.B. King's* just beyond as the street's busiest nightspot. A little further along, **A. Schwab's Dry Goods Store**, at no. 163, looks much as it must have done when it opened in 1876, with an incredible array of such voodoo paraphernalia, familiar from the blues, as Mojo Hands and High John the Conqueror lucky roots in fragrant oil, as well as 99¢ neckties and Sunday School badges (closed Sun). Next door, the free **Memphis Police Museum**, open around the clock, holds an assortment of old photos, newspapers and crime-fighting accoutrements – great fun at night after club-hopping.

A fairly new arrival to the city at Beale and Third streets is the **Gibson Guitar Plant**, 145 Lt George W. Lee Ave, which has guided tours ($10; call ☎901/543-0800 for times and reservations) where visitors can watch the craft-workers construct six-string and bass guitars. Upstairs is the **Rock'n'Soul: Social Crossroads**, formerly The Memphis Music Hall of Fame (Mon–Sun 10am–6pm; $8.50), an excellent audio-visual display, presented in collaboration with the Smithsonian Institution, which puts issues such as migration, racism, civil rights and youth culture in a musical context.

East along Beale at no. 352, the tiny former home of **W.C. Handy** (summer Tues–Sat 10am–5pm, Sun 1pm–5pm; winter Tues–Sat 11am–4pm; $1; ☎901/522–1556), who in 1910 was the first man to publish blues tunes (often blues in name only: see p.596). His *Memphis Blues* – originally *Mr Crump* – was the theme song for the 1909 mayoral election of Edward H. Crump, whose crooked political machine was to run the city until the early Fifties.

The excellent, but peripatetic **Center for Southern Folklore** (daily 11am–6pm, Sat & Sun 11am–11pm; free; ☎901/525–3655), at 119 S Main St, celebrates the music, food, storytelling and crafts of the people of the mid-South. A small stage puts on high-quality live music most afternoons or evenings, with gospel groups and choirs on Sundays, and there's also an espresso café, an exhibition area and a good giftshop that sells folk art, blues cassettes and quilts. The Center is also home to the **Shrine of the Elvis Impersonators** (drop a quarter into the slot to see an assortment of would-be Elvises light up and revolve in a glittery spectacle). The comments book makes entertaining reading: in amongst the teen angst, drug-fueled poetry and satirical doodles is the eternal question, "If Elvis was so great, why is he buried in the back garden like a hamster?"

Sun Studio

At **Sun Studio**, ten minutes' walk east of Beale Street at 706 Union Ave (10am–6pm daily), every hour on the half-hour, twenty-minute "tours" of its single room, measuring just eighteen feet by thirty feet and focusing around Elvis's original mike stand, plus a drum kit and stand-up bass, feature tapes of the legendary recording sessions. Sun Records moved out in 1959, and although the building was briefly a scuba-diving store – not surprisingly, a commercial failure – all its soundproofing remained in place when it was restored as a studio in 1987. One room of the building, which Elvis knew as *Mrs Taylor's Café*, still functions as an atmospheric diner, selling burgers and peanut-butter-and-banana sandwiches, and there's a well-stocked giftshop upstairs.

The National Civil Rights Museum

The **National Civil Rights Museum**, a few blocks south of Beale Street at 450 Mulberry St (Mon–Sat 9am–5pm, Sun 1–5pm, June–Aug 9am–6pm; $8.50), has been built around the remains of the *Lorraine Motel*, specifically the room where **Dr Martin Luther King Jr** was assassinated by James Earl Ray on April 4, 1968. In increasingly hardline speeches, Dr King had explicitly linked black poverty with military spending in Vietnam. He was killed by a single bullet the evening before he was due to lead a march in Memphis in support of a strike by black sanitation workers.

The struggle for civil rights is traced from A. Philip Randolph of the Brotherhood of Sleeping Car Porters, who originally called for a march on Washington in 1941, through to the Nation of Islam and the Black Panthers. Great resources have been devoted to an impressive exposition of the movement's

The sound of Memphis

Since the start of the twentieth century, Memphis has been a meeting place for black musicians from the Mississippi Delta and beyond. During the Twenties, its downtown pubs, clubs and street corners were alive with the sound of the blues. **Jug bands**, in which singers were given a bass accompaniment by a musician blowing across the neck of a jug, were a specialty. Several songs by **Gus Cannon's Jug Stompers** – such as *Walk Right In* – became hits for white artists during the folk revival of the Sixties. **Bukka White**, **Memphis Slim** and guitarist **Memphis Minnie** appeared at nightspots like *Mitchell's Hotel* and *Pee Wee's Saloon*, all long since defunct. After World War II, young musicians and radio DJs experimented by blending the traditional blues sound with jazz, adding electrical amplification to create **rhythm'n'blues**. Pioneers included **Bobby Bland** and **B.B. King**.

White promoter Sam Phillips started **Sun Records** in 1953, employing Ike Turner as a scout to comb the Beale Street clubs for new talent. Among those whom Turner helped introduce to vinyl were his own girlfriend, Annie Mae Bullock (later **Tina Turner**), **Howlin' Wolf** and **Little Junior Parker**, whose *Mystery Train* was Sun's first great recording. Phillips' conviction that "If I could find a white man who had the Negro sound and the Negro feel, I could make a billion dollars" was realized in 1954, during a coffee break, when he overheard a young white man who had hired the studio to record a disc for his mother – **Elvis Presley**. Phillips dropped his black artists right away, signing other white **rockabilly** singers like **Carl Perkins** and **Jerry Lee Lewis** to make classics such as *Blue Suede Shoes* and *Great Balls of Fire*. Elvis – who in the words of Carl Perkins had the advantage that he "didn't look like Mr Ed, like a lot of the rest of us" – was soon sold on to RCA (for just $35,000), and didn't record in Memphis again until 1969, when, with songs like *Suspicious Minds*, he produced the best material of his later career.

In the Sixties and early Seventies, Memphis's **Stax Records** provided a rootsy alternative to the poppier sounds of Motown. This hard-edged **southern soul** was created by a multiracial mix of musicians, **Steve Cropper**'s fluid guitar complementing the blaring **Memphis Horns**. The label's first real success was *Green Onions* by studio band **Booker T and the MGs**; further hits followed from **Otis Redding** (*Try A Little Tenderness*), **Wilson Pickett** (*Midnight Hour*), **Sam and Dave** (*Soul Man*) and **Isaac Hayes** (*Shaft*). The label eventually foundered in acrimony; the last straw for many of its veteran soulmen was the signing of the British child star Lena Zavaroni for a six-figure sum.

Memphis has been renowned for its **gospel** music since the Thirties, when Rev Herbert Brewster wrote **Mahalia Jackson**'s *Move On Up a Little Higher*. Following a religious revelation, the consummate soul stylist **Al Green**, who achieved chart success for **Hi Records** with *Let's Stay Together* and *Tired of Being Alone*, is now minister at the Full Gospel Tabernacle, at 787 Hale Rd in the leafy suburb of Whitehaven. Visitors are welcome at the 11am Sunday services, complete with four-piece rhythm section; continue a mile south of Graceland, then turn west (phone ahead to check he's in town; ☎901/396-9192).

history, along with a few effective exhibits – sitting on the front seat of a recon-structed Montgomery bus that triggers a recorded message instructing you to move to the back. However, for such an emotional subject, it's hardly surpris-ing that the museum has drawn its detractors, who argue that Memphis's role in Dr King's death should be a source of shame rather than a tourist attraction, and that his memory would have been better served by investment in social programs.

Graceland

In itself, Elvis Presley's **Graceland** was a surprisingly modest home for the world's most successful entertainer. It's certainly not the "mansion" you may have been led to expect, and while Elvis was clearly a man who indulged his tastes to the full, there's none of the pomposity that characterizes so many other showpiece Southern residences. Visits, run under the auspices of his widow Priscilla, are affectionate celebrations of the man; never exactly tongue in cheek, but not cloyingly reverential either.

Elvis was just 22 when he paid $100,000 for Graceland in 1957. It was then considered one of the most desirable properties in Memphis, though now the neighborhood is distinctly less exclusive, its main thoroughfare – **Elvis Presley Boulevard** – lined with motels, fast-food joints and surprisingly few Elvis-related souvenir shops. Tours start opposite the house in **Graceland Plaza**; excited visitors, kitted out with audio-cassette players, are ferried across the road in minibuses, which depart every few minutes and sweep through the musical gate in the "**Wall of Love**," scrawled with tens of thousands of mes-sages from fans.

The audio tours, peppered with spoken memories from Priscilla and rousing choruses from the King, allow you to spend as long as you wish – and press the rewind button as many times as you like – but it's not easy to get an accurate sense of the house's size and layout, as the upstairs rooms are out of bounds to visitors. The interior is a frozen tribute to the taste of the Seventies; choice moments include the Hawaiian-themed **Jungle Room**, with its waterfall and green shag-carpeted ceiling, where he recorded *Moody Blue* and other gems from his declining years, and the navy and lemon **TV Room**, mirrored and fitted with three screens that now show 1970s talk shows. In the separate **Trophy Room**, you parade past Elvis's platinum, gold and silver records, stage costumes, outfits from many of his 31 films, and his extensive gun collection; the tour of the interior ends with the racquetball court where he played on the morning he died. Strewn with flowers and soft toys sent daily from fans, Elvis (Jan 8, 1935 to Aug 16, 1977), his mother Gladys, his father Vernon and his grandmother are buried beside the swimming pool in the **Meditation Garden** outside; Elvis's body was moved here two months after his death,

Graceland attractions

Graceland is ten miles from downtown Memphis, at 3734 Elvis Presley Blvd, on bus route #13 from Third and Union streets. The ticket office is open April–Oct Mon–Sat 9am–5pm, Sun 9am–4pm; Nov–March Mon, Wed–Sun 10am–4pm, closed Tues. The last house tour starts at the ticket office's closing time while the other attractions remain open for roughly two more hours. Combined "Platinum" ticket to all attrac-tions (allow three hours) is $25; house tours only, $16 (closed Tues Nov–Feb); auto-mobile museum $7; airplanes $6; "Sincerely Elvis" (see overleaf) $5; parking fee $2. Reservations are recommended, especially in August (℡901/332-3322, ⊛www.elvis–presley.com).

when the security problems inherent in keeping it in the local cemetery became obvious, though there have been recent reports that his family want to move it to a private retreat away from Graceland.

The Plaza itself, resounding with nonstop Elvis hits and lined with giftshops selling velvet Elvises and heart-shaped *Love Me Tender* "dream pillows," holds several enjoyable related attractions: don't miss the wittily edited free film *Walk a Mile in My Shoes*, the "**Sincerely Elvis**" collection of personal belongings – which features a TV punctured by a bullet fired by Elvis himself (he also shot his fridge, his stereo and even Lisa Marie's slide), as well as the King's Hai Karate and Brut aftershave – and Elvis's personal **airplanes**, including the *Lisa Marie*, customized with 24-carat gold washroom and a blue suede bathroom. End your tour with a sit-down in the **Elvis Presley Automobile Museum**, which, quite apart from a Harley Davidson golf cart and powder pink Cadillac, has a reconstructed drive-in showing clips from his movies.

Midtown and East Memphis

The mile-long, heavily wooded expanse of **Overton Park**, three miles from downtown (#50 bus) on Poplar Avenue, holds the wide-ranging **Memphis Brooks Museum of Art** (Tues–Fri 10am–4pm, first Wed of each month free 10am–9pm, Sat 10am–5pm, Sun 11.30am–5pm; $5; ⊛ www.brooksmuseum.org), and the recently modernized **Memphis Zoo and Aquarium** (daily 9am–6pm, last visitors allowed to enter 5pm; $9.50). **Overton Square**, the city's top suburban entertainment, dining and shopping district, is within walking distance. Just past East Parkway, the **Memphis Pink Palace Museum and Planetarium** at 3050 Central Ave (Mon–Thurs 9am–4pm, Fri–Sat 9am–9pm, Sun noon–6pm; $7) centers on the pink marble mansion of Clarence Saunders, who founded America's first chain of self-service **supermarkets**, Piggly-Wiggly, in 1916. Saunders went bankrupt in 1923, and never actually lived here; instead the building has acquired several new wings in the process of becoming an all-embracing museum of Memphis history, holding all kinds of stuffed animals and oddities, including a miniature circus, an IMAX cinema and the **Sharpe Planetarium**, as well as a walk-through model of the first Piggly-Wiggly store, complete with 2¢ packets of Kellogg's Cornflakes and 8¢ cans of Campbell's Soup.

South of Overton Square, the tiny, hip **Cooper-Young** intersection is as yet little more than a handful of shops: vintage stores where the city's punks and hippies burrow through secondhand psychedelic Crimplene, and richer arty types muse over retro knickknacks. It's a lively place, quite different from downtown, where you're likely to stumble across poetry readings and yard sales, art exhibits and antique auctions.

Eating

Memphians are fond of their food, proclaiming their city to be the **pork barbecue** capital of the world, with over one hundred specialty restaurants. There's also a good selection of reasonably priced soul-food cafés, and a couple of cool *nouvelle* Southern places. **Downtown** has a good selection (including some lively cafés on Beale Street); for a bit of variety, try **Overton Square** or **Cooper-Young** midtown.

Arcade 540 S Main St ⊕ 901/526–5757. Over eighty years old, this unassuming landmark (featured in Jim Jarmusch's movie *Mystery Train*) serves up no-frills Southern lunches, dinners and big breakfasts.

Automatic Slim's Tonga Club 83 S 2nd St ⊕ 901/525–7948. Trendy Southwestern/Carribean restaurant and nightspot, complete with tumbleweed and excellent if pricey food.

Blues City Café 138 Beale St ⊕ 901/526–3637.

City branch of Mississippi soul-food specialist *Doe's Eat Place* (see p.595), open daily 11am–4am. Join musicians from nearby clubs for tasty tamales, catfish and stew.

Buntyn 4972 Park Ave ☎901/458-8776. Hugely atmospheric old-style diner, southeast of downtown, specializing in Southern fried chicken and an irresistible array of vegetables. Daily 11am–8pm.

Café Francisco 400 N Main St ☎901/578-80020. Deli-style café, with internet access, just a block from the Pyramid. Open till 10pm Mon–Sat, to 6pm on Sun.

Café Ole 959 S Cooper Ave ☎901/274-1504. Very popular Mexican restaurant in Cooper-Young with good fajitas and vegetarian specialties such as spinach and mushroom quesadillas.

Cielo 679 Adams ☎901/524-1886. Popular, though fairly pricey ($20+) restaurant in the Victorian Village district, serving cuisines from around the world – everything from seared fois gras to spinach-shiitake dumplings.

Interstate Bar-B-Que 2265 S 3rd St ☎901/775-2304. Legendary barbecue restaurant, south of downtown on the way to the Delta, and open daily for lunch and dinner.

Java Cabana 2170 Young Ave ☎901/272-7210.

The place in Memphis to drink coffee, featuring poetry readings and live music. Closed Mon.

Little Tea Shop 69 Monroe Ave ☎901/525-6000. Unusual downtown soul-food café, serving a health-conscious version of what is traditionally a very fatty cuisine. Mon–Fri 11.15am–2.15pm; lunches cost around $5.

The North End 346 N Main St ☎901/526-0319. Friendly bar-cum-restaurant in the Pinch District opposite the Pyramid, specializing in wild-rice dishes, stir-fries and a killer hot fudge pie. Open until 3am.

Otherlands 641 S Cooper Ave ☎901/278-4994. Funky midtown coffee bar with its own giftshop, colorful "naïve" art works, great lattes, bagels and cakes, and a laid-back crowd. Daily 7am–8pm.

The Rendezvous General Washburn Alley, 52 S 2nd St ☎901/523-2746. Downtown Memphis's top-rated pork barbecue joint, with huge helpings and a nice atmosphere. Open Tues–Sat.

Sleep Out Louie's 88 Union Ave ☎901/527–5337. Trendy oyster bar and grill that's a popular post-theater meeting place.

Tsunami 928 S Cooper Ave ☎901/274-2556. Seafood restaurant in the Cooper-Young district with delicious pan-Asian dishes on the menu.

Nightlife and entertainment

Though **live music** is at its best in Memphis during the city's many **festivals**, such as the month-long **Memphis in May** (which also features the Barbecue Cookout Competition) and October's **Blues Memphis Week**, the blues and soul clubs of Beale Street have plenty to offer fans all year round. The best sources of **listings** are the free weekly *Memphis Flyer*, Friday's *Memphis Commercial Appeal Playbook*, and the community **radio** station (90FM).

B.B. King's Blues Club 143 Beale St ☎901/524-5464. Despite accusations from purists of having "sold out," this is justifiably Beale's most popular club. Spacious and atmospheric, with barbecue ribs, catfish and beer, and nightly blues enjoyed by a wildly enthusiastic crowd who make good use of the dance floor. B.B. himself makes an appearance or two per year.

Blues City Café 138 Beale St ☎901/526-3637. This club stays active well after the others and while the band is beating away there's a choice of well-priced ribs, catfish, tamales and gumbo to chew on.

Elvis Presley's – Memphis 126 Beale St ☎1-800/238-2000. Lansky's, the tailors where Elvis bought his sharpest suits, has been transformed into a restaurant and bar with a heavily Elvis-themed menu and the financial clout to put on some of Memphis's best bands.

Flying Saucer Draught Emporium 130 Peabody

Place ☎901/523-8676. Appealingly laid-back beerhall, just north of Beale St, aimed at the grungy college crowd.

Huey's Midtown 1927 Madison Ave ☎901/726-4372. Popular Overton Square restaurant, famed for its great burgers, with live jazz on Sun afternoon, followed by an out-of-town blues band in the evening. There's also a downtown branch of this popular local chain at 77 S 2nd St ☎901/527-2700.

Kudzu's 603 Monroe Ave ☎901/525-4924. Great downtown bar with pool table and live weekend blues.

Rum Boogie Café 182 Beale St ☎901/528-0150. Usually one of Beale's most crowded venues, with resident blues bands every night 9pm–1.30am, plus Cajun cooking and ribs; $4 cover.

W.C. Handy Performing Arts Park Third Ave and Rufus Thomas Blvd ☎901/526-0110. An outdoor amphitheater featuring live music – most nights for free.

Wild Bill's 1580 Vollintine Ave ☎901/726-5473. North Memphis jook-joint with live music Fri–Sun. Willie Mitchell's Rhythm and Blues Club 326 Beale St ☎901/523-7444. One of Beale's smaller and less fancy clubs, owned by the daughters of legendary soul producer/songwriter Mitchell, and putting on consistently classy blues and R&B acts. Talent search Wed nights.

Shiloh National Military Park

Approximately 110 miles east of Memphis and twelve south of Savannah, Tennessee, via US-64 and Hwy-22, **SHILOH NATIONAL MILITARY PARK** (daily 8am–5pm; $2; ☎901/689-5275) commemorates one of the most crucial battles of the Civil War. After victories at Fort Henry and Fort Donelson, General Grant's confident Union forces were all but defeated by a surprise early-morning Confederate attack on April 6, 1862. A stubborn rump of resistance held on until around 5pm, and the Confederates elected to finish the task off the next morning rather than launching a twilight assault. However, Grant's decimated regiments were bolstered by the overnight arrival of new troops, and instead it was their dawn initiative that forced the tired and demoralized Confederates to retreat.

Shiloh was the first encounter on a scale that became common as the war continued, putting an abrupt end to the romantic innocence of many a raw volunteer soldier. Over 20,000 men in all were killed. Even the war-toughened General Sherman spoke of "piles of dead soldiers' mangled bodies . . . without heads and legs . . . the scenes on this field would have cured anyone of war."

The **visitor center** displays artifacts recovered from the battlefield and shows a twenty-minute film. A self-guided ten-mile driving tour takes in the **National Cemetery**, whose moss-covered walls contain thousands of unidentified graves.

Nashville

Set amid the gentle hills and fertile farmlands of central Tennessee, **NASHVILLE** attracts six million people each year – a mixture of devoted fans and the just plain curious – to immerse themselves in **country music**. They come to enjoy themselves, and the city makes sure that they do, offering not just the relatively mainstream **Country Music Hall of Fame** and **Grand Ole Opry**, but all the wonders of "Tacksville." To make the most of this facet of Nashville, you need to abandon any idea of detachment, and get out there among the nightspots and gift emporia, joining the quest for souvenir T-shirts, Stetsons, rattlesnake belts and photos of your favorite star.

However, there is a real city beneath the rhinestone glitter. Nashville has been the leading settlement in middle Tennessee since **Fort Nashborough** was established in 1779. State capital since 1843, it is now the **financial** and **insurance** center of the mid-South, as well as a fast-growing **manufacturing** base. Giant Nissan and Saturn motor plants have been attracted to its immediate hinterland, and rapid growth since World War II has transformed a once-compact city into a sprawling conurbation stretching out in all directions along the undulating roads, here known as **pikes**.

For all its blue-collar "Nash-Vegas" image, Nashville has maintained a strong reputation for **learning** since planter times, and is home to sixteen higher education establishments, including Vanderbilt University and the renowned black colleges of Fisk University and Meharry Medical School. The city likes to see itself as the "Athens of the South" – and, endearingly, has built a replica of the

Parthenon to bolster its claim. Even at night, Nashville offers more than country music, with enough going on to satisfy most tastes. It has also boosted its image by attracting an NFL team (the Tennessee Oilers) and NHL side (the Nashville Predators) here.

The other conspicuous element in Nashville's make-up is **religion**. There are over seven hundred churches, more per capita than anywhere else in the country. But what really earns it the tag of "Protestant Vatican" is the proliferation of colleges for training preachers and missionaries, church administrative offices and Bible-publishing plants.

Arrival, information and getting around

Nashville International Airport is eight miles southeast of downtown. Metropolitan Transit Authority **buses** into town (weekdays 8.13am–5.33pm; weekends 6.49am-4.19pm; ☎615/862-5950) leave every half-hour and cost $1.45. The Gray Line shuttle (every 15min 6am–11pm; $11 one-way $17 round-trip; ☎1-800/669-9463) drops off at most downtown hotels. Taxis are probably the quickest option but will set you back around $25. Greyhound buses arrive in a seedy part of downtown at 200 Eighth Ave S; there's no Amtrak service.

Nashville is so spread out that a **car** is a good option. However, the one-way system can be maddening, and the roads change name without warning. MTA runs **buses** until midnight to most parts of the county, from the transit mall on Deaderick Street and Fifth Avenue ($1.45 flat fare), and **trolleys,** leaving Broadway and 9th Street (Tues–Sat noon & 2pm, Sun 1–3pm), that cover the entire downtown area plus Music Row for a fare of $1 (an unlimited 1-day pass is $5; a similar 3-day pass is $8). To get out to the Opryland area MTA offer a city bus express #34 that leaves from 5th Street and Broadway about every hour Mon–Fri 10am–8.30pm, Sat–Sun 10am-6pm. Another system of trolleys runs between the Opry mills mall, the *Opryland Hotel* and the various attractions in Music Valley. Grand Ole Opry Tours (☎615/889-9490), Gray Line (☎615/883-5555) and Johnny Walker Tours (☎615/834-8585), among others, offer a variety of both cultural and specialist country music **bus tours**. Expect to pay $25 for a three-hour trip, not including admission to attractions. Alternatively you can hop on the "Big Pink Bus" with the singing guides of NashTrash Tours (Sat & Sun 11am & 2pm; other days by arrangement; $20; ☎615/226-7300), who dig up the dirt on the country stars. Nashville Black Heritage Tours offers **walking tours** concentrating on the city's considerable African-American history (☎615/890-8173; call to arrange at least 3 days in advance). The city also produces a handy CityWalk map of downtown, following two miles of painted blue lines around the major historic sights. These maps, as well as discount tickets to attractions, are available from the **visitor center**, next to the massive Nashville Arena at 501 Broadway (daily daylight hours; ☎615/259-4747 or 1-800/657-6910, ⓦwww.nashvillecvb.com).

Accommodation

Well-priced **rooms** are not too hard to find in Nashville, with budget **motels** gathering a couple of miles north of downtown, off the I-65 Trinity Lane/Brick Church Pike exit. Rates are usually higher in June during the country music Fan Fair festival (see p.576). **B&B** agencies include B&B About Tennessee, PO Box 110227, TN 37222 (☎615/331-5244), which arranges rooms from $55. There's **camping** at *Opryland KOA*, 2626 Music Valley Drive (☎615/889-0282), set in 27 attractive acres and with free live music shows in the summer.

Days Inn at the Coliseum 211 N 1st St ☎615/254-1551, ⒡15/256-0758, ⓦwww .daysinn.com. Inexpensive hotel with good view of the city skyline and close to downtown. ❸

Hampton Inn – Hillsboro 2324 Crestmoor Rd ☎615/777-0001, ⒡615/986-5200. Located among the Green Hills of Hillsboro. Suites come with fully equipped kitchens and the complimentary continental breakfast with "do-it-yourself" Belgian waffles. ❺

Opryland Hotel McGavock Pike ☎615/889-1000, ⒡615/871-7741, ⓦwww.oprylandhotel.com. Unbelievably vast and expensive 2000-room place (costing up to $3500) set out around tropical gar-

dens and glass-roofed courtyards. ❼

Ramada Inn 920 Broadway ☎615/244-0150, ⒡615/244-0445, ⓦwww.ramadainn.com. Reasonably priced downtown convention hotel, with pool. ❻

Days Inn – Downtown/Convention Center 711 Union St ☎615/242-4311, ⒡615/889-0090, ⓦwww.daysinn. Excellent central downtown location, and good weekend rates. ❸

Shoney's Inn – Music Row 1521 Demonbreun St ☎615/255-9977, ⒡615/242-6127, ⓦwww.shoneysinn. Good-value accommodation complete with complimentary continental breakfast. Close to all the record labels. ❹

The City

Downtown Nashville looks much like any other regional business center, dominated by office blocks and parking lots, and dotted here and there with major flagship structures like the gigantic **Nashville Arena** sports and entertainment complex at Fifth Avenue and Broadway, and the **Country Music Hall of Fame** at Fifth and Demonbreun streets. It's perfectly possible to spend a busy day in Nashville without coming into contact with country music. A good starting point is **Riverfront Park** at First Street and Broadway, a thin stretch of grass and terracing dipping down to the **Cumberland River**. A replica of the wooden **Fort Nashborough** (Tues–Sun 9am–5pm; free) stands on a promontory above the river as a monument to the city's founders of 1779. A few blocks away, the worthy **Tennessee State Museum** at 505 Deaderick St (Tues–Sat 10am–5pm, Sun 1–5pm; free) is strongest on the Civil War, highlighting the hardships of the ill-clad, ill-fed soldiers, of whom 23,000 out of 77,000 died at Shiloh alone. Other displays in this huge space focus on frontier life and on black Tennesseans, looking at slavery, Reconstruction, the founding of the Ku Klux Klan and the civil rights movement.

Marking downtown's northern boundary at Sixth and Charlotte avenues, the resplendent **Tennessee State Capitol** (Mon–Fri 9am–4pm; free), modeled on an Ionic temple, looks out across the city from its hilltop perch. Early in the twentieth century, this area was yet another "Hell's Half Acre," notorious for its drinking holes, gambling clubs, sex shows and dope dens; it's considerably tamer now, housing hotels and offices.

At the 1897 Tennessee Centennial Exposition, Nashville's "Athens of the South" exhibit featured a full-size wood-and-plaster replica of the Parthenon, which proved so popular with Nashville residents that the present permanent structure, in the middle of **Centennial Park** southwest of downtown at West End and 25th avenues, was built in 1931. This impressive edifice – familiar to moviegoers from the finale of Robert Altman's not-always-flattering *Nashville* – is now home to Nashville's premier **art museum** (Tues–Sat 9am–4.30pm; April–Sept also Sun 12.30–4.30pm; $3.50). The lower level contains American paintings; the upper hall is dominated by a 42ft replica of Phidias's statue of Athena.

Just across West End Avenue, weather-beaten Gothic structures sit alongside more modern utilitarian buildings on the campus of prestigious **Vanderbilt University**. This bastion of conservatism was one of the very few colleges to witness student demonstrations in *support* of US involvement in Vietnam. Nearby **Fisk University** is one of the nation's oldest black colleges, and on

DOWNTOWN NASHVILLE

N

Opryland & Grand Ole Opry

Centennial Park & The Parthenon

Museum of Tobacco Art & History

State Capitol

State Library

State Supreme Court

Fort Nashborough

Tennessee State Museum & Performing Arts Center

ARCADE

PRINTERS ALLEY

Riverfront Park

River Taxis

Ryman Auditorium

Hatch Show Print

Nashville Convention Center

Nashville Arena

Bus Station

MUSIC ROW

Country Music Hall of Fame

0   200 yds

ACCOMMODATION

Days Inn – Downtown/Convention Center   1
Ramada Inn   2
Shoney's Inn – Music Row   3

RESTAURANTS AND BARS

Bourbon Street Blues & Boogie Bar   A
Prime Cut Steakhouse   B

---

campus is the excellent **Van Vechten Gallery**, at Jackson Street and D.B. Todd Boulevard (Tues–Fri 10am–5pm, Sat & Sun 1–5pm; closed Sun in summer; donation). In addition to works by Picasso, Cézanne and Renoir, and a wide array of pieces by Georgia O'Keeffe, there are changing exhibits, many of them with an African-American theme.

Of the many buildings erected by Nashville's antebellum elite, none was more elaborate than the **Belmont Mansion**, a mile southeast of the Parthenon at 1900 Belmont Blvd (June–Aug Mon–Sat 10am–4pm, Sun 1pm–4pm; Sept–May Tues–Sat 10am–4pm; $7). This 36-room Italianate 1850 villa looks out across ornamented gardens that once kept bears and a lake stocked with alligators.

The Grand Ole Opry

Nashville's radio station **WSM** ("We Shield Millions," the slogan of its insurance-company sponsor) first broadcast on October 5, 1925. Two years later, at the start of his *Barn Dance* show, compere George D. Hay announced "for the past hour we have been listening to music taken largely from Grand Opera, but from now on we will present *The Grand Ole Opry*." This piece of slang became the name of America's longest-running radio show, still going out to millions every Friday and Saturday evening on WSM-AM (650); the original "hillbilly" jam session has become country music's elite showcase.

Swiftly outgrowing the WSM studios, the show moved in 1943 to a former tabernacle – the **Ryman Auditorium**. There it acquired a make-or-break reputation; up-and-coming singers could only claim to have made it if they had gone down well at the Opry. Among thousands of hopefuls who tried to get on the show was Elvis Presley, advised by an Opry official in 1954 to stick to truck-driving. The first appearance of **Hank Williams**, in 1949, commanded an unequaled six encores. Within four years, the Opry audience was singing his evangelical *I Saw the Light* on the news of his drink- and drug-induced death.

In 1974 the show moved on again, this time to a new purpose-built 4424-seat theater in what was the **Opryland** theme park (now the **Opry Mills** mall) – one of many Opry spin-offs, including hotels, TV stations and a record label. Among more than sixty stars currently on the Opry roster are old-timers like Hank Snow and Charlie Louvin, perennial superstars like Dolly Parton, and current country chart-toppers such as Garth Brooks and Alison Krauss. However, many of the younger artists are busy touring, so most shows are dominated by stars whose best days have past.

Throughout the year, two performances on Saturday night at 6.30pm and 9.30pm and one on Friday night at 7.30pm feature up to twenty acts. During the summer there's an extra Friday night show and matinee on Tuesday. The line-ups are usually announced at the box office on the preceding Thursday. Tickets are $23–25 and not too hard to get, especially if you book in advance. Contact the box office at 2808 Opryland Drive, Nashville, TN 37214 (☎615/889-3060).

Country music Nashville

The status of Nashville as country music's capital city dates back to the Twenties and the arrival of thousands of migrants fleeing rural poverty. The music they brought with them, rooted in the folk songs of Tennessee's first Irish and British settlers, soon mutated in the urban environment into something new, incorporating elements of Tin Pan Alley musicals, religious hymns and the songs of ex-slaves.

As radios and record players became widely available for the first time, the **recording industry** began to take off, and Nashville became the obvious geographical base for the musicians of the mid-South. Radio station WSM had championed the country sound since 1925, and its live weekly *Grand Ole Opry* concerts (see box above) spearheaded the city's burgeoning **live music** scene.

The first big commercial boom came in the decade of prosperity after World War II. Nashville proliferated with recording studios, publishing companies and artists' agencies. The big labels recognized that a large slice of the (white) record-buying public wanted something a bit safer than rockabilly. The easy-listening **Nashville Sound** they came up with, pioneered by Patsy Cline and Jim Reeves, perpetuated by the likes of Barbara Mandrell and Kenny Rogers and virtually preened free of twang by Shania Twain and Garth Brooks, remains the clean-cut face of country – though country music has always had its earthier side – and the concentration of stars and music-biz executives has turned

Nashville into something of a downmarket Hollywood.

Though Nashville's country scene is both conspicuous and accessible, submerging yourself in it takes time and quite a lot of money; prices are set at what the industry knows enthusiastic fans will pay. In addition to the daytime attractions mentioned below, country music venues are listed in the "Nightlife" section overleaf.

Downtown at 116 Fifth Ave, you can take a self-guided tour of the **Ryman Auditorium** (daily 8.30am–4pm; $6; ☏615/254-1445), the former home of The Grand Ole Opry. With its wooden church pews and glass cases filled with flowered frocks and bootlace ties belonging to the stars, it's certainly an evocative place to visit – it also presents live performances in the evening. Around the corner, among the Broadway honky-tonks, **Hatch Show Print** at no. 316 (Mon–Fri 9.30am–5.30, Sat 10.30am–5.30pm, hours vary on Sun; ☏615/256-2805) has been in business since 1879. It still prints and sells evocative posters from the early days of country and rock'n'roll, using the original blocks, along with probably the best postcards in the USA. Flamboyant leather and sequined garments are sold in **Dangerous Threads**, at the foot of Second Avenue nearby at no. 105, but to see some really outlandish stage costumes, visit **Manuel's Exclusive Clothing** up toward Music Row at 1922 Broadway.

Blue route trolleys run along Broadway to the **Country Music Hall of Fame**, at 222 Fifth Ave S (daily 9am–5pm; $10.75). This is packed with costumes, guitars and personal possessions of the stars, including Boxcar Willie's hobo hat, Gram Parsons' acoustic guitar and Elvis's gold Cadillac, whose forty coats of paint contain crushed diamonds and fish scales. Film and TV clips abound to help to clarify the arcane distinctions between bluegrass, cowboy, rockabilly, honky-tonk, Cajun and western swing.

Music Row is the heart of Nashville's recording industry, with companies like Warner Bros., Mercury and Sony operating out of plush office blocks. Almost adjacent are the garish souvenir shops on Demonbreun Street, and several tacky "museums."

With the exception of the **Grand Ole Opry** itself (see box, opposite), **Opryland**, the area nine miles northeast of downtown on Briley Parkway, just off the I-40 E loop, isn't all that country. The old theme park has been ripped down and replaced by **Opry Mills**, a giant series of malls filled with flagship stores, restaurants and cinemas. Also leaving from here are paddlesteamer trips on the beautifully restored **General Jackson Showboat** ($25–65; ☏615/871-6100). You can ride a bus #34X to nearby **Music Valley**, opposite the *Opryland* hotel, which boasts the popular *Nashville Palace* (see overleaf), along with a museum dedicated to **Willie Nelson** and others, that showcases wax dummies and surplus cars of the stars. A factory outlet mall, various stores and movie theaters all compete to snatch the tourist dollar.

Eating

Nashville has its share of awful chain restaurants, but it also offers many down-home Southern joints, as well as upmarket places well suited for expense account dining. Many live music venues (see overleaf) also serve food. If you have a car, be sure to get out to *The Loveless Café*, quite simply one of the best **country restaurants** in the South.

Brown's Diner 2102 Blair Blvd ☏615/269-5509. A classic diner where the cheeseburgers are to-die-for. Order one with everything on it – a perfect hangover "cure."

Cock o' the Walk 2624 Music Valley Drive ☏615/889-1930. Fantastic catfish served in cheery environs. Open daily until 9pm; until 10pm at the weekend.

The Loveless Café 8400 Hwy-100, 20 miles south of town ☎615/646-9700. Friendly motel café famed for its superb country food. Breakfasts are best: hunks of salty ham with gravy, eggs, toast and fluffy biscuits slicked with succulent homemade jams.

Nashville Deli 1918 Broadway ☎615/329-6674. Huge sandwiches and wicked shakes until midnight on Fri and Sat in this student-friendly haunt.

Pancake Pantry 1796 21st Ave ☎615/383-9333. One of Nashville's most popular breakfast spots – expect to wait for a table. Close to Vanderbilt University and Music Row in the likeable Hillsboro Village district. Open daily 6am–4pm.

Prime Cut Steakhouse 170 2nd Ave ☎615/242–3083. Generous-sized steaks and huge portions of Texas Toast at reasonable prices in a stylish yet relaxed atmosphere.

Sammy B's 26 Music Square E ☎615/256-6600. A smart-looking music industry hangout, but the great-tasting lunch plates of grilled chicken and fish are excellent value ($8–10).

Sunset Grill 2001 Belcourt Ave ☎615/386-3663. Stylish restaurant in Hillsboro Village, serving upmarket food such as fresh fish in smoky sauces. The terrace is great for people-watching. Around $30 per head; all food half-price after 10pm Mon–Thurs and after midnight Fri–Sat.

Wild Boar 2014 Broadway ☎615/329-1313. A nationally renowned French restaurant with an impressive wine list. Slightly pretentious, with entree prices touching $30.

Nightlife

Of all Nashville's country music venues, the main ones to **avoid** are the ersatz clubs along the much-hyped and tacky downtown **Printers Alley**. The **honky-tonks** on Broadway, between Second and Fourth avenues, are more genuine and down-to-earth, though steer clear if you're on your own. Dine-and-dance places like the *Nashville Palace* offer good-quality mainstream country music (and more crowds), while up-and-coming progressive country bands play smaller venues like the *Bluebird Café*. Every June, the **Fan Fair** is a week-long series of concerts and opportunities to meet the stars (☎615/770-2040, ⊛www.fanfair.com). Every Thursday evening in summer, the free **Dancin' in the District** event in Riverfront Park features talent from various genres.

For **listings** of upcoming gigs and events, check the free weekly *Nashville Scene*, Thursday's *Nashville Banner*, or Friday's and Saturday's *Tennessean*. If you're looking for music other than country, **Second Avenue** is a popular downtown hangout for both locals and tourists, offering everything from bluegrass to funk and punk, and various interesting venues can be found around Vanderbilt's campus.

Nashville's prime venue for theater, dance and classical music is the **Tennessee Performing Arts Center** at 505 Deaderick St (☎615/726-3372). Its **symphony orchestra** also puts on concerts in **Centennial Park**, at West End and 25th avenues by Vanderbilt University, from June to August.

Bluebird Café 4104 Hillsboro Rd ☎615/383-1461. Intimate café, six miles west of downtown, which has become *the* place to see the latest honky-tonk and country artists. Early evening entertainment is free, but a cover of $7–15 is charged for the second show. Reservations recommended.

Bourbon Street Blues & Boogie Bar 220 Printers Alley ☎615/242-5837. Consistently good blues in the otherwise awful downtown Printers Alley.

Ernest Tubb's Record Store Midnight Jamboree Texas Troubadour Theatre, 2414 Music Valley Drive ☎615/889-2474. A live radio show, recorded every Sat from midnight to 1am, next to Tubb's store, in a purpose-built theater that puts out musical and other productions most evenings.

Features genuinely promising newcomers as well as major Opry stars.

Exit/In 2208 Elliston Place ☎615/321-4400. Very popular venue for rock, reggae and country, with the occasional big name; serves beer and pizza. Tues–Sat until late; $5–20 cover after 9pm.

Nashville Palace 2400 Music Valley Drive ☎615/885-1540. Resident country bands, and Oprey acts on summer Mon; good country food. Cover around $5.

Robert's Western World 416 Broadway ☎615/244-9552. The best of Broadway's country music by far, which also doubles up as a cowboy boot store.

South from Nashville

As you head southeast from Nashville, large nineteenth-century plantation homes line US-31 between suburban Brentwood and the historic town of **FRANKLIN**, eighteen miles out. One of the bloodiest battles of the Civil War occurred here on November 30, 1864, when 8500 men fell in less than an hour. Despite forcing the Union troops back to Nashville, huge losses meant that the Southerners could not follow up their victory. Among several strategic buildings open to visitors is **Carnton Plantation** (April–Oct Mon–Sat 9am–5pm, Sun 1–5pm; Nov–March Mon–Sat 9am–4pm, Sun 1–4pm; $7; ☎615/794-0903), about a mile southeast of the town on Hwy-431, a former Confederate hospital where bloodstains are still visible on the floor. The town's entire fifteen-block center, now full of antique and specialty shops, is listed in the National Register of Historic Places. Several country stars favor the area, among them Billy Ray Cyrus, who owns a 400-acre ranch outside the town.

Jack Daniel's at Lynchburg

The change-resistant village, **LYNCHBURG**, seventy miles southeast of Nashville, is home to **Jack Daniel's Distillery** (daily 9am–4.30pm; free). Founded in 1866, this is the oldest registered distillery in the country (hence the famous "No. 1" appellation). Entertaining seventy-minute tours lead you through every step of the sour-mash whiskey-making process – but you can't actually sample the stuff, as you're in a dry county, though you can buy special edition bottles of the stuff in the giftshop, every day but Sunday.

Lynchburg itself is a pretty hamlet, laid out around a neat town square with a redbrick courthouse and a number of old-fashioned stores. One enjoyable throwback is *Miss Mary Bobo's Boarding House*, which serves enormous **Southern dinners** (fried chicken, turnip greens, country ham and the like) at group tables in a lovely 1805 home (reservations are essential; ☎615/759-7394).

Eastern Tennessee

Until the creation of the Tennessee Valley Authority, the opening of Great Smoky Mountains National Park and the building of the interstate highways, life had continued in the remote hills and valleys of **eastern Tennessee** in much the same way as it had ever since the arrival of the first pioneers. Now visitors flock here for its endless expanses of natural beauty; and as a result, especially in the fall, the Smokies can get clogged with traffic. Most communities are small, and either over-touristed or just bland. The two main cities, modern **Knoxville** and picturesque **Chattanooga**, have much in common, including healthy post–World War II industrial growth, thanks to cheap TVA power.

Knoxville

Surrounded by the backwoods wilderness of the Great Smoky, the Cumberland and the Blue Ridge mountains, **KNOXVILLE**, the original capital of Tennessee, is a rather quiet city of 180,000. Modern skyscrapers, older brick buildings and a riverfront at the bottom of steep bluffs combine to give **downtown** an attractive edge, but specific places of interest are thin on the ground. On the northern fringe, the **Old City**, centered on Central Street and Jackson

Avenue, is a small area of shops, galleries, restaurants and nightspots in Victorian warehouses.

On the western edge of downtown, the **World's Fair Park** is dominated by the futuristic **Sunsphere**, a huge glass ball mounted on a round concrete tower. There is an observation deck on the lower level of the sphere (Mon–Sat 9am–4.30pm; free). The **Knoxville Museum of Art**, in the park at 1050 World's Fair Park Drive, hosts visiting exhibits and features a small permanent collection of paintings and a cleverly designed sculpture garden focused on a 200-year-old elm tree (Tues–Thurs & Sat 10am–5pm, Fri 10am–9pm, Sun noon–5pm; $7; ☎865/525-6101). Follow Cumberland Avenue up a few blocks and you come to the sprawling campus of the **University of Tennessee**. Lined with bars and diners, frequently bedecked in the orange and white colors of the Volunteers football team, the campus has two theaters and the **Frank H. McClung Museum** at Circle Park, which features displays on the city's archeology, art and history (Mon–Sat 9am–5pm, Sun 1–5pm; free).

The **Gateway Regional Visitor Center**, 900 Volunteer Landing Lane (daily 9am–5pm; ☎1-800/727-8045), celebrates east Tennessee's natural resources and its technological (predominantly nuclear) achievements. It stands among the waterfalls and foliage of the revitalized Volunteer Landing, which boasts riverside restaurants and a marina complex.

Practicalities

Greyhound **buses** stop at the depot on Magnolia Street; K-Trans city buses run a free trolley to the campus. The **visitor center** is on the Riverfront at 900 Volunteer Landing Lane (☎423/523-7263 or 1-800/727-8045, ⓦwww.knoxville.org). The comfortable *Days Inn – Campus*, 1706 W Cumberland Ave (☎423/521-5000, ⓕ865/540-3866, ⓦwww.daysinn.com; ❸/❹), is fairly central, and there's a *Comfort Inn* further out at 5334 Central Ave Pike (☎423/688-1010,

---

Dollywood

Born in 1946, one of twelve children, **Dolly Parton** lived in several modest homes around Pigeon Forge, the most isolated of them two miles from the nearest neighbor and over four miles from the mailbox. As a child she sang every week on local radio, before leaving for Nashville on the day she finished at Sevier County High School. Her first success, duetting with Porter Wagoner, came to an acrimonious end in the early Seventies, but she scored a major country hit in 1976 with *Jolene*. She then crossed over to a poppier sound, and into Hollywood films like *9 to 5* and *The Best Little Whorehouse in Texas*. Her songs have been acclaimed for their readiness to address issues like rural poverty, and a refusal to tag along with the Nashville stereotype of subservient females.

Dollywood, Dolly Parton's "homespun fun" theme park, blends ersatz mountain heritage with the glamour of its celebrity shareholder. One section showcases Appalachian **crafts**, making everything from lye soap to horse-drawn carriages; a museum looks at Dolly herself in entertaining detail; and music shows are constantly on the go. The rides, however, are mostly unspectacular, and although they've moved with the times by installing the $8 million **Tennessee Tornado** roller coaster, the whole place can get insufferably precious.

Dollywood is at 700 Dollywood Lane at the north end of Pigeon Forge (April weekends 9am–6pm; May to mid-June Mon, Wed & Fri–Sun 9am–6pm; mid-June to Aug daily 9am–9pm; Sept–Nov Mon, Wed & Fri–Sun times vary; Dec daily times vary; $35, children (age 4–11) $24, April–Oct; Nov & Dec $25, children $12; ☎423/428-9488). Local **radio station** WDLY, 105.5FM, is another Dolly Parton enterprise.

ⓟ865/687-4235, ⓦwww.comfortinn.com; ❸), while the *Holiday Inn Select*, 525 Henley St (ⓣ423/522-2800, ⓕ865/523-0738, ⓦwww.holiday-inn.com/tys-downtown; ❹), is one of the more reasonably priced hotels near the downtown convention center. Rooms are at a premium when the Tennessee Volunteers are playing at home.

Knoxville's favorite **restaurant**, the rib specialists *Calhoun's*, overlooks the river downtown at 400 Neyland Drive (ⓣ423/673-3355). In the Old City, *Barley's*, 200 Jackson Ave, serves hand-tossed pizza and grilled food, has 43 beers on tap and hosts live music most nights. *Tomato Head* in the downtown Market Square Mall (ⓣ423/637-4067) is a wildly popular place for pizza and super-stuffed sandwiches throughout the day and evening.

Toward the Great Smoky Mountains

The usual way to approach the Smokies from the west is on the billboard-lined US-441 that sweeps past the small market center of **SEVIERVILLE**, whose well-preserved center is tucked just off the highway and evokes days gone by with its wooden-floored general stores and small cafés serving mountains of Southern food to hungry farmers. A statue of **Dolly Parton** stands on the lawn outside the courthouse. Sevierville merges almost seamlessly into the six-mile strip of motels, fast-food places, factory discount outlets, themed family attractions and souvenir shops at the dry town of **PIGEON FORGE**. This is the spot to race go-carts in places like the Rebel Yell Speedway, visit an Elvis museum and absorb regional entertainment at numerous barn-sized haunts including **Elwood Smooch's Hillbilly Hoedown**. Five miles further along US-441, a heavy layer of kitsch all but submerges the genuine Germanic heritage of the more upmarket "wet" tourist town of **GATLINBURG**. The long, narrow main street is packed to the point of claustrophobia with gimmicky souvenir shops, wax museums, and stalls selling sickly sweet taffy. An alternative, if you're approaching from the east, is to drive along the pretty Foothills Parkway through woods and across misty mountains, and turn east for seven miles or so to **TOWNSEND**, a peaceful strip where the motels are laid-back and the air is clear.

Practicalities

Sevierville (ⓣ1-800/255-6411), Gatlinburg (ⓣ1-800/568-4748) and Pigeon Forge (ⓣ1-800/251-9100) all have visitor centers on the main drag. **Accommodation** prices in the foothill towns fluctuate seasonally, from $20 up to $80 and also vary radically between weekdays and weekends.

As the furthest of the towns from the Smoky Mountains National Park, **Sevierville** has the best-value **motels**, and most of the major mid-price chains are represented. The *Calico Inn*, 757 Ranch Way (ⓣ865/428-3833 or 1-800/235-1054; ❺), is an award-winning **B&B** with great breakfasts. The town center offers several good spots for lunch including *Virgil's*, 109 Bruce St (ⓣ865/453-2782), a 1950s diner serving up big plates of burgers and home cooking.

Pigeon Forge has literally dozens of motels, such as the *Parkview*, 2806 Parkway (mid-March to Dec; ⓣ865/453-5051 or 1-800/239-9116; ❸), and the comfortable, friendly *Shular Inn*, 2708 Parkway (ⓣ865/453-2700 or 1-800/451-2376, ⓕ865/429-3069; ❸). If you prefer neon lights to wilderness trails and own a trailer you can **camp** at *Z Buda's Smokies Campground*, 705 S Parkway (April–Oct; ⓣ865/453-4129), where tentsites start from $12. A good **breakfast** place is the *Smoky Mountain Pancake House* at 4160 Parkway (ⓣ865/453-1947).

Gatlinburg offers the quickest access to the park and so tends to be the most expensive place to stay, but *Bales*, 221 Bishop Lane (☎865/436-4773 or 1-800/458-8249, ℻865/436-7341, ⓦwww.balesmotel.com; ❸), and *Bon Air Mountain Inn*, 950 Parkway (☎865/436-4857, ⓦwww.smokymountainresorts .com; ❹), are competitively priced. There's also an unaffiliated **youth hostel**, *Wa-Floy Mountain Retreat* at 3610 E Parkway (☎865/436-7700; $15). Gatlinburg is, however, the best choice for **food**: *Linebergers*, 903 Parkway (☎865/436-9284), at traffic light #8, is strong on seafood while *Calhoun's*, 1004 Parkway (☎865/436-4100), is a local chain renowned for decent barbecue.

In **Townsend** motels are strung along Hwy-321: try the peaceful *Highland Manor*, 7766 E Lamar Alexander Parkway (☎865/448-2211, ℻865/448-2312, ⓦwww.highlandmanor.com; ❷/❹), a friendly place with great views. Perhaps the best option in the entire area is the rustic cabins and lodges at the *Wonderland Lodge*, 3889 Wonderland Way (☎865/428-0779, ℻865/774-5011; ❸/❹), between Pigeon Forge and Townsend, where the idyll is maintained in the telephone-free rooms. The *Hearth and Kettle*, 7767 E Lamar Alexander Parkway (☎865/448-6059), opposite the *Highland Manor* motel, dishes up fresh trout and crispy fried chicken in a country store atmosphere.

Great Smoky Mountains National Park

The northern boundary of the **GREAT SMOKY MOUNTAINS NATIONAL PARK**, which stretches for seventy miles along the Tennessee–North Carolina border (see also p.515), is just two miles south of Gatlinburg on US-441. Don't expect immediate tranquility, however: the roads, particularly in the fall, can be lined almost bumper-to-bumper with cars, and if you're not staying in Gatlinburg it's best to use the well-marked bypass rather than drive through the town.

The Smokies, within a day's drive of the major urban centers of the east coast and the Great Lakes – and of two-thirds of the entire US population – attract over nine million visitors per year, more than twice as many as any other national park. These heavily contorted peaks are named for the **bluish haze** that hangs over them, made up of moisture and hydrocarbons released by the lush vegetation (a mature tree emits up to 900 gallons on a summer day). Since the Sixties, however, **air pollution** has been adding sulphates to the filmy smoke, and has cut back visibility by thirty percent. More than 120 tree species and over 1400 flowering plants clothe the mountains and meadows in color from early spring to late fall. Sixteen peaks rise above 6000ft, their steep elevation accounting for dramatic changes in climate.

The most popular **times to visit** are between late March and mid-May, for the delicate spring flowers, and during the second half of October, when the hills are shrouded in a magnificent canopy of glaring reds, subtle yellows and faded browns. During June and July, rhododendrons blaze fiercely in the sometimes stifling summer heat.

Just inside the park on US-441, the main artery running through to North Carolina, **Sugarlands Visitor Center** (summer daily 8am–7pm; fall and spring daily 8am–6pm; winter daily 8am–5pm) is a useful source of leaflets covering hiking trails, driving tours, forests and wildlife. From here a ten-mile drive rises to Newfound Gap on the state line, where a seven-mile spur road winds its way up to **Clingman's Dome**, at 6643ft the highest point in the park and in all Tennessee. A surreal concrete spiral walkway on top affords a panoramic, though hazy, view of the mountains, rather spoiled by the fact that virtually all the mature balsam firs in the area have been killed off by insect infestation.

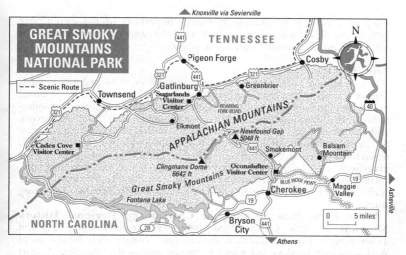

Asheville

The scenic **Little River Road** branches off back at Sugarlands toward **Cades Cove**, where another visitor center (mid–April to Oct 9am–7pm; call ☎865/436-1230 for winter hours) is situated halfway round an eleven-mile driving loop, always jam-packed with cars in summer and fall. Along the route, deserted barns, homesteads, mills and churches stand as a reminder of the farmers who carved out a living from this wilderness, before having to move out when national park status was conferred in 1934. Quieter **Hwy-321**, on the other side of Sugarlands, branches off onto a gravel road toward the beautiful Greenbrier area.

If you really want to get away from it all, escape onto the eight hundred miles of **hiking** trails. On the **Appalachian Trail**, however, you can now only camp in designated areas, caged in behind iron bars to keep out the bears.

Practicalities

Hikers intending to stay out overnight will need to obtain **backcountry permits**, available free from visitor centers (except in Cades Cove). The park also has ten developed **campgrounds**, of which the three most popular – *Cades Cove*, *Elkmont* and *Smokemont* – are always fully booked. Reserve in advance (☎1-800/365-CAMP) if you want a space in summer or fall. For details of the North Carolina side of the park, see p.515. For other enquiries contact the park headquarters (☎865/436-1230).

On Saturday, from dawn until 10am, the Cades Cove loop is reserved for **cyclists**. Bikes can be rented at the *Cades Cove Campground* (☎865-448-9034).

Chattanooga

Few cities are so identified with a song as **CHATTANOOGA**, in the southeast corner of Tennessee. Though visitors expecting Tex Beneke's and Glenn Miller's *Chattanooga Choo-Choo* may be let down to find that there is no longer even an Amtrak service, the town continues to celebrate its railroad history, and has plenty more to offer besides – not least its beautiful location on a deep bend in the **Tennessee River**, walled in by forested plateaus on three sides. This setting led John Ross, of Scottish and Cherokee ancestry, to found a trading post on the spot in 1815, and its strategic importance made it a great prize during the Civil War; victories here in 1863 were the springboard for Sherman's march through Georgia (see p.533).

The Town

The centerpiece of Chattanooga's twenty miles of reclaimed riverfront is **Ross's Landing** (the town's original name), a park at the bottom of Broad Street. Here the splendid five-story **Tennessee Aquarium** traces the aquatic life of the Mississippi from its Tennessee tributaries to the Gulf of Mexico, and also shows giant IMAX movies ($12.95, IMAX $7.25, combined ticket $17; call for hours and reservations ☎423/265-0695 or 1-800/262-0695, ⓦwww.tnaqua.com). A variety of different cruises on the *Southern Belle* **riverboat** (☎423/266-4488), from the bottom of nearby Chestnut Street, include the daunting experience of bobbing around in the bottom of a huge lock on Chickamauga Lake. Prices start from $10 for a daytime sightseeing tour.

A few blocks from the river, the **Chattanooga Regional History Museum** at 400 Chestnut St (Mon–Fri 10am–4.30pm, Sat–Sun 11am–4.30pm; $4) takes a look at the area's rich history, with displays on its steel, soft-drink bottling and power industries, and on the Cherokee. A short walk further along are the grand old c.1900 buildings of the lively business district, such as the eye-catching Tivoli Theatre at 709 Broad St.

The further Chattanooga sprawls back from the river, the more run-down it becomes, but it's well worth heading the two miles up to the **Choo-Choo complex**, where the 1909 Beaux Arts-style **Southern Railroad Terminal**, at 1400 Market St (☎423/266-5000), is now a *Holiday Inn* – the *Chattanooga Choo-Choo Hotel*. The impressive high-domed waiting room serves as the lobby, leading through to the former platform area, where restored carriages act as hotel suites. Giftshops and cafés share space with a steam engine similar to the original Choo-Choo (the name given by the local paper to the first passenger train to come in from Cincinnati in 1880). You're free to roam around; admission to the world's largest model railway display, on site, is $2.75. A free shuttle runs between the Choo-Choo complex and the Aquarium.

The authentic **steam trains** of the **Tennessee Valley Railroad** offer stunning six-mile rides, crossing the river, running through deep tunnels, and turning round on a giant turntable. The two main stations, restored to their 1930s look, are at 2200 N Chamberlain Ave in east Chattanooga and 4119 Cromwell Rd (I-75 exit 4 to Hwy-153); some routes pick up at the *Choo-Choo Hotel* ($10.50; for schedule call ☎423/894-8028 or visit ⓦwww.tvrail.com).

Practicalities

A taxi downtown from Chattanooga's **airport** (☎423/855-2200), three miles east, costs around $12. Greyhound connections with Nashville, Knoxville and Atlanta arrive on Broad Street downtown. The **visitor center**, adjacent to the Tennessee Aquarium (daily 8.30am–5.30pm; ☎423/756-8687 or 1-800/322-3344, ⓦwww.chattanoogafun.com), provides the usual range of help, along with a useful guide for travelers with disabilities. Budget **motels** downtown, such as the *Days Inn Rivergate*, 901 Carter St (☎423/266-7331, ⓕ423/266-9357, ⓦwww.daysinn.com; ❹), tend to be in rather dismal areas; far more atmospheric, if you can get a room on the train, is the *Choo-Choo* (☎423/266-5000 or 1-800/872-2529, ⓕ423/265-4635, ⓦwww.choo-choo.com; ❺), and there are countless inexpensive options along the interstates, such as the *Super*

8, at 1410 Mack Smith Rd off I-75 S, exit 1 (☎423/892-3888, ☞423/499-0677, ⓦwww.super8.com; ❷). There's **camping** at *Raccoon Mountain Campground*, 319 West Hills Drive (☎423/821-9403, ☞423/825-1289, ⓦwww.raccoonmountain .com; cabins ❶/❷, tentsites $12.95).

The obvious place to **eat** in Chattanooga is the *Choo-Choo* complex, where the enclosed but well-lit *Gardens Restaurant* serves standard meals for around $10; the more romantic *Silver Diner* serves steaks and seafood in a railroad car permanently parked on the platform behind, and there's also an *Espresso Café* (all ☎423/266-5000). For inventive Southern cooking in a stylish atmosphere, try the *Southside Grill*, 1400 Cowart St (☎423/266-9211). The *Big River Grille & Brewing Works*, 222 Broad St (☎423/267-2739), is a cavernous brewpub and restaurant near the Aquarium.

Lookout Mountain

The name Chattanooga comes from a Creek word, meaning "rock rising to a point"; six miles from downtown is the rock itself, the 2215ft **Lookout Mountain**. To reach the top, you can either drive the whole way along a complicated, poorly signed road or catch the world's steepest **incline railway**, which grinds its tentative way up through a narrow gash in the lush forest from 3917 St Elmo Ave near the foot of the mountain (on bus route #15), tackling nerve-racking gradients of up to 72.7 percent (daily: summer 8.30am–8.50pm; rest of year 9am–5.50pm; 3 trips per hour; $9; ☎423/821-4224). Once there, a steep five-minute walk through **Point Park** brings you to **Point Lookout**,

The Cherokee and the Trail of Tears

During the eighteenth and early nineteenth centuries, the **Cherokee** were the most powerful Indian tribe in the tristate region of Tennessee, Georgia and North Carolina. They forged close links with white pioneers, adopting white methods in schooling and agriculture, intermarrying – and owning African slaves. The only Native Americans to develop their own written language, they had a regular newspaper, *The Cherokee Phoenix*. They even supplied soldiers for Andrew Jackson's US forces against the Creek Indians and the British in 1814, hoping to buy influence with the federal government.

Thirteen years later, against a background of aggressive territorial claims by settlers, the Cherokee produced a written constitution modeled on that of the US, stating their intention to continue to be a self-governing nation. John Ross, founder of Ross's Landing, and at most one-eighth Cherokee, was elected as their first Principal Chief in 1828 in an effort to appease and negotiate with national and state governments over their lands. However, as white demand for land increased, their former ally **Jackson**, now US president, was pressurized by the Georgians into "offering" the Cherokee western lands in exchange for those east of the Mississippi. Although the tribal leadership refused, a minority faction accepted, giving the government the get-out clause they wanted. The Cherokee were ordered to leave within two years, and 14,000 of them were forcefully removed to Oklahoma in 1838 along the horrific **Trail of Tears**: 4000 died of disease and exposure on the way. In the meantime, their land was sold by lottery and Ross's Landing was renamed Chattanooga. One thousand Cherokee managed to avoid removal by escaping into the mountains, and their descendants now occupy a small reservation in North Carolina (see p.516).

The **Red Clay State Historic Park**, twenty miles east of Chattanooga off Hwy-317, recounts the old Cherokee way of life, with replica houses, tools and household implements. Its balsamic Sacred Council Spring was once a meeting place for Cherokee elders.

the northern promontory of the mountain, which commands a not-to-be-missed view of the city and the meandering Tennessee River. This is part of the **Chickamauga and Chattanooga National Military Park**, covering several sites around the city and in nearby Chickamauga, Georgia, that witnessed fierce fighting in the fall of 1863. The battle here that November, in which Confederate forces which had been besieging Chattanooga were finally forced to withdraw, was also known as the "Battle Above the Clouds"; thick mantles of fog often obscure the city below to this day. Among the many memorials in Point Park is the only statue in the country to show Union and Confederate soldiers shaking hands.

Alabama

Just 250 miles from north to south, **ALABAMA** ranges from the fast-flowing rivers, waterfalls and lakes of the **Appalachian foothills** to the subtropical bayous and white beaches of the **Gulf Coast**. Most of its industry is concentrated in the **north**, around rejuvenated **Birmingham**, and **Huntsville**, first home of the nation's space program. The sun-scorched farmlands of middle Alabama envelop sober **Montgomery**, the state capital. Away from the French-influenced coastal strip around attractive **Mobile**, fundamentalist Protestant attitudes have traditionally backed a succession of right-wing demagogues, such as **George Wallace**, the four-time state governor who received ten million votes in the 1968 presidential election.

Times have moved on since the epic **civil rights** struggles in Montgomery, Birmingham and **Selma**. Monuments and civic literature celebrate the achievements of the campaigners, and even Wallace renounced his racist views, courting – and winning – black votes in his successful campaign for governor in 1982.

Getting around Alabama

Considering its rural nature, **public transportation** is relatively good in Alabama. Daily Amtrak **trains** from New York and Atlanta to New Orleans stop at Anniston, Birmingham and Tuscaloosa, while the line from Jacksonville to New Orleans passes through Mobile; Amtrak **buses** connect Birmingham and Mobile by way of Montgomery, and Greyhound serves the major towns and cities. Mobile, Montgomery, Huntsville and Birmingham all have small airports.

Northern Alabama

Northern Alabama, on the trailing edges of the Appalachians, is brightened up by the mountain lakes, rivers and canyons of the **Tennessee River Valley**. The area's first white settlers were small farmers who had little in common with the big plantation owners further south, and attempted to dissociate from the Confederacy during the Civil War. Substantial postwar mineral finds led to an industrial boom that peaked in the early Thirties.

Huntsville

Many Southern cities aspire to blend the old with the new; few achieve it as dramatically as **HUNTSVILLE**, a hundred miles south of Nashville just inside the Alabama border. Its sleepy center still recalls the days when it was dominated by cotton merchants and railroad owners, a history absorbingly recounted in the **Huntsville Depot Museum**, 320 Church St (Tues–Sat 9am–5pm; closed Jan & Feb; $7). **Twickenham** – the community's original name in 1808, before anti-British sentiment in the run-up to the 1812 War dictated that it should be renamed for its first settler, a Virginian named John Hunt.

Time was when Huntsville was content to be the "Watercress Capital of the World"; the great leap forward came after World War II, when the army consolidated its **rocket and missile research** efforts in the city. Spearheading the project were **Dr Wernher von Braun** and 118 other German scientists, who came to Huntsville after a token period of rehabilitation. Von Braun's contribution of the V-2 ballistic missile to the Nazi war effort is ignored by the city, which prefers to laud his later space-age achievements, such as **Explorer I**, the nation's first satellite, and the mighty **Saturn V**.

The giant **US Space and Rocket Center**, five miles west of downtown on Hwy-20, off I-65 (summer daily 9am–6pm; $15), contains a mind-boggling array of technological exhibits, hands-on displays and weightlessness simulators, as well as a giant IMAX cinema. Outdoors, in the surreal Rocket and Space Shuttle parks, redundant rockets protrude skywards in the blazing Alabama sunshine; the 120-yard, four-story *Saturn V* rocket is laid on its side to emphasize its immensity.

Practicalities

Huntsville's **visitor center** is at 700 Monroe St (Mon–Sat 9am–5pm; ☏256/551-2230 or 1-800/843-0468, ⊛www.huntsville.org). Chain **motels** on the outskirts include a *Best Value Inn*, near the Space Center at 2201 N Memorial Parkway (☏256/536-7441; ❷). Of the **restaurants**, *Ol' Heidelberg*, 6125 University Drive NW (☏256/922-0556), offers German specialties including sauerkraut and Wiener schnitzel. *Eunice's Country Kitchen*, on the western fringes of downtown at 1006 Andrew Jackson Way (☏256/534-9550; closed Tues), is an inexpensive rendezvous for home-cooked Southern breakfasts.

Birmingham

The rapid transformation of farmland into the city of **BIRMINGHAM** began in 1870, when two railroad routes met in the Jones Valley, a hundred miles south of Huntsville. What attracted speculators was not the scenery, but what lay under it – a mixture of iron ore, limestone and coal, perfect for the manufacture of iron and steel. The expansion of heavy industry was finally brought to an abrupt halt by the Depression. Today iron and steel production account for only a few thousand jobs, but new service and medical industries have helped transform this once smog-filled metropolis into a prosperous and pleasant city.

Being known as the "Pittsburgh of the South" might seem like faint praise; however, Birmingham also earned the label of the "Johannesburg of

America" for the brutality and intolerance of its police force. An intense civil rights campaign in 1963 was the turning point, setting Birmingham on the road to smoother race relations. Since 1979, under five-term black mayor Richard Arrington, the city has slowly but surely turned itself around, and the 1990s in particular saw a growing self-confidence in Birmingham's potential to be the "next Atlanta." Nonetheless, even a short stroll around downtown leaves the rather depressing impression that a lot remains to be done.

Arrival, information and getting around

Birmingham Airport is just three miles from downtown; call Yellow Cabs ($12) on ☎205/252-1131. Amtrak pulls in at 1819 Morris Ave, downtown, and the Greyhound station is at 19th Street N, between Sixth and Seventh avenues – a rough area at night. Public transportation is poor, and most of the attractions are well spread out, so you'll need a car to see the city properly. The **visitor center** can be found at 2200 Ninth Ave N (Mon–Fri 8.30am–5pm; ☎205/458-8000 or 1-800/458-8085, ⊛www.sweetbirmingham.com). The city has two free listings magazines: *The Birmingham Weekly* and the bi-weekly *Black and White*.

Accommodation

Many of Birmingham's wide range of places to **stay** offer advantageous weekend rates. The nearest place to **camp** is the *Birmingham South KOA* (☎205/664-8832; $14 per tentsite), eight miles south in Pelham, off I-65 S.

Civil rights in Birmingham

In the first half of 1963, civil rights leaders chose Birmingham as the target of "Project C" (for confrontation), aiming to force businesses to integrate lunch counters and employ more blacks. Despite threats from Police Chief **"Bull" Connor** that there would be "blood running down the streets of Birmingham," pickets, sit-ins and marches sparked mass arrests. Over 2000 protesters flooded the jails; one was Dr Martin Luther King Jr, who wrote his *Letter from a Birmingham Jail* after being branded as an extremist by local white clergymen. Connor's use of high-pressure hoses, cattleprods and dogs against demonstrators acted as a potent catalyst of support. Pictures of snarling German shepherds sinking their teeth into the flesh of schoolkids were transmitted around the world, and led to an agreement between civil rights leaders and businesses in June 1963. Success in Birmingham sparked demonstrations in 186 other cities, which culminated in the 1964 Civil Rights Act prohibiting racial segregation.

The headquarters for the campaign, the 16th Street Baptist Church, on the corner of Sixth Avenue, was the site of a sickening Klan bombing on September 15, 1963, which killed four young black girls attending a Bible class. Open daily, the church's basement contains a small shrine dedicated to the murdered girls, and displays a number of related art works. Across the road, prettily landscaped Kelly Ingram Park, the site of many huge rallies during the Sixties and now home to some of the city's dispossessed – many of them African Americans – has a Freedom Walk, lined with several impressive sculptures that memorialize the city's turbulent history of race relations.

Nearby, the admirable **Civil Rights Institute**, 520 16th St (Tues–Sat 10am–5pm, Sun 1–5pm; $6), is an affecting attempt to interpret the factors that led to such violence and racial hatred in the US. Exhibits re-create life in a segregated city, complete with a burned-out bus and heart-rending videos of bus boycotts and the March on Washington.

Civic Center Inn 2230 Civic Center Blvd
☎205/328-6320, ℻205/439-0499. Downtown
hotel opposite the Sports Hall of Fame; continental
breakfast included. ❸/❹
Crown Plaza Inn Redmont 2101 5th Ave N
☎205/324-2101, ℻205/313-2649,
ⓦwww.crownplazabirminghamtheredmont.com.
Modernized downtown hotel a few blocks northeast of Amtrak. ❻/❼
Pickwick Hotel 1023 S 20th St ☎205/933-9555

or 1-800/255-7304, ℻205/933-7852,
ⓦwww.thepickwick.com. Charming hotel within
easy walking distance of Five Points South, with
comfortable rooms and all the amenities. Also
offers complimentary continental breakfast and
free shuttle service to and from the airport. ❺
Radisson 808 S 20th St at University Blvd
☎205/933-9000, ℻205/933-0920, ⓦwww.raddi-
son.com. Luxury hotel in upbeat, upmarket Five
Points South district. ❺

The City

Downtown Birmingham extends north from the railroad tracks at Morris
Avenue to Tenth Avenue N, bounded to the east and west by 25th and 15th streets.
The landscaped greenery of **20th Street**, overlooked by a collection of early skyscrapers, is not enough to save these one-hundred-plus blocks from anonymity,
with shopping now firmly anchored in the malls and suburbs. If you're just passing through, you'd do better to head straight for the much livelier **Five Points
South** district, a mile or so south of the tracks on 20th Street; thanks to the proximity of the university, its narrow streets and alleys are packed with bars and
restaurants, and throng with revelers – mostly students – every weekend.

The concrete colossus of the Birmingham-Jefferson Civic Center, at 22nd
Street and Tenth Avenue N, contains the **Alabama Sports Hall of Fame**
(Mon–Sat 9am–5pm, Sun 1–5pm; $5), a tribute to sporting greats such as 1936
Olympic hero **Jesse Owens**, **Le Roy "Satchel" Paige** – legendary Negro
League pitcher – and boxer **Joe Louis**. There's even a space for George Wallace,
on the excuse that he was state amateur boxing champion. Weave your way past
the monotonous white-walled legal buildings to the nearby **Museum of Art**,
2000 Eighth Ave N, which is strong on Oriental art, American landscapes and,
oddly enough, Wedgwood pottery (Tues–Sat 10am–5pm, Sun noon–5pm; free).

A few blocks from the edge of downtown, at First Avenue N and 32nd Street,
stand the massive sheds and tall chimney stacks of **Sloss Furnaces**, which produced pig iron to feed the city's mills and foundries from 1882 until 1971. Self-
guided tours through the boilers, stoves and casting areas vividly portray the
harsh working conditions endured by the ex-slaves, prisoners and unskilled
immigrants. Imagining the searing heat, cramped space, the heavy loads and the
putrid gaseous emissions, it's easy to appreciate why one former Sloss worker
claimed "if mules had to do this work they would have banned it" (Tues–Sat
10am–4pm, Sun noon–4pm; free; guided tours Sat & Sun 1pm, 2pm & 3pm).

Eating and drinking

Birmingham has a couple of fantastic **barbecue** joints; for something a little
more upmarket, the best bet is to ignore downtown in favor of **Five Points
South**.

Bottega 2240 Highland Ave S ☎205/933-2001.
Elegant 1920s clothing store that now houses one
of Five Points South's classiest restaurants, serving
luscious, garlic-rich Mediterranean cuisine; prices
are slightly lower in the adjoining *Café*. Closed
Sun.
Dreamland Barbecue 14th Ave S ☎205/933-
2133. Superlative barbecue in huge, cheery
restaurant. Place your order for a big plate of ribs
with white sliced bread and sauce – the only dish

on the menu – and watch as they barbecue in
front of your eyes.
The Mill 1035 20th St S ☎205/939-3001. Bakery,
brewery and general snackery, with outdoor patio,
in Five Points South. Ideal for morning coffees and
inexpensive lunches.
Ollie's Barbecue 515 University Blvd ☎205/324-
9485. Wonderful smoky pork in a peppery sauce;
unusually for this part of the country, there's beef and
chicken too. Mon 10am–3pm, Tues–Sat until 8pm.

West of Birmingham

Just west of Birmingham city limits, I-20/59 passes **BESSEMER**, a likeable small town named in 1887 after Sir Henry Bessemer, the English engineer who perfected the steel-making process. The **Hall of History Museum** here, in the 1916 Southern Railroad depot at 1905 Alabama Ave, displays Native American artifacts alongside exhibits from the industrial pioneer years (Tues–Sat 9am–12pm & 1–4pm; free). *Bob Sykes*, 1724 Ninth Ave (☎205/426-1400), is a mouthwatering takeout **barbecue** joint in town.

TUSCALOOSA, home of the lively main campus of the University of Alabama, but little else of interest, lies 32 miles southwest of Bessemer. If you're hungry, combine eating with a view of the **Black Warrior River** at *Henson's Cypress Inn*, 501 Rice Mine Rd N (☎205/345-6963), which specializes in keenly priced seafood and catfish. Sixteen miles south on US-69, the **Moundville Archeological Park** (8am–8pm) preserves twenty earthen mounds, carpeted in lush grass, with the largest supporting a rebuilt Native American temple. An estimated three thousand people lived here on the banks of the Black Warrior during the twelfth century; the on-site museum (daily 9am–5pm; $4) exhibits items found in burial grounds, including jewelry, ceremonial vessels and a few skeletons.

South central Alabama

Southern Alabama – memorably depicted in Harper Lee's child's-eye view of racial conflict, *To Kill a Mockingbird* – still consists mostly of small, sleepy, God-fearing rural communities. Only state capital **Montgomery**, with a population of just over 200,000, achieves metropolitan status. It lies in the heart of the **Black Belt**, originally named for the rich loamy soil, but these days more usually taken to refer to the region's ethnic make-up. Cotton was the major earner here until the boll weevil infestation of 1915. Now it has been supplanted (officially) by soybeans, corn and peanuts – though surveys suggest that the leading cash crop is, in fact, marijuana.

Montgomery

MONTGOMERY's Black Belt position, 90 miles south of Birmingham and 160 west of Atlanta, made it a natural political center for the plantation elite, leading to its adoption as state capital in 1846 and temporary capital of the Confederacy fifteen years later. Despite its administrative importance, Montgomery is strangely quiet, largely because many businesses have relocated to the suburbs. Most neighborhoods are either exclusively white or totally black; integration sadly does not appear to be on the social agenda in the city that saw the first successful mass civil rights activity in 1955–56.

Arrival and information

Dannelly Field Airport (☎334/281-5040) is fifteen miles from downtown on US-80, but the Greyhound station is much more conveniently located at 210 S Court St.

The **visitor center** is at 300 Water St (Mon–Fri 8.30am–5pm, Sat 9am–4pm, Sun noon–4pm; ☎334/261-1100 or 1-800/240-9452, ⊛www.visiting montgomery.com). Tours start at **Old Alabama Town**, an area of restored houses and museums immediately behind (Mon–Sat 9am–3.30pm, Sun 1–3.30pm; $7). All places of interest downtown are easily reached on foot.

Civil rights in Montgomery

During the Fifties, Montgomery's **bus system** was a miniature model of segregated society – as was the norm in the South. The regulation ordering blacks to give up seats to whites came under repeated attack from black organizations, culminating in the call by the Women's Political Council for a mass boycott after **Rosa Parks** was arrested on December 1, 1955, for refusing to give up her seat. Black workers were asked to walk to work, while black-owned taxis carried those who lived further away for the same 10¢ fare as buses. The protest attracted over ninety percent support, and the Montgomery Improvement Association (MIA), set up to coordinate activities, elected the 26-year-old **Dr Martin Luther King Jr** as its chief spokesperson. Meanwhile, the laid-off white bus drivers were employed as temporary police officials. Despite personal hardships, bombings and jailings, the boycott continued for eleven months, until in November 1956, the US Supreme Court declared segregation on public transportation to be illegal.

King remained pastor at the small brick **Dexter Avenue King Memorial Baptist Church**, surprisingly central at 454 Dexter Ave (call for tours 1 week in advance; Mon–Thurs 10am & 2pm, Fri 10am, Sat 10.30am & 1.30pm; $2; walk-through only on Sat 1.30–2pm), until his move to Atlanta in 1960. A mural along a basement wall chronicles his life, while the upstairs sanctuary, much as it was during his ministry, contains his former pulpit. One block away at the corner of Washington Avenue and Hull Street, in front of the Southern Poverty Law Center (which specializes in helping victims of racial attacks), the deeply moving **Civil Rights Memorial** (designed by Maya Lin) consists of a black granite table that records the names of forty martyrs murdered by white supremacists and police. Cool water pumps slowly and evenly across it, and the wall behind is engraved with the quotation used so often by Dr King, "(we will not be satisfied) until justice rolls down like waters and righteousness like a mighty stream."

Accommodation

There are several good-value places to stay in and around downtown Montgomery: a couple of homely **B&Bs** in town and the usual **motels** alongside the highways.

Ramada Statehouse Inn 924 Madison Ave ☎334/265-0741, ℻334/834-6126, ℗www.ramada.com. Central if anonymous downtown hotel, with pool and restaurant. ❸

Capitol Inn 205 N Goldthwaite St ☎334/265-3844, ℻334/265-3844. Old-fashioned motel in a somewhat bleak but central location, perched on a small hill fifteen minutes' walk from downtown. ❷

Lattice Inn 1414 S Hull St ☎334/832-9931 or 1-800/525-0652. Lovingly restored B&B complete with a pool located in the historic garden district a mile from downtown. ❹

Red Bluff Cottage 551 Clay St ☎334/264-0056. Friendly B&B near the capitol, with comfortable accommodation and good food. ❹

The City

Although 1993 saw Alabama's state flag finally replace the Confederate flag over the white-domed Greek Revival **State Capitol** at the top of Dexter Avenue, downtown Montgomery still bears reminders of its white-supremacist past. A bronze star marks the spot where Jefferson Davis was sworn in as president of the Confederacy on February 18, 1861 (see p.1325). Other "attractions" in this vein include the **Alabama Department of Archives and History**, next door, notable only for the lavish use of marble in its interior (Mon–Fri 8am–5pm, Sat 9am–5pm; free), and the **First White House of the Confederacy**, 644 Washington Ave, the temporary home of Jefferson Davis, now crammed with sentimental Confederate oddments (Mon–Fri 8am–4.30pm; free).

On a different note, Montgomery was jammed with mourners in 1954 for the funeral of 29-year-old country star **Hank Williams**, who died of a heart attack on his way to a concert on New Year's Eve 1953. An Alabama native from Butler County, Williams was as famous for his drink- and drug-sustained lifestyle as he was for writing honky-tonk classics like *Your Cheating Heart* and *I'm So Lonesome I Could Cry*. His hit single at the time of his death was *I'll Never Get Out of This World Alive*. The **Hank Williams Memorial**, a large white-marble headstone complete with song lyrics and an image of the singer, dominates the Oakwood Cemetery Annex, 1304 Upper Wetumpka Rd, near downtown; Hank's statue stands at Lister Hill Plaza on N Perry Street. There's also the **Hank Williams Museum**, at 118 Commerce St, complete with the 1952 Cadillac in which he made his final journey (Mon–Sat 9am–6pm, Sun 1–4pm).

Reminiscent of the grounds of an English stately home, the stunningly landscaped **Blount Cultural Park** gives some credence to the city's claim to be a regional center for the arts. Situated off Woodmere Boulevard, ten miles southeast of the city, it's home to the Alabama Shakespeare Festival (Aug–Nov; ☎334/271-5353 or 1-800/841-4273), which also performs contemporary works in the sumptuous Renaissance-style Carolyn Blount Theatre. The equally slick **Montgomery Museum of Fine Arts** (Tues–Sat 10am–5pm, Sun noon–5pm; free) spans more than two hundred years of American art.

Eating and drinking

Downtown Montgomery is dotted with cheap cafés selling burgers or soul food; a few minutes' drive southeast, suburban **Cloverdale** offers a good selection of eating places to suit every price range. Especially in the center, things get quiet at night.

Amy's Young House 231 N Hull St ☎334/262-0409. Southern cooking in an 1850 house, next to the visitor center and Old Alabama Town. Serves lunch only.

Farmers' Market Café 315 N McDonough St ☎334/262-9163. Just off downtown, next to the busy marketplace, this is Montgomery's best spot for Southern-style breakfasts. Mon–Fri 5.30am–2pm.

Jubilee Seafood Co 1057 Woodley Rd, Cloverdale ☎334/262-6224. Tiny fish restaurant that serves an extensive and deliciously creative menu for less than $20 for two entrees. Closed Sun & Mon.

Martha's Place 458 Sayre St ☎334/263-9135. Superb downtown Southern food, from collard greens to fried chicken. Serves lunch only; closed Sat.

Vintage Year 405 Cloverdale Rd, Cloverdale ☎334/264-8463. One of Alabama's most highly rated restaurants, with haute cuisine for $30 plus (two entrees). Dinner only, reservations recommended; closed Sun & Mon.

Selma

The tidy market town of **SELMA**, fifty miles west of Montgomery, became in the early Sixties the focal point of a national voting rights campaign. Demonstrations, meetings and attempts to register were repeatedly met by police violence, before the murder of a black protester by a state trooper prompted the decision to organize the historic **march from Selma to Montgomery**. On "Bloody Sunday," March 7, 1965, six hundred marchers set off across the steep incline of the imposing, narrow **Edmund Pettus Bridge**. As they went over the apex of the bridge, a line of state troopers fired tear gas without warning, lashing out at the panic-stricken demonstrators with nightsticks and cattleprods. This violent confrontation, broadcast all over the world, is credited with having directly influenced the passage of the **Voting Rights**

Act the following year. The full story is told in the **National Voting Rights Museum**, beside the bridge at 1012 Water Ave (Tues–Sat 1–5pm; $4). Outside the 1965 campaign headquarters at the **Brown Chapel AME Church**, 410 Martin Luther King St, a bust of Dr King forms part of a monument to the struggle that also includes explanatory plaques along the street.

Selma's history stretches back well before the Sixties; its huge arsenal and ship-building plant were prime targets for Union troops who looted and burned most of the buildings in March 1865. One of the few remaining plantation homes is **Sturdivant Hall**, 713 Mabry St (Tues–Sat 9am–4pm, closed Sun; $5), an attractively furnished house with an accessible cupola and lovely grounds.

Lined with independently owned stores and cafés, **Broad Street** is the town's busy main thoroughfare, running into the wide riverfront **Water Avenue**, which still feels set in the Forties with its frontier-style storefronts, seed warehouses and garages. Just a few blocks away stand the beautiful homes of the town's Historic District.

Practicalities

Downtown Selma is very short of inexpensive places to **stay**; if the grand **St James Hotel**, close to the river at 1200 Water Ave (☎334/872-3234; ⑤), is beyond your budget, head for the *Holiday Inn*, three miles west on US-80 at 1806 W Highland Ave (☎334/872-0461; ⑥). Among the pick of the soul-food restaurants is the unfriendly *Downtowner*, 1114 Selma Ave (☎334/872-5933), open for breakfast and lunch but beware, you may not get served if you're from New York. *Major Grumbles*, near the *St James* at 1 Grumbles Alley (☎334/872-2006), is an upmarket riverside pub with hot sandwiches such as the almondine flounder, but don't be put off by the disturbing "Indian giant" skeleton draped in a Confederate flag. The **visitor center** at 2207 Broad St (Mon–Sat 8am–8pm; ☎334/875-7485), north of town at the junction with Hwy-22, has tour brochures for the Historic District and black heritage sites.

Alabama's Gulf Coast

Alabama's narrow share of the **Gulf coastline** is blessed with an abundance of fine white-sand beaches, laundered by clear blue waters. The coast veers sharply inward to the port city of **Mobile**, featuring hundreds of antebellum buildings in a tree-shaded center. Away from the water's edge, agriculture, dominated by pecan, peach and watermelon growing, flourishes on the gently sloping coastal plain.

Mobile

The busy port and paper manufacturing city of **MOBILE** (pronounced *Mobeel*) traces its origins back to a French community founded in 1702. These early white settlers brought with them **Mardi Gras**, celebrated in Mobile continuously since 1704 – several years before New Orleans. Virtually every street is transformed in early spring by the delicate colors of azaleas, camellias and dogwoods – a beautiful complement to the many early eighteenth-century Spanish and colonial-style buildings. Parallels with New Orleans are everywhere you look, from wrought-iron balconies to street names like Conti and Bienville and gumbo specials in the restaurants.

Mobile survived the torches of the Union army during the Civil War, and possesses enough antebellum buildings to designate four sizeable areas as historic districts. Even so, the city is unlikely to hold your attention for more than a day. The obvious place to start exploring is **Fort Conde** (daily 8am–5pm; free), a reconstruction of the city's 1724 French fort that was constructed to mark the Bicentennial in 1976. Dioramas in its low-ceilinged rooms cover local history, while its ramparts provide a good view of the World War II battleship **USS Alabama** permanently moored nearby (fort & ship daily 8am–6pm; $10, parking $2). Fanning out north of the fort, the **Church Street Historic District** holds 59, mostly pre-Civil War, buildings, as well as two museums (both Tues–Sat 10am–5pm, Sun 1–5pm; free). The **Museum of Mobile**, 111 S Royal St (Mon–Fri 9am–6pm, Sun noon–5pm), displays glittering Mardi Gras costumes and lavish horse-drawn carriages, while steam-powered fire engines, resplendent in original livery, shining brass bells and trumpets, are the stars of the **Phoenix Fire Museum**, 750 S Clairborne St (Mon–Fri 10am–5pm, Sat–Sun 1–5pm).

Downtown Mobile's lack of action outside of Mardi Gras is made up for by an amazing display of greenery, particularly down its main thoroughfare, **Government Street**, which is shaded by a canopy of adjoining oaks, and central **Bienville Square**, a popular picnic spot with free lunchtime concerts every Wednesday during summer.

Practicalities

Downtown Mobile is somewhat under the shadow of I-10, as it sweeps to meet I-65 a few miles west. Amtrak, 11 Government St, and Greyhound, at no. 2545, are both central. Mobile's resourceful **visitor center**, located in Fort Conde, 150 S Royal St (daily 8am–5pm; ☎334/434-7304, ⓦwww.mobile.org), can provide valuable **accommodation** discount vouchers. Downtown, the *Lafayette Plaza* is a very central fifteen-story round tower at 301 Government St (☎334/694-0100, Ⓕe334/694-0160, ⓦwww.lafayette.com; ❸), while the *Malaga Inn*, 359 Church St (☎334/438-4701; ❹), is an 1862 twin townhouse with huge rooms and serving continental breakfast.

Unsurprisingly, Mobile abounds in **places to eat fish**: *Wintzels' Oyster House*, 605 Dauphin St (☎334/432-4605), serves good-value seafood platters and fresh oysters in a determinedly eccentric atmosphere, while *Gus's* at no. 751 (☎334/433-4877) has an array of seafood and steaks at reasonable prices. At night, downtown Mobile is largely deserted with the exception of a few blocks of Dauphin Street; *The Bicycle Shop*, at no. 661 is a popular **pub** with a laid-back atmosphere and an extensive drink selection. However, if your mood is a little more alternative, look to *Grand Central*, 256 Dauphin St, where an array of eclectic bands play nightly for no cover charge.

Around the bay area

Twenty miles south of Mobile, off I-10, the 65 acres of landscaped color that make up **Bellingrath Gardens** – once the home of a Coca-Cola magnate – include a quarter of a million azaleas (daily 8am–sunset; $8). Fifteen miles further south on Hwy-193 are the quiet beaches and undisturbed pine forest of sunny **Dauphin Island**, which has a **campground** (☎334/861-2742; from $13 per tentsite) on its eastern tip.

The Mobile Bay Ferry links Dauphin with the larger **Pleasure Island**, five miles away (round-trip $3, cars $25; ☎334/434-7345). The real gem here, and indeed on the entire Alabama Gulf Coast, lies twenty miles east, in the shape of **GULF SHORES**, a stunning **beach** where ultramarine waters sweep gently over blinding snow-white sands, just beyond the junction of Hwy-59 and Hwy-182. Although it never gets overcrowded, the beach is particularly busy on a Sunday, when young people from all over LA – as Lower Alabama is known locally – choose the resort over those of the more expensive Florida Panhandle. A smattering of lively cafés specialize in freshly caught **shrimp**, particularly the lurid and popular *Pink Pony Pub* (☎334/948-6371).

Tourism is Gulf Shores' only trade; if you get bored with the beach and the bars, there's not a lot else to do. **Accommodation** is pricey and often booked up at summer weekends, though the *Holiday Inn White Sands Resort*, a mile or so west at 365 E Beach Blvd (☎334/948-6191, ☎251/948-8240, ⊕www.whitesandsresort; ❸), is good value and has its own stretch of sand. Otherwise expect to pay in excess of $80 for a double, or **camp** three miles further east at the *Gulf State Park Resort* (☎334/948-7275), where tentsites are $13. The Gulf Coast **visitor center** (☎334/968-7511 or 1-800/745-SAND), on Hwy-59 near Gulf Shores, provides comprehensive information.

Mississippi

When cotton was king – and slavery was as yet unchallenged – **MISSISSIPPI** was the nation's fifth wealthiest state. Since the Civil War, however, it has been the poorest, its dependence on cotton now a handicap that makes it victim to the vagaries of the commodities market. Widespread poverty has long endured alongside pockets of enormous riches, and white Mississippi was notorious for violent resistance to black political participation. Not until the early Seventies did the church bombings and murders come to an end, and no one could claim that racial tension has ceased to exist. To some extent, the economy has regenerated since Mississippi's first Republican governor in a century, **Kirk Fordice**, decided to legalize gambling; the giant casinos may be lumbering eyesores that seem pitifully out of place on the sweeping Delta flatlands, but they're sucking considerable revenues across the state line from Memphis, Tennessee. Even today, you only have to take a detour down some rural side road to encounter pockets of truly scandalous black poverty, but with the profits from gaming being ploughed into education in Mississippi's poorest counties, the state may finally manage to shake off its appalling reputation for inequality.

While the major city is the capital, **Jackson**, historic river towns like **Vicksburg** and **Natchez** provide good reasons to stay off the interstates, and **blues** fans will need no encouragement to go exploring sleepy **Delta** settlements such as Alligator or Yazoo City.

Getting around Mississippi

Although Greyhound serves most of Mississippi, including the Delta, only along the coastal stretch are services at all frequent. Jackson has the only **airport** of any size, while Amtrak **trains** from New Orleans head north to Memphis by way of

Jackson and Greenwood; northeast to Atlanta, passing through a succession of unexciting small towns; and along the coast to Florida, stopping at Biloxi. Trips on the Mississippi itself are run on expensive luxury cruisers (see p.563).

The Delta

That Delta. Five thousand square miles, without any hill save the bumps of dirt the Indians made to stand on when the river over-flowed.

William Faulkner, Sanctuary

"That Delta" is not in fact a delta at all; technically it's an alluvial flood plain, a couple of hundred miles short of the mouth of the Mississippi. The name stems from its resemblance to the fertile delta of the Nile (which also began at a city named **Memphis**); the extravagant meanderings of the river on its way down to **Vicksburg** deposit enough rich topsoil to make this one of the world's finest cotton-producing regions.

The Delta is a land of scorching sun, parched earth, flooding creeks and thickets of bone-dry evergreens, best seen at dawn or dusk, when the glassy-smooth Mississippi waters reflect the sun and the foliage along the banks. Just containing the sheer volume of water is a never-ending battle, with giant levees struggling to protect the farmland. Though the main thoroughfare south is the legendary **Hwy-61**, exploring is best done on the back roads, which are characterized by huge, silent empty views interrupted only by roadside shacks, tiny churches and the sound of the blues.

Clarksdale

CLARKSDALE, the first significant town south of Memphis, has an unquestionable claim to consider itself the home of the blues. Its quite phenomenal roll call of former residents – stretching from Muddy Waters, John Lee Hooker, Howlin' Wolf and Robert Johnson up to Ike Turner and Sam Cooke – is celebrated in the **Delta Blues Museum**, housed at 1 Blues Alley (Mon–Sat 9am–5pm, closed Sunday; $6; ☎662/627-6820, ⓦ www.deltabluesmuseum.org). The centerpiece among the photos, instruments, personal possessions, videos and recordings is the "Muddywood" guitar, created by ZZ Top using wood from Waters' old cabin. Each year, around the second weekend in August, the town holds the **Sunflower River Blues and Gospel Festival** (free; ☎1-800/626-3764).

Practicalities

Clarksdale's strangest **accommodation** has to be at the *Riverside Hotel*, 615 Sunflower Ave (☎662/624-9163; ❷), which, until the early 1940s, was a hospital, famous as the site of **Bessie Smith**'s death in 1937 after a car crash. Now it's a basic hotel/rooming house, on the wrong side of the tracks in the town's black "New World" district, which, nonetheless, has hosted more than its share of notable guests. If you do stay, be sure to talk to "Rat," the son of the original owner, and learn the "true history of the blues". You can find accommodation with more amenities, albeit less character, along US-61, known in town as State Street, at the *Econo Lodge* at no. 350 S (☎662/621-1110, ⓕ662/621-9838; ❸), the *Hampton Inn* at no. 710 S (☎662/627-9292, ⓕ662/624-4763, ⓦ www.hampton-inn.com; ❹), and the *Southern Inn* at no. 1904 N (☎662/624-6558; ❷). A good central **restaurant** is *Abe's*, a barbecue joint at 616 S State St

(☎662/624-9947). *Sarah's Kitchen*, 208 Sunflower Ave (☎662/627-3239), is open irregular hours, but has a great blues jukebox.

The most famous of Clarksdale's **jook-joints**, *The Red Top Lounge* (aka *Smitty's*), 377 Yazoo Ave (no phone), still has occasional live music.

Delta towns

GREENVILLE, seventy miles south of Clarksdale, is the largest town on the Delta. Still an important riverport, it hosts the **Mississippi Delta Blues Festival** (☎1-888/812-5837, ⊛www.deltablues.org) on the third weekend of September. Tree-lined avenues lead from the characterless outskirts into the business district, beyond which pallid warehouses stand in the shadow of a huge levee. If you're **staying** overnight, the hotels near the river and the casinos would probably be the safest option. For a place **to eat**, try the original *Doe's*, at the safer end of Nelson Street at no. 502 (☎662/334-3315) – arguably the best in the entire Delta for down-home cooking.

Leland, seven miles east of Greenville off US-82, is where Mississippi native **Jim Henson** created Kermit the Frog, naming him after his childhood playmate, Kermit Scott. The exhibit, located on the banks of Deer Creek, at the intersection of Hwy-82 and Hwy-61, is small, but well worth a stop, with displays following Henson's life, Muppet memorabilia, and videos showing much of his work, including his early efforts (Mon–Sat 10am–4pm; free; ☎662/686-2687).

Sixteen miles farther east on US-82, **INDIANOLA** is the home of the largest catfish processing company in the world, Delta. **B.B. King**, who was born here, plays an open-air hometown show once a year under the auspices of *Club Ebony*, 404 Hannah Ave (☎662/887-9915).

GREENWOOD, a sleepy town of 20,000 people, forty miles east on US-82, is the country's second largest cotton exchange after Memphis. The nineteenth-century offices of downtown's Cotton Row overlook the shady Yazoo River, and graceful mansions line pretty Grand Boulevard. The **Cottonlandia Museum** (Mon–Fri 9am–5pm, Sat & Sun 2–5pm; $4), about two miles west of the town center on the US-82 W bypass, is a rag-tag collection of old hardware, Native American beads, stuffed birds and oddly long wooden benches polished by the tongues of mules – not one word on slavery or black history, but there's some intriguing artwork. Although Greenwood has recently begun to play on its Robert Johnson connection (he died here), the **Cotton Capital Blues Festival** in October is the city's current contribution to the Delta Blues music legacy.

Of the many **motels** along US-49 and US-82, the *Travel Inn* at no. 623 US-82 W (☎662/453-8810, ☎662/453-1277; ❷) is basic, clean and good value, with an outdoor pool. By far the best **place to eat** in Greenwood, and one of the finest in the South, is *Lusco's*, on the wrong side of the railway tracks at 722 Carrolton Ave (☎662/453-5365). Each table in this eccentric old place is hidden away in a small booth, veiled from other diners, and waiters, by chintz curtains – an arrangement dating from the days of Prohibition, when *Lusco's* was the renowned haunt of cotton barons who came here to drink moonshine. Its Italian/Cajun food is superlative, especially the pompano, lightly grilled in a garlicky lemon butter.

The Delta blues

As recently as 1900, much of the **Mississippi Delta** remained an impenetrable wilderness of cypress and gum trees, roamed by panthers and bears and plagued with mosquitoes. Bit by bit land was cleared for cotton plantations, but, though the soil was fertile, white laborers could not be enticed to work in this godforsaken backcountry. After emancipation, the economy came to depend on black **share-croppers**, who would work a portion of the land on a white-owned plantation in return for a share (often pitifully small) of the eventual crop. As a rule, this lifestyle ensured long periods of poverty and debt interspersed with occasional windfalls; but in the Delta the returns tended to be greater than elsewhere, and blacks moved here from all over Mississippi.

In 1903, W.C. Handy, often credited as "the Father of the Blues" but at that time the leader of a vaudeville orchestra, found himself waiting for a train in Tutwiler, fifteen miles southeast of Clarksdale. At some point in the night, a ragged black man carrying a guitar sat down next to him and began to play what Handy called "the weirdest music I had ever heard." Using a pocketknife pressed against the guitar strings to accentuate his mournful vocal style, the man sang that he was "Goin' where the Southern cross the Dog."

This was the **Delta blues**, characterized by the interplay between words and music, with the guitar aiming to parallel and complement the singing rather than simply provide a backing. Though a local, place-specific music – the "Southern" and the "Dog" were railroads that crossed a short way south at Moorhead – it did not simply appear from nowhere, but combined traditional African instrumental and vocal techniques and the "field hollers" chanted by slaves and the reels and jigs then at the basis of popular entertainment.

The blues started out as young people's music; the old folk liked the banjo, fife and drum, but the younger generation were crazy for the wild showmanship of bluesmen such as **Charley Patton**. Born in April 1891, Patton was the classic itinerant bluesman, moving from plantation to plantation and wife to wife, and playing Saturday-night dances with a repertoire that extended from rollicking dance pieces to documentary songs such as *High Water Everywhere*, about the bursting of the Mississippi levees in April 1927. The enigmatic **Robert Johnson** was rumored to have sold his soul to the Devil in return for a few brief years of writing songs such as *Love in Vain* and *Stop Breakin' Down*. His *Crossroads Blues* spoke of being

Northeastern Mississippi

Cutting its way south through Mississippi, I-55 acts as an approximate boundary between the Delta and the luscious green forests of the **northeast**. Of the area's small market towns, the most appealing are the old-style shopping center of **Columbus**, and **Holly Springs**, whose oak-lined streets hide one of the most extraordinary attractions in the state. The only other places of major interest in the region are genteel **Oxford** and tidy blue-collar **Tupelo**, birthplace of **Elvis Presley** and **John Lee Hooker**.

Holly Springs

Centering on a neat courthouse square, **HOLLY SPRINGS** is a time-warped little town that's said to have changed hands 62 times during the Civil War; the minutiae of its otherwise uneventful history fill three splendidly eclectic floors in the local **museum** at 220 E College Ave (Mon–Fri 10am–5pm, Sat 10am–2pm; $3). Were it not for **Graceland Too**, 200 E Gholson Ave (open 24hrs year-round; $5), however, Holly Springs would today be of little note.

stranded at night in the chilling emptiness of the Delta; themes carried to metaphysical extremes in *Hellhound on My Trail* and *Me and the Devil Blues* – "you may bury my body down by the highway side/So my old evil spirit can catch a Greyhound bus and ride."

Both Patton and Johnson died in the 1930s. However, within a few years the Delta blues had been carried north to **Chicago** by men such as **Muddy Waters** and **Howlin' Wolf**. Their electrified urban blues was the most immediate ancestor of rock 'n' roll.

In addition to towns such as Clarksdale and Helena, blues enthusiasts may want to search out the following rural sites:

Stovall Plantation Stovall Road, 7 miles northwest of Clarksdale. Where tractor-driver Muddy Waters was first recorded; his cabin is still (just) standing.
Sonny Boy Williamson II's Grave Outside Tutwiler, 13 miles southeast of Clarksdale.
Parchman Farm Junction US-49 W and Hwy-32. Mississippi State penitentiary, immortalized by former prisoner Bukka White.
Dockery Plantation On Hwy-8, between Cleveland and Ruleville. One of Patton's few long-term bases, also home to Howlin' Wolf and Roebuck "Pops" Staples.
Charley Patton's Grave New Jerusalem Church, Holly Ridge, off US-82 6 miles west of Indianola.
Robert Johnson's Grave Payne Chapel in Quito, off Hwy-7, roughly 6 miles southwest of Greenwood, where he was poisoned.

Getting to hear live blues music

Managing to hear live blues music in the Delta is rarely straightforward. Half the time nobody seems to know who is playing where, let alone when, and many of the jook-joints themselves – which can be dark, rudimentary, even intimidating places, making few concessions to decor or comfort – don't have phones. Most "jookin" gets done at weekends; we've listed a few likely venues under the specific Delta towns. With public transportation – even taxis – being all but nonexistent, a car is essential. Useful sources of information are the **Delta Blues Museum**, (☎662/627-6820; see also p.594) in Clarksdale, the Memphis **Blues Foundation** (☎901/527-2583), **Shangrila Records**, 1916 Madison Ave (☎901/274-1916), also in Memphis, and the websites ⊛www.bluesfestivals.com and ⊛www.bluesbytes.com.

The home of Paul McLeod and his son, Elvis Aaron Presley McLeod, this shrine to the King is a quite remarkable labor of love. Walls, ceiling and stairwells are crammed with memorabilia from the kitsch to the priceless, and, just as in Graceland, the upper floor is blocked off – the stairs lined with glassy-eyed mannequins kitted out in Elvis and Priscilla outfits. The McLeods insist that this is above all an archive and research center; as well as collecting records, cuttings and books, they work around the clock to monitor and log every reference to Elvis transmitted on TV and radio. Tours last up to three hours, depending on the mood of your hosts and how busy they are compiling Elvis info. During the tour everyone has their photo taken to be entered into a record of those visited; you can also have your photo taken with both McLeods and also buy infinitesimal snips of rug from Graceland's Jungle Room.

There's no reason to spend a night in Holly Springs, but it's well worth pausing for a **meal**. Housed in a former "blind tiger" (brothel) beside the railroad tracks east of town, *Phillips Grocery*, 541 E Van Dorn Ave (☎662/252-4671), is a ramshackle old grocery store that serves sublime fresh–ground hamburgers and Southern vegetables.

Oxford

Twelve thousand residents and eleven thousand students enable **OXFORD**, an enclave of wealth in a predominantly poor region, to blend rural charm with a busy nightlife. Its central square is archetypal smalltown America, but the leafy streets have a vaguely European air – the town named itself after the English city as part of its campaign to persuade the **University of Mississippi**, known as Ole Miss, to locate its main campus here.

It's an undeniably pretty, appealing place today, but this leafy campus was, in September 1962, the site of the most bitter display of racial hatred seen in Mississippi. After eighteen months of legal and political wrangling, federal authorities ruled that **James Meredith** should be allowed to enroll as the first black student at Ole Miss. The news that Meredith had been sneaked into college by federal troops sparked a riot that left three dead and 160 injured. Despite constant threats, Meredith graduated the following year, wearing a "NEVER" badge (the segregationist slogan of Governor Ross Barnett) upside down. The university boasts a Confederate monument, but no statue, not even a plaque, mentioning Meredith. However, in recent years a group of motivated students drew attention to the lack of a civil rights monument, and development is under way of one which will include Meredith.

The **Blues Archive** (Mon–Fri 9am–5pm; call ☎662/232-7753) on campus holds thousands of recordings and B.B. King's personal memorabilia, while the **Center for the Study of Southern Culture** looks at Southern folkways (Mon–Fri 8.00am–5pm; free; ☎662/915-5993).

From Ole Miss, a ten-minute walk through lush Bailey Woods leads to secluded **Rowan Oak**, the former home of novelist **William Faulkner**, preserved as it was on the day he died in July 1962 (Tues–Fri 10am–noon & 2–4pm, Sat 10am-4pm, Sun noon–4pm; free). The fictional Deep South town of Jefferson in Yoknapatawpha County, where the Nobel Prize-winner set his major works, was based heavily on Oxford and its environs. Each year, in the last week in July, the University holds a Faulkner and Yoknapatawpha Conference (for more info call ☎662/915-5993).

In town, a walk around the **square** brings you to Neilson's, a delightfully old-fashioned department store (the oldest in the South in fact), little changed since 1897. You can pick up a piece of quirky Mississippi folk art at one of the off-beat giftshops there, or join the students sipping lattes and reading on the balcony of the exemplary Square Books, at Van Buren and Lamar streets.

Practicalities

Oxford's **visitor center** (Mon–Fri 9am–5pm; ☎662/234-4680 or 1-800/758-9177, ⊛www.touroxfordms.com), next to Neilson's in the town square, hands out good walking tour leaflets. The adjacent tourist information center opens up on weekends (Sat 10am-4pm, Sun 1-4pm). **Accommodation** options nearby include the *Downtown Inn*, 400 N Lamar St (☎662/234-3031; ❹), and the comfortable B&B *Oliver-Britt House*, 512 Van Buren Ave (☎662/234-8043; ❸/❹). Nearer campus, try the friendly *Ramada*, 2201 Jackson Ave W (☎662/234-7013, ☎662/236-4378; ❸). Prices may go up during graduation, the Faulkner conference and at weekends when there are football games. You can **eat** home-style selections on the town square at *Ajax Diner*, 118 Courthouse Square (☎662/232-8880), or try the popular *Pearl St Pasta*, 308 S Lamar St (☎662/234-7525); the *Bottletree Bakery*, 923 Van Buren Ave (☎662/236-5000), is a friendly café with soup and sandwiches along with local arts and crafts.

Oxford's lively **nightlife** focuses in and around the town square, with a younger crowd frequenting the eastern portion of **Harrison**. At *Two Stick*, 1007 Harrison Ave (☎662/236-6639), you can hear an eclectic range of live music, while *Proud Larry's* at 211 S Lamar St (☎662/236-0050) books popular regional acts. However, there are several places to choose from, and the free *Oxford Town* paper should give a good idea of local events. Keep in mind, though, that Sunday is a dry day.

Tupelo

On January 8, 1935, **Elvis Presley** and his twin brother Jesse were born in **TUPELO**, an industrial town in northeastern Mississippi. Jesse died at birth, while Elvis grew up to be a truck driver. Their parents, Gladys and Vernon Presley, who lived in poor, white East Tupelo, found it hard to make ends meet. Such was the financial strain of rearing the young Elvis that his sharecropper father was reduced to forgery in a desperate attempt to raise cash, and was jailed for three years. Their home was repossessed, and the family moved to Memphis in 1948.

Tupelo **CVB**, 399 E Main St (☎662/841-6521 or 1-800/533-0611, ⓦwww.tupelo.net), has details of a four-mile driving tour that takes in Elvis's first school and the shop where he bought his first guitar. The town doesn't go in for overkill, however; Main Street is a long, placid stretch of faceless buildings with not a giftshop to be seen. The actual **Elvis Presley Birthplace**, 306 Elvis Presley Drive (Mon–Sat 9am–5.30pm, Sun 1–5pm; $2), is tiny. A two-room shotgun house, built for $150 in 1934, it has been refurnished to look as it did when Elvis was born, with the judicious addition of a large can of lard in the kitchen and a love-seat swinging from the porch. The separate **museum** alongside (same hours; $5) is filled with memorabilia collected by a family friend of the Presleys, Janelle McComb, and includes her photos of, poems about, and shrines to the King, as well as selling everything from matchbooks to Elvis pendulum clocks with swinging legs (Mon–Sat 9am–5pm, Sun 1–5pm; $1). Nearby, a modern **meditation chapel** was built with donations from fans, but oddly the pews and altar remain roped off to visitors.

Among local **motels**, there's a central *Comfort Inn*, 1190 Gloster St (☎662/842-5100, ⓕ662/844-0554, ⓦwww.comfortinn.com; ❸), and other chain accommodations close by. **Main Attraction**, 214 W Main St (☎662/842-9617), is a vintage clothing store with eccentric accessories that also holds a **coffee bar**, while there's more substantial Italian and Greek **food** at *Vanelli's*, 1302 Gloster St (☎662/844-4410).

South central Mississippi

South of the Delta, the rich woodlands and meadows of **central Mississippi** are heralded by steep loess bluffs, holding engaging historic towns such as **Vicksburg** and **Natchez**. Driving is a real pleasure, especially along the unspoiled **Natchez Trace Parkway** – devoid of trucks, buildings and neon signs – which runs through Jackson and on up to Tupelo.

Jackson

JACKSON, poised two hundred miles from both Memphis and New Orleans, has been Mississippi's state capital since 1821. Only in the twentieth century, however, did it become the largest conurbation in the state, flourishing as a center for health and technological industries.

The **Old Capitol**, now the **State Historical Museum** (Mon–Fri 8am–5pm, Sat 9.30am–4.30pm, Sun 12.30–4.30pm; free), charts Mississippi's unenviable history, with excellent displays on civil rights and slavery; note the chilling notices for slave auctions. The "new" **Mississippi State Capitol**, 400 High St (Mon–Fri 8am–5pm; free), built in 1903 as a Beaux Arts-style show-piece, is much more ornate. In true rebel fashion, the gilt eagle on the roof looks away from Washington. A block west at 528 Bloom St, the unmissable **Smith-Robertson Museum and Cultural Center**, in Jackson's first public school for blacks (1894–1971), tells the story of black Mississippians since the French first imported slaves in 1719. Subjects covered include "folk architecture" – black homesteads built in the same period as the grand antebellum homes so beloved of the tourist boards, but left to decay – and patterns of migration after the Civil War. Photos and personal testimony show how Mississippians survived the onslaught of Jim Crow laws through their institutions of school, church and family (Mon–Fri 9am–5pm, Sat 10am–1pm, Sun 2–5pm; $1).

Practicalities

Greyhound **buses** arrive at 201 S Jefferson St, while Amtrak is at 300 W Capitol St. JATRAN runs a reasonable in-town bus service until 6pm (75¢ flat fare). The main **visitor center** is at 921 N President St (Mon–Fri 8.30am–5pm; ☎601/960-1891 or 1-800/354-7695, ⓦwww.visitjackson.com).

There are central **rooms** a few blocks west of the State Capitol at the *Holiday Inn Express*, 310 Greymont Ave (☎601/948-4466, ⓕ601/352-9368; ❹), or the *Hampton Inn*, 320 Greymont Ave (☎601/352-1700; ❺). Downtown Jackson more or less closes down at 6pm, with the exception of *Hal & Mal's Restaurant & Brewery*, at 200 S Commerce St (closed Sun; ☎601/948-0888), which spe-cializes in New Orleans cuisine and puts on live bands throughout the week. Out in the suburbs, *Poet's*, 1855 Lakeland Drive (closed Sun; ☎601/982-9711), does great things with redfish and has live music as well.

Vicksburg

The historic port of **VICKSBURG** straddles a high bluff on a bend in the Mississippi, 44 miles west of Jackson. During the Civil War, its domination of the river halted Union shipping, and led Abraham Lincoln to call Vicksburg the "key to the Confederacy." It was a crucial target for General Ulysses S. Grant, who eventually landed to the south in the spring of 1863, circled inland and attacked from the east. After a 47-day siege, the outnumbered Confederates sur-rendered on the Fourth of July – a holiday Vicksburg declined to celebrate for the next hundred years – and Lincoln was able to rejoice that "the Father of Waters again goes unvexed to the sea." **Vicksburg National Military Park** (daily: summer 8am–7pm; rest of the year 8am–5pm; $4 per car), entered on US-80 (Clay St) just northeast of town, preserves the main battlefield. A sixteen-mile loop drive through the rippling green hillsides traces every contour of the Union and Confederate trenches, punctuated by statues, refurbished cannons and over 1600 state-by-state monuments. Also at the site are the substantial remains of the iron-clad **USS Cairo**, sunk by a mine in the Yazoo River, along with artifacts found when it was salvaged a century later, and the **Vicksburg National Cemetery**, where 13,000 of the 17,000 Union graves are simply marked "Unknown."

Vicksburg today is a bare but attractive city of precipitous streets, steep terraces and wooded ravines, its Victorian riverfront as yet unaffected by the impact of at least two floating **casinos**. As well as nineteenth-century homes, it offers the fascinating **Old Court House Museum**, 1008 Cherry St (summer Mon–Sat 8.30am–5pm, Sun 1.30–5pm; rest of year Mon–Sat 8.30am–4.30pm, Sun 1.30–4.30pm; $3), focusing largely on the siege; the victorious Grant, who returned as president in 1869, addressed thousands of ex-slaves from its balcony. At 1107 Washington St, a small museum (Sat 10am–4pm, Sun 1-4pm) marks the spot where Coca-Cola was first bottled, with vivid displays on how this came about.

Practicalities

Vicksburg's main **visitor center** is opposite the Military Park, at Clay Street and Old Highway 27 (daily 8am–5pm, summer extended to 5.30pm; ☎601/636-9421 or 1-800/221-3536, ⓦwww.vicksburgcvb.org). This is also the prime area for **motels**, such as the spartan *Hillcrest*, 4503 Hwy-80 E (☎601/638-1491; ●), which has a pool, and the comfortable *Battlefield Inn*, near the park at 4137 I-20 Frontage Rd (☎601/638-5811; ●/●), which includes use of the pool, two free cocktails and a free breakfast buffet. A central and very appealing **B&B**, is the 1868 Victorian-Italianate mansion *Annabelle*, located in the Historic Garden District, 501 Speed St (☎601/638-2000 or 1-800/791-2000, ⓕ601/636-5054 ⓦwww.annabelle.com; ●). You can **camp** at the *Magnolia RV Park*, 211 Miller St (☎601/631-0388; $11 per tentsite).

When it's time to **eat**, tuck into superb all-you-can-eat fried chicken and other Southern delicacies from overladen Lazy Susans at *Walnut Hills*, 1214 Adams St at Clay (lunch only); or else stop by *Goldie's Trail BBQ*, 4127 S Washington St near the river (☎601/636-9839), for ribs, pork, chicken and sausage. If you can resist plunking money down at the tables of the *Ameristar Casino*, 4116 Washington St (☎601/638-1000), invest it instead in their buffet dinner for around $15 and listen to live music in their *Blues Bar*. At *The Biscuit Company*, 1100 Washington St (☎601/631-0099), you can eat pizza or poboys, drink till late and hear live jazz or blues most weekends.

Natchez

Sixty miles south of Vicksburg, the river town of **NATCHEZ**, the oldest permanent settlement on the Mississippi River, was home to prehistoric Indians, sun-worshipping Natchez Indians, French, British and Spanish colonists before it first flew the Stars and Stripes in 1798. Yet despite its cosmopolitan ambience, the town abounds in Greek Revival antebellum mansions with meticulously maintained gardens. Fourteen homes stay open all year round, including the elaborate octagonal **Longwood**, 140 Lower Woodville Rd (daily 9am–5pm; $6), with its huge dome, snow-white arches and columns, and the palatial **Stanton Hall**, 401 High St (daily 9am–5pm; $6). In March and October each year, most of the rest can be seen on the **Natchez Pilgrimage** – tours, led by women wearing massive hoopskirts, which start from 200 State St ($24 per half-day tour, $16 off-peak season; ☎601/446-6631 or 1-800/647-6742). At the Presbyterian Stratton Chapel, 405 State St, a fascinating collection of **photographs** gives an idea of life in Natchez spanning from the Civil War era to World War II (Mon–Sat 10am–5pm, Sun 1–5pm; suggested donation $3). There is also a **hot–air balloon** race the third weekend in October.

Down below the town proper, raucous **Natchez Under-the-Hill**, once known as the "Sodom of the Mississippi," now houses, along with some perfectly respectable bars and restaurants, the 24-hour *Isle of Capri* riverboat **casino**, a cacophony of slot machines and craps tables.

Ceremonial mounds, reconstructed dwellings, and a small museum can be seen at the **Grand Village**, 400 Jefferson Davis Blvd (Mon–Sat 9am–5pm, Sun 1.30–5pm; free), the main ceremonial center of the local Natchez Indians, who by the mid-sixteenth century had built a flourishing commercial empire, which they later defended in bitter running battles with the French.

Each year, on the third weekend in April, the **Blues on the Bluff Festival** (☎601/442-2988, ⓦwww.natchezbluffbluesfest.com), a "city-wide house party" held in some fifteen different venues, celebrates an eclectic mix of regional blues styles.

Natchez's rich African-American heritage – Richard Wright, the author of *Native Son*, was born nearby and lived in the town as a small boy – is chronicled in an excellent 26-page free booklet, available from the Visitor Center.

Practicalities

Natchez's **visitor center** is at 640 S Canal St (daily: March–Oct 8am–5pm; rest of year 8.30am–5pm; ☎601/446-6345 or 1-800/647-6724, ⓦwww.natchez .ms.us). **Rooms** can be had at the *Days Inn*, 109 US-61 S (☎601/445-8291, ⓕ601/442-4861; ❸), and *Ramada Hilltop Inn*, 130 John R. Junkin Drive at the Mississippi River bridge (☎601/446-6311, ⓕ601/446-6321; ❹), while the downtown *Radisson Natchez Eola*, 110 N Pearl St (☎601/445-6000 or 1-800/ 333-3333, ⓕ601/446-5310, ⓦwww.radisson.com; ❸–❺), listed on the National Register of Historic Places, is a venerable hotel of considerable charm that has occasional discounted rates from October through March. For a quintessential Natchez experience, however, splash out on a historic **B&B**. The friendly *Highpoint*, 215 Linton Ave (☎601/442-6963 or 1-800/283-4099; ❺), offers good-value accommodation; others, such as *The Burn*, 712 N Union St (☎601/442-1344 or 1-800/654-8859; ❻), with its beautiful pool, reach into extraordinary realms of opulence. Ratings generally will rise during the fall and spring pilgrimages and some other special events. For **food**, *Cock of the Walk*, on the bluff at 200 N Broadway (☎601/446-8920), serves irresistibly tasty catfish. *Fat Mama's Tamales*, 500 S Canal St (☎601/442-4548), is a lively joint that serves Mexican and Cajun cuisine and is renowned for their "nock-u-naked" margaritas and fiery chili; while *Biscuits and Blues*, 315 Main St (☎601/446-9922), serves up salads and hamburgers to live music each Friday and Saturday night.

Mississippi's Gulf Coast

Mississippi's hundred-mile strip of **coast** is utterly unlike the rest of the state, culturally as well as physically – a strong Mediterranean (Catholic) heritage is conspicuous amid the subtropical beauty. Some of the towns are scarred by hurricanes, but the **beaches** are often superb. Along the **Gulf Islands National Seashore**, four beautiful barrier islands boast brilliant white sand and clear blue waters, while the 26-mile artificial **Harrison County Beach** runs parallel with the busy coast road between **Biloxi**, the major resort, and laid-back **Pass Christian**, with its fine live oaks.

Biloxi

Neon-lit **BILOXI** *(Bi-lux-ee)*, sprawling alongside a busy four-lane highway, cannot claim to be the prettiest resort in the world. But it's less expensive than Florida, it's near New Orleans, and it has sufficient diversity to satisfy local beach poseurs, senior citizens and families alike. Although Biloxi has experienced something of an economic boom since the state's legalization of gambling – the seafront is lined with permanently moored **casinos**, several of which have spawned large hotels on drier land nearby – it's really not a place that's likely to appeal for long to international visitors.

Old Biloxi, starting at the far end of Lameuse Boulevard, consists of narrow streets of stuccoed buildings, in a tree-shaded tranquility that seems miles from the hustle of US-90. Across the highway, shrimp and oyster fleets unload their catch at the **Small Crafts Harbor**. You can rent boats to visit windblown **Deer Island**, half a mile offshore, or just to go fishing (70–minute shrimping tours; $11; ☎228/385-1182). A mile west, a glut of the usual shops selling T-shirts, seashells, trinkets and other ephemera marks the approach to the most popular stretch of **Harrison County Beach**, in front of the *Broadwater Resort East*.

Five miles west of Main Street, the compact white raised cottage of **Beauvoir** (March–Oct 9am–5pm, Nov–Feb 9am–4pm; $7.50), set in beautiful wooded grounds across from the ocean, was the final home of Confederate President Jefferson Davis, who lived here until his death in 1889. Though not sponsored by the federal government, a **presidential library** has been opened there in honor of Davis, and includes an interesting museum chronicling his life. The area's role as a shrine for unrepentant Confederates is typified by the grandiose title of the Civil War museum – "Experiment in Nationalism" – and a bookstore that's bursting with back issues of *Southern Partisan*, a magazine featuring such editorials as "Why the South Was Right."

West Ship Island

Hailed by *USA Today* as one of the nation's top ten beaches, the barrier island of **West Ship** was only created in 1969, when the 200mph winds and 30ft tide of Hurricane Camille ripped Ship Island in half. It's basically a giant sandbank, dotted with inland ponds (home to a family of alligators), marshlands, sand dunes and warm tidal pools. Everywhere you come across delicate sea oats; even touching them incurs a heavy fine, as their elaborate root structure is all that holds the island together.

The small, idyllic **beach** boasts fine white sand, free showers and a reasonable café, though umbrella and deckchair rental is expensive. D-shaped **Fort Massachusetts** alongside was built in 1859 and captured by the Union navy early in the Civil War. Free tours give a wonderful panoramic view from its grass-topped roof.

West Ship is the only barrier island served by regular **ferry**, at **Gulfport Yacht Harbor**, at the intersection of US-90 and US-49 (summer daily 9am & noon; March to mid-May, Sept & Oct Mon–Fri 9am, Sat & Sun 9am & noon; $18; ☎228/864-1014 or 1-800/388-3290).

Practicalities

Biloxi's **visitor center** is at 710 Beach Blvd at Main Street (☎228/374-3105 or 1-800/245-6943, ��www.biloxi.ms.us). Greyhound **buses** from New Orleans and Mobile come in at 322 Main St, very near the Amtrak station on the New Orleans–Miami line. Coast Area Transit (☎228/896-8080) runs an hourly **trolley** service, the Beachcomber line, along the coast to the unspectacular business center of Gulfport; all-day passes cost $4.

Room rates vary considerably according to season and ocean view, but the most convenient area to stay is near the **Loop**. Options along Beach Boulevard include the *Sun Tan Motel* at no. 780 (☏228/432-8641; ❸/❹), and the *Gulf Beach Resort* at no. 2428 (☏228/385-5555; ❹). You can **camp** at the *Southern Comfort Camping Resort*, 1766 Beach Blvd; tentsites start from $13. *McElroy's Harbor House*, at 695 Beach Bvd (☏228/435-5001), is a cheery place for good **seafood**. You can also get great lunch specials and drink a local specialty, Barq's Root Beer, from the original long-necked bottles, at the homey *Ole Biloxi Schooner's Restaurant*, 159 E Howard Ave (☏228/374-8071), or enjoy excellent upscale dining at the 1737 *Mary Mahoney's Old French House*, 116 Rue Magnolia (☏228/374-0163, reservations recommended).

Arkansas

Historically, **ARKANSAS** belongs very much to the American South. It sided firmly with the Confederacy in the Civil War and its capital, Little Rock, was, in 1957, one of the most notorious flashpoints in the struggle for civil rights. Geographically, however, it marks the beginning of the Great Plains. Unlike the other Southern states, on the far side of the Mississippi River, Arkansas remained very sparsely populated until almost a century ago. Westward expansion was blocked by the existence of the Indian Territory in what's now Oklahoma, and not until the railroads opened up the forested interior during the 1880s did settlers stray in any numbers from their small riverside villages. Only once the Depression and mechanization had forced thousands of farmers to leave their fields did Arkansas begin to develop any significant industrial base. In 1992, local boy Bill Clinton's accession to the presidency catapulted Arkansas into national prominence. Four towns lay claim to him: Hope, his birthplace; Hot Springs, his "home town"; Fayetteville, where he and Hillary married; and, of course, Little Rock, the state capital. Of the four, only sleepy **Little Rock** and the nearby spa resort of **Hot Springs** are worth a trip, whatever the tourist brochures may say.

Though Arkansas encompasses the **Mississippi Delta** in the east, oil-rich timber lands in the south, and the sweeping **Ouachita** (*Wash-i-taw*) **Mountains** in the west, the cragged and charismatic **Ozark Mountains** in the north are its most scenic asset, where the main attractions for tourists are the uncrowded parks and unspoiled rivers. Incidentally, "Arkansas" is a distorted version of the name of a small Indian tribe; the state legislature declared once and for all in 1881 that the correct pronunciation is *Arkansaw*.

Getting around Arkansas

It's extremely difficult to venture beyond Little Rock and Hot Springs using public transportation. Greyhound runs intermittent services, while Amtrak cuts diagonally east–west through the state, calling at Little Rock, which also holds the only sizeable **airport**. To see the Ozarks you'll need a car.

Eastern Arkansas

What's surprising about the eastern Arkansas deltalands is that they are far from totally flat: **Crowley's Ridge**, a narrow arc of windblown loess hills, breaks up the uniform smoothness, stretching 150 miles from southern Missouri to the atmospheric river town of **Helena**. Despite scenic rivers and sleepy bayous, the pine-clad woodlands of the Gulf Coastal Plain in southern Arkansas are of little real interest.

Helena

The small Mississippi port of **HELENA**, roughly sixty miles south of Memphis, was once the shipping point for Arkansas's cotton crop, when Mark Twain described it as occupying "one of the prettiest situations on the river." A small historic district bordered by Holly, College and Perry streets reflects that brief period of prosperity, before the arrival of the railroad left most of the river towns obsolete; today Helena's central core is little more than the slightly run-down Cherry Street on the levee.

That said, there are three good reasons to visit Helena. Musicians among its large black population have ensured that the town is an important stop for **Delta blues** enthusiasts – no great distance from Clarksdale, Mississippi (see p.594), it hosts one of the country's leading blues festivals every October. Radio station KFFA (1360AM) with living legend "Sunshine" Sonny Payne, a DJ who started out in 1941, still broadcasts the long-running *King Biscuit Time Show* (Mon–Fri 12.15–12.45pm) from the foyer of the **Delta Cultural Center**, in the old train station at 95 Missouri St, at the end of Cherry Street; visitors are welcome. Helena was for many years the home of harmonica great **Sonny Boy Williamson II ("Rice" Miller)**, and featured in intimate detail in many of his (usually extemporized) recordings. He used to advertise Sonny Boy's Biscuit Meal on the radio show, and it continues to maintain the illusion that he is present in the studio. Each fall, on the weekend before Columbus Day, the city holds the **King Biscuit Blues Festival** (℡870/338-4350, ⊛www.kingbiscuitfest.org/), which is free and attracts some big name performers.

The **Cultural Center**, 141 Cherry St, itself is excellent, covering, among other things, the first settlers of this soggy frontier, contemporary racism and, of course, the region's musical heritage (Tues–Sat 10am–5pm, Sun 1–5pm; free; ℡870/338-4350, ⊛www.deltaculturalcenter.com). You can buy – and hear – a great assortment of blues records at Bubba Sullivan's Blues Corner, nearby in the small mall at 105 Cherry St (℡870/338-3501): Bubba himself is a mine of friendly information on local music gigs and events.

For some unexpected historic artifacts stop by the **Phillips County Museum** on 623 Pecan St, adjoining the library (Tues–Sat 10am–4pm; free; ℡870/338-7790). Here, besides paintings, period clothing, Native American arrowheads, a working model phonograph and a variety of other items on display, you'll find letters written by General Lafayette, Charles Lindbergh and Robert E. Lee, as well as Samuel Clemens (Mark Twain).

Practicalities

The best of the few places to stay, the *Edwardian Inn*, 317 Briscoe St, on the main highway into town north of the Mississippi Bridge (℡870/338-9155 or 1-800/598-4749, ℻870/338-4215, ⊛www.edwardianinn.com; ➍), is an opulent **B&B** with large wood-paneled rooms, slightly marred by views from the front over a chemical plant on the river. For **food**, *Pasquale's*, 211 Missouri St, opposite the cultural center (☎1-800/390-3992), serves nationally marketed homemade tamales.

Central and western Arkansas

Quiet **Little Rock** stands right in the middle of the state, just fifty miles west of the rejuvenated spa town of **Hot Springs**, which marks the eastern gateway to the remote **Ouachita Mountains**. The rippling farmland of the **Arkansas River Valley** is sandwiched by the Ouachita crests on the south side and the craggy ridges of the Ozarks to the north. Mining and logging communities dot the east–west roads, and former frontier towns like **Fort Smith** and **Van Buren** retain their Old West flavor. Fayetteville and Hope are both in west Arkansas; there's nothing to see in either.

Little Rock

The geographical, political and financial center of Arkansas, **LITTLE ROCK** is at the meeting point of its two major regions, the northwestern hills and the eastern Delta. The town today has a relaxed, open feel, a far cry from the dramatic events of 1957 (see box, opposite). In the rapidly expanding **River Market District**, 500 E Markham St, the **Museum of Discovery**, geared largely toward kids (Mon–Sat 10am–5pm, Sun 1–4.30pm; $5.95, free first Fri each month 5pm–9pm; ☎501/396-7050), is a welcome and fun addition. This area contains the majority of Little Rock's activity, with a series of restaurants, bars and the actual farmers' market on the river. Behind the museum is **Riverfront Park**, a thin strip of greenery and fountains that runs for several blocks – here, a commemorative sign marks the "little rock" for which the city is named, which is not particularly striking.

In MacArthur Park the **Arkansas Art Center** features work by local and international artists (Mon–Sat 10am–5pm, first Fri of every month 10am–8.30pm, Sun 11am–5pm; free). Also in the park is a **Military Museum** that has exhibits from the Civil War on forward.

The white **Old State House Museum**, 300 W Markham St, surrounded by smooth lawns and shaded by evergreens, backs onto the Arkansas River. Inside, displays cover all periods of Arkansas history, but the most impressive rooms are the two senate chambers, restored to their original grandeur (Mon–Sat 9am–5pm, Sun 1–5pm; free). This was where Clinton announced his bid for the presidency on October 3, 1991, and made his acceptance speech thirteen months later. There's now a special exhibit in the museum on his path to the presidency.

Practicalities

Greyhound arrives at 118 E Washington Ave in North Little Rock. Amtrak enjoys a more central location at Markham and Victory streets. **Taxis** don't pick up on the street, so call Black and White (☎501/374-0333); from Greyhound to downtown costs around $7. The **visitor center** is located in the Convention Center at Markham and Main streets (Mon–Fri 8.30am–4.30pm, open on occasional weekends; ☎501/376-4781 or 1-800/844-4781, ⓦwww.littlerock.com).

Finding a **room** downtown should be no problem. The best **budget** option is just outside of downtown at the *Masters Inn*, 707 I-30 (☎1-800/633-3434, Ⓕ501/372-1732, ⓦwww.mastersinn.com; ❷), while the *Rosemont B&B*, 515 W

In 1957, Little Rock unexpectedly became the battleground in the first major conflict between state and federal government over **race relations**. At the time, the city was generally viewed as progressive by Southern standards. All parks, libraries and buses were integrated, a relatively high thirty percent of blacks were on the electoral register, and there were black police officers. However, when the Little Rock School Board announced its decision to phase in **desegregation** gradually – the Supreme Court having declared segregation of schools to be unconstitutional – James Johnson, a candidate for state governor, started a campaign opposed to interracial education. Johnson's rhetoric began to win him support, and the incumbent governor, **Orval Faubus**, who had previously shown no interest in the issue, jumped on the bandwagon himself.

The first nine black students were due to enter Central High School that September. The day before school opened, Faubus reversed his decision to let blacks enroll "in the interest of safety," only to be overruled by the federal court. He ordered state troopers to keep out the black students anyway; soldiers with bayonets forced Elizabeth Eckford, one of the nine, away from the school entrance into a seething crowd, from which she had to jump on a bus to escape. As legal battles raged during the day, at night blacks were subject to violent attacks by white gangs. Three weeks later, President Eisenhower somewhat reluctantly brought in the 101st Airborne Division, and, amidst violent demonstrations, the nine were at last able to enter Central High. Throughout the year, they experienced immense intimidation; when one retaliated, she was expelled. The graduation of James Green, the oldest, at the end of the year, seemed to put an end to the affair, but Faubus, up for re-election, renewed his political posturing by closing down all public schools in the city for the 1958–59 academic year – and thereby increased his majority.

The school itself is an enormous brown, crescent-shaped structure, more like a fortress, at 1500 S Park Ave, about a mile from the capitol on bus route #9. There is a **visitor center** across the street from Central in a historically restored former Mobil gas station that has an interesting exhibit titled, "All the World Is Watching Us: Little Rock and the 1957 Crisis" (Mon–Sat 10am–4pm, Sun 1–4pm; free; call ☎501/374-1957 for details on special tours).

15th St (☎501/374-7456, ☞501/374-2111, ⓦ www.rosemontoflittlerock.com; ❹/❺), is conveniently situated in the downtown historic district. Near the River Market District is the *Doubletree*, 424 W Markham (☎501/372-4371, ☞501/372-0518; ❹). As for **eating**, *Trio's-Rivermarket*, 225 E Markham St (☎501/301-8000), has an interesting global/New American menu. *Juanita's Cantina*, 1300 S Main St (☎501/372-1228), an atmospheric and imaginative Mexican place, also hosts live bands.

Hot Springs

Fifty miles southwest of Little Rock, the spa town of **HOT SPRINGS** nestles in the heavily forested Zig Zag Mountains on the eastern flank of the Ouachitas. Its thermal waters have attracted visitors since Native Americans used the area as a neutral zone to settle disputes. Early settlers fashioned a crude resort out of the wilderness, and after the railroads arrived in 1875 it became a European-style spa. During the Twenties and Thirties, the mayor reputedly ran a gambling syndicate worth $30 million per annum, and punters included Al Capone and Bugsy Malone. However, Hot Springs's popularity waned when new cures for arthritis appeared during the Fifties, and all but one of the bathhouses closed down. There was a surge of interest after Clinton's election – he lived here between 1953 and 1964 – and the **visitor center** at Central Avenue and Court Street (☏501/321-2277) provides a glossy leaflet marking his favorite haunts.

Downtown Hot Springs is crammed into a looping wooded valley, barely wide enough to accommodate Central Avenue. Eight magnificent buildings here, behind a lush display of magnolia trees, elms and hedgerows, make up Bathhouse Row. Between 1915 and 1962, the grandest of them all was the **Fordyce Bathhouse**, at the 300 block of Central, which reopened in 1989 as the **visitor center** for **HOT SPRINGS NATIONAL PARK** – the only national park to fall within city limits. The interior of the Fordyce is a strange mixture of the elegant and the obsolete; the heavy use of marble, mosaic-tile floors and the stained-glass ceiling of the Sun Room lend it a decadent feel (daily 9am–5pm; free; ☏501/624-3383).

It's still possible to sample the old-time luxury of Hot Springs by taking a **bath**. The only establishment on Bathhouse Row still open for business is the Buckstaff, where a thermal mineral bath costs $14 (Mon–Fri 7–11.45am & 1.30–3pm, Sat 7–11.45am; ☏501/623-2308). Full bathing facilities are available at several hotels. To taste the water, which lacks the strong sulphuric taste often associated with thermal springs, fill up a container at the drinking fountain at Central and Reserve.

To the rear of the Fordyce, two small **springs** have been left open for viewing. The **Grand Promenade** from here is a half-mile red-and-yellow-brick walkway overlooking downtown. Trails of various lengths and severity lead up the steep slopes of **Hot Springs Mountain**. To reach the summit, take a short drive or any of several different trails, including a testing two-and-a-half-mile hike through dense woods of oak, hickory and short-leafed pine. The observation decks of **Mountain Tower** at the top offer superb views of the town, the Ouachitas and surrounding lakes (daily summer 9am–9pm; times vary in winter and also toward the end of summer; $5; ☏501/623-6035).

Practicalities

Most places of interest are within walking distance of the town's central accommodation, and local **buses** provide a reasonable hourly service to most parts of the city. **Bikes** can be rented from Parkside Cycles, 719 Whittington Ave (☏501/623-6188).

Though rates can rise by up to 25 percent in the long high season (Feb–Nov), luxury **accommodation** is surprisingly inexpensive. Dominating the town center, the elegant twin-towered *Arlington Resort/Spa* at 239 Central Ave is where Capone stayed when in town – and where President Clinton attended his Junior and Senior proms (☏501/623-7771, ☏501/623-2243, ⊛www.arlingtonhotel.com; ❹/❺; bath and massage $45). The *Margarete Motel*, 217 Fountain St (☏501/623-1192, ☏501/624-6043; ❷), is one of several neighboring budget motels. The nearest place to **camp** is *Gulpha Gorge Campground* ($10; ☏501/624-3383), in the national park, two miles out on Hwy-70 B, off Hwy-70 E.

Hidden among the usual family **restaurants** is the breakfast only *Pancake Shop*, 216 Central Ave (☏501/624-5720), whose stuffed pancakes make a filling start to the day. Other renowned eateries are *McClard's Bar-B-Q*, 505 Albert Pike (☏501/624-9586 or 623-9665), and *Coy's Steak and Seafood*, 300 Coy St (☏501/321-1414).

Western Arkansas

West of Hot Springs, US-270 cuts through the **Ouachita Mountains**, unique to the continent in that they run east–west rather than north–south. On its way to Oklahoma, the road passes over uneven crests separated by wide valleys speckled with tiny communities, so isolated that, in the Thirties, hill-dwellers supposedly spoke a form of Elizabethan English. Separating the Ouachitas from the northerly Ozarks, the **Arkansas River Valley**, a natural east–west path for bison, was used for centuries by Native Americans and white hunters before steamboats arrived in the 1820s.

Fort Smith

Now an industrial city of roughly 70,000 people, **FORT SMITH**, on the Oklahoma border, maintains a pronounced Western feel. Until Isaac C. Parker – the "Hanging Judge" – took over in 1875, this was a rowdy pioneer town uncomfortably close to Indian Territory, a sanctuary for robbers and bandits. Parker sent out two hundred marshals to round up the fugitives; in 21 years he sentenced 160 to death and saw 79 go to the gallows. **Fort Smith National Historic Site** on Rogers Avenue features remains of the original fort, Parker's courtroom, the dingy basement jail and a set of gallows (daily 9am–5pm; $3). **Old Main Street** in **Van Buren**, on the opposite bank of the Arkansas River, is a stretch of over seventy restored buildings that has been used in numerous Westerns.

Fort Smith's **visitor center**, Miss Laura's, 2 North B St (Mon–Sat 9am–4pm, Sun 1–4pm, ☎1-800/637-1477), is oddly housed in a restored former brothel and offers $1 trolley tours of the city (Mon–Sat 9.30am–3.30pm; every 45min). **Lodgings** in Fort Smith include the central *Holiday Inn*, 700 Rogers Ave (☎501/783-1000, ℉501/783-0312, ⓦwww.holiday-inn.com/ftsmithar; ④/⑤). For good-value, tasty home-cooked Italian **food**, try *Taliano's*, 201 N 14th St (☎501/785-2292).

The Ozark Mountains

Although the highest peak fails to top 2000 feet, the **Ozark Mountains**, which extend beyond northern Arkansas into southern Missouri, are characterized by severe steep ridges and jagged spurs. Hair-raising roads weave their way over the precipitous hills, past rugged lakeshores and pristine rivers. When ambitious speculators poured into Arkansas in the 1830s, those who missed the best land etched out remote hill farms that was no better than what they'd left behind in Kentucky or Tennessee. They remained utterly isolated until the last few decades; the Ozarks have now become the fastest-growing rural section of the US, a major tourist and retirement destination. Much-needed cash has flooded in, bringing with it the cafés and souvenir shops that have converted centers such as **Harrison** into cookie-cutter American towns.

The word *Ozark* is everywhere, used to entice tourists into music shows or gift emporia, which owe more to Nashville and Taiwan than to these mountains. With all the hype, it's getting increasingly difficult to tell the genuine article from imitations, which is a good reason for visiting the state park at **Mountain View**, a serious attempt to preserve traditional Ozark skills and music. The most visited town in the region, **Eureka Springs**, just inside the Missouri border, is a pretty mountainside Victorian spa town, though not one where you should expect to learn much about Ozark life.

Mountain View

Roughly sixty miles due north of Little Rock, the state-run **Ozark Folk Center** (℡870/269-3851, Ⓦwww.ozarkfolkcenter.com), two miles north of the town of **MOUNTAIN VIEW** on Hwy-14, is a living history museum that attempts to show how life used to be in these remote hills, not reached by paved roads until the Fifties. Homestead skills are displayed in reconstructed log cabins, and folk musicians and storytellers perform throughout the park. Every weekday night in season live Ozark music concerts are held at 7.30pm (mid-April to early Nov; concerts $8, craft displays $8, combination ticket $13.50). Additionally, there are two major festivals: the **Spring Folk Festival**, in the third weekend in April, and the **Bean Festival**, the fourth weekend in October; book accommodations well in advance during these times.

There's a **visitor center** at 199 Peabody St (April–Nov Mon–Sat 9am–5pm, Sun noon–3pm; Dec–March Mon–Fri 9am–5pm; ℡870/269-8068, Ⓦwww .mtnviewcc.org). There are **rooms** at the *Dry Creek Lodge* (℡870/269-3871, Ⓕ870/269-2909; ❸) in the center's grounds, and the pretty *Inn at Mountain View*, 812 Washington St (℡1-800/535-1301, Ⓦwww.innatmountainview .com; ❹), which serves a full country breakfast. Good **restaurants** include the Folk Center's *Iron Skillet Restaurant* (℡870/269-3139) and *Tommy's Famous...*, an award-winning pizzeria at 204 Carpenter St, four blocks west of the square (℡870/269-3278). For Saturday night entertainment, even in winter, it's hard to beat the friendly jam sessions in Mountain View's town square.

The **Buffalo River** – a prime destination for whitewater canoeing – flows across the state north of Mountain View. Buffalo Camping and Canoeing (℡870/439-2386) provides canoes and equipment, and runs a free shuttle bus to the river, which is at its most spectacular around **Pruitt Landing**, thirteen miles south of unremarkable Harrison.

Eureka Springs

Picturesque **EUREKA SPRINGS**, set on steep mountain slopes in Arkansas's northwestern corner, began life a century ago as a health center. As that role declined, its striking location turned it into a regular tourist destination, given a kitsch edge by its specialty in weddings and honeymoons. It's an enjoyable place to stroll around, filled with tasteful Victorian buildings, and you can ride on the **Eureka Springs and North Arkansas Railway** through wooded Ozark valleys. Rolling stock includes a magnificent "cabbage-head" wood-burning locomotive, and trips depart on the hour from the depot at 299 N Main St (mid-April to Oct Mon–Sat 10am–4pm; ℡501/253-9623).

Three miles east of town, an incredible religious complex includes the seven-story **Christ of the Ozarks** – a surreal statue of Jesus with a 60ft arm span – a **Bible Museum** ($2.50) and a **Sacred Arts Center** ($2.50). Elna M. Smith, whose Foundation runs the whole show, was so worried that the holy sites of the Middle East would be destroyed by war that she decided to build replicas in the Ozarks, safe from Arab attacks. Minibuses whisk visitors through the two-and-a-half hour **New Holy Land Tour** (last Fri in April to last Sat in Oct Mon–Sat 9am–3.30pm, Wed 9am–12.45pm; $9 admission includes all attractions) past scaled-down versions of the Sea of Galilee, the River Jordan and Golgotha. Christ's last days on earth are re-enacted with a cast of almost two hundred in the **Great Passion Play**, in a 4100-seat amphitheater (last Fri in April to Oct nightly except Sun and Wed 8.30pm, after August 7.30pm; $15.75–17.75; ℡1-800/882-7529).

Practicalities

In town US–62 and Van Buren are the same road. **Accommodation** rates vary seasonally, but you can usually find inexpensive lodging just over a mile from downtown on US–62 E. More central is the *Best Western Eureka Inn* (℡501/253-9551, 🅵501/253-9692, 🆆www.eurekabw.com; ❹), at the junction of US-62 and S Main Street. The local **visitor center** is at 137 W Van Buren (daily 9am–5pm; ℡501/253-8737).

For **food**, *Sparky's Road House Café*, 147 E Van Buren (℡501/253-6001), is atmospheric with an inexpensive menu and good beer selection. *Pancake's Family Restaurant*, 2055 E Van Buren (℡501/253-5289), serves tasty well-priced food and is open until 11pm. *Mama Sarah's Spaghetti House* at 3094 E Van Buren is exactly what it says. Just off the well-worn tourist paths, *Chelsea's Corner*, 10 Mountain St, off Spring Street (℡501/253-6723), has live **music** most evenings.

CHAPTER 7

Highlights

* **Ocean Drive, Miami**
South Beach's finest Art Deco showpiece, buzzing with cosmopolitan cafés, flashy vintage cars and wannabe models. See p.625

* **Mangrove Mama's, Sugarloaf Key**
Quintessential Florida Keys food joint, serving super-fresh conch fritters and Key Lime pie. See p.632

* **Little Havana, Miami**
Lunch on Cuban specialties and café con leche in this Hispanic enclave. See p.621.

* **Key West** Funky, anything-goes town, which feels like it's at the end of the world. See p.632

* **St Augustine** Sixteenth-century Spanish town packed with historic interest and a handful of lovely beaches. See p.644

* **Walt Disney World, Orlando** Pure entertainment, planned down to the last detail, yet irresistible all the same. See p.652

* **Everglades National Park** Bike or hike through the vast sawgrass plains of the legendary Everglades, or canoe through alligator-filled mangrove swamps. See p.669

Florida

Brochure images of tanning flesh and Mickey Mouse give an inaccurate and incomplete picture of **FLORIDA**. Although the aptly nicknamed "Sunshine State" is indeed devoted to the tourist trade, it's also among the least-understood parts of the US. Away from its overexposed resorts lie forests and rivers, deserted strands filled with wildlife, vibrant cities and primeval swamps.

In many respects Florida is still evolving. Seven hundred people a day move to the state, now the fourth most populous in the nation. Changing demographics are eroding the traditional Deep South conservatism: the new Floridians tend to be a younger, more energetic breed, while Spanish-speaking enclaves provide close ties to Latin America and the Caribbean – links as influential in creating wealth as the recent arrival of the movie industry in central Florida, fresh from Hollywood.

The essential stop is cosmopolitan, half-Latin **Miami**, from where a simple journey south brings you to the **Florida Keys**, a hundred-mile string of islands known for sports fishing, coral-reef diving, and the sultry town of **Key West**, legendary for its sunsets and anything-goes attitude. North from Miami, much of the **east coast** is disappointingly urbanized, albeit with miles of unbroken beaches flowing alongside. The residential stranglehold is lessened further north, where communities such as **Daytona Beach** have become subservient to the local sands. Farther along, historical **St Augustine** stands as the longest continuous settlement in the US.

In **central Florida** the terrain turns green, though it's no rural idyll: this is where you'll find **Orlando** and **Walt Disney World**, one of the world's leading tourist destinations. From here it's just a skip north to the forests of the **Panhandle**, Florida's link with the Deep South, or to the towns and beaches of the **west coast**. To the south, and also easily accessible from Miami, stretches the **Everglades**, a swampy sawgrass plain filled with camera-friendly (but otherwise unfriendly) alligators.

In at least one way it makes little difference **when you visit**: warm sunshine and blue skies are almost always a fact of life. Florida does, however, split into two **climatic zones**: subtropical in the south and warm temperate in the north. Orlando and points south have very mild winters (October to April), with warm temperatures and low humidity. This is the peak tourist season, when prices are at their highest. The southern summer (May to September), on the other hand, brings high humidity and afternoon storms – the rewards for braving the mugginess are lower prices and fewer tourists. Winter is the off-peak period north of Orlando; while snow has been known to fall in the Panhandle, daytime temperatures are generally comfortably warm. During the northern Florida summer, the crowds arrive, and the days – and the nights – get hot and sticky. Also, there is a potentially ominous time of the year – the **"hurricane season"** – June to November.

Finally, although Florida has struggled with its reputation for **crimes** against (and even murders of) tourists, the state's been very successful in reducing such attacks. It's definitely no longer the den of "Miami Vice" it once was, but, as when visiting all big cities, it pays to be wary.

Some history

The **first European sighting** of Florida, just six years after Christopher Columbus reached the New World, is believed to have been made by John and Sebastian Cabot in 1498, when they spotted what is now Cape Florida, on Key Biscayne in Miami. At the time, the area's 100,000 inhabitants formed several distinct **tribes**: the Timucua across northern Florida, the Calusa around the southwest and Lake Okeechobee, the Apalachee in the Panhandle and the Tequesta along the southeast coast.

In 1513, a Spaniard, **Juan Ponce de León**, sighted land during *Pascua Florida*, the Festival of the Flowers, and named what he saw *La Florida* – or "Land of Flowers." Eight years later he returned with a mandate from the Spanish king to conquer and colonize the territory, the first of several Spanish incursions prompted by rumors of gold hidden in the north of the region. When it became clear that Florida did not harbor stunning riches, interest waned; but the arrival of French Huguenots in 1562 forced the Spanish into a more determined effort at settlement. Three years later, Pedro Menéndez de Avilés founded **St Augustine** – the longest continuous site of European habitation on the continent. In 1586 St Augustine was razed by a British naval bombardment led by Francis Drake. The ensuing bloody confrontation for control of North America was eventually settled when the British captured the crucial Spanish possession of Havana, and Spain willingly parted with Florida to get it back. By this time, indigenous Floridians had been largely wiped out by disease. Florida's Native American population now largely comprised disparate tribes arriving from the west, collectively known as the **Seminoles**, who were generally left undisturbed in the inland areas.

Following American independence, when Florida was returned to Spain, the US began to think in terms of controlling the state. In 1814 a US general, Andrew Jackson, marched south, killing hundreds of Indians and triggering the **First Seminole War** – on the pretext of subduing the Seminole but with the actual intention of taking the region. Spain formally **ceded Florida to the US** in 1819, with Jackson sworn in as Florida's first American governor and Tallahassee selected as the new administrative center. Eleven years later, the **Act of Indian Removal** decreed that all Native Americans in the eastern US should be transferred to reservations in the Midwest. Most Seminole were determined to stay and the **Second Seminole War** broke out, with the Indians steadily driven south, away from the fertile lands of central Florida and into the Everglades, where they eventually agreed to remain.

Florida **became a state** on March 3, 1845, coinciding with the prosperity brought by the railroads. As a member of the Confederacy during the **Civil War**, Florida's primary contribution was the provision of food – a foretaste of its post-war economic role after being readmitted to the Union. As northern speculators began to invest in Florida, the country's newspapers extolled the curative virtues of its climate. These early efforts to promote Florida as a **tourist destination** brought in the wintering rich: Henry Flagler opened luxury resorts on the northeast coast and extended his Florida East Coast Railroad south, giving birth to communities such as Palm Beach. Henry Plant connected his own railroad to Tampa, turning it into a thriving port city. Florida's climate enabled citrus fruits to be grown during the winter and sold to the cooler north, and the state became a major beef producer. After World War I, it seemed that everyone in America wanted a piece of Florida, and chartered trains brought in thousands of eager buyers. But most deals were on paper only, and in 1926 the banks began to default. The **Wall Street Crash** then made paupers of the millionaires whose investments had helped shape the state.

7

FLORIDA

What saved Florida was **World War II**. Thousands of troops arrived to guard the coastline, empty tourist hotels provided ready-made barracks, and – most importantly – the soldiers got a taste of Florida that would entice many of them to return. In the mid-Sixties, the state government bent over backward to help the Disney Corporation turn a sizable slice of central Florida into **Walt Disney World**, the biggest theme park ever known. Its enormous commercial success helped solidify Florida's place in the international tourist market: directly or indirectly, tourism makes up 20 percent of the total state economy.

Behind the optimistic facade, however, lie many **problems**. There's a broadening gap between the relative liberalism of the big cities and the arch-conservatism of the rural Bible Belt: while Miami promotes its multicultural makeup, the Ku Klux Klan holds picnics in the Panhandle. Gun laws remain notoriously lax, and the multimillion-dollar **drug trade** shows few signs of abating – at least a quarter of the cocaine entering the US is said to arrive via Florida. **Racial issues** continue, too, with tension on several fronts: between Anglo-Americans and nouveau riche Cubans, blacks and whites, blacks and Hispanics, police and the inner-city poor. However, increased protection of the state's **natural resources** has been a more positive feature of the last decade and impressive amounts of land are under state control – overall, wildlife is less threatened now than at any time since white settlers first arrived.

The 2000 presidential election fiasco brought unwelcome attention to the state. Both Gov. George Bush of Texas (Republican) and Vice President Al Gore (Democrat) needed Florida's 25 electoral votes to win. Bush led by a few hundred votes on the morning after the election in unofficial returns. For five weeks top lawyers on both sides slugged it out in the courts. Disputes raged over such issues as whether ballots with "hanging chads" (partially punched out holes) should be counted. Ultimately, the US Supreme Court issued a ruling that effectively halted the recounts, and Bush won the state by 537 votes out of some six million cast.

Getting around Florida

Florida is surprisingly compact, and easy to get around by car: crossing between the east and west coasts takes a couple of hours, and one of the longest trips – between the western extremity of the Panhandle and Miami – can be done in a day. **Public transportation**, on the other hand, requires adroit advance planning. Greyhound buses link all major towns and cities, with both Miami and Orlando well served; but many rural areas and some of the most enjoyable sections of the coast are not covered.

Florida's **railroads** were built to service boomtowns in the Twenties, and consequently some rural nooks are well-linked. Amtrak runs west from **Jacksonville** via New Orleans all the way to LA, while connections with New York are good. However, in some areas Amtrak buses have replaced the trains; these can be very expensive, so check in advance. Passengers with cars can use the daily **Auto Train** from Lorton, Virginia (just south of Washington, DC), to Sanford, north of Orlando. The southeast coast boasts an elevated **TriRail** system that ferries commuters between Miami, Fort Lauderdale, Boca Raton and Palm Beach.

Although inadvisable in the cities, **cycling** is a great way to see large parts of Florida – miles of cycle paths follow the coast, and long-distance bike trails cross the state's interior. Forget **hitching**: always dangerous (especially for women), it's illegal in Miami (where you'd be lucky to live to regret it) and on the outskirts of many other cities.

Miami

Far and away the most exciting city in Florida, **MIAMI** is a stunning and often intoxicatingly beautiful place. Awash with sunlight-intensified natural colors, there are moments – when the neon-flashed South Beach skyline glows in the warm night and the palm trees sway in the breeze – when a better-looking city is hard to imagine. Even so, people, not climate or landscape, are what make Miami unique. Half of the two million population is Hispanic, the vast majority Cubans. Spanish is the predominant language almost everywhere – in many places it's the only language you'll hear, and you'll be expected to speak at least a few words – and news from Havana, Caracas or Managua frequently gets more attention than the latest word from Washington, DC.

Just a century ago Miami was a swampy outpost of mosquito-tormented settlers. The arrival of the railroad in 1896 gave the city its first fixed land-link with the rest of the continent, and cleared the way for the Twenties property boom. In the Fifties, Miami Beach became a celebrity-filled resort area, just as thousands of Cubans fleeing the regime of Fidel Castro began arriving in mainland Miami. The Sixties and Seventies brought decline, and Miami's reputation in the Eighties as the vice capital of the USA was at least partly deserved. As the cop show *Miami Vice* so glamorously underlined, drug smuggling was endemic; as well, in 1980 the city had the highest murder rate in America. Since then, though, much has changed for two very different reasons. First, the gentrification of South Beach helped make tourism the lifeblood of the local economy again in the early Nineties. Second, the city's determined wooing of Latin America brought rapid investment, both domestic and international: many US corporations run their South American operations from Miami and certain neighborhoods, such as Key Biscayne, are now home to thriving communities of expat Peruvians, Colombians and Venezuelans.

Arrival, information and getting around

Miami International Airport (☎305/876-7000) is six miles west of the city. A cab from the airport should cost around $24, or you can take one of the 24-hour SuperShuttle minivans, which will deliver you to any address in Miami for $9–15 (☎305/871-2000, ⓦ www.supershuttle.com). From the airport, take the #7 Metrobus to downtown, a trip of 30 minutes or so ($1.25, exact fare required; every 40min Mon–Fri 5.30am–8.30pm, Sat & Sun 7am–7pm), or the 'J' Metrobus ($1.25 plus a 25¢ surcharge to South Beach; every 30min daily 5.30am–11.30pm) to Miami Beach farther on. If you arrive late at night, the Airport Owl shuttle runs in a loop through South Beach, downtown and back to the airport ($1.25; once hourly, 11.50pm–5.50am). **Greyhound's** Miami West station is a short cab ride from the airport, while the other major terminal is downtown at 100 W 6th St (☎305/374-6180 or 1-800/231-2222, ⓦ www.greyhound.com). The **Amtrak** station, 8303 NW 37th Ave, is seven miles northwest. To get downtown or to Coconut Grove or Coral Gables from here, take Metrobus #L to the Metrorail, eight blocks away (see overleaf).

A good place for **information and maps** is the **Greater Miami Convention and Visitor Bureau**, 1920 Meridian Ave (Mon–Fri 9am–5pm,

Sat & Sun 10am–4pm; ☏305/672-1270, ⊛www.tropicoolmiami.com). In South Beach, at the Art Deco Welcome Center, 1001 Ocean Drive (Mon–Fri 10am–5pm; ☏305/672-2014, ⊛www.mdpl.org), the **Miami Beach Art Deco Preservation League** has details on walking tours and events, and a great line in retro gifts.

City transportation

Driving is the most practical way to get around Miami. Though the safety warnings handed to visitors as they pick up their rental cars can make unnerving reading, the much publicized tourist-targeted car-jackings of the early 1990s are now no more of an issue here than in any major city. Watch out for road signs marked with an orange sun on a blue background; they identify the most useful routes to the main attractions. Tourist police patrol in cars with the same logo.

With a lot of time and patience, it is possible to make your way around Miami on **public transportation** run by Metro-Dade Transit (☏305/770-3131 or ⊛www.co.miami-dade.fl.us/transit/ for route information). **Metrorail** trains (5am–midnight) run, slowly, along a single line between the northern suburbs and South Miami; useful stops are Government Center (for downtown), Coconut Grove, and Douglas Road or University (for Coral Gables). Single-journey fares are $1.25. Downtown Miami is also ringed by the **Metromover** (5.30am–midnight; flat fare 25¢), a monorail that doesn't cover much ground but gives a great bird's-eye view. **Metrobuses** cover the entire city, but services dwindle at night; the flat-rate single-journey fare is $1.25, with a 25¢ surcharge for transfers. **Route maps** and **timetables** for all Metro-Dade Transit services can be had at Government Center Station, and at the Metrorail station at NW First Avenue & First Street.

Taxis, cycling and tours

Taxis are abundant; try Central Cab (☏305/532-5555) or Metro Taxi (☏305/888-8888). Otherwise, get the free Miami on Two Wheels leaflet from the CVB and **rent a bike** from one of the many outlets, such as the Miami Beach Cycle Center, 601 5th St (Mon–Sat 10am–7pm, Sat & Sun 10am–5pm; ☏305/531-4161). For an informed stroll, take one of **Dr Paul George's Walking Tours** from the **Historical Museum of South Florida** (no tours July & Aug; $37; ☏305/375-1621, ⊛www.historical-museum.org). Or, try the various excellent **Art Deco walking tours** of South Beach (Thurs at 6.30pm & Sat at 10.30am; $10), which begin at the Miami Design Preservation League Welcome Center on Ocean Drive (see p.625). The latter also offers a self-guided audio walking tour of the district (daily 10am–4pm; 1hr–1hr 15min; $5).

Accommodation

Accommodation is not a problem in Miami except during the Boat Show (February). Otherwise, there are rooms to suit every taste and budget, with the majority of travelers opting for any one of the numerous Art Deco **South Beach** hotels. Elsewhere, **Coral Gables** is appealing but expensive; **downtown Miami** is filled with chain hotels; and the stylish high-rises of **Coconut Grove** are a jet-setter's preserve. Prices are steepest from December through April; the rest of the year you may have some luck negotiating – in any case, bargains can be found year-round in several well-run **hostels** in Miami Beach.

Banana Bungalow 2360 Collins Ave, Central Miami Beach ☏ 305/538-1951 or 1-800/746-7835. Yearning for a perpetual spring break? Go for the nightly movies in the plush video room, organized land and water tours and the cheapest tiki bar on the strip. Choose from bunk beds or private rooms. ❶/❷

Brigham Gardens Guesthouse 1411 Collins Ave, South Beach ☏ 305/531-1331. The large rooms have either basic or fully equipped kitchens. A tropical garden patio and friendly atmosphere help make this one of the most pleasant places to stay in South Beach. ❸/❹

Clay Hotel and Hosteling International 1438 Washington Ave, South Beach ☏ 305/534-2988 or 1-800/379-2529. The beautiful converted monastery serves as the city's best budget hotel and youth hostel. ❶/❷

Hotel Place St Michel 162 Alcazar Ave, Coral Gables ☏ 305/444-1666. The small, romantic hotel just off the Miracle Mile displays Laura Ashley decor and copious European antiques. Rates include a continental breakfast. ❺

Indian Creek 2727 Indian Creek Drive at 28th St, Miami Beach ☏ 305/531-2727. This fantastic restored Art Deco hotel is a 10min walk from South Beach. Amenities include simple, stylish, comfortable rooms, a peaceful garden and pool and fine dining in the hotel's restaurant, *Luna Rossa*. Highly recommended. ❸

Marlin 1200 Collins Ave, South Beach ☏ 305/534-2135 or 1-800/OUTPOST. The eleven costly but cozy suites come with a Caribbean-island theme. The rooftop doubles as a sun deck. If you can't afford to stay here, at least have a drink at the futuristic bar or a jerk chicken sandwich in the haremesque *Shabeen Lounge*. ❼

The Mermaid 909 Collins Ave, South Beach ☏ 305/538-5324. This tiny, sociable guesthouse with funky cabana-style rooms is hidden in a lush garden. It can be noisy, but the prices and atmosphere make up for it. ❹

Miami River Inn 118 SW South River Drive, Little Havana ☏ 305/325-0045. Minutes from downtown on the river, the inn offers lovely rooms in buildings dating from 1908, tropical gardens and a large pool. Don't wander round the area at night. ❸

Park Central 640 Ocean Drive, South Beach ☏ 305/538-1611. The glamorous Art Deco hotel on the strip has a charismatic lobby and bar. ❹–❻

Pelican 826 Ocean Drive, South Beach ☏ 305/673-3373 or 1-800/7PELICAN. Quirkily themed rooms range from the wild "Me Tarzan, You Vain" to the bizarre dentist office "With Drill," and the most requested, "Best Whorehouse," draped in red velvet and tassels. Totally fun. ❻

Shelley 844 Collins Ave, South Beach ☏ 305/531-3341 or 1-800/414-0612. An original Art Deco hotel with impeccably clean rooms, it is just across the street from Ocean Drive and the beach. ❺

The City

Many of Miami's **districts** are officially cities in their own right, and each has a background and character very much its own. Most people head straight to **Miami Beach**, specifically the **South Beach** strip, where many of the city's famed Art Deco buildings have been restored to their former stunning splendor, all pastels, neon and wavy lines. Though touted as the chic gathering place for the city's fashionable faces, it's not as exclusive as you might expect, especially on weekend afternoons when families and out-of-towners join the washboard stomachs and bulging pecs. Make time, too, for **Key Biscayne**, a smart, secluded island community with some beautiful beaches, five miles off the mainland but easily reached by a causeway.

On the mainland, **downtown** has a few good museums but little else of interest to visitors. **Little Havana**, to the west, is the best spot to head for a Cuban lunch, while immediately south the spacious boulevards of **Coral Gables** are as impressive now as they were in the 1920s, when the district set new standards in town planning. Independently minded but equally wealthy **Coconut Grove** is also worth a look, thanks to its walkable center and a couple of Miami's most popular attractions.

Map labels:

Miami International Airport

DOWNTOWN MIAMI

Gibson Park

N.W. 13TH STREET

N.E. 14TH STREET

N.E. 13TH STREET

395

Bicentennial Park

Biscayne Bay

N.E. 11TH STREET

N.E. 10TH STREET

N.E. 9TH STREET

N.E. 8TH STREET

N.E. 7TH STREET

N.E. 6TH STREET

N.E. 5TH STREET

95

N.W. 8TH STREET

N.W. 7TH STREET

N.W. 6TH STREET

N.W. 5TH STREET

Overtown Greyhound Bus Station

N.W. 1ST STREET

N. MIAMI AVENUE

BISCAYNE BOULEVARD

Greyhound Terminal

Freedom Tower

STATE PLAZA/ARENA

EDCOM

Bayside Marketplace

Miami Marina

COLLEGE/BAYSIDE

Lummus Park

Miami River

N.W. 3RD AVENUE

N.W. 2ND AVENUE

N.E. 3RD STREET

GOVERNMENT CENTER

Miami-Dade Cultural Center

Historical Museum of Southern Florida

Bayside Amphitheater

FIRST STREET

Bayfront Park

S.E. 2ND AVENUE

S.E. 1ST AVE.

Miami Art Museum

FLAGLER STREET

MIAMI AVE.

S.E. 1ST ST.

FT. DALLAS PARK

BAYFRONT PARK

N

Miami River Inn

S.E. 1ST STREET

S.E. 2ND STREET

S.E. 3RD STREET

S.E. 4TH STREET

S.E. 5TH STREET

S.E. 6TH STREET

S.W. 7TH STREET

S.W. 8TH STREET

S. RIVER DRIVE

KNIGHT CENTER

S.E. 2ND STREET

RIVERWALK

S.W. 2ND AVENUE

MIAMI AVENUE

S.E. 5TH ST.

S.E. 6TH ST.

BRICKELL AVE.

S.E. 8TH STREET

Little Havana

Coral Gables

W. FLAGLER ST.

0   400 yds

Metrorail
Metromover
Metro station

Downtown Miami

More like Buenos Aires than Boston, it's perhaps **DOWNTOWN MIAMI** that shows the city at its most Latin. Downtown divides into distinct halves: big business and big buildings line Brickell Avenue south of the Miami River, while the commercial bazaar around Flagler Street to the north hums with jewelers, fabric stores and cheap electronics outlets. Latin culture is comfortably dominant here – from office workers grabbing a midmorning *cafecito*, or Cuban coffee, from tiny streetside cafés to the bilingual signage in almost every store. If at first it may seem overwhelming, persevere: downtown is compact, holds two of Miami's best museums and provides the clearest idea of Cuba's continuing influence on the city.

Flagler Street is downtown's loudest, brightest, busiest strip; at its western end is the **Metro–Dade Cultural Center**, an ambitious attempt by architect Philip Johnson to create a postmodern Mediterranean-style piazza. Art shows, historical collections and a library frame the courtyard, but Johnson overlooked the power of the south Florida sun: rather than pausing to rest and gossip, most people scamper across the open space toward the nearest shade. The center's

Historical Museum of Southern Florida at 1010 W Flagler (Mon–Wed, Fri & Sat 10am–5pm, Thurs 10am–9pm, Sun noon–5pm; $5, $6 combination ticket with Center for Fine Arts; see also under "Tours") provides a comprehensive peek into the region's history. It has a strong section on refugees and immigration since 1960. A few yards away, the **Miami Art Museum of Miami–Dade County** houses a strong collection of post-1940 art, and showcases outstanding international traveling exhibits (Tues–Fri 10am–5pm, third Thurs each month 10am–9pm, Sat & Sun noon–5pm; $5, $6 combination ticket with Historical Museum; ☎305/375-5000).

Beside **Biscayne Boulevard** (part of Hwy-1), on the eastern edge of downtown, is the **Bayside Marketplace**, a large pink shopping mall enlivened by street entertainers and food stands. Across Biscayne Boulevard, the **Freedom Tower**, built in 1925 and modeled on a Spanish bell tower, earned its name by housing the Cuban Refugee Center in the 1960s. Between December 1965 and June 1972, ten planes a week brought over 250,000 Cubans allowed to leave the island by Fidel Castro. While US propaganda hailed them as "freedom fighters," most of the arrivals were simply seeking the fruits of capitalism, and, as Castro astutely recognized, any that were seriously committed to overthrowing his regime would be far less troublesome outside Cuba. Currently undergoing renovation, it is scheduled to open as a museum of Cuban-American history in 2002.

Fifteen minutes' walk from Flagler Street, the **Miami River** marks the southern limit of downtown. Around 1900, the millionaire oil baron Henry Flagler extended his railroad, which had opened up Florida's east coast, to reach Miami from Palm Beach. His *Royal Palm Hotel* (on the site of today's *Hotel Inter-Continental*) did much to put Miami on the map. One of the landowners was William Brickell, who ran a trading post on the south side of the river, an area now dominated by **Brickell Avenue** – *the* address in 1910s Miami. While the original grand homes have largely disappeared, money is still the avenue's most obvious asset: its half-mile parade of **bank buildings** is the largest grouping of international banks in the US. The rise of the banks was matched by new condominiums of breathtaking proportions (and expense) but little architectural merit.

Little Havana

The impact on Miami of **Cubans**, unquestionably the largest and most visible ethnic group in the city, has been incalculable. Unlike most Hispanic immigrants to the US, who trade one form of poverty for another, Miami's first Cubans had already tasted the good life when they arrived during the late Fifties and were soon enjoying more of the same here. Some now wield considerable clout in the running of the city.

The initial home of the Miami Cubans was a few miles west of downtown in what became **LITTLE HAVANA**, whose streets, if the tourist brochures are to be believed, are filled by old men playing dominoes while puffing on fat, fragrant cigars, and exotic restaurants whose walls vibrate to the pulsating rhythms of the homeland. Naturally, the reality is quite different. Little Havana's parks, memorials, shops and food stands all reflect the Cuban experience but the streets are quieter than those of downtown Miami (except during the Little Havana Festival in early March). Many successful Cuban-Americans have moved to Coral Gables or elsewhere in the city, to be replaced by immigrants from elsewhere in Central America, especially Nicaragua. By all means make a beeline here for lunch at one of the many small restaurants on SW 8th Street,

During the mid-Fifties, when opposition to Cuba's Batista dictatorship began to assert itself, a trickle of Cubans started arriving in a predominantly Jewish section of Miami called Riverside. The trickle became a flood when Fidel Castro took power in 1959, and the area became Little Havana, populated by the affluent Cuban middle classes who had the most to lose under communism. These original immigrants were joined by a second Cuban influx in May 1980, when the **Mariel boatlift** brought 125,000 islanders from the port of Mariel to Miami in only a few days. These arrivals were poor and uneducated, and a fifth of them were fresh from Cuban jails – incarcerated for criminal rather than political crimes. Bluntly, Castro had dumped his misfits on Miami. The city reeled and then recovered from this mass arrival, but it left Miami's Cuban community utterly divided. Even today, older Cuban Americans claim that they can pick out a *Marielito* from the way he or she walks or talks.

Local division gives way to fervent agreement when it comes to Fidel Castro: he's universally detested. Even though few would now seriously think about returning to the island once Castro is gone, passions within the exile political community run remarkably high and allow for little debate. In Miami, Cubans have been killed for being *suspected* of advocating dialogue with Castro, and one museum was bombed in 1989 for displaying the work of Castro-approved artists. The 1999–2000 case of six-year-old **Elián González**, who was returned to his father in Cuba after his mother was drowned while attempting to reach America with her son, is a telling example. Mention of the case still rouses loathing for Bill Clinton in Miami's Cuban community. The lawyer who defended Elián's right to stay in America was elected mayor of Miami in 2001 despite little political experience. The biggest test, though, will come when the Cuban-exile leadership is eventually able to return to the island, and Miami's armchair politicians face the daunting task of governing a country that will be very different from the one they left behind.

or *Calle Ocho* (its main drag), but don't expect monuments and museums – Little Havana's a neighborhood geared toward those who live and work, rather than visit, there.

There is, however, a cluster of memorials between 12th and 13th avenues along Calle Ocho that underscores the Cuban-American experience in Miami. Here, the simple stone **Brigade 2506 Memorial** remembers those who died at the Bay of Pigs on April 17, 1961, during the abortive invasion of Cuba by US-trained Cuban exiles. Veterans of the landing, aging men dressed in combat fatigues, gather here for each anniversary and make all-night-long pledges of patriotism.

Coral Gables

All of Miami's constituent cities are fast to assert their individuality, but none has a better case than **CORAL GABLES**, southwest of Little Havana. Twelve square miles of broad boulevards, leafy side streets and Spanish and Italian architecture form a cultured setting for a cultured community. Coral Gables' creator was a local aesthete, **George Merrick**, who raided street names from a Spanish dictionary to plan the plazas, fountains and carefully aged stucco-fronted buildings. Following the first land sale in 1921, $150 million poured in, which Merrick channeled into one of the biggest advertising campaigns ever known. However, Coral Gables took shape just as the Florida property boom ended. Merrick was wiped out, and died as Miami's postmaster in 1942. Coral Gables never lost its good looks, though, and remains an impressive place to explore. Merrick wanted people to know they'd arrived somewhere special, and eight grand **entrances** were planned on the main approach roads (though only four were completed). Three of these stand along the western end of *Calle Ocho* as you arrive from Little Havana.

The best way into Coral Gables is along SW 22nd Street, known as the **Miracle Mile**. Dominated by department stores, travel agents, and a staggering number of bridal shops, it gets more and more expensive and exclusive as you proceed west. Note the arcades and balconies, and the spirals and peaks of the **Colonnade Building**, nos. 133–169, completed in 1926 to accommodate George Merrick's office. Further west, along Coral Way, the **Merrick House**, no. 907 (Sun & Wed 1–4pm; $5; ☏305/460-5361), was George's boyhood home. In 1899, when he was twelve, his family arrived here from New England to run a 160-acre farm, which was so successful that the house quickly grew from a wooden shack into an elegant dwelling of coral rock and gabled windows (thus inspiring the name of the future city).

While his property-developing contemporaries left ugly scars across the city after digging up the local limestone, Merrick had the foresight to turn his biggest quarry into a sumptuous swimming pool. The **Venetian Pool**, 2701 De Soto Blvd, opened in 1924, is today an essential stop on a steamy Miami afternoon. Its pastel stucco walls hide a delightful spring-fed lagoon, with vine-covered loggias, fountains, waterfalls, coral caves and plenty of room to swim. The café isn't bad, either (call for hours; April–Oct $8.50, Nov–March $5.50; ☏305/460-5356).

Wrapping its broad wings around the southern end of De Soto Boulevard, Merrick's crowning achievement was the fabulous **Biltmore Hotel**, 1200 Anastasia Ave. With a 26-story tower visible across much of low-lying Miami, everything about the *Biltmore* was over-the-top: 25ft fresco-coated walls, vaulted ceilings, immense fireplaces, custom-loomed rugs, and a massive swimming pool hosting shows by such bathing belles and beaux as Esther Williams and Johnny Weissmuller. Today, it costs upward of $200 a night to stay here, but a fascinating free tour leaves from the lobby every Sunday (1.30pm, 2.30pm & 3.30pm; ☏305/445-1926 for more information). A short way south at 130 Stanford Ave is the **University of Miami**, site of the **Lowe Art Museum** (Tues–Wed, Fri–Sat 10am–5pm, Thurs noon–7pm, Sun 12–5pm; $5), whose diverse permanent collection ranges from European Old Masters to Native American artifacts and Guatemalan textiles.

Coconut Grove

COCONUT GROVE has come a long way since the 1960s, when it was peopled by down-at-heel artists and writers: these days, it rivals South Beach in trendiness, with a glittering cluster of art galleries, fashionable cafés and restaurants, and towering bay-view apartments.

There's more to "the Grove," – on Biscayne Bay about four miles southwest of downtown – than people-watching, however. A century ago, a strange mix of Bahamian salvagers and New England intellectuals laid the foundations of a fiercely individual community, separated from the fledgling city of Miami by a dense wedge of tropical foliage. In 1914, farm machinery mogul James Deering blew $15 million on re-creating a sixteenth-century Italian villa within this jungle. A thousand-strong workforce completed his **Villa Vizcaya**, 3251 S Miami Ave (daily 9.30am–4.30pm; $10), in just two years. Deering's madly eclectic art collection, and his concept that the villa should appear to have been inhabited for four hundred years, result in a thunderous clash of Baroque,

Renaissance, Rococo and Neoclassical fixtures and fittings; the fabulous landscaped **gardens**, with their fountains and sculptures, are just as excessive. Frequent **guided tours** (45min) leave from the entrance loggia and provide solid background, after which you're free to explore at leisure.

Blatant statements of wealth predominate as you approach central Coconut Grove. The marina on **Dinner Key** sports lines of million-dollar yachts, and the neighboring **Coconut Grove Exhibition Center** is usually consumed by top-of-the-range trade shows. It was at the Dinner Key Auditorium (a forerunner of the Exhibition Center) in 1969 that **Jim Morrison**, singer with the Doors, dropped his leather trousers during the band's first – and last – Florida show, bringing the band more infamy than they knew what to do with.

About two miles south along the coast, the 83-acre **Fairchild Tropical Garden**, at 10901 Old Cutler Rd (daily 9.30am–4.30pm; guided tours hourly 10am–4pm; $8), is the largest tropical botanical garden in the continental US. The entire range of tropical environments has been reproduced, and there's a good section on native south Florida areas.

Miami Beach

A long slender arm of land between Biscayne Bay and the Atlantic Ocean, three miles off mainland Miami, **MIAMI BEACH** was an ailing fruit farm in the 1910s when its Quaker owner, John Collins, formed an unlikely partnership with a flashy entrepreneur, Carl Fisher. With Fisher's money, Biscayne Bay was dredged. The muck raised from its murky bed provided the landfill to transform this wildly vegetated barrier island into a carefully sculptured landscape of palm trees, hotels and tennis courts. After a hurricane in 1926 devastated the city and especially the beach, damaged buildings were replaced by grander structures in the new Art Deco style and Miami Beach as we know it appeared. Since then, its history has been checkered: by the 1980s, crack dens and retirement homes were equally commonplace in South Beach, but the 1990s saw a renaissance spearheaded by a few savvy hoteliers and Miami's gay community.

One of the groups that remained in Miami Beach through it all was its sizable Jewish population, including many Holocaust survivors and their families. The **Holocaust Memorial** at 1933 Meridian Ave (daily 9am–9pm; free; ☏305/538-1663), at Dade Boulevard and Meridian Avenue opposite the visitor center, is a complex, uncompromising monument to their experience. From a distance, the impression is of a giant, defiant hand punching into the sky; as you approach, however, you make out the mass of wailing people scrabbling

---

The beaches of Miami Beach

If you took away the Art Deco, the beautiful people and the glittering nightlife, you'd still be left with the simple truth that Miami has a fabulous **choice of beaches**, twelve miles of calm waters, clean sands, swaying palms and candy-colored lifeguard towers – even if much of the sand in Lummus Park was shipped in from the Bahamas. The young and the beautiful soak up the rays between 5th and 21st, a convenient hop from the juice bars and cafés on Ocean Drive. **Lummus Park**, from 6th to 14th, is the heart of the South Beach scene, and there's an unofficial gay section roughly around 18th. North of 21st it's more family-oriented, with a **boardwalk** running between the shore and the hotels up to 46th. To the south, **Ocean Park** and **South Pointe** are favored by Cuban families, and are especially convivial at weekends. For **swimming**, head up to 85th, a quiet stretch usually patrolled by lifeguards.

up the wrist. Following the wall of names, inscribed with a relentless list of Holocaust victims, brings you to the foot of the sculpture, hidden from the road, where distressing statues portray more writhing, emaciated human figures. The whole, brutal, ensemble is underscored by the accompanying quote from Anne Frank: "Ideals, dreams and cherished hopes rise within us only to meet the horrible truth and be shattered."

A few blocks northeast is the prestigious **Bass Museum**, in a lovely Art Deco building at 2121 Park Ave (☎305/673-7530 for opening times and prices). The museum has been undergoing major renovations, overseen by the Japanese architect Arata Isozaki, and its reopening has been put back several times: at time of publication, it was scheduled for early 2002. The museum's permanent collection consists of fine, if largely unremarkable, European paintings, although its temporary exhibitions are often lively and worth visiting.

South Beach

Occupying the southernmost three miles or so of Miami Beach is gorgeous **SOUTH BEACH**, with its hundreds of dazzling pastel-colored Twenties and Thirties buildings. Concentrated between 5th and 23rd streets, Euclid Avenue and the ocean, the area referred to as the **Deco district** actually incorporates a variety of styles: take one of the excellent walking or cycling tours from the **Miami Design Preservation League Welcome Center** (see p.618) to learn the difference between Streamline, Moderne and Art Deco proper.

The most famous buildings lie along **Ocean Drive**, where revamped hotels have made much of their design heritage. One of the newest hotels is the reconverted **Casa Casuarina** at the corner of 10th Street. It was formerly the home of Italian fashion designer Gianni Versace, one of the first people to rediscover the pleasures of South Beach in the 1980s only to be shot on the steps of his home in a shocking murder in 1997. By night, the ten blocks of Ocean Drive became one of the liveliest stretches in Miami, as terrace cafés spill across the specially widened sidewalk, crowds of tourists and locals saunter by the beach and Jazz Age neon illuminates the starry sky. Behind Ocean Drive are **Collins Avenue**, lined with more Deco hotels and fashion chains, and **Washington Avenue**, which tends more toward funky thrift stores and cool coffee bars. At 1001 Washington Ave, the imaginative **Wolfsonian–Florida International University Museum** (Mon–Tues & Fri–Sat 11am–6pm, Thurs 11am–9pm, Sun noon–5pm; $5, free Thurs 6–9pm) houses an eclectic collection of decorative arts from the late nineteenth century to 1945. The displays of old books, photos, paintings, posters and all manner of domestic objects are impressive, if a bit muddled.

Key Biscayne

A compact, immaculately manicured community, **KEY BISCAYNE**, five miles off mainland Miami, is a great place to live – if you can afford it. The moneyed of Miami fill the island's upmarket homes; Richard Nixon had a presidential winter house here. The only way onto Key Biscayne is along the four-mile **Rickenbacker Causeway** ($1 toll), a continuation of SW 26th Road just south of downtown, which soars high above Biscayne Bay, giving a gasp-inducing view of the Brickell Avenue skyline.

Crandon Park Beach, a mile along Crandon Boulevard (the continuation of the main road from the causeway), is one of the finest landscaped beaches in the city, with crystal-clear waters, barbecue grills and sports facilities (daily 8am–dusk; $4 per car; ☎305/361-7385). Three miles of yellow-brown beach

SOUTH BEACH

Holocaust Memorial

The Bass Museum of Art

Collins Park

ⓘ

Miami Beach Post Office

Flamingo Park

Wolfsonian-FIU Museum

Beach Patrol Station

Versace Mansion

Art Deco Welcome Center

Lummus Park

ATLANTIC OCEAN

Star Island

MACARTHUR CAUSEWAY

Terminal Island

Causeway Island

Miami Beach Marina

First Street Beach

Biscayne Bay

Government Cut

South Pointe Park

Fisher Island

N

ACCOMMODATION

Banana Bungelow	1
Brigham Gardens Guesthouse	5
Clay Hotel and Hostelling International	4
Indian Creek	3
Marlin	6
Mermaid	7
Park Central	10
Pelikan Hotel	9
Hotel Place St Michel	2
Shelley	8

RESTAURANTS

Bambu	C
Big Pink	I
da Leo Trattoria	A
Gino's	F
Joe's Stone Crabs	J
Lario's on the Beach	E
News Café	E
Puerto Sagua	G
Sanloco	D
Tap Tap	H
Yuca	B

Electrowave Shuttle route

0   200 yds

fringe the park, and give access to a sand bar enabling knee-depth wading far from shore.

Crandon Boulevard terminates at the entrance to the **Bill Baggs Cape Florida State Recreation Area**, four hundred wooded acres covering the southern extremity of Key Biscayne (daily 8am–dusk; $3.25 per car; ☎305/361-5811). Hurricane Andrew took a devastating toll on the area in 1992, but most of the destroyed trees are beginning to grow back thanks to aggressive replanting, and the trails and boardwalks have been repaired. An excellent swimming **beach** lines the Atlantic-facing side of the park, and a boardwalk cuts around the wind-bitten sand dunes toward the 1820s **Cape Florida lighthouse**. Only with the ranger-led tour can you climb through the 95ft structure – attacked by Seminoles in 1836 and incapacitated by Confederate soldiers aiming to disrupt Union shipping during the Civil War.

Eating

Cuban food is what Miami does best, and it's not limited to the traditional haunts in **Little Havana** – the hearty, comfort food, notably rice and beans, fried plantains and shredded pork sandwiches, is found in every neighborhood. It is, however, complemented by sushi bars, American home-style diners, Haitian restaurants, Italian eateries and Indian venues, among a handful of other ethnic cuisines. **Coral Gables** stakes its claim in upmarket cafés and ethnic Italian and Greek restaurants, while **Coconut Grove** features American, Spanish, New Floridian – a mix of Caribbean spiciness and fruity Florida sauces – and even British. **Seafood** is equally abundant; succulent grouper, yellowfin tuna and wahoo, a local delicacy, are among five hundred species of fish thriving offshore. **Stone crab claws**, served from October to May, are another regional specialty. A tropical climate provides Florida with a juicy assortment of standard orange and grapefruit citrus, as well as the exotic flavors of the **lychee**, **mango**, **papaya**, **tamarind** and **star fruits** – many of which are used in sauces and *batidos* (light milkshakes). You'll also want to drink Cuban coffee: choose between *café cubano*, strong, sweet and frothy, drunk like a shot with a glass of water; *café con leche*, with steamed milk, and particularly good at breakfast with *pan cubano* (thin, buttered toast); or *café cortadito*, a smaller version of the *con leche*.

Ayestaran 706 SW 27th Ave, Little Havana ☎305/649-4982. The sprawling Cuban restaurant offers hearty daily specials and superb *café con leche* that you can mix to your liking.

Bambu 1661 Meridian Ave, Miami Beach ☎305/531-4800. Celebrity eateries are big business in Miami, and this one is co-owned by the actress Cameron Diaz. But the draw at this place is the food – great Asian fusion sushi and the occasional celebrity sighting make it a good place to splash out.

Big Fish Mayaimi 55 SW Miami Ave, downtown ☎305/373-1770. A lively spot on the Miami River, it has great fish dishes and a splendid view. The menu includes home-cooked fish sandwiches and fresh seafood chowder.

Big Pink 157 Collins Ave, South Beach ☎305/531-0888. Big portions of comfort food – mashed potatoes, ribs, macaroni and cheese, and classic "TV dinners" at 1950s prices – are served up.

David's Café 1058 Collins Ave, South Beach ☎305/534-8736. Cuban restaurant with two locations on the beach (the other is at 16th & Meridian Ave), where suited Cuban businessmen doing deals sit alongside *cholo* teenagers. The food is authentic and there's eat-in and take-out at both restaurants.

Fishbone Grille 650 S Miami Ave, downtown ☎305/530-1915. The busy, friendly restaurant serves excellent seafood with creative starters like shrimp potato fritters and smoked fish mousse.

Gino's 731 Washington Ave, Miami Beach ☎305/673-2837. Open 24 hours a day, it serves true New York-style pizza to shift workers and clubbers alike. It's famous, too, for a dedication to staying open, even in the face of hurricanes.

Greenstreet Café 3468 Main Highway, Coconut Grove ☎305/444-0244. Its terrific breakfasts make this café a real scene at weekends. It has a large number of outdoor tables for watching the world go by.

Joe's Stone Crabs 227 Biscayne St, South Beach ☎305/673-0365. A legendary restaurant, it is always packed for its superb stone crabs – if you're impatient, do as the locals do and head to the takeout window. Crabcakes, fresh fish and crispy fried chicken are also good. Open mid-Oct to mid-May.

Larios on the Beach 820 Ocean Drive, South Beach ☎305/532-9577. It is better known for being owned by singer Gloria Estefan rather than for its sophisticated – and surprisingly affordable – "Nuevo Cubano" food served in a Latin nightclub atmosphere.

Monty's 2560 S Bayshore Drive, Coconut Grove. ☎305/854-7997. Skip the pricey indoor restaurant and head for *Monty's Raw Bar* on the waterfront. Sit in the tiki huts eating fresh fish and sipping well-priced drinks.

News Café 800 Ocean Drive, Miami Beach ☎305/538-6397. The established, fashionable sidewalk café has front-row seating for the South Beach promenade – although the food's unremarkable. Open 24hr at weekends.

Puerto Sagua 700 Collins Ave, South Beach ☎305/673-1115. The Cuban diner serves great, rich black bean soup and other filling meals.

La Sandwicherie 229 W 14th St, South Beach ☎305/532-8934. Don't be put off by the silly name. This place serves serious sandwiches start-ing at around $6 from its open-air lunch counter; each giant French loaf doorstop could make two meals, and it's open until 5am.

Tap Tap 819 5th St, South Beach ☎305/672-2898. Haitian food is at its tastiest and most attractive in one of the best-looking restaurants in Miami Beach, hung with local art.

Versailles 3555 SW 8th St, Little Havana ☎305/444-0240. At this legend in Little Havana, very little English is spoken. Local families, Cuban businessmen and backpackers congregate here for the wonderfully inexpensive Cuban dishes, served by one of the friendliest staffs in Miami.

Yambo 1643 SW 1st St, Little Havana ☎305/642-6616. Try the good, inexpensive Nicaraguan food at an undiscovered gem. Step out of the USA and into Central America without leaving Miami.

Yuca 501 Lincoln Rd, South Beach ☎305/532-9822. Discover Nuevo Cubano cooking at its best – and most expensive. Expect to pay at least $50 a head. Latin music at weekends.

Drinking, nightlife and entertainment

Miami's nightlife is still unsurpassed. **Drinking** tends to take second place to eating and partying, but a number of friendly local bars double as very good **live music** venues. **Reggae** is particularly strong; Miami has a sizable Jamaican population, and local as well as flown-in acts appear regularly. Miami's **clubs** – especially those specializing in salsa or merengue and hosted by Spanish-speaking DJs – are among the hippest in the world, with most of the action at South Beach. Door policies are notoriously obnoxious at current in-spots; the places listed below include laid-back local haunts and some of the hotter bars.

Friday's *Miami Herald* carries full weekend entertainment **listings**; the free weekly *New Times* has reliable information on cafés and clubs, while the free *TWN* (*The Weekly News*) is the key source of **gay and lesbian info**.

If you want to try out the local **sports** scene, the **Marlins** pro **baseball** team, who won the World Series in 1997 in only their fourth season, and the **Dolphins**, Miami's pro **football** team, play at the Pro Player Stadium, sixteen miles northwest of downtown at 2269 Dan Marino Boulevard (box office Mon–Fri 10am–6pm; ☎305/620-2578).

Bars and live music

The Abbey Brewing Company 1115 16th St, South Beach ☎305/538-8110. The small yet homey spot is South Beach's only microbrewery. (Try the creamy Oatmeal Stout – their best and most popular brew.) Happy hour Mon–Fri 1–7pm.

Churchill's Hideaway 5501 NE 2nd Ave, Little Haiti ☎305/757-1807. A British enclave within Little Haiti with soccer and rugby matches on video and UK beers on tap.

Club Deuce 222 W 14th St, South Beach ☎305/531-6200. This grimy, noisy grunge bar is a rem-nant from pre-fabulous South Beach. Drinks are cheap, and there's a dartboard, pool table and an alternative crowd.

Delano Pool Bar *Delano Hotel*, 1685 Collins Ave, South Beach ☎305/672-2000. An antidote to the super-exclusivity of the hotel, this poolside bar offers reasonably priced drinks for anyone who knows it's back there. It's still a good place for celebrity-spotting, too.

Hungry Sailor 3426 Main Hwy, Coconut Grove ☎305/444-9359. The unpretentious, male-dominated bar features a nautical theme and occasional live reggae.

Lost Weekend 218 Espanola Way, South Beach
☎305/672-1707. The preppy clientele plays pool
and enjoys a great happy hour and the ladies'
night drink specials.

Pearl Restaurant and Champagne Lounge
above Nikki Beach at 1 Ocean Drive, South Beach
☎305/538-1231. Swathed in orange lights, this
neo-Space Age all-white bar has a champagne bar
in the center of the main room. Drinks are pricey,
so stay for one glass, then head elsewhere for the
rest of the evening.

Rumi 330 Lincoln Road, South Beach ☎ 305/672-
4353. The undisputed bar of the moment has a strict
door policy and a huge crowd clamoring to get in
most nights. It morphs into a mini-nightclub around
11pm, when the music gets louder and funkier.

Tobacco Road 626 S Miami Ave, downtown
☎305/374-1198. The friendly bar – Miami's oldest
– is a favorite with locals for its exceptional live
blues, jazz and R&B.

Wet Willie's 760 Ocean Drive, South Beach
☎305/532-5650. From this welcome antidote to
the chic scene in Miami Beach, customers take the
bargain $5 jumbo frozen drinks back to the beach.

Clubs

B.E.D. 929 Washington Ave, Miami Beach
☎305/532-9070. This restaurant serves its meals
on curtained beds where everyone lounges,
Roman-style, to try the so-called

FrancoFloribbeAsian food: get there early to snag
one of the beds. B.E.D. stands for
Beverage.Entertainment.Dining – and so this
restaurant becomes a club come midnight, with
Wednesdays the hippest night.

Club Tropigala *Fontainebleu Hotel*, 4441 Collins
Ave, South Beach ☎305/538-2000. This superb,
popular Latin supper club features live acts and an
orchestra, with shows Wed–Sat 8.30pm and Sun
8pm ($20). Dress up to the nines and salsa the
night away with a friendly, varied crowd amid a
fabulously camp decor.

Crobar 1445 Washington Ave, South Beach
☎305/531-8225. At this superclub, hardcore dancers
and a loved-up crowd get started around 4am.

N Nightclub 743 Washington Ave, South Beach
☎305/695-9299. It's most famous as a former
investment of Madonna's and also for the story
that the actress Jennifer Lopez came in to party
one New Year's Eve – only to have the owners ask
her to leave.

Nikki Beach Club One Ocean Drive, South Beach
☎305/538-1231. The place to be on Sunday
nights, an outdoor club right on the sand of the
beach, it features tiki torches and VIP tepees you
can reserve for a little privacy.

Opium 136 Collins Ave, South Beach ☎305/695-
4204. At this giant open-air club, a tent covers the
dance floor and multilevel spaces are accessed
from the main bar.

The Florida Keys

Fiction, films and folklore have given the **FLORIDA KEYS** – a hundred-mile
chain of islands that runs to within ninety miles of Cuba – an image of glamorous intrigue they don't really deserve. Instead, this is an outdoor-lover's paradise, where fishing, snorkeling and diving dominate. Terrific untainted natural
areas include the **Florida Reef**, a great band of living coral just a few miles off
the coast. But for many, the various keys are only stops on the way to fascinating **Key West**. Once the richest town in the US, and the final dot of North
America before a thousand miles of ocean, Key West has lush, Caribbean-style
streets with plenty of congenial bars in which to waste away the hours, watching the famous spectacular **sunsets**.

Wherever you are on the Keys, you'll experience distinctive **cuisine**, served
for the most part in funky little shacks where the food is fresh and the atmosphere laid-back. Conch, a rich meaty mollusc, is a specialty, served in chowders
and fritters. And as for the Key Lime Pie, the delicate, creamy concoction of
limes and condensed milk bears little resemblance here to the lurid green
imposters served in the rest of the country.

Traveling through the Keys could hardly be easier. There's just one route all the way through to Key West: the **Overseas Highway (US-1)**. The road is punctuated by **mile markers (MM)** – starting with MM127 just south of Miami and finishing with MM0 in Key West.

Key Largo

The first and largest of the keys, **Key Largo** boasts a fine opportunity to visit the Florida Reef, at the **John Pennekamp Coral Reef State Park** at MM102.5 (daily 8am–dusk, visitor center 8am–5pm; $5 for two people and car, plus 50¢ each additional person). This protected 78-square-mile section of living coral reef is rated as one of the most beautiful in the world. If you can, take the **snorkeling tour** (9am, noon & 3pm; $25.95 plus equipment rental; ☎305/451-1621), or the **guided scuba dive** (9:30am & 1:30pm; $39; ☎305/451-6322 or 1-977/LETS-DIVE); the **glass-bottom boat tour** (9.15am, 12.15pm & 3pm; $18; ☎305/451-1621) is less demanding.

Even from the glass-bottom boat, you're virtually certain to spot lobsters, angelfish, eels and jellyfish along the reef, and shoals of silvery minnows stalked by angry-faced barracuda. The reef itself is a delicate living thing, comprising millions of minute coral polyps extracting calcium from the seawater and growing from one to sixteen feet every thousand years. Sadly, it's far easier to spot signs of death than life: white patches show where a carelessly dropped anchor, or diver's hand, has scraped away the protective mucous layer and left the coral susceptible to terminal disease.

Key Largo town and Tavernier

South of the park, the people of Rock Harbor recognized a good thing when they saw one and changed the name of their community to **KEY LARGO** after the success of the 1948 film in which Humphrey Bogart and Lauren Bacall grappled with Florida's best-known features – crime and hurricanes. The movie's title suggested somewhere exotic, but the film, though set here, was almost entirely shot in Hollywood. Nonetheless, Key Largo, and its neighbor **TAVERNIER**, ten miles further on, make nice enough stops on the Upper Keys. You can almost feel urban stresses and strains slip away as you take in the turquoise sea and waving palms.

The **Florida Keys visitor center**, MM106 (daily 9am–6pm; ☎305/451-9949 or 1-800/822-1088, ⓦwww.fla-keys.com), has information on local accommodation, diving and attractions. Most **motels** offer diving packages: try *Ed & Ellen's Efficiencies*, 103365 Overseas Hwy (☎305/451-4712; ❸), which has a two-night minimum; the beach cottages at the *Sea Farer Hotel*, MM97.8 (☎305/852-5349; ❸); or the *Kona Kai Resort*, MM97.8 (☎305/852-7200; ❺), with huge chalets and its own hotel art gallery. For fresh **seafood**, try *Ballyhoo's*, MM97.8 opposite the Sea Farer (☎305/852-0822), the *Fish House*, MM102.4 (☎305/451-4665), and the tiny *Crack'd Conch*, MM105 (☎305/451-0732).

Islamorada

At **ISLAMORADA**, some five miles south of Tavernier on Upper Matecumbe Key, the **Theater of the Sea**, MM84.5 (daily 9.30am–4pm; $17.25; ☎305/664-2431), offers sea shows, glass-bottom boats, snorkel tours and swim-with-the-dolphin programs (9.30am, noon, 2pm; $125). There's good hiking at **Long Key State Recreation Area**, MM68, a 965-acre expanse of tropical foliage and mangroves that also has one of the best beaches on the Keys (daily 8am–dusk; $3.25 per car plus 50¢ per passenger; ☎305/664-4815), and excellent deep-sea fishing.

Good-value **accommodation** includes the prettily landscaped *Chesapeake Bay Resort*, MM83.5 (⊕305/664-4662; ❹), with two pools, a lagoon and water sports; and the serene, oceanside *Drop Anchor* motel at MM85 (⊕305/664-4863 or 1-888/664-4863; ❸). As for **eating**, *Lazy Days*, MM79.9 (⊕305/664-5256), does fabulous things with fresh fish and *Uncle's*, MM81 (⊕305/664-4959), offers good-value mainstream cuisine for around $20. But for a change from Keys cuisine (though they do make a delectable Key Lime Pie), try *Manny and Isa's*, MM81.6 (⊕305/664-5019), a simple Cuban diner where superb Spanish food comes with copious strong, sweet sangria.

The Middle Keys

Once over Long Key Bridge, you're into the **Middle Keys**. At the not-for-profit **Dolphin Research Center**, on **Grassy Key** at MM59 (daily 9am–4pm; $15; ⊕305/289-0002), you can swim with the dolphins for $135 (reservations must be made at least one month in advance).

The largest of several islands, **Key Vaca** holds the nucleus of the area's major settlement, **MARATHON**. Here you'll find a couple of small beaches – rare in the Keys – and great **fishing** and **water sports**. **Sombrero Beach**, along Sombrero Beach Road (off the Overseas Highway near MM50), has good swimming waters and shaded picnic tables; **Key Colony Beach** four miles north is prettier and quieter.

Nestled inside the 64-acre tropical forest of **Crane Point Hammock**, the **Museum of Natural History of the Florida Keys** provides an excellent introduction to the history and ecology of the area at MM50.5 (June–Oct Mon–Sat 10am–5pm, Sun noon–5pm; Nov–May Mon–Sat 9am–5pm, Sun noon–5pm; $7.50; ⊕305/743-9100). Follow the quarter-mile **nature trail** past the hammock forest, an area of dense hardwood trees characteristic of the Keys. At the end of the trail are the reconstructed remnants of a nineteenth-century village established by settlers from the Bahamas.

Marathon has several well-equipped **resorts**, such as the lush, luxurious *Banana Bay*, MM49.5 (⊕305/743-3500; ❹–❺), and indulgent *Cheeca Lodge & Spa*, MM82 (⊕305/664-4651 or 1-800/327-2888; ❺). Cheaper motels include the simple *Sea Cove*, MM54 (⊕305/289-0800; ❷), which has house-boat rooms in high season. For **eating**, *Herbie's*, MM50.5 (⊕305/743-6373), is justly busy on account of its inexpensive seafood, chowder and fritters. The tiny, laid-back *Seven-Mile Grill*, by the bridge of the same name, serves delicious conch and creamy Key Lime Pie to locals, sea salts and tourists (closed Wed & Thurs; ⊕305/743-4481). *The Quay*, MM54 (⊕305/289-1810), has good fish sandwiches for $5 in a waterfront tiki bar behind the pricey main restaurant, and *Porky's*, MM47.5 (⊕305/289-2065), offers cheap, traditional barbecue dishes and burgers, along with conch fritters and other local seafood special-ties. Take a free sunset cruise whether you eat there or not.

The Lower Keys

Starkly different from their northerly neighbors, the **Lower Keys** are quiet, heavily wooded and predominantly residential. Built on a limestone rather than a coral base, these islands have a flora and fauna all their own. It feels very quiet as you head south: everyone's gone fishing or is snoozing in a hammock.

The first place of consequence you'll hit after crossing Seven Mile Bridge is **Bahia Honda State Park** at MM37 (daily 8am–dusk; cars $4, pedestrians and cyclists 50¢; ⊕305/872-3210), one of the Keys' prettiest spots. Its lagoon has a beckoning natural beach and pristine, two-tone ocean waters, which can be

FLORIDA | The Florida Keys

enjoyed on a leisurely **kayak ride** ($20 per hour). Divers should head for the Looe Key Marine Sanctuary, signposted from the Overseas Highway on **Ramrod Key** – a five-square-mile protected reef area, easily the equal of the John Pennekamp Coral Reef State Park (see p.630). The sanctuary office (Mon–Fri 8am–5pm) can provide free maps, but to visit the reef you'll need the services of a dive shop, like the neighboring *Looe Key Dive Center* at MM27.5 (☎1-800/942-5397).

In the main Lower Keys settlement, **BIG PINE KEY**, the **visitor center** is at MM31 (Mon–Fri 9am–5pm, Sat 9am–3pm; ☎305/872-2411). Of the nearby **motels**, *Looe Key Reef Resort*, MM27.5 (☎305/872-2215; ❸), is a favorite with divers, an ideal base for visiting the marine sanctuary. There are also a couple of luxurious, secluded **B&Bs** along Long Beach Drive, off the Overseas Highway; you'll need to book ahead. Try *Deer Run*, MM32.5 (☎305/872-2015; ❹), or *Barnacle*, MM32.5 (☎305/872-3298; ❹). Exceptionally friendly, even for the Keys, *Mangrove Mama's*, MM20 on **Sugarloaf Key** (☎305/745-3030), serves stupendous local cuisine in a cheery shack with a tropical garden.

Key West

Much closer to Cuba than to mainland Florida, **KEY WEST** often seems rather tenuously bound to the rest of the US. Famed for their tolerant attitudes and laid-back lifestyles, the thirty thousand islanders seem adrift in a great expanse of sea and sky, and – despite a million tourists a year – the place resonates with an individual spirit that hits you the instant you arrive. In particular, liberal attitudes have stimulated a large **gay** influx. Yet as wild as it may at first appear, Key West today is far from being the hippy hangout of a decade ago. Much of the sleaziness has been brushed away through a steady process of restoration, setting the course for the advent of a sizable holiday industry. Even so, the sense of isolation from the mainland is best appreciated by adjusting to the mellow pace: amble the gorgeous, lushly vegetated streets, make meals last for hours, and pause regularly for refreshment in the numerous bars.

Arrival, information and getting around

The **airport** (☎305/296-5439) is four miles east of town, with the **Greyhound** station (☎305/296-9072) adjacent to its entrance. A taxi into town costs $10.

Both the **Welcome Center**, 3840 N Roosevelt Blvd (daily 9am–7pm; ☎305/296-4444, ⓦwww.keywestwelcomecenter.com), and the **Key West Chamber of Commerce**, Mallory Square, 402 Wall St (daily 8.30am–6.30pm; ☎305/294-2587), can give precise dates for Key West's annual **festivals**. The best are the Old Island Days (Jan–April) celebrating Key West's history; the Conch Republic Celebration in April; and the Fantasy Fest in late October, a gay-dominated version of Mardi Gras. The **Key West Business Guild**, 424 Fleming St (☎305/294-4603, ⓦwww.gaykeywestfl.com), is a good source of **gay information**.

It's best to explore the narrow streets of the mile-square **Old Town** – which contains virtually everything that you'll want to see – on foot. You could do it in little more than a day, though dashing about isn't the way to enjoy the place. The excellent *Sharon Wells' Walking and Biking Guide*, free in local restaurants and bars, details a number of self-guided routes through the Old Town, and lists

△ Key West beach

Wells' own regular walking tours (☎305/294-8380). **Bikes** ($8 per day with $150 deposit) can be rented from *The Bike Shop*, 1110 Truman Ave (Mon–Sat 9am–6pm, Sun 10am–4pm; ☎305/294-1073). For a (bright pink) **taxi**, call ☎305/296-6666.

Accommodation

It's essential to make a **reservation** in Key West during the winter; call the place directly as early as possible. In summer, competition for rooms is less fierce, and prices drop by almost fifty percent.

Alexander Palms Court 715 South St ☎305/296-6413. The comfortable rooms in this gorgeous, serene small hotel range around a lush, fairy-lit courtyard and pool. ❹

Angelina Guest House 302 Angela St ☎305/294-4480. There are simple rooms at good prices; spending a little more brings you kitchenettes and suites, good value for four people sharing. Rates include continental breakfast. ❸

Bananas Foster 537 Caroline St ☎305/294-9061 or 1-800/653-4888. The charming, centrally located B&B has beautifully decorated rooms, delicious breakfasts, a heated spa pool and the friendliest staff in the Keys. ❺

Blue Parrot Inn 916 Elizabeth St ☎305/296-0033.

Dating from 1884, the inn provides comfortable and nicely furnished rooms, a heated pool, continental breakfast and a "clothing optional" area. ❹

Eden House 1015 Fleming St ☎305/296-6868. At one of Key West's most relaxing hideaways, peaceful rooms surround the pool and numerous giant hammocks are surrounded by lush gardens and fish ponds. The cheaper rooms have shared bath; the priciest have Jacuzzis. ❹

Marrero's Guest Mansion 410 Fleming St ☎305/294-6977 or 1-800/459-6212. At a well-known haunted guesthouse the former owner, the late Mrs Marrero, rates guests' character by swaying the chandelier in the foyer. Ghost-hunters should ask for room 18, as that's where most of

the paranormal activity has been reported. ❹
Rainbow House 525 United St ☏ 305/292-1450.
This women-only accommodation has good rooms,
a pool, Jacuzzi and continental breakfast. ❺
Red Rooster 709 Truman Ave ☏ 305/296-6558.
The friendly, comfortable, gay-oriented B&B has a
good cappuccino bar and pretty garden. ❺
Tropical Inn 812 Duval St ☏ 305/294-9977. The
large, airy rooms in a charming restored "conch"

house are at the center of the action. Most rooms
sleep three, and the more expensive ones have
balconies. ❹
Wicker Guesthouse 913 Duval St ☏ 305/296-
4275. The rooms, though simple (and noisy at the
front), are very good value. Prices increase the farther you get from the road. Enjoy the huge garden,
pool, kitchen facilities and complimentary continental breakfast. ❺

Around the Old Town

Anyone who saw Key West in 1990 would now barely recognize the Old
Town's main promenade, the mile-long swath of **Duval Street**. Teetering just
on the safe side of seedy for many years, much of the street has been transformed into a tacky tourist strip of boutiques and beachwear shops. For a sense
of the locals' town, foray into the side streets, where gnarled banyans, tall
skinny palms, creepers and unruly exotic blooms threaten to overtake the faded
wooden houses. Make sure to get to the **Bahamian Quarter**, centering on
Thomas and Petronia streets. Originally settled by Cubans and African-
Bahamians, this unrestored, untouristed corner of town is an atmospheric
patchwork of single-story cigar-makers' cottages, Cuban groceries and ramshackle old churches, all covered by a rich green foliage.

Numerous **museums** in town concern themselves with "wrecking": the salvaging of cargo from the many vessels that foundered on these treacherous shores, and the industry on which Key West's earliest good times were based. The friendly little **Wrecker's Museum**, 322 Duval St (daily 10am–4pm; $5; ☎305/294-9502), illuminates the lives of the wreckers, portraying them as brave, uninsured heroes who risked all to save cargoes, ships and lives. Judging by the choice furniture that fills the house – the oldest in town – owned by Captain Watlington, the wrecker who lived here from the 1830s, they did pretty well for their pains.

Farther up, at 516 Duval St, the **San Carlos Opera House** (daily 9am–5pm; $3; ☎305/294-3887) has played a leading role in Cuban exile life since it opened as the San Carlos Institute in 1871. Financed by a grant from the Cuban government, the present building dates from 1924. Cuban architect Francisco Centurion designed the two-story building in the Cuban baroque style of that period. Soil from Cuba's six provinces covers the grounds. A cornerstone was taken from the tomb of Cuban independence campaigner José Martí. Now, operas are staged here, and the building has a first-rate exhibition on the history of Cubans in the US.

As you approach the southern end of Duval Street, everything, whether house, motel, gas station or restaurant, advertises itself as "the Southernmost . . ." Accurately, the **southernmost point** in Key West, and consequently in the continental US, is at the intersection of Whitehead and South streets. A daft-looking buoy marks the spot. Watch out for people who'll kindly offer to take your photograph, and then expect tipping for the pleasure.

In the early 1800s, thousands of dollars' worth of salvage was landed at the piers, stored in the warehouses, and flogged at the auction houses on **Mallory Square**, just west of the northern end of Duval Street. By day, the square is a souvenir market, with overpriced ice cream, trinkets and T-shirts. Each night, at an eminently missable tourist-oriented **sunset celebration**, fire-eaters and other entertainers do their stuff for the crowds as the sun sets. At the adjacent **Key West Aquarium**, 1 Whitehead St (daily 10am–6pm; $8; ☎305/296-2051), porcupine fish and longspine squirrel fish leer out from behind glass, and small sharks are known to jump out of their open tanks during the otherwise somewhat boring **guided tours** (11am, 1pm, 3pm, 4.30pm).

Mel Fisher's Treasure Exhibit, 200 Greene St (daily 9.30am–5.30pm; $6.50; ☎305/296-9936), now run by his children after his death in 1998, showcases diamonds and pearls, countless vases and daggers and an impressive emerald cross alongside the obligatory cannon, pulled up from two seventeenth-century wrecks. Fisher ran a surf shop in California before he arrived in Florida armed with old Spanish sea charts. In 1985, he discovered the *Nuestra Señora de Atocha* and *Santa Margarita*. Both sank during a hurricane in 1622, forty miles southeast of Key West. It's a romantic story, and the flabbergasting haul is said to be worth millions of dollars. If you're not satisfied with simply lifting a gold bar (chained to the wall, naturally), and fancy some for yourself, the gift shop sells affordable souvenirs alongside expensive salvage relics.

For all the atmosphere of the streets and alleys, Key West's most popular tourist attraction is the **Hemingway House**, at 907 Whitehead St (daily 9am–5pm; $8; ☎305/294-1136). The compulsory half-hour **guided tour** deals, sadly, more in fantasy than fact: although Ernest Hemingway owned this large, vaguely Moorish house for thirty years, he lived in it for barely ten, and even the authenticity of the furnishings is disputed by his former secretary. Hemingway bought the house in 1931, when it was seriously run-down. Some of his most acclaimed novels, including *For Whom the Bell Tolls* and *To Have and Have Not*, were produced in the study (in the hayloft of a carriage house that Hemingway entered by way of a rope bridge). Divorced in 1940, he boxed up his manuscripts and moved them to a back room at the original *Sloppy Joe's* before heading off for a house in Cuba with his new wife, journalist Martha Gellhorn. Today some fifty cats pad contentedly around the gardens, all of them descendants of Hemingway's own; look out for those with six toes, traditionally used as ship mascots.

Eating

In Key West, it's *de rigueur* to sample **conch fritters**; the stand at David Walkowsky and Wall streets (entrance to Mallory Square) does the best in town for under two dollars. Also, don't leave without tasting **Cuban food**, as there are several excellent restaurants in town – for the best **café con leche** this side of Miami, try the *M&M* laundromat at Virginia and White.

Blue Heaven 729 Thomas at Petronia, in the Bahamian Quarter ☎305/296-8666. At this excellent bar and restaurant in a colorful shack, rooster chicks peck at your feet as you eat fresh fish, jerk chicken and fabulous fruit-packed breakfasts.

BO's Fish Wagon 801 Caroline St ☎305/294-9272. The over-the-counter fish'n'chips and legendary conch fritters are some of the cheapest in town.

Café des Artistes 1007 Simonton St ☎305/294-7100. Upscale and rather more elegant than other places, this spot is well worth a splurge for its exquisite French-Caribbean cuisine. The upstairs deck is more casual, with simpler, cheaper food.

Camille's 1202 Simonton St ☎305/296-4811. Great breakfasts and brunches, perhaps shrimp cakes, blueberry pancakes or French toast with mango coconut cream sauce for $10.

El Siboney 900 Catherine St ☎305/296-4184. This no-frills family diner serves inexpensive and enormous Cuban dishes and good daily specials. Closes 9pm.

Half Shell Raw Bar Land's End Marina, at the Gulf end of Margaret St ☎305/294-7496. At a

dockside restaurant in an old fish market, locals flock to eat conch fritters, smoked fish, beer-steamed shrimp and fresh catch on the breezy wooden deck.

Island Wellness 530 Simonton St ☎305/296-7353. Health food store featuring sumptuous veggie specials, including burritos and smoothies.

Kelly's 301 Whitehead St ☎305/293-8484. Actress Kelly McGillis of *Top Gun* fame owns this excellent and reasonably priced restaurant featuring gourmet Floridian cuisine, an on-site microbrewery and the best key lime pie in Key West – prepared with a dense crushed-Oreo base.

Louie's Backyard 700 Waddell Ave ☎305/294-1061. This very popular, laid-back oceanfront restaurant serves typical Key West cuisine. The outside deck is the place to be; Sun brunch is especially good.

Mo's 1116 White St ☎305/296-8955. A locals' favorite serves up inexpensive food in a friendly atmosphere. Closed Sat and Mon.

Sippin 424 Eaton St ☎305/293-0555. Check out the cool cats' coffee house – overstuffed velvet sofas, board games, books and papers.

Drinking and nightlife

The anything-goes nature of Key West is exemplified by the **bars** that make up the bulk of the island's nightlife. Gregarious, rough-and-ready affairs, many stay open as late as 4am and feature regular live music. The most popular places are grouped around the northern end of Duval Street, no more than a few minutes' stagger from one another. For something a little less macho, keep south of the 500 block of Duval.

Bull & Whistle Bar 224 Duval St ☎305/296-4565. Loud and rowdy, this bar features the best of local musicians each night. Check the list on the door to see who's playing – or just turn up to drink.

Captain Tony's Saloon 428 Greene St ☎305/294-1838. Rustic fishermen's saloon that was the original *Sloppy Joe's* (see opposite), a noted hangout of Ernest Hemingway. Live music of various kinds nightly.

Green Parrot Bar 601 Whitehead St ☏ 305/294-6133. This Key West landmark since 1890 draws locals to its pool tables, dartboard and pinball machine. Live music at weekends.

Rumrunners 218 Duval St ☏ 305/294-1017. This multibar joint features cheap and tasty food, a big dance floor and reggae music until all hours. An open deck looks over Duval St.

Sloppy Joe's 201 Duval St ☏ 305/294-5717.

Despite the memorabilia and the crowds, this rowdy bar – with live music nightly – is not the one Hemingway made famous (see *Captain Tony's*, opposite), nor one that many locals set foot in.

Wax 422 Appelrouth Lane ☏ 305/296-6667. The closest Key West comes to a traditional nightclub – overstuffed red sofas and bead curtains decorate a chic, dimly lit space. Come only if you want to dance – the music's too loud to talk.

The East Coast

Florida's **east coast**, facing the Atlantic Ocean, runs for more than three hundred miles north from the northern fringe of Miami. The palm-dotted beaches and warm ocean waves bring to reality the sun-soaked playground of popular imagination. However, the first fifty or so miles lie deep within the sway of Miami, with one city offering little to distinguish it from the next. Despite its outdated party-town reputation, **Fort Lauderdale** these days is a sophisticated yachting center. **Boca Raton** and **Palm Beach** to the north are even more exclusive, their Mediterranean-Revival mansions inhabited almost exclusively by multimillionaires. North of here, the coast is still substantially unspoiled, although the **Space Coast**, centering on the **Kennedy Space Center**, and **Daytona Beach** both go all out to draw the crowds. The one genuinely characterful town in the entire stretch is **St Augustine**, still recognizable as the spot where Spanish settlers established North America's earliest foreign colony.

By car, the scenic route along the coast is **Hwy-A1A**, which sticks to the ocean side of the **Intracoastal Waterway**, formed when the rivers dividing the mainland from the barrier islands were joined and deepened during World War II.

Fort Lauderdale

A single low-budget Hollywood movie changed **FORT LAUDERDALE** from a mild-mannered little town that happened to adjoin seven miles of palm-shaded white sands into a byword for uninhibited beach life. Following the 1960 teen-exploitation movie *Where the Boys Are*, Fort Lauderdale instantly became the number-one Spring Break venue in the US, drawing hundreds of thousands of frenzied students each year. Having fueled its economic boom on underage drinking and lascivious excess, however, the city promptly turned its back on the revelers. By the end of the 1980s, it had imposed enough restrictions on boozing and wild behavior to put an end to the bacchanal, and Fort Lauderdale has transformed itself into a thriving pleasure port, catering to individual yacht-owners and major cruise liners alike, that's also one of the fastest-growing residential areas in the country.

Arrival, information and getting around

Both of Fort Lauderdale's public transit terminals are close to downtown. Greyhound **buses** pull in at 515 NE 3rd St, while the Amtrak and Tri-Rail **train** station (☎1-800/TRI-RAIL, ⊛www.tri-rail.com) is two miles west at 200 SW 21st Terrace – take bus #22 into town. The main local **visitor center** is in Port Everglades at 1850 Eller Drive (Mon–Fri 8.30am–5pm; ☎954/765-4466 or 1-800/227-8669, multilingual **entertainments/attractions hotline** on ☎954/527-5600, ⊛www.sunny.org).

Local bus #11 runs twice hourly along Las Olas Boulevard between downtown and the beach, and you can also call for a **water taxi** (daily 10am until late; one way $7.50, round-trip $14, all-day pass $16; ☎954/467-6677) to take you almost anywhere along Fort Lauderdale's many miles of waterfront.

Accommodation

Although Fort Lauderdale is moving inexorably upscale, plenty of **motels** near the beach offer a reasonable room for around $50 in summer, more like $75 in winter. The tourist office's free annual *Superior Small Lodgings Guide* holds full listings.

Floyd's Youth Hostel ☎954/462-0631. This friendly, well-kept private hostel in central Port Everglades vets would-be guests on the phone before revealing its address; $16 dorms and budget private rooms are available. A pickup is available from anywhere in Fort Lauderdale during the day. Floyd has recently opened a branch in a similar price range a few hundred yards from the beach. ❶/❷

Ocean Hacienda Inn 1924 N Atlantic Blvd ☎954/564-7800 or 1-800/562-8467. A great oceanfront hotel with a tropical garden and heated pool, it has surprisingly inexpensive rooms. ❸
Pillars Waterfront 111 N Birch Rd ☎954/467-9639 or 1-800/800-7666. Attractive, spacious resort facing the waterway rather than the ocean, but in the heart of the beach area, with a nice pool and full breakfast included. ❻–❽

The Town

For visitors, Fort Lauderdale contains two main areas of interest. **Downtown** focuses on a few blocks between E Broward and E Las Olas boulevards, which cross US-1 a couple of miles east of I-95. Heavily prettified with parks and promenades, it's a surprisingly pleasant place for a stroll, especially if you follow the half-mile pedestrian **Riverwalk** along the north shore of the **New River. Las Olas Boulevard** itself, the main **shopping district**, remains busy day and night, with boutiques, galleries, restaurants, bars and sidewalk cafés in abundance. It's also home to the stimulating **Museum of Art**, 1 E Las Olas Blvd (Tues–Sat 10am–5pm, Fri 10am–8pm, Sun noon–5pm; $10; ☎954/525-5500). The largely modern collection features several of the twentieth century's biggest names, but also celebrates 1960s work by the CoBrA movement of artists from Copenhagen, Brussels and Amsterdam. Not far west, the simulators and interactive displays at the **Museum of Discovery and Science**, 401 SW 2nd St (Mon–Sat 10am–5pm, Sun noon–6pm; $12.50 including one IMAX film; ☎954/467-6637), should pacify kids pining for Disney with a blockbuster 3D IMAX theater (call for showtimes).

Most visitors, nonetheless, still come for the **beach**. Cross the arching intra-coastal waterway bridge, about two miles along Las Olas Boulevard from downtown, and the mood changes appreciably. Where Las Olas ends, **beachside Fort Lauderdale** begins – T-shirt, sunscreen and beachwear stores are suddenly everywhere. Along the seafront, Fort Lauderdale Beach Boulevard once bore the brunt of Spring Break partying, but only a few beachfront bars suggest the carousing of the past, and the attractive new promenade draws an altogether healthier crowd of joggers, in-line skaters and cyclists.

Eating and drinking

The two main drags for eating and drinking in Fort Lauderdale are Las Olas and Sunrise boulevards. There are also some fun **bars** near the ocean, as well as a burgeoning restaurant district on West Broward Boulevard in the Old Town.

The Floridian 1410 E Las Olas Blvd, downtown ☎954/463-4041. Old Fort Lauderdale at its finest: formica furniture, peeling autographed pictures lining the walls and outstanding diner food at rock-bottom prices.

La Cantina 2870 E Sunrise Blvd ☎954/565-3839. The giant margaritas are $9, and enormous, cheap portions of authentic Mexican food make this a good stop on the beach.

Mark's Las Olas 1032 E Las Olas Blvd, downtown ☎954/463-1000. A top-notch dinner-only downtown restaurant, it serves contemporary south Floridian food – lots of sesame-crusted and pan-seared fish – at premium prices.

Nick's 3496 N Ocean Blvd, at the beach ☎954/563-6441. This low-key Italian restaurant serves fresh, hefty portions of pasta. Open until 4am, it's a scene by 1am when waiters from nearby restaurants descend for their own dinner.

Southport Raw Bar 1536 Cordova Rd ☎954/525-2526. South of downtown near Port Everglades, this boisterous local bar specializes in succulent crustaceans and well-prepared fish dishes.

Tom Jenkins' Bar-B-Q 1236 S Federal Highway (US-1), downtown ☎954/522-5046. Check out the outstanding barbecue and side dishes at inexpensive prices.

Boca Raton

BOCA RATON (literally "the mouth of the rat"), twenty miles north of Fort Lauderdale, is noteworthy mostly for its abundance of Mediterranean Revival **architecture**, a style prevalent here since the 1920s and kept alive in the **downtown** area by strict building codes. New structures must incorporate arched entranceways, fake bell towers and red-tiled roofs whenever possible, ensuring a consistent and distinctive "look." It all goes back to **Addison Mizner**, the "Aladdin of architects" (see box, overleaf), who swept in to Boca Raton on the tide of the Florida property boom and bought up 1600 acres of farmland. Mizner's vision of gondola-filled canals, luxury hotels and even a great cathedral never came to fruition, but the few buildings he completed left an indelible mark. His million-dollar *Cloister Inn*, for example, grew into the present $200-a-night **Boca Raton Resort and Club**, 501 E Camino Real, a pink palace of marble columns, sculptured fountains and carefully aged wood (☎561/447-3000 or 1-888/491-BOCA; ❻–❾). In its legendary confines at **Mizner Park**, off US-1 between Palmetto Park Road and Glades Road, the open-air plaza is adorned with palm trees and waterfalls. The park is also home to the **International Museum of Cartoon Art**, 201 Plaza Real (Tues–Sat 10am–6pm, Sun noon–6pm; $6; ☎561/391-2200), worth a stop for its expensive collection of political cartoons and comic strip exhibits. The collection has an interactive area geared toward kids.

A mile north of Hwy-798 (which links downtown with the beach) at 1801 N Ocean Blvd/Hwy-A1A, the **Gumbo Limbo Nature Center** (Mon–Sat 9am–4pm, Sun noon–4pm; $2 donation) covers twenty acres inhabited by osprey, brown pelicans and sea turtles. Night turtle-watching tours are offered between May and July; book well in advance (☎561/338-1473).

Boca Raton's most explorable **beachside** area is **Spanish River Park** (daily 8am–dusk; cars $8 Mon–Fri, $10 Sat, Sun & hols, pedestrians and cyclists free), a couple of miles north of downtown. Most of these fifty acres of vivid vegetation and high-rise greenery are only penetrable on trails through shady thickets.

Practicalities

Greyhound does not stop in Boca Raton. **Tri-Rail** stops off Yamato Road west of I-95 (⊕1-800/TRI-RAIL). The **Chamber of Commerce** is at 1800 N Dixie Hwy (Mon–Thurs 8.30am–5pm, Fri 8.30am–4pm; ⊕561/395-4433). The best-value **motels** near the beaches are *Shore Edge*, 425 N Ocean Blvd (⊕561/395-4491; ❸–❺), and *Ocean Lodge*, 531 N Ocean Blvd (⊕561/395-7772; ❸).

As for **eating**, *Max's Grill*, 404 Plaza Real (⊕561/368-0080), has good, reasonably priced standard American fare. Boca Raton has a rather subdued **nightlife**, but local bar *Flanigan's Guppys*, 45 S Federal Hwy (⊕561/395-4324), stays lively most of the week.

Palm Beach

A small island town of palatial homes and gardens, and streets so clean you could eat your dinner off them, **PALM BEACH** has been synonymous for nearly a century with the kind of lifestyle only limitless loot can buy. The nation's nobs began wintering here in the 1890s, after Henry Flagler brought his East Coast railroad south from St Augustine and built two luxury hotels on this then-secluded, palm-filled island. Since then, tycoons, sports aces, aristocrats, rock stars and CIA directors have flocked here, eager to become part of the Palm Beach elite and enjoy its aloofness from mainland, and mainstream, life. Joe Kennedy – father of John, Robert and Edward – bought the so-called Kennedy Compound here in 1933.

Summer in Palm Beach is very quiet, and the least costly time to stay. The winter months, from November to May, see a whirl of elegant balls, fundraising dinners and charity galas, as well as the **polo** season – watching a chukka or two is the only time Palm Beach denizens show themselves in the less particular environs of West Palm Beach (on the mainland).

Worth Avenue, close to the southern tip of the island, is filled with designer stores, high-class art galleries and ultraformal restaurants, and cruised by Rolls Royces, Mercedes and Jaguars. Its most appealing aspect is its **architecture**: stucco walls, Romanesque facades, and passageways leading to small courtyards where miniature bridges cross nonexistent canals and spiral staircases climb to the upper levels.

Addison Mizner: architect of Palm Beach

A former miner and prizefighter, **Addison Mizner** was an unemployed architect when he arrived in Palm Beach in 1918. Inspired by the medieval buildings he'd seen around the Mediterranean, Mizner built the **Everglades Club**, at 356 Worth Ave – the first public building in Florida in the Mediterranean Revival style. The success of the club, and the house he subsequently built for society bigwig Eva Stotesbury, won Mizner commissions all over Palm Beach as the wintering wealthy decided to swap suites at one of Henry Flagler's hotels for a "million-dollar cottage" of their own.

Brilliant and unorthodox, Mizner designed loggias and U-shaped interiors that made the most of Florida's pleasant winter temperatures, while his twisting staircases to nowhere became legendary. Mizner used untrained workmen to lay crooked roof tiles, sprayed condensed milk onto walls to create an impression of centuries-old grime and fired shotgun pellets into wood to imitate wormholes. By the mid-1920s, Mizner had created the Palm Beach Style, and he later fashioned much of Boca Raton.

Where Cocoanut Row and Whitehall Way meet, the white Doric columns fronting Whitehall are those of the **Flagler Museum** (Tues–Sat 10am–5pm, Sun noon–5pm; $8), the most overtly ostentatious home on the island – a $4 million wedding present from Henry Flagler to his third wife, Mary Lily Kenan. As in many of Florida's first luxury homes, the interior design was lifted from the great buildings of Europe: among the 55 rooms are an Italian library, a French salon, a Swiss billiard room, a hallway modeled on St Peter's, and a Louis XV ballroom. All are stuffed with ornamentation, but they lack aesthetic cohesion. Informative 45-minute guided tours depart frequently from the 110ft hallway and provide a background for Flagler's fascinating rise to success and a glimpse of the Gilded Age in which he flourished.

Built in 1926 in the style of an Italianate palace, **The Breakers** hotel, on South County Road off the main strip (℡561/655-6611 or 1-888/273-2537; ❾), operates as the last of Palm Beach's swanky resorts. Its design includes elaborate painted ceilings and huge tapestries. Take the free guided tour on Wednesday at 3pm (call ℡561/655-6611 ext 7560 for information).

Practicalities

Palm Beach's **Chamber of Commerce** is at 45 Cocoanut Row (summer Mon–Fri 10am–4.30pm, rest of year 9am–5pm; ℡561/655-3282). You'll need plenty of money to **sleep** here: prices of $200 a night are not uncommon. The elaborate, antique-furnished *Palm Beach Historic Inn*, 365 S County Rd (℡561/832-4009; ❸–❹), offers some of the best rates in town, but you'll need to book early. Otherwise come between May and December, when similarly grand options such as *The Chesterfield*, 363 Cocoanut Row (℡561/659-5800 or 1-800/243-7871; ❹–❾), and *The Plaza Inn*, 215 Brazilian Ave (℡561/832-8666 or 1-800/232-2632; ❹–❼), are at their least expensive.

As for **eating**, *TooJay's*, 313 Royal Poinciana Way (℡561/659-7232), is a bakery and deli open for breakfast onward, with omelettes under $6, while the lunch counter at *Green's Pharmacy*, 151 N County Rd (℡561/832-0304), keeps up a steady supply of diner food. If money is no object – and you're dressed to kill – make for *Café L'Europe*, 331 S County Rd (℡561/655-4020). Spend less than $50 a head in this super-elegant French restaurant and you'll still be hungry.

The Space Coast

The so-called **Space Coast**, the base of the country's space industry, occupies a flat, marshy island bulging into the Atlantic. Many visitors are surprised to find that the land from which the Space Shuttle leaves earth is also a sizable wildlife refuge. The general information hotline is ℡321/452-INFO or 1-800/93-OCEAN.

The Kennedy Space Center

The largest attraction in the area, the **Kennedy Space Center**, is the nucleus of the US space program and here NASA seizes every opportunity to enthuse young minds with the enduring glamour of outer space. The center remains a working facility, where space vehicles are developed, tested, and blasted into orbit. **Merritt Island** has been the center of NASA's activity since 1964, when the launch pads at Cape Canaveral US Air Force base, across the water, proved too small to cope with the giant new Saturn V rockets.

Careful planning by visitors is recommended. Allow an entire day for everything the Space Center has to offer. Crowds are thinner on weekends and in May and September. Check the weather: thunderstorms may force some attractions to close. Go first to the **visitor center/museum** (daily 9am–6pm; adults $25, children $15; the price includes admission to visitor complex exhibits, a bus tour and IMAX screening), reached via Hwy-405 from Titusville or Hwy-3 off Hwy-A1A. Museums and galleries in the main complex include an open-air **Rocket Garden** of spindly fireworks-like rockets from the 1950s. After you've examined the mission capsules, space suits and satellites and clambered through the mock-up Space Shuttle flight deck you'll want to watch an **IMAX movie** or join a two-hour guided **bus tour**. The bus passes the 52-story **Vehicle Assembly Building** and stops at the impressive **Apollo/Saturn V Center**, where multimedia displays re-create the excitement of the first moon landings and the Apollo 8 launch.

For the dates and times of **launches** from the Space Center, or to arrange $15 viewing passes, call ☎321/449-4444. Tickets can also be bought online at ⓦwww.kennedyspacecenter.com. However, you get almost as good a view from anywhere within forty miles of the Space Center.

Near the Space Center, at 6225 Vectorspace Blvd, Titusville, the **US Astronaut Hall of Fame** (daily 9am–5pm; $13.95) offers the full space explorer's experience, with G-force, shuttle-landing and flight simulators.

Staying over: Cocoa Beach

The Space Center holds a number of fast-food cafés, but the closest **motels** are on the mainland along US-1, or, if you're looking for a bargain rate, in **COCOA BEACH**, a few miles south on a ten-mile strip of shore washed by some of the biggest surfing waves in Florida. Options here include the *Luna Sea*, 3185 N Atlantic Ave (☎1-800/586-2732; ❹), a *Motel 6*, 3701 N Atlantic Ave (☎321/783-3103; ❸), and *Fawlty Towers*, 100 E Cocoa Beach Causeway (☎321/784-3870; ❸).

Merritt Island National Wildlife Refuge

NASA doesn't have Merritt Island all to itself, but shares it with the **Merritt Island National Wildlife Refuge** (daily dawn–dusk; free), reached via Hwy-402, a separate approach road from Titusville. The refuge is promoted, disconcertingly, with the slogan "Where Nature Meets Technology." Alligators, armadillos, raccoons and bobcats – and one of Florida's greatest gatherings of birdlife – live out their primeval existence beside some of the human world's most advanced hardware. Winter is the best time to visit: the skies are alive with birds migrating from the frozen north and mosquitoes are nowhere to be found. At any other time, especially in summer, the Mosquito Lagoon is worthy of its name: bring repellent.

Seven miles east of Titusville on Hwy-406, the six-mile **Black Point Wildlife Drive** gives a solid introduction to the basics of the island's ecosystem; pick up the free leaflet at the entrance. Be sure to walk in the refuge, too. Off the wildlife drive, the five-mile **Cruickshank trail** weaves around the edge of the Indian River. Drive a few miles farther east along Hwy-402 – branching from Hwy-406 just south of the wildlife drive – and take the half-mile **Oak Hammock** trail or the two-mile **Palm Hammock trail**, both accessible from the same parking lot.

Daytona Beach

The consummate Florida beach town, with its T-shirt shops, amusement arcades and wall-to-wall motels, **DAYTONA BEACH** owes its existence to twenty miles of light brown sand where the only pressure is to strip off and enjoy yourself. Once a favorite Spring Break destination when half a million college kids would indulge in underage drinking and libido liberation, Daytona Beach now discourages such activity, leaving it free to focus on its true love: motor sports. Life in this down-to-earth resort now revolves around three major festivals: February's **Daytona 500**, **Bike Week** in early March, and the relatively new **Biketoberfest**.

Pioneering auto enthusiasts, including Louis Chevrolet, Ransom Olds and Henry Ford, came to Daytona's firm sands in the early 1900s to race prototype vehicles beside the ocean. The land speed record was smashed five times by the British millionaire Malcolm Campbell who, in 1935, roared along at 276mph. When high speeds made racing on the sands unsafe, the **Daytona International Speedway**, an ungainly configuration of concrete and steel, was built three miles west of downtown along International Speedway Boulevard (buses #9A and #9B).

Opened in 1959, it seats 150,000 and hosts several major race meetings each year, starting in early February with the **Rolex 24**, a 24-hour race for GT prototype sports cars. A week or so later the qualifying races start for the year's biggest event, the **Daytona 500** stock-car race in mid-February. Tickets sell out well in advance (a weekend package from $220; ☎904/253-7223); book accommodation at least six months ahead. Though they can't capture the excitement of a race, **guided van tours** (daily except race days 9.30am–5pm, every half-hour; $6) take you around the remarkable curves, whose gradients make this the fastest racetrack in the world.

Immediately outside the Speedway, **Daytona USA** (daily 9am–7pm; $12) exhibits one of Campbell's many Bluebirds, the car in which he broke the land speed record at Ormond Beach in 1931, as well as interactive displays on the great races. A mile west, the **Klassix Auto Museum** at 2909 W International Speedway Blvd (daily 9am–6pm; $8.50) displays pristine examples of every Corvette design from 1953 on, plus vintage motorcycles and a 1938 Woody Wagon that boasts a top speed of 50mph.

For all the excitement that racing generates, the best thing about Daytona is the seemingly limitless beach: 500ft wide at low tide and fading dreamily into the heat haze. Lined with an all-but-endless procession of enormous but surprisingly low-priced motels, oceanfront Atlantic Avenue holds little to lure you away from the water. At the landward end of Main Street Pier, a $3 ride up the candy-striped **Space Needle** enables you to look down on the surrounding morass of low-rent bars and tattoo parlors. You can't get to the far end of the pier, though, because Hurricane Floyd knocked out 280ft of it in 1999.

Practicalities

As Ridgewood Avenue, **US-1** steams through mainland Daytona Beach, passing the Greyhound station at no. 138 S. Trolleys run the length of the beach from January to August only ($1). The **visitor center** is at 126 E Orange Ave (Mon–Fri 9am–5pm; ☎1-800/854-1234, ⊕www.daytonabeach.com).

Any of these Atlantic Avenue **motels** makes a good beach base: the *Driftwood Beach Motel* at no. 657 S (☎1-800/490-8935; ❶/❹); the *Streamline Hotel* at no. 140 S (☎386/258-6937; ❶); *Sunglow Resort* at no. 3647 S (☎877-332-4569, ⊕www.sunglowresort.com; ❹); or the welcoming *Tropical Manor Motel* at no.

2237 S (☎1-800/253-4920, ⊛www.visitdaytona.com/tropicalmanor/; ❷/❹).

Good places to **eat** include *Julian's*, 88 S Atlantic Ave (☎386/677-6767), a dimly lit, mock-Tahitian lounge with great food, and *Lighthouse Landing* (☎386/761-9271), beside the **Ponce Inlet Lighthouse**, for fresh fish. Or try the more elegant *Inlet Harbor*, 133 Inlet Road, Ponce Inlet (☎386/767-5590); eat right on the marina while local bands play their hearts out. The *St Regis Restaurant and Patio Bar*, 509 Seabreeze Blvd (☎386/252-8743), is a local culinary favorite, serving New American fare, the highlight of which is the chicken piccata. For beachside action, the bars in and around the *Adams Mark Daytona Beach Resort*, 100 N Atlantic Ave, are good bets.

St Augustine

Forty miles north of Daytona Beach, **Hwy-1** passes through the heart of **ST AUGUSTINE**. Few places in Florida are as immediately engaging as this old city, with the size and even some of the looks of a small Mediterranean town. The oldest permanent settlement in the US, with much from its early days still intact along its narrow streets, it also offers two alluring lengths of beach just across the bay.

Ponce de León touched ground here in 1513, but European settlement began when Spain's Pedro Menéndez de Avilés put ashore on St Augustine's Day in 1565. Sir Francis Drake's ships razed the town in 1586, the first of many battles before Florida was eventually ceded to Britain in 1763. By then the town was a major social and administrative center, soon to be capital of east Florida. Subsequently, Tallahassee (see p.671) became the capital of a unified Florida, and St Augustine's fortunes waned. Expansion largely bypassed the town – a fact inadvertently facilitating the restoration program that has turned this quiet community into a fine historical showcase.

Arrival, information and getting around

The Greyhound **bus** station, 100 Malaga St, is a fifteen-minute walk from the center. St Augustine is best seen on foot, though a **sightseeing train** tours the main landmarks (daily 8.30am–5pm; $12; tickets from 170 San Marco Ave or the visitor center). There's no public transportation, so if you want to get to the beaches two miles away and you don't have a car you'll have to either rent a bike from the youth hostel (see opposite), or take a **taxi** (Ancient City Cabs; ☎904/824-8161). The **visitor center**, 10 Castillo Drive (daily 8am–5.30pm; ☎1-800/653-2489, ⊛www.visitoldcity.com), shows a free film on the history of the town, has recommendations for a variety of tours and information on the numerous local festivals. Harbor **cruises** (☎904/824-1806; $8.50) leave five or six times a day from the City Yacht Pier, near the foot of King Street. The well-organized and informative Tour St Augustine (☎1-800/797-3778) leads historical and ghost walking tours. Gamsey Carriage Co. (☎904/829-2391; $15) offers horse-drawn carriage tours both day and night.

Accommodation

The Old Town has many excellent restored inns offering **bed and breakfast**, and there are cheap motels outside the center along San Marco Avenue. For the best prices, avoid the busy period between May and October, when rates rise by $15–25.

Best Western 6 Castillo Drive ☎1-800/528-1234.
Reliable chain's Spanish-style villa, provides a
pool, a hot tub for night-time star-gazing and complimentary breakfast. ❸–❻
Carriage Way 70 Cuna St ☎1-800/908-9832,
ⓦwww.carriageway.com. One of the Old Town's
best-priced B&Bs, in a pretty, centrally located
Victorian building. Some rooms offer four-poster
beds and fireplaces. ❹–❼
Casa Monica 95 Cordova St ☎1-800/648-1888,
ⓦwww.casamonica.com. Elegant Spanish-style
hotel established in the heart of the old city in
1888 and magnificently restored. ❻–❼
Coquina Gables 1 F St ☎904/461-8727,
ⓦwww.coquinagables.com. This beautiful and
relaxing oceanfront B&B in St Augustine Beach has
a pool and spa. It offers a variety of rooms, including three king rooms with ocean views and decorated with antiques. ❻
Pirate Haus 32 Treasury St ☎904/808-1999,
ⓦwww.internationalhaus.com. The town's only
hostel accommodation is popular with travelers
and near the plaza. It has a giant kitchen and a
common room stuffed with guidebooks. Air condi-
tioned dorms from $15, and some private rooms.
❶
Kenwood Inn 38 Marine St ☎904/824-2116,
ⓦwww.oldcity.com/kenwood. Handily positioned,
this charming, sizable Old Town inn near the
waterfront features individually decorated rooms,
some with four-poster or canopy beds, as well as
a pool, terrace and complimentary continental
breakfast. ❺
Vilano Beach Motel 50 Vilano Rd ☎904/829-
2651. This laid-back Art Deco motel is a great
base for enjoying the North Beach. ❷–❺

The Old Town

St Augustine's historic area – or **Old Town** – along St George Street and south
of the central plaza holds the well-tended evidence of its Spanish period. It may
be small, but there's a lot to see: an early start, around 9am, will give you a lead on
the tourist crowds and should allow a good look at almost everything in one day.

Given the fine state of the **Castillo de San Marcos National Monument**
(daily 8.45am–4.45pm; $4; regular free talks on the fort and local history), on
the northern edge of the Old Town beside the bay, it's difficult to believe that
the fortress was started in the late 1600s. Its longevity is due to its design: a diamond-shaped rampart at each corner maximized firepower, and 14-foot-thick
walls reduced vulnerability to attack. Inside, there's not a lot beyond small cases
of exhibits in echoing rooms, but venturing along the 35ft ramparts gives good
views across the city and the bay.

The eighteenth-century **City Gate** marks the entrance to **St George Street**,
once the main thoroughfare and now a tourist-trampled strip. You'll find a lot
of places called "The oldest. . ." in St Augustine; the **Oldest Wooden
Schoolhouse**, set in lush gardens at 14 St George St (daily 9am–5pm; $2.75),
is one of the most atmospheric, a restored wooden shack with jerky animatronic
dummies portraying nineteenth-century schoolchildren. A fair-sized plot at St
George and Cuna is taken up by the excellent **Spanish Quarter Living
Museum** (Sun–Thurs 9am–6pm, until 7pm Fri & Sat; $6.50). In its seven
reconstructed homes and workshops, volunteers dressed as Spanish settlers go
about their business at spinning wheels, anvils and foot-driven wood lathes.

For a more intimate look at local life during a slightly later period, head for
the **Peña Peck House**, 143 St George St (Mon–Sat 10am–4.30pm, Sun
12.30–4.30pm; $4.50 suggested donation). Thought to have originally been the
Spanish treasury, by the time the British took over in 1763 this was the home
of a physician and his gregarious spouse, who turned the place into a high society rendezvous. Nearby on Cordova Street, the evocative, overgrown **Tolomato
Cemetery** (9am–6pm) stands on the site of an eighteenth-century Christian
Indian village; most graves date from the 1900s.

In the sixteenth century, the Spanish king decreed that all colonial towns
must be built around a central plaza; thus St George Street runs into **Plaza de
la Constitucion**, a marketplace from 1598. On the plaza's north side, the
Basilica Cathedral of St Augustine (daily 7am–5pm; donation) adds a

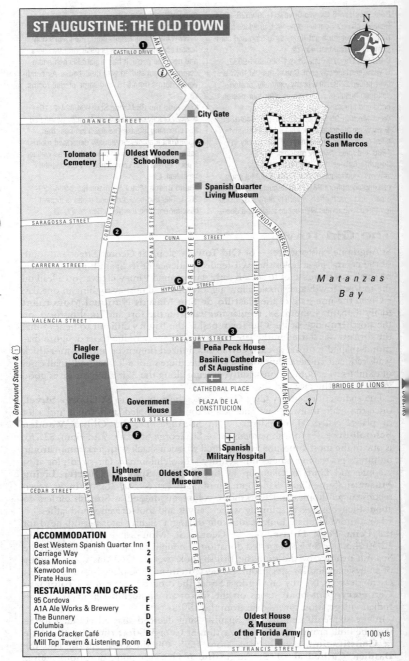

ST AUGUSTINE: THE OLD TOWN

N

CASTILLO DRIVE

1

ⓘ

City Gate

ORANGE STREET

A

Castillo de San Marcos

Tolomato Cemetery

Oldest Wooden Schoolhouse

Spanish Quarter Living Museum

AVENIDA MENENDEZ

SARAGOSSA STREET

2

CORDOVA STREET

SPANISH STREET

CUNA STREET

ST. GEORGE STREET

Matanzas Bay

CARRERA STREET

B

CHARLOTTE STREET

C

HYPOLITA STREET

D

VALENCIA STREET

TREASURY STREET

3

Peña Peck House

Basilica Cathedral of St Augustine

CATHEDRAL PLACE

AVENIDA MENENDEZ

BRIDGE OF LIONS

⚓

Flagler College

PLAZA DE LA CONSTITUCION

Government House

KING STREET

4 **F**

E

Spanish Military Hospital

GRANADA STREET

Lightner Museum

Oldest Store Museum

AVILES STREET

CHARLOTTE STREET

MARINE STREET

CEDAR STREET

AVENIDA MENENDEZ

ST GEORGE STREET

5

BRIDGE STREET

Oldest House & Museum of the Florida Army

ST FRANCIS STREET

0   100 yds

▲ Greyhound Station & ⓘ

ACCOMMODATION
Best Western Spanish Quarter Inn	1
Carriage Way	2
Casa Monica	4
Kenwood Inn	5
Pirate Haus	3

RESTAURANTS AND CAFÉS
95 Cordova	F
A1A Ale Works & Brewery	E
The Bunnery	D
Columbia	C
Florida Cracker Café	B
Mill Top Tavern & Listening Room	A

7

FLORIDA | St Augustine

646

touch of grandeur, although it's largely a Sixties remake of the late eighteenth-century original. Tourist numbers lessen as you cross **south of the plaza** into a web of quiet, narrow streets, just as old as St George Street. The **Government House Museum**, 48 King St (daily 9am–5pm; $2.50), gives an admirably concise and clear history of the changing demography of the colony. Nearby, opposite **Flagler College**, the classy **Lightner Museum** (daily 9am–5pm, last admission 4.30pm; $6) displays fine and decorative arts in the former Alcazar Hotel, one of the most fabulous resorts of the late nineteenth century. Rather more prosaically, the **Oldest Store Museum** at 4 Artillery Lane (Mon–Sat 9am–5pm, Sun noon–5pm; $5) re-creates a general store of the 1880s, filled to the rafters with more than 100,000 items from dusty top hats, bootscrapers and medicines to cigar molds and wooden washing machines.

More substantial history is unfurled a ten-minute walk away at the fascinating **Oldest House**, 14 St Francis St (daily 9am–5pm; $5), which is indeed the oldest house in town, dating from the early 1700s. Its rooms are furnished to show how the house – and people's lives – changed as new eras unfolded.

The beaches

Some fine **beaches** – busiest at weekends – lie just a couple of miles from the Old Town. Across the bay, **St Augustine Beach** is family terrain, with some good restaurants and a fishing pier, but the **Anastasia State Recreation Area** (daily 8am–dusk; cars $4.25, cyclists and pedestrians $1) on Anastasia Island offers a thousand protected acres of dunes, marshes and scrub, linked by nature walks. North of Old Town (take May St, off San Marco Ave), the broad orange **Vilano Beach** pulls a younger crowd.

Eating and drinking

Eating in the Old Town is expensive, and a number of its cafés and restaurants are closed in the evening. Many people head out to the oceanfront places for dinner, or settle instead for a long night's drinking at one of the nice old bars.

95 Cordova at the *Casa Monica* (see p.645) ☎904/810-6810. This luxurious and elegant restaurant's menu is an eclectic blend of American, Asian, Mediterranean, Caribbean and Moroccan influences.

A1A Ale Works 1 King St ☎904/829-2977. The convivial, good-looking bar/restaurant is popular with locals for its excellent, creative New World cuisine and home-brewed beers.

The Bunnery 121 St George St ☎904/829-6166. Tempting homemade food is served on a relaxing courtyard of this old Spanish bakery.

Columbia 98 St George St ☎904/824-3341. Lively New Orleans atmosphere, with a traditional Spanish/Cuban menu all served up in a sumptuous setting of fountains and candlelit arcades.

Florida Cracker Café 81 St George St ☎904/829-0397. Serves a blend of combo salads, sandwiches, entrees and homemade desserts. Favorites include hot artichoke and parmesan dip and conch fritters.

Mill Top Tavern 19 1/2 George St ☎904/829-2329. This historic local bar, with deck seating, in a nineteenth-century mill boasts a great view of the Castillo and harbor. Excellent live music helps make the place a local favorite.

The Oasis 4000 Ocean Trace Rd ☎904/471-3424. This beach bar is famous for its burgers. Try the "Gonzo Burger," served with three kinds of cheese and piles of extras.

Jacksonville and its beaches

Situated in the great double loop of the St Johns River and with long established lumber and coffee industries, **JACKSONVILLE**, the largest city in the US – 841 square miles – is suspicious of anything that might upset its hardworking tradition. Pleasure seekers are expected to stick to the beaches. Even the film industry, which came here seeking a base in the 1910s, was scared off by the religious zeal of the locals and settled in California instead. The growing size of the white-collar sector has eased the visual blight of years of heavy industry, and efforts have been made to enhance Jacksonville's appeal by creating parks and riverside boardwalks. However, the sheer size of the city dilutes its character and makes it impossible to walk around and get a real feel for the city.

To get an overview of downtown Jacksonville, take the **Skyway monorail** (daily 6.30am–7.30pm; 35¢) from the Convention Center to Hemming Park, a ten-minute journey at eye level with the high-rise offices. One noteworthy building on the north bank of the St John's River is the **Florida Theater**, 128 Forsyth St. Elvis Presley arrived in 1957 for his first appearance on an indoor stage, an event noted by *Life* magazine because a juvenile court judge sat through the whole performance to ensure it wasn't too suggestive. Crossing over to the south bank – try taking the River taxi ($2 one-way; $3 round-trip) – you'll find the **Museum of Science and History**, 1025 Museum Circle (Mon–Fri 10am–5pm, Sat 10am–6pm, Sun 1–6pm; $6), with its hands-on exhibits and planetarium. Or, for a break from the commerce and industry of the city, visit the **Jacksonville Museum of Modern Art**, 333 N Laura St (Tues–Fri 11am–2pm; $5), which has a permanent collection of modern art and hosts traveling exhibitions.

Just south of the Fuller Warren River bridge (I-95), the **Cummer Museum of Art and gardens**, 829 Riverside Drive (Tues & Thurs 10am–9pm, Wed, Fri & Sat 10am–5pm, Sun 2–5pm; $6; free Tues after 4pm), stands on the former Cummer family estate. The spacious rooms and sculpture-lined corridors contain works by prominent European masters.

From all over Jacksonville you can see the floodlights of the 73,000-seat **Jacksonville Jaguar Stadium**, 1 Altel Stadium Place, home to the National Football League franchise, and also the scene of the Florida–Georgia college football clash each autumn – an excuse for 48 hours of citywide drinking and partying.

The beaches

Traveling north from Jacksonville on Hwy-A1A, you'll first hit the **Ponte Verda Beach**, whose crowd-free sands and million-dollar homes form one of the most exclusive communities in northeast Florida. However, travel a few more miles farther north and you'll discover the much less snooty **Jacksonville Beach**. Although Hurricane Floyd destroyed the pier in 1999, the area around it remains the center of activity. A rebuilding program is scheduled for completion by 2003. If you tire of watching the novice surfers here and want some action of your own, **Adventure Landing**, 1944 Beach Blvd (Feb–May & Sept–Nov, Sun–Thurs 10am–midnight, Fri & Sat 10am–1am; ☎904/246-4386; $18.99), offers an uphill water coaster, wave pool go-carts and an amusement park. Two miles north of the old pier, the more commercialized **Neptune Beach** blurs into the identical-looking Atlantic Beach. Both are best visited for eating and socializing only.

Practicalities

The Greyhound **bus** station, 10 N Pearl St, is an easy walk from the **Convention and Visitors Bureau**, 201 E Adams St (Mon–Fri 8am–5pm; ☎1-800/733-2668, ⓦwww.jaxcvb.com), while the train station is an awkward six miles northwest of downtown at 3570 Clifford Lane. The best value **accommodation** can be found at the motels on the city's perimeter. Try the *Comfort Suites*, 1180 Airport Rd (☎904/741-0505; ❸). For downtown accommodation, *Extended Stay America*, 1413 Prudential Drive (☎904/396-1777; ❸), is one of the cheaper options. Or, consider the scenic but pricey *Radisson Riverwalk Hotel*, 1515 Prudential Drive (☎904/396-5100; ❹). For **accommodation at the beaches** try the *Pelican Path B&B By the Sea*, 11 N 19th Ave (☎904/249-1177; ❹), which has a pool and bicycles, or the *Best Western Inn*, 305 N 1st St (☎904/249-4949; ❻).

For **eating downtown**, the best breakfast and lunch options can be found near the Jacksonville Landing Mall. Check out *Biscotti's Expresso Café*, 3556 St John's Ave (☎904/387-2060). Alternatively, on the south bank, the *Loop*, 4000-21 St John's Ave (☎904/384-7301), has good-priced pizzas, while the *River City Brewing Co.*, 835 Museum Circle (☎904/398-2299), offers home-brewed beer and live music. Good **eating options at Jacksonville Beach** are *Billy's*, 1728 N 3rd St (☎904/246-8099), for good food and a large selection of beers, and *Ellen's Kitchen*, 1824 S 3rd St (☎904/246-1572), where the locals line up every day.

Central Florida

Encompassing a broad and fertile expanse between the east and west coasts, most of **central Florida** was farming country when vacation-mania first struck the beachside strips. From the 1970s on, this picture of tranquility was shattered: no section of the state has been affected more dramatically by modern tourism, and the most visited part of Florida can also be one of the ugliest. A clutter of freeway interchanges, motels and billboards arches around the small city of **Orlando**, where a tourist-dollar chase of Gold Rush magnitude was sparked by **Walt Disney World**, the biggest and cleverest theme-park complex ever created. The rest of central Florida is quiet by comparison, and, north of Orlando particularly, rural towns like **Ocala** typify the state before the arrival of the highways and of vacations spun around "attractions."

Orlando and the theme parks

ORLANDO, a quiet farming town in 1970, now has more visitors than any other place in the state. The reason, of course, is **Walt Disney World**, which, along with **Universal Studios Escape**, **Sea World** and a host of themed attractions, pulls more than 25 million people a year to a previously featureless plot of scrubland. Few people head to Orlando proper, choosing instead one of the countless motels along **Hwy-192**, fifteen miles south, or **International Drive**, five miles southwest. Despite enormous expansion over the last decade, the town itself remains free of the commercialism that surrounds it.

Arrival and information

The **international airport** is nine miles south of downtown Orlando; collect brochures and discount coupons at the official **information booth** (daily 7am–11pm). **Shuttle buses** (24hr; best prices offered by Mears or Transtar) run to any hotel in the Orlando area for around $15, while a **taxi** to downtown, International Drive or the motels on Hwy-192 costs around $30. **Buses** and **trains** arrive downtown at the Greyhound terminal, 555 N John Young Parkway, and the Amtrak station, 1400 Sligh Blvd.

Pick up discount coupons and promotional offers at the efficient **Visitor Information Center**, 8723 International Drive (daily 8am–7pm; ☎407/363-5872 or 1-800/643-9492, ◍www.go2orlando.com).

Getting around: visiting the theme parks

You have to be very determined to get to the theme parks without a car, but it can be done. Local Lynx **buses** (☎407/841-8240, ◍www.golynx.com) converge on the downtown Orlando terminal between Central and Pine streets; route #50 heads to Walt Disney World, but it's a somewhat patchy service and takes about an hour. The pricier Mears Transportation Service runs private **shuttle buses** (☎407/423-5566) between the main accommodation areas, the airport and Walt Disney World, Sea World and Universal Studios ($10–12 round-trip) – phone at least a day ahead to be picked up, or check at your hotel or hostel. **Taxis** are the best way to get around at night – try Yellow Cab Co. (☎407/699-9999). Along International Drive, between SeaWorld Orlando and

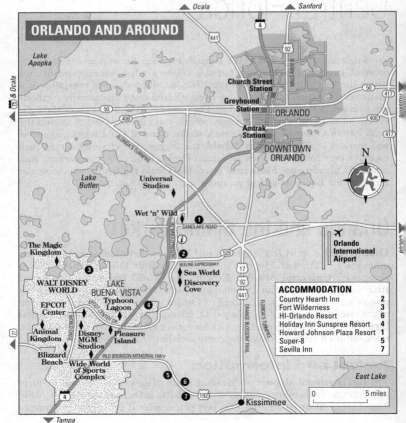

Universal Studios, the **I–Ride** trolley service (☎407/354–5656) operates every few minutes daily from 7am to midnight, costing 75¢ one way. The immense **convention center**, several blocks in length, stretches along International Drive amid the attractions.

Accommodation outside Walt Disney World

If you're on a budget, or want to spend time visiting Universal Studios and the other parks, you'd do best to stay **outside Walt Disney World**. Once you've decided to do so, location is pretty much irrelevant – the parks and attractions are so scattered that wherever you stay you'll spend a lot of time driving back and forth between them.

Competition is fierce, and quoted **rates** can often be negotiated down; independent travelers who show up on spec during the slow winter periods may well find some bargains. The motels line **Hwy–192** between Walt Disney World and Kissimmee (10–20min drive to Walt Disney World). The chain hotels on **International Drive** (about 20min drive from Walt Disney World) are a shade more upmarket, with good restaurants and shops within walking distance. Closest to Walt Disney World are the places around **Lake Buena Vista** (5–20min drive).

Country Hearth Inn 9861 International Drive ☎407/352-0008, ✉www.countryhearth.com. The plain rooms come in a kitsch building dripping with Southern Victoriana. Pool and continental breakfast. ❺

HI-Orlando Resort 4840 W Hwy-192, Kissimmee ☎407/396-8282, ✉www.hiorlando.org. The clean, friendly, efficient hostel has a pool, dorms ($16) and private rooms. Lynx stops nearby and shuttles run to the parks, airport and Orlando's bus and train stations. ❶/❷

Holiday Inn Sunspree Resort Lake Buena Vista 13351 Hwy-535 ☎407/239-4500, ✉www.kid-suites.com. Situated one mile from Walt Disney World, this comfortable and kid-friendly motel has a large pool, restaurant and entertainment. ❺

Howard Johnson Plaza Resort at the Universal Gateway 7050 Kirkman Rd ☎1-800/327-3808, ✉www.hojo.com. Close to International Drive, this motel is a good base for exploring Universal Studios. Free shuttle to other parks. ❸/❹

Sevilla Inn 4640 W Hwy-192, Kissimmee ☎1-800/367-1363, ✉www.sevillainn.com. The good-value attractive motel has clean rooms and a nice pool. ❷/❸

Super-8 4880 W Hwy-192, Kissimmee ☎407/396-1144, ✉www.super8.com. Comfortable, clean, reliable and cheap. ❷

Accommodation within Walt Disney World

Prices at the fabulously designed **Walt Disney World resorts** scattered around the complex (all ☎1-800/828-0228, ✉www.disneyworld.com) are much higher – sometimes more than $300 per night – than you'll pay elsewhere. However, the benefits (top-notch facilities, free transportation, early access to the parks, brunch with Goofy) can make it worth the extra. Note that rates drop by $25–50 during the "**value seasons**" (roughly in January and from September to December, excluding holidays).

Though rooms may be available at short notice during the quieter times, you should book as far ahead – nine months is not unreasonable – as possible. If you do arrive on spec, the **Disney Information Center** off I-75 in Ocala (daily 9am–6pm; ☎352/854-0770) can offer discounts on rooms for that night.

A good option if you're **camping**, the *Fort Wilderness Resort and Campground* is set on a lovely 700-acre forested site near the Magic Kingdom. Here you can hook up your RV or pitch your tent for $47–65, or rent a six-berth trailer for around $279, and still enjoy the privileges of being a Disney guest.

All-Star Resorts Three resorts, in the Disney-MGM area near Blizzard Beach, are themed around sports, music and movies. ④/⑤

Caribbean Beach Resort Five lodges on the EPCOT grounds, each with a pool, are beautifully landscaped. ⑥/⑦

Port Orleans Resort Gaze from your wrought-iron balcony across the mini New Orleans French Quarter re-created in this resort's courtyard, in Disney Village. ⑥/⑦

Wilderness Lodge This site features a frontier log cabin, an Old Faithful geyser and waterfalls. ⑦–⑨

Walt Disney World

As significant as air conditioning in making the state what it is today, **WALT DISNEY WORLD** turned a wedge of Florida cow fields into one of the world's most lucrative vacation venues. The immense and astutely planned empire also pushed the state's media profile through the roof: from being a down-at-the-heel mixture of cheap motels, retirement homes and tacky alligator zoos, Florida suddenly became a showcase of modern international tourism.

Walt Disney World is the pacesetter among theme parks: it goes way beyond Disneyland, which opened in Anaheim, California, in 1955 (see p.1080) – delivering escapism at its most technologically advanced and psychologically brilliant across an area twice the size of Manhattan. Its four main theme parks are quite separate entities and, ideally, you should allow a full day for each. The **Magic Kingdom** is the Disney park of popular imagination, where Mickey mingles with the crowds – very much the park for kids, though at its high-tech best capable of thrilling even the most jaded of adults. Known for its giant, golfball-like geosphere, **EPCOT Center** is Disney's celebration of science and technology; this sprawling area involves a lot of walking, and may bore young children. **Disney–MGM Studios** suits almost everyone: its special effects are enjoyable even if you've never seen the movies they're based on. The newest of the four, Disney's **Animal Kingdom**, brings all manner of African and Asian wildlife to the theme park setting, perhaps the lone entry that can be explored fairly quickly.

The Magic Kingdom

The **Magic Kingdom** follows the formula established by California's Disneyland, dividing into **Tomorrowland**, **Frontierland**, **Fantasyland** and **Adventureland** (roughly in declining order of merit). Some rides are identical to their California forebears; others are greatly improved. In Tomorrowland, old favorite **Space Mountain** offers a gut-churning roller-coaster trip around distant galaxies on a ferocious starlit switchback. More chilling is the high-tech, adrenalin-fueled **Extra TERRORestrial Alien Encounter**, where you're involved in an experiment that goes horrifically wrong. In the witty, fast-paced **Timekeeper**, an animatronic mad professor and feisty robots take you on a dizzying trip through time, relayed convincingly on an enormous 360° cinema screen.

Rides in Frontierland are gentler, though just as much fun. On **Splash Mountain**, a lazy boat ride through Brer Rabbit land culminates in a shriek-inducing 50ft drop. People with weak hearts steer towards the less frenetic run-away train of **Big Thunder Mountain Railroad**, or, if the rides are getting too much, to the hokey **Country Bear Jamboree**, where you can hoedown with furry, dungareed grizzlies. In **Liberty Square**, between Frontierland and Fantasyland, make time for **Haunted Mansion**, a seriously spooky ghost ride with spectacular holograms.

Fantasyland, heralded by **Cinderella**'s exceptionally pink castle, is very much old-style Disney, with a lot of stuff for kids. For adults the most endearing ride is the very 1970s **It's a Small World**, a bizarre boat jaunt advocating brotherly

One-day one-park tickets cost $48.76 (children aged 3–9 $39.22), and allow unlimited access to all shows and rides in one park only, for that day only. Park-Hopper Passes buy you entry to all four parks, in any combination, as many times as you like, over any four or five days. Four-day passes cost $186.56 ($150.52); five-day passes cost $218.36 ($177.02). A Park-Hopper Plus Pass, available for five ($250.16/$203.52), six ($281.96/$230.02) and seven ($313.76/$266.52) days, gives you the same options as the Park-Hopper Pass, but also features admission to the water parks, Pleasure Island or the Wide World of Sports complex, depending on the number of days on your ticket. Unused days and options never expire. If possible, buy tickets well in advance, over the phone, on the internet, or at a Disney store. If you must buy them at the gate, arrive at least an hour before opening time. The parking lots cost $6 a day, but are free if you're staying at a Walt Disney World resort. Also, keep your eyes open for discount vouchers that can be picked up from motels, tourist information centers and other businesses in the area.

Each park is open daily from 9am and closes between 6pm and midnight, depending on the time of year; pick up the current schedule when you arrive. However, all parks open earlier than the published hours, so turning up around 8am should ensure that you get to see the most popular rides before the hordes pour in. Upon arrival, the best tactic is either to rush to the far end of the park and work backwards, or to head straight for the big rides, getting them out of the way before the mid-afternoon crush.

At its worst, waiting time can be well over an hour, but the excitement in the line, the atmosphere and the cleverly devised entertainment usually make the time fly by. However, Disney has introduced Fastpass to alleviate the problem of long lines: Place your admission ticket into a machine at the entrance of the attraction; the machine returns it with another ticket that gives you a time to return to the attraction, usually about two hours later; you simply show up, hand your new ticket to the attendant and scoot to the front of the line.

love. Adventureland feels similarly quaint; **Pirates of the Caribbean**, a boat ride through a town invaded by debauched robotic figures, looks distinctly tame compared to the newer rides in Tomorrowland.

EPCOT Center

Even before the new Magic Kingdom opened, Walt Disney was developing plans for **EPCOT Center**, or Experimental Prototype Community of Tomorrow, conceived in 1966 as a real community experimenting with the new ideas and materials of the technologically advancing US. The idea failed to shape up as Disney had envisioned: EPCOT didn't open its gates until 1982, when global recession and ecological concerns had put a damper on the belief in the infallibility of science. One drawback of this park is simply its immense size: twice as big as the Magic Kingdom and very sapping on the feet.

Inside the unmissable 180ft geosphere (unlike a semicircular geodesic *dome*, the *geosphere* is completely round), **Future World**, a reminder of the park's original concept, details the history and possible advances to be made in agriculture, transportation, energy and communications. The best of the rides – all corporately sponsored, so don't expect any mention of alternative power or global warming – are the superb **Test Track**, a radical combination of simulator and switchback ride in which you test a high-speed car of the future; **Body Wars**, a fast-paced simulator voyage through the body's immune system; and the 4D cinematic thrill of **Honey, I Shrunk the Audience**. Occupying the largest area in the park is the **World Showcase**, with eleven different "countries"

When the brilliant illustrator and animator Walt Disney devised the world's first theme park, California's **Disneyland** (see p.1080), he left himself with no control over the hotels and restaurants that quickly engulfed it, preventing growth and erasing profits Disney felt were rightly his. Determined not to let that happen again, the Disney corporation secretly bought up 27,500 acres of central Florida farmland, acquiring by the late Sixties a site a hundred times bigger than Disneyland. With the promise of a jobs bonanza for Florida, the state legislature gave the corporation the rights of any major municipality – empowering it to lay roads, enact building codes, and enforce the law with its own security force.

Walt Disney World's first park, the Magic Kingdom, which opened in 1971, was a huge success. Unveiled in 1982, the far more ambitious EPCOT Center represented the first major break from cartoon-based escapism, but its rose-tinted look at the future received a mixed response. Partly due to this, and some cockeyed management decisions, the Disney empire (Disney himself died in 1966) faced bankruptcy by the mid-1980s. Since then, the corporation has sprung back from the abyss, and it now steers a tight and competitive business ship, always looking to increase Walt Disney World attendance figures of 100,000 visitors and stay ahead of its rivals. It may trade in fantasy, but where money matters, the Disney Corporation's nose is firmly in the real world.

represented by street sets. The **restaurants** here are the best in Walt Disney World, and it's a great place to watch the spectacular nighttime sound and light show, **Illuminations**.

Disney-MGM Studios

When the Disney corporation began making films and TV shows for adults – most notably *Who Framed Roger Rabbit* – they also set about devising a theme park to entertain adults as much as kids. Buying the rights to the Metro-Goldwyn-Mayer (MGM) oeuvre of films and TV shows, Disney acquired a vast repertoire of instantly familiar images to mold into shows and rides. Opening in 1990, **Disney–MGM Studios** served to mute the opening of Florida's Universal Studios (see opposite), and at the same time found an extra use for the real film studios based here. The people you'll see laboring over storyboards aren't there for show, they really are making films.

There are more stage shows and tours than rides as such, though thrill-seekers will be more than happy with the delightfully sadistic **Twilight Zone Tower of Terror**, set in a haunted, cobweb-strewn hotel, or the new **Rock & Roller Coaster**, which, with a 2.8 second 0–60 mph launch, is Disney World's wildest ride. **Star Tours**, a flight-simulator trip piloted by Star Wars characters R2D2 and C-3PO, is toothless in comparison, and the **Great Movie Ride**, with actors and robotic figures re-creating scenes from classic Hollywood movies in an ersatz Mann's Chinese Theatre, is a tad disappointing.

Don't miss the half-hour **Backstage Studio Tour**, climaxing with the special-effects bonanza *Catastrophe Canyon*: the interest level fluctuates but you won't get your money's worth if you miss it. The same applies to **Magic of Disney Animation**, an enlightening trip through the animation studios, and **Jim Henson's Muppet Vision 3D** show – enormous fun, with some great surprises. Capping them off is the twice-nightly **Fantasmic**, a 25-minute special effects-laden show in which Mickey battles the products of his own imagination.

Disney's Animal Kingdom

Disney's **Animal Kingdom** was opened in 1998 as an animal-conservation theme park with Disney's patented over-the-top twist. The park is divided into five major "lands" – **Africa**, **Camp Minnie-Mickey**, **Dinoland USA**, **Safari Village** and **Asia** – though the true tribute here is to the versatility of concrete, which is colored, imprinted upon and formed into an endless variety of shapes to help create mock-authentic ambiences for each land.

Once within the park, visitors have four major stops. The best is **Kilimanjaro Safaris**, where "lorries" of tourists ride past giraffes, zebras, elephants, lions, gazelles and rhinos, all passing what feels like authentic African wildlands (local oak trees have been trimmed to look like African acacias). Crossing over to "Asia," visitors walk through dense vegetation and village ruins to see giant fruit bats, Asian birds and possibly tigers in the **Maharajah Jungle Trek**. The park's only thrill ride is in DinoLand USA: **Countdown to Extinction**, a roller-coaster-style vehicle that makes small drops and short stops in the dark as dinosaurs pop out of nowhere and roar.

The remainder of the park requires no more than casual exploration. The **Flights of Wonder** bird show exhibits parrots, hawks and other unusual birds, and classic Disney characters in appropriate attire sign autographs in **Camp Minnie-Mickey**, where you can also catch *Festival of the Lion King*, a participatory production of upbeat music with some nifty acrobatics, loosely based on its namesake film.

Universal Studios

For some years, it seemed that US TV and film production would move away from California to Florida, which, with its lower taxes and cheaper labor, was more amenable, and the opening of Universal Studios Escape in 1990 appeared to confirm that trend. So far, for various reasons, Florida has not proved to be a fully realistic alternative, but that hasn't stopped the Universal enclave here, now known as **Universal Studios** (park opens daily at 9am, closing times vary; one-day pass $48.76, children 3–9 $39.22, under-3s free; two-day pass $84.75/$68.85; parking $7; ☏1-800/837-2273, ⊛www.universalstudios.com) from becoming a major player in the Orlando theme park arena. While Disney still holds court, Universal has drawn much attention, adding the hi-tech, special effects-laden **Islands of Adventure** and **CityWalk**, an earthier lure for nightlife dollars than Downtown Disney. Universal is also aspiring to full-fledged resort status with the *Portofino Bay Hotel* and plans for other accommodation. For access to all areas, park in the garage half a mile north of exits 29 and 30B off I-94.

Universal Studios Florida

Like its competitor Disney-MGM, Universal is a working studio, filling more than four hundred acres with the latest in TV and movie production technology. Unlike MGM, there's more emphasis on movie-related rides than backstage shows. Universal's top rides are **Back to the Future**, a bone-shaking flight-simulator trip from 2015 to the Ice Age (not for claustrophobes); the breathtaking **Terminator 2: 3D**, a dark, dizzying combination of high-speed live action, superb robotics and 3D morphing effects (for maximum enjoyment, sit in the middle of the auditorium, five or six rows from the front), and the flabbergasting **Twister**, where you're pitted against a tornado. **Men in Black: The Ride** will allow you, with others, to control the fate of each ride.

Of the other rides, **Jaws**, a boat trip through shark-infested waters, plays wickedly with audience suspense; **Kongfrontation** has you scooped up and shaken by the angry six-ton brute; and **Earthquake** takes you on a subway

Universal Studios Escape, Wet'n'Wild and Sea World have teamed together to create a pass that permits access to each park over a period of seven consecutive days. The Orlando Flex-Ticket costs $169.55 (ages 3–9 $135.63), or $209.05/$167.65 including Tampa's Busch Gardens (see p.661), which is good for ten days.

ride through chaos, flooding and collisions. **ET** is gentler, a superb, undulating bike ride to save ET's home planet – be sure to listen when the little tyke says goodbye. Elsewhere, there are attempts to demystify production techniques, the most successful being **Alfred Hitchcock: The Art of Making Movies**, with surprising insights into Hitch's famed visual trickery. The two-man **Gory, Gruesome and Grotesque Horror Makeup Show**, played for laughs, is as notable for its tour-de-force performances as for its educational content.

Universal Studios Islands of Adventure

As the latest entry in the Orlando game of one-upmanship, **Islands of Adventure** stakes its claim as the leader in state-of-the-art, edge-of-your-seat thrill rides. Though there are plenty of diversions for the less daring, this is what brings the crowds, and long lines are typical for many of the attractions, even if they thin out as the evening goes on.

The park's five "islands" – **Marvel Super Hero Island**, **Toon Lagoon**, **Jurassic Park**, **The Lost Continent** and **Seuss Landing** – surround a lagoon. Marvel Super Hero Island is home to three major rides. The **Incredible Hulk Coaster** begins with a thrust, supposedly equal to that of a US Air Force F-16 fighter jet, and continues for more than two minutes of incognizant intensity. **Doctor Doom's Fearfall** provides a great panoramic view of the park before dropping 200ft, but is not worth waiting the usual half-hour or so. **The Amazing Adventures of Spiderman** is arguably the best ride in the park and should not be missed, despite a not uncommon hour's wait. In a first-ever combination of moving ride vehicles, filmed 3D action and pyrotechnic special effects, you are to help Spidey get back the Statue of Liberty from a gaggle of villains. Try going during the closing fireworks show, although as far as lines go, this one is the most enjoyable as the ride's story is presented in the queuing area.

Continuing on to Toon Lagoon, **Dudley Do-Right's Ripsaw Falls** and **Popeye & Bluto's Bilge-Rat Barges** are good for getting a midday drenching. From here, **Jurassic Park** is a takeoff on the popular film and includes the visitor center used in the movie. The **Jurassic Park River Adventure** is an atmospheric trip through dino-land that ends with an 85-foot plunge – the steepest and fastest to date for a water ride. At The Lost Continent, one island over, the highlight is the intertwining set of inverted roller coasters, **Dueling Dragons**. Finally, although Seuss Landing is more directed towards kids, the playful architecture is right out of a Dr. Seuss book and the **fireworks show** at the end of the night is worth sticking around for.

Universal Studios CityWalk

Not to be outdone by Downtown Disney and Church Street Station, the **Universal Studios CityWalk** looks to cash in on those lucrative evening dollars with thirty acres of restaurants, live music, dance clubs, theaters and shops. CityWalk is free to enter but many bars and clubs will have a cover as the night progresses (Ⓦwww.citywalkorlando.com). Try the featured drink at *Jimmy*

FLORIDA | Orlando and the theme parks

7

Buffett's Margaritaville. Choose among the cuisines of twenty-one Latin American nations. Jazz lovers should take pleasure in **CityJazz**, a compound created in part by members of the Thelonious Monk Institute of Jazz. Or, you can visit **Bob Marley – A Tribute to Freedom**, a re-creation of the Jamaican musician's home.

Sea World

Sea World, at Sea Harbor Drive, near the intersection of I-4 and the Bee Line Expressway, the cream of Florida's sizable crop of marine parks, should not be missed; allocate a day to see it all (daily 9am–7pm or later; longer hours in summer; $50.83, ages 3–9 $41.29; ☎1-800/327-2424, ⊛www.seaworld.com). The big event is the **Shamu Adventure** show – beginning with a pre-show film attempting to justify the twenty minutes of tricks then performed by killer whales. The **Wild Arctic** complex, complete with artificial snow and ice, shows off beluga whales, walruses and a couple of claustrophobic-looking polar bears; the experience is topped off by a thrilling simulated helicopter flight through an Arctic blizzard. The park's first thrill ride, **Journey to Atlantis**, is part fantasy, part waterslide, part roller coaster, and has a sixty-foot drop. You will get drenched – by the ride and by other tourists who pay for the privilege of spraying you. With substantially less razzmatazz, plenty of smaller tanks and displays explain more than you need to know about the undersea world. Among the highlights, the **Penguin Encounter** attempts to re-create Antarctica with scores of waddling birds scampering over an iceberg; the occupants of the **Dolphin Pool** assert their advanced intellect by flapping their fins and soaking passersby; and **Terrors of the Deep** includes a walk through a glass-sided tunnel, offering the closest eye-contact you're ever likely to have with a shark and live to tell the tale.

Orlando's waterparks

Of the three Disney-owned **waterparks**, **Blizzard Beach**, on World Drive north of the *All-Star Resorts*, is the most creative, based on the fantasy that a hapless entrepreneur has opened a ski resort in Florida and the entire thing has started to melt. Star of the show is **Summit Plummet**, which shoots you down a 120ft vertical drop at more than fifty miles per hour. Gentler rides include toboggan-style slalom courses and covered raft rides. As well as the slides, **Typhoon Lagoon**, at Lake Buena Vista (one-day pass, one-park $28.57/$22.79), features geysers and a rainforest, a huge surfing pool and a shark reef, where you can snorkel among tropical fish. **River Country** is older, smaller and quieter (one-day pass $16.91/$13.25)

Wet 'n' Wild, 6200 International Drive (hours vary, call ☎1-800/992-9453, ⊛www.wetnwild.com; $29.95/$23.95, parking $4), defends itself admirably in the face of the Disney competition, with a range of excellent slides including the challenging seven-story Bomb Bay and the almost vertical Der Stuka. Lines are shorter, too.

Discovery Cove

Discovery Cove, the second of Sea World's theme parks, is a much more exclusive venture, limiting visitors to those with reservations (and who can afford the high admission prices that start at $109; ☎1-877/4DISCOVERY, ⊛www.discoverycove .com). This will entitle you to swim and play with dolphins, snorkel up to sharks and barracudas behind a clear partition and feed tropical birds in a resort-like setting.

Eating in the Orlando area

Downtown and its environs hold the pick of the locals' **eating** haunts; most visitors, however, head for International Drive's inexpensive all-day buffets and gourmet restaurants. There's a strict embargo on taking food into any of the theme parks, where the best restaurants are in **Epcot's World Showcase** – head for Japan, Morocco or Mexico.

Bahama Breeze 8849 International Drive ☎407/248-2499. Decent Caribbean food in an upbeat atmosphere.

The Globe 25 Wall St Plaza ☎407/422-1669. This is a perfect place for inexpensive Nouveau American snacks and light meals, such as pan-seared salmon salad and veggie burgers. Open 24 hours.

Le Coq au Vin 4800 S Orange Ave ☎407/851-6980. French restaurant with surprisingly low prices for top-notch food.

Magic Mining Company 7763 W Hwy-192 ☎407/396-1950. Colorful steak and seafood mountain-themed joint.

Ming Court 9188 International Drive ☎407/351-9988. An exceptional Chinese restaurant, serving delicious potstickers, dim sum and fragrant noodles, is not as costly as you might expect.

Numero Uno 2499 S Orange Ave ☎407/841-3840. Inexpensive, downtown Cuban restaurant.

Race Rock Supercharged Restaurant 8986 International Drive ☎407 248-9876. A race-car-themed restaurant with auto memorabilia on walls serves such eclectic American choices as burgers, milkshakes and malts at super-reasonable prices.

TuTu Tango 8625 International Drive ☎407/248-2222. This lively restaurant is done out like an artist's studio. Painters and sculptors work as you eat superb pan-Asian, New World and Mediterranean food, including seared tuna sashimi or black bean soup.

White Wolf Café 1829 N Orange Ave ☎407/895-5590. The down-to-earth café/antique store is known for creative sandwiches and generous salads.

Nightlife and entertainment

Though you'll probably be so exhausted from a long day at the parks that boozing and boogying with thousands of others will be the last thing on your mind, the Orlando area is just bursting with themed **nightspots** of every persuasion, from medieval banquets to piano bars and country and western clubs. It's all relentless good, clean fun, sanitized to the hilt.

From around 9pm, each **Walt Disney World** park holds some kind of closing-time bash, usually involving fireworks and fountains. There's also **Pleasure Island**, exit 26B off I-4 (in the Disney Village Marketplace), a remake of an abandoned island, whose pseudo-warehouses are the setting for shops, themed bars and night-clubs (daily 10am–7pm; after 7pm $21 gains access to all bars and clubs). The most enjoyable are the *Comedy Warehouse* and the *Adventurers' Club*, loosely based on a 1930s gentlemen's club. Take ID and a fat wallet.

In a similar vein, in downtown Orlando at 129 W Church St, the restored Victorian buildings of **Church Street Station** enclose a mall-like cluster of restaurants, bars, clubs and shows with a vaguely Old South theme (daily 11am–2am; after 6pm $19 gains access to all bars and clubs).

The West Coast

In three hundred miles from the state's southern tip to the border of the Panhandle, Florida's **west coast** embraces all the extremes. Buzzing, youthful towns rise behind placid fishing hamlets; mobbed holiday strips are just minutes from desolate swamplands. Surprises are plentiful, though the coast's one constant is proximity to the Gulf of Mexico – and sunset views rivaled only by those of the Florida Keys.

The largest city, **Tampa**, has more to offer than its corporate towers initially suggest – not least the exemplary **nightlife** scene at Cuban Ybor City and the Busch Gardens theme park. For the mass of visitors, though, the Tampa Bay area begins and ends with the **St Petersburg beaches**, whose miles of sea and sand are undiluted vacation territory. South of Tampa, a string of barrier-island beaches runs the length of the Gulf, and the mainland towns that provide access to them – such as Sarasota and Fort Myers – have enough to warrant a stop. Inland, the wilderness of **the Everglades National Park** is explorable on simple walking trails, by canoeing, or by spending the night at backcountry campgrounds with only the gators for company.

Tampa

TAMPA, the business hub of the west coast, has been one of the major beneficiaries of the flood of people and money into Florida – and boasts an impressive cultural diet envied by many larger rivals. A small, stimulating city with an infectious, upbeat mood, it's well worth a stop: in addition to its fine **museums** and **Busch Gardens**, one of the most popular theme parks in the state, it boasts in **Ybor City** the West Coast's hippest and most culturally eclectic quarter.

Tampa began as a small settlement beside a US Army base built to keep an eye on the Seminoles in the 1820s. In the 1880s the railroad arrived, and the Hillsborough River on which the city stands was dredged to allow seagoing vessels to dock. Tampa became a booming port, simultaneously acquiring a major tobacco industry as thousands of Cubans moved north from Key West to the new cigar factories of neighboring Ybor City. The Depression ended the economic surge, but the port remained one of the busiest in the country and tempered Tampa's postwar decline. While the social problems that blight any decent-sized US city are evident, little seems to stand in the way of Tampa's continued emergence as a forward-thinking and financially secure community.

Arrival, information and getting around

The city's **airport** (℡813/870-8700, ⓦwww.tampaairport.com) is five miles northwest of downtown: local HART bus #30 is the least costly connection (Mon–Fri every 30min 5.48am–8.18pm, weekends less frequent; $1.15; ℡813/623-5835), or use the 24hr Limo Inc. vans (℡813/572-1111 or 1-800/282-6817, ⓦwww.supershuttle.com; about $15 to downtown). **Taxis** (try United; ℡813/253-2424) to downtown or a Busch Boulevard motel cost $13–24; to St Petersburg or the beaches, $30–45. Greyhound **buses** come in downtown at 610 Polk St; trains arrive at 601 N Nebraska Ave N.

The downtown **visitor center**, 400 N Tampa St, suite 1010 (Mon–Sat 9am–5pm; ℡813/223-2752, ⓦwww.tampa.com), and the **Ybor City Chamber of Commerce**, 1800 E Ninth Ave (Mon–Fri 9am–5pm; ℡813/248-3712, ⓦwww.ybor.org), give out useful leaflets and maps.

Although both downtown Tampa and Ybor City are easily covered on foot, to travel between them without a car you'll need the HART **local buses**, ($1.15, one-day pass $2.50, five-day pass $12; ℡813/254-4278, ⓦwww .hartline.org). Useful bus numbers are #8 to the Florida Aquarium and Ybor

City, #5, #8 or #39 to Busch Gardens, #6 to the Museum of Science and Industry and #30 to the airport. Rush-hour commuter PSTA/HART express buses run **between Tampa and the coast** (Mon–Fri; $1.50) – #100 (PSTA ☎727/530-9911, ⓦwww.psta.net) to St Petersburg and #200 (HART) to Clearwater.

Accommodation

Tampa is not generously supplied with low-cost **accommodation**; you'll almost certainly save money by sleeping in St Petersburg or at the beaches. There are some good deals, though, in the motels along Busch Boulevard, six miles north.

Best Western Resort 820 E Busch Blvd ☎813/933-4011. Close to Busch Gardens and a reasonable base for seeing the city by car, this motel also offers a happy hour every afternoon and free breakfast. ❹–❺

Days Inn 2522 N Dale Mabry Hwy ☎1-800/448-4373. This chain is ten minutes' walk from downtown and provides a shuttle bus to the airport. Features two pools, one with a waterfall, and a tropical fish garden. ❸–❺

Days Inn Busch Gardens/Maingate 2901 E Busch Blvd ☎813/933-6471. Comfortable and reliable, with a 24hr restaurant. ❸–❹

Don Vincentre de Ybor Historic Inn 1915

Republica de Cuba ☎813/241-4545, ⓦwww .donvicente.com). The most luxurious B&B in Ybor City offers a fine restaurant and cigar- and-martini bar that features live entertainment most nights. ❻

Gram's Place 3109 N Ola Ave ☎813/221-0596, ⓦwww.grams-inn-tampa.com. This laid-back inn offers both private rooms (all themed in different musical styles) and youth hostel-style accommodation. ❶/❹

Riverside 200 N Ashley Drive ☎813/223-2222. If you're dependent on public transport, this downtown business traveler-oriented hotel is highly convenient.

Downtown Tampa

Aside from riverside warehouses in various states of dilapidation around the northern end of **Franklin Street** (once the district's main drag and still the best place to get your bearings), recalling the city's past is largely left to plaques detailing everything from the passage of sixteenth-century explorer Hernando de Soto to the site of Florida's first radio station. None of the contemporary buildings in downtown Tampa better reflects the city's cultural striving than the highly regarded **Tampa Museum of Art**, on the banks of the Hillsborough River at 600 N Ashley Drive (Tues, Wed, Fri & Sat 10am–5pm, Thurs 10am–8pm, Sun 1–5pm, closed Mon; $5; free Thurs 5–8pm & Sat 10am–noon; ☎813/274-8130, ⓦwww.ci.tampa.fl.us/dept_museum). The museum specializes in classical antiquities and twentieth-century American art. Selections from the permanent modern stock are cleverly blended with prime loaned specimens of recent US painting, photography and sculpture.

From **Curtis-Hixson Park** you'll see the silver minarets and cupolas on the far side of the river, sprouting from the main building of the University of Tampa – formerly the 500-room **Tampa Bay Hotel**, financed by steamship and railroad magnate Henry B. Plant. To reach it, walk across the river on Kennedy Boulevard and descend the steps into Plant Park.

The structure is as bizarre a sight today as it was at its opening in 1891. Plant had been buying up bankrupt railroads since the Civil War, steadily inching his way into Florida to meet his steamships unloading at Tampa's harbor, and was rich enough to put his fantasies of creating the world's most luxurious hotel into practice. But lack of care for the fittings and Plant's death in 1899 hastened its transformation from the last word in comfort to a pile of crumbling plaster. The city bought it in 1905 and leased it to Tampa University 23 years later; today, in one wing, the **Henry B. Plant Museum**, 401 W Kennedy Blvd (Tues–Sat

10am–4pm, Sun noon–4pm; $5), holds what's left of the hotel's furnishings.

The splendid **Florida Aquarium**, 701 Channelside Drive, in Tampa's dock-land area (daily 9.30am–5pm; $13.75, ☏813/273-4000, ⓦwww.flaquarium .org), houses lavish displays of Florida's fresh- and saltwater habitats, from springs and swamps to beaches and coral reefs. Residents include an impressive variety of fish and birds, otters, turtles and alligators.

Ybor City

In 1886, as soon as Henry Plant's ships had ensured a regular supply of Havana tobacco into Tampa, cigar magnate Don Vincente Martinez Ybor cleared a patch of scrubland three miles northeast of present-day downtown Tampa and laid the foundations of **YBOR CITY**. About twenty thousand migrants, mostly Cuban, settled here and created a Latin American enclave, producing the top-class, hand-rolled cigars that made Tampa the "**Cigar Capital of the World.**" However, mass-production, the popularity of cigarettes and the Depression proved a fatal combination for skilled cigar-makers: as unemployment struck, Ybor City's tight-knit blocks of cobbled streets and redbrick buildings became surrounded by drab, low-rent neighborhoods.

Today, Ybor City is in the midst of a revival; it buzzes with tourists and at night the atmosphere reaches carnival proportions, especially on weekends. It is trendy and culturally diverse, yet the city's Cuban roots are immediately apparent and explanatory background texts adorn many buildings. The **Ybor City State Museum**, 1818 Ninth Ave (Tues–Sat 9am–5pm; $2; ☏813/247-6323, ⓦwww.ybormuseum.org), helps you grasp the main points of Ybor City's creation and its multiethnic makeup. The museum also offers cigar-rolling demonstrations on Friday and Saturday from 10am to 1pm, historic walking tours (Fri 11am) and walking ghost tours of Ybor City (Sat 10.30am; $4). The old cigar-rolling factory is now converted into shops, restaurants and bars as **Ybor Square Mall**, between 13th and 14th streets and Eighth and Ninth avenues. Standing on the factory's steps in 1893, the Cuban poet and independence fighter José Martí called for "money, machetes and manpower" for the country's anti-Spanish struggles. Expatriate cigar workers responded by contributing ten percent of their earnings.

The Museum of Science and Industry, and Busch Gardens

A twenty-minute drive northeast from downtown Tampa takes you to the colossal **Museum of Science and Industry** (MOSI), at 4801 E Fowler Ave (daily 9am, closing times seasonal, call ☏813/987-6100; $13 including IMAX; ⓦwww.mosi.org), where topics such as health, the environment, and space and the stars are tackled through hands-on activities and a program of shows. Plan your day around the **Challenger Learning Center** (more space adventure where you can defy the laws of gravity), the 75mph **Gulf Coast Hurricane** and the **IMAX** shows.

Nearby, at Busch Boulevard and 40th Street, **Busch Gardens**, one of Florida's most popular theme parks (daily 9.30am–6pm; longer hours in high season; adults $48.76, children $39.22, parking $5–10; ☏813/987-5082, ⓦwww .buschgardens.com), offers the Southeastern US's fastest, largest, most nerve-jangling roller coasters, incongruously set in an interpretation of colonial-era Africa. A sedate monorail journey allows inspection of a variety of African wildlife, but by far the most popular of the twenty-odd rides is **Gwazi**, a dou-ble wooden roller coaster that pits the two against each other in a race to finish first. Other winners include the nerve-jangling **Montu** and the enormous **Kumba**. For those weary of the G forces, the water rides **Stanley Falls** and **Congo River** are a refreshing alternative on a hot afternoon.

Eating

There are plenty of good places to eat in Tampa, with a huge concentration of lively restaurants in Ybor City.

Bernini 1702 7th Ave, Ybor City ☎813/248-0099. An Italian joint that serves up wood-fired pizza and pasta in the lovely old Bank of Ybor City.
Café Creole 1330 E 9th Ave, Ybor City ☎813/247-6283. Good Creole food comes at reasonable prices – the Creole sampler platters will give you a taste of everything for $12.25.
Café Pepé 2006 W Kennedy Blvd ☎813/253-6501. This moderately priced restaurant has been a Tampa landmark for years. Enjoy Spanish and Cuban favorites like filete salteado and paella.
Castillo's 1823 7th Ave, Ybor City ☎813/248-1306. One of the best places to sample real Cuban sandwiches and invigorating Cuban coffee.

The Columbia 2117 E 7th Ave, Ybor City ☎813/248-4961, ⊛www.columbiarestautant.com. A tourist institution, the city's oldest restaurant serves fine Spanish and Cuban food. It also offers flamenco dancing six nights a week. Reservations recommended.
Joffrey's Coffee House 1616 7th Ave, Ybor City ☎813/248-5282. The delectable aromas of fruit, coffee and chocolate are always thick in the air at this reasonably priced coffee house.
Shells 11010 N 30th St ☎813/977-8456. Convenient for the hotels near Busch Gardens, this cheap and cheerful seafood restaurant serves consistently good fresh fish to an enthusiastic crowd.

Nightlife and entertainment

Ybor City is the only place to be at night, though new clubs open and close like wildfire. The free *Weekly Planet* (⊛www.weeklyplanet.com) has **nightlife listings**, as does the Friday *Tampa Tribune*.

Amphitheater 1609 E 7th Ave, Ybor City ☎831/248-2331, ⊛www.amphitheaterybor.com. A live music favorite featuring everything from retro to techno.
Castle 2004 16th St at 9th Ave ☎813/247-7547. A Gothic inspired drinking joint.
Irish Pub 1721 E 7th Ave, Ybor City ☎813/248-

2099. Convivial spot for late-night drinking.
Masquerade at The Ritz 1503 E 7th Ave, Ybor City ☎813/247-3319. A lively high energy dance club.
Skipper's Smokehouse 910 Skipper Rd ☎813/971-0666. Blues and reggae rule at this family-oriented live music venue.

St Petersburg

Situated on the eastern edge of the Pinellas Peninsula, **ST PETERSBURG** may be only twenty miles from Tampa, but location is about the only thing these cities share. Declared the healthiest place in the US in 1885, it wasted no time in wooing the recuperating and the retired, at one point putting five thousand green benches on its streets to take the weight off elderly legs. Although it remains a mecca for the retired, St Petersburg has worked hard to attract young blood. In addition to rejuvenating the pier, which now offers something for every age, its diverse selection of museums and plethora of art galleries has contributed to its emergence as one of Florida's richest cultural cities. Most remarkable of all, the town has acquired a major collection of works by Salvador Dali – making St Petersburg a good option if you are looking for a break from the beaches nine miles west on the Gulf Coast.

The **Salvador Dali Museum**, 1000 S 3rd St (Mon–Sat 9.30am–5.30pm, Sun noon–5.30pm; $8; ☎727/822-6270; ⊛www.salvadordalimuseum.org), stores more than a thousand paintings from the collection of a Cleveland industrialist,

A. Reynolds Morse, who struck up a friendship with the artist in the 1940s. **Free tours** begin whenever sufficient people gather, and trace a chronological path around the works, from the artist's early experiments with Impressionism and Cubism to the seminal Surrealist canvas *Persistence of Memory*.

Once you've done Dali, the quarter-mile-long **pier**, jutting from the end of Second Avenue N, is the town's central focus. It often hosts browsable arts and crafts exhibitions, and the inverted-pyramid-like building at its head holds five stories of restaurants, shops and fast-food counters. The pier is also home to **Great Explorations** (Mon–Sat 10am–8pm, Sun 11am–6pm; $4), a hands-on science museum for all ages. At the foot of the pier, the **Museum of History** (Mon–Sat 10am–5pm, Sun 1–5pm; $5) modestly recounts St Petersburg's early twentieth-century heyday as a winter resort. Nearby, the **Museum of Fine Arts**, 255 Beach Drive NE (Tues–Sat 10am–5pm, Sun 1–5pm; $6, free on Sun), holds a superlative collection ranging from pre-Columbian art through Asian and African to European Old Masters. The **Florida International Museum**, half a mile east of the pier at 100 2nd St (daily during exhibition periods 9am–6pm; $14.50; reserve on ☎1-800/777-9882, ⓦwww.floridamuseum.org), occupies an entire block and, for about a year at a time, displays exhibitions from renowned museums all over the world.

Practicalities

The Greyhound **bus** station is north of downtown between 18th and 19th avenues, at 180 9th St N. An Amtrak bus link from Tampa pulls in some way out of town at the Pinellas mall on 7200 Hwy-19. The **Chamber of Commerce** is at 100 Second Ave N (Mon–Fri 8am–5pm; ☎727/821-4715, ⓦwww.stpete.com). **Staying** in St Petersburg can be less costly than at the beaches. There is one **youth hostel** (members of any hostel organization pay $15): the *St Petersburg International Youth Hostel*, in the *Bay Park Arms*, 326 First Ave N, with some private rooms from $39 per night or $125 a week (☎727/822-4141; ❶/❷). Of the dozens of cheap **motels** along Fourth Street (Hwy-92), the *Kentucky* at no. 4246 (☎727/526-7373; ❷) is a good option. The area is also rich in charismatic bed and breakfasts such as *Orleans Bishop Bed and Breakfast*, 256 First Ave N (☎727/894-4312; ❹). Downtown, the restored *Hotel Ponce De Leon* at 95 Central Ave (☎1-877/5-DELEON or ☎727/822-4139; ❷-❸) is good value. For great, inexpensive Cuban **food**, head for *Tangelo's Grill*, 226 First Ave N (☎727/894-1695). For a more stylish dinner try the *Moon Under Water*, 332 Beach Drive NE (☎727/896-6160); overlooking the waterfront, this inexpensive British tavern is well known for its cocktails and curries.

The St Petersburg beaches

Drab suburbs stretch west from St Petersburg, covering virtually all of the Pinellas peninsula, a bulky thumb of land poking between Tampa Bay and the Gulf of Mexico. Framing the Gulf side of the peninsula, a 35-mile chain of barrier islands forms the **St Petersburg Beaches**, one of Florida's busiest coastal strips. When the resorts of Miami Beach lost some of their allure during the 1970s, the St Petersburg beaches grew in popularity with Americans and have since evolved into an established destination for package-holidaying Europeans. The beaches themselves are beautiful, the sea is warm, and the sunsets are fabulous, yet this in no way is Florida at its best.

All **buses** ($1; ☎727/530-9911, ⓦwww.psta.net) to the beaches originate in

St Petersburg at the **Williams Park terminal**, on First Avenue N and Third Street N; an information booth there has route details.

The southern beaches

In twenty-odd miles of heavily touristed coast, only **PASS-A-GRILLE**, at the very southern tip of the barrier island chain, has the look and feel of a genuine community – two miles of tidy houses, cared-for lawns, small shops and a cluster of bars and restaurants. At weekends, informed locals come to enjoy one of the area's liveliest set of sands. A mile and a half north of Pass-a-Grille, the painfully luxurious **Don Cesar Hotel**, 3400 Gulf Blvd (☎727/360-1881, ⓦwww.doncesar.com; ❼), is a grandiose pink castle, filling seven beachside acres. Opened in 1928, and briefly busy with the likes of Scott and Zelda Fitzgerald, it enjoyed a short-lived glamour: during the Depression part of the hotel was used as a warehouse, and later as the spring training base of the New York Yankees baseball team.

Continuing north on Gulf Boulevard brings you into the main section of **St Pete Beach**, a string of uninspiring hotels, motels and eating places. Further north, **Treasure Island** is even less varied tourist territory. An arching drawbridge leads to **Madeira Beach**, essentially more of the same – although, if you can't make it to Pass-a-Grille, the beach here justifies a weekend fling.

The northern beaches

Much of the northern section of **Sand Key**, the longest barrier island in the St Petersburg chain and one of the wealthiest portions of the coast, is taken up by stylish condos and time-share apartments. It ends with the pretty **Sand Key Park**, where tall palm trees frame a scintillating strip of sand. Among the nearby high-rises that somewhat mar the view is the *Sheraton Sand Key Resort*, venue of the liaison between TV evangelist Jim Bakker and church secretary Jessica Hahn in 1987, which led to the media preacher's fall from grace and, for a time, greatly boosted the hotel's business.

Sand Key Park occupies one bank of **Clearwater Pass**, across which a belt of sparkling white sands marks the holiday town of **CLEARWATER BEACH**, whose streets still retain an endearing small-town feel. The staff of a well-positioned **hostel** here will help plan excursions around the area. *HI-Clearwater Beach*, 606 Bay Esplande (☎727/443-1211, ⓔemagillr1@juno.com; ❶/❸), has dorms and some private rooms. Regular buses (#80 and #60) provide links to the mainland town of Clearwater – across the two-mile causeway – where you'll find connections to St Petersburg and a Greyhound station.

Beach practicalities

Hotels here tend to be filled with package tourists, and are always pricier than the **motels** that line mile after mile of Gulf Boulevard – typically $80 in the high season, anywhere between $50 and $80 in the low. Remember, too, that you'll pay $5–10 extra for a room on the beach side of Gulf Boulevard compared with an identical room on the inland side. At St Pete Beach the best bets are the *Ritz*, 4237 Gulf Blvd (☎727/360-7642, ⓦwww.rask.com/ritz; ❹), or the secluded old *Florida Dolphin*, 6801 Sunset Way (☎727/360-7233; ❹).

It's easy to find a decent place to **eat** around the beaches. *Hurricane Seafood Restaurant*, 807 Gulf Way (☎727/360-9558), has a well-priced menu of the freshest seafood. *Pep's Sea Grille*, 5895 Gulf Blvd (☎727/367-3550), creates inspired combinations of moderately priced pasta and seafood. In Clearwater Beach, *Frenchy's Shrimp and Oyster Café*, 41 Baymont St☎727/446-3607), cooks up good grouper burgers and shrimp sandwiches.

Sarasota

Rising on a gentle hillside beside the blue waters of Sarasota Bay, **SARASOTA** is one of Florida's better-off and better-looking towns, and also one of the state's leading cultural centers. It's home to numerous writers and artists, and the base of several respected performing arts companies. The community is far less stuffy than its wealth might suggest, and downtown Sarasota is fairly lively, with cafés, bars and eateries complementing the excellent grouping of bookstores for which the place has been known. Most visitors stop by to see the Ringling estate on the town's northern edge – home of the art-loving millionaire from whom modern Sarasota takes its cue – and the barrier island beaches, a couple of miles away across the bay.

Northern Sarasota: the Ringling Museum Complex

Don't fail to visit the house and art collections of **John Ringling**, a multimillionaire who gave Sarasota a taste for fine arts that it's never lost. One of the owners of the fantastically successful Ringling Brothers Circus, which toured the US from the 1890s, Ringling acquired a fortune estimated at $200 million (see also p.382). Recognizing Sarasota's investment potential, he built the first causeway to the barrier islands and made this the winter base for his circus. His greatest gift to the town, however, was a Venetian Gothic mansion and an incredible collection of European Baroque paintings, displayed in a purpose-built museum beside the house.

The **Ringling Museum Complex**, which includes the mansion (daily 10am–5.30pm; $9, admission to the art galleries free on Sat), is at 5401 Bay Shore Rd, three miles north of downtown beside US-41. Begin your exploration by walking through the gardens to the former winter residence of John and Mable Ringling, **Ca' d'Zan** ("House of John," in Venetian dialect), a gorgeous piece of work serenely situated beside the bay and a triumph of taste and proportion. On trips to Europe to scout for new circus talent, Ringling became obsessed with Baroque art and acquired more than five hundred Old Masters: a gathering now regarded as one of the finest collections of its kind in the US. To display the paintings, a spacious **museum** was built around a mock fifteenth-century Italian palazzo. As with Ca' d'Zan, the very concept seems absurdly pretentious but, like the house, it works: the architecture matches the art with great aplomb. Five enormous paintings by Rubens, commissioned in 1625, and the painter's subsequent *Portrait of Archduke Ferdinand*, are the highlights, though there's also a wealth of talent from Europe's leading schools of the mid-sixteenth to mid-eighteenth centuries. Free guided tours depart regularly from the entrance.

The Sarasota beaches

Increasingly the stamping ground of European package tourists spilling south from the St Petersburg beaches, the white sands of the **Sarasota beaches** are gradually losing much of their scenic appeal to towering condos. For all that, they're worth a day of anybody's time, with the two islands on which they lie, Lido Key and Siesta Key, accessible from the mainland. There is, however, no direct link between them. The third island, Longboat Key, is primarily residential.

The Ringling Causeway crosses the yacht-filled Sarasota Bay from the foot of Main Street to **Lido Key** and flows into **St Armand's Circle**, a roundabout ringed by upmarket shops and restaurants dotted with some of Ringling's replica classical statuary. Continuing south along Benjamin Franklin Drive you come to the island's most reachable beaches, ending after two miles at the more attractive **South Lido Park** (daily 8am–dusk; free), a belt of daz-zlingly bright sand beyond a large, grassy park.

The bulbous northerly section of tadpole-shaped **Siesta Key**, reached by Siesta Drive off US-41, about five miles south of downtown Sarasota, holds the bulk of the island's residents, with streets that twist around a network of canals. To escape the crowds at **Siesta Key Beach**, beside Ocean Beach Boulevard, continue south past Crescent Beach, and follow Midnight Pass Road for six miles to **Turtle Beach**, a small body of sand that has the island's only campground.

Practicalities

In downtown Sarasota, Greyhound **buses** stop at 575 N Washington Blvd (℡941/955-5735). The Amtrak bus from Tampa pulls up at the local bus ter-minal on Lemon Avenue, between First and Second. Catch the buses here for the Ringling house or the beaches. Call at the **visitor center**, 655 N Tamiani Trail (Mon–Sat 9am–5pm, Sun 11am–3pm; ℡941/957-1877 or 1-800/522-9799, ⊛www.sarasotafl.org), for discount coupons and leaflets.

On the mainland, **motels** run the length of US-41 (N Tamiani Trail) between the Ringling estate and downtown Sarasota, typically charging $40 to $60. Prices are higher at the beaches. Try the *Flamingo Colony Motel*, 4703 N Tamiani Trail (℡941/355-5135; ❸), or the *Lido Vacation Rentals* on Lido Key at 528 S Polk Drive (℡941/388-1004; ❹), which has friendly service and access to an Olympic-sized swimming pool.

Eating options along Main Street include the healthful salads, sandwiches and smoothies at *Nature's Way*, no. 1572 (℡941/954-3131), and excellent pizza at *Il Panificio*, no. 1703 (℡941/366-5570). *Café Kaldi*, no. 1568 (℡941/366-2326), is a hip coffee house with delicious pastries, internet facilities and live music some evenings. Opposite the Ringling Museum, the friendly *Café of the Arts*, 5230 N Tamiani Trail (℡941/351-4304), serves good European food for lunch and dinner.

Fort Myers

FORT MYERS, fifty miles south, may lack the élan of Sarasota, but it's nonetheless one of the up-and-coming communities of the southwest coast. Fortunately, most of its recent growth has occurred on the north side of the wide Caloosahatchee River, which the town straddles, allowing the tradition-al center, along the waterway's south shore, to remain relatively unspoiled.

Once across the river, US-41 strikes **downtown** Fort Myers, picturesquely nestled on the water's edge. Here, the **Fort Myers Historical Museum**, 2300 Peck St (Tues–Sat 9am–4pm; $2.50), provides thorough insights into the town's past, including the exploits of Dr Franklin Miles, the local man who developed Alka Seltzer.

In 1885, six years after inventing the light bulb, **Thomas Edison** collapsed from exhaustion and was instructed by his doctor to find a warm working environment or face an early death. Vacationing in Florida, the 37-year-old Edison bought fourteen acres of land on the banks of the Caloosahatchee and cleared a section of it to spend his remaining winters (he lived to be 84) at what became the **Edison Winter Home**, 2350 McGregor Blvd, a mile west of downtown (Mon–Sat 9am–5pm, Sun noon–5pm; guided tours every half-hour; $12; an extra $2 allows you entry into the Ford Winter Home, see oppo-site). The tours begin in the gardens, planted with such exotics as African

Sausage trees and wild orchids. The house (which you can glimpse only through the windows), though, is an anticlimax, its plainness probably due to the fact that Edison spent most of his waking hours inside the **laboratory**, attempting to turn the latex-rich sap of *Solidago edisonii* (a strain of goldenrod weed he developed) into rubber. However, when the tour reaches the engrossing **museum** the full impact of Edison's achievements becomes apparent: a design for an improved ticker-tape machine provided him with the funds for the experiments that led to the creation of the phonograph in 1877, and financed research that resulted in the incandescent light bulb. Here, too, you'll see some of the ungainly cinema projectors derived from Edison's Kinetoscope – which brought him a million dollars a year in royalties from 1907. Next door, the uninspiring **Ford Winter Home**, bought by Henry Ford in 1915, is open for viewing (tours as for Edison Home). The banyan tree outside the ticket office is the largest tree in the state, grown by Edison from a seedling.

The Fort Myers beaches

Still being discovered by the holidaying multitudes, the **Fort Myers beaches** on **Estero Island**, fifteen miles south of downtown, are appreciably different in character from the west coast's more commercialized beach strips, with a cheerful seaside mood. Accommodation is plentiful on and around Estero Boulevard – reached by San Carlos Boulevard, which runs the seven-mile length of the island. Most activity revolves around the short fishing pier and the **Lynne Hall Memorial Park**, at the island's north end.

Estero Island becomes increasingly residential as you press south, Estero Boulevard eventually swinging over a slender causeway onto the barely developed **San Carlos Island**. A few miles ahead, at the **Lovers Key State Recreation Area** (daily sunrise to sunset; $3.25 per carload, $1 for pedestrians and cyclists), a footpath picks a trail over a couple of mangrove-fringed islands and several mullet-filled creeks to **Lovers Key**, a secluded beach. If you don't fancy the walk, a free trolley will transport you between the park entrance and the beach.

The islands of **Sanibel** and **Captiva** are virtually impossible to visit unless you have a car and are reached only by crossing a causeway ($3 toll). However, if you have a spare day the islands offer a wildlife refuge, mangroves and shell-strewn beaches – for which the island is widely renowned. In contrast with the smooth beaches along the gulf side of Sanibel island, the opposite edge comprises shallow bays and creeks, and a vibrant wildlife habitat under the protection of the **J.N. "Ding" Darling National Wildlife Refuge** (daily except Fri sunrise–sunset; cars $5, cyclists and pedestrians $1; ☎941/472-1100). The main entrance and **information center** are just off the Sanibel–Captiva Road.

Practicalities

Greyhound is at 2275 Cleveland Ave; there are also daily Amtrak **buses** from Tampa. The **visitor center** is at Suite 100, 2180 W 1st St (Mon–Fri 8am–5pm; ☎941/338-3500 or 1-800/237-6444, ⊛www.fortmyers.com). Distances are large, and you'll struggle without a car, though it is possible – just – to reach the beaches on local LeeTran **buses** (☎941/275-8726 or 1-800/237-6444, ⊛www.lee-county.com), whose downtown terminal is at Monroe Avenue and MArtin Luther King Jr Boulevard.

Accommodation costs in and around Fort Myers are low between May and mid-December, when 40–50 percent gets lopped off the standard rates. In high season however, prices skyrocket and spare rooms are rare. **Downtown**, look along First Street – *Sea Chest*, no. 2571 (☎941/332-1545; ❷–❸), is among the cheapest. At the **beaches**, Estero Boulevard is your best bet: the *Beacon*, no. 1240 (℡941/463-5264; **❷**–**❺**), the *Gulf*, no. 2700 (℡941/463-9247; **❸**/**❹**), and *Laughing Gull*, no. 2890 (℡941/463-1346; three-night minimum; **❸**/**❹**), sometimes offer midweek discounts. Of all the **campgrounds**, only *Red Coconut*, 3001 Estero Blvd (℡941/463-7200), is an easy walk from the beach. For downtown **food**, try the *Casa De Guereto*, 2288 First Ave (℡941/332-4674), for excellent Mexican food from $9. At the beaches, sample the seafood at *Top O' The Mast*, 1028 Estero Blvd (℡941/463-9424), or the *Café de Monde*, 1740 Estero Blvd (℡941/463-8088), and the all-you-can-eat nightly specials at *The Reef*, 2601 Estero Blvd (℡941/463-4181).

The Everglades

Whatever scenic excitement you might anticipate from one of the country's more celebrated natural areas – whether you arrive west from Miami or south from Fort Myers, seventy miles along US-41 from either direction – there's nothing to herald your arrival in the **Everglades.** The most dramatic sights are small pockets of trees poking above a completely flat sawgrass plain, yet these wide-open spaces resonate with life, forming part of an ever-changing ecosystem, evolved through a unique combination of climate, vegetation and wildlife.

Appearing as flat as a table-top, the oolitic limestone on which the Everglades stand actually tilts very slightly towards the southwest. For thousands of years, water from summer storms and the overflow of nearby Lake Okeechobee has moved slowly through the Everglades towards the coast. The water replenishes the sawgrass, growing on a thin layer of soil formed by decaying vegetation, and gives birth to the algae at the foot of a complex food chain that sustains much larger creatures, most importantly **alligators**. After the floodwaters have reached the sea, drained through the bedrock or simply evaporated, the Everglades are barren except for the water accumulated in ponds – or "gator holes" – created when an alligator senses water and clears the soil covering it with its tail. Besides nourishing the alligator, the pond provides a home for other wildlife until the summer rains return. Sawgrass covers much of the Everglades, but where natural indentations in the limestone fill with soil, fertile tree islands – or "**hammocks**" – appear, just high enough to stand above the floodwaters.

Several **Native American tribes** once lived hunter-gatherer existences in the Everglades. The shell mounds they built can still be seen in sections of the park. In the nineteenth century, the Seminoles, fleeing white settlers from the north, also lived peaceably in the area. By the late 1800s, a few towns had sprung up, peopled by settlers who, unlike the Indians, looked to exploit the

Visitors and the environment

The activities of tourists can exacerbate the **environmental problems** in this fragile area. Airboat tours are synonymous with the Everglades, however, and many of the operators who tout rides along Hwy-41 are more concerned with profit than preservation; visitors are advised to seek out ranger-led trips instead (see opposite). The shortage of clean water is also a problem; much of it from the area is siphoned away to quench the thirst of urban areas such as Miami. Visitors therefore are requested to do all that they can to preserve water, such as not taking unnecessary baths or showers.

land. As Florida's population grew, the damage caused by hunting, road building and draining for farmland gave rise to a significant **conservation** lobby. In 1947, a section of the Everglades was declared a national park, but unrestrained commercial use of nearby areas continues to upset the Everglades' natural cycle. The 1500 miles of canals built to divert the flow of water away from the Everglades and toward the state's expanding cities, the poisoning caused by agricultural chemicals from local farmlands, and the broader changes wrought by global warming could yet turn Florida's greatest natural asset into a wasteland.

Everglades National Park

Throughout the last century the Everglades' boundaries were steadily pushed back by urban development, and **EVERGLADES NATIONAL PARK** bestows federal protection to only a comparatively small section around Florida's southeastern corner. In the park, the vital links holding the Everglades together become apparent: the all-important cycle of wet and dry seasons; the ability of alligators to discover water; the tree islands that provide sanctuaries for animals during the floods; and the forces, such as human demands for farmland and fresh water, that threaten to tear them apart.

Everglades City and around

Purchased and named in the 1920s by an advertising executive dreaming of a subtropical metropolis, **EVERGLADES CITY**, three miles south off US-41 along Route 29, now has a population of just under five hundred. Most who visit are solely intent on diminishing the stocks of sports fish living around the mangrove islands – the aptly titled **Ten Thousand Islands** – arranged like scattered jigsaw-puzzle pieces around the coastline.

For a closer look at the mangroves, which safeguard the Everglades from surge tides, take one of the park-sanctioned **boat trips**. Try either the Everglades National Boat Tours (☎941/695-2591), or Everglades Rentals and Eco Adventures (☎941/695-4666, ⓦwwwevergladesadventures.com), at the *Ivey House B&B* (see below). Trips leave from the dock on **Chokoloskee**, a blob of land – actually a Native American shell mound – marking the southern end of Route 29. The dockside **Gulf Coast visitor center** (daily 8.30am–5pm; ☎941/695-3311) provides details on the cruises and the excellent ranger-led **canoe trips**. In Chokoloskee, you can rent an RV by the night for \$50–70 at Outdoor Resorts (☎941/695-2881). In Everglades City try the charming and clean *Ivey House*, 107 Camellia St (☎941/695-3299, ⓦwwwiveyhouse.com; open Nov–April – booking advisable; ❷), or the eccentric *The Banks of the Everglades*, 201 W Broadway (☎941/695-3151, ⓦwww.banksoftheeverglades.com; ❷–❺), housed in what once was the first bank in Collier County.

Shark Valley

Driven out of central Florida by white settlers, several hundred Seminoles retreated to the Everglades during the nineteenth century, and their descendants – the **Miccosukees** – still live here, though the coming of US-41 brought a fundamental change in their lifestyle.

A mile east of the Miccosukee Indian Village, **Shark Valley** (daily 9am–5pm; \$5) epitomizes the Everglades' "River of Grass" tag. From here, dotted by hardwood hammocks, the sawgrass plain stretches as far as the eye can see. Aside from a few simple walking trails close to the **visitor center** (daily 8.30am–5.15pm, reduced hours during the summer; ☎305/221-8455), you can see Shark Valley only from a fifteen-mile loop road, ideally covered by renting a

bike ($3.25 per hour, return by 4pm). Alternatively, a highly informative two-hour **tram tour** (daily departures in summer; $9.50; reservations necessary March–July on ☎305/221-8455) stops frequently to view wildlife – but won't allow you to linger in any particular place, as you'll certainly want to do.

Flamingo

The **Flamingo** section of the park – at the end of the main park road and perched on Florida's southern tip – holds virtually everything that makes the Everglades tick: spend a day or two in this southerly portion of the park and you'll quickly grasp the fundamentals of its complex ecology. From the main **park entrance** (always open; cars $10, pedestrians and cyclists $5), the road passes the main **visitor center** in the Pine Island section of the park (daily 8am–5pm; ☎305/242-7700) and continues for 38 miles to the tiny coastal settlement of **FLAMINGO**, a former fishing colony now comprising a marina, hotel and campground. A century ago, the only way to get here was by boat – the place was so remote that it didn't even have a name until the opening of a post office made one necessary. Then "Flamingo" was chosen, supposedly because of the abundant roseate spoonbills – pink-plumed birds that the locals failed to identify correctly as they killed them for their feathers.

Flamingo now does a brisk trade servicing the needs of sports fishing enthusiasts. On land, the **visitor center** (summer daily 9am–5pm, but staffed intermittently; rest of year daily 7.30am–5pm; ☎941/695-2945) and the marina of the *Flamingo Lodge* (ⓦwww.flamingolodge.com), the park's only hotel, are the centers of activity. From the marina, the informative **Backcountry Cruise** ($16; reservations on ☎941/695-3101) makes a two-hour foray around the mangrove-enshrouded Whitewater Bay; the **Florida Bay Cruise** ($10; same number), a must for bird watchers, is a ninety-minute trip through the marine feeding and nursery grounds of Florida Bay.

Park practicalities

US–41 skirts the northern edge of the park, providing the only land access to the Everglades City and Shark Valley park entrances. To reach the Flamingo entrance, you'll need to touch the edge of Miami and head south. There's no **public transportation** along US–41, or to any of the park entrances. **Entering the park** is free at Everglades City, although you can travel only by boat or canoe. At Shark Valley it's $8 per car and $4 for pedestrians and cyclists; at the main entrance it's $10 and $5 respectively. Tickets are valid for seven days.

The park is **open all year**, but the most favorable time to visit is **winter** (Nov–April), when the receding floodwaters cause wildlife to congregate around gator holes, ranger-led activities are frequent and the mosquitoes are bearable. In **summer** (May–Oct), afternoon storms flood the prairies, park activities are substantially reduced and the mosquitoes are a severe annoyance. Visiting between seasons is also a good bet.

There are well-equipped **campgrounds** at Flamingo and Long Pine Key ($14) and many backcountry spots on the longer walking and canoe trails (permit $10 for up to six people). Spare space at Flamingo (which fills quickly) can be checked on the board just inside the park entrance. The only **rooms** within the park are at *Flamingo Lodge* (☎941/695-3101; ⓦwww.flamingolodge.com; ④–⑤); for winter stays, make reservations months in advance. Ten miles outside the park in Florida City, *The Everglades International Hostel*, 20 SW 2nd Ave (☎1-800/372-3874, ⓦwww.gladeshostel.com), may be the best option for budget-minded travelers who want to maximize their time in the park. Beds go for $13 a night and private rooms are available.

The Panhandle

Rubbing hard against Alabama in the west and Georgia in the north, the long, narrow **Panhandle** has much more in common with the states of the Deep South than with the rest of Florida, and city sophisticates have countless jokes lampooning the folksy lifestyles of the people here. Hard to credit, then, that just a century ago, the Panhandle was Florida. At the western edge, **Pensacola** was a busy port when Miami was still a swamp. Fertile soils lured wealthy plantation owners south and helped establish **Tallahassee** as a high-society gathering place and administrative center – a role which, as the state capital, it retains. But the decline of cotton, the chopping down of too many trees, and the coming of the East Coast railroad eventually left the Panhandle high and dry. Much of the inland region still seems neglected, and the **Apalachicola National Forest** is perhaps the best place in Florida to disappear into the wilderness. The **coastal Panhandle**, on the other hand, is enjoying better times and, despite rows of hotels, much is still untainted, with miles of blindingly white sands.

Tallahassee and around

State capital it may be, but **TALLAHASSEE** is a provincial city of oak trees and soft hills that won't take more than two days to explore in full. Around its small grid of central streets – where you'll find plenty of reminders of Florida's formative years – briefcase-clutching bureaucrats mingle with some of Florida State University's 250,000 students, who brighten the mood considerably and keep the city awake at night.

Though built on the site of an important prehistoric meeting place and taking its name from Apalachee Indian (*talwa* meaning "town", and *ahassee* meaning "old"), Tallahassee's **history** really began with Florida's incorporation into the US, and its selection as the state's administrative base – the local Native Americans, the Tamali tribe, being unceremoniously dispatched to make room for the trio of log cabins in which the first Florida government sat in 1823. The scene of every major wrangle in Florida politics – including the controversial ballot recount of the 2000 presidential election – Tallahassee has seen its fortunes hindered by the lightning-paced development of south Florida. Oddly distanced from most of the people it governs, the city has a slow tempo and a strong sense of the past – the city remains a conservative place.

Arrival, information and accommodation

The Greyhound **bus** terminal is at 112 S Tennessee St, within walking distance of downtown and opposite the local Taltran bus station (℡850/891-5200 or 1-800/955-8771; ⊛www.state.fl.us/citytlh/taltran/index.html). You can get a **free ride** into downtown Tallahassee from the bus station on the **Old Town Trolley**, which runs to the Civic Center (near the New Capitol Building) and back (every 20min Mon–Fri 7am–6pm). Otherwise, downtown Tallahassee is best seen on **foot**. For stacks of background information, visit the **Visitor Information Center**, 106 E Jefferson St (Mon–Fri 8am–5pm, Sat 9am–1pm, closed Sun; ℡1-800/628-2866, ⊛www.seetallahassee.com). **Accommodation** in Tallahassee is in short supply only during the sixty-day sitting of the state legislature from early April, and on fall weekends during home football games of the Florida State Seminoles. **Hotels** and **motels** on N Monroe Street, about three miles from downtown, are far cheaper than those downtown. To get out of the city altogether, consider the wonderful *Wakulla Springs Lodge*, fifteen miles to the south (see opposite).

Governors Inn 209 S Adams St ☎850/681-6855 or 1-800/342-7717. Every room in this splendid downtown inn is decorated with antique furniture reflecting the period of the governor each is named after. ❻—❽

Quality Inn 2020 Apalachee Parkway ☎850/877-4437. This recently renovated inn features bright and modern rooms and offers free evening cocktails. ❸

Super 8 2702 N Monroe St ☎850/386-8818 or 1-800/800-8000. A good option for the budget traveler, this motel offers simple rooms with basic amenities. ❷

The Town

A fifty-million-dollar eyesore dominates the square mile of **downtown Tallahassee** – the vertical vents of the towering **New Capitol Building**, at Apalachee Parkway and Monroe Street (Mon–Fri 8.30am–5pm; free). Florida's growing army of bureaucrats had previously been crammed into the 1845 **Old Capitol Building** (Mon–Fri 8am–5pm; free; ☎850/488-6167) that stands in the shadow of its replacement. For a more rounded history – easily the fullest account of Florida's past anywhere in the state – visit the **Museum of Florida History**, 500 S Bronough St (Mon–Fri 9am–4.30pm, Sat 10am–4.30pm, Sun noon–4.30pm; free). Detailed accounts of Paleo-Indian settlements, and the significance of their burial and temple mounds – some of which have been found on the edge of Tallahassee – are valuable tools in comprehending Florida's prehistory. The imperialist crusades of the Spanish are outlined with copious finds. There's little on the nineteenth-century Seminole Wars – one of the bloodier skeletons in Florida's closet – but plenty on the crucial c.1900 railroads.

It's well worth making the trip out to the **Florida A&M University** campus west of downtown, where the **Black Archives Research Center and Museum** (Mon–Fri 9am–4pm; free) holds one of the largest and most important collections of African-American artifacts in the nation, with oral histories and music stations, as well as an awe-inspiring group of Ethiopian crosses.

Eating

With so many politicos passing through, there's plenty of good food in Tallahassee; the presence of 47,000 students at its two universities keeps it affordable.

Andrew's Adams Street Café/Andrew's Second Act 228 S Adams St ☎850/222-3444. This stylish lunch spot has pricier gourmet evening meals and live jazz upstairs.

Barnacle Bill's 1830 N Monroe St ☎850/385-8734. Low-cost fresh fish and seafood are served in a riotous atmosphere.

Café Cabernet 1019 N Monroe St ☎850/224-1175. For light, inexpensive California-style eating, this café has the biggest wine selection in town. Live jazz can be heard here in the evening.

La Fiesta 911 Apalachee Parkway ☎850/656-3392. Try this eatery for the very best Mexican food in the city.

Mom and Dad's 4175 Apalachee Parkway ☎850/877-4518. Delicious homemade Italian food; dinner only.

Wakulla Springs State Park

Fifteen miles south of Tallahassee off SR-61 on SR-267, **Wakulla Springs State Park** (daily 8am–dusk; cars $3.25, pedestrians and cyclists $1.25) holds what is believed to be one of the biggest and deepest natural springs in the world. It pumps up half a million gallons of crystal-clear pure water from the bowels of the earth every day – though you'd never guess it from the calm surface.

It's refreshing to **swim** in the cool pool (in a small roped-off area – this is gator territory), but to learn more about the spring, take the thirty-minute **glass-bottom boat tour** ($4.50), and peer down to the swarms of fish hovering around the 180ft cavern through which the water comes. Forty-minute **river cruises** ($4.50) let you glimpse some of the park's inhabitants: deer, turkeys, turtles, herons, egrets and the inevitable alligators. The lovely wooden *Wakulla Springs Lodge* (☎904/224-5950; ❹–❺) is a serene 1930s hotel, with an excellent **restaurant** (call to reserve) serving home-baked country food, and a marble-topped soda fountain for sandwiches and coffee.

The Apalachicola National Forest

With swamps, savannahs and springs dotted liberally about its half-million acres, the **Apalachicola National Forest** is the inland Panhandle at its natural best. Several roads enable you to drive through a good-sized chunk, with many undemanding spots for a rest and a snack. To see deeper into the forest you'll need to make an effort: exploring at length, following one of the hiking trails, canoeing on one of the rivers, or simply spending a night under the stars at one of the basic campgrounds. Driving through the forest on Hwy-65, or around it on Hwy-319, you'll eventually pass the large and forbidding **Tate's Hell Swamp**. This is a breeding ground for the deadly water moccasin snake, and though gung-ho locals sometimes venture in hoping to catch a few to sell to zoos, you're well advised to stay clear.

The main **entrances** to the forest are off Hwy-20 and Hwy-319; three minor roads, routes 267, 375 and 65, form cross-forest links between the two. **Accommodation** is limited to camping; apart from Silver Lake (nine miles west of Tallahassee; $4), all the campgrounds are free, with very basic facilities (no running water). For more information call the **ranger stations** at Apalachicola (☎850/643-2282) or Wakulla (☎850/926-3561).

Panama City Beach

Follow Hwy-98 fifty miles west from Apalachicola and you'll hit the orgy of motels, go-kart tracks, mini-golf courses and amusement parks that is **PANAMA CITY BEACH**. This beach is entirely without pretension, but it capitalizes blatantly on the appeal of its 27-mile stretch of white sand. The whole place is as commercial as can be, but with the shops, bars and restaurants all trying to undercut one another, there are some great bargains to be found. That said, throughout the lively summer (the so-called 100 Magic Days), accommodation costs are high and bookings essential. In winter, prices drop and visitors are fewer; most are Canadians and – increasingly – Europeans, many of whom have no problems sunbathing and swimming in the cool temperatures.

Getting a tan, running yourself ragged at beach sports and going hammer-and-tongs at the nightlife are the main concerns in Panama City Beach. If you get restless, try go-karting, jet-skiing or parasailing; otherwise, visit one of the amusement parks (usually $18 for a go-on-everything day ticket) or go on a fishing trip (from around $30 a day). For scuba-divers, several explorable shipwrecks litter the area; get details from any of the numerous dive shops.

Practicalities

Places to stay, while plentiful, fill with amazing speed, especially at weekends. As a general rule, **motels** at the east end of the beach are smarter and slightly pricier than those in the center. Those at the west end are quiet and family oriented. The *Sugar Sands Motel*, 20723 Front Beach Rd (℡1-800/367-9221, ⓦwww.sugarsands.com; ❸–❹), is an excellent-value oceanfront motel away from the noise. The cheapest places to eat are the buffet restaurants on Front Beach Road, which charge $5–10 for all you can manage. Or, try one of the regular **lunch or dinner** restaurants: *Shuckum's Oyster Pub & Seafood Grill*, 15618 W Hwy-98 (℡850/235-3214); *Mike's Diner*, 17554 Front Beach Rd (℡850/234-1942), also open for breakfast and serving tasty Southern-style food; or *The Treasure Ship*, 3605 Thomas Drive (℡850/234-8881), a seafood restaurant that looks like a wooden sailing ship.

Pensacola

You might be inclined to overlook **PENSACOLA**, tucked away as it is at the west end of the Panhandle. The city, on the northern bank of the broad Pensacola Bay, is five miles inland from the nearest beaches, and its prime features are a naval aviation school and some busy dockyards. Pensacola is, however, worth a visit – its white beaches are relatively untouched, and it is an historic center: occupied by the Spanish from 1559. Only the hurricane two years later that ended their settlement prevented it becoming the oldest city in the US. It repeatedly changed hands among the Spanish, French and British before becoming the place where Florida was officially ceded by Spain to the US in 1821.

Pensacola was already a booming port by c.1900, when the opening of the Panama Canal was expected to boost its fortunes still further. The many new buildings that appeared in the **Palafox District**, around the southerly section of Palafox Street, in the early 1900s – with their delicate ornamentation and attention to detail – reflect the optimism of the era. Between 1870 and 1930, Pensacola's professional classes took a shine to the area called **North Hill**, just across Wright Street from Palafox, commissioning elaborate homes in a plethora of fancy styles. Strewn across the fifty-block area are Neoclassical porches, Tudor Revival cottages, low-slung California bungalows, and the rounded towers of the finest Queen Anne homes. Though none is open to the public, you can see them on special tours (see below).

In earlier times, Native Americans, pioneer settlers and seafaring traders had gathered to swap, sell and barter on the waterfront of the **Seville District**, about half a mile east of Palafox Street. Those who did well took up permanent residence, and many of their homes remain in fine states of repair, forming – together with several museums – the **Historic Pensacola Village** (Tues–Sat 10am–4pm; $6). Each ticket is valid for two days and allows access to all of the museums and former homes in an easily navigated four-block area. Inside the US naval base on Navy Boulevard, about eight miles southwest of central Pensacola, the **Museum of Naval Aviation** exhibits US naval aircraft. They range from the first flimsy seaplane acquired in 1911 to the Phantoms and Hornets of more recent times (daily 9am–5pm; free, IMAX $5.50; ℡1-800/247-6289, ⓦwww.naval-air.org).

Santa Rosa Island

On the other (east) side of the bay from the city lie Pensacola's real attractions: the glistening beaches and windswept sand dunes of **Santa Rosa Island** (the barrier island that runs sixty miles from Fort Walton). **Pensacola Beach** in particular has everything you'd want from a Gulf Coast beach: mile after mile of fine white sands, water sports rental outlets, a busy fishing pier and a sprinkling of motels, beachside bars and snack stands. A short way west, at the **Gulf Islands National Seashore**, on Fort Pickens Road (9am–dusk; cars $4, pedestrians and cyclists $2), vibrant white sands are walled by a nine–mile–long stretch of high, rugged dunes, and the only reminder of civilization is a foliage-encircled campground.

Practicalities

The Greyhound station is seven miles north of the city center at 505 W Burgess Rd; bus #10 links it to Pensacola proper. Pensacola is a stop on Amtrak's *Sunset Limited* to LA; the **train station** is at 980 E Heinberg St. Local **taxi** firms include Yellow Cab (⊕904/433-3333). ECAT **buses** serve the city but not the beach; the main terminal is at 1515 W Fairfield Drive (⊕850/595-3228, ⓦwww.ecat.pensacola.com).

At the foot of the three-mile Pensacola Bay Bridge into the city (on the city side), the **visitor center**, at 1401 E Gregory St (daily 8am–5pm; ⊕1-800/874-1234, ⓦwww.visitpensacola.com), has the usual worthwhile handouts. Plenty of budget chain **hotels**, charging $30–50 per night, line N Davis and Pensacola boulevards, the main approach roads from I-10. Central options are the *Seville Inn*, 223 E Garden St (⊕1-800/277-7275; ❷), and *Days Inn*, 710 N Palafox St (⊕904/438-4922; ❸). At the beach try along Via De Luna Drive: the airy *Hampton Inn*, no. 2 (⊕850/932-6800, ⓦwww.hamptonbeachresort.com; ❺), offers great value.

For **eating** in town, try *McGuire's Irish Pub*, 600 E Gregory St (⊕850/433-6789); it serves up hearty portions and home-brewed ale. For beachside dining, at the *Great Brit Inn*, 49 Via De Luna Drive (⊕850/916-1288), get standard pub fare while gazing at the front ends of a Triumph TR6, a white MG and an old Jag that jut from the walls.

CHAPTER 8

Highlights

* **Jackson Square, New Orleans** The heart of the French Quarter, where you can enjoy some of the world's best brass band and jazz music – for free. See p.686

* **Sunset over the Mississippi, New Orleans** Settle yourself down on a wooden bench and watch the sky turn violet over one of the world's great rivers. See p.693

* **Uglesich's** The best seafood in the world dished up in a down-home New Orleans shack. See p.697

* **Napoleon House, New Orleans** This gorgeous old bar is just the place to pass a steamy New Orleans night. See p.699

* **Southwest Louisiana Zydeco Festival, Plaisance** The very best in black Cajun music, food, arts and crafts in the heart of Cajun country. See p.708

* **Eunice** Welcoming little Cajun prairie town that's at the heart of the region's enduring music scene. See p.712

* **Swamp tours in Cajun Country** Local guides take you in small boats through ghostly, Spanish moss-shaded bayous. See p.712

8

Louisiana

Swathed in the romance of pirates, voodoo and Mardi Gras, **LOUISIANA** is undeniably special. Its history is barely on nodding terms with the view that America was the creation of the Pilgrim Fathers; its way of life is proudly set apart. This is the land of the rural, French-speaking **Cajuns** (descended from the Acadians, eighteenth-century French-Canadian refugees), who live in the prairies and swamps in the southwest of the state, and the Creoles of jazzy, sassy **New Orleans**. (The term **Creole** was originally used to define anyone born in the state to French or Spanish colonists – famed in the nineteenth century for their masked balls, family feuds and duels – as well as native-born, French–speaking slaves, but has since come to define anyone or anything native to Louisiana, and in particular its black population.) Louisiana's spicy home-cooked **food**, regular **festivals** and lilting French-based dialect – and above all its **music** (jazz, **R&B**, **Cajun** and its bluesy black counterpart, zydeco) – draw from all these cultures. Oddly enough, **north Louisiana** – Protestant Bible Belt country, where old plantation homes stand decaying in vast cottonfields – feels more "Southern" than the marshy bayous, shaded by ancient cypress trees and laced with wispy trails of Spanish moss, of the Catholic south of the state.

The **French** first settled Louisiana in 1682, braving swamps and plagues to harvest the abundant cypress, but the state was sparsely inhabited before its first permanent settlement, the trading post of **Natchitoches**, was established in 1714. In 1760, Louis XV secretly handed all French territory west of the Mississippi, to his **Spanish** cousin, Charles III, as a safeguard against the British. Louisiana remained Spanish until it was ceded to Napoleon in 1801, under the proviso that it should never change hands again. Just two years later, however, Napoleon, strapped for cash to fund his battles with the British in Europe, struck a bargain with president Thomas Jefferson known as the **Louisiana Purchase**. This sneaky agreement handed over to the US all French lands between Canada and Mexico, from the Mississippi to the Rockies, for a total cost of $15 million. The subsequent "Americanization" of Louisiana was one of the most momentous periods in the state's history, with the port of New Orleans, in its key position near the mouth of the **Mississippi River**, growing to become one of the nation's wealthiest cities. Though the state seceded from the Union to join the Confederacy in 1861, there were important differences between Louisiana and the rest of the slave-driven South. The **Black Code**, drawn up by the French in 1685 to govern Saint-Domingue (today's Haiti) and established in Louisiana in 1724, had given slaves rights unparalleled elsewhere, including permission to marry, meet socially and take Sundays off. The black population of New Orleans in particular was

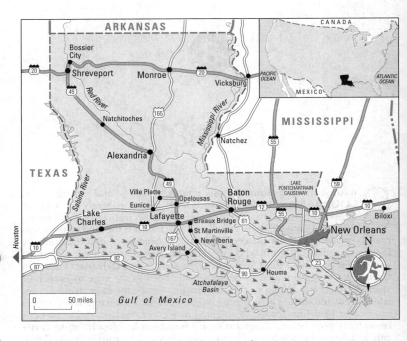

renowned as exceptionally literate and cosmopolitan.

Though Louisiana was not physically scarred by the Civil War, with few important battles fought on its soil, its economy was ravaged, and its social structures all but destroyed. The **Reconstruction** era, too, hit particularly hard here, with the once great city of New Orleans suffering a period of unprecedented lawlessness and racial violence. In time the economy, at least, recovered, benefiting from the key importance of the mighty Mississippi River and the discovery of offshore oil, but over the last century Louisiana has come to rely more and more heavily upon **tourism**, centered around New Orleans and Cajun country. And it's not hard to see why: whether canoeing along a moss-tangled bayou, dining in a crumbling Creole cottage on spicy, buttery crawfish, or dancing on a steamy starlit night to the best live music in the world, few visitors fail to fall in love with Louisiana.

Getting around Louisiana

Louisiana is crossed east–west by two major **interstates**, I-20 in the north and I-10 in the south. New Orleans is the hub, traversed by I-10 and served by I-55 and I-59 from Mississippi. I-49 sweeps across southeast to northwest, connecting Cajun country with the north.

The international **airport** is in New Orleans; regional airlines serve the rest of the state and surrounding areas. Amtrak **trains** link New Orleans with New York, Chicago and Memphis, and Los Angeles via Lafayette. Greyhound **buses** connect the major towns with the rest of the country, and are supplemented by smaller local lines. In addition to the Mississippi's bridges and causeways, **ferries** cross the river at New Orleans, St Francisville in Cajun country, and at various points along the River Road to Baton Rouge.

New Orleans

There's a lot more to **NEW ORLEANS** – the "Big Easy," the "city that care forgot" – than its tourist image as a nonstop party town. At once sordid and sublime, it careers along under an infuriating doublethink. While having enormous amounts of fun, you're liable to be repeatedly struck by the divisions between rich and poor (and, more explicitly, between white and black). Even so, the city's vitality and *joie de vivre* are real, buffeted but not beaten by the vagaries of commercialism and poverty. The melange of cultures and races that built the city still gives it its heart; not "easy," exactly, but quite unlike anywhere else in the States – or the world.

New Orleans began life in 1718 as a **French–Canadian** outpost, an unlikely set of shacks on a disease-ridden marsh. Its prime location near the mouth of the **Mississippi River**, however, led to rapid development, and with the first mass importation of African **slaves**, as early as the 1720s, its unique demography began to take shape. Despite early resistance from its Francophone population, the city benefited greatly from its period as a **Spanish** colony between 1763 and 1800. By the end of the eighteenth century, the **port** was flourishing, the haunt of smugglers, gamblers, prostitutes and pirates. Newcomers included Anglo-Americans escaping the American Revolution and aristocrats fleeing revolution in France. The city also became a haven for refugees – whites and free blacks, along with their slaves – escaping the slave revolts in Saint-Domingue. As in the West Indies, the Spanish, French and free people of color associated and formed alliances to create a distinctive **Creole** culture with its own traditions and ways of life, its own patois, and a cuisine that drew influences from Africa, Europe and the colonies. New Orleans was already a many-textured city when it experienced two quick-fire changes of government, passing back into French control in 1801 and then being sold to **America** under the Louisiana Purchase two years later. Unwelcome in the Creole city – today's French Quarter – the Americans who migrated here were forced to settle in the areas now known as the **Central Business District** (or **CBD**) and, later, in the **Garden District**. Canal Street, which divided the old city from the expanding suburbs, became known as "the neutral ground" – the name still used when referring to the median strip between main roads in New Orleans.

Though much has been made of the antipathy between Creoles and Anglo-Americans, in truth economic necessity forced them to live and work together. They fought side by side, too, in the 1815 **Battle of New Orleans**, the final battle of the War of 1812, which secured American supremacy in the States. The victorious general, **Andrew Jackson**, became a national hero – and eventually US president; his ragbag volunteer army was made up of Anglo-Americans, slaves, Creoles, free men of color and Native Americans, along with pirates supplied by the notorious buccaneer **Jean Lafitte**.

New Orleans' antebellum "**golden age**" as a major port and finance center for the cotton-producing South was brought to an abrupt end by the Civil War. The economic blow wielded by the lengthy Union occupation – which effectively isolated the city from its markets – was compounded by the social and cultural ravages of **Reconstruction**. This was particularly disastrous for a city once famed for its large, educated, free black population. As the North industrialized and other Southern cities grew, the fortunes of New Orleans took a downturn.

Jazz exploded into the bars and the bordellos around 1900, and, along with the evolution of **Mardi Gras** as a tourist attraction, breathed new life into the city. And although the Depression hit here as hard as it did the rest of the nation it also, spearheaded by a number of local writers and artists, heralded the resurgence of the **French Quarter**, which had disintegrated into a slum. Even so, it was the less romantic duo of **oil** and **petrochemicals** that really saved the economy – until the slump of the 1950s pushed New Orleans well behind other US cities. The oil crash of the early 1980s gave it yet another battering, a gloomy start for near on two decades of high crime rates, crack deaths and widespread corruption, but by the end of the century the tide had begun to turn, and the city now finds itself in relatively stable condition with a strengthening economy based on **tourism**.

Arrival, information and getting around

Louis Armstrong New Orleans International Airport, eighteen miles northwest on I-10, has an information booth (8am–9pm) in its baggage claim area. Flat-rate **taxi** fares into town are $24 for up to two people, $10 each for three or more, and **shuttles** (T504/592-0555) will take you to your hotel (every 10min; tickets available 24hr in the baggage claim area or from the bus driver; $10 to downtown hotels). There's also a **public bus** from the airport to Tulane Avenue in the CBD (daily 6am–6.30pm; every 15–25min; $1.50), but it holds carry-on luggage only. **Greyhound** buses arrive next to **Amtrak** at the Union Passenger Terminal, 1001 Loyola Ave, near the Superdome. This area, in the no-man's-land beneath the elevated Pontchartrain Expressway, is dangerous at night; take a **cab** to your lodgings. United Cabs is by far the best firm (T504/522-9771).

Information

Before you leave home, it's worth contacting the **New Orleans CVB** (T1-800/672-6124, W www.neworleanscvb.com); they mail out stacks of glossy brochures, and the website features some useful downloadable discount coupons. Once you've arrived, the best information, including self-guided walking tours, free **maps** and a variety of discount vouchers can be found at the **Welcome Center**, on Jackson Square at 529 St Ann St in the French Quarter (daily 9am–5pm; T504/566-5031).

The **post office** is at 701 Loyola Ave (Mon–Fri 7am–11pm, Sat 7am–8pm, Sun noon–5pm; zip code 70140); an equivalent service, along with fax, FedEx, photocopying and phone rental, is offered by the French Quarter Postal Emporium, 1000 Bourbon St (Mon–Fri 9.30am–6pm, Sat 10am–3pm; T504/525-6652).

Staying safe

Although the heavily touristed French Quarter is comparatively safe, to wander unwittingly beyond it – even just a couple of blocks – can place your **personal safety** in serious jeopardy. Be careful, and at night always take a cab when traveling any distance outside the Quarter.

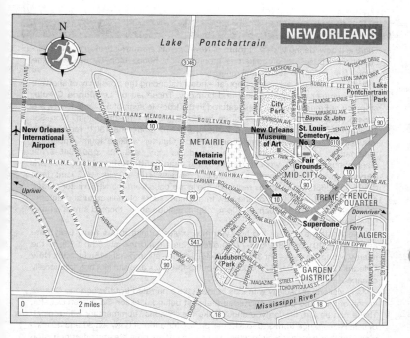

N

Lake Pontchartrain

NEW ORLEANS

New Orleans
International
Airport

Upriver

Downriver

LOUISIANA | New Orleans

8

0   2 miles

City transportation

Though New Orleans' most visited neighborhoods are a dream to **walk** around, getting from one to another is not always easy on foot, and if you're traveling anywhere outside the Quarter after dark you'd be better off calling a **cab**. The Regional Transit Authority (RTA) runs a network of **buses** ($1.25, exact fare required; 24hr information ☎504/248-3900). The most useful **routes** include "Magazine" (#11), which runs from Canal Street in the CBD to Audubon Park; and "Esplanade" (#48) from the edge of the Quarter up to City Park. You're more likely to use the handsome **St Charles streetcar** (a National Historic Monument, dating back around 100 years) that rumbles a thirteen-mile loop from Canal Street, along St Charles Avenue in the Garden District, past Audubon Park to Carrollton uptown ($1.25 each way; 25¢ transfers; exact fare). The cars trundle along at an average speed of 9mph; it takes about 45 minutes for a full one-way trip. Though the streetcar runs around the clock, services fall off after dark. There's a newer streetcar along the **riverfront**, where trolleys make ten stops between the Convention Center and Esplanade Avenue (Mon–Fri 6am–11pm, Sat & Sun 7am–11pm; every 15min; $1.50; exact fare). It's a total trip of less than two miles, however, and of most interest for its pretty river views. VisiTour **passes**, available from the welcome center and most major hotels, give unlimited travel on all streetcars and buses ($5 per day, $12 for three consecutive days).

There is a bewildering variety of **tours** of New Orleans, from whistlestop jaunts in air-conditioned buses to preposterous moonlit ghost-hunts; stop by the Welcome Center (see p.680) to see the full range.

Walking tours are especially popular – notwithstanding the possibility of showers and, in summer, debilitating heat and humidity. Those led by **Le Monde Creole**, stopping at French Quarter sites featured in the true-life saga of a Creole family, are superb. They set off from their store at 624 Royal St (2hr–2hr 30min; Mon–Sat 10.30am & 2.30pm, Sun 10am & 2.30pm; $17.50; ☎504/568-1801; reservations required). The **Bienville Foundation**'s French Quarter walking tours emphasize "alternative" history (2hr–2hr 30min; schedules vary; $18–20; ☎504/945-6789; reservations essential), while those led by the **Jean Lafitte National Historic Park Service** give scholarly and accessible overviews (1hr 30min; 10.30am; free; ☎504/589-2636; reservations required). Collect a pass from the NPS visitor center, 419 Decatur St, after 9am on the day. In addition, some of their cultural programs (30–45min; 9.30am, 11.30am, 1.30pm & 3pm) include short, themed strolls around the Quarter (see p.686).

If the weather's bad, or too hot, you may prefer to take a **bus tour**. Gray Line (☎504/569-1401 or 1-800/535-7786) offers trips around the city (2hr; $23), to the nearby plantations (4hr–7hr 30min; $33–45), and the swamps (3hr 15min; $38). **New Orleans Tours** (☎504/592-0560 or 1-800/543-6332) are similar, but fractionally cheaper.

Many visitors, especially with kids in tow, take a narrated trot through the Quarter in one of the **mule-drawn carriages** that wait behind Jackson Square on Decatur. These can be fun, though you should take the "historic" commentary with a pinch of salt. Rates range from $10 to $12 per person for a trip of between 30 and 45 minutes. Another pleasant way to while away a few hours on a steamy afternoon is on a **river cruise**. The *Natchez* steamboat is by far the best. Leaving from behind Jackson Brewery, it heads seven miles or so downriver before turning back near the Chalmette battlefield (2hr; daily 11.30am & 2.30pm; $15.75 or $21.75 with lunch and live jazz; ☎504/586-8777). The *John James Audubon* riverboat allows you to combine a cruise with a trip to the aquarium (see p.693) or the zoo (p.695), or both. It leaves daily from the aquarium at 10am, noon, 2pm and 4pm, and from the zoo an hour later (1hr one-way; $11.75 one-way, $14.50 round-trip, children half-price; ☎504/586-8777). The only boat that stops at Chalmette, site of the Battle of New Orleans, is the *Creole Queen* (10.30am & 2pm; 2hr 30min; $16, $22 with lunch; ☎504/524-0814), which leaves from the Plaza d'España. Tickets for all cruises are sold at booths behind Jackson Brewery and the aquarium.

For details on **ghost**, **voodoo** and **cemetery tours**, see p.689.

Accommodation

New Orleans has some fantastic **places to stay**, from rambling old guesthouses seeping faded grandeur to swanky tower hotels. **Room rates**, never low (you'll be pushed to find anything half decent for less than $50), increase considerably for Mardi Gras, Jazz Fest and the Sugar Bowl, when prices can go up by as much as 200 percent and rooms are booked months in advance. This is not a city in which you want to be stranded without a room, and though it's possible to take a chance on last-minute cancellations and deals, you should ideally make **reservations**. If you do turn up on spec, head immediately for the **Welcome Center** (see p.680), where you'll find racks of **discount leaflets** offering savings on same-day bookings (weekdays only).

△ Louisiana swamp

Most people choose to stay in the **French Quarter**, in the heart of things. Many accommodations here are in atmospheric **guesthouses**, most of them in old Creole townhouses. Outside the Quarter, the **Lower Garden District** offers budget options near the streetcar line, while the funky **Faubourg Marigny** specializes in bed and breakfasts and the **Garden District** proper has a couple of gorgeous old hotels. The **CBD** is the domain of the city's upmarket chain hotels, catering mostly to conventioneers.

French Quarter

Biscuit Palace 730 Dumaine St ☎504/525-9949, ⓦ www.biscuit-palace.com. Atmospheric, friendly and individualistic hotel, housed in an 1820 mansion with a flagstoned courtyard, fishpond and tropical plants. Characterful rooms, many of them suites, with balconies and antique baths. ❺

Chateau Hotel 1001 Chartres St ☎504/524-9636, ⓦ www.chateauhotel.com. Simple, clean rooms in the quieter part of the Quarter. Some are better than others, so if you feel yours is too small or a bit dark, check to see what else is available. There's an outdoor café-bar by the pool, and rates include continental breakfast. ❺

A Creole House 1013 St Ann St ☎504/524-8076, ⓦ www.acreolehouse.com. Unfussy guesthouse,

bordering on shabby in places, with rooms ranging from cozy nooks with shared bath to antique-filled suites. Rates include continental breakfast. ❸–❻

Dauphine Orleans 415 Dauphine St ☎504/586-1800 or 1-800/508-5554, ⓦ www.dauphineorleans.com. Gorgeous upmarket hotel with rooms in restored brick cottages around tranquil, lush courtyards. There's a pool, cozy bar, library and fitness room; rates include breakfast and afternoon tea. ❻

Olivier House 828 Toulouse St ☎504/525-8456. Though a bit dark in places, this atmospheric, rambling Creole house offers good value. The 42 rooms (all with bath) vary, but most have funky antique furniture and shuttered windows; room 112 has its own garden and fountain. There's a tropical courtyard, and a tiny pool. ❺–❽

Hotel Provincial 1024 Chartres St ☎504/581-4995 or 1-800/535-7922, ⓦwww.hotelprovincial.com. This sprawling – yet somehow intimate and relaxed – place is set in a quiet part of the Quarter, with antique-filled rooms opening onto peaceful, gaslit courtyards. Has two outdoor pools and a bar. ❺

Rue Royal Inn 1006 Royal St ☎504/524-3900 or 1-800/776-3901, ⓦwww.rueroyalinn.com. Good-value, gay-friendly hotel. The enormous, brick-walled, high-ceilinged rooms easily sleep four, and all have bath, fridge and minibar. Rates include continental breakfast, which you can eat in the courtyard. ❹

Outside the French Quarter

Columns Hotel 3811 St Charles Ave ☎504/899-9308, ⓦwww.thecolumns.com. Wonderfully louche Garden District hotel and bar (see p.699) in an 1883 mansion. Characterful rooms; some come with bath and balcony, but no TVs. Complimentary continental breakfast. Rates increase by 200 percent at Mardi Gras. ❺–❽

The Frenchmen 417 Frenchmen St ☎504/948-2166 or 1-800/365-2275, ⓦwww.acreolehouse.com/frenchmen.html. Gay-friendly Faubourg Marigny B&B with 25 rooms spread across two 1860 townhouses, overlooking a tropical patio. There's a small pool on site and a jacuzzi. Rates include breakfast. ❹–❻

HI-New Orleans Marquette House 2253 Carondelet St ☎504/523-3014, ⓦwww.hiayh.org/hostels/louisiana/neworl.htm. Official hostel a block from the streetcar near the Garden District. Dorm beds go for $17–21; there are doubles and apartments, a few with kitchens, in a separate building. Day use allowed and no curfew. Reservations recommended. ❶–❸

India House Hostel 124 S Lopez St ☎504/821-1904, ⓦwww.indiahousehostel.com. Funky backpackers' hostel well off the beaten track in Mid-City. Owned and run by keen travelers, it's the friendliest, and booziest, of the city's hostels, with regular pool parties and two pet alligators in the back yard. Dorm beds $14, plus a few basic rooms with shared bath for around twice the price. The area isn't great at night. ❶

La Salle Hotel 1113 Canal St ☎504/523-5831 or 1-800/521-9450, ⓦwww.lasallehotelneworleans.com. Reliable, popular budget option in the CBD near the Quarter. Few frills, just plain rooms – some with bath – free coffee and daily papers. The area, on the fringes of Tremé, can feel unsafe at night. ❷–❹

Maginnis Mansion 2127 Prytania St ☎504/566-1515, ⓦwww.henryhowardinn.com/mmansion.html. Budget accommodation in a Greek Revival mansion in the Lower Garden District. Rooms with private bath are good value, but standards vary, so if you're not happy with yours, ask to see something else. Full breakfast is served at the *Henry Howard Inn*, a sister property next door, where there are more rooms (not as nice) and a TV lounge. ❷

Royal Street Inn 1431 Royal St ☎504/948-7499 or 1-800/449-5535, ⓦwww.royalstreetinn.com. Hip Faubourg Marigny lodging above the funky *R-Bar* (see p.699), and run by the same people. The five rooms (all with bath) are decorated on themes ranging from Art Deco to bordello; the four-person suites are good value. It's favored by a young crowd who hang out in the bar; rates include two drinks per night. ❹–❻

St Charles Guest House 1748 Prytania St ☎504/523-6556, ⓦwww.stcharlesguesthouse.com. Bohemian Lower Garden District guesthouse offering a variety of rooms, none with phone or TV. Backpackers choose the basic 6ft by 8ft "cabins" for $35, but for the pricier en-suite doubles you can get better value elsewhere. It's friendly enough, though, with a pool and free breakfast. They give student discounts, but ask for deposits with reservations. No smoking. ❷–❹

St Vincent's Guest House 1507 Magazine St ☎504/566-1515, ⓦwww.stvincentsguesthouse.com. Lower Garden District lodging, run by the same people as the *Maginnis Mansion*, with more than seventy budget rooms in a huge 1861 orphanage. The atmosphere is cheery, if institutional, and there's a small pool. ❸

The City

One of New Orleans' many nicknames is "the **Crescent City**," because of the way it nestles between the southern shore of Lake Pontchartrain and a dramatic horseshoe bend in the Mississippi River. This unique location makes the city's layout confusing, with streets curving to follow the river, and shooting off at odd angles to head inland. Compass points are of little use here – locals refer instead to **lakeside** (towards the lake) and **riverside** (towards the river), and, using Canal Street as the dividing line, **uptown** (or upriver) and **downtown** (downriver).

Most visitors spend most time in the battered, charming old **French Quarter** (or *Vieux Carré*), site of the original settlement. On its fringes, the funky **Faubourg Marigny** creeps northeast from Esplanade Avenue, while the Quarter's lakeside boundary, **Rampart Street**, marks the beginning of the historic, run-down African-American neighborhood of **Tremé**. On the other side of the Quarter, across **Canal Street**, the **CBD** (Central Business District), bounded by the river and I-10, spreads upriver to the Pontchartrain Expressway. Dominated by offices, hotels and banks, it also incorporates the revitalizing **Warehouse District** and, towards the lake, the gargantuan **Superdome**. A ferry ride across the river from the foot of Canal Street takes you to the suburban west bank and the residential district of old **Algiers**.

Back on the east bank, it's an easy journey upriver from the CBD to the rare-fied **Garden District**, an area of gorgeous old mansions, some of them in delectable ruin. The **Lower Garden District**, creeping between the expressway and Jackson, is quite a different creature, its run-down old houses filled with impoverished artists and musicians. The best way to get to either neighborhood is on the streetcar along swanky **St Charles Avenue**, the Garden District's lakeside boundary; you can also approach it from **Magazine Street**, a six-mile stretch of galleries and antique stores that runs parallel to St Charles riverside. Entering the Garden District, you've crossed the official boundary into **uptown**, which spreads upriver to encompass **Audubon Park and Zoo**.

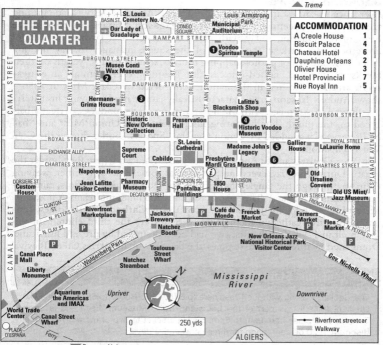

The French Quarter

The heartbreakingly beautiful **French Quarter** is where New Orleans began in 1718. Today, battered and bohemian, decaying and vibrant, it's the spiritual core of the city, its fanciful cast-iron balconies, hidden courtyards and time-stained stucco buildings exerting a haunting fascination that has long caught the imagination of artists and writers. Official tours are useful for orientation, but it's most fun simply to wander – and you'll need a couple of days at least to do it justice, absorbing the jumble of sounds, sights and smells. Early morning, in the pearly light from the river, is a good time to explore, as sleepy locals wake themselves up with strong coffee in the neighborhood patisseries, shops crank open their shutters and all-night revelers stumble home.

The Quarter is laid out in a grid, unchanged since 1721. At just thirteen blocks wide – smaller than you might expect – it's easily walkable, bounded by the Mississippi River, Rampart Street, Canal Street and Esplanade Avenue, and centering on lively **Jackson Square**. Rather than French, the famed **architecture** is predominantly Spanish colonial, with a strong Caribbean influence. Most of the buildings date from the late eighteenth century, after much of the old city had been devastated by fires in 1788 and 1794. **Commercial activity** – shops, galleries, restaurants, bars – is concentrated in the blocks between Decatur and Bourbon. Beyond Bourbon, up towards Rampart Street, and in the Lower Quarter, downriver from Jackson Square, things become more peaceful – quiet, predominantly residential neighborhoods where the Quarter's **gay** community lives side by side with elegant dowagers and scruffy artists.

Jackson Square

Ever since its earliest incarnation as the Place d'Armes, a dusty parade ground used for public meetings and executions, **Jackson Square** has been at the heart of the Quarter. Today, with its iron benches, neat lawns and blaze of flowerbeds, the park at the centre of the square manages to stay tranquil despite the streams of photo-snapping tourists, school groups, waiters on their breaks and the odd crashed-out casualty. Presiding over them all, an **equestrian statue** – the first in the nation, constructed by Clark Mills in 1856 – shows Andrew Jackson in uncharacteristically jaunty mode, waving his hat. It's a sculptural masterpiece, with the horse, rearing on its hind legs, perfectly balanced on the plinth. The hectoring inscription, "The Union Must and Shall be Preserved" was added by Union General "Spoons" Butler during the Civil War occupation.

St Peter, Chartres and St Ann streets are pedestrianized where they border the square. During the day, everyone passes by at some time or another, weaving their way through the tangle of artists, Lucky Dog hot dog vendors, rainbow-clad palmists, magicians, shambolic brass bands and blues musicians. A postcard-perfect backdrop for the Jackson statue, **St Louis Cathedral** is the oldest continuously active cathedral in the United States. It's the third church on this spot, built in 1794 after the first two had been destroyed by fire and hurricane. Dominated by three tall slate steeples, the facade, which marries Greek Revival

---

The Louisiana State Museum

The Cabildo – along with the Presbytère (p.687), 1850 House (p.687), and the Old US Mint (p.690) – is part of the **Louisiana State Museum**. Each site is **open** Tuesday to Sunday from 9am to 5pm; buying a ticket to two or more gives a total **discount** of 20 percent, good for three consecutive days.

symmetry with copious French arches, is oddly two-dimensional, like some elaborate stage prop. Though the cathedral has always been central to the life of this very Catholic city – Andrew Jackson laid his sword on the altar in thanks for victory at the Battle of New Orleans; voodoo queen Marie Laveau (see p.688) was baptized and married here – the interior offers little to get excited about.

On the upriver side of the cathedral, the **Cabildo** ($5) was built as the Casa Capitular, seat of the Spanish colonial government. The building – which cuts an impressive dash with its colonnade, fan windows and wrought-iron balconies – is now part of the **Louisiana State Museum** (see opposite). Inside, the outstanding history museum ably picks its way through the complex tangle of cultures, classes and races that binds together Louisiana's history, starting with the Native Americans and winding up with the demise of Reconstruction. In keeping with the city's fascination with matters morbid, there's a room devoted to disease, death and mourning, while another displays the viciously racist parade float designs put out by the Mardi Gras krewes (see p.702) during Reconstruction – Union generals portrayed as vermin and newly liberated blacks as simian fools. Black history is well-represented throughout, with as much emphasis on the free people of color as on the city's role as the major slave-trading center of the South.

On the second floor you can see the bronze **death mask of Napoleon**, along with the reconstructed **Sala Capitular**, where the Louisiana Purchase was signed in 1803, and where in 1892, the historic *Plessy vs Ferguson* case, which effectively legalized segregation throughout the South, was first argued.

Forming a matching pair with the Cabildo, the **Presbytère** ($5), on the downriver side of the cathedral, was designed in 1791 as a rectory. It was never used as such, however; and after completion in 1813 went on to serve as a courthouse. Today it's an unmissable **Mardi Gras museum**, which covers carnival from every conceivable angle. Full of odd treasures, among them jewel-encrusted costumes, primitive masks, posters and bizarre dance cards, with videos, interactive themed rooms, music stations and lots of great captioning, it manages perhaps more than any other city museum to give a real sense of what makes this unique city tick. It would take days to see the place in its entirety; if you do have to skim a section or two, though, make sure to leave time to play dress-up. There's a jumble of satiny clown ensembles by the exit that you're free to try on, and a photo-booth where you can pose for a souvenir snap.

The elegant three-story **Pontalba Buildings**, which line St Peter and St Ann streets where they border the square, were commissioned by the formidable Baroness Pontalba, who, having returned from France in 1849 to find her real estate palling in comparison to the American sector across Canal Street, dreamed of replacing the shabby buildings around the Place d'Armes with elegant colonnaded structures resembling those she'd seen in Paris. Planned as both business and residential units, they are still used as such, and remain some of the city's most desirable places to live. These were not, as is commonly claimed, the first apartment buildings in the US, but they were innovative in their use of mass-produced materials and, in particular, of **cast iron** – indeed, it was these very balconies that sparked off the citywide fad for lacy ironwork, which soon came to replace the plainer iron hand-wrought locally by African slaves. Part of the state museum (see opposite), the cordoned-off rooms of the restored **1850 House**, 523 St Ann St ($3), recreate the tastes of the well-to-do Creole families who lived in these fashionable apartments. Unfortunately, though the self-guided tours draw attention to every piece of Vieux Paris china and fine crystal – a treat for decorative arts fans – they leave you with little sense of how the family might have lived.

Voodoo

Voodoo, today practiced by around fifteen percent of the city's population, was brought to New Orleans by African slaves via the French colonies of the Caribbean, where tribal beliefs were mixed up with Catholicism to create a cult based on spirit-worship. French, and later, Spanish authorities tried to suppress the religion (voodoo-worshipers had played an active role in the organization of slave revolts in Haiti), but it continued to flourish among the city's black population. Under American rule, the weekly slave gatherings at **Congo Square** (in what is now Louis Armstrong Park; see p.692), which included ritual ceremonies, turned into a tourist attraction for whites, fueled by sensationalized reports of hypnotized white women dancing naked.

Unlike in the West Indies, where the cult was dominated by male priests, New Orleans had many voodoo priestesses. The most famous was **Marie Laveau**, a hair-dresser of African, white and Native American blood. Using shrewd marketing sense and inside knowledge of the lives of her clients, she was in high demand for her **gris-gris** – spells or potions – which she prepared for wealthy Creoles and Americans, as well as Africans. Laveau died in 1881, after which another Marie, believed to be her daughter, continued to practice under her name. The legend of both Maries lives on, and their **tombs** are popular tourist attractions (see opposite).

Today voodoo is big business in New Orleans, with numerous gift shops selling ersatz *gris-gris* – pouches carried for good luck, filled with amulets, charms and herbs – and exotic voodoo dolls; these can be fun, but if you're interested in the reality, you'd do better to head to the **Voodoo Spiritual Temple**, 828 N Rampart St (daily 10am–8pm; ☎504/522-9627), which holds an open service on Thursday evening and offers tours and consultations. Visitors are asked to make a donation.

The Historic Voodoo Museum, 724 Dumaine St (daily 10am–8pm; $7), is a rag-bag collection of ceremonial objects, paintings and *gris-gris*. Its aim, to debunk the myths that surround this misunderstood religion, is undermined somewhat by the self-consciously spooky atmosphere, not to mention its resident 12ft python, crum-bling rat heads and desiccated bats. The gift shop sells *gris-gris* and voodoo dolls, while the gallery features more expensive folk art. Ask about their readings, rituals and city tours.

The Cities of the Dead

There is no architecture in New Orleans, except in the cemeteries . . .

Mark Twain, Life on the Mississippi

So much of New Orleans is at, or below, sea level that early settlers who buried their dead – and there were many of them – found that during the frequent flooding great waves of moldy coffins would float to the surface of the sodden earth. Eventually, graves began to be placed, Spanish-style, in above-ground brick and stucco vaults, surrounded by small fences. These **cemeteries** grew to resemble cities, laid out in "streets"; today, as the tombs crumble away amid the overgrown foliage, they have become atmospheric in the extreme. The creepiness isn't totally imaginary, either – though armed muggers, rather than ghosts, are the danger these days. You should **never** venture here alone. Nearly all the city tours (see p.682) include a trip around one of the graveyards; some (see opposite) specialize in them.

Lafayette Cemetery No. 1, Washington Ave and Prytania. Built in 1833, by 1852 – when 2000 yellow fever victims were buried here – the Garden District cemetery was filled to capacity. Today it is an eerie place, with many tombs sinking into the ground, and some of them slowly opening in the shadow of tangled trees. It's no sur-prise that all this decaying grandeur should capture the imagination of local author Anne Rice, who has used the place in many of her books – she even staged a mock funeral here, to launch publication of *Memnoch the Devil*; the corpse was herself, wearing an antique wedding dress, in an open coffin carried by pall bearers.

St Louis Cemetery No. 1, 400 Basin St between Conti and St Louis. The oldest City of the Dead, dating from 1789, this small graveyard is full of crooked mausolea jutting into narrow pathways. On the fringes of the Quarter, it is a regular stop on the tour bus circuit, and you will invariably come across a crowd by the tomb of "voodoo queen" **Marie Laveau**, graffitied with brick-dust crosses. They're usually being told how if you knock on the slab and mark a cross, her spirit will grant you any favor. The family who own it have asked that this bogus tradition should stop, not least because people are taking chunks of brick from other tombs to make the crosses. Voodooists – responsible for the candles, plastic flowers and rum bottles surrounding the plot – deplore the practice, too, regarding it as a desecration that chases Laveau's spirit away.

St Louis Cemetery No. 2, 200 N Claiborne Ave between Iberville and St Louis. One of the most desolate Cities of the Dead, hemmed in between a Tremé housing project and the interstate. Built in 1823, it's a prime example of local cemetery design, with a dead-straight center aisle lined with grandiose Greek Revival mausolea. A second Marie Laveau, thought to be *the* Marie Laveau's daughter, has a tomb here, also daubed with red-chalk crosses.

St Louis Cemetery No. 3, 3421 Esplanade Ave, Mid-City. A peaceful burial ground, built in 1856 on the site of a leper colony, St Louis No. 3 is mostly used by religious orders; all the priests of the diocese are buried here, and fragile angels balance on top of the tombs.

A Haunted House

The striking French Empire **LaLaurie Home**, at 1140 Royal St on the corner with Gov Nicholls, is New Orleans' most famous **haunted house** (not open to the public). In the nineteenth century it belonged to the LaLauries, a doctor and his socialite wife Delphine, who, although seen wielding a whip as she chased a slave girl through the house to the roof, was merely fined when the child fell to her death. Whispers about the couple's cruelty were horribly verified when neighbors rushed in after a fire in 1834 – believed to have been started intentionally by the shackled cook – to find seven emaciated slaves locked in the attic. There they saw men, women and children choked by neck braces, some with broken limbs; one had a worm-filled hole gouged out of his cheek. The doctor's protestation that this torture chamber was, in fact, an "experiment," met with vitriol; the next day the pair escaped the baying mob outside their home, and fled to France. Since then, many claim to have heard ghostly moans from the building at night; some say they have seen a little girl stumble across the curved balcony beneath the roof.

Tours

New Orleans' image as a Gothic, vampire-stalked city has really taken off in recent years, and the choice of **tours** promising **magic**, **voodoo**, **vampires** and **ghosts** has become dizzying. Among the high-camp, the overpriced and the plain silly, there are, nonetheless, a few worth joining. **Historic New Orleans Walking Tours** (☎504/947-2120) will lead you to St Louis Cemetery No. 1, Congo Square, Marie Laveau's home, and a voodoo temple; meet at *Café Beignet*, 334 Royal St (Mon–Sat 10am & 1pm, Sun 10am; 2hr; $15; no reservations; arrive 15min before the tour is due to begin). **Save Our Cemeteries** (☎504/525-3377; call for meeting points and to reserve) is a nonprofit restoration organization leading fascinating tours of Lafayette No. 1 (Mon, Wed & Fri 10.30am; 1hr; $6) and St Louis No. 1 (Sun 10am; 1hr 30min; $12). Call for meeting points and to reserve. Finally, if you're less worried about authenticity and more concerned with whooping it up, consider the **New Orleans Ghost and Vampire Tour**, complete with magic tricks and "psychic demonstrations." Ghost tours leave from Washington Artillery Park, across Decatur St from Jackson Square (daily 8pm; around 2hr; $15), while for the cemeteries you should meet at *CC's Coffee House* on Royal and St Philip in the Quarter (Mon–Sat noon, Sun 10.30am; around 2hr; $15). No reservations are needed.

Decatur Street and Esplanade Avenue

Something of an anomaly among Upper Decatur's brassy T-shirt shops and theme restaurants, the **Jean Lafitte National Historic Park Visitor Center**, 419 Decatur St, is not only a starting point for excellent **walking tours** (see p.682), but also a great introduction to Louisiana's delta region. **Listening stations** let you eavesdrop on natives expounding, in a variety of accents, on the meaning of all those weird local expressions, while **touch screen monitors** feature classic footage of Louis Armstrong, Mahalia Jackson and Professor Longhair, among others. It's pot luck as to what you'll get during the daily **cultural programs** (9.30am, 11.30am, 1.30pm & 3pm; 30–45min) but whatever it is – a walking tour, a talk, a slide show – it'll be good, covering one of a hundred subjects as varied as the modern port, women in New Orleans, or cast versus wrought iron.

Downriver along Decatur, the specialty shops of the restored **French Market**, said to be on the site of a Native American trading area and certainly active since the 1720s, sell tourist knickknacks; for stalls, head towards the old **Farmers' Market**, just off Decatur on N Peters Street, where fresh produce, spices, hot sauce and the like are sold around the clock. Next door, the weekend **flea market** is full of bargain oddities, as are the funky thrift and **rummage stores** opposite on Decatur.

The **New Orleans Jazz National Historical Park Visitor Center** (Wed–Sun 9am–6pm; free), hidden away in the French Market, is a must for music fans. Though the National Park itself is still a twinkle in its planners' eyes, the center's light, airy room is a superb, informal place to attend the frequent concerts and workshops, with good acoustics and an intimate scale; afterwards, check out the rare photos, information sheets and the **bookstore**.

Continuing downriver, you'll come to the outer boundary of the Quarter, **Esplanade Avenue**, an exquisite, oak-shaded boulevard lined with crumbling nineteenth-century Creole mansions. Part of the state museum (see p.686), the **Old US Mint**, on the 400 block near the river, houses the understated **Jazz Museum**, which traces the history of the music that New Orleans calls its own through photographs, sheet music, old letters – among them a pencil-written fan letter to pianist Armand Hug from a ten-year-old Harry Connick Jr – and posters. The highlights are, of course, the musical instruments, whose battered, well-worn contours are enough to bring tears to the eyes of any jazz buff. There are some real treasures here: among them a bugle played by the young **Louis Armstrong** while learning his craft at the Waif's Home; Kid Ory's trombone; Sidney Bechet's soprano sax, and a beautifully engraved horn played by Bix Beiderbecke.

Across Esplanade from the Quarter you come to arty **Faubourg Marigny**, a low-rent area of Creole cottages. Though the Faubourg is gentrifying, and its bars, coffee shops and restaurants are expanding further and further beyond the Quarter, it's best **not to wander** too far beyond the blocks around Decatur and Frenchmen, the district's main drag. Even Elysian Fields – the street where Stanley and Stella lived in Tennessee Williams' *A Streetcar Named Desire* – can feel distinctly dodgy, despite its heavenly name.

Chartres and Royal streets

A left turn at the 600 block of Esplanade Avenue brings you to the **Old Ursuline Convent** at 1114 Chartres St (tours Tues–Fri hourly except noon 10am–3pm, Sat & Sun 11.15am, 1pm & 2pm; $5). Built in 1745, this is the only intact French colonial structure in the city, and quite possibly the oldest building in the Mississippi valley. It's one of the many places in the Quarter that are said to be haunted, its corridors roamed by specters of the "casket girls" – white virgins shipped over in the early days of the colony, who were kept here before being sold off as wives in an attempt to stop the increasing number of couplings between French settlers and African or Native American women. Inside the wonderfully peaceful building you can see a mishmash of religious paraphernalia, including the "Doorway to Heaven," a heavy wooden table on which bishops lay in state in St Louis Cathedral. The **Beauregard–Keyes House**, opposite at no. 1113 (tours hourly Mon–Sat 10am–3pm; $5), owes its name to Confederate General Pierre Beauregard – who ordered the first shot of the Civil War at Fort Sumter and rented a room here during Reconstruction – and to popular novelist Frances Parkinson Keyes. She refurbished this "raised cottage" (with the basement at ground level) as her winter home in the 1940s, and her possessions now fill what is essentially a museum of decorative arts. Keyes' novels – including *Madame Castel's Lodger*, a romance about the house's "Beauregard period"– are on sale in the gift shop.

A block north at 1132 Royal St, the handsome **Gallier House**, dating from 1857, is a fascinating little museum (tours every 30min Mon–Fri 10am–3.30pm; $6, $10 with the Hermann-Grima House, see overleaf). James Gallier Jr was a leading architect of the day, and the innovative features he designed for his home, such as the outdoor cistern and cooling system, indoor plumbing and above-ground storage, soon became essential for anyone wanting to live in comfort in this swampy climate. Meanwhile, the house's filigree cast-iron balconies would have been the last word in chic. Tours, which focus as much on social history as fine furniture, are some of the liveliest in the Quarter.

A rare example of the French Quarter's early, West Indies-style architecture, **Madame John's Legacy**, just off Royal at 628 Dumaine St (Tues–Sun 9am–5pm; $3), was rebuilt after the fire of 1788 as an exact replica of the 1730 house that had previously stood on the site. It was constructed using the *briquete entre poteaux* technique, in which soft red brick is set between hand-hewn cypress beams, and raised off the ground on stucco-covered brick pillars. The deep wraparound gallery provided extra living space, cooler and airier than the indoor rooms. It's now home to an intriguing **museum** of Southern folk art, with an interpretative exhibition details the house's various inhabitants and changes in fortune. For an account of the **Historic Voodoo Museum**, across Royal at 724 Dumaine, see p.688.

Back on Royal Street, beyond Jackson Square at no. 533, the superb **Historic New Orleans Collection** stands proud among the neighboring antique stores and chichi art galleries. Entry to the streetfront gallery (Tues–Sat 10am–4.30pm), which holds temporary exhibitions, is free, but to see the best of the collection you'll need to take a guided tour (10am, 11am, 2pm & 3pm; $4). These might cover the galleries upstairs, where fascinating exhibits – including old maps, drawings and early publicity posters – fill a series of themed rooms, or they might venture into the Williams House, behind the museum beyond a courtyard. The Williamses, prominent citizens in the 1930s, filled their home with unusual, exotic objects – Chinese burial art, samovar lamps, antique maps – and the house is a must for anyone interested in design and decorative arts.

The quirky **Historical Pharmacy Museum**, in an old apothecary a block towards the river at 514 Chartres St (Tues–Sun 10am–5pm; $2; free with a Le Monde Creole walking tour, see p.682), offers intriguing snippets into the history of medicine. On the ground floor, hand-carved rosewood cabinets are cluttered with *gris-gris*, dusty jars of leeches for blood-letting (to remove irritability) and various unpleasant-looking drills and corkscrews; upstairs there's a whole section devoted to women's medicine – with a fine range of Creole "tonics" used to cure "all the various form of female weakness" – that's enough to make your eyes water.

In 1910, when the Quarter was at its most run-down, an entire block, bounded by Royal, St Louis, Chartres and Conti, was demolished to make way for a colossal new courthouse. A Beaux Arts behemoth of marble and terracotta, in the 1950s the building was abandoned in favor of more modern premises in the CBD, and eventually fell into disuse. It's currently being restored to house the **Louisiana Supreme Court**, and though the sheer scale of the place is an incongruous sight in the narrow streets of the Quarter, its glossy veined marble facade, gleaming behind huge green palms, makes it an undeniably handsome one.

Bourbon Street

Continuing lakeside up Conti Street brings you to world-renowned **Bourbon Street**. Though you'd never guess it from the hype, there are two faces to this much-mythologized drag. The touristy, booze-swilled stretch spans the seven blocks from Canal to St Ann: a frat-pack cacophony of daiquiri stalls, novelty shops and dimly lit girlie bars. This enclave is best experienced after dark, when a couple of its **bars** and **clubs** – though by no means all – are worth a look, and the sheer mayhem takes on a bacchanalian life of its own. When the attraction of fighting your way through the crowds of weekending drunks starts to pall, however, it's easy to dip out again into the quieter parallel streets to regain some sort of sanity. If you do manage to make it as far as St Ann, you come to a kind of crossroads, beyond which Bourbon transforms into an appealing, predominantly gay, residential area.

Beyond Bourbon Street: Rampart Street and Tremé

Beyond Bourbon Street, tourists are outnumbered by locals dog-walking, jogging, or chatting on stoops. Though these quiet streets are fringed by some of the Quarter's finest **vernacular architecture**, "sights" as such are few. Half a block north of Bourbon, at 820 St Louis St, the restored 1831 **Hermann-Grima House** (Mon–Fri tours every 30min 10am–3.30pm; $6; $10 with the Gallier House, see overleaf) illustrates the lifestyle of middle-class Creoles in antebellum New Orleans – with cooking demonstrations in the kitchen every Thursday from October to May – while at the cheesy **Musee Conti Wax Museum** at 917 Conti St (Mon–Sat 10am–5.30pm, Sun noon–5pm; $7) you can enjoy a variety of high-camp tableaux portraying the city's history.

Rampart Street, the run-down strip separating the Quarter from **Tremé**, is a boundary rarely crossed by tourists. Though it's home to a couple of popular clubs (*Donna's* and *Funky Butt*; see p.700), both of which are just a short walk from the heart of the Quarter, it can feel hairy at night, and only slightly less so during the day, partly due to the proximity of some of the city's poorest housing projects. However, in the last few years, as the city as a whole has grown more stable and crime rates begun to fall, Rampart has slowly started to shed its dismal image. Much of this is thanks to the revitalization of **Louis Armstrong Park** as a place to hear music. In general, the park entrance, a huge twinkling arch clearly visible the length of St Ann St, promises more than the park itself delivers, and it's not recommended to wander around alone during the day. It's a different story during the occasional weekend **music festivals**, however, many of which, continuing its long tradition of black music and celebration, are held in **Congo Square**, the small paved area to the left of the entrance arch. Near the park, the church of **Our Lady of Guadalupe** at 411 N Rampart St is notable for its statue of "Saint Expedite," mysteriously delivered here, so the legend goes, in a crate simply stamped *expedite*.

Tremé itself, the historic African-American neighborhood where jazz was developed in the bordellos of Storyville – long since gone – has two small museums worth a look. The fascinating **Backstreet Cultural Museum**, in an old funeral parlor at 1116 St Claude (Tues–Sat 10am–5pm; $3), celebrates local street culture, including jazz funerals, while the **African-American Museum**, 1418 Gov Nicholls (Mon–Sat 9am–5pm; $4), displays art works from Africa and the diaspora in three old houses spread across flower-filled courtyards. It's safe enough, using common sense and caution, to venture to these museums on foot during the day, but if you're heading for one of Tremé's music clubs (see p.700) be sure and take a cab.

Outside the French Quarter

Along with the Mint (see p.690), the gray granite **Custom House**, 423 Canal St, was key in New Orleans' grand antebellum building program. In order to handle the volume of commerce coming through the port, and to celebrate its value to the city, work started in 1848 on what was to be the largest federal building in the nation; rooting such a monster in the city's soggy soil proved difficult, however, and what with the break during the Civil War – when the half-finished building was used by Union General "Beast" Butler as a prison for Confederate soldiers – the Custom House was not completed until 1881. Mark Twain had a point when he dismissed the foreboding Classical interior as "inferior to a gasometer," but fans of Greek Revival architecture should head to the second floor, where a huge **marble hall**, illuminated by a 54ft skylight, poignantly recalls the lofty aspirations and optimism of the city's golden age.

The lakeside edge of the **Central Business District** or CBD, a tangle of busy gray highways, would be pretty lifeless without the colossal home of the

New Orleans Saints football team, the **Superdome**. At 52 acres, with 27 stories and a diameter of 680ft, this is one of the largest buildings in the world. You can't really appreciate the sheer enormity of the place until you venture inside, either by seating yourself with 76,999 others to see a **game** (Aug–Dec $25–50), or second-best, by joining one of the superlatives- and statistics-heavy **tours** (Mon, Wed & Fri 10.30am, noon & 1.30pm, except during special events; $6; ☎504/587-3808).

Spreading upriver from the World Trade Center, at the foot of Canal Street, the revitalizing **Warehouse District** is being heralded as a thriving arts community. However, though it may be a desirable place to stick a cutting-edge gallery, the attractions are not always immediate for the casual visitor. Most of the sights are concentrated in the **Arts District**, the outcrop of art spaces concentrated around Julia and Camp streets. Hub of the scene is the **Contemporary Arts Center**, 900 Camp St (Tues–Sun 11am–5pm; ground-floor galleries free; changing exhibitions $5; ⓦwww.cacno.org). It's a beautifully designed space, and there's always something interesting going on, from the temporary shows on the ground floor to major exhibitions upstairs, along with avant-garde performances, classic and art-house movies, free lectures and workshops – plus a free **cybercafé**.

Around the corner, the impressive – and colossal – **National D-Day Museum**, 945 Magazine St (daily 9am–5pm; $7), opened on June 6, 2000, the 56th anniversary of the Allied invasion of Europe. Though its collection concentrates on the events of that devastating day, the museum also does a good job covering D-Day invasions in the Pacific. For all but diehard military buffs, the quantity of hardware and uniforms on show may seem a bit much, but luckily there is enough film footage, background material and, especially, oral testimony from both sides of the conflict to make the place thoroughly engaging.

It can be all too easy to forget that easy-living New Orleans has its roots entrenched in the Deep South; anyone who needs reminding should take a look at the **Confederate Museum**, 929 Camp St at Lee Circle. A gloomy Romanesque Revival hulk, designed in 1891 as a place for Confederate veterans to display their mementos, this so-called "Battle Abbey of the South" is a relic from a bygone age. Inside the church-like hall, glass cases are filled with swords, mess-kits, uniforms and helmets. The sepia photos – of the wealthy, muddy antebellum city, and sad-eyed youths awkward in uniform – are undeniably affecting, and there remains a funereal air about the place, with its bittersweet remembrances of long-lost generals and their forgotten families.

Next door, the **Ogden Museum of Southern Art** (Mon–Fri 10am–5pm; free) is due to open in 2002. You can get tasters of the eclectic collection, which runs the gamut from rare eighteenth-century watercolors to contemporary photography in its temporary residence at 603 Julia St, but this represents just a drop in the ocean compared to what will be in the purpose-built five-story gallery.

The Garden District and Audubon Park

Pride of uptown New Orleans, the **Garden District**, which drapes itself seductively across a thirteen-block area two miles upriver from the French Quarter, was developed as a residential area in the 1840s by an energetic breed of Anglo-Americans who wished to display their ever-accumulating cotton and trade wealth by building sumptuous mansions in huge gardens. Shaded by jungles of subtropical foliage, the glorious houses – some of them spick-and-span showpieces, others now in ruins – evoke a nostalgic vision of the Deep

South in a profusion of porches, columns and balconies. It's a ravishing spectacle, if somewhat Gothic – you can see it on any number of official or self-guided tours, but the homes are only open to the public during the Spring Fiesta (see p.703).

The historic **St Charles streetcar** is still by far the best way to get to and around the area, affording front-row views of "the avenue," as St Charles, the Garden District's lakeside boundary, is locally known. From the streetcar, look out for the **Brown House** at no. 4717, and the 1941 replica of **Tara**, the house in *Gone with the Wind*, at no. 5705. You can't miss the **Wedding Cake House** at no. 5809 – an ostentatious Colonial-Greek Revival building, frosted with a layer of balconies, cornices and columns.

Just before the streetcar takes a sharp turn at the river bend, it stops at peaceful **Audubon Park**, a lovely space shaded by Spanish moss-swathed trees and looped by cycling and jogging paths. The best thing about **Audubon Zoo**, a fifteen-minute walk or short shuttle ride from the park's St Charles entrance (daily 9.30am–5pm; summer Mon–Fri 9.30am–5pm, Sat & Sun 9.30am–6pm; $9, children $4.75; zoo and aquarium $17.50, children $9.25), is its beautifully recreated **Louisiana swamp**, complete with Cajun houseboats, wallowing alligators and knobbly cypress knees poking out of the emerald green water. You can also see white tigers, white alligators and Komodo dragons, along with recreated habitats including an African savannah, an "Asian domain," and a "jaguar jungle" set among Mayan ruins.

Algiers and Blaine Kern's Mardi Gras World

A free ferry ride from Canal Street brings you within ten minutes or so to the west bank and **Algiers**, a quiet residential neighborhood of pastel stucco Creole architecture and subtropical terraces. The main attraction is **Blaine Kern's Mardi Gras World**, 223 Newton St (daily 9.30am–4.30pm; $11.50), where year-round you can see artists preparing, constructing and painting the enormous floats used in the Mardi Gras parades. It's a surreal experience wandering these massive warehouses past piles of dusty, grimacing has-beens from parades gone by. In keeping with the carnival spirit, there is plenty of opportunity to dress up, fool about and take photos – you're free to try on colossal Nixon and Marilyn papier maché heads, velvet cloaks and towering plumed headdresses. A complimentary minibus picks up and drops off at the ferry landing.

Elsewhere in the city

Towards the lake, in the vast area known as **Mid-City**, New Orleans' 1500-acre **City Park** is crisscrossed with roads, and by no means as peaceful as Audubon Park. Nonetheless, it's impressively landscaped, streaked with lagoons and shaded by centuries-old live oaks. Chief attraction is the **New Orleans Museum of Art** (Tues–Sun 10am–5pm; $6), which includes works by Degas, Picasso and Dufy, Rodin sculptures, pre-Columbian pieces, African works, Asian ceramics and paintings, and a fabulous collection of Fabergé jeweled eggs.

The **Chalmette battlefield** (daily 8am–5pm; free), six miles downriver from Canal Street, is where Jackson's ragtag army defeated the British at the Battle of New Orleans in 1815. The battle is commemorated by a 110ft obelisk and an exhibit – a source of delight to war buffs but probably too much of a good thing for casual visitors. Park rangers give short talks (11.15am & 2.45pm; 15min) for visitors who have arrived on a *Creole Queen* **river cruise** (see p.682); if you've come under your own steam, along Hwy-46, you'll have more time to wander around the site (a loop of a mile and a half) and to watch the thirty-minute video which details the events that led up to the War of 1812.

Eating

New Orleans is a gourmand's dream. The **food**, commonly defined as **Creole**, is a spicy, substantial – and usually very fattening – blend of French, Spanish, African and Caribbean cuisine, mixed up with a host of other influences including Native American, Italian and German. It tends to be rich, and fragrant, using heaps of herbs, peppers, garlic and onion. Some of the simpler dishes, like red beans and rice, reveal a strong West Indies influence, while others are more French, cooked with long-simmered sauces based on a **roux** (fat and flour heated together) and herby stocks. Many dishes are served **étouffé**, literally "smothered" in a tasty Creole sauce (a roux with tomato, onion and spices), on a bed of rice. Note that what passes for **Cajun** food in the city is often a modern hybrid, tasty but not authentic; the "blackened" dishes, for example, slathered in butter and spices, that were made famous by chef Paul Prudhomme in the 1980s.

The mainstays of most menus are **gumbo** – a thick soup of seafood, chicken and vegetables (*gumbo* comes from the Bantu for okra, a prime ingredient) – and **jambalaya**, a paella jumbled together from the same ingredients. Other specialties include **po-boys**, French-bread sandwiches crammed with oysters, shrimp or almost anything else, along with spicy sauces or gravy, and **muffulettas**, the Italian version, stuffed full of aromatic meats and cheese and dripping with olive and garlic dressing. **Seafood** is abundant and can be very cheap. Along with shrimp and soft-shell crabs, you'll get famously good **oysters**; they're in season from September to April. **Crawfish**, or mudbugs (which resemble langoustines and are best between March and October), are served in everything from omelets to bisques, or simply boiled in a spicy stock. To eat them, tug off the overlarge head, pinch the tail and suck out the juicy, very delicious flesh.

Finally, European-influenced New Orleans has always been *the* American city for **coffee**; drunk in copious amounts, fresh, strong and aromatic, and often laced with chicory, it's been a big part of life here since long before Seattle got trendy, and locals drink twice the national average.

French Quarter

Acme Oyster House 724 Iberville St ☎504/522-5973. Noisy, characterful neighborhood restaurant popular with tourists, cops and business people alike, all of them guzzling inexpensive po-boys, salty fresh crawfish or plump, briny oysters.

Café Angeli 1141 Decatur St ☎504/566-0077. A favorite with hipsters, night owls and bar flies, this big, dimly lit room is an extension of the groovy Lower Decatur scene outside. The hours are a welcome rarity in the Quarter, and the Mediterranean salads, sandwiches and pasta are just the thing after a wild night out.

Croissant d'Or 617 Ursulines St ☎504/524-4663. Peaceful, absurdly cheap little local place serving delicious French pastries and stuffed croissants, plus quiches, salads and steaming café au lait, in a pretty, tiled building.

Galatoire's 209 Bourbon St ☎504/525-2021. Splendid, top-of-the-range Creole food in landmark, mirror-lined dining room. It's best at lunchtime, on Fri or Sun especially, when long, convivial hours are spent gorging on turtle soup, oysters en brochette, crabmeat maison and filet mignon. No reservations, so expect a wait. Jacket and tie required after 5pm and all day Sun.

Girod's Bistro 500 Chartres St ☎504/524-9752.

Wonderful, romantic restaurant, linked to the *Napoleon House* (see p.699) and hidden away beside its pretty courtyard. Like the bar, the bistro is all cracked plaster, candlelight and ancient paintings – the perfect setting to linger over robust, creative Creole food with Mediterranean and Caribbean accents. Prices are reasonable and portions are huge.

Mr B's 201 Royal St ☎504/523-2078. Casually chic bistro with dark-wood booths, a relaxed, chatty buzz and excellent food. The garlic chicken is the city's finest, served with wild rice drowned in a satiny reduction; the same accolade could go to the signature barbecue shrimp. Reservations advised.

Peristyle 1041 Dumaine St ☎504/593-9535. Incongruously set on Rampart Street, this elegant restaurant – *very* New Orleans, all dark wood, checked tile floors and mismatched mirrors – is one of the hottest places in town to eat contemporary French–Creole–New American cuisine. Reservations essential.

Port of Call 838 Esplanade Ave ☎504/523-0120. Strung with tatty nets and lifebuoys, this lively neighborhood bar is *the* place in town for delicious fresh half-pound burgers, served with mushrooms or cheese and a buttery baked potato, and best eaten at the bar.

Rita's 945 Chartres St ☎504/525-7543. Cozy, inexpensive local place for hearty soul food and Creole favorites; try fried chicken with beans, or a combo of jambalaya–crawfish pie–filé gumbo, and leave room for the bread pudding and warm praline sauce.

Tujague's 823 Decatur St ☎504/525-8676. Unpretentious, atmospheric and with a quintessential New Orleans ambience, "Two Jacks," 150 years old, is the second oldest restaurant in the city. The prix fixe menu – shrimp remoulade and beef brisket in secret sauce – has changed little over the years; though it's not on the menu, ask nicely and they might prepare you a delicious chicken Bonne Femme. The old stand-up bar is particularly lively at Sunday lunchtime.

Outside the Quarter

Casamento's 4330 Magazine St ☎504/895-9761. Spotless and wonderfully old-fashioned, this uptown oyster bar serves inexpensive ice-fresh oysters and seafood; the overstuffed "loaves" are especially good.

Commander's Palace 1403 Washington Ave ☎504/899-8221. Exceptional haute Creole cuisine in a Garden District mansion. The heart-thumpingly rich food is pricey (dinner entrees $25–30), but the prix fixe menus prove good value (lunch from $15).

Jacket required for dinner and Sun lunch. Reservations essential.

Jacques Imo's 8324 Oak St ☎504/861-0886. Funky uptown restaurant with a colorful patio. The cooking, an inventive Creole–Cajun take on soul food, is astounding and very good value – from the fried oysters and chicken livers to the buttery blackened redfish. It's a great place to fill up before a gig at the *Maple Leaf* a couple of doors away (see p.701), and well worth a trip any time. Reservations advised.

Juan's Flying Burrito 2018 Magazine St ☎504/569-0000. Mainstay of the Lower Garden District boho scene, this Tex-Mex joint serves low-priced tacos, burritos and overstuffed quesadillas in a convivial neighborhood atmosphere.

Lola's 3312 Esplanade Ave ☎504/488-6946. Cozy little place between Tremé and Mid-City. It's a firm local favorite for cheap, mouthwatering and authentic Spanish food, with great garlic soup and a paella to die for. No reservations; expect a wait. No credit cards. BYOB.

Metro Bistro 200 Magazine St ☎504/529-1900. Buzzy, welcoming CBD bistro wth excellent French-influenced food; entrees include duck cassoulet, Burgundian beef stew with wild mushroom bread pudding, grilled fish on corn *choux*, and a tangy bouillabaisse. Lunch is cheaper.

Palace Café 605 Canal St ☎504/523-1661. Casually elegant restaurant in a grand old music store building on the French Quarter–CBD border. The contemporary Creole food is mouthwatering; signature dishes include creamy crabmeat cheesecake and a fabulous oyster pan roast.

Uglesich's 1238 Baronne St ☎504/523-8571. The "Yew-gle-sitch-es" draw on Eastern European traditions to create the best food in the city, served in a shabby Lower Garden District seafood joint. Everything is delicious, from the oyster brie soup to the spicy "sizzling shrimp Gail." Feast on raw oysters while you wait for a table (which can be a long time). No credit cards. No reservations.

Coffee bars and picnic food

Café du Monde 800 Decatur St ☎504/581-2914 Despite the hype, the crowds and the sugar-sticky table tops, this is an undeniably atmospheric place to drink steaming café au lait with chicory, and snack on piping hot beignets for a couple of dollars – apart from orange juice and hot chocolate, they serve little else. Daily 24hr.

CC's 941 Royal St ☎504/581-6996. Perch yourself at the counter or linger for hours in plump leather armchairs in this light, airy space. The brews are good and strong, especially the mochasippi, a creamy iced espresso.

Central Grocery 923 Decatur St ☎504/523-1620. Fragrant old Italian deli famed for the best muffulettas in town, unfeasibly overstuffed and succulent with garlic dressing.

La Marquise 625 Chartres St ☎504/524-0420. Neighborhood patisserie, sister shop to the *Croissant d'Or* (see p.696), a croissant's throw from Jackson Square. Though the coffee's no great shakes, the French pastries are irresistible, and they do inexpensive salads and quiches.

PJs 634 Frenchmen St; other branches around town ☎504/949-2292. Friendly local place that's a firm favorite for its expertly made coffee (try it iced), muffins, bagels and gourmet sandwiches.

Rue de la Course 3128 Magazine St; other branches around town ☎504/899-0242. With their pressed-tin walls, café-au-lait-colored decor, ceiling fans and reading lamps, the *Rue* coffee shops have an old Europe ambience, buzzing with a mixed, local crowd. The coffee is great, as are the biscotti and bagels.

Entertainment and nightlife

New Orleans positively reels under the energy of its ever-present **live music**. From lonesome street musicians, through the shambling, joyous brass bands, to international names like Dr John and the Neville Brothers, music remains integral to the economy and the ideology of the Crescent City.

While the French Quarter has its share of atmospheric clubs and bars, there are plenty of good venues elsewhere. And visitors making a beeline for **Bourbon Street**, hoping to find it chock-a-block with cool jazz clubs, will be disappointed. That said, even this tawdriest of streets has a couple of good places to hear jazz and blues.

To decide where to go, check the **listings papers** (especially the superb music monthly *Offbeat*), collect fliers in French Quarter **record stores** such as Magic Bus, 527 Conti St, or Louisiana Music Factory, 210 Decatur St, and keep an ear tuned to the fabulous local **radio station** WWOZ (90.7 FM), which features regular gig information and ticket competitions.

Music in New Orleans often doesn't get going until late. However, many venues put on **two sets** a night, often by different performers, so with a little creative club-hopping you could easily see three outstanding gigs in one evening. Another distinctive feature of New Orleans' nightlife is that many shows can be seen – and heard – from the street. If you hear something you like, but don't want to pay the **cover charge** – low or nonexistent in bars, but as much as $20 in some clubs – it's perfectly acceptable to stand outside with a "beer to go" (see below) from another bar, moving on when the fancy takes you.

Bars

As befits its image as a hard-drinking, hard-partying town, New Orleans has dozens of truly great **bars**. However, though **24hr-drinking licenses** are common, don't expect every bar to be open all night – even on Bourbon Street many close whenever they empty, which can be surprisingly early during slow periods. It is also, unlike in any other American city, legal to **drink alcohol in the streets** – for some visitors it's practically *de rigueur* – though not from a glass or bottle. Simply ask for a plastic "**to go**" cup in any bar and carry it with you. You'll be expected to finish your drink before entering another bar, however. The **legal drinking age** is 21; you should carry ID, though few bartenders bother asking for it.

French Quarter bars

Lafitte's Blacksmith Shop 941 Bourbon St
T 504/523-0066. Ancient, tumbledown bar frequented by artists and writers (how they see by the candlelight remains a mystery), and a few lively tourists. A front for Lafitte's plottings, it's practically unchanged since the 1700s, with beamed ceilings and a blackened brick fireplace. In the evenings, a gloriously cheesy piano player pounds out cocktail-lounge standards – there's a patio for those who want a quieter time.

Molly's at the Market 1107 Decatur St
T 504/525-5169. Once famed for being a haunt of politicos and media stars, *Molly's* Irish bar is quintessential French Quarter, pulling a happy crowd of locals, rowdy tourists, service industry workers and grungy street punks. There's Guinness on tap, a burger kitchen at the back, and a photo booth in the corner.

The Napoleon House 500 Chartres St
T 504/524-9752. Ravishing old bar – all crumbling walls, shadowy corners and flickering candles – exuding a classic, relaxed New Orleans elegance. On a warm night the courtyard is one of the best places on earth to be. The building was the home of Mayor Girod, who schemed with Jean Lafitte to rescue Napoleon from exile.

Port of Call 838 Esplanade Ave T 504/523-0120. Unpretentious drinking hole haunted by a noisy mix of Quarterites, Faubourg denzens and in-the-know tourists who put the world to rights around the large wooden bar or at the small tables. Great burgers, too (see p.697).

Bars elsewhere in the city

Columns Hotel 3811 St Charles Ave T 504/899-9308. Gorgeous hotel bar seeping faded Southern grandeur; on warm evenings, make for the columned veranda, which overlooks the streetcar line. It's also a local favorite for occasional live jazz, when there's a small cover. For more on the hotel, see p.684.

R-Bar 1431 Royal St T 504/948-7499. Bohemian Faubourg Marigny bar with funky thrift-store decor and a pool table played by some of the coolest sharks in town. It's popular with a youngish set, which includes visitors staying at the guesthouse upstairs (see p.684).

Sazerac Bar *Fairmont Hotel*, 123 Baronne St
T 504/529-4733. Historic, very classy Art Deco bar in a grand old CBD hotel. Serving champagne, fine wines, tip-top cocktails and desserts, it attracts a well-dressed uptown and business traveler clientele.

Snake and Jake's Christmas Club Lounge
7612 Oak St T 504/861-2802. Dilapidated uptown bar, with perennial Yuletide decorations fading in the gloom. Nothing much happens before 2am, when it fills up with a jubilant local crowd of musicians, journalists and students. The jukebox is superb.

Jazz

It is generally agreed that **jazz** was born in New Orleans, shaped in the early twentieth century by the twin talents of **Louis Armstrong** and **Joe "King" Oliver** from a diverse heritage of African and Caribbean slave music, Civil War brass bands, plantation spirituals, black church music and work songs. It suits the city well: hard to define, improvisational, and ranging from melancholic to jubilant, upmarket to downright seedy.

In 1897, in an attempt to control the prostitution that had been rampant in the city since its earliest days, a law was passed that restricted the brothels to a fixed area bounded by Iberville and Lower Basin streets. The area, which soon became known as **Storyville** after the alderman who pronounced the ordinance, filled with newly arrived ex-plantation workers, seamen and gamblers, and, from the "mood setting" tunes played in the brothels to bawdy saloon gigs, there was plenty of opportunity for musicians – in particular the solo piano players known as "professors" – to develop personal styles. Children too young to enter the bars set up makeshift "spasm bands" in the streets. Their legacy lives on in the streetwise ragamuffins on every corner, tap dancing, shoe-shining and playing trumpet.

Jazz was originally looked down upon by the white establishment as the "filthy" music of poor blacks, and, after Storyville was officially closed in 1917

– which coincided with a clampdown on live music played throughout the city – there was a mass exodus of musicians to Chicago and New York. Many more jazz artists left the city or gave up playing altogether during the Depression (King Oliver died an impoverished janitor); but in the 1950s the city fathers literally changed their tune and began to promote jazz as a tourist attraction. The double-edged nature of the music – indigenous and authentic, and at the same time a commercial construction – persists, but it remains a living, evolving art form, and you're spoiled for choice for places to see it. The quality ranges from good to exceptional; thankfully, the best is not confined to the tourist traps.

Local, world-class **musicians**, including the multitalented Marsalis family and trumpeters Terence Blanchard, Irvin Mayfield and Nicholas Payton all perform regularly. Of the pianists, don't miss Henry Butler – whose superb, superfast modern jazz is matched by his mean R&B and blues repertoire. Two of the city's best-loved performers, trumpeters Kermit Ruffins and younger pup James Andrews, can always be counted on for a good show. Both cut their teeth in local **brass bands**, the ragtag groups who blast out New Orleans' homegrown party music, born from the city's long tradition of street parades. Regulars on the circuit include the ReBirth (Ruffins' old crew); the Lil Rascals, New Birth and Hot 8 brass bands, whose ear-splitting spin on traditional tunes is as big a hit in the parades as in the jazz clubs; Soul Rebels and Coolbone, who mix a cacophony of horns with hard funk, hip-hop and reggae, have a fresh "street" sound.

Jazz venues

Donna's 800 N Rampart St ☎504/596-6914. Funky barbecue joint on the fringe of the Quarter. Hosting all the best brass bands, it feels like a locals' place – there's no stage, and you have to fight your way through the blasting horns to get to the bathroom – but it attracts a big out-of-town crowd, and it's the *only* place to be on Monday nights, when a host of local stars drop in to jam. Cover varies; one drink minimum.

Funky Butt 714 N Rampart St ☎504/558-0872. Stylish, intimate club near *Donna's*. The eclectic decor resembles an Art Deco bordello-cum-speakeasy, while the music – cool jazz, piano and R&B – is great. Cover varies, rising to $15, but you can drink in the bar for free.

Joe's Cozy Corner 1532 Ursulines St ☎504/561-9216. Few tourists head out to this Tremé bar, where on Sunday nights Kermit Ruffins plays a lively end-of-week set to a mixed group of friends, family and New Orleanians from all over town. This part of Tremé is dangerous; take a cab there and back.

Palm Court Jazz Café 1204 Decatur St ☎504/525-0200. The aficionados' favorite: top-notch traditional jazz played while you dine in elegant French Quarter surroundings. New Orleans jazz memorabilia adds atmosphere, and they sell collectors' items and records. Reservations recommended for dinner; cover varies, but a seat at the bar costs nothing.

Preservation Hall 726 St Peter St ☎504/523-8939. Shabby old room – with no seats, bar, air conditioning or toilets – long lauded as the best place in New Orleans to hear trad jazz. Though the studied dereliction is a bit hokey – the hall has only been open since the 1960s – the music can't be beat, and gets better as the night goes on. Sets every 45min 8.30–11.45pm. The $5 cover allows you to stay as long as you like.

Snug Harbor 626 Frenchmen St ☎504/949-0696. Sophisticated Faubourg Marigny jazz club in a small, two-story space. Shows at 9pm and 11pm, but the restaurant (serving pasta, burgers and the like) and bar (where you can watch the gigs on closed-circuit TV) stay open late. Regulars include Astral Project, who play cool modern jazz, Charmaine Neville, and Ellis Marsalis. Cover $8–25.

Vaughan's 4229 Dauphine St, in the Bywater ☎504/947-5562. Tiny neighborhood bar that fills on Thursday, Kermit Ruffins' night. The band is crammed up against the audience – a mixed bunch of locals, students and the players' friends and family; between sets, help yourself to free beans and rice. Take a cab. Cover $10 (Thurs only).

Other live music

There's far more to New Orleans than jazz alone. Though the "**New Orleans sound**," an exuberant, carnival-tinged hybrid of blues, parade music and R&B, had its heyday in the early 1960s, many of its greatest stars are still going strong. Check listings papers for gigs by the Neville Brothers, Eddie Bo, and "soul queen of New Orleans" Irma Thomas.

In recent years, the **swing** revival has taken off in a big way in New Orleans, along with **Latin** music and **funk**. **Blues** fans should look out for guitarists Snooks Eaglin and Walter "Wolfman" Washington, the younger, urban bluesman Kipori "Baby Wolf" Woods, and, for powerful gospel-blues, the formidable Marva Wright.

Though many people associate New Orleans with **Cajun** music, it's not indigenous to the city: that said, locals do love to *fais-do-do* (the Cajun two-step) and there are a couple of fantastic places to dance to **zydeco**, its bluesier black relation. The city has also taken **klezmer** to its heart, and in particular the local Klezmer Allstars, who bang out a frenzied blend of Yiddish folk, jazz and funk. Finally, for something unique, scour the listings for **Mardi Gras Indians** (see p.702) such as the Wild Magnolias or Golden Eagles, whose rare gigs – you're most likely to catch them around Mardi Gras or Jazz Fest – are the funkiest, most extraordinary performances you're ever likely to see.

Café Brasil 2100 Chartres St ☎504/949-0851. Minimalist, arty club at the heart of the Faubourg scene, with eclectic live music (Latin, jazz, klezmer, reggae, world), poetry readings and a small bar. The crowd often spills onto Frenchmen St, creating a bohemian street party. Cover varies.

Circle Bar 1032 St Charles Ave ☎504/588-2618. Painfully hip bar in a crumbling old house at Lee Circle. With an inspired, eclectic booking policy, it's becoming renowned for resurrecting jazz and R&B legends from ignominy, and always pulls a hard-partying crowd. Cover varies.

Dragon's Den 435 Esplanade Ave ☎504/949-1750. Opium-den style bar/club above a Thai restaurant in the Faubourg. It's tiny, packed with bright young things lolling on cushions or dancing like demons to R&B, blues, jazz and brass. There's a poetry slam on Thurs. Low or no cover.

House of Blues/The Parish 225 Decatur St ☎504/529-2583. Sleek French Quarter venue, part of the national chain. If you can stomach its un-New Orleans attitude and high prices, it's worth checking out for big names; smaller, local acts play at the intimate *Parish* upstairs. Cover varies.

Maple Leaf 8316 Oak St ☎504/866-9359. Friendly uptown bar with pressed-tin walls, large dance floor and a patio. It's a New Orleans favorite for really great blues, Cajun, zydeco, R&B and brass bands; Rebirth's Tues night gigs are legendary. There's chess and pool too, and poetry on Sun afternoons. Cover varies.

Matador 504 Esplanade Ave ☎504/569-8631. The decor – pressed tin, red velvet, Spanish kitsch

and a huge circular bar to drape yourself over – is pure New Orleans, as is the oddball crowd. Music varies from flamenco through Europop to trad jazz; Wed night is Soul Rebels night – unmissable. Cover varies.

Mid-City Lanes 4133 S Carrollton St ☎504/482-3133. Eccentric and very good fun bowling alley-cum-music venue in an unprepossessing Mid-City mall. Though it's especially heaving on Wed and Thurs – zydeco nights – they also book great local R&B blues and Latin music. Take a taxi. Cover varies.

Red Room 2040 St Charles Ave ☎504/528-9759 Swanky, very scarlet, cocktail bar, restaurant and music venue on the fringes of the Garden District. Featuring cool jazz, swing and Latin bands, with DJ nights at the weekend, it attracts a superhip uptown set. Cover varies.

Shim-Sham Club 615 Toulouse St ☎504/565-5400. A decadent cabaret lounge in old Bourbon Street style, *Shim-Sham* is a little dark and slightly daring, without ever taking itself too seriously. Among the punk'n'porno and Eighties nights, look out for the sexy ShimShamettes burlesque review, various cabaret and swing titans, and wildly popular trad jazz combos. Cover varies.

Tipitina's 501 Napoleon Ave ☎504/891-8477. Legendary uptown venue, named after a Professor Longhair song, with a consistently good funk, R&B, brass and reggae lineup. The Cajun *fais-do-do* (Sun 5–9pm) is fun, too, with free red beans and rice. Cover varies.

New Orleans' **carnival season** – which starts on Twelfth Night and runs for the six weeks or so until Ash Wednesday – is unlike any other in the world. Though the name is used to define the entire season, **Mardi Gras** itself, French for "Fat Tuesday," is simply the culmination of a whirl of parades, parties, street revels and masked balls, all inextricably tied up with the city's labyrinthine social, racial and political structures. Mardi Gras was introduced to New Orleans in the 1740s, when **French** colonists brought over the European custom, established since medieval times, of marking the imminence of Lent with masking and feasting. Their slaves, meanwhile, continued to celebrate **African** and **Caribbean** festival traditions, based on musical rituals, masking and elaborate costumes, and the three eventually fused. From early days carnival was known for cavorting, outrageous costumes, drinking and general bacchanalia, and little has changed. However, although it is the busiest tourist season – when the city is invaded by millions – Mardi Gras has always been, above all, a party that New Orleanians throw for themselves. Visitors are wooed, welcomed, and showed the time of their lives, but without them carnival would reel on regardless, dressing wildly, drinking and dancing its bizarre way into Lent.

It was in the mid-nineteenth century that **official carnival** took its current form, with the appearance in 1857 of a stately moonlit procession calling itself the *Krewe of Comus, Merrie Monarch of Mirth*. Initiated by a group of Anglo-Americans, the concept of the "**krewes**," or secret carnival clubs, was taken up enthusiastically by the New Orleans aristocracy, many of them white supremacists who, after the Civil War, used their satirical float designs and the shroud of secrecy to mock and undermine Reconstruction. Nowadays about sixty official krewes equip colorful floats, leading huge processions on different – often mythical – themes. Each is reigned over by a King and Queen (an older, politically powerful man and a debutante), who go on to preside over the krewes' closed, masked balls. There are women-only krewes; "super krewes," with members drawn from the city's new wealth (barred from making inroads into the gentlemen's club network of the old-guard krewes); gay krewes and important **black** groups. The best known of these is **Zulu**, established in 1909 when a black man mocked Rex, King of Carnival, by dancing behind his float with a tin can on his head; today the Zulu parade on Mardi Gras morning is one of the most popular of the season. There are also many alternative, or **unofficial krewes**, including the anarchic **Krewe du Vieux** (from Vieux Carré, another term for the French Quarter), whose irreverent parade and "ball" (a polite term for a wild party, open to all) is the first of the season. And then there's the parade of the **Mystic Krewe of Barkus**, made up of dogs, hundreds of whom, during what is surely the campest parade of the season, can be seen trotting proudly through the French Quarter all spiffed up on some spurious theme.

Tourists are less likely to witness the **Mardi Gras Indians**, African-American groups who, in their local neighborhoods, organize themselves into "tribes" and, dressed in fabulous beaded and feathered costumes, gather on Mardi Gras morning to compete in chanting and dancing. As in Sydney and Rio, the **gay** community also plays a major part in Mardi Gras, particularly in the French Quarter, where the streets teem with strutting drag divas.

One important New Orleans Mardi Gras ritual is the flinging of "**throws**" from the floats. Teasing masked krewe members scatter beads, beakers and doubloons (toy coins) into the crowds, who beg, plead and scream for them. Souvenirs vary in worth: the bright, cheap strings of beads are least valuable, while the bizarrely garbed coconuts handed out by Zulu are worth their weight in gold. When the parade is over, tourists embark upon a frantic **bead-bartering** frenzy, which has given rise to the famed "Show Your Tits!" phenomenon – young co-eds pulling up their shirts in exchange for strings of beads and roars of boozy approval from the goggling mobs. Anyone keen to see the show should head for Bourbon Street.

The two weeks leading up to Mardi Gras are filled with processions, parties and balls, but excitement reaches fever pitch on **Lundi Gras**, the day before Mardi Gras. Some of the city's best musicians play at **Zulu's** free party in Woldenberg Park, which climaxes at 5pm with the arrival of the king and queen by boat. Following this, you can head to the **Plaza d'España**, where, in a formal ceremony unchanged for over a century, the mayor hands the city to Rex, King of Carnival. The party continues with more live music and fireworks, after which people head off to watch the big **Orpheus** parade, or start a frenzied evening of clubbing. Most clubs are still hopping well into Mardi Gras morning.

The fun starts early on Mardi Gras day, with **walking clubs** striding through uptown accompanied by raucous jazz on their ritualized bar crawls. Zulu, in theory, sets off at 8.30am (but can be as much as two hours late), followed by Rex. Ironically, by the time Rex turns up, many people have had their fill of the official parades. The surreal **St Ann walking parade** gathers outside the *R-Bar* (see p.699) at around 11am, while the gay costume competition known as the **Bourbon Street awards** gets going at noon. In the afternoon, hipsters head to the Faubourg, where **Frenchmen Street** is ablaze with bizarrely costumed carousers. The fun continues throughout the Quarter and the Faubourg until **midnight**, when a siren wail heralds the arrival of a cavalcade of mounted police that sweeps through Bourbon Street and declares through megaphones that Mardi Gras is officially over. Like all good Catholic cities, New Orleans takes carnival very seriously. Midnight marks the onset of Lent, and repentance can begin.

Other New Orleans festivals

St Joseph's Day, March 19. Sicilian saint's day, at the mid-point of Lent. Families build massive altars of food in their homes, inviting the public to come and admire them and to share food. The Sunday closest to St Joseph's ("Super Sunday") is the only time outside Mardi Gras that the Mardi Gras Indians (see opposite) take to the streets.

Spring Fiesta, March/April (week after Easter). Five-day festival when many of the loveliest homes in the French Quarter and Garden District are open to the public. It's all rather genteel, with guides rigged up in hooped skirts and a classical concert series. Contact ☏504/581-1367.

French Quarter Festival, early April. Free three-day music festival that rivals Jazz Fest for the quality and variety of music on offer. Stages and food stalls, a jazz brunch in Jackson Square, tours of private patios, free evening gigs, parades and talent contests. Contact ☏504/522-5730 or ⊛www.frenchquarterfestivals.org.

Jazz and Heritage Festival (Jazz Fest), end of April/start of May at the Fairgrounds Race Track. Fabulous, enormous festival, with stages hosting jazz, R&B, gospel, African, Caribbean, Cajun, blues, reggae, funk, Mardi Gras Indian and brass band music, with evening performances in clubs all over town. Also crafts and fantastic food stalls. Contact ☏504/522-4786 or ⊛www.nojazzfest.com.

Cajun Country

Cajun country stretches across southern Louisiana from Houma in the east, via **Lafayette**, the hub of the region, into Texas. It's a region best enjoyed away from the larger towns, by visiting the many old-style hamlets that despite modernization can still be found cut off from civilization in soupy bayous, coastal marshes and inland swamps.

Cajuns are descended from the French colonists of Acadia, part of Nova Scotia, which was taken by the British in 1713. The Catholic **Acadians**, who had quietly fished, hunted and farmed for more than a century, refused to renounce their faith and swear allegiance to the English king, and in 1755 the British expelled them all, separating families and burning towns. About 2500 ended up in French Louisiana, where they were given land to set up small farming communities, enabling them to rebuild the culture they had left behind. Hunting, farming and trapping, they lived in relative isolation until the 1940s, when major roads were built, immigrants from other states poured in to work in the **oil** business, and **Cajun music**, popularized by local musicians such as accordionist Iry Lejeune, came to national attention. Since then, the history of the Cajuns has continued to be one of struggle. The whole region was hit hard by the oil slump; the erosion of coastal wetlands threatens the existence of towns like Houma and Morgan City; the silting up of the Atchafalaya Basin is having adverse effects on fishing and shrimping; and many coastal towns are in the firing line of the devastating hurricanes that hurtle up from the Gulf of Mexico.

However, the favorite Cajun phrase, *lache pas la patate* – "don't let go of the potato" – is an encouragement not to give up that suits this enduring culture to a tee. The popular image of the Cajuns as partying, fun-loving people is borne out at their many local dances, or *fais-do-dos*, held mostly at weekends. These singing, dancing celebrations, where everyone is welcome to trip a quick two-step, are good places to encounter this unique culture at close hand, and visitors will find plenty of opportunity to join one. After Roosevelt's administration decreed that all American children should speak English in schools, French was practically wiped out in Louisiana, and the local Creole patois of the older inhabitants, with its strong African influences, was kept alive primarily by music. Since the 1980s, CODOFIL (the Council for Development of French in Louisiana) has been devoted to preserving the region's indigenous **language** and culture.

Although **Baton Rouge**, the capital of Louisiana, is not actually in Cajun country, heading out this way from New Orleans, via the **plantations** on the banks of the Mississippi, makes a good approach.

Northwest from New Orleans: plantation country

The fastest roads out from New Orleans toward the west are the major I-10 and US-61; you can also drive along the **River Road**, which hugs both banks of the Mississippi all the way to Baton Rouge, seventy miles upriver. It's not a particularly eventful drive, winding through flat, fertile farmland, but a series of bridges and ferries allow you to crisscross the water, stopping off and touring several restored antebellum **plantation homes** along the way. In the nineteenth century, these spectacular homes were the focal points of the vast estates from where wealthy planters – or rather, their slaves – loaded cotton, sugar or indigo onto steamboats berthed virtually at their front doors. Today many of them offer luxurious **B&B** accommodation.

To get to the River Road from New Orleans, take I-10 west to exit 220, turn on to I-310 and follow it to **Hwy-48**, on the east bank (*above* the river on the map). It shortly becomes **Hwy-44**, or the River Road. For the west bank (*below* the river), cross Destrehan Bridge onto **Hwy-18** rather than branching onto Hwy-48. The levee runs the length of the banks, blocking the river from view, and though you'd never guess it from the tourist brochures, it's the hulking chemical plants that dominate the River Road **landscape**. There are rural stretches where wide sugarcane fields are interrupted only by moss-covered shacks – the prettiest views are to be found around the small town of **Convent**, on the east bank – but you'll more often find yourself driving through straggling communities of boarded-up lounges and laundromats, scarred by scrap piles and smokestacks.

From **Edgard**, 25 miles along on Hwy 18, you can cross the river to the **San Francisco House** (daily 10am–4.30pm; $8), two miles upriver of **Reserve** on Hwy-44. Built in a style dubbed "Steamboat Gothic" by novelist Frances Parkinson Keyes, its rails, awnings and pillars were designed to recreate the ambience of a Mississippi showboat. The elaborate facade is matched by a gorgeous interior – a riot of pastoral trompe l'oeils, floral motifs and Italian cherubs. Crossing the river at **Lutcher**, the settlement a few miles beyond San Francisco, brings you to Vacherie and the fascinating **Laura plantation** (daily 9.30am–4pm; $10). Rather than dwelling lovingly on priceless antiques, tours here, which draw upon a wealth of historical documents – from slave accounts and photographs to private diaries – sketch a vivid picture of day-to-day plantation life in multicultural Louisiana. Nine miles upriver from Laura, **Oak Alley** is the quintessential image of the antebellum plantation home. It's a splendid Greek Revival mansion dating from 1839 – the magnificent oaks that form a canopy over the driveway are 150 years older (daily: March–Oct 9am–5.30pm; Nov–Feb 9am–5pm; $10). The **restaurant** serves Cajun lunches, and you can **stay** in pretty B&B cottages in the grounds (☎504/265-2151; ❺).

The restored **plantation cottages** at **Tezcuco** (daily: March–Oct 9am–5pm, Nov–Feb 10am–4pm; $8), some 25 miles upriver from San Francisco, offer B&B accommodation, complete with porches, rocking chairs and, in some cases, fireplaces and libraries (☎225/562-3929; ❸–❽). Rates include a bottle of wine, breakfast in your room and a tour of the main house, an antebellum raised cottage built in Greek Revival style. Tezcuco is also notable for its small **African-American Museum** (Wed–Sat 10am–5pm, Sun 1–5pm).

Eighteen miles south of Baton Rouge on the west bank, **Nottoway** is the largest surviving plantation home in the South, a huge white Italianate edifice of 64 rooms, 200 windows and 165 doors. Tours (daily 9am–5pm) cost $10, but you can get a peep at this "white castle" from the road. The house now also holds an **inn** (☎225/545-2730; ❼) and **restaurant** (daily 11am–3pm & 6–9pm).

8

LOUISIANA | Cajun Country

Baton Rouge

When French explorers first came upon the site of **BATON ROUGE** in 1699, they found poles smeared in animal blood to designate the separate hunting grounds of the Houmas and Bayougoulas Indians. The area on these shallow bluffs therefore appeared on French maps as *Baton Rouge* – "red stick." Now capital of Louisiana and the fifth biggest port in the US, Baton Rouge is an easygoing city for its size.

Louisiana State Capitol

Surrounded by fifty acres of showpiece gardens, the magnificent Art Deco **Louisiana State Capitol** (daily 8am–4.30pm; free) serves as a monument to **Huey Long**, the "Kingfish," the larger-than-life state governor who ordered its construction in 1931 and was assassinated in its corridors just four years later. First elected governor in 1928 after a vehemently anti-big-business campaign, Long swiftly concentrated power into his own hands. His massive program of public works included financing charity hospitals by levying heavy taxes on the big oil and gas corporations. Variously labeled a demagogue, communist and fascist, he set himself apart from other Southern populists of the time by refusing to exploit the race issue. Just as his appeal – with slogans like "Every Man a King" – began to reach national proportions, with a bid for the presidency in the offing, he was shot by a local doctor whose exact motives remain unknown.

Other controversial figures to have worked in the building include the segregationist country singer **Jimmie Davis**, better remembered for writing *You Are My Sunshine* and riding his horse up the steps of the capitol than for any political skills, and **David Duke**, a former Grand Wizard of the Ku Klux Klan, who was elected as a state representative in 1989 and was the unsuccessful Republican candidate for governor in 1991.

Tours of this stunning building, with its huge murals and sculptures, are enlivened by remnants of Louisiana's maverick political history. Guides point out stray bullets in the marble pillars of the ground-floor corridor and a pencil embedded in the ceiling of the legislative chamber by an exploding bomb. Long decreed that nothing in Baton Rouge could be taller than the 450ft capitol, so its 27th-floor observation deck (closes 4pm) is the best vantage point to look out over miles of greenery and the sluggish Mississippi.

The riverfront

Mark Twain referred to Baton Rouge's **Old State Capitol** (in use from 1850 to 1932) as "that monstrosity on the Mississippi." A grey crenellated structure on a lumpy mound overlooking the river, penned in by an ugly wrought-iron fence, it looks like a cross between a castle and a cathedral, without the particular merits of either. Inside, the entertaining **Center for Political and Governmental History** explores Louisiana's scandal-ridden political history (Mon–Sat 10am–4pm, Sun noon–4pm; $4).

The splendid **LSU Rural Life Museum**, 4560 Essen Rd at I-10 (daily 8.30am–5pm; $5), re-creates pre-industrial Louisiana life through its carefully restored buildings – among them a plantation house, slave cottages and a grist mill – spread over 25 acres in a sultry garden setting.

One-hour harbor tours leave from the end of Florida Boulevard, passing under the **Baton Rouge Bridge**. This was perhaps the most ingenious of Huey Long's constructions; his stipulation that it should have a clearance of just 65 feet ensured that big boats could go no further north, thereby boosting the port trade of Baton Rouge several times over.

Cajun music

It's easy to "pass a good time" in Cajun country, especially if you're here at the weekend, when the *fais-do-dos* are traditionally held. Though things are quieter during the week, you'll still be able to enjoy authentic local music at many of the restaurants. Cajun music is a jangling, infectious melange of nasal vocals backed by jumping accordion, violin and triangle, fueled by traces of country, swing, jazz and blues. Zydeco is similar, but more blues-based, and more often played by black musicians. The patois heard in both bears only a passing resemblance to the language spoken in France. Music is never performed without space for dancing; everyone from the smallest child to most aged grandparent can join in. As well as the popular restaurants *Mulate's*, *Prejean's* and *Randol's* (reviewed on p.711), venues include simple dance halls, record stores, river landings and the streets themselves. Check the comprehensive music listings in the free *Times of Acadiana* or simply look out for signs saying "French dance here tonight."

Bourque's Club on Leo Lane, Lewisburg, 10 miles south of Opelousas ☎337/948-9904. One of the few remaining old-style dance halls, featuring live music Fri & Sat 8pm–midnight, and jam sessions (with free dinner) Wed 7–10pm.

El Sid O's Zydeco Club 803 Martin Luther King Drive, Lafayette ☎337/235-0647. Dancing Fri & Sat, with great zydeco and blues bands. They also serve food.

Fred's Lounge 420 6th St, Mamou ☎337/468-5411. Extremely welcoming home of the locally famed radio show "Live from Fred's Lounge" (KVPI 1050 AM), with music, dancing and lots of drinking. Sat only, 9.15am until well into the afternoon.

Prairie Acadian Cultural Center 250 W Park Ave, Eunice ☎337/457-8499. Splendid cultural center (see p.712) that hosts local musicians, storytelling and cookery demonstrations on Sat afternoons from 3pm.

Rendezvous des Cajuns Liberty Center for Performing Arts, S 2nd St

and Park Ave, Eunice ☎337/457-7389. Live Cajun/zydeco radio and TV show, mostly in French, every Sat 6–7.30pm. Family-oriented and hugely popular. Cover $5.

Richard's Hwy-190, eight miles west of Opelousas in Lawtell ☎337/543-6596. Incredibly congenial place for zydeco bands; regular Sat evening dances plus occasional events on Fri & Sun.

Savoy Music Center Accordion Factory 4413 Hwy-190, three miles west of Eunice ☎337/457-9563. Cajun record shop, where accordions are made in the back room. The store is open Tues–Fri 9am–5pm, but you should aim to be here for the joyous jam sessions on Sat 9am–noon.

Slim's Y-Ki-Ki Washington Rd, Hwy-182, Opelousas ☎337/942-6242. Famed shack-style venue for zydeco music and dancing. Fri & Sat only.

Whiskey River Whiskey River Landing, Henderson. ☎337/228-8567. Live Cajun music venue doubling as the starting point for a popular swamp tour (see box on p.712). Sun 4–8pm.

Arrival, information and accommodation

Connecting **buses** from New Orleans' Amtrak station and regular Greyhound buses come in to Baton Rouge at 1253 Florida St, fifteen minutes from downtown. Local buses, run by Capital City Transportation (☎225/336-0821), are infrequent. The **visitor center** is located inside the state capitol building (daily 9am–4.30pm; ☎225/342-7317).

Downtown offers few decent places to **stay**; most of the chains lie along I-12 or on I-10. There's a *KOA-Baton Rouge* campground (☎1-800/562-5673, ⓦ www.koakampgrounds.com; $19 per tentsite) seven miles east of the city on I-12, which offers free swimming, hot tub and firewood.

Best Western Chateau Louisianne All-Suite Hotel off I-10 at 710 Lobdell Ave ☏ 225/927-6700 or 1-800/256-6263, ⓦ www.bestwestern.com. Large rooms are arranged around a pretty atrium, and there's a gym and outdoor pool onsite. ❹

Mount Hope Plantation 8151 Highland Rd ☏ 225/761-7000, ⓦ www.mthopeplantation.com. Pretty, homey B&B in a comparatively welcoming part of town. ❹

Sheraton Baton Rouge 102 France St ☏ 225/242-2600, ⓦ www.sheraton.com. Unmistakably a chain offering but close proximity to riverboat gambling makes up for lack of character. ❺

The Stockade 8860 Highland Rd ☏ 225/769-7358, ⓦ www.thestockade.com. Friendly B&B on the grounds of a former Civil War stockade. Don't miss the garlic cheese grits. ❹

Cajun festivals

Authentic Cajun festivals, held almost daily it seems, are a wonderful way to experience the food and music of the region. For some of the larger events, it's a good idea to book a room in advance; the rest of the world is catching on to the fun, and Lafayette, especially, gets crowded. The following is merely a sampler; for full details, check with your tourist office in the area.

Mardi Gras, Feb/March. Second only to the New Orleans bash, this pre-Lenten party begins with street dancing on the Saturday before "Fat Tuesday." Cajun Mardi Gras differs from its city cousin; although there are private balls and parties, it is a far more pagan affair. Villages around Lafayette, like Eunice, Church Point and Mamou, are the scene of the *Courir du Mardi Gras* (see p.713).

World Championship Crawfish Étouffé Cookoff, last Sun in March (the Sun before if Easter falls on a Sun), Eunice. *The* place to taste the very best mudbugs, accompanied by great local music and a fierce spirit of competition among the fifty or so teams (☏ 337/457-7389).

Festival International de Louisiane, last full week in April. Huge, five-day festival in Lafayette, with participants from all over the French-speaking world, including Africa and the Caribbean. Particular emphasis on indigenous music and food (☏ 337/232-8086, ⓦ www.festivalinternational.com).

Breaux Bridge Crawfish Festival, first full weekend of May (Fri–Sun), Parc Hardy, Breaux Bridge. Crawfish-eating and peeling contests, crawfish *étouffé* cookoffs and crawfish races, along with music, crafts stalls, rides and dancing (☏ 337/332-6655).

Louisiana Shrimp and Petroleum Festival, Labor Day weekend, Morgan City. The Cajun coast honors its local industries – shrimp and oil — with a blessing of the local fishing fleet, as well as a shrimp cookoff, coronation ball and lots of dancing (☏ 985/385-0703, ⓦ www.shrimp-petrofest.org).

Southwest Louisiana Zydeco Music Festival, Fri evening & Sat before Labor Day at the Southern Development Farm, 457 Zydeco Rd, Hwy-167, Plaisance, near Opelousas. Top zydeco performers play "black Creole" music; with regional cuisine and African-American arts and crafts (☏ 337/942-2392, ⓦ www.zydeco.org).

Festivals Acadiens, third week of Sept in Lafayette. Huge, three-day festival, with Cajun, zydeco and traditional French bands, and indigenous crafts and food. (☏ 337/232-3808 or 1-800/346-1958).

Prairie Cajun Folklife Festival, in Eunice in late October. One day of free music, crafts, storytelling, cooking demonstrations and *Rendezvous des Cajuns* broadcasts (☏ 337/457-7839).

Mamou Zydeco and Blues Festival, first full weekend in Oct. Local music, food and dancing. Fri from 6pm, Sat from 9am (☏ 337/468-2370).

Louisiana Yambilee, last weekend in Oct. Opelousas goes all out to celebrate the sweet potato, with food stalls, sweet potato auctions, music and Miss Yambilee and Lil' Miss Yum Yum contests (☏ 337/948-8848 or 1-800/210-5298, ⓦ www.members.tripod.com/yambilee/yambilee.htm).

Eating, drinking and nightlife

Downtown Baton Rouge virtually shuts down on weekends; for coffee bars, funky diners and the bulk of the city's **nightlife**, you'll need to head to the shopping centers out on I-10 or to the area around the LSU campus, along College Drive, Chimes Street and Highland Road.

The Bayou 124 W Chimes St ☎225/346-1765. A trendy bar with pool tables and live music, catering to a rowdy local crowd.

Chelsea's Café 148 W State St ☎225/387-3679. Great local bands and an eclectic open mic night on Mon, plus table soccer and two separate bars.

The Chimes 3357 Highland Rd ☎225/383-1754. Well-heeled regulars come to watch televised sports events and choose from a humbling selection of over 120 beers. Next door to the *Varsity* (see below).

Mike Anderson's Seafood Restaurant 1031 W Lee Drive ☎225/766-7823. Serves the area's best seafood gumbo, along with lots of Cajun-inspired fish dishes.

Juban's 3739 Perkins Rd ☎225/346-8422. The place for pricey (entrees around $18) but inventive Creole-style seafood, such as blackened crawfish cakes and pecan-crusted snapper.

Ralph and Kacoo's 6110 Bluebonnet Blvd ☎225/766-8634. Lunch with the politicos in the capitol's dining room, where breaded seafood ranges from catfish to crawfish for around $12.

Varsity Theatre 3353 Highland Rd ☎ 225/383-7018. A live music venue with the permanent party vibe of a fraternity-sorority mixer, the *Varsity* hosts some decent rock and country acts as well as the ubiquitous LSU pre-game party.

Lafayette and around

LAFAYETTE, 135 miles northwest of New Orleans on I-10, is geographically central in Cajun country, and is the key city for its **oil** business. Originally named Vermilionville, after the orangey bayou nearby, it was renamed in 1844 in honor of the Marquis de Lafayette. Today Lafayette is a quiet place, a city with a small-town feel and no real centre. It does, however, offer some lively Cajun history and good restaurants – and makes the best base for exploring the swamps, bayous and dance halls of the surrounding region.

Arrival, information and getting around

Greyhound arrives in Lafayette at 315 Lee Ave and Amtrak a few blocks north at 133 E Grant St at Jefferson. There's an **airport** south of town on Hwy-90. The **local bus** system is of little use to visitors; to get the best out of the area you'll need a **car**, as the dance halls, restaurants and hotels are spread out some distance from each other. If you need a **taxi**, try Yellow Checker Cab (☎318/237-6196). The Lafayette Parish **CVB** is at 1400 Evangeline Thruway at Willow Street (Mon–Fri 8.30am–5pm, Sat & Sun 9am–5pm; ☎337/232-3737 or 1-800/346-1958, ⓦwww.lafayettetravel.com).

Accommodation in and around Lafayette

Scores of chain **hotels** line Evangeline Thruway just south of I-10, and US-90 and Hwy-182 toward New Iberia. Alternatively, **B&Bs** are welcoming and reasonably inexpensive, but you must book ahead. You can **camp** at *KOA Lafayette* (☎337/235-2739, ⓦwww.koakampgrounds.com; ❶–❷), five miles west of town, which also has a few simple cabins.

Bayou Cabins 100 W Mills Ave/Hwy-94, Breaux Bridge ☎337/332-6158, ⓦwww.bayoucabins.com. Eight rustic cabins – most of which date from the nineteenth century – on Bayou Teche. Run by the

owners of *Bayou Boudin and Cracklin'* (see p.711); rates include a free taster of their fantastic Cajun food and a full breakfast. ❸

Blue Moon Guest House 215 E Convent St,

Lafayette ☎ 337/654-1444, ⓦ www.bluemoonhostel
.com. Cheerful new hostel downtown, near the
University of Louisiana at Lafayette, with five dorm-
style guestrooms and one private suite. ❶–❸
Maison des Amis 140 E Bridge St, Breaux Bridge
☎ 337/507-3399, ⓦ www.cafedesamis.com. Four
B&B rooms in a Creole house, with two more at
Chez des Amis, a Cajun cottage. Complimentary
breakfast served at *Café des Amis* (see opposite). ❺

The Town

In the center of Lafayette, such as it is, stands the Romanesque **St John's Cathedral**, 914 St John St, and the old **cemetery**, where the crumbling raised graves include that of **Jean Mouton**, the town's Cajun founder. Each of the magnificent branches of the 500-year-old **Cathedral Oak** opposite, spreading over 200ft, weighs seventy tons. Three blocks north, the small **Lafayette Museum**, at 1122 Lafayette St (Tues–Sat 9am–4.30pm, Sun 1–4pm; $3), was the "Sunday home" – a townhouse used after Mass, before the family returned to their plantation – of Jean's son Alexandre, Louisiana's first Democratic governor. It's now filled with family memorabilia, Civil War relics and Cajun Mardi Gras costumes.

The campus of the **University of Louisiana at Lafayette**, south of the center next to the Student Union, boasts a swamp – complete with alligators, turtles, water birds and tattered Spanish moss. Its **art museum** showcases local artists and Southern folk art (Tue–Fri 9am–4pm, Sun 2–5pm; $2).

The great energies Lafayette has put into tourism since the oil slump have created two excellent reconstructions of early Cajun communities. **Vermilionville**, at 1600 Surrey St across from the airport, is the most accessible, and impressive, of the two, extending its scope to explore the culture of the early Creoles as well as the Cajuns (Tues–Sun 10am–4pm; $8). Set in 23 attractive acres on the Bayou Vermilion, it's a living history site, filled with craftspeople demonstrating traditional skills. A large replica of a rice mill serves as a **theater**, hosting storytellers, plays and noisy *fais-do-dos*, while in the simple chapel you can hear talks on religious traditions, from voodoo to the *traiteurs*, or Cajun healers. Cooking demonstrations are staged several times a day (10.30am, 12.30pm & 1.30pm), and the **restaurant** next to the theater serves good Cajun lunches (Mon–Fri 11am–2pm, Sat & Sun 11am–3pm).

Ten miles or so from the CVB, Lafayette's other folk-life museum, the smaller **Acadian Village** at 200 Greenleaf Drive (daily 10am–5pm; $7), depicts early nineteenth-century Cajun life along the bayous. Original homes and reproductions of other structures – including a blacksmith's shop and a chapel – line a sluggish bayou set in gardens and woodlands, and are filled with traditional furnishings and crafts.

Eating in and around Lafayette

They say a Cajun cooks every part of a pig but its squeal, and it's true that **Cajun dishes** are packed with a jumble of flavors, textures and, well, anything that's good and fresh. Though it bears resemblances to the Creole cuisine you'll find in New Orleans – lots of seafood, rice, rich tomatoey sauces and gumbos – this is rustic food, often spicy, and yes, pork features highly on many menus. It's very difficult to eat badly around here, and prices are generally low. At lunchtime, takeout *boudin* (spicy sausage) goes down a treat, as do finger-licking specialties like rich pork cracklin' and salty hogshead cheese. Often, however, eating in Cajun country is inseparable from **dancing** and **music**; evening – or afternoon, or morning – entertainment revolves around restaurants that double as dancehalls. Even if you don't feel like two-stepping yourself, it's great fun to watch all the old-timers and young sweethearts whirling around the room while you gorge on a delicious dinner of spicy seafood with a frosty beer.

Bayou Boudin and Cracklin' 100 Mills Ave, Hwy-94, Breaux Bridge, exit 109 from I-10 ☏337/332-6158. Nineteenth-century Cajun-country cottage on Bayou Teche – the crawfish capital of the world – selling takeout seafood boudin, hogshead cheese-smothered chicken and crawfish balls, all prepared on the spot from traditional recipes. Tues–Sun 7am–6pm.

Cafe des Amis 140 E Bridge St, Breaux Bridge ☏337/332-5273. Cozy, atmospheric country store serving tasty Cajun-Creole food. The traditional breakfasts are highly recommended. Wed–Fri 8am–10pm, Sat 7.30am–10pm, Sun 7.30am–3pm.

Cafe Vermilionville 1304 W Pinhook Rd, Lafayette ☏337/237-0100. Superlative French-Cajun restaurant in an elegant 1818 building, specializing in fresh seafood served in creative sauces; try the fantastic turtle soup. Mon–Fri 11am–2pm & 5.30–10pm, Sat 5.30–10pm.

Dean-O's 305 Bertrand Drive, Lafayette ☏337/233-5446. Unprepossessing downtown pizza joint, a local institution for its delicious pies topped with succulent shrimp and seafood. Mon–Thurs 11am–11pm, Fri & Sat 11am–12am, Sun 4–11pm.

Mulate's 325 Mills Ave, Breaux Bridge ☏337/332-4648 and 1-800/422-2586. Touristy, fun Cajun restaurant, where you'll find seafood, catfish and gumbo for less than $15; the Cajun music is thrown in for free. Dancing nightly, and daily at noon on weekends. Fifteen minutes from Lafayette on Hwy-94, a mile off I-10. Daily 11am–10pm.

Poupart's 1902 W Pinhook Rd, Lafayette ☏337/232-7921. Superb French bakery serving good coffee, quiches, continental breakfasts and sandwiches. Try the exquisite pastries and crawfish pies. Tues–Sat 7am–6.30pm, Sun 7am–4pm.

Prejean's 3480 I-49 N, Lafayette ☏337/896-3247. Fabulous, reasonably priced Cajun food in lively dance-hall surroundings. The menu is huge, but you can't go wrong with the fish or seafood – and don't miss the stuffed oysters. Mon–Thurs & Sun 6am–10pm, Fri & Sat 11am–11pm; live music begins at 7pm.

Randol's 2320 Kaliste Saloom Rd, Lafayette ☏337/981-7080. Locally famed dancehall serving fresh steamed seafood dinners (boiled softshell crabs are a specialty). The nightly *fais-do-dos* are occasionally televised. Sun–Thurs 5–10pm, Fri & Sat 5–11pm.

Richard's Seafood Patio 1516 S Henry St, Abbeville, 20 miles south of Lafayette ☏337/893-1693. Top-notch seafood focusing on regional standards like boiled crabs, gumbo and grilled shrimp. Mon–Sat 5pm until the last person leaves.

Touring Cajun country

North of Lafayette, the **Cajun Prairie** has been described by folklorist Alan Lomax as the "Cajun Cultural Heartland." A patchwork of rice and soybean fields scattered with crawfish ponds, the region has a few tiny towns where you'll be greeted with genuine warmth and interest by locals.

GRAND COTEAU, off I-49 ten miles north of Lafayette, is a picture-perfect little town, with whitewashed buildings – including a dazzling white chapel – and prettily winding roads. Since 1866, when a dying woman was miraculously healed by the intercession of a saint in the **Academy of the Sacred Heart**, 1821 Academy Rd, devout Cajun Catholics have made pilgrimages here. You can see the old classrooms of this beautifully columned school, and follow a long path through the ornate gardens, canopied by huge old oaks (Mon–Fri by appointment; $5; ☏337/662-527, ⊛www.ashcoteau.org).

The 1831 **Chretien Point Plantation**, in **SUNSET**, ten miles north of Lafayette on Hwy-93 just off I-10, is one of Louisiana's oldest Greek Revival buildings (daily 10am–4pm; $6.50). Its main staircase was the model for Tara's in *Gone with the Wind*. Mrs Chretien, left to run the plantation after her husband's death in 1832, was very much in the Scarlett O'Hara mode. She scandalized the community by drinking, smoking, gambling and sitting with the men after dinner, and once shot an intruder, whose ghost is said to roam the corridors. Bullet holes in the front door date from 1863, when Mrs Chretien's son showed a Masonic sign to an attacking Union general, who thereupon directed fire over the roof. The plantation has five luxurious **B&B** rooms (☎ 337/662-5876; ❻).

Sweet little **OPELOUSAS**, twenty miles north of Lafayette on I-49, has four claims to fame. It was the boyhood home of Jim Bowie, Texas Revolutionary hero and inventor of the Bowie knife, the first place in the world to produce an offset newspaper (in 1915), the birthplace of the great zydeco musician **Clifton Chenier**, and today, even more excitingly, it's the **yam** capital of the universe (see p.708 for a festival celebrating this achievement). You can find out more about it at the quirky **Opelousas Museum and Interpretive Center**, 315 N Main St (Mon–Sat 9am–5pm; free), which displays such relics of local history as the barber's stool on which outlaw Clyde Barrow got his last shave before being shot dead by the FBI in northern Louisiana. Stop by the 1920s *Palace Café*, on the central square at 167 W Landry Ave (Mon–Sat 6am–9pm, Sun 7am–3pm; ☎ 337/942-2142), for shrimp, crawfish and gumbo in immaculate **diner** surroundings, and if you're tempted to stay the night, head for one of the small cluster of chain hotels outside town on I-49; both the *Best Western* (☎ 337/942-5540, ⓦ www.bestwestern.com; ❸) – just south of town – and the *Holiday Inn* (☎ 337/948-3300, ⓦ www.holiday-inn.com; ❹) – just north – are relatively new.

To learn a little about the Cajun Prairie, head for friendly **EUNICE**, about 20 miles west of Opelousas. The exemplary **Prairie Acadian Cultural Center** at the **Jean Lafitte National Historical Park**, 250 W Park Ave (daily 8am–5pm; free), holds far-reaching displays on local life, ranging across family, language, food and farming, with live Cajun music at weekends. If time is limited, choose this place over the **Eunice Museum**, 220 S C.C. Duson Drive (Tues–Sat 8am–noon & 1–5pm; free) – though this too has its charms; it's an old

Swamp tours

Swamp tours are available from many landings in the **Atchafalaya Basin**; you'll pass numerous signs pinned to the old cypress trees along the roadside. The basin is an eerie place: almost all its cypresses were harvested last century, and now just the twisted silhouettes of their stumps poke out of the sluggish waters. In some places cars cut right across on the enormous concrete I-10 above, and old houseboats lie abandoned, or get used simply for weekend retreats. The best tours take you further out, to the backwoods; wherever you go you'll see scores of fishing boats and plenty of wildlife, including sunbathing alligators. Tours are conducted by Cajuns who see the basin as more than just a tourist attraction and provide fascinating personal commentaries.

Angelle's Atchafalaya Basin Swamp Tours Whiskey River Landing, 1365 Henderson Levee Rd, Henderson (☎337/228-8567, ⓦwww.angelleswhiskeyriver.com). Twenty-five minutes from Lafayette, along I-10 to exit 115, then highways 347 and 332, this quiet landing is also host to a great *fais do-do* Sun 4–8pm. Swamp tours daily 10am, 1pm & 3pm; 90min; no reservations required; $12.

The Atchafalaya Experience 338 N Sterling St, Lafayette ☎337/233-7816. The father-son team that runs these lengthy swamp tours includes a geologist; both guides are lifelong explorers of the swamp. Daily 9am & 4pm; 3hr; reservations required; $40.

McGee's Swamp Tours McGee's Landing, 1337 Henderson Levee Rd, Henderson (☎337/228-2384, ⓦwww.McGeesLanding.com). Leisurely tours run from Henderson Swamp, a top fishing spot. Daily 8am, 10am, 1pm & 3pm; no tours in Jan; 90min; reservations recommended; $12.

train depot crammed with an eccentric ragbag of toys, musical instruments, farming implements and Native American artifacts. However long you're here, don't miss out on Eunice's splendid down-home **food** – *Johnson's Grocery,* 700 E Maple Ave (T337/457-9314), serves fat, juicy boudin and spicy hogshead cheese from 6am, while *Allison's Hickory Pit,* 501 W Laurel St (Fri–Sun; T337/457-9218), specializes in pork, chicken, steak and brisket smothered in a mean barbecue sauce. Although there's little else to see in Eunice, it's at the hub of the region's **music scene** (see p.707); the regular *Savoy Accordion Factory* and *Liberty Center* bashes are supplemented by the riotous annual **Courir du Mardi Gras**, when masked horsemen gallop through the countryside before parading through downtown, where the drinking and dancing continues all day. *Potier's Prairie Cajun Inn*, at 110 W Park Ave (T337/457-0440; ❹), next door to the Liberty Center for the Performing Arts, is a 1920s hospital restored as a friendly **place to stay**.

From here it's twenty miles north to **VILLE PLATTE**, and Floyd's Music Store, 434 E Main St (Mon–Fri 8.30am–5.30pm, Sat 8.30am–5pm; W www.floydsrecords.com), owned by dashing Floyd Soileau, the world's chief distributor of **South Louisiana music**, and stocking everything from zydeco reissues to contemporary swamp pop. If Mr Soileau isn't around, you could well find him listening to the rocking jukebox a couple of doors down at the *Pig Stand*, 318 E Main St (daily till late; T337/363-2883), where giant plates of fried chicken, smothered sausage and ribs come heaped with rice, gravy, black-eyed peas and potato salad. The place is famed for its pork barbecue (served Tues, Thurs, Sat & Sun only).

South of Lafayette

South of Lafayette the towns are less immediately welcoming than those in the Prairie, but the surroundings are undeniably atmospheric: this is **bayou country**, a marshy expanse of rivers and lakes dominated by the mighty Atchafalaya swamp, where the soupy green waters creep right up to the edges of the highway. Unsurprisingly, the economy is based on fishing and shrimping, with hunting in the forests and sugar fields, but it's also a semi-industrial landscape, with a web of oil pipelines running beneath the waterways, and refineries and corrugated-iron shacks sharing space with neat white Catholic churches.

Settled in 1765, old **ST MARTINVILLE** on the Bayou Teche, off US-90 and 18 miles south of Lafayette, was a major port of entry for exiled Acadians. Hard to believe now, but in the nineteenth century this country town grew to become known as "le petit Paris," filled with French Royalists fleeing the Revolution and re-creating a glittering city life of soirees and balls. It was later decimated by yellow fever, fire and hurricane, and is now a peaceful hamlet, kept going by a trickle of tourists. You'll see a lot of references to "Evangeline". To find out why, head for **Evangeline Oak Park**, on Evangeline Boulevard where it meets the bayou. Here stands the **Evangeline Oak**, where real-life Acadian **Emmeline Labiche**, the inspiration for Longfellow's *Evangeline*, disembarked after her hard journey from Nova Scotia, only to hear that her lover, Gabriel, was engaged to another. You may find a small group of musicians or storytellers around the tree. Nearby in the park the **Museum of the Acadian Memorial** (daily 10am–4pm; free) pays tribute to the 3000 refugees displaced from Canada to Louisiana between 1764 and 1788, with a "Wall of Names" listing the settlers. The adjacent **African American Museum** (daily 10am–4pm; free) focuses on the arrival of Africans, as slaves, into Southwest Louisiana during the 1700s. Further along the bayou boardwalk is the **Acadian Memorial** itself, with a 30-foot mural marking the Acadians' arrival in Louisiana and a Wall of Names honoring the 3000 refugees.

Other sights, such as they are, can be found on or around the town square. The eighteenth-century St Martin de Tours **Catholic church**, at 133 Main St, contains a gold and silver sanctuary light and intricate carved font said to have been gifts from Louis XVI and Marie Antoinette; next door, the off-beat **Petit Paris Museum** exhibits fabulous local Mardi Gras costumes (daily 10am–4pm; $2; tours of museum and church $5). Behind the church, the bronze **Evangeline Monument** was donated by the producers of the 1929 movie *The Romance of Evangeline*, and is modeled on Dolores del Rio, its star. Just north of town on Hwy-31, the **Longfellow-Evangeline State Commemorative Area** (daily 9am–5pm; $2) on the bayou contains an 1815 **Creole Plantation House**, made with the *bousillage* mixture (mud, Spanish moss and animal hair) characteristic of early Louisiana buildings, and held together by wooden pegs. If St Martinville's sleepy charm wins you over you might want to **stay**: the *Old Castillo,* 220 Evangeline Blvd next to the Evangeline Oak (T 337/394-4010 or 1-800/621-3017; ❸), is a comfortable mid-nineteenth-century B&B. Its **restaurant** serves good home cooking (Mon & Tue 8am–5pm, Wed–Sat 8am–9pm, Sun 8am–2pm).

AVERY ISLAND, ten miles southwest of the bayou town of **New Iberia** along a toll road, is not an island at all, but rather the tip of a massive salt dome. **Tabasco sauce** is still prepared from a family recipe in the McIlhenny factory here, using the red-hot local peppers (daily 9am–4pm; free). The steamy, 200-acre **Jungle Gardens and Bird City** (daily 8am–5pm; $5.75) are full of exotic camellias, azaleas and irises, and serve as a sanctuary for blue herons, black ibises and snowy egrets.

North Louisiana

North Louisiana is at the heart of the region known as the **Ark-La-Tex**, where the cottonfields and soft vocal drawl of the Deep South Bible-belt merges with the ranches, oil and country music of Texas and the forested hills (resplendent in the fall) of Arkansas. Settled by the Scottish and Irish after the Louisiana Purchase, the area is strongly Baptist, with less of a penchant for fun than south Louisiana, though it does share its profusion of **festivals**.

Natchitoches

Tiny **NATCHITOCHES** (pronounced "Nakitish"), in the sleepy cottonfields of the Cane River, is the oldest European settlement in Louisiana, having begun life as a French trading post in 1714. A Catholic oasis in a Protestant desert, it was swiftly fortified when its Spanish and Native American customers started to combine aggression with commerce.

With its lovingly restored Creole architecture, Natchitoches's exquisite **Front Street**, on the river, bears a passing resemblance to New Orleans' French Quarter, with its lacy iron balconies, spiral staircases and cobbled courtyards complemented by friendly, old-style stores. The 1717 **Church of the Immaculate Conception**, at Second and Church streets, has many of its original French features, including glass chandeliers and a hand-carved font. Fleur de lis on the nearby **Walk of Honor** commemorate celebrities with local connections, such as John Wayne, Clementine Hunter (see below), and the cast of the movie *Steel Magnolias*, which was set and filmed here in 1988. **Fort St Jean Baptiste**, at Moreau and Mill streets (daily 9am–5pm; $2), is a five-acre reconstruction of the town's 1716 fort, with rough wooden and adobe buildings, enclosed by a tall wooden fence.

The quirky **Bayou Folk Museum** in novelist **Kate Chopin**'s old home in **CLOUTIERVILLE** (Mon–Sat 10am–5pm, Sun 1–5pm; $5), is filled with all manner of oddities of local interest, along with exhibits relating to Chopin herself, whose nineteenth-century novel *The Awakening*, about a married woman's desire for independence, shocked the nation.

Practicalities

Natchitoches lies 150 miles northeast of Lafayette, on Hwy-6 off I-49. Greyhound comes in on the southeast side of town, on Hwy-1; the town has **no public transportation** or taxis, so to avoid being stranded, you should reserve accommodation in advance at a **B&B**, and arrange to be collected. One of the most appealing is the Judge Porter House at 321 Second St (℡318/352-9206 or 1-800/441-8343, ⓦwww.judgeporterhouse.com; ⑤), with its romantic porch and antique-stuffed rooms; *Chateau d'Terre*, just outside of downtown Natchitoches at 109 Jamar Drive (℡318/354-7929 or 1-888/798-6599, ⓦwww.chateaudterre.com; ⑤), offers a tranquil lake view and an endless supply of delicious cookies and biscuits.

The **visitor center**, 781 Front St (Mon–Fri 8am–6pm, Sat 9am–5pm, Sun 10am–3pm; ℡1-800/259-1714, ⓦwww.historicnatchitoches.com), provides self-guided tours and can help find accommodation. The best place to **eat** is *Lasyone's Meat Pie Kitchen* (Mon–Sat 7am–6.30pm; ℡318/352-3353), around the corner at 622 Second St, which specializes in meat pies (spicy, flaky and lightly fried), cream pies, red beans and sausage, and fresh, crumbly cornbread.

Cane River National Heritage Area

Just south of Natchitoches, the rural **Cane River roads** are dotted with ramshackle houses and small farms. As you drive past farmers sitting on porches and women hanging out the wash, you'll come across many **plantation homes**, some overgrown and in sad disrepair, others beautifully restored.

The **Cane River National Heritage Area**, a collection of restored plantation homes, churches and forts, stretches for 35 miles south from Natchitoches. Head first for the fascinating **Melrose Plantation** (daily noon–4pm; $6), on Hwy-119, which was granted in 1794 to Marie Therese Coincoin, a freed slave, by her owner, Thomas Metoyer – the father of ten of her fourteen children. With remarkable resourcefulness Coincoin assembled the original grounds and additional land grants into an 800-acre plantation; she was later able to buy freedom for two of her children and one of her grandchildren. Around 1900, enterprising Melrose owner "Miss Cammie" Henry – a collector and patron of local writing – turned the crumbling Melrose into an arts community, visited by painters and writers such as William Faulkner and John Steinbeck, and in the 1940s a black Melrose cook, **Clementine Hunter**, began to use materials discarded by visiting artists to paint vivid images of life on and around the plantation. She carried on painting until her death at the age of 101, and her works have since become valuable pieces of folk art. Many of them are on show in the 1800 **African House**, which resembles a Congo mud hut and was used as the slave jail, and in the Big House, a typical plantation home, made from brick and *bousillage*.

CHAPTER 9 Highlights

* **The Menil Collection, Houston** Houston's premier gallery boasts a magnificent collection of ancient and modern artworks, plus the sombre Rothko Chapel. See p.723

* **Johnson Space Center, Houston** Send your imagination into orbit with a trip to Mission Control, the nerve center for the Apollo moon missions. See p.726

* **The River Walk, San Antonio** Texas offers few more romantic experiences than a riverside stroll through the heart of San Antonio. See p.733

* **The Sixth Floor Museum, Dallas** Decide for yourself whether Oswald really did shoot JFK, as you overlook Dealey Plaza. See p.750

* **The Stockyards, Fort Worth** Watch a cattle drive, or tuck into a colossal steak in this cowboy heaven. See p.754

* **Rafting the Santa Elena Canyon** The Rio Grande rushes through this narrow gorge in remote Big Bend National Park. See p.765

* **Starlight Theater** Enjoy the stars – in the sky and on stage – in this glorious desert bar in the tiny West Texas ghost town of Terlingua. See p.766

Texas

Still cherishing the memory that it was from 1836 to 1845 an independent nation in its own right, **TEXAS** stands apart from the rest of the United States. While its sheer size – eight hundred miles from east to west and nearly a thousand from top to bottom – gives it a great geographical diversity, is firmly bound together by a shared history, culture and ideology. Independence is key to the Texan mentality, from the overriding distrust of government – any government – to the absence of unionized labor. As the old anti-litter campaign put it, "Don't mess with Texas."

Preconceived ideas about what exactly is "Texan" are soon shattered. It's actually one of the most eclectic and cosmopolitan states in the Union and each of the major tourist destinations has its own distinct character. Hispanic **San Antonio**, for example, with its Mexican population and historic importance, has a laid-back feel absent from the big-city neurosis of **Houston** or **Dallas**, while trendy **Austin** revels in a lively music scene and intellectualism found nowhere else in the state.

Regional differences are vast. The swampy, forested **east** is more like Louisiana than the pretty **Hill Country** or the agricultural plains of the **Panhandle**, and the tropical **Gulf Coast** has little in common with the mountainous **deserts** of the west. Changes in **climate** are equally dramatic: snow is common on the Panhandle, whereas the humidity of Houston, in particular, is only made bearable by nonstop high-power air conditioning.

One thing shared by the whole of Texas is the constant boasting – everything has to be bigger and better than anywhere else. Such chauvinism is tempered both by a delight in self-parody and by the state's melting pot of cultures. The much-cited Texan **friendliness** is not imaginary; to be unwelcoming would simply be unpatriotic. Texas is, after all, named for a Native American word meaning friend, *tejas*, and a visit here, especially to the Panhandle or the Hill Country, is not for those who want to be alone.

Some history

Early inhabitants of Texas included the Caddo in the east and nomadic Coahuiltecans further south. The **Comanche**, who arrived from the Rockies in the 1600s, soon found themselves at war when the **Spanish** ventured in, looking for gold. In the 1700s, threatened by French hopes of westward expansion from Louisiana, the Spanish began to build **missions** and forts, although these had minimal impact on the indigenous population's nomadic way of life. When Mexico won its independence from Spain in 1821, taking Texas with it was part of the deal. At first, the Mexicans were keen to open up their land, and offered generous incentives to settlers. Stephen Austin ("the father of

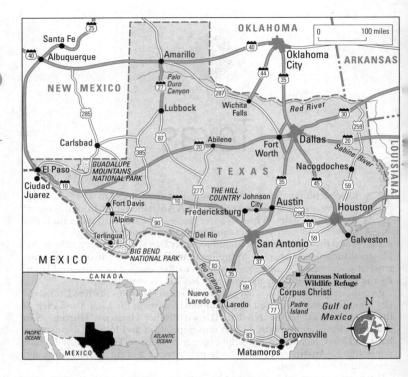

Texas") established Anglo-American colonies in the Brazos and Colorado River valleys. However, the Mexican leader, Santa Anna, soon became alarmed by Anglo aspirations to autonomy, and his increasing restrictions led to the eight-month **Texan Revolution** of 1835–36. The romance of the Revolution draws legions of tourists to **San Antonio**, site of the legendary **Battle of the Alamo**, which, though a military disaster, presaged independence. Today's street names echo the conflict: Crockett, Travis and Bowie were all heroes at the Alamo, and Houston was the general who finally led the army to victory at San Jacinto.

The short-lived **Republic of Texas**, which included territory now in Oklahoma, New Mexico, Colorado, Kansas and Wyoming, served to define the state's identity, and in 1845 Texas joined the Union on the understanding that it could secede whenever it so wished. This is still written into its constitution, as is the proviso that it can, at any time, divide itself into five separate states. Texans display an unmatched measure of state pride: Texas schoolchildren are as familiar with the heroes of the Alamo as the heroes of the Revolutionary War, and you'll see a ubiquitous state symbol – the **Lone Star** – emblazoned on everything from advertising to architecture.

The influence, especially in the north and east, of settlers from the Southern states and their attendant slave-centered cotton economy resulted in Texas joining the **Confederacy**. No major Civil War battles were fought on Texan soil, however, and it remained relatively unscathed. During Reconstruction, settlers from both the North and the South began to pour in, and the phrase

"Gone to Texas" was familiarly applied to anyone fleeing the law, bad debts or unhappy love affairs. This was also the period of the great cattle drives, when the longhorns roaming free in the south and west of Texas were rounded up and taken to the railroads in Kansas. The Texan – and national – fascination with the romantic myth of the **cowboy** has its roots in this era, and still prevails; today his regalia – Stetson, boots and bandana – is virtually a state costume, especially in Fort Worth and the west.

Along with ranching and agriculture, **oil** has been crucial. After the first big gusher in 1901, at Spindletop on the Gulf Coast, the focus of the Texan economy – and culture – shifted almost overnight from agriculture toward rapid industrialization. Boom towns flew up as wildcatters chased the wells, and millions of dollars were made as ranchers, who had previously thought their land only fit for cattle, sold out at vast profit. Texas today produces one-third of all the oil in the United States, and the sight of nodding pump jacks is one of the state's most potent images.

Getting around Texas

Texan distances are best negotiated by **car**; in fact, in the larger cities like Dallas or Houston driving is all but essential. **Greyhound** routes are concentrated between the major cities of the east and the central region, though buses also serve the Gulf Coast, the Rio Grande Valley, West Texas and, to a lesser extent, the Panhandle. Two **Amtrak** trains pass through Texas: The *Texas Eagle* travels between Chicago and San Antonio, stopping in Dallas and Austin; while the *Sunset Limited* stops in Houston, Alpine and El Paso on its way between Orlando and Los Angeles. An Amtrak Thruway bus links San Antonio with Laredo. **Flying** saves time and can be very cheap; look out for price wars between airlines such as Southwest and smaller local carriers.

Where Texas really falls down is on **public transportation** within the cities themselves; mass transit has proved impractical in a state where long distances – in Houston many people travel at least thirty miles to work – and low gasoline prices make the love affair with the car almost inevitable. **Cycling** only really makes sense within cities like Austin and San Antonio.

Southern Texas and the Gulf Coast

The coastline of **south Texas**, which state residents half-jokingly refer to as the "Third Coast," curves from Port Arthur on the Louisiana border (a shipping and petrochemical town and the birthplace of Janis Joplin) on the much-touristed **Gulf Coast**, down past the urban monster of Houston, to the Rio Grande, the border with Mexico. Giant, cosmopolitan **Houston** dominates everything; its great wealth has led to a thriving arts scene, but ultimately it overpowers, rather than relates to, the rest of the region. Geographically and culturally, this area has two distinct faces. To the east are the seaside resorts of the prairie, rolling away from the hills and forests of east Texas. Much of the coast is feeling the strain of rapid property development, but there are still unspoiled stretches along the **Padre Island National Seashore**. In the south, a Hispanic influence spreads north from the fertile Rio Grande Valley. The border towns here have little charm and are only of interest as points of entry into Mexico for cheap shopping and entertainment. Uniting south Texas is the hot, swampy climate; Houston, especially, is unbearable in the summer, one reason for the mass exodus to the coast.

Houston

HOUSTON is an ungainly beast of a city, confused by overdevelopment during the oil boom and then traumatized by the sudden slump of the early 1980s. It's a suffocating place, choking with traffic and high on humidity, yet for all this, its sheer energy, its relentless Texan pride, and above all its refusal to take itself totally seriously, give it a perverse appeal, while its well-endowed museums and rich nightlife mean there is always something to do. That Howard Hughes came from Houston makes absolute sense; eccentric, domineering and sordid, the millionaire typified all that makes the city intriguing.

There is no good reason why Houston exists at all; it was founded on a muddy mire in 1837 by two brothers from New York who hoped it would become the capital of the new Republic of Texas. For all their wild claims about its potential as a port, and its (imaginary) urban attractions, the more promising site of Austin was made capital in 1839. However, by then Houston had somehow established itself as a commercial center. Oil – discovered in 1901, and, like the city itself, unpredictable and heading for obsolescence – became the foundation, along with cotton and real estate, of vast private fortunes. Among the most famous of the philanthropists responsible for the development of downtown Houston was the cruelly named Ima Hogg. Her city improvement projects were largely cosmetic, however, and the contradictions of urban life are still writ large here, where abject poverty (not least among the blacks who migrated here from the rural South in the 1960s) coexists with ostentatious wealth.

Arrival, information and getting around

Downtown Houston is at the intersection of I-10 (San Antonio–New Orleans) and I-45 (Dallas–Galveston), with most of what you'll want to see encircled by Loop 610, now widened on the west to include the huge Galleria mall. **George Bush Intercontinental Airport** (☎281/230-3000), 23 miles north, is the main hub for Continental Airlines, while the smaller, domestic **William P. Hobby Airport** (☎713/641-7770), is seven miles southeast of downtown, just west of I-45 and a major hub for the budget Southwest Airlines. Both are served by the Airport Express **shuttle** (☎713/523-8888), which drops off at the Galleria and downtown hotels ($19 from Intercontinental and Hobby), and Metro **buses** (from Intercontinental on route #101 or #102: Mon–Fri 5.30am–midnight, Sat and Sun 5.20am–12.30am; $1.50; from Hobby on route #101 or #50: daily 5am–midnight; $1.50; ⊛www.ridemetro.org) which run downtown approximately every half-hour. **Taxis** cost $35 to $45 from Intercontinental, with the downtown fare from Hobby priced at $25 – though the fare to the Galleria from here is $35. With these prices, renting a **car** makes sense for some, and all major companies are represented at the airports.

Amtrak arrives at 902 Washington Ave, on the western fringes of downtown. Have your camera ready for a splendid view of the skyline, though the station itself is small, isolated and barely served by taxis. Try to arrive here, or at the large and modern **Greyhound** terminal, 2121 Main St, during daylight hours, as the immediate surroundings can feel a bit threatening.

The main **tourist office**, a huge space with touch-screen computers and other visual displays, is on the first floor of City Hall, 901 Bagby St (daily 9am–4pm; ☎713/227-3100 or 1-800/365-7575, ⊛www.houston-guide.com).

City transport

There are few options for nondrivers in Houston. The Metro buses are predominantly for commuters; **taxis** (the most reliable firm is Yellow Cabs; ☎713/236-1111) at $4 for the first mile and $1.65 for each additional mile, are expensive; and the humid climate and huge distances make walking unappealing. However, in the face of crippling traffic congestion, efforts are being made to encourage public transportation; a light rail system is in the works linking downtown to key tourist destinations. Maps of the city's **bus** routes are available from the Customer Service Center, 813 Dallas Ave (Mon–Fri 7.30am–5.30pm). Local fares are $1 (with free transfers), while the downtown trolleys are free. For more information call ☎713/635-4000.

Gray Line Tours (☎713/670-3254, ☻www.grayline.com) and Texas Bus Lines (☎713/523-8888) offer several **sightseeing tours** from $25.

Accommodation

Although hostelers are reasonably well catered for, there's little call for budget **accommodation** in central Houston, where most visitors will have cars; inexpensive hotels are concentrated near the Astrodome and outside the Loop, and motorists should try along I-45 or I-10.

You might also arrange **bed and breakfast** accommodation in advance; the human touch can be welcome in a city as potentially alienating and standards are high.

Angel Arbor B&B 848 Heights Blvd ☎713/868-4654 or 1-888/810-0092, ☻www.angelarbor.com. Redbrick Georgian home just northwest of downtown which hosts "Murder Mystery Dinner Parties." ❻

Grant Palm Court Inn 8200 S Main St ☎1-800/255-8904. Reliable motel near the Astrodome, with a small pool but relatively large rooms. ❷

Houston International Hostel 5302 Crawford St ☎713/523-1009, ☻www.houstonhostel.com. Near Hermann Park in a pleasant neighborhood; dorm beds $12 for members, $14 for others. ❶

Lancaster Hotel 701 Texas Ave ☎713/228-9500, ☻www.lancaster.com/hotel.htm. Small English-flavored hotel in the Theatre District. Expensive, but weekend rates go down to around $145. ❾

Lovett Inn 501 Lovett Blvd ☎713/522-5224 or 1-800/779-5224, ☻www.lovettinn.com. Located on a leafy avenue on the edge of the Montrose district, this historic house offers first-class service and Southern hospitality. ❹

Sara's Bed and Breakfast 941 Heights Blvd ☎713/868-1130 or 1-800/593-1130, ☻www.saras.com. Less than four miles northwest of downtown, near Memorial Park. A sweet Victorian house with a fine view of downtown Houston, serving continental breakfasts on the porch. ❹

YMCA 1600 Louisiana Ave ☎713/659-8501. Clean downtown rooms with shared bathrooms, a cut above the usual YMCA standards, for around $30 plus a $10 key deposit. ❶

The City

It's demoralizing and unwise to try and see too much of Houston in one go; best to concentrate on **downtown** or the **Museum District**, which can be walked around at leisure. Houston's human face is most evident in the **Montrose** area, on the way to yuppification but still home to eccentrics and bohemians.

Downtown

Since the oil crisis in the early 1980s, the frenzy of skyscraper-building has slowed down, but Houston's skyline remains an unforgettable monument to an earlier age of certainty. Observation floors at the **Chase Tower**, 600 Travis St, and the **Texaco Plaza** offer views of the endless plateau over which the city sprawls. Just to the north, the area now covered by the reflecting pool in front

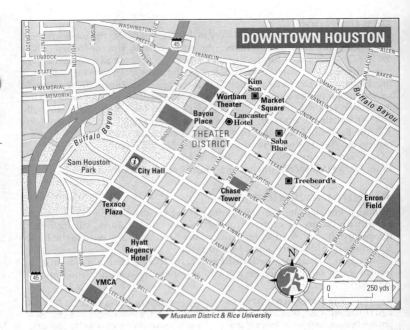

DOWNTOWN HOUSTON

Museum District & Rice University

of **City Hall** was granted to the city by a characterful rancher on the condition that no one could ever be arrested there for public intoxication, so it attracts a somewhat varied crowd.

Most people escape the Houston heat by staying underground, in the nearly seven miles of air-conditioned **tunnels** entered from the *Hyatt Regency* and the Main Street banks. However, they're a confusing and visually unappealing way to get around, despite the city's pride in their shops and restaurants. One consequence of this bustling subterranean world is a surreal, dreamlike isolation above ground, as few pedestrians emerge into the sunlight long enough to enjoy the various modern sculptures installed along the sidewalks (such as the Mirós outside the Chase Tower).

Nestling below the skyscrapers, **Sam Houston Park** on Bagby Street (Mon–Sat 10am–4pm, Sun 1–5pm; $6) contains restored structures such as a church and shop, while **Market Square** features some of the original buildings at the heart of the early city.

Even if you don't make it to a performance in the **Theater District**, west of Milam Street between Preston and Rusk streets, visit the **Wortham Theater Center**, 500 Texas St (☎713/237-1439), which houses the city's opera and ballet. The beautifully sculpted interior, perfect acoustics and secluded private bars take the breath away, as does the knowledge that the whole set-up cost $70 million.

Baseball fans won't want to miss **Enron Field,** home of the Houston Astros (ⓦwww.astros.com). The park, which opened in 2000, features a retractable roof that can withstand hurricane conditions and close in twelve minutes. Tours of the field are available (during the season Mon–Fri 10am, noon, 2pm, 4pm; no 4pm tour on Sat or game days; off-season Mon–Sat 10am, noon, 2pm; $7; ☎713/259-8687).

The Museum District and the Rice University area

Five miles southwest of downtown, the oak-lined, student-thronged boulevards of the **Museum** and **Rice** districts are enjoyable to explore on foot, full of interesting exhibition spaces and several good bookstores.

A magnificent purpose-built gallery at 1515 Sul Ross St – designed by Renzo Piano, who contributed to the Pompidou Centre in Paris – houses the private **Menil Collection** (Wed–Sun 11am–7pm; free; ☎713/525-9400, ⓦwww.menil.org). The superb works, gathered by oil millionaires John and Dominique de Menil, are displayed in spacious rooms, white-walled and naturally lit. Pieces range from paleolithic carvings dating from 15,000 BC, and a female idol from the "Mother Goddess" civilization of Catal Huyuk in Turkey, right up to modern sculptures such as Barnett Newman's 1950 *Here 1*. Artists with rooms to themselves include Max Ernst – look for the bronze *The King Playing with the Queen* – and René Magritte, while there's also a fine array of African art, including woodcarvings from Mali and ivories from Benin. One block east, the minimalist Ecumenical **Rothko Chapel**, 3900 Yupon St at Sul Ross (daily 10am–6pm; ☎713/524-9839, ⓦwww.menil.org/rothko.html), contains fourteen morose paintings commissioned by the Menils from Mark Rothko shortly before his death. The artist, who worked with architect Philip Johnson in designing the chapel, considered these to be his most important works, but many people today deride the building's resemblance to a nuclear bunker. The broken obelisk in the small park outside is dedicated to Dr Martin Luther King Jr. Diagonally opposite, the **Byzantine Fresco Chapel Museum**, 4011 Yupon St (Wed–Sun 11am–6pm; free; ☎713-521-3990, ⓦwww.menil.org/byzantine.html), houses a pair of thirteenth-century Cypriot frescoes in a contemporary structure with a somber, subdued ambience.

At the intersection of Bissonet and Main streets, the expansive **Museum of Fine Arts** (Tues, Wed, & Sat 10am–7pm, Thurs & Fri 10am–9pm, Sun 12.15–7pm; $5, free Thurs; ☎713-639-7300, ⓦwww.mfah.org) features an eclectic collection from all eras, with Renaissance art especially well represented. Crane your neck upward from the Matisses and Rodins in the pine-shaded **Cullen Sculpture Garden** outside to the downtown skyline.

Hermann Park, three miles south of downtown, is a pleasant green space with its own Japanese meditation garden. Exhibits on natural history at its excellent **Houston Museum of Natural Science** (Mon–Sat 9am–6pm, Sun 11am–6pm; $5, free Tues after 2pm; ☎713/639-4629, ⓦwww.hmns.org) include the Cullen Hall of Gems and Minerals, with its fascinating spangly array of diamonds and other jewels. The **Cockrell Butterfly Center** (additional $4) is a giant three-story greenhouse where you can walk among lurid, exotic butterflies as they flutter around a rainforest environment, and even watch them emerge from their cocoons. There's also an IMAX theater (hourly Mon–Thurs 10am–6pm, Fri & Sat 10am–8pm, Sun 11am–6pm; $6.50), a stunning gem collection, a *McDonald's* on the premises and a sundial fountain lapping a map of the Texas coastline. Be aware that the park is best avoided at night.

A short walk away, the **Contemporary Art Museum**, 5216 Montrose Blvd (Tues–Wed 10am–5pm, Thurs 10am–9pm, Fri–Sat 10am–5pm, Sun noon–5pm; free; ☎713/284-8250, ⓦwww.camh.org), is worth a look if only for its striking architecture, notably its huge windowless corrugated-steel facade. The **Holocaust Museum Houston**, 5401 Caroline St (Mon–Fri 9am–5pm, Sat & Sun noon–5pm; free; ☎713-942-8000, ⓦwww.hmh.org), is housed in another architecturally striking building, with a massive black funnel emerging from a triangular glass wedge. A chilling movie, *Voices*, is on permanent play and installations focus on concentration camps and those local people who survived.

The Reliant Astrodome and the Orange Show

Around three miles farther south from the Museum District, down Kirby Drive, Houston's legendary **Reliant Astrodome** was the first domed, climatized stadium in the world when it was built in 1965, and lends its name to astroturf which was first laid down here. It was home to the NFL's Oilers before they relocated to Nashville a few years ago and, with the Astros having played their last baseball season here in 1999, its sparse usage is now restricted to big-wheel truck racing, trade shows and, in March, the Houston Livestock Show and Rodeo – predictably, the world's largest. Pro sports is set to return to the area in 2002, upon completion of a football stadium for the Houston Texans. A few hundred yards beyond, on the far side of the Loop, the big attraction at the **Six Flags AstroWorld** theme park is yet another mighty roller coaster, the suspended-looping "megacoaster" Serial Thriller (opening hours vary; $37.99; ☎713/799-8404, ⊛www.sixflags.com).

Despite the dreams of its creator, **The Orange Show**, five miles east at 2401 Munger Ave, just off I-45 at the Telephone Road exit, is an altogether lower-key affair (March–Dec Sat & Sun noon–5pm; summer also Wed–Fri 9am–1pm; $1). Promoted as Houston's most original piece of folk art, it's not really a show, but a suburban house transformed by the monomania of former salesman and would-be inventor Jeff McKissack into a paean to the orange. With one simple purpose – "to get more people to eat more oranges" – McKissack spent twenty years covering his home with celebratory tiles, ironwork and slogans, with placards displayed by such oddball mannequins as the son of Santa Claus. The fabric of the place is solid ("weak construction would make the orange look weak"), but much of the mosaic work is surprisingly delicate, and it's not quite as garish as it might sound. When he finally opened it to the public in May 1979, McKissack confidently predicted that eight out of every ten Americans would visit. Depressed at the lack of crowds, the author of *How You Can Live 100 Years . . . And Still Be Spry* (in which oranges played a starring role) died in June 1980 aged 77.

The Galleria and around

The ultramodern **Galleria** hypermall lies just west of the Loop, on Westheimer Road. Its three hundred or so smart shops, movie theaters and restaurants, plus skating rink and health club (with indoor tennis courts!), and ornate street lamps and signage, exemplify Houston's love of modern architecture, upmarket style and Texan tack. Across the way, a waterfall-sized fountain cascades outside the 64-story, black-glass **Williams Tower**, particularly breathtaking when lit at night.

Montrose

Bohemian and fun **Montrose** begins at the junction of Smith and Elgin streets. It's all quirky sleaze, chock-full of tattoo parlors, vintage clothing stores, experimental art galleries, and junk shops selling barbed-wire cacti and other curiosities. While the forces of gentrification are evidently at work, don't think it's all gone Gap. Though the teenagers who once cruised the streets on Saturday night have been forced elsewhere and the strip joints have closed down, this has long been the base of a very visible **gay** community, and a high concentration of gay bars and clubs remains.

Eating

There's plenty of variety in Houston's **food**: the large immigrant population has left its mark. Look out for Mexican, Vietnamese and even Indian restaurants, and the many good delis – such as the sixteen outlets of *Antone's Deli* – serving huge salads and sandwiches with an international flavor.

Benjy's 2424 Dunstan Rd, off Kirby Rd ☎713/522-7602. Modern American food with an ethnic bent and inventive desserts in California-style decor near Rice University.

Black Labrador 4100 Montrose Ave ☎713/529-1199. Open fireplaces, oak beams and superb English comfort food (bangers, shepherd's pie and the like) with great black-and-tans and imported Yorkshire bitter.

Goode Company 5109 Kirby Rd ☎713/522-2530. Fabulous barbecue on the road to the Astrodome, with creative menu, outdoor seating and C&W atmosphere.

Kim Son 2001 Jefferson St ☎713/222-2461 or 300 Milam St ☎713/222-2790. Massive Vietnamese restaurant with a long menu. Best at lunch for the good-value buffet.

La Strada 322 Westheimer Rd ☎713/523-1014. Very tasty Italian dishes with an innovative and spicy Texan twist, near downtown.

Ruggles Grill 903 Westheimer Rd ☎713/524-3839. One of the best places for a big night out in Montrose, with eclectic regional food at around $18 per entree. Reservations are advisable.

Saba Blue 416 Main St ☎713/228-7222. Fusion-based cuisine (think calamari, wasabi, sesame-crusted tuna) in a hip atmosphere smack in the middle of the revitalized downtown strip.

La Tapatia 1749 Richmond Ave ☎713/521-3144. This Mexican diner looks uninviting but its big, low-cost portions are a hit with Montrose residents.

This Is It 207 W Gray St ☎713/659-1608. Heaps of soul food at budget prices in this downtown favorite.

Treebeard's 1117 Texas St ☎713/229-8248. Cheap and tasty Cajun food; good for a downtown lunch (stick to the vegetable plates rather than the stews), and don't miss the simple, delicious butter bread.

Entertainment and nightlife

There's no shortage of things to do in Houston; just check the listings in the free *Houston Press* (🌐www.houstonpress.com). **Cajun** and **zydeco** music have been significant in the city since a wave of migration from rural Louisiana in the early 1960s; and there's a strong **blues** tradition, while rootsy Texan **country** is another favorite. The Montrose area supports a very visible **gay** scene, and most of the clubs tend to be very male-dominated. **Miller Outdoor Theatre** in Hermann Park, at 2020 Hermann Drive (☎713/284-8354), has free symphony concerts, swing and opera on summer evenings, a "Juneteenth Blues" festival and a Shakespeare Festival in August. Downtown's **Theatre District** holds considerable options including the nationally renowned **Alley Theater** at 615 Texas Ave (☎713/228-8421, 🌐www.alleytheatre.org), which offers last-minute discount seats, and the **Wortham Theater Center**, on the same street (see p.722), is home to Houston's opera and ballet companies. **Bayou Place** at Bagby between Texas and Capitol streets, is a relatively new – and ever-expanding – entertainment and restaurant complex that used to be a convention hall; one of its more interesting residents is the **Angelika Film Center** (☎713/225–5232, 🌐www.angelika.com), a multiscreen cinema complex that shows many art movies and has a good late night coffee house.

Bars and clubs

Big Easy Social and Pleasure Club 5731 Kirby Dr ☎713/523-9999. The city's best blues, plus occasional zydeco nights in the University area.

Emo's 2700 Albany St ☎713/523-8503. A little hard to find on the edge of Montrose, but this slacker bar gets in the first-rate alternative bands from the US and around the world. Beer prices are below average, too.

Engine Room 1515 Pease St ☎713/654-7846. Pool tables and aggressive indie line-up (think Limp Bizkit on the way up), plus a crowd that seems culled from more than one economic class.

Fabulous Satellite Lounge 3616 Washington Ave

⊕713/869-2665, ⊛www.fabsat.com. Hosts the cream of Texan roots bands and singer-songwriters.

The Last Concert Café 1403 Nance St ⊕713/226-8563. East of downtown, in an arty and isolated area. Good, cheap Tex-Mex food and live rock and roots bands in the back garden.

McGonigel's Mucky Duck 2425 Norfolk St ⊕713/226-8563. A great folk club featuring national acts, as well as a terrific Irish jam session on Wed.

Rudyard's 2010 Waugh Dr ⊕713/521-0521. Solid

indie bands amid the raucous atmosphere make up for somewhat surly service.

Sam's Boat and Sam's Place 5720 Richmond Ave ⊕713/781-2628. If you were wondering about the Richmond scene, here's its zenith, in all its post-college glory. Yes, it's the bar shaped like a boat.

Spotlight Karaoke 5901 Westheimer Rd ⊕713/266-7768. A popular karaoke joint seemingly frozen in 1978, with a great selection of songs and a dedicated crowd.

Around Houston

Houston's double-edged status as having both historical importance and all the trappings of a hyper-modern "space city" is exemplified by two major attractions, both about twenty miles south of the city.

San Jacinto Battleground State Historical Park

San Jacinto Battleground, 22 miles east of Houston off I-10, was the site of an eighteen-minute fight, two months after the Alamo in 1836, in which the Texans all but wiped out the superbly trained Mexican army. You see little but miles of flat land from the observation deck ($3) of the tallest stone column **monument** in the world (570ft, topped by a 34ft Lone Star), but the **Museum of History** inside is more interesting, with the stirring 35-minute movie *Texas Forever!* (hourly 9am–5pm; museum daily 9am–6pm; $3.50; ⊛www.sanjacinto-museum.org).

NASA

NASA has been controlling space flight from the **Johnson Space Center**, 25 miles south of Houston off I-45 (bus #246 from downtown), since the launch of *Gemini 4* in 1965 – locals love to point out that the first word ever spoken on the moon was "Houston." As a working facility, it's not fully geared to tourists, but three tram tours will give you a glimpse into different parts of the grounds. Start with an impressive array of hands-on exhibits at the **Space Center Houston** (summer daily 9am–7pm, rest of year Mon–Fri 9am–5pm, Sat & Sun 10am–7pm; $14.95; ⊕281-244-2100, ⊛www.spacecenter.org); you get to try on space helmets, inspect moonrocks and some remarkably rickety-looking rocket replicas, join astronauts and scientists in the cafeteria, and stock up on gimmicky space-themed merchandising.

The Gulf Coast

You only have to look at the number of condo developments along the **Gulf Coast** to see that this is a major tourist destination. The climate ranges from balmy at Galveston to subtropical at the Mexican border, but everywhere it's windy: Corpus Christi rivals Chicago as the gustiest city in the States, and a devastating hurricane in 1900 all but leveled the city of Galveston. The fierce tide, progressively gnawing away at the beaches, may pose a threat to tourism, but for now **Galveston** offers history, shopping and low-key relief from uptight Houston, while **Corpus Christi** to the south makes the best base for the beaches of Padre Island National Seashore. **Rockport**, a weathered resort on Hwy-35, is convenient for the **Aransas National Wildlife Refuge**, sheltering endangered whooping cranes, armadillos and alligators.

Galveston

In 1890 **GALVESTON** – on the northern tip of Galveston Island, the southern terminus of I-45 – was a thriving port, far larger than Houston fifty miles northwest; many newly arrived European immigrants chose to stay here in the so-called "Queen of the Gulf." However, the building of Houston's Ship Canal, after the hurricanes of 1900 killed more than six thousand people and washed away much of the land, left the coastal town to fade slowly away. Thanks to its pretty historic district and its popularity with Houston residents seeking a summer escape, Galveston's undergone a certain revitalization, but the occasionally gritty city still seems to be laboring under the psychic weight of its past calamities.

The **Strand** downtown, the 19th-century "Wall Street of the Southwest," has been fitted with gaslights, upmarket shops, restaurants and galleries. The **Texas Seaport Museum**, in amongst a complex of shops and restaurants on Pier 21, just off Water Street (daily 10am–5pm; $6; ☎409-763-1877, ⊛www.tsm-elissa.org), focuses on the port's role in trade and immigration during the nineteenth century; admission includes boarding the *Elissa*, an 1877 tall ship. **Harbor tours** (Sat 8.30am, 10.30am & 1.30pm; $12) leave from the adjacent Pier 22, taking a 90-minute look at the town's trading history.

Between the Strand and the beaches, old houses are everywhere, among them the ostentatious **Bishop's Palace**, 1402 Broadway (summer Mon–Sat 10am–5pm, Sun noon–5pm; rest of year daily noon–4pm; $6), with its stained glass, mosaics and marble; the antebellum **Ashton Villa**, 2328 Broadway (Mon–Sat 10am–4pm, Sun noon–4pm; $5), which shows a film about the 1900 hurricane and tours starting on the hour; the 1839 **Samuel May Williams Home**, 3601 Ave P (Sat & Sun noon–4pm; $3), a New England residence moved here from Maine; and the city's oldest building, the **Michel B. Menard Home**, 1605 33rd St (Fri–Sun noon–4pm; $6), an imposing wooden structure built in 1838 which now holds a good collection of American antiques. Galveston's old Santa Fe depot, at 25th Street and the Strand, is now a **Railroad Museum** (daily 10am–4pm; $5), displaying steam trains, Pullman cars and endless train-travel-related artifacts in a skillful evocation of a lost era. Eerie white statues stand around in the waiting room; pick up a telephone and listen to their conversations.

On the west side of town, **Moody Gardens**, at I-45 61st St exit (summer daily 10am–9pm, winter Mon–Thurs & Sun 10am–6pm, Fri & Sat 10am–9pm; $7.95 per attraction, $28.95 day pass to all attractions; ☎800.582.4673, ⊛www.moodygardens.com), is an environmental research facility where you can happily while away a few hours. The complex is centered around three giant glass pyramids: the Rainforest Pyramid houses exotic plants, birds and fish from around the world; the Discovery Pyramid is a good-quality science museum with an IMAX cinema; and the impressive Aquarium Pyramid is one of the largest aquariums in the world. Also in the ever-growing complex are themed outdoor gardens, pleasant walking trails along the shore of scenic **Offatt's Bayou**, where you can take a cruise on a paddlewheeler, and Palm Beach, a popular spot for families where kids can play on a giant yellow submarine. It's worth visiting more than one attraction, especially as the box office (☎409/744-4673 or 1–800/582-4673) offers an array of discounted combo tickets.

The downtown **beaches** of Seawall Boulevard are a constant reminder of Galveston's struggle simply to exist: murky, rocky and protected behind a ten-mile-long seawall from the ever-encroaching tides and the threat of further hurricanes. **Stewart Beach Park**, the most convenient beach for downtown, is geared toward family fun and gets very crowded; the wide **R.A. Apfell Park**, further east, is marginally quieter during the week, but has live music some weekends and a lively bar. Both of these beaches charge $5 per car.

Arrival, information and accommodation

Greyhound takes about ninety minutes to cover the fifty miles from Houston, arriving at 714 25th St (around $6 by taxi from downtown). There is no Amtrak service. **Trolleys** (daily 10am–6.30pm; $1; ☎409/797-3900, ⓦwww.islandtransit.net) rattle past the historic homes and other sights between the **visitor centers** at 2215 the Strand and 2428 Seawall Blvd (daily 8.30am–5pm; ☎1-888/425-4753, ⓦwww.galveston.com).

Hotels in Galveston are pricey in summer and at weekends, but bargains can be found at other times; rates along Seawall Boulevard can drop below $40 per night. Within easy walking distance to the Strand, the town's **East End Historic District** holds some relaxing **B&Bs**.

Commodore on the Beach 3618 Ship's Mechanic Row ☎409/763-2375 or 1-800/231-9921, ⓦwww.commodoreonthebeach.com. Nicer than *Treasure Isle* and has a large pool; adequate, inexpensive rooms overlook the Gulf. ❹–❻

Gaido's Seaside Inn 3800 Ship's Mechanic Row ☎409/762-9625 or 1-800/525-0064. A clean, popular choice, with a good fish restaurant attached. ❹

Hotel Galvez 2024 Ship's Mechanic Row ☎409/765-7721. Classy hotel built in 1911, with a beautiful pool and swim-up bar. ❺–❼

Garden Inn 1601 Ball St ☎409/770-0592 or 1-888/770-7298. Built in 1887, a very pretty

Victorian B&B in the historic district featuring well-appointed rooms and a hammock in the backyard. ❺

Queen Anne B&B 1915 Sealy Ave ☎409/763-7088 or 1-800/472-0930, ⓦwelcome.to/queenanne. Pleasant B&B built in 1905. ❺

Treasure Isle Inn 1002 Ship's Mechanic Row ☎409/763-8561. One of the best values at the lower end of the spectrum. ❸

Tremont Hotel 2300 Ship's Mechanic Row ☎409/763-0300. Landmark hotel and the grandest place to stay on the island, with tastefully uncluttered Victorian decor in the rooms. ❻–❾

Eating and drinking

Dining out in Galveston will likely mean settling in at one of the many low-key seafood restaurants along Seawall Boulevard – they're unassuming, yes, but the often delicious fresh fish dishes and unapologetically kitschy decor are strangely intoxicating. **Nightlife** in Galveston basically amounts to cover bands, but there are several good noisy bars along Post Office Street between 20th and 23rd streets.

Casey's 3800 Seawall Blvd ☎409/762-9625. A less expensive option offering local Gulf seafood.

Clary's 8509 Teichman Rd, off I-45 on Offat's Bayou ☎409/740-0771. Somewhat pricey, but recommended for the excellent fresh seafood.

Evolution 2214 Mechanic St ☎409/763-4212. A boisterous nightclub that's a good place to dance off some excess energy — and one of the few places open very late (4 am on weekends).

Old Quarter Acoustic Café 413 20th St ☎409/762-9199. Presents hard-edged folk music; the late Texan singer-songwriter Townes Van Zandt

wrote *Rex's Blues* about the café's owner, musician Rex Bell.

21 2102 Post Office St ☎409/762-2101. Classy, subdued bar with a menu of over twenty varieties of martinis.

Phoenix 2228 Ship's Mechanic Rd ☎409/763-4611. Bakery and popular breakfast spot; don't leave without trying the yummy beignets.

Yaga's Café 2314 the Strand ☎409/762-6676. Serves delicious Caribbean food in gaudy surroundings amid reggae and calypso music.

Corpus Christi

The unabashed and much larger resort town of **CORPUS CHRISTI** is reached along the coast on Hwy-35 from Houston or Galveston, or on I-37 from San Antonio. Originally a rambunctious trading post, it too was hit by a fierce hurricane, in 1919, but recovered, transforming itself into a center for naval air training, petroleum and shipping. Much of the population is Hispanic, and the community was devastated in March 1995, when the 23-year-old singer **Selena** was shot dead in a motel parking lot by the former president of her fan club. Selena was on the verge of becoming the first major cross-over star of **Tejano** music, a hybrid of Mexican rhythms, German polka and reggae-influenced Colombian *cumbia*, and fifty thousand fans turned out for her funeral. In addition to the Selena Auditorium at the Bayfront Convention Center, there's a memorial to the singer just south of Peoples Street on Shoreline Boulevard; a new **Selena Museum**, 5410 Leopard St, is stuffed with Selena memorabilia, from her famously extravagant gowns to her Porsche (Mon–Fri 9–11.45am & 1–6pm; free). The visitor center (see below) can supply a free map of Selena-centric stops.

Apart from fishing, sailing and water sports across the channel on Padre Island (see p.730), there's not a great deal to do in Corpus Christi. The impressive collection of the Philip Johnson-designed **South Texas Institute for the Arts**, 1902 N Shoreline Blvd (Tues–Sat 10am–5pm, Sun 1–5pm, first Thurs of the month until 9pm; $3; ☎361/825-3500, ⓦwww.stia.org), includes pieces by Monet and Picasso. Further along N Shoreline Boulevard, at no. 2710, is the massive **Texas State Aquarium** (summer Mon–Sat 9am–6pm, Sun 10am–6pm; rest of year until 5pm; $9; ☎361/881-1200 or 1-800/477-GULF, ⓦwww.texasstateaquarium.org), which nonetheless feels cramped compared to the aquarium in Galveston. Adjacent is the **USS Lexington** (summer daily 9am–6pm; rest of year until 5pm; $10; ⓦwww.usslexington.com), a World War II aircraft carrier that's impressive to walk around, though the few exhibits on board are weak. The **Corpus Christi Museum of Science and History**, 1900 N Chaparral St (daily: summer 9am–6pm; rest of year 9am–5pm; $8; ☎361/883-2862, ⓦwww.ci.corpus-christi.tx.us/services/museum), specializes in hands-on natural history exhibits, on topics ranging from shipwrecks to shells to, curiously, the building of the Selena memorial. Moored in the harbor a short walk from the museum, the **Columbus Fleet** (included in the museum admission) consists of life-size replicas of Christopher Columbus's *Santa Maria* and *Pinta*.

Practicalities

Greyhound arrives at 702 N Chaparral St downtown. The **visitor center** (☎361/881-1888 or 1-800/678-OCEAN, ⓦwww.corpuschristi-tx-cvb.org) is further along N Chaparral at no. 1823 (daily 9am–5pm; ☎361/561-2000 or 1-800/766-2322). A daytime **trolley** (☎361/289-2600; 50¢) connects the major attractions with area hotels (except Sun); other services include a free downtown "Beach Shuttle" **tram** service (summer only) and a harbor ferry from the art museum to the Texas State Aquarium ($1).

Budget **motels**, inaccessible without a car, line Leopard Street in the northwest. Along N Shoreline Boulevard, the *Bayfront Inn* at no. 601 is a good deal (☎361/883-7271 or 1-800/456-2293; ❸), while the *Omni Bayfront*, at no. 900, offers rooms with a view of the water (☎361/887-1600 or 1-800/843-6664, ⓦwww.omnihotels.com; ❺). Downtown Corpus's main concentration of **restaurants** is in Water Street Market at 309 N Water St, where the *Water Street*

Oyster Bar (☎361/881-9448) serves fresh seafood. *Wahoos*, 415 N Water St (☎361/888-8522), serves excellent Cajun food to a background of zydeco beats. Just across the JFK Causeway is *Snoopy's* at 13313 S Padre Island Drive (☎361/949-8815), with ridiculously good fried seafood and crabmeat-stuffed jalapeño peppers.

South toward Mexico

The barrier islands of **Padre Island National Seashore** (🌐www.nps.gov/pais) stretch just offshore for 110 miles south of Corpus Christi, almost down to the Mexican border. The frontier between **Brownsville** and **Matamoros** is not very interesting, however; for a brief taste of Mexico, head almost due west from Corpus one hundred miles to **Laredo**. (US-83 runs along the Rio Grande between Brownsville and Laredo.) Away from the coast, the fertile landscape begins to dry out and citrus groves give way to the brush and mesquite of a region of huge ranches, where Mexican *vaqueros* once held sway.

Padre Island National Seashore and Brownsville

Padre Island National Seashore is not quite as unspoiled these days as its reputation might suggest, with its ranks of condos advancing steadily, but it remains a good destination for bird-watching, beachcombing and camping. Pick up details at the **visitor center** at 20402 Park Road 22 (daily: summer 8.30am–6pm, rest of year 8.30am–4.30pm; ☎361/949-8068). The park is easily accessed by car, but cab services in Corpus Christi will make the trip for around $30 (Star Taxi ☎361/884-9451). The park itself is open 24 hours, with a $10 admission charge per vehicle, good for one week. Camping on the beach is free, but permits are $5 for the primitive Bird Island Basin and $8 for the semi-primitive *Malaquite Beach Campground*. Note that an impassable canal divides the island, meaning that the pricier and much more touristy **South Padre Island** in the south can only be reached from the mainland – it's a three-hour drive from Corpus Christi.

BROWNSVILLE, just across from South Padre Island, is a scruffy, semitropical resort, populated by retired Texans on winter vacation, where you'll hear more Spanish spoken than English. To cross the border into **MATAMOROS**, walk across Gateway Bridge at International Boulevard. Wealthier than Brownsville, and considerably larger, the Mexican city is not terribly inspiring, but it has a good market, Mercado Juarez, on calles 9 and 10, and an untouristy main plaza at Calle 5, dominated by the cathedral. If you're intending to stay in Mexico or venture further than twenty miles or so, you must pick up a tourist card from the Mexican Consulate at Twelfth Avenue and Washington Street in Brownsville.

Laredo

The dusty, downtrodden and rather isolated smuggling center of **LAREDO**, over one hundred miles from the coast, has seen greater days even though it's the fastest-growing city in the state. Santa Anna marched his troops through in 1836, and in 1840 the city was the center of Zapata's Mexican separatist protest. The capitol of Zapata's short-lived republic still stands on Zaragoza Street in the historic district, now housing the small **Republic of the Rio Grande Museum** (Tues–Sat 9am–4pm, Sun 1–4pm; $1). San Agustin Plaza, the site of the original Spanish settlement, has been restored with cobbled streets and Victorian buildings, as has El Mercado, on San Agustin Avenue, the former hub of downtown activity.

Nuevo Laredo: Mexican border crossing

It's an easy walk across the bridge from San Agustin Plaza in Laredo (see opposite) to the typical Mexican border town of **NUEVO LAREDO**; so easy that this is the most popular crossing along the entire frontier, with most visitors coming simply for evening meals and weekend shopping. There is a lively atmosphere, with all the tourist shops and restaurants concentrated near the bridge, on "the strip," Avenida Guerrero. Most take American dollars, and bargaining is acceptable at some.

Seven blocks down Avenida Guerrero, the main plaza is the social center of town. **Hotels** include the good-value *Nuevo Romano*, at Doctor Mier 800 (☎871/12-26-94; ❶), with rooms for around US$15, while the *Reforma*, on Avenida Guerrero at Calle Canales (☎871/12-26-50; ❶) is cleaner and better, but you'll still get change from thirty bucks. The *El Dorado Bar*, at Avenida Ocampo and Belden (☎871/12-00-15), was the first of the town's **bars** and **restaurants** to encourage tourism here, serving drinks to Texans escaping Prohibition. It's a bit tacky now; better to head for *El Rancho*, 2124 Avenida Guerrero (☎871/14-87-53), for *cabrito* (barbecued goat), guacamole and cold beer. For a more expensive treat, try the patio at *Victoria 3020*, 3020 Victoria St (☎871/13-30-20). As a whole, though, Nuevo Laredo lacks real charm, and can be particularly depressing after dark; have a meal but give the nightlife a miss.

As with all border crossings, expect to undergo full immigration procedures when you re-enter the United States.

Greyhound arrives at 610 Salinas St. The **visitor center** is at 501 San Agustin Ave (Mon–Fri 8am–5pm, Sat 9am–3pm; ☎956/795-2200 or 1-800/361-3360). **Hotels** include *La Quinta*, 3610 Santa Ursula Ave (☎956/722-0511, ⓦ www.laquinta.com; ❹), and the more central *La Posada*, 1000 Zaragoza St (☎956/722-1701, ⓦ www.laposadahotel-laredo.com; ❺), just east of the international bridge, where the dining room offers a big lunch buffet and good steaks. *Toños*, 1202 E Del Mar Blvd (☎956/717-4999) is especially popular at lunch for its Tex-Mex standards, and *Cotulla-Style Pit Bar-B-Q*, 4502 McPherson St (☎956/724-5747), serves a regional spicy type of barbecue as well as other Mexican dishes.

Central Texas

Central Texas stretches from the prairies of the northeast through the green and fertile Hill Country into the chalky limestone landscape of the west, and includes two of Texas's most pleasant cities: San Antonio and Austin. Austin in particular, the capital city and home to the progressive University of Texas, helps to give the region an intellectual and political feel uncharacteristic of the rest of the state.

Agriculture has been the mainstay of the economy here ever since the resistant Comanche population was finally packed off to reservations in the 1840s. The slave-driven cotton plantations of the south and east have gone, but the small communities set up by Polish, Czech, Norwegian and Swedish immigrants in the **Hill Country** maintained, even until very recently, the traditions, architecture and languages of their homelands. Great cattle drives came trampling through after the Civil War and played a large part in the development of San Antonio.

San Antonio

With neither the modern skyline of an oil town, nor the tumbleweed-strewn landscape of the Wild West, attractive and festive **SAN ANTONIO** looks nothing like the stereotypical image of Texas – despite being pivotal in the state's history. Standing at a geographical crossroads, it encapsulates the complex social and ethnic mixes of all Texas. Although the Germans, among others, have made a strong contribution to its architecture, cuisine and music, today's San Antonio is predominantly **Hispanic**: abundant Tex-Mex restaurants, the prevalent Catholicism, the newly expanded Mexican Cultural Institute and advertising billboards in Spanish all attest to a long history of "Texican" culture.

Founded in 1691 by Spanish missionaries, San Antonio became a military garrison in 1718, and was settled by the Anglos in the 1720s and 1730s under Austin's colonization program. It is most famous for the legendary **Battle of the Alamo** in 1836, when the Mexican General Santa Anna, seeking to curb the aspirations of the Anglo-Americans, wiped out a band of Texan volunteers: hence San Antonio's claim to be the "birthplace of the revolution," borne out by its role during Texas's ten subsequent years of independence. After the Civil War, it became a hard-drinking, hard-fighting "sin city," at the heart of the Texas **cattle** and **oil** empires. Drastic floods in the 1920s wiped out much of the downtown area, but the sensitive WPA program which revitalized two of the city's prettiest sites, **La Villita** and the **River Walk**, laid the foundations for its future as a major tourist destination. San Antonio is now the eighth largest city in the US, but it retains an unhurried, organic feel, thanks to a winning combination of small town warmth, respect for diversity and a self-confidence rooted in its own history.

Arrival, information and getting around

San Antonio International Airport (☎210/207-3411, ⓦwww.ci.sat.tx.us/ aviation/) is just north of the I-410 loop which encircles most of the sights. SA Trans Shuttle (☎1-800/868-7707) makes the twenty-minute journey downtown ($9 one-way, $16 round-trip; every 10-15min 4am–1am), while normal city buses cost only 75¢ but take nearly an hour to make the same trip. Taxis cost about $15 (Yellow Cabs ☎210/226-4242). Amtrak arrives centrally at 350 Hoefgen St, while Greyhound operates from 500 N St Mary's St. Pick up information on **city transport** from the **visitor center** at 317 Alamo Plaza directly across from the Alamo (daily 8.30am–6pm; ☎210/207-6748 or 1-800/447-3372, ⓦwww.sanantoniocvb.com), or call the VIA Metropolitan Transit Service (☎210/362-2020, ⓦwww.viainfo.net). **Buses** are reliable; journeys within the I-410 loop cost 75¢, and many downtown routes run until 10.30pm. Four downtown **streetcar** routes serve the major attractions for 50¢, from Alamo Plaza. A Day Tripper pass available from the VIA Downtown Information Center, 112 Soledad St, costs $2 and can be used on all buses, including express services, and trolleys. Gray Line's **bus tours** (☎210/226-

1706, @www.grayline.com) are only really of much use as a way to see the most distant missions (3 1/2 hr; $22), though VIA's #42 service from the Alamo does stop at the San Jose mission. The very enjoyable $5.25 **boat tours** (☎210/244-5700), which do a leisurely 35-minute circuit of the River Walk, depart from two locations, just below the bridges on Commerce Street and Market Street. You can rent **bicycles** from Abel's Mobile Bicycle Shop, 1119 Ada St (☎210/533-9927).

The downtown **post office** is next to the Alamo at 615 E Houston St (Mon–Fri 8.30am–5.30pm; (☎210/212-8046; zip code 78205).

Accommodation

The pleasure of a moonlit amble along the river back to your hotel is one of the joys of visiting San Antonio, so it's worth making a determined effort to stay in the center. However, downtown is monopolized by luxury hotels, and a car is virtually a prerequisite for finding budget lodgings. There are clusters of reasonably priced **motels** just north of Brackenridge Park on Austin Highway, or, convenient to the airport, on I-35 north toward Austin.

The Crockett Hotel 320 Bonham St ☎210/225-6500, @www.hotelsanantoniotx.com. Historic hotel with modern facilities, in an excellent location just opposite the Alamo. ❻

Days Inn (Alamo-River Walk) 902 E Houston St ☎210/227-6233, @www.daysinn.com. Standard chain motel rooms, two blocks from the Alamo and the River Walk. ❹

Hampton Inn River Walk 414 Bowie St ☎210/225-8500, @www.hamptoninn.com. Good, clean rooms in a central location. ❺

HI-San Antonio 621 Pierce St ☎210/223-9426, @www.hiayh.org/hostels/texas/sanant.htm. Across from Fort Sam Houston, two miles north of downtown (bus #11 or #15). Friendly proprietors make up for out-of-the-way location; a pool and kitchen are nice extras. Dorm beds $16.25 members, $19.25 others) and a few private rooms are available at $59. Call ahead to reserve in summer.

La Quinta – San Antonio Market Square 900 Dolorosa St ☎210/271-0001, @www.laquinta.com. Decent motel next to bustling Market Square. ❹

Menger Hotel 204 Alamo Plaza ☎210/223-4361, @www.historicmenger.com. Texas's most famous hotel of the great cattle drives; Teddy Roosevelt recruited his "Rough Riders" here in 1898 for the Spanish–American War. Inexplicably, the bar is furnished to re-create the tap-room at the British House of Lords. ❻

Motel 6 – San Antonio Downtown 211 N Pecos St ☎210/225-1111, @www.motel6.com. Clean but slightly worn rooms near Market Square, with a small pool. ❸

A Yellow Rose 229 Madison St ☎210/229-2903, www.ayellowrose.com. A relaxed, welcoming accommodation in the B&B-choked Historic King William District, with beautiful antique-laden rooms. ❺

The Town

Since mission times, the **San Antonio River** has been the key to the city's fortunes. Destructive floods in the 1920s, and subsequent oil drilling, reduced its flow, leading to plans to pave the river over. Instead, a careful landscaping scheme, started in 1939 by the WPA, created the Paseo del Rio, or **River Walk**, now the aesthetic and commercial focus of San Antonio. Below street level, the walk is reached by steps from various spots along the main roads and crossed by humpbacked stone bridges. Cobbled paths, lined with tropical plants and shaded by pine, cypress, oak and willow, wind for two and a half miles (twenty-one blocks) beside the jade-green water, with much of the city's eating and entertainment concentrated along the way. You can catch a river taxi at a number of places, but strolling is cheaper and just as much fun, for the view of the river slowly changing character between the lively Rivercenter Mall and the quieter, more park-like outskirts.

SAN ANTONIO

Bus Station

Alamo Visitor Center

The Alamo

Buckhorn Museum

San Fernando Cathedral

Spanish Governors Palace

Rivercenter Mall

La Villita

HemisFair Park

Mexican Cultural Institute

Tower of the Americas

KING WILLIAM HISTORIC DISTRICT

0   1 mile

N

RESTAURANTS, BARS AND CLUBS						ACCOMMODATION			
Bonham Exchange	A		Mi Tierra	G		A Yellow Rose	7	La Quinta	6
Boudro's	F		Paesano's	D		The Crockett Hotel	4	Menger Hotel	5
Casa Rio	H		Polly Esther's	C		Days Inn	3	Motel 6	1
El Mirador	J		Swig	E		Hampton Inn	2		
Jim Cullum's The Landing	B		Zuni Grill	I					

While the **Alamo** (see p.736) is the main attraction in the downtown area, the surreal **Buckhorn Museum**, 318 E Houston St (Sun–Thurs 10am–5pm, Fri & Sat 10am–6pm; $8.99), takes a pleasingly kitsch look at Americana. During San Antonio's heyday as a cowtown, cowboys, trappers and traders would bring their cattle horns to the original *Buckhorn Saloon* in exchange for a drink. The entire bar has been transplanted to this downtown location, which boasts an extra floor of exhibition space and, as well as thousands of horns on display, mounted as trophies, chandeliers and chairs, there are many stuffed animals, including "Blondie", an unforgettable two-headed lamb.

La Villita ("little town"), on the River Walk opposite Hemisfair Park, was San Antonio's original settlement, occupied in the mid- to late eighteenth century by Mexican "squatters" with no titles to the land. Only when its elevation enabled it to survive fierce floods in 1819 did this rude collection of stone and adobe buildings become suddenly respectable. It is now a National Historic District, turned over to a dubious "arts community" consisting mostly of over-priced craftshops (daily 10am–6pm). It's at its best off-season or at dusk, when the crowds dwindle and the muted colors, smells and noises are more evoca-tive of earlier times. In contrast, the 25-block **King William Historic District** southwest, between the river and S St Mary's Street, contains the ele-gant late nineteenth-century homes of German merchants. A pleasant incon-gruity in this Mexican-feeling city, it remains a fashionable residential area and has some stylish B&Bs (see p.733).

The best of several museums in **HemisFair Park** is the **Institute of Texan Cultures**, 801 S Bowie St (Tues–Sun 9am–5pm; $5), which maps the social histories of 26 diverse "Texan" cultures, with especially pertinent African-American and Native American sections, and an intriguing corner devoted to short-lived attempts to introduce the camel to West Texas as a beast of burden. The **Mexican Cultural Institute** (daily 10am–5pm; free) recently underwent a mammoth renovation, expanding into seven gallery spaces and a theatre, while retaining its focus on historic and contemporary Mexican art. The ugly 750ft **Tower of the Americas** is devoid of interest, save for the views from its observation deck (Sun–Thurs 9am–10 pm, Fri & Sat 9am–11pm; $3).

West of the river at 115 Main Plaza, the 1731 **San Fernando Cathedral** is the oldest cathedral in the US, though, contrary to the claims of the tourist board, nobody really believes that the Alamo heroes are buried here. Mariachi Masses are held on Saturday at 5.15pm, when crowds overflow onto the plaza. Two blocks west at 105 Plaza de Armas, the beautifully simple whitewashed **Spanish Governors Palace** (Mon–Sat 9am–5pm, Sun 10am–5pm; $1.50) was once home to Spanish officials during the mission era. Just one story tall, it's hardly a palace, but its flagstone floors, low doorways and beamed ceilings, religious icons and ornate wooden carvings give it a wonderful atmosphere, and it provides an illuminating glimpse of the lifestyles of the civil and religious authorities in this remote outpost. Don't miss the sweet cobbled courtyard, with its fountain, mosaic floor and lush palms.

Market Square (daily: summer 10am–8pm; rest of year 10am–6pm), a cou-ple of blocks further northwest, dates from 1840. Its outdoor restaurants and bustle are still at the heart of the city's life; fruit and vegetables are on sale early in the morning, while the shops are a compelling mix of color and kitsch. **El Mercado**, an indoor complex, is meant to resemble a traditional Mexican market, selling tourist-oriented gifts, jewelry and oddities. A few of the shops are great, even if the air conditioning and piped music undermine the authen-ticity of the venture.

It's also worth getting to the beautiful **McNay Art Museum**, 6000 N New Braunfels Ave at Austin Highway (Tues–Sat 10am–5pm, Sun noon–5pm; free). This exquisite Moorish-style villa, complete with tranquil garden, was built in the 1950s to house the art collection of millionaire and folk artist Marion Koogler McNay, which includes modern sculpture, Gothic and medieval works, as well as a sprinkling of major players (Picasso, Monet and Van Gogh). Buses #11 (Nacogdoches) and #14 (Thousand Oaks) serve the museum from downtown. On the way there, bus #11 passes the **San Antonio Museum of Art**, 200 W Jones Ave (Tues 10am–9pm, Wed–Sat 10am–5pm, Sun noon–5pm; $5, free on Tues 3–9pm), which occupies the old Lone Star Brewery, but it's the added Rockefeller Center for Latin American Art wing that holds most inter-est, with its particularly fine exhibit on folk art.

The Alamo and the other missions

The Alamo (☎210/225-1391, ⊛www.thealamo.org) is the most famous – for reasons that have nothing to do with its original purpose – of a trail of Catholic missions established by the Spanish along remote stretches of the San Antonio River early in the eighteenth century. San Antonio's most distinctive landmark, it is smack in the center of downtown, but for a real sense of early Spanish influence in Texas, it's important to make an effort to get out and see the more distant, less visited missions. Each was laid out like a small fortified town, with the church as aesthetic and cultural focus. The goal was to strengthen Spanish control by "converting" the indigenous Coahuiltecan – in practice, using them as workforce and army. The missions flourished from 1745 to 1775, but couldn't survive the ravages of disease and attack from the Apache and Comanche, and fell into disuse early in the nineteenth century. To get a sense of the history of the Alamo, you could head first for the nearby **Rivercenter Mall**, where the battle is re-enacted on a six-story, Texas-scale IMAX screen (call ☎210/225-4629 for showtimes; $8.95); fact and sentiment may converge during the 45-minute presentation, but it takes a callous viewer not to be affected by the rousing patriotism of the finale.

The main **visitor center** (daily 9am–5pm; ☎210/932-1001) for the string of missions is next to Mission San Jose (see opposite) and contains a movie theater, small museum and giftshop.

The Alamo

All that is left of the original fort of the **Alamo** – at the meeting of Houston, Crockett, Bonham and Alamo streets – is the **chapel**, with a large arched facade of delicately carved sandstone, and the **Long Barracks**, now a **museum** (Mon–Sat 9am–5.30pm, Sun 10am–5.30pm; free). The first of the Spanish missions, established as San Antonio de Valero in 1718, it only became known as the Pueblo del Alamo in 1801, after secularization, when it was named for the Mexican home town of a Spanish cavalry unit which used it as a base. The **battle**, immortalized in film and song, occurred on March 6, 1836, when all of the 189 men who had held out for thirteen days against the five-thousand-strong Mexican troops were killed, a massacre dismissed by the Mexican General Santa Anna as "but a small affair." The rebels consisted of a few native – Hispanic – Texans, and a majority of volunteers (adventurers like Davy Crockett and Jim Bowie, and aspiring colonists from other states), dreaming of Texan autonomy and driven by the battle cry of "Victory or Death!"

Though a constant stream of bus tours makes visits crowded and hectic, seeing the Alamo is crucial to understanding Texan pride and stubbornness. The battle memorabilia in the **chapel** is undeniably emotive, with poignant letters sent home by soldiers preparing to die, and the **Long Barracks Museum**, hidden away southwest of the shrine's main entrance, presents a 20-minute video on the history of the missions and the battle. Take time also to sit in peace in the four-acre grounds, a haven from the downtown commotion just outside the walls, dotted with lush blooms, palms and cacti, and holding an irrigation ditch filled with fat fish.

The other missions

The **Mission Trail** runs ten miles south along the river from Alamo Street, down S St Mary's Street and onto Mission Road. Mission Concepción and Mission San José can be reached via Texas Trolley from the Alamo Visitor Center (210/212-5395; $28); missions San Juan and Espada require a car. Each

△ The Alamo

of the remaining four missions has been restored to act as an **interpretive center** illustrating some aspect of mission life (daily 9am–5pm; free), while the churches themselves still serve active parishes.

Mission Concepción, 807 Mission Rd, with its distinctive twin towers and cupola, was built between 1731 and 1751. Colorful scraps of original frescoes can still be seen, along with bullet holes from rougher days. Exhibits here concentrate on the religious function of the missions. The 1720 **Mission San José**, 6701 San Jose Drive, which interprets the mission as a social and defense center, is the most complete of all, restored in the 1930s by the WPA. Other notable features include the beautiful carved-stone ornamentation, especially the ornate rose window. A Mariachi Mass is held here each Sunday at noon. Of the two smaller and more isolated missions, **Mission San Juan**, 9101 Graf Rd, has displays on agriculture (as well as a unique delicate bell tower), while **Mission San Francisco de la Espada**, 10040 Espada Rd, looks back on ranching at the missions.

Eating

Not surprisingly, San Antonio has good **Tex–Mex** food in all price ranges. Many visitors head straight for the Mexican restaurants on the River Walk, but, charming as it is to eat alfresco beside the river, don't be seduced to such an extent that you never venture above ground. There are many good places downtown and the floor of the **Rivercenter Mall** is packed with assorted fast-food stalls (head straight for *Ninfa's Express*).

Boudro's 421 E Commerce St ☎210/224-8484. One of the best places on the River Walk; look for the tasty, unusual entrees (i.e. quail) and don't miss the prickly pear margaritas.

Casa Rio 430 E Commerce St ☎210/225-6718. The oldest, most established restaurant on the River Walk, offering cheap but excellent Mexican food: a huge "deluxe dinner" costs around $7.

El Mirador 722 S St Mary's St ☎210/225-9444. Wonderful Mexican breakfasts and lunches for under $5, and pricier Southwestern cuisine in the evening. Specialties include *xocetl* (chicken broth) and *azteca* (spicy tomato) soups. Closed Sun and Aug.

The Guenther House 205 E Guenther St ☎210/227-1061. Delicious cookies and cakes in a cool green flour mill-cum-museum in the King William District. Good breakfasts and lunches, too.

Mi Tierra 218 Produce Row ☎210/225-1262. Expansive 24-hour joint serving superb, inexpensive Tex-Mex. In a bustling old Market Square building.

Paesano's 111 W Crockett St ☎210/227-2782. Lively Italian restaurant on the River Walk, near the *Hard Rock Café*. The *shrimp paesano* is delectable.

Rudy's BBQ 24152 I-10 ☎210/698-2141. Fabulous BBQ on the way out of town, well worth making the exit off the interstate.

Zuni Grill 511 River Walk ☎210/227-0864. Creative Southwestern fare in one of the most stylish River Walk restaurants. Main courses around $14.

Entertainment and nightlife

With its abundance of picturesque settings, San Antonio is a great city for **festivals**. The year's biggest event is April's ten-day **Fiesta San Antonio** (Ⓦwww.fiesta-sa.org), marking Texas's victory in the Battle of San Jacinto, with parades, cookouts and Latin music concerts filling the streets. Also in May is the **Tejano Conjunto Festival** at Rosedale Park and at the Guadalupe Cultural Arts Center on Guadalupe Street (☎210/271-3151, Ⓦwww.guadalupeculturalarts.org/tcf.html), west of downtown, which celebrates the German–Mexican country music of south and central Texas. During June's **Texas Folklife Festival** at the Institute of Texan Cultures, ten stages reflect the state's huge diversity of music, ranging from gospel to Lebanese. Finally, the **San Antonio Stock Show & Rodeo** (Ⓦwww.sarodeo.com) in early February celebrates cowboy and King of the Hill culture with two weeks of rodeo events and country music.

Check the free weekly *Current* (Ⓦwww.sacurrent.com) for gigs, films and events. The live jazz and flamenco in the restaurants along the **River Walk** tend to be rather sanitized, while **N St Mary's Street** (just beyond the bus station toward the art museum) is the main strip for college clubs and bars. The outdoor **Arneson River Theatre**, opposite La Villita, where the river separates the audience from the stage, hosts Mexican folk music and dance during the summer. The outlying areas hold some great old **country dance halls**, the best of which is *Greune Hall*.

Bonham Exchange 411 Bonham St ☎210/271-3811. Popular mixed gay club with good house and garage DJs.

Floore Country Store 14464 Old Bandera Rd, downtown Helotes ☎210/695-8827. Old country dance hall, with outdoor dancing.

Gruene Hall 1281 Gruene Rd, Gruene ☎210/606-1281. Dominating this small town (pronounced *green*), 30 miles northeast of downtown San Antonio, is the oldest remaining dance hall in Texas, with top country stars playing here at weekends.

Jim Cullum's The Landing 123 Losoya St under the *Hyatt Regency* ☎210/223-7266. Traditional jazz every night in a club that's been running for over thirty years.

Polly Esther's 212 College St ☎210/220-1972. Sure, it's a chain, but it's also undeniably fun and enlivened by an ultra-energetic crowd spilling out from the club all over the River Walk.

Swig 111 W Crockett St ☎210/476-0005. The best martinis in the city, with an attractive crowd looking to mingle in a jazzy, classy space.

Tycoon Flats 2926 N St Mary's St ☎210/737-1929. A variety of live music with no cover charge. Patio restaurant serves good vegetarian food for about $5 per plate. Closed Mon.

White Rabbit 2410 N St Mary's St ☎210/737-2221. The main venue for touring indie bands, drawing a raucous, young crowd.

Austin

AUSTIN was only a tiny community on the verdant banks of the (Texas) Colorado River when Mirabeau B. Lamar, president of the Republic, suggested in 1839 that it would make a better capital than swampy and disease-ridden Houston. Early building had to be done under armed guard, as angry Comanche watched from the surrounding hills, but despite its perilous location, the city thrived.

These days it wears its status as capital of Texas very lightly; sightseeing rates as a low priority against simply hanging out. Since the 1960s, this laid-back and progressive city has been a haven for artists, musicians and writers. Many visitors come specifically for the **music**. Local musicians are renowned for their innovative reworkings of Texas's country, folk and R&B heritage, often severing their rural roots to use Austin's enthusiastic environment as a springboard to national recognition. Janis Joplin had her start here in the early 1960s, and at the end of that decade, Austin was second only to San Francisco in its adherence to the "turn on, tune in, drop out" philosophy, with locals coining the term "headneck" to describe themselves. Musicians hungry for fame still tumble out of buses from all over Texas to seek their fortunes in the literally hundreds of live venues.

Austin is one of the few cities in the state where cycling is a viable alternative to driving. It may not have completely avoided the usual problems of urban growth – thanks to a sizeable population leap, ugly suburbs have shot up to threaten its small-town ambience – but it feels wonderfully safe for visitors, even women traveling alone, and the presence of the vast UT campus adds to the atmosphere, even if almost every shop and streetlamp is adorned with the unsightly brown and white colors of the college's Longhorns football team.

Within the city limits a great park system offers numerous hiking and biking trails and a wonderful spring-fed swimming pool. Looking further afield, Austin makes a fine base for exploring the green **Hill Country** that rolls away to the west.

Arrival, information and getting around

Austin spreads about twenty miles north–south and eighteen miles east–west, severed by I-35 (between Dallas and San Antonio) to the east. The Colorado River runs south of downtown. Flights come in at the tasteful **Austin-Bergstrom International Airport** (⊕512/530-2242). Eight miles southeast of downtown at the intersection of highways 71 and 183, it takes about twenty minutes to get downtown by **taxi** (Yellow Checker Cabs; ⊕512/472-1111; around $25) or by SuperShuttle vans (⊕512/258-3826, ⊛www.supershuttle .com; $11) while the #100 **bus** runs approximately once an hour to the campus and downtown (Mon–Fri 5am–11pm, Sat 7am–11pm, Sun 8am–10.30pm) for a bargain fare of 50¢.

Austin has a good **public transportation** system. The Capital METRO **bus** runs downtown, crosstown and through the campus for a flat fare of 50¢ (express services charge a dollar), with additional shuttle routes for students – distinguishable by the Longhorn emblem beside the route number (Mon–Fri 5.30am–12.30am, times vary widely on Sat & Sun). Schedules are available from the Customer Service Center at 801 Congress Ave (Mon–Fri 8am–5pm), or you can call the METRO information line on ⊕512/474-1200. The Dillo, also run by METRO, is a free downtown **trolley** system, running along five routes, including three out to the UT campus, every ten to forty minutes between 6.30am and 8.30pm on weekdays; limited schedule on weekends. **Bicycles** can be rented from Bicycle Sport Shop, 1426 Toomey Rd (Mon–Fri 10am–7pm, Sat 9am–6pm, Sun 11am–5pm; ☎512/477-3472). Walking is an easy and pleasant way of getting around; organized **walking tours** leave from the south entrance of the capitol (March–Nov Sat 2pm, Sun 9am; ☎512/478-0098).

The **visitor center** is at 201 E Second St (Mon–Fri 8.30am–5pm, Sat & Sun 9am–5pm; ☎512/478-0098 or 1-800/926-2282, ⓦwww.austintexas.org) and there's a State Tourist Information Center (daily 9am–5pm; ☎512/305-8400) in the foyer of the state capitol (free), with changing exhibits of Texacana and a video presentation. The **post office** is at 510 Guadalupe St (Mon–Fri 7am–6.30pm, Sat 8am–3pm; ☎512/494-2210; zip code 78701).

Accommodation

I-35 and Congress Avenue are Austin's budget **hotel** strips, but **B&Bs** are better options; there are good ones in most areas of the city.

Austin Motel 1220 S Congress Ave ☎512/441-1157, ⓦwww.austinmotel.com. Basic rooms just south of the bridge, a favorite with visiting musicians. Opposite the *Continental Club*. ❸

Carrington's Bluff 1900 David St ☎512/477-0711. Very good B&B, central but countrified, a block from Lamar Blvd at Martin Luther King Blvd. Shady veranda, friendly hosts and gourmet breakfast. ❹

Driskill Hotel 604 Brazos St ☎512/474-5911, ⓦwww.driskillhotel.com. Grand historic hotel in a great location, with glittery clientele. ❽

La Quinta Inn Austin Capitol 300 E 11th St ☎512/476-1166, ⓦwww.laquinta.com. Comfortable, central rooms and an outdoor pool. ❹

Sixth Street Hostel 604 E 6th St ☎1-800/HOSTEL-6, ⓦwww.6thstreethostel.com. Bargain rates right in the middle of the bustling 6th Street corridor. Private rooms also available. ❶–❷

Woodburn House 4401 Ave D ☎1-888/690-9763, ⓦwww.woodburnhouse.com. Small B&B in the leafy Hyde Park area, within walking distance of the university. Reservation and deposit required. ❺

The Town

The Texas **State Capitol**, at 13th Street and Congress Avenue, is over 300ft high, taller than the national capitol in Washington, with a red sunset granite dome that dominates the downtown skyline. The chandeliers, carpets and even the door hinges of this colossal building are emblazoned with lone stars and other Texan motifs, a theme continued in the recent extension, a sleek maze of marble halls (daily 9am–5pm; public tours every 15min; free). Nearby, the antebellum **Governor's Mansion**, 1010 Colorado St, contains displays on Texan history (free tours Mon–Fri every 20min 10am–noon). **Congress Avenue**, a stretch of 1950s shops and muted office buildings that slopes south from the capitol down to the river, is worthy of a stroll; at dusk 1.5 million **bats** – the world's largest urban bat colony – emerge in a large cloud from their hangouts under the bridge. **6th Street**, also known as Old Pecan Street, runs west from I-35 to Congress Street, and is the focus of much of the city's nightlife, as well as featuring many renovated buildings, galleries and hip shops. The elegant Romanesque **Driskill Hotel**, on the corner with Brazos Street, has its own self-guided walking tour, with a glossy leaflet recounting the hotel's many links with government since 1886. Between 5th and 6th streets, just west of Lamar Boulevard, the 600-year-old **Treaty Oak** is the last of the Council Oaks where treaties were signed with Native Americans; unfortunately, someone chose to poison the tree in 1989, and only one-third of it remains.

The recently opened **Bob Bullock Texas State History Museum**, at Martin Luther King Jr Boulevard and North Congress Avenue should satisfy

AUSTIN

N

University of Texas

Bob Bullock
Texas State
History Museum

MARTIN LUTHER KING JR.

W. 18TH — E. 18TH

W. 17TH

W. 16TH — E. 17TH

W. 15TH — E. 16TH

W. 14TH — E. 15TH

W. 13TH — E. 14TH

E. 13TH

State Capitol

W. 12TH — E. 12TH

W. 11TH — E. 11TH

Governor's Mansion

W. 10TH — E. 10TH

W. 9TH — E. 9TH

W. 8TH — E. 8TH

W. 7TH — E. 7TH

Driskill Hotel

W. 6TH — E. 6TH

W. 5TH — E. 5TH

W. 4TH — E. 4TH

W. 3RD — E. 3RD

W. 2ND — E. 2ND

W. CESAR CHAVEZ — E. CESAR CHAVEZ

DRISKILL

0   500 yds

Town Lake

Bat Colony

Shoal Creek

Zilker Park

RIO GRANDE · NUECES · SAN ANTONIO · GUADALUPE · LAVACA · COLORADO · CONGRESS · BRAZOS · SAN JACINTO · TRINITY · NECHES · RED RIVER · SABINE · HOSPITAL · OLANDER · UNIVERSITY · WICHITA · SPEEDWAY · 35

ACCOMMODATION

| Driskill Hotel | 2 |
| La Quinta Inn | 1 |

RESTAURANTS, BARS AND CLUBS

Antone's	F
Black Cat	E
Club de Ville	B
Emo's	D
Las Manitas	I
La Zona Rosa	G
Mezzaluna	H
Scholz Garden	A
Stubb's BBQ	C

anyone's curiosity for Texas arcana. Exhibits include the diary of Stephen F. Austin, generally considered the founder of the state, and a Bible that saved the life of Sam Houston Jr, during the Civil War; a bullet is still lodged in its pages (Mon–Sat 9am–6pm; $5). The **Elisabet Ney Museum** at 304 E 44th St is a German-influenced castle-like building in a leafy, historic residential area. It preserves the last studio, with marquettes and finished marbles, of Austin's most celebrated sculptor (Wed–Sat 10am–5pm, Sun noon–5pm; free).

Zilker Park, across the river from Amtrak and southwest of the center, is one of the best of the many fine parks in the city, a perfect retreat on sweaty Austin afternoons. One of its main attractions is the spring-fed (and deliciously cold) **Barton Springs Pool**, a 1000ft turquoise rectangle shaded by pecan trees (daily 5am–10pm; $2.50 Mon–Fri, $2.75 Sat & Sun). You can paddle in the pebbly creek below the pool free of charge, and you'll also find hiking and biking trails, a miniature railroad winding beside the river (daily 10am–7pm; $2.75), and, to the west, the wildlife garden of the **Austin Nature and Science Center** (Mon–Sat 9am–5pm, Sun noon–5pm; free; ☎512/327-8181, ⓦwww.ci.austin.tx.us/nature-science). South of the Barton Springs Pool on Robert E. Lee Road, the **Umlauf Sculpture Garden** (Wed–Fri 10am–4.30pm, Sat & Sun 1-4.30pm; $3.50; ☎512/445-5582, ⓦwww.umlaufsculpture.org) is a tranquil, grassy enclave dotted with more than one hundred works in bronze, terracotta, wood and marble. More outdoor relief can be found farther north on the banks of the Colorado River. Don't miss **Mayfield Park**, a peaceful idyll complete with water lilies and peacocks. Nearby **Mount Bonnell** gives great views over the city and surrounding countryside.

The **Austin Museum of Art** is in the process of relocating from its Laguna Gloria location, at 3809 W 35th St, to a permanent facility downtown, scheduled to open in 2004. In the meantime, many exhibits are on view at a separate downtown location, at 823 Congress Ave (Tues–Sat 10am–6pm, Thurs until 8pm, Sun noon–5pm; $3; ☎512/495-9224, ⓦwww.amoa.org).

The University

Having its own oil well (the drilling rig Santa Rita No. 1 on San Jacinto Blvd) has made the **University of Texas** one of the world's richest universities. Its unparalleled collection of manuscripts by contemporary authors is available to scholars amid tight security in the **Harry Ransom Center**; stories abound of the sums lavished to acquire work from relative unknowns who might someday achieve fame. The Center, in the southwest corner of the campus, also houses an **art gallery** (Mon–Fri 9am–5pm, Sat 9am–noon; free), with a Gutenberg Bible as well as contemporary Latin American and American paintings. Student-guided tours of the main campus building and its tower are offered frequently; call ☎512/475-6633 for details.

The stretch of **Guadalupe Street** running along campus north from Martin Luther King Boulevard to 24th Street is known as "**the Drag**." A focus of student activity, and lined with cafés, vintage clothes shops and bookstores, it was the location for much of Richard Linklater's 1991 movie, *Slacker*.

The **LBJ Library and Museum** (daily 9am–5pm; free; ☎512-916-5137, ⓦwww.lbjlib.utexas.edu), on the northeast edge of campus at 2313 Red River St, traces the career of the brash and egotistical Lyndon Baines Johnson from his origins in the Hill Country to the House of Representatives, the Senate and the White House. The curious circumstances surrounding his first senatorial election in 1948 (his primary victory was confirmed only after some "overlooked" votes – all written in the same hand – were found three days after his opponent had apparently won the Democratic nomination) go unmentioned. John Kennedy is said to have made Johnson his vice president to avoid his establishing a rival power base; but in the aftermath of Kennedy's assassination, Johnson's administration (1963–69) was able to push through a far more radical program than Kennedy ever attempted. Johnson's nemesis, Vietnam, is presented here as an awful mess left by Kennedy for him to clear up, at the cost of great personal anguish. There's a replica of the Johnson Oval Office in the White House, as well as gifts presented to the president, including a 1910 Model T from Henry Ford.

Eating

Radical Austin has many more vegetarian and wholefood **restaurants** than is usual in Texas; even chicken–fried steak can be found prepared healthily. There are plenty of good budget restaurants near the university, especially along Guadalupe Street – look for the crowds. Many of the music venues also serve up decent food.

El Sol y La Luna 1224 S Congress Ave ☎512/444-7770. A fun, family-run Mexican joint on the funky strip of shops and clubs just south of downtown. Serves great breakfasts.

Jovita's 1619 S 1st St ☎512/447-7825. Reliable Tex-Mex food, with occasional sets by top local country musicians (among them Don Walser) on the porch.

Las Manitas 211 Congress Ave ☎512/472-9357. Authentic, great-value Mexican food and decor right downtown. Offers breakfast and lunch only – get there early to beat the politicians to a space.

Magnolia Café 2000 S Congress Ave and 2304 Lake Austin Blvd ☎512/478-8645. A local favorite for breakfast. Open 24hr.

Mezzaluna 310 Colorado St ☎512/472-6770. A moderate to expensive traditional Italian restaurant in the warehouse district between 6th St and the river.

Salt Lick 18300 Farm Road-1826 ☎512/858-4959. The standard answer for anyone wondering where the city's best BBQ is. Fabulous ribs soaked in a near-perfect BBQ sauce.

Scholz Garden 1607 San Jacinto Blvd ☎512/474-1958. Big portions of German sausage and Tex-Mex food at an Austin legend that also puts on good live music.

Stubb's BBQ 801 Red River St ☎512/480-8341. Great Texan-style brisket, sausage and ribs, plus bands of national repute playing the indoor and outdoor stages.

Threadgill's 6416 N Lamar Blvd ☎512/451-5440. An Austin institution since Kenneth Threadgill was given the first license to sell beer in the city after Prohibition. Real home cooking at bargain prices, with free seconds of vegetables like black-eyed peas and okra. Lively atmosphere, with occasional live fiddle music, folk or country-and-western bands. There's also a new downtown branch at 301 W Riverside Drive ☎512/472-9304. Not to be missed.

West Lynn Café 1110 W Lynn ☎512/482-0950. Stylish vegetarian food from around the world at one of the city's most popular restaurants.

Nightlife

The only problem you'll have with Austin **nightlife** is being spoiled for choice. On 6th Street in particular, virtually every building houses a club or a bar, and many of these have become rather over–commercialized. It's much better to venture just off 6th where you'll find some of the best clubs, or take a cab to some of the further-flung joints. Three first-rate local newspapers, the *Daily Texan*, the UT paper (Thurs; ⓦwww.dailytexanonline.com), the "XLent" supplement to the *Austin American-Statesman* (Thurs; ⓦwww.austin360.com), and the *Austin Chronicle* (Fri; ⓦwww.auschron.com) carry listings.

There's usually something to catch on campus. Big drama and dance names appear in the **Performing Arts Center**, 23rd Street and Robert Dedman Drive (☎512/471-1444, ⓦwww.utpac.org), and you can see **independent movies** at the Dobie Theater, 2021 Guadalupe and 21st streets. *The Velveeta Room*, 521 E 6th St ($5 cover; ☎512/469-9116, ⓦwww.thevelveetaroom.com), showcases comedy open mic on Wednesday nights. On the same block is *Esther's Pool*, 525 E 6th St (around $15; ☎512/320-0553, ⓦwww.esthersfollies.com), home of *Esther's Follies*, Austin's hippest and funniest cabaret, which combines spoofs of local and national politicians with Texas–style singing and dancing.

Live music

Although Austin's folk revival in the 1960s attracted enough attention to propel **Janis Joplin** on her way from Port Arthur, Texas, to stardom in California, the city first achieved prominence in its own right as the center of "**outlaw country**" music in the 1970s. **Willie Nelson** and **Waylon Jennings**, disillusioned with

Nashville, spearheaded a movement which reworked sentimental country-and-western with an incisive injection of rock'n'roll. The audiences in Austin, far removed from the hard-drinking honky-tonk crowds of West Texas, provided an environment which encouraged and rewarded risk-taking and experimentation. These days the predominant "**Austin sound**" is a melange of country, folk, blues, psychedelic and "alternative" influences, very much reliant on acoustics and guitars, though that's not to say the scene is anything but eclectic (with swing particularly popular at the moment); this, after all, is the city that spawned the Butthole Surfers.

The tradition of black Texas bluesmen such as Blind Lemon Jefferson and Blind Willie Johnson, as well as the rocking bar blues of Stevie Ray Vaughan, still lives on; *Antone's Blues Club* on Guadalupe Street is the place to hear **live blues**, while **folk** music, traditional or with a punk twist, is also thriving, with the annual **Kerrville Folk Festival** at Rod Kennedy's *Quiet Valley Ranch* in **KERRVILLE**, a hundred miles west of Austin on I-10 (☎830/257-3600). The ten-day **South by Southwest Festival**, held in the third week of March, features the best bands from Texas and around the world, along with tons of movies; passes are $475 (in advance) for all film, music and interactive events; a music-only pass is $325; call ☎512/467-7979 or visit ⊛www.sxsw.org for information).

Antone's 213 W 5th St ☎512/474-5314. Hot, sweaty and crowded; the best blues club in the city, with big-name national and local acts nightly.

The Backyard 13101 W Hwy 71 ☎512/263-4146. Out-of-the-way club that plays host to engaging folk- and country-tinged acts.

Black Cat 309 E 6th St (no phone). Small, dark space promoting local rock and roots bands through residencies. A nicely uncommercial contrast to much of 6th St.

The Broken Spoke 3201 S Lamar Blvd ☎512/442-6189. Neighborhood restaurant (good chicken-fried steak) and stomping country-music hall, with all the trappings but well away from the center. The barn-like dance floor regularly attracts the best acts on the Texas circuit. Two-stepping begins at 9pm.

Cactus Café, Texas Union, 24th and Guadalupe sts ☎512/475-6515. At UT's student union, one of Austin's favorite venues putting on consistently good country, rock and folk music; a regular showcase for new acts.

Club de Ville 900 Red River St ☎512/457-0900. Excellent cocktails and a superb patio setting in this stylish bar just a few minutes from the 6th St morass.

Continental Club 1315 S Congress Ave ☎512/441-2444. The premier place to hear hard-edged country sung the Austin way. Attracts top-notch artists.

Emo's 603 Red River St ☎512/477-EMOS. Launchpad for Austin's best alternative bands, with a friendly, tattooed and pierced crowd. Cover varies, patrons under 21 pay extra.

La Zona Rosa 612 W 4th St ☎512/472-2293. Great venue for rootsy bands and also serves decent Southwestern food.

Symphony Square Red River Rd and 11th St ☎512/476-6064. Rough-hewn outdoor amphitheater, below street level on the river, hosting good jazz and classical concerts in summer.

The Hill Country

The rolling hills, lakes and valleys of the **Hill Country**, north and west of Austin and San Antonio, were inhabited mostly by Apache and Comanche until after statehood, when German and Scandinavian settlers arrived. Many of the log-cabin farming communities they established are still here, such as **New Braunfels** (famous for its sausages and pastries) and Luckenbach. You may still hear German spoken, and the German influence is also felt in local food and music; *conjunto*, for example, is a blend of Tex-Mex and accordion music.

The whole region is a popular retreat and resort area, with some wonderful hill views and lake swimming, and a lot of good places to camp.

The Lyndon B. Johnson Historical Park

Sixty-five miles west of Austin on US-290, the **Lyndon B. Johnson State and National Historical Park** preserves LBJ's birthplace (1908) and the ranch house where Lady Bird Johnson continued to live long after her husband's death in 1973 (daily 10am–4pm; 1hr 15min tours leave from the visitor center; $3). The Sauer-Beckmann Farmstead, a "living history" farm, depicts German family life in the early 1900s.

The **visitor center** (daily 8.45am–5pm; ☎830/868-7128) and Johnson's boyhood home (daily 9am–4pm; free guided tours every 30min) are at sleepy **JOHNSON CITY**, fourteen miles further east; for a good lunch, stop off here at the *Hill Country Cupboard* (☎830/868-4625), at the junction of US-281 and US-290.

Fredericksburg

FREDERICKSBURG, smack in the middle of the Hill Country, might at first glance look like a pastiche of a German village, overrun by Biergartens and gingerbread storefronts. In fact it's still pretty much the town founded by six hundred enterprising Germans in 1846. They managed to make – and, uniquely, keep – treaties with the local Comanche, and their community, based on hard work and perseverance, survived through epidemics and civil war.

At the weekend, crowds of day-trippers from San Antonio and Austin visit Main Street's galleries, craft shops, antique stores and numerous fancy tearooms. Several original structures make up the **Pioneer Museum** at 309 W Main St, including a church and a store (Mon–Sat 10am–4pm, Sun 1–5pm; ⓦ www.pioneermuseum.com; free). The **National Museum of the Pacific War**, 340 E Main St, incorporates the *Nimitz Steamboat Hotel* with its looming tower that really does look like a steamboat, and features a peace garden and an historical trail that leads past aircraft, tanks and heavy artillery (daily 10am–5pm; ⓦ www.nimitz-museum.org; $5). Look out also for the quirky limestone and pink-granite Bank of Fredericksburg.

Practicalities

Like the rest of the Hill Country, Fredericksburg has no Amtrak service, but Greyhound stops at 758 S Washington. The **CVB**, in the Market Square at 106 N Adams St (Mon–Fri 8.30am–5pm, Sat 9am–noon & 1-5pm, Sun 1–5pm; ⓦ www.fredericksburg-texas.com; ☎830/997-6523), has details of the budget **hotels** along E Main Street; of these, the pool-equipped *Sunday House* at no. 501 (☎830/997-4484, ⓦ www.sundayhouseinn.com; ❺) is one of the more luxurious. **Bed and breakfast** is big business in historic Fredericksburg; contact B&B of Fredericksburg, 619 W Main (☎830/997-4712, ⓦ www.bandbfbg.com; ❷–❻). There's **camping** in the Lady Bird Johnson Municipal Park, three miles southwest on Hwy-16 S, or in the Enchanted Rock State Natural Area.

Restaurants and bakeries line Main Street, many of them doing cheap lunch specials. *Dietz Bakery*, at no. 218 (☎830/997-3250), is the oldest in town, good for tasty breads and biscuits. You can eat more substantially at *Friedhelm's Bavarian Inn* at no. 905 (☎830/997-6300; closed Mon), which specializes in starchy plates of dumplings and sauerkraut.

North and east Texas

Early immigration into **north and east Texas**, during the days of the Republic and following the devastation of the Civil War, was largely from the Southern states. In the 1930s, the northeastern oil fields near **Tyler** (a drab town only redeemed by its beautiful rose gardens) proved to be the richest ever found in the US. In addition to oil, agriculture has become a prime source of commerce, with logging important in the densely forested east. The grand exception is, of course, the **Metroplex** – the area which includes **Dallas** and **Fort Worth**. The main tourist attractions and cultural life of the region are concentrated here; but if you enjoy exploring small-town America, and have a car, the north and east can yield more subtle pleasures. The **national forests** of Angelina, Davy Crockett, Sabine and Sam Houston in the east offer unsurpassed opportunities for outdoor living: the forest supervisor (☎713/632-4446) in Lufkin, midway between Davy Crockett and Angelina on US-59, has details of free and private **camping** facilities. Fans of the movie will want to check out **Paris**, **Texas**, northeast on US-82.

East Texas

The tall pine forests of **east Texas** bear more relation to Louisiana than to the rest of the state; while undeniably Texan, the locals also identify themselves culturally and geographically with the adjacent corners of Arkansas and Louisiana – the "**Arklatex**" – and you'll find jambalaya and gumbo in restaurants along with standard Texan dishes.

Burial sites and reconstructed dwellings of the sophisticated **Caddo** Indians, an early southeastern mound-building culture, can be seen at the **Caddoan Mounds State Historic Site**, thirty miles west of Nacogdoches on Hwy-21. Active between the ninth and fourteenth centuries, the site includes a self-guided walking tour and videos on Caddoan history (Mon & Thurs–Sun 9am–4pm; $3 per car, $1 for pedestrians and cyclists; ☎936/858-3218).

Big Thicket National Preserve

The **Big Thicket National Preserve**, south of the Piney Woods on US-96, is a remarkable composite of natural elements from the southwestern desert, central plains and Appalachian Mountains, with swamps and bayous to boot. The area once offered ideal refuge for outlaws, runaway slaves and gamblers; now it just hides a huge variety of plant and animal life, including deer, alligators, armadillos, possums, hogs and panthers, and over three hundred species of birds. Wild flowers, orchids and towering trees share space with cacti and yucca.

Check in at the visitor center (daily 9am–5pm; ☎409/246-2337, ⓦwww.nps.gov/bith), south of Angelina National Forest off US-69, before entering the site; casual rambling isn't allowed, and hiking or canoeing is best done with the Preserve guides. There is primitive **camping** in designated areas.

Nacogdoches

NACOGDOCHES, north of Angelina National Forest on US-59, claims to be the oldest town in Texas. One of the state's first five Spanish **missions** was established here in 1716, to keep a watchful eye on the French in Louisiana, and a pyramidal **Caddo Indian Mound** in the 500 block of Mound Street testifies to more ancient history. The **Sterne–Hoya House**, 211 S Lanana St, the town's oldest surviving and unreconstructed home, illustrates early pioneer life (Mon–Sat 9am–noon & 2–5pm; free).

La Hacienda, 1411 North St (℡936/564-6487), is the best place to **eat** in town, serving Mexican food in a prairie-style ranch home. If you want to **stay**, the *Jones House*, 141 N Church St (℡936/559-1487; ❹), offers good **bed and breakfast** in a cottage close to downtown, while *Mound Street B&B*, 408 N Mound St (℡936/569-2211, ⓦwww.moundstreet.com; ❺), features big rooms in a Victorian home. The downtown **hotel**, the *Fredonia*, 200 N Fredonia St (℡936/564-1234; ❹), is venerable but clean. The **Chamber of Commerce** is at 200 E Main St (Mon–Fri 9am–5pm, Sat 10am–4pm, Sun 1–6pm; ℡936/564-7351 or 1-888/564-7351, ⓦwww.visitnacogdoches.org).

Dallas

Contrary to popular belief, there's no oil in glitzy, status-conscious **DALLAS**. Since its foundation as a prairie trading post, by Tennessee lawyer John Neely Bryan and his Arkansan friend Joe Dallas in 1841, successive generations of **entrepreneurs** have amassed wealth here through trade and finance, using first cattle and later oil reserves as collateral. One early group of European settlers of the 1850s – a group of French intellectuals and artists known as the La Reunion co-operative – had to pack up and move on after a series of summer droughts and a harsh winter; the few who stayed would include a future mayor of Dallas. The city still prides itself on their legacy of arts and high culture.

The power of **money** in Dallas was demonstrated in the late 1950s, when its financiers threw their weight behind integration. Potentially racist restaurant owners and bus drivers were pressured not to resist the new policies, and Dallas was spared major upheavals. The city's image was, however, catastrophically tarnished by the **assassination** of President Kennedy in 1963, and it took the building of the giant Dallas/Fort Worth International Airport in the 1960s, and the twin successes of the *Dallas* TV show and the Cowboys football team in the 1970s to restore confidence. Then boom turned to crash once more. Unemployment and the demise of the fictional Ewings, not to mention an appalling crime rate, all took their toll, but the indomitable entrepreneurial spirit remains. After a slump in the late 1980s, the Cowboys are back in the big time, though their off-field antics have provided the nation's papers with some anti-Dallas copy once again.

Competitive with Houston, and smug about its cowtown neighbor Fort Worth, Dallas boasts of its "sophistication" and its "old" wealth. For all that, the stuffiness is tempered by a typically Texan delight in self-parody, and there's still fun to be had if you know where to look – especially in the alternative **Deep Ellum** district, with its superb restaurants and nightlife.

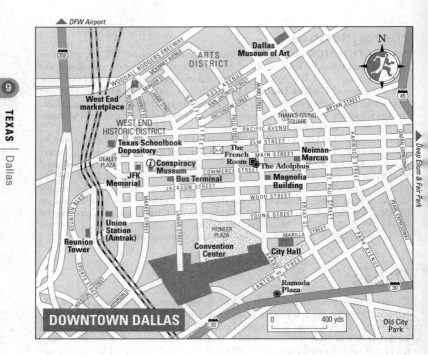

DOWNTOWN DALLAS

Arrival, information and getting around

Dallas is served by two major **airports**. **Dallas/Fort Worth** (DFW) (☎972/574–4420, ⓦwww.dfwaiport.com), as big as Manhattan and the world's second busiest airport, is exactly midway between the two cities (around 17 miles from each). Telephones in the baggage claim area link up to a variety of different **shuttle buses**, such as Super Shuttle (☎817/329-2000, ⓦwww.supershuttle.com) and Discount Shuttle (☎817/267-5150, ⓦwww.shuttleservice.com), all charging around $15 to downtown; **taxis** cost around $40 (Yellow/Checker ☎214/426-6262). The other major airport, **Love Field** (☎214/670-6080), used mostly by Southwest Airlines, lies about nine miles northwest of Dallas, from where taxis to downtown cost around $15, shuttles charge $9, or you can take bus #39 to downtown for a total of $1. Greyhound is at 205 S Lamar St downtown, while Amtrak's 1916 Union Station is further west at 400 S Houston St. The Trinity Railway Express service goes east to Richland Hills; once construction is completed, the service will continue to downtown Fort Worth.

Dallas proper is circled by Inner Loop 12 (or Northwest Highway) and the Outer Loop I-635 (which becomes LBJ Freeway). A **car** makes sense in a city this size, though the main sights of downtown's Central Business District are easy to tour on foot. The downtown **visitor center** is at the "Old Red" Courthouse, 100 S Houston St, in the thick of the Kennedy-related sights (daily 9am–6pm; ☎214/571-1300, ⓦwww.dallascvb.com). The city also runs a 24–hour Events Hotline (☎214/571-1301).

DART, the Dallas Area Rapid Transit system (☎214/979-1111, ⓦwww.dart.org), operates the city's **buses** ($1 local services, $2 express buses and trains) and a swish **light rail** network that links downtown and the Dallas

Convention Center with the West End and various sights (fares $1 local, $2 express; all–day pass $2). Both DART buses and trains operate every day from 5am to 12.30am. The McKinney Trolley (☏214/855-0006, ⊛www.mata.org) runs north from the downtown Dallas Museum of Art to the historic McKinney Avenue area (every 30min daily 10am–10pm; one–way $1.50, all–day pass $3).

The **post office** is at 1201 Main St (Mon–Fri 6am–4pm, Sat 6am–2pm; ☏214/752-5654; zip code 75202).

Accommodation

Room rates in downtown Dallas are firmly geared toward the business travel-er, though the swanky hotels do some reasonable **weekend** deals. Chain **motels** are concentrated a long way out, on the freeways; there's a large group on LBJ Freeway near the Galleria mall, a dozen miles north, for example. **Bed and breakfast** can be arranged through B&B Texas Style (☏979/696-9222 or 1-800/899-4538, ⊛www.bnbtexasstyle.com; from ❸). There's **camping** in the pretty Lake Park on the Kingfisher Trail, a mile east of I-35 in Lewisville (☏979/219-3550).

The Adolphus 1321 Commerce St ☏214/742-8200, ⊛www.hoteladolphus.com. Stunning historic hotel downtown, decorated with antiques. When built in 1912, it was said to be the most beautiful building west of Venice, Italy; today it is still by far Dallas's most glamorous place to stay. ❽

American Dream Bed and Breakfast Marsh Lane off I-635 exit 24 ☏214/357-5636 or 1-800/373-2690, ⊛www.dallas-bed-breakfast.com). A pleasant B&B with ultra-attentive hosts, providing easy access to downtown and DFW. ❸

Best Western Market Center 2023 Market Center Blvd ☏214/741-9000 or 1-800/275-7419, ⊛www.bestwestern.com. Chain motel two miles from downtown, offering complimentary breakfast. ❹

La Quinta North Park 10001 N Central Expressway/Hwy-75 ☏214/361-8200, ⊛www.laquinta.com. Decent-priced rooms, quite near the ever-popular Galleria and the burgeoning Lower Greenville shopping and entertainment district. ❹

The Mansion on Turtle Creek 2821 Turtle Creek Blvd ☏214/559-2100, ⊛www.mansiononturtle-creek.com). Considered one of the finest hotels in the world, you can anticipate absolute luxury on a gorgeous landscaped hillside. ❾

Ramada Plaza 1011 S Akard St ☏214/421-1083, ⊛www.ramada.com. Reliable rooms and a heated pool near the Convention Center. ❹

Stoneleigh Hotel 2927 Maple Ave ☏214/871-7111. Classy, comfortable hotel in the Turtle Creek area, three miles north of downtown. ❼

The City

Downtown Dallas is a hymn to commerce. Many of its skyscrapers are land-marks in themselves; at night the red neon Mobil Pegasus on the 1921 Magnolia Building on Akard and Commerce streets appears to gallop over the city, while over two miles of green argon tubing delineate the 72-story Bank of America building. The original **Neiman Marcus** department store, set up in 1907 by sister and brother Carrie Neiman and Herbert Marcus and famed for its glamorous Christmas catalog, is still there on Main Street (Mon–Sat 10am–6pm, Thurs until 8pm). One refuge is the **Center for World Thanksgiving** at **Thanksgiving Square** at the intersection of Akard, Ervay and Bryan streets and Pacific Avenue (Mon–Fri 9am–5pm, Sat & Sun 1–5pm), with its meditation garden, fountains and modern spiraling chapel – though even here pealing bells boom out at regular intervals. South of the square on Ervay Street looms the precarious upside-down pyramid of **City Hall**, possibly familiar as the police station in *Robocop*.

On the north edge of downtown, the **Arts District** boasts the huge and wide-ranging **Dallas Museum of Art**, 1717 N Harwood St (Tues–Sun 11am–5pm, Thurs until 9pm; free, around $5 for special exhibits; ☎214/922-1200, ⓦwww.dm-art.org), which has plenty of European works downstairs, including a good range of Mondrians, and an especially impressive pre-Columbian collection in the Gallery of the Americas upstairs. Two blocks east, at 2301 Flora St, the magnificent **Morton H. Meyerson Symphony Center**, designed by I.M. Pei, is the home of the symphony orchestra. The vast geometries of glass, onyx and wood inside cost $80 million, as the tour guides won't let you forget.

Tourists flock to the restored redbrick warehouses of the **West End Historic District**, the site of the original 1841 settlement on Lamar and Munger streets, for the eighty stores and twenty restaurants here. The indoor **marketplace** has become something of an amusement arcade, with a *Planet Hollywood*, tacky giftshops, crazy golf, and fast-food outlets.

A couple of blocks south and west of here lies **Dealey Plaza**, forever associated with the Kennedy assassination (see box on p.752). A small park beside Houston Street's triple underpass, it remains unchanged since the fateful day – in fact, since it was designed by a committee which included LBJ, in the late 1930s – and must be one of the most recognizable urban streetscapes in the world. The **Texas Schoolbook Depository** itself, at 411 Elm St, is now the Dallas County Administration Building, the penultimate floor of which houses **The Sixth Floor Museum** (daily 9am–6pm; $9, or $12 with audio tour; ☎214/747-6660 or 1-888/485-4854, ⓦwww.jfk.org). Displays build up a suspenseful narrative, with the infamous blurred 8mm images of Kennedy crumpling into Jackie's arms left until the end, at which point there's likely to be much sobbing from moved visitors, who can exorcize their grief by writing in the "memory book." The "gunman's nest" has been re-created and, whatever you feel about Oswald's guilt, it is undeniably chilling to look down at the streets below and imagine the mayhem the shooter must have seen that day.

One block west of Dealey Plaza, in the Dallas Historical Plaza on Main and Market streets, an open cenotaph, designed by Philip Johnson and enclosing an 8ft flat granite block, stands as the **John F. Kennedy Memorial**. Alongside, at 110 S Market St, the **Conspiracy Museum** (daily 10am–6pm; $7) is a dreadful waste of money. It strives to impress with its CD-ROM technology, but in fact displays the usual amateurish hand-drawn diagrams and wild accusations, interpreting virtually every public act in America since the late 1950s as the work of the Professional War Machine.

A little further south and east is the city's main business and administrative district, focused around City Hall on Marilla Street. **Pioneer Plaza**, at Young and Griffin streets, holds the world's largest bronze sculpture, a monument to the cattle drives that depicts forty longhorn steers under the guidance of three cowboys.

You can see all of these and much more from the 51st-story observation deck in the **Reunion Tower**, 300 Reunion Blvd (daily 10am–10.30pm; $2), on the east side of downtown next to the Amtrak station. The *Dome Lounge*, in the Tower, provides a good place to sip some liquor.

Farther southeast, across I-30, near Harwood Street at 1717 Gano St, Dallas's first park, **Old City Park**, now serves as both recreational area and museum, charting the history of the city from 1840 to 1910 through more than thirty buildings relocated from towns in north Texas, among them a farmhouse, a bank, a train station, a store, a church and a schoolhouse (Tues–Sat 10am–4pm, Sun noon–4pm; tours Tues–Sat 11.30am and 1.30pm, Sun 12:30pm and 2:30pm; $7; 214/421-5141, ⓦ www.oldcitypark.org).

Deep Ellum

Dallas's coolest district is **Deep Ellum**, five blocks east of downtown between the railroad tracks and I-30 at Elm and Main streets. Famous in the 1920s for its jazz and blues clubs (and supposedly named by Blind Lemon Jefferson, though it's more likely to stem from the Southern pronunciation of "elm"), the old warehouse district now accommodates avant-garde galleries, theaters, hip clothes stores and excellent restaurants and clubs. To the despair of its original inhabitants, prices are rocketing as the area drifts mainstream. However, rebellious and nonconformist nature makes a great antidote to the prevalent stuffiness of Dallas.

Fair Park

Not far southeast of Deep Ellum, **Fair Park**, a gargantuan Art Deco plaza bedecked with endless Lone Stars, was built to house the Texas Centennial Exposition in 1936, and hosts the annual State Fair of Texas, the biggest event of its kind in the US. Among its plethora of fine museums are the **Dallas Museum of Natural History** (daily 10am–5pm; ℡214/421-DINO, ⓦ www.dallasdino.org; $6.50), which boasts reconstructions of the 20,000-year-old "Trinity River Mammoth" and a lagoon nature walk; the hands-on **Science Place** (Mon–Sat 9.30am–5.30pm, Sun 11.30am–5.30pm; $7.50; ℡214/428-5555, ⓦ www.scienceplace.org), which sets out to teach kids and adults about physics and dinosaurs and the like, hosts lively lavish temporary exhibits, and has its own IMAX screen ($6.50); and the **Dallas Aquarium** (daily 9am–5pm; $3; ℡214/670-5656, ⓦ www.dallas-zoo.org).

The **Women's Museum** (Tues 10am–9pm, Wed–Sun 10am–5pm; $5), is the latest addition to a collection of museums in Fair Park. Young girls will likely benefit the most from the rah–rah attitude on display, from the Electronic Quilt – a video project highlighting achievements in women's history – to the Wall of Words, featuring inspirational quotes from female leaders. The nearby **African–American Museum** (Tues–Fri noon–5pm, Sat 10am–5pm, Sun 1–5pm; suggested donation $2; ℡214/565-9026) features a superb collection of **folk art** in its permanent collection,complete with detailed biographies of the artists responsible. These include Clementine Hunter, a Louisiana field hand who used materials left over by artists visiting the wealthy plantation where she worked; Charles Williams, known as Artist Chuckie, from Shreveport, Louisiana, who was "discovered" in 1989 when a neighbor's house burned down and he refused to leave his mother's home until his 700 paintings were brought out; and the real stand-out, Bessie Harvey, who died in 1994. She worked with found pieces of wood, spray-painting them and sticking on other materials to produce scenes such as the extraordinary *Jonah and the Whale* and *Two Heads Are Better Than One*. Changing exhibits here focus primarily on African art.

The centerpiece of the park, however, has to be the magnificent **Hall of State Building**, an Art Deco treasure of bronze statues, blue tiles, mosaics and murals, with rooms decorated to celebrate the different regions of Texas. The park also holds the **Cotton Bowl** stadium (℡214/638-BOWL, ⓦ www.swbellcottonbowl.com), home of the annual college football classic, while for three weeks in October, Fair Park spills over with more than three

The assassination of President Kennedy

It was 12.30pm on November 22, 1963, as John F. Kennedy greeted the crowds of Dallas from his ceremonial motorcade, when the shots rang out over Dealey Plaza that killed the president and ended the "Camelot" era.

Within hours, a gunman's nest was discovered in the nearby Texas Schoolbook Depository, and one of its employees, **Lee Harvey Oswald**, was arrested. Two days later, he in turn was shot and killed in a police station by nightclub owner **Jack Ruby**, who said he wanted to spare Kennedy's wife Jackie from having to testify at Oswald's trial. The **Warren Commission**, which investigated the assassination, concluded that Oswald had acted alone, but **conspiracy** theories have flourished ever since. Most accept that Oswald (an ex-Marine who defected to Russia and returned with a Russian wife) fired the shots, but see him as the fall guy in a larger plot, variously attributed to the Mafia, anti-Castroists, Cuba, the KGB and US government agencies. Claims by witnesses to have heard shots on the famous **Grassy Knoll** on the north side of Elm Street remain unsubstantiated, but visitors can usually be found sniffing around here for clues – along with self-styled guides, ready to engage them in costly conversation. Senate inquiries were finally closed down by the Justice Department in 1988, arguing that there was no "persuasive evidence" of any plot.

million revelers enjoying the riotous **State Fair** (☎214/565-9931, ⓦwww.texfair.com) itself.

Southfork Ranch

The former TV home of the *Dallas* soap's wheeling-and-dealing Ewing clan, **Southfork Ranch** (daily 9am–5pm; $7.95) lies about 25 miles northeast of Dallas, beyond I-75 at 3700 Hogge Drive, in Parker. Having lain dormant for two years from 1991, it was purchased by a private firm and has since been kitted out as a convention center-cum-Western mini-theme park, with a **museum** in which you can see the gun that shot JR and Jock Ewing's original 1978 Lincoln Continental. There are also plenty of Stetson-dominated giftshops and *Miss Ellie's Deli*. The **Ranch House** itself is surprisingly small – all the show's interior scenes were shot in California, and the exterior views used a very wide-angled lens. Most recommended for those very serious about their kitsch.

Eating

Many of the less expensive – and least extravagant – of Dallas's five thousand restaurants are concentrated in **Lower Greenville Avenue**, which runs northeast of downtown parallel to I-75, and trendier **Deep Ellum**, where even the excellent New American cuisine won't break the bank.

Café Brasil 2815 Elm St ☎214/747-2730). Open 24hr on weekends with great omelets, crepes and enchiladas.

Deep Ellum Café 2706 Elm St ☎214/741-9012. The first restaurant in the area and still the benchmark for the rest. Very popular, serving delicious, casual food (think waffles, crepes, sandwiches) for around $10. Open until 2am on Fri and Sat.

El Fenix 1601 McKinney Ave ☎214/747-1121. Don't let its ubiquity within the Metroplex stop you from trying out this ultra-reliable Tex-Mex favorite; don't miss the tortilla soup.

Firehouse 1928 Greenville Ave ☎214/826-2468). Inventive (if a bit pricey) menu – think antelope tenderloin – smack in the middle of Lower Greenville.

The French Room *The Adolphus* 1321 Commerce St ☎214/742-8200. Perhaps the best restaurant in the state, with prices to match the top-notch French food and exquisite decor (hand-blown crystal chandeliers, marble floors and so on).

Gloria's 600 W Davis St ☎214/948-3672. Catfish ceviche, hot banana-leaf tamales and other low-priced, top-quality El Salvadorean dishes.

Green Room 2715 Elm St ☎214/748-7666. Post-modern decor, with up-to-the-minute American cuisine downstairs, and pizzas on the roof with views across Deep Ellum to downtown.

Mia's 4322 Lemmon Ave ☎214/526-1020. A family-run Mexican restaurant, a favorite with the Dallas Cowboys.

Monica's Aca y Alla 2914 Main St ☎214/748-7140. Wood-grilled *nouvelle* Mexican food, with dashes of Mediterranean and Asian influences, in a Deep Ellum hot spot jumping with live salsa and mambo on weekends.

Samba Room 4514 Travis Walk ☎214/522-4137. Sexy, Cuban-themed space with fabulous mojitos and a beautiful patio.

Sonny Bryan's Smokehouse 2202 Inwood Rd ☎214/357-7120. The original location – it still looks like a shack – of a favorite local barbecue chain, but get there in good time as the meat can be all snapped up by early afternoon.

Entertainment and nightlife

The two nightlife destinations in Dallas have to be offbeat **Deep Ellum** – where among the trendy clubs the innovative **Pegasus Theater**, 3916 Main St (☎214/821-6005, ⓦwww.pegasustheatre.org), puts on avant-garde and independent plays – and the ever-so-slightly gritty **Lower Greenville**. Elsewhere nightlife is pretty formal. Mainstream attractions include the **Dallas Symphony Orchestra** at the showpiece Morton H. Meyerson Symphony Center (☎214/670-3600, ⓦwww.dallassymphony.com), and the **Dallas Black Dance Theater** at 2627 Flora St (☎214/871-2376, ⓦwww.dbdt.com). In June and July, free **Shakespeare in the Park** performances are held in Samuell-Grand Park, east of downtown near the intersection of I-30 and Hwy-87 (☎214/559-2782, ⓦwww.shakespearedallas.org).

For a real Wild West night out, head to the **Mesquite Championship Rodeo**, well out of town on I-635 at Military Parkway (April–Oct Fri & Sat 8pm; $10–28; ☎972/285-8777, ⓦwww.mesquiterodeo.com).

Full **listings** can be found in Thursday's *Dallas Observer* (ⓦwww.dallasobserver.com), Friday's *Dallas Morning News* (ⓦwww.dallasnews.com), or the events information line (☎214/571-1301).

Adair's 2624 Commerce St ☎214/939-9900. A country-music bar that attracts both old-timers and students with its hard-edged honky-tonk music.

Bar of Soap 3615 Parry Ave ☎214/823-6617. Groovy pub-cum-laundromat on the outskirts of Deep Ellum, opposite Fair Park. Open daily 3pm–2am, no cover.

Club Clearview 2803 Elm St ☎214/939-0077. Four-in-one Deep Ellum warehouse; a cool dance club, blacklight room, endless bars, and big touring acts, plus a great rooftop deck.

Club DaDa 2720 Elm St ☎214/744-DADA. Famed Deep Ellum club where Edie Brickell and the New Bohemians began their days. Open mic on Sundays, live bands and club nights.

Muddy Waters 1518 Greenville Ave ☎214/823-1518). Generally acknowledged as the city's best down-home blues bar, with live acts at weekends.

Sons of Hermann Hall 3414 Elm St ☎214/747-4422. Delightfully old-school country venue where the Texan masters come to play as well as respectful young outfits channelling the masters.

Tejano West 6532 E Northwest Highway ☎214/361-6083. A welcome break from the sometimes over-busy Deep Ellum scene, with great music and a laid-back, festive crowd.

Trees 2709 Elm St ☎214/748-5009. Deep Ellum warehouse turned auditorium, popular with up-and-coming indie rock bands.

Fort Worth

Yes, Dallas does have something Fort Worth doesn't have – a real city thirty miles away.

Amon Carter, publisher, philanthropist, Fort Worthian

FORT WORTH, often dismissed as some kind of poor relation to Dallas, in fact has a rush and energy largely missing in its more complacent neighbor thirty miles east. Unlike comparably cosmopolitan Dallas, this is one of the most "Western" cities in Texas. In the 1870s it was the last stop on the great cattle drive to Kansas, the **Chisholm Trail**; when the railroads arrived, it became a livestock market in its own right, with its own packing houses, while remaining a haven for cowboys and outlaws. The **cattle** trade is still a major industry, after aviation and defense, but the city can also pride itself on its thriving cultural life. Unlike the more anxious Dallas, Fort Worth doesn't feel the need to brag about its many excellent **museums**. For a place so wealthy (the grand **Western Hills** area claims to have proportionately more millionaires than any other US locale), it's surprisingly laid-back.

Arrival, information and getting around

The main road between Fort Worth and Dallas, **I-30**, cuts the city north–south; Loop 820 encircles it. An Airporter express **bus** (daily 5am–midnight, every half-hour at peak times; $10; ☎817/334-0092) runs to and from DFW International Airport, seventeen miles northeast (see p.748); a taxi costs around $45. Amtrak pulls in four times per week in either direction just southeast of downtown in the lovely red 1899 Santa Fe Depot, 1501 Jones St (☎817/332-2931). Greyhound operates out of the depot at 901 Commerce St, next to the Convention Center. The city's public transportation system, **The T**, operates **bus service** throughout the city, as well the tourist-oriented **Longhorn Trolley**, which travels between the major attractions and some downtown hotels ($1 for the bus, $2 for the trolley; ☎817/871-6200, ⊛www.the-t.com).

There are three **visitor centers**: in the **Stockyards** at 130 E Exchange Ave (daily 9am–6pm; walking tours are $2, call for times; ☎817/624-4741, ⊛www.stockyardsstation.com), downtown in the **CVB** at 415 Throckmorton St (Mon–Fri 8.30am–5pm, Sat 10am–4pm; ☎817/336-8791 or 1-800/433-5747), and in the Cultural District at the **Will Rogers Memorial Center** at 3401 W Lancaster Ave (Mon–Thurs 9am–5pm, Fri–Sat 9am–6pm, Sun noon–4pm; ☎817/882-8588). The downtown Sundance Square and Stockyard areas are well patrolled and safe to walk around after dark; for a **taxi** between the two, call Yellow Cab Co ☎817/534-5555.

Accommodation

Fort Worth is blessed with plenty of mid-priced **accommodation**, even downtown. The liveliest places to stay are around Sundance Square downtown, or in the Stockyards; more standard motel rooms can be found along I-35 both to the north and the south of the city.

Clarion Hotel 600 Commerce St ☎817/332-6900 or 1-800/252-7466). Excellent location with bright, comfortable rooms; steps away from Sundance Square and the bus station. ❺
Etta's Place B&B 200 W 3rd St ☎817/654-0267.

Ten great rooms in the heart of the Sundance Square area, offering three-course breakfast, several patios and lounges. Named after the schoolteacher girlfriend of the Sundance Kid. ❻
Miss Molly's Bed and Breakfast 109 W Exchange

Ave ☎817/626-1522 or 1-800/996-6559. Quirkily furnished old former bordello in the heart of the Stockyards, bursting with cowboy kitsch. Friendly hosts serve up gourmet breakfast. ❺
Park Central Hotel 1010 Houston St ☎817/336-2011, ⓦwww.parkcentralhotel.com. Centrally located, convenient for downtown. ❸
Ramada Plaza 1701 Commerce St ☎817/335-7000,ⓦwww.ramada.com. Geared more to confer-ence trade it's nevertheless a relatively inexpensive option on the edge of downtown. ❻
Stockyards Hotel 109 E Exchange Ave ☎817/625-6427 or 1-800/423-8471. Historic Stockyards hotel, reputedly a favorite haunt of Bonnie and Clyde, with Western, Mountain Man, Indian and Victorian themed rooms. *Booger Red's Saloon* boasts funky saddle barstools. ❻

The City

Fort Worth's main attractions fall tidily into a triangle anchored by downtown with the Cultural District and the Stockyards two miles away to the west and north respectively. The chief focus of **downtown** Fort Worth is **Sundance Square**, a leafy, redbrick-paved fourteen-block area of shops, restaurants and bars between First and Sixth streets, ringed by glittering skyscrapers and pervaded with a genuine enthusiasm for the town's rich history. It owes its existence to vast injections of cash from the Bass family; the whole ensemble is dominated by the two gleaming glass skyscrapers of the Bass-owned **City Center Towers**, while the extremely tasteful **Nancy Lee & Perry R. Bass Performance Hall** (☎817/212-4325, ⓦwww.basshall.com) is evidence of its continuing development. Notice the carvings of longhorn skulls everywhere, and the many trompe l'oeil murals – especially the Chisholm Trail mural on Fourth Street between Main and Houston streets. The **Sid Richardson Collection of Western Art**, tucked away at 309 Main St (Tues–Wed 10am–5pm, Thurs–Fri 10am–8pm, Sat 11am–8pm, Sun 1–5pm; free; ☎817/332-6554, ⓦwww.sidrmuseum.org), has a small but excellent collection of late works by Remington, including some of his best black-and-white illustrations, and early elegiac cowboyscapes by Charles Russell.

Naming the square after the Sundance Kid isn't particularly appropriate; he, and other outlaws such as Bonnie and Clyde, spent their time a few blocks south, just north of I-30 at the city's original settlement. Even into the 1950s "**Hell's Half Acre**" was renowned for bawdy lawlessness; these days it's much less exciting, although the bubbling fountains and pools of its central **Water Gardens** offer refreshing respite.

The **Cultural District**, two miles west of downtown, is an impressive area of museums and art galleries. The finest collection is at the small **Kimbell Art Museum**, 3333 Camp Bowie Blvd (Tues–Thurs 10am–8pm, Fri noon–8pm, Sat 10am–5pm, Sun noon–5pm; free, around $5 for special exhibits; ☎817/332-8451, ⓦwww.kimbellart.org/), a splendid vaulted, naturally lit building designed by Louis Kahn. Downstairs displays concentrate on pre-Columbian and African pieces, with some noteworthy Mayan funerary urns, while upstairs, as well as canvases by Gauguin, Cézanne, Picasso and Monet, you can admire a seventh-century Khmer figure of a Hindu deity, ancient Chinese bronzes and a fourteenth-century Japanese polychrome wood statue of En no Gyoja. The museum café itself is adorned with relief sculptures by Henri Matisse.

American art in the recently renovated and expanded **Amon Carter Museum**, just up the hill at 3501 Camp Bowie Blvd (Tues–Sat 10am–5pm, Sun noon–5pm; free; ☎817/738-1933, ⓦwww.cartermuseum.org), includes great photographs of Western landscapes, as well as a fine assortment of Remingtons and Russells and works by Winslow Homer and Georgia

O'Keeffe. The **Modern Art Museum of Fort Worth**, 1309 Montgomery St (Tues–Fri 10am–5pm, Sat 11am–5pm, Sun noon–5pm; free; ☏817/738-9215, ⓦwww.mamfw.org), which specializes in twentieth-century abstract art, is being moved to a larger facility to be unveiled in 2002. South of here, the wide-ranging **Fort Worth Museum of Science and History** (Mon–Thurs 9am–5.30pm, Fri–Sat 9am–8pm, Sun noon–5.30pm; $6.50; ☏817-255-9300, 1-888/255-9300, ⓦwww.fwmsh.org) includes a planetarium and an IMAX theater. The museum's most popular exhibits include ExploraZone – a kid-friendly area for exploring topics like magnetism, weather, math, etc – and DinoDig, where amateur paleontologists can dig through an "outdoor discovery zone" for dinosaur bones.

The lively, interactive **Cattle Raiser's Museum** is, for now, slightly farther north at 1301 W Seventh St (Mon–Sat 10am–5pm, Sun 1–5pm; $3) – it's scheduled to be relocated to the Cultural District by 2004. The changing economic face of the cattle trade is traced from the days of the open range, via the great cattle drives, to modern ranching and latterday cowboys – with displays of spurs, assorted tangles of barbed wire and some interesting history on the travails of early women pioneers. After the move, the museum will be adjacent to the **National Cowgirl Museum and Hall of Fame**, set to open in 2002.

However, museums, no matter how good, aren't necessarily what you want from a cowtown. The ten-block **Stockyards Area**, with its wooden sidewalks and old storefronts centered on Exchange Avenue two miles north of downtown, is a glorious evocation of the days when Fort Worth's stockyards made this "the richest little city in the world." It's much more than a cynical creation for cowboy-hungry tourists and even the daily march down East Exchange Avenue of the fifteen or so Texan Longhorn cattle (with six-feet horn spans) is done in good, educational taste. The drives occur, weather permitting, at 11.30am from the corrals behind the Livestock Exchange Building (see below) with the herd arriving back around 4pm; one of the best views can be found directly in front of the visitor center.

Along with the restaurants and bars, the **stores** will have Western-wear obsessives in heaven. Look out for Fincher's rodeo equipment store and M.L. Leddy's expansive saddle shop; and check out the Maverick Trading Post, packed with hip, bright cowgirl regalia, and a bar serving good cold beers. They encourage you to drink first and buy later; this is not a good idea. If all the authenticity is too much to bear, there's a nearby mall with a slightly more tourist-friendly orientation: the shops and restaurants in the **Stockyards Station**, a brick-floored enclave in the old hog pens, are squeaky clean; one of the best is the Ernest Tubb Record Shop, next to the Stockyards Wedding Chapel. From here the magnificent *Tarantula* **steam train** puffs along to Eighth Avenue downtown (departs Wed–Sat noon, Sun 3pm; 30min; $10; ☏817/625-RAIL, ⓦwww.tarantulatrain.com).

The Stockyards no longer host live **cattle auctions**; instead, images are beamed by satellite into the huge 1902 **Livestock Exchange Building** at 131 E Exchange Ave, home of the **Stockyards Collections Museum** (Mon–Sat 10am–5pm; free), packed with meaty memorabilia. The mission-style **Cowtown Coliseum** next door, used for rodeos (☏817/625-1025, ⓦwww.cowtowncoliseum.com; ticket prices vary) and concerts, is fronted with a bust of Bill Pickett, the black rodeo star who invented the unsavory but effective practice of "bulldogging" – stunning the bull by biting its lip.

Eating

If you love **steak**, Fort Worth is for you. Meat here is hefty, fresh and prepared with tender loving care, especially in the Stockyards area, where the many good home-cooking cafés are frequented as much by cattle ranchers as by visitors. Mex and Tex-Mex tastes are well covered though vegetarians will do less well; try the upmarket restaurants downtown. The **café** in the Kimbell Art Museum (see p.755) makes for a pleasant place to snack or eat lunch.

Angelo's Barbecue 2533 White Settlement Rd ☎817/332-0357. Venerable westside restaurant open for lunch and dinner and cited by locals as the best in the city.

Angeluna 215 E 4th St ☎817/334-0080. Tasty Caribbean-Asian-Southern fusion food across the street from Bass Hall.

Cattlemen's Steak House 2458 N Main St ☎817/624-3945. Dim lighting and wall-sized portraits of prize steers. A Fort Worth institution thanks to its steaks and margaritas. Dinner is around $20.

J & J Oyster Bar 612 N University Drive ☎817/335-2756. Try the fresh crab and oysters at this local institution near the Cultural District.

Joe T Garcia's Mexican Dishes 2201 N Commerce St ☎817/626-4356. Nationally famed Mexican restaurant in the owners' 1930s home, serving hefty set tortilla/fajita dinners (around $10) and frosty margaritas. Outdoor seating available next to the family swimming pool.

Mi Cocina 509 Main St ☎817/877-3600. Healthy Tex-Mex dishes in a modern, eclectically decorated joint.

Star Café 111 W Exchange Ave ☎817/624-8701. Neon-lit café serving some of the least expensive steaks – not just in the Stockyards but in the entire city. They also know how to chicken-fry steak well.

Nightlife and entertainment

You'd be hard pushed not to find something to your taste amid Fort Worth's late-night drinking and carousing. This is a truly cosmopolitan city, where roustabouts will happily down a few beers with modern jazz fans. Bar crawling is safe and fun, and there's a great mix of live music venues (though the pick-up joints in the Stockyards are best avoided). Check the *Fort Worth Weekly* (Ⓦ www.fwweekly.com) or the *Fort Worth Star-Telegram* (Ⓦ www.star-telegram.com) for listings. The **Nancy Lee & Perry R. Bass Performance Hall** (☎817/212-4280) is the new downtown home of the city's orchestra, opera, theater and dance companies and hosts visiting spectacles.

In addition to the regular cowboy venues below, the **Chisholm Trail Round-Up** (mid-June; Ⓦ www.chisholmtrail.org) and **Pioneer Days** (September) are two hugely enjoyable annual Western-style celebrations in the Stockyards. Cowtown Coliseum holds a championship **rodeo** (Fri and Sat 8pm; $8.50; ☎817/625-1025, Ⓦ www.cowtowncoliseum.com) and special events throughout the year.

Billy Bob's Texas 2520 Rodeo Plaza ☎817/624-7117). The largest honky-tonk in the world, down in the Stockyards, with bull-riding (Fri & Sat 9pm & 10pm), pool tables, bars, restaurants and stores, and big-name concerts. Live music nightly; open until 2am. Tours Mon–Sat 11am, 2pm & 4pm, Sun 2pm & 4pm. Cover Mon–Thurs & Sun $3–5, Fri & Sat $5–10.

The Caravan of Dreams 312 Houston St ☎817/877-3000. A superb downtown club in a beautiful building with a cactus garden. Attracts a friendly, stylish crowd and regular big-name acts. Cover $12–60, though access to the *Rooftop Grotto Bar* is free.

Casa Mañana Theater 3101 Lancaster Ave ☎817/332-6221. Alternative comedy and plays in the Cultural District, with a great selection of kid-friendly plays as well.

8.0 111 E 3rd St ☎817/336-0880. Highly popular downtown bar in Sundance Square, flamboyantly decorated inside and with sidewalk tables.

Flying Saucer 111 E 4th St ☎817/336-7468.

Over 200 beers, often with enticing promotional prices, in a fun Sundance Square setting, with live music Tues–Sun.

J&J Blues Bar 937 Woodward Ave ☎817/870-BEER. Westside joint with regional blues acts Thurs–Sat.

J&Js Hideaway 3305 W 7th St ☎817/877-3363. Good neighborhood bar in the Cultural District, and a welcome respite from the more aggressively Western-themed outlets.

White Elephant Saloon 106 E Exchange Ave ☎817/624-1887. Notoriously wild and authentic Stockyards saloon with a cowboy hat hall of fame; prop yourself up at the long wooden bar and listen to cowboy singer and owner Don Edwards. $4 cover Fri. Open till midnight weekdays, 2am Fri & Sat.

Wreck Room 3208 W 7th St ☎817/870-4900. Underground westside hangout with occasional leftfield rock bands.

Toward the Panhandle

Routes west from central Texas lead you through the state's "backyard," where farmlands and rough-cut, juniper-covered hills give way to treeless, sandy landscapes. Of the towns, only **Abilene** and **Sweetwater**, both on I-20 toward El Paso, are even marginally interesting to be possible stopovers for long-distance drivers. In theory, this is rich, oil-bearing land, but the cities have taken a battering since the slump.

Abilene and Sweetwater

ABILENE has a certain curiosity value as an oppressively God-fearing Bible city and home to three Christian universities. There's not much reason to stop here, though a downtown stroll reveals a few places along **Cypress Street** worth a look. At no. 102 the **Grace Museum** (Tues–Wed & Fri–Sat 10am–5pm, Thurs 10am–8.30pm; $3, free after 5.30pm Thurs; ☎915/673-4587, ⦿www.thegrace museum.org) occupies what was once the grandest hotel in this former railroad town and is divided into three distinct sections: regional art, local history and a children's museum. The **Center for Contemporary Arts** at no. 220 (Tues–Sat 11am–5pm; ☎915-677-8389, ⦿www.abilene.com/art/cca) exhibits work by local artists and is free, while the beautiful **Paramount Theatre** at no. 352 (☎915/676-9620, ⦿www.paramount-abilene.org) is open for self-guided tours of its elaborate Moorish interior on weekdays between 1pm and 5pm. Evening shows range from theater productions to classic and art films. If you have to stay, there are plenty of interstate **motels**, including the well-kept *Executive Inn*, 1650 I-20 E (☎915/677-2200; ❷), while downtown, *BJ's*, 508 Mulberry St, offers homey, comfortable **B&B** rooms (☎915/675-5855; ❹). Cypress Street is the place to go for **food** with the *Cypress Street Station* at no. 158 (☎915/676-3463) offering a more eclectic menu than you would expect from a restaurant in this locale.

Dozy **SWEETWATER**, further west on I-20, began as a general store for buffalo hunters in 1877, and since 1958 has been mildly notable for its **rattlesnake roundup** (⦿www.rattlesnakeroundup.com) on the second full weekend of March, when you can try fried snake (tough but tasty) or buy a transparent toilet seat with a rattler coiled in it. As well as the serious business of the farmers ridding their land of the diamondbacks, there are parades, cookouts, a Miss Snake Charmer Queen contest and snake-handling demonstrations. Of the motels along Georgia Street, one of the nicest is the *Ranch House Motel and Restaurant* (☎915/236-6341; ❷).

The Panhandle

The inhabitants of the **Panhandle**, the southernmost portion of the Great Plains, call it "the real Texas"; it certainly fulfills the fantasy of what Texas should look like. When Coronado's expedition passed this way in the sixteenth century, the gold-seekers drove stakes into the ground across the vast and unchanging vista, despairing of otherwise finding their way home. Hence the name *Llano Estacado*, or staked plains, which still persists today.

Once the buffalo – and the natives – had been driven away from what was seen as perilous and uninhabitable frontier country, the Panhandle began, around the 1870s, to yield great **natural resources**. Helium – especially in Amarillo – and oil, as well as **agriculture**, have brought wealth to the region, home to some of the world's largest **ranches**.

The Panhandle may hold few actual tourist attractions, but what appeals are its rural charm, its quirkiness and its distance from the eastern cities. **Music** has particular significance in an area famous for songwriters such as Buddy Holly, Roy Orbison, Waylon Jennings, Mac Davis, Joe Ely and Natalie Maines from the Dixie Chicks, although most musicians relocate to cosmopolitan centers like Austin. Above all, the exceptionally hospitable **people** of the Panhandle make it special, along with the starkly romantic landscape, strewn with tumbleweeds and mesquite trees.

Lubbock

LUBBOCK, the largest city in the Panhandle, has long been the center of its commerce and transportation, roughly one hundred miles northwest of Abilene and the same distance south of Amarillo. At first this was cattle-grazing land, but the discovery of copious underground water made agriculture profitable.

The prosperity of the city was built on cotton. In recent years, while farmers have been perpetually plagued by economic struggles, the town's economy now also relies on manufacturing and retail outlets; you may, however, still see solitary cottonfields standing defiantly on the outskirts, where farmers have refused to sell out.

With its fields, farms, lumpen bungalows and faceless block buildings, Lubbock is relentlessly ordinary-looking, its muted downtown area dotted with fading 1950s shopfronts. Which is not to say that it's dull; though Southern Baptism has left its mark, Lubbock has a uniquely Texan sense of fun, clearly evident in its love of music, rodeos, and having a good time.

Arrival, information and getting around

Loop 289 circles Lubbock proper, with the **airport** (☏806/775-2035) a few minutes north; city buses don't come out here, so taxis are the only option (Yellow Taxi ☏806/765-7474) to downtown costs $10. **Buses** come in downtown at 1313 13th St (☏806/765-6641). The **citibus** system (☏806/762-0111, ⓦwww.citibus.com) runs commuter routes within the Loop, stopping at around 6.15pm (Mon–Sat only). The **visitor center** is at 1301 Broadway (Mon–Fri 8am–5pm; ☏806/747-5232 or 1-800/692-4035, ⓦwww.lubbocklegends.com).

Buddy Holly

Lubbock's claim to world fame is as the birthplace of Charles Hardin Holley on September 7, 1936. Inspired by the blues and country music of his childhood – and a seminal encounter with the young Elvis Presley, gigging in Lubbock at the *Cotton Club* – **Buddy Holly** was one of rock'n'roll's first singer-songwriters. The Holly sound, characterized by steady strumming guitar, rapid drumming and his trademark hiccuping vocals, was made famous by hits such as *Peggy Sue*, *Rave On*, *Not Fade Away*, *Oh Boy!* and *That'll Be the Day*; but Buddy himself was killed at the age of 22 by the Iowa plane crash of February 3, 1959 ("the day the music died") that also claimed the Big Bopper and Ritchie Valens.

In September 1999, the city opened the **Buddy Holly Center** at 19th Street and Avenue G (Tues–Fri 10am–6pm, Sat 11am–6pm; ☏806-767-2686, ⓦwww.buddyhollycenter.org), an impressive space that holds Lubbock's collection of Holly memorabilia (contracts, clothes, rare records, autographed items, and yes, those glasses) plus the Texas Music Hall Of Fame and various temporary exhibition galleries. All exhibits are free except for the Holly collection ($3).

An 8ft bronze **Buddy Holly Statue**, on Eighth Street and Avenue Q, towers over a **Walk of Fame** of plaques to local performers like Roy Orbison and Waylon Jennings (the bassist for Buddy's final concert). **Buddy's birthplace**, at 1911 Sixth St, is now a vacant lot, but more substantial sites around town include:

J.T. Hutchinson Junior High School 3102 Canton Ave. Buddy and friend Bob Montgomery performed here in the sixth grade.

Lubbock High School 2004 19th St. Buddy and Bob, who graduated in 1955, won the school's "Westerners Round Up" with *Flower of My Heart*. Souvenirs are on sale.

Tabernacle Baptist Church 1911 34th St. A percentage of Buddy's royalties still go to the church that saw his baptism, wedding and funeral.

Radio Station KRLB 6602 Martin Luther King Jr Blvd. Opened in 1953, this was the first full-time country music station in the US. Buddy and bandmate Jack Neal had their own show.

Fair Park Coliseum 10th St and Ave A. Where Buddy opened shows for Bill Haley and Elvis Presley. His "discovery" here in 1955 led to a contract with Decca.

Buddy's grave, in Lubbock cemetery at the end of 34th St. Take the right fork inside the gate, and the grave, decorated with flowers and guitar picks, is on the left.

Accommodation

Prices are very reasonable in this region, and rooms are plentiful, so there should be no problem finding someplace to stay. Avenue Q has a string of good, reliable chain hotels.

Coronado Inn 501 I-27 N ☏806/763-6441. Northside motel with clean rooms for thirty bucks. ❶

Holiday Inn – Civic Center 801 Ave Q ☏806/763-1200, ⓦwww.holiday-inn.com. Popular downtown hotel with pool and other facilities. ❹

La Quinta Inn – Civic Center 601 Ave Q ☏806/763-9441, ⓦwww.laquinta.com. Free coffee and decent rooms, adjacent to a 24hr restaurant

and just across from the Buddy Holly Statue. ❸

Lubbock Inn 3901 19th St ☏806/792-5181, ⓦwww.lubbockinn.com. Basic motel featuring a restaurant and a pool with waterfalls. ❸

Woodrow House B&B 2629 19th St ☏806/793-3330 or 1-800/687-5235, ⓦwww.woodrowhouse.com. Eight rooms, each with a Texan theme, in a mansion-style house opposite Texas Tech. ❹

The Town

Downtown Lubbock, and the university, are on the northern side of town. Few buildings of interest survive, thanks to the construction boom of the 1950s and a tornado in 1970. However, you can get a stimulating overview of local history at the university's **Ranching Heritage Center**, Fourth Street and Indiana Avenue (Mon–Sat 10am–5pm, Sun 1–5pm; free). Over thirty original ranch buildings, from simple cowboy huts to grand overseers' houses, are set in a harsh landscape spiked with cactuses and mesquite. There's an excellent museum on pioneer and cowboy history, and demonstrations on making lye soap, sourdough and quilts. The adjacent **Texas Tech Museum** (Tues, Wed, Fri, Sat 10am–5pm, Thurs 10am–8.30pm, Sun 1–5pm; free) has further Southwestern displays and Buddy Holly memorabilia.

Nearby, the **Lubbock Lake Landmark State Historical Park** archeological site (Tues–Sat 9am–5pm, Sun 1–5pm; free; ⓦ www.ttu.edu/~museum/lll) has yielded an impressive array of artifacts spanning 12,000 years, although to the untrained eye it resembles little more than a dry gravelly site buzzing with gigantic Texan insects. As indeed does **Prairie Dog Town**, in Mackenzie State Park, where six hundred of the cuddly little rodents are attempting to repopulate the world and gain their revenge for the attempts of government officials and irate ranchers in the 1930s to poison them into extinction.

Three miles east of the Loop on Farm Road 1585, the **Llano Estacado winery** started as the hobby of two university professors. It might look incongruous, set amid scrubby pastureland and cottonfields, but its success has led Lubbock to pin great hopes on the potential of wine to revitalize and diversify its flagging economy. Visitors are given a guided tour and free tasting (Mon–Sat 10am–5pm, Sun noon–5pm; ☎806/745-2258, ⓦ www.llanowine.com).

Eating

Lubbock has a surprising variety of **eating places**, with good barbecue and Tex-Mex and even some New American restaurants, with a particular concentration along Buddy Holly Avenue (Avenue H). However, many of even the most upmarket restaurants close before 10pm.

Abuelo's 4401 82nd St ☎806/794-1762. Lubbock's best Mexican restaurant, with some great fish dishes, punch-packing margaritas, and live music on the patio in summer.

The County Line half a mile west of I-27 in Escondido Canyon ☎806/763-6001. First-rate barbecue in Lubbock, with all-you-can-eat specials for around $15. Outside, ducks and peacocks saunter around freely.

Hub City Brewpub 1807 Buddy Holly Ave ☎806/747-1535. Lively and youthful, with decent grill food and beers.

Pancake House 510 Ave Q ☎806/765-8506. Popular downtown joint for breakfast.

Santa Fe 401 Ave Q ☎806/763-6114. Bulging enchiladas, gargantuan burritos and standard Tex-Mex favorites, in a peaceful family atmosphere.

Entertainment and nightlife

The best entertainment the Panhandle has to offer is at its **annual events**. After having been designated the "Music Crossroads of Texas" by the state legislature in 1999, the city changed the name of the annual Buddy Holly Music Festival to the catchy mouthful of the Music Crossroads of Texas Labor Day Weekend Music Festival (MCOTLDWMF for short?) – and now it's simply September Fest. Whatever it's called in the following years, it'll likely still attract big Texan names like Joe Ely and Tanya Tucker, as well as those playing a straight homage to Mr Holly. **Rodeos** are always rip-roaring fun; Texas Tech holds one each October in Fair Park, and the **ABC Rodeo** (☎806/793-5800, ⓦ www.abcrodeo.com) is at Lubbock Municipal Coliseum every spring. In the same spirit, there are twirling contests, bull-riding, big-name country performers and livestock exhibits at the **Panhandle South**

Plains Fair (⊛www.southplainsfair.com) in late September and early October.

Despite its rich musical heritage there isn't a great deal of **nightlife** in Lubbock; most of the local musicians decamp to Austin. The buzz zone is the downtown Historical Depot District, which spreads out for a few blocks from 19th Street and Hwy-27, and has a mix of crass chain bars and sports bars. The oddly named *Lubbock Avalanche–Journal* (⊛www.lubbockonline.com) carries listings.

9

Cactus Theatre 1812 Buddy Holly Ave ⊕806/762-3233. Insists on putting on a mix of variety shows as syrupy musical nostalgia shows with frequent nods to you-know-who.

Midnight Rodeo 7301 S University Ave at Loop 289 ⊕806/745-2813. Huge C&W club, featuring karaoke, lanky cowboys and big-haired Texan belles. Great fun.

Amarillo

AMARILLO may seem cut off from the rest of Texas, up in the northern Panhandle, but it stands on one of the great American cross-country routes – I-40, once the legendary **Route 66** – roughly 300 miles east of Albuquerque and 250 miles west of Oklahoma City. The name comes from the Spanish for "yellow," the color of the soil characteristic in these parts. An early promoter of the city was so delighted with its potential as a site for lucrative buffalo hunting (for those who braved the Apache and Comanche threat) and as excellent ranching land that he painted all the buildings bright yellow.

Today, sitting on ninety percent of the world's helium and hosting a world-class cattle market, Amarillo is a prosperous but surprisingly uneventful city. The small "**old town**" consists of a few tree-lined streets and staid old homes; some of the less twee antique stores along **Sixth Street** (the old Route 66, known locally as "Old San Jacinto") serve equally well as museums of pioneer life. Following I-40 six miles west to exit 60 (Arnot Road) brings you to **Cadillac Ranch** (⊛www.libertysoftware.be/cml/cadillacranch/crmain.htm). An extraordinary vision in the middle of nowhere, ten battered roadsters stand upended in the soil, their tail fins demonstrating the different Cadillac designs from 1949 to 1963. Since the cars were installed in 1974, they have been subject to countless makeovers at the hands of graffiti artists, photographers and members of the public (encouraged by owner and patron, eccentric helium millionaire Stanley Marsh III, on whose land the cars are planted); occasionally they're shiny blue or red after having been painted for a photo shoot. In 1997 the whole installation was moved two miles west to this present site as the city had begun to encroach and spoil the horizon.

Amarillo is also host to the world's stompingest, snortingest **livestock auction** (⊕806/373-7464), in the stockyards at S Manhattan and Third avenues, on the east side of town. The auction proper, held on Tuesday morning, is open to the public, as is the adjacent *Stockyard Café* (⊕806/374-6024).

If you enjoy playing cowboys, it's fun to visit one of the many grand old Panhandle **ranches** to have diversified into tourism. Some just open for the day; others provide (usually expensive) accommodation (call Amarillo's CVB for particulars). The ranchers who entertain you are often natural showmen and women, whose welcome is utterly genuine, though they'd rather be working the animals for real than running a theme park.

Practicalities

Eight local bus lines connect downtown Amarillo with outlying attractions (Mon–Sat 6.30am–6pm; 75¢; ☎806/342-9144), but the city is easier to navigate by car. Greyhound comes in downtown at 700 S Tyler St (☎806/374-5371). The **CVB** is at 1000 Polk St (Mon–Fri 8am–5pm; ☎806/374-1497 or 1-800/692-1338, ⓦwww.amarillo-cvb.org).

Innumerable budget **hotels** are concentrated along I-40. For a little luxury, *Ambassador Hotel*, 3100 I-40 W, is good value (☎806/358-6161; ⑤) while *Auntie's House*, 1712 S Polk St (☎806/371-8054 or 1-888/661-8054, ⓦwww.auntieshouse.com; ④) is a sweet, welcoming **B&B**. Texana fans will love the tongue-in-cheek Western charm of the *Big Texan Steak House Motel*, 7701 I-40 E at exit 75 (☎806/372-5000 or 1-800/657-7177, ⓦwww.bigtexan.com; ③). Its restaurant, as well as serving fried rattlesnake and ostrich burgers, offers the 72oz steak challenge: if you can **eat** it all within an hour, you get it free (losers pony up $54.13). Other popular Amarillo restaurants include *Arnold Burgers*, 1611 S Washington St (☎806/372-1741), which serves enormous beef patties (up to 24 inches); *Tacos Garcia*, 1412 S Ross (☎806/371-0411), for reliable Mexican food in a festive environment; and the self-consciously bohemian *OHMS Gallery Café*, 619 S Tyler St (☎806/373-3233), with a decidedly international menu – think lasagne, shepherd's pie and enchiladas.

Canyon

The one "sight" in the former cattle town of **CANYON**, fifteen miles south of Amarillo on I-27, is a must. The **Panhandle–Plains Historical Museum** (daily 9am–6pm, Sun 1–6pm; $4; ⓦwww.panhandleplains.org) has exhibits on restored pioneer buildings, the history of Texas ranching, natural history displays, a collection of Western art, and even the oldest known assembly line automobile (a 1903 Model A Ford). Even the history of the oil and gas industry is made interesting. For **food**, try the *Chuckwagon Restaurant* (☎806/488-2152) just off the park road on the Canyon floor; it's impossible to miss.

Palo Duro State Canyon Park

Palo Duro Canyon, twelve miles east of Canyon and twenty miles southeast of Amarillo, is one of Texas's best-kept secrets. Plunging 1000 feet from rim to floor, it splits the plains wide open and offers breathtaking views and colors, especially at sunset and in spring, when the whole chasm is scattered with wild flowers. Pillars of sturdy sandstone loom over the flame-colored rocks, which Coronado's explorers named "Spanish Skirts" on account of their resemblance to stripy flounces.

The **park** itself is located in the most scenic part of the 130-mile canyon (park daily 8am–10pm, visitor center and interpretive center daily 9am–5pm; $3 per person). You can explore the depths on **horseback** ($12 per hour; reservations ☎806/488-2180), though backpackers and hikers may want to escape the tourist busloads by following the Prairie Dog Town fork into more remote sections of the park. To **camp**, advance reservations are recommended (☎806/488-2227).

You may balk at heart-warming musical spectaculars, but the outdoor production *TEXAS* has an undeniable pull in an area not exactly throbbing with nightlife, with the dramatic prairie sky as a ceiling, a 600ft cliff as a backdrop, and genuine thunder and lightning (mid-June to late Aug Thurs–Tues 8.30pm; $8–23; pre-show chuckwagon barbecue 6pm; ☎806/655-2181, ⓦwww.texasmusicdrama.com).

West Texas

West Texas is the stuff of Wild West fantasy: parched deserts, ghost towns, looming mesas, and above all a sense of utter isolation. Although the area south from the Panhandle down to Del Rio on the Rio Grande is, for convenience, also known as West Texas, the fantasy really begins west of the River Pecos; you can drive for hours without a sign of life to **El Paso**, Texas's shabby western-most city. Most travelers only venture into the desolation to explore **Big Bend National Park**, nearly three hundred miles southeast of El Paso in the curve of the Rio Grande.

Minimal rainfall and harsh land were not the only hindrances to settlement. The **Apache** and **Comanche**, though accustomed in the 1820s to trading with Mexican *comancheros*, were infuriated when hapless white pioneers began to trickle in during the 1830s. With their horsemanship and ability to find scarce water supplies, the Native Americans posed a real threat; upon statehood, a string of cavalry forts was set up with the help of federal money to protect Mexican and Anglo settlers from attack. As trading posts and cattle ranges began to spring up after the Civil War, the paramilitary **Texas Rangers** were sent out on violent vigilante missions. Eventually, as in the Panhandle, a brutal program of buffalo slaughter, supported by the US Army, starved the natives out. Not long afterwards, **oil** was discovered in West Texas and boom towns appeared, with all the attendant lawlessness, gunslinging and brawling.

The Davis Mountains

The temperate climate of the verdant **Davis Mountains**, south of the junction of I-10 and I-20, makes them a popular summer destination for sweltering urban Texans, while the glassy, starry nights facilitate the work of the **McDonald Observatory** about twenty miles north of Fort Davis on Hwy-118 (guided tours of dome and 107-inch telescope daily 11.30am and 2.30pm, $4; self-guided tours daily 9am–5pm, free; ☎915-426-3640, ⊛www.as.utexas .edu/mcdonald/mcdonald.html). Nocturnal "star parties" here provide the opportunity to look at the constellations for yourself (Tues, Fri & Sat, time depends on sunset). **Fort Davis National Historic Site** (summer daily 8am–6pm; rest of year daily 9am–8pm; $2 per person, $4 per vehicle; ☎915/426-3224 ext 20, ⊛www.nps.gov/foda), which starts on the northern edge of the town along Hwy-17, offers good hiking, and fishing and swimming at the foot of the canyon in Limpia Creek. Rooms at its adobe *Indian Lodge* are clean and com-fortable – and often booked up, so call in advance (☎915/426-3254; ❸).

FORT DAVIS, a one-street town with less than a thousand residents, at the junction of highways 118 and 17, is a peaceful base for exploring the state park, en route to or from Big Bend. *The Old Texas Inn*, above a wood-fronted drug-store, has clean, colorful **B&B**-style rooms; breakfast is served in the café down-stairs, accompanied by country tunes on the jukebox (☎915/426-3118, ⊛www.oldtexasinn.com; ❸). The more expensive *Hotel Limpia*, opposite (☎915/426-3237 or 1-800/662-5517; ❺), serves home-cooked dinners in its cozy dining room. There's pleasantly little to do in Fort Davis at night, though you can buy "membership" to the hotel's bar for $3. The town's **visitor cen-ter** (☎915/426-3015, ⊛www.fortdavis.com) offers regional information including road maps for the 75-mile scenic loop of the Davis Mountains.

Big Bend National Park

The **Rio Grande**, flowing through 1500ft gorges, makes a ninety-degree bend south of Marathon to form the southern border of **BIG BEND NATIONAL PARK** – thanks to its isolation one of the least visited of the US national parks, and very much of a kind with the great desert parks of the Southwest.

The Apache, who forced the Chisos Indians out three hundred years ago, told that this hauntingly beautiful wilderness was used by the Great Spirit to dump all the rocks left over from the creation of the world. A breathtaking million-acre expanse of pine-forested mountains and ocotilla-dotted desert, Big Bend has been home to prospectors and smugglers, a last frontier for the true-grit pioneers at the end of the nineteenth century, who took advantage of the rich cinnabar deposits for mercury mining. Today there is camping in specific areas, and some trailer parks, but much of the park remains barely charted territory, the ruins of primitive Mexican and white settlements testament to its power to defeat earlier visitors. Wild animals have fared somewhat better: coyotes, road-runners and javelinas (an odd-looking bristly black pig with a pointy snout) all roam free. Violent contrasts in topography and temperature result in dramatic juxtapositions of desert and mountain plant and animal life. Despite the dryness, tangles of pretty wild flowers and blossoming cactuses, including peyote, erupt into color each April.

The most interesting route into Big Bend is from the west. You can't follow the river all the way from El Paso, but Hwy-170 – the **River Road**, reached on Hwy-67 south from Marfa, where James Dean made *Giant* – runs through spectacular desert scenery for around thirty miles west from Ojinaga, climbing stark buttes from where you can peep down to the river below. Before reaching the park boundary just beyond Study Butte, you pass through the haunting communities of Lajitas and Terlingua (see overleaf).

Once in the park, unless you're prepared to do some strenuous hiking, there are few opportunities to see the river itself; the main road is obliged to run across the desert, north of the outcrop of the Chisos Mountains. A spur road starting west of the headquarters at **Panther Junction** leads south for six miles, up into the alpine meadows of the **Chisos Basin**, ringed by dramatic (though not amazingly high) peaks. The one gap in the rocky wall here is the **Window**, looking out over the deserts and reached by a relatively simple trail. Driving twenty miles southeast of Panther Junction brings you to the riverside **Rio Grande Village** – unless you choose to detour just before, to bathe in some rather dilapidated natural **hot springs** that feed into the river. A foot-bridge crosses from near the village to the Mexican hamlet of Boquillas; or you can pay $1 to be rowed across the river, then ride a donkey into nearby Bouquillas for a meal and a beer.

At three separate stages within the park boundaries the river runs through gigantic **canyons**. The westernmost, the **Santa Elena**, is the most common **rafting trip**, being accessible from a put-in at Lajitas. Although there is virtually no whitewater, it boasts the technically challenging Rock Slide, and two ethereal Mexican side canyons that can be hiked, as well as stretches where the river swirls between awesome high rock walls, striated at an angle that makes it seem like you're plunging into an abyss. It's possible to drive within the park to the eastern end of the canyon, where the towering cliffs suddenly come to an end and the river meanders through marshy fields; a short hike from here shows the gorge in all its splendor.

The ease of crossing the **international frontier** adds to the thrill of the Big Bend experience, although you can get no further into Mexico than sandbanks populated by browsing burros. This area is so remote that casual traffic across the river is regarded as insignificant; police checks for illegal immigrants take place roughly fifty miles north of Big Bend, on each of the main roads.

Practicalities

The park headquarters at **Panther Junction** (daily 8am–5pm; ☎915/477-2251), where you pay the $10-per-vehicle entrance fee, has orientation exhibits and a daytime gas station. Camping is first-come, first-served. **Rio Grande Village** also has a visitor center, hot shower facilities in the grocery store, a laundry and a daytime gas station. Camping permits here and at **Chisos Basin** (see below) are $8. Further free primitive **campgrounds** are scattered along the 36 marked hiking trails. These have no facilities, and you'll need a wilderness permit from Panther Junction, plus a map, compass, flashlight and first-aid kit before you can venture onto the trails.

The **Chisos Basin**, which has a visitor center, a store and a post office, is the site of the park's only roofed accommodation. The motel-style *Chisos Mountains Lodge* (reservations essential; ☎915/477-2291, ⊛www.chisosmountainslodge .com; ❹) offers balcony rooms with gorgeous views; you'll often hear javelinas snuffling for food outside your door. Its adequate cafeteria restaurant closes at 8pm.

Terlingua and Lajitas

Some of the long-abandoned mercury mining communities on the fringes of Big Bend are now stuttering back to life as alternative tourist centers. **TERLINGUA** in particular, a strangely appealing little ghost town scattered across the scrubby hills along Hwy-170, is populated by the adventurous types who work for the local rafting companies, along with assorted drifters lured by the solitary desert life. Near its fly-blown cemetery, against a backdrop of evocative ruins, the hugely atmospheric *Starlight Theater, Bar and Restaurant* (☎915/371-2326), with its postmodern reinterpretation of Southwestern decor, is the perfect place to enjoy a cold beer and soak up the haunting desert view; it also serves food, and puts on evening shows in summer. A mile or so east along the highway is the only other place to eat in the evening: *La Kiva* (☎915/371-2250), attached to the RV-oriented *Big Bend Travel Park*, is carved into the rock, and attracts a young crowd to its New Age bar, restaurant and evening gigs. The *Chisos Mining Company Motel* on Hwy-170 (☎915/371-2254; ❷) has reasonable **rooms**.

Allow around $125 for a full day's **rafting** along Santa Elena Canyon (see overleaf); canyons further out can cost up to $150. Far Flung Adventures, based next door to the *Starlight* in Terlingua, runs all the Big Bend routes, as well as many other Southwestern rivers, and also does memorable multiday music trips with renowned Texan musicians (☎915/371-2325 or 1-800/359-4138, ⊛www.farflung.com).

LAJITAS, west of Terlingua, is the main put-in for rafting trips, but has largely been taken over by the somewhat ersatz *Lajitas on the Rio Grande* resort complex, with its five separate hotels (☎915/424-3471, ⊛www.lajitas.com; ❹). However, it attempts to pull in the tourists with its distinguished political figurehead – Clay Henry III, a beer-drinking goat who beat four other candidates – including a wooden Indian and a real person – for the mayoral post. Look for his pen, littered with empty Lone Star Longneck bottles, outside the adobe Lajitas Trading Post.

El Paso

Back when Texas was still *Tejas*, **EL PASO**, the second oldest settlement in the United States, was the main crossing on the Rio Grande. It still plays that role today, its 700,000 residents joining with another 1.7 million across the river in **CIUDAD JUAREZ**, Mexico, to form the largest binational (and bilingual) megalopolis in North America. At first sight it's not an especially pretty place – massive railyards fill up much of downtown, the belching smelters of copper mills line the riverfront, and the northern reaches are taken up by the giant Fort Bliss military base, where two museums trace the military history of the city from adobe Spanish outpost to largest air defense center in the Western world. Its dramatic setting, however, where the Franklin Mountains meet the Chihuahua desert, gives it a certain bold, rough pioneer edge, bearing more relation to old rather than new Mexico, with little of the pastel softness of the Southwest US. Local legend has it that when Wyatt Earp arrived in sharp-shooting El Paso, he thought it too wild for him, and boarded the first train to Tombstone.

Arrival, information and getting around

El Paso's **airport** is about twenty minutes' drive northeast of downtown; Sun Metro bus route #33 (☎915/533-3333) will take you downtown until 9pm Mon–Sat and 7pm Sun for $1; it's a $15 cab ride, although most downtown hotels offer free van rides. Greyhound **buses** stop at 200 W San Antonio Ave, while Amtrak **trains** pull in to the Daniel Burnham-designed Union Station at 700 San Francisco St, slightly to the west.

For full information on El Paso and its Mexican neighbor, contact the downtown **visitor center** (daily 8am–5pm; ☎915/544-0062 or 1-800/351-6024, ⊛www.visitelpaso.com), at 5 Civic Center Plaza in the Convention Center complex.

Accommodation

Prices in El Paso tend to be reasonable and there's a good range of choices, from hostels, functional old downtown hotels and swanky joints to the usual chain motels along the interstate.

Gardner Hotel & Hostel 311 E Franklin St ☎915/532-3661. Atmospheric hotel where John Dillinger bedded down in the 1920s. The hostel costs $14 for members and an extra buck for others. Rooms vary from dorms to singles with shared bath to clean en-suite doubles. ❶–❷

Hilton Camino Real 101 S El Paso St ☎915/534-3000, ⊛www.hilton.com. El Paso's luxury option. If you can't stay here at least visit its elegant Southwestern restaurant or the wonderfully romantic *Dome Bar*, topped with a colorful Tiffany dome and surrounded by rose and black marble. ❹

Microtel Inn 2001 Airway Blvd ☎915/772-3650, ⊛www.microtelinn.com. A new, inexpensive chain offering near the airport, providing a great base for the Mission Trail east of downtown. ❸

Sunset Heights B&B Inn 717 W Yandell Drive ☎915/544-1743. Welcoming Victorian B&B, a few minutes from downtown, that serves excellent multi-course breakfasts. ❹

Travelodge City Center 409 E Missouri Ave ☎915/544-3333, ⊛www.travelodge.com. Large, downtown motel rooms and there's a passable Mexican restaurant on the premises. ❷

The Town

Downtown El Paso holds surprisingly little to see apart from a couple of passable art museums; what character it has continues to be shaped by the **US–Mexico border**. In times past outlaws and exiles from either side of the border would take refuge across the river, and today's traffic remains considerable and not entirely uncontroversial. Manual workers come north to find undocumented jobs, and US companies secretly dump their toxic waste on the south side. The border itself, the Rio Grande, has caused its share of disagreements: the river changed course quite often in the 1800s, and it was not until the 1960s, when it was run through a concrete channel, that it was made permanent. An attractive park, the **Chamizal National Memorial** (daily 8am–5pm; free), on the east side of downtown off Paisano Drive, was built to commemorate the settling of the border dispute and provides a pleasant place to picnic. The **Border Patrol Museum**, 4315 Transmountain Rd at Hwy-54 (Tues–Sun 9am–5pm; free), is a small but engrossing museum explaining the work of the patrollers and highlights the ingenuity of smugglers. The **Cordova Bridge** heads across the river into Mexico, where there's a larger park and a number of museums; there are no formalities, so long as you have a multiple-entry visa for the US and don't travel more than twenty or so miles south of the border. The El Paso–Juarez "Border Jumper" trolley departs hourly from the visitor center; the $12 round-trip ticket is steep but does provide a pretty comprehensive tour of the city.

Although El Paso is predominantly Hispanic, there is also a substantial population of **Tigua Indians**, a displaced Pueblo tribe, based in a reservation (complete with the almost statutory **casino**) on Socorro Road, southeast of downtown. The reservation's arts and crafts center is open to the public, selling pottery and textiles. Adjacent to the reservation, the simple **Ysleta del Sur**, the oldest mission in the United States, marks the beginning of a **mission trail** (information office ☎915/534-0677, ☜www.missiontrail.com) running alongside scruffy cotton, alfalfa, chili, onion and pecan fields. Two miles east, the **Socorro mission**, moved from its original seventeenth-century site on the river, shows an unusually heavy Native American influence; the crenelation on either side of the bell tower represents a Tigua rain god. Still an active church, inside it is relatively unadorned, with hand-carved ceiling beams and lattices; major renovation efforts, replacing crumbling concrete, will continue through 2003. Off the beaten track, six miles further along the trail, the cathedral-style **San Elizario** was the chapel for the Spanish military, with whitewashed walls, jewel-colored stained glass and a decorative tin ceiling. Splendid views of three states and two countries can be seen from the southern rim of the Franklin Mountains, either from Scenic Drive or from the vertigo-inducing Wyler Aerial Tramway (summer Mon & Thurs noon–6pm, Fri–Sun noon–9pm; rest of year Mon, Thurs & Fri noon–6pm, weekends noon–9pm; $7; ☎915/566-6622, ☜www.tpwd.state.tx.us/park/tram), which climbs 946 feet to Wyler Observatory.

In **Concordia cemetery**, just northwest of the I-10 and Hwy-54 intersection, a shambling collection of crumbling stones and plain wooden crosses commemorates assorted pioneers and desperados. The grave of **John Wesley Hardin**, much romanticized gunslinger, is marked by a crooked headstone northwest of the Chinese graveyard, a section walled off since the Chinese built the railroads in the 1880s. El Paso is also the home of Tony Lama, makers of top-quality **cowboy boots**, available at substantial discounts at three outlets across town.

Dining and nightlife

Dining is understandably dominated by Mexican cuisine. After dark, El Paso offers an uninspiring mix of **clubs** and **bars**. The *Camino Real Hotel*'s beautiful *Dome Bar* offers a pleasant drinking atmosphere. Alternatively, head across the border to **Ciudad Juárez**: two solid options are the Hemingway-esque *Kentucky Club Cantina*, 629 Av Juárez, just south of the Santa Fe Street bridge, and the more relaxed *Viva Mexico* restaurant, at the Pueblito Mexicano Mall, with its live mariachi music. The latter is considerably more comfortable for women travelers.

9

Azulejos *Hilton Camino Real,* 101 S El Paso St ☎915/534-3020. Without doubt the most pleasant dining space in the city, though the prices of the Tex-Mex and regional fare do reflect the location.

Cattleman's Steakhouse Indian Cliffs Ranch, Fabens, TX ☎915/544-3200. A regional legend about 25 miles east of El Paso, serving superb food – plus you can wander around the working ranch. To get here take I-10 east to exit 49, turn right and drive five miles north.

H&H Coffee Shop & Car Wash 701 E Yandell Drive ☎915/533-1144. These adjacent businesses just off downtown work well together; stop by in the morning for their wicked huevos rancheros. Reportedly a favored stop for President Bush and assorted governors.

Puerto Vallarta Grill 1611 Montana Ave ☎915/544-8169. Unassuming local favorite with delicious, seafood-centric Mexican fare.

Guadalupe Mountains National Park

Roughly one hundred miles east of El Paso, Hwy-62/180 climbs toward Carlsbad Caverns along the southern fringes of the **GUADALUPE MOUNTAINS**, once a stronghold of the Mescalero Apache. The national park here (headquarters ☎915/828-3251, ⓦ www.nps.gov/gumo) is very much a hiking and camping destination, barely penetrated by roads and without accommodation, food or even gas. It's possible to hike right to the top of Guadalupe Peak, at 8749ft the highest point in Texas, but most walkers head instead for the painlessly flat trek through **McKittrick Canyon**, passing from bare desert into lush mountain forests beside sheer canyon walls.

CHAPTER 10   # Highlights

* **Woolaroc Ranch, Bartlesville, OK** Fascinating museum of Western art and history. See p.777

* **Hannibal, MO** This delightful Mississippi River town is still recognizable as the setting for Mark Twain's epic tales of boyhood. See p.784

* **Live music in Kansas City, MO** Choose from a host of venues, from downhome blues joints to slick jazz clubs. See p.797

* **Dodge City Days and Rodeo, KS** A good ol' time with some good ol' boys in late July and early August. See p.805

* **Carhenge, Alliance, NE** America's crazy vehicular Stonehenge, planted in a Nebraska wheat field. See p.818

* **Badlands, SD** This spooky moonscape offers great camping and hiking – and a monument to the Ghost Dancers at Wounded Knee. See p.823

* **Black Hills, SD** Superb camping, the overblown monuments of Mount Rushmore and Crazy Horse, and wandering bison; the all-American destination. See p.825

The Great Plains

T HE GREAT PLAINS, stretching west of the Mississippi through **OKLAHOMA**, **MISSOURI**, **KANSAS**, **IOWA**, **NEBRASKA** and **SOUTH** and **NORTH DAKOTA**, are lumped together in the popular imagination as an unappealing expanse of unvarying flatness and conservative "Middle American" values, a huge national joke to be passed through as fast as possible. Once, however, this was the **West**, a vast empty canvas on which outlaws, fur trappers, buffalo hunters and cowboys painted their dreams. In the 1870s, the wide open range of the lone prairie, which had originally been known as the **Great American Desert** but was then promoted as a bountiful Garden of Eden, inspired such fascination that General Custer was moved to call it "the fairest and richest portion of the national domain." As well as the main routes west (the Oregon and Santa Fe trails through Missouri, Kansas and Nebraska), the plains were crisscrossed by the Pony Express, cattle trails and railroads. Today the massive Gateway Arch in **St Louis** celebrates the traders, explorers and pioneers who followed their destinies further and further west.

Early maps show the "Desert" as uninterrupted by towns or roads; even today there are fewer towns, spaced further apart, on the plains than anywhere else in the nation. One sinister note echoes through this openness and emptiness: most of the nation's **nuclear missiles** – marked by unprepossessing concrete blocks fenced into empty fields – sit beneath a land already ravaged by greed.

The plains, today so apparently uneventful, share a troubled history. The systematic destruction by white settlers of the awesome herds of **bison** presaged the virtual eradication of the **Plains Indians**. Reservations, agencies and "assigned lands" dwindled as the natural resources of the area attracted white settlement; after 1874, when **gold** was discovered in the Black Hills, the fate of the Native Americans was practically sealed. However, thanks to warriors like **Crazy Horse** and **Sitting Bull**, the struggle for control of the plains was by no means as easy as the Hollywood Westerns imply. Today the region is ambivalent about this history: many of its museums and monuments to Native Americans seem almost like a veiled celebration of the destruction of their culture.

The plains are more comfortable playing **cowboys**, glorying in a romantic myth of the Wild West and flaunting sanitized versions of wicked old cowtowns like **Deadwood** in South Dakota, **Dodge City** (once called the "Beautiful, Bibulous Babylon of the Frontier") in Kansas, and **St Joseph**, Missouri, the birthplace of the Pony Express. **Calamity Jane**, **Wild Bill Hickok**, **Billy the Kid** and **Annie Oakley** all left their mark here when this was the wild frontier, and today, in the sandy scrublands of northern Nebraska and North

Dakota, you can still see real cowboy and cattle country.

After Reconstruction, Southern blacks came here in search of an egalitarian future, and black colonies sprang up all around the region. The dreams soon died, though, and there are few black faces to be seen nowadays. There is, however, more evidence of nineteenth-century **Russian** and **German** settlement: many of the oldest families on the plains are descendants of European

Mennonites who escaped religious persecution in the 1870s, bringing with them new farming methods that heralded the region's great agricultural prosperity. The Great Plains still provide the nation with much of its food and export two-thirds of the world's **wheat**, seas of which wave over the flat fields of Iowa, Nebraska and Kansas. The economy has also long been dependent on oil, especially in Oklahoma, and gold in the Dakotas.

Defining the geographical limits of the plains is difficult, and the term itself is almost a misnomer – there are vast flat expanses and long uninterrupted roads, but there are also canyons, forests and splashes of unexpected color, as well as two of the nation's mightiest rivers: the **Missouri**, which weaves its course southeast from North Dakota, and the **Mississippi**, which it joins at St Louis. Since the 1950s, the siphoning of the underground Ogallala aquifer from Nebraska to Oklahoma has transformed much that was once dusty desert into verdant fields; the consequences of overuse (ensuring the depletion of the reservoir in another fifty-odd years) remain to be seen.

The woods, caves and springs of the **Ozarks**, the lunar landscapes of South Dakota's **Badlands**, and stately **Mount Rushmore** are the region's most visited areas. Otherwise, there are few immediate attractions, and only St Louis stands out as an urban destination. Drama comes instead in the form of such unpredictable **weather** as freak blizzards, dust storms, lightning storms and the notorious "twister" tornadoes. Images of the devastating Thirties' dustbowl Depression (when topsoil was whisked as far away as Washington, DC) remain as potent as the fantasy of Dorothy and Toto being swept up from Kansas by a tornado to the land of Oz, while **flooding** is a constant threat – huge swaths of Iowa and Missouri were swamped in 1993.

A **car** is practically obligatory in the plains, where distances are long, roads straight and seemingly endless, and the population sparse. The main routes (I-94, I-90, I-80, I-70, I-40) cross from east to west, while north-south travel is often limited to quiet, curving byways. Greyhound **buses** travel the interstates, but often bypass the small towns that provide a real sense of the region. Subsidiary bus lines include Jack Rabbit in South Dakota, and the Jefferson Line, which covers Iowa, Kansas, Missouri and Oklahoma. True to their image as a crossroads rather than a destination, the plains are crossed by Amtrak **trains** almost exclusively at night, with South Dakota not covered at all. St Louis, Missouri, has the major **airport**, while Wichita, Kansas, is a regional hub.

Oklahoma

Often ridiculed by the rest of the country as dust-filled and boring, **OKLA-HOMA** has had a traumatic and far from dull history. In the 1830s all this land, held to be useless, was set aside as **Indian Territory**; a convenient dumping ground for the so-called Five Civilized Tribes who blocked white settlement in the southern states. The Choctaw and Chickasaw of Mississippi, the Seminole of Florida, and the Creek of Alabama were each assigned a share, while the rest (though already inhabited by indigenous Indians) was given to the Cherokee from Carolina, Tennessee and Georgia, who followed in 1838 on

the four-month trek notorious as "the Trail of Tears" (see p.583). Today the state
has a large Native American population – *oklahoma* is the Choctaw word for
"red man" – and even the smallest towns tend to have museums of Native
American history.

Once white settlers realized that Indian Territory was, in fact, well worth
farming, they decided to stay. The Indians were relocated once more, and in a
series of manic free-for-all scrambles starting in 1889, entire towns sprang up
literally overnight. Those who jumped the gun and claimed land illegally were
known as Sooners; hence Oklahoma's nickname, the **Sooner State**. White settlers didn't have an easy life, however, facing, after great oil prosperity in the
1920s, an era of unthinkable hardship in the 1930s. The desperate migration,
when whole communities fled the dust bowl for California, has come to
encapsulate the worst horrors of the Depression, most famously in John
Steinbeck's novel (and John Ford's film) **The Grapes of Wrath**, but also in
Dorothea Lange's haunting photos of itinerant families, hitching and camping
on the road, and in the sad yet hopeful songs of Woody Guthrie. After the
slump of the early Thirties, improved farming techniques brought life, and
people, back to Oklahoma. Today the state is known for its staunch conservatism; as the Bible Belt stronghold, bars and liquor stores close early, while tattoo parlors are banned altogether.

Oklahoma is not the flat and unchanging expanse of popular imagination.
Most of its places of interest, such as attractive Tulsa, lie in the hilly wooded
northeast; only the sparse and treeless west is devoid of appeal, on the far side
of the central "tornado alley" prairie grassland which holds the state's revitalized capital, **Oklahoma City**. The lakes and parks of the south, which bears
more than a passing resemblance to neighboring Arkansas (complete with
mountains, foliage and bluegrass music), have made tourism Oklahoma's second industry after oil.

Getting around Oklahoma

Car travel is the only way to explore Oklahoma. Amtrak serves Oklahoma City
with one train a day from Fort Worth, Texas. Greyhound **buses** speed along I-
35 and I-40, which converge on Oklahoma City, but public transportation
within the towns is minimal. Tulsa and Oklahoma City have **airports**. **Route
66**, which passes through both cities on its way from Missouri to Texas, is
no longer a national highway, but if you have plenty of time (and sturdy tires;
much of the road is in a bad way), makes a nostalgic alternative to the interstates. Travel literature detailing the small communities and ghost towns on the
way is plentiful at roadside information centers or contact the Oklahoma
Route 66 Association (☎405/258-0008, ⓦwww.oklahomaroute66.com).

Eastern Oklahoma

Eastern Oklahoma includes the "Green Country" of the northeast, patterned
with the foothills of the Ozarks, and woods, streams, lakes and rivers that make
it a popular camping destination. Art Deco Tulsa is its cultural center;
Tahlequah and Pawhuska are the capitals of the Cherokee and Osage nations
respectively.

Tulsa

TULSA is a good-looking city, thanks in part to the striking Art Deco architecture that dates from its Twenties heyday as an immensely wealthy oil town. Despite – or possibly because of – its pleasant atmosphere, two excellent museums, and thriving art scene, the city tends towards complacency. In addition, fundamentalist Christian attitudes are hard to ignore; Tulsa is known as the "Buckle of the Bible Belt."

Arrival, information and getting around

Tulsa International Airport (☎918/838-5000) lies a few minutes by cab ($20) east of downtown. Hwy-169 from Kansas City skirts its east side; I-44, which gives access from the south, is also the main route east-west across town. Greyhound comes in downtown at 317 S Detroit Ave. The **CVB**, 616 S Boston Ave (Mon–Fri 8am–5pm; ☎918/585-1201 or 1-800/558-3311, ⓦwww.visittulsa.com), provides information on a self-guided walking tour of downtown, as well as local **bus** schedules; services operate between 5am and 8.30pm, with no Sunday service ($1, transfers 5¢). Web surfers can visit the Public Library at 400 Civic Center, or *Schlotzsky's Deli* at 3348 S Peoria Ave, for free **internet** access.

Accommodation

Most of Tulsa's **budget hotels** are on the interstates and along W Skelly Drive, forking southwest from I-44. There's **camping** at the *KOA*, 19605 E Skelly Drive (☎918/266-4227). There are a few **B&Bs** in town, including the *Dream Catcher B&B* (☎918/743-6704); check the CVB website (see above) for listings.

Best Western Trade Winds East Inn 3337 E Skelly Drive ☎918/743-7931. Comfortable rooms. ❹
Doubletree Hotel 616 W 7th St ☎918/587-8000. Good downtown location. ❺

Lexington Hotel Suites 8525 E 41st St ☎918/627-0030. Luxury doubles, with breakfast. ❹
YMCA 515 S Denver Ave ☎918/583-6201. Men-only downtown accommodation for $20 per bed.

The City

Downtown Tulsa's most obvious landmark is the ornate Art Deco **Union Depot**, on the First Street and Boston Avenue Overpass, built in the early 1930s and now housing offices. The **320 Boston Building** on Boston Avenue, known in the 1920s as the "Oil Bank of America," is worth a look for its huge brass doors, gargoyles and hand-painted ceilings. Further along the other side of the road, another distinctive Twenties skyscraper, the **Philtower**, 527 S Boston Ave, has a green and red tiled sloping roof and crouching gargoyles, a lobby richly decorated in brass and marble, and a small gallery of Tulsa history. **Lyon's Indian Store**, an old trading post a few blocks east at 401 E 11th St, sells authentic goods made by more than thirty Oklahoman tribes, including feather headdresses, bead work, rugs and jewelry. The huge and gloriously exuberant Art Deco **Boston Avenue Methodist Church**, 1301 S Boston Ave – at 255ft in height, it's practically cathedral-sized – offers good views of the city from its fourteenth story (free tours Mon–Fri 9am–4pm, Sun 12.15pm).

Black life in Tulsa was traditionally centered around what is now the **Greenwood Historic District**, a small section of narrow streets north of downtown. In 1921, a brutal race riot erupted outside the city courthouse after a black man was accused of assaulting a white woman in a downtown elevator. The commotion spread to Greenwood, and houses, businesses and churches were burnt to the ground. Other properties fell victim to urban renewal in the mid-1960s, but community leaders managed to save a small grouping of buildings along Greenwood Avenue and Archer Street. The Greenwood Cultural Center, at 322 N Greenwood Ave (Mon–Fri 9am–5pm; free), houses the **Goodwin-Chappelle Gallery**, a photographic portrait of the neighborhood's history, and the **Oklahoma Jazz Hall of Fame**, a fascinating tribute to jazz greats who were either residents of the state (Wardell Gray, Charlie Christian) or passed through on national tours (Cab Calloway, Dizzy Gillespie, Count Basie) to jam with local talent.

Outside downtown, to the south, the 75ft **Creek Council Oak**, 18th Street and Cheyenne Avenue, marks the spot where the Creek Indians ended their tortuous migration from Alabama in 1836, and founded Tulsa on the Arkansas River. The tree became a tribal meeting site, used ceremonially until 1896. The airy and stylish **Philbrook Museum of Art**, 2727 S Rockford Rd, in the house of oil man Waite Phillips in the well-heeled suburb of Mapleridge, is a Florentine-style mansion set amid an oasis of fountains and greenery (Tues, Wed, Fri & Sat 10am–5pm, Thurs 10am–8pm, Sun 11am–5pm; tours Thurs, Sat & Sun; $5). Though displays include Native American pottery, African sculpture, Chinese jades and Renaissance paintings, the house itself is every bit as decorative as the art, with ostentatious marble floors, indoor fountains and sweeping staircases.

Oral Roberts University, 7777 S Lewis Ave, is a must for kitsch obsessives. The campus, which bears a striking resemblance to Disneyland, welcomes visitors with a 60ft-high monument of hands in prayer. The University and television station concept was inspired by visionary Oral Roberts – who back in 1987 announced that God had decided to "call him home" unless he could raise $4.5 million before a certain deadline. Roberts retreated to a lonely vigil at the top of his **Prayer Tower**, a kind of B-movie space ship until he got his money, though his credibility was dented when the tower was allegedly struck by lightning at the moment of the deadline. In the base of the tower, you can now see a sycophantic exhibition, to the strains of a heavenly choir, on the great man's life (Mon–Sat 9am–5pm, Sun 1–5pm). In the upper level, the Abundant Life Prayer Group works 24 hours a day to answer phone calls from faith seekers worldwide.

The **Gilcrease Museum**, 1400 Gilcrease Museum Rd, just northwest of downtown, is set in the gently rolling **Osage Hills**, with a fine vista from the back and good view of downtown from the front. Thomas Gilcrease, of Indian heritage, grew very rich after oil was found on his land. His private collection of Western art includes Native American works, as well as excellent Remingtons, Russells and Morans (Mon–Sat 9am–5pm, Sun 11am–5pm; summer Thurs until 8pm; winter closed Mon; free tours daily at 2pm; $3 donation).

Eating

Tulsa's **restaurants** are diverse and scattered; good options can be found along E 15th Street and S Peoria Avenue in the fashionable **Brookside** district, while downtown holds several down-home diners.

The Bistro At Brookside 3523 S Peoria Ave ☎918/749-7737. Inventive dishes and an extensive wine list in trendy Brookside. The Sunday brunches are well worth sampling.
Bourbon Street Café 1542 E 15th St ☎918/583-5555. Extensive Cajun menu, featuring excellent $5 gumbo. Live jazz Sunday at 7pm.
Camerelli's 1536 E 15th St ☎918/582-8900. Inexpensive but tasty Italian meats and pasta.

Casa Bonita 2120 S Sheridan Rd ☎918/836-6464. Strolling mariachis liven up this enormous restaurant, where large spicy dinners are served in rooms featuring a 20ft waterfall and an "erupting" volcano, among other things.
Metro Diner 3001 E 11th St ☎918/592-2616. Fifties-style diner east of downtown, serving good home-baked pies and chicken-fried steaks, as well as great ice cream sodas.

Nightlife and entertainment

There is even less to do in downtown Tulsa after dark than during the day; 15th and Cherry streets just south of downtown, and S Peoria Avenue by the river, are much livelier. If you visit in early September, try to catch the zydeco music and Creole cooking at the **Backdoor Cajun Music Festival**. Newspapers like the *Urban Tulsa Weekly* and *Tulsa World* carry full nightlife listings.

The ID 3430 S Peoria Ave ☎918/743-0600. Hip live bands, and a youthful crowd. Open Wed–Sat.

Discoveryland! 10 miles west of downtown on W 41st St ☎918/742-5255 or 1-800/245-6552. Outdoor venue for performances of Rodgers and Hammerstein's *Oklahoma!* Mon–Sat, June–Aug; $15; pre-show barbecue 5.30pm, $9.

The Majestic Brady St and Boston Ave ☎918/584-9494. Live music in a converted warehouse; cover charge also gets you into *The*

Bowery, a smaller bar one block up at 201 N Main St.

Spotlight Theatre 1381 Riverside Drive ☎918/587-5030. This Art Deco building has been hosting the melodrama *The Drunkard* for the past fifty years – accompanied by pretzels and sandwiches, every Sat at 8.15pm.

Steamroller Blues Barbeque 18th St and Boston Ave ☎918/583-9520. Popular live venue, with the best performances at weekends.

Claremore

Thirty miles northeast of Tulsa on Route 66, **CLAREMORE**, the birthplace of **Will Rogers**, populist comedian, journalist and Twenties film star, is a shrine to a man being slowly forgotten as his films are no longer seen. His career began with a vaudeville show that included lassoing a horse and its rider, while giving a witty commentary, and he was renowned for his pithy and good-natured one-liners. Incredibly, when he died in a plane crash in 1935 there was a nationwide thirty-minute silence. One of his most famous declarations, "I never met a man I didn't like," is inscribed on his statue at the **Will Rogers Memorial**, 1720 Will Rogers Blvd (daily 8am–5pm; free), which displays his possessions, such as his "gag book," together with stills and clips from his films. In September, the **Chili Cookoff and Bluegrass Festival** comes to town with its spicy chili competitions, clogging and bluegrass gigs.

Bartlesville

For forty miles north of Tulsa, the monotony of the plains is relieved only by clumps of spindly scrub oaks. Then comes quiet **BARTLESVILLE**, dominated by the extraordinary **Price Tower** (Tues–Sat 10am–5pm), designed by Frank Lloyd Wright in 1956 – an ugly, cantilevered green oddity at Sixth Street and Dewey Avenue, resembling a tall tree. The **Frank Phillips Home**, 1107 SE Cherokee Ave, built in 1908 by the founder of Phillips Oil, displays oil wealth at its gaudiest, with gold faucets, mirrored ceilings and marble floors (Wed–Sat 10am–5pm, Sun 1–5pm; donation). More impressive is his **Woolaroc Ranch**, thirteen miles southwest in the Blackjack Hills, now a wildlife refuge and museum of Western art and history, where over sixty thousand artifacts are scattered through seven huge rooms. Paintings and decorative art line the walls, from Native American works to the epic Western scenes of Remington and Russell, while artifacts belonging to various tribes, pioneers and cowboys are gathered in too great an abundance to take in. Look out for the 95-million-year-old dinosaur egg, exquisite Navajo blankets, scalps taken by Native Americans, and Buffalo Bill's weathered saddle (June–Aug daily 10am–5pm; rest of year closed Mon; $5).

For **lodging**, choose between the *Travelers Motel*, 3105 SE Frank Phillips Blvd (☎918/333-1900; ❹), and the more upmarket *Hotel Phillips*, 821 S Johnstone Ave (☎918/336-5600 or 1-800/331-0706; ❹).

Tahlequah

A seventy-minute drive southeast from Tulsa on Hwy-51, **TAHLEQUAH** is the capital of the **Cherokee** nation, formed in 1839 when the Trail of Tears finally reached its end. The sophisticated Cherokee had a written constitution, published the first newspaper in Indian Territory (in both Cherokee and English) and set up the Cherokee female seminary, the first higher education school for women west of the Mississippi. The seminary stands today on the campus of **Northeastern State University** on Hwy-82, which has more Native American students than any other academic institution in the US.

Tahlequah itself is uncommercialized, and the **Cherokee Heritage Center**, three and half miles south off US-62, presents Native American culture with more dignity than might be expected. The museum is largely interactive, leading the visitor across the Trail of Tears with the use of powerful audiovisual displays (Mon–Sat 10am–5pm, Sun 1–5pm; closed Jan). The entrance fee ($8.50) also gets you into a reconstructed seventeenth-century Indian village that offers arts and crafts demonstrations (Mon–Sat 10am–4pm, Sun 1pm–5pm; closed Jan). Summer performances are put on at the Tsa-La-Gi Amphitheater (℡1-888-999-6007, ⓦwww.cherokeeheritage.org), including the gripping Trail of Tears drama.

For a town with such a lovely Main Street, Tahlequah has a pretty poor selection of hotels. The best is the *Holiday Inn Express*, 1 Holiday Drive (℡918-456-7800; ❸), which has a pool. The not-so-exciting, but slightly cheaper, *Tahlequah Motor Lodge* at 2501 S Muskogee Ave (℡918/456-2350; ❸), is another choice. The *Restaurant of the Cherokees,* on US-62 (℡918/456-2070), serves American-style buffet and is located next to the excellent Cherokee Nation Gift Shop.

Muskogee

The Creek Indians, relocated to **MUSKOGEE** in the 1830s, established the town as the central meeting place of the Civilized Tribes, fifty miles southeast of Tulsa; decades later in 1905, Native American leaders gathered here to draw up a plan for their own separate state, which was never to be. The arrival of the railroad in the 1870s and the discovery of oil in 1903 both guaranteed that the town would be usurped by white settlers. The **Five Civilized Tribes Museum**, Honor Heights Drive, Agency Hill, tells the Native Americans' story through costumes, documents, photographs and jewelry, along with a reconstructed trading post and a printing room (Mon–Sat 10am–5pm, Sun 1–5pm; $2). The other unlikely attraction in town is the **USS Batfish**, a WWII-era submarine moored in the Oklahoma grass, 3500 Batfish Rd (Mon, Wed, Thurs, Fri, Sat 9am–5pm, Sun noon-5pm; $4).

Muskogee is an appealing place, with a dozen **motels** within a few blocks along US-69, including a *Days Inn* at 900 S 32nd St (℡918/683-3911; ❸). It also makes a good base for the crystal-clear **Lake Tenkiller**, thirty miles southeast on US-64. Surrounded by woods, cliffs and quiet beaches, the lake is perfect for fishing, boating, swimming and scuba-diving, and has camping facilities, but is (unsurprisingly) very touristy; call ℡918/457-4403 for full details. The Muskogee Tourism Center, Hwy-69 at Shawnee Street (℡918-684-6363 or 1-888/687-6137, ⓦwww.muskogee.org/tourism), can provide details about the popular azalea festival held in April.

Oklahoma City and beyond

Oklahoma City and Tulsa are separated by one hundred surprisingly green miles along the Will Rogers Turnpike and the famed **Route 66**. The Blue Whale in Catoosa and the Round Barn in Arcadia are classic landmarks along the "mother road." West of the state capital, I-40 carries you across empty agricultural communities, the tedium only broken by the worthwhile Route 66 Museum in Clinton. I-44 to Wichita Falls passes near the ruggedly beautiful **Wichita Mountains Wildlife Refuge**; to the north, in the Oklahoman Panhandle, ranches and tiny hamlets are the only signs of life.

Oklahoma City

OKLAHOMA CITY was created in a matter of hours on April 22, 1889, after a single gunshot signaled the opening of the land to white settlement. What was barren prairie at dawn was by nightfall a city of ten thousand. In 1911 the capital was moved here from nearby Guthrie, and in 1928 oil was discovered. Sitting on one of the nation's largest oilfields, the city was brought up short by the slump in the 1980s, but it remains the largest stocker and feeder cattle market in the world. The economy came alive again in the 1990s, aided by tourism development and an inflated sales tax that funded redevelopment in run-down neighborhoods.

However, the devastating **bombing** of the Alfred P. Murrah Federal Building on April 19, 1995, which killed 168 people, nineteen of them children, literally tore the heart out of the city; the massive community rescue effort has since helped Oklahoma City regain some of its self-confidence, though it will be a while before the city is fully healed. In June 2001, ex-military recluse Timothy McVeigh was executed for the crime; his accomplice, Terry Nichols, is serving a lifetime sentence in jail for his part. A permanent landscaped memorial has been constructed at the former site of the Murrah building, while the Journal Record Building next door has been turned into the **Museum and Institute for the Prevention of Terrorism**.

Arrival, information and getting around

Will Rogers World Airport, 7100 Terminal Drive (☎405/680-3200), lies southwest of the city and is connected to downtown by Airport Shuttle (☎405/681-3311; $13 one-way). The **CVB** is downtown at 189 W Sheridan Ave (Mon–Fri 8.30am–5pm; ☎405/297-8912 or 1-800/225-5652, ⊛www.visitokc.com), not far from Greyhound at no. 427; there's also a station at the airport. Amtrak comes in once a day from Fort Worth at historic Sante Fe Station, on Sante Fe Street. The **post office** is at 320 SW 5th St (Mon–Fri 6am–8pm, Sat 9am–noon; zip code 73125), and the Public Library, which provides **internet** access, is downtown at 131 Dean A. McGee St.

The city bus depot is temporarily located downtown at 200 N Shartel (☎405/235-7433), and will be moved in late 2002 to 5th St and North Hudson Avenue in the northwest part of downtown. **Buses** run daily except Sunday from 6am until 6pm ($1). The Oklahoma Spirit Streetcars run from the hotel strip in the Meridian and the stockyards to downtown, and up to the Cowboy Museum and Lincoln Park (Mon–Sat 9am–11pm, Sun 10am–6pm; 50¢). You can rent **bikes** from Miller's Cycling and Fitness Center, 215 W Boyd for $10 a day (☎405/360-3838).

Accommodation

Rooms are very cheap; try along the interstates, especially I-35 S, for chain motels. **B&Bs** are a good deal, but even the downtown luxury hotels can be affordable. There is a *KOA* campground (☎405/391-5000) 15 miles east of downtown on I-40 at exit 166.

Best Western Saddleback Inn 4300 SW 3rd St ☎405/947-7000. One block north of I-40, on the west side of town. Pseudo-Indian decor, with luxurious touches like poolside service. ❹

Brass Lantern Inn 700 NW 9th St ☎405/232-0505. Dimly lit, slightly worn, but fairly priced rooms near downtown, across from St Anthony Hospital. ❷

Howard Johnson Lodge Airport 400 S Meridian Ave ☎405/943-9841. Standard rooms close to the

freeway, with breakfast included. ❸

Plaza Inn I-35 and 29th St ☎405/672-2341. No-frills accommodation to suit a backpacker's budget. ❷

Ramada Inn Airport South 6800 I-35 S ☎405/631-3321. Functional accommodation directly east of the airport. ❸

Westin Oklahoma City 1 N Broadway ☎405/235-2780. Smart rooms with amazingly comfortable beds in the heart of downtown. ❻

The City

Tumbleweeds no longer roll through downtown Oklahoma City, but the city center remains a quiet affair, with low-key skyscrapers and little in the way of commercial activity. The hub of activity is around the renovated warehouses of **Bricktown**, on Sheridan Avenue east of the Santa Fe Railroad, which has developed into a reasonable eating and nightlife center. **Myriad Gardens** on Sheridan Avenue, prettily landscaped with hills, gardens and waterways, gives great views across to the brick-towered downtown skyline, and on a sunny day the **Crystal Bridge** tropical botanical garden, in a glass tube in the middle of the park, abounds in garish exotic blooms (daily 9am–6pm; $4).

A few blocks north, at 620 N Harvey Ave, where the Federal Building stood until its 1995 bombing, throngs of tourists mill somberly about the **Oklahoma City National Memorial** (open 24hrs; free). The site, which dominates the center of the city, includes a field of 168 empty bronze and glass chairs, and a black reflecting pool flanked by two massive gold barriers marking 9.01–9.03am – the moment of destruction. Nearby, an elm tree that continued to bloom after the blast stands as a lone sentinel. The Memorial Center Museum behind it (Mon–Sat 9am–6pm, Sun 1–6pm; $7), is also worth a visit, recounting the tragedy in gruesome detail, with TV news coverage from the day, interviews with survivors and items pulled from the wreckage, such as shredded clothing, cracked coffee mugs and twisted filing cabinets. Other sections describe the ensuing FBI investigation and McVeigh trial, and on the ground floor are tributes to the victims, and gift shop. Outside, the complex is surrounded by a chain link fence weighed down by tokens and talismans left by grief-stricken mourners.

Just northeast of downtown, a working oil well pumps crude from underneath the Capitol Building (Mon–Fri 8am–4.30pm; free), which, at the time of publication, was being fitted with a $22 million dome, slated for completion in late 2002. The Capitol Complex includes the **State Museum of History** (Mon–Sat 8am–5pm; free), which is expected to move in 2003 to a new building across from the Governor's Mansion. The Heritage Hills area nearby, where the cattle barons, oil millionaires and bankers used to live, is worth a visit for the Victorian-style **Overholser Mansion**, 405 NW 15th St (Tues–Sat 10am–4pm, Sun 2–4pm; hourly tours $3), the **Oklahoma Heritage Center**, 201 NW 14th St (Mon–Sat 9am–5pm, Sun 1–5pm; $3), is not as impressive, but the **Harn Homestead Museum**, 313 NE 16th St (Mon–Fri 10am–4pm; $3), is worth a wander for its old barn, wagons and general pioneer spirit.

DOWNTOWN OKLAHOMA CITY

Memorial Center Museum
Public Library
Oklahoma City National Memorial
Metro Transit Bus Terminal
Myriad Convention Center
Myriad Gardens
Union Bus Depot
Amtrak/Santa Fe Train Depot
SW Bell Bricktown Ballpark
Bricktown Canal

★ Oklahoma Spirit trolley stops

5TH ST.
4TH ST.
DEAN A. McGEE AVE.
ROBERT S. KERR AVE.
COULTER DR.
COLCORD DR.
MAIN ST.
CALIFORNIA AVE.
DEWEY AVE.
LEE AVE.
SHERIDAN AVE.
SHARTEL AVE.
RENO AVE.
WALKER AVE.
HUDSON AVE.
HARVEY AVE.
PARK AVE.
ROBINSON AVE.
BROADWAY AVE.
E. K. GAYLORD DR.
5TH ST.
3RD ST.
2ND ST.
OKLAHOMA AVE.
MAIN ST.
SHERIDAN AVE.
PARK AVE.
BYERS AVE.
STILES AVE.
RENO AVE.
COMPRESS
2ND ST.

0   250 yds

OKLAHOMA CITY

World of Wings Pigeon Center
The Omniplex
Oklahoma Firefighters Museum
National Cowboy & Western Heritage Center
Lincoln Park
State Capitol
State Museum of History
Ham Homestead & 1889ER Museum
Henry Overholser Mansion
Oklahoma Heritage Center
Union Station
Oklahoma State Fair Park
Stockyards City

MARTIN LUTHER KING AVENUE
63RD STREET
50TH STREET
36TH STREET
LINCOLN BOULEVARD
23RD STREET
KELLEY AVENUE
SANTA FE AVENUE
WESTERN AVENUE
CLASSEN BOULEVARD
PENNSYLVANIA AVENUE
10TH STREET
RENO AVENUE
MAY AVENUE
PORTLAND AVENUE
MACARTHUR BOULYEVARD
MERIDIAN AVENUE
10TH STREET
RENO AVENUE
ROCKWELL AVENUE
COUNCIL ROAD

North Canadian River

35
40
44
3
77
235
270
66

See Inset

▲ 5
▶ 6 & Norman
▶ 6 & Will Rogers World Airport
◀ Amarillo (TX)
To96, Home (07) & 77

N

0   1 mile

ACCOMMODATION

Best Western Saddleback Inn   4
Brass Lantern Inn   2
Howard Johnson Lodge Airport   3
KOA Campground   5
Plaza Inn   6
Westin Oklahoma City   1

RESTAURANTS, BARS AND CLUBS

Bricktown 54   C
Bricktown Brewery   A
Cattleman's Steakhouse   F
In Cahoots   G
Sushi Neko   D
Tapwerks Ale House & Cafe   B
VCD's Restaurant and Club   E

The **National Cowboy Hall of Fame and Heritage Center** at 1700 NE 63rd St is a real treat (June–Aug daily 8.30am–6pm; Sept–May daily 9am–5pm; $8.50). Sitting atop Persimmon Hill overlooking Route 66, it combines "high art" and popular art in one loving collection. In the works of Remington and Russell the link between Western art and Western movies is very clear. The paintings look like film stills, and titles such as *Waiting for Trouble* evoke the cinema's endlessly reworked myths of the West. Large exhibitions focus on contemporary Native American work, much of it colorful, bitter and subversive. John Wayne's collection is a delight for the cowboy fetishist, and the Western Performers Hall of Fame pays homage to movie cowboys and cowgirls in hilariously reverent oil paintings and memorabilia. The poignant *End of the Trail* sculpture, eighteen feet high, portrays an Indian slumped exhausted – or dead – over his horse. You can also venture into Prosperity Town (a mock-up of a Western town with details down to hoof marks in the road), the American Rodeo Gallery and a learning center for little buckaroos. In the garden, dotted with horse graves, corny epigraphs give the much-loved deceased beasts a fitting send-off to "Hoss Heaven."

Lincoln Park, squeezed between Martin Luther King Drive and Hwy-35, contains the **Firefighter's Museum**, **City Zoo**, and the **Omniplex** (ten acres of futuristic exhibits, and an aquarium and planetarium). On the northern end, the modest **World of Wings Pigeon Center** (Mon–Fri 10am–4pm; free) specially breeds homing pigeons for racing. You can inspect the small museum and aviary that houses racing breeds and "fancy" pigeons bred for their looks.

Oklahoma City's **stockyards**, on Agnew Avenue and Exchange Street, are the busiest in the world, having sold over one hundred million cattle since 1910. They're well worth a visit, though vegetarians and animal-lovers should steer clear. This is the real thing, stomping, snorting and smelly, with scrawny animals shunted in and out of tiny pens for auction. The roughnecks that spend their lives here, smoking, chatting, even sleeping, take no apparent notice of the quick-fire auctioneer, but nonetheless millions of head of cattle are bought and sold each year, and it can make for addictive entertainment. Morning sales, starting at 8am (Monday and Tuesday only), are the most intense and fizzle out by late afternoon.

Eating

Beef is, of course, good in Oklahoma City, especially around the stockyards. The warehouse restaurants of **Bricktown** are popular with the after-work and singles crowd.

Cattleman's Steakhouse 1309 S Agnew Ave ☏ 405/236-0416. Cattlemen from the adjacent stockyards eat in this comfortable, pub-like restaurant, which has served great steaks since 1910. (It was allegedly won in a craps game.) Lunchtime specials are a good deal.
Sonic Drive-in, branches throughout the city. Waitresses on roller skates serve up cheap and fast burgers and fries.
Sushi Neko 4318 N Western Ave ☏ 405/528-8862. Trendy Japanese restaurant with excellent sushi and outside seating.
TapWerks Ale House and Café 121 E Sheridan Ave ☏ 405/319-9599. Very popular Bricktown restaurant with a British-influenced menu and a long list of beers. Open late.

Nightlife and entertainment

Newly established progressive restaurants and clubs, especially those in Bricktown, attempt to part Oklahoma City from its cowtown image. The **Crown Heights** district north of downtown pulls in a younger crowd, but perhaps your best bet is to head for the campus nightlife of **Norman**, a thirty-minute drive south, which is home to the University of Oklahoma. Wednesday's *Oklahoma Gazette*, along with lively articles, carries good listings.

Bricktown Brewer 1 Oklahoma Ave ☎405/232-BREW. Large brewpub, with giant tanks of beer on show in its restaurant and live jazz most nights.
Bricktown 54 7 Mickey Mantle Drive ☎405/235-5454. A dance club for trendy singles crowd, featuring '70s and '80s disco; also has a dress code.
In Cahoots 2301 S Meridian Ave ☎405/686-1191. Popular dance hall and saloon with nightly live music ranging from country to indie rock, R&B

to rap. Quite a way southwest of downtown, but worth the trip. Hours and cover vary.
Oklahoma Opry 404 W Commerce Ave ☎405/232-8322. Venue for authentic country music shows, Sat 8pm. $6.
VCD's Restaurant and Club 4200 N Western ☎405/524-4203. Cheap and varied food by day, including artichoke spinach dip and grilled tuna steak salad, and grungy rock music by night.

Guthrie

GUTHRIE, thirty miles north of downtown Oklahoma City on I-35, was the capital from statehood in 1907 until 1911. Today the 1400-acre **Guthrie Historical District** forms a remarkably complete collection of tastefully restored Victorian architecture. The **State Capitol Publishing Museum**, 301 W Harrison Ave (Tues–Fri 9am–5pm, Sat 10am–4pm, Sun 1–4pm; donation), exhibits printing technology dating back to the earliest newspaper printed in Oklahoma Territory. The ornate **Doric Scottish Rite Masonic Temple**, 900 E Oklahoma Ave, is the largest Masonic complex in the world, featuring hundreds of bright stained-glass windows (tours Mon–Fri 10am & 2pm, Sat 10am; $5). Guthrie is also home to the **Lazy E Arena**, four miles east of downtown, a huge site which hosts world champion rodeos and roping competitions, as well as big-name concerts (☎405/282-3004).

Guthrie has several good **B&Bs**, including the *Haunted Stone Lion Inn*, 1016 W Warner Ave (☎405/282-0012; ❹), a 1907 Victorian mansion with clean rooms and antique claw-footed tubs. The *Harrison House*, 124 W Harrison Ave (☎405/282-1000 or 1-800/375-1001; ❹), is larger than most B&Bs but still charming and is housed in Guthrie's first bank building. Cheaper is the *Townhouse Motel*, 223 E Oklahoma Ave (☎405/260-2400; ❷). The *Blue Belle Saloon*, 224 W Harrison, is Oklahoma's oldest saloon and boasts that Tom Mix tended bar here before going on to Hollywood fame. The **visitor center** is at 212 W Oklahoma Ave (☎405/282-1947 or 1-800/299-1889, ⓦwww.guthrieok.com).

Missouri

The state of **MISSOURI**, where the forest meets the prairie and the Mississippi River meets the Missouri River, has just two significant cities. Dominant **St Louis** sits midway down its eastern fringe; **Kansas City** is almost directly across on the western border. The pair are linked by I-70, but there's not much in between to warrant stopping off. In contrast, the **south** features the beautiful hillsides, streams and ragged lakes of the **Ozark Mountains**, as well as the booming country-and-western town of **Branson**; while in the **east**, small river towns such as **Hannibal** and serene **Ste Genevieve** brighten the course of the Mississippi. The **northwest**, home of the Pony Express and outlaw Jesse James, still strikes up images of frontier times.

Although the first French colonists honored the claims of local Native Americans, such as the original Missouri, when the area was sold to the US in 1803 as part of the Louisiana Purchase, the Indians were driven west by a great rush of settlers. In the 1840s and 1850s immigrants from Germany and Ireland flooded into eastern Missouri. Outnumbering their pro-slavery predecessors, they swung the balance in favor of staying in the Union during the Civil War. However, Confederate guerrilla forces attracted considerable support among slave-owners in the west of the state. Meanwhile Missouri, and St Louis in particular, was establishing itself as an important gateway to the West. Today, the "**Show Me State**" (so called because of the supposed skepticism of the typical Missourian) retains a conservative air, particularly in the rural areas.

Getting around Missouri

The central corridor between St Louis and Kansas City is well served by **Greyhound**; the journey takes around six hours. Chicago and Memphis are both five hours from St Louis. Infrequent Greyhound buses run through the southeast, to Springfield and a few Ozark towns, but you'll need a car to see the mountains and the river towns in the north. St Louis (TWA's main hub) and Kansas City have major **airports**. Daily Amtrak **trains** from Chicago run to St Louis, from where direct connections can be made to Kansas City, San Antonio, Fort Worth and Little Rock. For keen cyclists, there's the popular **Katy Trail**, which stretches 230 miles from St Charles to Clinton.

Eastern Missouri

The Mississippi defines Missouri's eastern border, absorbing as major tributaries the Missouri, Ohio, Illinois and Des Moines rivers. Innumerable towns sprang up along the river, their aspirations reflected by such classical names as Alexandria, Antioch and Athens. **Hannibal**, the boyhood home of Mark Twain, is the largest in the northeast, while Gallic **Ste Genevieve** is the prettiest in the south. All have, however, decreased in importance with the growing pre-eminence of **St Louis**. Away from the river, the land rises to the Ozark Plateau, whose deep green valleys are cut by swift, clear streams.

Hannibal

HANNIBAL might well have been just another medium-sized river settlement, had not Samuel Langhorne Clemens, who renamed himself **Mark Twain** after the cry of pilots on the Mississippi, spent his boyhood here. Although Hannibal does have other industries, downtown is little more than a Twain theme park, with attractions such as museums, period buildings and wax displays. Just about every business in town is flogging souvenirs featuring Twain's ashen visage, or is named for the scribe, including Huck's Taxi Service, Injun Joe Campground and even the Mark Twain Roofing Company.

Mark Twain wrote surprisingly little about his home town in his extensive nonfiction works; you could say he spoke with his feet when he left for good at seventeen to become a journeyman printer, riverboat pilot, journalist and writer. However, those of his books most specifically set in Hannibal – *The Adventures of Tom Sawyer* and the sequel *The Adventures of Huckleberry Finn* – provide vivid accounts of growing up in the rowdy frontier riverport he renamed St Petersburg for his books.

The Town

Hannibal's riverside location and historical buildings make it almost disturbingly picturesque. Squeezed between two steep bluffs – Tom Sawyer's "**Cardiff Hill**" to the north and **Lover's Leap** to the south – the once-busy community is now quiet except for the occasional creaking of a crane loading cement. You can get an intimate look at the Mississippi aboard the slow-moving **Mark Twain riverboat** (1hr tour 11am, 1.30pm & 4pm, $9; 2hr dinner cruise by reservation, 6.30pm, $26; ☎573/221-3222). Twain's youthful stomping ground was the short, cobbled incline of **Hill Street**, at the north end of town. Adjoining the restored **Mark Twain Boyhood Home**, a simple white-clapboard house where Twain lived between 1844 and 1853, the **Mark Twain Museum** (summer daily 8am–6pm; rest of year times vary; $6; ☎573-221-9010) includes such memorabilia as first editions, letters, photos, original artwork and one of his trademark white coats. Immediately opposite, there's a bookstore in the original home of Laura Hawkins (the model for Tom Sawyer's first love, Becky Thatcher), who visited Twain in Connecticut in 1908 and lived on in Hannibal until 1928. Nearby stands the law office of Twain's father, a JP who died of pneumonia while the writer was still a boy. Antique, souvenir and gift stores stretch away from here down **Main Street**, where the **New Mark Twain Museum** opened in 1997. Included in the admission price to the original museum and home, the exhibits here re-create scenes from Twain's books, the cave and Huck Finn's raft among them.

Upstairs are the fifteen original Norman Rockwell paintings commissioned for limited editions of Twain's most popular titles. About two miles south of town is the **Mark Twain Cave** (summer daily 8am–8pm, times vary rest of the year; $12; ☎573/221-1656) where one-hour tours recall Tom's and Becky's frightening misadventure in the dark.

South of Hannibal, Hwy-79 towards St Louis offers one of the most **scenic drives** along the Mississippi, continually broken by thin, elongated, thickly wooded islands and bounded by towering limestone bluffs.

Practicalities

Pick up full details on Hannibal from the **visitor center** at 505 N Third St (April–Oct daily 8am–6pm; Nov–March Mon–Fri 8am–5pm, Sat & Sun limited hours; ☎573/221-2477, ⊛www.visithannibal.com). For **internet access** visit the Public Library, 200 S 5th St. **Motel** rates vary wildly according to season. The very central *Best Western Hotel Clemens*, 401 N Third St (☎573/248-1150; ❹), with a pool, is pretty good value, while the *Hannibal Inn*, US-61 at Market St (☎573/221-6610; ❸), on the edge of town, is more basic. *Lula Belle's*, 111 Bird St (☎573/221-6662 or 1-800/882-4890; ❸–❼), has **B&B** rooms of varying degrees of luxury, including some with river views, and serves tasty **food**; while the *Mark Twain Dinette & Family Restaurant*, just up from the museum at 400 N Third St (☎573/221-5300), has classic American fare and Twain paraphernalia on the walls. You can camp at the shaded *Mark Twain Campground* (☎573/221-1656 or 1-800/527-0304; $17.50 for tents, $21.50 for RVs), a mile south of town on Hwy-79.

St Louis

Perched just below the confluence of the Mississippi and Missouri rivers, three hundred miles south of Chicago and north of Memphis, cosmopolitan **ST LOUIS** (pronounced, whatever any song might say, as Lewis) owes its vaguely European air to its history and developed cultural infrastructure. Any city

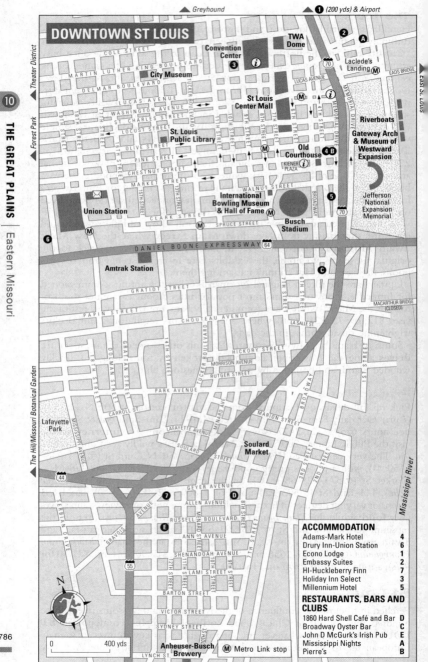

DOWNTOWN ST LOUIS

▲ Greyhound   ▲ ● ❶ (200 yds) & Airport

❷ Ⓐ

TWA Dome

Convention Center ❸ ⓘ

Laclede's Landing Ⓜ

EADS BRIDGE

◀ Theater District

City Museum

COLE STREET

MARTIN LUTHER KING BOULEVARD

DELMAR BOULEVARD

LUCAS AVENUE

LUCAS AVENUE

WASHINGTON AVENUE

Ⓜ ⓘ

St Louis Center Mall

ST CHARLES STREET

LOCUST STREET

St. Louis Public Library

OLIVE STREET

Ⓜ

Old Courthouse

❹ Ⓑ

Riverboats

Gateway Arch & Museum of Westward Expansion

◀ Forest Park

PINE STREET

CHESTNUT STREET

KIENER PLAZA ⓘ

MARKET STREET

WALNUT STREET

Union Station

✉

International Bowling Museum & Hall of Fame Ⓜ

❺

Jefferson National Expansion Memorial

CLARK STREET

SPRUCE STREET

Busch Stadium

Ⓜ

Ⓜ

❻ Ⓜ

DANIEL BOONE EXPRESSWAY 64

Amtrak Station

Ⓒ

GRATIOT STREET

PAPIN STREET

MACARTHUR BRIDGE (CLOSED)

CHOUTEAU AVENUE

LA SALLE ST

◀ The Hill/Missouri Botanical Garden

HICKORY STREET

MORRISON AVENUE

RUTGER STREET

BROADWAY

PARK AVENUE

CARROLL ST

Lafayette Park

MARION STREET

LAFAYETTE AVENUE

SOULARD STREET

44

Soulard Market

Mississippi River

GEYER AVENUE

❼ Ⓓ

ALLEN AVENUE

Ⓔ

RUSSELL BOULEVARD

ANN STREET

SHENANDOAH AVENUE

55

LAMI STREET

BARTON STREET

VICTOR STREET

SYDNEY STREET

N

0   400 yds

Anheuser-Busch Brewery

LYNCH ST.

Ⓜ Metro Link stop

ACCOMMODATION

Adams-Mark Hotel	4
Drury Inn-Union Station	6
Econo Lodge	1
Embassy Suites	2
HI-Huckleberry Finn	7
Holiday Inn Select	3
Millennium Hotel	5

RESTAURANTS, BARS AND CLUBS

1860 Hard Shell Café and Bar	D
Broadway Oyster Bar	C
John D McGurk's Irish Pub	E
Mississippi Nights	A
Pierre's	B

capable of producing two of the twentieth century's greatest poets – T.S. Eliot and Chuck Berry – probably has a lot going for it.

St Louis was founded in 1764 by the French fur trader **Pierre Laclede**, but the American immigration that followed its sale to the US under the Louisiana Purchase all but extinguished the refinement it had gained during French and Spanish rule. It subsequently became crucial as the major gateway for pioneers on the wagon trails westward. Transportation – first steamboats, then trains and now air haulage – has long been the basis of its considerable industrial strength. However, St Louis has not always had an easy ride. Downtown reached a nadir during the 1970s, but the years since then have seen a remarkable turnaround, with attractions on the revitalized **riverfront** including the magnificent **Gateway Arch** and the restored warehouses of **Laclede's Landing**.

Try not to leave without sampling the outlying districts. To the west lie arty **Central West End** and student **University** (or "U") **City**, on either side of prodigious **Forest Park** with its museums and playing fields. The blue-collar **southside** features the markets, antique shops and jazz pubs of **Soulard** and the Italian shops and cafés of **the Hill**. Directly across the river in Illinois, **East St Louis**, once the stomping ground of jazz stars like Miles Davis and John Coltrane, has very little to offer visitors.

Arrival, information and getting around

Lambert–St Louis International Airport (☏314/426-8000) is a dozen miles northwest of downtown – $27 by taxi or $3 by bus or Metro Link. Some Greyhound **buses** call at the airport, though their main terminal is downtown at 1450 N 13th St. **Amtrak** stops at 550 S 16th St and Market Street downtown. The Bi–State Transit System (☏314/231-2345) operates the Metro Link, a **light rail system** serving the airport and most of the significant tourist sights; rides cost $1.25 (free in downtown Mon–Fri 11am–1.30pm). BSTS

The Poets of St Louis

Thomas Stearns Eliot, who as a naturalized Englishman won the 1948 Nobel Prize for Literature, was born in St Louis on September 26, 1888. His family were Unitarian aristocrats who traced their ancestry back to the earliest days of settlement in New England; his grandfather, the Rev William Eliot, founded St Louis' Washington University. Eliot lived in the city until he was seventeen, and went to school at Smith Academy on Union Avenue, a period which he later referred to as one of the happiest of his life. The "Prufrock" of his first major poem, *The Love Song of J. Alfred Prufrock*, was a St Louis furniture dealer; "the yellow fog that rubs its back upon the window-panes" was the smog drifting across the Mississippi from the city's factories.

Once Eliot had moved to Boston, to attend Harvard University, and then on to Europe, he rarely returned, and he deliberately threw off his drawling St Louis accent. The house in which he was born, at 2635 Locust St, has long since been torn down, and the only memorial to him in the city is the incongruous brass star set into the sidewalk of Delmar Boulevard as part of the St Louis Walk of Fame.

Another honoree of the Walk of Fame, **Chuck Berry**, first saw the light of day on October 18, 1926, at 2520 Goode Ave – echoed in his most famous song, *Johnny B Goode*. Berry played his earliest gigs at the Cosmopolitan Club at 17th and Bond in East St Louis. Initially seen as a bizarre hybrid, a black hillbilly singing country-and-western, within a few months of his first recording for Chess Records in Chicago (*Maybellene*, in 1955) Chuck Berry's blend of razor-sharp lyrics and incisive guitar-playing – not to mention his legendary business acumen – had made him the definitive rock 'n' roll songwriter.

buses also go to all of the city's suburbs, but service can be slow and infrequent. Big Shark Bicycle Company, near Forrest Park at 6681 Delmar Blvd (☎314/862-1188; $5 per hour or $20 per day), rents **bikes**.

The city runs **visitor centers** at 308 Washington Ave, near the riverfront (daily 9.30am–4.30pm; ☎314/241-1764), at the America Center in the massive Cervantes Convention Center, a few blocks back (Mon–Fri 9am–5pm; ☎1-800/916-0092), and at Kiener Plaza (Mon–Fri 9am–5pm, Sat 9am–2pm, closed Jan–Feb; ☎314/231-0336). The post office is at 1720 Market St (Mon–Fri 6.30am–2.30pm, Sat 7am–2pm; ☎1-800/275-8777; zip code 63155). You can access the **internet** at the St Louis Public Library, 1301 Olive St (Mon 10am–9pm, Tues–Fri 10am–6pm, Sat 10am–5pm), or inside Union Station at Big Fat Wow! computer terminals. For the latest events, visit ⓦwww.explorestlouis.com.

Accommodation

St Louis may be a business center – complete with huge convention hall – but good-value lodging can still be found downtown, with appealing weekend rates. For **B&Bs**, contact the Greater St Louis Reservation Service, PO Box 30069, MO 63119 (☎314/961-2252).

Best Western Inn at the Park 4630 Lindell Blvd ☎314/367-7500 or 1-800/373-7501. Good chain motel on northeast corner of Forest Park, right by the cafés of Central West End. ❺

Drury Inn – Union Station 201 S 20th St ☎314/231-3900 or 1-800/325-8300. Very tastefully restored accommodation. ❺

Econo Lodge Downtown 1100 N 3rd St ☎314/421-6556. The least expensive downtown option, just a few strides from Laclede's Landing, though it's not a pleasant walk late at night. ❸

Econo Lodge Airport 4575 N Lindbergh Blvd ☎314/731-3000. Clean rooms and friendly staff. Very close to the airport. ❸

Embassy Suites 901 N 1st St ☎314/241-4200. Comfortable suites in the heart of Laclede's Landing, with buffet breakfast included. ❼

HI-Huckleberry Finn 1904–1908 S 12th St ☎314/241-0076. Dorms (members $15, non-members $18) and single rooms without air-conditioning. On the edge of a dodgy area in Soulard, so take bus #73 or #30 from downtown. Office hours 8–10am and 6–10pm. ❶

Holiday Inn Select 811 N 9th St ☎314-421-4000. Comfortable rooms and an indoor pool. Next to the Convention Center in downtown. ❺

Millennium Hotel 200 S 4th St ☎314/241-9500 or 1-800/325-7353. Ideal downtown setting; with all the facilities you'd expect from a hotel of its size. ❹–❼

Napoleon's Retreat 1815 Lafayette Ave ☎314/772-6979. Attractive B&B near Lafayette Square, with appealing rates. ❹–❺

The riverfront

The one-and-a-half-mile cobbled granite **wharf** along the Mississippi used to lie in the shadow of a dense tangle of warehouses and factories. When river trade decreased these became an embarrassing eyesore. Though most were ripped down, some restored structures between Eads and Martin Luther King bridges now form **Laclede's Landing Historic District**, their cast-iron facades fronting antique stores, office suites, restaurants and live music venues. In late August, the district hosts the **Big Muddy Blues Festival**, featuring artists of national prominence and a great party atmosphere (information on ☎314/241-5875, ⓦwww.lacledeslanding.org).

On the waterfront itself, where roustabouts once handled cargoes of cotton and ores, assorted permanently moored vessels hold museums, theater shows, a heliport and casinos. **Cruises** aboard replica paddle-wheelers leave from under the Gateway Arch (April–Nov daily 10am–4.15pm; $9; dinner cruises depart at 7pm, $32.50; ☎314/621-4040 or 1-800/878-7411).

Ten minutes' walk south, more than thirty blocks of derelict buildings were torn down to clear space for the **Jefferson National Expansion Memorial**, dedicated to the US president who negotiated the Louisiana Purchase and thereby opened up the West, and to the pioneers who journeyed along the Oregon and Santa Fe trails. Its highlight, the **Gateway Arch**, designed by Eero Saarinen, was completed in 1965, a 630ft stainless steel parabola of majestic symmetry; in technical terms it's a weighted catenary curve, the outline formed by a heavy cable hanging freely from two points. The arch is at its most striking when its gleaming coat catches a stray reflection – perhaps a rich red sunset or a fireworks display.

So long as you're not claustrophobic, it's fun to take the four-minute **tram ride** up the hollow curving arch. Tiny five-seater capsules carry you to a viewing gallery, repeatedly shifting position as they go so you don't arrive at the top upside down. The views of the Midwestern plains, St Louis and the mighty Mississippi are spectacular, though looking straight down will make you dizzy. Lengthy queues build up during summer, but you can pick up a numbered ticket earlier in the day and come back at the allotted time. Still, you'll have to wait in another queue for the elevator so expect a 45-minute round-trip (daily summer 8.30am–9.20pm; rest of year 9.30am–5.20pm; $7).

In a massive bunker beneath the arch, the **visitor center** (summer daily 8am–10pm; rest of year daily 9am–6pm; ☎314/982-1410; $6 one film, $10 for two) shows a riveting film about the construction of the monument, and another on the Lewis and Clark Expedition, which set off from St Louis in 1804 to explore the Missouri River and water communications to the Pacific Ocean. It returned two years later with details of trade routes, Native American settlements and observations on animal and plant life. The spacious **Museum of Westward Expansion** (free) recounts the story, drawing heavily on the pair's very readable journals. The **Arch Odyssey Theater**, in the same building, beams IMAX epics onto a four-story screen.

Central downtown

One block from the arch along St Louis' main east–west thoroughfare, Market Street, old photographs at the stately **Old Courthouse Museum** (daily 8am–4.30pm; free) record the development of the city and the settling of the West. Two restored courtrooms were the site of the trial of **Dred Scott**, a black slave who argued that having spent time with his owner in nonslave Illinois and Wisconsin, he had the right to be set free. His case was upheld in 1850, but overturned two years later. On appeal, the Supreme Court declared that Scott, born a slave in a slave state, might like any other chattel be taken anywhere his master chose to go. The decision, which meant that the US Constitution saw slaves as legitimate personal property, sent shock waves through the corridors of government and hastened the onrush of the Civil War. Scott himself, by now a nationally known figure, was voluntarily freed by his new owner, but died a year later.

The **International Bowling Museum and Hall of Fame**, at 111 Stadium Plaza (summer Mon–Sat 9am–5pm, Sun noon–5pm; rest of year daily 11am–4pm; $6, includes four free frames), is devoted to the favorite sport of such diverse figures as Martin Luther and Homer Simpson, tracing its history from ancient Egypt to the present. Bowling was not always the slick commercial sport it is today; excessive betting on games got it denounced by the Church in fifteenth-century Germany and, three centuries later, the behavior of drunken fans led to all alleys being shut down in London.

See the world's largest pair of underpants and witness the mystic power of the corndog at the whimsical **City Museum**, 701 N 15th St (Wed–Fri 9am–5pm, Sat–Sun 10am–5pm; $7.50). The exhibits, made almost entirely of junk, often

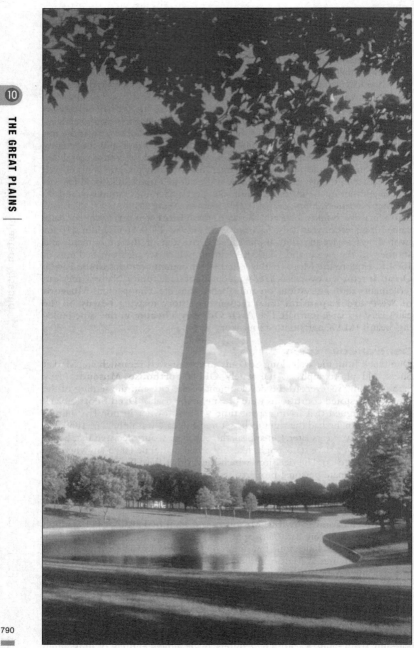

△ Gateway Arch

border on the bizarre, as one floor is devoted to secret passages and dead ends. On entering, you will be informed, "Have fun, and don't lose your adult." Over on Market Street at 18th Street, the focal point of the giant Romanesque **Union Station** is a 230ft clock tower. The station, erected in 1884, was transformed in the early 1980s into a huge complex of shops, cafés, bars and a hotel. An artificial lake, where you can rent boats, is in the back. The *Hyatt Hotel*'s ornate lobby, once the station's main waiting room, is well worth visiting for a coffee or just a look.

West of downtown

Three miles west of downtown, the St Louis theater district, called **Grand Center**, is staked out with ornate street lamps along Grand Avenue between Lindell and Delmar boulevards. Bright posters advertise the current shows at the **Fabulous Fox Theater**, 527 N Grand Ave, where you can have a look at the magnificent Siamese-Byzantine interior and massive Wurlitzer organ (tours Tues, $5; Thurs & Sat, $8 including a special organ performance, at 10.30am; ☏314/534-1111).

About a mile further west, on the edge of Forest Park, trendy shops, wine bars and c.1900 mansions line the leafy thoroughfares of the **Central West End** district. A few blocks away at 4431 Lindell Blvd, the Romanesque-Byzantine **Cathedral of St Louis**, referred to by locals as the New Cathedral, houses the world's largest collection of mosaic art (May–Sept daily 7am–7pm; Oct–April daily 7am–5pm; free).

The decision to put **Forest Park** four miles directly west of downtown (served by Metrolink every ten minutes) aroused much criticism during the 1870s, with opponents claiming that its inaccessibility would make it merely a pleasure ground for the local rich. It's larger than New York's Central Park, and every bit as full of attractions; in summer, the 12,000-seat amphitheater is regularly filled for the Broadway-style musical theater productions (June–Aug; ☏314/361-1900, ⓦwww.muny.com). Shuttle Bugs – bright-red buses with black spots – scurry around the park's roadways ($1.25 or free if you arrive on a metro/bus ticket).

Standing on **Art Hill** in the central western section of the park, the striking **Beaux Arts St Louis Art Museum** (Tues 1.30–8.30pm, Wed–Sun 10am–5pm; tours at 1.30pm; free), is the only surviving structure from the 1904 World's Fair. Its brief – to cover international art from prehistoric times onwards – may be ambitious, but none of the galleries can be considered as weak points or fillers. It houses one of the world's most extensive collections of **German Expressionism**, devoting an entire gallery to the powerful, spiraling and jagged images of Max Beckmann, and its pre-Columbian art works cover every significant style, medium and culture from Mexico to Peru.

In addition to the animals in its "cageless displays," the **St Louis Zoo** (daily 9am–5pm, in summer open until 8pm on Tues; free), set in beautiful grounds, boasts a "Living World" exhibit in which an animatronic robot of Charles Darwin gives synopses of his theories.

The main strengths of the **History Museum**, on the northern fringe of the park (Tues 9.30am–8.30pm, Wed–Sun 9.30am–5pm; free), are the thematic collections of old photos of St Louis, documenting river life, black music in the city and Charles Lindbergh's 1927 flight in the *Spirit of St Louis* (sponsored by the city's aircraft industry) from New York to Paris. The **St Louis Science Center** (winter daily 9am–5pm, Fri open until 9pm; summer daily 9am–6pm, Tues until 9pm; free) straddles I-64 and can be entered from either side of the freeway; use one of the radar guns on the covered access bridge to check the speed of cars on the freeway below. General admission is free, but it costs a few dollars a time to get into the planetarium, OMNIMAX Theater and other major exhibits.

Southside

The tens of thousands of **Germans** who came to St Louis in the mid-eighteenth century settled mostly in the **southside**, which has retained a noticeable Teutonic influence. They were skilled brewers; only one of the breweries they opened from the 1850s onwards still stands, but it does happen to be the largest in the world. The **Anheuser–Busch plant**, at 12th and Lynch streets (summer Mon–Sat 9am–5pm, Sun 11.30am–5pm; winter 9am–4pm, Sun 11.30–1pm; free), produces a sizeable proportion of the company's 14.3 million barrels of beer each year, including Budweiser and Michelob. The buildings themselves are architecturally interesting: over one hundred intricate redbrick structures. The free eighty-minute tours are mostly company PR, but they're still good fun, and you get two glasses of the company product at the end, before you're shunted into the gift shop.

A few blocks towards downtown, the colorful **Soulard Market** (Wed–Fri 8am–5.30pm, Sat 6am–5.30pm), at Broadway and Lafayette Avenue, is a great place to pick up picnic items and fresh fruit, especially on a Saturday. The terraced streets behind it hold the city's best blues and jazz pubs.

Red-, white-and-green fire hydrants let you know that you're in the thirty-square-block **Hill district**, a small, neat Italian community three miles east of Soulard. At its heart, **St Ambrose Church** displays a statue of Italian immigrants; all around, the aroma of freshly baked bread drifts out of the small specialty bakeries that share the area with one-room grocery stores and dozens of restaurants.

Just east of the Hill District at 4344 Shaw Blvd, the 79-acre **Missouri Botanical Garden** (9am–5pm daily, summer also Mon 9am–8pm; $7) is a haven of peace and tranquility, just a few hundred yards from busy I-44. The grounds contain everything from a magnificent Japanese garden through scented rose and English woodland gardens to the Climatron, a huge greenhouse that re-creates a tropical rainforest complete with waterfalls and cliffs.

St Charles

The beautiful little river town of **ST CHARLES**, 25 miles northwest of downtown St Louis and forever threatened by flooding – in 1993 it briefly became an island in the swirling waters – remains redolent with lazy charm, despite the advent of its first riverboat casino. Three small though distinct **historic districts** are crammed with antique shops, specialty outlets and good cafés and restaurants, including the *Trailhead Brewery*, 921 S Riverside Dr. (☎636/946-2739), a modern pub housed in an 18th-century grist mill. Lewis and Clark set up strategic camp here in 1804, and are remembered in the interesting small **museum**.

St Charles's **CVB**, 230 S Main St (☎636/946-7776 or 1-800/366-2427, ⓦwww.historicstcharles.com), has details of downtown's growing range of elegant and amply porched **B&Bs**. The popular **Katy Trail**, which hugs "Big Muddy" along the route of an old railroad before turning west to Clinton, is excellent for hiking or cycling. Ride Me Recycles (☎314/707-7433 or 1-888-274-4626, ⓦwww.justrideme.com) rents bikes and provides pick up and drop off along the trail, as does Touring Cyclist (☎636/949-9430). Gambling and showboats are anchored along the riverbanks, while the *St Charles Princess* operates sightseeing, lunch and dinner **cruises** from Frontier Park (☎636/946-4995).

Eating

Italian food dominates St Louis cuisine, from humble salami sellers upwards. Otherwise most of the friendly Irish pubs serve beef sandwiches and stew, while University City's **Delmar Boulevard** offers African, Middle Eastern, Chinese, Indian and other ethnic places. More expensive cafés are located in **Laclede's Landing**, and the **Central West End** has acquired a scattering of upmarket espresso bars such as the *Coffee Cartel*, 2 Maryland Plaza.

Duff's 392 N Euclid Ave, Central West End ☎ 314/361-0522. Small, relaxed and moderately priced, with a French-flavored international menu, homemade desserts and Sunday brunch. Outdoor seating available.

John D McGurk's Irish Pub 1200 Russell Blvd at 12th St, Soulard ☎ 314/776-8309. Freshly baked soda bread, corned beef'n'cabbage, Irish stew and imported Guinness on offer. Live Irish music every night.

O'Connell's Pub 4652 Shaw Ave at Kingshighway Blvd ☎ 314/773-6600. The best burgers in the city, and the beef sandwiches aren't bad either. Near the Hill district.

Red Sea 6511 Delmar Blvd, U City ☎ 314/863-0099. Cheap and cheerful Ethiopian restaurant, serving berbere sauce with everything. The decor is basic and the service slow, but the food's excellent.

Rigazzi's 4945 Daggett Blvd, the Hill ☎ 314/772-4900. Popular trattoria, famous for "frozen fish bowls" of beer. Over thirty different pasta dishes on the menu, from $9, plus pizzas, veal, chicken and steak.

Saleem's 6501 Delmar Blvd, U City ☎ 314/721-7947. "Where garlic is king" and St Louisians reckon you get the best ethnic food in the city. Lebanese and continental menu.

Ted Drewes Frozen Custard 6726 Chippewa Ave ☎ 314/481-2652 and 4224 S Grand Blvd ☎ 314/352-7376. A legendary slice of Americana. Try a "concrete" – an ice cream so thick it won't budge if you turn your cup upside down. Open March–Dec.

Nightlife and entertainment

Downtown St Louis' highest concentration of **bars** and **clubs** can be found in **Laclede's Landing**, with nightly jazz, blues, rock and reggae. Some of the outlying districts are well worth checking out in the evening; these include the Loop in U City, whose bars and cafés are not just popular with students, and the slightly more upmarket cafés and wine bars of **Central West End**. Unpretentious **Soulard** is the place to go for good jazz and blues. Every spring, the four-day **Mid–America Jazz Festival** (☎ 314/241-1888) brings the top names together for performances all over St Louis.

Don't forget also to check out **Grand Center**, centered on North Grand Boulevard in midtown, home to stage shows and the St Louis Symphony Orchestra (☎ 314/534-1700). Excellent listings can be found in the free weekly *Riverfront Times*.

Blueberry Hill 6504 Delmar Blvd, U City ☎ 314/727-0880. Crammed full of memorabilia, with the downstairs dedicated to Elvis and a jukebox acclaimed by *Cashbox* magazine as the best in the country. The drinks and burgers are good, and live entertainment is offered every weekend (Chuck Berry comes in for monthly cameos).

Broadway Oyster Bar 736 S Broadway, downtown ☎ 314/621-8811. Cramped, crowded and dark blues club, in an atmospheric old bar.

1860 Hard Shell Café & Bar 1860 S 9th St, Soulard ☎ 314/231-1860. One of the liveliest bars in Soulard with dancing to blues, R&B and soul bands. Also serves good Cajun and fish dishes.

Mississippi Nights 914 N 1st St, Laclede's Landing ☎ 314/421-3853. The city's top venue for nonstadium bands.

Pageant 6161 Delmar Blvd, U City ☎ 314/726-6161. Large bar and live entertainment venue that brings in big name rock groups.

Pierre's 4th and Chestnut, downtown ☎ 314/342-4690. Open Thurs–Sat . "Cigar smoking encouraged" in this classy jazz bar in the *Adams-Mark Hotel*.

Riddles Penultimate 6307 Delmar Blvd, U City ☎ 314/725-6985. Very lively bar in the heart of U City, with a young crowd and some sidewalk seating.

South of St Louis

Missouri's oldest community, the French and German heritage of tiny **STE GENEVIEVE**, sixty miles south of St Louis, retains its eighteenth-century charm through historic cottages, a redbrick square and summer festivals. A perennial favorite of Mississippi flood waters, the town, with a population of 4500, has recently been sheltered by a $50 million levee, a measure taken to ensure the safety of homes that pre-date the American Revolution. The *St Gemme Beauvais*, 78 N Main St (☎573/883-3562 or 1-877/272-5588; ❸), is a nineteenth-century Greek Revival inn downtown, while Amish variations on catfish, chicken and seafood are on the menu in the *Anvil Saloon*, 43 S Third St (☎573/883-7323).

CAPE GIRARDEAU, responsible for giving Rush Limbaugh to the airwaves of the world, looks down on the Mississippi from a rocky ledge 55 miles downriver. Among its antebellum and Victorian buildings, the *Port Cape Girardeau*, 19 N Water St (☎573/334-0954), serves tasty ribs. The *Sands Motel* at 1448 N Kings Hwy (☎573/334-2828; ❷), with a decent restaurant, is good value. You can **camp** ten miles north of town at the Trail of Tears State Park (☎573/334-1711, $7 per tent site). The **visitor's center** at 100 Broadway (Mon–Fri 8am–5pm, Sat 10am–4pm; ☎1-800/777-0068, ⓦwww.capegirardeaucvb.org) also has **internet** access. The road continues south to Arkansas through reclaimed swamplands, rich in wheat, corn and melons, but little else.

Kansas City

KANSAS CITY, 250 miles due west of St Louis, straddles the state line between Kansas and Missouri. Virtually all its main points of interest are on the Missouri side, where the fountains, boulevards, and Art Deco and Mediterranean-style buildings, and the encouraging revitalization of downtown, are unusual and welcome features in a Midwestern city. Kansas City, Kansas, on the other hand, is a dull sprawl of suburbs that doesn't have much to attract visitors.

Kansas City was a convenient staging post for 1830s wagon trains heading west. Its consequent prosperity – and rough and tumble "sin city" image – was brought to an abrupt end by the Civil War. However, its fortunes revived in the 1870s, when the railroads brought the boom in meat packing that was responsible for the development of the huge stockyards, which finally closed down in 1992.

Thanks to political boss Tom Pendergast, an outrageous figure with whom the city had a love-hate relationship, its many jazz clubs continued to sell alcohol during Prohibition. As in Chicago and New Orleans, speakeasies, brothels and gambling dens went hand in hand with superlative **jazz** – and, to a lesser extent, blues – spawning the careers of Count Basie, Duke Ellington and, in the Fifties, Charlie Parker. KC's resurgent jazz scene, fine restaurants, professional football and baseball teams, and theme parks help make it a popular short-break destination for the people of the western heartland.

Arrival, information and getting around

From the **airport** (☎816/243-5237), twenty miles northwest of downtown, a convenient forty-minute **shuttle bus** (half-hourly 6am–11.55pm; ☎816/243-5000) heads to major downtown hotels ($13) and Westport ($14). The equivalent taxi ride costs around $43 (Yellow Cab ☎816/471-5000).

The isolated Greyhound terminal lies well out from downtown in a miserable area at 12th Street and Troost Avenue. Amtrak is in the Union Station at

23rd and Main streets, opposite Crown Center. The Metro Buses system
(☎816/221-0660) covers downtown and routes out to Independence. In addition, seasonal trolleys loop continuously between downtown, Crown Center,
Westport and the Country Club Plaza ($7 all-day pass, $10 two-day pass).

The city's main **visitor center** is tucked away on the 25th floor of City
Center Square at 1100 Main St (Mon–Fri 8.30am–5pm; ☎816/221-5242 or
1-800/767-7700, ⓦwww.gointokansascity.com); additional information
offices are housed in the Country Club Plaza at 4709 W Central St (daily
8am–6pm; ☎816/691-3800) and in the Grand Hallway of Union Station.
There's also a State Welcome Center on the grounds of the Truman Sports
Complex, off exit 9 on I-70 in Independence (daily 8am–5pm, closed
Dec–Feb; ☎816/889-3330). The main **post office** is close to Amtrak at 315
W Pershing Rd (Mon–Fri 8am–6pm, Sat 8am–3.30pm; ☎1-800/275-8777;
zip code 64108). You can access the **internet** at the Public Library, 311 E
12th St (☎816/701-3400) or at the Westport Coffee House at 4010
Pennsylvania St.

Accommodation

Kansas City's budget motels lie along the interstates or out towards
Independence, but reasonable central options do exist. The Kansas City Visitor
Center is the best place to inquire about **B&Bs**. Depending on which direction you are coming from, **camping** choices are the *Trailside Camper's Inn*
(☎816/229-2267 or 1-800/748-7729; $17) at I-70 exit 24, 24 miles east of
downtown in Grain Valley, or the *Cottonwood RV Park* (☎913/422-8038) on
Hwy-7 just off I-70 exit 224, 24 miles west of downtown in Bonner Springs.

Historic Suites of America 612 Central St
☎816/842-6544 or 1-800/733-0612. Beautiful
large rooms with fully equipped kitchens in the
heart of the Garment District. Includes free breakfast and cocktails. ⑥–⑧
Holiday Inn Express Westport 801 Westport Rd
☎816/931-1000. Reasonable lodgings on the

edge of the trendy Westport district. ⑤
Plaza Hotel at Westport 4309 Main St
☎816/561-9600. Very central, close to
Westport. ④
Super 8 Independence 4032 S Lynn Court
☎816/833-1888. Clean budget motel, east of the
city in Independence. ②–④

The City

Kansas City is doing a good job of reinvigorating its **downtown**, and wandering past the restored lofts and small businesses of the **Garment District**,
between Sixth and Ninth streets, makes a nice walk to City Hall, 414 E 12th
St, a fine Art Deco building with an observation deck on its thirtieth floor
(Mon–Fri 8.30am–4.15pm; free). Also downtown is the redeveloped historic
district known variously as **River Market** or City Market, on the banks of the
Missouri. As well as colorful shops, cafés and a lively farmers' market at Fifth
and Walnut streets, there's a good museum in the complex – **The Treasure of
the Steamboat Arabia** – which tells the story behind the 1988 salvaging of
a side-wheeler that sank on its way to Council Bluffs in 1856. Perfectly preserved artifacts – china, guns, gold and Kentucky bourbon to name a few –
afford unexpected and intriguing insights into frontier life (Mon–Sat
10am–6pm, Sun noon–5pm; $7.50).

The sprawling concrete **Crown Center**, on Grand Avenue and Pershing
Road, owned by Hallmark Cards, calls itself "a city within a city," and houses
apartments, shops, restaurants, offices, hotels, cinemas and an ice rink.
Interesting displays in its splendidly awful **Hallmark Visitors Center**
(Mon–Wed & Sat 10am–6pm, Thurs–Fri 10am–9pm, Sun noon–5pm; free)

trace styles of greetings cards along-side political and cultural changes; designs from the 1940s, for example, featured stars and stripes, and Uncle Sam. There are also demonstrations of dying and engraving techniques. The nearby **Union Station** is a Kansas City landmark: huge, beautifully renovated and home to **Science City** (daily 10am–6pm; $12.50), an incredible arena of futuristic games, movies and exhibits.

The **18th and Vine Historic Jazz District**, south of I-70 as it sweeps east-west, was the hub of the city's 1930s jazz scene. Formerly an unsafe area of empty lots and boarded-up shops, a huge revitalization project in the 1980s culminated with the opening of the **Negro Leagues Baseball Museum**, 1616 E 18th St (Tues–Sat 9am–6pm, Sun noon–6pm; $6). This enthralling collection of photographs, interactive exhibits and game equipment traces the turbulent history of black baseball in America, which was segregated from the white major leagues for the first half of the twentieth century. In 1920, Kansas City hosted the key meeting that founded the Negro National League – an institution that paved the way for the likes of Jackie Robinson to enter the major leagues. In the same complex is the **American Jazz Museum** (Tues–Thurs 9am–6pm, Fri–Sat 9am–9pm, Sun noon–6pm; $6), which tells the history of jazz through interactive exhibits; profiling some of its greatest performers, including Kansas City native Charlie Parker and others who cut their teeth in the smoky halls of 18th and Vine. *The Blue Room* functions as a working jazz bar, with Monday night jam sessions bringing many stars out of the woodwork.

Westport, an attractive district of good restaurants, cafés and trendy shops between 39th and 45th

DOWNTOWN KANSAS CITY

ACCOMMODATION
Historic Suites of America 1
Holiday Inn Express Westport 2
Plaza Hotel at Westport 3

RESTAURANTS, BARS AND CLUBS
Arthur Bryant's C
Blayney's M
The Cup and Saucer A
Gates Bar-B-Q G
The Grand Emporium I
Hereford House E
The Hurricane L
Jazz/A Louisiana Kitchen J
Jerusalem Café N
Kiki's Bon Ton Maison O
Lamar's Donuts H
Lidia's F
Mutual Musicians Foundation D
Phoenix Piano Bar and Grill B
Westport Coffee House K

streets, was the original jumping-off point for the Santa Fe Trail. Stop off for a drink at the city's oldest building, *Kelly's Westport Inn*, 500 Westport St, a shabby but friendly redbrick bar. Five miles south of downtown, beginning at 47th and Main streets, the elegant **Country Club Plaza** dates from the early 1920s. Tree-shaded and upmarket (with branches of Eddie Bauer and Saks), its tiling, mosaics, fountains and orange trees evoke the streets of Spain, and a replica Sevillan tower completes the effect.

Highlights at the extensive **Nelson–Atkins Museum of Art**, a few blocks east at 4525 Oak St (Tues–Thurs 10am–4pm, Fri 10am–9pm, Sat 10am–5pm, Sun noon–5pm; $5, free on Sat), include superb Oriental exhibits, with figurines from Tang and Egyptian tombs, plus canvases by Titian, Caravaggio (*St John the Baptist*) and Monet, and twelve Henry Moore sculptures in a landscaped setting. The pretty **Toy and Miniatures Museum**, further south at 5235 Oak St (Wed–Sat 10am–4pm, Sun 1–4pm; $4), houses an offbeat collection of antique toys, games and puppets.

When the Midwestern humidity gets too much, head for the tropically themed water world **Oceans of Fun**, or the adjoining **Worlds of Fun**, with its 140-plus rides, out at exit 54 of I-435 (late May–early Sept daily, hours vary; $22.95 for Oceans, $33.50 for Worlds).

Eating

Barbecue, once the unfashionable food of the poor, is big news in Kansas City – cheap, cheerful, hickory-smoked and served with tasty sauces. The **Country Club Plaza** has some great places, but they tend to be overpriced and some require formal dress. The restaurants in Crown Center and around Westport are more casual.

Arthur Bryant's 1727 Brooklyn Ave ☎816/231-1123. *The* place for barbecue, a mile east of downtown in a desolate area. Serving the largest portions you've ever seen of barbecue and beans; the combo plate easily feeds two hefty appetites. This is serious business – be sure not to dawdle in the queue, as novices are given short shrift.

Gates Bar-B-Q 3201 Main St ☎816/753-0828. Massive portions of BBQ served on platters in a family style atmosphere.

Hereford House 20th and Main streets ☎816/842-1080. KC's top steak house, in a handy downtown spot.

Jerusalem Café 431 Westport Rd ☎816/756-2770. Small Middle Eastern restaurant serving superb falafel and kebabs.

LaMar's Donuts 240 E Linewood Blvd ☎800/533-7489. A KC institution, now with branches in several states; this one is the original.

Lidia's 101 W 22nd St ☎816/221-3722. Popular spot housed in an old freight house. Excellent pastas and an extensive wine selection – at affordable prices.

River Market Brewing Company 500 Walnut St ☎816/471-6300. A billiards room and full bar are added attractions to the American-style menu and house brew. Located near City Market.

Stroud's 1015 E 85th St ☎816/333-2132. Classic roadhouse, a long way southeast of downtown, and renowned for its fried chicken. A favorite with Rush Limbaugh among others.

The Cup and Saucer 412B Deleware St ☎816/474-7375. A unique sandwich and coffee shop that transforms into a bar by night, where weekend jazz jams are popular.

Nightlife and entertainment

Check out Kansas City's reviving **jazz** and **blues** scene, especially the authentic dives holding wonderful jam sessions into the early hours. The Friday and Sunday editions of the *Kansas City Star* carry listings, as does the freebie *Pitch Weekly*. You can also call the Jazz Hotline (☎816/753-JASS) or check ⓦ www.jazzkc.org. Downtown is otherwise pretty dead by mid-evening, and most people head to Westport for nightlife from country-and-western to alternative rock.

Blayney's 415 Westport Rd ☎816/561-3747. A good Westport venue with live blues Tues & Wed; open until 3am.

The Grand Emporium 3832 Main St ☎816/531-7557. R&B, blues, reggae and jazz, with superb Cajun and Jamaican food. Twice voted the best blues club in America by the National Blues Foundation.

The Hurricane 4048 Broadway ☎816/783-0884. Trendy dance club in Westport operating until the wee hours.

Jazz/A Louisiana Kitchen 1823 W 39th St ☎816/531-5556. Cajun cuisine and live jazz and blues.

Kiki's Bon Ton Maison 1515 Westport Rd ☎816/931-9417. Louisiana-style food, plus Cajun and zydeco music on Wed & Sat.

Mutual Musicians Foundation 1823 Highland Ave ☎816/471-5212. National Historic Landmark in the 18th and Vine district. Fierce jam sessions begin 1.30am Fri & Sat, with musicians competing in a frenzy for hours. Things can get a bit rough, and is not recommended for women alone.

Phoenix Piano Bar and Grill 302 W 8th St at Central Ave ☎816/472-0001. Downtown jazz piano venue featuring Sat afternoon sessions.

Independence and Liberty

Bus #24 from Kansas City goes to the small town of **INDEPENDENCE**, twenty minutes east of the city and most famous as the former home of President Harry S. Truman. The **Truman Presidential Museum and Library** on US-24 and Delaware Street (Mon–Wed & Sat 9am–5pm, Thurs 9am–9pm, Sun noon–5pm; $5) includes a reconstruction of his White House office, and chilling documents pertaining to the development of the atomic bomb. The **Victorian Truman Home**, a mile south at 219 N Delaware St, is decorated as it was when it functioned as the summer White House (daily 8.30am–5pm, in winter closed Mon; $3).

Jesse James staged the first ever daylight bank robbery in 1866 in what's now the **Jesse James Bank Museum**, on the Old Town Square of **LIBERTY**, fifteen miles northeast of downtown Kansas City (Mon–Sat 9am–4pm; $4). Among the memorabilia and dusty relics of early banking, you can see the vault and the safe that he raided.

St Joseph

Sixty miles north of Kansas City, **ST JOSEPH** boomed as a supply depot for the California Gold Rush, and today is still a busy manufacturing town. For a brief eighteen months, starting in 1860, it was the home of the legendary **Pony Express**, which took ten days to deliver mail all the way to Sacramento, California, by continuous horseback relay. The Pony Express was a financial disaster, driven out of business by its inability to compete with the transcontinental telegraph, but riders such as Buffalo Bill Cody went on to become legends. Charlie Miller, the last of the riders, rode from New York to San Francisco in 1931, and died aged 105 in 1955. The full story is told in lively dioramas at the **Pony Express Museum**, 914 Penn St, attractively set in the company's original stables (Mon–Sat 9am–5pm, Sun 1–5pm; $4).

It was in St Joseph, on April 3, 1882, that the notorious Jesse James was shot in the back by Robert Ford, a twenty-year-old member of his own gang who had negotiated a $10,000 reward from the governor. Countless books and films have portrayed Jesse James as a latter-day Robin Hood; in fact, he spent most of the Civil War riding with a band of Confederate guerrillas. The **Jesse James Home Museum**, the one-story frame cottage where James was living incognito (naturally) while he planned his next bank job, now stands at 12th and Penn streets, having been moved closer to the main highway in the hope of attracting sightseers (April–Oct Mon–Sat 10am–5pm, Sun 1–5pm; Nov–March Mon–Sat 10am–4pm, Sun 1-4pm; $2). A ragged hole in the wall is pointed out as the spot where the bullet supposedly hit, after striking James as he was hanging a picture; you can also see where bloodstained splinters were chiseled from the floor to be sold as souvenirs. As for the assassin, Ford was himself gunned down ten years later, and his killer in turn was also shot.

There are thirteen museums, most about the Old West, but there's not much reason to linger. If you do want to leave the drive to Kansas City or Omaha for another day, you'll find **motels** strung along I-29 as it passes east of downtown, including a *Motel 6* (℡816/232-2311; ❷) and a *Days Inn* (℡816/279-1671; ❸) at the intersection with Frederick Boulevard. The **Old Town Smokehouse & Pub**, 1120 Penn St (℡816/232-1899), serves huge sandwiches at appealing prices and is a must if you want lunch in St Joseph.

Southwest Missouri – Ozark country

There's little to see south of Kansas City before the **Ozark Mountains**. Occupying most of southern Missouri and northern Arkansas (see p.609), the area remained frontier territory until the timber companies moved in at the end of the nineteenth century. When they moved on, the hill-dwellers were left to eke out a living from the denuded terrain. Severe droughts forced many to leave for the cities. For those who remain, fishing resorts and tourist attractions supply some work, though the region remains poor and economically backward. None of the Ozark peaks is particularly high, but the roads through switch, dip, climb and swerve to provide stunning views of steep hillsides, thick with oak, elm, hickory and redbud that are quite resplendent in the fall.

Springfield is the region's main city, 130 miles south of Kansas City, but the gateway to the Ozarks, the country music town of **Branson**, is more popular by far.

Branson

Nestled among beautiful Ozark lakes, the resort of **BRANSON** (year-round population 5000), forty miles south of Springfield on US-65, is one of the top auto destinations in the country. Over seven million visitors a year are attracted to what's become known as the "Ozark Disneyland" by thirty-plus music venues (almost all of a country bent), a few theme parks and lots of good ol' family fun.

"**The Strip**," until recently merely Hwy-76, looks like it was thrown together with a pitchfork – a hideous agglomeration of theme parks and theaters owned and/or performed in by big-name stars. The spectrum ranges from Japanese fiddler Shoji Tabuchi and ancient crooner Andy Williams, to banal mountain humor joints like *Baldknobbers* and *Presleys'* (not that Presley). Lesser lights include Russian comedian Yakov Smirnoff, and Jim Spiders and Snakes Stafford's place. Tickets for a two-hour show are fairly priced, at around $20, and there's no shortage of takers in summer for most, if not all, of the town's 57,000 seats – a figure said to exceed that of Nashville. Branson shows are firmly geared toward families; you won't find anything remotely progressive or avant-garde, although the new *Ripley's Believe It or Not* performance is a step in a new direction.

The Strip, once dubbed "the world's longest parking lot" because of the mass of cars that crammed here each night, has been somewhat eased with road improvements, but try to avoid driving at night. When you've had it with Branson, escape to nearby **Table Rock Lake**, a beautiful area offering hiking, biking, camping, water-skiing and world-class fishing.

Practicalities

Greyhound connects Branson with Springfield, Kansas City and Memphis. Call ahead, or drop in at the local **Chamber of Commerce**, at the intersection of Hwy-65 and Hwy-248 (Mon–Sat 8am–5pm, Sun 10am–4pm; ☎417/334-4136 or 1-800/214-3661, ⓦ www.explorebranson.com), for a copy of their show guide detailing performance schedules of all the theaters. During the main season (May–Oct), hotel prices rise, especially on weekends, but you can still find some deals. Branson Vacation Reservations (☎1-800/221-5692) will try to sell you a package deal, but can also book you into a motel, including one of five *Best Westerns* (☎1-800/528-1234; ❹). The *Ozark Mountain Country B&B*, Box 295, Branson, MO 65616 (☎1-800/695-1546), is another reliable reservation service, but if you're visiting in the main season call at least a week in advance. Table Rock State Park (☎417/334-4704) has campsites for $7. Most places to eat are of the family diner ilk, though it's worth searching out the fat-free menu at *McGuffey's* on the Strip, and the down-home cookin' at *The Farmhouse Restaurant*, downtown.

Kansas

Today's cutesy, gingham-pinafore image of **KANSAS**, associated with *Little House on the Prairie* and *The Wizard of Oz*, is a far cry indeed from the troubled history that made it known as "bleeding Kansas." It took three hundred years after Coronado came in search of gold in 1541 before pioneers established trails across the region, and Kansas's bid for statehood in 1861 is often cited as the catalyst for the Civil War. The 1854 Kansas–Nebraska Act, which gave both territories the right to self-determination over slavery, led to fierce clashes between Free Staters and pro-slavery forces. Runaway slaves from the South were given passage through the area, aided by abolitionist John Brown, and Kansas eventually joined the Union as a free state.

After the war, the mighty cattle drives from Texas made towns like Abilene, Wichita and Dodge City centers of the "**Wild West**." The debauched, male image of the West, spawning such "heroes" as Wyatt Earp and Wild Bill Hickok, is, however, challenged in Kansas, which as well as being the first state to give women the vote in municipal elections, boasts the nation's first female mayor and senator, as well as aviator Amelia Earhart and the battling Prohibitionist Carry Nation.

In 1874, Russian Mennonites brought the grain that was to transform the state into the bountiful "bread basket" that now harvests most of the nation's wheat. However, only in the west do miles of golden corn sway in Kansas's infamous gusty wind. The green and hilly northeast, patterned with woods and lakes, is home to the unattractive industrial city of Topeka, liberal college town **Lawrence**, and the dull suburbs of Kansas City (though downtown lies across the state line in Missouri). The wild and sparse northwest is pioneer country, while the once-wicked cowtown **Dodge City** is in the southwest. **Wichita**, the state's largest city, lies in the south central area.

Getting around Kansas

Greyhound **buses** run to all Kansas's main cities, supplemented by erratic smaller companies; services to the west and southwest are especially poor. The most frequent routes run from Kansas City to Albuquerque via Wichita (about 3 daily; 20–23hr), with one or two buses per day along I-70 to Denver. Amtrak **trains** head east-west between LA and Chicago through the center of the state, calling, usually in the middle of the night, at Lawrence, Topeka, Emporia, Newton (for Wichita, but without a connecting service), Dodge City and Garden City. Wichita has the state's biggest **airport**.

East Kansas

Undulating **east Kansas** is laced with lakes, streams and rivers. The northeast, once crossed by the Oregon, Santa Fe and Smoky Hill trails, and now home to both Topeka and Lawrence, is more heavily visited than the southeast, where the major attraction is the Little House on the Prairie historical site, located 13 miles southwest of Independence on Hwy-75. The heritage of Kansas's four Indian tribes comes alive in annual powwows, held in major towns as well as the northwestern reservations.

Lawrence

The mellow town of **LAWRENCE** lies on the Kansas River, roughly halfway between Kansas City and Topeka, around thirty miles from either. Tree-lined streets, a welcoming historic downtown and an aura of old-hippie artsiness make it an appealing destination, with a cultural energy owed in part to the University of Kansas (home of the Jayhawk, the mythical bird which is the emblem of its sports teams), and a long liberal and intellectual history. Founded by the New England Emigrant Aid Company in 1854, and a center of Free State activities, Lawrence was the site of a violent Civil War skirmish in 1863, when Missourian Confederate guerrilla Quantrill led about 300 men on the town, killing over 150, wounding hundreds more and setting the place alight. Rebuilding was quick, however, as evidenced by the limestone and brick buildings of today's downtown, centered on Massachusetts Street, and the State University campus, which stands on a steep, tree-covered grassy bank known as Mount Oread.

The Town

Studded with cafés and eclectic shops, downtown Lawrence is a delight to walk around – and just as busy outside of term time, when day-trippers flock in from less congenial Kansan cities. However, most of the town's formal attractions are congregated on campus. The **University of Kansas Natural History Museum**, on Jayhawk Boulevard at 14th Street (Mon–Sat 10am–5pm, Sun noon–5pm; free), holds a chronological panorama of North American flora and fauna, as well as the now stuffed horse Comanche, the lone survivor of Custer's cavalry at the Battle of Little Bighorn. Across the road, the **Museum of Anthropology**, in Spooner Hall, presents African and Eskimo artifacts (Mon–Sat 9am-5pm, Sun 1–5pm; free). The **Spencer Museum of Art**, at 1301 Mississippi St (Tues, Wed, Fri & Sat 10am–5pm, Thurs 10am–9pm, Sun noon–5pm; free), specializes in world art, with an Oriental gallery, Old Masters and a Pre-Raphaelite masterpiece. Graphic art (shown by appointment) from the Sixties includes some Warhols and exceptional photographs, from Diane

Arbus's disturbing portraits to Weegee's documentary exposés of New York City life. Its gift shop does a great line in surreal and offbeat postcards.

Native American traditions are preserved and packaged for the public each year by the exhibitions of the **Lawrence Indian Arts Show**, held throughout the city from mid-September to the end of October. One venue is the **Haskell Indian Nations University** at 23rd and Massachusetts streets, where the **Hiawatha Visitor Center and American Indian Athletic Hall of Fame** are open year-round by appointment (☏785/749-8404).

Arrival, information and accommodation

Amtrak comes into Lawrence at 413 E 7th St, and Greyhound arrives at 2447 W 6th St. The kitsch Fifties-style Lawrence Bus Co runs local buses. The **visitor center** is north of downtown in the renovated Union Pacific Depot at N 2nd and Locust streets (Mon–Sat 8.30am–5.30pm, Sun 1–5pm; ☏785/865-4499 or 1-888/LAWKANS, ⓦ www.visitlawerence.com). You can find **internet** terminals at the Lawrence Public Library, 707 Vermont St or *Café Nova* (☏785/841-3282) at 745 New Hampshire St.

Adequate but dull budget **rooms** can be found near the bus station at the *Virginia Inn*, 2907 W 6th St (☏785/843-6611; ❸), while the *Super 8* at 515 McDonald Drive (☏913/842-5721; ❸) is a reliable fall-back. If you have a little extra cash, head instead to the lovely all-suite *Eldridge Hotel*, at 7th and Massachusetts streets (☏785/749-5011 or 1-800/527-0909; ❺/❻); twice burned down by pro-slavery forces, it has been restored to an evocative faded elegance, and houses the stylish *Shalor's* restaurant (☏785/749-1005) and the atmospheric *Jayhawker* bar in the lobby. You can **camp** near downtown at *KOA*, 1473 Hwy-40 (☏785/842-3877; $20 per tent site), or three miles out along W 23rd Street at Clinton Lake State Park, where the vehicle fee is $5 and a tent site $6.50 (☏785/842-8562).

Eating, drinking and entertainment

Lawrence's **nightlife** is dominated by students, found in their droves along Massachusetts Street. One of the better places to investigate is Liberty Hall at 642 Massachusetts St (☏745/749-1912). Once a social and political center, this building housed Lawrence's first newspaper until it was burned down by pro-slavery agitators in 1863. Today it puts on art-house films, plays and concerts.

Buffalo Bob's Smokehouse 719 Massachusetts St ☏785/841-6400. Hickory-smoked barbecue pork, chicken and ribs for those who can't wait until Kansas City. Tater curl french fries and apple fritters included.

Free State Brewing Co 636 Massachusetts St ☏785/843-4555. Trendy brewpub serving award-winning amber beer and robust steaks.

Jazzhaus 926 Massachusetts St ☏785/749-3320. As the name suggests, this dimly lit bar hosts weekend jazz gigs.

Paradise Café 728 Massachusetts St ☏785/842-5199. Veggie burgers, soups, salads, fish specials and breakfast too.

Teller's 746 Massachusetts St ☏785/843-4111. Excellent nachos and pizza served in a beautifully restored bank building.

Yellow Sub 624 W 12th St ☏785/841-3268. Good sandwiches and lunch specials in a laid-back atmosphere with sweeping views. It's campus location keeps it busy during the school year.

West through Kansas

Further west across Kansas, three towns re-create the state's Wild West heritage, although only in the westernmost, Dodge City, does the scrubby landscape conform to the cowboy-movie image. **Abilene**, if less famous than Dodge

City, has as many outlaw and gunslinger stories, and **Wichita**, about 200 miles southwest of Kansas City, holds an excellent, authentic reconstruction of frontier days in its Old Cowtown Museum.

Abilene

Like all the old cattle-trail cowtowns, **ABILENE**, 115 miles west of Lawrence on I-70, claims to have been the most riproaring of the lot. By the time legendary lawman Wild Bill Hickok became its marshal in 1871, the unruly behavior was already dying down, and little today reminds you of those raucous days. Doing its best, though, is **Old Abilene Town**, at SE Sixth and Kuney streets (May–Sept daily 9am–8pm; free), a replica of the town during its cattle boom. Gunfights and cancan performances are still held when tourists turn up, but the place has seen better days – most buildings are falling apart or boarded up – it's up for sale and no longer touted by the local tourist office.

These days, Abilene prefers to stress its connections with Dwight Eisenhower. The **Eisenhower Center**, 201 SE Fourth St (May–August daily 8am–5.45pm; Sept–April daily 9am–4.45pm), encompasses his boyhood home, with its original furnishings, the obligatory film show and many photos and papers on display in the spacious museum ($3.50). The former president and his wife are buried in the meditation chapel.

Abilene's **visitor center** is at 201 NW Second St (☎785/263-2231 or 1-800/569-5915). Most of the town's budget **motels** are off I-70 at Hwy-15. The very basic *Diamond*, at 1407 NW Third St (☎785/263-2360; ❷), is an option. But the best rates are at the *White House Hotel*, 101 NW 14th St (☎785/263-3600; ❶), a slightly faded but clean motel not far from the I-70 exit.

Wichita

WICHITA, about 165 miles southwest of Lawrence on I-35, is the largest city in Kansas, severed by the Arkansas River, which forks just north of downtown into the Big and Little Arkansas rivers (incidentally, Kansans take umbrage if you pronounce it "Arkansaw"; pronounce it here the way it is spelled). Originally settled by the Wichita Indians, who by 1865 had been relocated to Oklahoman Indian Territory, Wichita grew up as a stop on the Chisholm Trail, a Texas-to-Kansas cattle route celebrated in frontier lore and cowboy ballads. Its glory days were to be short-lived, however, as farmers, angry about the damage done by stampeding cattle, erected fences which forced the drives onto different trails further west, creating new cowtowns such as Dodge City. Today three of the world's major aircraft manufacturers (Cessna, Raytheon and Learjet) are based here, and the city, already with a rich arts scene, has been invigorated with a downtown revival.

The City

Downtown Wichita is enlivened mainly by the public art and sculpture that pops up unexpectedly all over the place, in empty lots and even in tree stumps. The exceptional **Wichita–Sedgwick County Historical Museum**, 204 S Main St (Tues–Fri 11am–4pm, Sat & Sun 1–5pm; $2), is in **Old City Hall**, a heavy stone building decorated with turrets, gargoyles and arches. The cozy interior is crammed with exhibits on everything from the Wichita Indians through decorative art to Carry Nation, whose initial zeal for singing hymns to errant drunks grew into a campaign against everything from tobacco to corsets. The stately church with vivid stained-glass windows at 601 N Water St houses the **Kansas African American Museum** (Tues–Fri 9am–5pm, Sun 2–6pm; free), an eclectic antidote to more mainstream views of Great Plains history, with details on Buffalo Soldiers, inventors from across the country and early black Wichitans, and some African art.

Excellent museums in the Riverside stretch of parkland (which also holds walking and bike trails) include the **Indian Center and Museum**, 650 N Seneca Drive (Tues–Sat 10am–5pm, Sun 1–5pm; $3). The 44ft *Keeper of the Plains* statue, facing east at the confluence of the Little and Big Arkansas rivers, was designed in the 1970s by a Kiowa-Comanche artist, Blackbear Bosin, and dedicated by Native Americans and city officials smoking the peace pipe. It's an eerie sight at dusk, reaching into the sky with some unknown offering. The museum itself is small, with changing exhibits of traditional and contemporary Native American art.

Western artist C.M. Russell is the best represented of the veritable who's who of American painters assembled at the **Wichita Art Museum**, 619 Stackman Drive (Tues–Sat 10am–5pm, Sun noon–5pm; free). **Old Cowtown Museum**, 1871 Sim Park Drive (March–Oct Mon–Sat 10am–5pm, Sun noon–5pm; $7), is a seventeen-acre riverside exhibit re-creating the buildings of 1870s Wichita. Looking and feeling like a movie set, the area includes – along with some docile longhorns – the city's first one-room jail, a schoolroom, a store, a smithy, churches and stables, and old homes.

To the north of the city, the surreal geodesic **Bright Spot for Health Center**, 3100 N Hillside Ave (Mon–Thurs 8am–5.30pm; $4), houses the Garvey Center for the Improvement of Human Functioning, which aims, by using holistic medicine, to find a cure for cancer. It's all very worthy, but weird: road signs, for example, tell you to "de-stress to 25," and there's a 39ft food guide pyramid. In the southeast of the city, the products of Wichita's plane industry are on display at the **Kansas Aviation Museum**, in the old Art Deco air terminal at 3350 George Washington Blvd (Tues–Fri 9am–4pm, Sat 1–5pm; $2). A more interesting detour is to **Hutchinson** (on Hwy-50, 45 miles northwest of Wichita), for the **Kansas Cosmosphere and Space Center** (Mon–Sat 9am–9pm, Sun noon–9pm; $5.50 museum admission, $13 includes IMAX and Planetarium) which features, among other aerospace paraphernalia, the Apollo 13 command module.

Practicalities

Domestic **flights** arrive at the Mid-Continent Airport (☏316/946-4700), five miles southwest of downtown on Hwy-54 (W Kellogg Drive). Amtrak stops at Newton, a small Mennonite town 25 miles north, with a local bus connection to Wichita throughout the day; Greyhound comes in to 312 S Broadway Ave, two blocks east of Main Street. City transportation consists of **buses** (WMTA; ☏316/265-7221; $1 per ride), and, more appealingly, **trolleys**, which run at lunchtimes and on Saturdays for just 50¢. The resourceful **CVB** is in the heart of downtown at Douglas Avenue and Main Street (Mon–Fri 8am–5pm; ☏316/265-2800 or 1-800/288-9424, ⊛www.wichita-cvb.org). An additional **information office** is housed in the Wichita Boathouse at 335 W Lewis St (daily 9am–5pm; ☏316/337-9088). City trolley tours ($8) depart from here Mon–Sat at 10am. You can surf the **web** at the Wichita Public Library, 223 S Main St.

Budget l**odgings** in Wichita are plentiful, especially near the airport on W Kellogg Drive – try the *Ramada* at no. 6245 (☏316/945-5261; ❸). On the opposite flank of the city is a good *Fairfield Inn* at 333 S Webb Rd (☏316/685-3777; ❸). The *Hotel at Oldtown,* at First and Mosley streets (☏316/267-4800;

❺–❼) has a stylish turn of-the-century flavor and perfect location. In the east is the *Mainstay Suites*, 9444 E 39th St (☎316/631-3773; ❹), comfortable and self-contained. *Blasi Campground*, 11209 W Hwy-54 (☎316/722-2681), offers tent sites ($17) nine miles from town.

Until recently considered just another boring Midwestern city, life has come to downtown Wichita. There is suddenly a hoard of new **restaurants**, **clubs** and **bars** around the quaint Old Town Marketplace such as the *River City Brewing Co*, 150 N Mosley St (☎316/263-2739), which has good Kansas steaks, locally brewed beer and veggie pasta dishes. If you are here on Saturday morning the Wichita Farm and Art Market Plaza is a good place to pick up fresh produce. There's great sandwiches and Southwestern food at the *Old Mill Tasty Shop*, by the railroad tracks at 604 E Douglas Ave (☎316/264-6500), complete with marble soda fountain. Or you can dip into one of the thirteen *Pizza Huts* around town, including one with a café at 7700 E Kellogg Drive (☎316/683-1311); the chain started here in 1958. *The Brickyard* at 129 N Rock Island St (☎316/263-4044) is an American-style restaurant with a huge patio where rock, jazz and blues bands perform most nights; while the biggest discotheque is *America's Pub*, at 900 E 1st St (☎316/267-1782).

Dodge City

DODGE CITY, 150 miles west of Wichita, is perhaps the most famous of all America's cowtowns. It has certainly been committed to celluloid more times than any other, especially in 1930s Westerns like *My Darling Clementine* and *Dodge City*. However, this wildest of Wild West cities had a heyday of only a decade, from 1875 until 1886. Established in 1872 with the Santa Fe Railroad, which transported the hides of millions of plains buffalo, by 1875 the town of traders, trappers and hunters had to find a new economic base – the buffalo had been exterminated. The era of the great cattle drives was already underway, and Dodge City became a den of iniquity where gambling, drinking and general lawlessness were the norm. Such wickedness led to gunfights galore, and the notorious Boot Hill cemetery (where the villains were buried with their boots on) was kept busy by charismatic lawmen such as Bat Masterson and Wyatt Earp.

The Town

Dodge City today is rather more staid, with its old downtown area enveloped by a hinterland of railroad tracks and giant silos. Outside of the two-week **Dodge City Days and Rodeo** (🌐www.dodgecityroundup.com), held near the end of July, it is content to replay its movie image in the **Boot Hill Museum**, 500 Wyatt Earp Blvd (June–Aug daily 8am–8pm; Sept–May Mon–Sat 9am–5pm, Sun 1–5pm; $7, $18 family ticket, covering admission only). The museum centers on the single-sided **Historic Front Street**, which was constructed in 1958 and has been acquiring old buildings from all over the West ever since. There's a bank and a grocer, stagecoach rides, a funeral parlor, a smithy, and even a full-sized railroad station, as well as the *Long Branch Saloon*, scene of a variety show with cancan dancers every night at 7.30pm ($6). Gunfights and showdowns break out with alarming regularity. **Boot Hill cemetery** itself is higher up the hill, still on museum grounds; there's just a sorry little patch of lawn on one corner of the original site, which was in any case abandoned in 1879 after just six years and thirty-four burials. The bodies were reinterred elsewhere, and as the graves were never marked in the first place, the jokey wooden crosses in the cemetery are more than a little bogus.

Other sights in town include the **Home of Stone**, 112 E Vine St (June–Aug Mon–Sat 9am–5pm, Sun 2-4pm; free), an emotive memorial to pioneer mothers, often forgotten amid the macho Wild West myth-making. The house looks pretty much as it would have when built in 1881, with domestic memorabilia that belonged to early plainswomen. **El Capitan**, at Second Street and Wyatt Earp Boulevard, is a massive bronze longhorn, facing south towards an identical north-facing statue in Abilene, West Texas. Together they mark the beginning and the end of the cattle drives.

Practicalities

Greyhound **buses** from Wichita arrive twice daily at 2405 W Wyatt Earp Blvd. Amtrak comes right into downtown, to the historic and renovated Santa Fe Station at Central Avenue and Wyatt Earp Boulevard. The **CVB** at Third St and Wyatt Earp Boulevard (Mon–Fri 8.30am–5pm; ☎620/225-8186 or 1-800/OLD-WEST, ⊛www.dodgecity.org) can offer advice on tourist activities; they also have a **visitor center** at 400 W Wyatt Earp Blvd (summer 8.30am–6.30pm; winter Mon–Fri 8.30am–5pm). The Dodge City Trolley runs narrated town **tours** four times a day from a booth on the Boot Hill parking lot ($5). You can use the **internet** at the Public Library, 1001 2nd Ave (☎620/225-0248).

Most of Dodge City's **motels** are strung out roughly a mile west of downtown along US-50, still known here as Wyatt Earp Boulevard. The *Astro* at no. 2200 (☎620/227-8146; ❷) is inexpensive but a little noisy, and offers free rides to the train and bus stations; the *Dodge House* at no. 2408 (☎620/225-9900; ❸–❺) has a reliable restaurant. The *Econo Lodge* at no. 1610 has an indoor pool and sauna area (☎620/225-0231; ❷–❸). **Camping** is an option even for the car-less: the lakeside *Water Sports Campground Recreation*, 500 Cherry St (☎620/225-8004; $6 tent sites), lies ten blocks south of Front Street. If you feel like bustin' your own bronco, head for the *Marchel Ranch*, 10873 W Hwy-50 (☎620/227-7307 or 877/631-6196, ⊛www.marchelranch.com), a small ranch offering horse rides, chuckwagon dinners and cozy rooms.

As for **food**, *Café at the Plaza*, 100 Military Ave (☎620/227-6151), doesn't have much in the way of atmosphere, but the roast beef sandwiches and soups are pretty good and reasonably priced. *Peppercorns*, out near the motels at 1301 W Wyatt Earp Blvd (☎620/225-2335), is a conventional highway steakhouse with meals for about $13.

Iowa

Although at times serene, and almost always verdant, nothing about **IOWA** truly stands out: this 55,000-square-mile chunk of the Great Plains doesn't even manage to be completely flat, it just wobbles up and down a little. The state is the very essence of smalltown America, close to the geographical center of the mainland US, and ranking decidedly average in size, population and level of personal income. Even the cities seem at times to be merely villages grown large.

Iowa's history, too, has been relatively uneventful. It was opened for settlement after the Black Hawk Treaty of 1832, a one-sided exercise in negotiations with the Sauk Indians, conducted after many of them had been chased down and slaughtered in neighboring Wisconsin and Illinois. The Northern European immigrants who replaced them made agricultural development their prime concern, turning Iowa into the "**Foodbasket of America**" – a role it generally achieves with scrupulous efficiency.

Tourist attractions in Iowa are few and far between; its most visited destination is the throwback Germanic enclave of the **Amana Colonies**. However, the state does also hold a few oddball sites, such as the original locations for the movies *The Bridges of Madison County* (in south central **Winterset**, birthplace of John Wayne) and *Field of Dreams* (near Dubuque in the northeast).You can also see, but not enter, the original house that featured in Grant Wood's much-parodied *American Gothic* painting (at Eldon in the southeast, and now owned by the state).

Getting around Iowa

Greyhound **buses** out of Chicago call at all Iowa's major towns, with at least seven services per day in each direction along I-80. St Louis is also well served by six daily buses from Des Moines and Iowa City; these towns are connected less frequently with Minneapolis/St Paul. Amtrak's east-west route misses the cities, stopping instead at assorted small communities in the south, though a bus usually makes the short trip to Des Moines from Osceola.The only sizeable **airport** is in Des Moines. Somewhat surprisingly, Iowa is a good place for **cycle touring**. Each year the extremely popular cross-state bike ride – the **RAGBRAI** – attracts thousands of entrants, any of whom can tell you that the plains aren't always flat (tour details ☎1–800/474–3342, ⓦ www.ragbrai.org).

Eastern Iowa

EASTERN IOWA, in the Mississippi River hinterland, is liberally sprinkled with agribusiness towns that display the continuing influence of their central and northern European pioneers, plus **religious communities** – Amish, Mennonite and the Amana Colonies. All are easily accessible from **Iowa City**; as home to a huge university it's one of the state's livelier centers. Riverside towns such as northerly **Dubuque** and Burlington, near the Missouri state line, have been enlivened since 1991 by gambling, though so far low-stake poker and roulette games can only be played on board Mississippi paddlewheelers, decked out in less-than-authentic Mark Twain-era trimmings.

Dubuque

The handsome town of **DUBUQUE**, overlooked by rocky bluffs on the Mississippi around 150 miles west of Chicago, was founded as the first white settlement in Iowa by French-Canadian leadminers in 1788. In the nineteenth century it became a boisterous riverport and logging center. Buildings from this era still stand, but the companies that use them are now in meat packing and other food industries.

A complex of buildings at Third Street in the old Ice Harbor area, cut off from downtown by Hwy-61, includes an assortment of river-related museums (daily 10am–5.30pm; $6). Precisely which exhibits are housed in the **Mississippi River Museum**, in the **Riverboat Museum**, and in the

National Rivers Hall of Fame (which focuses on "Pathfinders" such as Lewis and Clark, rather than the rivers themselves) seems to vary, but together they tell the story of Mississippi navigation from the days of Robert Fulton's first commercial steamboat in 1807 until the floods of 1993. The fifteen-minute introductory film **"River of Dreams"** is a good starting point for your explorations. At the time of writing the complex was undergoing a $188 million renovation and by 2003 will feature an aquarium, hotel and entertainment complex among other attractions.

Once your appetite has been whetted, you can travel along the high-banked Mississippi on a *Spirit of Dubuque* **paddle-wheeler** cruise (May–Sept daily; $9.50 for 90min; ☎319/583-8093 or 1-800/747-8093), or on board one of the more expensive gambling boats. Alternatively, what's said to be the world's shortest and steepest **cable-car** ride grinds its way in summer from Fourth Street downtown up a sheer bluff to Fenelon Place, a residential street of old money and Victorian architecture. The top offers a sweeping view across the Mississippi to Illinois and Wisconsin (April–Nov daily 8am–10pm; 75¢). If cable cars don't appeal, then head north to the lovingly maintained, 164-acre **Eagle Point Park** (daily 7am–10pm; $1) set on bluffs high above the river.

Film buffs who enjoyed the 1989 baseball fantasy **Field of Dreams** can meet like-minded souls in surprising numbers at the original movie location, three miles north of Dyersville, which is 25 miles west of Dubuque on US-20. True to the movie's slogan – "if you build it they will come" – crowds still gather on the bleachers to watch phantom games at the edge of the cornfields, and buy souvenirs from two rival family concerns (April–Nov daily 9am–6pm).

Practicalities

The **Iowa Welcome Center** at 300 Main St (daily 9.30am–5.30pm; ☎319/566-4372 or 1-800/798-8844, ⓦwww.traveldubuque.com) is the best place to pick up information on Dubuque. **Internet** access is available at the Carnegie-Stout Public Library, 360 W 11th St, and you can rent a bike at the Bike Shack, 3250 Dodge St (☎319/582-4381; $15 per four hours, $5 each additional hour). As for **places to stay**, try the *Richards House B&B*, 1492 Locust St (☎319/557-1492; ❹), if you want something well-managed and veering toward old-world luxury. Bargain hunters might want to stay at the grand redbrick *Julien Inn*, 200 Main St (☎319/556-4200 or 1-800/798-7098; ❶–❸), which was once owned by mobster Al Capone who used it as his "safe house" when trouble was brewing in Chicago. A major renovation project, set for 2003, should restore its Victorian grandeur. Picturesque **campsites** can be found at Miller Riverview Park, off Greyhound Park Road (☎319/589-4238; $6 per tent site). The *Shot Tower Inn*, at the foot of the cable car at Fourth and Locust streets (☎319/556-1061), serves a standard menu of pizzas and meat dishes.

Cedar Rapids

Seventy miles southwest, **CEDAR RAPIDS**, home of Quaker Oats, is Iowa's industrial leader. In the late 1840s, a meat-packing boom lured thousands of Czechs here. The **Czech Village**, 16th Avenue SW and First Street, features the excellent *Sykora's* bakery, gift shops, traditional houses and a new museum of national costumes and immigrant artifacts (Tues–Sun 9.30am–4.00pm; $5; ☎319/362-8500). The very modern **Museum of Art**, 410 Third Ave SE, boasts a comprehensive collection of paintings by Grant Wood, best known for his depictions of 1930s farmlife (Tues, Wed, Fri & Sat 10am–4pm, Thurs

10am–7pm, Sun noon–4pm; $4).

Cedar Rapids' **CVB** is based at 119 First Ave SE, downtown (Mon–Fri 8am–5pm; ☎319/398-5009 or 1-800/735-5557, ⓦwww.cedar-rapids.com). For reasonably priced **rooms**, there's the *Best Western Cooper's Mill*, 100 F Ave NW (☎319/366-5323 or 1-800/858-5511; ➌).

The Amana Colonies

The **Amana Colonies** spread from the intersection of Hwy-151 and Hwy-220, midway between Cedar Rapids and Iowa City. They were founded in 1855 by the **Community of True Inspiration**, pacifist German refugees (not linked to the Amish or Mennonites) who believed that God spoke through prophets – themselves, for example – rather than ordained ministers. Members led a simple, collective lifestyle: each family lived in its own home, but they all ate together and shared profits from the farms. During the Depression, communal ownership became increasingly difficult to maintain, and in 1932 stock was redistributed among all the adults. However, they did keep up their commitment to close family ties, a sense of community and religious principles. On Sunday mornings, you can still see women church members wearing the traditional black cap, shawl and apron, with men dressed in equally sombre attire. Church services for visitors take place at 10am every Sunday in Middle Amana.

The Amana Colonies today, consisting of seven separate villages set in an immaculate, serene valley, feel like a cross between a ski resort with no mountains and a reservation for Midwestern pioneers. Their prosperity is very evident, though as well as tasteful clapboard houses standing on well-groomed lawns, and neat plank fences dividing rolling meadows, you'll also come across factories, pizza parlors and even a golf course. It's geared less for families and more toward Iowan couples on a weekend getaway. The twee streets of the largest village, **AMANA**, are lined with restaurants and craft shops, a brewery, several wineries and a woolen mill – plus a small and somewhat self-congratulatory **Museum of History** (Mon–Sat 10am–5pm, April–Nov also Sun noon–5pm; $5). Picturesque and less commercialized **HOMESTEAD**, three miles south of Amana, is enhanced by a 3.5-mile walking trail around a dam on a scenic bend of the Iowa River, built centuries ago by Indians to concentrate fish into one area and thus allow them to be caught more easily.

Practicalities

Conventional addresses are seldom used in the Amana Colonies, but points of interest are well signposted. The **visitor center**, near the junction of Hwy-151 and Hwy-220 (Mon–Sat 9am–5pm, Sun 10am–5pm; ☎319/622-7622 or 1-800/245-5465, ⓦwww.amanacolonies.com), hosts evening **theater** five nights a week ($19.50) and has details of **B&Bs** such as *Judy's Guest Haus* (☎319/622-3599; ➌), a restored 1890 colony home in the heart of Amana. Across the road from the visitor center are **tent spaces** at the *Amana Colonies RV Park* (☎319/622-7616; $10 per tent site).

Probably the most compelling reason to visit the colonies is their undeniably excellent old-style German food. Apple-cheeked serving staff at the *Amana Barn Restaurant* (☎319/622-3214) in Amana village dish up huge portions of country ham, beef schnitzel and the like, with pickled baby vegetables; for a lighter snack, call in at *Hahn's Hearth Oven Bakery* in Middle Amana (☎319/622-3439). South Amana's *Market Place Restaurant* (☎319/622-3225) offers sausages galore. As alcohol is not proscribed, some eating establishments, like the *Ronnenberg Restaurant and Bar* (☎319/622-3641), are also popular for locally produced wine.

Iowa City

IOWA CITY, on I-80 55 miles west of the Mississippi, is refreshingly young at heart. The restored gold-domed **Old Capitol** is a reminder of its days as state capital, before government was transferred to the more central Des Moines. Residents were placated by getting the University of Iowa instead. The arty shops and sidewalk cafés of the compact downtown touch the east end of campus, but its red and gray buildings, closeted by tall dark trees, remain aloof from the rest of the town. About 12 miles east of Iowa City, the tiny Quaker town of West Branch attracts a steady stream of traffic from I-80 for its **Herbert Hoover Library & Museum** (daily 9am–5pm; $2). Informative exhibits and a documentary film cover Hoover's youthful adventures in China, his presidential victory and subsequent disgrace when the nation blamed him for the Great Depression, and his comeback after WWII as the leader of the European humanitarian relief effort. A walking tour includes Hoover's birthplace, a replica of his father's blacksmith shop and the Friends Meetinghouse where he attended Sunday services.

Greyhound stops at 404 E College St, just off downtown. The **CVB** is at 408 First Ave in Coralville, a mile northeast of downtown (☎319/337-6592 or 1-800/283-6592, ⊛www.icccvb.org). The Iowa City Public Library, 123 S Linn St. has **internet** access.

Iowa House is a comfortable central **hotel** in the Union building, beside the river on Madison Street (☎319/335-3513; ❸). To the west, inexpensive **motels** in Coralville include a very clean and good-value *Super 8*, 611 First Ave (☎319/337-8388; ❸). The Coralville Park, three miles north of I-80 at exit 244 (☎319/338-3543), is a good place to cast a fishing line, has a Devonian-era fossil bed and offers grassy **tent sites** for $8. Bargain **food** is easy to find, be it soup in a sourbread bowl at *Quinton's*, 215 E Washington St (☎319/354-7074); the pastries and espressos served on long comfortable sofas at *Java House*, nearby at 211 E Washington St; or the burgers at *Micky's*, 11 S Dubuque St (☎319/338-6860), a friendly, dimly lit Irish bar.

Central and western Iowa

Pigs outnumber people in central Iowa. The only city among the cornfields, state capital **Des Moines** struggles to lift the monotony, and many visitors may prefer the college town of **Ames**. The humdrum west has little to offer.

Des Moines

DES MOINES, near the center of Iowa amid tree-covered hills at the confluence of the sluggish Des Moines and Raccoon rivers, owes its origins to a military fort set up in 1843. It had already grown into a trading center for farmers by the time the eighteen-year-old Frederick Hubbell arrived in 1855; within a decade he had founded the Equitable Life and Insurance Corporation to service their need for investment capital. Other companies soon realized the potential of agrarian business, and today the city is the world's third largest **insurance** center, behind London and Hartford, Connecticut. Illustrious former denizens of Des Moines include **Ronald Reagan**, who started out as a sportscaster on Radio WHO, and **John Wayne**, born and raised in nearby Winterset.

Arrival and information

Des Moines' Greyhound station is just northwest of downtown at 1107 Keosauqua Way. From the very efficient transfer depot at Sixth Avenue and Walnut Street, MTA **buses** (℡515/283-8100) run practically everywhere in the city. The **visitor center** is at 405 6th Ave, Suite 201 (Mon–Fri 8.30am–5pm; ℡515/286-4960 or 1-800/451-2625, ⓦwww.seedesmoines.com).

Accommodation

Downtown Des Moines caters mostly for insurance company business, but still offers some fairly inexpensive **places to stay**. You can **camp** in summer at the *Iowa State Fairgrounds Campgrounds*, E 30th Street and Grand Avenue (℡515/262-3111; $12). Better is the *Walnut Woods State Park*, off Hwy-35 (exit 68), where tent sites are $9.

Best Western Starlite Village 929 3rd St ℡515/282-5251. Reasonably priced downtown rooms. ❹

Hotel Fort Des Moines 1000 Walnut Ave at 10th St ℡515/243-1161 or 1-800/532-1466. Exquisite, historical downtown gem with old-world elegance and exemplary service. The indoor swimming pool/spa area won awards for its tasteful design. Highly recommended. ❹–❻

Motel 6 4817 Fleur Drive ℡515/287-6364. Clean rooms near the airport. ❷

YMCA 101 Locust St at 1st Ave ℡515/288-0131. Slightly faded, men-only downtown rooms for $25; weekly rates available. ID required (passport or social security card only). ❶

YWCA 717 Grand Ave ℡515/244-8961. Clean, dorm-style rooms for women in a safe part of downtown; $10 per bed per night with discount for weekly stays. ❶

The City

The steel-and-glass skyline of **downtown** Des Moines, most of which shot up during the 1980s, is testimony to its ever-growing insurance trade. Towering above all is the boxy, 44-story **801 Grand** building, headquarters of the Principal Financial Company. For such a fast-track financial center, the streets are curiously empty; pedestrians instead use the **Skywalk**, a three-mile network of air-conditioned corridors linking twenty blocks of offices, banks, parking lots, restaurants, hotels and movie theaters.

Most businesses stand on the west bank of the Des Moines River, which cuts downtown in two. In 1857, a group of speculators attempted to shift the commercial hub to the east side by bribing commissioners to site the **state capitol** at E Ninth Street and Grand Avenue (they apparently offered more than the Westsiders were willing to dish out). Their hopes of huge spin-offs were dashed when the nationwide financial crash later that same year saw property prices collapse. As a result, the five-domed Italian Renaissance-style mass, on the crest of a steep hill, is now detached from the heart of the city (Mon–Fri 8am–4.30pm, Sat & Sun 8am–4pm; free; call for tour times ℡515/281-5591). A short walk downhill, displays in the futuristic pink-and-brown **State of Iowa Historical Building** (Tues–Sat 9am–4.30pm, Sun noon–4.30pm; free) at E Sixth and Locust streets, cover Indian civilization, pioneer times and the development of Iowan farming, along with plenty of solemn portraits of former governors.

Three miles west, the impressive **Des Moines Art Center**, in a leafy suburb on 4700 Grand Ave (Tues, Wed, Fri & Sat 11am–4pm, Thurs 11am–9pm, Sun noon–4pm; free), is housed in a trio of buildings designed by world renowned architects Eliel Saarinen, I.M. Pei and Richard Meier. Works by Matisse, Picasso and Renoir stand alongside twentieth-century Americans such as Wood, Hopper and O'Keeffe. The most dynamic exhibits are in the Meier wing, and include a gigantic and disturbing Anselm Kiefer canvas.

Eating, drinking and nightlife

That Iowans **eat** well is reflected in the quality – and quantity – of food on offer in Des Moines' restaurants.

Buzzard Billy's 100 Court Ave ☏515/280-6060. Offers good Cajun cuisine, including alligator dishes; catfish, shrimp and oyster meals are also a specialty. It's packed on Thursdays for "Crappy Beer Night."

Java Joe's 214 4th St ☏515/288-5282. Late-closing coffee bar and sandwich place attached to an artist's gallery, featuring live entertainment at weekends. Internet access available. Open until 11:30pm on weekdays, 1am on weekends.

Papa's Planet 208 3rd St ☏515/284-0901. This bar/nightclub is a favorite weekend gathering place for young locals, with guitar bands at low cover charges and an outdoor street patio.

Spaghetti Works 310 Court Ave ☏515/243-2195. Spacious Italian outfit with original interior decor (it has variously served as a glove factory, hat millinary and fruit market). The all-you-can-eat pasta dishes from $5 are great value.

Stella's Blue Sky Diner 400 Locust St, in the Capitol Square building ☏515/246-1953. Kitsch diner decked out in lurid pinks, turquoises and yellows. Wash down burgers and fries ($4) with divine chocolate, peanut butter and banana malts. A must for lunch, but be prepared for long lines. Mon–Sat 8am–6pm.

Around Des Moines

Thirty miles north of Des Moines, **AMES** is the home of Iowa State University. Smaller and slightly less trendy than Iowa City, it's still a lively little community (by Iowan standards at least). The **visitor center**, 1601 Golden Aspen Drive, Suite 110 (☏515/232-4032 or 1-800/288-7470, ⊕www.acvb.ames.ia.us), can advise on concerts and area attractions. **Room** rates are reasonable out at the *Super 8*, I-35 and Hwy-30 (☏515/232-6510; ❸), three miles from campus; *Godfather's Pizza*, 414 Lincoln Way (☏515/232-9000), is popular.

Ten miles west of downtown Des Moines (I-80 exit 125), the **Living History Farms** in Urbandale (May–Oct daily 9am–5pm; $10) trace the evolution

---

The Bridges of Madison County

The fortunes of Winterset, the county town of Madison County, have taken an unexpected turn for the better in the years since the publication of Robert Waller's bestselling tearjerker **The Bridges of Madison County**. Fans attracted by the 1995 movie version, which was filmed in and around Winterset and starred Clint Eastwood and Meryl Streep, will be delighted to find everything looking just as it did on screen. *National Geographic* may never have published a feature about them – fictional photographer Robert Kincaid's assignment in the book and film – but there really are six (out of an original nineteen) nineteenth-century **covered bridges** in the immediate neighborhood, of which the two that were most prominent in both book and film are most worth seeing. None charges for admission or has formal opening hours. For a full list and **driving map**, drop in at Winterset's visitor center on Courthouse Square.

Roseman Bridge, where Kincaid was guided by housewife Francesca Johnson, crosses the Middle River around six miles southwest of town, and can be reached via a bewildering succession of country roads (head south from Hwy-92 eight miles west of Winterset if you want to follow the undulating dirt track seen during the credits). Built on this spot in 1883, and supposedly haunted, it was restored in 1992 at a cost of over $150,000, only to be thoroughly aged again for the movie. It's far too frail to support vehicles, but you can walk out on its knotted planks, and decipher the ever-multiplying sets of carved initials on its peeling timbers.

The sturdier **Cedar Bridge**, the only one still used by traffic, was moved in 1921 from what is now Hwy-169, and today stands to one side of Hwy-G4R, a couple of miles northeast of town. The scene of Kincaid's and Johnson's final tryst, it is the focus of a small county park and picnic area.

of agriculture on the plains. Self-guided tours lead from the oval bark homes of an eighteenth-century Iowan settlement, through an 1850s homestead, to a look at the high-tech methods of today. If you want to continue the rural theme, eat colossal portions of meat loaf and chops in the *Iowa Machine Shed Restaurant* (☎515/270-6818), or stay in the country-style *Comfort Suites Hotel* (☎515/276-1126; ❹); both are next to the farm entrance.

Winterset

Until Robert Waller's *The Bridges of Madison County* changed everything, sleepy, rundown **WINTERSET**, 25 miles southwest of Des Moines, seemed a long way off the beaten track. Its one tourist attraction was the modest former home of the local pharmacist at 216 S Second St, run as a museum as a tribute to his son, Marion Robert Morrison (daily 10am–4.30pm; $2.50). Born in 1907, he grew up to become Hollywood hardman John Wayne. His first lead role was in 1930 but real stardom, as the Ringo Kid in John Ford's *Stagecoach*, didn't come for another nine years. Three decades later, Wayne claimed his only Oscar as Rooster Cogburn, the drunken one-eyed marshal in *True Grit*. Among the photos, personal belongings and mementos is a glowing personal endorsement of "the Duke" from his buddy Ronald Reagan, who shared his political views, if not perhaps his acting abilities.

These days Winterset's **visitor center**, on Courthouse Square in the heart of town (Mon–Fri 9am–5pm, Sat 9am–4pm, Sun 11am–4pm; ☎515/462-1185 or 1-800/298-6119, ⓦwww.madisoncounty.com), has become accustomed to handling inquiries from all over the world about the locations for Waller's tale, including hundreds of couples wanting to marry on the bridges themselves. If you don't want to go that far, you can drive out to view the covered bridges (see box opposite), or at least have a meal in the old-style *Northside Café*, a few doors along from the visitor center, where Clint was made to feel decidedly uncomfortable in the movie. You can also visit the late 1800s homestead that was used as Francesca Johnson's farm in the movie at 3271 130th St (May–Oct 10am–6pm or by appointment; $5; ☎515/981-5268). A good time to visit Winterset is the second full weekend of October for the **Bridge Festival** featuring local bands and artists. Accommodation possibilities nearby include the *Village View Motel*, Hwy-92 E (☎515/462-1218 or 1-800/862-1218; ❸), and *A Step Away*, 104 W Court St (☎515/462-5956; ❹), a snug little B&B. There is a small **campground** at the Winterset City Park on the east end of town (☎515/462-3258; $8). Behind the CVB, at 222 N John Wayne Drive, is the computer store i-rule.net, which has **free internet** access.

Nebraska

Hell, I thought I was dead too. Turns out I was just in Nebraska.

Gene Hackman in *Unforgiven*

Though modern transcontinental travelers tend to see **NEBRASKA** in much the same light as did the early pioneers, heading west during the Gold Rush –

as just another dreary expanse of prairie to get through as fast as possible – this flat and sparsely populated state in fact encompasses quite a few places of interest. However, its most appealing cities, commercial **Omaha** and the livelier state capital, **Lincoln**, are separated by a good three hundred miles of underwhelming, livestock-rearing flatlands from the western Panhandle, where the landscape finally erupts into giant sand hills and valleys, broken by towering rocky columns and hemmed in by sheer-faced buttes.

Western Nebraska was still embroiled in vicious and bloody battles against Native Americans long after the east had been settled; from the first serious uprising in 1854, it was 36 years before the US Army could make white control unchallengeable. Close to the South Dakota state line, **Fort Robinson**, where Crazy Horse was murdered, remains one of the West's most evocative historic sites.

Without navigable rivers, Nebraska had to rely on the **railroads** to help populate the land. During the 1870s and 1880s, rail companies, encouraged by grants that allowed them to accumulate one-sixth of the state, laid down such a comprehensive network of tracks that virtually every farmer was within a day's cattle drive of the nearest halt. Thus the buffalo-hunting country of the Sioux and Pawnee was turned into high-yield farmland, which today has few rivals in terms of **beef** production.

Getting around Nebraska

Omaha **airport** offers the best domestic links, though planes from other cities in the region also fly to Lincoln. Several Greyhound **buses** traverse I-80 each day on the coast-to-coast marathon, stopping at all the major towns. Amtrak **trains**, traveling through the night, follow a similar route and call at Omaha, Lincoln, Hastings, Holdredge and McCook. **Driving** on I-80 can get tedious; if you're not in a rush, Hwy-2 is a good alternative.

Eastern Nebraska

The silt-laden **Missouri River** separates Nebraska from Iowa and Missouri to the east. There are few natural ports on this stretch, and **Omaha** remains the only riverfront community of any size. **Lincoln**, 58 miles southwest, is the state's capital and seat of its university.

Omaha

Although **OMAHA**, Nebraska's largest and most easterly city, is visibly a prosperous place, with a great zoo, several museums and a lively entertainment district, the atmosphere remains sedate and predominantly suburban. As a major terminus on the first transcontinental railroad, Omaha made a logical alternative to distant Chicago as a marketplace for Wyoming and Nebraska ranchers to sell their herds of cattle. By 1900 massive stockyards had spread along the southern edge of town, and the city still handles well over one million head of livestock per year.

In **downtown** Omaha you'll find good bars and cafés along the cobbled streets of the **Old Market** district, plus interesting specialist shops such as the Antiquarian Bookstore, 1215 Harney St (☎402/341-8077), packed with dusty volumes (and local bohemians). The nearby **Heartland Park of America**, at Eighth and Douglas streets – ideal for a picnic – holds a huge, water-blasting fountain. Train buffs will be impressed with the **Durham Western Heritage**

Museum, converted from the Union Pacific Railroad station, at 801 S 10th St. (Tues–Sat 10am–5pm; $5). Old train cars and huge model train sets are featured alongside a gallery of Omaha history. Behind its pink-marble Art Deco exterior, the **Joslyn Art Museum**, 2200 Dodge St (Tues–Sat 10am–4pm, Sun noon–4pm; $6, free Sat before noon), contains an eclectic selection of Indian art and twentieth-century American paintings.

The **Great Plains Black Museum**, in the city's predominantly black north side at 2213 Lake St (Tues–Sat 10am–2pm; free), presents the history of African American people on the prairies. One stimulating section focuses on blacks in the frontier army: where recently freed slaves, who could find no work in the Deep South after the Civil War, were often sent as advance parties into the most hostile and dangerous regions. It was Native American warriors who first called them "**buffalo soldiers**," because of their tightly curled hair and the color of their skin.

Malcolm X was born in Omaha in May 1925, though his family moved to Michigan immediately thereafter, in the face of Ku Klux Klan death threats to his father, a preacher who followed the back-to-Africa teachings of Marcus Garvey. Omaha tourist authorities don't promote his birthsite, at 34th and Evans streets (formerly 3448 Pinkney St), perhaps because the residents of the surrounding neighborhood use it as a dumping ground for old TVs, bent car parts, shredded furniture and other debris. Years of debate over how to develop the site have yielded a solitary placard, hidden behind some trees, offering a brief biography. By way of contrast, the lavish birthplace of President **Gerald R. Ford**, at 32nd St and Woolworth Avenue, is also open to the public; he too moved to Michigan as an infant, after his parents separated (Tues–Fri 1pm–4pm; $2).

The **Henry Doorly Zoo**, 3701 S 10th St (daily 9.30am–5pm; $8), rightfully considers itself one of the best zoos in America. It started off with two buffalo borrowed from Buffalo Bill; now there's a gigantic free-flying aviary, some rare white Siberian tigers, a magnificent bear canyon, and the large Kingdoms of the Seas aquarium.

Twenty-nine miles southwest of Omaha at exit 426 on I-80 is a welcome diversion for those seeking relief from pioneer museums. The **Strategic Air and Space Museum** (daily 9am–5pm; $7) is inside two huge hangers containing giant 1950s- and 1960s-era war planes designed and built by the Martin Bomber Company of Omaha. Films, photos and exhibits concentrate on WWII and the Cold War, the latter highlighted by various weapons including an Atlas-D Intercontinental Ballistic Missile, located outside the museum entrance.

Practicalities

Omaha's Greyhound station is at 1601 Jackson St; Amtrak **trains** depart very late at night, and arrive long before the city wakes up, at 1003 S Ninth St. Both depots are well placed for downtown; however, local public transportation is poor.

The **CVB** is at 6800 Mercy Rd, exit 459 from I-80, near the old race track (Mon–Fri 8.30am–4.30pm; ☎402/444-4660 or 1-866/937-6624, ⓦwww .visitomaha.com). There's also a **welcome center** for Nebraska as a whole, just off I-80 exit 454, across from the zoo at Tenth Street and Deer Park Boulevard (May–Oct daily 9am–5pm; ☎402/595-3990). **Internet** access is available at the *Latte Lounge* at 15418 Weir St (☎402/891-6633), Borders bookstore at 72nd St and Dodge St (☎402/393-5576), and the main library at 215 S 15th St (402/444-4800). Hotel rates are good, except in mid-June when the college baseball World Series comes to town. **Rooms** at the circular, almost cute, and certainly pretty unusual *Satellite Motel*, 6006 L St (☎402/733-7373; ❷–❸), come clean and at good prices. The *Riverview Garden B&B*, 9641 N 29th St (☎402/455-4623; ❸), has comfortable rooms in a quiet neighborhood that overlooks the Missouri River. The well-kept *Best Western White House Inn* at 305 N Fort Crook Rd (☎402/293-1600 or 1-800/962-4601; ❸) offers good rates about five miles south of downtown. Located next to the SAC Museum, the **Eugene T. Mahoney State Park** (☎402/944-2523) has **campsites** ($7), cabins and a lodge (❸/❹), in a family oriented setting.

The **Old Market** district, centered on Tenth and Howard streets, has the liveliest **restaurants** and **bars**. The *Indian Oven*, 1010 Howard St (☎402/342-4856), a superb Asian restaurant, features paneer and vegetable dishes on its extensive menu. *M's Pub*, at 422 S 11th St (☎402/342-2550), serves renowned baked casseroles and a long list of salads, while *The Upstream Brewing Company*, 514 S 11th St (☎402/344-0200), has excellent beers and a standard American menu. Whether you fancy terrific desserts or a light meal, the *Garden Café*, 1212 Harney St (☎402/422-1574), won't break the bank. Omaha is a bar town, with not much in the way of dance clubs, but *Mr Toad's*, 1002 Howard St (☎402/345-4488), is a reliable **jazz venue** with good jam sessions on Sundays.

Lincoln

Tiny Rochester was selected to be state capital in 1867 – on the condition that it change its name to **LINCOLN** in honor of the recently assassinated president. Such was the disappointment in the territorial seat of government, Omaha, that state officials had to smuggle documents, books and office furniture out of the city in the middle of the night to avoid armed gangs.

Lincoln, 58 miles southwest of Omaha, now serves as an oasis of culture for a large chunk of the plains. At night, when the students emerge, its compact downtown comes into its own. Of its alphabetical array of broad boulevards, O Street (the subject of Allen Ginsberg's poem *Zero Street*) is the main drag; 13th and 14th streets are packed with bars and places to eat.

Dwarfing the rest of **downtown**, the central tower of the 1932 **Nebraska state capitol**, 1445 K St (Mon–Fri 9am–4pm, Sat 10am–4pm, Sun 1-4pm; tours every half-hour; free), protrudes 400ft into the sky. Topped by a 20ft statue of a sower on a pedestal of wheat and corn, its remarkably phallic appearance – an adventurous departure from the usual architecture of state capitols – has prompted the nickname "penis of the prairies." For once there's no golden dome, and the superb iridescent murals in the foyer are a welcome alternative to old portraits, flags and emblems. From the fourteenth-floor observation deck you can survey the flatness of the surrounding farmland.

Twelve thousand years of life on the plains are covered at the **Museum of Nebraska History**, 15th and P streets (Mon–Fri 9am–4.30pm, Sat 9am–5pm, Sun 1.30–5pm; free), where displays focus on anthropology rather than history. The Elephant Hall, a gallery of towering mammoth, mastodon and four-tusker skeletons, is the highlight of the **University of Nebraska State Museum** at 14th and U streets (Mon–Sat 9.30am–4.30pm, Sun & holidays 1.30-4.30pm; $2). A few blocks away, the **Sheldon Memorial Art Gallery**, 12th and R streets (Tues, Wed & Fri 10am–5pm, Thurs & Sat 10am–5pm & 7–9pm, Sun 2–9pm; free), traces the development of American art, and has a twenty-piece sculpture garden. The 76,000-seater **Memorial Stadium** (tickets ☎402/472-3111 or 1-800/8BIGRED), at the northern end of campus on Vine Street, is where the brutal "Big Red" Cornhuskers invariably thrash the footballing opposition.

Practicalities

Lincoln's Greyhound station is downtown at 940 P St, while Amtrak passes through 201 N 7th St at crazy early-morning hours. Star-Tran (☎402/476-1234) runs good local **buses** (85¢). The **visitor center** is in Lincoln Station, right next to Amtrak (June–Sept Mon–Fri 9am–8pm, Sat 8am–5pm, Sun noon–5pm; rest of year Mon–Fri 9am–6pm, Sat 10am–4pm, Sun noon–5pm; ☎402/434-5348 or 1-800/423-8212, ⊛www.lincoln.org). Except on football weekends, it's easy to find inexpensive **accommodation** out by the airport, off I-80 exit 399 – at the *Inn 4 Less* motel (☎402/475-4511; ❷), for example. Downtown, however, has a shortage of budget rooms: the *Holiday Inn*, 9th and O streets (☎402/475-4011; ❹), is good value; the *HI-Cornerstone* **hostel**, 640 N 16th St (☎402/476-0355; ❶), in a church on the edge of campus, offers basic bunks; members $10, nonmembers $13. The Branched Oak State Park, off Raymond Road from Hwy-79, has tent sites for $3–7; the more expensive sites have showers.

The downtown restaurants tend to be less than compelling, with grills, pizzerias and family diners predominating. *The Oven*, 201 N 8th St (☎402/475-6118), offers Indian cuisine with a range of cheap breads and inventive specials, while the Italian menu at cafeteria-style *Valentino's*, 232 N 13th and Q streets (☎402/475-1501), is fast and well priced. *The Zoo*, 136 N 14th St (☎402/435-8754), attracts big-name jazz and blues acts who drop in en route between Chicago and Kansas City; *Duffy's Bar*, 1412 O St (☎402/474-3543), pulls in a younger crowd and some good rock bands. Across the street at 1329 O St, *O'Rourke's Lounge* (☎402/435-8052) is a lively, well-priced hangout. The **Historic Haymarket District**, down by the Amtrak station, holds a further selection of bars and restaurants, including *The Mill*, at 800 P St, which offers good coffee and **internet** access.

Western Nebraska

After the unerringly flat journey across eastern Nebraska, the far west comes as a refreshing change. In the **Panhandle**, as it's often called, wave upon wave of rumpled sandy hills, thinly coated with prairie grass, back off toward the horizon like a sea in constant turmoil. Early pioneers wrote the area off as unproductive, and it remained barren until massive irrigation work at the start of the twentieth century enabled agricultural settlement. In the northwest the sand hills yield to classic John Ford-style Western scenery: pancake-flat valleys, crisscrossed by dry meandering riverbeds and corraled by crusty, contorted bluffs under the constant shadow of fast-moving clouds. Emigrants on the **Oregon Trail** used the bizarre outcrops which sprout along the way as "road signs" as a way of knowing that their trek across the plains was coming to an end.

Along I-80

Interstate-80 is one of the most popular coast-to-coast routes simply because it's the shortest. Scenery is not its strongest suit, and the central swath through 450 miles of Nebraskan farmland is not always a prospect drivers cherish. If time doesn't matter, then it's better to head northwest at dreary Grand Island, 93 miles west of Lincoln, onto Scenic Hwy-2 (see overleaf) for a lonesome yet exhilarating drive through the Sandhills.

If you stick to I-80, decent pull-off points are few and far between. It's hard to miss the newest attraction at **KEARNEY** – the new Grand Platte River

Road Archway Monument (daily 8am–8pm; $8.50) actually spans the Interstate near exit 272. Exhibits inside tell the story of a transient nation and re-creates the hardships of life on the westward trail. The town of Kearney is pleasant enough and offers a strip of inexpensive restaurants and studenty bars. Just over halfway across the state at exit 177, **NORTH PLATTE** makes a big deal about its **Buffalo Bill Ranch Historical Park** (April–May & Sept–Oct daily 9am–5pm; June–Aug daily 10am–8pm; closed Nov–March; $2.50 per car), another property of the ubiquitous William "Buffalo Bill" Cody. Today the ranch is run by the state, which places more emphasis on history than tacky folklore. Cody's mansion and various barns can be examined and an excellent documentary film shows movie clips of his "Wild West Show" which toured America and Europe for 30 years. The park offers horse rides ($12 per hour) and camping ($3 per night). *The Rambler Motel*, 1420 Rodeo Rd (☎308/532-9290; ❷), has comfortable **rooms** and an outdoor pool, while the authentic Mexican cantina, *La Casita*, at 1911 E Fourth St (☎308/534-8077), boasts an irresistible Elvis room, littered with tacky souvenirs honoring The King.

Thirty miles west, another restaurant sets out to entertain bored drivers, in the one-horse hamlet of **PAXTON**, off exit 145. *Ole's Big Game Lounge & Grill* (☎308/239-4500) serves tasty fried food, with over two hundred wildlife trophies from around the world mounted on walls, cabinets and shelves. Fascinating, but not a place for the animal rights activist.

At **OGALLALA**, twenty miles further along, Old West outlaws were interred at **Boot Hill Cemetery** (10th St and Parkhill Rd; free) in the 1880s. The town sits just nine miles south of "Big Mac" – **Lake McConaughy** reservoir, famous for fishing, water sports and the sandy beaches along its 105 miles of shoreline. From Ogallala, it's 165 miles to Cheyenne, Wyoming, though Sidney (exit 59) takes you into rugged Oregon Trail country (see opposite).

Scenic Hwy-2 and Alliance

Scenic **Hwy-2** meanders and dips for over 330 miles from I-80 to South Dakota's Black Hills. It passes through the **Sandhills** – a mesmerizing landscape carpeted with short-grass prairie and softened by delicate wild flowers and shiny ponds. Apart from a few farmsteads, grain silos and tiny churches, all you're likely to see on the open road are lazing cattle, a few sluggish rivers and the occasional mile-and-a-quarter-long freight train weaving its way through the hills. It's a long, desolate, yet incredibly beautiful drive through an anachronistic corner of the US, where small towns are all spick-and-span and everyone could well know each other's name; **Broken Bow**, 77 miles north of I-80, features one of the neatest town squares in the heartland.

The road dawdles for another 200 miles through scattered villages before drifting into **ALLIANCE** – a nice enough little prairie town, which pulls in over 50,000 visitors per year for its one big attraction. **Carhenge**, two and a half miles north on State Hwy-87, is a rough copy of Stonehenge, made with old cars rather than stone. Erected in a cornfield during a family reunion in 1987, this intriguing collection of Chevys, Cadillacs and Plymouths, painted a brooding battleship grey and tilted at unusual angles, has to be the best picnic site in America's heartland. To some it's an ingenious piece of Pop Art; others view it as great black humor, or an appalling eyesore. After it was built, a few fundamentalist Christians feared it was a Satanic shrine. Certainly, the Nebraska Department of Roads saw nothing amusing about the project. They rapidly declared it a junkyard, and ordered the city of Alliance to remove it, forcing locals to form **Friends of Carhenge**, whose work seems to have secured the monument's future (always open; free).

The helpful downtown **CVB** office, 124 W Third St (☎308/762-1520) provides information and sells Carhenge souvenirs. There is no reason to linger in Alliance, but if you arrive late, try the *Days Inn*, 117 Cody Ave, just off Third Street (☎308/762-8000; ❸), or the *Super 8*, 1419 W Third St (☎308/762-8300; ❷). For **food**, there's *Ken & Dale's*, 123 E Third St (☎308/762-7252), which serves succulent all-day breakfasts and great pecan pancakes.

The Oregon Trail landmarks

Two of the first landmarks encountered by travelers on the **Oregon Trail**, which in western Nebraska paralleled the route of modern US-26, were the lumpy **Courthouse and Jail rocks**, which lie four miles beyond the likeable little town of **Bridgeport**, 36 miles south of Alliance. Fourteen miles west, along Hwy-92, the much-painted and photographed **Chimney Rock** rises almost 500ft above the North Platte River. Although this phallic outcrop's nineteenth-century stature may have been chipped away by erosion and lightning, it remains one of the most recognizable and memorable landmarks in the West.

The twin towns of **GERING** and **SCOTTSBLUFF**, 25 miles further west, are the commercial center for the farmlands of western Nebraska. Southwest of Gering, the rugged 800ft rampart of **Scotts Bluff National Monument** (summer daily 8am–7pm; rest of year daily 8am–5pm; $4 per car) stands like a Nebraskan Gibraltar. Known to the Sioux as Me-a-pa-te ("hill that's hard to get around"), it earned its anglicized name in 1828 after fur trader Hiram Scott was mysteriously found dead at its base. Treks (by foot or shuttle bus) to the top are rewarded with a magnificent view, and the entrance fee includes the absorbing **Oregon Trail Museum**, which relates the experiences of the early emigrants. Just outside Gering, to the southwest, the spiky **Wildcat Hills** hold some delightful vistas and hiking terrain.

Well-kept **rooms** are available in the *Lamplighter American Inn*, 606 E 27th St, Scottsbluff (☎308/632-7108; ❸); the fully licensed *Woodshed*, 18 E 16th St (☎308/635-3684), is the best spot for family-style **food**. The towns' **visitor center** can be found at 1517 Broadway, Scottsbluff (☎308/632-2133).

Fort Robinson State Park

Some eighty miles north of Scottsbluff, just west of Crawford village, **Fort Robinson State Park**, beside 1000ft crenelated cliffs in the inhospitable White River Valley, preserves the spot where the US Army coordinated its campaign to rid the gold-rich Badlands of the native Sioux. Today, it's a cross between a dude ranch and a living history village; a cosmeticization which makes the memories of the obliteration of an entire way of native life all the more poignant.

Restored fort buildings contain period furnishings, and there are two small museums. A simple stone marks the spot where **Crazy Horse** was killed; the tour train (three per day; $3) acknowledges it with a mere ten-second halt. Good-value **horseback rides** pass some wondrously weird rock formations, and *Fort Robinson Lodge* (☎308/665-2900; ❹) has nice **rooms** as well as bargain cottages; the Lodge's **restaurant** serves cheap **buffalo tacos** and other beef and bison dishes. There is good **camping** for $8 per person, or you could really rough it, at the beautiful but remote Toadstool Geological Park, 25 miles to the north.

The town of **CHADRON**, 23 miles east of Fort Robinson, is worth a visit principally for the small **Museum of the Fur Trade**, four miles east on US-20 (summer daily 8am–5pm; $2.50) – a valuable historical archive illustrating the unique barter system that operated between fur traders and local Native Americans.

Crazy Horse

The life of Oglala Sioux leader **Crazy Horse** is shrouded in confusion, misinterpretation and controversy. So thoroughly did the most enigmatic figure in Plains Indian history avoid contact with whites outside battle that no photograph or even sketch of him exists; unlike other Indian chiefs, he refused to visit Washington, DC or talk to reporters.

Crazy Horse earned his title as a youth, after he single-handedly charged rival Arapahoe and took two scalps. The finest moment in a brilliant military career came in June 1876, when he led a thousand warriors in inflicting a stinging defeat on the superior forces of General George Crook at the Battle of the Rosebud River. Just eight days later Crazy Horse headed the attack at the Battle of Little Bighorn, where Custer and his entire company were killed (see p.903).

After Little Bighorn, US Army efforts to round up the Indians redoubled. In May 1877, Crazy Horse surprised friend and foe alike by leading nine hundred of his people into Fort Robinson. They gave up their weapons and Crazy Horse, keen to stay in his native land (unlike Sitting Bull, who had retreated to Canada), demanded that the buffalo grounds along the Powder River should remain in Indian hands. Tensions at the army camp rose after a rumor went around the barracks that the Sioux chief had come to murder General Crook. Crazy Horse was arrested on September 5, 1877; during a tussle outside the fort jail, he was bayoneted three times, dying the next morning.

Quite why this undefeated warrior should have surrendered without a fight, and whether he fell victim to a deliberate assassination, remains unclear. What is certain is that his death signaled the closing chapter of the Indian Wars. The Oglala Sioux were forcibly moved to the poor hunting country of Missouri, and settlers immediately swept in their thousands into western Nebraska, South Dakota, Wyoming and Montana.

Crazy Horse, so one story goes, was buried by his family in an unmarked grave in an out-of-the-way creek called **Wounded Knee** – the very place where thirteen years later three hundred Sioux men, women and children were slaughtered in the bloody finale to over half a century of barbarism (see p.825).

South Dakota

The wide-open spaces of the Great Plains roll away to infinity to either side of I-90 in **SOUTH DAKOTA**. Though the land is more green and fertile east of the Missouri River, vast numbers of high-season visitors speed straight on through to the spectacular southwest, site of the **Badlands** and the adjacent **Black Hills** – two of the most dramatic, mysterious and legend-impacted tracts of land in the US. For whites, they encapsulate a wagonload of American notions about heritage and the taming of the West. To Native Americans they are ancient, spiritually resonant places.

The science-fiction severity of the Badlands resists fitting into easy tourist tastes. The bigger, more user-friendly Black Hills, home of that most patriotic of icons, **Mount Rushmore**, have been subjected to greater exploitation (dozens of physical, historical and downright commercial attractions, and the mining of gold and other metals), but encourage more active exploration (via hiking trails, mountain lakes and streams, and scenic highways).

Time and Hollywood have mythologized the larger-than-life personalities for whom the Dakota Territory served as a stomping ground: **Custer** and **Crazy Horse** battled here for supremacy over the plains, while **Wild Bill Hickok** and **Calamity Jane** were denizens of the once-notorious Gold Rush town of **Deadwood**. On a more contemporary note, Kevin Costner's award-winning **Dances with Wolves** (1990), shot in the state, boosted South Dakota's tourism image, though Costner's own ambitious development plans for the Black Hills have meant that he himself has fallen foul of the Sioux.

Sioux tribes dominated the plains from the eighteenth century, having gradually been pushed westwards from the Great Lakes by the encroaching whites. To these nomadic hunters, unlike the gun-toting Christian settlers and federal politicians, the concept of owning the earth was utterly alien. They fought hard to stay free: the Sioux are the only Indian nation to have defeated the United States in war and forced it to sign a treaty (in 1868) favorable to them. Even so, they were compelled, in the face of a gung-ho gold rush, to relinquish the sacred Black Hills, and ultimately the choice lay between death or confinement on reservations. For decades their history and culture were outlawed; until the 1940s it was illegal to teach or even speak their language, Lakota. More Sioux live on South Dakota's six reservations now than dwelled in the whole state during pioneer days, but their prospects are often grim. Nowhere is the legacy of injustice better symbolized than at **Wounded Knee**, on the Oglala Sioux **Pine Ridge Reservation** – scene of the infamous 1890 massacre by the US Army, and also of a prolonged "civil disturbance" by the radical American Indian Movement in 1973.

Today Native American traditions are celebrated by music, dance and socializing at **powwows**, held in summer on the reservations; the state tourist office can supply dates and locations. Apart from powwows, South Dakota summers are taken up with historical celebrations, volksmarches (a friendly sort of community walking exercise), ethnic festivals and rodeos. The 200th anniversary of the **Lewis and Clark expedition** will be celebrated between 2003 and 2006; check ⓦ www.travelsd.com for event details. The state has 170 parks and recreation areas for hikers and campers. In winter, downhill **skiing** is limited to Terry Peak and Deer Mountain outside **Lead** in the Black Hills; cross-country skiing and snowmobiling are more prevalent.

Getting around South Dakota

You'll be hard put to see much of South Dakota without a **car**. Amtrak routes bypass the state entirely, while Jefferson (☎1-800/444-6287) **bus** lines serve points between Rapid City and Sioux Falls, sites of the two major **airports**. Powder River buses (☎1-800/442-3682) serve Black Hills I-90 towns such as Rapid City, Spearfish and Sturgis, as well as making the two-hour trip to Cheyenne, Wyoming.

East of the Missouri

For tourists, little in eastern or central South Dakota can be considered essential. **Sioux Falls**, the state's biggest city, is faceless but handy. As one of the country's quietest and smallest capitals, **Pierre** has its charms. **Mitchell** has a few curiosities, while **Yankton**, comfortably ensconced beside the Missouri across from Nebraska, is a gem-like historic town draped with parks and picket fences, with the excellent Lewis and Clark Recreation Area on its doorstep. The town marks the start of an alternative cross-state route to I-90, trundling through nearby **Vermillion**, home to the exceptional Shrine to Music Museum (where the collection of musical instruments from all over the world now includes one of Bill Clinton's saxophones), plus the Rosebud and Pine Ridge reservations. About sixty miles northwest of Sioux Falls, **De Smet** is known as "Little Town on the Prairie" thanks to the autobiographical books of Laura Ingalls Wilder. You can tour eighteen sites she mentions for smatterings of history, pretty scenery and homely pride. **Chamberlain**, where I-90 shoots down a steep bluff and over the Missouri River, provides the most spectacular vistas in the eastern part of the state and is home to the worthwhile Akta Lakota Museum and Cultural Center.

Mitchell

MITCHELL makes a mildly diverting stop on the seemingly endless drive along I-90. **The Corn Palace** at 604 N Main St (summer daily 8am–9pm; winter Mon–Fri 8am–5pm; free) has been pegged as "the world's largest bird-feeder"; the first Corn Palace was built in 1892 to encourage settlement and to display local agricultural products. Topped with brightly painted onion-shaped domes and minarets, this kitsch Moorish transplant to the Corn Belt is decorated annually (at a cost of about $125,000) with large murals depicting farming and other outdoor scenes. The artists' materials consist exclusively of native corn, grains and grasses of varying natural colors; further examples of such rural folk art are found inside. Mitchell's **visitor center**, 601 N Main St (Mon–Fri 9am–5pm; ☎605/996-5567 or 1-800/257-CORN, ⓦ www.cornpalace.com), is across the street, and the *Hard Drive Central* internet café (318 N Main St; 20¢ per minute) is two blocks south.

Other places where you can while away time in Mitchell include a gallery devoted to a Yanktonai Sioux painter; a surprisingly engaging museum of dolls, including a salt-carved Shirley Temple; a pioneer museum; and a prehistoric Native American village. Both the *Best Western*, 1001 S Burr St (☎605/996-5536; ❸) and *Super 8* (☎605/996-9678; ❸) **motels** lie just off I-90 at exit 332. The *Lake Mitchell Campground*, one mile north of town on Hwy-37 (☎605/995-8457), has grassy tent sites ($11) that overlook the water. The railroad-themed *Depot*, 210 S Main St (☎605/996-9417), is a fun place to grab a meal.

Pierre

Straggling along the east bank of the Missouri River at the center of South Dakota, **PIERRE** is the second smallest and by far the least sophisticated of all the US state capitals. With none of the plush hotels or fancy restaurants catering to power-broking politicos that you find in other capital cities, Pierre (pronounced "peer") is instead a typical South Dakota town, whose 15,000 residents do their best to ignore the fact that it's the seat of state government.

Apart from the black-domed **Capitol** itself, which sits in a pleasant park at the northeast edge of downtown and is open for tours (daily 8am–10pm; free), there's not a lot to detain you here. One exception is the worthwhile **Cultural Heritage Center** (Mon–Fri 9am–4.30pm, Sat & Sun 1–4.30pm; $3), located high on a hill, half a mile north of the capitol, and modeled on traditional Plains Indian dwellings. Repository for the usual barrage of pioneer implements and prehistoric artifacts, the museum is one of few to do more than pay lip service to the state's significant Native American cultures.

Pier 347, 347 S Pierre St (☎605/224-2400), offers creative bagels and lattes, while the fast-food chains line up along Sioux Avenue, which also holds the bulk of the town's **motels**, including the clean and comfortable *Governor's Inn*, 700 W Sioux Ave (☎605/224-4200 or 1-800/341-8000; ❸). Rollins Library at 1000 Church St near the Capitol has **internet** access. The **visitor center** is at 108 E Missouri St (☎605/224-7361 or 1-800/962-2034, ⓦwww.pier-rechamber.com).

The Badlands

The White River **BADLANDS** could be considered a pocket-sized cousin to Arizona's Grand Canyon. Beyond the family resemblance, what's most impressive about the "Badlandscape" is not its scale, as at the Canyon, but rather its sheer strangeness. More than 35 million years ago this area of southwest South Dakota was a saltwater sea; later it became a marsh, into which sank the remains of such prehistoric mammals as sabre-toothed cats and three-toed horses, to be covered with white volcanic ash. Drying as it evolved, the terrain became unable to support the deep-rooted shrubs or trees that might have preserved it, and over the last few million years erosion has slowly eaten away layers of sand, silt, ash, mud and gravel, to reveal rippling gradations of earth tones and pastel colors. The crumbly earth is carved into all manner of shapes: pinnacles, precipices, pyramids, knobs, cones, ridges, gorges or, if you're feeling poetic, lunar sandcastles and cathedrals. The Sioux dubbed these incredible contortions of nature *Mako Sica*, literally "land bad"; early French trappers echoed that with *Mauvaises Terres à Traverser*, or "bad lands to travel across"; they have also been aptly described as "hell with the fires out." Despite this daunting reputation, animals such as bighorn sheep, mule deer and prairie dogs are at home here, while on average a million visitors pass through each year.

The most spectacular formations can be found within the **Badlands National Park**, particularly its northern sector, while the southern stretches are encompassed by the poverty-stricken Pine Ridge Indian Reservation. Clean-cut **Wall**, just a few miles north of the park boundaries, is the most visited commercial center in the region.

Badlands National Park

About one-tenth of the Badlands – the most amazing parts – were declared a national park (open year-round) in the 1970s. Its two most accessible entrances are off I-90 at exits 131 (northeast entrance) and 109–110 (at the town of Wall), and connected by the forty-mile paved loop of Hwy-240, peppered with scenic overlooks. Visitors can backpack or climb just about anywhere; among the best of the marked **hiking trails** are the Door Trail, a half-hour loop that enters the eerie wasteland through a natural "doorway" in the rock pinnacles ten miles south of the northeast entrance, and the even shorter Fossil Exhibit Trail, ten miles further on. The Badlands' rainbow colors are most vibrant at dawn, dusk and just after rainfall.

Adjoining the **Ben Reifel visitor center** (June–Aug daily 7am–8pm; rest of year daily 8am–5pm; $10 per vehicle for seven days; ☎605/433-5361), five miles from the northeast entrance, is the only in-park **accommodation** option. *Cedar Pass Lodge*, which has its own restaurant (mid-March to Oct; ☎605/433-5460; cabins ❸, cottages ❹), is operated by the Oglala Sioux, who use it as a base for assorted tours into the Pine Ridge Reservation (see below), and offer all-inclusive lodging-and-tour packages. Another **visitor center** – White River (June–Aug only, daily 10am–4pm) – stands on Hwy-27 in the less visited and less spectacular southern end of the park. A handful of seasonal **campgrounds** operate both in the park and in Wall. Short scenic **helicopter** rides leave from outside the northeast entrance (from $15; ☎605/433-5322).

Wall

The town of **WALL**, eight miles north of the Badlands, may look like nothing special, yet thanks to **Wall Drug**, begun modestly in 1931 as a pharmacy and veterinary supplies shop on Main Street, it's known around the world. You'll learn about Wall Drug's presence long before you reach town. Over five hundred billboards along I-90 tout its wares, including the **free ice water** that was its original sales gimmick. By the time you get to exit 110 (the one with the 85ft Wall Drug dinosaur), you'll be compelled to pull off and see what all the fuss is about.

Behind the hype lies a kitschy emporium that serves up to twenty thousand visitors per day. You can fill up on steaks or cakes in the 520-seat café-cum-Western art gallery, or just enjoy the wall-to-wall collection of photos, memorabilia, animal trophies and mechanical automata like the Cowboy Orchestra and the Chuckwagon Quartet. The merchandise runs the gamut from quality (an excellent Western bookstore and a complete trail outfitters) to junk (anyone for a rattlesnake mold?). Most compelling, though, is the crackpot cornucopia atmosphere of this ultimate family store, a downmarket, down-home Disneyland wallowing in nostalgia. Beyond the Wall Drug billboards lie the impressive **Buffalo Gap National Grasslands,** an empty and remote portion of South Dakota so bleak it's almost beautiful. The **National Grasslands Visitor Center**, at 708 Main St (daily 8am–6pm), makes a good jumping-off point and will provide maps.

There's absolutely no reason to spend the night in Wall, but if you're stuck try the *Best Western Plains Motel*, 712 Glenn St (☎605/279-2145; ❹), or the slightly less expensive *Super 8* across the road at 711 Glenn St (☎605/279-2688 or 1-800/843-1991; ❹). The *Cactus Café and Lounge* on Main Street (☎605/279-2561) offers a mixed menu of reasonably priced Mexican, Italian and American food.

Pine Ridge Indian Reservation

Pine Ridge, the second largest Indian reservation in the United States (after Arizona's Navajo Nation – see p.991), overlaps the southern Badlands. It is also located in the nation's poorest county. Its prefab homes and beat-up trucks blend sadly and uneasily with the surrounding dry grasslands, rocky bluffs and tree-lined creeks.

The largest town, also called **PINE RIDGE**, comprises a collection of shabby, paint-stripped structures. Though the emergence of the profitable Prairie Wind casino in Oglala has improved life here, in many ways the reservation towns are an even more bitter pill to swallow than places like the nearby site of the Wounded Knee massacre: nowhere is America's disparity of wealth and opportunity so evident as in this area, which posts the highest poverty- and alcohol-related death statistics on the continent and where the average lifespan is just 52 years. Internal strife continues to plague the tribe; in 2000 the entire tribal council was ousted and some members jailed in a money laundering scandal that put the reservation $5 million in the hole. A group of vigilante elders temporarily took over the tribal HQ but were later forced out by a court decision. The locally produced *Black Hills People's News* (Ⓦhttp://members.tri-pod.com/GrassRootsOyate/) follows the on-going dispute.

Red Cloud Indian School, four miles north of the town of Pine Ridge on US-18, is named after a former chief whose fight against the US forced the closure of military forts on Sioux hunting grounds. The school holds an Indian art show each summer featuring work by tribes in the US and Canada; it also has a permanent display of star quilts (a Sioux tradition), paintings and a gift shop (daily 8am–5pm; free). Red Cloud, who later signed a peace treaty with the US and invited Jesuits to teach his tribe "the ways of the white man," is buried in a cemetery on a nearby knoll. The **Oglala Nation Fair**, on the first weekend in August, features a powwow and rodeo. For details, contact the Oglala Sioux Tribe, Box H, Pine Ridge, SD 57770 (Ⓣ605/867-6121). For news and both traditional Lakota and contemporary American music, tune in to KILI 90.1 FM, "the Voice of the Lakota Nation."

Wounded Knee

No other atrocity against Native Americans remains so potent and poignant as the massacre at **WOUNDED KNEE**. On December 29, 1890, the US Army delivered a coup de grâce to the vestiges of Plains Indian resistance, killing several hundred unarmed Sioux men, women and children. Most were **Ghost Dancers**, followers of a messianic cult who believed that by trance-inducing dancing and singing they could recover their lost way of life. The massacre was triggered by a misunderstanding during a tribal round-up. A deaf Indian, asked to surrender his rifle along with his peers, instead held it above his head, shouting that he'd paid a lot for it. An officer grabbed at the gun, it went off, and the troops started shooting.

A commemorative stone monument, surrounded by a chain-link fence, marks the victims' collective gravesite, off Hwy-27 toward the bottom of Pine Ridge Reservation. Somehow it has an intangible feeling of grief and anger, the mass murder here having left an indelible scar on all First Americans. Eighty-three years later, members of the radical American Indian Movement (AIM) grabbed headlines by occupying Wounded Knee in a dispute over the federal imposition of a tribal government; they were eventually dispersed by armed FBI agents and a paramilitary unit. More peaceably, since the mid-1980s the **Sitanka Wokiksuye** movement has organized an annual pilgrimage to the site, arriving in harsh winter weather by horse and travois, to symbolically release the spirits of their dead ancestors. The tribe has so far refused federal funds to turn the site into a glossy national monument, wanting instead to leave it uncommercialized; a concrete block nearby offers a few souvenirs and local knowledge.

The Black Hills

Our people knew there was yellow metal in little chunks up there, but they did not bother with it, because it was not good for anything.

Black Elk, Oglala Sioux holy man

The timbered, rocky **BLACK HILLS** rise like an island from a sea of rolling hills and flat, grain-growing plains, stretching for a hundred miles between the Belle Fourche River in the north and the Cheyenne to the south, and varying in width from forty to sixty miles. For many generations of Sioux, their value was and still is immeasurable. The Hills are "the heart of everything that is," a kind of spiritual safe, a place of gods and holy mountains where warriors went to speak with Wakan Tanka (the Great Spirit) and await visions. They were dubbed Paha Sapa, or Black Hills, even though they are actually mountains (the highest, Harney Peak, rises 7242ft), and the blue spruce and Norway pine trees that cover them only appear to be black from a distance.

Imagining the Hills to be worthless, the United States government drew up a treaty in the mid-nineteenth century that gave them and most of the land west of the Missouri River to the Indians. All such treaties were destined to be broken when the discovery of gold turned the Indians' Eden into the white explorers' El Dorado, and fortune-hunters came pouring in. The story has an incomplete postscript: in 1980, the US Supreme Court ordered the federal government to pay the Sioux $105 million in **compensation** for the illegal seizure of the Hills in 1877. After heated debate among Native American representatives, this settlement was rejected and a steering committee subsequently formed to campaign for the return of the Hills themselves to the tribes. The legal battle continues, often hindered by a lack of consensus among the tribes.

The Hills these days are a major tourist destination, albeit attracting more Midwesterners, driven stir-crazy by the endless plains, than international travelers for whom forested hills may be less of a novelty. As yet, however, despite the real danger of the entire area becoming an ersatz Western theme park – as evidenced by its T-shirt stores, pseudo-historical wax museums, cowboy supper shows and water slides – marketing and merchandising aren't so extensive as to rob the Hills of all their beauty or dignity.

The more thickly wooded north is noted more for urban activities, with the casino town of **Deadwood** its busiest spot. No place in the Hills is much more than ninety minutes from the four presidential heads carved into **Mount Rushmore**, but even more remarkable is **Crazy Horse Mountain**, the world's most ambitious work-in-progress. In the shade of these great monuments, the less spoiled southern hills are home to the bison of **Custer State Park** and **Wind Cave National Park**, along with the town of **Hot Springs**.

Finally, a word about **gold**. Numerous outlets sell gold pendants of the area's distinctive grape-leaf design. The Hills variety has a frosted finish and comes in three shades – yellow, green and pink; the last two are alloys, made by mixing gold with silver and copper or zinc.

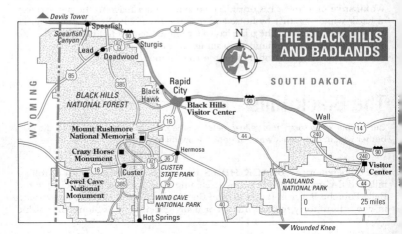

The North Hills

The predominantly privately owned northern **Black Hills** are more commercialized than their southern siblings, with **Rapid City**, the hub, surrounded by more interesting smaller towns, such as Sturgis, Spearfish and **Deadwood**. The back roads, especially in the **Spearfish Canyon** area, form a network of prime driving and cycling country. **The Black Hills Information Center**, exit 61 off I-90 (June–Aug daily 8am–8pm; rest of year Mon–Fri 8am–5pm, Sat–Sun 9am–5pm; ☎605/355-3700), is just outside of Rapid City and has an abundance of information on the Black Hills, the Badlands and Native American points of interest.

Rapid City

Though South Dakota's second largest town, **RAPID CITY** is all but swamped with family-fun attractions, but it makes a convenient base for exploring the charms of the Black Hills' lesser communities. In town, the **Journey Museum**, 222 New York St (daily 9am–5pm; $6), leads you through time, beginning with the geologic evolution of the Plains and the era of dinosaurs, right through the life of the Plains Indians to the pioneers who invaded their territory.

Rapid City offers the cheapest **lodgings** in the Black Hills, although summer rates top $50 almost everywhere. The Bavarian wood trimmings and Sioux soft furnishings of the delightful *Hotel Alex Johnson*, 523 Sixth St (☎605/342-1210 or 1-800/888-2539; ❸–❺), provide a great escape from dull corporate decor prevalent in Rapid City, while the *Ramkotta Inn*, I-90 exit 59, (☎605/343-8550; ❹), is clean and right off the highway. *Robert's Roost*, 627 South St (☎605/341-3434; ❶), is a little-known youth **hostel** with comfortable beds for $16 a night. Both the food and beer at *Firehouse Brewing Co*, 610 Main St (☎605/348-1915) – which has plenty of outdoor seating – are worth sampling; while *B&L Bagels*, 512 Main St (☎605/399-1777), is a convenient bakery and deli. Greyhound comes in at 333 Sixth St. The **visitor center** is located in the Civic Center, 444 Mount Rushmore Rd N (Mon–Fri 8am–5pm; ☎605/343-1744 or 1-800/487-3223, ⓦwww.rapidcitycvb.com). There's **internet access** at the Prince and Pauper Bookstore, 902 Mount Rushmore Rd (☎605/342-7964) or at the Public Library, 610 Quincy St.

Sturgis

The sleepy town of **STURGIS**, thirty miles north of Rapid City, comes to life in a big way during the first full week of August, when the world-famous **Sturgis Rally and Races** (PO Box 507, SD 57785; ☎605/347-9158, ⓦwww.sturgismotorcyclerally.com) packs out virtually every motel and campground in the region with motorcycle enthusiasts. For the rest of the year, bikers have to make do with an abundance of Harley souvenirs in the downtown stores and the worthy **Sturgis Motorcycle Museum and Hall of Fame**, 1344 Main St (Mon–Fri 9am–6pm, Sat 10am–4pm; $3). East of town, off Hwy-34, the volcanic outcrop which dominates **Bear Butte State Park** stands as a lonely sentinel, detached from the rest of the hills. Hundreds of Native Americans come to this site on retreat each year – to avoid disturbing anyone, check with the park's **visitor center** (☎605/347-5240) before setting out on its excellent **hike** to the summit. Campers can secure a tent site within the park for $6.

Of the wide range of **motels** in Sturgis, the reasonably central *National 9 Junction Inn*, 1802 S Junction Ave (☎605/347-2506; ❸), represents the best value. The lure of breakfast, burgers and overpriced souvenirs is hard to resist at the garish *Roadkill Café*, 1333 Main St (open only during summer; ☎605/347-4502). The Sturgis **visitor center** (☎605/347-2556, ⓦwww.sturgis -sd.org) lies off I-90 exit 32.

Deadwood

One of the West's wildest Gold Rush towns, **DEADWOOD**, in a deep gulch high in the hills 42 miles northwest of Rapid City, has the rare accolade of being a National Historic Landmark in its entirety. Within a year of the discovery of **gold** here in 1876, six thousand gold-diggers had swarmed in to stake their claims; con artists, outlaws and other dubious frontier types were not far behind. Among them were James Butler, aka **Wild Bill Hickok** – sometime spy, scout, bullwhacker, stagecoach driver, sheriff and gambler, who spent only a few weeks in Deadwood prior to his murder by a young drifter named Jack McCall – and Martha "**Calamity Jane**" Canary Burke, an illiterate alcoholic whose checkered career included stints as a dishwasher, muleskinner, scout, prostitute, nurse and Wild West Show performer. She died penniless in 1903, her last wish to be buried beside Hickok in **Mount Moriah Cemetery**, a short but blustery hike from town.

Gambling was outlawed in Deadwood in 1889, the year South Dakota achieved statehood, but betting parlors and brothels flourished well into the twentieth century. Now the old ghosts have been revitalized, since the passing of limited-stake gambling legislation in 1989. With a residential population of only 2000, Deadwood is now booming again, the old gaming dens and flophouses transformed for the sake of tourism into flash casinos and rustic saloons. Corny but entertaining gunfights, sing-alongs and community theater are shown sporadically; check with the **CVB**, 735 Main St (☎800/999-1876, ⓦwww.deadwood.org), for details.

For an overview of Deadwood past and present, start by visiting the **History and Information Center**, in the heart of town at 3 Siever St (May–Oct daily 8am–8pm; rest of year daily 9am–5pm; ☎605/578-2507). Main Street boasts several grand old **hotels**, including the *Bullock* at no. 633 (☎605/578-1745 or 1-800/336-1876; ❹–❻), and the *Franklin Hotel* at no. 700 (☎605/578-2241 or 1-800/688-1876; ❹–❻) which has an elegant old-world dining room. **Budget motels** are found a mile south of town on Hwy-85 towards Lead, including the *Thunder Cove Inn* (☎800/209-7361; ❸). *The Penny Motel*, 818 Main St (☎605/578-1842, ⓦwww.pennymotel.com/; ❶), offers excellent **hostel** accommodation at $12 for members and $15 for nonmembers as well as bike rental, shuttle service and **internet** access. You can also access the internet at the Carnegie Public Library, 435 Williams St. *Saloon #10*, 657 Main St (☎605/578-3346), has cold **beer**, sawdust floors and lots of memorabilia. Above the door is the chair in which Hickok was sitting when he was shot dead, while holding two aces, a pair of eights and the nine of diamonds – forever after christened the Dead Man's Hand. Several casinos along Main Street aim to lure in the punters with cut-price **buffets**, but Deadwood's finest dining is at the dinner-only *Jake's*, on the top floor of Kevin Costner's Midnight Star casino, 677 Main St (☎605/578-1555).

Spearfish Canyon area

Aspen, birch and white spruce spread over the towering limestone cliffs above the nineteen-mile **Spearfish Canyon National Scenic Highway**, which starts on Hwy-14A half an hour's drive west of Deadwood, and threads past sights such as Bridal Veil and Roughlock falls. The route reveals almost as many gastronomic pleasures as it does scenic ones. Twenty minutes out of Deadwood, the *Latchstring Restaurant* (☎605/584-3333) treats those who have been exploring the site of the nearby winter camp from *Dances with Wolves* with steak, pasta, shrimp and excellent rainbow trout almandine. Marking the southern mouth of the canyon at Hwy-14A and Hwy-85, the *Cheyenne Crossing Country Store* (☎605/584-3510) is a must if you have a hearty appetite; popular menu items include all-day breakfasts with buffalo sausage, enormous Indian tacos and traditional Indian fry bread.

Marking the canyon's north end, **SPEARFISH** itself reels in the crowds each summer for the **Black Hills Passion Play** (June–Aug Tues, Thurs & Sun 8pm; tickets $10–18; ☎605/642-2646 or 1-800/457-0160). Burgers and inventive snacks are served in the restaurant at *Lown House B&B* at 745 Fifth St (☎605/642-5663; ❹–❻), which also has good-value rooms (the loft sleeps six comfortably). The quiet *Best Western Downtown Spearfish*, 346 W Kansas St (☎605/642-4676 or 1-800/843-6358; ❸), is also recommended. *Sanford's*, 545 Jackson St (☎605/642-3204), is a lively, student-oriented pub and restaurant; for a morning-after coffee, call in at *Common Grounds*, 111 E Hudson St (☎605/642-4292). The **visitor's center** is at 106 W Kansas St (☎605/642-2626 or 1-800/626-8013, ⓦwww.spearfish.sd.us). For **internet** access, try the Public Library, 625 Fifth Ave.

From Spearfish, the spectacular **Devils Tower** stands just an hour's drive away across the Wyoming state line (see p.886).

The South Hills

The **southern Black Hills** encompass lower foothills and wooded pastureland; from a purely physical standpoint they are more attractive than the north, drawing visitors for their scenery and wildlife rather than kitsch or gambling. The two big mountain carvings, **Mount Rushmore** and **Crazy Horse**, mark the northern end of the region, **Custer State Park** and **Wind Cave National Park** account for much of the central zone, and the pleasant town of **Hot Springs** sits on the southern edge.

Mount Rushmore National Memorial

America's two largest stone carvings are a mere seventeen miles apart, spitting distance when you consider the scale on which they're conceived. The better-known **Mount Rushmore National Memorial**, originally dubbed The Shrine of Democracy, is the linchpin of the Hills' tourist circuit (summer daily 8am–10pm; rest of year daily 8am–5pm). It's an easy 24-mile drive southwest of Rapid City, though by far the most impressive approach is to take **Iron Mountain Road** (US-16A) from **Custer State Park** (see p.831), which runs for seventeen miles up and over 5500ft Iron Mountain.

In 1923, state historian Doane Robinson and the sculptor Gutzon Borglum, known for carvings such as the leaders of the Confederacy in Stone Mountain, Georgia (see p.537), talked over the possibility of turning the imposing fingers of granite known as the Needles into dramatic patriotic sculpture. They discussed depictions of such heroic figures of the West as Lewis and Clark, Buffalo Bill Cody and Jim Bridger. Borglum opted for a nearby mountain named after New York attorney Charles E. Rushmore, upon which he would fashion the faces and heads of four certifiably great American presidents: **George Washington**, **Thomas Jefferson**, **Abraham Lincoln** and Borglum's buddy, **Theodore Roosevelt**.

Borglum talked, dreamed and worked big. "American art ought to be monumental, in keeping with American life," he opined. Sixty when the project began in 1927, he died fourteen years later, $200,000 in debt, just a few months prior to the dedication of the last head – Roosevelt's – in 1939. Inclement weather and uncertain funding had meant that the actual sculpting took about six and a half years, at a total cost of $993,000. Half a million tons of rock were removed to reach the softer, more malleable granite from which the heads were dynamited, drilled and chiselled into recognizable shape.

The Big Four gaze out impassively, cheek by jowl, arguably a greater engineering feat than an artistic one. Each head is about sixty feet from chin to crown. (The Statue of Liberty's head is only seventeen feet.) Lincoln, Borglum's favorite, has an eighteen-foot-long nose and the glint in each eleven-foot-wide eye is thirty inches. If he and his fellow presidents had been done full-figure to scale, they'd stand 465ft tall and be able to stride across the Potomac River in Washington, DC without getting their knees wet.

The best time to view Rushmore is dawn or dusk, when there are fewer people and better lighting. Patriots flock here for a massive **fireworks display** on July 3. Although there is no admission charge, by congressional decree, an $8 **parking fee** has been introduced since the construction of a hideous new multilevel parking lot and high-tech visitor center; you can, however, park for free at a lot a quarter of a mile away. The café, complete with panoramic windows, as seen in Hitchcock's *North by Northwest*, serves full meals and "Monumental Breakfasts" of hash browns, eggs, country-fried steak with gravy and a biscuit piled on one plate. With alternative bases such as Rapid City or Custer State Park so close to hand, there's no particular reason to stay in the nearest town, **Keystone** – a once quiet mining town turned T-shirt hawker's paradise.

Crazy Horse Mountain Monument

In 1939, prompted by the sight of the Rushmore monument nearing completion, Sioux leader Henry Standing Bear wrote to Korczak Ziolkowski, who had just won first prize for sculpture at the New York World's Fair, proclaiming that Indians "would like the white man to know that the red man has great heroes, too." The chief invited him to take on a similar project, and less than a decade later, pushing forty and with just $174 to his name, the New Englander moved permanently to the Black Hills to undertake a vastly more ambitious scheme than Rushmore – the **Crazy Horse Mountain Monument**, on US-16, six miles north of Custer.

The subject, the revered warrior Crazy Horse on horseback (see p.820), so appealed to Ziolkowski that he set out to make his monument the biggest statue in the world, larger even than the Great Pyramid. The work he began on Thunderhead Mountain in 1948 – five Native American survivors of the battle at Little Bighorn attended the dedication ceremony – didn't stop with his death in 1982; his widow, children and grandchildren continue to realize his vision. National and international interest has greatly increased as the monument finally starts to take recognizable shape; the 90ft high face was completed in time for the fiftieth anniversary celebrations in 1998, although it could well be another fifty years before the project is finished. The sheer scale of the thing is phenomenal; it's hard to believe that the main viewing terrace at the **visitor center** is a full mile from the carving itself, and that the 20ft scale model on show there is 34 times smaller than the end result, which will be 563ft high and 641ft long. An estimated four thousand people could stand atop Crazy Horse's outstretched arm, while all four Rushmore heads could fit in his head, from which will jut a 44ft stone feather. Nor do the plans stop with the carving: Ziolkowski's descendants hope to build a North American Indian museum, university and medical training center on the land stretching between the visitor center and the monument.

The Bison of the Great Plains

In the fifteenth century, the Great Plains were roamed by one hundred million shaggy, short-sighted American bison (popularly known as buffalo, a corruption of the French *boeuf*). Apart from eating their flesh, Native Americans used the fur and hide for clothing and shelter, the bones for weapons, utensils and toys, and the droppings for fuel. Eliminating the bison en masse was a mercilessly effective way to deplete the Indians as well. By 1900 there were fewer than one thousand bison left in North America.

Custer State Park was instrumental in helping to raise that meager number to a head count of 250,000 in the US and Canada. Its one thousand bison constitute the country's second largest publicly owned herd, beaten only by Yellowstone National Park. However, over ninety percent of bison in the US are now privately owned – the meat, higher in protein and lower in cholesterol than either chicken or tuna, is becoming something of a cross between a novelty and a delicacy item in restaurants (you can try it in burger form at the *State Game Lodge* in Custer State Park and dozens of other places around South Dakota). The Triple U Ranch, outside Pierre, South Dakota – the stage for several scenes in *Dances with Wolves* – boasts a herd of 3500 strong, though Ted Turner owns around 20,000, split between his ranches in several western states.

The Custer State Park bison are free to roam where they please until either the last Monday of September or the first Monday in October, when the park stages its annual **roundup**. From selected viewing points, the public is welcome to witness one of the Midwest's more thrilling occasions. Modern technology has invaded cowboy territory. Helicopters, jeeps and pickup trucks, as well as riders on horseback, steer the often recalcitrant herd down a six-mile "corridor" and into a series of pens. There the calves are branded and vaccinated, and the whole herd sorted to determine which five hundred will be auctioned off on the third Saturday in November. Proceeds from the sale account for twenty percent of the park's annual revenue.

Don't let the tranquil, easygoing appearance of North America's biggest mammal lull you into a false sense of security. An average bull can stand six feet high at the hump, weigh up to a ton, outrun a horse, turn on a dime and gore a human most efficiently.

Ziolkowski himself raised and spent $4 million on the project. His belief in free enterprise has meant that Crazy Horse has received no federal or state funds, instead relying entirely on admissions and contributions. He twice turned down $10 million in federal funds, claiming the government had no right to be involved after all the treaties it had broken with the Sioux. The site, open dawn to dusk year-round (and illuminated for an hour each night), is free to Native Americans. Everyone else over six pays $8 each; carloads are let in for $19. Apart from the monument, the premises include a huge lodge full of Native American artifacts and crafts, a Native American Education and Cultural Center, the *Laughing Water Café* (May–Oct only), and an extensive gift shop. Coffee and souvenir stones are free. On the first weekend in June, the public is invited to walk to the top of the mountain and see the work close-up.

Custer State Park

The 73,000 sublime, billboard-free acres of **Custer State Park** fill much of the southern central Black Hills, a perfect antidote to the commercial crassness elsewhere. **The Needles Highway** (Hwy-87; open mid-April to mid-Oct) winds for fourteen miles through pine forests and past the eponymous jagged granite spires in the park's northwestern corner, between Sylvan and Legion lakes. Not far out of Sylvan Lake, as you pass close to the summit of Harney

Peak (at 7242feet South Dakota's highest point), look south to spot the Needle's Eye, a slender gap in one of the pinnacles that measures three to four feet wide and fifty to sixty feet tall. The eighteen-mile **Wildlife Loop** (separate from the Needles Highway) undulates through the rolling meadows along the park's southern edge. Sunrise and sunset are prime times to spy such critters as elk, bighorn sheep, antelope, deer, burros, and the most plentiful species, bison. Finally, **Iron Mountain Road** (US-16A), to the northeast, makes a dramatic route to Mount Rushmore (see p.829). This is the most likely place to bump into the park's famous "begging burros": tame and disarming four-legged panhandlers who stick their snouts through the windows of passing vehicles in search of handouts.

For a fuller appreciation of the beauty of Custer State Park, forsake your car and set off into the wilderness. Rangers at the park entrances – where you're required to pay **entrance fees** of $5 per person, $8 per vehicle (the pass remains valid for a week and gets you into all other state parks) – can advise on **hiking** and **biking** trails, while concession firms offer horseback rides, boat rental and cross-country drives in open-topped jeeps. Good short hikes also include the one-hour **Stockade Lake Trail** in the west, which climbs to give distant views across the lake to Harney Peak and the Needles, and the two-hour **Lovers Leap Trail**, which starts from the park's main Peter Norbeck **visitor center** (summer daily 8am–8pm; rest of year daily 9am–5pm; ☎605/255-4464) on Hwy-16A in the east.

As long as nightlife isn't high on your agenda, the park's four state-run resorts make it a splendid **place to stay** (for reservations call ☎1-800/658-3530). The finest is the *State Game Lodge* (☎605/255-4541) on Hwy-16A not far from the visitor center, which operates a motel-style lodge (④) and also has some lovely individual cabins (④) at the edge of the woods; the Pheasant Dining Room offers hearty (as opposed to heart-healthy) meaty meals. President Coolidge planned to stay for a week when he arrived here in 1927, but found it so much to his liking that he hauled his aides over from DC and ran the country from the lodge for the entire summer. Tucked in the northwest corner on its own artificial lake, the *Sylvan Lake Resort* (☎605/574-2561; ③–⑤) similarly offers 31 comfy cabins, more traditional rooms in its tasteful main building, and the upscale Lakota Dining Room. Custer State Park also has eight **campgrounds** (☎1-800/710-2267), costing $12–16 a night plus park entrance fees.

Custer

In little **CUSTER**, five miles west of the park on US-16, the *Bavarian Inn* on the main highway has classic German dining and rooms (☎605/673-2802 or 1-800/657-4312; ④), while the *Custer Motel*, 109 Mount Rushmore Rd (☎605/673-2876; ③), is one of the cheapest in the Black Hills. Of many garish **campgrounds**, *Flintstones Bedrock City* (☎605/673-4664), with its own small theme park, manages to steal the show. The **visitor center** is at 615 Washington St (☎605/673-2244 or 1-800/992-9818, ⓦwww.custersd.com). Twelve miles west of Custer is the **Jewel Cave National Monument** (daily 8.30am–6pm; $8–20 for 1–4hr tours; ☎605/673-2288, ⓦwww.nps.gov/jeca) where spelunkers are sure to receive a layer of manganese dust; call ahead for tour details.

Wind Cave National Park

Beneath wide-open rangelands, **WIND CAVE NATIONAL PARK**, ten minutes north of Hot Springs, comprises over 100 miles of mapped underground passages etched out of limestone. One of the largest caves in the US, it was discovered in 1881 when a loud whistling noise on the plains led a settler to a hole in the ground – the cave's only natural opening. The wind, caused by differences between atmospheric pressures in the cave and outside, was apparently enough to blow the discoverer's hat off. Nowadays rangers lead a variety of cave **tours** ($6–20 based on length of tour) from the **visitor center** (June to mid-Aug daily 8am–7.30pm; May & mid-Aug to Sept daily 8am–6pm; Oct–April daily 8am–4.30pm; ☎605/745-4600, ⓦwww.nps.gov/wica/), pointing out delicate features such as frostwork and boxwork along the way. If you come in summer, forget the standard walking tours and opt for the ones that allow you to crawl around in the smaller passages, or explore the caves by candlelight (call ahead).

Even if you lack the time or inclination to delve into the Dakotas' dank bowels, simply **driving** through the park is yet another unmissable Black Hills experience. Its native grass prairieland is home to deer, antelope, elk, coyote, prairie dogs and a sizeable herd of buffalo.

Hot Springs

The Black Hills' southern anchor, **HOT SPRINGS**, differs from other regional towns in that it hasn't tarted up its downtown to look like a movie set. It doesn't need to. Several dozen utilitarian yet handsome sandstone structures dominate its center, through which flows the sprightly Fall River.

Battles over the town's thermal pools have caused as much grief as the clamor for gold. Before white settlement, the Sioux drove out the Cheyenne, and later landowners, speculators and settlers dodged and outwitted each other for ownership of the springs. The disputes ceased in 1890 when Fred Evans incorporated numerous small springs and one mammoth hot water pool into a spa center. Today, **Evans Plunge**, on the north edge of town at 1145 N River St, is a popular family-fun center, where three great slides zoom down into the 87°F waters (summer daily 8am–10pm; rest of year times vary; $8; ☎605/745-5165).

The unique **Mammoth Site** on Hwy-18 By-Pass is the only *in situ* display of mammoth fossils in the US. In 1974, building on a housing project came to an abrupt halt when a tractor driver unearthed a seven-foot tusk. Paleontologists soon declared that the workers had discovered the 26,000-year-old grave of Columbian and Woolly mammoths – 52, all male, have been found to date. Inside the dome, fascinating tours explain how these ten-ton mammoths, along with camels, bears and rodents, were trapped in a steep-sided sinkhole (a pond formed by a collapsed underground cave) and were gradually covered by sediment. Complete skeletons are easy to pick out in the excavation site, which is still being uncovered slowly by groups of summer volunteers (mid-May–Aug daily 8am–8pm; rest of year times vary; $5.50).

Seven miles south of Hot Springs, the huge reservoir of the **Angostura Dam State Recreation Area** ($3 per person), set against contorted sandstone bluffs, is a picture-perfect spot for boating and jet skiing. Equipment can be rented from Breakers Beach Club, a small hut offering beer, snacks and beach volleyball, at the north entrance.

Information for visitors to Hot Springs is available from the cabin at 630 N River St or from the CVB, 801 S Sixth St (May–Sept Mon–Fri 9am–7pm, Sat 9am–6pm, Sun 1–5pm; rest of year Mon–Fri 8am–5pm; ☎605/745-4140 or 1-800/325-6991, ⓦwww.hotsprings-sd.com). **Accommodation** rates are a bit more reasonable than in the hectic northern towns. The *Super 8 Motel*, 800 Mammoth St (☎605/745-3888 or 1-800/800-8000; ❹), is unusual in having a bar and restaurant, both of which are recommended; alternatives include the old, faded, riverside *Braun Hotel*, 902 N River St (☎605/745-3187; ❹/❺), and the sumptuous *Villa Teresa B&B*, 801 Almond St (☎605/745-4633; ❹). *Yogi's Den*, 625 N River St (☎605/745-5949), a lively lounge, fries up good burgers, while the *Elkhorn Café*, 310 S Chicago St (☎605/745-6556), serves sandwiches and salads on a sunny terrace.

North Dakota

NORTH DAKOTA has no nationally recognizable landmarks, nor is the state's history particularly lurid or glamorous. It seems like somebody's quiet afterthought, a place to pass through. Grain silos loom on the horizon; the haystacks resemble loaves of bread. In the summer, with the sun baking in a defiantly blue sky and the wind raking strong fingers through tall fields of golden wheat and flax, North Dakota epitomizes all things rural American. Charming, picturesque – and a bit maddening.

The influx of Europeans into the Dakota Territory, spurred by the Homestead Act of 1862, precipitated a population and agricultural boom that lasted into the twentieth century. As in South Dakota, the fertile east is more thickly settled than the west, where vast cattle and sheep ranges predominate, and it was the east that was hardest hit by the so-called **500-year flood** of 1997, when 1.7 million low-lying acres of farmland were inundated, and the entire state was declared a disaster area. Lately, North Dakotan lawmakers, ashamed of their state's reputation as an arctic wasteland, have proposed that the "North" be dropped from the state's title, leaving just "Dakota", a suggestion most locals vehemently protest.

From **Fargo**, the state's largest city, I-94 passes through the central capital of **Bismarck**, and on to the **Bad Lands** of the west, once cherished by President Theodore Roosevelt. Though the national park bearing his name is a key destination, Roosevelt would surely not be pleased about the continuing disfiguration of much of western North Dakota by strip mining operations.

Getting around North Dakota
Amtrak runs one **train** per day in each direction between Fargo and Williston in the northwest, via Grand Forks. Greyhound is the major interstate **bus** operator: three or four buses per day make the ten-hour trip from Minneapolis/St Paul to Bismarck via Grand Forks and Fargo, before heading west along I-94 into Montana.

East of the Missouri

Far more of North Dakota lies east of the big winding **Missouri River**, its uneven dividing line, than west. The **Red River Valley**, the state's furthest eastern strip, is home to two sizeable cities, easygoing **Grand Forks** and the less attractive **Fargo**. Pelicans, geese, swans, prairie chickens and ring-necked pheasants live off the sloughs and potholes of the rolling, glaciated prairie of south central North Dakota, while lakes and woodland dominate the north and the Canadian border. **Spirit Lake Sioux Indian Reservation** at Devils Lake is midway between Grand Forks and the low-slung Turtle Mountains, which are topped by Lake Metigoshe and the **International Peace Garden** (more of a political symbol than a compelling sight).

Grand Forks

GRAND FORKS sits eighty miles north of I-94, right next to Minnesota, a mere 75 miles south of the Canadian border. Even before its foundation a century ago, fur traders had used the area to rest and barter during their travels between Winnipeg and Minneapolis. It's a small, friendly, outdoorsy city, with nineteen parks and several tree-lined avenues of fine homes. Furious construction has rebuilt the downtown area, ravaged in the 1997 floodwaters. But the disaster shook investors' confidence and most of the new buildings lie empty, save for their "for lease" signs posted across the windows.

The most interesting distractions can be found on the redbrick main campus of the **University of North Dakota**. The **North Dakota Museum of Art** (Mon–Fri 9am–5pm, Sat & Sun 1–5pm; donations) offers an eclectic assortment of contemporary art and top touring exhibits. Fascinating tours of the **John D. Odegard School of Aerospace Sciences**, one of the largest civilian pilot-training schools in the world, take in flight simulators, the air-traffic control room and an altitude chamber.

Practicalities

The **visitor center** is at 4251 Gateway Drive (℡701/746-0444 or 1-800/866-4566, ⓦwww.grandforkscvb.org). Greyhound is at US-81 and Hwy-2; Amtrak at no. 5555 W Demers Ave. **Internet access** is available at the Public Library, 2110 Library Circle. Triangle Transportation (℡218/773-2631) runs **buses** into Minnesota out of East Grand Forks from the Greyhound station.

Downtown's *Best Western Town House*, 710 First Ave N (℡701/746-5411; ❸), is Grand Forks' most luxurious **motel**; for about $20 less you can stay in the kitsch splendor of the *Fabulous Westward Ho* on US-2 (℡701/775-5341; ❷), and swim in its cowboy-boot-shaped pool, while nearby there's a *Super 8*, 1122 N 43rd St (℡701/775-8138; ❷). The most serene place to **camp** is 20 miles west on US-2, in the grounds of Turtle River State Park (reservations recommended; ℡701/594-4445; $11). The *Red River Café*, 315 Demers Ave (℡701/772-3900), is good for lunch and also features reminders from the 1997 flood, including lines on the wall marking the height of the river at its crest.

Devils Lake

The scruffy town of **DEVILS LAKE**, ninety miles west of Grand Forks on US-2, shares its name with the state's largest natural body of water, which has two state parks and two private campgrounds along more than 300 sprawling, irregular and growing miles of shoreline. The damming of rivers in the northern part of the state inadvertently caused Devils Lake to rise; so far it has gone up 25 feet and quadrupled in area since 1997. Pastureland has been submerged, dikes built, roads raised, and one town, nearby Churchs Ferry, evacuated. Embarrassed engineers, nervous politicians and a frustrated public are still at a loss about how to stem the tide – $300 million has already been spent on relief. Downtown, now saved by a seven-mile-long dike, holds a smattering of nineteenth-century buildings and a few rough-and-ready bars. Most of the **places to stay**, such as the *Super 8* (☎701/662-8656; ❸), are strung along US-2; the Woodland Resort (☎701/662-5996, ⓦ www.woodlandresort.com; ❷–❸) on Creel Bay, about six miles from town, rents boats, pontoons and fishing gear. You can camp three miles east of town on Hwy-2 at Shelver's Grove State Park (☎701/766-4015) for $7 per person, $4 per vehicle, but if the lake rises another six inches you will be swimming in your tent. For more info, contact the **Devils Lake CVB** on Hwy-2 E next to the *Great American Inn*.

Spirit Lake Sioux Indian Reservation, fifteen miles south of town, is the site of **Fort Totten Military Post** (daily 8am–5pm; $4), one of the best-preserved frontier military posts in the country. During the last weekend in July, the reservation hosts the thrilling **Spirit Lake Oyate Wacipi Powwow and Rodeo** (daily $5, $10 for a weekend pass). It's an impassioned, alcohol-free, multitribal party at which hundreds of magnificently clothed dancers of all ages compete for cash prizes.

The West

Anyone with a hankering to play cowboy could do worse than follow in the footsteps of **Theodore Roosevelt**, who declared "I never would have been President if it had not been for my experiences in North Dakota." Roosevelt initially came to the state in search of spiritual and physical renewal after the deaths (on the same day) of his mother and first wife. He dubbed what he discovered during his few years in this "grimly picturesque" area, with its clear skies, panoramic views and weird, colorful landforms, a "perfect freedom." The national park named after him is the choicest destination in the **North Dakota Bad Lands** (distinct from South Dakota's Badlands) that dominate the state's western half.

The **Missouri River** wriggles like a giant raggedy worm out of Montana, down past the capital, **Bismarck**, and into South Dakota. En route it is transformed into Lake Sakakawea, a virtual inland sea nearly two hundred miles long that's the state's premier water playground. Scenic state **highways 1804 and 1806** follow the routes mapped out by the Lewis and Clark expedition in those respective years.

Bismarck and Mandan

The West seems to begin as soon as you cross the Missouri River from **BIS-MARCK**, a capital city with a small-town feel, to Mandan. Both were founded in 1872, Bismarck as a military camp to protect railroad crews from hostile Indians and outlaws. Its original name, Edwinton, was changed by the secretary of the Northern Pacific Railroad, both in honor of German Chancellor Otto von Bismarck and in the hope of attracting Teutonic settlers. Though the scheme failed, the name stuck. The city survived an early lawless period (present-day Fourth Street was once dubbed "Murderers' Gulch") and a major fire to become first the territorial and then the state capital.

Contemporary Bismarck is pretty much contained within the oblong between I-94 in the north and Main Avenue to the south. Locals are proud of their nineteen-story limestone **Capitol**, 600 E Boulevard Ave, dating from the mid-1930s and set at the crest of a public park. The interior, a model of spatial economy and marbled Art Deco elegance, is open for free guided tours on weekdays. Across the street, the superb **North Dakota Heritage Center**

(Mon–Fri 8am–5pm, Sat 9am–5pm, Sun 11am–5pm; donation) divides the state's past into six resonant sections, from the dinosaurs onwards. Look out for Sitting Bull's painted robe and the bison "smell box," which offers homesick cowboys and curious tourists a whiff of buffalo dung.

The major reason to venture into **MANDAN** is **Fort Lincoln State Park** ($4), five miles south of downtown via Hwy-1806, where the centerpiece is the **Custer House** (May–Sept daily 9am–7pm; Oct–April daily 1–5pm; $4), an admirable reconstruction of the 1874 original designed by the brutally ambitious, indefatigable horseman himself. The guided tour supplies nuggets of quirky information about him (he loved to eat raw onions), his wife and their household prior to his death at Little Big Horn in 1876. Nearer the river, four earthlodge reconstructions stand on the site of the once-vast On-a-Slant village, occupied by the Mandan (or River Dweller) tribe from about 1610 to the late 1700s. After the Mandan abandoned On-a-Slant village, they moved upstream and settled on the site that became Fort Mandan, where in 1804 the explorers Lewis and Clark came into contact with the Shoshone woman **Sakakawea** (aka Sacajawea), who helped guide them west towards the Pacific. The site and adjacent historical museum (summer daily 9am–7pm, Sept daily 9am–5pm, Oct daily 1–5pm; Nov–Apr by appointment; free with purchase of Custer House ticket) sit below a bluff topped with replicas of the Fort Lincoln infantry post. If you don't have a car you can reach the park via **trolley** from 200 SE 3rd St (summer daily 1–5pm; $5 round-trip; ☎701/663-9018).

Practicalities

Bismarck's Greyhound terminal is at 3750 E Rosser Drive; its **visitor center** is at 1600 Burnt Boat Drive (Mon–Fri 7.30am–7pm, Sat 8am–6pm, Sun 10am–5pm; ☎701/222-4308 or 1-800/767-3555, Ⓦwww.bismarck-mandancvb.org). The Public Library, 515 N 5th St (☎701/222-6410), has free **internet** access. For clean, though small, downtown doubles, try the *Budget Inn Express*, 122 E Thayer Ave (☎701/255-1450; ❷). Great rooms, a pool and breakfast are on offer at *Fairfield Inn*, which has two locations, one near the airport at 135 Ivy Ave (☎701/223-9293; ❸), the other near the I-94/US-83 interchange at 1120 E Century Ave (☎701/223-9077; ❸). For **camping** off the beaten track, try the excellent Cross Ranch State Park (☎701/794-3731; vehicle fee $4, campsites $5–11), thirty minutes north of Bismarck on Route 1806. Overlapped by a six-thousand-acre Nature Preserve, the park features sixteen miles of trails. Alternatively, you can camp in Fort Lincoln State Park.

Dining and nightlife are plentiful in Bismarck. *Peacock Alley*, 422 E Main St (☎701/255-7917), in a downtown hotel that was once the headquarters of the progressive Non-Partisan League, serves Cajun, Italian and American cuisine, with lunch specials in the classy adjoining bar. In Mandan, the *Drug Store and Soda Fountain*, 316 W Main St (☎701/663-5900), is a good place to grab a cheap lunch, espresso or ice cream. There is fine dining at *Meriwether's Restaurant* at the Port of Bismarck (☎701/224-0455), where the *Lewis & Clark* riverboat takes tourists on narrated **historical rides** (☎701/255-4233, $12 daytime, $30 dinner cruise).

Theodore Roosevelt National Park

The **THEODORE ROOSEVELT NATIONAL PARK**, a huge tract of multihued rock formations, rough grassland and lazy streams, is split into north and south units approximately seventy miles apart, the area between comprising a checkerboard of federal, state and privately owned territory. Exploring the park's seventy thousand acres is like entering different rooms: from desert to woods to mountains. Both units are at their subtlest at sunrise or sundown, the best times to observe such fauna as elk, antelope, bison and several fascinating, closely knit prairie dog communities (both open daily dawn–dusk; vehicles $10, pedestrians $5).

Your first taste of the larger, more popular southern unit is likely to be at the breathtaking **Painted Canyon**, seven miles east of the town of Medora off I-94, exit 32. Here and elsewhere in the park, the land is like a sedimentary layer cake that for millions of years has been beaten by hard, infrequent rains, baked by the sun into a kaleidoscope of colors and cut through to the base by erosive streams and rivers. A mile-long nature hike begins at the end of the canyon's boardwalk.

The **southern unit**'s main **visitor center** in Medora (daily: June to early Sept 8am–8pm; early Sept to May 8am–4.30pm; ☎701/623-4466) counts as park headquarters, and runs tours, nature walks and lectures by campfire in high season. Out back, the simple cabin was used by the young Roosevelt while a partner in the Maltese Cross Ranch (free guided tours daily until 4.15pm). A highlight of the scenic 36-mile loop road is the sublime view from **Wind Canyon**, ten miles out of Medora. Peaceful Valley Ranch (☎701/623-4496), seven miles from Medora and a mile from the park's first-come, first-served *Cottonwood Campground* ($10 per tent site), arranges **horseback tours** in summer for $12 per hour.

The **northern unit**, off Hwy-85 near **Watford City**, receives only a tenth as many visitors and is smaller but more spectacular than its southern counterpart, the highlight being **Oxbow Overlook**, at the end of a fifteen mile scenic drive. Its **visitor center** is open daily (9am–5.30pm; ☎701/842-2333) and closes a half hour earlier in winter months. Keep in mind that the northern unit is on Central time while the southern unit is on Mountain time.

Medora

MEDORA, the southern gateway to Theodore Roosevelt National Park, languished in obscurity until the early 1960s, but has become one of North Dakota's principal attractions, an inoffensively touristy place with enough to keep you busy, and reasonably interested, for most of a day. The biggest noise in town is the **Medora Musical** (daily 8.30pm; $19–21; ☎1-800/MEDORA-1), a pseudo-Western, super-Americana variety show staged beneath the stars in a vast, modern amphitheater. There is a lot of clogging and yodeling, plenty of accolades to a certain 26th US President, and special guest appearances that range from Chinese chair-stackers to double-jointed Lithuanians. The extravaganza is preceded by a fantastic feed whereby 240 steaks are simultaneously fondued on pitchforks inside giant oil vats (6.30pm; $18). A better idea is to take to the hills on a mountain bike – the **Maah Daah Hey Trail** dips and curves through spectacular country for 120 miles. Rent from Rough Riders Dakota Cyclery in Medora (☎701/623-4808). Or if TR has inspired your cowboy within, make for the *Dakotah Lodge Guest Ranch* to join an authentic cattle drive (reservations strongly recommended; ☎800/508-4897, ⓦwww.dahkotahlodge.com). If the $1000 seems a bit much to spend, you can take two-day pack trips ($400) or rent horses by the hour ($20). For accommodation, you can pitch your own tent for $20 and use the facilities or stay in homey, ranch-style rooms (❸–❹).

The conservative Theodore Roosevelt Medora Foundation owns and operates most of the town and its attractions, including the quaint and central *Rough Rider Hotel* (☎701/623-4444; ❹), as well as the *Medora* (☎701/623-4422; ❸) and *Badlands* (☎701/623-4422; ❹) motels, both of which have outdoor pools. While these hotels only operate from May to September, the *Americinn Motel* (☎701/623-4800 or 1-800/634-3444; ❹) is open year-round. The *Medora Campground* (☎701/623-4435) caters to both tents ($15) and RVs ($24).

CHAPTER 11

Highlights

* **Durango & Silverton Narrow Gauge Railroad, CO** This steam train ride corkscrews through spectacular mountains to the mining town of Silverton. See p.873

* **Cheyenne Frontier Days, WY** Wyoming's premier annual event features the world's most prestigious outdoor rodeo. See p.880

* **Buffalo Bill Historical Center, WY** Centering on an extraordinary museum, the town of Cody celebrates the life and times of Buffalo Bill. See p.889

* **Old Faithful, WY** Photograph the 150-foot water jet of the world's most famous geyser, in Yellowstone National Park. See p.895

* **Little Bighorn Battlefield, MT** Hard now to believe that these windswept grasslands witnessed the last great flourish of Native American resistance. See p.903

* **Going-to-the-Sun road, Glacier National Park, MT** The hairpin turns along this fifty-mile stretch offer staggering mountain views. See p.926

* **Sawtooth Mountains, ID** Of all Idaho's 81 mountain ranges, the Sawtooth summits make for the most awe-inspiring scenic drive. See p.921

The Rockies

xploring the Rocky Mountain states of **COLORADO**, **WYOMING**, **MONTANA** and **IDAHO** could literally take forever. Stretching over one thousand miles from the virgin forests on the Canadian border to the desert of New Mexico, America's rugged spine encompasses an astonishing array of **landscapes** – geyser basins, lava flows, arid valleys and huge sand dunes – each in its own way as dramatic as the magnificent white-topped peaks. The geological grandeur is enhanced by wildlife such as bison, bear, moose and elk, and the conspicuous legacy of the miners, cowboys, outlaws and Native Americans who fought over the area's rich resources during the nineteenth century.

Apart from the **Ancestral Puebloan** cliff-dwellers, who lived in southern Colorado until around 1300 AD, most **Native Americans** in this region were nomadic hunters. They inhabited the western extremities of the Great Plains, the richest buffalo-grazing land in the continent. Spaniards, groping through Colorado in the sixteenth century in search of gold, were the first whites to venture into the Rockies. But only after the territory was sold to the US in 1803 as part of the **Louisiana Purchase** was it thoroughly charted, starting with the **Lewis and Clark expedition** that traversed Montana and Idaho in 1805. As a result of the team's reports of abundant game, the fabled "**mountainmen**" had soon trapped the beavers here to the point of virtual extinction. They left as soon as the pelt boom was over, however, and permanent white settlement did not begin until gold was discovered near Denver in 1858. Within a decade, speculators were plundering every accessible gorge and creek in the four states in the search for valuable ores. The construction of transcontinental rail lines and the establishment of vast cattle ranches to feed the mining camps led to the slaughter of millions of buffalo, and conflict with the Native Americans became inevitable. The **Sioux** and **Cheyenne**, led by brilliant strategists like Sitting Bull and Crazy Horse, inflicted decisive victories over the US Army, most notably at Little Bighorn – "**Custer's Last Stand**." However, a massive military operation had cleared the region of all warring tribes by the late 1870s.

Most of those who came after the Native Americans saw the Rockies strictly in terms of profit: they took what they wanted and left. Small communities in this isolated terrain remain exclusively dedicated to coal, oil or some other single commodity, and all too often the uncertain tightrope walk between boom and bust is evident in their run-down facades.

Each of the four states has its own distinct character. **Colorado**, with fifty peaks over 14,000ft, is the most mountainous and populated, as well as the economic leader of the region. Friendly, sophisticated **Denver** is the only major metropolis in the Rockies. It's also the most visited, in part because it's that much more accessible, but tourist numbers remain low enough not to detract from its role as a summer paradise for cyclists and whitewater enthusiasts, and as home to the best ski resorts in the country. Less touched by the tourist circus is vast, brawny **Montana**, where the "Big Sky" looks down on a glorious verdant manuscript scribbled over with gushing streams, lakes and tiny communities.

Away from gurgling, spitting **Yellowstone**, adjacent **Grand Teton** park and the nearby **Bighorn Mountains**, vast stretches of scrubland fill **Wyoming**, the country's least populous state. Rugged, remote and desolate **Idaho** holds some of the Rocky Mountains' last unexplored wildernesses, most notably the mighty **Sawtooth** range.

You can expect **temperatures** in the high sixties all the way up to a hundred degrees Fahrenheit, between early June and early September, depending on whether you are in the high desert of Wyoming, the plains of Idaho, or the mountains of Colorado. In the mountains, you should be prepared for wild variations – and, of course, the higher you go the colder it gets. The altitude is high enough to warrant a period of acclimatization, while the intensity of the sun at these elevations can be uncomfortably fierce. Spring (the "mud season"), when the snow melts, is the least attractive time to visit the Rockies, and while the delicate golds of quaking aspen trees light up the mountainsides in early fall, by October things are generally a bit cold for enjoyable hiking or sports. Most **ski** runs are open by late November and operate well into March – or even June, depending on snow conditions. The coldest month is January, when temperatures below 0°F are common.

Attempting to rush around every national park and major town is a sure way to miss out on one of the Rockies' real delights – coaxing a car along the tight switchback roads that wind up and over precipitous mountain passes. At some point it's worth forsaking motorized transportation, though, to see at least some of the area by **bike**; the Rockies contain some of the most challenging and rewarding cycling terrain on the continent. And of course, you cannot count yourself a visitor to the area without embarking on a hike or two.

Colorado

COLORADO is one of the least geographically homogenous of the United States, ranging from the flat, endless plains of the east to the colossal mountains of the west. In the north, **Native Americans** hunted and trapped in lush mountain valleys in summer, and returned to the prairies for the winter; in the south, the Ancestral Puebloans of Mesa Verde grew corn on their isolated mesas and shared in the great early civilization of the southwest.

Different parts of what's now Colorado accrued to the US at different times: the east and north were acquired under the **Louisiana Purchase** in 1803, while the south was won 45 years later in the war with **Mexico**. (Land grants issued under Mexican rule were honored by the Americans, which accounts for a still-strong Hispanic influence.) Gold-hungry Spaniards came through in the sixteenth century, and US Army Colonel Zebulon Pike ventured into the mountains on an exploratory expedition in 1806, but the Native American way of life only became seriously threatened with the discovery of **gold** west of Denver in 1858. At that time Colorado was still part of Kansas Territory; it became a territory in its own right in 1861, and a state in 1876. The distractions of the Civil War gave the Native Americans the opportunity to fight back, but they were soon overwhelmed. From then until the end of the century, Colorado boomed; the quantities of gold and silver extracted from the mountains did not really compare with the riches found in California, but they were sufficient to fuel a rip-roaring frontier lifestyle. At first, too, absentee landlords attempted to exploit massive **ranches** on the plains, but their disregard for conservation ensured that the droughts and storms of 1886 and 1887 swept away the topsoil.

For the modern visitor, the obvious first port of call is **Denver**, at the eastern edge of the Rockies and the biggest city for six hundred miles. Outside Denver, the northern half of the state holds the most popular destinations, starting with the dynamic college town of **Boulder** and the spectacular **Rocky Mountain National Park**. The majority of the resorts that have made Colorado the continent's foremost **skiing** destination snuggle into the mountains to the west of Denver: **Summit County** attracts the most visitors, **Vail** is considered best for terrain, and **Aspen** boasts the glitziest après-ski scene. The far west of the state stretches onto the red-rock deserts of the Colorado Plateau. **Pikes Peak** towers over the enjoyable city of **Colorado Springs**, but the rest of the state's **southeast** quarter is mostly agricultural plains. To the **southwest** untouched old mining towns like **Crested Butte** and **Durango** stand in the mountains, while **Mesa Verde National Park** preserves perhaps the most impressive of all the cliff cities left by the ancient Ancestral Puebloan civilization.

Getting around Colorado

By far the largest **airport** in Colorado is in Denver. Shuttle buses radiate from there to all the main towns and ski resorts – as do commuter-style aircraft. Denver is also a major hub for Greyhound **buses** to all neighboring states. Amtrak **trains** run straight across the middle of Colorado, timed in both directions to pass through magnificent Glenwood Canyon in daylight hours, but are so slow that they're barely more efficient than the hugely enjoyable tourist train, the Durango & Silverton Narrow Gauge Railroad, in the southwest.

Colorado is also one of the best destinations in the world for **cyclists**, hosting numerous on- and off-road championships. For excellent **maps and guides** to cycle routes in the state, contact the State Department of Transportation (☎719/530-0051).

Denver

Its skyscrapers marking the final transition between the Great Plains and the American West, **DENVER** stands at the threshold of the **Rocky Mountains**. Despite being known as the "**Mile High City**," and serving as the obvious point of arrival for travelers heading into the mountains, it is itself uniformly flat. The majestic peaks are clearly visible, but they only begin to rise roughly fifteen miles west of downtown, and Denver has, during the last century, had plenty of room to spread out.

Mineral wealth has always been at the heart of the city's prosperity, with all the fluctuations of fortune that this entails. Though local resources have been progressively exhausted, Denver has managed to hang on to its role as the most important commercial and transportation nexus in the state. Its original "foundation" in 1858 was by pure chance; this was the first spot where small quantities of **gold** were discovered in Colorado. There was no significant river, let alone a road, but prospectors came streaming in, regardless of prior claims to the land – least of all those of the **Arapahoe**, who had supposedly been confirmed in their ownership of the area by the Fort Laramie Treaty of 1851. Various communities had their own names for the settlement; with the judicious distribution of whiskey, one faction persuaded the rest to agree to "Denver" in 1859. The hope was to ingratiate themselves with the governor of the Kansas Territory, James Denver, but it turned out he had already resigned. The newspaperman Horace Greeley passed through in the early days, and described the place as a "log city of 150 dwellings, not three-fourths completed nor two-thirds inhabited, nor one-third fit to be."

There was actually very little gold in Denver itself; the infant town swarmed briefly with disgruntled fortune-seekers, who decamped when news came in of the massive gold strike at Central City. Denver survived, however, prospering further with the discovery of **silver** in the mountains. All sorts of shady characters made this their home; Jefferson "Soapy" Smith, for example, acquired his nickname here, selling bars of soap at extortionate prices under the pretence that some contained $100 bills. When the first railroads bypassed Denver – the death knell for so many other communities – the citizens simply banded together and built their own connecting spur.

These days, Denver is a welcoming and enjoyable, though conservative city. Tourism is based on getting out into the wide open spaces rather than on sightseeing in town, but somehow its isolation, a good six hundred miles from any conurbation of even vaguely similar size, gives its two-million population a refreshing friendliness; and in a city which is used to providing its own entertainment there always seems to be something going on.

Arrival, information and getting around

The colossal, ultra-high-tech **Denver International Airport** lies 24 miles northeast of downtown, out on the plains beyond Stapleton. Regular SkyRide **buses** can take you downtown ($6 one-way, $10 round-trip) and to Boulder ($8 one-way, $13 round-trip). Buses are available outside exit 506 in the East terminal and 511 in the West terminal. There are also a number of independent shuttle service options, which can be arranged within the terminal.

Amtrak **trains** arrive on the northwest side of downtown Denver at the beautiful old **Union Station** on Wynkoop Street, and the Greyhound **bus terminal** is every bit as close to the action at 1055 19th St.

The best place to pick up **information** about the city is the visitor information center, which can be found in the **Tabor Center**, 1668 Larimer St (Mon–Fri 8am–5pm, Sat 9am–1pm; ☎303/892-1112, ⓦwww.denver.org), though there's also an informal morning-only advice center for travelers arriving at the Greyhound terminal. The main downtown **post office** is at 951 20th St (Mon–Fri 8am–5pm; zip code 80201).

The Colorado Division of Parks and Recreation (☎303/866-3437) has information and maps for cycling in the city and the mountains, while GrayLine (☎303/289-2841, ⓦwww.coloradograyline.com) operates bus tours of Rocky Mountain National Park and the surrounding area (mid-May to mid-Oct).

City transportation

Downtown Denver is fairly easily negotiated on foot, with the occasional help of the very regular **free buses** that run for a mile up and down the 16th Street pedestrian mall at its heart (daily 6am–1am). RTD **buses** (Mon–Fri 6–9am & 4–6pm, $1.25; other times 75¢), with frequent services to Boulder, sports arenas

---

Colorado shuttles

Numerous **direct bus services** run from Denver airport to many of **Colorado's most popular resorts**, making it unnecessary to rent a car if you're based in just one place. For services to Aspen, see p.863; Boulder p.852; Colorado Springs, p.870; Estes Park (for Rocky Mountain National Park), p.856; Steamboat Springs, p.858; Summit County, p.859; Vail, p.866; and Winter Park, p.857. Note that these should be booked as far in advance as possible.

and the airport, leave from the underground **Market Street Station** at Market and 16th streets. They are supplemented by a **light rail tram line** that runs five miles through downtown from I-25 and Broadway, across the 16th Street mall and up to Five Points in the northeast (same fares as buses). From June to September, you can also buy a hop-on, hop-off day pass on the **Cultural Connection Trolley** (every 30min 9.30am–10pm; $3), which links Denver's main points of interest. For information and detailed schedules of the entire RTD network, call ☏303/299-6000 or visit ⓦwww.rtd-denver.com.

Accommodation

Denver has a good selection of central budget **accommodation**, ranging from hostels to motels and homey B&Bs, as well as various grand historic downtown hotels. One specialist **agency** with reasonably priced properties in Denver and throughout Colorado is B&B Colorado, PO Box 6061, Boulder, CO 80306 (☏303/494-4994).

Adam's Mark Hotel 1550 Court Place ☏303/893-3333, ⓦwww.adamsmark.com. Giant, luxurious hotel with excellent facilities, adjacent to the 16th Street mall. ⑥/⑦

Broadway Plaza Motel 111 Broadway ☏303/893-0303. Within walking distance of downtown, this plain but friendly motel has large and clean rooms (with phones and cable TV), free parking and reasonable daily and weekly rates. ④

Brown Palace Hotel 321 17th St ☏303/297-3111 or 1-800/321-2599, ⓦwww.brownpalace.com. Beautifully maintained downtown landmark dating from 1892, with elegant dining rooms and public areas. Step inside and marvel at the eight-story cast-iron atrium, and relax in the comfortable red leather armchairs. ⑧/⑨

Capitol Hill Mansion 1207 Pennsylvania St ☏303/296-666, ⓦwww.capitolhillmansion.com. Luxurious B&B in an old Victorian mansion. ⑤–⑦

Comfort Inn Downtown 401 17th St ☏303/296-0400. Very central comfortable chain hotel, with good continental breakfast. ⑤

Denver International Youth Hostel 630 E 16th Ave ☏303/832-9996, ⓦwww.youthhostels.com/Denver. Dorm beds for $8.50, four blocks from the capitol, in a not entirely safe area. Office hours are 8–10am & 5–10.30pm. No curfew.

Hampton Inn DIA 6290 Tower Rd, next to the airport ☏303/371-0200, ⓦwww.hamptoninn-suites.com. A comfortable place with continental breakfast and airport shuttle included. ⑤

Melbourne Hostel 607 22nd St ☏303/292-6386, ⓦwww.denverhostel.com. A run-down old hostel with no ventilation. An easy – if not all that safe – walk from the center. Dorms from $10. No curfew.

Oxford Hotel 1600 17th St ☏303/628-5400 or 1-800/228-5838. Very grand, traditional Western hotel dating from 1891. ⑦

Queen Anne Inn 2147 Tremont Place ☏303/296-6666, ⓦwww.queenannebnb.com. Central and very hospitable nineteenth-century B&B near a peaceful park; each of the 14 rooms is tastefully decorated to an individual theme. ④–⑦

YMCA 25E 16th Ave ☏303/861-8300. Clean, secure and comfortable, with plain private rooms (most en-suite) in a prime downtown location. Staying entitles free use of the excellent fitness center. Weekly rates available, reservations advised. ③

The City

Though oil money brought a spate of high-rise construction in the early 1980s, creating the "17th Street canyon," **downtown Denver** remains recognizable as the Gold Rush town of the 1860s. It's very easy to pick out the oldest sections on a map; though an endless regimental grid stretches for miles in all directions, at its heart one small area of tightly packed streets stands at a sharp angle to the rest. Much of the day-to-day activity centers on the shops and restaurants of **16th Street**, which but for its free buses is a pedestrian zone; there's also a range of galleries, brewpubs, shops and lofts in the revitalized district bordered by 14th and 20th, and Wynkoop and Larimer streets, known as **LoDo**, or Lower Downtown. It was in the **Larimer Square** district, around Market Street between 14th and 15th, that William Larimer built Denver's

Coors Field

Union Station
(Amtrak)

DOWNTOWN DENVER

Black American
West Museum

Market Street Station
(Local Buses)

Long-distance
Bus Terminal

WRITER
SQUARE

LARIMER
SQUARE

16TH STREET MALL

Performing
Arts Center

Cherry Creek

Colorado
Convention
Center

16TH STREET MALL

Civic Center
Station
(Local Buses)

US Mint

Civic Center
Park

State
Capitol

Molly Brown House

Denver
Art Museum

Colorado
History
Museum

0   400 yds   — ⊙ — Light Rail Transit

Cherry Creek Mall

THE ROCKIES | Denver

ACCOMMODATION				RESTAURANTS			
Adam's Mark Hotel	7	Denver International Youth Hostel	8	Delhi Darbar	E	St Mark's Coffeehouse	F
Broadway Plaza Motel	10	HI-Melbourne Hostel	2	Kapre Lounge	B	Tom's Diner	H
Brown Palace Hotel	5	Oxford Hotel	1	Mercury Café	D	Vesta Dipping Grill	A
Capitol Hill Mansion	9	Queen Anne Inn	3	Racine's	I	Wazee Supper Club	C
Comfort Inn	4	YMCA	6	Rocky Mountain Diner	G		

original log cabin. That burned down in a general conflagration within a few years, whereupon a city ordinance decreed that all new construction should be in brick. Restored to its late Victorian appearance, Larimer Square provides another lively focus for shops, bars and restaurants.

For a quick appreciation of Denver's geographical position, head for the **State Capitol** at Broadway and E Colfax Avenue. The thirteenth of the steps up to its entrance is exactly one mile above sea level; turn back and look west, and you get a commanding view – zealously protected by building regulations – of the Rockies swelling on the horizon. The capitol is a rather predictable copy of the one in Washington, DC, but the free tours (Mon–Fri 9.30am–3.30pm) are pleasantly informal, and you can climb its dome for an

△ mining camp in Leadville, ninety miles west of Denver

even better view. The world's entire available supply of red onyx was used to make its wainscoting.

Civic Center Park, right in front of the capitol, is flanked by two of Denver's finest museums. The glass-tile-covered **Denver Art Museum** at 100 W 14th Ave (Tues–Sat 10am–5pm, Sun noon–5pm; $4.50, free Sat; ⓦ www.denverartmuseum.org) has a solid collection of paintings from around the world, but is most noteworthy for its superb examples of Native American craftwork, with marvelous beadwork by Plains tribes and some finely detailed Navajo weavings. Some of the pre-Columbian art from Central America – particularly the extraordinary Olmec miniatures – is also spectacular.

The most interesting features of the **Colorado History Museum** at 1300 Broadway (Mon–Sat 10am–4.30pm, Sun noon–4.30pm; $4.50; ⓦ www .coloradohistory.org) are to be found in the downstairs galleries. Several dioramas, made under the auspices of the WPA in the 1930s, show historical scenes in fascinating detail, starting with the Ancestral Puebloans of Mesa Verde, following up with trappers meeting with Indians at a "fair in the wilderness" in the early 1800s, and a model of Denver in 1860. An exhaustive archive of **photographs** of the early West showcases the work of W.H. Jackson, who died in 1942 at the age of 99.

Free tours of the **US Mint**, a short walk northwest at 320 W Colfax Ave (Mon–Fri 8am–2.45pm; every 20min; ⓦ www.usmint.gov), reveal millions of fresh coins gushing from the presses in a flurry of flashing metal; avaricious fantasies are checked, though, once you notice the machine-gun turrets on the exterior, mounted in the depth of the Depression.

The **Molly Brown House**, 1340 Pennsylvania Ave (June–Aug Mon–Sat 10am–3.30pm, Sun noon–3.30pm; Sept–May same schedule, closed Mon; $6; ⓦ www.mollybrown.org), was home to the "unsinkable" Molly Brown, who is most famous for surviving the sinking of the *Titanic* (she'd already lived through a typhoon in the Pacific) and raising money for the survivors and their families. Interestingly, "Molly" is a moniker picked up after her death – she was known as Maggie during her lifetime. A poor Irish girl who went West to marry a millionaire, she ended up mixing with high society in Denver; after the *Titanic* brought her notoriety, she went on to become a suffragette and eventually ran for senator. Sadly, the house tours concentrate more on what the Browns owned and what the preservationists have managed to authenticate than on illuminating her extraordinary life.

Denver's black community is most prominent in the old **Five Points** district, northeast of downtown, created to house black railroad workers in the 1870s. The **Black American West Museum** at 3091 California St (summer Mon–Fri 10am–5pm, Sat & Sun noon–5pm; rest of year Wed–Fri 10am–2pm, Sat & Sun noon–5pm; $3; ⓦ www.coax.net/people/lwf/bawmus.htm) has intriguing details on black pioneers and outlaws. Perhaps the most interesting section is on cowboys, which debunks a lot of Western myths: one-third of all cowboys are thought to have been black, many of them slaves freed after the Civil War who left the South and found work as cattle hands.

Two or three miles east of downtown en route to the airport, the enormous **City Park** is home to the **Denver Museum of Nature and Science**, 2001 Colorado Blvd (daily 9am–5pm; museum and planetarium $6, IMAX $6, all three for $9; ⓦ www.dmns.org). As with many such museums, its brief extends beyond the (very good) dinosaur exhibits and wildlife displays to include anthropological material on Native Americans, which, though fascinating, does seem rather out of place. There's also a large **zoo** nearby (daily: April–Oct 9am–6pm; rest of year 10am–5pm; $8; ⓦ www.denverzoo.org), whose four thousand inmates include a couple of huge lowland gorillas in a large, thickly wooded sanctuary.

Denver's **Six Flags Elitch Gardens** theme park, on the western edge of downtown at 2000 Elitch Circle (summer Sun–Thurs 10am–10pm, Fri & Sat 10am–11pm; rest of year hours vary; $33 aged 6 and above; ☎ 303/595-4386, ⓦ www.sixflags.com/elitchgardens), is not only unusual for being so close to the city center (accessible by a cycle path along Cherry Creek or on the Cultural Connection Trolley), but also in having a state-of-the-art **water park** attached. There are some great white-knuckle rides here, including the Mind Eraser, that catapults you at 60mph through terrifying corkscrew loops; the Tower of Doom, a freefall vertical drop of 70ft; and the Sidewinder, which spins you round an impossibly tight loop and then, sadistically, does it again – backwards.

If you're looking for something a little quieter, the glitzy **Cherry Creek Mall**, a few miles southeast of downtown, is second only to the 16th Street mall as Denver's most popular shopping center. Opposite its main entrance is one of the best **bookstores** in the US, the Tattered Cover Bookstore at 2955 E First Ave (☎ 303/322-7727), which spreads over four extremely well-stocked floors. Even more tranquil is the **Denver Botanical Gardens**, 1005 York St (daily 9am–5pm; $3; ⓦ www.botanicgardens.org), where an excellent array of beautifully displayed plant life thrive, including a rock alpine garden featuring local mountain flora.

Finally, twenty miles west of downtown, high above the Coors Brewery town of Golden, **Buffalo Bill's Memorial Museum and Mountain Parks** on Lookout Mountain (May–Oct daily 9am–5pm; Nov–April Tues–Sun 9am–4pm; $3) is the final resting place of William Cody, famed frontiersman, buffalo-hunter, army scout and showman, who died in Denver in 1915 (see also p.888). Though now surrounded by huge electricity pylons, the gravesite offers great views in both directions, over the city and out to the mountains. The adjacent museum does a thorough job of outlining Buffalo Bill's past, and one of the more gruesome elements on display is a pistol whose handle has been fashioned from human bone.

Eating

As well as plenty of Western-themed steak and barbecue places, Denver has a cosmopolitan selection of international restaurants. Of the several distinct restaurant districts, the **Larimer Square** area is the most easily accessible on foot and has a wide selection. Several of the city's famed **brewpubs** serve good quality meals, too.

Casa Bonita 6715 W Colfax Ave ☎303/232-5115. Absolutely wild Mexican place, seating 1200 diners, a long way out on Colfax. Gunfights, cliff divers, abandoned mines to explore . . . the only weak link is the food itself, but it's all a lot of fun (especially for kids) and far from expensive.

Cherry Cricket 2641 E 2nd Ave ☎303/322-7666. Excellent burgers and Mexican food served up in a generally dingy sports-bar ambience make this a great place (near Cherry Creek Mall) to nurse a hangover – or even work on getting one (120 different beers on offer) while watching televised sports. Open 11am–2am.

Delhi Darbar 1514 Blake St ☎303/595-0680. Relaxed haunt with decent Indian food and a well-priced lunch buffet.

Fourth Story Restaurant & Bar 2955 E 1st Ave ☎303/322-1824. Relaxed American restaurant gracing the top floor of the Tattered Cover Bookstore, with overstuffed couches and chairs. Sunday brunch served with live music.

Kapre Lounge 2729 Welton St ☎303/295-9207. Exceptionally good Southern-fried chicken in a an old, established Five Points soul-food restaurant.

Mercury Café 2199 California St ☎303/294-9281. A lot of healthy choices, many vegetarian, but with some meat options as well. A good value.

The Palace Arms 321 17th St ☎303/297-3111. This small and classy restaurant tucked in the *Brown Palace Hotel* (see p.846) is the ultimate splurge in town, with a menu of mostly seasonal game specialties, and decorated mostly in antiques from the Napoleonic period – including a pair of Napoleon's dueling pistols.

Racine's 850 Bannock St ☎303/595-0418. Just south of downtown, this large, laid-back place is a Denver institution. Housed in a former auto showroom, the inexpensive restaurant serves excellent egg-based breakfasts, with imaginative pastas, reliably good sandwiches and spicy Mexican entrees later in the day.

Rocky Mountain Diner 1800 Stout St ☎303/293-8383. Continental food served up in a festive Western-style atmosphere.

St Mark's Coffeehouse 1416 Market St ☎303/446-2925. The small frontage of this trendy café hides a huge, art-filled room where regulars play chess and hang out day and night – from 7am to midnight. Brews excellent espresso.

Tom's Diner 601 E Colfax Ave (and Pearl). Wonderfully gritty and authentic 24hr diner, providing cheap deals on big portions of stock diner food at the seedy end of town.

Vesta Dipping Grill 1822 Blake St ☎303/296-1970. Attractive restaurant in a renovated LoDo warehouse serving tasty food in unusual combinations, based around the "art" of dipping. You can personalize each entrée – including a range of kebab-style meat or veggies – in a spectrum of flavors (Mediterranean, Asian, Mexican).

Wazee Supper Club 1600 15th St ☎303/623-9518. Well-established LoDo dining room, serving good cheap burgers, deli sandwiches and superb pizzas, plus a full range of beers, in a retro, art-deco atmosphere. One of the few places open really late (1.30am most nights).

Nightlife and entertainment

Though business still booms for Denver's numerous downtown brewpubs, an onslaught of sports bars in the LoDo district, particularly near Coors Field, have mostly taken over as the city's liveliest nightlife area. And if sports bars don't appeal, there are plenty of other more stylish or relaxing places to drink here, too. Most places close around 1am. For news of **musical** happenings, consult Wednesday's free *Westword*, the hip free monthly *Freestyle*, or the "Weekend" section in the *Denver Post*.

The remarkable **Red Rocks Amphitheater** (☎303/694-1234, ⓦwww.red-rocks.com), twelve miles west of downtown Denver, has been the setting for thousands of rock and classical concerts; U2 recorded *Under a Blood Red Sky* here. This 9000-seater venue is squeezed between two 400-foot red-sandstone rocks that seem to glow in early morning and late evening. The park is open free of charge during the day.

Denver's pride and joy, the modern **Denver Performing Arts Complex** on 14th and Curtis streets (☎303/893-4100 or 1-800/641-1222, ⓦwww.denvercenter.org), is home to the Denver Center Theater Company, Colorado Symphony Orchestra, Opera Colorado and the Colorado Ballet, and hosts performances nightly. Facilities in the complex include eight **theaters**, as well as the **Symphony Hall** (which is in the round, giving it superb acoustics).

In the hunt for **tickets**, both Ticketmaster (☎303/830-8497) and Ticketman (☎303/430-1111) can usually help. You can also try the Ticket Bus, parked on 16th and Curtis, in person (daily: 10am–6pm), where you'll often find last-minute deals on shows that have yet to sell out.

Breckenridge Brewery 2220 Blake St ☎303/297-3644. Atmospheric brewpub opposite Coors Field, you can watch the beers being brewed on site. Serves good pub grub as well.
Brendan's 1624 Market St ☎303/595-0609. Small basement pub in the LoDo with regular live blues; big-name acts pop by a few times a month and cover is rarely more than $10.
Comedy Works 1226 15th St ☎303/595-3637. Right off Larimer Square, Denver's major comedy venue is the most likely place to find visiting big-name stand-up acts. Closed Mon.
Cruise Room Bar *The Oxford Hotel*, 1600 17th St ☎303/628-5400. This place is a replica of the Art Deco bar on the *Queen Mary* ocean liner. Worth a stop for the atmosphere alone.
El Chapultepec 20th and Market sts ☎303/295-9126. Tiny, popular LoDo venue near Coors Field, with nightly live jazz and occasional big names.
The Church 1160 Lincoln St ☎303/832-3528. A dance club inside a gutted cathedral, combining a downtown nightlife landmark, a wine bar, sushi bar and three invariably busy dance floors. Plays mostly hard-house or garage. $5–15 cover.
Grizzly Rose 5450 N Valley Highway ☎303/295-1330. Celebrated Country and Western venue a ten-minute drive north of downtown on I-25 (exit 215). The massive venue has bands every night

and attracts famous names regularly. Cover $5–10.
Herman's Hideaway 1578 S Broadway ☎303/777-5840. One of Denver's favorite rock clubs, in a homey little bar just south of I-25, with live music from Wed–Sat.
Mercury Café 2199 California St ☎303/294-928. When there's not jazz on here, there's swing dancing, poetry readings or some other form of entertainment. The club is combined with a good-value restaurant, which serves lots of healthy choices, many vegetarian.
Polly Esthers 2301 Blake St ☎303/382-1976. Enormous and consistently popular club with '70s and '80s hits playing on two floors. Cover $5–10.
The Soiled Dove 1949 Market St ☎303/299-0100. Hugely popular bar with an often rowdy rooftop overlooking Market Street. There's an eclectic variety of live music almost every night; from local to national names and from jazz to rock.
The Stampede 2430 S Havana St and Park Road ☎303/337-6909. The massive antique saloon bar is the centerpiece of this Country and Western pick-up joint in suburban Aurora.
Wynkoop Brewing Co 1634 18th St ☎303/297-2700. Good home-brewed beers and bar food in the state's first brewpub, in LoDo opposite Union Station. There's an elegant pool hall upstairs, and live entertainment in the comedy lounge.

Northern Colorado

The major attraction for visitors in the Denver area is **Rocky Mountain National Park** to the northwest. Though on the map the distances involved may not look that great, it would be a mistake to attempt to see the whole park on a day-trip from Denver. Segments of the loop drive along the way can be very slow and laborious, and in a single day it's more realistic just to dip a few miles into the park's eastern fringes.

The lively foothill town of **Boulder** can be used as a base, though the smaller mountain towns give you more time in the wilds: **Grand Lake**, near the western entrance, makes a more attractive stopover than overblown **Estes Park** on the east, while **Winter Park** is an affordable, enjoyable ski resort. Further west, midway across the state on either side of the I-70 freeway, you'll find the famous Rocky Mountain ski resorts of **Vail**, **Aspen** and the rest, and the evocative mining town of **Leadville**. Continuing towards the Utah border, the landscape dips and rises in a patchwork of granite peaks, raging rivers and red-sandstone canyons, winding up at **Grand Junction** and the memorable scenery of **Colorado National Monument** and **Dinosaur National Monument**.

Boulder

BOULDER, just 27 miles northwest of Denver on US-36, is one of the liveliest college towns in the country, filled with a young population that seems to divide its time between phenomenally healthy daytime pursuits and almost equally unhealthy nighttime activities – the town is often referred to as "7 miles surrounded by reality." It was founded in 1858 by a prospecting party who felt that the nearby Flatiron Mountains, the first swell of the Rockies, "looked right for gold"; in fact they found little, but the community grew anyway.

With an easygoing, forward-looking atmosphere and plenty of great places to eat and drink, Boulder makes an excellent place to return each night after a day in the mountains. Downtown centers on the leafy pedestrian mall of **Pearl Street**, lined with all sorts of lively cafés, galleries and stores – including several places where you can rent **mountain bikes**. The most obvious short excursion is to drive or hike up nearby **Flagstaff Mountain**, for views over town and further into the Rockies; any road west joins up with the Peak to Peak Highway, which heads through spectacular montane scenery to Estes Park and Rocky Mountain National Park. For rock climbing, **Eldorado Canyon State Park** offers many opportunities and The Boulder Mountaineer (℡303/442-8355) can answer any questions and, of course, provide gear.

The adventurous **University of Colorado** offers a mixed bag of **events**, including in summer the Colorado Music Festival (℡303/449-1397), in the Chautauqua Auditorium (℡303/449-2413), and the seven-week Colorado Shakespeare Festival (℡303/492-0554).

Practicalities

Local and long-distance **buses** come into Boulder at the Transit Center, 14th and Walnut streets (℡303/442-1044); there are regular services from Denver and the airport (every 30min 8am–6pm, hourly 5–8am & 6–11pm; 75¢ local fare, $3 to Denver, $8 to airport; ℡303/299-6000). The Boulder Airporter also runs shuttles from Denver International Airport (hourly 8am–11pm; $14; ℡303/444-0808). Boulder's **local shuttle** bus, the HOP (every 15min Mon–Wed 7am–9pm, Thurs–Sat 7am–2.30am; 75¢), links downtown, the university and the trendy student district known as "the Hill." The hospitable **visitor center** is at 2440 Pearl St (Mon–Fri 9am–5pm; ℡303/442-2911 or 1-800/444-0447).

Even if you're not **staying** in the historic *Hotel Boulderado*, wonderfully located near Pearl Street at 2115 13th St (℡303/442-4344, ⓦwww.boulderado .com; ⑦), it's an atmospheric place to wander into for a drink and to listen to the free evening jazz. Nearby, in another grand old restored building, the *Pearl Street Inn*, 1820 Pearl St (T303/444-5584 or 1-888/810-1302, Wwww.pearlstreet.com; ⑤), offers elegant B&B-style accommodations. The *Foot of the Mountain*, 200 Arapahoe Ave (T303/442-5688; ④), is a friendly, log-cabin-style **motel**, nine blocks from downtown beside Boulder Creek. There's a welcoming **youth hostel** in a Victorian building at 1107 12th St, near the campus (T303/442-0522; ②); dorm beds cost $15, and there are lots of private rooms ($35 single, $42 double).

You won't have any problem finding **bars** and **restaurants** downtown, especially around the Pearl Street area. Two local papers, the *Boulder Planet* and the *Boulder Weekly*, are replete with dining and boozing information. *May Wah Cuisine*, 2500 Baseline Rd (T303/499-8225), is a good-value Chinese restaurant with cheap lunch specials, while *The Harvest Restaurant and Bakery*, 1738 Pearl St (T303/449-6223), is a must for any vegetarian, or anyone who appreciates healthy fare – though they do serve some flesh. A good upmarket choice is the *Flagstaff House*, 1138 Flagstaff Rd (T303/442-4640), where the menu frequently changes but often includes gamey "Rocky Mountain Cuisine." The *Hotel Boulderado* (see opposite) has two popular **nighttime** haunts: the *Corner Bar*, with armchair seating, a patio and pub food, and the *Catacombs*, which features nightly live blues, jazz and acoustic guitar music. The *West End Tavern*, 926 Pearl St (T303/444-3535), is a great venue for live jazz and comedy, with local microbrews and spectacular **Flatiron** mountain views from the roof terrace. For getting your groove on, *Round Midnight* at 1005 Pearl St is your best bet; there's a packed dance floor on the weekends (T303/442-2176).

Rocky Mountain National Park

You don't have to go to **ROCKY MOUNTAIN NATIONAL PARK** to appreciate the full splendor of the Rockies; it is simply one small section of the mighty range, measuring roughly twenty-five by fifteen miles. A tenth of the size of Yellowstone, it attracts the same number of visitors – around three-and-a-half million per year – and with the bulk of those coming in high summer, the one main road through the mountains can get incredibly congested. However, it is undeniably beautiful, straddling the Continental Divide at elevations often well in excess of ten thousand feet. A full third of the park is above the tree line, and large areas of snow never melt; the name of the **Never Summer Mountains** speaks volumes about the long, empty expanses of arctic-style tundra. Lower down, among the rich forests, are patches of lush greenery; you never know when you may stumble upon a sheltered mountain meadow flecked with flowers. Parallels with the European Alps spring readily to mind – helped, of course, by the heavy-handed Swiss and Bavarian themes of the region's motels and restaurants.

This is not an area that humans have ever made their home, though it lies on the route of old Indian trails, and the Ute would come here to hunt in summer. Early white mining ventures came to nothing, and the region was dedicated as a national park in 1915. The original proposal was for it to be much bigger, extending from Wyoming to Pikes Peak; the existing boundaries were drawn up as a compromise, after long negotiations with Colorado's powerful logging and mining interests.

Approaching the park

Approaching the park from the **east**, you barely penetrate the foothills of the Rockies before you arrive at the gateway town of **ESTES PARK**, 65 miles

THE COLORADO ROCKIES

WYOMING

Laramie

Cheyenne

Dinosaur
National
Monument

Steamboat
Springs

ROCKY MOUNTAIN
NATIONAL PARK

Grand Lake

Estes Park

Boulder

Winter Park

Central
City

Golden

Glenwood
Springs

Dillon/
Silverthorne

Denver

Colorado River

Vail

Frisco

Breckenridge

Grand
Junction

Redstone

Aspen
closed in winter

Leadville

Colorado
Springs

Colorado
National
Monument

Grand
Mesa

Crested
Butte

Hotchkiss

Buena Vista

Cripple
Creek

Black Canyon of the
Gunnison

Gunnison

Montrose

COLORADO

Sangre de

Ouray

Great Sand Dunes
National Monument

Telluride

San

Silverton

Juan

Cristo

Durango-Silverton
Railroad

Range

Monte Vista

Cortez

Range

Durango

N

MESA VERDE
NATIONAL PARK

Aztec

NEW MEXICO

0   25 miles

Taos

northwest of Denver and 90 miles southwest of Cheyenne. At the end of the nineteenth century, Estes Park was the private hunting preserve of the Irish Earl of Dunraven; once he was squeezed out, the town took on the more democratic function it still serves, of providing visitors with food, lodging and other services. In itself, it's not an attractive place, but its presence does at least ensure that all the necessary evils of mass tourism are confined into one neat valley. The **park headquarters** and main **visitor center** (daily: June–Aug 8am–9pm; Sept–May 8am–5pm; admission $15 per vehicle, $5 pedestrians and bikes; information ☎970/586-1206; weather ☎970/586-1333) is a couple of miles north, on US-36.

To reach the **western** entrance, 85 miles from Denver, turn north off I-70 onto US-40, a small detour beyond the junction takes you to the former mining community of **GEORGETOWN**, one of the best preserved Victorian mining towns in Colorado. The town is however most known as the starting point of the **Georgetown Loop Railroad**, 1106 Rose St (summer daily every 80min 10am–3.20pm; $12.95; ☎303/569-2403 or 1-800/691-4386). On the line, 1920s steam trains run a tortuous six-mile round-trip to Silver Plume, on a route that loops in big arcs – added to enable the engines to overcome the six percent climb – and includes a trip across a precarious trestle above Clear Creek.

Back on US-40. the highway negotiates **Berthoud Pass** en route to **GRAND LAKE**, a more low-key version of Estes Park. This unlikely **yachting** center, high in the mountains, consists of one main boardwalk-lined street beside the lake, lined with family amusements, lodgings and restaurants. The **Kawuneeche Visitor Center** of Rocky Mountain National Park is a mile north of town (daily: May–Sept 8am–6pm, Oct–April 8am–5pm; ☎970/627-3471).

Exploring the park

The showpiece of the park is **Trail Ridge Road**, between Estes Park and Grand Lake. This 45-mile stretch of US-34, said to be the highest highway in the world, affords a succession of tremendous views, and several short trails start from parking lots along the way. There are no services en route, and rangers advise that you allow three to four hours' driving time. The road is normally open from late May to mid-October. As winter deepens and the snow falls, it is blocked progressively lower down, but you can always expect to get as far as **Many Peaks Curve** from the east or the **Colorado River Trailhead** from the west. Snowfall is typically heaviest during March and April. The definite highlight is the stretch of road on both sides of the Alpine visitor center; here the peaks and alpine tundra will take your breath away.

While many people do little more than the drive along Trail Ridge Road, the park is best appreciated by getting out of the car and hiking. Recommending any one **hiking** trail above another isn't necessary as there are dozens of superb hikes to choose from. Instead, think about the kind of experience you're after – photographing a particular animal, for instance, or hiking across the Continental Divide – and plan around this with a ranger's help. While a hike on the wild, wind-blown tundra is (literally) the high spot of any visit, the ecosystem is so delicate that it is essential to stay on the paths. Be watchful of your own system at this altitude: dehydration and altitude sickness affect some park visitors each year, so plan hikes conservatively and drink plenty of fluids.

Between June and September, the informative **Alpine Visitor Center**, halfway along Trail Ridge Road at Fall River Pass, marks the center of the park; it has good exhibits on the alpine tundra (summer only daily 9am–5pm).

You can also drive here in summer along the unpaved **Old Fall River Road**; completed in 1920, the first road to be built in the park. This runs one-way only (east–west) along the bed of a valley carved into a U-shape by glaciers. While it doesn't have open mountain vistas, it's much quieter than the Trail Ridge, and there's far more chance of spotting **wildlife**. Roaming the park are moose, coyote, mountain lions and a total population of perhaps thirty black bears, which with a plentiful natural food supply tend to avoid contact with humans. The central and southern tracts of this wilderness are all but impenetrable; only a well-planned hiking expedition can get you into the remoter forests and valleys.

Just inside the park, near the Estes Park entrance, a spur road, open year-round, leads south to two small and pristine alpine lakes. On the way, the **Moraine Park Museum** (summer only daily 9am–5pm) has a well-laid-out set of exhibits on the park's natural history. Beyond here, to ease the traffic in summer, a free and very regular **shuttle bus** from the Glacier Basin parking area runs the last few miles up to **Bear Lake** (every 15–30min from approximately 8:30am until 5.30pm; check at the visitor centers for the day's schedule), which is the park's most definitive viewpoint, with the mountains framed to perfection beyond the cool, still waters. **Sprague Lake**, lower down, has been landscaped to provide access for disabled visitors: a dead-level paved path encircles the shore, and there are special camping facilities for up to twelve people plus six wheelchairs (contact the park HQ for details; see overleaf).

Park practicalities

Public transportation to Estes Park from Denver International Airport is provided by Estes Park Shuttle ($39 one-way; ☎970/586-5151 or 1-800/950-3274). To get around the park if you're not driving, you can either pick up a **tour** from Estes Park, which with admission (not always included in the quoted price) should cost around $70 a day or $35 a half-day, or you can make the trip from Denver, with Gray Line (see p.845).

Five official **campgrounds**, at Moraine Park, Glacier Basin, Aspenglen, Longs Peak and Timber Creek, provide the only accommodation within the park ($16 per night). All fill early each day; in summer, reservations are essential for Moraine Park and Glacier Basin (☎301/722-1257 or 1-800/365-2267, ⓦwww.reservations.nps.gov), while the others are first-come first-served. Longs Peak imposes a maximum stay of three days, the rest allow one week. For **backcountry camping** you need a permit ($15 fee May–Oct only), valid for up to seven days, and available from park headquarters or the Kawuneeche Visitor Center (see overleaf).

Estes Park abounds in lodges, motels and places to eat; the **Chamber of Commerce**, 500 Big Thompson Ave (May–Sept Mon–Sat 8am–8pm, Sun 9am–5pm; Oct–April Mon–Sat 8am–5pm, Sun 10am–4pm; ☎970/586-4431 or 1-800/443-7837, ⓦwww.estesparkresort.com), has full details. Options include the *Alpine Trail Ridge Inn*, 927 Moraine Ave (☎970/586-4585 or 1-800/233-5023; ❸), *Lazy T Motel*, 1340 Big Thompson Ave (☎970/586-4376 or 1-800/530-8822; ❷), and the glamorous 1909 *Stanley Hotel*, in a fantastic mountainside location at 333 Wonderview Ave (☎970/586-3371 or 1-800/976-1377; ❼). The *Colorado Mountain School*, 351 Moraine Ave (☎970/586-5758; $20 per bed), is the nearest thing to a hostel in town, with dorm beds in cramped rooms and no cooking facilities. The relaxed *Molly B*, 200 Moraine Ave (☎970/586-2766), has an extensive all-day menu, while the excellent dinner buffet at the historic *Baldpate Inn*, 4900 S Hwy-7 (☎970/586-6151; reservations essential), includes hearty soups, freshly baked gourmet breads and a range of salads, for only $11.

Grand Lake has a highly recommended **youth hostel**: the gorgeous, rambling log-built *Shadowcliff Lodge*, perched high in the woods on Tunnel Road (June–Sept only; ☎970/627-9220; ❷). Run by the United Methodist Church, it offers budget dorms for $10–12; clean, comfortable motel rooms with great views; big, hummingbird-visited terraces; and a serene chapel open to all. Among a number of moderately priced **motels** are the *Western Riviera Motel*

& Cabins, in an attractive spot down by the lake at 419 Garfield St (☎970/627-3580; ❹), and *Waconda Motel*, 725 Grand Ave (☎970/627-8312; ❸/❹), whose central location and well-reputed breakfast menu make it a popular choice; note that during summer, some places in Grand Lake insist on a minimum three-night stay. One of the better places to eat is *EG's Garden Grill*, serving quality Mediterranean-style food at moderate prices in a cozy, colorful dining room on the boardwalk at 1000 Grand Ave (☎970/627-8404) – you can also sit in the beer garden (happy hour Mon–Sat 5–7pm); don't miss the fabulous $7 breakfast buffet at *Grand Lake Lodge*, 15500 US-34 (☎970/627-3185; open June to mid-Sept).

Winter Park

The former railroad center of **WINTER PARK**, 67 miles northwest of Denver, may not be Colorado's trendiest resort, but its wide, ever-expanding variety of ski and bike terrain, friendly atmosphere and good-value lodgings draw over one million visitors a year. As the only publicly owned resort in the state, it has great facilities for kids and disabled skiers – and the 200-acre **Discovery Park**, an excellent, economical area for beginners. Experienced skiers, in turn, relish the mogul runs on the awesome **Mary Jane Mountain**, the fluffy snows of the Parsenn Bowl, and the backcountry idyll of **Vasquez Cirque**.

In addition to skiing, you can **snowmobile** the Continental Divide on a one-hour tour with Trailblazers in Fraser ($35; ☎970/726-8452), or around a 25-mile course at Mountain Madness ($35 per hour; ☎970/726-4529), just north of town. **Summer** visitors can enjoy six hundred miles of **mountain bike** trails, some of the best of which are accessible from the chair-lift ($21 for an adult day bike pass), in addition to the super-fun mile-and-a-half-long **Alpine Slide** ($6) and several contemporary music festivals.

Practicalities

Year-round service to Winter Park is provided by Greyhound, stopping downtown outside the **visitor center** at the junction of Hwy-40 and Vasquez Road (daily 8am–5pm; ☎970/726-4118 or 1-800/903-7275, ⓦwww.winterpark-info.com), by Amtrak, five miles north in Fraser, and on Home James shuttles from Denver International Airport ($34; ☎303/726-5060 or 1-800/451-4844). The **Winter Park Ski Train** does round-trips from Denver every Saturday and Sunday during ski season, leaving at 7.15am and starting back at 4.15pm ($35; 2hr; reservations required; ☎303/296-4754, ⓦwww.skitrain.com). An excellent network of free **shuttle buses** means that a car is not essential in town. Trail maps and general outdoor information are available at the visitor center.

Winter Park offers the best choice of **rooms** among Colorado resorts. As well as **condos** (bookable through Winter Park Central Reservations; ☎970/726-5587 or 1-800/453-2525, ⓦwww.winterparkresort.com; ❹ and up), inexpensive **motels** include the downtown *Viking Lodge* (☎970/726-8885 or 1-800/421-4013; ❷–❹). The *YMCA Snow Mountain Ranch*, a few miles north on Hwy-40 (☎970/726-4628; ❸–❺), has good group rates, an indoor pool, library and guide-led activities. On the face of it, Winter Park's six **ski lodges**, like downtown's *Arapahoe Ski Lodge* (☎970/726-8222 or 1-800/338-2698; ❹–❼), may seem expensive, but these delightful old-style inns offer unmatched comfort, facilities and value, and are often full-board.

Nightlife starts at the base of the ski lifts at *The Slope* (☎970/726-5727), before progressing downtown to the likes of *Carlos and Maria's* in Cooper

Creek Square (☎970/726-9674), good for low-cost margaritas and Mexican food, and *Deno's* (☎970/726-5332), with its hundred-plus beers and tasty pasta.

Steamboat Springs

Surrounded by wide valleys, **STEAMBOAT SPRINGS**, 65 miles north of Vail, looks like no other Colorado mountain resort. Its roots are in ranching rather than mining, and its downtown area still evokes a pioneer feel – until you spot the upmarket boutiques. In this ski-mad town, rancher-types judge the quality of snowfall by the number of fence wires it covers; they're usually satisfied with a three-wire winter, which corresponds to its average snowfall of 325 inches per year.

The town's top-notch **ski resort** (lift tickets $59 per day), snuggled into Mount Werner four miles south of downtown, is boosted by such activities as dogsled expeditions, hot-air ballooning and snowmobiling, available in and around town. A favorite year-round activity is to let all the stress seep out at the secluded 105°F **Strawberry Park Hot Springs** (daily; 10am–midnight; $5–10), six miles north of town but only accessible by 4WD in winter. If you prefer to stay in town, the **Steamboat Springs Health and Recreation Center** offers hot mineral pools (6.30am–10pm; $5), as well as workout facilities. In the summertime, opportunities for **mountain biking**, **whitewater rafting** and **horseback riding** abound. Outfitters throughout the town can assist you with gear and guides.

Practicalities

Most winter visitors fly into **Yampa Valley Airport**, 22 miles out from Steamboat Springs, though it's possible to drive, weather permitting, from Denver over scenic **Rabbit Ears Pass**, or take the Alpine Taxi shuttle direct from Denver International Airport (☎970/879-8294 or 1-800/343-7433; $60). Visitor information is at 1255 Lincoln Ave, two miles east of downtown (Mon–Sat 9am–6pm, also Sun 9am–6pm during peak times in summer and winter; ☎970/879-0880, ⓦwww.steamboat-chamber.com).

From town, free SST **buses** (☎970/879-3717) run the four miles to the ski resort. Slopeside **lodging**, such as the comfortable *Best Western Ptarmigan Inn* (☎970/879-1730 or 1-800/538-7519; winter ❻, summer ❺), costs more than downtown options like *Rabbit Ears Motel* (☎970/879-1150 or 1-800/828-7702, ⓦwww.rabbitearsmotel.com; winter ❺, summer ❹), or *Nite's Rest Motel* (☎970/879-1212 or 1-800/828-1780, ⓦwww.nitesrest.com; winter ❺, summer ❸). Steamboat Central Reservations (☎1-800/922-2722) can supply information on lodging and packages. You can **camp** at the *Steamboat Springs KOA Campground* (☎970/879-0273; tents $20, hookups $26), two miles west of downtown on US-40.

For **food**, *Azteca Taqueria*, 402 Lincoln Ave (☎970/870-9980), has great inexpensive Mexican takeout; for a casual atmosphere and deli-bakery delights try *Winona's*, 617 Lincoln Ave (☎970/879-2483); and for more stylish dining, *Antares*, 57-and-a-third 8th St (☎970/879-9939), is one of Steamboat's very best, serving an eclectic range of fish and meat dishes. If you've got money to spare, try the delicious dinner at *Hazie's*, up on the mountain (open Tues–Sat for lunch and dinner during ski season, Fri and Sat nights during summer; ☎970/879-6111), which includes a free gondola ride; best of all is their superb $26 summer-only Sunday brunch. Microbrews and decent pub food are available near the ski area at *The Tugboat Grill and Pub* (☎970/879-7070), which also has live music and a dance floor; *The Cellar Lounge*, 703 Lincoln Ave (☎970/871-8917), is a good downtown venue for live bands too.

Summit County

The mix of purpose-built ski resorts, old mining towns, snow-covered peaks, alpine meadows and crystal lakes that make up **Summit County** lie alongside I-70, around seventy miles west of Denver. Before white settlement, the Ute hunted here every summer: the swanky Keystone Ranch Golf Club now occupies the meadow where they pitched their tepees. During the late nineteenth century the county witnessed several gold-mining booms; dilapidated **ghost towns** cling to the mountainsides, but one settlement that survived is **BRECK-ENRIDGE**, whose streets are lined with brightly painted Victorian houses, shops and cafés. This is the liveliest of Summit County's four towns; **FRISCO**, stretching sedately along a quiet valley, appeals to those looking for a less hectic pace. Both the other towns, **DILLON** and **SILVERTHORNE**, are dull, though the latter contains dozens of cut-price factory outlet stores. The villages at the resorts of **Keystone** and **Copper Mountain** are also unexciting.

Arrival and information

By **car**, Summit County is about two hours from Denver. Greyhound **buses** stop at the Frisco Transit Center ($11 one-way) from where free buses radiate to Copper Mountain, Keystone and Breckenridge. There are also **shuttles** from **Denver International Airport**. Resort Express serves Silverthorne and Breckenridge ($40; ☎970/468-7600 or 1-800/334-7433), while Supershuttle (☎1-800/258-3826) and Colorado Mountain Express (☎1-800/222-2112) run a more expensive door-to-door service to your hotel in Breckenridge. Summit Stage (☎970/453-1241) provides free **local transportation** around the county, and the Breckenridge Downtown Trolley (☎970/453-5000) runs through town and up to the resort. The main **visitor center** (daily 9am–5pm; ☎970/668-2051 or 1-800/424-1554, ⓦwww.townoffrisco.com) stands by the lake at the end of Frisco's Main Street, and there's a small welcome center in Breckenridge at 309 N Main St (☎970/453-6018).

Accommodation

Lodgings in Summit County cover all price ranges, with prices doubling in winter. Frisco has the best-priced inns and **motels**, with places like the *Sky-Vue* (☎970/668-3311; ❸–❺) and *Snowshoe* (☎970/668-3444; ❸–❺) as well as the excellent *Frisco Lodge* (see below). There are a few downtown **B&Bs** in Breckenridge, where otherwise accommodation usually means a slopeside condo; The Breckenridge Resort Chamber (Mon–Fri 8am–5pm; ☎970/453-6018 or 1-800/221-1091, ⓦwww.gobreck.com; ☎0800/897491 in the UK) can advise on prices and package deals. Resort accommodation at both Copper Mountain (☎1-800/458-8386, ⓦwww.skicopper.com) and Keystone (☎1-800/222-0188, ⓦwww.keystoneresort.com; ☎0800/898727 in the UK) is first class, but so too are the prices; virtually nothing costs under $100 a night, unless you find an unusual package deal.

Fireside Inn 114 N French St, Breckenridge ☎970/453-6456. Cozy B&B rooms, as well as a few bunk beds costing $25–30 per night in winter, $20 in summer. Winter ❻, summer ❸.

Frisco Lodge 321 Main St, Frisco ☎970/668-0195. Simple, motel-style accommodation in an old railroad inn. With kitchenette and access to a hot tub. Winter ❺, summer ❸.

HI-Alpen Hütte 471 Rainbow Drive, Silverthorne ☎970/468-6336. Clean bunkrooms in comfortable environs, and there's a midnight curfew. Winter $15–25, summer $12. Private, motel-style rooms are also available. ❹.

Ridge Street Inn 212 N Ridge St, Breckenridge ☎970/453-4680. Comfortable, luxurious B&B in the heart of the historic downtown area. Winter ❻, summer ❸/❹.

Outdoor activities

Winter is still the busiest time in Summit County. **Breckenridge Ski Area**, the oldest of the four top-class resorts, spans four peaks and offers ideal terrain for all skiers – and snowboarders, with a six-acre park with half-pipe – as does the plush **Keystone Resort**, where the biggest night-ski operation in the US permits skiing until 10pm. The smallest resort in the county, **Arapahoe Basin** (generally known as "A-Basin"), offers great above-tree line bowl skiing. All three are owned by the same company and covered by one lift ticket ($47 per day), making this one of the best-value deals in the country. The slopes at the other ski area, the ingenious **Copper Mountain** ($45 for one day), are divided into three clear sections to keep beginners, intermediates and experts out of each other's way. You can find out about conditions by calling ☎970/453-6118.

In summer, mountain-bikers and road racers alike will be happy with the opportunities for **cycling**, particularly the stretch between Frisco and Breckenridge; Racer's Edge at 114 N Main in Breckenridge (☎970/453-0995) rents out the best bikes. Each resort runs chair-lift or **gondola rides** to the top of the mountains, which, as well as stunning views, provide access to great **hiking** and cycling trails. Breckenridge also offers toboggan rides down the dry **Superslide** (summer daily 9am–5pm; $8), mini-golf ($6) and a giant maze ($4).

Eating

With the exception of Keystone Resort, Summit County hasn't developed a reputation for fine **dining**, though there's no end of good-value places to eat, especially in Breckenridge.

Alpenglow Stübe Keystone Mountain ☎970/496-4386. The best dining experience in Summit County – take the free gondola ride to the top of 11,444ft North Peak and feast on New American cuisine with a Bavarian edge in beautiful surroundings. It doesn't come cheap though – the six-course meals run around $70.

Blue Moose 540 S Main St, Breckenridge ☎970/453-4859. Inventive café menu, with lots of vegetarian dishes for well under $10. Open for breakfast, when good inexpensive wheat pancakes are on offer, and for lunch, when sandwiches, soups and salads take over.

Mi Casa, 600 S Park Ave, Breckenridge ☎970/453-2071. The best Mexican food in Summit County, including fine *chile rellenos*. The tangy fajitas are good value, as is the daily 3–6pm happy hour.

Mountain Java 118 S Ridge St, Breckenridge ☎970/453-1874. Cozy, book-lined coffee house serving healthful lunches, low-fat muffins and gourmet breads along with steaming espresso drinks.

Pika Bagel Bakery & Café 500 S Main St, Breckenridge ☎970/453-6246; also at 401 Main St, Frisco (☎970/668-0902). Friendly outlets for a fruit smoothie and a bagel sandwich.

The Prospector 130 S Main St ☎970/453-6858. Tasty traditional home-cooked breakfasts (including a spicy and excellent *huevos rancheros*) and lunches including roasts and meatloaf. Prices are among the lowest in town.

Rasta Pasta 411 S Main St, Breckenridge ☎970/453-7467. Good, fairly cheap pasta with a Caribbean twist and served to a soundtrack of reggae music.

Uptown Bistro 304 Main St, Frisco ☎970/668-4728. This is an elegant, upscale restaurant with seafood and Asian specialties.

Drinking

Immediate après-ski boozing is good at the slopeside bars of all four resorts. As the night wears on, Breckenridge offers the most choice, with several late-night music venues, though Frisco too has its moments.

Breckenridge Brewery 600 S Main St, Breckenridge ☎970/453-1550. This huge brew-pub, one of the first in Colorado and now a landmark at the southern edge of town, serves good-quality microbrews and hearty pub food.

Dillon Dam Brewery 100 Little Dam Rd ☎970/262-7777. Good microbrew ales and inexpensive quality bar food – salads, burgers and pasta – with entrees from around $8.

Downstairs at Eric's 111 S Main St ☎970/453-1401. Lively basement sports bar, with a good range of microbrews and filling bar food.
Gold Pan 103 N Main St, Breckenridge ☎970/453-5499. The only place you could get a drink in Colorado during Prohibition. Nowadays it's a lively saloon and pool hall. Daily happy hour 4–7pm, and they serve burritos, pizzas and soup.

Moose Jaw 208 Main St ☎970/668-3931. Dark wooden bar serving mediocre burgers and a dreary selection of beers until 2am – but a popular local hangout nevertheless.
Shamus O'Toole's Roadhouse 115 S Ridge St, Breckenridge ☎970/453-2004. Dingy-looking bar attracting a motley crew of bikers, bohemians and boozers. Rowdy, fun, and with a generous happy hour.

Leadville

Standing at an elevation of over ten thousand feet, south of I-70 and eighty miles west of Denver, the wonderfully atmospheric old mining town of **LEADVILLE** is the highest incorporated city in the US, with a magnificent view across to broad-shouldered, ice-laden mounts **Elbert** (14,433ft) and **Massive** (14,421ft), Colorado's two highest peaks. As you approach from the south, your first impression is likely to be of giant slag heaps and disused mining sheds, but don't let this put you off: Leadville is rich in character and romance, its old redbrick streets abounding with tales of gunfights, miners dying of exposure and graveyards being excavated to get at the seams.

In the light of this, visiting Leadville's rambling **National Mining Hall of Fame and Museum**, 120 W Ninth St (summer daily 9am–5pm; rest of year Mon–Fri 10am–2pm; $3), is a patchy experience: skip the baffling dioramas and outdated mine-shaft models in favor of the lurid globs of precious minerals and the atmospheric old photos of weather-beaten prospectors and rough-and-ready sluicers. For a more illuminating romp through the town's grim early history, head for the **Heritage Museum**, just around the corner at 102 E Ninth St (summer daily 10am–6pm; $2.50). Glass cases hold snippets on local fraternal organizations, quack doctors, music-hall stars and the like, while a host of smoky photographs portray the lawless boomtown that in two years grew from a mining camp of 200 people into Colorado's second largest city.

Of all Leadville's extraordinary tales, perhaps the most compelling is that of **Horace Tabor**, a storekeeper who supplied goods to prospectors in exchange for a share in potential profits, and hit lucky when two prospectors developed a silver mine that produced $20 million inside a year. Tabor collected a one-third share and left his wife to marry local waitress **"Baby Doe"** McCourt in the socialite wedding of 1883 in Washington, DC, attended by President Chester Arthur. By the time of his death in 1899, Tabor was financially ruined. Baby Doe survived Tabor by 36 years, living a hermit-like existence in the godforsaken wooden outhouses on his only remaining mine – the **Matchless Mine**. The buildings still stand, two miles out on Seventh Street, and in the crude wooden shack in which she died, emaciated and frostbitten, guides recount the story of Baby Doe's bizarre life in full, fascinating detail (daily 9am–4.15pm; $3). Also on Seventh Street is the **Leadville, Colorado & Southern Scenic Railroad**, (depot at 326 E 7th St; $27; ☎719/486-3936), which takes passengers on a two-and-a-half-hour scenic trip to Fremont Pass.

Back in town, don't miss the **Tabor Opera House**, 308 Harrison Ave (Sun–Fri 9am–5.30pm; $4), where you're free to wander onto the stage, through the ranks of red velvet and gilt seats, and around the eerie, dusty old dressing rooms, while recorded oral histories tell tales of the theater's golden days. They give no details, sadly, of the time in 1882 when Oscar Wilde, garbed in black velvet knee britches and diamonds, addressed a host of dozing miners on the "Practical Application of the Aesthetic Theory to Exterior and Interior House Decoration with Observations on Dress and Personal Ornament."

Outdoor activities

Leadville is an ideal base for some superb **mountain** biking, hiking and skiing. Bill's Sport Shop, 225 Harrison Ave (☎719/486-0739), rents and repairs bikes, while Leadville Ski Country, 116 E Ninth St (☎719/486-3836), has a full range of ski gear and snowmobiles, and can organize local ski packages. The resort of **Ski Cooper** (☎719/486-2277), ten miles north, offers good downhill, cross-country and backcountry skiing, as well as lessons.

Practicalities

Leadville's **visitor center** is at 809 Harrison Ave (summer daily 10am–5pm; ☎719/486-3900 or 1-800/939-3901). A good **place to stay** is the historic landmark *Delaware Hotel*, 700 Harrison Ave (☎719/486-1418 or 1-800/748-2004; ④–⑤), an atmospheric Victorian place where rates include a full breakfast; south of town on US-24 you'll find a string of cheaper motels, among them the dependable *Super 8* (☎719/486-3637; ④). Leadville has a gratifying choice of places to **eat and drink**. *Cloud City Coffee House and Deli*, 711 Harrison Ave (☎719/486-1317), serves bagels, buns and espresso in a grand old hotel lobby, while further along the street at no. 612, *Columbine Café* (☎719/486-3599) dishes up imaginative fresh food with lots of vegetarian options, in simple diner surroundings. There's great Mexican and Southwestern food at the spartan *La Cantina*, a mile south on Hwy-24 (☎719/486-9021), which also has dancing at the weekends. Among Leadville's fine **bars**, the *Pastime Saloon*, 120 W Second St (☎719/486-9986), is a local favorite, with a great mountain view from its patio, and delicious wings and burgers. After his performance at the Opera House (see overleaf), Oscar Wilde drank at the wood-paneled *Silver Dollar Saloon*, 315 Harrison Ave (☎719/486-9914); today, it's a welcoming, atmospheric place, filled with Irish memorabilia.

Aspen

Coffee-table magazines might have you believe that a tollgate outside **ASPEN** only admits film stars and the super-rich. This elite **ski resort**, two hundred miles west of Denver via Leadville, is indeed home to the likes of Cher, Jack Nicholson and Goldie Hawn, but it can be an affordable and very appealing place for anyone visit in summer – unless you're on an absolute shoestring budget. Visiting in winter requires more cash, though you can save money by commuting to the slopes from Glenwood Springs (see p.868), less than fifty miles away.

From inauspicious beginnings in 1879, this pristine mountain-locked town developed slowly, thanks to its remote location, to become one of the world's top silver producers. By the time the silver market crashed fourteen years later, it had acquired tasteful residential palaces, grand hotels and an opera house. In the 1930s, when the population slumped below seven hundred, it was, ironically, the anti-poverty WPA program that gave the struggling community the cash to build its first crude ski lift in 1936. Entrepreneurs seized the opportunity presented by the varied terrain and plentiful snow, and the first chairlift was dedicated on Aspen Mountain (now known as **Ajax**) in 1947. Skiing has since spread to three more mountains – Aspen Highlands, Snowmass and Buttermilk Mountain, and the jet set arrived in force during the 1960s. **Development** is a burning political issue: tight architectural constraints have been placed on businesses (*McDonald's* is forbidden to have a neon sign), but the last decade has seen yet more Scandinavian-style lodges, condo blocks and giant houses that remain empty for most of the year.

Arrival and information

In winter, **Independence Pass** on Hwy-82 from Leadville, which provides the quickest access to Aspen, is closed, and the detour through Glenwood Springs adds an extra seventy miles to the trip from Denver. The **airport** is four miles north of town on Hwy-82, served by local buses; if you fly into **Denver**, connecting flights bought in advance only cost another $60 or so. Or you can take a door-to-door shuttle from the airport (be sure to book in advance); companies include Supershuttle (T 1-800/258-3826) and Colorado Mountain Express (T 1-800/222-2112). Numerous airlines fly into **Eagle County Airport** near Vail, eighty minutes from Aspen by car or by Colorado Mountain Express.

Once in Aspen, there's no problem **getting around**: the Roaring Fork Transit Agency (T 970/925-8484) runs a free skiers' shuttle between the four mountains and serves the airport and outlying areas. The main **Rubey Park transit center** terminal is in the center of town on Durant Avenue.

Aspen's **visitor center** is at 425 Rio Grande Place (Mon–Fri 9am–5pm; T 970/925-1940 or 1-800/290-1324). The free *Aspen Daily News* ("If you don't want it printed, don't let it happen") is an excellent source of local gossip, news, and food and drink offers.

Accommodation

Aspen Central Reservations (T 970/925-9000 or 925-4444) runs a superb service, and doesn't balk if you ask for the cheapest available room. It also arranges package deals combining accommodation with lift tickets. Rates vary considerably even in winter; the least expensive times to come are in the "**value seasons**" (last week in Nov, first two weeks of Dec and first two weeks of April). Between mid-December and January 4, you'll do well to find a double for less than $140. If you're traveling in a group, money can be saved by renting a **condo**; for which the Aspen Skiing Company (T 970/925-1220 or 1-800/525-6200) and Affordable Aspen (T 970/527-6451 or 1-800/243-9466) are good sources. In summer, camping is also an attractive and inexpensive option; the ranger station, at 806 W Hallam Rd (Mon–Fri 8am–4.30pm; T 970/925-3445), can advise on free wilderness sites and campgrounds. There are several campgrounds on Maroon Creek Road, south of Aspen, and some smaller options out toward Independence Pass. Call the US Forestry Service at T 877/444-6777 for reservations and information.

Hotel Durant 122 E Durant St T 970/925-8500, W www.preferredlodging.com. Small hotel a couple of blocks from the town center and one of Aspen's cheapest deals; includes a hot tub, use of a cozy communal lounge area and a continental breakfast. Winter ❼, summer ❹
Hotel Jerome 330 E Main St T 970/920-1000 or 1-800/331-7213, W www.hoteljerome.com. Stately downtown landmark built at the height of the 1880s silver boom. Spacious rooms feature period wallpaper, antique brass and cast-iron beds, and a gamut of modern amenities. The lobby elegantly combines Victorian splendor and Rocky

Mountain chic and is worth a look even if you're not staying. ❾
Innsbruck Inn 233 W Main St T 970/925-29880, W www.preferredlodging.com. Bright basic rooms in an Austrian-style lodge with hand-carved beams, a few blocks from downtown. Continental breakfast is included in rates. Winter ❼, summer ❹
L'Auberge 435 W Main St T 970/925-8297, W www.preferredlodging.com. Idyllic little cabins, superbly outfitted with kitchens and fireplaces close to downtown. Winter ❼, summer ❺
Mountain Chalet, 333 E Durant Ave, Snowmass T 970/925-7797. Friendly, lodge-style

863

accommodation, with large comfortable rooms, pool, hot tub, gym and fine buffet breakfast. Winter ❼, summer ❹

St Moritz Lodge 334 W Hyman Ave ☎970/925-3220 or 1-800/817-2069, ⓦwww.stmoritzlodge .com. Lodge five blocks from downtown housing

Aspen's unofficial youth hostel; the private rooms and dorms are some of the best bargains in town and hard to get. Facilities include a small heated pool and a comfortable common room. Continental breakfast included. Winter ❻, summer ❸

The town and the mountains

Despite the virtually limitless recreation opportunities in the surrounding mountains, there's not all that much to do in Aspen itself. Even so, sitting around the town's leafy pedestrianized streets, watching the world go by, or browsing in the chichi stores and galleries is a pleasant way to spend a couple of hours. In summer, the Aspen Historical Society Museum, 620 W Bleeker St (☎970/925-3721), offers **walking tours** of Aspen and nearby ghost towns. The **Aspen Art Museum** at 590 N Mill St (☎970/925-8050) holds changing exhibits, lectures and special events; **Aspen Center for Environmental Studies**, 100 S Puppy Smith St (☎970/925-5756), is a wildlife sanctuary, which gives guided nature tours of some of the taller peaks in the Elk Mountain Range.

Aspen's four mountains are run by the **Aspen Ski Co** (☎970/925-1220 or 1-800/525-6200, ⓦwww.aspensnowmass.com); call ☎1/888-ASPENSNO

RESTAURANTS, BARS & CLUBS

Boogie's Diner	J
Double Diamond	K
Explore Booksellers & Bistro	C
J-Bar	A
Little Annie's	G
Main Street Bakery Café	B
Mezzaluna	L
Red Onion	I
Shooters	D
Su Casa	F
Takah Sushi	E
Wienerstube	H

ASPEN

ACCOMMODATION

Hotel Durant	5
Hotel Jerome	1
Innsbruck Inn	3
L'Auberge D'Aspen	2
Mountain Chalet	6
St Moritz Lodge	4

0   250 yds

for conditions. The mogul-packed monster of **Aspen Mountain**, looming over downtown, is for experienced skiers only; **Buttermilk** is great for beginners, with an excellent ski school that offers a three-day guaranteed "Learn to Snowboard" program; the wide-open runs of **Snowmass**, though mostly for intermediate skiers, feature some testing routes. **Aspen Highlands** has some new high-speed lifts and offers excellent extreme skiing terrain. Daily **lift tickets** for all mountains cost $45 (up to 27 years) or $65 (27 years and older). **Rental** of skis, boots and poles usually costs around $18 a day – you can also rent snowshoes in which to trek up and down the mountains. However, the town's best value has to be its fifty miles of groomed **Nordic ski trails** – one of the most extensive free cross-country trail networks in the US.

Cycling is the main **summer** pursuit; The Hub, 315 E Hyman Ave (T970/925-7970), has a wide range of bikes, while Timberline, 204 S Galena St (T970/925-9237), is the cheapest for mountain bikes, and also organizes tours. The **Roaring Fork River**, surging out of the Sawatch range, is excellent for kayaking and rafting, but sections can be dangerous and every summer sees a few fatalities. Blazing Paddles ($55 for a half-day float trip; T970/925-5651) is not the lowest-priced company, but it does have a good safety record.

If you fancy **walking** in the mountains, the Silver Queen **gondola** climbs from 601 Dean St to the summit of **Ajax** (daily 10am–4pm; $18), where guided nature walks set off on the hour from 11am to 3pm. Occasional free lunchtime concerts and talks are held up here, and there's a good restaurant. Even more alluring is the landscape around the twin purple-gray peaks of the **Maroon Bells**, fifteen miles southwest, soaring above the dark-blue Maroon Lake. The road is closed between 8.30am and 5pm, except for overnight campers with permits, travelers with disabilities and RFTA buses, which leave daily from the Rubey Park transit center (every 30min 9am–4.30pm; $5 round-trip, or $19 combination ticket with gondola ride). Details on hiking are available from the **ranger station** (see p.863).

Eating and drinking

Many of Aspen's classy cafés and restaurants charge over $25 for a main course, but good budget places exist and competition is keen. New restaurants open and close with alarming regularity; the list below consists of tried and trusted favorites. Note, too, that many of Aspen's bars serve good, reasonably priced food (see overleaf).

Boogie's Diner 534 E Cooper Ave (T970/925-6610). Airy second-floor atrium lined with vinyl and chrome for an inexpensive 50s-style diner experience; great meatloaf and killer shakes, but also few imaginative tofu-rich veggie options too.

Explore Booksellers and Bistro 221 E Main St (T970/925-5336). Great bookstore with high-quality creative vegetarian food, good espresso and pastries, and a shady roof terrace.

Little Annie's 517 E Hyman Ave (T970/925-1098). Lively, popular and unpretentious saloon-style restaurant. Potato pancakes and hearty stews for lunch, with huge trout, chicken, beef or rib dinner platters for around $15.

Main Street Bakery Café 201 E Main St (T970/925-6446). Scrumptious, inventive New American cuisine, and an excellent wine list in a

casual, chatty setting. Always busy in the morning for massive, fresh fruit-packed breakfasts.

Mezzaluna 624 E Cooper Ave (T970/925-5882) Mid-priced Northern Italian dishes for lunch or dinner, including wood-fired pizzas.

Poppycocks 609 E Cooper Ave (T970/925-1245). Open from 7am until 2pm, serving tasty crepes and smoothies.

Takah Sushi 420 E Hyman Ave (T970/925-8588). Phenomenally good sushi and pan-Asian cuisine, in a buzzing, cheerful atmosphere. Highly recommended yet quite expensive.

Wienerstube 633 E Hyman Ave (T970/925-3357). The best breakfast in Aspen: eggs Benedict, Austrian sausage and Viennese pastries among other things. A great value. Tues–Sun 6.30am–2.30pm.

Entertainment and nightlife

Going out in Aspen, the capital of **après-ski**, is fun year-round and need not be expensive. Check the free papers for special offers. In summer, downtown hosts several top-notch festivals. The flagship event is the nine-week-long **Aspen Music Festival**, between late June and late August, when orchestras and operas feature well-known international performers, as well as promising students who come to learn from musical masters (☎970/925-9042); July and early August see the **DanceAspen** festival (☎970/925-7718), which showcases reliably good contemporary shows.

Double Diamond 450 S Galena St ☎970/920-6905. Aspen's top live rock music venue, occasionally featuring nationally known acts. Usually free before 10pm and the drink prices are reasonable.

J-Bar 330 E Main St, in the *Hotel Jerome* ☎970/920-1000. This grand bar is a good place to soak in the hotel's atmosphere and rub elbows with well-heeled hotel guests.

Red Onion Cooper St Mall ☎970/925-9043. Aspen's oldest bar, serving big portions of Mexican food and good burgers. A popular après-ski spot,

especially for its lethal line in jello shots.

Shooters 220 S Galena St ☎970/925-4567. Swinging Country and Western bar that also holds a popular Tuesday night non-Country disco.

Woody Creek Tavern Upper River Rd, Woody Creek ☎970/923-4585. Unpretentious local bar, where ranch hands and rock stars shoot pool, guzzle fresh lime-juice margaritas and eat good Tex-Mex. The bar is in tiny Woody Creek – seven miles north of Aspen along Hwy-82, right on River Road, and then first left.

Vail

Compared to most other Colorado ski towns, **VAIL**, 122 miles west of Denver off I-70, is a new creation. Only a handful of farmers lived here before the resort – a collection of fake Tyrolean-style chalets and concrete-block condominiums – opened in 1952. During the Ford administration, it served as the western White House; Gerald Ford and his wife still live here, hosting annual celebrity golf and skiing competitions.

According to *SKI* magazine, Vail is the top **ski** destination in the US. What lures the ultra-rich (more conspicuous here than in Aspen) is the exceptional quality of the snow, the sheer variety of terrain, and the huge number of lifts (expensive at $62 a day, though the ticket also lets you ski Beaver Creek, ten miles west and home to America's top-rated ski school). You can also speed down a 3000ft **bobsled run** for $20 a time, or, in summer, go **mountain biking**: one good option is to use the two available gondolas (mid-June to Aug daily 10am–4.30pm; $12, $19 with bike) to carry your bike, then ride back down the mountain.

Practicalities

From **Denver International Airport**, several companies offer door-to-door shuttle service to Vail and Beaver Creek, including Supershuttle (☎1-800/258-3826) and Colorado Mountain Express (☎1-800/222-2112). **Eagle County Airport**, used by American Airlines among others, lies just 35 miles from the resort. Vail Valley Transportation (☎970/476-8008 or 1-800/882-8872) offers shuttles from the airport to Vail for $32.

Vail spreads for eight miles along the narrow valley floor, with successive adjoining villages from east to west at Vail Village, Lionshead, Cascade Village and West Vail. Beaver Creek, home of the Fords, lies a further ten miles west. The entire complex is **pedestrianized**; there's no charge for the parking lots in summer, and Vail Buses run free year-round shuttles (☎970/328-8143).

For information on skiing and accommodation, contact Vail Reservations (☎1-800/427-8308; ☎0800/891772 from the UK), or call a **visitor center** at either Vail Village (☎970/479-1394) or Lionshead (☎970/479-1385). Finding an affordable place to **stay** can be a problem. By Vail standards at least, the condos in **Avon**, just below Beaver Creek, are inexpensive. Rates in **Vail Village**, the main social center, are higher; try *Tivoli Lodge* (☎970/476-5615 or 1-800/451-4756; winter ❼, summer ❺), where rates include a continental breakfast and use of an outdoor pool, whirlpool and sauna; or the sumptuous *Mountain Haus* (☎970/476-2434 or 1-800/237-0922; winter ❼, summer ❻). The *Eagle River Inn*, 145 N Main St (☎970/827-5761 or 1-800/344-1750; winter ❼/❽, summer ❺), is a B&B decked out in tasteful Santa Fe style in the hamlet of **Minturn**, seven miles south of Vail on US-24.

Eating out can also prove expensive. *Jackalope* in West Vail Mall (☎970/476-4314) is a lively saloon and pool hall serving basic food (entrees around $9), and *Vendetta's*, 291 Bridge St in Vail Village (☎970/476-5070), offers fine Italian lunch specials and pasta dinners (around $15).

Nightlife revolves around **The Circuit** on Bridge Street, Vail Village. Most people tour between the bars and discos. The checklist of places to see and be seen includes *The Club* (☎970/479-0556), a basement bar with loud rock; the *Hong Kong Café*, 227 Wall St (☎970/476-1818), a small venue where crowds spill outside and loud music rules upstairs at *Vendetta's* (the ski patrol hangout); and *Nick's* (☎970/476-5011), below *Russell's Restaurant*, which plays reasonable dance music.

Glenwood Springs

Bustling, touristy **GLENWOOD SPRINGS** sits at the end of impressive Glenwood Canyon, 160 miles west of Denver and within easy striking distance of Vail and Aspen. Just north of the confluence of the Roaring Fork and Colorado rivers, the town offers endless recreational opportunities. Long used by the Ute as a place of relaxation, the **hot springs** here were the target for unscrupulous speculators who broke treaties and established resort facilities in the 1880s. North from downtown and across the Eagle River, is the town's main attraction, the **Glenwood Hot Springs Pool**, 410 N River St (summer daily 7.30am–10pm; rest of year daily 9am–10pm; $8), announced by its sulphurous smell. Billed as the "world's largest outdoor mineral hot springs pool," it sports an exhilarating water slide and special "jacuzzi" seats into which water is jetted. Next door, you can de-stress in the natural subterranean steam baths of the **Yampah Spa Vapor Caves** at 709 E Sixth St (daily 9am–9pm; $8.75), where cool marble benches are set deep in ancient caves.

Some of the West's most colorful characters came here in the early days, including Dr John R. **"Doc" Holliday**, a dentist better known as a gambler, gunslinger and shooter in the gunfight at the OK Corral (see p.970). A chronic tuberculosis sufferer, Holliday came to the springs for a cure but died just a few months later in November 1887, at the age of 35. He is buried on a bluff overlooking the town in the picturesque Linwood Cemetery. In the paupers' section lies the grave of Harvey Logan, alias bank robber Kid Curry, a member of Butch Cassidy's notorious Hole-in-the-Wall gang (see p.883).

Whitewater Rafting, I-70 exit 114 (☎970/945-8477), arranges good float trips and whitewater rides along a fairly placid twenty-mile stretch of the Colorado River. **Hiking** and **mountain biking** trails alongside streams and waterfalls crisscross the White River National Forest surrounding the town, and offer good fishing opportunities. The nearby, family-oriented **Sunlight Mountain Resort** offers some of the least expensive **skiing** in the region, accessible by shuttle from Glenwood Springs (☎970/945-7491; $1).

Practicalities

Amtrak arrives at 413 Seventh St, at the end of a scenic route through the canyons, gorges and valleys of central Colorado. Greyhound, traveling along the less inspiring I-70, stops close to downtown at the *Ramada Inn*, 124 W 6th St. The **visitor center**, 1102 Grand Ave (open 24hr; ☎970/945-6589, ⓦwww.glenscape.com) stocks the very useful *Glenwood Springs Official Guide*. Regular RFTA **buses** link the town with Aspen (daily 6am–10pm; 1hr; $6; call for schedule ☎970/925-8484).

The enthusiastically run *HI-Glenwood Springs Hostel*, near downtown at 1021 Grand Ave (☎970/945-8545 or 1-800/9-HOSTEL), has spacious dorms (beds $12–14), cheap private rooms (❶), plus kitchen facilities, a giant record collection and a wealth of local knowledge. They also arrange tours and whitewater trips, and are closed from 10am–4pm. Reasonable **motels** include the *First Choice Inn of Glenwood Springs*, 51359 Sixth St (☎970/945-8551 or 1-800/332-2233; ❸/❹), at the west end of town, which has striking mountain views, a guest laundry and a free, good breakfast. The *Daily Bread Café and Bakery*, downtown at 729 Grand Ave (☎970/945-6253), has delicious breakfasts, soups and salads. For dinner, *Rick's*, upstairs at 710 Grand Ave (☎970/945-4771), serves elegant continental food and boasts an extensive wine list. *Fiesta Guadalajara*, 503 Pine St (☎970/947-1670), is a decent family-run Mexican place near the hot springs and offers a huge variety of filling options, with its many combination plates priced around $9. A block away in the *Hotel Denver*, the *Glenwood Canyon Brewpub*, 402 Seventh St (☎970/945-1276), will certainly quench your thirst, with its great hand-crafted microbrews.

Grand Junction

GRAND JUNCTION, 246 miles west of Denver on I-70, is often neglected as a destination, even though its immediate environs abound with outdoor opportunities, and within a fifty-mile stretch you can trace the transition from fertile valley to full-blown desert. Another town that sprang into life in the 1880s with the arrival of the railroads, it now makes its living primarily through the oil and gas industries. Although initial impressions are bound to be unfavorable – an unsightly sprawl of factory units and sales yards lines the I-70 Business Loop – downtown is much better, with leafy boulevards encircling a small, tree-lined, historic and retail district.

Although the Colorado section of Dinosaur National Monument (see p.1025) is ninety miles north of Grand Junction along Hwy-139, the town itself holds the superb **Dinosaur Valley Museum**, 362 Main St (summer daily 9am–5pm; rest of year Tues–Sat 10am–4.30pm; $4.50), which houses a collection of reconstructed reptiles and giant bones excavated in the region.

But the main local attraction around town is the splendid local network of trails, many through parched, rugged and desolate desert country. Especially enticing for **hikers** is the remarkable scenery of the **Colorado National Monument**, while **mountain bikers** flock to the smooth rolling single-track trails around **Fruita**. Both activities are possible year-round, and are in fact generally more pleasant in the winter months. Trail information and rental bikes (front suspension $28 per day) are to be had from Over the Edge Sports, 202 E Aspen Ave (☎970/858-7220), a block east of the roundabout at the center of Fruita or from several shops in Grand Junction including Bicycle Outfitters, 248 Ute Ave (☎970/245-2699). The area is also a **rock climber's** dream; Summit Canyon Mountaineering, 549 Main St (☎970/243-2847), can supply you with the necessary information and gear.

Practicalities

Amtrak stops at Second Street and Pitkin Avenue. Greyhound buses serve Durango, Denver and Salt Lake City from 230 S Fifth St. The helpful **visitor center** is at 740 Horizon Drive (☎970/244-1480 or 1-800/962-2547, ⓦwww.grand-junction.net). Budget **motels** on the interstate – such as the *Best Western Horizon Inn*, 754 Horizon Drive (☎970/245-1410; ❸), with pool, spa, and continental breakfast – offer great rates; alternatives include the downtown *HI-Grand Junction* in the historic *Hotel Melrose*, 337 Colorado Ave (☎970/242-9636 or 1-800/430-4555), where bunks cost $12 and private rooms start at around $30. *Daniel's Motel*, at 333 North Ave, is basic but cheap and clean, and convenient to downtown (☎970/243-1084; ❷).

You can **eat** casually and inexpensively at the busy *Blue Moon Bar & Grill*, 120 N Seventh St (☎970/242-5406), which serves sandwiches, salads and bar food, or at *The Rockslide Brew Pub*, 401 Main Grand Junction (☎970/245-2111), offering filling portions of tasty bar food (burgers $7; Cobb salad $8) alongside a good variety of local beers.

Colorado National Monument

Millions of years of wind and water erosion have gouged out the brightly colored rock spires, domes, arches, pedestals and balanced rocks along a line of cliffs to form the **COLORADO NATIONAL MONUMENT**, just four miles west of Grand Junction. This painted desert of warm reds, stunning purples, burnt oranges and browns is also home to a high arid vegetation of piñon pine, yucca, sagebrush and Utah juniper.

The Monument has two entrances ($5, valid for seven days) at either end of the twisting, 23-mile **Rim Rock Drive** that passes through it (a 39-mile round trip from Grand Junction). The best of many overlooks along the rim drive is the **Book Cliff View**, or the **Parade of the Monoliths**, just off the rim road at the sign for Window Rock Trail. Short hikes include the one-hour **John Otto's Trail**, affording close-up views of several monoliths; longer trails get right down to the canyon floor. One of the best trails is the **Monument Canyon Trail** weaving through a series of scenic spots, while **Unaweep Canyon** is another beautiful area, with excellent **rock climbing.** You can **camp** for $8 in the park's only campsite, the basic *Saddlehorn Campground*, or pitch a tent anywhere more than a quarter of a mile off the road for free. For detailed information on trails, call in at the **visitor center** at the north end of the park (June–Aug 8am–7pm; Sept–May 9am–5pm; ☎970/858-3617, ⓦwww.nps.gov/com).

Grand Mesa

The **Grand Mesa**, thirty miles east of Grand Junction on Hwy-65, via I-70, is at 10,000ft the world's largest flat-topped mountain, created over a period of 600 million years by the erosion of the softer rock that surrounded the hard rock of this one-time massive lava flow. Though its full extent can only really be grasped from thirty miles away, visitors who ascend the twisting Hwy-65 to the plateau are rewarded by a tranquil landscape, covered by pine and aspen groves with over two hundred lakes. **Lands End Road**, an eleven-mile dirt track, ends at a stunning panorama: lakes, plains, sand hills and smaller mesas separate thick forest on the left from desert on the right, with the snow-crested San Juan peaks far off in the background.

The helpful **visitor center** near the Cobbet Lake junction of USFS Rd 121 and Hwy-65 on the southern side of the Mesa, can suggest good places to mountain bike and where to head out on cross-country skis or snowshoes in winter. Pretty campgrounds, open summer only, dot the east side near

Alexander Lake (details from the **ranger office** at 764 Horizon Drive in Grand Junction; ☎970/242-8211), as do a motel and some basic cafés. At the bottom of the Mesa, five miles north of **Cedaredge**, the hospitable *Llama's B&B* on Hwy-65 (☎970/856-6836; ❹) offers fantastic breakfasts served on a sun deck, and the chance to meet some llamas.

Southeast Colorado

The gently undulating plains of **southeast Colorado** come as a surprise to travelers expecting the ski resorts and alpine splendor that characterize the rest of the state. Here instead are hundreds of small farming towns and endless acres of grassland, much of which looks as it did 150 years ago, when traders and early explorers crossed the region along the Santa Fe Trail, following the Arkansas River between Missouri and Mexico.

The southeast's most popular destination is the engaging small city of **Colorado Springs**, which sits at the foot of towering **Pikes Peak** and provides access to the old gold-mining country around **Cripple Creek**.

Colorado Springs and around

Seventy miles south of Denver on I-25, **COLORADO SPRINGS** was originally developed as a vacation spot in 1871 by railroad tycoon William Jackson Palmer. He attracted so many English gentry to the town that it earned the nickname of "Little London." Despite sprawling for ten miles alongside I-25, modern Colorado Springs, a bastion of conservatism compared to liberal Denver, still retains much of Palmer's vision, thanks to a high military presence, fundamentalist religious organizations, the exclusive Colorado College and a well-to-do Anglo-American community.

Motorists whisk through the incredible **Garden of the Gods**, on the west edge of town off US-24 W, without bothering to get out of their vehicles. This gnarled, twisted and warped red sandstone rockery was lifted up at the same time as the nearby mountains (around 65 million years ago), but has since been eroded into finely balanced overhangs, jagged pinnacles, massive pedestals and mushroom formations. The **visitor center**, at the park's eastern border (☎719/634-6666, ⓦwww.gardenofgods.com), has details on hiking and mountain biking **trails**.

At the **Pro Rodeo Hall of Fame**, 101 Pro Rodeo Drive, off I-25 exit 147 (daily 9am–5pm; $6; ⓦwww.prorodeo.com), videos and displays explain the sport's various disciplines (calf roping, barrel racing and the like). Other local exhibits of note include the painting and sculpture gardens of the **Colorado Springs Fine Arts Center**, 30 W Dale St (Tues–Fri 9am–5pm, Sat 10am–5pm, Sun 1–5pm; $6), ranging from Native American art to Post-Modern pieces; the displays and demonstrations of specialized mining equipment at the **Western Museum of Mining and Industry**, east of I-25 exit 156A (Mon–Sat 9am–4pm, Sun noon–4pm; $6); and the town's history museum, the **Colorado Springs Pioneer Museum**, 215 S Tejon St (Tues–Sat 10am–5pm, Sun 1–5pm; free), part of which is a restored courtroom, location for a number of Perry Mason episodes.

Practicalities

From **Denver International Airport** there are a number of inexpensive **flights**, or you can book the Colorado Springs Shuttle (☎719/578-5232; $27).

Greyhound **buses** stop at 120 S Weber St downtown. Colorado Springs' **visitor center** is at 104 Cascade St (summer daily 9am–5pm; rest of year daily 10am–4pm; ☎719/635-7506 or 1-800/368-4748). The best value **accommodation** in the area is four miles west in Old Colorado City, at the inexpensive and well-worn *Amarillo Motel*, 2801 W Colorado Ave (☎719/635-8539; ❷). There are plenty more motels nearby; two blocks east of the *Amarillo Motel* is the elegant, rustically themed *Old Town Guesthouse*, 115 S 26th (☎719/632-9194 or 1-888/375-4210, ⓦwww.bbonline.com/co/oldtown), where hors d'oeuvres at check-in and a turn-down service are among the many personal touches. In summer, the neat, sociable and busy *Garden of the Gods Campground*, 3704 W Colorado Ave (☎719/475-9450; ❶), has $35 cabins for two, and a $23 campground.

Appealing places to **eat** downtown include the excellent *Olive Branch*, 23 S Tejon Ave (☎719/475-1199), with good vegetarian food. The *Phantom Canyon Brewing Co*, 2 E Pikes Peak Ave (☎719/635-2800), is a great place for some microbrews and authentic pub food. Out in Old Colorado City, the family-owned *Henri's Mexican*, 2427 W Colorado Ave (☎719/634-9031), pulls in the crowds for home-style food and superb margaritas. Nearby is one of the best **bars** in the city, *Meadow Muffins*, 2432 W Colorado Ave (☎719/633-0583), festooned with movie memorabilia, and serving good burgers, sandwiches and salads. It also hosts live music and stays open late (until 2am Fri & Sat).

Pikes Peak

Though there are thirty taller mountains in Colorado alone, **Pikes Peak**, just west of Colorado Springs, is probably the best known – largely because the view from its summit inspired Katherine Lee Bates to write the words to *America The Beautiful*. The 14,110ft peak was first mapped by Zebulon Pike in 1806, who never climbed it himself. By the end of the century gondola trails had been built to carry rich tourists like Ms Bates to the top. In 1929 it took Bill Williams, a Texan, twenty days and 170 changes of trousers to scale the mountain, pushing a peanut with his nose.

You can reach the top by a long **hike**, or by a difficult **toll road** (summer 7am–7pm, rest of year 9am–3pm; $10 per person or $35 per car; ☎719/385-7325 or 1-800/318-9505, ⓦwww.pikespeakcolorado.com). The thrilling **Pikes Peak Cog Railway** grinds its way up an average of 847ft per mile on its ninety-minute journey to the summit; from 11,500ft onward it crosses a barren expanse of tundra, scarred by giant scree flows. From the bleak and windswept top, it's possible to see Denver seventy miles north, and the endless prairie to the east, while to the west mile upon mile of giant snowcapped peaks rise into the distance. The train leaves from 515 Ruxton Ave in **Manitou Springs**, six miles west of Colorado Springs (mid-May to Nov; $22, reservations advised; ☎719/685-5401, ⓦwww.cograilway.com).

Great Sand Dunes National Monument

Fifty square miles of silky shifting sands huddled against the craggy Sangre de Cristo mountains, the **Great Sand Dunes National Monument** is around 170 miles southeast of Colorado Springs along I-25 and Hwy 160. Dunes have appeared in this surprising montane location thanks to millions of years of westerly winds blowing fine glacial sands from the San Juan mountains east to be trapped beside the Sangre de Cristos. Looking for a way through the mountains, the prevailing winds have been channelled towards the lower part of the range – near the Music, Medano and Mosca passes – where winds have been buffeted against the mountains, dropping their load at their base and forming the dunes.

Winds blow here every day, so whilst footprints aren't left for long, the dampness of the sand only a foot below the surface means that the general shape of the dunes has remained unchanged for centuries. A strange, eerie, yet beautiful place, the dunes harbor a number of small, endemic creatures, including the giant sand-treader camel cricket and the small kangaroo rat. Most visitors go little further than the "beach" beside Medano Creek, which runs along the eastern and southern side of the dune mass; but the climb up the dunes themselves, though incredibly tiring, is not to be missed – for the fun slide down (bring your own dune board) as much as for the views of the amazing desolate scenery. A walk along sandy trails, squeezed between the dunes and the mountains, and a night spent out at one of the underused backcountry campsites are also worthwhile.

The monument **visitor center** is three miles beyond the park entrance ($4 per vehicle; ☎719/378-2312, ⓦwww.nps.gov/grsa). Behind the visitor center is the **Mosca picnic area** – the main gateway for exploring the dunes. The most unforgettable way to stay at the dunes, and one that will leave sand in your gear for weeks, is to pitch on the dune mass itself. For this you'll need to pick up a free **backcountry permit** from the visitor center. A backcountry permit is also needed to use the seven lightly used primitive backcountry sites ($10) in the park. Most campers, however, stay at the large *Pinyon Flats Campground* ($10), the only site in the park accessible by car and usually crowded with RVs. It is run on a first-come, first-served basis, and is often full in July and August. The *Great Sand Dunes Oasis Store* (☎719/378-2222; ❶) just before the monument entrance offers showers, laundry and arid tent sites ($10) as well a small number of basic cabins (❸). Behind the store, the *Great Sand Dunes Lodge* (☎719/378-2900, ⓦwww.gsdlodge.com; ❺) has a restaurant, an indoor pool and pleasant rooms with dunes views.

Southwest Colorado

The high mountain passes of **southwest Colorado** are classic mining territory; dotted through the valleys you'll find all sorts of well-preserved late-Victorian frontier towns. As the pioneers moved in, first illegally and then backed by the federal government, they drove the Ute away into the poorer land of the far southwest.

From **Durango**, the main town of southwest Colorado, the dramatic **San Juan Skyway** completes a loop of over two hundred miles through the mountains, north along US-550 and then back via Hwy-145 and US-160. The stretch of road north of Durango, negotiating its way over stunning high passes, is known as the **Million Dollar Highway** for the gold-laden gravel that was used in its construction. Remote **Crested Butte**, to the north of the San Juan Mountains, is a gorgeous nineteenth-century mining village turned ski resort and one of Colorado's major attractions.

Durango

DURANGO is the largest town in southwest Colorado and the best hub for exploring the Four Corners region. Founded in 1880 as a refining town and rail junction for Silverton, 45 miles north, steam trains continue to run along the spectacular old mining route through the Animas Valley, though nowadays tourists, not sacks of gold, are the money-making cargo. The **Durango & Silverton Narrow Gauge Railroad** runs up to four round-trips daily between May and October, from a depot at 479 Main Ave at the south end of town (all leave in early morning; $53 round-trip; reserve tickets at least two weeks in advance; ℡970/247-2733). Shorter excursions, covering the most scenic areas of the route, run between late November and early May (daily 10am; $42).

Durango has also become one of the West's latest boomtowns, attracting a large influx of long-distance computerized teleworkers. Combine them with the local population of students from **Fort Lewis College** and outdoors enthusiasts who come to ride their mountain bikes in the area, and you end up with a town which has a youthful, energetic buzz.

Greyhound services between Denver and Albuquerque call in at 275 E Eighth Ave. Durango's **visitor center**, near the train station (summer Mon–Fri 8am–7pm, Sat 10am–6pm, Sun 11am–5pm; rest of year Mon–Fri 8am–6pm, Sat 8am–5pm, Sun 10am–4pm; ℡970/247-0312 or 1-800/525-8855, Ⓦwww.durango.com), has full lists of **accommodation**, topped by the landmark *Strater Hotel* at 699 Main Ave (℡970/247-4431 or 1-800/247-4431, Ⓦwww.strater.com; ❻), and rounded off by the $13 dorms at the shabby *Durango Youth Hostel*, downtown at 543 E Second Ave (℡970/247-9905; ❶). The innumerable **motels** north of town along Main Avenue double their rates in summer; try the good-value *Siesta* at no. 3475 (℡970/247-0741; ❸), on the northern fringes of town, or the small, comfortable **End O' Day Motel**, 350 E 8th Ave (℡970/247-1722; ❸) only a ten-minute walk southeast from downtown. The *Scrubby Oaks*, three miles east at 1901 Florida Rd (℡970/247-2176; ❹), is a good-value mountain-view **B&B**. There are plenty of places to **eat** and **drink**: *Carver's Bakery & Brewpub*, 1022 Main Ave (℡970/259-2545), opens at 6.30am for breakfast, serves Southwestern lunches and dinners, and keeps buzzing later on in its brewpub role. *Steamworks Brewing Co*, 801 E Second Ave (℡970/259-9200), is another good choice to sample local brews and also serves good food.

Silverton

Journey's end for the narrow-gauge railroad from Durango comes at **SILVERTON**, spread across a small flat valley surrounded by high mountains. It's one of Colorado's most atmospheric mountain towns, with wide, dirt-paved streets leading off towards the hills to either side of its one main road. Silverton's zinc and copper mining days only came to an end in 1991, and while the population has dropped since then, those that remain have so far resisted suggestions that its future lies in gambling to draw in the tourists. They are, however, extremely reliant on the seasonal tourist train; so while the false-fronted stores along "Notorious Blair Street" are a reminder of the days when **Wyatt Earp** dealt cards in the Arlington saloon, the town is defined by the restaurants and gift shops that fill up between 11am and 2pm when tourists are deposited in town.

Although tourism makes Silverton tick, it's pretty quiet here in the evenings as most visitors are on day-trips with the train. Bargain **accommodation** is to be had at the *Triangle Motel*, 848 Greene St (℡970/387-5780; ❸), at the south end of town, which also offers good-value two-room suites and jeep rental, though the old-style, central *Grand Imperial Hotel*, 1219 Greene St (℡970/387-5527 or 1-800/341-3340; ❹), with its forty creaky, antique-furnished rooms, is not much more expensive. The tin-walled *Silverton Hostel*,

1025 Blair St (check-in daily 8–10am & 4–10pm; ☎970/387-0015; ❶), has $11 dorm beds. For **food**, there's the *French Bakery*, 1250 Greene St (☎970/387-5976), serving sandwiches and soups through to full meals, while *Romero's*, 1151 Greene St (☎970/387-0123), is an enjoyable Mexican cantina with a menu of tasty, authentic food, plus fantastic salsa.

Ouray

The equally attractive mining community of **OURAY** lies 23 miles north of Silverton, on the far side of the 11,018ft **Red Mountain Pass**, where the bare rock beneath the snow really is red, thanks to mineral deposits. The Million Dollar Highway twists and turns, passing abandoned mine workings and rusting machinery in the most unlikely and inaccessible spots; back roads into the mountains offer rich pickings, for hikers or drivers with four-wheel drive.

Ouray itself squeezes into a narrow but verdant valley, with the commercially run **Ouray Hot Springs** beside the Uncompahgre River at the north end of town. A mile or so south, a one-way loop dirt road leads to Box Canyon Falls Park (daily 8am–7pm; $2), where a straightforward 500ft trail, partly along a swaying wooden parapet, leads into the dark, narrow Box Canyon. At the far end, the falls thunder through a tiny cleft in the mountain.

The local **visitor center** is on the northern edge of town beside the hot springs (daily 8am–6pm; ☎970/325-4746 or 1-800/228-1876). At *Box Canyon Lodge*, an old-style timber **motel** at 45 Third Ave below the park (☎970/325-4981 or 1-800/327-5080; ❸), you can bathe in natural hot tubs; the luxurious B&B *St Elmo Hotel*, 426 Main St (☎970/325-4951; ❺), holds a good **restaurant**, and the *Ouray Coffee House*, next to the springs at 960 Main St (☎970/325-4001), has an appealing patio for light lunches.

Telluride

Lying at the flat base of a bowl of vast steep-sided mountains, **TELLURIDE**, 120 miles northwest of Durango on Hwy-145, is located in one of the most stupendously picturesque valleys in the Rockies. Another former mining village, in the 1880s the town was briefly home to the young Butch Cassidy, who robbed his first bank here in 1889. These days Telluride is better known as the home of a top-class **ski resort** that rivals Aspen as the prime winter destination for the stars. It has, however, achieved this status without losing its character, exemplified by the low-slung buildings on the wide main street, beautifully preserved as a National Historic District. Healthy young bohemians with few visible means of support but top-notch ski or snowboarding equipment seem to form the bulk of the 1200 inhabitants, while most of the glitzy visitors tend to hang out two miles above the town in **Mountain Village**; the two places are connected by a free year-round gondola service. In summer, the **hiking** opportunities are excellent; one three-mile round-trip walk leads from the head of the valley, where the highway ends at Pioneer Mill, up to the 365ft **Bridal Veil Falls**, the largest in Colorado.

Accommodation is much less expensive in summer than during ski season, though prices do go up for the Bluegrass Festival in June, the Jazz Festival at the beginning of August and the Film Festival at the start of September. As well as being the town's official **information service**, Telluride Central Reservations, 666 W Colorado Ave (summer daily 9am–7pm; rest of year Mon–Fri 9am–5pm; ☎970/728-4431 or 1-800/525-3455, ⓦwww.telluridemm.com), coordinates **lodging** and package deals, with free lift tickets for the first month of the season for guests in certain lodges. Skiing comes half-price if you stay in any of seven neighboring towns. Of specific places, the 1895 *New Sheridan Hotel*, 231 W Colorado Ave (☎970/728-4351 or 1-800/200-1891; winter ❻, summer ❸), offers some bargain rooms with shared bath, and the *Victoria Inn*, 401 W Pacific Ave (☎970/728-6601 or 1-800/611-9893; ❺), has clean, motel–style doubles.

Eddie's, a sports bar at 300 W Colorado Ave (☎970/728-5335), serves good Italian **food** and home-brewed ales; *Smugglers Brewpub and Grille*, at San Juan Avenue and Pine Street (☎970/728-0919), is a lively evening hangout with a wide-ranging menu and some good local brews.

Crested Butte

The beautiful Victorian mining village of **CRESTED BUTTE**, 150 miles northwest of Telluride and 230 miles southwest of Denver, almost died off in the late 1950s when its coal deposits were exhausted. However, the development of 11,875ft **Mount Crested Butte** into a world-class **ski resort** in the 1960s, and a **mountain–bikers'** paradise two decades later, means that today it can claim to be the best year-round resort in Colorado. The old town is resplendent with gaily painted clapboard homes and businesses, and zoning laws ensure that condos and chalets are confined to the resort area, tucked behind the foothills three miles up the road. The rapid transition from near-ghost town to sporting heaven has lured young people here from throughout the West, to produce an addictive laid-back atmosphere.

Arrival and information

Crested Butte is not an easy place to get to, especially in winter and spring when **roads** can be cut off by snow and avalanches. Most skiers **fly** in: ten flights per day from Denver, and at least one per week from Atlanta, Dallas and Houston, touch down at **Gunnison Airport**. From here, Alpine Express ($40 round-trip; ☎970/641-5074) will drive you the 28 miles to your accommodation. Once in Crested Butte there's no need for a car: free **buses** ply the three-mile route between the town and resort every fifteen minutes. The **visitor center** is at Elk Avenue and Sixth Street (daily 9am–5pm; ☎970/349-6438 or 1-800/545-4505, ⓦwww.cbinterative.com).

Accommodation

The choice in Crested Butte lies between staying up at the ski area or downtown; you're likely to flit between the two areas every day, so it's only worth staying at the mostly more expensive mountainside lodgings if you're obsessed with getting first tracks. Crested Butte Vacations (☎970/349-2222 or 1-800/544-8448; ☎0800/894085 from the UK) can book accommodation and advise on money-saving package deals. In any case, be sure to reserve a room in advance during winter.

Claim Jumper B&B 704 Whiterock Ave ☎970/349-6471. Six variously themed rooms amid a jumble of Americana make this historic log home one of the most enjoyable B&Bs in Colorado. ❺

Crested Butte International Hostel 615 Teocalli Ave ☎970/349-0588. Large, friendly hostel, where dorm beds are $17 in summer, and $24 – assuming you manage to get one – in winter. ❶

Crested Butte Lodge Crested Mountain Village ☎970/349-4660 or 1-800/544-8448. Built in the 1960s, this is the oldest and most characterful place to stay in the resort, with its own indoor pool and spa. Winter ❺, summer ❹

Forest Queen Hotel & Restaurant 129 Elk Ave ☎970/349-5336. Built in 1881, the "Queen" has seven clean and basic hotel rooms. Located in the center of Crested Butte. ❸

The town and mountain

Despite the presence of a pretty and well-preserved Victorian downtown core, people come to Crested Butte only to head out again into the surrounding mountains where the skiing and mountain biking in particular are world-class.

In skiing and snowboarding circles the Butte is best known for its extreme terrain, with lifts serving out-of-the-way bowls and faces that would only be accessible by helicopter at other resorts. It's no surprise then that the resort hosts both the US extreme skiing and snowboarding championships. That said, there are plenty of long intermediate runs mixed in over the mountain's thousand skiable acres, keeping the slopes accessible to all. Fourteen chairlifts (adult day lift passes $55) link 86 runs, which are usually uncrowded thanks to the resort's isolated location. Cross-country, especially telemark, skiing attracts thousands, while snowmobiling ranks as a great way to rest your legs. For something a little different, try a **horseback ride** through the snow with Fantasy Ranch ($85; ☎970/349-5425).

In summer, **mountain bikes** all but outnumber cars around the town, especially during **Fat Tire Week** in July, one of the oldest festivals in the young sport and one that according to local legend evolved from a race over the rocky 21-mile **Pearl Pass** to Aspen on newspaper bicycles in the 1970s. You can still ride this route – 190 miles shorter than the road – but some of the most exciting trails are much nearer town and include the gorgeous 401 trail with wide open vistas, the Dyke Trail thickly wooded with aspens and the long, varied and occasionally challenging Deadman's Gulch. The visitors' information center can help out with a basic map and route description for main trails, and local bike shops like The Alpineer, 419 6th St (☎970/349-5210, ⓦwww.alpineer.com), are well-equipped with route maps and rental bikes.

Eating and drinking

Crested Butte lays claim to a surprising number of gourmet **restaurants**, which charge much less than their equivalents in the more glitzy resorts. Good, reasonably priced food is also easy to find; even around the ski lifts, a filling lunch can be had for $5. The early après-ski center is *Rafters*, right by the lifts. By early evening most visitors have found their way to downtown, for no-nonsense local bars such as *Kochevars* and *The Talk of the Town*.

Bakery Café 3rd St and Elk Ave ☎970/349-7280. Oven-fresh muffins, breads and pastries, plus a great selection of coffees and juices make this the best place in town for breakfast.
Idlespur Brewpub 226 Elk Ave ☎970/349-5026. Definitive, cavernous Colorado microbrewery, with roaring fire in winter and hearty, inexpensive bar food.

Le Bousquet 201 Elk Ave ☎970/349-5808. Excellent, imaginative and expensive French cuisine.
Powerhouse 130 Elk Ave ☎970/349-5494. The Mexican food is comparable to nearby *Donita's Cantina* at no. 330, but this restaurant's setting – a fondly restored 1880s generating station with a huge wooden bar and 65 varieties of tequilla – gives *Powerhouse* the edge.

Cortez

The town of **CORTEZ**, in the far southwest corner of Colorado, consists basically of one long curve of highway (US-160), roughly 25 miles up from the **Four Corners Monument** that marks the meeting place of Colorado, New Mexico, Arizona and Utah. Its primary function is as an overnight stop for visitors to Mesa Verde National Park, heading to or from the canyonlands of northern Arizona. Nothing in town commands much attention, though the giant **Sleeping Ute Mountain** to the southwest, visible from all over, makes a dramatic backdrop, looking uncannily like a warrior god asleep with his arms folded across his chest.

The **visitor center** at 928 E Main St (daily 8am–6pm; ☎970/565-4048 or 1-800/253-1616) has information on the entire state. **Motels** include the clean and basic *Aneth Lodge*, 645 E Main St (☎970/565-3453 or 1-877/263-8454; ❸), and the bland but reliable *Budget Host Inn*, 2040 E Main St (☎970/565-3738; ❸). *Dry Dock Restaurant*, 200 W Main St (☎970/564-9404), dishes up great seafood in its pleasant garden, while *Main Street Brewery*, 21 E Main St (☎970/564-9112), serves bar food. *Francisca's*, 125 E Main St (☎970/565-4093), is the best place in town for authentic Mexican food, and is often packed.

Mesa Verde National Park

MESA VERDE NATIONAL PARK, the only national park in the US devoted exclusively to archeological remains, is set high in the plateaus of southwest Colorado, off US-160 halfway between Cortez and Mancos. It's an astonishing place, so far off the beaten track that its extensive **Ancestral Puebloan ruins** were not fully explored until 1888.

Between the time of Christ and 1300 AD, Ancestral Puebloan civilization expanded to cover much of the area known as the "**Four Corners**." Their earliest dwellings were simple pits in the ground, but before they vanished from history they had developed the architectural sophistication needed to build the extraordinary complexes of Mesa Verde. Most of the best-preserved Ancestral Puebloan relics are in modern New Mexico, Arizona and Utah; see p.941 for more background information and a list of other sites.

Mesa Verde is a densely wooded plateau, cut at its southern edge by sheer canyons that divide the land into narrow fingers. The Ancestral Puebloans are thought to have been the only inhabitants the region has ever had: no one has lived here since the thirteenth century, and neither have any traces been found of a human presence before 500 AD. The people who built the first pit-houses here in the sixth century were already skilled potters leading a stable agricultural life; they owned domesticated turkeys and grew corn. After several hundred years, they moved off the mesa tops and began to construct spectacular multistory apartments and entire communities, nestling in rocky alcoves high above the canyons. Why they did so is not clear, though recent evidence suggests that Ancestral Puebloan culture was not quite as peaceful as previously imagined; in any case the soil at Mesa Verde ultimately appears to have been depleted, and they are thought to have migrated into what's now New Mexico to establish the pueblos where their descendants still live.

Touring the park

The access road to Mesa Verde climbs south from US-160 ten miles east of Cortez. Once past the entrance station (fee of $10 per vehicle), the road climbs and twists for fifteen miles to the **Far View visitor center** (late April to late Oct daily 8am–5pm; ☎970/529-4461). Exhibits inside cover Navajo, Hopi and Pueblo crafts and jewelry. Immediately beyond, the road forks south to the two main constellations of remains: Chapin Mesa to the south, and Wetherill Mesa to the west. To tour any of the major ruins you must buy **tickets** at the visitor center; $1.75 for each attraction, valid for one specific time only. On Chapin Mesa, Cliff Palace is usually open between 9am and 5pm daily from late April until early November, and Balcony House for the same hours between late April and mid-October; at busy times, you can't tour both on the same day. On Wetherill Mesa, generally accessible between late May and early September, tours of Long House operate between 9am and 4pm daily.

Six miles toward **Chapin Mesa** from the visitor center, the **Archeological Museum** holds the park's best displays on the Ancestral Puebloans, and also sells tour tickets for the remainder of the season after the visitor center closes in late fall (summer daily 8am–6.30pm; rest of year daily 8am–5pm). It's also the starting point for the short, steep hike down to **Spruce Tree House**, the only ruin that can be seen in winter – a neat little village of three-story structures, snugly molded into the recesses of a rocky alcove and fronted by open plazas.

Beyond the museum, Ruins Road (April to early Nov daily 8am–dusk) consists of two one-way, six-mile loops. If you're pressed for time, follow the eastern one only, to reach **Cliff Palace**, the largest Ancestral Puebloan cliff dwelling to survive anywhere. Tucked a hundred feet below an overhanging ledge of pale rock, its 217 rooms once housed over 200 people. Even if you don't have a tour ticket (see overleaf), you can get a great view from the promontory where tour groups gather, below the parking lot. Entering the ruin itself, especially on a quieter day, provides a haunting evocation of a lost and little-known world, as you walk through the empty plazas, and peer down into the mysterious *kivas* (circular, stone-lined ceremonial pits or buildings). Fading murals can still be discerned inside some of the structures.

Balcony House, a little further on, is one of the few Mesa Verde complexes that was clearly geared towards defense; access is very difficult, and it's not visible from above. Guided tours involve scrambling up three hair-raising ladders and crawling through a narrow tunnel, teetering all the while above a steep drop into Soda Canyon. Park authorities present it as more "fun" than the other ruins, but unless you share the fearless Ancestral Puebloan attitude to heights, you might prefer to give it a miss.

From the end of the tortuous twelve-mile drive onto **Wetherill Mesa** (daily late May to early Sept 8am–4.30pm; excluding large vehicles like RVs and cycles), a free miniature train loops around the tip of the mesa to reach the **Long House**, the park's second largest ruin, set in its largest cave. Hour-long tours descend sixty or so steps to reach its central plaza, then scramble around its 150 rooms and 21 *kivas*.

Park practicalities

Mesa Verde gets very crowded in high summer; the best months to visit are May, September and October. The park remains open all year, though most of the sights are inaccessible in winter, as detailed overleaf, and concessions such as gas, food and lodging only operate between late April and mid-October.

Most visitors stay in nearby towns; the only **rooms** in the park itself are at the summer-only *Far View Motor Lodge*, near the visitor center (Box 277, Mancos, CO 81328; ☎970/529-4421 or 1-800/449-2288; call ☎970/533-7731 in winter; ⑤), which has its own restaurant. **Food** is also available year-round at *Spruce Tree Terrace* near the Chapin Mesa museum. You can **camp** at the pleasant and very large *Morefield Campground*, four miles up from the entrance (late April to mid-Oct; $10; ☎970/529-4421), and there are also several commercial campgrounds nearby.

Ute Mountain Tribal Park

Abutting Mesa Verde National Park to the south is the Ute Mountain Indian Reservation, in which Ancestral Puebloan **cliff dwellings** spread over the inaccessible but utterly enthralling **Ute Mountain Tribal Park**, including the eighty-room **Lion House** and the precarious **Eagle's Nest Cliff** perched in a cavernous natural alcove. The only way to visit the dwellings is by joining a

Ute-led tour, arranged at the tribe's **visitor center** (no fixed hours; ☎970/565-3751 ext 282 or 1-800/847-5485), housed in a former gas station at the intersection of US-160 and US-666. Full-day tours (8.30am–4.30pm) cost $30, and involve walking three miles and climbing five tall ladders; easier half-day trips, on which you see petroglyphs but no cliff dwellings, are $20. Bring water and food as there's none on sale in the park. You're welcome to drive your own (sturdy) vehicle on the tours, but paying $5 extra entitles you to ride in the guide's jeep.

Wyoming

Pronghorn antelope all but outnumber people in wide-open **WYOMING**, the ninth largest but least populous state in the union, with just 460,000 residents. Above all, this is classic **cowboy country** – the inspiration behind *Shane*, *The Virginian* and countless other Western novels – where the days of the open range are evoked by rodeos, country-and-western dance halls and ranch-wear stores. The state emblem, seen everywhere, is a hat-waving cowboy astride a bucking bronco.

Northern Wyoming is the prime tourist goal, with well over three million per year heading for the simmering geothermal landscape of **Yellowstone National Park**, and the craggy mountain vistas of the adjacent, and equally outstanding, **Grand Teton National Park**. Wedged in between Yellowstone and South Dakota to the east are the helter-skelter **Bighorn Mountains**, likeable Old West towns such as **Buffalo**, and the otherworldly outcrop of **Devils Tower**.

The meager supply of buffalo in early Wyoming caused fierce intertribal wars over hunting grounds and kept the **Native American** population down to around 10,000. However, Sioux, Cheyenne and Blackfoot combined to inflict notable defeats on the US Army before it could clear the way for pioneer settlement in the 1870s. The cattle ranchers and sheep-farming homesteaders who followed engaged in violent **range wars** over grazing rights to the wiry grasslands.

Unlikely as it may seem, this rowdy, heavily male-dominated state was the first to grant women the vote in 1869 – a full half-century before the rest of the country, on the grounds that the enfranchisement of women would attract settlers and increase the population, thereby hastening statehood. A year later Wyoming appointed the country's first women jurors, and the "Equality State" elected the first female US governor in 1924.

The absence of rivers to irrigate farmland has effectively put a lid on agricultural and population growth. These days, any weather-beaten, denim-clad stranger is more likely to be an oil roustabout than a genuine cowboy, fuel and mineral extraction having replaced livestock as the mainstay of the economy in the early part of the twentieth century.

Getting around Wyoming

Greyhound **buses** operate along I-80 through the south. The rest of the state is covered only patchily by regional bus companies; it takes considerable time and planning to get where you want to go, so your own car is definitely the best option. Jackson has the state's largest **airport**, though flights also go to Casper and Cheyenne. **Cycling** across northern Wyoming can be great fun, although if you're crossing the Bighorns you'll need to pick your routes carefully, as roads here have incredibly steep gradients.

South and central Wyoming

State capital **Cheyenne** is the only town of real note in the lower two-thirds of Wyoming. Set in the heart of rich prairie – a surprise after the scrubland, mountain and desert of most of the region – it has closer economic ties with Omaha or Denver than with the rest of Wyoming, a point the more northerly oil city of **Casper** stressed in its unsuccessful bids to become the seat of government. West of Cheyenne, smaller **Laramie** possesses an agreeable frontier feel, while the spectacular wilderness of the **Wind River Range**, accessible from **Pinedale** and **Lander**, accounts for most of the west central portion of the state.

Cheyenne

The approach into **CHEYENNE**, dropping into a wide dip in the plains, leaves enduring memories for most travelers. With the snow-crested Rockies looming in the distance and short, sun-bleached grass encircling the town, the sky suddenly appears gargantuan, dwarfing the city's leafy suburbs and everything else below it.

A quick walk around reveals a diverse community, shaped by railroads, state politics, and even nuclear arms. When the Union Pacific Railroad reached this site in 1867, soldiers had to drive out the "**Hell on Wheels**" brigade of gamblers, moonshiners and hard-drinking gunmen who stayed one step ahead of the railroads, claiming land and then selling it for huge profit before moving on to the next proposed terminal. Union Pacific's sprawling yards and fine old terminus now mark the eastern edge of downtown, while to the west the city's longstanding military installation was expanded in 1957 to house the first US intercontinental ballistic missile base. Cowboy culture is big here, too, as the ranchwear stores and honky-tonks dotted around town attest. Along with the world's largest outdoor rodeo, the nine-day **Cheyenne Frontier Days** festival (℡307/778-7222 or 1-800/227-6336, ⓦwww.cfdrodeo.com/) in late July attracts thousands of people to its concerts with top country stars, parades, chuckwagon races, air shows and free pancake breakfasts. The rest of the year, it's pretty quiet; would-be cowboys have to make do with the **Old Cheyenne Gunfight**, at 16th Street and Carey Avenue (summer Mon–Fri 6pm, Sat "high noon"; free), in which gunslingers act out incidents from the town's turbulent first decade.

Sixteenth Street, or Lincolnway, is the retail and entertainment heart of Cheyenne. Five minutes' walk north up leafy Capitol Avenue near the unspectacular State Capitol, the **Wyoming State Museum**, at no. 2320, takes a sober look at Wild West history (June–Aug Mon–Fri 8.30am–5pm, Sat 9am–4pm, Sun noon–4pm; Sept–May Mon–Fri 8.30am–5pm, Sat noon–4pm; free). The **Cheyenne Frontier Days Old West Museum**, five minutes' drive from downtown at 4501 N Carey Ave (Mon–Fri 9am–5pm, Sat & Sun 10am–5pm; $3), is more lighthearted, telling how the railroad came to town, with some great old engines and well-presented temporary exhibits. Much of the place is devoted to the Frontier Days celebrations, with photos, costumes and videos evoking the annual frenzy.

Practicalities

Greyhound **buses** run east and west along I–80 and south to Denver, while Powder River buses travel through eastern Wyoming to Colorado, Montana and South Dakota. Both companies share the depot at 1209 S Greeley Hwy (US-85), along I–80 a mile south of town. The **visitor center**, at 309 W Lincolnway (June–Aug daily 8am–6pm; rest of year Mon–Fri 8am–5pm; ☎307/778-3133 or 1-800/426-5009, ⓦwww.cheyenne.org), has a free detailed map of the city, and operates a two-hour **trolley tour** of Cheyenne in summer ($8 for adults, $4 for children) as well as **ghost tours**. For information on the state in general, stop by the Wyoming Travel Information Center, perched at the windy highway junction of I–25 and College Drive (daily 8am–5pm, closed holidays; ☎307/777-2883 or 1-800/225-5996).

Although places to **stay** are normally inexpensive, prices double during the Frontier Days festival. Budget motels line up along West Lincolnway, like the *Atlas Motel* at no. 1524 (☎307/632-9214; ❷), and there are inexpensive rooms downtown in the historic *Plains Hotel*, 1600 Central Ave (☎307/638-3311; ❷). Best of the upmarket options is the *Nagle Warren Mansion*, 222 E 17th St (☎637-3333 or 1-800/811-2610, ⓦwww.naglewarrenmansion.com; ❺), which offers superb bed and breakfast in opulent surroundings. **Campers** should head for *AB Camping* at 1503 W College Drive (March–Oct; ☎307/634-7035; $13 per tent site).

Cheyenne has no shortage of **diners** serving cowboy-sized breakfasts, lunches and Mexican food; try *Los Amigos*, 620 Central Ave (☎307/638-8591). *Sanford's*, 115 E 17th St (☎307/778-2739), is a big, lively **brewpub** with great food and a mixed crowd, and comedy and live music downstairs. Between June and August the Terry Bison Ranch, some ten miles south of town, holds a **night rodeo** on Tuesdays and Saturdays ($7, prices vary; ☎307/634-4171).

Laramie and around

LARAMIE lies fifty miles west of Cheyenne on I–80, or slightly further via the spectacular Happy Jack Road (Hwy-210), which slices through plains studded with bizarrely shaped boulders and outcrops. At first Laramie seems typical of rural Wyoming, but behind downtown's quaint Victorian facades lurk hard-rocking record stores, day spas, vegetarian cafés and secondhand bookstores – unusual for rodeo land, and due to the **University of Wyoming**, whose campus spreads east from the town center.

The centerpiece of the ambitious **Wyoming Territorial Park**, west of town at 975 Snowy Range Rd (mid-May to Sept daily 10am–6pm; $6), is the old territorial **prison**. A touch over-restored, it holds informative displays on the Old West and women in Wyoming, and huge mugshots of ex-convicts, among them Butch Cassidy, who was incarcerated here for eighteen months in 1896, for – as was the crime of most of the inmates – cattle-rustling.

The Wyoming Children's Museum and Nature Center at 412 S Second St (Tues–Fri 9am–5pm, Sat 10am–4pm; $2 for adults, $3 for kids; ☎307/745-6332) is a great hands-on experience, with gold panning, a crawl-through beaver lodge and some live reptiles. The University of Wyoming visitor center, 1408 Ivinson Ave (Mon–Fri 8am–5pm, Sat 9am–1pm; ☎307/766-4075), can direct you to several free museums and sights of interest on campus, including the Anthropology Museum, the Museum of Geology, the University Art Museum and the Rocky Mountain Herbarium.

Practicalities

Greyhound pulls in at Tumbleweed Express gas station in Bluebird Lane, 2.5 miles east of downtown beside Grand Avenue. The **visitor center** at 800 S 3rd St (Mon–Fri 8am–5pm; ☎307/745-7339 or 1-800/445-5303, ⓦwww .laramie-tourism.org) is staffed by volunteers and is supplemented on summer weekends by a bright yellow railway caboose by the I-80 underpass (Sat & Sun 8am–5pm). **Room** rates are good at the downtown *Travel Inn*, 262 N 3rd St (☎307/745-4853 or 1-800/227-5430; ❸), while the *Motel 6* at 621 Plaza Lane (☎307/742-2307; ❷) is cheaper still, and clean and pleasant to boot. *Corona Village*, 421 Boswell Drive (☎307/721-0167), serves authentic and inexpensive Mexican **food**; great for vegetarian choices, including lasagna, and salad and sandwich combos (entrees $6–10), is the menu at the buzzing *Jeffrey's Bistro*, 123 Ivinson Ave (☎307/742-7046). *Lovejoy's Bar and Grill*, at 101 Grand Ave (☎307/745-0141), has great all-American food and tasty desserts. *Coal Creek Coffee Co*, 110 Grand Ave, is a friendly student hangout, and serves good espresso, bagels, muffins and lunch specials. Students, yuppies and bikers pack out the frontier-style *Buckhorn Bar*, 114 Ivinson Ave (☎307/742-3554), for live rock bands, while the friendly *Cowboy Saloon*, 108 S 2nd St (☎307/ 721-3165), is a fun place to go to hear country music.

The Medicine Bow Mountains

Just outside Laramie, **Hwy-130** dips into the huge wind-gouged bowl of **Big Hollow**, passes through rustic **Centennial** and starts the steep climb up the **Medicine Bow Mountains**, one of Wyoming's most picturesque drives. Overlooks at the top of the 10,847ft Snowy Range Pass (closed in winter) present picturesque alpine lakes and meadows, tight against steep mountain faces, and at lower levels there are plenty of good places to stop – pack a picnic and sit by **Marie Lake**, where the snowcapped peaks are reflected in the dark glassy waters.

Some 21 miles west of Laramie, in the shadow of the Snowy Mountain range at 2091 Hwy-130, the superb **Vee-Bar Guest Ranch** (☎307/745-7036 or 1-800/483-3227) is one of the best in the country, offering week-long summer packages for would-be cowhands of all ages. Accommodation is in luxurious log cabins by a rushing stream, and rates include all meals, your own horse, a camp-out, mountain tours, river tubing and fishing – or you're free simply to sit on your deck and take in the views. In winter they offer wonderful bed and breakfast (❻).

Forty-nine miles out from Centennial, sleepy **SARATOGA** is hemmed in by the Snowy and Sierra Madre ranges. The **Hobo Hot Springs** on Walnut Avenue is a free outdoor pool fed by natural 114°F springs. Easily the best place to **stay** is the antique-furnished *Wolf Hotel*, 101 E Bridge Ave (☎307/326-5525; ❸), which has a good restaurant and bar, and you can get subs, salads and low-priced lunch specials at *Stumpy's*, 218 N First St.

Southwest Wyoming

The long and monotonous drive across southern Wyoming on I-80 – the route also followed by the old train track – holds little to delight the eye, though geologists and fossil enthusiasts will be in their element, and it may provide some travelers with their first glimpse of the red-rock scenery of the West.

Rawlins

There would be little reason to stop at the tiny prairie town of **RAWLINS**, a hundred miles west of Laramie, but for one extraordinary sight: the unmissable

Butch Cassidy & the Sundance Kid

Without doubt the two most engaging characters to roam the Rocky Mountains of northern Colorado and southern Wyoming, **Butch Cassidy** and the **Sundance Kid** remain legends of the Old West – thanks in large part to the classic 1969 Hollywood film *Butch Cassidy and the Sundance Kid* (which starred Paul Newman and Robert Redford).

Butch Cassidy was born George LeRoy Parker in the town of Beaver, Utah, on 6 April, 1866. Taught the art of cattle-rustling by ranch-hand Mike Cassidy, Parker borrowed his mentor's last name, then picked up the handle "Butch" while working as a butcher in Rock Springs, Wyoming. He pulled his first bank job in Telluride, Colorado, in 1889, and soon found himself in the company of a like-minded group of outlaws known as the **Wild Bunch**, among them Harry Longabaugh – the Sundance Kid. The gang's resume would include horse-rustling as well as the robbing of trains, banks and mine payrolls; they gave away a fortune in gold to friends and even strangers in need, hence their reputation as latter-day "Robin Hoods".

The image of a dashing, philanthropic band of outlaws did not sit well with authorities, who mustered teams of lawmen – and gunmen – to go after them. The gang took to laying low through the winter months in **Brown's Hole**, a broad river valley in remote northwest Colorado, and they were known to visit the southern Wyoming towns of Baggs, Rock Springs and Green River. The gang were eventually undone by their own vanity, when, during a visit to Fort Worth, Texas, five of the men posed for a group photo in smart suits and derby hats; the photographer proudly placed the photo in his shop window the following day, where it was seen by a detective from the famous Pinkerton's agency.

Wearying of life on the run, Butch and Sundance sailed for **South America** in 1902, and were soon trying their hand at gold-mining, while robbing the occasional bank or train. The Hollywood version was true enough to this point, but Butch Cassidy did not die in a hail of bullets at the hands of Bolivian soldiers in 1909 as depicted in the film – although it seems that Harry Longabaugh did. The last say belongs to Josie Morris, an old girlfriend from Butch's Brown's Hole days, who insisted that he came to see her on his return from South America, and claimed furthermore that he died an old man in Johnny, Nevada, some time during the 1940s.

Wyoming Frontier Prison, at Fifth and Walnut streets (hourly tours 8.30am–5.30pm June–Aug, by reservation only the rest of the year; $4.25; ☎307/324-4422). In service until 1981, this huge, creepy jail with dark, neglected cells, peeling walls and echoing corridors is as different from Laramie's Wyoming Territorial Park (see p.881) as it is possible to be. While the whole experience is troubling – not least due to the fascinating life stories and anecdotes told with aplomb by the exceptional guides – the darkest moment comes as the gas chamber (in use from 1937 until 1965) is revealed. The *Sunset Motel*, 1302 W Spruce (☎307/324-3448 or 1-800/336-6752; ❷), offers clean rooms, and there's very good authentic Mexican food at *Rose's Lariat*, 410 E Cedar St (Tues–Sat 11am–7pm, ☎307/324-5261).

Just to the west, the Continental Divide briefly splits into two in the **Great Divide Basin**. In theory, rain that falls here should remain here, unable to flow toward either ocean – unfortunately virtually all of it evaporates, and the brick-red hell of the **Red Desert** stretches implacably away to the horizon.

Rock Springs and Green River

ROCK SPRINGS, the largest town in southwest Wyoming, is also wholly unremarkable, a down-at-heel mining community that experienced its latest short-lived boom in the 1980s. If you need to **stay**, there's the *Knotty Pine*

Lodge at 1234 Ninth St (℡307/362-4515; ❶); not far away, the *Santa Fe Trail Restaurant* at 1635 Elk St (℡307/362-5427) serves fresh Tex-Mex.

Ramshackle **GREEN RIVER** is fourteen miles west. Wedged between high buttes, and sliced through by the railroad, the interstate and the Green River itself it's not an easy place to find your way around. *Embers*, 95 E Railroad Ave (℡307/875-9983), is the most popular **eating** spot, while the *Coachman Inn*, 470 E Flaming Gorge Way (℡307/875-3681; ❶/❷), is a good-value **motel**. **Campers** should note that both Green River and Rock Springs lie within easy reach of **Flaming Gorge National Recreation Area** (covered on p.1026). Roads south from either town run through the empty hills, looking out over incandescent orange rocks and a dramatic artificial lake.

Fossil Butte National Monument

Roughly seventy miles northwest of Green River – and reached by turning north from I-80 just west of the "world's largest service station" at Little America – **Fossil Butte National Monument** preserves a fossilized cross-section of the fish population of a lake that existed here 50 million years ago. From a distance, you can clearly see the corresponding pale limestone strata on the flat-topped Butte itself, but the various trails turn out to show you less than the displays at the **visitor center** (daily: June–Aug 8am–7pm; Sept–May 8am–5pm; free; ℡307/877-4455). Fossil enthusiasts will be more stimulated by the open quarry face at Dinosaur National Monument, around two hundred miles southeast (see p.1025).

Twelve miles east of the monument, and isolated from the world by fifty miles of open rangeland in every direction, **KEMMERER** was the unlikely home of the first of more than 1900 J.C. Penney stores. It's still there on Main Street, along with assorted fossil shops.

Casper

Dreary **CASPER**, halfway up Wyoming on I-25, may not seem an obvious place to visit, but at a good 150 miles from anywhere of similar size it makes a likely pit stop. Originally at the spot where the Oregon Trail crossed the North Platte River – you can visit a reconstruction of the 1860s **Fort Caspar** which gave it its (misspelled) name – Casper has been the center of Wyoming's oil region since 1890. Its population (and appearance) fluctuates between periods of high and low demand; right now, the economy is ticking along, though with the exception of a couple of retail blocks along E Second Street downtown, still hasn't completely shaken off the signs of harder times.

Casper's biggest bright spot is the **Nicolaysen Art Museum**, 400 E Collins Drive (Tues, Wed, Fri & Sat 10am–5pm, Thurs 10am–8pm, Sun noon–4pm; $3). Housed in a disused power station, it displays old and new art by Wyoming artists. For a portrayal of life at an Oregon Trail Outpost, visit the **Fort Caspar National Historic Place**, on the North Platte River west of downtown.

Practicalities

Powder River **buses**, serving Cheyenne, Denver, Cody, Billings and Rapid City, have a base at the *Parkway Plaza Hotel*, 123 W E St (℡307/266-1904 or 1-800/442-3682), south of the **visitor center** at 500 N Center St (summer Mon–Fri 8am–5pm, Sat & Sun 9am–6pm; rest of year Mon–Fri 9am–5pm; ℡307/234-5362 or 1-800/852-1889, ⓦwww.casperwyoming.org). Of Casper's bargain **motels**, the downtown *National 9 Showboat Motel*, 100 W F St (℡307/235-2711 or 1-800/524-9999; ❷), with its flashing neon lights and waterbeds, is pleasantly kitsch. *Antelope Campground* at 1101 Prairie Lane, Bar Nunn, exit 191 off I-25, offers **camping** for $12 a tent site (☎307/577-1664); they have a pool, hot tub and laundry to boot. The *Cheese Barrel*, 544 S Center St (☎307/235-5202), serves great breakfasts and sticky cheese bread; while *La Casacita*, at 633 W Collins Drive (☎307/234-7633), is a good bet for Mexican food.

The Wind River range

Roads to Grand Teton and Yellowstone national parks from southern Wyoming skirt the **Wind River Mountains**, the state's longest and highest range, with some of the Rockies' most beautiful and challenging backpacking terrain. No roads cross the mountains; you can either see them from the **east**, by driving through the Wind River Indian Reservation on US-26/287, or from the less accessible **west**, by taking US-191 up from I-80 at Rock Springs.

Wind River Indian Reservation

The **Wind River Indian Reservation** occupies a large (and largely forgotten) swath of west central Wyoming, overshadowed by the high snowcapped peaks to the west and south. It is the only Indian reservation in Wyoming, and extends roughly seventy miles from the natural spa of **Thermopolis** in the east, through arid grasslands and desiccated uranium-rich badlands, to **Dubois** in the west, with the rich fishing grounds of the cottonwood-lined Wind River at its heart. The reservation was created in 1863 as a permanent home for the Eastern Shoshone, but due to US government imposition, it soon came to accommodate the Northern Arapaho as well; and these days the Arapaho account for more than double the Shoshone population. Near **Fort Washakie** – named for the centenarian Chief Washakie, who held the Shoshone together throughout the period of white expansion – is the likely grave of **Sacagawea**, the guide of Lewis and Clark's expedition. **Powwows** – gatherings that have both spiritual and social significance to Native Americans – are held throughout the year, and are open to the public. Contact the Shoshone Tribal Cultural Center, 31 Black Cole St, Fort Washakie (Mon–Fri 8am–5pm; ☎307/332-9106), for details on how to join in.

The friendly one-horse town of **LANDER**, southwest on US-287, makes an appealing base, with a string of cheap motels along Main Street and an excellent **B&B** at the Art Nouveau *Blue Spruce Inn*, 677 S Third St (☎307/332-8253 or 1-888/503-3311; ❹). Good places to **eat** include the locals' favorite *Gannett Grill*, 126 Main St (☎307/332-8228), for a great burger or a few beers at the bar next-door; the *Ranch*, 148 Main St (☎307/332-7388), for family-style dining and local microbrews; or *Amoretti's*, 202 Main St; (☎307/335-8500), which offers upscale Italian food. The funky *Magpie Coffee House*, 159 N Second St, is the place for espresso, light breakfasts, lunches and, most vitally, dessert.

In nearby **Sinks Canyon State Park**, the Popo Agie River plunges underground, only to re-emerge half a mile later in a huge spring (trail information from the ranger office at 333 S Hwy-789 in Lander).

Dubois

The former logging town of **DUBOIS** ("dew-boys"), squeezed into the northern tip of the Wind River valley, and an oasis among the badlands, turned to tourism after its final sawmill closed in 1987. Given a head start by being just fifty miles southeast of Grand Teton National Park (via the dramatic **Togwotee Pass**), Dubois is home to the biggest herd of bighorn sheep in the lower 48 states, and celebrates that fact with its **National Bighorn Sheep Center**, a half-mile northwest of town on US-26/287 (daily: summer 9am–8pm; rest of year 9am–5pm; closed for part of winter; $2; ☎307/455-3429).

Dubois is a bargain alternative to Jackson (see p.900), thanks to **motels** such as the log-built *Branding Iron*, 401 W Ramshorn St (☎307/455-2893 or 1-888/651-9378, ✉brandingiron@wyoming.com; ❷/❸), with its kitchenettes and the beautifully restored historic **B&B** *Twin Pines Lodge and Cabins*, 218 Ramshorn St (☎307/455-2600 or 1-800/550-6332, ✉twinpines@wyoming.com; ❸/❹). The evening pastime is listening to country crooners in classic Western bars like the *Rustic Pine*, 119 E Ramshorn St (☎307/455-2772), which also serves steaks. *The Hang-Out*, 8 Stalnaker St (☎307/455-3800), is good for sandwiches, soup and coffee.

Pinedale
On the western side of the Wind River range, tiny well-to-do **PINEDALE** on US-191 offers unrivaled access to the mountains. Once a major logging center, it now attracts second-homeowners and hikers. The excellent **Museum of the Mountain Man**, 700 E Hennick Rd (May–Sept daily 10am–6pm; rest of year by appointment only; $4; ☎307/367-4102), commemorates the town's role as a rendezvous for fur trappers in the 1830s.

A sixteen-mile road winds east from Pinedale past Fremont Lake to **Elkhart Park**, from where trails lead past beautiful **Seneca Lake** and along rugged Indian Pass to the glaciers and 13,000ft peaks; the Pinedale Ranger Station office at 29 Fremont Lake Rd (June–Aug Mon–Sat 8am–5pm; rest of year Mon–Fri 8am–5pm; ☎307/367-4326), can give information on good hiking routes.

There are clean, basic **rooms** at the *Sun Dance Motel*, 148 E Pine St (☎307/367-4336 or 1-800/833-9178; ❸/❹). Any one of the three **saloons** in town – *Calamity Jane's World Famous Corral Bar*, *The Cowboy* and *Stockman's* – may have a live country or blues band or just general rowdiness from a mob of cowboys. *McGregor's Pub*, 21 N Franklin Ave (☎307/367-4443), offers a good pint, a wide range of moderate to expensive dishes and a pleasant patio; *Wrangler Café*, 905 W Pine St (☎307/367-4233), has big, inexpensive roast dinners, a salad bar and a huge range of pies for dessert.

Northwest and north central Wyoming

Northern Wyoming has a lot more to offer than just a handy route between the Black Hills and Yellowstone. The surreal volcanic monument of **Devils Tower**, the abrupt **Bighorn Mountains** and the desertscape of the **Bighorn Basin** are the major natural attractions in a land steeped in the history of Native American wars, outlaw activity and pioneer hardships. Small towns such as unassuming **Buffalo** and the more commercialized **Cody**, developed by Buffalo Bill himself, are potential stopovers.

Devils Tower National Monument
Though Congress designated **DEVILS TOWER**, in far northeastern Wyoming, as the country's first national monument in 1906, it took Steven Spielberg's inspired use of it as the alien landing spot in *Close Encounters of the Third Kind* to make this eerie 867ft volcanic outcrop a true national icon.

Plonked on top of a thickly forested hill, itself a full six hundred feet above the peaceful Belle Fourche River, it resembles a giant wizened tree stump; but, painted ever-changing hues by the sun and moon, it can be hauntingly beautiful. Sioux legend says the tower was formed after three young girls jumped onto a boulder to escape a vicious bear. They were rescued when the great god, seeing their plight, made the rock rise higher and higher; the bear's desperate efforts to climb up scored the sides of the column.

Four short trails loop the tower, beginning from the **visitor center** (mid-June to mid-Sept daily 8am–7.45pm; mid-Sept to mid-June weather dependent; ☎307/467-5283) at its base, three miles from the main gate. There will invariably be a few foolhardy souls attempting to scale the tower, despite objections from local Native American communities for whom this is a sacred place. If you feel otherwise inclined, then rockclimbing opportunities abound. For guide and route information, contact Tower Guides Climbing School (☎307/467-5589 or 1-888/345-9061). The **entrance fee** per car is $8, and until October you can **camp** for $12 a night – arrive early or you'll end up paying more than twice that at one of the nearby commercial campgrounds.

Buffalo

Snuggled among the southeastern foothills of the Bighorn Mountains, quiet, attractive **BUFFALO** remains largely unaffected by the bustle of the nearby I-90/I-25 intersection. Although **Main Street**, now lined with frontier-style stores, used to be an old buffalo trail, the place was actually named after Buffalo, New York. The **Jim Gatchell Museum**, 100 Fort St, stacked full of Old West curiosities pertaining to soldiers, ranchers and Native Americans, is well worth a visit (June–Aug daily 8am–8pm; May, Sept & Oct Mon–Fri 8am–5pm; $2).

Pick up information from the **visitor center**, 55 N Main St (summer Mon–Fri 8am–6pm, Sat & Sun 10am–6pm; rest of year Mon–Fri 8am–5pm; ☎307/684-5544 or 1-800/227-5122, ⓦwww.buffalowyo.org). The **Clear Creek Trail System**, which runs through town, makes for a nice stroll, while a drink at the lovingly restored c.1880 *Occidental Hotel* – which once changed hands in a high-stakes poker game – is a must. Decent **rooms** can be had at the cozy, log-built *Mountain View Motel*, 585 Fort St (☎307/684-2881; ❷), and the historic *Mansion House Motel*, 313 N Main St (☎307/684-2218 or 1-888/455-9202; ❸); the latter's rates include a continental breakfast. *Tom's*, 41 N Main St, is an excellent local diner, while the best restaurant in town is the *Winchester Steakhouse*, 117 E Hwy-16 (☎307/684-8636).

Through the Bighorn Mountains

Of the three scenic highways through the **Bighorn Mountains**, US-14A from **Burgess Junction**, fifty miles west of Victorian **Sheridan**, is the most spectacular. The massive and heavily wooded Bighorns soar abruptly from the plains to over 9000ft; the loftiest peaks, protruding above the timberline, seem bald beside their dark-coated neighbors. The road edges its way up **Medicine Mountain**, on whose windswept western peak the mysterious **Medicine Wheel** – the largest such monument still intact – stands protected behind a wire fence. Local Native American legends offer no clues as to the original purpose of these flat stones, arranged in a circular "wheel" shape with 28 spokes and a circumference of 245ft – though the pattern suggests sun-worship or early astronomy. To get there, you'll have to drive along a precipitous dirt

Buffalo Bill

The much-mythologized exploits of **William Frederick "Buffalo Bill" Cody**, born in Iowa in 1846, began at the age of just eleven, when the murder of his father forced him to take a job as an army dispatch rider. An early escape from ambush brought Cody fame as the "Youngest Indian Slayer of the Plains"; four years later, he became the youngest rider on the legendary **Pony Express**. After a stint fighting for the Union, Cody found work – and a lifelong nickname – supplying buffalo meat to workers laying the transcontinental railroad. He killed over 4200 animals in just eighteen months, before rejoining the army in 1868 as its chief scout. In the next decade, when the Plains Indian Wars were at their peak, he earned a Congressional Medal of Honor and a remarkable record of never losing any troops in ambushes. Among battles in which he took part was the 1877 encounter with Sioux forces when he killed – and scalped – Chief Yellow Hand.

By the late 1870s, exaggerated accounts of Cody's adventures were appearing back east in the "dime novels" of Ned Buntline, and with the Indian Wars all but over he took to guiding Yankee and European gentry on buffalo hunts. He referred to the vacationers as "dudes," and called his camps "dude ranches." The theatrical productions he laid on for his rich guests developed into the world-famous **Wild West Show**. First staged in 1883, these spectacular outdoor carnivals usually consisted of a re-enactment of an Indian battle such as Custer's Last Stand, featuring Sioux who had been present at Little Bighorn, trick riders, buffalo, clowns, and exhibition shooting and riding by the man himself. The show spent ten of its thirty years in Europe, and made Buffalo Bill "the most famous and recognized man in the world." Dressed in the finest silks and sporting a well-groomed goatee, Cody stayed in the grandest hotels and dined with heads of state; Queen Victoria was so enthusiastic in her admiration that rumors circulated of an affair between them.

In later life, a mellowing Cody played down his past activities, to the point of urging the government to respect all Native American treaties and put an end to the wanton slaughter of buffalo and game. Although the Wild West Show was reckoned to have brought in as much as one million dollars per year, his many investments failed badly, and, in January 1915, a penniless 69-year-old Buffalo Bill died at his sister's home in Denver. His grave can be found atop Lookout Mountain, outside Golden, Colorado (see p.849).

track (past an incongruous radar dome) to within a mile of the site and hike the rest of the way. Even if US-14A isn't closed by snow (usually Nov–May), or even if the Medicine Wheel isn't being used by local Native Americans for religious ceremonies, you might still find the dirt track impassable due to bad weather.

The route down the west side, with gradients of ten to twenty percent and three awesome runaway truck ramps, is said to have cost more to build per mile than any other road in America. Tight hairpin bends will keep the driver's eyes off the magnificent overlooks, but the best view comes near the bottom, when the road lets you out into the **Bighorn Basin**. This ultra-flat, sparsely vegetated valley, walled in by mighty mountains on three sides and ragged foothills to the north, can strike you as a land that time forgot.

Bighorn Canyon National Recreation Area

Before US-14A gets to Lovell, Hwy-37 turns north to the **Bighorn Canyon National Recreation Area**, an unexpected red-rock wilderness straddling the border between Wyoming and Montana. No road runs the full length of the canyon which, since being flooded by the 525ft Yellowtail Dam (only accessible from Montana), has become primarily the preserve of water-sports enthusiasts. In summer, **boat tours** leave from **Horseshoe Bend**, where the marina (☎307/548-7230) rents out assorted equipment, and a shadeless beach of red sand offers swimming in the most bizarre of settings. The **Devil's Canyon overlook**, just off Hwy-37 three miles over the border into Montana, affords landlubbers an opportunity to gauge the knee-knocking 1000ft-plus drop into the abyss.

A **visitor center** just east of Lovell on US-14A (daily 8.30am–5pm; ☎307/548-2251) supplies information on local activities, and has maps of the Medicine Wheel area.

Cody

CODY, 79 miles east along US-14 and the North Fork of the Shoshone River from Yellowstone, was the brainchild of investors who, in 1896, persuaded "Buffalo Bill" Cody to get involved in their development company, knowing his approval would attract homesteaders and visitors alike. During summer, tourism is big business, but underneath all the Buffalo Bill-linked attractions and paraphernalia, Cody manages to retain the feel of a rural Western settlement. It's certainly not a place where you'd expect avant-garde painter **Jackson Pollock** to have been born and raised.

The wide, dusty main thoroughfare, **Sheridan Avenue**, holds an array of souvenir and ranchwear shops, and is the scene of parades and rodeos during the annual **Cody Stampede**, held on the weekend of July 4. Between June and August there's a **rodeo** every night at the open-air stadium on the road to Yellowstone, at 421 W Yellowstone Ave (8.30pm; $10–12; ☎307/587-5155).

Buffalo Bill Historical Center

The nation's most comprehensive collection of Western Americana, Cody's giant **Buffalo Bill Historical Center** at 720 Sheridan Ave comprises several distinct museums (April daily 10am–5pm; May daily 8am–8pm; June to mid-Sept daily 7am–8pm; mid-Sept to Oct daily 8am–5pm; Nov–March Tues–Sat 10am–3pm; $10 ticket is valid for two consecutive days; ☎307/587-4771 or 1-800/227-8483).

At the **Buffalo Bill Museum** artifacts from William Cody's various careers, such as guns, gifts from European heads of state, billboards, clothes and dime novels, trace the years of the Pony Express, Civil War, Indian Wars and Wild West shows. The lives of western Native Americans are celebrated in the **Plains Indian Museum**: many of the ceremonial garments are in stunning condition; one prize exhibit is a brightly decorated shirt that belonged to Red Cloud, a Lakota Sioux chief who visited Washington in the 1870s to petition for peace on behalf of his people. A superb bear-claw necklace is another standout, and there's also a poignant display of Ghost Dance shirts, worn for the ritual song and dance that would hasten the day when all whites would be buried by a heaven-sent fall of soil. The US Army condemned Ghost Dances as unacceptable shows of resistance, and mobilized troops to disrupt ceremonies.

In the beautifully laid-out **Whitney Gallery of Western Art,** the contrasting styles of Frederic Remington and Charles M. Russell command the most attention. The propagandist Remington dwells on conflict, depicting the Indian as a savage in the path of progress, while Russell's work shows a consistent respect for the Native American way of life.

Practicalities

For information and accommodation reservations, contact Cody's **visitor center** at 836 Sheridan Ave (summer Mon–Sat 8am–7pm, Sun 10am–3pm; rest of year Mon–Fri 8am–5pm; ☎307/587-2777, ⓦwww.codychamber.org). Cody is the site of the **Yellowstone Regional Airport**. Powder River Coaches arrive at Daylight Donuts, 1452 Sheridan Ave (☎1-800/442-3682), and also offer one-day Yellowstone tours; **float trips** on the Shoshone are available from, among others, Wyoming River Trips (☎307/587-6661 or 1-800/586-6661).

Cody's showpiece Western **hotel**, the *Irma* at 1192 Sheridan Ave (☎307/587-4221 or 1-800/745-4762; ❹/❺), was named for Buffalo Bill's daughter in 1902, and retains a superb original cherrywood bar. Among good-value motels, the friendly *Skyline Motor Inn*, high above town on the main through highway at 1919 17th St (☎307/587-4201 or 1-800/843-8809; ❷–❹), stands out. Sheridan Avenue is the place for an evening's **eating** and **entertainment**.

You may need a cowboy hat to really feel comfortable at *Cassie's*, 214 Yellowstone Ave, where entertainment ranges from line-dancing classes to country and country-rock bands, and you can settle in for a full evening including dinner, although the menu is surprisingly expensive. After a steak at the always-packed *Irma's*, call in for a drink at the *Proud Cut Saloon*, at no. 1227. *Peter's Café Bakery,* at no. 1191, is the morning place for coffee or a full breakfast.

Wapiti Valley

The drive west from Cody to Yellowstone is a superb preparation for the splendors of the park itself, skirting the artificial lake created by the Buffalo Bill Dam before running alongside the Shoshone River through the open, high **Wapiti Valley**, the heart of Wyoming's "beef country," and finally climbing through the rugged mountains to Sylvan Pass. Lodges and campgrounds appear at intervals without spoiling the magnificence of the landscape. The *Elephant Head Lodge*, along US-14/16/20 (☎307/587-3980; ❹), is one such option, should you need a place to stay.

Yellowstone National Park

Millions of visitors each year come to **YELLOWSTONE NATIONAL PARK**, America's oldest national park and the largest in the lower 48 states, to glory in its magnificent mountain scenery and abundant wildlife, and above all to witness hydrothermal phenomena on a unique scale. Measuring roughly sixty by fifty miles, and overlapping slightly from Wyoming's northwestern corner into Idaho and Montana, the park centers on a 7500ft-high plateau, the caldera of a vast volcanic eruption that occurred some 600,000 years ago. Into it are crammed more than half the world's **geysers**, in which the rain and snow that seep through the bedrock escape the pressure-cooker conditions under the surface in intermittent spectacular blasts, plus thousands of **fumaroles** jetting plumes of steam, **mud pots** gurgling with acid-dissolved muds and clays, and **hot springs**.

Yellowstone amounts to an extraordinary experience, combining the **colors** of the Grand Canyon of the Yellowstone, limpid Yellowstone Lake, the wild flower meadows and the rainbow-hued geyser pools; the **sounds** of subterranean rumblings, belching mud pools, and steam hissing from the mountainsides; and the constant **smells** of drifting sulphurous fumes, with the presence of browsing bull moose, shambling bears, heavy-bearded bison, herds of elk and ubiquitous scurrying **marmots**. It is, however, very popular; if you let yourself get frustrated by the inevitable crowds and expense, you risk missing something very special. The key to appreciating the park is to take your time, and to plan carefully; above all, try to allow for a stay of at least three days.

GALLATIN
NATIONAL
FOREST

Livingston

Gardiner
N Entrance

Mammoth
Hot Springs

MONTANA

GALLATIN RANGE

Cooke
City

Silver
Gate

NE
Entrance

ABSAROKA RANGE

SHOSHONE
NATIONAL
FOREST

Tower Roosevelt

Lamar Valley

Mount
Washburn
(10,243ft)

Grand Canyon
of the
Yellowstone

WYOMING

Norris

Canyon
Village

Artist
Point

Caldera Boundary

Lamar River

W Entrance

West
Yellowstone

Gibbon River

Madison River

Madison

Hayden Valley

White
Lake

Lower Geyser
Basin

Midway Geyser
Basin

Lake Village

Fishing
Bridge

E Entrance

Upper Geyser
Basin

Firehole River

Old
Faithful

CONTINENTAL DIVIDE

Craig Pass
(8262ft)

West Thumb
Geyser Basin

Yellowstone
Lake

Sylvan Pass
8530 ft

Cody

IDAHO

Grant Village

ABSAROKA RANGE

Eagle Peak
(11,358ft)

Shoshone
Lake

Lewis
Lake

Heart
Lake

Yellowstone River

WYOMING

Lewis River

CONTINENTAL DIVIDE

S Entrance

Snake River

Road closed in winter

GRASSY LAKE ROAD closed in winter

BRIDGER-TETON
NATIONAL FOREST

0   10 miles

GRAND TETON
NATIONAL PARK

YELLOWSTONE NATIONAL PARK

Arrival and information

Two of the five main **entrances** to Yellowstone are in Wyoming, via **Cody** in the east and **Grand Teton National Park** to the south. The others are in Montana: **West Yellowstone** (west), **Gardiner** (north) and **Cooke City** (northeast). Most roads are open from late May to October only (see box, overleaf). **Admission** ($20 per car, $10 for pedestrians or cyclists) is good for seven days, and includes entry to the Grand Teton park.

The **park headquarters** are at **Mammoth Hot Springs**, near the north entrance (daily: June–Sept daily 8am–7pm; Oct–May 9am–5pm; ☎307/344-2263). Tune into 1610 AM for weather information, and consult the free newspaper *Yellowstone Today* for activities and current regulations. Other, summeronly **visitor centers** are located approximately every twenty miles along the main **Loop Road**. Each issues backcountry hiking permits, and has an exhibit on a different aspect of the park – natural and human history (Mammoth Hot Springs), geothermal activity (Old Faithful and Norris), the National Park

Winter in Yellowstone

Blanketed in four feet of snow between November and April, Yellowstone takes on a whole new appearance in winter: a silent and bizarre world where waterfalls freeze in mid-plunge, geysers blast towering plumes of steam and water into the cold, crisp air, and buffalo, beards matted with ice, stand around in huddles. Only the road from Gardiner to Cooke City via Mammoth Hot Springs is kept open (the Beartooth Highway is closed), and you can only stay at the *Mammoth Hot Springs Hotel* or the *Old Faithful Snow Lodge* (accessible by snowmobile).

Winter vacationing in Yellowstone took off in a big way in the 1960s. Amfac/TW Services (℡307/344-7311, ⓦwww.travelyellowstone.com) runs **snowcoach** tours of the park from West Yellowstone, Flagg Ranch at the southern entrance, Old Faithful and Mammoth Hot Springs ($110–130). Yellowstone Alpen Guides (℡406/646-9591 or 1-800/858-3502) runs slightly cheaper excursions out of West Yellowstone ($100). **Snowmobile** rental, generally cheapest in West Yellowstone, costs around $120 a day (note that snowmobiling is likely to be banned from the park by 2004). Much less expensive is **cross-country skiing**; several miles of groomed trails explore the park's west side. Call ℡307/344-7311 for full details.

---

service (Norris), wilderness areas and the 1988 fires (Grant Village), wildlife (Fishing Bridge) and bison (Canyon). Excellent National Park Service leaflets (50¢ each), which can be found at major sights as well as visitor centers, cover the important landmarks, marking trails and points of interest.

To get to Yellowstone by **bus**, take Karst Stage (℡406/586-8567) from Bozeman, via West Yellowstone or Gardiner; Powder River Coach (℡1-800/442-3682), which runs tours and day-trips from Cody; or Amfac/TW Services (℡307/344-7311) from West Yellowstone, Gardiner or Billings, which also runs day tours inside the park in summer. Similar services are offered by 4X4 (℡1-800/517-8243) from Gardiner, Cooke City, West Yellowstone and Bozeman; Buffalo Bus Co. (℡406/646-9353 or 1-800/426-7669) from West Yellowstone; Greyhound runs as far as Bozeman and West Yellowstone (for details call ℡402/330-8552 or 1-800/229-9424).

Accommodation in the park

All accommodation within the park is run by Amfac Parks and Resorts (PO Box 165, Yellowstone National Park, WY 82190; ℡307/344-7311, ⓦwww.travelyellowstone.com). **Reservations**, strongly recommended from June through September, are essential over public holiday weekends. Prices beyond the park boundaries are a little lower, but staying inside can be wonderfully relaxing; none of the rooms has a TV, and only a few après-hike revelers stay up past midnight. Every location has a lodge building offering dining facilities (closing at 9.30pm) and sometimes a laundromat, grocery store, gift shop and gas station.

Canyon Lodge and Cabins Simple frame cabins, all en-suite, half a mile from the Grand Canyon of the Yellowstone. ❸/❹
Grant Village Spartan en-suite rooms on the southwest shore of Yellowstone Lake, and the southernmost accommodation in the park. ❹
Lake Yellowstone Hotel and Cabins Grand colonial-style hotel rooms, and dark, dingy en-suite cabins. The "Sun Room," looking over the lake, is a great place for an evening drink. ❹/❺

Mammoth Hot Springs Hotel & Cabins 1930s lodging right at the north end of the park offering very basic cabins, without shower or toilet, en-suite cabins, and hotel rooms with or without bath. Especially popular in winter. ❸–❹
Old Faithful Inn and Lodge The most beautiful lodge in the US and consequently very popular. The amazing 1903 inn – said to be the world's largest log building – has assorted rooms plus budget and en-suite cabins. You can watch Old

Faithful erupt from the terrace bar. ❸–❻

Old Faithful Snow Lodge and Cabins Along with *Mammoth Hot Springs Hotel*, this is the only accommodation open in the winter. Built in 1998, the lodge has a modern hotel feel about it, while the en-suite cabins are pretty basic but well sealed against the cold. Open May to mid-Oct &

mid-Dec to early March. ❺

Roosevelt Lodge Cabins The most basic of these cabins is a rustic wooden shelter with no bedding and communal bathroom facilities; en-suite cabins are also available. Cozy lounge and bar with a roaring fireplace. ❷–❸

Accommodation in gateway towns

In addition to **Jackson** (see p.900) and **Cody** (p.889) in Wyoming, the small towns just outside the park's western and two northern gates offer alternative and somewhat cheaper lodging, as well as more nightlife. **West Yellowstone**, the largest town, at the west entrance, is disfigured by gift stores and fast-food joints, but the surrounding national forest lands are well worth exploring. **Gardiner** lies next to the northwest entrance, just five miles from Mammoth Hot Springs; prices here tend to be a little higher than elsewhere. More developed **Cooke City** is ten miles from the northeast entrance on US-212.

High Country Motel US-212, Cooke City ☎406/838-2271. Good value, if basic, motel rooms, some with kitchens for an extra $10. ❷

Hillcrest Cottages 200 Scott St, Gardiner ☎406/848-7353. Comfortable cottages with kitchenettes. Good value, especially the larger ones which will accommodate up to six people. ❹

Hoosier's Motel US-212, Cooke City ☎406/838-2241. Comfortable modern motel with its own popular bar. Mid-May through October. ❸

Round Up Motel and Dude Motor Inn 3 Madison Ave, West Yellowstone ☎406/646-7301 or 1-800/833-7669, ⓔroundup@wyellowstone .com. Located in one of the quieter parts of town but only a block from all the action, the rooms here are clean and well maintained, and some have two bedrooms and kitchenettes. ❹

Sleepy Hollow Lodge 124 Electric St, West Yellowstone ☎406/646-7707, ⓔsleepyhollow@ wyellowstone.com. Attractive log cabins with fully equipped kitchens and a free continental breakfast, plus a fly-tying bench for anglers. Good value. ❹

Stage Coach Inn 209 Madison Ave, West Yellowstone ☎406/646-7381 or 1-800/842-2882, ⓔsci@wyellowstone.com. One of the town's oldest and most historic buildings, with comfortable rooms, an attractive lobby and reading area, a hot tub and sauna and a good restaurant. Open year-round and there are some great off-season deals, with rooms for under $40. ❺

West Yellowstone International Hostel at Madison Hotel 139 Yellowstone Ave ☎406/746-7745 or 1-800/838-7745. A real boon for budget travelers, this is one of the very few hostels in Montana. The attractive log-hewn building dates back to 1912 and has rooms with bunks for up to four people ($20 each) and private rooms for around $50. Open late May–early Oct.

Yellowstone Village Inn corner Main and 2nd streets, Gardiner ☎406/848-7417 or 1-800/228-8158, ⓦwww.yellowstoneVinn.com. Forty basic but clean and comfortable rooms, with kitchen suites. There's also an indoor pool, and horseback riding, fishing and rafting can be organized for you. ❺

Camping

Amfac Parks and Resorts operates twelve **campgrounds** in Yellowstone, including one for RVs only. Of these campgrounds, seven operate on a first-come, first-served basis; you have to arrive early in the day to get a site during June–August as most are full by 11am. The remaining five campgrounds – Bridge Bay, Canyon, Fishing Bridge, Grant Village and Madison – accept **reservations** (☎307/344-7311, same-day reservations ☎307/344-7901, ⓦwww.travelyellowstone.com). **Fees** range from $10–15 per night for tent camping, and upwards of $27 for RVs, and campgrounds operate from mid-May or early June through to September, October or November. Though all campgrounds have toilet facilities, not all have showers. RV owners should note that generators are not allowed at the following campgrounds: Indian Creek, Pebble Creek, Slough Creek and Tower Fall.

To camp in the **backcountry**, you'll need a permit – free from visitor centers, information stations and ranger stations; these can be collected no earlier than 48 hours in advance of your camping trip. You can also camp at commercial grounds in the gateway towns and in neighboring national forests such as Gallatin (℡307/344-7381) to the northwest and Shoshone (℡307/527-6241) to the east.

Touring the park

All of Yellowstone's major sights are labeled and signposted within a few hundred yards of the 142-mile **Loop Road**, a figure-of-eight circuit fed by roads from the five entrances. Although the **speed limit** is a radar-enforced 45mph, the traffic makes journey times hard to predict. To get the most out of a visit, even if you're short of time, choose one or two areas to explore thoroughly. Only in the early morning is **cycling** bearable or safe; there are no mountain bike trails. Though you can expect to **walk** considerable distances along

A brief human history of Yellowstone

Although Native Americans had long hunted in what is now **Yellowstone National Park**, they were decimated by disease (and, in their absence, the wildlife thrived) by the time the first white man arrived in 1807 – **John Colter**, a veteran of the Lewis and Clark expedition (see also p.907). His account of the exploding geysers and seething cauldrons of "Colter's Hell" was widely ridiculed. However, as ever more trappers, scouts and prospectors hit upon Yellowstone, the government eventually sent out survey teams in 1870. Just two years later, Yellowstone was set aside as the first **national park**, in part to ensure that its assets were not entirely stripped by hunters, miners and lumber companies.

At first, management of the park was beset by problems; Congress devoted enthusiasm but little funding towards its protection. Irresponsible tourists stuck soap down the geysers, ruining the intricate plumbing; bandits preyed on stagecoaches carrying rich excursionists; and the Nez Percé even killed two tourists as they raced through the park (see p.924). Congress took the park out of civilian hands in 1886, and put the army in charge. By the time they handed it over to the newly created National Park Service in 1917, the ascendancy of the automobile in Yellowstone had begun.

The conflict between tourism and wilderness **preservation** has raged ever since. The elimination of predators such as mountain lions and wolves allowed the elk herd to grow unsupportably large; the former policy of permitting bears to feed from tourist scraps resulted in maulings. Most of these issues have since been addressed, but ecologists now warn that the park cannot stand alone as some pristine paradise, and must be seen as part of a much larger "Greater Yellowstone Ecosystem"; this notional ecosystem encompasses Yellowstone, the Tetons, the Snake River Valley south of Jackson to just over the Idaho border, and the northern Wind River Mountains. In 1995, amid vociferous complaints from local ranchers fearing a subsequent loss of livestock, several packs of **wolves** were reintroduced to the park. They've since made an emphatic comeback, and from the original fourteen animals released, there are now more than 150 wolves comprising fifteen packs roaming the Greater Yellowstone area.

The **fires** that razed 36 percent of the park in 1988 also brought Yellowstone's environmental policies into focus. Despite President Reagan's dismay, park authorities insisted that the burn was a natural part of the forest's ecocycle, clearing out 200-year-old trees to make way for new growth. The scarred mountainsides are slowly but surely recovering, as evidenced by forests of young saplings.

the canyon and geyser trails, it's worth leaving the backcountry hiking for the more scenically rewarding **Grand Teton National Park**.

The following account runs clockwise around the Loop Road, from Old Faithful to the Yellowstone Lake area, both of which lie in the southern reaches of the park.

Geyser country: from Old Faithful to Mammoth Hot Springs

For well over a century, the dependable **Old Faithful** has been the most popular geyser in the park, erupting more frequently than any of its higher or larger rivals. As a result, a half-moon of concentric benches, backed by visitor facilities including the gigantic log-built *Old Faithful Inn*, now surround it at a respectful distance on the side away from the Firehole River. On average, it "performs" for the expectant crowds every 78 minutes, with a minimum gap of half an hour and a maximum of two hours; approximate schedules are displayed in the nearby visitor center and in the lobby of the inn. The first sign of activity is a soft hissing as water splashes repeatedly over the rim. After several minutes, a column of water shoots to a height of 100 to 180ft, the geyser spurting out a total of 11,000 gallons.

Two miles of boardwalks lead from Old Faithful to dozens of other geysers in the Upper Basin. If possible, try to arrive when **Grand Geyser** is due to explode. This colossus blows its top on average just twice a day, for twelve to twenty minutes, in a series of four powerful bursts that climb to 200ft. Other highlights along the banks of the Firehole River, usually lined with browsing buffalo, include the fluorescent intensity of the **Grand Prismatic Spring** at **Midway Geyser basin**, especially breathtaking in the early evening when human figures and bison herds are silhouetted against plumes of mineral spray.

Thirty miles north of Old Faithful, in the less crowded **Norris Geyser Basin**, two separate trails explore a pallid landscape of whistling vents and fumaroles. **Steamboat** is the world's tallest geyser, capable of forcing near-boiling water over 300ft into the air; full eruptions are entirely unpredictable (the two most recent were on May 2, 2000, and October 2, 1991), but it usually delivers lesser bursts of ten to forty feet a couple of times a day. The **Echinus Geyser** is the largest acid-water geyser known; every 35 to 75 minutes it spews crowd-pleasing, vinegary eruptions of forty to sixty feet. The **Emerald Spring** is a 27ft-deep pool where the vivid blue water combines with the yellow of the crater to create a stunning, jewel-like color.

At **Mammoth Hot Springs**, at the northern tip of the Loop Road, terraces of barnacle-like deposits cascade down a vapor-shrouded mountainside. Tinted a marvelous array of grays, greens, yellows, browns and oranges by algae, they are composed of travertine, a form of limestone which, having been dissolved and carried to the surface by boiling water, is deposited as tier upon tier of steaming stone.

Tower and Roosevelt areas

The main landmark of Yellowstone's **Tower** and **Roosevelt** areas, east of Mammoth Hot Springs, is **Mount Washburn**, one of the park's highest peaks, whose lookout tower can be reached by an enjoyable all-day hike or a grueling cycle ride. A more manageable trail leads down to the spray-drenched base of **Tower Fall**. From Tower Junction, US-212 wanders away east through the meadows of serene **Lamar Valley**, where moose and buffalo graze, toward the ice-packed peaks of the **Beartooth Mountains**.

The Grand Canyon of the Yellowstone River

The Yellowstone River roars and tumbles for 24 miles between the sheer golden-hued cliffs of the 1540ft **Grand Canyon of the Yellowstone**, its course punctuated by two narrow but striking **waterfalls**: the 109ft **Upper Falls** and the thunderous **Lower Falls**, plummeting 308ft. Both rims of the canyon offer superb vistas, short trails and intense scenery, but the north side is the more popular, as sightseeing can be combined with a visit to the nearby stores and snack bars. To try to see some bears, stake out a roadside spot just south of Tower Junction at dawn or dusk.

On the south rim, **Artists' Point** looks down 700ft to the river, which swirls between mineral-stained walls. Nearby, **Uncle Tom's Trail** descends steeply into the canyon, to a gently vibrating, spray-covered platform right in the face of the Lower Falls. A few miles south, the river widens to meander over tranquil, marshy **Hayden Valley**. Buffalo, elk and deer congregate here, so it's an unsuitable place to go on foot.

Yellowstone Lake

North America's largest alpine lake, the deep and (usually) deceptively calm **Yellowstone Lake** fills the eastern half of the Yellowstone caldera. At 7733ft above sea level it's high enough to be frozen for half the year, but in summer it's filled with tourists out on cruises (one hour; $7.30), rowboats ($6 per hour), motor launches ($30 per hour) and fishing expeditions ($55 for two hours). Boat tours leave from the Bridge Bay Marina near Lake Village.

At the **West Thumb Geyser** basin, north of Grant Village, hot pools empty into the tranquil waters and fizz away into nothing, and it's easy to see why early tourists would have made use of the so-called **Fishing Cone** by cooking fresh-caught fish in its boiling waters.

The ominous rumblings and sulphurous stench of the **Mud Volcano** area, north of the lake, make it the moodiest and ugliest of the park's thermal regions. A one-mile boardwalk winds through gurgling pools of sickly brown and yellow mud, past trees that have been steamed to death, to the bleak, barren shores of **Sour Lake**: an unnerving sight at the best of times, at dusk it makes a chemical waste dump look appealing. Joining a free ranger-led tour here gives you the chance to get off the boardwalk and into the backcountry, where the **Big Gumper**, which blew into existence in the 1970s, bubbles with big gray globs of smelly mud.

Snack bars and **restaurants** inside the park aren't cheap, but given where you are they're not hideously expensive either. Buying food at the general stores can get pricey. There's not a lot of menu variation among the **restaurants**, which are located at *Old Faithful Inn*, *Old Faithful Snow Lodge*, *Roosevelt Lodge*, *Lake Yellowstone Hotel*, *Mammoth Hot Springs Hotel*, *Canyon Lodge* and *Grant Village*; however, *Old Faithful Inn* and *Lake Yellowstone Hotel* are the clear standouts for location, mood and ambience. Entrees ($14–22) run from salmon and steak to roast dinners and lighter choices such as burgers or Caesar salads ($8), with desserts ($4–5) and a basic range of beers and wines available too. Note that **dinner reservations** are required during summer at *Old Faithful Inn* (℡307/545-4999), *Lake Yellowstone Hotel* (℡307/242-3899) and *Grant Village* (℡307/242-3499); you won't get a table without one. The restaurants are also open for lunch and **breakfast**; they usually offer a breakfast buffet that includes fresh fruit, cereals, pastries and standard cooked breakfast items, all for around $7.

The gateway towns hold few culinary delights, but do offer cheaper prices and more variety. In **West Yellowstone**, *Nancy P's*, 29 Canyon St (℡406/646-9737), is good for breakfast, and *Rustlers's Roost*, 234 Firehole Ave (℡406/646-7622), offers local wild game, including elk and bison, with tasty dinners starting around $15. The lively and friendly *Town Café* (T 406/848-7322) on Park Street in **Gardiner** serves good filling breakfasts, and the stylish *Beartooth Café* in **Cooke City** is probably the best place for breakfast, burgers and inexpensive dinners in any of the peripheral towns.

Within the park, the dining room at the *Old Faithful Inn* (T 307/545-4999) serves high-quality meals (entrees $14–22) in an unforgettable rustic setting, with log walls and ceilings, and huge chandeliers lighting the elegant table settings.

Grand Teton National Park and Jackson Hole

The classic triangular peaks of **GRAND TETON NATIONAL PARK**, which stretches for fifty miles between Yellowstone and Jackson, are every bit as dramatic as the mountains of its congested neighbor, and a visit should be more than an afterthought on the route south. Though not especially high or extensive by Rocky Mountain standards, these sheer-faced cliffs make a magnificent spectacle, rising abruptly to tower 7000ft above the valley floor. A string of gem-like lakes is set tight at the foot of the mountains; beyond them lies the broad, sagebrush-covered **Jackson Hole** (a "hole" was the pioneers' term for a flat, mountain-ringed valley), broken by the winding Snake River.

The Shoshone people knew the mountains as the *Teewinot* ("many pinnacles"), but their present name, meaning large breast, was bestowed by over-imaginative French-Canadian trappers in the 1830s. After Congress set the mountains aside as a national park in 1929, it took another 21 years of legal wrangling for Grand Teton to reach its current size – local ranchers protested that the economy of Jackson Hole would be ruined if further land was surrendered to tourism. Meanwhile, John D. Rockefeller Jr bought up a large swath of Jackson Hole and presented it to the government for free (on the condition that the Grand Teton Lodge Company, which he then owned, would be the exclusive operator of park concessions).

Seeing the park

No road crosses the Tetons, but those that run along their eastern flank were designed with an eye to the mountains, affording stunning views at every turn. Two excellent side trips are the **Jenny Lake Scenic Loop**, leading to a face-to-face encounter with towering, partly hunchbacked **Grand Teton Mountain**, and the narrow track up **Signal Mountain**, which gives a fine view of the five main Teton pinnacles and Jackson Hole.

Hiking trails, too, have been laid out so that no time is wasted in getting to the highlights. One easy and popular walk is along the sandy beaches of **Leigh Lake**, where the imposing 12,605ft **Mount Moran** bursts out dramatically from the lake shores. Also very accessible are the cascading **Hidden Falls**, reachable by a two-mile walk along the south shore of Jenny Lake; it's also fun to take the shuttle boat ($5 round-trip) across the lake, and walk the remaining 800 yards. For the more adventurous, the rocky nine-mile trail from Hidden Falls through U-shaped **Cascade Canyon** leads to aptly named **Lake Solitude**. Another strenuous hike, and an excellent way to reach the tree line in a short distance, is the five-mile trail from **Lupine Meadows**, just south of

YELLOWSTONE NATIONAL PARK

Falls River

Grassy Lake Reservoir

Lake of the Woods

TARGHEE NATIONAL FOREST

JOHN D. ROCKEFELLER JR. MEMORIAL PARKWAY

Flagg Ranch

Snake River

89

GRAND TETON NATIONAL PARK

Moose Creek

TETON NATIONAL FOREST

Jackson Lake

Colter Bay Visitor Center

Two Ocean Lake

Emma Matilda Lake

Jackson Lake Lodge

Jackson Lake Junction

PACIFIC CREEK RD

Moran Canyon

TARGHEE NATIONAL FOREST

Signal Mountain (7593ft)

Moran Junction

Moran Entrance Station

Leigh Canyon

Leigh Lake

Snake River

TETON PARK ROAD

Grand Targhee Resort

Cascade Canyon

Jenny Lake

Grand Teton (13,770ft)

Jenny Lake Visitor Center

Middle Teton (12,804ft)

Garnet Canyon

South Teton (12,514ft)

Bradley Lake

Avalanche Canyon

Taggart Lake

191

TETON NATIONAL FOREST

Death Canyon

Moose Visitor Center

Moose Entrance Station

Phelps Lake

Moose Junction

GROS VENTRE ROAD

Lower Slide Lake

Open Canyon

Granite Canyon

Jackson Hole Airport

Gros Ventre River

Teton Village

Jackson Hole Ski Area

Gros Ventre Junction

NATIONAL ELK REFUGE

TETON NATIONAL FOREST

N

Teton Pass (8429ft)

Wilson

22

MOOSE WILSON RD

191

National Museum of Wildlife Art

Jackson

GRAND TETON NATIONAL PARK

0   5 miles

Jenny Lake, which skirts small glacial pools like Amphitheater and Surprise lakes.

On the flat roads of the Hole, **cycling** is a joy; rent a bike down in Jackson ($25–30). To admire the Tetons from **water**, take a float trip along the Snake River (see overleaf) or rent a rowing boat from Colter Bay or Signal Mountain marinas ($25). In winter, all hiking trails are open to cross-country **skiers**, and **snowmobiles** can be rented from various outlets in Jackson. Excellent **rock climbing** opportunities exist within the park. Contact the Jenny Lake Visitors Center (☎307/739-3343) for climbing details. **Climber's Ranch**, within the park on **Teton Park Road**, has basic dorm accommodation for climbers only (June–Sept only; ☎307/733-7271; $7).

Practicalities

Shuttle buses to the park run from Jackson and Yellowstone. The **visitor centers** are just off the main road in **Moose** (daily: mid-May to June 8am–6pm; June–Sept 8am–7pm; Sept to mid-May 8am–5pm; ☎307/739-3399) to the south, and at **Colter Bay** (May 10–18 & Sept daily 8am–5pm; May 18 to June daily 8am–7pm; June–Aug daily 8am–8pm; ☎307/739-3594), halfway up, on the east shore of Jackson Lake. There are smaller centers at **Jenny Lake** (June–Sept daily 8am–7pm; ☎307/739-3343) and **Flagg Ranch** (June–Sept daily 9am–6pm). The **Indian Arts Museum** (daily: summer 8am–8pm; spring & fall 8am–5pm; free) at Colter Bay has an extensive collection of Plains Native American craftwork.

The free *Teewinot* newspaper gives details of trails, facilities and ranger-led activities. The **entrance fee** of $20 per car ($10 for pedestrians and cyclists) also covers Yellowstone.

Most **rooms**, services and activities within the park are managed by the Grand Teton Lodge Co. (☎307/543-3100 or 1-800/628-9988, ⊛www.gtlc.com) and reservations are essential in summer. Prices for the comfortable rooms in *Jackson Lake Lodge* (❺–❼) depend on whether or not you want a mountain view; *Colter Bay Village Cabins* (❶, en-suite ❸, four-person cabins ❺) are more utilitarian, and in high summer they also have $32 "tent cabins" – canvas cabins each with four bunk beds (no bed linen supplied), a wood-burning stove and outdoor barbecue grill – potentially pretty cold at night. There's good accommodation otherwise at *Signal Mountain Lodge* (☎307/733-5470, ⊛www.signalmtnlodge.com; ❹–❻), which has bland motel-style units with two double beds, bathroom and fridge, or much nicer rustic log cabins with two doubles plus private bath. All of the five summer-only park **campgrounds** work on a first-come, first-served basis ($12 per site). Visitor centers or entrance stations can advise on availability, or you can call (☎307/739-3603) for recorded information. Individual campgrounds tend to fill in July and August in roughly the following order: Jenny Lake (8am; 49 sites, tents only), Signal Mountain (10am; 86 sites), Colter Bay (noon; 306 sites), Lizard Creek (2pm; 60 sites) and Gros Ventre (evening; 360 sites); Gros Ventre is the only campground suitable for large RVs. For backcountry camping, you need a **permit**, available free from the Moose and Colter Bay visitor centers and the Jenny Lake Ranger Station, near the Jenny Lake Visitor Center. The park **restaurants and snack bars**, especially at Colter Bay, are good but a little pricey. *Dornan's Original Moose Chuckwagon* (☎307/733-2415), however, just outside the southern entrance in Moose, serves all-you-can-eat pancake breakfasts and rib dinners for a song. For the ultimate in relaxation, have an early-evening **drink** in *Jackson Lake Lodge's Blue Heron Lounge*, where you can recline in comfortable chairs and watch the ever-changing blues, grays, purples and warm pinks of Mount Moran through huge picture windows.

Jackson

The overgrown community of **JACKSON** is tucked in at the end of **Jackson Hole**, ten miles from Teton park's southern gate. Hunched around a tree-shaded square, marked by an arch of tangled elk antlers at each corner, the Old West-style boardwalks of **downtown** front designer boutiques, craft shops and over thirty galleries. Every summer evening, except Sundays, an amateurish shoot-out is staged in the town square (6.30pm). In winter, time is better spent visiting the **National Elk Refuge** on the north edge of town, where you can take a horse-drawn sleigh ride among a 10,000-strong herd of elk (late Dec to late March daily 10am–4pm; $12 for adults and $8 for kids); rides leave from the National Museum of Wildlife Art, and a combined museum-and-sleigh-ride ticket is good value at $15 adults/$11 kids.

Jackson is home base for two of Wyoming's best ski areas: **Snow King** (℡733-5200 or 1-800/522-5464, Ⓦwww.snowking.com) is Jackson's family-friendly hill, also lit for night-skiing, while **Jackson Hole Mountain Resort** (℡733-2292 or 1-888/333-7766, Ⓦwww.jacksonhole.com) is a massive mountain with a huge vertical drop and terrain best suited to upper intermediate-to-extreme downhillers. Summer visitors can enjoy **chairlift** rides (up 7751ft Snow King Mountain from Snow King Avenue, six blocks from the town square (daily 9am–6pm; $7), and come down by hiking, cycling or taking the thrilling 2500ft **Alpine Slide** ($6 a turn), a summer toboggan run. Out at **Teton Village**, home of **Jackson Hole Mountain Resort** (℡307/733-2292), aerial **trams** swoosh their way 10,536ft to the top of Rendezvous Mountain where there's a spectacular panorama of the valley and mountain ranges (daily: June–Aug 9am–7pm; May & Sept 9am–5pm; $16).

Arrival, information, tours and activities

Jackson's **airport** is actually within the national park, eight miles north; it's linked to town by the All Star Transportation van service (℡307/733-2888; $8 one-way), while the regular **taxi** fare is around $20. Jackson Hole Express (℡307/733-1719 or 1-800/652-9510) operates two direct **shuttle services** daily between the international airport in **Salt Lake City** and Jackson (around 5hr; $47 one-way); pick-up and drop-off in Jackson is at the MiniMart beside *Burger King* on West Broadway.

Jackson's excellent **Wyoming Information Center**, 532 N Cache St (daily: summer 8am–7.30pm; rest of year 9am–5pm; ℡307/733-3316, Ⓦwww.jacksonholechamber.com), has detailed statewide information. Nearby, the **Bridger–Teton National Forest Headquarters**, 340 N Cache St (Mon–Fri 8am–4.30pm; ℡307/739-5500), has details of hiking and backcountry camping.

Transport around Jackson Hole is provided by START **buses** (℡307/733-4521, Ⓦwww.startbus.com), which also run to Teton Village, twelve miles northwest. The **visitor center** has racks of leaflets detailing **bus tours** of Jackson and the parks: Gray Line, 330 N Glenwood St (℡307/733-4325 or 1-800/443-6133), will pick you up at your hotel and take you through either Teton or Yellowstone park on a brisk one-day drive for $60. Guided **bike tours** in the area are run by Teton Mountain Bike Tours (℡307/733-0712 or 1-800/733-0788), and cost $55 for a half-day tour including equipment.

Dozens of companies in Jackson offer **float trips** and whitewater **rafting** on the Snake River (half-day around $35, full-day $60). Try Dave Hansen Whitewater, 455 N Cache St (℡733-6295 or 1-800/732-6295) or, Jackson Hole Whitewater, 650 W Broadway (℡733-1007 or 1-800/700-7238); Leisure

Sports, 1075 Hwy-89 S (☎307/733-3040), offers reasonable rental rates for rafts, kayaks, tubes and bikes.

Accommodation

Accommodation in Jackson is fairly expensive in summer; rates in winter drop by around 25 percent, making this potentially good value for a ski vacation. The only in-town **camping** is at *Wagon Wheel Campground*, 525 N Cache St, behind the *Wagon Wheel Motel* (☎307/733-4588; $16).

The Alpine House 285 N Glenwood St ☎307/739-1570 or 1-800/753-1421, ⓦ www.alpinehouse.com. B&B accommodation in a bright, cheerful 21-room house. Winter packages, including ski passes or cross-country expeditions, are good value. Summer ⑥, winter ⑤

Antler Inn 43 W Pearl St ☎307/733-2535. Very central, but reasonably quiet, with sauna and hot tub. Some rooms have log fires. ❸/❹

Best Western Lodge at Jackson Hole 80 S Scott Lane, Teton Village ☎307/739-9703 or 1-800/458-3866. Some rooms have log fires, kitchenettes and hot tubs. Rates include an excellent continental breakfast, and there's a pool and jacuzzi. Look out for the whimsical carved bears climbing all over the log-built exterior. ❻

Bunkhouse in the Anvil Motel 215 N Cache St ☎307/733-3668. Mid-range motel a block from the town square that also has beds in a large, dreary dorm (no kitchen facilities to speak of). Summer ❹, winter ❸, dorm $22.

Hostel X Teton Village ☎307/733-3415. Excellent slopeside hostel accommodation; amenities include a lounge fireplace, TV and games room, ski lockers and storage, microwave oven, free tea and coffee but no kitchen. Summer dorm bed $19, double $45, four-bed room $55; winter (five-night minimum stay) double room $48; four-bed room $61. ❷

Virginian Lodge 750 W Broadway ☎733-2792 or 1-800/262-4999. The 170 rooms are pretty basic but complemented by a big outdoor pool and a hot tub that sits in the middle of a grass-covered courtyard. There's a family-style restaurant on-site, a saloon, liquor store and guest laundry too. Summer ❸, winter ❹

The Wort Hotel 50 N Glenwood St ☎733-2190 or 1-800/322-2727, ⓦ www.worthotel.com. Jackson's most venerable high-end property, combining old-world style with modern facilities that include two large hot tubs, a grill-bistro and an attractive bar. Summer ❼, winter ❻

Eating and nightlife

The year-round tourist trade makes Jackson Wyoming's liveliest nighttime community, with an ever-changing cast of **restaurants** and **nightspots**.

Anthony's 62 S Glenwood St ☎307/733-3717. Imaginative Italian food at fair prices by Jackson standards (entrees $15–20).

Bubba's Bar-B-Que Grill 515 W Broadway. Inexpensive dinners offering babyback ribs, sandwiches, steaks and such – it's also the premier breakfast spot for locals, and a double stack of plate-size blueberry pancakes is top choice at $3.

The Bunnery 130 N Cache St ☎307/733-5474. Great breakfasts, baked goodies, espressos, stuffed omelets and sandwiches.

Cadillac Grill 55 N Cache St ☎307/733-3279. Fancy Art Deco restaurant on the main square, serving up huge burgers, as well as buffalo, wild boar, caribou, antelope and seafood entrees for $15–22. Reservations recommended.

Harvest Natural Foods Café 130 W Broadway ☎307/733-5418. Earnest health food store with a veggie food counter: burgers, tofu, baked goods and fruit smoothies to eat in or take out.

Mangy Moose Teton Village ☎307/733-4913. Jackson Hole's legendary ski-bum hangout, the

Moose is famed for its après-ski sessions that segue into rowdy evenings of live rock or reggae (cover charge for live bands $5–10). The bustling upstairs dining room serves decent basic fare like burgers, chicken and pasta; the *Moose's Belly* downstairs dishes up a pretty ordinary $7 skiers' breakfast buffet.

Million Dollar Cowboy Bar 25 N Cache St ☎307/733-2207. Hugely touristy Western-themed bar, with saddles for seats, a large dance floor, karaoke and big steaks.

Mountain High Pizza Pie 120 W Broadway ☎307/733-3646. Offers casual, low-priced and healthy pizza, calzones and salads.

Old Yellowstone Garage 175 Center St ☎307/734-6161. One of Jackson's finest restaurants, offering flawless service and an Italian-themed menu that changes daily. Sunday night features all-you-can-eat pizza for just $10. Reservations essential.

Pearl Street Bagels 145 W Pearl Ave ☎307/739-1218. It's all in the name: a plethora of fresh and tasty bagels, from tomato-herb to cinnamon-raisin. Daily 6.30am–6pm.

Thai Me Up 75 E Pearl St ☎307/733-0005. Red, green and yellow curries featured alongside interesting seafood variations and noodle dishes (entrees $12–16) at Jackson's only Thai restaurant.

The Rancher 20 E Broadway ☎307/733-3886.

Dollar drinks every Tuesday night at this local pool-hall hangout.

The Silver Dollar Bar 50 N Glenwood St ☎307/733-2190. The closest thing to an upscale bar in town, but still pretty relaxed and casual; hosts singers and piano players of variable quality. The silver dollars embedded in the bar-top number 2032.

Montana

MONTANA is Big Sky country. The nickname is no empty cliché: the entire state is blessed with a huge blue roof that both dwarfs the beautiful countryside and complements it perfectly. A magnificent northernmost cap for the US Rockies, this is a region of snowcapped summits, turbulent rivers, spectacular glacial valleys, heavily wooded forests and sparkling blue lakes, at their most dramatic in **Glacier National Park**. By contrast, the **eastern** two-thirds is high prairie: sun-parched in summer and wracked by icy blizzards each winter.

Preconceptions of a desolate land populated by cowpokes are soon shattered: each of Montana's small cities has its own proud identity. The university and sawmill community of **Missoula**, for example, possesses a high-culture feel absent from the heavily Irish, copper-mining town and union stronghold of **Butte**, while elegant state capital **Helena** still harks back to its prosperous gold mining years, and **Bozeman**, just to the south, is one of the hippest mountain towns in the US.

The fur trappers and gold miners who were the first whites to brave this inhospitable terrain soon moved on, but as white settlers invaded Native American hunting grounds, conflict was inevitable. A key plank of army strategy was to starve the Native Americans into submission: "For the sake of a lasting peace let them [professional hunters] kill, skin and sell until the buffalo are exterminated. Then your prairies can be covered by the speckled cow and the festive cowboy," declared General Philip Sheridan. By the late 1870s the buffalo were almost gone, and most of Montana had been cleared for settlement.

The speckled cow and festive cowboy were not in for an easy time. The horrendous winter of 1886 wiped out many herds, and the "sodbusters" who planted wheat in the wake of bankrupt ranchers often fared little better. Plagues of grasshoppers, droughts, falling wheat prices and erosion of the topsoil caused farms to fail everywhere in the 1920s, during which time Montana was the only state to record a population decline.

Wheat has since made a revival, and now, with lumbering and coal mining, forms the base of Montana's economy. Tourism is currently the state's second biggest earner, though, apart from skiing, the harsh climate generally restricts the season to the months between June and September.

Getting around Montana

Considering Montana's size and sparse population, transportation connections are not bad. Greyhound and regional **bus** companies like Intermountain (north from Butte and Missoula to Glacier) and Rimrock serve towns on I-90 and I-15. Delta Air Lines and Northwest offer the most **flights** to Montana, landing in seven towns. Amtrak **trains** cross the north, stopping east and west of Glacier National Park without making it easier to see the park itself. Western Montana, in particular, is great **cycling** territory; the Adventure Cycling organization, whose national headquarters are in Missoula (see p.911), can provide special maps.

However, the best way to **get around** this huge state is by car, with practically every interstate exit in the west leading to areas of mountain solitude, interesting landmarks or small communities. Montana's "Basic Rule" used to state that, as long as you drive in a "reasonable and prudent manner," you're free to go at whatever speed you wish. However, much to the chagrin of locals, Montana now has posted speed limits, usually of 75mph.

Eastern Montana

Before ranchers and farmers settled the flat prairie of **eastern Montana**, it was prime **buffalo** territory: one early traveler waited three nights while a massive herd crossed his path. Native Americans fought hard to hold onto their land; the crushing defeats they inflicted on the US Army include the legendary victory at **Little Bighorn**.

The eastern Montana plains are intermittently broken by mountains, of which the most impressive are the icy **Beartooth Range**, crammed between the town of Red Lodge and Yellowstone. Don't expect much from the region's towns; most are lazy farm-supply centers, and **Billings**, Montana's largest city with a population of over 90,000, doesn't have a great deal to offer.

Little Bighorn Battlefield National Monument

In June 1876, massive US Army detachments were sent to southeastern Montana to subjugate the Sioux and Cheyenne. A key unit in the campaign was the crack **Seventh Cavalry**; at its head was the flamboyant **Lt Col George Armstrong Custer**.

Few if any US soldiers have achieved the fame or opprobrium of Custer. During an erratic career, he graduated last in his class at West Point in 1861; was the US Army's youngest-ever major general; was suspended for ordering the execution of deserters from a forced march he led through Kansas primarily to see his wife; and became notorious for allowing the murder in 1868 of almost 100 Cheyenne women and children.

On June 25, 1876, Custer's was the first unit to arrive in the **Little Bighorn Valley**. Disdaining to await reinforcements, he set out to raze a tepee village along the Little Bighorn River – which turned out to be the largest-ever gathering of Plains Indians. As a party of his men pursued fleeing women and children, they were encircled by two thousand Sioux and Cheyenne warriors emerging from either side of a ravine. The soldiers dismounted to attempt to shoot their way out, but were soon overwhelmed; simultaneously, Custer's command post on a nearby hill was wiped out. Archeologists have discounted the idea of **Custer's Last Stand** as a heroic defiance in which Custer was the last cavalryman left standing; the battle lasted less than an hour, with the white soldiers being systematically and effortlessly picked off. The most decisive Native American victory in the West – led by Sitting Bull – was also their final great show of resistance. An incensed President Grant piled maximum resources into a military campaign that brought about the effective defeat of all Plains Indians by the end of the decade.

The **monument** is 56 miles southeast of Billings, with the entrance one mile east of I-90 on US-212. You can trace the course of the battle on a five-mile self-guided driving tour through the grasslands (daily: 8am–dusk; $10 per car), following the high ridge overlooking the valley, or on a narrated bus tour (spring–fall; $10). White-marble tablets mark where individual soldiers fell, and a sandstone obelisk stands above their mass grave on "Last Stand Hill" (Custer himself lies in West Point Military Academy). Dioramas in the **visitor center and museum** (mid-April to May 8am–6pm; June–Aug 8am–8pm; rest of year 8am–4.30pm; $10 per vehicle; ☎406/638-2621) outline the battle, while the US military **cemetery** nearby holds soldiers from all America's wars (free passes available).

Hardin

Little Bighorn is the focus of the Crow Indian Reservation. Little **HARDIN**, thirteen miles northwest, makes its living from tourists seeking authentic Native American artifacts and other Western mementos. Each year, on the weekend closest to the battle's June 25 anniversary, the **Little Bighorn Days** festival centers around re-enactments of the battle at a site eight miles west of the town (*not* at the original battlefield). Other activities include Native American dancing, downtown parades, dinner dances and a rodeo.

The least expensive place to **stay** is the *Western Motel*, off Hwy-313 at 831 W Third St (☎406/665-2296; ❸/❹). *The Purple Cow*, Hwy-47 N (☎ 406/665-3601), is a cheerful family **diner** serving home-cooked feasts.

Billings

By Montana standards, **BILLINGS** is a big city. Its dramatic setting, bounded on its north and east sides by the 400ft crumpled sandstone cliffs of the **Rimrock**, certainly makes it something more than a pockmark on the prairie. The town has made an attempt to spruce itself up with the development of an attractive and quite lively row of galleries, bars and restaurants along Montana Avenue. However, scarring the west side of downtown are the tracks and warehouses of the Northern Pacific Railroad, whose president, Frederick Billings, gave the city its name.

Just north of Montana Avenue you'll find a massive selection of cowboy paraphernalia at Lou Taubert, 123 N Broadway (☎406/245-2248), which specializes in all things Western. An enormous selection of hats, boots, shirts, jeans and jackets will make dressing up like John Wayne never look more appealing.

A couple of blocks northeast is **Yellowstone Art Museum**, 401 N 27th St (Tues, Wed, Fri & Sat 10am–5pm, Thurs 10am–8pm, Sun noon–5pm; $5 adults, $3 seniors, $2 children; ☎406/256-6817, ⊛http://yellowstone.artmuseum.org). Partly housed in the town's 1910 jail, it specializes in regional and Western exhibits, including an absorbing display of book illustrations, paintings and posters by cowboy illustrator Will James.

Billings' **bus station**, served by Greyhound along I-90 and I-15, and Powder River, heading north from Wyoming, is at 2501 First Ave N (☎406/245-5116).

The Dude Rancher, 415 N 29th St (☎1-800/221-3302 or 406/259-5561; ❸), is a reasonably-priced bright and cheerful motel with a good restaurant and coffee shop attached. Cheaper options line I-90, off exit 446, including a *Super 8* at 5400 Southgate Drive (☎406/248-8842; ❸). *Billings KOA* is half a mile south of I-90 in an attractive spot beside the Yellowstone River with good shady campsites for $17. This was America's first *KOA* and the facilities include a store, outdoor pool, laundry and mini-golf course.

Downtown, hearty meals can be found at *The Beanery Bar and Grill,* 2314 Montana Ave (☎406/896-9200), tucked inside the restored old Northern Pacific Depot. *Casey's Golden Pheasant*, 109 N Broadway (☎406/256-5200), is a lively jazz and blues **bar** with good Cajun food. For coffee and something sweet, try *Café Jones* at 2712 Second Ave (☎ 406/259-7676).

Red Lodge and the Beartooth Scenic Highway

The atmospheric mountain town of **RED LODGE**, sixty miles south of Billings at the foot of the awesome Beartooth Mountains and originally founded to dig coal for the transcontinental railroads, makes an altogether more pleasant stop. During winter, it acts as a base for skiers using the popular **Red Lodge Mountain**, six miles west on US-212 (☎ 406/446-2610, lodging reservation service ☎1-800/444-8977, ⓦwww.redlodgemountain .com), where ski-lift passes cost $36 a day ($28 Mon & Tues from early Jan).

Red Lodge faced extinction in 1924, when its largest coal mine closed, but its future was secured by the construction of the 65-mile **Beartooth Scenic Highway** to Cooke City at the northeastern entrance to Yellowstone National Park (see p.890). Other roads in the Rockies may be higher, but none gives quite such a top-of-the-world feeling as this succession of tight switchbacks, steep grades and exciting overlooks. Even in summer the springy tundra turf of the 10,940ft **Beartooth Pass** is covered with snow that (due to algae) turns pink when crushed. All around are gem-like corries, deeply gouged granite walls, stretches of scree and huge blocks of roadside ice.

Though Red Lodge boasts plenty of reasonable **motels** grouped south of town – the *Yodeler*, 601 S Broadway (☎406/446-1435, ⓦwww.wtp.net/yodeler; ❸), is friendly, clean and central. By far, the nicest place to stay is the lovely historic *Pollard Hotel*, 2 N Broadway (☎406/446-000 or 1-800/POLLARD; ❺–❽), with a pool, sauna, comfortable old library and superb restaurant (see below). One of the best B&Bs in town, *Bear Bordeaux*, 302 S Broadway (☎406/446-4408; ❹), is a well-decorated downtown home with bright, colorful rooms and great mountain views. There's a hot tub, filling breakfasts and an enormous video library (each room has a VCR). **Camping** at the *KOA* (June–Sept; ☎406/446-2364), four miles north, costs $18. Or you can rent a cabin for $36.

Undoubtedly the best **food** in town, if not in the entire Rocky Mountain region, is served at the *Pollard*, where *Greenlee's* (☎406/446-0001) features sublime, simple, European dishes in a wonderfully serene wood-lined dining room. Also on Broadway, *Bogart's* at no. 11 S (☎406/446-1784) is popular for its Mexican and Californian cuisine, and the nearby *Red Lodge Pizza Company,* 123 S Broadway (☎406/446-3933), is a lively combination pizza joint and brewhouse with one of the largest ranges of beers in town. Red Lodge has a cheerful **nightlife** scene, especially in winter – get a real feel for the town at the *Snow Creek Saloon*, 124 S Broadway, an always-busy bar popular with locals and visitors alike.

Western Montana

The **western** third of Montana sees the state at its best – from Big Timber westwards, I-90 squeezes between dramatic mountain ranges, making an exhilarating approach to Yellowstone country, replete with outdoor opportunities and bustling communities. The only mining camps to grow into substantial permanent settlements were state capital **Helena** and craggy **Butte**, which made its money from copper. Between them they conjure up more of a feel for the rambunctious times, the lust for profit and the post-bust hardships of the era than all the hyped-up ghost towns in the Rockies combined.

Bozeman

Pretty, tree-lined **BOZEMAN** lies at the north end of the lush Gallatin Valley, 142 miles west of Billings and a mere ninety miles north of Yellowstone. Founded by farmers in 1863, it's the only sizeable town in Montana not to owe its roots to mining, railroading or lumbering. The smart-looking storefronts along the busy Main Street just beg to be window-shopped, and you may just bump into one of the Hollywood celebrities who have set up home or business in this increasingly trendy town.

South of downtown, as **Montana State University** peters out into a beautiful wilderness in the shadow of the mountains, the huge, impressive **Museum of the Rockies** at S Seventh Avenue and Kagy Boulevard (summer daily 8am–8pm; rest of year Mon–Sat 9am–5pm, Sun 12.30–5pm; $7) holds impressive dinosaur finds, Native American weapons and a fine selection of Western landscape paintings; there's also a **planetarium**. Though far smaller in scale, the **Pioneer Museum**, 317 W Main St (June–Sept Mon–Fri 10am–4.30pm, Sat 1–4pm; Oct–May Mon–Fri 11am–4pm, Sat 1–4pm; free) is also very good, with an intriguing, well-presented selection of locally gathered historic objects, including cartoons drawn by local boy Gary Cooper in his pre-movie star days. The excellent photo selection features some great old images of early tourism at Yellowstone; many of the prints are for sale. Striking a modern note, the **Compuseum,** 234 E Babcock St (June–Aug Mon–Sun 10am–4pm; Sept–May Tues, Wed, Fri & Sat noon–4pm; $3), follows the evolution of computers, from their bulky, awkward beginnings to the modern compact incarnations of today; also on display are some well-intentioned inventions that never quite hit mainstream America.

Bozeman is well placed for those in search of **outdoor activities**, particularly in rugged Hyalite Canyon just south of town, which has top-notch hiking and mountain biking in summer and excellent ice climbing in winter, or at the challenging ski spot, Bridger Bowl (lift tickets $31; ☎406/587-2111). An hour's drive south down the beautiful Gallatin Valley is Big Sky Resort (lift tickets $56; ☎1-800/548-4486, ⓦwww.bigskyresort.com), with plenty of top-quality powder and steep slopes on 11,166ft Lone Mountain to challenge skiers at all levels.

For more details on outdoor activities, the ranger office, 3710 Fallon St (Mon–Fri 8am–5pm; ☎406/587-6920; 24hr recreation recording ☎406/587-9784), provides information on local walking trails, and Chalet Sports at 108 W Main (☎406/587-4595) rents out mountain bikes and ski equipment.

Practicalities

Greyhound and Rimrock cruise the interstates from 625 N Seventh St (☎406/587-3110), while Amfac/TW Services runs a bus a day to Yellowstone (see p.891); and from the same spot you can also take the Karst Stages bus service (☎406/586-8567) each morning and evening in summer to Big Sky and West Yellowstone. The Downtown Bozeman Association **Visitor Center** at 224 E Main St (☎406/586-4008, ⓦwww.historicbozeman.com) has loads of maps and info plus limited free **internet** access, which is also available at the **pubic library** at 220 E Lamme St. Central **motels** lining Seventh Avenue include the *Rainbow* at no. 510 N (☎406/587-4201; ❸); the *Bozeman Inn* at no. 1235 N (☎406/587-3176 or 1-800/648-7515; ❹) is more luxurious. Main Street also has a few worthy options: the rambling *Lewis and Clark*, no. 824 W (☎406/586-3341 or 1-800/332-7666; ❸), though gaudy, is very good value and centrally located, with pool, sauna, gym and hot tub. The friendly *International Backpackers Hostel*, 405 W Olive St (☎406/586-4659; ❶), has bunk beds for $12 and a fully equipped kitchen. More upmarket is the lovely *Voss Inn*, 319 S Willson Ave (☎406/587-0982, ⓕ585-2964, ⓦwww.bozeman-vossinn.com; ❺), a lovely Victorian home featuring period furniture in each room.

Bozeman boasts plenty of good **places to eat**. The *Community Co-op* on Ninth Avenue and Main Street (☎406/587-4039) serves terrific fresh veggie food and mouth-watering desserts in its pretty roadside garden, while the *McKenzie River Pizza Co.* at 232 E Main St (☎406/586-0055); pulls in a crowd with fresh and somewhat unusual toppings. The *Spanish Peaks Brewery* at Main and Church streets (☎406/585-2296) offers Italian cuisine at moderate prices alongside home-brewed beers like Black Dog Ale and Spanish Peaks Porter, but even more choices are available at *Montana Aleworks*, 611 E Main St (☎406/587-7700), with over forty microbrews on tap. For something milder, try the gourmet coffee and pastries at *The Leaf and Bean* at 35 W Main St.

Other places to **drink** include *Molly Brown's* and the *Haufbrau*, both at Eighth Avenue and Main Street, and both good rowdy bars. For live music, the *Zebra Lounge* on Rouse Avenue S offers an eclectic mix. The *Tributary* and *BoZone* are both good for local entertainment listings.

Missouri Headwaters State Park

Officially, the Missouri River begins its circuitous journey to the Mississippi, and eventually the Gulf of Mexico, at the confluence of the Jefferson, Madison and Gallatin rivers. Three miles north of I-90, halfway between Bozeman and Butte, and maintained as the **Missouri Headwaters State Park** ($3 per vehicle; camping $5), these marshy grasslands beneath a shallow bluff were identified by Lewis and Clark in July 1805. Three years later, **John Colter**, a veteran of that expedition who was the first to describe Yellowstone (see box p.894), was captured here by a party of Blackfoot, who, after killing his companion, stripped him and made him run for his life. Colter killed the one pursuer who kept up with him, hid under a snag on the river, and reached safety on the Bighorn River eleven days later. Fur trappers who followed in the wake of Lewis and Clark included Kit Carson; traces remain of the nineteenth-century town they created.

Butte

Eighty miles west of Bozeman, copper-mining **BUTTE** is bunched on a steep, almost treeless hillside where massive black headframes of long-abandoned pits soar up among paint-bare homes, stark gray business premises, and a ring of surface workings and dirty-yellow slag heaps. It's an oddly compelling landscape, best appreciated at dusk, when the golden pink light casts a glow on the mine-scoured hillsides, and the old neon signs illuminate uptown's historic brick buildings.

Exploration of this friendly, atmospheric town soon reveals a community rich in ethnic and trade union culture. Among immigrants to leave their mark were the **Irish** – Butte still hosts the biggest St Patrick's Day celebrations in the Rockies, with an estimated 40,000 customers passing through the famous old *M&M Bar* every March 17 – and miners from **Cornwall**; the traditional meat-and-potato pasty (*PAST-ee*) is still served in most cafés.

From its early days, Butte stood out as a "Gibraltar of Unionism" in the anti-union West. Miners used their collective strength to obtain a minimum wage and an eight-hour day, and it became impossible to get work without a union card. Such confidence bred radicalism, and Butte sent the largest delegation to the founding convention of the IWW (the "Wobblies") in 1906. The eventual consolidation of mining operations under the huge Anaconda Company led to inter-union rivalries and rioting, and in 1983 the last mine closed. Today conflicts rage between the clean-up lobby (the town's largest disused mine, the Berkeley Pit, is slowly filling with heavily poisoned groundwater) and the traditionalists, keen to develop new methods to exploit the mineral-rich seams that once made Butte the "richest hill on earth." To take a look at the ecological disaster that is the 700ft by mile-long **Berkeley Pit**, head for Continental Drive. Here, a viewing platform surveys the whole horrifying mess, the most toxic stretch of water in the United States (summer daily 8am–9pm; free).

Uptown lies Butte's extensive **historic district**. On W Park Street, the excellent, although rather grandly named, **World Museum of Mining** (daily 9am–6pm April–Oct; $4) is packed with fascinating memorabilia from the local boom years. Outside, beyond the scattered collection of rusting machinery – baffling to all but experts – its 35-building **Hell Roarin' Gulch** re-creates a cobbled-street mining camp, complete with saloon, bordello, church, schoolhouse and Chinese laundry. Above it all looms the blackened headframe of the 3200-foot-deep Orphan Girl mineshaft.

In an old noodle parlor at 17 W Mercury St, the tiny **Mai Wah Museum** (June–Aug Tues–Sat 11am–3pm; free) focuses on the history of Butte's Chinese community with its small, intriguing collection of photos, cooking implements, kites, fireworks, menus and books. At the end of the nineteenth century the narrow strip between Galena and Mercury streets was known as China Alley, the bustling heart of a 600-strong community; by the 1940s widespread racism had reduced the number to just a few families. At the other end of the cultural spectrum is the **Dumas Brothel Museum**, 45 E Mercury (May–Sept daily 9am–5pm; tours $3.50; ☏406/782-3808, ⓦwww.dumasbrothel.com). The Dumas was built as a brothel in 1890 and stayed in business until 1982. It's the only surviving building in what was once a thriving red-light district, and the guided tour gives you a good insight into what life was like for the occupants and their clients during Butte's heyday. The tour takes in the building's underground "bedrooms," accessible through tunnels that connected with the uptown business district.

At night the 90ft **Our Lady of the Rockies** statue is illuminated by floodlights. Built entirely by voluntary labor – there had just been a major layoff at one of the mines – it was set in place on top of the Continental Divide, some 3500ft above Butte, by helicopter.

Practicalities

Greyhound and Intermountain Transit **buses** drop off downtown at 101 E Front St. From June to September, ninety-minute **trolley tours** of town

⑪

(11am, 1.30pm, 3.30pm; $6) leave from the **Chamber of Commerce**, 1000 George St (May–Aug daily 8am–8pm; Sept & Oct daily 8am–5pm; Oct–May Mon–Fri 9am–5pm; ☎406/723-3177 or 1-800/735-6814). The chain **motels** line the interstate, out on the "Flat." The efficient *Best Western Butte Plaza*, 2900 Harrison Ave (☎406/494-3500 or 1-800/543-5814; ➍), has good rooms, an excellent pool, steam room and gym, and generous continental breakfast; uptown, the historic *Finlen Hotel*, 100 E Broadway (☎406/723-5461; ➌), has rooms in the original 1920s building and a more modern annex. The *Scott Inn*, 15 W Copper (☎406/723-7030; ➍/➎), is a charming B&B in a historic old manor.

Butte has plenty of good places to **eat and drink**, most of them uptown. The funky, friendly *Blue Venus* coffee house, 124 Main St, serves good espresso, light breakfasts and lunches, while *Metals Banque*, 8 W Park (☎406/723-6160), offers tasty Tex-Mex in an old bank vault complete with enormous metal safe. More upscale, though still relatively informal, the *Uptown Café*, 47 E Broadway (☎406/723-4735), serves fixed five-course gourmet meals, particularly strong on Mediterranean-style seafood. Savings on decor allow the roomy *M&M Bar*, 9 N Main St (☎406/723-7612,) to serve the cheapest grease-laden breakfasts in town; it's also an atmospheric place for a beer. *The Copper King Saloon,* at 1000 S Montana St (☎406/723-9283), is a lively place to spend an evening.

Helena and around

In 1864 a party of disheartened prospectors working over the present site of **HELENA**, more or less halfway between Yellowstone and Glacier, decided to have one final dig along a likely-looking ravine – and struck lucky on what is now **Last Chance Gulch**, the town's attractive main street. More than $20 million of gold was extracted, but Helena retained an orderly appearance, set neatly at the foot of two rounded mountains with a fine view over the golden-brown **Prickly Pear Valley**. Over fifty successful prospectors remained here as millionaires, and their palatial residences still enhance the west side of town. Hollywood star Gary Cooper was born and brought up in this quintessentially Western town; actress Myrna Loy also lived here as a child, and is commemorated by the **Myrna Loy Center for the Performing Arts** at 15 N Ewing St (☎406/443-0287).

Inside the massive Neoclassical **State Capitol**, atop a small hill surrounded by lawns at Sixth and Montana avenues, huge murals by "cowboy artist" C. M. Russell depict scenes from Montana's history (daily 8am–6pm; free). You can see more of his work at the excellent **Montana Historical Society Museum**, 225 N Roberts (June–Aug Mon–Fri 8am–6pm, Sat & Sun 9am–5pm; rest of year Mon–Fri 8am–5pm, Sat 9am–5pm; free), as well as early photographs of pioneer life. The majestic red-tiled spires of the **Cathedral of St Helena** rise 230ft at 530 N Ewing St; elaborate Bavarian stained glass, white-marble altars and gold leaf decorate the interior. Also worth a visit is the **Holter Museum of Art**, 12 E Lawrence St (June–Sept Mon–Sat 10am–5pm, Sun noon–5pm; Oct–May Tue–Fri 11.30am–5pm, Sat & Sun noon–5pm; free), which exhibits painting, sculpture, photography and ceramics. West of downtown, the **Archie Bray Foundation**, 2915 Country Club Ave (☎406/443-3502), hosts world-renowned ceramic artists who hone their craft while you watch.

Practicalities

Between them, Intermountain and Rimrock (which links with Greyhound), offer connections throughout Montana from Helena's **bus station** at 3122

Prospect Ave (☎406/442-5860). Between mid-May and September the Historical Society runs imitation steam train **tours** three times a day from the corner of Sixth Avenue and Roberts Street ($5; ☎406/442-1023 or 1-888/423-1023). There's a **visitor center** at 225 Cruse Ave (Mon 9am–5pm, Tues–Fri 8am–5pm; ☎406/442-4120) where you can pick up a free visitor's map, and look out for the free *Lively Times* – a good source of local listings. Information and maps on local hiking trails and camping is available from Helena National Forest Ranger Station, 2001 Poplar St (☎406/449-5490).

The northernmost blocks of Last Chance Gulch form a low-key pedestrian-ized mall, decorated with mining-themed sculptures and fountains, enlivened by bars, sidewalk coffee shops and restaurants. The *Budget Inn Express*, 524 Last Chance Gulch (☎1-800/862-1334 or 406/442-0600; ❺), offers comfortable rooms in a good-value downtown location, or for something more traditional and stylish try *The Barrister Bed & Breakfast*, 416 N Ewing (☎406/443-7330, ☎1-800/823-1148, Ⓦwww.wtp.net/go/montana/sites/barrister.html; ❺), a lovely Victorian mansion dating back to 1874 situated beside the cathedral, and originally used as priest's quarters. Campers should head for *Helena Campground and RV Park*, 5820 N Montana Ave (☎406/458-4714, Ⓕ458-6001), situated about 3.5 miles north of town with sites for $16.

For **breakfast** head for *The Bagel Co*, 735 N Last Chance Gulch (☎406/449-6000), which is open for breakfast bagels and coffee from 6am (Sun 7am). *Bert and Ernie's*, at 361 Last Chance Gulch (☎406/443-5680), serves classy lunches and has a popular saloon bar; while the *Windbag Saloon* at no. 19 (☎406/443-9669) is a big old barn of a place that serves a reasonable pint of Guinness, and good burgers and steaks. A little more upscale, *On Broadway*, 106 Broadway (☎406/443-1929), offers excellent Italian food and wine.

Gates of the Mountains

Sixteen miles north of Helena off I-15, you can take a two-hour **boat tour** through the **Gates of the Mountains** (daily June–Sept; ☎406/458-5241; $8.50). This dramatic stretch of the Missouri River, which enters a gorge between sheer 1200ft cliffs that rise abruptly from the northern shores of a tranquil lake, was named by Meriwether Lewis (of the Lewis and Clark expedition). This area offers excellent hiking and backpacking opportunities. The Helena National Forest Office (☎406/449-5201) can provide maps and local **camping** information.

Missoula

Blue-collar and academic cultures converge in **MISSOULA**, framed by the Bitterroot and Sapphire mountains, to produce one of the most vibrant and friendly small towns in the country. It's a town of contrasting faces – truck sales yards and bookstores, continental cafés and gun shops – where nearly everyone seems to be connected to either the city's huge sawmills or the 10,000-student University of Montana.

The **visitor center**, across the river from the campus, at 825 E Front St (☎406/543-6623), can provide details on **trails** such as the grueling one leading from its office up **Mount Sentinel**, embellished by a huge concrete letter "M." The top gives a great view of the area, especially the rugged Hellgate River Canyon. Other worthwhile trails traverse the **Rattlesnake Wilderness**, which, despite its name, is serpent-free. The most developed of the city's two small **ski** areas is **Montana Snowbowl**, twelve miles northwest, which has a good range of slopes for all abilities and boasts a summer **chairlift** (Fri, Sat & Sun

Missoula and cycling

Missoula has enjoyed close ties with **cycling** since 1896, when it became home to the 25th Infantry Bicycle Corps, founded to test the military potential of bikes as a means of transporting troops in mountainous regions. Its tasks included a 1900-mile ride to St Louis, where the army decided against the use of cycles and the soldiers came home by train.

Today Missoula is one of the best cities in the country for cycling, offering dozens of great road and dirt bike routes. The council even employs a bicycling coordinator (☎406/523-4626), but the best source of **information** and trail maps is the Adventure Cycling Association, 150 E Pine St (☎406/721-1776; see also p.903). The Bicycle Hangar, 1801 Brooks Ave (☎406/728-9537), rents out good-quality cycles.

noon–5pm; ☎406/549-9777; $6, $2 for bikes). **Marshall Mountain**, 7 miles east of Missoula (☎406/258-6000), is geared toward the novice.

Tours of the Forest Service **Smokejumper Center**, ten miles out of town on US-93, look at the methods used to train smokejumpers, highly skilled fire-fighters who parachute into forested areas to stop the spread of wildfires. A small visitor center explains their work (Memorial Day–Labor Day 10am–5pm; free; ☎406/329-4934).

Missoula is home to a number of **authors**, among them Norman *A River Runs Through It* MacLean, crime writers James Lee Burke and James Crumley, and several good bookstores, including Fact & Fiction, 220 N Higgins St (☎406/721-2881).

Practicalities

Greyhound, Rimrock and Intermountain share the **bus depot** at 1660 W Broadway (☎406/549-2339). **Motels** along East Broadway, between downtown and campus, include the *Downtown Motel* at no. 502 (☎406/549-5191; ❷); the *Campus Inn* at no. 744 (☎406/549-5134 or 1-800/232-8013; ❹); and, for more luxury, the spacious *Holiday Inn Express Riverside* at no. 1021 (☎406/549-7600; ❹). *Goldsmith's B&B*, 809 E Front St (☎406/721-6732; ❹/❺), beside the river across from the campus, offers comfortable rooms and award-winning food. The only **campground** in Missoula is the *Missoula KOA*, 3695 Tina Ave (exit 101 off I-90) – just follow the signs from W Broadway. Sites are $25.

Morning espressos and gooey pastries are the specialty at *Break Espresso*, 432 N Higgins St (☎406/728-7300); you can pick up the best picnic lunch in town over the road at *Wordens* deli, Higgins and Spruce streets (☎406/549-1293). For tasty Italian food, join the inevitable line at *Zimorino's Red Pies Over Montana*, 424 N Higgins St (☎406/728-6686); try the white pizza or any of the specialty sauces. The *Mustard Seed*, 419 W Front St (☎406/728-7825), is popular for its tasty pan-Asian food, including a passable sushi – no mean feat in Montana, and *The Raven*, 130 E Broadway (☎406/829-8188), with good coffee and a great jukebox is one of the best hangouts in town.

Bars and entertainment

When Milo Milodragonovitch, the heavy-drinking, coke-snorting private eye in James Crumley's *Dancing Bear*, was left battered and bleeding miles from Missoula, he was consoled by the knowledge that he would soon be back in what he considered to be "the town with the best bars in a state of great bars." It's hard to argue with either claim. Pick up a copy of the weekly *Independent* or Friday's *Missoulian* for local happenings and live music listings.

The **bar** Milodragonovitch uses as an impromptu office is based on *Charley B's*, 428 N Higgins St – a dark but lively no-frills local now known as the *Dinosaur Café*. *The Blue Heron Club*, 140 W Pine St (☎406/543-2525), is Missoula's newest and coolest live music venue, usually featuring the Northwest's better rock and indie bands. Also worth checking out are *The Oxford Saloon*, 337 N Higgins St (☎406/549-0117), a Montana institution and a friendly joint with as varied a clientele as any bar in Montana, and the *Rhinoceros*, 158 Ryman St (☎406/721-6061), which serves over fifty beers from around the world.

The Flathead Valley

The sheer splendor of the remote 28-mile-long **Flathead Lake** provides a welcome diversion on the long route north towards Glacier National Park, reached by following US-93 north from I-90 to the Flathead Indian Reservation. Before reaching the lake, stop off and view the bison herds at the **National Bison Range** (mid-May to late Oct daily 8am–8pm; late Oct to mid-May 8am–4.30pm; $5 entrance fee; ☎406/644-2211). The main entrance is at the small town of Moiese, 20 miles west of St Ignatius off Hwy-212.

Between Polson in the south and Somers in the north, US-93 follows the Flathead Lake's western shore, while the smaller Hwy-36 runs up the east, scrunched beneath the Mission Mountains. Both offer superb views of the deep alpine waters; US-93's curve around Elmo in the west, where conical **Wild Horse Island** rises starkly from the crystal-blue depths, is especially memorable.

Flathead Lake is a major destination for **water-sports** enthusiasts, with the prime spot for launching fishing and pleasure boats being **Bigfork** in the northeast. If you feel more comfortable on an organized cruise, summer options include the *Far West* (☎406/857-3203) from Somers, and the *Port Polson Princess* ($10–16; ☎406/883-2448) from *Best Western KwaTaqNuk Resort* at Polson.

General **information** on the Flathead Valley can be found on ☎1-800/543-3105. **POLSON** has the most extensive range of facilities. Here, the Flathead tribe owns the *Best Western KwaTaqNuk Resort*, which has a pool and its own marina with boat rentals, at 303 US-93 E (☎406/883-3636 or 1-800/882-6363; ❹/❺); the *Port Polson Inn*, also overlooking the lake from US-93 E (☎406/883-5385 or 1-800/654-0682; ❸/❹), is slightly less expensive. If you're passing through, it's worth pausing at *Watusi*, 318 Main St (☎406/883-6200), for its delicious, healthy lunches.

Kalispell

Thirty miles southwest of Glacier, and fifteen miles north of Flathead Lake, largish **KALISPELL** corners a significant portion of the tourist trade en route to Glacier. There's not much to do here, but in high season it may be the closest place to the park you'll get to stay.

A stylish **accommodation** option is the venerable *Kalispell Grand Hotel*, 100 Main St (☎406/755-8100 or 1-800/858-7422; ❹); the *Hilltop Inn*, 801 E Idaho St (☎406/755-4455; ❸), has clean, comfortable, reasonably good-value rooms with queen beds; and *Cavanaugh's West Coast Kalispell Center*, 20 N Main St (☎406/752-6660, ☎1-800/843-4667), is one of the best-appointed hotels in town with a restaurant, indoor pool, sauna and hot tub.

For excellent **food**, try the Chinese dishes at the *Alley Connection* in the *Kalispell Hotel*; the game and seafood dishes at *Café Max*, 121 Main St (☎406/755-7687); or *Montana Coffee Traders*, 328 W Center St (☎406/756-2326). If you're looking for a lively night out, the *Hellroaring Saloon & Eatery* on Big Mountain above Whitefish is the place to be – especially during ski season.

Whitefish
The resort and lumber village of **WHITEFISH**, seventeen miles north of Kalispell, has a lively vibe summer or winter. Hacked out of thick forests, it lies on the south shore of beautiful **Whitefish Lake** in the shade of the *Big Mountain Ski Resort* (lift tickets $44; ☎406/862-1900). The narrow roads round the lake and foothills deserve to be **cycled** – bikes can be rented from Glacier Cyclery, 336 E 2nd St (☎406/862-6446) – and the surrounding mountains provide great outdoor action year-round. Big Mountain is the second biggest ski hill in the state, and is also open in summer for great lift-accessed hiking and mountain biking ($12).

Amtrak drops off downtown on Central Avenue, en route to and from Glacier National Park, and there's a useful **tourist information counter** in the depot building; while Intermountain **buses** call in at Your C-stop gas station at 403 Second St on their way between Missoula and Glacier during summer.

Whitefish has two **hostels**, a rare commodity in Montana. The *Bunkhouse Travelers Inn & Hostel*, 217 Railway St (☎406/862-3377), has bunk accommodation ($13) or private rooms ($30) and the smaller *Non-Hostile Hostel*, 300 W 2nd St (☎406/862-7447), has bunks for four people ($15 each).

Of the inexpensive **motels** lining US-93, *Allen's Motel*, no. 6540 (☎406/862-3995; ❹), is a decent choice a mile south of downtown; **B&Bs** in the area include the friendly little *Duck Inn*, 1305 Columbia Ave by the river (☎406/862-3825 or 1-800/344-2377; ❺), and the rural *Crenshaw House*, three miles south of town at 5465 US-93 (☎406/862-3496 or 1-800/453-2863; ❹–❼).

For dining, the *Great Northern Bar and Grill*, 27 Central Ave (☎406/862-2816), is a busy, friendly spot with pool tables, deli meals and live music, while *Truby's* at 115 Central Ave (☎406/862-4979) is an excellent choice for pizza and pasta. *Whitefish Times*, 344 Central Ave (☎406/862-2444), is a great place to relax with coffee, cakes and a wide range of complimentary magazines and newspapers.

Glacier National Park

Two thousand lakes and a thousand miles of rivers, threading between thick forests and glorious meadows, weave a blue-and-green carpet below the tightly packed peaks of **GLACIER NATIONAL PARK** – a haven for bighorn sheep, mountain goats, black bears and threatened grizzlies, wolves and mountain lions. Though the park still holds fifty small glaciers, its name comes from the fact that these immense valleys were carved by huge flows of ice, millennia ago. Crisp air, freezing waterfalls and year-round snow combine to give the impression of being very close to the Arctic Circle; in fact, the latitude here is lower than that of London.

Arrival and information
There are **visitor centers** just inside the park's **western** entrance at **Apgar**, on the shores of gorgeous McDonald Lake, twenty miles east of Whitefish and just 35 miles south of the Canadian border (May–Oct; various hours, but open at least 9am–4:30pm daily and until 8pm in summer) and at the main **east** gate at **St Mary**, seventy miles west of **Shelby** (daily: late May to late June, early Sept to mid-Oct 8am–5pm; late June to early July 8am–9pm; early July to early Sept 7am–9pm). Another visitor center (early June to mid-Oct; various hours, but always open at least 10am–5pm daily) stands at the top of **Logan Pass** on

the Going-to-the-Sun road – the one through-road between the two entrances, usually only passable between early June and mid-October. The park itself is open year-round, however, and it's well worth entering as far as Lake McDonald or St Mary's Lake even when the road is blocked and the visitor center is closed. The **entrance fee** of $10 per vehicle is good for seven days; for **park information** call ☎ 406/888-7800, or go to Ⓦ www.nps.gov/glac.

Glacier combines with the adjacent, much smaller Waterton Lakes National Park (☎ 403/859-2224) in Canada to form the **Waterton–Glacier International Peace Park**, though Going-to-the-Sun road does not pass that way. Both parks operate their own fees and regulations, and to get to Waterton's separate entrance, north of St Mary, you have to pass customs and pay a $4 entrance fee.

The southern border of the park is skirted by the low-lying US-2, which remains open all year and constitutes an attractive alternative drive. Amtrak **trains** follow the same route, stopping at West Glacier, a short walk from the west gate, and in the south at East Glacier (thirty miles south of St Mary) and Essex Park.

Intermountain (☎ 406/563-5246) operates a fairly frequent summer bus service from Missoula, Kalispell, Whitefish and, to the east, Great Falls. Travelers arriving by public transportation are faced with the problem of how to see the actual park: bright red vintage "jammer" buses (so called because of the need to jam the gears into place) run throughout the park on narrated **sightseeing tours** from the main lodges (May–Oct; ☎ 406/888-9817). They also offer shuttles from the Amtrak station at West Glacier to the *Village Inn* and *Lake McDonald Lodge,* hikers' shuttles from *Many Glacier Hotel* to the various trailheads including Logan Pass, The Loop and Siyeh Bend, and a number of one-way tours and connections. Sun Tours (☎ 406/226-9220 or 1-800/786-9220) offers tours given by members of the Blackfeet Indian tribe, providing a historical perspective to the park's beauty.

Accommodation within the park

Accommodation options within the park, along with the *Glacier Park Lodge* in East Glacier, are run by Glacier Park Inc. (May–Sept: East Glacier Park, MT 59434, ☎ 406/226-5551; rest of year: Viad Corporate Center, Phoenix, AZ 85077; ☎ 602/207-6000).

Most rooms cost over $80, though you can stay more cheaply at the *Swiftcurrent Motor Inn* at Many Glacier on the upper east side (June–Sept; ❹, basic cabins ❷); the lakeside *Rising Sun Motor Inn* (June–Sept; ❹/❺), seven miles in from the east gate at St Mary; and the *Village Inn* (mid-May to Sept; ❺/❻) in Apgar, which fronts onto Lake McDonald with stunning views. Nearby, the lovely *Lake McDonald Lodge* has a few relatively affordable motel rooms (June–Sept; ❺/❻), but these, like the better rooms, are in the lodge itself and need to be booked well in advance. Or you could try the more upscale *Prince of Wales Hotel* in Waterton (May–Sept; ❽/❾) or the *Many Glacier Hotel* (June to mid-Sept; ❻–❽).

The park's thirteen **campgrounds** – all first-come, first-served, ranging from $12 to $17 – fill up by late morning during July and August; ask at any visitor center for locations and availability, or call ☎ 406/888-7800. For advanced reservations, call ☎ 1-800/365-CAMP. Most are open from late May to mid-September, though Apgar, Bowman Lake, Kintla Creek, Logging Creek, Many Glacier, Quartz Creek, St Mary and Two Medicine are open for very basic camping in winter ($6), when facilities are absolutely minimal and may not include water. For overnight backpacking, get a permit from any visitor center.

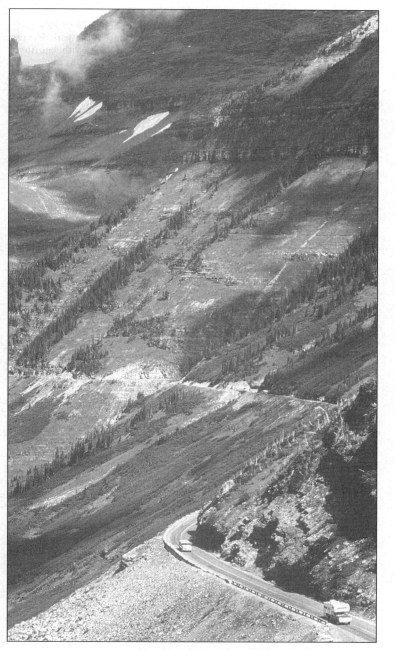

915

△ Going-to-the-Sun road

Accommodation outside the park

Another Glacier Park Inc. operation, the massive log-built *Glacier Park Lodge* (mid-May to Sept; ❻–❽), off US-2 at the **eastern edge** of the park, is a terrific place to stay, with simple rooms, a cozy lobby lined with enormous Douglas fir pillars, a veranda with mountain views, a swimming pool, and a very good restaurant. Though very near the lovely Two Medicine Lake area, it's a long drive from the park entrances at St Mary and Many Glacier. Two miles outside the **western entrance**, the *Vista Motel* (☎406/888-5311 or 1-800/831-7101; ❸) has affordable rooms and an outdoor pool, while the beautifully refurbished 1910 *Belton Chalet* (❻) offers tastefully appointed rooms with period furniture and without phones or TV to disturb. On the southern boundary at **Essex**, the *Izaak Walton Inn* (☎406/888-5700; ❺), halfway between the east and west gates, is an atmospheric 1939 building, originally used to house railroad workers charged with keeping the lines clear in winter – to this day, Amtrak stops at the front door. There are two **hostels** in the village of **East Glacier Park**. *HI-Brownie's* at 1020 Hwy-49 (☎406/226-4426; ❶) has dorms for $20 and some private doubles, while the simpler *Backpackers' Inn* (☎406/226-9392; ❶), behind *Serrano's Mexican Restaurant*, offers shared dorm space for $10–12; both are near the Amtrak station. Up in **Polebridge**, the *Northfork Hostel* (☎406/888-5241) is extremely cozy, with no electricity. Beds cost $15 dollars and cabins start at $30.

Information on other **lodging** in the immediate vicinity is available from Glacier Country (☎1-800/338-5072), while popular alternative bases to the west of the park include **Whitefish** and **Kalispell** (see pp.912–913).

Exploring the park

Driving the fifty-mile **Going-to-the-Sun road** from west to east (which can take several hours, even when summer restrictions on vehicle size – aimed primarily at banning RVs – are in force) creates the illusion that you'll be climbing forever. After a stealthy ascent of the foothills, when the road appears to be heading straight into the huge bare mountain that fills the entire windscreen, each successive hairpin confronts you with a new colossus. At the east end of ten-mile **Lake McDonald**, the road starts to climb in earnest. Snowmelt from waterfalls gushes across the road, spilling over the sheer drops on the other side. The winding route nudges over the **Continental Divide** at **Logan Pass** (6680ft) – a bewildering area where the peaks that looked so unscaleable from the valley floor are now mere hillocks of ice. Four miles on, there's an overlook at **Jackson Glacier**, one of the few glaciers visible from the roadside. Once you get down to the east gate, continue about five miles southeast on US-89 for a stunning view of the start of the Great Plains, which stretch 1600 miles east to Chicago.

Glacier National Park is a hiker's paradise, with exceptionally beautiful views at every turn. Good short **trails** start from **Avalanche Creek** on the west flank of the Divide. The mile-long **Trail of the Cedars** loop leads through dark forest to a wall of contoured vivid red sandstone, from where a four-mile path continues gently uphill, past several waterfalls, to glacier-fed **Avalanche Lake**. The most popular trail in the park – it can be teeming at weekends and holidays – begins at Logan Pass, following a boardwalk for a mile and a half across beautiful wild flower alpine meadows framed by extraordinary craggy peaks en route to serene **Hidden Lake**.

At **Swiftcurrent Lake**, north of the east entrance and reached by the minor Many Glacier entrance, an easy two-mile loop trail runs along the lakeshore, and an exciting nine-mile trail heads to **Iceberg Lake**, so called for the blocks of ice that float on its surface even in midsummer.

From **St Mary Lake**, you can weave a mile and a half up through fir forest to the crashing, frothing **St Mary Falls** and on to the taller **Virginia Falls**; combined with an early-morning boat trip from the Rising Sun launch to the trailhead, this can be an experience verging on the sublime.

Down in the quiet southeastern end of the park, the two-mile **Aster Park** trail gives access to some of Glacier's most astounding scenery. Starting at Two Medicine Lake, framed by the ever-receding massifs, it leads through spruce forest into flower-filled meadows, passing a couple of beaver ponds before ascending steeply through the forest to a small outcrop. From here there are fantastic views of the mighty Sinopah and Rising Wolf mountains, and the calm lakes below.

Tour boats explore all of the large lakes, charging $8–10 for one-hour trips, including sunset cruises on Lake McDonald and St Mary Lake. You can also rent canoes, rowboats and outboards. The lakes, teeming with cutthroat trout, are excellent for **fishing**; regulations are outlined in a free pamphlet available from visitor centers.

Both Glacier Raft Co. (☎406/888-5454 or 1-800/235-6781) and Wild River Adventures (☎1-800/700-7056), based outside the west gate, offer half-day (around $30) and full-day (around $70) **float trips** down the middle fork of the Flathead River, which runs along the park boundary.

Eating and drinking

Food in the park, served in the various hotel dining rooms, is nothing special. The best place to head in the immediate vicinity – outside the lodges – is East Glacier Park, where *Serrano's*, 29 Dawson Ave (mid-April to mid-Oct; ☎406/226-9392), serves delicious Mexican food and microbrews. On the east side of Hwy-49, next to *Brownie's*, is the cozy *Whistlestop Café*, which has a great menu featuring terrific huckleberry pie. On the northeast side of Glacier the funky *Two Sisters Café* on Hwy-89 in Babb (☎406/732-5535) is obvious from the "Aliens Welcome" sign on the roof, and the food is top notch.

Idaho

IDAHO, sandwiched in between Washington, Oregon and Montana, was the last of the states to be penetrated by whites, and rivals Alaska in the sheer scale of its barely explored **wilderness** areas. Though much of its scenery amply deserves national park status, its citizens have long been suspicious of encroachment by federal government and tourism alike, and only now is its potential for adventurous travel being appreciated.

With a marked absence of urban centers (the pleasant state capital **Boise**, in the south, being the only real exception), Idaho is very much a destination for the outdoors enthusiast. Natural wonders in its five-hundred-mile stretch include **Hell's Canyon**, America's deepest river gorge, the dramatic **Sawtooth National Recreation Area** and the black, barren **Craters of the Moon**. Beyond these, **hikers** and **backpackers** have the choice of no fewer than 81 mountain ranges, interspersed with virgin forest and lava plateau, while the mighty **Snake and Salmon rivers** offer endless scope for **fishing** and **white-water rafting**.

In 1805, **Lewis and Clark** declared central Idaho's bewildering labyrinth of razor-edge peaks and wild waterways to be the most difficult leg of their mammoth journey from St Louis to the Pacific. Only their Shoshone guides enabled them to get through; to this day, there is no east–west road across the heart of the state. Reports of game animals tripping over each other in their profusion attracted the usual legions of itinerant trappers, but the Gold Rush of the 1860s and white pressure for land hastened the violent end of traditional life: four hundred Shoshone men, women and children were killed along the Bear River in 1863, the Nez Percé were driven out (see box p.924), and by the end of the 1870s the "Indian problem" had been eradicated. The name "Idaho," incidentally, was invented by a mining lobbyist, who felt it sounded Indian; it was originally proposed for what is now Colorado.

The central wilderness still divides the state into two distinct halves. The heavily forested **north**, interspersed with glacial lakes now fronted by resorts like **Sandpoint** and **Coeur d'Alene**, has always had strong trading links with Spokane in Washington; in the **south**, irrigation programs begun in the 1880s – partly instigated by Mormons – have transformed the scrubland to either side of the Snake River into the fertile fields responsible for the state's license-plate tag of "Famous Potatoes." Idaho's isolation, and small (1 million) population, have kept it largely out of the mainstream of recent US history; indeed, its remoteness has attracted assorted unwelcome guests – neo-Nazi survivalists awaiting the Second Coming and/or nuclear holocaust.

Getting around Idaho

Bus services between northern and southern Idaho are very poor, and a car is essential for extensive travel. Only one **Amtrak** route crosses the state, ultimately linking Seattle with Chicago, and stopping only at Sandpoint in northern Idaho, though Spokane is not far across the border. Boise also has an **airport**, though Spokane and Salt Lake City can be more convenient for northern and southern Idaho respectively.

Southern Idaho

To drivers on the interstates, **southern Idaho** appears to consist of little more than miles of vegetable fields and a few rocky or sandy desert stretches; only state capital **Boise** provides any urban interest. A trip into the interior along US-20, however, brings you to the spectacular ragged outcrops of the **Sawtooth Mountains**. During summer, the much-hyped **Sun Valley** ski resort is a good base for mountain bikers, rafters and hikers, and has the best bars and restaurants in this remote zone – in winter it has the most glitzy ski scene in the northern Rockies.

Idaho Falls

Of the two largest towns in southeast Idaho, **IDAHO FALLS** makes a better overnight stop than down-at-heel Pocatello, being approximately 100 miles from Craters of the Moon to the west and Yellowstone and Grand Teton to the northeast. The first sign you see of this likeable but quiet community, as you approach along I-15, sixty miles north of Pocatello, is its seven-tier wedding-cake Mormon temple, rising from the flat Snake River Valley. The falls for which the town was named are now entirely tamed, with a long, low concrete dam running diagonally across the river very near downtown – but they form a pleasant focus for the greenbelt of parkland that lines both banks of this agricultural town.

Much of the country en route to Yellowstone is every bit as spectacular as in the national parks, and far less crowded; the magnificent **Mesa Falls**, for example, are a worthwhile brief detour along Hwy-47, roughly forty miles short of West Yellowstone.

Practicalities

Hotels and **restaurants** are congregated on the west bank of the river, near the interstate, while the old downtown area on the east side retains a fair number of shops. The **visitor center** at 505 Lindsay Blvd (☎208/523-1010 or 1-800/634-3246) has information on the whole area, including a large relief model of the entire valley. The bizarre towering *Holiday Inn-West Bank* at 475 River Parkway (☎208/523-8000 or 1-800/465-4329; ❺) has some of the most expensive rooms in town. *Best Western Cotton Tree Inn*, 900 Lindsay Blvd ☎208/523-6000 or 1-800/662-6886; ❺), has large, comfortable rooms with internet connections, a pool, hot tub and fitness center, while the large *Days Inn Stardust* nearby at no. 700 (☎208/522-2910; ❸) offers cheaper accommodation and very good-value **food** at its *Snake River Smokehouse* (☎208/523-1865). Other good restaurant choices include the *Brownstone Restaurant & Brewpub* on River Parkway (☎208/535-0310) with a more sophisticated feel than many of its neighbors and *Jaker's Steak, Ribs & Fish House,* 851 Lindsey Blvd (☎208/524-5240). Downtown, *DD Mudd*, 439 A St (☎208/535-9088), does good coffee, in a pleasant interior of brick and galvanized zinc plus free newspapers and magazines.

Craters of the Moon National Monument

The eerie **CRATERS OF THE MOON NATIONAL MONUMENT** is around ninety miles west of Idaho Falls, less than twenty miles beyond Arco. At first sight, these 83 square miles look like a sooty-black wasteland, but closer inspection reveals a surreal cornucopia of lava cones, tubes, buttes, craters, caves and splatter cones. Here and there, sagebrush clings to the bleak soil, and trees have been battered by the fierce winds into bonsai-like contortions. All these features were formed without the aid of a volcano as such; instead, at roughly two-thousand-year intervals over the last thirteen thousand years, successive waves of lava have oozed from gaping wounds in the earth's crust. The next wave is thought to be due any time now.

The park **visitor center** is on US-20 (summer daily 8am–6pm; rest of year daily 8am–4.30pm; ☎208/527-3257). entrance is $5 per car, $2 bicycles, and spaces at the *Lava Flow* **campground** cost $10 (May–Oct). A seven-mile loop road, open late April to mid-November, leads to assorted cones and monoliths with trails of varying difficulty – don't stray from the trails, as the rocks are razor-sharp and can reach temperatures of 200°F. In winter, the road is open for **cross-country skiing**; for a conditions report, call ☎208/527-3257. "**Caves**" formed by molten lava tubes can be explored, alone or on frequent ranger-led tours.

Halfway between the park and Idaho Falls on US-20, the unassuming red-brick Experimental Breeder Reactor No. 1 (**EBR-1**) – in lay terms, the **world's first nuclear power station** – stands just south of the 890-square-mile Idaho National Engineering Laboratory. Even the first prototype nuclear submarine was built and tested here. Now decommissioned, it's a free museum.

Sun Valley

Although these days **Sun Valley** is the common label for the entire Wood River Valley area – in the center of southern Idaho, 150 miles west of Idaho Falls and east of Boise – technically it is just the name of a **ski resort**. This was the 1930s brainchild of Union Pacific Railroad chairman Averell Harriman, who, on discovering his railroad was obliged to maintain a passenger service, decided an alpine ski center would be an ideal stimulus to tourism. His scout, Austrian ski champion Count Schaffgotsch, set out to find dry powder snow on open treeless slopes, sheltered by higher mountains and not at too strenuous an elevation. Having turned down Aspen for being too high, he decided **Dollar** and **Bald mountains** fitted the bill, here in the relatively gentle foothills of the Sawtooths near the old sheep-ranching village of **KETCHUM**. The Sun Valley name was chosen because the snow remained even in the brightest winter sun; early brochures showed skiers stripped to the waist. The world's first chairlift was built here in 1936, and the resort was an instant success.

Sun Valley's season runs from late November through to April; as well as downhill skiing (daily lift pass $63 at Bald Mt, $25 at Dollar Mt), you can also set off cross-country. Ketchum itself is a lively little town with plenty of accommodation, and an oasis of nightlife in this otherwise thinly populated zone. Up to a point, it resembles the Colorado ski towns, though summer trade is not quite as busy. Among summer outdoor activities are **cycling** along thirty miles of excellent trails – including the former railroad tracks, long since paved over – **mountain biking** on the superb lift-accessed trails on Bald Mountain and **rafting** on the rivers to the north (see opposite). The **Sports Complex** (℡208/622-2387) on Sun Valley Road, south of Dollar Road, offers a Nordic ski center, tennis, ice skating, winter sleigh rides and guided horseback rides.

Ernest Hemingway completed *For Whom the Bell Tolls* as a celebrity guest in the resort in 1939, and lived in Ketchum for the last two years of his life, before his suicide; his very plain grave can be found in the town cemetery.

Practicalities

There's a free in-town shuttle service between 7.30am and midnight. Ketchum's **visitor center**, on the corner of 4th and Main streets, runs a free reservation service for **accommodation** (daily 9am–5pm; ℡208/726-3423 or 1-800/634-3347, ⓦvisitsunvalley.com). Room rates everywhere are highest in the heavy summer and winter seasons. You can save a bundle by staying in nearby Hailey, twelve miles south of Ketchum.

The luxurious 600-room *Sun Valley Lodge* resort is very expensive in season, though worth every cent in spring and fall (℡208/622-4111 or 1-800/786-8259; winter & summer ❼–❽, spring & fall ❹); also run by the resort is the *Sun Valley Inn* (winter & summer ❺–❼). A cheaper option in Ketchum is the comfortable, welcoming *Lift Tower Lodge,* 703 S Main St (℡208/726-5163 or 1-800/462-8646; ❺); the more upmarket, opulently furnished *River Street Inn*, 100 River St (℡208/726-3611), is also a good choice with cozy, intimate rooms, a hot tub and excellent breakfasts. The reasonably luxurious *Best Western Tyrolean Lodge* (℡208/726-5336 or 1-800/333-7912; ❺) is also a fine, good-value choice. The *Dining Room* at the *Sun Valley Lodge* (℡208/622-2150) serves some of the best and most elegant **meals** in Idaho, while in Ketchum, the *Ketchum Grill*, 520 East Ave (℡208/726-4460 or 726-7434), has plenty of delicious vegetarian options. The village also has a number of decent **drinking** spots; *Whiskey Jacques* at 206 N Main St (℡208/726-3200) is a good local watering hole, as is the busy *Grumpy's* at 860 Warm Springs Rd, a popular burger and beer joint.

Sawtooth National Recreation Area

North of Ketchum and Sun Valley, Hwy-75 climbs through ever-larger mountains and forests to top out after twenty miles at **Galena Summit**, one of the most spectacular panoramic viewpoints in all the Rockies. Spreading out far below, the meadows of the Sawtooth Valley stretch northwards, bearing minimal traces of the long-abandoned gold-mining settlements. The simple road meanders beside the young **Salmon River**, whose headwaters rise in the forbidding icy peaks to the south; and the serrated ridge of the **Sawtooth Mountains** forms an impenetrable barrier along the western horizon.

Backpackers are guaranteed solitude in these high fastnesses, dotted with remote lakes – pick up details of primitive **camping** sites and hiking trails at the **Sawtooth National Recreation Area headquarters** (☎208/726-7672 or 1-800/260-5970), eight miles out of Ketchum.

Beside **Redfish Lake**, just east of Hwy-75, sixty miles north of Sun Valley, the attractive and deliberately low-key *Redfish Lake Lodge* offers accommodation in motel rooms and cabins (June to early Oct; ☎208/774-3536; ❸–❺).

At tiny **STANLEY**, a few miles north, dirt roads radiate from the junction of Hwy-75 and Hwy-21, with assorted **motels** such as the large *Mountain Village Lodge* (☎208/774-3661 or 1-800/843-5475; ❹) with sixty comfortably furnished rooms and a natural hot springs spa, and the more rustic *Valley Creek Motel* (☎208/774-3606; ❹/❺). The *Rod and Gun Club Saloon*, on Ace of Diamonds Avenue, is a lively local **bar** that also serves decent pub grub. Out of season Stanley virtually closes up; in summer its main activity is organizing **rafting trips** (check in advance; weather conditions – such as heavy snowmelt – can make conditions too dangerous). Operators include The River Company (☎208/774-2244).

Boise

Anywhere in the US, the verdant community of **BOISE** (pronounced *Boy-zee*) would come across as a bustling and likeable small city; located in arid southwestern Idaho, it's all the more appealing. The town straddles I-84, just 350 miles from Salt Lake City to the southeast and a trifling 490 miles from Seattle in the northwest.

The town grew up under the protective wing of Fort Boise, established in 1862 for the benefit of pioneers using the Oregon Trail. After adapting (or misspelling) the name originally given to the area by French trappers – *les bois*, the woods – the earliest residents boosted the town's appearance by planting hundreds more trees.

The Town

To explore Boise's compact, friendly **downtown**, start at the central **State Capitol** at Jefferson Street and Capitol Boulevard. This squat replica of the national capitol exhibits gemstones such as the star garnet, found only in Indo-China and Idaho. **Old Boise Historic District**, nearby, is an elegant area of brick houses, shops and restaurants that has undergone major restoration. The unusual **Idaho Basque Museum and Cultural Center** at 607–611 Grove St (Tue–Fri 10am–4pm, Sat 11am–3pm; $1),) is located in a former boarding house that was for many years home to Basque immigrants fresh from the western Pyrenees, who came to central Idaho, with its equally mountainous terrain, to employ their shepherding skills. The museum traces the Basque cultural heritage and hosts regular traditional dance nights.

It's impossible not to be impressed by the contrast between the urban greenery and the humpy desert hills all around. The city is rightly proud of the **Greenbelt**, some nineteen miles of paths that crisscross the tranquil **Boise River** to link nine separate parks. In **Julia Davis Park**, the **Idaho Historical Museum** (Mon–Sat 9am–5pm, Sun 1–5pm; donation) chronicles Native American and Basque history, as well as the experience of the Chinese miners of the 1870s and 1880s, who picked over mines long since abandoned by whites. The state legislature, controlled by unreconstructed Confederates who had fled the South after the Civil War, did nothing to stamp out racial violence, and forced the Chinese to pay $4 a month, a considerable amount at the time, just to live in the Territory.

The **Old Idaho Penitentiary** nestles beneath desert hills at 2445 Old Penitentiary Rd, off Warm Springs Avenue (summer daily 10am–6pm; rest of year daily noon–5pm; $4). This imposing sandstone-walled citadel feels like a desolate outpost, despite being just a mile from downtown. Constructed in 1870 to hold robbers, rustlers and other desperadoes, it remained open until 1974. Self-guided tours take you through the cramped solitary confinement unit, and the gallows room where the last hanging in Idaho was carried out in 1957. Restoration work has sensibly avoided trying to make this brutal prison look more palatable. A small museum displays confiscated weapons and mugshots of former inmates, including one Harry Orchard, who blew up the state governor in 1905 and served out his sentence here, dying in 1954 at the age of 88. Oddly adjacent to the penitentiary, the **Idaho Botanical Gardens** (mid-April to mid-Oct Mon–Fri 10am–3pm, Sat & Sun 10am–5pm) has nine themed gardens.

Practicalities

Greyhound **buses** and the Boise–Winnemucca/Northwestern Stage Lines stop at 1212 W Bannock St. The city's Boise Urban Services (BUS) (☎208/336-1010) run a fairly extensive local bus service – fares are 75¢ adults, 50¢ youths (6–18 yrs), 35¢ flat fare on Saturday. The **visitor center** (April–Sept Mon–Fri 10am–6pm; Oct–March Mon–Fri 10am–3.30pm; ☎208/344-5338, ⓦwww.boise.org) is in the **Boise Center** next to The Grove plaza. Downtown's best **place to stay** is either *The Grove Hotel*, 245 S Capitol Blvd (☎208/333-8000 or 1-800/426-0670; ❻), which has luxury accommodation in large, well-appointed rooms, many with great views over the city and mountains beyond, or the *Owyhee Plaza Hotel*, 1109 Main St (☎208/343-4611 or 1-800/233-4611; ❺), a renovated, older hotel in the heart of downtown with an outdoor pool and free airport shuttle. If you're on a tight budget try *Sands Motel,* 111 W State St (☎208/343-2533; ❷), within easy walking distance of downtown, although the rooms are a bit tatty and it can be noisy. The best B&B is the *Idaho Heritage Inn B&B*, 109 W Idaho St (☎208/342-8066), a lovely Victorian building that was once the residence of Governor Chase Clark and later Senator Frank Church. If you're **camping**, head a couple of miles northwest of downtown to *On The River RV Park*, 6000 N Glenwood (☎208/375-7432 or 1-800/375-7432), which has shady tent sites for $15 beside the Greenbelt and Boise River.

You're spoilt for choice when it comes to **eating** in Boise. *Milford's Fish House* in the Eighth Street Marketplace, 405 S 8th St (☎208/342-8382), serves good fresh fish and has a wide selection of beers; popular among locals is *Goldy's*, 128

S Capitol (☎208/345-4100), where you can create your own breakfast combos. Of the city's many good **ethnic restaurants**, try *Aladdin*, 111 Broadway (☎208/368-0880), for Egyptian food and belly dancing on Fridays or *Bar Gernika*, 202 Capitol Blvd (☎208/344-2175), for Basque specialties – particularly good are the range of tapas. Other fine downtown bars and restaurants include the bustling *Bittercreek Alehouse*, 246 N 8th St (☎208/345-1813), with its huge selection of beers; the *Grape Escape Wine Bar,* 800 W Idaho St (☎208/368-0200), serving good-value Latin dishes; and *Bardenay Restaurant & Distillery*, 610 Grove St (☎208/426-0538), which meticulously distills its own gin, rum and vodka in America's first legal distillery/pub, and features an excellent menu. After dining, check out *The Big Easy,* 416 9th St (☎208/367-1212), one of Idaho's top rock venues.

Northern Idaho

The wilderness peaks and pinnacles of the Sawtooth, Salmon River and Clearwater mountains make traveling through the heart of Idaho impossible. There are only two routes from south to north: up the eastern fringe from Idaho Falls, or, more enjoyably, along US-95 via Hwy-55 out of Boise. At first barren and infertile, not until just before Lewiston does the scenery unfold into superb pastoral farmland. The **Nez Percé** hunted buffalo, gathered berries and fished here for hundreds of years, until gold was discovered and they were forced to beat a bloody retreat.

The heavily forested far north of the Idaho Panhandle is broken by hundreds of deep glacial lakes, the largest of which have resort towns such as **Coeur d'Alene** and **Sandpoint**. While not major destinations, they can make good one- or two-day stops.

Hell's Canyon Region

From the busy but not over-commercialized little water-sports and ski resort of **McCALL**, 110 miles north of Boise, Hwy-55 climbs steadily to merge with US-95 and follow the turbulent **Little Salmon River**. Just south of the hamlet of Riggins, thirty miles on, comes the only good opportunity to see **Hell's Canyon** from Idaho. With an average depth of 5500ft this is the deepest river gorge in the USA, though its low-relief formation, hemmed in by a series of gradually ascending false peaks, means that it lacks the impact of the steep-walled Grand Canyon. Nevertheless, it is impressive, with Oregon's Wallowa and Eagle Cap ranges rising behind it and the river glimmering far down below. Hwy-241 leads towards the overlooks; the final few miles of dirt road require a 4WD vehicle and permission from the Riggins forest ranger office on Hwy-95 (Mon–Fri 8am–5pm; ☎208/628-3916). The canyon is also accessible by road from Oregon (see p.1237) and by boat from Lewiston.

RIGGINS itself reclines in a steeply rising T-shaped canyon. This is prime **white-water rafting** country, and outfitters, spread along a one-mile stretch of the one-street village, outnumber cafés and shops. The **Chamber of Commerce** (☎208/628-3441) has details. From Riggins, US-95 heads north along the Salmon River Valley for thirty miles to the rumpled terrain around **White Bird**, the start of Nez Percé country.

There are few compelling reasons to visit industrial **LEWISTON**, 110 miles

The Nez Percé

The first whites to encounter the **Nez Percé** were the weak, hungry and disease-ridden Lewis and Clark expedition in 1805. Though the Native Americans had the explorers at their mercy, they gave them food and shelter, and cared for their animals until the party was ready to carry on westward.

Relations between the Nez Percé (so called by French-Canadian trappers because of their shell-pierced noses) and whites remained excellent for over half a century – until the discovery of gold, and white pressure for space, led the government to persuade some renegade Nez Percé to sign a treaty in 1863, taking away three-quarters of tribal land. As settlers started to move into the hunting grounds of the Wallowa Valley in the early 1870s, the majority of the Nez Percé, under the leadership of **Chief Joseph**, refused to recognize the agreement. In 1877, after much vacillation, the government decided to enact its terms and gave the tribe thirty days to leave. The Nez Percé asked for more time to round up their livestock and avoid crossing the Snake River at a dangerous time; the general in charge refused.

The ensuing tensions resulted in skirmishes that caused the deaths of a handful of settlers – the first whites ever to be attacked by Nez Percé – and a large army force began to gather to round up the Nez Percé. Chief Joseph then embarked upon the famous **Retreat of the Nez Percé**. Around 250 warriors (protecting twice as many women, children and old people) outmaneuvered army columns many times their size, launching frequent guerrilla attacks in a series of hair-breadth escapes. After four months and 1700 miles, the Nez Percé were cornered just thirty miles from the relative safety of the Canadian border. Chief Joseph then (reportedly) made his much-quoted speech of surrender:

Hear me my chiefs! I am tired. My heart is sick and sad.
From where the sun now stands I will fight no more forever.

The Native Americans had been told that they would be put on a reservation in Idaho; instead, they were taken to Oklahoma, where the marshy land caused a malaria epidemic. Chief Joseph died in 1904 on the Colville reservation in Washington, but decades later the Nez Percé were allowed to return to the northwest, where today some 1500 live in a reservation between Lewiston and Grangeville – a minute fraction of their original territory.

The **Nez Percé National Historic Park**, containing 24 separate sites, is spread over 12,000 square miles of north central Idaho. At the visitor center in **Spalding**, ten miles east of Lewiston (℡208/843-2261), the **Museum of Nez Percé Culture** (daily summer 8am–5.30pm; rest of year 8am–4.30pm; free) is good on arts and crafts but weak on history; the heavily ravined **White Bird Battlefield**, seventy miles further south on US-95, was where the Native Americans inflicted 34 deaths on the US Army at no cost to themselves, in the first major battle of the retreat. Further exhibits on Nez Percé history can be found in the Wallowa County Museum in Joseph, Oregon (see p.1236).

north of Riggins (which was Territorial capital for one brief year before Boise took over). One is to drive down the old road into town from the top of Lewiston Hill, just north – what seems like an intricate network of roads crisscrossing a series of mounds is, in fact, a single tarmac ribbon, which twists and turns for several miles down the steep hillside. Another is the **Lewiston Round-up**, a massive rodeo held on the second weekend of September.

For the rest of the year, the main reason to subject yourself to the nasty smells emanating from the local paper mills is for the fantastic journey down

Hell's Canyon on the Salmon River. Boats sail past abandoned mine shafts and Native American caves, with mountain goats, bobcats, snakes and birds of prey adding further interest. Of the various outfitters, Snake River Adventures, 227 Snake River Ave (℡1-800/262-8874), offers the best value: an all-day, wet-and-wild trip to Granite Creek costs around $120 including lunch. Contact the **visitor center** on the north side of the Clearwater River at 313 N 2nd St (May–Sept Mon–Fri 9am–5pm; ℡208/746-5172) for other options.

Moscow

The thirty miles of US-95 between Lewiston and **MOSCOW** wind through the beautiful rolling hillsides of the fertile Palouse Valley – a patchwork of green lentils, bright yellow rape, soft white wheat and (100ft-thick) black topsoil. Roadside red barns and farmhouses complete a marvelous rural picture.

With ten thousand year-round residents and a similar number of **University of Idaho** students, Moscow is a friendly, culturally rich town that makes a good overnight stop. Bookstores, galleries, bars and sidewalk cafés line up along tree-shaded, part-pedestrianized **Main Street**, the only shopping thoroughfare. Theater, music and avant-garde cinema are on offer throughout the year, while summer sees a sprinkling of big-budget arts festivals.

The town's name might raise a few eyebrows, but it's pretty ordinary compared to the first settlers' choice of Hog Heaven. A proposal to rename it Paradise was seen as a trifle over-the-top; the present title comes from one early resident's hometown in Pennsylvania.

Practicalities

Moscow's **visitor center** is at 411 S Main St (℡208/882-1800 or 1–800/380-1801); Northwest Trailways (a Greyhound affiliate) stops at the basic *Royal Motor Inn*, 120 W Sixth St (℡208/882-2581; ❷). For a bit more comfort, try the *Mark IV Motor Inn*, 414 N Main St (℡208/882-7557 or 1–800/833-4240; ❸), which has a nice pool and hot tub. The *West 4th Bar and Grill*, in the *Moscow Hotel*, 313 S Main St (℡208/882-0743), offers good **food** served in a bright, arty atmosphere.

Coeur d'Alene

When US Army Chief of Staff William Tecumseh Sherman set up camp in 1877 on the present site of **COEUR D'ALENE**, fifty miles north of Moscow on US-95, he found the sparkling blue lake, surrounded by wild flower borders and lush forest, so appealing that he ordered a fort to be built here. Another large structure now stands on the beautiful shoreline of long, narrow Lake Coeur d'Alene; looking not unlike an office block, the phenomenally expensive **Coeur d'Alene Resort**, which boasts the world's only floating golf green, completely dominates downtown (℡208/765-4000 or 1–800/688-5253; ❺–❾). Not surprisingly, it's a bitter local debating point.

Downtown is unremarkable despite its reasonably appealing sidewalk cafés and rather pricey shops. Directly east of the resort, a small public beach backs onto a balmy park area. Scenic **lake cruises** leave from the nearby City Dock (three daily in summer; $13; ℡208/765-4000). You can also see the lake on a twenty-minute **sea plane flight** from here, for $40 with Brooks Seaplane (℡208/664-2842).

Greyhound **buses** stop at 157 Spruce St (☎208/664-3343), situated a couple of miles north of downtown, especially inconvenient as there's no public transport within the town. The **Coeur d'Alene Visitor and Convention Services**, at 3rd and Spruce streets (Mon–Fri 8:30am–5pm; ☎1-877/782-9232, ⊛www.coeurdalene.org), has a good range of free helpful publications. Along Sherman Avenue, the *Flamingo Motel* at no. 718 (☎208/664-2159 or 1-800/955-2159; ❹) is close to downtown, while one of the best B&Bs is *Amor's Highwood House*, 1206 Highwood Lane (☎208/667-4735; ❹), located in a quiet residential area near the lake and also within walking distance of downtown. For **eating** out, *Las Palmitas*, 201 N 3rd St (☎208/664-0581), is a lively, moderately priced Mexican restaurant and bar set in the town's old railroad depot. Of the bars, *Moon's Saloon*, 204 N 2nd St (☎208/664-6747), is one of the more interesting, featuring a stuffed grizzly among the decor, a good selection of microbrews, burgers for under $10 and occasional live music and/or comedy. Somewhat more upmarket is *Beverly's*, a top choice for seafood and meat in the *Coeur d'Alene Resort* (☎208/765-4000).

East from Coeur d'Alene on I-90

Travelling east on I-90 towards Missoula, Montana (see p.910), you pass the surprisingly good ski hill of Silver Mountain (☎208/783-1111 or 1-800/204-6428) at Kellogg, some forty miles from Coeur d'Alene. It has the world's longest single-stage gondola (3.1 miles), which is open year-round for fine skiing in winter ($31), and some good mountain biking and hiking in summer ($11).

A further ten miles east on I-90 are the authentic western-style streets of friendly **WALLACE,** where most of the town's buildings are listed on the National Register of Historic Buildings, and evoke strong images of its silver mining days. See them on the 75-minute **Sierra Silver Mine Tour** which leaves from 420 N Fifth St every half-hour and is a fun trolley-car trip that takes you to the mine via the town's streets; at the mine you descend a thousand feet underground on a guided tour (summer daily 9am–4pm; $7). In town, check out the unusual *Oasis Rooms Bordello Museum*, 605 Cedar St (May–Oct daily 10am–5pm, Nov & Dec Wed–Sun noon-4.30pm; $5; ☎208/753-0801), a former brothel that has been left exactly as it was when raided and closed down by the FBI in 1987. For **eating** call in at *The Jameson Hotel,* 304 Sixth St (☎208/556-1554), where you can enjoy lunch or dinner surrounded by vintage furnishing and decor.

Sandpoint

Forty-four miles north of Coeur d'Alene in the shadows of the spiky Selkirk Mountains, **SANDPOINT**, northern Idaho's most attractive resort, is at the northwestern end of Lake Pend Oreille (pronounced "Pon-duh-ray"). Smaller and less commercialized than Coeur d'Alene, Sandpoint's lazy downtown is brightened by **Cedar Street Bridge Public Market**, a covered mall of stalls, shops and cafés overlooking placid Sandy Creek. At the south end of the lake, **Farragut State Park**, 13400 Ranger Rd (cars $3; ☎208/683-2425), a former naval training base, is a popular spot for hiking, camping and the like.

Accommodation possibilities include the comfortable *Lakeside Inn*, beside the lovely white sandy beach at 106 Bridge St (☎208/263-3717 or 1-800/543-8126; ❹/❺); the *K2 Inn at Sandpoint*, 501 N Fourth Ave (☎208/263-3441; ❹); and *Coit House*, 502 N Fourth Ave (☎208/265-4035; ❺), a tastefully restored Victorian

B&B house within walking distance of downtown and the lake. One of the best bars in town is **Eichardts**, 212 Cedar St (☏208/263-4005), which has a dozen microbrews to choose from and good bar food. Local rock bands perform on weekends. Amtrak passes through early in the morning in both directions.

Looking down on Sandpoint from the Selkirk Mountains to the northeast, **Schweitzer Mountain Resort** is northern Idaho's best ski and summer resort (☏208/263-9555, ⓦwww.schweitzer.com). Lift tickets are $37, night skiing is also available ($10) and in summer you can use one of the lifts for hiking and mountain biking ($8).

CHAPTER 12

Highlights

✳ **Santa Fe, NM** Great museums, fascinating history, atmospheric hotels – New Mexico's capital is a must on any Southwest itinerary. See p.934

✳ **The Havasupai Reservation, AZ** This little-known offshoot of the Grand Canyon remains home to its original Native American inhabitants and stunning turquoise waterfalls. See p.989

✳ **Monument Valley, AZ** The eerie sandstone monoliths of Monument Valley are familiar the world over – but still take every visitor's breath away. See p.993

✳ **Canyon de Chelly, AZ** Ruined Ancestral Puebloan "cliff dwellings" pepper every twist and turn of this stupendous sheer-walled canyon. See p.994

✳ **Scenic Hwy-12, UT** Crossing the heart of Utah's red-rock wilderness, Hwy-12 is perhaps the most exhilarating drive in the US. See p.1008

✳ **Bellagio, Las Vegas, NV** Las Vegas' most opulent hotel must be seen to be believed, and its sumptuous buffet is the best in town. See p.1033

12

The Southwest

The four sparsely populated Southwestern desert states of **NEW MEXICO**, **ARIZONA**, **UTAH** and **NEVADA** are extraordinary, unforgettable and unique. They stretch from Texas to California across an elemental landscape ranging from towering monoliths of stark red sandstone to snowcapped mountains, on a high desert plateau that repeatedly splits open to reveal yawning canyons. The raw power of the scenery, uninterrupted from horizon to horizon, is overwhelming, and is complemented by the emphatic presence of numerous Native American cultures and the palpable legacy of America's Wild West frontier.

Among the earliest inhabitants were the **Ancestral Puebloans** (the former name for whom, "**Anasazi**," has now fallen into disrepute; see p.941). The remains of their cliff palaces and cities, abandoned around seven hundred years ago, are scattered throughout the region, but their direct descendants, the **Pueblo** peoples of New Mexico and the **Hopi** in Arizona, still lead much the same lifestyle, in the same general vicinity.

Less sedentary tribes, such as the **Navajo** and the **Apache**, are thought to have migrated into the Southwest from the fourteenth century onwards. They adopted local agricultural and craft techniques and appropriated vast tracts of territory, which they in turn soon had to defend against bands of European immigrants. The first such, in 1540, was a party of **Spanish** explorers led by Coronado, who spent two years searching for mythical El Dorado-style cities of gold. Sixty years later, Hispanic colonists founded the province of **New Mexico**, an ill-defined region that covered not only all of the Southwest but much of modern California and Colorado; many of the Catholic missions they established remain intact. Not until 1848 – by which time New Mexico had spent thirty years as a neglected backwater of the newly independent nation of Mexico – was the region forcibly taken over by the **United States**. Almost immediately, large numbers of outsiders began to pass through on their way to Gold Rush California.

Thereafter, increasingly violent confrontations took place between the US government and the Native Americans. The entire **Navajo** population was rounded up and forcibly removed to the barren plains of eastern New Mexico in 1864 (though they were soon allowed to return to northeastern Arizona), and the **Apache**, under warrior chiefs Cochise and Geronimo, fought extended battles with the US cavalry. Though the nominal intention was to open up Indian lands to newly American settlers, few ever succeeded in extracting a living from this harsh terrain.

One exception were the **Mormons** (or the Church of Jesus Christ of Latterday Saints), whose flight from religious persecution brought them by the late 1840s to the alkaline basin of Utah's **Great Salt Lake**. Through sheer hard work, and the cooperative management of limited water resources, they established what amounted to an independent country, with outlying communities all over the Southwest. Even here they met with resistance, and until the Civil War intervened, there was a real possibility that the US might declare war on them. They still constitute seventy percent of Utah's population and maintain virtual control of the state's government.

Despite their common heritage, each of the four Southwestern states remains quite distinct. New Mexico bears the most obvious traces of long-term settlement, the Native American pueblos of the north coexisting alongside towns such as Santa Fe, Albuquerque and Taos, which clearly retain their Spanish colonial identity. In Arizona, the history of the Wild West is more conspicuous, in towns such as **Tombstone**, site of the legendary shoot-out at the OK Corral. Over a third of the state belongs to Native American tribes, such as the

Apache, Hopi and Navajo, most of whom live in the red-rock lands of the northeast corner, notably amid the splendor typified by the **Canyon de Chelly** and **Monument Valley**.

The canyon country of northern Arizona – even the immense **Grand Canyon** – won't prepare you for the uninhabited but compelling landscape of southern Utah, where **Zion** and **Bryce canyons** are just the best known of a string of national parks and monuments. **Moab**, poised in the east between majestic **Canyonlands** and the surreal **Arches**, has become a top destination for youthful outdoors enthusiasts. Nevada, on the other hand, is nothing short of desolate; gamblers are lured in the millions by the bright lights of **Las Vegas**, but away from the casinos there's little to see or do.

You can count on warm sunshine anywhere in the Southwest for nine months of the year, with incredible sunsets most evenings. Summer is the peak tourist season, for no good reason – air temperatures topping 100°F can make outdoor life unbearable, while in late summer awesome thunderstorms sweep in without warning, causing flash floods and forest fires. By October, perhaps the best time to come, the crowds are gone and in the mountains and canyons the leaves turn red and gold. Winter brings snow to higher elevations – there's excellent skiing in **northern Utah** and in the **Sangre de Cristo Mountains** of New Mexico – while spring sees wild flowers bloom in otherwise barren desert. Note that the climate varies sharply according to elevation, with mountains often 30°F cooler than the plains.

More than almost anywhere in the US, the backcountry wildernesses of the Southwest are ideal for (well-planned) **camping** and backpacking expeditions. It's vital to be prepared for the harshness of the desert, where even the most basic needs can be hard to fill: always carry water, and if you venture off the beaten track let someone know where you're going and when you'll return.

Unless you have your own vehicle, many of the most fascinating corners of the region are utterly inaccessible. Scheduled public **transportation** runs almost exclusively between the big cities – which are not at all where you should aim to spend your time.

New Mexico

Settled in turn by Native Americans, Spaniards, Mexicans and Yankees, **NEW MEXICO** is among the most ethnically and culturally diverse of all the states in the US. Each successive group has built upon the legacy of its predecessors; their various histories and achievements are closely intertwined, and in some ways the late-coming white Americans from the north and east have had comparatively little impact. Signs of the region's rich heritage are everywhere, from ancient pictographs and cliff dwellings to the design of the state's license plates, taken from a **Zia** Indian symbol for the sun – the one near-constant fact of life in this arid land.

New Mexico's indigenous peoples – especially the **Pueblo Indians**, as the name suggests clear descendants of the **Ancestral Puebloans** – provide a sense of cultural continuity. Despite the **Pueblo Revolt** of 1680, which forced a temporary Spanish withdrawal into Mexico, the missionary endeavor here was in general less brutal than elsewhere. The proselytizing padres eventually co-opted the natives without destroying their traditional ways of life, as local deities and celebrations were incorporated into Catholic practice. Somewhat bizarrely to outsiders, grand churches still stand at the center of many Pueblo settlements, often adjacent to the underground ceremonial chambers known as *kivas*, and almost always built in the local adobe style.

The Americans who took over from the Mexicans in 1848 saw New Mexico as a useless wasteland. But for a few mining booms and range wars – such as the Lincoln County War, which brought **Billy the Kid** to fame (see p.959) – New Mexico was left relatively undisturbed until it finally became a state in 1912. During World War II, it was the base of operations for the top-secret **Manhattan Project**, which built and detonated the first atomic bomb, and since then it has been home to America's premier weapons research outposts. By and large, people here work close to the land – mining, farming and ranching – with tourism increasingly underpinning the economy.

Northern New Mexico centers on the magnificent landscapes of the **Rio Grande Valley**, which contains its two finest cities: **Santa Fe**, the adobe-fronted capital, and the artists' colony and winter resort of **Taos**, with its nearby pueblo. More than a dozen **Pueblo** villages can be found in the mountainous area between the two, while to the west lie the evocative ancient ruins at **Bandelier** and **Puyé**. The broad swath of **central New Mexico** along I-40 – the interstate highway that succeeded the old **Route 66** – pivots around the state's biggest city, **Albuquerque**, with the extraordinary mesa-top Pueblo village of **Acoma** ("Sky City") an hour's drive to the west. In wild and wide-open **southern New Mexico**, the deep **Carlsbad Caverns** are the main attraction, while you can still stumble upon old mining and cattle-ranching towns that have somehow hung on since the end of the Wild West.

For many visitors, the defining feature of New Mexico is its **adobe architecture**, as seen on homes, churches, and even shopping malls and motels. Adobe bricks are a sun-baked mixture of earth, sand, charcoal and chopped grass or straw, set with a mortar of much the same composition, and then plastered over with mud and straw. The color of the soil used dictates the color of the final building, and thus subtle variations can be seen all across the state. However, adobe is a far from convenient material: it needs replastering every few years and turns to mud when water seeps up from the ground, so that many buildings have to be sporadically raised and bolstered by the insertion of rocks at their base. These days, most of what looks like adobe is actually painted cement or concrete, but even this looks attractive enough in its own semi-kitsch way, and hunting out such superb old adobes as the remote **Santuario de Chimayó** on the "**High Road**" between Taos and Santa Fe, the formidable church of **San Francisco de Asis** in Ranchos de Taos, or the multitiered dwellings of **Taos Pueblo**, can provide the focus of an enjoyable New Mexico tour.

You'll also become familiar with another New Mexico trademark, the bright-red *ristras*, or strings of dried **chili peppers**, that adorn doorways throughout the state; festooned on restaurant entrances, they serve as warnings of the fiery delights that await within.

Getting around New Mexico

Public transportation is rare in New Mexico; Santa Fe, for example, does not have a rail service. Amtrak **trains** do, however, pass through Albuquerque, pit stop for transcontinental Greyhound **buses** and site of the only major **airport** – linked by shuttle services with the rest of the state. Texas' **El Paso** (see p.767) is a more convenient transportation hub for Carlsbad. A few companies offer guided **coach tours** in the Santa Fe and Taos area, but as usual getting around is really best done by **car**.

Northern New Mexico

The mountainous north is the New Mexico of popular imagination, with its pastel colors, vivid desert landscape and adobe architecture. Even **Santa Fe**, the one real city is, with well under 100,000 residents, hardly metropolitan in scale, and the narrow streets of its small, historic center, though thronged with tourists, retain the feel of bygone days. Ranging along the headwaters of the Rio Grande 75 miles northeast, the amiable frontier town of **Taos** – immortalized by Georgia O'Keeffe and D.H. Lawrence – is remarkable chiefly for the stacked dwellings of neighboring **Taos Pueblo**.

An hour's drive west from Taos or Santa Fe brings you to **Bandelier National Monument**, where ancient cliff dwellings were carved out of the same forested volcanic plateau that now holds the eerie **Los Alamos National Weapons Laboratory**. Alternatively, the hills to the east of the Rio Grande hold a succession of characterful Hispanic hamlets, strung along a scenic mountain highway known as the **High Road**.

Santa Fe

Since the early 1980s, **SANTA FE** has ranked among the chic-est destinations in the US, regularly voted the country's most popular city by upmarket travelers. That appeal rests on a very solid basis: it's one of America's oldest and most beautiful cities, founded by Spanish missionaries as their northernmost colonial capital in 1609, a full ten years before the Pilgrims reached Plymouth Rock. Spread across a high plateau at the foot of the stunning Sangre de Cristo Mountains, New Mexico's capital still glories in the adobe houses and Baroque churches of its original architects, while its newer museums and galleries attract art-lovers from all over the world.

As upward of a million and a half tourists every year descend upon a town of just sixty thousand inhabitants, Santa Fe has inevitably grown somewhat overblown; long-term residents bemoan what's been lost, while first-time visitors are inclined to wonder what all the fuss is about. The urban sprawl as you approach from the interstate makes for a lousy introduction, while the rigorous insistence that every downtown building should look like a seventeenth-century Spanish colonial palace takes a bit of getting used to. This is the only city in the world where what at first glance appears to be a perfectly preserved ancient adobe turns out to be a high-rise parking lot, and it would be illegal to build a gas station that didn't resemble an Indian prayer chamber.

There's still a lot to like about Santa Fe, however, with its compact, peaceful downtown and walkable streets. Though Santa Fe style may have become something of a cliché, that cliché is changing; the pastel-painted, wooden coyotes that were the obligatory souvenir ten years ago have, for example, been replaced by cast-iron sculptures of Kokopelli, the hunch-backed Ancestral Puebloan flute-player. In a town where the *Yellow Pages* list over 250 art galleries, you'll get plenty of opportunities to buy one.

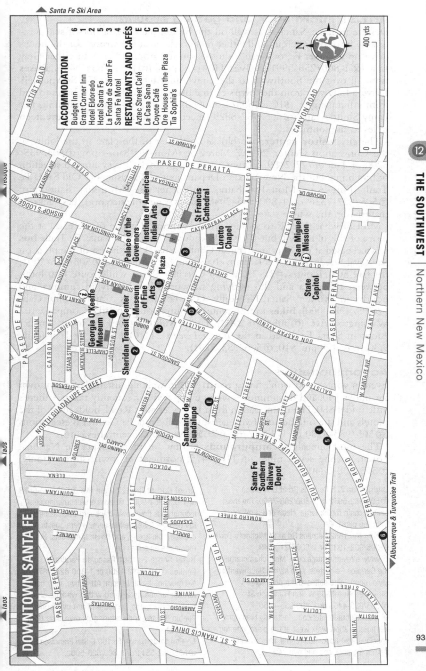

DOWNTOWN SANTA FE

▲ Santa Fe Ski Area

N

0   400 yds

ACCOMMODATION
Budget Inn   6
Grant Corner Inn   1
Hotel Eldorado   2
Hotel Santa Fe   5
La Fonda de Santa Fe   3
Santa Fe Motel   4

RESTAURANTS AND CAFÉS
Aztec Street Café   E
La Casa Sena   C
Coyote Café   D
Ore House on the Plaza   B
Tia Sophia's   A

ARTIST ROAD

BISHOP'S LODGE RD

KEARNEY AVE

MAGDALENA

OTERO ST

PASEO DE PERALTA

CIENEGA ST

CASTILLO

FAITHWAY ST

CANYON ROAD

St Francis Cathedral

Institute of American Indian Arts

Palace of the Governors

CATHEDERAL PLACE

EAST ALAMEDA STREET

ORCHARD DR

E. MARCY ST

WASHINGTON AVE

LINCOLN

SHERIDAN AVE

W. MARCY ST

SOUTH FEDERAL PLACE

GRANT AVE

CATRON LN

CATRON STREET

GRIFFIN

STAAB STREET

McKENZIE STREET

CHAPELLE STREET

JOHNSON ST

Georgia O'Keeffe Museum

Sheridan Transit Center

Museum of Fine Arts

Plaza

PALACE AVE

SAN FRANCISCO STREET

BURRO ALLEY

SHELBY STREET

WATER STREET

GALISTEO ST

ORTIZ ST

DON GASPAR AVENUE

Loretto Chapel

SANTA FE TRAIL

F. DE VARGAS

OLD SANTA FE TRAIL

San Miguel Mission

State Capitol

PASEO DE PERALTA

E. SANTA FE AVE

SANTA FE AVE

W. SANTA FE AVE

GALISTEO STREET

PASEO DE PERALTA

JEFFERSON STREET

NORTH GUADALUPE STREET

SANDOVAL ST

PARK AVENUE

JOSE

DURAN

ELENA

QUINTANA

CANDELARIO

JIMENEZ

MASCARAS

CHUCITAS

W. WATER ST

DEFOURI ST

CAMINO DEL CAMPO

DOLORES

POLACO

DODMOW ST

W. DE VARGAS

AZTEC ST

Santuario de Guadalupe

MONTEZUMA STREET

GARFIELD ST

READ STREET

E. MANHATTAN AVE

CERRILLOS ROAD

SOUTH GUADALUPE STREET

Santa Fe Southern Railway Depot

ALTO STREET

DON FELIX STREET

CLOSSON STREET

CASADOS

BARELA

ROMERO STREET

AGUA FRIA

ALTO ST

AMBROSIO

DUNLAP

CLEVELAND

IRVINE

WEST MANHATTAN AVENUE

HICKOX STREET

ALAMO STREET

MONTEZ PLACE

AMADO ST.

LOLITA

JUANITA

NINITA

HOSTIA

S. ST. FRANCIS DRIVE

ALTO

PASEO DE PERALTA

▲ Taos

▲ Taos

▲ Andreva

▼ Albuquerque & Turquoise Trail

Arrival, information and getting around

Despite its fame, Santa Fe is well off the beaten track. Most out-of-state visitors fly into Albuquerque, and either rent a vehicle at the airport for the hour's drive up to Santa Fe, or catch a shuttle van for around $25 with either Gray Line (☎1-800/256-8991) or Twin Hearts Express (☎1-800/654-9456). **Buses** from all over the Southwest to the Greyhound terminal at 858 St Michael's Drive, a long way from the town's central plaza, include four daily buses to and from Albuquerque ($10; ☎505/471-0008). There's no direct **rail** link, but Lamy Shuttle vans (☎505/982-8829) meet Amtrak trains to Lamy, seventeen miles to the southeast.

The city **visitor center**, two blocks northwest of the plaza in the lobby of the Convention Center, 201 W Marcy St (Mon–Fri 8am–5pm; ☎505/955-6200 or 1-800/777-2489, ⓦwww.santafe.org), stocks a very limited selection of brochures, but the New Mexico Department of Tourism, 491 Old Santa Fe Trail (June–Aug Mon–Fri 8am–7pm, otherwise Mon–Fri 8am–5pm; ☎505/827-7336 or 1-800/545-2040, ⓦwww.newmexico.org), has racks of material on the whole state.

Most of what there is to see lies within walking distance of the plaza at the heart of the old town, but it's worth knowing about the Santa Fe Trails **bus** service, based at the Sheridan Transit Center, a block northwest of the plaza on Sandoval Street (Mon–Fri 6.30am–10.30pm, Sat 8am–8pm; ☎505/955-2001; flat fare 50¢). Routes #21–23 run up Cerrillos Road, while route #10 loops between the plaza and the outlying museums, half-hourly in summer and hourly in winter. Santa Fe's only **taxi** company is Capital City Cabs (☎505/438-0000); **bikes** can be rented at Sun Mountain Bike Company, 107 Washington Ave (☎505/820-2902). For a **walking tour** of town, contact Afoot in Santa Fe, based in the *Inn at Loretto*, 211 Old Santa Fe Trail (daily 9.30am & 1.30pm; $10; ☎505/983-3701).

Accommodation

Even in winter, you won't find a **room** within walking distance of downtown for under $50, and in summer – when every bed is frequently taken – there's little under $80. The main road in from I-25, Cerrillos Road, holds most of the motels and the one hostel. If you get stuck, call Santa Fe Central Reservations (☎505/983-8200 or 1-800/776-7669, ⓦwww.santafecentralres.com).

The most appealing **campgrounds** nearby are in the Santa Fe National Forest, starting seven miles up Hwy-475, northeast of town (summer only; ☎505/438-7840).

Budget Inn 725 Cerrillos Rd at Don Diego ☎505/982-5952 or 1-800/288-7600. The most central chain motel; large, clean and a mile or so from the plaza. ❹

El Rey Inn 1862 Cerrillos Rd at St Michael's Drive ☎505/982-1931 or 1-800/521-1349, ⓦwww.elreyinnsantafe.com. Most characterful of the Cerrillos Rd motels, with stylish Southwestern-style rooms, nice suites and a pool. ❹

Eldorado Hotel 309 W San Francisco St ☎505/988-4455 or 1-800/955-4455, ⓦwww.eldoradohotel.com. Tastefully tiled upmarket hotel, a short walk west of the plaza, offering spacious well-appointed rooms, plus a rooftop swimming pool, spa and gym. ❽

Grant Corner Inn 122 Grant Ave ☎505/983-6678 or 1-800/964-9003, ⓦwww.grantcornerinn.com. Incongruous downtown clapboard B&B, alongside the Georgia O'Keeffe Museum, where guests enjoy considerable luxury, and lavish breakfasts. Not all rooms are en suite. ❺

Hotel Santa Fe 1501 Paseo de Peralta at Cerillos ☎505/982-1200 or 1-800/825-9876, ⓦwww.hotelsantafe.com. Attractive, very comfortable adobe hotel (just) within walking distance of the plaza, owned and run by Picuris Pueblo Indians and featuring its own *Blue Corn Café*. ❺

La Fonda de Santa Fe 100 E San Francisco St ☎505/982-5511 or 1-800/523-5002, www.lafondasantafe.com. Gorgeous old inn on the southeast corner of the plaza. Marking the end of the Santa Fe Trail, it features hand-painted murals and stained glass throughout. Each opulently furnished room is different, and there's a good restaurant, plus a lounge with live entertainment and a rooftop bar. ❽

Santa Fe International Hostel 1412 Cerrillos Rd at Alta Vista ☏505/988-1153. Old-style HI-AYH hostel, housed in ramshackle motel a couple of miles out, which can be damp and cold in winter.

Dorm beds for $15, private rooms from $33 for singles to $43 for doubles. ❶/❷

Santa Fe Motel 510 Cerrillos Rd at Paseo de Peralta ☏505/982-1039 or 1-800/745-9910, www.santafemotelinn.com. Small, quiet, pleasant adobe motel near downtown. No connection to the *Hotel Santa Fe* next door. ❹

Silver Saddle 2810 Cerrillos Rd at Siler ☏505/471-7663, www.motelsantafe.com. Busy, down-to-earth, but surprisingly characterful motel, well out from downtown. ❸

Downtown Santa Fe: around the plaza

Santa Fe's old central **plaza** is still the focus of town life, especially during the annual **Indian Market** on the weekend after the third Thursday in August, when buyers and craftspeople come from all over the world, and during the Labor Day weekend for the **Fiestas de Santa Fe**. Apart from an influx of art galleries and stylish restaurants, the web of narrow streets around the plaza has changed little through the centuries. When the Yankees took over in 1848, they neglected the adobes and chose instead to build in wood, but many of the finer adobe houses have survived. Since a preservation campaign in the 1930s, almost every non-adobe structure within sight of the plaza has been designed or redecorated to suit the city-mandated Pueblo Revival mode, with rounded, mud-colored plaster walls supporting roof beams made of thick pine logs. Santa Fe today, in fact – at least at its core – looks much more like its original Spanish self than it did a hundred years ago.

The **Palace of the Governors** fills the entire northern side of the plaza. Part of the Museum of New Mexico (see box, below), this low-slung and initially unprepossessing structure is actually the oldest public building in the US. Originally sod-roofed, it was constructed in 1610 as the headquarters of Spanish colonial administration; the name may now seem misleadingly grand, but the building was once much larger. Its well-preserved interior, organized around an open-air courtyard, holds excellent displays on New Mexican history, plus photos showing that until 1913 the palace itself looked like a typical, formal, territorial building, with a square tower at each corner. Its subsequent adobe "reconstruction" was based on pure conjecture. The arcaded adobe veranda along its front, offering protection from both sun and wind, serves as a market for local Native American crafts-sellers.

Just west of the palace, the **Museum of Fine Arts** is housed in a particularly attractive adobe, with ornamental beams and a cool central courtyard. It's also one of the few major art museums to be established by artists, as opposed to educators or collectors, and focuses on changing exhibits of contemporary painting and sculpture by mostly local artists. The showpiece **Georgia O'Keeffe**

The New Mexico State Museums

The Museum of New Mexico is made up of four individual museums, two – the Palace of the Governors and the Museum of Fine Arts – in the heart of downtown Santa Fe, and two – the Museum of International Folk Art and the Museum of Indian Arts and Culture – close together a couple of miles away. Admission to each museum costs $5; a more economical option is a $10 ticket, valid for four days in all four museums. All are open daily except Mondays between 10am and 5pm, and also between 5pm and 8pm on Fridays, when admission is free.

Museum, a block northwest at 217 Johnson St (Nov–June Mon, Tues, Thurs, Sat & Sun 10am–5pm, Fri 10am–8pm; July–Oct also open Wed noon–8pm; $5, free Fri 5–8pm), owns the largest collection of O'Keeffes in the world, including many of the desert landscapes she painted near **Abiquiu**, forty miles northwest of Santa Fe, where she lived from 1946 until her death in 1986. In its permanent collection, housed in its first two galleries, some less familiar New York cityscapes make a surprising contrast among the sun-bleached skulls and iconic flowers, as sold in print galleries throughout the Southwest. However, most of the museum is given over to touring exhibitions devoted to differing aspects of O'Keeffe's work, typically on show for three to four months, so there's little guarantee as to which precise pieces may be displayed at any one time.

Across the tiny Santa Fe River to the southwest, three blocks along Guadalupe Street, you'll find a less celebrated but equally attractive little district, centered around the small **Santuario de Guadalupe** (May–Oct Mon–Sat 9am–4pm; Nov–April Mon–Fri 9am–4pm; donation). Complete with a fine Baroque reredos (altarpiece), the shrine was built at the end of the eighteenth century to mark the end of the **Camino Real** highway from Mexico City. Old warehouses and small factory premises nearby, such as the **Sanbusco Centre** on Montezuma Avenue, have been converted to house boutiques, art galleries and restaurants.

Follow the river upstream, or walk two blocks east from the plaza, and you approach **St Francis Cathedral**, looming at the top of San Francisco Street. The first church west of the Mississippi to be designated a cathedral, it was commissioned in 1869 in the formal – and, frankly, dreary – Romanesque style popular in France by **Archbishop Lamy**, the French-educated title figure in Willa Cather's novel *Death Comes for the Archbishop*. The nearby **Loretto Chapel**, a block away at the start of Old Santa Fe Trail, is known for its so-called "Miraculous Staircase," an elegant spiral built without nails or obvious means of support. During construction, the church's designer is said to have been killed by Lamy's cousin, so that for years there was no way up to the choir loft. According to legend, an unknown carpenter arrived in answer to the nuns' prayers, built the stairs and then disappeared.

Two blocks south, across the river along the Old Santa Fe Trail, is the ancient **San Miguel Mission** (Mon–Sat 9am–5pm, Sun 1.30–4pm; $1). Only a few of the massive adobe internal walls survive from the original 1610 building, most of which was destroyed in the 1680 Pueblo Revolt. The chapel is the heart of the old **Barrio de Analco** workers' district, whose many two-hundred-year-old houses now form one of Santa Fe's most appealing residential neighborhoods.

Not far away to the east, gallery-lined **Canyon Road** – which stakes a claim to being the oldest street in the US, dating from Pueblo days – climbs a steady but shallow incline along the riverbed and is lined by dozens of fine adobes.

The outlying museums

On a slightly raised plateau two miles southeast of the town center, with extensive views of the hills and mountains that almost entirely surround the city, stands Santa Fe's other concentration of museums, reachable by Santa Fe Trails bus #10. The delightful **Museum of International Folk Art**, part of the New Mexico State Museum, focuses on a huge collection of clay figurines and models from around the world, arranged in colorful dioramas that include a Pueblo Feast Day with dancing *kachinas* and camera-clicking tourists. The Hispanic Heritage Wing is an engaging reminder of just how close New

Mexico's ties have always been with Mexico itself, while the museum's gift shop sells some unusual ethnic souvenirs. The **Museum of Indian Arts and Culture**, across the attractively landscaped plaza and also part of the Museum of New Mexico, holds a superb array of Native American pottery, ranging from **Ancestral Puebloan** pieces right up to the works of twentieth-century revivalists, and covers contemporary Southwestern cultures in fascinating detail.

Fifteen miles southwest of the city, three miles from exit 276 off I-25, the **Rancho de las Golondrinas** (June–Sept Wed–Sun 10am–4pm; $5) preserves the eighteenth-century "Ranch of the Swallows." As well as the main adobe farmstead, once a fortified outpost on the Camino Real, this living-history complex includes a water mill, a Penitente chapel, and several other early Hispanic structures – and it's also a lovely spot in its own right.

Eating

Santa Fe has been renowned as a culinary hot spot since the 1980s, when a stupendous feat of marketing managed to make dishes such as banana-crusted sea bass seem quintessentially Southwestern, and now has more quality **restaurants** per head than any other US city. Even if you don't pay the wallet-busting prices of the big-name attractions, there's some memorable dining to be had, and the sheer inventiveness of the city's menus makes up for its lack of interesting ethnic alternatives.

Aztec Café 317 Aztec St ℡505/983-9464. Counterculture hangout off Galisteo Street, offering a travelers' notice board and a nice patio, plus coffees, pastries, light meals and live music.

Coyote Café 132 W Water St ℡505/983-1615. Celebrity chef Mark Miller's showcase restaurant, just off the plaza. The à la carte prices are ferocious, but the $42.50 set meal provides a good-value sampler with dishes such as lamb fig sausage tamale and red-banana-crusted sea bass. For a cheaper taste, try the less-expensive rooftop café.

Geronimo 724 Canyon Rd ℡505/982-1500. Canyon Road's classiest option, with a streetfront patio and a cool inner courtyard, serves contemporary fusion cuisine with Mexican touches; dinner entrees are mostly $18–27.

La Casa Sena 125 E Palace Ave ℡505/988-9232. Lovely courtyard restaurant, a block from the plaza; zestful Southwestern lunches, with entrees around $10, are the best deal, though the $42 set dinners are consistently good. La Cantina,

adjoining, is a little cheaper and its staff perform Broadway showsongs as they work.

Mu du noodles 1494 Cerrillos Rd ℡505/983-1411. Largely but not exclusively vegetarian place, near the hostel. Its pan-Asian menu may not always be authentic, but it's still tasty. Closed Sun.

Ore House on the Plaza 50 Lincoln Ave ℡505/983-8687. "Nueva Latina" restaurant, where the menu ranges from $5 green-chili stews to elaborate $26 dinner entrees, and the on-plaza location, complete with ristra-garlanded balcony, is unbeatable.

Tecolote Café 1203 Cerrillos Rd at Cordova ℡505/988-1362. Inconspicuous joint, two miles south of downtown, renowned for great breakfasts – burritos, huevos rancheros and the like. Daily except Mon 7am–2pm.

Tia Sophia's 210 W San Francisco St ℡505/983-9880. Spicy, very inexpensive Mexican diner west of the plaza that's a huge hit with lunching locals. Daily except Mon 7am–2pm.

Nightlife and entertainment

Santa Fe has the range of **nightlife** you'd expect in a small city rather than a major metropolis, though its cultural scene livens up in summer. For full listings of what's going on, check the free weekly *Reporter* or the "Pasatiempo" section of Friday's *New Mexican*. The much-anticipated Santa Fe Opera season runs through July and August in a magnificent renovated amphitheater seven miles north of town (℡505/986-5900 or 1-800/280-4654, ⓦwww.santafeopera.org).

Some of the most atmospheric places to **drink** in town are in the old hotels – the downstairs lounge and rooftop bar of *La Fonda* on the plaza spring to mind – but otherwise conventional bars are surprisingly few and far between.

Catamount Bar 125 E Water St ☎505/988-7222. Downtown bar with plenty of microbrewed beers on tap, and live rock or blues most nights.
Cowgirl Hall of Fame 319 S Guadalupe St ☎505/982-2565. Very busy country-and-western-themed restaurant and bar, with regular live music.
The Dragon Room *Pink Adobe*, 406 Old Santa Fe Trail ☎ 505/983-7712. Classy, atmospheric bar in romantic 300-year-old adobe restaurant facing the San Miguel Mission, with eccentric décor and an eclectic mix of regulars.
El Farol 808 Canyon Rd ☎505/983-9912. Historic bar-cum-restaurant that serves Spanish tapas to a musical accompaniment from blues to flamenco.
Evangelo's 200 W San Francisco St ☎505/982-9014. The only good bare-bones bar in easy walking range of the plaza, with a pool table, a jukebox, and occasional live music.
The Paramount and Bar B 331 Sandoval St ☎505/982-8999. Cool, glamorous former restaurant that's become Santa Fe's premier venue for clubbing and alternative live music; the smaller *Bar B* programs its own specialized-appeal events.

Bandelier National Monument

Cut into the forested mesas of the Pajarito Plateau, 35 miles northwest of Santa Fe, the cliff dwellings and Ancestral Puebloan ruins of **BANDELIER NATIONAL MONUMENT** ($10 per vehicle) are spread across fifty square miles of pine woods and deep stream-cut gorges. Named after archeologist Adolph Bandelier, who publicized the place in the 1880s, they date from around 1300 AD, at the very end of the Ancestral Puebloan period (see box, opposite). Various itinerant groups, seeking sanctuary from drought and invasion, gathered here to build a community that amalgamated their assorted cultures. At the end of the narrow switchbacking road down from Hwy-4, the **visitor center** provides an excellent overview of the site (summer daily 8am–6pm; rest of year daily 8am–5pm; ☎505/672-0343, ⊛www.nps.gov/band).

The first stop along the paved 1.5-mile trail beyond, looping through **Frijoles Canyon**, is **Tyuonyi**, a circular, multistory village of which only the ground floor and foundations survive. A side path leads up to dozens of **cave dwellings**, their rounded chambers scooped out of the soft volcanic rock; you can scramble up to, and even enter, some of them, to peer out across the valley. The main trail continues to the **Long House**, an 800ft series of two- and three-story houses built side by side against the canyon wall. Though most of the upper stories have collapsed, you can still see the holes that held the roof beams, and the rows of petroglyphs carved above them. Half a mile beyond that, protected by a rock overhang 150ft above the canyon floor, a reconstructed *kiva* sits in **Ceremonial Cave**. To reach it you have to climb a succession of rickety ladders and steep stairs cut into the crumbly rock.

Los Alamos

If you approach Bandelier from the east, you'll pass **Los Alamos National Laboratory**, the main US center for the research and development of **nuclear weapons** (as well as neurobiology, computer science, and solar and geothermal energy). Virtually all the work at this, one of the foremost scientific research establishments in the world, is military-based, and consequently most of the complex is off limits – the small and over-simplified **Bradbury Science Museum** (Tues–Fri 9am–5pm, Sat–Mon 1–5pm; free) is the only part you can visit. What's both remarkable and unnerving about the place is that the people who work here seem oblivious to the fact that not everybody has learned to love the Bomb. The local radio station is called KBOM, and museum guides glow with excitement as they describe their weapons' devastating power. Judging by the visitors' register, a sizeable percentage of visitors come here as a sort of pilgrimage from Hiroshima and Nagasaki.

The Ancestral Puebloans

Few visitors to the Southwest are prepared for the awesome scale and beauty of the desert cities and cliff palaces left by the **Ancestral Puebloans**, as seen all over the high plateaus of the **"Four Corners"** district, where Colorado, New Mexico, Arizona and Utah now meet.

The earliest humans reached the Southwest around 10,000 BC, but the Ancestral Puebloans first appeared as the **Basketmakers**, near the San Juan River, more like two thousand years ago. Named for their woven sandals and bowls, they lived in pits in the earth, roofed with logs and mud. Over time, the Ancestral Puebloans adopted an increasingly settled lifestyle, becoming expert farmers and potters. Their first free-standing houses on the plains were followed by multistoried **pueblos**, in which hundreds of families lived in complexes of contiguous "apartments." The astonishing **cliff dwellings**, perched on precarious ledges high above remote canyons, which they began to build around 1100 AD, were the first Ancestral Puebloan settlements to show signs of defensive fortifications. Competition for scarce resources became even fiercer toward the end of the thirteenth century, and recent research suggests that warfare and even cannibalism played a role in their ultimate dispersal. Moving eastward, they joined forces with other displaced groups in a coming-together that eventually produced the modern **Pueblo Indians**. Hence the recent change of name, away from "Anasazi," a Navajo word meaning "ancient enemies", in favor of "Ancestral Puebloan".

Among the most significant **Ancestral Puebloan sites** are:

Mesa Verde – Magnificent cliff palaces, high in the canyons of Colorado; see p.877.

Bandelier National Monument – Large riverside pueblos, and cave-like homes hollowed from volcanic rock; see opposite.

Chaco Canyon – The largest and most sophisticated freestanding pueblos, far out in the desert; see p.955.

Wupatki – Several small pueblo communities, built by assorted tribal groups; see p.979.

Walnut Canyon – Numerous canyon-wall houses above lush Walnut Creek; see p.980.

Betatakin – Canyon-side community set in a vast rocky alcove in the Navajo National Monument; see p.993.

Canyon de Chelly – Superbly dramatic cliff dwellings in glowing sandstone canyon; now owned and farmed by the Navajo; see p.994.

Hovenweep – Enigmatic towers poised above a canyon; see p.1019.

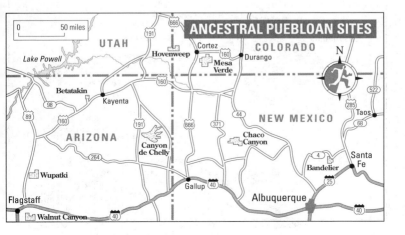

From Santa Fe to Taos: the pueblos

The quickest route between Santa Fe and Taos follows US-84 as far as the Rio Grande, then continues northeast along the river on Hwy-68 – not that the switch from one to the other, at **Española,** is discernible to the naked eye. US-84 passes through the heartland of the **northern pueblos**, a cluster of tiny Tewa-speaking communities that have survived for over five centuries.

To reach the most beautifully sited village, leave US-84 at **Pojoaque**, twelve miles north of Santa Fe, and head east, uphill, for five miles. Apart from a large *kiva*, not much remains in **NAMBE PUEBLO**'s old plaza area, but the tripledecker **Nambe Falls**, another four miles on, are well worth seeing (April, May & Oct daily 7am–7pm; June–Sept daily 6am–9pm; $4). There's riverside **camping** below the falls ($20).

The main reason to visit **SANTA CLARA PUEBLO** – five miles west of the largest town along US-84, Española, which is itself five miles north of Pojoaque –is to see the ancestral home of its people: the dramatic **PUYÉ**

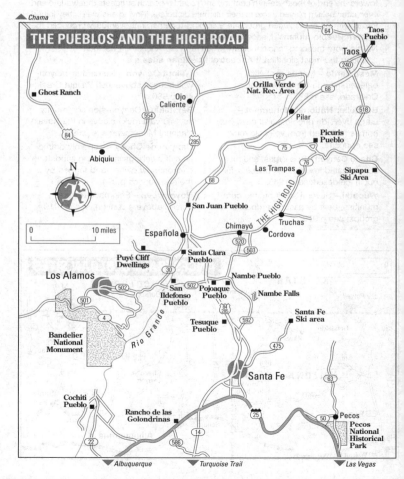

Visiting the Rio Grande Pueblos

The first Spaniards to explore what's now New Mexico were greeted by a settled population of around a hundred thousand people, living in perhaps a hundred villages and towns. However, the people the Spaniards named the **Pueblo Indians** (*pueblo* is Spanish for "village") soon grew to resent the imposition of Catholicism and the virtual enslavement of Pueblo laborers. In the **Pueblo Revolt** of 1680, the various tribes banded together and ousted the entire colonial regime, killing scores of priests and soldiers and sending hundreds more south to Mexico. After the Spanish returned in 1693, the Pueblos showed little further resistance, and they have coexisted surprisingly amicably ever since, accepting aspects of Catholicism – most pueblos have a large adobe church at their core – without giving up their traditional beliefs and practices.

New Mexico is now home to around forty thousand Pueblo Indians, with each of its nineteen autonomous pueblos having its own laws and system of government. All have been modernized to some extent, and the recent explosion of Native American gaming has seen many open their own **casinos**, at sites usually located along the major highways well away from the residential areas. However, all also proudly retain the "Old Ways." Saints' days, major Catholic holidays such as Easter and the Epiphany, and even the Fourth of July, are celebrated with a combination of Native American traditions and Catholic rituals, featuring elaborately costumed dances and massive communal feasts.

Most pueblos are not the tourist attractions they're often touted to be. The best known, **Taos** and **Ácoma**, retain their ancient defensive architecture, but the rest tend to be dusty adobe hamlets scattered around a windblown plaza. Unless you arrive on a feast day, or are a knowledgeable shopper in search of Pueblo crafts (most have their own specialties), visits are liable to prove disappointing. In addition, you'll certainly be made to feel unwelcome if you fail to behave respectfully – don't go "exploring" places that are off limits to outsiders, such as shrines, *kivas* or private homes.

Fifteen of the pueblos are concentrated along the Rio Grande north of Albuquerque, with a longstanding division between the seven **southern pueblos**, south of Santa Fe, most of which speak Keresan, and the group to the north, which mostly speak Tewa (pronounced *tay-wah*) and jointly promote themselves as the **Eight Northern Indian Pueblos** (☎505/852-4265 or 1-800/793-4955, ⓦwww.indianpueblos.org). Visitors to each are required to register at a visitor center; some charge an admission fee of around $3, and all charge additional fees of up to $25 for still photography, $15–50 for video cameras and up to $100 for sketching. There's no extra charge for feast days or dances, but photography is often forbidden on special occasions.

CLIFF DWELLINGS in Santa Clara Canyon, an eleven-mile drive on paved roads west of the pueblo (April–Sept daily 8am–8pm; Oct–March daily 9am–4.30pm; $5, or $7 for a guided tour, summer Mon–Fri 9am).

Like the similar ruins at Bandelier (see p.940), the ancient community of **Puyé** was set against the south-facing cliffs at the edge of the Pajarito Plateau and was occupied between 1250 and 1550. Two tiers of "apartments" were hollowed into the upper canyon wall, while a large freestanding pueblo occupied the mesa-top just above. The trail up from the visitor center is easy at first, but eventually involves climbing at least one steep ladder, plus some deeply worn "staircases" in the rock. What seem like cozy little cave dwellings were originally interior rooms in larger complexes; each was fronted by several adobe-walled rooms, as the countless holes that once supported roof-beams now testify.

If you're reluctant to tear yourself away from this gorgeous spot, a **café** in the visitor center serves snacks on weekdays, and it's even possible to **camp** six miles further along Santa Clara Canyon (April–Oct; ☎505/753-7326; $8).

The High Road

The satisfying if circuitous drive along the "**High Road**" enables you to combine a tour of the Pueblo region with the trip from Santa Fe to Taos. Leaving US-68/84 a dozen miles north of Santa Fe, near Nambe Pueblo, it leads high into the pines and aspens of the **Sangre de Cristo Mountains**, passing a number of pueblos as well as several timeless Hispanic villages. Dotted with isolated, tin-roofed shacks and barns, these hills are said to be the heartland of the secretive **Penitentes**, fanatical Catholics who, in the nineteenth century, were renowned for forming Lenten processions along the ridges, flagellating themselves with yucca whips while chanting prayers.

Chimayó

The quaint mountain village of **CHIMAYÓ**, 25 miles north of Santa Fe at the junction of Hwy-503 and Hwy-76, is the site of New Mexico's most famous Spanish colonial church, the 1816 **Santuario de Chimayó** (daily May–Sept 9am–6pm; Oct–April 9am–4pm). Known as the "Lourdes of America" for the devotion of its many pilgrims, this round-shouldered, twin-towered adobe beauty squats behind an enclosed courtyard; a pit in the floor of a small room to one side holds the "holy dirt" for which the site is venerated. A smaller and more ramshackle chapel nearby contains a diminutive statue of *Santo Niño*, the Lost Child – more of a doll, if truth be told – to whom expectant mothers bring gifts such as tiny pairs of shoes.

Two properties belonging to the Jaramillo family, resident since 1695, make Chimayó an appealing overnight destination. The *Restaurante Rancho de Chimayó*, Hwy-503 (☎505/351-4444), must be the best traditional New Mexican **restaurant** in the state, serving superb *flautas* and mouth-watering *sopaipillas*, stuffed with meat and chilis, on a lovely sun-drenched outdoor patio. Across the road, the rambling adobe *Rancho de Chimayó* (PO Box 11, Chimayó, NM 87522; ☎505/351-2222, ⓦwww.rachdechimayo.com; ❹) has lovely **B&B** rooms.

Taos

Still home to one of the longest-established Native American populations in the United States, though transformed by becoming first a Spanish colonial outpost, and more recently a hangout for bohemian artists and New Age dropouts, **TAOS** (which rhymes with *mouse*) has become famous out of all proportion to its size. Just six thousand people live in its three component parts: **Taos** itself, around the plaza; sprawling **Ranchos de Taos**, three miles to the south; and the Native American community of **Taos Pueblo**, two miles north.

Beyond the usual unsightly highway sprawl, Taos is a delight to visit. As well as museums, galleries and stores to match Santa Fe, it still offers an unhurried pace and charm, and the sense of a meeting place between Pueblo, Hispanic and American cultures. Its reputation as an **arts colony** began at the end of the nineteenth century, with the arrival of painter Joseph Henry Sharp. He was soon joined by two young New Yorkers, Bert Phillips and Ernest L. Blumenschein; legend has it that their wagon lost a wheel outside Taos as they headed for Mexico in 1898, and they liked it so much they never got round to leaving. The three men formed the nucleus of the **Taos Society of Artists**, established in 1915. Soon afterwards, society heiress and arts patron Mabel Dodge arrived, and married an Indian from the Pueblo to become Mabel Dodge Luhan. She in turn wrote a fan letter to English novelist **D.H. Lawrence**, who visited three times in the early 1920s; his widow Frieda made her home in Taos after his death. New generations of artists and writers have "discovered" Taos ever since, but the most famous of all was **Georgia O'Keeffe**, who stayed for a few years at the end of the 1920s. Her renditions of the church at Ranchos de Taos in particular were a major influence on contemporary Southwestern art.

Arrival, information and getting around

Two daily Greyhound and TNM&O **buses** from Albuquerque ($22) and Santa Fe ($11) arrive at **Taos Bus Center** (☎505/758-1144), opposite the well-equipped local **visitor center**, two miles south of the plaza at the intersection of Hwy-68 and US-64 (daily 9am–5pm; ☎505/758-3873 or 1-800/816-1516, ⓦwww.taoschamber.com). Faust Transportation (☎505/758-3410) also connects Taos with Santa Fe ($25) and the Albuquerque airport (one-way $35, round-trip $65).

Walking is the best way to get around the compact center, while Chile Line **buses** (☎505/751-4459) cover a twelve-mile route along the highway, and **trolley tours** visit the main attractions (Historic Taos Trolley Tours; May–Oct twice daily from visitor center and plaza; $33; ☎505/751-0366). Another option is to rent a **bike** from Cottam's, 207A Paseo del Pueblo Sur (☎505/758-2822).

Accommodation

Taos has **accommodation** to meet all needs, at prices well below those of Santa Fe (though thanks to the local ski resort midwinter rates are no lower than midsummer). There are no budget options near the plaza, but a couple of local **hostels** offer bare-bones bunks. Otherwise, chain motels line Hwy-68 south of town, while three or four amusingly adobe-styled motels on Kit Carson Road just east of the plaza provide quieter alternatives. Taos Central Reservations (☎505/758-9767 or 1-800/821-2437, ⓦwww.taoswebb.com/plan/tcr) can reserve lodging in advance.

The best places to **camp** are the nine summer-only campgrounds in **Carson National Forest** (☎505/758-6200), reached by following Kit Carson Road east.

Abominable Snowmansion Hostel/HI-Taos Taos Ski Valley Rd, Arroyo Seco ☎505/776-8298, ⓦwww.taoswebb.com/hotel/snowmansion. Pleasant, friendly, independent hostel-cum-ski lodge, at a tight curve in the road up to Taos Ski Valley, five miles north of downtown. Office hours daily 8–11am & 4–10pm. Dorm beds $13–18; bargain private rooms and camping space. ❶–❸

Best Western Kachina Lodge de Taos 413 Paseo del Pueblo Norte ☎505/758-2275 or 1-800/522-4462, ⓦwww.kachinalodge.com. Large, tasteful, family motel at the Taos Pueblo turnoff, with lots of Southwestern art, a good restaurant, live music, and nightly Pueblo dance performances in summer. ❹

Historic Taos Inn 125 Paseo del Pueblo Norte ☎505/758-2233 or 1-888/519-8267, ⓦwww.taosinn.com. Rambling, ravishing – and very Southwestern – central hotel. Each of its 37 rooms plays a variation on the Pueblo theme, while both *Doc Martin's* restaurant (see opposite) and the *Adobe Bar* are packed nightly. ❸–❼

Indian Hills Inn 233 Paseo del Pueblo Sur ☎505/758-4293 or 1-800/444-2346, ⓦwww.taosnet.com/indianhillsinn. The only cheapish highway motel within walking distance of the plaza; be sure to get a room away from the street. ❸

Mabel Dodge Luhan House 240 Morada Lane ☎505/751-9686 or 1-800/846-2235, ⓦwww.mabeldodgeluhan.com. Gorgeous 200-year-old adobe B&B complex, not far northeast of the plaza off Kit Carson Lane, where the lovely guest rooms are named in honor of creative former guests such as Willa Cather and Ansel Adams. Two rooms, including the light-filled solarium, share a bathroom painted by D.H.Lawrence, while there's also a cheaper lodge annex with more modern fittings. ❹/❺

La Fonda de Taos 108 South Plaza ☎505/758-2211 or 1-800/833-2211, ⓦwww.hotellafonda.com. Throwback 1930s hotel on the plaza, long a Taos landmark, that has lost only a little of its former charm during recent modernizations. ❺

Quail Ridge Inn Resort Taos Ski Valley Road
℡505/776-2211 or 1-800/624-4448,
ⓦwww.quailridge.com. Rooms and suites in
mountain-view adobe cottages five miles north of
town, with a good on-site restaurant and pool. ❸
Rio Grande Gorge Hostel Hwy-68 ℡505/758-

9072. Attractive hostel-cum-B&B, perched above
the Rio Grande at Pilar, 15 miles southwest of
Taos. Dorm beds cost $9.50 in summer, when
reservations are essential, and $11.50 in winter;
private rooms are $29.

Taos plaza and the museums

The old Spanish **plaza**, still at the heart of Taos, is now ringed by jewelry
stores, art galleries and restaurants; all conform to the predominant Pueblo
motif of rounded brown adobe. Specific sights are few – a small **museum** off
the lobby of the *La Fonda de Taos* hotel has a collection of sexy but amateurish
paintings by D.H.Lawrence, and the tree-filled square itself is often animated
by guitar-toting buskers – but the surrounding streets are perfect for an aimless stroll, and it's easy to spend half a day just mooching around. Some of the
best places to eat or drink, as well as a number of top-notch art and crafts galleries, are on **Bent Street**, a block north of the plaza. Bent Street takes its name
not from any irregularities, but from the first American governor of New
Mexico, Charles Bent; his house here, in which he was murdered in 1847, has
been preserved as a **museum of frontier Taoseño life** (daily: summer
9am–5pm; winter 10am–4pm; $2). A single $20 ticket, valid for a year, grants
admission to both this and six other Taos museums, including the four large
enough to be described below.

Just east of the plaza, across the highway at the end of Taos's sole surviving
stretch of wooden boardwalk, is the dusty but evocative adobe abode that was
home to mountain man, mason and part-time US cavalry officer **Kit Carson**
(see p.1350) for 25 years in the mid-1800s. It too is now a **museum**, filled with
saddles, rifles and Wild West paraphernalia (daily: May–Oct 8am–6pm;
Nov–April 9am–5pm; $5). Two blocks south of the plaza at 222 Ledoux St, the
much-restored 1790 **house** of artist and collector **Ernest L. Blumenschein**,
co-founder of the town's 1920s arts colony, displays paintings and furniture
(daily: April–Oct 9am–5pm; Nov–March 10am–4pm; $5).

Two miles north of the Taos Pueblo turning, reached by a dirt road that angles
into a tricky five-way intersection, the **Millicent Rogers Museum** (April–Oct
daily 10am–5pm; Nov–March daily except Mon 10am–5pm; $6) shows off a
superb collection of craft works. Objects range from Ancestral Puebloan and
Mimbres pottery to the contemporary black-on-black ceramics of San Ildefonso
Pueblo potter Maria Martinez, plus Hopi *kachinas* (see p.998) and beautiful
Navajo blankets. Affecting exhibits trace the development of Spanish colonial
religious art in the New World; the highlight is a "Death Cart," in which a skeleton holding a bow and arrow rides in a rickety wooden carriage.

Ranchos de Taos

South of the central plaza area, to either side of Hwy-68, **Ranchos de Taos**
was originally a separate community, composed of the farms that fed the town
of Taos. Each *rancho* had its own main house, or *hacienda*; one has been restored
as a **museum** of colonial life. The **Hacienda Martínez** (daily: April–Oct
9am–5pm; Nov–March 10am–4pm; $5), two miles southwest of the plaza on
Ranchitos Road, was built in 1804 by Don Antonio Martínez, an early mayor
of Taos. Within its thick, windowless, adobe walls – sealed like a fortress against
still-prevalent Indian raids – two dozen rooms are wrapped around two patios,
holding animal pens and a well. Trade goods of the kind Don Antonio once
carried south along the Rio Grande are displayed alongside tools, looms and
simple furnishings.

In Ranchos' small unpaved plaza, the mission church of **San Francisco de Asis** turns its broad shoulders, or more accurately its massive adobe buttresses, to the passing traffic on Hwy-68. Built around 1776, it's one of colonial New Mexico's most splendid architectural achievements, with subtly rounded walls and corners disguising its underlying structural strength. Though the ever-changing interplay of light and shade across its golden exterior has fascinated painters from Georgia O'Keeffe onward, the interior is equally intriguing, with a magnificently ornate green-and-red reredos (altarpiece) framing several naïve paintings.

Taos Pueblo

Continuously inhabited for perhaps eight hundred years, the two multistory adobes at **Taos Pueblo**, two miles north of Taos plaza and half a mile east of Hwy-68, constitute the most impressive Native American dwelling place still in use. The 150 full-time residents of Hlauuma, the north house, and Hlaukwima, the south house – separated by the Rio Pueblo de Taos, which flows down the hills from the sacred Blue Lake, inaccessible to outsiders – have made few concessions to the modern world, living without toilets, running water or electricity.

Each day between 9am and 6pm, whenever sufficient visitors are waiting, short **tours** of the complex provide an introduction to its traditions and culture; though you do not enter the actual adobes, several smaller buildings are open as craft shops. Car and camera fees are charged ($10, plus $10 for still photography and $20 for a video camera; ☎505/758-1028 or ⓦwww.taospueblo.com).

For most of the year, Pueblo life continues with scant regard for the intrusion of tourists, but feast days and dances, held throughout the summer, can be spectacular. The biggest parties are the **Corn Dances** in June and July and the **Feast of San Gerónimo** at the end of September, when outsiders flock to join the general revelry. The pueblo is sometimes closed during tribal events, however; check before you visit.

Taos Ski Valley

Fifteen miles north of Taos, reached via an attractive road that winds up through a narrow gap in the mountains from the village of Arroyo Seco, lie the challenging slopes of **Taos Ski Valley**. Located on the north flank of **Wheeler Peak**, the highest point in New Mexico at 13,161ft, the demanding runs are usually open to skiers – snowboarding, incredibly, continues to be banned on the slopes – between late November and early April (lift tickets $45; ☎505/776-2291, resort reservations ☎1-800/992-7669, ⓦwww.skitaos.org).

Eating, drinking and nightlife

Taos is too small to offer much **nightlife**, but it does have a fine selection of **restaurants** in all price ranges, and several coffee houses. If your main priority is to **drink**, the *Adobe Bar* in the *Taos Inn* is the coziest spot in town, while *Eske's*, a short way south at 106 Des Georges Lane (☎505/758-1517), is a lively brewpub.

Apple Tree Restaurant 123 Bent St ☎505/758-1900. Eclectic international café, based around a courtyard just north of the plaza, where the inexpensive menu ranges from Thai to Mexican.
Bent Street Deli & Café 120 Bent St ☎505/758-5787. Airy, partly outdoor place, just north of the plaza; good-value breakfasts, sandwich lunches,

and tasty dinners for under $20. Closed Sun.
Caffe Tazza 122 Kit Carson Rd ☎505/758-8706. Trendy, central café with nice sunlit terrace, selling coffees and light veggie meals to students and assorted crazies. Next door to Taos Book Shop.
Doc Martin's *Taos Inn*, 125 Paseo del Pueblo Norte ☎505/758-1977. Delicious, inventive New

Mexican food in romantic adobe inn, on the main road just east of the plaza. Most dinner entrees, such as *piñon*-crusted salmon or smoked lamb sirloin, are $16–23.

Island Coffees and Hawaiian Grill 1032 Paseo del Pueblo Sur ☎505/758-7777. Friendly, very inexpensive Hawaiian-themed café near the visitor center, serving Kona coffee plus noodle dishes,

curries and sandwiches, and offering cut-rate internet access.

Outback in Taos 712 Paseo del Pueblo Norte ☎505/748-3112. Hard-to-find pizzeria, a mile north of town, with a welcoming youthful ambience and huge portions of great food – the $9 calzones are amazing.

Chama

Eighty-five miles northwest of Taos on US-64 – which crosses the dramatic Rio Grande Gorge Bridge – beyond Abiquiu and the red rocks around Ghost Ranch, tiny **CHAMA** is the base for trips on the **Cumbres and Toltec Scenic Railroad** (June to mid-Oct; ☎505/756-2151, ⓦwww.cumbrestoltec.com), an exhilarating high-mountain ride, following the course of the Los Piños Gorge. Daily excursions run through the High Brazos mountains on the border with Colorado; you can either take a motor coach to Antonito, Colorado, and return by train (depart Chama 8.30am; $60), go by train and return by coach (depart Chama 10am; $60), or take a round-trip for the day by train to a point halfway along (depart 10am; $40).

Modern timber lodges like the *Elkhorn Lodge* (☎505/756-2105; ❸) line the river south of town, while the *Gandy Dancer* is a three-bedroom B&B in a purple-clapboard mansion, near the station at 299 Maple St (☎505/756-2191 or 1-800/424-6702, ⓦwww.gandydancerbb.com; ❹).

From Santa Fe to Albuquerque

Driving from **Santa Fe to Albuquerque**, you have three options. One route loops through the mountains to the west via **Bandelier** (see p.940) and the appealing village of Jemez Springs, while another follows the slumbering **Turquoise Trail** through the ghost towns further east. Even the direct sixty-mile sprint down **I-25** has its moments, with views of Sandia Crest to the east and the sprawling Rio Grande to the west.

The Turquoise Trail

The "**Turquoise Trail**," less glamorously known as Hwy-14, is a detour off I-25 that leads between the Sandia and Ortiz mountains, and a couple of the long-abandoned mining camps along the way still just about rank as towns in their own right.

The dusty rolling hills that surround the northernmost town, **CERRILLOS**, hold one of the world's greatest concentrations of **turquoise**. Archeologists estimate that ninety percent of the turquoise treasures seized by the Spanish when they conquered the Aztec capital of Tenochtitlan came from this unprepossessing spot. Prehistoric Indians scooped hundreds of tons of rock from the hillsides with the most basic of tools; after the **Pueblo Revolt** many shafts were buried to conceal them from the Spanish, and tales of fabulous "lost mines" still abound.

With its unpaved roads and old wooden buildings, Cerrillos made an atmospheric location for the filming of the bratpack Western *Young Guns* in 1988. There's still a bit of life in the old town; as recently as 1983 robbers made off with $500,000 worth of gold from the nearby Ortiz Mines. Tourists, however, have to content themselves with the **Casa Grande Trading Post**, **Turquoise Mining Museum and Petting Zoo**, an endearing shop–cum–museum that offers a random assortment of old bills and letters, porcupine quills, rattlesnake skins and petrified wood, plus the chance to pull on a string to make a plaster Indian hammer on a rock.

A dozen miles further on, the New Agey village of **MADRID** (pronounced *MAD-rid*) consists of a straggle of wooden cottages on either side of the narrow highway. Several hold interesting crafts and antiques stores; if you're close enough to home to carry furniture, there are some real bargains to be had. One attractive old mining home, *Java Junction* (℡505/438-2772 or 1-877/308-8884, Ⓦwww.java-junction.com; ❸), houses a **coffee shop** downstairs and a **B&B** apartment upstairs, with full kitchen and bathroom facilities. Behind the lively *Mine Shaft Tavern* (℡505/473-0743), there's an accessible mine shaft.

Coronado State Monument

If you do drive the I-25 route, be sure to stop off along the way at **Coronado State Monument**, just off the freeway on the far side of the Rio Grande, eighteen miles north of Albuquerque (daily: 8am–5pm; April–Oct $3, Nov–March $2). Named after the Spanish explorer who wintered here in 1540 (and who, in frustration at not finding any of the vast riches he was searching for, tortured and brutally murdered a number of local Indians), the monument consists of a large **adobe pueblo** beside the Rio Grande. You can enter its restored *kiva* to see reproductions of its multihued murals. The originals, preserved in the **visitor center**, include scenes of a rabbit hunt – the animals are still abundant in the undergrowth by the river.

The small town of **ALGODONES**, five miles north on the east bank of the river, holds one of New Mexico's most relaxing rural **B&Bs**, *Hacienda Vargas*, set in a lovely, restored adobe trading post at 1431 El Camino Real (℡505/867-9115 or 1-800/261-0006, Ⓦwww.haciendavargas.com; ❹).

Albuquerque and central New Mexico

Although to most travelers **central New Mexico** is an area to be raced through as quickly as possible, it does hold isolated pockets of interest, with the scenery, at least in the west, the main attraction. Dozens of all-American small towns hang on to the last remnants of **Route 66**, the winding old "Chicago-to-LA" transcontinental highway which has by and large been superseded by high-speed Interstate 40.

Albuquerque – New Mexico's largest city, with a third of the state's population – sits dead center, at the intersection of I-40 and I-25. It's also a main stop for Amtrak and Greyhound, and holds New Mexico's only major **airport**. Though the area **east of Albuquerque**, stretching along I-40 toward Texas, is among the most desolate parts of the Southwest, one or two towns merit a quick detour off the interstate, thanks largely to **Wild West** heroes such as Kit Carson and Billy the Kid. The mountainous region to the **west of Albuquerque** has more to see – above all **Ácoma Pueblo**, the mesa-top community known as "Sky City."

East of Albuquerque: Tucumcari and Fort Sumner

The long line of truck stops, diners and motels at **TUCUMCARI**, the biggest town between Albuquerque and Amarillo, Texas (see p.762), has made it a favorite I-40 pit stop, punctuated with neon signs. During the day you can while away an hour at the mind-boggling **Tucumcari Historical Research**

Institute Museum, at 416 S Adams St (Mon–Sat 9am–6pm, Sun 1–6pm; $2), which boasts one of the world's greatest collections of barbed wire. Literally hundreds of inexpensive **rooms** lie along this stretch of old Route 66; the *Rodeway Inn East*, 1023 E Tucumcari Blvd (☎505/461-0360; ❷), is a cut above the many cheaper dives. The *Big Dipper*, 101 Second St at Main (☎505/461-4430), is an appealingly old-fashioned downtown diner.

FORT SUMNER, south of I-40 some way short of Tucumcari, means different things to different people. To the Navajo, it's where frontiersman and US Army colonel **Kit Carson** dragged them in 1864 after destroying their orchards and burning their villages in Arizona (see p.995). What little is left of the reservation is now the **Fort Sumner State Monument**, seven miles east of the modern town (daily 8.30am–5pm; $1). To Wild West fanatics, Fort Sumner is a pilgrimage spot because legendary outlaw **Billy the Kid** was gunned down here by Pat Garrett in 1881. His grave stands behind the **Old Fort Sumner Museum** (daily 9am–5pm; $3), his tombstone shielded from memento-seekers by a steel cage.

Albuquerque

Sprawling at the heart of New Mexico, where the main east–west road and rail routes cross both the Rio Grande and the old road south to Mexico, **ALBU-QUERQUE** is, with half a million people, the state's only major metropolis. Though many tourists dash straight from the airport up to Santa Fe, without a thought for Albuquerque, the **"Duke City"** has a good deal going for it. Like Phoenix, it's grown a bit too fast for comfort in the last fifty years, but the original Hispanic settlement is still discernible at its core, and its diverse, cosmopolitan population gives it a rare cultural vibrancy. Even if its architecture is often uninspired, the setting is magnificent, sandwiched between the Rio Grande – lined by stately cottonwoods – and the dramatic, glowing **Sandia Mountains**. Specific highlights for visitors include the intact **Spanish plaza**, the neon-lit **Route 66** frontage of Central Avenue and the excellent **Indian Pueblo Cultural Center**; while every October Albuquerque hosts the nation's largest **hot-air balloon** rally, attracting upward of 100,000 people to its mass ascensions.

Arrival and information

Albuquerque's **International Sunport** is four miles southeast of downtown. All the major **car rental** chains have outlets here, while a **taxi** into town with the Albuquerque Cab Co. (☎505/883-4888) costs around $10, and Airport Express (☎505/765-1234) runs door-to-door shuttles at similar rates. Many hotels and motels also have their own free shuttles, while both Gray Line (☎1-800/256-8991) and Twin Hearts Express (☎1-800/654-9456) send regular shuttle vans on the 70-minute drive north to Santa Fe, costing around $25.

The modern Greyhound/TNM&O **bus** terminal, 300 Second St SW, is located in an otherwise deserted area, five easy minutes' walk south of downtown. It's used by long-distance east–west services, as well as four daily buses up to Santa Fe ($10) and Taos ($22), and has good-sized left-luggage lockers. Amtrak **trains** call in at a small temporary station immediately behind, at 214 First St.

Maps and free listings magazines are available from the **tourist office** downtown in the Galeria mall, 20 First Plaza at Second and Tijeras (Mon–Fri 8am–5pm; ☎505/842-9918 or 1-800/284-2282, ⓦwww.abqcvb.org). Further information kiosks can be found in the Plaza Don Luis on Romero NW in Old Town (daily: April–Oct 9am–5pm; Nov–March 9.30am–4.30pm), and at the airport (Sun–Fri 9.30am–8pm, Sat 9.30am–4pm).

Accommodation

The twenty-mile length of **Central Avenue**, the old Route 66, is lined with the flashing neon signs of dozens of $30-a-night **motels**. If you want to escape your car for a while, you'll have to pay a little extra to stay in the heart of Old Town – which holds few accommodation options – or downtown. Larger convention hotels are congregated along the interstates, and out near the airport.

Albuquerque Hilton 1901 University Blvd NE ☎505/884-2500 or 1-800/821-1901. Midtown highrise, near the intersection of I-40 and I-25. Good rooms, three restaurants – the *Casa Chaco* serves tasty Southwestern cuisine – and several busy bars. ❺

Casas de Sueños 310 Rio Grande Blvd SW ☎505/247-4560 or 1-800/242-8987, ⓦwww.casasdesuenos.com. Beautifully furnished, exotic and friendly B&B, very close to Old Town, with themed cottages and smaller rooms. One of New Mexico's most appealing places to stay. ❹–❽

Comfort Inn – Airport 2300 Yale Blvd SE ☎505/243-2244 or 1-800/221-2222. Good-value motel, served by free shuttles from the airport across the road, and with complimentary breakfasts. ❸

El Vado Motel 2500 Central Ave SW ☎505/243-4594. Vintage adobe Route 66 motel, within easy reach of Old Town. ❷

La Posada de Albuquerque 125 2nd St NW ☎505/242-9090 or 1-800/777-5732. Historic, elegant hotel in convenient downtown location, built in Mexican style by Conrad Hilton in 1939. Plush, renovated rooms, a superb restaurant and a spacious, atmospheric bar. ❹

Monterey Nonsmokers Motel 2402 Central Ave SW ☎505/243-3554 or 1-877/666-8379, ⓦwww.nonsmokersmotel.com. Clean, fifteen-room motel, two blocks west of Old Town, with pool, laundry and a strict nonsmoking policy. ❸

Route 66 Hostel 1012 Central Ave SW ☎505/247-1813, ⓦhttp://members.aol.com /route66hos. Albuquerque's only hostel, a friendly place on the outskirts of Old Town, a mile west of downtown, offers dorm beds for $14, kitchen facilities and bargain private doubles. Office hours daily 7.30–10.30am & 4–11pm. ❶

Old Town

Once you've cruised up and down **Central Avenue**, looking at the flashing neon and 1940s architecture of this twenty-mile stretch of Route 66 (Sun Tran buses do it all day for 75¢), most of what's interesting about Albuquerque is concentrated in **Old Town**, the recently tidied-up old Spanish heart of the city. As the billboards on the interstate nearby rightly proclaim, "it's darned old and historic." The tree-filled **main plaza** is overlooked by the twin-towered adobe facade of **San Felipe de Neri church**, and circled by horse-drawn carriages that you can hop on for a short tour ($5). It's a very pleasant place to wander or have a meal, even if there's not a whole lot otherwise to do. One of the more bizarre of the many knickknack shops is the **Rattlesnake Museum** southeast of the plaza at 202 San Felipe St NW (daily 10am–6pm; $2), which has live rattlers on display. Nearby, Gus's Trading Post, at 2026 Central Ave NW, is one of the best-value shops in the Southwest for buying the perfect bolo tie or other pieces of Indian **jewelry**.

Still on Central Avenue, in the Old Town Shopping Center half a block west of the plaza, the intriguing little **Turquoise Museum** (Mon–Sat 9.30am–5.30pm; $2) may look like just another mall store, but turns out to be more of a fortified bank vault, filled with rare and beautiful turquoise nuggets. The **New Mexico Museum of Natural History**, four blocks northeast of the plaza at 1801 Mountain Rd NW (daily 9am–5pm; closed Mon in Jan & Sept; $5), has full-scale, animated models of dinosaurs, a simulated volcanic eruption and a replica of an Ice Age snow cave, as well as an engaging, touchable collection of fossils and dinosaur bones.

The riverfront

The Rio Grande has shifted its course in the last three hundred years, so there's an unexpectedly low-key gap west of Old Town, much of it left undeveloped in deference to the unruly river. Along the wooded eastern riverbank, the **Bio Park** holds two attractions that focus on the natural world. Not for the squeamish, the **Albuquerque Aquarium** (June–Aug Tues–Fri 9am–5pm, Sat & Sun 9am–6pm; Sept–May daily except Mon 9am–5pm; $9) offers such diverse experiences as eating in a restaurant beside a glass-walled tank filled with live sharks and walking through a tunnel surrounded on all sides by fierce-eyed moray eels. Across the way, the **Rio Grande Botanic Garden** (same hours; same ticket) consists of two large conservatories – one holding rare plants from the Sonoran and Chihuahua deserts, the other more temperate Mediterranean species – plus a series of walled gardens.

At the lower-key **Rio Grande Nature Center** (daily 8am–5pm; $1.50), two miles north of Old Town on Rio Grande Boulevard, informative displays describe Albuquerque's wildlife, and two short but enjoyable nature trails along the riverside feel far removed from the city.

Indian Pueblo Cultural Center

The **Indian Pueblo Cultural Center**, at 2401 12th St NW, one block north of I-40 (daily 9am–5.30pm; $4; ☎505/843-7270 or 1-800/766-4405, ⓦwww.indianpueblo.org), is a stunning museum and crafts market owned and run as a cooperative venture by the diverse Pueblo Indians of New Mexico. Its horseshoe-shaped design deliberately echoes the architecture of the Ancestral Puebloan city of Pueblo Bonito, in Chaco Canyon (see p.995), and the central courtyard is the venue for free Pueblo dances, every Saturday and Sunday at 11am and 2pm.

This is New Mexico's one major museum about Native Americans curated by Native Americans, and the displays downstairs have a clear and distinct point of view. The shared Ancestral Puebloan heritage at the root of Pueblo culture is explained in detail, as is the impact of the Spanish conquistadors. Describing the **Pueblo Revolt** of 1680 as the "first civil war," it states that by allowing the defeated Spaniards to leave unharmed, the Pueblo peoples "showed them more mercy than they showed us." There's also as good an explanation as you're ever likely to get of a topic Pueblo Indians rarely discuss with outsiders: how indigenous Pueblo religion has managed to coexist with imported Catholicism. Videos illustrate modern Pueblo life, and the stores upstairs sell outstanding pottery and jewelry. A good-quality **café** serves assorted Pueblo specialties.

Sandia Crest

The forested 10,500ft peaks of the **Sandia Crest** tower over Albuquerque to the east, affording particularly beautiful views from the top at and after sunset, when the city lights sparkle below. In summer it's a good 25°F cooler up here than in the valley, and in winter you can go downhill or cross-country **skiing** (lift tickets $34 per day; ☎505/242-9133). If you don't want to drive the scenic but twisting twenty-mile route from Albuquerque, take the **Sandia Peak Tramway** (daily: summer 9am–10pm; rest of year shorter hours; $15), the world's longest single-span tramway at 2.7 miles; it leaves from the end of Tramway Road at the city's northeast edge.

Eating

The chefs of Santa Fe may be trying to redefine Southwestern cuisine, but Albuquerque still knows what it likes – mountainous Mexican meals. This is the place to get to grips with what real New Mexican food is all about, with family diners all over the city competing to create the spiciest chiles rellenos, enchiladas and sopaipillas.

Artichoke Café 424 Central Ave SE ☎505/243-0200. Simple but classy restaurant in the heart of downtown, with indoor and outdoor seating. Good, varied menu of California-influenced modern American cuisine; most entrees well under $20. Closed Sun.

Conrad's *La Posada de Albuquerque*, 125 2nd St NW ☎505/242-9090. Classic Art Deco hotel diner, modernized and serving expensive but excellent Hispanic-influenced dishes, including tasty salads and tapas, plus the signature dish, a superb seafood paella, complete with lobster and saffron rice.

Double Rainbow 3416 Central Ave SE ☎505/255-6633. University-district coffee bar, with a stupendous array of breads and pastries, full cooked breakfasts and a huge stock of maga-zines. Daily 6am–midnight.

Duran Central Pharmacy 1815 Central Ave NW ☎505/247-4141. Mexican dining counter attached to a working drugstore, not far from Old Town, with delicious, inexpensive tortillas, enchiladas and plenty of chile. Closed Sun.

High Finance 40 Tramway Rd NE ☎505/243-9742. Pricey seafood and steak place in unparalleled location, at the top of the Sandia Peak Tramway – see opposite – with eagle's-eye sunset views. Open daily for dinner only.

Kanome 3128 Central Ave SE ☎505/265-7773. Bright, colorful, modern pan-Asian diner near the University, where few of the Thai, Chinese or Japanese entrees cost over $10. Open daily for dinner only.

Drinking and nightlife

Downtown Albuquerque has been revitalized in recent years by the emergence of a host of **bars** and **nightclubs**, many of which double as small theaters or music venues. Free magazines such as the weekly *Alibi* or *Crosswinds*, and the monthly *On The Scene*, can tell you all you need to know about what's coming up or going down.

Assets Grille & Southwest Brewing Company 6910 Montgomery Blvd NE ☎505/889-6400. Lively microbrewery with indoor and outdoor seating, plus Italian food. Closed Sun.

Caravan East 7605 Central Ave NE ☎505/265-7877. Enormous honky-tonk, where tenderfeet can do the two-step with throngs of urban cowboys.

Club 211 211 Gold Ave SE ☎505/766-9601. Extravagant, outrageous downtown dance club. Closed Sun.

El Rey Theater 620 Central Ave SW ☎505/764-2624. Live music from salsa to country and all points in between; the adjoining *Golden West* *Saloon* is the venue of choice for Albuquerque's metal maniacs.

KiMo Theatre 423 Central Ave NW ☎505/848-1370. Gorgeous, city-owned "Pueblo Deco" theater, dating from the late 1920s, which puts on an eclectic program of opera, dance and theater performances, kids' movie shows and also regular live bands.

The Launchpad 618 Central Ave SW ☎505/764-8887. Dance and live music space that showcases touring indie, reggae and blues bands, and also has a cluster of pool tables.

West of Albuquerque: I-40 to Arizona

Driving between Albuquerque and Arizona, you could easily be so put off by the parade of billboards and hoardings offering cut-price cigarettes and Indian jewelry that you'd miss out on some of central New Mexico's most interesting places, such as **Ácoma Pueblo** and **Chaco Canyon**, which lie south and north of I-40 respectively.

Ácoma Pueblo

The amazing **ÁCOMA PUEBLO**, south of I-40 fifty miles west of Albuquerque, encapsulates a thousand years of Native American history. Its focus is the ancient village known as "**Sky City**," perched atop a magnificent isolated mesa, 367ft high and 7000ft above sea level. Probably occupied by Chacoan migrants between 1100 and 1200 AD, when the great pueblos of Chaco Canyon were still in use, Ácoma has adapted to repeated waves of invaders ever since, while retaining its own strong identity. As the Acomans have long been happy to take the tourist dollar – they run a large casino beside the interstate, and have hosted the Miss America Pageant – visitors seldom feel the awkwardness possible at other pueblo communities. Nonetheless, Ácoma is the real thing, and its sense of unbroken tradition can reduce even the least culturally sensitive traveler to awestruck silence.

To see Sky City, you have to join one of the hour-long guided **bus tours** (April–Oct daily 8am–6pm, except July 10–13 & first or second weekend in Oct; Nov–March daily 8am–4.30pm; $9, plus $10 for photo permit; ☏505/469-1052 or 1-800/747-0181), which leave regularly from the small visitor center at the base of the mesa. The main stop is at the **San Esteban del Rey** mission, a thick-walled adobe church completed in 1640. Its earthenfloored nave is capped by a roof made of pine logs, which are said to have been carried here from the top of Mount Taylor, twenty miles away, without once touching the ground. Catholicism did eventually take root among the Pueblo people, but tales of the early mission days often speak of the Spanish priests as harsh and unfeeling taskmasters, many of whom came to rather sticky ends. The sheer visual impact of the building is undeniable – due in part to its sheer incongruity – and it's striking that the Acomans obviously never felt inclined to follow its architectural example. Instead they went on constructing the multistory stone and adobe houses around which the tour then proceeds. Only thirteen families live permanently on the mesa; most Acomans prefer to reside down below, where they can get electricity, running water, and jobs. Villagers do, however, come up here during the day to sell pottery and fry-bread, and maintain their family homes for occasional use.

Instead of taking the bus back down, you can walk along the old path, scrambling over boulders and through narrow clefts. Away to the east, legend has it that the forbidding **Enchanted Mesa** once held its own Pueblo community; the only access to the top was via a system of ropes strung between the mesa itself and an adjoining rock pillar. When that pillar collapsed one day while the men were away from the village, the women and children were left stranded, their cries for help fading as they starved away.

Grants

The old Route 66 town of **GRANTS**, fifteen miles west of Ácoma, holds half a dozen budget motels, including a good *Super 8*, 1604 E Santa Fe Ave (☏505/287-8811; ❷). In the heart of town, the *Mission at Riverwalk*, 422 W Santa Fe Ave (☏505/285-4632), is an appealing converted church that now doubles as a community theater and healthy café, serving sandwiches, smoothies and coffee. The local **visitor center** doubles as the comprehensive and enjoyable **New Mexico Museum of Mining** at 100 N Iron Ave (May–Sept Mon–Sat 9am–5pm, Sun 9am–4pm; Oct–April Mon–Sat 9am–5pm; $3; ☏505/287-4802, ⓦ www.grants.org), offering a chance to descend into a mock-up of one of the region's many **uranium mines**.

El Morro National Monument

Hidden away on Hwy-53 south of the Zuni Mountains, 42 miles west of Grants, **EL MORRO NATIONAL MONUMENT** feels as far off the beaten track as it's possible to be in the modern US. Incredibly, however, this pale-pink sandstone cliff was a regular rest stop for international travelers before the Pilgrims landed at Plymouth Rock, thanks to a cool, perennial pool of water that collects at the base of a tumbling waterfall. This spot was first recorded by Spanish explorers in 1583 – *el morro* means "the headland" – and in 1605, Don Juan de Oñate, the founder of New Mexico, carved the first of many messages that earned it the American name of **Inscription Rock**.

Translations and explanations of El Morro's graffiti are displayed in the **visitor center** (daily: summer 9am–7pm; rest of year 9am–5pm; $4 per vehicle; ☏505/783-4226, ⓦwww.nps.gov/elmo). You can see the real thing on a half-mile trail, which stays open until an hour before the visitor center closes. Not far beyond some **Ancestral Puebloan petroglyphs**, scraped into the desert varnish, Don Juan's chiseled signature celebrates "the discovery of the South Sea"; he was returning from an expedition that had taken him all the way to the mouth of the Colorado River.

Chaco Canyon

For casual visitors, the long, bumpy ride to the Ancestral Puebloan ruins of **CHACO CANYON**, north of I-40 between Grant and Gallup, may seem more bother than it's worth. True, the site protected as the **Chaco Culture National Historic Park** is the largest pre-Columbian city in North America; for beauty and drama, however, it can't compete with lesser settlements such as Canyon de Chelly (see p.994). The low-walled canyon is a mere scratch in the scrubby high-desert plains, and the Chaco Wash that runs through it is often completely dry.

Once you accept that you won't have amazing photos to show the folks back home, however, there's still plenty about Chaco to take your breath away. Over 3600 separate sites have been logged in the canyon, of which the thirteen principal ones are open to visitors. Six, arrayed along the canyon's north wall, are what are known as "Great Houses" – self-contained pueblos, three or four stories high, whose fortress-like walls concealed up to eight hundred rooms.

Both the routes to Chaco Canyon entail driving twenty miles over rough but passable dirt roads. Open all year, these should not be attempted during or within a day of a rainstorm. Whether you approach from the south, by following Hwy-57 up from **Seven Lakes**, eighteen miles northeast of **Crownpoint**, or from the north or east, by turning off Hwy-44 at **Nageezi**, 36 miles south of **Bloomfield,** you enter the park at its southeast corner, close to the **visitor center** (daily: summer 8am–6pm; rest of year 8am–5pm; $8 per vehicle; ☏505/786-7014, ⓦwww.nps.gov/chcu). The basic first-come, first-served *Gallo* **campground** ($10), a short way east, is the only visitor facility in the park; from April to October it's usually full by 3pm.

The gates of the canyon's eight-mile one-way **loop road** are immediately north of the visitor center, and open the same hours. The major stop is at the far end, where **Pueblo Bonito** ("Beautiful town" in Spanish) – said to have been the biggest single building in America until structural steel was developed in 1898 – can be explored on an easy half-mile trail. Work on this four-story D-shaped structure, which is almost perfectly aligned east–west, started in 850 AD and continued for three hundred years. Entering the ruin via its lowest levels, the path reaches its central plaza, which held at least three **Great Kivas** – ceremonial chambers thought to have been used by entire communities rather than individual clans or families. From there, you can walk through the passageways and chambers of the pueblo proper, where the rows of neatly finished doorways, each framed by the next, are Chaco's most photographed feature.

Gallup

Just half an hour from the Arizona border, 65 miles west of Grants, the famous **Route 66** town of **GALLUP** is a handy but uninteresting I-40 pit stop. A five-mile line of the old Route 66 frontage contains some of the least expensive **motels** in the US, ranging from the *Ambassador*, 1601 W 66 Ave (☏505/722–

3843; ❶), and the *Blue Spruce Lodge*, 1119 E 66 Ave (☎505/863-5211; ❶), to the pricier national chains. Unless you're falling asleep at the wheel, the only place really worth stopping for in Gallup is the lovely *El Rancho Hotel*, 1000 E 66 Ave (☎505/863-9311 or 1-800/543-6351, ⓦwww.elranchomotel.com; ❷/❸), built in 1937 by the brother of movie director D.W.Griffith as a home away from home for the many Hollywood stars filming nearby. Nowadays you can ogle their signed photos in the spacious Spanish Revival lobby, grab a bite in its decorative restaurant or spend the night in the *Ronald Reagan Room*, the *Marx Brothers Room* or the *Mae West Room*. Some guestrooms are in the original ranchhouse, the rest in a two-story motel building alongside.

The Navajo and other local Native Americans come together in **Red Rock State Park**, four miles east, on the second weekend in August for the **Inter-Tribal Indian Ceremonial**, the largest such gathering anywhere. Four days of dances and craft shows have as their highlight a Saturday morning parade through the town.

Southern New Mexico

Most of the travelers who come to **southern New Mexico** are here to visit **Carlsbad Caverns National Park**. Crassly commercialized it may be, but, like the Grand Canyon, it's too amazing a geological spectacle to miss. Northwest of Carlsbad, the **Sacramento** and **Jicarilla mountains** – home to the **Mescalero Apache** reservation as well as some rough-and-ready resorts with alpine settings to match Taos – rise from the desert plains once roamed by Billy the Kid and other Wild West heroes. The desolate dunes of the **White Sands** – half national park, half missile and bombing range – spread west of the mountains with the rolling hills of the **Rio Grande Valley** beyond. The little-visited southwest corner is among the most attractive reaches of the Southwest, with dozens more ghost towns and some fine scenery, plus the undisturbed pre-Columbian remains of the **Gila Cliff Dwellings National Monument**.

Carlsbad Caverns National Park

CARLSBAD CAVERNS NATIONAL PARK consists of a tract of the Guadalupe Mountains that's so riddled with underground caves and tunnels as to be virtually hollow. Tamed in classic park-service style with concrete trails and electric lighting, this subterranean wonderland is now a walk-in gallery, where tourists come in droves to marvel at its intricate limestone tracery. Though the summer crowds can get pretty intense, in a strange way that's part of the fun – coming to Carlsbad feels like a real throwback to the great 1950s boom in mass tourism. Before you decide whether to join in, however, be sure to grasp that the park is a *long* way from anywhere else – three hundred miles southeast of Albuquerque and 150 miles northeast of El Paso, Texas.

To reach the park, follow the narrow, twisting seven-mile road that leaves US-62/180 at **White's City**, twenty miles southwest of the town of **CARLS-BAD**. This ends at the **visitor center** – part of a complex that includes a restaurant, a gift shop, a day-care center and even a kennel – where you can pay entrance fees and pick up details of the day's schedule of tours (daily: June to mid-Aug 8am–7pm; mid-Aug to mid-Oct and mid-March to April 8am–5.30pm; mid-Oct to mid-March 8.30am–5pm; ☎505/785-2232, ⓦwww.nps.gov/cave).

Almost all park visitors confine their attention to the main cave, **Carlsbad Cavern** itself, and the standard park fee of $6 per person for three days covers access to this cave only; note that Golden Eagle passes (see p.48) are not accepted. Direct elevators drop to the Cavern's centerpiece, the **Big Room**, 750 vertical feet below the visitor center (summer first down 8.30am, last up 6.30pm; rest of year first down 8.30am, last up 4.55pm), but you can choose instead to walk down via the **Natural Entrance Route** (last entry summer 3.30pm; rest of year 2pm). This steep, paved footpath switchbacks into the guano-encrusted maw of the cave, taking fifteen minutes to reach the first of the formations and another fifteen to reach the Big Room. All visitors are obliged to ride the elevator back out.

Measuring up to 1800ft long and 250ft high, the Big Room is festooned with stalactites, stalagmites and countless unnameable shapes of swirling liquid rock. All are a uniform stone gray; the rare touches of color are provided by slight red or brown mineral-rich tinges, improved here and there with gentle pastel lighting. Most visitors take an hour or so to complete the reasonably level trail around the Room's perimeter. Whatever the weather up top – summer highs exceed 100°F – the temperature down here is always a cool 56°F, so dress warmly.

Adjoining the Big Room, the **Underground Lunchroom** is a vast formation-free side cave paved over in the 1950s to create a diner-cum-souvenir-shop that sells indigestible lunches in polystyrene containers, plus Eisenhower-era souvenirs like giant pencils and Viewmaster reels. To modern eyes, this strange installation seems absurd, but moves to close it down have been stymied by its place in popular affections.

The main appeal of walking down used to be that the trail meandered through beautiful side caves such as the **King's Palace**, filled with translucent "draperies" of limestone, but these are now open to guided tours only, which start from the Big Room (summer daily 9am, 10am, 11am, 1pm, 2pm & 3pm; less frequent during rest of year; $8). Longer tours explore less accessible, more demanding caves within the complex such as the **Hall of the White Giant** (Sat 1pm; $20) and **Spider Cave** (Sun 1pm; $20). It's also possible to take a two-hour tour of **Slaughter Canyon Cave**, 25 miles southwest of the visitor center (usually summer daily 10am & 1pm; call for exact schedule; $15). To get there, drive five miles south of White's City on US-62/180, then eleven miles west on Hwy-418, and finally hike the steep half-mile up to the cave entrance.

The recesses of Carlsbad Caverns are the summer home of around a million Mexican free-tailed **bats**. Each evening, at dusk or a little later, having slept all day suspended from the ceiling of the imaginatively titled Bat Cave – to which there's no public access – they emerge in cloud-like spirals, and disperse across the desert in search of delectable insects. Park visitors watch the spectacle from the amphitheater seating that faces the cave mouth, while rangers give a free and informative "Bats aren't as bad as you think" presentation.

Practicalities

No matter how you get to Carlsbad Caverns, you have to cross seemingly endless miles of the **Llano Estacado**, the deathly flat rangeland that covers southeast New Mexico and the Texas Panhandle. The route from El Paso, Texas, has the advantage of passing through **Guadalupe Mountains National Park**, a beautiful though little-visited complement to Carlsbad, which offers superb camping (see p.769).

WHITE'S CITY is not so much a town as a privately owned tourist complex, which as well as featuring a little water park provides the closest **accommodation**

and **camping** to the national park, including the mock-adobe *Best Western Cavern Inn* (T505/785-2291 or 1-800/CAVERNS, W www.whitescity.com; ❹); the *White's City RV Park* (same number), which has tent camping space; and the *Velvet Garter Restaurant* (same number). The town of **CARLSBAD** itself, 25 miles north of White's City, holds little of interest outside its many motels, such as the central *Holiday Inn*, 601 S Canal St (T505/885-8500 or 1-800/742-9586; ❺), and the clean, comfortable *Super 8*, 3817 National Parks Hwy (T505/887-8888; ❸). *Lucy's*, 701 S Canal St (closed Sun; T505/887-7714), serves good Mexican food.

Roswell

Seventy-five miles north of Carlsbad, the small ranching town of **ROSWELL** is renowned because an alien spaceship supposedly crash-landed nearby on July 4, 1947. The commander of the local air force base authorized a press statement announcing that they had retrieved the wreckage of a flying saucer, and despite a follow-up denial within a day – claiming that it was in fact a weather balloon – the story has kept running. In 1997, as 100,000 *X-Files* fanatics descended upon Roswell for a six-day festival to mark the "Incident's" fiftieth anniversary, the US government revealed that the errant weather balloon had crashed while monitoring the atmosphere for evidence of Soviet nuclear tests. Nonetheless, their imaginations further stimulated by the TV series *Roswell High*, UFO theorists remain unconvinced.

Despite its best intentions, and the wishful thinking of the truly weird clientele who drift in from the plains, the central **International UFO Museum**, 114 N Main St (daily: May–Sept 9am–5pm, Oct–April 10am–5pm; free), inadvertently exposes the whole tawdry business as transparent nonsense. Its showpiece is a model of the notorious "alien autopsy"; built for the movie *Roswell*, you can't help suspecting it was also featured in the grainy "documentary" autopsy footage that created a brief international sensation in 1995.

By way of contrast, the longstanding **Roswell Museum**, 100 W 11th St (Mon–Sat 9am–5pm, Sun 1–5pm; free), boasts an excellent, multifaceted collection with nary an alien corpse to be seen. Its most sensational section celebrates pioneer rocket scientist Robert Goddard (1882–1945), while historical artifacts elsewhere range from armor and pikes brought by Spanish conquistadors to astronaut Harrison Schmitt's spacesuit. A huge gallery also displays Southwestern art by Henriette Wyeth, Peter Hurd and Georgia O'Keeffe.

Roswell's **visitor center** is at 426 N Main St (Mon–Sat 9am–5pm; T505/624-0889, W www.roswellcvb.com). The finest **motel** in town, the *Best Western Sally Port Inn*, 2000 N Main St (T505/622-6430 or 1-800/600-5221; ❺), also has a good **restaurant**; the *Super 8*, 3575 N Main St (T505/622-8886 or 1-800/800-8000; ❸), and the *Frontier Motel*, 3010 N Main St (T505/622-1400 or 1-800/678-1401; ❷), are cheaper.

Ruidoso

The **Sacramento**, **Capitan** and **Jicarilla mountains**, which rise at the western edge of the Llano Estacado, 85 miles northwest of Carlsbad, form a rare respite from the scrubby flatness. Spread out along winding roads that cut through dense groves of pine, fir and aspen, the main town here, **RUIDOSO** – named for the Ruidoso ("Noisy") River – is the fastest-growing resort in the Southwest.

The **Ruidoso Downs** racetrack, just east of town, plays host to a 77-day racing season that culminates on Labor Day with the **All-American Futurity**, one of the world's richest horse races. Alongside, the **Hubbard Museum of the American West** (daily 10am–5pm; $6) holds displays on the natural and human-related history of horses, with a selection of memorabilia from around the world such as horse-drawn Russian sleighs, English road coaches and Wild West stagecoaches.

In winter, attention turns to the 12,000ft slopes of **Ski Apache** (℡505/336-4565, Ⓦwww.skiapache.com), a downhill ski area northwest of town where lift tickets cost around $43 per day. Though operated by the Mescalero Apache, it's not on tribal land – they bought it as a going concern.

Brochures from Ruidoso's **visitor center**, 720 Sudderth Ave (Mon–Sat 9am–5pm, Sun 1–4pm; ℡505/257-7395 or 1-800/253-2255, Ⓦwww.ruidoso.net), list dozens of **motels**, such as the inexpensive *Apache*, 344 Sudderth Ave (℡505/257-2986 or 1-800/426-0616; ❷), but supply still fails to meet demand on big race days. The real local showpiece, however, is the glitzy *Inn of the Mountain Gods* (℡505/464-5141 or 1-800/545-9011, Ⓦwww.innofthe-mountaingods.com; ❻), located three miles southwest of town on Carrizo Canyon Road. Also owned and run by the Mescalero Apache, the resort offers ski packages, casino gambling, golf, fishing, tennis and horseback riding, plus the excellent *Dan Li Ka* **restaurant**.

Lincoln

One of the most enduring of New Mexico's many legendary Wild West figures was a Brooklyn-born one-time bus boy named William Bonney, better known as **Billy the Kid**. Many towns lay claim to him, but he first came to fame as an eighteen-year-old in the **Lincoln County War**, which erupted in 1878 in the frontier town of **LINCOLN** – on Hwy-380 halfway between Carlsbad and Albuquerque – when rival groups of ranchers and merchants fought to gain control of the town and the hundreds of square miles of grazing lands surrounding it. Since those days, no new buildings have joined the venerable false-fronted structures that line Main Street, and the entire town is now the **Lincoln State Monument**. Visitors can stroll its length at any time, while admission to its various historical sites is via a joint ticket sold at each (daily 8.30am–5pm; $6; ℡505/653-4372). Displays in the modern **Lincoln County Historical Center**, at the east end of town, cover Hispanics, cowboys, "Buffalo Soldiers" – the black cavalrymen stationed at nearby Fort Stanton – and Apaches, as well as the Lincoln County War. Billy the Kid's most famous jailbreak is commemorated at the **Lincoln County Courthouse**, at the other end of the street; waiting here under sentence of death, he shot his way out and fled to Fort Sumner, where Sheriff Pat Garrett eventually caught up with him (see p.950). On the first weekend of August, the town fills up, and its streets echo with gunfire once again, during the three-day **Old Lincoln Days** festival.

Near the courthouse, the *Wortley Pat Garrett Hotel* – once owned by Sheriff Pat Garrett – offers eight plain but appealing **hotel** rooms (open late April to mid-Oct only; PO Box 96, Lincoln, NM 88338; ℡505/653-4300 or 1-8777/WORTLEY, Ⓦwww.patgarretthotel.com; ❸), and its **dining room** serves simple stews and sandwiches at lunchtime only. If you like a bit more comfort, head to the nearby *Casa de Patrón* **B&B** (PO Box 27, Lincoln, NM 88338; ℡505/653-4676 or 1-800/524-5202, Ⓦwww.casapatron.com; ❹/❺), where the more expensive rooms are in a separate but less atmospheric modern annexe.

White Sands National Monument

Filling a broad valley west of Ruidoso and the Sacramento Mountains, the **White Sands** are 250 square miles of glistening, three-story-high dunes, not of sand but of finely ground gypsum eroded from the nearby peaks. Unfortunately, most of the desert valley is under the control of the US military, who use it as a missile range and training ground for pilots, and as a landing site for the **space shuttle**; only the southern half of the dunes is protected within **WHITE SANDS NATIONAL MONUMENT** (and even that is often closed for an hour or two at a time while missile tests are underway). The best place to start is at the **visitor center**, just off US-70, which illuminates the unique plants and animals that dwell here (daily: summer 8am–7pm; rest of year 8am–4.30pm; ⓦ www.nps.gov/whsa). An eight-mile paved road ($3) stretches into the heart of the dunes, where you can scramble and slide in the sheer white landscape.

ALAMOGORDO, which sits at the base of the Sacramento Mountains, sixteen miles east of the Monument along US-54, holds the nearest food and lodging.

Las Cruces and Mesilla

From White Sands, US-70 heads southwest across the Tularosa Valley to **LAS CRUCES** – "the Crosses" – a large, modern farming community on the Rio Grande at the junction of I-10 and I-25. The town takes its name from the dozens of white crosses set up in the sands to mark the graves of early travelers killed by the Apache, but any real sense of its history is pretty well buried by motels and fast-food franchises.

The little-changed Hispanic colonial village of **MESILLA**, just south of I-10 two miles west, was until the 1870s one of the Southwest's largest towns, with upward of eight thousand inhabitants. During the Civil War, it even served briefly as the Confederate capital of New Mexico and Arizona, but it went into swift decline when the railroad bypassed it in favor of Las Cruces in 1881. Mesilla's delightful Old-West **plaza** has a real frontier feel to it, even though most of the old adobes that surround it – including the former courthouse where Billy the Kid was tried and sentenced to death in 1881 – now house art galleries and souvenir shops. **Restaurants** include the steak-oriented *Double Eagle* (☎505/523-6700) and *El Patio*, a Mexican cantina (closed Sun; ☎505/524-0982), while the *Mesón de Mesilla*, 1803 Av de Mesilla (☎505/525-2380 or 1-800/732-6025, ⓦ www.mesondemesilla.com; ❷–❺), a gorgeous "boutique resort" **hotel** five minutes' walk east, has a top-class dining room, plus fifteen guest rooms offering widely varying facilities.

The southwest corner

I-10 heads west from Las Cruces across the wide-open rangeland that fills out the southwest corner of New Mexico, also known as the "**Bootheel**" for the way it steps down toward Mexico. It's so sparsely inhabited that there are roughly three square miles per person. Towns are few and far between: **DEMING**, sixty miles west of Las Cruces, has a few motels and cafés and is one of two stops for Amtrak trains. Even if you're racing through on the interstate, make time for the very good **Luna Mimbres Museum** (Mon–Sat 9am–4pm, Sun 1.30–4pm; free), which relates the region's Native American and Wild West past, and has a great show of minerals and gemstones. **LORDSBURG**, too, on I-10 twenty miles short of Arizona, has a string of gas stations, cafés and motels but little else.

Silver City

Rarely visited and almost entirely wilderness, the semi-arid, forested, volcanic **Mogollon** and **Mimbres mountains** soar above the high desert plain of southwest New Mexico to over ten thousand feet. But for a number of copper mines, the area is protected within the **Gila National Forest**. The mountains are some of the most remote in the US, little altered since Apache warrior **Geronimo** was born here at the headwaters of the Gila River.

Halfway up the mountains, the biggest settlement, **SILVER CITY**, lies 45 miles north of I-10 at the junction of US-180 from Deming and Hwy-90 from Lordsburg. The Spanish came here in 1804, sold the Mimbreño Indians into slavery, and opened the **Santa Rita copper mine**, just east of town below the Kneeling Nun monolith; but the town was re-established in 1870 as a rough-and-tumble silver camp – **Billy the Kid** spent most of his childhood here. A fine selection of ornate old buildings is scattered along elm-lined avenues and across the surrounding hills. The excellent **Silver City Museum** at 312 W Broadway (Tues–Fri 9am–4.30pm, Sat & Sun 10am–4pm; free) tells the boom-and-bust tales, and holds fine specimens of **Casas Grandes pottery**, beautiful Navajo rugs, and basketry from all the major Southwest tribes. Three blocks east, the original Main Street was washed away in a great flood and has become the cottonwood-shaded **Big Gulch Park**.

In downtown Silver City, the *Carter House*, 101 N Cooper St (℡505/388-5485; ●–●), is a HI-AYH **youth hostel** that doubles as a **B&B**, with $13 dorm beds ($16 nonmembers) and five en-suite private rooms; be sure to call in advance, however, as the house was up for sale as this book went to press. Just outside town, *Bear Mountain Guest Ranch* (℡505/538-2538 or 1-877/620-BEAR, ⓦwww.bearmountainlodge.com; ●) is a large 1920s ranch, now run as a B&B by the Nature Conservancy, that makes a great base for bird-watching, cycling, mountain biking or cross-country skiing. Bullard Street in the heart of town holds atmospheric **saloons and cafés** like the *Silver Café* at 514 N Bullard (℡505/388-3480).

Gila Cliff Dwellings National Monument

Beautiful, twisting Hwy-15 threads north from Silver City into the mountains, passing the picturesque old mining camp of Pinos Altos during its fifty-mile, two-hour climb to the **GILA CLIFF DWELLINGS NATIONAL MONUMENT**. A mile beyond the monument's **visitor center**, a further mile-long trail (daily: summer 8am–6pm; rest of year 9am–4pm; $3; ℡505/536-9461, ⓦwww.nps.gov/gicl) sets off beside a year-round stream.

Only once you've followed the stream for half a mile do you get your first glimpse of the ancient pueblo, abandoned seven centuries ago by the **Mogollon** peoples. What look from below like three separate caves turn out, when you climb the hillside, to be a single deep alcove with three entrances. Each entrance was sealed with stones and mortar, but behind them lay around forty interconnected rooms, sharing a communal plaza at the rear. While they may not be as architecturally impressive as those of Mesa Verde (see p.887), exploring them alone – you can wander freely through the chambers – allows you to imagine yourself as one of the original occupants.

The monument maintains four small, free **campgrounds** in the immediate vicinity, including the *Forks* beside the Gila River, which is equipped with running water in summer only.

Arizona

The tourism industry in **ARIZONA** has, literally, one colossal advantage – the **Grand Canyon** of the Colorado River. It's the single most awe-inspiring spectacle in a land of unforgettable geology, and one of the few places in the world that you absolutely have to see at least once in your life. However, the Grand Canyon is by no means the most interesting or memorable destination in the state. Indeed, in comparison to its inhuman scale, other parts of Arizona have a more abiding emotional impact, precisely because of the sheer drama of human involvement in this forbidding but deeply resonant desert landscape.

Over a third of the state still belongs to the **Native Americans** who have lived here for centuries, and who outside the cities form the majority of the population. In the so-called **Indian Country** of northeastern Arizona, the reservation lands of the **Navajo Nation** hold the stupendous **Canyon de Chelly** and dozens of other marvellously sited **Ancestral Puebloan ruins**, as well as the stark rocks of **Monument Valley**. The Navajo surround the homeland of one of the most stoutly traditional of all Native American peoples, the **Hopi**, who live in remote **mesa-top villages**. The third main tribal group are the **Apache**, in the harshly beautiful southeastern mountains – the last Native Americans to give in to the overwhelming power of the white American invaders.

Away from the reservations, **Wild West** towns like **Tombstone**, site of the famed gunfight at the OK Corral, give a clear sense of Arizona's characteristically rough-and-ready, pioneer mentality; this was the last of the lower 48 states to join the Union, in 1912. The **cities**, however, are not much fun. In **Phoenix**, the capital, well over a million souls are scattered over a 500-square-mile morass of shopping malls and tract-house suburbs; **Tucson** is a bit more civil, but still wears thin after a day or so.

Though the open spaces of southern Arizona can be harsh and violent – most of the southwestern quarter, along the parallel I-8 and I-10 highways, is used as a bombing range – the bleakness is balanced somewhat by the many nature reserves which protect its amazing flora and fauna, such as **Saguaro National Park**, just outside Tucson, with its giant cactuses, real-life roadrunners and rare Gila monsters.

Getting around Arizona

Arizona is better served by public transportation than much of the Southwest, but it's still an effort to get around without a car. Greyhound **buses** stop at all the major cities and at most towns along the interstates, while Amtrak **trains** cross the state on two of their transcontinental routes (via Tucson in the south, or Flagstaff further north). Seeing the backcountry, however – and especially the reservations – is all but impossible without a car. The largest airport is at Phoenix, and assorted good-value, short-hop **flights** cover the principal destinations. The only worthwhile **bus tours** visit the area around Flagstaff.

Tucson, Phoenix and southern Arizona

Most of Arizona's compelling natural attractions are in its northern reaches, but the **southern** half of the state holds ninety percent of its people, all its significant cities and several important historic sites. Apart from a couple of Spanish missions, the bulk of what there is to see is frontier Americana, especially in **Tombstone**, in the southeast corner. **Phoenix**, the state capital, is huge, sprawling and dull; **Tucson** makes a better base for visiting this part of the world and for trips south of the border into Mexico.

Tucson and around

After serving as a colonial outpost under the Spanish and Mexicans, and then as territorial capital for both the US and Confederate governments, **TUCSON** (pronounced *TOO-sonn*) – a mere sixty miles north of Mexico on the cross-country I-10 – has grown into a modern mini-metropolis of nearly a million people without entirely sacrificing its historic quarters. Now equal parts college town and retirement community, it's one of the more attractive big cities of the Southwest – which admittedly isn't saying much. Although it suffers from the same Sunbelt sprawl as Albuquerque and Phoenix, it does have a wanderable center, some enjoyable restaurants and a pretty good nightlife, energized by the 35,000 students at the University of Arizona. It is also redeemed by having so much superb landscape within easy reach, from the forested flanks of **Mount Lemmon** to the rolling foothills of **Saguaro National Park**.

Arrival and information

Tucson International Airport, eight miles south of downtown, receives far fewer long-distance flights than Phoenix. It's connected to the city by the slow Sun Tran bus #11 or #6 ($1), and the $15 Arizona Stagecoach shuttles (☎520/889-1000). For **taxi** service, call Allstate Cabs (☎520/798-1111). The Amtrak station, downtown at 400 E Toole Ave, is served by three **trains** weekly in each direction (east–west), with connecting buses running north to Phoenix. Greyhound **buses** also stop very centrally, at 2 S Fourth Ave.

Tucson's downtown **visitor center**, 110 S Church Ave (Mon–Fri 8am–5pm, Sat & Sun 9am–4pm; ☎520/624-1817 or 1-800/638-8350), has free maps and information. North of the university, Tucson Map & Flag Center, 3239 N First Ave (☎520/887-4234), stocks Arizona's best selection of maps and local guides. Great Western Tours (☎520/572-1660) offer three-hour city tours for $35, and an extensive program of trips further afield.

Accommodation

Tucson offers a broader range of **accommodation** than Phoenix, with plenty of reasonably priced hotels and motels in the central area, as well as some atmospheric **B&Bs** both in the historic center and out in the surrounding desert. It also has its fair share of **resorts** and **dude ranches**. Rates drop when the mercury rises, and some places are open only in the peak winter and spring seasons.

Best Western Ghost Ranch Lodge 801 W Miracle Mile ☎520/791-7565 or 1-800/456-7565, ⓦwww.ghostranchlodge.com. Charming, old-fashioned motel/resort in the center of town, with south-of-the-border stylings, a cactus-filled garden and a logo designed by Georgia O'Keeffe. ④
Catalina Park Inn 309 E First St ☎520/792-4541 or 1-800/792-4885, ⓦwww.catalina-parkinn.com. A beautiful but not overly fussy historic bed and breakfast across from a quiet park but within walking distance of the university and

happening Fourth Avenue. ⑤/⑥
Clarion Santa Rita Hotel & Suites 88 E Broadway Blvd ☎520/622-4000 or 1-877/526-7737, ⓦwww2.choicehotels.com/hotel/AZ121. Large if anonymous hotel that's an unexpected downtown bargain, and has the good Mexican *Café Poca Cosa* downstairs. ④/⑤
Hotel Congress 311 E Congress St ☎520/622-8848 or 1-800/722-8848, ⓦwww.hotcong.com. Bohemian downtown hotel, an easy walk from Amtrak, with vintage Art Deco furnishings. $18

hostel beds for HI-AYH members (no reservations) and simple private rooms for just over $30. There's a small café and a lively bar downstairs, and at night it's one of the hottest music venues in town. ❶–❸

Roadrunner Hostel 346 E 12th St ☏520/628-4709. Small and very central independent hostel in a downtown home, offering singles space in six-bed dorms for $16 per night or $95 per week, $35 for a double room, plus internet access and bicycles for rent.

Tanque Verde Ranch 14301 E Speedway Blvd ☏520/296-6275 or 1-800/234-DUDE,

Ⓦwww.tanqueverderanch.com. One of Arizona's most appealing dude ranches, an irresistibly romantic 400-acre spread adjoining Saguaro National Park twenty miles east of downtown; offers luxury accommodation in individual *casitas* and a stable of over a hundred horses. Rates include all meals and a full program of rides. ❾

Westward Look Resort 245 E Ina Rd ☏520/297-1151 or 1-800/722-2500, Ⓦwww.westwardlook.com. Updated historic resort on attractive landscaped grounds in the northern section of the city, offering extra-large rooms and suites. ❼–❾

The Town

Tucson has two main historic centers: the **downtown core** along the (usually bone-dry) Santa Cruz River, bisected by Congress Street, and the quarter around the **University of Arizona** campus, a mile to the east. The city was founded in the late 1700s by Catholic missionaries who came from Mexico, then a Spanish colony, to convert the Pima Indians. Nothing very substantial remains from this era, but hundreds of artifacts are now displayed inside the many historic adobe homes in and around the **El Presidio** district of cafés, art galleries and B&Bs, two blocks north of Broadway. Access to much of El Presidio is controlled by the **Tucson Museum of Art and Historic Block** complex, 140 N Main Ave (June–Aug Tues–Sat 10am–4pm, Sun noon–4pm; Sept–May Mon–Sat 10am–4pm, Sun noon–4pm; $5, free Sun). The main building displays changing exhibitions of modern paintings and sculpture, while an adjoining adobe holds an excellent collection of folk art and pre-Columbian artifacts. The district's oldest house, La Casa Cordova, showcases the city's Mexican heritage.

Three blocks south, engulfed by the Tucson Convention Center complex, the adobe **Sosa-Carrillo-Frémont House**, 151 S Granada Ave (Wed–Sat 10am–4pm; free), is the sole survivor of a neighborhood torn down during the 1960s. Built for merchant Leopoldo Carrillo in 1858, it was briefly rented by former explorer John C Frémont when he was Governor of Arizona in 1878. Though much restored, it offers a vivid sense of the more civilized side of frontier life.

Tucson's other main area of interest, around the University of Arizona, spreads between Sixth Street and Speedway Boulevard, a mile east of downtown. Its highlights are the on-campus **Arizona State Museum** (Mon–Sat 10am–5pm, Sun noon–5pm; free), where an exceptionally comprehensive assembly of Native American artifacts from the very earliest days traces the evolution of the various Southwest tribes, and the **Center for Creative Photography** (Mon–Fri 9am–5pm, Sat & Sun noon–5pm; $2), featuring work by Ansel Adams, among other modern masters.

Arizona-Sonora Desert Museum

Part zoo, part garden, the top-quality **Arizona-Sonora Desert Museum** is fourteen miles west of the university along Speedway Boulevard, in **Tucson Mountain Park** (daily: March–Sept 7.30am–5pm; Oct–Feb 8.30am–5pm; adults $9.95 Nov–April, $8.95 May–Oct, ages 6–12 $1.75; Ⓦwww.desertmuseum.org). Indoor displays, including a walk-through cave and mine, highlight regional geology and history, and a series of glass-fronted cages are occupied

TUCSON

N

0   3 miles

Mt. Lemmon ▲

SANTA CATALINA MOUNTAINS

MOUNT LEMMON HWY

SABINO CANYON ROAD

TANGERINE

NARANJA

LA CHOLLA ROAD

THORNEYDALE ROAD

LAMBERT

HARDY RD

MAGEE RD

INA ROAD

ORANGE GROVE ROAD

SKYLINE DRIVE

SUNRISE DR

Tohono Chul Park

Tucson Mall

RIVER

LA CANADA ROAD

WETMORE RD

ROGER ROAD

ORACLE RD

FORT LOWELL BLVD

CAMPBELL AVE

STONE AVE

GRANT ROAD

DOWNTOWN

University of Arizona

SPEEDWAY BLVD

'A' Mountain

W. ANKLAM

GATES PASS RD

Old Tucson

KINNEY ROAD

TUCSON MOUNTAINS

GOLF LINKS ROAD

OLD TUCSON

Arizona-Sonora Desert Museum

SAGUARO NATIONAL PARK (WEST)

GOLDEN GATE RD

PICTURE ROCKS ROAD

AVRA VALLEY ROAD

86

10

TANQUE VERDE BLVD

SPEEDWAY BLVD

FREEMAN ROAD

BROADWAY

HARRISON ROAD

PANTANO ROAD

KOLB ROAD

WILMOT ROAD

CRAYCROFT ROAD

SWAN ROAD

COUNTRY CLUB RD

FIRST

AVENUE

SIXTH AVENUE

TWENTY-SECOND RD

ALVERNON WAY

AJO WAY

DREXEL ROAD

VALENCIA ROAD

MISSION ROAD

CAMINO D'OESTE

19

OLD SPANISH TRAIL

FREEMAN ROAD

HOUGHTON

HARRISON ROAD

IRVINGTON ROAD

OLD SPANISH TRAIL

GOLF LINKS ROAD

WILMOT RD

SAGUARO NATIONAL PARK (EAST)

RINCON MOUNTAINS

10

by tarantulas, rattlesnakes and other creepy-crawlies. In enclosures along the looped path beyond – a hot walk in high summer – bighorn sheep, mountain lions, jaguars and other seldom-seen desert denizens prowl in credible simulations of their natural habitats, and a colony of impish prairie dogs goes about its impenetrable business. Hawks and bald eagles fly about their own large aviary, thankfully separated from a greenhouse-full of hummingbirds. The museum also serves as an animal rescue center: almost all the animals you see were injured in some way before ending up here, and would be unable to survive on their own.

Saguaro National Park

Flanking Tucson to either side, the two sections of **SAGUARO NATIONAL PARK** offer visitors a rare and enthralling opportunity to stroll through strange desert "forests" of monumental, multi-limbed **saguaro** (pronounced *suh-WAH-row*) cactuses. Each saguaro can grow up to fifty feet tall and weigh up to eight tons, but it takes around 150 years to do so. Whatever you may have seen in the movies, you can drive a long way in Arizona without seeing one; saguaro are unique to the Sonora Desert, and so the thrill when you finally encounter a thousand at once is deeply satisfying. Both segments of the park tend to be seen on short forays from the city: in summer, it's far too hot to do more than pose for photographs, dwarfed beneath some especially eccentric specimen, and there is in any case no lodging, or even permanent campground, in either segment.

The **Tucson Mountain District**, which stretches north from the Desert Museum around fifteen miles west of downtown Tucson, on the far side of the mountains, charges no admission fee. Beyond the **visitor center** (daily 8.30am–5pm; ☎520/733-5158, ⓦwww.nps.gov/sagu), the nine-mile **Bajada Loop Drive** – not fully paved, but always passable to ordinary vehicles – loops through a wonderland of weird saguaro, offering plentiful short hiking trails and photo opportunities. Signal Hill is especially recommended, for its petroglyphs and superb sunset views.

To reach the eastern section of the park, the **Rincon Mountain District** ($6 per vehicle; ☎520/733-5153), drive seventeen miles east of town, first along Broadway Boulevard and then Old Spanish Trail. Here, too, short trails such as the quarter-mile Desert Ecology Trail lead off the eight-mile **Cactus Forest Drive** (daily 7am–sunset), but many visitors come specifically to hike far from the road, up into the mountains. The saguaro cactuses thin out almost as soon as you start climbing the Tanque Verde Ridge Trail, which leads in due course to a hundred-mile network of remote footpaths through thickly forested canyons.

Eating, drinking and nightlife

Though downtown Tucson shuts down pretty early each evening – it's hard to find anywhere open after 9pm – the city has a fine selection of **restaurants**. Mexican joints and cowboy-style Wild-West steakhouses abound in the central districts, while fancier restaurants are found in the exclusive St Phillips Plaza and other parts of the Foothills, a few miles north, as well as in the resort hotels. Most of the arty **cafés** and **nightclubs** on Congress Street downtown double as bars and restaurants, while several student-oriented places can be found in the university area. There are half a dozen country-and-western saloons on the outskirts of town. For a full rundown, check the listings in the free *Tucson Weekly*.

Blue Willow 2616 N Campbell Ave ☎520/327-7577. Tasty, fruity breakfasts and light lunches and dinners, served on a pleasant garden patio.

Club Congress *Hotel Congress*, 311 E Congress St ☎520/622-8848. Hectic, trendy, late-opening bar, with live music a couple of nights each week; the *Cup Café*, off the hotel lobby, is a jazzy café, straight out of the 1930s but updated to include an espresso bar, which serves a bewilderingly broad menu from 7am until 11pm during the week, until 1am weekends.

El Charro 311 N Court Ave ☎520/622-1922. Housed in the same El Presidio building since 1922, this claims to be the oldest Mexican restaurant in the US, and now has its own lively bar next door. The moderately-priced food is good, though not especially fiery; specialties include fine chimichangas.

Gentle Ben's Brewing Co 865 E University Blvd ☎520/624-4177. Microbrewery serving simple food; regularly packed out with students.

J-Bar *Westin La Paloma Resort*, 3770 E Sunrise Blvd ☎520/615-6000. Terrific southwest-Mex cuisine by Tucson's nationally acclaimed chef Janos Wilder at half the price of his upscale restaurant, *Janos*, next door. That and the view make it work the trip north to the Foothills.

Kingfisher 2564 E Grant Rd ☎520/323-7739. One of the few restaurants in town with a late-night menu, specializing in relatively expensive seafood. Very cool bar, too, and music on the weekends.

Maverick, King of Clubs 4702 E 22nd St ☎520/748-0456. Old-fashioned country-music honky-tonk, a bit out from the center and brimming with Stetsons.

The Rialto Theatre 318 E Congress St ☎520/740-0126. A 1920s vaudeville theater that's re-opened as Tucson's hottest venue for touring bands.

Tohono Chul Tea Room Tohono Chul Park, 7366 N Paseo del Norte ☎520/797-1222. Attractive adobe café in small desert park on the northern fringes of town. Open daily 8am–5pm; ideal for breakfast, a light lunch or a scones-and-jam afternoon tea.

Biosphere 2

The giant Plexiglass bubble known as **BIOSPHERE 2** looms out of the desert thirty miles north of Tucson, in a high-security compound at mile marker 96.5 on Hwy-77 and near the town of **Oracle**. On its completion in 1991, this vast complex was trumpeted as a major laboratory for experiments in applied environmental science. Containing five separate "biomes," or self-contained ecosystems – rainforest, marsh, savannah, desert and a 25ft-deep ocean – it was designed as a miniature working model of Biosphere 1, planet Earth itself, and stocked like a real-life Noah's Ark with almost four thousand species of plants and animals. Backed by a hundred million dollars' worth of support from Texas oil tycoon Ed Bass, this far-fetched scheme was intended as a step toward the eventual colonization of Mars.

Eight "Biospherians" were sealed into Biosphere 2 in September 1991, their "mission" being to survive in isolation for two full years. This they more or less did, although emergency oxygen twice had to be pumped in as carbon dioxide levels rose. Much of what transpired was replete with irony; hungry Biospherians soon found themselves planting bananas and papayas in what was supposed to be the inviolate wilderness of the rainforest, and destroying parts of the desert to boost oxygen, while the ocean proved impossible to keep clean. By the time the next crew moved in, conditions at Biosphere 2 had degenerated into farce. Two of the original crew, who had been acrimoniously fired, sneaked back and broke the Biosphere's seals from the outside, thus aborting the second mission after just six months; they later sued for wrongful dismissal and won compensation. Since 1996 Biosphere 2 has been taken over by Columbia University, which seems to be frantically trying to think of something to do with its vast new "campus."

In its brief heyday, Biosphere 2 was one of Arizona's most popular tourist destinations. Now that no one is locked inside, the crowds have dwindled, but the two-and-a-half-hour guided tours are still worth taking (daily 8am–5pm; $12.95; ⓦ www.bio2.edu). Most of that time is spent peering into the greenhouses hoping to spot any sign of life larger than an ant, and marveling at the fact that, whatever you may have assumed, Biosphere 2 is not solar powered but depends on an external natural-gas power plant. Visitors are also allowed into the Biospherians' futuristic living quarters, tacked like a space capsule onto the back of the main block, where they appear to have suffered no privations whatsoever. For an extra $10, a 45-minute "Under the Glass" tour gets you through the massive airlock doors and into the giant terrarium itself.

The all-day *Cañada del Oro* restaurant serves good meals on an appealing terrace. There's also a cybercafé, and good-value **lodging** at the on-site *Inn at Biosphere 2* (T 520/825-6222; May–Sept ❸, Oct–April ❺) – especially worth it if you come for one of the new on-site astronomy programs (an observatory was added in 2001) and don't want a late-night drive back into town.

South to the border: the Mission Trail

South from Tucson, I-19 heads straight for the Mexican border, 65 miles away, passing some tangible reminders of the region's Spanish and Mexican heritage. The first of these, the **MISSION SAN XAVIER DEL BAC** – the best-preserved mission church in the United States – lies just west of the freeway, nine miles south of downtown Tucson on the fringe of the vast arid plain of San Xavier Indian Reservation. It was built for the Franciscans between 1783 and 1797, and even today its white-plastered walls and towers seem like a dazzling desert mirage; how much more dramatic they must have been two centuries ago, when to Christian missionaries and Apache warriors alike they symbolized the Spanish quest to subdue and convert the native peoples of the Southwest. No one knows the name of the architect responsible for its Spanish Baroque, even Moorish lines – it consists almost entirely of domes and arches, making only minimal use of timber – let alone the O'odham craftsmen who embellished its every feature. Recently restored with the help of Vatican experts previously responsible for work on the Sistine Chapel, it attracts a constant stream of tourists (daily 9am–6pm; donation). The ideal time to come is on Sunday morning, when four separate Masses draw large congregations from the reservation.

Fifty miles further south, barely twenty miles north of the border, stands the evocative ruin of another eighteenth-century mission church, preserved as **TUMACÁCORI NATIONAL HISTORICAL PARK** (daily 8am–5pm; $4 per vehicle), topped by a restored whitewashed dome, and home only to the birds that fly down from the Patagonia Mountains. Behind its red-tinged, weather-beaten facade, the plaster has crumbled from the interior walls to reveal bare adobe bricks. A few traces of a mural can still be discerned in the raised sanctuary, but little remains of the priests' living quarters alongside. A very good museum is housed in the small **visitor center** at the entrance, and a self-guiding tour map ($1) tells the mission story.

Nogales, Arizona and Nogales, Mexico

Twenty miles south of Tumacácori, an hour from Tucson, sits the largest of the Arizonan-Mexican border towns, **NOGALES** – in effect two towns, one in the US and one across the border in Mexico. Known jointly as *Ambos Nogales* (both Nogales), they welcome considerable numbers of tourists, though with cheap Mexican crafts now so widely available in the US, day-trippers these days tend to be looking for cut-price medicines rather than rugs or hammocks.

There's nothing in particular to see on either side of the border, though the contrast between the orderly streets of the American town and the jumbled white-washed houses clinging to the slopes in Mexico hits you as soon as you come in sight. Nogales, Arizona – the birthplace of iconoclastic jazz great **Charles Mingus** – is a dreary little community, while Nogales, Mexico, is basically a lively, large-scale street market.

Crossing the border is straightforward, as Mexican visas are only required by travelers heading more than 21km south of the border. US citizens should, however, ideally carry their passports or birth certificates – drivers' licenses are not always sufficient – while foreign visitors should check that their visa status entitles them to re-enter the US; if you're on or eligible for the Visa Waiver Scheme (see p.17), you're fine. If driving, leave your car on the US side; you'll see lots of cheap lots as you approach the border, and it'll save you the hassle of finding parking and waiting on long car lines to return. There's no need to change money; US dollars are freely accepted by stores and businesses across the border.

None of the Arizona-side **motels** stands within a mile of the border; the closest is the *Best Western Siesta Motel*, 673 N Grand Ave (☎520/287-4671 or 1-888/215-4783; ➋). Most visitors prefer to **eat** in Mexico, where abundant cafés and diners line the busy central streets. Classier dining is offered by the unusual *La Roca*, hollowed into the rocky hillside just east of the railroad, a couple of blocks from the border at c/Elias 91, where a full seafood meal costs under $20.

The southeast corner

Among thousands of acres of unspoiled and magnificent wilderness, southeast Arizona contains numerous well-preserved and highly atmospheric **ghost towns**. I-10 buzzes towards the New Mexico border, but for a grand tour of the region you can detour south instead along the more scenic US-80. Even if you're racing through this barren country, set aside an hour at least for the excellent **Amerind Foundation Museum** (June–Aug Wed–Sun 10am–4pm; Sept–May daily 10am–4pm; $3), a mile from I-10 exit 318, 65 miles east of Tucson. It's one of the better anthropological museums in the US, broad in scope and focusing in turn on the diverse native cultures of the Southwest, the Pacific Northwest, and Central and South America. Nearby, the town of **BENSON** has been gearing itself up for several years for the opening of **Kartchner Caverns State Park**, a labyrinth of subterranean wonders that finally debuted in 2000. It's not quite up to the hype that preceded it, being a lot smaller than Carlsbad Caverns in New Mexico (see p.956) and a bit more expensive ($14 adults, $6 ages 7–13). And, especially considering the delays made in the name of keeping the caves pristine, the corny sound-and-light show at the end is a tacky add-on. Nevertheless, the caves are worth seeing – and very popular. Reservations (☎520/586-CAVE) are a must.

Tombstone

Perhaps the most famous town in the Wild West, **TOMBSTONE** lies 22 miles south of I-10 on US-80, 67 miles southeast of Tucson. More than a century has passed since its mining days came to an end, but "The Town Too Tough to Die" clings to an afterlife as a tourist theme park. With its dusty streets, wooden sidewalks and swinging saloon doors, it's surprisingly unchanged. Most adults, however, have seen too many inauthentic replicas and movie re-creations for the real thing to retain much appeal, and so Tombstone is reduced to trying to divert kids with tacky dioramas and daily shoot-outs. The best time to visit is during **Helldorado Days** in late October, when the air is cooler and the sun less harsh, but the streets are full of gun-toting strangers acting out gun battles and stagecoach robberies.

Tombstone only began life as a silver-boomtown in 1877, and by the end of the 1880s it was all but deserted again. However, on the day that gave it the notoriety that's kept it alive, its population stood at more than ten thousand. It was 2pm on October 26, 1881, when **Doc Holliday**, along with **Wyatt Earp** and his brothers Virgil and Morgan (who all served as local sheriffs), confronted a band of suspected cattle rustlers, the Clantons, in the legendary **Gunfight at the OK Corral**. Within a few minutes, three of the suspects were dead. The Earps were accused of murder, but charges were eventually dropped.

Although the gunfight in fact took place on Fremont Street, the **OK Corral** itself remains the major attraction for visitors (daily 8.30am–5pm; $2.50), despite the fact that it holds little more than crude dummies that show the supposed locations of the Earps and the Clantons, in complete contradiction to contemporary reports of the fight. A couple of blocks along Allen Street, the **Bird Cage Theater** (daily 8am–6pm; $5) was Tombstone's leading venue for entertainment of all kinds. Seven "bird cages," much like theater boxes but curtained off and said to have been used by prostitutes, hang from either side of the main hall. The dusty, cluttered theater now holds a motley collection of curiosities, including a revolting foot-long "merman" from China, while downstairs you can see the old gaming tables and bordello rooms. The exhibits are real enough, but there's little historical accuracy to many of the makeshift signs. You might want to skip it entirely in favor of **Tombstone Courthouse State Historic Park** on Toughnut and Third streets, just off the main drag (daily 8am–5pm; $2.50). This one-time seat of Cochise County features the little-changed courtroom where several well-known trials took place. Excellent exhibits include two detailed alternative versions of what might have actually happened at the OK Corral.

Central **motels** include the *Adobe Lodge*, 505 Fremont St (☎520/457-2241 or 1-888/457-2241; ❸), while the classier mountain-view *Best Western Lookout Lodge* is a mile north on US-80 W (☎520/457-2223 or 1-800/652-6772; ❸/❹), just across from the Boot Hill Graveyard. Among old-style **saloons** serving burgers and beer in as raucous an atmosphere as they can are the *Crystal Palace* at Fifth and Allen, and *Big Nose Kate's* at 417 E Allen St, where you can still join an ongoing card game.

Bisbee

Crammed into a narrow gorge 25 miles south of Tombstone, the town of **BISBEE** is rivaled only by Jerome, near Sedona, as Arizona's most atmospheric Victorian relic. Like Jerome, its fortunes were built on a century of mining mundane, dependable copper from the surrounding mountains, rather than a few ephemeral years of gold and silver. Its solid brick buildings still stand as an enduring testament to the days when Bisbee's population of twenty thousand outstripped both Phoenix and Tucson to make it the largest city between New Orleans and San Francisco. Phelps Dodge finally closed down its Bisbee operations in 1975, having extracted more than six billion dollars' worth of metals. As the miners moved away, however, artists and retirees moved in, preserving Bisbee's original architecture while turning it into a thriving, friendly little community that caters to tourists without being overwhelmed by them.

Walking Bisbee's narrow central streets, lined with galleries and antiques stores, is a pleasure in itself, but if you'd like to know more of the background it's well worth calling in at the **Bisbee Mining and Historical Museum**, 5 Copper Queen Plaza (daily 10am–4pm; adults $4, under-18s free).

The best **place to stay** is the venerable *Copper Queen Hotel*, 11 Howell Ave

(☎520/432-2216 or 1-800/247-5829; ⑤), with a plush bar and a good **restaurant** with terrace seating.

Southwest Arizona: Yuma

There's virtually nothing in the vast desert plain of southwest Arizona to tempt you off the twin freeways that sprint to California. The US Army stages tank battles in its Yuma Proving Grounds between I-10 and I-8, while the air force drops bombs and tests Stealth technology in the more mountainous region bordering Mexico. The largest town, **YUMA**, is little more than an oversized pit stop for freight trains and cross-country truckers. **Yuma Territorial Prison**, now a state park (daily 8am–5pm; $3) beside the Colorado River, was known a century ago as the "Hell Hole of Arizona," holding over a hundred of the Wild West's most violent criminals. Its first inmates were forced to build the adobe walls that later contained them; there's a small museum, and you can wander around the grounds and cell blocks at will.

Neon-lit budget **motels** along the main drag include the good-value *Yuma Cabana*, 2151 S Fourth Ave (☎928/783-8311 or 1-800/874-0811; ②), while the *Crossing*, 2690 S Fourth Ave (☎928/776-5551), is typical of several run-of-the-mill **diners**.

Phoenix

The state capital and largest city in Arizona, **PHOENIX** holds only minimal appeal for tourists. When it began life in the 1860s, it must have seemed like a good idea. The sweltering little farming town stood in the heart of the large Salt River Valley, with a ready-made irrigation system left by ancient Indians (the name Phoenix honors the fact that the city rose from the ashes of a long-vanished **Hohokam** community). Within a century, however, Phoenix had turned into what writer Edward Abbey called "the blob that is eating Arizona," acquiring as it did so the money and political clout to defy the self-evident absurdity of building a huge city in a virtually waterless desert. Now the sixth largest city in the US, it has filled the entire valley, engulfing the neighboring towns of **Scottsdale**, **Mesa** and **Tempe** in the process, with over a million people within the city boundaries and more than two million in the metropolitan area. Arizona's financial and industrial epicenter may just be getting into its stride; boosters claim the megalopolis will one day stretch 150 miles, from Wickenburg to Tucson.

The city's phenomenal rise was originally fueled by its image as a healthy oasis, where the desert had been tamed and transformed into a suburban idyll. While retirees still flock to enclaves such as **Sun City**, Phoenix now has a deserved reputation as the most unpleasant city in the Southwest – Las Vegas with no casinos, or LA with no beach. Above all, it's **hot**; between June and August daytime highs average over 100°F, making it the hottest city outside the Middle East.

In winter, when temperatures rarely drop below 65°F, tourists from colder climes arrive in large numbers. They pay vast sums to warm their bones in the luxury resorts and spas, concentrated especially in Scottsdale, that are the modern equivalent of the 1930s dude ranches. Unlike golf, tennis and shopping, sightseeing rarely ranks high on the agenda – which is just as well, since there's a good deal of truth in the charge laid by Phoenix's older arch-rival, Tucson, that the city is sorely lacking in culture and history. Apart from the **Heard Museum**'s excellent Native American displays, and Frank Lloyd Wright's architecture studio at **Taliesin West**, Phoenix is short of must-see attractions.

ACCOMMODATION

Budget Lodge Motel	3
HI-Phoenix	2
San Carlos	4
YMCA	1

RESTAURANTS

Alice Cooper'stown	C
Pizzeria Bianco	B
Sam's Cafe	A

DOWNTOWN PHOENIX

In fact, if you're on a touring vacation, you'd miss little if you bypassed it altogether; a day at one of the city's plentiful upscale malls is probably as authentic and enjoyable an experience as Phoenix has to offer.

Arrival, information and getting around

Sky Harbor International Airport (☎602/273-3321), three miles east of downtown, is connected by Valley Metro **buses** (☎602/253-5000) with downtown, Tempe and Mesa, but it's easier to take a door-to-door shuttle bus, at $14 for downtown destinations or around $20 for Scottsdale, with a company such as SuperShuttle (☎602/244-9000 or 1-800/BLUEVAN, ⓦwww.supershuttle .com). Arizona Shuttle Services (☎928/795-6671 or 1-800/888-2749, ⓦwww.arizonashuttle.com) runs an hourly service south to Tucson, costing $24.

There's no longer an Amtrak **train** service to Phoenix, but Greyhound **buses** arrive at 2115 E Buckeye Rd (☎602/389-4200 or 1-800/231-2222), close to the airport. Getting around without a car is not ideal – it can take hours to cross town – but it's not impossible. Valley Metro's commuter routes charge $1.25 per ride; pick up a schedule at the downtown terminal, at First and Washington. Tourists are more likely to use the free purple DASH buses (Mon–Fri 6.30am–11pm), which ply between the Arizona Center and the

Capitol downtown. For a **taxi**, call Checker Cab (☎602/257–1818).

Phoenix's main **visitor center** is at Adams and Second downtown (Mon–Fri 8am–5pm; ☎602/254–6500 or 1-877/255-5749; 24hr hotline ☎602/252-5588, ⊛www.phoenixcvb.com); there's also an office at 24th Street and Camelback, at the northeast corner of the Biltmore Fashion Park (Mon–Sat 10am–9pm, Sun noon–6pm). The main **post office** is at 4949 E Van Buren St, though the branch at 522 N Central Ave is more convenient for downtown.

Accommodation

Metropolitan Phoenix is so huge that it's worth paying a bit extra to ensure that your **accommodation** is near the places you want to visit. Oddly enough, downtown Phoenix is not one of the more expensive areas, with cheap motels lining the somewhat run-down W Van Buren Street a few blocks north of the center. The summer room rates, shown below, rise significantly in winter, when snowbirds from all over the US fill the upscale resorts of Scottsdale in particular. If you're having trouble finding a place, **Phoenix Scottsdale Hotel Reservations** (☎602/954-1425, ⊛www.phoenixhotel-res.com) offers a free reservation service.

Arizona Biltmore Resort & Spa 24th St & Missouri Ave ☎602/955-6600 or 1-800/950-0086, ⊛www.arizonabiltmore.com. Extraordinarily lavish 500-room resort, built under the influence of Frank Lloyd Wright in the 1930s, and renovated while retaining its Art-Deco trimmings. ❾

Budget Lodge Motel 402 W Van Buren St ☎602/254-7247. Reasonably attractive rooms at very attractive rates – not far from downtown, but you'll feel safer if you drive rather than walk. ❷

Days Inn Resort at Fashion Square Mall 4710 N Scottsdale Rd, Scottsdale ☎480/947-5411 or 1-800/325-2525, ⊛www.scottsdaledaysinn.com. Standard hotel, well priced by local standards, and handily located within walking distance of downtown Scottsdale. ❹

Fiesta Inn Resort 2100 S Priest Drive, Tempe ☎480/967-1441 or 1-800/528-6481, ⊛www.fiestainnresort.com. Long-established, well-priced resort, offering spacious rooms, along with tennis courts and a pool, not far from the airport (served by free shuttle buses) and university. ❹

HI-Phoenix *The Metcalf House*, 1026 N 9th St above Roosevelt ☎602/254-9803. Dorm beds at $12 for HI-AYH members, $15 others; a 15min walk north of the Arizona Center downtown. No phone reservations, but space is usually available. No curfew, cheap bike rental.

Holiday Inn SunSpree Resort 7601 E Indian Bend Rd, Scottsdale ☎480/991-2400 or 1-800/852-5205, ⊛www.holiday-inn.com/scottsdale-rst. Scottsdale's least expensive full-fledged resort, with its own lake and golf course as well as good restaurants, is particularly good value for summer visitors. ❹

Hotel San Carlos 202 N Central Ave ☎602/253-4121 or 1-800/528-5446. Atmospheric, very central Twenties hotel, with tasteful good-value rooms, a nice café, and a rooftop swimming pool. ❹

Royal Inn Motel 2934 N Scottsdale Rd, Scottsdale AZ 85251 ☎480/947-5885 or 1-800/341-8000. Surprisingly inexpensive, perfectly adequate traditional motel, a few blocks south of Old Scottsdale. ❷

Scottsdale's Fifth Avenue Inn 6935 5th Ave, Scottsdale ☎480/994-9461 or 1-800/528-7396, ℻480/947-1695. Good-value motel with pool, on the edge of Scottsdale's shopping district. ❸

Tempe Super 8 Motel 1020 E Apache Blvd, Tempe ☎480/967-8891 or 1-800/800-8000. Chain motel, within half a mile of the university and 5 miles of the airport. ❸

YMCA 350 N 1st Ave ☎602/253-6181. Grungy but central single rooms for men and women, with shared bathrooms. Very low weekly rates. No reservations: first-come, first-served. ❶

Central Phoenix

Downtown Phoenix – defined as the few blocks east and west of Central Avenue, and north and south of Washington Street – is too hot, too run-down, and too spread out to walk around in any comfort. The only time it's buzzing is when the World Series-winning Arizona Diamondbacks are playing at the Bank One Ballpark. At other times, life tends to revolve around the modern

Arizona Center mall, on Van Buren Street between Third and Fifth, which is nonetheless a pale imitation of the mega-malls further north.

What little remains of Phoenix's nineteenth-century architecture now constitutes **Heritage Square**, a couple of blocks southeast of the Arizona Center at 115 N Sixth St. Rather than original adobe ranchhouses, however, it preserves a quaint assortment of Victorian homes, converted into tearooms and toy museums. You can get a better impression of the early days at the **Phoenix Museum of History**, across the street at 105 N Fifth St (Mon–Sat 10am–5pm, Sun noon–5pm; $5), which features the city's first jail – a rock with a chain attached. Twenty sun-baked blocks west, the sparkling copper dome of the disused **Arizona State Capitol** dominates the low-level sprawl. Documents in the dull, dry museum within do little to bring the state's political history to life (Mon–Fri 8am–5pm; free).

Two more significant attractions lie a mile or so north of downtown. Thanks to extensive remodeling, the **Phoenix Art Museum**, 1625 N Central Ave (Tues, Wed, Sat & Sun 10am–5pm, Thurs & Fri 10am–9pm; $6, free Thurs 5–9pm), has plenty of space to display its permanent collection, which includes paintings by Georgia O'Keeffe and Rufino Tamayo, as well as de rigueur Western art by Russell and Remington and some middleweight Old Masters, and features stimulating temporary exhibitions. Three blocks north and a block east, the **Heard Museum**, 22 E Monte Vista Rd (daily 9.30am–5pm; $7), has also been greatly enlarged, while still showcasing the lovely old buildings in which it was founded. It provides a fascinating introduction to the Native Americans of the Southwest, and their arts and crafts in particular. There's an especial emphasis on the Hohokam, with plenty of artifacts from the large town, now known as "La Ciudad," which occupied the site of modern Phoenix during the twelfth century. Elsewhere, the superb pottery collection ranges from stunning Mimbres bowls to modern Hopi ceramics, but the real highlight is a refrigerated room filled with **kachina dolls** – 400 of them donated by the late Arizona senator Barry Goldwater – arranged according to the Hopi sacred calendar.

If Phoenix gets too hot to bear, the coolest place to beat the heat is on the east side of town at the Big Surf **water park**, 1500 N McClintock Ave (May–Sept only: Mon–Sat 10am–6pm, Sun 11am–7pm; $16), where you can ride 5ft waves or careen down waterslides into a giant freshwater lagoon.

Taliesin West and the Cosanti Foundation

Whatever its general appearance may suggest, Phoenix has managed to attract some visionary designers. Notable among them is **Frank Lloyd Wright**, who came to the city to work on the *Biltmore Hotel*, and stayed for most of the 25 years before his death in 1959. His winter studio, **Taliesin West** – located at 114th Street and Frank Lloyd Wright Boulevard, at Scottsdale's northeastern edge – is now an architecture school and a working design studio, with regular multimedia exhibits of the man's life and work (Sept–June daily 9am–4pm; July & Aug daily except Tues & Wed 9am–4pm; ☏480/860-2700). Three different guided tours operate according to complicated seasonal schedules: hourlong "Panorama" tours ($16), 1hr 30min "Insights" ($22), and less frequent 3hr "Behind The Scenes" tours ($35).

Less well known, but in many ways more compelling, is the **Cosanti Foundation**, four miles west of Taliesin at 6433 Doubletree Rd (daily 9am–5pm; $1 donation). The buildings, designed by **Paolo Soleri**, an Italian-born ex-student of Wright, and constructed out of rammed earth and concrete, have a much more organic feel than Taliesin. Crafts workshops make bells and cast bronzes, and a small museum shows drawings and models of Soleri's life's work: **Arcosanti**, a space-age, environmentally sensitive project designed to be (someday) an entirely self-sufficient community of five thousand people, which emerges from the desert just an hour's drive north, a mile east of I-17 at Cordes Junction. Three-hour guided tours are given throughout the day ($8 donation; ☎520/632–6217, ⊛ www.arcosanti.org), and an airy and spacious café serves healthy and tasty meals.

Eating

Most of the **restaurants** in greater Phoenix seem to have retreated to the malls in recent years, so unless you're prepared to pay resort prices, it's hard to find a good restaurant with very much atmosphere. The mall places aren't at all bad, however, and there's plenty of variety. Apart from a block or two in central Scottsdale, no area of the metropolis is small enough to walk around while you look for a place to eat, but if you're happy to drive, neighborhood diners – especially Mexican – can still be found.

Alice Cooper'stown 101 E Jackson St ☎602/253-7337. Barbecue restaurant-cum-sports bar, owned by the rock star and alongside downtown's America West Arena, where the food's better than you'd expect, and the atmosphere is fun, with the staff bedecked in full face paint. Lunch and dinner daily.

Ed Debevic's Short Orders Deluxe 2102 E Highland Ave ☎602/956-2760. Burgers and fries, malts and cokes, served amid frenetic retro-Americana that includes a mini-jukebox on every table.

House of Tricks 114 E 7th St, Tempe ☎480/968-1114. Tiny, smart, romantic modern-American place in the university district, with lots of vegetarian options. Closed Sun.

Monti's La Casa Vieja 101 W Rio Salado Parkway, Tempe ☎480/967-7594. Tempe's oldest adobe house, built in 1873, is now an atmospheric Western-themed diner, serving a conventional steak-and-chicken menu at extraordinarily low prices. Lunch and dinner daily.

Pizzeria Bianco Heritage Square, 623 E Adams St ☎602/258-8300. Good quality pizzas in very con-

venient downtown location. Dinner only, daily except Mon.

MacAlpine's Nostalgic Soda Fountain 2303 N 7th St ☎602/252-7282. Classic downtown soda fountain; wash down your breakfast special or deli sandwiches with an old-style soda.

Roxsand Biltmore Fashion Park, 2594 E Camelback Rd ☎602/381-0444. Eclectic, futuristic restaurant in upmarket uptown mall. Entrees drawn from the major world cuisines – especially Asian, with plenty of spicy Thai and Chinese sauces – start at around $20, and the desserts are great.

Roy's 7001 N Scottsdale Rd, Scottsdale ☎602/905-1155. Ravishing Pacific Rim restaurant in very chic dining district. Meaty entrees, mostly at $20–25, include Szechuan barbecued pork ribs or rack of lamb, while specials usually include Hawaiian fish dishes. Open daily for dinner only.

Sam's Café Arizona Center, 455 N 3rd St ☎602/252-3545. Hectic downtown mall joint, with patio seating, that's nonetheless a great place to try out modern Southwestern cuisine at old-fashioned prices. Lunch and dinner daily.

Nightlife, entertainment and sports

Not surprisingly, **nightlife** in Phoenix tends toward cowboy dance halls and Top 40 discos in the big hotels. For a rundown of what's on musically, pick up the free weekly *New Times* in local record- or bookstores, or check out the bars and clubs listed overleaf. Both the Phoenix Symphony Hall, 225 E Adams St (☎602/495–1117), and the Scottsdale Center for the Arts, 7380 E Second St (☎602/994–2787), put on **classical music**, **theater** and **ballet**. The **Arizona Diamondbacks** have been playing major league baseball beneath the retractable roof of the Bank One Ballpark since 1998 (☎602/514–8500), while the **Phoenix Suns** play NBA basketball at the America West Arena, 201 E Jefferson St (☎602/379–2000), and football's **Arizona Cardinals** are based at the university's Sun Devil Stadium (☎602/379–0102).

Balboa Café 404 S Mill Ave, Tempe ☎ 480/966-1300. Jazz, offbeat rock and acoustic music – plus internet access – near the university.

Char's Has The Blues 4631 N 7th Ave ☎ 602/230-0205. Phoenix's longest-standing, best-loved blues venue, attracting big-name touring stars and featuring live acts nightly.

Coyote Springs Brewing Company Town & Country Shopping Center, 4883 N 20th St ☎ 602/256-6645. Mall microbrewery that puts on R&B several nights of the week.

Mr Lucky's 3660 NW Grand Ave ☎ 602/246-0686. Massive country-music honky-tonk, featuring real-life bull-riding at weekends.

Phoenix Live! Arizona Center, 455 N 3rd Ave ☎ 602/252-2502. Anodyne but very central alliance of three separate clubs under a single roof, with a single cover charge.

East of Phoenix: the Superstition Mountains

Relief from the tedious Phoenix sprawl is provided by the **Superstition Mountains** that rise to the east. The main route through the angular mountains, Hwy-88 (popularly known as the **Apache Trail**), is full of cars on summer weekends; the road cuts off northeast from US-60 about ten miles east of downtown Phoenix. Despite the many dams along the Salt River, it makes for a pleasant drive, with lots of picnic spots and campgrounds. The road turns to gravel just beyond the funky hamlet of **Tortilla Flat**, before reaching the cliff dwellings of **Tonto National Monument** (daily 8am–5pm; $3 per vehicle; Ⓦ www.nps.gov/tont), where the remains of a large pueblo built in the mid-fourteenth century by Salado Indians are preserved in the mouths of three distinct caves.

Hwy-88 rejoins US-60 at the nondescript mining town of **Globe**, on the western edge of the two-million-acre San Carlos Apache Indian Reservation, roughly sixty miles south of the awesome **Salt River Canyon**.

Central Arizona

The I-40 interstate crosses the center of Arizona, skirting the **Navajo Reservation** that fills the northeastern corner of the state. Though the narrow strip of land to either side can be extraordinarily beautiful, with double rainbows reaching across the desert plain and fiery dawns blazing along the horizon, it holds few specific places worth stopping for until you come to the **Flagstaff** area. Itself a pleasant town, Flagstaff makes a base for several interesting excursions – to ancient **Native American sites** and the New Age mecca of **Sedona**, but above all to the **Grand Canyon**. Beyond Flagstaff to the west, there is once again little of interest.

East of Flagstaff

The widely touted **Meteor Crater** (daily: summer 6am–6pm; winter 8am–5pm; $8; Ⓦ www.meteorcrater.com), six miles south of the interstate on a well-marked road nearly forty miles east of Flagstaff, might have been interesting 22,000 years ago, when a meteorite blasted a huge hole, nearly a mile across and over five hundred feet deep, into the scrubby plateau. These days, however, it's a privately run tourist operation, managed in mock-Park Service style and absurdly overpriced. Visitors cannot hike into the actual crater.

Two old Route 66 towns, **WINSLOW** and **HOLBROOK**, are kept alive by transcontinental truckers. Each town consists of little more than a strip of motels, such as the *Best Western Adobe Inn* in Winslow at 1701 N Park Drive

(T928/289-4638; ❸), and the concrete teepees of the *Wigwam Motel* at 811 W Hopi Drive in Holbrook (T928/524-3048; ❷). In addition, Winslow is now graced once more by the restored splendor of the 1929 *La Posada Hotel*, at 303 E Second St (T928/289-4366, Wwww.laposada.org; ❹).

Petrified Forest National Park

At **PETRIFIED FOREST NATIONAL PARK**, which straddles I-40 a dozen miles east of Holbrook, a fossilized prehistoric forest of gigantic trees has been unearthed by erosion. The original cells of the wood have been replaced by multicolored crystals of quartz. Cross-sections, cut through with diamond saws and polished, look stunning, and can be seen in the two **visitor centers**, thirty miles apart at the north and south entrances. On the ground, however, the trees are not all that exciting: segmented, crumbling and very dark. Here and there rough concrete walkways have been laid over the terrain – and often over the tree trunks themselves. The **Long Logs Walk** near the southern entrance is probably the best section; but they're still just a bunch of logs lying in the sand, even if they are stone logs.

The northern section of the national park – site of the main visitor center and **entrance station** (daily 8am–5pm; $10 per vehicle; T928/524-6228, Wwww.nps.gov/pefo) – is renowned for its views of the **Painted Desert**, an undulating expanse of solidified sand dunes, which at different times of day take on different colors (predominantly bluish shades of gray and reddish shades of brown).

Flagstaff

Redolent with the charm of both the nineteenth-century Wild West and the twentieth-century heyday of **Route 66**, the small college town of **FLAGSTAFF** ranks among the most atmospheric and attractive places to stay in the entire Southwest. It's split in two by the twin east–west routes of the main drag, Santa Fe Avenue, which was once Route 66, and before that the pioneer trail west, and the tracks of the **Santa Fe Railroad** whose mournfully whistling trains still reverberate through the desert night. Immediately north lies the characterful downtown area, while the lively, low-rent blocks to the south are predominantly the preserve of the town's student population.

Flagstaff's first Anglo settlers arrived in 1876, lured from Boston by widely publicized accounts of mineral wealth and fertile land, but they soon moved on, disappointed, towards Prescott. However, they stayed long enough to celebrate the centenary of American independence by flying the Stars and Stripes from a towering pine tree. This flagpole became a familiar landmark on the route west, and as the community grew it inevitably became known as Flagstaff. Right from the start, it was a cosmopolitan town, with a strong black and Hispanic population working in the (originally Mormon-owned) lumber mills and in the cattle industry, and with Navajo and Hopi Indians heading in from their nearby reservations to trade. Today, Flagstaff makes an ideal base for travelers, with hotels, restaurants, bars and shops aplenty within easy strolling range of the center (and a number of food and lodging chains a couple of miles away beside the interstate). There's not all that much actually to see in the town itself, but the countryside in every direction is very much worth exploring.

Arrival and information

As the nearest town of any size to the **Grand Canyon**, seventy miles northwest, Flagstaff remains a major junction for road and rail passengers. Daily

Amtrak **trains** heading both east and west pull in at the station in the very center of town, part of which doubles as a very helpful **visitor center** (Mon–Sat 7am–6pm, Sun 7am–5pm; ☎928/774-9541 or 1-800/842-7293, ⓦwww .flagstaffarizona.org). As this book went to press, the company that previously ran bus connections to the Grand Canyon ceased operations; contact the visitor center to see whether, as planned, they've arranged an alternative shuttle service. The least expensive **car rental** is Budget Rent-a-Car, 100 N Humphreys St (☎928/779-0307); Avis, Hertz and National also have outlets.

Accommodation

Flagstaff's dozens of **motels** and **B&Bs** provide reasonable value, while budget travelers can benefit from a couple of high-quality **hostels**. Most of the chain motels are congregated well to the east, along Butler Avenue and Lucky Lane, but staying nearer downtown is much more fun.

DuBeau International Hostel 19 W Phoenix Ave ☎928/773-1656 or 1-800/398-7112. Welcoming independent hostel just south of the tracks, whose converted en-suite motel rooms serve as four-person dorms at $16 per bed in summer, $14 in winter, or private doubles at $35. It also runs $18 one-way shuttle rides to the Grand Canyon (full-day tours $43), and $25 tours down to Sedona and Montezuma Castle.

Econolodge West 2355 S Beulah Blvd ☎928/774-2225 or 1-800/490-6562, ⓦwww.travelsouthwest.com. Relatively appealing chain motel, in white clapboard style with large rooms and suites, south of downtown near the interstate. ❸

Grand Canyon International Hostel 19 S San Francisco St ☎928/779-9421 or 1-888/442-2696, ⓦwww.grandcanyonhostel.com. Independent hos-

tel, under the same friendly management as the similar nearby *DuBeau*, and offering the same tours, plus dorm beds at $16 in summer, $12 in winter, and private rooms at $25. Tours to the Grand Canyon ($38) and Sedona ($20), and car rental discounts.

The Inn at Four Ten 410 N Leroux St ☎928/774-0088 or 1-800/774-2008, ⓦwww.inn410.com. Bright ranch home that's now an antique-furnished B&B; all eight rooms are en-suite. ❺

Hotel Monte Vista 100 N San Francisco St ☎928/779-6971 or 1-800/545-3068, ⓦwww.hotelmontevista.com. Atmospheric little 1920s hotel in the heart of downtown, where the assorted restored rooms, with and without attached bathrooms, are named for celebrity guests from Bob Hope to Michael Stipe. Rates rise by up to $20 at weekends. ❸–❺

The Town

Flagstaff's appealing **downtown** stretches for a few redbrick blocks north of the railroad. Filled with cafés, bars, and stores selling Route 66 souvenirs and Indian crafts, it's a fun place to stroll around, even if it holds no significant tourist attractions or historic buildings. Your most lasting impression is likely to be of the magnificent San Francisco Peaks, rising smoothly from the plains on the northern horizon, and topped by a jagged ridge.

The exceptional **Museum of Northern Arizona**, however, three miles northwest of downtown on US-180, rivals Phoenix's Heard Museum as the best museum in the state (daily 9am–5pm; $5). Its main emphasis is on documenting Native American life, with an excellent run-through of the Ancestral Puebloan past and contemporary Navajo, Havasupai and Hopi cultures, and also actively encourages the development of traditional and even new skills among Native American craftworkers. The exquisite inlaid silver jewelry now made by the Hopi, for example, is the result of a museum-backed program to find work for Hopi servicemen returning from World War II. At all times, marvellous pots, rugs and *kachina* dolls are on display – a pleasant surprise after the low standards often seen elsewhere – but the time to come is for one of the Indian Craftsmen Exhibitions each summer. The Zuni show lasts for five days around Memorial Day weekend in late May; the Hopi show is on the weekend closest to July 4; and the nine-day Navajo event is at the end of July and the start of August, with every item for sale.

Eating and nightlife

There's enough money around in Flagstaff to support several upscale **restaurants**, while the area around San Francisco Street, both north and south of the tracks, must be the liveliest **nightspot** between Las Vegas and Santa Fe, filled with vegetarian cafés, espresso bars and pubs.

Alpine Pizza 7 N Leroux St ☏928/779-4109. Raucous student hangout downtown, with decent pizzas and lots of beer.

Beaver Street Brewery & Whistle Stop Café 11 S Beaver St ☏928/779-0079. Inventive sandwiches and salads, wood-fired pizzas, and outdoor barbecue in the beer garden in summer.

Black Barts 2760 E Butler Ave ☏928/779-3142. Enjoyable Western-themed steakhouse on the east edge of town, with a delicious smell of burning wood, and waiting staff who sing and dance on stage in between serving up barbecued steaks, ribs and chickens, for $15–20.

Café Espress 16 N San Francisco St ☏928/774-0541. Great vegetarian breakfasts, then salads, sandwiches and veggie specials for the rest of the day, plus espresso coffees.

Downtown Diner 7 E Aspen Ave ☏928/774-3492. Classic Route 66 diner a block north of the main drag, featuring leatherette booths and hefty burgers and sandwichs.

Flagstaff Brewing Company 16 E I-40 ☏928/773-1442. Popular downtown pub, with outdoor seating, big windows, and live music Wed–Sat.

Macy's European Coffee House & Bakery 14 S Beaver St ☏928/774-2243. Not merely superb coffee, but heavenly pastries to go with it, plus more substantial vegetarian dishes such as black bean pizza, and even couscous for breakfast.

The Museum Club 3404 E I-40 ☏928/526-9434. A real oddity; this log-cabin taxidermy museum somehow transmogrified into a classic Route 66 roadhouse, saloon and country music venue, that's a second home to hordes of dancing cowboys.

Around Flagstaff

The area around Flagstaff is extraordinarily rich in natural and archeological wonders, with three national monuments – **Sunset Crater**, **Wupatki** and **Walnut Canyon** – within 25 miles. Of these, only Sunset Crater has even a campground, and none has indoor lodgings. There's no scheduled public transportation, so if you don't have your own vehicle you'll have to take a guided tour.

Sunset Crater and Wupatki national monuments

North of Flagstaff, the **San Francisco Volcanic Field** of around four hundred volcanoes is prominent on the western horizon from the Hopi Mesas, and its peaks are said to be the home of their powerful *kachina* spirits. Several hiking trails lead into the San Francisco Peaks, and a chairlift operates in summer ($10; May–Oct daily 10am–4pm) from the **Arizona Snowbowl** almost to the summit of Mount Agassiz (12,350ft), though you can't hike any further from there. For a brief period each winter this becomes a mildly hectic ski area.

Some of the volcanoes are still active, though the most recent eruption was that of **SUNSET CRATER** (twelve miles from Flagstaff on US-89) in around 1066 AD. The crater was named by John Wesley Powell for the many colors of its cone, which swells from a black base through reds and oranges to a yellow-tinged crest. It's too unstable for walkers to be allowed onto the rim, but a trail passes through lava tubes around its base. The national monument's **visitor center** is nearby (open all year, at least 8am–5pm; $4 per person), opposite the *Bonito* **campground** (late May to mid-Oct; ☏928/526-0866).

A dozen miles further north, the ancient ruins at **WUPATKI NATIONAL MONUMENT** appear to show different tribal groups living side by side in harmony (daily: summer 8am–6pm; rest of year 8am–5pm; same ticket as

Sunset Crater). The **Sinagua** were joined here by many others, including the **Ancestral Puebloans**, when the Sunset Crater explosion deposited a rich new layer of topsoil. The specific site known as Wupatki (meaning "tall" or "big house"), standing proud on its natural foundations of red sandstone, is just the largest of innumerable sites.

Walnut Canyon National Monument

Between 1100 and 1250 AD, **WALNUT CANYON**, ten miles east of Flagstaff just south of I-40, was home to a thriving Sinagua community. Literally hundreds of their **cliff dwellings** can still be seen nestling beneath overhangs in the sides of the canyon. They simply walled off alcoves where the softer levels of the striated rock had eroded away, and then put up partitions to make separate rooms.

A large scenic window in the **visitor center** (daily: summer 8am–6pm; rest of year 9am–5pm; $4 per person) gives an excellent overall view. Beyond it, a short trail of steep steps leads across a narrow causeway to an isthmus of rock high above a gooseneck of Walnut Creek. Along the path, you can go inside several Sinagua homes; note the T-shaped doorways that could only be entered headfirst and the ceilings blackened by the smoke of generations of fires. No accommodation, and only minimal snack food, is available.

Sedona and Red Rock Country

US-89A threads its way south from Flagstaff down the spectacular **Oak Creek Canyon** to emerge after 28 miles at **Sedona**, on the threshold of the extraordinary **Red Rock Country**. Up from the valley rise giant mesas and buttes of stark red sandstone, where Zane Grey set a number of his Wild West adventures. The boom-and-bust mining town of **Jerome** looks down from a mountainside to the south, while back beside I-17 toward Phoenix are further haunting Sinagua ruins.

Sedona

Though local boosters make much of its setting, amid some definitive Southwestern canyon scenery, the New Age resort of **SEDONA** adds nothing to the beauty of its surroundings. Architecturally, it's a real mess, with several miles of ugly redbrick sprawl interrupted by the occasional mock-historical mall monstrosity. To the artists, healers, walking wounded and wealthy retirees who have flocked here in the last two decades, however, Sedona is "the next Santa Fe." Whether you love it or hate it will probably depend on whether you share their wide-eyed awe for angels, crystals and all matters mystical – and whether you're prepared to pay over-the-odds prices for the privilege of joining them.

Established in 1902 by one Theodore Schnebly, and named after his wife, Sedona remained for most of the twentieth century a small farming settlement, unmarked on most maps. German surrealist painter Max Ernst moved here in the 1940s – the bizarre backdrops of his later canvases seem less surreal once you've seen where they were painted – and Hollywood movie-makers filmed in the area from the 1950s onward. However, Sedona's big break came in 1981, when Page Bryant, author and psychic, "channeled" the information that Sedona is in fact "the heart *chakra* of the planet." Since she pinpointed her first **vortex** – a point at which, it is claimed, psychic and electromagnetic energies can be channeled for personal and planetary harmony – the town has achieved its own personal growth, and blossomed as a focus for **New Age** practitioners of all kinds.

Vortex Tours of Red Rock Country

As few of the side roads around Sedona are paved – in part because the town's ardent libertarians would not pay the necessary taxes – there's a booming business in **off-road tours**, run by companies such as Earth Wisdom Tours ($42 and up; ☎928/282-4714 or 1-800/482-4714), who teach their clients "the ancestral secrets of the Medicine Wheel," and the garish Pink Jeep Tours ($32–75; ☎928/282-5000 or 1-800/873-3662, ⓦwww.pinkjeep.com). Nonetheless, a lot of the best scenery is visible from the highway, and many of the jeep roads are perfectly passable in ordinary vehicles. So long as you're happy to remain in ignorance as to which rocks are really electromagnetic tuning forks vibrating in harmony with Alpha Centauri, there's no great need to take a commercial tour. At Legends of Sedona Ranch (☎928/282-6826 or 1-800/848-7728), where "horses are free . . . but rides ain't," an hour on **horseback** costs around $40.

If you don't have much time to spend exploring, a cruise along US-89A enables you to see most of the sights, albeit from a distance; the best parts are south along Hwy-179 within Coconino National Forest. The closest **vortex** to town is on **Airport Mesa**; turn left up Airport Road from US-89A as you head south, about a mile past the downtown junction known as the **"Y"**. The vortex is at the junction of the second and third peaks, just after the cattle grid. Further up, beyond the precariously sited airport, the **Shrine of the Red Rocks** looks out across the entire valley.

Sedona's **visitor center**, just north of the "Y," has full listings of lodgings and tour operators (Mon–Sat 8.30am–5pm, Sun 9am–3pm; ☎928/282-7722 or 1-800/288-7336, ⓦwww.sedonachamber.com). It's an expensive place to **stay**; what pass for budget **motels** include the *Sedona Motel*, close to the "Y" at 218 Hwy-179 (☎928/282-7187; ❹), and the renovated *Canyon Portal*, a little further north at 210 N US-89A (☎928/282-7125 or 1-800/542-8484; ❺). The luxurious *Enchantment Resort*, 525 Boynton Canyon Rd (☎928/282-2900 or 1-800/826-4180, ⓦwww.enchantmentresort.com; ❾), has taken over ravishing Boynton Canyon eight miles west.

Lots of expensive Southwestern-style **restaurants** – not all of them particularly good – cater to tourists, and there's still a smattering of old-fashioned diners. *Fournos*, 3000 W Hwy-89A (reservations compulsory; ☎928/282-3331), is a lovely little Greek restaurant, open for dinner at 6pm and 8pm from Thursday to Saturday, and for brunch on Sunday at noon, while the *Sedona Coffee House & Bakery*, 293 N Hwy-89A (☎928/282-2241), is a popular breakfast hangout near the "Y," serving espresso coffees and pastries, and graduating to soup and salad later on.

Jerome

The former mining town of **JEROME**, high above the Verde Valley on US-89A about thirty miles south of Sedona, is conspicuous from quite a distance: an enormous letter "J" is etched deep into the hillside above it, and a large chunk of that hillside is missing altogether, having been blown apart for **opencast copper mining**. This land abounds in mineral wealth – thick veins of copper are interspersed with gold and silver, and an endless supply of limestone is still extracted for cement – but serious exploitation only started in 1876. The **United Verde** mine was partly financed by New Yorker Eugene Jerome (a cousin of Winston Churchill's mother, Jennie Jerome), who insisted that the new town bear his name. Until the current tortuous road was built, the only way up to Jerome was the precipitous rail line connecting the mine with the world's largest copper smelter at Clarkdale.

From the early 1950s, when the mines closed down, until as recently as the 1970s, Jerome was a **ghost town** in which it was possible to turn up and move into an empty house. Many who did so are still here, making a living from arts and crafts, and the town itself has made a dramatic recovery. It's a bit of a tourist trap, but is nonetheless fascinating to explore. The hillside is so steep that the stone houses (it was far too expensive to haul timber up here) tend to have two stories at the front and four or five at the back. Under the repeated concussion of more than two hundred miles of tunnels being blasted into the mountainside, the whole town used to slip downhill at the rate of five inches per year, and the **Sliding Jail** on Hull Avenue came to rest 225ft from where it was built.

The old-style *Inn at Jerome*, 309 N Main St (℡928/634-5094 or 1-800/634-5094, ⓦwww.innatjerome.com; ❸/❹), has five themed B&B **rooms**, with and without private bathrooms, as well as a **bar**, and operates a **café**, the *Jerome Grille*. The *English Kitchen* (℡928/634-2132) has been at 119 Jerome Ave since 1899. Under Chinese ownership, it was an opium den; later the Wobblies held their meetings downstairs. Now it's open for breakfast and lunch every day except Monday, and its terrace offers a commanding view of the valley. Many of the **shops** stock only souvenirs, but interesting crafts showrooms around town include the Knapp Gallery on Lower Main Street and, next door, Made in Jerome Pottery.

Montezuma Castle National Monument

In an idyllic setting just above Beaver Creek and just east of I-17, around 25 miles from Sedona, **MONTEZUMA CASTLE NATIONAL MONUMENT** focuses on a superbly preserved Sinagua **cliff dwelling** (daily: summer 8am–7pm, rest of year 8am–5pm; $2; ⓦwww.nps.gov/moca). Filling an alcove in the hillside with a wall of pink adobe, its five stories taper up to fit the contours of the rock. Apparently, the fingerprints of the masons are still visible on the bricks, and the sycamore beams remain firmly in place, but visitors are not permitted to climb up. The ruins of an even larger dwelling "next door," which was burned out around 1400, can be examined more closely. This had 45 rooms, as well as little "cupboards" recessed into the walls.

West of Flagstaff: I-40 to California

Everything along I-40 west of Flagstaff is dominated by the road's function as the main route between Las Vegas and the Grand Canyon. The first town you reach, **WILLIAMS**, seems to exist solely to capture the passing tourist trade, with a historic **railroad** running north to the Canyon (see p.984 for more details). Things here, though, do liven up come winter, when the slopes of Mount Williams and the rest of the surrounding **Kaibab National Forest** offer good skiing, particularly for cross-country aficionados. Forty-five miles further west at the town of **SELIGMAN**, one of the longest surviving stretches of the old Route 66 heads off on a northern loop through the **Hualapai Indian Reservation** and a dozen quickly fading towns, **PEACH SPRINGS** in particular, that look like they're straight out of *The Grapes of Wrath*. This makes a great detour on what is otherwise a very dull drive; it also provides the best access to the less visited western reaches of the Grand Canyon, around **Havasu Canyon** (see p.989).

Unless you need to fill your tank, or fill up on fast food, there's little reason to stop at **KINGMAN**, the largest town in western Arizona, from where US-93 branches north to Las Vegas and I-40 continues to Los Angeles.

Lake Havasu City

Forty miles southwest of Kingman, ten miles from the California border, a detour south brings you to one of the more bizarre sights of the American desert – the old gray stone of **London Bridge**, reaching out to an artificial island across the stagnant waters of the dammed Colorado River at **LAKE HAVASU CITY**. It has to be said that it looks a hell of a lot better here, with the Chemehuevi Mountains as a backdrop, than it ever did on the River Thames. The resort's developer, Robert P. McCulloch, bought the bridge (under the impression it was Tower Bridge – or so the story goes) for 2.4 million dollars in the late 1960s, and painstakingly shipped it across the Atlantic chunk by chunk before reassembling it over a channel dug to divert water from Lake Havasu, creating an island on the other side of the bridge known as Pittsburgh Point.

  Motels are abundant: the *Windsor Inn Motel,* 451 London Bridge Rd (☎928/855-4135 or 1-800/245-4135; ❷), has especially low rates, while the *Ramada at Lake Havasu,* 271 S Lake Havasu Ave (☎928/855-5169 or 1-800/528-5169; ❸), is a little fancier. Among several good-value **restaurants** is *Shugrue's,* in the Island Fashion Mall at the end of London Bridge (☎928/453-1400), which serves fresh fish, salads and pasta.

The Grand Canyon

Although five million people come to see the **GRAND CANYON OF THE COLORADO** every year, it remains beyond the grasp of the human imagination. No photograph, no set of statistics, can prepare you for such vastness. At more than one mile deep, it's an inconceivable abyss; varying between four and eighteen miles wide, it's an endless expanse of bewildering shapes and colors, glaring desert brightness and impenetrable shadow, stark promontories and soaring, never-to-be-climbed sandstone pinnacles. Somehow it's so impassive, so remote – you could never call it a disappointment, but at the same time many visitors are left feeling peculiarly flat. In a sense, none of the available activities can quite live up to that first stunning sight of the chasm. The **overlooks** along the rim all offer views that shift and change unceasingly from dawn to sunset; you can **hike** down into the depths on foot or by mule, hover above in a **helicopter** or raft through the **whitewater rapids** of the river itself; you can spend a night at **Phantom Ranch** on the canyon floor, or swim in the waterfalls of the idyllic **Havasupai Reservation**. And yet that distance always remains – in some sense the Grand Canyon stands apart.

  Until the 1920s, the average **visitor** would stay for two or three weeks. These days it's more like two or three hours – of which forty minutes are spent actually looking at the canyon. The vast majority come to the **South Rim** – it's much easier to get to, there are far more facilities (mainly at **Grand Canyon Village**), and it's open all year round. There is another lodge and campground at the **North Rim**, which by virtue of its isolation can be a lot more evocative, but at one thousand feet higher it is usually closed by snow from mid-October until May. Few people visit both rims; to get from one to the other demands either a two-day hike down one side of the canyon and up the other, or a 215-mile drive by road.

  Finally, there's a definite risk that on the day you come the Grand Canyon will be invisible beneath a layer of **fog**, thanks to the 250 tons of sulphurous emissions pumped out every day by the Navajo Generating Station, seventy miles upriver at Page.

Admission to the park, valid for seven days on either rim, is $20 per vehicle or $10 for pedestrians and cyclists.

Getting to the Canyon

Nearly all visitors make their way to the South Rim by heading north of I-17 from either **Williams** (58 miles south) or **Flagstaff** (81 miles southeast). Most of the route is through thick ponderosa pine forests, so the ride up from Williams on the restored **steam trains** of the Grand Canyon Railway is not especially scenic (departs Williams daily 10am; from $55 round-trip; ℡928/773-1976 or 1-800/843-8724, Ⓦwww.thetrain.com). For details of buses from Flagstaff, to connect with Amtrak's rail service, see p.978.

The small **airport** at Tusayan – six miles from the South Rim, and used primarily by "flight-seeing" tour companies (see p.988) – also welcomes scheduled services, especially from Las Vegas, with operators such as Scenic Airlines (from $60 one-way; ℡702/739-1900 or 1-800/634-6801, Ⓦwww.scenic.com).

Arrival and information

For the century following the arrival of the railroad in 1901, **GRAND CANYON VILLAGE** was the main center for tourism at the South Rim. By 2000, however, it had become woefully ill-equipped to handle its daily deluge of visitors, and the Park Service was forced to implement an ambitious scheme to reduce traffic congestion in the vicinity. The first stage was to build the large

---

Geology and history of the canyon

Layer upon layer of different rocks, readily distinguished by color, and each with its own fossil record, recede down into the Grand Canyon and back through time, until the strata at the river bed are among the oldest exposed rocks on earth. And yet how the canyon was **formed** is a mystery. Satellite photos show that the Colorado actually runs through the heart of an enormous hill (which native Americans called the *Kaibab*, the mountain with no peak); experts cannot agree on how this could happen. Studies show that the canyon still deepens, at the slow rate of 50ft per million years. Its fantastic sandstone and limestone formations were not literally carved by the river, however; they're the result of erosion by wind and extreme cycles of heat and cold. These features were named – **Brahma Temple**, **Vishnu Temple**, and so on – by Clarence Dutton, a student of comparative religion who wrote the first Geological Survey report on the canyon in 1881.

While it may look forbidding, the Grand Canyon is not a dead place. All sorts of desert **wildlife** survive here – sheep and rabbits, eagles and vultures, mountain lions, and, of course, spiders, scorpions and snakes. The **human** presence has never been on any great scale, but signs have been found of habitation as early as 2000 BC, and the **Ancestral Puebloans** were certainly here later on. A party of **Spaniards** passed through in 1540 – less than twenty years after Cortés conquered the Aztecs – searching for cities of gold, and a Father Garcés spent some time with the Havasupai in 1776. **John Wesley Powell**'s expeditions along the fearsome and uncharted waters of the Colorado in 1869 and 1871–72 were what really brought the canyon to public attention. A few abortive attempts were made to mine different areas, but facilities for tourism were swiftly realized to be a far more lucrative investment. With the exception of the Indian reservations, the Grand Canyon is now run exclusively for the benefit of visitors; although even as recently as 1963 there were proposals to dam the Colorado and flood 150 miles of the Canyon, and the Glen Canyon dam has seriously affected the ecology downstream.

THE GRAND CANYON

0   25 miles

N

UTAH
ARIZONA

NEVADA
ARIZONA

Lake Powell

Page
Glen Canyon Dam
Lees Ferry
Marble Canyon
Echo Cliffs
Colorado River
Vermilion Cliffs

Kanab
Fredonia

ZION NATIONAL PARK
Pipe Springs Nat. Mon.

St George
Colorado City

Jacob Lake
Kaibab Lodge
Closed in winter

North Rim
Pt. Imperial
Walhalla Plateau
Cape Royal
Desert View

Phantom Ranch
Grand Canyon Village
Tusayan

Supai

Havasupai Indian Reservation

GRAND CANYON NATIONAL PARK

Lake Mead

Hoover Dam

Colorado River

Las Vegas

Laughlin

Kingman

Peach Springs

Seligman
Ash Fork

Williams

Valle

Tuba City
Cameron

Wupatki National Monument
Little Colorado River
Sunset Crater National Monument

SAN FRANCISCO PEAKS

Flagstaff
Phoenix

and very impressive **Canyon View Information Plaza** near Mather Point (daily: May to mid–Oct 8am–6pm; mid-Oct to April 8am–5pm; Ⓦwww.nps .gov/grca), where the open-air displays and trail guides are complemented by a visitor center staffed by helpful rangers, and a separate bookstore. Stage two, however – the construction of a light rail system to ferry visitors to the plaza from huge parking lots at **TUSAYAN**, just outside the park six miles south – has yet to materialize, and appears to have been postponed indefinitely. At some point, a new bus system may serve that purpose, but for the moment the plaza is peculiarly inaccessible, in that it has no parking lot of its own, and there are only a few spaces at Mather Point itself, a few hundred yards' walk away.

Currently, free **shuttle buses** run on three routes: one connects the new plaza with Grand Canyon Village; one heads east along the East Rim; and the other sets off west from the village along the West Rim. Private vehicles are still allowed on the East Rim, and into Grand Canyon Village (so overnight guests can reach their lodgings), but only along the West Rim in winter.

Grand Canyon accommodation

All the "lodges" in Grand Canyon Village are operated by the park conces-sionaire, Amfac, and charge similar prices, with no budget **accommodation** alternative. In terms of seeing the canyon, it makes little difference where in the village you stay. Even in the "rim-edge" places – the magnificent 1905 *El Tovar Hotel* (➎) and the *Bright Angel* (rooms ➌, rim-side cabins ➍), *Thunderbird* and *Kachina* lodges (both ➎) – few rooms offer much of a view, and in any case it's always dark by 8pm. Further back are *Maswik Lodge* (cabins ➌, rooms ➍), *Yavapai Lodge* not far from the information plaza (➍), and *Moqui Lodge* at the park entrance (mid-April to mid-Oct; ➍).

Camping facilities (and a laundry) are available at the *Mather* campground and RV park ($15), near the information plaza, at least one section of which is open year-round. If you arrive on foot, you don't need a reservation; all vehi-cles should, however, check in well in advance (you can book through Biospherics on Ⓣ1-800/365-2267). The summer-only *Desert View* camp-ground, 26 miles east, is first-come, first-served, costs $10, and has no hook-ups. It's also possible to camp inside the canyon itself, if you first obtain a per-mit from the **Backcountry Reservations Office** near *Maswik Lodge* (daily 8am–noon & 1–5pm; Ⓣ928/638-7875); each permit costs $10, plus $5 per person per night.

If all the park accommodation is full, the nearest alternative is the under-whelming service village of **Tusayan**. *Seven Mile Lodge* (Ⓣ928/638-2291; ➌) offers the least expensive rooms; the new *Grand Hotel* (Ⓣ928/638-3333 or 1-888/634-7263, Ⓦwww.gcanyon.com; ➎) is more stylish. Much the most popular of the commercial **campgrounds** outside the park – with families, at least – is *Flintstone's Bedrock City* (mid-March to Oct; Ⓣ928/635-2600; $14–18), 22 miles south at the junction of Hwy-64 and Hwy-180, which has its own little prehistoric theme park.

All in-park **accommodation reservations** – for the lodges on both the South and the North rims, as well as for Phantom Ranch and RV camping – are handled by Amfac Parks & Resorts, 14001 East Iliff, #600, Aurora, CO 80014 (same-day Ⓣ928/638-2631, advance Ⓣ303/297-2757, Ⓦwww.grandcanyonlodges.com). The best rooms are often booked as much as a year in advance, and your chances of turning up without a reservation and finding a place in summer are minimal.

Grand Canyon eating

Due to the canyon's remoteness and lack of water, **food prices** tend to be well above average; if you're on a tight budget, bring your own. However, *Yavapai* and *Maswik* lodges have reasonable basic caféterias, open until 10pm. *Bright Angel Lodge* has its own **restaurant**, as well as the *Arizona Steakhouse*, both also open until 10pm, and both costing $15–30. At *El Tovar*, where the dining room looks right out over the canyon, the sumptuous menu is enormously expensive. Breakfast is the most affordable meal; lunch and dinner can easily cost upwards of $40. In **Tusayan**, *We Cook Pizza & Pasta* (☎928/638-2278) is good but pricey.

Exploring the South Rim

The fact that these days most visits to the South Rim start at the Canyon View Information Plaza, at **Mather Point**, rather than in Grand Canyon Village, doesn't mean you're missing out. In fact the canyon panorama that spreads out below Mather Point is more comprehensive than any obtainable from the village. The views to the east in particular are consistently stupendous; it's hard to imagine a more perfect position from which to watch the **sunrise** over the canyon.

The Colorado is visible from various vantage points along the rim-edge footpath near Mather Point. In addition, if you walk west for around ten minutes – that is, turn left along the rim from the information plaza – you'll come to **Yavapai Point**. From here, you can see two separate tiny segments of the river, one of which happens to include both the suspension footbridge across the Colorado and Phantom Ranch (see p.989). Nearby, if you can tear your eyes away from its panoramic bay windows, the **Yavapai Observation Station** (daily: summer 8am–7pm, winter 8am–5pm; free) has illuminating displays on how the canyon may have been formed.

The **West** and **East Rim drives** extend along the South Rim for several miles in either direction from the information plaza and Grand Canyon Village, paralleled by the paved **Greenway Trail** on the very lip of the canyon. No one overlook can be said to be the "best", but there are far too many to stop at them all. Obvious short walks include an excursion to see the **sunset**, which is particularly magical at Hopi Point, to the west.

Driving or taking a shuttle bus along the East Rim Drive opens up further dramatic views. **Desert View**, 23 miles out from the village, is, at 7500ft, the highest point on the South Rim. Visible to the east are the vast flatlands of the **Navajo Nation**; to the northeast, **Vermillion** and **Echo Cliffs**, and the gray bulk of **Navajo Mountain** ninety miles away; to the west, the gigantic peaks of **Vishnu** and **Buddha temples**, while through the plains comes the narrow gorge of the **Little Colorado**. The odd-looking construction on the very lip of the canyon is **Desert View Watchtower**, built by Fred Harvey in 1932 in a conglomeration of Native American styles and decorated with Hopi pictographs. It contains a **gift shop**, as does the general store a few yards away. Groups of tarantulas are often seen in the evenings at Desert View, scuttling back into the warmth of the canyon for the night.

Into the Canyon

Hiking any of the trails that descend **into the Grand Canyon** offers something more than just another view of the same thing. Instead you pass through a sequence of utterly different landscapes, each with its own distinct climate, wildlife and topography. However, while the canyon can offer a wonderful wilderness experience, it's essential to remember that it can be a hostile and very unforgiving environment, grueling even for expert hikers.

The South Rim is 7000ft above sea level, an altitude that for most people is fatiguing in itself. Furthermore, all hikes start with a long, steep descent – which can come as a shock to the knees – and unless you camp overnight you'll have to climb all the way back up again when you're hotter and wearier.

If you're day-hiking, the golden rule is to keep track of how much time you spend hiking down, and allow twice that much to get back up again. Average summer temperatures inside the canyon exceed 100°F; to hike for eight hours in that sort of heat, you have to drink an incredible thirty pints of water. Always carry at least a quart per person, and much more if there are no water sources along your chosen trail. You must have food as well, as drinking large quantities without also eating can cause water intoxication (see p.52 of Basics).

There's only space here to detail the most popular trail, the **Bright Angel**. Many of the others, such as the **Hermit**, date from the days prior to 1928, when the obstreperous Ralph Cameron controlled access to the Bright Angel and many other rim-edge sites by means of spurious mining claims, and the Fred Harvey Company had to find other ways to get its customers down to the Colorado. These other trails tend to be overgrown now, or partially blocked by landslides; check before setting out.

Bright Angel Trail

The **BRIGHT ANGEL TRAIL**, followed on foot or mule by thousands of visitors each year, starts from the wooden shack in the village which was once the Kolb photographic studio. The trail switchbacks for 9.6 miles down to **Phantom Ranch** beside the river, but park rangers have a simple message for all would-be hikers: don't try to hike down and back in a single day. It might not look far on the map, but it's harder than running a marathon. Instead, the longest feasible day-hike is to go as far as **Plateau Point** on the edge of the arid Tonto Plateau, an overlook above the Inner Gorge from which it is not possible to descend any further – a twelve-mile round-trip that will probably take you at least eight hours. In summer, water can be obtained along the way.

Grand Canyon tours

The Fred Harvey Company (contact the "transportation desks" in the South Rim lodges, or call ☎928/638-2401) runs at least two short daily **coach tours** along the **rim** to the west ($14) and east ($25) of the village, **sunrise** and **sunset** trips to Yavapai Point ($10), and **mule** rides to Phantom Ranch (from $315; see opposite). It also operates a five-hour **Smooth Water River Raft Excursion** through Marble Canyon ($87); whitewater rafting trips in the canyon proper – such as those run by Western River Expeditions (☎801/942-6669 or 1-800/453-7450, wwww.westernriver.com) – are booked up literally years in advance, so this is probably your only chance of a trip along the river at short notice.

    Airplane tours cost from around $75 for 30min ($45 child) up to as long as you like for as much as you've got. Operators include Air Grand Canyon (☎928/638-2686 or 1-800/AIR-GRAND) and Grand Canyon Airlines (☎928/638-2407 or 1-800/528-2413). **Helicopter tours**, from $100 for 30min, are offered by AirStar Helicopters (☎928/638-2622) and Papillon Helicopters (☎928/638-2419), who also operate $440 day-trips to the Havasupai Reservation. Unless otherwise specified, all the companies are in **Tusayan**, at or near the airport.

The first section of the trail was laid out by miners a century ago, along an old Havasupai route, and has two short tunnels in its first mile. After another mile, the **wildlife** starts to increase (deer, rodents and the ubiquitous ravens), and there are a few **pictographs** which have been all but obscured by graffiti.

At the lush **Indian Gardens** almost five miles down, where you'll find a ranger station and campground with water, the trails split to Plateau Point or down to the river via the **Devil's Corkscrew**. The latter route leads through sand dunes scattered with cactuses and down beside **Garden Creek** to the Colorado, which you then follow for more than a mile to get to Phantom Ranch.

Phantom Ranch

It's a real thrill to spend a night at the very bottom of the canyon, at the 1922 **Phantom Ranch**. The **cabins** are reserved exclusively for the use of excursionists on Fred Harvey two-day mule trips ($315 per person for one night, $429 for the winter-only two-night trips). Beds in the four ten-bunk **dorms** ($22) are usually reserved way in advance, through Amfac (see p.986), but it's worth checking for cancellations at the Bright Angel transportation desk as soon as you reach the South Rim. Do not hike down without a reservation, and even if you do have one, reconfirm it the day before you set off. All supplies reach Phantom Ranch the same way you do (an all-day hike on foot or mule), so **meals** are expensive, a minimum of $15 for breakfast and $18 for dinner.

The **suspension bridge** here was set in place in 1928 (hanging from twin cables carried down on the shoulders of 42 Havasupai). The delta of **Bright Angel Creek**, named by Powell to contrast with the muddy **Dirty Devil** upriver in Utah, is several hundred feet wide here, and strewn with boulders. All the water used on the South Rim now comes by pipeline from the North Rim, and crosses the river on the 1960s Silver Bridge nearby.

The Havasupai Reservation

The **HAVASUPAI RESERVATION** really is another world. A 1930s anthropologist called it "the only spot in the United States where native culture has remained in anything like its pristine condition"; things have changed a little since then, but the sheer magic of its turquoise waterfalls and canyon scenery makes this a very special place. Traditionally, the Havasupai would spend summer on the canyon floor and winter on the plateau above. However, when the reservation was created in 1882, they were only granted land at the bottom of the canyon, and not until 1975 did the concession of another 251,000 acres up above make it possible for them to resume their ancient lifestyle.

Havasu Canyon is a side canyon of the Grand Canyon, about 35 miles as the raven flies from Grand Canyon Village, but almost two hundred miles by road. Turn off the interstate at Seligman or Kingman, onto AZ-66, which curves north between the two, stock up with food, water and gas, and then turn on to Arrowhead Hwy-18. Plans to build a road – or even a tramway – down into Havasu Canyon have always been rejected, in part because much of the income of the five or six hundred Havasupai comes from guiding visitors on foot, mule or horseback. Instead, the road ends at **Hualapai Hilltop**, from where an eight-mile trail zigzags down a bluff and leads through the stunning waterless Hualapai Canyon to the village of **SUPAI**. Riding down costs $50 one-way, $80 round-trip, while hiking is free; all visitors, however, pay a $15 entry fee on arrival at Supai.

Beyond Supai the trail becomes more difficult, but leads to a succession of spectacular waterfalls, including **Havasu Falls**, one of the best for swimming, and **Mooney Falls**, which was named after an unfortunate prospector who dangled here for three days in the 1890s, at the end of a snagged rope, before falling to his death.

A **campground** (☎928/448-2141) stretches between Havasu and Mooney Falls, and Supai itself holds the **motel**-like *Havasupai Lodge* (☎928/448-2111; summer ❹, winter ❸), along with a **café**, a **general store** and the only **post office** in the US still to receive its mail by pack train. From time to time Supai is hit by freak floods, which can result in the temporary closure of the camp-ground and hotel.

To the North Rim

The 215-mile route by road from Grand Canyon Village to the **North Rim** follows AZ-64 along the East Rim Drive to Desert View, then passes an over-look into the gorge of the Little Colorado, before joining US-89 fifty miles later at **CAMERON**. The Cameron Trading Post has the best selection of Native American crafts in the Grand Canyon area, and remains a trading cen-ter for the Navajo Nation. It also has a good-quality **motel** and **restaurant** (☎928/679-2231 or 1-800/338-7385, 🌐www.camerontradingpost,com; ❹).

Fifteen miles north of Cameron is the junction with US-160, which heads northeast via Tuba City toward Monument Valley and Colorado. Continuing north, after another forty miles of barren wasteland, US-89 branches off to climb the mesa to the right, heading for Page and Glen Canyon Dam (see p.1019).

Lees Ferry

The direct route to the North Rim, now US-89A, crosses the Colorado at last over the single arch of **Navajo Bridge**, almost five hundred feet above the river. There are in fact two Navajo Bridges, the 1929 original, now reserved for pedes-trians, having been supplanted by a wider facsimile in 1995. Until the first was built, a ferry service operated at **LEES FERRY**, six miles north. This was estab-lished in 1872, at the instigation of the Mormon Church, by John D. Lee, at the only spot within hundreds of miles to offer easy access to the banks of the river on both sides. The Colorado, however, could still be a raging torrent, and the crossing was carried out in both directions by casting out and struggling across while being swept downstream. Lee himself was on the run after the **Mountain Meadows Massacre** in Utah in 1857, when a wagon train of would-be settlers was slaughtered by an armed white band clumsily disguised as Indians.

Lees Ferry is the launching point for **whitewater rafting** trips – boats set-ting off from here can't leave the canyon before Diamond Creek, twelve days away by muscle power – and the end of Fred Harvey's smooth water trips from Glen Canyon Dam (see p.988). It still holds the atmospheric remains of Lee's Lonely Dell ranch, as well as a **campground** (☎928/355-2334), while back on US-89A beneath the red of the **Vermillion Cliffs** you'll find a succession of **motels** – *Marble Canyon Lodge* (☎928/355-2225 or 1-800/726-1789; ❸), *Cliff Dweller's Lodge* (☎928/355-2228; ❸) and the beautifully located, rustic *Lees Ferry Lodge* (☎928/355-2231; ❸). All have **restaurants**.

The turning south to get to the North Rim, off US-89A onto AZ-67, comes at **JACOB LAKE**, home to the *Jacob Lake Inn* (☎928/643-7232; ❸) and a **campground**, but not much else. From here – along a road that's closed in winter – it's 27 miles to *Kaibab Lodge* (☎928/638-2389; ❸) and another four-teen to the canyon itself.

The North Rim

Higher, bleaker and far less accessible than the South Rim, the **NORTH RIM** of the Grand Canyon receives less than a tenth as many visitors. While that doesn't mean you'll have the place to yourself, it can still make you feel as though you're venturing into unexplored wilderness. The basic principle, however, is the same as at the South Rim, with a cluster of venerable park-service buildings where the main highway reaches the canyon, and a handful of rim-edge roads where drivers can take their pick from additional lookouts. Only one hiking trail sees much use, the **North Kaibab Trail**, which follows Bright Angel Creek down to Phantom Ranch.

Tourist facilities on the North Rim, concentrated at **Bright Angel Point**, open for the season on May 15 and close on October 15. **Accommodation** at the *Grand Canyon Lodge* (④) is in cabins that spread back along the ridge from the *Lodge* entrance, very few of which have canyon views. Advance reservations are essential, and are handled by the same agents as for the South Rim: Amfac Parks & Resorts, 14001 E Iliff Ave, #600, Aurora, CO 80014 (same-day ☏928/638-2631, advance ☏303/297-2757, ⓦwww.grandcanyonlodges.com). Just over a mile north is the *North Rim Campground*, where $15 spaces can be reserved – though it's not necessary for backpackers – through Biospherics (☏1-800/365-2267). The *Lodge* also holds a reasonable **restaurant**, plus a saloon and an espresso bar; ask at the information desk for details of **mule rides** (1hr $20, half-day $45, full-day canyon expeditions $100; ☏435/679-8665), and **van tours** along the rim.

The park itself remains open for day-use only after October 15, but no food, lodging or gas is available, and visitors must be prepared to leave at a moment's notice. It's shut down altogether by the first major snowfall of winter, which usually comes toward the end of October.

Northeastern Arizona: Indian Country

The deserts of northeastern Arizona, popularly known as **INDIAN COUNTRY**, hold some of the most fascinating **pre-Columbian ruins** in North America, in the most striking settings imaginable. The cliff palaces of **Canyon de Chelly**, and **Betatakin** and **Keet Seel** in the Navajo National Monument, are among the greatest architectural achievements of the **Ancestral Puebloans**, made that much more special by the fact that the lands on which they stand are still lived on and worked by their heirs, the Hopi and Navajo.

The **NAVAJO NATION**, the largest Native American reservation in the US, fills most of the region, lapping over into western New Mexico and stretching to include the majestic sandstone pillars of Monument Valley in southernmost Utah. Although the migrant Navajo have embraced the American Way – driving pickup trucks and wearing baseball caps – you get a very real sense of traveling through a foreign country here. Everyone can speak English, but Navajo, a language so complex that it was used as a secret military code during World War II, is still the lingua franca. Supermarkets mark their prices in Navajo, and the reservation follows its own rules over Daylight Savings; in frontier-style towns like Tuba City, the time on the clock can vary according to whether you're in an American or a Navajo district. Tune into the Navajo Nation **radio station**, KTNN 740AM, for a sense of the Navajo–American melange.

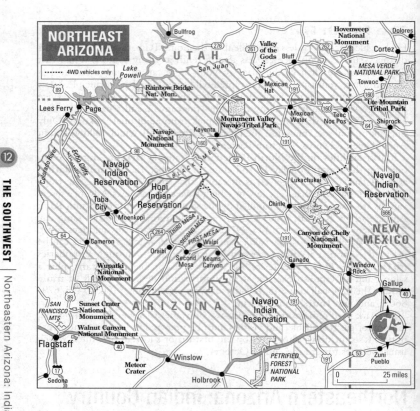

NORTHEAST ARIZONA

······· 4WD vehicles only

When white immigrants began to arrive in force during the early nineteenth century, the Navajo – who call themselves *Dineh*, "The People" – had lived in Arizona for hundreds of years; within a generation, they lost almost everything. When the Yankees took over from the Mexicans, things just got worse, hitting bottom in 1864 when Kit Carson rounded up every Navajo he could find and forced them all to move to Fort Sumner in the desolate plain of eastern New Mexico (see p.949). A few years later, the Navajo were allowed to return, the US government granting them most of the vast acreage they hold today (lawsuits arising from territorial disputes with the **Hopi**, their neighbors and predecessors, have dragged on ever since). Most of the 250,000-plus Navajo today work the land as shepherds and farmers on widely scattered smallholdings, though many craftspeople also live by selling their wares from small stands set up along highways and in tourist stops.

Visiting this region can be fascinating and rewarding, but it's important to respect the people and places you encounter. The Ancestral Puebloans, the region's first occupants, have long since vanished, but many of the relics they left behind are on land that is still of spiritual significance to their modern counterparts – Native Americans come here from all over the Southwest and beyond to take pride in their heritage. Similarly, it is offensive to photograph or otherwise intrude upon people's lives without permission; one reason why the Hopi, for example, banned photography was because it was such an inter-fering nuisance.

On a practical note, don't expect extensive **tourist facilities**. Most towns exist solely as bureaucratic outposts that only come alive during the annual tribal fairs and rodeos, and have little to offer visitors beyond a handful of places to eat and even fewer hotels and motels. For more information, call the **Navajo Nation Tourism Office** on ☏928/871-6436.

Navajo National Monument

NAVAJO NATIONAL MONUMENT, in the northwest quarter of the reservation, protects two of Arizona's biggest and most beautifully sited cliff dwellings. From behind the good **visitor center** (summer daily 8am–6pm; rest of year daily 8am–5pm; ☏928/672-2366, ⦿www.nps.gov/nava; free) at the end of paved Hwy-564, ten miles north of US-160, a ten-minute trail crosses the plateau to a viewpoint overlooking **Betatakin**, an exceptionally well-preserved 135-room masonry structure tucked away in a large natural alcove halfway up the 700ft high, brilliant-red sandstone on the far side of a canyon. It's only possible to hike down to Betatakin – which feels as though it was abandoned seven years, not seven centuries, ago – by joining one of the unfor-gettable six-hour ranger-guided hikes (May–Sept; daily 9am), which leave from the visitor center. Numbers are limited, and no advance bookings are taken, so get here as early as possible on the day – or stay the previous night at the very attractive free **campground** in the forest beside the visitor center.

In summer, you can also visit the even larger Ancestral Puebloan site of **Keet Seel**. However, the seventeen-mile round-trip hike from the visitor center is too grueling to attempt in a single day, so you'll have to sleep in the small **campground** near the site, having obtained a permit from the visitor center at least a day in advance.

Most people pass through this area on their way somewhere else, so there aren't many **places to stay**. However, **TUBA CITY**, west of the monument, has the large, modern *Quality Inn Tuba Trading Post* (☏928/283-4545 or 1-800/644-8383; ❹), while the coal and uranium mining town of **KAYENTA**, 22 miles northeast of the monument at the junction of US-160 and US-163, holds the *Best Western Wetherill Inn* (☏928/697-3231, ⦿www.gouldings.com; ❹) and the *Holiday Inn* (☏928/697-3221; ❹), which has a distinctive and good-value **restaurant**.

Monument Valley

The classic Wild-West landscape of stark sandstone buttes and forbidding pin-nacles of rock, poking from an endless expanse of drifting red sands, has become an archetypal image. Only when you arrive at **MONUMENT VAL-LEY** – which straddles the Arizona–Utah state line, 24 miles north of Kayenta and 25 miles southwest of Mexican Hat – do you realize how much your per-ception of the West has in fact been shaped by this one spot. Such scenery does exist elsewhere, of course, but nowhere is it so perfectly concentrated and dis-tilled. While movie-makers have flocked here since the early days of Hollywood – this was where John Ford made John Wayne a star – the sheer majesty of the place still takes your breath away. Add the fact that it remains a stronghold of **Navajo** culture, little affected by tourism, and Monument Valley can be the absolute highlight of a trip to the Southwest.

The biggest and most impressive of the monoliths are a pair called **The Mittens**, one East and one West, each of which has a distinct thumb splintering off from its central bulk. The taller of the two rises a thousand feet above the valley floor, with sand dunes lapping at its base. Over a dozen other spires are spread around nearby, along with **rock art panels** and an assortment of minor but nicely sited **Ancestral Puebloan ruins**.

You can see the buttes for free, towering alongside US-163, but the four-mile detour to enter **Monument Valley Tribal Park** is rewarded with much closer views (May–Sept daily 7am–7pm; Oct–April daily 8am–5pm; $4). A rough, unpaved road drops from behind the visitor center to run through Monument Valley itself. The 17-mile **self-drive route** makes a bumpy but bearable ride in an ordinary vehicle, and takes something over an hour to complete (open summer daily 8am–6pm; rest of year daily 8am–4.30pm). You're allowed to stop en route to stretch your legs, but not to hike for any distance. However, the Navajo-led **jeep** or **horseback tours** into the backcountry are very much recommended; a two-hour jeep trip costs from around $20 per person if arranged at the visitor center, slightly more if organized through *Goulding's Lodge* (see below). As well as stopping at such movie locations as the **Totem Pole** (atop which Clint Eastwood had some perilous moments in *The Eiger Sanction*), these pause so you can watch weavers at work in a Navajo *hogan* (traditional eight-sided dwelling).

The *Haskeneini* (☎928/871-4602) is a reasonable **restaurant** at the visitor center, not far from the very exposed *Mitten View* **campground** (first-come, first-served; summer only; $10). The only **accommodation** in the immediate vicinity is six miles west, in Utah; *Goulding's Lodge* (☎435/727-3231 or 1-800/874-0902, ⓦwww.gouldings.com; ❺), is a 1920s trading post that now offers pricey motel rooms with magnificent views, a fairly good restaurant, a general store and gas station, a small movie museum and its own campground (mid-March to Oct; $14; same phone).

Canyon de Chelly National Monument

A short distance east of **CHINLE**, sixty miles southwest of Kayenta and seventy miles north of I-40, twin sandstone walls emerge abruptly from the desert floor, climbing at a phenomenal rate to become the awesome thousand-foot cliffs of **CANYON DE CHELLY NATIONAL MONUMENT**. Between these sheer sides, the meandering course of the Chinle Wash can be discerned by its fringe of cottonwoods as it winds through grasslands and planted fields. Here and there a Navajo *hogan* stands in a grove of fruit trees, a straggle of sheep is penned in by a crude wooden fence, or ponies drink at the water's edge. And everywhere, perched above the valley on ledges in the canyon walls and dwarfed by the towering cliffs, are the long-abandoned adobe and stone dwellings of the **Ancestral Puebloans**.

There are two main canyons, which branch apart a few miles upstream: **Canyon de Chelly** (pronounced *de shay*) to the south and **Canyon del Muerto** to the north. Each twists and turns in all directions, scattered with vast rock monoliths, while several smaller canyons break away. The whole labyrinth threads its way upward for thirty miles into the Chuska Mountains.

Canyon de Chelly is a magnificent place, easily on a par with the best of the Southwest's national parks. Its relative lack of fame owes much to the continuing presence of the **Navajo**, for whom the canyon retains enormous symbolic significance (although they did not build its cliff dwellings). Casual visitors are restricted to peering into the canyon from above, from overlooks along the two "rim drives." There's no road in, and, apart from one short trail, you can only enter the canyons with a Navajo guide.

Some history

The first known inhabitants of the canyon were **Ancestral Puebloan** Basketmakers, around 300 AD. During the next thousand years, they advanced from living in pit houses dug into the soil to building elegant cliff dwellings, and developed fine pottery and weaving. For some centuries after the Ancestral Puebloans left the area (see p.941), the **Hopi** came here to farm each summer, returning for the winter to the mesas to the east, but as time went by, **Navajo** migrants from the north and west eventually displaced the Hopi altogether.

From 1583 onward, the Navajo were locked with the Spanish in a bloody cycle of armed clashes and slave raids. The US Army in turn failed in repeated attempts to dislodge the Navajo, but no treaty could restrain the rapacious hunger for land by New Mexican settlers. The end appeared to have come with the brutal round-up and deportation (the "**Long Walk**") of the entire Navajo people, completed by Kit Carson in 1864 when he starved the last of them down from Navajo Rock and destroyed their homes and livestock. So barbaric was the Navajo's imprisonment at Fort Sumner, however, that Congress soon allowed them to return. To this day, 25 Navajo families still farm the Canyon de Chelly in summer, the matrilineal descendants of the women between whom it was reapportioned in the 1870s.

The view from above: the rim drives

Each of the two "rim drives" from the visitor center offers a succession of spectacular overlooks; allow two to three hours for each of the forty-mile round-trips. Thefts from cars have been a major problem, so it's wise to heed the prominent warnings.

The first significant stopping point along the **South Rim Drive** is **Junction Overlook**, after four miles, far above the point where the two main canyons branch their separate ways; as you scramble across the bare rocks you can see Canyon de Chelly narrowing away, with a *hogan* immediately below. Two miles further along, by which time the canyon is 550ft deep, **White House Overlook** looks down on the highly photogenic **White House Ruins**. This is the only point from which unguided hikers can descend to the canyon floor, taking perhaps 30 to 45 minutes to get down and a good hour to get back up. The beautiful if precarious trail, at times running along ledges chiseled into the slick rock, culminates with a close-up view of the ruins; the most dramatic dwellings, squeezed into a tiny alcove sixty feet up a majestic cliff, were once

Into the Canyons

Tours of the canyon floor, organized by *Thunderbird Lodge* (see overleaf), zigzag along the washes, which vary from two- or three-feet deep during the spring thaw to completely dry in summer. For most of the year, the bone-shaking tours are in open-top flatbed trucks, lurching over the rutted earth, and the heat can be incredible; in winter they carry on in glass-roofed army vehicles with caterpillar tracks. To reach as far as Spider Rock, you have to take the full-day tour ($63.50), but the half-day trip at $39 still enables you to see a wide variety of sites and terrain, including the White House Ruins.

The visitor center also arranges highly recommended 4.5-mile, four-hour **group hikes**, which cost $15 per person. The precise schedule varies, but usually includes a morning trip via the White House Trail and an afternoon hike in the Canyon del Muerto; separate **night hikes** last just two hours but cost slightly more. Justin's Horse Rentals (☎928/674-5678) and Twin Trail Tours (☎928/674-8425) organize horseback trips for $10 per person per hour, plus $10 an hour for a guide.

reached via the rooftops of now-vanished structures. Visitors are forbidden to walk for more than a hundred yards in either direction beyond the site. Back up on the South Rim Drive, twelve miles along, the view from **Sliding House Overlook** reveals more Ancestral Puebloan ruins seemingly slipping down the canyon walls toward the ploughed Navajo fields below, while eight miles further on the road ends above the astonishing **Spider Rock**, where twin 800ft pinnacles of rock reach to within 200ft of the canyon rim.

The **North Rim Drive** runs twenty miles up Canyon del Muerto to **Massacre Cave**, where the Spanish expedition of 1805, led by Lieutenant Narbona, killed around one hundred Navajo women, children and old men. The "cave" is just a pitifully exposed ledge, upon which the huddled group were easily picked off by the Spanish, using ricochets off the overhang above. Visible from the nearby **Mummy Cave Overlook** is the **House Under The Rock**, with its central tower in the Mesa Verde style – the single most striking ruin in the monument. Of the two viewpoints at **Antelope House Overlook**, one is opposite Navajo Fortress, an isolated eminence atop which the Navajo were besieged for three months in 1863, while the other looks down on the ruins of Antelope House, and the **Tomb of the Weaver** across the wash, where the embalmed body of an old man was found wrapped in golden eagle feathers.

Practicalities

The Canyon de Chelly **visitor center**, on the road from Chinle (May–Sept daily 8am–6pm; Oct–April daily 8am–5pm; ☎928/674-5500, ⓦwww.nps.gov/cach), has informative displays, and provides guides for unorthodox hiking or motorized expeditions. Facilities nearby are overstretched, so it's essential to book your **accommodation** well in advance. The most appealing options are the *Thunderbird Lodge* (☎928/674-5841 or 1-800/679-2473, ⓦwww.tbird-lodge.com; ❹), very near the canyon entrance – which arranges the standard sightseeing tours and has an adequate caféteria – and the *Holiday Inn* (☎928/674-5000; ❺), slightly further back towards Chinle, where the food is a lot better. The free, minimally equipped *Cottonwood* **campground** has pleasant sites among the trees alongside *Thunderbird Lodge*. Chinle itself is a brief nondescript straggle on the highway, with service stations, *Taco Bell*, *Kentucky Fried Chicken*, a post office and a laundry.

Window Rock

The seat of the Navajo Tribal Council, the reservation's governing body, is on its eastern edge, along the New Mexico border. It was based for fifty years at Fort Defiance, a US cavalry outpost, until in the 1930s **WINDOW ROCK** was established as a new capital. Named for the natural stone arch on its northern side, it's not a great place to get a grasp of Navajo culture, but it does at least have gas stations, shops and a **motel**, the showpiece *Navajo Nation Inn* at 48 W Hwy-264 (☎928/871-4108 or 1-800/662-6189; ❸). The adjacent **Navajo Tribal Museum** (summer Mon–Fri 8am–5pm & Sat 10am–4pm; rest of year Mon–Fri 8am–5pm; donation) gives the background on tribal history and displays high-quality crafts.

The Hopi Mesas

The **Hopi** people are virtually unique in the United States, in that they have lived continuously in the same place for over eight hundred years. Some invaders have come and gone in that time, others have stayed; but the villages on **First**, **Second** and **Third mesas** have endured, if not exactly undisturbed then at least unmoved.

To outsiders, it's not obvious why, with the whole Southwest to pick from, the Hopi should have chosen to live on three barren and unprepossessing fingers of rock, poking from the southern flanks of **Black Mesa** in the depths of northeast Arizona. There are two simple answers. The first is that while Black Mesa has no perennial streams, its subterranean rocks are tilted at just the correct angle to deliver a tiny but dependable trickle of water, and that the "black" in its name comes from the coal that gives the Hopi limitless reserves of fuel. The second is that the Hopi used to farm and hunt across a much wider area, and have only been restricted to their mesa-top villages by the encroachment of their Navajo neighbors. While the Hopi are celebrated for their skill at "**dry farming**," managing to preserve enough precious liquid to grow corn, beans and squash on hand-tilled terraces, this precarious and difficult way of life has nonetheless been forced upon them.

By their very survival, not to mention the persistence of their ancient beliefs and ceremonies, the Hopi have long been a source of fascination to outsiders. While visitors are welcome, the Hopi have no desire – or need, as the tribe has finally begun to earn considerable amounts from mineral leases – to turn themselves into a tourist attraction. Although stores and galleries on the reservation provide plenty of opportunity to buy crafts such as pottery, basketwork, silver overlay jewelry and hand-carved *kachina* dolls, tourists who arrive in the hope of extensive sight-seeing – let alone spiritual revelations – are likely to leave disappointed, and quite possibly dismayed by what they perceive as conspicuous poverty.

Visiting the Hopi Mesas

The essential first stop for visitors is the modern, mock-Pueblo **Hopi Cultural Center** below Second Mesa, which holds a **museum** (summer Mon–Fri 8am–5pm, Sat & Sun 9am–3pm; rest of year Mon–Fri 8am–5pm; $3), as well as a **caféteria** and **motel** (☎928/734-2401, ⓦ www.hopionline .com; ❹). In summer, its unexotic but adequate rooms are usually booked solid a week or more in advance.

Unless your visit coincides with a social event that's open to tourists (see box, overleaf), the only way to see the mesa-top villages is to take a **guided tour** of the most impressive one, **WALPI** (summer Mon–Fri 9am–6pm; winter Mon–Fri 9.30am–4pm; $5). By Hopi standards, Walpi is not in fact that old; it was hastily thrown together in the immediate aftermath of the Pueblo Revolt of 1680, when the people of First Mesa decided to move to a more secure site in the face of possible Spanish or Navajo attack. The spot they chose is absolutely stunning, standing alone at the narrow southernmost tip of the mesa, and connected to the other First Mesa villages by the merest slender neck of stone, with a drop of three hundred feet to either side. It's now home to around 35 people, who do without electricity or running water.

To see Walpi, take Hwy-264 to modern **POLACCA**, at the foot of First Mesa, then drive a mile up the twisting paved road until it ends in **SICHOMOVI**. The tours assemble in Sichomovi's small community center, setting off at regular intervals for a half-hour walk to and around Walpi. Depending on the time of year, you'll either be in a group of twenty or so, or on your own, but either way there's plenty of opportunity to ask questions, and to buy pottery, *kachina* dolls, and fresh-baked *piiki*, a flatbread made with blue cornflour.

Hopi ceremonies

The Hopi feel neither the urge nor the obligation to divulge details of their religious beliefs and practices to outsiders. To that end, they have resisted attempts to make Hopi a written language, or to expose it to scrutiny by teaching it in schools. As a result, Hopi spirituality has been repeatedly misrepresented to the world, whether as barbarous devil-worship or New Age guff. There is in any case no single unified Hopi religion; ceremonials vary from clan to clan and village to village. The most basic common element is the role of the *kachinas*. These "spirit messengers," which may represent the spirits of the dead, live in the San Francisco peaks north of Flagstaff.

There are over three hundred different *kachinas*. At one time, they visited the mesas in person; now they come in the form of masked dancers. Not every village follows the same ceremonial calendar, but in general the *kachinas* arrive each year in early February for the Powamuya ceremony, or **Bean Dance**. They continue to visit throughout the growing season, before returning home after the Niman ceremony or **Home Dance** in July.

The Hopi do not worship the *kachinas*; their main significance is as examples and allegories for the children. All Hopi babies receive *tihus* – what outsiders know as *kachina* dolls, which have become very popular crafts objects – at their first Niman ceremony, and the girls receive further dolls at each Powamuya and Niman ceremony thereafter.

For much of the twentieth century, Hopi **ceremonies** were promoted as tourist attractions. Even after cameras were banned in 1916, occasions such as the **Snake Dance**, when members of the Snake clan dance with live snakes between their teeth, attracted as many as 2500 outsiders. In recent years, however, the Hopi have moved toward the exclusion of non-Native Americans. By 1989, Second Mesa had closed all its ceremonies to outsiders, and it was joined by all the First Mesa villages in 1992 after the publication of a Marvel comic that characterized the *kachinas* as violent avengers.

While spectators are now very unlikely to be allowed at any *kachina* dances, however, some **social dances**, held between August and January when the *kachinas* are away from the mesas, may still be "open." Held in the village plazas, these usually take place at the weekends, so that Hopi who live off the reservation can return. Specific timings tend not to be announced until a few days in advance; for information, contact the Cultural Center. If you do get the chance to attend, wear clothing that fully covers your body, keep your distance, and do not photograph, sketch or question either dancers or audience.

Utah

With the biggest, most beautiful and most pristine landscapes in North America, **UTAH** has something for everyone: from brilliantly colored canyons, across endless desert plains, to thickly wooded and snow-covered mountains. This unmatched range of terrain, almost all of which is public land, makes Utah *the* place to come for **outdoor pursuits**, whether your tastes run to hiking, off-track mountain biking, whitewater rafting or skiing.

Southern Utah has more **national parks** than anywhere else in the US; in fact it has often been suggested that the entire area should become one vast national park. The most accessible parts – such as **Zion** and **Bryce Canyon** – are by far the most visited, but lesser-known parks like **Arches** and **Canyonlands** are every bit as dramatic. Huge tracts of this empty desert, in which beautiful pre-Columbian pictographs and Ancestral Puebloan ruins lie hidden, are all but unexplored; seeing them in safety requires a good degree of advance planning and self-sufficiency.

In the **northeast** of the state, the **Uinta Mountains** remain uncrossed by road and form one of the most extensive wilderness areas in the US outside Alaska, while **Flaming Gorge** and **Dinosaur** preserve more desert splendor. Though the **northwest** is predominantly flat and dry, the granite mountains of the **Wasatch Front** tower over state capital **Salt Lake City** – a surprisingly attractive and enjoyable stopover – while Alta, Snowbird and the resorts around Park City offer some of the best **skiing** in North America.

Led by Brigham Young, Utah's earliest Anglo settlers – the **Mormons** – arrived in the Salt Lake area in 1847, and set about the massive irrigation projects that made their agrarian way of life possible. At first they provoked great suspicion and hostility back east; Congress turned down their first petition for statehood in 1850, in part because of the religious significance of the proposed name, **Deseret**, a Mormon word meaning "honeybee" (the state symbol is still a beehive, to denote industry). The Republican convention of 1856 railed against slavery and polygamy in equal measure – had the South not intervened, civil war with the Mormons was a real possibility. Relations eased when the Mormon church realized in 1890 that it had better drop polygamy on its own terms before being forced to do so. Statehood followed in 1896, and a century on, seventy percent of Utah's two-million-strong population are Mormons. The Mormon influence is responsible for the layout of Utah's towns, where residential streets are as wide as interstates, and all are numbered block-by-block according to the same logical if ponderous system.

Despite Brigham Young's early opposition to the search for mineral wealth, Mormon businessmen became renowned as fiercely pro-mining and anti-conservation. Only since the early 1980s – once the uranium bonanza was definitely over – has tourism been appreciated as a major industry, and former mining towns such as **Moab** developed facilities for wide-eyed travelers smitten by the lure of the desert. Increased tourism has also led to a relaxation of Utah's notoriously arcane **drinking laws**; In most towns, at least one restaurant will be licensed to sell beer, wine and mixed drinks to diners, and it may also be licensed to sell beer in its bar or lounge. Beer is also sold in a few other locations, but to drink stronger liquor you'll have to become a member of a **"private club"**; most sell temporary membership for a token fee. Take-out bottled drinks, including beer, can only be purchased in State Liquor Stores.

Getting around Utah

It's nearly impossible to get anywhere in Utah without your own **car**. Amtrak and Greyhound serve Salt Lake City and a few provincial towns, but practically nowhere else. However, a couple of firms offer **bus tours** of the national parks, and if you're feeling adventurous, southern Utah also has an unbeatable range of mountain biking, river rafting, even hot-air ballooning opportunities: see p.1016 for a list of companies.

Southern Utah: the national parks

Southern Utah is a peculiar combination of the mind-boggling and the mundane. Its **scenery** is stupendous, a stunning geological freakshow where the earth is ripped bare to expose cliffs and canyons of every imaginable color, unseen rivers gouge mighty furrows into endless desert plateaus, and strange sandstone towers thrust from the sagebrush. By contrast, however, the tiny **Mormon towns** scattered across this epic landscape are almost without exception boring in the extreme, so most visitors spend as much time as possible **outdoors**.

While Southern Utah's five national parks are complemented by countless lesser-known but equally dramatic wildernesses, they make the most obvious targets for travelers. In the southwest, **Zion National Park** centers on an awe-inspiring canyon, backed by barren highlands of white sandstone, while **Bryce Canyon** is a roaring inferno of orange pinnacles. Over to the east, **Arches** holds an eroded desertscape of graceful red-rock fins and spurs, all on a more manageable scale than the astonishing hundred-mile vistas of neighboring **Canyonlands**. Both lie within easy reach of **Moab**, a disheveled former mining town turned Utah's hippest destination. The fifth park, **Capitol Reef**, stretches through the middle of the state, pierced by slender, ravishing canyons.

The defining topographical feature of southwest Utah is the **Grand Staircase**. Named by pioneer river-runner John Wesley Powell, it consists of a series of plateaus, stacked tier upon tier, that climb from the North Rim of the Grand Canyon. The **Chocolate Cliffs**, near the border with Arizona, are followed by the dazzling **Vermillion Cliffs**, then the **White Cliffs** – a 2000ft wall of Navajo sandstone, best seen at Zion – the **Grey Cliffs**, and finally the **Pink Cliffs** of Bryce. Although it took a billion years of sedimentation for these rocks to form, the staircase itself has only been created in the last dozen million years, by the general upthrust of the **Colorado Plateau**, which stretches away to the east.

This is a tough land, and a rough one for travelers: with fewer roads than anywhere else in the US, almost nobody gets far into the deep backcountry. Even within the national parklands, overground access is more often than not limited to heavy-duty, high-clearance **four-wheel-drive vehicles**, **hikers** and, increasingly, to **mountain bikes**. The best way of all to experience the region is as the first explorers did: by **water**, along such rivers as the Colorado and the Green. Dozens of companies offer river-rafting trips, floating downstream and camping out under the clear night sky to experience the sights, sounds and smells of the desert.

St George and Cedar City

Southern Utah's two biggest towns, **St George** and **Cedar City**, lie fifty miles apart on I-15 en route between Las Vegas and Salt Lake City. Both make reasonably pleasant and serviceable bases, if not ones that are likely to detain you for very long.

St George

ST GEORGE was the winter home of Brigham Young and other early Mormon leaders, who basked in the comparatively mild climate of "Utah's Dixie." Set at the foot of a broad, reddish-brown sandstone cliff, it's a pretty enough town, centering around the fine 1877 **LDS Temple** at 440 South 300

SOUTHERN UTAH

N

0   25 miles

◄ Las Vegas

◄ Salt Lake City

◄ Grand Junction

Fillmore

Richfield

Sevier

Junction

Beaver

Parowan

Brian Head

Cedar City

Pine Valley

Mountain Meadows Massacre Site

St. George

Hurricane

Virgin

Colorado City

Fremont Indian S.P.

UTAH

AQUARIUS PLATEAU

Loa

Bicknell

Torrey

CAPITOL REEF NATIONAL PARK

Hanksville

Goblin Valley State Park

SAN RAFAEL REEF

Green River

Moab

Cisco

Colorado River

ARCHES NAT. PARK

Dead Horse Point

Horseshoe Canyon

CANYON-LANDS NATIONAL PARK

Dirty Devil River

HENRY MOUNTAINS

Hite

Bullfrog

Halls Crossing

Monticello

Blanding

Natural Bridges Nat. Monument

Grand Gulch

San Juan River

Goosenecks

Valley of the Gods

Mexican Hat

Bluff

Four Corners Monument

Hovenweep Nat. Mon.

Monument Valley

Navajo Indian Reservation

Kayenta

Navajo Nat. Mon.

Rainbow Bridge Nat. Mon.

Lake Powell

Wahweap

Page

GLEN CANYON NATIONAL RECREATIONAL AREA

BURR TRAIL

HOLE-IN-THE-ROCK ROAD

KAIPAROWITS PLATEAU

Grand Staircase-Escalante National Monument

Kodachrome Basin

Escalante

Boulder

Tropic

BRYCE CANYON NAT. PARK

Panguitch

Hatch

Glendale

Mt. Carmel Jct

Kanab

Fredonia

Jacob Lake

Lees Ferry

Jacob Lake

Cedar Breaks Nat. Mon.

Kolob Canyons

ZION NATIONAL PARK

Springdale

Coral Pink Sand Dunes

Pipe Springs Nat. Mon.

A R I Z O N A

Virgin River

Flagstaff ►

East, the oldest still in use anywhere. The rest of the town holds quaint pioneer homes, including Brigham Young's much-restored **adobe house** on 200 North First West (daily 9am–dusk; free).

Travelers driving up I-15 can call in at the **Utah Visitor Center**, just inside the state line (daily: summer 8am–9pm; winter 8am–5pm; ☏435/673-4542). Virtually all St George's commercial life takes place along the main drag, St George Boulevard, where the twenty or so **motels** include the popular *Dixie Palm* at no.185 E (☏435/673-3531; ❶). Among various good **restaurants** in the Ancestor Square development is the *Pizza Factory*, 1 W St George Blvd (☏435/628-1234). The St George Shuttle bus (☏435/628-8320) connects with Las Vegas and Salt Lake City on request.

Cedar City

CEDAR CITY, 53 miles north of St George and approximately half its size, is no more worthy of a stop. Founded as an iron mining town in the late 1850s, it's now kept alive by the Southern Utah State College on its western fringe, and by the flood of theater-goers who come to watch the enthusiastic productions of the **Utah Shakespeare Festival**, held on campus every summer (☏435/586-7878).

The large local **visitor center** stands at 581 N Main St (Mon–Fri 8am–5pm; ☏435/586-5124, ⓦwww.scenicsouthernutah.com). **Main Street** is handy for food and lodging; motels with pools include two *Best Westerns*, the *El Rey Inn* at no.80 S (☏435/586-6518, ⓦwww.bwtowncountry.com; ❸–❻), and the smart *Town and Country Inn* at no.200 N (☏435/586-9900; ❹). *Godfathers Pizza* at no.241 N (☏435/586-1111) offers Italian specialties in a lively atmosphere, while *Sulli's* at no.301 S (☏435/586-6761) is part steakhouse, part coffeeshop.

Zion National Park

With its soaring cliffs, riverine forests and cascading waterfalls, **ZION NATIONAL PARK** is the most conventionally beautiful of Utah's parks. On first glance, it's also the least "Southwestern"; its centerpiece, **Zion Canyon**, is a lush oasis that feels far removed from the otherworldly desolation of Canyonlands or the downright weirdness of Bryce. Like California's Yosemite Canyon, it's a spectacular gorge, squeezed between mighty walls of rock and echoing to the sound of running water; also like Yosemite, it can get claustrophobic in summer with its approach roads clogged with traffic and its limited facilities crammed with sweltering tourists.

Too many visitors see Zion Canyon as a quick half-day detour off the interstate, as they race between Las Vegas (158 miles southwest) and Salt Lake City (320 miles northeast). Beautiful though the **Scenic Drive** through the canyon may be, Zion deserves much more of your time than that. Even the shortest hiking trail within the canyon can help you escape the crowds, while a day-hike will take you away from the deceptive verdure of the valley and up onto the high-desert tablelands beyond.

Summer is by far the busiest season. That's despite temperatures in excess of 100°F, and violent thunderstorms concentrated in August and a week or so to either side. If you can, come in April or May, to see the spring flowers bloom – though the mosquitoes are also at their peak – or in September and October, to enjoy the fall colors along the river. The **admission charge** for Zion, valid in all sections of the park for seven days, is $20 per vehicle, or $10 for motorcyclists, cyclists and pedestrians.

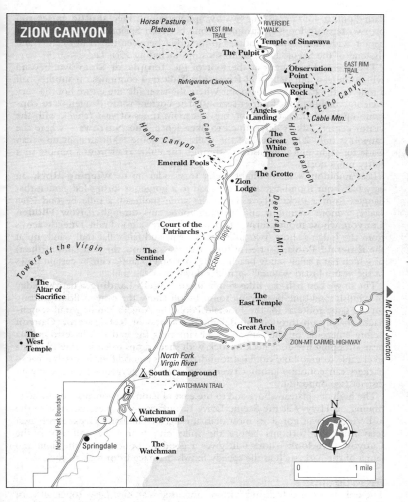

ZION CANYON

Horse Pasture
Plateau
WEST RIM
TRAIL
RIVERSIDE
WALK
Temple of Sinawava
The Pulpit
EAST RIM
TRAIL
Observation
Point
Refrigerator Canyon
Weeping
Rock
Echo Canyon
Behunin Canyon
Angels
Landing
Cable Mtn.
Heaps Canyon
The
Great
White
Throne
Hidden Canyon
Emerald Pools
The Grotto
Zion
Lodge
Deertrap Mtn.
Court of the
Patriarchs
SCENIC DRIVE
Towers of the Virgin
The
Sentinel
Mt Carmel Junction
The
Altar of
Sacrifice
The
East Temple
9
The
Great Arch
ZION-MT CARMEL HIGHWAY
The
West
Temple
North Fork
Virgin River
South Campground
WATCHMAN TRAIL
National Park Boundary
9
Watchman
Campground
N
Springdale
The
Watchman
0   1 mile

Visiting Zion Canyon

In **Zion Canyon**, mighty walls of Navajo sandstone rise nearly half a mile above the groves of box elders and cottonwoods that line the loping North Fork of the **Virgin River**. The awe of the early Mormon settlers who called this "Zion" is reflected in the names of the stupendous slabs of rock along the paved six-mile **Scenic Drive** from the park entrance – the **Court of the Patriarchs**, the **Great White Throne** and **Angel's Landing**.

Although Hwy-9 remains open to through traffic all year, the Scenic Drive is accessible to private vehicles during the winter only. Between April and October, all visitors, other than guests staying at *Zion Lodge* (see overleaf), are obliged to leave their vehicles either in Springdale or at the large new **visitor center** just inside the park (daily: April–Oct 8am–7pm; Nov–March

8am–5pm; ☎435/772-3256, ⓦwww.nps.gov/zion). Free **shuttle buses** run on two separate loops in summer – one between Springdale and the visitor center, with nine stops en route, and the other between the visitor center and the end of the Scenic Drive, with six stops including *Zion Lodge*.

The Scenic Drive ends at the foot of the **Temple of Sinawava**, beyond which the easy but delightful **Riverside Walk** trail continues on another half a mile up the canyon, to the point where the river fills the entire floor (a very welcome bathing spot in drier seasons). The current is too dangerous to continue upstream from this point, but at certain times of year (check with the visitor center), hikers determined to experience **The Narrows** – where the canyon is only 20ft across and the walls tower some 800ft straight up – can wade for eight miles downstream through the chilly river from a remote spot thirty miles north.

Less ambitious walkers might prefer to wander up to **Weeping Rock**, an easy half-hour round-trip from the road to a gorgeous spring-fed garden that dangles from a rocky alcove. From the same trailhead, a mile beyond *Zion Lodge*, a more strenuous and exciting route cuts through narrow **Hidden Canyon**, whose mouth turns into a waterfall after a good rain. Directly across from the lodge a short (two-mile round-trip) and fairly flat trail winds up at the **Emerald Pools**, a series of three clearwater pools, the best (and furthest) of which has a small sandy beach at the foot of a gigantic cliff; at certain times of the year a broad waterfall sprinkles down over the trail.

The single best half-day **hike** climbs up to **Angel's Landing**, a narrow ledge of whitish sandstone protruding some 1750ft above the canyon floor. Starting on the same route as for the Emerald Pools, the Angel's Landing trail switchbacks sharply up through the delightful coolness of **Refrigerator Canyon** before emerging on the canyon's west rim; near the end you have to cross a heart-stopping five-foot neck of rock with sheer drops to either side (there's a steel cable to grab hold of). That round-trip takes a good four hours, but backpackers can continue another twenty miles to the gorgeous Kolob Canyons district (see opposite).

The high dry plateau above and to the **east** of Zion Canyon, reached by continuing on Hwy-9 at the Scenic Drive turnoff, is a complete contrast to the lush Virgin River gorge. Its most dramatic sight is the blind **Great Arch**, best seen from the turnouts before the mile-long tunnel, beyond which the **Canyon Overlook** nature trail gives a good introduction to the flora and fauna of the park, such as the speedy lizards that race from rock to rock.

Practicalities

The only **food and lodging** within Zion itself is at *Zion Lodge* (open all year; ☎435/772-2001, reserve through Amfac Parks & Resorts, 14001 E Iliff Ave, #600, Aurora, CO 80014; ☎303/297-2757, ⓦwww.zionlodge.com or ⓦwww.amfac.com; ⑤), set amid rolling and well-shaded lawns near the Great White Throne. Even if you can't get a room here – they're often booked up by tour groups – it's well worth stopping for lunch on the terrace of the fine old wooden dining room. The *Lodge* is also the base for **horseback** excursions, with regular one-hour rides costing $15 per person (☎435/772-3810). Two good **campgrounds**, both charging $14 per night, are located alongside the visitor center; the *Watchman* accepts reservations in summer (☎1-800/365-2267, ⓦhttp://reservations.nps.gov), while the *South* is first-come, first-served.

The best alternatives to the in-park lodge are in the appealing small town of **SPRINGDALE**, set among the riverbank cottonwoods half a mile south of the park entrance. Budget **motels** along Hwy-9, known here as Zion Park

Boulevard, include the friendly *El Rio Lodge*, no. 995 (☎435/772-3205 or 1-888/772-3205, ⓦwww.elriolodge.qpg.com; ❷), while two pricier modern alternatives, the *Best Western Zion Park Inn* at no. 1215 (☎1-800/934-7275 or 435/772-3200, ⓦwww.zionparkinn.com; ❺), and the *Desert Pearl Inn*, no. 707 (☎435/772-8888 or 1-888/828-0898, ⓦwww.desertpearl.com; ❹), offer good views and pools. The *Switchback Grille* (☎435/772-3700), adjoining *Zion Park Inn,* is the grandest local **restaurant**, while as well as being the liveliest **bar** for miles, the *Bit and Spur Saloon* opposite (no. 1212; ☎435/772-3498), serves very good Mexican food.

The Kolob Canyons

Although the immaculate **KOLOB CANYONS** are just three miles off I-15, twenty miles south of Cedar City, this section of Zion receives far fewer visitors than Zion Canyon itself. Here, too, the focus is on **red-rock canyons**, which in the Kolob seem somehow redder, and the trees greener, than those down below.

The view from the five-mile paved road that heads up from the small but worthwhile **visitor center** (daily: May–Sept 8am–7pm; Oct–April 8am–6pm; ☎435/586-9548) is amazing, but hiking off along either of two main trails will give you a feeling for what makes this place so special. The first and shorter of the two starts two miles from the visitor center and follows Taylor Creek on a five-mile round-trip to **Double Arch Alcove**, a spectacular natural amphitheater roofed by twin sandstone arches; there's also a small waterfall a quarter of a mile further along. The other trail starts from the north side of the parking area at Lee Pass, four miles beyond the visitor center, and follows a well-marked route for seven miles past LaVerkin Falls to **Kolob Arch**, which at over 300ft across rivals Landscape Arch in Arches (see p.1015) as the world's longest natural rock span. There are no permanent campgrounds in the Kolob Canyons, but two dozen backcountry sites are allotted by rangers each day.

Cedar Breaks National Monument

The shortest drive between Zion and Bryce, along the Virgin River and then north on US-89 across the high plain of Long Valley, is spectacular enough, but the longer route through the maple and aspen groves of the **Dixie National Forest** is even more dramatic. Halfway between Cedar City and US-89, Hwy-148 cuts sharply north through the eerie fringes of **CEDAR BREAKS NATIONAL MONUMENT** ($4 per vehicle), where the soft sandstone has crumbled away from the edge of a high wooded plateau to create a fairyland amphitheater of bizarre and brilliantly colored formations.

Cedar Breaks is in a sense just a pocket version of Bryce Canyon to the east, but that's no reason not to come. Most of the plateau is over 10,000ft high, so it's usually quite cold; in fact the roads through are often blocked by snow until June. **Point Supreme**, with a small summer-only **visitor center** (June to mid-Oct daily 8am–6pm; ☎435/586-9451), **snack bar** and **campground** ($10), is a mile into the park from the south, and has the best view.

East of Cedar Breaks, Hwy-143 passes through pine forests and across lava flows, then drops past Panguitch Lake to reach the broad Sevier River valley at the squeaky-clean Mormon farming town of **PANGUITCH**. This holds eight gas stations, twenty-odd **motels**, such as the *Marianna Inn*, 699 N Main St (☎435/676-8844 or 1-800/331-7407, ⓦwww.mariannainn.com; ❷–❹), and not much else.

Bryce Canyon National Park

The surface of the earth can hold few weirder-looking spots than **BRYCE CANYON**. Named for Mormon settler Ebenezer Bryce, who memorably declared that it was "a helluva place to lose a cow," it is not in fact a canyon at all. Along a twenty-mile shelf on the eastern edge of the thickly forested **Paunsaugunt Plateau**, 8000ft above sea level, successive strata of dazzlingly colored rock – yellows, reds, whites and flaming oranges – have slipped and slid and washed away to leave a menagerie of multihued and contorted **stone shapes**.

Like Cedar Breaks, the formations here have been eroded out of the muddy sandstone by a combination of icy winters (the temperature drops below freezing 200 nights out of the year) and summer rainstorms. The racks of top-heavy pinnacles known as "**hoodoos**" were formed when the harder upper layers of rock stayed firm as the lower levels were worn away beneath them. These hoodoos – **Thor's Hammer**, visible from Sunset Point, is the most alarmingly precarious – look down into technicolor ravines, all far more vivid than the Grand Canyon and much more human in scale. The whole place is at its most inspiring in winter, when the figures stand out from a blanket of snow.

The park approach road runs south from Hwy-12 about twenty miles east of Panguitch. Between October and mid-June, the **entrance fee** to Bryce is $10 per vehicle, valid for a week. In summer, things get more complicated. Motorists have the choice of either paying $20 to take their own vehicles into the park, or parking at the highway junction and paying $15 to ride a **shuttle bus** system. The Blue bus line carries you as far as the visitor center, four miles in (April–Oct daily 8am–8pm; Nov–March daily 8am–4.30pm; ☎435/834-5322, ⓦ www.nps.gov/brca), from where the Red bus ferries you another couple of miles south to Bryce Amphitheater. If that's as far as you want to go – and for most people, even keen hikers, it's entirely sufficient – then there's no reason to use your own car. If you want to get as far as Rainbow Point, however, the Green bus to the end of the road runs only twice a day at most, so using your own car is preferable.

Of the succession of scenic overlooks into **Bryce Amphitheater**, at the heart of the park, the two most popular are on either side of *Bryce Canyon Lodge* (see p.1008): the more northerly, **Sunrise Point**, is 350yd from the parking lot and so is slightly less crowded than **Sunset Point**, where most of the bus tours stop. A network of **hiking trails** also drop abruptly from the rim down into the amphitheater – bear in mind that you'll have to walk back up the same distance that you go down. One good three-mile trek switchbacks steeply from Sunset Point through the cool 200ft canyons of **Wall Street**, where a pair of 800-year-old fir trees stretch to reach daylight. It then cuts across the surreal landscape into the basin known as the **Queen's Garden**, where the stout and remarkable likeness of Queen Victoria sits in majestic condescension – pointed out by a brass plaque – before climbing back up to the rim at Sunrise Point. A dozen trails crisscross the amphitheater, but it's surprisingly easy to get lost, so don't stray from the marked routes.

Sunrise and Sunset points notwithstanding, the best view at both sunset and dawn (which is the best time for taking pictures) is from **Bryce Point**, at the southern end of the amphitheater. From here, you can look down not only at the Bryce Canyon formations but also take in the grand sweep of the whole region, east to the **Henry Mountains** and north to the Escalante range. The park road then climbs another twenty miles south, by way of the intensely colored **Natural Bridge**, an 85ft rock arch spanning a steep gully, en route to its dead end at **Rainbow Point**.

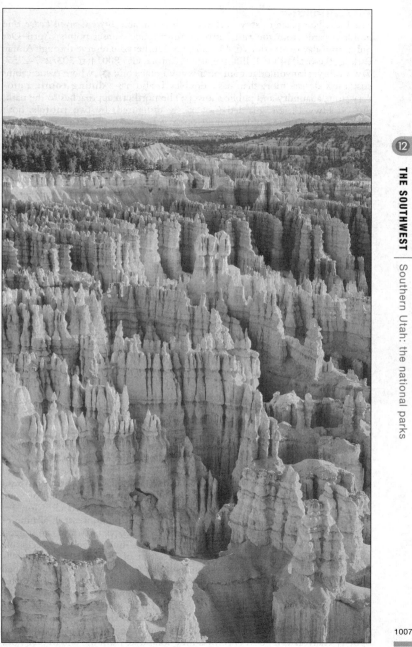

△ Bryce Canyon

Practicalities

Much the best place to **stay** in Bryce is the venerable *Bryce Canyon Lodge*, one hundred yards from the rim between Sunrise and Sunset points (April–Oct only; same-day reservations ℡ 435/834-5361, otherwise reserve through Amfac Parks & Resorts, 14001 E Iliff Ave, #600, Aurora, CO 80014; ℡ 303/297-2757, Ⓦ www.brycecanyonlodge.com or Ⓦ www.amfac.com; ❹), where rustic cabins cost a few dollars more than basic doubles. It also has a **dining room**, a grocery store, a laundry and public showers. The northern approaches to the park, just off Hwy-12, are guarded (not to say disfigured) by two **motels**, both owned by the same company and open year-round; the large *Best Western Ruby's Inn* (℡ 435/834-5341 or 1-800/468-8660, Ⓦ www.rubysinn.com; summer ❹, winter ❷), and the cheaper, newer (and misleadingly named) *Bryce View Lodge* (℡ 435/834-5180 or 1-888/279-2304, Ⓦ www.bryceviewlodge.com; ❷). *Ruby's Inn* has its own **campground** ($14), and there are also two first-come, first-served campgrounds within the park, which charge $10 per night; *Sunset Campground*, close to Sunset Point, and *North Campground*, near the visitor center. Backpackers can choose from dozens of sites below the rim, all south of Bryce Point; pick up the required permit at the visitor center, and take lots of water.

Bryce Canyon to Capitol Reef: Highway 12

Turning its back on the grand amphitheater of Bryce Canyon, the tiny hamlet of **TROPIC**, which strings along Hwy-12 eight miles east of the park entrance, seems almost embarrassed about the flamboyant geological phenomena ranged along the ridge above it. The practical-minded people of this Mormon farming community (population 380) don't especially concern themselves with tourists, but they have restored Ebenezer Bryce's log cabin, which stands next to the *Bryce Pioneer Village* **motel–cum–restaurant** (℡ 435/679-8546 or 1-800/222-038, Ⓦ www.bpvillage.com; ❷–❹). An unmarked road heads west from the cabin two miles to the park boundary, from where it's a two-mile hike up to the main formations.

   Hwy-12 then curves along the edge of the Table Cliff Plateau before dropping down into the remote canyons of the **Escalante River**, the last river system to be discovered within the continental US and site of some of the finest **backpacking** routes in the Southwest. As soon as you walk even a hundred yards off the main highway, you're in a wilderness that few travelers ever see.

   ESCALANTE, 33 miles east of Cannonville, was just another roadside town, until it was given a new lease on life in 1996 by the surprise Presidential proclamation that created the vast **Grand Staircase-Escalante National Monument** (free). The **interagency visitor center** at the west end of town (mid-March to Oct daily 7.30am–5.30pm; Nov to mid-March Mon–Fri 8am–4.30pm; ℡ 435/826-5499, Ⓦ www.ut.blm.gov/monument), is a mine of up-to-date information on all the public lands in the vicinity, and can suggest **hiking** or **mountain biking** trips into the backcountry. The most accessible local highlight is **Calf Creek**, sixteen miles east of Escalante, where a well-marked trail leads just under three miles upstream to a gorgeous shaded dell replete with a 125ft waterfall, and there's a nice undeveloped **campground** ($5). More ambitious trips start from trailheads along the dusty but usually passable **Hole-in-the-Rock Road**, which turns south from Hwy-12 five miles east of town. A trio of slender, storm-gouged **slot canyons**, including the delicate, graceful Peek-a-Boo Canyon and the downright intimidating Spooky Canyon, can be reached by a mile-long hike from the end of Dry Fork

Road, 26 miles along, while from **Hurricane Wash**, 34 miles along, you can hike five miles to reach Coyote Gulch, and then a further five miles, passing sandstone bridges and arches, to the Escalante River. Under normal conditions, two-wheel-drive vehicles should go no further than **Dance Hall Rock**, 36 miles down the road, a superb natural amphitheater sculpted out of the slick-rock hills. The pick of Escalante's **motels** is unquestionably the *Prospector Inn*, 380 W Main St (☎435/826-4653; ❸), which adjoins the friendly, high-quality *Ponderosa Restaurant*, 400 W Main St (☎435/826-4658).

Until the mid-1980s, when it was paved through to Capitol Reef, Hwy-12 ended at **BOULDER**, thirty miles beyond Escalante. **Anasazi State Park** (summer daily 8am–6pm; rest of year daily 9am–5pm; $2), which holds the excavated and partially reconstructed remains of a small Ancestral Puebloan village, is set on a shallow knoll overlooking Boulder Creek. Beyond Boulder, Hwy-12 makes a gorgeous drive up onto the Aquarius Plateau, with marvelous vistas to the east across waves of gold- and red-sandstone outcrops; there's a lovely **campground** (☎435/425-3702; $10) at Oak Creek, fifteen miles along. Due east from Boulder, all except twenty miles of the old dirt **Burr Trail** has (controversially) been paved, providing easy access to the southern reaches of **Capitol Reef National Park** and down to **Lake Powell**.

Capitol Reef National Park

CAPITOL REEF sounds more like something you'd find off the coast of Australia than in the heart of the Utah desert, but in most respects its towering ochre-, white- and red-**rock walls** and deep **river canyons** are of a piece with the rest of the region. The outstanding feature is a multilayered, 1000ft-high reef-like wall of uplifted sedimentary rock, a section of which reminded an early traveler of the grand dome of the US Capitol. Stretching for over a hundred miles north to south, but only a few miles across, the seemingly impenetrable barrier of the **Waterpocket Fold** was warped upward by the same process that lifted the Colorado Plateau, and the sharply defined sedimentary layers on display here trace over two hundred million years of geological activity. The Waterpocket Fold is sliced through in a number of places by deeply incised river canyons – some only twenty feet wide, but hundreds of feet deep – often accessible only by foot.

The one paved road through the park, Hwy-24, cuts across the northern half of the Fold, following the deep canyon of the **Fremont River**; motorists who stick to this road do not incur an entrance fee. Beneath the enormous and very prominent **Castle**, the **visitor center** (daily: June–Sept 8am–7pm; Oct–May 8am–4.30pm; ☎435/425-3791, ⓦwww.nps.gove/care) has explanatory exhibits and an irresistible campground ($10), set amid the cherry, apple and peach orchards of the abandoned Mormon community of **FRUITA**; in season, you can pick all the fruit you can gobble down. To the west, the **Goosenecks Overlook** gazes down 500ft into the entrenched canyons cut by Sulphur Creek. Further east, beyond Fruita's former schoolhouse, are some extraordinary **Fremont petroglyphs**, figures of bighorn sheep and stylized space-people chipped into the varnished red rock a thousand years ago; a five-minute radio broadcast (AM 1540) describes their makers. Another four and a half miles along, one of Capitol Reef's best **day-hikes** heads up along the gravelly riverbed through **Grand Wash** – a beautiful (and usually quite cool) canyon where, it's said, Butch Cassidy and his gang used to hide out.

Few other paved routes run through the park, so to reach the spectacular backcountry canyons you may have to put up with many miles of dusty and spine-rattling roads – renting a mountain bike is a good idea. The paved, popular **Scenic Drive** ($4 per vehicle) heads twelve miles south from the visitor center, past the top of Grand Wash to **Capitol Gorge** and back. A more adventurous sixty-mile loop trip explores **Cathedral Valley** in the north, while a 125-mile southern route starts at the foot of the volcanic **Henry Mountains**, then follows the Burr Trail through **Muley Twist Canyon**, and continues west to Boulder (see p.852).

The nearest **food and lodging** to Capitol Reef is eleven miles west, in the rapidly growing small town of **TORREY**, where options include *Austin's Chuckwagon*, 12 W Main St (☎435/425-3335 or 1-800/863-3288, ⓦwww.austinschuckwagonmotel.com; ❸–❺), the *Wonderland Inn*, at the intersection of Hwy-12 and Hwy-24 (☎435/425-3775 or 1-800/458-0216, ⓦwww.capitolreefwonderland.com; ❸), and the *Capitol Reef Inn*, 360 W Main St (☎435/425-3271, ⓦwww.capitolreefinn.com; ❸), which has a small café.

Goblin Valley

Fifty fairly desolate miles east of Capitol Reef along Hwy-24, you reach the tiny crossroads of **Hanksville**. Twenty miles north on Hwy-24, a right turn takes you onto a 32-mile dirt road to a real anthropological and artistic wonder – the rock paintings of **Horseshoe Canyon**, a remote subsection of Canyonlands National Park (see p.1013).

Half a mile further north on Hwy-24, a side road to the east veers off to **GOBLIN VALLEY STATE PARK** (open 24hr; $4), where thousands of gnome-like figures loom out of the soft Entrada sandstone. The **Carmel Canyon** trail loops for over a mile through a throng of misshapen rock pillars, many of which seem to have eyes and other human features; in the 2000 movie spoof *Galaxy Quest*, the entire valley comes to life. Stay at the well-equipped **campground** (☎1-800/322-3770; $10) if you want to see the place by moonlight, when it looks especially spooky.

Green River

The uneventful riverside town of **GREEN RIVER**, just east of the Hwy-24 junction on I-70, is the largest community on a 200-mile stretch of interstate. One good reason to visit is the **John Wesley Powell River History Museum**, 885 E Main St (daily: summer 8am–8pm; rest of year 8am–5pm; $2), which features the anything-but-dry personal accounts of the men who first successfully navigated the Colorado River from near its source all the way through the Grand Canyon. In summer, **raft trips** from the museum – which also doubles as the local **visitor center** – float downriver to the **Crystal Geyser**, a 100ft cold-water gusher, and every Memorial Day hundreds of boats set out on weekend-long convoy trips that cruise down the Green River to its confluence with the Colorado, then head upriver to Moab.

Green River holds several bargain-rate **motels**, including the *Book Cliff Lodge*, 395 E Main St (☎435/564-3406 or 1-800/493-4699; ❷), which also has a handy **café**.

Canyonlands National Park

CANYONLANDS NATIONAL PARK, the largest and most magnificent of Utah's national parks, is as hard to define as it is to map. Its closest equivalent, the Grand Canyon, is by comparison simply an almighty crack in an otherwise relatively flat plain; the Canyonlands area is a bewildering tangle of canyons, plateaus, fissures and faults, scattered with buttes and monoliths, pierced by arches and caverns, and penetrated only by a paltry handful of dead-end roads.

The 527 square miles of the park are just the core of a much larger wilderness that stretches to the horizon in every direction. To nineteenth-century explorers, this was the epitome of useless desolation; only since uranium prospectors blazed crude trails across the trackless wastes in the 1950s has it become at all widely known. Even after the park was created in 1964, it took a couple of decades before tourists arrived in appreciable numbers.

Canyonlands focuses on the Y-shaped confluence of the **Green** and **Colorado rivers**, buried deep in the desert forty miles southwest of Moab. There's only one spot from which you can see the rivers meet, however, and that's a five-mile hike from the nearest road. With no road down to the rivers, let alone across them, the park therefore splits into three major sections. The **Needles**, east of the Colorado, is a red-rock wonderland of sandstone pinnacles and hidden meadows that's a favorite with hardy hikers and 4WD enthusiasts, while the **Maze**, west of both the Colorado and the Green, is a virtually inaccessible labyrinth of tortuous, waterless canyons. In the wedge of the "Y" between the two, the high, dry mesa of the **Island In The Sky** commands astonishing views across the whole park and beyond, with several overlooks that can easily be toured by car. Getting from any one of these sections to the others involves a drive of at least a hundred miles.

Canyonlands is not a place that lends itself to a short visit. With no lodging, and little camping, inside the park, and no loop road to whisk you through it, it takes a full day to have even a cursory look at a single segment. If you're among the many visitors who find the conditions too grueling to spend much time out of your car – summer temperatures regularly exceed 100°F, and most trails have no water and little shade – then the Island In The Sky is the most immediately rewarding option. On the other hand, if you fancy a long day-hike you'd do better to set off into the Needles.

Island In The Sky and Dead Horse Point State Park

Reached by a good road that climbs steadily up from US-191, 21 miles south of I-70, the **ISLAND IN THE SKY** district looks out over hundreds of miles of flat-topped mesas that drop in 2000ft steps to the river. Four miles along from its **visitor center** (daily 8am–5pm; ☎435/259-4712), the **Mesa Arch**

Trail is the area's best short hike, looping for a mile around the mesa-top hillocks to the edge of the abyss, where long, shallow Mesa Arch frames an extraordinary view of the **La Sal Mountains**, 35 miles northeast. The definitive vantage point, however, is **Grand View Point Overlook**, another five miles on at the southern end of the road. An agoraphobic's nightmare, it commands a hundred-mile prospect of layer upon layer of naked sandstone, here stacked thousands of feet high, there fractured into bottomless canyons. The Island In The Sky's only developed **campground**, the first-come, first-served and waterless *Willow Flat* ($5), is just back from the **Green River Overlook**, reached by forking right shortly after the Mesa Arch trailhead.

On the way in to Island In The Sky, a turnoff long before the visitor center cuts across south to the smaller but equally breathtaking **DEAD HORSE POINT**, located at the tip of a narrow mesa, which looks straight down 2000ft to the twisting Colorado River. Cowboys used the mesa as a natural corral, herding up wild horses then blocking them in behind a piñon pine fence that still marks its 90ft neck. One band of horses was left here too long and died – hence the name. As a Utah state park, Dead Horse Point charges its own $5 admission fee, and national-park passes cannot be used. The new **visitor center** (summer daily 8am–6pm; rest of year daily 8am–5pm; $5) stands two miles short of the point itself, and there's also a **campground** ($11; advance reservations on ☎1-800/322-3770).

The Needles and Newspaper Rock

Taking its name from the thousands of colorful sandstone pillars, knobs and hoodoos that punctuate its many lush canyons and basins, the **NEEDLES** district allows a more intimate look at the Canyonlands environment than does Island In The Sky. Here you're not always gazing thousands of feet downward or scanning the distant horizon; instead you can wander through seemingly endless acres of stone figures.

The road ends with a great collection of mushroom-shaped hoodoos at the **Big Spring Canyon Overlook**. A memorable and demanding eleven-mile round-trip hike from here remains the only way to get to the **Confluence Overlook**, 1000ft above the point where the Green River joins the muddy waters of the Colorado, to flow together, parallel but separate, toward fearsome **Cataract Canyon**. Various short walks head off the road at selected viewpoints; one of the best is **Pothole Point**, a mile before **Big Spring Canyon**. A longer day-trip, or a good overnight hike, leaves from near the *Squaw Flat* **campground** ($10) to the green meadow of **Chesler Park**, cutting through the narrow cleft of the Joint Trail. Check in at the **visitor center** (daily 8am–5pm; ☎435/259-4711) near the park boundary to get up-to-date information, as well as backcountry permits if you plan to camp out. The only way to **reach the river** from within the park is by taking the hot and dry trail down through Lower Red Canyon to **Spanish Bottom**; this is the start of the Cataract Canyon rapids, so don't try to swim across.

The 35-mile drive in to the Needles from US-191 is among the prettiest in the state, winding along Indian Creek through deep red-rock canyons lined by pines and cottonwoods. **NEWSPAPER ROCK**, twelve miles in, is the best of many similarly named sites; here hundreds of tiny **petroglyphs**, many of which show deer, antelope, bear claws and helmeted human figures, have been etched in the jet-black desert varnish of a red-sandstone boulder by centuries of passing hunters and travelers. There's a lovely (free) streamside **campground** just across the road.

The Maze and Horseshoe Canyon

Only about one in a hundred of the half-million visitors who come to Canyonlands every year makes it into the harsh backcountry of the remote **MAZE** district. Filling up the western third of the park, on the far side of the Colorado and Green rivers, the Maze is noted for its ancient rock-art panels and for its many-fingered box canyons, accessible only by jeep or by long, dry hiking trails. If you're tempted, call into the Hans Flat **ranger station**, 46 miles east of Hwy-24 (daily 8am–5pm; ☎ 435/259-2652).

Pretty, tree-lined **HORSESHOE CANYON**, reached halfway down a long, long dirt road that loops south from Green River itself to join Hwy-24 just south of Goblin Valley (see p.1010), contains the greatest concentration of **ancient rock art** in the Southwest. Allowing at least an hour's driving from the highway both before and after, plus five hours for the six-mile round-trip hike down into the canyon itself, you'll need a full day to spare, but it's well worth the effort, both for the joy of the walk and for the sight of the "**Great Gallery**" at the far end. Hundreds of mysterious, haunting pictographs – mostly life-sized human figures, albeit weirdly elongated, or draped in robes and adorned with strange, staring eyes – were painted onto these red-sandstone walls, probably between 500 BC and 500 AD. Rangers from Hans Flat (see above) lead guided hikes into Horseshoe Canyon on summer weekends (April–Oct Sat & Sun 9am).

Arches National Park

The writer Edward Abbey, who spent a year as a ranger at **ARCHES NATIONAL PARK** in the 1950s, wrote in *Desert Solitaire* that its arid landscape was as "naked, monolithic, austere and unadorned as the sculpture of the moon." It certainly is one of the least terrestrial places on this planet. Massive fins of red and golden sandstone stand to attention out of the bare desert plain, and over 1800 natural arches of various shapes and sizes have been cut into the rock by eons of erosive weathering. Apart from the single ribbon of black asphalt that snakes through the park, there's nothing even vaguely human about it. The narrow, hunching ridges are more like dinosaurs' backbones than solid rock, and under a full moon, at twilight, or watching the lightning strikes of a distant thunderstorm, you can't help but imagine that the landscape has a life of its own.

While you could race through in a couple of hours, to do Arches justice you should plan to spend a whole day here at the very least. A twenty-mile road cuts uphill sharply from US-191 and the park **visitor center** (daily: mid-April to Sept 7.30am–6.30pm; Oct to mid-April 8am–4.30pm; $10 per vehicle, or $25 for pass also covering Canyonlands, Hovenweep & Natural Bridges; ☎ 435/719-2299, ⊛ www.nps.gov/arch), where exhibits explain the fairly simple process by which the arches are formed and point out some of the more photogenic examples. The first possible stop is the south trailhead for **Park Avenue**, an easy trail leading one mile down a scoured, rock-bottomed wash. If you stay on the road, the **La Sal Mountains Viewpoint** provides a grandstand look at the distant peaks rising over 12,000ft above the surrounding desert, as well as the huge red chunk of **Courthouse Towers** closer at hand. Beyond the Towers, the road follows the foot of the salmon-hued sandstone of the **Great Wall**.

From **Balanced Rock** – a 50ft boulder atop a slender 75ft pedestal – a turning to the right winds for two miles through the **Windows** section, where a half-mile trail loops through a dense concentration of massive arches, some

ARCHES NATIONAL PARK

N

DEVILS
GARDEN

KLONDIKE
BLUFFS

Dark Angel

Double O Arch

Landscape
Arch

Devils Garden
Trailhead

Salt Valley

Broken Arch

Sand Dune Arch

FIERY
FURNACE

Delicate
Arch

Fiery Furnace Viewpoint

Salt Valley Overlook

Wolfe Ranch

Delicate
Arch
Viewpoint

Panorama
Point

Cove of Caves
Double Arch

Balanced
Rock

North Window

Turret Arch

South Window

THE WINDOWS
SECTION

Petrified Dunes
Viewpoint

Courthouse Towers
Viewpoint

COURTHOUSE
TOWERS

La Sal Mountains
Viewpoint

PARK
AVENUE

Park
Headquarters

Colorado River

Jackson Canyon

Negro Bill Canyon

Moab

4WD vehicles only

0   2 miles

POTASH ROAD

Dead Horse Point and Island in the Sky

over 100ft high and 150ft across. A second trail, fifty yards beyond, leads to **Double Arch**, a staunch pair of arches that together support another arch overhead.

Beyond Balanced Rock, the main road drops downhill for two miles past Panorama Point and the turnoff to **Wolfe Ranch**, where a century-old log cabin now serves as the trailhead for the exposed three-mile round-trip hike up to **Delicate Arch**, which, as a freestanding crescent of rock perched at the brink of a deep canyon, is by far the most impressive arch in the park. Three miles beyond the Wolfe Ranch turnoff, the deep, sharp-sided mini-canyons of the **Fiery Furnace** section form a (usually quite cool) labyrinth through which rangers lead regular hikes in spring, summer and fall ($6; reserve in advance at the visitor center).

The road continues on to the **Devil's Garden** trailhead, from which an easy one-mile walk leads to a view of the astonishing 306ft span of **Landscape Arch**, now too perilously slender to approach more closely. Several other arches lie along short spur trails off the main route; seeing them all, and returning from **Double O Arch** via the longer primitive trail, requires a total hike of just over seven miles. Arches' only **campground** ($10; water only available mid-March to Oct) is across from the trailhead; all its first-come, first-served sites tend to be occupied by early morning in season. Permits for **backcountry camping**, allowed anywhere that's a mile from the road and half a mile from any trail, are issued at the visitor center.

Moab

Founded in the late 1800s, **MOAB** was hardly a speck until the 1950s, when prospector Charlie Steen discovered uranium in the nearby hills. When the ensuing mining boom finally waned, the conservative hold of Moab's industrialists and landowners waned with it, and the town threw in its lot with tourism. In barely ten years, it has transformed itself into the Southwest's number one adventure-vacation destination.

Moab still isn't a large town – the population has yet to reach ten thousand – and neither is it an attractive one. The setting is what matters. With two national parks on its doorstep, plus millions more acres of public land, Moab is an ideal base for outdoors enthusiasts. At first, it was a mecca for **mountain bikers**, lured by the legendary **Slickrock Bike Trail**. Then the **jeep** drivers began to turn up, and the **whitewater rafting** companies moved in. These days it's almost literally bursting, all year, with legions of Lycra-clad vacationers from all over the world.

Perhaps the main reason Moab has grown so fast is that out-of-state visitors tend to find Utah's other rural communities so irredeemably boring. As soon as Moab emerged from the pack, it became a beacon in the desert, attracting tourists ecstatic to find a town that stayed up after dark. Moab amounts to little more than a few miles of motels, restaurants and bars, but that's enough to make it the only southern-Utah town where you can stay for a week and still feel that you haven't seen everything, and everyone, a dozen times. The only sight-seeing to speak of is provided by the **Moab Skyway**, an incongruous new chairlift that climbs a thousand feet above town to the northern tip of the Moab Rim, for superb views across the Colorado to Arches and beyond (daily 9am–9pm; $8).

Arrival and information

Moab's superb **visitor center**, in the heart of town at Center and Main (summer daily 8am–9pm; rest of year daily 8am–5pm; ☎435/259-8825 or 1-800/635-6622, ⓦwww.discovermoab.com), carries stacks of information on Moab itself, plus brochures and maps for the nearby parks and public lands. ARK Bighorn Express (☎801/328-9920 or 1-888/655-7433, ⓦwww.goark.com) run daily shuttle **buses** between Salt Lake City and Moab, continuing on to Blanding, while the nearest Amtrak station is at Green River.

Accommodation

If you've already been in Utah for a while when you reach Moab, its glittering neon **motel** signs will come as a big surprise. At last count, there were 28 motels and a dozen B&Bs in town, but every one of the thousand-plus rooms

Adventure travel outfitters in southeast Utah

Moab is the main center for companies running **adventure trips** through the back-country and along the raging waters of southwest Utah. Varying from half-day jaunts to week-long expeditions, such trips not only get you to places you'd never otherwise reach, but also provide a sense of the region's natural splendor that can't be had from a car or on foot.

River trips
Among Moab's dozen licensed operators offering motorized one-day trips along the Colorado River for around $45 and up are: Western River Expeditions (☎801/942-6669 or 1-800/453-7450, ⊛www.westernriver.com), Adrift Adventures (☎435/259-8594 or 1-800/874-4483, ⊛www.adrift.net) and Tag-a-Long Expeditions (☎435/259-8946 or 1-800/453-3292, ⊛www.tagalong.com). The short trips start northwest of Moab, near the butte known as Fisher Towers, and arrive near town in the afternoon; many companies give passengers the chance to float quieter stretches in two-person kayaks. **Oar-powered** trips are slower but much quieter, and less expensive than motorboat trips. Longer (2- to 7-day) trips head through Cataract Canyon and other wild Canyonlands spots.

Mountain biking
While the Moab area is ideally suited to mountain-bike touring, only experienced riders should attempt its most challenging route, the famous **Slickrock Bike Trail**. This ten-mile, half-day loop starts atop the mesa about three miles east of Moab, threading its way among the sandstone knobs with views of the La Sal Mountains and the Colorado River; wear a **helmet**, take lots of **water**, and keep an eye and an ear out for motorcyclists, who are also allowed on the trail. A more relaxing alternative is to explore the dirt roads leading through the red-rock country of Kane Creek, west of town.

Bike shops offering daily rental and guided tours include Rim Tours, 1233 S Hwy-191 (☎435/259-5223 or 1-800/626-7335, ⊛www.rimtours.com), Kaibab & Moab Cyclery, 391 S Main St (☎435/259-7423 or 1-800/451-1133, ⊛www.kaibabtours.com), and Poison Spider, 497 N Main St (☎435/259-7882 or 1-800/635-1792, ⊛www.poisonspiderbicycles.com).

Jeep tours
Most of the thousands of miles of **jeep trails** around Moab were built years ago by miners and haven't been maintained since. The visitor center has a free map and guide to some of the more popular ones, and you can rent a 4WD jeep or pickup truck for around $100 per day from Slickrock 4x4 Rentals at 284 N Main St (☎435/259-5678 or 1-888/238-5337). **Guided jeep tours** ($60–80 per person per day) are offered by Lin Ottinger Tours (☎435/259-7312) and Tag-a-Long Expeditions (see above).

Scenic Flights
From a small airfield twenty miles north of Moab on US-91, Redtail Aviation (☎435/259-7421 or 1-800/842-9251, ⊛www.moab-utah.com/redtail) runs unforgettable **flights** over the Canyonlands area and beyond: a perfect opportunity to appreciate the labyrinthine complexity of the Maze, to see the confluence of the two great rivers, and even to pick out inaccessible Ancestral Puebloan ruins – and well worth the $80 per-person rate for a one-hour reconnaissance.

is taken on many nights between mid–March and October – when you'd be lucky to find anything below $60 – so reservations are strongly recommended. Agencies such as Moab/Canyonlands Central Reservations (☎435/259-5125 or 1-800/505-5343) can help.

Commercial **campgrounds** nearby include the well-shaded *Slickrock Campground*, 1301 N Hwy-191 (☎435/259-7660 or 1-800/448-8873,

@ www.slickrockcampground.com; $15), a mile north of town; if you're happy to put up with far more primitive facilities to escape the crowds, head instead for the BLM's **Sand Flats Recreation Area**, along the top of the mesa to the east of town, near the Slickrock Bike Trail, at 1924 S Roadrunner Hill (T 435/259-2100; $8).

Aarchway Inn 1551 N Hwy-191 T 435/259-2599 or 1-800/341-9359, @www.moab-utah.com /aarchway/inn.html. New, well-equipped motel with a nice pool, not far from the Colorado at the north end of town. ❹

Gonzo Inn 100 W 200 South T 435/259-2515 or 1-800/791-4044, @www.gonzoinn.com. Luxurious if rather self-consciously "hip" inn, complete with kitsch retro furnishings, quirky artworks, and in-house espresso bar. ❺

Inca Inn Motel 570 N Main St T 435/259-7261, @www.moab-utah.com/inca/inn.html. Clean, minimally equipped but adequate budget motel. ❷

Lazy Lizard International Hostel 1213 S Hwy-

191 T 435/259-6057. Amiable, appealing and laid-back independent hostel, well south of the center, with $8 beds in six-person dorms, $6 camping and private cabins for $22, plus hot tub, kitchen and internet access.

Moab Valley Inn 711 S Main St T 435/259-4419 or 1-800/831-6622, @www.moabvalleyinn.com. Modern, large and well-equipped motel at the south end of town, with pool, hot tub, and on-site car and 4WD rental. ❸

Sleep Inn 1051 S Main St T 435/259-4655 or 1-800/753-3746. Comfortable chain motel, whose location a mile south of downtown means it offers highly competitive rates. ❸

Eating and drinking

Moab offers by far the greatest range of **restaurants** in southern Utah, and for once most places make the effort to cater for vegetarians. With two pubs and a winery, there's also no problem getting a **drink**, while **coffee bars** are springing up everywhere. Note that many local restaurants, tired of low-tipping foreign customers, have taken to including a fifteen percent service charge on all checks.

Buck's Grill House 1393 N Hwy-191 T 435/259-5201. Belying its stockade-like exterior, this "American Western Food" joint is actually a sophisticated affair, serving rich, classy Southwestern food, such as game hen or pork ribs, at very reasonable prices. Open for dinner nightly.

Center Café 60 North 100 West T 435/259-4295. Expensive but exquisite restaurant, offering gourmet dining with a Pacific twist. Entrees, at around $20, range from Asian barbecue salmon to rack of lamb. Open for dinner nightly; closed Dec–Feb.

Eddie McStiff's 57 S Main St T 435/259-2337. Central pub, next to the visitor center, which serves some interesting beers, including raspberry and blueberry varieties, and also a varied and inexpensive menu of salads, pizzas and pastas.

Mondo Café 59 S Main St T 435/259-5911. Groovy all-day hangout next to *Eddie McStiff's*, serving espresso coffees and the odd pastry or sandwich.

Jailhouse Café 101 N Main St T 435/259-3900. Very popular central café, open for breakfast only, until noon on weekdays and 1pm at weekends. There's indoor and outdoor seating year-round, and great specials like ginger pancakes and eggs Benedict.

Sunset Grill 900 N Hwy-191 T 435/259-7146. Charlie Steen's luxury hilltop home is now a fine restaurant, with meat and seafood entrees for $13–20, great desserts and stunning views. The tortuous if short approach road from the north end of town means it's no place to drink and drive.

Natural Bridges National Monument

One of the prettiest and least-traveled highways in southern Utah, **Hwy–95** runs for over a hundred miles southeast from Capitol Reef, through dozens of red-rock canyons and across the Dirt Devil and Colorado rivers, before topping out on the sagebrush plains of San Juan County. En route it gives access to the marvellous collection of sandstone spans at **NATURAL BRIDGES NATIONAL MONUMENT**, forty miles west of US-191. Three canyons come together here, and at each junction the streams that carved them have also formed sandstone bridges. The largest, **Sipapu Bridge**, is 268ft across at its base and over 200ft high, and can be seen from the nine-mile paved road that loops through the monument; hike less than a mile down into the canyon for a closer look. **Kachina Bridge**, the next along the road, is nearly as high but twice as thick, and has Ancestral Puebloan pictographs at its base. The oldest, slimmest and most fragile bridge – **Owachomo**, a mile and a half up Armstrong Canyon – spans 180ft but is only nine feet thick at its thinnest point. A strenuous eight-mile trail along the canyon bottom leads past all three bridges.

Admission to the monument is $6 per vehicle. The **visitor center** (summer daily 8am–6pm; rest of year daily 8am–4.30pm; ☎435/692-1234, ⓦwww.nps.gov/nabr), four miles off Hwy-95, has free trail guides and a slide show explaining how the bridges are formed, as well as a brief introduction to the Ancestral Puebloan sites. Camping is allowed only in the small **campground** ($10) near the visitor center, which also has the only drinkable water in the monument.

Monticello

The small town of **MONTICELLO** stands 56 miles south of Moab on US-191, sixteen miles beyond the turnoff for the Needles section of Canyonlands (see p.1012). Its strip of budget **motels** includes *Canyonlands Motor Inn*, 197 N Main St (☎435/587-2266 or 1-800/952-6212; ❷), and a *Super 8*, 649 N Main St (☎435/587-2489; ❸). Good, large, standard **meals** can be had at the *MD Ranch Cookhouse*, 380 S Main St (☎435/587-3299). Information on the town, and on the parks and public lands in the vicinity, can be picked up from the **visitor center**, in the courthouse at 117 S Main St (April–Oct Mon–Fri 8am–5pm, Sat & Sun 10am–5pm; Nov–March Mon–Fri 8am–5pm; ☎435/587-3235 or 1-800/574-4386, ⓦwww.southeastutah.com).

The San Juan River, Mexican Hat and Bluff

From Natural Bridges and the Grand Gulch area, Hwy-261 runs south for some 25 miles before coming to what looks like a dead end at the edge of Cedar Mesa. From here, high above the eerie sandstone towers of the **Valley of the Gods** (where much of *Thelma and Louise* was filmed), the road turns to gravel before dropping over a thousand feet in little over two twisting, hairpin-turning miles down the "**Moki Dugway**." Six miles from the foot of the switchbacks, the barely marked Hwy-316 shoots across what seems like a flat valley floor to yet another overlook, this time high above the **SAN JUAN RIVER** at the extraordinary and aptly named **Goosenecks State Reserve** (open 24hr; free). A textbook example of what geologists call an entrenched meander, the river, a thousand feet below, snakes around in such convoluted twists and turns that it flows six miles in total for every one mile west.

Back on Hwy-261 and just south, sleepy **MEXICAN HAT**, briefly a frenzied gold-mining camp, takes its name from a riverside **sandstone hoodoo**, just north of town, that looks more than a little like a south-of-the-border sombrero. More of a cluster of buildings on the banks of the river than a town, it's good fun and makes a good base for visiting Monument Valley, twenty miles south (see p.993). The best **place to stay** is the *San Juan Inn* (☎435/683-2220 or 1-800/447-2022; ❸), right on the river, which has its own grocery store and trading post, where the amiable *Olde Bridge Bar and Grill* offers cold beers and Navajo tacos. Just up the road, *Mexican Hat Lodge* (☎435/683-2222; ❸) has an atmospheric steakhouse.

The rafts you may see emerging from the water at Mexican Hat went in at **BLUFF**, twenty miles upstream. US-163, the road between, doesn't follow the river very closely but is still an enthralling drive, and when you get there the town itself has a number of **Mormon pioneer houses** along its backstreets. Places to **eat** in Bluff include the *Twin Rocks Café* (℡435/672-2341) and the *Cottonwood Steakhouse* (℡435/672-2282), while an excellent new motel at the south end of town, the *Desert Rose Inn*, 701 W Hwy-191 (℡435/672-2303 or 1-888/475-7673, Ⓦwww.desertroseinn.com; ❸), holds thirty attractively designed and well furnished rooms.

Hovenweep National Monument

Hidden in the no-man's-land that straddles the Utah–Colorado border, the remote **Ancestral Puebloan ruins** at **HOVENWEEP NATIONAL MONUMENT** – 25 miles east of US-191 along Hwy-262, which branches off halfway between Bluff and Blanding, and 35 miles west of Cortez, Colorado (see p.876) – offer a haunting sense of timeless isolation. Hovenweep preserves six distinct conglomerations of ruins, sprouting from the rims of shallow desert canyons and dwarfed by the distant mountains, but easy access is restricted to the **Square Tower Group**, behind the small **ranger station** (daily 8am–5pm; entrance fee $6; ℡435/719-2100, Ⓦwww.nps.gov/hove). The half-mile **Tower Loop Trail**, offers good views of the largest ruins, including the grandly named **Hovenweep Castle**, constructed around 1200 AD.

No accommodation, gasoline or food is available at or anywhere near Hovenweep, but (funding permitting) the 31-site **campground** beside the ranger station remains open all year ($10; no reservations).

Lake Powell and Glen Canyon Dam

The mighty rivers and canyons of southern Utah come to an abrupt and ignoble end at the Arizona border, where the **Glen Canyon Dam** stops them dead in the stagnant waters of **LAKE POWELL**. Ironically, the lake is named for John Wesley Powell, the first white man to explore the canyonlands in depth, and the first of any color to run the Colorado River through the Grand Canyon. The roaring torrents with which he battled are now lost beneath these placid blue waters, and the blocked-up Colorado, Green, Dirty Devil, San Juan and Escalante rivers are now a playground for houseboaters and waterskiers. The construction of the dam in the early 1960s outraged **environmentalists** (Edward Abbey's *Monkey Wrench Gang* made their first big splash here, sabotaging bulldozers and simulating huge cracks in the dam at the opening ceremonies) and **anthropologists** (innumerable Ancestral Puebloan pictographs are submerged hundreds of feet below the surface). It has created one of the most peculiar – and utterly unnatural – landscapes imaginable, the deep and tranquil lake a surreal contrast with the surrounding dry slickrock and sandstone buttes.

Lake Powell has 1960 miles of shoreline, which is more than the entire Pacific coast of the US, and 96 water-filled side canyons. The water level fluctuates considerably, so for much of the time the rocks to all sides are bleached for many feet above the current waterline, with a dirty-bath tidemark sullying the golden sandstone. Most of the many summer visitors bring their own boats, or rent a vessel from one of the four marinas that fringe the lake.

If you're passing through, by far the most accessible stop is **WAHWEAP MARINA**, just off US-89 on the way between Zion and the Grand Canyon, where *Wahweap Lodge* (℡602/278-8888 or 1-800/528-6154, Ⓦwww .visitlakepowell.com; ❻) has comfortable lakeside rooms and some of the best

Rainbow Bridge National Monument

The spectacular and extremely remote **Rainbow Bridge National Monument**, the world's largest natural bridge, can be visited on **guided boat tours** from Wahweap ($89 full-day, $69 half-day), Bullfrog ($83 full-day only) and Hall's Crossing ($89 full-day only). It lies roughly fifty miles by water from either direction, including a final mile or two down the narrow, winding side channel of Forbidding Canyon. From the unappealing jetty where the boats moor, bobbing in a morass of pond scum, a ten-minute walk leads to the astonishing giant sandstone gateway, springing up nearly 300ft from just above the waterline, with Navajo Mountain visible through its magnificent smooth curve. Its upper section is composed of Navajo sandstone, while the base belongs to the harder Kayenta formation, not as easily cut by flowing water; despite the increase in tourism since the creation of the lake, it remains an inspiring sight, and a place of special importance to the Navajo.

food within a day's drive. The same company arranges **houseboat rental** from Wahweap or other Lake Powell marinas; boats sleep four or more people and cost from $675 for three nights in winter, $1200 in summer. There's **camping** on the shore of the lake at each of the marinas. The nearest **budget accommodation** is across the Arizona border in **PAGE**, home of the usual assortment of chain motels and diners, including the *Navajo Trail Motel*, 800 Bureau St (☎928/645-9508; ❸).

GLEN CANYON DAM itself, in between Page and Wahweap, can be seen on half-hour self-guided tours that start from the **visitor center** (May–Sept daily 8am–7pm; Oct–April daily 8am–5pm; free) and climb down to the huge 1.1 million kilowatt hydroelectric turbines.

The cheapest way to get out on the waters of Lake Powell is to take the **ferry** ($9 per car) between **Halls Crossing** and **Bullfrog** marinas, two-thirds of the way up the lake; from here the Burr Trail heads west toward Capitol Reef (see p.1009), while Hwy-276 runs northeast to Natural Bridges.

Northern Utah

Compared to the scenic splendor of the southern half of the state, northern Utah holds little to interest the tourist, although **Salt Lake City**, the capital, is by far the state's largest and most cosmopolitan urban center. The dramatic Wasatch Mountains that line Salt Lake's eastern horizon do however come into their own in winter, as they constitute one of the nation's premier **ski destinations**. The **northeast corner** has coal mines, old railroad towns and, along the Wyoming border, the **Uinta Mountains**, uncrossed by road and showing hardly a sign of civilization. From the **northwest**, the harshly alkaline **Great Basin** plain stretches uneventfully west across Nevada to California.

Salt Lake City

Disarmingly pleasant and easygoing, **SALT LAKE CITY** is well worth a stopover of a couple of days. It's not a particularly thrilling destination in itself, but its setting is superb, towered over by the **Wasatch Front**, which marks the dividing line between the comparatively lush eastern and the bone-dry western halves of northern Utah, and which offers great hiking or cycling in summer and fall and, in winter, some of the world's best skiing. Salt Lake City's bid to raise its international profile by hosting the **2002 Winter Olympics** resulted in a major building program both in the city itself and in the surrounding ski valleys, plus an unwelcome notoriety following the taint of corruption that surrounded its selection. Nonetheless, though people elsewhere in the US still tend to imagine Salt Lake City as decidedly short on spontaneous public fun, so long as you're willing to switch gears and slow down, its unhurried pace, and the positive energy and lack of pretence of its people, can make for a surprisingly enjoyable experience.

Arrival, information and getting around

Salt Lake City International Airport (☎801/575-2400) is a mere four miles west of downtown. A **cab** into town costs around $15; cheaper **shuttle vans** to downtown destinations are run by Xpress Shuttles (☎801/596-1600 or 1-800/397-0773; reserve 24hrs in advance), while Canyon Transportation (☎801/255-1841) serves the ski areas. Long-distance Greyhound-Trailways **buses**, 160 W South Temple Blvd (☎801/355-9579), and Amtrak **trains**, 320 S Rio Grande Ave, arrive downtown. Local buses, and also TRAX trams, are

SALT LAKE CITY

ACCOMMODATION
Marriott Downtown 2
Monaco 3
Motel 6 5
Peery 4
Travelodge-Temple Square 1

RESTAURANTS & CAFÉS
Lamb's Restaurant B
Market Square Grill F
Martine's A
Oasis Café C
Orbit Café D
Rio Grande Café E

operated by the Utah Transit Authority (℡801/743-3882); journeys within the immediate downtown area are free.

Gray Line (℡801/521-7060) offers **bus tours** ranging from city jaunts to multiday trips to the national parks. To reach the best parts of the surrounding mountains, however, you'll need a **car** – all the rental companies are represented at the airport – or a cycle and strong legs. **Bikes** can be rented from Utah Ski Rental, 134 W 100 South St (℡801/355-9088).

Visitor centers supplying information on the city itself can be found downtown at 90 S West Temple Blvd in the Salt Palace Convention Center (Mon–Fri 8.30am–5pm, Sat & Sun 9am–5pm; ℡801/521-2822, ⓦwww.saltlake.org), or in Terminal 2 of the airport (daily except Sat 9am–9pm). For details on the rest of Utah, stop by the Utah Travel Council, which occupies the imposing Council Hall across from the capitol at 300 N State St (Mon–Fri 9am–6pm; ℡801/538-1030). The downtown **post office** is at 230 W 200 South St (Mon–Fri 8am–5.30pm, Sat 8am–1.30pm; ℡801/978-3001; zip code 84101).

Accommodation

Salt Lake City is well equipped with **accommodation**, with downtown options that range from budget motels and B&B inns to rather more luxurious hotels, and the usual mid-range places near the airport and along the interstates. There's so much capacity for business travelers that weekend rates can be real bargains.

Brigham Street Inn 1135 E South Temple Blvd ℡801/364-4461 or 1-800/417-4461, ⓦwww.brighamstreetinn.citysearch.com. Luxurious, peaceful – and inconspicuous – B&B a few blocks east of downtown toward the mountains. ❺

Holiday Inn Airport 1659 W North Temple Blvd ℡801/533-9000 or 1-800/HOLIDAY, ⓦwww.bristolhotels.com. Well-equipped, well-priced hotel, served by free airport shuttles and not too far from downtown. ❸

Hotel Monaco 15 W 200 South ℡801/595-0000 or 1-877/294-9710, ⓦwww.monacosaltlakecity.com. Extremely hip, very upscale downtown hotel, housed in a former bank. ❺

Motel 6 176 W 600 South St ℡801/531-1252. Budget downtown motel, handy for Amtrak. ❷

Peery Hotel 110 W 300 South St ℡801/521-4300 or 1-800/331-0073, ⓦwww.peeryhotel.com. 1910 downtown landmark, entirely renovated in 1999, offering very tasteful, comfortable rooms. ❺

Salt Lake City Marriott Downtown 75 S West Temple Blvd ℡801/531-0800. Very central, characterful and attractively furnished hotel, facing the visitor center and equipped with a good pool. ❻

Travelodge – Temple Square 144 W North Temple Blvd ℡801/533-8200. Most central and least expensive of three local *Travelodges*. ❸

Ute Hostel, 21 E Kelsey Ave ℡801/595-1645, ⓦwww.infobytes.com/utehostel. Much the better of Salt Lake City's two hostels, this small private establishment, a few miles south of downtown, offers $15 dorm beds and a couple of private rooms, plus bike rental, a hot tub and free airport pickup.

Temple Square

The geographical – and spiritual – heart of Salt Lake City is **Temple Square**, the world headquarters of the **Mormon Church** (or the Church of Jesus Christ of Latterday Saints – LDS). Its focus, the monumental **Temple** itself, was completed in 1893 after forty years of intensive labor. The multispired granite edifice rises to 210ft above the city – it's not the tallest building on the mainly flat skyline but, thanks to its crisply angular silhouette, it's just about the only interesting one. Only confirmed Mormons may enter the Temple, and even they do so only for the most sacred LDS rituals – marriage, baptisms and "sealing," the joining of a family unit for eternity.

Wander through the gates of Temple Square, however, and you'll swiftly be snapped up by one of the many waiting Mormons, and shepherded to join a free 45-minute **tour** of the various sites within. As well as monuments to Mormon pioneers, you'll be ushered into the odd oblong shell of the **Mormon Tabernacle**. No images of any kind adorn its interior, which is home to the world-renowned Mormon Tabernacle Choir; a helper at the lectern laconically displays its remarkable acoustic properties by tearing up a newspaper and dropping a nail. There's free admission to the choir's 9.30am Sunday broadcast, and its rehearsals on Thursday evenings at 8pm.

The primary aim of the tours is to awaken your interest in the Mormon faith; differences from Christianity are played down in favor of a soft-focus video of Old Testament scenes. The tour ends in the northern of the Square's two **visitor centers**, where an array of touch-screen computers provide woolly answers to questions like "What is the purpose of life?" and "Who was Joseph Smith?" In the southern visitor center, a surprisingly good free movie tells the story of the arrival of Salt Lake City's first Mormon settlers.

Downtown Salt Lake City

A block east of Temple Square along South Temple Boulevard, the **Beehive House** (Mon–Sat 9.30am–4.30pm, Sun 10am–1pm; free) is a plain white New England-style house, with wraparound verandas and green shutters. Erected in 1854 by church leader **Brigham Young**, it's now a small museum of Young's life, restored to the style of the period. Free twenty-minute tours, which you have to join to see much of the house, are given at least every half-hour.

The **Family History Library**, across West Temple Boulevard from Temple Square (Mon 7.30am–6pm, Tues–Sat 7.30am–10pm; free; ⓦ www.family-search.org), is intended to enable Mormons to trace their ancestors, and then baptize them into the faith by proxy, but it's open to everyone. The world's most exhaustive genealogical library is surprisingly user-friendly, giving immediate access, through CD-ROMs and banks of computers, to birth and death records from over sixty countries, some dating back as much as five hundred years. All you need is a person's place of birth, a few approximate dates, and you're away; volunteers provide help if you need it, but leave you alone until you ask. Next door to the library, the **Museum of Church History and Art** (Mon–Fri 9am–9pm, Sat & Sun 10am–7pm; free) charts the rise of the Mormon faith in art and artifact.

The area southwest of Temple Square, now the site of the massive Salt Palace convention center and sports arena (home of the Utah Jazz basketball team), has undergone a rapid transformation. The surrounding district of brick warehouses around the Union Pacific railroad tracks is quickly filling up with designer shops and art galleries, signs that even Mormons can be yuppies.

Capitol Hill

Quite why the Mormons chose not to put their Temple on the gentle hill that stands above today's Temple Square is anyone's guess. As a result, when Utah was granted statehood in 1896, it was free to become the site of the imposing, domed **Utah State Capitol** (summer Mon–Sat 6am–8pm; rest of year Mon–Sat 6am–6pm; free). Along with the plaques and monuments you might expect, the corridors of power are packed full of earnest and rather diverting exhibits of great Utah moments.

Now called **Capitol Hill**, the neighborhood around the capitol holds some of Salt Lake City's grandest c.1900 homes, with dozens of ornate Victorian houses lining Main Street and Quince Street to the northwest; **walking tour maps** of the district are available from the Utah Heritage Foundation, 355 Quince St.

Eating

Though Salt Lake City has a perfectly good selection of **restaurants**, it lacks an atmospheric – let alone hip – dining district. If you like to compare menus, the only downtown area with much potential is the block or two to either side of West Temple Street, south and east of the Salt Palace.

Bambara *Hotel Monaco*, 15 W 200 South ☎801/363-5454. Chic, post-Deco and pricey downtown restaurant, with a fabulous menu ranging from buffalo carpaccio or crab cakes to lamb sirloin on du Puy lentils.

Lamb's Restaurant 169 S Main St ☎801/364-7166. Great breakfasts, best eaten at the long shiny counter, and excellent-value set meals throughout the day. Closed Sun.

Market Street Grill 48 Market St ☎801/322-4668. As close as Salt Lake City comes to a New York City bar and grill. Fresh seafood, especially oysters, plus steaks in all shapes and sizes. $8 lunch specials, full dinners $15–30.

Martine's 22 E 100 South ☎801/363-9328. Formal, dimly-lit but high-class Southwestern restaurant, in central location facing the ZCMI mall; most menu items can be served as "tapa" (appetizer) or entree. Closed Sun.

Oasis Café 151 S 500 East ☎801/322-0404.

Classy but inexpensive café, serving very good food (dinner entrees $13–20) with plenty of appealing vegetarian options. Live acoustic music or jazz in the evening.

Orbit Café 540 W 200 South ☎801/322-2808. Large, (post)modern diner, which serves tasty sandwiches and ethnic specials for lunch, and then fancier late-night meals (until 4am Fri & Sat).

Rio Grande Café 270 S Rio Grande ☎801/364-3302. Spirited and stylish Mexican cantina in the old Denver and Rio Grande railroad station, still used by Amtrak, three blocks west of downtown.

Ruth's Diner 2100 Emigration Canyon Rd ☎801/582-5807. Good-value indoor and patio dining, often accompanied by live music, set in and around old railroad carriages in a narrow canyon just three miles east of town. Wide selection of fresh dishes, great salads and Utah's best breakfasts. For more sophisticated and expensive fare, *Ruth's* sister restaurant, the *Santa Fe*, is next door.

Drinking and nightlife

Salt Lake City doesn't roll up the sidewalks when the sun goes down. Many **drinking** venues are technically private clubs, in which a nominal membership fee entitles the cardholder and up to five guests to two weeks' use of the facilities, but there are also a handful of **brewpubs**, for which membership is not required. To find out about the broad range of **fringe** art, music and clubland happenings, pick up free papers such as *City Weekly* or the monthly *Catalyst*, or tune to radio station KRCL 91FM.

Dead Goat Saloon 165 S West Temple Blvd ☎801/328-4628. Raucous, semi-subterranean saloon, with live loud music most nights.

Squatters Pub 147 West Broadway ☎801/363-2739. Casual, friendly brewpub with a range of beers available until 1am every day, plus a simple menu.

Zephyr Club 301 S West Temple Blvd ☎801/355-2582. Salt Lake's premier live music venue, with semi-famous jazz, blues, country or rock names most nights. Upmarket clientele, elegant decor, cover $5–15.

Park City

Despite Brigham Young's strictures against prospecting for precious metals – he feared a Gentile "Gold Rush" – the first mining camp at **PARK CITY**, just thirty miles east of downtown Salt Lake City along I-80 through the mountains, was established in the late 1860s. In 1872 George Hearst laid the foundations of the Hearst media empire by paying $27,000 for a claim that became the Ontario Silver Mine, worth $50 million. These days, the **Park City Mountain Resort** (☎435/649-8111 or 1-800/222-7275, ☼www.parkcitymountain.com), and the nearby **The Canyons** (☎435/649-5400 or 1-888/226-9667, ☼www.thecanyons.com) and (skiers-only) **Deer Valley** (☎435/649-1000 or 1-800/424-3337, ☼www.deervalley.com) resorts constitute Utah's largest **ski area**, with the season usually running from mid-

November to mid-April. Daily lift passes for each resort cost around $60; equipment rental outlets include Park City Sport (☎1-800/523-3922) and Gart Brothers (☎1-800/284-4754). In addition, Park City hosts the prestigious **Sundance Film Festival**, held over the second half of January each year.

Park City has for many years been engulfed by an ever-growing sprawl of new condos, factory outlets and other developments, and has become completely unrecognizable since being overhauled for the 2002 Winter Olympics. Its restored **Main Street** now makes only token gestures towards mimicking the mountain mining community it used to be, its shops and restaurants striving instead to emulate the chic resorts of Colorado.

Practicalities

Park City's **visitor center**, 528 Main St (May & Oct daily noon–5pm; rest of year Mon–Sat 10am–7pm, Sun noon–6pm; ☎435/649-6100 or 1-800/453-1360, ⓦwww.parkcityinfo.com), doubles as an enjoyable museum of town history, and stands above the town's original jailhouse. Lewis Bros Stages (☎435/649-2256 or 1-877/491-8111, ⓦwww.lewisbrothers.com) runs scheduled **shuttles** from downtown Salt Lake City ($25) and the airport (up to $50), and mountain **bikes** can be rented from White Pine Touring, 363 Main St (daily 10am–7pm; ☎801/649-8710).

Accommodation rates double in the ski season; the CVB can provide full listings of resorts and other lodgings. The *Old Miners' Lodge*, right next to the ski lift at 615 Woodside Ave (☎435/645-8068 or 1-800/648-8068; ❹), is an 1893 lodge restored as a comfortable B&B; the unassuming *Chateau Apres-Ski*, 1299 Norfolk Ave (☎435/649-9372 or 1-800/357-3556; ❶–❹), is a cheap, cozy alternative with some $28 dorm beds. *Morning Ray Café*, 268 Main St (☎435/649-5686), serves good breakfasts and has a wide-ranging lunch menu, while the dinner-only *Chimayo*, 368 Main St (☎435/649-6222), offers cutting-edge contemporary Southwestern cuisine. The *Wasatch Brew Pub*, nearby at 250 Main St (☎435/645-0900), is open until midnight daily.

Northeast Utah

Most of Utah's **northeastern corner** – due east of Salt Lake City, as Wyoming takes a bite out of its otherwise perfect rectangle – is taken up by the forbidding **Uinta Mountains**, very much of a piece with the rest of the Rockies. However, to the east of the mountains the terrain reverts to the classic Southwestern desert plains, with the small town of **Vernal** serving as the base for explorations of the wildernesses of **Flaming Gorge** and **Dinosaur**.

Dinosaur National Monument

DINOSAUR NATIONAL MONUMENT straddles the border between Utah and Colorado in a remote area only conceivably visitable in your own vehicle. Divided into two separate sections, it was created to preserve a rock stratum in its Utah half, seven miles north of Jensen on Hwy-149, east of Vernal, which has over the years provided brontosaurus skeletons and other astonishing remains to museums around the world. Uniquely, in the **Dinosaur Quarry** building, a tilted layer of sandstone has been painstakingly exposed to display an incredible three-dimensional jigsaw of fossilized dinosaur bones, left in situ for imaginative visitors to piece together.

The other half of the monument is a 25-mile drive north of the flyblown and unattractive little town of Dinosaur, Colorado, the site of the main **visitor center** (summer daily 8am–7pm; winter daily 8am–4.30pm; $10 per vehicle; ☎435/789-2115, ⓦwww.nps.gov/dino). At the end of the road **Harpers**

Corner provides a phenomenal view of the goosenecks of the Green and Yampa rivers, approaching their confluence at imposing **Steamboat Rock**.

Flaming Gorge

It took a major controversy in the 1950s to spare the Green and Yampa confluence from submergence by a new dam. **FLAMING GORGE**, starting around 25 miles north of Vernal, was not so lucky; the damming of the Red Canyon of the Green River in 1964 has turned it into a National Recreation Area, another "splendid recreational playground" for water-sports enthusiasts, anglers and hikers.

Ambivalence about its creation can't obscure its continuing beauty, which can be appreciated from various points on the loop drive that circles the canyon, calling at Green River, Wyoming, at its northern end (see p.884). The **Gorge** itself is an incandescent wall of red rock named by John Wesley Powell and best seen from the **Antelope Flat** marina-cum-campground on the eastern side. **Red Canyon visitor center** (summer daily 9.30am–5pm) to the west is another good stop, with a dramatic overlook and the attractive nearby *Red Canyon Lodge*, a complex of new and restored cabins offering varying degrees of luxury (℡435/889-3759, ⓦwww.redcanyonlodge.com; ❷–❺). The actual dam is not all that exciting.

Vernal

Although **VERNAL**, thirty miles west of the Colorado border on US-40 as it heads to Salt Lake City, is the largest community in northeast Utah, and holds a mildly diverting dinosaur museum, for most visitors it's only significant as an overnight stop. Budget **motels** lining Main Street include the *Sage* at no. 54 W (℡435/789-1442 or 1-800/760-1442, ⓦwww.vernalmotels.com; ❷), which has its own adjacent **restaurant**, and the *Best Western Antlers Motel* at no. 423 W (℡435/789-1202; ❸).

Nevada

NEVADA is without doubt the most desolate state in the US, consisting largely of endless tracts of bleak, empty desert. Its flat sagebrush plains are cut intermittently by angular mountain ranges, and the lack of rainfall or fertile soil has ensured its maintenance as untouched wilderness. Apart from the huge acreages given over to mining and to grazing cattle and sheep, much of Nevada is under the control of the **military**, who use it to test aircraft and weapons systems, including Stealth fighters and atomic bombs. Dozens of intriguing small communities are scattered around the state, some showing signs of strong Basque influence. Many more are decrepit roadside ghost towns, often little more than a gas-station-cum-general-store, flanked by a saloon and perhaps a brothel – Nevada is the only US state not to have outlawed **prostitution**, though it is illegal in Las Vegas.

Though millions of people pass through on their way to and from California, there's only one real reason why anyone ever *visits* Nevada, and that is to

gamble: as soon as you cross the state border, you'll be attacked by a 24-hour onslaught of neon signs and gimmicky architecture, each advertising the best odds and biggest jackpots, nowhere more than in the surreal oasis of **Las Vegas**. Even the smaller and more down-to-earth settlements of **Reno** and state capital **Carson City** revolve around the casino trade. At least the casinos' energetic pursuit of passing trade keeps rooms and especially food inexpensive, so the towns make good places to break a long journey – and, with Nevada's relaxed marriage and divorce laws, make or break a relationship.

Getting around Nevada

As there's almost nothing in Nevada outside of Las Vegas and Reno, it's hardly surprising that getting around the state's vast empty spaces is nearly impossible without a car. Las Vegas is no longer served by Amtrak, but Reno still welcomes daily trains between San Francisco and Salt Lake City; both Las Vegas and Reno have **airports**.

Las Vegas

Shimmering from the desert haze of Nevada like a latter-day El Dorado, **LAS VEGAS** is the most dynamic, spectacular city on earth. At the start of the twentieth century, it didn't even exist; now it's home to over one million people, and boasts fourteen of the world's fifteen largest hotels, whose flamboyant, no-expense-spared **casinos** lure in over thirty million tourists each year. Las Vegas has been stockpiling superlatives since the 1950s, but never rests on its laurels for a moment. Long before they lose their sparkle, yesterday's showpieces are blasted into rubble, to make way for ever more extravagant replacements. A few years ago, when the fashion was for fantasy, Arthurian castles and Egyptian pyramids mushroomed along the legendary Strip; now Vegas demands nothing less than entire cities, and boasts pocket versions of New York, Paris, Monte Carlo and Venice.

While Las Vegas has certainly cleaned up its act since the early days of Mob domination, there's little truth in the notion that it's become a **family** destination. In fact, for kids, it's not a patch on Orlando. Several casinos have added theme parks or fun rides to fill those odd non-gambling moments, but only five percent of visitors bring children, and the crowds that cluster around the exploding volcanoes and pirate battles along the Strip remain almost exclusively adult. Neither is Vegas as consistently **cheap** as it used to be. It's still possible to find good, inexpensive rooms, and the all-you-can-eat buffets offer unbeatable value, but the casino owners have finally discovered that high-rollers happy to lose hundreds of dollars per night don't mind paying premium prices to eat at top-quality restaurants and stay in plush hotels.

Your first hours in Las Vegas are like entering another world, where the religion is luck, the language is money, and time is measured by revolutions of a roulette wheel. Once you're acclimatized, the whole spectacle can be absolutely exhilarating – assuming you haven't pinned your hopes, and your savings, on the pursuit of a fortune. Las Vegas is an unmissable destination, but one that palls for most visitors after a couple of (hectic) days. If you've come solely to gamble, there's not much to say beyond the fact that all the casinos are free, and open 24 hours per day, with acres of floor space packed with ways to lose money: million-dollar slots, video poker, blackjack, craps, roulette wheels and much, much more.

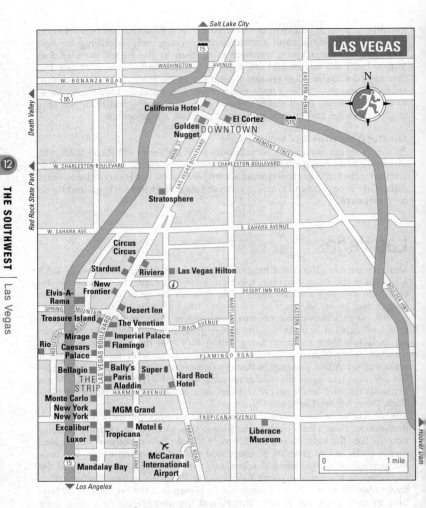

A history of Las Vegas

The name *Las Vegas* – Spanish for "the meadows" – was originally applied to a group of natural springs that from 1829 onwards served as a way-station for travelers on the Old Spanish Trail. In 1900, the valley had a population of just thirty people. Things changed in 1905, with the completion of the now-defunct rail link between Salt Lake City and Los Angeles.

Though Nevada was the first state to outlaw gambling, in 1909, it was made legal once more in 1931, and the workers who built the nearby **Hoover Dam** flocked to Vegas to bet away their pay-packets. Providing abundant cheap electricity and water, the dam amounted to a massive federal subsidy for the infant city. Hotel-casinos such as the daring 65-room *El Rancho* began to appear in the early 1940s, and mobster Bugsy Siegel raised $7 million to open the *Flamingo* on the Strip in December 1946.

By the 1950s, Las Vegas was booming. The military had arrived – mushroom clouds from **A-bomb tests** in the deserts were visible from the city, and visitors would drive out with picnics to get a better view – and so too had big guns like **Frank Sinatra**, who debuted at the *Desert Inn* in 1951, and **Liberace**, who received $50,000 to open the *Riviera* in 1955. As the stars gravitated towards the Vegas honeypot, nightclubs across America went out of business, and the city became the nation's undisputed live-entertainment capital.

The beginning of the end for Mob rule in Vegas came in 1966, after reclusive airline tycoon **Howard Hughes** sold TWA for $500 million and moved into the *Desert Inn*. When the owners tired of his non-gambling ways, he simply bought the hotel, and his clean-cut image encouraged other entrepreneurs to follow suit. **Elvis** arrived a little later; the young rock'n'roller had bombed at the *New Frontier* in 1956, but started a triumphant five-year stint as a karate-kicking lounge lizard at the *International* (now the *Las Vegas Hilton*) in 1969.

Endless federal swoops and stings drove the Mob out of sight by the 1980s, in time for Vegas to reinvent itself on a surge of junk-bond megadollars. The success of Steve Wynn's *Mirage* in enticing a new generation of visitors, from 1989 onwards, spawned a host of imitators. The 1990s kicked off with a spate of casino building, including *Excalibur* and the *MGM Grand*, that has barely let up since, with *Luxor* and *New York–New York* followed into the new millennium by the opulent quintet of *Bellagio*, *Mandalay Bay*, the *Venetian*, *Paris* and the revamped *Aladdin*. Beneath the glitz, however, **gambling** remains the bedrock, and Las Vegas' pre-eminence seems little dented by the spread of casinos elsewhere in the US. City boosters point out that only fifteen percent of Americans have so far seen Vegas, and they're confidently expecting the rest to turn up any day now.

Arrival, information and getting around

Las Vegas's busy **McCarran International Airport** is a mile east of the southern end of the Strip, and four miles from downtown (☏702/261-5211). Some hotels run free shuttle buses for guests, while Bell Trans (☏702/380-7060, ⓦ www.bell-trans.com) runs a **minibus** service to the Strip ($3.50) and downtown ($5); a **cab** to the Strip costs from $10 for the southern end up to $20 for casinos further north.

If you plan to see more of Vegas than the Strip, a **car** is invaluable. **Public transport** does exist, however. The oak-veneered streetcars of the **Las Vegas Strip Trolley** (☏702/382-1404) ply the Strip between *Mandalay Bay* and the *Stratosphere*, for a flat fare of $1.50, while the similar **Downtown Trolley** (☏702/229-6024) loops between the *Stratosphere* and downtown for 50¢. CAT buses (☏702/228-7433) serve the whole city; #301 and #302 connect the Strip to downtown ($1.50). Greyhound's long-distance buses use a terminal at 200 S Main St downtown. Several Strip casinos are also connected by free **monorail systems**, but these don't link up with each other, and most require you to walk through the full length of the casinos in order to use them. Amtrak trains no longer serve Las Vegas, but a new high-speed service between LA and Las Vegas is rumored to be coming soon.

Any number of local freesheets and magazines provide local information. There's also a **visitor center** at 3150 Paradise Rd (Mon–Fri 8am–6pm, Sat & Sun 8am–5pm; ☏702/892-7575 or 1-800/332-5333, ⓦ www.vegasfreedom.com), half a mile east of the Strip in the Convention. There can be no easier city in which to **change money**: the casinos gladly convert almost any currency, and their walls are festooned with every conceivable ATM machine.

Getting married in Las Vegas

Second only to making your fortune as a reason to visit Las Vegas is the prospect of **getting married**. Over a hundred thousand weddings are performed here each year, many so informal that bride and groom just wind down the window of their car during the ceremony, and a Vegas wedding has become a byword for tongue-in-cheek chic.

You don't have to be a local resident or take a blood test to get wed in Las Vegas. Assuming you're both at least eighteen years old and carrying picture ID, and neither of you is already married, simply turn up at the Clark County Marriage License Bureau, downtown at 200 S Third St (Mon–Thurs 8am–midnight, and continuously from 8am on Fri to midnight on Sun; ☎702/455-4415), and buy a marriage license for $35 cash.

Wedding chapels claim to charge as little as $50 for their most basic ceremonies, but at that sort of rate even the minister is regarded as an "extra" costing an additional $40. Reckon on paying at least $100 for the bare minimum, which is liable to be as romantic a process as checking in at a hotel, and to take about as long. The full deluxe service ranges up to around $500.

Candlelight Wedding Chapel, 2855 Las Vegas Blvd S; ☎702/735-4179 or 1-800/962-1818, ⍟www.candlelightchapel.com. Busy little chapel across from *Circus Circus*, where you get a carnation bouquet with the $179 wedding package, or a garter with the $499 option.

Graceland Wedding Chapel, 619 Las Vegas Blvd S; ☎702/382-0091 or 1-800/824-5732, ⍟www.gracelandchapel.com. Home of the King – if you take the $495 package, an Elvis impersonator will act as best man, give the bride away or serenade you, but unfortunately he can't perform the service.

Little Church of the West, 4617 Las Vegas Blvd S; ☎702/739-7971 or 1-800/821-2452, ⍟www.littlechurchlv.com. Once part of the *Last Frontier* casino, this fifty-year-old chapel is on the National Register of Historic Places, and has moved progressively down the Strip to its current site south of *Mandalay Bay*. Among the more peaceful and quiet places to exchange your Vegas vows – if that's really what you want.

Little White Chapel, 1301 Las Vegas Blvd S; ☎702/382-5943 or 1-800/545-8111, ⍟www.alittlewhitechapel.com. Where Bruce Willis and Demi Moore married each other, and Michael Jordan and Joan Collins married other people. Open all day every day, with the "The One & Only 24hour Drive-Up Wedding Window," if you're in a major hurry.

Accommodation

Although Las Vegas has well over 100,000 hotel rooms, it's best to book accommodation ahead if you're on a tight budget, or arriving on Friday or Saturday. Whatever you may have heard, Las Vegas hotels no longer offer incredibly cheap deals at the drop of a hat. It is true that serious gamblers can get their accommodation free, but to count as "serious" you'd have to commit yourself to gambling several thousand dollars, which is a strange definition of "free."

Precise **room rates** are dictated by supply and demand, and have been especially volatile since the September 11 attacks; the price codes listed opposite can only be taken as a broad guide. Even if you stay in the same room for several consecutive days, you'll be charged a different rate for each day, depending on the day of the week, and what's going on in town. The only sure-fire way to get a cut-price room is to **visit during the week**; rates everywhere rise enormously on Friday or Saturday. On top of that, many hotels won't accept Saturday arrivals.

Bellagio 3600 Las Vegas Blvd S ☏ 702/693-7111 or 1-888/987-6667, ⓦwww.bellagiolasvegas.com. Extremely luxurious rooms, with plush European furnishings and marble bathrooms; amazing pool complex; and the best restaurants in town. Sun–Thurs ❼, Fri & Sat ❾

Caesars Palace 3570 Las Vegas Blvd S ☏ 702/731-7110 or 1-800/634-6661, ⓦwww.caesars.com. Right in the heart of the Strip, the epitome of 1960s luxury continues to offer the last word in pseudo-Roman splendor, with top-class restaurants and shops. Sun–Thurs ❺, Fri & Sat ❻

California Hotel 12 Ogden Ave at 1st St ☏ 702/385-1222 or 1-800/634-6255, ⓦwww.the-cal.com. Almost all the guests in this mid-range downtown casino are Hawaiian, and Hawaiian food and drink dominate the bars and restaurants. The actual rooms are plain but adequate. ❸

Circus Circus 2880 Las Vegas Blvd S ☏ 702/734-0410 or 1-800/634-3450, ⓦwww.circuscircus-lasvegas.com. Venerable Strip hotel popular with budget tour groups. Kids love the theme park and (almost) nonstop circus acts, adults love the low room rates. ❸

El Cortez Hotel 600 E Fremont St ☏ 702/385-5200 or 1-800/634-6703, ⓦwww.elcortez.com. Veteran downtown casino, with adequate cut-price rooms in the main building, good-value mini-suites in the new tower, and bargain-basement accommodation in *Ogden House* across the street. ❶/❷

Imperial Palace 3535 Las Vegas Blvd S ☏ 702/731-3311 or 1-800/634-6441, ⓦwww.imperialpalace.com. Behind its hideous facade, one of the Strip's best-value options. Its standard rooms are adequate if not exciting – all have balconies – while the "luv tub" suites, at $30 extra, offer huge beds, even bigger sunken baths, and mirrors everywhere you can imagine. Sun–Thurs ❸, Fri & Sat ❺.

Las Vegas International Hostel 1208 Las Vegas Blvd S ☏ 702/385-9955, ⓦwww.lasvegashostel.com. Bare-bones AAIH hostel in a small former motel, in an insalubrious area on the fringes of downtown. Dorm beds cost $14, rooms with shared bath under $30, and there's internet access. Demand is heavy, especially in summer.

Luxor Las Vegas 3900 Las Vegas Blvd S ☏ 702/262-4000 or 1-800/288-1000, ⓦwww.luxor.com. A night in this vast smoked-glass pyramid is one of the great Las Vegas experiences. All the 2000 enjoyably Egyptian-themed rooms in the pyramid itself face outwards, with tremendous views. Sun–Thurs ❸, Fri & Sat ❺

Main Street Station 200 N Main St at Ogden ☏ 702/387-1896 or 1-800/465-0711, ⓦwww.mainstreetcasino.com. Downtown's best-value option, two short blocks from Fremont Street, with four hundred large guestrooms plus a brew-pub and an assortment of good restaurants. ❸

MGM Grand 3799 Las Vegas Blvd S ☏ 702/891-7777 or 1-800/929-1112, ⓦwww.mgmgrand.com. The world's largest hotel; waiting for any kind of service, especially check-in, can be horrendous, but you get a good standard of accommodation for the price, and it holds several of Las Vegas's finest restaurants. Sun–Thurs ❹, Fri & Sat ❺

New York–New York 3790 Las Vegas Blvd S ☏ 702/740-6969 or 1-800/693-3763, ⓦwww.nynyhotelcasino.com. Rooms at the most exuberantly enjoyable Strip casino are very nice, if a bit small, and filled with Art Deco furnishings and flourishes. Sun–Thurs ❹, Fri & Sat ❻

Paris-Las Vegas 3655 Las Vegas Blvd S ☏ 702/946-7000 or 1-888/266-5687, ⓦwww.paris-lv.com. Flamboyant French-themed casino, where the rooms and services are pitched slightly below those of Las Vegas's most upscale joints, but the location, views and general ambience are superb. ❺

USA Hostels Las Vegas 1322 E Fremont St ☏ 702/385-1150 or 1-800/550-8958, ⓦwww.usahostels.com. Well-kept independent hostel in a grim neighborhood ten blocks east of downtown, offering dorm beds for $15 and private double rooms for $45, plus use of a good pool, internet access, and shuttle buses. No curfew.

The Venetian 3355 Las Vegas Blvd S ☏ 702/414-1000 or 1-888/283-6423, ⓦwww.venetian.com. Even the standard rooms at this upscale Strip behemoth are split-level suites, offering antique-style canopied beds on a raised platform, plus roomy living rooms. Sun–Thurs ❻, Fri & Sat ❼

The City

Though the Las Vegas sprawl measures fifteen miles wide by fifteen miles long, most tourists stick to the six-mile stretch of Las Vegas Boulevard that includes the downtown area, slightly southeast of the intersection of I-15 and US-95, and the Strip, home to the major casinos. In between lie two somewhat seedy miles of gas stations, fast-food drive-ins and wedding chapels, while the rest of town is largely residential, and need barely concern you.

The Strip

For its razor-edge finesse in harnessing sheer, magnificent excess to the deadly serious business of making money, there's no place like the **Las Vegas Strip**. It's hard to imagine a time when Las Vegas was an ordinary city, and Las Vegas Boulevard a dusty thoroughfare scattered with the usual edge-of-town motels. After five decades of capitalism run riot, with every new casino-hotel setting out to surpass anything its neighbors ever dreamed of, the Strip seems to be locked into a hyperactive craving for thrills and glamour, forever discarding its latest toy in its frenzy for the next jackpot.

Each casino is a self-contained fantasyland of high camp and genuine excitement. Almost against your will, huge moving walkways sweep you in from the sidewalk; once inside, it can be almost impossible to find your way out. The action keeps going day and night, and in this sealed and windowless environment you rapidly lose track of which is which. Even if you do manage to get back onto the streets during the day, the scorching heat is liable to drive you straight back in again; night is the best time to venture out, when the neon's blazing at its brightest.

As the Strip pushes deeper into the desert, the newest casinos tend to rise at its southern end, not far west of the airport. The procession kicks off with the glowing gilded tower of **Mandalay Bay**, which opened in 1999. Financed through the profits from its neighbors, *Luxor* and *Excalibur*, *Mandalay Bay* is more upmarket than either, though all it has to offer casual sightseers is Shark Reef, a walk-through aquarium loacted near the pool at the back of the property (daily 10am–11pm; $14). With an excellent assortment of restaurants as well as the *House of Blues* music venue, however, it's lively at night.

From the palm-fringed avenue of sphinxes guarding the entrance onwards, the 36-story smoked-glass pyramid of **Luxor** next door plays endless variations upon Egyptian archeology. These range from a meticulous reconstruction of the Tomb of Tutankhamun (Sun–Thurs 9am–11pm, Fri & Sat 9am–11.30pm; $6) – a slightly odd exercise in view of the fact that the original remained undiscovered for millennia precisely because it was so small and pokey – to the "IMAX ride-film" *In Search of the Obelisk* (same hours; $7).

Luxor's architect, Veldon Simpson, had previously designed **Excalibur**, immediately north. A less-sophisticated mock-up of a medieval castle, complete with drawbridge, crenellated towers, and a basement stuffed with fairground-style sideshows for the kids, it's usually packed out with low-budget tour groups. Its brief reign as the world's largest hotel, from 1990 to 1993, ended when the five-thousand-room **MGM Grand** – another Simpson creation – opened across the street. At that time, Las Vegas was in the midst of its misguided attempt to restyle itself as a destination for kids, and the *MGM Grand* sold itself on the strength of having its own theme park. That's long gone, but the *Grand* is prospering nonetheless, with replacements including a steady stream of Elvis impersonators on a giant stage, and the **Lion Habitat**, a walk-through wooded zoo where real lions lounge around a ruined temple beneath a naturally-lit dome. Admission is free (daily 11am–11pm), while for $20 you can have a degrading photo taken with a cute little lion cub (daily except Tues 11am–5pm).

Excalibur and the *MGM Grand* are not the only giants facing off across the intersection of Las Vegas Boulevard and Tropicana Avenue, said to be the busiest traffic junction in the US. The northwest corner, diagonally opposite the veteran *Tropicana*, is occupied by the exuberantly meticulous **New York–New York**. This miniature Manhattan – created, like the original, in response to space limitations – boasts a skyline featuring twelve separate skyscrapers, and is fronted by the Statue of Liberty. Unusually, the interior is every bit as carefully realized, with a lovely rendition of Central Park at dusk. In one respect, it even surpasses New York itself; for $10 you can swoop around the whole thing at 65mph on the hair-raising *Manhattan Express* **roller coaster**.

North again, the **Aladdin** re-opened following a complete re-building in 2000, with the casino at its core encircled by the very upscale, but as yet far from busy, **Desert Passage** shopping mall. **Paris**, next door, was the 1999 handiwork of the same team of designers as *New York–New York*. With a half-size Eiffel Tower straddling the Arc de Triomphe and the Opera, it all feels a little compressed, but once again the attention to detail is a joy, with a fine selection of top-notch French restaurants along its cobbled streets. Elevators soar through the roof of the casino and up to the summit of the Eiffel Tower, for stunning views of the city, at their best after dark (daily 9am–1am; $9).

The Eiffel Tower was cheekily positioned to enjoy perfect views of **Bellagio**, opposite, *Mirage* owner Steve Wynn's 1998 attempt to build the best hotel in world history. *Bellagio* is undeniably a breathtaking achievement, but Wynn set himself a pointless and self-defeating task. While casino theming has always been playful – you're not supposed to think that being in *Luxor* is like being in ancient Egypt, just that it's fun to pretend – *Bellagio* wants to be real, and somehow more authentic than its original models. The trouble is that *Bellagio* is not in Europe, it's in Las Vegas, and it's stuffed full of slot machines. Inlaid with jewel-like precision into marble counters, perhaps, but still slot machines. *Bellagio*'s proudest boasts are the **Via Bellagio**, a covered mall of impossibly glamorous designer boutiques, and its opulent **Conservatory**, where a network of flowerbeds beneath a Belle Epoque canopy of copper-framed glass is replanted every few weeks with ornate seasonal displays. When Steve Wynn was bought out by MGM in 2000, he took the permanent collection from his ground-breaking **Bellagio Gallery of Fine Art** with him, so it now hosts changing and not very enthralling temporary exhibitions (daily 8am–10pm; $12).

Across Flamingo Road from *Bellagio*, **Caesars Palace** still encapsulates Las Vegas at its best. Here the walkway delivers you past grand marble staircases that lead nowhere, and full-sized replicas of Michelangelo's *David*, into a vast labyrinth of slots and green baize, peopled by strutting half-naked Roman centurions and Cleopatra-cropped waitresses. Above the stores, restaurants and "living statues" of the extraordinary **Forum**, the blue-domed ceiling dims and glows as it endlessly cycles from dawn to dusk and back again. The Forum is also home to **Race for Atlantis**, Las Vegas's only 3-D IMAX simulator ride (Sun–Thurs 10am–11pm, Fri & Sat 10am–midnight; $9.50). What you pay is expensive for what you get – shaken to smithereens in front of a short sci-fi B-feature – but few kids leave disappointed. *Caesars* itself has its own giant-screen OMNIMAX movie theater ($7), as well as the elaborate Magical Empire, a dinner-cum-magic-show for which tickets cost $75.

Nighttime crowds jostle for space on the sidewalk outside the glittering **Mirage**, beyond *Caesars*, to watch the somewhat half-hearted volcano that erupts every fifteen minutes, spewing water and fire into the lagoon below. Inside, a couple of Siegfried and Roy's white tigers lounge dopily in a glass-fronted enclosure near the main entrance. Next door, a pirate galleon and a British frigate, crewed by actors, do noisy battle outside **Treasure Island** (every ninety minutes; daily 4–11pm). Around the back, behind the Fashion Show Mall at 3401 Industrial Road, you can admire (if not step on) the King's very own blue suede shoes at **Elvis-A-Rama** (daily 9am–7pm; $14). As well as a stunning array of Elvis memorabilia, the museum puts on hourly impersonator shows, included in the admission price.

12

THE SOUTHWEST | Las Vegas

Across the Strip, the facade of another 1999 newcomer, the **Venetian**, includes loving facsimiles of six major Venice buildings. The main emphasis in the casino itself is on the lavish **Grand Canal Shoppes**, reached via a stairwell topped by vivid frescoes copied from yet more Venice originals. The ludicrous re-creation of the **Grand Canal** at the top, complete with gondolas and singing gondoliers (Sun–Thurs 10am–10.30pm, Fri & Sat 10am–11.30pm; $12.50 a ride), is quintessential Las Vegas, and as such utterly irresistible – for God's sake, it's *upstairs*. Set on the second and third floors of the *Venetian*'s Library, the first US outpost of **Madame Tussaud's** renowned waxwork museum eschews boring old history in favor of styling itself as the **Celebrity Encounter** (Sun–Thurs 11am–7pm, Fri & Sat 11am–10pm; $13.50, ages 4–12 $11). Unless you've always dreamed of shaking hands with a wax model of the wife of chef Wolfgang Puck, or Liberace, the whole experience is seriously overpriced, its token animatronic showpieces not a patch on the free shows at *Caesars*. Fall 2001 saw the opening of two Guggenheim museums within the Venetian, both built in an ultra-modern style that's deliberately out of keeping with the classical Italian flourishes of the Venetian proper (both daily 9am–11am; $15 each). The **Guggenheim Hermitage** is a collaboration with St Petersburg's legendary State Hermitage Museum that's designed to provide much-needed funds for the Russian museum in return for displaying some of its finest treasures on a six-monthly changing rotation. Its russet steel walls and magnetic frames may be futuristic, but the paintings themselves are masterpieces to rank with any gallery in the world. If its inaugural exhibition of "The Art of the Motorcycle" is anything to go by, on the other hand, the **Guggenheim Las Vegas** aims much more firmly at the traditional gimmick-seeking Las Vegas crowd.

The family-oriented **Circus Circus**, another mile north, uses live circus acts to pull in the punters – a trapeze artist here, a fire-eater there – and also has an indoor theme park, **The Adventuredome** (Mon–Thurs 10am–6pm, Fri & Sat 10am–midnight, Sun 10am–8pm), where you pay separately for each roller coaster or river-ride. If you really want to cool off, you'd do better to head on to the flumes and chutes of Vegas's one purpose-built water park, **Wet'n'Wild**, 2601 S Las Vegas Blvd (summer daily 10am–8pm; $24).

Meanwhile, the **Las Vegas Hilton**, half a mile east of *Circus Circus* at 3000 Paradise Rd, is home to the very busy **Star Trek Experience** (daily 11am–11pm; $25). In a museum-like atmosphere, glossy display panels recount a wordy Star Trek chronology that takes in World War III in 2053, and the birth of Spock in 2230, while diminutive Ferengi stroll among you. The whole thing culminates when you're sent on a mildly vomitous motion-simulator ride through deep space, to emerge in a shopping area you could have reached without paying anyway, where memorabilia prices boldly go to well over $2000 for a leather jacket.

Circus Circus has traditionally marked the northern limit of the Strip, though the 1996 opening of the **Stratosphere**, half a mile towards downtown, tried to change that. At 1149 feet, the *Stratosphere* is the tallest building west of the Mississippi, and the outdoor deck and indoor viewing chamber in the sphere near the summit offer amazing panoramas across the city ($6). Two utterly demented thrill rides can take you even closer to heaven; the world's highest roller coaster swirls around the outside of the sphere, while the ludicrous *Big Shot* shunts you to the very top of an additional 160-foot spire, from which you freefall back down again ($15 for both).

Downtown and the Liberace Museum

As the Strip has gone from strength to strength, **downtown** Las Vegas, the city's original core, has by comparison been neglected. Long known as "Glitter Gulch," and consisting of a few compact blocks of lower-key casinos, it has recently embarked upon a revival. Between Main Street and Las Vegas Boulevard, five entire blocks of Fremont Street, its principal thoroughfare, have been roofed with an open-air mesh to create the **Fremont Street Experience**. This "Celestial Vault" is studded with over two million coloured light bulbs, choreographed by computer in dazzling nightly displays (hourly, 8pm–midnight; free), but there's a long way to go before the district as a whole can compete with the Strip once again.

Almost all Las Vegas's handful of museums are eminently missable, with one unarguable exception: the **Liberace Museum**, two miles east of the Strip at 1775 E Tropicana Ave (Mon–Sat 10am–5pm, Sun 1–5pm; $8). Popularly remembered as a beaming buffoon who knocked out torpid toe-tappers, Liberace, who died in 1987, started out playing piano in the rough bars of Milwaukee during the 1940s. A decade later, he was being mobbed by screaming adolescents and ruthlessly hounded by the scandal-hungry press. All this is recalled by a yellowing collection of cuttings and family photos, along with electric candelabra, bejewelled quail eggs with inlaid pianos, rhinestone-covered fur coats, glittering cars and more. The music, piped into the scented toilets, may not have improved with age, but the museum is a satisfying attempt to answer the seminal question "how does a great performer top himself on stage?"

Eating

Little more than a decade ago, the **restaurant** scene in Las Vegas was governed by the notion that visitors were not prepared to pay for gourmet food, and the only quality restaurants were upscale Italian places well away from the Strip. Now, however, the situation has reversed, as the major casinos compete to attract culinary superstars from all over the country to open Vegas outlets. Many tourists now come to the city in order to eat at the best restaurants in the United States, without having to reserve a table months in advance or pay sky-high prices.

Nonetheless, almost every casino still features an all-you-can-eat **buffet**. The better buffets tend to be in casinos that are neither on the Strip nor downtown, and depend on locals as well as tourists. By contrast, those at the largest casinos, like *Excalibur* and the *MGM Grand*, only have to be good enough to ensure that the crowds already in the building don't leave, while also coping with a daily deluge of customers.

Buffets

The Buffet *Bellagio*, 3600 Las Vegas Blvd S ☎702/791-7111. Far and away Las Vegas's best buffet. With other buffets, you may rave about what good value they are; with this one, you'll rave about what good food it is. Breakfast is $10; lunch is $14, and can include sushi, sashimi and dim sum; and dinner, with choices like lobster claws, fresh oysters and venison, is $23.

Carnival World Buffet *Rio*, 3700 W Flamingo Rd ☎702/252-7777. Excellent value, half a mile west of the Strip. The variety is immense, including Thai, Chinese, Mexican and Japanese stations as well as the usual pasta and barbecue, and even a fish'n'chip stand. $8 for breakfast, $11 for lunch, and $15 for dinner.

Garden Court Buffet *Main Street Station*, 200 N Main St ☎702/387-1896. Downtown's best-value buffet, ranging from fried chicken and corn at "South to Southwest," to tortillas at "Ole," and pork chow mein and oyster tofu at "Pacific Rim." Breakfast is $5, lunch $7, while dinner is usually $11, but rises to $14 for Friday's seafood spread.

Le Village Buffet *Paris*, 3655 Las Vegas Blvd S ☏702/967-7000. Superb French-only cuisine, with great seafood, succulent roast chicken, and super-fresh vegetables. The setting is a little cramped, squeezed into a very Disneyesque French village, but the food is *magnifique*. Breakfast is $12, lunch $17, and dinner $22.

Restaurants

America *New York–New York*, 3790 Las Vegas Blvd S ☏702/740-6451. Cavernous 24-hour diner, with a vast 3-D "map" of the United States curling from the ceiling, and a staggeringly eclectic menu. At any hour of day or night, at any price there really is something for everyone, and it's all surprisingly good.

Binion's Horseshoe Coffee Shop *Binion's Horseshoe*, 128 E Fremont St ☏702/382-1600. The 24-hour Las Vegas coffee shop of your dreams, in the basement of a veteran downtown casino. Between 10pm and 5am, a steak dinner costs just $3, but even at prime time, 4.45–11.45pm, a 16oz T-bone is only $6.75. Breakfast is highly recommended.

Commander's Palace *Aladdin*, 3667 Las Vegas Blvd S ☏702/892-8272. The first-ever outpost of New Orleans' finest (and most expensive restaurant) abuts the Strip at the front of the Desert Passage mall. The decor is formal but redolent of Louisiana atmosphere, and the food is sumptuous. Open daily for lunch and dinner.

Il Fornaio *New York–New York*, 3790 Las Vegas Blvd S ☏702/740-6403. The nicest place to enjoy the atmosphere of *New York–New York*, this rural-Italian restaurant is a real joy. Grab a pizza for around $10, or linger over a full meal of soft-shell crab ($9) or carpaccio of beef ($8) to start, followed by gnocchi with smoked salmon ($14), baked sea bass with cherry tomatoes ($18.50), or rotisserie chicken ($14.50).

Margarita's Mexican Cantina *New Frontier*, 3120 Las Vegas Blvd S ☏702/794-8433. Appealingly old-fashioned bar-cum-restaurant, with the best-value Mexican food on the Strip.

Mr Lucky's 24/7 *Hard Rock Hotel*, 4455 Paradise Rd ☏702/693-5592. Stylish 24-hour coffee shop, with an open kitchen, faux-fur booths, and subdued tan-and-cream paintjob, where the food is well above average.

Olives *Bellagio*, 3600 Las Vegas Blvd S ☏702/693-8181. *Bellagio*'s finest restaurant may be the kind of place that calls a $10 pizza an "individual oven-baked flatbread," and your food is more likely to be arranged vertically than horizontally, but the largely Mediterranean menu is uniformly fresh and superb. Great for lunch, at under $20; dinner is pricier.

Wolfgang Puck Café *MGM Grand*, 3799 Las Vegas Blvd S ☏702/895-9653. Designer-diner-cum-café, where they'll whisk you through your meal in the blink of an eyelid, but you won't be disappointed with the food. No reservations. Open daily for lunch and dinner.

Bars and clubs

Alcohol is very easy indeed to come by in Las Vegas. All the casinos have plenty of bars, but if you want a drink, there's no need to look for one; instead, a tray-toting waitress will come and find you. As for **live music**, check newspapers like *City Life* and the *Las Vegas Review Journal* to see who's appearing when you're in town. In general, it'll help if your tastes are rooted in the 1960s or even earlier, but some of the newer breed of casinos are orienting themselves towards younger audiences.

The Beach 365 Convention Center Drive ☏702/731-1925. 24-hour dance club, just east of the Strip, which attracts a very young crowd to the massive dance floor downstairs, and sports bar upstairs.

Gipsy 4605 Paradise Rd ☏702/731-1919. High-profile gay dance club, whose success has spurred the emergence of the surrounding gay business district. There's normally some form of live entertainment, and there are beer busts most nights too.

House of Blues *Mandalay Bay*, 3950 Las Vegas Blvd S ☏702/632-7600. The Strip's premier live music venue, the voodoo-tinged, folk-art-decorated *House of Blues* has a definite but not exclusive emphasis towards blues, R&B, and black music in general. Prices range up to $75 for big-name stars.

rumjungle *Mandalay Bay*, 3950 Las Vegas Blvd S ☏702/632-7408. You have to run a gauntlet of go-go dancers and volcanic gas jets just to get into this hybrid bar-restaurant-nightclub. Inside, the leopardskin-clad staff serve well-priced cock-tails, plus a vast menu of rums, and it's too loud to do anything more than watch, or join, the dance-floor action.

VooDoo Lounge *Rio*, 3700 W Flamingo Rd ☎702/252-7777. Las Vegas's hottest bar, with amazing 51st-floor views and super-cool atmosphere.

Entertainment

There was a time when Las Vegas represented the pinnacle of any showbusiness career. In the early 1960s, when Frank Sinatra's Rat Pack were shooting hit movies like the original *Ocean's 11* during the day then singing the night away at the *Sands*, the city could claim to be the capital of the international entertainment industry. It was even hip. Now, however, although the money is still there, the world has moved on. As the great names of the past fade from view, few of the individual performers popular with traditional Vegas visitors are considered capable of carrying an extended-run show. The tendency instead is to rely on lavish stunts and special effects. A fair number of old-style Vegas revues are still soldiering on, but there are more stimulating contemporary productions than you might imagine.

Lance Burton *Monte Carlo*, 3770 Las Vegas Blvd S ☎702/730-7160. The best family show in Las Vegas, featuring master magician Lance Burton. Most of it consists of traditional but very impressive stunts with playing cards, handkerchiefs and doves, but large-scale illusions include the disappearance of an entire airplane and a narrow escape from hanging. Tues–Sat 7pm & 10pm. $55 and $60.

Legends in Concert *Imperial Palace*, 3535 Las Vegas Blvd S ☎702/794-3261. Enjoyable celebrity-tribute show, with a changing roster of stars that ranges from the Righteous Brothers to Shania Twain. Daily except Sun 7.30pm & 10.30pm. $34.50, including 2 drinks, ages 12 and under $19.50.

Mystère *Treasure Island*, 3300 Las Vegas Blvd S ☎702/796-9999. Fabulous Cirque du Soleil showcase, with tumblers, acrobats, trapeze artists, pole climbers, clowns and strongmen, but no animals apart from fantastic costumed apparitions. Wed–Sun

7.30pm & 10.30pm. $88, ages 12 and under $44.

O *Bellagio*, 3600 Las Vegas Blvd S ☎702/796-9999. Las Vegas's most expensive show is a remarkable testament to how much is possible when the budget is barely an issue. Any part of the stage at any time may be submerged to any depth. One moment a performer can walk across a particular spot, the next someone may dive head-first into it from the high wire. From the synchronized swimmers onwards, the Cirque du Soleil display their magnificent skills to maximum advantage. Mon, Tues & Fri–Sun 7.30pm & 10.30pm. $99 and $121.

The Rat Pack is Back *Sahara*, 2535 Las Vegas Blvd S ☎702/737-2515. Las Vegas's hottest ticket takes its audience back to 1961; December 12 in fact, and Frank Sinatra's 46th birthday party. The impersonations are spot-on, but you'll probably only enjoy it if your nostalgia is genuine rather than tongue-in-cheek. Mon & Wed 6.30pm & 9pm, Tues & Fri–Sun 8pm. $40.

Lake Mead and the Hoover Dam

Almost as many people as go to Las Vegas visit **LAKE MEAD**, the vast reservoir thirty miles southeast of the city that was created by the construction of the Hoover Dam. As with the similarly incongruous Lake Powell (see p.1019), it makes a bizarre spectacle, the blue waters a vivid counterpoint to the surrounding desert, but it gets excruciatingly crowded all year round.

Though the Lake Mead National Recreation Area straddles the border between Nevada and Arizona, the best views come from the Nevada side. Even if you don't need details of how to sail, scuba-dive, water-ski or fish from the marinas along the five-hundred-mile shoreline, call in at the Alan Bible visitor center (daily 8.30am–4.30pm; ☎702/293-8990, @www.nps.gov/lame), four miles northeast of Boulder City on US-93, to enjoy a sweeping prospect of the whole thing.

Eight miles on, beyond the rocky ridges of the Black Mountains, US-93 reaches the **HOOVER DAM** itself. Designed to block the Colorado River and provide low-cost electricity for the cities of the Southwest, it's among the tallest dams ever built (760ft high), and used enough concrete to build a two-lane highway from the west coast to New York. It was completed in 1935, as the first step in the Bureau of Reclamation program that culminated with the Glen Canyon Dam (see p.1020). Informative half-hour guided tours of the dam leave from the **Hoover Dam Visitor Center** on the Nevada side of the river (daily 9am–5.30pm; $10, plus $5 parking; ☎702/293-1824). Gray Line's five-hour **bus tours** from Las Vegas cost around $24 (☎702/384-1234).

Crossing Nevada

The bulk of Nevada – the largest but least populated state in the Southwest – is made up of dry, flat plains sliced by knife-edge volcanic mountain ranges. Called the **Great Basin** because its rivers and streams have no outlet to the ocean, the land has a certain eerie, even hypnotic, beauty. Its attractions are hard to pinpoint, but there's an indefinable, very American sense of the endless frontier, of wide-open space.

The main route across Nevada, **I-80**, shoots from Salt Lake City to Reno, skirting dozens of bizarrely named small towns – Winnemucca, Elko, Battle Mountain – packed with casinos, bars, brothels, motels and little else. The other main route, **US-50**, has a reputation as the loneliest highway in America, with the least traffic and roadside life. Older and slower than I-80, it follows much the same route as did the riders of the Pony Express in the 1860s, though many of the towns along it have faded away, and some have been entirely abandoned. US-50 passes by Nevada's sole national park, **Great Basin National Park** in the eastern mountains, before it links up with I-80 at Reno, and then cuts off to the southwest to circuit magnificent **Lake Tahoe**. One last main route, **US-95**, links Reno and Las Vegas, passing near Death Valley (see p.1098), as well as Nevada's most famous and most evocative ghost town, **Goldfield**.

Great Basin National Park

Just across the border from Utah, **GREAT BASIN NATIONAL PARK** was created in 1986 by the amalgamation of the Lehman Caves National Monument with the Wheeler Peak Scenic Area. It's a distillation of the range of scenery the Nevada desert offers, from angular peaks to high mountain meadows cut by fast-flowing streams. The **Lehman Caves** are some of the most extensive and fascinating limestone caves in the country, not as big as Carlsbad Caverns, but if anything more densely packed with intriguing formations. Guided tours leave regularly throughout the day, costing $2 for 30min, $6 for 1hr, or $8 for 90min, from the **visitor center** near the mouth of the caves (summer daily 8am–5pm; winter daily 8.30am–4.30pm; ☎775/234-7331, ⓦwww.nps.gov/grba), five miles west of the hamlet of **Baker**.

From the Lehman Caves, a twelve-mile road climbs the east flank of the bald and usually snowcapped **Wheeler Peak**, and trails lead past alpine lakes and through a grove of gnarled, ancient bristlecone pines to the 13,063ft summit. Few people ever come here, but in winter the mountains and meadows make for excellent off-track cross-country skiing. The nearest real town, **ELY**, an hour's drive away, has two worthwhile museums – the entertaining **Nevada Northern Railway Museum** (daily except Mon 11am–1pm; $2.50), which offers $16 rides on a restored steam train, and the **County Museum** (daily 9am–4pm; free) – as well as a dozen **motels** (try *Motel 6*, 770 Avenue O; ☎775/289-6671; ❷) and a handful of **casinos** and **restaurants**.

Elko

One of the few Nevada towns worth aiming for, if you're here at the right time of year, is **ELKO**, a straggling highway town a hundred miles from the Utah border. The self-proclaimed last real cowtown in the West is the center of one of the largest open-range cattle ranching regions in the US, and the fitting home of the annual **Cowboy Poetry Gathering**, held here every January. People get together in a sort of celebration of folk culture, telling stories around campfires, singing about the lonesome life on the range, and keeping alive the dying traditions and tales of the Wild West.

During the 72-hour party of the **National Basque Festival**, each Fourth of July weekend, hulking men throw huge logs at each other amid a whole lot of carousing and downing platefuls of Basque food. The food is available year-round in restaurants like the *Star Hotel*, two blocks south of the main drag at 246 Silver St (☎775/738-9925). Greyhound and Amtrak both stop in Elko, and there are dozens of budget motels, such as the *Holiday Motel*, 1276 Idaho St (☎775/738-7187; ❷). Elko's **visitor center** is at 700 Moren Way (Mon–Fri 9am–5pm; ☎775/738-4091 or 1-800/248-ELKO, ⓦwww.elkocva.com).

Reno and around

If you don't make it to Las Vegas, you can get a feel for the nonstop, neon-lit gambler's lifestyle by stopping in **RENO**, on I-80, very near the California border. "The biggest little city in the world," as it likes to call itself, is a some-what downmarket version of the glitz and glamour of Vegas, with miles of gleaming slot machines and poker tables, surrounded by tacky wedding chapels and quickie divorce courts. While the town itself may not be much to look at, its setting – at the foot of the snowcapped **Sierra Nevada**, with the Truckee River winding through the center – is superb.

There are three things to do in Reno: gamble, get married and get divorced. The **casinos** are concentrated in the downtown area, along Virginia Street either side of the railroad tracks. To get **married**, the requirements are the same as in Las Vegas (see p.1030), though here you obtain your **marriage license** at the **Washoe County Court**, Virginia and Court St (daily 8am–midnight; ☎775/328-3275). Wedding chapels all around the city will help you tie the knot; across the street from the courthouse, the *Starlight Chapel* – "No Waiting, Just Drive In" – does the job for under $50, providing a pink chintz parlor full of plastic flowers and heart-shaped seats (☎775/786-4949).

Practicalities

Reno's Cannon International **airport** is a couple of miles southeast of down-town, a twenty-minute ride on local bus #24. Greyhound **buses** use the terminal at 155 Stevenson St; daily Amtrak **trains** call at 135 E Commercial Row downtown, six hours out of San Francisco en route for Salt Lake City.

The downtown **visitor center**, in the National Bowling Stadium at 300 N Center St (daily 8am–6pm; ☎1-888/HIT-RENO), should be able to help you find an inexpensive **place to stay**, though rates tend to double at weekends. All the big casinos offer accommodation – the pick of them are the *Atlantis*, 3800 S Virginia St (☎775/825-4700; ❸), *Silver Legacy*, 407 N Virginia St (☎775/329-4777 or 1-800/687-7733, ⓦwww.silverlegacyresort.com; ❸), and *Circus Circus*, 500 N Sierra St (☎775/329-0711 or 1-800/648-5010; ❸) – while the *Gatekeeper Inn*, 221 W Fifth St (☎775/786-3500 or 1-800/822-3504; ❷), is a clean, safe and reliable motel. Reno's best **buffet** is at the *Eldorado*, 345 N Virginia St (☎775/786-5700 or 1-800/648-5966; ❸).

Carson City

US-395 heads south from Reno along the jagged spires of the **High Sierra**, past **Mono Lake**, **Mount Whitney** and **Death Valley**. Just thirty miles south of Reno, **CARSON CITY**, state capital of Nevada, is small by comparison but has a number of elegant buildings, some excellent historical museums and a handful of world-weary casinos.

Carson City was named after frontier explorer Kit Carson in 1858, and is still redolent with Wild West history. A good introduction is the **Nevada State Museum** at 600 N Carson St (daily 8.30am–4.30pm; $3). Housed in the former Carson Mint, it covers the geology and natural history of the Great Basin desert, from prehistoric times up through the heyday of the 1860s, when the silver mines of the nearby Comstock Lode were at their peak. Amid the many guns and artifacts is the reconstructed **Ghost Town**, from which a tunnel allows entry down into a full-scale model of an **underground mine**.

Greyhound **buses** between Reno and Los Angeles stop once a day in each direction, at 111 E Telegraph Ave. Among budget **motels** are the *Super 8* at 2829 S Carson St (☎775/883-7800; ❷), and the *Hardman House Motor Inn* at 917 N Carson St (☎775/882-7744 or 1-800/626-0793; ❹). The **visitor center**, on the south side of town at 1900 S Carson St (Mon–Fri 8am–5pm, Sat & Sun 10am–3pm; ☎775/687-7410), can help with practical details and provide maps for self-guided architectural walking and driving **tours** of the town, taking in the State Capitol, the museums, and many of the fine 1870s Victorian wooden houses and churches on the west side.

Virginia City

Much of the wealth on which Carson City – and indeed San Francisco – was built came from the silver mines of the **Comstock Lode**, a solid seam of pure silver discovered underneath Mount Hamilton, fourteen miles east of Carson City off US-50, in 1859. Raucous **VIRGINIA CITY** grew up on the steep slopes above the mines, and a young writer named Samuel Clemens made his way here from the east with his older brother, the acting Secretary to the Governor of the Nevada Territory, to see what all the fuss was about. His descriptions of the wild life of the mining camp, and of the desperately hard work men put in to get at the valuable ore, were published years later under his pseudonym, **Mark Twain**. Though Twain also spent some time in the Gold Rush towns of California's Mother Lode, on the other side of the Sierra –

which by then were all but abandoned – his tales of Virginia City life, collected in *Roughing It*, form a hilarious eyewitness account of the hard-drinking life of the frontier miners. There's not much to Virginia City nowadays, since all the old storefronts have been taken over by hot-dog vendors and tacky souvenir stands, but the surrounding landscape of arid mountains still feels remote and undisturbed.

CHAPTER 13 **Highlights**

* **San Diego Zoo, San Diego** As humane and "natural" a zoo as you'll find anywhere, with a vast collection of rare species. See p.1050

* **Mono Lake** The blue waters of remote Mono Lake are prime bird-watching territory; it's also a spectacle in its own right. See p.1102

* **Joshua Tree National Park** The eerie "arms" of Joshua trees beckon visitors to explore this long-abandoned mining country. See p.1096

* **Hearst Castle, San Simeon** A million visitors a year now tramp through "Citizen Kane"'s opulent unfinished home. See p.1106

* **Highway 1** Thrilling drive along the US's west coast, with pounding Pacific surf as far as the eye can see. See p.1107

* **Yosemite National Park** Giant sequoias, towering waterfalls, the sheer face of Half Dome – your eyes will hardly get a rest. See p.1119

* **The streets of San Francisco** Get the flavor of the Beats in North Beach, flower power in Haight-Ashbury, and gay pride in the Castro. See p.1134

California

Publicized and idealized all over the world, **CALIFORNIA** really does live up to the myth. More than just a terrestrial paradise of sun, sand and surf, it has high mountain ranges, fast-paced glitzy cities, primeval old-growth forests and vast stretches of deserts. The landscape is imbued with history, ranging from rock carvings left by indigenous Native Americans to the eerie ghost towns of the Gold Rush pioneers.

In some ways, the west coast is the ultimate "now" society. Anywhere so vulnerable to the constant threat of the Big One – a massive **earthquake** of unimaginable terror – is bound to have a sense of living for the moment. However, its supposed superficiality is largely fictitious. Although home to such reactionary figures as Ronald Reagan and Richard Nixon, it has also been the source of some of the country's most progressive **political movements**. The fierce protests of the Sixties may have died down, but California remains the heart of liberal America, at the forefront of environmental awareness, gay pride and social permissiveness, and increasingly a bulwark of the Democratic Party. **Economically**, too, the region is crucial, whether in the film industry, the music business, the financial markets, or the all-consuming sector of real-estate development.

California is too large to be fully explored in a single trip, but in an area so varied it's hard to pick out specific highlights. **Los Angeles** is far and away the biggest and most stimulating city: a maddening collection of freeways, beaches, seedy suburbs, upscale neighborhoods and extreme lifestyles. From Los Angeles you can head south to the growing metropolis of **San Diego**, with its broad, welcoming beaches and easy access to Mexico; or push inland to the **desert areas**, most notably **Death Valley**, a barren and inhospitable landscape of volcanic craters and salt pans that in summer becomes the hottest place on earth.

Most people, though, follow the shoreline north up the **central coast**: a gorgeous run that takes in lively small towns like **Santa Barbara** and **Santa Cruz**. California's second city, **San Francisco**, at the top end, is about as different from LA as it's possible to get: the oldest, most European-styled city in the state, set on a series of steep hills, its wooden houses tumbling down to water on three sides. It is also well placed for the national parks to the east, such as **Yosemite**, where waterfalls cascade into a sheer glacial valley, and **Sequoia/Kings Canyon** with its gigantic trees, as well as the ghost towns of the **Gold Country**. **North** of San Francisco the countryside becomes wilder, wetter and greener, approaching Oregon through spectacular and almost deserted volcanic tablelands.

The **climate** in **southern California** consists of seemingly endless days of sunshine and warm dry nights, with occasional bouts of torrential flooding in the winter. LA's notorious smog is at its worst when the temperatures are high-est, from July through September. All along the **coast** mornings can be hazily overcast, especially in May and June; in exposed San Francisco it can be chilly all year, and fog rolls in to ruin many a sunny day. Much more so than in the south, winter in northern California can bring rain for weeks on end, causing massive mudslides that wipe out roads and hillside homes. Most hiking trails in the **mountains** are blocked between October and June by the snow that keeps California's ski slopes among the busiest in the nation.

Some history

Around half a million people – almost half the population of what is now the US – were living in tribal villages along the west coast when the Spaniard **Juan Cabrillo** first sighted San Diego harbor in 1542, and named **California** after an imaginary island (inhabited by Amazons) from a Spanish novel. **Sir Francis Drake** landed near Point Reyes, north of San Francisco, in 1579, where the "white bancks and cliffes" reminded him of Dover. In 1602 **Sebastián Vizcáino** bestowed most of the place-names that still survive; his exaggerated description of **Monterey** as a perfect harbor led later colonizers to make it the region's military and administrative center. The Spanish occu-pation began in earnest in 1769, combining military expediency with mis-sionary zeal. Father **Junípero Serra** first established a small mission and *pre-sidio* (fort) at San Diego, before arriving in June 1770 at Monterey. By 1804 a chain of 21 missions, each a long day's walk from the next along the dirt path of *El Camino Real* (The Royal Road), ran from San Diego to San Francisco. Native Americans were either forcibly converted into Catholicism or killed; though not all gave up without a fight, disease ensured that they were soon wiped out.

When Mexico gained its independence in 1821, in theory it also acquired control of California. However, **Americans** were already starting to arrive, despite the immense difficulty of getting to California – three months by sea via Cape Horn, or four months overland in a covered wagon. Though the non-native population was a mere ten thousand in 1846, the growing belief that it was the **Manifest Destiny** of the United States to cover the continent from coast to coast, evident in the aggressively imperial policies of President James K. Polk, soon led to the **Mexican–American War**. Virtually all the fighting took place in Texas; Monterey was captured by the US Navy without a shot being fired, and by January 1847 the Americans controlled the entire west coast. In 1850 California became the 31st US state.

By chance, a mere nine days before the signing of the treaty that ended the war, flakes of **gold** were discovered in the Sierra Nevada. Prospectors flooded west, in the most madcap migration in history; it took just fifteen years to pick the goldfields clean. The completion of the **transcontinental railroad** in 1869, built using Chinese laborers, was a major turning point. The crossing from New York now took just five days, and a railroad rate war brought fares down to as little as $1 for a one-way ticket.

California was perceived as immune to the worst effects of the **Great Depression** of the 1930s – thanks in part to the images of prosperity prom-ulgated by its now-established **film industry**. From the Dust Bowl Midwest, entire families of "**Okies**" packed up everything they owned and set off for the farms of the Central Valley, though they often found bleak terrain and a hos-tile attitude to newcomers. Heavy industry came during **World War II**, in the form of shipyards and airplane factories, and many workers and military per-sonnel stayed on afterwards.

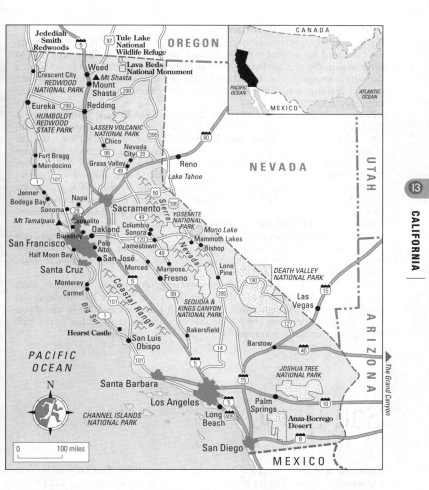

As home to the **Beats** in the Fifties and the **hippies** in the Sixties, and a host of radical political and ecological movements since, California was at the cutting edge of cultural change. However, the illusions of the Flower Power days were shattered by the violence of the 1969 rock concert at Northern California's Altamont Speedway, and once the anti-Vietnam War struggle was over, popular culture seemed to withdraw into smug self-satisfaction. The **junk–bond boom** of the Eighties, however, crash-landed in a tangled mess of scandal, and for California the Nineties kicked off with a stagnant property market, rising unemployment, escalating gang violence and racial tensions in LA, and an appalling death toll from AIDS in San Francisco – compounded by **earthquakes**, **drought** and **flooding**. Yet despite all the problems, and with more-conservative Californians fleeing the state for more hospitable climes in Colorado and Arizona, at the turn of the millennium the state continues to attract countless **new migrants** from the rest of the US and the world, who continue to provide much of the economic growth and cultural vitality of this dynamic, ever-changing place.

If you want to explore and enjoy California to the full, you'll need a **car**. A city such as Los Angeles couldn't exist without the automobile, and in any case to drive down the coastal freeways invites irresistible mental images of Beach Boys-style cruising. Car **rental** in California is among the cheapest in the country and the savings made by easy access to campgrounds and chain motels can easily offset the initial cost.

Frequent Amtrak **trains** connect **LA** and **San Diego**, with a stop at Fullerton for buses to Disneyland, and one daily service runs up the coast from LA, stopping at **Oakland** and **Emeryville**, the nearest stations to San Francisco, and continuing via Sacramento to Seattle. Another line from Oakland runs along the Central Valley, but only connects with LA by bus. **Cross-country** routes leave LA for Florida (the *Sunset Limited* via Tucson, Houston and New Orleans) and for Chicago (the *Southwest Chief* daily via Flagstaff, Albuquerque and Kansas City). Oakland has its own direct service to Chicago. Foreign visitors can cut fares greatly by using the **Rail Pass** program. Greyhound and Green Tortoise **buses** link all the main cities.

For quick hops between the major cities – especially LA and San Francisco – you can't beat **flying**. Services are extremely frequent, and prices competitive – if your plans are flexible enough to take advantage of off-peak deals. Regular scheduled fares are high.

If you plan to do any **long-distance cycling**, traveling from north to south can make all the difference – the wind blows this way in the summer, and besides, you're on the right side of the road for the best views. Be careful if you cycle along the coast on Hwy-1: despite its stunning views, it has heavy traffic, tight curves and is prone to fog.

San Diego

Relatively free from smog and byzantine freeways, **SAN DIEGO**, set around a gracefully curving bay, represents the acceptable face of southern California. The second biggest city in California may be affluent and conservative, but it's also easygoing and far from smug. Although it was the site of the first mission in California, the city only really took off with the arrival of the Santa Fe Railroad in the 1880s, and in terms of trade and significance it has long been in the shadow of Los Angeles. However, during World War II the US Navy made San Diego its Pacific Command Center, and the military continues to dominate the local economy, along with tourism.

Arrival, information and getting around

Both **trains** and **buses** leave you in the heart of downtown San Diego: Greyhound at Broadway and First Avenue is more central than Amtrak's Santa Fe Depot, at the west end of Broadway. **Lindbergh Field Airport** is only two miles out, on bus #2 ($1.50).

Getting around without a car, by day at least, is comparatively easy. Seven companies operate the integrated **Metropolitan Transit System** (bus tickets

$1.25–2.50; ⓦ www.sdcommute.com); the Transit Store, 102 Broadway (Mon–Sat 8.30am–5.30pm; ⓣ619/234–1060), has detailed timetables and sells a **Day Tripper Transit Pass** for one- to four-day visits ($5, $8, $10 and $12, accordingly). The passes apply also to the tram-like **San Diego Trolley**, which runs throughout the area (tickets $1–2.50) and covers the sixteen miles from the Santa Fe Depot to the Mexican border crossing at San Ysidro. It's a 45-minute journey ($4 round-trip; every 15min from 5am–midnight), and the last trolley back leaves at 1am on Saturday night. **Bicycle** rental shops include Rent-a-Bike, 523 Island St (ⓣ619/232-4700), and Hamel's Action Sport Center, 704 Ventura Place, Mission Beach (ⓣ619/488-5050).

The **International Visitors Information Center** is downtown at 11 Horton Plaza, F Street at First Avenue (Mon–Sat 8.30am–5pm; ⓣ619/236-1212, ⓦ www.sandiego.org). The poste restante, or general delivery, **post office** is at 2535 Midway Drive, between downtown and Mission Beach (Mon 7am–5pm, Tues–Fri 8am–5pm, Sat 8am–4pm; ⓣ1-800/275-8777; zip code 92138).

Accommodation

Accommodation is plentiful throughout San Diego, with budget travelers especially well served. The best-placed, though mall-like, **campground** is *Campland on the Bay*, 2211 Pacific Beach Drive (ⓣ1-800/4BAY-FUN), linked to downtown by bus #30, where a basic site costs a little more than $20. For a more serene camping option, there's **San Elijo Beach State Park**, Rte-21 south of Cardiff-by-the-Sea (ⓣ1-800/444-7275; sites from $17–25).

Hostels

Banana Bungalow 707 Reed Ave, Pacific Beach ⓣ858/273-3060 or 1-800/5-HOSTEL, ⓦ www.bananabungalow.com/sub/bbsd.html. Friendly, with slightly scruffy rooms, but the proximity to the beach – coupled with the free breakfasts, keg nights, barbecues, bonfires and other groovy attractions – draws a party-all-night, sleep-all-day crowd. There is no better value in San Diego if you want to be right on the beach. Dorm beds for $18. Bus #34 takes you there. ❶/❷

Grand Pacific Hostel 726 5th Ave, downtown ⓣ619/232-3100 or 1-800/438-8622. Well-placed hostel on the edge of the Gaslamp District. Converted from an 1890s-era hotel, with 6 to 8 beds per room, sheets and continental breakfast, for $18. Doubles for $40. Free bike use, organized tours to Tijuana, Sea World and the Zoo, and a handy shuttle to LA. ❶/❷

HI-San Diego Metropolitan Hostel 521 Market St at 5th Ave, downtown ⓣ619/525-1530 or 1-800/909-4776, ⓦ www.hostelweb.com /sandiego/downtown.htm. Handy for the Gaslamp District and Horton Plaza. HI members $18, non-members $21, and private doubles from $40. Free coffee and bagels. No curfew. ❶/❷

HI-San Diego Pt Loma/Elliott Hostel 3790 Udall St, Ocean Beach ⓣ619/223-4778 or 1-800/909-4776, ⓦ www.hostelweb.com/sandiego/pointlo-ma.htm. A couple of miles back from the beach and minus the relentless party-time atmosphere that prevails elsewhere, offering a large kitchen, patio, and common room with TV. Well-run and friendly, with $15–18 dorm beds, private rooms for three people or more, $20 per person. Bus #35 from downtown. ❶

Hotels, motels and B&Bs

Bahia Resort Hotel 989 West Mission Bay Drive, Mission Bay ⓣ1-888/576-4229, ⓦ www.bahiaho-tel.com. Prime beachside accommodation with expansive ocean views, water-sport rentals, pool and jacuzzi. Rooms range from cozy but pleasant rooms in a palm-garden setting to pricier bayside suites. ❻–❾

Balboa Park Inn 3402 Park Blvd, Hillcrest ⓣ619/298-0823, ⓦ www.balboaparkinn.com. Elegant, gay-oriented B&B, within walking distance of Balboa Park and museums. All are romantic one- and two-bedroom suites with coffeemakers and mini-fridges. ❺–❻

Beach Haven Inn 4740 Mission Blvd, Pacific Beach ⓣ858/272-3812 or 1-800/831-6323, ⓦ www.beachhaveninn.com. Nice rooms around a pool and spa; continental breakfast included. With air conditioning, kitchenettes and cable TV, it's one of the better values at the beach. ❺–❻

Crystal Pier Hotel and Cottages 4500 Ocean Blvd, Pacific Beach ⓣ858/483-6983 or 1-800/748-5894, ⓦ www.crystalpier.com.

Beautiful, deluxe cottages situated on Pacific Beach pier. All units are suites with private deck, and most have kitchenettes. ⑦–⑧

Horton Grand 311 Island Ave at 3rd Ave ☎619/544-1886 or 1-800/542-1886, Ⓦwww.hortongrand.com. Classy, modernized amalgam of two century-old hotels, with fireplaces in most rooms and friendly staff clad in Victorian attire. ⑥

J Street Inn 222 J St, downtown ☎619/696-6922. Near the Gaslamp District, Greyhound station and waterfront, this little-known bargain has units with microwaves, refrigerator and cable TV. ④

Ocean Beach Motel 5080 Newport Ave, Ocean Beach ☎619/223-7191. Not too pretty, but right across the street from the sand, with ocean view and kitchenettes available. ③

Surf & Sand Motel 4666 Mission Blvd, Pacific Beach ☎858/483-7420. Clean, comfortable motel close to the beach; offers pool, cable TV, mini-fridges or kitchenettes. ⑤–⑥

US Grant Hotel 326 Broadway, downtown ☎619/232-3121 or 1-800/237-5029, Ⓦwww.usgranthotel.com. Across from Horton Plaza, an elite favorite from 1910 onward, with neoclassical styling, countless chandeliers, marble floors and cozy but elegant rooms. ⑦

Wyndham Emerald Plaza 400 Broadway, downtown ☎619/239-4500, Ⓦwww.wyndham.com /EmeraldPlaza. Upscale, high-rise lodging with spacious rooms oriented toward business travelers, with pool, spa and exercise facilities. ⑦–⑨

The City

With its mix of laid-back libertarians and military-minded conservatives (drawn from its adjacent naval base), San Diego embodies both work-hard and play-hard lifestyles. With an easily navigable central area, scenic bay, 42 miles of beaches and plentiful parks and museums, the city is hard not to like from the moment you arrive.

Downtown San Diego and Coronado

Always vibrant and active, **downtown** San Diego is the best place to start exploring. Since the late 1970s, several blocks of 1920s architecture have been stylishly renovated, with the sleek modern bank buildings symbolizing the city's growing economic importance on the Pacific Rim. Downtown is safe by day, but can be unwelcoming at night, as much of it shuts down after business hours, and you should confine your after-dark visits to the restaurants and clubs of the comparatively well-lit and well-policed Gaslamp District.

The tall Moorish archways of the **Santa Fe Railroad Depot**, at the western end of **Broadway**, built in 1915 for the Panama-California Exposition, still evoke a sense of grandeur. Broadway slices through the middle of downtown, at its most hectic between Fourth and Fifth avenues. Shoppers, sailors, yuppies and slackers linger around the fountains outside **Horton Plaza** (Mon–Sat 8.30am–5pm, summer Mon–Sat 10am–9pm, Sun 11am–7pm; Ⓦhorton-plaza.shoppingtown.com), San Diego's major upmarket shopping venue, with a somewhat dated postmodern style that borrows heavily from Art Deco designs and motifs. Head for the open-air eating places on its top level; though the cuisine may be more expensive than in the streets – and offers little more than the standard fast-food fare of other shopping zones – it's fun to sit over a coffee and watch the parade of tourists go by. Take time on your way out to visit the 21ft-tall **Jessop Clock** on level one, made for the California State Fair of 1907.

South of Broadway, a few blocks and yet a world away from Horton Plaza, the sixteen-block **Gaslamp District**, heart of frontier San Diego, is now filled with smart streets lined with classy cafés, antique stores, art galleries, and, of course, gas lamps – now powered by electricity. A tad artificial it may be, but its late-nineteenth-century buildings are intriguing to explore. Worth a peek is the **Horton Grand**, 311 Island Ave, a reconstruction of two nineteenth-

DOWNTOWN SAN DIEGO

Tramline

A & B — Little Italy (1 block) — Hillcrest (25 blocks)

Balboa Park

CEDAR STREET
BEECH STREET
ASH STREET
A STREET
B STREET
C STREET

Maritime Museum **C**

San Diego County Administration Center

Santa Fe Railroad Depot & American Plaza

San Diego Bay Ferry Docking Stage

Greyhound Station

Transit Store **1**

Library

Horton Plaza

D
E F G
1 **2** **H**
J

Newtown Park

GASLAMP DISTRICT

MARKET STREET

K **3**

William Heath Davis House

L **4**

ISLAND AVENUE

Seaport Village

EMBARCADERO

HARBOR DRIVE

5

San Diego Convention Center

Embarcadero Marina Park

0   200 yds

N

East San Diego & Coronado ▼

ACCOMMODATION		RESTAURANTS, BARS AND CLUBS			
Grand Pacific Hostel	2	Anthony's Star of the Sea Room	C	The Casbah	B
HI-San Diego Metropolitan		Bella Luna	J	Croce's Restaurant and Jazz Bar	G
Hostel	3	Blue Tattoo	D	Filippi's Pizza Grotto	A
Horton Grand	4	Café Lulu	E	Fio's Cucina Italiana	F
J Street Inn	5	Café Seville	K	Gas Haus	H
US Grant Hotel	1	Café 222	L	Sammy's	I

century hotels originally located a few blocks away, with Old World decor and hotel staff in Victorian costumes.

West of downtown, the **Embarcadero** pathway follows the curve of the bay, and leads to the **Maritime Museum**, 1306 N Harbor Drive (daily 9am–8pm, summer closes at 9pm; $6; @ www.sdmaritime.com), where the most interesting of three vintage sailing craft is the *Star of India*, built in 1863 and now the world's oldest still-afloat merchant ship.

Across San Diego Bay from downtown, the isthmus of **Coronado** is a well-scrubbed resort community with a major naval station occupying its western end. It's of somewhat limited interest, save for the majestically modern **Coronado Bay Bridge**, a curving 11,000-foot span that's one of the area's signature images ($1 toll for southbound travelers without passengers), and the historic **Hotel del Coronado**, around which the town grew. The massive Victorian-turreted "Del" is where Edward VIII (then Prince of Wales) first met Mrs Simpson (then a Coronado housewife) in 1920 and where *Some Like It Hot* was filmed in 1958, posing as a Miami Beach hotel. The simplest and most scenic way to get to Coronado is on the **San Diego Bay ferry** ($2 each way; ☏619/234-4111) which leaves Broadway Pier daily on the hour between 9am and 9pm (10pm Fri & Sat). Tickets are available at **San Diego Harbor Excursion**, 1050 N Harbor Drive (Ⓦwww.sdhe.com).

Balboa Park and San Diego Zoo

Sumptuous **Balboa Park** contains one of the largest groups of **museums** in the US, scattered either side and to the south of El Prado, the road that bisects the park. Yet its greatest charms are its trees, gardens, statues, traffic-free promenades and Spanish Colonial-style buildings. Within easy reach of downtown by **buses** #7, #16 or #25, the park is large but fairly easy to **get around on foot** – if you tire, there's a free tram. The $30 **Balboa Park Passport**, which allows one-time admission to all twelve of the park's museums and its Japanese garden (though not the zoo), is available from the **visitors information center** (daily 9am–4pm; Ⓣ619/239-0512), inside the beautifully reconstructed House of Hospitality. Most of the museums are closed on Mondays, and most are free on varying Tuesdays.

Minor works by Rembrandt and El Greco and a stirring collection of Russian icons make the stifling formality of the **Timkin Museum of Art** (Tues–Sat 10am–4.30pm, Sun 1.30–4.30pm; closed Sept; free; Ⓦgort.ucsd.edu /sj/timken) worth enduring. The **San Diego Museum of Art** (Tues–Sun 10am–4.30pm; $8; Ⓦwww.sdmart.org) has few individually striking items in its permanent collection, save for a small selection of 17th-century Dutch works by Hals and Rembrandt, but it's the main venue for touring shows and offers some exquisitely crafted pieces from China and Japan. Outside, don't miss the free **Sculpture Court and Garden**, with formidable works by Henry Moore and Alexander Calder. The **Museum of Man** (daily 10am–4.30pm; $6; Ⓦwww.museumofman.org), which straddles El Prado, veers from banal crafts demonstrations to excellent Native American displays, artifacts, folklore and physical remains.

The child-oriented **Reuben H. Fleet Science Center** (Mon & Tues 9.30am–6.30pm, Wed–Sun 9.30am–9pm; science center $6.50, with theater or simulator $9, all three $11; Ⓦwww.rhfleet.org), close to the Park Boulevard end of El Prado, is notable mainly for its Space Theater's huge IMAX screen and virtual reality simulator, which take you on stomach-churning trips into outer and inner space. Across the plaza, the **Natural History Museum** (daily 9.30am–4.30pm; $6; Ⓦwww.sdnhm.org) has a great collection of fossils and pulls no punches in its coverage of threatened species. Just behind, in the **Spanish Village Art Center** (daily 11am–4pm; free), craftspeople in 37 studios and galleries practice skills such as painting, sculpture, pottery and glass-working.

The enormous **San Diego Zoo** (daily: mid June–early Sept 7am–10pm; early Sept–mid June 9am–dusk; last entry an hour before closing; Ⓦwww.sandiegozoo.org), immediately north of the main museums, is one of the world's best. Its wide selection of animals, many of them rare, are restrained in "psychological cages," without bars. (Don't depend on the much-hyped but usually sleeping Chinese pandas for entertainment, however.) Basic **admission**, including the children's zoo, is $18.50 (kids 3–11 $9.50); a Deluxe Tour ticket ($28.50, kids $16.50) includes a bus tour and a round-trip ride on the Skyfari overhead tramway.

Old Town San Diego and Presidio Hill

In 1769, Spanish settlers chose **Presidio Hill** as the site of the first of California's missions. They soon began to build homes at the foot of the hill, which was dominated in turn by Mexican officials and then by early arrivals from the eastern US. **Old Town San Diego**, reachable from downtown via the Trolley, is now a state historical park holding a number of original adobe dwellings, plus the inevitable souvenir shops. The stores and restaurants stay open until 10pm or later, but the **best time** to be around is during the afternoon, to enter the more interesting of the adobes on the daily **free walking tour** (2pm), which leaves from the **Seeley Stable**, just off the central plaza, home to many nicely preserved horse-drawn carriages and wagons from the nineteenth century. Details are available from the **visitors center**, 4002 Wallace St (daily 10am–5pm; ☏858/220-5422).

The Spanish-style building now atop Presidio Hill is only a rough approximation of the original mission – moved in 1774 – but its **Serra Museum** (Thurs–Sun 10am–4.30pm; $5) is an intriguing examination of Junipero Serra, the padre who led the Spanish colonization and Catholic conversion of California. The **Mission San Diego de Alcalá** itself was relocated six miles north to 10818 San Diego Mission Rd (daily 9am–5pm; $3 donation), to be near a water source and fertile soils – and to be safer from attack. The present building (on bus #43 from downtown) is still a working parish church, a peaceful complex with a small **museum** that holds craft objects and historical articles from the mission, including the crucifix held by Serra at his death in 1834.

Hillcrest, Ocean Beach and Point Loma

North of downtown and on the northwest edge of Balboa Park, **Hillcrest** is a lively and artsy area at the center of the city's **gay community**. Go there either for something to eat – there's a selection of interesting cafés and restaurants around University and Fifth streets – or simply to stroll around the fine gathering of Victorian homes.

Ocean Beach, six miles northwest of downtown and reached by bus #35, rivals Pacific Beach in its surfing and party atmosphere, although Ocean Beach has a more down-to-earth, bohemian feel, and is replete with excellent secondhand music shops. Despite being a former, notorious Hell's Angels hangout, this has become one of the most sought-after San Diego addresses, with **Newport Street** the prime spot where most young backpackers spend their time, among rows of cheap snack bars, surf and skate shops and T-shirt stalls.

The **Cabrillo National Monument** (daily 9am–5.15pm; 7-day pass $5 per car, pedestrians and cyclists $2), at the southern extremity of the hilly and very green peninsula of **Point Loma**, stretches south from Ocean Beach. It was at its southern extremity where Cabrillo and crew became the first Europeans to land in California. That's as far as the historical interest goes, for they quickly reboarded their vessel and sailed away again. The startling views from this high spot, however, across San Diego Bay to the downtown skyline and right along the coast to Mexico, easily repay the journey here. From the western cliffs of the park, a platform makes it easy to view the November-to-March **winter whale migration**, when scores of gray whales pass by en route to their breeding grounds off Baja California, Mexico.

Mission Bay, Mission Beach, Pacific Beach and La Jolla

North of Ocean Beach, you come to **Mission Bay** and San Diego's most popular tourist attraction. Exhibits and events at **Sea World** (mid June–Aug daily 9am–dusk; rest of year 10am–dusk; $41.95, kids $31.95, parking $7; ⓦ www.seaworld.com) range from "performances" by killer whales and dolphins to the eerie sight of the heads of hundreds of moray eels protruding from the hollow rocks of the "Forbidden Reef." Sharks circle menacingly in the Shark House; the Penguin Exhibit is a mock Antarctica; the Wild Arctic exhibit simulates the North Pole with polar bears and walruses; and the Manatee Rescue provides a close-up glimpse of the white, bulbous freshwater herbivores.

Anyone of a nervous disposition, or with a physique inappropriate for bathing apparel, might find nearby **Mission Beach** – the peninsula that separates Mission Bay from the Pacific Ocean – and its seamless northern extension, **Pacific Beach**, an intimidating spot, with scads of scantily clad torsos and surf-board-clutching hunks. Despite first impressions, though, the city authorities are endeavoring to limit its anarchic hedonism – more families are using the area, but little impact has been made on the beach's freewheeling character.

A more pretentious air prevails in **La Jolla** (always "la-hoya"), an elegant beach community just to the north that mystery writer Raymond Chandler once described as "a nice place – for old people and their parents." Stroll its immaculate, gallery-filled streets, fuel up on some California cuisine at one of the many sidewalk cafés or visit the La Jolla site of the **Museum of Contemporary Art**, 700 Prospect St (Tues & Thurs–Sat 10am–5pm, Wed 10am–8pm, Sun noon–5pm; $4; Ⓦwww.mcasandiego.org), which has a huge – and regularly changing – stock of paintings and sculptures from 1955 onwards, with California pop and minimalism some of the highlights. On the seaward side of the museum lies the small, exquisitely tasteful **Ellen Scripps Browning Park**, named after the philanthropist whose Irving Gill–designed home now houses the museum. Where the park meets the coast is the popular **La Jolla Cove**, with clear waters perfect for snorkeling, as long as you can secure a parking space.

Eating

Wherever you are in San Diego, you'll have few problems finding somewhere to **eat** good food in a fun atmosphere at reasonable prices. Everything from crusty coffee shops to stylish ethnic restaurants is in copious supply, with seafood at its best around Mission Beach and the Gaslamp District, and the latter home to the greatest concentration of restaurants, aimed at both tourists and locals alike.

Anthony's Star of the Sea Room 1360 N Harbor Drive, downtown ☎619/232-7408. Pricey Franco-California-style preparations of seafood, justly famed for its freshness and variety, served on a terrace on the waterfront.

Bella Luna 748 5th Ave, downtown ☎619/239-3222. This romantic, moon-adorned restaurant serves up wonderful, familiar Italian dishes to a relaxed artsy crowd.

Berta's 3928 Twiggs St, Old Town ☎619/295-2343. A far cry from the area's many touristy Mexican restaurants, offering low-priced, authentic cooking from all over Latin America.

Café 222 222 Island Ave at 2nd Ave, downtown ☎619/236-9902. Industrially decorated café serving some of the city's best breakfasts and lunches – mainly fresh twists on staples like sandwiches, burgers and salads – and at reasonable prices. Open daily 7am–1.45pm.

Chilango's Mexican Grill 142 University Ave, Hillcrest ☎619/294-8646. Gourmet food for under $8, with solid emphasis on Mexican-vegetarian cooking. Tiny storefront locale is popular with locals and packed to the rafters in the evenings.

Crest Café 425 Robinson Ave, Hillcrest ☎619/295-2510. Old-fashioned American staples at low prices, with a fair selection of homemade desserts.

Croce's Restaurant and Jazz Bar 802 5th Ave, downtown ☎619/233-4355. Devoted to the life and work of folk-rock troubadour Jim Croce, with a pricey but excellent range of pastas and salads; the Sunday jazz brunch is renowned for its tasty mix of music and munchies.

Filippi's Pizza Grotto 1747 India St at Date St, Little Italy ☎619/232-5094. Great pizzas and a handful of scrumptious pasta dishes served in a convivial small room at the back of a Little Italy grocery.

Fio's Cucina Italiana 801 5th Ave at F St, downtown ☎619/234-3467. Stylish, high-priced Italian
cuisine aimed for business clientele and special
events.
Ichiban 1449 University Ave, Hillcrest ☎619/299-
7203. A good spot to enjoy quality, reasonably
priced Japanese cuisine, and especially good for
combo platters.
Kono's 704 Garnet Ave, Pacific Beach ☎858/483-
1669. Crowded, tourist-centric place for breakfast
or lunch on the boardwalk. Serves inexpensive,
hefty portions of eggs, sandwiches, hamburgers
and other all-American favorites.
Living Room Coffeehouse 1010 Prospect St, La
Jolla ☎858/459-1187. Great sandwiches, soups,
quiches and pastries in a living room-like setting – a
bit comfier than its other three San Diego locations.
Mexican Village Restaurant 120 Orange Ave,
Coronado ☎935/435-1822. Good for cheap,
south-of-the-border staples and renowned for its

authentic music and mind-numbing margaritas.
Mission Café and Coffeehouse 3795 Mission
Blvd, Mission Beach ☎858/488-9060. Mexican
breakfasts and lunch offerings, plus beer, specialty
coffees, shakes and smoothies. Open late.
Point Loma Seafoods 2805 Emerson St, Ocean
Beach ☎619/223-1109. Fast, inexpensive counter
serving San Diego's freshest fish'n'chips and oversized sandwiches. Often crowded, especially on
weekends.
Sammy's 770 4th Ave, just outside of Horton
Plaza ☎619/230-8888. California cuisine in a
Mediterranean-style atmosphere. Pizza, pasta, salads, seafood and chicken are the highlights, along
with local favorites like rich, messy sundaes.
Taste of Thai 527 University Ave, Hillcrest
☎619/291-7525. Terrific Thai for reasonable
prices in the center of Hillcrest; expect a wait on
weekends.

Nightlife

Although San Diego's money is lavished on **classical music**, **opera** and **theater** (half-priced tickets and information available at the **Times Arts Tix**
booth at 28 Horton Plaza; ☎619/497-5000), the crowds flock to beachside
discos and boozy **music venues**. For full listings, pick up the free *San Diego
Reader* from numerous shops, bars and cafés around town.

Blind Melons 710 Garnet Ave, Pacific Beach
☎858/483-7844. College-oriented spot with live
rock, blues and reggae bands nightly.
Blue Tattoo 835 Fifth Ave, downtown ☎619/238-
7191. Stylish debauchery with ass-shaking tunes,
"foam parties" with copious bubbles, and a snooty
door policy that keeps slackers at bay. Make sure
to come clad in your hippest clubwear.
Café Lulu 419 F St, downtown ☎619/238-0114.
A popular coffee bar that's good for late-night kib-
bitzing and consuming a wide range of java concoctions.
Café Sevilla 555 4th Ave, downtown ☎619/233-
5979. Traditional Spanish cuisine upstairs, hip
Latin American-flavored dance club downstairs.
Brings in a trendy European crowd.
The Casbah 2501 Kettner Blvd, downtown
☎619/232-4355. Fun, unpretentious hangout with
a varying roster of blues, funk, reggae and indie
bands.
Emerald City 945 Garnet Ave, Pacific Beach
☎858/483-9920. Lively disco with drink specials
at weekends, and the popular underworld industrial
and Gothic night on Sun.
The Flame 3780 Park Blvd, Hillcrest ☎619/295-
4163. The city's premier lesbian club, with pool

tables and dancing, and live musical acts from
early evening to early morning. Tuesday becomes
"Boys' Night."
Gas Haus 640 F St, downtown ☎619/232-5866.
Alcohol-free café with eclectic decor and stocked
with teens, students and aging hippies. Lounge on
deep-set couches or take in a casual game of
pool.
La Jolla Brewing Company 7536 Fay Ave, La
Jolla ☎858/456-2739. One of the few decent
choices for nightlife in this buttoned-down burg,
with tasty microbrewed beer and surfboard decor.
Red Fox Room 2223 El Cajon Blvd, near Hillcrest
☎619/297-1313. A retro piano bar and steak joint
with a swell atmosphere of mellow newcomers
and boozy old-timers.
Rich's 1051 University Ave, Hillcrest ☎619/295-
2195. Gay club with heavy dance beats Fri and
Sat, and more casual "Hedonism" night on Thurs,
with house music and tribal rhythms.
Winston's Beach Club 1921 Bacon St, Ocean
Beach ☎619/222-6822. A former bowling alley,
this local club has rock bands most nights, with
occasional reggae and 1960s-style acts as well.
Close to the pier.

Out from San Diego:
the Anza-Borrego Desert

Most of eastern San Diego County, which otherwise consists largely of sleepy suburban communities, is taken up by the more than 600,000-acre **Anza-Borrego Desert**, much of it a **state park** (free; $5 per vehicle). Some of it can be covered by car, although four-wheel-drive vehicles are necessary for the more obscure – and most interesting – routes. The best **time to come** is winter, when daytime temperatures stay around the mid-eighties. In the fiercely

Tijuana: a taste of Mexico

You could hardly find a more intriguing day-trip out from San Diego than **Tijuana**, just over the border in Mexico. While far from the most culturally rich place in Mexico, every year twenty million people cross here from the US. Most of them are Californians and tourists on day-long shopping expeditions, seeking somewhere cheap and colorful to spend money on blankets, pottery, cigarettes, tequila, dentistry, car repair, and, more recently, pharmaceutical drugs – available through many of the town's cut-rate pharmacies and usually without a prescription. Keep in mind, though, that while everything is lower-priced in Tijuana than in the US, the quality and safety of the merchandise are sometimes questionable.

Although you can't help but be made aware of the vast economic gulf separating the two countries – you're immediately confronted by shabbily dressed food vendors and children selling woven bracelets and gum – Tijuana is, in fact, one of the wealthiest Mexican cities, and somewhat safer than it was a decade ago. The main streets and shopping areas are a few blocks from the border in downtown, where the major thoroughfare is Avenida Revolución. Stroll around for a while to get the mood and then retire to one of the many bars and watch the tourist throngs lubricate themselves with potent margaritas. At night, the action mostly consists of inebriated North American youths dancing themselves silly in flashy discos and rowdy rock'n'roll bars. **Iguanas-Ranas** (Avenida Revolución at Calle 3; ℡66/85-14-22) is a good example, and for big food and revelry, check out **Tia Juana Tilly's** (Avenida Revolución at Calle 7; ℡66/85-60-24), where you can sample traditional Mexican specialties such as roast pig and chicken mole (mo-lay).

Heavy traffic, and insurance problems, make crossing into Mexico **by car** a risky business; from San Diego you can take either the Trolley ($4 round-trip; p.1047) or bus #932 from Santa Fe Railroad Depot. However, if you do decide to drive into Mexico, invest in **auto insurance**, which can be had for as little as $10 per day in San Ysidro. Dollars are accepted as readily as pesos, so there's no need to **change money**, though prices are better if you do. **Border formalities** are minimal: you only need a Mexican Tourist Card (free from consulates in the US or at the Mexican Customs office just inside the Tijuana side of the border) if you're planning to go further than 75 miles into the country or stay for more than three days. Returning to the US, however, even within a single day, immigration procedures are stringent – even joking about smuggling weapons or illegal drugs can bring a humiliating interrogation, so be wary of saying or doing anything foolish. **Hotels** are cheap, with many low-cost lodgings close to the center. At the lowest end of the price scale is *Hotel Jaliscense*, Calle 1 #7925 (℡66/85-34-91; ①); slightly more upmarket, *La Villa de Zaragoza*, Avenida Madero 1120 (℡66/85-18-32; ③; ⓦmembers.aol.com/hotellavilla/tijuana.html), has clean rooms with air conditioning and cable TV; and *Camino Real*, Paseo de los Heroes 10305 (℡66/33-40-01, ⓦwww.caminoreal.com/tijuana; ⑤), best of all, has plush rooms and two fine restaurants and bars.

hot summer, it's best left to the lizards, but when the desert **blooms**, between March and May, scarlet ocotillo, orange poppies, white lilies, purple verbena and other wild flowers paint a memorable, and fragrant, picture. To find out more information, and begin your trip at a good jumping-off point, stop by the **park visitors center**, near park headquarters at 200 Palm Canyon Drive (daily 8am–5pm, weekends only during summer; ☎760/767-4205).

Historical reminders in the desert span Native American tribes, early white explorers and Gold Rush fortune-hunters. Approaching from the west, Hwy-78 descends to Scissors Crossing, the junction with Hwy-22, which follows the **Butterfield Stage Route**, the first regular line of communication between the East and the newly settled West, which began service in 1857. Further on, the old adobe rest stop of **Vallecito** (vy-ay-SEE-toe) **Stage Station** gives a good indication of the privations of early desert travel. To the south, around Imperial Valley in the least-visited portion of Anza-Borrego, there's a vivid and spectacular clash as gray rock rises from the edges of the red desert floor. Along Hwy-22, east of Borrego Springs, is a memorial to Peg Leg Smith, an infamous local spinner of yarns from the Gold Rush days who is celebrated by the **Peg Leg Liars Contest** on the first Saturday in April; anybody can get up before the judges and fib their hearts out.

The only substantial settlement in the desert is **BORREGO SPRINGS**, at the northern end of Hwy-S3 along Hwy-S22, which is a good base for the area's canyon walks, some with free but waterless **campgrounds**. Camping is also available at the *Borrego Palm Canyon* campground, near the Anza-Borrego park visitors center. From here, a 1.5-mile trail takes you to a small oasis with palms and a waterfall. **Hotels** in town are fairly pricey; only the *Oasis* at 366 W Palm Drive (☎760/767-5409; ❸) and *Hacienda del Sol* (☎760/767-5442; ❸), on Palm Canyon Drive, are even close to affordable.

Los Angeles

The rambling metropolis of **LOS ANGELES** sprawls across the thousand square miles of a great desert basin, knitted together by an intricate network of congested freeways between the ocean and the snowcapped mountains. Its colorful melange of shopping malls, palm trees and swimming pools is both mildly surreal and startlingly familiar, thanks to the celluloid self-image that it has spread all over the world.

LA is a young city; in the mid-nineteenth century, it was a community of white American immigrants, poor Chinese laborers and wealthy Mexican ranchers, with a population of less than fifty thousand. Only on completion of the transcontinental railroad in the 1880s did it really begin to grow, as a national mecca for good health, clean living, plentiful sunshine and endless acres of citrus crops. The biggest group of transplants were refugees from the Midwest, who created a new political ruling class to replace the old Mexican elite. The old ranchos were soon subdivided, the population grew rapidly, and the enduring symbol of the city became the family-sized suburban house (with

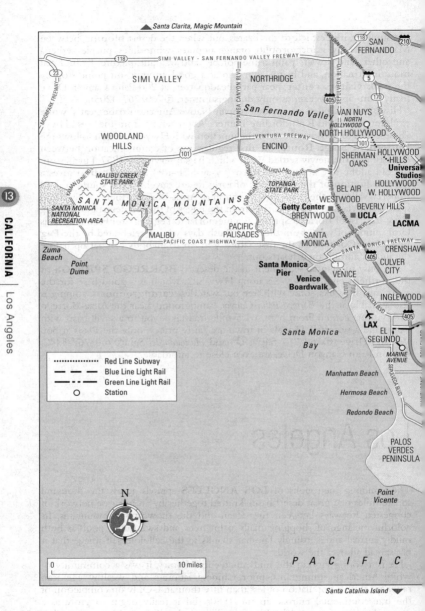

Santa Clarita, Magic Mountain

SIMI VALLEY

SAN FERNANDO

SIMI VALLEY - SAN FERNANDO VALLEY FREEWAY

NORTHRIDGE

San Fernando Valley

VAN NUYS

NORTH HOLLYWOOD

NORTH HOLLYWOOD

WOODLAND HILLS

VENTURA FREEWAY

ENCINO

SHERMAN OAKS

HOLLYWOOD HILLS

Universal Studios

MULHOLLAND DRIVE

HOLLYWOOD W. HOLLYWOOD

MALIBU CREEK STATE PARK

SANTA MONICA MOUNTAINS

TOPANGA STATE PARK

BEL AIR

WESTWOOD

Getty Center

BRENTWOOD

UCLA

BEVERLY HILLS

LACMA

SANTA MONICA NATIONAL RECREATION AREA

MALIBU

PACIFIC PALISADES

SANTA MONICA

PACIFIC COAST HIGHWAY

CRENSHAW

Zuma Beach

Point Dume

Santa Monica Pier

Venice Boardwalk

VENICE

CULVER CITY

INGLEWOOD

Santa Monica Bay

LAX

EL SEGUNDO

MARINE AVENUE

Manhattan Beach

Hermosa Beach

Redondo Beach

·········· Red Line Subway
– – – Blue Line Light Rail
–·–·– Green Line Light Rail
○ Station

PALOS VERDES PENINSULA

Point Vicente

N

0   10 miles

P A C I F I C

Santa Catalina Island

swimming pool and two-car garage). The biggest boom came after World War II with the mushrooming of the aeronautics industry – which, until post–Cold War military cutbacks, accounted for one in four jobs.

The first-time visitor may well find Los Angeles thrilling and threatening in equal proportions; it's a place that picks you up and sweeps you along whether

TUJUNGA

FOOTHILL FREEWAY

LA CAÑADA
FLINTRIDGE

BURBANK

ANGELES NATIONAL FOREST

GLENDALE

134

**Rose
Bowl**

PASADENA

San Gabriel Valley

5

GLENDALE FWY

VENTURA FREEWAY

MONROVIA

210

Old Pasadena

FOOTHILL FREEWAY (ROUTE 66)

210

Griffith
Park

2

**Norton Simon
Museum**

SAN MARINO

ARCADIA

HUNTINGDON DR.

AZUSA AVE.

101

SILVER
LAKE

GOLDEN STATE FREEWAY

PASADENA FREEWAY

SOUTH
PASADENA

**Huntington
Library & Gardens**

605

WEST COVINA

210

FOOTHILL FREEWAY

110

HIGHLAND PARK

19

SAN BERNARDINO FREEWAY

10

*WILSHIRE &
WESTERN*

MID-
WILSHIRE

Union Station

MONTEREY
PARK

EL MONTE

60

CITY OF
INDUSTRY

13

xposition
Park

*SEVENTH STREET/
METRO CENTER*

DOWNTOWN

EAST LA

60

POMONA FREEWAY

▶ *Palm Springs*

VERNON

HARBOR FREEWAY

SLAUSON AVENUE

ROSEMEAD BOULEVARD

San Gabriel River

SAN GABRIEL RIVER FREEWAY

WHITTIER

SOUTH
CENTRAL
LA

42

MANCHESTER AVENUE

5

SANTA FE
SPRINGS

LA HABRA

CALIFORNIA | Los Angeles

WATTS

Watts Towers

CENTURY FREEWAY

105

Los Angeles River

LONG BEACH FREEWAY

IMPERIAL HIGHWAY

90

**Nixon
Library**

AWTHORNE

WILMINGTON

COMPTON

19

*605/105 FREEWAY
INTERCHANGE*

SANTA ANA FREEWAY

YORBA LINDA

ARDENA

91

REDONDO BEACH FWY

ARTESIA FREEWAY

91

BUENA
PARK

RIVERSIDE FREEWAY

91

SAN DIEGO FREEWAY

ORRANCE

LAKEWOOD

605

57

55

EPULVEDA

WILMINGTON

405

LAKEWOOD BLVD.

CARSON ST.

LINCOLN AVENUE

LOS ALAMITOS

ANAHEIM

22

GARDEN GROVE FREEWAY

1

BOULEVARD

PACIFIC COAST HIGHWAY

○ *LONG BEACH PLAZA*

Disneyland

5

GARDEN GROVE

**LA
Harbor**

Queen Mary

LONG BEACH

SEAL
BEACH

405

**ORANGE
COUNTY**

SAN PEDRO

BEACH BOULEVARD

COSTA MESA FREEWAY

Point
Fermin

1

PACIFIC COAST HIGHWAY

Huntington Beach

HARBOR BLVD.

SAN DIEGO FREEWAY

55

IRVINE

405

O C E A N

Newport Beach

73

you want it to or not. While it has its fine-art museums, California cuisine and a few old-fashioned urban plazas, what people really come here for is to experience the city that has come to epitomize the American Dream – the fantasy worlds of **Disneyland** and **Hollywood**, as well as the gilded opulence of **Beverly Hills** and **Malibu**.

Arrival, information and getting around

All European and many domestic **flights** use Los Angeles International Airport – always known as **LAX** (℡310/646-5252, ⊕www.los-angeles-lax.com) – sixteen miles southwest of downtown. Free 24-hour **shuttle buses** (line "C") connect with the LAX Transit Center at Vicksburg Avenue and 96th Street, where you can pick up **local buses**. Minibuses such as LAX Chequer Shuttle (℡1-800/545-7745, ⊕www.laxchequer.com), SuperShuttle (℡310/782-6600 or 1-800/554-3146, ⊕www.supershuttle.com) and Coast Shuttle (℡310/417-3988) run all over town, delivering you to your door. Fares are generally around $20–30 (plus tip), with a journey time of between 30 and 45 minutes. **Taxis** from the airport are always expensive: around $25 to downtown and West LA, $30 to Hollywood and as much as $90 to Disneyland.

If you're arriving from elsewhere in the US, or from Mexico, you might just land at one of the **other airports** in the LA area – at Burbank, Long Beach, Ontario, or Orange County's John Wayne Airport. MTA buses (℡213/626-4455 or 1-800/COMMUTE, outside LA ℡1-800/2-LARIDE, ⊕www.mta .net) serve them all – phone on arrival and tell them where you are and where you're going.

The main **Greyhound** bus terminal, at 1716 E Seventh St (℡213/629-8401, ⊕www.greyhound.com), is in a seedy section of downtown, but access is restricted to ticket holders so it's safe enough inside. LA's other Greyhound stations handle fewer services: 1409 Vine St, in Hollywood; 11239 Magnolia Blvd, North Hollywood; 645 E Walnut St, Pasadena; 464 W 3rd St, Long Beach; and 100 W Winston Rd, Anaheim.

Arriving in LA by **train** you'll be greeted with the Mission Revival architecture of Union Station, 800 N Alameda St (℡213/624-0171), on the north side of downtown, from which you can also access the city's MTA bus lines.

Information

LA has a number of **visitors centers**. The downtown one is at 685 S Figueroa St (Mon–Fri 8am–5pm, Sat 8.30am–5pm; ℡213/689-8822, ⊕www .lacvb.com); others, all open normal weekday working hours, are in Santa Monica at 1400 Ocean Ave (℡310/393-7593, ⊕www.santamonica.com); near Disneyland at 800 W Katella Ave (℡714/999-8999, ⊕www.anaheimoc.org); in Beverly Hills at 239 S Beverly Drive (℡310/248-1015, ⊕www.beverly-hillscvb.com); and in Hollywood at Janes House, 6541 Hollywood Blvd (℡323/689-8822). All supply free local **maps**, but you'd do better to spend $2.95 on Gousha Publications' fully indexed *Los Angeles CityMap*, available from machines in visitors centers and hotel lobbies.

For general delivery/poste restante, use the main downtown **post office** at 760 N Main St (Mon–Fri 8am–7pm, Sat 8am–4pm, pick up letters Mon–Fri 8am–3pm; zip code 90012; ℡1-800/275-8777).

City transport

The sheer scale of LA – its detractors call it "nineteen suburbs in search of a city" – means that it really *is* difficult to get around without a car. Even though the traffic is often bumper-to-bumper, the freeways are the only way to cover long distances quickly. If you're driving yourself, avoid traveling at rush hours and phone ahead for directions whenever possible. Otherwise, try to relax on the fastest alternative, **express buses**.

Guided tours

Some of your best bets for touring downtown and other spots are the two-and-one-half hour **walking tours** offered by the LA Conservancy (Sat 10am; $8; ☏213/623-CITY, ⓦwww.laconservancy.org), which concentrate on various aspects of the city's architecture, history, murals and culture. If you'd rather take a ride, innumerable **bus tours** introduce the city, though only the specialists below show you anything you couldn't see more cheaply yourself. Costs are $30 minimum; most will collect you from your hotel. The **mainstream** bus tours whiz you past the main sights and the **homes of the stars** (though you often don't see much more than the gate at the end of the driveway), padding out the experience with views of palm trees and wide boulevards. Operators include **Casablanca Tours**, at the *Hollywood Roosevelt* hotel, 6362 Hollywood Blvd (☏323/461-0156, ⓦwww.casablancatours.com), which focuses on the golden age of cinema; **Tour Coach**, 6922 Hollywood Blvd (☏323/463-3333), which points out the houses of Marilyn Monroe, Barbra Streisand and Charlie Chaplin, and also runs shopping trips to the Mexican border town of Tijuana; and **Hollywood Fantasy Tours**, 6671 Hollywood Blvd (☏323/469-8184), which shows off Beverly Hills and Hollywood only. Even if you don't call or drop by their offices, you can pick up a tour flyer or brochure by standing outside Mann's Chinese Theatre, 6925 Hollywood Blvd, where discarded advertisements litter the sidewalk.

Specialist tours

Black LA Tours ☏323/750-9267. Black historical and entertainment tours of once-famed Central Avenue and key African-American history museums and cultural attractions.

The California Native 6701 W 87th Place (☏310/642-1140 or 1-800/926-1140, ⓦwww.calnative.com). Go sea-kayaking, tour the uninhabited islands off the coast of California. Adventure tours $195 and up.

Googie Tours (☏323/980-3480). Groovy treks to space-age glass and formica diners, quirky cocktail lounges and classic fast-food joints, as well as touring tributes to LA's primo pop architecture.

Haunted Hearse Tours PO Box 461145, Hollywood (☏323/782-9652, ⓦwww.tour-landusa.com). Better have a strong taste for the morbid to spend two and a half hours in the back of a Cadillac hearse, tracking down the location of every eventful death, scandal, perverted sex act and drug orgy ever to have tainted Hollywood.

Neon Cruises 501 W Olympic Blvd, downtown (☏213/489-9918, ⓦwww .neon-mona.org /cruise.html). Three-hour-long, eye-popping evening tours of LA's best remaining neon art, once a month on Saturdays, sponsored by the Museum of Neon Art.

SPARC tours: the Murals of LA 685 Venice Blvd, Venice (☏310/822-9560, ⓦwww.sparcmurals.org). Expert tours through the "mural capital of the world." Pointing out remarkable neighborhood landmarks all over the city – community art in a cultural context.

Some people are surprised to find sidewalks in LA, let alone pedestrians, but within districts such as downtown, Santa Monica, Pasadena, Beverly Hills and central Hollywood, **walking** is the best way to explore.

Public transportation

Hampered by construction scandals and budget cuts, LA's long-anticipated **Metrorail** train system was envisioned to cover the whole of Los Angeles County, but is currently made up of only three lines, each distinguished by color. Centering on the Seventh Street Metro Center Station, the **Red Line** stretches from Union Station through Hollywood to North Hollywood in the San Fernando Valley. The **Green Line** goes from Hawthorne to Norwalk along the Century Freeway, and the most complete route, the **Blue Line**, connects downtown through Watts to the Pacific Transit Mall in Long Beach. Tickets cost $1.35, or 75¢ at night from 9pm–5am, and trains run every five to fifteen minutes (and more infrequently at night).

Car-less Angelenos are still most well served, however, with **buses**, most of which are run by the LA County Metropolitan Transit Authority (MTA or "Metro"; ⓦwww.mta.net), still sometimes abbreviated to its old name, the RTD. For information, phone ☎213/626-4455 or 1-800/COMMUTE, or show up in person at 515 S Flower St, downtown (level C of Arco Plaza; Mon–Fri 7.30am–3.30pm), 5301 Wilshire Blvd (Mon–Fri 9am–5pm), or 6249 Hollywood Blvd (Mon–Fri 10am–6pm). Buses on the major arteries between downtown and the coast run roughly every fifteen minutes between 5am and 2am; other routes, and the **all-night services** along the major thoroughfares, are less frequent. At night, be careful not to get stranded alone downtown waiting for a connection.

The standard **single fare** is $1.35; **transfers** cost 25¢ more, but must be made within an hour; **express buses**, and any others using the freeway, are $1.85 up to $3.85. A **monthly pass** costs $42, slightly more to include express buses, with weekly passes for $11 and a student pass for $30. Smaller **DASH** buses run five routes around downtown, and a Hollywood service weekdays and Saturdays (25¢ flat fare).

You'll be hard pressed to find an available **taxi** cruising the streets, so call ahead; among the more reliable companies are the Independent Cab Co. (☎1-800/521-8294), LA Taxi (☎1-800/200-1085) and United Independent Taxi (☎1-800/411-0303). Fares include a base charge of around $2; add $1.60 per mile and tack on another $2.50 if you're getting picked up from LAX.

Major LA bus routes (MTA)

From downtown to:
Burbank Studios #96
Exposition Park #38, #81
Forest Lawn Cemetery, Glendale #90, #91
Huntington Library #79, #379
LAX #42, #439
Long Beach #60
Orange County, Knott's Berry Farm, Disneyland #460 (express)
Pasadena #401, #402
San Fernando Valley #424, #425, #522
San Pedro #445, #446, #447 (all express), transfer to LADOT #142 for Catalina terminal
Santa Monica #20, #22, #320, #322, #434 (express)
Venice #33, #333, #436 (express)

To and from downtown:
Along Hollywood Blvd #1
Along Melrose Ave #10, #11
Along Santa Monica Blvd #4, #304
Along Sunset Blvd #2, #3, #302
Along Wilshire Blvd #20, #21, #22, #320 (limited stops, but faster than #20)

From LAX to:
Downtown #42, #439
Getty Center/San Fernando Valley #561
Hollywood #220 (then transfer to #4 at Santa Monica Blvd)
Long Beach #232
San Pedro #225
West Hollywood #220

Cycling

Cycling in LA may sound perverse, but there are great coastal bike paths between Santa Monica and Redondo Beach, and nice routes at the Orange County coastline, Griffith Park and Pasadena. More disturbingly, the LA River route is only intended for daring cyclists who don't mind the sight of broken glass, mounds of trash and grim industrial vistas.

Accommodation

Finding a **place to stay** in LA is easy; finding somewhere inexpensive and well located is difficult, though not impossible. Downtown has both upscale and budget hotels; Hollywood has a wide range of cheap motels; and West LA, Santa Monica, Beverly Hills and Malibu are predominantly mid- to upper-range. If you're not driving, you'll want to choose your base carefully to avoid lengthy cross-town journeys between these areas, or divide your stay between them. The nearest **campgrounds** to LA are along the Orange County coast, such as *Bolsa Chica* in Huntington Beach (☎1-800/444-7275), and in the mountains and beaches around Malibu, notably Malibu Creek State Park (☎1-800/706-8809) and Leo Carrillo State Beach (☎1-818/706-1310). Expect to pay $14–21 per campsite.

Hostels

Hostels are dotted all over the city, though some limit stays to a few nights. Colleges and fraternity houses let out space during summer; for details call UCLA's Interfraternity Council (☎310/825-7878) and USC's off-campus housing office (☎1-800/USC-4632).

Banana Bungalow 2775 Cahuenga Blvd W ☎323/851-1129 or 1-800/446-7835, ⓦwww.bananabungalow.com. Huge, party-oriented hostel in the Hollywood Hills near Hwy-101. Dorms $18–21; singles or doubles $60 and up. Free shuttle buses to Venice Beach, Universal Studios and Magic Mountain. Every other night, you get as much beer as you can drink for $3. ❶/❷

HI-Anaheim/Fullerton 1700 N Harbor Blvd, Fullerton ☎714/738-3721, ⓦwww.hostelweb .com/losangeles/fullerton.htm. Spacious and comfortable, 5 miles north of Disneyland. Summer check-in 5–11pm; rest of year 4–11pm. Mornings open 7.10am–noon. Orange County Transit Authority bus #43 stops outside. Members $14, nonmembers $17. ❶

HI-Los Angeles/Santa Monica 1436 2nd St, Santa Monica ☎310/393-9913, ⓦwww.hostel-web.com/losangeles/los_angeles.htm. Huge new hostel in well-restored old building, a few strides from the Santa Monica sands. Members $24, non-members $27. Open 24hr. ❶

HI-Los Angeles/South Bay 3601 S Gaffey St, #613 ☎310/831-8109,

ⓦwww.hostelweb.com/losangeles/south_bay.htm. In the South Bay area, overlooking the ocean. MTA bus #446 passes close by but it's a 2hr journey from downtown, or take SuperShuttle from LAX. There's a pool, and free trip to the local aquarium. Open 7am–midnight. Members $14, nonmembers $17; private rooms $36. ❶

Hollywood Orange Drive Manor 1764 N Orange Dr ☎323/850-0350, ⓦwww.orangedrivehostel .com. Centrally located spot behind the Chinese Theatre, with tours to film studios, theme parks and homes of the stars. Old-fashioned hostel features movieland antiques recalling its days as a celebrity-friendly hotel in the 1950s. Members $16, nonmembers $18. ❶

Hostel California 2221 Lincoln Blvd, Venice ☎310/305-0250. Built for the 1984 Olympics, with six-bed dorms, free shuttle bus to LAX, big-screen TV and cable. Members $15, nonmembers $17; $100 per week. ❶

Huntington Beach Colonial Inn Hostel 421 8th St, Huntington Beach ☎714/536-3315, ⓦwww .huntingtonbeachhostel.com. Four blocks from the beach; mostly double rooms. Open

8am–11pm. Key rental after 1pm $1 (plus $20 deposit). Dorms $20, private rooms $22.50 per person. ❶

Jim's at the Beach 17 Brooks Ave, Venice ☎310/399-4018. Beachside dormitory rooms on production of a passport. $19 per night, $120 per week. ❶

Share-Tel Hostel 20 Brooks Ave, Venice ☎310/392-0325. Rooms for 6 to 8 people sharing facilities and bedrooms. $15 per night including breakfast and dinner Mon–Fri. Private rooms $20. Rates jump $5 during summer. ❶

Venice Beach Cotel 25 Windward Ave, Venice ☎310/399-7649, ⓦwww.venicebeachcotel.com. Located in a historic beachside building, this colonnaded hostel (or "cotel") has dorm rooms from $15–17, and private rooms $35–48. ❶/❷

Hotels, motels and B&Bs

There are no booking agencies, and visitors centers do not reserve accommodation, so to be sure of a **hotel** or **motel** room you should reserve direct as early as possible (and don't be afraid to haggle).

Downtown and around

Biltmore 506 S Grand Ave ☎213/624-1011 or 1-800/222-8888, ⓦwww.thebiltmore.com. Neoclassical 1923 architecture combined with modern luxury to make your head swim. Cheaper by far at weekends. ❾

City Center Motel 1135 W 7th St ☎213/628-7141. Small and informal, with tacky 1960s decor, but a free continental breakfast and airport shuttle bus. ❷

Figueroa 939 S Figueroa St ☎213/627-8971 or 1-800/421-9092, ⓦwww.figueroahotel.com. Well-placed mid-range hotel with pleasant rooms, 24hr coffee shop, pool and jacuzzi. ❺

Kawada 200 S Hill St at 2nd ☎213/621-4455 or 1-800/752-9232, ⓦwww.kawadahotel.com. Comfortable, clean but drab rooms in renovated hotel near Civic Center. Business-oriented but still one of the city's better bargains. ❹–❺

Miyako Inn 328 E 1st St ☎213/617-2000, ⓦwww.miyakoinn.com. Don't let the concrete-box look fool you; this is a comfortable spot with spa, karaoke bar and clean rooms with fridges. ❻

New Otani 120 S Los Angeles St ☎213/629-1200 or 1-800/421-8795, ⓦwww.newotani.com. Affordable luxury hotel with spacious suites, top-notch restaurant and authentic Japanese garden. ❻/❼

Orchid 819 S Flower St ☎213/624-5855 or 1-800/874-5855. Cozy place with a concierge. A simple walk to anywhere in downtown. Weekly rates. ❷

Park Plaza 607 S Park View St ☎213/384-5281. Sumptuous lobby (popular with filmmakers) and grand ballroom, but ordinary rooms. ❹

Westin Bonaventure 404 S Figueroa St ☎213/624-1000 or 1-800/228-3000, ⓦwww.westin.com. Luxury masterpiece or shiny nightmare, depending on your point of view. Five glass towers, six-story lobby – with a lake. Suites top $2000. ❽–❾

Hollywood

Best Western Hollywood Hills 6141 Franklin Ave ☎323/464-5181, ⓦwww.bestwesterncalifornia.com. Small and pleasant place with a heated pool and cable TV, in the heart of Hollywood. ❹

Chateau Marmont 8221 Sunset Blvd ☎ 323/656-1010, ⓦwww.chateaumarmont.com. Dark Norman castle was the former haunt of Greta Garbo et al. Largely suites and bungalows. ❽

Dunes Sunset Motel 5625 Sunset Blvd ☎323/467-5171. An acceptable, no-frills spot along a grim stretch on the east side of Hollywood. Good for reaching downtown. ❸

Holiday Inn Hollywood 1755 N Highland Ave ☎323/462-7181 or 1-800/465-4329, ⓦwww.holiday-inn.com. Massive, expensive but well-placed near the Chinese Theatre. Cheaper rates if three share a room. ❻

Hollywood Metropolitan 5825 Sunset Blvd ☎323/962-5800 or 1-800/962-5800, ⓦwww.metropolitanhotel.com. A sleek highrise with good rooms, decent views, and disabled access. The best at this price. ❺

Hollywood Roosevelt 7000 Hollywood Blvd ☎323/466-7000, ⓦwww.hollywoodroosevelt.com. The first hotel built for the movie greats in 1927, revamped and reeking with atmosphere, with jacuzzi, fitness room and swimming pool – though the rooms are drab. ❻

West LA

Hotel Bel Air 701 Stone Canyon Rd ☎310/472-1211 or 1-800/648-1097, ⓦwww.hotelbelair.com. The nicest hotel in LA bar none – and the only one in Bel Air – tucked up in a lushly overgrown canyon above Beverly Hills. Go for a beautiful brunch by Swan Lake if you can't afford the rooms, which reach a dizzying $450 a night. ❾

Beverly Hilton 9876 Wilshire Blvd ☎310/274-7777 or 1-800/922-5432, ⓦwww.hilton.com.

Centrally located, Merv Griffin-owned Beverly Hills hotel with many luxurious amenities. ⑧

Le Montrose 900 Hammond St, West Hollywood ☎310/855-1115, ⒲www.lemontrose.com. Elegant hotel with Art Nouveau styling, featuring rooftop tennis courts, pool and jacuzzi. Most rooms are suites. ⑧

Le Reve 8822 Cynthia St ☎310/854-1114 or 1-800/835-7997, ⒲www.lerevehotel.com. A few blocks north of Santa Monica Boulevard, offering many nice suites in the style of a French provincial inn, but others with stripped-down amenities. ⑥

The Standard 8300 Sunset Blvd, West Hollywood ☎323/654-2800, ⒲www.standardhotel.com. The biggest name on the local hipster hotel scene, with ultra-cool decor (looking like a 1970s rec room), jaded staff, outdoor pool with bar and surprisingly basic rooms. ⑥

Santa Monica, Venice and Malibu

Cadillac 8 Dudley Ave ☎310/399-8876, ⒲www.thecadillachotel.com. Restored 1930s Art Deco hotel and hostel right on Venice Boardwalk. Bright, airy atmosphere and friendly staff. Dorms ❶, hotel rooms ❹

Channel Road Inn 219 W Channel Rd ☎310/459-1920, ⒲www.channelroadinn.com. Fourteen-roomed romantic getaway built in 1910, nestled in lower Santa Monica Canyon, with ocean view, hot tub and free bike rental. ⑥–⑧

Inn at Venice Beach 327 Washington Blvd ☎310/821-2557 or 1-800/828-0688, ⒲www.innatvenicebeach.com. Located near Venice Beach and the canals, with simple rooms with balconies and fridges. ⑥

Loew's Santa Monica Beach 1700 Ocean Ave ☎310/458-6700, ⒲www.loewshotels.com/santa-monicahome.html. One of Santa Monica's chicest hotels, overlooking Santa Monica pier and often in demand as a film set. The best rooms top $400, but others are more cramped. ⑨

Malibu Surfer Motel 22541 Pacific Coast Hwy ☎310/456-6169, ⒲www.malibusurfmo.qpg.com. King-size beds, refrigerators and TVs make this roadside joint an excellent budget stop, despite the nasty retro decor. ❹

Shangri-La 1301 Ocean Ave ☎310/394-2791. Wonderfully restored Art Deco treasure overlooking Palisades Park and the Santa Monica beach, with clean and sleek, if basic, rooms. ⑥

Near LAX

Days Inn 901 W Manchester Blvd ☎310/649-0800 or 1-800/231-2508, ⒲www.the.daysinn.com/inglewood04020. Outdoor

pool, free parking and airport shuttle. ❹

Quality Inn 5249 W Century Blvd ☎310/645-2200 or 1-800/228-5151, ⒲www.qualityhotellax.com. Good-value motel, with ten floors of comfortable, fully equipped rooms, plus restaurant and bar. Free shuttle buses to LAX every 15min. ❸

Travelodge LAX South 1804 E Sycamore Ave ☎310/615-1073, ⒲www.travelodge.com. Five minutes south of LAX, ideal for South Bay. Pool, free tea, coffee and breakfast. ❸

The South Bay and Harbor Area

Barnabey's 3501 N Sepulveda Blvd, Manhattan Beach ☎310/545-8466, ⒲www.barnabeyshotel.com. One of the best hotels in the area, with nice rooms, whirlpool and LAX airport transit. ⑥

Broadlind 149 Linden Ave, Long Beach ☎562/436-5526, ⒲www.beachcalifornia.com/broadlx.html. Near a string of overpriced chain hotels, this no-frills antique is an amazing bargain for the area – as long as you can handle small rooms and no phones, parking or maid service. ❷

Seahorse Inn 233 N Sepulveda Blvd ☎310/376-7951 or 1-800/233-8050. Typical roadside motel, but clean and comfortable. A few blocks from the sands. ❸

Around Disneyland

Desert Palm Inn and Suites 631 W Katella Ave ☎1-800/635-5423, ⒲www.anaheimdesertpalm.com. Large, comfortable rooms feature refrigerators, microwaves, VCRs and continental breakfast. ❺

Disneyland 1150 W Cerritos Ave ☎714/956-6400, ⒲disneyland.disney.go.com/disneyland-dresort. The price does not include admission to the park, although the Disneyland monorail does stop outside. Hardly a good deal: cookie-cutter rooms without much charm. Still, an irresistible stop for many. ⑨

Park Place Inn 1544 S Harbor Blvd ☎714/776-4800, ⒲www.stovallshotels.com/park_place. *Best Western* hotel across from Disneyland, with the standard clean rooms and no-frills amenities. ❹

Pavilions 1176 W Katella Ave ☎714/776-0140, ⒲www.stovallshotels.com/pavilion. Convenient chain hotel with fridges, spa, pool, sauna and shuttle to Disneyland. ❹

The San Gabriel and San Fernando valleys

Artists Inn 1038 Magnolia St, South Pasadena ☎1-800/799-5668, ⒲www.artistsinns.com. Themed B&B honoring various painters. Most attractive is the Italian Suite with a sun porch. ⑥

The City

With only limited space between the desert, the mountains and the ocean, LA has long since filled in the gaps between what were once small and isolated towns. As a result, it's a massive conglomeration of interconnected, amorphous districts, often with little in common.

If LA has a heart, however, it's **downtown**, in the center of the basin. It offers a taste of almost everything you'll find elsewhere around the city, from upscale avant-garde art along Bunker Hill to the abject dereliction of Skid Row in the Eastside, compressed into an area of small, easily walkable blocks. The area **around downtown** contains some decaying Victorian suburbs, 1920s Art Deco buildings and the center of LA's enormous and growing Hispanic popu-lation.

Heading west from downtown to the coast, the first major district you come to, **Hollywood**, has streets caked with movie legend – even if the genuine glamour is long gone. Adjoining **West LA** is home to the city's newest money, shown off in Beverly Hills and along the Sunset Strip. **Santa Monica and Venice** to the west are the quintessential seafront LA of palm trees, white sands and laid-back living, while the coastline itself stretches another twenty miles northwest to glamorous **Malibu**, home to the movieland elite.

Suburban **Orange County**, to the southeast, holds little of interest apart from **Disneyland** and a handful of laid-back beach towns. On the far side of the northern hills lie the **San Gabriel and San Fernando valleys**, or sim-ply "the Valley," seen by mainstream Los Angeles as nothing more than depress-ing tract homes and endless strip malls – not unlike the generic LA stereotype viewed by the rest of America.

Downtown LA

Downtown LA embraces LA's every social, economic and ethnic division. It's not the highrise megalopolis you might expect; only a small clutch of tower-ing office blocks punctuate its skyline. During the postwar boom, as business-es spread out across the basin, it seemed to be heading for dilapidation and decay, but recent corporate revitalization and piles of urban renewal dollars have given it a new life, at least economically.

The whole area can easily be seen in a day on foot, aided by the odd 25¢ ride on a DASH, or LADOT, **bus** (Ⓣ 213/808-2273, Ⓦ www.ladottransit.com). LA's original settlement on the **Northside** is the obvious first stop, before crossing into the brasher and more modern **Westside**, and continuing through the chaos along **Broadway**.

The Northside: Olvera Street

To see downtown LA, begin at the city's beginning. **El Pueblo de Los Angeles**, off Alameda Street and south of **Chinatown**, was the site of the original late-eighteenth-century Mexican settlement of Los Angeles, and a few

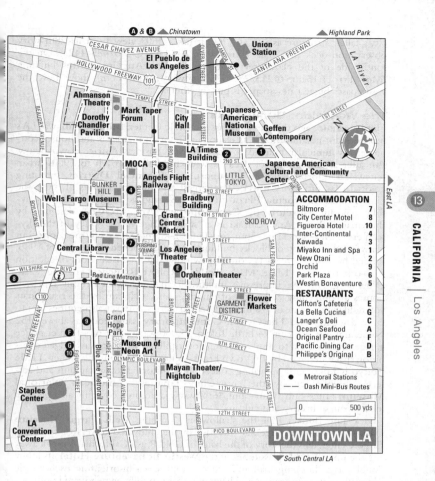

Union Station
Highland Park
Ⓐ & Ⓑ ▲ Chinatown

CESAR CHAVEZ AVENUE

El Pueblo de
Los Angeles

HOLLYWOOD FREEWAY
101

Ahmanson
Theatre

Dorothy
Chandler
Pavilion

Mark Taper
Forum

City
Hall

Japanese
American
National
Museum

Geffen
Contemporary

LA Times
Building

Japanese American
Cultural and Community
Center

MOCA

Angels Flight
Railway

LITTLE
TOKYO

Bradbury
Building

SKID ROW

Wells Fargo Museum

Library Tower

Grand
Central
Market

Central Library

PERSHING
SQUARE

Los Angeles
Theater

Orpheum Theater

Red Line Metrorail

WILSHIRE   BLVD

GARMENT
DISTRICT

Flower
Markets

Grand
Hope
Park

Museum of
Neon Art

OLYMPIC BOULEVARD

Mayan Theater/
Nightclub

PICO BOULEVARD

Staples
Center

LA
Convention
Center

ACCOMMODATION

Biltmore	7
City Center Motel	8
Figueroa Hotel	10
Inter-Continental	4
Kawada	3
Miyako Inn and Spa	1
New Otani	2
Orchid	9
Park Plaza	6
Westin Bonaventure	5

RESTAURANTS

Clifton's Cafeteria	E
La Bella Cucina	G
Langer's Deli	C
Ocean Seafood	A
Original Pantry	F
Pacific Dining Car	D
Philippe's Original	B

● Metrorail Stations
‒ ‒ Dash Mini-Bus Routes

0   500 yds

DOWNTOWN LA

▼ South Central LA

evocative early buildings remain in situ. The plaza church **La Placita**, the city's
oldest, serves as a sanctuary for Central American refugees and the site of some
enjoyable Sunday "Mariachi Masses" (11.30am & 4.30pm). **Olvera Street**,
which runs north from the plaza, contrived in part as a pseudo-Mexican village market, is saved only by its cheery grouping of food and craft stalls and by
the historic **Avila Adobe** (daily Mon–Sat 10am–5pm; free), technically the
city's oldest building, although it's been completely rebuilt in the last thirty
years.

The magnificent Mission Revival **Union Station** nearby is chiefly used as a
Metrorail and Amtrak terminal, although it was once the site of **Chinatown**,
which now sits a few blocks to the north and primarily offers a host of fine
restaurants. Across the Santa Ana Freeway at the **Civic Center**, plodding office
buildings surround the lifeless plaza of the Music Center, home to LA's
high-culture investments and near the future site of **Disney Hall** (Ⓦwww
.disneyhall.org), a long-awaited Frank Gehry–designed concert hall. The main
attraction of this zone is the Art Deco **City Hall** (Ⓦwww.lacityhall.org); the

city's tallest structure as late as 1960, it has a 360° view from its 28th-story observation deck (free daily tours 10am & 11am; ☎213/485-4423). On the south side of the plaza, free tours of the **Los Angeles Times** building (Mon–Fri 11.15am; ☎213/237-5757, ⓦwww.latimes.com) show how the west coast's biggest newspaper is put together.

The Westside: Bunker Hill

Until a century ago the area south of the Civic Center, **Bunker Hill**, was LA's most elegant neighborhood, its elaborate Victorian mansions and houses connected by funicular railroad to the growing business district down below. But after a half-century of decay, a wrecking-ball approach to 1960s urban renewal transformed it into an amorphous **Financial District**, sprouting colossal new fifty-story towers. The largest and most ambitious of these, the billion-dollar **California Plaza** on Grand Avenue, is based around the playfully colorful **Museum of Contemporary Art** (**MOCA**), designed by showman architect Arata Isozaki as a "small village in the valley of the skyscrapers" (Tues–Sun 11am–5pm, free Thurs 5–8pm; $8; ⓦwww.moca.org), but really a reddish array of blocky buildings. MOCA opened at the end of 1986, funded by a one-percent tax on all new downtown construction. In addition to work by Franz Kline, Mark Rothko, Robert Rauschenberg and Claes Oldenburg, and the impressive multimedia memorials of Antoni Tapiès, it houses a compelling collection of paintings and sculpture by the rising stars you're likely to come across in trendy city galleries. A ticket also entitles you to same-day entry into **The Geffen Contemporary** (same hours as above), 152 N Central Ave, adjacent to Little Tokyo, 55,000 square feet of a former police garage initially used to display MOCA overspill, now a more raw-edged exhibition space, designed by LA's own Frank Gehry. Across from the Geffen, **Little Tokyo** is a pleasantly appealing collection of historic sites, restaurants and galleries, highlighted by the compelling **Japanese American National Museum** (Tues–Sun 10am–5pm; $6; ⓦwww.janm.org), covering all aspects of local Japanese history and culture.

Back atop Bunker Hill, the shallow but amusing **Wells Fargo Museum** (Mon–Fri 9am–5pm; free), at the base of the shiny red towers of the Wells Fargo Center, tells the story of the bank of Gold Rush California. A block away rise the unmistakable glass tubes of the **Westin Bonaventure Hotel**. Its lobby doubles as a shopping mall and office complex – a disorienting Escher-style labyrinth of spiraling ramps and balconies that can only be negotiated with frequent recourse to the color-coded map.

Broadway

Although it's hard to picture now, **Broadway** was once LA's most fashionable shopping and entertainment district. Today it's largely taken over by the cash-rich hustle and bustle of Hispanic clothing and jewelry stores, all to a soundtrack of blaring salsa music. Its most vivid taste is to be had amid the pickled pigs feet and sheep brains inside the **Grand Central Market**, on Broadway between Third and Fourth streets. Right alongside, the whimsical terracotta facade of the 1918 **Million Dollar Theater** mixes buffalo heads with bald eagles, and was seen in the film *Blade Runner*, like the neighboring 1893 **Bradbury Building**, no. 304. While the moviehouse has since become a church, the **Los Angeles Theater** at 615 S Broadway still shows movies during the annual "Last Remaining Seats" film festival (ⓦwww.laconservancy.org for details), and is even more extravagant, built in ninety days for the world premiere of Charlie Chaplin's *City Lights* in 1931. The best old moviehouse still in regular use, though, is the **Orpheum**, no. 630, a neo-French Renaissance marvel of grand staircases and chandeliers. A few blocks south and west, don't miss the **Museum of Neon Art**, 501 W Olympic Blvd (Wed–Sat 11am–5pm, Sun noon–5pm; $5; ⓦwww.neonmona.org), featuring modern neon designs and a range of strange kinetic art, plus some great old theater signs, such as the one for the Melrose, with its sweeping, streamlined letters.

Around downtown

The LA sprawl begins as soon as you leave downtown, whose diverse environs tend to be forgotten quarters, cut through by freeways and with large distances separating their few points of interest. It makes little sense to see them consecutively, as each is ten to thirty minutes by car or bus from the next.

MacArthur Park and around

Reachable on the Red Line subway, the dilapidated patches of green and large lake of **MacArthur Park** are the nearest open spaces to the sidewalks of downtown, and teem with immigrant street vendors, homeless people and busy residents, under the disused old sign of the Westlake Theatre. On a nearby street, the **Grier-Musser Museum**, 403 S Bonnie Brae St (Wed–Fri noon–4pm, Sat 11am–4pm; $6; ⓦpeople.we.mediaone.net/gmuseum), provides a vivid glimpse of the old days when this was a middle-class suburb of downtown, and the area's Victorian houses boasted neo-Gothic turrets, Italianate windows and gingerbread ornament. Surprisingly enough, some homes in the neighborhood still do. Just don't jump out of your car to investigate; the crime rate is among the city's highest. Half a mile west in a safer zone, the seminal **Bullocks Wilshire** department store, 3050 Wilshire Blvd, is the most perfectly realized example of late 1920s Art Deco in LA, with a colossal copper tower, and has recently been reincarnated as the law library of adjacent **Southwestern University**.

Inside the **Ambassador Hotel**, 3400 Wilshire Blvd, the *Cocoanut Grove* club flourished from the Twenties to the Forties, and the large ballroom (now closed) featured in the 1937 and 1954 versions of *A Star Is Born*. The kitchen, however, was the scene of the hotel's most notorious event. **Bobby Kennedy** was fatally shot here on June 5, 1968, after his victory in the California Democratic Primary. Converted into a filmmaking location, nowadays the *Ambassador* is also closed to public view (ⓦwww.cocoanutgrove.org for more details).

The so-called "Miracle Mile" continues west from the *Ambassador* into the Mid-Wilshire district that runs along that boulevard into West LA. South of Wilshire, along Olympic Boulevard between Vermont and Western, **Koreatown** is five times larger – and far more genuine and lively – than the more tourist-oriented Chinatown and Little Tokyo, and is home to the largest concentration of Koreans outside Korea.

Exposition Park

Across Exposition Boulevard from the USC campus, south of downtown, is the sizeable **Exposition Park**, one of the most appreciated parks in LA. It retains a real sense of community, bolstered by its function as a favorite lunchtime picnic spot. The **California Science Center** here, off Figueroa Street (daily 10am–5pm; $5; ⓦwww.casciencectr.org), contains enjoyable working models and thousands of gadgets – recently improved thanks to a multimillion-dollar renovation, though the museum remains as familiar as other science-and-industry museums around the US. Just outside, an IMAX Theater attracts youthful patrons of nature documentaries, while nearby the **Aerospace Hall** recalls LA's once-dominant industry, though the building is more notable for its architect, Frank Gehry, who affixed a jet plane to its outer wall. Exhibitions on the history, art and culture of America's black communities are at the **California African American Museum** (daily except Mon 10am–5pm; free; Ⓦ www.caam.ca.gov).

The **Natural History Museum of Los Angeles County** (Mon–Fri 9.30am–5pm, Sat & Sun 10am–5pm; $8; Ⓦ www.nhm.org) is the nicest building in the park, with its echoey domes and travertine columns. Its tremendous stock of dinosaur skeletons includes the skull of a Tyrannosaurus rex, and a Diatryma – a huge flightless bird. Other displays include Mayan pyramid murals and the complete contents of a Mexican tomb (albeit a reconstruction). The last major sight in the park is the **LA Coliseum**, familiar as the site of the 1932 and 1984 Olympics and for its towering headless statues, and always proposed as the next home for an LA football franchise, if ever the city gets one.

South Central LA

South Central LA hardly ranks on the tourist circuit, but it's a large and integral part of the city, whatever wealthy white LA might prefer to think. The population has historically been mostly black, but is increasingly Hispanic and Asian, joined here and there by poor and working-class whites. It doesn't look so run-down at first sight, mostly made up of detached bungalows enjoying their own patch of palm-shaded lawn, but just about all its residents get an abysmal deal in schooling and employment, and have little chance of climbing the social ladder and escaping. If you pass through, every block for twenty-odd miles looks much like the last, littered with fast-food outlets, noxious liquor stores and abandoned factory sites, and burned-out, vacant lots still undeveloped a decade after the 1992 **riots** following the Rodney King verdict.

A crumbling reminder of the old days of black LA can be found along **Central Avenue** running south from downtown, where hot jazz clubs and fine hotels and restaurants once thrived. Only a few spots enliven the general gloom, including the wildly Streamline Moderne **Coca-Cola Bottling Plant**, 1334 S Central Ave, in the form of a giant white ocean liner, and the **Dunbar Hotel**, 4225 S Central Ave, the first US hotel built specifically for blacks and patronized by almost every prominent African American from the 1930s to the 1950s. Although you can only see its restored lobby and facade – the structure is now used for elderly housing – the hotel is the site for the Central Avenue Jazz Festival in August (☎ 213/847-3169 for details) and you can find out more about the building from the nearby OASIS senior center, at no. 4207 (☎ 323/231-6220).

The district of **Watts**, on the southernmost fringe of downtown, achieved notoriety as the scene of the six-day **Watts Riot** of August 1965, which left 36 dead and innumerable buildings in charred ruins, and of the 1975 gun battle which put an end to the Symbionese Liberation Army (SLA) kidnappers of publishing heiress Patti Hearst. It's also the site of the Gaudíesque **Watts Towers**, striking pieces of folk art which stand alongside railroad tracks at 1765 E 107th St. The towers are usually open on Saturdays, but the schedule can be erratic; call the adjacent Watts Towers Arts Center, 1727 E 107th St (Wed–Sun 10am–4pm, free; ☎ 213/847-4646, Ⓦ artscenecal.com/WattsTowers.html), for more details. Recently celebrated as the former home of tennis phenoms Venus and Serena Williams, **Compton** is renowned as the "crib" of many of LA's **rappers**, but outsiders should not attempt to sniff out the local music scene.

Hollywood

If a single place-name encapsulates the LA dream of glamour, money and overnight success, it's **Hollywood**. Millions of tourists arrive on pilgrimages; millions more flock here in pursuit of riches and glory. Hollywood blurs the edges of fact and fiction, simply because so much seems possible – and yet, for most people, so little actually is. Those who do strike it rich here get out as soon as they can, just as they always have; the big film companies, too, long ago relocated well away, leaving Hollywood a blend of prostitutes and petty criminals with visiting tourists and slumming hipsters – all under the shadow of grand old movie palaces and dive hotels.

Central Hollywood

The myths, magic, fable and fantasy splattered throughout **Central Hollywood** create a rich sense of nostalgia, giving it an appeal no measure of tourists or souvenir postcard stands can diminish. Although you're more likely to find a porno theater than spot a real star, the decline which blighted Hollywood from the early 1960s is fast receding, with all manner of new investment and redevelopment projects, most prominently the **Hollywood and Highland** theater and retail complex, at the corner of those boulevards, due to open in November 2001 and begin hosting the Oscars as well. Nevertheless, this section of town can still get hairy after dark, with adolescents cruising Hollywood Boulevard in customized cars and pickpockets on the prowl for the odd pocketbook.

The natural place to begin exploring Hollywood Boulevard is the junction of **Hollywood and Vine** – the classic location for budding stars to be mythically "spotted" by big-shot directors and whisked off to fame and fortune. At 6608 Hollywood Blvd, the purple and pink **Frederick's of Hollywood** has

---

A brief history of Hollywood

Once the home of what was allegedly the country's largest Presbyterian church, Hollywood started life as a temperance colony in 1887, intended to provide a sober, God-fearing alternative to raunchy downtown LA, eight miles away by rough country road. The film industry was drawn here from the east coast by the guaranteed sunshine, low taxes, cheap labor and diverse assortment of natural locations, and as a way of dodging Thomas Edison's restrictive motion picture patents. Nearby Silver Lake was the first (temporary) location for the movie business; the first permanent studio opened in Hollywood in 1911, and within three years the place was packed with filmmakers such as Cecil B. DeMille, who shared his barn-converted office space with a horse (now reincarnated as the Hollywood Heritage Museum, 2100 N Highland Ave; Sat & Sun 10am–3.30pm; $4; ⓦwww.hollywoodheritage.org).

The industry expanded fast, and eager new arrivals soon swamped the original small-scaled community. Once movie-making had proved itself to be a financially secure business – with the success of D.W. Griffith's racist epic *The Birth of a Nation* in 1914 – film production became conglomerated and highly specialized. Small companies either went bust or were incorporated into big studios. Hollywood's enduring success is in making slick, pleasurable movies that sell – from the hard-bitten film noir of the 1940s to the uncommon creativity of filmmakers such as Francis Ford Coppola and Quentin Tarantino to the mindless shoot-'em-ups and teenage sex comedies of today.

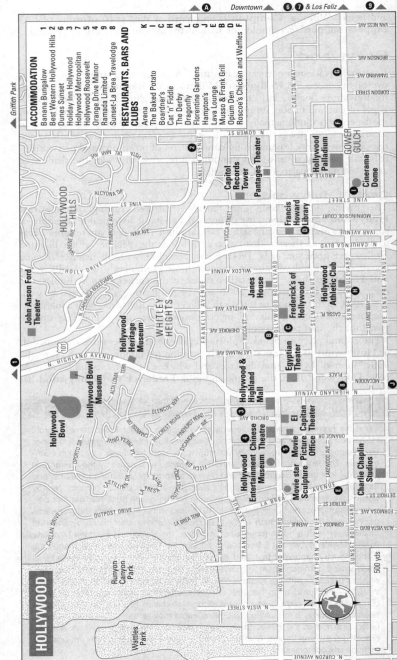

HOLLYWOOD

ACCOMMODATION

Banana Bungalow	1
Best Western Hollywood Hills	2
Dunes Sunset	6
Holiday Inn Hollywood	3
Hollywood Metropolitan	7
Hollywood Roosevelt	5
Orange Drive Manor	4
Ramada Limited	9
Sunset-La Brea Travelodge	8

RESTAURANTS, BARS AND CLUBS

Arena	K
The Baked Potato	I
Boardner's	C
Cat 'n' Fiddle	H
The Derby	A
Dragonfly	G
Florentine Gardens	J
Hampton's	E
Lava Lounge	B
Musso & Frank Grill	D
Opium Den	D
Roscoe's Chicken and Waffles	F

Downtown ▲   6, 7 & Los Feliz ▲   9 ▲

Griffith Park ▲

John Anson Ford Theater

HOLLYWOOD HILLS

Capitol Records Tower

Pantages Theater

Hollywood Bowl Museum

Hollywood Bowl

Hollywood Heritage Museum

WHITLEY HEIGHTS

Francis Howard Library

Janes House

Frederick's of Hollywood

Hollywood Athletic Club

Hollywood & Highland Mall

Egyptian Theater

Hollywood Entertainment Museum

Chinese Theatre

El Capitan Theater

Movie Picture Office

Movie star Sculpture

Runyon Canyon Park

Charlie Chaplin Studios

Hollywood Palladium

Cinerama Dome

GOWER GULCH

Wattles Park

N

500 yds

Sunset Strip & West Hollywood ▲

been (under-) dressing Hollywood's sex goddesses since 1947, as well as mortal bodies all over the world via mail order. Inside, the **lingerie museum** (Mon–Sat 10am–9pm, Sat closes at 7pm, Sun 11am–6pm; free) displays some of the company's best corsets, bras and panties, donated by happy big-name wearers ranging from Lana Turner to Cher.

A little further on, the **Egyptian Theater** at no. 6712 was financed by impresario Sid Grauman, in a modest attempt to re-create the Temple of Thebes. The very first Hollywood premiere (*Robin Hood*) took place here in 1922. Now owned by the city, Grauman's Thebes has recently been reborn as home to American Cinematheque (ⓦ www.americancinematheque.com), a film preservation and exhibition group that offers inspired film festivals and a less impressive, touristy documentary extolling the fact and fantasy behind Hollywood (hour-long shows Tues–Sun 2pm & 3.30pm; $7). No Hollywood visitor will want to miss the mundane yet magical foot and hand prints in the concrete concourse of Mann's **Chinese Theatre** at 6925 Hollywood Blvd (ⓦ www.manntheatres.com/chinese.html). Actress Norma Talmadge (supposedly by accident) trod in wet cement while visiting the construction site, and the practice has continued ever since, from Mary Pickford and Douglas Fairbanks Sr, at the 1927 opening of *King of Kings*, to modern ceremonies for stars like Anthony Hopkins. For many decades, this has long been the spot for movie premieres, and as for the building, it's an odd version of a classical Chinese temple, replete with quasi-Chinese motifs and upturned dragon tails.

The **Roosevelt Hotel**, opposite at no. 7000, was movieland's first luxury hotel, its *Cinegrill* restaurant hosting the likes of W.C. Fields and F. Scott Fitzgerald, not to mention hangers-on like Ronald Reagan and the alleged ghost of 1950s-era actor Montgomery Clift. In 1929 the first Oscars were presented here, beginning the long tradition of Hollywood rewarding itself in the absence of honors from elsewhere. Across the street, television fans may want to stop in at the **Hollywood Entertainment Museum**, no. 7021 (daily 11am–6pm, closed Wed during winter; $7.50; ⓦ www.hollywoodmuseum .com), whose collection of media memorabilia is highlighted by the set from *Cheers* and the bridge of the Starship Enterprise.

Despite the beliefs of some of their more ardent fans, even the biggest Hollywood stars have been mortal; the LA cemeteries that hold their tombs get at least as many visitors as the city's museums. In the southeast corner of the **Hollywood Memorial Cemetery**, near Santa Monica Boulevard and Gower Street, a mausoleum contains the resting place of **Rudolph Valentino**, the celebrated screen lover who died aged just 31 in 1926. To this day on each anniversary of his passing (August 23), at least one "Lady in Black" – as his posthumous devotees are known – will likely be found mourning. The achingly ostentatious memorial to **Douglas Fairbanks Sr**, who with his wife Mary Pickford did much to introduce social snobbery among movie-making types, is just outside. Also on view are the graves of Hollywood's more recently deceased inhabitants: an increasingly large population of Russian and Armenian immigrants.

Griffith Park

The greenery and mountain slopes that make up vast **Griffith Park** northeast of Hollywood (daily 5am–10.30pm, mountain roads close at dusk; free) are a welcome escape from the mind-numbing hubbub of the metropolis, providing lush fern and azalea gardens, a bird sanctuary, a Greek Theatre showing outdoor concerts, and many miles of fine trails. The landmark **Observatory** (Tues–Fri 2–10pm, Sat & Sun 12.30–10pm, summer daily 12.30–10pm; free; Ⓦwww.GriffithObs.org) here has appeared in innumerable Hollywood films, most famously *Rebel Without a Cause*, and the surrounding acres add up to the largest municipal park in the country. Above the landscaped flat sections, the hillsides are rough and wild, marked by foot and bridle paths, leading into desolate but appealingly unspoiled terrain that gives great views over the LA basin and out to the ocean, provided the city smog isn't too thick. One way to explore is on a **rented bike** from *Spokes 'n' Stuff*, near the park ranger station, at 4400 Crystal Springs Rd (daily during daylight hours; Ⓣ323/662-6573). Definitely worth a look is the **Gene Autry Museum of Western Heritage**, 4700 Western Heritage Way, devoted to true Wild West history and its Hollywood interpretation (Tues–Sun 10am–5pm, Thurs closes at 8pm; $7.50; Ⓦwww.autrymuseum.org). The park is safe by day, but has a fearsome reputation for after-dark violence.

The Hollywood Hills

The views from the **Hollywood Hills** take in a bizarre assortment of opulent properties, perhaps most famously the so-called **Chemosphere**, or "UFO House," at 776 Torreyson Drive. Around these canyons and slopes, which run from Hollywood itself into Benedict Canyon above Beverly Hills, mansions are so commonplace that only the half-dozen fully blown castles (at least, Hollywood-style castles) really stand out. On Mulholland Drive are Rudolph Valentino's extravagant **Falcon Lair** (1436 Bella Drive) and Errol Flynn's **Mulholland House** (7740 Mulholland Drive). Guided tours (see box p.1059) can point out which is which, but for the most part you can't get close to the most elaborate dwellings anyway, and none is open to the public. For an up-close look at some of the area's iconic architecture, take in a concert at the **Hollywood Bowl**, 2301 N Highland Blvd (information at Ⓣ323/850-2000, Ⓦwww.hollywoodbowl.org), the massive concrete bandshell that's been built and reconstructed three times in the last eighty years. Although the summer music offerings are rarely highbrow, it's as good a spot as any to hear the familiar roar of the *1812 Overture*.

From more or less anywhere in Hollywood, you can see the **Hollywood Sign**, erected as a property advertisement in 1923 (when it spelled "Hollywoodland"; the "land" was removed in 1949). The sign is also famous as a suicide spot, though few have followed the 1932 example of would-be movie star Peg Entwhistle, who started out at Beachwood Drive (a route that affords a fine view of the sign) and picked a path slowly upwards through the thick bush, to leap to her death from the 50ft "H." For the first time in its nearly seventy-year existence, the sign is now insured against earthquake damage, and infrared cameras and radar-activated zoom lenses have been installed to catch graffiti writers. Innocent tourists who can't resist a close look are liable for a steep fine.

West LA

LA's so-called "Westside" begins immediately beyond Hollywood in **West LA**, bordered by the foothills of the Santa Monica Mountains to the north and the Santa Monica Freeway to the south. West LA is at the sharp end of all that's new and happening in the city, though tucked away behind the showcase streets, the usual long residential blocks are only marginally less drab than is normal in LA.

Continued Success
to Sid Grauman
The Master Showman

Janet Gaynor

5-29-29

Harold Llo
Hand and foot prints
Nov. 21. 27

To Sid.— Following
in My FATHERS
FOOTSTEPS

△ Mann's Chinese Theatre

The LA County Museum of Art

The **Miracle Mile**, between La Brea and Fairfax avenues along Wilshire Boulevard, was the premier property development of the 1930s. Many of the businesses have moved out, but recent development has created a "Museum Mile" in their place. Although the enormous **LA County Museum of Art**, or **LACMA** (Thurs–Tues noon–8pm, Fri closes at 9pm, weekends opens at 11am; $7, free second Tues of the month; Ⓦwww.lacma.org), comprises an unimpressive set of blocky buildings, its collections are among the best in the world. Despite the loss of Armand Hammer's stock of paintings to his own museum in Westwood (see p.1076), it justifies a lengthy visit. The **Fearing Collection** of funereal masks and sculpted guardian figures from pre-Columbian Mexico is highly impressive, but where the museum really excels is in its specializations: **German Expressionist** prints and drawings, scrolls and ceramics in the **Pavilion for Japanese Art**, and entire rooms devoted to Auguste Rodin, 17th-century Dutch masters, rare jewelry and porcelain, and Hollywood fashion designers. An astonishing assortment of prehistoric bones has been recovered from the adjacent **La Brea Tar Pits**. For thousands of years animals who tried to drink from the deceptive layer of water that covers this pool of smelly and still-seeping tar have found themselves stuck fast; it is now surrounded by life-size models of such victims as mastodons and saber-toothed tigers, more of which are on display at the site's impressive **George C. Page Museum** (Mon–Fri 9.30am–5pm, weekends opens at 10am; $6; Ⓦwww.lam.mus.ca.us/page).

Further west, the **Petersen Automotive Museum**, 6060 Wilshire Blvd, pays sumptuous if superficial homage to the automobile (Tues–Sun 10am–6pm, also open Mon during holidays; $7; Ⓦwww.petersen.org). It fails to explain the reasons behind the collapse of LA's early public transportation system and the city's subsequent obsession with what Tom Wolfe called the "Kandy-Kolored Tangerine-Flake Streamline Baby," but it has enough mint-condition classic models to make the car-crazy delirious with joy.

West Hollywood

Between Fairfax Avenue and Beverly Hills, **West Hollywood** was for many years notorious for after-hours vice clubs and general debauchery. Since its 1984 incorporation as a city, however, it's become much more upmarket, home to Los Angeles's prominent – and affluent – gay community, as well as rent-controlled pensioners and newly arrived Russian immigrants. **Melrose Avenue**, LA's trendiest shopping street and one of the unmistakable symbols of Southern California, runs parallel to the seedier main drag, **Santa Monica Boulevard**, looking at times like something out of a low-budget 1950s sci-fi feature. Neon and Art Deco abound among a fluorescent rash of designer and secondhand boutiques, exotic antique shops and avant-garde galleries. **La Brea Avenue**, a less-heralded, but no less appealing shopping strip runs perpendicular to the east side of the Melrose district, offering more space, fewer tourists, and a host of chic clothing stores, upscale restaurants and even trendier galleries.

Above West Hollywood, on either side of La Cienega Boulevard, is the two-mile-odd conglomeration of restaurants, plush hotels and nightclubs on Sunset Boulevard known as the **Sunset Strip**, one of LA's best areas for nightlife. Its clubs first appeared in the early 1920s, along what was then a dusty dirt road linking the Hollywood movie studios with the West LA "homes of the stars." With the rise of TV the Strip declined, only reviving in the Sixties when a scene developed around the landmark **Whisky-a-Go-Go** club, no. 8901, which featured seminal psychedelic rock bands such as The Doors, Love and Buffalo Springfield, and later in the 1970s around the **Sunset Hyatt** hotel, no. 8401, the infamous "Riot House" where Led Zeppelin raced motorcycles in the hallways and rock stars committed countless acts of eye-popping debauchery. Greta Garbo was only one of many stars to appreciate the quirky, if gloomy, Norman castle that is the **Chateau Marmont Hotel**, towering over the east end of the Sunset Strip at no. 8221. Howard Hughes used to rent the entire penthouse so he could keep an eye on the bathing beauties around the pool below, and comedian John Belushi died of a heroin overdose here, in the hotel bungalow he used as his LA home.

Beverly Hills

Beverly Hills is one of the world's wealthiest residential areas, revealed and glorified by immaculate shops (such as those on **Rodeo Drive**, squeaky-clean streets and the odd ostentatious display – notably the mock-European shopping alley **Rodeo Two**, perhaps LA's height of pretension. Still, there are a number of worthwhile and unassuming spots for visitors interested in things other than commodities. The **Museum of Television and Radio** (Wed–Sun noon–5pm; $6; ⓦ www.mtr.org) is a welcome addition, chronicling fifty years of the boob tube, while the **Beverly Hills Trolley** (daily noon–4pm during summer, otherwise Sat; $5) offers tourists a 40-minute glimpse of the city's highlights, departing hourly from the corner of Dayton Way and Rodeo Drive. For a view of the city's finest art and architecture, a 50-minute trolley tour takes you to a number of less familiar, though still compelling sights (11am Sat only; $5).

Palatial estates lie hidden behind landscaped security gates in the verdant canyons and foothills above Sunset Boulevard. **Benedict Canyon Drive** climbs past a good number. Some, like the lavish **PickFair** mansion, 1143 Summit Drive, are long gone, while others survive, including Harold Lloyd's **Green Acres** (1740 Green Acres Drive), with its secret passageways and large private screening room, though much of its spacious grounds, with a waterfall and nine-hole golf course, has been broken up into smaller lots.

Just outside Beverly Hills, the **Simon Wiesenthal Center**, **Beit HaShoa Museum of Tolerance**, 9786 W Pico Blvd (April–Oct Mon–Thurs 11.30am–4pm, Fri 11.30am–3pm, Sun 11am–5pm; Nov–March closes 1pm on Fri; $9; ⓦ www.wiesenthal.com/mot; is the most technologically advanced institution of its kind, using videotaped interviews to provide LA's frankest examination of the 1992 riots, looking at international hate and intolerance in general, and showing the rise of Nazism with a harrowing look at a replica gas chamber.

Westwood

West of Beverly Hills, north of Wilshire Boulevard, **Westwood** is one of LA's more user-friendly neighborhoods, a grouping of low-slung redbrick buildings that went up in the late 1920s around Broxton Avenue, along with the nearby campus of the University of California at Los Angeles (UCLA). Known then as "Westwood Village," it's an area that is easily explored on foot, and one very much shaped by the proximity of the university campus, the lifeblood of the area. Once LA's prime movie-going district, Westwood Village has lost some of its cinematic eminence due to a 1980s gang scare and a real lack of parking, but remains the most densely packed movie-theater district in the country, and its 1931 **Westwood Village Theater**, 961 Broxton Ave, is still often used for premieres or special "sneak" previews to gauge audience reactions.

South of Westwood, Wilshire Boulevard exploded in the 1970s with oil-rich highrise developments; now modest detached houses sit next to twenty-story condominium towers in which penthouse apartments with private heliports sell for upwards of $20 million. Inside one such tower, on the corner with Westwood Boulevard, is the **UCLA Hammer Museum** (Tues–Sat 11am–7pm, Thurs closes at 9pm, Sun 11am–5pm; $4.50, free Thurs 6–9pm; Ⓦwww.hammer.ucla.edu), amassed over seven decades by Armand Hammer, the flamboyant boss of Occidental Petroleum, and now administered by the university. The works by Rembrandt and Rubens are less stunning than those at LACMA, but Van Gogh's intense and radiant *Hospital at Saint Rémy* is a jewel.

Outside the museum, behind the tiny Avco cinema, Hammer's marble tomb in **Westwood Memorial Park**, 1218 Glendon Ave, stands near the lipstick-covered plaque that marks the resting place of **Marilyn Monroe**.

The Getty Center

Opened in 1997, the **Getty Center** near the Sepulveda Pass north of Wilshire Boulevard (Tues–Wed 11am–7pm, Thurs–Fri 11am–9pm, Sat–Sun 10am–6pm; free; Ⓦwww.getty.edu) towers over the surrounding area. Designed by Richard Meier at a cost of $1 billion, this towering modernist temple (clad in countless acres of travertine) is LA's most recent, and most obvious, attempt to make a mark on the international art scene, its various buildings devoted to conservation, acquisition and other philanthropic tasks, and its surrounding gardens arranged with rigid geometric precision. Drivers must pay a $5 fee, though parking reservations are no longer required for off-peak hours (such as weekdays and nonholiday periods); otherwise, take MTA bus #561, which stops on Sepulveda Boulevard.

Two years after the original Malibu museum opened in 1974 (see p.1078), oil magnate John Paul Getty died, leaving it $1.3 billion. Obliged to spend a set percentage of its now $3.5 billion endowment every year, it can outbid anyone to get what it wants, which is usually anything except contemporary art – a real deficiency in the museum's collections.

Still, the quality of the **exhibits** is extraordinary, especially in the rooms devoted to decorative arts, where you can indulge in a feast of ornate French furniture from the reign of Louis XIV, with clocks, chandeliers, tapestries and gilt-edged commodes filling several overwhelmingly opulent chambers. Although Getty himself was much less interested in painting, a sizeable collection has been amassed since his death, featuring all the major names from the thirteenth century on, including Van Gogh's *Irises* and several Rembrandt portraits. Photography is well represented with works by Man Ray, Moholy-Nagy and many others.

Santa Monica, Venice and Malibu

Set along an unbroken twenty-mile stretch of white-sand beaches, the small, self-contained communities that line **Santa Monica Bay** feature some of the best LA has to offer, with none of the smog or searing heat that can make the rest of the metropolis unbearable. The entire area is well served by public transportation, near (but not too near) the airport, and a wide choice of accommodation makes it a good base for seeing the rest of the city.

Venice

Venice was laid out in the marshlands of Ballona Creek in 1905 by developer Abbot Kinney as a romantic twenty-mile network of canals, lined by sham palazzos and waterfront homes. The original plan to create a west coast art-and-culture zone failed, followed by a more successful turn as an amusement park;

however, the coming of the automobile finished it off altogether. Most of the canals were filled in, and the area fell into disrepair, being taken over by oil wells. Orson Welles's film *Touch of Evil* starred the then-derelict Venice as a seedy Mexican border town. Kinney was, however, ahead of his time. A fair bit of the original plan survives, and the pseudo-European atmosphere has made Venice one of the coast's trendier spots. Chic cafés and restaurants abound near the beach, an alternative art scene centers on the **Beyond Baroque Literary Arts Center**, 681 Venice Blvd (Ⓦ www.beyondbaroque.org), and the easy, laid-back vibe attracts countless slackers and slummers.

The town's main artery, **Windward Avenue**, runs from the beach into what was the Grand Circle of the canal system. Its original Romanesque **arcade**, around the intersection with Pacific Avenue, is alive with health-food shops, secondhand record stores and roller-skate rental stands, although less and less of the arcade remains with each passing year. Nearby, the few remaining **canals** display renovated white bridges and pedestrian-friendly footpaths, along with a bevy of the latest neo-modern and postmodern housing designs. A one-way street, **Dell Avenue**, enters the area from its intersection at Washington Boulevard, and is the best way to take a closer look at the canals.

Southerly **Venice Beach** itself is the reason most people come here. Nowhere else does LA parade itself quite so openly as along the wide pathway of **Venice Boardwalk**, ever packed with jugglers, fire-eaters, roller-skating guitar players and people-watchers, though increasingly on the verge of gentrifying into a corporate-sanitized shopping district. South of Windward is **Muscle Beach**, a legendary outdoor weightlifting center where serious-looking hunks of muscle pump some serious iron, and high-flying gymnasts swing on the adjacent rings and bars. Outlets along Washington Street near the pier – such as *Spokes 'n' Stuff* (Ⓣ 310/395-4748) – rent out **bikes** for $5–7 per hour or $12–20 per day.

At night Venice Beach is alive with street gangs and drug dealers. Walking on the beach after dark is illegal, and you should be very cautious in the vicinity.

Santa Monica

Immediately north of Venice, **Santa Monica** is the oldest and biggest of LA's resort areas, perched on palm-tree-shaded bluffs, or "the palisades," above the blue Pacific. Once a wild beachfront playground, it's now a self-consciously healthy and liberal community, with a large expatriate British contingent of writers and rock stars, ranging from Rod Stewart to John Lydon.

The Santa Monica beachfront grew into a giant funfair city when it was linked to downtown LA by the suburban streetcar system. It was the location for many of the underworld stories of Raymond Chandler, most memorably as "Bay City" in *Farewell My Lovely*, but today Chandler wouldn't recognize the place. The gambling ships and bathing clubs have gone, and Santa Monica is now well known for its tight rent control policy and stringent planning and development regulations. For these perceived infractions, local right-wingers refer sneeringly to the city as the "People's Republic."

Santa Monica reaches nearly three miles inland, but most things of interest are within a few blocks of the beach. The **visitors center** (daily 10am–4pm; Ⓣ 310/393-7593, Ⓦ www.santamonica.com), in a kiosk at 1400 Ocean Ave, makes a good first stop. It can be found in **Palisades Park**, the enjoyable, cypress-tree-lined green strip along the top of the bluffs, where the homeless mix with the yuppie elite and the whole area seems to be under constant threat of eroding down to the beach below. Two blocks east of Ocean Avenue, the **Third Street Promenade**, a pedestrianized stretch popular with street vendors and itinerant evangelists, is the closest LA comes to having an urban energy, though colorless chain stores are crowding out many of the quirky boutiques and oddball shops – especially north of Arizona Avenue, now a fully corporatized dead zone. On weekend nights the Promenade brings together visitors and Angelenos of all ages and accents, and it's by far the best place to come for alfresco dining, beer-drinking or people-watching.

The real focal point of Santa Monica life is down below, on the **beach** and around the once-decaying and recently refurbished **Santa Monica pier**, which boasts a well-restored 1922 wooden **carousel** (daily 9am–6pm; 50¢ – featured, along with Paul Newman, in the 1973 movie *The Sting*. Although the familiar thrill rides of **Pacific Park** (Mon–Fri 11am–6pm daily, weekends closes at midnight; $16, kids $9), the pier's walled-off amusement zone, may first attract the eye, save your money for the **UCLA Ocean Discovery Center** (weekends 11am–5pm, summer also Tues–Fri 3-6pm; $3; Ⓦwww.odc.ucla.edu), just below the pier at 1600 Ocean Front Walk, where you can find out about local marine biology and get your fingers wet touching sea anemones and starfish. The grand beach houses just to the north of the pier were known as Hollywood's "Gold Coast"; the largest, now the **Sand and Sea** beach club, was built as the servants' quarters of a massive 120-room house, now demolished, that belonged to William Randolph Hearst. In the adjacent villa of MGM boss Louis B. Mayer, the Kennedy brothers were later rumored to have had liaisons with Marilyn Monroe.

Five miles north along the curving **Pacific Coast Highway (PCH)** from Santa Monica, a huge mock French chateau inadvertently marks the easily missed entrance to the opulent **Getty Villa**, 17985 PCH (Ⓦwww.getty.edu/museum/villa.html), the original site of the Getty museum. A fake Roman villa poised high above the ocean, the complex is currently closed until 2002, when it will re-emerge as a showcase for Getty antiquities.

Malibu

Malibu, at the top of the bay twenty miles north of Santa Monica, is a whole other world, its beach-colony houses owned by those famous enough to need privacy and rich enough to afford it. It's not all that impressive on arrival, however, with ramshackle surf shops, fast-food stands and real-estate agents scattered along PCH around the graceful **Malibu Pier**, 23000 PCH. **Surfrider Beach** here was the surfing capital of the world in the 1950s and early 1960s, as seen in the *Beach Blanket Bingo* movies of Annette Funicello and Frankie Avalon (the surf is at its best in late summer). Just beyond is **Malibu Lagoon State Park** (daily 9am–7pm; parking $6), a nature reserve and bird refuge, and nearby is the **Adamson House** (daily 8am–sunset; $3), a stunning Spanish Colonial home, mixed with Moorish and Mission Revival elements, featuring opulent decor and colorful tilework.

Most Malibu residences are tucked away in an insular community in the narrow canyons on the fringes of town. There's very little to see, despite tourists' futile attempts to peek into the exclusive **Malibu Colony** celebrity retreat, located along an unmarked stretch near PCH. You'd do better to visit **Malibu Creek State Park**, on Las Virgenes Road to the north near Mulholland Drive, once used by 20th Century-Fox, which filmed many Tarzan pictures here, as well as the TV show *M.A.S.H.* The 4000-acre park includes a large lake, some waterfalls and nearly fifteen miles of hiking trails. Another park further west, the **Paramount Ranch**, 2813 Cornell Rd, provided that movie studio's exterior sets, and still features a faux-Western town that may be familiar to viewers of TV's *Dr Quinn Medicine Woman*.

Five miles along the coast from Malibu Pier, **Zuma Beach** is the largest and most crowded of the Los Angeles County beaches. Adjacent **Point Dume State Beach**, below the imposing promontory of Point Dume, is a lot more relaxed, and the rocks at its southern tip, **Pirate's Cove**, are a good place to view seals and migrating gray whales in winter.

The South Bay

Heading south from LA along PCH, beyond the runways of LAX and the oil refineries of El Segundo, begins the eight-mile coastal strip of the quieter and less pretentious South Bay beach towns: **Manhattan Beach**, **Hermosa Beach** and **Redondo Beach**. Each has a beckoning strip of white sand – much more open to the public than those around Malibu – and Manhattan and Hermosa are especially well equipped for surfing and beach sports. They're also well connected by the regular #439 bus to downtown LA. To the south are **Long Beach** and **Catalina Island**.

Long Beach

Thanks to a billion-dollar clean-up, downtown **Long Beach** is not the seedy stomping grounds of off-duty sailors that it was twenty-odd years ago. **Pine Avenue** is an enjoyable stretch of restored architecture and bargain antique stores, but the only reason most tourists cross to the far side of LA's massive harbor is to see the **Queen Mary** (daily 10am–6pm; $19 guided tours, kids $15). The Cunard flagship from the 1930s until the 1960s, the *Queen Mary* is now a luxury hotel, and guided tours present a sentimentalized version of its days of elegance and refinement. The huge geodesic dome nearby housed Howard Hughes's *Spruce Goose* airplane until it was sold and moved to Oregon in 1992, but this tourist loss has been more than remedied by the opening of the **Aquarium of the Pacific** (daily 10am–6pm; $17; Ⓦwww .aquariumofthepacific.org), along Shoreline Drive, a terrific exploration of aquatic flora and fauna in three distinct geographic and climatic zones from around the world. As you drive along the coast of Long Beach, don't be fooled by the sight of the bright pastel **islands** just off shore; far from natural, they're actually oil-drilling platforms in disguise.

Santa Catalina Island

The enticing island of **Santa Catalina**, twenty miles offshore, has been in private ownership since 1811, when the resident Gabrieleño Indians were forced to resettle on the mainland. It remains a wilderness, devoted to the conservation of unique species such as the **Catalina shrew** (so rare that it's only been sighted twice), and tourism has been held largely at bay. Hotels are unobtrusive among the whimsical architecture, and cars are largely forbidden; the two thousand islanders walk, ride bikes or drive electric golf carts. **Ferry** trips to Catalina run several times daily from San Pedro and Long Beach ($30–42; operators are Catalina Cruises, ☎562/436-5006, and Catalina Express, ☎1-800/481-3470, Ⓦwww.catalinaexpress.com). From Newport Beach, the Catalina Passenger Service (☎949/673-5245) runs a $30 daily round-trip.

The island's one town, **AVALON**, can be fully explored on foot in an hour, and you can rent bikes at a stand on Bay Shore Drive. Pick up a map at the Chamber of Commerce (☎310/510-1520, Ⓦwww.visitcatalina.org), at the foot of the ferry pier, and begin at the sumptuous Art Deco **Avalon Casino**, 1 Casino Way, built in the 1920s by William Wrigley Jr (of the Chicago chewing-gum dynasty and one-time owner of the island), which runs regular movie showings and irregular silent film displays. The collections at the adjoining **museum** (daily 10.30am–4pm, Jan–March closed Thurs; $1.50) include Native American artifacts from Catalina's past. On the slopes above, the **Zane Grey Pueblo Hotel**, 199 Chimes Tower Rd (☎310/510-0966, ⓦ www.zanegreyhotel.com; ❹–❺), is the former home of the Western author, who visited Catalina to film *The Vanishing American* and liked the place so much he never left. The hotel's seventeen rooms are each themed around a Zane Grey story, and there's a pool in the shape of an arrowhead.

Hotel **accommodation** in Avalon is much in demand, and pricey – upwards of $95: the least expensive is usually the *Atwater* (☎1-800/626-1496; ❸) and the most, the sumptuous, six-room *Inn on Mount Ada* (☎310/510-2030; ❽), whose sweeping ocean views once belonged to Wrigley himself. The only budget options are one mountainside and three seaside **campgrounds** (☎310/510-8368, ⓦ www.scico.com/camping; $12 per person, kids $6).

Anaheim: Disneyland and around

In the early 1950s, cartoonist Walt Disney conceived a theme park where his already hugely popular characters – Mickey Mouse, Donald Duck and the rest – could come to life, to enchant children and make their Uncle Walt even richer. **ANAHEIM** was chosen as the location for **Disneyland** on the basis that these acres of orange groves, thirty miles southeast of downtown LA, would become Southern California's next major focus of population growth – which indeed they did. The whole area is now so completely overrun with shameless souvenir shops, chain hotels and fast-food restaurants that it's long since spun out of the control of the Disney grasp and makes for a surprisingly seedy environment (outside the park itself, of course). When Disney opened his next theme park, in Florida – see p.652 – he made sure he owned all the land, hotels and commercial properties, not making the same mistake he made here of only buying a few square miles. If you're not coming to visit Disneyland, or the similar spectacle of carnival rides and historical hokum, **Knott's Berry Farm** (8039 Beach Blvd; $40), you may as well give the town a miss: it hasn't an ounce of interest in itself.

Disneyland

To make the most of **Disneyland** – the ultimate corporate-escapist fantasy and the blueprint for countless imitations worldwide – throw yourself right into it. Don't think twice about anything and go on every ride you can. The shockingly high admission price ($43, kids $33; ⓦ disneyland.disney.go.com) includes them all, although during peak periods each one can entail hours of waiting in line. Remember, too, that the emphasis is on family fun; the authorities take a dim view of anything remotely anti-social and eject those they consider guilty.

Over four hundred "Imagineers" worked to create the *Indiana Jones Adventure*, based on the Steven Spielberg movie franchise. Two hours of waiting are built into the ride, with an interactive archeological dig and 1930s-style newsreel show leading up to the main feature – a giddy journey along 2500ft of skull-encrusted corridors in which you face fireballs, falling rubble, venomous snakes and, inevitably, a rolling boulder finale. Disney claims that, thanks to computer engineering, no two *Indiana Jones* rides are ever alike. Judge for yourself.

Among the best of the older **rides** are two in **Adventureland**: the *Pirates of the Caribbean*, a boat trip through underground caverns, giving you the chance to sing along with animatronic pirates; and the *Haunted Mansion*, a riotous "doom buggy" tour in the company of the house spooks. **Fantasyland** consists mainly of low-tech fairy-tale rides that won't scare the kiddies, but is much better than the tedious, dumbed-down **Toontown** to the north, a real snooze for adults. **Tomorrowland** is Disney's vision of the future, where the *Space Mountain* roller coaster zips through the pitch-blackness of outer space, and the *Star Tours* ride simulates a journey into the world of George Lucas. This section of the park has been updated in the last few years with space probes and "rocket rods," which underscores how Cold War-era this area still remains in its outlook.

The latest adjunct to Disneyland, taking over a large chunk of its former parking lot, is the **California Adventure**, technically a separate park but quite connected in architecture, style and spirit – it does for California's history and culture what Epcot Center does for the world's, namely sanitize most of the fun out of it. Aside from its more exciting roller coasters and slightly better food, the Adventure is really just another "land" to visit on your Disney trek, albeit a much bigger and more expensive one: you cannot get access to both parks with a single-day admission ticket. Instead, you either have to shell out another $43 or spend $111 for a three-day pass that covers both – hardly a deal, considering that an annual pass to either park only runs $28 more.

As for accommodation, try to visit just for the day and spend the night somewhere else. Most of the hotels and motels nearby cost well in excess of $75 per night (see p.1063 for reasonable choices). You're not permitted to bring your own **food** to either park; you can only consume the fast-food sold on the premises.

Both Disneyland and the California Adventure are at 1313 Harbor Blvd, Anaheim, 45 minutes by **car** from downtown using the Santa Ana Freeway. In summer, the parks are open daily between 8am and 1am; otherwise opening hours are weekdays 10am to 6pm, Saturday 9am to midnight, and Sunday 9am to 10pm. Arrive early; traffic and ride queues quickly become nightmarish, especially in the summer. For further **information**, including public transportation details, call ☏714/781-4565.

Yorba Linda: the Richard Nixon Library and Birthplace

Mickey Mouse may be its most famous resident, but conservative Orange County's favorite son is former president **Richard Milhous Nixon**, born in 1913 in what's now the freeway-caged **Yorba Linda**, about eight miles northeast of Disneyland at 18001 Yorba Linda Blvd (Mon–Sat 10am–5pm, Sun 11am–5pm; $5.95; ⓦwww.nixonfoundation.org). His birthplace – and final resting place, as he's buried in the grounds – is a shrine to a man who forged a career from lies and secrecy, and finally resigned from the world's most powerful job in total disgrace. In the shadow of a 12ft high, 600lb chunk of the Berlin Wall, oversized gifts from world leaders, amusing campaign memorabilia and a laugh-a-line collection of obsequious letters written by and to Nixon form the core of the exhibition, but the man's distinctive persona is best enjoyed in the constantly running archive radio and TV recordings.

Nixon's face leers down in Big Brother fashion from almost every wall, but only inside the **Presidential Auditorium** do you get the chance to ask him a question, although the choice is limited to a small pre-programmed selection. Nixon's gaunt features fill the overlarge screen and provide the stock replies – as oily as ever.

The San Gabriel and San Fernando valleys

The northern limit of LA is defined by two long, wide valleys lying over the hills from the central basin, starting close to one another a few miles north of downtown and spanning outwards in opposite directions – east to the deserts around Palm Springs, west to Ventura on the central coast. You wouldn't miss an awful lot by not visiting the valleys at all, but they do give a picture of life in LA's suburbs.

The San Gabriel Valley

Spreading east from Pasadena, ten miles north of Los Angeles, the **San Gabriel Valley** was settled by farmers and cattle ranchers on the lands of the eighteenth-century Mission San Gabriel. **PASADENA** itself is as much the home of the *grandes dames* of LA society as it is to the "little old lady from Pasadena" of the Jan and Dean song. A luxury resort in the 1880s, it then became a residential area and underwent a major renovation in the 1980s, with modern shopping centers slipping in behind 1920s facades, and the blocks around the so-called **Old Pasadena** of Colorado Boulevard, now fashionable for their restaurants, cinemas and bookstore.

Aside from its famous **Rose Parade** in January, Pasadena's two best offerings are the splendid collection at the **Norton Simon Museum**, 411 W Colorado Blvd (Wed–Sun noon–6pm, Fri closes at 9pm; $6; Ⓦ www.nortonsimon.org), one of LA's greatest and least heralded institutions, with a prime selection of old masters and modern works (including Rembrandt, Hals, Monet and Picasso), and the **Gamble House**, 4 Westmoreland Place (hour-long tours Thurs–Sun noon–3pm; $8; Ⓦ gamblehouse.usc.edu), a Craftsman-styled mansion with Arts and Crafts decor and Japanese-inspired design elements. Maps and booklets of Pasadena are available at the **Convention and Visitors Bureau**, 171 S Los Robles Ave (Mon–Fri 8am–5pm, Sat 10am–4pm; Ⓣ 626/795-9311, Ⓦ www.pasadenavisitor.org).

South of Pasadena, in the dull, upper-crust little suburb of **San Marino**, the **Huntington Museum and Library**, off Huntington Drive at 1151 Oxford Rd (Tues–Fri noon–4.30pm, Sat–Sun 10.30am–4.30pm; suggested donation $10; Ⓦ www.huntington.org), contains numerous manuscripts and rare books, such as a Gutenberg Bible and the Ellesmere Chaucer, an illuminated manuscript of *The Canterbury Tales* from around 1410. Paintings include Gainsborough's *Blue Boy* and Reynolds' *Mrs Siddons as the Tragic Muse*, and the whole complex is set off by acres of beautiful themed **gardens**, of which the centerpiece is a neoclassical **mausoleum** containing the museum's founder Henry Huntington himself – and said to be the inspiration for the Jefferson Memorial in Washington, DC.

The San Fernando Valley

The San Fernando Valley, spreading west, is "the Valley" to most Angelenos: a sprawl of tract homes, mini-malls, fast-food drive-ins and auto parts stores. It has more of a middle-American feel than anywhere else in LA, inhabited – at least, in the popular LA imagination – by macho men and bimboesque "Valley Girls," speaking their own fractured dialect. In the gateway town of **GLENDALE**, eight miles north of downtown, **Forest Lawn Cemetery** at 1712 S Glendale Ave (daily 9am–5pm; free) was immortalized with biting satire by Evelyn Waugh in *The Loved One*. Those buried here include Errol Flynn, Walt Disney (contrary to urban legend, not frozen), Clara Bow, Nat King Cole, Chico Marx, Clark Gable and Jean Harlow, in a marble-lined room paid for by her fiancé William Powell. If seeing the gravesites of the famous isn't enough for you, check out the replicas of the highlights of art history (such as a stained-glass *Last Supper*) spiced with a healthy dollop of religious kitsch, all rendered with maximum vulgarity.

Burbank and the studios

The name of Hollywood may be synonymous with the movies, but the studios themselves moved out of Tinseltown long ago; the nitty-gritty business of actually making films goes on over the hills in otherwise hot and boring **Burbank**. **Studio tours** include a solid look inside **NBC**, 3000 W Alameda St, Burbank (Mon–Fri 9am–3pm; $7; ☎818/840-3537), the rather uninspired walk-through for **Paramount Studios**, 5555 Melrose Ave, Hollywood (Mon–Fri 9am–2pm; $15; ☎323/956-4552, ⊛www.paramount.com/studio), and the technically oriented trek into **Warner Bros Studios**, 4000 Warner Blvd, Burbank (Mon–Fri 9am–4pm; $33; ☎818/972-TOUR, ⊛www.burbank .com/warner_bros_tour.shtml). The largest of the old backlots belongs to **Universal Studios**, whose four-hour tours (summer daily 8am–10pm; rest of year daily 9am–7pm; $43; ☎818/508-9600, ⊛www.universalstudioshollywood .com) are more like a trip around an amusement park, with high-tech rides and "evening spectaculars" often based on current movies. The shows are without exception cheesy, but for fans of explosions and pratfalls, they're an absolute must.

Eating

LA **eating** covers every extreme: whatever you want to eat and however much you want to spend, you're spoiled for choice. Try to take at least a few meals in the more acclaimed restaurants, if only to watch the city's many self-appointed food snobs going through their paces. If you simply want to fill up quickly and inexpensively, the options are almost endless, and include terrific burger stands where you can scarf down mountains of fried favorites, and the many restaurant and bar happy hours where you can get a range of good, free food available for the price of a drink. LA is also littered with **celebrity-owned** outfits – like Steven Spielberg's submarine-shaped sandwich store *Dive!* and *Planet Hollywood* (where displays include Forrest Gump's box of chocolates) in Beverly Hills – but the food is usually unremarkable, as many visitors soon discover.

Downtown

Buffet Palace 3014 Olympic Blvd ☎213/480-8949. Authentic Korean restaurant in the heart of Koreatown, good for spicy barbecued beef.

Clifton's Cafétéria 648 S Broadway ☎213/627-1673. A cafeteria complete with redwood trees, waterfall and mini-chapel, and serving good, inexpensive American staples.

El Cholo 1121 S Western Ave ☎323/734-2773. One of LA's first big Mexican restaurants and still one of the best, despite the drunken frat-rats from USC.

La Bella Cucina 949 S Figueroa St ☎213/623-0014. Fabulous pizzas and homemade pastas, with the accent on Northern Italian cuisine, and a predictably high price tag.

Langer's Deli 704 S Alvarado ☎213/483-8050. Over twenty types of hot pastrami sandwiches draw the crowds to this classic eatery, despite the grim surroundings.

Ocean Seafood 750 N Hill ☎213/687-3088. Cavernous and often crowded Chinese restaurant serving low-priced, excellent food – try the abalone, crab, shrimp or duck.

The Original Pantry 877 S Figueroa St ☎213/972-9279. Mayor Riordan owns this classic old diner serving huge pork chops and American breakfasts served 24hrs a day.

Pacific Dining Car 1310 W 6th St ☎213/483-6000. Starched linen and very expensive steaks in a former railroad carriage styled after the hushed tones of an English supper club. Good-value breakfasts available. Open until 2am.

Philippe's Original 1001 N Alameda St ☎213/628-3781. Since 1908, the home of delicious French dip sandwiches, stuffed with pork, beef and lamb; invented right here as well.

Hollywood

Casa Carnitas 4067 Beverly Blvd ☎323/667-9953. Tasty, cheap Mexican food from the Yucatan, with dishes inspired by Cuban and Caribbean cooking; lots of seafood, too.

Citrus 6703 Melrose Ave ☎323/857-0034. Trendy, upmarket restaurant, serving good California cuisine using fish, duck, and rack of lamb. Reservations are essential; lunch for two will be at least $65.

French Quarter 7985 Santa Monica Blvd ☎323/654-0898. Inside the French Market Place, a gay-run, New Orleans-themed Cajun restaurant that's at least as much fun as Disneyland.

Gloria's Café 3603 W Sunset Blvd ☎323/664-5732. Popular, gay-friendly local hangout that's great for dinner, especially Cajun food.

Hampton's 1342 N Highland Ave ☎323/469-1090. Over fifty styles of gourmet hamburger on the menu.

Mexico City 2121 Hillhurst Ave ☎323/661-7227. Spinach enchiladas and other Californian versions of Mexican standards served in red booths, with a great view of the street from the wall-length window and a young crowd. You're allowed to smoke in the adjoining bar, a rarity in LA.

Musso and Frank Grill 6667 Hollywood Blvd ☎323/467-7788. Since 1919, all the Hollywood bigwigs have frequented this landmark restaurant – but at $15 for bacon and eggs, you're better off having a cocktail in the bar.

Roscoe's Chicken and Waffles 1514 N Gower St ☎323/466-7453. Mind-blowingly caloric delights at this always-packed spot, highlighted by hefty helpings of the eponymous comfort food.

Shibucho 3114 Beverly Blvd ☎323/387-8498. Excellent sushi bar in the heart of Little Tokyo; go with someone who knows what to order, as the waiters don't speak English.

Tommy's 2575 Beverly Blvd ☎310/389-9060. Often called LA's best burgers: loaded with thick beef, toppings and, most importantly, grease. But watch the dicey neighborhood.

Yukon Mining Co 7328 Santa Monica Blvd ☎323/851-8833. Colorful coffee shop catering to local drag queens, Russian immigrants, and residents of the neighboring senior citizens' home. Open 24hr.

West LA

Apple Pan 10801 W Pico Blvd ☎310/475-3585. Grab a spot at the counter and enjoy great pies and fresh, juicy hamburgers. A much better choice than the adjacent Westside Pavilion mall's food court.

Campanile 624 S La Brea Ave ☎323/938-1447. Expensive Northern Italian restaurant with indoor fountain and pleasing pastries from *La Brea Bakery* next door.

Canter's Deli 419 N Fairfax Ave ☎323/651-2030. Waitresses in pink uniforms and running shoes serve kosher soup and sandwiches in a kitsch, white-vinyl setting, featuring its own bizarre cabaret.

Chung King 11538 W Pico Blvd ☎310/477-4917. The best neighborhood Chinese restaurant in LA, serving spicy Szechuan food: don't miss out on the *bum-bum* chicken.

El Coyote 7312 Beverly Blvd ☎323/939-2255. Heavy portions of Mexican staples in a gloomy setting. Watch soccer and down the legendary cheap margaritas in the bar.

Georgia 7250 Melrose Ave ☎323/933-8420. Chic and upscale decor, but authentically downhome, Southern cooking at this celebrity-owned hot spot.

The Gumbo Pot 6333 W 3rd St in the Farmers' Market ☎323/933-0358. Delicious and dirt-cheap Cajun cooking amid hordes of tourists; try the *gumbo yaya* of chicken, shrimp and sausage, and the fruit-and-potato salad.

Mishima 8474 W 3rd St ☎323/782-0181. Some of LA's best miso soup and *udon* noodles, at surprisingly affordable prices.

Shamshiry 1916 Westwood Blvd ☎310/474-1410. The best of the Iranian restaurants in town, offering reasonably priced fine kebabs, pilafs and exotic sauces.

Swingers 8018 Beverly Blvd ☎323/653-5858. Basic and cheap American food served in a mildly surreal and trendy motel environment, loaded with hipsters and slackers.

Tail o' the Pup 329 N San Vicente Blvd ☎310/652-4517. A pop architecture favorite shaped like a hot dog. Munch on savory red hots before shopping at the nearby Beverly Center mall.

Tommy Tang's 7313 Melrose Ave ☎323/937-5733. Excellent Thai food in a very popular restaurant. Incongruous biweekly drag nights, with glammed-up waiters and a few customers as well.

Santa Monica, Venice and Malibu

Café 50s 838 Lincoln Blvd, Venice ☎310/399-1955. No doubts about this place: Ritchie Valens on

the jukebox and hot 'n' juicy burgers on the tables.
Café Montana 1534 Montana Ave, Santa Monica ☎310/829-3990. Good breakfasts, excellent salads and grilled fish in this art gallery-cum-café on a new upmarket shopping strip.
Chaya 110 Navy St, Venice ☎310/396-1179. Coolly elegant culinary crossroads serving Japanese and Mediterranean foods to a smart clientele. Try the huge California roll platter for two.
Chinois on Main 2709 Main St, Santa Monica ☎310/392-9025. One of LA's most renowned restaurants, run by chef Wolfgang Puck, and serving nouveau Chinese dishes like fresh fish in garlic and ginger. Very expensive, with lunches from $25.
Inn of the Seventh Ray 128 Old Topanga Canyon Rd, just off Topanga Canyon ☎310/455-1311. The ultimate New Age restaurant, serving vegetarian and wholefood dishes in a relatively secluded environment. Excellent desserts, too.
Lighthouse Buffet 201 Arizona Ave, Santa Monica ☎310/451-2076. All-you-can-eat sushi; indulge to your heart's content for $10 at lunchtime or $20 in the evening.
Norm's 1601 Lincoln Blvd, Santa Monica ☎310/450-0074. The prototypical LA diner, with colorful 1950s architecture and ample $4 breakfasts.
Rae's Diner 2901 Pico Blvd ☎310/828-7937. Another classic retro diner popular with the late-night crowd. Check out the film *True Romance* for a better look.
Valentino 3115 Pico Blvd ☎310/829-4313. Some call it the finest Italian restaurant in the US – and definitely in LA. Expect to max out your credit card.

Disneyland and around

Angelo's 511 S State College Blvd, Anaheim ☎714/533-1401. Straight out of *Happy Days*, a drive-in complete with roller-skating car-hops and good burgers. Open until 2am at weekends.

Belisle's 12001 Harbor Blvd, Garden Grove ☎714/750-6560. Open late with sandwiches, sweet and meat pies, and plenty of baked goods.
Knott's Chicken Dinner Restaurant 8039 Beach Blvd, located just outside Knott's Berry Farm ☎714/220-5080. Famous for fried chicken long before Disneyland was around – serving cheap and tasty meals for about 70 years. Park admission not required.
Ruby's 1 Balboa Pier, Newport Beach ☎949/675-RUBY. A solid spot for burgers and fries – the only eatery on this popular pier and one of the few cheap spots in this upscale burg.

The San Gabriel and San Fernando valleys

Dr Hogly-Wogly's Tyler Texas Bar-B-Q 8136 Sepulveda Blvd, Van Nuys ☎818/780-6701. Queue up for the chicken, sausages, ribs and beans – some of the best in LA.
Fair Oaks Pharmacy and Soda Fountain 1526 Mission St, South Pasadena ☎626/799-1414. Serving good fountain drinks and diner food since the hallowed days of Route 66. Preserved with plenty of period detail.
Genmai Sushi 4454 Van Nuys Blvd, Van Nuys ☎626/986-7060. Japanese-style vegetarian restaurant with brown rice, sushi and seasonal macrobiotic dishes.
Merida 20 E Colorado Blvd, Pasadena ☎626/792-7371. Mexican restaurant with dishes from the Yucatan; try the spicy pork wrapped and steamed in banana leaves.
Sea Star 2000 W Main St, Alhambra ☎626/282-8833. Affordable dim sum at its best: pork, *baos*, potstickers and dumplings, and delicious sweets.
Wolfe Burger 46 N Lake St, Pasadena ☎626/792-7292. A great place for chili, tamales and burgers, with huevos rancheros served for breakfast.

Nightlife and entertainment

Exploring the jungle of LA's **nightlife** can be great fun. Everyone you meet claims to be either a rock star or in the movies. Even the quietest venue offers a chance to eavesdrop on a bit of vapid *Less Than Zero* dialogue; the most raucous ones will take your breath away. In all the pubs, clubs and discos, you'll need to be 21 and will almost certainly be asked for ID.

The best sources of **listings** are *LA Weekly* and the "Calendar" section in the *LA Times* on Fridays.

Bars, pubs and coffeehouses

LA's **bars and pubs** are rarely the scruffy boozing places found elsewhere in the US, due in part to the generally high degree of health consciousness – not to mention the very early (daybreak) starting time of the movie business working day. As elsewhere along the west coast, **coffee houses** are established all over the city as popular meeting places.

Barney's Beanery 8447 Santa Monica Blvd, West Hollywood ☎213/654-2287. Well-worn pool-hall bar popular with graying rebels and sullen youth, stocking over 200 beers. It also serves food of marginal quality.

Boardner's 1652 N Cherokee Ave, Hollywood ☎323/462-9621. A likeably unkempt neighborhood bar with a mix of salty old-timers and hip newbies.

Cat 'n' Fiddle 6530 Sunset Blvd, Hollywood ☎323/468-3800. Boisterous British expat pub with good beers and live music.

The Dresden Room 1760 N Vermont Ave, Hollywood ☎323/665-42984. Wed night is open mike, otherwise the resident husband-and-wife lounge act takes requests from the crowd.

El Adobe 5536 Melrose Ave, Mid-Wilshire ☎323/462-9421. An old favorite for potent margaritas, B-list celebs and a laid-back So-Cal vibe, though the Mexican food is rather insipid.

Gotham Hall 1431 Third St Promenade, Santa Monica ☎310/394-8865. Purple-felt pool tables and mind-numbing cocktails are the main draw for the youthful clientele here. Also draws its share of inquisitive tourists from the Promenade.

Insomnia 7286 Beverly Blvd, West LA ☎323/931-4943. One of the more chic and trendy coffee joints in the area, with amateur art on the walls and not too many poseurs.

King's Road Espresso House 8361 Beverly Blvd, Hollywood ☎323/655-9044. Sidewalk café popular day and night with West Hollywood's neo-beatnik crowd.

Lava Lounge 1533 N La Brea, Hollywood ☎323/876-6612. Cheesy, retro decor, glowing cocktails and plenty of rock and surf music, along with Brubeck jazz and lounge favorites.

Little Frida's 8730 Santa Monica Blvd, West Hollywood ☎310/854-5421. Art, coffee, and pastries served to a mixed straight and gay crowd; also with comedy and music acts.

The Novel Café 212 Pier Ave, Santa Monica ☎310/396-8566. Stacks of used books and high-backed wooden chairs at this fairly unpretentious café, with good coffees, teas and pastries, and funky old sofas on the mezzanine to curl up in.

The Red Setter Irish Pub 2615 Wilshire Blvd, Santa Monica ☎310/828-9839. Plenty of darts and beer, and a mixed crowd of locals and expats.

Tiki-Ti 4427 W Sunset Blvd, Hollywood ☎323/669-9381. Tiny grass-skirted cocktail bar straight out of *Hawaii Five-0*. The Filipino owners mix deadly concoctions at about $6 a hit.

Ye Olde Kings Head 116 Santa Monica Blvd, Santa Monica ☎310/451-1402. Prime LA spot for English expats playing darts, swigging British brews and munching on steak-and-kidney pie.

Clubs and discos

LA's **clubs** are among the wildest in the country, ranging from absurdly faddish hangouts to industrial noise cellars. The trendier side of the club scene is, as always, hard to pin down; check the *LA Weekly* before setting out.

Dragonfly 6510 Santa Monica Blvd, Hollywood ☎323/466-6111. Disco and house music, with the odd bit of rock at this established hipster hangout featuring two large dance floors and a so-called "eye-contact" bar.

Florentine Gardens 5951 Hollywood Blvd, Hollywood ☎323/464-0706. A fun, unpretentious dance club catering to the under-21 set. Stuck between the Salvation Army and a porno theater in a seedier section of Hollywood.

Mayan 1038 S Hill St, downtown ☎213/746-4287. Get past the doorman and you're in with LA's coolest, eager to shake a leg to Latin, fusion and salsa in gorgeous and historic surrounds done up in pre-Columbian style.

Playroom 836 N Highland Ave, Hollywood ☎323/461-8301. Where LA goth-rockers and

industrial noise-makers come out to play, with plenty of aggressive, ear-popping sounds.

Sugar 814 Broadway, Santa Monica ☎310/899-1989. The entire range of electronic beats, from house to hip hop, can be found at this sleek glass-and-steel-styled club.

Union 8210 Sunset Blvd, West Hollywood ☎323/654-1001. Relaxed supper club with funk, soul and R&B groove room. Centrally located on the Sunset Strip and frequented by the young actor crowd on Tuesday nights.

The Viper Room 8852 Sunset Blvd, West Hollywood ☎310/358-1881. Stellar live acts playing house to swing to disco to jazz, and a famous owner to boot. Best known as the spot where River Phoenix met his end. Cover varies.

Lesbian and gay LA

Although proportionately not as big as that of San Francisco, the **gay scene** in LA is no less prominent. While West Hollywood is synonymous with the (affluent white) gay lifestyle, not just in LA but all over California, there are many other spots where intolerance is kept at bay. The other major gay community is Silver Lake, most evidently along Hyperion Boulevard, home to working-class blacks, whites and Hispanics, while other places like Venice, Los Feliz, Studio City and even Laguna Beach in Orange County are comfortable gay and lesbian locales. We've listed gay-friendly accommodations, restaurants, bars and clubs in the relevant listings sections.

The city's best known gay and lesbian bookshop is **A Different Light**, 8853 Santa Monica Blvd (℡310/854-6601, ⊛www.adlbooks.com), with monthly art shows, readings and musical events. Magazines with good listings sections include *Nightlife*, *Edge* and *Frontiers*. **The Gay Community Yellow Pages** (℡323/469-4454) is a comprehensive annual directory ($5) of gay businesses, publications, services and gathering places; it also publishes a gay restaurant guide. The **Gay and Lesbian Community Services Center**, 1625 N Schrader Blvd (℡323/993-7400), is the community's prime resource for counseling, health testing and information.

Gay and lesbian bars and clubs

Arena 6655 Santa Monica Blvd, Hollywood ℡323/462-0714. Many clubs under one huge roof, large dance floors throbbing to funk, Latin and hi-NRG grooves. At the same address, *Circus* is mostly men at Pink Feather night on Tuesdays; gay men and women on Fridays.

Detour 1087 Manzanita St, Silver Lake ℡323/664-1189. A friendly and quite inexpensive denim and leather bar in a bleak stretch of town.

Jewel's Catch One 4067 W Pico Blvd, Mid-Wilshire ℡323/734-8849. Sweaty dance barn covering two floors, with gay men on Wednesdays, lesbians on Thursdays.

The Palms 8572 Santa Monica Blvd, Hollywood ℡310/652-6188. Mostly house and dance nights at West Hollywood's longest-established lesbian bar.

Queen Mary 12449 Ventura Blvd, Studio City ℡818/506-5619. A regular gay crowd at the back and straight visitors at the front at this well-established drag club in the San Fernando Valley.

Rage 8911 Santa Monica Blvd, West Hollywood ℡310/652-7055. Very flashy gay men's club playing the latest hi-NRG hits. Drinks are inexpensive. Great Forties tea dance on Sundays.

Revolver 8851 Santa Monica Blvd, West Hollywood ℡310/659-8851. Sleek bar, intimate lounge, and regular karaoke and drag shows. Oriented toward gay men.

Rudolpho's 2500 Riverside Drive, Silver Lake ℡323/669-1226. Every second Saturday of the month the "dress up, drag down" dance club, *Drag Strip 66*, has a different theme. Otherwise a gay-friendly Mexican restaurant.

Live music

LA has an overwhelming choice of venues for **live music**. Ever since the nihilistic punk bands – Circle Jerks, X, Black Flag – drew the city away from its laid-back west coast country-folk scene in the late Seventies and early Eighties, LA's **rock music** has been excellent, with up-and-comers traditionally getting their first break in clubs on the Sunset Strip. Authentic **country music** is also fairly prevalent, at least away from trendy Hollywood. **Jazz**, too, is played in a few genuinely authentic downbeat dives, though more commonly found being used to improve a restaurant's atmosphere. **Reggae**, though popular with many, is much less common. **Salsa** is pervasive among LA's Hispanic population, and is found in the male-oriented bars of East LA and increasingly in some of the clubs of the Westside. In many of these clubs, **cover charges** can vary widely, depending on the prominence of the headliner and the night of the week, so call ahead.

Babe and Ricky's Inn 4339 Leimert Blvd, South Central ☎323/295-9112. One of LA's best venues for blues, where nationally known acts drop in on occasion.

The Baked Potato 6266 Sunset Blvd, Hollywood t323/461-6400. A small but legendary contemporary jazz spot, where many reputations have been forged.

B.B. King's Blues Club 1000 Universal Center Drive, Universal City ☎818/6-BBKING. Get past the garish exterior of Universal's CityWalk mall, and it's all catfish, deep-fried pickle and Southern hospitality. The club room called *Lucille's* features acoustic blues at the weekend.

The Conga Room 5364 Wilshire Blvd, Mid-Wilshire ☎323/938-1696. A high-profile celebrity investment results in a surprisingly appealing feast of Cuban food and Latin music, heavy on the mambo and salsa.

The Derby 4500 Los Feliz Blvd, Hollywood ☎323/663-8979. Swing, rockabilly and bebop, with dance lessons to get you up to speed. Drinks are club-pricey, but the circular bar, domed wooden ceiling and swing are hard to resist.

Doug Weston's Troubadour 9081 Santa Monica Blvd, West Hollywood ☎310/276-6168. Less heavy metal than of old, featuring a newer blend of acoustic and alternative acts, but still a good place for heavy riffs and shaggy manes.

El Floridita 1253 N Vine St, Hollywood ☎323/871-8612. Don't let the mini-mall setting deter you; this is a prime spot for Cuban and salsa acts, and also has good Mexican food.

The Foothill Club 1922 Cherry Ave, Signal Hill ☎562/984-8349. A glorious country dance hall from the days when hillbilly was cool. Punk, surf and roots-rock Thurs to Sat. Also offers the occasional dose of garage bands and dance music.

Gabah 4658 Melrose Ave, Mid-Wilshire ☎323/664-8913. Located in one of the truly abysmal corners of the city sprawl, this eclectic spot mixes reggae, dub, funk and rock – fun despite the surrounding gloom.

Golden Sails Hotel 6285 E Pacific Coast Hwy, Long Beach ☎562/596-1631. Has some of the best reggae bands from LA and beyond on Fridays and Saturdays. Located in an anonymous Long Beach hotel setting.

House of Blues 8430 Sunset Blvd, West Hollywood ☎323/848-5100. Incongruous mock sugar shack, with excellent but pricey live music nightly. Good local-name hip hop, R&B and blues. Always very popular with tourists.

Kingston 12 814 Broadway, Santa Monica ☎310/451-4423. Reggae tunes on periodic weekends in a nice and small venue.

Largo 432 N Fairfax Ave, Mid-Wilshire ☎323/852-1073. Intimate cabaret venue with some of LA's more interesting rock bands.

Luminarias 3500 Ramona Blvd, Monterey Park, East LA ☎323/268-4177. A hilltop Mexican restaurant where the live salsa is as good as the spicy food. Fri and Sat shows.

McCabe's 3103 W Pico Blvd, Santa Monica ☎310/828-4497. The back room of LA's premier acoustic guitar shop; long the scene of excellent and unusual folk and country shows.

Opium Den 1605 1/2 N Ivar Ave, Hollywood ☎323/466-7800. A strip club turned nightclub with an array of upcoming rock and punk acts taking turns on the overly small stage.

The Roxy 9009 Sunset Blvd, West Hollywood ☎310/276-2222. The showcase of the rock industry's new signings, intimate and with a great sound system.

Rusty's Surf Ranch 256 Santa Monica Pier ☎310/393-PIER. Loaded with out-of-towners, but still good for live folk and country, along with karaoke and, of course, surf music.

Whisky-a-Go-Go 8901 Sunset Blvd, West Hollywood ☎310/652-4202. Thanks to the Doors, for many years LA's most famous rock'n'roll club, nowadays featuring mainly hard rock.

Classical music, opera and dance

While not blessed with the same institutional largesse of east coast cities, LA has an increasing number of **classical music** venues. The **Los Angeles Philharmonic** (☎213/850-2000, ⓦwww.laphil.org), the city's only major name, performs regularly during the year with nationally known conductor Esa-Pekka Salonen at the helm. San Francisco has more of an opera scene (see p.1148), although **LA Opera** (☎213/972-8001, ⓦwww.laopera.org) stages productions between September and June, as does Orange County's **Opera Pacific** (☎1-800/34-OPERA, based in Costa Mesa; ⓦwww.operapacific.org), which performs both grand opera and operettas. Perhaps the city's most exciting company is the **Long Beach Opera** (☎562/439-2580, ⓦwww.lbopera .com), which is anything but provincial, putting on challenging but well-regarded performances of modern and lesser-known operas.

January

1 Tournament of Roses in Pasadena. A parade of floral floats and marching bands along Colorado Boulevard.

Mid Martin Luther King Parade and Celebration. Activities honoring the civil rights hero throughout town, notably in King Park and the Baldwin Hills mall.

February

First full moon after 21st Chinese New Year. Three days of dragon-float street parades, based in Chinatown.

Late Mardi Gras. Across LA, the spectacle of this Brazilian fun fest plays out, but nowhere as colorfully as in West Hollywood.

March

Mid St Patrick's Day. Related events all over the city, with some bars serving green beer.

End The Academy Awards are presented at the Hollywood & Highland theater complex beginning in 2002; legendary citywide parties ensue.

April

Early California Poppy Festival. Worth a trip to the distant northern burg of Lancaster to see the thousands of acres of eye-popping orange blossoms at this poppy reserve. (Call ☎661/723-6077 or visit ⊛www.poppyfestival.com for more details.)

Early The Blessing of the Animals. A long-established ceremony of Mexican origin thanking animals for their services to humans. Pets are blessed in Olvera Street, followed by a parade.

May

5 Cinco de Mayo. Day-long commemoration of the Mexican victory at the battle of Puebla. With several blocks closed to downtown traffic, the celebration features a spirited parade in Olvera Street and celebrations with Mexican food, drink and music in most LA parks.

June

Late Gay Pride. Parades throughout town, but notably on Santa Monica Boulevard in West Hollywood, where carnival atmosphere features spirited marchers and male cheerleaders in drag.

Early Lotus Festival. A long-standing favorite in Echo Park, just northwest of downtown, with dragon boats, ethnic food, pan-Pacific music, and plenty of resplendent lotus blossoms.

4 Independence Day. The *Queen Mary* in Long Beach hosts the biggest fireworks display.

August

First two weeks International Surf Festival. South Bay party where globally famed surfers compete amid crowds of tourists and beach volleyball players.

Mid Long Beach Jazz Festival. Held in Rainbow Lagoon Park near downtown Long Beach, a great chance to see excellent regional, and some national performers.

September

4 LA's birthday. A civic ceremony and assorted street entertainment around El Pueblo de Los Angeles to mark the founding of the original pueblo in 1781.

Late LA County Fair in distant Pomona, in the San Gabriel Valley. The country's biggest; with livestock shows, pie-eating contests, rodeos and carnival rides.

October

Early Watts Jazz Festival. Two days of free music with the Watts Towers as a backdrop.

Mid LA Street Fair and Carnival. Free rock music, fringe theater and comedy on the streets of downtown. Held at the same time as the West Hollywood Street Festival, a display of handmade arts and crafts in that city.

November

Late Doo-Dah Parade. Surprisingly popular, quintessential LA event, with a cast of absurdly costumed characters parading their way through Pasadena.

End Hollywood Christmas Parade. The first and best of the many Yuletide events, with a cavalcade of mind-boggling floats.

December

Mid Christmas Boat Parade. A flotilla of yachts and powerboats gets decorated in bright holiday lights and then cruises around Marina del Rey.

13

CALIFORNIA | Los Angeles

The last twenty years have seen an increase in smaller-scaled **chamber music** and **period performance** groups, most prominently the **LA Baroque Orchestra** (T310/458-0425) and **Los Angeles Chamber Orchestra** (T213/622-7001, Wwww.laco.org), and an upsurge in **dance** activity as well, with UCLA's **Dance Kaleidoscope** (T323/343-5120, Wwww.performingarts .ucla.edu), running two weeks in July, as one of the artistic highlights.

The Dorothy Chandler Pavilion in the Music Center, 135 N Grand Ave, downtown T213/972-7211 or 972-7460, Wwww.musiccenter.org. Home to the LA Philharmonic from October until May. Also used by the LA Opera and even the Oscars, presented biannually here.

The Hollywood Bowl 2301 N Highland Ave, Hollywood T323/850-2000, Wwww.hollywood-bowl.org. The LA Philharmonic gives open-air concerts Tues–Sat evenings from July to Sept, leaning toward familiar pops offerings.

Japan America Theatre 244 S San Pedro St, downtown T213/680-3700, Wwww.jaccc.org /jat/jat.html. Dance and performance works drawn from Japan and the Far East.

John Anson Ford Theater 2850 Cahuenga Blvd, Hollywood T323/461-3673, Wwww.lacount-yarts.org/ford.html. As well as UCLA's summer "Dance Kaleidoscope," this open-air venue also has one-off productions by local groups.

Orange County Performing Arts Center 600 Town Center Drive, Costa Mesa T714/556-ARTS, Wwww.ocpac.org. Home of the Pacific Symphony Orchestra and Opera Pacific, as well as touring big names in pop and jazz.

Pacific Amphitheater 100 Fair Drive, Costa Mesa T949/740-2000. A big open-air venue drawing mainstream crowds, Orange County's answer to the Hollywood Bowl.

Pasadena Dance Theater 1985 Locust Ave, Pasadena T626/683-3459, Wwww.pasade-nadance.org. A prominent San Gabriel Valley dance venue, hosting diverse groups throughout the year.

Royce Hall on the UCLA campus T310/825-9261 or 825-2101. Classical concerts throughout the college year, often involving big names. Usually Sept–June.

The Shrine Auditorium 665 W Jefferson Blvd T213/749-5123, box office at 655 S Hill St. A striking white-Islamic domed complex hosting regular performances by choral gospel groups and alternate Academy Awards ceremonies.

UCLA Center for the Performing Arts T310/825-4401, Wwww.performingarts.ucla.edu. Coordinates a wide range of touring companies, and also runs the experimentally inclined "Art of Dance" series between September and June.

Comedy clubs

The **comedy** scene in LA has long been known as the national proving ground for aspiring funnymen and -women, and it's also a good place to catch live performances by established television names like Jay Leno and Drew Carey.

Acme Comedy Theater 135 N La Brea Ave, West Hollywood T323/525-0202. A broad range of sketch and improv comedy, hosting the odd big name.

Comedy & Magic Club 1018 Hermosa Ave, Hermosa Beach T310/372-1193. Strange couplings of magic acts and comedians, highlighted by Jay Leno occasionally testing material.

The Comedy Store 8433 W Sunset Blvd, West Hollywood T323/656-6225. Popular comedy showcase spread over three rooms; you can usually get in, even on weekends.

Groundlings Theater 7307 Melrose Ave, Hollywood T323/934-9700. Only the gifted survive at this pioneering improvisation venue, where Pee Wee Herman got his start.

The Improvisation 8162 Melrose Ave, West Hollywood T323/651-2583. Prime destination for out-of-town comedy-lovers – so book ahead. Peer through the dark to see big names watching their buddies perform.

LA Connection 13442 Ventura Blvd, Sherman Oaks T818/784-1868. An improvisation showcase for highly rated specialists in the art of being obnoxious. Seldom less than memorable.

Theater

We've listed a few selections from LA's very active **theater** scene; ticket services like Times Tix (T310/659-3678) and Theater LA (T213/614-0556,

@ www.theatrela.org) provide full- and half-price tickets and offer reservations. The *LA Weekly* and the *LA Times* "Calendar" section have full listings and reviews. Expect to pay $10–25 for smaller shows, and $30 and up for the big touring productions.

Alex Theater 216 N Brand Blvd, Glendale ☎1-800/872-8997. Gloriously restored movie palace that now features a fine range of musical theater, comedy, film and one-person shows.

The Complex 6476 Santa Monica Blvd, Hollywood ☎323/469-9338. An association of six small theaters putting on edgy, innovative works you may not see anywhere else.

Coronet Theater 368 N La Cienega Blvd, West Hollywood ☎310/657-7377. Home of the LA Public Theater; productions include a famous name or two. Also home to the Youth Academy of Dramatic Arts.

Geffen Playhouse 10886 Le Conte Ave, Westwood ☎310/208-5454. Small theater across from UCLA with frequent one-person shows.

Showcased playwrights have included comedian Steve Martin.

Mark Taper Forum 135 N Grand Ave, downtown ☎213/972-0700. Theater in the three-quarter round, sometimes putting on innovative new plays but mostly known for its conservatism and adherence to the established repertoire.

Powerhouse Theater 3116 2nd St, Santa Monica ☎310/396-3680. Experimental, alternative shows, located in a former electrical station for the Red Car transit line.

Shubert Theater 2020 Avenue of the Stars, Century City ☎1-800/447-7400. The only good thing about Century City is that you can come here to ogle the big razzmatazz musicals.

Film

Feature films are often released in LA months (or years) before they play anywhere else in the world. Short seasons of **foreign–language films** are screened at the eight Laemmle Theaters. If you're after a golden-age **atmosphere**, head for one of the historic downtown movie palaces along Broadway, where the delirious furnishings may hold your attention longer than the all-action double bills. You can catch mainstream **new releases** in one of the many mall-based multiplexes, like the Beverly Center Cineplex, 8500 Beverly Blvd, West LA (☎310/652-7760), AMC Century 14, 10250 Santa Monica Blvd, Century City (☎310/553-8900) or the Universal City 18, at Universal Studios' CityWalk, San Fernando Valley (☎818/508-0588).

Bing Theater at the LA County Art Museum, 5905 Wilshire Blvd, Mid-Wilshire ☎323/857-6010. Afternoon screenings of many neglected Hollywood classics. Matinees cost just $2, evening shows $8.

Chinese Theatre 6925 Hollywood Blvd, Hollywood ☎323/464-8186. Landmark cinema with stylish decor, giant screen and six-track stereo sound – absolutely the best place to see a big-budget flick; on opening weekends draws a cheering crowd.

Egyptian Theater 6712 Hollywood Blvd, Hollywood ☎323/466-FILM. Renovated showcase for classic and foreign films, in the middle of Hollywood, offering a wild design and frequent film festivals with an eclectic selection.

El Capitan Theater 6834 Hollywood Blvd, Hollywood ☎323/467-7674. Another legendary Hollywood venue, restored to full glory and recently renovated for a second time. Expect to see plenty of animated and live-action Disney fare.

New Beverly Cinema 7165 Beverly Blvd, Mid-

Wilshire ☎323/938-4038. Imaginative double bills for cult, art and classic films.

Nuart Theater 11272 Santa Monica Blvd, West LA ☎310/478-6379. Rare classics, foreign films and documentaries. Often the December screening room of choice for Oscar hopefuls, so be prepared for a lengthy line outside.

Orpheum 842 S Broadway, downtown ☎213/239-0939. The grandest of the remaining downtown movie palaces open to the public. The action-oriented fare may be insipid, but the French Renaissance and Baroque decor is not.

Rialto 1023 Fair Oaks Ave, South Pasadena ☎626/799-9567. Aging Moorish and pre-Columbian revival palace, famed as the spot where Tim Robbins tracks down and kills a screenwriter in *The Player*.

Silent Movie 611 N Fairfax Ave, West LA ☎323/655-2510. As its name suggests, showings of silent Chaplin, Laurel and Hardy, Ramon Navarro thrillers and so on. Every show is accompanied by an organist.

Shopping

You can buy virtually anything, anywhere, anytime in LA. The big **department stores** or the exclusive **Rodeo Drive** (see p.1075) will have it if the ubiquitous run-of-the-mill retailers don't, and if all else fails try LA's massive **malls**, which often resemble self-contained city suburbs as much as shopping precincts. The antiseptic **City Walk** mall at Universal Studios distills a dozen LA neighborhoods into cutout facades fronting all the national chain stores, complete with a sandy beach. At the central seven-acre **Beverly Center**, at Beverly and La Cienega boulevards, you'll find designer stores, fourteen cinemas and ample opportunities for star-spotting, all above a giant parking garage. Another local favorite is the **Century City Mall**, 10250 Santa Monica Blvd, Century City, aimed at middle-class and upscale – but unpretentious – buyers. West Hollywood and **Melrose Avenue** hold many of the city's trendier boutiques, but if you're after a first edition of Shirley MacLaine's autobiography, old movies stills or a rare Beatles "butcher cover" LP in mint condition, try one of the places listed below.

Books

Acres of Books 240 Long Beach Blvd, Long Beach ☏562/437-6980. LA's largest, and most disorganized and confusing, secondhand collection – well worth a trip down the Blue Line.

Book Soup 8818 Sunset Blvd, West Hollywood ☏323/659-3110. Packed to the gills with an eclectic selection, this shop is as good for spotting celebs as it is for browsing.

Either/Or 124 Pier Ave, Hermosa Beach ☏310/374-2060. Known for its fiction and New Age sections, and once the haunt of Thomas Pynchon. Open until 11pm nightly.

Hennessey and Ingalls 1254 Third St Promenade, Santa Monica ☏310/458-9074. An impressive range of expensive, hard-to-find art and architecture books, plus rare posters and catalogs.

Koma Books 1764 N Vermont Ave, Hollywood ☏323/665-0956. Mayhem, true crime, fanzines and loony conspiracy theories; everything the others are too shocked to sell. A small shop with a large mail-order clientele, favored by tabloid TV researchers. Now publishing its own authors.

Larry Edmunds Book Shop 6644 Hollywood Blvd, Hollywood ☏323/463-3273. Stacks of books on every aspect of film and theater, plus movie stills and posters.

Midnight Special 1318 Third St Promenade, Santa Monica ☏310/393-2923. Excellent for lefty politics, social sciences and general fiction and literature; open late.

Norton Simon Museum Bookstore 411 W Colorado Blvd, Pasadena ☏626/449-6840. Inexpensive prices for art books, given the pricey LA market. Good selection, too.

Samuel French Theatre & Film Bookshop 7623 Sunset Blvd, Hollywood ☎ 323/876-0570. Famed for its performing arts selection, the best in town, with a prime selection of cinema books as well.
Sisterhood Bookstore 1351 Westwood Blvd ☎ 310/477-7300. Westside landmark selling music, cards, jewelry and books, pertaining to all aspects of the women's movement.

Records

Aron's Records 1150 N Highland Ave, Hollywood ☎ 323/469-4700. One of the best places in LA for secondhand discs – huge stock, all styles, all prices.
Moby Disc 28 E Colorado Blvd, Pasadena ☎ 626/449-9975. Secondhand and deletions, cen-trally located in Old Pasadena shopping district.
Record Surplus 11609 W Pico Blvd, West LA ☎ 310/478-4217. Hands down the best spot for used music in LA, or anywhere for that matter, loaded with ancient LPs, out-of-print CDs, new releases and all manner of assorted junk you have to see to believe – even 8-tracks.
Rhino Records 1720 Westwood Blvd, West LA ☎ 310/474-8685. The biggest selection of interna-tional independent releases, plus the full selection of Rhino's music catalog.
Vinyl Fetish 7305 Melrose Ave, Hollywood ☎ 323/935-1300. Besides the punk and post-punk merchandise, a good place to discover what's new on the LA music scene and purchase a cheesy T-shirt or two.

The Deserts

The **deserts** of Southern California occupy a quarter of the state. Untouched but for the three million acres used for military bases, this hot and often inhos-pitable wilderness exerts a powerful fascination for venturesome travelers. There are two distinct regions: the **Colorado** or **Low Desert** in the south, which is the most easily reached from LA, containing the opulent artificial oasis of **Palm Springs** and the primeval expanse of **Joshua Tree**; and the **Mojave** or **High Desert**, dominated by **Death Valley** and stretching along Hwy-395 up to the sparsely populated **Owens Valley**, infamous as the place from which the city of Los Angeles stole its water.

It is impossible to do justice to this area without your own wheels. Palm Springs can be reached on public transportation, but only the periphery of Joshua Tree is accessible and it's a long hot walk to anywhere very interesting. You can get as far as Barstow on Greyhound and Amtrak, but no transporta-tion traverses Death Valley, leaving only the Owens Valley with its daily Greyhound service between LA and Reno.

The Low Desert

Most visitors to the Low Desert have no intention of getting away from it all. They head straight for where it's at – the irrefutable capital of the desert, bastion of right-wing politics and sun-scorched refuge of the Hollywood elite, **Palm Springs**. In these few square miles, overrun with the famous and the star-struck, the average age and average temperature are said to be about the same – a steady 88. Still, it's got a gorgeous setting and you'll find it hard to avoid: it's the first stopping point east from LA on I-10, at the center of the **Coachella Valley**, part of the most intensively productive agricultural area in the world, growing dates, oranges, lemons and grapefruits in vast quantities.

The sublime landscape of **Joshua Tree National Park**, well worth a weekend spent taking in the sunsets and the howls of coyotes at twilight, lies one hour's drive east of Palm Springs, three and a half from LA.

Palm Springs

Sitting in lush farming land, replete with manicured golf courses, condominiums and millionaires, **PALM SPRINGS** does not conform to any typical image of the desert, embodying a strange mix of Spanish Colonial and mid-century modern styling. The massive bulk of Mount San Jacinto looms over its low-slung buildings, casting a welcome shadow over the town in the late afternoon. Ever since Hollywood stars first came here in the 1930s, laying claim to ranch-style estates and holing up in elite hotels, the clean dry air and sunshine, just 120 miles east of LA, have made Palm Springs irresistible. For years, high-school kids arrived in their thousands for the drunken revelry of Spring Break, until civic zeal ran them out of town, while others come specifically to sober up: the **Betty Ford Center** in nearby Rancho Mirage draws a star-studded patient list to its booze- and drug-free environment, attempting to undo a lifetime's worth of behavioral disorders in an $11,000 28-day stay. The town is also regarded as the country's largest gay resort.

Palm Springs wasn't always like this. Once it was the domain of the **Cahuillan Indians**; they were allocated this land in the 1890s, but exact zoning wasn't settled until the 1940s, by which time the development of hotels and leisure complexes was well under way. Under an odd checkerboard system, every other square mile of Palm Springs forms part of the **Agua Caliente** (Spanish for "hot water") **Indian Reservation**, and high rents have made this the second richest tribe in America, worth more than $2 billion – wealth that's been increasing with the new Casino Morongo, right in the heart of town.

Arrival, information and getting around

Arriving by car, you drive into town on N Palm Canyon Drive, passing the visitors center at no. 2781 (daily 9am–5pm; ☎1-800/34-SPRINGS). Greyhound **buses** (17 daily from LA) come in at 311 N Indian Canyon Drive, while Amtrak **trains** from LA (two daily) stop just south of I-10 at N Indian Avenue, about ten minutes from downtown. Sun Buses (6am–8pm; ☎760/343-3451, ⓦwww.sunline.org) circulate in all the local resort towns, costing 75¢ for a typical trip and $3 for a day pass.

Companies such as Palm Springs Celebrity Tours, 4751 E Palm Canyon Drive (☎760/770-2700), offer **celebrity tours** from $15 for a basic, hour-long trip to $20 for more involved treks. You could do it yourself, with a map of the stars' homes ($6) from the visitors center – but you'd miss out on the sharp anecdotal commentary.

Accommodation

Luxury **hotels** outnumber the affordable variety in Palm Springs, but prices drop by as much as seventy percent as temperatures rise in summer. The north end of town, along Hwy-111, holds many of the lower-priced places, including countless motels, virtually all of which have pools and, of course, air conditioning. The prices below are **summer rates**.

Bee Charmer Inn 1600 E Palm Canyon Drive ☎760/778-5883, ⓦwww.beecharmer.com. Lesbian-oriented motel a mile or so south of downtown, offering continental breakfast, pool, and mini-fridges and microwaves in the rooms. ➍

Casa Cody 175 S Cahuilla Rd ☎760/320-9346 or 1-800/231-2639, ⓦwww.casacody.com. Attractive, well-located Southwestern-style B&B in a shady garden. ➍
Desert Lodge 1177 S Palm Canyon Drive

760/325-1356 or 1-800/385-6343, Ⓦwww.desertlodge.com. Spacious motel-style place with free continental breakfast and in-room movies. Closed July and Aug. ❸

Hampton Inn 2000 N Palm Canyon Drive ☎760/320-0555. Features a beautiful outdoor pool, a must-have in the desert, plus free continental breakfast and comfortable rooms. ❹

Ingleside Inn 200 W Ramon Rd ☎760/325-0046 or 1-800/772-6655, Ⓦwww.inglesideinn.com. Historic but expensive downtown option, with a guest list that has included Dalí, Garbo and Brando. Many rooms have antiques, fireplaces,

whirlpool tubs and patios. ❻

Mira Loma 1420 N Indian Canyon Drive ☎760/320-1178. Small, welcoming place with well-appointed rooms around a central pool. Marilyn Monroe stayed in Room Three in 1949, just before she hit it big. ❷

The Willows 412 W Tahquitz Canyon ☎760/320-0771, Ⓦwww.thewillowspalmsprings.com. The perfect spot to discover why celebrities were first attracted to Palm Springs in the 1930s: a stunning historic hangout for the Hollywood elite that provides great views, richly decorated rooms and lush appointments. ❾

Downtown Palm Springs

Downtown Palm Springs stretches for half a mile along **Palm Canyon Drive**, a wide, bright and modern strip of upscale boutiques that has engulfed the town's original Spanish village–style structures. Shops run the gamut from Saks Fifth Avenue to tacky T-shirt emporia and bookstores devoted exclusively to dead Hollywood stars.

The luxuriously housed **Desert Museum**, 101 Museum Drive (Tues–Sat 10am–5pm, Sun noon–5pm; end of July through end of Sept, Fri–Sun only, 10am–5pm; $7.50; Ⓦwww.psmuseum.org), is strong on Native American and Southwestern art, though its only permanent display is the late actor William Holden's collection of Asian and African works. Some interesting natural science exhibits focus on the animal and plant life of the desert, demonstrating that it's not all sandstorms and rattlesnakes. There is a modern art gallery and some lovely sculpture courts on the museum grounds, and the museum hosts performances in the 450-seat **Annenberg Theater** (tickets available at ☎760/325-4490, Ⓦwww.palmsprings.com/annenberg). The major cultural center in the desert is the **McCallum Theater**, 73000 Fred Waring Drive, Palm Desert, presenting films, live music, opera, ballet and plays (☎760/340-2787, Ⓦwww.palmsprings.com/mccallumtheatre).

Not to be missed is the striking **Tramway Gas Station**, 2901 N Palm Canyon Drive, a classic gem of pop architecture with an upswept roof and boomerang-modern design, since converted into the **Montana St Martin art gallery**, which hosts a wide range of sculptural and design exhibits (daily 11am–5pm, weekends open at 9am; ☎760/340-2787, Ⓦwww.montana-st-martin.com). There's also an anarchic piece of landscape gardening at **Moorten Botanical Gardens**, 1701 S Palm Canyon Drive (Mon–Sat 9am–4.30pm, Sun 10am–4pm; $2.50), a strange cornucopia of every desert plant and cactus, in settings designed to simulate their natural environments, but lumped together in no particular order.

Around Palm Springs

Most visitors to Palm Springs never leave the poolside, but desert enthusiasts still visit to **hike** and **ride** in the **Indian Canyons** (daily 8am–5pm, summer schedule varies; $6; ☎760/325-5673), three miles southeast of downtown along S Palm Canyon Drive. Centuries ago, ancestors of the Cahuilla developed extensive communities here, growing melons, squash, beans and corn. The canyons are about fifteen miles long, and can be toured by car, although it's worth walking at least a few miles; the easiest trails lead past the waterfalls, rocky gorges and palm trees of **Palm Canyon** and **Andreas Canyon**. Some areas are set aside for **trailblazing** in jeeps and four-wheel-drives; rent a vehicle from Off-Road

Rentals, four miles north of town at 59755 Hwy-111 (Sept–June only; $30 per hour; ☎760/325-0376, ⓦwww.offroadrentals.com), or take a guided jeep adventure around the Santa Rosa Mountains with Desert Adventures, 67555 E Palm Canyon Drive, Cathedral City ($89 for 3hr trip, $109 for 4hr; ☎760/324-JEEP, ⓦwww.red-jeep.com/jeep_tours.html).

If the desert heat becomes too much to bear, large cable cars grind and sway over eight thousand feet up the **Palm Springs Aerial Tramway**, Tramway Road, just off Hwy-111 north of Palm Springs (daily 10am–9.45pm, weekends open at 8am; $20.80, kids 3–12 $13.80; ☎760/325-1391, ⓦwww.pstramway .com), passing through five climatic zones on the way to the 10,815ft summit of Mount San Jacinto, where there's a **bar** and **restaurant** at the Mountain Station.

Eating and drinking

Although most of the more famous **restaurants** in Palm Springs are ultra-expensive, more reasonable options can be found with a little effort; alternatively, head to gay-oriented **Cathedral City** ("Cat City"), five miles east along Hwy-111.

Agua Bar & Grill 110 N Indian Canyon Drive ☎760/778-1515. Elegant setting with fine American/eclectic menu and swank piano bar. Located at downtown's Spa Resort Casino.

El Gallito 68820 Grove St, Cathedral City ☎760/328-7794. Busy Mexican cantina that has the best food for miles and often a wait to match – get there around 6pm to avoid the crowds. Closed in Aug.

Las Casuelas 368 N Palm Canyon Dr ☎760/325-3213. Local Mexican favorite popular for its hefty portions and laid-back atmosphere. The best bet in a local chain.

Le Vallauris 385 W Tahquitz Way, next to Desert Museum ☎760/325-5059 – reservations only. Excellent Californian/French/Italian hybrid dishes, though the price is around $80 per head, with a

swank atmosphere popular with faded movie stars.

Native Foods 1775 E Palm Canyon Drive ☎760/416-0070. One of the town's better and cheaper choices for vegetarian cuisine, offering natural ingredients and healthy meals that even manage to be tasty on occasion.

Shame on the Moon 69950 Frank Sinatra Drive, Rancho Mirage ☎760/324-5515. Pasta, seafood and meat on a mid-priced menu, in a contemporary setting that attracts an upscale gay clientele. Excellent service.

Thai Smile 651 N Palm Canyon Drive ☎760/320-5503. Uninspiring decor but great, authentic Thai food, especially good for curry and noodle dishes, all at very reasonable prices. Open daily.

Joshua Tree National Park

In a unique transitional area, where the lower Colorado Desert meets the high Mojave northeast of Palm Springs, **JOSHUA TREE NATIONAL PARK** protects 800,000 acres of grotesquely gnarled and ragged trees (familiar as the cover of the eponymous U2 record). The trees can reach up to forty feet in height, but they have to contend with extreme aridity and rocky soil, and the strain of their struggle to survive is evident. All around lie great heaps of boulders, pushed up by the Pinto Mountain fault, their edges rounded and smoothed by flash floods and winds.

This unearthly landscape is ethereal at sunrise or sunset, when the desert floor is bathed in red light; at noon it can be a threatening furnace, with temperatures sometimes topping 125°F in summer, and rising even higher in the Low Desert section of the park below 3000ft. The name "Joshua Tree" was given by Mormons in the 1850s, who saw the craggy branches of the trees as the arms of Joshua pointing them to the promised land. Nowadays, Joshua Tree is appreciated by campers, day-trippers and rockclimbers for its unspoiled beauty, gold-mine ruins, ancient petroglyphs and incredible rock formations.

Be selective in your explorations. As with any desert area, the heat can be punishing and, for a good part of the year, an ambitious schedule is impossible. Brief yourself at the visitors centers, and never venture anywhere without a map. On unmarked roads restricted to four-wheel-drive vehicles, don't think about taking a normal car – you'll soon grind to a halt, and it could be quite a few panic-stricken hours before anybody finds you. When hiking, **stick to the trails**. Joshua Tree is full of abandoned gold mines: watch for loose gravel around openings, stay away from the edges, never trust the safety of ladders or timber, and bear in mind that the rangers rarely check mines for casualties. Even on the simpler trails, allow around an hour per mile.

One of the easiest hiking routes leads one and a half miles from Canyon Road, six miles from the visitors center at Twentynine Palms, to **Fortynine Palms Oasis** (2–3hr), accessible only on foot. To the west of the oasis, quartz boulders tower around the *Indian Cove* campground; a trail from the eastern branch of the campground road heads to **Rattlesnake Canyon**, where, after rainfall, the streams and waterfalls break an otherwise eerie silence among the monoliths.

Moving south into the main body of the park, the **Wonderland of Rocks** features rounded granite boulders that draw rockclimbers from around the world; **Hidden Valley** (an hour-long hike) offers a glimpse of where cattle rustlers used to hide out; and, to the east (1hr hike), rain-fed **Barker Dam** provides Joshua Tree's crucial water supply, built by cattlemen around 1900. One negotiable trail climbs past abandoned mining sites, where some buildings and equipment are still intact, to **Lost Horse Mine** (3hr), 450ft up – which once produced an average of $20,000 worth of gold a week, and now consists of crumbling foundations and old-time mining equipment.

A brilliant desert panorama of badlands and mountains is to be had from the 5185ft **Keys View** nearby, from where Geology Tour Road leads down to the east through the best of Joshua Tree's **rock formations** and, further on, to the **Cholla Cactus Garden**.

Practicalities

Hwy-62 from Palm Springs leads to the park's West Entrance, near the town of Joshua Tree, and its North Entrance, which is close to the **Oasis Visitors Center**, 74485 National Park Drive, Twentynine Palms (daily 8am–5pm; ☎760/367-5500, ⓦwww.joshuatree.org), offering maps and information on cheap local accommodations. There's another entrance and visitors center at **COTTONWOOD**, seven miles north of I-10 (daily 8am–4pm; ☎760/367-5500).

The park has nine established **campgrounds**, all in the northwest except for one at Cottonwood. Only two have water – *Black Rock Canyon* ($12) and *Cottonwood* ($10) – and except for *Indian Cove* ($10), all the others are free. You can reserve sites at *Black Rock* and *Indian Cove* by calling *Destinet* (☎1-800/365-2267, related info at ⓦwww.joshua.tree.national-park.com/camping.htm). The rest are operated on a first-come, first-served basis. Come prepared – gathering firewood is not allowed, and you should stock up on water. There are good **motels** and decent restaurants in **TWENTYNINE PALMS**, a desolate but friendly spot just two minutes' drive from the park. The best place to stay is the pleasantly historic *Twentynine Palms Inn*, 73950 Inn Ave (☎760/367-3505, ⓖ), although the *El Rancho Dolores*, nearby at no. 73352 (☎760/367-3528; ②), provides cheaper, no-frills accommodation. You can grab a snack at *The Finicky Coyote*, 73511 Twentynine Palms Hwy (☎760/367-2429), or basic Mexican fare at *Ramona's*, nearby at no.

72115 (☎760/367-1929). Morongo Basin Transit Authority **buses** (☎760/367-7433 or 1-800/794-6282) run twice daily between Palm Springs and Twentynine Palms ($7 one-way, $11 round-trip), but inconveniently not into the park itself.

The High Desert

The stretches of the **Mojave Desert** that most people tend to see from the road conform to the stereotype of the earth's arid regions – barren, lifeless and desolate. Consequently few visitors are inspired to explore further, but this High Desert – all of it above 2000ft – offers some of the most dramatic scenery in the southern part of the state, rolling with lush grasses, startling volcanic formations, large stands of Joshua trees and even, in some spots, piñon pines.

Death Valley National Park

DEATH VALLEY is utterly inhuman: the hottest place on earth and almost entirely devoid of shade, much less water – carry plenty for both car and body. Its sculpted rock layers form deeply shadowed, eroded crevices at the foot of sharply silhouetted hills, their exotic mineral content turning million-year-old mudflats into rainbows of sunlit phosphorescence. It was named by a party of white settlers who stumbled through in 1849, looking for a short cut to the Gold Rush towns; they survived despite running out of food and water.

Throughout the summer, the air temperature in Death Valley averages 112°F, and the ground can reach near boiling point. Better to come during the spring, when the wild flowers are in bloom, or from October to May, when it's generally mild and dry.

The central north–south valley for which the park is named contains its two main outposts: **Stovepipe Wells** and **Furnace Creek**, where the **visitor center** (daily 8am–6pm; ☎760/786-2331, ⓦwww.nps.gov/deva) is located. A $10 per vehicle entrance fee (valid for seven days) is payable at the **park entrance ranger stations**, close to the park boundaries, which provide free maps and information on tours and activities.

Many of the most unusual sights are located south of Furnace Creek. A good first stop, seven miles along Hwy-178/Badwater Road, is the **Artist's Palette**, an eroded hillside covered in an intensely colored mosaic of reds, golds, blacks and greens. Ten miles further south, **Badwater** is an unpalatable but nonpoisonous 30ft-wide pool of water, loaded with chloride and sulphates, that's the only home of the soft-bodied Death Valley snail. A four-mile hike across the hot valley floor drops a further two feet down to the **lowest point in the western hemisphere**, 282ft below sea level.

Zabriskie Point, overlooking Badwater and the Artist's Palette off Hwy-190, four miles south of Furnace Creek, was the inspiration for Antonioni's eponymous 1970 film. The view is best during the early morning, when the pink-and-gold Panamint Mountains across the valley are highlighted by the rising sun.

Near Stovepipe Wells, some thirty miles northwest of Furnace Creek, spread fifteen rippled and contoured square miles of ever-changing **sand dunes**. A ten-mile dirt road west of the campground leads to sheer black-walled **Marble Canyon**, scratched with mysterious ancient petroglyphs.

Hordes of overheated tourists wait patiently to wander through the surreal luxury of **Scotty's Castle**, forty miles north of Stovepipe Wells. It was built in the 1920s as the desert retreat of Chicago insurance broker Albert Johnson, but named after "Death Valley" Scotty, who managed the construction and claimed the house was his own, financed by a hidden gold mine. **Tours** (daily on the hour 9am–5pm; $8; reserve your place on ☎760/786-2392) take in the ornate wooden ceilings, indoor waterfalls and a remote-controlled player piano. The house remains as it was when Johnson died in 1948. Scotty himself lived here until 1954, and is buried just behind the house.

Eight miles west gapes the half-mile-wide **Ubehebe Crater**, the rust-tinged result of a massive volcanic explosion; half a mile south sits its thousand-year-old younger brother, **Little Hebe**. Beyond the craters the road continues south for another twenty dusty miles to **Racetrack Valley**, a two-and-a-half-mile mudflat across which giant boulders seem slowly to be racing, leaving faint trails in their wake.

Practicalities

Death Valley is a long way from anywhere and has no scheduled public transportation. If you plan to **stay**, you must reserve ahead. AMFAC (☎1-800/236-7916 or 760/786-2345, ⓦwww.furnacecreekresort.com) operates two hotels on natural oases at Furnace Creek – the expensive but gorgeous *Furnace Creek Inn* (winter ❽, summer ❻), and the ordinary (and still pricey) *Furnace Creek Ranch* (winter ❻, summer ❺), about half a mile north, which has two **restaurants** and a nice bar. Far more reasonable is *Stovepipe Wells Motel* (☎760/786-2387, ⓕ786-2389; ❸) on Hwy-190 about thirty miles northwest of Furnace Creek. **Camping** in one of the many National Park Service campgrounds costs $10–16 depending on facilities and location, or is free if you don't mind being up in the Panamint Range, far from the valley's sights: the only campground to take reservations is *Furnace Creek* (☎1-800/365-2267, ⓦwww.furnacecreekresort.com).

The High Sierra and the Owens Valley

The towering **eastern** peaks of the **High Sierra** drop abruptly to the empty landscape of the **Owens Valley**, sixty miles west of Death Valley. Almost the entire range is wilderness: well-maintained roads lead to trailheads at over ten thousand feet, providing access to the stark terrain of spires, glaciers and clear mountain lakes. US-395 is the lifeline of the area connecting several small towns, all with plenty of budget motels. Because the long-standing US-395 Greyhound service was cancelled in late-2001 you will really need a car to explore fully.

Mount Whitney and Lone Pine

Rising out of the northern Mojave Desert, the mountainous backbone of the Sierra Nevada announces itself with a bang two hundred miles north of Los Angeles at 14,494ft **Mount Whitney**, the highest point in the lower 48 states. A silver-gray ridge of pinnacles forms a nearly sheer wall of granite, dominating the small roadside town of **LONE PINE** eleven thousand feet below. **Motels** here include the *Dow Villa Motel/Historic Dow Hotel* at 310 S Main St (☎760/876-5521 or 1-800/824-9317, ⓦwww.dowvillamotel.com; ❸), where John Wayne always stayed when filming in the area, and the *Best Western Frontier Motel*, 1008 S Main St (☎760/876-5571 or 1-800/528-1234; ❷). Those headed north might want to push on sixteen miles to Independence, where the slightly run-down but atmospheric *Winnedumah Hotel*, 211 N Main St (℡760/878-2040, ⓦwww.winnedumah.com; ❷), operates as an HI-**hostel** with $18 beds which includes breakfast. You can **camp** at *Tuttle Creek* campground (free; no water) on Horseshoe Meadow Road some four miles west of Lone Pine beyond the Alabama Hills (see below). The *Pizza Factory*, 301 S Main St (℡760/876-4707), and the diner-style *Mt Whitney Restaurant*, 227 S Main St (℡760/876-5751), are decent places to **eat**. The **Eastern Sierra Interagency Visitor Center**, a mile south of town on US-395 at the junction of Hwy-136 (daily: June–Aug 8am–6.50pm; Sept–May 8am–5.50pm; ℡760/876-6222), is a great source of information about the Owens Valley.

Many early Westerns, and the epic *Gunga Din*, were filmed in the **Alabama Hills** to the west, a rugged expanse of bizarrely eroded sedimentary rock. Some of the oddest formations are linked by the **Picture Rocks Circle**, a paved road that loops around from Whitney Portal Road, passing rocks shaped like bullfrogs, walruses and baboons.

Two thousand eager souls make the strenuous 22-mile round-trip **hike** (12–16hr; 6100ft ascent) to the summit of Mount Whitney each summer. Permits are needed and are awarded by lottery: ensure your application (available at ⓦwww.r5.fs.fed.us/inyo/vvc/permits.htm) is postmarked February and sent to the Wilderness Reservation Office, Inyo National Forest, 873 N Main St, Bishop, CA 93514 (℻760/873-2484). On a trial basis, cancelled reservations are available by phone from 1 to 5pm, Monday to Friday at ℡760/873-2483. All hikers pay a $15 fee.

One-day ascents start at dawn from either the *Whitney Portal* **campground** (mid-May to mid-Oct; ℡1-877/444-6777; $13), or the one-night-only first-come-first-served *Whitney Trailhead* site ($8) at the end of twisting Whitney Portal Road, reachable via trailhead shuttle (℡760/876-5518). The trail cuts up to boulder-strewn Trail Crest Pass, the southern end of the 220-mile John Muir Trail to Yosemite, then climbs along the top of vertical cliffs. At the rounded summit, a stone cabin serves as an emergency shelter – though not one you'd choose to be in during a lightning storm.

Big Pine and the White Mountains

Nearly fifty miles north, hikes lead from the end of Glacier Lodge Road, ten miles west of nondescript **BIG PINE**, up to the **Palisades Glacier**, the southernmost glacier in the northern hemisphere. Along the opposite wall of the five-mile-wide Owens Valley, the ancient, bald and dry **White Mountains** are home to the gnarled **bristlecone pines**, the oldest living things on earth. Occupying a narrow band at around ten thousand feet, and often covered in snow until mid-June, some of these gnarled trees have been alive for over four thousand years. Battered and beaten by the harsh environment into contorted but beautiful shapes, even when dead they hang on without decaying for upwards of another thousand years, slowly being eroded by wind-driven ice and sand.

Schulman Grove ($2) was named after dendrochronologist Dr Edmund Schulman, who revealed the extreme longevity of the trees in the mid-1950s. It is the most accessible collection, 24 twisting but paved miles from Big Pine off Hwy-168, and centers on the newly enlarged **visitor center** (late May-Aug daily 10am-5pm or later; Sept & Oct Sat & Sun 10am-5pm; recorded into on ℡760/873-2500). Two trails radiate from here: the mile-long **Discovery Trail**, which passes some photogenic examples; and a longer loop which passes but intentionally fails to identify the oldest tree, the 4700-year-old Methuselah.

Patriarch Grove, twelve miles further, along a dusty dirt road that gives spectacular views of the Sierra Nevada and the Great Basin ranges, contains the largest and comparably ancient bristlecone.

In the White Mountains there's the free, waterless *Grandview* **campground**, or you can retreat to the **motels** along US-395 in Big Pine – the *Big Pine Motel*, 370 S Main St (☎760/938-2282; ❷), and the *Starlight Motel*, 511 S Main St (☎760/938-2011; ❷).

Bishop

BISHOP, to a Californian, means outdoor pursuits. The largest town (population 3500) in the Owens Valley, it's an excellent base for cross-country skiing, fly-fishing and especially rock-climbing. **Motels**, such as the *El Rancho*, 274 W Lagoon St (☎760/872-9251 or 1-888/872-9251; ❷), the *Thunderbird*, 190 W Pine St (☎760/873-4215; ❷), and bargain restaurants can be found within a block of US-395. The **visitor center** at 690 N Main St (Mon–Fri 9am–5pm, Sat & Sun 10am–4pm; ☎760/873-8405. ⓦwww.bishopvisitor.com) can provide details of the many **adventure travel specialists** based in town. For **hiking** and **camping** information, the White Mountain Visitor Center, 798 N Main St (mid-June to Aug daily 8am–5pm; rest of year Mon–Fri 8am–4.30pm; ☎760/873-2500), will be more use.

Mammoth Lakes

Forty miles north along US-395 from Bishop then five miles west on Hwy-203, the resort town of **MAMMOTH LAKES** offers the state's premier ski slopes outside the Lake Tahoe basin, and in summer hosts on- and off-road bike races. The setting is stunning, but the town is pricey and prone to testosterone overload. To ski **Mammoth Mountain** (ⓦwww.mammothmountain.com), which looms up behind the resort, pick up **lift tickets** ($56 per day) from the Main Lodge on Minaret Road, where you can also rent **equipment** ($26 for basic skis, boots and poles), and book three-hour **lessons** ($48). In summer, fifty miles of snow-free slopes transform themselves into the 3500-acre **Mammoth Mountain Bike Park** ($28 a day for trail access and ski lifts, $47 for 4hr bike rental plus two lift rides).

One appealing summer-only destination is the **DEVIL'S POSTPILE NATIONAL MONUMENT**, seven miles southwest of the bike park, reached by shuttle bus ($9.50). A collection of slender, blue-gray basaltic columns, some scaling sixty feet, the Postpile was formed as lava from a volcanic eruption cooled and fractured into multisided forms. From here, a two-mile hike along the San Joaquin River leads to **Rainbow Falls** which refract the midday sun perfectly.

Practicalities

The daily Greyhound stops in the *McDonald's* parking lot on Hwy-203. During the ski season, get around on the five-line Mammoth Shuttle (☎760/934-3030). For information, go to the combined US Forest Service and Mammoth Lakes **visitor center** (daily 9am–5pm; ☎760/924-5500 or 1-888/466-2666, ⓦwww.visitmammoth.com) on the main highway half a mile east of the town center.

Mammoth's plentiful **accommodation**, which includes two hostels, are costliest in winter. *Mammoth Mountain Inn* on Mammoth Mountain (☎760/934-2581 or 1-800/228-4947; ❺), is a touch sterile but it's at the heart of all the ski and bike action, while the *White Stag Inn*, at Main and Minaret

(☏760/934-7507 or 1-888/376-4134, ✉wstag@qnet.com; ❸), is reasonably priced and central. *Davison St Guesthouse*, 19 Davison St (☏619/544-9093; ❶), offers mountain views from its four-bed rooms and dorms. There are **campgrounds** ($12) close to Devil's Postpile National Monument, and free waterless sites in the Inyo National Forest off US-395 around eleven miles north.

Restaurants tend to be expensive but casual: *Giovanni's*, in the Minaret Village Mall (☏760/934-7563), is popular for pasta and pizza, with great lunchtime deals; *Sierra Sundance*, at the Mammoth Mall (☏760/934-8122), serves great juices and shakes from inside this health food store; and *The Lakefront Restaurant*, at Tamarack Lodge (☏760/934-3534), offers superb lake views and good food - for a price. *Whiskey Creek*, at Main and Minaret (☏760/934-2555), is a lively **bar** and restaurant, with its own good microbrews.

⑬

Mono Lake, Lee Vining and Bodie Ghost Town

The blue expanse of **Mono Lake** sits in the midst of a volcanic desert tableland at the north end of the valley. It looks like a science-fiction landscape, with two large islands, one light colored, the other black, surrounded by salty, alkaline water. Strange sandcastle-like formations of **tufa** (calcium deposited from springs) have been exposed over the fifty years since the City of Los Angeles extended an aqueduct into the Mono Basin through an eleven-mile tunnel, dropping the **water level** by over forty feet and creating the biggest environmental controversy in California. Mono Lake is the primary nesting ground for the state's **California gull** population – twenty percent of the world total – and a prime stopover point for thousands of grebes and phalaropes. As the water levels dropped, the islands in the middle of the lake, where the seagulls lay their eggs, became peninsulas, and the colonies fell prey to coyotes and other mainland predators. The landlocked water became increasingly alkaline, threatening the unique ecosystem. Though the California Supreme Court ruled in 1983 that Mono Lake must be saved, it wasn't until 1991 that emergency action was taken.

For more details about Mono Lake and the fight for its survival, stop by the **Mono Lake Committee Information Center** (daily 9am–5pm, often until 10pm in July & Aug; ☏760/647-6595, 🌐www.leevining.com), in the small town of **LEE VINING** on US-395, or a mile north at the excellent **Mono Basin Visitor Center** (May–Oct daily 9am–5.30pm; Nov–April Thurs–Mon 9am–4pm; ☏760/647-3044). **Motels** along US-395 include *El Mono Motel* (☏760/647-6310; ❸) and *Murphey's* (☏760/647-6316 or 1-800/334-6316; ❹). *Nicely's Restaurant* (☏760/647-6477) is a Fifties vinyl palace that opens at 6am; the more upscale *Mono Inn Restaurant*, five miles north along US-395 (☏760/647-6581), is owned by Ansel Adams' granddaughter.

Northeast of Lee Vining, in a remote, high desert valley, stands a well-preserved and evocative relic of the gold-mining 1870s. The **Bodie State Park** (open all year but often inaccessible by car in winter; $2 per person; ☏760/647-6445) is perhaps the best **ghost town** in the US, with many of its structures still intact but not gussied up for tourists. With thirty saloons and dance halls and a population of ten thousand, it was once the raunchiest and most lawless mining camp in the west; over 150 wooden buildings survive in a state of arrested decay around the intact town center, littered with old bottles, bits of machinery and old stagecoaches. The ruins of the mines themselves, in the hills east of town, are off limits to visitors except on the frequent tours.

The Central Coast

After the hustle of LA and San Francisco, the four hundred miles of coastline in between – the **central coast** – is a welcome respite, sparsely populated outside the few medium-sized cities and lined by clean sandy beaches. It is at its most dramatic along **Big Sur**, one of the most rugged, savagely beautiful stretches of coastline in the world, where the brooding Santa Lucia Mountains rise steeply out of the thundering Pacific surf. The two largest towns are poles apart: **Santa Barbara** in the south is a wealthy resort colony, full of old and new money, while **Santa Cruz** to the north is a coastal town redolent of the Sixties – where the local collegians are officially known as the "Banana Slugs." In between, languorous **San Luis Obispo** makes a good base for visiting **Hearst Castle**, the hilltop palace of publishing magnate William Randolph Hearst, and the inspiration for the Xanadu pleasure palace in the film *Citizen Kane*.

Almost all of the towns grew up around Spanish **missions**, each a long day's walk from the next, and once enclosed within thick walls to prevent Native American attack. **Monterey**, a hundred miles south of San Francisco, was California's capital under Spain and Mexico, and still has attractive early-nineteenth-century architecture.

Amtrak's *Coast Starlight* **train** runs along the coast up to San Luis Obispo before cutting inland north to San Francisco and up to Seattle; Greyhound **buses** stop at most of the towns, especially along the main highway, US-101.

Santa Barbara

The six-lane coastal freeway that races past oil wells and offshore drilling platforms slows to a leisurely pace a hundred miles north of Los Angeles at **SANTA BARBARA**. Beautifully sited on gently sloping hills above the Pacific, the town's ubiquitous red-tiled roofs and white stucco walls of its low-rise buildings form a backdrop to some fine Spanish Revival architecture, while the golden beaches are wide and clean, lined by palm trees along a curving bay. Although a large portion of downtown has been replaced by a vast, upscale shopping mall, Santa Barbara has managed to retain its quaintly upscale yet relaxed character.

The mission-era feel of Santa Barbara is no accident. Following a devastating earthquake in 1925, the entire town was rebuilt in the image of an apocryphal Spanish Colonial past, with numerous arcades linking shops, cafés and restaurants, and a pedestrian-friendly layout that serves visitors well – a far cry from LA's all-consuming auto-worship. **State Street**, the main drag, is home to an appealing assortment of diners, bookshops, coffee bars and nightclubs. The few remaining genuine mission structures are preserved as **El Presidio de Santa Barbara** (daily 10.30am–4.30pm; suggested donation). At its center, the 200-year-old barracks, **El Cuartel**, stands two blocks off State Street on Perdido Street; the second-oldest building in California, it now houses historical exhibits and a scale model of the small Spanish colony. The more recent past is recounted in the nearby **Santa Barbara Historical Museum**, 136 E de la Guerra St (Tues–Sat 10am–5pm, Sun noon–5pm; suggested donation), full of Spanish and Victorian memorabilia.

State Street leads half a mile down from the town center to wooden **Stearns Wharf**. Built in 1872, it was nearly destroyed in November 1998, when a third of the pier was engulfed in flames; restoration efforts have now made it home to an array of shopping stalls and food vendors, with magnificent **beaches** stretching in either direction.

In the hills above the town is the beautiful **Mission Santa Barbara** (daily 9am–5pm; $4), with a colorful twin-towered facade, the so-called "Queen of the Missions," though it was one of the later ones constructed in California. A small **museum** displays artifacts from the mission archives. Other missions in the area are Santa Inés, just outside the kitsch Danish town of **Solvang** heading north on US-101, and La Purísima, the most completely restructured of all the missions, about twenty miles northwest of Solvang on Hwy-1.

Arrival, information and accommodation

Greyhound **buses** from LA and San Francisco stop every two hours downtown at 34 W Carrillo St; **trains** arrive at the old Southern Pacific station at 209 State St, a block west of US-101. The **visitors centers** are at 12 E Carrillo St (Mon–Sat 9am–5pm; ☎805/966-9222 or 1-800/676-1266, ⓦwww.santabarbaraca.com) and 1 Santa Barbara St, East Beach (Mon–Sat 9am–5pm, Sun 10am–5pm; ☎805/965-3021). You can walk to most places, although a frequent **shuttle bus** (25¢ per ride) loops around Santa Barbara during the day, with the Santa Barbara Metropolitan Transit District (☎805/683-3702, ⓦwww.sbmtd.gov) covering the outlying areas into the evening.

Although there are a few reasonable places to **stay** in town, most hotels are expensive and hard to find. The nearest useful **camping** spots are ten miles south of Santa Barbara at Carpinteria State Beach (☎805/684-2811 or 1-800/444-7275; $18), and El Capitan State Beach to the north (☎805/968-1033 or 1-800/444-7275; $18).

Banana Bungalow Hostel 210 E Ortega St ☎805/963-0154 or 1-800/3-HOSTEL, ⓦbananabungalow.com/sub/bbsb.html. Dorm beds here are both cheap and comfortable ($18), if you don't mind a nonstop party atmosphere. ❶
Bayberry Inn 111 W Valerio St ☎805/569-3398, ⓦwww.bayberryinnsantabarbara.com. Lovely little spot offering eight comfortable B&B rooms decked out with canopy beds and Victorian furnishings, each named after a type of berry. ❼
Cheshire Cat B&B 36 W Valerio St ☎805/569-

1610, ⓦwww.cheshirecat.com. Fairly upscale spot with hot tubs, free bike use and an Alice-in-Wonderland theme. ❻
Harbor View Inn 28 W Cabrillo Blvd ☎805/963-0780 or 1-800/755-0222. Casually luxurious option with pleasant rooms and a quiet, elegant atmosphere. ❼
Hotel State Street 121 State St ☎805/966-6586. An old mission-style establishment located near the beach and offering complimentary breakfast. ❷

Eating, drinking and nightlife

Although Santa Barbara, as a college town, has plenty of places for munching on comfort food and swilling beer, the unquestioned center for local and tourist activity is **State Street**, lined with a number of good **restaurants**, **bars** and **clubs**.

Chad's 625 Chapala St ☎805/568-1876. Features a modern American menu in the intimate atmosphere of a historic Victorian home.
Citronelle 901 Cabrillo Blvd ☎805/963-4717. Perhaps the most swank dining of all, nouveau French and American cuisine with only a hint of pretension.
Coffee Bean & Tea Leaf 811-A State St ☎805/966-2442. A solid café and a great place to watch the evening clubgoers parade back and

forth on the strip.
El Paseo 10 El Paseo ☎805/962-6050. Upscale Mexican restaurant with a festive fountain courtyard.
Madhouse Martini Lounge 434 State St ☎805/962-5516. Mellow spot that cashes in on the retro-cocktail craze with easygoing style and modern decor.
Mousse Odile 18 E Cota St ☎805/962-5393. Pricey French cuisine with a California flair.

Natural Café 508 State St ☎ 805/962-9494.
Offers scrumptious veggie meals and prime vistas
for people-watching.
Pascucci 729 State St ☎ 805/963-8123. Serving
tremendous portions of innovative Italian dishes at
reasonable prices.

Rose Café 424 E Haley St ☎ 805/966-3773.
Popular no-frills cantina offering tasty Mexican
specialties at great prices.
Zelo 630 State St ☎ 805/966-5792. Popular
restaurant and club hosting spirited DJs with
eclectic tastes.

San Luis Obispo

SAN LUIS OBISPO, 160 miles north of Santa Barbara and halfway between
LA and San Francisco, is a few miles inland, but makes the best base for exploring the surrounding coastal regions. Still primarily an agricultural market center, it holds more nineteenth-century architecture than any other Californian
city (especially around Buchon Street), plenty of good restaurants, a couple of
pubs, and – outside summer holiday weekends – plenty of accommodation.

The compact core of San Luis is eminently walkable, centered around the late
eighteenth-century **Mission San Luis Obispo de Tolosa** (daily 9–4pm,
June–Oct closes at 5pm; suggested donation), a dark and unremarkable church
that was the prototype for the now ubiquitous red-tiled roof, developed to
replace the original, flammable thatch in response to Native American arson
attacks.

Between the mission and the visitors center, **Mission Plaza**'s terraces step
down along San Luis creek, along which footpaths meander, crisscrossed by
bridges every hundred feet and overlooked by shops and outdoor restaurants
on the south bank. The undeniable highlight is the stunning pink **Fremont
Theater**, 1035 Monterey St, an Art Deco marvel that becomes a riot of splashy
neon at night and still plays movies. **Higuera Street**, a block south of Mission
Plaza, is the main drag, and springs to life on Thursday afternoons for the
Farmers' Market, when the street is closed to cars and filled with vege-table
stalls, mobile barbecues and street-corner musicians.

Arrival, information and accommodation

The Greyhound depot is at 150 South St, while Amtrak trains stop at the end
of Santa Rosa Street, half a mile south of the business district. The **chamber
of commerce** is at 1039 Chorro St (☎ 805/781-2777, ⓦ www.slochamber
.org), and local bus rides will cost you 75¢ (information at ☎ 805/541-2277,
ⓦ www.rideshare.org).

Monterey Street was the site of the world's first (since long gone) **motel** –
the *Motel Inn*. Rates for its modern counterparts are generally low, though if
you want a nice view of the ocean, you're better off taking a short drive south
to **Pismo Beach**, a pleasant beach community that's little more than a
stopover.

Best Western Shorecliff Lodge 2555 Price St,
Pismo Beach ☎ 805/773-4671, ⓦ www.shorecliff
.com. Has a dramatically situated swimming pool
and a cliff-hugging gazebo over the Pacific. ➏
Campus Motel 404 Santa Rosa St ☎ 805/544-
0881. Basic motel, but with complimentary breakfast. ➌
Economy Motel 652 Morro St ☎ 805/543-7024.
A particularly good value, clean and cozy, with the
usual amenities. ➋

Edgewater 280 Wadsworth Ave, Pismo Beach
☎ 805/773-4811, ⓦ www.edgewater-inn.com.
Right on the beach, offering hot tubs, a heated
pool, and kitchenettes in some rooms. ➍
Hostel Obispo 1617 Santa Rosa St ☎ 805/544-
4678, ⓦ www.hostelobispo.com. At $20 a night,
this hostel is the best value around, offering a convenient central location, cheap bike rentals and
complimentary pancake breakfasts. ➊

Eating and drinking

Higuera Street is the prime place to **eat**, especially during the farmers' market on Thursday, with a nice range of unassuming restaurants and **bars**. Other fine dining choices can also be found throughout town, along with a few upstart microbreweries.

Buona Tavola 1037 Monterey St ☎805/545-8000. Features a great selection of Northern Italian bistro-style food and wine.

SLO Brewing Company 1119 Garden St ☎805/543-1943. The first brewery/restaurant in the city since Prohibition.

Splash Café 197 Pomeroy Ave, Pismo Beach ☎805/773-4653. Oriented toward seafood, and offering a fine clam chowder.

Taj Palace 795 Foothill Blvd ☎805/543-0722. The city's top choice for Indian cuisine.

Hearst Castle

Forty-five miles northwest of San Luis Obispo, the hilltop **Hearst Castle** is one of the most extravagant houses in the world. The home where publisher **William Randolph Hearst** held court over such guests as Winston Churchill, Charlie Chaplin, George Bernard Shaw and Charles Lindbergh now brings in over a million visitors a year. Its interior combines walls, floors and ceilings ripped from European churches and castles with Gothic fireplaces and Moorish tiles, while nearly every room bursts with Greek vases and medieval tapestries. Ironically, the same financial power and public infamy which allowed Hearst to hoard these artifacts have made them viewable to more people than they would have had they remained in the lands where they were created.

Work on Hearst's 250,000-acre ranch began in 1919, managed by architect Julia Morgan (also famous for designing the Spanish Colonial newspaper complex housing Hearst's own *Los Angeles Herald Tribune*), who designed each room and building in the spirit of the works destined to be housed inside. The castle was never truly completed: rooms were torn out as soon as they were finished in order to accommodate yet more acquired booty. The main facade, a twin-towered copy of a Mudejar cathedral, stands atop steps curving up from the world's most photographed swimming pool, filled with spring water and lined by a massive neoclassical colonnade – the height of aesthetic glory, or irredeemably vulgar kitsch, depending on your taste.

W.R. Hearst – Citizen Kane

Often portrayed as a power-hungry monster – most memorably by Orson Welles in his thinly veiled *Citizen Kane* – **William Randolph Hearst** was born in 1863 as the only son of a multimillionaire mining engineer, learning the newspaper trade in New York under Joseph Pulitzer, the inventor of "Yellow Journalism," of which Hearst became its greatest practitioner. When he published his own *Morning Journal*, Hearst fanned the flames of American imperialism to ignite the Spanish–American War of 1898. As he told his correspondents in Cuba: "You provide the pictures, and I'll provide the war." Hearst eventually controlled an empire that during the 1930s sold twenty-five percent of the nation's newspapers – and sixty percent of those sold in California.

Despite his war-mongering and nationalism, Hearst was middle-of-the-road politically, a lifelong Democrat who served two terms in the House of Representatives but failed to be elected mayor of New York, let alone president. Besides his many newspapers, Hearst owned eleven radio stations and two movie studios, which he used to make his mistress, Marion Davies, a star. The Depression forced him to sell off most of his holdings, but he continued to exert power and influence until his death in 1951, aged 88.

The most dramatic time to visit is in the morning when the coastal fog hides the world below. Four different, two-hour guided **tours** (summer daily 8am–4pm; rest of year 8.20am–3.20pm; $10 unless specified; ☎1-800/444-4445, ⓦwww.hearst-castle.org) leave from the visitors center just off Hwy-1. A tour is essential, as are reservations; new visitors are directed to the so-called "Experience Tour" ($14) which provides a basic overview of the castle and its treasures. In the spring and fall, the evening tour series ($20) is guided by docents in period dress leading visitors through the castle, speaking of Hearst in the present tense.

The Big Sur coast

Starting just north of Hearst Castle, the ninety wild and undeveloped miles of rocky cliffs of the **Big Sur coast** form a sublime landscape at the edge of the continent, where redwood groves line river canyons and the Santa Lucia Mountains rise straight out of the blue-green Pacific. Only the occasional out-post interrupts the tortuous, exhilarating route of **Hwy-1**, carved out of bedrock cliffs 500ft above the ocean, and **public transportation** is limited to the MST bus (☎831/899-2555, ⓦwww.mst.org), which runs south from Monterey to Nepenthe twice daily during the summer. Summer weekends see the roads and campgrounds packed to overflowing, and hardly anyone braves the turbulent winters when violent storms can erode cliffsides and toss sections of the highway into the sea. The southern coastline of Big Sur is relatively gentle, with sandy beaches hiding below crumbling ochre cliffs.

Roughly midway along the Big Sur coast, **ESALEN** is named after the long-gone Native Americans who once enjoyed its natural **hot spring**, on a clifftop high above the raging Pacific surf. Since the 1960s, when people came to Big Sur to smoke pot and get back to nature, Esalen has been at the forefront of the New Age movement, and the spring is now owned and operated by the Esalen Institute, which offers workshops on "potentialities and values of human existence" (by reservation only; ☎831/667-3005, ⓦwww.esalen.org), although most yuppies simply come for the yoga and massage treatments.

Three miles north on Hwy-1, **Julia Pfeiffer Burns State Park** (daily dawn–dusk; $6 parking), has some of the best day-hikes in the Big Sur area, including a ten-minute walk along the cliffs to see McWay Falls crashing down onto the beach, and, two miles north below Hwy-1, a 200ft-long tunnel gets you to **Partington Cove**, rare beach access for this rugged spot. As with other Big Sur-area parks, Pfeiffer Burns provides camping sites for $12–14 a night (reservations on ☎831/667-2315, ⓦwww.reserveamerica.com/usa/ca/juli), while private operations like nearby *Ventana Campground* (☎831/667-2712, ⓦwww.ventanawildernesscampground.com) offer campsites for $25, including bath houses with hot water and electricity. Seven miles north of Pfeiffer Burns, lovely old *Deetjen's Big Sur Inn* (☎831/667-2377; ⑥) has rooms hand-crafted from thick redwood planks and in-room fireplaces, as well as fine breakfasts and fish and veggie meals in its dining room.

Further north at **NEPENTHE**, the rooftop *Nepenthe* restaurant, just off Hwy-1, offers pricey steaks and seafood, though you can find more impressive views, and more affordable prices, at *Café Kevah* (☎831/667-2344), serving breakfast and lunch on a terrace. Just across the highway, at the **Henry Miller Library** (Wed–Sun 11am–6pm; suggested donation), books by the author, who lived in the area intermittently until the 1960s, are displayed and sold. Two miles north along Hwy-1, the unmarked Sycamore Canyon Road leads a mile west to Big Sur's best beach, **Pfeiffer Beach**; the white sand here is dominated by a hump of rock whose color varies from brown to red to orange in the changing light.

Big Sur River valley

Immediately north of the Pfeiffer Beach turnoff, Hwy-1 drops into the valley of the Big Sur River, where the majority of the accommodation and restaurants are dotted sporadically along six miles of the highway. First stop should be at the US Forest Service **ranger station** (daily 8am–6pm; ☎831/667-2315), which issues the camping permits required for the Ventana Wilderness in the mountains above.

In sheltered **Pfeiffer Big Sur State Park**, deep, clear swimming holes form in the steepwalled river gorge during late spring and summer, and a hiking trail leads half a mile up a canyon shaded by redwoods to the sixty-foot **Pfeiffer Falls**. The **campgrounds** here charge $12–18 and are often full on summer weekends; book through the California State Parks' Reservation Service (☎831/667-2315 or 1-800/444-7275, ⊛www.reserveamerica.com/usa/ca/pfei).

The cluster of shops, lodgings and restaurants known as **The Village**, sited just north of Pfeiffer Big Sur State Park, is the most feasible base for seeing Big Sur. **Accommodation** fills up in summer, but if you can afford it, it's worth spending a night in one of the rustic riverside rooms at the *Big Sur River Inn Resort* (☎831/667-2700 or 1-800/548-3610, ⊛www.bigsurriverinn.com; ❹–❼), which has a fine **restaurant** featuring seafood staples and solid American cuisine. There are also good-sized cabins in the *Big Sur Lodge* (☎831/667-3100 or 1-800/424-4787, ⊛www.bigsurlodge.com; ❹–❻). Alternatively try the cabins at *Big Sur Campgrounds and Cabins*, a mile north of Pfeiffer Big Sur State Park (☎831/667-2322; ❷).

The Monterey Peninsula

On rocky headlands of the **Monterey Peninsula**, gnarled cypress trees amplify the collision between the cliffs and the sea, marking the northern edge of the Big Sur coast, a hundred miles south of San Francisco. The lively harbor town of **Monterey** was the capital of California under the Spanish and briefly under the Mexicans, and retains many old adobe houses and places of genuine historic appeal alongside the requisite tourist traps. **Carmel**, on the other hand, three miles to the south, is a self-consciously quaint village of million-dollar holiday homes, famous for once having elected Clint Eastwood as its mayor.

Arrival, information and getting around

If you're coming from the south, Greyhound **buses** will drop you at the Exxon station on the Monterey waterfront, 1042 Del Monte Ave, while Amtrak requires you to change in the sprawling agricultural town of **Salinas** inland, and take a further 55-minute trip on the hourly local bus #21 into Monterey. **Getting around** the peninsula itself is surprisingly easy, on Monterey-Salinas Transit buses (☎831/899-2555, ⊛www.mst.org). The most useful routes from Monterey are #4 and #5 to Carmel, #21 to Salinas, #1 to Pacific Grove, and #22 along the Big Sur coast to Nepenthe (twice a day, summer only). There's also a free shuttle bus, the WAVE, from downtown to the Aquarium on Cannery Row.

Another option is to **rent a bike** ($25–30 a day): good-quality mountain bikes are offered by *Adventures by the Sea*, 201 Alvarado Mall (☎831/372-1807), and outside the Maritime Museum, *Bay Bikes*, 640 Wave St on Cannery Row (☎831/659-5824).

The Monterey **Visitors Center** is at 401 Camino El Estero at Franklin Street (daily Mon–Sat 9am–6pm, winter closes at 5pm; Sun 9am–5pm, winter 10am–4pm; ☎831/649-1770); the less busy **Chamber of Commerce**

tourist office is at 380 Alvarado St (Mon–Fri 8.30am–5pm; ☎831/648-5360, Ⓦwww.mpcc.com); and, in Carmel, the **Monterey County Visitors Center**, 137 Crossroads Blvd (daily 9.30am–6pm; ☎1-888/221-1010, Ⓦwww.montereyinfo.org), has information on the entire peninsula and will help with hotel reservations.

Accommodation

Hotel and **B&B** rates average $140 a night, but cheaper **motels** cluster along Fremont Street and Munras Avenue, two miles north of the center. The nearest **camping** is in Veterans Memorial Park, site of Steinbeck's fictional *Tortilla Flat*, in the hills above town. All listings are for Monterey, unless otherwise stated.

Bide-a-Wee Motel 221 Asilomar Ave, Pacific Grove ☎831/372-2330. Excellent value for the area, with no-frills rooms, and a few with kitchenettes. 2min walk to the ocean. ❸
Carmel Resort Inn Carpenter St and 2nd Ave, Carmel ☎831/624-3113 or 1-800/454-3700, Ⓦwww.carmelresortinn.com. Considering its cozy elegance and central location, this is one of the

least expensive properties in town; cottage rooms come with fireplaces. ❺
Carmel River Inn Rio Rd at Hwy-1, Carmel ☎831/624-1575 or 1-800/882-8142, Ⓦwww.carmelriverinn.com. Features rooms with kitchenettes and fireplaces, a heated pool and riverside location. ❹
Del Monte Beach 1110 Del Monte Ave, Monterey

831/649-4410. A bargain B&B close to the center of Monterey. All the usual trappings for half the normal cost, with shared baths and continental breakfast. ❸

Green Gables Inn 104 5th St, Pacific Grove ℡831/375-2095 or 1-800/722-1774, ⓦwww.foursisters.com/inns/greengablesinn.html. Top-of-the-line Queen Anne jewel with plush doubles in one of the prettiest homes in town, on the waterfront a few blocks from the Aquarium. ❻

Mariposa Inn 1386 Munras Ave, Monterey ℡831/649-1414 or 1-800/283-5663. The best deal in town. Cozy rooms with fireplaces and full amenities at reasonable rates. ❸/❹

Pacific Grove Motel Lighthouse Ave at Grove Acre, Pacific Grove ℡831/372-3218 or 1-800/858-8997. Nice, small motel in marvelous setting, 100 yards from the sea, offering heated pool, hot tub and in-room refrigerators. ❹

Monterey

Named by the Spanish merchant and explorer Vizcaino in 1602, **MONTEREY** was not colonized until 1770, founded as the military and administrative center of a territory that extended east to the Rockies and north to Canada (with a non-native population of less than seven thousand). By the mid-nineteenth century era of the US takeover and the Gold Rush, Monterey had become a forgotten backwater, hardly affected by the fresh waves of California immigration.

Impressive vernacular colonial **buildings** now stand unassumingly in the compact town center, within a few blocks of the tourist-thronged waterfront. A loosely organized **Path of History** connects the 37 sites of the **Monterey State Historic Park**. Most can't be entered unless you're part of a ninety-minute guided historic **walking tour** (daily 10am–3pm; $5), leaving hourly from the park's Stanton Center.

The best place to get a feel for life in old Monterey is the **Larkin House**, on Jefferson Street a block south of Alvarado (entered only as part of the walking tour), home of the first and only American Consul to California. The New England-born Thomas Larkin, who was influential in persuading the Californians to turn towards the US and away from Mexico, is credited with developing the now-common Monterey style of architecture, mixing adobe walls, balconies of Greek Revival Southern plantations and a Yankee taste for ornament. The house, the first two-story adobe in California, is filled with millions of dollars' worth of antiques and memorabilia, and is surrounded by gorgeous gardens as well.

The **Stevenson House**, a short way east at 530 Houston St (entry as for Larkin House, above), is filled with memorabilia of Scottish author Robert Louis Stevenson, who passed through in 1879 and foresaw that Monterey's Mexican-influenced lifestyle was no match for the "Yankee craft" of the "millionaire vulgarians of the Big Bonanza." At the foot of the otherwise tacky **Fisherman's Wharf**, the Colonial Revival **Pacific House** (daily 10am–5pm; $2) has been a courthouse, rooming house and dance hall since its construction in 1847, and is now the best of the local **museums**, with displays on Monterey history and a pretty fair collection of Native American artifacts. While in the area, wander by the historic balconies of the **Customs House** (daily 10am–5pm; free), the oldest governmental building on the west coast, with portions built by Spain in 1814, Mexico in 1827, and the US in 1846 – though it hasn't collected duties for 135 years.

A **bike path** runs the two miles to Pacific Grove, along **Cannery Row** – named after John Steinbeck's literary portrait of the rough-and-ready workers of its fish canneries. During World War II some 200,000 tons of sardines were caught and canned each year, but the stocks were exhausted by 1945. The abandoned canneries reopened in the 1970s as malls and restaurants, and now teem with tourists instead of fish.

The engaging **Monterey Bay Aquarium**, 886 Cannery Row (daily 10am–6pm, summer opens at 9.30am; $15.95, kids 3–12 $7.95; ☎831/648-4888 or 1-800/756-3737, ⓦwww.mbayaq.org), is reputed to have one of the largest displays of underwater life in the world. Book tickets well in advance and allow a day for your visit. Highlights include a 335,000 gallon Kelp Forest tank, a touch pool where you can pet bat rays, a two-story exhibit devoted to sea otters, and a "Drifters Gallery," with striking, multicolored jellyfish dipping and swirling before your very eyes.

Pacific Grove

A few miles north of Monterey along the peninsula, **PACIFIC GROVE** – or "Butterfly Town USA," as it likes to call itself – began as a campground and Methodist retreat in 1875, where Christian revivalists prohibited booze, bare skin and reading the Sunday newspapers, and which still holds ornate wooden **cottages** from those long-forgotten days. One of the few other reminders of that pious period is the Gothic Revival church **St Mary's by the Sea**, Central Ave at 12th Street, an 1887 redwood marvel with a signed Tiffany window near the altar. **Ocean View Boulevard** circles the coast around the town, passing the headland of **Lovers Point** – originally called Lovers of Jesus Point – where preachers used to hold sunrise services. Surrounded in early summer by the colorful red-and-purple cloaks of blooming ice plant, it's one of the peninsula's best **beaches**. Every year, from November through early March, hundreds of thousands of golden Monarch **butterflies** come to Pacific Grove to escape the winter chill, forming orange and black blankets on the **Butterfly Trees**, on Ridge Road, a block west of Lighthouse Avenue. At the end of the avenue, near the tip of Monterey Peninsula, stands the 150-year-old **Point Piños** lighthouse (Thurs–Sun 1–4pm; free), the oldest continuously operating lighthouse on the California coast and, perhaps contrary to grander expectation, is basically a charming little farmhouse with a revolving light poking out from its roof.

Carmel

Set on gently rising headlands above a sculpted rocky shore, **CARMEL** is well known for its ridiculously inflated real-estate prices, neat rows of quaint shops and miniature homes along Ocean Avenue, and a largely untouched coastline. Unfortunately, the town also has a thick air of stultifying pretension, peppered with tacky galleries and mock-Tudor tearooms, and lacking any authentic sense of small-town culture. Even so, **Carmel Mission Basilica**, 3080 Rio Rd (Mon–Sat 9.30–4pm, Sun 10am–4pm; $2), provides a rare hint of genuine historical interest, with Moorish bell towers, a sandstone facade, three small museums featuring antiques and memorabilia, and an eerie **cemetery** containing the graves of over 3000 Native Americans.

The area's natural appeal is much greater than its cultural offerings. **Carmel Beach**, for one, is a tranquil cove of blue water bordered by soft white sand and cypress-covered cliffs (the tides are deceptively strong and dangerous, so be careful if you chance a swim). **Point Lobos State Reserve**, two miles south of Carmel on Hwy-1 (daily: summer 9am–6.30pm; winter 9am–5pm; $3 per vehicle; ⓦhttp://pt-lobos.parks.state.ca.us), has plenty of natural attractions to support its title of "the greatest meeting of land and water in the world." Spread along 1250 acres, and with more than 250 bird and animal species along the area's hiking trails, the sea here is one of the richest underwater habitats in California. Gray whales are often seen offshore, migrating south in January and returning with young calves in April and early May. Because the point juts so far out into the ocean, chances are good of seeing them from as little as a hundred yards away.

Eating

There are many excellent places to **eat** all over the peninsula. If you're on a tight budget, the best cheap eats are on the north side of Monterey, along Fremont Street and just south of Cannery Row on and around Lighthouse Avenue.

Bookworks 667 Lighthouse Ave, Monterey ☎831/372-2242. Unpretentious café serving light lunch fare at reasonable prices. Open until 11pm on weekends.

Fishwife 1996 Sunset Drive at Asilomar Blvd, Pacific Grove ☎831/375-7107. Longstanding local favorite, serving great seafood dished at reasonable prices – about $10 a plate.

La Boheme Dolores and Seventh streets, Carmel ☎831/624-7500. Cozy French provincial and Parisian offerings in swank, quasi-European setting. Dinner around $20 per person.

Old Monterey Café 489 Alvarado St, Monterey ☎831/646-1021. More-than-you-can-eat breakfasts, with hefty pancakes and omelets, plus tasty sandwiches. Closed Mon.

Paolina's San Carlos St between Ocean Ave & 7th St, Carmel ☎831/624-5599. Fresh homemade pastas in a casual courtyard setting. Less expensive than other area eateries.

Papa Chano's Taqueria 462 Alvarado St, Monterey ☎831/646-9587. Delicious and cheap Mexican food, featuring burritos. Nearby chicken rotisserie branch, two doors down, also offers inexpensive fare.

Pasta Mia Trattoria 481 Lighthouse Ave, Pacific Grove ☎831/375-7709. Tasty homemade pastas, grilled seafood and veal, starting at $12, served up in a rustic, homey setting.

Pepper's Mexicali Café 170 Forest Ave, Pacific Grove ☎831/373-6892. Gourmet Mexican seafood done in a California style, and reasonably priced.

Sardine Factory 701 Wave St, Monterey ☎831/373-3775. California seafood cuisine served in French château splendor, with entrees around $20.

Schooners in the *Monterey Plaza Hotel*, 400 Cannery Row, Monterey ☎831/372-2628. Colorful California bistro in a historic hotel with views over the bay.

Drinking and nightlife

Monterey has always been better known as a sleepy, romantic getaway than as a hub of hip nightlife, but the **Monterey Jazz Festival** in mid-September (☎1–800/307-3378, ⓦ www.montereyjazzfestival.org) is the oldest continuous jazz festival in the world and draws crowds from afar.

Crown and Anchor 150 W Franklin St, Monterey ☎831/649-6496. All your English favorites, from fish'n'chips to bangers'n'mash, at this unpretentious local pub, best known for its wide selection of brews.

Franco's Norma Jean Club 10639 Merritt St, Castroville ☎831/633-2090. On the route to Santa Cruz, this disco serves up Latin, house and techno to local trendies.

Lighthouse Bar & Grill 281 Lighthouse Ave, Monterey ☎831/373-4488. Friendly gay pub where the locals hang out, with a pool table and Sunday "beer bust" starting at 2pm.

The Mucky Duck 479 Alvarado St, Monterey ☎831/655-3031. Sip a 20oz Guinness around the fire, at the bar or at a table on the patio out back. Occasional live folk, Celtic and rock music; DJ on the back patio.

Planet Gemini 625 Cannery Row, Monterey ☎831/373-1449. Mixed music and comedy venue usually with cheap cover. Closed Mon.

Santa Cruz

After the overcharged tourism of Monterey, the unassuming community of **SANTA CRUZ**, 75 miles south of San Francisco, comes as a surprise. Although in many ways the quintessential Californian coastal town, spread at the foot of thickly wooded mountains beside a clean sandy beach, it has grown considerably in the last few years, having recovered from the destruction wrought by the 1989 earthquake. In the Sixties, the Merry Pranksters turned the local youth on to LSD long before it defined a generation in San Francisco's Summer of Love, and the area is still among the most politically and socially progressive in California. It's also surprisingly untouristy. No hotels spoil the miles of coastline; most of the land is agricultural; and roadside stands are more likely to sell apples or sprouts than postcards and souvenirs.

The **Santa Cruz Boardwalk**, one of the last surviving beachfront amusement parks on the west coast, is the main focus for visitors (May–Aug daily 11am–10pm; rest of year hours vary; $1.80–3.60 per ride, unlimited rides $22.95). Although it can get packed on weekends with teenagers on the prowl, most of the time it's a friendly funfair, where barefoot hippies mix with mushroom farmers. The star attraction is the 80-year-old **Giant Dipper**, a wild and rickety wooden roller coaster that has been ridden by more than 45 million people.

The **beach** next to the boardwalk is good but can get rowdy (and dirty). For more peace and quiet, follow the coast out of town to one of the smaller beaches such as Capitola or New Brighton. From **West Cliff Drive**, you'll see some of the biggest waves in California, not least at **Steamer Lane**, beyond the Municipal Pier. Cowell's Beach, just north of the Municipal Pier, is the best place to give surfing a try; Club Ed (☎831/459-9283) in the parking lot, will rent boards ($7 per hour, $20 per day) and assist with lessons. The ghosts of surfers past are animated at the **Surfing Museum** (daily except Tues noon–4pm; donation) in the old Abbott Memorial lighthouse on the point, where surfboards range from early 12ft redwood planks to modern high-tech multifinned cutters. A clifftop cycle path runs two miles to **Natural Bridges State Beach** (daily 8am–dusk; $6 per car), where waves have cut holes through the coastal cliffs, forming delicate stone arches (though three of its four eponymous bridges have now collapsed due to erosion and visitors walking across them).

Twenty-five miles up the coast from Santa Cruz, the beginning of the San Francisco Peninsula is marked by **Pigeon Point Lighthouse** (☎650/879-0633, ⓦwww.pigeonpointlighthouse.org; ❶/❷), where you can spend the night in the old lighthouse keeper's quarters and soak your bones in a hot tub, cantilevered out over the rocks. The 52 dorm beds cost $16 and there are also four private doubles. Pigeon Point took its name from the clipper ship *Carrier Pigeon*, which broke up on the rocks off the point, one of many shipwrecks that led to the construction of the lighthouse in the late nineteenth century.

Just before Pigeon Point, at the foot of beautiful **Big Basin Redwoods State Park** ($6 parking), giant blubbery elephant seals congregate every December and January to mate in the **Año Nuevo State Reserve** (daily 8am–dusk; $6 parking). Even without the spectacle of the seals, the surrounding coastal area has beautiful **hiking**; when the fog rolls in (as it often does), head for the redwood tree-shaded trails of Big Basin.

Arrival, information and accommodation

Greyhound **buses** from San Francisco, Oakland and San Jose stop five times a day at 425 Front St, in the center of town. Santa Cruz has an excellent **public transportation** system known as the Metro, on which the basic fare is $1 and an all-day pass $3 (information at ☎831/425-8600, ⓦwww.scmtd.com). The Bicycle Rental Center, 131 Center St (☎831/426-8687), rents **bikes** from $7 an hour or $25–30 per day. The **Santa Cruz Visitors Council** is at 701 Front St (Mon–Sat 9am–5pm, Sun 10am–4pm; ☎831/425-1234 or 1-800/833-3494, ⓦwww.santacruzca.org).

Off season, Santa Cruz has plenty of inexpensive places to **stay**, though rates can be much higher on weekends. The best **campground** is at *New Brighton State Beach* (☎831/464-6330 or 1-800/444-7275, ⓦwww.reserveamerica .com/usa/ca/newb; $12–14 per night), three miles south near the beachfront village of Capitola.

Capitola Venetian 1500 Wharf Rd, Capitola ⓣ831/476-6471, ⓦwww.capitolavenetian.com. Beach hotel offering one- to three-bed rooms, some with stoves, fridges, fireplaces and ocean views. Rates vary wildly; it's much cheaper during winter and on weekdays. ❸–❽

Capri Motel 337 Riverside Ave ⓣ831/426-4611. The cheapest motel near the boardwalk, with basic but clean rooms. ❷

Cliff Crest B&B Inn 407 Cliff St ⓣ831/427-2609, ⓦwww.cliffcrestbedandbreakfast.com. At the top of Beach Hill, an 1887 refurbished Queen Anne with elegant rooms, set among its own lovely gardens. Winter ❹, summer ❽

HI-Santa Cruz 321 Main St ⓣ831/423-8304, ⓦwww.hi-santacruz.org. Well-sited hostel offering dorm beds from $15, easily the best bargain in town. ❶

Eating, drinking and nightlife

The main drag of **Pacific Avenue**, peppered with many relaxed **restaurants** and **bars**, is easily the best spot in town for watching locals parade past. Santa Cruz has the central coast's rowdiest **nightlife**, ranging from coffee houses to nightclubs where the music varies from surf-thrash to reggae to the rock of local resident Neil Young and sometimes all on the same dance floor. Consult the free *Good Times* magazine for what's on.

Blue Lagoon 923 Pacific Ave ⓣ831/423-7117. Supposedly a major gay hangout, but really draws a mixed crowd for its techno and hip-hop DJs on weekends.

The Catalyst 1011 Pacific Ave ⓣ831/423-1336. Medium-sized club that's one of the best bets for catching big-name touring artists and up-and-coming locals.

Club Dakota 1209 Pacific Ave ⓣ831/454-9030. Gay and lesbian bar popular with locals and the occasional out-of-towner.

Gabriella Café 910 Cedar St ⓣ831/457-1677. Elegant Californian cuisine in a comfortable setting.

Kuumbwa Jazz Center 320 Cedar St ⓣ831/427-2227. Friendly and intimate spot showcasing both traditional and modern jazz.

Miramar Fish Grotto 45 Municipal Wharf ⓣ831/423-4441. One of several good seafront restaurants on the wharf, with stunning oceanside views.

Palookaville 1133 Pacific Ave ⓣ831/454-0600. A local club favorite, home to touring bands and rising regional talent.

Zachary's 819 Pacific Ave ⓣ831/427-0646. One of the many casual cafés along this stretch, with good vistas for people-watching.

The Central Valley

The vast **interior** of California is split down the middle by the **Sierra Nevada** (Spanish for "snowy range"), or High Sierra, a sawtooth range of snow-capped peaks that stands high above the semi-desert of the Owens Valley (see p.1099). The wide **Central Valley** (aka the San Joaquin Valley) in the west was made super-fertile by irrigation projects during the 1940s, and is now almost totally agricultural. Even if the nightlife begins and ends with the local ice-cream parlor, after the big cities of the coast it can all be quite refreshing. However, the real reason to come here is to reach the **national parks** of **Sequoia** and **Kings Canyon** – whose huge trees form the centerpiece of a rich natural landscape – and **Yosemite**, where towering walls of silvery granite are invigorated by waterfalls. Few roads penetrate the hundred miles of wilderness to the east, but the entire region is crisscrossed by hiking trails leading up into the pristine alpine backcountry.

The arrow-straight I-5 barrels straight up from LA to San Francisco. Four daily **trains** and frequent Greyhound **buses** run through the valley, calling at the towns along Hwy-99, in particular Merced, which has bus connections to Yosemite but otherwise doesn't merit a look-in.

Bakersfield

The first town you come to across the rocky peaks north of Los Angeles, looming unappealingly out of a forest of oil derricks, is the flat and featureless **BAKERSFIELD**. This is the unlikely home of one of the liveliest **country music** scenes in the nation, stemming from the arrival during the Depression of Midwestern farmers, with their hillbilly instruments and campfire songs. In the mid-Sixties, the gutsy honky-tonk style of Bakersfield artists such as Merle Haggard and Buck Owens challenged the slick commercial output of Nashville, and hopes of luring the major country music record labels to "Nashville West" foundered with the emergence of rivals like Austin, Texas.

Nevertheless, the numerous honky-tonks of Bakersfield are still jumping every Friday and Saturday night. There's seldom a cover charge, and live sets usually entail one band playing for four or five hours from around 8pm, with a fifteen-minute break every hour. Stetson hats and Nudie shirts are the sartorial order of the day, and audiences span generations. Most venues are hotel lounges or restaurant backrooms; don't miss the country bar *Trouts*, 805 N Chester Ave (☎661/399-6700). Closer to town, you might also try the *Buck Owens Crystal Palace*, 2800 Buck Owens (☎661/328-7560, ☎www.buckowens.com), where the $6 cover includes a show (Buck himself plays on Friday and Saturday nights), and a museum of Buck Owens memorabilia, or the clubbier *Rockin' Rodeo*, 3745 Rosedale Hwy (☎661/323-6617), with a New Country or rock DJ every night.

Practicalities

You have to come to Bakersfield from LA by Amtrak Thruway bus to catch the train through the valley to San Francisco and northern California. Several Greyhound routes require changes here too, calling at 1820 18th St. The handiest visitor center is at 1725 Eye St (Mon 9am–5pm Tues–Fri 8am–5pm; ☎661/327-4421). Bargain overnight stays include the *EZ-8*, 2604 Pierce Rd (☎661/322-1901 or 1-800/326-6835; ❶), and the adjacent *La Quinta*, 3232 Riverside Drive (☎661/325-7400 or 1-800/531-5900; ❸), both pool-equipped and a short stagger from *Buck Owens Crystal Palace*. For eating, *Zingo's* at 2625 Pierce Rd (☎661/324-3640) is a 24-hour truckstop where frilly-aproned waitresses deliver plates of diner staples; *24th Street Café*, 1415 24th St (☎661/323-8801), does top-rate breakfasts; *Joseph's*, hidden back off the road at 3013 F St (☎661/322-7710), serves huge calzone and other Italian dishes; and the *Noriega Hotel*, 525 Sumner St (☎661/322-8419), offers excellent all-you-can-eat Basque meals at long communal tables.

Sequoia and Kings Canyon

The southernmost of the Sierra Nevada national parks, preserving ancient forests of giant sequoia trees, are Sequoia and Kings Canyon. As you might expect, **Sequoia National Park** contains the thickest concentration – and the biggest specimens – of sequoias to be found anywhere, tending (literally) to overshadow its assortment of meadows, peaks, canyons and caves. **Kings Canyon National Park** has few big trees but compensates with a gaping canyon gored out of the rock by the Kings River as it cascades down from the High Sierra. The few established sights of both parks are near the main roads, leaving the vast majority of the landscape untrammeled and unspoiled, but well within reach for willing hikers.

Arrival and information

No **public transportation** of any kind serves the parks, but by **car** things are simple: the closest large town is **Visalia**, just under fifty miles distant on Hwy-198, or a slightly longer, but faster, drive uses Hwy-180 from Fresno: note that there is **no gas** in the parks. The **entrance fee** ($10 per car, $5 per hiker or biker: valid 7 days) entitles you to a detailed map of the paired parks, and a copy of *Sequoia Bark*, detailing accommodation, **guided hikes** and other activities. The two parks are separate but jointly run; for activities, **road** and **park information** call ☏559/565-3730 or look at ⓦwww.nps.gov/seki.

Sequoia National Park

While trees are seldom scarce in **SEQUOIA NATIONAL PARK** – where the giant sequoias can't grow there are thick swaths of pine and fir – the scenery varies. Paths lead through forests and meadows; longer treks rise above the tree line to the barren peaks of the High Sierra. Soon after entering the park from the south, Hwy-198 becomes the **Generals Highway** and climbs swiftly into the dense woods of the aptly labeled **Giant Forest**, where displays in the new **Giant Forest Museum** explain the lifecycle of the giant sequoias and what's being done to protect the remaining groves. From here you can explore along Crescent Meadow Road, which spurs east past the **Auto Log** – a fallen sequoia chiseled flat for motorists to drive onto. Just beyond, a loop road leads to the granite monolith of **Moro Rock** (a three-mile marked trail leads from Giant Forest), which streaks wildly upward from the green hillside. Views from its remarkably level top can stretch 150 miles. A hewn staircase makes it easy to climb the rock in fifteen minutes, although the altitude can be a strain.

Continuing east along Crescent Meadow Road, you pass under the **Tunnel Log**, which fell across the road in 1937 and had a vehicle-sized hole cut through it. At the end of the route, **Crescent Meadow** is, like other grassy fields in the area, more accurately a marsh, too wet for the sequoias that form an impressive boundary around. A perimeter trail leads to **Tharp's Log**, a cabin hollowed out of a fallen sequoia by Hale Tharp who, while searching for a summer grazing ground for his sheep, was led here by Native Americans in 1856. He was not only the first white man to see the giant sequoias but the first to live in one. Just north of Giant Forest, back on the Generals Highway, is the biggest sequoia of them all, the 3000-year-old, 275ft **General Sherman Tree**. While it's certainly a thrill to see what is held to be the largest living thing on the planet, its extraordinary dimensions are hard to grasp alongside the almost equally monstrous sequoias around.

Whatever your plans, you should stop at **Lodgepole Village**, three miles north of the Sherman Tree, for the geological displays and film shows at the **visitor center** (mid-May to Aug daily 8am–6pm; rest of year daily 8am–4.30pm). You can explore the glacial canyon on the **Tokopah Valley Trail** (2hr), which leads to the base of Tokopah Falls, beneath the 1600ft **Watchtower** cliff. The top of the Watchtower is accessible by the fatiguing but straightforward seven-mile **Lakes Trail**.

Kings Canyon National Park

Kings Canyon National Park is wilder and less visited than Sequoia, with a maze-like collection of canyons and a sprinkling of isolated lakes – the perfect environment for careful self-guided exploration. To reach the main canyon

N

SEQUOIA AND KINGS CANYON NATIONAL PARKS

JOHN MUIR WILDERNESS

McClure Meadow 9600 ft

JOHN MUIR TRAIL AND PACIFIC CREST TRAIL

Muir Pass 11955 ft

Bishop Pass 11972 ft

INYO NATIONAL FOREST

JOHN MUIR WILDERNESS

LeConte Canyon

Big Pine

SIERRA NATIONAL FOREST

Spanish Mountain 10051 ft

KINGS CANYON NATIONAL PARK

395

Monarch Wilderness Area

Kings Canyon Lodge

Hume Lake

Kings Canyon

Cedar Grove

Boyden Cave

Rae Lakes

Independence

Princess

Hume Lake

SEQUOIA NATIONAL FOREST

Cedar Grove

JOHN MUIR TRAIL

Charlotte Lake

Grant Grove

Grant Grove Big Stump

Buck Rock

Big Meadows

Lone Pine (15 miles)

Big Stump Entrance

245

Montecito-Sequoia Lodge

Stony Creek

Badger

Stony Creek

198

Dorst

Wuksachi Village

Lodgepole

Mt Whitney

Whitney Portal

Crystal Cave

GENERALS HIGHWAY

Giant Forest Museum

Lodgepole

General Sherman Giant Sequoia

JOHN MUIR TRAIL

Crescent Meadow

Bearpaw Meadow

HIGH SIERRA TRAIL

PACIFIC CREST TRAIL

Hospital Rock

Moro Rock

Potwisha

Buckeye Flat

Ash Mountain Entrance

Foothill Visitor Center

Three Rivers

Mineral King

Lake Kaweah

Atwell Mill

Cold Springs

Lemon Cove

198

Lookout Point Entrance Station

SEQUOIA NATIONAL PARK

INYO NATIONAL FOREST

0   5 miles

South Fork

SEQUOIA NATIONAL FOREST

Golden Trout Wilderness Area

13

CALIFORNIA | Sequoia and Kings Canyon

proper, you have to pass through the hamlet of **Grant Grove**, where there's a useful **visitor center** (daily: mid-May to Aug 8am–6pm; rest of year 8am–4.30pm) and the 2.5-mile **Big Stump Trail** shows off the remains of the logging which took place in the 1880s. Several massive trees from these parts were sliced up and sent to the Atlantic seaboard to convince cynical easterners that such enormous trees really existed. A mile west of Grant Grove, a large

1117

stand of sequoias contains the **General Grant** and **Robert E. Lee** trees, which rival the General Sherman further south.

Kings Canyon Highway (Hwy-180; May–Oct only) descends from Grant Grove into the steep-sided Kings Canyon, cut by the furious gushings of various forks of the Kings River. Whether or not this is the deepest canyon in the US, as some would have it, its wall sections of granite and gleaming blue marble and the yellow pockmarks of yucca plants are magnificent. It's extremely perilous to wade into the river: people have been swept away even when paddling close to the bank in a seemingly placid section.

Once into the national park proper, the canyon sheds its V-shape and gains a floor. **Cedar Grove Village** here is named for its proliferation of incense-cedars. There's a **ranger station** across the river (June–Aug daily 9am–5pm; May, Sept & Oct hours reduced). Apart from the scenery, you should look out for the **flowers** – leopard lilies, shooting stars, violets, lupins and others – and **birdlife**. The longer hikes beside the creeks, many seven or eight miles long, are fairly strenuous. An easy alternative is to wander around the green **Zumwalt Meadow**, four miles from Cedar Grove Village and a short walk from the road, beneath the forbidding gray walls of Grand Sentinel and North Dome.

Just a mile further on, Kings Canyon Road comes to an end at **Copper Creek**. Thirty years ago it was decided that vehicles should not be allowed to penetrate further. Instead the multitude of canyons and peaks which constitute the Kings River Sierra are networked by **hiking paths**, almost all best enjoyed armed with a tent, provisions and a wilderness permit from the trailhead ranger station.

Accommodation and eating in the parks

The least expensive **rooms** are in the motels near the park entrances: *Sierra Inn Motel* (℡559/338-2144, ℱ338-0789; ➍), fourteen miles west of the southern entrance on Hwy-180 and, near the southern entrance on Hwy-198, *Gateway Lodge* (℡559/561-4133, ℱ561-3656; ➍). Inside the parks, all facilities are managed by Kings Canyon Park Services (KCPS; ℡559/335-5500 or 1-866/522-6966, ⓦwww.sequoia-kingscanyon.com; ➎/➏) who operate cabins and hotel units at Stony Creek, Grant Grove and Cedar Grove; and Delaware North Parks Services (DPNS; ℡559/253-2199 or 1-888/252-5757, ⓦwww.visitsequoia.com; ➏/➐) who run the upmarket *Wuksachi* in Sequoia. Space is at a premium during the high season (May to mid-Oct), but you can usually pick up cancellations on the day. Summer prices range from $50 for basic cabins without bath to $160 for stylish modern hotel rooms. In winter the cheaper cabins are too cold; and only those at Grant Grove drop their prices below $50.·

Recorded **camping** information for both parks is on ℡559/565-3341. Campgrounds are dotted all over both parks, charging an average of $14 a pitch, though there are a couple of free, waterless sites in the national forest between the two. In **Sequoia**, the busiest is *Lodgepole*, which you can book up to eight weeks in advance through the National Park Reservation System (℡1-800/365-2267, ⓦwww.reservations.nps.gov). In **Kings Canyon**, the bulk of the sites are around Grant Grove, with another at Cedar Grove – again, all cost around $14. For **backcountry** camping, get a free permit from a visitor center or ranger station. And remember this is **bear country**: in established campgrounds use the bearproof food boxes, in the backcountry rent bear canisters from the stores in Cedar Grove, Grant Grove and Lodgepole.

There are pricey **food** markets and cafeterias in the various villages, and a couple of restaurants, notably bargain buffets at the *Montecito-Sequoia Lodge* in the national forest between the two parks. Three Rivers, on the southern approach to Sequoia, has the best range of places to eat nearby.

The Sierra National Forest

The entire gaping tract of land between Kings Canyon and Yosemite is taken up by the less-visited **Sierra National Forest**. If you want to hike and camp in complete solitude, this is the place to do it. But don't try lone exploration without thorough planning – public transportation is nonexistent, and roads and trails are often closed due to bad weather. The best-placed source of information is the **Pineridge Ranger Station** (daily 8am–4.30pm; ☎559/855-5360), located along Hwy-168 at Prather, five miles west of the forest entrance.

Of the forest's two main regions, the Pineridge district, forty miles east from Fresno using Hwy-168, is the best to explore. The popular Shaver Lake and Huntington Lake, rich in campgrounds (reserve in summer on ☎1-800/280-2267), soon give way to the isolated alpine landscapes beyond the 9200ft Kaiser Pass. The sheer challenge posed by the rugged, unspoiled terrain of the adjoining John Muir Wilderness can make the national parks look like holiday camps. You can bathe outdoors at the nearby Mono Hot Springs, although the *Mono Hot Springs Resort* here (mid-May to mid-Oct; ☎559/325-1710, ⓦwww.monohotsprings.com; ❷/❸) has indoor mineral baths along with its self-catering cabins. The road narrows and twists on to Edison Lake and the *Vermillion Valley Resort* (☎559/855-6558, ⓦwww.edisonlake.com; ❸/❹), from where you can catch a small ferry across the lake to the trailheads. Ranger stations (daily 8am–4.30pm) at Huntington Lake on Hwy-168, and another twenty miles east at Shaver Lake issue free backcountry permits and have camping and wilderness information.

Yosemite National Park

More gushing adjectives have been thrown at **YOSEMITE NATIONAL PARK** than at any other part of California. However excessive the hyperbole may seem, the instant you turn the corner that reveals **Yosemite Valley**, you realize it's actually an understatement – this is one of the world's most dramatic geological spectacles. Just seven miles long and at most one mile across, it is walled by near-vertical three-thousand-foot cliffs, streaked by tumbling waterfalls and topped by domes and pinnacles that form a jagged silhouette against the sky. At ground level, grassy meadows are framed by oak, cedar and fir trees; deer, coyotes and even black bears are not uncommon. Tourists are even commoner, but the park is big enough to absorb the crowds: you can visit at any time of year, even in winter when the waterfalls ice up and the trails are blocked by snow, and out of summer the valley itself is rarely overcrowded.

Yosemite Valley was made by glaciers gouging through the canyon of the Merced River: the ice scraped away the softer granite but only scarred the harder sections, which became the existing cliffs. The lake which formed when the glaciers melted eventually silted up to create the present valley floor. Native Americans lived here in comparative peace until the mid-nineteenth century, when the threatening approach of Gold Rush settlers led them to launch raiding parties. In 1851 Major James Savage's Mariposa Battalion trailed the Native Americans into the foothills and beyond, becoming the first whites to set foot

YOSEMITE NATIONAL PARK

Lake Eleanor

Saddlebag Lake

Hetch Hetchy Reservoir

Tuolumne River

Hetch Hetchy

120 (closed in winter)

Tioga Lake

Tioga Pass Entrance Station

San Francisco, 120

YOSEMITE NATIONAL PARK

TUOLUMNE MEADOWS

White Wolf

Tuolumne Meadows Visitor Center

Tuolumne Meadows

TIOGA ROAD (closed Nov–May)

Porcupine Flat

Carlon

Middle Fork

Big Oak Flat Entrance Station

Yosemite Creek

Tenaya Lake

John Muir Trail

Merced Lake

Hodgdon Meadow

Valley Visitor Center

Tamarack Flat

Crane Flat

Yosemite Falls

Half Dome

El Capitan

Yosemite Valley

Little Yosemite Valley

Glacier Point

Arch Rock Entrance Station

Bridalveil Fall

GLACIER POINT ROAD (closed Nov–May)

INYO NATIONAL FOREST

El Portal

Yosemite West

Badger Pass Ski Area

Bridalveil Creek

N

SIERRA NATIONAL FOREST

Wawona Information Center

Wawona

Mariposa Grove

0   5 miles

South Entrance Station

Fish Camp

Fresno, 41

Lower Yosemite Fall

Valley Visitor Center

Village Store

Ahwahnee Hotel

Mirror Lake

Half Dome

Yosemite Falls Trail

Yosemite Lodge

Camp 4

Merced River

Housekeeping Camp

LeConte Memorial

Curry Village

Lower Pines

North Pines

Tenaya Creek

One Way

Upper Pines

One Way

Four Mile Trail

Glacier Point

Nature Center at Happy Isles

Emerald Pool

Vernal Fall

0   800 yds

Sentinel Dome

Mist Trail

Nevada Fall

John Muir Trail

in Yosemite Valley, and the native community were soon forced out to make way for farmers, foresters and tourists. In 1864 Yosemite became the country's first national park.

John Muir, a Scottish immigrant who traveled the entire area on foot, spearheaded the conservation movement that led to the founding of the Sierra Club, with the express aim of preserving Yosemite. In 1913, the construction of a dam in the Hetch Hetchy Valley just north, to provide water for San Francisco, was a setback; but the publicity actually aided the formation of the present National Park Service in 1916, which promised – and has since provided – greater protection.

Getting there

Getting to Yosemite by car is straightforward, though the only road in from the east, Hwy-120 from Lee Vining, is closed from early November to around the beginning of June. **Gas** is pricey in the park and unavailable in Yosemite Valley. **Public transportation** into the Park centers on the Amtrak-accessible Central Valley town of Merced, from where YARTS **buses** (℡209/388-9589 or 1-877-989-2787, ⓦwww.yarts.com) make the two-hour run to Yosemite Valley four or five times a day, charging $10 each way. All services call at the Merced Transport Center, 710 W 16th St, for Greyhound connections, and at the Amtrak station, 324 W 24th St at K Street, where two of the services connect with trains from San Francisco. YARTS also runs a once-daily summer-only service over the Tioga Pass road from Mammoth Lakes and Lee Vining ($20 round-trip).

Bus fares are inclusive of **park entry**, which otherwise costs $20 per vehicle, $10 per cyclist or hiker, and is valid for seven days.

If you need somewhere to stay overnight before heading to Yosemite, consider the *HI–Merced Home Hostel* (℡209/725-0407; members $14, nonmembers $17), where the staff pick you up from the train or bus and drop you off at the appropriate station the following morning. If you'd rather be closer to the park, try the lively *Yosemite Bug Hostel & Lodge*, 6979 Hwy-140 (℡209/966-6666, ⓕ966-6667, ⓦwww.YosemiteBug.com; rooms ❸, bunks $15), at **Midpines**, on the YARTS bus route, with an excellent bar and café.

For recorded **park**, **road** and **weather information** phone ℡209/372-0200.

Yosemite Valley

The three roads from the Central Valley end up in the center of the park's 1200 square miles, in the natural splendor of **Yosemite Valley**. This is the busiest part of Yosemite, with **Yosemite Village** holding the main shops and the useful **visitor center** (daily: June–Sept 8am–6pm; mid-Oct to May 8am–5pm; ℡209/372-0299).

There's little in the village of any great interest; the reason to come here is to explore the valley itself. One of the most popular trails is the **Mist Trail** (3 miles round-trip; 2–3hr; 1000ft ascent), which winds up so close to the sensual **Vernal Fall** that during the spring snowmelt period (mid-April to mid-June) hikers are drenched by the spitting water but rewarded by vivid rainbows framing the fall. Vernal Fall always has some water flowing over it, but like all those in the valley, the falls are at their most dramatic in spring; by August they can be reduced to a trickle, and others disappear altogether.

The more strenuous trail to **Upper Yosemite Fall** (7 miles round-trip; 4–7hr; 2700ft ascent) leads up along a steep switchback path from behind the *Camp 4* campground, near *Yosemite Lodge*. This almost continuous ascent is very sapping on the leg muscles, but you get fine views over the valley on the way up, and after about two miles, a chance to appreciate the power (and volume) of the water as it crashes almost 1500ft in a single cascade. A mile and a half further on the same trail, you reach the top of the fall, more spectacular views and riverside spots for a much deserved picnic.

Of the two major cliffs visible from the valley, the 3600-foot **El Capitan** is one of the world's biggest pieces of exposed granite, so large that rock-climbers on its face are virtually invisible to the naked eye. **Half Dome**, the sheerest cliff in North America, is only seven percent off the vertical. You can hike up past Vernal Fall, making the final ascent by way of a steel staircase hooked on to its curving back (late May to mid-Oct only); if you plan a one-day assault, you'll need to start at the crack of dawn.

The most spectacular views of Yosemite Valley are from **Glacier Point**, the top of a 3200ft almost-sheer cliff, 32 miles by road from the valley. It's possible to get there on foot using the vertiginous **Four-Mile Trail** (4.8 miles one-way; 3–4hr; 3200ft ascent) though the lazy prefer to take the bus up (details below) and the trail down. The valley floor lies directly beneath the viewing point, and there are tremendous views across to Half Dome and the distant snowcapped summits of the High Sierra.

Practicalities

Prices within Yosemite are uniformly higher than outside the park, but not unaffordable. Of the **hotels** in the valley, try *Yosemite Lodge* (❺) or *Curry Village*, a mile from Yosemite Village, which has similarly priced rooms, plus fixed tent cabins (❸) and cabins (❹/❺); it also offers showers for nonguests ($2). For hotel information and reservations, call ☎559/252-4848 or visit Ⓦwww.yosemitepark.com.

Camping in the valley is only permitted in campgrounds, such as *Camp 4* walk-in ($5 per person), just west of *Yosemite Lodge*, which is popular with rock-climbers and has a bohemian reputation; it lacks showers and can only be reserved on the day at the kiosk on site. Other valley campgrounds cost $18 per site, and you can book up to five months ahead in summer (☎1-800/436-7275; from outside the US or Canada ☎301/722-1257): reserve as far in advance as you can, though there are occasionally cancellations.

As for **food**, there are expensive and generally poor stores, diners and snack bars in Yosemite Village, the best of which is *Degnan's Deli*, where massive sandwiches cost around $6. The *Garden Terrace Buffet* at *Yosemite Lodge* and the *Curry Pavilion* at *Curry Village* both have all-you-can-eat buffets for $8-12, while the baronial *Ahwahnee Dining Room* (☎209/372-1489) has the best (and most expensive) food in Yosemite and a great $32 Sunday brunch: jacket required for dinner. *Curry Village* has a great deck where you can order pizza, and margaritas.

Once in Yosemite Valley, **getting around** is easy, but **cars** spoil everybody's fun. If you drive in for the day, park at *Yosemite Village* and ride the frequent, free **shuttle buses** which loop around the valley in summer (daily 7.30am–10pm), calling at all points of interest. A number of **bicycle paths** cross the valley floor but **bike rental** is limited to outlets at *Yosemite Lodge* and *Curry Village* ($20 a day). There are also **guided tours** (☎209/372-1240), **hikes** and **horseback trips**.

Outside the valley

The **Mariposa Grove**, close to the park's southern entrance, is the biggest and best of Yosemite's groves of **giant sequoia** trees. To get to the towering growths, walk the 2.5-mile loop trail from the parking lot at the end of the road, which is also served by a free bus from the park entrance. The most renowned of the grouping, well marked along the route, is the **Grizzly Giant**, thought to be over 2700 years old.

On the eastern edge of the park, **Tuolumne** (June–Oct only) has an atmosphere quite different from the valley; here, at 8600 feet, you almost seem to be level with the tops of the surrounding snow-covered mountains. The air always has a fresh, crisp bite, and early summer reveals a plethora of colorful wild flowers. It's a better starting point than the valley for backcountry hiking into the High Sierra, where eight hundred miles of trails, both long and short, crisscross their way along the Sierra Nevada ridges. To spend a night in the backcountry, you must get a free **wilderness permit**, available up to 24 weeks in advance from the Wilderness Center, Box 545, Yosemite, CA 95389 (ⓦwww .nps.gov/yose/wilderness), or no more than 24 hours in advance from the nearest visitor center. There are tent cabins at *Tuolumne Meadows Lodge* (☎559/ 252-4848, ⓦwww.yosemitepark.com; ❸) and camping at the Tuolumne Meadows campground for $18 per site if you have a vehicle, $5 per person if you're hiking.

San Francisco

SAN FRANCISCO proper occupies just 48 hilly square miles at the tip of a slender peninsula, almost perfectly centered along the California coast. Arguably the most beautiful, certainly the most liberal city in the US, it remains true to itself: a funky, individualistic, surprisingly small city whose people pride themselves on being the cultured counterparts to their cousins in LA – the last bastion of civilization on the lunatic fringe of America. It's a compact and approachable place, where downtown streets rise on impossible gradients to reveal stunning views of the city, the bay and beyond, and blanket fogs roll in unexpectedly to envelop the city in mist. This is not the California of monotonous blue skies and slothful warmth – the temperatures rarely exceed the seventies, and even during summer can drop much lower.

The original inhabitants of this area, the **Ohlone Indians**, were all but wiped out within a few years of the establishment in 1776 of the **Mission Dolores**, the sixth in the chain of Spanish Catholic missions that ran the length of California. Two years after the Americans replaced the Mexicans in 1846, the discovery of gold in the Sierra foothills precipitated the rip-roaring **Gold Rush**. Within a year fifty thousand pioneers had traveled west, and east from China, turning San Francisco from a muddy village and wasteland of sand dunes into a thriving supply center and transit town. By the time the **transcontinental railroad** was completed in 1869, San Francisco was a lawless, rowdy boomtown of bordellos and drinking dens, something the moneyed elite – who hit it big on the much more dependable silver Comstock Load – worked hard to mend, constructing wide boulevards, parks, a cable car system and elaborate Victorian redwood mansions.

In the midst of the city's golden age, however, a massive **earthquake**, followed by three days of fire, wiped out most of the town in 1906. Rebuilding began immediately, resulting in a city more magnificent than before; in the decades that followed, writers like Dashiell Hammett and Jack London lived and worked here. Many of the city's landmarks, including Coit Tower and both the Golden Gate and Bay bridges, were built in the 1920s and 1930s. By World War II San Francisco had been eclipsed by Los Angeles as the main west coast city, but it achieved a new cultural eminence with the emergence of the Beats in the Fifties and the hippies in the Sixties, when the fusion of music, protest, rebellion and, of course, drugs that characterized 1967's "Summer of Love" took over the Haight-Ashbury district.

In a conservative America, San Francisco's reputation as a liberal oasis continues to grow, attracting waves of resettlers from all over the US. It is estimated that over half the city's population originates from somewhere else. It is a city in a constant state of evolution, fast gentrifying itself into one of the most high-end towns on earth – thanks, in part, to the disposable incomes pumped into its coffers from its sizeable singles and gay contingents. Gay capital of the world, San Francisco has also been the scene of the dot.com revolution's rise and fall. The resultant wealth at one time made housing prices skyrocket – often at the expense of the city's middle and lower classes – but the closure of hundreds of start-up IT companies has brought real-estate prices back down to (almost) reasonable levels. Despite the city's current economic ebbs and flows, your impression of the city likely won't be altered – it remains one of the most proudly distinct places to be found anywhere.

Arrival and information

All international and most domestic flights arrive at **San Francisco International Airport** (SFO), inconveniently located about fifteen miles south of the city. San Mateo County Transit (SamTrans) **buses** leave every half-hour from the lower level of the airport; the #KX express ($3) takes around 30 minutes to reach the Transbay Terminal downtown, while the slower #292 ($1.10) stops everywhere and takes nearly an hour. On the #KX, you're allowed only one carry-on bag; on the #292, you can bring as much as you want provided you can carry it onto the bus yourself. The SFO Airporter bus ($12) picks up outside each baggage claim area every fifteen minutes and travels to Union Square and the Financial District. The blue **SuperShuttle**, **American Airporter Shuttle** and **Bay Shuttle** minibuses depart every five minutes from the lower level of the circular road and take passengers to any city-center destination for around $14 a head. Be ruthless – competition for these and the several other companies running shuttle service is fierce and queues nonexistent. **Taxis** from the airport cost $30–35 (plus tip) for any downtown location, more for East Bay and Marin County – definitely worth it if there is more than one of you. If you're planning to drive, the usual **car rental** agencies operate free shuttle buses to their depots, leaving every 15 minutes from the upper level, but you have to load and unload your bags yourself. The car rental depot is located north of SFO and is too far to walk to. A shuttle train, now under construction, will alleviate this inconvenient system.

Several domestic airlines (Jet Blue and Southwest are two) and United fly into **Oakland International Airport** (OAK; see p.1151 for details), across the bay. This is actually closer to downtown San Francisco than SFO, and is efficiently connected with the city by the $2 AirBART shuttle bus, which drops you at the Coliseum BART station. Get on BART and San Francisco's downtown stops are fifteen minutes away ($2.75).

By bus and train

All San Francisco's **Greyhound** services use the **Transbay Terminal** at 425 Mission St, south of Market Street, near the Embarcadero BART station. **Green Tortoise** buses stop behind the Transbay Terminal on First and Natoma. **Amtrak** trains stop across the bay in **Richmond** (with easy BART transfers) and continue to **Oakland**, from where free shuttle buses run across the Bay Bridge to the Transbay Terminal, or you can take BART. Though technically closer to San Francisco, don't get off at the stop before Oakland, **Emeryville**, as consistent public transportation to the city doesn't exist.

Information

The **San Francisco Visitor Information Center**, on the lower level of Hallidie Plaza at the end of the cable car line on Market Street (Mon–Fri 8.30am–5pm, Sat & Sun 9am–3pm; ℡ 415/391-2000, ⓦ www.sfvisitor.org), has free maps of the city and the Bay Area, and can help with lodging and travel plans. Its free *San Francisco Book* provides detailed, if somewhat selective, information about accommodation, entertainment, exhibitions and stores.

San Francisco's two main **post offices**, with telephone and general delivery facilities, are at Sutter Street Station, 150 Sutter St (Mon–Fri 8.30am–5pm), and Rincon Station, 180 Steuart St (Mon–Fri 7am–6pm, Sat 9am–2pm).

City transportation

San Francisco is a rare American city where you don't need a car to see everything. In fact, given the chronic shortage of parking downtown, horrible traffic and zealous meter maids who love to give expensive parking tickets, going carless makes sense. The public transportation system, **MUNI**, though much maligned by locals for its unpredictable schedule, covers every neighborhood

San Francisco Public Transport

Useful bus routes

#5 From the Transbay Terminal, west alongside Haight-Ashbury and Golden Gate Park to the ocean.

#7 From the Ferry Terminal (Market St) to the end of Haight St and to Golden Gate Park.

#15 From Third St (SoMa) to Pier 39, Fisherman's Wharf, via the Financial District and North Beach.

#20 (Golden Gate Transit) From corner of Mission and First streets to the Golden Gate Bridge ($1.75).

#22 From the Marina up Pacific Heights and north on Fillmore.

#28 and **#29** From the Marina through the Presidio, north through Golden Gate Park, the Richmond and the Sunset.

#30 From the Caltrain depot on Third Street, north to Ghirardelli Square, via Chinatown and North Beach, and out to Chestnut Street in the Marina district.

#38 From Geary St via Civic Center, west to the ocean along Geary Blvd through Japantown and the Richmond, ending at Cliff House.

Muni train lines

Muni F-MARKET LINE Restored vintage trolleys from other cities run downtown from the Transbay Terminal and Fisherman's Wharf, up Market Street and into the heart of the Castro.

Muni J-CHURCH LINE From downtown to the edge of the Castro and on to the Mission and Noe Valley.

Muni K-INGLESIDE LINE From downtown through the Castro to Balboa Park.

Muni L-TARAVAL LINE From downtown west through the Sunset to the zoo and Ocean Beach.

Muni M-OCEAN VIEW From downtown west by the Stonestown Galleria shopping center and San Francisco State University.

Muni N-JUDAH LINE From downtown west through the Inner Sunset and to Ocean Beach, via the outer Haight.

From the Muni N-Judah line or buses #5 and #38, you can connect to **bus #44** that goes by the **De Young Museum, Japanese Tea Garden, California Academy of Sciences** and **Steinhart Aquarium** in Golden Gate Park. A Muni transfer will get you **discounts** at these places.

inexpensively via its system of cable cars, buses and trolleys. Bikes are a good option, as marked bike routes – with lanes – direct riders to all major points of interest. Walking the compact metropolis is the best bet, with each turn revealing surprises. Often these are in the form of stunning homes and bustling marketplaces, but on killer hills, some angled at 30 degrees and all punishment on the legs. Wear comfortable shoes.

Muni

The city's public transportation is run by the **San Francisco Municipal Railway**, or Muni (☎415/673-6864). A comprehensive network of **buses**, **trolleybuses** and **cable cars** run up and over the city's hills, while the underground **trains** become **streetcars** when they emerge from the downtown metro system to split off and serve the suburbs. On buses and trains the flat **fare** (correct change only) is $1; with each ticket you buy, ask for a **free transfer** – good for another two rides on a train or bus, and a fifty-percent reduction on cable cars if used within ninety minutes. Local groceries have begun to vend **single-ride tokens** (80¢), which save money and take care of the annoyance of not having correct change. Cable cars cost $2 one-way (no transfers). Most of the streetcar lines (J, K, L, M and N) require proof-of-payment (meaning they can check your ticket), so hold on to a valid ticket, pass or transfer (they often do check) or you may be subject to a steep fine.

If you're staying a few days, the Muni **Passport** is available in one-day, three-day and seven-day denominations ($6, $10, $15) and is valid for unlimited travel on the Muni system and BART stations (see below) within the city limits. A **Fast Pass** costs $35 for a full calendar month. Muni trains run **throughout the night** on a limited service, except those on the M-Ocean View line, which stop around 1am. **Buses** run all night, but services are greatly reduced after midnight. For **more information**, pick up the handy Muni map from the Visitor Information Center or bookstores.

Bikes are allowed on MUNI buses equipped with bicycle racks (on the front of the bus) and on Bay Area Rapid Transit, **BART**, except during peak commute hours.

Other transportation services

Various other public transportation networks serve San Francisco and the Bay Area. Along Market Street downtown, Muni shares the station concourses with BART, which runs to the East Bay – including downtown Oakland and Berkeley – and outer suburbs. The **Caltrain** commuter railway (depot at Fourth and King, South of Market) links San Francisco along the peninsula south to San Jose. **Golden Gate Ferry** boats (☎415/923-2000) leave from the Ferry Building at the Embarcadero, crossing the bay past Alcatraz to Sausalito and Larkspur in Marin County. **Blue & Gold Fleet** (☎415/773-1188) sails to Sausalito and Tiburon from Pier 41 at Fisherman's Wharf. The **Alameda–Oakland ferry** (☎510/522-3300) sails between Oakland's Jack London Square, the Ferry Building, Fisherman's Wharf and Pac Bell Park ($5 one-way) and, in summer, to Angel Island ($12 round-trip; daily late May–Oct).

Taxis ply the streets, and you can flag one down (especially downtown), but finding one can be a pain. Phoning around, try De Soto (☎415/970-1300) or Yellow Cab (☎415/626-2345). Fares (within the city) are roughly $1.70 for the first mile and $1.80 per mile thereafter.

If you fancy **cycling**, Avenue Cyclery, 640 and 756 Stanyan St (☎415/387-3155) in the Haight, near Golden Gate Park, rents mountain or city bikes for

$5 per hour, $25 per day. Downtown, for Golden Gate Bridge rides, try New World Sports, 1365 Columbus Ave, near Fisherman's Wharf (℡415/776-7801), and Blazing Saddles, on Fisherman's Wharf on Pier 41 and at 1095 Columbus Ave in North Beach (℡415/202-8888, ⓦwww.blazingsaddles.com); both rent bikes for $5 per hour, $25-28 per day.

Organized tours

One way to orient yourself is an **organized tour**. Gray Line Tours (℡415/558-9400), for example, take you around the city in four fairly tedious hours for around $37 a head. Considerably more exciting are the 60-minute **bay cruises** operated by the Blue & Gold Fleet ($17; ℡415/705-8203) from pier 39 and pier 41 – though be warned that everything may be shrouded in fog. Excruciatingly expensive **aerial tours** of the city and Bay Area in light aircraft or helicopters are available from several operators, such as San Francisco Helicopter Tours (℡1-800/400-2404, ⓦwww.sfhelicoptertours.com), which offers spectacular flights over the Bay Area for $95 per passenger.

The best of the **walking tours** include City Guides, sponsored daily by the San Francisco Public Library (free; ℡415/557-4266); Cruisin' the Castro ($40; ℡415/550-8110, ⓦwww.webcastro.com/castrotour), an absorbing and witty tour of the gay community; Footnotes (℡925/672-5908, ⓦwww.footnotes-tour.com), a rigorous walk and storytelling centered around the city's Barbary Coast days; and All About Chinatown ($25; ℡415/982-8839), an insider's cultural perspective on this lively quarter (optional dim sum lunch, $12 extra). Three Babes and a Bus ($35, which includes all cover charges; ℡415/552-CLUB, ⓦwww.threebabes.com) takes a luxury coachload of people looking for a good time to different nightclubs around the city. There are also special mural tours of the Mission by Precita Eyes taking in the district's distinctive street art (see p.1138 for details).

Accommodation

Annual visitors far outnumber San Francisco's 800,000 people, and the city isn't short on lodging, but be sure to book in advance, sometimes several months in advance for visits in the summer and fall. Some thirty thousand beds are available in the city, at prices ranging from $15 for dormitory-style accommodation to a whopping $575 for a suite at the *Ritz*. The **hotels and motels** have a good reputation for comfort and cleanliness. Hotels in the developing South of Market area and the very seedy Tenderloin start at around $30 per night or $120 a week, without a private bath or even a toilet. In the groomed areas around Union Square and Nob Hill it's hard to find a place for under $125 a night.

For **B&Bs**, the city's fastest-growing source of accommodation, consult the list overleaf, or contact a specialist agency such as Bed and Breakfast California (12711 McCartysville, Saratoga, CA 95070; ℡408/781-3774 or 1-800/872-4500, ⓦwww.bbintl.com) or Bed and Breakfast San Francisco (PO Box 420009, San Francisco, CA 94142; ℡415/931-3083). British visitors can reserve rooms through **Colby International** (℡0151/220 5848.) San Francisco Reservations (360 22nd St, Suite 300, Oakland, CA 94612; ℡1-800/677-1500, ⓦwww.hotelres.com) will find you a room from around $90 a double. If all else fails and you've got a car, **motels** are legion along the highways and bigger roads throughout the Bay Area, at a standard rate of $40–50 a night. In all cases, bear in mind that all quoted room rates are subject to a **fourteen percent room tax**.

Camping isn't an option in San Francisco itself, though throwing down a bag in Golden Gate Park or the Presidio may seem tempting. Camping is illegal within the city, and can be dangerous as well.

Hostels and YMCAs

Globe Hostel 10 Hallam Place ☎415/431-0540. Lively South of Market hostel with young clientele and no curfew. $21 per person; doubles $60 for one or two people; $25 per person after that. **①**–**③**

Green Tortoise Hostel 494 Broadway ☎415/834-1000, ⊛www.greentortoise.com. Funky North Beach hostel amongst strip clubs but near cheap food in Chinatown and North Beach. Dorm beds $22 per night, double rooms $56; both options include complimentary breakfast, use of sauna and Internet access. **①**–**③**

HI-San Francisco City Center 685 Ellis ☎ 415/474-5721, ⊛www.norcalhostels.org. New hostel in a restored building close to the theater and nightspots. Dorm beds from $22 for members, $25 for nonmembers; two- and four-person rooms with en suite bathrooms are $66 a night. **①**–**③**

HI-San Francisco Downtown 312 Mason St ☎ 415/788-5604, ⊛www.norcalhostels.org. Large, excellent downtown hostel with dorm beds from $22 for members, $25 for nonmembers (which is really a day membership for $3). Along with its sister HI-SF City Center, it is the cleanest and most central of the bunch. **①**

HI-San Francisco Fisherman's Wharf Building 240, Fort Mason ☎415/771-7277, ⊛www.norcalhostels.org. On the waterfront between the Golden Gate Bridge and Fisherman's Wharf with great views. One of the most comfortable hostels around, though not an easy walking distance to downtown. Open 24hr, 170 beds, free parking. $22 per person. Includes breakfast, and because it is on federal land, no membership fee. **①**

Pacific Tradewinds Guesthouse 680 Sacramento St ☎415/433-7970. Great location in Chinatown, no curfew, laundry and a host of other services. $24 per person or $22 per person sharing a double. **①**

San Francisco International Guest House 2976 23rd St ☎415/641-1411. Popular with European travelers, this Mission District Victorian house has dorms and a few private rooms. $15 per person daily, 5-day minimum stay; $13 a day if you stay a month. Two kitchens; no curfew, and no reservations accepted. **①**

YMCA Central Hotel 220 Golden Gate Ave ☎415/345-6700. Good central single and double rooms, two blocks from Civic Center. Rates include breakfast and use of gym, pool and sauna. $50.50 single, $68 double. **②**/**③**

Hotels, motels and B&Bs

Abigail 246 McAllister St ☎415/861-9728, ⊛www.abigailhotel.com. Comfortable, stylish and affordable, this Civic Center hotel caters to travelers performing at the nearby arts centers. **⑤**/**⑥**

Andora Inn 2438 Mission at 20th ☎415/282-2608 or 1-800/967-9219, ⊛www.andorainn.com. Fully restored 12-room Victorian manor located in the heart of the Mission with an awesome staff. Guestrooms start at $79; deluxe room and suites for $119 to $249. **④**–**⑨**

Archbishop's Mansion 1000 Fulton St ☎415/563-7872 or 1-800/543-5820, ⊛www.archbishopsmansion.com. Once a school for wayward Catholic boys, this grandly camp Alamo Square mansion is an appealing, gay-friendly B&B. Attentive personalized service, rooms named after operas, the ballroom chandelier from *Gone With the Wind*, and everything from fitness training to image consulting are all available. **⑦**–**⑨**

Beresford Arms 701 Post St ☎415/673-2600 or 1-800/533-6533, ⊛www.beresford.com/berarms.html. Luxury B&B in the heart of town. **⑥**–**⑨**

Clarion Bedford 761 Post St ☎415/673-6040 or 1-800/252-7466, www.hotelbedford.com. Charming old-world mid-sized hotel offering tremendous value in the traditionally pricey Theater District. **⑥**/**⑦**

Fairmont 950 Mason St ☎415/772-5000, ⊛www.fairmont.com. The most famous of the top-notch hotels, this over-ornate palace with two restaurants and two lounges, and fantastic views from the rooms was the site of the US TV series *Hotel*. Entirely renovated in 2001, it is worth checking out the terrace garden and the splendid cheesiness of the Tonga Room, in the basement. **⑨**

Grant Plaza 465 Grant Ave ☎415/434-3883 or 1-800/472-6899, ⊛www.grantplaza.com. Clean, comfortable Chinatown hotel. One of the best values in San Francisco. **①**–**④**

Harbor Court 165 Steuart St ☎415/882-1300 or 1-800/695-8284. Smart hotel in the Embarcadero district. On the waterfront; bay-view rooms get a panorama. **⑥**–**⑨**

Hotel Del Sol 3100 Webster St ☎415/921-5520 or 1-877/433-5765, ⊛www.thehoteldelsol.com. Bright, sunny refurbished 1950s motor lodge in the heart of the Marina, near Union and Fillmore Street shopping. A delight to the eye. **⑤**–**⑧**

Huntington 1075 California St ☎415/474-5400. Understated and quietly elegant compared to its

Nob Hill counterparts, this is the hotel for the wealthy who don't need to flash it about. ⑨

Inn at the Opera 333 Fulton St ☎415/863-8400 or 1-800/325-2708. Very fancy, small hotel with a classical music theme. Across the street from the Opera House. ⑥–⑨

Jackson Court 2198 Jackson St ☎415/929-7670, ⓦwww.jacksoncourt.com. Lovely converted Pacific Heights mansion. ⑦/⑧

La Quinta Inn 20 Airport Blvd ☎650/583-2223. Overnight laundry service and a pool make this a good option if you need to be near the airport. Free shuttle service to the airport. ⑥

Mansions 2220 Sacramento St ☎415/929-9444. Luxurious Victorian mansion, perched high up in the fancy reaches of Pacific Heights. ⑥–⑨

Monaco 501 Geary St ☎415/292-0100 or 1-866/622-5284, ⓦwww.monaco-sf.com. Best of the new wave of San Francisco hotels offering great style and décor plus Nintendo in every room. Unfortunately, prices have risen in recent years. ⑥–⑨

Nob Hill 835 Hyde St ☎415/885-2987 or 877/662-4455, ⓦwww.nobhillhotel.com. Inexpensive accommodation in the lower Nob Hill area. Small, clean and comfortable rooms. Discounted weekly rates. ⑥/⑦

Pension San Francisco 1668 Market St ☎415/864-1271. A good, clean and basic base near the Civic Center, walkably close to SoMa and the Castro. ③

The Phoenix 601 Eddy St ☎415/776-1380, ⓦwww.thephoenixhotel.com. Converted Fifties-style motel in a slightly dodgy neighborhood on the edge of the Tenderloin with bungalow rooms around a pool, but the hip music-biz crowd who lounge around the pool drinking cocktails don't seem to mind. Next to the hip *Backflip* (see p.1145). ⑥/⑦

The Red Victorian Bed, Breakfast and Art 1665 Haight St ☎415/864-1978, ⓦwww .redvic.com. Bang in the middle of Haight-Ashbury, a lively New Agey B&B, which also calls itself the *Peace Travelers Center*, with a hippie art gallery. A real Sixties relic. Discounts for longer stays. ④/⑤

Renoir 45 McAllister between 7th and Market sts ☎415/626-5200, ⓦwww.renoirhotel.com. Good location just opposite the Civic Center. Glitzy lobby and large, comfy rooms. ⑥–⑦

Ritz-Carlton 600 Stockton St ☎415/296-7465. Incredible Beaux Arts structure – immaculate, expensive and yet somehow soulless. ⑥–⑨

San Remo 2237 Mason St ☎415/776-8688 or 1-800/352-7366, ⓦwww.sanremohotel.com. Pleasant, old-fashioned rooms (shared bath, no phones, no televisions) in nice North Beach Victorian house. Friendly staff, good bar and

restaurant. ④

Sir Francis Drake 450 Powell St ☎415/392-7755 or 1-800/795-7129, ⓦwww.sirfrancis-drake.com). Don't be put off by the Beefeaters outside, this is a colonial California hotel whose greatest attraction is the 21st-floor *Harry Denton's Starlight Room*, offering jazz, smart drinks and great views to a good-time crowd. ⑦–⑨

Stanyan Park 750 Stanyan Ave ☎415/751-1000, ⓦwww.stanyanpark.com. Gorgeous small Victorian hotel in a great setting across from Golden Gate Park, with friendly staff and free continental breakfast. ⑤–⑥

Triton 342 Grant Ave ☎1-800/433-6611, ⓦwww.hotel-tritonsf.com. Very stylish, very comfortable and very central hotel, across from the Chinatown Gateway, two blocks from Union Square. Suites include one dedicated to the Grateful Dead's Jerry Garcia. ⑥/⑦

Washington Square Inn 1660 Stockton St ☎415/981-4220. Cozy B&B right on North Beach's lovely main square. Nonsmokers only. ⑤/⑥

Westin St Francis 335 Powell St ☎415/397-7000 or 1-800/WESTIN1. This completely renovated landmark hotel in the heart of Union Square has a sumptuous lobby, three restaurants, a bar and a fitness center, but disappointingly plain rooms. ⑨

York 940 Sutter St ☎415/885-6800 or 1-800/808-9675. Quiet, older hotel on the western edge of downtown; location for the dramatic stairway scenes in *Vertigo*. ⑥–⑨

Women's and gay men's accommodation

Andora Inn 2438 Mission St at 20th ☎415/282-2608 or 1-800-967-9219. Lovingly restored Victorian manor in the lively Mission district. Free continental breakfast, and wine and cheese in the evenings. ④–⑨

Archbishop's Mansion 1000 Fulton St ☎415/563-7872 or 1-800-543-5820 ⓦwww.archbishopsmansion.com. Over-the-top, gay-friendly B&B. (See earlier listing opposite.) ⑦–⑨

Hayes Valley 417 Gough St ☎415/431-9131 or 1-800/930-7999, ⓦwww.hayesvalleyinn.com. Homey place with shared baths, popular with a rowdy crowd. Pets allowed if arranged in advance. ③/④

Inn on Castro 321 Castro St ☎415/861-0321, ⓦwww.innoncastro2.com. Luxury B&B – though a single with shared bath can be had for $100 a night – well worth the price for the larger rooms and good breakfasts. Smack in the middle of the Castro. Discounts for longer stays. ④–⑦

Mary Elizabeth Inn 1040 Bush St ☎415/673-6768, ⓦwww.meinn.org. Run by the United Methodist Church; a safe but unexciting place for women. Weekly rates available, breakfast and dinner included. ❸–❹

Queen Anne 1590 Sutter St ☎415/441-2828 or 1-800/227-3970, ⓦwww.queenanne.com. Very much a gay hotel with overdone decor and complimentary afternoon tea and sherry. ❻–❼

24 Henry Guesthouse 24 Henry St ☎415/864-5686. Quiet, intimate guesthouse near the heart of the Castro. ❹ with shared bath, ❺–❻ with private bath.

Village Guesthouse 4080 18th St ☎415/864-5686. Branch of the above; 24 Henry handles bookings for both. Right in the heart of the Castro. ❻

The Willows 710 14th St ☎415/431-4770, ⓦwww.willowssf.com. Affordable, well furnished and near the Castro. Rooms have shared bath. ❹–❺

Women's Hotel 642 Jones St ☎415/775-1711. Comfortable, secure, women-only building, unfortunately situated in the shabby Tenderloin district. Weekly rates only: $185 per week for a shared bath, $225 per week for a private bath. Another person in the room is another $50 per week. ❶–❷

The City

San Francisco is a city of hills and distinct neighborhoods. As a general rule, geographical elevation means wealth – the higher up you are, the less fog you endure, resulting in better views. Commercial square-footage is surprisingly small and mostly confined to the downtown area, and the rest of the city is made up of primarily residential neighborhoods with street-level shopping districts, easily explored on foot. Armed with a good map and strong legs, you could plough through much of the city in a day, but the best way to get to know San Francisco is to dawdle.

Union Square

The city's heart can be found around **Union Square**, located north of Market Street and bordered by Powell and Stockton streets. Cable cars clank past bustling shoppers and theater-goers who gravitate to the district's many upscale hotels, department stores and boutiques. The statue in the center commemorates

Cable cars

It was the invention of the **cable car** that made high-society life on San Francisco's hills possible and practical. Since 1873, these little trolleys have been an integral part of life in the city, thanks to Scots-born Andrew Hallidie's concern for horses. Having watched a team struggle and fall, breaking their legs on a steep San Franciscan street, Hallidie designed a pulley system around the thick wire rope his father had patented in England. A transportation revolution followed. At their peak, just before the 1906 earthquake, over six hundred cable cars traveled 110 miles of track throughout the city; over the years, usage dwindled and, in 1964, nostalgic citizens voted to preserve the last seventeen miles (now just 10) as a moving historic landmark.

Today there are three lines. Two of them, the Powell & Mason and the Powell & Hyde lines run from Hallidie Plaza off Union Square at Powell and Market streets to Fisherman's Wharf. The Powell & Hyde is the steepest, reaching a hair-raising 21-degree grade between Lombard and Chestnut streets. The oldest route, the California line, climbs Nob Hill along California Street from the Embarcadero, rattling past the fanciest hotels in the city. The cars fasten onto a moving two-inch cable, which runs beneath the streets, gripping on the ascent then releasing at the top and gliding down the other side. You can see the huge motors that still power these cables in the **Cable Car Museum and Powerhouse**, at 1201 Mason at Washington Street (free; daily 10am–6pm; ⓦwww.cablecarmuseum.com).

East Bay & Sausalito ▶

Pac Bell Park ▶

Caltrain Depot ▼

Admiral Dewey's success in the Spanish–American War, though the square takes its name from its role as gathering place for stumping speechmakers during the US Civil War. (The woman who posed for the monument became a local celebrity, marrying into the wealthy Spreckels family.) The square witnessed the attempted assassination of President Gerald Ford outside the (now Westin) **St Francis Hotel** in 1975, and was also the location of Francis Ford Coppola's film *The Conversation*, where Gene Hackman spied on strolling lovers. Many of **Dashiell Hammett's** detective stories, such as *The Maltese Falcon*, are set partly in the *St Francis*, in which he worked as a Pinkerton detective during the Twenties. Hammett fans should check out *John's Grill*, 63 Ellis St, for Sam Spade's favorite eating spot (though it probably won't be yours), and **Burritt Alley**, two blocks north of the square on Bush Street, near Stockton Street. Here's where Spade's partner, Miles Archer, met his end, shot by Brigid O'Shaughnessy. A plaque marks the spot.

On Geary Street, on the south side of the square, the **Theater District** is a pint-sized Broadway of restaurants, tourist hotels and serious and "adult" theaters. On the eastern side of the square, **Maiden Lane** is a chic urban walkway that before the 1906 earthquake and fire was one of the city's roughest areas, where homicides averaged around ten a month. Nowadays, aside from some prohibitively expensive boutiques, its main feature is San Francisco's only **Frank Lloyd Wright** building (now occupied by the Xanadu Tribal Art Gallery), an intriguing circular space which was a try-out for the Guggenheim in New York.

The Financial District

North of the city's main artery, Market Street, the glass-and-steel skyscrapers of the **Financial District** have sprung up in the last twenty years to form its only real high-rise area. Sharp-suited workers clog the streets and coffee kiosks during business hours, but after 6pm, the area pretty much shuts down. Stop at the corner of Kearny and Market streets to admire the just-refurbished **Lotta's Fountain**, San Francisco's most treasured artifact. It was around here that people gathered to hear news following the 1906 earthquake and fire, and also where famed soprano Luisa Tetrazinni gave a free concert on Christmas Eve, 1910.

Once cut off from the rest of San Francisco by the double-decker Embarcadero Freeway – damaged in the 1989 earthquake and finally torn down in 1991 – the **Ferry Building**, at the foot of Market Street, was modeled on the cathedral tower in Seville, Spain. Before the bridges were built in the 1930s it was the arrival point for fifty thousand cross-bay commuters daily. A few ferries still dock here (see p.1126), but the characterless office units inside do little to suggest its former importance. The area in front of the Ferry Building is the site of the much-loved **Ferry Plaza Farmers' Market** (Tues 11am–3pm, Sat 8am–1.30pm), a great place to buy or merely gawk at the colorful local produce.

Since the freeway was pulled down, the area around it, known as **The Embarcadero**, has experienced a dramatic renaissance – from an area of charmless office blocks into a swanky waterfront district with the city's most fashionable restaurants and hotels springing up beside palm trees and views of the bay.

From the vast and unimaginative **Embarcadero Center** shopping mall and the fountains of **Justin Herman Plaza** at the foot of Market it's a few blocks down to **Montgomery Street**, where the grand pillared entrances and banking halls of the post-1906 earthquake buildings era jostle for attention with a mixed bag of modern towers. For a hands-on grasp of modern finance, the **World of Economics Gallery** in the **Federal Reserve Bank**, 101 Market St (Mon–Fri 9am–6pm), is unbeatable: computer games allow you to engineer your own inflationary disasters, while exhibits detail recent scandals and triumphs. The **Wells Fargo History Museum**, 420 Montgomery St (Mon–Fri 9am–5pm; free), traces the far-from-slick origins of San Francisco's big money, right from the days of the Gold Rush, with mining equipment, gold nuggets, photographs, and a genuine retired stagecoach. Tucked discreetly in a nondescript building at 121 Steuart St is the little-known **Jewish Museum San Francisco** ($5, free first Mon of month and Thurs 6-8pm; Sun–Wed 11am–5pm, Thurs 11am–8pm), which, far from being the somber trudge through history its name suggests, has an impressive collection of contemporary work by Jewish artists. The museum will be moving to a new building in Yerba Buena Gardens in 2003.

Jackson Square and the Barbary Coast

A century or so ago, the eastern flank of the Financial District formed part of the **Barbary Coast**, an area of land that grew due to the hundreds of ships that lay abandoned by sailors heading for the Gold Rush. Enterprising San Franciscans used the dry ships as hotels, bars and stores. This then-rough-and-tumble waterfront district gave The City an unsavory reputation as **Baghdad by the Bay**, packed as it was with saloons and brothels where hapless young males were given Mickey Finns and shanghaied into involuntary servitude on merchant ships. William Randolph Hearst's *Examiner* lobbied frantically to shut down the quarter, resulting in a 1917 California law prohibiting prostitution. Remains of the cradle of San Francisco can be seen in the **Jackson Square Historic District**, not an actual square but an area bordered by Washington, Columbus, Sansome and Pacific streets.

The landmark **Transamerica Pyramid**, at the foot of diagonal Columbus Avenue and Washington, serves as a useful dividing point between the various downtown areas. The 48-story structure, capped by a colossal 212ft hollow spire, arose amid a city-planning furor that earned it the name of "Pereira's Prick," after its LA-based architect William Pereira. Since then it's been indisputably the signature of San Francisco's skyline, in these days of plump speculative buildings, a rare example of architecture that sacrifices the pragmatic for the symbolic. From a real-estate perspective, the building is a nightmare – as the structure tapers upward, the floors that fetch the highest rents diminish in area – the pyramid would be far more valuable upside down. Rudyard Kipling, Robert Louis Stevenson, Mark Twain and William Randolph Hearst all rented office space in the Montgomery Block that originally stood on this site, and regularly hung around the notorious *Bank Exchange* bar within. Legend also has it that Sun Yat-sen – whose statue is in Chinatown, three blocks away – wrote the Chinese constitution and orchestrated the successful overthrow of the Manchu Dynasty from his second-floor office here. Next door is the pleasant **Transamerica Redwood Park** with fountains perfect for an outdoor lunch. Across the street from the park, **Hotaling Place**'s winding brickwork and antique lamps recall the past, and some original redbrick buildings can be seen, now serving as office space for upscale design firms. Heading west on Jackson or Pacific streets from the area leads you back to Columbus and the green-copper siding of the **Columbus Tower**, 906 Kearney, the de facto beginning of North Beach. Director and San Francisco native Francis Ford Coppola owns the building, and his *Neibaum-Coppola Café* on the ground floor serves sandwiches, pasta and his wine from the nearby vineyards.

Chinatown

Its 24 square blocks smack in the middle of San Francisco make up the second-largest Chinese community outside Asia. Almost entirely autonomous, with its own schools, banks and newspapers, it has its roots in the migration of Chinese laborers to the city after the completion of the transcontinental railroad, and the arrival of Chinese sailors keen to benefit from the Gold Rush. The city didn't extend much of a welcome: they were met by a tide of vicious racial attacks and the 1882 Chinese Exclusion Act. Nowadays they have been joined by Vietnamese, Koreans, Thais and Laotians: by day the area seethes with activity, by night it's a blaze of neon. Overcrowding is compounded by a brisk tourist trade – sadly, however, Chinatown boasts some of the tackiest stores and facades in the city, making it more similar to shopping in a bad part of Hong Kong than in Beijing. Indeed, Chinese tourists are often disappointed in the neighborhood's disorder, and the new, some say true, Chinese neighborhood is in the Richmond district along Clement Street.

Gold ornamented portals and brightly painted balconies sit above the souvenir shops and restaurants of narrow **Grant Avenue**; pass under the entrance arch at Bush Street to be met by an assault of plastic Buddhas, cloisonné "health balls," noisemakers and chirping mechanical crickets in every doorway. **Old St Mary's Church**, on Grant and California, was one of the few San Francisco buildings to survive the 1906 earthquake and fire, and they have a good photo display of the damage to the city in the entranceway of the beautiful church.

Parallel to Grant Avenue, **Stockton Street** is crammed with exotic fish and produce markets, bakeries and herbalists. Inside the **Ellison Herb Shop** at no. 805 Stockton St, Chinatown's best-stocked herbal pharmacy, you'll find clerks filling orders the ancient Chinese way – with hand-held scales and abacuses – from drug cases filled with dried bark, roots, sharks' fins, cicadas, ginseng and other staples. Here, between Grant and Stockton, jumbled alleys hold the most worthwhile stops in the area. The best of these is Waverly Place, a two-block corridor of brightly painted balconies that was lined with brothels before the 1906 catastrophe and now home to three opulent but skillfully hidden **temples** (nos. 109, 125 and 146), their interiors a riot of black, gold and vermilion, still in use and open to visitors. North of Waverly Place, between Jackson and Washington streets, Ross Alley features the **Golden Gate Fortune Cookie Company**, no. 56, specializing in X-rated fortunes, and next door, a barber who will cut your hair to resemble that of any Hollywood star's.

Some of the hundred-plus **restaurants** (see p.1142 for recommendations) are historical landmarks in themselves. *Sam Wo*, at 813 Washington St, is a cheap and churlish ex-haunt of the Beats where Gary Snyder taught Jack Kerouac to eat with chopsticks and had them both thrown out with his loud and passionate interpretation of Zen poetry.

North Beach

Resting in the hollow between Russian and Telegraph hills, and split by Columbus Avenue, **North Beach** likes to think of itself as the happening district of San Francisco. It has been a focal point for anyone vaguely alternative ever since the **City Lights Bookstore** opened in 1953. The first paperback bookstore in the US stands amid the flashing neon and sleazy clubs of Columbus Avenue at Broadway, open until midnight seven days a week, and is still owned by poet and novelist Lawrence Ferlinghetti. The **Beat Generation** made this the literary capital of America, achieving overnight notoriety when charges of obscenity were leveled at Allen Ginsberg's poem *Howl* in 1957, which he first performed over in Cow Hollow at 3119 Fillmore St. It was the hedonistic antics of the Beats, as much as their literary merits, that struck a chord, and North Beach came to symbolize a wild and subversive lifestyle. The roadtrips and riotous partying, the drug-taking and embrace of Eastern religions were emulated nationwide; tourists poured into North Beach for "Beatnik Tours."

Next to the bookstore, **Vesuvio's**, an old North Beach bar where the likes of Dylan Thomas and Kerouac would get loaded, remains a haven for the lesser-knowns to pontificate on the state of the arts. At the crossroads of **Columbus and Broadway**, poetry meets porn in a raucous assembly of strip joints, coffee houses and drag queens. Most famous, the *Condor Club* was where Carol Doda's revealing of her silicone-implanted breasts started the topless waitress phenomenon. Now reincarnated as the (fully-clothed) *Condor Sports Bar*, the landmark site still preserves her nipples, once immortalized in neon above the door, in its museum, along with photos and clippings from the *Condor Club's* heyday.

As you continue north on Columbus Avenue, you enter the heart of the old **Italian neighborhood**, an enclave of narrow streets and leafy enclosures. Explorations lead to small landmarks like the **Café Trieste**, where the jukebox blasts out opera classics to a heavy-duty art crowd, toying with cappuccinos and browsing slim volumes of poetry. From Columbus's **Washington Square**, head up the very steep steps on Filbert Street to reach Telegraph Hill and the **Coit Tower**, featuring grand views of the city and beyond.

To the west of Columbus, **Russian Hill** was named for Russian sailors who died here in the early 1800s. In the summer, there's always a long line of cars waiting to drive down the tight curves of **Lombard Street**. Surrounded by palatial dwellings and herbaceous borders, Lombard is an especially thrilling drive at night, when the tourists leave and the city lights twinkle below. Even if you're without a car, the journey up here is worth it for a visit to the **San Francisco Art Institute**, 800 Chestnut St (free; daily 8am–9pm), the oldest art school in the west, where the **Diego Rivera Gallery** has an outstanding mural created by the painter in 1931. Walking south from the institute for four blocks on Jones Street, you'll find **Macondray Lane**, a pedestrian-only "street" thought to be one of the inspirations for Armistead Maupin's *Tales of the City* (see p.1347).

Alcatraz

Before the rocky islet of **Alcatraz** became America's most dreaded **high-security prison**, in 1934, it had been home to little more than the odd pelican (*alcatraz* in Spanish). Surrounded by the freezing, impassable water of San Francisco Bay, it made an ideal place to hold the nation's most wanted criminals – men such as Al Capone and Machine Gun Kelly. The conditions were inhumane: inmates were kept in solitary confinement, in cells no larger than nine by five feet, most without light. They were not allowed to eat together, read newspapers, play cards or even talk; relatives could visit for only two hours each month. Escape really was impossible. Nine men managed to get off the rock, but there is no evidence that any of them made it to the mainland.

Due to its massive running costs, the jail finally closed in 1963. The island remained abandoned until 1969, when a group of Native Americans staged an occupation as part of a peaceful attempt to claim the island for their people, citing treaties which designated all federal land not in use as automatically reverting to their ownership. Using all the bureaucratic trickery it could muster, the government finally ousted them in 1971, claiming the operative lighthouse qualified it as active.

At least 750,000 tourists each year take the excellent hour-long, self-guided audio **tours** of the abandoned prison, which include some sharp anecdotal commentary and even the chance to spend a minute (it feels like forever) locked in a darkened cell.

Boats to Alcatraz leave from pier 41 ($13.25 including audio tour, $10 without; frequent departures from 9.30am, last boat leaves Alcatraz at 6.30pm). Advance reservations strongly recommended, especially in peak tourist season (allow two weeks; ☎415/705-5555, ⓦwww.nps.gov/alcatraz). Night tours are also available in the summer, from Thursday to Sunday departing at 6.20pm and 7.05pm and returning at 8:15pm and 9.30pm.

Fisherman's Wharf

San Francisco rarely tries to pass off pure, unabashed commercialism as a worthy tourist attraction, but with **Fisherman's Wharf** and the nearby waterfront district, it makes an exception.

An inventive use of statistics allows the area to proclaim itself the most-visited tourist attraction in the entire country; in fact, this crowded and hideous ensemble of waterfront kitsch and fast-food stands makes a sad and rather misleading introduction to the city. It may be hard to believe, but this was once a genuine fishing port; the few fishing vessels that can still afford the exorbitant mooring charges are usually finished by early morning and get out before the tourists arrive. The shops and bars here are among the most overpriced in the city, and crowd-weary families do little to add to the ambience.

If you wish to get out on the water, 60-minute **bay cruises** depart several times a day from piers 39 and 41 (see p.1127). Better instead to head to the museums of **Fort Mason** and on to the expanse of green parkland along the **Marina district**, affording excellent views of the Golden Gate Bridge.

Nob Hill

From Nob Hill, looking down upon the business wards of the city, we can decry a building with a little belfry, and that is the stock exchange, the heart of San Francisco; a great pump we might call it, continually pumping up the savings of the lower quarter to the pockets of the millionaires on the hill.

Robert Louis Stevenson

If the Financial District is representative of new money in the city, the posh hotels and Masonic institutions of **Nob Hill** exemplify San Francisco's old wealth; it is, as Joan Didion wrote, "the symbolic nexus of all old California money and power." Once you've made the stiff climb up (or taken the California cable car), there are very few real sights as such, but nosing around is pleasant enough, taking in the aura of luxury and enjoying the views over the city and beyond.

The area became known as Nob Hill after the robber-baron industrialists who came to live here while running the Central Pacific Railroad. **Grace Cathedral** here is one of the biggest hunks of sham-Gothic architecture in the US. Construction began soon after the 1906 earthquake, but most of it was built, of faintly disguised reinforced concrete, in the early Sixties. The entrance is adorned with faithful replicas of the fifteenth-century Ghiberti doors of the Florence Baptistry. A block east, be sure to go inside the **Fairmont Hotel**, 950 Mason St, to get a sense of the opulence that once ruled the hill. Take its elevators up for a great view of the city. Across from the *Fairmont*, the brownstone of the **Pacific Union Club** was the only original Nob Hill structure left standing after the 1906 fire.

The Tenderloin, Civic Center and South of Market

While parts of San Francisco can almost seem to be an urban utopia, the adjoining districts of **the Tenderloin** and **Civic Center** reveal harsher realities and are a gritty reminder that not everybody has it so easy. However, **South of Market** (aka SoMa) has, like the Embarcadero, taken a previously unimaginable upswing. A new entertainment complex surrounding Yerba

Buena Gardens – anchored by the high and low culture appeals of the San Francisco Museum of Modern Art and Sony's Metreon mall – has transformed it from a bleak post-industrial wasteland into a thriving extension of the crowded downtown area.

The majestic federal and municipal buildings of **Civic Center**, squashed between the Tenderloin and SoMa, can't help but look strangely out of sync, both with their immediate neighbors and with San Francisco as a whole. Their grand Beaux Arts style is at odds with the quirky wooden architecture of the rest of the city. At night, when the ritzy **War Memorial Opera House**, 301 Van Ness Ave, and the aquarium-like **Louise M. Davies Symphony Hall**, Grove Street at Van Ness Avenue, swarm with well-heeled patrons of the ballet, opera and symphony, it all looks distinctly more impressive than by day.

It was at the huge, green-domed **City Hall**, on the northern edge of the dismal **United Nations Plaza**, that Mayor George Moscone and gay Supervisor Harvey Milk were assassinated in 1978 (see p.1138). The recently restored gold plate dome is an impressive relic of Gold Rush-era largess.

Formerly one of San Francisco's least desirable neighborhoods, **SoMa**, the district South of Market, has been enjoying a renaissance since the 1980s. It's reminiscent in a way of New York's SoHo several years ago: many of its abandoned warehouses have been converted into studio spaces and art galleries, and the neighborhood is now home to artists, musicians, hep-cat entertainers and trendy restaurants. This may well be short-lived however: SoMa is a prime piece of central real estate, and during the dot.com heyday, the bulldozers moved in and many artists were squeezed out. It remains to be seen which direction the district will go as the dot.com revolution grinds to a halt. Still, the new home of the **SF Museum of Modern Art**, 151 Third St ($10, free first Tues of month; Mon, Tues & Fri–Sun 11am–6pm, Thurs 11am–9pm, open an hour earlier May–Sept), opened here in January 1995. Major works include paintings by Jackson Pollock, Frida Kahlo and Diego Rivera. The temporary exhibitions are the museum's strongest suit; with newly acquired financial muscle it can snap up the better touring works. However, the allegation that the building, designed by Swiss architect Mario Botta, is far more beautiful than anything inside, is pretty hard to dispute – flooded with natural light from a soaring, truncated, cylindrical skylight, it's a sight to behold.

Opposite the museum is the other totem of civic pride, the **Yerba Buena Center for the Arts** ($6, free first Tues of month; daily except Mon 11am–6pm, Thurs–Fri 11am–8pm), bounded by Third and Fourth streets, Mission and Folsom. A spectacular $44 million project featuring a theater and three galleries, the center's best feature is its parklike setting – five and a half acres of lovely gardens with a 50ft Sierra granite waterfall memorial to Martin Luther King Jr. Dominating the Gardens' south side is the **Sony Metreon**, a combination movie theater and multimedia entertainment mall.

An incredible addition to the city's waterfront is **Pac Bell Park**, down Third Street at King, home to the **San Francisco Giants**. The faux-old brick building offers superb views of the bay beyond the outfield fences, some of the finest food to ever grace a ballpark, as well as the chance to see the odd home run splash into the bay.

Above all, SoMa is the nucleus of **clubland**, where the city's wildlife is at its best. Folsom Street was until recently a major gay strip, the center for much lewder goings-on than the Castro; in recent years the mix has become pretty diverse, though never tame.

The Mission

Vibrant, hip and ethnically mixed, **the Mission** is easily San Francisco's funkiest neighborhood. A mile or so south of downtown, it is also the warmest, eluding the summer fogs. As the traditional first stop for immigrants, the Mission serves as a microcosm of the city's history and, for the time being, ensures that the neighborhood never transcends the "transitional" stage it has been in for years.

The area takes its name from the old **Mission Dolores**, at 16th and Dolores ($3 suggested donation; daily 9am–4pm, until 4.30pm May–Oct), the oldest building to survive the 1906 earthquake and fire. Founded in 1776, it was the sixth in a series of missions built along the Pacific coast as Spain staked its claim to California; the graves of the Native Americans it tried to "civilize" can be seen in the cemetery next door, along with those of white pioneers. Go early in the morning to avoid the tour buses.

The heart of the Mission lies east of Mission Street between 16th and 24th streets. Here you'll absorb the district's original Latin flavor, with Nicaraguan, Salvadoran, Costa Rican and Mexican stores and restaurants, along with markets selling tropical fruits and *panaderias* baking traditional pastries.

In the last few years, however, the "in" crowd has descended on a strip of Valencia south of 16th, site of a new crop of hip bars, cafés and restaurants. The profusion of independent bookstores and thrift stores around here makes for heavenly browsing and the vicinity of 22nd Street has become a new gourmet-dining ghetto. Worth a visit is the **Levi Strauss & Co factory**, at 250 Valencia St, built after the original factories were destroyed in the 1906 earthquake. Though tours have been discontinued, you can admire the yellow brick facade of where the world's most famous jeans are made.

What really sets the Mission apart from other neighborhoods, though, are its **murals** – there are over two hundred in all. A brilliant tribute to local hero **Carlos Santana** adorns three buildings where 22nd Street meets South Van Ness, while every possible surface on **Balmy Alley**, between Folsom and Harrison off 24th Street, has been covered with murals depicting the political agonies of Central America. The mural organization, Precita Eyes, hosts weekend **mural tours** by foot, bike or bus ($10 to $50; ☎415/285-2287, Ⓦwww.precitaeyes.org). A visitor's center is also located at 2981 24th St.

The Castro

Progressive and celebratory, but also increasingly comfortable and wealthy, **the Castro** is the city's gay capital, providing a barometer for the state of the grown-up and sobered gay scene. Some people insist that this is still the wildest place in town, others reckon it's a shadow of its former self; all agree that things are not the same as ten or even five years ago, when a walk down the Castro would have had you gaping at the revelry. Most of the same bars and hangouts still stand, but these days they're host to an altogether different and more conservative breed. Cute shops and restaurants lend a young professional feel to the place. A visit to the district is a must if you're to get any idea of just what San Francisco is all about, though in terms of visible street life, the few blocks around Castro and Market streets contain about all there is to see.

Harvey Milk Plaza, by the Castro Muni station, is dedicated to the assassinated gay supervisor (or councilor), who owned a camera store in the Castro. The man who shot Milk and Mayor George Moscone, Dan White, was a disgruntled ex-supervisor who resigned in protest at their liberal policies. At the trial, his plea of temporary insanity caused by harmful additives in his fast food

Gay and lesbian San Francisco

San Francisco is still the undoubted **gay capital of the world**, but the gay scene hasn't had much to celebrate in the last few years and there's been a definite move from the outrageous to the mainstream. The increasing number of gay activists in public office have become more conservative in approach, if not in policy. However, gay parties, parades and street fairs still swing better than most. If you're here in June, you'll coincide with the Gay and Lesbian Film Festival, Gay Pride Week and the Gay Freedom Day Parade. Come October, the street fairs are in full swing and Halloween, for years the zenith of the Castro's social calendar, traditionally sees the beautiful of body and ballgown out in force – although in the last couple of years city officials have tried to move it to Civic Center, where there's better crowd control and safety.

Although the 1980s saw the flowering of a **lesbian** culture to rival the male 1970s upsurge, the bars for women have all but closed down (the exception being the Mission's *Lexington Club*, see p.1146) and the nightlife revolves around a handful of women's club nights. Lesbian culture is more in evidence in the bookstores.

The Sentinel, *Oblivion*, *The Bay Area Reporter* and *Gay Times* are all free **publications** listing events, services, clubs and bars, found in Castro bars and cafés. *On Our Backs* and *Girlfriends* are of particular use to lesbians. Gay men could not do better than purchase a copy of *Betty and Pansy's Severe Queer Review of San Francisco* ($11), available in gay bookstores – as is *The Lavender Pages*, a free telephone-cum-resource book. The AIDS/HIV Hotline (℡415/863-2437) provides counseling and advice. You'll find gay **accommodation** and **bars** listed on pp.1129 and 1145 respectively.

– the "Twinkie defense" – won him a sentence of five years' imprisonment for manslaughter. The gay community reacted angrily; the riots that followed were among the most violent San Francisco has ever witnessed, with protesters marching into City Hall, burning police cars as they went.

Before heading down Castro Street into the heart of the neighborhood, take a short walk to the former location of the **Names Project** at 2363A Market St, which sponsored the creation of "**The Quilt**" – a gargantuan blanket in which each panel measures six feet by three feet (the size of a grave site) and bears the name of a person lost to AIDS. Made by lovers, friends and families, the panels are stitched together and regularly tour the country and the world; it has been spread on the Mall in Washington, DC several times to dramatize the epidemic. The 54-ton Quilt and Names Project Foundation moved to a permanent home in Atlanta in 2001; San Francisco will continue to be recognized as the birthplace of the Quilt and efforts are underway to come up with the best way to mark the project's local history.

The junction of **Castro and 18th Street**, known as the "gayest four corners of the earth," marks the Castro's center, cluttered with bookstores, clothing stores, cafés and bars. The side streets offer a slightly more exclusive fare of exotic delicatessens, fine wines and fancy florists, and enticingly leafy residential territory.

Haight-Ashbury

The fame of **Haight–Ashbury**, two miles west of downtown San Francisco, far outstrips its size. No more than eight blocks in length, centered around the junction of Haight and Ashbury streets, "The Haight" was a run-down Victorian neighborhood until it transmogrified into the epitome of cool during the 1960s. Since then the area has become gentrified, but it retains a collection of radical bookstores, laid-back cafés, record stores and secondhand

The hippies

During the heady days of the massive "be-in" in Golden Gate Park in 1966 and the so-called "Summer of Love" the following year, no fewer than 75,000 pilgrims turned the busy little intersection of Haight-Ashbury into the mecca of alternative culture. Where Beat philosophy had emphasized self-indulgence, the **hippies**, on the face of it at least, stressed such concepts as "universal truth" and "cosmic awareness." Characters like Ken Kesey and his Merry Pranksters set a precedent of wild living and challenging authority. The use of drugs was seen as an integral – and positive – part of the movement. **LSD**, especially, which was not then illegal, was claimed as an avant-garde art form, pumped out in private laboratories and distributed by Timothy Leary and his supporters with a prescription – "Turn on, tune in, drop out" – that galvanized a generation into inactivity. Life in the Haight took on a theatrical quality: Pop Art found mass appeal, light shows became legion and dress flamboyant. The psychedelic music scene, spearheaded by the Grateful Dead, Jefferson Airplane and Janis Joplin, became a genuine force nationwide, and it wasn't long before kids from all over America started turning up in Haight-Ashbury for the free food, free drugs and free love. Money became a dirty word, the hip became "heads," and the rest of the world were "straights."

clothing emporia, not to mention a collection of characters still flying the counterculture's rather worn flag.

All there is to do in the Haight today is to stroll around what is one of the best areas in town to **shop**. It shouldn't take more than a couple of hours to update your record collection, dress yourself up and blow money on books and beer. The eastern end of Haight Street, around the crossing with Fillmore Street, is the funkiest corner of the district. Known as the **Lower Haight**, and for decades a primarily black neighborhood, it was reborn a few years ago – thanks to low rents – as a stomping ground for young hipsters. Though its trend appeal has since been surpassed by the Mission, it remains home to a small glut of DJ shops and a boisterous Brit-heavy population of club kids.

Golden Gate Park

In a city with an abundance of green space, **Golden Gate Park** stands out as not just the largest, but also the most beautiful, and safest, of its parks. Spreading three miles or so west from the Haight as far as the Pacific, it was constructed on what was then an area of wild sand dunes, buffeted by the spray from the ocean. Despite the throngs of joggers, polo players, roller-skaters, cyclists and strollers, it never seems to get overcrowded and you can always find a spot to be alone.

Of the park's several museums, two are under construction as we go to press. The **M.H. de Young Museum**, with its large and diverse range of painting and sculpture, is in the midst of a massive rehaul and not due to reopen until 2005. The similarly under-construction **Asian Art Museum** is moving locations entirely. It will re-open within the old Main Library space (next to the new Main Library in the Civic Center district) in the fall of 2002. It is considered one of the largest and most impressive museums devoted only to Asian art in the Western Hemisphere. (You can check on the status of its development at ⓦ www.asianart.org.) The **California Academy of Sciences** ($8.50, $2.50 discount with Muni transfer, free first Wed of month; summer daily 9am–6pm; rest of year daily 10am–5pm; ⓦ www.calacademy.org) opposite is a good place to amuse restless children, with its 30ft dinosaur skeleton, life-size replicas of elephant seals and other California wildlife, and live colony of black-footed penguins. Over 6,000 specimens of aquatic life can be viewed in its **Steinhart**

Aquarium (admission included in museum ticket; daily 10am–5pm), the best are the alligators and other reptiles lurking in a simulated swamp. Sky shows in its **Morrison Planetarium** cost $2.50 more. Slightly to the west is the **Japanese Tea Garden** ($3.50; daily 9am–6.30pm), dominated by a massive bronze Buddha. Bridges, footpaths, pools filled with carp, bonsai and cherry trees lend a peaceful feel. Busloads of tourists pour in; by far the best idea is to get here early for a breakfast of tea and fortune cookies in the tea house ($3.50 anytime).

The beautiful **National AIDS Memorial Grove** is in the eastern end of the park, near the tennis courts. Inaugurated in 1991, it is a pleasant and thought-provoking place to stroll. Tours take place Thursdays from 9.30am to 12.30pm (☎415/750-8340, ⊛ www.aidsmemorial.org).

The Golden Gate Bridge and beyond

The orange towers of the **Golden Gate Bridge**, perhaps the best-loved symbol of San Francisco, are visible from almost every high point in the city. The bridge, which spans 4200ft, had taken only 52 months to design and build when it was opened in 1937. Some quarter of a million people turned up for a sunrise party to celebrate its fiftieth anniversary in 1987; the winds were strong and the bridge buckled, but fortunately did not break. **Driving** across is a real thrill, racing under the towers, while the half-hour **walk** across allows you to take in its enormous size and absorb the views. It's also a favorite with the suicidal – in a typical year dozens jump to their deaths. Those jumping are said to hit the water at a speedy 80mph – few have survived the leap.

The **Fort Point National Historic Site** beneath the bridge gives a good sense of the place as the westernmost outpost of the nation. This brick fortress, built in the 1850s, has a dramatic site, the surf pounding away beneath the great span of the bridge high above – a view made famous by Kim Novak's suicide attempt in Alfred Hitchcock's *Vertigo*. A small **museum** (Thurs–Mon 10am–5pm; free) inside the fort displays some rusty old cannons and artillery.

San Francisco's best waters are to be found at the **beaches** at the tip of the peninsula, but beach culture doesn't exist here the way it does in southern California. Dangerous riptides and excruciatingly cold water make it impossible to swim with any confidence, and nude sunbathing is about as adventurous as things get.

Inland, **Lincoln Park**, at 34th Avenue and Clement Street, primarily an unusually dramatic golf course, offers striking views of the Marin headlands and is home to the remote, white-pillared **California Palace of the Legion of Honor** ($8, $2.50 off with Muni transfer, free every Tues, surcharge for special exhibitions; daily except Mon 9.30am–5pm; ⊛ www.legionofhonor.org). Re-opened in late 1995 after extensive renovation, the museum is arguably San Francisco's best and most staggeringly majestic building. Its isolated, windswept location, high on a bluff overlooking the ocean, is unsurpassably romantic, and deters the hordes that swarm the MoMA and the museums in the park. The emphasis is on fine art, with the **Renaissance** represented by the works of Titian and El Greco, hung in spacious, high-ceilinged, well-lit marble halls. Some great canvases by Rembrandt and Hals, as well as Rubens' magnificent *Tribute Money*, are highlights of the seventeenth-century **Dutch** and **Flemish** collection. The **Impressionist** and **Post-Impressionist** galleries contain works by Courbet, Manet, Monet, Renoir, Degas and Cézanne. Several galleries are devoted to **Rodin** sculptures – bronze, porcelain and stone pieces including *The Athlete*, *Fugit Amor* and a small cast of *The Kiss*. A highlight of the museum, *The Thinker*, greets visitors in the museum's front courtyard.

Eating

With well over three thousand restaurants crammed onto the small peninsula, and scores of bars and cafés open all day, **eating** in San Francisco is never difficult. Eating is *the* culture in this town, with excellent food often at modest prices. Be warned, though – San Francisco closes early, and you'll be struggling to get served much after 10pm. **Mexican** food is big in the Mission, **Italian** places abound in North Beach, and, of course, Chinatown naturally has plenty of **Chinese**, while **Japan Center** – the heart of Japantown, located at Post between Geary, Laguna and Fillmore, a mile west of Union Square – boasts a few fine Japanese places. In health–conscious San Francisco you'll find **vegetarian** entrees on every menu and quite a few entirely vegetarian restaurants. With the vineyards of Napa and Sonoma Valley on the city's doorstep, quality **wines** have a high profile in most San Francisco restaurants. State law prohibits **smoking** in all restaurants, cafés and bars, as evidenced by crowds of people puffing illicitly on the pavements.

Downtown

Aqua 252 California St ℡415/956-9662. The city's best seafood restaurant (and some say, best restaurant, period) with an amazing wine list. Open for lunch and dinner, make reservations and bring your credit card: a meal here won't be cheap. Entrees start around $30.

Boulevard 1 Mission St ℡415/543-6084. Outstanding French/California cuisine in this chic brasserie catering to a smart crowd. Prices keep it a special occasion for most. Reservations strongly recommended.

Café Claude 7 Claude Lane, Union Square ℡415/392-3505. More than any of the other imitations in town, the great old furnishings of this one make it *feel* like Paris. A young, loose crowd listens to jazz with their $20 dinners.

Farallon 450 Post St, Union Square ℡415/956-6969. Sumptuously styled as an undersea grotto, serving highly creative seafood dishes in small portions. Definitely worth a splurge if you're into elegant dining experiences.

House of Nanking 919 Kearny St ℡415/421-1429. One of the city's most popular Chinese restaurants, despite the lack of decor and elbow room. You wait ages for a table, but the inexpensive food doesn't disappoint.

Plouf 40 Belden Place, off Bush between Kearny and Montgomery ℡415/986-6491. Convivial South-of-France seafood bistro, with sidewalk seating in good weather. The garlicky mussels – the house specialty – are the best in the city.

Tadich Grill 240 California St ℡415/391-2373. The oldest restaurant in California, and a wood-paneled San Francisco institution. Grilled fresh seafood and excellent desserts.

The Marina, Embarcadero, Fisherman's Wharf, North Beach and Chinatown

Café Marimba 2317 Chestnut St ℡415/776-1506. Not a bad choice if you're down in the Marina district, *Marimba* tries to replicate authentic

---

Late-night eating

For that midnight snack or 3am binge, check out the following **24-hour** dependables.

Allstar Donuts 2095 Chestnut St at Steiner, Marina (℡415/441-9270).

Bagdad Café 2295 Market St at 16th, Castro (℡415/621-4434).

Denny's 1700 Post St at Webster, Japantown (℡415/563-1400) and 495 Beach St at Jones, Fisherman's Wharf (℡415/776-3700)

International House of Pancakes 2299 Lombard St at Pierce, Marina (℡415/921-4004).

Lori's Diner 336 Mason St at Geary and O'Farrell, Downtown (℡415/392-8646).

Orphan Andy's 3991 17th St at Market and Castro, Castro (℡415/864-9795).

Pine Crest 401 Geary St at Mason, Downtown (℡415/885-6407).

Sparky's 242 Church St, Castro (℡415/626-8666).

Mexican regional cuisine, achieving excellent salsas and moles. Packed with young professionals.

Capp's Corner 1600 Powell St ☎415/989-2589. Funky, family-style Italian restaurant in North Beach, with a fashionable clientele lining up for the big portions.

Empress of China 838 Grant Ave ☎415/434-1345. The poshest Chinese place in town. An incredible selection of dishes and amazing views over North Beach. $13 to 25 for a main course.

Fior d'Italia 601 Union St ☎415/986-1886. This is where to go when you're tired of trendy Italian cooking with attitude and just want the real thing. Good old-timer scene at the bar.

Gaylord Ghirardelli Square, 900 North Point, Fisherman's Wharf ☎415/771-8822. The best of San Francisco's very few Indian restaurants. Expect to pay around $15 for a main course.

Greens Building A, Fort Mason Center, Fort Mason ☎415/771-6222. The city's only Zen Buddhist restaurant, with delicious macrobiotic and vegetarian food, plus a gorgeous view of the bay. Book ahead; $38 for a five-course dinner.

Little Joe's 523 Broadway ☎415/433-4343. Always a line for tables, but worth it for the low-cost, enormous portions of well-cooked food in this North Beach institution.

Maye's Oyster House 1233 Polk St ☎415/474-7674. One of the oldest restaurants in town still serves classic seafood dishes such as Oysters Rockefeller, along with hearty Italian dishes. Open for dinner only.

Rose Pistola 532 Columbus ☎415/399-0499. A staple of North Beach's "Cal-Ital" dining scene, headed by one of the city's hottest chefs. Menu selections include a range of eclectic tapas and thin-crust pizzas that won't break the bank.

Sam Wo 813 Washington St ☎415/982-0596. The space is unpleasantly cramped, the food is mediocre and the service downright unpleasant. So why bother? It's open late and back in the Fifties this was the spot Jack, Allen and the rest of the Beats used to come when they were too wired to go to bed.

Yank Sing 427 Battery St ☎415/781-1111. A cavernous spot that regularly tops locals' list for the best dim sum in the city. Despite being routinely packed during lunch hours, the waitstaff can almost always find a spot for you in the seemingly endless warren of dining rooms. You might need their help to get out, as well.

Yuet Lee 1300 Stockton St ☎415/982-6020. Cheap and cheerful Chinese restaurant with a good seafood menu and enthusiastic diners. Surprisingly good food served as late as 3am. Closed Tuesdays.

Zinzino 2355 Chestnut St ☎415/346-6623. Lively Marina bistro done out like a Roman piazza, combining tasty Italian cuisine – try the wild mushroom lasagne – with San Francisco pizzazz.

Civic Center, Tenderloin, SoMa and the Mission

Asia SF 201 9th St ☎415/255-2742. More of an "experience" than a restaurant, this only-in-San Francisco spot features an all-drag-queen staff who put on a nightly revue. Though it can't compete with the show, the food's not half bad, either.

Café Delle Stelle 395 Hayes St ☎415/252-1110. Serving strong renditions of the hearty cooking of northern Italy, with an emphasis on rich flavors and roasted meats.

Delfina 3621 18th St ☎415/552-4055. Friendly service and fantastic Italian cooking for $15 an entree. Well loved by locals, this tiny spot is packed on a nightly basis, so call ahead.

Harveys 1582 Folsom St ☎415/626-1985. Rowdy restaurant, where punky waiting staff serve up burgers, sandwiches and several vegetarian options for less than $10.

La Rondalla 901 Valencia St ☎415/647-7474. Lively, late-night Mission Mexican festooned in Christmas lights. Killer margaritas and good live mariachi music. Open till 3am. Doesn't accept credit cards.

La Taqueria 2889 Mission St ☎415/285-7117. The best place in town for a taco. Slightly pricier than average, it still consistently packs in a crowd by simply focusing on the basics and getting them right every time.

Manora's Thai Cuisine 1600 Folsom St ☎415/861-6224. Massively popular: you may have to wait, but it's worth it for light, spicy and fragrant Thai dishes at around $7 each.

Millennium 246 McAllister St in the *Abigail Hotel* ☎415/487-9800. You'd swear it couldn't be done, but this restaurant has managed to make delicious meals for vegans and is consistently rated as one of the best restaurants around. Stylish decor inside.

Pancho Villa 3071 16th St ☎415/864-8840. Though locals tend to scoff at the largely out-of-neighborhood clientele, the Mexican food here is consistently fresh and flavorful. Open til midnight.

Shalimar 532 Jones St ☎415/982-0333. A happy find in the downtrodden Tenderloin, this divey spot serves delicious, cheap Indian food, all of it made to order before your eyes, so you know it's fresh.

Slanted Door 584 Valencia St ☎415/861-8032. One of the trendiest restaurants in town, serving upscale Vietnamese to customers thankful for having successfully made reservations.

Suppenküche 601 Hayes St ☎415/252-9289. Satisfying and delicious German cooking near Civic Center in a loud, lively bar/restaurant decked out like a traditional Bavarian pub. Don't miss the potato pancakes appetizer – it's enough alone for a light supper.

Truly Mediterranean 3109 16th St ☎415/252-7482. Fast-threatening to overtake the beloved burrito as the locals' favorite portable dinner item, this hole-in-the-wall's version of the falafel comes wrapped in thin, crispy bread. A second location can be found at 1724 Haight St.

Tulan 8 6th St ☎415/626-0927. If you can brave the seedy Tenderloin neighborhood, you can stuff your face with fresh Vietnamese food for $4. Open daytime only.

Vicolo 20 Ivy St, off Franklin ☎415/863-2382. Superlative pizza in a crowded, café-like place in Hayes Valley, near Civic Center.

Zuni Café 1658 Market St ☎415/552-2522. Chic place to be and be seen, with California cuisine portions as minimal as the decor for around $35 with wine. The staff can be a bit snooty.

The Castro, Haight-Ashbury and Japantown

Axum Café 698 Haight St ☎415/252-7912. Neighborhood coffee shop where you can chow down on well-made Ethiopian specialties in a relaxed, homey atmosphere.

Cha Cha Cha 1805 Haight St ☎415/386-5758. Bright, colorful, noisy Cuban restaurant that serves up delicious dishes and great cocktails at reasonable prices.

Chow 215 Church St ☎415/552-2469. New eatery serving wonderful, lovingly made, eclectic Italian dishes on the cheap – a real find. Entrees $8 and under.

Citrus Club 1790 Haight St ☎415/387-6366. Enormous helpings of Pan-Asian noodles with veggies and a choice of meats and seafood. Home-

brewed beer and sake martinis round out a meal. Come early and plan on standing in line at this popular and inexpensive spot.

Eos Restaurant & Wine Bar 901 Cole St ☎415/566-3063. The best place to sip a glass of wine and enjoy Euro-Asian inspired cuisine. The restaurant is very pricey, so stick to the wine bar for a similar experience at a lower price. Come early to get a seat at the bar.

Spaghetti Western 576 Haight St ☎415/864-8461. Best breakfasts in town and a lively Lower Haight crowd to look at while you chow down.

Thep-Phanom 400 Waller St ☎415/431-2526. Delicate decor and beautifully prepared Thai dishes in the Lower Haight. Only $8 for a main course, but expect to wait for a table.

Yoshida-Ya 2909 Webster St ☎415/346-3431. Genuine sushi bar; kick off your shoes and eat at low tables on futon floors. Expect to pay around $25 a head, with a few drinks.

The Sunset and Richmond

Beach Chalet 1000 Great Hwy ☎415/386-8439. A combination brewpub and restaurant located in a pretty WPA-era building, with Lucien Labaudt murals and mosaics, along the windy stretches of Ocean Beach.

Coriya Hot Pot City 852 Clement St ☎415/387-7888. Also in Richmond, this popular Taiwanese restaurant lets you load up all you can eat and cook it yourself at the table. Go early to grab a table.

Ebisu 1283 9th Ave ☎415/566-1770. Generally considered the best sushi in town. They don't take reservations and standing out in the evening breeze can get more than chilly, but the freshness of the fish should more than compensate.

Kabuto Sushi 5116 Geary Blvd ☎415/752-5652. Richmond favorite where the eccentric owner prepares sushi at a manic pace. Perfect for sitting at the bar and picking.

Nightlife and entertainment

Compared to many US cities, where you need money and attitude in equal measure, San Francisco's **nightlife** scene demands little of either. It is not unusual for restaurants to provide live music and you can often eat and be entertained for no extra cost. This is no 24-hour city, and the approach to socializing is often surprisingly low-key, with little of the pandering to fads and fashions that goes on in New York or LA. For $30 you can get a decent night out, including cover charge and a few drinks. Always have your ID with you, otherwise you cannot get past the bouncers at all clubs and music venues. Though smoking is technically illegal in all bars and clubs, the law is routinely flouted by locals willing to risk a ticket.

The Sunday *Chronicle*'s "Pink Pages" supplement, along with the free weekly *Bay Guardian* or the *San Francisco Weekly*, are the best sources of **listings**. Ticketmaster (☎415/421-8497, ⓦwww.ticketmaster.com) is the major **ticket** agency, with outlets in Tower Records and Rite Aid stores. Tickets.com (☎415/478-2277, ⓦwww.tickets.com) is also worth a try.

Bars

Since its lawless, boomtown days, San Francisco has been a **drinking** town. Even as the rest of California cleans up its act, San Franciscans continue to indulge; the city's bars vary from seedy late-night dives to rooftop piano lounges touting glittering views.

Backflip *Phoenix Hotel*, 601 Eddy St, Tenderloin ☎415/771-3547. Fantastically retro bar adjacent to the hotel's pool patio. Black-vinyl-clad waitstaff, entirely blue decor and a menagerie of bizarre and lively patrons. To write home about.

Brainwash 1122 Folsom St, SoMa ☎415/861-FOOD. Great idea – café/bar and laundromat where you can have breakfast and beer while you do your washing. Popular with the young and novelty-conscious.

Edinburgh Castle 950 Geary St, Tenderloin ☎415/885-4074. The best place in the city for British-style pints, fish and chips (still wrapped in newspaper) and a game of darts. The bar was prominently featured in the cult film, *So I Married an Axe-Murderer*.

Gordon Biersch Brewery 2 Harrison St, Embarcadero ☎415/243-8246. Bayfront microbrewery in a converted coffee warehouse. Great selection of beers pulls in a downtown twenty-something crowd.

Harry Denton's Starlight Room top floor, *Sir Francis Drake Hotel*, 450 Powell St, downtown ☎415/395-8595. Join the dressed-up, grown-up, moneyed crowd and drink martinis to live-jazz accompaniment.

Occidental Grill 56 Belden Place, downtown ☎415/834-0484. Re-opened in a new location due to a fire, this Barbary Coast-style den is supposedly the birthplace of the martini, though that's open to more than some debate. However, they certainly do make a mean one. Their second business, the Occidental Cigar Club, is around the corner at 471 Pine St.

Red Room 827 Sutter St, Tenderloin ☎415/346-7666. Like the name implies, everything – including the walls, the furniture, the glasses and many of the drinks – is red in this popular faux-dive.

The Tonga Room basement of the *Fairmont*, 950 Mason St, Nob Hill ☎415/772-5278. A must for fans of the ludicrous or just the very drunk. It's decked out like a Polynesian village, complete with a pond and simulated rainstorms, and a grass-skirted band plays terrible jazz and pop covers from a raft in the middle of the water. Cover $3 after 8pm, outrageously priced cocktails, but worth every cent.

Tosca Café 242 Columbus St, North Beach ☎415/391-1244. A beautiful old bar with tiled floors, bow-tied bartenders and opera as the soundtrack. Come early as the bass from the nightclub upstairs can be bothersome.

The Up & Down Club 1151 Folsom St, SoMa ☎415/626-2388. This small, popular split-level club-cum-bar has earned a solid reputation for first-rate drinks and live music.

Vesuvio's 255 Columbus St, North Beach ☎415/362-3370. Legendary Beat haunt in the 1950s, next to City Lights Bookstore. Still draws an arty, friendly crowd who prop up the bar into the small hours.

Zeitgeist 199 Valencia, the Mission ☎415/255-7505. A biker bar largely populated with nonmotorized bicycle messengers. A large patio makes it a haven for smokers.

Gay and lesbian bars

San Francisco's **gay and lesbian bars** are many and varied, ranging from cozy cocktail lounges to no-holds-barred leather-and-chain hangouts. The scene may no longer be quite as wild as its reputation would have you believe, but at its best it can still be hard to beat.

Badlands 4121 18th St ☎415/626-9320. A Western-style bar with a small dance floor and happy hour every weeknight (4–7pm). Very popular and recently re-vamped.

Café Flore 2298 Market St ☎415/621-8579. Very much the "in" spot before dark. Attractive café with leafy outdoor area and no shortage of people sizing each other up.

Eagle Tavern 398 12th St ☎415/626-0880. Legendary SoMa biker bar. Not for wimps.

Women's San Francisco

The flip side of San Francisco's gay revolution has in some women's circles led to a separatist culture, and women's resources and services are sometimes lumped together under the lesbian category. While this may be no bad thing, it can be hard to tell which organizations exist irrespective of sexuality. Don't let this stop you checking out anything that sounds interesting; nobody is going to refuse you entry or help if you're not a lesbian.

Contacts and resources

Lyon-Martin Women's Health Services 1748 Market St at Valencia, Suite 201 (℡415/565-7667). Low-cost health care and referral service. Drop-in hours Mon–Fri from 8.30am to 5pm; appointments available at other times.

Osento Bathhouse 955 Valencia St (℡415/282-6333). More than a bathhouse, this is the heart of San Francisco's women's community. Girls of all shapes, sizes, colors and persuasions. Open 1pm–1am.

San Francisco Women Against Rape (℡415/647-7273 or 647-RAPE). 24-hour crisis line based within the Women's Building.

Women's Building 3543 18th St (℡415/431-1180). Central stop in the Mission for women's art and political events. A great place to get information – the women who staff the building are happy to deal with the most obscure of inquiries.

Esta Noche 3079 16th St ℡415/861-5757. Gay discomania Latin-style. Young men and their admirers dance to a hi-NRG disco beat.

Harvey's 500 Castro St ℡415/431-4278. A central and convivial gay bar in The Castro drawing a friendly, community-oriented mixed gay and lesbian crowd. Serves food, too.

Hole in the Wall 289 8th St ℡415/431-HOWL. A biker and rock club that deliberately recalls the days when gay bars hid in dark alleys. Beware: the clientele can occasionally be found completely nude. However, it's all in good fun (and quite popular) but occasionally a little rough.

Lexington Club 3464 19th St at Lexington ℡415/863-2052. The first neighborhood bar for women in a long time, packed with lesbians of all stripes and their male friends. Good jukebox.

Martunis 4 Valencia St at Market ℡415/241-0205. A swank place in which to drink martinis and sing show tunes around the piano, from 9pm on.

Midnight Sun 4067 18th St ℡415/861-4186. Young, white boys dressed to the nines and cruising like maniacs in this noisy Castro video bar.

The Mint 1942 Market St ℡415/626-4726. The best karaoke bar in the city, packed with a boisterous, thirtysomething crowd of songsters.

Rawhide 280 7th St ℡415/820-1621. If men in chaps are your scene, look no further than this dimly lit SoMa bar/dance club that plays country-and-western and bluegrass favorites. A legendary SF venue.

The Stud 399 9th St ℡415/252-7883. An oldie but a goodie. A favorite gay dancing spot with lesbian nights on certain days. Energetic, uninhibited dancing and good times.

Live music: rock, jazz and folk

San Francisco's **music scene** reflects the character of the city: laid-back, eclectic and not a little nostalgic. The options for catching live music are wide and the scene is definitely on the up and up, with the city regularly spawning good young bands. Check the *San Francisco Bay Guardian* and *SF Weekly* free weeklies, and the *San Francisco Chronicle*, for listings.

Bimbo's 365 Club 1025 Columbus Ave ℡415/474-0365. Classy lounge with tableside drink service (2 minimum) and a varied high quality menu of music styles from jazz to ska.

Biscuits & Blues 401 Mason St ℡415/292-2583. Lively blues supper club with inexpensive Southern cuisine and hot blues acts nightly. Reservations recommended for dinner shows.

Blue Lamp 561 Geary St ℡415/885-1464.

Quintessential dive close to downtown that features good acoustic acts (blues & jazz).

Boom Boom Room 1601 Fillmore St ℡415/673-8000, ⓦ www.boomboomblues.com. Once owned by the late blues legend John Lee Hooker, this small, intimate bar delivers straight-ahead jazz or classic blues acts nightly; $3 cover weekdays and $7-$10 weekends.

Bottom of the Hill 1233 17th St ℡415/621-4455.

Potrero Hill hangout for rock & country music, live seven nights a week, drawing a late-twenty- to thirtysomething crowd. There's an outdoor all-you-can-eat barbecue on the patio Sun. Cover for shows $4–7.

Bruno's 2389 Mission St ☎ 415/648-7701. Swank jazz and swing bar/restaurant pulling the kind of attractive young things who are titillated to be in the Mission's seedy section. Cover about $7.

Butterfly 1710 Mission St ☎ 415/864-5575. A sophisticated jazz and dining spot, with occasional poetry and performance art pieces. The food is very good (served till 1am), but come for the jazz.

Café du Nord 2170 Market St ☎ 415/861-5016. This popular bar is quite the place to experience live swing, jazz, Latin and blues over good food, or just have a beer and shoot some pool.

Elbo Room 647 Valencia St ☎ 415/552-7788. The birthplace of acid jazz, a smoothed out instrumental sound that provides upbeat background music for an intense pick-up scene.

The Fillmore 1805 Geary at Fillmore ☎ 415/346-6000, ⓦ www.thefillmore.com. The revitalization of a San Francisco institution, the Fillmore features big and little acts alike, for about $20–$25 a pop. A great place to imagine what it was all like in the 1960s.

Great American Music Hall 859 O'Farrell ☎ 415/885-0750. Historic former bordello and saloon that has been converted into a popular venue for rock, blues, and world music acts.

Lou's Pier 47 300 Jefferson St ☎ 415/771-0377. An old favorite, and about the only decent place on the Wharf. Lou's blues pulls a good crowd most nights.

Paradise Lounge 308 11th St ☎ 415/861-6906. Good SoMa venue to see up-and-coming rock bands (usually three per night), or take a break for a game of pool upstairs.

The Saloon 1232 Grant St ☎ 415/989-7666. North Beach's best spot for R&B. Always packed, it creaks nightly as blues bands and crowds of enthusiastic dancers do their thing.

Tongue & Groove 2513 Van Ness Ave ☎ 415/928-0404. Local bands ranging from rock and funk to Seventies retro and alternative. Cover $4–8.

Clubbing

While **clubbing** in San Francisco may not have the feverish following of other cities, the clubs that exist are encouragingly inexpensive, and you can leave your attitude at home. A recent spate of police raids has put something of a damper on the scene and forced several popular spaces to shut down. But with a population as young and hip as this city's, odds are it will be impossible to keep a good party down for long. The greatest concentration of clubs is in **SoMa** and, recently, the **Mission**. You must bring your ID to get in to all clubs; most require you to be at least 21 except for a few 18-and-over clubs. Expect to pay a cover charge ranging anywhere from $3 to $7 and up to $15 for the huge dance caverns like *Ten15*.

Club Townsend 177 Townsend St ☎ 415/974-1156. Site of long-running gay and lesbian dance parties (Club Q for women, Club Universe and Pleasuredome for men) on the first Fri of every month, Sat and Sun respectively. Call their information line for the latest events.

DNA Lounge 375 11th St ☎ 415/626-1409. The music changes nightly, but the young hipsters are the same. Large dance floor downstairs, comfy sofas in the mezzanine.

El Rio 3158 Mission St ☎ 415/282-3325. Mixed crowds gather for changing nightly entertainment and some great giveaways, like oysters on the half-shell on a Friday. The popular live salsa on summer Sun afternoons draws a predominantly female crowd.

EndUp 401 6th St at Harrison ☎ 415/357-0827. Long after other places close, this is where everyone ends up. Certain nights attract gay or lesbian crowds like Girl Spot (Sat) and Fag (Fri). Good for the hardcore party animal – especially the all-day,

all-night Sunday T-dance beginning at 5am.

Justice League 628 Divisadero St ☎ 415/289-2038, ⓦ www.justiceleaguelive.com. Hosting top-notch hip-hop and salsa acts, in addition to regular stints by adventurous DJs and poetry slams.

The Make-Out Room 3225 22nd St at Mission ☎ 415/647-2888. The hipster's meeting place of choice featuring DJs just about every night. Tuesdays and Fridays are free starting at 10pm; otherwise plan on a $5–10 cover.

Nickie's 460 Haight St ☎ 415/621-6508. This place rocks every night. Whether it's Grateful Dead night, African, Latin or Seventies funk, *Nickie's* is for the very lively.

Sound Factory 525 Harrison St ☎ 415/979-8686. Huge multilevel 18-and-over place with three rooms for simultaneous house, hip-hop and Latin dance parties.

Ten15 1015 Folsom ☎ 415/385-1015. Another huge club for serious sweating: 6 rooms with different music in each, especially deep jungle

house, and cool laser light shows. You may have to wait in a long line Thurs–Sat.
330 Ritch 330 Ritch St ☎415/541-9574. Low-ceilinged and crowded with slender SoMa types.

Serves food until 10pm, then DJs spin funk, soul, disco and British pop music on different nights. Live jazz on Satuday and a live swing band and free swing lessons on Wednesday.

Classical music, opera and dance

Though the San Francisco arts scene has a reputation for provincialism, this is the only city on the west coast to boast its own professional **symphony**, **ballet** and **opera** companies. These companies rely entirely on private contributions for their survival and low-priced tickets are rare, if not nonexistent. Look out in summer for the **free concerts in Stern Grove** (at 19th Avenue and Sloat Boulevard), where the symphony, opera and ballet give open-air performances for ten successive Sundays (starting in June). Last-minute standing room tickets provide a cheaper option for those on a budget.

The **San Francisco Opera Association** (ticket and schedule information ☎415/864-3330) has been performing in the opulent **War Memorial Opera House**, 301 Van Ness Ave at Grove, since the building opened in 1932, pulling in big names like Placido Domingo and Kiri Te Kanawa on a regular basis. Its main season runs from the end of September for thirteen weeks, and its opening night is one of the principal social events on the west coast. Also housed here is the **San Francisco Ballet** (☎415/865-2000), whose regular season starts in February, while performances of *The Nutcracker* occur during the Christmas season.

The **Louise M. Davies Symphony Hall**, 201 Van Ness Ave (☎415/864-6000), is the permanent home of the San Francisco Symphony, hosting a year-round season of classical music and sometimes performances by other, often offbeat musical and touring groups.

Theater

The majority of the **theaters** in downtown's Theater District are not especially innovative, but tickets are reasonably inexpensive – up to $20 a seat – and there's usually good availability. The TIX Bay Area ticket booth in Union Square (Tues–Thurs 11am–6pm, Fri & Sat 11am–7pm; ☎415/433-7827) regularly has day-of-performance tickets for half price and full-price advance sales. It's also an outlet for Ticketmaster and sells Muni tickets.

American Conservatory Theater Geary Theater, 415 Geary St ☎415/749-2228. The Tony award-winning ACT puts on eight major plays each season in the city's best serious theater venue.

Beach Blanket Babylon Club Fugazi, 678 Green St ☎415/421-4222. This legendary musical spoof, filled with celebrity impersonations and towering hats, has been running since 1974. Highly recommended, but remember to book in advance.

Exit Theatre 156 Eddy St ☎415/673-3847. Avant-garde and experimental, the Exit is the place to go when you've wearied of the Broadway retreads.

Golden Gate Theater 1 Taylor St ☎415/551-2000. San Francisco's most elegant theater (in its least elegant neighborhood), with marble flooring, Rococo ceilings and gilt trimmings. A pity the program doesn't live up to the surroundings – generally a mainstream diet of touring musicals.

Lorraine Hansberry Theater 620 Sutter St ☎415/474-8800. The mainstay of African-American theater in San Francisco. Traditional theater as well as contemporary political pieces and jazz/blues musical revues.

The Magic Theater Fort Mason Center, Building D ☎415/441-8001. Specializes in contemporary American playwrights and emerging new talent: Sam Shepard premieres his work here.

Theatre Rhinoceros 2926 16th St ☎415/861-5079. San Francisco's leading gay theater group. Lighter, humorous productions, as well as those that confront gay issues.

Theatre on the Square 450 Post St ☎415/433-9500. Converted Gothic theater with drama, musicals, comedy and mainstream theater pieces. San Francisco's main fringe venue.

Comedy Clubs

Bay Area Theatresports Bayfront Theatre, Bldg B, Third floor, Fort Mason Center (Marina Blvd at Buchanan St) ☎415/474-6776. An acting-based improv group that can be hilariously spontaneous. Definitely a less predictable comedy night out than at your average club.

Cobb's Comedy Club *The Cannery*, 2801 Leavenworth St ☎415/928-4320. Pricey and usually full of tourists, but the standard of the acts is fairly consistent. Worth a look if everything else is booked up.

Punchline Comedy Club 444 Battery St ☎415/397-7573. Frontrunner of the city's "polished" cabaret venues. Intimate, smoky feel; ideal for downing expensive cocktails and laughing your head off. The bigger names in the world of stand-up perform here, and it's always packed.

Shopping

While boasting the large-scale facilities and international names you'd expect in a major city, San Francisco's shopping scene is low-key and unpretentious. This means prices are slightly lower, and shopping here is a pleasant, relatively stress-free activity.

If you want to run the gauntlet of designer labels, or just watch the style brigade consume, **Union Square** is the place to be. The heart of the city's shopping territory, it has a good selection of big-name and chic stores – Neiman Marcus, whose prices have earned it the nickname "Needless Markup," Nordstrom, Saks Fifth Avenue, Gump's and a completely redesigned Macy's – worth a few hours if you're into serious dollar-dropping.

SoMa is home to the new Sony Metreon mall at Fourth Street and Mission, a form of "shopper-tainment" with its technology-driven stores and state-of-the-art movieplex.

Books

The Booksmith 1644 Haight St ☎415/863-8688. Good general Haight-Ashbury bookstore with an excellent stock of countercultural titles.

Borders Books and Music 400 Post St ☎415/399-1633. Massive, emporium-style chain stocking over 160,000 book titles as well as a music department with over 60,000 choices. It's a day's work getting through this lot, but there's a café within the store to refresh yourself.

Bound Together Book Collective 1369 Haight St ☎415/431-8355. Haight-Ashbury store specializing in radical and progressive publications.

City Lights Bookstore 261 Columbus Ave ☎415/362-8193. America's first paperback bookstore, and still San Francisco's best. The range of titles includes house publications.

A Different Light 489 Castro St ☎415/431-0891. Well-stocked and diverse gay bookstore.

Good Vibrations 1210 Valencia St ☎415/974-8980. A comfortable, decidedly unsleazy place to buy sex books and erotica, specializing in women's sexuality. Also sells a bewildering array of sex toys, condoms and the like.

Green Apple Books & Music 506 Clement ☎415/387-2272. In the heart of the Richmond district, this relaxed and welcoming store features new and used books (rare out-of-print volumes as well as standards) plus a well-priced selection of CDs and vinyl recordings.

Modern Times 888 Valencia St ☎415/282-9246. Alternative community bookstore in the Mission. Good selection of Latin American literature, women's issues and hard-to-find contemporary cultural studies.

Rand McNally 595 Market St at 2nd ☎415/777-3131. Travel guides, maps and paraphernalia for the person on the move.

Stacey's Booksellers 581 Market St ☎415/421-4687. A big store with a big selection, yet dedicated to independent booksellers and the community. The store sponsors author events and can order anything that you can't find yourself. Also features a large selection of magazines.

Music

Amoeba Music 1855 Haight St ☎415/831-1200. A massive, independent record and CD store with one of the largest and best used collections you'll ever find (over one million new and used). They also host live performances within the store.

Aquarius Records 1055 Valencia St ☎415/647-2272. Small neighborhood store with friendly, knowledgeable staff and a good range of indie rock, jazz, and things experimental and obscure.
CD & Record Rack 3897 18th St ☎415/552-4990. Castro emporium with a brilliant selection of dance music including a few 1970s 12-inch singles.
Jack's Record Cellar 254 Scott St ☎415/431-3047. The city's best source for American roots music – R&B, jazz, country and rock'n'roll – especially on LP.
Mission Music Center 2653 Mission St ☎415/648-1788. Mission store selling music from all over the continent, but especially South America.
Rooky Ricardo's 448 Haight St ☎415/864-7526. Secondhand store specializing in soul, funk and jazz from the Fifties to the Seventies. Vinyl only.
Streetlight Records 3979 24th St ☎415/282-3550. A great selection of used records, tapes and CDs. The perfect opportunity to beef up your collection on the cheap.
Virgin Megastore 2 Stockton at Market ☎415/397-4525. Three floors of books, videos and music.

Sports in San Francisco

San Francisco's dedication to its **professional sports** teams can verge on the obsessive. Tickets for the big events can sell out, but it's usually possible to show up on the day, and it needn't cost all that much: an outfield seat to watch baseball from the "bleachers" goes for around $7, with seats closer in topping the scale at around $15. The Oakland team runs a promotion called "Buck Days" when select seats and all hot dogs are $1 on Wednesdays. Advance tickets for all Bay Area sports events are available through the Ticketmaster charge-by-phone ticket service (☎415/421-TIXS, ⓦwww.ticketmaster.com), or through the teams' headquarters.

Baseball: The **Oakland A's** play at the usually sunny Oakland (aka Network Associates) Coliseum (☎510/638-0500), which has a BART stop in front. The **San Francisco Giants** play at Pac Bell Park, where home runs sometimes splash into the bay (☎415/972-2000). There are 500 tickets made available two-and-a-half hours before game time and long lines form early and often. Walk up to the ticket booths at 24 Willie Mays Plaza, near Third and King, to get them.

Football: The **San Francisco 49ers**, many-time Super Bowl champions, also play at 3Com Park, where you may have to pay as much as $100 (☎415/656-4900), and the **Oakland Raiders**, blue-collar heroes, bash heads at the Oakland Coliseum (☎1-800/949-2626).

Basketball: The reliably awful **Golden State Warriors** play at newly renovated Oakland Arena (☎1-888/479-4667).

Ice hockey: The **San Jose Sharks** (☎408/287-7070) play at their own arena in San Jose.

Soccer: The **San Jose Earthquakes** (☎408/260-6300, ⓦwww.sjearthquakes.com), major league soccer champs in 2001, draw large crowds at San Jose State's Spartan Stadium. Women's soccer, also played at Spartan Stadium, is represented by the **Bay Area CyberRays** (☎408/535-0980, ⓦwww.bayareacyberrays.com), who won the WUSA championship in 2001, the first year of the league's inception.

Stanford Stadium, scene of six matches in soccer's **1994 World Cup**, is on the campus of Stanford University, 27 miles south of San Francisco and not far north of San Jose. The Stanford Cardinal football team plays here during the fall.

The Bay Area

Of the six million people who make their home in the vicinity of San Francisco, only a lucky one in eight lives in the city itself. Everyone else is spread around the **Bay Area**, a hodgepodge of either very rich or very poor towns located down the peninsula or across one of the two impressive bridges that span the chilly waters of the exquisite natural harbor. In the **East Bay** are industrial Oakland and intellectual Berkeley. To the south lies the gloating new wealth of the **Peninsula**, known as "Silicon Valley" because of its multibillion-dollar computer industry. Across the Golden Gate Bridge to the north is the woody, leafy landscape and rugged coastline of **Marin County**, America's richest suburb.

The East Bay

The largest and most-traveled bridge in the US, the **Bay Bridge** heads east from San Francisco, part graceful suspension bridge and part heavy-duty steel truss. Now recovered from its partial collapse during the 1989 earthquake, the Bay Bridge works a lot harder for a lot less respect than the more famous (and better-loved) Golden Gate: a hundred million vehicles cross it each year. The heart of the East Bay is **Oakland**, a blue-collar city that was badly scarred by the firestorm of October 1991. Just north is the image-conscious, progressive university town of **Berkeley**; the two communities all but merge into one city, with the hills above them topped by a twenty-mile string of forested **regional parks**.

Arrival, information and getting around

Flights direct to the East Bay touch down at **Oakland Airport**, just outside town. The AirBART Shuttle van ($2; every 15min) runs to the Coliseum BART station, and there are also door-to-door shuttle buses such as BayPorter Express ($15-19; ☎415/467-1800 or 1-877/467-1800). The **Greyhound** station is in a dodgy part of northern Oakland on San Pablo Avenue at 21st Street. **Amtrak** terminates at Second Street near Jack London Square in West Oakland, but a better option is to get off at Richmond and change onto the ultramodern **BART** trains. Three of these underground lines link San Francisco with the East Bay (fares $2.75-3.10; Mon–Fri 4am–midnight, Sat 6am–midnight, Sun 8am–midnight), heading their separate ways from downtown Oakland. The revamped AC Transit (☎510/839-2882) buses cover the entire East Bay area, with a more limited service running to Oakland and Berkeley from the Transbay Terminal in San Francisco.

There are **visitor centers** at 550 Tenth St near the 12th Street BART station in downtown Oakland (Mon–Fri 8.30am–5pm; ☎510/839-9000, ⓦwww.oaklandcvb.com), and in Berkeley at 2015 Center St (Mon–Fri 9am–12.30pm and 1.30–5pm; ☎510/549-7040, ⓦwww.visitberkeley.com).

East Bay accommodation

The East Bay's **motels** and **hotels**, at between $60 and $90 a night, are barely better value for money than their San Francisco equivalents. However, they give visitors the chance to stay just outside of the city's hubbub whilst affording easy access to it.

Bancroft Hotel 2680 Bancroft Way, Berkeley ☎1-800/549-1002 or 510/549-1000. Small hotel – just 22 rooms – with good location and service.

Breakfast included. ❺

Berkeley YMCA 2001 Allston Way at Milvia St, a block from Berkeley BART ☎510/848-6800.

Berkeley's best bargain accommodation. Singles cost $43, doubles $55; rates include use of gym and pool. ❷/❸

The Claremont Resort & Spa 41 Tunnel Rd, Berkeley ☎1-800/551-7266 or 510/843-3000, ⓦwww.claremontresort.com. The lap of luxury among Berkeley hotels in a 1915 building. Standard rooms start at $260 and go up steeply from there; spa sessions begin at $112/hour for facials or massages. ❾

Dean's Bed and Breakfast 480 Pedestrian Way, Rockridge ☎510/652-5024, ⓦwww.bbonline.com/ca/deans. A hidden gem with swimming pool and Japanese garden. $95 for a single or double. ❹.

Durant 2600 Durant Ave, Berkeley ☎1-800/238-7268 or 510/845-8981, ⓦwww.hoteldurant.com. Fairly plain but well worn and comfortable, and very handy for the UC Berkeley campus. ❻/❼

Jack London Inn 444 Embarcadero W, Oakland ☎510/444-2032. Kitschy motorlodge located next to Jack London Square. ❺

Shattuck 2086 Allston Way, Berkeley ☎510/845-7300. Comfortable, central rooms in a well-restored older hotel. ❹/❺

Waterfront Plaza Hotel 10 Washington St, Oakland ☎510/836-3800 or 1-800/729-3638, ⓦwww.waterfrontplaza.com. Plush, modern hotel moored on the best stretch of the Oakland waterfront. ❼/❽

Oakland

OAKLAND, the workhorse of the Bay Area, is one of the largest ports on the west coast. It has also been the breeding ground of revolutionary **political movements**. In the Sixties, the city's fifty percent black population found a voice through the militant Black Panthers, and in the Seventies the Symbionese Liberation Army, kidnappers of heiress Patty Hearst, obtained a ransom of free food for the city's poor. It's not all hard graft, though: the climate is often sunny and mild when San Francisco is cold and dreary, and there's great hiking in the redwood- and eucalyptus-covered hills above the city.

Despite this, there's not all that much to see within the city, the major concession to the tourist trade being the waterfront Jack London Square, an aseptic collection of national chains that have nothing to do with the writer. At the far eastern end of the promenade, however, you will find **Heinhold's First and Last Chance Saloon**, a slanting tiny bar built in 1883 from the hull of a whaling ship. Jack London really did drink here, and the collection of yellowed portraits of him on the wall are the only genuine thing about the writer you'll find on the square. A half-mile north up Broadway from the waterfront, Oakland's restored downtown is anchored by chain stores and the gargantuan open-air **City Center** complex of offices and fast food. Beside it, at Broadway and 14th Street, the massive green space of **Frank Ogawa Plaza** offers a good place for people-watching. A bit east on Tenth and Oak streets, the **Oakland Museum of California** ($6; Wed–Sat 10am–5pm, Sun noon–5pm) has a good exhibit of California history, including the Beat Generation.

Gertrude Stein, who was born in Oakland at around the same time as the macho and adventurous London, is barely commemorated – perhaps because she wrote "what was the use of me having come from Oakland, it was not natural for me to have come from there yes write about it if I like or anything if I like but not there, *there is no there there*" – a quote which has haunted Oakland ever since. Nonetheless, the majority of Oakland residents are proud of their city, and would argue that there is indeed a *there* there, notably in the small and trendy communities of **Rockridge** and **Piedmont Avenue**, and the lively **Grand Avenue** neighborhood.

Joaquin Miller Park, the most easily accessible of Oakland's hilltop parks, stands above East Oakland. It was once home to the "Poet of the Sierras," Joaquin Miller, who made his name playing the eccentric frontier American in the salons of 1870s London. His poems weren't exactly acclaimed (his greatest poetic achievement was rhyming "teeth" with "Goethe"), but his prose account of the time he spent with the Modoc Indians near Mount Shasta (see p.1174) remains invaluable. His house, a small white cabin called **The Abbey**, still survives, as do the thousands of trees he planted.

Berkeley

BERKELEY (pronounced as for Busby, though named after the English philosopher-theologian George Berkeley) is dominated by the **University of California**, one of America's most famous – and infamous – universities. Its grand buildings and thirty thousand students give off an energy that spills south down raucous **Telegraph Avenue**, where ageing hippies peddle rainbow bracelets in front of vegetarian restaurants, music stores and pizza joints. The very name of Berkeley conjures up images of dissent. **Sproul Plaza**, in front of the school's entranceway, Sather Gate, is where the Free Speech Movement began, and, too, argue some historians, the experience known as the Sixties. Among the sites of the almost-daily pitched battles of the Sixties and early Seventies, part of the broad campus revolt against the Vietnam War, was the now-seedy **People's Park**. Things have calmed down considerably, and now the campus prides itself on its high academic rankings and Nobel-laureate-laden faculty. In recent years, the biggest cause célèbre on campus was the plight of Naked Man, an undergraduate who refused to wear clothing while attending class, and the attempted shutting down of local radio station KPFA. Today's students yell profanities and shout down Bible-thumpers on Sproul Plaza, unaware of the irony of it all; feel free to stroll around the campus's tree-shaded pathways and contemplate the dissent of years long gone.

Telegraph Avenue holds most of the student hangouts, and several excellent bookstores. Older students congregate in **Northside**, popping down from their woodsy hillside homes to partake of goodies from "Gourmet Ghetto" – the restaurants, delis and bakeries on Shattuck Avenue. North of here, on the hills, **Tilden Regional Park** has good trails and a fine rose garden. Along the bay itself, at the **Berkeley Marina**, you can rent windsurfing boards and sailboats, or just watch the sun set behind the Golden Gate.

Eating

As befits the birthplace of California cuisine, the East Bay offers a choice of good **restaurants**. Berkeley is both an upmarket diner's paradise and a student town where you can eat cheaply and well, especially on and around Telegraph Avenue.

Breads of India 2448 Sacramento St, Berkeley ☎510/848-7684. A consistently craved and cramped Indian spot, particularly big at lunchtime. Leave lots of room for the breads, the restaurant's specialty.

Café Intermezzo 2442 Telegraph Ave near Haste, Berkeley ☎510/849-4592. Huge sandwiches on homemade bread, even bigger salads, and great coffee.

Café Rouge 1782 4th St, Berkeley ☎510/525-1440. Southern French and Northern Italian food specializing in delicately prepared organic meats. They have their own butcher shop. Dinner entrees are about $16; lunch is cheaper.

Cha-Am 1543 Shattuck Ave, North Berkeley ☎510/848-9664. Climb the stairs up to this unlikely, always crowded small restaurant for deliciously spicy Thai food at bargain prices.

Cheeseboard Pizza 1512 Shattuck Ave, North Berkeley ☎510/549-3055. Incredibly good designer pizza at incredibly low prices: $1.75 a slice.

Chez Panisse 1517 Shattuck Ave, North Berkeley ☎510/548-5525. First and still the best of the modern Californian cuisineries – although at $45, $55 and $65 a head prix fixe (plus wine) on Mondays, Tuesdays–Thursdays and Fridays respectively, you may prefer to try the comparatively inexpensive *Café* upstairs, especially if you don't have the obligatory three-months-in-advance reservation.

Fenton's Creamery 4226 Piedmont Ave, Oakland ☎510/658-7000. The ultimate old-style ice cream parlor in which to indulge in sweet cravings. Sandwiches, fries and other snacks are available to offset the sundae-buzz.

Homemade Café 2454 Sacramento St, Berkeley ☎510/845-1940. Nontraditional Californian-style

Jewish food served for breakfast and lunch – at shared tables when it's crowded. Next to *Breads of India*, overleaf.

Juan's Place 941 Carleton St, West Berkeley ☎510/845-6904. The original Berkeley Mexican restaurant, with great food (tons of it) and an interesting mix of people.

La Mediterranee 2936 College Ave, Berkeley ☎510/540-7773. Great Middle Eastern food in a relaxed atmosphere.

La Note 2377 Shattuck Ave, Berkeley ☎510/843-1535. The appropriately sunny cuisine of Provence isn't the only flavor you'll find in this petite dining room: students and teachers from the jazz school next door routinely stop in for casual jam sessions.

Tropix Backyard Café 3814 Piedmont Ave, Oakland ☎510/653-2444. Large portions of fruity Caribbean delicacies at reasonable prices, with authentic jerk sauce and thirst-quenching mango juice. Outside seating on the patio.

Zachary's Chicago Pizza 5801 College Ave, Oakland ☎510/655-6385. Locals flock to this collegial standby for stuffed pizzas, available with whole-wheat crust. Come early; it gets very busy. Open for lunch, dinner and take-out.

Cafés and bars

The many bohemian **cafés** of Berkeley are full from dawn to near midnight with earnest characters wearing their intellects on their sleeves; if you're not after a caffeine fix, you can generally get a glass of beer or wine. For serious drinking you're better off in one of the many **bars**, particularly in rough-hewn Oakland. Grittier versions of what you'd find in San Francisco, they're mostly blue-collar, convivial, and almost always less expensive.

The Alley 3325 Grand Ave, Oakland ☎510/444-8505. A piano bar where locals come specifically to sing. With local Rod Dibble at the piano (he's not famous, he should be), the boozy conviviality and the right melody, you will too. Music starts at 9pm.

Bison Brewing Company 2598 Telegraph Ave, Berkeley ☎510/841-7734. Eat and drink at great prices on the terrace, where some of the best Bay Area beers are brewed. Noisy bands on weekends.

Caffe Mediterraneum 2475 Telegraph Ave, Berkeley ☎510/841-5634. Berkeley's oldest café, straight out of the Beat generation archives: beards and berets optional, books de rigueur, and people come specifically to smoke.

Heinhold's First and Last Chance Saloon Jack London Square, Oakland ☎510/839-6761. Authentic waterfront bar that's hardly changed since around 1900, when Jack London himself drank here. They've never even bothered to fix the slanted floor that was caused by the 1906 earthquake.

Jupiter 2181 Shattuck Ave, Berkeley ☎510/843-8277. Many, many beers to select from at this local favorite. Live jazz on weekends and an outdoor beer garden.

Mama Bears 6536 Telegraph Ave, North Oakland ☎510/428-9684. Women's bookstore, doubling as a café and meeting place. Open daily 10.30am–7pm, later for regular author readings.

Pyramid Brewery 901 Gilman St, Berkeley ☎510/528-9880. Great microbrewed beers in a popular pub.

Starry Plough 3101 Shattuck Ave, Berkeley ☎510/841-2082. Convivial Irish bar where you can argue the latest cease-fire over darts. Bargain-price live rock and country many evenings.

The White Horse 6551 Telegraph Ave at 66th St, North Oakland ☎510/652-3820. Oakland's oldest gay bar – a smallish, friendly place, with mixed dancing for men and women nightly.

Live music and entertainment

Nightlife is where the East Bay really comes into its own. **Discos** are virtually nonexistent; however, dance music – this is, after all, the home of Hammer, En Vogue and Digital Underground – is thriving, and **live music venues** range from smoky jazz cafés to sweaty R&B dives.

Berkeley's **Pacific Film Archives** at 2575 Bancroft Ave (☎510/642-5249 for tickets), perhaps the best **cinema** in California, puts on contemporary international films, plus old favorites. The free *East Bay Express* has the most comprehensive **what's on** listings.

Ashkenaz 1317 San Pablo Ave, Berkeley ☎510/525-5054. World music and dance café. Acts from modern Afrobeat to the best of the Balkans.

Kids and under-21s welcome. Cover $7–12.

Freight and Salvage 1111 Addison St, West Berkeley ☎510/548-1761. Singer-songwriters in a coffee house setting. Cover $6–20.

Gilman Street Project 924 Gilman St, West Berkeley ℡510/525-9926. On the outer edge of the hardcore punk, indie, and experimental scene, this institution helped launch Green Day and Sleater-Kinney. No booze, all ages; cover $3–5.

Kimball's East 5800 Shellmound, off Powell St in the Emerybay Public Market, Emeryville ℡510/658-2555. The prime jazz and blues venue in the entire Bay Area, with big-name players in an intimate setting. Cover $15–20.

Stork Club 2330 Telegraph Ave, Oakland ℡510/444-6174. The historic club is presently a favorite with DJs and indie bands. The jukebox specializes in country tunes. Cover $5–8.

Yoshi's Restaurant and Nitespot 510 Embarcadero W, Oakland in Jack London Square ℡510/238-9200. The centerpiece of Oakland's revived Jack London Square, this combination jazz club and sushi bar routinely attracts the biggest names in jazz. Cover $10–30.

The Peninsula

The city of San Francisco sits at the tip of a five-mile-wide neck of land commonly referred to as the **Peninsula**. Home of old money and new technology, the peninsula stretches for fifty miles of relentless suburbia south from San Francisco along the bay, winding up in the futuristic roadside landscape of the so-called "Silicon Valley" near **San Jose**.

There was a time when the region was largely agricultural, but the continuing computer boom – spurred by Stanford University in **Palo Alto** – has replaced the orange groves and fig trees of yesteryear with office complexes and parking lots. Surprisingly, however, most of the land along the **coast** – separated from the bayfront sprawl by a ridge of redwood-covered peaks – remains rural and undeveloped; it also contains some of the best **beaches** in the Bay Area, well worth a day-trip from San Francisco.

Palo Alto

In recent years, **Palo Alto**, home of high-brow **Stanford University**, has become somewhat a social center for Silicon Valley's nouveaux riches, as evidenced by the trendy cafés and chic new restaurants that have popped up along its main drag, **University Avenue**. The town doesn't offer a lot in terms of sights other than Spanish colonial homes, but it's a great place for a lazy stroll and a gourmet meal. Wash down a California-style Greek dish from *Evvia*, 420 Emerson St (℡650/326-0983), or a heaping plate of Cajun-influenced food from *Nola*, 535 Ramona St (℡650/328-2722), with a microbrewed beer from the *Gordon Biersch Brewery*, 640 Emerson St (℡650/323-7723), or a latte from *Caffe Verona*, 236 Hamilton Ave (℡650/326-9942). The old-style malt and burger joint, *The Peninsula Creamery*, Hamilton and Emerson streets (℡650/323-3131), is a favorite with Apple co-founder Steve Jobs. *MacArthur Park*, 27 University Ave (℡650/321-9990), is a great barbecue restaurant with more than two hundred wines on offer. Surprisingly affordable **rooms** are available at the *Cardinal Hotel*, 235 Hamilton Ave (℡650/323-5101, Ⓦwww.cardinalhotel.com; ❸–❼).

San Jose

Burt Bacharach could easily find **SAN JOSE** today simply by heading south from San Francisco and following the heat and smog. Although one of the fastest-growing cities in California, it is not strong on identity – though in area and population it's close to twice the size of San Francisco. Sitting at the southern end of the peninsula, San Jose has in the past 25 years emerged as the civic heart of Silicon Valley, surrounded by miles of faceless high-tech industrial parks where the next generations of computers and websites are designed and crafted. Ironically, it's also acknowledged as the first city in California, though the only sign of this is the eighteenth-century **Mission Santa Clara de Asis**, on the pleasant campus of the Jesuit-run Santa Clara University.

Its most famous landmark is the **Winchester Mystery House**, 525 S Winchester Blvd, just off I-280 near Hwy-17 ($12.95–22.95; daily 9am–5pm, until 7pm June–Sept). Sarah Winchester, heiress to the Winchester rifle fortune, was convinced upon her husband's death that he had been taken by the spirits of men killed with Winchester rifles, and believed that unless a room was built for each of the spirits and the sound of hammers never ceased, the same fate would befall her. Work on the mansion went on 24 hours a day for the next thirty years – stairs lead nowhere, windows open on to solid brick. The **Rosicrucian Museum**, 1342 Naglee Ave (Tues–Fri 10am–5pm, Sat–Sun 11am–6pm; $9), houses a brilliant collection of Assyrian and Babylonian artifacts, while the revamped **Tech Museum of Innovation** (daily 10am–5pm; $9), downtown at 201 S Market St, contains hands-on displays of high-tech engineering.

San Jose's **visitor center** is at 333 W San Carlos St, Suite 1000 (Mon–Fri 8am–5.30pm, Sat & Sun 11am–5pm; Ⓣ408/295-9600 or 1-800/SAN-JOSE, Ⓦwww.sanjose.org), and also has a branch in the convention center across the street. Downtown **accommodation** is grossly overpriced, serving as it does high-tech executives and conventioneers. Options include the *Valley Inn*, 2155 The Alameda (Ⓣ408/241-8500; ❺), and the slightly more expensive *San Jose Convention Inn*, 455 S Second St (Ⓣ408/298-3500; ❹–❻). The *Executive Inn Suites*, 3930 Monterey Rd (Ⓣ408/281-8700; ❺/❻), offers basic rooms fifteen minutes outside downtown. Good old-fashioned American **food** is dished up at *Original Joe's*, 301 S First St (Ⓣ408/292-7030). Grab a stool at the counter or settle into one of the comfy booths and enjoy a burger or a plate of pasta at this San Jose institution, where $10 goes a long way. For fresh coffee and pastries, head to *Café Matisse*, 371 S First St (Ⓣ408/298-7788), in the heart of the popular "SOFA" district.

The coast

The **coastline** of the peninsula south from San Francisco is a world away from the valley of the inland: mostly undeveloped, with a few small towns, and countless beaches that run 75 miles south to the mellow cities of Santa Cruz and **Capitola**. Past Daly City just south of San Francisco, Hwy-1 hugs the precipitous cliffs of Devil's Slide to the clothing-optional sands of **Gray Whale Cove State Beach** (daily 8am–sunset). Despite the name, it's not an especially great place to look for migrating gray whales, but there is a stairway from the bus stop down to a fine strand of sand. Two miles south, the red-roofed buildings of the 1875 **Point Montara Lighthouse**, set among the windswept Monterey pine trees at the top of a steep cliff, have been converted into a **youth hostel** (Ⓣ650/728-7177, Ⓦwww.norcalhostels.org/pointmontara-lighthouse.html; ❶). Just south of the hostel, down California Street, the **Fitzgerald Marine Reserve** (Ⓣ650/728-3584; free) has three miles of diverse oceanic habitat, peaceful trails and, at low tide, the best tidal pools. But continue a tiny bit further for the historic **Moss Beach Distillery** (Ⓣ650/728-5595), a great place to grab a snack and a beer on its windswept patio. They provide enormous blankets to help brave the fog. Continuing a few miles south on Hwy-1, the hamlet of **El Grenada** has other good roadside lunch stops like the *Highway One Diner*, and its beaches are always clogged with surfers and crowds of spectators watching them. There's a long breakwater here you can walk out on. The next town, growing **Half Moon Bay**, allows camping on a first-come, first served basis on some of its beaches ($12; Ⓣ650/726-8820). Gas up here; fuel stations are rare for the next fifty miles to Santa Cruz.

Marin County

Across the Golden Gate from San Francisco, **Marin County** is an unabashed introduction to Californian self-indulgence: a pleasure zone of conspicuous luxury and abundant natural beauty, with sunshine, sandy beaches, high mountains and thick redwood forests. Often ranked as the wealthiest county in the US, Marin has attracted a sizeable population of wealthy young professionals to its swanky waterside towns, though in the past the region served as logging headquarters.

The modern **ferries** that travel across the bay from San Francisco can make a great start to a day out. Boats to the chic bayside settlement of **Sausalito** leave from the Embarcadero ($5.30 each way; Golden Gate Ferry; 7.40am–8pm, half-hourly during rush hour, less often during the rest of the day, and every two or so hours on weekends; ☎415/923-2000, ⊛www.goldengate.org) or Pier 41 at Fisherman's Wharf (Blue & Gold Fleet Ferries; $6.75 each way; 6–7 trips daily; ☎415/705-8200). **Biking** over here makes for a beautiful ride over the Golden Gate Bridge (pending fog) and allows you to explore the headlands freely. Bikes are allowed on the ferry back to San Francisco.

Across the Golden Gate: the Marin Headlands

The largely undeveloped **Marin Headlands**, across the Golden Gate from San Francisco, afford some of the most impressive views of the bridge and the city behind. The coastline is much more rugged than it is on the San Francisco side, and it makes a great place for an isolated clifftop scramble, in among the concrete remains of old forts and gun emplacements. Heading west on Bunker Hill Road takes you up to the brink of the headlands before snaking down to Fort Barry, and wide, sandy **Rodeo Beach**, from which numerous hiking trails branch out. Check in at the Marin Headlands Visitor Center (daily 9.30am–4.30pm; ☎415/331-1540) above Rodeo Lagoon for free maps. The largest of the fort's old buildings has been converted into the spacious but homey *HI-Marin Headlands* **hostel** (☎415/331-2777, ⊛www.norcalhostels.org; ❶), an excellent base for more extended explorations of the inland ridges and valleys.

Sausalito

Pretty, smug little **SAUSALITO**, along the bay below US-101, was once a gritty community of fishermen and sea traders, full of bars and bordellos. Now exclusive restaurants and pricey boutiques line its picturesque waterfront promenade, and expensive, quirky houses climb the overgrown cliffs above Bridgeway Avenue, the main road and bus route through town. Ferries from San Francisco arrive next to the Sausalito Yacht Club in the town center. If you have **sailing** experience, split the $130 daily rental fee of a four- to six-person sailboat at Cass's Marine, 1702 Bridgeway (☎415/332-6789).

Aside from walking, shopping and sucking in the sea air, Sausalito has a one-of-a-kind exhibit in the **Bay Model Visitor Center**, 2100 Bridgeway (Tues–Fri 9am–4pm, Sat & Sun 10am–5pm; donation), where elevated walkways in a huge building lead you around a scale model of the entire bay, surrounding deltas and its aquatic inhabitants.

Casa Madrona at 801 Bridgeway Ave (☎415/332-0502 or 1-800/567-9524, ⊛www.casamadrona.com; ❼–❾), a deluxe **hotel** hideaway in the hills above the bay, also houses *Mikayla*, a delectable seafood **restaurant**. Less expensive food can be found near the waterfront; *Gatsby's*, 39 Caledonia St (☎415/332-4500), at the north end of town, is a reasonably priced pizza parlor, while *Caffe*

DiVino, 37 Caledonia St (☎415/331-9355), serves a tasty variety of organic salads, toasted focaccio sandwiches and some great coffee. The *no name bar*, 757 Bridgeway Ave (☎415/332-1392), is a smoky ex-haunt of the Beats hosting frequent live jazz.

Mount Tamalpais and Muir Woods

Mount Tamalpais dominates the skyline of the Marin peninsula, hulking over the cool canyons of the rest of the county in a crisp yet voluptuous silhouette, and dividing the county into two distinct parts: the wild western slopes above the Pacific coast and the increasingly suburban communities along the calmer bay frontage. The Panoramic Highway branches off from Hwy-1 along the crest above Mill Valley, taking ten miles to reach the center of **Mount Tamalpais State Park**, which has some thirty miles of hiking trails and many campgrounds. While most of the redwood trees that once covered its slopes have long since been chopped down to build San Francisco's Victorian houses, one towering grove remains, protected as the **Muir Woods National Monument** (daily 8am–sunset; $2). It's a tranquil and majestic spot, with sunlight filtering three hundred feet down from the treetops to the laurel and fern-covered canyon below. Being so close to San Francisco, Muir Woods is a popular target, and the paved trails nearest the car park are often packed with coach-tour hordes; more secluded hiking paths include the Matt Davis Trail, leading south to Stinson Beach and north to Mount Tamalpais.

Mill Valley

From the east peak of Mount Tamalpais, a quick two-mile downhill hike follows the Temelpa Trail through velvety shrubs of chaparral to the town of **MILL VALLEY**, the oldest and most enticing of the inland towns of Marin County. This was originally a logging center, from where the destruction of the surrounding redwoods was organized, but for many years the town has made a healthy living out of tourism and October's annual Mill Valley Film Festival, which draws area stars and up-and-coming directors alike.

The restored town centers today around the redwood-shaded square of the *Depot Bookstore and Café* (Mon–Fri 7am–8pm, Sat & Sun 8am–9pm; ☎415/383-2665), a popular bookstore, café and meeting place at 87 Throckmorton Ave; there's a small **visitor center** in the same building (Mon, Tues, Thurs & Fri 10am–noon and 1–4pm; ☎415/388-9700). Far and away the best place to **stay**, if you can afford it, is the *Mill Valley Inn*, 165 Throckmorton Ave (☎415/389-6608 or 1-800/595-2100, ⓦwww.millvalleyinn.com; ❼–❾), a gorgeous European-style inn with elegant rooms and two private cottages. They've also opened a branch along the waterfront: sumptuous *Acqua Hotel*, 555 Redwood Hwy (☎415/380-0400 or 1-888/662-9555, ⓦwww.acquahotel.com; ❼/❽), on Richardson Bay. *Piazza D'Angelo*, at 22 Miller Ave (☎415/388-2000), has very good pizzas and pastas. *Sunnyside Café*, 31 Sunnyside Ave (☎415/388-5260), claims "the customers are rarely right" but serves large, affordable breakfasts and lunches nonetheless. *Sweetwater*, at 153 Throckmorton Ave (☎415/388-2820, ⓦwww.sweetwatersaloon.com), is a comfortable saloon which doubles as Marin's prime **live music** venue, with gigs ranging from jazz and blues all-stars to Jefferson Airplane survivors.

Point Reyes National Seashore

The westernmost tip of Marin County comes at the end of the **Point Reyes National Seashore**, a near-island of wilderness bordered on three sides by over fifty miles of isolated coastline – pine forests and sunny meadows hemmed in by rocky cliffs and sandy, windswept beaches. This wing-shaped landmass is a rogue piece of the earth's crust that has been drifting steadily northwards along the San Andreas Fault, having started out some six million years ago as a suburb of Los Angeles. When the great earthquake of 1906 shattered San Francisco, the land here, at the epicenter, shifted over sixteen feet in an instant, though damage was confined to a few skewed cattle fences.

The **Bear Valley visitor center** (Mon–Fri 9am–5pm, Sat, Sun & hols 8am–5pm; ☎415/464-5100, ⓦwww.nps.gov/pore), two miles southwest of Point Reyes Station in Olema, has engaging displays on local geology and natural history, plus details of hiking trails. Just to the north, Limantour Road heads six miles west to the *HI-Point Reyes* **hostel** (closed 10am–4.30pm; ☎415/663-8811, ⓦwww.norcalhostels.org/pointreyes.html; ❶) in an old ranch house. Nearby **Limantour Beach** is good (and cold) for swimming.

Eight miles west of the hamlet of Inverness, a small road leads down to **Drake's Beach**, the presumed landing spot of Sir Francis Drake in 1579. Appropriately, the coastline resembles the southern coast of England – cold, wet and windy, with chalk-white cliffs rising above the wide sandy beach. The road continues southwest another four miles to the very tip of Point Reyes. A precarious-looking **lighthouse** (Thurs–Mon 10am–4.30pm; ☎415/669-1534) stands firm against the crashing surf, and the bluffs are excellent for watching sea lions and, from mid-March to April and late December to early February, migrating gray whales.

The Gold Country

Over 150 years before international techies invaded California in search of Silicon gold, rough and ready **49ers** came to the **Gold Country** of the Sierra Nevada, 150 miles east of San Francisco, to look for the real thing. The area ranges from the foothills near Yosemite to the deep gorge of the Yuba River two hundred miles north, with **Sacramento** as its largest city. Many of the mining camps that sprung up around the Gold Country vanished as quickly as they appeared, but about half still survive. Some are bustling resorts, standing on the banks of whitewater rivers in the midst of thick pine forests; others are just eerie ghost towns, all but abandoned on the grassy rolling hills. Most of the mountainous forests along the Sierra crest are preserved as near pristine wilderness, with excellent hiking, camping and backpacking. There's great skiing in winter, around the mountainous rim of **Lake Tahoe** on the border between California and Nevada, aglow under the bright lights of the nightclubs and casinos that line its southeastern shore.

Sacramento

California's state capital, **SACRAMENTO**, in the flatlands of the Central Valley, was founded in 1839 by the Swiss John Sutter. He worked hard for ten years to build a busy trading center and cattle ranch, only to be thwarted by the discovery of gold at a nearby sawmill in 1848. His workers quit their jobs to go prospecting, and thousands more flocked to the goldfields of the Central Mother Lode, without any respect for Sutter's claims to the land. Sacramento became the main supply point for the miners, and remained important as the western headquarters of the transcontinental railroad. Flashy office towers and hotel complexes have now sprung from its rather suburban streetscape, enlivening the flat grid of leafy, tree-lined blocks, and going some way towards resurrecting the rowdy, free-for-all spirit of the city's Gold Rush past.

Sacramento is not especially prominent on most travelers' itineraries. There's not a great deal to see, though the wharves, warehouses, saloons and stores of the historic core along the **riverfront** have been restored and converted into the touristy shops and restaurants of **Old Sacramento**. On the northern edge of the old town, the **California State Railroad Museum** (daily 10am–5pm; $3) brings together a range of lavishly restored 1860s locomotives, with "cow-catcher" front grilles and bulbous smokestacks. The old passenger station and freight depot, a block south on Front Street, now serve as the summer depot for a refurbished **Central Pacific Railroad steam train** (summer weekends 11am–5pm; $6), which makes a seven-mile, 45-minute round-trip along the river.

Further east, and isolated from downtown, the dome of the **state capitol** stands proudly in a spacious green park two blocks south of K Street Mall. Recently restored to its original elegance, and still the seat of state government, the luxurious building brims over with finely crafted details. Although you're free to walk around, you'll see a lot more if you take one of the free hourly **tours** (daily 9am–5pm).

Sutter's Fort State Historic Park (daily 10am–4.30pm; $3), on the east side of town at 27th and L streets, is a re-creation of Sacramento's original settlement, dating back to 1839. An adobe house displays relics from the Gold Rush, and on summer weekends volunteers dress up and act out scenes from the 1850s.

Practicalities

Most tourists arrive in Sacramento by car, taking a logical break from driving on Rte-80. **Trains** come in at Fifth and I streets, near Old Sacramento, while an almost continuous stream of Greyhound **buses** arrives at Seventh and L streets. The **airport** is twelve miles northwest: SuperShuttle Sacramento vans ($10; ☎1-800/BLUE-VAN) take you directly to your downtown destination.

Sacramento's most accessible **visitor information center** is at 1101 Second St (daily 10am–5pm; ☎916/442-7644). Besides the central *HI-Sacramento Hostel*, 900 H St (☎916/443-1691; ❶), there are plenty of **places to stay** within walking distance of the city center – the best value is the *Econo Lodge*, 711 16th St (☎916/443-6631 or 1-800/553-2666; ❷–❹), while *Hartley House Inn*, 700 22nd St (☎916/447-7829 or 1-800/831-5806, ⓦwww.hartleyhouse .com; ❻/❼), offers nineteenth-century elegance in the heart of Sacramento's liveliest local neighborhood. *Savoyard Bed & Breakfast*, 3322 H St (☎916/442-6709 or 1-800/772-8692, ⓦwww.savoyard.com; ❺/❻), is another beautiful night's stay, across from the city's Rose Garden, or *On the Bluffs*, 9735 Mira Del Rio (☎916/363-9933, ⓦwww.onthebluffs.com; ❺/❻), is out-of-the-way but offers rooms with river views. *Paesano's*, at 1806 Capitol Ave (☎916/447-8646), is a delicious and popular pizza **restaurant**; *Virga's*, at 1501 14th St near O (☎916/442-8516) offers scrumptious Italian fare and was selected best restaurant in local polls; *Centro Cocina Mexicana*, 454 28th St near J Street (☎916/442-2552), offers innovative Californian-Mexican fusion cuisine. Local indie bands play at the down-to-earth *Café Paris*, 2326 K St (☎916/442-1557). Pick up the free weekly, *Sacramento News & Review*, for more entertainment specifics.

The Mines

In the romantically rugged landscape of the **Gold Country**, overshadowed by the 10,000ft granite peaks of the Sierra Nevada, fast-flowing rivers cascade through steeply walled canyons. During the fall, the flaming reds and golds of poplars and sugar maples on the slopes stand out against an evergreen background of pine and fir. The camps of the **southern mines** of the Gold Country were the liveliest and most uproarious of all the Gold Rush settlements, and inspired most of the popular images of the era: Wild West towns full of gambling halls, saloons and gunfights in the streets. Freebooting prospectors in these "placer" mines sometimes panned for nuggets of gold in the streams and rivers; further **north**, the diggings were far richer and more successful, but the gold was (and is) buried deep underground, and had to be pounded out of hardrock ore.

Sonora, Columbia, Jamestown and Mariposa

The center of the southern mining district is **SONORA**, set on steep ravines roughly a hundred miles east of San Francisco. This friendly and animated logging town boasts numerous Victorian houses and false-fronted buildings on its main **Washington Street**. The Tuolumne County Visitors Bureau, 542 West Stockton Rd off Hwy-49 (℡209/533-4420 or 1-800/446-1333, ⓦwww.thegreatunfenced.com), is the best source of **information**.

Sonora's onetime arch-rival, **COLUMBIA**, three miles north on Parrots Ferry Road, is now a ghost town (and a state historic park), with a carefully restored Main Street that gives an excellent – if slightly contrived – idea of what Gold Rush life might have been like. In 1854 it was California's second largest city, and it missed becoming the state capital by two votes – just as well, since by 1870 the gold had run out and the town was abandoned.

The **Railtown 1897 State Historic Park**, on the corner of Fifth and Reservoir streets along the way to Sonora, in **JAMESTOWN**, holds an impressive collection of old steam trains including the one used in *High Noon* (daily 9.30am–4.30pm; ⓦwww.csrmf.org). Further south, after a breathtaking drive over the Don Pedro Lake and Merced River, is **MARIPOSA**, gateway to Yosemite and one of the last Gold Rush towns on Hwy-49. Its **California State Mining & Mineral Museum** ($1; daily 10am–4pm; summer daily 10am–6pm), south a mile or so of the historic downtown, has a working 1860s stamp mill model and hundreds of mineral samples.

Practicalities

In downtown Columbia, the best **place to stay** is right on the historic Main Street in the balconied *City Hotel* (℡209/532-1479 or 1-800/532-1479, ⓦwww.cityhotel.com; ❹/❺); in Sonora, *Sterling Gardens* is a comfortable B&B with four rooms among 10 acres at 18047 Lime Kiln Rd (℡209/533-9300 or 1-800/510-2225, ⓦwww.sterlinggardens.com; ❹/❺), or try the *Gunn House Hotel* (℡209/532-3421; ❷/❸), right in town at 286 S Washington St; motels on Hwy-49 between Sonora and Jamestown include the good-value *Miner's Motel* (℡209/532-7850 or 1-800/451-4176; ❷). Jamestown's Main Street is lined by old Gold Rush hotels such as the fantastic *Jamestown Hotel* (℡209/984-3902 or 1-800/205-4901, ⓦwww.jamestownhotel.com; ❹–❻), which boasts an impressive restaurant while being close to other good options, including *Morelia Mexican*, across the street. Sonora has a wide variety of **places**

to eat along Washington Street: locals love *Alfredo's* for Mexican food at no. 123 S Washington St and *Josephine's* at the historic *Gunn House Hotel* (see overleaf), for romantic Italian.

Grass Valley, Nevada City and Downieville

The compact communities of **GRASS VALLEY** and **NEVADA CITY**, four miles apart in the Sierra Nevada Mountains, were the most prosperous and substantial of the gold mining towns. Since the 1960s, artists and craftspeople have settled in the elaborate Victorian homes of the surrounding hills and gorges. In Grass Valley, the **North Star Mining Museum** (donation; May–Oct daily 10am–5pm) at the south end of Mill Street is housed in what used to be the power station for the North Star Mine. Its giant water-driven **Pelton wheel**, fitted with a hundred or so iron buckets, once powered the drills and hoists of the mine. Dioramas show the day-to-day working life of the miners, three-quarters of whom had emigrated here from the depressed tin mines of Cornwall (bringing the Cornish pasty with them).

The last mine in California to shut down was its richest, the **Empire Mine**, now preserved as a state park in the pine forests a mile southeast of Grass Valley (daily 10am–5pm; summer 9am–6pm; $1). It closed in 1956, after more than six million ounces of gold had been recovered, when the cost of getting the gold out of the ground exceeded $35 an ounce, the government-controlled price at the time. Machinery sold off when the mine closed has been replaced from other disused workings and now augments the excellent and very informative **museum** at the entrance.

The excellent Grass Valley **visitor center** at 248 Mill St (Mon–Fri 9.30am–5.30pm, Sat 10am–3pm; ☎530/273-4667 or 1-800/655-4667) is in a replication of Lola Montez's original home. Lola was an Irish entertainer and former mistress of Ludwig of Bavaria, who retired here after touring America with her provocative "Spider Dance" and kept a grizzly bear in her front yard.

Towns don't get much quainter than **Nevada City**. Amid all the shops and restaurants in the city center, the newly restored **Old Firehouse** at 214 Main St, a lacy, balcony and bell-towered piece of gingerbread, houses a small **museum** of local social history (donation; May–Oct daily 11am–4pm; Nov–April Thurs–Sun 11am–4pm).

Several daily Amtrak Thruway **buses** from Sacramento and Auburn stop on Sacramento Street in Nevada City and on West Main Street in Grass Valley. The Gold Country Stage connects the two towns every half-hour (Mon–Fri 8am–5pm, Sat 9.15am–5.30pm; $1, $2 for a day-pass; ☎530/477-0103).

North on Hwy-49, an hour's drive from Nevada City, you'll head into the most rugged and beautiful part of the Gold Country, where waterfalls tumble over black rocks bordered by pines and maples. **DOWNIEVILLE** is in the midst of an idyllic setting and particularly popular with mountain bikers; it abuts an extensive trail system with moderate to extreme bike trails. Oddly, as the only mining camp to have ever hanged a woman, the town has restored a gallows to commemorate that grisly passage of its history.

Accommodation

Accommodation in the revamped old Gold Rush **hotels** doesn't come cheap, but if you can afford to splash out on a B&B, Nevada City has some excellent options.

Holbrooke Hotel 212 W Main St, Grass Valley ☎530/273-1353 or 1-800/933-7077. Historic hotel, once visited by Mark Twain, and right in the center of town. Breakfast included. ❸/❹

Holiday Lodge 1221 E Main St, Grass Valley
℡530/273-4406 or 1-800/742-7125.
Comfortable, basic accommodation with perks
such as a swimming pool, free breakfast and free
local calls. **❸/❹**

Outside Inn 575 E Broad St, Nevada City
℡530/265-2233, ⓦ www.outsideinn.com. Quiet,
1940s motel with swimming pool, and only a
10min walk from the center of town. **❸—❺**

The Parsonage 427 Broad St, Nevada City
℡530/265-9478. Century-old Victorian B&B with
great breakfasts and helpful hosts. Conveniently
located. **❹—❻**

Swan-Levine House 328 S Church St, Grass
Valley ℡530/272-1873. Attractively decorated,
sunny rooms in an old Victorian hospital run by
two artists. **❸/❹**

Eating and drinking

Both Grass Valley and Nevada City have good places to eat, as well as many bars
and saloons, where you'll often be treated to free live music.

Broad Street Books & Espresso 426 Broad St,
Nevada City ℡530/265-4204. Pastries, light fare,
and espresso with wonderful tree-shaded outdoor
seating.

Café Mekka 237 Commercial St, Nevada City
℡530/478-1517. Relaxed, fabulously decorated
coffee shop.

Main Street Café 213 W Main St, Grass Valley
℡530/477-6000. Casual but refined and slightly
expensive restaurant. An eclectic menu, from lunch
sandwiches and pastas to Cajun specialties.
Recommended for grilled meats and fresh fish.

Marshall's Pasties 203A Mill St, Grass Valley
℡530/272-2844. Vast array of fresh takeout pasties.

Lake Tahoe

One of the highest, largest, deepest, cleanest and coldest lakes in the world,
Lake Tahoe is perched high above the Gold Country in an alpine bowl of
forested granite peaks. Longer than the English Channel is wide, and more
than a thousand feet deep, it's so cold that perfectly preserved cowboys who
drowned over a century ago have been recovered from its depths. The lake lures
weekenders from the Bay Area and beyond with sunny beaches in the summer,
snow-covered slopes in the winter and bustling casinos year-round.

Arrival, information and getting around

Daily Greyhound buses from San Francisco and Sacramento stop at Harrah's
casino in **Stateline**, Nevada. From there, local STAGE **buses** serve the communities of Tahoe City and South Lake Tahoe. Amtrak Thruway buses arrive
several times daily from Sacramento, heading for Carson City. You can rent
bicycles from the Mountain Sports Center (℡530/542-6584, ⓦ www.cam-
prichardson.com) in South Lake Tahoe's Camp Richardson Resort and from
Olympic Bike Shop (℡530/581-2500) in Tahoe City. There are **visitors centers** around the lake, in California at 1156 Ski Run Blvd, South Lake Tahoe
(℡530/544-5050 or 1-800/288-2463), and at 950 North Lake Blvd in Tahoe
City (℡530/583-3494); in Nevada at 969 Tahoe Blvd in Incline Village
(℡778/831-4440) and on Hwy-50 (℡775/588-4591, ⓦ www.tahoecham-
ber.org) in Round Hill, just across the state line. The Tahoe Central
Reservation Service can be reached at ℡1-800/288-2463 or ⓦ www.virtual-
tahoe.com.

Accommodation

There are dozens of bargain **motels** along the Southshore, though weekday
rates from $50 can easily double at weekends and in summer. In Tahoe City,
there are fewer budget choices, but as prices skyrocket around the lake, you'll

rarely find a great deal in any direction. The South Lake Tahoe Visitors Authority (℡ 1-800/288-2463) runs a free **room reservation service**, which can also help you with Northshore and Reno reservations.

Blu Zu Hostel 4140 Pine Blvd, South Lake Tahoe ℡ 530/542-0705, ⓦ www.hostels.com/us.ca.es.html. A near-lakeside hostel with a Native American bent. Dorm beds are $15 a night and come with free coffee and beach pass. There's also a full kitchen and laundry facilities as well as 24-hour access. ❶

Forest Inn Suites 1 Lake Parkway, South Lake Tahoe ℡ 530/541-6655 or 1-800/822-5950, ⓦ www.forestinn.com. Prices are reasonable for guest rooms and suites with all the modern conveniences, a fitness center and a hot tub on site. Definitely a cut above any of the motels on the strip and quieter, too. They often offer special package deals. ❺–❼

River Ranch Hwy-89 and Alpine Meadows Rd, Tahoe City ℡ 530/583-4264 or 1-800/535-9900, ⓦ www.riverranchlodge.com. Historic lodge on the Truckee River with one of the lake's best restaurants. ❻

Sierrawood Guest House 12 miles from Southshore on Hwy 89, Tahoe Paradise ℡ 530/577-6073 or 1-800/700-3802. This chalet is just a few minutes drive from the casinos' glitter. Jacuzzi, exercise room, fireplace and free snowmobiling on premises. Breakfast and dinner are included in the price of a room. ❻

Stardust Lodge 4061 Lake Tahoe Blvd, South Lake Tahoe ℡ 530/544-5211 or 1-800/262-5077, ⓦ www.stardust-tahoe.com. Simple suites and guest rooms with kitchenettes. An easy walking distance to the casinos and the lake. ❹–❻

Tahoe City Inn 790 North Lake Blvd, Tahoe City ℡ 530/581-3333 or 1-800/800-8246, ⓦ www.tahoecityinn.com. This place can cost as little as $49 midweek in the low season. Central location. ❷–❹

Tamarack Lodge 2311 North Lake Blvd, Tahoe City ℡ 530/583-3350 or 1-888/824-6323, ⓦ www.tamarackattahoe.com. One of the best deals anywhere on the lake. Comfortable and clean cabins and rooms. ❷–❺

South Lake Tahoe and around

In **South Lake Tahoe**, the lakeside's largest community, ranks of restaurants, modest motels, and pine-bound cottages stand cheek by jowl with the high-rise gambling dens of Stateline, just across the border in Nevada. If you happen to lose your money at the tables and slot machines, you can always explore the beautiful hiking trails, parks and beaches that populate the surrounding area.

Not far away, the prettiest part of the lake is along the southwest shore, at **Emerald Bay State Park**, ten miles from South Lake Tahoe, which has a number of good shoreline **campgrounds**. A mile from the parking lot, **Vikingsholm** is an unlikely reproduction Viking castle (summer daily 10am–4pm, hourly tours; $3). In **Sugar Pine Point State Park**, two miles north, the huge **Ehrman Mansion** (daily 11am–4pm; $3) is decorated in Thirties-era furnishings; the extensive lakefront grounds were seen in *The Godfather II*.

The rest of the 75-mile **drive** is lovely enough, though certainly not the "most beautiful drive in America" as one locally produced brochure touts; a better way to see it is to take a **paddlewheel boat cruise** on the *MS Dixie II*, from Zephyr Cove (three departures daily in summer, one in winter, call for times; $23–49; ℡ 775/588-3508, ⓦ www.tahoedixie2.com), reached on a free shuttle from South Lake Tahoe, or sign up for other boat tours through one of the larger casinos.

Tahoe City

Tahoe City, the hub on the lake's northwestern shore, does not escape the tourists, but nevertheless manages to retain a more relaxed small-town attitude. Hwy-89 meets Hwy-28 at Lake Tahoe's only outlet, the **Truckee River**. The **Gatekeeper's Cabin Museum** (Wed–Sun 11am–5pm May–mid-June; daily 11am–5pm mid-June to mid-Oct; $2), at the mouth of the river, is a well-presented hodgepodge of artifacts from the nineteenth century, and has a good collection of native basketware. **Rafting** down the Truckee is a common activity in summer.

A couple of miles south along Hwy–89, 500 yards past the Kaspian picnic grounds, **hike** ten minutes up the unmarked trail to the top of **Eagle Rock** for amazing panoramic views of the royal–blue lake. Several miles further along the highway is popular **Chamber's Beach**.

Squaw Valley, the site of the 1960 Winter Olympics, is situated five miles west of Tahoe City off of Hwy–89, although the original facilities (except the flame and the Olympic rings) are now swamped by the rampant development which has made this California's largest ski resort (see box below).

Lake Tahoe skiing

Lake Tahoe has some of the best **downhill skiing** in North America, with some of its larger resorts rivalling their Rocky Mountain counterparts. Although skiing is certainly not cheap – the largest ski areas charge at least $50 for the privilege of using their mountain for a single day – many resorts offer decent-valued rental/lift ticket/lesson packages or multiday discounts. **Snowboarding** has, of course, caught on in a big way, and the same resorts that once scoffed at the sport have now installed massive snow parks with radical half-pipes and jumps. **Cross-country skiing** is also popular. Most resorts **rent** skis for about $30 and snowboards for $35.

Downhill skiing

Squaw Valley USA, Squaw Valley Rd, halfway between Truckee and Tahoe City (℡530/583-6955 or 1-800/766-9321, ⓦwww.squaw.com). Thirty lifts service over 4000 acres of unbeatable terrain at the site of the 1960 Winter Olympics. Nonskiers can take the cable lift ($16) and use the ice-skating/swimming pool complex for the day. Lift tickets are $54.

Heavenly, reachable by shuttle from Southshore, two miles from the casinos, or via a newly completed gondola right on Hwy 50, next to the state line (℡775/586-7000 or 1-800/243-2836, ⓦwww.skiheavenly.com). Prime location and sheer scale (82 runs and 27 lifts) make this one of the lake's most frequented resorts, and also offers the highest vertical skiing served by a lift. Nonskiers can take a scenic gondola ride for the view ($20) in winter or summer. Lift tickets are $57.

Homewood, 6 miles north of Tahoe City on Hwy–89 (℡530/525-2992 or 1-800/824-6348, ⓦwww.skihomewood.com). Smaller and more relaxed than its massive resort neighbors, Homewood boasts some surprisingly good skiing with unbeatable views of the lake and reasonable prices. Lift tickets go for $42; as low as $25 mid-week.

Kirkwood Ski Resort, 35 miles south of South Lake Tahoe on Hwy-88 (℡209/258-6000, ⓦwww.kirkwood.com). A bit out of the way if you're in Tahoe but worth the trip as a destination in itself for numerous recreational possibilities including excellent hiking and biking trails. Lift tickets are $49.

Cross-country skiing

Royal Gorge, in Soda Springs, 10 miles west of Truckee (℡530/426-3871 or 1-800/500-3871, ⓦwww.royalgorge.com). The largest and best of Tahoe's cross-country resorts has 204 miles of groomed trails. $24.50 trail fee, $17.50 rental fee, and $20 for group lessons, $30 for private.

Spooner Lake, in Nevada at the intersection of Hwy-50 and Hwy-28 (℡775/749-5349, ⓦwww.spoonerlake.com). The closest cross-country resort to South Lake Tahoe has lake views and 63 miles of groomed trails. Trail fees are $16.50, rentals are $16, and lessons are $36.

Eating and drinking

Fast food and casino all-you-can-eat buffets are standard in Southshore. Tahoe City has a better range of moderately priced restaurants as well as a couple of good bars, all within a few minutes of each other.

Lakehouse Pizza 120 Grove St, Tahoe City ☏530/583-2222. Tahoe's best place for pizza is also a popular spot for cocktails on the lake at sundown.

Pierce Street Annex in the back of the Lighthouse Center, Tahoe City ☏530/583-5800. The place for drinking and dancing on the Northshore.

Red Hut Waffle Shop 2749 Lake Tahoe Blvd, South Lake Tahoe ☏530/541-9024. Ever-popular coffee shop, justifiably crowded early winter mornings with carbo-loading skiers.

River Ranch Hwy-89 and Alpine Meadows Rd, Tahoe City ☏530/583-4264 or 1-800/535-9900. Historic lodge on the Truckee River with excellent New American cuisine served in a relaxed, comforting atmosphere.

Rosie's Café 571 North Lake Blvd, Tahoe City ☏530/583-8504. Cozy restaurant with a vaulted ceiling and fireplace serving delicious grilled

meats, fresh sandwiches and filling breakfasts.

Sprouts 3123 Lake Tahoe Blvd near Alameda Ave, South Lake Tahoe ☏530/541-6969. Almost, but not completely, vegetarian, with good organic sandwiches, burritos and smoothies.

Sunnyside Restaurant and Lodge 1850 West Lake Blvd, near Tahoe City ☏530/583-7200. One of the most popular places to have cocktails at sunset on the deck overlooking the lake.

Tahoe Restaurant & Bäckerei Hwy-89, 1/2 mile south of Hwy-28, Tahoe City ☏530/583-1377. Family-style bakery and restaurant popular with locals.

Taj Mahal 3838 Lake Tahoe Blvd in the *Quality Inn*, South Lake Tahoe ☏530/541-6495. Basic Indian fare with a daily 11-course lunch buffet.

Tep's Villa Roma 3450 Hwy-50, South Lake Tahoe ☏530/541-8227. Longstanding Southshore institution serves large portions of hearty Italian food.

Donner Lake

Twenty-five miles north of Lake Tahoe, **Donner Lake**, surrounded by alpine cliffs of silver-gray granite, was the site of a gruesome tragedy in 1846, when the **Donner Party**, heading for the Gold Rush, found their route blocked by early snowfall. They stopped and built crude shelters, hoping that the snow would melt; it didn't. Fifteen of their number braved the mountains in search of help from Sutter's Fort in Sacramento; only two men and five women made it, surviving by eating the bodies of the men who died. A rescue party set off immediately, only to find more of the same: thirty or so half-crazed survivors, living off the meat of their fellow travelers. The horrific tale is recounted in the small **Emigrant Trail Museum** (daily 9am–5pm; $1), just off Donner Pass Road in Donner State Park.

Northern California

The massive and eerily silent volcanic lands of **northern California** have more in common with Oregon and Washington than with the rest of the state. Its small settlements live by logging, fishing and farming, though locals have been joined in recent years by New Agers, ex-hippies, and an ever-growing contingent of tourists. Once you're past the atypically lush valleys of the **Wine Country**, the **coast** stretches for four hundred miles of rugged bluffs and forests. Aside from the beautiful deserted beaches that stripe the coast, trees are the big attraction, thousands of years old and hundreds of feet high, dominating a landscape swathed in swirling mists. The **Redwood National Park** teems with campers and hikers in summer, but out of season it can be idyllic. The remote wildernesses of the **interior** can be enchanting, especially around the **Shasta Cascade** and **Lassen Volcanic National Park**.

Public transportation is, not surprisingly, scarce, though Greyhound buses run from San Francisco and Sacramento up and down I-5 and US-101.

The Wine Country

The warm and sunny hills of **Napa** and **Sonoma valleys**, an hour north of San Francisco, are by reputation, if not statistically, at the center of the American wine industry; their 29,000 grape-acres turn out vintages to satisfy a snobbery every bit as rampant as in Europe. In summer, cars jam Hwy-29 through its heart, as visitors embark on a day's free drinking, thinly disguised as an avid interest in wine.

The Napa Valley

A thirty-mile strip of gently landscaped hillsides, the **Napa Valley** looks more like southern France than a near-neighbor of the Pacific Ocean. The one anomaly is the town of **Napa** itself, a sprawling, ungainly city of 60,000 best avoided in favor of the wineries and small towns north on Hwy-29. Nine miles north, first up is **YOUNTVILLE**, named in honor of the valley's pioneer, George C. Yount. Today the town is anchored by **Vintage 1870**, 6525 Washington St (daily 10.30am–5.30pm), a shopping and wine complex in a converted winery that rents bikes, helmets and a map of wine country for $20 per day.

Of the large wineries at the valley's southern end, **Robert Mondavi**, at 7801 St Helena Hwy in Oakville (daily 10am–5pm; $10; Ⓦ www.mondavi.com), offers the most informative and least sales-driven tours and tastings.

A little further up the valley past the pretty village of **ST HELENA**, **Beringer Vineyards,** at 2000 Main St (daily 9.30am–4.30pm; $5; Ⓦ www.beringer.com), is modeled on a German Gothic mansion and has graced the cover of many a wine magazine. Spacious lawns and a grand tasting room, heavy on the dark wood, make for quite a regal experience.

Homey **CALISTOGA**, at the very tip of the valley, is well known for its mud baths, whirlpools and mineral water, though its wineries are just as appealing. South of town, **Clos Pegase**, 1060 Dunaweal Lane (daily 10.30am–5pm; Ⓣ 707/942-4981, Ⓦ www.clospegase.com), is a flamboyant, high-profile winery that emphasizes the link between fine wine and fine art, with an excellent sculpture garden around buildings designed by postmodern architect Michael Graves. Tastings are $2.50, and there are tours at 11am and 2pm. The **Chateau Montelena**, 1429 Tubbs Lane (Ⓣ 707/942-5105, Ⓦ www.montelena.com), just north of town, is one of the valley's oldest and smallest wineries, with an impressive medieval facade and a reputation for first class chardonnays. This is where the 'Judgment of Paris' came down. A mile further up the road, the **Old Faithful Geyser** (daily 9am–6pm; $6; Ⓣ 707/942-6463) spurts boiling water sixty feet into the air at forty-minute intervals. The water source was discovered while drilling for oil here in the 1920s, when search equipment struck a force estimated to be up to a thousand pounds per square foot.

Practicalities

From San Francisco there are daily Gray Line **bus tours** ($55; ☎415/558-7300 or 1-800/826-0202) to the Wine Country; otherwise take the Blue & Gold Fleet tour which leaves daily from Fisherman's Wharf and includes a ferry trip across the bay past Alcatraz as well as a bus trip through Napa and Sonoma valleys with stops at three wineries ($54.50; ☎415/705-8200). Napa itself doesn't offer much for budget lodging; you're better off in Sonoma, where at least the cost of a room is offset by a pleasant surrounding.

In **St Helena**, *Hotel St Helena*, 1309 Main St (☎707/963-4388; ❼–❾), provides cozy rooms right in the center of town. Also a working vineyard set on 20 acres of grapes, *Sunny Acres Bed & Breakfast*, 397 Main St (☎707/963-2826; ❻/❼), continually books its three sumptuous rooms. St Helena's restaurants range from the California fusion cooking of *Pinot Blanc*, 641 Main St (☎707/963-6191), to the 400-plus list of wines at the gigantic *Wine Spectator Greystone Restaurant*, 2555 Main St (☎707/967-1010).

In **Calistoga**, *Dr Wilkinson's Hot Springs*, 1507 Lincoln Ave (☎707/942-4102, ⓦwww.drwilkinson.com; ❺–❼), is a legendary health spa and hotel; less expensive lodgings (and spa facilities) lining the main drag, Lincoln Avenue, include the quiet, modern *Comfort Inn* at no. 1865 (☎707/942-9400; ❹/❺ weekdays, ❻/❼ weekends). Downtown's most enticing hotel can be found at 1457 Lincoln in the historic *Mount View Hotel and Spa* (☎707/942-6877 or 1-800/816-6877, ⓦwww.mountviewhotel.com; ❻/❼ double, ❽/❾ cottage with patio and jacuzzi). Creative cuisine featuring unheard-of combinations such as chile rellenos with walnut pomegranate sauce make dining at the *Wappo Bar Bistro*, 1226 Washington St (☎707/942-4712), a delicious adventure. The *Calistoga Inn*, 1250 Lincoln Ave (☎707/942-4101), serves great seafood appetizers, including spicy Cajun prawns and crispy crabcakes, plus a wide range of wines, microbrewed beers and excellent desserts. *Brannan's Grill*, 1374 Lincoln Ave (☎707/942-2233), serves fresh oysters, salmon and pecan-stuffed quail in an airy wood-interior bistro.

The Sonoma Valley

On looks alone, the crescent-shaped **Sonoma Valley** beats Napa hands down. This altogether more rustic valley curves between oak-covered mountain ranges from the Spanish colonial town of **SONOMA** to Glen Ellen, a few miles north along Hwy-12. It's far smaller than Napa, and many of its wineries are informal, family-run businesses, where a charge for tasting is still frowned upon and visitors are few.

The restored **Mission San Francisco Solano de Sonoma** (daily 10am–5pm; $3), just east of the spacious plaza in Sonoma, was the last and northernmost of the California missions, and the only one established in northern California by the nervous Mexican rulers, who were fearful of expansionist Russian fur traders. The plaza was also the sight of the Bear Flag Revolt, the 1846 action that propelled California into independence from Mexico, and then statehood. Sonoma's wineries are concentrated a mile east, within walking distance, and include the grand old **Buena Vista Winery**, 18000 Old Winery Rd (free tasting daily 10.30am–4.30pm; historical tours daily 2pm; ☎1-800/926-1266, ⓦwww.buenavistawinery.com), which has champagne cellars, tunnels of oak caskets and a high-ceilinged tasting room. A 10-minute drive further north, in charming Glen Ellen, takes you to the **Benziger Family Winery**, 1883 London Ranch Rd (daily 10am–5pm; $10 for five tastings; ☎1-888/490-2739, ⓦwww.benziger.com). A do-it-yourself tour explains how wine grapes are cultivated and flavored, and four times daily a vineyard tram ride tour takes you around the vineyard along the side of Mount Sonoma. A half-mile up London Ranch Road begins **Jack London State Park** (daily 9.30am–5pm, till 7pm in summer; $3 per car), which holds the author's final resting place along with a decent museum that houses a collection of souvenirs he picked up while traveling the globe.

Practicalities

On weekdays, Sonoma County Transit (℡707/576-7433, Ⓦwww.sctransit.com) **buses** link the town to Napa, and to Santa Rosa in the north. **Accommodation** is pricey, though the *Sonoma Hotel*, 110 W Spain St (℡707/996-2996; ❼), has antique-crammed doubles and a good bar, and the *Swiss Hotel*, 18 W Spain St (℡707/938-2884, Ⓦwww.sterba.com/sonoma/swiss; ❻/❼), is both historical and whimsical. Good shopping and cafés abound on the square; *La Casa*, 121 E Spain St (℡707/996-3406), is a friendly, festive and inexpensive Mexican **restaurant** across from the mission, while nearby, at 2 Spain St, the *Sonoma Cheese Factory* sells solid Sonoma Jack cheeses and other ingredients perfect for putting together a picnic basket.

The northern coast

The fog-bound towns and windswept, craggy beaches of the **northern coast** couldn't be farther removed from Southern California's sandy, sunny strip of ocean. Stretching north of San Francisco to the Oregon border, the area is better suited for hiking and camping than sunbathing, with a climate of cool temperatures year-round and a huge network of national, state and regional parks preserving magnificent **redwood** trees. Throw on your hiking boots and get out onto the trails that sweep past lolling seals, migrating whales, and some of the oldest, tallest trees on Earth.

The Sonoma coast and Russian River

Despite the weekend influx from San Francisco, the villages of the **Sonoma coast** and **Russian River Valley** seem all but asleep for most of the year. Tucked along the slow, snaking Hwy-1, towns include **BODEGA BAY**, where Hitchcock filmed *The Birds*. From here, a great thirteen-mile hike leads along the rugged cliffs to busy **Goat Rock Beach**, where the Russian River joins the ocean. A prime seal- and whale-watching spot, the beach is less than a mile from equally pleasing **JENNER**, which is a good place for clam chowder and ocean-staring.

About ten miles inland on Hwy-116, towards the warm and pastoral Russian River Valley, **GUERNEVILLE** is a well-established gay resort. It offers plenty of **places to stay** – though many are expensive. *The Willows*, 15905 River Rd (℡707/869-2824 or 1-800/953-2828, www.willowsrussianriver.com; ❹–❻), provides luxurious rooms alongside the river, while the **campground** at *Johnson's Resort* on First Street has cabins, as well as a lively nightlife (℡707/869-2022, Ⓦwww.johnsonsbeach.com/home.htm; ❶). The *Russian River Resort* ("Triple R"), 16390 Fourth St (℡707/869-0691 or 1-800/4-1RESORT, Ⓦwww.russianriverresort.com; ❸–❻), and *River Business Inc*, 16225 Main St (℡707/869-3400), are both popular places to eat and drink. The **Armstrong Redwoods State Reserve** ($2 per car, pedestrians free), two miles north, contains 750 very dense acres of enormous redwoods, interspersed by trails – horseback riding is particularly recommended. Guided expeditions run by the Armstrong Woods Pack Station (℡707/887-2939, ⓦwww.redwoodhorses.com) vary in length from half a day ($50 and up) to three-day pack trips ($675).

MONTE RIO, three miles back down the river towards the coast, is a lovely old resort town, at the entrance to the 2500-acre **Bohemian Grove**, where the richest and most powerful men in the country traditionally gather in privacy each July for two weeks of (supposedly male-only) high jinks.

The Mendocino coast

The coast of **Mendocino County**, 150 miles north of San Francisco, is a dramatic extension of the Sonoma coastline – the headlands a bit sharper, the surf a bit rougher, but otherwise more of the same. **MENDOCINO** itself looks like a transplanted New England fishing village: weathered and charming, with plenty of art galleries and boutiques. Just south of town, hiking and cycling trails weave through the unusual **Van Damme State Park**, on Hwy-1 ($2–3; ℡707/937-5804), where the ancient trees of the **Pygmy Forest** are stunted to waist height because of poor drainage and soil chemicals. Two-hour sea cave tours through the park are available through Lost Coast Kayaking (three times daily; $45; ℡707/937-2434).

The *Sea Gull Inn*, 44960 Albion St (℡1-888/937-5204 or 707/937-5204, ⓦwww.mcn.org/a/seagull; ❷–❻), is the best of the affordable accommodations in the center of town, though the antique-filled rooms at *The Mendocino Hotel and Garden Suites*, 45080 Main St (℡1-800/548-0513 or 707/937-0511, ⓦwww.mendocinohotel.com; ❹–❾), are more luxurious. The town's oldest **bar** is *Dick's Place* on Main Street, the closest thing you'll find to a local hangout. Of Mendocino's **restaurants**, the best and most famous is *Café Beaujolais*, 961 Ukiah St (℡707/937-5614), which specializes in organic California cuisine. *955 Ukiah Street* (℡707/937-1955) serves some of the best food in town: entrees are considered a steal for $15–25 a plate (daily from 6pm; closed Tues). For slightly cheaper fare, try the *Mendocino Café*, 10485 Lansing St (℡707/937-2422), serving an eclectic mix of salads, pastas and sandwiches, daily until 9pm. *Tote Féte Bakery*, behind the deli of the same name at 10450 Lansing St (℡707/937-3140; daily until 4pm), produces delicious breads, pastries and muffins, which you can eat outside on the tree-shaded deck.

The Humboldt coast

Humboldt is by far the most beautiful of the coastal counties: almost entirely forestland, overwhelmingly peaceful in places, in others plain eerie. The impassable cliffs of **Kings Range** prevent even the sinuous Hwy-1 from reaching the "Lost Coast" of its southern reaches. To get there you have to travel US-101 through the deepest redwood territory as far as **GARBERVILLE**, a one-street town with a few good bars, at the center of the "Emerald Triangle" that produces the majority of California's largest cash crop, marijuana. Every August, the town hosts the enormous **Reggae on the River** festival (information on ℡707/923-4583, ⓦwww.reggaeontheriver.com).

Redwood country begins in earnest a few miles north, at the **Humboldt Redwoods State Park**, California's largest redwood park. The serpentine **Avenue of the Giants** weaves for 33 miles through trees that block all but a few strands of sunlight, but you can exit at numerous points to get back on US-101. This is the habitat of *Sequoia sempervirens*, the coastal redwood, with ancestors dating back to the dinosaurs. Some are over 350ft tall. Three campgrounds fill up

Bigfoot country

Willow Creek, forty miles east of Arcata, is the self-proclaimed gateway to "**Bigfoot Country**." Reports of giant 350- to 800-pound humanoids wandering the forests of northwestern California have circulated since the late nineteenth century, fueled by long-established Indian legends, but weren't taken seriously until 1958, when a road maintenance crew found giant footprints. Thanks to their photos, the Bigfoot story went worldwide. Since then, there have been over forty separate sightings of Bigfoot prints. At the crossroads in Willow Creek is a huge wooden replica of the man-ape, with slanted forehead, flared nostrils and short ears, an identikit of the creature who in recent years has added kidnapping to his list of alleged activities. A small **visitor center** here has details of Bigfoot's escapades, as well as information on the adjacent **Hoopa Valley Indian Reservation**, which has often been the site of violent confrontation between Native Americans and whites over fishing territory.

quickly in summertime ($12; reserve through PARKNET at ☏1-800/444-7275 or call ☏707/946-2409 for information, ⓦwww.humboldtredwoods.org).

Tiny **SAMOA**, a few minutes by car over the bay from **EUREKA**, holds the last remaining cookhouse in the west. Lumbermen came to the *Samoa Cookhouse* (☏707/442-1659) to eat gargantuan meals after a day of felling redwoods; the oilskin tablecloths and burly workers have gone, but the lumbercamp style remains, with long tables and colossal portions of red meat.

ARCATA, twelve miles north of Eureka, a small college town with an earthy, mellow pace, has a grassy central plaza surrounded by good restaurants, and some excellent white-sand, windswept beaches to the north. The *Fairwinds Motel*, 1674 G St (☏707/822-4824; ❷/❸), is probably the best deal in town. More upscale, the *Hotel Arcata*, 708 Ninth St (☏707/826-0217 or 1-800/344-1221, ⓦwww.hotelarcata.com; ❸–❻), is central and offers standard rooms and nicer suites. The working *Humboldt Brewery*, 856 Tenth St, maker of the not uncontroversial Humboldt Hemp Ale, has its own bar and low-priced restaurant.

Redwood National Park

Thirty miles north of Arcata, the small town of **ORICK** marks the southern limit, and busiest section, of the **Redwood National Park**. **Tall Trees Grove** here is home to one of the world's tallest trees – a mighty 367-footer. Many visitors hike to it on the 8.5-mile trail from the **information center** (daily 9am–5pm; ☏707/464-6101), from which you can obtain the needed free permit to drive and camp the back roads leading to the tree.

Of the three state parks within the Redwood National Park area, **Prairie Creek** is the most varied and popular, and while bear and elk roam in plain sight, you can also be taken around here by the rangers for a **tour** of the wild and damp profusion. Highlights include the meadows of **Elk Prairie** in front of the **ranger station** (summer daily 8am–6pm; rest of year daily 9am–5pm; ☏707/464-6101), where herds of Roosevelt Elk, massive beasts weighing up to four hundred pounds, wander freely, protected from poachers.

Spectacular coastal views can be had from trails in the **Klamath** area, especially the **Klamath Overlook**, on Requa Road about three-quarters of a mile down to the sea. You can drive through, jump over, or lumber under all the sculpted **Trees of Mystery** (daily in summer 8am–8pm, 9am–5pm in winter; $15), except the impressive **Cathedral Tree**, where nine trees have grown from one root structure to form a spooky circle. The HI-Redwood National Park **hostel** (☏707/482-8265, ⓦwww.norcalhostels.org; ❶) on US-101 has dorm beds from $13–15.

The park headquarters are in **CRESCENT CITY** at 1111 Second St (daily 9am–5pm ℡707/464-6101), but you can pick up information all over the park. There are **campgrounds** everywhere; three that have showers and water are *Prairie Creek* on US-101; *Mill Creek*, eight miles south of Crescent City; and *Jedediah Smith*, five miles north of Crescent City on the Smith River. If you must come in summer, make reservations through PARKNET (℡1-800/444-7275) and if things get really desperate, head up US-101 and look for **motels** around Crescent City.

The northern interior

The remote **northern interior** of California, cut off from the coast by the **Shasta Cascade** range and dominated by forests, lakes and mountains, is largely uninhabited too, and infrequently visited. I-5 leads through the heart of this near wilderness, forging straight through the unspectacular farmland of **Sacramento Valley** to **Redding** – the region's only buses follow this route. Redding isn't much of a place in itself, but it's a good base for the **Whiskeytown–Shasta–Trinity area** and the more demanding **Lassen National Volcanic Park**. Mountaineers and the spiritually-minded flock to **Mount Shasta**, which is close enough to the volcanic **Lava Beds** at the very northeastern tip of the state for them to be a long but feasible day's car trip.

Chico

Charming little **CHICO**, about midway between Sacramento and Redding, some twenty miles east of I-5, is a good stop-off if you don't want to attempt to cover the whole valley from top to bottom in one day, or if you're here to visit Lassen Volcanic National Park (see opposite) and need somewhere to stay. Home to **Chico State University**, the laid-back town is loved by mountain bikers for its many trails. Cheap rooms downtown exist at *Holiday Inn*, 685 Manzanita Court (℡530/345-2491 or 1-800/310-2491; ❸/❹), and there are several good restaurants, notably *La Hacienda Inn*, 2635 Esplanade (℡530/893-8270), a Mexican spot famed for its special pink sauce, known as "Heroin Sauce" for its addictive sweet flavor.

Redding and Shasta

A sprawling expanse of chain stores with a shopping mall in its heart and a poured-concrete convention center at its gate, **REDDING** sticks out as an anomaly amidst the natural splendor that makes up the northern interior. The region's largest city, with 70,000 people, it's acted as a northern nexus since the late-nineteenth century, when the Central Pacific railroad came through. Today it remains a crossroads, bulging with cookie-cutter motels and diners. Along Market Street (Hwy-273): *Best Western Hospitality House*, 532 N Market St (℡530/241-6464 or 1-800/700-3019; ❸/❹), is a typical option; the *Deluxe Inn*, 1135 Market St (℡530/243-5141; ❷/❸), is slightly less luxurious but close to the Greyhound station.

  SHASTA, six miles west of Redding and not to be confused with Mount Shasta, is more appealing, though barely. These half-ruined brick buildings were once a booming gold-mining town, literally at the end of the road from San Francisco and on the very edge of the wilderness. The **courthouse** has been turned into a museum (Wed–Sun 10am–5pm; $2) full of historical California artwork and mining paraphernalia; the gallows and prison cells are a grim reminder of the once daily executions.

Precipitous Hwy-299 climbs from Shasta into the **Whiskeytown-Shasta-Trinity National Recreation Area**, where the artificial beaches, forests and camping facilities at three lakes – Clair Eagle, Whiskeytown and Shasta – meet the needs of waterskiers, sailors and wilderness hikers. Sadly, during summer it's completely congested, as windsurfers, motorboats, jet skis and recreational vehicles block the narrow routes which serve the lakes. An extensive system of tunnels, dams and aqueducts directs the plentiful waters of the Sacramento River in to California's central valley to irrigate cash crops. The lakes are pretty enough, but residents complain they're not a patch on the wild waters that used to flow from the mountains before the Central Valley Project came along in the 1960s.

Lassen Volcanic National Park

About fifty miles over gently-sloping plains east from Red Bluff on Hwy-36, or forty miles east from Redding on Hwy-44, the 106,000 acres that make up the pine forests, crystal-green lakes and boiling thermal pools of the **LASSEN VOLCANIC NATIONAL PARK** are one of the most unearthly parts of northern California's forbidding climate, which brings up to fifty feet of snowfall each year, keeping the area pretty much uninhabited outside the brief summer season. **Mount Lassen** itself last erupted in 1915, when the peak blew an enormous mushroom cloud some seven miles skyward, tearing the summit into chunks that landed as far away as Reno; scientists predict that it is the likeliest of all the west coast volcanoes to blow again.

The thirty-mile tour of the park along Hwy-89 from **Manzanita Lake** in the north should take no more than a few hours. There is a $10 access fee per vehicle to the park. The Mount Lassen explosion denuded the devastated area, ripping out every tree and patch of grass. Slowly the earth is recovering a green blanket, but the most vivid impression is one of complete destruction. Marking the halfway point, **Summit Lake** is a busy camping area set around a beautiful icy lake, close to which are the park's most manageable hiking trails. From a parking area to the south (8000ft up), the steep, five-mile ascent to Lassen Peak begins. Experienced hikers can do it in four hours, but wilderness seekers will have a better time pushing east to the steep trails of the **Juniper Lake** area.

Continuing south along Hwy-89, Lassen's indisputable show-stealers are **Bumpass Hell** and **Emerald Lake**, the former (named after a man who lost a leg trying to cross it) a steaming valley of active pools and vents which bubble away at a low rumble all around. The trails are sturdy and easy to manage, but you should never venture off them. The crusts over the thermal features are often brittle, and breaking through could plunge you into very hot water. Before leaving the park at **Mineral**, make an effort to stop at **Sulphur Works**, an acrid cauldron of steam vents. A magnificent but grueling trail leads for a mile around the site to the avalanche-prone summit at **Diamond Peak**, with great views over the entire park and forestland beyond.

The Park Service has its **headquarters** in Mineral (Mon–Fri 8am–4.30pm; PO Box 100, Mineral, CA 96063; ☎530/595-4444, ⓦ www.nps.gov/lavo), where you can get free maps and information (there's a box outside when it's closed, and they'll leave your backcountry permits here if you arrive late), including the *Lassen Park Guide*. Another **visitor center** (summer daily 9am–5pm; ☎530/595-4444 ext 5180) is at Manzanita Lake, just inside the northern entrance, and includes the Loomis Museum, which documents the park's eruption cycle.

Mount Shasta City and Mount Shasta

Roughly sixty miles north of Redding, a scenic road branches off I-5 to the tiny town that describes itself as "the best kept secret in California": **MOUNT SHASTA CITY**, hard under the enormous bulk of the 14,162ft **Mount Shasta**. Still considered active despite not having erupted for two hundred years, this lone peak dominates the landscape for a hundred miles around, and its "energies" attract New Agers by the score. If you want to climb to the summit (10hr; crampons and ice axe needed most of the year), or simply to explore the flanks of the mountain along the many trails, you must obtain a free permit from the **ranger district office**, 204 W Alma St (April–Oct Mon–Sat 8am–4.30pm; rest of year Mon–Fri 8am–4.30pm; ☎530/926-4511), or you can self-issue one at the main trailheads.

Greyhound buses on the Redding–Oregon run stop on N Mount Shasta Boulevard, a couple of blocks from the **Chamber of Commerce**, 300 Pine St (summer daily 9am–5pm, in winter daily 10am–4pm; ☎530/926-4865 or 1-800/397-1519, Ⓦwww.mtshastachamber.com). There's budget **accommodation** at the excellent *Alpenrose Cottage Guest House*, 204 E Hinkley St (☎530/926-6724, Ⓦwww.hostels.com/alpenrose; ❶–❸), and the *Best Western Tree House Motor Inn*, 111 Morgan Way (☎1-800/545-7164 or 530/926-3101; ❹/❺). Nicer still, the *McCloud Hotel Bed & Breakfast*, 408 Main St, McCloud (☎1-800/964-2823 or 530/964-2822), has rooms with Jacuzzis (❻/❼) and without (❹/❺). *Lake Siskiyou Campground* (☎530/926-2618) is four miles west of town.

Some of the town's best food can be found at *Lily's*, 1013 S Mount Shasta Blvd (☎530/926-3372), which serves Mexican fare, prime rib and, surprisingly, a wide range of vegetarian dishes, and big Sunday brunches. For Italian and cocktails, head for *Mike and Tony's*, 501 S Mount Shasta Blvd (☎530/926-4792). Breakfast, or bagels anytime, can be found at the New Agey *Bagel Café and Bakery*, 315 N Mount Shasta Blvd (☎530/926-1414).

Lava Beds National Monument

Lava Beds National Monument, in the far northeastern corner of the state, is the most remote and forgotten of California's parks, and also one of its most interesting. The history of these volcanic caves and huge black lava flows is as violent as the natural forces that created them. Before the Gold Rush the area was home to the **Modoc** Indians, but repeated and bloody confrontations with miners led the government to order them into a reservation shared with another, traditionally enemy, tribe. After only a few months the Modocs drifted back to the isolation of the lava beds, and in 1872 the army was sent in. Fifty-two Modoc warriors, under the leadership of "Captain Jack," held back an army twenty times the size of theirs for five months from a natural fortress of passageways now known as **Captain Jack's Stronghold**, at the park's northern tip. You can retrace the conflict and the US press's pressure on the Army to abandon its cause, through well-detailed self-guided trails in the park as well as an exhibit at the **visitor center** (summer daily 8am–6pm; rest of year daily 8am–5pm; ☎530/667-2282, Ⓦwww.nps.gov/labe).

The bulk of the lava tube caves are close to the visitor center from where you can opt for the free ranger-led tours (daily 9am & 2pm) or, with some nerve and a good light source (free to borrow from the visitor center), explore the caves alone. You can camp near the visitor center, but there are no shops nearby, so bring everything you need with you. Nearby is the **Modoc Ranger Station** (Mon–Fri 9am–5pm; ☎530/233-5811) with general information on the Modoc National Forest. North and west of Lava Beds, the **Klamath Basin**

National Wildlife Refuge ($3 permit needed; self-issuing boxes on premises) hosts millions of birds migrating along the Pacific Flyway. The **visitor center** (Mon–Fri 8am–4.30pm, Sat & Sun 10am–4pm; ☎530/667-2231) is off Hill Road near the northwest entrance for Lava Beds. Surprisingly, the best way of spotting the wildlife is by driving along designated routes; getting out of the car and walking scares the birds off.

CHAPTER 14

Highlights

* **Pike Place Market, Seattle, WA** This regenerated market holds Seattle's liveliest assortment of stalls and street entertainers. See p.1183

* **Vashon Island, WA** Just a short ferry ride from downtown Seattle, this tranquil little island is home to the Northwest's loveliest youth hostel. See p.1192

* **Quinault Rainforest, WA** Sublime hiking trails meander through this dense lakeside forest in Olympic National Park. See p.1203

* **Mount St Helens, WA** Still a haunting sight two decades after it blew its top, despite the rehabilitation of wildlife. See p.1207

* **Sandcastle Competition, OR** By far the best time to visit Cannon Beach is in summer, for its annual eruption of seaside sculpture and tomfoolery. See p.1228

* **Crater Lake, OR** Cradled in what's left of a hollowed-out volcano, this sheer blue lake makes a stunning year-round destination. See p.1232

* **Hells Canyon, OR** Even deeper than the Grand Canyon, this remote gorge offers white-water rafting in summer. See p.1236

The Pacific Northwest

The Pacific Northwest states of **WASHINGTON** and **OREGON**, while similar in climate, topography and generally liberal politics, are quite different in their attitude toward expansion and progress. Since the 1990s, Washington has been home to high-tech businesses, sprawling growth, bustling military bases and notorious freeway gridlock, while Oregon remains lower-scaled in both design and temperament, thanks in no small measure to its stringent land-use laws and "urban-growth boundaries" surrounding its larger cities.

Significantly cooler than California to the south, both are split by the great north–south spine of the **Cascade Mountains**, with their western sides more appealing by far. Throughout these hilly **western** regions, the ocean rains have created a verdant landscape, thick with woodlands that on the **Olympic Peninsula** become localized rainforests. This fertile land is where the population is most heavily concentrated, although the principal cities are not along the exposed coast itself, which remains – in Oregon at least – remarkably pristine, scattered with remote, rugged beaches. Both **Seattle** and **Portland** lie roughly fifty miles from the Pacific Ocean along the I-5 Interstate, running from Canada to California. Seattle, the commercial and cultural capital of the Northwest, is a major national port perched on the edge of the beautiful, island-strewn **Puget Sound**, with a busy network of local and long-distance ferries among the container traffic. Portland lies adjacent to the rich farmlands of the Willamette Valley, long the historic heartland of Oregon.

Across the Cascades, the **east** is far drier and less hospitable, peppered with desert and scrubland, much of which is prone to drought and periodic wildfires, which have become increasingly common in recent years. Of the towns, only **Spokane** is of any appreciable size, though the booming resort town of **Bend** is a far more appealing destination, as its Cascade-straddling location makes it a useful base for sampling the mountains, desert and, especially the beautiful **Columbia River Gorge**. Of outstanding interest also is the scarred territory between Seattle and Portland around **Mount St Helens**, which erupted with devastating effect in 1980.

Some history

The **first inhabitants** of the Pacific Northwest are believed to have reached the continent across a land bridge over what is now the Bering Strait between Siberia and Alaska, from 12,000 to 20,000 years ago near the end of the last Ice Age. It wasn't until the early nineteenth century that was there a significant white presence in the region, and even that was very much confined to trading and exploration along the coast rather than to permanent settlement.

During that time, Russian trappers began to make their way down from the north, Canadians from the northeast, while European sea captains such as Cook and Vancouver came in search of the fabled **Northwest Passage**, an ice-free route between the Atlantic and the Pacific. A brief period of hectic competition, in which entrepreneurs of many nationalities vied for fur-trading profits, came to an end only when the whole coast was all but "trapped out."

Explorers Meriwether Lewis and William Clark, who came along the Columbia River Gorge in 1804 in search of the Pacific, were the first whites to cross the interior of the continent, and within forty years American settlers were streaming in along the **Oregon Trail**. This legendary period of immigration gave de facto control of the region to the United States, and official title followed in 1846 with the signing of a land pact with Britain that established a territorial boundary for the US and Canada at the 49th Parallel.

During the forty years after that, the railroads reached Portland and Seattle, Chief Joseph of the Nez Percé made his last bid on behalf of the displaced Native Americans (see p.924), and both Oregon and Washington achieved statehood.

Washington

Although **Seattle** is one of America's most likeable and vibrant cities, well worth a few days of anybody's time, perhaps its greatest asset for visitors is its proximity to the glorious rural scenery of **Puget Sound**. The islands here are stepping stones to the **Olympic Peninsula** to the west, whose mountains are home to rare elk and lush vegetation that merges into rainforest, and whose wilderness beaches have remained unchanged for centuries. The **Olympic National Park**, which occupies the bulk of the peninsula, is dazzling, and a hike along one of its clearly laid-out trails can be a highlight of any trip. Just make sure that you don't mind the wet, often stormy **weather** of western Washington, which only offers predictably warm temperatures and blue skies during the summer.

Not quite as rainy as the mountains to the northeast, the **southern coast** is flatter and more accessible but not as appealing, littered with industrial towns and glum holiday resorts. The nearest worthwhile destination lies a few hours east, where you can marvel at the wasted volcanic scenery of **Mount St Helens**.

Much drier and more desolate, the sprawling prairie-plateau that makes up most of **eastern Washington** is a long, slow grind with little of interest, though if a cross-country trek takes you through **Spokane**, the **Grand Coulee Dam** is worth a detour. Otherwise you're only likely to come out here if you're traveling the Cascade loop, a memorable 400-mile round-trip through the stunning **Cascade Mountains**.

Getting around Washington

Seattle is well served by both **trains** and **buses**. Amtrak (☎1-800-USA-RAIL, ⓦ www.amtrak.com) runs its Coast Starlight train once daily south to LA, while its Cascades line runs four times per day south to Eugene, Oregon, and north to Vancouver in British Columbia. Amtrak's daily Empire Builder route heads east (to Chicago), just as Greyhound (☎1-800/229-9424) provides bus service east across the Cascades to **Spokane** and beyond, with other routes to Wenatchee (for Chelan), Ellensburg, Yakima and Walla Walla. Areas not covered by Greyhound are usually accessible on local buses, though this can be time-consuming and inconvenient.

Getting to and along the coast is more difficult and requires some planning. **Ferries** from Seattle shuttle across to Winslow, on **Bainbridge Island**, from where Kitsap Transit services link with Jefferson Transit for access to Port Angeles, Port Townsend and Olympic National Park. In the Seattle and Puget Sound area, ferries (mostly run by Washington State Ferries; Washington: ☏206/464-6400 or 1-888/808-7977; British Columbia: ☏250/381-1551, ⓦwww.wsdot.wa.gov/ferries) are a reliable and enjoyable method of getting to such places as Whidbey Island and the San Juan Islands. There are also long-distance services, to Canada from Seattle, Anacortes and Port Angeles, and to Alaska from Bellingham; see p.1192.

Seattle

Curved around the shore of Elliott Bay, with Lake Washington behind and the snowy peak of Mount Rainier hovering faintly in the distance, **SEATTLE** has a magnificent setting. The insistently modern skyline of glass skyscrapers gleams across the bay, an emblem of three decades of aggressive urban renewal.

Seattle's beginnings were inauspiciously muddy. Flooded out of its first location on the flat little peninsula of Alki Point, in the 1850s the town shifted to what's now Pioneer Square, renaming itself after the Native American Chief Sealth (hence Seattle). This was soggy ground, and the small logging community built its houses on stilts. As the surrounding forest was gradually felled and the wood shipped out, Seattle grew slowly until the Klondike Gold Rush of 1897 put it firmly on the national map. World War I boosted shipbuilding, and the city was soon a large industrial center. Trade unions, based around the shipworkers, grew strong, and the Industrial Workers of the World, or "Wobblies," coordinated the US's first general strike here on February 6, 1919.

Since the beginning of the twentieth century, the **Boeing** airline corporation was crucial to the city's wellbeing, booming during World War II and employing one in five of Seattle's workforce by the 1960s. The prosperity that Boeing and more recent success stories such as **Microsoft** and internet shopping site **Amazon.com** have brought the city is obvious, reflected in a restored old center, a nationally acclaimed arts scene with vibrant movie and music industries, and a flood of coffee houses and excellent seafood restaurants. No longer overshadowed by the two big California metropolises, Seattle now regularly tops magazine surveys of desirable places to live, attracting migrants across the social and economic spectrum, which has led to both exponential growth and increasingly nightmarish traffic jams. As if to round out the turbulent decade, a February 2001 **earthquake** shook Seattle's foundations, and reminded its residents that they're just as prone to Pacific Rim tremors as their southern counterparts in the Golden State.

Despite the dizzying expansion, the city's more established neighborhoods remain distinctive, and Seattle has a pleasantly down-to-earth ambience. However, its new-found affluence jars uncomfortably with a visible street community of teenage runaways and homeless people – as well as a growing **radical scene** that splashed across the world's newspapers and TV screens with the WTO trade conference in 1999, an event that saw black-clad anarchists rioting amidst peaceful protesters in turtle outfits.

Arrival, information and getting around

Flights land at Seattle/Tacoma's **Sea-Tac Airport** (☎206/431-4444, ⓦwww
.seatac.org), on Hwy-99 (the Pacific Highway) fourteen miles south of downtown. Outside, the Gray Line Airport Express bus ($8.50 one-way, $15 round-
trip; ☎206/626-6088, ⓦwww.graylineofseattle.com) leaves every twenty
minutes for the 25-minute journey to various hotels downtown.
ShuttleExpress (☎206/622-1424 or 1-800/487-RIDE, ⓦwww.shuttleexpress
.com) offers door-to-door service for $18–30. Metro express city bus #194
($1.10, peak hours $1.75) takes thirty minutes to reach downtown's Transit
Tunnel. A **taxi** to the city center costs $25-30.

The Amtrak station at Third Avenue and Jackson Street, just south of downtown, and the Greyhound bus terminal at Eighth Avenue and Stewart Street to
the east, are both an easy bus ride from downtown. A couple of blocks towards
downtown from Greyhound is the **visitors bureau**, on the Galleria level inside
the Washington State Convention Center at Seventh Avenue and Pike Street
(Mon–Fri 8.30am–5pm, summer also Sat–Sun 10am–4pm; ☎206/461-5840,
ⓦwww.seeseattle.org). The main **post office** is downtown at Union Street and
Third Avenue (Mon–Fri 8am–5.30pm; ☎1-800/275-8777; zip code 98101).

City transportation

It's best to **get around** either on foot or on the free downtown buses. Cross
out of the free zone – bordered by Jackson and Battery streets, 6th Avenue, and
the waterfront – and you pay as you get off; come back in and you pay as you
enter. Single fares vary between $1 and $1.75, and tickets are valid for an hour.
Day–passes ($2; bought from the driver) are available on weekends and holi-
days: ticket books (for 10 and 20 rides; $10 and $20) can be purchased from
the **Metro Customer Assistance Offices** at the Metro Transit Tunnel,
Westlake Station, Fifth Avenue and Vine Street (Mon–Fri 9am–5.30pm), or in
the King Street Center, 201 S Jackson St (Mon–Fri 8am–5pm; call 24-Hour
Rider Information ☎206/553-3000 or Bus-Time ☎206/287-8463 for automated schedule, ⓦtransit.metrokc.gov), and can be used on the overhead
monorail ($1.25) between downtown and the Seattle Center, and on the
waterfront streetcar ($1 off-peak, $1.75 peak).

Washington State **ferries** run to Bainbridge Island and Bremerton; tickets
from Pier 52, Colman Dock (☎206/464-6400, ⓦwww.wsdot.wa.gov/ferries).
Gray Line (☎206/626-5208) organizes guided half-day **bus tours** ($27), or
three-hour **boat tours** ($33), which are also offered by other local operators,
the best choice being Argosy's Locks Cruise tour from Pier 57 (2 1/2 hrs, $30;
☎206/623-4252, ⓦwww.argosycruises.com).

Accommodation

While there's no shortage of hotel space in Seattle, it can be difficult to find
the middle ground between smart, expense-account-oriented places and seedy
dives. The best choices are downtown. Also of good value are the city's hostels
and B&Bs, the latter of which are especially prevalent around the Capitol Hill
district. Three specialist **B&B agencies** are A Pacific Reservation Service
(☎206/439-7677 or 1-800/684-2932, ⓦwww.seattlebedandbreakfast.com),
Washington Bed and Breakfast Guild (2442 NW Market St, #355, Seattle, WA
98107; ☎1-800/647-2918, ⓦwww.wbbg.com), and Travelers' Reservation
Service (14716 26th Ave NE, Seattle, WA, 98155; ☎206/364-5900); all provide
lodging throughout the state.

Hotels, motels and B&Bs

Alexis 1007 1st Ave ☎ 206/624-4844 or 1-800/426-7033, ⓦ www.alexishotel.com. A posh nineteenth-century hotel situated between Pike Market and Pioneer Square. With hot tubs and fireplaces, as well as an Aveda spa, fitness center and cigar bar. ❽

Claremont 2000 4th Ave ☎ 206/448-8600 or 1-800/448-8601, ⓦ www.claremonthotel.com. An intimate, European-style hotel in downtown Seattle, with weekend rates for basic rooms significantly lower than weekday rates for suites. Complimentary continental breakfast included. ❻–❽

Hotel Seattle 315 Seneca St ☎ 206/623-5110, ⓦ www.thehotelseattle.com. A good deal for those looking for a central location and modern, but not antiseptic, ambience in the upper-middle price range. Centrally located near the Seattle Art Museum. ❹–❺

Kings Inn 2106 5th Ave ☎ 206/441-8833 or 1-800/546-4760, ⓦ www.kingsinnseattle.com. Clean and basic downtown motor lodge with some spacious suites. ❸–❹

Monaco 1101 4th Ave ☎ 206/621-1770 or 1-800/945-2240, ⓦ www.monaco-seattle.com. A luxurious "boutique" hotel in the old Pacific Northwest Bell switching office, with striking lobby, elegant suites, and pet-friendly policy. Complimentary goldfish included during your stay. ❽

Paramount 724 Pine St ☎ 206/292-9500, ⓦ www.westcoasthotels.com/paramount. Solid entry in national chain of stylish modern hotels, with central location and midweek specials for around $160. Otherwise ❽.

Pioneer Square Hotel 77 Yesler Way ☎ 206/340-1234, ⓦ www.pioneersquare.com. A restored nineteenth-century hotel in Pioneer Square. Good value accommodation with a nice level of comfort. Saloon and juice bar on the lobby floor. ❻

Sorrento 900 Madison St ☎ 206/622-4400 or 1-800/426-1265, ⓦ www.hotelsorrento.com. Seattle's oldest hotel is a small luxury accommo-dation on the east side of I-5 from downtown. The regal exterior surrounds a circular courtyard with palm trees. ❽–❾

University Inn 4140 Roosevelt Way NE, University District ☎ 206/632-5055 or 1-800/733-3855, ⓦ www.universityinnseattle.com. Average modern hotel just off University Way. Some rooms have kitchens; there's also a pool and whirlpool spa. ❻

W Seattle 1112 4th Ave ☎ 206/264-6000, ⓦ www.whotels.com. The height of ultra-chic accommodation, where youthful hipsters can pose in the dark, stylish lobby, and the Gen-X elite can enjoy rooms with designer carpets and bedding, copious entertainment options and internet access, and the chance of spotting a B-list celebrity arriving with his "posse." ❾

Hostels

Green Tortoise 1525 2nd Ave, between Pike and Pine ☎ 206/340-1222 or 1-888/424-6783, ⓦ www.greentortoise.net/gtmain.html. Old-style hotel digs now functioning as a hostel, with dorm beds ($18, or $21 in summer) and some private rooms ($55–75). Free breakfast, internet access, and pickups at Amtrak, Greyhound or ferries.

HI-Seattle 84 Union St, behind Pike Place Market ☎ 206/622-5443 or 1-888/662-5443, ⓦ www.hiseattle.org. Modern and well-equipped hostel popular with families. Dorm rooms start at $24, with private rooms from $60–95. Open 24hr. Reservations are strongly advised in summer.

Vincent's Backpackers Guest House 527 Malden Ave E ☎ 206/323-7849. Comfortable house in Capitol Hill with 38 beds, most in six-bunk dorm rooms ($14), but a few doubles for $49. Bathroom with showers in all rooms, kitchen facilities and a backyard with picnic tables. Free pickup from Greyhound, Amtrak, ferry terminals and anywhere downtown if you call in advance.

YWCA 1118 5th Ave ☎ 206/461-4888, ⓦ www.ywcaworks.org. Large, clean women-only singles and doubles in a good central location. $33 single occupancy with shared bath.

The City

Downtown Seattle's main attractions are the busy stalls and cafés of **Pike Place Market** and the restored nineteenth-century **Pioneer Square**, lined with restaurants and taverns. A stroll along the more touristy **waterfront** lets you enjoy fabulous views of Elliott Bay. At the **Seattle Center** in the north, the **Space Needle** presides over cultural institutions and carnival rides, as well as the city's latest draw, the **Experience Music Project**. Several outlying districts are often livelier than downtown: **Capitol Hill**'s cafés and bars are the heart of

DOWNTOWN SEATTLE

▲ *Mukilteo Ferry*

◀ Victoria BC

◀ Bainbridge Island

◀ Bremerton

◀ Vashon

▶ 2 & Capitol Hill

▶ 7

▶ International District

ACCOMMODATION

Alexis	13
Claremont	4
Green Tortoise	6
HI-Seattle	8
Kings Inn	3
Monaco	12
Paramount	5
Pioneer Square	14
Hotel Seattle	10
Sorrento	7
University Inn	1
Vincent's Backpackers Guest House	2
W Seattle	11
YWCA	9

Elliott Bay

N

0 _____ 500 yards

RESTAURANTS, BARS AND CLUBS

Alibi Room	K	Dutch Ned's		Old Timer's	
Assaggio	F	Saloon	P	Tavern	R
Campagne	I	Gravity Bar	A	Place Pigalle	M
Copacabana	L	Jazz Alley	B	Showbox	J
Crocodile Café	E	Nikko	G	Speakesy Café	C
Dahlia Lounge	H	Noodle Ranch	D	Wild Ginger	N
Doc Maynard's		OK Hotel Cafe	O		
Public House	Q				

▼ *Museum of Flight & Airport*

the city's hipster and gay scene, and the **University District** is a student area with inexpensive cafés and uptempo nightlife.

Pike Place Market and the waterfront

Pike Place Market is the oldest continuous working public market in the US. Farmers first brought their produce to the market in 1907, lowering food prices by selling straight from the barrow. The market prospered during the Depression, but by the 1960s it was shabby and neglected, and the authorities decided to flatten the area altogether. Following vigorous protests, Seattlites voted overwhelmingly to preserve this as the affordable domain of the elderly and poor. The restoration has been highly successful: the whole place, stretched over several city blocks, bustles with energy, and a real attempt has been made to keep it true to its roots, even though upscale restaurants are beginning to creep in and sanitize away all the former seediness. Still, there's plenty to enjoy, with street entertainers playing to busy crowds, the aroma of coffee drifting from cafés, and stalls offering piles of lobsters, crabs, salmon, vegetables, fruit and flowers. Further into the long market building, handmade jewelry, wood-carvings and silk-screen prints are on sale, while small shops close by stock a massive range of ethnic foods.

Also nearby, the **Seattle Art Museum** at 100 University Street and First Avenue (Tues–Sun 10am–5pm, Thurs open until 9pm; $7 ticket includes entry to the Seattle Asian Arts Museum on Capitol Hill; free first Thurs of month; Ⓦwww.seattleartmuseum.org) occupies a Robert Venturi–designed building – noteworthy for its giant engraved letters – and features international touring exhibitions and eclectic collections of African, Pacific and Native American work, with a more limited selection of modern art. Outside the main entrance is the 48ft "**Hammering Man,**" a kinetic sculpture by Jonathan Borofsky, which has become the museum's enigmatic emblem.

Stairs in the market lead down to the steep staircase of the **Pike Place Hillclimb**, and to the waterfront below. Almost opposite the Hillclimb, **Pier 59**, an old wooden jetty that once served tall ships, now houses the underwater viewing dome of the **Seattle Aquarium** (daily 10am–5pm; summer closes at 7pm; $9, kids $6.25; Ⓦwww.seattleaquarium.org). A combined ticket also admits you to the 3-D **Omnidome** next door (daily shows starting 10am; $7; combined ticket $13; Ⓣ206/622-1869 for program info; Ⓦwww.seattleimaxdome .com), where 70mm films on the huge curved screen include the always-popular *Eruption of Mount St Helens*. On Pier 54 to the south, the most famous of the waterfront's fish-and-chip stands, *Ivar's Acres of Clams*, has its own special stop ("Clam Central Station") on the restored vintage **waterfront streetcar** ($1, peak hours $1.75). **Colman Dock** at Pier 52 is the terminal for Washington State Ferries (see p.1181).

Pioneer Square and around

A few blocks inland from the ferry terminal, the **Pioneer Square** area, Seattle's oldest district, was nearly destroyed in the 1960s, but has since been renovated, with bookshops and galleries adding a veneer of sophistication to the old red-brick, wrought iron and shady trees. Things get more raucous at night, when rock music booms out from assorted taverns and panhandlers become more aggressive.

By far the most interesting way to find out about the city's seamy past is on a 90-minute **Underground Tour** from *Doc Maynard's* tavern, 610 First Ave ($9, kids $5; Ⓣ206/682-4646, Ⓦwww.undergroundtour.com). After a disastrous fire in 1889, this area was rebuilt with the street level raised by one story, so what used to be the ground-level floors of its brick buildings are now underground, linked by subterranean passageways. A couple of blocks north from *Doc Maynard's*, at 117 S Main St, the **Klondike Gold Rush National Historical Park** (daily 9am–5pm; free; Ⓦwww.nps.gov/klse) is not a park, but a small museum celebrating the days when, thanks to a formidable campaign to promote Seattle as the gateway to Alaskan gold, prospectors streamed in and traders (and con artists) made their fortunes. The dog population fared less well as many a hapless mutt was harnessed to a sledge so that gold-seekers could practice "mushing" up and down Seattle's streets before facing Alaskan snow (see Jack London's novel *The Call of the Wild*). Just as interesting, the nearby cobblestoned square of **Occidental Park**, between Main and Washington streets at Occidental, holds four totem poles carved with mythical creatures from Northwest Native American legends. Two blocks northeast, on the edge of Pioneer Square, the 1914 white-terracotta **Smith Tower** was the city's first skyscraper, as well as its longtime visual icon – until the Space Needle appeared in the 1960s to become the city's main postcard symbol.

A few blocks south of Pioneer Square, football fans can check out a Seahawks game at **Washington State Public Stadium** (℗1-888/635-4295, ⓦwww.seahawks.com), while baseball enthusiasts can visit **Safeco Field**, further south at First Avenue and S Atlantic Street, to take in a Seattle Mariners game (℗206/622-HITS, ⓦwww.mariners.mlb.com).

The Museum of Flight

The biggest of Seattle's museums, the **Museum of Flight**, a twenty-minute bus ride (#174) south of downtown at 9404 E Marginal Way (daily 10am–5pm, until 9pm on Thurs; $9.50, kids $5; ⓦwww.museumofflight.org), is partly housed in the magnificently restored 1909 "Red Barn" that was the original Boeing manufacturing plant. Displays of 54 airplanes lead from ancient prototypes to the Wright Brothers, from the growth of Boeing to a gallery hung with twenty full-sized aircraft and a replica of John Glenn's 1962 Mercury space capsule. One unmistakable highlight is the chance to sit in the cockpit of an SR-71 Blackbird, the type of spy plane once used to fly 80,000 feet above the jungles of Vietnam.

Belltown

The resurgently chic **Belltown** area (also referred to as the Denny Regrade) has left its grunge legacy behind and is now choked with bohemian cafés, vintage clothing stores, used record shops and alternative galleries. Belltown casually blends the swank and avant-garde, beginning just to the north of Pike Street Market and extending one mile in the same direction towards the Seattle Center, with the heart of Belltown being the five-block area of Second Avenue between Stewart and Battery. Godfathers of the neighborhood, **Sub Pop Records**, famous for promotion of the early 1990s grunge scene with releases by Nirvana, Mudhoney and Soundgarden, began its operations on the edge of Belltown, where it still occupies several floors of the Terminal Sales Building. You can get the best sense of the local bohemian scene, though, at the **Center on Contemporary Art**, 65 Cedar St (Tues–Sat 11am–6pm; $5; ⓦwww.cocaseattle.org), which focuses on edgy regional works with a satirical flair.

The Seattle Center

The **Seattle Center** (ⓦwww.seattlecenter.com) dates from the 1962 World's Fair, whose theme was "Century 21" (hence the rather outdated architecture and spindly, 600ft flying-saucer-tipped Space Needle tower). Since then the 74-acre complex has become a sort of culture park, staging major sporting events, concerts and festivals, as well as a longstanding site for ancient-looking carnival rides aimed at the pre-teen set. Amid this strange hodgepodge stands the Pacific Science Center, Seattle Opera (closed until 2003), Children's Museum, Experience Music Project, and various theaters. The Center is best reached by the **monorail**, which runs from the third floor of Westlake Center at Fifth Avenue and Pine Street downtown ($1.25 one-way; ⓦ www.monorail .org) and drops you close to the **Space Needle**, the Space Age-modernist city icon, which is most appealing at night when it's lit up. The panoramic view from the observation deck, where there's a bar, is unmatched (daily 8am–midnight; $11; kids $5; ⓦ www.spaceneedle.com).

Southwest of the needle, the **Pacific Science Center** (daily 10am–5pm, weekends and summer open until 6pm; $8; ⓦ www.pacsci.org) is easily recognizable by its modernist white arches and shallow, stagnant "lake." The hands-on adventure park is full of science-related exhibits for children, and includes a planetarium and IMAX theater. Nearby lies the Frank Gehry-designed **Experience Music Project** (daily 9am–9pm, weekends open until 11pm; $19.95; ⓦ www.experience.org), a giant burst of colored metal made of sweeping aluminum curves – into which the monorail passes – that opened in June 2000. Inside is an 80,000-piece strong collection of rock memorabilia divided up into exhibits on different phases of popular music history, along with a gallery-shrine to the original Seattle guitar-god, Jimi Hendrix. As much an interior amusement park as a bona fide museum (check out the Sound Lab, where you can bang on drums and keyboards to your heart's delight), the "EMP" never loses the sense of freewheeling pleasure associated with 1960s rock and pop.

Capitol Hill

A fifteen-minute bus ride to the top of a steep hill east of downtown takes you to **Capitol Hill**, the city's alternative center since young gays, hippies and assorted radicals moved in during the 1960s and 1970s. Today it exemplifies the city's diverse lifestyles and, despite a fair bit of gentrification driving up the rents, remains a good choice for munching on ethnic food, listening to old LPs, and hitting the club scene. The shops and cafés around **Broadway** are abuzz with neo-bohemian activity and are littered throughout with storefront coffee vendors and espresso carts. East of Broadway from Twelfth to about Ninth avenues, the **Pike/Pine Corridor** is filled with all-night coffee houses, live music venues and some of Seattle's best nightspots.

By contrast, the northern end of the district features mansions built on Gold Rush fortunes that sit sedately around **Volunteer Park** (named after Spanish–American War veterans). Here you'll find the 1912 **Conservatory**'s hothouses, home to flowers, shrubs and orchids from jungle, desert and rainforest landscapes (daily 10am–4pm, summer closes at 7pm; free), as well as the old **Water Tower** that provides a free, sweeping view of Seattle through wire mesh. In the same area, the **Seattle Asian Art Museum**, 1400 E Prospect St (Tues–Sun 10am–5pm, Thurs closes at 9pm; $3, free first Thurs of month; ⓦ www.seattleartmuseum.org), boasts a 7000-piece collection of ceramics, jade and snuff bottles from Japan, China, Korea and Southeast Asia. Ten blocks east, **Washington Park** stretches to the north, encompassing the **University of Washington Arboretum**, a lush showcase for indigenous Puget Sound vegetation, with plenty of charming footpaths and different varieties of regional trees. At the south end of the park, the immaculately landscaped **Japanese Gardens** flash banks of pink flowers beside neat little pools with exotically colored carp (March–Nov daily 10am–dusk; $2.50).

The University District

Across Union Bay from the park, the **University District**, or the "U" District, is a busy hodgepodge of coffee houses, cinemas, and clothes, book and record stores catering to the University of Washington's 35,000 students.

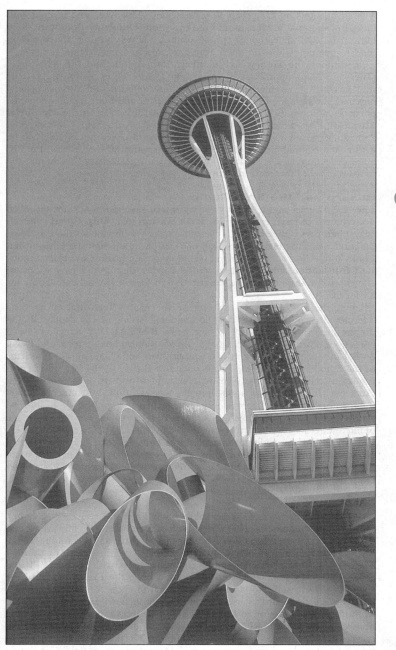

△ Space Needle

The area centers on University Way, known as "**The Ave**," and is lined with inexpensive ethnic restaurants and the cavernous University Bookstore, 4326 University Way NE. Although the sidewalks are always bustling, the area lacks the late-opening clubs and music venues of nearby Capitol Hill.

On campus, the **Henry Art Gallery**, 15th Avenue and NE 41st Street (Tues–Sun 11am–5pm, Thurs closes at 8pm; $6, free Thurs 5–8pm and for any student with ID; Ⓦwww.henryart.org), houses American and European paintings and photography from the last two centuries, and hosts rotating contemporary exhibitions focusing on regional art in all forms. The **Burke Memorial Museum**, 17th Avenue and NE 45th Street (daily 10am–5pm, Thurs closes at 8pm; $5.50; Ⓦwww.washington.edu/burkemuseum), presents exhibits on the natural and cultural history of the Pacific Rim and displays selections from its huge collection of 2.75 million fossils and Ice Age skeletons, including the remains of a 12,000-year-old sloth.

Ballard and the Ship Canal

The "U" District and Seattle's other northern neighborhoods are sliced off from the rest of town by water; the **Lake Washington Ship Canal** connects Lake Union with the sea to the west and Lake Washington to the east. Near the mouth of the canal, a procession of boats passes through the **Chittenden Locks** (bus #17 from downtown), where migrating salmon and trout negotiate a **fish ladder** laid out with viewing windows, through which you can see enormous fish leaping up (late summer season for salmon, fall and early winter for trout).

Behind the locks is Salmon Bay, with **Fisherman's Terminal** on its south side, crowded with Seattle's fishing fleet and stalls selling freshly caught fish. On the northern side of Salmon Bay, blue-collar **BALLARD** (reached by several buses from downtown) is undergoing gentrification and the historic Old Town, on Ballard Avenue, is now home to galleries, bars and restaurants. The heritage of the Scandinavian fishermen who settled in Ballard in the late nineteenth-century is celebrated at the **Nordic Heritage Museum**, 3014 NW 67th St (Tues–Sat 10am–4pm, Sun noon–4pm; $5; Ⓦwww.nordicmuseum.com), offering memorabilia and folk art associated with their long journey from the Old World through Ellis Island and eventually to the West Coast. The only other site of interest in the area lies further east, on the north shore of Lake Union, where **Gasworks Park** provides an unexpected delight. A former gas plant turned postmodern park, children now play on grassy hills that were once slag heaps and decaying, graffiti-covered machines offer surreal evidence of the site's previous industrial incarnation.

Fremont

North of downtown Seattle across Lake Union, **Fremont** is a consciously hip, mostly white middle-class area, with a spate of used bookshops and artsy cafés. The hub is the stretch of Fremont Avenue N that runs, beginning at the Fremont Bridge, from N 34th to N 37th streets, where the **Fremont Sunday Market** (April–Nov 10am–5pm) fills up a parking lot with produce stalls and a flea market. In summer, the neighborhood hosts the **Fremont Outdoor Cinema** (Ⓦwww.outdoorcinema.com), which projects classic films against a building wall on Saturdays at dusk, with live music and entertainment before all shows. A big attraction in Fremont's industrial section is the *Trolleyman Pub* housed in the historic **Redhook Brewery** building, 3400 Phinney Ave N, where beer is no longer brewed on site, but where you can still order a pint or taste a few samples to find your match. Additionally, fans of public art should check out the curious local **sculptures**, the best of the bunch being the **Fremont Troll** lurking under the Aurora Bridge at 36th Street and Aurora Avenue.

Eating

You won't have to spend a fortune in Seattle's elegant French restaurants to eat well: among the coffee shops of Capitol Hill, ethnic restaurants of the University district and, above all, Pike Place Market, there are many excellent choices. **Seafood** is the specialty, ranging from salmon and crab to trout and mussels to classic clam chowder.

Much social interaction in the city is fueled by **coffee**, and we list some of the best places to get the buzz. Along with being good spots to sip java, Seattle's coffee houses host much of its social scene, and are inexpensive choices for whiling away the time. Corporate giant *Starbucks* started here in the early 1970s (in a still-extant location in the Pike Place Market), though you're better off sampling a local brew that you can't find in your hometown minimall. Other big names include *Seattle's Best Coffee*, *Tully's* and *Torrefazione Italia*, but if you want a true taste of the city, check out one of the 200-plus **espresso carts** scattered about town, each colorfully styled and uniquely designed.

Restaurants and cafés

Assaggio 2010 4th Ave, downtown ☎206/441-1399. A fine, mid-priced Italian joint, where you can consume a wide range of tasty, inventive pastas, as well as a good selection of pizzas and salads.

Café Flora 2901 E Madison St, Capitol Hill ☎206/325-9100. Tasty, filling vegetarian restaurant strong on desserts, soups, and creative entrees like mashed potato tacos and wild mushroom curry.

Café Septieme 214 Broadway E, Capitol Hill ☎206/860-8858. A trendy, bustling European-style bistro. Sophisticated and imaginative homemade food, at moderate prices. Great desserts.

Campagne 86 Pine St ☎206/728-2800. Superb French provincial cooking near the market, with delicious foie gras and excellent desserts. A less expensive branch, *Café Campagne*, can be found downstairs at 1600 Post Alley, and is often packed with gourmands.

Copacabana 1520 Pike Place ☎206/622-6359. Inside the market, the fine South American dining here is highlighted by shrimp soup and corn pie. The always-popular balcony seating offers a good view of the crowds.

Crocodile Café 2200 2nd Ave ☎206/441-5611. Best known as Belltown's prime nightlife haunt for alternative music and poetry readings, it is also a diner by day, serving the biggest breakfasts in town for about $7.

Dahlia Lounge 1904 4th Ave, downtown ☎206/682-4142. Beautifully presented, Asian-influenced seafood dishes, and the prices to match – dinner will cost around $50 per person.

Gravity Bar 415 Broadway E ☎206/325-7186. Described as a "fern bar on smart drugs," this industrial-chic eatery is the last word in postmodern vegetarian cuisine, with familiar veggie staples and a whole range of novel juice drinks – highlighted by the pepper/garlic/citrus concoction called the "Liver Flush."

Nikko 1900 5th Ave ☎206/322-4641. Sushi and barbequed dishes are the main attractions at this downtown Japanese restaurant, where you can save a few bucks by eating from the lunch buffets.

Noodle Ranch 2228 2nd Ave, Belltown ☎206/728-0463. Affordable pan-Asian cuisine – in the $10 range – lures in hungry souls for the fine noodle dishes and scrumptious satays.

Piroshki 124 Broadway E, Capitol Hill ☎206/322-2820. Closet-sized eatery serving up some of the town's best "piroshki": scrumptious Russian pastries stuffed with all kinds of meat and veggies, and handmade by the owner.

Place Pigalle 81 Pike St, on the staircase behind the fish market ☎206/624-1756. Great seafood offerings – mussels, crab, sturgeon – with fine French cuisine make this small, one-time bar an excellent choice, despite the pricey fare.

Saigon Deli 4142 Brooklyn Ave NE, University District ☎206/634-2866. Tiny diner with scrumptious Vietnamese fare, most of it for under $6. A good option for take-out.

Wild Ginger 1400 Western Ave, downtown ☎206/623-4450. An extremely popular, well-designed, upscale restaurant with an extensive menu of fiery dishes from Southeast Asia, India and China.

Coffee houses

Allegro 4214 University Way ☎206/633-3030. One of the better spots to taste local brews around the University, where the other prime draws are internet access via three computer terminals (customers only) and watching the quasi-bohemian clientele strike intellectual poses.

Bauhaus Books & Coffee 301 E Pine St ☎206/625-1600. A Capitol Hill hangout for the dressed-in-black crowd with large tables, an artsy used-book section – focusing on art and architecture volumes – and good coffee.

Online Coffee Company 1720 E Olive Way ☎206/328-3731. Check your email here on Capitol Hill – large black monitors and stylish wooden desks set the tone for serious surfing.

First 30 minutes free with a coffee purchase – otherwise $6 per hour.

Speakeasy Café 2304 2nd Ave ☎206/728-9770. A favorite Belltown hangout that offers more than just coffee (or tea, beer, salads and desserts), with a wide range of poetry readings, live music and movies.

Still Life in Fremont Coffeehouse 709 N 35th ☎206/547-9850. As expected in Seattle, the coffee is excellent; plus *Still Life* serves up great baked goods, hearty fritatta breakfasts, and lunch specials like corn tortilla pies.

Torrefazione Italia 320 Occidental Ave ☎206/624-5847. Excellent roast coffees and outdoor seating are the main draws at this Pioneer Square java house, part of one of the better regional chains.

Nightlife and entertainment

Seattle's **nightlife** doesn't quite live up to the expectations aroused by the city's musical notoriety, but it's still compelling and not bad for a **beer** or two, either – like other West Coast cities, Seattle boasts an excellent selection of microbrewed beers. *The Pike Pub & Brewery,* 1415 First Ave, and *Pyramid Brewery & Ale House,* 1201 First Ave S, both make unique hand-crafted brews, and the Irish pubs *Kells*, 1916 Post Alley, and *Tir na nog*, 801 First Ave, serve fine pints of Guinness plus the usual selection of European ales. Note, though, that in the state of Washington **taverns** sell beer and wine but not spirits, while **bars** sell everything but must be attached to a restaurant. The tavern scene is most accessible, and touristy, in **Pioneer Square**, where lively establishments like *Doc Maynard's, Old Timer's Café* and the *Central Saloon* host jazz, reggae and blues bands. Look out for "joint cover nights" ($10 weekends/$5 weeknights), when you can get into about ten different live music venues. Although Seattle's grunge heyday is long gone, there's still a thriving **music** scene. The better-known bands play at the old, atmospheric **Moore Theater** downtown, 1932 Second Ave (Ⓦwww.themoore.com), or the **Seattle Center Arena**.

As far as more refined entertainment goes, the **Seattle Center** (Ⓦwww .seattlecenter.com) is the base for most of the city's cultural institutions: the **Pacific Northwest Ballet** (☎206/441-2424, Ⓦwww.pnb.org) and the **Seattle Opera** (☎206/389-7699, Ⓦwww.seattleopera.com) performed in the Opera House, which is closed for renovation until 2003 (re-opening as Marion Oliver McCall Hall). Until then, you can catch performances for both groups at the adjacent Mercer Arts Arena. The **Seattle Symphony Orchestra** has a new stylish home in the glass-walled **Benaroya Concert Hall**, 3rd and Union streets (☎206/215-4747, Ⓦwww.seattlesymphony.org). Tickets tend to sell out in advance, but there are sometimes half-price tickets on the day of the performance for students and seniors.

Seattle has numerous **theaters**; the longest-established small company is the **Seattle Repertory Company** (☎206/443-2222, Ⓦwww.seattlerep.org) at the Seattle Center. Next door, the **Intiman Theater** (☎404/815-1888 or 206/269-1900, Ⓦwww.intiman.org) performs classics and premieres of innovative new works; **On the Boards** presents contemporary performances (☎206/217-9888, Ⓦwww.ontheboards.org); and big-name musicals open at the **Fifth Avenue Theatre** (☎206/625-1418, Ⓦwww.5thavenuetheatre.org) or the restored **Paramount** (☎206/682-1414, Ⓦwww.theparamount.com).

For a much larger-scaled event, **Bumbershoot**, the Seattle Arts Festival, hosts more than 2000 artists from around the world at 25 stages, exhibit halls and performance venues on Labor Day weekend ($40 four-day pass; Ⓦ www.bumbershoot.org). In May, the **Seattle International Film Festival** (Ⓦ www.seattlefilm.com) centers on independent venues such as the Art Deco **Egyptian**, in the Masonic temple at 801 E Pine St (Ⓣ 206/323-4978), and the **Harvard Exit** on 807 E Roy near Broadway in Capitol Hill (Ⓣ 206/323-8986). **Seafair**, held from late July to early August (Ⓦ www.seafair.com), is Seattle's answer to Mardi Gras, complete with pirates, parades and the gay-inspired "Unofficial Seafair Tacky Tourist Queen City Cruise" through the Ship Canal.

For what's on **listings** throughout the year, *Seattle Weekly*, free from boxes on the streets and many cafés and stores, is good for reviews and theater, cinema and arts listings, as is the Friday edition of the *Seattle Post Intelligencer*. Free papers *The Stranger* and *The Rocket* provide excellent coverage of the regional music scene.

Bars and clubs

Alibi Room 85 Pike St Ⓣ 206/623-3180. Swank martini bar tucked in a dramatic alley behind the Pike Street Market. Excellent food in café-type rooms upstairs, DJs spinning tunes on the dance floor downstairs, and a good selection of film scripts in the library.

Comet Tavern 922 E Pike St, Capitol Hill Ⓣ 206/323-9853. The oldest bar on Capitol Hill, and a grunge institution, is not surprisingly a smoky dive and a bit of a rocker's hangout with pool tables.

Doc Maynard's Public House 610 1st Ave S Ⓣ 206/682-4649. Fun, restored 1890s Pioneer Square saloon popular with tourists and featuring live reggae, classic and alternative rock music.

Dutch Ned's Saloon 201 1st Ave S Ⓣ 206/340-8859. The main draw of this friendly Pioneer Square bar is the Seattle Slam poetry night on Wednesdays ($3), when raucous locals come to cheer their favorite frantic wordsmiths.

Linda's Tavern 707 E Pine St, Capitol Hill Ⓣ 206/325-1220. Immensely popular with musicians mainly for its jukebox stocked with classics and current indie rock acts. DJs also pop up several times a week.

Old Timer's Tavern 620 1st Ave S Ⓣ 206/623-9800. Narrow and crowded tavern with nightly blues and jazz acts.

Tractor Tavern 5213 Ballard Ave NW Ⓣ 206/789-3599. A popular music joint in Ballard with great character and especially good microbrewed beers.

Music venues

Baltic Room 1207 Pine St E, Capitol Hill Ⓣ 206/625-4444. Stylish alternative music venue and jazz club, comprising three different sections, and selling beer, wine and cigars.

Breakroom 1325 E Madison St, Capitol Hill Ⓣ 206/860-5155. Regional alternative acts mixed with a few big names make this a solid offering on the local music scene.

Crocodile Café 2200 2nd Ave Ⓣ 206/441-5611. A hip alternative joint in Belltown promoting everything from rock to avant-garde jazz and spoken word. Also a good diner (see p.1189).

Jazz Alley 2033 6th Ave Ⓣ 206/441-9729. Best jazz spot in town, showcasing international jazz acts, as well as up-and-coming brilliants. Tickets start around $20.

OK Hotel Café 212 Alaskan Way S Ⓣ 206/621-7903. Once the mosher's favorite, this lively venue near Pioneer Square mixes grunge with avant-garde and poetry. Good for local bands and new jazz.

Showbox 1426 1st Ave Ⓣ 206/628-3151. A good alternative choice for regional rock acts, and quite affordable compared to the bigger-name venues. Near the Pike Place Market.

Out from Seattle: Bainbridge and Vashon islands

For a brief escape from Seattle, the half-hour ferry ride across Elliott Bay to **Bainbridge Island** provides a relaxing, scenic experience. Washington State Ferries leave from Pier 52 ($4.50 round-trip for foot passengers; $8 round-trip per car and driver, or $10 during peak periods; hourly – avoid rush hours; Ⓣ 206/464-6400) for the 35-minute journey, docking in the town of

Onward to Canada and Alaska

Victoria on Vancouver Island in Canada is just two to three hours by the high-speed, passenger-only *Victoria Clipper* from Seattle's Pier 69 (summer four daily, winter one daily; $56–68 one-way, $90–110 round-trip; ☎206/448-5000, ⓦwww.victoriaclipper .com). Other services to Vancouver Island from Washington State run out of Anacortes (see p.1196), Port Angeles (see p.1201) and Bellingham (see p.1198). Kenmore Air schedules five flights daily from downtown Seattle on Lake Union to Victoria (☎1-800/543-9595; $110 one-way, $181 round-trip; ⓦwww.kenmoreair.com), as well as six flights to the San Juan Islands ($96 one-way, $159 round-trip).

The much more expensive **Alaska Marine Highway** (☎360/676-0212 recorded schedule information, ☎360/676-8445 administrative office, ⓦwww.akmhs.com; winter $256, summer $282) is a three-day ferry ride that winds between islands and a fjord-lined coast from **Bellingham**, ninety miles north of Seattle, to Skagway, Alaska (see p.1253).

BAINBRIDGE ISLAND (formerly Winslow), which is small and charming but provides little reason to linger. This green and rural island, occupying less than fifty square miles, is mostly private land, but if you want to pitch a tent, there's **camping** at the far end in Fay Bainbridge State Park ($12; ☎206/842-3931). Otherwise, accommodation is limited to **B&Bs**, details of which can be obtained from the **visitor center** at 590 Winslow Way E (☎206/842-3700, ⓦwww.bainbridgechamber.com). The *Streamliner Diner*, 397 Winslow Way (☎206/842-8595), with its huge breakfasts and sandwiches, is the best place to **eat** in the daytime.

Nine daily Washington State Ferries from Seattle and West Seattle also make the short trip to pleasant, bicycle-friendly **Vashon Island**. Ferries from downtown Seattle's Pier 50 are passenger-only ($5.50), while West Seattle trips are also for vehicles (car and driver $10 round-trip, or $13 during peak hours; passengers $2.90 round-trip). A few beaches lie along the coast of this island, where the community of **VASHON** is little more than a hamlet. The *AYH Ranch Hostel* at 12119 SW Cove Rd (☎206/463-2592, ⓦwww.vashonhostel .com; ❶/❷), six miles from the Seattle–Vashon ferry dock at the north end of the island, is in an amiable wooded spot and features log cabins, covered wagons or tepees as accommodation. Phone ahead to make a reservation and arrange a free pickup at the jetty. There are also a number of good **B&Bs**, among them *Artist's Studio Loft,* 16592 91st Ave SW (☎206/463-2583, ⓦwww.asl-bnb.com; ❺), and the *Swallow's Nest Guest Cottages*, 6030 SW 248th St (☎206/463-2646, ⓦwww.vashonislandcottages.com; ❺). Good **places to eat** are *Emily's Café,* 17530 Vashon Hwy SW, an espresso bar and bakery with good vegetarian meals, *Casa Bonita*, 17623 100th Ave SW, offering solid Mexican fare, and *Rock Island Pub & Pizza,* 17322 Vashon Hwy SW, which has gourmet pizzas and microbrews.

Puget Sound

The broad and deep **Puget Sound** hooks far into Washington, a clutter of tiny islands and ragged peninsulas teeming with yachts, oceangoing ships, fishing trawlers and even nuclear submarines. At first, the dense forest deterred homesteaders, but soon small logging communities sprang up, and the Sound became a vital waterway. As more settlers arrived, the demand for land grew, and in the

1850s treaties confining Native Americans to reservations were put before tribal leaders. Some signed, including Chief Sealth of the Suquamish, but others refused and accusations of forgery flew. A legacy of injustice was created, with which modern courts still struggle.

The southern end of the Sound is increasingly urban, and from the colorless vantage point of the I-5 freeway, this is all that less inquisitive visitors see of it. Although there's little to attract visitors to industrial **Tacoma** or the small state capital of **Olympia**, all around are appealing mountains, forests and lakes. Popular weekend escapes include rural parts of **Whidbey Island**, and the beautiful **San Juan Islands** further north.

Tacoma

It's hard to avoid passing through **TACOMA** on the main Seattle–Portland route, and passing through may be all you wish to do, given the city's bad reputation as a military-oriented industrial town with pervasive pollution – and a toxic brew of chemicals still lingering in Commencement Bay. In recent years, though, the massive **Tacoma Dome** has become a major concert venue (ⓦwww.tacomadome.org), and the downtown historical district has slowly been renovated, improving it somewhat. The two-block-long **Antique Row** on Ninth Avenue and Broadway features some great Victorian buildings worth perusing if you have the time.

Among the smattering of new galleries and theaters in the city center is the **Tacoma Art Museum**, 1123 Pacific Ave (Tues–Sun 10am–5pm, Thurs closes at 8pm; $5, free third Thurs of month; ⓦwww.tacomaartmuseum.org), which hosts decent touring exhibitions to augment a pedestrian permanent collection, highlighted mainly by the colorful works of local glassblower Dale Chihuly. Another attraction of sorts is the copper-domed **Union Station**, built in 1911, which has been impressively restored as a courthouse. Next door at 1911 Pacific Ave, the huge **Washington State History Museum** (summer Mon–Wed & Fri–Sat 10am–6pm, Thurs 10am–8pm, Sun 11am–6pm; rest of year Tues–Wed & Fri–Sat 10am–5pm, Thurs 10am–8pm, Sun 11am–5pm; $7; ⓦwww.wshs.org/wshm) has fine exhibits on frontier towns, railroads, logging, Native American and twentieth-century regional history.

Hotels tend to be either too smart or too grim, but are usually significantly less expensive than their counterparts in Seattle. The downtown *Tacoma Sheraton*, 1320 Broadway (☎253/572-3200 or 1-800/325-3535, ⓦwww.sheratontacoma .com; ❼), has the best rooms in town. The usual **motel** chains line the freeways, or you can **camp** in **Dash Point State Park**, 5700 SW Dash Point Rd, Federal Way ($19; ⓦwww.parks.wa.gov/reserve.asp), five miles northeast of Tacoma, which has wide beaches and some decent hiking trails. For **B&B**s, contact the Greater Tacoma Bed & Breakfast Reservation Service (☎253/759-4088 or 1-800/406-4088, ⓦwww.tacoma-inns.org). If hungry, the *Ram Restaurant and Big Horn Brewery,* 3001 Ruston Way (☎253/756-7886), has better than average pub fare. *Antique Sandwich Shop*, 5102 N Pearl St (☎253/752-4069), near the large **Point Defiance Park**, is an authentic luncheonette filled with locals, and *Engine House no. 9,* 611 N Pine St (☎253/272-3435), is a friendly tavern that's a solid bet for beer and pizza.

Olympia and around

Just a muddy little logging community when picked as Washington's territorial capital in 1853, **OLYMPIA** has never really become the metropolis its founders had hoped, instead continuing to remain somewhat a backwater locale despite government efforts to spruce it up. Its downtown area is small, with a few blocks of stores and restaurants presided over by the neo-Romanesque **Old Capitol** at Seventh Avenue between Washington and Franklin, home mainly to bureaucratic offices. Nevertheless, it's quite a busy little town, with state employees knocking around during the day and students from the Evergreen State College, a popular liberal arts school, pepping up the nightlife. There's a well-established **Farmers' Market** downtown at 401 N Capitol Way (April–Dec weekends, and occasional weekdays; Ⓦ www.farmers-market.org), north of which is a boardwalk with some decent places to **eat**.

The state offices are arranged around neat lawns on the **Capitol Campus**, just south of downtown. It's worth taking a tour of the imposing neoclassical **Legislative Building** (daily 10am–3pm; free; Ⓦ www.ga.wa.gov/visitor) completed in 1928 after more than three decades of work, if only to wonder at the sheer energy of the pioneers who set out to construct a close replica of the Capitol building in Washington, DC, in what was then a backwoods on the far side of the continent. Eight blocks south, the small **State Capitol Museum**, 211 W 21st Ave (Tues–Sun 10am–4pm, weekends opens at noon; $2; Ⓦ www.wshs.org/wscm), juxtaposes a restored dining room with displays of Native American basketwork and local natural history.

A short drive south of Olympia, tiny **TUMWATER** was Washington's first pioneer community, settled in 1845 by a group that included Bing Crosby's grandparents. Its name comes from the tumbling water of the Deschutes River, which is still used at the **Olympia Brewery**, Schmidt Place and Custer Way off I-5 exit 103 (tours Mon–Sat 9am–4.30pm; free). As the last remaining national brewery in the region (ironically producing Rainier and Henry Weinhard brews, two of its former rivals, which were swallowed up by current owner Miller Beer), the Olympia complex overlooks **Tumwater Falls**, now part of a park but once a rich salmon-fishing site for the Nisqually tribe.

Practicalities

The **Greyhound** station is at 107 Seventh Ave at Capitol Way, five blocks north of the Capitol Campus in Olympia; the **Amtrak** station is about eight miles southeast and not on the bus route. Intercity Transit (IT) (☎ 360/786-1881, Ⓦ www.intercitytransit.com) runs **local buses**, providing a free service between downtown and the Capitol Campus (75¢, one-day pass $1.50).

Olympia's **visitors center** (Mon–Fri 8am–5pm; ☎ 360/586-3460) is on the Capitol Campus, 14th Avenue and Capitol Way. In-town **accommodation** is geared towards business travelers; the *Golden Gavel Motor Hotel*, 909 Capitol Way S (☎ 360/352-8533, Ⓦ www.goldengavelmotel.com; ❸), usually has the cheapest deals, while the *Harbinger Inn*, 1136 E Bay Drive (☎ 360/754-0389, Ⓦ www.harbingerinn.com; ❹), is a pleasant nineteenth-century **B&B**, offering five rooms with period furnishings a mile from downtown. The new *Phoenix Inn*, 415 Capitol Way (☎ 360/570-0555, Ⓦ www.phoenixinnsuites.com; ❻), is perhaps the best choice overall, with fridges and microwaves in each room. For real budget rooms you'll have to go further out to one of Tumwater's motels, such as the *Holly Motel*, 2816 Martin Way (☎ 360/943-3000; ❷), east of town at exit 109 off I-5. There's also **camping** at forested **Millersylvania State Park**, 12245 Tilley Rd, south of Olympia, two miles east of I-5 exit 99.

Of places to **eat**, the *Urban Onion*, 116 Legion Way (☎ 360/943-9242), has delicious burgers for the vegetarian and carnivore alike, while a few blocks away, *The Spar* at 114 Fourth Ave (☎ 360/357-6444), is a diner which has catered to Olympia's working class since 1935.

Whidbey Island

With sheer cliffs and craggy outcrops, rocky beaches and prairie countryside, **Whidbey Island** is a favorite retreat for Puget Sound's city-dwellers. In its north is a naval base, but in the southern and central parts, narrow country roads wind through farmland and small villages.

Although it's possible to reach the island by road – Hwy-20 off I-5 drops into the north end of Whidbey, some 85 miles north of Seattle – the **ferry** is often a better option. The quickest route from Seattle is to head thirty miles north to Mukilteo and catch the ferry to Whidbey's southern tip (every half-hour; $2.50 per person round-trip; $4.50 one-way for driver and vehicle, or $6 during peak season). From Port Townsend on the Olympic Peninsula (see p.1199) an hourly ferry goes to **Keystone**, in the middle of the island just south of the town of Coupeville (one-way $2 per person; $6.50 with a car, $8.50 peak season; Ⓦwww.wsdot.wa.gov/ferries). Whidbey's **bus** system, Island Transit (Ⓣ360/321-6688, Ⓦwww.islandtransit.org), runs the length of the island for free.

The Mukilteo ferry lands at the small town of Clinton, but **LANGLEY**, further around the east coast, makes a better place to linger, with its old-West main street of wooden storefronts set on a picturesque bluff overlooking the water. The **visitors center** is at 208 Anthes St (daily 9am–5pm; Ⓣ360/221-6765, Ⓦwww.langley-wa.com/chamber). Among the limited food options, the *Café Langley*, 113 Main St (Ⓣ360/221-3090), is a decent **restaurant** with unsurprising fare.

The middle part of the island contains the **Ebey's Landing National Historic Reserve** (Ⓦwww.nps.gov/ebla), which some may find worthwhile for its preserved World War II-era military garrisons **Fort Ebey** and **Fort Casey**. More appealing, though, is charming little **COUPEVILLE**, with its Victorian sea captains' mansions – and is certainly preferable to **OAK HARBOR**, Whidbey's largest town and the site of a naval air station and a slew of motels. To the north, at **Deception Pass State Park**, a steel bridge arches gracefully over the narrow gorge between Whidbey and Fidalgo Island, connecting point for the San Juans beyond.

On the edge of Coupeville, you'll find **accommodations** at the appealing *Captain Whidbey Inn*, 2072 W Captain Whidbey Inn Rd, two miles west of Coupeville on Penn Cove (Ⓣ360/678-4097, Ⓦwww.captainwhidbey.com; ❻), a lovely nautical-themed **hotel** serving superb food. The *Anchorage Inn*, 807 N Main St (Ⓣ360/678-5581, Ⓦwww.anchorage-inn.com; ❹), however, is in a more central location. The local **Chamber of Commerce**, 302 N Main St (Ⓣ360/678-5434, Ⓦwww.whidbey.net/coup), has lists of **B&Bs**, or visit the Whidbey Island Bed & Breakfast Association website at Ⓦwww.whidbeyisland.com/bandb. You can also **camp** in any of four state parks, including **Fort Ebey State Park** ($14; Ⓣ360/678-4636).

The San Juan Islands

North and west of Whidbey Island, midway between Seattle and Vancouver, the beautiful **San Juan Islands** are scattered across the northern reaches of Puget Sound. Every summer brings more visitors than the islands can easily accommodate, especially on the largest ones, San Juan and Orcas, so you'll need to book in advance.

Getting there

Washington State Ferries runs a dozen boats per day – or up to fifteen in summer – to the islands from the harbor a few miles west of **ANACORTES**, a gritty fishing port 75 miles north of Seattle at the end of Hwy-20. The ferry stops at four of the 172 islands (Lopez, Shaw, Orcas and San Juan; ⓦ www.wsdot.wa.gov/ferries), and the slow cruise through the archipelago is a delight. Motorists should get to the port early, as there's often an hour's wait or more to get vehicles onto a summer crossing; pedestrians and cyclists have less of a hassle. Fares to San Juan – $6.80 for foot passengers on a round-trip and $22.50 for a car and driver, with an additional $6 for the latter in summer – are collected only on the westbound journey and there is no charge for foot passengers on inter-island trips. One ferry a day (two in summer) goes on to Sidney in British Columbia. A **passenger–only** service to Orcas and San Juan islands runs from Bellingham (see p.1198) during the summer months. Kenmore Air (ⓣ206/486-1257 or 1-800/543-9595, ⓦ www.kenmoreair.com) runs **seaplane flights** from Seattle to five harbors in the San Juans for $110 (one-way) and $162 (round-trip). Harbor Airlines (ⓣ253/851-2381 or 1-800/359-3220) offers flights from Sea-Tac Airport to Friday Harbor, and West Isle Air (ⓣ360/293-4691 or 1-800/874-4434, ⓦ www.westisleair.com) flies between Anacortes or Bellingham and San Juan and Lopez islands.

If you want to catch an early ferry (the first one leaves before 6am) from Anacortes, you may as well stay the night. The *Islands Inn*, 3401 Commercial Ave (ⓣ360/293-4644; ⓦ www.islandsinn.com; ❹), is one of several roadside **motels**, while the grand old 1889 *Majestic*, 419 Commercial Ave (ⓣ360/293-3355 or 1-800/950-3323; ❺), has the best restaurant and bar in Anacortes. Gas on the islands is considerably more expensive than on the mainland, so fuel up before arriving.

San Juan Island

San Juan, the ferry's last stop before Canada, is the only island where the ferry drops you in something resembling a town. Though small, **FRIDAY HARBOR** is the only incorporated place in the archipelago and the best spot to sort out the necessary transportation. San Juan Shuttle circles between twelve communities and points of interest on the island, and a daily hop-on, hop-off pass costs a reasonable $10 ($17 for two days; ⓦ www.sanjuantransit.com). *The Inn* at Friday Harbor, 680 Spring St (ⓣ360/378-3031 or 1-800/752-5752, ⓦ www.theinns .com), rents out **cars** and runs tours, while **bikes** can be had from Island Bicycles at 380 Argyle St (ⓣ360/378-4941), and **mopeds** from Susie's Mopeds at First and A streets (ⓣ360/378-5244 or 1-800/532-0087). Maps, essential on such twisting and badly marked roads, are available at the unattended **tourist information booth** on A Street, just across from where the cars line up for the ferry. Further information is available from the main office of the San Juan Island Historical Park at First and Spring streets (summer daily 8am–5pm; rest of year daily 8.30am–4.30pm; ⓣ360/378-2240, ⓦ www.nps.gov/sajh).

Friday Harbor's cafés, shops and waterfront make for pleasant wandering, and the small **Whale Museum**, 62 First St N (daily 10am–5pm, summer opens at 9am; $5; ⓦ www.whale-museum.org), offers an interesting look at the sights and sounds of local cetaceans. To see the real thing, head past the coves and bays on the island's west side to **Lime Kiln Point State Park**, named after the site's former lime quarry. Orca ("killer") whales come here in summer to feed on migrating salmon, and there's usually at least one sighting a day. San Juan Tours (ⓣ360/378-3499) is one of several companies offering three-hour **whale-watching cruises** (May–Sept only; $39; ⓦ www.whaletour.com).

Camping is a good choice on San Juan Island; there's a pleasant cyclists-only campground called the *Pedal Inn* at 1300 False Bay Drive (☎360/378-3049; $5), and *Lakedale Campground* (☎1-800/617-2267, ⓦwww.lakedale .com; $8) is six miles from the ferry on Roche Harbor Road, accessible by bus. In Friday Harbor, *Friday's*, 35 First St (☎360/378-5848 or 1-800/352-2632, ⓦwww.friday-harbor.com/lodging.html; ❺), is a cozy central inn, or you can stay in one of two cabins on a former sailboat parked in Slip K-13 in the port, now converted into the charming *Wharfside* B&B (☎360/378-5661, ⓦwww.slowseason.com; ❻). *Blair House* at 345 Blair Ave (☎360/378-5907 or 1-800/899-3030, ⓦwww.fridayharborlodging.com/blair; ❺) offers seven pleasant, traditional B&B rooms, though it's more enjoyable – and roomier – to rent their on-site cottage for $175 a night. The Bed & Breakfast Association of San Juan Island (PO Box 3016, Friday Harbor, WA 98250; ☎360/378-3030, ⓦwww.san-juan-island.net) can hook you up with a room, though most places start at around $100 in high season. It's essential to **book ahead** in summer for rooms in Friday Harbor, especially during the popular **San Juan Island Jazz Festival** (☎360/378-5509), the last weekend in July.

Of Friday Harbor's plentiful places to **eat**, *Bella Luna*, 175 First St, is good for Italian fare, the *Hungry Clam,* 130 First St, serves excellent fish'n'chips and burgers, *Angie's Cannery House*, 174 First St, offers steak and seafood with a terrace view, and the *San Juan Donut Shop*, 209 Spring St, provides hefty breakfasts from 5am.

Orcas Island

Horseshoe-shaped **Orcas Island** is quieter than San Juan, its several holiday resorts tucked away in distant coves. Tiny **ORCAS** itself, where the ferry lands, is mainly interesting for its grand Victorian *Orcas Hotel* (☎360/376-4300, ⓦwww.orcashotel.com; e). You can rent **bicycles** and **mopeds** (around $25 and $50 per day respectively) around the ferry dock area.

Most visitors head ten miles north to the rather drab main town of **EAST-SOUND**, where the **visitor information kiosk** on North Beach Road, just past Eastsound Square, provides maps. Places to **eat** include *Doty's A-1 Café* (☎360/376-2593), a block inland from the waterfront, and the more eclectic and upscale restaurant at the *Outlook Inn* (☎360/376-2200, ⓦwww.outlook-inn .com; ❺), west of the center. Two miles west, at the end of West Beach Road, the *Beach Haven Resort* (☎360/376-2280, ⓦwww.beach-haven.com; ❺) is a great place to **stay**, its 50-year-old beachfront log cabins lined up along a densely wooded, sunset-facing cove; in summer they are only available by the week.

The island's real highlight is **Moran State Park**, where over thirty miles of hiking trails wind through dense forest and open fields to freshwater lakes, and to the summit of the 2409ft **Mount Constitution**, where there are great views to be had from an observation tower. The park's four **campgrounds** (around $14; ⓦwww.orcasisle.com/moran) fill up early in summer; book ahead through Reservations Northwest (☎360/376-2326). The lovely *Doe Bay Village Resort & Retreat,* Star Rte-86, 18 miles east of Eastsound on Horseshoe Hwy (☎360/376-2291, ⓦwww.doebay.com; ❶–❺), is tucked into a secluded bay and offers everything from primitive campsites to modern cabins. As for **food**, *Café Doe Bay* offers vegetarian dishes and seafood, with a good selection of beer on tap. Nearby, in tiny **Olga**, *Café Olga* (☎360/376-5098) serves great pies, but is often swamped by people visiting the adjoining art gallery.

Lopez Island

Much more tranquil than the two larger atolls is modest **Lopez Island**, whose rolling hills also make it the most enjoyable place to cycle. The delightful and spacious *Lopez Islander* resort hotel (℡360/468-2233 or 1-800/736-3434, Ⓦwww.lopezislander.com; ⑥) sits on the edge of **Lopez Village**, about four miles from the ferry dock, and not far from the excellent *Bay Café Restaurant* (℡360/468-3700). For a change of pace, and a quiet respite in the woods, *Blue Fjord Cabins* (℡1-888/633-0401, Ⓦwww.interisland.net/bluefjord; ④) offers two cozy, secluded cabins for reasonable rates.

Bellingham

BELLINGHAM – a happy blend of industry, Victorian architecture and college-town liveliness – runs ten miles along a broad curve of Bellingham Bay, 85 miles north of Seattle and just eighteen miles south of the Canadian border. Its notoriety is largely due to its being the southern terminus of the **Alaska Marine Highway** (see box, p.1192). The ferries sail from the Cruise Terminal on the edge of the brick-and-sandstone **Fairhaven** district – three miles south of downtown (I-5 exit 250) – which, with its hip bookstores, cafés and clothing stores, is easily Bellingham's most appealing area. In contrast, **downtown** itself (I-5 exit 253) is fairly mundane, but likeable enough and has a few good restaurants.

Bellingham's chief attraction, however, is its access to a wide range of excellent parks – set among the bluffs and forests surrounding the city, with myriad hiking trails – and, further east, the foothills of **Mount Baker**, 56 scenic miles along Hwy-542. Lummi tribal myths have the mountain as a sort of Ararat, surviving the Great Flood to provide sanctuary for a Native American Noah in his giant canoe, but it's better known today for its skiing, with a seven-month season from early November until late May (ski information on ℡360/734-6771, Ⓦwww.mtbakerskiarea.com; daily lift tickets $34 on weekends, $25 midweek).

Practicalities

Greyhound **buses** and Amtrak **trains** pull in at the **Bellingham Cruise Terminal** in the Fairhaven district. San Juan Island Shuttle Express (℡360/671-1137, Ⓦwww.orcawhales.com) runs a passenger-only service to Orcas and San Juan Island in summer ($20 one-way fares, $33 round-trip), and Victoria–San Juan Cruises (℡360/738-8099 or 1-800/443-4552, Ⓦwww.whales.com) operates a similar summer service to San Juan Island and Victoria in British Columbia ($49 one-way fares, $79 round-trip). Local WTA **buses** (℡360/676-RIDE, Ⓦwww.ridewta.com) ply thirty routes for a fare of 50¢, with the **transit center** at E Magnolia and Railroad Ave. The **visitor center** is at 904 Potter St, off I-5 exit 253 (℡360/671-3990 or 1-800/487-2032, Ⓦwww.bellingham.org).

The best **rooms** in Bellingham are at the gabled Victorian *North Garden Inn*, 1014 N Garden St (℡360/671-7828 or 1-800/922-6414, Ⓦwww.northgardeninn.com/ngi; ④), a beautiful B&B near downtown and just off I-5, with first-class breakfasts and a great view of the bay. Also off I-5 (exit 253) is the reliable *Best Western Bellingham Lakeway Inn*, 714 Lakeway Drive (℡360/671-1011, Ⓦwww.bellingham-hotel.com; ④). There's also the *HI-Bellingham Hostel* in Fairhaven, 107 Chuckanut Drive (℡360/671-1750), where you can get a dorm room for $15. The best place to **camp** is **Larrabee State Park**, seven miles south of Bellingham on Hwy-11, but there are numerous campgrounds along the highway to Mount Baker as well.

Downtown has several decent places to **eat** and **drink**, including *Dirty Dan Harris'*, 1211 11th St (☎360/676-1011), for solid prime rib and steaks, and *Dos Padres*, 1111 Harris Ave (☎360/733-9900), for good Mexican food. **Fairhaven** is the best bet for whiling away a few hours: *Tony's*, at 1101 Harris Ave (☎360/733-6319), is a hip coffee shop, sometimes hosting live music, while inside Village Books at 1208 11th St is the *Colophon Café* (☎360/647-0092), which is open in the evening until 9 or 10pm and serves good meals and great desserts.

The Olympic Peninsula

The broad mass of the **Olympic Peninsula** projects across Puget Sound, sheltering Seattle from the open sea. Small towns are sprinkled sparingly along US-101, which loops the peninsula's coast, but at the core the Olympic Mountains thrust upwards, shredding rain clouds as they drift in from the Pacific and drenching the surrounding area. In the western river valleys, the dense vegetation thickens into rainforest, and the forests and unspoiled Pacific beaches provide habitat for a huge variety of wildlife and seabirds.

Although much of the peninsula is now protected land, and large areas of national forest surround the rugged and verdant preserve of **Olympic National Park**, the legacy of timber clear-cutting provides an all-too-visible scar on the landscape, especially if you venture off the main roads into an ecological dead zone riddled with ugly stumps and uprooted vegetation. The lumber trade brought the first Western settlers here in the nineteenth century, and while almost every town has a sawmill, the industry is in crisis and ecologists favor tourism as the lesser environmental evil.

Port Townsend

With its brightly painted Victorian mansions, convivial cafés and vigorous cultural scene, **PORT TOWNSEND** has always had aspirations beyond its small-time logging roots. Gothic mansions sprang up above the flourishing port in the 1890s, when confident predictions of a railroad terminus lured in the rich. Unfortunately for the investors, the trains never arrived, and the town was left with a glut of stylish residences and a very small business district.

Port Townsend's physical split – half on a bluff, half at sea level – reflects nineteenth-century social divisions, when wealthy merchants built their houses uptown, far above the rowdy clamor and working-class color of the port below. The downtown area is at the base of the hill, its shops and pleasant cafés centering on **Water Street** – lined with proud 1890s brick and stonework. In recent times the old mansions have been restored, and the town has mellowed into an artsy community with hippie undertones and a fair amount of charm. For a more detailed look at the area's rich history, check out the museum of the **Jefferson County Historical Society**, 540 Water St (daily 11am–4pm, Sun opens at 1pm; $2; ⓦwww.jchsmuseum.org), which offers more information about the town's historic Victorian structures.

Though fairly bustling year-round, the town is busiest during its summer **music festivals** – principally Jazz Port Townsend in late July, and American Fiddle Tunes in early July – which take place at the state park at **FORT WORDEN**, the remains of a military encampment two miles north of town.

Practicalities

Pick up a map and information in Port Townsend at the helpful **visitor center**, 2437 E Sims Way (Mon–Fri 9am–5pm; ☎360/385-2722 or 1-888/365-6978, ⓦwww.ptchamber.org), about twelve blocks south of the Ferry Terminal on Hwy-20. There's a good choice of **places to stay** in town, but prices are fairly high – with the exception of the *HI-Olympic Hostel,* 272 Battery Way (☎360/385-0655 or 1-800/909-4776; $17 per person), in Fort Worden State Park – and vacancies rare in the height of summer. The town's specialty is its **B&Bs**, the best of which occupy grand mansions uptown, such as the bluffside *James House*, 1238 Washington St (☎360/385-1238 or 1-800/385-1238, ⓦwww.jameshouse.com; ⑥), and the delightful *Quimper Inn*, 1306 Franklin St (☎360/385-1060 or 1-800/557-1060, ⓦwww.olympus.net/quimper; ⑤). There are also several fine, nineteenth-century downtown **hotels**, the best being the renovated *Palace Hotel*, 1004 Water St (☎360/385-0773 or 1-800/962-0741, ⓦwww.olympus.net/biz/palace; ❸–⑤), a surprisingly affordable spot with bayside views and elegant period furnishings. Even cheaper, several **motels** are available, such as *The Tides Inn,* 1807 Water St (☎360/385-0595 or 1-800/822-8696, ⓦwww.tides-inn.com; ④), located on the waterfront.

Port Townsend, the peninsula's best place to **eat and drink**, has no shortage of excellent restaurants. The *Salal Café*, 634 Water St (☎360/385-6532), is a local favorite with decent omelettes and lunches at modest prices, while the best baked goods can be found at *Bread & Roses,* 230 Quincy St (☎360/385-1044), serving great sandwiches and displaying the work of local artists as well. More upmarket alternatives include *The Fountain Café*, 920 Washington St (☎360/379-9343), with innovative regional cuisine, and the *Silverwater Café*, 237 Taylor St (☎360/385-6448), with good fresh seafood. In the nearby beach town of **Port Hadlock**, the *Ajax Café*, 271 Water St (☎360/385-3450), serves up inventive Northwest seafood dishes and occasional live music.

Port Angeles

Originally named "Puerto de Nuestra Señora de los Angeles" by the Spanish in 1791 (the postal service later insisted one Los Angeles was enough), **PORT ANGELES** is the peninsula's main town and the most popular point of entry into Olympic National Park. Like many other similarly sized towns in the Pacific Northwest, the community is a paradoxical mixture of timber-industry grittiness and picturesque beauty, which sometimes collide in strange and unexpected ways – such as the working-class harbor streaked with industrial chimneys and backdropped by striking mountains.

Though it's preferable to stay inside the park, Port Angeles has a number of inexpensive chain **motels** near its uninspiring one-way main drags, First Street and Front Street. These include the *Best Western Olympic Lodge,* 140 Del Guzzi Dr (☎1-800/600-2993, ⓦwww.portangeleshotelmotel.com; ❸), and *Traveler's Motel,* 1133 E First St (☎360/452-2303, ⓦwww.travelersmotel.net; ❷). For more upscale accommodation, try the *Red Lion Inn*, 221 N Lincoln St (☎360/452-9215, ⓦwww.redlion.com; ⑥), or *Domaine Madeleine,* 146 Wildflower Lane (☎360/457-4174, ⓦwww.domainemadeleine.com; ⑥–❽), a B&B with themed rooms and a lovely five-acre garden. If you are staying inside the park, at any of the seventeen excellent **campgrounds** (☎360/452-4501, $8–12 per night), you'll need your own vehicle. Try *Heart o' the Hills*, six miles south of Port Angeles, along Hurricane Ridge Road, or further west, *Elwah* and *Altaire* campgrounds are equally good with access to the numerous hiking trails.

For **breakfast** or **lunch**, head for the tiny *First Street Haven*, 107 E First St and Laurel (☎360/457-0352); for **dinner**, the upscale *Bella Italia*, 118 E First St (☎360/457-5442), has seafood and authentic Italian cuisine.

Port Angeles has the peninsula's best **transportation connections**. Olympic Bus Lines (☎360/452-3858) offers daily trips to Seattle and Sea-Tac Airport, while Clallam Transit buses (☎360/452-4511 or 1-800/858-3747) go west from Port Angeles around the peninsula to Lake Crescent, Neah Bay and Forks and east to Sequim, connecting with Jefferson Transit (☎360/385-4777) buses to Port Townsend. Black Ball Transport (☎360/457-4491) runs **ferries** to Victoria in Canada (2–4 daily, except in Feb) for a bargain $8 walk-on one-way fare, $30 for a car, and Victoria Express (☎360/452-8088 or 1-800/633-1589) operates a faster passenger-only service (2–3 daily) for $20–25. The **visitors center**, at 121 E Railroad St, beside the ferry terminal (summer daily 7am–6pm; rest of year Mon–Fri 10am–4pm; ☎360/452-2363, Ⓦwww.portangeles.org), stocks information on the entire peninsula and can put you in touch with local river-rafting and sea-kayaking firms.

Neah Bay, the Makah Indian Reservation and Cape Flattery

Whereas US-101 takes a turn inland from Port Angeles to skirt Olympic National Park (see overleaf), Hwy-112 clambers along the coast for seventy miles to **NEAH BAY**, the tiny fishing village that is home to the **Makah Nation**, seagoing Native Americans almost wiped out by a smallpox epidemic in 1850. "Makah," a name given to the tribe by their neighbors, means "generous with food," though in recent years their name has also been synonymous with controversy. A series of court battles between the tribe and environmentalists over the resumption of tribal **whale hunting** was recently resolved in favor of the Makah – though this hasn't stopped eco-protestors from trying to stop the hunts on the high seas.

In 1970, tidal erosion near Cape Alava uncovered an ancient Makah settlement that had been buried by a mudslide some 500 years ago. The first witnesses encountered bizarre scenes of green alder leaves, lying where they had fallen centuries ago, shriveling as soon as they were exposed. The Ozette Dig, one of the most significant archeological finds in North America, uncovered thousands of artifacts: harpoons, intricately-carved seal clubs, watertight boxes made without metal, bowls, toys – all belonging to a period before trade with Europeans. The site itself was reburied in 1981, but the finds are displayed at Neah Bay's **Makah Cultural and Research Center** (Wed–Sun 10am–5pm; summer daily; $4; Ⓦwww.makah.com/museum.htm), a superbly curated museum which includes marine dioramas, dugout cedar canoes, fishing gear, and a life-size replica of a fifteenth-century Makah longhouse.

At the northern corner of the Makah Reservation is **Cape Flattery**, a remote headland accessible on an unpaved road from Neah Bay. A half-mile hike from the road through the rainforest leads to the cape which once "flattered" Captain Cook with the hope of finding a harbor. It is the continental US's northwesternmost point. Below the cape, the waves have worn caves into the sheer rock of the cliff face, while opposite, on Tatoosh Island, the Coast Guard runs a remote lighthouse.

You can get to Neah Bay on Clallam Transit (see above), though there are few worthwhile options for **accommodation**. Given the area's drab **motels**, you'll have to head seventeen miles back east to **SEKIU**, a popular sports fishing town, to find the waterside *Van Riper's Resort*, 280 Front St

(℡ 360/963-2334, Ⓦ www.olypen.com/vanrip; ❸), one of the only appealing spots in the vicinity. A better selection can be found further south near Forks, or in Port Angeles.

Olympic National Park

The stunning **OLYMPIC NATIONAL PARK** – covering much of the peninsula's mountainous interior and a detached 57-mile strip of the Pacific coast – was created in 1938 by Franklin D. Roosevelt, partly to ensure the survival of the rare Roosevelt elk; it now has the largest remaining herd in the US. More than two hundred miles of wild rivers wind through the park, while the valleys of the Quinault, Queets and Hoh rivers contain sizeable tracts of **temperate rainforest** – one of the world's rarest types of climatic forest, seen elsewhere only in Patagonia and New Zealand.

The main **visitors center**, just outside Port Angeles at 600 East Park Ave at the top of Race Street en route to Hurricane Ridge (daily 9am–4pm, summer closes at 8pm; ℡ 360/452-0330, Ⓦ www.nps.gov/olym), has useful brochures and trail maps, with smaller centers located at **Hurricane Ridge**, **Hoh Rainforest**, **Kalaloch** and **Quinault Lake**. The **weather** is consistently erratic and often rainy – there's even a fair amount of snow as late as June. No roads cross the park, but many run into it, so you'll probably end up making several forays into different sections around the peninsula's western rim.

Hurricane Ridge and Lake Crescent

The main visitor center marks the start of a winding, precipitous road that climbs seventeen miles to daunting **Hurricane Ridge**, where the jagged peaks and sparkling glaciers of the Olympic Mountains are spread majestically before you. A new **day lodge** on the ridge (May–Oct) has tourist facilities and information. Where the road ends, the hiking trails begin. Hurricane Hill Trail (three miles round-trip) is a moderate hike, climbing through wild-flower meadows to the peak where, on a clear day, Cape Flattery, the Straits of Juan de Fuca, Vancouver Island and the Cascade Mountains are all in view. In winter, Clallam Transit **buses** (℡ 360/452-4511, Ⓦ www.clallamtransit.com) climb up to the ridge for excellent cross-country skiing.

Ten miles west of Port Angeles, the glacially carved **Lake Crescent** is popular for trout fishing and has good shoreline trails. *Lake Crescent Lodge* (May–Oct; ℡ 360/928-3211, Ⓦ www.lakecrescentlodge.com; ❹–❻) is superbly located among dense forest on the lake's south shore. The lodge is the best place to stay on the peninsula, though the *Sol Duc Hot Springs Resort* (early April to late Sept; ℡ 360/327-3583, Ⓦ www.northolympic.com/solduc; ❺), set deep in the park twelve miles off US-101, is a close rival, with free guest access to **Sol Duc Hot Springs** ($7.50) – mineral-rich waters bubbling out of the ground at 100-to-108F° and channeled into three bathing pools.

Forks

Beyond the Sol Duc turnoff, US-101 cuts across Olympic National Forest to dreary **FORKS**, a logging burg nestled between the Olympic Mountains and coastal sections of the park. Despite its neighboring temperate rainforests draped with moss and world-class river fishing, there's little reason to visit the town itself, other than as a base for touring the mountains. Decent **accommodation** is available at *Miller Tree Inn*, 654 E Division St (℡ 360/374-6806, Ⓦ www .millertreeinn.com; ❹–❻), with Victorian-styled suites and pleasant guest rooms, and at the large *Olympic Suites*, 800 Olympic Drive (℡ 360/374-5400 or

1-800/262-3433, ⓦwww.olympicgetaways.com/olympicsuites; ❸/❹), with spacious one- and two-bedroom units. The town's **visitors center** is at 1411 S Forks Ave (☎360/374-2531 or 1-800/44-FORKS, ⓦwww.forkswa.com).

The Hoh Rainforest
One of the park's most popular areas, the **Hoh Rainforest** is situated nineteen miles along Upper Hoh River Road, which branches off from US-101 twelve miles south of Forks. There are two short **trails** to explore: the Hall of Mosses Trail, and the slightly longer Spruce Trail, following along the glacier-fed Hoh River. More energetic hikers can undertake the 36-mile Hoh River Trail up to the base of 8000ft Mount Olympus. Climbing the ice-covered peak is a major undertaking; if you just want to camp along the route, check in with the rangers and get a backcountry permit ($5–7) for one of the ninety sites. Keep in mind that cougars and other beasts are still very much present in the park and in winter Roosevelt elk from higher elevations gather here. For more information, nineteen miles inland is the **visitors center** (daily 9am–4pm, summer closes at 6.30pm; ☎360/374-6925).

South to Kalaloch: the peninsula's ocean beaches
Beyond the Hoh turnoff, US-101 dips down to the Pacific coast where the wild **beaches** retain their rugged looks: black rocks jut out of a tumultuous sea, whose strong currents, floating tree trunks and dramatic tides make the waters unsuitable for swimming. The hiking can be magnificent, though, and a series of short, appealing trails head down to and along the seashore – **Ruby Beach**, named for its red-and-black-pebbled sand, is the unmistakable highlight. Near the end of the park's coastal strip, **KALALOCH** has a few campgrounds and the impressive *Kalaloch Lodge* (☎360/962-2271, ⓦwww.visitkalaloch.com; ❺/❻), offering a good restaurant and large ocean-view rooms. The **ranger station** here has lots of information and suggestions for hiking trips (☎360/962-2283).

Queets River Rainforest
South of Kalaloch, US-101 turns inland to circumvent the wilderness of the Quinault Indian Reservation before reaching the 25-mile dirt road that branches northeast to the **Queets River Rainforest**. Although it's the least visited of the three main rainforest areas, it's worthwhile for its rustic, accessible trails – and especially for the luxuriant flora and fauna along the well-marked trail at the end of the turnoff. Here you can also get a glimpse of the **world's tallest Douglas fir tree** – 220feet tall and 45feet around.

Lake Quinault and the Quinault Rainforest
The most accessible, and beautiful, of all the rainforests is the **Quinault Rainforest**, around the shores of glacier-carved Lake Quinault just off US-101. The lake itself was already a popular resort area when Teddy Roosevelt visited in the 1900s and decided to proclaim it part of an expanded Olympic National Park. Thick and impressive groves fan off from the road, explored by a series of hiking trails: one of the best is the half-mile **Maple Glade Trail** on the north shore, leading through some textbook rainforest vegetation. Longer and more difficult trails, such as the dark, four-mile **Quinault Loop Trail** through looming stands of old growth, take hikers up the forested river valley and into the Olympic Mountains.

Of Lake Quinault's three **hotels**, the best is the charming 1926 *Quinault Lodge* (☎360/288-2900 or 1-800/562-6672, ⓦwww.visitlakequinault.com;

THE PACIFIC NORTHWEST | The Olympic Peninsula

), a National Historic Landmark on the shores of Lake Quinault. There are also five lakeside **campgrounds**, information for which is available at the **ranger station** (☎360/288-2525, ⓦwww.olympus.net/onf), located footsteps from the lodge.

Aberdeen and further south

Heading south on US-101 from Lake Quinault, leaving the national park, it's about forty hilly miles through clear-cut timber land to industrial **ABERDEEN**. Once a major seaport, Aberdeen has little claim to fame nowadays, except as the hometown of Nirvana. After Kurt Cobain's suicide some spoke of erecting a statue of him in the waterfront park, but the idea was rejected as tasteless.

At Aberdeen there's a choice of routes: US-12/Hwy-8 lead east towards Olympia (see p.1193), while Hwy-101 pushes on south over the hills, threading along the shore of muddy Willapa Bay to the base of the **Long Beach Peninsula**. The peninsula is known for a handful of popular spots, including **OYSTERVILLE**, a forested collection of rusting old buildings near the peninsula's tip; the main draw, **Oysterville Sea Farms** (☎360/665-6585), is recognizable by its bayside piles of discarded shells and worth a visit for its freshly packaged oysters ($4 a dozen).

Down at the far southwestern corner of Washington, near the mouth of the Columbia River, the last points of interest are within **Fort Canby State Park** (ⓦwww.parks.wa.gov/ftcanby.htm). The site includes the evocative **North Head Lighthouse** (summer daily 11am–3pm; $1), now over a century old, and the informative historical displays of the **Lewis and Clark Interpretive Center** (daily 10am–4pm; free), which tell all about the historical hazards of navigating the Columbia River. Luckily, you'll be spared any such difficulty as you travel south on Hwy-101 over the 1966 span of the **Astoria Bridge**, crossing the state boundary into Oregon (see p.1227).

The Cascade Mountains

The idyllic beauty of the snowcapped and pine-covered **Cascade Mountains** actually conceals awesome volcanic power – as demonstrated by the 1980 explosion of **Mount St Helens**. But away from the truncated, rocky stump resulting from the blast, the Cascades offer mile upon mile of forested wilderness, stretching from Canada down to Oregon, traversed by a skein of beautiful trails – which, for all but a few summer months, you'll need snowshoes to follow. The most popular access point is **Mount Rainier**, set in its own national park some ninety miles southeast of Seattle, while the protected zone around Mount St Helens also rewards a visit for its eerie scenery. Further north, the **North Cascades National Park** demands more time; Hwy-20, the high mountain road that crosses the Cascades, is by far the most spectacular route to eastern Washington.

The North Cascades and the Cascade Loop

When Hwy-20 opened up the rugged **North Cascades** to an admiring public in 1972, the towns of the eastern foothills got together and created the **Cascade Loop**, a 350-mile round-trip that channeled tourist traffic their way, along highways 20, 153, 97 and 2 (Ⓦwww.cascadeloop.com). The complete trip is only feasible during the summer, since at other times snow closes the mountain passes, and can be rather exhausting if driven all at once. Unless you have at least three days to explore the territory in full, you're better off choosing a few selected treks through the gorgeous scenery. The towns themselves are best taken simply as bases for your travels, rather than as compelling destinations in their own right.

Hwy-20 begins its long journey inland at **Anacortes**, from where it crosses the coastal flatlands – passing the **North Cascades National Park Information Center** (Mon–Fri 8am–4.30pm, open daily in summer; ☎360/856-5700, Ⓦwww.ncascades.org) at Hwy-9 near Sedro Woolley. From here the highway threads through high mountain passes to tiny **WINTHROP**, an old mining town decked out in a Wild West get-up. As the original setting for Owen Wister's *The Virginian*, the burg's Western theme has proved popular with passing motorists, and if you'd like to **stay** look to either the *Hotel Rio Vista*, 285 Riverside Ave (☎509/996-3535 or 1-800/398-0911, Ⓦwww.hotelriovista.com; ❹), or the *Cascade Inn*, 960 Hwy-20 (☎509-996-3100 or 1-800/468-6754, Ⓦwww.winthropwa.com; ❹), which both provide clean and basic rooms. As for **eating** options, the *Winthrop Brewing Co*, 155 Riverside Ave (☎509/996-3183), offers solid microbrews like the excellent, unpasteurized *Outlaw Pale Ale*, and the *Duck Brand Cantina*, 248 Riverside Ave, (☎509/996-2192) serves up cheap and tasty Mexican fare. The nearby **visitors center**, 202 Riverside Ave (☎509/996-2125), has a good range of tourist information and backcountry permits.

Chelan

The trim resort of **CHELAN**, some sixty miles south of Winthrop, nestles at the foot of Lake Chelan, a spectacular lake set in a glacially-carved trough deep in the mountains. Of several good **lodgings**, *Campbell's Resort*, 104 W Woodin Ave (☎509/682-2561 or 1-800/553-8225, Ⓦwww.campbellsresort.com; ❹, summer ❽), is the most appealing for its attractive lakeside rooms. Cheaper accommodation is available at the *Apple Inn Motel*, 1002 E Woodin Ave (☎509/682-4044, Ⓦwww.chelanvalley.com/appleinnmotel.htm; ❸). Spots to **eat** include *Peter B's Bar & Grill,* 116 E Woodin Ave (☎509/682-1031), and *Deepwater Brewing & Public House,* 225 Highway-20 (☎509/682-2720). For hiking trail maps, the **ranger station** is at 428 W Woodin Ave (☎509/682-2576).

The *Lake Chelan Boat Company*, 1418 W Woodin Ave (☎509/682-2224 info, ☎509/682-4584 reservations, Ⓦwww.ladyofthelake.com), runs a passenger ferry service to the head of Lake Chelan, with scheduled stops at Field's Point, Lucerne and Stehekin. Leaving from the jetty a mile west of town on Woodin Avenue, the *Lady of the Lake II* ferry takes four hours to cruise the 55 miles of the nation's deepest gorge, leaving daily (May–Oct) at 8.30am and returning at 6pm ($16 one-way, $25 round-trip). There's also the year-round *Lady Express* ($28 one-way, $44 round-trip) which reaches Lake Chelan's mountainous western tip in half the time, and the *Lady Cat*, a high-speed catamaran that takes you on a thrilling one-hour jaunt (June–Sept only; $56.50 one-way, $89 round-trip). These cruises feature 60- to 90-minute layovers at **STEHEKIN** (pop. 70), an isolated village otherwise accessible only by a Chelan Airways **seaplane** ($80 one-way, $120 round-trip; ☎509/682-5555, Ⓦwww.chelanairways.com). At Stehekin there are **campsites** and trailheads leading to superb hiking and backpacking in the North Cascades. Bikes and canoes are available from the *North Cascades Stehekin Lodge* (reserve well ahead; ☎509/682-4494,

ⓦwww.stehekin.com; ❺). For camping and hiking information (and, for some of the trails, a wilderness permit), visit the **Golden West Visitor Center** near the Stehekin jetty (Apr–Oct only; ⓣ360/856-5700, ⓦwww.nps.gov/noca).

Leavenworth
A few miles south of Chelan, the Cascade Loop turns west along US-2 at **Wenatchee**, the drab center of Washington's embattled apple industry, suffering from a recent market glut of fruit from Asia. From there, the loop heads for pocket-sized **LEAVENWORTH**, a Bavarian theme town where even the *Safeway* and *McDonald's* are decked out in high gables and half-timbered woodwork. It only takes about an hour to explore the place, but there are plenty of outdoor activities to be had in the spectacular mountain setting – though the hills may look a little charred after the area's recent rash of wildfires. The **ranger station**, just off US-2 at 600 Sherbourne St (daily 7.45am–4.30pm; ⓣ509/782-1413), provides trail guides and hiking information, and **bikes**, **canoes** and **kayaks** can be rented from several outlets, including *Leavenworth Ski and Sports*, US-2 at Icicle Road (ⓣ509/548-7864). The **visitors center**, 894 Hwy-2 (ⓣ509/548-5807, ⓦwww.leavenworth.org), has copious listings of places to **stay** and **eat**. Downtown options include the arch-Teutonic suites of the *Hotel Pension Anna*, 926 Commercial St (ⓣ509/548-6273, ⓦwww .pensionanna.com; ❺), and the comparable *Enzian Motor Inn*, 590 Hwy-2 (ⓣ509/548-5269 or 1-800/223-8511, ⓦwww.enzianinn.com; ❺). The *Andreas Keller*, 829 Front St (ⓣ509/548-6000), serves up hefty helpings of gut-busting German cuisine.

West of Leavenworth, US-2 crosses the mountains over Stevens Pass, but the principal east–west highway, I-90, lies further to the south, connecting Seattle with the fertile Yakima Valley. Near I-90 is the 268-foot **Snoqualmie Falls** and the luxurious *Salish Lodge,* 6501 Railroad Ave SE (ⓣ425/888-2556 or 1-800/826-6124, ⓦwww.salishlodge.com; ❾), where much of the David Lynch television series *Twin Peaks* was filmed.

Mount Rainier National Park
Set in its own national park, glacier-clad **MOUNT RAINIER** is the highest (14,410ft) and most accessible peak in the Cascades. Recurrent puns characterize its name as a description of its weather: often very wet, with heavy snowfalls during the long winter season (except if joking, pronounce the name as "ray-neer"). Not until midsummer does the snowpack melt enough to unblock roads, and then the deer, mountain goats and marmots reappear, the alpine meadows become ablaze with dazzling wild flowers, and Mount Rainier makes for some perfect – and not necessarily strenuous – hiking.

If you only have a day to explore the park, consider traversing the south and east sides from Nisqually entrance to **Paradise**, with a side trip to **Sunrise**. The stunning 80-mile drive winds through river valleys and lowland forests with glaciated peaks and magnificent vistas. There are numerous **trails** radiating from Paradise, such as the 5-mile Skyline Trail to Glacier Overlook, the perfect spot to ponder the awesome Nisqually Glacier. In Mount Rainier National Park, there are more than three hundred miles of trails, ranging from short, simple interpretive walks, to the Pacific Crest Trail that cuts through the park's eastern edge, to the 93-mile Wonderland Trail that encircles Mount Rainier itself.

Climbing Mount Rainier itself is hazardous and should only be undertaken by experienced climbers with the necessary equipment, and who are physically fit. The long-established guide service, *Rainier Mountaineering*, in Paradise (☎360/569-2227 or 253/627-6242 in winter, ⓦwww.rmiguides.com), offers climbing courses and guided climbs – one day's practice, then the two-day climb – for $600, with equipment rental for around $300.

Park practicalities

Admission to the park is $10 per vehicle, $5 per person, for a one-week pass. The park has four **entrances**: **Nisqually** in the southwest corner, **Stephen's Canyon** in the southeast, **White River** in the northeast, and **Carbon River** in the northwest. Only the Nisqually entrance is open year-round (for cross-country skiing; the others open May–Oct). For map and trail conditions, stop by the **visitor centers** at Longmire, Paradise and White River (ⓦwww.nps .gov/mora). During the summer, you can drive the 240 miles of roads that almost circumnavigate Mount Rainier National Park to the various entrances. The Nisqually entrance is the only part serviced by public transportation – either on a day-trip with *Gray Line* from Seattle (May–Sept; ☎206/624-5077 or 1-800/426-7505), or from Sea-Tac Airport to Paradise via *Rainier Shuttle* (☎360/569-2331) or through *Ashford Mountain Center* (mid-May to Oct; ☎360/569-2604). There is no public transportation within the park.

Two national park lodges provide **accommodation**: *National Park Inn* (☎360/569-2275, ⓦwww.guestservices.com/rainier; ❹), nestled in a forest at Longmire, is a small lodge open year-round, and further up the mountain, *Paradise Inn* (mid-May to early Oct; ☎360/569-2275; ❹), is a massive 1917 wooden lodge, where the striking views, not the functional rooms, are the main draw. Make reservations well in advance. Rustic *Cougar Rock* and *Ohanapecosh* **campgrounds** are available by reservation only from July–Aug (☎1-800/365-CAMP, ⓦwww.americanparknetwork.com/reserve; $12-15), while *White River, Sunshine Point* and *Ipsut Creek* campgrounds are first-come, first-served. For overnight backpacking, pick up a required wilderness permit, free from Longmire, White River or Paradise ranger stations (☎360/569-2211).

Mount St Helens

The Klickitat Indians who called **Mount St Helens** *Tahonelatclah* ("Fire Mountain") knew what they were talking about. A snowcapped peak long popular with scout camps and climbing expeditions, Mount St Helens erupted on May 18, 1980, leaving a scorched area of near-total destruction. Its blast wave flattened the surrounding forests, heavy clouds of ash settled as far away as Portland, and a massive mudflow sent an avalanche of debris down the Toutle River Valley. Since then, the forests have started to grow again, and many animal species have made a surprisingly quick recovery, while others have seemingly vanished for good. With the scarred landscape testifying to the awesome force of nature, Mount St Helens has justifiably become a major tourist attraction.

Located in a remote pocket of Gifford Pinchot National Forest, there are three entry routes into the region. Most visitors arrive along Hwy-504, off I-5 roughly halfway between Olympia and Portland. The road snakes through dark green forests, until bald, spiky trees signal a sudden change: thousands of gray tree-skeletons lie in combed-down rows, knocked flat in different directions as the blast waves bounced off the hillsides. At the end is the **Johnson Ridge Observatory** (May–Sept daily 10am–6pm; ☎360/274-2140), offering breathtaking views of the still-steaming lava dome and crater, plus state-of-the-art interpretive displays, an exciting film of the eruption of Mount St Helens

The eruption of Mount St Helens

From its first rumblings in March 1980, **Mount St Helens** drew the nation's attention. Residents and loggers were evacuated and roads were closed, but by April the entrances to the restricted zone around the steaming peak were jammed with reporters and sightseers. But the mountain didn't seem to be doing much, and impatient residents demanded to be allowed back to their homes. Even the official line became blurred when Harry Truman, operator of the *Lodge at Spirit Lake* who refused to move out, became a national celebrity and was, incredibly, congratulated on his "common sense" by Washington's governor.

A convoy of homeowners was waiting at the barriers, about to go and collect their possessions, when the explosion finally came on May 18 – not upwards but sideways, ripping a great chunk out of the mountainside. An avalanche of debris slid into Spirit Lake, raising it by two hundred feet and turning it into a steaming cauldron of mud, as dark clouds of ash buried Truman and suffocated loggers on a nearby slope. Altogether, 57 people died on the mountain: a few were there officially, but most, like Harry Truman, had ignored the warnings. The wildlife population was harder hit: about a million and a half animals – deer, elk, mountain goats, cougar and bears – were killed, and thousands of fish were boiled alive in sediment-filled rivers. There were dire economic effects, too, as falling ash devastated the land, and millions of feet of timber were lost.

and powerful testimonials by blast survivors. On bright summer days, views of the mountain can be both unexpectedly picturesque and starkly ominous. The only real disadvantage with the Hwy-504 approach to Mount St Helens is its popularity – you can expect long caravans of SUVs on any fair-weather day.

One alternative is to take Hwy-503 from Portland (or I-5) to **COUGAR**, on the mountain's southern periphery, from where challenging, summer-only forest roads, USFS-90, -25 and -99, wind along its flanks to **Windy Ridge** viewpoint on the northeast side of the mountain. Attracting only a fraction of the tourists swarming on Johnson Ridge, this is the best place to view the volcanic apocalypse up close, with shocking views of shattered trees and torn-up hillsides. Windy Ridge can also be accessed from the north from **RANDLE** along USFS-25 and -99, which provides access to what remains of Spirit Lake and passes through lava flows with numerous viewpoints en route.

Mount St Helens National Monument charges a $6 **admission fee** that allows visitors access to all the sites, good for one week. En route to **Windy Ridge** from Hwy-503 is the **Mount St Helens Volcanic Monument Headquarters** (℡360/247-3900, ⓦwww.fs.fed.us/gpnf/mshnvm) in Amboy, which has information and issues backcountry permits ($15; reserve at ℡360/247-3961). Just off the I-5 near Castle Rock is the **Mount St Helens Visitor Center** (daily 9am–5pm; ℡360/274-2103), complete with informative exhibits. The **Coldwater Ridge Visitor Center** (daily 10am–6pm; ℡360/274-2131) focuses on the ways plants and animals have successfully recolonized in the blast zones. There are also areas in the Monument where you can **hike** and **camp**.

Eastern Washington

Big, dry and hot, **eastern Washington** has little in common with the green, western side of the state: faded olive-colored sagebrush covers many acres, and massive red rocks loom over the prairies, while huge bare patches of basalt and torn-away groundcover (from centuries of Ice Age floods) give the area the unattractive geological moniker of the "**channeled scablands**." Further south, the lower Yakima Valley is a vast agricultural belt with miles of orchards and farms that flank the Yakima River. With over 300 sunny days a year, this region is the largest producer of apples in the world, though that claim is increasingly threatened by cheap fruit imports from the Far East. In the last 20 years, however, this has also become one of the Northwest's major wine regions. The area towns are agricultural and commercial centers, and only **Spokane** has any degree of cultural life. Nevertheless, some are excellent bases for winery tours or outdoor activities such as rafting, fishing, hiking, paragliding and skiing.

Ellensburg

If you're traveling by Greyhound east of the mountains along I-90, your first major stop will be **ELLENSBURG**, a dusty little town with fetching nineteenth-century red-brick architecture, a state police training academy, a regional university, and not much else except for the **Ellensburg Rodeo**, held over Labor Day weekend. Featuring Stetson-wearing cowhands roping steers, riding bulls, and braving bucking broncos, the rodeo is a rather big deal for the area. To get tickets (starting at $10), call the Rodeo Ticket Office (T 509/962-7831 or 1-800/637-2444, W www.ellensburgrodeo.com).

Greyhound stops at Okanogan St and Eighth Avenue. The **visitors center**, 801 S Ruby St (Mon–Fri 8am–5pm, Sat 10am–2pm; T 509/925-3137, W www .ellensburg-chamber.com), provides maps and hotel options; a safe choice is *Ellensburg Inn*, 1700 Canyon Rd (T 509/925-9801; ④). The art-deco *Valley Café*, 103 W Third Ave (T 509/925-3050), is the nicest place in town to eat.

Yakima and Toppenish

The agricultural hub of **YAKIMA**, to the south, is rather grim terrain: the railroad yard is pretty much its aesthetic high point. Though its attractions are few, it is an excellent base to visit the tasting rooms of the award-wining wineries scattered throughout the Yakima Valley (for information call the Yakima Valley Wine Growers Association, T 1-800/258-7270, W www.yakimavalleywine.com). The only appealing part of downtown is among the brightly painted railroad cars at Yakima Avenue at N First Street, where **Track 29** houses a small collection of shops and food stalls.

Wine-tour maps, as well as lodging and dining information, can be found at the **visitor center**, 10 N Eighth St (Mon–Fri 8.30am–5pm, also summer weekends 9am–4pm; T 509/575-3010 or 1-800/221-0751, W www.visityakima .com). Greyhound stops nearby at 602 E Yakima Ave. **Motels** and diner-type **restaurants** abound along N First Street. Located in the old train depot is America's first brewpub, *Grant's Brewery Pub*, 32 N Front St (T 509/575-2922), which serves quality hand-crafted ales and tasty pub food, just as *Gasparetti's*, 10 N First St (T 509/248-0628), provides solid, affordable Italian fare. *Santiago's*, 111 E Yakima Ave (T 509/453-1644), is a decent Mexican restaurant, but for the real thing, super cheap, check out *Salsita Antojitos Mexicanos*, N Second St at Yakima Ave (T 509/425-9515). There's **camping** across the Yakima River on Hwy-24 at **Sportsman State Park** (T 509/575-2774 or 1-800/562-0990).

Twenty miles south of Yakima, **TOPPENISH**, the main town on the Yakima Indian Reservation, has a Wild West feel enlivened by buildings with historic Western murals. The **visitors center**, 11 S Toppenish Ave (T 509/865-3262, W www.toppenish.org), supplies brochures on the murals and has a list of local

accommodation. The modern and comfortable *Toppenish Inn Motel*, 515 S Elm St (℡509/865-7444 or 1-800/222-3161; **❸**), is the best choice, and there are also a few good Mexican restaurants, notably *Los Murales,* 202 W First Ave (℡509/865-7555). In nearby Sunnyside, *Snipes Mountain Brewery & Restaurant,* 905 Yakima Valley Hwy (℡509/837-BREW), serves great regional food and wine.

Walla Walla: the Whitman Mission

WALLA WALLA, about 120 miles east of Yakima along I-82 and US-12, is an uneventful college and agricultural town, known best for its sweet onions, eaten raw like apples. There's little to see now, but this was the place where the missionary **Dr Marcus Whitman** arrived from the East Coast in 1836. Unsuccessful in his bid to convert the local Cayuse into crop-growing Christians, he turned his attention to white settlers. In 1843, Whitman helped guide the first wagon-train across the Oregon Trail, and his mission became a refuge for sick and orphaned travelers. The Cayuse eyed the ever-increasing emigrants warily, and when measles spread among the tribe, suspicions grew that they were being poisoned, particularly as Dr Whitman could help (some) whites but few of the natives – who had no natural immunity to the disease, which led to the death of half the tribe. Despite the native tradition that medicine men were liable for the deaths of their patients, Whitman continued to take on even hopeless cases. In November 1847, a band of Cayuse murdered Whitman, his wife and eleven others. Fifty more, mostly children, were taken captive, and although they were later released, angry settlers raised vigilante bands against the Cayuse. When the story hit the newspapers back East, it generated such a tide of fear about Native American uprisings that the government finally declared the Oregon land (then including Washington) a US territory, which meant the army could be sent in to protect the settlers – with drastic implications for all of the area's tribes.

The site where the **Whitman Mission** was burned down (daily 8am–4.30pm, summer closes at 6pm,;℡509/522-6360, ⓦwww.nps.gov/whmi; $2), in a lovely little dell seven miles west of town off US-12, has simple marks on the ground to illustrate its layout; a visitor center shows a film on Whitman and exhibits the weapon thought to have polished him off. Of more quasi-historical interest, the **Fort Walla Walla Museum**, 755 Myra Rd (Apr–Oct Tues–Sun 10am–5pm; ⓦwww.fortwallawallamuseum.org; $4), is a curious mock-up of a pioneer village, with sixteen old shacks loaded with antiques and Old West dioramas.

Greyhound stops at 315 N Second St, a couple of blocks from the **visitors center**, 29 E Sumach (Mon–Fri 9am–5pm; ℡509/525-0850 or 1-800/743-9562, ⓦwww.wwchamber.com). The *Walla Walla Suites*, 7 E Oak (℡509/525-4700; **❹**), provides good basic **accommodation**, while the *Green Gables Inn,* 922 Bonsella St (℡1-888/525-5501, ⓦwww.greengablesinn.com; **❺**), is a comfortable **B&B** in an old mansion on the east side of town, with private baths in all rooms. There are a few good eateries, mostly downtown: *Merchants Ltd French Bakery*, 21 E Main St (℡509/525-0900), is a decent spot for espresso and pastries.

Spokane

The wide-open spaces and drab little towns of eastern Washington don't prepare you for **SPOKANE** ("spo-CAN"). A few miles from the Idaho border, it's the region's only real city, and its scattering of grandiose late-nineteenth-century buildings – built on the spoils of Idaho silver mines – sport some unexpectedly elegant touches. But its heyday came and went, and shades of the dreary freight town it became still haunt the modern city. It's not a place to linger long, but its pleasant parks and unusual architecture can easily fill a day.

The town's nexus is the hundred-acre **Riverfront Park** (ⓦ www.spokane-riverfrontpark.com), sprawling over two islands in the middle of the Spokane River. Originally planned by Frederick Olmsted of Central Park fame, the park was not laid out as specified until just before Spokane hosted the 1974 World's Fair. Bisecting the park, the river tumbles down a series of rocky shelves known as the **Spokane Falls**, once a fishing site for native peoples and later the home of the first pioneers. Attractions include an ice-skating rink which shares space with the IMAX theater, the charming hand-carved **Looff Carousel**, and the **Gondola Skyride** cable cars (summer Sun–Thurs 11am–8pm, Fri & Sat 11am–10pm; $4.75) which run above the falls from the west end of the park.

Most of the relics of Spokane's early grandeur can be found several blocks southwest on W Riverside Avenue, where neoclassical facades cluster around Jefferson Street. The city's nineteenth-century highlights include the **Davenport Hotel**, the **Clark Mansion**, and the Tudor Revival **Campbell House** (Tues–Sun 10am–5pm, Sun opens at 1pm; $4), part of the **Cheney Cowles Museum** at 2316 W First Ave (ⓦ www.cheneycowles.org), a regional history museum holding an impressive collection of artifacts.

Practicalities

Amtrak, Greyhound, Northwestern Trailways (☎ 509/838-5262, ⓦ www.nwadv.com/northw) and local bus lines share the **transit center** at 221 W First Ave. The **visitors center** is at 201 W Main St (Mon–Fri 8.30am–5pm; ☎ 509/747-3230 or 1-800/776-5263, ⓦ www.visitspokane.com). Central, moderately priced **accommodations** include the basic *Towne Center Motel*, 901 W First Ave (☎ 509/747-1041; ❸), the *Travelodge*, 33 W Spokane Falls Blvd (☎ 509/623-9727, ⓦ www.spokanetravelodge.com; ❹), and the *West Coast Ridpath Hotel*, 515 W Sprague Ave (☎ 509/838-2711, ⓦ www.westcoasthotels.com; ❺), a 350-room hotel with good views over the city. There's also a string of generic motels along I-90, and **camping** in Riverside State Park (☎ 509/456-3964, ⓦ www.riversidestatepark.org), located six miles northwest off Hwy-291.

Downtown, there's solid Italian **food** and "world famous" lasagna at *Luigi's*, 245 W Main St (☎ 509/624-7444), and innovative vegetarian cuisine at *Mizuna*, 214 N Howard St (☎ 509/747-2004), including a mean orange pepper tofu.

The Grand Coulee Dam and around

The huge **Grand Coulee Dam** – the largest concrete structure in the world – is eighty miles west of Spokane. When work began in 1933, it was as much a political icon as it was an engineering feat. Probably the most ambitious scheme of Roosevelt's New Deal, this massive dam provided jobs for hundreds of workers from all over the country, including folk singer **Woody Guthrie**, who also worked on the Bonneville Dam in the Columbia Gorge (see p.1222) and was commissioned to write twenty songs about the Columbia project. These were originally played at local rallies, held to raise investment money and combat propaganda from private power companies that wanted to monopolize power production. The dam's unquestioned heyday, though, was during World War II, when its waterpower was harnessed into the making of aluminum that became essential to the production of war materiel.

Grand Coulee Dam is now the world's biggest producer of hydroelectricity, and has certainly controlled flooding lower down the Columbia. Unfortunately, power-guzzling agricultural and industrial demands have made this dam, like others along the Columbia, a potent symbol of the decline of native salmon species, whose migration routes have largely disappeared in recent decades, thanks to the looming turbines and concrete walls in their way.

The earlier, heroic story of power production is detailed in the **visitor center** (℡ 509/633-9265, Ⓦ www.grandcouleedam.org; free), on Hwy-155 on the west side of the dam, which also runs free tours of the dam and its generating plants (summer daily 9am–9pm; rest of year daily 9am–5pm). The **dam** itself is initially something of an anticlimax; because of its horizontal layout, it just doesn't look that big – a trick of the hugely scaled scenery that surrounds it. On summer nights it's lit up by a laser show that takes place from 8.30pm to 10pm, depending on the month.

The neighboring towns of **Coulee Dam**, **Grand Coulee** and **Electric City** have a few **motels** and fairly dire **restaurants**. More appealingly, over thirty **campgrounds** are scattered around the long, spindly reservoir of Lake Roosevelt, which becomes more woody and secluded as you get further north. The more noteworthy spots include *Spring Canyon Campground*, located on the lake itself (℡ 509/725-2715), and *Steamboat Rock State Park*, 12 miles south of Grand Coulee (℡ 509/633-1304).

Oregon

For nineteenth-century pioneers, driving in covered wagons over the mountains and deserts of the arduous Oregon Trail, the **Willamette Valley** was the promised land. Rich and fertile, it became the home of Oregon's first settlements, and the valley is still the heart of the state's social, political and cultural existence. **Portland**, the biggest city, has a cozy European feel; **Salem**, the state capital, maintains a small-town air; and **Eugene**, at the southern foot of the valley, is a likeable college community.

East of Portland, waterfalls cascade down mossy cliffs along the **Columbia River Gorge**, south of which the twisting path of an old pioneer road leads through more beautiful scenery around **Mount Hood**. Central Oregon, and its increasingly popular recreation hub, **Bend**, is located on a high chaparral desert with sage and juniper trees, with close access to the southern Cascades, as well as numerous lakes and rivers dropping into striking canyons. Further south, around **Grants Pass** the major rivers drain to the Pacific, carving steep gorges and making for some excellent whitewater rafting, while the liberal hamlet of **Ashland** offers a splash of culture with its annual Shakespeare Festival.

Several highways link the Willamette Valley to the rugged coast, whose most northerly town, **Astoria**, enjoys a magnificent setting strewn with imposing Victorian homes. South along the coast, wide and protected expanses of sand are broken by jagged black monoliths; white lighthouses look out from stark headlands; and rough cliffs conceal small, sheltered coves. With its sand dunes, dense forests, and sheer variety, the coast is every bit as appealing as its Californian counterpart, albeit not as warm.

The rugged deserts and lava fields of **Eastern Oregon** are more remote and were only settled on any scale once the prime land in the west had already been taken. The settling process involved not only ferocious "Indian campaigns" but also the bitterly violent range wars between sheep-farmers and terrorist "sheep-shooters" (associations of cattle ranchers). Sheep and cows now graze in peace, and some small towns still celebrate their cowboy roots with annual rodeos.

Getting around Oregon

Portland is well connected by **train** and **bus** along the I-5 freeway to Seattle in the north and California to the south. Amtrak (℡1-800-USA-RAIL, ⓦwww.amtrak.com) runs its *Coast Starlight* train once daily north to Seattle or south to LA, while its Cascades line runs four times daily between **Eugene** and Vancouver, BC. Bus routes radiate from Portland out to Spokane in Washington, across southern and central Oregon and to the coast. There's also a twice-daily service from Portland to San Francisco along US-101, and another following the line of I-84 east from Portland as far as Pendleton, and then south towards Boise in Idaho.

Local bus companies serve communities north of Lincoln City in sporadic fashion, but the coast is also excellent for **cycling**, if a bit windy. There are many great opportunities for **hiking**, though having your own vehicle can make it easier to access the more remote spots. **Hitchhiking**, inadvisable anywhere in the US, is illegal in Oregon.

Portland

Having been spared the kind of aggressive, remorseless development that many Seattle residents have come to loathe, **PORTLAND** still retains a pleasant, small-city feel, both for its well-preserved Beaux Arts architecture and walkable urban core, as well as its easygoing atmosphere. That said, there's not a lot to keep intrepid tourists here for more than a day, with most of the city's handful of major attractions located within close walking distance of each other on the short city blocks – half the size of most American cities. On the other hand, while Portland's unpretentious bohemian flavor may be lost on more gung-ho travelers, the city remains an excellent spot for casual visitors to slack around for weeks at a time, with a wealth of good diners, microbreweries, clubs, bookstores and coffee houses to keep you occupied.

The city was named after Portland, Maine, following a coin toss between its two East Coast founders in 1845 ("Boston" was the other option). Its location on a deep part of the Willamette River, just 78 miles from the Pacific and surrounded by fertile valleys, made it a perfect trading port, and it grew quickly, replacing its clapboard houses with ornate facades and Gothic gables. Nevertheless, throughout the nineteenth century it remained a raunchy, bawdy place, notorious for gambling, prostitution and opium dens. By the 1970s, Portland's historic buildings had decayed or were sacrificed to parking lots and expressways, but since then, it has salvaged what was left of its past, replacing concrete with red brick, and introducing folksy statues and murals. Although the city's rehabilitation, along with its "urban growth boundary" to limit unrestrained development, has done much for Portland's reputation nationwide, most residents are ambivalent about the praise and would prefer you move anywhere – preferably Seattle – but here.

Arrival and information

Portland International Airport (PDX) is a thirty-minute drive from downtown, by either the Gray Line Airport Express bus (every 45min 5am–midnight; $15; Ⓦ www.grayline.com), which drops off at major hotels, or the cheaper MAX light-rail line (4 hourly, 7am–11.30pm; $1.55), which connects to the airport near Terminal C and takes about forty minutes to reach downtown. A **cab** from the airport into town costs $25–30. Greyhound at 550 NW Sixth Ave and Amtrak close by at 800 NW Sixth Ave are conveniently situated within easy walking distance of the center; if you arrive at night take a cab though – this part of town is not safe after dark. Pacific Trails (Ⓣ 503/292-4437) runs buses from Portland to the Oregon Coast.

The **visitor center**, by the river in the World Trade Center, 26 SW Salmon St at Front Avenue (May–Oct daily 9am–5pm; Nov–Apr Mon–Fri 9am–5pm, Sat 10am–2pm, Ⓣ 503/275-9750 or 1-800/962-3700, Ⓦ www.pova.org), has plenty of maps and information on both the city and the state. Portland's main **post office** is at 715 NW Hoyt St (Ⓣ 503/294-2124; zip code 97205).

Getting around

Although you can see much of the compact city center on **foot**, or along the city's impressive, extensive network of **cycling** paths and trails, Portland also has an excellent public transit network. Portland's **light rail system**, Metropolitan Area Express (MAX), moves tourists around central downtown and Old Town, and carries commuters over the river to the eastern suburbs, also tunneling under Washington Park and the zoo. The Tri-Met **bus system** is based at the downtown **transit mall** along Fifth Avenue (southbound) and Sixth Avenue (northbound). Each bus shelter is labeled with a symbol – brown beaver, blue snowflake and so on – serving as a code for a block of bus routes in a particular area of the city. Although excellent for transportation, the mall is not a place to linger: it's well-known as a drug-dealing zone. The **Tri-Met Info Bureau** on Pioneer Courthouse Square (Mon–Fri 8am–5pm; Ⓣ 503/238-7433, for disabled customers Ⓣ 503/238-4952, Ⓦ www.tri-met .org) offers free transit maps and sells all-zone day tickets ($4), "Quik Tik" six-hour passes ($3), books of ten tickets ($11.50), and monthly passes ($45) with special student rates ($16). Buses and MAX trains are **free** in the downtown zone – "Fareless Square" – edged by the Willamette to the east, Irving Street to the north, and I-405 to the south and west. Outside here, fares are between $1.05 and $1.55 – pay the bus driver exact change; **transfers** for onward travel within the same zone (there are three fare zones altogether) are free.

The brightly colored cars of the new **Portland Streetcar** line ply a tourist-oriented route between Portland State University and Northwest Portland, covering most downtown sights on NW and SW 10th and 11th streets. Fares are free inside Fareless Square, otherwise $1.25 (Ⓦ www.portlandstreetcar.org). Portland's **taxis** don't stop in the street; you'll have to either get one at a hotel or call (Broadway Cabs Ⓣ 503/227-1234, Portland Taxi Co Ⓣ 503/256-5400).

Accommodation

Scads of flavorless **motels** line the interstates and Sandy Boulevard northeast of the city center, but for a few dollars more you're far better staying downtown, where you'll find **hostels**, **B&Bs** and a good range of **hotels**, the pick of which occupy grand and elegantly restored old buildings.

Hotels, motels and B&Bs

Benson 309 SW Broadway ☎503/228-2000 or 1-888/523-6766, ⓦwww.westcoasthotels.com/benson. The typical spot for visiting dignitaries and celebs, this classy hotel has a superb walnut-paneled 1912 lobby, and swank bedrooms with modern appointments. ❽

Days Inn City Center 1414 SW 6th Ave ☎503/221-1611 or 1-800/899-0248, ⓦwww.daysinn.com. Great location with smart, well-tended motel rooms. Excellent value for downtown. ❺

Edgefield 2126 SW Halsey Rd ☎503/669-8610 or 1-800/669-8610, ⓦwww.mcmenamins.com/edge. Fifteen minutes east of the airport, this unique brewery-resort features a Georgian Manor, restaurants, bars, winery and tasting room, distillery, movie theater, gardens, and an 18-hole British golf course. ❹

General Hooker's House B&B 125 SW Hooker St ☎503/222-4435 or 1-800/745-4135, ⓦwww.generalhookers.com. Four attractive Victorian guestrooms, a 20-min walk from downtown. ❹

Heathman Hotel 1001 SW Broadway at Salmon St ☎503/241-4100 or 1-800/551-0011, ⓦwww.heathmanhotel.com. Occupies a finely restored Neoclassical building, with an elegant, teak-paneled interior and much marble and brass. Splendid rooms, excellent restaurant, and popular lobby-lounge where you can swill among the swells. ❼

Heron Haus 2545 NW Westover Rd ☎503/274-1846, ⓦwww.heronhaus.com. Stylish 1904 Tudor B&B, whose large suites feature fireplaces and cozy sitting areas. Excellent continental breakfast and close hiking access to Portland's expansive Forest Park. ❼

Kennedy School 5736 NE 33rd Ave ☎503/249-3983 or 1-888/249-3983, ⓦwww.mcmenamins.com/kennedy. Thirty-five B&B rooms, each in a refurbished schoolroom with chalkboards and cloakrooms, plus modern conveniences. Excellent breakfast, multiple brewpubs, movie theater, outdoor bathing pool, and "detention bar." ❺

Mallory Hotel 729 SW 15th Ave ☎503/223-6311 or 1-800/228-6857, ⓦwww.malloryhotel.com. Stylish lobby, but rather plain – though affordable – rooms in this old Portland favorite, well placed along the MAX tracks. ❺

Vintage Plaza 422 SW Broadway ☎503/228-1212 or 1-800/243-0555, ⓦwww.vintageplaza.com. An intimate boutique hotel with oversized rooms and a calm, relaxed atmosphere. Wine is offered in the afternoons in the lobby. ❻

White Eagle Hotel 836 N Russell St ☎503/282-6810, ⓦwww.mcmenamins.com/eagle.html. Hands-down Portland's best bargain, a refurbished old hotel converted into a hip brewpub in an industrial-bohemian neighborhood. Rooms are clean and simple, and surprisingly cheap. Live music nightly. ❷

Hostels

HI-Portland 3031 SE Hawthorne Blvd ☎503/236-3380, ⓦwww.portlandhostel.com. Hostel facilities in a cheery Victorian house, well located in the heart of the Hawthorne District. Occasional live performances. $18 dorms, $45 private rooms.

HI-NW Portland International Hostel 1818 NW Glisan ☎503/241-2783, ⓦwww.2oregonhostels.com. Located in a nineteenth-century home in Northwest Portland, near the popular *Mission Theatre & Brewpub*. Contains espresso bar and family rooms. $19 dorms, private rooms (only two) $50.

The City

The Willamette River divides Portland in half: the downtown area lies between the river's west bank and the I-405 freeway, forming the bulk of the city's southwest quadrant; the east is mostly residential. Surrounded by historic terracotta buildings downtown, **Pioneer Courthouse Square** is the indisputable center of Portland, its curving brick steps filled with music and people, and is named after the adjacent **Pioneer Courthouse**, a squat 1868 structure that still maintains its judicial function. Within easy walking distance are the city's leading theaters, museums and department stores (notably **Nike Town**, 930 SW Sixth Ave, a flashy corporate theme store with high retail prices) – a

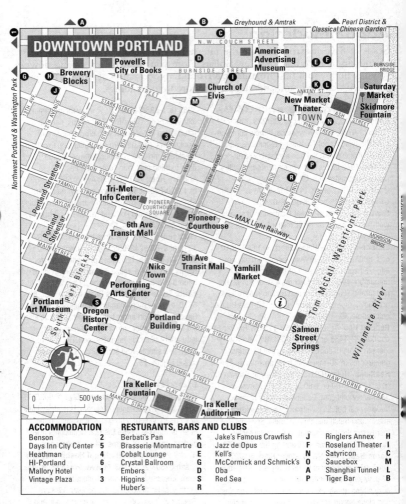

DOWNTOWN PORTLAND

Northwest Portland & Washington Park

Greyhound & Amtrak

Pearl District & Classical Chinese Garden

N.W. COUCH STREET

Powell's City of Books

American Advertising Museum

BURNSIDE BRIDGE

Brewery Blocks

BURNSIDE STREET

OAK STREET

Church of Elvis

Saturday Market

New Market Theater

Skidmore Fountain

STARK STREET

WASHINGTON STREET

OLD TOWN

ALDER STREET

MORRISON STREET

Tri-Met Info Center

PIONEER COURTHOUSE SQUARE

Pioneer Courthouse

MAX Light Railway

6th Ave Transit Mall

MORRISON BRIDGE

TAYLOR STREET

SALMON STREET

Nike Town

5th Ave Transit Mall

Yamhill Market

MAIN STREET

Performing Arts Center

Portland Art Museum

Oregon History Center

Portland Building

MADISON STREET

Tom McCall Waterfront Park

Salmon Street Springs

Willamette River

JEFFERSON STREET

COLUMBIA STREET

Ira Keller Fountain

CLAY STREET

HAWTHORNE BRIDGE

Ira Keller Auditorium

MARKET STREET

0   500 yds

ACCOMMODATION		RESTURANTS, BARS AND CLUBS					
Benson	2	Berbati's Pan	K	Jake's Famous Crawfish	J	Ringlers Annex	H
Days Inn City Center	5	Brasserie Montmartre	Q	Jazz de Opus	F	Roseland Theater	I
Heathman	4	Cobalt Lounge	E	Kell's	N	Satyricon	C
HI-Portland	6	Crystal Ballroom	G	McCormick and Schmick's	O	Saucebox	M
Mallory Hotel	1	Embers	D	Oba	A	Shanghai Tunnel	L
Vintage Plaza	3	Higgins	S	Red Sea	P	Tiger Bar	B
		Huber's	R				

melange of old and new, where fading plasterwork and ceramic reliefs face concrete and glass, punctuated by small grassy parks.

Broadway epitomizes Portland's mix of early grandeur and new wealth, with prestigious hotels sharing space with cultural institutions, such as the grand old *Paramount* theater, restored as part of the impressive **Portland Center for the Performing Arts**, at 1111 SW Broadway (Ⓦwww.pcpa.com). One block west, the **Portland Art Museum** (Tues–Sat 10am–5pm, Sun noon-5pm; $7.50; Ⓦwww.pam.org) hosts touring exhibitions, plus a wide-ranging collection of Northwest Native American masks, Mexican statues and ancient Chinese figures – and recently acquired the modernist personal collection of critic Clement Greenberg, parts of which are on display intermittently. A block away, decorated with huge trompe l'oeil pioneer murals, the **Oregon History Center**, 1200 SW Park Ave (Tues–Sat 10am–5pm, Sun noon–5pm; $6;

Ⓦwww.ohs.org), is primarily a research facility, but has some imaginative exhibits exploring different facets of the state's history. Between the museum and the history center run the **South Park Blocks**, a twelve-block green belt and favorite Portland hangout, where retirees commingle with teen slackers and the homeless – all under the shadow of statues of Teddy Roosevelt riding on to victory at San Juan Hill and Abe Lincoln standing rigidly with a long, dark expression.

A five-minute walk away, at the junction of Madison and Fifth avenues, is one of Portland's few notable architectural sights – Michael Graves' **Portland Building**, a monumental concrete box with "ironic" blue ribbons. Several blocks east, Portland's riverfront has been rescued from a century of burial beneath wharves, warehouses and, more recently, an express highway. The area is now lined by another favorite urban oasis, the two-mile-long **Tom McCall Waterfront Park** (created by demolishing the highway), where flocks of Canadian geese abound on the grass and young and old alike dash through the fountains of **Salmon Street Springs**. As a cheap and fun way to get wet, the springs are second only in popularity to the user-friendly **Ira Keller Fountain**, a huge concrete water sculpture just west of the riverfront at SW Third and Clay streets. Further north, the small **Yamhill Historic District** is lined with 1890s buildings, and the **Yamhill Marketplace** (built in 1982), SW second at Yamhill street, has a couple of produce stalls and cafés, though most of its interior has been turned into a gym.

Old Town, Chinatown, Pearl District and Northwest Portland

Old Town, the area around and just south of the Burnside Bridge, is where Portland was founded in 1843. The area tended to flood, however, and when the railroad came in 1883 the town center soon shifted away; its big, ornate buildings became warehouses and it plummeted down the social scale. These days, missions for the homeless coexist with galleries, brewpubs and boutiques. The **Saturday Market** (March–Dec Sat 10am–5pm, Sun 11am–4.30pm; Ⓦwww.portlandsaturdaymarket.com) packs the area south of, and under, the Burnside Bridge with arts and crafts stalls, eclectic street musicians, spicy foods and lively crowds, all crammed cheek-to-jowl by the MAX tracks. At First and Ankeny stands the **Skidmore Fountain**, a bronze basin raised by caryatids above a granite pool, designed to provide European elegance for the citizens and water for hard-working nineteenth-century horses. Across the fountain's angular plaza, an ornamental colonnade stretches from the side of the **New Market Theater**, a restored theater-cum-vegetable market that is now full of cafés. A few blocks west, the **24–Hour Church of Elvis**, 720 SW Ankeny St ("most hours"; ℡503/226-3671, Ⓦwww.churchofelvis.com; donation), is an only-in-Portland attraction: a storefront, walk-through maze of Styrofoam and plastic monstrosities, many dedicated to Mr Presley. Church of Elvis marriage certificates – and other Presley paraphernalia – are usually available from the coin-operated display in the window, and marriages can be arranged, complete with a serenade from Portland's premier Elvis impersonator.

Nearby along west Burnside, the ornamental gate at Fourth Avenue marks **Chinatown**, once the second-largest Chinese community in the US until white unemployment in the 1880s led, as elsewhere, to racist attacks and forced most Chinese workers to leave. There's still enough of a community here to support a range of cheap ethnic restaurants and bars, along with numerous rock and dance clubs – this stretch is the city's nexus for nightlife. Other notable sights include the **American Advertising Museum**, 211 NW Fifth Ave

(Wed–Sun noon–5pm; $3), giving a fascinating account of the rise of advertising, from posters to tapes of old radio and TV ads, and the **Classical Chinese Garden**, NW Third Ave at Everett (daily Apr–Oct: 9am–6pm; Nov–Mar 10am–5pm; $6), a Suzhou-styled garden with traditional vegetation, ponds and walkways.

North of Burnside lies the chic **Pearl District**, an old industrial zone now gentrified with upscale lofts, galleries, restaurants and boutiques. The biggest recent redevelopment is the so-called **Brewery Blocks**, NW 11th Avenue between Burnside and Davis streets, a monumental renovation of the former Blitz-Weinhard brewery into high-end restaurants, retail shops and condos – due to be mostly completed by the end of 2002. Nearby is the famous **Powell's City of Books**, 1005 W Burnside St (daily 9am–11pm; ⓦwww.powells.com). With over a million new, used and rare books, Powell's occupies an entire block, as well as separate annexes around town, and provides free maps so customers can find their way around. At the store's **Anne Hughes Coffee Room** (ⓣ503/228-4651), you can pore over a book or magazine before you buy.

Further west, the Nob Hill district is better known to locals as **Northwest Portland**, stretching from W Burnside Street along a dozen blocks of NW 23rd and NW 21st avenue, choked with fine restaurants and boutiques, where the population density is the state's highest and the street parking is notoriously bad on weekends. The assortment of multicolored Victorian piles adds a San Franciscan tinge – and the food is as good as it gets north of California.

The West Hills and Washington Park

Directly west of Northwest Portland, the wooded bluffs of the West Hills contain the massive **Forest Park**, the country's largest urban green space, interlaced with countless hiking trails, including the 26-mile loop of the Wildwood Trail. Just to the south, the elegant houses of Portland's wealthy include the ever-popular **Pittock Mansion**, 3229 NW Pittock Drive (Feb–Dec noon–4pm; $5; ⓦwww.pittockmansion.com), a 1914 Renaissance Revival creation whose most attractive attribute is its stunning – and free – view of the city from the front lawn. Beyond the mansion, forested **Washington Park** is home to a number of Portland's most popular attractions. These include the expansive city views from the **International Rose Test Gardens** (daily 7am–9pm; free), featuring a wide array of bright summertime blooms; the tranquil **Japanese Garden** (daily: Apr–Sept 10am–7pm; Oct–Mar 10am–4pm; $6; ⓦwww.japanesegarden.com), actually a collection of five gardens with traditional ponds, bridges, foliage, and sand patterns; and the **Oregon Zoo** (daily: Apr–Sept 9am–6pm; Oct–Mar 9am–4pm; $6.50; ⓦwww.zooregon.org), whose most unusual feature is its Elephant Museum, detailing the biological and cultural history of pachyderms – and decorated with a giant mastodon skeleton. Close by, the rather staid **World Forestry Center** (daily 10am–5pm; $4.50; ⓦwww.worldforestry.org) uses interactive exhibits to explain forest management from a timber industry perspective. Most Washington Park attractions have convenient access to a MAX light-rail station, which is buried deep underground and accessible only by elevator.

East of the river

While the west side of the Willamette River provided a deep port, the east side was too shallow for shipping, and so the area remained undeveloped for the first fifty years of Portland's life. The Morrison Bridge crept across at the end of the nineteenth century; since then, most of Portland's population has lived here at some point, in various neighborhoods that are almost entirely residential.

Perhaps the best reason to venture in this direction is to walk or bike the 2.3-mile loop of the **Eastbank Esplanade**, a new $30-million concourse that connects from the Hawthorne to the Steel bridge on floating walkways and cantilevered footpaths, offering striking views of downtown and close-up perspectives on the city's industrial zone. Near the south end of the esplanade, the splashy exhibits of the **Oregon Museum of Science and Industry**, 1945 SE Water Ave (June–Aug daily 9.30am–7pm, rest of year Tues–Sun 9.30am–5.30pm; $6.50; ⓦ www.omsi.edu), are primarily geared toward children, with hundreds of interactive booths, toys and kiosks aimed at those with only a sketchy knowledge of science.

More appealing, two miles further east, the **Hawthorne District** is Portland's best alternative culture zone. With Hawthorne Boulevard as its axis between 34th and 45th streets, and dominated by the sparkly, quasi-Moorish *Bagdad Theatre/Brewpub* at 37th street, the area teems with bookstores, hip cafés, dive bars, cheap ethnic restaurants, and as yet only a handful of corporate chain stores. Six blocks north, **Belmont Avenue** is a historic corridor thick with boutiques and ethnic restaurants, centered around the neon lights of the *Avalon Theatre*, at no. 3451, while a mile southwest around 26th Avenue, **Clinton Street** is home to several good diners, funky bars and vintage clothiers (the best being *Xtabay*, at no. 2515). Finally, only sports fans and conventioneers should bother to visit the overly hyped **Rose Quarter**, west of I-5 between the Steel and Broadway bridges (ⓦ www.rosequarter.com), where a green-spired convention center and basketball stadium are the only points of interest amid a clutch of overpriced restaurants and dreary chain motels.

Eating

As in Seattle, Portland's Pacific Northwest cuisine is a mix of international cooking styles and fresh regional produce, and the city offers many excellent **dining** options for all palates and pocketbooks. Downtown, the Pearl District and Northwest Portland have swank cocktail bars, sedate bistros, brewpubs and Pacific-fusion and vegan-friendly restaurants, while Hawthorne Boulevard has the best inexpensive grub and ethnic restaurants. Downtown also has an abundance of **food carts** that crank out Mexican food, Italian panini, vegetarian Indian cuisine, and rice-bowl bentos – typically cheap and tasty fare.

Bangkok Kitchen 2534 SE Belmont St ☎503/236-7349. Forget the higher-priced joints downtown (two miles west of here): this dreary-looking spot has Portland's best – and cheapest – Thai food. And if you don't like the ugly red-vinyl booths or kitschy decor, just order take-out.

Bombay Cricket Club 1925 Hawthorne Blvd ☎503/231-0740. Not just another excellent Indian restaurant, the *Cricket Club* also adds a Muslim-inspired Middle Eastern element to the usual fare. A mile west of the main Hawthorne scene.

Brasserie Montmartre 626 SW Park Ave ☎503/224-5552. The city's most popular French bistro, with tasty pasta and free live jazz on most evenings. The favorite lunching spot for shoppers at nearby Nordstrom.

Dot's Café 2521 SE Clinton St ☎503/235-0203. In the center of the small-but-hip Clinton district, a cheap late-night spot decked out in primo garage-

sale decor, offering the classic bacon cheese-burger, vegan burritos and the best grilled-cheese sandwich in Portland.

Higgins 1239 SW Broadway ☎503/222-9070. One of the city's finest restaurants, where fresh Northwest cuisine and scrumptious desserts are served in cozy quarters just south of the city's main attractions.

Jake's Famous Crawfish 401 SW 12th Ave ☎503/226-1419. Portland's landmark restaurant for over a hundred years. A staggering choice of fresh fish, including Columbia River Sturgeon, Depot Bay Dungeness Crab, and spicy crawfish cakes. The innocuous-sounding "Bag of Chocolate" is an infamously delicious, gut-busting dessert.

McCormick and Schmick's 235 SW 1st Ave at Oak St ☎503/224-7522. Excellent fish restaurant, with fresh nightly specials and a lively oyster bar with a happening singles scene. Entrees around $15.

Oba 555 NW 12th Ave ☎ 503/228-6161. Flashy, Nuevo Latino eatery in the Pearl District that fuses flavors from all over Latin America to create food you won't find anywhere else in Portland.

Papa Haydn 701 NW 23rd Ave, Northwest Portland ☎ 503/223-7317. Expect at least a half-hour wait for a table at this upscale eatery on weekend nights – worth it for a taste of the

hundred-odd desserts on the menu, with the best on view behind glass.

Toney Bento 1423 SE 37th Ave ☎ 503/234-4441. A lively Hawthorne spot with giant bowls of tasty, inexpensive noodle concoctions, and delicious sushi – made by a master first-generation chef.

Wildwood 1221 NW 21st Ave ☎ 503/248-9663. Trendy Northwest Portland restaurant with a warm interior, friendly staff and imaginative food. Fresh local ingredients rule.

Drinking, nightlife and entertainment

Portland's smart cocktail lounges and dive bars easily rival those of Seattle. The city is a beer-drinker's haven, with over thirty local **microbreweries**. *BridgePort Ale House,* 3632 SE Hawthorne Blvd (☎ 503/233-6540), and *BridgePort Brewing Co,* 1313 NW Marshall St (☎ 503/241-3621), are two solid choices, and the *McMenamins* "concept" brewpubs sell their own locally-brewed ales in unique settings, such as former schoolhouses and renovated hotels (see "Accommodation," p.1215; ⓦ www.mcmenamins.com). The **coffee**-swilling scene looms large, but without Seattle's ubiquitous coffee carts – naturally, though, *Starbucks* is everywhere. For **music**, the place to head is downtown, with the coolest venues centered around Burnside.

The art scene in Portland revolves around the **Portland Center for the Performing Arts**, 1111 SW Broadway (☎ 503-248-4335 or 224-4000, ⓦ www.pcpa.com), a dynamic complex consisting of two main buildings – the **Arlene Schnitzer Concert Hall** and the New Theater Building, containing the **Dolores Winningstad Theater** and **Newmark Theater**. The "Schnitz" is a sumptuously restored 1928 vaudeville and movie house that presents big musical extravaganzas, opera and theater, hosting performances by the **Oregon Symphony Orchestra** (☎ 503/228-1353), **Portland Opera** (☎ 503/241-1407) and **Oregon Ballet Theater** (☎ 503/222-5538), amongst others. Several blocks east at SW 3rd Avenue between Market and Clay streets, the **Ira Keller Auditorium** (☎ 503-274-6560) is home to traveling musicals.

As for **festivals**, Portland State University hosts the mid-July **Portland International Performance Festival** (ⓦ www.extended.pdx.edu/pipf) for contemporary dance and theater productions. During the summer, **free concerts** are held at Pioneer Courthouse Square, Tom McCall Waterfront Park, and the zoo.

The free *Willamette Week* (ⓦ www.wweek.com), available on any street corner, carries **listings** of what's on and where, as does the Friday edition of *The Oregonian*, the main local newspaper (ⓦ www.oregonian.com). *Just Out* is the chief gay/lesbian publication (ⓦ www.justout.com).

Bars, brewpubs and coffee houses

Café Lena 2239 SE Hawthorne Blvd ☎ 503/238-7087. A mile west of the main Hawthorne district, this joint attracts an alternative crowd for its open-mike poetry and acoustic guitar performances. Late-night weekend menu served until 1am.

Cobalt Lounge 32 NW 3rd Avenue ☎ 503/225-1003. A fun, retro-style club in Old Town with stiff drinks and a party crowd. Breakfast served from 4pm to 2am daily.

Coffee People 533 NW 23rd Ave, Northwest Portland ☎ 503/221-0235. Splendid range of coffees – arguably the best in town, though now part of a chain. Visually striking spot attracts more locals – and fewer motorcyclists – than the *Starbucks* across the street.

Embers 11 NW Broadway ☎ 503/222-3082. An often crowded club with drag shows in the gay-oriented front room and high-energy dancing in the straight-leaning room in back. Cool fish-tank bar top.

Goose Hollow Inn and Tavern 1927 SW Jefferson St ☎503/228-7010. Great microbrews, the city's best Reuben sandwich, and convenient location near the MAX tracks (a mile west of downtown) make this a solid bet. Keep watch for colorful owner Bud Clark, once the town mayor.

Huber's 411 SW 3rd Ave ☎503/228-5686. Portland's oldest bar is an elegant room with arched stained-glass skylight, mahogany paneling and terrazzo floor. Famous for roast turkey sandwiches and flaming Spanish coffees.

Kell's 112 SW 2nd Ave ☎503/227-4057. A long-standing favorite Irish bar, with fine authentic cuisine and a range of microbrews, imported beers, and of course, Irish (and Scotch) whiskey.

Lucky Lab Brewpub 915 SE Hawthorne Blvd ☎503/236-3555. Just across the river from downtown, this unpretentious brewpub occupies a huge warehouse space with an outdoor patio. Fresh ales, great sandwiches, BBQ specials, and a delicious peanut curry bento.

Produce Row 204 SE Oak St ☎503/232-8355. Be one of the few tourists at this local favorite, stuck in an unglamorous location by the railroad tracks, across the river in an industrial zone, but boasting thirty brews on tap and a nice range of live music.

Ringlers Annex 1223 SW Stark St ☎503/525-0520. Great people-watching in the cavernous basement of the ornate wedge-shaped 1917 Flatiron Building. Companion bar, *Ringlers*, is two blocks away at 1332 W Burnside St.

Shanghai Tunnel 211 SW Ankeny St ☎503/220-4001. Located just off Burnside Street, this subterranean bar is popular with hipsters and offers Asian-style soul food.

The Tao of Tea 3430 SE Belmont St ☎503/736-0119. More than 120 different kinds of teas are served in an exquisite room with Zen-like decor and a somewhat pretentious air. Elegant meals of affordable vegan and Indian food.

Tiger Bar 317 NW Broadway ☎503/222-7297. An über-hip, swank lounge with a tiger-striped bar and long banquettes. Dark, sultry and smoke-friendly, with late-night food.

Music venues

Berbati's Pan 10 SW 3rd Ave ☎503/248-4579. Mediterranean food is just the entrée, with pool, pinball and ping pong, as well as a reconstructed nineteenth-century European bar in back and nightly eclectic music selections in the nightclub.

Crystal Ballroom 1332 W Burnside St ☎503/778-5625. Just above the *Ringlers* bar, a nineteenth-century dance hall with a "floating" floor on springs. Bands range from hippie to hip-hop, local to national, and feature the best of Portland's indie rock and good DJs in "Lola's Room" upstairs.

Dante's 1 SW 3rd Ave ☎503/226-6630). Perhaps the city's hippest nightspot, where cabaret acts and live rock and electronica music are mixed in with the lounge's signature "Karaoke from Hell" Mondays and "Sinferno" Sunday strip shows.

Jazz de Opus 33 NW 2nd Ave ☎503/222-6077. Cozy, low-key atmosphere with excellent live jazz and grilled food. No cover most nights.

Ohm 31 NW 1st Ave ☎503/223-9919. Located near Saturday market, a top spot for electronica and hip-hop music, with both live acts and DJs. Weekends are packed and stuffy, so come during midweek for a more relaxed environment.

Parchman Farm 1204 SE Clay St ☎503/235-7831. Located a half-mile across the river from downtown, this intimate club features good pizza, great jazz, and no cover.

Red Sea 318 SW 3rd Ave ☎503/241-5450. Dine on African/Middle Eastern cuisine while you groove to reggae and African tunes on weekends. Also offers the occasional belly dancer.

Roseland Theater 8 NW 6th Ave ☎503/224-2038. Located in one of the city's dicier corners, this is a top spot for rock and alternative acts, drawing a mostly young, tattooed and pierced crowd.

Satyricon 125 NW 6th Ave ☎503/243-2380. Diverse acts with an emphasis on punk rock. Good bar food.

Saucebox 214 SW Broadway ☎503/241-3393. Easily missable spot features great pan-Asian cuisine, colorful cocktails, and eclectic nightly music that attracts black-clad poseurs and serious hipsters.

Around Portland: the Columbia River Gorge and Mount Hood

Due east of Portland along the I-84 interstate, the **Columbia River Gorge** is a striking, almost forbidding setting with gusty winds, craggy rocks and incredible views resembling the heroic landscapes of Albert Bierstadt. Scoured into a deep U-shape by huge Ice Age-era floods that also carved up Eastern Washington, the gorge is a nationally protected scenic area, where foamy waterfalls tumble down its sides and fir and maple trees turn fabulous shades of gold and red in the fall. Much more rugged in the nineteenth century before the arrival of modern dams, this was the ominous final leg of the Oregon Trail, where many pioneers met a dark end negotiating perilous rapids on flimsy wooden rafts.

The most dramatic part of the gorge, between Troutdale and the town of Hood River, is just north of snow-capped Mount Hood. The ideal way to explore it is by driving along the narrow, winding **Historic Columbia River Highway** (accessible at exits 22 or 35 off I-84,), which boasts several excellent vistas, particularly **Crown Point** – a marvelous WPA structure perched high above the gorge about ten miles east of Troutdale. Further east, some highway sections are now closed to automotive traffic due to the road's difficulty in handling modern traffic loads, and are designed more for hikers and cyclists.

Back on I-84 below, the most spectacular of the waterfalls en route is **Multnomah Falls** (accessed by an unexpected left-lane exit), whose waters plunge over 530ft down a rock face, collect in a pool, and then drop another seventy feet. Be warned: this is the state's most popular attraction and the crowds can get quite thick. Further east, **Bonneville Dam** (daily 9am–5pm; ☎541/374-8820) is the Oregon counterpart of Washington's Grand Coulee, a huge New Deal project that generates regional electricity and offers a viewing chamber where you can see salmon making their way upstream – although the numbers dwindle each year.

To the south along Highway 35, **Mount Hood** is a dormant volcano rising about eleven thousand feet, the tallest of the Oregon Cascades. The **Mount Hood Loop** – a combination of highways 35 and 26 – takes in both the mount and the gorge, and one of the joys of the area is to explore it by foot along some of the trails. The highest point on the loop at some 4000ft, **Barlow Pass** is named after Sam Barlow, a wagon-train leader who blazed the first "road" around the mountain, which became the unpleasant alternative to the even more dangerous Columbia River route on the Oregon Trail. Much of the Barlow Road is still followed by the loop, including the steep ridges where wagons frequently skidded out of control and plummeted downhill. You can still see deep gashes on some of the trees where ropes were fastened to check the wagons' descent.

Near the intersection of Hwy-35 and US-26, a turn-off leads to the rough-hewn stone of **Timberline Lodge** (☎503/272-3311 or 1-800/547-1406, ⓦ www.timberlinelodge.com; ❺), a New Deal structure which is part of the year-round *Timberline* ski resort (☎503/219-3192; lift tickets $38), and the exterior setting for Stanley Kubrick's *The Shining*. Two other downhill ski areas – Mount Hood Meadows (ⓦ www.skihood.com; $44) and Mount Hood SkiBowl (ⓦ www.skibowl.com; $39) – offer nighttime **skiing** from November to April (around $20). There are also many miles of cross-country skiing trails throughout the **Mount Hood National Forest**.

Hood River

Adjacent to the Columbia River, north of Mount Hood, charming little **HOOD RIVER** is a gusty center for river windsurfing and mountain biking, with outfitters' shops lining the streets and a riverfront park to take in the local sporting scene. It's a good base for exploring the gorge; one of the most exquisite **places to stay** in the entire region is the *Columbia Gorge Hotel*, 3000 Westcliff Drive (☎541/386-5566 or 1-800/345-1921, ⓦ www.columbiagorge hotel.com; ❽), whose impressive rooms and garden overlook the gorge just off I-84 at the far west end of town. More central, and less expensive options include the *Hood River Hotel*, 102 Oak Ave (☎541/386-1900 or 1-800/386-1859, ⓦ www.hoodriverhotel.com; ❺), built in 1913 and featuring a good

Italian restaurant, and the basic but clean *Love's Riverview Lodge*, 1505 Oak St (℡541/386-8719 or 1-800/789-9568, ⓦ www.riverviewforyou.com; ❸). The *Full Sail Brewing Co*, 506 Columbia St (℡541/386-2247), is a popular spot in the evening, and there are several inexpensive places to **eat**, the best bet being the *6th Street Bistro*, at Sixth and Cascade streets (℡541/386-5737), whose flavorful burgers are the main draw. The town's **visitors center** is by the river in Port Marina Park (℡1-800/366-3530, ⓦ www.hoodriver.org).

South through the Willamette Valley

South of Portland, I-5 approaches California along a series of inland valleys, bypassing historic **Oregon City**, the first state capital, at the end of the Oregon Trail. Today, the split-level town consists of a short main street, connected by steps, steep streets and a cliff-face elevator to an uptown area of old wooden houses set on a bluff. The highlight is unquestionably the **John McLoughlin House**, 713 Center St (Tues–Sat 10am–4pm, Sun 10am–1pm; $3.50), the dwelling of an Oregon Trail pioneer that's loaded with many artifacts and details on local history.

The Willamette Valley has a diverse agriculture scene, but is best known for its grapes. Hwy-99 W, the scenic route through wine country, accesses more than two dozen acclaimed **wineries,** most of which pour superb Pinot noirs, Chardonnays and Rieslings. Pick up a wine-country tour map from any local visitor center (or from ⓦ www.oregonwine.org) – and expect the odd traffic delay in little burgs like **Dundee**, now a well-known draw for vino. The Valley also has some of the best examples of **covered bridges**, with thirty-four in the state spanning creeks near Scio, Albany and Cottage Grove (check out the directory at ⓦ coveredbridges.stateoforegon.com).

Salem

The main – and perhaps the only – reason to visit **SALEM** is to see the modern, white Vermont-marble **State Capitol** (Mon–Fri 7.30am–5.30pm, Sat 9am–4pm, Sun noon–4pm; free), whose cupola is topped by a large gold-leaf pioneer, axe in hand, eyes to the West. At the entrance, there's a marble carving of explorers Lewis and Clark processing regally towards the Willamette Valley. There are hourly summer **tours** of the building as well (9am–4pm; free). Nearby, tree-lined **Willamette University** is the oldest university in the West. Historic **Mission Mill Village**, 1313 Mill St SE (Tues–Sat 10am–3pm; $5), is also worth seeing for its collection of historic pioneer buildings.

Greyhound is convenient at 450 Church St NE, as well as Amtrak at 13th and Oak. The **visitors center** (℡503/581-4325 or 1-800/874-7012, ⓦ www.scva .org) is in Mission Mill Village. There are plenty of decent **motels**, among them the central *Travelodge*, 1555 State St (℡503/581-2466; ❷), and *Phoenix Inn*, 4370 Commercial St SE (℡503/588-9220, ⓦ www.phoenixinn.com; ❹). *The Marquee House*, 333 Wyatt Court NE (℡503/391-0837 or 1-800/949-0837, ⓦ www.marqueehouse.com; ❹), is a nice **B&B** close to downtown. If you're **camping**, head for the huge waterfalls and lush forests of **Silver Falls State Park** (℡503/873-8681; $18–20), 26 miles east of Salem via highways 22 and 214, justifiably the state's most popular park.

The university area is not a great scene for **food**; you're better off downtown, where the *Dairy Lunch Café*, 347 Court St at Liberty (℡503/363-6433), is a classic 1960s diner with tasty entrees; *Jonathan's Oyster Bar and Long Bar*, 120

Liberty St (☎503/362-7219), serves fresh seafood, Cajun and Southwestern cuisine; and the pleasant *Arbor Café*, 345 High St NE (☎503/588-2353), has a nice range of pasta, sandwiches and salads.

Eugene

A lively mix of students, professionals, hippies and blue collars, **EUGENE** is Oregon's second largest city and a liberal enclave where the late Ken Kesey and some of his Merry Pranksters came to live after their retreat from central California. On a slightly different note, the town was also the filming location for much of the movie *Animal House*.

Although short on sights, Eugene is an energetic cultural center, to which the **University of Oregon** in the city's southeast corner lends a youthful bohemian feel, especially along hip 13th Avenue just west of campus. The **Hult Center for Performing Arts**, Sixth Avenue and Willamette Street (☎541/682-5746, ⓦwww.hultcenter.org), is home to several arts organizations including the Eugene Opera, Eugene Symphony, Eugene Ballet Company, and renowned Oregon Bach Festival.

The city has two big markets: the weekly **Saturday Market**, around Eighth Avenue and Oak Street (Apr–Dec 10am–5pm; ⓦwww.eugenesaturdaymarket .org), is a thirty-year institution and something of a neo-hippie carnival, thanks to the live music and street performers. Tie-dye and wholefoods set the tone, but rastas, skateboarders, punks and students join in, too. **Fifth Street Market** is a staid boutique mall, with a handful of interesting arts, crafts and clothes stores.

Eugene is also a prime spot for sports. Trails and paths abound for walkers and cyclists in the city center, along the river banks, and up imposing Spencer's Butte; you can rent bikes from Pedal Power, 535 High St (☎541/687-1775).

Practicalities

Greyhound lets off at 987 Pearl St at Tenth Avenue, while Amtrak stops at Fourth Avenue and Willamette Street. Eugene has a terrific regional bus system, the LTD (☎541/687-5555, ⓦwww.ltd.org), based in an expansive bus mall downtown, and the **visitor center** is also downtown at 115 W Eighth Ave (Mon–Fri 8.30am–5pm, Sat 10am–4pm; ☎541/484-5307 or 1-800/547-5445, ⓦwww .visitlanecounty.org). The best **places to stay** include the *Eugene Hilton*, 66 E 6th Ave (☎541/342-2000 or 1-800/937-6660, ⓦwww.eugene.hilton.com; ❺), useful for being close to the Hult Center, and *Campbell House*, 252 Pearl St (☎541/343-1119 or 1-800/264-2519, ⓦwww.campbellhouse.com; ❺), offering great hospitality in an elegant 1892 Victorian home with eighteen rooms. *Franklin Inn*, 1857 Franklin Blvd (☎541/342-4804; ❸), has affordable rooms near the university, while the *Eugene International Hostel*, 2352 Willamette St (☎541/349-0589; $19), is clean, safe and comfortable.

With thousands of students to feed, Eugene has plenty of places to **eat**. *Café Zenon*, 898 Pearl St (☎503/343-3005), has an eclectic menu filled with various international dishes; *Chanterelle*, 207 E Fifth Ave (☎541/484-4065), is an intimate French bistro; *Morning Glory Café*, 448 Willamette (☎541/687-0709), serves hearty vegan breakfasts all day; and the *Steelhead Brewery*, 199 E 5th Ave (☎541/686-2739), is a choice microbrewery.

Live **music** is big in town. *Jo Federigo's*, 259 E Fifth Ave (☎541/343-8488), has nightly jazz and serves Italian cuisine in a great late-night atmosphere, while funky, downscale *WOW Hall*, 291 W 8th Ave (☎541/687-2746), showcases up-and-coming rockers. For a taste of the music scene near the university, stroll along 13th Avenue.

The **Oregon Country Fair** (☎541/343-4298, ⓦ www.oregoncountryfair
.org) is a big, hippie-flavored festival of music, arts, food and dancing, held in
VENETA, ten miles west on US-126, during the second weekend in July.
Traffic then is heavy, and even if you have a car it's easier to travel there by bus
– Eugene's LTD system operates special services.

South to California

South of Eugene along I-5, not too far from the California border, unenticing
GRANTS PASS depends on the Rogue River – tumbling vigorously from the
Cascades – for its living. Half a day of **whitewater rafting** costs around $45, a
full day $65 – the **visitors center**, just off I-5 at 1995 NW Vine St (☎1-800/547-
5927 or 541/476-7717, ⓦ www.visitgrantspass.org), can provide brochures from
more than two dozen licensed (and thus safer) river guides. Beyond Grants Pass,
I-5 dips southeast through **Ashland**, taking a mountainous inland route to
California, whilst US-199 heads southwest to the California (and south Oregon)
coast, passing near the **Oregon Caves**.

Oregon Caves National Monument

Thirty miles southwest of Grants Pass along US-199, at the dull burg of **Cave
Junction**, Hwy-46 veers east twenty miles to the **OREGON CAVES
NATIONAL MONUMENT**. Tucked in a wooded canyon at the end of a
narrow, twisting road, it's actually one enormous cave, with smaller branching
passages. The dripping marble walls are covered with elaborate stalactites, stalagmites and flowstone. Organized (and very cold) tours of the caves run year-
round (75min; $8; ☎541/592-2100 for schedule, ⓦ www.nps.gov/orca).

Close to the cave entrance, surrounded by forest, is the appealing *Oregon
Caves Lodge,* 2000 Caves Hwy (mid-May to Oct; ☎541/592-3400, ⓦ www
.visitoregoncaves.com; ❺), an elegant 1930s structure with grand public
rooms; reservations are advised. Alternatively, there are plainer lodgings back
in Cave Junction – try the *Holiday Motel*, 24810 Redwood Hwy (☎541/592-
3003; ❸) – or the several **campgrounds** dotted along Hwy-46, with
Grayback and *Cave Creek* being the closest to the monument (☎541/592-
2166 for reservations).

Ashland and the Shakespeare Festival

Throughout Oregon, the hamlet of **ASHLAND**, forty miles southeast of
Grants Pass, is identified with William Shakespeare – a real anomaly among the
rest of the timber and dairy-farming towns. Since 1945, the **Oregon
Shakespeare Festival** has been held here between February and October,
packing audiences into the half-timbered **Elizabethan Theatre** in Lithia
Park. Its setting, between the Cascade and the Siskiyou mountains, is magnificent; there's good skiing in the winter and river rafting in summer; there's also
some excellent contemporary fringe theater – not to mention pleasant cafés,
galleries and a friendly atmosphere throughout.

The **Angus Bowmer Theatre**, adjacent to the Elizabethan Theatre, stages
both Shakespearean and more recent works, while the appropriately named
New Theatre has a mostly modern repertoire. The three theaters share the
same box office (☎541/482-4331, ⓦ www.orshakes.org) and tickets average
around $40, sometimes half-price on the day; standing room at the Elizabethan
Theatre costs $10. For a further helping of contemporary drama, try the
Actors Theater, three miles north in the tiny town of **TALENT**, at Main and
Talent streets (☎541/535-5250, ⓦ www.actors-theatre.com), or the **Oregon**

Cabaret Theater, in a renovated pink church at First and Hargadine streets (Feb–Dec; ☎541/488-2902, ⊛www.oregoncabaret.com).

The **visitors center** is at 110 E Main St (Mon–Fri 9am–5pm; ☎541/482-3486, ⊛www.ashlandchamber.com), and there's a seasonal information kiosk – with longer hours – at the entrance to Lithia Park off Main Street. Greyhound **buses** drop passengers on the edge of town near the I-5 freeway exit. Ashland has over sixty **B&Bs** (❹–❼), most of which are in charming Victorian homes. Ashland B&B Network (☎1-800/944-0329, ⊛www.abbnet .com) or Southern Oregon Reservation Center (☎1-800/547-8052, ⊛www .sorc.com) can get you a room (and theater tickets). Perhaps the finest B&B overall is the *Mount Ashland Inn*, five miles south at 550 Mt Ashland Ski Rd (☎541/482-8707, ⊛www.mtashlandinn.com; ❼), offering five marvelous suites in a scenic wooden lodge, with fireplaces, hot tubs, and fine breakfasts. In town, nice local **hotels** include the restored *Ashland Springs Hotel*, 212 E Main St (☎541/488-1700, ⊛www.ashlandspringshotel.com; ❹–❻), easily the town's most prominent building, with a charming, two-story lobby, day spa, afternoon tea, and nicely appointed rooms; and the cheaper *Windmill Inn*, 2525 Ashland St (☎1-800/547-4747, ⊛www.windmillinns.com/ash.htm; ❹–❺), with complimentary breakfast, spa, swimming pool, and convenient location near I-5. For budget options, the *Ashland Hostel*, 150 N Main St (☎541/482-9217, ⊛www.ashlandhostel.com; $18), is friendly, clean and well-located, while the no-frills *Palm Motel*, 1065 Siskiyou Blvd (☎541/482-2636, ⊛www.palmmotel.com; ❸), is one of the better **motels** on this stretch of road.

The main choices for **eating** and **drinking** can be found along east and north **Main Street**, near the entrance to Lithia Park. The choices vary wide-ly, from the good and affordable *Ashland Bakery Café*, 38 E Main St (☎541/482-2117), to the pricey, eclectic entrees of *The Firefly*, 23 N Main St (☎541/488-3212), and the upscale French *Chateaulin,* 50 E Main St (☎503/482-2264). Overall, your best bet is *Greenleaf*, 49 N Main St (☎541/482-2808), an inexpensive but excellent eatery with standards like pasta, burgers, salads, and seafood nicely crafted with fresh, tasty ingredients.

The Oregon Coast

The **Oregon coast** is as beautiful as any stretch of coastline in America. While the California sun draws off the tan-seeking masses (Oregon summers are gen-erally mild), Oregonians are left to hike and clam-dig along their own secluded four hundred miles, almost all of it public land. State parks and campgrounds abound, and extensive and often isolated beaches offer numerous free activities, from beachcombing to shell-fishing and whale-watching. Although Oregon hasn't escaped commercialism (only lucky travelers find budget rooms without booking ahead in July and August), the state's shoreline could well be consid-ered the least exploited, or developed, in the entire US.

A dozen coastal state parks offer novel accommodation in the form of **yurts** – Mongolian-style domed circular tents with wooden floors, electricity and lock-able doors, as well as bunk beds and a futon ($25 per night for five people; details from the State Park Information Line, ☎1-800/452-5687, ⊛www.oregon stateparks.org). Alternatively, you can **camp** for $15–20 at sites on the coast.

For the most scenic transportation along the waves, **cycling** is always a good option, whether within the state parks, along US-101 (following the coastline to the California border), or on the many smaller "scenic loop" roads. Pick up the *Coast Bike Route Map* from any major visitor center.

Astoria

Set near the mouth of the Columbia River, **ASTORIA** was founded in 1811 as a private venture – a base for exporting furs to Asia – by the millionaire John Jacob Astor. "Fort Astoria" survived only a painful year and a half, beset by natural disasters and internal feuds, before it was sold to the British: Washington Irving made the best of the saga in his novel *Astoria*. A small replica of the old fort stands at 15th and Exchange streets, but nowadays many of Astoria's canneries and port facilities have vanished – the disused railroad tracks now gather rust along the water – and the city is trying to reinvent itself for tourists interested in nautical history and working-class Northwest color.

Arriving from Portland, the main road into Astoria, **Marine Drive**, runs parallel to the waterfront, once crammed with saloons and brothels in the nineteenth century, many equipped with built-in trap doors for "shanghaiing" drunken customers, who might wake up halfway across the Pacific. Eventually, workers at quayside canneries carried guns to get themselves safely through the night shift. Things are tamer now, but exhibits from Astoria's seafaring past are on display at the **Columbia River Maritime Museum**, 1792 Marine Drive (daily 9.30am–5pm; $5), which also features impressive displays of scrimshaw, native artifacts and reconstructed ships.

From Marine Drive, numbered streets climb towards the fancy Victorian mansions of the uptown area, many now renovated B&Bs (see overleaf). Beyond, on top of Coxcomb Hill, the **Astoria Column** is decorated with a mural depicting pioneer history, and offers stunning views for anyone willing to climb its gloomy spiral stairs. Back in town, further west, the **Flavel House**, 441 8th St (daily 10am–5pm; $5; ⓦwww.clatsophistoricalsociety.org), is one of the grandest of the city's mansions, the 1880s home of sea captain George Flavel. While the main rooms are set up as period dioramas featuring the furniture and decor of the nineteenth century, more interesting is the ungainly display of local castoffs like bank-teller windows, farm tools and horse carriages hiding down in the basement.

A few miles southwest of town is **Fort Clatsop** (daily 8am–5pm, summer closes at 6pm; $2; ⓦwww.nps.gov/focl), a reconstruction of the stockade/winter quarters Lewis and Clark built here in 1808. In the summer, exhibitions by docents in pioneer costumes are given on subjects like the proper ways to shoot a flintlock musket, pour molten bullets, and make beef-tallow candles. Further west, also off US-101, **Fort Stevens State Park** (ⓣ503/861-1671) offers trails, camping and miles of beaches, on which you can find the rusting hulk of the *Peter Iredale*, a 1906 shipwreck slowly sinking into the sand, but still enough of a marvel to clamber over at low tide. Although Fort Stevens was developed as a Union post in the Civil War, **Battery Russell** is its most significant military relic. The fort was shelled during World War II by a passing Japanese submarine, which makes it, incredibly, the only military installation on the mainland US to have been fired on by a foreign power since 1812.

Practicalities

Pacific Trails (ⓣ503/692-4437) operates a once-daily **bus** service from Portland to Astoria (and subsequently Seaside). The **visitors center**, 111 W Marine Drive (summer daily 8am–6pm; winter Mon–Fri 9am–5pm, Sat & Sun 10am–2pm; ⓣ503/325-6311, ⓦwww.oldoregon.com), is near the base of the

US-101 bridge over the Columbia. You can **camp** at Fort Stevens State Park (see overleaf), or stay in one of the mundane **motels** along Marine Drive, but the town's most distinctive offerings are its **B&Bs**, many of which occupy splendidly refurbished Victorian mansions. *Franklin St Station*, 1140 Franklin St (T 503/325-4314 or 1-800/448-1098, W www.franklin-st-station-bb.com; ⑤), has seven rooms with balconies overlooking town; the *Rosebriar*, 636 14th St (T 503/325-7427 or 1-800/487-0224, W astoria-usa.com/rosebriar; ④), is a renovated 1902 convent with great river views; and the *Benjamin Young Inn*, 3652 Duane St (T 503/325-6172, W www.benjaminyounginn.com; ④), has five charming rooms and high tea on Saturdays.

Downtown has a handful of good places to **eat**. *Columbian Café*, 1114 Marine Drive (T 503/325-2233), offers gourmet seafood and vegetarian meals, and the *Home Spirit Baking Company*, 1585 Exchange (T 503/325-6846), serves hearth-stone-baked sourdough and homemade ice cream in a lovely Victorian home. If all else fails, make like the locals and head to *Pig 'n Pancake*, unavoidable at 146 W Bond St (T 503/325-3144), where you can get your fill of delightfully greasy, gut-busting breakfasts.

Seaside

Seventeen miles down the coast from Astoria, **SEASIDE** is a rather seedy resort, the one spot on the Oregon coast nature-lovers try assiduously to avoid as it's an amalgamation of crude carnival rides and depressing chain motels. Surprisingly, it was here that the Lewis and Clark expedition had to take a tedious turn boiling seawater to make salt – vital to preserve meat for the return journey. The reconstructed **salt works** – a few boulders and pans – are located near the south end of town and are mildly interesting, or at least bet-ter than observing the endless parade of pimply teenagers and middle-aged burnouts patrolling the town's central concrete walkway, **the Prom**.

As for **accommodation**, there's no good reason to spend a lot of money in Seaside. The *Riverside Inn*, 430 S Holladay Dr (T 503/738-8254 or 1-800/826-6151, W www.riversideinn.com; ③), officially a B&B, is a good cut above the average motel, though the ten Victorian guest rooms of the 1893 *Gilbert Inn*, 341 Beach Dr (T 503/738-9770, W www.gilbertinn.com; ⑤), are worth the extra cost. There's also the *HI-Seaside Hostel*, 930 N Holladay Drive (T 503/738-7911, W 2oregonhostels.com; $18), just four blocks from the ocean. Places to **shop** and **eat** are concentrated along Broadway. Seaside is on the once-daily *Pacific Trails* (T 503/692-4437) bus route south from Astoria. The **visitor center** is at 7 N Roosevelt Dr (T 503/738-6391 or 1-800/444-6740, W www.seasidechamber.com).

Cannon Beach

Nine miles south from Seaside, the more upmarket and pleasant **CANNON BEACH** manages to retain its small-town air despite decades of relentless commercialism. The place is at its liveliest during the annual **Sandcastle Competition** (W www.cannon-beach.net/sandcastle.html), a one-day event held in late May or early June, whose most notable sandworks have included dinosaurs, sphinxes, and even the Crucifixion. Cannon Beach's best natural draw is its 240ft **Haystack Rock**, a black monolith crowned with nesting seagulls – accessible at low tide, though definitely not climbable. To escape the town's inevitable crush of tourists, head four miles north to **Ecola State Park**, where dense conifer forests decorate the basaltic cliffs of Tillamook Head, or south to **Oswald West State Park** where there is a beautiful beach, rocky headland and coastal rainforest. *Oswald West* (☎1-800/551-6949), a tent-only campground popular with surfers, has wheelbarrows to transport your gear to the site.

Accommodation is tight, especially at competition time. *Cannon Beach Hotel*, 1116 S Hemlock St (☎503/436-1392, ⓦwww.cannonbeachhotel.com; ➎), is a petite, European-style hotel, while the popular *Waves Motel* is right on the seafront at 188 W Second St (☎503/436-2205 or 1-800/822-2468, ⓦwww.thewavesmotel.com; ➎). For **food**, *Midtown Café*, 1235 S Hemlock St (☎503/436-1016), has the best breakfast in town; the *Bistro*, 263 N Hemlock St (☎503/436-2661), doles out a fine range of seafood; and *Heather's Café,* 271 N Hemlock St (☎503/436-9353), makes a mean grilled-cheese sandwich.

Lincoln City and Tillamook

There's no avoiding **LINCOLN CITY** if you're driving; the ugliest town on the Oregon coast, it sprawls along the highway for seven congested, dreadful miles – the legacy of consolidating five beach towns in the 1960s. In the unlikely event you decide to stay, there's plenty of cheap **accommodation** to choose from – the **visitor center**, on US-101 (☎541/994-8378 or 1-800/452-2151, ⓦwww.lincolncity.org), has the full list. For somewhere to **eat**, you're better off headed south to Newport or further north to **TILLA-MOOK**, whose main draw is the **Tillamook Cheese Factory** (daily 8am–6pm; free; ⓦwww.tillamookcheese.com), north of town on US-101, where you can watch cheese being made while devouring a cone from one of the factory's two ice-cream counters. Tastier cheese can be had just to the south at the **Blue Heron** (daily 9am-5pm; free; ⓦwww.bluehe023oregon.com), an increasingly popular spot where you can sample the company's pepper-encrusted brie before heading out back to have a close encounter with a rooster or donkey in a quasi-petting zoo.

Newport

Thirty miles south of Lincoln City, **NEWPORT** is one of several Oregon ports laboring to turn itself into a resort – more successfully than most, perhaps. The place has an artsy feel, manifest in a pair of **arts centers** – one performing, the other visual (more information at ⓦwww.coastarts.org) – on uncrowded **Nye Beach**, a quiet oceanside gem. A more traditional attraction is the impressive **Oregon Coast Aquarium**, across the bridge at 2820 SE Ferry Slip Rd (summer daily 9am–6pm; rest of year daily 10am–5pm; $10.50; ⓦwww.aquarium.org), home to sea otters, seals, the tufted puffin, and all sorts of aquatic species. The aquarium's latest attraction, *Passages of the Deep* (a shark-oriented underwater tunnel), replaces its former big draw, Keiko the Killer Whale – the star of the movie *Free Willy*, now shipped off to an Icelandic cove. Just north of town, Newport's other top attraction is **Yaquina Head** (daily dawn–dusk; $5), home to a marine-science center (free with the $5 admission), striking cape lighthouse, and manmade tidepools constructed from the remains of a quarry.

The Greyhound station is just off US-101 on SW Bayley Street, and the **chamber of commerce** is at 555 SW Coast Hwy (☎541/265-8801 or 1-800/262-7844, ⓦwww.newportchamber.org). The most prominent place to **stay** is the *Sylvia Beach Hotel*, on Nye Beach at 267 NW Cliff St (☎541/265-5428, ⓦwww.sylviabeachhotel.com; ➍–➏), whose twenty rooms bear the name of a famous writer (it also has dorm beds; ➊). Every evening, mulled wine is served in the upstairs library. Less pretentious is the neighboring *Nye*

Beach Hotel (☎541/265-3334, ⓦwww.nyebeach.com; ➎), with six great oceanfront rooms featuring stove heating, balconies and hot tubs. Cheap lodgings include the *Penny Saver Motel*, 710 N Coast Hwy (☎541/265-6631; ➌), among countless other **motels** near US-101.

There's a cluster of first-rate **cafés** and **restaurants** in the Historic Bayfront on Bay Boulevard. The *Whale's Tale* (☎541/265-8660) has a good seafood menu and isn't quite as crowded as *Mo's Original* (☎541/265-2979) or *Mo's Annex* (☎541/265-7512), two decent chain seafood restaurants that are always thick with tourists. *Rogue Ales House* (☎541/265-3188) is the liveliest spot for food and beer, and on Nye Beach, *April's*, 749 NW 3rd St (☎541/265-6855), offers fine Italian cuisine – the town's best restaurant by default.

Bandon

At the mouth of the Coquille River, twenty miles south of industrial Coos Bay, easygoing **BANDON** combines old-town restoration with a strong New Age, arts-and-crafts presence. It was originally a Native American settlement, swamped by the onset of the Gold Rush. The twentieth century began rather ominously, when townsfolk dynamited Tupper Rock, a sacred tribal site, to build the sea wall, and the town was cursed to burn down three times: it's happened twice so far, in 1914 and 1936, and the superstitious are still waiting for the final conflagration.

Bandon's main attraction today is its rugged **beach**, strewn with unusual rock formations and magnificent in stormy weather, when giant tree stumps are tossed up out of the ocean like matchsticks. In calmer conditions, clammers head off to the river's mudflats, crabbers gather at the town dock, and the whole scene makes for a delightful stroll. The **visitor center** is centrally located at 300 SE Second St (☎541/347-9616, ⓦwww.bandon.com), and there's oceanfront **accommodation** just south of town at the outstanding *Sunset Motel*, 1755 Beach Loop Drive (☎541/347-2453 or 1-800/842-2407, ⓦwww.sunsetmotel.com; ➌–➐), which comprises motel rooms, condos and, best of all, seafront cabins. In town, the place to stay is the *Sea Star Guest House*, 375 Second St (☎541/347-9632, ⓦseastarbandon.com; ➌), part of which is given over to the *HI-Sea Star Hostel* (dorm beds $18). West of town, there's great **seafood** at *Bandon Boatworks*, at the end of Jetty Road (☎541/347-2111), and at various eateries along First and Second streets in the center of town. You can **camp** just north of town at **Bullards Beach State Park** (☎541/347-2209), where the disused Coquille River Lighthouse casts a romantic silhouette over miles of windswept sands.

South to California

Towns are fewer and farther between as you travel south along US-101, with the coastline at its prettiest beyond **PORT ORFORD** – known principally for its unusual **dry dock**, on which a crane hoists boats aloft – where forested mountains sweep smoothly down to the sea. These mountains mark the western limit of the **Siskiyou National Forest**, a vast slab of remote wilderness best explored by boat along the turbulent Rogue River from workaday **GOLD BEACH**. The town's **visitor center**, on the main road at 29279 S Ellensburg (☎541/247-7526 or 1-800/525-2334, ⓦwww.goldbeachchamber.com), has details of rafting and powerboat excursions plus prices for the town's various motels and hotels. Finally, at the state's far southwestern corner, **BROOKINGS** has a warmer "banana belt" climate, and is best visited as a base for exploring northern California's **Redwood National Park**. Contact the local

visitors center (Mon–Fri 9am–5pm; ☎541/469-3181, Ⓦwww.brookings
-harbor.com) for more details.

Central and eastern Oregon

East of the Cascades, Oregon grows warmer, drier and wilder; green valleys give
way to the high desert with sageland, juniper trees, bare hills and stark rock formations broken up by the occasional tract of pine forest. The volcanic landscape
has cracked lava flows, abrupt cone-like hills, and high craters such as beautiful
Crater Lake in the south. The east, though seldom visited, can be surprisingly
beautiful: the **John Day Fossil Beds** along US-26, and the remote, snowcapped
Wallowa Mountains – overlooking the deep slash of **Hells Canyon** – are both
overwhelmingly dramatic landscapes, and not to be missed if you have a lot of
time to drive around the outback from one isolated sight to another.

Bend and around

BEND is easily the most useful base for visiting central Oregon, giving access
both to Cascade grandeur and the eerie landscape of Oregon's Lava Lands. Packed
with restaurants, microbreweries and outdoor gear shops, its roots are firmly set in
outdoor pursuits. Greyhound buses from Portland and Eugene arrive a mile east
of town at Hwy-20. The **visitors center** is on Hwy-97, just north of the center
(☎541/382-3221 or 1-800/905-2363, Ⓦwww.bendchamber.org), while the
Central Oregon Welcome Center, 63085 N US-97 (☎541/389-8799 or 1-
800/800-8334, Ⓦwww.covisitors.com), has brochures and accommodation listings. Beyond recreation, the area's main attraction is undoubtedly the **High
Desert Museum**, 59800 US-97 (daily 9am–5pm; $8.50; Ⓦwww.highdesert.org),
a fascinating collection of artifacts from Native American and pioneer history,
along with displays of regional flora and fauna, and a reconstructed pioneer homestead and sawmill out back.

Budget **motels** – often full – are strung out along US-97 (also known as
Third Street), including the plain but clean *Dunes Motel*, 1515 NE Third St
(☎541/382-6811; ❸). However, the compact town center, with its old villas
dotting the banks of the Deschutes River, is a much more attractive destination and home to several smart **B&Bs**. Try the *Lara House*, 640 NW Congress
St (☎541/388-4064, Ⓦwww.larahouse.com; ❹), or the slightly pricier *Sather
House*, 7 NW Tumalo Ave (☎541/388-1065 or 1-888/388-1065, Ⓦwww
.satherhouse.com; ❺). The *Bend Cascade Hostel*, 19 SW Century Drive (☎541/
389-3813), has dorm beds for $15 and is only a short walk from the free ski
shuttle to Mount Bachelor (see overleaf). You can camp in **Tumalo State
Park** (☎541/388-6055, Ⓦwww.reserveamerica.com/usa/or/tuma), a wooded
dell by the Deschutes River five miles northwest along US-20, which offers
the domed tents called **yurts** as well as large canvas-covered **tepees** (both $27).

Bend has some great **restaurants** and **microbreweries**. *Pine Tavern
Restaurant*, 967 NW Brooks St (☎541/382-5581), *Deschutes Brewery and Public
House*, 901 SW Simpson St (☎541/385-8606), and *Bend Brewing*, 1019 NW
Brooks St (☎541/383-1599), all serve microbrewed ales and stouts and solid
American cuisine. *West Side Café & Bakery*, 1005 NW Galveston (☎541/382-
3426), has filling breakfasts and *Cup of Magic*, 1304 NW Galveston
(☎541/330-5539), has great coffee and baked goods.

Mount Bachelor and the Cascades Lake Highway

The Northwest's largest ski resort is **Mount Bachelor** (☎541/382-2442 or 1-800/829-2442; ⓦwww.mtbachelor.com; lift tickets $42), 22 miles southwest of Bend, its Olympic-standard facilities open from mid-November to late-May, snowfall permitting. Mount Bachelor is also the first stop on the **Cascade Lakes Highway**, known as "Century Drive" – a hundred-mile mountain loop road giving access to trailheads into the **Three Sisters** or, further south, the **Diamond Peak** wilderness areas and a sprinkling of campgrounds. Get details from **Deschutes National Forest Ranger Station**, just outside of Bend at 1645 E Hwy-20 (☎541/388-2715), or in Bend at 1230 NE Third St (☎541/388-5664).

The Lava Lands

The so-called **Lava Lands** cover a huge area of central Oregon, with the greatest concentration of sizeable lava formations – conical buttes, craggy caves and the rocky molds of tree trunks – in the Bend area located at **Newberry National Volcanic Monument** (dawn–dusk; five-day parking passes $5; ⓦwww.fs.fed.us/r6/centraloregon). Dating back seven thousand years to the eruption of Mount Newberry, the monument is actually a huge, sloping crater laced with hiking paths, nature trails, campgrounds, and prime fishing spots. Some of the rugged highlights (most free with monument admission) include the chilly, mile-long **Lava River Cave** (summer daily 9am–5pm; $3, plus $2 for a lamp), an eerie but walkable subterranean passage made from a hollow lava tube; the **Lava Cast Forest**, a strange walk through the basalt casts of trunks of trees burnt by lava before they could fall; and the surreal landscape of the **Big Obsidian Flow**, huge hills of volcanic black glass that native tribes throughout the Northwest once used to make arrowheads. As the rock is still quite sharp and brittle – and especially rare – you're strongly advised not to take home any geological souvenirs. The **Lava Lands visitors center** (summer daily 9am–5pm; ☎541/593-2421; $5), eleven miles south of Bend on US-97, is an excellent source of maps and information on hiking trails.

Crater Lake National Park

Despite its stunning natural beauty, Oregon has only one national park, located just over a hundred miles south of Bend. The shell of Mount Mazama holds the deep, blue, resoundingly beautiful **CRATER LAKE** (seven-day access fee $10; ⓦwww.nps.gov/crla), formed after an explosion 42 times greater than that of Mount St Helens (see p.1207). The biggest island on the lake, **Wizard Island**, is actually the tip of a still-rising cinder cone. In its snowy isolation, the lake, at a depth of nearly two thousand feet, is awe-inspiring; in summer, too, it's spectacular, when wild flowers bloom along its desolate rim. The most popular, though still strenuous, hike is up **Garfield Peak**, an 8,054ft mountain that offers a tremendous view of the lake and is particularly striking – and harder to reach – during winter. More intrepid hikers can explore the marginally better views offered by the park's tallest outcrop, **Mount Scott**, rising to almost nine thousand feet.

You need a car to get to the park, though only the southern roads (the US-62 from Medford off I-5 or Klamath Falls off US-97) are open year-round. The northern access road (off Hwy-138) is closed from mid-October to June, as is the spectacular, 33-mile "Rim Drive" around the crater's edge. Regular **boats** cruise the lake (late June–mid-Sept daily 10am–4.30pm; $12.50), reached via the sheer, mile-long **Cleetwood Cove trail**, which provides the only access to the lakeshore. The trail is on the north shore, but visitor facilities are clustered on the south at tiny **RIM VILLAGE**, where the summer-only **visitors center** is a few steps from *Crater Lake Lodge* (mid-May to mid-Oct; ℡541/830-8700, ⓦwww.crater-lake.com; ❻), a grand old lodge that's recently been refurbished at massive expense; ask for a room overlooking the lake – the lodge perches on the rim of the caldera. *Mazama Village* (early June to mid-Oct; ℡541/830-8700; ❹) is a **motel** with an adjoining **campground** ($10) in a quiet wooded setting about seven miles south of the rim. There are also several wilderness campsites. The **park headquarters** are at the Steel Information Center (daily 9am–5pm; ℡541/594-2211, more information at ⓦwww.crater.lake.national-park.com), a year-round facility a few miles south of the rim on the main access road.

Klamath Falls

Sixty miles southeast of Crater Lake, industrial **KLAMATH FALLS** makes an easy day-trip – a useful option if the weather deteriorates in the mountains. It's not particularly pretty (only appearing in the national news as the site of angry water-shortage protests by local farmers), but it does boast the **Favell Museum**, 125 W Main St (Mon–Sat 9.30am–5.30pm; $4; ⓦwww.favellmuseum.com), housing a fine collection of native artifacts and a large assortment of frontier paintings.

Klamath Falls sits in the middle of **Klamath Basin**, whose low-lying lakes and marshes once formed a vast wetland stretching far beyond the California border. Much of the basin has been drained for cattle grazing, but six areas are now protected as **national wildlife refuges**, with the resident bird population increased to upwards of a million during spring and fall migrations. The town's **visitor center** at 1451 Main St in the Klamath County Museum (daily 9am–4.30pm; ℡541/884-0666, ⓦwww.klamathcountytourism.com), issues detailed maps of the basin and its bird sanctuaries.

East on US-26: the John Day Fossil Beds

Hwy-140 trudges on monotonously from Klamath Falls into southeast Oregon, though a better route is via US-97, then Hwy-126/26 from Bend, where you'll emerge from a brief passage through the **Ochoco National Forest** into a bare, sun-scorched landscape of ochre and beige. Many features here are named after **John Day**, an employee of fur trapper John Jacob Astor (see p.1227). Of special importance are the **John Day Fossil Beds**, which hold some of the most revealing fossil formations in the US, preserved in a layer of volcanic ash as the Cascades sputtered into being, just after the extinction of the dinosaurs sixty-five million years ago. There are three fossil-bed sites, the most westerly of which is the **Painted Hills**, six miles off US-26 down a paved side road. Striped in shades of rust and brown, the surfaces of the sandcastle-like hills are quilted with rivulets worn by draining water. Back on US-26, thirty miles east, is the **Sheep Rock** unit, just north of the junction with Hwy-19. Here, the **visitors center** (Mon–Fri 9am–5pm; ℡541/987-2333, ⓦwww.nps.gov/joda) is in an old rancher's homestead and has a modest selection of fossils. A mile further north is the **Blue Basin**, a natural amphitheater where a mile-long trail leads past fossil replicas like a tortoise that hurtled to its death millions of years ago, and a saber-toothed cat.

John Day

The largest town along US-26 between Baker City and Prineville is charmless **JOHN DAY**, which would be easily missable if it weren't the unexpected home of one of Oregon's key historical sights. The fascinating **Kam Wah**

Chung & Co. Museum (May–Oct Mon–Thurs 9am–noon & 1–5pm, Sat & Sun 1–5pm; $3; Ⓦ www.oregonstateparks.org/park_8.php) was once the home, opium den and general store of famed Chinese herbalist Ing Hay, whose apothecary wares – five hundred herbs, dried lizard, bear claw, bottle of rattlesnakes – have been preserved and are still on display. Providing one of the truly authentic glimpses of Oregon's pioneer history, the museum is well worth a look if you're in the area.

Baker City

In the forested hills east of John Day, US-26 turns southeast for the long run down to Idaho. More enjoyable is the far shorter drive on Hwy-7 through the southern reaches of the **Wallowa–Whitman National Forest** to red-brick **BAKER CITY**, a Gold Rush boomtown and now the commercial center for the surrounding cattle lands. The **Oregon Trail Interpretative Center** (daily: Apr–Oct 9am–6pm; Nov–Mar 9am–4pm; $5; Ⓣ 541/523-1843, Ⓦ www.or .blm.gov/nhotic) at Flagstaff Hill, five well-signposted miles east of town, was built to commemorate the 150th anniversary of the trail in 1993. As well as audiovisual displays, the complex has around four miles of original trails featuring well-preserved wagon ruts and other points of interest. Back in town, the **Oregon Trail Regional Museum**, 2480 Grove St (Apr–Oct daily 9am–4pm; $3.50), has artifacts from pioneer days, but is most notable for its fine collection of rocks, petrified wood, and fluorescent geodes glowing under ultraviolet light.

Baker's Main Street has many handsome early twentieth-century buildings, but the bulk of the available **accommodation** is on the town periphery in routine motels along Tenth or Campbell: the *Quality Inn*, 810 Campbell St (Ⓣ 541/523-2242 or 1-800/228-5151, Ⓦ www.qualityinn.com; ❸), and the *Welcome Inn*, 175 Campbell St (Ⓣ 541/523-3431, Ⓦ www.welcomeinn.com; ❸), are typical. The vast Wallowa–Whitman National Forest, stretching east and west of town, has many **campgrounds**; get details from the **visitors center**, 490 Campbell St, beside I-84's exit 304 (Ⓣ 541/523-3356 or 1-800/523-1235, Ⓦ www.visitbaker.com). Good **restaurants** include the cheap *Front Street Café*, 1840 Main St (Ⓣ 541/523-0223), and the solid pub fare at *Barley Brown's Brewpub*, 2190 Main St (Ⓣ 541/523-4266). Greyhound **buses**, 515 Campbell St, connect to Portland.

North on I-84: La Grande and Pendleton

The **Grande Ronde Valley**, north of Baker City on I-84, is large, round, flat and rimmed by mountains. Now mostly drained to become farmland, this was once marshland, fatally boggy to pioneer wagons, forcing the Oregon Trail to keep to the higher but tougher ground around the hills as it headed northwest to the Blue Mountains.

The valley's hub is **LA GRANDE**, a lumber-and-university town linked with Portland by Greyhound buses, which pull in at 2108 Cove Ave. The **chamber of commerce**, 1912 Fourth St (Ⓣ 541/963-8588 or 1-800/848-9969, Ⓦ www.visitlagrande.com), has maps and information. Look to the *Greenwell Motel*, 305 Adams Ave (Ⓣ 541/963-4134 or 1-800/772-0991; ❷), and the *Royal Motor Inn,* 1510 Adams Ave (Ⓣ 541/963-4154 or 1-800/990-7575; ❷), for cheap **motel** rooms. Decent **restaurants** include *Mamacita's*, 110 Depot St (Ⓣ 541/963-6223), with solid Mexican food, and *Sunflower Books*, 1114 Washington Ave (Ⓣ 541/963-5242), good for browsing with coffee and a pastry.

The Oregon Trail

Between the 1840s and 1870s, more than a quarter-million Americans journeyed by wagon train from the Midwest to Oregon in search of a new start. Ever since Lewis and Clark completed their successful survey of the Oregon Country (the coastal region between Russian Alaska and Spanish California) in 1806, the ideal of "manifest destiny" had both politicians and prospective settlers keen to see their country grow from coast to coast. The first migrants were also inspired by the missionaries who went to try to Christianize Native Americans in the 1830s, and who sent back glowing reports of the region's fine climate, fertile soil, dense forests, fish-rich rivers and absence of malaria.

With the promise of generous land grants, in spring 1843 more than one thousand would-be migrants gathered at Independence and Westport on the banks of the Missouri, preparing for the "**Great Migration**." The pioneers were a remarkably homogenous bunch, nearly all experienced farmers, traveling with their families in ox-pulled wagons with flimsy canvas roofs.

Traversing almost two thousand miles of what is now Missouri, Nebraska, Wyoming and Idaho, the movers forced their wagons across rivers, over mountain passes and through virgin forests, pausing at the occasional army fort or missionary station to recuperate. They also bartered supplies with Native Americans in return for rafts and local knowledge. After three months on the trail, they arrived at what is now the town of The Dalles. From here the group had a difficult choice to make before reaching the lush Willamette Valley. Some people built rafts and risked the treacherous currents of the Columbia River, while others took the hazardous Barlow Road around Mount Hood (see p.1222), notorious for its swiftly changing weather.

Over the next thirty years further waves of settlers swelled the population of the Willamette Valley by fifty thousand, with others moving into Washington and California. The migration spawned a cottage industry of specialist suppliers and wagon builders, and traffic on the trail was such that the route was miles wide in parts. Inevitably, there are precious few surviving signs of the passing of the migrants, but they are commemorated by several museums, the best of which is near Baker City.

Pendleton

From La Grande, I-84 follows the Oregon Trail route northwest to **PENDLE-TON**, where Stetsons and pick-up trucks abound. Unsurprisingly then, this is home to the immensely popular, annual four-day **Pendleton Round-Up** in mid-September, combining traditional rodeo with extravagant pageantry; get tickets from the Round-Up Association, PO Box 609, Pendleton, OR 97801 ($12–15 per rodeo session; ☏541/276-2553 or 1-800/45-RODEO, ⓦwww.pendletonroundup.com). The **Round-Up Hall of Fame**, 1205 SW Court Ave (June–Aug Mon–Sat 10am–4pm; $2), is stuffed with associated memorabilia. The famed **Pendleton Woolen Mills**, 1307 SE Court Pl (tours Mon–Fri 9am, 11am, 1.30pm & 3pm; free; ⓦwww.pendleton-usa .com), will mainly appeal to those interested in textile manufacture, although you can always pick up a sweater while there.

The fascinating **Pendleton Underground**, 37 SW Emigrant at First Street (Mon–Sat 9am–4.30pm; $10; ⓦwww.pendletonundergroundtours.org), lets you tour the town's extensive network of subterranean passageways, used during Prohibition as saloons, card rooms and brothels – and as a refuge for the area's much-abused Chinese population. The **chamber of commerce**, 501 S Main St (Mon–Fri 9am–5pm; ☏541/276-7411 or 1-800/547-8911, ⓦwww.pendleton-oregon.org), is a short walk from the Greyhound station.

Accommodation options include the five Victorian rooms of the *Parker House B&B*, 311 N Main St (℡541/276-8581, 🕸www.parkerhousebnb.com; ❹), and the plain *Chaparral Motel*, 620 SW Tutuilla St (℡541/276-8654; ❷). Be sure to book early at Round-Up time. As would be expected, most **restaurants** dole out hefty portions of all-American fare, although *Raphael's*, 400 SE Dorian Ave (℡541/276-8500), offers a touch of upscale, nouveau-regional cuisine – welcome relief from the ubiquitous burgers and fries.

Joseph and the Wallowa Mountains

The **Wallowa Mountains**, reached by leaving I-84 at La Grande and heading east on Hwy-82, are one of eastern Oregon's loveliest and least-discovered areas. At the northern tip of the glacially-carved **Wallowa Lake**, the tiny town of **JOSEPH** is a perfect spot to spend the night. **Motels** such as the *Indian Lodge Motel*, 201 S Main St (℡541/432-2651, 🕸www.eoni.com/~gingerdaggett; ❸), are inexpensive, and the friendly *Chandlers' Bed, Bread and Trail Inn*, 700 S Main St (℡541/432-9765, 🕸www.eoni.com/~chanbbti; ❹), offers five rooms, a garden, and solid breakfasts. Also on Main Street are many antique and craft stores and the small **Wallowa County Museum**, 110 S Main St (summer daily 10am–5pm; donation; 🕸www.co.wallowa.or.us/museum), where the story of the Nez Percé (see p.924) is presented along with a limited collection of pioneer artifacts.

A mile or so south of Joseph, **Wallowa Lake** is inhabited by the Native American legend of the Wallowa Lake Monster, a great horned beast known to some as "Wally." At its far end, the state park has **camping** ($18; 🕸www.wallowalake.net), and the **Mount Howard Tramway** whisks visitors to the top of the mountain, where short trails lead to magnificent overlooks (June–Aug daily 10am–4pm; weekends only in May & Sept; $16 round-trip; 🕸www.wallowalaketramway.com). Much of the mountain scenery behind Joseph makes up the **Eagle Cap Wilderness**, whose lakes, streams and peaks are accessible only via hiking trails. Backcountry camping and hiking around here is strikingly remote – contact the **Wallowa Mountains Visitor Center**, 88401 Hwy-82 (℡541/426-5546), for details of the Eagle Cap and Hells Canyon (see below), or look on 🕸www.wallowacounty.org for more information.

Hells Canyon

East of Joseph, marking the Idaho border, the **Snake River** has cut the deepest canyon on the continent, a thousand feet deeper than the Grand Canyon, with the Seven Devils mountains rising behind and the river glimmering in its depths. Perhaps best known as the site of an ill-fated 1974 motorcycle jump by daredevil Evel Knieval, **Hells Canyon** is a 130-mile gorge edged by a series of gradually ascending false peaks, which doesn't quite have the overwhelming impact of the steeper-walled Grand Canyon.

Formerly a winter retreat for the Nez Percé, the canyon zone is preserved as the **Hells Canyon National Recreation Area**: deer, otters, mink, black bears, mountain lions and elk live here, along with rattlesnakes and black widow spiders. Mechanical vehicles are banned above water-level in much of the canyon (motorized boats on the Snake are allowed), so you can only explore on foot or horseback. The forest roads that skirt the recreation area are rough and slippery, and many are closed by snow much of the year. If you intend to use them, check the official site at 🕸www.fs.fed.us/r6/w-w/hcnra.htm or with the **rangers** in Enterprise (℡541/426-5546) or Baker City (℡541/523-6391) before you go

– bear in mind that summers aren't much easier as temperatures here regularly reach 100°F.

Of the two ways to approach the canyon from Oregon, the more difficult begins in Joseph. From here, Little Sheep Creek Highway leads to **IMNAHA** where a narrow and extremely precipitous graveled Forest Service road leads to the ultimate view from **Hat Point**, site of a campground and lookout tower. Beyond Hat Point, the road fades into a trail that leads to the bottom of the canyon, but to undertake this trek you must be very fit and well-equipped. The easier approach is at the south end of the canyon, along Hwy-86 east from Baker City. On the way, tiny **HALFWAY** (formerly named Half.com, after a website paid for the town's naming rights) makes a good stop-off, with **accommodation** at *Halfway Motel*, 170 S Main St (℡541/742-5722, Ⓦwww.halfwayor.com/motel-rvpark; ❷), and the five rooms in the rustic farmhouse of the *Clear Creek Farm B&B*, 48212 Clear Creek Rd (℡541/742-2238, call for directions; Ⓦwww.neoregon.com/ccgg; ❺).

From Halfway, Hwy-86 heads to the canyon, meeting the Snake River at Oxbow Dam, where a rough Forest Service road leads to **Hells Canyon Dam**, the launching-point for jet boat and raft trips through the canyon. Hells Canyon Adventures (℡541/785-3352 or 1-800/422-3568, reservations required; Ⓦwww.hellscanyonadventures.com) and other companies run sight-seeing **tours** in summer ($30 per person for a two-hour trip). Skimming over the rapids, the boats take you between deceptively low, bare hills to an old pioneer homestead. They also operate a "drop-off" service, taking you to hiking trails along the canyon and picking you up the same day or later in the week ($25–30 per person).

14

CHAPTER 15 Highlights

- **Sitka** Russian influence blended with Native heritage and fabulous coastal scenery make this one of Alaska's most diverting towns. See p.1246

- **The Chilkoot Trail** Follow in the (frozen) footsteps of the Klondike prospectors on this demanding 33-mile trail near Skagway. See p.1255

- **Talkeetna** Every Alaska visitor's favorite small town is the base for superb flightseeing trips around Mount McKinley. See p.1270

- **Denali National Park** Alaska's finest park offers superb mountain scenery and incomparable wildlife spotting around the highest peak in North America. See p.1271

- **Aurora borealis** The spectacular after-dark displays of the Northern Lights are at their best around Fairbanks. See p.1277

- **Dalton Highway** This lonely and grueling 500-mile road leads north from Fairbanks to the Arctic Ocean. See p.1277

Alaska

No other region in North America possesses the mythical aura of **ALASKA**; even the name – a derivation of *Alayeska*, an Athabascan word meaning "great land of the west" – fires the imagination. Few who see this land of gargantuan ice fields, sweeping tundra, glacially excavated valleys, lush rainforests, deep fjords and occasionally smoking volcanoes leave unimpressed. **Wildlife** may be under threat elsewhere, but here it is abundant, with Kodiak bears standing twelve feet tall, moose stopping traffic in downtown Anchorage, wolves prowling through national parks, bald eagles circling over the trees, and rivers solid with fifty-plus-pound salmon.

Alaska's sheer size is hard to comprehend: more than twice the size of Texas, it contains America's **northernmost**, **westernmost** and, because the Aleutian Islands stretch across the 180th meridian, its **easternmost** point. If superimposed onto the Lower 48 (the rest of the continental United States) it would stretch from the Atlantic to the Pacific, and its coastline is longer than the rest of the US combined. All but three of the nation's twenty highest peaks are found within its boundaries and one glacier alone is twice the size of Wales.

A mere 600,000 people live in this huge state – over forty percent of them in **Anchorage** – of whom only one-fifth were born here: as a rule of thumb, the more winters you have endured, the more Alaskan you are. Often referred to as the **"Last Frontier,"** Alaska in many ways mirrors the American West of the nineteenth century: an endless, undeveloped space in which to stake one's claim and set up a life without interference. Or at least that's how Alaskans would like it to be. Throughout this century tens of thousands have been lured by the promise of wealth, first by gold and then by fishing, logging and, most recently, oil. However, Alaska's 86,000 **Native peoples**, who don't have the option of returning to the Lower 48 if things don't work out, have been greatly marginalized, though Native corporations set up as a result of pre-oil boom land deals have increasing economic clout.

Traveling around Alaska still demands a spirit of adventure, and to make the most of the state you need to have an enthusiasm for striking out on your own and roughing it a bit. Binoculars are an absolute must, as is bug spray; the **mosquito** is referred to as the "Alaska state bird" and it takes industrial-strength repellent to keep it away. On top of that there's the **climate**, though Alaska is far from the popular misconception of being one big icebox. While winter temperatures of -40°F are commonplace in Fairbanks, the most touristed areas – the southeast and the Kenai Peninsula – enjoy a maritime climate (45–65°F in summer) similar to that of the Pacific Northwest, meaning much more rain (in some towns 180-plus inches per year) than snow. Remarkably, the summer temperature in the Interior often reaches 80°F.

Alaska is far more expensive than most other states: apart from two dozen hostels there's little budget accommodation, and **eating** and **drinking** will set you back at least twenty percent more than in the Lower 48 (perhaps fifty percent in more remote regions). Still, experiencing Alaska on a **low budget** is possible, though it requires planning and off-peak travel. From June to August room prices are crazy; May and September, when tariffs are relaxed and the weather only slightly chillier, are just as good times to go, and in April or October you'll have the place to yourself, albeit with a smaller range of places to stay and eat. Ground **transportation**, despite the long distances, is reasonable, with backpacker shuttles ferrying budget travelers between major centers. **Winter**, when hotels drop their prices by as much as half, is becoming an increasingly popular time to visit, particularly for the dazzling **aurora borealis**.

Some history

Alaska has been inhabited for longer than anywhere else in the Americas; it was here, across the broad plains of the "land bridge" that is now submerged below the Bering Sea, that humans first reached the "New World," most likely around 14,000 years ago. These first settlers can be classified into four groups, which lived within well-defined regions until whites arrived. The **Aleut**, in the inhospitable Aleutian Islands, built underground homes and hunted sea mammals such as walrus for food and clothing, while the nomadic **Athabascan** herded caribou in the Interior. The warrior **Tlingit** lived in the warmer coastal regions of the southeast, where food was plentiful, in contrast to the **Eskimos** (or, more correctly, Yupik and Inupiat), who inhabited the northwestern coast, living off fish and larger marine life. Descendants of all these groups remain in Alaska today; a few live in much the same way as their ancestors, though most have been integrated into the modern American way through conquest, rape, marriage and religion.

In 1741, Danish explorer **Vitus Bering**, working for the Tsar of Russia, became the first Caucasian to set foot on Alaskan soil and found huge numbers of fur seals and **sea otters** – whose treasured pelts were made into hats. Russians, and later Britons and Spaniards, joined in the ensuing slaughter, both of the otters and the Aleut, who were enslaved and forced to hunt on behalf of the fur traders. By 1799 the Russians had established their Alaskan capital at present-day Sitka, pushed down the coast as far as northern California and, in the process, decimated the sea otter colonies.

During the 1860s, limited returns and domestic economic problems forced Russia to sell its lands to America. On October 18, 1867, Secretary of State William Seward purchased what was disparagingly known as "**Seward's Folly**" or "Seward's Icebox" for $7.2 million – less than 2¢ per acre. Alaska soon turned out to be a literal **gold mine** with major discoveries at Juneau (1880), Nome (1898), and Fairbanks (1902). With logging companies and commercial fishing operations also descending upon Alaska, the government began to take a more active interest in its affairs and in 1959 Alaska became the **49th state**.

Alaska's next boom followed the discovery of oil at Prudhoe Bay on the Arctic Ocean, and fortune-seekers headed to Alaska in the mid-1970s to build the **trans–Alaska pipeline**. Today, Alaska still derives about eighty percent of its wealth from oil and gas; indeed, each resident receives an annual dividend check of almost $2000. But the state is still in economic transition and continues to be prone to extreme boom-and-bust cycles. Once lucrative fishing and lumber industries are fast giving way to tourism as a source of income, and the ethical question of how best to use Alaskan lands in the future has led to bitter controversy, not least over the oil reserves under the Arctic National Wildlife Refuge.

Getting to Alaska

Alaska is a long way from the rest of the United States, and whichever way you get there is going to be **expensive**. Once you accept that, however, there is no question as to which is the most **enjoyable** method – the memorable ferry trip on the Alaska Marine Highway.

By air

Anchorage is no longer the major air crossroads it once was, but it's still easy to **fly** to Alaska. It is, however, very expensive. Most but not all flights from the Lower 48 are routed through Seattle. The most frequent service from the west coast is operated by Alaska Airlines/ERA Aviation (☎1-800/252-7522, Ⓦ www.alaskaair.com), whose money-saving package enables you to fly to towns like Juneau, Sitka, Cordova and Fairbanks at little extra cost. Round-trip fares from Seattle to Anchorage are around $460 if bought three weeks in advance, but occasional short-notice deals turn up for under $200 – check the website. Better still, foreigners traveling from outside North America can make use of the "Best of the West" airpass (see opposite).

By sea

The **ferries** of the state-run **Alaska Marine Highway System** (☎1-800/642-0066, Ⓦ www.state.ak.us/ferry) cover many areas unreachable by car, currently operating in two separate regions with an occasional "inter-tie" trip linking them. The popular **southeast** route runs a thousand miles from Bellingham, just north of Seattle, through a wonderland of pristine waters, narrow fjords and untouched forests to Skagway, at the northern end of the **Inside Passage** stopping at Ketchikan, Wrangell, Sitka, Juneau and Haines. The whole trip takes three days and costs $277 for walk-on passengers, $624 for a small car, $224 for a motorbike and $45 for bicycles and canoes. It is possible to sleep – and even to pitch a tent – on the "solarium," a covered, heated upper deck, while a two-berth cabin costs from $235. The **southwest** ferry system connects the Kenai Peninsula and Prince William Sound to the Aleutians, and the new Kennicott ferry now links the two systems by running between Juneau and Seward once a month in summer. Throughout the system, section passenger fares depend on distance traveled: $180 from Bellingham to Ketchikan; $59 from Ketchikan to Sitka; $29 from Sitka to Juneau; and $166 from Juneau to Seward. While the ferry is a bargain for foot passengers prepared to rough it, an extended voyage with vehicle and an overnight cabin (both of which should be booked in advance) becomes very expensive. If you're driving up from the Lower 48, consider boarding a ferry at Prince Rupert in British Columbia, a day's drive north of Seattle. This saves the cost of one day at sea from Bellingham without missing much of the natural spectacle.

By road

For many people, the drive up to Alaska through Canada is one of the major highlights of a visit to the state. Originally built by the military in just eight months, and with a fearsome reputation, the 1500-mile **Alaska Highway** is now fully paved (though long sections are often under repair) and equipped with sufficient service stations, campgrounds and hotels along the way. It remains as beautiful as ever, and still demands a spirit of adventure from drivers who attempt it.

No direct **buses** run to Alaska, though for around $380 (sometimes considerably less) you can hop on a Greyhound in Seattle and, after a few transfers over two grueling days, reach Whitehorse in the Yukon, from where Alaskon Express (see below) continues to Haines or Skagway in the southeast, or on the longer haul to Fairbanks and Anchorage.

Getting around Alaska

Getting around Alaska on the cheap can be tough; **public transportation** is limited, and many areas are only accessible by boat or plane, which is quick and convenient but invariably pricey. With little traffic, **hitching** is hard work, but is more acceptable, and safer, than elsewhere.

With the exception of the ferry system (see opposite), **Anchorage** is very much the hub of Alaska with several **bus** companies running to major destinations: Seward with Seward Bus Line (☎907/224-3608, ⊛www.alaskaone .com/sewardbus; $35); Homer with Homer Stage Lines (☎907/235-2252; $45); Denali ($49) and Fairbanks ($69) with the Parks Highway Express (☎1-888/600-6001, ⊛www.alaskashuttle.com); and Valdez ($71) and Whitehorse, Yukon ($206) with Gray Line's Alaskon Express (☎1-800/544-2206, ⊛www.graylinealaska.com).

The expensive **Alaska Railroad** runs nearly five hundred miles from Seward north through Anchorage to Fairbanks, with a spur to Whittier for ferries to Valdez. One-way **fares** from Anchorage are: Denali, $125; Fairbanks $175; and Seward $55.

Driving around Alaska in summer requires no special skills, though the less traveled routes often have a gravel surface and caution is required. Be aware, however, that wildlife, especially moose, can be a danger any time. In spring and fall you should be prepared for snow, and it is wise to carry a **survival kit**, particularly in winter, as traffic can be sparse even on major routes. Conditions on the roads can change rapidly – call ☎907/456-7623 for information, or ☎1-800/478-7656 for a pre-recorded hotline.

Travel by **plane** is not always more expensive than other methods, especially if you can map out your itinerary in advance with the state's largest operator, Alaska Airlines (see opposite), which flies to most major communities and uses subcontractors such as ERA Aviation (☎1-800/866-8394, ⊛www.eraaviation.com), Reeve Aleutian (☎1-800/544-2248, ⊛www.reeveair.com), and PenAir (☎1-800/448-4226, ⊛www.penair.com) to get to smaller towns. If you are traveling from outside North America, consider pre-purchasing an Alaska Airlines "Best of the West" **airpass** that allows you to reserve up to ten one-way flights either within Alaska ($99 each leg), or from outside the state (essentially Seattle or LA to Anchorage; $149), or any combination of these. **Chartering a plane** might sound extravagant but can be an inexpensive alternative for groups of four or more, and may be the crowning glory of an Alaskan

---

The Alaska Pass

If you are planning to keep up a frenetic pace you may make savings by buying an **Alaska Pass**, PO Box 351, Vashon, WA 98070 (☎206/463-6550 or 1-800/248-7598, ⊛www.alaskapass.com), which allows unlimited surface transport on participating ferries, trains and buses throughout Alaska, British Columbia and Yukon Territory. There are two types of Alaska Pass: one is valid for a number of **consecutive days of travel** (15 days for $649; 22 days for $749); the other covers a number of travel days over a longer period (8 days in 12 for $549; 12 days in 21 for $699).

vacation. To arrange this, contact any operator of small planes (every town has at least one). ERA Aviation, Reeve Aleutian and PenAir are good places to start, though they may refer you to another company.

Southeast Alaska

Southeast Alaska – also known as the panhandle – is archetypal Alaska; an awesome six-hundred-mile-long tableau of fjords, mountains, glaciers, a thousand islands, and thick conifer forests lining the **Inside Passage**. All of its communities have their economic base in lumber, fishing and tourism and are set amid magnificent scenery. The state's southernmost town, **Ketchikan**, rich in native heritage, makes a pretty introduction, tiny **Wrangell** emits a pioneer air, while **Sitka** retains a Russian influence. Further north are swanky **Juneau**, the capital; **Haines**, with its mix of old-timers and arty newcomers; and **Skagway**, thoroughly redolent of the old gold-mining days. You could spend months exploring here, but most are content to focus on the highlights, particularly the towns of Sitka and Skagway, and **Glacier Bay National Park**, an expensive side trip from Juneau that penetrates one of Alaska's most stunning regions.

The region's first settlers, the **Tlingit** (*Hlin-git*), were joined somewhat violently by Russian expansionists at the end of the eighteenth century. A steady stream of freelance profiteers, keen on tapping the region's gold, fur, fish and lumber, soon followed, and today its small communities resound with tales of endurance, folly and cruelty.

With no roads connecting towns, by far the best way to travel is by **ferry**, though at some stage make sure you take a **floatplane** ride. For a true outdoor adventure, you can rent a **cabin** in the huge Tongass National Forest – which encompasses most of southeast Alaska – for around $35 per night; details from the visitor centers in Juneau (see p.1249) and Ketchikan (see opposite), or through the NRRS reservation service (⊕www.ReserveUSA.com).

Ketchikan and around

KETCHIKAN, five hundred miles north of Seattle, is Alaska's "first city," and as the first port of call for many cruise ships, its historic downtown, wedged between water and forested mountains, becomes saturated in summer with elderly tourists. Beyond the souvenir shopping it can be a delight, built into steep hills and partly propped on wooden pilings, with boardwalks, wooden staircases and totem poles dotted throughout.

By 1886, white settlers had opened the first of dozens of canneries in what was soon to be the "salmon capital of the world." Forests of cedar, hemlock and spruce, which had provided timber for Tlingit homes and totems, also fed the town's sawmills. The timber and fishing industries have declined, and with the closure of the antiquated pulp mill in 1997 the town's economy is in a state of flux.

The state's fourth largest city is a strong contender for the nation's wettest; annual precipitation averages 165 inches. The tourist board shrugs it off as "liquid sunshine" and, indeed, Ketchikan's perennial drizzle and sporadic showers won't spoil your visit.

Arrival and information

Ferries dock two miles north of downtown on Tongass Highway; city **buses** stop here every 30 minutes until 9.30pm (Sun 3.30pm). Alaska Airlines serve the **airport**, which is on an island and is linked to town by half-hourly ferries

($2.50). The **visitor center** stands downtown at 131 Front St (daily 7am–5pm; ℡907/225-6166 or 1-800/770-3300, ⓦwww.visit-ketchikan.com), and for information about the surrounding Tongass forests visit the **Southeast Alaska Discovery Center**, 50 Main St (daily 8am–5pm; ℡907/228-6220, ⓦwww.fs.fed.us/r10/ketchikan), a striking cedar-framed building which houses absorbing displays ($4) of the region's natural habitats and native culture.

Scores of companies run **sightseeing excursions**, among them Alaska Sourdough Tours (℡907/225-4081 or 1-888/801-7596), which takes you around town and to the two major totem pole sites at Saxman and Totem Bight. Promech Air (℡907/225-3845 or 1-800/860-3845) and Taquan Air (℡907/225-8800 or 1-800/770-8800) offer **floatplane** trips from just $60, while Southeast Sea Kayaks (℡907/225-1258 or 1-800/287-1607) or Southeast Exposure, 515 Water St (℡907/225-8829), will take you **sea kayaking** along the fjords; a four-hour trip costs around $80 with day rental for experienced paddlers from $30. The latter also rents **bikes**.

Accommodation

Hotels in Ketchikan vary widely, and the closest **campgrounds** to town ($10) are in the attractive Ward Lake Recreation Area, five miles northwest of the ferry terminal.

Cape Fox Lodge 800 Venetia Way ℡907/225-8001 or 1-800/544-0970. The grandest hotel in town, located on a hill above the town with international standard rooms, many with water views glimpsed through the spruce and hemlocks. ❽

HI-Ketchikan in the United Methodist Church, 400 Main St ℡907/225-3319. Very basic youth hostel with beds for $10 (nonmembers $13), June–Aug only. ❶

Innside Passage B&B 114 Elliot St, above the main road just north of town ℡ & ℗907/247-3700, ⓦwww.innsidepassagebedandbreakfast.com. Rooms and an apartment close to the ferries, with good views across the Narrows. Apartment ❺, rooms ❹

The New York Hotel 207 Stedman St ℡907/225-0246 or 1-866/225-0246, ⓦwww.thenewyorkhotel.com. Nicely refurbished hotel by the small-boat harbor with cozy but tastefully decorated rooms and a good café. ❺

The town and around

The bulk of Ketchikan's historic buildings lie on **Creek Street**, a rickety-looking boardwalk along Ketchikan Creek. This was a red-light district until 1954; now all the former houses of ill-repute are given over to gift shops and arty cafés. **Dolly's House**, 24 Creek St, once the home and workplace of Dolly Arthur, the town's most famous madam, is now a small museum stuffed with saucy memorabilia (hours vary; $4).

Most of the totem poles you see around town are authentic replicas, but the **Totem Heritage Center**, 601 Deermount St (daily 8am–5pm; $4), exhibits the largest collection of original totem poles in the US: 33 mostly nineteenth-century examples recovered from abandoned Native villages. The Tlingit-run **Saxman Totem Park**, three miles south of town, displays the world's largest standing collection of poles and an authentic tribal house. Admission, including a chance to see sculptors at work, is free, but two-hour **guided tours** (several daily; $30) will help to decipher the images. Fourteen of the best replica totem poles and a rebuilt tribal house stand in **Totem Bight State Park**, breathtakingly set on a forested strip of coast overlooking the Narrows, ten miles north of town on the Tongass Highway. On the way back, take some time out to do the easy but enjoyable boardwalk trail up to **Perseverance Lake**, starting at Ward Cove, four miles north of town.

Twenty-two miles east of Ketchikan on the mainland, the awe-inspiring **MISTY FIORDS NATIONAL MONUMENT** consists of 2.3 million acres of deep fjords flanked by sheer 3000ft glacially scoured walls topped by dense rainforest. As befits its name, the monument is at its most atmospheric when swathed in low-lying mists. No roads lead here, but the kayak and float-plane operators listed in "Arrival and information" do. Four-hour cruise-in/fly-out tours are run by Alaska Cruises (T 907/225-6044 or 1-800/225-1905, W www.goldbelttours.com; $198). Fourteen rustic cabins (mostly $35) are rented out by the Forest Service (T 1-877/444-6777).

Eating and drinking

Inexpensive **food** in Ketchikan tends to be rather good, a rare combination in Alaska. The place is also renowned for its hard **drinking**. Steer clear of the *First City Tavern*, a favorite with commercial fishers and cannery workers eager to forget the sight and smell of raw fish.

Annabelle's Keg & Chowder House 326 Front St T 907/225-6009. Classy but relaxed atmosphere. Good espresso, sourdough pancakes and seafood at moderate to high prices.

Arctic Bar 509 Water St. Basic, dark boozing bar with a great view over the water once the cruise ships have left.

Diaz Chinese Restaurant 335 Stedman St T 907/225-2257. Great inexpensive diner food with some tasty Filipino dishes.

Pizza Mill 808 Water St T 907/225-6646. Ketchikan's oldest pizza joint is a great low-key place for gourmet pizzas (known here as Yuppie Pies; from $10 for a 12-inch), subs, burgers ($6–8), burritos ($6–7), salads and draft beer. No credit cards.

Steamers 76 Front St T 907/225-1600. Large, bustling restaurant opposite the cruise-ship dock with great views and seafood to match – not to mention a well-stocked bar with a plethora of beers on tap and occasional live music.

Wrangell

With a population of just 2600, **WRANGELL**, the second stop on the ferry system, is altogether quieter than Ketchikan and has a distinctly old-fashioned feel. Right in the busy harbor, accessible by a short boardwalk, **Chief Shakes Island** holds an excellent collection of totem poles and a replica tribal house filled with Tlingit blankets. The ancient rock carvings at **Petroglyph Beach**, half a mile or so north of town along Evergreen Avenue, date back as far as 7500 years and are only obscured during high tide.

Ferries dock right in town but seldom stop over long enough to allow explorations of the sights, so you may want to stay: try the **campground** at *City Park* (one night max; free), less than two miles south on Zimovia Highway, or the clean and central *Wrangell Hostel*, 220 Church St (T 907/874-3534; ❶), a Presbyterian Church where $15 gets you a thin mattress on the floor. The **airport**, with daily connections to other Southeastern towns, is a mile and a half north of town, and you'll find the **visitor center** (Mon–Fri 10am–4pm; T 907/874-3901) inside the *Sitkine Inn* on Front Street.

Sitka

One of the highlights of an Inland Passage ferry ride is negotiating the 46 tight turns of the 22-mile-long **Wrangell Narrows** between Wrangell and the "Norwegian" fishing town of Petersburg on the route north. At times it feels like you can reach out and touch the steep-walled shore, and at night the ferry has to negotiate a slalom course of navigation lights.

Perched on the seaward edge of the Inside Passage and eleven hours from Petersburg, **SITKA** ranks as one of Alaska's prettiest and most historic towns. The Fuji-like **Mount Edgecumbe** volcano rises menacingly across Sitka Sound from the spot where Russian colonists established a fort in 1799. Three years later Tlingit warriors massacred the imperialist troops and their Aleut slaves, but were themselves cannoned into submission in 1804. Under Russian occupation the town was rebuilt and christened **Novaya Archangelsk** (New Archangel), the capital of Russian America – a role it retained beyond the 1867 transfer of ownership to the US, until federal powers passed control to Juneau in 1906. Sitka today earns its keep mostly from fishing and tourism; it's all too keen to flog tacky "Russiocana" – you'll find more nesting dolls here than the rest of the US put together – but the town also has a wealth of great outdoor opportunities and a fine reputation for its festivals, especially the chamber-oriented **Summer Music Festival** each June and the **Alaska Day Festival** (celebrating the Russia–US transfer) on the days leading up to October 18.

Arrival, information and accommodation

Ferries visit Sitka around five times per week, mooring seven miles northwest of town on Halibut Point Road (☎907/747-3300), from where Sitka Tours **shuttles** (☎907/747-8443; $7 round-trip) run downtown; they also do three-hour tours of town ($10). Alaska Airlines runs a daily service on the Seattle–Juneau–Anchorage route from the airport on Japonski Island, a pleasant half-hour walk from downtown or $3 ride with Sitka Tours. **Mountain bikes** can be rented from Yellow Jersey Cycles, 805 Halibut Point Rd (☎907/747-6317), and Baidarka Boats, 201 Lincoln St (☎907/747-8996, ⓦwww.kayaksite.com), rents single and double **kayaks** ($35/50 a day) as well as organizing day-long guided trips on the Sound ($65). The **CVB** office is in the Centennial Building, 330 Harbor Drive (daily 8am–5pm; ☎907/747-3220, ⓦwww.sitka.org).

Sitka has a good range of **accommodation**: the spartan *HI-Sitka* hostel, 303 Kimshan St (☎907/747-8661; ❶; closed Sept–May), in a Methodist church a mile from downtown, has beds for $10 (nonmembers $13); the historic *Sitka Hotel*, 118 Lincoln St (☎907/747-3288, ⓦwww.sitkahotel.com; ❹), offers a touch of old-fashioned class and good-value rooms that come with and without bathrooms; *Finn Alley Inn B&B*, 711 Lincoln St (☎907/747-3655, Ⓕ747-5007, ⓦwww.ptialaska.net/~seakdist/finn.htm; ❺), is well located and its large half-basement apartment has private entrance, full kitchen and a continental breakfast delivered to the room; and the *Westmark Shee Atika*, 330 Seward St (☎907/747-6241 or 1-800/544-0970, ⓦwww.westmarkhotels.com; ❼), owns the flashest rooms in town. **Campers** should head a mile north of the ferry dock to the *Starrigavan* campground (☎907/747-4216; $8) or seven miles east of Sitka to the free but basic *Sawmill Creek* site.

The Town

The best place to get a grasp of Sitka's Russian past and the lay of the land is from the rocky vantage point of **Castle Hill**, where Alaska was officially transferred to the US on October 18, 1867; an informative plaque marks the spot. A two-minute stroll to the heart of downtown leads to **St Michael's Cathedral** on Lincoln Street. A fine piece of rural Russian church architecture, completed in 1848 and rebuilt after a disastrous fire in 1966, it displays priceless original icons (daily 9am–4pm when cruise ships are in town; $2). Guided tours take in the restored chapel, schoolroom and living quarters of the large mustard-colored 1842 **Russian Bishop's House**, by the harbor – a log structure that is the oldest standing building in Alaska (summer daily 9am–1pm & 2–5pm; rest of year by appointment; ☎907/747-6281; $3).

Four blocks further along at 104 College Drive, the **Sheldon Jackson Museum** (summer daily 9am–5pm; rest of year Tues–Sat 10am–4pm; $4) houses a compact but extensive accumulation of Native artifacts. All of the tools, utensils and craft objects from Aleut, Athabascan, Tlingit and especially Aleut peoples were collected by the Rev Dr Sheldon Jackson on his wide-ranging travels throughout Alaska as a missionary and the territory's first General Agent for Education.

At the end of Lincoln Street, in a verdant copse between ocean and creek, **Sitka National Historic Park** embraces both the town's Tlingit heritage and its days of Russian rule. When Tsarist troops attacked a Tlingit fort on this site in 1804, the natives withstood bombardment for six days, but after running out of gunpowder, decided to abandon the fort silently at night. The next day Russians stormed the stockades only to find them empty except for a few dead children, whom they alleged were murdered to accomplish the retreat in complete silence. Nothing remains of the fort except a grassy clearing, but the evocative air is enhanced by several vividly painted **totem poles** alongside the footpaths, all replicas of nineteenth-century classic designs. A **visitor center** (summer daily 8am–5pm; free) features good interpretive displays on what is commonly called the "Battle of Sitka," as well as hosting Native craft workshops.

Sitka's **trail system** ranges from shoreside strolls to harder climbs up Gavan Hill and steep Mount Verstovia: for more information visit the **Forest Service office**, 201 Katlian St (☎907/747-4220).

Eating

Sitka's **restaurants** aren't exactly going to set gourmet tongues wagging, though there are several decent places to dine out. The best bargain in town is the *Sheldon Jackson College Dining Room*, David Sweetland Hall, a simple cafeteria-style place with all-you-can-eat breakfast (6.30–8am; $5), lunch (11.30am–1pm; $5), and dinner (4.45–6pm; $10): follow the road opposite the entrance to the Sheldon Jackson Museum. For great coffee, tasty sandwiches, pastries and light lunches duck through Old Harbor Books at 201 Lincoln St to *The Backdoor* (☎907/747-8856) or try the small organic café in *Evergreen Natural Foods*, 2a Lincoln St (☎907/747-6944). The *Bayview Restaurant*, upstairs at 407 Lincoln St (☎907/747-5440), offers great sea views and well-prepared dishes on its standard Alaskan menu, with additional Russian treats such as borscht; and the *Channel Club*, four miles west of town at 2906 Halibut Point Rd (☎907/747-9916), is the place to go for steak: there's a free shuttle from downtown. For evening **drinks**, join the crowds in the *Westmark Shee Atika's* bar, or the down-to-earth *Pioneer Bar* on colorful Katlian Street.

Juneau

The sophisticated and vibrant city of **JUNEAU** is unlike any other state capital in the nation. Accessible only by sea or air, it is exceptionally picturesque, hard against the **Gastineau Channel**, with steep, narrow roads clawing up into the rainforested hills behind. Gold features heavily in its history. In 1880, two prospectors – one of them Joe Juneau – made **Alaska's first gold strike** in the rainforest along the banks of the Gastineau Channel. Named Gold Creek, the camp grew rapidly. Until the last mine was shut down in 1944, this was the world's largest producer of low-grade ore – all the flat land in Juneau, stretching from downtown to the airport, is landfill from mine tailings.

Arrival, information and getting around

The **ferry terminal** is fourteen miles northwest of downtown at Auke Bay; ferries often arrive at unearthly hours, so getting into town can be a problem. Apart from taking a $30 taxi ride, the only transport is with the MGT **shuttle**

(☎907/789-5460 between 6pm and 8pm only, ⊛www.mightygreattrips.com) which meets ferries and drops off at the airport and downtown (both $5). Alternatively, walk a mile and a half to Mendenhall Loop Road and catch the Capital Transit bus #3 or #4 (☎907/789-6901; $1.50). It's part of the town **bus service**, which runs hourly from 7am until 11pm (limited service on Sun). The ferry dock is not to be confused with the **cruise-ship terminal**, right downtown. Alaska Airlines land daily at Juneau's **airport**, nine miles out towards the ferry terminal; grab a $20 cab, or pick up Capital Transit buses into town from Mallard Street, behind the nearby Nugget Mall: for details and schedules see the Juneau Visitors Information Desk at the airport on the ground floor, which is open for all arrivals.

The main **visitor center** (May–Sept Mon–Fri 8.30am–5pm, Sat & Sun 9am–5pm; Oct–April Mon–Fri 9am–5pm; ☎907/586-2201 or 1-888/581-2201, ⊛www.traveljuneau.com) is at 134 Third St, and when a cruise ship's in there are **information booths** at Marine Park on the waterfront, and by the cruise-ship dock. The **Tongass National Forest visitor center** at 101 Egan Drive (Mon–Fri 8am–5pm; ☎907/586-8751) has exhibits and videos on the region's ecology and is the place to book forest cabins.

Popular **hikes** from Juneau include the undemanding Perseverance Trail and, over the bridge on Douglas Island, the Treadwell Mine Historic Trail. Mountain Gears, 210 N Franklin St (☎907/586-4327), rents out **mountain bikes** and offers customized area tours. Alaska Discovery (☎907/780-6226 or 1-800/586-1911) or Auk Ta Shaa (☎907/586-8687 or 1-800/820-2628) organizes **sea-kayaking trips** amid wondrous scenery from around $100 per day.

Accommodation

Juneau has the widest range of accommodation in Southeast Alaska, and some fine **camping** either at the *Mendenhall Lake Campground* ($10), spectacularly situated near the glacier and accessible by buses #3 or #4 and a short hike, or at the basic *Thane Road Tent Camping* ($5), just a mile south of downtown. All of the places listed blow are handy for downtown.

Alaskan Hotel and Bar 167 S Franklin St ☎907/586-1000 or 1-800/327-9374. Pleasant old hotel with a salacious past and a fine bar in the heart of downtown. Twelve doubles with shared or private bath. ❹

Cashen Quarters B&B 303 Gold St ☎907/586-9863 or 1-888/543-5701, ⊛www.cashenquarters.com. Central B&B with five rooms and continental breakfast brought to you. ❺

Driftwood Lodge 435 Willoughby Ave ☎907/586-2280 or 1-800/544-2239. One block from the waterfront, with large rooms including kitchenettes. Courtesy bus to airport and ferry. ❺

HI-Juneau 614 Harris St ☎907/586-9559, ✉juneauhostel@gci.net. Clean, comfortable and relaxed hostel, in an old home near downtown, with dorm beds for $7 (nonmembers $10), an inconvenient daytime lock-out (10am–5pm) and an 11pm curfew. ❶

Silverbow Guest Inn 120 2nd St ☎907/586-4146 or 1-800/586-4146, ⊛www.silverbowinn.com. Attractive small hotel linked to the restaurant and bakery of the same name, with smallish but nicely furnished and tastefully decorated rooms, each with TV and phone, and with a good continental breakfast included. ❻

Downtown Juneau

From the kiosk in Marine Park, it takes an hour and a half to follow the self-guided Juneau **walking tour**. Many original buildings stand in the **South Franklin Street Historic District** – Juneau managed to avoid the fires that destroyed many other gold towns in Alaska. The onion-domed **St Nicholas Russian Orthodox Church**, on Fifth and Gold (Mon–Sat 9am–6pm; $1 donation), contains icons and religious treasures, while the excellent **Alaska State Museum**, 395 Whittier St (Mon–Fri 9am–6pm, Sat & Sun 10am–6pm;

$5), covers native culture, the Russian heritage and the first gold strikes. Its pride and joy is the logbook in which Bering reported his first sighting of Alaska. The smaller **City Museum**, 155 S Seward St (summer Mon–Fri 9am–5pm, Sat & Sun 10am–5pm; rest of year Fri & Sat noon–4pm; $3), displays relics from the mining era.

The best views of town are from the top of the **Mount Roberts Tramway** (summer daily 9am–9pm; $20), which careers up from the cruise-ship dock 1700 feet up Mount Roberts, where there's a nature center and some easy trails.

Mendenhall Glacier and Tracy Arm Fjord

There are certainly bigger and more spectacular glaciers in Alaska, but the twelve-mile-long, one-and-a-half-mile-wide **Mendenhall Glacier**, thirteen miles from downtown, is easily the most accessible. Should your knowledge of cirques and striations be a little rusty, the **visitor center** (built on a point occupied by the glacier as recently as 1940) has all you need to know (summer daily 8am–6pm; rest of year Sat & Sun 10am–4pm; ☎907/789-0097). Hiking trails include the West Glacier Trail, on which, with extreme caution and without official approval, you can explore the ice caves.

Capital Transit buses leave for Mendenhall hourly from downtown; get off at Glacier Spur Road for the visitor center, or Montana Creek Road for the West Glacier trail. Alaska Travel Adventures runs three-hour **float trips** on the Mendenhall River (☎907/789-0052 or 1-800/791-2673; $97), while Temsco (☎907/789-9501; $160) offers one-hour **helicopter trips** with 25 minutes on the glacier itself.

One of the best day-trips out of Juneau is up the narrow, twisting **Tracy Arm Fjord**, with waterfall-fringed cliffs and common sightings of whales and seals. Day-long **cruises** with Auk Nu Tours' stable twin-hulls (☎907/586-8687 or 1-800/820-2628; $109) or with Adventure Bound Alaska (☎907/463-2905 or 1-800/228-3875; $99) are both worthwhile.

Eating and drinking

Downtown's excellent places to **eat and drink** fill up very quickly when cruise ships are in town.

Alaskan Hotel and Bar 167 S Franklin St ☎907/586-1000. Great old bar, with live music most weekend nights.

Armadillo 431 S Franklin St ☎907/586-1880. Justly popular Tex-Mex café and microbrewery serving huge plates of *huevos rancheros* ($8) and *chicken fajitas grande* ($14).

Bacar's corner 4th and Franklin sts ☎907/463-5091. Quirky hard-to-find restaurant worth seeking out for last-all-day breakfasts ($5–9), clam chowder and burger lunches ($8–10), and dinners that include a wonderful chicken fried steak ($19) and liver, bacon and onions ($15). Closed Mon & Tues. No credit cards.

Hanger on the Wharf Merchants Wharf ☎907/586-5018. Renovated, historic floatplane hanger right on the wharf with a tremendous view of the waterfront and over twenty beers on tap, plus pool tables on the mezzanine, and a lively atmosphere, especially at weekends when there is live rock or jazz. Food extends from wraps and burgers at lunch to items like jambalaya and halibut tacos ($8–11) later on.

Silverbow Bakery and Restaurant 120 2nd St ☎907/586-4146. Out front there's a wonderful bakery and coffee bar with big windows that catch the morning sun (if you're lucky enough to see any). Traditionally boiled and baked bagels and superb pastries bolster a menu of homemade breads used to make hot and cold deli sandwiches ($5–11). The restaurant (closed Mon) itself has one of the most varied and imaginative menus in town, from salads and soups ($6–9) to kielbasa and pierogies ($11), Indonesian peanut pasta with either tofu or chicken ($12), and pesto and red pepper burgers ($9); and some evenings you can even stick around for the movie.

Uncle Sam's Cafeteria 2nd Floor, 709 W 9th St ☎907/586-3430. Low cost dining with a view, inside the Federal Building. Open for breakfast ($4) from

7am, then lunches including daily specials ($6) such as taco salad or chicken fried steak. Closes 4pm.
Red Dog Saloon 278 S Franklin St ☎907/463-3777. Straightforward sawdust-on-the-floor tourist trap and merchandising empire masquerading as a raucous, historic bar. Musicians get the cruise ship crowd going from around 2pm. Pretty quiet once the boats leave.

Glacier Bay National Park

When Captain George Vancouver sailed through Icy Strait in 1794, **GLACIER BAY** didn't exist. Since then the Grand Pacific Glacier has receded 65 miles, to reveal a tranquil world of deep fjords lined by rock walls and fed by fifteen other receding tidewater glaciers. The flora of the bay ranges from mature spruce forests to delicate plant life, while brown and black bear, moose, mountain goats, sea otters, humpback whales, porpoise, seals and a colorful array of birds have made the area their home. Most, if not all of them can be seen on a **day–cruise** through Glacier Bay (the only way to access the area). The most spectacular moment comes when the boat, having negotiated its way through three miles of icebergs, comes face to face with the massive wall of the Grand Pacific Glacier.

AMHS ferries don't go to **GUSTAVUS**, the nearest town to the otherwise inaccessible park, so the cheapest way to get there is with Alaska Airlines who fly in once each afternoon in summer from Juneau for a bargain $32 each way if booked well in advance. Smaller operators such as LAB (☎766-2222 or 1-800/426-0543) have more flights but charge around $60 from Juneau and connect Gustavus directly with Haines and Skagway. You might want to fly out and cruise back on the daily Juneau-to-Gustavus **ferry** run by Auk Nu Tours (2hr 15min; ☎1-800/478-3610, ⓦwww.goldbelttours.com; $45 one-way, bikes $10, kayaks $40).

The ferry and flights are met by a bus ($10) which takes you ten miles to Bartlett Cove, site of the **park headquarters** and the dock for the all-day **cruise** on the *Spirit of Adventure* ($157) – the principal way of experiencing the park's wonders short of paddling. Also here is the park's only **hotel**, *Glacier Bay Lodge* (☎1-800/451-5952; rooms ❼, bunks ❸) with tasteful hotel rooms and bunks in poky dorms with no cooking facilities. A better budget alternative is the first-come-first-served campground (free) beside the fjord.

If you want a roof over your head, the best bet lies in Gustavus in the form of *Bear's Nest B&B* (☎907679-2440, ⓔriddlephilip@hotmail.com; ❺), a completely self-contained and fully-furnished cabin with a double bed upstairs and a single futon down. Breakfast ingredients are provided though you'll have to bring everything else from Juneau, or wander next door to the *Bear's Nest Café*.

Haines

The small community of **HAINES** sits on a peninsula between the Chilkat and the Chilkoot inlets at the northern end of the longest and deepest fjord in the US, Lynn Canal. The town tends to be overshadowed by its brasher neighbor, Skagway, but it remains a real Alaskan experience nonetheless. When the weather is clear, it is nothing short of spectacular, with snow-covered **Mount Ripinsky** rising up behind, the **Chilkoot and Chilkat mountains** hemming it in on either side, and glaciers spilling out into the deep fjord. The community itself is an interesting mix of unreconstructed rednecks and urban escapees from the Lower 48.

The Tlingit fished and traded here for years before 1881, when the first missionaries arrived and renamed the settlement for a prominent Presbyterian, Mrs F. Haines. Today the town survives on fishing and tourism, and though cruise ships tend to press on to Skagway, it remains a popular spot, which in mid-August hosts the cookouts, crafts and log-rolling of the **Southeast Alaska Fair**. The fairgrounds also hold **Dalton City**, a small pioneer theme park notable only in that its buildings came from the movie sets of Jack London's *White Fang*, which was filmed in the Haines area in 1989.

Arrival and information

Haines's **ferry** terminal is five miles north of town, with a daily service to and from Juneau and Skagway. Local **taxis** meet all ferry arrivals; downtown costs $5. Two private ferry operators, Haines–Skagway Water Taxi (☎1-888/766-3395) and Chilkat Cruises (☎1-888/766-2103), undertake the one-hour run up the fjord to Skagway for around $36 round-trip.

From town, the Haines Highway runs 151 miles to the Alaska Highway in Canada; a weekly minivan service, by RC Shuttles (☎907/479-0079 or 1-877/479-0079, ⓦwww.rcshuttles.com), runs routes to Fairbanks (from Fairbanks on Mon, from Haines on Tues; $130 to Fairbanks).

The **visitor center**, at Second and Willard (summer Mon–Fri 8am–8pm Sat & Sun 10am–4pm; rest of year Mon–Fri 8am–5pm; ☎907/766-2234 or 1-800/458-3579, ⓦwww.haines.ak.us), has all kinds of maps and information.

Accommodation

As well as the usual mid-range **accommodation**, Haines has half a dozen handy **campgrounds**. The best two are the tent-only *Portage Cove*, on a great beach less than a mile from Fort Seward on S Front Street (no vehicles; $6), and the peaceful *Port Chilkoot Camper Park*, Mud Bay Road beside Fort Seward (☎907/766-2000 or 1-800/542-6363; $8.50), pay-showers and a laundromat on site.

Haines Hostel and Bear Creek Cabins Small Tract Road ☎ 907/766-2259, ⓦkcd.com/hostel. Good hostel over a mile south of Fort Seward with coin-op laundry, bike rentals for $8 a day, no lock-out or curfew, and $3 rides from the ferry terminal. Campers ($6–8) can use hostel facilities. Dorms $14, cabins ➋.

Hotel Hälsingland 13 Fort Seward Drive ☎907/766-2000 or 1-800/542-6363, ⓦwww.haines.ak.us/halsingland. The town's grandest hotel with original features in some rooms, but well past its best: ask to look at a few rooms. B&B ➏, rooms ➎, shared bath ➍.

The Summer Inn B&B 117 Second Ave ☎907/766-2970, ⓦwww.summerinn.wytbear.com. Immaculately kept downtown B&B with shared-bath rooms, some with good sea views and a good cooked breakfast. It's all light and airy, and amenities include clawfoot baths, quilts and fresh flowers. ➎

Mountain View Motel 57 Mud Bay Road ☎907/766-2900 or 1-800/478-2902, ⓦwww.mtnviewmotel.com. Nine comfortable rooms with cable TV, free coffee, and most with functional kitchenettes. ➍

The Town

In the center of town, the **Sheldon Museum & Cultural Center**, 11 Main St (summer daily 1–5pm; rest of year Mon, Wed & Sun 1–4pm, Tues, Thurs & Fri 3–5pm; ⓦwww.sheldonmuseum.org; $3), does a great job of showing how Haines fits into its Chilkat environment and the wider Tlingit world, and exhibits fine examples of woodwork, clothing and the distinctive yellow and black Chilkat blanket in wolf, raven and killer whale designs.

Half a mile away, grassy **Fort William H. Seward** was established in 1903 to contain general Gold Rush lawlessness, and territorial disputes with Canada. It is now the site of the **Chilkat Center for the Arts** (mid-May to mid-Sept Mon–Thurs at 7.30pm; $10; ☎907/766-2160), where Chilkat Dancers do a forty-minute performance in traditional costumes.

Nearby, the stuffed birds of the **American Bald Eagle Foundation**, Second Avenue and Haines Highway (summer daily 9am–5pm; $2.50), make a poor substitute for seeing the world's largest gathering of **bald eagles**, which flock to the banks of the Chilkat River each fall. They arrive to feed on an unusually late chum salmon run (delayed by an upwelling of groundwater that keeps the river from freezing), and by November over three thousand of these once-endangered rare birds – as many as two dozen to a tree – are gathered along a five-mile sand bar at the **Chilkat Bald Eagle Preserve**, nine miles north of town on the Haines Highway.

Two great, wild **state parks** – Chilkoot Lake and Chilkat – are a mere half-hour cycle ride to the north and south of town respectively. Chilkat in particular has some good trails and vistas, while well-tramped treks lead from town to the summits of Mount Riley and the much more difficult Mount Ripinsky. Haines is also a popular starting point for **rafting trips**: Chilkat Guides on Beach Road (☎907/766-2491, ⓦraftalaska.com) is one of many operators to offer four-hour **float trips** ($82) down the Chilkat River, ideal for viewing eagles and other wildlife.

Eating and drinking

Haines's most exciting **bars** and **restaurants** can be found in the Fort Seward area. In the evening visitors converge on the friendly bar at the *Hotel Hälsingland* while some locals stick to the more raucous joints downtown.

Bamboo Room 11 2nd St near Main ☎907/766-2800. Standard diner popular for its well-prepared meals (especially the locally-caught halibut and chip dinner), and fresh-baked pies.

Mountain Market 312 3rd Ave at Haines Hwy ☎907/766-3340. Combined natural food grocery and espresso bar that's one of the best morning spots in town thanks to a $6.50 bagel breakfast, similarly priced tortilla wraps or just a muffin with your mocha.

Fireweed Bakery and Café Building 37, Blacksmith Road ☎907/766-3838. Coffee, pastries, breakfasts, sandwiches and great pizza served inside or out. Closed Sun.

Port Chilkoot Potlatch Parade Grounds, Fort Seward ☎907/766-2003. All-you-can-eat salmon bake on summer evenings ($22) in the fort's replica tribal house.

Skagway

SKAGWAY, the northernmost ferry stop on the southeast route, sprang up overnight in 1897 as a trading post serving **Klondike Gold Rush** pioneers about to set off on the five-hundred-mile ordeal. It was also the last stop before the harrowing White Pass Trail, known as the "Dead Horse Trail," on which over three thousand horses perished during the winter of 1897–98 from severe weather, rugged ground and exhaustion. Having grown from one cabin to a town of twenty thousand in three months, Skagway, rife with disease and desperado violence, was reported to be "hell on earth." It boasted over seventy bars and hundreds of prostitutes, and was controlled by organized criminals, including the notorious **Jefferson "Soapy" Smith**, renowned for cheating hapless prospectors out of their gold. One of his scams was to operate a bogus telegraph office through which he concocted false messages from loved ones in the Lower 48 urgently demanding money, which Soapy, of course, took responsibility for sending. He finally met a nasty end in 1898 after a shoot-out with Frank Reid, head of a vigilante group.

By 1899, the Gold Rush was over, but the completion in 1900 of the White Pass and Yukon Railway from Skagway to Whitehorse, the Yukon capital, ensured Skagway's survival. Today, the town's 800 residents have gone to great lengths to maintain the original appearance of their home, much of which lies in the **Klondike Gold Rush National Historic Park**, and in summer as many as five cruise ships a day call in to appreciate the effort.

Arrival, information and getting around

Ferries (℡907/983-2229) and two independent operators (see p.1252) arrive daily from Haines at the foot of the main thoroughfare, Broadway, and just a block from the **train station** from where two to five trains a day run over the White Pass to Fraser, British Columbia. Here you can connect with buses to Whitehorse, Yukon. Alaska Direct **buses** (℡1-800/780-6652) also run daily in summer direct to Whitehorse ($35), from where trips run to Anchorage ($145) and Fairbanks ($120) three times a week; Alaskon Express offers a similar service from the *Westmark Inn* on Third Avenue (℡907/983-2241).

Skagway is very compact, and most of the sights can easily be seen on foot. The Klondike Gold Rush National Park **visitor center**, Broadway at second Avenue (May & Sept daily 8am–6pm; June–Aug daily 8am–8pm; ℡907/983-2921, ⓦwww.nps.gov/klgo), holds talks, leads walking tours, and has historical displays and an impressive movie about the Gold Rush, as well as maps and information on the Chilkoot Trail. Skagway's **visitor center** (summer daily 8am–6pm; ℡907/983-2854 or 1-888/762-1898, ⓦwww.skagway.org) is on Broadway between Second and Third avenues in the Arctic Brotherhood Hall building.

Accommodation

In such a touristy little town, prices run slightly higher, and places often book up far in advance. For camping there's the pleasantly secluded *Mountain View RV Park*, Broadway at 12th (℡907/983-3333 or 1-888/778-7700, ⓦwww.alaskarv .com; $12.50), a large RV-dominated site with all the expected facilities, full RV hookup ($21) and dry RV sites ($15.50).

Cindy's Place Mile 0.2 Dyea Rd ℡907/983-2674 or 1-800/831-8095, ⓦwww.alaska.net/~croland. Three cabins in the woods two miles from downtown Skagway, one budget, two more luxurious log-built affairs with private bathrooms (one with a wood-burning stove), phone and cooking equipment. All guests have free use of the hot tub and mountain bikes, and there are thoughtful touches like a dozen varieties of tea and coffee in the cabins, and homemade jams and jellies for breakfast. Deluxe ⑥, budget ❸.

Skagway Inn B&B 7th Ave and Broadway ℡907/983-2289 or 1-888/752-4929, ⓦwww.skagwayinn.com. Former bordello with a lovely ambience and fresh-baked breakfasts in one of Alaska's very best small inns. ⑥.

Golden North Hotel Broadway at 3rd Ave ℡907/983-2294 or 1-888/222-1898,

ⓦwww.goldennorthhotel.com. Alaska's oldest and Skagway's most famous hotel, recently restored with considerable aplomb. Splurge on a deluxe room (⑦) or settle for a standard (⑥), with claw-foot bath, or even a shared-bath room (⑤). ⑤–⑦

Gold Rush Lodge 6th Ave at Alaska St ℡907/983-2831, ⓦalaskaone.com/goldrush. Immaculately kept and tastefully decorated motel where the smallness of the rooms is compensated by appointments like cable TV with VCR, phone, fridge, microwave and coffee pot. ⑤

Skagway Home Hostel 3rd Ave and Main St ℡907/983-2131. In-with-the-family hostel in a century-old building with bunks in single-sex dorms ($15) and one private room (②). There's a communal feel, ample supplies for cooking (honesty box) and an 11pm curfew. ❶

The Town

Strolling up Broadway you can't miss the eye-catching facade of the 1899 **Arctic Brotherhood Hall**, decorated with over ten thousand pieces of driftwood and housing the Skagway Visitor Center. Many of the other buildings hereabouts form part of the **Klondike Gold Rush National Historic Park**, notably the former **Mascot Saloon** on Broadway (May & Sept daily

8am–6pm; June–Aug 8am–8pm; free), and **Moore House**, Fifth Avenue at Spring Street (May–Sept daily 10am–noon & 1–5pm; $2), now a city museum. There's further detail in the recently refurbished **Skagway Museum and Archive** (May–Sept daily 9am–5pm; $2) which contains the Trail of 98 Museum.

About a mile and a half north of town, the **Gold Rush Cemetery** is the final resting place of many of the stampeders. Among them are Soapy Smith and Frank Reid, who, according to his gravestone, "gave his life for the honor of Skagway"; a local prostitute, on the other hand, is remembered for "giving her honor for the life of Skagway."

If you've had enough of Soapy and his cronies, you may feel like **hiking**; one of the best short trails leads from the cemetery to the 300ft high Reid Falls. The useful *Skagway Trail Map*, available from the visitor center, details other walks in the area, including those in the Dewey Lakes system, which pass pretty subalpine lakes and tumbling waterfalls, and the more difficult scramble uphill to Denver Glacier. Sockeye Cycles, 5th Avenue and Broadway (☎907/983-2851, ⑩www.cyclealaska.com), rents out well-maintained **mountain bikes**, and the neighboring Mountain Shop (☎907/983-2544) rents and sells backpacking supplies.

A lazier way to take in the scenery is on the **White Pass and Yukon Route** railway (early May to late Sept; 3–7 departures daily; ☎907/983-2217 or 1-800/343-7373, ⑩www.whitepassrailroad.com), which follows the gushing Skagway River upstream past waterfalls and ice-packed gorges and over a 1000ft high wooden trestle bridge, stopping at the Canadian border ($82 round-trip) before occasionally continuing on to Lake Bennett, British Columbia ($128). There's no shortage of riders, so get there early and grab a seat on the left-hand side going up. The company also offers a through bus service to Whitehorse after a train ride to Fraser, British Columbia ($95 one-way).

The Chilkoot Trail

Alaska's most famous trail, the 33-mile **Chilkoot Trail**, is a hike through one huge wilderness museum following the footsteps of the original Klondike prospectors. Starting in **DYEA**, nine miles from Skagway, and ending in **BENNETT** in Canada, the trail climbs through rainforest to tundra often strewn with haunting reminders of the past, including ancient boilers that once drove aerial tramways, and several collapsed huts.

The three- to five-day hike can be strenuous, especially the final ascent up from Sheep Camp (1000ft) to Chilkoot Pass (3550ft). You must be self-sufficient for food, fuel and shelter, and be prepared for foul weather. Campgrounds line the trail, as well as emergency shelters with stoves and firewood. There are also ranger stations at Dyea, Sheep Camp and Lindeman City. Dyea is accessible by road, and the White Pass and Yukon Railway runs a service for hikers returning to Skagway for $65.

The main hiking season runs from July to early September, when there is a quota system: for details call Parks Canada (☎867/667-3910 or 1-800/661-0486) or consult ⑩www.nps.gov/klgo/chilkoot.htm. Whether you have a reservation or not, you must first visit the Skagway **Trail Center**, Broadway at 1st Avenue (late May to early Sept daily 8am–4.15pm), where rangers make sure you understand the challenges and dangers, and can advise on weather conditions and current bus and train schedules for the trip back to Skagway. While here you must also pay out a rather extravagant Can$40 for a Canadian permit.

Eating and drinking

Most of Skagway's **bars** and **restaurants** line the touristy part of Broadway. A few blocks away, at the corner of Sixth Avenue and Broadway, the *Days of 98 Show* is an entertaining historical musical about Soapy Smith ($12).

Corner Café State St at 4th Ave ☏907/983-2155. Daytime diner much favored by Skagway's outdoor set serving stuffed croissants with salad or soup for $7, or halibut burger for $8.

Mabel G Smith's 342 5th Ave at Broadway ☏907/983-2609. Low-key espresso bar with the best coffee in town and glazed pumpkin cookies that have a reputation throughout the north.

Red Onion Saloon Broadway at 2nd Ave ☏907/983-2222. An 1898 bar and former bordello with heaps of character, draft beers and excellent pizza.

Stowaway Café 205 Congress Way ☏907/982-3463. Quality daytime take-outs such as hot soup (from $3), wraps or a blackened chicken Caesar ($5.50), then evening meals with harbor views: expect seafood gumbo ($17), sweet and sour vegetables ($15), and pecan pie ($6).

Anchorage

Wedged between the two arms of Cook Inlet and the imposing Chugach Mountains, **ANCHORAGE** is home to over forty percent of Alaska's population, and serves as the transportation center for the whole state. This sprawling city on the edge of one of the world's great wildernesses often gets a bad press from those who live elsewhere in Alaska – derided as being "just half an hour from Alaska" – but it has its attractions, and with its beautiful setting can make a pleasant one- or two-day stopover.

By the time Captain James Cook came up what is now Cook Inlet in 1778, in search of a Northwest Passage to the Atlantic, Russian fur trappers had already started to settle the area, trading copper and iron for fish and furs with the Native Americans. Though Cook was sure that the inlet was not the Passage, he sent boats out in a southeasterly direction to investigate. When they were forced to turn back by the severe tides, Cook named this gloriously scenic stretch **Turnagain Arm**.

Anchorage itself began life in 1915 as a tent city for construction workers on the Alaska Railroad. During the 1930s, hopefuls fleeing the Depression came pouring in from the Lower 48, and World War II – and the construction of the Alaska Highway – further boosted the city's size and importance. The opening of the airport established Anchorage – equidistant between New York and Tokyo – as the "Crossroads of the World," and statehood in 1959 brought in yet more optimistic adventurers.

Arrival, information and accommodation

Anchorage Airport, seven miles southwest of town, is served by the Borealis Shuttle service (☏907/276-3600 or 1-888/436-3600) which costs $10 for two to downtown: a taxi costs around $15. The **train station** is downtown at 411 W First Ave (☏907/265-2494 or 1-800/544-0552), and the major sights are easily reached on foot. People Mover **buses** cover the city daily between 6am and 10pm for a $1.25 flat fare ($2.50 day-pass from the driver), though they're a rare sight on Sundays.

The **Log Cabin Visitor Center**, downtown at Fourth and F (daily: April, May & Sept 8am–6pm; June–Aug 7.30am–7pm; Oct–March 9am–4pm; ☏907/274-3531, ✆www.anchorage.net), has all the brochures you could need and details of an easy self-guided downtown walking tour. Across the street, the **Alaska Public Lands Information Center** (June–Aug daily 9am–5.30pm;

rest of year Mon–Fri 10am–5.30pm; ☏907/271-2737, ⓦwww.nps.gov/aplic) has an excellent natural history display plus maps and more brochures. It can help plan trips into the Interior, and make reservations both for accommodation and the shuttle bus to Denali National Park – important in summer.

Accommodation

Inexpensive **accommodation** in Anchorage can be hard to find, especially in summer, and many places are reserved months in advance. **Campers** should head for the central *Ship Creek Landings RV Park*, 150 N Ingra (☏907/227-0877, ⓦwww.alaskarv.com; $15), or the more woodsy *Centennial Park* (☏907/333-9711; $13), five miles north on Glenn Highway.

Alaskan Samovar Inn 720 Gambell St ☏907/277-1511 or 1-800/478-1511. No-nonsense motel close to downtown with cable TV and spa baths. ❺

Anchor Inn 326 L St ☏907277-2624, ⓔanchorin@alaska.net. Small B&B with tree-obscured views of Cook Inlet and rooms each with a large bed, sofa, cable TV, and most with a kitchenette. There's an enticing deck out the front and internet access is available. ❻

Earth B&B 1001 W 12th Ave ☏907/279-9907, ⓦwww.alaskaone.com/earthbb. A B&B unlike any other, enthusiastically and liberally run by multilingual Dutch émigré, Margriet, who makes the place a home-away-from-home for Denali-bound climbers during the season and a broad cross-section of folk for the rest of the year. Bus #6, #36 or #60 from downtown. ❺

HI-Anchorage 700 H St ☏907/276-3635, ⓕ907/276-7772, ⓦwww.alaska.net/~hianch. Functional and very central hostel with luggage storage, internet access and laundry along with a daytime lockout and evening curfew. Dorm beds $16 (nonmembers $19). Reserve well ahead in summer. ❶

Inlet Inn 539 H St ☏907-277-5541, ⓕ907/277-3108. The cheapest rooms downtown, with airport transfer, cable TV and free local calls, though the decor leaves a bit to be desired. ❹

Qupqugiac Inn 640 W 36th Ave, midtown ☏907/562-5681, ⓦwww.qupq.com. Great budget hotel with clean, simple rooms each with phone and satellite TV, and a communal lounge area with self-catering facilities. Bus #9 from downtown passes within a block, along Arctic Blvd. Rooms with bath ❺, without ❹

Spenard Hostel 2845 W 42nd Place ☏907/248-5036, ⓦwww.alaskalife.net/spnrdhstl/hostel.html. Well-organized and friendly hostel in a residential suburb with nearby mall just a mile and a half from the airport (bus #6). $10 bike rental, no curfew or lockout, and dorm beds for $15. ❶

Voyager Hotel 501 K St at 5th Ave ☏907/277-9501 or 1-800/247-9070, ⓦwww.voyagerhotel.com. The best of the mid- to upper-range hotels featuring spacious rooms (with a kitchenette) and most of the facilities of the large business hotels at much lower cost. Reserve well in advance in summer. ❽

The City

Travelers eager to rush off into the "real" Alaska tend to overlook cosmopolitan Anchorage – a blend of old and new, urban blight and rural parks – but there is plenty to see, and it's worth spending some time here experiencing big-city Alaska. The city is laid out on a grid; numbered avenues run east–west, lettered streets north–south.

Your first stop should be the **Anchorage Museum of History and Art**, 121 W Seventh Ave (summer Sun–Fri 9am–9pm, Sat 9am–6pm; rest of year Tues–Sat 10am–6pm, Sun 1–5pm; $6.50), an excellent overview of the state and its history told through intricate dioramas, alongside beautiful examples of carved ivory and basketware. The art gallery is notable for the works by Alaska's best known painter, Sydney Laurence, particularly his monumental oil painting of Mount McKinley.

The rest of the downtown sites are more modest: the **Imaginarium**, 737 W Fifth Ave (daily: June to early Sept 10am–6pm; early Sept to May Mon–Sat 10am–6pm, Sun noon–5pm; $5), has hands-on displays telling you all about glaciers, the Northern Lights, polar bears and the private life of the dopey-looking

ANCHORAGE

Fish Hatchery
OIL WELL ROAD
Native Heritage Centre

POST RD
REEVE BLVD
COMMERCIAL DR
Ship Creek
GLENN HIGHWAY
Centennial Park

See 'Downtown Anchorage' map
E. 3RD AV
W 3RD AV
W 5TH AV
E 5TH AV
GAMBELL ST
INGRA ST
St Innocent Russian Orthodox Church

Knik Arm

Merrill Field
Russian Jack Springs Park
DEBARR RD
DEBARR RD

15TH AV
C STREET
A STREET

Westchester Lagoon
Tony Knowles Coastal Trail

Earthquake Park
FIREWEED LANE
A
Chester Creek Greenbelt
Chester Creek

NORTHERN LIGHTS BLVD
B
W 36th AV
E 36th AV
C
Lake Otis
NORTHERN LIGHTS BLVD
Goose Lake
NORTHERN LIGHTS BLVD

Fish Creek
SPENARD
2

Lake Hood
3
Lake Spenard
TUDOR ROAD
University of Alaska Anchorage
Alaska Native Medical Center
TUDOR ROAD

Seaplane Base
INTERNATIONAL AIRPORT ROAD
North Fork Campbell Creek
TUDOR RD

International Airport
W. RASPBERRY ROAD
C STREET
SEWARD HIGHWAY
Bicentennial Park

Sand Lake
Campbell Field

OWL LAKE ROAD
MINNESOTA DR
LAKE OTIS PKWY
ABBOTT LOOP ROAD
South Fork Campbell Creek

Jewel Lake
E. DIMOND BLVD
Hillside Park Ski Area

Dimond Transit Center
ABBOTT ROAD
BIRCH ROAD
HILLSIDE DRIVE
UPPER HUFFMAN RD

W. DIMOND BLVD
ABBOTT LOOP RD

Campbell Lake
C STREET
MINNESOTA DRIVE
O MALLEY ROAD
Zoo

ACCOMMODATION
Qupqugiac Inn — 2
Ship Creek Landing RV Park — 1
Spenard Hostel — 3

RESTAURANTS & CLUBS
Chilkoot Charlie's — A
Moose's Tooth — C
Mr. Whitekey's Fly by Night Club — B

O MALLEY ROAD
Little Campbell Creek
N
0 — 1 mile

BRAGAW STREET
LAKE OTIS HWY
HUFFMAN ROAD
HUFFMAN RD
DE ARMOUR ROAD
DE ARMOUR RD
Rabbit Creek

Girdwood (25 miles) & Seward (115 miles) ▼

DOWNTOWN ANCHORAGE

W. 1ST AVE
Train Station
0 — 200 yards

W. 2ND AVE
W. 2ND AVE
N

Tony Knowles Coastal Trail
Captain Cook Monument — D
W. 3RD AVE
Public Lands Information Center (APLIC)
Hilton Hotel
Saturday Market

Resolution Park
4
Elderberry Park

Oscar Anderson House
W. 4TH AVE
Imaginarium
4th Avenue Theatre
Egan Center
Bronze Dog Sled Statue
Cyrano's Off-Center Playhouse

E
F
i
Town Square Park
Alaska State Trooper Museum
Wolf Song

5
W. 5TH AVE
6
G
Performing Arts Center
H
I
Anchorage Museum of History and Art

W. 6TH AVE
Oomingmak Musk Ox Producers' Co-op
Transit Center
Alaska Experience Center
J
Federal Building

ACCOMMODATION
Alaskan Samovar Inn — 7
Anchor Inn — 4
Earth B&B — 9
HI-Anchorage — 8
Inlet Inn — 6
Voyager Hotel — 5

W. 7TH AVE
8
W. 8TH AVE

RESTAURANTS & BARS
Bernie's Bungalow — I
Darwin's Theory — G
Federal Building Cafeteria — J
Glacier Brewhouse — F
Humpy's — H
The Marx Bros Café — D
Snow City Cafe — E

W. 9TH AVE
Delaney Park (aka The Park Strip)
▼ 9 & L'Aroma (400 yds)

moose; the period-furnished 1915 **Oscar Anderson House Museum**, 420 M St (June to mid-Sept Tues–Sat 11am–4pm ; $3), illustrates early Anchorage life; and the **Alaska Experience Center**, Sixth Avenue and G Street (summer daily 9am–9pm; $10), presents forty minutes of Alaska's best scenery, shot from choppers and beamed onto a 180° wraparound screen, and the admission price includes a film of the devastating 1964 Good Friday earthquake that leveled much of downtown – 9.2 on the Richter scale and North America's strongest-ever quake.

Six miles to the east on the outskirts of town lies the new **Alaska Native Heritage Center**, Muldoon Road exit from the Glenn Hwy (May–Sept daily 9am–9pm; $20). It is expensive and still finding its feet, but provides an excellent introduction to the state's five main ethnic groups. Each is represented by a typical house where Native guides interpret their culture. Throughout the day, cultural groups perform in the main auditorium where there is also an instructive introductory film. The 4th Avenue Trolley runs here hourly from downtown for $6.

On long summer days it is better to stay outside, perhaps strolling (or biking) along the **Tony Knowles Coastal Trail** that offers restorative views of Turnagain Arm, or exploring the mountains and lakes of the 495,000-acre **Chugach State Park**, just fifteen minutes' drive east from Anchorage. Challenging trails traversing the park include an often treacherous scramble to the summit of the 4500ft Flattop Mountain, a spectacular vantage point from which to view the city and Cook Inlet.

Eating, drinking and nightlife

Nowhere in Alaska will you find a more diverse range of places to eat. That's not to say you'd make a special journey for its culinary wonders, but after a few weeks in the state's interior the scene here can seem like heaven. For groceries, make for Carr's supermarket at the junction of Northern Light Boulevard and Minnesota Drive (bus #3, #4 or #36), which has a good deli section.

Good **bars** abound in downtown Anchorage, and the atmosphere varies as much as the clientele. Also visit the lively (and somewhat edgy) neighborhood of **Spenard** – on Spenard Road between Northern Lights Boulevard and International Airport Road – which can be fun as long as you're careful. Women travelers may not find the "bohemian" side of macho Anchorage quite as endearing as many locals seem to think it is, with some innocent-looking bars turning out to be strip joints. Shows, plays, opera and concerts take place at the **Center for Performing Arts** (☎907/263-2787).

Bernie's Bungalow 626 D St at 7th Ave ☎907/276-8808. A very un-Alaskan hangout featuring the "lounge-a-licious" martini and a cocktail bar fashioned from an old wooden house. Latin and jazz grooves the smartly dressed set. Stylish seating is in short supply, so come early.

Chilkoot Charlie's 2435 Spenard Rd ☎907/272-1010. Sawdust-strewn barn that packs them in nightly for pricey drinks, pool, foosball, two floors of DJ-led dance and live music from 9.30pm.

Darwin's Theory 426 G St at 4th Ave ☎907/277-5322. Straightforward local bar good for moderately priced boozing and neighborly encounters with colorful local characters.

The Federal Building Cafeteria 222 W 7th at C St ☎907/277-6736. Breakfast and lunch cafeteria that's about the best budget value downtown, certainly a cut above the fast-food joints and more filling. Steaming clam chowder or one of their entrees cost around $5.

Glacier Brewhouse 737 W 5th St ☎907/274-2739. Hugely popular restaurant, bar and micro-brewery serving wonderful food and drink. At least half a dozen toothsome house-brewed beers accompany alder-wood-baked gourmet pizza ($11), spit-grilled three-peppercorn prime rib ($20), or steamed Alaskan King crabs ($30).

Humpy's 610 W 6th Ave ☎907/276-2337. Popular watering hole with live music and a strong college bar feel. The likes of charbroiled salmon, burgers, soups and salads (mostly under $10) are helped down with local microbrews plus English and Belgian bottled beers, and over thirty top-shelf single malts.

L'Aroma at New Sagaya's City Market 900 W 13th Ave at I St ☎907/274-6173. Trendy and spendy grocery store, deli and café with a great selection that ranges from organic vegetables and great cheeses to pizza, wraps, Thai dishes and good coffee. The nearest groceries to downtown.

The Marx Bros. Café 627 W 3rd Ave ☎907/278-2133. The best all-round fine dining downtown served up in a historic house with views of the water. Start on the likes of sautéed alligator with crawfish tails followed by their signature baked halibut rolled in a macadamia nut crust and curry sauce and chutney. Entrees are around $25.

Moose's Tooth 3300 Old Seward Hwy at 33rd Ave ☎907/258-2537. A perennial favorite, always alive with diners tucking into some of the town's best gourmet pizza.

Mr Whitekey's Fly By Night Club 3300 Spenard Rd at 32nd Ave ☎907/279-7726. Zany cabaret and live music venue which, throughout summer, hosts *The Whale Fat Follies* (June to mid-Sept Tues–Sat 8pm; $12–18; 16 and over only), a satirical and occasionally bawdy slant on Alaska.

Snow City Café 1034 W 4th Ave ☎907/272-6338. Foremost among the city establishments that successfully manage to combine several roles drawing in the coffee set, lunching office workers and pre-theater diners. All-day breakfast – French toast for $5, granola for $3 – are supplemented by Thai halibut, rosemary chicken, cedar plank salmon or vegetarian meatloaf. Live music on Friday night.

Kenai Peninsula and Kodiak Island

South of Anchorage, the Seward Highway hugs the shore of **Turnagain Arm** past the ski resort of **Alyeska** to **Girdwood**. Just beyond, a side road cuts to the ever-popular **Portage Glacier**, and continues through a new tunnel to **Whittier**, little more than a ferry dock for accessing Prince William Sound (see p.1266).

Beyond Portage, the Seward Highway enters the **Kenai Peninsula**, "Anchorage's playground," which at over nine thousand square miles is larger than some states. The peninsula offers up an endless diversity of activities and scenery, mostly concentrated around major communities such as **Seward**, the base for cruises into the inspirational **Kenai Fjords National Park**, and artsy **Homer**, where the waters and shorelines of the glorious **Kachemak Bay State Park** are the main destination.

Most Alaskans come to the Kenai Peninsula to **fish**: the Kenai, Russian and Kasilof rivers host "combat fishing," with thousands of anglers standing elbow to elbow using strength and know-how to pull in thirty-pound-plus king salmon. **Campgrounds** along the rivers fill up fast, especially in July and August.

A hundred miles beyond Homer in the Gulf of Alaska, the "Emerald Isle" of **Kodiak Island** offers some of Alaska's most uncommon and pleasing landscapes, and is home to the **Kodiak bear**, an overgrown subspecies of the grizzly.

Girdwood and Portage Glacier

Outdoorsy **GIRDWOOD**, 37 miles south of Anchorage, lies two miles inland in the shade of the **Alyeska Resort** (ⓦwww.alyeskaresort.com; $45), Alaska's largest winter sports complex and the lowest-elevation ski resort in the world – Mount Alyeska's 3939ft summit rises from just 270 feet above sea level. Downhill runs and an extensive night-skiing operation run from November to mid-April, and in summer you can ride the Alyeska Tramway ($16) up to stunning views and some good hiking territory. Girdwood Ski and Cyclery, Mile

1.5 Alyeska Highway (☎907/783-2453; closed Mon & Tues), rent mountain **bikes** ($25 a day) to explore the surrounding trails, and Class V Whitewater (☎907/783-2004, ⊛www.alaskanrafting.com) run a range of **rafting** trips from gentle scenic float trips on the Portage River (3hr; $50) to serious Class III–V whitewater on the Six-Mile River ($65–130).

The resort's *Alyeska Prince Hotel* (☎907/754-1111 or 1-800/880-3880; ❼) is a grand ski lodge with half a dozen good restaurants and service to match. Alternatively, try the Austrian-run *Alyeska View B&B*, Vail Drive (☎907/783-2747, ⊛www.alyeskaview.com; ❺), or *Alyeska Home Hostel* (☎907/783-2099; ❶), with $10 loft beds. There's inexpensive **food** at *Chair Five* in Girdwood (☎907/783-2500; daily 11am–2am) or the unmissable *Double Musky Inn* on Crow Creek Road (☎907/783-2822): budget on $25 a head and a meal to remember.

Eleven miles south of Girdwood, a road leads to Whittier, past **Portage Glacier**, an unbearably popular day-tour from Anchorage. Frustratingly, you can't see the glacier from the parking lot; instead you must pay Gray Line $25 for a cruise around the lake's corner to the glacier's snout. Two USFS **campgrounds** ($10) can be found two or three miles back down the road.

Seward and the Kenai Fjords National Park

SEWARD, ringed by glaciers and mountains 127 miles south of Anchorage, sprang to life in 1903 after engineers declared this ice-free port the ideal starting point for railroad tracks to the Interior. Since then it has been a key freight terminal, but tourism – particularly cruises into Kenai Fjords National Park – is now its most conspicuous business.

Seward's main activities are enjoying the scenery and visiting the wonders at the waterfront **SeaLife Center** (daily: summer 8am–8pm; rest of year 10am–5pm; $12.50), a successful marriage of marine research and visitor education partly funded by the Exxon Valdez oil spill settlement. The center offers the chance to watch ongoing cold water research in action and marvel at the underwater antics of stellar sea lions, harbor seals and adorable puffins. After a visit to the center, another good local option is the four-hour hike up nearby **Mount Marathon** for some glorious views. The trail here is also the scene of an annual Fourth of July race thanks to the antics of two pioneers who, in 1909, bet each other to run up and down the 3022-foot mountain – the current race record is 43 minutes 23 seconds.

Most visitors also drive thirteen miles out to **Exit Glacier**, one of the few in the state you can approach on land. From the ranger station at the end of the track, a short stroll leads to the still-active glacier, though signs warn you back from the ice wall and its inviting blue clefts. Exit Glacier is part of the **KENAI FJORDS NATIONAL PARK**, a magnificent 580,000-acre region of peaks, glaciers and craggy coastline. Its towering mountains are mantled by the prodigious three-hundred-square-mile Harding Icefield, feeding the three dozen retreating glaciers that have exposed the dramatic fjords after which the park is named.

Eight of these tidewater glaciers "calve" icebergs into the sea with thunderous booms, and the fjords also hold a wealth of **marine wildlife** – sea otters, porpoises, seals, stellar sea lions, plus orca, gray, humpback and minke whales – as well as the seabird rookeries on the cliffs of the Chiswell Islands. The best of the **cruises** from Seward are conducted aboard the large boats of Kenai Fjords Tours (☎1-800/468-8068; $54–139); pay out for the longer day-tours which go right up to the calving tidewater glaciers.

The park's **visitor center**, 1212 Fourth Ave in Seward's small-boat harbor (summer Mon–Fri 8am–6pm, Sat 9am–5pm, Sun 9am–4pm; rest of year Mon–Fri 8am–5pm; ☎907/224-8051), provides maps, film shows and details on regional hikes.

Practicalities

Trains from Anchorage arrive and depart daily (☎1-800/544-0552; $90 round-trip) at the depot next to the dock for **ferries** from Valdez and Kodiak. Seward Bus Line (☎907/224-3608) charges $30 for a one-way ride from Anchorage. Seward's two hubs of activity, the small-boat harbor and downtown, are joined by the mile-long Fourth Avenue; if you don't feel like walking, hop on the **local trolley** (daily 10am–7pm every 30min; $1.50, day-pass $3). The main **visitor center** is at Mile 2 Seward Highway (summer Mon–Fri 8am–5pm, Sat 8am–6pm, Sun 9am–4pm; rest of year Mon–Fri 8am–5pm; ☎907/224-8051, ⓦwww.seward.net/chamber).

One of the best downtown **accommodation** options is the *Sauerdough Lodging*, 225 4th Ave (☎907/224-8946 or 1-877/224-8946, ⓦwww.sauerdoughlodging.com; ❺–❼), with small and highly individual shared-bath rooms as well as suites with clawfoot baths and twelve-foot ceilings: all come with a sumptuous continental breakfast. For something cheaper try the *Moby Dick Hostel*, 432 Third Ave (☎907/224-7072, ⓦwww.mobydickhostel.com; ❶ & ❹), with bunks ($16.50), limited kitchen facilities, and private rooms (some with kitchenettes). Or head out to the lovely log *Alaska's Treehouse B&B*, off Timber Street at Mile 7 Seward Highway (☎907/224-3867, ⓦseward.net/treehouse; ❹), which offers a hot tub and sauna and great breakfasts. There's also the excellent and central *Beachfront* **campground** (☎907/224-4055; $6), off Ballaine Boulevard on the shores of Resurrection Bay.

Eating in Seward is fairly reasonably priced: for a coffee or light meal make for *Resurrect Art*, 320 Third Ave, a coffee house and gallery in a former church. More substantial eating is best done at the seafood oriented *Harbor Dinner Club* on Fifth Avenue (☎907/224-3012), or the upscale *Ray's Waterfront Bar and Grill*, by the harbor (summer only; ☎907/224-3012), which has nice views and big steak and seafood dinners for around $20.

Homer

HOMER, 226 miles south from Anchorage, is the Kenai Peninsula's southernmost road-accessible town. It commands a truly magnificent setting, spread beneath gently sloping verdant bluffs with a four-mile finger of land – **The Spit** – slinking out into the dark waters of Kachemak Bay, into which flow crystal-blue glaciers, framed by dense black forest. With abundant activities, a lively nightlife, and a varied, youthful population that supports a thriving arts community, it's so appealing you'll probably want to scrap your itinerary and linger a few days extra.

Russians, drawn by the abundance of coal, were the first whites to reach the area, and by the mid-1800s several American companies had followed suit. In 1896, **Homer Pennock**, a gold-seeker from Michigan, set up the community that still bears his name. Every summer in recent years, young people from the Lower 48 have arrived here in droves to work on the halibut boats or in the cannery, many living in an impromptu tent city on the beach.

Arrival, information and getting around

Ferries arrive at the end of the Spit from Seldovia, Kodiak and Seward. Homer Stage Lines (☎907/235-2252) runs a daily **bus** service between Anchorage and Homer for $45 each way.

Most hotels, restaurants and shops are in town, while almost all of the fishing charter and tour operators can be found along the twee boardwalks of the Spit. In summer, the infrequent Homer Trolley links the two, though it may be quicker to hitch or rent a mountain bike from Homer Saw & Cycle, 1532 Ocean Drive (☏907/235-8406; $25 per day). The main **visitor center** is at 135 Sterling Hwy (summer Mon–Fri 9am–8pm, Sat & Sun 10am–6pm; ☏907/235-7740, ⊛homeralaska.org).

Accommodation

Homer's good-value **hotels** and **B&Bs** are often fully booked in midsummer; the visitor center, though, can help if you arrive without reservations. There's **camping** on the Spit beach for $6 and at the wooded *Karen Hornaday Hillside Campground*, Campground Road (☏907/235-1583; $6).

Chocolate Drop Inn Mile 6 East End Rd ☏907/235-3668 or 1-800/530-6015, ⊛www .chocolatedropinn.com. Homer's finest inn, located on a hillside facing Kachemak Bay and with a spacious lounge, recreation room, sauna and hot tub and gorgeous breakfasts. One room ❻, others ❼–❽.

Driftwood Inn 135 W Bunnel Ave ☏907/235-8019 or 1-800/478-8019, ⊛www.thedriftwoodinn .com. Characterful older hotel with an extensive and varied range of rooms, RV parking, and a communal TV lounge with video library. Breakfast is not included, though there is free tea and coffee and breakfast is available. Private bath ❹–❺, shared bath ❸–❹

Historic Old Town B&B 106 W Bunnell Ave ☏907/235-7558, ⊛www.xyz.net/~oldtown.

Beautiful B&B located in a 1936 building, with wooden-floor rooms all with a restrained antique decor and tremendous sea views. Breakfast is served in the *Two Sisters* bakery downstairs. ❻

Seaside Farm Hostel Mile 5 East End Rd ☏907/235-7850. Excellent hostel on a small farm with a large outdoor cooking and lounge area, camping ($6), bunks ($15) and some great cabins (❷). Closed Oct to May. ❶–❷

Sun Spin 358 Lee Drive ☏907/235-6677 or 1-800/391-6677, ⊛www.sunspin.com. Spacious B&B with accommodation in a shared bunkroom ($28 per person), and private rooms (❹–❺). There's a barbecue area, and rates include airport or ferry pickup and a large breakfast ($6 extra if you are in a bunkroom). ❶–❺

The Town and around

The downtown **Pratt Museum**, 3779 Bartlett St (daily 10am–6pm; $6), features high-quality works by local craftspeople, as well as Inuit and other Native artifacts, aquariums and historic Homer oddities. Many of Homer's most popular activities, however, revolve around the Spit. To Alaskan anglers, Homer is "Halibut Central": a full day's fishing excursion with any of the charter companies begins at around $140. If you don't mind joining the crowds, it's cheaper and simpler to visit the **Fishing Hole**, a tiny bight on the Spit, which is stocked with salmon and offers good fishing from mid-May to mid-September.

The prime tourist attraction in the Homer area is exploring the 250,000 acres of forested mountains, glaciers, pristine fjords and inlets that comprise **Kachemak Bay State Park**, directly across the bay from Homer. Bird species here include puffin, auklets, kittiwakes and storm petrels, and marine creatures such as seals, sea otters and whales are also plentiful. Rainbow Tours on Cannery Row (☏907/235-7272) operates two-hour sightseeing cruises ($20) to **Gull Island** – a 15,000-strong rookery. The most popular destination is the gorgeous hamlet of **Halibut Cove**, where boardwalks link art galleries and *The Saltry* restaurant: the *Danny J* ferry (☏907/235-7847) makes two daily trips to Halibut Cove, on the south shore of the bay, via Gull Island rookery, for $44 round-trip, $22 if you book in for an evening meal.

The area's best trails, most of them manageable in a day, are those in the Kachemak Bay State Park on the south side of Kachemak Bay: pick up the park's hiking trails leaflet ($1) and other information from the **Alaska National Marine Wildlife Refuge**, 202 Pioneer Ave in Homer (☎907/235-6546). The most-traveled route, up to **Grewingk Glacier**, is an easy three-and-a-half-mile trek above the spruce and cottonwood forest to the foot of the glacier, from where you get splendid views of the bay.

Eating and drinking

Not surprisingly, Homer's culinary scene focuses most on fresh fish. For **nightlife**, head out to a colorful bar or to the relaxed **Pier One Theater** (May–Sept; ☎907/235-7333), next to the fishing hole on the Spit.

Cactus Café The Spit ☎907/235-0721. Great take-out café with some outdoor seating for tucking into your halibut burrito ($6), ginger curry tofu wrap ($6), fruit smoothie ($3.50) or espresso. Closed Sun.

Café Cups 162 Pioneer Ave ☎907/235-8330. Relaxing yet vibrant café serving some of the best coffee and great sandwiches and salads.

Two Sisters Espresso/Bakery 106 W Bunnell Ave ☎907/235-2280. Great little spot for that morning coffee either in the diminutive bakery or at tables out on the small deck. Good too for pizza, soups and quiches at moderate prices.

The Homestead Mile 8.2 East Rd ☎907/235-

8723. Open for dinner nightly for crab-and-shrimp cakes ($13) followed by Mediterranean pasta ($20), half a pound of King crab ($23) or sautéed scallops ($21).

Lands End Resort at the end of the Spit ☎907/235-0400 or 1-800/478-0400. Plush and pricey restaurant offering an absolutely wonderful view of the bay. Breakfast is a must.

Salty Dawg The Spit. No self-respecting drinker should pass up a few jars in the *Dawg* with its dark interior, life preservers pinned to the wall, and what is reliably claimed to be the only surveyors' benchmark located in a bar in the US.

Kodiak

A nine-hour ferry ride connects Homer with **KODIAK ISLAND**, the second largest island in the US (after Hawaii's Big Island). In the north it is thick with spruce forests, but the interior is carpeted by wild grasses studded with marshes, lumpy knolls and reeded lakes. This is prime territory for the renowned **Kodiak bear**, a subspecies of the brown/grizzly, which weighs up to 1500 pounds. Streams chock-full of spawning salmon allow these monsters to thrive in the **Kodiak National Wildlife Refuge**, covering the southwestern two-thirds of the island. Roughly ten bears inhabit each square mile around Red and Fraser lakes, and bear-watching trips are big business. In addition to *Ursus*, the Emerald Isle provides a favorable habitat for **bald eagles**, and as many as two million seabirds nest along the fjords, bights and bays. Accommodation in the nine **wilderness cabins** ($35 a night) dotted throughout the island is drawn by lottery each year; for details, contact Kodiak NWR, 1390 Buskin River Rd, Kodiak, AK 99615 (April–Sept Mon–Fri 8am–4.30pm, Sat noon–4.30pm; ☎907/487-2600).

The warm **Japanese Current** that flows around the island supports a mild maritime climate along with plenty of rain and fog, creating poor flying conditions and the distinct possibility that your stay could be extended by a day or two. If you want to avoid peak-season prices, note that May and June are notoriously wet but September weather is usually fairly reliable.

All but two thousand of the island's 12,000 inhabitants live in and around its only major town, the likeable and busy fishing port of **KODIAK** on the northeastern tip. Before Russian explorers established a community here in 1792, Aleut and Alutiiq had fished the area for millennia. After Alaska was transferred to the US, Kodiak survived as a center for trappers, whale-hunters and salmon-fishers, and in 1939 was just another sleepy Alaskan village when a massive war base was established here and the population rocketed to around 50,000. However, most of Kodiak's wealth comes from fishing the rich waters of the Gulf, and the town maintains a fleet of over 2700 fishing vessels. Tourism definitely plays second fiddle; few cruise ships stop, but this bustling little town has a splendid range of activities, good B&Bs and a lively nightlife.

Arrival, information and getting around

Ferries dock downtown once a week. Alaska Airlines and ERA Aviation jointly dispatch eight one-hour flights a day from Anchorage at around $290 round-trip. The local bus runs five miles into town roughly every ninety minutes (not Sun) for $2. The most practical way to explore the island is to **fly**; Uyak Air's Kodiak trips (☎907/486-3407 or 1-800/303-3407), which guarantee close-up views of bears or your money back, have never had to refund the $400-plus fee.

The helpful **visitor center** is by the ferry dock at 100 Marine Way (June–Aug daily 8am–5pm and later if there is a late ferry arrival; Sept–May Mon–Fri 8am–5pm; ☎907/486-4782, ⓦwww.kodiak.org) and the **Kodiak National Wildlife Refuge Visitor Center**, close to the airport, four miles south of town (April–Sept Mon–Fri 8am–4.30pm, Sat noon–4.30pm; ☎907/487-2600), stocks a wealth of information on bears and the backcountry.

Accommodation

Most **lodging** in Kodiak is expensive, but the hotels and B&Bs are generally very good. The best place to **camp** is in *Fort Abercrombie State Historical Park*, four miles north of town ($10). There's no hostel, so the cheapest rooms are at the *Shelikof Lodge*, 211 Thorsheim Ave (☎907/486-4141; ❹), though you may prefer the well-located *Harborview B&B*, 312 W Rezanof Drive (☎907/486-2464 or 1-888/283-2464, ⓦwww.ptialaska.net/~kodiakfk; ❹), with home-cooked breakfast, cable TV, and one room (❻) with a wonderful view of the harbor. The flashest rooms are at the *Best Western Kodiak Inn*, 236 W Rezanof Drive (☎907/486-5712 or 1-888/563-4254, ⓦwww.ptialaska.net/~kodiakin; ❼), with all the expected amenities.

The Town and around

Downtown Kodiak is usually lively, with plenty of comings and goings in the small-boat harbor and adjacent bars and cafés on Marine Way. The small **Baranov Museum** (June–Aug Mon–Fri 10am–4pm, Sat & Sun noon–4pm; Sept–Jan, March–May Mon–Wed & Fri 10am–4pm, Sat noon–3pm; $2), in an old Russian house opposite the dock, holds Aleut, Russian and American pioneer artifacts, including an impressive collection of whale bones. Nearby, the small but beautifully formed **Alutiiq Museum**, 218 Mission Rd (June–Aug Mon–Sat 10am–6pm, Sun 11am–4pm; Sept–May Tues–Sat 10am–4pm; $2), centers on the life and culture of the island's native people.

Etched out of lush rainforest, less than four miles north, **Fort Abercrombie State Historical Park** is a great place to do some seabird- and **whale-watching**, camp or take a shoreline hike: a meadow at the north end provides a dazzling blaze of color in summer. Other moderately easy **hiking trails** originating near town go to the top of Pillar Mountain and Termination Point. However, most trails are not maintained and can be confusing; get precise details from the visitor center or the rangers at Fort Abercrombie. The undulating and unpaved **Chiniak Highway** runs for 48 miles to Cape Greville and the *Road's End Café*, sweeping through tightly bunched spruce and passing many abandoned World War II defenses, plus prime vistas of Chiniak Bay.

Eating and drinking

Food in Kodiak is generally good, and not overpriced: *Harborside Coffee & Goods*, 216 Shelikof St (☎907/486-5862), offers coffee, pastries, soups and muffins; *El Chicano*, 103 Center Ave (☎907/486-6116), presents faintly Americanized Mexican dishes at very reasonable prices; and *The Chart Room*, inside the *Best Western* at 236 W Rezanof Drive (☎907/486-5712), has Kodiak's most formal dining, serving king crab legs ($30) or halibut steaks ($17) with good harbor views. *Henry's Great Alaskan Restaurant*, 512 Marine Way (☎907/486-3313), is the downtown entertainment hub, open from 11am until the fun runs out.

Prince William Sound

Prince William Sound, a largely unspoiled wilderness of steep fjords and mountains, glaciers and rainforest, rests calmly at the head of the Gulf of Alaska. Sheltered by the Chugach Mountains in the north and east, and the Kenai Peninsula in the west, and with its sparkling blue waters full of whales, porpoise, sea otters and seals, the Sound has a relatively low-key tourist industry. The only significant settlements, spectacular **Valdez**, at the end of the trans-Alaska oil pipeline, and to a lesser extent **Cordova**, a fishing community only accessible by sea or air, are the respective bases from which to see the **Columbia** and **Childs glaciers**.

The region's first settlers, the Chugach Eskimos, were edged out by the more aggressive Tlingit, who in turn were displaced first by Russian trappers in search of sea otter pelts, and then by American gold prospectors and fishers. The whole glorious show was very nearly spoiled forever on Good Friday 1989, when the **Exxon Valdez** spilled its cargo of 11 million gallons of crude oil. Although the long-term effects have yet to be fully determined, the spill fortunately affected just a fifth of the Sound and today no surface pollution is visible.

Valdez

VALDEZ, 304 road miles from Anchorage and the northernmost ice-free port in the western hemisphere, lies at the head of a fjord that reaches inland twelve miles from Prince William Sound. Known as "Little Switzerland" due to its stunning backdrop of steep mountains, glaciers and waterfalls, and a record annual snowfall of over forty feet, Valdez (pronounced *val-Deez*) offers great hiking, rafting, sea kayaking, wildlife-viewing and, of course, fishing.

The 1890s **Gold Rush** transformed Valdez from a remote whaling station into a flourishing settlement, when thousands of prospectors arrived to head over the deadly Valdez and Klutina glaciers on the Valdez Trail to the mines in the Yukon. Only three hundred of the 3500 miners who set out made it to the goldfield – those that did not perish from frostbite and starvation gave up. Valdez came to depend on fish canneries, logging and occasional military use for its economic survival, and nature conspired to finish it off on Good Friday 1964: the epicenter of North America's largest **earthquake** (see p.1259) was just 45 miles away. Shockwaves turned the ground to quivering jelly, snapping roads, toppling buildings and killing 33 residents. However, the citizens of

Valdez refused to be intimidated, and moved sixty-odd buildings to the more stable present site four miles away.

The town's fortunes rose again during the 1970s, when oil was found beneath Prudhoe Bay, and Valdez became the southern terminus of the 800-mile **trans-Alaska pipeline**, which carries up to two million barrels of oil per day. Although winds and tides ensured that no oil from the *Exxon Valdez* made it into the port of Valdez, ironically the spill triggered an economic boom for the city as it was the most accessible site from which to direct the massive **cleanup**. The operation, which lasted into 1991, cost Exxon and the government over one hundred billion dollars, and called on eleven thousand workers in over one thousand boats and three hundred planes to scour the beaches.

Arrival and information

One of the most exciting things about Valdez is getting here; both car and ferry rides are unforgettable. The **Richardson Highway** holds epic scenery: restful alpine meadows, angry-looking waterfalls, mountain glaciers, the icy summit of **Thompson Pass** and the waterfall-fringed **Keystone Canyon**. Alaskon Express, based at the *Westmark Hotel*, 100 Fidalgo Drive (☎907/835-4391), plies the ten-hour route to Anchorage daily in high season for $71. **Ferries** from Cordova, Whittier or Seward dock at the end of Hazelet Avenue (☎907/835-4436). If the weather is clear, the ride offers superb views of the Columbia Glacier. ERA/Alaska Airlines flies two to four times daily to Anchorage (one-way $85) from the **airport** five miles north. From there, **taxis** (☎907/835-2500) run downtown for around $5.

The central **visitor center** (summer daily 8am–8pm; ☎907/835-4636 or 1-800/770-5954, ⊛www.valdezalaska.org) is at 200 Fairbanks St.

Accommodation

Valdez's **accommodation** gets snapped up pretty quickly, though a free phone (summer only) outside the visitor center connects with some of the fifty-plus **B&Bs**. **Campers** can choose between the central but busy *Bear Paw* campground (☎907/835-2530; $18), and the inconvenient *Valdez Glacier Campground* ($10), seven miles from town past the airport. Fortunately there's also the *Valdez Hostel*, 139 Altina St (☎907/835-2155, ⊛valdezhostel.com; ❷), with three bunks to a room ($22 per person), free tea and coffee, and excellent cooking facilities. For rooms, try the renovated *Keystone Hotel*, 144 Egan Drive (☎907/835-3851 or 1-888/835-0665, ⊛www.alaskan.com/keystonehotel; ❺), which has comfortable rooms with bath and continental breakfast; the motel-style *Downtown B&B*, 113 Galena Drive (☎907/835-2791 or 1-800/478-2791, ⊛www.alaskaone.com/downinn; ❺); *Blueberry Mary's*, 810 Salmonberry Way (☎907/835-5015, ⊛www.alaska.net/~bmary; ❺), a secluded B&B a mile from town with stupendous views of Valdez Arm, comfortable rooms, a sauna and breakfast pancakes with blueberries from the local hillside.

The Town and around

The **Valdez Museum**, 217 Egan Drive (summer daily 8am–6pm; $3), carries just the right amount of detail on the Gold Rush, glaciation, the oil pipeline that supports the town's economy, and a display on the oil spill; and an **annex**, 426 Hazelet St (summer daily 9am–4pm; $1.50), covers the 1964 earthquake at length. Oil industry aficionados will want to take the two-hour **Alyeska Marine Terminal** bus tour (summer 2–4 daily; $16; ☎907/835-2686), which leaves a small visitor center at 212 Tatitlek Street and takes you around the fjord into the $1.4 billion Alyeska pipeline terminal where crude from the arctic is pumped into waiting tankers.

You'll need transport to get to the **Alaskan Cultural Center**, at the airport (daily 9am–6pm; $4), with its astounding collection of carved ivory and an assortment of dead beasts, including a couple of moose hides with Alaskan scenes burned into them by an early pioneer. If you fancy something more active, **mountain bikes** can be rented at Beaver Sports, 316 Galena St (☎907/835-4727), and Keystone Raft and Kayak Adventures, at Mile 17 on the Richardson Highway (☎907/835-2606 or 1-800/328-8460), can take you **rafting** ($50) along the Lowe River as it surges through Keystone Canyon. Out in the Sound, Anadyr Adventures (☎907/835-2814) offers **sea kayaking** among the ice floes and whales from around $90.

While here, you should take a cruise out into Prince William Sound, principally to see the spectacular **Columbia Glacier**, nearly four miles wide at its face and towering three hundred feet above the sea. Unfortunately it is receding rapidly and the fjord is now so choked with ice that you can't get close to the face. You can see it at long range from the Alaska Marine Highway **ferries** running between Valdez and Whittier, but for a closer look at this calving giant go with Prince William Sound Cruises and Tours (☎907/835-4731 or 1-800/992-1297, ⊛www.princewilliamsound.com), who pick their way through a floating icefield and point out such sights as Bligh Reef, where the *Exxon Valdez* ran aground. Choose between a nine-hour cruise that includes a salmon bake, for $119, and a six-hour cruise at $74.

Eating

Don't schedule a gourmet night out while in Valdez, but the **dining** selection will satisfy for the night or two you're here. The best all-round restaurant is *Oscar's*, 143 N Harbor Drive (☎907/835-4700), with its harbor views and varied menu of diner favorites, fast food, and a nightly all-you-can-eat barbecue ($15). Next door, *Mike's Palace* (☎907/835-2365) dishes up Italian-oriented fare along with burgers and Mexican dishes, and oil-boom survivor *The Pipeline Club*, 136 Egan Drive (☎907/835-4332), is worth a try for top-quality steak and seafood, and its lively dark bar.

Cordova and the Copper River Delta

Far quieter than Valdez, and only accessible by sea or air, **CORDOVA** is an unpretentious fishing community set in forests and mountains on the southeastern edge of the Sound. In 1906, the Irish engineer **Michael J. Heney** chose Cordova as the port from which to ship the copper mined in Kennicott (see p.1273), a hundred miles northeast, and gambled on cutting a path between two active glaciers for his proposed Copper River and Northwestern Railroad – the CR&NW – ridiculed at the time as the "Can't Run & Never Will." Nonetheless, in 1911 he spanned the Copper River with the elaborate "**Million Dollar Bridge**" and the railroad was completed. Despite the effort, the mines were exhausted just 27 years later and Cordova shifted its dependency to fishing, which itself was dealt a potentially fatal blow in 1989 with the grounding of the *Exxon Valdez*. For the next two seasons, the community reeled from the effects of the **oil spill**; since then fortunes have improved.

Today the "Million Dollar Bridge," heavily battered by the 1964 earthquake, cuts a lonely figure at the end of the Copper River Highway, a 48-mile gravel road that traverses the wondrous wetlands of the **Copper River Delta**, a major breeding ground for America's migratory birds backed by the Chugach

Mountains. It is a tranquil spot for fishing, bird-watching or **hiking** along many of the excellent trails, such as the difficult trek up to Crater Lake. The road ends right next to the bridge and beside the incredibly active **Childs Glacier**.

By far the best way to experience the bridge is in your own vehicle rented (for around $75 a day, unlimited mileage) from either the *Reluctant Fisherman Inn* (℡907/424-3272) in town or Cordova Auto Rentals (℡907/424-5982) at the airport. Alternatively, Copper River/Northwest Tours (℡907/424-5356) runs a six-hour tour to the bridge for $45 including lunch.

Cordova itself has few sights; the **small-boat harbor** is the core of the town's activity, particularly when the fleet is in, from May until September. The **Cordova Historical Museum** on First Street and Adams Avenue (summer Mon–Sat 10am–6pm, Sun 2–4pm; rest of year Tues–Fri 1–5pm, Sat 2–4pm; $1 donation) has quirky exhibits on local history, including the evolution of the little **ice worm** that lives in the glaciers, and the funky annual festival that celebrates its existence.

Practicalities

There is no road access to Cordova; daily **flights** from Anchorage and Juneau land at the airport twelve miles down the Copper River Highway. A **bus** runs from the airport for $10. Thrice-weekly **ferries** dock a mile north of town. The tiny **Chamber of Commerce** office is on First Street (summer only Mon–Fri 10am–5.30am; ℡907/424-7260, ⓦwww.cordovachamber.com).

Cordova has no **hostel** and the only tent **camping** close to town is at the scruffy *Odiak Camper Park* on Whitshed Road, half a mile south of town (℡907/424-6200; $3 per person). The cheapest option is the low standard *Alaskan Hotel*, 600 First St (℡907/424-3299; ❸), though you may prefer the *Northern Nights Inn*, 501 Third Ave (℡907/424-5356; ❹), or the *Cordova Rose Lodge*, 1315 Whitshed Rd, a mile east of downtown (℡907/424-7673; ❹), built into a permanently dry-docked barge filled with nautical artifacts.

For **food**, check out the popular *Killer Whale Café* on First Street (℡907/424-7733), above the Orca Bookshop, or the superb seafood at the pricier *Reluctant Fisherman Inn*, 407 Railroad Ave (℡907/424-3272). Wash it all down afterwards with a drink at the *Alaskan Hotel's* **bar**.

Interior and northern Alaska

Interior and northern Alaska cannot fail to live up to expectations of the "great land." For the most part it's a rolling plateau divided by the Alaska and Brooks ranges, crisscrossed by river valleys, punctuated by glaciers and with views of imposing peaks, including ever present Mount McKinley, the nation's highest. Even in high summer, when RVs clog the George Parks Highway, people are still hugely outnumbered by game: moose, Dall sheep, grizzly bears and herds of caribou sweep over seemingly endless swathes of taiga (birch woodland) and tundra.

Heading north from Anchorage the first essential stop is the tiny town of **Talkeetna**, which has great views of Mount McKinley and the opportunity to fly around it. The mountain is at the heart of **Denali National Park**, the jewel of the Interior. If you prefer your wilderness with fewer people and regulations, head east for the vast and untrammeled world of **Wrangell–St Elias National Park**.

Fairbanks, Alaska's second city, is diverting in its own right and serves as the hub of the North, with roads fanning out to **hot springs** and the **Dalton Highway**, threading five hundred miles to the Arctic Ocean at **Prudhoe Bay**.

Weather in the region can vary enormously from day to day, with even greater seasonal variations: in winter temperatures can drop to -50°F for days at a time, while summer days reach a sweltering 90°F. However, the major problem during the warmer months is huge mosquitoes; don't forget to bring insect repellent.

Talkeetna

A hundred miles north of Anchorage, **TALKEETNA** has a palpable small-town Alaska feel: rumor has it that this eclectic hamlet was the model for Cicely in TV's *Northern Exposure*, but to its credit Talkeetna doesn't use this as tour-bus bait. The town is lent an international flavor by the world's mountaineers, who come here to scale the 20,320-foot **Mount McKinley**, which in Alaska is usually referred to by its original Athabascan name of **Denali**, "the Great One." Whatever you choose to call it, North America's highest mountain rises from 2000ft lowlands, making it the world's tallest from base to peak (Everest et al rise from high terrain).

Though central to Denali National Park (see opposite) the mountain is best seen from Talkeetna, where the **overlook** just south of town reveals the peak's transcendent white glow, in sharp contrast to the warm colors all around.

From mid-April to mid-July Denali climbers amass in Talkeetna to be flown to the mountain: only half of the 1200 attempting the climb each year succeed, due to extreme weather conditions. Air taxi companies also run **flightseeing** trips ranging from a spectacular one-hour ($115) flight to the full ninety-minute grand tour ($165) completely encircling the mountain. K2 Aviation (☎907/733-2291 or 1-800/764-2291, ⓦwww.alaska.net/~flyk2), the choice of most climbing expeditions, offers the widest range of options, including glacier landings (extra $40) in planes fitted with skis.

Talkeetna's famed **Moose Dropping Festival** falls on the second weekend of July; little brown balls can be purchased (with a sanitary coat of varnish) for use as earrings, necklaces and so on, throughout the town. In addition to these highly desirable lumps of Alaskana, the festival features dancing, drinking and a moose-dropping throwing competition and some more drinking.

Practicalities

Talkeetna is at the end of a fourteen-mile spur off the George Parks Highway, which can usually be hitched. Bus services avoid Talkeetna except for The Park Connection (daily from Anchorage; $41; ☎1-800/208-0200); Anchorage to Denali **trains** stop half a mile south of the center of Talkeetna once a day. Information is widely available from shops around town and from the **Talkeetna Ranger Station**, on B Street (summer daily 8am–6pm; ☎907/733-2231).

For a town of just three hundred, Talkeetna teems with good **accommodation**, the cheapest being central *Talkeetna Hostel International* on I Street (☎907/733-4678, ⓦwww.akhostel.com; bunks $23, rooms ❸). Dating back to 1917, the central *Talkeetna Roadhouse* (☎907/733-1351, ⓦwww.talkeetnaroadhouse.com; ❹), bolsters its old-style atmosphere with some great home cooking and rooms with shared bathrooms. Easily the fanciest hotel hereabouts is the *Talkeetna Alaskan Lodge* (☎733-9500 or 1-888/959-9590, ⓦwww.talkeetnalodge.com; ❽), on the hill to the south of town. **Campers** can stay at the

Talkeetna River Park ($10), at the western end of Main Street, but most stroll a hundred yards further west from the latter and (unofficially) pitch on the river flats.

Good places to **eat** include the bakery/diner at the *Talkeetna Roadhouse* (see opposite), and the *McKinley Deli* at Main and C streets (☎907/733-1234), which serves pizza. And make sure you stop for a **drink** in the wonderfully ancient *Fairview Inn* on Main Street.

Denali National Park

The six-million-acre **DENALI NATIONAL PARK**, 240 miles north of Anchorage, is named after the Athabascan word for its most famous denizen, **Mount McKinley**, which is often shrouded in cloud, and only around one-quarter of visitors actually get to see the snow-covered massif. The mountain is far from being the park's only attraction, however. A ride through Denali on a shuttle bus offers a glimpse of a vast world of tundra and taiga, glaciers, huge mountains and abundant wildlife – the Park Service reports that 95 percent of visitors see **bears**, **caribou** and **Dall sheep**, 82 percent moose, and over one-fifth **wolves**, along with porcupine, snowshoe hare, red foxes, and over 160 bird species.

Visiting Alaska without trying to see Denali is unthinkable for most travellers, and therein lies the park's problem. In the height of summer, the visitor center and the service hotels out on the Parks Highway are a stream of RVs, tour buses and the like. Things pick up in the park itself, and backcountry hiking, undertaken by only a tiny fraction of visitors, remains a wonderfully solitary experience.

In **winter**, Denali is transformed into a ghostly, snow-covered world. Motorized vehicles are banned and transportation, even for park personnel, is by snowshoe, skis or dogsled as temperatures dive and northern lights glitter over the snows.

Getting to the park

Driving to Denali Park takes about five hours from Anchorage, three from Fairbanks, and **hitching** is quite easy with twenty hours of summer daylight. Several **bus** companies run services from Anchorage to Fairbanks via Denali: Parks Highway Express (☎1-888/600-6001, ⑯www.alaskashuttle.com) charges $49 from Anchorage and $34 from Fairbanks. One Denali-bound **train** a day leaves Anchorage (8.15am; $125) and Fairbanks (8.15am; $50), depositing you at 4pm and noon respectively at the train station a mile and a half inside the park entrance. **Park entry** costs $5 per person and is valid for a week.

Accommodation and eating

With the exception of several exclusive lodges deep in the heart of the park, there are no hotels in Denali, so your choice is among camping, the $150-a-night gaggle of summer-only hotels a mile north of the park entrance, or the cheaper offerings ten miles further north in the little coal-mining town of **HEALY**. The cheapest place by the park entrance is *Denali Sourdough Cabins* (☎907/683-2773; mid-June to mid Aug ❼, rest of summer ❺), whose comfy cabins are surrounded by spruce trees. In Healy there's the compact, spotless and very popular *Denali Hostel*, Mile 1.3 Otto Lake Rd (☎907/683-1295, ⑯www.denalihostel.com; room ❹), which has $23 bunks, private rooms and offers a complimentary shuttle ride to the park twice a day. Nearby try the high-quality *Motel Nord Haven*, Mile 249.5 Parks Hwy (☎907/683-4500 or 1-800/683-4501, ⊛www.ptialaska.net/~nordhavn; ❻), or the comfortable *Alaskan Chateau* B&B, Sulphide Road (☎907/683-1377; ❺).

Camping is the best way to experience Denali up close, with most of the park's eight campgrounds open from mid-May to mid-September. The best sites are at **Wonder Lake** ($12) with a stunning view of McKinley; failing that, **Igloo Creek** ($6) is good for spotting Dall sheep, while **Riley Creek** ($12) near the entrance is open year-round. All sites (except the $6 *Morino* walk-in close to the train station and park entrance, where you can self-register) are bookable at the main visitor center or on ☎1-800/622-7275. If you don't do this you may have to wait for up to three days to get a spot. The best alternative is *Denali Grizzly Bear Cabins & Campground*, Mile 231.1, seven miles south of Denali (☎907/683-2696, ⊛www.alaskaone.com/dengrzly/; ❶–❹), set in the trees close to the Nenana River with simple but attractive cabins all around.

Eating is expensive hereabouts, with only a limited range of grocery stores for those preparing their own meals, and a small selection of fairly pricey restaurants close to the park entrance, such as the *Black Bear Coffee House* (☎907/683-1656), serving light meals; and *Lynx Creek Pizza and Pub* (☎907/683-2548), where the menu includes pasta dishes and Mexican specialties, as well as pizza and draft microbrews.

Sightseeing, hiking and other activities

To preserve flora and fauna, the only vehicles allowed on Denali's narrow, unpaved ninety-mile road are a few tour buses and green **shuttle buses**, for which you'll need to reserve well in advance (☎907/622-7275 or 1-800/622-7275). You can try for a seat up to two days in advance from the **visitor center** (late April to Sept daily 7am–8pm; ☎907/683-1266), just inside the park entrance, where you can pick up a free copy of the *Denali Alpenglow* paper and a wide range of literature, and join ranger-led activities including short hikes and the popular, and free, dogsled demonstration held daily at 10am, 2pm and 4pm.

Shuttle buses run to either the **Eielson Visitor Center** at Mile 66 ($23), where rangers lead one-hour tundra tours each day at 1.30pm, or to the aptly named **Wonder Lake** at Mile 84 ($30); round-trips take about eight and ten hours respectively. The shuttle drivers don't give guided tours, but with forty pairs of watchful eyes on board, you're almost guaranteed to see the big mammals. You can also hop off at any point for a day-hike (no permits required) and return to the road to flag down the next bus back, if it has room. Buses run 6–8 times daily, and there are also buses used mainly by campers that will pick up stragglers at the end of the day.

Overnight backcountry camping is the best way to appreciate Denali's scenery and its inhabitants. Don't expect it to be easy though, there are no formal trails, and with thick spongy tundra and frequent river crossings even hardy hikers find themselves limited to five miles a day. The park is divided into 43 units and only a designated number of hikers is allowed into each section at a time. Free permits are available, one day in advance, from the visitor center's **Backcountry Desk** (daily 7am–8pm), though high demand means you should be prepared to hike in the less popular areas. The Backcountry Desk will also teach you about avoiding run-ins with bears and issue you with bear-resistant containers for food storage. Special camper buses reserved for those with campground or backcountry permits cost $15. It's not a bad idea to reconnoitre the park on a full-day bus trip in order to choose where you might like to hike on subsequent days. If there's room, buses also carry bikes; cyclists can be dropped off wherever they like, but are obliged to keep to the road.

An alternative to going it alone is to join a **narrated tour** (☎1–800/276–7234) along the park road: either the three-hour Natural History Tour ($37) or the full-day Tundra Wildlife Tour ($71), which penetrates as far as Mile 53, stopping frequently to observe wildlife.

Just outside the park entrance, several **rafting** companies offer two-hour trips down the Nenana River: all offer a gentle "scenic float" and an eleven-mile "Canyon Run" through Class III and IV rapids – they cost around $60 individually and $80 for a joint run. Denali Outdoor Center (☎907/683-1925 or 1-888/303-1925, ⊛www.denalioutdoorcenter.com) charges a couple of dollars more than some of the others but offers a quality experience and the luxury of dry-suits.

Wrangell-St Elias National Park

As Denali becomes more crowded, people are increasingly making the trip to more out-of-the-way **WRANGELL-ST ELIAS NATIONAL PARK** in the extreme southeast corner of the Interior. Here, four of the continent's great mountain ranges – the Wrangell, St Elias, Chugach and Alaska – cramp up against each other, and even the usually reserved National Park Service literature breaks ranks by saying, "Incredible. You have to see Wrangell-St Elias . . . to believe it – and even then you won't be so sure." Everything is writ large: glacier after enormous glacier, canyon after dizzying canyon and nine of the sixteen highest peaks in the US, all laced together by braided rivers and idyllic lakes where mountain goats, Dall sheep, bears, moose and caribou roam.

The first whites in the area came in search of gold but instead hit upon one of the continent's richest copper deposits. The mines closed in 1938, after 27 frantic years of production, and today **Kennicott**, with over thirty creaking, disused buildings, is a virtual ghost town. You can visit the mill complex on fascinating two-hour **walking tours** run by St Elias Alpine Guides ($25; ☎1-888/933-5427, ⊛www.steliasguides.com), which is based in nearby **McCarthy**, the main social hub and base for outfitters. They also run a number of hikes, ice climbing trips, mountain bike rides, raft trips and even glacier skiing out into what is essentially a trailless park.

Practicalities

Half the fun is getting to McCarthy along 58 rugged miles of the McCarthy Road, which follows the trackbed of the long abandoned railroad that once linked the Kennicott mill to the port at Cordova. Take it slow (old rail spikes can still cause punctures) and stop often to admire the scenery and abandoned trestle bridges. At the end of the road you cross the Kennicott River on a footbridge and continue half a mile to McCarthy on foot, from where a shuttle bus runs along the rough five-mile dirt road to Kennicott. Hitching along the McCarthy Road can be a hit-or-miss affair; if you haven't got a vehicle you can take a McCarthy Kennicott Shuttle (mid-May to mid-Sept Mon–Sat; ☎907/822-5292 or 1-800/478-5292) from Glenallen ($105 round-trip).

There's free **camping** (no water) a mile before the road ends and $25 beds in four-bunk cabins nearby at the *Kennicott River Lodge and Hostel* (☎907/554-4441, ⊛www.ptialaska.net/~grosswlr; ❸). Showers cost $5; bring a sleeping bag and food to prepare. In McCarthy, try the very pleasant and atmospheric *Ma Johnson Hotel/McCarthy Lodge* (☎907/554-4402; ❻). In Kennicott there's the upscale *Kennicott Glacier Lodge* (☎907/554-4477, ⊛www.kennicottlodge.com;

❼), which also has the town's one restaurant (reserve for dinner). The park's **visitor center** is at the Copper Center turnoff at Mile 111 on the Richardson Highway (summer daily 8am–6pm; ☎907/822-7261).

Fairbanks

FAIRBANKS, 358 miles north of Anchorage, is at the end of the Alaska Highway from Canada and definitely at the end of the road for most tourists. Though flat and somewhat bland, its central location makes a great base for exploring a hinterland of gold mines and hot springs, and a staging point for both the tiny villages scattered around the surrounding wilderness, and for journeys along the **Dalton Highway** (aka the "Haul Road") to the Arctic Ocean oil community of **Prudhoe Bay**.

Alaska's second most populous town was founded accidentally, in 1901, when a steamship carrying E.T. Barnette, a merchant with all his wares on board, ran aground in the shallows of the Chena River. Unable to transport the supplies he was carrying, Barnette set up shop in the wilderness and catered to the few trappers and prospectors trying their luck in the area. The following year, with the beginnings of the **Gold Rush**, a tent city sprang up on the site, and Barnette made a mint. In 1908, at the height of the gold stampede, Fairbanks had a population of 18,500, but by 1920 the population had dwindled to only 1100. To thwart possible Japanese attacks during World War II, several huge **military bases** were built and the population rebounded, getting a further boost in the mid-1970s when it became the transportation center for the **trans-Alaska oil pipeline** project: construction and other oil-related activities brought a rush of workers seeking wages of up to $1500 per week and the population reached an all-time high. The city's economy dropped dramatically with the oil crash, and unemployment hit twenty percent before government spending put the city back on track.

The spectacular **aurora borealis** is a major winter attraction, as is the **Ice Festival** in mid-March, with its ice sculpting competition and open sled dog race on the frozen downtown streets. Summer visitors should try to catch the three-day **World Eskimo-Indian Olympics** in mid-July when contestants from around the state compete in the standard dance, art and sports competitions, as well as some unusual ones like ear-pulling, knuckle hop, high kick and the blanket toss, where age and wisdom often defeat youth and strength.

Fairbanks suffers remarkable extremes of climate, with winter temperatures dropping to -70°F and summer highs topping 90°F. Proximity to the Arctic Circle means over 21 hours of sunlight in midsummer, when midnight baseball games take place under natural light, and 2am bar evacuees are confronted by bright sunshine.

Arrival, information and getting around

Alaska Airlines, Delta and United all offer daily services from Anchorage to **Fairbanks Airport**, four miles southwest of downtown; the MACS **bus** Yellow Line (Mon–Sat; $1.50) runs downtown but the long wait between services means you'll probably want to grab a **taxi** (around $12) or the Airlink Shuttle (☎907/452-3337), which charges $7 (for two) to your accommodation. The airport is also a gateway for flights into the bush; Frontier Flying Service (☎907/474-0011) operates a reliable service. Daily **trains** stop downtown at 280 N Cushman Rd, but are far more expensive than the minibus companies that run here from Anchorage and Valdez and drop you off at your accommodation.

The best way to get around is by car, but the five **bus lines**, run by MACS (☎907/459-1011), provide a reasonable service; call for information or collect a schedule from the visitor center (see below). Airlink Shuttle (see opposite) offers transport to sights within the city for $5. Among the companies that can whisk you off into the surrounding bush and fly you to the **Arctic Circle**, the widest choice is with the Northern Alaska Tour Company (☎907/474-8600, ⓦwww.alaskasarctic.com).

The **visitor center**, at 550 First Ave (summer daily 8am–8pm; rest of year Mon–Fri 8am–5pm; ☎907/456-5774 or 1-800/327-5774, ⓦwww.explore-fairbanks.com), carries a vast amount of information on lodging and activities. For information on the area's parks, including Denali, stop by the useful **Alaska Public Land Information Center** (APLIC) at 250 N Cushman St (summer daily 9am–6pm; rest of year Tues–Sat 10am–6pm; ☎907/456-0527).

Accommodation

The motels and hotels in downtown Fairbanks tend to be either quite pricey or pretty dodgy. **B&B**s are plentiful, with rooms from $65 a night; the visitor center offers free phone calls and all the brochures. Thankfully there are plenty of hostels, each close to a good bus route. For campers, the best choice is the tranquil *Tanana Valley Campground*, 1800 College Rd at Aurora Drive (mid-May to mid-Sept; ☎907/456-7956; $8), on the MACS bus Red line and with free bikes for guests to use.

Ah, Rose Marie 302 Cowles St at 3rd Ave ☎907/456-2040, ⓦwww.akpub.com/akbbrv/ahrose.html. Small but well-run and justly popular B&B where a hearty breakfast is served on the glassed-in veranda. Some single rooms for ❸, shared bath ❹, private bath ❺.

Billie's Backpackers 2895 Mack Rd ☎ & ⓕ 907/479-2034. Welcoming though somewhat cramped hostel, in a nice area and handily placed on the bus route between downtown and the university. Bikes and internet access available. Bunks $20, camping $10. ❶

Fairbanks Exploration Inn 505 Illinois St ☎907/451-1920 or 1-888/452-1920, ⓦwww.feinn.com. Former gold company bungalows turned into a classy B&B with very comfy rooms and a large buffet breakfast. Two-bedroom suites ❽, rooms ❼.

Fairbanks Hotel 517 3rd Ave ☎907/456-6411, ⓦwww.alaska.net/~fbxhotl. Good-value downtown hotel done in ersatz Miami Beach Deco style, with cheerily decorated rooms each with cable TV and a washstand. Shared bath ❺, private bath ❻

Golden North Motel 4888 Old Airport Way ☎1-800/447-1910, ⓔgoldennorthmotel@alaska.com. Spotlessly clean motel near the airport with cable TV and continental breakfast. Courtesy pickups are available, but inconveniently located unless you have your own wheels. ❺

Grandma Shirley's 510 Dunbar St ☎907/451-9816. Clean and tidy hostel run by Grandma Shirley, who makes up the $16 beds on arrival (linen provided), and generally runs a tight ship. Guests can use the family kitchen and bikes are available. The MACS bus Purple line passes within a block. ❶

Midge's Birch Lane B&B 4335 Birch Lane ☎907/388-8084 or 1-800/479-4895, ⓔmidge@alaska.net. Relaxed, welcoming and spacious house in the quiet University district. Rooms with and without private bathrooms. ❺

The Town

Besides the visitor centers, the only point of interest **downtown** is the small **Fairbanks Community Museum**, 450 Cushman St at 5th Avenue (summer Mon–Sat 10am–5pm; donation requested), containing locally donated trapping and mining and dogsled racing equipment. The museum also acts as the public face of the **Yukon Quest** dogsled race – a grueling thousand-mile marathon between Fairbanks and Whitehorse – selling related books, videos and T-shirts. A similarly wintry theme is pursued at the **Ice Museum**, 500 2nd Ave at Lacey Street (summer daily 10am–6pm; $8), a year-round chance to get a taste of the annual Ice Sculpting competition by way of a slide show and walk-in refrigerators housing some small ice carvings.

A couple of miles west on the banks of the Chena River, the **Alaskaland** complex celebrates Alaskan history in a very touristy, but not unpleasant way; admission is free, though different attractions charge small fees. Two reasonable **museums** cover the early pioneering days, and a miniature railway encircles the entire park; there's plenty here for the kids to do.

From the downtown area, College Road heads west past **Creamer's Field**, thick with sandhill cranes and Canada geese, especially in spring and fall. Further out, the **University of Alaska Fairbanks (UAF) Museum** (summer daily 9am–5pm, closing times vary; $5; ☎907/474-7505), occupies a corner of the attractive campus on the northeastern edge of town and houses some of the state's best examples of Native Alaskan artifacts and pioneer relics, as well as natural and human history displays.

Unashamedly touristy but great fun and very popular is a four-hour **cruise** down the Chena River on the "Riverboat Discovery" ($40; ☎907/479-6673), which includes a visit to a mock Native village.

Eating and nightlife

Fairbanks's **eating** options are varied, with good Thai particularly prevalent. They're also well scattered, with downtown and College Road, toward the university, having the greatest concentrations. For groceries try the 24-hour Carr's supermarket downtown at 526 Gafney Rd. Fairbanks has its decent **nightspots**, though none lie in hard-drinking downtown.

Blue Loon Mile 353.5 Parks Hwy ☎907/457-5666, ⊛www.theblueloon.com. Late-closing hotspot five miles west of Fairbanks that's always good for a convivial drink. Hosts local and touring bands (sometimes a DJ) several nights a week, and screens cult and art-house movies. Closed Sun.

The Diner 244 Illinois St ☎907/451-0613. Reliable joint serving diner fare cooked to perfection at good prices.

Gambardella's Pasta Bella 706 2nd Ave, downtown ☎907/456-3417. Fairbanks's best Italian and not wildly expensive, with a pleasant outdoor area for those endless summer evenings.

Gulliver's Books Café 3525 College Rd ☎907/474-9574. Pleasant spot above a bookstore, serving chicken tarragon wraps, pesto turkey melts, bagels, biscotti and coffee all at reasonable prices, and offering free internet access to boot.

Howling Dog Saloon Mile 11 Old Steese Hwy, Fox ☎907/457-8780. An inconvenient eleven miles north of town, but perhaps the best bar in the north – unassuming, unpretentious and fun. Live rock and R&B bands perform and it's the ideal place to play volleyball under the midnight sun.

The Marlin 3412 College Rd ☎907/479-4646. Poky wood-paneled cellar bar that defines the cutting edge of Fairbanks's music scene with live bands – blues, jazz and rock – playing most evenings from around 9pm and only a small cover charge, if any.

Pump House Mile 1.3 Chena Pump Rd ☎907/479-8452. A local favorite in a historic pumphouse, stuffed with gold mining paraphernalia and set by the Chena River with a deck to watch river life go by. Great for steak, seafood and burgers, and also pulls in a substantial drinking crowd.

Souvlaki 1119 2nd Ave, downtown ☎907/452-5393. Bargain Greek and American dishes served in spartan surroundings. Stuffed vine leaves are only 50¢ each, Greek salad and *spanakopita* are both under $4, and crab quiche and souvlaki barely break $6. Closed Sun.

Thai House 526 5th Ave, downtown ☎907/452-6123. A small but ever-popular restaurant serving the usual range of Thai dishes, but all done to perfection and at very modest prices for around $9. The green and red curries with zucchini, peas and peppers are especially good. Closed Sun.

Around Fairbanks: two hot springs

Chena Hot Springs, the most accessible and developed resort in the area, stands in a clearing sixty miles east of Fairbanks amid a wonderfully bucolic swath of **muskeg** (grassy swampland) and forest traversed by good hiking trails

The Northern Lights

The **aurora borealis**, or "Northern Lights," an ethereal display of light in the upper-most atmosphere, give their brightest and most colorful displays in the sky above Fairbanks. For up to one hundred winter nights, the sky appears to shimmer with dancing curtains of color ranging from luminescent greens to fantastic veils that run the full spectrum. Named after the Roman goddess of dawn, the aurora are caused by an interaction between the earth's magnetic field and the **solar wind**, an invisible stream of charged electrons and protons continually blown out into space by the innate violence of the sun. The earth deflects the solar wind like a rock in a stream, with the energy released at the magnetic poles – much like a neon sign.

The Northern Lights are at their most dazzling from December to March, when nights are longest and the sky darkest, but late September can be good for summer visitors.

and teeming with moose. Nonguests can use the indoor pool and hot tubs for $8 a day, or stay at the fully equipped resort (☎907/452-7867 or 1-800/478-4681, @www.chenahotsprings.com; ❻), where camping costs $20. The resort also rents out canoes and mountain bikes, as well as offering rafting float trips.

The traditional favorite for folks from Fairbanks has been the more rustic **Arctic Circle Hot Springs**, 130 miles northeast of the city along scenic Steese Highway. It's a long drive through pristine scenery beside the Chatanika River to the tiny mining village of **Central**, then eight miles to the resort (☎907/520-5113; ❶–❹), where you can camp ($5), take a $20 dorm bed or stay in deluxe rooms.

The Dalton Highway

Built in the 1970s to service the **trans-Alaska pipeline**, the gravel-surfaced **Dalton Highway**, or Haul Road, runs from Fairbanks five hundred miles to the oil facility of Prudhoe Bay on Alaska's north coast, some three hundred miles beyond the Arctic Circle. It is a long, bumpy and demanding drive, so be prepared with spare tires, gas, provisions and, ideally, a sturdy 4WD: regular rentals aren't permitted up here. Just beyond the Fairbanks city limits you start to get glimpses of the pipeline snaking up hills and in and out of the ground. At 188 miles a sign announces that you've just crossed the **Arctic Circle**. The **Northern Alaska Tour Company** (☎907/474 8600, @www.alaskasarctic.com) will drive you up in a minibus and fly you back down to Fairbanks for around $219 (you can save $100 by taking the minibus back, but it makes for a long day).

Most people are happy to return south at this point, but the highway plugs on through increasingly barren territory, finally dispensing with trees as you climb through the still largely unmapped and unexplored **Brooks Range**, a 9000ft chain mostly held within the **Gates of the Arctic** National Park. From the crest at Atigun Pass you descend through two hundred miles of grand glaciated valleys and blasted arctic plains to the end of the road at dead-boring **Deadhorse**. You can't stroll by the ocean or camp here so your choices are confined to staying in one of the $120 per night hotels and taking a $25 tour of the adjacent – and otherwise off-limits – **Prudhoe Bay** oil facility, worth it just for the sight of the Arctic Ocean after the long drive.

By far the best way to do it is with Northern Alaska, which runs a three-day tour to Prudhoe Bay for around $650.

CHAPTER 16 # Highlights

* **Waikiki Beach, Oahu** Learn to surf, or just sip a cocktail on the world's most famous beach. See p.1286

* **Pearl Harbor, Oahu** Relive December 7, 1941 – the "day that will live in infamy" – by visiting the sunken USS Arizona. See p.1287

* **Kilauea Eruption, Big Island** The Big Island gets bigger day by day, thanks to the spectacular eruption of its youngest volcano, Kilauea. See p.1299

* **Lahaina, Maui** This former whaling port ranks among the most characterful historic towns in Hawaii. See p.1302

* **Downhill biking, Maui** Freewheel forty miles down the slopes of Maui's mighty Haleakala volcano. See p.1304

* **Lumahai Beach, Kauai** This superb, if dangerous, beach has featured in countless movies. See p.1309

* **Kalalau Trail, Kauai** The magnificent Na Pali coastline of Kauai can be admired from one of the world's greatest hiking trails. See p.1309

Hawaii

The islands of **HAWAII**, with their **volcanoes**, palm-fringed **beaches**, verdant **valleys**, glorious **rainbows** and awesome **cliffs**, hold some of the most spectacularly beautiful scenery on earth. However, despite their isolation, two thousand miles out in the Pacific, they belong very definitely to the United States. If you expect your South Seas idyll to be completely unspoiled, forget it; the fantasy of a dream holiday in Paradise remains firmly rooted in the creature comforts of home. With seven million tourists per year, including honeymooners from all over the world, frequent fliers cashing in their mileage, and almost two million Japanese, the islands can seem like a gigantic theme park.

Honolulu, by far the largest city of the fiftieth state, and with its resort annex of **Waikiki** also the main tourist center, is on **Oahu**. The biggest island, **Hawaii** itself, is known as the **Big Island** in a vain attempt to avoid confusion. **Maui** and **Kauai** also attract mass tourism, while smaller **Molokai** remains far quieter. All the islands share a similar topography and **climate**. Ocean winds from the northeast shed their rain on the **windward** coast, keeping it wet and green; the southwest, **leeward** (or "Kona") coasts can be almost barren, and so make ideal locations for big resorts. While temperatures remain consistent throughout the year at between 70°F and 85°F, rainfall is heaviest from December to March. That is nonetheless the most popular time to visit, enabling mid- to upper-range hotels to add a premium of at least $30 per night to their standard room rates. A visit to Hawaii doesn't have to cost a fortune, however; there are plenty of **budget** facilities if you know where to look. The one major expense you really can't avoid, except possibly on Oahu, is car rental – rates are very reasonable, but gas is pricey.

Some history

Each of the Hawaiian islands was forced up like a vast mass of candle drippings by submarine volcanic action, all fueled by the same "hot spot," which has remained stationary as the Pacific plate drifted above. The oldest islands are now mere atolls way off to the northwest; the process is continuing at Kilauea on the Big Island, with lava exploding into the sea to add new land day by day. Until two thousand years ago, these unknown specks in the ocean were populated only by the descendants of what few organisms had been carried here by wind or wave. The first known human inhabitants were the **Polynesians**, who arrived in two separate migrations: one from the Marquesas in the eighth century, and another from Tahiti four or five hundred years later.

No Western ship chanced upon Hawaii until **Captain Cook** arrived at Kauai in January 1778. He was amazed to find a civilization sharing a culture

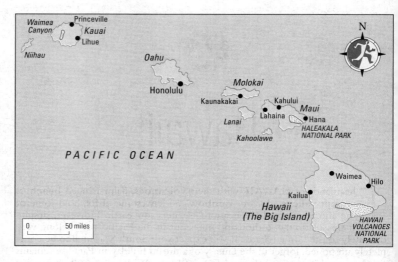

– and language – with the peoples of the South Pacific. The Hawaiians, too, were amazed, having long since lost contact with the outside world. Cook himself was killed in Hawaii in 1779 (see p.1298), but he had started an irreversible process of change. The first Polynesians had brought the plants and animals necessary to create a self-sufficient way of life. Westerners took things further, and in reshaping the islands to suit their economic and agricultural needs decimated most of the indigenous flora and fauna – as well as the Hawaiians themselves. Cook's men estimated that there were a million islanders; the population today is roughly the same, but a mere eight thousand **pure-blood Hawaiians** are left.

As well as bringing venereal and other diseases, Cook's voyage opened the fur trade between the Pacific Northwest and China. Passing ships traded arms to the Hawaiians, and within a few years, **Kamehameha** became the first king to unite all the islands. The sudden advent of capitalism was devastating. When the fur traders realized that Hawaiian **sandalwood** fetched enormous prices in China, the mass of the population abandoned taro-farming and fishing.

With the dislocation of traditional ways, Hawaiian **religion** fell apart. After the death of Kamehanuha in 1819, the female regent Kaahumanu set out to break the **kapu** (*taboo*) system that held society together. Her public defiance of the injunctions forbidding women to eat alongside men, or to eat bananas or pork, threw the islands into moral anarchy – just as the first Puritan **missionaries** arrived from New England in 1820. Their wholehearted capitalism and harsh strictures on the easygoing Hawaiian lifestyle might have been calculated to compound the chaos. White advisers and ministers soon dominated the government, and the children of the missionaries became Hawaii's wealthiest and most powerful class.

Although the Civil War severely disrupted **whaling**, which once the forests were denuded had supplanted sandalwood as the island's main source of revenue, it triggered a Hawaiian **sugar** boom, to replace Southern sugar in the markets of the north. From then on, the machinations of the sugar industry to get favorable prices on the mainland moved Hawaii inexorably towards **annexation** by the US. In 1887 an all-white group of "concerned businessmen" forced King David Kalakaua to surrender power to an assembly elected by property owners (of any nationality) rather than citizens. When, after his death, his sister Liliuokalani announced her desire to proclaim a new constitution, the businessmen called in the US warship *Boston* and declared a provisional government. US President Cleveland (a Democrat) responded that "Hawaii was taken possession of by the United States forces without the consent or wish of the government of the islands . . . (It) was wholly without justification . . . not merely a wrong but a disgrace." The provisional government found defenders in the Republican US Congress, however, and declared itself a republic on July 4, 1894.

On August 12, 1898, Hawaii was formally **annexed** as a territory of the United States. At this point there was no question of Hawaii becoming a state; the whites were outnumbered ten to one, and had no desire to afford the natives the protection of US labor laws, let alone to give them the vote. Consequently, Hawaii was for the first half of the twentieth century the virtual fiefdom of the **Big Five**, conglomerations started by the missionary families and rooted in their massive landholdings. By controlling agriculture, they also dominated transportation, banks, utilities, insurance – and government. The inevitable integration of Hawaii into the American mainstream was hastened by its crucial role in the war against Japan, and the expansion of tourism thereafter. The islands finally became the fiftieth of the United States in 1959, after a plebiscite showed a seventeen-to-one majority in favor. The only group to oppose statehood were the few remaining native Hawaiians.

Support has been growing over the last couple of decades for the concept of **Hawaiian sovereignty**, on the basis that those of Hawaiian descent should gain at least the rights already held by Native American nations on the mainland. In 1993, the US Congress and President Clinton issued a formal apology to native Hawaiians "on the occasion of the 100th anniversary of the illegal overthrow of the Kingdom of Hawaii"; debate rages as to what form restitution might take, with some campaigners arguing for a complete restoration of **independence**.

Modern Hawaii

Roughly sixty percent of the million-plus modern Hawaiians were born here. Around one-third are Caucasian (many of them US military personnel), one-third Japanese and one-sixth Filipino, with 200,000 claiming at least some Hawaiian ancestry. The traditional reliance on agriculture seems to be in terminal decline, with sugar and pineapple plantations closing one after the other, and the need to import virtually all the basics of life has resulted in an extraordinarily high **cost of living**. In particular, the cost of housing is so high that many islanders find themselves either obliged to work at two jobs, or simply to sleep on the beaches.

Visitors in search of the **ancient Hawaii** will find that few vestiges remain. What is presented as "historic" usually postdates the missionary impact. Although the ruins of temples (*heiaus*) to the old gods still stand in some places – notably on the Big Island – and committed campaigners work to revive traditional philosophies, the "old towns" are pure nineteenth-century Americana, with false-front stores and raised wooden boardwalks. The two biggest **festivals** are the Big Island's week-long **Merrie Monarch Festival**, honoring King David Kalakaua (mid-April), and the statewide **King Kamehameha** events (around June 11). Authentic **hula** dancing is a powerful art form, but you're far more likely to encounter it bastardized in a **luau**. Primarily tourist money-spinners, these "traditional feasts" provide an opportunity to sample Hawaiian **foods** such as *kalua* pig, baked underground, and local fish such as *ono, ahi, mahi mahi* and *lomi-lomi* (raw salmon). *Poi* — a paste made from mashed taro root — remains a staple of the diet, much as it was when one of Captain Cook's men described it as "a disagreeable mess."

The Hawaiian **language** endures in place names and music. At first glance it looks unpronounceable — especially as it is written using a mere twelve letters (the five vowels, plus *h, k, l, m, n, p* and *w*). Usually, each letter is enunciated individually — glottal stops indicate a pause for breath. Long words often break down into repeated sounds, such as "*meha-meha*" in "Kamehameha." Hawaii itself is more correctly written (and pronounced) *Hawai'i*, but for visual clarity we've omitted the glottal stops in this book.

Getting to and around Hawaii

Honolulu, just under six hours by plane from the US west coast, is one of the world's busiest centers for air traffic; return fares from **LA**, **San Francisco** and **Seattle** start at around $350. There are also direct flights from the mainland to Maui, the Big Island and Kauai. Many flights to the US from **Australia** – such as those on Continental – include free stopovers in Hawaii. **European** travelers should buy all-inclusive tickets from Europe.

The principal **inter-island carriers** are Hawaiian Airlines (Oahu ☎1-808/838-1555, US ☎1-800/367-5320, ⓦwww.hawaiianair.com) and Aloha Air (Oahu ☎808/484-1111, US ☎1-800/367-5250, ⓦwww.alohaairlines .com), together with its subsidiary Island Air (Oahu ☎808/484-2222, US ☎1-800/323-3345). They connect all the major islands several times per day, with standard one-way fares of around $85. Discount travel agents, and virtually all resorts, hotels, B&B agencies and even hostels in Hawaii can arrange discounts on inter-island flights.

All the airports have car rental outlets; with the exception of Oahu, **bus** services on the islands barely exist.

Oahu

Three-quarters of Hawaii's population live on **OAHU**, which has monopolized the islands' trade and tourism since the first European sailors realized that **Honolulu** offered the safest in-shore anchorage in thousands of miles of ocean. Over eighty percent of visitors to Hawaii still arrive in **Honolulu** – albeit by air now, rather than by sea – and most remain for their entire vacation. Oahu effectively confines tourists to the tower-block enclave of **Waikiki**, just east of downtown Honolulu; there are few rooms anywhere else. In much the same way, the **military** are closeted away in relatively inconspicuous camps. On any one day, the numbers of military personnel and tourists on Oahu are roughly the same.

Overcrowding and rampant development mean Oahu can't be recommended over the **Neighbor Islands** (as the other Hawaiian islands are known), but it can still give a real flavor of Hawaii. There are some excellent **beaches**, with those on the north shore a haven for **surfers** and campers, and the **cliffs** of the windward side are awesome.

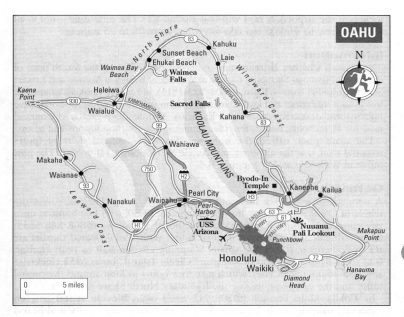

Honolulu

Until the Europeans came, **HONOLULU** was insignificant; soon so many for-eign ships were frequenting its waters that it had become Kamehameha's capi-tal, and it remains the economic center of the island. The city covers a long (if narrow) strip of southern Oahu, but **downtown** is a manageable size, and a lot quieter than its glamorous image might suggest. The tourist hotels, and most of Honolulu's hustle, are concentrated among the skyscrapers of very distinct **WAIKIKI**, a couple of miles east.

The setting is beautiful, right on the Pacific and backed by dramatic cliffs and the extinct volcanoes of **Punchbowl** (a military cemetery) and **Diamond Head**; but then beauty is not so rare a commodity on Hawaii, and you can see this sort of scenery in plenty of other places without a city in the middle of it. What attracts most visitors to stay in Honolulu, and especially Waikiki, is the sheer **hedonism** of shopping, eating and generally hanging out in the sun. It's also the center of an exemplary **public transportation** system, facilitating exploration of the whole island.

Arrival, information and getting around

The runways of Honolulu's **International Airport**, just west of downtown, extend out to sea on a coral reef. **Car rental** outlets abound, but a car is not especially desirable in Honolulu, what with city traffic and hefty parking fees in Waikiki. The Waikiki Airport Express (one-way $8, round-trip $13; ☎808/566-7333) is typical of the many **shuttle services** that run on request to any Waikiki hotel. Regular buses **#19** and **#20** connect Waikiki with the airport, but don't allow large bags, cases or backpacks (there are left-luggage lockers at the airport). A **taxi** will cost around $20. The nine-mile – not at all scenic – drive to Waikiki can take anywhere from 25 to 75 minutes.

Information

The **Hawaii Visitors Bureau** runs an information office on the fourth floor of the Royal Hawaiian Shopping Center in Waikiki, at Kalakaua Avenue and Lewers Street (Mon–Fri 8am–4.30pm; ☎808/923-1811), but you're unlikely to need it: free listings magazines and leaflets are everywhere you turn, and all the hotels have information desks. Kiosks around Kalakaua Avenue offer greatly discounted rates for island tours, helicopter rides, dinner cruises, surfing lessons and so on.

The main **post office**, the only one that takes general delivery (poste restante) mail, is at the airport (3600 Aolele St, Honolulu, HI 96820). The post office in Waikiki is at 330 Saratoga Rd.

Getting around

A network of over sixty **bus** routes, collectively named TheBus, covers the whole of Oahu. All journeys, however long, cost $1.50, with free transfers onto any connecting route if you ask as you board (enquiries ☎808/848-5555, ⓦwww.thebus.org). The most popular routes with Waikiki-based tourists are **#2** to downtown, **#8** to Ala Moana Shopping Center, **#20** to Pearl Harbor, **#22** to Hanauma Bay, and the bargain "**Circle Island**" buses (**#52** clockwise and **#55** counterclockwise), which take four hours to loop around the central valley and the east coast, passing the legendary North Shore surf spots.

In Waikiki, Aloha Funway (☎808/942-9696) offers **bicycle rental** at seven locations, charging $20 for 24 hours. Among companies running **city and island bus tours** from around $25 for a full day, as well as off-island packages, are Polynesian Adventure Tours (☎808/833-3000, ⓦwww.polyad.com) and Roberts (☎808/539-9400, ⓦwww.roberts-hawaii.com). Honolulu TimeWalks (☎808/943-0371) runs a changing program of themed **walking tours** of the city.

Accommodation

All the accommodation listed below is in or near **Waikiki**; very little is available in central Honolulu. Waikiki accommodation covers a wide range, and the highest rates will bring absolute luxury, but it's possible to find comfortable lodging for much less. It's also such a tiny place that there's little point paying the $50-plus premium on top of usual rates to get an ocean view.

Aloha Punawai 305 Saratoga Rd ☎808/923-5211, ⓦwww.alternative-hawaii.com/aloha-punawai/. Miniature hotel, opposite the post office, offering kitchenette apartments and studios with and without air-conditioning. ❹

Banana Bungalow Waikiki Beach Hostel 2463 Kuhio Ave ☎808/924-5074 or 1-888/2-HOSTEL, ⓦwww.bananabungalow.com. Central tower block that doubles as both hostel and budget hotel. All sixty or so rooms have en-suite bathrooms, balconies, phones and TVs; half are dorms at $18 per person, the rest are $55 private doubles. Free airport pick-up available, plus island tours several days per week. ❶–❸

Hale Aloha Hostel (Hostelling International Waikiki) 2417 Prince Edward St ☎808/926-8313. Official but informal youth hostel in the heart of Waikiki, a couple of minutes from the beach, and charging HI-AYH members $17, nonmembers $19 for a dorm bed. Reserve in advance, especially for the four private double rooms. ❶/❷

Hale Pua Nui 228 Beach Walk ☎808/923-9693. Small, clean hotel that's among central Waikiki's best deals. Simple studio apartments with two twin beds, kitchenettes and free local calls. Reserve well ahead. ❹

Island Hostel Hawaiian Colony Building, 1946 Ala Moana Blvd ☎808/924-8748. Good-value independent hostel in western Waikiki. No curfew, dorm beds $17, plus doubles with kitchenette and TV. ❶/❸

New Otani Kaimana Beach Hotel 2863 Kalakaua Ave ☎808/923-1555 or 1-800/421-8795, ⓦwww.kaimana.com. Intimate, Japanese-toned beachfront hotel half a mile east of central Waikiki. ⑤ Outrigger and Ohana linked hotel chains with numerous locations around Waikiki, mostly skyscrapers (reservations *Outrigger* ☎1-800/688-7444, Ⓦwww.outrigger.com, *Ohana* ☎1-800/462-6262, Ⓦwww.ohanahotels.com). Choices include the *Ohana Maile Sky Court*, 2058 Kuhio Ave (⑤), or the slightly more luxurious *Ohana Waikiki Surf*, 2200 Kuhio Ave (⑤); most of the other *Ohanas* have rooms for around $110, while the *Outriggers*, such as the *Reef on the Beach*, 2169 Kalia Rd (⑧), are more expensive. ⑤–⑨

Polynesian Hostel Beach Club 2584 Lemon Rd ☎808/922-1340, Ⓦwww.hostelhawaii.com. Clean private hostel, a block from the sea. Some rooms have en-suite bathrooms; some hold four $16 bunk beds, some serve as good-value private dou-

bles. Free snorkels, boogie boards and internet access are available; and meals are served in the communal area some nights. ❶–❷

The Royal Hawaiian 2490 Kalakaua Ave ☎808/922-7311 or 1-800/782-9488, Ⓦwww.sheraton-hawaii.com. 1920s "Pink Palace," commanding the beach, which is one of Waikiki's best-loved landmarks. The original building looks out across terrace gardens to the sea, but is now flanked by a less atmospheric tower block, which holds the most expensive suites. ❽

Waikiki Prince 2431 Prince Edward St ☎808/922-1544. Drab but adequate central budget hotel. All rooms offer air-conditioning, en-suite baths and cooking facilities, but no phones; the "very small" and "small" categories work out even cheaper than "economy". ❸

The City

Downtown Honolulu is surprisingly small, set back a little from the sea and centering around a spacious plaza on King Street that includes **Iolani Palace** and the **state capitol**. The palace was built for King David Kalakaua in 1882, but, apart from its *koa*-hardwood floors, contains little that is distinctively Hawaiian (Tues–Sat 9am–2.15pm; $15). Across the road is a flower-bedecked, gilt statue of Kamehameha the Great.

To reach the nearby ocean, pedestrians have to negotiate fearsome traffic. Although the sea may be turquoise, the shorefront is concrete, not beach, and you can't wander along it for any distance due to excessive recent construction works. The **Aloha Tower** on Pier 9 used to be the city's tallest building; the area around its base has been converted into an expensive shopping and dining mall, fronting onto the city docks. The view from the top of the tower is little short of ugly, but is good for orientation (daily: April–Sept 9am–7.30pm; Oct–March 9am–7pm; free). The **Hawaii Maritime Center** (daily 8.30am–5pm; $7.50), just east of Aloha Tower, documents Hawaii's seafaring past in superb detail, from ancient migrations through to white contact, nineteenth-century trade and twentieth-century cruises. A stunning film from 1922 (with Clara Bow in a bit part) shows the true-life drama of whaling, and there's a wall of gigantic historic surfboards. In the adjacent dock are the fully rigged four-master *Falls of Clyde* and the replica Polynesian canoe *Hokulea*, whose voyages to Tahiti and New Zealand over the last two decades have inspired tremendous interest in traditional methods of navigation.

Though few tourists seem to know about it, Honolulu residents take great pride in the stunning fine art on display at the **Academy of Arts**, half a mile east of the capitol at 900 S Beretania St (Tues–Sat 10am–4.30pm, Sun 1–5pm; $5). Highlights of the superb collection of paintings include Van Gogh's *Wheat Field*, Gauguin's *Two Nudes on a Tahitian Beach* and one of Monet's *Water Lilies*. The Academy also holds some fascinating depictions of Hawaii by visiting artists, including a pencil sketch of Waikiki drawn in 1838, and vivid, stylized studies of Maui's Iao Valley and Hana coast by Georgia O'Keeffe, plus magnificent ancient **Chinese** ceramics and bronzes.

Chinatown

TheBus #2 from Waikiki drops you at Hotel and Bishop streets, in front of the gleaming high-tech Executive Center in downtown Honolulu. Just five minutes' walk away down Hotel Street, the faded green-clapboard storefronts of **Chinatown** seem like another world. Traditionally the city's red-light district, the narrow streets leading down to the Nuuanu Stream are still characterized by pool halls, massage parlors and heavy-duty bars.

It's well worth delving into a few of Chinatown's inconspicuous alleyways. Some of its old walled courtyards are now modern malls, but the businesses remain much the same as ever, and you can still find herbalists weighing out dried leaves in front of vast arrays of bottles. Pig snouts and salmon heads are among the food specialties at **Oahu Market**, on N King and Kekaulike streets.

Bishop Museum

The anthropological collection at the **Bishop Museum** at 1525 Bernice St (daily 9am–5pm; $15) – well away from both the ocean and downtown, near the foot of the Likelike Highway – showcases real Polynesian culture, as opposed to the fakery of Waikiki. Three floors of one of Hawaii's oldest houses display ancient carved stone and wooden images of gods, magnificent feather *leis* and cloaks, and a full-sized *hale* (traditional hut) brought here from Kauai, in addition to Japanese samurai armor and a full-size sperm whale hanging in the central well. There are also excellent special exhibitions for kids, and a planetarium. TheBus #2 from Waikiki stops two blocks away on Kapalama Street.

Punchbowl

High above Honolulu, lush lawns growing in the caldera of an extinct volcano are the emotive setting for the **National Memorial Cemetery of the Pacific** (daily: March–Sept 8am–6.30pm; Oct–Feb 8am–5.30pm), in which are buried the dead of all US Pacific wars, including Vietnam. The Hawaiian shuttle astronaut Ellison Onizuka is also here. This spot is said to have held an ancient sacrificial temple, and is on TheBus route #15 from town.

Waikiki

Built on a reclaimed swamp, **Waikiki** is very nearly an island, all but separated from Honolulu between the sea and the Ala Wai canal (which provides the drainage to make its incredible highrise profusion possible). Once home to Kamehameha the Great, the site may be venerable, but these days its *raison d'être* is rampant commercialism. You could, just about, survive here with very little money, buying snacks from the omnipresent ABC convenience stores, but there would be no point – there's nothing to see, and the only thing to do apart from surf and sunbathe is to stroll along the seafront **Kalakaua Avenue** and shop.

The most striking thing about the parallel **Waikiki Beach** is how narrow it is, a thin but nonetheless attractive strip of shipped-in sand. Compared to other Hawaiian beaches, it's overcrowded and small, but the fact that it's lined by a pedestrian walkway, with several pleasant gardens en route, make this, relatively speaking, a refuge from the resort frenzy nearby.

Two possible diversions on the eastern fringes of Waikiki are **Honolulu Zoo** (daily 8.30am–5.30pm; $6), where you can walk through a mock African savannah set against the magnificent backdrop of Diamond Head, and the more expensive oceanfront **Waikiki Aquarium** (daily 9am–5pm; $7) which, as well as holding sharks and monkfish seals, has a tank devoted to the many-hued reef fish of Hanauma Bay (see opposite).

Diamond Head

Waikiki's most famous landmark is the pinnacle of **Diamond Head**, another extinct volcano just to the east. The lawns of the crater interior are oddly bland,

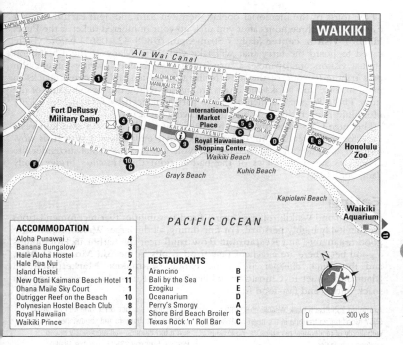

Fort DeRussy Military Camp

International Market Place

Royal Hawaiian Shopping Center

Waikiki Beach

Gray's Beach

Kuhio Beach

Kapiolani Beach

Honolulu Zoo

Waikiki Aquarium

PACIFIC OCEAN

N

0   300 yds

ACCOMMODATION

Aloha Punawai	4
Banana Bungalow	3
Hale Aloha Hostel	5
Hale Pua Nui	7
Island Hostel	2
New Otani Kaimana Beach Hotel	11
Ohana Maile Sky Court	1
Outrigger Reef on the Beach	10
Polynesian Hostel Beach Club	8
Royal Hawaiian	9
Waikiki Prince	6

RESTAURANTS

Arancino	B
Bali by the Sea	F
Ezogiku	E
Oceanarium	D
Perry's Smorgy	A
Shore Bird Beach Broiler	G
Texas Rock 'n' Roll Bar	C

but a straightforward hiking trail leads up a mile or so to the summit, and a panorama of the whole coast, passing through a network of tunnels built during World War II. TheBus #22 and #58 stop on the road nearby.

Hanauma Bay

A few miles to the east, magnificent crescent-shaped **Hanauma Bay**, formed when the wall of a crater collapsed and let in the sea, is renowned as Oahu's best place to **snorkel**. Though it makes a nice excursion, and the sea is full of brightly colored fish, overuse has killed off most of the coral near the shore, and the feeding of fish has led to a decline in the range of species. Tour parties were banned in 1991, and access is now controlled via a visitor center that shows educational videos about the bay's fragile ecology (daily except Tues 9am–6pm; $3). TheBus #22 ("The Beach Bus") runs by the bay from Waikiki every forty minutes.

Pearl Harbor

Almost the whole of **Pearl Harbor**, the principal base for the US Pacific fleet (just over one hour west of Waikiki, beyond the airport, on TheBus #20), is off limits to visitors. However, the surprise Japanese attack of December 7, 1941, which an official US enquiry called "the greatest military and naval disaster in our nation's history," is commemorated by a simple white memorial set above the wreck of the battleship **USS Arizona**, still discernible in the clear blue waters. More than 1100 of its crew – who had earned the right to sleep in late that Sunday morning by coming second in a military band competition – are entombed there.

Free tours of the memorial operate between 8am and 3pm each day, but it can be two or three hours after you pick up your numbered ticket at the **Pearl Harbor visitor center** (daily 7.30am–5pm; ☎808/422-0561) before you're called to board the ferry that will take you there. Many of the 1.5 million annual visitors are Japanese; a surprisingly even-handed twenty-minute film pays tribute to "one of the most brilliantly planned and executed attacks in naval history," and books and charts are on sale telling the Japanese side of the story. The *USS Arizona* memorial was partly financed by Elvis Presley's 1961 Honolulu concert, his first show after leaving the army.

The huge **USS Missouri**, which survived the attack and was used four years later for the ceremony in Tokyo Harbor that ended World War II, is now moored alongside the *Arizona*. Guided visits include the actual surrender site as well as sweeping views of the harbor from the *Missouri*'s bridge (daily 9am–5pm; $14).

Eating

Honolulu and Waikiki offer so many **food** possibilities that recommendations are inevitably highly personal. For fine dining, all the larger Waikiki hotels have good restaurants, and **Restaurant Row mall** near the harbor in Honolulu is a good bet. There are excellent **fast-food malls** in the **Ala Moana Center**, and the much cheaper and more exotic **Maunakea Marketplace** on Maunakea Street in Chinatown, while Waikiki's Kuhio Avenue is lined with snack outlets and fast-food franchises.

Arancino 255 Beach Walk, Waikiki ☎808/923-5557. Good Italian trattoria in the heart of Waikiki, with plenty of moderately priced pasta, pizza and seafood specialties.

Bali by the Sea *Hilton Hawaiian Village*, 2005 Kalia Rd, Waikiki ☎808/941-2254. Highly refined gourmet restaurant, with irresistible views of the full length of Waikiki and very tasteful (and expensive) "Pacific Rim" cuisine.

Ezogiku 2546 Lemon Rd ☎808/923-2013. Plain and very inexpensive Japanese diner, with three branches in Waikiki – the others are at 2420 Koa Ave and 2146 Kalakaua Ave. Ramen soups plus rice and curry dishes, all at $6–7, to eat in or take out.

Kakaako Kitchen Ward Center, 1200 Ala Moana Blvd ☎808/596-7488. Mall diner that dishes up high-quality Hawaiian-style fast food; pretty much everything, from the hamburger stew to the signature dish chicken linguine, costs $6–9, and there's a menu of daily $7.25 specials like meat loaf or pot roast.

Maxime 1134 Maunakea St ☎808/545-4188. Bright, clean, pastel-pink Chinatown restaurant serving very inexpensive Vietnamese food, especially *pho* (noodle soups).

Oceanarium *Pacific Beach Hotel*, 2490 Kalakaua Ave, Waikiki ☎808/922-6111. Simply furnished restaurant with a big gimmick: you gorge yourself beneath the goggling eyes of 400 live fish, plus the occasional scuba diver. Open for all meals, with noodles, burgers and sandwiches, and full surf'n'turf dinners – all moderately priced.

Perry's Smorgy 2380 Kuhio Ave, Waikiki ☎808/926-0184. All-you-can-eat buffets, indoors and alfresco (with hordes of scavenging birds). Bargain prices – $5 breakfast (7–11am), $6 lunch (11.30am–2.30pm), $9 dinner (5–9pm) – but the food is bland in the extreme. A second location is at the *Ohana Coral Seas*, 250 Lewers St.

Sam Choy's Breakfast, Lunch and Crab 580 N Nimitz Hwy ☎808/545-7979. Copious quantities of modern Hawaiian cuisine, plus a microbrewery, a mile or two west of downtown Honolulu.

Sansei Restaurant Row, 500 Ala Moana Blvd ☎808/536-6286. The central Honolulu setting may not be particularly attractive, but whether you go for the full Pacific Rim menu or stick to the sushi bar, the food is excellent and very well priced.

Shore Bird Beach Broiler *Outrigger Reef on the Beach*, 2169 Kalia Rd, Waikiki ☎808/922-2887. Open-air oceanfront restaurant that serves an $8 breakfast buffet, and dinner with an open salad bar for $13–19, depending on choice of entree. Guests cook their own meat or fish on a communal grill.

Texas Rock 'n' Roll Sushi Bar *Hyatt Regency Hotel*, 2424 Kalakaua Ave, Waikiki ☎808/923-7655. A high-concept, postmodern restaurant/bar, with a bizarre menu that combines traditional sushi at reasonable prices with duck, barbecued beef and chicken.

Yakiniku Canellia 2494 S Beretania St ☎1-800/331-9698. Korean buffet restaurant a mile

north of Waikiki, where you select slices of marinated beef, chicken or pork and grill it yourself at the gas-fired burners set into each table. Open daily for lunch ($10) and dinner ($16).

Entertainment and nightlife

Most of Honolulu's **nightlife** is concentrated in Waikiki, where fun-seeking tourists set the tone. On the whole, the available entertainment is on the bland side. Hawaii tends to be off the circuit for touring musicians, so if you enjoy live music you'll probably have to settle for little-known local performers (rising stars of contemporary Hawaiian music tend to prefer to keep their credibility by not playing in Waikiki too often). Look out also for special events at downtown's beautifully restored Hawaii Theater, 1130 Bethel St (☎808/528-0506). As for **bars**, Chinatown has the most raucous in town, but they're way too hair-raising for most tastes.

Chai's Island Bistro Aloha Tower Marketplace, 101 Ala Moana Blvd ☎808/585-0011. Sumptuous and very expensive Thai restaurant, where the very finest Hawaiian musicians perform for diners nightly 7–8.30pm.

Duke's Canoe Club *Outrigger Waikiki on the Beach*, 2335 Kalakaua Ave ☎808/923-0711. Smooth Hawaiian sounds wash over this ocean-front Waikiki cocktail bar nightly from 4pm to 6pm and 10pm to midnight – including big-name "Concerts on the Beach" Fri–Sun 4–6pm. No cover charge.

Hula's Bar and Lei Stand *Waikiki Grand Hotel*, 134 Kapahulu Ave ☎808/923-0669. Waikiki's most popular gay venue occupies a suite of ocean-view rooms across from the Honolulu Zoo. As well as a state-of-the-art dance bar equipped with giant video screens, there's also a more casual lounge area. Daily 10am–2am.

La Mariana Sailing Club 50 Sand Island Access Rd ☎808/848-2800. Waterfront restaurant with a wonderful 1950s feel, hidden away amid Honolulu's docks, and featuring live Hawaiian music at weekends. Daily 11am–11pm.

Ocean safety

Drownings in Hawaii are all too common. Waves can sweep in from two thousand miles of open ocean onto beaches magnificent to look at but unprotected by any reef. Not all beaches have lifeguards and warning flags; unattended beaches are not necessarily safe. Watch the sea carefully before going in, and never take your eyes off it thereafter. Fierce **rogue waves** can appear from the blue to drag waders – or even those walking along the shore – far out to sea in seconds, and powerful **undertows** may not be detectable until too late. If you do get swept out, don't fight the big waves; wait for the current to die down before trying to swim back to shore.

Sea creatures to avoid include black spiky **sea urchins**, Portuguese man-of-war **jellyfish**, and **coral** in general, which can give painful infected cuts. **Shark attacks** are much rarer than popular imagination suggests; those that do occur are usually due to "misunderstandings," such as surfers idling on their boards looking a bit too much like turtles from below.

Ocean Fun

The nation that invented **surfing** – long before the whites came – remains its greatest arena. The sport was popularized early in the twentieth century by Olympic swimmer Duke Kahanamoku, using a 20ft board; these days most are around six feet. Smaller **boogie boards** make an exhilarating initiation. **Windsurfing**, too, is rapidly growing, often using the same favorite beaches, usually on the north shore of each island. **Snorkeling** and **diving** are top-quality, although Hawaii's **coral** has fewer brilliant hues than those in warmer equatorial waters.

Wave Waikiki 1877 Kalakua Ave ☏ 808/941-0424. In so far as Waikiki has an alternative rock scene, this is it, with a bar upstairs and dance floor down below, and DJs rather than live bands most nights. Daily 9pm–4am.

World Café Nimitz Business Center, 1130 N Nimitz Highway ☏ 808/599-4450. Three-level club not far west of Chinatown that boasts Hawaii's largest dance floor. Hip hop, house and trance music predominate, and as one of the few clubs to admit under-21s it tends to be crammed with hyped-up youngsters. Daily 9pm until late.

Windward Oahu

The most spectacular moment of a tour of Oahu comes as you cross the Koolau Mountains on the **Pali Highway** (Hwy-61) to see the sheer green cliffs of the windward side of the island, veiled by swirling mists. The highest spot, just four miles out of Honolulu heading northeast, is the **Nuuanu Pali Lookout**. Kamehameha the Great finalized his conquest of Oahu here in 1795, forcing hundreds of enemy warriors over the edge of the cliffs; Mark Twain saw the battlefield seventy years later, littered with skulls.

The wide highway is barely adequate for its role as a major commuter thoroughfare connecting Honolulu with **Kailua** and **Kaneohe**. Apart from the Japanese Buddhist **Byodo-In Temple**, in a spectacular setting against the mountains off Hwy-83 (daily 8.30am–4.30pm; $2), there's little worth seeing. The best way to get a close-up view of the inaccessible inland cliffs is on the attractive hiking trails in **Kahana Valley State Park** (no opening hours or fee), a dozen miles short of the island's northernmost tip.

Oahu's leading paying attraction, with one million annual visitors, is the **Polynesian Cultural Center**, slightly further north at Laie (Mon–Sat 12.30–9pm; $27). This haphazard mixture of real and bogus Polynesia – in which the history is firmly on the latter – is owned by the Mormons, and staffed by students from the adjacent Brigham Young University, who perform tired music and dance routines. TheBus #52 takes roughly two hours to get this far.

North Shore Oahu

The **surfing beaches** of northern Oahu are famous the world over, but they're barely equipped for tourists. **Waimea**, **Sunset** and **Ehukai** beach parks (the latter is home of the Banzai Pipeline, the most famous surfing spot in the world) are all laid-back roadside stretches of sand, where you can usually find a quiet spot to yourself. Sunset is best for savoring the atmosphere, though surfers can be an exclusive bunch. The tame summer waves may make you wonder what all the fuss is about; if you see them at full tilt in the winter, you'll have no doubts.

HALEIWA is the main surfers' hangout, combining alternative shops and cafés with upfront tourist traps. Most of the **food** around is vegetarian; at the back of the Celestial Natural Foods store, 66-443 Kamehameha Hwy, the *Paradise Found Café* (☏ 808/637-4640) serves breakfast and lunch for about $6 a time, while *Cholo's Homestyle Mexican*, in the North Shore Marketplace across the street (☏ 808/637-3059), is a busy, plain but very lively Mexican joint.

For **accommodation**, you'll have to head five miles northeast to the *Backpacker's Vacation Inn*, at 59-788 Kamehameha Hwy by Waimea Bay (☏ 808/638-7838, ⓦ www.backpackers-hawaii.com; ❶–❹), which has dorm beds for $17 a night, as well as some great-value ocean-view private rooms and studios.

△ Culture

The Big Island

The **Big Island of Hawaii** is well named – it could hold all the other islands put together, with room to spare. The entire island has the population of a medium-sized town, with 150,000 people (half what it was in Captain Cook's day) and a low level of tourism compared to Oahu or Maui; despite its fair share of restaurants, bars and so on, this is basically a rural community. The development that will surely come may put an end to that, but for the moment there are sleepy old towns all over the island, unchanged for a century. The few resorts are in the least beautiful areas, built on the barren lava flows of the **Kona** coast to catch maximum sunshine.

The Big Island is, in fact, growing, its southern shore inching ever further out to sea, thanks to the **Kilauea** volcano, which has destroyed roads and even towns, and spews out pristine beaches of jet-black sand. **Hawaii Volcanoes National Park**, which includes **Mauna Loa** as well as Kilauea (though not **Mauna Kea**, which is further north and higher than either at 13,796ft), is absolutely compelling; you can explore steaming craters and cinder cones, venture into the rainforest, and at times approach within feet of the eruption itself. The summits of Mauna Loa and Mauna Kea have the clearest air on earth – and astronomical observatories to take advantage of it – but down below, when the tradewinds drop, the island is prone to a choking sulphurous haze known as "**vog**."

As befits the birthplace and base of **King Kamehameha**, more of the ancient Hawaii survives on the Big Island than anywhere else in the islands. **Puuhonua O Honaunau National Historical Park** preserves a "place of refuge" for *kapu*-breakers and defeated warriors, and there are further temples north along the Kohala coast, while **Waipio Valley**, where Kamehameha spent his youth, remains as lush and green as ever.

Flights to the Big Island arrive at **Hilo** on the rainy east coast, or the much less genuine but inoffensive resort of **Kailua** (often referred to as Kona) on the west. If you don't rent a **car**, you may not get to the interesting sites; one bus daily links Hilo and Kailua, and organized bus tours go to specific attractions, but public transportation is all but nonexistent.

Windward Hawaii

Almost all the rain that falls on the slopes of Mauna Kea flows down to the sea on the eastern side of the Big Island. As a result, myriad streams and waterfalls nourish dense jungle-like vegetation, ensuring that the main road north along the coast from Hilo – the only sizeable base for travelers – is alive with flowering trees and orchids.

Hilo

Although it's the Big Island's capital, and largest town, just 45,000 people live in **HILO**, which remains endearing and unpressured. Mass tourism has never taken off here; basically it rains too much. However, the rain falls mostly at night, and America's wettest city blazes with tropical blooms, set against a backdrop of rainbows.

Hilo has always been at the mercy of fire and water. Cataclysmic *tsunami* killed 96 people in April 1946, and a further 61 in May 1960. Countless lava flows have also threatened to engulf it; in 1881 Princess Ruth (see p.1297) summoned up all her spiritual power to halt one on the edge of town, while in 1984 another flow stopped just eight miles short.

Arrival, information and getting around

Downtown Hilo is compact and very walkable. However, the urban area extends for several miles, and the **airport** at **General Lyman Field** (☎808/935-4782), on the eastern outskirts, is well beyond walking distance. If you're not renting a car at the airport, a taxi into town is your only alternative, costing around $8.

The **Hawaii Visitors Bureau** is at 250 Keawe St (Mon–Fri 8am–noon & 1–4.30pm; ☎808/961-5797). Hilo's HeleOn Bus Company (☎808/961-8744) operates a small-scale **city bus** service, plus one service each to Kailua (Mon–Sat) and down to Hawaii Volcanoes National Park (Mon–Fri) from the Mooheau Bus Terminal on Kamehameha Avenue.

Accommodation

Hilo, and the whole east coast, has fewer major resort hotels than usual in Hawaii, but there are several **accommodation** options; the less expensive ones tend to be in town rather than around the loop of **Banyan Drive** on the seafront near the airport.

Arnott's Lodge and Hostel 98 Apapane Rd ☎808/969-7097, ⓦwww.arnottslodge.com. Laid-back accommodation in a two-story lodge, tucked away in the woods 2 miles southeast of downtown. Call from the airport for free pickup. 12-bed dorms ($17 a bed) and private rooms, plus organized island tours. ❶/❸

Dolphin Bay Hotel 333 Iliahi St ☎808/935-1466, ⓦwww.dolphinbayhilo.com. Very nice, very friendly little hotel, just across the river from downtown. Spotlessly clean one- and two-bedroom suites with kitchens. ❸

Shipman House B&B Inn 131 Kaiulani St ☎808/934-8002 or 1-800/627-8447, ⓦwww.hilo-hawaii.com. Magnificent Victorian mansion, converted into a plush B&B. Three grand antique-furnished en-suite rooms in the main house, plus two more in a guest cottage. ❻

Uncle Billy's Hilo Bay Hotel 87 Banyan Drive ☎808/961-5818 or 1-800/367-5102, ⓦwww.unclebilly.com. Family-run hotel, the oldest on Banyan Drive, with pleasantly relentless Polynesian decor and budget restaurant. ❺

Downtown Hilo

There is a simple and tragic reason why **downtown Hilo** looks so appealingly low-key, with its modest streets and wooden stores: all the buildings that stood on the seaward side of Kamehameha Avenue were destroyed by the two *tsunami* of 1946 and 1960. After 1960, no attempt was made to rebuild "little Tokyo," which had housed Hilo's predominantly Japanese population, and the seafront is now occupied by a succession of pleasant gardens. The story is told in the high-tech **Pacific Tsunami Museum**, on Kamehameha Avenue at Kalakuaua Street (Mon–Sat 10am–4pm; $5). A scale model shows how the city looked before the 1946 disaster; contemporary footage and personal letters bring home the full impact of the tragedy. The section devoted to the wave of 1960 is even more poignant. Locals had several hours' warning that it was on its way, but many flocked to the seafront to watch it come in; photos show them waiting excitedly for the cataclysm that was about to engulf them.

The focus of the two-part **Lyman Museum** at 276 Haili St (Mon–Sat 9am–4.30pm; $7) is the original 1830s **Mission House**, furnished in dark *koa* wood, which belonged to Calvinist missionaries David and Sarah Lyman. The museum next door starts with a fascinating set of ancient weapons and then documents Hawaii's various ethnic groups, including the Portuguese shipped in in 1878 from the overpopulated but similarly volcanic Azores, whose *braginha* became the ukelele.

A couple of miles up Waianuenue Avenue, at **Rainbow Falls**, just to the right of the road, a spectacular wide waterfall plummets 100ft across the mouth of a huge cavern. Continue another two miles to reach the bubbling, foaming pools known as the **Boiling Pots**.

Eating and nightlife

Most of Hilo's (eminently missable) **nightlife** is in the Banyan Drive hotels, though there are a few shows at downtown's restored Palace Theater. As well as its **restaurants**, early risers will enjoy the daily 7am **Suisan Fish Auction**, at Banyan Drive and Lihiwai Street, where you can buy from the night's catch of marlin and other big fish.

Bears Coffee 110 Keawe St ☏ 808/935-0708. Hilo's most bohemian breakfast hangout, one block back from the ocean in the heart of downtown.

Café Pesto 130 Kamehameha Ave ☏ 808/969-6640. Large, Pacific-influenced Italian restaurant, facing the ocean from downtown Hilo, serving tasty calzones and pizzas.

Pescatore 235 Keawe St ☏ 808/969-9090.

Formal Italian dining opposite the visitor center, with lunch specials ($7–10) and wonderful fish stews for dinner ($25).

The Seaside Restaurant 1790 Kalanianaole Ave ☏ 808/935-8825. Located just over two miles southeast of town, this superb, if plain, fish restaurant presides over thirty-acre fishponds brimming with trout, mullet and catfish. A full fish supper costs under $20.

North from Hilo

The **Belt Road** (Hwy-19) follows the **Hamakua coast** north of Hilo, clinging to the hillsides and crossing ravines on slender bridges. At first the fields are crammed into narrow rain-carved "gulches"; further north the land spreads out. For a glimpse into the interior, head into the mountains after fifteen miles to the 450ft **Akaka Falls**. A short loop trail through the forest, festooned with wild orchids, offers views of Akaka and other jungle-like tropical waterfalls.

Waipio Valley

Hwy-240, which turns north off the Belt Road at **HONOKAA**, comes to an abrupt end after nine miles at the edge of **Waipio Valley**. As the southernmost of six successive sheer-walled valleys, this is the only one accessible by land – and it's as close as Hawaii comes to the classic South Seas image of an isolated and self-sufficient valley, dense with fruit trees and laced by footpaths leading down to the sea. Spectacular waterfalls cascade down the valley's flanks, but recurrent tidal waves have ensured that only a few taro farmers now live here.

It's perfectly possible to walk down the steep, mile-long track into Waipio, but most visitors take tours, either in the four-wheel-drive vehicles of the Waipio Valley Shuttle (Mon–Sat 9am–4pm; ☏ 808/775-7121; $40), at the Waipio Valley Art Works in Kukuihaele, a mile from the end of the road; in horse-drawn wagons (☏ 808/775-9518; $40); or on horseback (☏ 808/775-0419; $75). It's permissible to **camp** discreetly for free on the beach, for which you need a permit from the Bishop Estate (☏ 808/322-5300).

North Kohala

On the green slopes of **Kohala Mountain**, at the northern tip of the Big Island, traditional plantation towns such as **HAWI** survive virtually unchanged – run-down in an appealing sort of way, the all-purpose stores still floored with creaking planks. Call in at the spacious *Bamboo Restaurant and Bar* (☎808/889-5555) to enjoy one of the friendliest and most Hawaiian restaurants in the state.

Polulu Valley, where North Kohala's main artery, Hwy-270, comes to a dead end, is the last of the chain of inaccessible valleys, and for the moment is every bit as pristine as Waipio. The fear of *tsunami*, which led the Hawaiians to abandon these once densely populated valleys, is probably their best defense against the rapacity of the developers.

Waimea and the interior

The **interior** of the Big Island comes as a surprise: pastoral meadows roll over gentle hills where once stood forests of sandalwood. This is cattle-ranching country, most of it – ten percent of the island – owned by the United States's largest private ranch, the **Parker Ranch**.

WAIMEA (also known as **Kamuela**) is not the company town it once was – the Parker Ranch now employs just one hundred of its eight thousand inhabitants – but more of a sophisticated country-town resort, which retains traces of its cowboy past. Though you can no longer tour the ranch itself, the ranch has an interesting **visitor center** (Mon–Sat 9am–5pm; $6) in town; the nearby **Kamuela Museum** is enjoyably eclectic and eccentric, with an extensive range of ancient Hawaiian artifacts (daily 8am–5pm; $5).

Waimea practicalities

B&Bs are a booming business in Waimea; in fact there's little else. Barbara Campbell runs her own very appealing *Waimea Gardens Cottage* (☎808/885-4550 or 1-800/262-9912; ❻), and also coordinates Hawaii's Best B&Bs (PO Box 563, Kamuela, HI 96743, ⓦwww.bestbnb.com), a selection of properties on all the islands. The main alternative is the refurbished *Kamuela Inn* (☎808/885-4243; ❹), which is part inn, part luxury hotel. *Merriman's* in Opelo Plaza (☎808/885-6822) wins awards for its innovative **cuisine**, but if paying $20 for an entree puts you off, cross the street and walk a few yards to the *Waimea Coffee Co* in Parker Square (☎808/885-4472), which offers good coffees and vegetarian specials.

The Saddle Road

The fifty-mile **Saddle Road** cuts across the Big Island from Hilo to Kona, between Mauna Kea and Mauna Loa. Even locals consider it dangerous, especially at night, as there are no facilities, and it's a winding, foggy drive. If you do choose to chance it (in the daytime), you get some great views of the volcanoes – and a good deal of mist even then. Strictly speaking, though, rental-car companies forbid their clients from driving on it.

The Kona coast

Hawaii's leeward **Kona coast** divides into two distinct areas. To the north of its only sizeable community, **Kailua**, barren lava trails down to the sea from the third highest of the Big Island's volcanoes, Hualalai. Thanks to the relentless sun on its magnificent beaches, luxury hotels dot the shoreline, incongruous green patches in the wasteland. To the south, the hillsides are more fertile, and although the condos are spreading, you can still get a real feel for the old Hawaii, in the land where Captain Cook met his end.

North Kona and the resorts

The best of the spectacular sandy beaches along the Kona coast – safe for summer swimming, though with tempestuous winter surf – lie to the north of Kailua. **Hapuna Beach**, almost forty miles up the coast, is deservedly the most famous, despite being overshadowed by the giant *Hapuna Prince Beach Hotel* (℡808/880-1111 or 1-800/882-6060, Ⓦwww.hapunabeachprincehotel; Ⓞ); it's still possible to rent $20 beachside cabins (℡808/974-6200), but since opening in 1994 it has lost some of its charm. For real idyllic seclusion, head instead for **Kona Coast State Park** (daily except Wed 9am–8pm; free), reached via a bumpy dirt road just a couple of miles north of Keahole Airport.

Several extraordinary **resort hotels** lie in the district of South Kohala, thirty miles north of Kailua (see below). Three separate enclaves – Waikoloa, Mauna Kea and Mauna Lani – have been landscaped out of this inhospitable lava desert, each one a self-contained oasis holding two or three hotels, a beach or two, and nothing else. Although **Waikoloa** is the least exclusive of the three, it's home to the ludicrously ostentatious, mile-long *Hilton Waikoloa* (℡808/886-1234, Ⓦwww.hiltonwaikoloavillage.com; Ⓞ), said to consume seven percent of all the island's energy. Guests travel to and from their rooms by electric boats or monorail.

Kailua (Kona)

Although the Big Island's main resort is officially called **KAILUA**, and its postal address is "Kailua-Kona," you're likely to hear it referred to as **Kona** as often as not. It's reasonably attractive, and has played its part in Hawaiian history, but its summer-holiday seafront of fast-food restaurants and souvenir shops could be anywhere; and the wind-borne "vog" means that the atmosphere can be as bad as in Los Angeles or London.

Arrival

Open-plan **Keahole Airport**, on a field of black lava nine miles north of Kailua, has the usual car rental places; otherwise Speedi Shuttle (℡808/329-5433) into town costs around $20 per person. In Kailua, a regular **shuttle bus** runs the six-mile length of Alii Drive every ninety minutes (8.30am–9.30pm; $2; ℡808/961-8744). One daily bus follows Hwy-11 around the north of the island to Hilo, leaving Kailua just before 6am and returning in the evening.

Accommodation

Alii Drive is lined for about five miles south from Kailua with hotels and condos, but none offers much by way of budget accommodation. The listings opposite therefore include a couple of places a bit further along the coast.

King Kamehameha's Kona Beach Hotel 75-5660 Palani Rd ☎808/329-2911 or 1-800/367-6060, ⓦwww.konabeachhotel.com. Long-established landmark hotel at the northern end of oceanfront Kailua, centered around a picturesque little beach and the Ahuena Heiau (see below). ❺

Kona Seaside Hotel 75-5646 Palani Rd ☎808/329-2455 or 1-800/560-5558, ⓦwww.sand-seaside.com. Six floors of reasonable air-conditioned rooms, with and without kitchens, plus discounted car rental. ❻

Kona Tiki Hotel 75-5968 Alii Drive ☎808/329-1425. Bargain three-story motel, on the ocean a mile south of central Kailua. No phones or TVs, but some rooms have kitchenettes. ❸

Patey's Place 75-195 Ala Ona Ona ☎808/326-7018, ⓦwww.hawaiian-hostels.com. Chaotic, ramshackle and unappealing budget hostel that's nonetheless popular with backpackers and surfers. $18 beds in 4-person dorms, plus some private rooms with shared bath. ❶/❷

The Town

Hulihee Palace (Mon–Fri 9am–4pm, Sat & Sun 10am–4pm; $5) faces out to sea from the center of Kailua. Built as the governor's residence in 1838, it's not all that imposing from the outside. Within, it's notable for massive *koa*-wood furnishings, made to fit the considerable girth of the various members of the Hawaiian royal family who later lived here, such as the redoubtable 400-pound Princess Ruth. The 1836 **Mokuaikaua Church** directly opposite was the first in Hawaii, and part of it has been set aside as a museum of the early days of Hawaiian Christianity. A peculiar "sausage-tree" from Mozambique, named after the elongated fruit that dangles from its branches, grows in the church grounds. Nearby, *King Kamehameha's Kona Beach Hotel* (listed above) dominates the northern end of the bay. King Kamehameha's funeral rites were performed in the ancient temple of **Ahuena Heiau**, which juts into the sea in front of its beach.

Some of the world's best fishing, snorkeling and scuba spots are approached by sea from Kailua. Expensive two-hour tours on Atlantis Submarines ($79, under-12s half-price; ☎808/329-6626) descend one hundred feet to a coral reef, accompanied by the *Star Wars* theme, to see a frenzy of feeding fish and the occasional lurking shark. The catamaran *Fair Wind* ($80; ☎808/322-2788) goes to Kealakekua Bay, for snorkeling and a bit of scuba. If you fancy chartering a boat to fish for the big ones, contact the Charter Desk (☎808/329-5735, ⓦwww.charterdesk.com); rates start at $75 for a half-day.

Eating and drinking

Competition ensures that the bars and restaurants of central Kailua – especially those along the seafront – are well priced, though the relentless vacation atmosphere means the place can seem a bit unreal.

Cassandra's Greek Taverna Kona Plaza, 75-5719 Alii Drive ☎808/334-1066. Delicious and inexpensive Greek food, from light salads to substantial moussakas.

Huggo's 76-6828 Kuhakai St ☎808/329-1493. Lunch and dinner only served on a large ocean-view terrace. The menu includes burgers, salads and sandwiches, as well as Pacific Rim specialities, and there's often live evening entertainment.

Ocean View Inn 75-5683 Alii Drive ☎808/329-9998. Very inexpensive Hawaiian and Asian diner overlooking the sea, where the menu includes

roast beef dinners, traditional fish dishes and even Chinese cuisine. Closed Mon.

Oodles of Noodles Crossroads Shopping Center, 75-1027 Henry St ☎808/329-2222. Pan-Asian noodle joint, a mile up from the ocean near the highway, serving great dinners from around $15.

Sibu Café Banyan Court Mall, 75-5695 W Alii Drive ☎808/329-1112. Popular, informal Indonesian restaurant, with no views but some atmospheric outdoor seating. Serves $11–14 entrees, including a tasty shrimp *sate*.

Kealakekua Bay

Kealakekua Bay, a dozen miles south of Kailua, was where Captain Cook was killed on his second voyage to Hawaii (see box below). One of ancient Hawaii's major population centers, it's now barely inhabited, and the white **obelisk** on the death site – legally a small piece of England – is all but inaccessible. You can only get to within a mile of it by car, to the beach at **Napoopoo** across the bay, though you'll glimpse it from the road on the way down. The bay itself is the best place on the Big Island for **snorkeling**, even if there are sharks further out. It's also possible to hike down to the monument, but it's a grueling four-hour round-trip, for which you need to carry all your water and supplies. The trail starts just before the town of **CAPTAIN COOK**, which is also home to the bargain *Manago Hotel* (℡808/323-2642, Ⓦwww.managohotel.com; ❶/❷), offering comfortable ocean-view rooms amid flowering Japanese gardens.

This region, South Kona, is the prime source of **Kona coffee**, which sells here for around $20 a pound (including shipping). A mile south of Captain

---

The death of Captain Cook

When **Captain James Cook** sailed into Kealakekua Bay on January 17, 1779, he was on his second visit to Hawaii, after a year spent searching in vain for the fabled Northwest Passage. As he anchored his ship, the *Resolution*, in this sheltered harbor, a vast crowd of Hawaiians gathered to greet him – eyewitnesses claim that as many as ten thousand were out on the water. For three weeks, he was fed and feted by chief Kalaniopuu, attending temple ceremonies and wrestling matches, and replenishing his supplies.

The departure of the *Resolution*, amid declarations of friendship, might have been the end of things, had it not been forced to return just a week later, following a storm that left the ship in tatters. This time the islanders were not so hospitable, and far from keen to part with further scarce resources. On February 14, Cook led a landing party of nine men in a bid to kidnap Kalaniopuu and force the islanders to return a stolen small boat. In an undignified scuffle, surrounded by thousands of hostile warriors, including the future Kamehameha the Great, Cook was stabbed and died at the water's edge. His body was treated as befit a dead chief: the skull and leg bones were kept, and the rest cremated.

The legend soon grew that the Hawaiians had taken Cook to be the great god *Lono*; but Hawaiian commentators now argue that such tales say more about European attitudes to Cook than about Polynesian perceptions. To the European mentality of the time, it was self-evident that a noble figure of the Enlightenment such as Captain Cook must appear god-like to superstitious "natives." That Hawaiians prostrated themselves on the ground in front of Cook could only mean that they were worshipping him as a god – even though commoners were obliged to do so before any of their chiefs. It was in England, not Hawaii, that popular images appeared showing his ascent to heaven, borne by angels.

The major anomaly in the legend is quite why the Hawaiians would have killed this "god." Some proponents say it was a sacrifice, even though it happened in battle, while others argue that the man who struck the final blow "didn't know" that Cook was a "god." The usual explanation, that it was simply an accident, serves both to perpetuate the idea of Hawaiians as "innocent" savages, and to absolve Cook himself of any responsibility for his fate. What seems more likely is that his actions in peremptorily dismantling a temple at Napoopoo for use as firewood antagonized the priests, and when he infuriated the chiefs as well by seizing Kalaniopuu, deference gave way to defiance.

Cook, the *Coffee Shack* (daily 7am–3.30pm; ☎808/328-9555) serves wonderfully fresh coffee and smoothies on a terrace that enjoys staggering views all the way down to Kealakekua Bay.

Puuhonua O Honaunau – "The City of Refuge"

Puuhonua O Honaunau National Historical Park (daily 7.30am–5.30pm; $2; ⓦwww.nps.gov/puho), four miles on from Kealakekua, is the single most evocative historical site in all the Hawaiian islands, jutting into the Pacific on a small peninsula of jagged black lava. The grounds include a palace, with fishpond and private canoe landing, and three *heiaus*, guarded by large carved effigies of gods – reproductions, but still eerie in their original setting. An ancient "**place of refuge**" lies firmly protected behind the mortarless masonry of the sixteenth-century **Great Wall**. Those who broke ancient Hawaii's intricate system of *kapu* (taboo) – perhaps by treading on the shadow of a chief, or fishing in the wrong season – could expect summary execution unless they fled to the sanctuary of a place such as this. As chiefs lived on the surrounding land, transgressors had to swim through the shark-infested seas. If successful, they would be absolved and released overnight.

Hawaii Volcanoes National Park

The Big Island's southernmost volcanoes, **Mauna Loa** and **Kilauea**, jointly constitute **HAWAII VOLCANOES NATIONAL PARK**, thirty miles from Hilo and eighty from Kailua. It's possibly the most dramatic of all the US national parks; as well as two active volcanoes, of which at least one is likely to be erupting at any given time, it includes desert, arctic tundra, and rainforest.

Evidence is everywhere of the awesome power of the volcanoes to create and destroy; no map can keep up with the latest whims of the lava flow. Whole towns have been engulfed, and what were once prized beachfront properties lie buried hundreds of yards back from the sea.

Kilauea Caldera

The main focus of the park is **Kilauea Caldera**, close to the rim of which both the **visitor center** (daily 7.45am–5pm; $10 per vehicle; ☎808/967-7311, ⓦwww.nps.gov/havo) and the fascinating **Jaggar Museum** of geology (daily 8.30am–5pm; free), on the eleven-mile **Crater Rim Drive**, offer basic orientation. Kilauea is said to be the home of the volcano goddess **Pele**, who has followed the "hot spot" from island to island. In 1824 Queen Kapiolani, a recent convert to Christianity, defied her by descending into the crater, reading aloud from her Bible, eating the *tabu* red *ohelo* berries, and throwing stones into the pit. When Mark Twain came here, he saw a dazzling lake of liquid fire; since a huge explosion in 1924 it's been shallower and quieter, a black dusty expanse dotted with hissing steam vents. Enthusiastic hikers should set time aside to follow the long trails that explore the caldera floor, now (mostly) solid. Both the **Halemaumau Trail**, a seven-mile round trip, and the **Kilauea Iki Trail**, a total of five miles, involve picking your way from cairn to cairn across an eerie landscape of cracked and jagged lava.

Among shorter routes, the mile-long **Devastation Trail** is a boardwalk laid across the scene of a 1959 eruption; scientists are monitoring how long vegetation takes to re-establish itself. Most of what you see is new growth – fresh lava is full of nutrients, and rainwater and seeds soon collect in the recesses – but a few older trees survived partial submersion in ash by growing "aerial roots" some way up their trunks.

A short drive from *Volcano House* (see below), and across the road from the crater, is a rainforest. Starting from close to the Devastation Trail, a ten-minute walk takes you through **Thurston Lava Tube**, created when the surface of a lava stream hardened on exposure to the air. It's now a damp empty tunnel, a segment of which is open and illuminated. Gigantic ferns grow over the top, and a few roots have worked their way through cracks in the rock to dangle from the ceiling.

Chain of Craters Road

Chain of Craters Road winds down to the sea from Crater Rim Drive, sweeping around a succession of cones and vents in an empty landscape where the occasional dead white tree trunk or flowering shrub pokes up. Fresh sheets of lava constantly ooze down the slopes to cover the road. When a new road is built on top of the flow, more lava covers it. Along the coast, the scale of the damage since 1983 has been too great to repair – over seven miles have been lost – so now the road is a dead end, and getting shorter year by year. One by one the landmarks along its seafront stretch – such as **Wahaula Heiau**, a temple where human sacrifice may have been introduced to Hawaii – have been destroyed, and before long it may not follow the shoreline at all.

Check current conditions at the visitor center when you arrive (see overleaf), and make sure you have enough gas. The end of the road is a fifty-mile round-trip from the park entrance, and there are no facilities of any kind along the way. For several years, depending on where current volcanic activity is concentrated, it has been possible at times to walk across the congealed lava blocking Chain of Craters Road to see molten rock gush from the earth – sometimes directly into the sea. The park's **Volcano Update line** (☎808/985-6000) has the latest details; for information on ranger-led tours, call the visitor center.

Practicalities

The national park operates two free **campgrounds** on a first-come, first-served basis, while the famous *Volcano House*, on the very edge of the crater within the park (PO Box 53; ☎808/967-7321; ❹), has spectacular views, and good food in the evening, although the prices for its simple motel-style rooms are rather high. Otherwise, the small and inconspicuous town of **VOLCANO**, just before the park entrance on the Hilo side, provides the best places to **stay** in the vicinity, with B&Bs such as *Hale* (PO Box 758; ☎808/967-7986, ⓦwww.haleohia.com; ❹), south of the highway across from the village. *Kilauea Lodge*, on the leafy main street (☎808/967-7366, ⓦwww.kilauealodge.com; ❺), is a comfortable inn with a good **restaurant**, and there's also good food at *Surt's* nearby (☎808/985-6711).

Maui

The island of **MAUI**, the second largest in the Hawaiian chain, is Oahu's fastest-growing rival, attracting roughly a third of all visitors to the state. Some would say that things have gone too far. What were once remote, unspoiled beaches, around **Kaanapali** and **Kihei** for example, have been swamped by sprawling resorts, and **Lahaina**, once "whaling capital of the world," is now little more than just another tourist trap.

On the other hand, the crowds come to Maui for the good reason that it's still beautiful. This is probably the best equipped of all the islands for **activity** holidays – whale-watching, windsurfing, diving, sailing, snorkeling and cycling. Temperatures along the coast can be searing, especially at Lahaina, but it's always possible to escape to somewhere cooler. **Upcountry Maui**, on the slopes of the mighty **Haleakala** volcano, is a delight, well away from the bustle; **Makawao** and **Paia** here make good alternative hangouts, although they're short on accommodation. Finally, the waterfalls and ravines along the tortuous road out west to **Hana** outclass anything on Oahu.

Kahului and Wailuku

Almost half of Maui's 120,000 inhabitants – the workers who keep this fantasy island going – live in the twin towns of **KAHULUI** and **WAILUKU**, to the north of the "neck" connecting its two mountainous sections. The land here can be so flat you fear the waves will wash right over it. Kahului is the main commercial center; Wailuku, if not aesthetically pleasing, is one of the few towns on Maui that feels like a genuine community, and with its budget hotels and restaurants – and the stunning **Iao Needle** nearby – makes a good central base.

Arrival and information

Virtually all visitors to Maui arrive at **Kahului Airport**, which is well placed for all the major destinations and has an information booth. Maui Airporter Shuttle **buses** (☎808/877-7308) connect the airport regularly with Lahaina and Kaanapali, for $13 per person, while TransHawaiian (☎808/877-0380) provides similar services to the rest of the island.

The offices of the **Maui Visitors Bureau** are hard to find, tucked away at 1727 Wili Pa Loop in Wailuku (Mon–Fri 8am–4.30pm; ☎808/244-3530); it's easier simply to pick up information in major hotels.

Accommodation

As most of the Maui resorts are long oceanfront strips of expensive hotels, where you have to drive just to get to a shop or restaurant, there's a lot to be said for a simple room in Wailuku.

Banana Bungalow 310 N Market St, Wailuku ☎808/244-5090 or 1-800/846-7835, ℡http://home1.gte.net/bungalow.htm. Extremely convivial, unofficial hostel with Maui's least expensive accommodation. $16 for a dorm bed; some bare, basic doubles are also available. Amenities include informal meals, organized trips and cut-price car rental. ❶/❷

Maui Seaside Hotel 100 W Kaahumanu Ave at the harbor ☎808/877-3311 or 1-800/560-5552,

www.mauiseasidehotel.com. Good-value rooms in a far from attractive setting, plus discounted car rental. ❺
Northshore Inn 2080 Vineyard St, Wailuku

☎808/242-1448, www.hawaii-hostel.com. $16 dorm beds, plus some plain private rooms. Has much the same communal feel as *Banana Bungalow*. ❶/❷

Exploring Kahului and Wailuku

There's no sightseeing to speak of in either Kahului or Wailuku, though you may well become familiar with both while shopping for food and other necessities, better value here than elsewhere on the island. **Market Street** in Wailuku contains several interesting curio and souvenir shops, and commands a view across to Haleakala.

Wailuku's Main Street heads straight into the **West Maui Mountains**, stopping three miles in at **Iao Needle**, a stunning 1200ft pinnacle of green-clad lava. It stands, head usually in the clouds, at the intersection of two lush valleys; you can't climb the needle itself, but hiking trails lead off in all directions, and as few visitors follow them for any distance you can soon be alone in the wilderness. Kamehameha won control of Maui here in 1790, in a battle determined by a cannonade directed by two European gunners.

Eating

While both Kahului and Wailuku hold a handful of good-value **restaurants**, neither has anything that could be considered fine dining.

Kakaako Kitchen Kaahumanu Mall, Kahului ☎808/893-0366. High-quality Hawaiian-style fast-food diner, where pretty much everything, at lunch and dinner alike, costs $6–9, with daily specials such as pot roast or seafood marinara.
Maui Coffee Roasters 444 Hana Hwy, Kahului ☎808/877-2877. Relaxed espresso bar serving

good breakfasts, lunch specials and, of course, coffees.
Saeng's 2119 Vineyard St ☎808/244-1567. Pleasant, plant-filled restaurant, serving top-quality Thai food at bargain prices (entrees come in well under $20).

West Maui

Despite the guaranteed sunshine that draws the vacationers, you can feel somewhat cut off if you choose to stay on Maui's **west coast**, while the prices are higher, and the long drive around is worsened by heavy traffic. The hotels and shopping centers are concentrated in the two main resorts, **Lahaina** and **Kaanapali**, although development has sensibly been restricted to the *makai* (oceanward) side of the Honoapiilani Highway, leaving the inland hills and valleys untouched except by drifting rainbows.

Lahaina

The square at the heart of modern **LAHAINA** is all but filled by a magnificent **banyan tree**, its aerial roots pushing down into the earth to become sturdy additional trunks. Just in front, in the small harbor, the replica square-rigged *Carthaginian* houses a lackluster **maritime museum** (daily 10am–5pm; $4). The **Pioneer Inn** nearby is Lahaina's main social center, great for a convivial, if not quiet, beer.

Otherwise, a walk up Front Street and back down Wainee Street covers most of what Lahaina has to offer. While it does hold some appealing nineteenth-century buildings, the concentration of tourist shops and fast-food places is

Whale-hunting and whale-watching

The first **whaling ships** arrived in Hawaii in 1820, the same year as the missionaries – and had an equally dramatic impact. With the ports of Japan closed to outsiders, Hawaii swiftly became the center of the industry. Any Pacific port of call must have seemed a godsend to the whalers, who were away from New England for three years at a time, and paid so badly that most were either fugitives from justice or just plain mad (see p.230). Hawaii was such a paradise that up to fifty percent of each crew would desert, to be replaced by native Hawaiians, born seafarers eager to see the world. Soon King Kamehameha IV had established his own whaling fleet, and the economy adapted to meet the sailors' needs. Cattle-raising began on the Big Island, and vegetables were grown on Maui.

Until the 1840s, Honolulu, which permitted drinking, was the whalers' favorite port. Then potatoes and prostitution lured them to **Lahaina** as well, which by 1857 stretched for several miles. The sea was calm enough for ships to dock along the open road, and a grassy marketplace stood beside a central canal. Both Lahaina and Honolulu soon became notorious for such diseases as syphilis, influenza, measles, typhoid and smallpox.

At the peak of the trade, almost six hundred whaling vessels docked in Honolulu in a single year. Decline came with the Civil War – when many ships were bought up in order to be sunk as a blockade of Confederate ports – and an 1871 disaster, when 31 vessels lingered in the Arctic too long, became frozen in, and had to be abandoned.

Whale-watching

Ironically, the waters just off western Maui now rate among the world's best areas for whale-watching and research. Between January and March each year, and for up to a month either side of that, **humpback whales** use the ocean channels here as both sanctuary and playground.

The whales are often clearly visible from the shore, but specific whale-watching trips can take you much closer (with money-back guarantees if you don't see one). Operators include the nonprofit Pacific Whale Foundation ($25; ☏808/879-8811).

phenomenal. The view out to sea, toward the island of **Lanai**, is a welcome respite. If you have the time, consider taking a ferry there for the day; there's little to see, but the main beach, at Hulopoe Bay, is a delight. Expedition provides five sailings daily, from Lahaina Harbor ($50 round-trip; ☏808/661-3756).

Accommodation

If you have the money to spend on resort-style **accommodation**, Lahaina and the coast to the north have some good options, but there's very little available for under $100 per night.

Aloha Lani Inn 13 Kauaula Rd ☏808/661-8040, ⓦwww.maui.net/~tony. Two small, simple rooms in a comfortable B&B near the beach. ❹.

Aston Maui Islander 660 Wainee St ☏808/667-9766 or 1-800/922-7866, ⓦwww.aston-hotels .com. Very central, low-key but attractively refurbished, mid-range accommodation. ❺

Best Western Pioneer Inn 658 Wharf St ☏808/661-3636 or 1-800/4575457, ⓦwww.pio-

neerinnmaui.com. Characterful and very lively old hotel, right in the thick of things. Tastefully furnished rooms come with private bath and air-conditioning. ❺

Old Lahaina House PO Box 10355, Lahaina, HI 96761 ☏808/667-4663 or 1-800/847-0761, ⓦwww.oldlahaina.com. Good-quality en-suite B&B rooms in friendly private home, complete with pool. ❹

Food and nightlife

Lahaina's harborside malls contain a tremendous selection of restaurants, national and local chain outlets and takeout places, not all of them good by any means, but covering a wider spectrum than the hotels.

Cheese Burger in Paradise 811 Front St ☎808/661-4855. Busy, crowded seafront restaurant, perched on stilts above the water. Very much what the name suggests, though as well as meaty $7–8 cheeseburgers they have fish sandwiches and spinach nutburgers at similar prices.

David Paul's Lahaina Grill *Lahaina Inn*, 127 Lahainaluna Rd ☎808/667-5117. Upmarket dinner-only restaurant with Maui's finest Pacific Rim cooking; it's slightly cramped and unatmospheric, but the food is great.

The Feast at Lele 505 Front St ☎808/667-5353. An inspired cross between a *luau* and a gourmet restaurant. Each of the five Polynesian courses consists of at least two dishes – a colossal amount of food, but it's excellent and unusual, and the beachfront setting is superb. The $89 charge, though steep, includes unlimited cocktails and other beverages. Reservations are essential. April–Sept Tues–Sat 6pm, Oct–March Tues–Sat 5.30pm.

Pacific 'O 505 Front St ☎808/667-4341. Pacific Rim cuisine served in an attractive oceanfront mall setting; try the amazing $28 Shrimp Nui.

Sunrise Café 693A Front St at Market St ☎808/661-8558. Small, laid-back and very central café, with outdoor seating beside its own tiny patch of beach. Espressos, smoothies, salads, sandwiches and daily specials, with prices starting at around $6.

Kaanapali

KAANAPALI, just a few miles north of Lahaina but reliably cooler, was never a town; fields of sugar cane here were replaced in the 1960s by high-rise hotels and condos, each no doubt comfortable enough but soulless en masse. Besides several perfect family **beaches** – swimming and snorkeling are best at **Black Rock**, in front of the *Sheraton* – the main attraction is the **whaling museum** in the Whalers Village mall (daily 9.30am–10pm; free). Grisly but fascinating exhibits include a cast-iron "try pot," used for reducing whale blubber at sea; such pots gave rise to the stereotyped but not entirely untrue image of cannibals cooking missionaries in big black cauldrons.

Maui activities

Promotional handouts and free newspapers advertise a wide range of tours and activities; agencies along Front Street in Lahaina can offer cut-rate deals.

Molokini

Maui's best-known **snorkeling** and **diving** spot is the tiny crescent of **Molokini** poking above the sea, all that's left of a once-great volcano. There's no beach, or landfall of any kind, but you do see a lot of fish, including deep-water species. Countless cruises leave early each morning (to avoid the worst of the heat) from Maalea Harbor; snorkelers can pay anything from $45 to $100 for a morning trip, and from $30 for a shorter afternoon jaunt. Vessels range from the forty-passenger *Blue Dolphin* (☎808/622-0075) up to the 150-seater *Prince Kuhio* (☎808/242-8777).

Downhill Cycle Rides

One of Maui's more unusual opportunities is to be taken by van to the top of **Haleakala**, watch the sun rise, and then ride a bicycle 39 miles down to Paia by the sea – without pedaling once. Serious cyclists may find the slow pace of the trip frustrating; complete novices or the unfit shouldn't try; the in-betweens will think it's great. Companies running trips for around $80 (including pickups) include Haleakala Bike Co (☎808/572-2200) and Maui Downhill (☎808/871-2155).

A free shuttle bus connects Kaanapali with Lahaina, and a trolley operates within the resort. The warnings of the car rental companies concerning the sinuous **Kahekili Highway**, which on the map looks like a good route to continue on around northwest Maui and back to Wailuku, should be taken seriously; it's an exceptionally dangerous drive. Two of Maui's most famous **surfing** spots, at Mokuleia Bay and Honolua Bay, are a few miles along, however, before the road gets too hair-raising.

Kihei and Wailea

Maui's other main resort area is south of Kahului, across the isthmus. The long strip of hotels, malls and condos begins at **KIHEI**, with the road heavily built up on both sides, but thins out beyond the manicured lawns of **WAILEA**, near some superb beaches. **Paluea Beach** is ideal for families, while **Little Beach**, reached by a trail from cactus-lined **Makena (or Big) Beach**, is famous for (illegal) nudism. Beyond that, the main road deteriorates to become a rough one-lane track with minimal visibility, and which peters out altogether just before **La Pérouse Bay**. Once a significant population center, the beach here is good for snorkeling, and **dolphins** regularly come to play with swimmers, though you're forbidden to encourage them.

Few of the **accommodation** options are geared toward budget travelers; *Wailana Inn*, 14 Wailana Place (℡808/874-3131 or 1-800/399-3885, Ⓦwww.wailanabeach.com; ❹), is a good-value motel-style building, while *Maui Vista*, 2191 S Kihei Rd (℡808/879-7966 or 1-800/535-008, Ⓦwww.marcresorts.com; ❺), is a bit more luxurious. For **food**, the *Pacific Café Maui*, 1279 S Kihei Rd (℡808/879-0069), offers some great Pacific Rim concoctions, while *Kihei Caffe*, 1945 S Kihei Rd (℡808/878-2230), has smoothies and inexpensive snacks.

Upcountry Maui

Hawaii is not always a land tarnished by civilization. **Central Maui**, in the nineteenth century "a dreary expanse of sand and shifting sandhills, with a dismal growth . . . of thornless thistles," is now a pastoral idyll, thanks to an ingenious system of irrigation channels.

The highway to the top of **Haleakala** rises higher, at a faster rate, than any road on earth. Starting in rich meadows, it climbs past purple-blossoming jacaranda, firs and eucalyptus to reach open ranching land, and then ascends in huge curves to the volcanic desert and the crater itself.

Haleakala

Though **HALEAKALA** – "the House of the Sun" – is the world's largest dormant volcano, you may not appreciate its full ten thousand feet until you're at the top. Shield volcanoes are not as dramatic as the classic cones, as lava oozes from fissures along broad flanks to create a long, low profile, and the summit is often obscured by clouds. That it hasn't erupted for two hundred years doesn't necessarily mean it won't ever again – in 1979, for example, Haleakala was thought more likely to explode than Mount St Helens (see p.1207).

The higher reaches of the mountain are a **national park**, which never closes (admission $10). Manhattan would fit comfortably into the awe-inspiring **crater**, almost eight miles across, which was for the ancient Hawaiians a site of deep spiritual power. The most popular time to come is for the **sunrise**; the **visitor center** at the top operates from just before dawn until 3pm (weather ☎808/871-5054, information ☎808/572-4400, ⓦwww.nps.gov/hale). Hiking trails of varying difficulty cross the crater floor, where **camping** is permitted in three remote cabins, awarded by lottery two months in advance, that require a hike of four to ten miles and a $40 fee per night. In addition, fifteen to twenty-five free tent sites outside the crater are available every day (first-come, first-served).

Makawao and Paia

Coming down from Haleakala, Hwy-365 leads north to two laid-back little country towns, populated mainly by old Californian hippies: **MAKAWAO**, five miles up from the ocean, and **PAIA**, Maui's first plantation town, near the great windsurfing beach of **Hookipa**. In the center of Makawao, the friendly Italian restaurant *Casanova's*, 1188 Makawao Ave (☎808/572-0220), puts on live music at night, courtesy of the local community of rock exiles. Fresh fish is the specialty in Paia, at *Paia Fishmarket*, 101 Hana Hwy (☎808/579-8030), and the more expensive but greatly recommended *Mama's*, 799 Poho Place (☎808/579-8488), set next to the sea a mile along the Hana Highway. Vegetarians will be glad of the top-quality food at *Vegan*, 115 Baldwin Ave, Paia (closed Mon; ☎808/579-9144).

The road to Hana

The rains that fall on Haleakala cascade down Maui's long windward flank, covering it in thick, jungle-like vegetation. Convicts in the 1920s hacked out a road along the coast that has become a major tourist attraction in its own right, twisting tortuously in and out of gorges, past innumerable waterfalls and over more than fifty tiny one-lane bridges. All year round, and especially in June, the route is ablaze with color, from orchids, rainbow eucalyptus and orange-blossomed African tulip trees.

The usual day's excursion is roughly fifty miles (three hours) each way from Paia, to **Oheo Gulch** just past Hana. Don't attempt it if it's raining; in good weather, this road of hairpin turns, while not too difficult, is not recommended for the potentially carsick.

Hana

The former sugar town of **HANA** itself might seem a disappointment at the end of the road; it's a pleasant enough little community that isn't especially interested in attracting tourists. Hasegawa's General Store is a friendly place to pick up supplies, and a delightful **red-sand beach** can be reached by a precarious trail from the end of Uakea Road. Rooms at the deluxe *Hotel Hana-Maui* (☎808/248-8211 or 1-800/3215-4262, ⓦwww.hotelhanamaui.com; ❽) *start* at around $400; *Joe's Place* on Uakea Road is a rudimentary but affordable alternative (☎808/248-7033; ❸). There's also **camping** beside the black-sand beach at lovely Waianapanapa State Park, four miles short of Hana ($5; ☎808/984-8109).

Beyond Hana

Ten miles out of Hana is the gorgeous **Oheo Gulch** – a far-flung outpost of Haleakala National Park (admission free), where waterfalls tumble down the hillside to oceanfront meadows. If you hike a mile or two in the hills, you'll soon escape the crowds and reach cool rock pools, ideal for swimming; most visitors stroll down to an attractive spot the tour operators persist in calling the **Seven Sacred Pools** – a groundless label discouraged by Hawaiians that in its time has been attached to other features along the way. If you're averse to going back the same way you came, in normal conditions (but *not* rain) it is possible to follow the road right around southern Maui, although it has several rocky and unpaved stretches that invalidate rental-car insurance. Eventually, after a thirty-mile climb up bleak lava fields, it rounds the corner to give spectacular views out to the island of **Kahoolawe** (a naval bombing range until 1990, which has now been returned for restoration to the Hawaiians). You're now back in upcountry Maui, and soon come to the **Tedeschi Winery** (daily 9am–5pm; free), Hawaii's only vineyard.

Kauai

Although no point on the tiny island of **KAUAI** is as much as a dozen miles from the sea, the variety of its landscapes is quite incredible. This is the oldest of the major islands, and erosion has spent that many more million years to sculpt it into fantastic shapes. The mist-shrouded extinct volcano **Mount Waialeale** at its heart is the world's wettest spot, draining into a high landlocked swamp, full of unique plants and animals. Nearby is the chasm of **Waimea Canyon**, while the north shore holds the vertiginous green cliffs of the awe-inspiring **Na Pali** coast, familiar to millions from films such as *Jurassic Park* and *South Pacific* but the sole preserve of adventurous **hikers**. Kauai is a place to be active, on sea and land; and if you only go on one **helicopter** flight in your life, this is where to do it, despite recent restrictions on how low they can fly.

Lihue

Flights to Kauai arrive at the capital, **LIHUE**, which stands slightly inland of little Nawiliwili Harbor. It's roughly at the midpoint of the round-island highway (prevented from completing a loop by the Na Pali cliffs), but as a base it's pretty undistinguished. The population is just five thousand, and downtown consists of a few tired plantation-town streets, well back from the sea and surrounded by anonymous malls.

The small **Kauai Museum** at 4428 Rice St (Mon–Fri 9am–4pm, Sat 10am–4pm; $5) traces the island's history from the mythical *menehune* (the most ancient Hawaiian people) through Captain Cook's 1778 landfall and on to its sugar-growing heyday. Kauai was the one island not conquered by Kamehameha the Great; he spent six years amassing a fleet that never sailed, and settled in the end for accepting economic tribute.

Practicalities

Lihue's **airport** is only two miles from downtown ($8 by **taxi**; Wailua or Kapaa cost more like $20). Along with the usual **car** rental outlets, it also has **helicopters** – Safari Helicopter Tours (℡808/246-0136) is typical, offering basic tours from $120. The **Hawaii Visitors Bureau** is in town at 4334 Rice St (Mon–Fri 8am–4.30pm; ℡808/245-3971, ⓦwww.kauaivisitorsbureau.org).

There's no real point staying in Lihue rather than along the coast. However, the *Garden Island Inn*, near the harbor at 3445 Wilcox Rd (℡808/245-7227 or 1-800/648-0154, ⓦwww.gardenislandinn.com; ❹), is a lovely refurbished three-story motel, dripping with purple bougainvillea. For a quick meal in the heart of town, call in at *Hamura's Saimin*, 2956 Kress St (℡808/245-3271), a family-run communal Japanese food counter, open very late and specializing in bowls of *saimin* (noodles) for $3.50. The *Hanamaulu Restaurant and Tea House* (℡808/245-2511), a mile or two east, is a delightful old place, complete with fishponds, that serves both Chinese and Japanese food.

East Kauai

Most Kauaians live between Lihue and the overlapping communities of **WAILUA**, **WAIPOULI** and **KAPAA**, whose malls, condos and hotels blend into each other a few miles north of the capital. All the way along there's an exposed thin strip of beach; only Wailua is especially aesthetic, and you have to go further north for snorkeling.

Accommodation

Most East Shore **hotels** are in the luxury bracket, but there are several possibilities on a more affordable scale.

Kauai Coast Resort (at the Beachboy) Coconut Plantation, Kapaa ℡808/822-3441 or 1-800/922-7866, ⓦwww.aston-hotels.com. High lava-rock walls make this property look a little forbidding, but lawns lead down from the comfortable rooms to an open beach. ❻

Kauai International Hostel 4532 Lehua St, Kapaa ℡808/823-6142, ⓦwww.hostels.com/kauaihostel.

Kauai's only hostel, across from Kapaa Beach and open to everyone except Hawaiian residents, with a maximum one-week stay. $20 dorm beds and a few private rooms. ❶/❷

Lae Nani 410 Papaloa Rd, Wailua ℡808/822-4938 or 1-800/367-7052. Irresistible complex of luxurious oceanfront apartments and condos, with lovely swimming alongside. ❻

Eating

Kapaa is the only one of the towns in east Kauai with anything like a center; you can windowshop for **restaurants** along its street of wooden stores, fronted by a beach park.

Caffè Coco 4-1639 Kuhio Hwy, Wailua ℡808/822-7990. Attractively ramshackle café, serving cheap and wholesome, if not entirely vegetarian, breakfasts and lunches for under $10, plus changing dinner specials. Closed Mon.

Korean Bar-B-Q Restaurant 4-3561 Kuhio Hwy, Wailua ℡808/823-6744. Unassuming barbecue diner serving excellent grilled meats and chicken; the best bet for a bargain meal, with large combos for under $8.

Mema 4-361 Kuhio Hwy, Wailua ℡808/823-0899. Large, attractive Thai/Chinese restaurant; great curries with fresh spices for around $10.

A Pacific Café 4-831 Kuhio Hwy, Kapaa ℡808/822-0013. Very popular for its exotic and utterly wonderful (if expensive; entrees $20–27) Pacific cuisine. Dinner only.

North Kauai

That part of northern Kauai that is unique and unspoiled seems to be diminishing all the time. The astonishing valleys of the **Na Pali coast** itself must surely remain inviolate – though accessible enough by canoe to sustain large Hawaiian populations, their awesome walls shield them from any attempt to build roads there. But the bulldozers are inching ever closer. Only temporarily did 1991's Hurricane Iniki manage to slow the growth of the resort of **Princeville**, which began life as a sugar plantation in 1860.

Long, golden **Secret Beach**, hidden away from the road up from Kapaa, is among Kauai's best-looking beaches, though swimming is usually unsafe. An unofficial center for campers and nudists, local landowners have been cracking down on long-term stays. To get there, drive up Hwy-56 from the south, pass **Kilauea** and then turn right at Kalihiwai. Take the second right onto a dirt track leading to a parking area, and the beach is a ten-minute walk down through the woods. At the far end a waterfall of beautiful fresh mountain water cascades down the cliffs, and there are often spinner dolphins just offshore, especially around the picturesque 1913 Kilauea **lighthouse**. The cliffs above are a bird sanctuary.

Hanalei

For the moment, major development stops beyond Princeville, mainly because the road then crosses seven successive one-lane bridges. The first is over the Hanalei River, where the valley stretching away inland is a National Wildlife Refuge. Here endangered Hawaiian ducks, coots and stilts are protected by the preservation of their major habitats – natural wetlands and taro ponds. As a result, this is a rare chance to see a Hawaiian landscape relatively unchanged since ancient times.

The small town of **HANALEI**, set around a magnificent bay, has some low-key apartments for rent, but otherwise little formal accommodation. Of local **restaurants**, the *Tahiti Nui* (☎808/826-6277) is particularly nice, with authentic Tahitian decor, rattan screens and old prints; go for the simple steak or fish entrees ($16). In the **Hanalei Center** mall, the busy *Hanalei Gourmet* (☎808/826-2524) is the ideal stop for breakfast or a sandwich lunch, and also has live music every night.

Gorgeous **Lumahai Beach**, at the western edge of Hanalei Bay, has starred in countless movies, among them *South Pacific*, but is too treacherous for swimming. All the roadside beaches from here on, however, are good for snorkeling. Just two miles from the start of the Na Pali coast (see below), the *Hanalei Colony Resort* (☎808/826-6235 or 1-800/628-3004, ⑩www.hcr.com; ❼) is Kauai's most dramatic waterfront property, within a few feet of the pounding surf; its units all have two bedrooms. The road finally comes to an end at **Kee Beach**, perhaps the loveliest spot of all.

The Na Pali coast

The lush valleys of the **Na Pali coast**, separated by knife-edge ridges of rock often thousands of feet high but just a few feet thick, make Kauai one of the world's great hiking destinations. Although many of the best views (other than from a helicopter) are from the trails in Kokee State Park (see overleaf) or boat trips out at sea, the **Kalalau Trail** along the shore is unforgettable. The full eleven miles to Kalalau Valley is arduous and gets progressively more dangerous;

in places you have to scramble along a precipitous (and shadeless) wall of crumbly red rock.

However, the first two miles of the trail, to **Hanakapiai Beach**, are probably the most beautiful. They're steep but straightforward, passing through patches of dense vegetation where you clamber over the gnarled root systems of the splay-footed *hala* (pandanus) tree. Creepers and vines hang down, and it's all exposed to the sun. From the beach, a further hour's arduous hike (off the main trail) leads inland to the natural amphitheater of the towering **Hanakapiai Falls**. It takes at least four and a half hours to get to the falls and back from the trailhead at Kee Beach, opposite the ten-mile marker at the end of the road. Hikers and campers doing anything more than a day-hike must obtain (free) permits from the State Parks Office (3060 Eiwa St, Lihue, HI 96766; Mon–Fri 8am–3.30pm; ☎808/274-3444). Accidents and drownings are not uncommon, and the staff need a record of who may be missing.

Until recently, **boat excursions** along the Na Pali coast were a major attraction for visitors to Hanalei. Fears that such trips were causing irreparable environmental damage have resulted in their suspension, though it's still possible to take rather longer and less exciting trips up the west shore of the island from near Waimea (see below).

South Kauai

POIPU, Kauai's principal beach resort, was hard hit by Iniki, but is now finally back to normal, offering great surfing and snorkeling. Its finest **hotel** is the sumptuous *Hyatt Regency*, 1571 Poipu Rd (☎808/742-1234 or 1-800/554-9288, Ⓦwww.kauai-hyatt.com; ❾), while *Grantham Resorts* (☎808/742-7220 or 1-800/325-5701, Ⓦwww.grantham-resorts.com; ❺–❾) quotes much lower prices for condos in the area than you'll be offered by individual properties. The best restaurants are two upmarket Pacific Rim options: *Casa di Amici*, 2360 Nalo Rd (☎808/742-1555), and *Roy's Poipu Bar & Grill* (☎808/742-5000), in the Poipu Shopping Village mall.

West Kauai

Two of the major scenic attractions in all Hawaii, the gorge of **Waimea Canyon** and **Kokee State Park**, with its views of the Na Pali cliffs to one side and the sodden Alakai Swamp to the other, can only be reached from the **west coast** of Kauai. The coast itself, however, is nondescript. **WAIMEA**, the largest town, is just one short street at the foot of the poorly marked road up to the canyon. The statue of **Captain Cook**, which commemorates his "discovery" of Hawaii here on January 20, 1778, is an exact replica of one in Cook's home town of Whitby, England. Western Kauai's only **accommodation** option is *Waimea Plantation Cottages* (☎808/338-1625, Ⓦwww.aston-hotels.com; ❻), set in an attractive coconut grove, and with a good restaurant and brewpub in the main plantation house.

Waimea Canyon and Kokee State Park

It's not unreasonable to call **Waimea Canyon** the "Grand Canyon of the Pacific." At three thousand feet, it may not be quite as deep as its Arizona rival, but the colors – all shades of green against the bare red earth – are absolutely breathtaking. Erosion by torrential rains created this landscape, but the process began when a massive geological fault almost split Kauai in two. The road from Waimea climbs beside the widening gorge, until after eight miles the mile-wide canyon can be seen in all its splendor. Each of the roadside lookouts is definitely worth stopping for.

Explore Kokee Park as early in the day as possible; by late morning the valleys may be filled with mist and clouds. Trails head off to both sides of the highway. Although the ranger station at **KOKEE**, the park headquarters, is often unstaffed, you can pick up detailed information from the small but informative **Kokee Natural History Museum** nearby (daily 10am–4pm; $1 donation), where displays center on the indigenous wildlife. Kauai is the only island where mongooses have not killed off most native **birds**, and at this height mosquitoes are no threat either, so some of the world's rarest species (such as the *o'o a'a*) survive here and nowhere else.

Kokee Lodge Housekeeping Cabins, next to the park headquarters, are rented by the day (PO Box 819, Waimea, Kauai, HI 96796; ☎808/335-6061; ❷), and there's free **camping**, with permits from the parks office in Lihue (see p.1308). For **food**, *Kokee Lodge* has lunch specials for around $8.

Awaawapuhi Trail

The **Awaawapuhi Trail** drops steeply from the road beyond Kokee, passing through three miles of dense forest before emerging abruptly to provide a staggering view of a valley open only to the ocean, tucked between the Na Pali cliffs. The sheer razorback ridges are almost vertical, though somehow covered with clinging vegetation.

Kalalau Lookout and Pihea Trail

A few miles further up, **Kalalau Lookout** stands over the valley where the Kalalau Trail ends – though to attempt a descent would be certain suicide. The **Pihea Trail** follows the course of a lunatic attempt to extend the road beyond its current end. At times it narrows to a few feet, with precipitous drops to either side, and visibility can drop to nothing as the clouds siphon across the ridges. Inland lies the **Alakai Swamp**, where the heaviest rainfall on earth collects in the volcanic rock; standing here above, you can listen to the shrills, whistles and buzzes of a jungle without mammals or snakes, and watch the darting flashes of color. Since Iniki, the trail through the swamp has had a boardwalk laid for almost its entire six-mile length, though in places the planks just rest on cloying black swamp mud. Giant ferns dangle above the trail, and orchids gleam from the undergrowth, while the trees – especially in June – erupt into brilliant flowering displays. If you make it all the way to the end, you're rewarded with a stupendous panorama of Hanalei Bay.

contexts

contexts

CONTEXTS

A brief history of North America

There's no room in these few pages to do more than briefly survey the peopling and political development of the disparate regions that now form the USA, and to show that there's much more to the history of America than the history of the United States alone. Many of the events and issues discussed below are covered in more detail in the relevant chapters, while the books listed on pp.1336–1348 are invaluable resources for serious students.

First peoples

The true pioneers of America, the first settlers to enter the pristine continent, are thought to have been nomadic **mammoth-hunters** from Siberia. Around 14,000 years ago, they gradually worked their way into Alaska, along the "**land-bridge**" that then followed the line of what is now the Bering Strait. The entire region was treeless tundra, no more appealing than it is today, but it supported sufficient quantities of large mammals to make hunting worthwhile. It's quite possible that only a small band of perhaps fifty individuals completed the journey; that could have been enough to spread and populate the entire continent. Their descendants advanced so quickly through the new territory that they had reached the southernmost tip of South America within a couple of thousand years. That may well be because everywhere they went, they swiftly drove the indigenous fauna – not just the mammoths, but also such defenseless creatures as giant ground sloths – to extinction, and they were forever obliged to press onwards in search of new sources of food. Behind them, several thousand years later, came at least two further groups, the Athapascans who made their way to the Great Plains, and the ancestors of the modern Inuit, who found their own niche in the frozen Arctic north.

Distinct groups settled in specific areas, and adapted to the challenges of their local environment. The first definite signs of a human presence in the territory of the modern United States, dating back 12,000 years, have been uncovered at Meadowcroft in southwest Pennsylvania. Five hundred years later, the Southwest was dominated by what archeologists call the **Clovis** culture, whose distinctive arrowheads were first identified at Clovis, New Mexico. Subsequent subgroups ranged from the Algonquin farmers of what's now New England to peoples such as the Chumash and Macah, who lived by catching fish, otters and even whales along the coasts of the Pacific Northwest.

Nowhere did a civilization emerge that could rival the wealth and sophistication of the great cities of ancient Mexico, such as Teotihuacan or Tenochtitlan. However, the influence of these far-off cultures does seem to have filtered north; the cultivation of crops such as beans, squash and maize made the development of large communities possible, and northern religious cults, including those that performed human sacrifice, are thought to owe much to Central American beliefs. The so-called **Moundbuilders** of the **Ohio** and **Mississippi** valleys developed sites such as the Great Serpent Mound in modern Ohio and Poverty Point in Louisiana. The most prominent of these early societies, now known as the **Hopewell** culture, flourished between around 1 and 400 AD. Later on, **Cahokia**, just outside present-day St Louis, became the largest pre-Columbian city in North America, centered on a huge mound topped by some form of temple, and reaching its peak between 1050 and 1250 AD.

In the deserts of the **Southwest**, the Hohokam settlement of Snaketown, near what's now Phoenix in Arizona and complete with Central American-style ball courts, set about grappling with the same problems of water management that plague the region today. Nearby, the **Ancestral Puebloan** "Basketmakers" developed the art of pottery around 200 AD, and began to gather into the walled villages later known as pueblos, possibly for protection against the threat of Athapascan invaders, such as the Apache, who were arriving from the north. Ancestral Puebloan "cities," such as Pueblo Bonito in New Mexico's Chaco Canyon – a center for the turquoise trade with the mighty Aztec – and the "Cliff Palace" at Mesa Verde in Colorado, are the most impressive monuments to survive from ancient America. Although the Ancestral Puebloans are no longer identifiable as a group after the twelfth century – they probably dispersed after a devastating drought – many of the settlements created by their immediate descendants have remained in use ever since. Through centuries of migration, war and changes of government, the desert farmers of the **Hopi Mesas** in Arizona (see p.996), and the pueblos of **Taos** and **Acoma** in New Mexico, have never been dispossessed of their homes.

While estimates of the total indigenous population before the arrival of the Europeans vary widely, the figure of twelve million is generally thought to be reasonable.

European contacts

The greatest seafarers of early medieval Europe, the **Vikings**, are known to have established a colony in Greenland around 982 AD. Under the energetic leadership of Erik the Red, this became a base for voyages of exploration and even colonization along the mysterious coastline that lay to the west. Traces of permanent Viking occupation have been uncovered at L'Anse aux Meadows in Newfoundland, though the exact location of their southernmost outpost, **Vinland**, will probably never be known. It seems likely, however, that they ventured as far as Maine, and that while the Algonquin may have been inquisitive enough to trade, they forcibly prevented permanent settlement.

The Vikings remained a presence in Greenland until about 1500 AD, by which time it appears that European **fishermen**, such as the British and the Spanish Basques, were already familiar with the cod-rich seas off Newfoundland. The world first took notice of the region when organized voyages dispatched in search of China began to return with news of a new continent. **Christopher Columbus** reached San Salvador in the Bahamas on October 12, 1492, and a mere four years later the English navigator John Cabot officially "discovered" Newfoundland. Soon British fishermen in particular began to set up makeshift encampments in what became known as **New England**, to spend the winter curing their catch.

Over the next few years various expeditions mapped the eastern seaboard. In 1524, for example, the Italian **Giovanni Verrazano** sailed past Maine, which he characterized as the "Land of Bad People" thanks to the inhospitable and contemptuous behavior of its natives, and reached the mouth of what would become the Hudson River. The great hope initially was to find a sea route in the Northeast that would lead to China – the fabled **Northwest Passage**. To the French **Jacques Cartier**, the St Lawrence Seaway seemed a distinct possibility, and successive expeditions explored and attempted (unsuccessfully) to settle the northern areas of the Great Lakes region from the 1530s onwards. Intrepid trappers and traders began to venture ever further west.

To the south, the Spaniards had started to nose their way up from the Caribbean in 1513, when **Ponce de Leon**'s expedition in search of the Fountain of Youth landed at what is now Palm Beach, and named the region of **Florida**. Spanish attentions for the next few years focused on the lucrative conquest of Mexico, but in 1528 they returned under Panfilo de Narvaez, whose voyage ended in shipwreck somewhere in the Gulf. One of his junior officers, **Cabeza de Vaca**, managed to survive, and together with three shipmates spent the next six years on an extraordinary odyssey across Texas into the Southwest. Sometimes held as slaves, sometimes revered as seers, they finally managed to get back to Mexico in 1534, bringing tales of golden cities deep in the desert, known as the **Seven Cities of Cibola**.

One of Cabeza de Vaca's companions was a black African slave called **Estevanico the Moor**, a giant of a man who had amazed the native peoples they encountered. Rather than return to a life of slavery, he volunteered to map the route for a new expedition; racing alone into the interior, with two colossal greyhounds at his side, he was killed in Zuni Pueblo in 1539. The following year, **Francisco Vázquez de Coronado**'s full party managed to prove to everyone's intense dissatisfaction that the Seven Cities of Cibola did not exist, encountering the Hopi and other pueblo peoples along the way and reached as far as the Grand Canyon. Hernán Cortés, the conqueror of the Aztec, had meanwhile traced the outline of the peninsula of Baja California, and in 1542 Juan Cabrillo sailed right up the coast of California, failing to spot San Francisco Bay in the usual mists.

It was the Spanish who established the **first permanent settlement** in the present United States, when they founded **St Augustine** on the coast of Florida in 1565 – permanent, at least, until it was burned to the ground by Sir Francis Drake in 1586. In 1598 the Spanish also succeeded in subjugating the pueblo peoples, and founded the colony of **New Mexico** along the Rio Grande. This was more of a missionary rather than military enterprise, and its survival always precarious due to the vast tracts of empty desert that separated the colony from the rest of Mexico. Nonetheless, the construction of a new capital, **Santa Fe**, began in 1609 (see p.934).

The growth of the colonies

The great rivalry between the English and the Spanish in the late sixteenth century extended right around the world. Freebooting English adventurers-cum-pirates contested Spanish hegemony along both coasts of North America. Sir Francis Drake staked a claim to California in 1579, five years before **Sir Walter Raleigh** claimed **Virginia** in the east, in the name of his Virgin Queen, Elizabeth I. The party of colonists he sent out in 1585 established the short-lived settlement of **Roanoke**; they were still there three years later, when they were reinforced, but the only trace of them left in 1590 was a single mysterious word carved on a tree – "Croatan."

The Native Americans encountered by the earliest settlers were seldom hostile at the outset. To some extent the European newcomers were obliged to make friends with the locals; most had crossed the Atlantic to find religious freedom or to make their fortunes, and lacked the experience or even the inclination to make a success of the mundane business of subsistence farming. Virginia's first enduring colony, **Jamestown**, was founded by Captain John Smith on May 24, 1607. He bemoaned "though there be Fish in the Sea, and Foules in the ayre, and Beasts in the woods, their bounds are so large, they are so wilde, and we so weake and ignorant, we cannot much trouble them"; not surprisingly, six out of every seven colonists died within a year of their arrival in the New World.

Gradually, however, the settlers learned the techniques necessary to cultivate the strange crops that grew in this unfamiliar terrain. As far as the English government was concerned, the colonies were strictly commercial ventures, intended to produce crops that could not be grown at home, and it was inconceivable to them that the colonists might have goals of their own. After early failures with sugar and rice, Virginia finally found its feet with its first **tobacco** harvest in 1615 (the man responsible, John Rolfe, is now better known as the husband of Pocahontas). A successful tobacco plantation requires two things in abundance: land, which intensified the pressure to dispossess the Indians, and labor. No self-respecting Englishman came to America to work for others; when the first **slave** ship called in at Jamestown in 1619, the captain found an eager market for his cargo of twenty African slaves. By that time there were already a million slaves in South America.

The 102 **Puritans** known to history as the "**Pilgrim Fathers**" were deposited on Cape Cod by the *Mayflower* in late 1620, and soon moved on to set up their own colony at Plymouth (see p.218). Fifty of them died during that winter, and the whole party might well have perished but for their fortuitous encounter with the extraordinary **Squanto**. This Native American had twice been kidnapped and taken to Europe and succeeded in making his way home; during his wanderings he had spent four years working as a merchant in the City of London, and had also lived in Spain. Having recently come home to find his entire tribe exterminated by smallpox, he decided to throw in his lot with the English. With his guidance, they finally managed to reap their first harvest, celebrated with the mighty feast of **Thanksgiving** that is still commemorated today.

Of greater significance to the history of New England was the founding in 1630 of a new colony, further up the coast at Naumkeag (which became Salem), by the Massachusetts Bay Company. Its governor, **John Winthrop**, soon moved to establish a new capital on the Shawmut peninsula – the city of **Boston**, complete with its own university of Harvard. His vision of a Utopian "City on a Hill" did not extend to sharing Paradise with the Indians; he argued that they had not "subdued" the land, and it was therefore a "vacuum" for the Puritans to use as they saw fit. While their faith helped individual colonists to endure the early hardships, the colony as a whole failed to maintain a strong religious identity (the Salem witch trials of 1692 did much to discredit the notion that the New World had any moral superiority to the Old), and breakaway groups soon left to create the rival settlements of Providence and Connecticut.

Between 1620 and 1642, sixty thousand migrants – which amounted to 1.5 percent of the population – left England for America. Those who came in pursuit of economic opportunities tended to join the longer-established colonies, where in effect they diluted the religious zeal of the Puritans. Groups hoping to find spiritual freedom were more inclined to start afresh; thus **Maryland** was created as a haven for Catholics in 1632, and fifty years later **Pennsylvania** was founded by the Quakers.

The English were not alone, however. After Sir Henry Hudson rediscovered Manhattan in 1609, it was "bought" by the **Dutch** in 1624 – though the Indians who took their money were passing nomads with no claim to it either. The Dutch colony of New Amsterdam, founded in 1625, lasted less than forty years before it was captured by the English and renamed **New York**; by that time, there was a strong Dutch presence on the lower reaches of the Hudson River.

From their foothold in the Great Lakes region, meanwhile, the **French** sent the explorers Joliet and Marquette to map the course of the Mississippi in 1673. They turned back once they had established that the river did indeed flow into the Gulf of Mexico, but their trip cleared the way for the foundation of the huge and ill-defined colony of **Louisiana** in 1699. The city of **New Orleans**, at the mouth of the Mississippi, was created in 1718.

While the Spanish remained firmly ensconced in Florida, things were not going so smoothly in the Southwest. In the bloody **Pueblo Revolt** of 1680, the pueblo peoples managed to drive the Spanish out of New Mexico altogether, only to have them return in force a dozen years later. Thereafter, a curious synthesis of traditional and Hispanic religion and culture began to evolve, and, but for hostile raids from the north, the Spanish presence was not seriously challenged.

With the arrival of the foreigners, things were also changing in the unknown hinterland. The frontier in the east was pushing steadily forward, as colonists seized Indian land, with or without the excuse of an "uprising" or "rebellion" to provoke them into bloodshed. The major killer of the indigenous peoples, however, was **smallpox**, which worked its way deep into the interior of the continent long before the Europeans. (Scientists speculate that the Native Americans may have had no equivalent "new" diseases to inflict on the newcomers because of the long period their ancestors had spent crossing the Arctic in subzero temperatures.) As populations were decimated, great migrations took place. In addition, around this time the **horse** arrived on the Great Plains. The original inhabitants of the region were sedentary farmers, who also hunted buffalo by driving them over rocky bluffs. The bow and arrow was discovered around the fifth century, but the acquisition of horses (probably captured from the Spanish, and known at first as "mystery dogs") made possible the emergence of an entirely new, nomadic lifestyle. Groups such as the Cheyenne and the Apache swept their rivals aside to dominate vast territories, and eagerly seized the potential offered by firearms when they were introduced in due course. This created a very dynamic, but fundamentally unstable culture, as they became dependent on trade with Europeans for the necessities of life.

The American Revolution

The American colonies prospered during the **eighteenth century**, with the cities of Boston, New York and **Philadelphia** in particular becoming home to a wealthy, highly educated and highly articulate middle class. Frustration began to mount at the inequities of the colonies' relationship with Britain. While they were allowed to trade among themselves, the Americans could otherwise only sell their produce to the British, and all transatlantic commerce had to be undertaken in British ships.

Although full-scale independence was not an explicit goal until late in the century, the main factor making it possible was the economic impact of the pan-European conflict known as the **Seven Years War**. Officially, the war in Europe lasted from 1756 to 1763, but fighting among the English, French and Spanish in North America broke out a little earlier. Beginning in 1755 with the mass expulsion of French settlers from Acadia in Nova Scotia (triggering their epic migration to Louisiana, where as the **Cajuns** they remain to this day), the British went on to conquer all of Canada. In forcing the **surrender of Québec** in 1759, General Wolfe brought the war to a close; the French ceded Louisiana to the Spanish rather than let it fall to the British, while Florida passed into British control for a year before reverting to the Spanish. All the European monarchs were left hamstrung by debts, and it became apparent to the British that colonialism in America was not as profitable a business as in those parts of the world where the native populations could be coerced into working for their overseas masters.

There was one other major player on the scene – the **Iroquois Confederacy**. Evidence of Iroquois culture, characterized by military expansionism and even human sacrifice, has been found in the Great Lakes region dating from around 1000 AD onwards. Forever in competition with the Algonquin and the Huron, the southern Iroquois had by the eighteenth century resolved themselves into a League of Five Nations – the Seneca, Cayuga, Onondaga, Oneida and Mohawk, all in what's now upstate New York. Wooed by both French and British, the Iroquois for most of the century charted an independent course between the two. During negotiations with the colonists in 1744, an Onondaga chief, unimpressed by the squabbling representatives of Pennsylvania, Virginia and Maryland, had recommended "by your observing the same methods our wise forefathers have taken, you will acquire fresh strength and power." Benjamin Franklin, who was present, wrote in 1751 that "It would be a very strange thing if . . . ignorant savages should be capable of forming a scheme for such a union . . . that has subsisted ages and appears indissoluble; and yet that a like union should be impracticable for ten or a dozen English colonies."

Shortly after the Seven Years War, an unsuccessful insurrection by the Ottawa tribe in 1763, led by their chief **Pontiac**, led the cash-strapped British to conclude that, while America needed its own standing army, it was not unreasonable to expect the colonists to pay for it.

In 1765, the British introduced the **Stamp Act**, which required duty on all legal transactions and printed matter in the colonies to be paid to the British Crown. Firm in the belief that there should be "no taxation without representation," delegates from nine of the colonies met in the Stamp Act Congress in October 1765. By that time, however, the British prime minister responsible for the Act had already been dismissed by King George III. Only briefly, in Georgia, were the offending stamps ever distributed, and the Act was repealed in 1766.

However, in 1767, Chancellor Townshend made political capital at home by proclaiming "I dare tax America" as he introduced a program of legislation that included the broadly similar Revenue Act. That led the merchants of Massachusetts, inspired by **Samuel Adams**, to vote to boycott English goods; they were subsequently joined by all the other colonies except New Hampshire. Townshend's Acts were repealed in turn by a new prime minister, Lord North, on March 5, 1770. By chance, on that same day a stone-throwing mob surrounded the Customs House in Boston; shots from the guards killed five people in what became known as the **Boston Massacre**. Even so, most of the colonies resumed trading with Britain, and the crisis was postponed for a few more years.

In May 1773, Lord North's **Tea Act** relieved the debt-ridden East India Company of the need to pay duties on exports to America, while still requiring the Americans to pay duty on tea. Massachusetts called for the colonies to unite in action, and its citizens took the lead on December 16 in the **Boston Tea Party**, when three tea ships were boarded and 342 chests thrown into the sea. As John Adams put it, "to let it be landed would be giving up the principle of taxation by Parliamentary authority."

The infuriated British Parliament thereupon began to pass a body of legislation collectively known as both the "Coercive" and the "Intolerable" Acts, which included closing the port of Boston and disbanding the government of Massachusetts. Thomas Jefferson argued that the acts amounted to "a deliberate and systematical plan of reducing us to slavery." To discuss a response, the first **Continental Congress** was held in Philadelphia on May 5, 1774, and attended by representatives of all the colonies except Georgia.

War finally broke out on April 18, 1775, when General Gage, the newly imposed governor of Massachusetts, dispatched four hundred British soldiers to destroy the arms depot at **Concord**, in order to prevent weapons from falling into rebel hands. Silversmith **Paul Revere** was dispatched by the citizens of Boston on his legendary ride to warn the rebels, and the British were confronted en route at Lexington by 77 American "Minutemen," and the resulting skirmish led to the "shot heard round the world."

Congress set about forming an army at Boston, and decided for the sake of unity to appoint a Southern commander, **George Washington**. One by one, as the war raged, the colonies set up their own governments and declared themselves to be states, and the politicians set about defining the society they wished to create. The writings of pamphleteer Thomas Paine – especially *Common Sense* – were, together with the *Confederacy of the Iroquois*, a great influence on the **Declaration of Independence**. Drafted by Thomas Jefferson, this was adopted by the Continental Congress in Philadelphia on July 4, 1776. The anti-slavery clauses originally included by Jefferson – himself a slave-owner – were omitted to spare the feelings of the Southern states, though the section that denounced the King's dealings with "merciless Indian Savages" was left in.

At first, the Revolutionary War went well for the British. General Howe crossed the Atlantic with around twenty thousand men, took New York and New Jersey, and ensconced himself in Philadelphia for the winter of 1777–78. Washington's army was encamped not far away at Valley Forge, freezing cold and all but starving to death. However, General Burgoyne's expedition, which set out from Canada to march on New England, was so harried by rebel guerrillas that he found himself obliged to surrender at Saratoga in October 1777. As the logistical difficulty of maintaining the British war effort became ever more apparent, other European powers took delight in coming to the aid of the Americans. Benjamin Franklin led a wildly successful delegation to France to request support, and soon the nascent American fleet was being assisted in its bid to cut British naval communications by both the French and the Spanish. The end came when Cornwallis, who had replaced Howe, was instructed to dig in at Yorktown and wait for the Royal Navy to come to his aid, only for the French to seal off Chesapeake Bay and prevent reinforcement. Cornwallis surrendered to Washington on October 17, 1781, just fifteen miles from the site of the first English settlement at Jamestown.

THE GROWTH OF THE UNITED STATES

N

The date of statehood for each state is shown in bold

NEW JERSEY 1787
DELAWARE 1787
CONNECTICUT 1788
MARYLAND 1788
MASSACHUSETTS 1788
NEW HAMPSHIRE 1788
RHODE ISLAND 1790
VERMONT 1791

MAINE 1820
N H
MASS
VT
CONN
R I
N Y
NEW YORK 1788
PENNSYLVANIA 1787
N J
DEL
MD
D C
VIRGINIA 1788
W VIRGINIA 1863
N CAROLINA 1789
S CAROLINA 1789
OHIO 1803
KENTUCKY 1792
TENNESSEE 1796
GEORGIA 1788
FLORIDA 1845
MICHIGAN 1837
INDIANA 1816
ILLINOIS 1818
ALABAMA 1819
MISSISSIPPI 1817
LOUISIANA 1812
WISCONSIN 1848
MINNESOTA 1858
IOWA 1846
MISSOURI 1821
ARKANSAS 1836
N DAKOTA 1889
S DAKOTA 1889
NEBRASKA 1867
KANSAS 1861
OKLAHOMA 1907
TEXAS 1845
MONTANA 1889
WYOMING 1890
COLORADO 1876
NEW MEXICO 1912
WASHINGTON 1889
OREGON 1859
IDAHO 1890
UTAH 1896
NEVADA 1864
CALIFORNIA 1850
ARIZONA 1912

CANADA

MEXICO

Oregon Territory established 1846
Ceded by Mexico 1848
Louisiana purchase 1803
Texas annexed 1845
Ceded by Spain 1819
Bought from Russia 1867
Annexed 1898

HAWAII 1959

ALASKA 1959

© **CONTEXTS** | A brief history of North America

1322

The ensuing **Treaty of Paris** granted the Americans their independence on generous terms – the British completely abandoned their Native American allies, including the Iroquois, to the vengeance of the victors – and Washington entered New York as the British left in November 1783. The Spanish were confirmed in their possession of Florida.

The victorious US Congress met for the first time in 1789, and the tradition of awarding political power to the nation's most successful generals was instigated by the election of George Washington as the first president. He was further honored when his name was given to the new capital city of **Washington DC**, deliberately sited between the North and the South.

The nineteenth century

In its first century, the territories and population of the new **United States of America** expanded at a phenomenal rate. The white population of North America in 1800 stood at around five million, and there were another one million African slaves (of whom thirty thousand were in the north). Of that total, 86 percent lived within fifty miles of the Atlantic, but no US city could rival Mexico City, whose population approached 100,000 inhabitants. (Both New York and Philadelphia reached that figure within twenty years, however, and New York had passed a million fifty years later.)

It had suited the British to discourage settlers from venturing west of the Appalachians, where they would be far beyond the reach of British power and therefore inclined to carry on independent existences. For George Washington, however, any agreement to follow such a policy had been a "temporary expedient to quieten the minds of the Indians." Adventurers such as **Daniel Boone** started to cross the mountains into Tennessee and Kentucky during the 1770s. Soon makeshift rafts, made from the planks that would later be assembled to make log cabins, were careering west along the Ohio River (the only westward-flowing river on the continent).

In 1801, the Spanish handed Louisiana back to the French, on the express undertaking that the French would keep it for ever. However, Napoleon swiftly realized that any attempt to hang on to his American possessions would involve spreading his armies too thinly. He chose instead to make the best of things by selling them to the United States for $15 million, in the **Louisiana Purchase** of 1803. The new territories extended far beyond the boundaries of present-day Louisiana (see map opposite), and for President Thomas Jefferson it was a matter of urgency to send the explorers **Lewis and Clark** to map them out. With the help of Sacagawea, their female Shoshone guide, they followed the Missouri and Columbia rivers all the way to the Pacific; in their wake, trappers and "mountain men" came to hunt in the wilderness of the Rockies. The **Russians** had already reached the Pacific Northwest by this time and established a network of fortified outposts to trade in the pelts of beaver and otter.

British attempts to blockade the Atlantic, primarily intended as a move against Napoleon, gave the new nation its first chance to flex its military muscles. Although British raiders succeeded in capturing Washington DC, and burned the White House to the ground, the **War of 1812** most significantly provided the US with a cover for aggression against the Native American allies of the British. Thus **Tecumseh** of the Shawnee was defeated near Detroit, and

Andrew Jackson moved against the Creek of the southern Mississippi. Jackson's campaign against the Seminole in Florida enabled the US to gain possession of the state from the Spanish; he was rewarded first with the governorship of the new state, and later by his election to the presidency. During his period in office, in the 1830s, Jackson went even further, and set about clearing all states east of the Mississippi of their native populations. The barren region that later became Oklahoma was designated as "Indian Territory," home to the "Five Civilized Tribes." The Creek and the Seminole, and the Choctaw and Chickasaw of Mississippi, were eventually joined by the Cherokee of the lower Appalachians there, after four appalling months on the forced march known as the "**Trail of Tears**."

For the citizens of the young republic, it took only a small step from realizing that their country might be capable of spreading across the whole continent to supposing that it had a quasi-religious duty – a "**Manifest Destiny**" – to do so. At its most basic, that doctrine amounted to little more than a belief that might must be right, but the idea that they were fulfilling the will of God inspired countless pioneers to set off across the plains in search of a new life.

Mexico had by now gained its independence from Spain. The Spanish territories of the Southwest had never attracted enough migrants to turn into full-fledged colonies, and the American settlers who arrived in ever-increasing numbers began to dominate their Hispanic counterparts. The Anglos of **Texas** rebelled in 1833, under the leadership of General Sam Houston. Shortly after the legendary setback at the **Alamo** (see p.736), in 1836, they defeated the Mexican army of Santa Ana, and Texas became an independent republic in its own right.

The ensuing **Mexican War** was a bare-faced exercise in American aggression, in which most of the future leading figures of the Civil War received their first experience fighting on the same side. The conflict resulted in the acquisition not only of Texas, but also of Arizona, Utah, Colorado, Nevada, New Mexico and finally California, in 1848. A token US payment of $15 million to the Mexican government was designed to match the Louisiana Purchase. Controversy over whether slavery would be legal in the new states was rendered academic when it turned out that, on virtually the same day the war ended, gold had been discovered in the Sierra Nevada of California. The resultant **Gold Rush** created California's first significant city, San Francisco, and brought a massive influx of free white settlers to a land that was in any case utterly unsuitable for a plantation-based economy.

Proponents of Manifest Destiny seem never to have given much thought to the **Pacific Northwest**, which remained nominally under the control of British Canada. However, once the Oregon Trail started to operate in 1841 (see p.1235), American settlers there swiftly outnumbered the British. In 1846, a surprisingly amicable treaty fixed the border along the 49th parallel, just as it already did across eastern Canada, and left the whole of Vancouver Island to the British.

The Civil War

From the moment of its inception, the unity of the United States had been based on shaky foundations. Great care had gone into devising a **Constitution** that balanced the need for a strong federal government with the aspirations for autonomy of its component states. That was achieved by giving Congress two separate chambers – the **House of Representatives**, in which the number of representatives from each state depended upon its population, and the **Senate**, in which each state, regardless of size, had two members. Thus, although in theory the Constitution remained silent on the issue of **slavery**, it allayed the fears of the less populated Southern states (where, of course, the slaves themselves did not have the vote) that the voters of the North might destroy their economy by forcing them to abandon their "peculiar institution." However, it gradually became apparent that the system only worked so long as there were roughly equal numbers of "Free" and slave-owning states. At first it seemed possible that the balance could be maintained – in 1820, under the Missouri Compromise, Missouri was admitted to the Union as a slave-owning state simultaneously with Maine as a free one.

Abolitionist sentiment in the North was not all that great before the middle of the nineteenth century. At best, after the importation of slaves from Africa ended in 1808, Northerners had vague hopes that slavery was an anachronism that might simply wither away. In fact, the profitability of the Southern plantations was dramatically boosted by the development of the cotton gin, and the increased demand for manufactured cotton goods triggered by the **Industrial Revolution**. What ultimately changed the situation was the rapid growth of the nation as a whole, making it ever more difficult to maintain a political balance between North and South.

There was a clear difference between tacitly acknowledging the existence of slavery in the Southern states as a matter for those states to decide, and being obliged to let it spread into one out of every two new states that joined the Union. In 1854, the **Kansas–Nebraska Act** brought matters to a head, sparking off guerrilla raids and mini-wars between rival settlers by allowing both prospective states self-determination on the issue. That same year, the **Republican Party** was founded, on the platform of resisting the further expansion of slavery. Escaped former slaves such as Frederick Douglass were by now inspiring Northern audiences to moral outrage, and Harriet Beecher Stowe's *Uncle Tom's Cabin* found unprecedented readership.

In October 1859, **John Brown** – a white-bearded, wild-eyed veteran of some of Kansas's bloodiest infighting – led a dramatic raid on the US Armory at Harpers Ferry, West Virginia, intending to secure arms for a slave insurrection (see p.458). Swiftly captured by forces under the command of Robert E. Lee, he was hanged within a few weeks, proclaiming that "I am now quite certain that the crimes of this guilty land will never be purged away but with blood."

The Republican candidate for the presidency in 1860 was the little-known **Abraham Lincoln** from Kentucky; he won no Southern states, but with the Democrats split into Northern and Southern factions he was elected with 39 percent of the popular vote. Within weeks, on December 20, South Carolina became the first state to secede from the Union; the **Confederacy** was declared on February 4, 1861, when it was joined by Mississippi, Florida, Alabama, Georgia, Louisiana and Texas. Its first (and only) president was Jefferson Davis, also from Kentucky; at their inauguration, his new vice-president remarked that their government was "the first in the history of the world based upon the great physical and moral truth that the negro is not equal to the white man." Lincoln was inaugurated in turn in March 1861, proclaiming that "I have no purpose, directly or indirectly, to interfere with the institution of slavery in the States where it exists. I believe I have no lawful right to do so, and I have no inclination to do so." He was completely inflexible, however, on one paramount issue: the survival of the Union.

The **Civil War** began just a few weeks later. The first shots were fired on April 12, when a much-postponed federal attempt to resupply Fort Sumter, in the harbor at Charleston, South Carolina, was greeted by a Confederate bombardment that forced its surrender. Lincoln's immediate call to raise an army against the South was greeted by the further secession of Virginia, Arkansas, Tennessee and North Carolina. Within a year, both armies had amassed 600,000 men; Robert E. Lee had been offered command of both and opted for the Confederacy, while George McLellan became the first leader of the Union forces. Although the rival capitals of Washington, DC and Richmond, Virginia, were a mere one hundred miles apart, over the next four years operations of war reached almost everywhere south of Washington and east of the Mississippi.

Tracing the ebb and flow of the military campaigns – from the Confederate victories of the early years, via Grant's successful siege of Vicksburg in 1863 and Sherman's devastating March to the Sea in 1864, to Lee's eventual surrender at Appomattox in April 1865 – it's easy to lose sight of the fact that it was not so much generalship as sheer economic power that won the war for the Union. It was the North that could maintain full trading with the rest of the world while diverting spare resources to the production of munitions, and could go on doing so despite matching Southern losses man for man. Conversely, defeat for the South spelled destruction for its economy; two-thirds of its wealth was lost, its share of national assets collapsed from thirty percent in 1860 to twelve percent in 1870, and one in four Southern white males of military age had been killed. Moreover, when Lincoln's wartime proclamation emancipating the slaves achieved full legal force under the Thirteenth Amendment in 1865, the plantation system was rendered inoperable.

Lincoln himself was assassinated within a few days of the end of the war, a mark of the deep bitterness that would almost certainly have rendered successful **Reconstruction** impossible even if he had lived. There was a brief period, after black men were granted the vote in 1870, when the Southern states elected black political representatives, but without a sustained effort to enable former slaves to acquire land, social relations in the South swiftly deteriorated. Thanks to white supremacist organizations such as the Ku Klux Klan, nominally clandestine but brazenly public, Southern blacks were soon effectively disenfranchised once more. Anyone working to transform the South came under attack either as a carpetbagger (a Northern opportunist who headed South for personal profit) or a treacherous scalawag (a Southern collaborator).

The aftermath of the Civil War can almost be said to have lasted for a hundred years. While the South condemned itself to a century as a backwater, the rest of the re-United States embarked on a period of expansionism and prosperity.

The Indian Wars

With the completion of the transcontinental railroad in 1867, Manifest Destiny became an undeniable reality. Among the first to head west were the troops of the federal army, with Union and Confederate veterans alike marching under the same flag to do battle with the remaining Native Americans. Treaty after treaty was signed, only to be broken as it became expedient to do so (usually upon the discovery of gold or precious metals). When the whites overreached themselves, or when driven to desperation, the Indians were capable of fighting back. The defeat of **General George Custer** at Little Bighorn in 1876, by **Sitting Bull** and his Sioux and Cheyenne warriors (see p.903), provoked the full wrath of the government. Within a few years, leaders such as **Crazy**

Horse of the Oglala Sioux and **Geronimo** of the Apache had been forced to surrender, and their people were confined to reservations. One final act of resistance came in the form of the visionary, messianic cult of the **Ghost Dance**, whose practitioners hoped that by correct ritual observance they could win back their lost way of life, in a land miraculously free of white intruders. Such aspirations were regarded as hostile, and military harassment of the movement culminated in the massacre at **Wounded Knee** in South Dakota in 1890.

A major tactic in the campaign against the Plains Indians was to starve them into submission, by eliminating the vast herds of bison that were their primary source of food. As General Philip Sheridan put it, "For the sake of a lasting peace . . . kill, skin and sell until the buffalo are exterminated. Then your prairies can be covered by the speckled cow and the festive cowboy." More significant than the activities of the much-mythologized cowboys, however, was the back-breaking toil of the miners up in the mountains, and the home-steading families out on the plains.

Industry and immigration

The late nineteenth century was an era of massive **immigration** to North America from the rest of the world, with influxes from Europe to the east coast paralleled by those from Asia to the West. As in colonial times, national groups tended to form enclaves in specific areas – examples range from the Scandinavian farmers of Minnesota and the northern Plains, to the Basque shepherds of Idaho, and the Cornish miners of Colorado. In the Southwest, where individual hard work counted for less than shared communal effort, the **Mormons** of Utah had fled persecution eastward across the United States to become the first white settlers to eke a living from the unforgiving desert.

The fastest growth of all was in the nation's greatest **cities**, especially New York, Chicago and Boston. Their industrial and commercial strength enabled them to attract and absorb migrants not only from throughout Europe but also from the Old South – particularly ex-slaves, who could now at least vote with their feet.

Now that it stretched "from sea to shining sea," the territorial boundaries of the US had reached almost their current form. In 1867, however, Secretary of State William Seward agreed to buy **Alaska** from the crisis-torn Russian government for $7.2 million. The purchase was at first derided as "Seward's Folly," but it was not long before the familiar Midas touch of the Americans was revealed by the discovery of gold there as well. Finally, the Kingdom of **Hawaii**, far out in the Pacific, was annexed in 1898 following the 1894 "Revolution," led by white American businessmen, which even then-President Cleveland condemned as "wholly without justification . . . not merely wrong but a disgrace."

The various US presidents of the day, from the victorious General Grant (a man palpably out of his depth) onwards, now seem anonymous figures compared to the industrialists and financiers who manipulated the national economy. These "**robber barons**" included such men as John D. Rockefeller, who controlled seventy percent of the world's oil almost before anyone else had realized it was worth controlling; Andrew Carnegie, who made his fortune introducing the Bessemer process of steel manufacture; and J.P. Morgan, who went for the most basic commodity of all – money. Their success was predicated on the willingness of the government to cooperate in resisting the development of a strong labor movement. A succession of widely publicized strikes

– such as those on the railroads in 1877, in the mines of Tennessee in 1891 and in the steel mills of Pittsburgh in 1892 – were forcibly crushed.

The nineteenth century had also seen the development of a distinctive American voice in **literature**, which rendered increasingly superfluous the efforts of passing English visitors – such as Charles Dickens, and the Trollopes, mother and son – to "explain" the United States. From the 1830s onwards, a wide range of writers set out to find new ways to describe their new world, with results as varied as the introspective essays of Henry Thoreau, the morbid visions of Edgar Allan Poe, the all-embracing novels of Herman Melville, and the irrepressible poetry of Walt Whitman, whose endlessly revised *Leaves of Grass* was an exultant hymn to the young republic. Virtually every leading participant in the Civil War wrote at least one highly readable volume of memoirs, while public figures as disparate as Buffalo Bill Cody and the showman P. T. Barnum also produced lively autobiographies. The boundless national self-confidence found its greatest expression in the vigorous vernacular style of **Mark Twain**, whose depictions of frontier life, whether in the journalistic *Roughing It* and *Life on the Mississippi*, or fictionalized in novels like *Huckleberry Finn*, gave the rest of the world perhaps its most abiding impression of the American character.

At the end of the century, despite an erratic boom-and-bust cycle that hit its lowest point in 1893, the United States had advanced to the point that it knew, even if the rest of the world wasn't yet altogether sure, that it was the strongest, wealthiest country on earth. As the empires of Europe embarked upon their long, slow disintegration, the United States was even toying with **colonialist ventures** of its own. For a brief period it seemed as if the Philippines might pass into permanent US control, while the escapades of Teddy Roosevelt's Rough Riders in Cuba presaged a century of ongoing US involvement in Latin America.

The twentieth century

It may not have been apparent to everyone at the time, but the first few years of the twentieth century witnessed the emergence of many of the features that came to characterize modern America. In 1903 alone, Wilbur and Orville Wright achieved the first successful powered **flight**, and Henry Ford established his Ford Motor Company. Ford's enthusiastic adoption of the latest technology in mass production – the assembly line – gave Detroit a head start in the new **automobile** industry, which swiftly became the most important business in America. Both **jazz** and **blues** music came to the attention of a national audience for the first time during that same period, while Hollywood acquired its first **movie** studio in 1911, and its first major hit in 1915 with D. W. Griffith's unabashed glorification of the Ku Klux Klan in *Birth of a Nation*.

This was also a time of growing **radicalism**. Both the NAACP (National Association for the Advancement of Colored People) and the socialist International Workers of the World ("the Wobblies") were founded in the early 1900s, while the campaign for women's suffrage also came to the forefront. Writers such as Upton Sinclair, whose *The Jungle* exposed conditions in Chicago's stockyards, and Jack London proselytized to the masses; contemporary improvements in the educational system suggest this may well have been the most literate period in US history.

President Wilson managed to keep the US out of the **Great War** for several years but, when the time came, American intervention was decisive. With the Russian Revolution illustrating the dangers of anarchy, the US also took charge of supervising the peace. However, although Wilson presided over the postwar negotiations that resulted in the Treaty of Versailles in 1919, isolationist sentiment at home kept the US from joining his pet scheme to preserve future world peace, the League of Nations.

Back home, the Eighteenth Amendment to the Constitution, in 1920, forbade the sale and distribution of alcohol, while the Nineteenth finally gave all American women the vote. Quite how **Prohibition** ever became the law of the land is something of a mystery; certainly, in the buzzing metropolises of the Roaring Twenties, it enjoyed little conspicuous support. There was no noticeable elevation in the moral tone of the country, and Chicago in particular became renowned for the street wars between bootlegging gangsters such as Al Capone and his rivals.

The Depression and the New Deal

By the middle of the 1920s, the US was enough of an industrial powerhouse to be responsible for more than half the world's output of manufactured goods. After leading the way into a new era of prosperity, however, it suddenly found itself dragging the rest of the world down into economic collapse. It's hard to say exactly what triggered the **Great Depression**; the consequences were out of all proportion to any one specific cause. Possible factors include American overinvestment in the floundering economy of postwar Europe, combined with high tariffs on imports that effectively precluded European recovery, as well as a quasi-superstitious faith in the stock market that had seen interest rates rise to a minimum of twelve percent in 1928. That faith was shattered by the **Wall Street Crash** of October 1929. On "Black Tuesday" alone, enough stocks were sold to produce a total loss of ten thousand million dollars – more than twice the total amount of money in circulation in the US. Within the next three years, industrial production was cut by half, the national income dropped by 38 percent and, above all, unemployment rose from 1.5 million to 13 million.

National self-confidence, however shaky its foundations, has always played a crucial role in US history, and President Hoover was not the man to restore it. Matters only began to improve in 1932, when the patrician figure of **Franklin Delano Roosevelt** accepted the Democratic nomination for president with the words "I pledge myself to a new deal for America," and went on to win a landslide victory. At the time of his inauguration, early in 1933, the banking system had all but closed down; it took Roosevelt the now-proverbial "Hundred Days" of vigorous legislation to turn around the mood of the country.

Taking advantage of the new medium of radio, he used his "Fireside Chats" to cajole America out of crisis; among his earliest observations was that it was a good time for a beer, and that therefore the experiment of Prohibition was over. The **New Deal** took many forms and worked through many newly created agencies, but was marked throughout by a massive growth in the power of the federal government, which only now seems to be under threat. Among its accomplishments were the National Recovery Administration, which created two million jobs; the Social Security Act, of which Roosevelt declared "no damn politician can ever scrap my social security program"; the Public Works Administration, which built dams and highways the length and breadth of the country; the Tennessee Valley Authority, which by generating electricity under public ownership for the common good was probably the closest the US has ever come to institutionalized socialism; and measures to legitimize the role of the unions and revitalize the "Dust Bowl" farmers out on the plains.

Roosevelt originally saw himself as a populist who could draw support from every sector of society. By 1936, however, business leaders were making it clear that as far as they were concerned he had done more than enough already to kick-start the economy. From then on, as he secured an unprecedented four consecutive terms as president, he was firmly cast as the champion of the little man.

After the work-creation programs of the New Deal had put America back on its feet, the deadly pressure to achieve victory in **World War II** spurred industrial production and know-how to new heights. Once again the US stayed out of the war at first, until it was finally forced in by the high-stakes gamble of the Japanese, who launched a pre-emptive strike on Hawaii's Pearl Harbor in December 1941. In both the Pacific and in Europe, American manpower and economic muscle eventually carried all before it. Roosevelt died early in 1945, after laying the foundations for the postwar carve-up with Stalin and Churchill at Yalta, and thus was spared the fateful decision, made by his successor Harry Truman, to use the newly developed atomic bomb on Hiroshima and Nagasaki.

The coming of the Cold War

With the war won, the United Nations was created amid much hopeful rhetoric, and the Marshall Plan was set up to speed the recovery of Europe, a goal in which it was far more successful than its predecessors 25 years earlier. However, as Winston Churchill announced in Missouri in 1946, an "Iron Curtain" had descended upon Europe, and Joseph Stalin was transformed from ally to enemy almost overnight.

The ensuing **Cold War** lasted for over four decades, at times fought in ferocious combat in scattered corners of the globe, and during the intervals amassing colossal resources in the stockpiling of ever more destructive arsenals. Some of its ugliest moments came in its earliest years; Truman was still in office in 1950 when war broke out in **Korea**. A dispute over the arbitrary division of the Korean peninsula into two separate nations, North and South, soon turned into a stand-off between the US and China (with Russia, in theory at any rate, lurking in the shadows). Two years of a bloody stalemate ended, with little to show for it, except that Truman had by now been replaced by the genial **General Eisenhower**, the latest war hero to turn president.

The Eisenhower years have come to be synonymous with bland complacency. Once **Senator Joseph McCarthy**, the "witch-hunting" anti-Communist scourge of the State Department and Hollywood, had finally discredited himself by attacking the army as well, the country lapsed into a wilful suburban stupor. Great social changes were starting to take shape, however. World War II had introduced vast numbers of women and members of ethnic minorities to the potential rewards of factory work, and it had shown many Americans the lifestyle that was attainable in other parts of their own country. The development of a national highway system, and a huge increase in automobile ownership, encouraged people to pursue the American Dream wherever they chose, and this led to another **mass migration** of blacks from the rural South to the cities of the North. The cities of **California** entered a period of exponential growth, with the aeronautical industries of Los Angeles in particular attracting thousands of prospective workers.

It was also during the 1950s that **television** reached every home in the country. Together with the LP record, it created an entertainment industry that seemed designed to promote mass conformity but which swiftly showed itself capable of addressing the needs of consumers who had previously been barely identified. **Youth culture** burst into public prominence from 1954 onwards, with Elvis Presley's recording of *That's Alright Mama* appearing within a few months of Marlon Brando's moody starring role in *On the Waterfront* and James Dean's in *Rebel Without a Cause*.

The civil rights years

Racial segregation of public facilities, which had remained the norm in the South ever since Reconstruction, was in 1954 finally declared illegal by the Supreme Court ruling on *Brown vs Topeka Board of Education*. Just as a century before, however, the Southern states saw the issue more in terms of states' rights than of human rights, and attempting to implement the law, or even to challenge the failure to implement it, required immense courage. The action of Rosa Parks in refusing to give up her seat to a white man on a bus in Montgomery, Alabama, in December 1955 triggered a successful mass boycott (see p.589), and pushed the 27-year-old **Rev Dr Martin Luther King Jr** to the forefront of the civil rights campaign. Further confrontation took place at the Central High School in Little Rock, Arkansas, in 1957 (see p.607), when the reluctant Eisenhower found himself forced to call in federal troops to counter the state's unwillingness to integrate its education system.

The election of **John F. Kennedy** to the presidency in 1960, by the narrowest of margins, marked a sea-change in American politics, even if in retrospect his policies do not seem exactly radical. At 43 the youngest ever president, and the first Catholic, he was prepared literally to reach for the moon, urging the US to victory in the Space Race in which it had thus far lagged humiliatingly behind the Soviet Union. Kennedy had won in part thanks to his spurious allegations concerning the "missile gap," and after years of peace under Eisenhower the Cold War soon began to heat up again. Fortunately, the US military spotted Soviet missile bases in Communist Cuba in 1962 before the missiles themselves had been installed, and Kennedy insisted they be withdrawn. Kennedy had had rather less success the previous year, however, in launching the abortive **Bay of Pigs** invasion of Cuba, and he also managed to embroil America in the ongoing war in Vietnam, by sending "advisers" to Saigon.

Another factor in Kennedy's election success had been a much-publicized telephone call to the wife of Dr King, during one of King's many sojourns in Southern jails, but as president he was rarely keen to identify himself with the civil rights movement. The campaign nonetheless made headway, given added momentum by the global impact of television news programs showing such horrific images as Birmingham police chief "Bull" Connor turning water cannons and dogs on peaceful demonstrators in 1963. The movement's defining moment came when Dr King delivered his eloquent "I Have a Dream" speech during the "March on Washington for Jobs and Freedom" later that summer. For his unwavering espousal of Gandhian principles of nonviolence, King was awarded the Nobel Peace Prize the following year. Nonetheless, part of the reason that middle America came to accept the need to address racial inequalities was the threat it perceived in the rhetoric of **Malcolm X**, who argued that black people had the right to defend themselves against aggression.

After Kennedy's assassination in November 1963 (see p.752), his successor **Lyndon Johnson** ("LBJ," in homage to Roosevelt's "FDR") was responsible for pushing through a body of legislation that enacted most of civil rights campaigners' key demands. Violent white resistance in the South continued, however, and only the long, painstaking and dangerous work of registering Southern black voters en masse eventually forced Southern politicians to mend their ways.

Johnson won a landslide victory over Republican Barry Goldwater in the election of 1964, but whether his dream of building a "Great Society" could ever have reached fruition is impossible to know. Instead he was soon brought low by the war in **Vietnam**, where American involvement had escalated beyond all reason or apparent control. Broad-based popular opposition to the conflict grew in proportion to the death toll of American soldiers, and the threat of the draft heightened the mood of youthful rebellion. San Francisco in particular responded to psychedelic prophet Timothy Leary's call to "turn on, tune in, drop out"; 1967's Summer of Love saw the lone beatniks of the Fifties transmogrify into an entire generation of hippies.

From the earliest days of the civil rights struggle, Dr King had argued that social justice could only be achieved through economic equality. That message was given a new urgency by riots in the ghettos of Los Angeles in 1965 and Detroit in 1967, and the emergence of the Black Panthers, an armed defense force in the tradition of the now-dead Malcolm X. King also began to denounce the Vietnam War; meanwhile, after refusing the draft with the words "No Vietcong ever called me nigger," Muhammad Ali was stripped of his title as world heavyweight boxing champion.

In 1968, not long after his plummeting popularity led LBJ to announce that he would not run again for the presidency, Dr King, in Memphis to support a garbage workers' strike, was gunned down in his motel. Shortly after, JFK's brother and former attorney general Robert, who had managed to redefine himself as spokesman for the nation's dispossessed, was fatally shot on the night that he emerged as Democratic front-runner. It didn't take a conspiracy theorist to see that the spate of deaths reflected a malaise in the soul of America.

Richard Nixon to Jimmy Carter

Somehow – perhaps because the brutally suppressed riots at the Chicago Democratic Convention raised the specter of anarchy – the misery of 1968 resulted in the election of Republican **Richard Nixon** as president. Eisenhower's vice-president while still in his thirties, Nixon had famously told the press after his failed bid for the governor of California in 1962 that "you won't have Nixon to kick around any more." Now he was back, and it soon became apparent that he had scores to settle with his countless perceived enemies, above all in the media. Nixon's impeccable conservative credentials enabled him to bring the US to a rapport with China, but the war in Vietnam dragged on, to claim a total of 57,000 American lives. Attempts to win it included the secret and illegal bombing of Cambodia, which raised opposition at home to a new peak, but ultimately it was simpler to abandon the original goals in the name of "peace with honor." The end came either in 1972 – when Henry Kissinger and Le Duc Tho were awarded the Nobel Peace Prize for negotiating a treaty, and Tho at least had the grace to decline the award – or in 1975, when the Americans finally withdrew from Saigon.

During Nixon's first term, many of the disparate individuals politicized by the events and undercurrents of the 1960s coalesced into activist groupings. Native Americans occupied the island of Alcatraz in San Francisco, in the genesis of the American Indian Movement; gay men in New York's *Stonewall* bar fought back after one police raid too many; feminists united to campaign for abortion rights and an Equal Rights Amendment; and even the prisoners in America's jails attempted to organize themselves, resulting in such bloody debacles as the 31 prisoners killed when the military stormed Attica prison in September 1971. Nixon directed various federal agencies to monitor the new radicalism, but his real bugbear was the antiwar protesters. Increasingly ludicrous covert operations against real and potential opponents culminated in the botched attempt to burgle Democratic National Headquarters in Washington DC's **Watergate** complex in 1972. It took two years of investigation before Nixon's role in the subsequent cover-up was proved conclusively, and in 1974 he resigned, one step ahead of impeachment by the Senate, to be succeeded by vice-president Gerald Ford.

With the Republicans momentarily discredited, former Georgia governor **Jimmy Carter** was elected to the presidency as a clean-handed outsider in the nation's bicentennial year of 1976. His victory showed how far the US had come in a decade, let alone two centuries; a crucial constituency of this new-style Southern Democrat was the recently enfranchised black population of the South. Carter's enthusiastic attempts to put his Baptist principles into practice on such issues as global human rights were soon perceived as naive, if not un-American. Misfortune followed misfortune. He had to break the unpleasant news to the nation that it was facing an energy crisis, following the formation of the OPEC cartel of Middle East oil producers. Worse still, the Shah of Iran, a close American ally, was overthrown, and the staff of the US embassy in Teheran was taken hostage by Islamic revolutionaries. Carter's failed attempts to arrange the hostages' release was seized upon by the Republicans as a sign of his weakness as a leader and all but destroyed his hopes of winning re-election in 1980. In fact, the tenacious refusal of the Iranians to release the hostages while Carter was still President, holding them until the very day he left office to be replaced by the former B-movie actor **Ronald Reagan**, led to accusations that the Republicans had struck a secret deal with the hostage-takers. Whatever the truth, the facts are that Carter's presidency ended with the taint of the hostage crisis still present, and Reagan's term started in an aura of celebration at their final return home.

The Reagan–Bush years

Ronald Reagan was a new kind of president. Unlike the obsessive workaholic Carter, he made a virtue of his hands-off approach to the job, joking for example that "they say hard work never killed anybody, but I figured why take the risk." This laissez-faire attitude extended to his domestic economic policies, under which the rich were left to get as rich as they could; his successors were left to cope with the explosion in the national debt that followed deregulation of the financial markets and the collapse of the Savings and Loan system. The common perception that Reagan was unaware of what went on around him ensured that his popularity remained undented through a succession of scandals, and he was re-elected in 1984. He did have his pet projects, however, such as the enormously expensive attempt to seal off American skies with the Strategic Defense Initiative ("Star Wars"), and a personal vendetta against Colonel Qaddafi of Libya. The administration's persistent maneuverings to destabilize the left-wing Sandinista government in Nicaragua culminated in the labyrinthine "Iran–Contra" affair, under which the profits from illegal arms sales to Iran were used to buy arms for the Contra rebels in Nicaragua (unbeknownst to Congress or the public). Like other conservatives before him, Reagan was adept at Cold War posturing, and was allowed greater leeway by his electorate than a Democrat might have been in arms-control negotiations with Mikhail Gorbachev, the new leader of what Reagan called the "Evil Empire."

In 1988, Reagan was replaced in office by his vice-president **George Bush**. For a moment, it seemed that Jesse Jackson, at the head of his multiracial "Rainbow Coalition," might become the first black presidential candidate of a major party, but after an early strong showing in the Democratic primaries, he lost the nomination to a more traditional – and, it was thought, more "electable" – Democrat, Massachusetts governor Michael Dukakis. During the ensuing race, Bush succeeded in labeling Dukakis a "card-carrying liberal," and voters responded to Bush's pledge, "read my lips – no new taxes," a vow that would help undo him a few years later.

Bush's one term in office was marked by the increasing influence of the US in foreign affairs, largely made possible by the sudden end of the Cold War, which was brought on by the collapse of the communist governments in Eastern Europe; the Berlin Wall came down in 1989, and the Soviet Union crumbled away. Bush was also president when Operation Desert Storm drove the Iraqis out of Kuwait in February 1991, an undertaking that lasted 100 hours and in which virtually no American lives were lost. Bush's unprecedented popularity at the moment of triumph in Kuwait convinced many that he was certain of a second term in office. His success was short-lived, however. During the 1992 election campaign it became clear that Americans were more concerned with domestic affairs than with what was happening overseas, and Bush appeared woefully out of touch with the common man when he was confused by the workings of a supermarket cash register during a campaign appearance. Twelve years of Republican government came to an end with the election of the Arkansas governor **Bill Clinton** in 1992.

Clinton and the end of the century

Bill Clinton's first term as president was marked by his failure to deliver on specific campaign promises – most obviously, his pledge to reform the nation's health-care system. His resultant unpopularity helped the Republican opposition to win sweeping victories in the 1994 congressional elections and made it nearly impossible for him to pass any of his favored legislation. The remaining years of his first term were characterized by protracted struggles with the Republican-dominated Congress, just the sort of "gridlock" that both parties had pledged to avoid. Through a better grasp of the popular mood, Clinton managed to assign most of the blame for the government's ineffectiveness to the Republicans and was elected to a second term with surprising ease.

But the "Comeback Kid" was to find holding on to his office somewhat more challenging than the re-election. Persistent allegations of adulterous liaisons finally came to a head in early 1998 with the revelation that Clinton had carried on an affair with a young White House intern named Monica Lewinsky. To make matters worse, he engaged in a series of dubious actions and made misleading statements that Republicans, behind appointed Special Prosecutor Kenneth Starr, interpreted as a far-reaching cover-up of the scandal. Starr's exhaustive investigation led to the technical **impeachment** of the President, on grounds of perjury and abuse of power. Despite being convicted by the lower house of Congress, Clinton was eventually saved by a close vote in the upper house of the Senate – largely because the American people were tired of the scandal, and did not feel Clinton's indiscretions were serious enough to merit removal. In fact, it was the Republicans who suffered losses in the 1998 congressional elections, while the President's popularity remained surprisingly high.

The new millennium

Despite the doomsaying predictions of technology analysts and religious fundamentalists, the much-feared Y2K computer bug turned out to be more a product of media hype than an actual threat. The real challenges for the US, however, were just beginning. By the middle of 2000, the **dot-com** bubble had burst, sending countless high-tech companies into bankruptcy and devaluing their stocks to mere pennies. Once-triumphant businesses like Pets.com and Kozmo disappeared overnight, and the technology sector started on a long, steep decline, taking other stocks down with it in a deepening **recession** that ended a decade of unprecedented growth and prosperity.

As the Clinton era drew to a close, the country became mired in the disputed **2000 presidential election**. Amid charges of improper ballot counting, the final verdict on the lackluster race between Texas governor and son of the 41st president **George W. Bush** and Vice President Gore was suspended for several months, while the nominees' parties frantically filed suits and countersuits to squeeze out every last advantage. The debacle ended in what amounted to a constitutional crisis, with the US Supreme Court deciding the winner for the first time in the nation's history. Despite a sizeable contingent doubting the legitimacy of the outcome, the Republican Bush – known for his linguistic blunders and a limited grasp of foreign affairs – took office on January 20, 2001, around the same time that Clinton was tacking on another scandal to his outgoing administration, centered on possible influence-peddling for presidential pardons.

That and any other affairs destined as news-of-the-month in 2001 were all subsumed by the events of **September 11**, when a wave of terrorist attacks brought George W. Bush his first serious challenge in office. Using only knives and box-cutters, hijackers took control of four planes and plowed two of them into the twin towers of the World Trade Center in New York City – resulting in their horrific collapse – and the third into the Pentagon; the fourth crashed in a Pennsylvania forest. All told, upwards of 3000 died, and the country entered a period of mourning, accompanied by a strident patriotic fervor.

The attacks were quickly linked to the al Qaida network of Saudi Arabian terrorist **Osama bin Laden**, and a month later President Bush retaliated by declaring an open-ended **war** against terrorism, first targeting bin Laden's Islamic fundamentalist protectors in Afghanistan, the Taliban. US air and ground strikes in Afghanistan, with the support of an international coalition, brought Bush unprecedented popularity at home, if not necessarily overseas, and within weeks he was pushing for measures to extend the legal boundaries for electronic surveillance and suspect questioning.

Still, the months following the terrorist attack were marked by serious worries: the stock market continued to falter and the airline industries were hit especially hard by the sudden drop in leisure travel; an **anthrax scare** gripped the public consciousness, as letters containing the lethal spores showed up in the offices of prominent figures; and a few scattered incidents at airports and on public transportation reminded people that no matter how many precautions were put in place, safety could never be fully guaranteed. That said, perhaps all the talk of a "changed world" was slightly overstated.

Books

It would be futile to attempt to provide a comprehensive overview of American literature in the limited space available. The following bibliography is, therefore, an idiosyncratic selection of books intended as a starting point for interested readers. Books tagged with the * symbol are particularly recommended.

History and society

★ **James Baldwin** *No Name on the Street, The Fire Next Time, Evidence of Things Not Seen*, and many others. The most brilliant prose stylist of twentieth-century America. Stunningly incisive accounts of the black experience in the cities of the USA, although Baldwin was such a powerful polemicist that he was occasionally swept away by his own rhetoric.

John Berendt *Midnight in the Garden of Good and Evil*. Voodoo, transvestism and murder; best-selling true-life tales of life and death in contemporary Savannah – see p.541.

Center of the American West *Atlas of the New West*. Admirable, well-illustrated volume, full of quirky facts, figures and personal essays that reveal the true colors of one of the most mythologized, rapidly changing regions in the nation.

Dee Brown *Bury My Heart at Wounded Knee*. A quarter of a century on from its first publication, this remains the best narrative of the impact of white settlement and expansion on Native Americans across the continent.

Bill Bryson *Made in America*. A compulsively readable history of the American language, packed with bizarre snippets, which does much to illuminate the history of the nation.

Peter Carroll and David Noble *The Free and the Unfree: a New History of the USA*. A good interpretive history of American political development, focusing on the wide gap between those who hold power and those who are disadvantaged on grounds of race, sex or class.

Jill Ker Conway (ed) *Written by Herself*. Splendid anthology of women's autobiographies from the mid-1800s to the present, including sections on African Americans, scientists, artists and pioneers.

★ **Mike Davis** *City of Quartz*. City politics, neighborhood gangs, unions, film noir and religion are drawn together in this award-winning, leftist, hyperbolic history of Los Angeles.

Joan Didion *The White Album, Slouching Toward Bethlehem, Miami* and others. Essays on the American way of life, drawing heavily on the late Sixties. A respected social commentator, Didion spoils the act at times by dropping too many names.

Frederick Douglass et al *The Classic Slave Narratives*. Compilation of ex-slaves' autobiographies, ranging from Olaudah Equiano's kidnapping in Africa and global wanderings to Frederick Douglass' eloquent denunciation of slavery. Includes Harriet Jacobs' story of her escape from Edenton, North Carolina – see p.498.

W.E.B. DuBois *The Souls of Black Folk*. Seminal collection of largely autobiographical essays examining the separation of the races in American society at the beginning of the twentieth century.

Brian Fagan *Ancient North America*. Archeological history of America's native peoples, from the first hunters to cross the Bering Strait up to European contact.

Frances Fitzgerald *Cities on a Hill*. Intelligent, sympathetic exploration of four of the odder corners of American culture, including San Francisco's gay Castro district and the Rajneeshi community in eastern Oregon.

Shelby Foote *The Civil War: a Narrative*. Epic, three-volume account containing anything you could possibly want to know about the "War Between the States."

U.S. Grant *Personal Memoirs*. Encouraged by Mark Twain, the Union general and subsequent president wrote his autobiography just before his death, in a (successful) bid to recoup his horrendous debts. At first the book feels oddly downbeat, but the man's down-to-earth modesty grows on you.

James R. Grossman *Land of Hope*. Scholarly yet moving account of the exodus of Southern blacks to Northern cities, specifically Chicago, during the early twentieth century. Though it focuses on the broader social and economic issues, it also manages to bring to life the individual stories involved.

Tony Horwitz *Confederates in the Attic: Dispatches from the Unfinished Civil War*. Strange meld of past and present, as journalist Horwitz explores the places in the South where die-hards keep the Civil War very much alive.

Frederick Hoxie (ed) *Indians in American History*. Eye-opening collection of essays focusing on the role of Native Americans in US history, presenting them as active and aware (if hopelessly outgunned) players rather than passive victims. Filled with illustrations and extensive quotes from journals and contemporary accounts of Native Americans from across the US.

J.B. Jackson *American Space*. Engagingly written work that traces the transition of America from a rural to an urban and industrialized nation in the crucial decade immediately after the Civil War.

William Loren Katz *The Black West*. Fascinating, scholarly and long-overdue exploration of the African-American experience of the opening of the West.

Roger G. Kennedy *Rediscovering America*. Collected essays by one of America's most readable historians, appointed by Clinton to run the National Park Service. Kennedy looks behind the gloss of conventional tellings to reveal something of the real story of how America came to be.

Meriwether Lewis and William Clark *The Original Journals of the Lewis and Clark Expedition, 1804–1806*. Eight volumes of meticulous jottings by the Northwest's first inland explorers, scrupulously following President Jefferson's orders to record every detail of flora, fauna and native inhabitant.

Clyde A. Milner II, Carol A. O'Connor and Martha A. Sandweiss, *The Oxford History of the American West*. Fascinating collection of essays on Western history, covering topics ranging from myths and movies to art and religion.

James M. McPherson *Battle Cry of Freedom*. Extremely readable history of the Civil War, which integrates and explains the complex social, economic, political and military factors in one concise volume. Highly recommended.

James Mooney *The Ghost Dance Religion and The Sioux Outbreak of 1890*. An extraordinary Bureau of Ethnology report, first published in 1890 but still available in paperback. Mooney persuaded his Washington superiors to allow him to roam the West in search of first-hand evidence, and even interviewed Wovoka, the Ghost Dance prophet, in person.

Roderick Frazier Nash *Wilderness and the American Mind*. Classic book, just recently reissued, which examines the American take on environmental and conservation issues over the past couple of hundred years. Especially good sections on John Muir and his battles to preserve Yosemite.

Stephen Plog *Ancient Peoples of the Southwest*. Much the best single-volume history of the pre-Hispanic Southwest, packed with diagrams and color photographs.

Marc Reisner *Cadillac Desert*. Concise but engaging account of the environmental and political impact on the West of the twentieth century's mania for dam-building and large-scale irrigation projects.

Witold Rybczynski *A Clearing in the Distance: Olmsted and America*. Well-told study of America's favorite landscape architect (responsible for NYC's Central Park, among many other accomplishments) that gets beyond Olmsted's green spaces and views him more as a historical and cultural touchstone.

Hunter S. Thompson *The Great Shark Hunt* and *Songs of the Doomed*.

Accessible and varied collections of the maverick Dr Gonzo's journalistic rantings on contemporary American life and politics. Spiced up by tales of his own anarchic love of good times, guns and gambling.

Sun Tracks & University of Arizona Press *Between Sacred Mountains*. Superb overview of Navajo history, culture and politics, written by Navajo teachers and parents as a sourcebook for Navajo students.

Stephen Trimble *The People*. Excellent introduction to all the Native American groups of the Southwest, bringing the history up to date with contemporary interviews.

★ **Mark Twain** *Roughing It*, *Life on the Mississippi*, and many others. Mark Twain was by far the funniest and most vivid chronicler of nineteenth-century America. *Roughing It*, which covers his early wanderings across the continent, all the way to Hawaii, is absolutely compelling.

John Unruh *The Plains Across*. A history of the wagon trains, drawing heavily on pioneer journals.

Mariann Voller *Ghosts in Mississippi*. This horrific account of the 1963 murder of civil rights leader Medgar Evers, and quite why it took thirty years to convict his self-proclaimed assassin, provides fascinating insights into how the Deep South has and has not changed.

Geoffrey C. Ward, with Ric and Ken Burns *The Civil War*. Marvelous illustrated history of the Civil War, designed to accompany the TV series and using hundreds of the same photographs.

Richard White *It's Your Misfortune and None of My Own*. Dense, authoritative and all-embracing history of the American West, that debunks the notion of the rugged pioneer by stressing the role of the federal government.

Juan Williams *Eyes on the Prize*. Informative and detailed accompaniment to the excellent TV series, covering the Civil Rights years from the early 1950s up to 1966, with lots of rare and some very familiar photos.

Edmund Wilson *Patriotic Gore*. Fascinating eight-hundred-page survey of the literature of the American Civil War, which in its own right serves as an immensely readable narrative of the conflict.

Biography and oral history

Maya Angelou *I Know Why the Caged Bird Sings*. First of a five-volume autobiography that provides an ultimately uplifting account of how a black girl transcended her traumatic childhood in 1930s Arkansas.

Paul Auster (ed) *True Tales of American Life* (UK)/*I Thought My Father Was God* (US). Anthology of true-life stories sent to Auster for a National Public Radio project. Arranged by subject, it's best dipped into at random; among the mawkish and the mundane are just enough quirky, touching and plain crazy tales to make it worth the while. A humanistic and accepting view of America and its people – complications, contradictions and all.

William F. Cody *The Life of Hon. William F. Cody, Known as Buffalo Bill*. Larger-than-life autobiography of one of the great characters of the Wild West. Particularly treasurable for the moment when he refers to himself more formally as "Bison William."

Henry Hampton and Steve Fayer *Voices of Freedom*. Hugely impressive oral history of the Civil Rights movement, heavily drawn from the TV series.

Joyce Johnson *Minor Characters*. Johnson, Jack Kerouac's girlfriend and "muse," tells her own story and those of the other women in the 1950s East Village scene, revealing the stiflingly reactionary male elitism of the Beats.

Florence King *Confessions of a Failed Southern Lady*. Hilarious autobiography of a girl who grows up with her faded Southern belle grandmother and foul-talking, heavy-smoking mother, only to effect the greatest rebellion of all by falling in love with a woman.

Malcolm X, with Alex Haley *The Autobiography of Malcolm X*. Searingly honest and moving account of Malcolm's progress from street hoodlum to political leadership. Written on the hoof over a period of years, it traces the development of Malcolm X's thinking before, during and after his split from the Nation of Islam. The conclusion, when he talks about his impending assassination, is painful in the extreme.

Edmund Morris *Theodore Rex*. Thoroughly engaging and superbly researched biography of Theodore Roosevelt, tracing the energetic and controversial president's far-reaching achievements between 1901 and 1909.

Muhammad Ali *The Greatest*. Powerful and entertaining autobiography of the Louisville boy who grew up to become world heavyweight boxing champion. The most memorable parts deal with his fight against the Vietnam draft and the subsequent stripping away of his world championship title.

Tony Parker *A Place Called Bird.* Fascinating oral history based on interviews with the inhabitants of a tiny town in the very center of Kansas, the heartland of the Midwest.

Ishbel Ross *Rebel Rose.* Evocative, rebel-yelling biography of Rose Greenhow, glamorous Washington socialite and remarkably brave Confederate spy. Works equally well as an exciting tale of political espionage and an impeccably detailed historical document.

Quinta Scott and Susan Croce Kelly *Route 66.* Moving oral histories and monochrome photographs trace the life of the now abandoned 2000-mile highway immortalized in film, novels and song.

Ralph Steadman *Scar Strangled Banner.* Warped, cynical and crazy underview of America, full of sketches and hacked-about photos, from sometime Hunter S. Thompson collaborator and illustrator.

Joanna L. Stratton *Pioneer Women.* Original memoirs of women – mothers, teachers, homesteaders and circuit riders – who ventured across the Plains from 1854 to 1890. Lively, superbly detailed accounts, with chapters on journeys, homebuilding, daily domestic life, the church, the cowtown, temperance and suffrage.

Studs Terkel *American Dreams Lost and Found.* Interviews with ordinary American citizens. As illuminating a guide to US life as you could hope for.

Geoffrey C. Ward, Dayton Duncan and Ken Burns *Mark Twain: An Illustrated Biography.* Tied in with the superb TV series, this classy and readable volume is filled with essays from various authors interspersed with Twain's own words, taken from published works, personal diaries and letters. These, along with the many rare photographs, shed vivid light on an extraordinarily prolific American icon.

★ **Frank Waters** *Book of the Hopi.* Extraordinary insight into the traditions and beliefs of the Hopi, prepared through years of interviews and approved by tribal elders.

Entertainment and culture

Kenneth Anger *Hollywood Babylon.* A vicious yet high-spirited romp through Tinseltown's greatest scandals, amply illustrated with gory and repulsive photographs, and always inclined to bend the facts for the sake of a good story. A shoddily researched second volume covers more recent times.

Joshua Berrett (ed) *The Louis Armstrong Companion: Eight Decades of Commentary.* Broad selection of

essays, interviews, letters, reviews and autobiography, revealing the world's most influential musician in all his complexity. A fine introduction to the subject, featuring lots of previously unpublished material: standouts include Armstrong's own lament about defeatism and negativity in his fellow black men.

Charlotte Greig *Will You Still Love Me Tomorrow?* Enthusiastic feminist appraisal of (predominantly

American) girl groups from the 1950s (the Chantels and the Crystals) through to 1980s rap stars like Salt 'n' Pepa. Though inevitably somewhat dated now, its many photos and personal recollections still make it a great read.

Peter Guralnick *Lost Highways, Feel Like Going Home* and *Sweet Soul Music*. Thoroughly researched personal histories of black popular music, packed with obsessive detail on all the great names. His more recent Elvis biographies, *Last Train to Memphis* and *Careless Love*, trace the rise and fall of the iconic star in a nonsensational but nonetheless gripping documentary manner, while also performing the rare trick of evaluating him seriously as a musician.

Gerri Hershey *Nowhere To Run: the History of Soul Music*. Definitive rundown on the evolution of soul music from the gospel heyday of the 1940s through the Memphis, Motown and Philly scenes to the sounds of the early 1980s. Strong on social commentary and political background and studded with anecdotes and interviews.

Greil Marcus *Dead Elvis*. Vastly entertaining overview of the many Elvis myths, if a little hastily put together from previously published articles. Marcus's *Mystery Train* is an intelligent and absorbing overview of American popular music, from Robert Johnson to Elvis Presley and Randy Newman.

Michael Ondaatje *Coming through Slaughter*. Extraordinary, dream-like fictionalization of the life of doomed New Orleans cornet player Buddy Bolden, written in a lyrical style that evokes the rhythms and pace of jazz improvisation.

Robert Palmer *Deep Blues*. Readable history of the development and personalities of the Delta Blues.

Randall Reise *Nashville Babylon*. Thrashes the squeaky-clean image of the country music scene. Cocaine, whiskey, infidelity, murder, rape and other skeletons are dug up from the closets of some unlikely characters.

Henry Rollins *Get in the Van*. Illustrated diary of a trek round the US and Europe with punk band Black Flag during the early 1980s. Rollins lives up to his malcontent reputation by criticizing almost everywhere he visits: Madison, Wisconsin, being about the only place he seems to like.

David E. Stanley *The Elvis Encyclopedia*. It might lack the authoritative analysis of Peter Guralnick's book (see above), but this well-illustrated tome, by Presley's stepbrother, is the most enjoyable of the many coffee-table trivia books on the subject. Interesting oddments include "Elvis's Iron Constitution."

Geoffrey C. Ward, Ken Burns et al *Jazz: A History of America's Music*. While the story peters out somewhat after bebop, this highly readable volume (linked to the TV series) boasts hundreds of illustrations and rare photographs, first-hand accounts and lively essays to provide a beautifully drawn picture of America's home-grown music and its icons.

John Williams *Into the Badlands*. Williams' interviews with a group of America's very best crime writers build a picture of the underbelly of US society from the Montana mountainsides of James Crumley to the mean streets of Elmore Leonard's Detroit. He lapses into sexism, however, when dealing with Chicago's Sara Paretsky, who "is learning as she goes along."

Travel writing

Edward Abbey *The Journey Home*. Hilarious accounts of whitewater rafting and desert hiking trips alternate with essays, by the man who inspired the radical environmentalist movement Earth First! All of Abbey's many books, especially *Desert Solitaire*, a journal of time spent as a ranger in Arches National Park, make great traveling companions.

James Agee and Walker Evans *Let Us Now Praise Famous Men*. A deeply personal but also richly evocative journal of travels through the rural lands of the Depression-era Deep South, complemented by Evans' powerful photographs.

Stephen Brook *New York Days, New York Nights*. An Englishman's dryly witty impressions of the Big Apple in the 1990s, with chapters on every aspect of the place, from flotation chambers to Jewish restaurants. Brook's *Honky Tonk Gelato* treats Texas in a similar, if sometimes patronizing vein.

Bill Bryson *The Lost Continent*. Using his boyhood home of Des Moines in Iowa as a benchmark, the author travels the length and breadth of America to find the perfect small town. Hilarious, if occasionally a bit smug. *A Walk in the Woods* applies his trademark irony to the Appalachian Trail from Georgia to Maine, but suffers from too much nature and too few quirky characters.

J. Hector St-John de Crèvecoeur *Letters from an American Farmer and Sketches of Eighteenth-Century America*. First published in 1782, a remarkable account of the complexities of Revolutionary America.

Robert Frank *The Americans*. The Swiss photographer's brilliantly evocative portrait of mid-century American life from coast to coast, with striking images contextualized by an introductory essay from Jack Kerouac.

★ **Ian Frazier** *Great Plains*. An immaculately researched and well-written travelogue containing a wealth of information on the people of the American prairielands from Native Americans to the soldiers who staff the region's many nuclear installations.

Jack Kerouac *On the Road*. Definitive account of transcontinental Beatnik wanderings, which now reads as a curiously dated period piece. Not as incoherent as you might expect.

James A. MacMahon (ed) *Audubon Society Nature Guides*. Attractively produced, fully illustrated and easy-to-use guides to the flora and fauna of seven different US regional ecosystems, covering the entire country from coast to coast and from grasslands to glaciers.

Virginia and Lee McAlester *A Field Guide to American Houses*. Well-illustrated and engaging guide to America's rich variety of domestic architecture, from pre-colonial to postmodern.

Melanie McGrath *Motel Nirvana*. Entertaining account of a British traveler's experiences in the Southwest, with some enjoyable swipes at various New-Age nonsense.

John McPhee *Encounters with the Arch Druid*. In three interlinked narratives, environmental activist and Friends of the Earth founder David Brower confronts developers, miners and dam builders, while trying to protect three different American wilderness areas – the Atlantic shoreline, the Grand Canyon and the Cascades of the Pacific Northwest.

William Least Heat Moon *Blue Highways*. Account of a mammoth loop tour of the US by back roads, in which the author interviews ordinary people in ordinary places. A good overview of rural America, with lots of interesting details on Native Americans. His next book, *Prairyerth*, opted for the microcosmic approach, taking six hundred loving pages over the story of Chase County, Kansas.

Jonathan Raban *Old Glory*. A somewhat pompous though always interesting account of Raban's journey on a small craft down the Mississippi River from the headwaters in Minnesota to the bayous of Louisiana.

Bernard A Weisberger (ed) *The WPA Guide to America*. Prepared during the New Deal as part of a make-work program for writers, these guides paint a fairly comprehensive portrait of 1930s and earlier America. Also available are state-by-state guides, most of them out of print but easily found in US libraries and secondhand bookshops.

Edmund White *States of Desire: Travels in Gay America*. A revealing account of life in gay communities across the country, focusing heavily on San Francisco and New York.

Fiction

General Americana

⭐ **Raymond Carver** *Will You Please Be Quiet Please?* Stories of the American working class, written in a distinctive sparse, almost deadpan style that perhaps owes something to Hemingway and certainly influenced untold numbers of contemporary American writers. The stories served as the basis for Robert Altman's film *Short Cuts*.

Don DeLillo *White Noise* and *Underworld*. The former is his best, a funny and penetrating pop culture exploration, while the latter is one of those typically flawed attempts to pack the twentieth-century American experience into a great big novel. Worthwhile, though.

John Dos Passos *USA*. Hugely ambitious novel (originally a trilogy) that grapples with the US in the early decades of the twentieth century

from every possible angle. Gripping human stories with a strong political and historical point of view.

Dennis Johnson *Jesus' Son*. Junkies and thieves and all the usual trappings of a Beat-era collection of stories, but from 1990s urban America.

William Kennedy *Ironweed*. Terse, affecting tale of a couple of down-on-their-luck drunks haunted by ghosts from a checkered past; excellent evocation of 1930s America, specifically working-class Albany, New York.

⭐ **Herman Melville** *Moby Dick*. Compendious and compelling account of nineteenth-century whaling, packed with details on American life from New England to the Pacific.

E. Annie Proulx *Accordion Crimes*. Proulx's masterly book comes as close to being the fabled "Great American Novel" as anyone could reasonably ask, tracing a fascinating history of immigrants in all parts of North America through the fortunes of a battered old Sicilian accordion.

New York City

Paul Auster *New York Trilogy*. Three Borgesian investigations into the mystery and madness of contemporary New York. Using the conventions of the detective novel, Auster unfolds a disturbed and disturbing picture of the city.

Truman Capote *Breakfast at Tiffany's* and *In Cold Blood*. The first story is about a fictional social climber in New York called Holly Go-Lightly; the second concerns the true-life stories of two serial killers in the heartland. The subject matter of these two stories could hardly be more different, but the degree of insight drawn from two uniquely American stories is equally high in both accounts.

Michael Chabon *The Amazing Adventures of Kavalier & Clay*. Pulitzer-prize winning novel charting the rise and fall of comic book-writing cousins in New York City – one a refugee from World War II Prague, the other a closeted Brooklynite.

Jonathan Franzen *The Corrections*. While it never quite lived up to the hype - what possibly could? – this ambitious saga, about a classically dysfunctional American family, manages to capture all that late twentieth-century navel searching in a nutshell. And it's very funny in places, too.

★ Chester Himes *Cotton Comes to Harlem*, *Blind Man with a Pistol*, and many others. Action-packed and uproariously violent novels set in New York's Harlem, starring the much-feared detectives Coffin Ed Johnson and Grave Digger Jones.

Jonathan Lethem *Motherless Brooklyn*. A hilarious crime caper starring Lionel Essrog, a Prince-loving private detective with Tourette's syndrome, on the trail of a killer in Brooklyn's characterful neighborhoods.

Grace Paley *Collected Stories*. Shrewd love–hate stories written over a lifetime by the daughter of Russian-Jewish immigrants, who published dead-on accounts of New York life in three installments: her first book of stories came out in the 1950s, her second in the early 1970s and her third in the late 1980s.

J.D. Salinger *The Catcher in the Rye*. Classic novel of adolescence, tracing Holden Caulfield's sardonic journey through the streets of New York.

New England

George V. Higgins *Penance for Jerry Kennedy*. Crime thriller written almost entirely in the dialogue of Boston lowlifes and crooked lawmen.

John Irving *The Cider House Rules*. One of Irving's more successful sprawling novels, weaving themes of love, suffering, and the many facets of the abortion debate against a Maine backdrop.

H.P. Lovecraft *The Best of H.P. Lovecraft: Bloodcurdling Tales of Horror and the Macabre*. Creepy New England stories from the author Stephen King called "the twentieth century's greatest practitioner of the classic horror tale."

Florida, The South

William Faulkner *The Reivers*. The last and most humorous work of this celebrated Southern author. *The Sound and the Fury*, a fascinating study of prejudice, set like most of his books in the fictional Yoknatapawpha County in Mississippi, is a much more difficult read.

Carl Hiaasen *Basket Case*, and many others. Hiaasen is the funniest crime writer on the scene – and a razor-sharp chronicler of Florida's weirder, wilder side. This one sees dead rock stars, a grumpy investigative reporter and a giant frozen lizard caught up in a fast-moving caper plot.

Zora Neale Hurston *Spunk*. Short stories celebrating black culture and experience from around the country, by a writer from Florida who became one of the bright stars of the Harlem cultural renaissance in the 1920s.

Harper Lee *To Kill a Mockingbird*. Classic tale of racial conflict and society's view of an outsider, Boo Radley, as seen through the eyes of children.

Cormac McCarthy *Suttree*. McCarthy is better known for his "modern Western" works like *Blood Meridian* and *All the Pretty Horses*, but this beautifully written tale, of a Knoxville, Tennessee scion opting for a hard-scrabble life among a band of vagrants on the Tennessee River, is his best.

Carson McCullers *The Heart Is a Lonely Hunter*. McCullers is unrivaled in her sensitive treatment of misfits, in this case the attitude of a small Southern community to a deaf-mute.

Margaret Mitchell *Gone with the Wind*. Worth a read even if you know the lines of Scarlett and Rhett by heart.

★ Toni Morrison *Beloved*. Exquisitely written ghost story by the Nobel Prize-winning novelist, which recounts the painful lives of a group of freed slaves after Reconstruction, and the obsession a mother develops after murdering her baby daughter to spare her a life of slavery.

Flannery O'Connor *A Good Man Is Hard to Find*. Short stories, featuring strong, obsessed characters, that explore religious tensions and racial conflicts in the Deep South.

Alice Walker *In Love and Trouble*. Moving and powerful stories of black women in the South, from the author of the much-acclaimed *The Color Purple*.

Eudora Welty *The Ponder Heart*. Quirky, humorous evocation of life in a backwater Mississippi town. Her most critically acclaimed work, *The Optimist's Daughter*, explores the tensions between a judge's daughter and her stepmother.

Bailey White *Mama Makes up Her Mind* and *Sleeping at the Starlight Motel*. Witty, touching tales of Georgian life. The eponymous, eccentric mother is the delightful central character of the former, while the fond portrayal of White's small home-town in the second is spot-on.

Louisiana

James Lee Burke *Black Cherry Blues*. Cajun cop Dave Robicheaux sets out to expose alliances between government and organized crime in the beautiful environs of Louisiana and Montana. A detective book that has it all.

George Washington Cable *The Grandissimes*. Romantic saga of Creole family feuds, written c.1900 but set during the Louisiana Purchase. Superb evocation of steamy Louisiana elite, the Creole lifestyle and the resistance of New Orleans to its Americanization. Apparently shocking at the time for its sympathetic portrayal of blacks.

★ **Kate Chopin** *The Awakening*. Subversive story of a bourgeois married woman whose fight for independence ends in tragedy. Swampy c.1900 Louisiana is portrayed as both a sensual hotbed for her sexual awakening and as her eventual nemesis.

★ **John Kennedy Toole** *A Confederacy of Dunces*. Anarchic black tragicomedy in which the pompous and repulsive anti-hero Ignatius J. Reilly wreaks havoc through an insalubrious and surreal New Orleans.

The Great Lakes, The Great Plains

★ **Willa Cather** *My Ántonia*. Stunning book set in Nebraska that provides a great sense of the pioneer hardships on the Plains.

Louise Erdrich *The Beet Queen*. Offbeat tale of passion and obsession among poor white North Dakota folk – particularly women – against the backdrop of an economy and culture changing with the introduction of sugar beet as a crop in the 1940s. Erdrich's other novels play through the tensions between tradition and "progress" in Native American communities.

Garrison Keillor *Lake Wobegon Days*. Wry, witty tales about a mythical Minnesota small town, poking gentle fun at the rural Midwest.

Elmore Leonard *Freaky Deaky*. One of the funniest of Leonard's many tough, brutal thrillers. Set in Detroit, it follows two former Sixties radicals who turn to crime.

Mari Sandoz *Old Jules*. Written in 1935, this fictionalized biography gives a wonderful insight into the life of the author's pioneer Swiss father on the Nebraskan plains. Sandoz's other major work, *Crazy Horse*, contains great historical overviews but is spoiled somewhat by her insistence on narrating it through Sioux eyes.

Richard Wright *Native Son*. The harrowing story of Bigger Thomas, a black chauffeur who accidentally kills his employer's daughter. The story develops his relationship with his lawyer, the closest he has ever come to being on an equal footing with a white.

The Rockies, The Southwest

James Crumley *The Wrong Case.* The lack of an intricate plot is more than compensated for by accounts of Montana scenery and the hapless detective Milo Milodragonovic, a man with a drinking problem and a knack for doing things the hard way. An enjoyable, easy read.

A.B. Guthrie Jr *Big Sky.* When first published in the Thirties it shattered the image of the mythical West peddled by Hollywood. Realistic historical fiction at its very best, following desperate mountain man and fugitive Boone Caudill, whose idyllic life in Montana was ended by the arrival of white settlers.

Tony Hillerman *The Dark Wind,* and many others. The adventures of Jim Chee of the Navajo Tribal Police on the reservations of northern Arizona, forever dabbling in dark and mysterious forces churned up from the Ancestral Puebloan past.

Norman MacLean *A River Runs through It.* Unputdownable – the best ever novel about fly-fishing, set in beautiful Montana lake country.

Annick Smith *Homestead.* Beautifully written episodes of a Montana life, a host of characters, and personal and cultural insights, all offset by Smith's tangible passion for that huge, awesome landscape.

California

★ **Raymond Chandler** *The Big Sleep* and *Farewell My Lovely.* The original incarnations of archetypal tough guy and iconic private eye Philip Marlowe are far more complex and beautifully written than the related movies would lead you to expect. This is pulp fiction at its finest – written by an American raised in London.

Armistead Maupin *Tales of the City.* Long-running saga comprising sympathetic and entertaining tales of life in San Francisco, that also work surprisingly well as suspenseful stand-alone novels. That many of its key characters are gay meant that over the years the series became a chronicle of the impact of AIDS on the city. Maupin's *Maybe the Moon* is the poignant true-life story of his friend, the short person who played ET in the movie but was never allowed to reveal her true identity.

Thomas Pynchon *The Crying of Lot 49.* Shorter, funnier and more accessible than *Gravity's Rainbow*, this novel of techno-freaks and potheads in Sixties California reveals, among other things, the sexy side of stamp collecting.

John Steinbeck *The Grapes of Wrath.* The classic account of a migrant family forsaking the Midwest for the Promised Land. Steinbeck's lighthearted but crisply observed novella *Cannery Row* captures daily life on the prewar Monterey waterfront, and the epic *East of Eden* updates and resets the Bible in the Salinas Valley and details three generations of familial feuding.

Nathanael West *The Day of the Locust.* West wrote dark novels wholly vested in the American experience; this one, set in LA, is an apocalyptic story of fringe characters at the edge of the film industry.

The Pacific Northwest

David Guterson *Snow Falling on Cedars*. Gripping, atmospheric mystery novel, evocatively capturing interracial tensions in the postwar Pacific Northwest.

Tobias Wolff *This Boy's Life*. A memoir that reads more like a novel, this mournful book – leavened by self-deprecating humor – recounts his tough upbringing in a small Washington State town.

Alaska

Tom Bodett *The End of the Road*. First novel by the broadcaster from Homer, Alaska, who shot to fame as the voice on *Motel 6* radio commercials. Funny, witty and certainly better than his often shallow collections of essays (*As Far As You Can Go without a Passport*), but for the best value invest in some of his taped books.

Jack London *The Call of the Wild and Other Stories*. London's classic tale, of a family pet discovering the ways of the wilderness while forced to pull sleds across Alaska's Gold Rush trails, is still essential reading before a trip to the far north.

Biographies

The following are some of the many personalities from American history whose names recur throughout this book. You can find detailed page references for all of them in the main index, which begins on p.1365.

Susan B. Anthony (1820–1906). Pioneer suffragette and president of the US suffragist society from 1892 to 1900, Anthony began her campaigning career in the temperance movement. She was also a committed abolitionist, published the New York liberal paper *The Revolution* (1868–70), and advocated equal pay for women, as well as donning bloomers to protest against the constrictive nature of women's clothing.

Louis Armstrong (1900–1971). New Orleans–based jazz trumpeter, known as Satchmo (from "satchel mouth"). Credited with devising the scat style of improvisational singing, and for his individualistic style, which foregrounded the solo performance above that of the band. Well known for his humor and affability, Armstrong also appeared in a number of Hollywood films.

Benedict Arnold (1741–1801). Revolutionary commander who shifted his allegiance to the British in 1779, but soon lost popularity with loyalists for leaving his British contact, Major John Andre, to be captured and hanged as a spy.

Chuck Berry (born 1926). Rock'n'roll pioneer born in (*Johnny B*) Goode Street, St Louis. Consummate lyricist, red-hot guitarist and sharp businessman.

Billy the Kid (1859–1881). The subject of innumerable Wild West legends, former busboy William Bonney made his name in the Lincoln County Wars in New Mexico. His brief and bloody career ended at the hands of Pat Garrett.

Daniel Boone (1735–1820). Legendary hunter, trapper and explorer. One of the first whites to cross the Appalachians and stake out Kentucky for settlement.

John Brown (1800–1859). Fervent white abolitionist who, as part of a grand plan to set up a free state for escaped slaves, seized the US Armory at Harpers Ferry. After a short battle, Brown was captured, tried and hanged for treason.

Calamity Jane (1852–1903). Bawdy frontierswoman, cook, dancer, prostitute and camp follower, who in 1876 took up as bullwhacker for the Gold Rush camps in South Dakota. "Calam" traveled with Wild West shows but was fired for boozing and brawling.

Al Capone (1899–1947). Bootlegger and gangster who controlled the Chicago underworld during the 1920s, and later died in Florida of syphilis.

Andrew Carnegie (1835–1919). Scots-born industrialist and philanthropist, responsible for major innovations in the steel industry. By the close of the nineteenth century, when US steel production outdid that in Britain, most of it came from Carnegie's "vertically integrated" company – which owned the coalfields and the ships and railroads for transport of the supplies to the mills.

Kit Carson (1809–1868). Carson, who moved to Taos in 1826 and became a guide on the Santa Fe Trail and "mountain man," was later instrumental in rounding up the Navajo from Canyon de Chelly.

William "Buffalo Bill" Cody (1846–1917). Pony Express rider and Indian scout immortalized by the dime novels of Ned Buntline. His Wild West show toured all over the world.

Francisco Vázquez de Coronado (1510–1554). Spanish explorer who traveled through the Southwest as far as Kansas in search of cities of gold. He threw in the towel in 1542 and returned to Mexico, only to face a series of indictments for his lack of success.

Crazy Horse Ta-Sunko-Witko (1842?–1877). Oglala Sioux leader, and one of the most able and determined Native American warriors. Prominent in the Fetterman Massacre, Battle of the Rosebud and Custer's Last Stand. Murdered at Fort Robinson, Nebraska.

Davy Crockett (1786–1836). Frontiersman, Indian fighter and Tennessee politician, who perished at the Alamo with all the other American volunteers. Popularly represented as a backwoods boy in a raccoon hat, with no education but the gift of the gab, Crockett was, in fact, less unconventional than his legend suggests.

George Armstrong Custer (1839–1876). Legendary US Cavalry general whose first big mistake – leading over two hundred troops into an ambush at Little Bighorn – was his last.

John Dillinger (1902–1934). Bank robber whose criminal activities earned him the title of Public Enemy Number One. After being set up by the legendary "Lady in Red," Dillinger was killed by FBI agents outside a Chicago movie theater.

Walt Disney (1901–1966). Inventor of Mickey Mouse, Donald Duck and Disneyland, Disney was also Hollywood's Last Tycoon, single-handedly controlling a vast media and entertainment empire.

Frederick Douglass (1817?–1895). Escaped slave who rose to prominence as a writer and orator in the abolitionist movement.

W.E.B. DuBois (1868–1963). Black intellectual and civil rights activist best known for his debates with Booker T. Washington (see p.1356) in the early part of the twentieth century, and his role in forming the National Association for the Advancement of Colored People. A longtime campaigner for the independence of African colonies, he joined the Communist Party in 1961 and emigrated to Ghana, where he renounced his US citizenship.

Bob Dylan (born 1941). North-country Minnesota boy who redefined himself first as Woody Guthrie-style folkie and later as enigmatic rock star. The endearing elliptical games of his youth have long since grown wearisome in a man in his sixties, but he can still write songs to equal his best.

Amelia Earheart (1897–1937). Pioneer aviatrix, the first woman to fly solo across the Atlantic (in 1932), and the first person ever to fly the perilous route from Hawaii to California (1935). Both she and her navigator vanished without trace on an attempted round-the-world flight, and were last contacted just near the international date line.

Thomas Edison (1847–1931). Mercurial inventor and entrepreneur who developed the light bulb, motion pictures and phonograph records. He also founded General Electric, still one of the largest US corporations.

Thomas Stearns Eliot (1888–1965). Born beside the Mississippi in St Louis, Eliot reversed the usual American pattern and moved east, first to Harvard and then England, where he was awarded the Nobel Prize for Literature for a body of poetry including *The Waste Land* and *The Four Quartets*.

Henry Ford (1863–1947). Michigan farmer's son and industrial genius who pioneered assembly-line production in his car factories. A vehement right-winger, particularly on trade union and racial issues.

Benjamin Franklin (1706–1790). Printer, inventor, diplomat and politician, responsible among other things for publishing *Poor Richard's Almanac* (a litany of mottoes advocating prudence and honesty), setting up America's first public library, the invention of bifocal glasses and early experiments with electricity. Franklin also helped draft the Declaration of Independence, and went to France to seek aid for the revolutionary cause.

Geronimo (1829–1909). Brilliant Chiricahua Apache leader who battled the US Army in Arizona and New Mexico throughout the 1880s. Despite US promises, after surrendering he and his people were deported to Florida.

Ulysses S. Grant (1822–1885). At the start of the 1860s, the 38-year-old Ulysses Grant was finding it difficult to hold down a part-time job in his brother's saddle shop; within ten years he had led the Union armies to victory in the Civil War and become president of the US.

William Randolph Hearst (1863–1951). Publishing magnate and role model for *Citizen Kane*, whose inflammatory "yellow journalism" kindled public support for the Spanish–American War.

Billie Holiday (1915–1959). Definitive song stylist – not quite blues, not quite jazz – who made her greatest recordings with Lester Young and Duke Ellington.

Buddy Holly (1936–1959). Bespectacled kid from Lubbock, Texas, who died at 22 but was the first and the greatest of rock's singer-songwriters.

Henry Hudson (1565–1611). English explorer whose expedition for the Dutch East India Company to find a route from Europe to Asia through the Arctic led to the discovery of the Hudson River in 1609 – which he mistakenly believed would lead to the Pacific – and formed the basis for Dutch colonization in the New World.

Howard Hughes (1905–1976). Business magnate and Hollywood film producer (*Hell's Angels*, 1930; *Scarface*, 1932), who became increasingly eccentric after a plane crash in 1946. Twenty years later, he sold his majority holding in TWA for $500,000,000 and lived from then on in complete seclusion in sealed-off hotel suites.

Andrew Jackson (1767–1845). Military general who was a major light in the Revolutionary War. His defeat of the British in New Orleans in 1815 led to huge popular support, and he was elected seventh US president (Democrat) in 1829. The first president from west of the Appalachians, Jackson had much grass-roots support in Tennessee, and his election is seen as the first truly democratic choice in the nation's history.

Rev Jesse Jackson (born 1941). Black religious and political leader whose Rainbow Coalition seemed briefly during the late 1980s to represent the most viable progressive alternative to the centrist Democratic Party.

Thomas Jefferson (1743–1838). Author of the Declaration of Independence, third US president and slave-owner, Jefferson was a strong advocate of freedom of the press and of religion, as well as being an accomplished architect.

Lyndon Baines Johnson (1908–1973). Brash Texan Democrat sworn in as president two hours after John Kennedy's assassination in 1963. Johnson pushed through liberal civil rights and social welfare bills, but his failure to deal with the increasingly horrific mess of Vietnam left him obliged not to seek re-election in 1968.

Robert Johnson (1911?–1938). Seminal Delta bluesman, whose songs were imbued with such a brooding aura that he was rumored to have sold his soul to the Devil. The clearest, earliest forerunner of rock'n'roll.

Kamehameha the Great (1760?–1819). The first man to unite the Hawaiian islands – by terror, force of personality and shrewd exploitation of European expertise.

Helen Keller (1880–1968). Despite being struck blind and deaf by scarlet fever as an infant, Keller's writings and activism made her an inspirational early leader in the movement for equal rights for disabled people.

John Fitzgerald Kennedy (1917–1963). When elected in 1960, Kennedy was the youngest ever, and the first Catholic, president. His liberal domestic policies (known as "new frontier" programs) and success in securing the nuclear test ban treaty with the USSR and Britain won him huge popularity, as did his superficially glamorous life with wife Jackie. His assassination in Dallas, on November 22, 1963, might be said to mark the beginning of a long period of disillusionment and hopelessness in the American psyche.

Dr Martin Luther King Jr (1929–1968). Baptist minister who was the main black spokesperson during the Civil Rights years, and was awarded the Nobel Peace Prize after his "I have a dream" speech. Remembered by a public holiday in most states, and a street name in most major cities.

General Marie Joseph Paul Yves Roch Gilbert du Motier Lafayette (1757–1834). French aristocrat, known as "the hero of two worlds" for supporting the Americans in the Revolutionary War, who went on to fight with the revolutionary bourgeoisie in France. A great friend of George Washington, Lafayette advocated religious tolerance and the abolition of slavery.

Robert Edward Lee (1807–1870). Confederate Civil War general, considered one of the outstanding military strategists of all time. Enjoyed early success by whipping the vastly superior Union forces under the incompetent McClellan, but crashed to defeat at Gettysburg.

Meriwether Lewis (1774–1809) and **William Clark** (1770–1838). Jointly famed as leaders of the first exploratory expedition west from the Mississippi to the Pacific in 1804–1805. Lewis's journals and

Clark's drawings are invaluable documents of the pre-conquest western US.

Rush Limbaugh (born 1951). Ultraconservative loudmouth turned political powerbroker, with daily talk-radio and TV shows.

Abraham Lincoln (1809–1865). To northerners at least, the most revered of all US presidents. The son of a Kentucky backwoodsman, he taught himself law and later entered Illinois politics, beating better-known opponents for the 1860 Republican presidential nomination. He led the Union through the Civil War, but was shot five days after the Confederate surrender.

Charles Lindbergh (1902–1974). In 1927, Lindbergh became the first person to complete a solo flight across the Atlantic, in the *Spirit of St Louis*, named for his home town. Ticker-tape parades feted him across the continent, and the "Lindy Hop" dance was named for him. The kidnapping and murder of his infant son was one of the most notorious crimes of the 1930s, but his pronounced Nazi sympathies lost him public support.

Huey Long (1893–1935). Flamboyant, populist governor of Louisiana known as the "Kingfish." His radical social welfare policies and tax reforms boosted the morale of poor rural whites during the Depression, and as senator, in the last three years of his life, he claimed his "Share the Wealth" program would make "every man a king." However, his corrupt and intimidating style of government made him plenty of enemies, and he was eventually assassinated in still-mysterious circumstances in Baton Rouge.

Joe Louis (1914–1981). Black Detroit heavyweight boxer who took the world championship from Mussolini-sidekick Primo Carnera in 1937 and retained it for twelve years.

Malcolm X (1925–1965). Not so successful burglar who in prison came into contact with the teachings of Elijah Muhammad's Nation of Islam, rose to become its leading minister and spokesperson, and then broke with the organization after a trip to Mecca and tour of Africa. Malcolm occasionally worked with Dr Martin Luther King Jr during his civil rights campaigns, and for many people his militant approach remains more persuasive than Dr King's.

Joseph McCarthy (1909–1957). Republican Senator for Wisconsin, notorious for his hysterical and unproven charges of Communist subversion in high government circles. President Truman called him a "pathological character assassin" and his career was ended when the Senate censured him for unconstitutional behavior.

J. Pierpoint Morgan (1837–1913). The quintessential New York financier, Morgan achieved sufficient wealth to buy out Andrew Carnegie and served as a broker between world governments.

Muhammad Ali (born 1941). Heavyweight boxer who upon winning the world title from Sonny Liston in 1964 announced that he was a member of the Nation of Islam. Within three years his antiwar stance – "no Vietcong ever called me nigger" – had cast him into the wilderness, but eventually America took him to its bosom once more.

Carry Nation (1846–1911). Temperance activist and suffragette whose tendency to take an axe to saloons after storming in, singing hymns and bellowing biblical insults, won her no popularity with the official temperance movement (although she made lots of money on lecture tours). Frequently imprisoned, she paid her fines from souvenir axe sales.

Richard Nixon (1913–1995). From his earliest days as Eisenhower's vice-president – a position obtained with the help of his maudlin "Checkers" speech, about his little puppy – Nixon was the man American liberals most loved to hate. That he emerged from the turmoil of 1968 as America's president made a mockery of the idea that the 1960s would turn out to be a progressive decade. The seemingly relentless progress of his rehabilitation following the disgrace of Watergate has much to do with the media's enduring and perverse fondness for him.

Annie Oakley (1860–1926). Performer with Buffalo Bill's Wild West show. Nicknamed "Little Miss Sure Shot," she once shot the cigar from the mouth of Kaiser Wilhelm.

Georgia O'Keeffe (1887–1986). Prolific painter whose stark, brightly colored abstractions of flowers and the Southwest desert won her acclaim as one of the greatest modern US artists.

Dolly Parton (born 1946). Country singer, movie star, perennial talk-show guest and part-owner of a theme park.

William Penn (1644–1718). British Quaker, often imprisoned in England for his beliefs. He gradually softened towards other doctrines, and campaigned strongly against any form of persecution, eventually establishing the colony of Pennsylvania as a refuge for religious minorities.

Pocahontas (1597?–1617). Daughter of a Native American chief, Pocahontas was instrumental in the successful establishment of the English colony at Jamestown, Virginia. After sparing the life of the captive Captain John Smith, in 1614 Pocahontas married colonist John Rolfe, who brought her (and tobacco) to England, where she died.

John Wesley Powell (1834–1902). After losing an arm in the Civil War, Powell headed west to lead the first group of white men through the rivers and canyons of the Colorado Plateau.

Elvis Presley (1935–1977). Poor white boy from Tupelo, Mississippi, who moved to Memphis and became the first and the greatest white rock'n'roll star. Whether you blame Colonel Tom Parker or Elvis himself, within a couple of years he was throwing away his magnificent voice on empty show-tunes, and embarking on the long road to Hamburger Heaven.

Paul Revere (1735–1818). Silversmith and unofficial political leader of the mechanic class in Boston in the period leading up to the Revolutionary War. As principal rider for Boston's Committee of Safety, in April 1775 he made the famed horseback journey from Boston to Concord to warn the rebels that the British were coming; thus started the War of Independence.

John D. Rockefeller (1839–1937). Petroleum magnate whose Standard Oil company dominated the US and international markets from the 1880s to 1911, when the government dissolved his monopoly. Also a great philanthropist, in his later years he gave away his money – over half a billion dollars.

Franklin Delano Roosevelt (1882–1945). Four-term Democratic president, crippled by polio in 1920, who steered the country through the Depression with the closest the US has ever come to having socialist policies: his "New Deal" provided work for the unemployed and enforced collective bargaining with unions. His wartime leadership was often criticized, especially, with hindsight, his appeasement of Stalin.

Theodore (Teddy) Roosevelt (1858–1919). Explorer, writer, soldier and Republican president from 1901 to 1909. His "square deal" policies, which included "trust busting" and government arbitration in wage disputes, were seen to serve the public interest over Big Business, and he won the Nobel Peace Prize in 1906 for mediating an end to the Russo–Japanese War. In 1912 he founded the Progressive Party and ran (unsuccessfully) for president as an independent, advocating a strong social service state.

Sacagawea (1788?–1812). A legendary figure in American history, Sacagawea was a young Shoshone woman who accompanied the Lewis and Clark expedition across the continent in 1805. Only seventeen years old, and carrying her newborn baby boy, "Pomp," she and her French fur-trapper husband Charbonneau were indispensable members of the "Corps of Discovery," and their presence helped convince the natives of the explorers' peaceful intentions.

Dred Scott (1795?–1858). Black slave who made constitutional history as the plaintiff in a widely publicized but unsuccessful test case, in which he sought his freedom on the grounds that his master had taken him to live in a free state. The ruling effectively allowed slavery in US territories and was a leading factor in the build-up to the Civil War.

William Tecumseh Sherman (1820–1891). The Union general who burned Atlanta and laid waste to Georgia, and boasted about it in his memoirs. The bane of his later life was to be greeted at all official functions with *Marching through Georgia*, a song he detested. His son, a Jesuit priest, had to be forcibly dissuaded from attempting his own march thirty years later.

Frank Sinatra (1915–1998). Italian boy from Hoboken, New Jersey, who made his name thrilling bobby-soxers with New York's Tommy Dorsey Band in the early 1940s and went on to become the most beloved voice of the twentieth century. One of the few singers to turn into a decent movie actor.

Sitting Bull Tatanka Iyotake (1834–1890). Chief of the Dakota Sioux and leader of the Native American forces at the Battle of Little Bighorn. Pursued by the army, he escaped to Canada but surrendered in 1881. He was killed by police in the attempt to suppress the 1890 Ghost Dance movement.

Bruce Springsteen (born 1949). New Jersey singer-songwriter known as "the Boss." His energetic and poignant articulations of white, male, working-class America are often dismissed as machismo; President Reagan missed the point completely in the 1980s and announced his approval of Springsteen's *Born in the USA*, mistaking its ironic blue-collar disillusionment for reactionary blue-eyed patriotism.

Harriet Beecher Stowe (1811–1896). Though she had little firsthand experience of the South, Stowe's *Uncle Tom's Cabin* aroused the world in fierce opposition to slavery. Abraham Lincoln greeted her with the words "so this is the little lady that made this big war."

Peter (Petrus) Stuyvesant (1592–1672). Early governor of all Dutch colonies in North America, known as "Peg-leg Pete" for his wooden leg. He arrived in New Amsterdam (now New York) in 1647, doubling the colony's size and population, but was so unpopular, ignoring all appeals for self-government, that in 1664 he was forced to surrender the colony to the British. His farm, the Bowerie, gave the district in New York City its name.

Harriet Tubman (1820–1913). Escaped from slavery in Maryland in 1849 to become the leading abolitionist voice in the pre-Civil War years. Led hundreds of slaves to freedom on the Underground Railroad and served as a nurse and spy for Union forces during the war.

Nat Turner (1800–1831). Black preacher who led five Virginia slaves on a murderous rampage, killing over fifty whites, mostly with knives and axes, in a single day. In reaction, whites murdered hundreds of blacks and enacted an even more repressive regime.

Mark Twain (1835–1910). The great humorist and novelist, whose works provide the most vivid imaginable account of pioneer days across the continent, was also a powerful polemicist for liberal causes, and pioneered white-suit chic long before writer Tom Wolfe. He pursued his desire to typeset his own books, and break free from the evil machinations of self-important publishers, almost to the point of bankruptcy.

George Wallace (1919–1998). Segregationist three-times Alabama governor; received 13 percent of the popular vote in the 1968 presidential election and looked set to increase his tally in the 1972 race before he was shot and paralyzed. Towards the end of his political career he eschewed his previous racist policies and was re-elected governor in 1982.

Booker Taliaferro Washington (1856–1915). Controversial self-taught black educationalist who founded Tuskegee University. His 1901 book *Up from Slavery* proposed that blacks should abandon campaigns for voting rights and instead learn skills to work for economic gains.

John Wayne (1907–1979). Alias "the Duke": movie macho man, legendary boozer, Reagan role model and right-wing crank.

Walt Whitman (1819–1892). Writer and poet whose *Leaves of Grass*, first published in 1848, is among the most original and passionate works of American literature.

Hank Williams (1923–1953). Country music legend whose compositions (*I Saw the Light, Jambalaya*, and others) are still Nashville standards. A drink- and drug-sodden lifestyle accounted for his premature death.

Frank Lloyd Wright (1867–1959). Prolific architect who came to prominence around 1900 with a series of prototypical suburban houses and went on to design such landmarks as New York's Guggenheim Museum.

Wilbur (1867–1912) and **Orville** (1871–1948) **Wright**. Bicycle shop proprietors from Dayton, Ohio, who went on to greater things at Kitty Hawk, North Carolina, when they made the world's first powered flight on December 17, 1903 – it lasted twelve seconds.

Brigham Young (1801–1877). The son of near-illiterate Vermont farmers, Young led the Mormons to Utah following the assassination of Joseph Smith in 1844, establishing a permanent home for his people.

Film

Since the 1910s, America's film industry has been centered in Hollywood and employed an assembly-line method of film production, which has resulted in countless cookie-cutter duds, but also a substantial number of classics. The list below focuses on key films in certain genres that have helped define the American experience for domestic and foreign audiences alike, cementing cultural stereotypes such as the gangster, cowboy and blonde chorus girl, as well as national iconography such as open prairies, open highways, big-city skyscrapers and suburban dream homes. Unlike these industrially produced fantasies, America's independent cinema has often presented dissenting themes, experimental techniques, and a more freewheeling approach to movie-making – sometimes with quiet financial backing from the big studios.

Films tagged with the ⊡ symbol are particularly recommended.

Music/Musicals

Gimme Shelter (Albert and David Maysles, 1969). Excellent documentary about the ill-fated Rolling Stones concert at Altamont. Its searing look at homegrown American violence and Vietnam-era chaos at the end of the 1960s also includes an on-camera stabbing.

Gold Diggers of 1933 (Mervyn LeRoy/Busby Berkeley, 1933). The most entertaining in a famous trio of 1933 films (including *42nd Street* and *Footlight Parade*), in which choreographer Berkeley pioneered the stunning overhead-crane shots of precision dance numbers featuring lines of glamorous chorines.

Meet Me in St Louis (Vincente Minnelli, 1944). Most famous for its Judy Garland number "The Trolley Song," this charming piece of nostalgia celebrates turn-of-the-century America through the ups and downs of a St Louis family during the 1903 World's Fair.

On the Town (Stanley Donen/ Gene Kelly, 1949). An exuberant musical tour of New York City, led by director Kelly and Frank Sinatra, who play sailors on shore leave.

⊡ **Singin' in the Rain** (Stanley Donen/Gene Kelly, 1952). Beloved musical comedy about Hollywood at the dawn of the sound era, featuring memorable tunes like "Make 'Em Laugh" and the title song, along with energetic performances by star Kelly, sidekick Donald O'Connor and a pixie-ish Debbie Reynolds.

Woodstock (Michael Wadleigh, 1969). *Gimme Shelter's* upbeat counterpart, documenting the musical pinnacle of the hippie era, showing a half-million flower children peacefully grooving to Jimi Hendrix, The Who, and Sly and the Family Stone while getting stoned, muddy and wild on an upstate New York farm.

Silent era

Birth of a Nation (D.W. Griffith, 1915). Possibly the most influential film in American history, both for its pioneering film technique (close-ups, cross-cutting and so on) and appalling racist propaganda, which led to a twentieth-century revival of the KKK and a resurgence in lynchings across the country.

★ **The General** (Buster Keaton, 1926). A fine introduction to Keaton's acrobatic brand of slapstick and his inventive cinematic approach, in which the Great Stone Face chases down a stolen locomotive during the Civil War.

The Gold Rush (Charlie Chaplin, 1925). Chaplin's finest film: the Little Tramp gets trapped in a cabin during an Alaska blizzard in an affecting story that mixes sentiment and high comedy in near-perfect balance.

Greed (Erich von Stroheim, 1923). An audacious scene-by-scene adaptation of Frank Norris's novel *McTeague*, a tragic tale of love and revenge in San Francisco at the end of the nineteenth century. Slashed from ten to two-and-a-half hours by MGM, the film remains a cinematic triumph for its striking compositions, epic drama and truly bleak ending.

Intolerance (D.W. Griffith, 1916). The greatest debacle of the silent era, a colossal bomb that helped destroy Griffith's career, but still fascinates for its multiple storylines, arch melodrama and stunning Babylonian set (a replica was built as part of a shopping mall in Hollywood; see p.1069).

Sunrise (F.W. Murnau, 1927). Among the most beautiful Hollywood productions of any era, the film's German émigré director employed striking lighting effects, complex traveling shots, and emotionally compelling performances in a tale of a country boy led astray by a big-city femme fatale.

Westerns

Man of the West (Anthony Mann, 1958). Reformed outlaw Gary Cooper returns to his former gang, led by psycho Lee J. Cobb, in this disturbing masterpiece by one of the genre's great directors.

McCabe and Mrs. Miller (Robert Altman, 1971). Often referred to as an anti-western because of its stark, snowy landscapes, soft-focus images and unromantic outlook, a story of entrepreneur Warren Beatty bringing prostitution to a Washington State town and trying to reinvent himself as a gunslinger.

Once upon a Time in the West (Sergio Leone, 1968). The quintessential spaghetti Western, actually filmed in Spain by an Italian director, steeped in mythic American themes of manifest destiny and rugged individualism.

Red River (Howard Hawks, 1948). Upstart Montgomery Clift battles beef-baron John Wayne on a momentous cattle drive through the Midwest. Prototypical Hawks tale of clashing tough-guy egos and no-nonsense professionals on the range.

★ **The Searchers** (John Ford, 1956). John Wayne relentlessly hunts down the Indian chief who massacred his friends and family in this highly influential production with vivid cinematography and epic scale, only one of the director's many iconic Westerns.

The Wild Bunch (Sam Peckinpah, 1969). A movie that says as much about the chaotic end of the 1960s as it does about the West, featuring a band of killers who hunt for women and treasure and wind up in a bloodbath unprecedented in film history.

Americana

⭐ **Citizen Kane** (Orson Welles, 1941). A masterpiece and arguably the greatest American movie ever, inverting the rags-to-riches saga: a poor country boy finds nothing but misery when he inherits a fortune.

ET (Steven Spielberg, 1982). Reagan-era blockbuster as well as a sentimental variation on 1950s monster flicks, courtesy of the director's ongoing interest in absentee fathers, suburban fantasies and otherworldly saviors. A fine example of American cinema's never-ending search for lost innocence.

Mr. Smith Goes to Washington (Frank Capra, 1939). Tub-thumping populist film that still resonates for its rosy belief in the goodness of the common man, dark view of political elites and earnest hope for America's future. Though less familiar, the director's *Meet John Doe* offers a grimmer variation on the tale.

Nashville (Robert Altman, 1975). A long, woolly epic, typical of Altman's style, about 24 characters adrift in the nation's capital of country music,

who come together at a concluding political rally and witness an unexpected assassination.

North by Northwest (Alfred Hitchcock, 1959). Not only an exciting chase film with international criminal James Mason hunting down ad-man Cary Grant, but also a fun travelogue that starts on New York's prestigious Madison Avenue and ends on the cliff-face of Mount Rushmore in South Dakota.

Rebel Without a Cause (Nicholas Ray, 1955). The apotheosis of adolescent angst, with James Dean lamenting the hypocrisies of family life and engaging in all manner of fisticuffs, deadly drag races and nighttime battles with the cops.

The Wizard of Oz (Victor Fleming, 1939). A cinematic institution and Technicolor extravaganza that shows Hollywood at its zenith, romanticizing small-town life in the Midwest and offering up eye-popping fantasies of good and evil witches, dancing dwarves, flying monkeys and Judy Garland sporting ruby shoes on a yellow-brick road.

Road Movies

Badlands (Terrence Malick, 1973). Midwest loner-loser Martin Sheen and girlfriend Sissy Spacek take a spellbinding tour of the heartland while on a random murder spree. A dark view of life on the road as a synonym for existential futility.

⭐ **Easy Rider** (Dennis Hopper, 1969). Peter Fonda and director Hopper head out in search of America while riding on a groovy set of wheels, pick up nerdy Jack Nicholson on the way, get high in a New Orleans cemetery and get

killed by gun-toting rednecks. A road movie as a metaphor for political and cultural conflict.

Lost in America (Albert Brooks, 1985). Hilarious take on the unbearable lightness of yuppiedom, in which a couple trades everything in for a motor home, the open road and a date with destiny in Las Vegas.

Thelma and Louise (Ridley Scott, 1991). The road movie as feminist manifesto, in which two friends (Susan Sarandon and Geena Davis) wind up on the run after one of them kills a would-be rapist. Plenty of striking images of the American Southwest from a stylish British director.

Two-Lane Blacktop (Monte Hellman, 1971). A slow, hypnotic narrative – closer to art than most Hollywood films – starring musicians James Taylor and Dennis Wilson as two burnouts who live to drag race, but couldn't care less for the nubile girl in their car or goofball racer Warren Oates.

Film noir and gangster films

Bonnie and Clyde (Arthur Penn, 1967). Warren Beatty and Faye Dunaway play Depression-era gangsters in a film that did much to destroy Hollywood's censorship code by ushering in an era of open sexuality and unmitigated blood and violence.

Visiting locations featured in American films

Although many memorable sights are off-limits to the public or exist only on the backlot tours of movie-studio theme parks, there are still countless **filmmaking locations** that widely advertise their Tinseltown appearances or make quiet efforts to accommodate visitors. This list provides an overview of notable films; you could conceivably make an entire vacation out of traveling from spot to spot.

2001: A Space Odyssey (Stanley Kubrick, 1968). Monument Valley, Arizona (p.993).

Back to the Future (Robert Zemeckis, 1985). Gamble House, Pasadena (p.1082).

Badlands (Terrence Malick, 1973). Badlands National Park, South Dakota (p.823).

Being There (Hal Ashby, 1979). Biltmore Estate, Asheville, North Carolina (p.514).

The Birds (Alfred Hitchcock, 1963). Bodega Bay, California (p.1169).

Blade Runner (Ridley Scott, 1982). Los Angeles: Union Station (p.1065), Bradbury Building (p.1066).

The Bridges of Madison County (Clint Eastwood, 1995). Winterset, Iowa (p.812).

Chinatown (Roman Polanski, 1974). Los Angeles: Santa Catalina island (p.1079), Biltmore Hotel (p.1062).

Citizen Kane (Orson Welles, 1941). Hearst Castle, California (p.1106) – inspiration for film's "Xanadu."

Close Encounters of the Third Kind (Steven Spielberg, 1978). Devils Tower, Wyoming (p.886).

Easy Rider (Dennis Hopper, 1969). New Orleans cemeteries (pp.688–689); Sunset Crater, Arizona (p.979).

Five Easy Pieces (Bob Rafelson, 1970). San Juan Islands, Washington (p.1195).

Grapes of Wrath (John Ford, 1940). Petrified Forest, Arizona (p.977).

Greed (Erich von Stroheim, 1923). Death Valley, California (p.1098).

High Plains Drifter (Clint Eastwood, 1972). Mono Lake, California (p.1102).

Intolerance (D.W. Griffith, 1916). "Babylon" set, Hollywood, California (p.1069).

Jaws (Steven Spielberg, 1975). Martha's Vineyard, Massachusetts (p.226).

Little Big Man (Arthur Penn, 1970). Custer State Park, South Dakota (p.831).

Manhattan (Woody Allen, 1978). Central Park (p.97), Brooklyn Bridge (p.80).

Midnight in the Garden of Good and Evil (Clint Eastwood, 1998). Savannah, Georgia (p.541).

Mr. Smith Goes to Washington (Frank Capra, 1939). Lincoln Memorial (p.413).

Chinatown (Roman Polanski, 1974). Jack Nicholson plays Jake Gittes, a morally aloof private eye whose dogged investigations reveal municipal corruption, racism and incest in the City of Angels. A darker twist on the older film noir style, in which the hero causes as many problems as he solves.

★ **Double Indemnity** (Billy Wilder, 1944). In many ways the quintessential noir film, in which suave insurance executive Fred MacMurray is corrupted by femme fatale Barbara Stanwyck, with stylishly dark photography and memorably fatalistic ending.

★ **The Godfather** (Francis Ford Coppola, 1972). The film that revived the gangster genre for modern times, avoiding the cartoonish mobsters and no-nonsense G-men of its predecessors and focusing instead on the family hierarchy of organized crime and its deep connections to all levels of American society.

Mystery Train (Jim Jarmusch, 1989). Memphis, Tennessee (p.560).

Nashville (Robert Altman, 1975). Parthenon (p.572), Grand Ole Opry (p.534).

North by Northwest (Alfred Hitchcock, 1959). United Nations, New York City (p.92); Mount Rushmore, South Dakota (p.829).

On the Town (Stanley Donen/Gene Kelly, 1949). American Museum of Natural History, New York City (p.103).

Paper Moon (Peter Bogdanovich, 1973). St Joseph, Missouri (p.798).

The Parallax View (Alan J. Pakula, 1974). Space Needle, Seattle (p.1186).

Planet of the Apes (Franklin J. Schaffner, 1968). Arizona: Page (p.962), Lake Powell, UT (p.1019).

Poseidon Adventure (Ronald Neame, 1972). Queen Mary, Long Beach (p.1079).

Rebel Without a Cause (Nicholas Ray, 1955). Griffith Observatory, Los Angeles (p.1072).

Return of the Jedi (Richard Marquand, 1983). Redwood National Park, California (p.1171).

Rocky (John G. Avildsen, 1976). Philadelphia Museum of Art (p.162).

The Searchers (John Ford, 1956). Monument Valley, Arizona (p.993).

Shane (George Stevens, 1953). Wyoming: Grand Teton National Park (p.897), Jackson Hole (p.900).

The Shining (Stanley Kubrick, 1980). Timberline Lodge, Oregon (p.1222).

Singin' in the Rain (Stanley Donen/Gene Kelly, 1952). Chinese Theatre, Hollywood (p.1071).

Some Like It Hot (Billy Wilder, 1959). Coronado Hotel, San Diego (p.1049).

The Sting (George Roy Hill, 1973). Santa Monica Pier, California (p.1078).

A Streetcar Named Desire (Elia Kazan, 1951). New Orleans, Louisiana (p.690).

Sunset Boulevard (Billy Wilder, 1950). Hollywood: Paramount Studios (p.1083), Sunset Boulevard (p.1074).

Thelma and Louise (Ridley Scott, 1991). Arches National Park, Utah (p.1013).

The Thing (Christian Nyby/Howard Hawks, 1951). Glacier National Park, Montana (p.913).

Touch of Evil (Orson Welles, 1958). Venice, California (p.1076).

Twin Peaks (David Lynch/ABC-TV, 1990–1991). Snoqualmie Falls/Salish Lodge, Washington (p.1206).

Vertigo (Alfred Hitchcock, 1958). San Francisco: Golden Gate Bridge (p.1141), Fairmont Hotel, Nob Hill (p.1136).

Witness (Peter Weir, 1985). Lancaster County, Pennsylvania (p.166).

Zabriskie Point (Michelangelo Antonioni, 1969). Death Valley, California (p.1098).

Kiss Me Deadly (Robert Aldrich, 1955). Outlandish portrait of vicious antihero Mike Hammer, a private eye searching LA for the great "whatsit," tormenting elfin vixens and half-witted thugs along the way, and winding up in a beachside nuclear fireball.

Maltese Falcon (John Huston, 1941). A forerunner of a spate of film noir pictures made later in the 1940s, in which Bogart plays his trademark role of Philip Marlowe, the cool and calculating detective who runs up against sexy schemer Mary Astor, low-life Peter Lorre, and evil flesh-pile Sydney Greenstreet.

Scarlet Street (Fritz Lang, 1945). A lesser-known noir that ranks among the genre's finest, in which Edward G. Robinson plays a frustrated painter sucked into a moral abyss with a crass hooker (Joan Bennett) and her violent pimp (Dan Duryea); the ending is merciless.

White Heat (Raoul Walsh, 1949). Gangster/noir hybrid featuring James Cagney as a mother-fixated criminal who's repeatedly conned by ostensible good-guy Edmond O'Brien and ends up atop a burning industrial plant, screaming unforgettably, "Look at me, Ma! Top o' the world!"

Independent and cult movies

Blue Velvet (David Lynch, 1986). A young man (Kyle Maclachlan) peers under the cheery facade of apple-pie America and finds a sinister netherworld of tortured lounge singers, vicious sex games and nitrogen-inhaling perverts.

Fargo (Joel Coen, 1996). Set amid the snowy landscapes of northern Minnesota and North Dakota, a quirky tale of a scheming car salesman whose plan to kidnap his own wife and keep the ransom money goes terribly wrong. Widely regarded as the Coen Brothers' best film (Ethan Coen co-wrote and produced).

Ghost World (Terry Zwigoff, 2001). Sardonic portrait of alienated high-schooler Thora Birch trying to find her place in a grim world of strip malls, dead-end jobs and adult hypocrisy. Based on an equally effective and groundbreaking comic strip of the same name.

Pulp Fiction (Quentin Tarantino, 1994). A touchstone for American independent cinema, composed of three vignettes involving drug-addicted hit men, conniving boxers and redneck rapists, and directed with stylish verve and audacity.

Shadows (John Cassavetes, 1967). An early example of a principled auteur working outside the Hollywood system. The semi-improvised film, featuring a fine cast of lesser-known actors, tells a powerful tale of racism's scabrous effect on a sibling relationship.

Slacker (Richard Linklater, 1990). Emblematic of the Generation X ennui to come in the 1990s, this indie great also manages to highlight 96 characters with episodic monologues over the course of 24 hours in Austin, Texas. Memorable alone for its collection of paranoid conspiracy rants.

★ **Taxi Driver** (Martin Scorsese, 1976). Robert De Niro does a memorable turn as Travis Bickle, a psychotic loner and would-be assassin whose infatuation with a teen prostitute (Jodie Foster) inspired the real-life attempted assassination of Ronald Reagan five years later.

index

and small print

Index

Map entries are in color

INDEX

INDEX

1369

I

Twenty Years of Rough Guides

In the summer of 1981, Mark Ellingham, Rough Guides' founder, knocked out the first guide on a typewriter, with a group of friends. Mark had been traveling in Greece after university, and couldn't find a guidebook that really answered his needs. There were heavyweight cultural guides on the one hand – good on museums and classical sites but not on beaches and tavernas – and on the other hand student manuals that were so caught up with how to save money that they lost sight of the country's significance beyond its role as a place for a cool vacation. None of the guides began to address Greece as a country, with its natural and human environment, its politics and its contemporary life.

Having no urgent reason to return home, Mark decided to write his own guide. It was a guide to Greece that tried to combine some erudition and insight with a thoroughly practical approach to travelers' needs. Scrupulously researched listings of places to stay, eat, and drink were matched by careful attention to detail on everything from Homer to Greek music, from classical sites to national parks, and from nude beaches to monasteries. Back in London, Mark and his friends got their Rough Guide accepted by a farsighted commissioning editor at the publisher Routledge and it came out in 1982.

The Rough Guide to Greece was a student scheme that became a publishing phenomenon. The immediate success of the book – shortlisted for the Thomas Cook award – spawned a series that rapidly covered dozens of countries. The Rough Guides found a ready market among backpackers and budget travelers, but soon acquired a much broader readership that included older and less impecunious visitors. Readers relished the guides' wit and inquisitiveness as much as the enthusiastic, critical approach that acknowledges everyone wants value for money – but not at any price.

Rough Guides soon began supplementing the "rougher" information – the hostel and low-budget listings – with the kind of detail that independent-minded travelers on any budget might expect. These days, the guides – distributed worldwide by the Penguin group – include recommendations spanning the range from shoestring to luxury, and cover more than 100 destinations around the globe. Our growing team of authors, many of whom come to Rough Guides initially as outstandingly good letter-writers telling us about their travels, are spread all over the world, particularly in Europe, the USA, and Australia. As well as the travel guides, Rough Guides publishes a series of dictionary phrasebooks covering two dozen major languages, an acclaimed series of music guides running the gamut from Classical to World Music, a series of music CDs in association with World Music Network, and a range of reference books on topics as diverse as the Internet, Pregnancy, and Unexplained Phenomena. Visit **www.roughguides.com** to see what's cooking.

Rough Guide Credits

Text editor: Yuki Takagaki
Series editor: Mark Ellingham
Editorial: Martin Dunford, Jonathan Buckley, Jo Mead, Kate Berens, Ann-Marie Shaw, Helena Smith, Judith Bamber, Orla Duane, Olivia Eccleshall, Ruth Blackmore, Geoff Howard, Claire Saunders, Gavin Thomas, Alexander Mark Rogers, Polly Thomas, Joe Staines, Richard Lim, Duncan Clark, Peter Buckley, Lucy Ratcliffe, Clifton Wilkinson, Alison Murchie, Matthew Teller, Andrew Dickson, Fran Sandham (UK); Andrew Rosenberg, Stephen Timblin, Yuki Takagaki, Richard Koss, Hunter Slaton, Julie Feiner (US)
Production: Susanne Hillen, Andy Hilliard, Link Hall, Helen Prior, Julia Bovis, Michelle Draycott, Katie Pringle, Mike Hancock, Zoë Nobes, Rachel Holmes, Andy Turner
Cartography: Melissa Baker, Maxine Repath, Ed Wright, Katie Lloyd-Jones
Picture research: Louise Boulton, Sharon Martins, Mark Thomas
Online: Kelly Cross, Anja Mutic-Blessing, Jennifer Gold, Audra Epstein, Suzanne Welles, Cree Lawson (US)
Finance: John Fisher, Gary Singh, Edward Downey, Mark Hall, Tim Bill
Marketing & Publicity: Richard Trillo, Niki Smith, David Wearn, Chloë Roberts, Demelza Dallow, Claire Southern (UK); Simon Carloss, David Wechsler, Kathleen Rushforth (US)
Administration: Tania Hummel, Julie Sanderson

Publishing Information

This sixth edition published May 2002 by **Rough Guides Ltd**,
62–70 Shorts Gardens, London WC2H 9AH.
Penguin Putnam, Inc., 375 Hudson Street, NY 10014, USA.
Distributed by the Penguin Group
Penguin Books Ltd,
80 Strand, London WC2R ORL
Penguin Putnam, Inc.
375 Hudson Street, NY 10014, USA
Penguin Books Australia Ltd,
487 Maroondah Highway, PO Box 157, Ringwood, Victoria 3134, Australia
Penguin Books Canada Ltd,
10 Alcorn Avenue, Toronto, Ontario, Canada M4V 1E4
Penguin Books (NZ) Ltd,
182–190 Wairau Road, Auckland 10, New Zealand
Typeset in Bembo and Helvetica to an original design by Henry Iles.

Printed in Italy by LegoPrint S.p.A

1416pp includes index
A catalogue record for this book is available from the British Library

ISBN 1-85828-878-9

The publishers and authors have done their best to ensure the accuracy and currency of all the information in **The Rough Guide to the USA**, however, they can accept no responsibility for any loss, injury, or inconvenience sustained by any traveler as a result of information or advice contained in the guide.

Help us update

We've gone to a lot of effort to ensure that the sixth edition of **The Rough Guide to the USA** is accurate and up-to-date. However, things change – places get "discovered," opening hours are notoriously fickle, restaurants and rooms raise prices or lower standards. If you feel we've got it wrong or left something out, we'd like to know, and if you can remember the address, the price, the time, the phone number, so much the better.

We'll credit all contributions, and send a copy of the next edition (or any other Rough Guide if you prefer) for the best letters. Everyone who writes to us and isn't already a subscriber will receive a copy of our full-color thrice-yearly newsletter. Please mark letters: "**Rough Guide USA Update**" and send to: Rough Guides, 62–70 Shorts Gardens, London WC2H 9AH, or Rough Guides, 4th Floor, 345 Hudson St, New York, NY 10014. Or send an email to:
mail@roughguides.co.uk or
mail@roughguides.com

Acknowledgments

Sam: Thanks to Yuki and Andrew at Rough Guides, Christine de Cuir at the New Orleans CVB, to all the researchers who worked so hard for this edition, and to Pam Cook, Jim Cook, and Greg Ward.

Greg: Thanks to Sam for the big adventure; to my father, mother, and family; and to Yuki Takagaki for holding the whole vast project together. A big thank you to Edie Jarolim, for all her invaluable help with southern Arizona, and also to Candy Aluli, Barbara Campbell, Marian Delay, Lynn Holt, Ron and Donna Katz, Steve Lewis, Lorraine Moore, Deanna Mukai, Pamela Westwood Kelly, and Sandi Yara.

Special thanks to Rachel Holmes, Julia Bovis, and Michelle Draycott for seamless production, Maxine Repath and The Map Studio, Romsey, Hants for precise maps, Melissa Krupanski for extensive photo research, Diane Margolis for diligent proofreading, Julie Feiner, Hunter Slaton and Donald Young for their editorial expertise and Andrew Rosenberg for overseeing it all with aplomb.

The authors and contributors would like to thank the visitor centers, state tourism offices, and others who were so generous with their help, specifically Charles Duncan, Donald Hall, Janene Charbeneu, HI-Angie's Guest Cottage Hostel, Donna Schorr, Sean Peter Genell, Martin Chester, Danie Donovan, Joan and Tom McHugh, Karen Ballard, Nancy Richardson, Pam Gosink, Todd Thesing, Rachel Roach, Derreck, Leslie Thompson, Rick Shaffer, Nancy Phillips, Sandy Pantlik, Faye Bleigh, Brandon Billings, Maxine Odell, Carol Jones, Sallie Vollmer, Stacy Linn, Donna Andrews, Sheri Boffa, Cathy Murphy, Lori Aberle, David Bernard-Stevens; the staffs of the Black Hills People's News, Theodore Roosevelt Medora Foundation, Mark Twain Cave, Museum of the Fur Trade, Buzzard Billy's and Ronneburg Restaurant and Bar; and the Lakota people of Pine Ridge Reservation, notably Charmaine White Face and the caretakers of the memorial at Wounded Knee.

SMALL PRINT

Readers' letters

A big thank you to the many readers who took the time to make suggestions for this guide: Ayad Andrews, Nicki Barry, Michele Borrelli, Zoe Brough, Jean Cartwright, Lucienne Cole, S. Connelly and L. Howarth, Maggie Coombs, Jan Cotterall, Ian Cripps, Andy Cunningham, Beatrix Davies, Eunhee Denton, Sharon Edmead, Jenniffer H. Edwards, Sarah Ellison, Mike Feintuck, Steve Fleming and Claire Thompson, Anthony Francis-Jones, Susan Grant, S. Grigg, Jonathan Harmer, Laura Hatfield, Jane Haycock, Annalisa Henderson, Edward Henry, William Houston, Margaret Knight, Alex Lattimore, Sandy LeMole, Rob Main, John McDonnell, G. Monkman, Matt Perkins, Alison Petch, Jill Prime, Danny Rhodes, Sarah Johnson and Matthew Santer, Christian Schweer, Louis Sherwood, Nicole Sherwood, Hans Spaans, Joanne Spensley, Alyson Steel, Michael Strutt, Deb Styer, Garry Telford, Patricia Thorpe, Brent C VanCamp, Neil Welch, Anne Wilkinson, David R. Williams, Adam Woog, Teri and Alan Zimbalist, and the many folks who contacted us by email but preferred to remain anonymous.

Photo credits

Jefferson Memorial across the Tidal Basin, Washington, DC © Melinda Berge/Network Aspen

Elvis' grave at Graceland, Memphis, TN © Andrew Rosenberg

Road sign © David Paler

Bison herd, Custer State National Park, SD © Geoffrey Clifford/Network Aspen

Louisiana hot sauce bottles, New Orleans, LA © Alan Becker/Network Aspen

Things not to miss

1. Grand Prismatic Hot Spring, Yellowstone National Park © David Hiser/Network Aspen
2. Highway 1 near Bixby Bridge © Robert Holmes
3. Monticello © Virginia Tourism Corporation
4. Sign at Wrigley Field © Rich McHugh
5. Airborne in The Canyons © Dan Campbell
6. Country Music Hall of Fame © State of Tennessee Photo Services
7. Fall foliage in Massachusetts © Alan Becker/Network Aspen
8. Glacier National Park © John Warden/Network Aspen
9. Florida alligator © Donald Young
10. Louisiana sternwheeler © Alan Becker/Network Aspen
11. Savannah mansion © Georgia Department of Tourism
12. South Philly cheesesteak © Terry Way
13. Aurora borealis © Johnny Johnson/AlaskaStock.com
14. South Beach Art Deco © Paul Chesley/Network Aspen
15. Masks at the Mardi Gras Museum © Alan Becker/Network Aspen
16. Lincoln Memorial, Washington Monument and the Capitol © Alan Becker/Network Aspen
17. Bridalveil Falls © Phil Schermeister/Network Aspen
18. Chicago skyline © Illinois Tourism
19. Niagara Falls © Bill Bachmann/Network Aspen
20. White House Ruin © Donald Young
21. Mount St Helens © Kirkendall/Spring
22. Churchill Downs © kentuckytourism.com
23. Richmond district © Phil Schermeister/Network Aspen
24. Mount Rushmore © Paul Chesley/Network Aspen
25. Rodeo grounds © Jeffrey Aaronson/Network Aspen
26. Birthplace of Dr Martin Luther King Jr © Georgia Department of Tourism
27. Sixth Street © Austin Convention and Visitors Bureau
28. Lava flowing into sea © Kirk Lee Aeder
29. Central Park © Geereint Tellem/Travel Ink
30. View from South Rim © Richard Reynolds/TDOC
31. Crabs © Doug Berry/Telluride Stock
32. Saguaro cactus, Saguaro National Park © John Warden/Network Aspen
33. Las Vegas Strip © Norman Godwin/Network Aspen
34. Walt Disney World © Peter Hammond/Network Aspen
35. Fish vendor, Pike Place Market © Norman Godwin/Network Aspen
36. The open road © Dawn Kish

Black and white photos

Carnegie Deli, New York City, NY © NYC and Company (p.66)

View of the Empire State Building New York City, NY © David Paler (p.91)

Boardwalk at Atlantic City, NJ © Drew Fellman (p.126)

Independence Hall, Philadelphia, PA © Terry Way (p.161)

Edgartown lighthouse, Martha's Vineyard, MA © Bill Bachmann/Network Aspen (p.194)

Pumpkin harvest, VT © J.C. Leacock/Network Aspen (p.213)

Lobster © Maine Tourism (p.271)

Birches and Maples, VT © T. Mackie, Trip (p.293)

Spoonbridge and Cherry, Minneapolis, MN © Paul Chesley/Network Aspen (p.296)

The Mall of America, Bloomington, MN © Paul Chesley/Network Aspen (p.391)

Crabs © Doug Berry/Telluride Stock (p.400)

Monticello, VA © Virginia Tourism Corporation (p.451)

Country Music Hall of Fame, Nashville, TN © State of Tennessee Photo Services (p.490)

A mill in Tennessee © State of Tennessee Photo Services (p.500)

Florida alligator © Donald Young (p.612)

Key West beach, FL © Florida Tourism (p.633)

French Quarter architecture detail, New Orleans, LA © Alan Becker/Network Aspen (p.676)

Anglers in a Louisiana swamp © Louisiana Department of Tourism (p.683)

Summit of Guadalupe Peak, Guadalupe Mountains National Park, TX © Kirkendall/Spring (p.716)

The Alamo, San Antonio, TX © Richard Reynolds (p.737)

Carhenge, NE © Dan Curran (p.770)